Volume 97 • Number 2A • March 2026

SRL Seismological Research Letters

Focus Section
Intraplate Earthquakes

Seismological Society of America

The Seismological Society of America is an international scientific society devoted to the advancement of seismology and the understanding of earthquakes for the benefit of society.

www.seismosoc.org
www.srl-online.org

SRL **Seismological Research Letters**

Volume 97 • Number 2A • March 2026

Focus Section

Intraplate Earthquakes

Guest Editors: Trevor I. Allen, Susan E. Hough, Oliver S. Boyd, Felix Waldhauser, and Marcelo Assumpção

Preface to the Focus Section on Intraplate Earthquakes Management Perspective 619
Trevor I. Allen, Susan E. Hough, Oliver S. Boyd, Felix Waldhauser, and Marcelo Assumpção

Late Quaternary Fault Activity Along the Eastern Margin Fault of the Daxing Uplift, Southeast Beijing, China, and Implications for the Rupture Behavior of Intraplate Earthquak 626
Yanbao Li, Zhengfang Li, Bengang Zhou, Jun Ma, and Mingming Han

Folding Growth Pattern of the Southern Tian Shan: Insights from the 2024 M_w 7.0 Wushi Earthquake and 2020 M_w 6.0 Jiashi Earthquake, Western China 637
Zhidan Chen, Nan Fang, Wenbin Xu, Yuan Yao, Peng Zhou, Lei Xie, and Lei Zhao

The Earthquake Swarms of Eastern Maine and Nearby New Brunswick Since 2006 651
John E. Ebel

Stress Constraints on Fault Activity in the 2020 M_w 5.1 Sparta, North Carolina, Earthquake and Aftershock Sequence 664
Will Levandowski

Source Complexity and Faulting Heterogeneity of the 2024 M_w 4.8 Zhongdian Earthquake, Yunnan, China 679
Zhenyu Wang, Chunmei Ren, Longtan Wang, Lijun Chang, and Yijian Zhou

AGMD: A Ground-Motion Database for the Australian Continental Crust 698
Hadi Ghasemi, Trevor Allen, Abhi Sunketa, Callum Mckenna, and Deepika Mani

On the Cover

Although the vast majority of earthquakes worldwide occur at plate boundaries, earthquakes can and do occur in intraplate regions far from these boundaries. This issue's focus section on Intraplate Earthquakes includes articles on intraplate earthquakes from every continent except Antarctica. These articles include the latest research aimed at better understanding these earthquakes, as well as new data sets to facilitate future research. The cover image shows the beautiful Stirling Ranges in southwestern Australia, an intraplate region discussed in an article by Pickle *et al.*

Image credit: iStock.com/Sahil Malhotra

Repeated Large-Magnitude Earthquakes in the Marianna Area of East-Central Arkansas During the Middle-Early Holocene and Possibly the Late Pleistocene 715
Martitia P. Tuttle, Haydar Al-Shukri, Hanan Mahdi, Rauf Hussein, Taher Ameen, Steven L. Forman, Kathleen Dyer-Williams, Kathleen Tucker, Martha Kopper, Muntadher Al-Kaabi, and Okba R. Al-Qadhi

The 2023 M_w 6.8 Al Haouz Lower Crustal Earthquake Buried in a Thick Crust Within a Thin Lithosphere Beneath the High Atlas Mountain Range (Morocco) 730
Hafid Ouammou, Abdelkrim Aoudia, Farhan Javed, Hari Ram Thapa, Abdelilah Tahayt, and Hua Wang

High-Resolution Imaging of the Crust Beneath the Proterozoic Aravalli–Delhi Fold Belt in Northwestern India: Evidence of Anomalous Crustal Thickening 743
Deepak Nayal, Gowthami Bandlamudi, and Mohan Gollapally

Ground-Motion Simulations for the 2024 M_w 4.8 Tewksbury, New Jersey, Earthquake 755
Oliver S. Boyd, Ebru Bozdağ, Haiyang L. Kehoe, and Morgan P. Moschetti

The 2019–2021 Xayaburi, Lao PDR, Intraplate Earthquake Sequence on a Previously Undocumented Active Fault Segment: Source Characteristics, Stress Transfer, and Regional Implications 767
Pansa Pholsonda, Passakorn Pananont, Kevin Furlong, Patinya Pornsopin, Kasian Prasertwongphilai, and Songsak Muangnoi

Characteristic Displacement and Paleoearthquake Activity of the Xiaojiang Fault Mapped from Historical Image Data and Tectonic Implications 784
Xingao Li, Zhongtai He, and Long Guo

A New High-Resolution Seismic Catalog for Southwestern Australia (2020–2025) and Analysis of Long-Term Clustering Behavior 805
Robert Pickle, Meghan S. Miller, Trevor Allen, Sima Mousavi, Ping Zhang, Huaiyu Yuan, and Ruth Murdie

Rapid Seismicity Monitoring After the March 2023 M_s 4.5 Earthquake Around the Xinfengjiang Reservoir, China 822
Linyang Xin, Ruijia Wang, Lipeng He, Zhen Guo, Lichun Yang, Zhengtao He, and Dixiang Zuo

Mailing & Subscription Information

Subscriptions to *Seismological Research Letters* (SRL): Information regarding institutional subscriptions can be found at https://www.seismosoc.org/publications/institutional-subscribers/. Members of the Seismological Society of American receive online access to SRL and may purchase a print subscription. For membership information visit https://www.seismosoc.org.

Seismological Research Letters (ISSN: 0895-0695) is published bimonthly in January, March, May, July, September, and November by the Seismological Society of America, 400 Evelyn Avenue, Suite 201, Albany, California 94706. Periodicals postage paid at Berkeley, California and at additional mailing offices.

Postmaster: Send address changes to Seismological Research Letters, 400 Evelyn Avenue, Suite 201, Albany, California 94706.

For information on submissions and instructions for authors, visit https://www.seismosoc.org/publications/srl. Communications regarding the journal apart from submission of manuscripts should be addressed to the Seismological Society of America at info@seismosoc.org.

Coseismic Rupture and Aftershock Migration Governed by Multiple Fault Geometries: The 2022 M_w 6.6 Menyuan Earthquake 832
Jun Li, Lihua Fang, Long Zhang, Chaoyong Peng, Yijian Zhou, Li Zhao, and Anne Replumaz

An Intraplate Seismic Swarm in the Karoo Basin, South Africa, Highlights the Presence of Critically Stressed Faults in an Area of Proposed Shale Gas Exploration 845
Benjamin A. Whitehead, Melody Janse van Rensburg, Diego A. Quiros, R. Alastair Sloan, and Beth Kahle

Looking for the Possible Epicenters and Magnitudes of Strong Prehistoric Earthquakes Near Boston, Massachusetts 860
John E. Ebel, Katrin Monecke, J. Bradford Hubeny, Francine M. G. McCarthy, Lindsay Theis, and Aaron Alderson

Earthquake Catalog for the Fairbanks Region of Central Alaska, 2014–2024, Based on Waveform Cross-Correlation 877
Nealey E. Sims, Carl Tape, Natalia A. Ruppert, and Michael E. West

Sub-Basalt Velocity Image of the Main Seismogenic Fault at Koyna, an Intraplate Active Region in Western India, Using Borehole Seismic Network 897
Dodla Shashidhar, Perugu Mahesh, Sandeep Gupta, and Kothamasu Mallika

Fault Intersections Control the Extremely Shallow 2020 M_w 5.1 Sparta, North Carolina, Earthquake Sequence 907
Kaiteng Huang, Sidao Ni, Jun Xie, Xiaohui He, and Wangwang Gu

The BELSHAKE Database of Earthquake Ground Motion in Belgium 918
Kris Vanneste, Mahsa Onvani, Giovanni Rapagnani, and Koen Van Noten

Seismogenic Crustal Stress in Intraplate North America: Slip Potential of Suspected Quaternary Faults in the Central and Eastern United States 934
Will Levandowski

Low Aftershock Productivity and Fault Geometry of the 2017 Delaware Earthquake 957
Karen M. Pearson, Vedran Lekic, and Lara Wagner

Articles

Coseismic Slip of the 2024 M_w 7.3 Hualien Earthquake Constrained by GNSS Observations and Its Implications for Fault Interactions 977
Chengfang Sang, Yan Hu, Siyuan Yang, Kai Wang, and Xin Cui

Coseismic Deformation and Slip Distribution of the 2024 M_w 7.0 Wushi, Xinjiang, Earthquake from High-Rate GNSS 986
Zhicai Li, Zhi Chen, Xiaodong Huang, Junli Wu, and Kaihua Ding

Increased Stress Along the Sumpur and Northern Sianok Segments of Sumatran Fault Due to the 25 February 2022 M_w 6.1 Pasaman, Indonesia, Earthquake 998
Endra Gunawan, Nanang T. Puspito, Andri Dian Nugraha, Sri Widiyantoro, Risya Fauziyyah, Medina Apriani, Nuraini Rahma Hanifa, Ekbal Hussain, Bayu Triyogo Widyantoro, and Sidik Tri Wibowo

Crustal Rheology and Fluid Migration Control the 2008 M_w 7.9 Wenchuan, China, Earthquake 1008
Xingpeng Dong, Dinghui Yang, and Weijuan Meng

The East Helanshan Fault: Revisiting the 1739 M 8 Pingluo Event and Earthquake Scenarios 1018
Boyang Sun, Yilong Li, Zijia Wang, Baizhou An, Xudong Zhou, and Zhenguo Zhang

Automated Classification of Volcanic Earthquakes Using Transformer Encoders: Insights into Data Quality and Model Interpretability 1032
Yugo Suzuki, Yohei Yukutake, Takao Ohminato, Masami Yamasaki, and Ahyi Kim

Ambient Noise Analyses at Broadband Ocean-Bottom Seismometers: Data Quality and Transfer Function Corrections 1048
Helen A. Janiszewski and Joshua B. Russell

Probing the Dead Sea Fault with the First Wireline-Free Hybrid DAS-Accelerometer Array in an Abandoned Well 1067
Ariel Lellouch and Nadav Wetzler

Meter- and Second-Scale Spatiotemporal Analysis of Anthropogenic Seismic Noise Source Distributions Using Deep Learning 1078
Jie Zhou, Binbin Mi, and Jianghai Xia

Imaging Shallow Complex V_s Structure Using F–J Surface-Wave Tomography with Partition Similarity Test: A Case Study at the San Jacinto Fault Zone 1089
Shuhao Song, Zhengbo Li, Juqing Chen, Fengjiang Ju, Chunquan Yu, and Xiaofei Chen

Surface-Wave Tomography with Transfer Learning and Moho Constraints: Method and Application to China Mainland 1104
Feiyi Wang, Xuezhen Zhang, and Xiaodong Song

Present-Day Segmented Kinematic Characteristics of the Keping Nappe System, Tian Shan, Inferred from Intensive GPS Observations 1123
Ling Zhang, Shiming Liang, Rui Li, and Jie Li

Late Pleistocene Kinematics of the Great Southern Puerto Rico Fault Zone, Puerto Rico 1136
Emerson M. Lynch, Jessica Thompson Jobe, Rich Briggs, M. Morow Tan, Victor Ortega Díaz, and K. Stephen Hughes

Eastern Section

Crustal Unloading as a Possible Source of Seismicity at Plainfield, Connecticut 1156
John E. Ebel, Sean Kondas, Parker Aubin, Justin Starr, and Jay J. Pulli

Electronic Seismologist

SURF: An Automated Method for Building Nonplanar 3D Fault Models from Earthquake Hypocenters 1174
Travis Alongi, Austin J. Elliott, Robert J. Skoumal, David R. Shelly, and Alexandra E. Hatem

Subduction Zone Earthquake Catalog Separation Tool: Implementation in the USGS 2025 Puerto Rico and U.S. Virgin Islands National Seismic Hazard Model 1191
Kirstie L. Haynie, Eric M. Thompson, Mike Hearne, Gavin P. Hayes, David R. Shelly, Allison M. Shumway, Andrea L. Llenos, Andrew J. Michael, and Peter M. Powers

Historical Seismologist

Demise of the Pilgrimage Town of Philippi (Northern Greece): Structural, Hydrogeological, Historical, and Seismological Implications of an Unrecorded, Seventh Century Strong Earthquake in a Low-Seismicity Region 1201
Stathis C. Stiros

Data Mine

Nodal Seismic Deployment on Mauna Loa Volcano, Hawai'i: Dataset and Preliminary Insights 1215
Xusong Yang, Guoqing Lin, Ninfa Bennington, and Elisabeth Gallant

Erratum

***Erratum* to Automated Classification of Volcanic Earthquakes Using Transformer Encoders: Insights into Data Quality and Model Interpretability** 1227
Yugo Suzuki, Yohei Yukutake, Takao Ohminato, Masami Yamasaki, and Ahyi Kim

SSA News and Notes 1228

Meeting Reports 1230

In Recognition 1233

Preface to the Focus Section on Intraplate Earthquakes

OPEN ACCESS

Trevor I. Allen*[1], Susan E. Hough[2], Oliver S. Boyd[3], Felix Waldhauser[4], and Marcelo Assumpção[5]

More than a half century after plate tectonics provided an overarching framework to explain earthquakes along active plate boundaries, numerous theories have been proposed to explain where, why, and how often earthquakes occur within continental crust, away from active plate boundaries. Even the classification of earthquakes away from active plate boundaries as "intraplate" raises issues, with potentially important distinctions between so-called "stable continental regions" (SCRs) and more actively deforming regions, including passive margins and failed rifts. Some of the largest known continental intraplate earthquakes themselves remain enigmatic, having occurred before the modern instrumental era. Although low levels of seismicity—and potentially low seismic hazard—are characteristic of intraplate regions, it does not necessarily follow that these regions have low seismic risk (e.g., Hobbs *et al.*, 2023). Because of the limited number of large damaging earthquakes in the historical period, numerous legacy structures in low-seismicity regions have been built to lower seismic design standards and will thus be more vulnerable to damage from future earthquakes. In addition, intraplate earthquakes within continental crust will commonly generate stronger ground shaking at mid to high frequencies, and the ground-shaking intensities will attenuate more slowly with distance relative to interplate regions (e.g., Nordenson and Bell, 2000; Bakun and McGarr, 2002; Petersen *et al.*, 2024; Bayless and Somerville, 2025). The lower occurrence rates of earthquakes, together with the stronger shaking intensities over larger distances, mean that probabilistic seismic hazard estimates calculated for intraplate regions commonly increase at faster rates with decreasing probabilities of exceedance—e.g., from 10% versus 2% probability of exceedance in 50 years—than in interplate regions (e.g., Leyendecker *et al.*, 2000; Allen, 2020). Earthquake hazard scientists can learn from the sparse historical observations of these events to improve community safety and resilience to rare large intraplate earthquakes that may occur in the future.

Seismic hazard assessments in continental intraplate regions are often data-limited: low fault-slip rates relative to landscape modification rates can result in poor identification of potentially active faults, challenging the characterization of seismic sources; the completeness and homogenization of instrumental earthquake catalogs using uncertain magnitude conversions can lead to uncertainties in earthquake recurrence; and limited strong-motion observations for large-magnitude events at near-source distances lead to uncertainties in the development and selection of ground-motion models for seismic hazard studies. Data from recent intraplate earthquakes around the world—from the moment magnitude (**M**) 7.6 2001 Bhuj, India, earthquake 25 yr ago (Hough *et al.*, 2003) to the 2024 **M** 4.8 Tewksbury, United States, earthquake (Boyd, Barnhart, *et al.*, 2024; Han *et al.*, 2024)—have yielded both new insights and new questions. The articles in this focus section discuss many of the long-standing challenges related to intraplate earthquake investigations and provide a snapshot of current research to advance our understanding.

Like earthquakes that occur on plate boundaries, intraplate earthquakes can occur in a wide variety of seismotectonic settings (e.g., Scholz *et al.*, 1986). Examples include regions with measurable crustal strain, moderate levels of seismicity and geological evidence for recurrent morphogenic earthquakes (Liu *et al.*, 2011; Kreemer *et al.*, 2014; Gahalaut *et al.*, 2019; Feng *et al.*, 2020; Chang *et al.*, 2025), and SCRs that have limited to no measurable strain, low rates of historical seismicity and where little geological evidence of prior morphogenic earthquakes may be present (e.g., Clark *et al.*, 2012, 2020; King *et al.*, 2019). Although the occurrence of the former "active intraplate" earthquakes can generally be understood in their geologic and seismotectonic setting, SCR earthquakes are more enigmatic (e.g., Assumpção *et al.*, 2025), with various theories proposed to describe their occurrence (e.g., Mazzotti *et al.*, 2005; Forte *et al.*, 2007; Sandiford and Egholm, 2008; Quigley *et al.*, 2010; Calais *et al.*, 2016; Jackson and McKenzie, 2022). So, too, the geographical definition of SCRs worldwide has continued to evolve over time (e.g., Johnston, 1994; Schulte and Mooney, 2005; Wheeler, 2011).

The focus section is global in scope, with contributions on intraplate earthquakes in Australia, Belgium, China, India, Laos, Morocco, South Africa, and the United States. In light of the challenges discussed, earthquakes can be investigated in different

1. Geoscience Australia, Canberra, Australian Capital Territory, Australia, https://orcid.org/0000-0003-3420-547X (TIA); 2. U.S. Geological Survey, Pasadena, California, U.S.A., https://orcid.org/0000-0002-5980-2986 (SEH); 3. U.S. Geological Survey, Golden, Colorado, U.S.A., https://orcid.org/0000-0001-9457-0407 (OSB); 4. Lamont Doherty Earth Observatory, Palisades, New York, U.S.A., https://orcid.org/0000-0002-1286-9737 (FW); 5. University of São Paulo, São Paulo, Brazil

*Corresponding author: trevor.allen@ga.gov.au

Cite this article as Allen, T. I., S. E. Hough, O. S. Boyd, F. Waldhauser, and M. Assumpção (2026). Preface to the Focus Section on Intraplate Earthquakes, *Seismol. Res. Lett.*, **97**, 619–625, doi: 10.1785/0220260004.

intraplate regions around the world, both those that are more classically described as SCRs and those that are in more active intraplate settings. A global approach not only brings more data to bear on outstanding problems; it also can identify both commonalities and differences that potentially shed light on physical earthquake properties. For example, earlier work by Liu *et al.* (2011) concluded that large historic earthquakes in intraplate regions in China have been distributed over a large region, with no evidence for multiple historical ruptures on the same fault segment over a 2000-year period. However, there is now abundant evidence for recurrent paleoearthquakes throughout central China (e.g., Feng *et al.*, 2020; Zou *et al.*, 2021; Zhang *et al.*, 2024). Furthermore, there is compelling evidence that the New Madrid Seismic Zone in central North America has experienced multiple sequences of large earthquakes in the late Holocene (Tuttle *et al.*, 2005, 2019). There is also paleoseismic evidence for multiple large earthquakes in the Charleston, South Carolina, seismic zone (Talwani and Schaeffer, 2001) and on the Cadell (Clark *et al.*, 2017), Lake George (Macphail *et al.*, 2015), Jindabyne (Griffin *et al.*, 2024), and Willunga (Clark *et al.*, 2024) faults in southeastern Australia. Evidence also suggests that earthquake rates can differ appreciably between low-strain-rate regions worldwide (Mazzotti, 2007), for example, with Australia experiencing a higher rate of **M** > 6.0 earthquakes than other Precambrian cratons in the historical period (Fenton *et al.*, 2006). In 2001, the Bhuj, India, earthquake was identified as a possible modern analog for large earthquakes in the New Madrid Seismic Zone (Ellis *et al.*, 2001). However, Stein *et al.* (2002) identified key differences between central North America and western India in that the Bhuj earthquake occurred within a zone of diffuse deformation related to plate boundary motion (e.g., Gahalaut *et al.*, 2019).

In the active intraplate region north of the Tibetan plateau—a transition between the Himalayan front and the stable interior of the Eurasian continent—Chen *et al.* (2025) proposed that basement faulting contributes to development of fold structures in the surface layers to accommodate crustal shortening, whereas Li *et al.* (2026) showed how changes in fault geometry limited the extent of the main coseismic rupture. Both articles showed how stress changes from the main rupture caused the largest aftershock and expanded the total rupture zone.

Our understanding of earthquake processes in intraplate regions has long been hampered by data limitations. Augmenting the record of known historical earthquakes, paleoseismic investigations have been used to extend the documented earthquake record further back in time. Where faults are identified at the surface, conventional paleoseismic investigations can help identify past earthquakes and slip rates on individual faults. Three articles in this focus section present results of such investigations in the Marianna area of east-central Arkansas (Tuttle *et al.*, 2026), the Xiaojiang fault in southwestern China (Li *et al.*, 2026), and the Daxing uplift in southeast Beijing (Li *et al.*, 2025).

Where there may be limited surface expression of morphogenic earthquakes, paleoliquefaction studies have been used to investigate historic and prehistoric earthquakes, notably in the New Madrid Seismic Zone (Tuttle *et al.*, 2005). Past studies have also focused on sediment disturbances in lakes, identifying earthquake-induced deformation that can identify prehistoric earthquakes (e.g., Doig, 1990; Brooks, 2015; Daxer *et al.*, 2022; Oswald *et al.*, 2022). Toward this end, Ebel *et al.* (2026) describe and interpret evidence from sediment disturbances in cores extracted from two small lakes in eastern Massachusetts: Sluice Lake and Walden Pond. The authors present evidence for earthquake-induced subaqueous mass wasting in both lakes around 1400 C.E., and in Walden Pond only around 1200 C.E. The estimated magnitude of the earthquake around 1400 C.E. might have been as large as **M** 6.7. A moderate earthquake, **M** 4.7 ± 0.3, can most plausibly explain the disturbance around 1200 C.E. in Waldon Pond. These results contribute to the body of knowledge about prehistorical earthquakes and seismic hazard in eastern Massachusetts and southeastern New Hampshire and suggest that studies of sediments in other small lakes may be used to further constrain seismic hazards in the region.

Complementing paleoseismic (and historical) investigations that offer an opportunity to extend the intraplate record back in time, well-recorded recent earthquakes offer an opportunity to investigate intraplate earthquakes and fault zones in detail. Several articles in this section present detailed results for notable recent intraplate earthquakes, including the 2019 **M** 6.3 Xayaburi, Laos (Pholsonda *et al.*, 2026); 2020 **M** 5.1 Sparta, North Carolina (Levandowski, 2025; Huang *et al.*, 2026); 2023 **M** 6.8 Al Haouz, Morocco (Ouammou *et al.*, 2026); and 2024 **M** 4.8 Zhongdian, China (Wang *et al.*, 2026), earthquakes. Studies of these earthquakes benefit from recent advancements in data analysis methods that yield improved earthquake source parameters, high-resolution aftershock hypocenter catalogs complete down to low magnitudes, and/or detailed information on the seismic velocity structure in the source region. These tools were also used by Sims *et al.* (2026) to map new and conjugate fault segments in Central Alaska that can improve tectonic and seismic hazard assessments. Shashidhar *et al.* (2026) used local earthquakes recorded on borehole seismic sensors to generate a sub-basalt velocity model for the Koyna Reservoir region, India. They identified a velocity signature of the Donichiwada fault at 6–10 km depth, coinciding with a dense cluster of seismicity. Looking deeper into the crust, Nayal *et al.* (2026) used *P*-wave receiver functions to image the Proterozoic Aravalli-Delhi fold belt in an intraplate region of northwestern India. They find evidence for varying crustal thickness and composition beneath the fold belt and explore possible scenarios for the crustal evolution within the region.

Although aftershock sequences in intraplate regions are commonly observed to endure over longer periods than interplate regions (e.g., Stein and Liu, 2009), Pearson *et al.* (2026)

investigate the 2017 **M** 4.2 Delaware earthquake and find that low aftershock productivity. Ebel (2025) revisits several swarms of small earthquakes in Maine, United States, and New Brunswick, Canada, to find common characteristics (i.e., shallow depths, small spatial extents, aseismic creep, locations within or near Devonian granitic plutons) that suggest that stress concentration within and along the edges of granitic bodies make them plausible hosts for swarm activity. Pickle *et al.* (2026) develop a high-resolution earthquake catalog using temporary array data in southwestern Australia and explore the behavior of high-productivity earthquake sequences. The authors introduce the notion of "drip-type" earthquake clusters (spatial clusters with no characteristic time-decay variation), which may infer the location of prehistoric seismicity and future seismic risk, potentially supporting the observations of Stein and Liu (2009).

The potential for induced seismicity from the impoundment of large water reservoirs, hydrocarbon extraction, and wastewater disposal (e.g., Foulger *et al.*, 2018) is also a key concern for intraplate regions. Xin *et al.* (2026) describe results from rapid seismicity monitoring of an aftershock sequence following the 2023 M_s 4.5 earthquake near the Xinfengjiang Reservoir, China, a region with a demonstrated history of reservoir-triggered earthquakes (e.g., Huang *et al.*, 2024). Further, Whitehead *et al.* (2026) explore an intraplate seismic swarm in the Karoo basin and highlight the presence of critically stressed faults in a region of proposed shale gas exploration in South Africa.

In addition to the challenge of quantifying earthquake sources, characterization of ground motions from large earthquakes in SCRs has been a long-standing separate challenge, with almost no instrumental recordings of large (**M** ≥ 6.0) earthquakes at distances of <50 km (e.g., McNamara *et al.*, 2019; Goulet, Bozorgnia, *et al.*, 2021; Allen *et al.*, 2024). Ground-motion models have been developed using relatively abundant recordings of moderate-magnitude earthquakes (**M** < 6.0; Goulet, Kishida, *et al.*, 2021; Thompson *et al.*, 2023) but have relied heavily on simulations (e.g., Goulet, Bozorgnia, *et al.*, 2021). This reliance has sometimes led to large frequency-dependent discrepancies between predicted and observed ground motions (e.g., Ramos-Sepúlveda *et al.*, 2024) that can be explained, to some extent, by the effects of thick sediments (Chapman and Guo, 2021; Boyd, Churchwell, *et al.*, 2024).

In this focus section, Ghasemi *et al.* (2026) and Vanneste *et al.* (2026) present high-quality ground-motion databases for Australia and Belgium, respectively, to help fill the gap in instrumental observations for SCR earthquakes. Together, these datasets provide thousands of new waveforms and engineering parameters for intraplate earthquakes up to **M** 6.6 (e.g., Allen *et al.*, 2024). Given the paucity of near-source ground motions from large-magnitude earthquakes in low-seismicity regions, simulations fill an important gap in being able to model the accelerations from larger magnitude events. Boyd *et al.* (2026) apply a 3D seismic velocity model to further constrain the source and ground motions of the 2024 **M** 4.8 Tewksbury earthquake. These validation studies can be used to advance ground-motion forecasting methods and provide confidence in the use of simulation approaches to underpin seismic hazard assessments.

Parallel investigations have focused on characterization of macroseismic intensity (e.g., Johnston, 1996; Hough and Bilham, 2024; Martin *et al.*, 2024). Macroseismic intensities have not only been used to constrain instrumentally determined ground-motion models, but they may provide a basis for comparison for earthquakes such as the 1886 Charleston, South Carolina, earthquake (Hough and Bilham, 2024).

Like the strain rates within intraplate regions, progress toward understanding intraplate earthquakes and their hazard remains slow. Efforts to characterize seismic hazard in these regions face challenges associated with considerable uncertainties (e.g., Stein *et al.*, 2015). In particular, if intraplate seismicity can be characterized as a stationary process, the rate of earthquakes is expected to vary substantially in short catalogs. Using simulated earthquake catalogs based on an epidemic-type aftershock sequence model and strain and seismicity rates for California, Page and Felzer (2015) showed that the long-term earthquake rate can only be estimated reliably from a catalog roughly three times the recurrence time of the largest earthquakes in the region. In eastern North America, the historical record is about twice as long as the historical record in California, but the earthquake and strain rates are at least a factor of 100 lower. However, ever-increasing resolution and sensitivity in geodetic and seismic observations result in improved mapping of present-day stress fields. To that end, Levandowski (2025) analyzes focal mechanisms and Quaternary features in eastern North America to distinguish faults compatible with the modern stress field from those unlikely to be seismogenic, improving interpretation of past earthquakes and future earthquake potential.

The contributions in this focus section discuss some of the recent seismological advances and observations from earthquakes in continental intraplate regions worldwide. There are still key challenges in understanding the seismic hazard potential in many of these regions, particularly in terms of seismic source and ground-motion characterization. Although many of these challenges can benefit from ongoing monitoring, field investigations, and research, opportunities remain to advance earthquake hazard science for intraplate regions. Continued efforts, such as those promoted in this focus section, can lead to improved seismic safety of our communities and ensure that the built environment and major infrastructure assets remain resilient to earthquakes into the future.

Data and Resources

There are no new data or resources to report for this article.

Declaration of Competing Interests

The authors acknowledge that there are no conflicts of interest recorded.

Acknowledgments

The authors are grateful to Jessica Thompson Jobe and Morgan Moschetti of the U.S. Geological Survey and Jonathan Griffin and James La Greca of Geoscience Australia for their thoughtful and constructive internal reviews of this preface. The *Seismological Research Letters* editorial team, Allison Bent and Miranda Bohl, are thanked for their guidance and support in compiling this focus section. Trevor Allen publishes with the permission of the chief executive officer, Geoscience Australia.

Any use of trade, firm, or product names is for descriptive purposes only and does not imply endorsement by the U.S. Government.

References

Allen, T. I. (2020). Seismic hazard estimation in stable continental regions: Does PSHA meet the needs for modern engineering design in Australia? *Bull. New Zeal. Soc. Earthq. Eng.* **53,** no. 1, 22–36, doi: 10.5459/bnzsee.53.1.22-36.

Allen, T. I., H. Ghasemi, and R. Ebrahimi (2024). Seismology down under: Developing engineering ground-motion databases in regions of low seismicity and sparse monitoring networks, *18th World Conf. on Earthquake Engineering*, Milan, Italy, 30 June–5 July, 12 pp.

Assumpção, M., M. Bianchi, J. Calhau, D. Rosa, J. Baksh, D. Assing, C. Basdeo, J. Zahradnik, F. Dias, R. Jolivet, *et al.* (2025). The 2021 M_w 5.6 earthquake in the Guyana shield, South America: An intraplate event with no reason to occur, *Seism. Rec.* **5,** no. 2, 228–238, doi: 10.1785/0320250002.

Bakun, W. H., and A. McGarr (2002). Differences in attenuation among the stable continental regions, *Geophys. Res. Lett.* **29,** no. 23, 2121, doi: 10.1029/2002GL015457.

Bayless, J., and P. Somerville (2025). Are ground motions in Australia different between cratonic and non-cratonic regions, and different from global models? *Australian Earthquake Engineering Society National Conference*, Melbourne, Victoria, 20–22 November, 14 pp.

Boyd, O. S., W. D. Barnhart, J. Bourke, M. Chapman, P. S. Earle, G. Huang, J. A. Thompson Jobe, W.-Y. Kim, F. Link, M. Litherland, *et al.* (2024). Preliminary observations of the 5 April 2024 M_w 4.8 New Jersey earthquake, *Seism. Rec.* **4,** no. 4, 240–250, doi: 10.1785/0320240024.

Boyd, O. S., E. Bozdağ, H. L. Kehoe, and M. P. Moschetti (2026). Ground-motion simulations for the 2024 M 4.8 Tewksbury, New Jersey earthquake, *Seismol. Res. Lett.* doi: 10.1785/0220250333.

Boyd, O. S., D. Churchwell, M. P. Moschetti, E. M. Thompson, M. C. Chapman, O. Ilhan, T. L. Pratt, S. K. Ahdi, and S. Rezaeian (2024). Sediment thickness map of United States Atlantic and Gulf Coastal Plain Strata, and their influence on earthquake ground motions, *Earthq. Spectra* **40,** no. 1, 89–112, doi: 10.1177/87552930231204880.

Brooks, G. R. (2015). An integrated stratigraphic approach to investigating evidence of paleoearthquakes in lake deposits of eastern Canada, *Geosci. Can.* **42,** no. 2, 247–261, doi: 10.12789/geocanj.2014.41.063.

Calais, E., T. Camelbeeck, S. Stein, M. Liu, and T. J. Craig (2016). A new paradigm for large earthquakes in stable continental plate interiors, *Geophys. Res. Lett.* **43,** no. 20, 10621–10637, doi: 10.1002/2016GL070815.

Chang, F., J. Fang, S. Dong, H. Yin, C. Rollins, J. R. Elliott, and A. J. Hooper (2025). Geodetic strain rates, slip deficit rates, and seismic potential in the Tianshan, Central Asia, *Geophys. Res. Lett.* **52,** no. 22, e2025GL118470, doi: 10.1029/2025GL118470.

Chapman, M. C., and Z. Guo (2021). A response spectral ratio model to account for amplification and attenuation effects in the Atlantic and Gulf Coastal Plain, *Bull. Seismol. Soc. Am.* **111,** no. 4, 1849–1867, doi: 10.1785/0120200322.

Chen, Z., N. Fang, W. Xu, Y. Yao, P. Zhou, L. Xie, and L. Zhao (2025). Folding growth pattern of the southern Tian Shan: Insights from the 2024 M_w 7.0 Wushi earthquake and 2020 M_w 6.0 Jiashi earthquake, western China, *Seismol. Res. Lett.* doi: 10.1785/0220250135.

Clark, D., J. Griffin, J. La Greca, M. Quigley, Z. Jacobs, S. Sellmann, D. Ninis, K. Kuang, and A. Wilson (2024). Large earthquake recurrence on the Willunga fault, South Australia: Earthquake chronology and co-seismic displacements, *Australian Earthquake Engineering Society 2024 Conference*, Adelaide, South Australia, 21–23 November, 14 pp.

Clark, D., A. McPherson, M. Cupper, C. D. N. Collins, and G. Nelson (2017). The Cadell fault, southeastern Australia: A record of temporally clustered morphogenic seismicity in a low-strain intraplate region, in *Seismicity, Fault Rupture and Earthquake Hazards in Slowly Deforming Regions*, A. Landgraf, S. Kübler, E. Hintersberger, and S. Stein (Editors), Geological Society of London, Special Publications 432, 163–185, doi: 10.1144/SP432.2.

Clark, D., A. McPherson, and R. Van Dissen (2012). Long-term behaviour of Australian stable continental region (SCR) faults, *Tectonophysics* **566–567,** 1–30, doi: 10.1016/j.tecto.2012.07.004.

Clark, D. J., S. Brennand, G. Brenn, M. C. Garthwaite, J. Dimech, T. I. Allen, and S. Standen (2020). Surface deformation relating to the 2018 Lake Muir earthquake sequence, southwest western Australia: New insight into stable continental region earthquakes, *Solid Earth* **11,** no. 2, 691–717, doi: 10.5194/se-11-691-2020.

Daxer, C., M. Ortler, S. C. Fabbri, M. Hilbe, I. Hajdas, N. Dubois, T. Piechl, C. Hammerl, M. Strasser, and J. Moernaut (2022). High-resolution calibration of seismically-induced lacustrine deposits with historical earthquake data in the eastern Alps (Carinthia, Austria), *Quat. Sci. Rev.* **284,** 107497, doi: 10.1016/j.quascirev.2022.107497.

Doig, R. (1990). 2300 yr history of seismicity from silting events, in Lake Tadoussac, Charlevoix, Quebec, *Geology* **18,** no. 9, 820–823.

Ebel, J. E. (2025). The earthquake swarms of eastern Maine and nearby New Brunswick since 2006, *Seismol. Res. Lett.* doi: 10.1785/0220250237.

Ebel, J. E., K. Monecke, J. B. Hubeny, F. M. G. McCarthy, L. Theis, and A. Alderson (2026). Looking for the possible epicenters and magnitudes of strong prehistoric earthquakes Near Boston, Massachusetts, *Seismol. Res. Lett.* doi: 10.1785/0220250310.

Ellis, M., J. Gomberg, and E. Schweig (2001). Indian earthquake may serve as analog for New Madrid earthquakes, *Eos* **82,** no. 32, 345–350, doi: 10.1029/01EO00211.

Feng, X., J. Ma, Y. Zhou, P. England, B. Parsons, M. A. Rizza, and R. T. Walker (2020). Geomorphology and paleoseismology of the Weinan fault, Shaanxi, central China, and the source of the 1556 Huaxian earthquake, *J. Geophys. Res. Solid Earth* **125,** no. 12, e2019JB017848, doi: 10.1029/2019JB017848.

Fenton, C. H., J. Adams, and S. Halchuk (2006). Seismic hazards assessment for radioactive waste disposal sites in regions of low seismic activity, *Geotech. Geol. Eng.* **24**, 579–592, doi: 10.1007/s10706-005-1148-4.

Forte, A. M., J. X. Mitrovica, R. Moucha, N. A. Simmons, and S. P. Grand (2007). Descent of the ancient Farallon slab drives localized mantle flow below the New Madrid seismic zone, *Geophys. Res. Lett.* **34,** no. 4, L04308, doi: 10.1029/2006GL027895.

Foulger, G. R., M. P. Wilson, J. G. Gluyas, B. R. Julian, and R. J. Davies (2018). Global review of human-induced earthquakes, *Earth Sci. Rev.* **178,** 438–514, doi: 10.1016/j.earscirev.2017.07.008.

Gahalaut, V. K., K. Gahalaut, R. K. Dumka, P. Chaudhury, and R. K. Yadav (2019). Geodetic evidence of high compression across seismically active Kachchh paleorift, India, *Tectonics* **38,** no. 8, 3097–3107, doi: 10.1029/2019TC005496.

Ghasemi, H., T. Allen, A. Sunketa, C. McKenna, and D. Mani (2026). AGMD: A ground-motion database for the Australian continental crust, *Seismol. Res. Lett.* doi: 10.1785/0220250316.

Goulet, C. A., Y. Bozorgnia, N. Kuehn, L. Al Atik, R. R. Youngs, R. W. Graves, and G. M. Atkinson (2021). NGA-East ground-motion characterization model Part I: Summary of products and model development, *Earthq. Spectra* **37,** no. S1 1231–1282, doi: 10.1177/87552930211018723.

Goulet, C. A., T. Kishida, T. D. Ancheta, C. H. Cramer, R. B. Darragh, W. J. Silva, Y. M. Hashash, J. Harmon, G. A. Parker, *et al.* (2021). PEER NGA-East database, *Earthq. Spectra* **37,** no. S1, 1331–1353, doi: 10.1177/87552930211015695.

Griffin, J., D. Clark, J. Kemp, M. Stirling, T. King, O. Kulesza, J. La Greca, A. Sharma, M. Quigley, *et al.* (2024). Large earthquake recurrence in the Snowy Monaro region: New findings to inform dam safety, *2024 Australian National Committee on Large Dams Conference*, Adelaide, South Australia, 11–14 November, 9 pp.

Han, S., W.-Y. Kim, J. Y. Park, M.-S. Seo, and Y. Kim (2024). Rupture model of the 5 April 2024 Tewksbury, New Jersey, earthquake based on regional *Lg*-wave data, *Seism. Rec.* **4,** no. 3, 214–222, doi: 10.1785/0320240020.

Li, X., Z. He, and L. Guo (2026). Characteristic displacement and paleoearthquake activity of the Xiaojiang fault mapped from historical image data and tectonic implications, *Seismol. Res. Lett.* doi: 10.1785/0220250326.

Hobbs, T. E., J. M. Journeay, A. S. Rao, M. Kolaj, P. LeSueur, M. Simionato, V. Silva, M. Pagani, K. Johnson, *et al.* (2023). A national seismic risk model for Canada: Methodology and scientific basis, *Earthq. Spectra* **39,** no. 3, 1410–1434, doi: 10.1177/87552930231173446.

Hough, S. E., and R. Bilham (2024). The 1886 Charleston, South Carolina, earthquake: Intensities and ground motions, *Bull. Seismol. Soc. Am.* **114,** no. 3, 1658–1679, doi: 10.1785/0120230224.

Hough, S. E., S. Martin, R. Bilham, and G. M. Atkinson (2003). A media-based assessment of damage and ground motions from the January 26th, 2001 M 7.6 Bhuj, India earthquake, *J. Earth Syst. Sci.* **112,** no. 3, 353–373, doi: 10.1007/BF02709262.

Huang, K., S. Ni, J. Xie, X. He, and W. Gu (2026). Fault intersections control the extremely shallow 2020 M_W 5.1 Sparta, North Carolina earthquake sequence, *Seismol. Res. Lett.* doi: 10.1785/0220250313.

Huang, R., X. Sun, P. Zhang, and Y. Deng (2024). Seismicity migration and the upper crustal structure in the Xinfengjiang Reservoir, *Seismol. Res. Lett.* **95,** no. 5, 2833–2843, doi: 10.1785/0220230369.

Jackson, J., and D. McKenzie (2022). The exfoliation of Cratonic Australia in earthquakes, *Earth Planet. Sci. Lett.* **578,** 117305, doi: 10.1016/j.epsl.2021.117305.

Johnston, A. C. (1994). Seismotectonic interpretations and conclusions from the stable continental region seismicity database, in *The Earthquakes of Stable Continental Regions, Volume 1-Assessment of Large Earthquake Potential*, A. C. Johnston, K. J. Coppersmith, L. R. Kanter, and C. A. Cornell (Editors), Electric Power Research Institute, Palo Alto, California, TR-102261-V1.

Johnston, A. C. (1996). Seismic moment assessment of earthquakes in stable continental regions—III. New Madrid 1811–1812, Charleston 1886, and Lisbon 1755, *Geophys. J. Int.* **126,** no. 2, 314–344, doi: 10.1111/j.1365-246X.1996.tb05294.x.

King, T. R., M. Quigley, and D. Clark (2019). Surface-rupturing historical earthquakes in Australia and their environmental effects: New insights from re-analyses of observational data, *Geosciences* **9,** no. 10, 408, doi: 10.3390/geosciences9100408.

Kreemer, C., G. Blewitt, and E. C. Klein (2014). A geodetic plate motion and Global Strain Rate Model, *Geochem. Geophy. Geosys.* **15,** no. 10, 3849–3889, doi: 10.1002/2014GC005407.

Levandowski, W. (2025). Stress constraints on fault activity in the 2020 M_W 5.1 Sparta, North Carolina, earthquake and aftershock sequence, *Seismol. Res. Lett.* doi: 10.1785/0220250309.

Leyendecker, E. V., R. J. Hunt, A. D. Frankel, and K. S. Rukstales (2000). Development of maximum considered earthquake ground motion maps, *Earthq. Spectra* **16,** no. 1, 21–40, doi: 10.1193/1.1586081.

Li, J., L. Fang, L. Zhang, C. Peng, Y. Zhou, and A. Replumaz (2026). Coseismic rupture and aftershock migration governed by multiple fault geometries: The 2022 M_W 6.6 Menyuan earthquake, *Seismol. Res. Lett.* doi: 10.1785/0220250355.

Li, Y., Z. Li, B. Zhou, J. Ma, and M. Han (2025). Late Quaternary fault activity along the eastern margin fault of the Daxing uplift, southeast Beijing, China, and implications for the rupture behavior of intraplate earthquakes, *Seismol. Res. Lett.* doi: 10.1785/0220250180.

Liu, M., S. Stein, and H. Wang (2011). 2000 years of migrating earthquakes in North China: How earthquakes in midcontinents differ from those at plate boundaries, *Lithosphere* **3,** 128–132, doi: 10.1130/L129.1.

Macphail, M., L. K. Fifield, B. Pillans, M. Davies, and G. Hope (2015). Lake George revisited: New evidence for the origin and evolution of a large closed lake, southern Tablelands, NSW, Australia, *Aust. J. Earth Sci.* **62,** no. 7, 853–871, doi: 10.1080/08120099.2015.1108365.

Martin, S. S., P. R. Cummins, J. D. Griffin, D. Clark, and T. I. Allen (2024). Resolving the location and magnitude of the 1918 Queensland (Bundaberg), Australia, earthquake, *Bull. Seismol. Soc. Am.* **114,** no. 6, 3202–3223, doi: 10.1785/0120240029.

Mazzotti, S. (2007). Geodynamic models for earthquake studies in intraplate North America, in *Continental Intraplate Earthquakes: Science, Hazard, and Policy*, S. Stein and S. Mazzotti (Editors), Geological Society of America Special Paper 425, 17–32, doi: 10.1130/2007.2425(02).

Mazzotti, S., T. S. James, J. Henton, and J. Adams (2005). GPS crustal strain, postglacial rebound, and seismic hazard in eastern North America: The Saint Lawrence Valley example, *J. Geophys. Res.* **110,** no. B11, doi: 10.1029/2004JB003590.

McNamara, D. E., M. D. Petersen, E. M. Thompson, P. M. Powers, A. M. Shumway, S. H. Hoover, M. P. Moschetti, and E. Wolin (2019). Evaluation of ground-motion models for USGS Seismic Hazard Forecasts: induced and tectonic earthquakes in the central and eastern United States, *Bull. Seismol. Soc. Am.* **109,** no. 1, 322–335, doi: 10.1785/0120180106.

Nayal, D., G. Bandlamudi, and M. Gollapally (2026). High resolution imaging of the crust beneath the Proterozoic Aravalli-Delhi fold belt in northwestern India: Evidence of anomalous crustal thickening, *Seismol. Res. Lett.* doi: 10.1785/0220250281.

Nordenson, G. J. P., and G. R. Bell (2000). Seismic design requirements for regions of moderate seismicity, *Earthq. Spectra* **16,** no. 1, 205–225, doi: 10.1193/1.1586091.

Oswald, P., M. Strasser, J. Skapski, and J. Moernaut (2022). Magnitude and source area estimations of severe prehistoric earthquakes in the western Austrian Alps, *Nat. Hazards Earth Syst. Sci.* **22,** no. 6, 2057–2079, doi: 10.5194/nhess-22-2057-2022.

Ouammou, H., A. Aoudia, F. Javed, H. Ram Thapa, A. Tahayt, and H. Wang (2026). The 2023 M_W 6.8 Al Haouz lower crustal earthquake buried in a thick crust within a thin lithosphere beneath the High Atlas Mountain range (Morocco), *Seismol. Res. Lett.* doi: 10.1785/0220250299.

Page, M. T., and K. R. Felzer (2015). Southern San Andreas fault seismicity is consistent with the Gutenberg–Richter law, *Bull. Seismol. Soc. Am.* **105,** no. 4, 2070–2080, doi: 10.1785/0120140340.

Pearson, K. M., V. Lekic, and L. Wagner (2026). Low aftershock productivity and fault geometry of the 2017 Delaware earthquake, *Seismol. Res. Lett.* doi: 10.1785/0220250322.

Petersen, M. D., A. M. Shumway, P. M. Powers, E. H. Field, M. P. Moschetti, K. S. Jaiswal, K. R. Milner, S. Rezaeian, A. D. Frankel, A. L. Llenos, *et al.* (2024). The 2023 US 50-State National Seismic Hazard Model: Overview and implications, *Earthq. Spectra* **40,** no. 1, 5–88, doi: 10.1177/87552930231215428.

Pholsonda, P., P. Pananont, K. Furlong, P. Pornsopin, K. Prasertwongphilai, and S. Muangnoi (2026). The 2019–2021 Xayaburi, Laos, intraplate earthquake sequence on a previously unmapped fault: Source characteristics, stress transfer, and regional implications, *Seismol. Res. Lett.* doi: 10.1785/0220250317.

Pickle, R. C., M. S. Miller, T. Allen, S. Mousavi, P. Zhang, H. Yuan, and R. Murdie (2026). A new high-resolution seismic catalog for southwestern Australia (2020–2025) and analysis of long-term clustering behavior, *Seismol. Res. Lett.* doi: 10.1785/0220250308.

Quigley, M. C., D. Clark, and M. Sandiford (2010). Tectonic geomorphology of Australia, in *Australian Landscapes*, P. Bishop and B. Pillans (Editors), Geological Society of London, Special Publications 346, 243–265, doi: 10.1144/SP346.13.

Ramos-Sepúlveda, M. E., J. P. Stewart, G. A. Parker, M. P. Moschetti, E. M. Thompson, S. J. Brandenberg, Y. M. A. Hashash, and E. M. Rathje (2024). Data-driven adjustments for combined use of NGA-East hard-rock ground motion and site amplification models. *Earthq. Spectra* **40,** no. 2, 1132–1157, doi: 10.1177/87552930241231825.

Sandiford, M., and D. L. Egholm (2008). Enhanced intraplate seismicity along continental margins: Some causes and consequences, *Tectonophysics* **457,** nos. 3/4, 197–208, doi: 10.1016/j.tecto.2008.06.004.

Scholz, C. H., C. A. Aviles, and S. G. Wesnousky (1986). Scaling differences between large interplate and intraplate earthquakes, *Bull. Seismol. Soc. Am.* **76,** no. 1, 65–70, doi: 10.1785/BSSA0760010065.

Schulte, S. M., and W. D. Mooney (2005). An updated global earthquake catalogue for stable continental regions: Reassessing the correlation with ancient rifts, *Geophys. J. Int.* **161,** no. 3, 707–721, doi: 10.1111/j.1365-246X.2005.02554.x.

Shashidhar, D., M. Perugu, S. Gupta, and M. Kothamasu (2026). Sub-basalt velocity image of the main seismogenic fault at Koyna, an intraplate active region in western India, using borehole seismic network, *Seismol. Res. Lett.* doi: 10.1785/0220250319.

Sims, N., C. Tape, N. A. Ruppert, and M. E. West (2026). Earthquake catalog for the Fairbanks region of central Alaska, 2014–2024, based on waveform cross-correlation, *Seismol. Res. Lett.* doi: 10.1785/0220250342.

Stein, S., and M. Liu (2009). Long aftershock sequences within continents and implications for earthquake hazard assessment, *Nature* **462,** 87–89, doi:10.1038/nature08502.

Stein, S., M. Liu, T. Camelbeeck, M. Merino, A. Landgraf, E. Hintersberger, and S. Kuebler (2015). Challenges in assessing seismic hazard in intraplate Europe, in *Seismicity, Fault Rupture and Earthquake Hazards in Slowly Deforming Regions*, A. Landgraf, S. Kuebler, E. Hintersberger, and S. Stein (Editors), Geological Society of London, Special Publications 432, 13–28, doi: 10.1144/SP432.7.

Stein, S., G. F. Sella, and E. A. Okal (2002). The January 26, 2001 Bhuj earthquake and the diffuse western boundary of the Indian plate, in *Plate Boundary Zones*, S. Stein and J. T. Freymueller (Editors), Vol. 30, Geodynamics Series, American Geophysical Union, 243–254, doi: 10.1029/GD030p0243.

Talwani, P., and W. T. Schaeffer (2001). Recurrence rates of large earthquakes in the South Carolina Coastal Plain based on paleoliquefaction data, *J. Geophys. Res.* **106,** no. B4, 6621–6642, doi: 10.1029/2000JB900398.

Thompson, E. M., O. S. Boyd, D. Churchwell, and M. P. Moschetti (2023). Central and eastern U.S. earthquake ground motion database: 2010 to 2020, *Center for Engineering Strong Motion Data (CESMD)*, doi: 10.5066/P9HX7MYG.

Tuttle, M. P., H. Al-Shukri, H. Mahdi, R. Hussein, T. Ameen, S. L. Forman, K. Dyer-Williams, K. Tucker, M. Kopper, *et al.* (2026). Repeated large magnitude earthquakes in the Marianna area of east-central Arkansas during the Middle-Early Holocene and possibly the Late Pleistocene, *Seismol. Res. Lett.* doi: 10.1785/0220250324.

Tuttle, M. P., E. S. Schweig III, J. Campbell, P. M. Thomas, J. D. Sims, and R. H. Lafferty III (2005). Evidence for New Madrid earthquakes in A.D. 300 and 2350 B.C., *Seismol. Res. Lett.* **76,** no. 4, 489–501, doi: 10.1785/gssrl.76.4.489.

Tuttle, M. P., L. W. Wolf, M. E. Starr, P. Villamor, R. H. Lafferty, J. E. Morrow, R. J. Scott, S. L. Forman, K. Hess, K. Tucker, *et al.* (2019). Evidence for large New Madrid earthquakes about A.D. 0 and 1050 B.C., central United States, *Seismol. Res. Lett.* **90,** no. 3, 1393–1406, doi: 10.1785/0220180371.

Vanneste, K., M. Onvani, and K. Van Noten (2026). The BELSHAKE database of earthquake ground motion in Belgium, *Seismol. Res. Lett.* doi: 10.1785/0220250321.

Wheeler, R. L. (2011). Reassessment of stable continental regions of southeast Asia, *Seismol. Res. Lett.* **82,** no. 6, 971–983, doi: 10.1785/gssrl.82.6.971.

Whitehead, B. A., M. Janse van Rensburg, D. A. Quiros, R. A. Sloan, and B. Kahle (2026). An intraplate seismic swarm in the Karoo basin, South Africa, highlights the presence of critically stressed faults in an area of proposed shale gas exploration, *Seismol. Res. Lett.* doi: 10.1785/0220250325.

Xin, L., R. Wang, L. He, Z. Guo, L. Yang, Z. He, and D. Zuo (2026). Rapid seismicity monitoring after the March 2023 M_S 4.5 earthquake around the Xinfengjiang Reservoir, China, *Seismol. Res. Lett.* doi: 10.1785/0220250262.

Zhang, Y.-H., H. Pan, J. Cheng, and M. Zhang (2024). Research on paleoearthquake and recurrence characteristics of strong earthquakes in active faults of mainland China, *Appl. Geophys.*, doi: 10.1007/s11770-024-1125-4.

Zou, J., H. He, Y. Yokoyama, A. D. Sproson, Y. Shirahama, Y. Zhou, Z. Wei, F. Shi, and S. Geng (2021). Identification of paleoearthquakes and coseismic slips on a normal fault using high-precision quantitative morphology: Application to the Jiaocheng fault in the Shanxi Rift, China, *Lithosphere* **2021,** no. S2, 550879, doi: 10.2113/2021/2550879.

Wang, Z., C. Ren, L. Wang, L. Chang, and Y. Zhou (2026). Source complexity and faulting heterogeneity of the 2024 M_W 4.8 Zhongdian earthquake, Yunnan, China, *Seismol. Res. Lett.* doi: 10.1785/0220250259.

Manuscript received 3 January 2026
Published online 10 February 2026

Late Quaternary Fault Activity Along the Eastern Margin Fault of the Daxing Uplift, Southeast Beijing, China, and Implications for the Rupture Behavior of Intraplate Earthquakes

Yanbao Li[1], Zhengfang Li[*1], Bengang Zhou[1], Jun Ma[1], and Mingming Han[2]

Abstract

The mechanisms of seismic rupture behavior for large intraplate earthquakes remain poorly resolved. One important reason is the lack of sufficient paleoseismic data to constrain the spatiotemporal patterns of late Quaternary fault activity. In this study, we used drilling, paleoseismic trenching, radiocarbon dating, and optically stimulated luminescence dating methods to first show that the blind eastern margin fault of the Daxing uplift (EFDU), southeast Beijing, has been active during the Holocene. The most recent paleoseismic event was constrained to have occurred at 6280 ± 250 cal B.P., whereas the fault has showed a low vertical slip rate of ~0.3 mm/yr since the late Pleistocene. Our results suggest that the fault did not rupture during the M 8 Sanhe–Pinggu earthquake in A.D. 1679, which was associated with the Xiadian fault to the north, indicating a fault segmentation rupture pattern between the two faults. Compared with these two faults and previous results for the North China Plain, we hypothesize that the slowly deforming intraplate active faults might have ruptured less regularly in terms of recurrence intervals. Considering the long-elapsed timing of the blind EFDU, future seismic risk should be a particular focus because of its location in the southern part of the densely populated Beijing Plain.

Cite this article as Li, Y., Z. Li, B. Zhou, J. Ma, and M. Han (2025). Late Quaternary Fault Activity Along the Eastern Margin Fault of the Daxing Uplift, Southeast Beijing, China, and Implications for the Rupture Behavior of Intraplate Earthquakes, *Seismol. Res. Lett.* **97**, 626–636, doi: 10.1785/0220250180.

Supplemental Material

Introduction

Large intraplate earthquakes have caused the most fatalities in human history (Dubar *et al.*, 1992), yet they remain poorly resolved, particularly with respect to the spatiotemporal deformational patterns of late Quaternary fault activity (Obermeier *et al.*, 1991; Stein and Newman, 2004, 2012; Hough, 2014; Calais *et al.*, 2016; Vallage and Bollinger, 2020). Moreover, large intraplate earthquakes may occur on blind active faults that might be more destructive in densely populated regions (Yin *et al.*, 2015). How these blind faults accommodate regional deformation and interact with each other in an intraplate setting remains uncertain (Liu, Stein, and Wang, 2011). Answering the aforementioned questions could help us better understand the deformational mechanism of active faults and be useful for systematic mitigation of large earthquakes.

The North China Plain, located in eastern China, features a complex blind fault system capable of generating destructive intraplate earthquakes (Yin and Nie, 1993; Liu, Stein, and Wang, 2011; Yu *et al.*, 2019). In the history of the region, many catastrophic earthquakes have occurred (Fig. 1a), such as the **M** 8½ Tancheng earthquake in A.D. 1668, the **M** 8 Sanhe–Pinggu earthquake in A.D. 1679, the **M** 7.2 Xingtai earthquake in A.D. 1966, and the **M** 7.8 Tangshan earthquake in A.D. 1976 (Department of Earthquake Disaster Prevention, China Earthquake Administration, 1995, 1999; Yin *et al.*, 2020). Among these earthquakes, the A.D. 1679 event has been a particular focus because its historically recorded epicenter occurs very close to Beijing, the capital of China, indicating enormous seismic risk in the future (Xu *et al.*, 1996, 2002; Guo *et al.*, 2011; Yu *et al.*, 2019) (Fig. 1b). It has been suggested that the Xiadian fault (XDF in Fig. 1b) caused the A.D. 1679 event (Xiang *et al.*, 1988; Ran *et al.*, 1997). However, the surface

1. State Key Laboratory of Earthquake Dynamics and Forecasting, Institute of Geology, China Earthquake Administration, Beijing, China, https://orcid.org/0000-0003-0513-1440 (YL); https://orcid.org/0000-0003-0667-7808 (BZ); https://orcid.org/0000-0002-8866-0833 (JM); 2. Chengdu Center of China Geological Survey, Geosciences Innovation Center of Southwest China, Chengdu, Sichuan, China

*Corresponding author: lizhengfang@ies.ac.cn

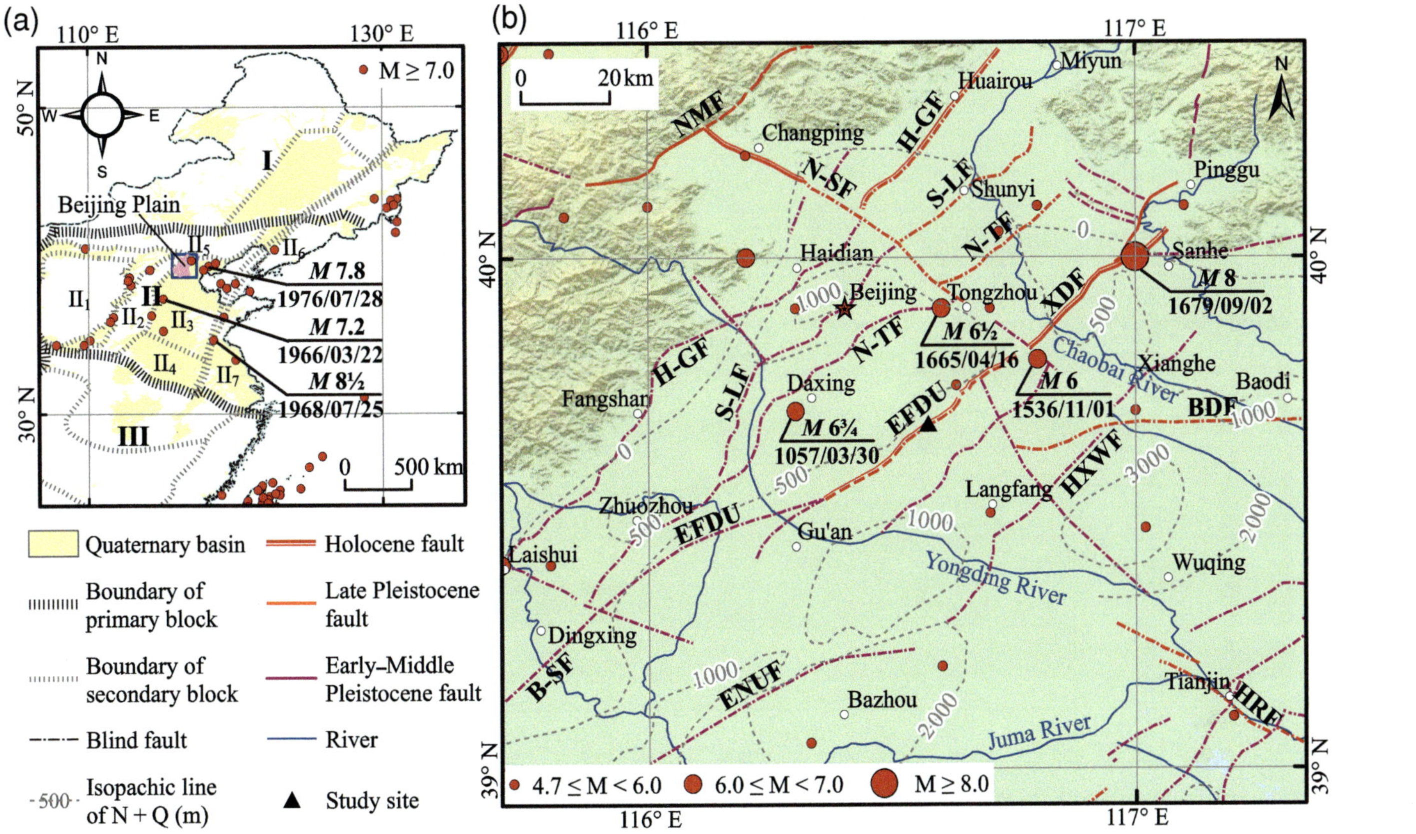

Figure 1. (a) Distribution of active blocks in the North China Plain. The rectangular box indicates the area of panel (b), and the purple polygon indicates the range of the Beijing Plain. (b) Tectonic and topographic map of the eastern margin fault of the Daxing uplift (after Deng *et al.* (2007)). **I** indicates northeast China block region; **II** indicates North China block region: II_1 indicates Ordos block, II_2 indicates Tai-hang Mountains block, II_3 indicates North China Plain block, II_4 indicates Hehuai Plain block, II_5 indicates Yinshan–Yanshan block, II_6 indicates Jiaoliao block, and II_7 indicates Jiangsu–Shanghai–South Yellow Sea block; and **III** indicates South China block region. B-SF, Baoding–Shijiazhuang fault; BDF, Baodi fault; EFDU, eastern margin fault of the Daxing uplift; ENUF, eastern Niutuozhen uplift margin fault; H-GF, Huangzhuang–Gaoliying fault; HRF, Hai River fault; HXWF, Hexiwu fault; N-SF, Nankou–Sunhe fault; N-TF, Nanyuan–Tongxian fault; NMF, Nankou Mountain piedmont fault; S-LF, Shunyi–Liangxiang fault; XDF, Xiadian fault. N + Q denotes the sum of Neogene and Quaternary deposits.

rupture length of earthquakes is only ~12 km (Xiang *et al.*, 1988; Yu *et al.*, 2019), which is obviously not consistent with the relationship between the earthquake magnitude and rupture length (Deng *et al.*, 1992; Wells and Coppersmith, 1994). The Daxing uplift, recognized as one of the distinctive basin-and-range structures within the North China Plain, has undergone development since the Eocene–Oligocene epoch (Xu *et al.*, 2001). Recent studies have shown that the blind eastern margin fault of the Daxing uplift (EFDU) (Fig. 1), connected to the XDF in southern China, was likely active during the late Quaternary period on the basis of geophysical prospecting and drilling data without trenching and precise dating constraints (Institute of Geology, China Earthquake Administration, 1985; Gao and Ma, 1993; Li *et al.*, 2024). Therefore, the following questions arise: has the seismogenic structure responsible for the A.D. 1679 earthquake been underestimated? Could the earthquake exhibit a cascaded rupture behavior along with the blind EFDU? How do these blind faults interact and accommodate regional deformation with the XDF? Determining the late Quaternary fault activity of the EFDU could be critical for resolving the aforementioned issues, which is also important for assessing the future seismic risk in Beijing.

Herein, we used a combination of drilling and paleoseismic trenching, radiocarbon (^{14}C), and optically stimulated luminescence (OSL) dating methods to reveal the fault activity of the blind EFDU. We suggest that the fault was active during the Holocene with a low deformation rate but did not rupture during the A.D. 1679 earthquake, which indicates that the two seismogenic faults might have been affected by the Nankou–Sunhe fault (N-SF) that potentially served as a structural boundary.

Geological Background

The Beijing Plain, located in the northern part of the North China craton, has been jointly surrounded by the

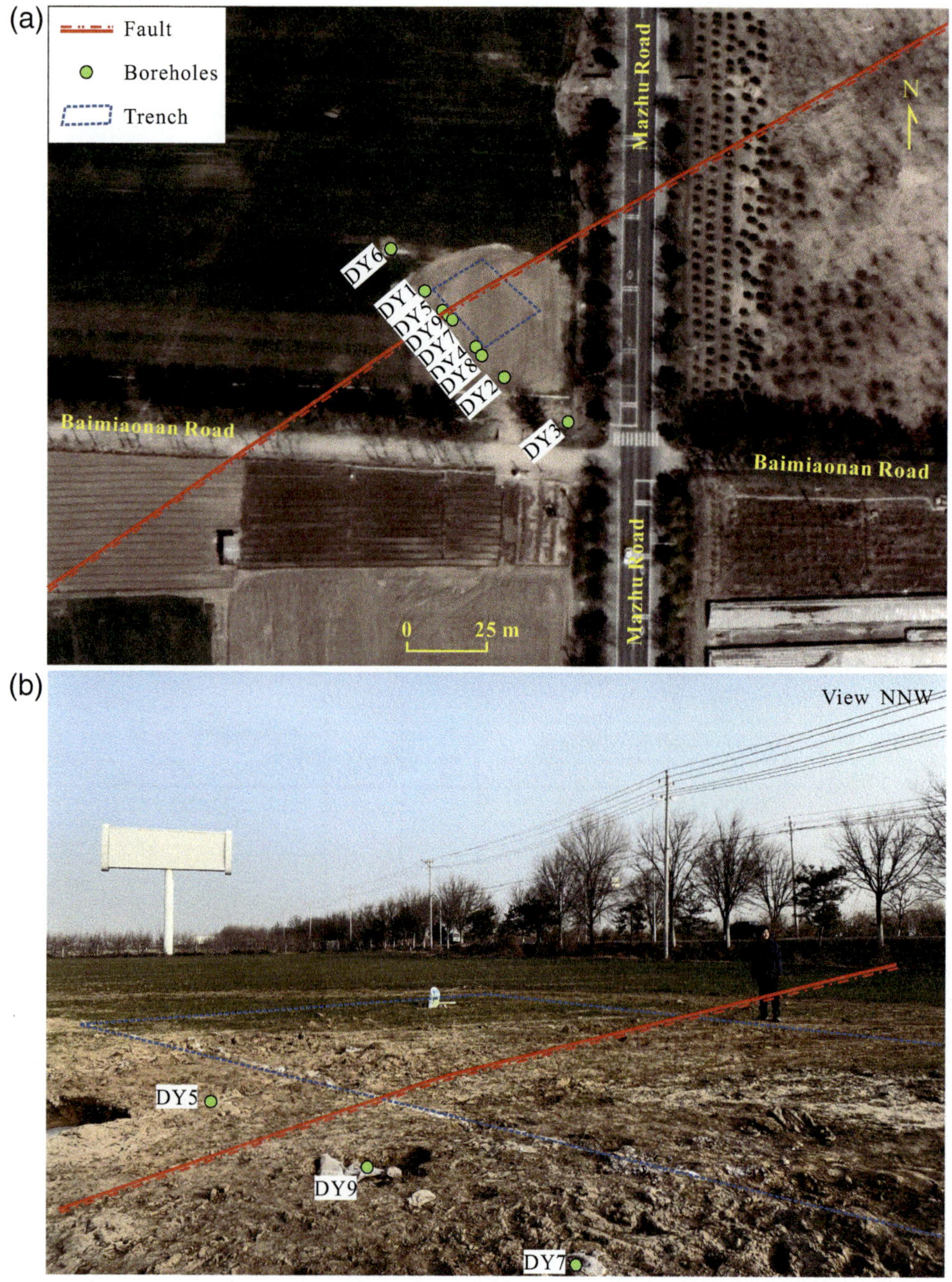

Figure 2. (a) Satellite image of the study site showing the locations of the EFDU, drill holes and trenches. (b) Photo of the study site. NNW, north-northwest.

east-northeast Taihang Mountain belt, the east–west Yanshan belt, and the North China Plain subsidence belt (Fig. 1a). The major seismogenic faults in this region are buried below thick (~300–1200 m) Quaternary sediments (Fig. 1) (Xu *et al.*, 1996, 2002; Guo *et al.*, 2011; Yu *et al.*, 2019). The distribution characteristics of the thicknesses of Neogene and Quaternary sediments indicate that these faults have experienced long-term structural deformation (Xu *et al.*, 1996). Geometrically, these faults can be divided into two groups based on fault strikes: northeast-striking faults and northwest-striking faults. The northeast-striking faults, encompassing more than five parallel faults, might have experienced more intense Holocene activity than the northwest-striking faults did, whereas the active northwest-striking N-SF fault offset most northeast-striking faults (Fig. 1b) (Deng *et al.*, 2007; Li *et al.*, 2024). The N-SF fault predominantly exhibits left-lateral strike-slip deformation, spanning a length of roughly 80 km. From drilling data and trenching studies (Zhang *et al.*, 2008; Zhao *et al.*, 2023), 13 paleoseismic events have been identified over the past 60,000 yr.

The XDF–EFDU fault zone, the largest northeast-striking fault in this area, controls the eastern margin of the Daxing uplift, which is characterized by shear deformation with a high dip angle at depth and offsets the Moho (Liu, Zhang, *et al.*, 2011; He *et al.*, 2013, 2020; Zhao *et al.*, 2013; Wang *et al.*, 2017). Moreover, previous studies have indicated that the EFDU demonstrates a similar deep-shallow fault structure and shows a seismic potential comparable to that of the XDF (Yu *et al.*, 2019; Niu *et al.*, 2023). Several historical recorded earthquakes, such as an **M** 6¾ earthquake in A.D. 1057, an **M** 6 earthquake in A.D. 1536, and an **M** 6½ earthquake in A.D. 1665, occurred near the EFDU (Department of Earthquake Disaster Prevention, China Earthquake Administration, 1995, 1999).

Interpretation of the Douying Drilling Data

To reveal the late Quaternary fault activity of the EFDU, we conducted drilling and paleoseismic trenching in farmland in the southern part of Douying village, Changziying town, Daxing District, Beijing (Fig. 2). Although the farmland

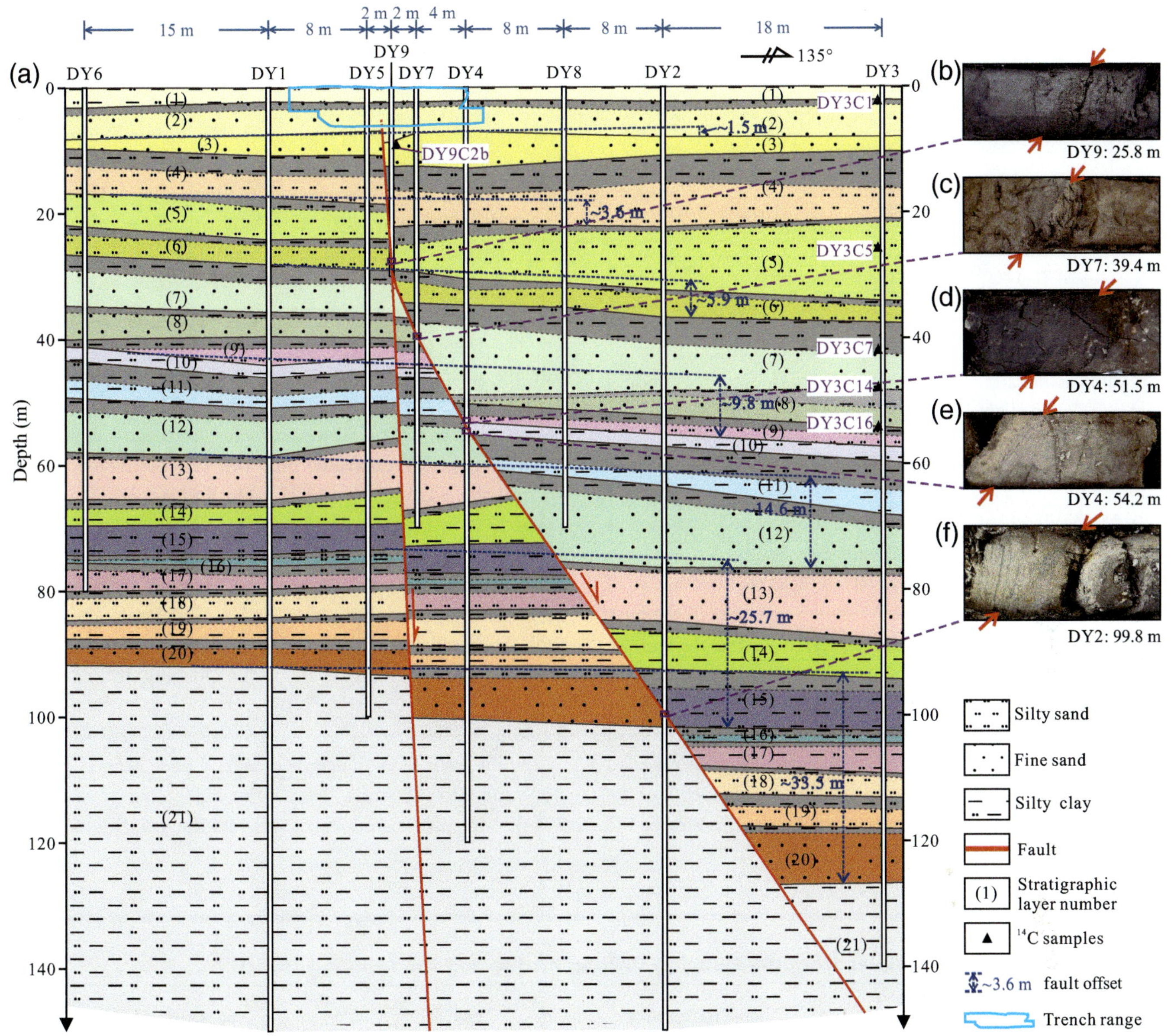

Figure 3. (a) Map showing the comprehensive interpretation of the Douying joint borehole geological profile (after Li *et al.*, 2024). (b–f) Close-up photographs showing fault details revealed in boreholes DY2, DY4, DY7, and DY9.

exhibits no fault-related geomorphic evidence, we chose the study site on the basis of the geophysical prospecting and drilling results of Li *et al.* (2024). The Douying drilling profile is 65 m long and comprises nine boreholes (DY1–DY9), each with a diameter of 108 mm. The minimum horizontal borehole spacing is 2 m, and the maximum and minimum drilling depths are ~150 and 30 m, respectively. The core recovery rate of the boreholes exceeded 90%.

The borehole cores revealed Quaternary sedimentary sequences dominated by fine-grained sand and silty clay, exhibiting well-defined cyclic stratigraphic features. No coarse-grained sediment (e.g., gravel or coarse sand) was observed in the boreholes. The fine sand was mainly yellow, locally gray, or green. The silty clay was mainly grayish-black and earthy yellow in the shallow part (above 60 m) and gradually became brownish yellow in the deep part. According to the lithology and cyclic stratigraphic features, the drilling strata can be divided into 21 layers, namely, layers (1)–(21) (from young to old), as shown in Figure 3. For the detailed descriptions of each layer, see Table S1, available in the supplemental material to this article.

In the boreholes, we collected a series of ^{14}C samples and obtained six dating results (Table 1). As shown in Figure 4, the age results indicated a linear relationship with the burial depth of the samples. According to the slope of the fitting curve shown in Figure 4, the average sedimentation rate has been ~1.7 mm/yr since the middle–late stage of the late Pleistocene (~35,000 yr ago). According to Zhao *et al.*

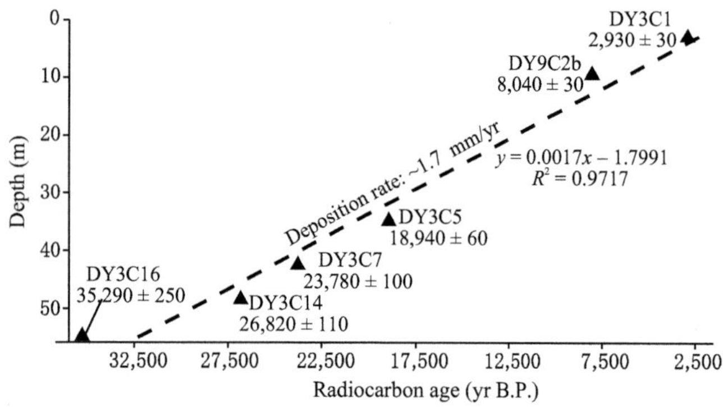

Figure 4. Diagram of the change in radiocarbon age with stratigraphic horizon. The dashed line denotes the fitted trend line, which is a linear fit, and its slope denotes the average formation deposition rate.

(2019), the depth of the Holocene bottom near this region is ~17.35 m, which is consistent with our results.

The Douying drilling boreholes revealed multiple pieces of evidence of fault deformation. As shown in Figure 3, the fault clearly offset the top of layer (3), which may have affected the bottom of layer (2), but the top of layer (2) is very flat. Because the strata indicate clear cycle characteristics, including composition and color, the offset of each stratum on the two sides of the fault can be compared. The measurement results revealed that the relationships between the offset and burial depth of the marker layers are consistent. In other words, the greater the burial depth is, the greater the cumulative offset of the fault. For example, the offset of layer (3) with the smallest burial depth was ~1.5 m; the offsets of layers (5), (7), (9), (12), and (15) with successively greater burial depths were 3.6, 5.9, 9.8, 14.6, and 25.7 m, respectively. The deepest buried layer (21) showed the maximum offset of ~33.5 m. In addition, fault planes were directly observed in boreholes DY2, DY4, DY7, and DY9 at depths of ~99.8, 54.2, 39.4, and 25.8 m, respectively (Fig. 3b–f).

Interpretation of the Douying Trench

On the basis of the Douying drilling profile, we could not directly determine whether the bottom of layer (2) was offset by the fault. Therefore, we opened the Douying trench to obtain more evidence. However, owing to trench collapse and water seepage, we excavated only two benches in the trench, which were ~18 m long, 18 m wide, and 6.0 m deep. Layer (1) and a large part of layer (2) exposed by the Douying drilling profile were also revealed in the trench (Figs. 3, 5, and 6). The stratigraphic units determined through trenching can be divided into 10 units, that is, U1–U10 (from bottom to top). Among them, U1–U8 and U9–U10 were consistent with layers (2) and (1), respectively, in the Douying drilling profile (Fig. 3). The characteristics of each unit are described in Table 2.

On the basis of evidence such as fault offset, sand liquefaction, and growth strata (McCalpin, 2009; Ran *et al.*, 2012, 2014), one paleoseismic event was identified in the two walls

TABLE 1
Radiocarbon and OSL Samples from the Douying Drilling Profile and the Douying Trench

Sample	Test Method	Dating Results	Material	Sample Location
DY3C1	^{14}C	2,930 ± 30 yr B.P.	Organic sediment	Layer (2), borehole DY3
DY9C2b	^{14}C	8,040 ± 30 yr B.P.	Organic sediment	Layer (3), borehole DY9
DY3C5	^{14}C	18,940 ± 60 yr B.P.	Organic sediment	Layer (5), borehole DY3
DY3C7	^{14}C	23,780 ± 100 yr B.P.	Organic sediment	Layer (7), borehole DY3
DY3C14	^{14}C	26,820 ± 110 yr B.P.	Organic sediment	Layer (8), borehole DY3
DY3C16	^{14}C	35,290 ± 2,500 yr B.P.	Organic sediment	Layer (9), borehole DY3
DYTC1	^{14}C	5,200 ± 30 yr B.P.	Organic sediment	U5, Douying trench
DYTC9	^{14}C	2,910 ± 30 yr B.P.	Organic sediment	Middle of U6, Douying trench
DYTC13	^{14}C	1,800 ± 30 yr B.P.	Organic sediment	Top of U6, Douying trench
DYTS1A	OSL	7.4 ± 0.8 yr	Fine sand	U2, Douying trench
DYTS2A	OSL	6.7 ± 0.4 yr	Fine sand	U3, Douying trench
DYTS5A	OSL	7.6 ± 1.1 yr	Fine sand	U2, Douying trench
DYTS6A	OSL	6.6 ± 0.5 yr	Fine sand	U3, Douying trench

Note: All samples were prepared and analyzed by staff at Beta Analytic, Inc. (Miami, Florida, United States). Radiocarbon ages are expressed as years B.P. relative to 1950. All the optically stimulated luminescence (OSL) samples were tested by staff at the Institute of Geology, China Earthquake Administration.

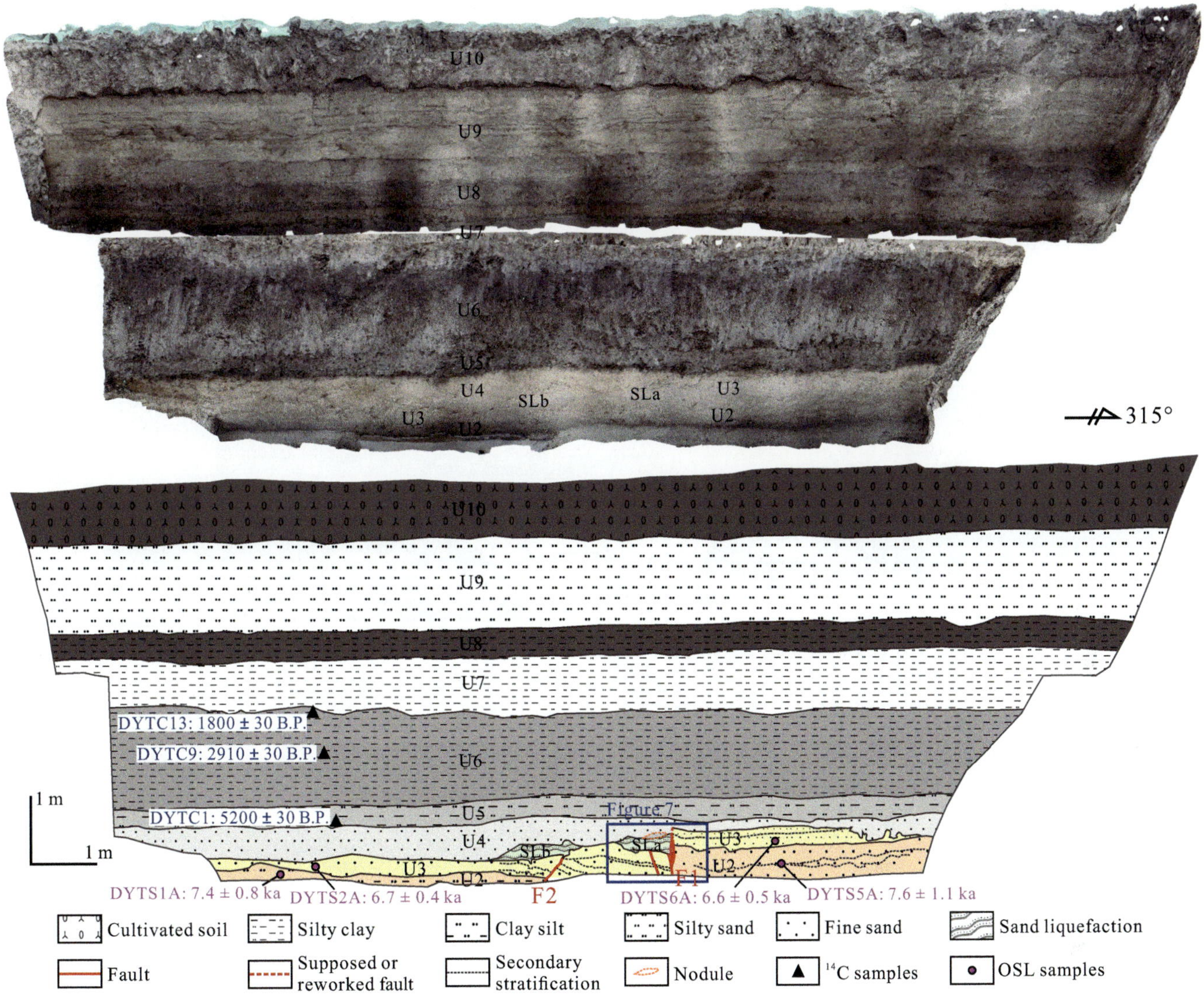

of the trench (Figs. 5–8). The evidence can be summarized as follows: (1) Two branch faults, namely, F1 and F2, were observed in the two walls (Figs. 5 and 6). Specifically, F1 developed into several branches locally and offset U3, which is unconformably covered by U4. (2) U3 was also offset by F2, which is supported by the depositional characteristics of U3 on both sides of the faults, namely, the color, particle size, and bedding direction differed. Moreover, the secondary thin subunit close to the fault demonstrated folding deformation. (3) Sandy lenses developed along F1 with alignment characteristics (Figs. 7 and 8). (4) The thickness of U4 increased gradually away from the fault, and the grain sizes were greater at the bottom with mixed sedimentary facies, which could be interpreted as a growth stratigraphic deposit associated with an earthquake. (5) Sand liquefaction was observed along both F1 and F2. Sand deformed through the fault and showed a mushroom shape, which indicates that the liquefaction event occurred after the deposition of U3. (6) As shown in Figures 7 and 8a, at the bottom of the trench, a fault zone with a width of ~30 cm affected by the fault branches of F1 caused deformation of U3, whereas the tops of U4 and the units overlying U4 were relatively complete, continuous, and flat, indicating that no surface rupture events occurred after the deposition of U4.

Figure 5. Photomosaic of the southwestern wall of the Douying trench and its interpretation. U denotes units. The blue font indicates the number and test results of the ^{14}C samples, and the purple font indicates the number and test results of the OSL samples. SLa and SLb indicate sand liquefaction units.

Slip Rate and Timing of Paleoseismic Events at the EFDU

We used the cumulative offset amount and the corresponding measured ages obtained from the Douying borehole profile to constrain the slip rate of the fault, which is represented by the estimated slope of the dashed line in Figure 9. Specifically, layers (3), (5), (7), (8), and (9) yielded ages of 8,040 ± 30 yr

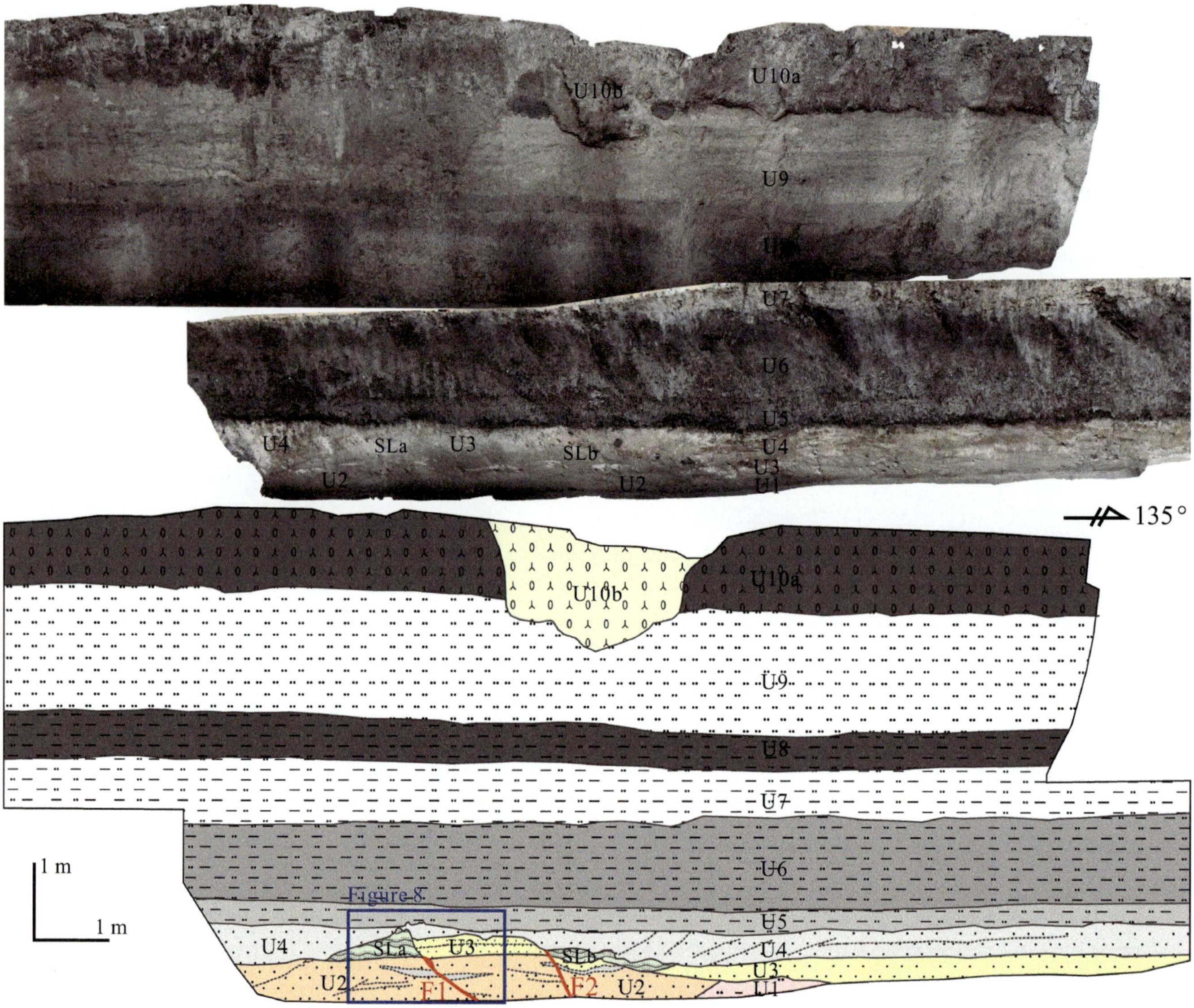

Figure 6. Photomosaic of the northeastern wall of the Douying trench and its interpretation. U denotes units. SLa and SLb indicate sand liquefaction units.

B.P., 18,940 ± 60 yr B.P., 23,780 ± 100 yr B.P., 26,820 ± 110 yr B.P., and 35,290 ± 250 yr B.P., respectively. The corresponding offsets of these layers were ~1.5, 3.6, 5.9, 6.6, and 9.3 m, respectively, which collectively determined the vertical slip rate of the EFDU (~0.3 mm/yr) since the late Pleistocene.

According to paleoseismic analysis of the Douying trench, the most recent seismic event ruptured the surface of the fault after the sedimentation of U3 and before the sedimentation of U4. U3 comprises a set of fine–medium–fine sand layers from which OSL samples were collected for dating. Two age results were obtained, namely, 6.6 ± 0.5 ka and 6.7 ± 0.4 ka, which were relatively stable and consistent with the two results for the lower unit, U2 (7.4 ± 0.8 ka and 7.6 ± 1.1 ka, respectively). Unfortunately, no age was obtained in U4, but a ^{14}C age of 5200 ± 30 yr B.P. was obtained in the overlying strata, U5. Similarly, the ^{14}C ages in the middle and upper layers of shallower unit U6 were 2910 ± 30 yr B.P. and 1800 ± 30 yr B.P., respectively, indicating a consistent stratigraphic sequence in ages. We used the OxCal 4.4 software (Ramsey, 2009) to recalibrate the age of sample DYTC1, which was initially measured at 5200 ± 30 yr B.P., resulting in a more precise age determination of 5965 ± 45 cal B.P. (Fig. S1). Consequently, when we combine this information with the age of the lower unit U3, which was dated at 6.6 ± 0.5 ka B.P. using the OSL sample DYTS6A, we further refine our estimate, concluding that the paleoseismic event occurred ~6280 ± 250 cal B.P. via the arithmetic mean method.

Discussion and Conclusions

Although our trench only constrains one paleoseismic event at the EFDU, the fault was constrained as a Holocene-active fault and did not rupture during the A.D. 1679 event associated with the XDF. Moreover, the Holocene-active N-SF crosses two

TABLE 2
Unit Description from the Douying Trench

Unit No.	Description
U1	This unit comprises gray–green clay silt, with horizontal bedding found only at the bottom of the northeast (NE) wall and is the darkest one among the sandy units revealed by the trench.
U2	This unit comprises light gray–green medium–fine sand (the color shows a tendency to darken with an increasing depth), with occasional nodules (<1 cm and the upper part of the unit contains a higher amount); cross-bedding development occurs.
U3	This unit comprises light grayish–white fine sand to medium–fine sand, containing a small amount of nodules (<0.5 cm), with local horizontal bedding and cross-bedding, and unstable thickness caused by faulting.
U4	This unit comprises yellow medium–fine sand; the bottom part contains more pebbles, the bottom deposit is more chaotic, and gradual upward bedding development is observed. The middle part exhibits cross-bedding development, and the top part exhibits obvious horizontal bedding. This unit in the southeastern plate of the fault is obviously thickened.
U5	This unit comprises gray–black sandy clay, containing more calcareous nodules (<1 cm), with obvious horizontal bedding, and the particles at the bottom are slightly coarser. The layer thickness remains relatively constant.
U6	This unit comprises a thick layer of gray–black sandy clay, with local yellowing and slightly lighter color than U5. A few black nodules and yellow brown nodules (<1 cm) occur, with no obvious bedding. The layer thickness remains relatively constant.
U7	This layer can be divided into two sections. The lower section is gray–black with a small amount of brownish-yellow clay; the upper section is earthy yellow medium–fine sand with obvious horizontal bedding. The color of this layer are slightly lighter than that of U6. The layer thickness remains relatively constant.
U8	This layer comprises gray–black silty clay, which is soft and loose, with darker color than that of U7 and horizontal bedding. The thickness remains constant.
U9	This unit comprises tick layers of yellow sand interlaced with thin layers of gray–yellow to gray–black silty clay (<1 cm thick) with obvious horizontal bedding and noticeably lighter color than U8.
U10	This unit comprises cultivated soil, with plant roots and no bedding structure. U10b in the NE wall comprises backfill material.

faults, namely, the XDF to the north of the N-SF shows surface deformation, whereas the EFDU to the south shows a blind fault structure (Yu *et al.*, 2019), which might indicate that these two faults show a segmentation rupture pattern controlled by the N-SF. Furthermore, the limited extent of ~12 km of coseismic surface ruptures associated with the **M** 8 Sanhe–Pinggu earthquake in A.D. 1679 could potentially be attributed to several factors: (1) The magnitude of the earthquake might have been overestimated based on historical accounts, consistent with the findings of Xu *et al.* (2018), who proposed that the magnitude of the 1303 C.E. Hongdong earthquake in the North China Plain was significantly lower than the previously estimated **M** 8; (2) the presence of a thick, hundred-order deposit layer could have hindered the propagation of coseismic ruptures to the surface, thereby predominantly reducing the length of the observed surface ruptures; and (3) a combination of these two factors.

Considering that parameters such as paleoseismic intervals and slip rates at the EFDU have not yet been reported, we compared our results with those of previous studies focused on the neighboring XDF to the north. Our paleoseismic trenching results suggested that the most recent paleoseismic event associated with the EFDU was constrained to have occurred at 6280 ± 250 cal B.P.. Compared with the XDF, Ran *et al.* (1997) suggested that the average recurrence interval of major earthquakes along the XDF is approximately 6561 ± 691 yr after 20 ka. Since the onset of the Holocene, slip rates along the XDF have been estimated at 0.34 mm/yr, increasing to 0.98 mm/yr over the period from 10 to 21 ka, and further rising to 1.2 mm/yr between 21 and 26 ka, demonstrating temporal variability along the fault (Xu *et al.*, 2000). Recently, Yu *et al.* (2019) excavated trenches that revealed evidence of eight paleoearthquakes, suggesting variable recurrence intervals with a median interval estimated at ~2820 ± 561 yr. Assuming that these two faults exhibit similar paleoseismic intervals, the elapsed time at the EFDU may significantly exceed the average interval of paleoseismic events observed along the XDF, thereby pointing to a heightened seismic risk in the future. Moreover, our drilling data indicate a slip rate of ~0.3 mm/yr at the EFDU since the late Pleistocene. If we conservatively consider a comparable slip rate to the 0.34 mm/yr observed since the Holocene, and given that the longest recurrence interval for the XDF is estimated at 5830 ± 500 yr (Xu *et al.*, 2000), the elapsed time at the EFDU also approaches this extended interval, further underscoring the potential for a significant seismic event.

The aforementioned results indicate that the two faults exhibit variations in paleoseismic rupture behavior with a

If so, the blind active fault in the North China Plain might be more dangerous because surface active faults released long-term strain accumulation related to historical record earthquakes, whereas those blind active faults without earthquake records might be ready to rupture, such as the active faults responsible for the 1966 **M** 7.2 Xingtai and 1976 **M** 7.8 Tangshan earthquakes, which were not known until after earthquake disaster occurrence and produced surface ruptures (Yin *et al.*, 2015).

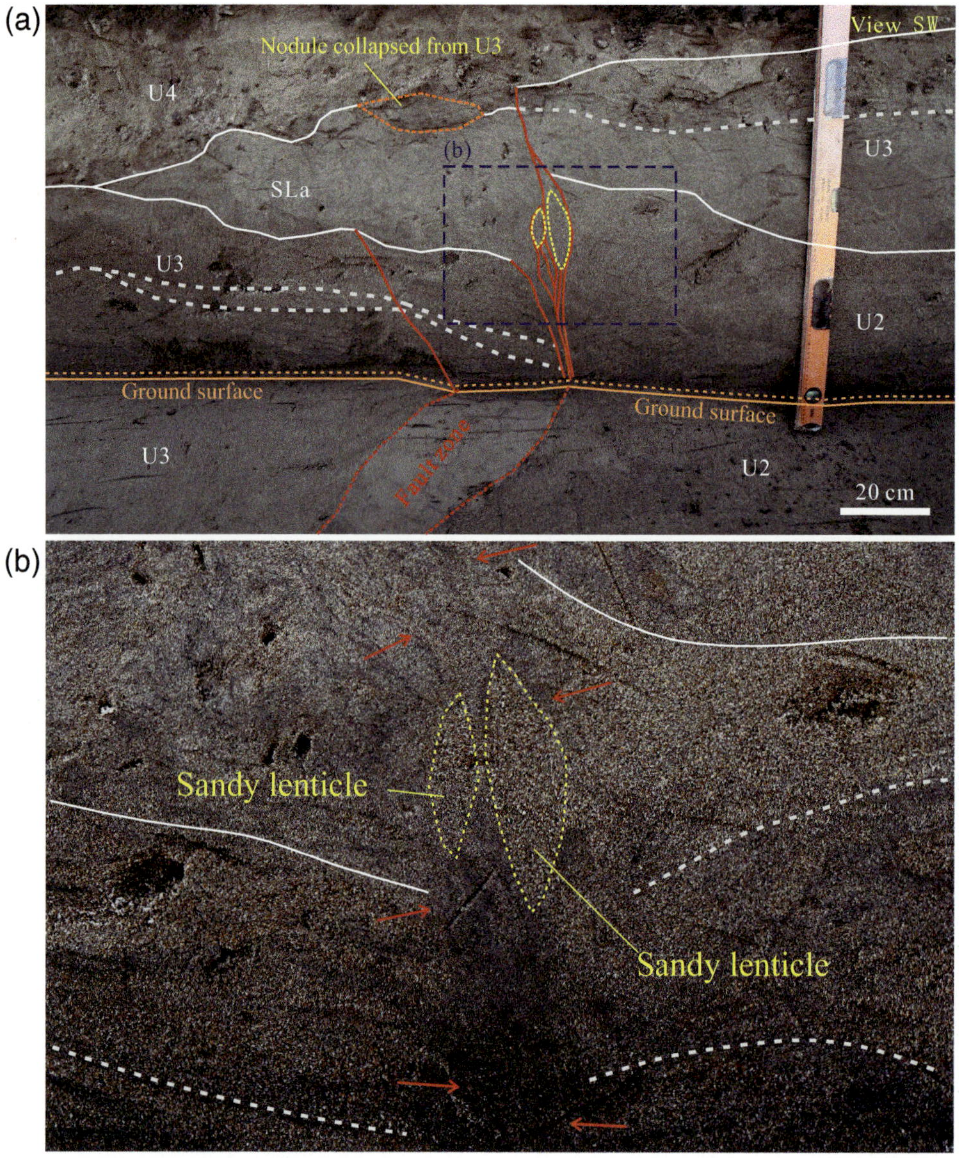

Figure 7. (a,b) Close-up views of the offsets revealed in the southwestern wall of the Douying trench. The solid white lines indicate stratigraphic boundaries, and the dashed lines indicate stratigraphic stratification. The red lines and arrows indicate faults. The brown double line indicates the ground plane. U denotes units. SLa indicates the number of sand liquefaction units. SW, southwest.

Data and Resources

Fault surface trace data were obtained from the Seismic Active Fault Survey Data Center (https://Activefault-datacenter.cn/map; last accessed May 2023). The locations of the earthquakes shown in Figure 1 were provided by the China Earthquake Administration, and they can be released to the public. Digital elevation model (DEM) data were obtained from the Shuttle Radar Topography Mission (SRTM; https://srtm.csi.cgiar.org/srtmdata/; last accessed October 2022). The supplemental material includes a table that provides detailed descriptions of the strata layers revealed by our drilling holes and a figure that provides the calibrated result of the OxCal software for the radiocarbon age.

low slip rate. Similarly, paleoseismic events along the Reelfoot fault in the slowly deforming New Madrid seismic zone, United States, also showed clustered paleoseismic intervals. Specifically, the trench results indicated a period of quiescence from at least 11 to 4.4 ka, followed by four major seismic events clustering in the 1811–1812 C.E. sequence (Gold *et al.*, 2019). Liu, Stein, and Wang (2011) summarized earthquake records from North China covering a 2000-year period and suggested that for intraplate earthquakes, slow tectonic loading is accommodated collectively by a complex system of interacting faults, each of which can remain active for a short period after long dormancy.

Declaration of Competing Interests

The authors acknowledge that there no conflicts of interest recorded.

Acknowledgments

This work was supported by the National Key Research and Development Program of China (Grant Number 2022YFC3003501). The authors sincerely acknowledge Qinjian Tian, Jian Wu, Wei Min, Shimin Zhang, Zhikun Ren, and Feng Li for their help and suggestions in the field. The authors give great thanks to Susan Hough, Seth Stein, and an anonymous reviewer for their constructive suggestions to improve this article.

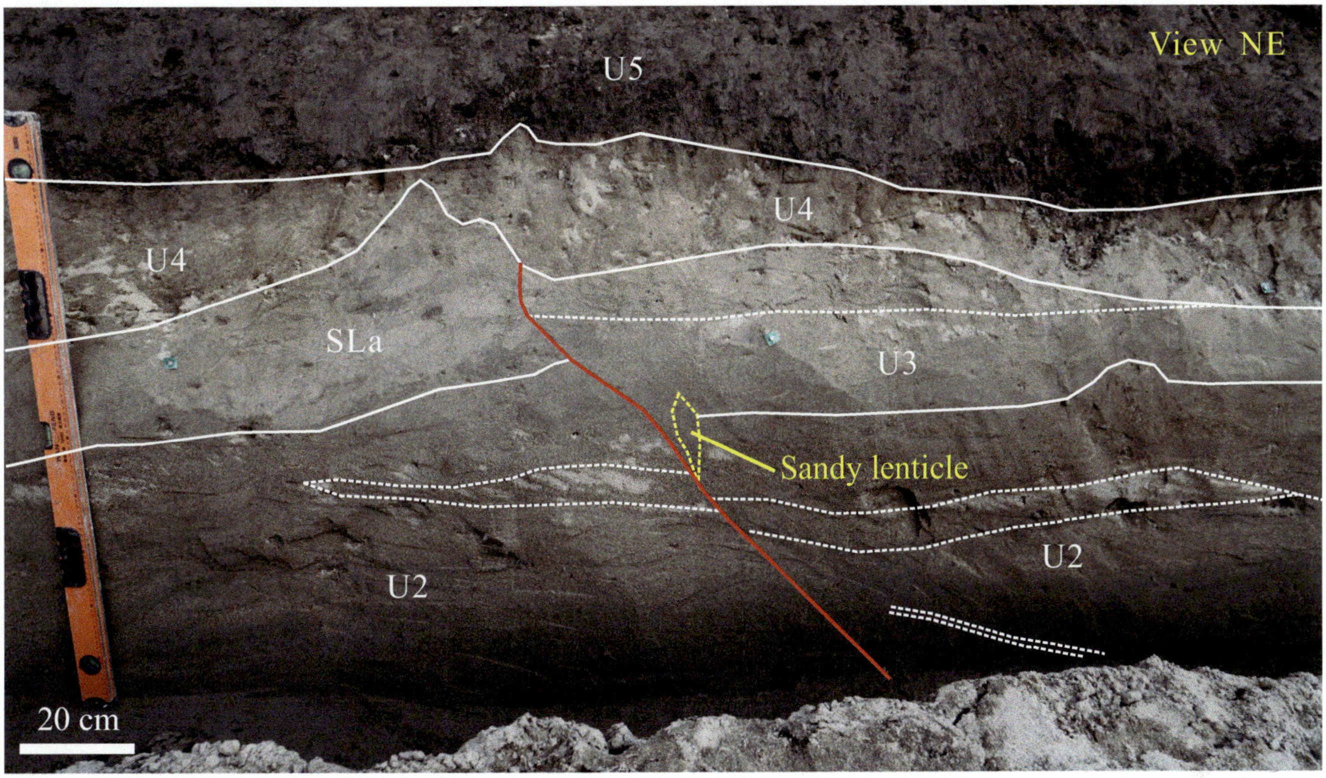

Figure 8. Close-up views of the offsets revealed in the northeastern part of the Douying trench. The solid white lines indicate stratigraphic boundaries, and the dashed lines indicate stratigraphic stratification. The red lines indicate faults. SLa indicates the number of sand liquefaction units. NE, northeast.

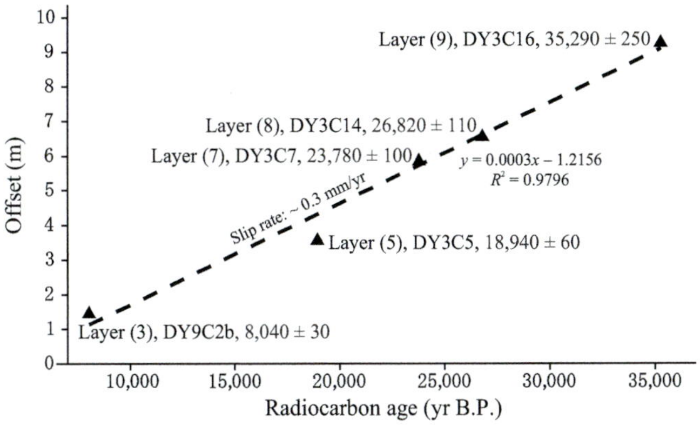

Figure 9. Diagram of the change in radiocarbon age with offset of stratigraphic layers at different burial depths. The dashed line denotes the fitted trend line, which is a linear fit, and its slope denotes the fault-slip rate.

References

Calais, E., T. Camelbeeck, S. Stein, M. Liu, and T. J. Craig (2016). A new paradigm for large earthquakes in stable continental plate interiors, *Geophys. Res. Lett.* **43,** 10,621–10,637.

Deng, Q., Y. Ran, X. Yang, W. Min, and Q. Chu (2007). *Active Tectonics Map of China*, Seismological Press, Beijing.

Deng, Q., G. Yu, and W. Ye (1992). *Study on the Relations Between Parameters of Surface Rupture and Magnitude*, Institute of Geology, China Earthquake Administration, Research on Active Fault, Seismological Press, Beijing, 247–294.

Department of Earthquake Disaster Prevention, China Earthquake Administration (1995). *Catalog of Chinese Historical Strong Earthquakes (2300 BC-1911 AD)*, Seismological Press, Beijing.

Department of Earthquake Disaster Prevention, China Earthquake Administration (1999). *Catalog of Earthquakes in Modern China (1912 AD ~ 1990 AD, Ms≥4.7)*, Seismological Press, Beijing.

Dubar, P. K., P. A. Lockridge, and L. S. Whiteside (1992). Catalog of significant earthquakes 2150 B.C.–1991 A.D. Including quantitative casual ties and damage, *National Geophysical Data Center Technical Rept. SE-49*, U.S. Department of Commerce, National Oceanic and Atmospheric Administration, Environmental Data and Information Service, National Geophysical Data Center, Boulder, Colorado.

Gao, W., and J. Ma (1993). *Seismo-Geological Background and Earthquake Hazard in Beijing Area*, Seismological Press, Beijing.

Gold, R. D., C. B. DuRoss, J. E. Delano, R. W. Jibson, R. W. Briggs, S. A. Mahan, R. A. Williams, and D. R. Corbett (2019). Four major Holocene earthquakes on the Reelfoot fault recorded by Sackungen in the New Madrid seismic zone, USA, *J. Geophys. Res.* **124,** 3105–3126.

Guo, H., W. Jiang, and X. Xie (2011). Late-quaternary strong earthquakes on the seismogenic fault of the 1976 Ms7.8 Tangshan earthquake, Hebei, as revealed by drilling and trenching, *Sci. China Earth Sci.* **54,** 1696–1715.

He, F., L. Bai, J. Wang, Y. Liu, X. Cai, Y. Sun, L. Zhang, T. Fang, and G. Guo (2013). Deep structure and quaternary activities of the Xiadian fault zone, *Seismol. Geol.* **35,** 490–505.

He, F. B., X. W. Xu, Z. J. He, X. L. Zhang, L. Y. Liu, W. Zhang, B. Wei, and J. B. Ni (2020). Research on neogene-quaternary stratigraphic structure and shallow tectonic features in the north section of Daxing fault zone based on shallow seismic reflection profiling, *Seismol. Geol.* **42,** 893–908.

Hough, S. E. (2014). *Intraplate Seismic Hazard: Evidence for Distributed Strain and Implications for Seismic Hazard,* Cambridge University Press, Cambridge, 303–327.

Institute of Geology, China Earthquake Administration (1985). *Neotectonic Map of Hebei Plain and Adjacent Regions,* Seismological Press, Beijing.

Li, Z., B. Zhou, and Y. Li (2024). Discovery of a buried active fault to the south of the 1679 M8. 0 Sanhe–Pinggu earthquake in the North China plain: Evidence from seismic reflection exploration and drilling profile, *Lithosphere* **2024,** doi: 10.2113/2024/lithosphere_2023_301.

Liu, B. J., X. K. Zhang, Y. Chen, S. Y. Feng, J. F. Ji, H. K. Yuan, and Y. Zuo (2011). Research on crustal structure and active fault in the Sanhe-Pinggu earthquake (M8. 0) zone based on single-fold deep seismic reflection and shallow seismic reflection profiling, *Chin. J. Geophys.* **54,** 1251–1259.

Liu, M., S. Stein, and H. Wang (2011). 2000 years of migrating earthquakes in North China: How earthquakes in midcontinents differ from those at plate boundaries, *Lithosphere* **3,** 128–132.

McCalpin, J. P. (2009). *Paleoseismology,* Academic Press, San Diego.

Niu, W. Z., F. B. He, and Z. H. Liu (2023). Determination of the northeast section of the Nanyuan–Tongxian fault in Beijing and research on its quaternary activity, *J. Geomech.* **29,** 879–887.

Obermeier, S. F., N. R. Bleuer, C. A. Munson, P. J. Munson, W. S. Martin, K. M. McWilliams, D. A. Tabaczynski, J. K. Odum, M. Rubin, and D. L. Eggert (1991). Evidence of strong earthquake shaking in the lower Wabash valley from prehistoric liquefaction features, *Science* **251,** 1061–1063.

Ramsey, C. B. (2009). Bayesian analysis of radiocarbon dates, *Radiocarbon* **51,** 337–360.

Ran, Y. K., Q. D. Deng, X. P. Yang, W. X. Zhang, R. C. Li, and H. F. Xiang (1997). Paleoearthquakes and recurrence interval on the seismogenic fault of 1679 Sanhe-Pinggu M8 earthquake, Hebei and Beijing, *Seismol. Geol.* **19,** 193–201.

Ran, Y. K., Y. B. Li, P. Du, L. C. Chen, and H. Wand (2014). Key techniques and several cases analysis in paleoseismic studies in mainland China (3): Rupture characteristics, environment impact and paleoseismic indicators on normal faults, *Seismol. Geol.* **36,** 287–301.

Ran, Y. K., H. Wang, Y. B. Li, and L. C. Chen (2012). Key techniques and several cases analysis in paleoseismic studies in mainland China (1): Trenching sites, layouts and paleoseismic indicators on active strike-slip faults, *Seismol. Geol.* **34,** 197–210.

Stein, S., and A. Newman (2004). Characteristic and uncharacteristic earthquakes as possible artifacts: Applications to the New Madrid and Wabash seismic zones. *Seismol. Res. Lett.* **75,** 173–187.

Stein, S., R. J. Geller, and M. Liu (2012). Why earthquake hazard maps often fail and what to do about it, *Tectonophysics* **562–563,** 1–25.

Vallage, A., and L. Bollinger (2020). Testing fault models in intraplate settings: A potential for challenging the seismic hazard assessment inputs and hypothesis? *Pure Appl. Geophys.* **177,** 1879–1889.

Wang, C., Q. Wu, Y. Duan, Z. Wang, and H. Lou (2017). Crustal and upper mantle structure and deep tectonic origin of large earthquakes in North China, *Sci. China Earth Sci.* **47,** 684–719.

Wells, D. L., and K. J. Coppersmith (1994). New empirical relationships among magnitude, rupture length, rupture width, rupture area, and surface displacement, *Bull. Seismol. Soc. Am.* **84,** 974–1002.

Xiang, H. F., Z. Fang, J. Xu, R. Li, S. Jia, S. Hao, J. Wang, and W. Zhang (1988). Seismotectonic background and recurrence interval of great earthquakes in 1679 Sanhe-Pinggu M= 8 earthquake area, *Seismol. Geol.* **10,** 29–37.

Xu, J., Z. Gao, J. Sun, and C. Song (2001). A preliminary study of the coupling relationship between basin and mountain in extensional environments—A case study of the Bohai Bay basin and Taihang Mountains, *Acta Geol. Sinica* **75,** 165–174.

Xu, J., L. F. Niu, C. H. Wang, and Z. J. Han (1996). Tangshan-Hejian-Cixian newly-generated seismotectonic zone, *Seismol. Geol.* **18,** 193–198.

Xu, X., F. Ji, G. Yu, W. Chen, F. Wang, and W. Jiang (2000). Reconstruction of paleoearthquakes sequence using stratigraphic records from drill logs: A study at the Xiadian fault, Beijing, *Seismol. Geol.* **22,** 9–19.

Xu, X., W. Wu, X. Zhang, S. Ma, W. Ma, G. Yu, M. Gu, and W. Jiang (2002). *Recent Crustal Tectonic Deformation and Earthquakes in the Beijing Capital Region,* Science Press, Beijing.

Xu, Y., H. He, Q. Deng, M. B. Allen, H. Sun, and L. Bi (2018). The CE 1303 Hongdong earthquake and the Huoshan Piedmont fault, Shanxi graben: Implications for magnitude limits of normal fault earthquakes, *J. Geophys. Res.* **123,** 3098–3121.

Yin, A., and S. Nie (1993). An indentation model for the North and South China collision and the development of the Tan-Lu and Honam fault systems, eastern Asia, *Tectonics* **12,** 801–813.

Yin, A., X. Yu, Z. K. Shen, and J. Liu-Zeng (2015). A possible seismic gap and high earthquake hazard in the North China basin, *Geology* **43,** 19–22.

Yin, X. F., G. M. Zhang, Z. G. Shao, P. Wang, and X. Z. Sun (2020). Research on activity characteristics of strong earthquakes in North China, *Earthquake* **40,** 11–33.

Yu, Z., H. Pan, H. Xi, Y. Zhang, and H. Chen (2019). Late quaternary paleoseismicity of the Xiadian fault in the North China plain with implications for earthquake potential, *J. Asian Earth Sci.* **184,** 103,997.

Zhang, S., D. Wang, X. Liu, G. Zhang, J. Zhao, M. Luo, J. Ren, R. Wang, and Y. Zhang (2008). Using borehole core analysis to reveal Late Quaternary paleoearthquakes along the Nankou-Sunhe fault, Beijing, *Sci. China Earth Sci.* **51,** 1154–1168.

Zhao, C. B., B. J. Liu, J. F. Ji, S. Y. Feng, and J. H. Shi (2013). Fine crustal structure in the south of Beijing revealed by deep seismic reflection profiling, *Chin. J. Geophys.* **56,** 1168–1176.

Zhao, S., Z. Li, Q. Jia, F. Li, Y. Meng, R. Qian, X. Zhou, M. Sun, Z. Qian, and W. Ceng (2023). Recent evidence of slip deformation of the Nankou-Sunhe fault based on paleoseismic results, *Technol. Earthq. Disaster Prev.* **18,** 736–744.

Zhao, Y., R. Li, B. Wei, C. Wang, Y. Sun, and T. Fang (2019). Magnetostratigraphy of borehole PGZ05 in southern Daxing uplift, Beijing plain, *Geoscience* **33,** 56–62.

Manuscript received 1 June 2025
Published online 12 September 2025

Folding Growth Pattern of the Southern Tian Shan: Insights from the 2024 M_w 7.0 Wushi Earthquake and 2020 M_w 6.0 Jiashi Earthquake, Western China

Zhidan Chen[1], Nan Fang[1], Wenbin Xu[*1], Yuan Yao[2], Peng Zhou[1], Lei Xie[1], and Lei Zhao[1]

Abstract

The 2024 M_w 7.0 Wushi and 2020 M_w 6.0 Jiashi earthquakes, two recent large events in the southern Tian Shan, provide rare opportunities for understanding the seismotectonic deformation patterns in compressional orogenic regimes. Here, we utilize Sentinel-1 satellite radar images and Differential Interferometric Synthetic Aperture Radar techniques to map coseismic deformation fields for the 2024 Wushi and 2020 Jiashi earthquakes, occurring at the front and root of the Kepingtage fold-and-thrust belt, respectively. A modified Bayesian nonlinear method is utilized to simultaneously invert fault geometry parameters and slip distributions. Our findings show that both Wushi and Jiashi earthquakes are predominantly characterized by reverse/thrust motions with minor strike-slip components. The spatial continuity of the interferometric fringes and coseismic deformation fields suggests shallow (< 5 km depth) folding deformation in response to deeper reverse/thrust faulting. Specifically, the Wushi earthquake produced a high-angle fault-propagation fold, with fault-slip penetrating into the crystalline basement, whereas the Jiashi earthquake formed a low-angle detachment fold developed within the cover layer. The M_w 5.7 aftershock following the Wushi mainshock compensated for the shallow coseismic slip deficit and generated positive flowerlike ruptures superimposed on the pre-existing mainshock fold deformation, explaining the observed opposite dip direction of the aftershock rupture compared to the mainshock mechanism. These two fold-type earthquakes demonstrate the dominance of folding deformation in accommodating crustal shortening and orogenic growth in the southern Tian Shan, elucidating compressional tectonic processes.

Cite this article as Chen, Z., N. Fang, W. Xu, Y. Yao, P. Zhou, L. Xie, and L. Zhao (2025). Folding Growth Pattern of the Southern Tian Shan: Insights from the 2024 M_w 7.0 Wushi Earthquake and 2020 M_w 6.0 Jiashi Earthquake, Western China, *Seismol. Res. Lett.* **97**, 637–650, doi: 10.1785/0220250135.

Supplemental Material

Introduction

The deformation patterns by which intracontinental compressional orogens accommodate crustal shortening are critical for understanding intraplate tectonic deformation, earthquake generation, long-distance stress propagation, and mountain building processes (Molnar and Tapponnier, 1975; Tapponnier and Molnar, 1979; Avouac and Tapponnier, 1993; Yin *et al.*, 1998; Zhang *et al.*, 2004; Royden *et al.*, 2008). As a typical intracontinental compressional orogenic belt, the Tian Shan ("Shan" means "mountains" in Chinese) orogenic belt has undergone substantial crustal shortening and consequent mountain building due to far-field impact induced by the ongoing India-Eurasia collision (Fig. 1a) (Avouac *et al.*, 1993; Sobel and Dumitru, 1997; Yin *et al.*, 1998). On both flanks of the Tian Shan, a series of nearly east–west-trending foreland fold-and-thrust belts have developed as a result of north–south compressional forces (Avouac *et al.*, 1993; Sobel and Dumitru, 1997; Yin *et al.*, 1998; Allen *et al.*, 1999; Deng *et al.*, 2003). These belts are deemed to accommodate most of the crustal shortening across the Tian Shan (Yang, Li, and Wang, 2008; Wu *et al.*, 2023). However, the relative contributions of folding versus faulting in accommodating crustal shortening and driving mountain uplift in the Tian Shan remain controversial.

The Kepingtage fold-and-thrust belt (FTB) is a key active structure accommodating crustal shortening of the Tian Shan, formed during the propagation of the orogenic belt toward the Tarim basin (Fig. 1b,c). Previous studies suggest

1. School of Geosciences and Info-Physics, Central South University, Changsha, China, https://orcid.org/0000-0001-6015-3963 (ZC); https://orcid.org/0000-0001-6461-7219 (NF); https://orcid.org/0000-0001-7294-8229 (WX); https://orcid.org/0000-0003-0398-1476 (LX); 2. Urumqi Institute of Central Asia Earthquake, China Earthquake Administration, Urumqi, China

*Corresponding author: wenbin.xu@csu.edu.cn

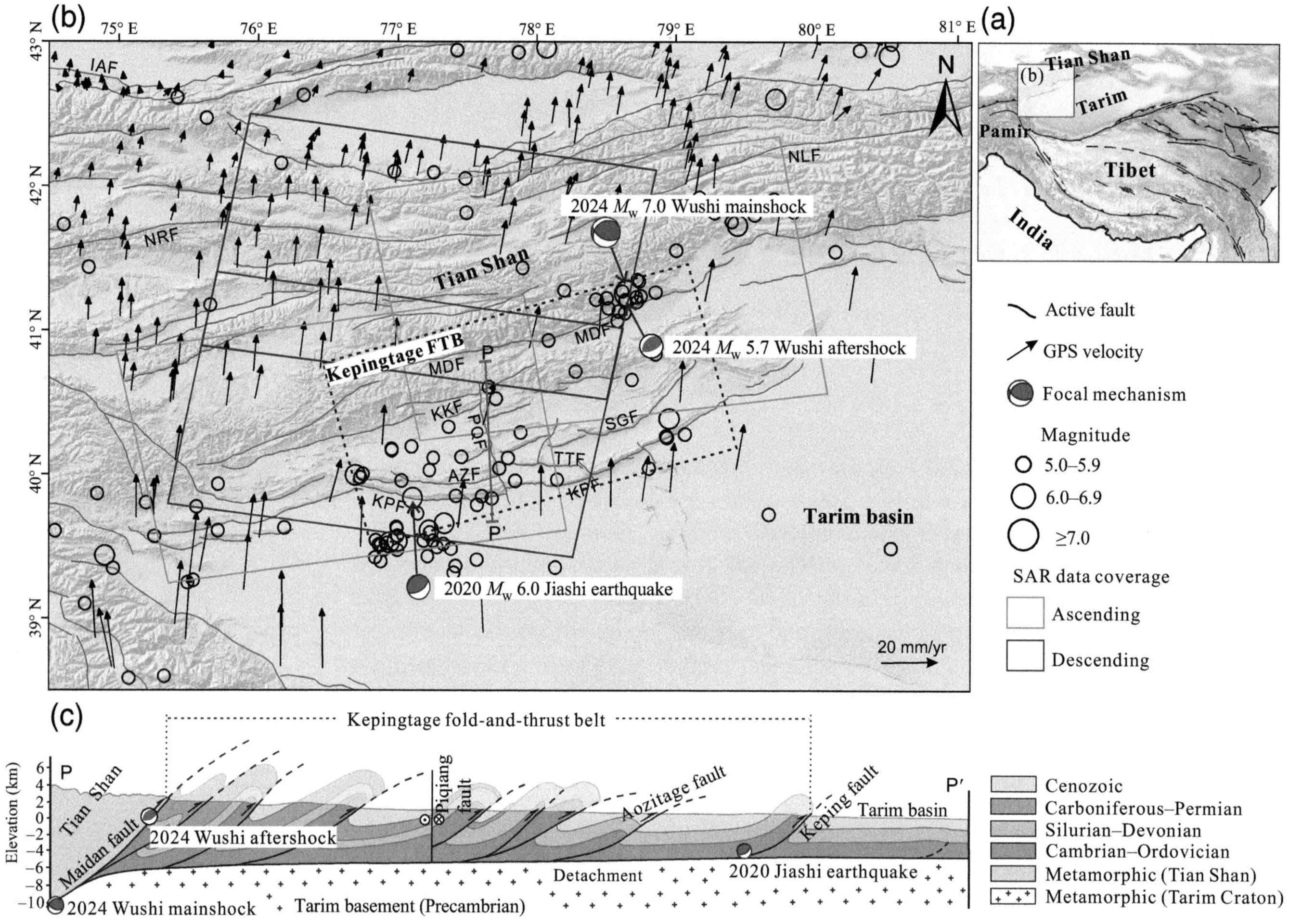

Figure 1. Seismotectonic framework of the study area. (a) Tectonic configuration of the India–Eurasia collisional system. (b) Active tectonics, Global Positioning System (GPS) velocity field and seismic activity in the southern Tian Shan. GPS velocities are relative to stable Eurasia and derived from Zheng *et al.* (2017). Focal mechanisms are from the U.S. Geological Survey (USGS). The hollow circles represent historical earthquakes with magnitudes 5+ since 1990, sourced from the USGS. The dashed rectangle marks the Kepingtage fold-and-thrust belt (FTB). The area of panel (b) is outlined by the white rectangle in panel (a). The gray curves denote the regional active faults, referenced from Deng *et al.* (2003) and Zelenin *et al.* (2022). AZF, Aozitage fault; IAF, Issyk-Ata fault; KKF, Kekebuke fault; KPF, Keping fault; NLF, Nalati fault; NRF, Naryn fault; MDF, Maidan fault; PQF, Piqiang fault; SGF, Saergantage fault; TTF, Tataiertage fault. (c) Cross-section P–P′ across the Kepingtage FTB showing the active structures and underlying rock layers (modified from Turner *et al.*, 2010), with the cross-section location depicted in panel (b). SAR, Synthetic Aperture Radar. The color version of this figure is available only in the electronic edition.

that crustal shortening is primarily absorbed by the piedmont fold-and-thrust belts (Yang, Deng, *et al.*, 2008; Zubovich *et al.*, 2010; Li *et al.*, 2021, 2022; Wu *et al.*, 2023). Geodetic observations show that the Kepingtage FTB absorbs a crustal shortening rate of 4–8 mm/yr, accounting for one-third of the total convergence across the western Tian Shan (Yang, Li, and Wang, 2008; Li *et al.*, 2022; Wu *et al.*, 2023). Structural analyses employing balanced cross sections and seismic reflection profiles consistently demonstrate that crustal shortening in these belts is accommodated through a combination of fault-related folding and reverse/thrust faulting (Allen *et al.*, 1999; Yang, Deng, *et al.*, 2008; Li *et al.*, 2018, 2023; Lü *et al.*, 2021), but which mechanism plays a more critical role in partitioning crustal shortening remains poorly understood.

Coseismic deformation investigations provide complementary tools for understanding tectonic deformation patterns because earthquake kinematics directly reflect the slip behavior of their causative faults and broader tectonic regimes. Two recent large earthquakes, namely the 2024 M_w 7.0 Wushi earthquake and the 2020 M_w 6.0 Jiashi earthquake (Fig. 1b), provide unique opportunities to elucidate folding or faulting contributions in absorbing crustal shortening in the Tian Shan, for these two events ruptured the root and front of the Kepingtage FTB, respectively (Fig. 1b,c). Between these two events lie a complex imbricate fold-and-thrust system that serves as a key region for revealing how the Tian Shan responds to crustal shortening.

Notably, the M_w 7.0 Wushi earthquake, on 23 January 2024, represents the first strong earthquake with magnitude 7+ in the southern Tian Shan over the past century (Fig. S1; Text S1, available in the supplemental material to this article) (Lü *et al.*, 2021; Zhao, Chen, *et al.*, 2024). The focal mechanisms from different organizations show that the 2024 Wushi earthquake is triggered by reverse motion with left-lateral strike-slip components (Table S1). Intriguingly, preliminary Interferometric Synthetic Aperture Radar (InSAR) observations indicate that the Wushi event caused notable surface uplift and subsidence but produced no clear surface ruptures, as evidenced by the smooth InSAR interference fringes and deformation fields (Zhao, Chen, *et al.*, 2024). However, subsequent investigations discovered an ~10-km-long surface rupture, with a maximum slip of ~0.4 m south of the epicenter (Qiu *et al.*, 2024; Zhang, Qian, *et al.*, 2024; Zheng *et al.*, 2024). Current interpretations suggest this rupture resulted not from the mainshock but from an M_w 5.7 aftershock a week later, on 30 January 2024 (Qiu *et al.*, 2024; Zheng *et al.*, 2024). Nevertheless, what factors led to the Wushi earthquake initially failing to produce surface ruptures but instead generating them during subsequent aftershock disturbances? This concern also makes the seismotectonic pattern of the southern Tian Shan subject to debate.

Here, we employ Differential Interferometric Synthetic Aperture Radar (D-InSAR) to derive the coseismic deformation fields of the 2024 Wushi and 2020 Jiashi earthquakes, respectively. A modified Bayesian nonlinear inversion method is utilized to constrain the geometry parameters and slip distributions of the causative fault (Zhao, Zhou, *et al.*, 2024). By integrating these results with regional geological data, we aim to clarify the seismogenic mechanisms and deformation patterns of the southern Tian Shan, providing new insights into tectonic deformation and mountain growth in compressional tectonic regimes.

Tectonic Background

The Tian Shan is a typical intracontinental orogenic belt rejuvenated during the late Cenozoic, extending ~2500 km long from east to west and 250–350 km wide from north to south in central Asia (Fig. S1) (Yin *et al.*, 1998; Xiao and Santosh, 2014; Wu *et al.*, 2023). This orogenic belt was initially formed by the subduction of the Paleo-Asian Ocean in the Paleozoic (Xiao *et al.*, 2020). The Cenozoic collision between Indian and Eurasian plates gave rise to the intense intracontinental deformation and orogeny in central Asia (Molnar and Tapponnier, 1975; Tapponnier and Molnar, 1979; Yin *et al.*, 1998; Deng *et al.*, 2003; Xiao and Santosh, 2014). Since the middle Miocene, north–south convergence between the Tian Shan and the Tarim basin has generated a series of nearly east–west-trending reverse faults within the Tian Shan and fold-and-thrust belts along its northern and southern frontal piedmonts (Text S2) (Yin *et al.*, 1998; Charreau *et al.*, 2009; Jia *et al.*, 2020). Global Positioning System (GPS) observations show the differential crustal shortening across the Tian Shan, with the shortening rates decreasing from west to east (Shen *et al.*, 2001; Wang *et al.*, 2001; Zubovich *et al.*, 2010; Zheng *et al.*, 2017; Li *et al.*, 2021; Wu *et al.*, 2023), showing ~20 mm/yr of north–south crustal shortening in the western Tian Shan and only 3–4 mm/yr in the eastern Tian Shan (Shen *et al.*, 2001; Zubovich *et al.*, 2010; Wu *et al.*, 2023).

The Kepingtage FTB along the southern Tian Shan front forms an imbricated thrust nappe structure, extending ~300 km from west to east and 60–140 km from north to south. This structure comprises five rows of east–west-trending thrust faults and fault-related anticlines (Fig. 1b) (Yang, Deng, *et al.*, 2008). These thrust faults converge to the same Precambrian basement detachment at a depth of 5–10 km (Fig. 1c) (Yin *et al.*, 1998; Allen *et al.*, 1999; Yang *et al.*, 2006; Yao *et al.*, 2020; Lü *et al.*, 2021). The Kepingtage FTB exhibits thin-skinned tectonic regimes near the frontal margin (closer to the basin) and thick-skinned regimes near the root zone (closer to the orogenic belt) (Allen *et al.*, 1999; Turner *et al.*, 2010). GPS measurements reveal a total shortening rate of 4.0 ± 1.5 mm/yr across the Kepingtage FTB, with higher rates in the east than in the west (Li *et al.*, 2022; Wu *et al.*, 2023). The inconsistency of shortening rates between the eastern and western parts is accommodated by the north-northwest-trending left-lateral Piqiang fault in the central Kepingtage FTB (Fig. 1b) (Yang *et al.*, 2006; Turner *et al.*, 2010, 2011).

The 2024 Wushi earthquake and the 2020 Jiashi earthquake ruptured the basin-mountain boundary fault (Maidan fault) and the frontal thrust fault (Keping fault) in the southern Tian Shan (Fig. 1b,c), respectively. The Maidan fault defines the topographic boundary between the Tian Shan and Tarim basin, extending more than 400 km in length (Fig. 1b), characterized by high-angle reverse slip with notable sinistral strike-slip components (Wu *et al.*, 2019; Zhao, Chen, *et al.*, 2024). This fault has been active since the late Quaternary and its long-term geological shortening rate is estimated to be 1–1.5 mm/yr (Wu *et al.*, 2019). The Keping fault, located at the southern front of the Kepingtage FTB, results from underthrusting of the Tarim basement beneath the Tian Shan orogenic belt (Fig. 1c) (Yin *et al.*, 1998; Allen *et al.*, 1999).

Data and Methods

Data and InSAR processing

InSAR technology has been widely utilized in monitoring surface deformation induced by earthquakes or tectonic activities based on the phase difference between radar signals reflected from the surface before and after tectonic events (Massonnet *et al.*, 1993; Bürgmann *et al.*, 2000; Fialko *et al.*, 2005; Meng *et al.*, 2024; Wang, Chang, *et al.*, 2024). This study collected pre- and post-earthquake Sentinel-1 ascending and descending radar images for the 2024 Wushi and 2020 Jiashi earthquakes (Table S2). The image data were downloaded from the Alaska Satellite Facility Data Search (see Data and Resources). We

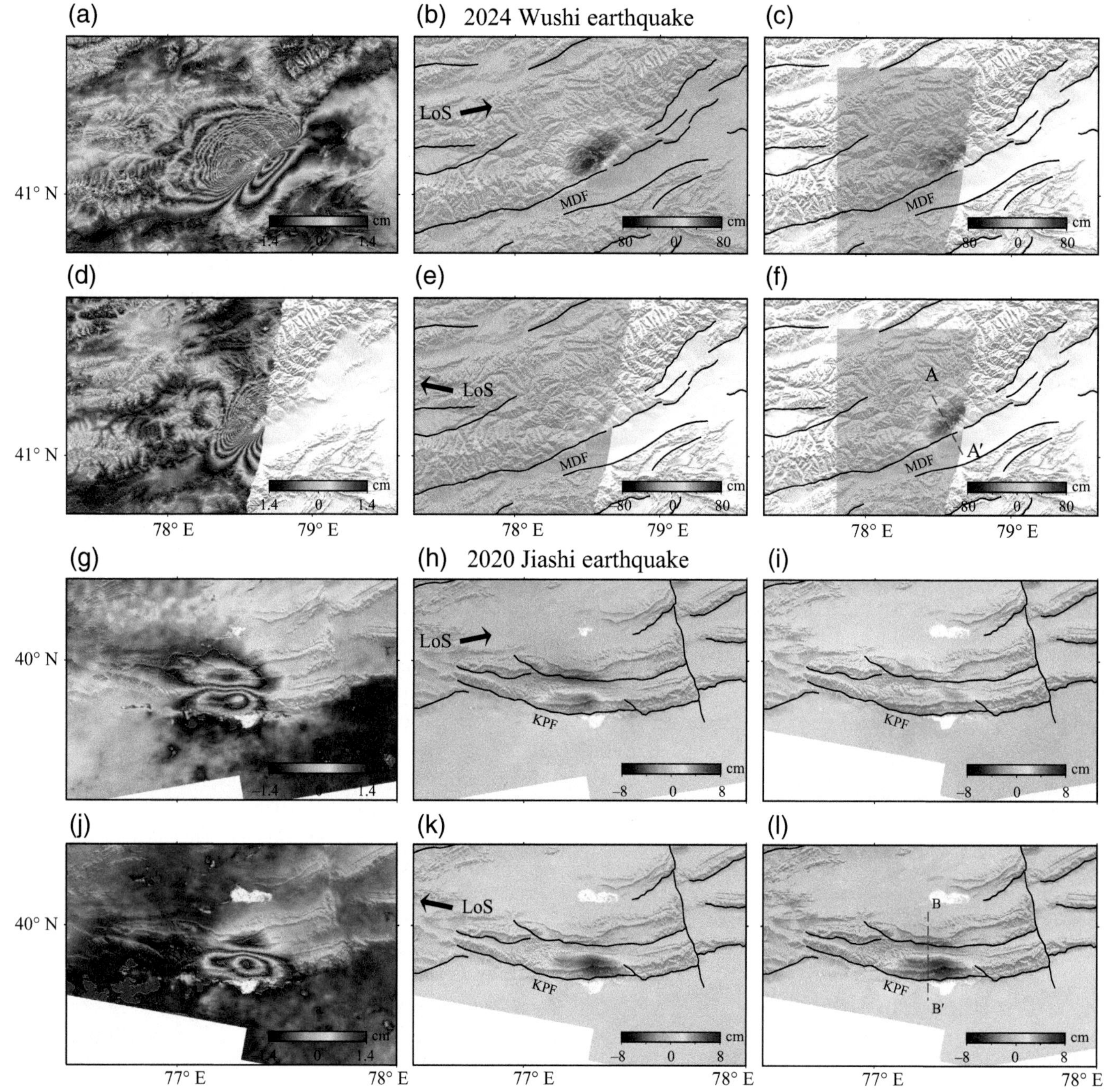

employed the software GAMMA to conduct D-InSAR processing. The interferograms are multilooked with a ratio of 10 : 2 (i.e., range : azimuth) to improve the signal-to-noise ratio. The 30 m resolution digital elevation model was utilized to simulate and correct the topographic phase. The interferograms were processed using the adaptive filtering algorithm and subsequently unwrapped via the minimum cost flow method (Goldstein and Werner, 1998). Long-wavelength atmospheric delays and orbital errors were removed through polynomial fitting (Fournier *et al.*, 2011; Xu *et al.*, 2018). Finally, we utilized SAR satellite parameters to transform the Synthetic Aperture Radar (SAR) coordinate into the geographical coordinate system and obtain the coseismic deformation fields (Fig. 2).

Figure 2. Interferometric Synthetic Aperture Radar (InSAR) coseismic deformation fields for the 2024 Wushi and 2020 Jiashi earthquakes. (a,b) The ascending and descending track interferograms of the 2024 Wushi earthquake. (c,d) The line-of-sight (LoS) deformation fields for the ascending and descending tracks of the Wushi earthquake. (e,f) The east–west deformation field and the vertical deformation field of the Wushi earthquake. (g–l) are similar to (a–f), but for the 2020 Jiashi earthquake. KPF, Keping fault; MDF, Maidan fault. The color version of this figure is available only in the electronic edition.

Given that the 2024 Wushi and 2020 Jiashi earthquakes are dominated by reverse or thrust motion, vertical deformation more accurately delineates their deformation features. We further decomposed the line-of-sight (LoS) deformation fields into vertical and horizontal deformation components. Currently, most SAR satellites employ near-polar orbits and right-looking imaging modes, resulting in variations in the accuracy of InSAR deformation monitoring in different directions, particularly rendering it insensitive to deformation in the north–south direction. Therefore, we extracted the east–west and vertical deformation components while neglecting the north–south displacement (Fig. 2). By integrating the ascending and descending LoS deformation fields, we calculated the east–west and vertical deformation fields based on the following geometric relationship:

$$\begin{bmatrix} D_{\mathrm{LOS}(AT)} \\ D_{\mathrm{LOS}(DT)} \end{bmatrix} = \begin{bmatrix} -\sin\theta\cos\alpha, \cos\theta \\ -\sin\theta\cos\alpha, \cos\theta \end{bmatrix} \begin{bmatrix} D_E \\ D_U \end{bmatrix}. \quad (1)$$

In equation (1), $D_{\mathrm{LOS}(AT)}$ and $D_{\mathrm{LOS}(DT)}$ represent the LoS deformation in the ascending and descending track directions, respectively. θ is the incidence angle, and α is the azimuth angle. D_E and D_U represent the east-west and vertical deformation components.

Inversion of fault geometry and slip distribution

The geometry parameters and slip distributions of the causative fault inverted from InSAR-derived surface deformation can reveal the fault kinematics, offering insights into the seismogenic mechanisms and energy release (Massonnet *et al.*, 1993; Goldstein and Werner, 1998; Jónsson *et al.*, 2002; Fukuda and Johnson, 2010; Wang, Chang, *et al*,. 2024). In this study, we employ a modified Bayesian approach (MF-J method) to simultaneously invert for fault geometry parameters and slip distributions using Okada solutions for rectangular dislocations in a homogeneous, elastic half-space, assuming a Poisson's ratio of 0.25 and a shear modulus of 30 GPa (Text S3) (Okada, 1985; Zhao, Zhou, *et al.*, 2024). First, the MF-J method assigns initial values following a uniform distribution for the nonlinear parameters and estimates the initial linear slip distribution and hyperparameters through the variance component estimation (VCE) method (Fan *et al.*, 2017). The nonlinear parameters include *Ex*, *Ey*, *Ez* (coordinates of the fault's upper left corner) as well as strike and dip angles. The two hyperparameters (Sig_d and Sig_a) represent the variance components of the actual and virtual observations, respectively (Text S3; Figs. S2 and S5). Second, the MF-J method calculates the corresponding posterior probability density function (PDF) using the equations from Fukuda and Johnson (2010). Third, the MF-J method perturbs the current parameter set by adding a random step (with step size scaled by a uniform random number) to generate a new candidate set of nonlinear parameters and hyperparameters. The new parameter set is used to invert the slip distribution with the VCE method, and then the new full posterior PDF is recalculated. Finally, the MF-J method determines the likelihood ratio *R* between the new PDF and the previous PDF and accepts the new group of linear and nonlinear parameters if min{*R*,1} exceeds a random value following a uniform distribution from 0 to 1 based on the Metropolis algorithm (Metropolis *et al.*, 1953). After sufficient iterations, the sampling results of the parameters are obtained. Initial samples (generally the first few thousand iterations) are discarded as the burn-in period until convergence is achieved. Then, we extract the stabilized samples after the burn-in period (Text S3).

To enhance the computational efficiency of the inversion process, we apply the quadtree sampling method for data set downsampling (Jónsson *et al.*, 2002). This method uses the deformation gradient as the indicator to allow dense sampling in the areas with large deformation gradients but coarse sampling in areas with small changes, which is suitable for coseismic deformation data reduction (Gao *et al.*, 2022). We obtain 956 and 789 data points for the 2024 Wushi ascending and descending deformation fields (Fig. S4). Based on the empirical relationship between the fault size and moment magnitude (Wells and Coppersmith, 1994), we set the fault length and width to 60 and 40 km, to allow an exhaustive search in the potential space. We discretize the fault plane into 600 patches with a size of 2 km × 2 km (Fig. 3). Then, we use the coordinates (78.649° E, 41.269° N) as a reference point to convert the fault's geographic coordinates into UTM coordinates. The initial values and bounds for the fault's geometric parameters are presented in Table S3. We constrain the fault strike between 200° and 300° and limit the fault dip between 1° and 60° based on previous studies (Qiu *et al.*, 2024; Zhao, Chen, *et al.*, 2024; Zheng *et al.*, 2024). We then execute the MF-J method for 15,000 iterations, considering the first 10,000 iterations as the burn-in period. After the burn-in period, we retain the fault geometric parameters, hyperparameters, and slip distribution every 25 iterations to ensure sample independence. Finally, we resolve the average and standard deviation of each parameter (Figs. S2 and S3; Table S3).

For the 2020 Jiashi earthquake, we acquire 523 and 530 data points for the ascending and descending deformation fields, respectively (Fig. S7). We set the fault dimensions of 40 km × 20 km for exhaustive parameter space exploration. The fault plane is discretized into 200 patches with a size of 2 km × 2 km (Fig. 4). Using the coordinates (77.27° E, 39.89° N) as the reference point, we transform the geographic coordinates to UTM. Initial values and bounds are listed in Table S4. The strike and dip angles are constrained to 200°–360° and 5°–30° based on previous studies (Yao *et al.*, 2020; Wu *et al.*, 2024). The MF-J inversion is conducted for 10,000 iterations (with 5,000 as burn-in), with parameters sampled every 25 iterations. Then, we calculate the average and standard deviation of each parameter (Figs. S5 and S6; Table S4). The program code for this inversion method and the processing results for the 2024 Wushi and 2020 Jiashi earthquakes are accessible on the GitHub platform (see Data and Resources).

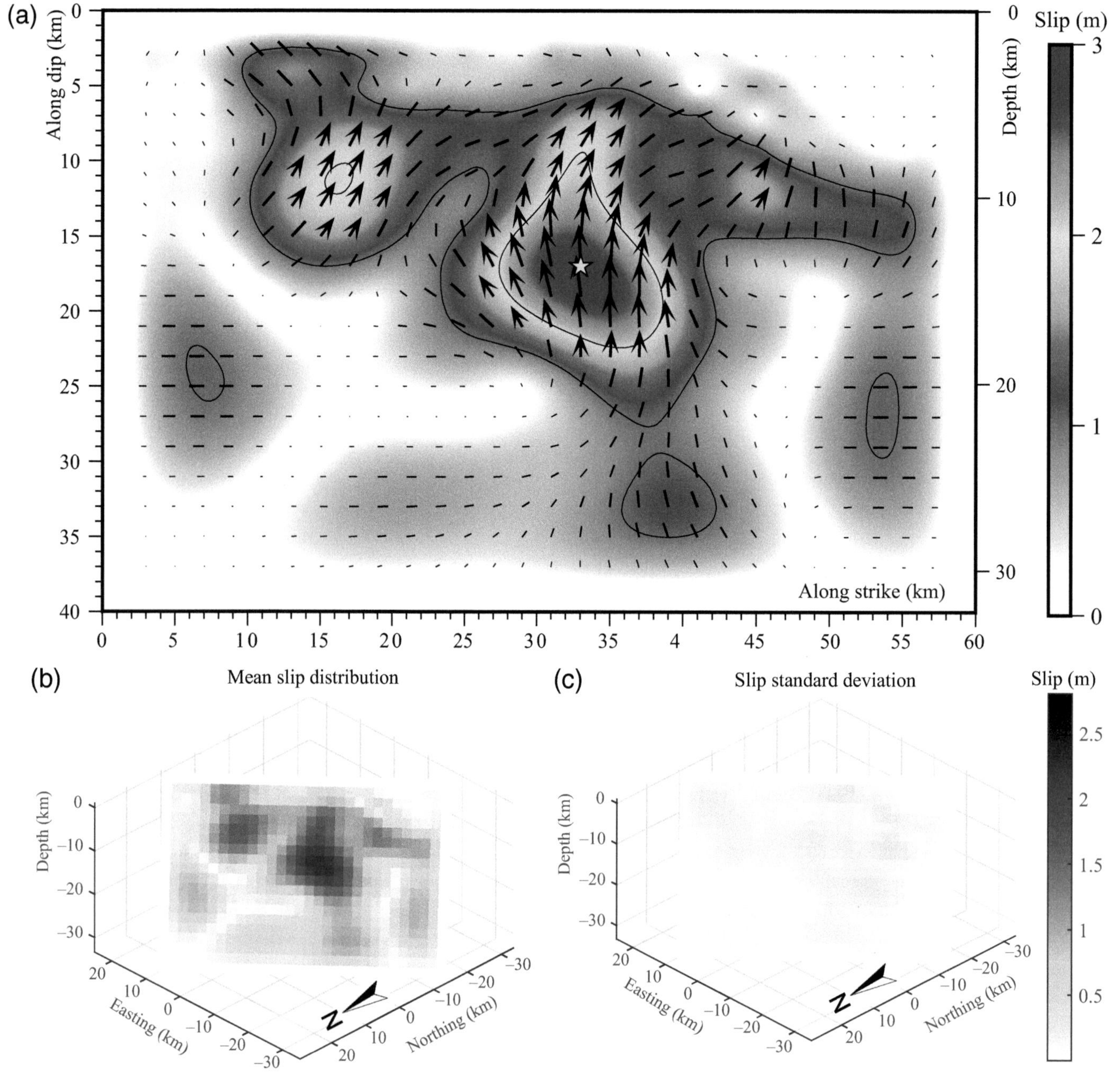

Figure 3. Slip distributions and slip standard deviation of the 2024 Wushi earthquake. (a) 2D slip distribution of the 2024 Wushi earthquake showing slip magnitudes and orientations. (b,c) 3D slip distribution and slip standard deviation (uncertainty) of the Wushi earthquake. The color version of this figure is available only in the electronic edition.

Results

Coseismic deformation fields and slip kinematics of the 2024 Wushi earthquake

The interferograms derived from ascending and descending tracks reveal two distinct elliptical deformation zones separated by the Maidan fault (Fig. 2a,b). The northern deformation zone exhibits significantly greater spatial extent and magnitude compared to the southern zone. The deformation ellipses are oriented along the east-northeast–west-southwest direction, consistent with both the focal mechanism solutions (Table S1) and the strike of the Maidan fault.

Both ascending and descending LoS deformation fields display similar deformation patterns (Fig. 2c,d), indicating dominant vertical motion induced by the Wushi earthquake. The northern side of the Maidan fault experienced uplift, while the southern side underwent subsidence. Specifically, the ascending track measured ~0.77 m uplift and ~0.10 m subsidence, whereas the descending track detected ~0.38 m uplift and ~0.14 m subsidence (Fig. 2c,d). The continuous fringe patterns in both interferograms suggest no surface rupture occurred during the earthquake (Fig. 2a,b). However, the denser interference

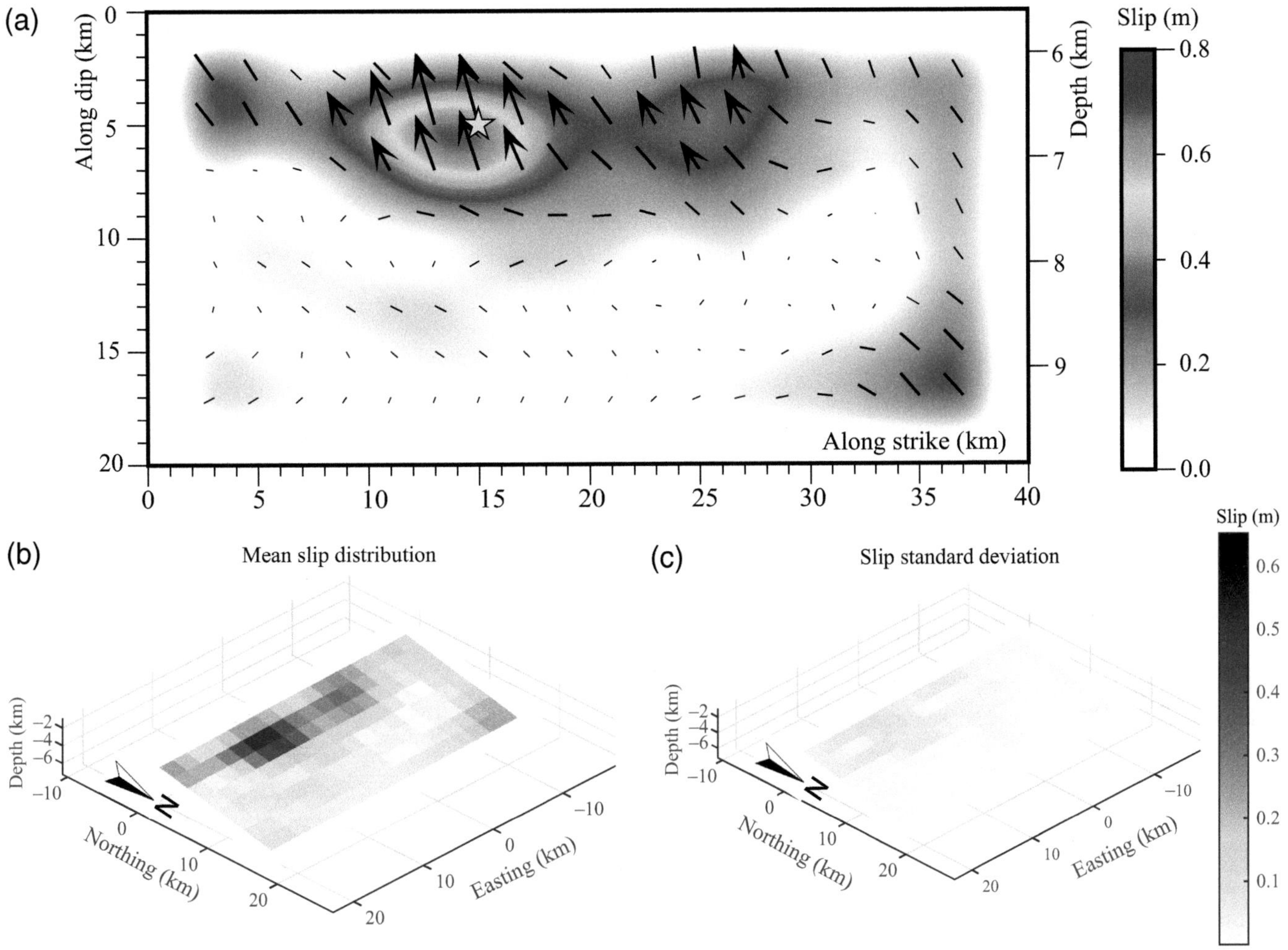

Figure 4. Slip distributions and slip standard deviation of the 2020 Jiashi earthquake. (a) 2D slip distribution of the 2020 Jiashi earthquake showing slip magnitudes and orientations. (b,c) 3D slip distribution and slip standard deviation (uncertainty) of the Jiashi earthquake. The color version of this figure is available only in the electronic edition.

fringes near the Maidan fault indicate a steep deformation gradient along the causative fault (Fig. 2a,b).

The east–west and vertical deformation fields further demonstrate that the Wushi earthquake is a primarily reverse-faulting event with a significant left-lateral component (Fig. 2e,f). The east–west deformation field indicates westward motion of the northern block relative to the southern block, with a left-lateral displacement of ~0.5 m (Fig. 2e). The vertical displacement field reveals that the hanging wall (northern block) was uplifted by a maximum of ~0.68 m relative to the footwall (southern block), which subsided by ~0.12 m, yielding a total vertical displacement of ~0.8 m (Fig. 2f). The transition between uplift and subsidence spatially coincides with the surface traces of the Maidan fault.

The Bayesian inversion yields a strike angle of 227.5° ± 0.6° and a dip angle of 53.7° ± 0.7°, dipping to northwest (Figs. S2 and S3). The slip distribution confirms that the earthquake is dominated by reverse faulting with a notable left-lateral component (Fig. 3a). The maximum slip amount is ~2.8 m at a depth of ~15 km below the surface (Fig. 3a). The seismic moment released by the rupture is 4.09×10^{19} N · m, equivalent to a moment magnitude M_w 7.0. The root mean square error (RMSE) between the predicted values based on the slip distribution model and the observed values are ~1.3 cm (Fig. S4).

Coseismic deformation fields and slip kinematics of the 2020 Jiashi earthquake

The interferograms from InSAR ascending and descending tracks, coupled with the LoS deformation fields, also identify two elliptical deformation zones induced by the 2020 Jiashi earthquake (Fig. 2g,h). The long axis of these ellipses align nearly east–west, consistent with the strike of the Kepingtage FTB. Although the ascending track reveals a near-symmetrical distribution of the two deformation ellipses (Fig. 2g), the descending track shows a larger southern ellipse compared to the northern one (Fig. 2h).

Unlike typical earthquakes where the causative fault lies at the intersection of deformation zones, the Jiashi earthquake exhibits an anomalous deformation pattern: the intersection of uplift and subsidence does not coincide with the Keping fault's traces. Instead, the fault traces are distributed along the southern margin of the entire deformation field, with the vast majority of the deformed area being confined to its hanging wall (Fig. 2i–l). Localized decoherence is observed along the fault traces (Fig. 2g,h), indicating small surface displacements along the Keping fault. Both ascending and descending LoS deformation fields consistently indicate vertical-dominated motion, characterized by uplift in the southern ellipse and subsidence in the northern ellipse (Fig. 2i,j). The interferograms and deformation fields demonstrate nearly continuous uplift and subsidence variation.

The east–west and vertical deformation fields show a pure thrust motion (Fig. 2k,l). The maximum uplift is measured to be ~0.07 m, whereas the maximum subsidence is ~0.03 m, yielding a total vertical displacement of ~0.1 m (Fig. 2l). The east–west deformation field exhibits a diffuse movement from the uplift center toward the edges, with the eastern part moving eastward and the western part westward (Fig. 2k).

The Bayesian inversion resolves a strike angle of 276° ± 1.4° and a dip angle of 12.5° ± 1.0°, dipping to north (Figs. S5 and S6). The slip distribution model further supports dominant thrust motion, with minor right-lateral strike-slip components (Fig. 4a). The maximum slip amount is ~0.65 m, located at a depth of ~6.8 km below the surface (Fig. 4a). The released seismic moment is 2.32×10^{18} N · m, equivalent to a moment magnitude $M_w \sim 6.18$. The RMSE between the predicted values and the observed values is ~0.43 cm (Fig. S7).

Discussion

Deformation patterns and seismogenic mechanisms of the 2024 Wushi and 2020 Jiashi earthquakes

The InSAR interferograms and the cross-fault deformation profiles reveal that the surface deformation caused by the 2024 Wushi earthquake exhibits good spatial continuity (Fig. 2a,b and 5a), indicating that this event did not rupture the surface (Ding *et al.*, 2024; Qiu *et al.*, 2024; Zhao, Chen, *et al.*, 2024; Zheng *et al.*, 2024). Notably, the interference fringe density and deformation gradient of the Wushi earthquake peak near the causative fault (Figs. 2a,b and 5a). For the 2020 Jiashi earthquake, the deformation gradient reaches its maxima within 5–10 km north of the causative fault (Fig. 5b), and localized subsidence was observed along the southern margin of the Keping fault, with a width not exceeding 2 km, which has been rarely reported in previous studies (Fig. 5b) (Yao *et al.*, 2020; He *et al.*, 2021; Wang *et al.*, 2022; Zhang *et al.*, 2023; Wu *et al.*, 2024). Although minor localized subsidence occurred, the Jiashi earthquake generally exhibits nearly continuous surface deformation (Fig. 5b).

The spatially continuous deformation fields of the Wushi and Jiashi earthquakes are interpreted as surface folding resulting from deep reverse/thrust faulting. Folding deformation generally refers to the bending or warping of layered rock strata under tectonic forces, leading to the formation of curved or wavelike surface structures (Suppe, 1983), which are often associated with distributed, off-fault inelastic deformation within the bulk crust. It is critical to acknowledge that our inversion model, which is based on dislocations in a purely elastic half-space (see the Data and Methods section), is by design only capable of inferring the geometry and slip of the underlying fault (Okada, 1985; Zhao, Zhou, *et al.*, 2024). Therefore, this model cannot directly quantify any potential contribution of distributed inelastic deformation to the observed surface folding deformation. Accordingly, we clarify that our interpretation of the term "folding" here refers primarily to the geomorphic expression and the kinematic pattern of deformation, rather than to a specific mechanical mechanism involving inelastic deformation.

The folding pattern of the Wushi earthquake shows an anticline feature, with an asymmetrical anticline on the hanging wall of the Maidan fault, featuring a gentle deformation gradient on the northern limb and a steep gradient on the southern limb (Fig. 5a). Conversely, the Jiashi earthquake displays a combination of anticline and syncline, with an anticline near the fault and a syncline more than 8 km away from it (Fig. 5b). The difference in fold styles between these two events may be attributed to the different dip angles of the causative faults. Fault geometry derived in this study suggests that the Wushi earthquake was triggered by a high-angle reverse fault with a dip angle of 53.7°, whereas the fault plane of the Jiashi earthquake exhibits a much gentler dip angle of only 12.5° (Table S1). Besides, the slip distribution of the Wushi fault shows an upward gradual reduction of slip along the fault plane, together with its asymmetric deformation gradient (a steeper forelimb and a gentler backlimb), indicating that the Wushi event conforms to the fault-propagation fold pattern (Fig. 5a) (Suppe, 1983; Yang *et al.*, 2006; Jabbour *et al.*, 2012). In contrast, the Jiashi earthquake slip core is concentrated at 6–7 km depth, consistent with the local detachment depth (Yin *et al.*, 1998; Allen *et al.*, 1999; Yang *et al.*, 2006). Therefore, the Jiashi event demonstrates a low-angle thrusting along the deep detachment surface, corresponding to the detachment fold pattern (Fig. 5b). However, unlike the symmetrical arch observed in typical detachment folds (Yang *et al.*, 2006; Contreras, 2010), the Jiashi earthquake displays a wavelike anticline–syncline complexity (Fig. 5b).

Seismic reflection profiles reveal the gradually evolving crustal structure in the southern Tian Shan (Lü *et al.*, 2021). The cover thickness of the Kepingtage FTB is ~5 km at its front edge and gradually increases northward to about 8 km at its root (Allen *et al.*, 1999; Yang *et al.*, 2006; Lü *et al.*, 2021). The fault-slip distribution inverted in this study shows that the focal depth of the Wushi earthquake reaches up to ~15 km, far exceeding the cover thickness. Consequently, the Wushi earthquake

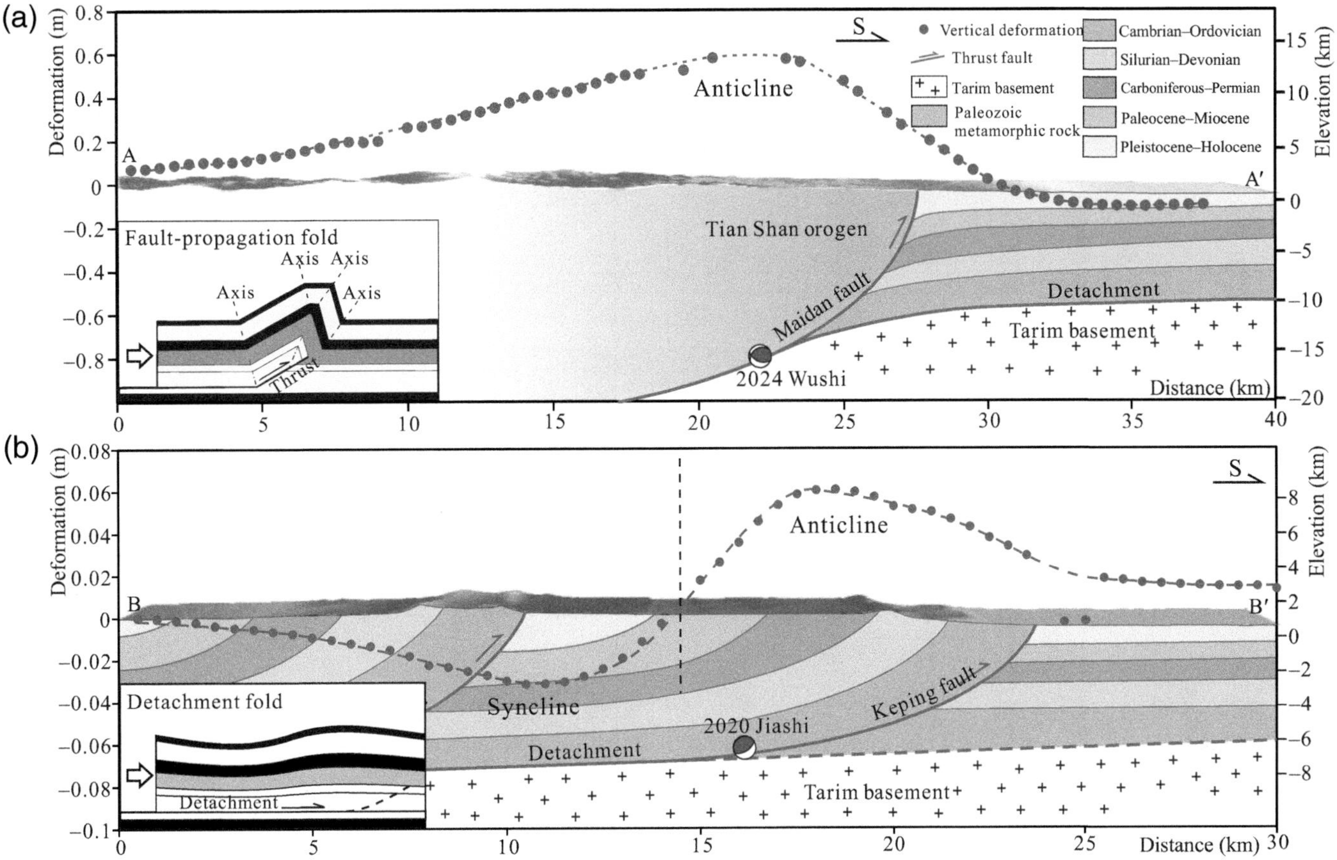

Figure 5. Deformation cross sections of the 2024 Wushi and 2020 Jiashi earthquakes. (a) Cross-section A–A′ showing the vertical deformation of the 2024 Wushi earthquake, topographic relief, active structures, and underlying rock layers, with the inset of the fault-propagation fold model (modified from Yang *et al.*, 2006). The cross-section location is depicted by the red-dashed line in Figure 2f. (b) Cross-section B–B′ showing the vertical deformation of the 2020 Jiashi earthquake, topographic relief, active structures, and underlying rock layers, with the inset of the detachment fold model. The cross-section location is depicted by the red-dashed line in Figure 2l. The color version of this figure is available only in the electronic edition.

simultaneously ruptured the Paleozoic metamorphic rocks of the Tian Shan orogen and the Precambrian crystalline basement of the Tarim basin (Fig. 5a). Given that the Tarim basement rocks have significantly greater strength than the sedimentary rocks in the overlying cover (Allen *et al.*, 1999; Yang *et al.*, 2006), the Maidan fault is more capable of accumulating strain compared to the Keping fault, thus generating larger magnitude earthquakes.

In addition, the Maidan fault is the basin–mountain boundary fault between the Tarim Craton and the Tian Shan orogen, exhibiting better geometry linearity and a higher degree of fault maturity (Wu *et al.*, 2019), making it prone to triggering longer ruptures. In contrast, thrust faults at the front of the Kepingtage FTB are intersected by multiple northwest-trending strike-slip faults, resulting in discontinuous fault geometry (Li *et al.*, 2019; Lü *et al.*, 2021; Wu *et al.*, 2024), thus limiting the rupture propagation and potentially explaining why the moderate-magnitude earthquakes such as the Jiashi earthquake are frequently observed in the Kepingtage FTB.

Surface rupture mechanism of the 2024 Wushi earthquake

A surface rupture was identified ~15 km south of the 2024 Wushi epicenter, stretching ~10 km in length and featuring a maximum vertical displacement of ~0.4 m (Qiu *et al.*, 2024; Zheng *et al.*, 2024; Zhang, Qian, *et al.*, 2024). Intriguingly, the surface rupture is characterized by a south-dipping reverse faulting, in contrast to the north-dipping mechanism of the Wushi mainshock (Zhang, Qian, *et al.*, 2024).

To ascertain whether the surface rupture was caused by the aftershock or mainshock, we re-extracted InSAR surface deformation fields, encompassing the M_w 5.7 aftershock solely (Fig. 6). Both ascending and descending deformation fields detected an ~10-km-long surface rupture (R1) on the northern side of the Maidan fault in the aftershock deformation fields (Fig. 6d,e), striking to the east-northeast direction, with a maximum displacement of ~0.5 m (Fig. 6f). The southern part of the rupture (R1) exhibits uplift relative to the northern part (Fig. 6d,e), contrasting with the mainshock deformation pattern (Fig. 6a,b), but consistent with the field observations (Zhang, Qian, *et al.*, 2024). The fault geometry inversion reveals that

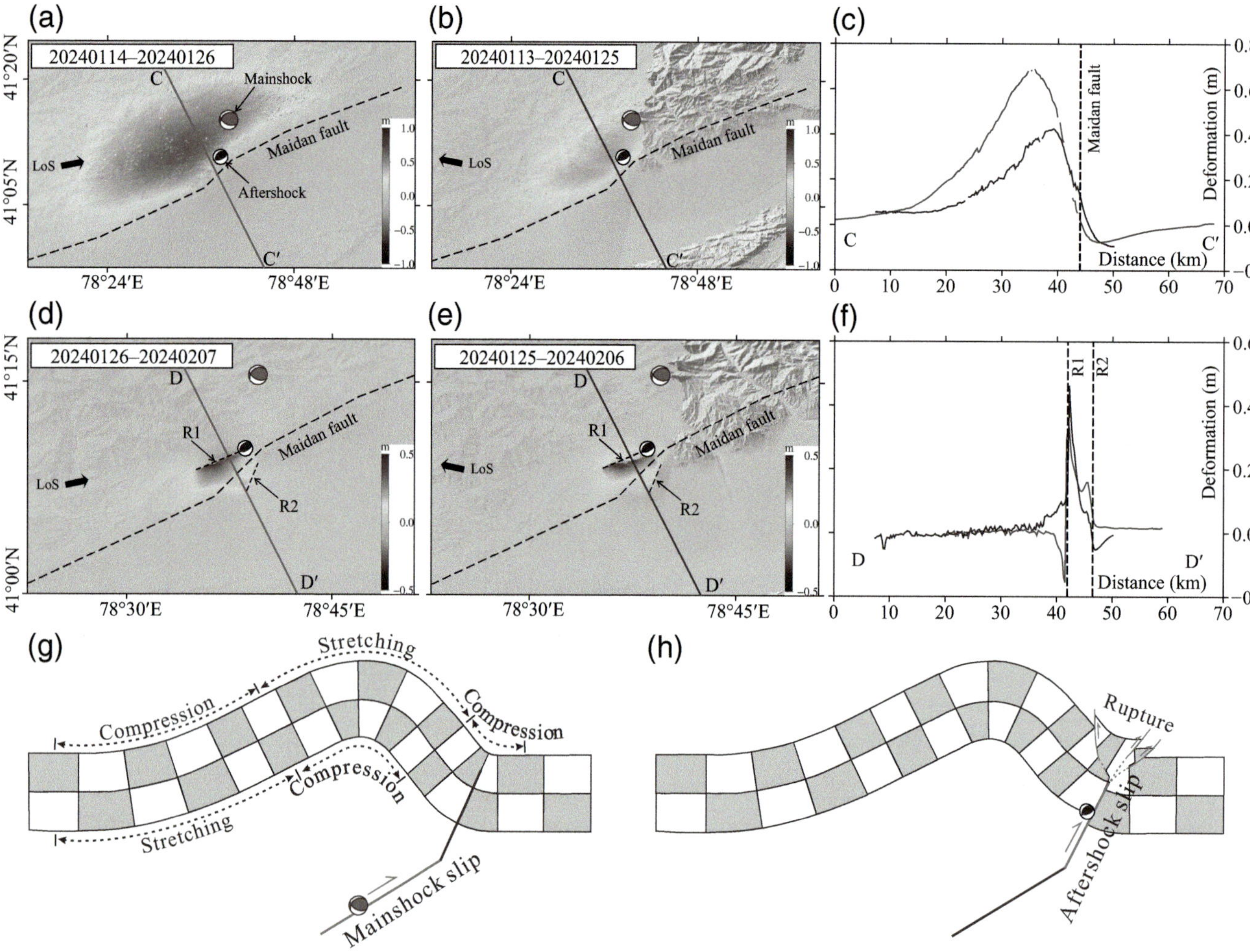

the aftershock rupture exhibits a strike of ~60°, dipping to the southeast, contrary to the mainshock mechanism (Qiu *et al.*, 2024; Zheng *et al.*, 2024; Famiglietti *et al.*, 2025). Some studies have attributed this rupture to the broad temporal span of InSAR observations, which may capture additional deformation resulting from aftershocks (Qiu *et al.*, 2024; Zheng *et al.*, 2024). However, the field survey conducted one day prior to the M_w 5.7 aftershock failed to observe the surface rupture, but immediately discovered it in the afternoon of the day that the M_w 5.7 aftershock occurred (Zhang, Qian, *et al.*, 2024), suggesting that this rupture was primarily induced by the M_w 5.7 aftershock. In addition, the aftershock deformation fields detected another minor surface rupture (R2) on the southern side of the Maidan fault (Fig. 6d,e), with a displacement of ~0.15 m (Fig. 6f). This rupture dips to the northwest, consistent with the mainshock mechanism (Qiu *et al.*, 2024).

Figure 6. InSAR deformation fields and deformation profiles of the M_w 7.0 Wushi mainshock and the M_w 5.7 Wushi aftershock. Panels (a–c) represent the ascending deformation field, descending deformation field, and deformation profile C–C′ of the M_w 7.0 Wushi mainshock. Profile C–C′ locations are marked by red and blue lines in panels (a) and (b). (d–f) represent the ascending deformation field, descending deformation field, and deformation profile D–D′ of the M_w 5.7 Wushi aftershock, showing two surface ruptures (R1 and R2). Profile D–D′ locations are outlined by red and blue lines in panels (d) and (e). (g) Schematic diagram showing the shallow fold deformation induced by deep mainshock slip. (h) Schematic diagram showing surface positive flowerlike ruptures generated by shallow aftershock slip (modified from Zhang, Li, *et al.*, 2024). Focal mechanisms are from the USGS. The color version of this figure is available only in the electronic edition.

The inverted fault-slip distribution reveals that the mainshock slip concentrated at depths exceeding 5 km below the surface, peaking at around 15 km, whereas the aftershock slip occurred in the shallow crust above 5 km and propagated to the surface (Fig. S8) (Qiu *et al.*, 2024; Zheng *et al.*, 2024). The nonpropagation of the mainshock slip to the surface could be attributed to variations in fault geometry, particularly the increasing dip angles toward the surface along the Maidan fault (Fig. 1c) (Zhang *et al.*, 2019; Lü *et al.*, 2021). Variations in dip angles along the fault plane prevent the mainshock rupture from propagating to the surface, while causing a slip deficit and Coulomb stress loading in the shallow crust (Fig. S8).

Therefore, we propose a two-stage model to explain the surface ruptures during the 2024 Wushi event (Fig. 6g,h):

First, the mainshock slip concentrated below 5 km caused shallow fold deformation without notable surface ruptures, but formed a compressive strain zone at the leading tip of the fold (Fig. 6g), generating a slip deficit zone in the shallow crust (Fig. S8a,c); second, the aftershock slip occurring above 5 km compensated for the shallow slip deficit, leading to positive flowerlike ruptures in the folded strain zone (Fig. 6h, Fig. S8b,d). This model explains why the aftershock rupture exhibits an opposite dip direction compared to the mainshock mechanism. In addition, because the aftershock ruptures were superimposed on the mainshock deformation fold, a portion of the compressive strain accumulated in the fold was released through surface rupturing, resulting in the actual displacement magnitude (~0.5 m) of the aftershock being larger than the seismically calculated magnitude (M_w 5.7) based on magnitude–displacement scaling relationships (Wells and Coppersmith, 1994).

Implications for seismicity and growth patterns of the southern Tian Shan

GPS measurements suggest that crustal shortening in the Tian Shan orogenic belt is predominantly absorbed by the foreland fold-and-thrust belts (Deng *et al.*, 2003; Yang, Li, and Wang, 2008). However, the 2024 Wushi earthquake and recent GPS/InSAR observations demonstrate that a portion of convergence strain is also absorbed within the Tian Shan interior (Li *et al.*, 2021; Lü *et al.*, 2021; Wu *et al.*, 2023; Wang, Xu, *et al.*, 2024). In spite of the limited crustal shortening rates within the Tian Shan, the high-angle reverse faults within the orogenic interior still have capacity to produce considerable strain accumulation and cause large-magnitude earthquakes. This seismic hazard potential arises because, under equivalent crustal shortening conditions, steeper-dipping reverse faults accumulate greater elastic strain than their gentler counterparts. In addition, recent geodetic studies have mapped the spatial distribution of interseismic coupling of the Maidan fault before the 2024 Wushi event and identified four locked segments with high seismic risks (Wang, Xu, *et al.*, 2024). However, although the Wushi earthquake ruptured only one of these segments, the remaining three segments retain the potential to generate M 7+ earthquakes.

Fault-bend folds triggered by seismic events may exhibit either elastic or inelastic deformation characteristics (Mallick *et al.*, 2021). Geophysical modeling suggests that distinguishing between the elastic and inelastic responses to fault slip is possible only during the postseismic period following large earthquakes (Mallick *et al.*, 2021). In the case of the Wushi event, the shallow fold induced by deep coseismic slip underwent partial postseismic recovery, manifested as surface ruptures in the shallow slip deficit zone (Fig. 6). Nevertheless, the surface deformation caused by the Wushi event remains characterized by folding deformation because the postseismic recovery produced only ~10-km-long surface ruptures, significantly shorter than the ~50-km-long coseismic deformation field (Fig. 6). Moreover, geodetic observations reveal that fault-bend folding develops not only during long-lasting postseismic phases (Zhou *et al.*, 2016), interseismic periods (Chong *et al.*, 2024), and aseismic slip episodes (Tsukahara and Takada, 2018), but also during instantaneous coseismic phases (Yao *et al.*, 2020; Qiu *et al.*, 2024), as observed in the 2024 Wushi and 2020 Jiashi events.

Both thrust/reverse faulting and folding contribute to mountain growth and outward expansion of compressional orogenic belts. The southern Tian Shan foreland hosts multiple imbricated fold-and-thrust belts that accommodate regional crustal shortening primarily through low-angle detachment folding along a uniform décollement (Yin *et al.*, 1998; Allen *et al.*, 1999; Yang *et al.*, 2006; Turner *et al.*, 2010; Tian *et al.*, 2016; Lü *et al.*, 2021). Recent paleoseismic investigations have identified multiple fold earthquakes within the southern Tian Shan (Zhang, Li, *et al.*, 2024). In this study, although localized surface ruptures were observed in the deformation fields, the Wushi and Jiashi events remain characterized as fold-dominated deformation features. Thus, we suggest that folding deformation plays a predominant role in accommodating crustal shortening in the southern Tian Shan, which is of great significance for understanding deformation patterns and mountain growth processes in intracontinental compressive orogenic belts.

Conclusion

The two powerful earthquakes that occurred in the southern Tian Shan, the 2024 M_w 7.0 Wushi earthquake and the 2020 M_w 6.0 Jiashi earthquake, provide critical cases for understanding tectonic deformation patterns in compressive tectonic regimes. This study employed Sentinel-1 radar images provided by the European Space Agency to capture the coseismic deformation fields of both events and then applied a modified Bayesian inversion method to derive the geometry parameters and the slip distributions along the fault planes. Our findings reveal that both Wushi and Jiashi earthquakes exhibit shallow fold deformation caused by deep reverse/thrust faulting. The high-angle reverse motion of the Wushi earthquake produced a fault-propagation fold in the shallow crust (<5 km depth), whereas the low-angle thrusting along detachment during the Jiashi earthquake generated a detachment fold within the sedimentary cover layer. The surface ruptures observed in the Wushi event resulted from positive flowerlike structures produced by the subsequent M_w 5.7 aftershock, explaining the opposite dip direction between the aftershock and mainshock mechanisms. The deformation patterns of the two earthquakes highlight the dominance of folding deformation in accommodating shallow crustal shortening in the southern Tian Shan.

Data and Resources

The Synthetic Aperture Radar (SAR) data used in this study was provided by the European Space Agency (ESA) through the ASF Data Hub website (https://search.asf.alaska.edu/). The earthquake focal mechanisms were obtained from the U.S. Geological Survey (USGS; https://earthquake.usgs.gov), Global Centroid Moment Tensor (Global CMT; https://www.globalcmt.org), China Earthquake Networks Centre (CENC; https://news.ceic.ac.cn/) and National Earthquake Data Center (NEDC; https://data.earthquake.cn/). The program code of the MF-J inversion method and the processing results for the 2024 Wushi and 2020 Jiashi earthquakes are accessible on the Github platform (https://github.com/XiongZhao0303/MF-J-method-to-simultaneously-solve-for-the-co-seismic-fault-geometry-and-slip-parameters/blob/main/MF-J/readme.txt). Some figures were drawn by Generic Mapping Tools (GMT; Wessel *et al.*, 2019). All websites were last accessed in January 2025. The supplemental material includes Text S1–S3, Figures S1–S8, and Tables S1–S4.

Declaration of Competing Interests

The authors acknowledge that there are no conflicts of interest recorded.

Acknowledgments

The authors are grateful to Zhao Xiong from Wuhan University for providing the MF-J inversion program code. The authors thank Rebetsky Y. L. from Institute of Physics of the Earth, Russian Academy of Science, for sharing the regional historical seismic data. This research was supported by National Natural Science Foundation of China (42174023, 42304037), Natural Science Foundation of Hunan Province (2024JJ3031), and Frontier Cross Research Project of Central South University (2023QYJC006). The authors sincerely thank Editor-in-Chief Allison Bent and the two anonymous reviewers for their constructive comments, which have significantly improved the quality of this work.

References

Allen, M. B., B. F. Windley, C. Zhang, Z. Y. Zhao, and H. R. Wang (1999). Late Cenozoic tectonics of the Kepingtage thrust zone: Interactions of the Tien Shan and Tarim, *Tectonics* **18,** no. 4, 639–654, doi: 10.1029/1999TC900019.

Avouac, J.-P., and P. Tapponnier (1993). Kinematic model of active deformation in central Asia, *Geophys. Res. Lett.* **20,** no. 10, 895–898, doi: 10.1029/93GL00128.

Avouac, J.-P., P. Tapponnier, M. Bai, H. You, and G. Wang (1993). Active thrusting and folding along the northern Tien Shan and Late Cenozoic rotation of the Tarim relative to Dzungaria and Kazakhstan, *J. Geophys. Res.* **98,** no. B4, 6755–6804, doi: 10.1029/92JB01963.

Bürgmann, R., P. A. Rosen, and E. J. Fielding (2000). Synthetic aperture radar interferometry to measure earth's surface topography, *Annu. Rev. Earth Planet. Sci.* **28,** 169–209, doi: 10.1146/annurev.earth.28.1.169.

Charreau, J., Y. Chen, S. A. Gilder, S. Dominguez, J. Lavé, W. M. Wang, and J.-P. Avouac (2009). Neogene uplift of the Tian Shan Mountains observed in the magnetic record of the Jingou River section (northwest China), *Tectonics* **28,** TC2008, doi: 10.1029/2007TC002137.

Chong, J.-H., B. Oryan, L. Shen, M. S. Steckler, and E. O. Lindsey (2024). Interseismic uplift of anticlines above the Rakhine-Bangladesh megathrust from ALOS-2 InSAR, *J. Geophys. Res.* **129,** no. 1, e2023JB030003, doi: 10.1029/2024JB030003.

Contreras, J. (2010). A model for low amplitude detachment folding and syntectonic stratigraphy based on the conservation of mass equation, *J. Struct. Geol.* **32,** no. 4, 566–579, doi: 10.1016/j.jsg.2010.03.006.

Deng, Q. D., P. Z. Zhang, Y. K. Ran, X. P. Yang, W. Min, and Q. Z. Chu (2003). Basic characteristics of active tectonics of China, *Sci. China Earth Sci.* **46,** no. 4, 356–372, doi: 10.1360/03yd9032.

Ding, Y., X. Liu, X. Dai, G. Yin, Y. Yang, and J. Guo (2024). D-InSAR-based analysis of slip distribution and coulomb stress implications from the 2024 M_w 7.01 Wushi earthquake, *Remote Sens.* **16,** no. 22, 4319, doi: 10.3390/rs16224319.

Famiglietti, N. A., D. Cheloni, R. Caputo, and A. Vicari (2025). Geodetic model of the 2024 January 22 M_w 7.0 Wushi (northwestern China) earthquake and M_w 5.7 aftershock from inversion of InSAR data, *Geophys. J. Int.* **241,** no. 2, 941–953, doi: 10.1093/gji/ggaf084.

Fan, Q., C. Xu, L. Yi, Y. Liu, Y. Wen, and Z. Yin (2017). Implication of adaptive smoothness constraint and Helmert variance component estimation in seismic slip inversion, *J. Geod.* **91,** 1163–1177, doi: 10.1007/s00190-017-1015-0.

Fialko, Y., D. Sandwell, M. Simons, and P. Rosen (2005). Three-dimensional deformation caused by the Bam, Iran, earthquake and the origin of shallow slip deficit, *Nature* **435,** no. 7040, 295–299, doi: 10.1038/nature03425.

Fournier, T., M. E. Pritchard, and N. Finnegan (2011). Accounting for atmospheric delays in InSAR data in a search for long-wavelength deformation in South America, *IEEE Trans. Geosci. Remote Sens.* **49,** no. 10, 3856–3867, doi: 10.1109/TGRS.2011.2139217.

Fukuda, J., and K. M. Johnson (2010). Mixed linear-non-linear inversion of crustal deformation data: Bayesian inference of model, weighting and regularization parameters, *Geophys. J. Int.* **181,** 1441–1458, doi: 10.1111/j.1365-246X.2010.04564.x.

Gao, H., M. S. Liao, X. G. Liu, W. B. Xu, and N. Fang (2022). Source geometry and causes of the 2019 Ms 6.0 Changning earthquake in Sichuan, China based on InSAR, *Remote Sens.* **14,** no. 9, 2082, doi: 10.3390/rs14092082.

Goldstein, R. M., and C. L. Werner (1998). Radar interferogram filtering for geophysical applications, *Geophys. Res. Lett.* **25,** no. 21, 4035–4038, doi: 10.1029/98GL02964.

He, Y., T. Li, S. Wen, and C. Wang (2021). The 2020 M_w 6.0 Jiashi earthquake: Coinvolvement of thin-skinned thrusting and basement shortening in shaping the Keping-Tage fold-and-thrust belt in southwestern Tian Shan, *Seismol. Res. Lett.* **92,** no. 6, 3216–3230, doi: 10.1785/0220210063.

Jabbour, M., D. Dhont, Y. Hervouët, and J.-P. Deroin (2012). Geometry and kinematics of fault-propagation folds with variable interlimb angle, *J. Struct. Geol.* **42,** 212–226, doi: 10.1016/j.jsg.2012.05.002.

Jia, L., J. Sun, L. Lü, J. Pang, and Y. Wang (2020). Late Oligocene-miocene intra-continental mountain building of the Harke Mountains, southern Chinese Tian Shan, *J. Asian Earth Sci.* **191,** 104,198, doi: 10.1016/j.jseaes.2019.104198.

Jónsson, S., H. A. Zebker, P. Segall, and F. Amelung (2002). Fault slip distribution of the 1999 M_w 7.1 Hector Mine, California, earthquake, estimated from satellite radar and GPS measurements, *Bull. Seismol. Soc. Am.* **92,** no. 5, 1970–1985, doi: 10.1785/0120000922.

Li, F., X. Cheng, H. Chen, X. Shi, Y. Li, J. Charreau, and R. Weldon (2023). Cenozoic shortening and propagation in the eastern Kuqa fold-and-thrust belt, South Tian Shan, NW China, *Tectonics* **38,** no. 1, e2022TC007447, doi: 10.1029/2022TC007447.

Li, J., Y. Yao, R. Li, S. Yusan, G. Li, J. T. Freymueller, and Q. Wang (2022). Present-day strike-slip faulting and thrusting of the Kepingtage fold-and-thrust belt in southern Tianshan: Constraints from GPS observations, *Geophys. Res. Lett.* **49,** no. 20, e2022GL099105, doi: 10.1029/2022GL099105.

Li, T., J. Chen, J. A. Thompson Jobe, D. W. Burbank, and W. Zheng (2018). Active bending-moment faulting: Geomorphic expression, controlling conditions, accommodation of fold deformation, *Tectonics* **37,** no. 10, 3820–3843, doi: 10.1029/2018TC004982.

Li, T., Z. Chen, J. Chen, J. A. Thompson Jobe, D. W. Burbank, Z. Li, X. He, W. Zheng, P. Zhang, and B. Zhang (2019). Along-strike and downdip segmentation of the Pamir frontal thrust and its association with the 1985 M_w 6.9 Wuqia earthquake, *J. Geophys. Res.* **124,** no. 9, 9890–9919, doi: 10.1029/2019JB017319.

Li, Y., M. Liu, M. Hao, L. Zhu, D. Cui, and Q. Wang (2021). Active crustal deformation in the Tian Shan region, central Asia, *Tectonophysics* **811,** 228,868, doi: 10.1016/j.tecto.2021.228868.

Lü, L., T. Li, Z. Chen, J. Chen, J. Thompson Jobe, and L. Fang (2021). Active structural geometries and their correlation with moderate (M 5.5-7.0) earthquakes in the Jiashi-Keping region, Tian Shan southwestern front, *Seismol. Res. Lett.* **92,** no. 6, 3087–3104, doi: 10.1029/2021TC006760.

Mallick, R., R. Bürgmann, K. Johnson, and J. Hubbard (2021). A unified framework for earthquake sequences and the growth of geological structure in fold-thrust belts, *J. Geophys. Res.* **126,** e2021JB022045, doi: 10.1029/2021JB022045.

Massonnet, D., M. Rossi, C. Carmona, F. Adragna, G. Peltzer, K. Feigl, and T. Rabaute (1993). The displacement field of the landers earthquake mapped by radar interferometry, *Nature* **364,** 138–142, doi: 10.1038/364138a0.

Meng, L. S., C. Yan, S. N. Lv, H. Y. Sun, S. H. Xue, Q. K. Li, L. F. Zhou, D. Edwing, K. Edwing, X. P. Geng, *et al.* (2024). Synthetic aperture radar for geosciences, *Rev. Geophys.* **62,** no. 3, RG2001, doi: 10.1029/2023RG000821.

Metropolis, N., A. W. Rosenbluth, M. N. Rosenbluth, A. H. Teller, and E. Teller (1953). Equation of state calculations by fast computing machines, *J. Chem. Phys.* **21,** 1087–1092, doi: 10.1063/1.1699114.

Molnar, P., and P. Tapponnier (1975). Cenozoic tectonics of Asia: Effects of a continental collision, *Science* **189,** no. 4201, 419–426, doi: 10.1126/science.189.4201.419.

Okada, Y. (1985). Surface deformation due to shear and tensile faults in a half space, *Bull. Seismol. Soc. Am.* **75,** no. 4, 1135–1154, doi: 10.1785/BSSA0750041135.

Qiu, J., J. Sun, and L. Ji (2024). The 2024 M_w 7.1 Wushi earthquake: A thrust and strike-slip event unveiling the seismic mechanisms of the South Tian Shan's thick-skin tectonics, *Remote Sens.* **16,** no. 16, 2937, doi: 10.3390/rs16162937.

Royden, L. H., B. C. Burchfiel, and R. D. van der Hilst (2008). The geological evolution of the Tibetan plateau, *Science* **321,** no. 5892, 1054–1058, doi: 10.1126/science.1155371.

Shen, Z.-K., M. Wang, Y. Li, D. D. Jackson, A. Yin, D. Dong, and P. Fang (2001). Crustal deformation along the Altyn Tagh fault system, western China, from GPS, *J. Geophys. Res.* **106,** no. B12, 607–621, doi: 10.1029/2001JB000349.

Sobel, E. R., and T. A. Dumitru (1997). Thrusting and exhumation around the margins of the western Tarim basin, *J. Geophys. Res.* **102,** no. B3, 5043–5063, doi: 10.1029/96JB03267.

Suppe, J. (1983). Geometry and kinematics of fault-bend folding, *Am. J. Sci.* **283,** no. 7, 684–721, doi: 10.2475/ajs.283.7.684.

Tapponnier, P., and P. Molnar (1979). Active faulting and Cenozoic tectonics of the Tien Shan, *J. Geophys. Res.* **84,** no. B7, 3425–3459, doi: 10.1029/JB084iB07p03425.

Tian, Z., J. Sun, B. F. Windley, Z. Zhang, Z. Gong, X. Lin, and W. Xiao (2016). Cenozoic detachment folding in the southern Tianshan foreland, NW China: Shortening distances and rates, *J. Struct. Geol.* **84,** 142–161, doi: 10.1016/j.jsg.2016.01.007.

Tsukahara, K., and Y. Takada (2018). Aseismic fold growth in southwestern Taiwan detected by InSAR and GNSS, *Earth Planets Space* **70,** 52, doi: 10.1186/s40623-018-0816-6.

Turner, S. A., J. W. Cosgrove, and J. G. Liu (2010). *Controls on Lateral Structural Variability Along the Keping Shan Thrust Belt, SW Tien Shan Foreland, China*, Geological Society of America, London Special Publications, Vol. 348, 71–85, doi: 10.1144/SP348.5.

Turner, S. A., J. G. Liu, and J. W. Cosgrove (2011). Structural evolution of the Piqiang fault zone, NW Tarim basin, China, *J. Asian Earth Sci.* **40,** no. 1, 394–402, doi: 10.1016/j.jseaes.2010.06.005.

Wang, C., L. Chang, X. Wang, B. Zhang, and A. Stein (2024). Interferometric synthetic aperture radar statistical inference in deformation measurement and geophysical inversion: A review, *IEEE Trans. Geosci. Remote Sens.* 12, no. 1, 8–35, doi: 10.1109/MGRS.2023.3344159.

Wang, Q., P. Z. Zhang, J. T. Freymueller, R. Bilham, K. M. Larson, X. Lai, and Q. Chen (2001). Present-day crustal deformation in China constrained by global positioning system measurements, *Science* **294,** no. 5542, 574–577, doi: 10.1126/science.1063647.

Wang, S., E. Nissen, L. Pousse-Beltran, T. J. Craig, R. Jiao, and E. A. Bergman (2022). Structural controls on coseismic rupture revealed by the 2020 M_w 6.0 Jiashi earthquake (Kepingtag belt, SW Tian Shan, China), *Geophys. J. Int.* **230,** 1895–1910, doi: 10.1093/gji/ggac159.

Wang, X., C. Xu, Y. Wen, X. Zhao, S. Wang, and G. Xu (2024). Distribution of interseismic coupling along the Maidan fault in Tianshan before the 2024 M_w 7.0 Wushi earthquake, *Geophys. Res. Lett.* **51,** no. 24, e2024GL111472, doi: 10.1029/2024GL111472.

Wells, D. L., and K. J. Coppersmith (1994). New empirical relationships among magnitude, rupture length, rupture width, rupture area, and surface displacement, *Bull. Seism. Soc. Am.* **84,** no. 4, 974–1002, doi: 10.1785/BSSA0840040974.

Wessel, P., J. F. Luis, L. Uieda, R. Scharroo, F. Wobbe, W. H. F. Smith, and D. Tian (2019). The Generic Mapping Tools version 6, *Geochem. Geophys. Geosys.* **20,** 5556–5564, doi:10.1029/2019GC008515.

Wu, C., P. Zhang, Z. Zhang, W. Zheng, B. Xu, W. Wang, Z. Yu, X. Dai, B. Zhang, and K. Zang (2023). Slip partitioning and crustal deformation patterns in the Tianshan orogenic belt derived from GPS measurements and their tectonic implications, *Earth Sci. Rev.* **238,** 104,362, doi: 10.1016/j.earscirev.2023.104362.

Wu, C., W. Zheng, P. Zhang, Z. Zhang, Q. Jia, J. Yu, H. Zhang, Y. Yao, J. Liu, G. Han, and J. Chen (2019). Oblique thrust of the Maidan fault and late Quaternary tectonic deformation in the southwestern Tian Shan, northwestern China, *Tectonics* **38,** no. 8, 2625–2645, doi: 10.1029/2018TC005248.

Wu, D., Z. Chen, and M. Zimin (2024). InSAR coseismic deformation field and seismogenic structure of the 2020 M_w 6.0 Jiashi earthquake and the implication for the moderate-magnitude seismicity in the southwestern Tian Shan, western China, *Front. Earth Sci.* **11,** 1305519, doi: 10.3389/feart.2023.1305519.

Xiao, W. J., and M. Santosh (2014). The western Central Asian Orogenic Belt: A window to accretionary orogenesis and continental growth, *Gondwana Res.* **25,** no. 4, 1429–1444, doi: 10.1016/j.gr.2013.08.017.

Xiao, W., D. Song, B. F. Windley, J. Li, C. Han, B. Wan, J. Zhang, S. Ao, and Z. Zhang (2020). Accretionary processes and metallogenesis of the central Asian orogenic belt: Advances and perspectives, *Sci. China Earth Sci.* **36,** 329–361, doi: 10.1007/s11430-019-9524-6.

Xu, W., G. Feng, L. Meng, A. Zhang, J. P. Ampuero, R. Bürgmann, and L. Fang (2018). Transpressional rupture cascade of the 2016 Mw 7.8 Kaikoura Earthquake, New Zealand, *J. Geophys. Res.* **123,** no. 3, 2396–2416, doi: 10.1002/2017JB015168.

Yang, S. M., J. Li, and Q. Wang (2008). The deformation pattern and fault rate in the Tianshan Mountains inferred from GPS observations, *Sci. China Earth Sci.* **51,** no. 8, 1064–1080, doi: 10.1007/s11430-008-0090-8.

Yang, X., Q. Deng, P. Zhang, and X. Xu (2008). Crustal shortening of major nappe structures on the front margins of the Tianshan, *Seismol. Geol.* **30,** no. 1, 111–131, (in Chinese with English abstract).

Yang, X., Y. Ran, F. Song, X. Xu, J. Cheng, W. Min, Z. Han, and L. Chen (2006). The analysis for crust shortening of kalpin thrust tectonic zone, south-western Tianshan, Xinjiang, China, *Seismol. Geol.* **28,** no. 2, 194–204 (in Chinese with English abstract).

Yao, Y., S. Wen, T. Li, and C. Wang (2020). The 2020 M_w 6.0 Jiashi earthquake: A fold earthquake event in the southern Tian Shan, northwest China, *Seismol. Res. Lett.* **92,** no. 2A, 859–869, doi: 10.1785/0220200146.

Yin, A., S. Nie, P. Craig, T. M. Harrison, F. J. Ryerson, Q. Xiang, and Y. Geng (1998). Late Cenozoic tectonic evolution of the southern Chinese Tian Shan, *Tectonics* **17,** no. 1, 1–27, doi: 10.1029/97TC03140.

Zelenin, E., D. Bachmanov, S. Garipova, V. Trifonov, and A. Kozhurin (2022). The active faults of Eurasia database (AFEAD): The ontology and design behind the continental-scale dataset, *Earth Syst. Sci. Data* **14,** 4489–4503, doi: 10.5194/essd-14-4489-2022.

Zhang, B., L. Qian, T. Li, J. Chen, J. Xu, Y. Yao, L. Fang, C. Xie, J. Chen, G. Liu, *et al.* (2024). Geological disasters and surface ruptures of the January 23, 2024 Ms7.1 Wushi earthquake, Xinjiang, China, *Seismol. Geol.* **46,** no. 1, 220–234, doi: 10.3969/j.issn.0253-4967.2024.01.013 (in Chinese with English abstract).

Zhang, L., A. Li, X. Yang, W. Huang, S. Li, and H. Yang (2024). Multiple fold earthquakes recorded by the paleoseismic surface ruptures of bending-moment faults in the Qiulitage Anticline, South Tianshan, China, *Seismol. Res. Lett.* **95,** no. 5, 2844–2858, doi: 10.1785/0220230388.

Zhang, P. Z., Z. K. Shen, M. Wang, W. J. Gan, R. Burgmann, P. Molnar, Q. Wang, Z. Niu, J. Sun, J. Wu, H. Sun, and X. You (2004). Continuous deformation of the Tibetan plateau from global positioning system data, *Geology* **32,** no. 9, 809–812, doi: 10.1130/G20554.1.

Zhang, X., J. Li, X. Liu, Z. Li, and N. Adil (2023). Coseismic deformation field and fault slip distribution inversion of the 2020 Jiashi Ms 6.4 earthquake: Considering the atmospheric effect with Sentinel-1 data interferometry, *Sensors* **23,** no. 6, 3046, doi: 10.3390/s23063046.

Zhang, Y., S. Yang, H. Chen, Y. Dilek, X. Cheng, X. Lin, and C. Wang (2019). The effect of overburden thickness on deformation mechanisms in the Keping fold-thrust belt, southwestern Chinese Tian Shan Mountains, *Tectonophysics* **753,** 79–92, doi: 10.1016/j.tecto.2019.01.005.

Zhao, L., Z. Chen, L. Xie, Z. Zhu, and W. Xu (2024). Coseismic deformation and slip model of the 2024 M_W 7.0 Wushi earthquake obtained from InSAR observation, *Rev. Geophys. Planet. Phys.* **55,** no. 4, 453–460, doi: 10.19975/j.dqyxx.2024-010 (in Chinese with English abstract).

Zhao, X., L. Zhou, C. Xu, G. Jiang, W. Feng, Y. Wen, and N. Fang (2024). Modified Bayesian method for simultaneously imaging fault geometry and slip distribution with reduced uncertainty, applied to 2017 M_w 7.3 Sarpol-e Zahab (Iran) earthquake, *J. Geod.* **98,** 106, doi: 10.1007/s00190-024-01906-6.

Zheng, G., H. Wang, T. J. Wright, Y. Lou, R. Zhang, W. Zhang, C. Shi, J. Huang, and N. Wei (2017). Crustal deformation in the India-Eurasia collision zone from 25 years of GPS measurements, *J. Geophys. Res.* **122,** no. 11, 9290–9312, doi: 10.1002/2017JB014465.

Zheng, R., R. Zou, R. Dong, Z. Fang, and Q. Wang (2024). The 2024 M_w 7.0 Wushi earthquake in southern Tianshan convergent zone: Finite-fault model for the coseismic rupture and aftershock, *Seismol. Res. Lett.* **95,** no. 2A, 816–827, doi: 10.1785/0220240126.

Zhou, Y., R. T. Walker, J. Hollingsworth, M. Talebian, X. Song, and B. Parsons (2016). Coseismic and postseismic displacements from the 1978 M_w 7.3 Tabas-e-Golshan earthquake in eastern Iran, *Earth Planet. Sci. Lett.* **452,** 185–196, doi: 10.1016/j.epsl.2016.07.038.

Zubovich, A. V., X.-Q. Wang, Y. G. Scherba, G. G. Schelochkov, R. Reilinger, C. Reigber, O. L. Mosienko, P. Molnar, W. Michajljow, V. I. Makarov, *et al.* (2010). GPS velocity field for the Tien Shan and surrounding regions, *Tectonics* **29,** no. 6, TC6014, doi: 10.1029/2010TC002772.

Manuscript received 30 April 2025
Published online 13 October 2025

The Earthquake Swarms of Eastern Maine and Nearby New Brunswick Since 2006

John E. Ebel*[1]

Abstract

Several earthquake swarms in Maine and nearby New Brunswick are analyzed to look for common features among the swarms. The swarms took place at Bar Harbor, Maine, in 2006–2007, at Searsport, Maine, in 2011, at McAdam, New Brunswick, in 2012 and 2015–2016, at Jonesboro, Maine, in 2022, at Dedham, Maine, in 2022–2023, and at Millinocket, Maine, in 2022–2023. The six earthquake swarms all had focal depths of 4 km or less, appear to have taken place within or at the edges of Devonian granitic plutons, and with one exception show spatial distributions that are parallel to trends in the local geology. The swarms all had spatial extents of 3 km or less. The time histories of most of the swarms in Maine and New Brunswick are generally consistent with the main part of the swarm being controlled by aseismic creep rather than by fluid diffusion. Modeling of a rock inclusion that is stiffer than the surrounding rock mass in a regional stress field shows that stress will concentrate within the rock inclusion as well as along some of its edges. This modeling suggests that granitic rock bodies in eastern North American could have stress concentrations that fail in earthquakes, although the size of the largest earthquake in any single granitic rock body cannot be assessed by the results of this study.

Cite this article as Ebel, J. E. (2025). The Earthquake Swarms of Eastern Maine and Nearby New Brunswick Since 2006, *Seismol. Res. Lett.* **97**, 651–663, doi: 10.1785/0220250237.

Supplemental Material

Introduction

Although most earthquakes in northeastern North America (NENA) occur either as single events or as part of a foreshock–mainshock–aftershock sequence, some smaller percentage of the earthquakes of this region takes place in earthquake swarms, where there is no clear mainshock–aftershock sequence and where the rate of seismicity with time does not follow Omori's aftershock law. Examples of some earthquake swarms in NENA were at Moodus, Connecticut, in the 1980s for which a small, short-duration microearthquake swarm was observed in 1981 (Ebel *et al.*, 1982) and for which four more significant earthquake swarms, each lasting several months and involving 10s to over 100 earthquakes, were documented in 1982, 1983, 1986, and 1987–1988 (Ebel, 1989). Among all of the Moodus swarms, the largest earthquake was only M_c 2.9. Even with a dense local network at the time to provide hypocenters to a precision of about 0.5 km, the association of the Moodus swarms of the 1980s with local geologic structures was ambiguous, as was the cause of these swarms (Woodward-Clyde Consultants, 1988; Ebel, 1989).

More recently, earthquake swarms have taken place in other parts of NENA. For example, Ebel *et al.* (2008) reported on an earthquake swarm at Bar Harbor, Maine, in 2006–2007, for which the largest earthquake was M_{Lg} 4.2. Napoli and Ebel (2017) analyzed a swarm of offshore earthquakes in the Gulf of Maine in 2012–2013, with the largest earthquake there being M_{Lg} 3.9. From even just the few examples discussed so far, as well as others that have been published, it appears that earthquake swarms occur in many different geologic settings in NENA.

The purpose of this article is to analyze several earthquake swarms in eastern Maine and nearby New Brunswick to look for common features among the swarms. In particular, the questions that were investigated are how the swarms relate to the local geology and whether there are any common geological conditions in the places where these swarms occurred. The answers to these questions might give some indications of what geologic structures might be seismically active in the region. It should be noted that the swarms of eastern Maine and New Brunswick took place in areas of metamorphosed bedrock that contains many intrusive igneous rock bodies, and there is no hydrocarbon production in the region because the rocks are not suitable for producing hydrocarbons. Furthermore, the rocks in which the swarms took place contain no waste disposal sites or impounded reservoirs. Thus, the swarms are inherently natural phenomena and are not anthropogenic.

1. Weston Observatory, Department of Earth and Environmental Sciences, Boston College, Weston, Massachusetts, U.S.A., https://orcid.org/0000-0003-1064-0629 (JEE)

*Corresponding author: ebel@bc.edu

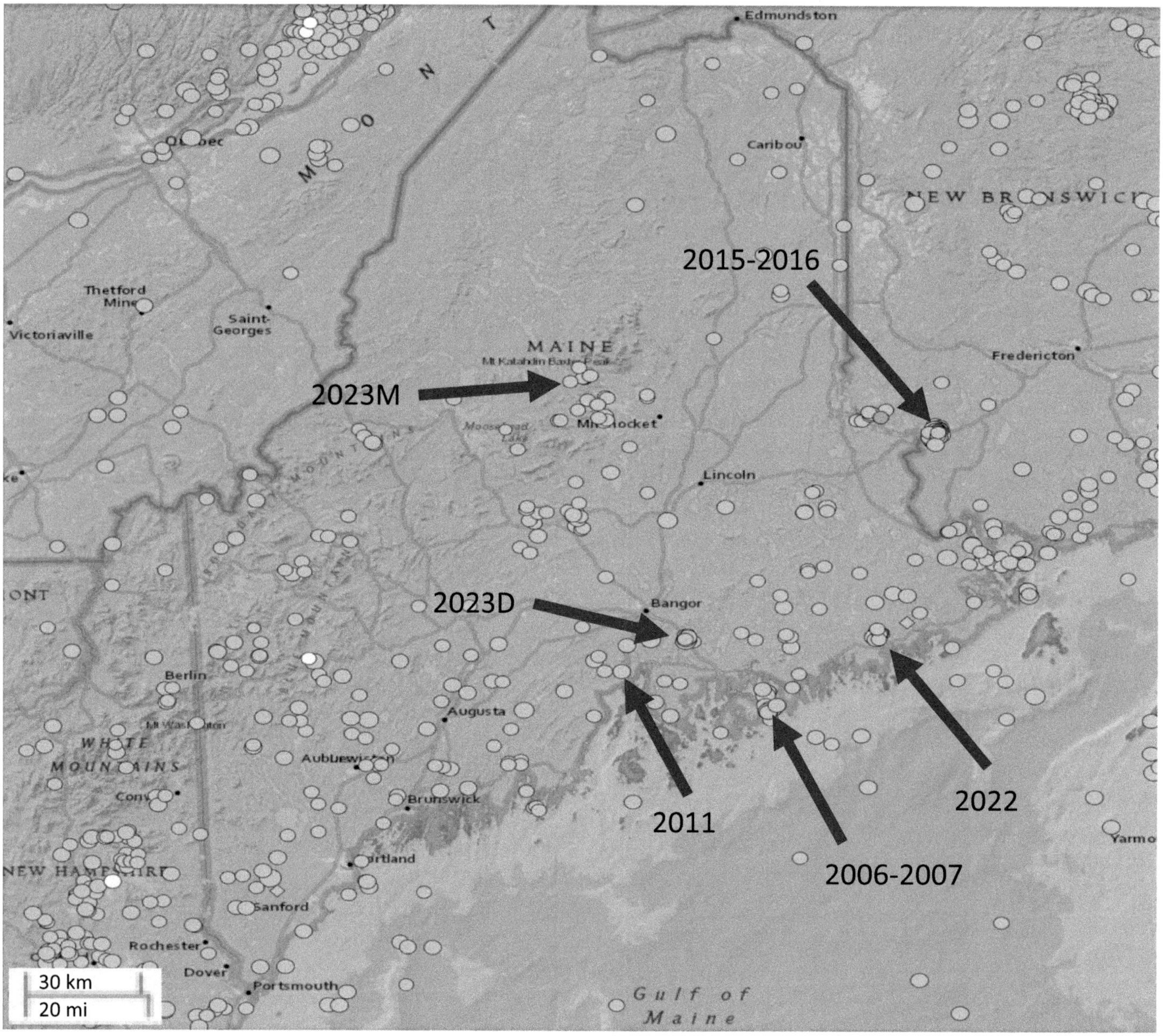

Figure 1. Map of the seismicity of Maine and surrounding areas from 2006 to 2023 from the U.S. Geological Survey (USGS) earthquake hazards program (see Data and Resources). The map extent ranges from 42.9° to 47.4° N and 71.9° to 66.3° W. The earthquake symbols are scaled to magnitude, with the magnitude values ranging from 1.0 to 4.7. The locations of the earthquake swarms discussed in this study are shown by the arrows, and the dates of the swarms are shown at the tails of the arrows. The earthquake swarms are 2006–2007, Bar Harbor; 2011, Searsport; 2015–2016, McAdam; 2022, Jonesboro; 2023D, Dedham; and 2023M, Millinocket. The color version of this figure is available only in the electronic edition.

Earthquake Swarms in Maine and New Brunswick Since 2006

A total of six earthquake swarms are discussed in this article. Details of three of the swarms, those at Bar Harbor, Maine, in 2006–2007 (Ebel *et al.*, 2008), at Searsport, Maine, in 2011 (Ebel, 2016), and at McAdam New Brunswick in 2012 and 2015–2016 (Bent *et al.*, 2017), have already been published. Three additional swarms are analyzed in this article, those at Jonesboro, Maine, in 2022, at Brewer, Maine, in 2022–2023, and at Millinocket, Maine, in 2022–2023. In the following sections, the spatial trend and the association with the local geology of each swarm are discussed. The locations of all of these swarms are shown in Figure 1. The spatial trends of the swarm events were determined using the relative location analysis method of Ebel *et al.* (2008). In this method, one earthquake is selected as a master event and the locations of all other events are found relative to the location of the master event. By ignoring the absolute locations of the events, the locations of the other events relative to the master event can be found with very high precision. For the relative location analyses reported on here, the epicentral

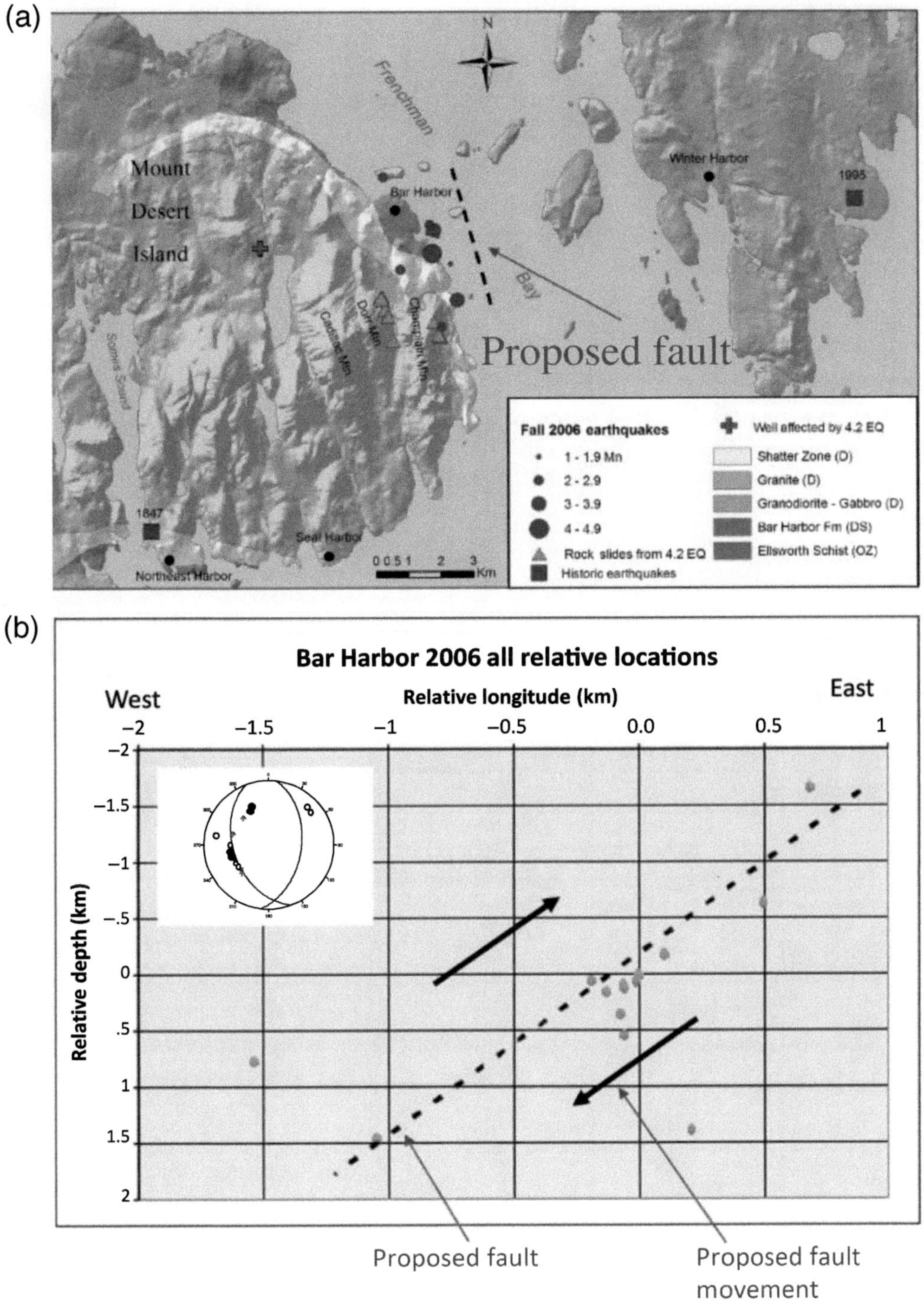

Figure 2. (a) Map of the bedrock geology of the area of the 2006–2007 Bar Harbor, Maine, earthquake swarm (locations of the swarm events are indicated by the red circles). The surface projection of the inferred fault is shown by the dashed line. (b) Results of the relative location analysis, showing an inferred fault that dips toward the west. The master event is at location (0,0). The focal mechanism of the M_{Lg} 4.2 earthquake is inset. Both figures are from Ebel *et al.* (2008). The color version of this figure is available only in the electronic edition.

uncertainties for events within about 500 m of the master event are typically 39–80 m, and the depth uncertainties are all less than 100 m. For events more than 500 m from the master event, the uncertainties of the relative epicentral locations range typically from <100 m to as much as 700 m for the most distant events based on a jackknife analysis, with a similar uncertainty profile for relative depth. The absolute locations of the best-located events in each of these swarms are less than 2 km, and those for which arrival times from local portable instruments were obtained are less than 1 km. Thus, both the relative location patterns and absolute locations of the events in this study are well constrained.

2006–2007 Bar Harbor, Maine, Swarm

The Bar Harbor swarm, located near the town of Bar Harbor, Maine (Fig. 2a), consisted of at least 41 events, with the largest being M_{Lg} 4.2 on 3 October 2006. Most of the events took place between September and December 2006, with a few events occurring in the first part of 2007. Ebel *et al.* (2008) showed that the earthquake swarm apparently took place on a west-dipping, north-striking thrust fault based on the focal mechanism of the M_{Lg} 4.2 earthquake and the relative locations of the swarm events, which have uncertainties of 100 m or less (Fig. 2b). The swarm events had focal depths of about 1–2 km based on data from two portable seismographs installed in Bar Harbor during the swarm, data from which were also used to help constrain the absolute locations of the swarm events to less than 1 km uncertainty. The inferred fault on which the earthquake swarm took place projects to the Earth's surface in Frenchman Bay to the east of the town of Bar Harbor (Fig. 2a). The length of the projected fault zone from the spread of epicenters in Figure 2a is about 5 km. If this zone had failed

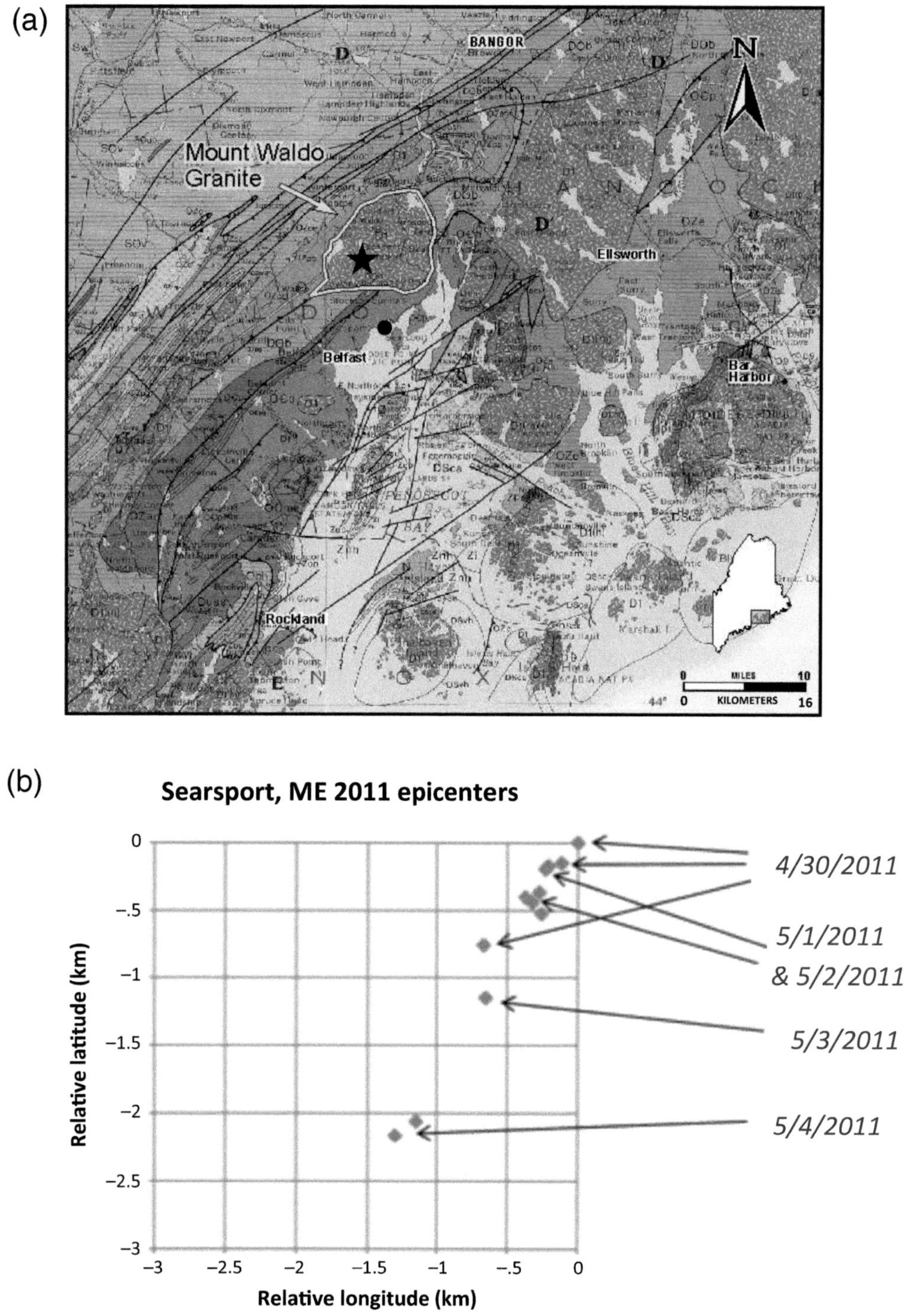

Figure 3. (a) Map of the bedrock geology of the area of the 2011 Searsport, Maine, earthquake swarm, with the swarm location indicated by the star. The black dot shows the location of the town of Searsport, with the size of the star indicating the uncertainty in the absolute locations of the swarm events. The Mount Waldo granite is a Devonian granitic pluton, which may be more than 7 km thick in the epicentral area of the 2011 swarm (Sweeney, 1976). (b) Results of the relative location analysis, showing the locations and dates of the swarm events. The master event is at location (0,0). Both figures are from Ebel (2016). The color version of this figure is available only in the electronic edition.

in a single earthquake, the earthquake would have had a magnitude of about M_w 5.4 using the scaling laws of Wells and Coppersmith (1994) and Leonard (2010). The fault dips toward the west beneath the rocks of Mount Desert Island, which is made up primarily of rocks of a Devonian granitic pluton. At its eastern edge, the pluton abuts a thin belt of sandstones of the Bar Harbor formation lying unconformably on much older Ellsworth schist along the coast where the earthquake swarm took place (Gilman *et al.*, 1988).

2011 Searsport, Maine, Swarm

A swarm of 17 small earthquakes took place over a 12 day period starting on 29 April 2011 near Searsport, Maine (Fig. 3a), with the largest being M_{Lg} 1.7 (Ebel, 2016). The focal depths of the events of the swarm were probably about 1.8 km based on data from some portable seismographs that were installed in the epicentral area and recorded some of the swarm events. Ebel (2016) computed relative locations of the larger of the swarm events and showed that the events progressed in a unilateral fashion from the northeast toward the southwest over a distance of about 2.5 km (Fig. 3b). The uncertainties in the relative location epicenters were <100 m for the events on 1 May, <200 m for the events on 2 May, <800 m for the events on 3 May, and <1000 m for the events on 4 May. The absolute locations of some later swarm events (not shown in Fig. 3b) were well constrained using *P*- and *S*-arrival-time readings from two portable seismographs that were installed in the epicentral area on 8 May. The data from these two portable stations allowed the absolute hypocentral location of the swarm event on 10 May at 17:51 UTC to be located with uncertainties of less than 1.0 km in epicenter and focal depth. The absolute hypocentral

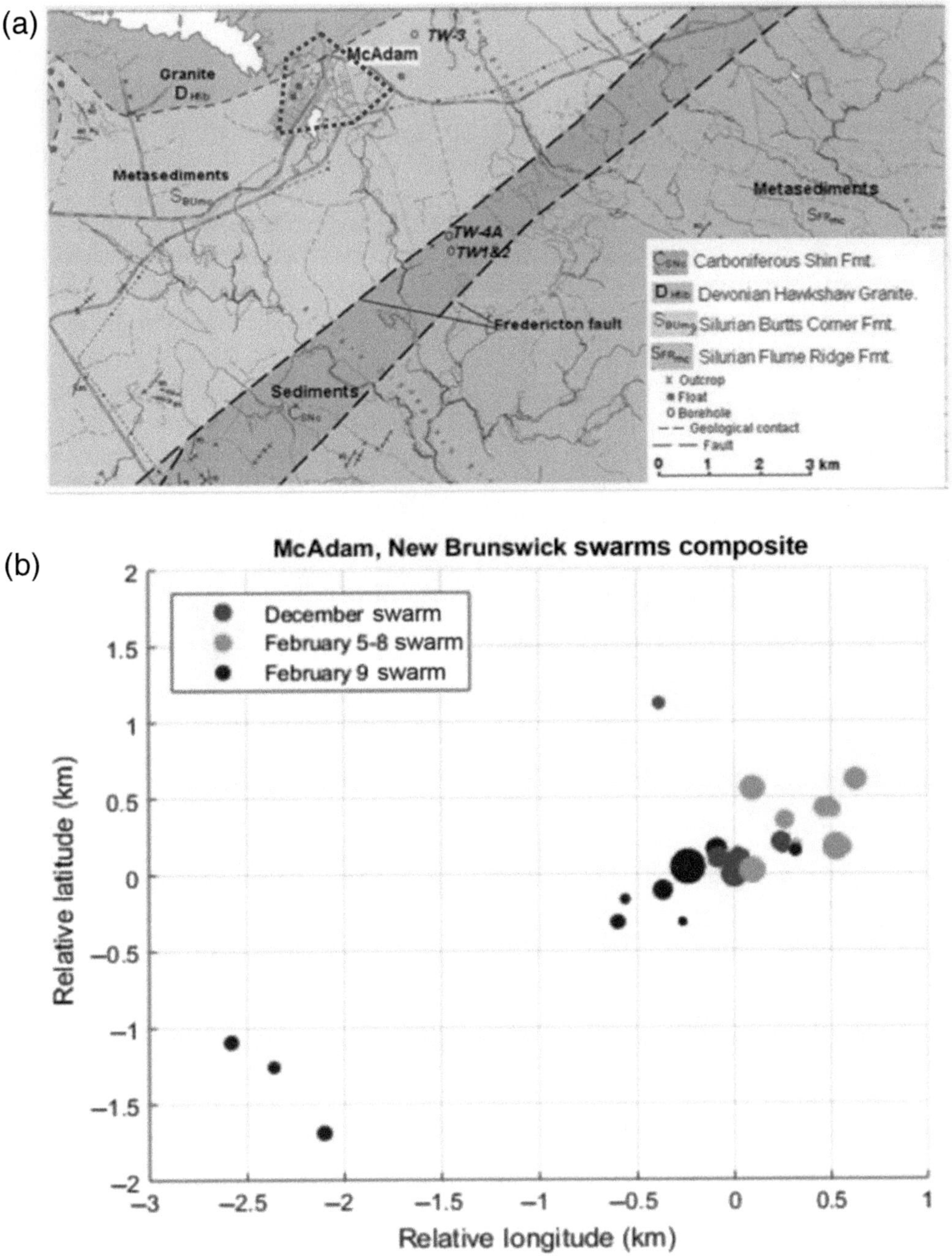

Figure 4. (a) Map of the bedrock geology of the area of the 2015–2016 McAdam, New Brunswick, earthquake swarm. The area of the well-located swarm events beneath the town of McAdam is outlined by the short-dashed polygon (from Bent *et al.*, 2017). (b) Results of the relative location analysis, showing the locations and dates of the swarm events, first presented by Pontrelli and Ebel (2017). The master event is at location (0,0). The color version of this figure is available only in the electronic edition.

calculations that included arrival times from the portable seismographs confirm that the swarm was located in the center of the granitic Mount Waldo Pluton, which is of Devonian age (Fig. 3a). Curiously, although no faults are mapped within the Mount Waldo Pluton itself, the spatial trend of the 2011 swarm as shown in Figure 3b is on-strike with a possible extension of a southwest–northeast fault that terminates on the southwestern tip of the pluton (Fig. 3a).

2012 and 2015–2016 McAdam, New Brunswick, Swarm

Two earthquake swarms, one from March to June 2012 and a second, larger swarm from December 2015 to June 2016, took place apparently under the town of McAdam in southwestern New Brunswick (Bent *et al.*, 2017; Fig. 4a). The 2012 swarm had 28 events that could be located, and many smaller events that were heard by local residents in McAdam but that were not detected on regional seismic network stations were also reported. The largest earthquake of this swarm had M_N 2.6. Another swarm in the same place had some precursory small events in December 2015, but the main swarm started on 5 February 2016. The largest event of this swarm had M_N 3.3 on 9 February, and over 160 events of this swarm had a sufficient number of seismographic readings that a hypocenter could be computed, with many more detected events that were too small to locate. Natural Resources Canada deployed portable seismographic instruments in the McAdam area for both swarms, and they confirmed that the events were coming from directly beneath the town with focal depths between 0 and 1.5 km, with most of the events having depths of less than 1 km. Epicentral uncertainties for locations that include *P* and *S* readings from the portable seismographs are 1.0 km or less.

Pontrelli and Ebel (2017) reported on a relative location analysis of some of the larger events of the 2016 swarm, using the relative location method of Ebel *et al.* (2008). Those relative locations are shown in Figure 4b, along with a map in Figure 4a of the local McAdam geology from Bent *et al.* (2017). The relative location analysis shows that the events of 5–8 February were located to the northeast of the December 2015 event locations,

(a)

(b)

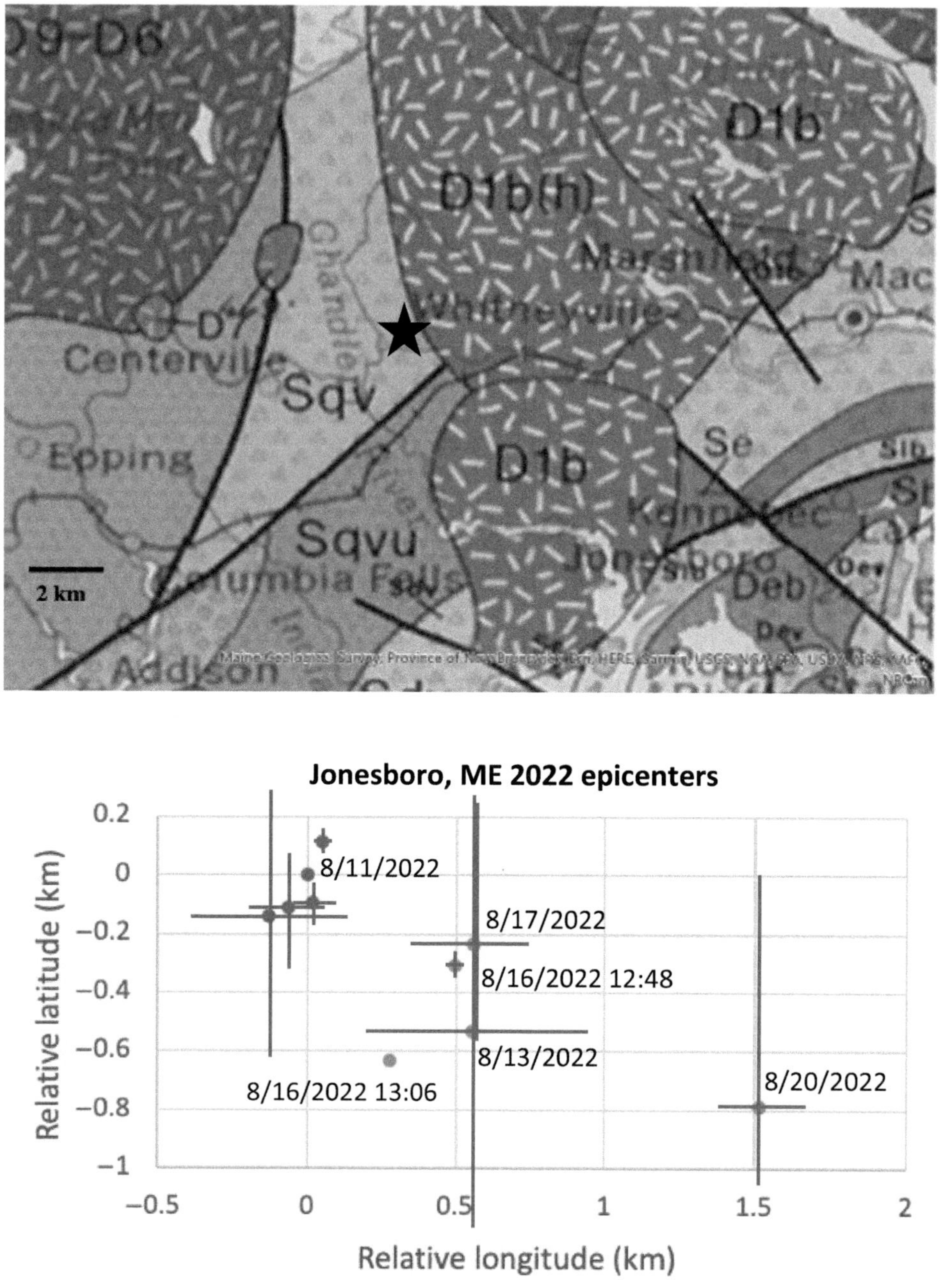

Figure 5. (a) Map of the bedrock geology of the area of the 2022 Jonesboro, Maine, earthquake swarm (from Osberg *et al.*, 1985), with the swarm location indicated by the star. The size of the star indicates the uncertainty in the absolute locations of the swarm events. Geologic units are: D1b and D1b(h), Devonian granite; D7, Devonian syenite; Deb, Devonian basalt; D9-06, Devonian grabbro; Se, Silurian tuff breccia; Sqv, Silurian mafic to ultramafic volcanic rock. (b) Results of the relative location analysis carried out for this study (given in Table S1). The master event is at location (0,0). The events on 11 August 2022 are one color and the events from 12 August 2022 to 20 August 2022 are a different color. Note that the epicentral uncertainties for the event on 13 August 2022 are for the location of this event relative to the master event of 11 August 2022. The uncertainties of the other events on 16–20 August 2022 and 20 August 2022 are relative to the master event of 13 August 2022. All epicentral uncertainties are from a jackknife analysis. There are no epicentral uncertainties given for the event on 16 August 2022 at 13:06 because it had too few arrivals for a jackknife analysis. The color version of this figure is available only in the electronic edition.

whereas on 9 February the swarm events spread to the southwest of the December event locations. The uncertainties of the epicenters of most of these relative locations are <300 m, although some are as large as 700 m. The relative locations of all events in Figure 4b are aligned approximately parallel to the trend of the two strands of the Fredericton fault a few kilometers southeast of McAdam as well as a contact between an early Devonian granitic pluton and metasedimentary rocks just northwest of the town itself (Bent *et al.*, 2017), suggesting that the local geology may play a role in controlling the direction of spread of the events during the swarm. The Devonian granitic pluton extends about 24 km to the northwest from the McAdam area. According to Bent *et al.* (2017), determinations of first-motion *P*-wave focal mechanisms, both single event and composite focal-mechanism determinations, did not find consistent focal mechanisms or fault planes. There are thrust events on northwest–southeast fault planes, on north–south fault planes, and perhaps even east–west fault planes. The greatest consistency among the fault-plane solutions seems to be a nodal plane that is oriented somewhere between north-northwest and north-northeast. It is challenging to reconcile the spatial trend of the relative locations in Figure 4b with the range of focal mechanisms in Bent *et al.* (2017).

2022 Jonesboro, Maine, Swarm

A swarm of 15 small earthquakes took place near Jonesboro, Maine (Fig. 5a), from 11

August 2022 to 1 September 2022, with two additional small shocks on 21 September 2022 and 18 December 2022. The swarm started with an earthquake of M_{Lg} 2.9 at 11:29 on 11 August. Another M_{Lg} 2.9 took place on 17 August, and earthquakes of M_{Lg} 2.8 took place on 11 and 16 August. The rest of the events in the swarm had smaller magnitudes. The relative location analysis method of Ebel *et al.* (2008) was applied to 10 events of this swarm, and the results are shown in Figure 5b. The earthquakes that took place on 11 August follow a northeast–southwest trend and spread out over a 300 m extent, with relative location and depth uncertainties of about 100 m or less. Starting on 13 August and extending to 17 August, a second northeast–southwest trend of earthquakes took place. This second set of events extends about 450 m and is offset about 450 m to the southeast of the events of 11 August, with relative location uncertainties of about 400 m or less. On 20 August, there took place an event that was displaced about 900 m to the southeast of the 13–17 August events with a relative location uncertainty of about 1000 m. Both the events in the 11 August trend and the 13–17 August trend included earthquakes of M_{Lg} 2.9 and 2.8. The waveform envelope modeling method of Dahal and Ebel (2019) was applied to the largest events of the 11 August trend and of the 13–17 August trend. In both cases, the focal depths of the events determined with the Dahal and Ebel (2019) method are 2 km and the moment magnitudes of the events are M_w 2.9. Although the waveform envelope modeling method of Dahal and Ebel (2020) was applied to the largest events in the swarm to look for the focal mechanisms of the events, no consistent moment tensors and therefore focal mechanisms were found. This is not surprising as Dahal and Ebel (2020) reported that only sometimes could reliable focal mechanisms be found for events with $M_w < 3.0$. Although no portable seismographs were installed to record this swarm, the density of regional seismic stations in eastern Maine allowed epicenters to be computed with an uncertainty of about 1.1–1.3 km. From Figure 5a, it can be seen that the Jonesboro swarm took place near the contact between Silurian mafic volcanic rocks and a Devonian granitic pluton. There is a northeast–southwest fault mapped a couple kilometers south of the epicentral region of this swarm. The fault bounds the Silurian mafic volcanic rocks to its north and terminates at the edge of the Devonian granitic pluton; the two easterly epicentral trends parallel that fault.

2022–2023 Dedham, Maine, Swarm

Starting on 27 November 2022 and extending into 19 January 2023, a swarm of small earthquakes took place at the south end of Phillips Lake in Dedham, Maine (Fig. 6a). In November and December 2022, there were seven small earthquakes with $M_{Lg} \leq 1.0$ that were recorded by the regional seismic network and several smaller events that were heard by local residents. The swarm restarted on 13 January 2023 with an M_{Lg} 1.5 event followed 18 hr later by the largest event in the swarm, M_{Lg} 3.2, on 14 January. Of the subsequent events in the swarm, four had $1.8 \leq M_{Lg} \leq 2.0$, with the rest having smaller magnitudes. Once again, residents reported hearing small booms that were not detected on the regional seismic network stations. The relative location analysis method of Ebel *et al.* (2008) was applied to nine events of this swarm, and the results are shown in Figure 6b. The uncertainties in the relative epicenters and depths are <100 m except for the southernmost event, which has an epicentral uncertainty of about 250 m. The relative depth uncertainties are generally less than 100 m except for the events on 15 December 2022 and on 14 January 2023 at 06:30. Although the relative epicentral distribution does not show any obvious alignment of the epicenters, the relative location analysis indicates that the events appear to have migrated from north to south during the swarm. The waveform envelope modeling method of Dahal and Ebel (2019, 2020) was applied to the largest event in the swarm. This analysis indicated a focal depth of about 4 km and a focal mechanism with strike, dip, and rake of about 300°, 40°, and 80°, respectively (Fig. 6a). The moment magnitude of the event is determined to be M_w 3.6. Strong *Rg* waves observed at stations EMMW (epicentral distance of 87 km, azimuth of 88°) and WVL (epicentral distance of 89 km, azimuth of 261°) confirm that the focal depth of this earthquake was likely less than about 4 km (Fig. 7; Kafka, 1990). Many felt and heard reports by local residents of events during the January part of the swarm were received, with only some of these reports corresponding to earthquake waveforms on nearby regional seismic network stations. The other reports were likely small earthquakes that were not recorded regionally.

No portable seismographs were installed to record this swarm, although the density of regional seismic stations in eastern Maine allowed epicenters to be computed with an uncertainty of about 1.2–1.5 km. The Dedham, Maine, earthquake swarm occurred in the middle of a Devonian granitic pluton (Fig. 6a). No bedrock faults are mapped within or at the edges of the pluton that might explain the focal mechanism of the M_{Lg} 3.2 mainshock. There are no faults in the vicinity of the earthquake epicenters, with the closest mapped fault about 8 km to the north. In addition, the pluton is mapped as cutting an older northeast–southwest thrust fault.

2022–2023 Millinocket, Maine, Swarm

The most recent of the swarms that is analyzed in this study took place near Millinocket, Maine (Fig. 8a) with one small event on 6 December 2022 and seven small earthquakes between 6 and 11 January 2023. Later small earthquakes took place on 31 August 2023 and 17 January 2024. Among these events, the largest magnitude was only M_{Lg} 1.5, with just four events of $M_{Lg} \geq 1.0$. The relative location analysis method of Ebel *et al.* (2008) was applied to five events of this swarm, and the results are shown in Figure 8b. The uncertainties in the relative epicenters of all of the events in Figure 8b are <90 m, with uncertainties in the relative focal depths less than 70 m. The events generally trend from northwest to southeast and

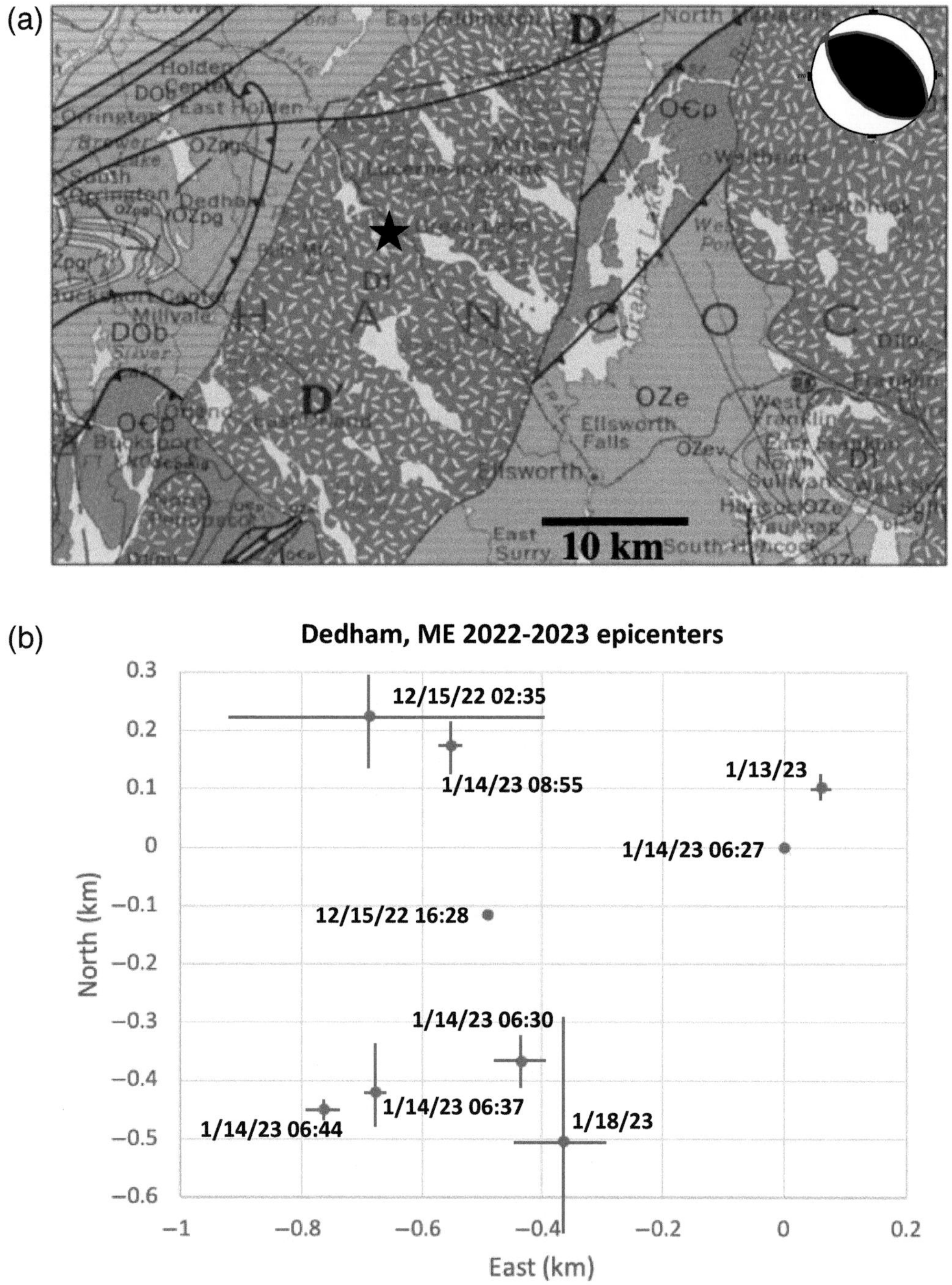

Figure 6. (a) Map of the bedrock geology of the area of the 2022–2023 Dedham, Maine, earthquake swarm (from Osberg *et al.*, 1985), with the swarm location indicated by the star. The size of the star indicates the uncertainty in the absolute locations of the swarm events. The focal mechanism of the largest event in the swarm is inset in the top right corner of the plot. Geologic units are: D1, Devonian granite; DOb, Silurian granofels; OCp, Cambrian shaly sediments; OZe, Cambrian schist; OZe b, Cambrian greenstone; OZpgs, Ordovician pelite and sandstone. (b) Results of the relative location analysis carried out for this study (given in Table S2). The master event is at location (0,0). The dates, and in some cases times, of each event are shown. All epicentral uncertainties are from a jackknife analysis. There are no epicentral uncertainties given for the event on 15 December 2022 at 16:20 because it had too few arrivals for a jackknife analysis. The color version of this figure is available only in the electronic edition.

also deepen in that same direction. All of the events in the swarm were too weak for the Dahal and Ebel (2019) method for determining the focal depths and moment magnitudes of the events. However, for the strongest event in the swarm, weak *Rg* waves were observed at a few stations, suggesting that this earthquake had a focal depth of less than about 4 km (Kafka, 1990). The low signal-to-noise ratios for the other, smaller events precluded a search for *Rg* waves.

Although no portable seismographs were installed to record this swarm, the density of regional seismic stations in Maine allowed epicenters to be computed with an uncertainty of about 1.0 km. As can be seen in Figure 8a, this swarm occurred in the center of a Devonian granitic pluton. The swarm took place near the southeastern end of a northwest-trending fault within the granitic pluton. The relative locations of the swarm events can be interpreted to have a northwest–southeast trend as seen in Figure 8b, perhaps implying that the swarm events are associated in some way with this mapped fault.

Discussion

There are some commonalities among all or most of the swarms discussed in this article that are worth enumerating. First, the events for all of the swarms had focal depths of 4 km or less, and many of the events had focal depths of 2 km or less. Second, in each of the swarms the spatial extent of the events is 3 km or less. Third, some of the swarm events extended bilaterally

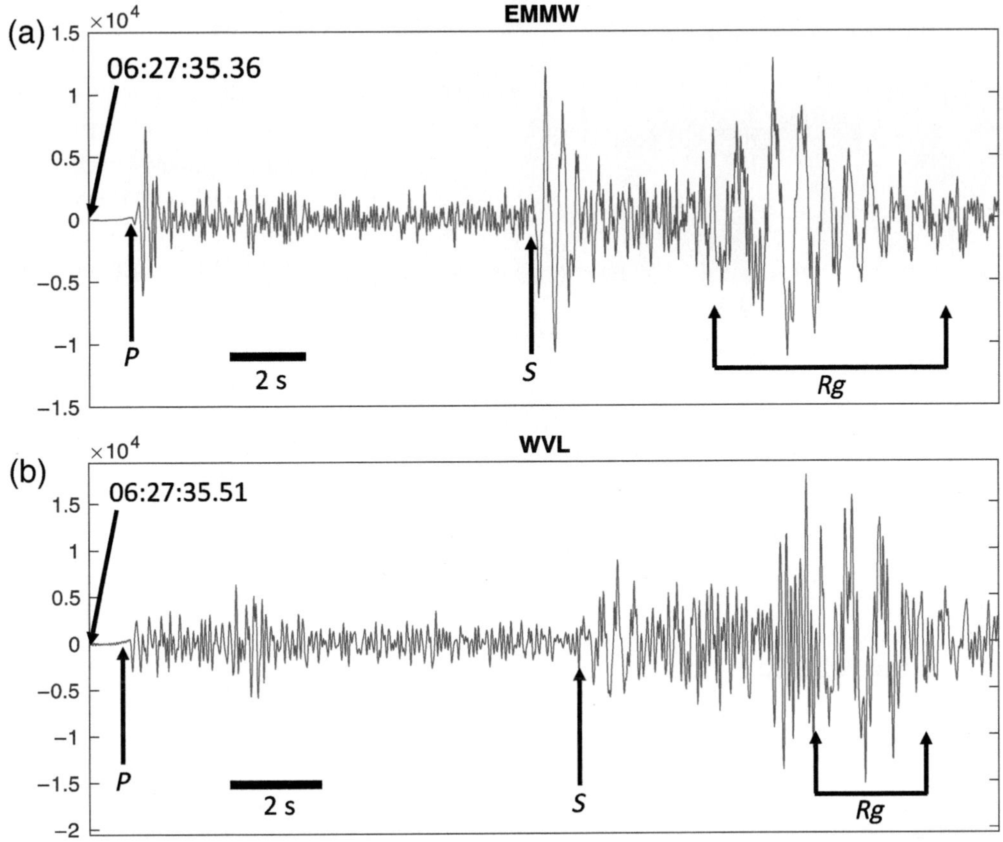

Figure 7. Waveforms from stations (a) EMMW and (b) WVL of the M_{Lg} 3.2 earthquake at Dedham, Maine, on 14 January 2023. The *P*- and *S*-arrival times as well as the time period with strong *Rg* waves are indicated. The original seismograms were band-pass filtered with a four-pole Butterworth filter with cutoff frequencies at 1 and 15 Hz. The color version of this figure is available only in the electronic edition.

from the location of the initial event, whereas in the 2011 Searsport swarm the events extended unilaterally from northeast to southwest. Fourth, three of the swarms (Searsport, Dedham, and Millinocket) apparently occurred within Devonian granitic plutons, and the other three swarms appear to have been located near the edges of other granitic plutons, all also of Devonian age. The thicknesses of the Maine Devonian plutons do not seem to have been documented, but similar plutons in New Brunswick extend to depths greater than 5 km (see Data and Resources), thus confirming the shallow swarms within the Maine mapped plutons are (almost certainly) within the pluton. The subsurface shape of the plutons is unknown, so it is possible that earthquakes that are a few kilometers deep but have epicenters outside the mapped pluton could be inside the pluton or just outside its edge. Finally, the Millinocket and Dedham swarms overlapped in time, and the primary Jonesboro swarm took place only a few months before these other two swarms, although the last event in the Jonesboro swarm overlapped in time with these other two swarms.

In addition to some earthquake swarms that were apparently associated with the impoundment of reservoirs (e.g., Talwani *et al.*, 1979; Secor *et al.*, 1982), there have been studies of several natural earthquake swarms in the eastern United States for comparison with the swarms that are the subject of this study. Stevenson *et al.* (2006) described three swarms of earthquakes in South Carolina, all of which were associated with granitic plutons. Earthquakes with M <2.0 were located near Rion from 1996 to 2003, with estimated focal depths from 1 to 4 km, although the focal depths are not well constrained. A swarm of over 100 earthquakes from 1982 to 1984 with magnitudes up to 2.6 were detected near the Newbury Pluton. The focal depths of these events were well constrained to within 2 km of the Earth's surface. Three earthquakes with M ≤2.5 were detected near the Neeses Pluton in 1992–1993. The focal depths could not be constrained. All three of these swarms took place at the mapped or inferred edges of granitic plutons, with the spatial extent of each of the three swarms being less than about 3 km. Another intense swarm of almost 100 earthquakes with M ≤3.6 took place between the towns of Elgin and Lugoff in South Carolina from 2021 to 2024 (Adeboboye *et al.*, 2024). The focal depths range from about 1.5 to 3.0 km. Precise locations of the seismicity show that the swarm has a spatial extent of about 3 km. This swarm occurred in the area of the East Piedmont fault system (EPFS), although the events of the modern earthquake swarm strike approximately north–south and dip west, which is different from the strike and dip of the EPFS.

A series of four earthquake swarms took place at Moodus, Connecticut, in 1981, 1982, 1986, and 1987–1988 (Ebel, 1989). The first two swarms had over 100 events each, and the last two had over 50 events each. The largest event in each swarm had coda magnitudes M_c 2.1, 2.9, 2.0, and 2.4, respectively. All four swarms appear to have originated from approximately the same place, and all had focal depths less than 2.4 km. Woodward-Clyde Consultants (1988) installed a dense network of portable seismographs to record the 1987–1988 swarm. They found that their well-located events ranged in focal depth from 1.3 to 1.9 km and with one exception spread over an area

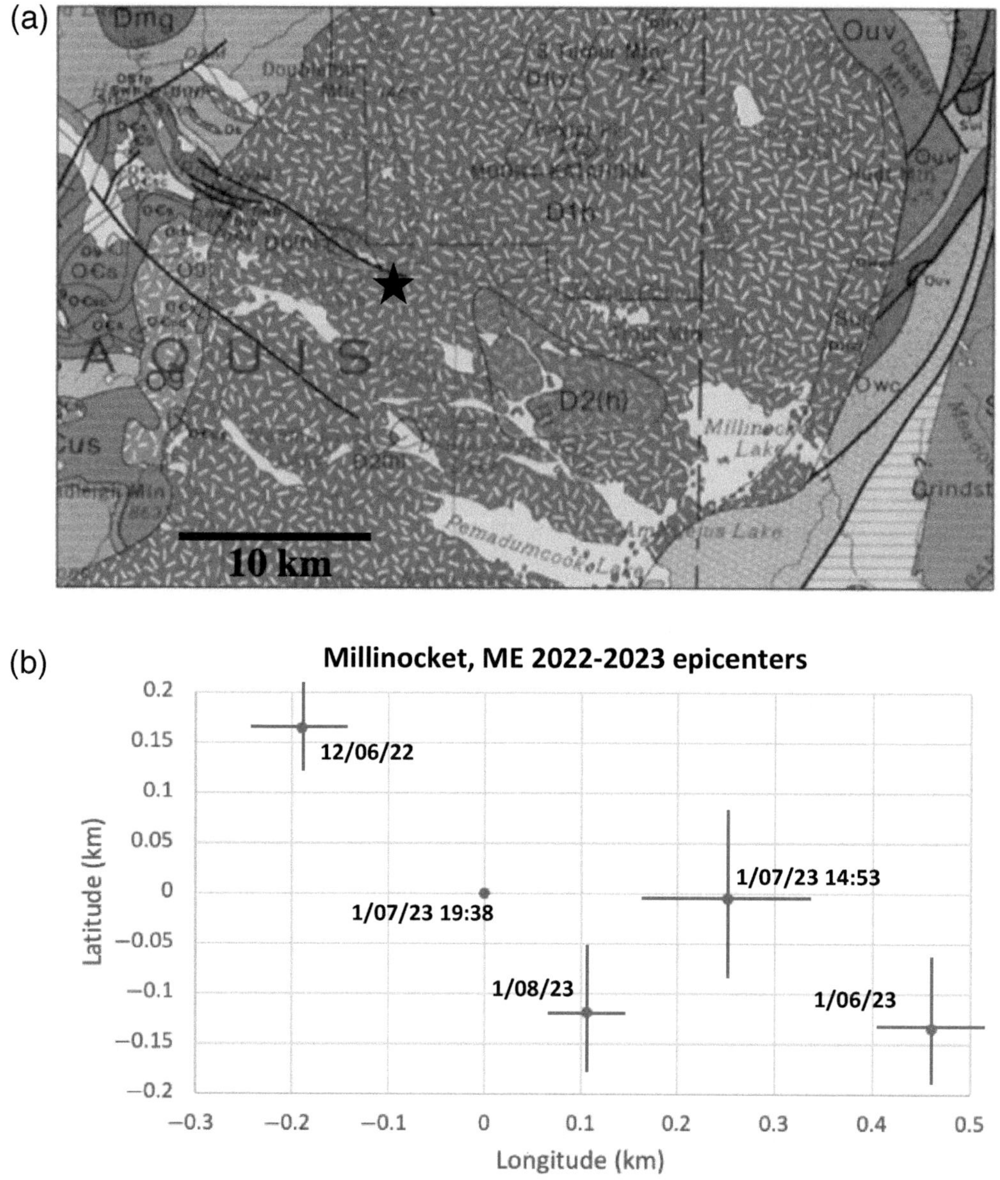

Figure 8. (a) Map of the bedrock geology of the area of the 2022–2023 Millinocket, Maine, earthquake swarm (from Osberg *et al.*, 1985), with the swarm location indicated by the star. The size of the star indicates the uncertainty in the absolute locations of the swarm events. Geologic units around the earthquake epicenters are: D1, D1h, and D1(y), Devonian granite; D2(h), Devonian granodiorite; D6(h), Devonian syenite. (b) Results of the relative location analysis carried out for this study (given in Table S3). The numbers next to each epicenter show the depth in kilometers relative to the depth of the master event at location (0,0). All epicentral uncertainties are from a jackknife analysis. The color version of this figure is available only in the electronic edition.

approximately 600 m in dimension. The events were all located in the Waterford Group gneisses, about 500 m below the Honey Hill fault. The high-quality locations from Woodward-Clyde Consultants (1988) of all of the events that they located are spread in an approximately circular shape in map view, with the earliest events perhaps showing a spatial trend that extended from northeast to southwest.

The only known earthquake swarms in the Appalachian area of the United States and Canada with focal depths below about 4 km of those mentioned in this study were those near Berne, New York, from 2007 to 2011 (Jacobi and Ebel, 2019). Five earthquake swarms were studied, each with 4–24 earthquakes and magnitudes ranging from M_{Lg} 1.0–3.1. Most of these earthquakes took place at focal depths below 14 km, with the shallowest event having a focal depth of 6 km. Each individual swarm was located at a slightly different place, and none of the swarms exceeded 1 km in spatial extent. Three of the swarms extended bilaterally from the first event location, but the events of the swarm of August 2011 spread unilaterally to the northeast. Given the foci of these events in the middle and lower crust, it is difficult to correlate the swarm locations with the local geology.

Jacquemond *et al.* (2024) reported on an analysis of an earthquake swarm of 188 events of M ≤2.0 that took place beneath the Tenée Valley of southern France immediately following the occurrence of a very heavy rainfall event (>600 mm) in 2020. The initial events were located at 3–4 km depth, although later events were deeper with depths that extended to 10 km. Jacquemond *et al.* (2024) argued that event spatial migration rates <100 m/hr suggest that the deformation associated with the earthquakes is due to fluid diffusion, whereas event migration rates of 100–1000 m/hr indicate that the events are being triggered by aseismic slip. The authors reported a northward migration of the initial Tenée Valley swarm events of ~130 m/hr, suggesting aseismic slip, whereas a later southern migration of events at ~5 m/hr suggests fluid pressure diffusion. They showed that a stress-driven model based on rate-and-state friction successfully explained the spatial evolution of the swarm events with time, as opposed to a fluid-diffusion model, which did not explain the time–space history of the data.

TABLE 1
Swarm Migration Rates

Swarm	Foreshock Duration (hr)	Foreshock Migration Rate (m/hr)	Initial Swarm Duration (hr)	Initial Swarm Migration Rate (m/hr)	Later Swarm Duration (hr)	Later Swarm Migration Rate (m/hr)
September 2006 Bar Harbor, Maine			5	**1600**		
October–December 2006 Bar Harbor, Maine					1868	*1.5*
2011 Searsport, Maine			1	**436**	1104	*23.1*
December 2015 McAdam, New Brunswick			4	*32.2*	20	*15.8*
February 2016 McAdam, New Brunswick	2	**130.6**	0.6	**649**		
2022 Jonesboro, Maine			0.4	**758**	48	*27*
2023 Brewer, Maine	720	*3.3*	2.5	**234**		
2023 Millinocket, Maine	739	*0.3*	34	*14.2*		
February 2009 Berne, New York			13	*10.6*	35	*5.9*
May 2009 Berne, New York			6.5	*43.9*		
December 2009 Berne, New York			0.8	**200**		
February 2010 Berne, New York			0.5	**467**	21	*28.3*
August 2011 Berne, New York			1.55	*45.9*	12.6	*9.7*
December 2021 Elgin, South Carolina			1.6	**109**	306	*36.2*
May 2022 Elgin, South Carolina			1.6	**200**		

The bolded values of migration rates are all above 100 m/h, whereas the italicized migration rates are all below 100 m/h.

For this study, Table 1 summarizes the migration rates of the events in the six swarms of this study along with the swarms at Berne, New York (Jacobi and Ebel, 2019). The event migration rates in Table 1 are divided up into three groups: foreshocks before the beginning of the main swarm (for those swarms that had foreshocks), initial swarm events, and later swarm events. The duration of each of these divisions was selected based on the data and vary from swarm to swarm. The migration rates of the initial swarm events for all swarms except McAdam in December 2015, Millinocket, and three of the Berne swarms are well above 100 m/hr, implying that the events in the swarms appeared to be spreading out due to aseismic creep. Of the five swarms where this was not true, three were at Berne, New York, with focal depths much deeper than the other swarms. Even at McAdam, although the events in the December 2015 swarm migrated only at 32 m/hr, the much larger number of events in the February 2016 swarm migrated at 649 m/s. Thus, only the Berne swarms and the Millinocket swarm deviate from the generalization that the initial swarms appear to migrate initially due to aseismic slip. It is also clear in Table 1 that the migration rates in the later parts of the swarms are all well below 100 m/hr, meaning that they could be due to the fluid diffusion model. For context, at Tenée Valley the initial swarm with a migration rate of ~130 m/hr lasted about 2 hr, and the later events that migrated at a rate of ~5 m/hr started about 8 hr after the commencement of the swarm (Jacquemond *et al.*, 2024). This pattern appears to be similar to the rate histories for the North American swarms in Table 1.

An explanation for the swarms in Maine and New Brunswick concentrating within or at the edges of granitic plutons has been provided by Campbell (1978), in which modeling of an inclusion of a rock body of a different stiffness than the surrounding rock is presented. Campbell (1978) considered intrusions that are both stiffer than the surrounding rock, such as a granite rock body, and less still than the surrounding rock, such as a serpentinized gabbro. The modeling shows that in a prevailing regional stress field the stiff inclusion has stress concentrations both within the inclusion and on its edges, and the differential stress within the stiff inclusion can be enhanced by as much as a factor of 1.35 depending on the shape of the inclusion relative to the prevailing maximum stress direction (Fig. 9). On the other hand, for a weak inclusion (not shown in Fig. 9), there are stress concentrations at some places outside the inclusion, with the locations of those stress concentrations depending on the orientation of the stress field and the shape of the inclusion. The locations of the swarms in Maine and New Brunswick as well as the swarms discussed by Stevenson *et al.* (2006) in South Carolina might be explained by this model if the earthquake swarms are occurring within or at

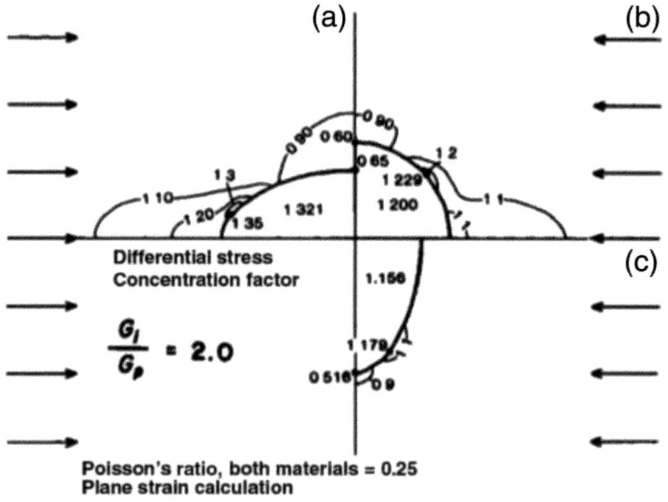

Figure 9. Contour plots of differential stress concentration factor near stiff inclusions in a plate under uniaxial compression (direction indicated by arrows): (a) elliptical inclusion with major axis parallel to uniaxial stress field, (b) circular inclusion, and (c) elliptical inclusion with major axis perpendicular to the uniaxial stress field. Each figure repeats through all four quadrants by symmetry. Here, the largest differential stress concentrations occur for case (a). Inside each inclusion the differential stress concentration is constant, and for still inclusions like these, almost as large as the highest differential stress concentration in the plate outside the inclusion. The ratio of the shear modulus inside the inclusion (G_i) to the shear modulus outside the inclusion (G_p) is 2.0 (from Campbell, 1978).

the edges of stiff inclusions within a less stiff surrounding geology. That appears to be the case for the earthquake swarms discussed in this article.

The stress model of Campbell (1978) can also explain the location of the Miramichi, New Brunswick, earthquakes of 1982 (Wetmiller *et al.*, 1984). This sequence of earthquakes included mainshocks of m_b 5.7 and 5.4, both with thrust mechanisms on north–south fault planes, and was followed by a very active aftershock sequence. The aftershock activity extended from about 7 km depth almost to the Earth's surface and extended approximately 6 km north–south, 6 km east–west, and to about 8 km depth (Basham and Adams, 1984; Ma and Motazedian, 2016). The earthquakes occurred in the Miramichi Anticlinorium, consisting of a series of granite plutons of Devonian age that were intruded into Ordovician and older metasediments and granites. According to Basham and Adams (1984), the Miramichi earthquakes in 1982 occurred in a Devonian granitic intrusion, with no known pre-existing faults in the vicinity of the area where the earthquakes took place. Campbell (1978) states that larger intrusives can host larger earthquakes. The Miramichi terrane where the 1982 earthquakes took place is about 85 km wide. This might explain why the 1982 Miramichi mainshocks were so much larger than the largest events of the swarms in this study because the Miramichi pluton is much larger than the plutons with the swarms in Maine and at McAdam, New Brunswick. It is unclear how large the earthquakes can be that take place in or near the smaller Devonian granitic plutons of Maine and at McAdam in southern New Brunswick.

Conclusions

The six earthquake swarms in Maine and New Brunswick discussed in this study all had focal depths of 4 km or less, appear to have taken place within or at the edges of Devonian granitic plutons, and with one exception show spatial distributions that are parallel to trends in the local geology. The swarms all had spatial extents of 3 km or less. The time histories of most of the swarms in Maine and New Brunswick are generally consistent with the initial part of the swarm being controlled by asesismic creep rather than by fluid diffusion. The spatial migration rates of the later events in the swarm are more consistent with the fluid diffusion model than with the aseismic creep model. Modeling of a rock inclusion that is stiffer than the surrounding rock mass in a regional stress field shows that stress will concentrate within the rock inclusion as well as along some of its edges. This suggests that granitic rock bodies in eastern North America have stress concentrations that fail in earthquakes. The size of the largest possible earthquake in any single granitic rock body cannot be assessed by the results of this study.

Data and Resources

Regional seismic network data used in this work came from the Earthscope Data Management Center (DMC) and are freely available from that center. All other data came from published sources. The U.S. Geological Survey (USGS) earthquake hazards program website is available at earthquakes.usgs.gov. The article "Magnetic and gravity models across terrane boundaries in southern New Brunswick, Canada" is available at https://cdnsciencepub.com/doi/epdf/10.1139/e04-046. Both websites were last accessed in July 2025. The supplemental material for this article includes the relative location data including the jackknife results used to create the plots in Figures 5b, 6b, and 8b.

Declaration of Competing Interests

The author acknowledges that there are no conflicts of interest recorded.

Acknowledgments

The author thanks the Department of Earth and Environmental Sciences at Boston College for supporting the publication of this research. The author thanks John Adams and an anonymous reviewer for their insightful suggestions to improve the first draft of this article, as it was submitted to the journal.

References

Adeboboye, O., L. Y. Chuang, M. Neves, Z. Peng, D. Frost, and S. Jaumé (2024). Localized west-dipping seismic structure defines the Elgin-Lugoff Swarm Sequence in South Carolina, *Seismol. Res. Lett.* **96,** no. 3, 2011–2026, doi: 1785/2020240302.

Basham, P. W., and J. Adams (1984). The Miramichi, New Brunswick earthquakes: Near-surface thrust faulting in the northern Appalachians, *Geosci. Canada* **11,** no. 3, 115–121.

Bent, A. L., S. Halchuk, V. Peci, K. E. Butler, K. B. S. Burke, J. Adams, N. Dahal, and S. Hayek (2017). The McAdam, New Brunswick, earthquakes swarms of 2012 and 2015-2016: Extremely shallow, natural events, *Seismol. Res. Lett.* **88,** no. 6, 1586–1600, doi: 10.1785/0220170071.

Campbell, D. L. (1978). Investigation of the stress-concentration mechanism for intraplate earthquakes, *Geophs. Res. Lett.* **5,** no. 6, 477–479.

Dahal, N., and J. E. Ebel (2019). Method for determination of depths and moment magnitudes of small-magnitude local and regional earthquake recorded by a sparse seismic network, *Bull. Seismol. Soc. Am.* **109,** 124–137, doi: 10.1785/0120180141.

Dahal, N., and J. E. Ebel (2020). Method for determination of focal mechanisms of magnitude 2.5 to 4.0 earthquakes recorded by a sparse regional seismic network, *Bull. Seismol. Soc. Am.* **110,** 715–726, doi: 10.1785/0120190170.

Ebel, J. E. (1989). A comparison of the 1981, 1982, 1986 and 1987-1988 microearthquake swarms at Moodus, Connecticut, *Seismol. Res. Lett.* **60,** 177–184.

Ebel, J. E. (2016). An enigmatic little earthquake swarm near Searsport, Maine, *Seismol. Res. Lett.* **87,** 207–214, doi: 10.1785/0220150167.

Ebel, J. E., A. M. Moulis, D. Smith, and M. Hagerty (2008). The 2006-2007 earthquake sequence at Bar Harbor, Maine, *Seismol. Res. Lett.* **79,** 457–468.

Ebel, J. E., V. Vudler, and M. Celata (1982). The 1981 microearthquake swarm near Moodus, Connecticut, *Geophys. Res. Lett.* **9,** 397–400.

Gilman, R. A., C. A. Chapman, T. V. Lowell, and H. W. Borns Jr. (1988). *The Geology of Mount Desert Island: A Visitor's Guide to the Geology of Acadia National Park*, Maine Geological Survey, Department of Conservation, Augusta, Maine, 50 pp.

Jacobi, R. D., and J. E. Ebel (2019). Seismotectonic implications of the Berne earthquake swarms west-southwest of Albany, NY, *Lithosphere* **11,** 750–764, doi: 10.1130/L1066.1.

Jacquemond, L., M. Godano, F. Cappa, and C. Larroque (2024). Interplay between fluid intrusion and aseismic stress perturbations in the onset of earthquake swarms following the 2020 Alex extreme rainstorm, *Earth Space Sci.* **11,** e2024EA003528, doi: 10.1029/2024EA003528.

Kafka, A. L. (1990). Rg as a depth discriminant for earthquakes and explosions: A case study in New England, *Bull. Seismol. Soc. Am.* **80,** 373–394.

Leonard, M. (2010). Earthquake fault scaling: Self-consistent relating of rupture length, width, average displacement, and moment release, *Bull. Seismol. Soc. Am.* **100,** 1971–1988, doi: 10.1785/0120090189.

Ma, S., and D. Motazedian (2016). Focal depth distribution of the 1982 Miramichi earthquake sequence determined by modelling depth phases, *Can. J. Earth Sci.* **54,** no. 4, doi: 10.1139/cjes-2016-0111.

Napoli, , V. J., and J.E. Ebel (2017). Relative location analysis and moment tensor inversion of the 2012 Gulf of Maine Earthquake Swarm, *Seismol. Res. Lett.* **89,** 229–240, doi: 10.1785/0220170131.

Osberg, P. H., A. M. Hussey II, and G. M. Boone (Editors) (1985). Bedrock geologic map of Maine, Maine Geological Survey, scale 1:500,000.

Pontrelli, M., and J. E. Ebel (2017). Evaluating McAdam, New Brunswick earthquake swarms: An analysis using double difference relative locations, *Seismol. Res. Lett.* **88,** no. 1, 257, doi: 10.1785/0220160205.

Secor, D. T., Jr, L. S. Peck, D. M. Pitcher, D. C. Powell, D. H. Simpson, W. A. Smith, and A. W. Snoke (1982). Geology of the area of induced seismic activity at Monticello Reservoir, South Carolina, *J. Geophys. Res.* **87,** no. B8, 6945–6957.

Stevenson, D., A. Gangopadhyay, and P. Talwani (2006). Booming plutons: Source of microearthquakes in South Carolina, *Geophys. Res. Lett.* **33,** L03316, doi: 10.1029/2005GL024679.

Sweeney, J. F. (1976). Subsurface distribution of granitic rocks, south-central Maine, *Geol. Soc. Am. Bull.* **87,** 241–249.

Talwani, P., D. Stevenson, D. Amick, and J. Chian (1979). An earthquake swarm at Lake Keowee, South Carolina, *Bull. Seismol. Soc. Am.* **60,** no. 3, 825–841.

Wetmiller, R. J., J. Adams, F. M. Anglin, H. S. Hasegawa, and A. E. Stevens (1984). Aftershock sequences of the 1982 Miramichi, New Brunswick, earthquakes, *Bull. Seismol. Soc. Am.* **74,** no. 2, 621–653.

Wells, D., and K. Coppersmith (1994). New empirical relationships among magnitude, rupture length, rupture width, rupture area, and surface displacement, *Bull. Seismol. Soc. Am.* **84,** 974–1002.

Woodward-Clyde Consultant (1988). Moodus, Connecticut borehole research project: The magnitude and orientation of tectonic stress in Southern New England, *Final Report, EP86-42*, prepared for Empire State Electric Energy Research Corporation, Northeast Utilities and Electric Power Research Institute.

Manuscript received 14 July 2025
Published online 18 November 2025

Stress Constraints on Fault Activity in the 2020 M_w 5.1 Sparta, North Carolina, Earthquake and Aftershock Sequence

Will Levandowski*[1]

Abstract

During the 2020 M_w 5.1 Sparta earthquake, sinistral-reverse slip reactivated the preexisting Little River fault (LRF), creating the first observed surface rupture in the eastern United States and an unprecedented opportunity to investigate intraplate fault reactivation under modern stress. This study examines the relationships between stress and faulting for the mainshock and 16 fore/aftershocks using stress inversions and geomechanical calculations. Sparta's N60°E–N68°E maximum compression direction and strike slip to transpressive regime (stress ratio: $\Phi = 0.17 \pm 0.05$) are both consistent with the broader eastern North America stress field. The LRF is well aligned for slip (normalized instability $I = 0.94 \pm 0.02$), as are 14 of the 16 fore/aftershocks ($I \gtrsim 0.9$). Constraints on active focal planes are then used to develop a kinematic model of the seismic cycle. This model suggests that interseismic strain accumulation was asymmetric about the seismogenic asperity, leading to asymmetric rupture with more coseismic offset east of the hypocenter than west. Following the mainshock, aftershocks were bimodal: The primary population on the higher-slip east side accommodated minor additional slip along the LRF, as is typical. Aftershocks on the low-slip west side, however, delineated the trailing edge of the coseismic slip patch, which parallels the dominant regional joint orientation but is poorly oriented for slip ($I = 0.24 \pm 0.08$). The west-side aftershocks provide a cautionary example that aligned aftershocks need not delineate an active fault. Although epicenters coalesce parallel to regional jointing, the focal planes are highly oblique to that trend. These are interpreted as en echelon faults that accommodate deformation on well-oriented planes within a pre-fractured belt. This interpretation contrasts with the typical assumption that active fault orientations can be inferred from planes fit to microseismic hypocenters. The Sparta sequence exemplifies reactivation of favorably oriented ancestral faults and highlights the importance of understanding crustal stress in identifying inherited faults prone to reactivation in the modern stress field.

Cite this article as Levandowski, W. (2025). Stress Constraints on Fault Activity in the 2020 M_w 5.1 Sparta, North Carolina, Earthquake and Aftershock Sequence, *Seismol. Res. Lett.* **97**, 664–678, doi: 10.1785/0220250309.

Supplemental Material

Introduction

The 2020 M_w 5.1 Sparta, North Carolina, earthquake was the largest by magnitude in the central and eastern United States (CEUS) since the 2011 M_w 5.8 near Mineral, Virginia, yet it occurred in an area of the Blue Ridge geologic and physiographic province with sparse historical seismicity (Fig. 1). With a hypocenter near 1 km depth, anomalously shallow slip on the previously unrecognized east-southeast-striking Little River fault (LRF) created the first surface rupture observed in the eastern United States and the first in the CEUS since the 1811/1812 New Madrid earthquakes (e.g., Figueiredo *et al.*, 2022). Although no casualties were reported in the mostly rural epicentral region, the earthquake caused more than $24 million in damage to roads, utility lines, and masonry buildings, and a water main ruptured. The outsized damage caused by even moderate-magnitude surface-rupturing earthquakes in low-strain-rate intraplate regions (e.g., 2019 M_w 4.9 Le Teil, France; Cornou *et al.*, 2021) motivates a better understanding of the processes responsible for these exceedingly rare events.

Geologic setting

The 2020 Sparta earthquake sequence occurred near the eastern edge of the Blue Ridge in the upper Precambrian Ashe and Alligator Back metamorphic suites (Raymond, 2015; Lynn, 2023) (Figs. 1 and 2). The primary structures in the region

1. Tetra Tech, Inc., Chapel Hill, North Carolina, U.S.A., https://orcid.org/0000-0003-4903-5012 (WL)

*Corresponding author: will.levandowski@tetratech.com

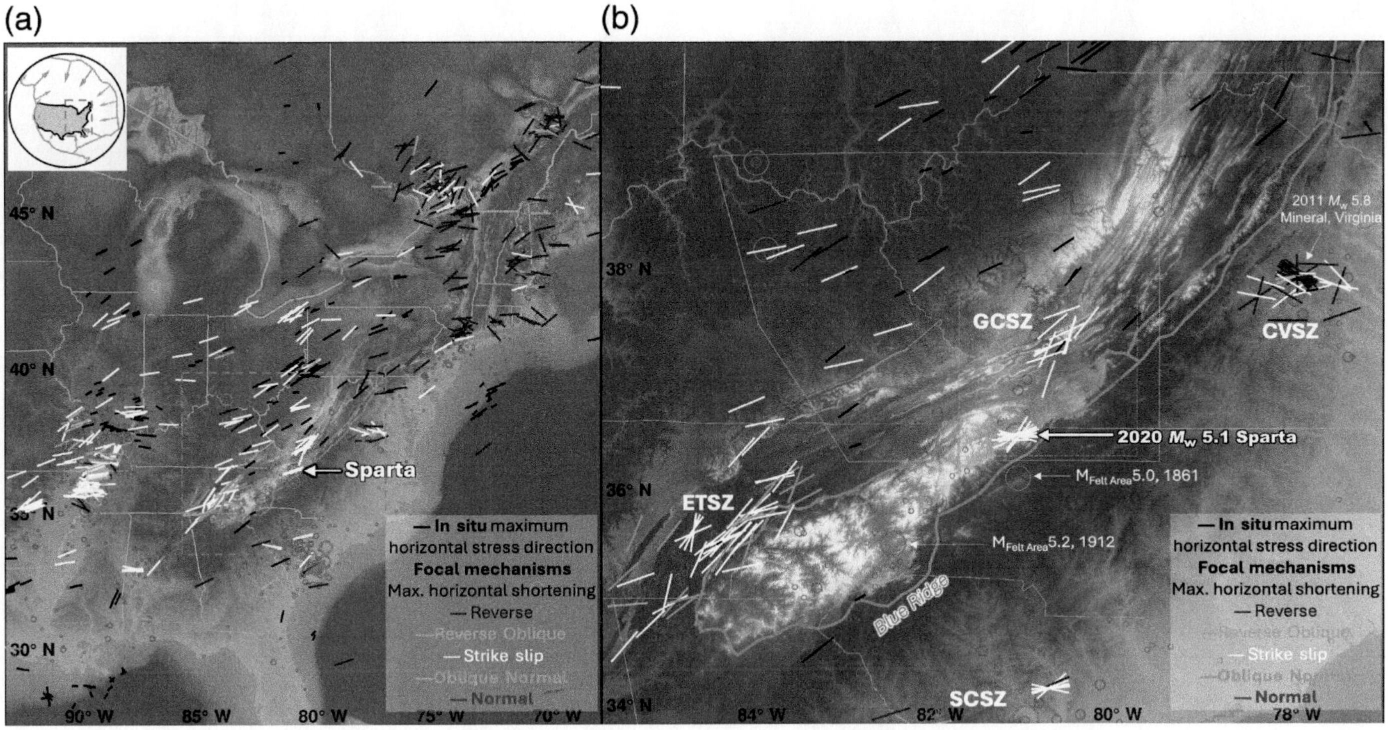

Figure 1. Seismotectonic setting of the central and eastern United States (CEUS). (a) CEUS focal mechanisms and seismicity. The green circles indicate M ≥ 3 from U.S. Geological Survey (USGS) Comprehensive catalog. The bars indicate focal mechanism maximum horizontal shortening direction $S_{H\max}$ (e.g., P axis), colored by faulting style (see Table 2). For clarity, these are smoothed with a 2.5-km Gaussian truncated at 25 km. The black bars indicate maximum horizontal stress $\sigma_{H\max}$ from in situ indicators (World Stress Map/Lundstern and Zoback, 2020). The orange box indicates the area shown in panel (b). The inset figure shows plate boundary tractions on North America: directions and relative magnitudes from Humphreys and Coblentz (2007). (b) Regional focal mechanisms and seismicity for the orange box in panel (a). Unlike panel (a), focal mechanisms are not smoothed. Otherwise, symbology is as in panel (a). Southeastern U.S. seismic zones: CVSZ, Central Virginia seismic zone; ETSZ, eastern Tennessee seismic zone; GCSZ, Giles County seismic zone; SCSZ, South Carolina seismic zone. The orange box indicates the area used for regional stress inversions. The orange dashed box indicates the area used for Sparta and GCSZ stress inversions. The color version of this figure is available only in the electronic edition.

are east-northeast-striking, top-to-northwest thrusts that were likely reactivated multiple times between the Proterozoic and Mississippian (Levine *et al.*, 2018). Recent mapping near Sparta documents a dominant east-northeast-striking foliation (063/57°) and bimodal joint trends northwest–southeast (145 or 325, ±10°) and north/south (005 or 185, ±5°) (Merschat and Carter, 2023). Notations in this study follow the convention that strike/dip (###/##°) are listed such that dip is to the right when looking in the strike direction, and trend/plunge (###/##°) are listed such that plunge is downward in the trend direction. Cardinal directions are abbreviated as follows: E, east; N, north; S, south; W, west.

2020 mainshock and aftershocks

The mainshock has been characterized with moment tensors (Table 1), broadband waveforms, Interferometric Synthetic Aperture Radar, and geodesy (Figueiredo *et al.*, 2022; Neves *et al.*, 2024; Pollitz, 2023; Szymanski *et al.*, 2024), as well as from the coseismic surface scarp (Hill *et al.*, 2020; Figueiredo *et al.*, 2022; Lynn, 2023). There is consensus that sinistral-reverse motion on the east-southeast-striking LRF occurred on an asymmetric patch spanning more than 2 km east from the hypocenter but less than 1 km west (Fig. 2), and resulting in a south-side-up coseismic scarp trending N110°E for 3.4 km. The maximum scarp height of 28 cm was measured from differential light detection and ranging (Lynn, 2023) at a location approximately up-dip from the hypocenter, near Figueiredo *et al.* (2022) trench T2 (Fig. 2b), and scarp height decreased along strike. Finite-fault models (Pollitz, 2023; Szymanski *et al.*, 2024) feature a maximum of 80 cm of reverse-oblique slip near the hypocenter and up-dip from it. In these models, a vaguely triangular patch moves east, north, and up relative to the footwall—effectively a clockwise rotation around the northeastern corner of the slip patch. Slip decreases along strike away from the hypocenter (Fig. 2b,c), mirroring the coseismic scarp height, and slip becomes more purely sinistral with distance eastward. By contrast, surface deformation features were primarily pure dip-slip and on low-angle reverse faults (Figueiredo *et al.*, 2020, 2022; Hill *et al.*, 2020). Trenching revealed that the low-angle reverse faults only penetrate ~20 cm into the subsurface, where they rotate and root into more steeply dipping pre-existing fabrics (Hill *et al.*, 2020).

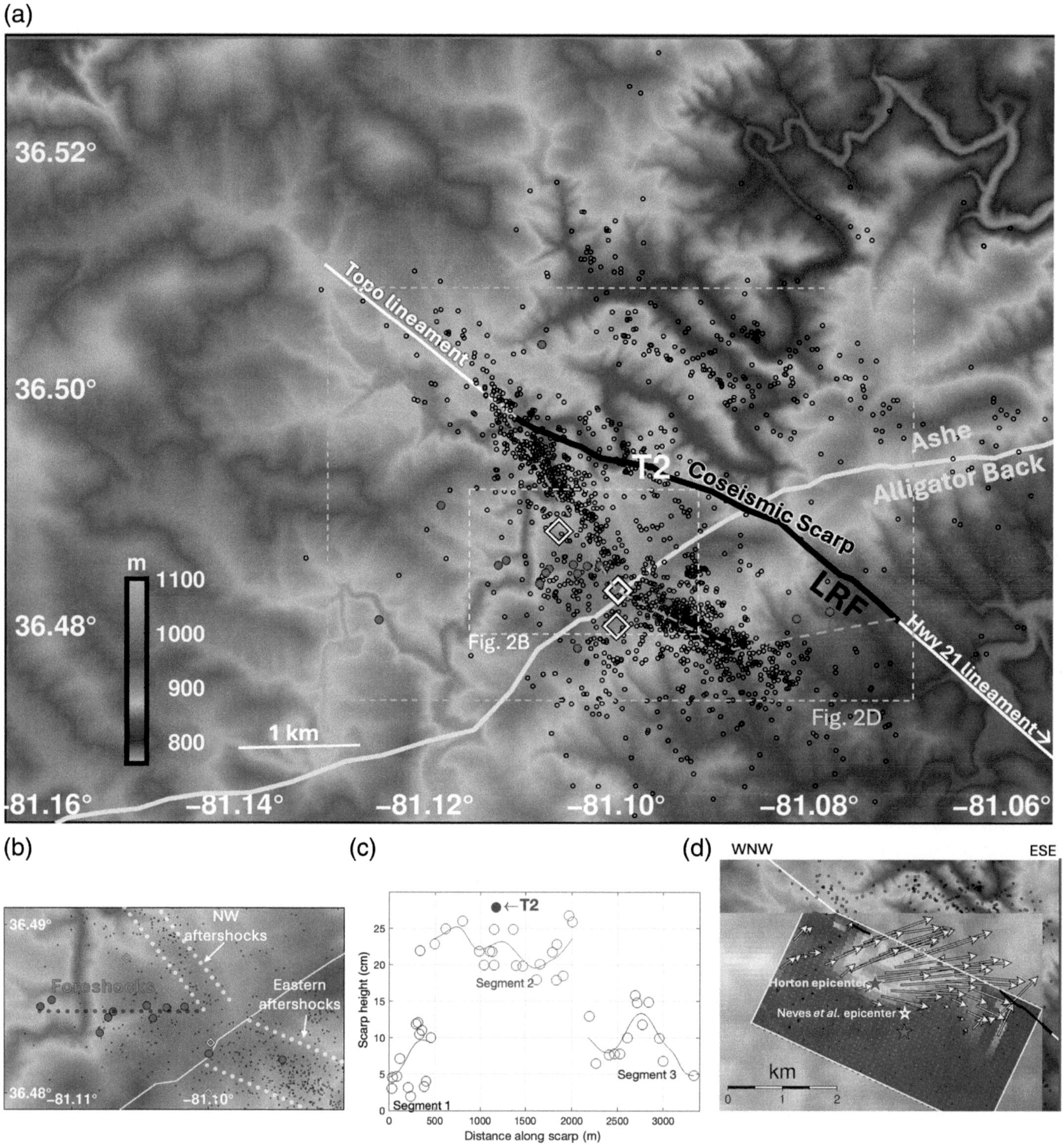

Figure 2. Coseismic deformation. (a) Epicentral region. Coseismic scarp (black) and longer topographic lineament (white) from Lynn (2023). Trench T2 (Figueiredo *et al.*, 2022) was excavated at the location of the peak scarp height. The black dots/magenta circles indicate aftershocks/foreshocks (relocated by Neves *et al.*, 2024). The diamonds indicate mainshock epicenter estimates (Horton *et al.*, 2021; Herrmann, 2025; Neves *et al.*, 2024). The white-dashed boxes indicate extents of panels (b) and (d). The yellow line indicates contact between Ashe and Alligator Back metamorphic suites. The cyan-dashed lines indicate schematic 3D outline of the hanging-wall slip patch. (b) Seismicity near the 2020 epicenter. Foreshocks (magenta) focused west of the mainshock along an east–west trend (black dotted line). The white-dotted lines indicate approximate outlines of the two primary aftershock clusters. (c) Coseismic scarp height along the rupture (black line in panel a). Scarp heights from Lynn (2023). (d) Slip model (Pollitz, 2023) overlain on basemap from panel (a). LRF, Little River fault. The color version of this figure is available only in the electronic edition.

TABLE 1
Mainshock Moment Tensors and Focal Mechanisms

Source	Strike/Dip/Rake (°)	Longitude*	Latitude*	Depth	Type†	P Axis
Center for Earthquake Research and Information (CERI) (Horton *et al.*, 2021; Figueiredo *et al.*, 2022)	108/60/24	−81.1060	36.488	0.6 km	SS/TS	068°/06°
Neves *et al.* (2024)	116/31/40	−81.0998	36.483	1.3 km	TF/TS	061°/22°
SLU (Herrmann, 2025)	115/50/40	−81.10	36.480	1.0 km	TF/TS	058°/06°
First motion, relocated (Neves *et al.*, 2024)	113/88/1	−81.0998	36.483	3.0 km	SS	067°/01°

SLU, St. Louis University; SS, strike slip; TF/TS, reverse slip.
*Significant figures as reported by the source.
†Defined by principal axis plunges (Table 2), allowing 10° uncertainty.

At the time of the mainshock, the nearest seismic station was ~50 km away. In the following days, the Center for Earthquake Research and Information of the University of Memphis deployed a temporary network of five seismic stations. Using this and other data, Neves *et al.* (2024) cataloged and relocated 1761 earthquakes—18 foreshocks in the two days prior to the M_w 5.1 and 1742 aftershocks.

Foreshocks showed different spatial patterns than the aftershocks. Foreshocks were deeper (5.3 ± 1.3 km) than the mainshock and aftershocks (1.6 ± 0.8 km). Average horizontal and vertical uncertainties are 442 m/454 m for foreshocks and 216 m/164 m for aftershocks. The majority (12 of 18) foreshocks occurred just west of the mainshock and delineated an east-trending band ~200 m wide. Some aftershocks did occur in this area, but far fewer than occurred east-southeast and northwest of the mainshock.

Aftershocks form two prominent clusters (Figs. 2a and 3a–d). One trends east-southeast from the mainshock and is approximately coplanar with the LRF (Fig. 3b). The other trends 325 (i.e., northwest) from the epicenter to the western rupture terminus, meaning that it traces the western edge of the slip patch (Fig. 2a,c). This northwest cluster appears nearly vertical in cross section, best fit by a plane oriented ~325/88°, yet seismicity shallows systematically from ~3 km depth near the epicenter to <100 m depth at the western surface-rupture terminus (Fig. 3a,c). The northwest cluster can thus be described as a southeast-plunging volume linking the down-dip limit of slip (near the hypocenter) with the western limit of slip, approximately delineating the western edge of the slip patch.

Focal mechanisms for the mainshock, 6 foreshocks, and 10 aftershocks (Fig. 3d) were determined from *P*-wave polarity and *S/P* amplitude ratios (Neves *et al.*, 2024). For both foreshocks and aftershocks, the nodal planes are characterized by steep dips (median 75°) and north-northeast–south-southwest or east-southeast–west-northwest strikes (Fig. 3d–f). The faulting type can be quantitatively categorized from the principal-axis plunges (following Zoback, 1992) (Table 2). Doing so, 14° out of 17° are classified as strike slip and one as reverse oblique. The remaining two focal mechanisms (IDs 2 and 15 in Fig. 3d) do not fall into any of Zoback's categories, yet subhorizontal rakes (179° and 19°) on the preferred nodal planes (determined below) indicate nearly strike-parallel slip.

TABLE 2
Focal Mechanism Categorization (Zoback, 1992)

P Plunge	N Plunge	T Plunge	Type	Inferred $S_{H\max}$
pl ≥ 52°		pl ≤ 35°	Normal (NF)	N trend
40° ≤ pl < 52°		pl ≤ 20°	Oblique normal (NS)	T trend + 90°
pl < 40°	pl ≥ 45°	pl ≤ 20°	Strike slip (SS)	T trend + 90°
pl ≤ 20°	pl ≥ 45°	pl < 40°	Strike slip (SS)	P trend
pl ≤ 20°		40° ≤ pl < 52°	Oblique reverse (TS)	P trend
pl ≤ 35°		pl ≥ 52°	Reverse (TF)	P trend

N, null vector, N-axis or B-axis; P, maximum shortening vector, or pressure axis; T, maximum stretching vector, or T axis.

Recurrent slip on the Little River fault

Geologic studies since 2020 have demonstrated prior activity on the LRF and suggest that the inherited fault extends beyond the limits of the 2020 rupture. Mapping as fine as 1:6000 scale (Lynn, 2023; Merschat and Carter, 2023) documented brittle deformation on clay-coated saprolite surfaces at locations near, yet beyond, the termini of the coseismic scarp. These offsets attest to slip along adjacent parts of the LRF since the formation of the clays, likely in the past 2 ka to 2 Ma (Lynn, 2023). East of the 2020 rupture, the LRF changes strike to ~N130°E and merges with a previously described 10 km trend of interpreted brittle deformation dubbed the Highway 21 lineament (Dennison and Stewart, 2001). Finally, both the LRF and Highway 21 lineament are part of a longer topographic lineament (Figueiredo *et al.*, 2022) (Fig. 2a).

Prior activity on the LRF was not limited to the modern tectonic regime. At one location in the eastern segment of

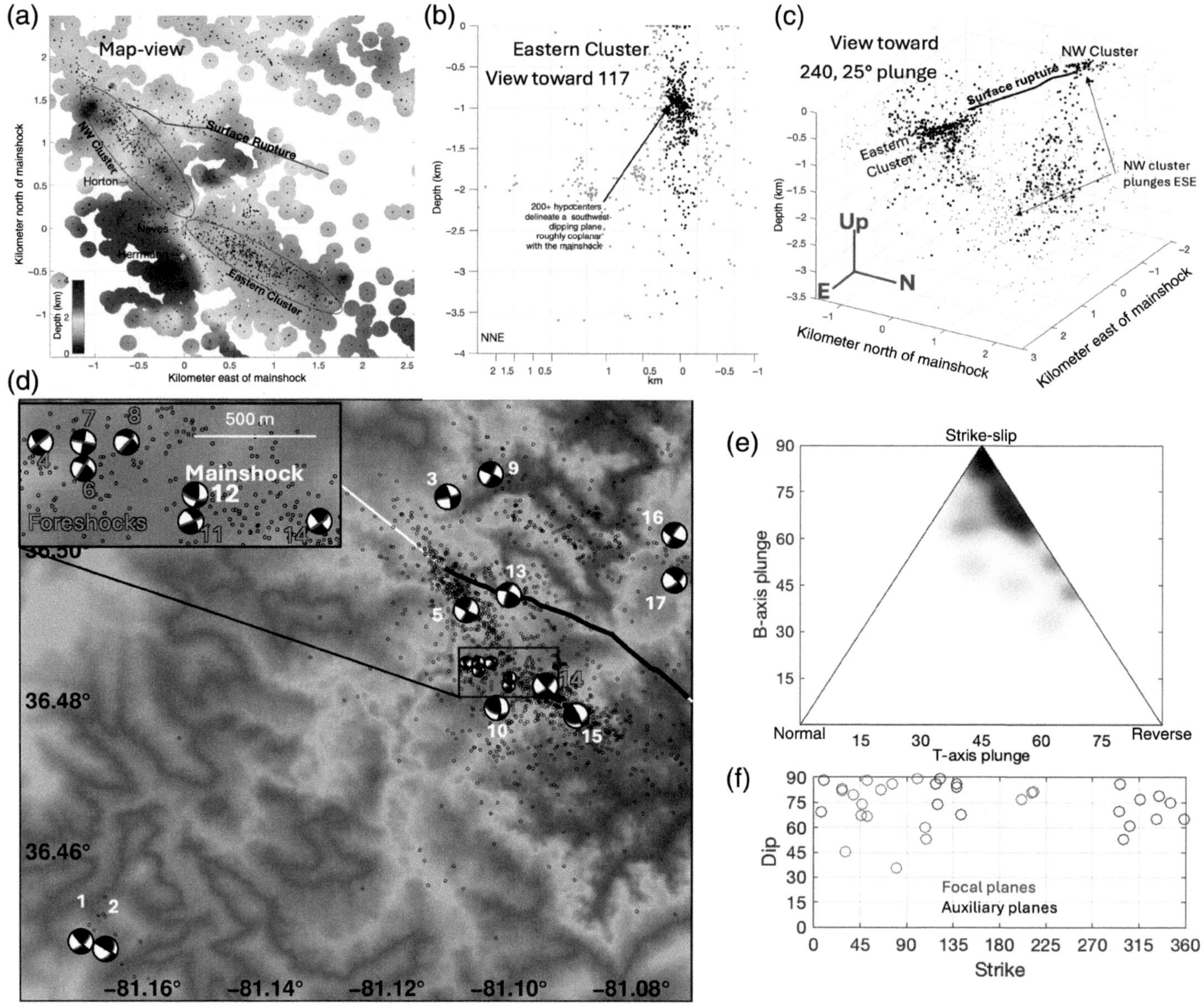

the 2020 rupture, the LRF dextrally offsets the contact between magnetic and comparatively nonmagnetic rocks (Lynn, 2023), the opposite sense of modern motion. In fact, kinematic indicators from brittle fault-related features elsewhere along the LRF mainly (78%) indicate northwest–southeast shortening that is nearly orthogonal to the modern regime, plus a secondary population (11%) consistent with modern northeast–southwest contraction (Lynn, 2023). In summary, the 2020 rupture was not the first along this stretch of the LRF, and the modern LRF is part of a longer corridor of suspected Cenozoic faulting that appears to be reactivating faults inherited from Paleozoic or earlier deformation.

Figure 3. Seismicity as relocated by Neves *et al.* (2024). (a) Map-view aftershocks. The color indicates the average hypocentral depth on a 10 m grid, smoothed with a 25 m Gaussian for clarity. The diamonds indicate epicenter location estimates. (b) Cross-sectional view of eastern cluster looking along strike. The black dots indicate events in the cluster, as defined by Neves *et al.* (2024). The green dots indicate events outside the cluster. (c) Oblique view of 3D seismicity. The northwest (NW) cluster plunges east-southeast (ESE), from near the surface at the western rupture terminus to ~3 km depth near the Neves *et al.* (2024) epicenter. (d) Focal mechanisms. The red indicates the preferred focal plane, as determined from instability. The inset figure indicates an expanded view of the epicenter and foreshock zone. (e) Heat map of faulting style of the 17 Sparta focal mechanisms, classified by P/T/B axis plunges (following Frohlich and Apperson, 1992). Strike slip with a secondary reverse component is dominant. (f) Nodal plane strike and dip. The red indicates the preferred focal planes. The black indicates the preferred auxiliary planes. The color version of this figure is available only in the electronic edition.

Stress and intraplate seismicity in the CEUS and Blue Ridge

Most intraplate earthquakes do occur by reactivation of inherited faults like the LRF in the modern stress field (e.g., Talwani, 2014), where modern stress may be the product of far-field tectonic processes. The CEUS lies some 3000 km from the nearest tectonic plate boundary, the Mid-Atlantic Ridge. Atlantic spreading pushes North America to the west-southwest, and this ridge push (and/or drag due to the motion it causes relative to the underlying asthenosphere) creates a dominant east-northeast–west-southwest compressive stress across intraplate eastern North America (Sbar and Sykes, 1973; Richardson, 1992; Lundstern and Zoback, 2020). Consistent with this boundary condition, CEUS earthquakes generally accommodate northeast–southwest to east–west horizontal shortening via reverse to strike-slip faulting (Fig. 1). Reverse faulting is more abundant along the East Coast, and strike-slip faulting dominates the Midcontinent; Sparta is located within that transition.

Despite the plate-scale forces thought to be responsible for them, intraplate earthquakes in the CEUS generally cluster in a handful of distinct seismic zones (Fig. 1). Sparta and the Blue Ridge are near, but outside of, several areas of active seismicity. The Giles County seismic zone, 100 km north-northeast of Sparta in the adjacent Valley and Ridge province, hosted the largest known earthquake in the southern Appalachians in 1897 ($M_{Felt-Area}$ 5.6) but has been comparatively quiescent in recent decades (e.g., Munsey and Bollinger, 1985). Abundant low-magnitude seismicity in the 300-km-long eastern Tennessee seismic zone (200 km west to 500 km southwest of Sparta), also in the Valley and Ridge, has not historically exceeded M_w 4.6. Farther away (350 km northeast), the Central Virginia seismic zone—site of the 2011 M_w 5.8 Mineral earthquake—has been recognized from historical seismicity since the nineteenth century, and the diffuse South Carolina seismic zone spans the piedmont and coastal plain (250–450 km south-southeast), including Charleston's catastrophic M_{we} 7.0 in 1886.

In contrast to these areas, earthquakes in the Blue Ridge are uncommon (Advanced National Seismic System Comprehensive Catalog [ComCat]: see Data and Resources). The nearest comparable earthquake within the Blue Ridge occurred 160 km southwest of Sparta in 1912 ($M_{Felt-Area}$ 5.2) (Fig. 1). An earthquake in 1926 with modified Mercalli intensity up to VII (Reinbold and Johnston, 1987; Stover and Coffman, 1993) toppled a chimney in Spruce Pine, North Carolina ~105 km southwest of Sparta. Finally, an $M_{Felt-Area}$ 5.0 event occurred 35 km south of Sparta in 1861, yet this epicenter was east of the Blue Ridge in the geologically distinct Piedmont.

Given the lack of instrumentally recorded seismicity, little is known about crustal stress in the Blue Ridge generally and near Sparta specifically. This leaves several open questions: Is local stress consistent with the broader CEUS tectonic stress field or anomalous near Sparta? Is the LRF well oriented for frictional slip, or might other factors be at play, such as low friction or high fluid pressure? What faults were active during the foreshock–mainshock–aftershock sequence, and how did these faults partition strain release through the seismic cycle?

In pursuit of answers to these questions, earthquake focal mechanisms from the Sparta sequence and regional seismicity are inverted to constrain crustal stress. The resulting stress models are used to quantify the slip potential of the LRF and other faults, and to infer the fault-plane orientations activated in the aftershock sequence. Improved understanding of crustal stress in the Blue Ridge will lay the foundation to proactively identify other inherited faults that are prone to reactivation and provide insight into strain partitioning across the intraplate earthquake cycle.

Stress

Disambiguating the focal and auxiliary planes of Sparta focal mechanisms may provide insight into the active fault network, with constraints that are independent from and complementary to relocated seismicity. To do so, the regional stress field is examined using focal mechanism inversions, and the stability of the nodal planes in that stress field is quantified.

Regional stress

The southern Appalachians lie within the transition from dominantly reverse faulting along the Atlantic margin to dominantly strike-slip faulting in the Midcontinent (Fig. 1; Table S1, available in the supplemental material to this article). Northeast of Sparta in the Giles County seismic zone, the 12 available focal mechanisms (Munsey and Bollinger, 1985; DePaolis and Chapman, 2018) are all strike slip, primarily on planes striking north-northeast/south-southwest or east–west, consistent with east-northeast–west-southwest $\sigma_{H\max}$. Northwest of Sparta, in eastern Kentucky and West Virginia 13 available focal mechanisms (Carpenter *et al.*, 2014; Carpenter, 2019; Herrmann, 2025) are also dominantly strike slip on north-northeast/south-southwest or approximately east/west planes, with reverse faulting on east-southeast/west-northwest planes in three events. To the southeast, South Carolina piedmont earthquakes also display strike-slip, reverse-oblique, and reverse mechanisms. To the southwest, the oblique extension in the ETSZ is distinct from the rest of the eastern United States (Levandowski *et al.*, 2023) so is excluded from this analysis and further discussion.

Focal mechanisms from the southern Appalachian region—the Sparta sequence, Giles County, West Viginia, and Kentucky (n = 42)—are inverted to constrain seismogenic stress. The stress inversion methods have been previously applied in the CEUS and elsewhere (Levandowski, Herrmann, *et al.*, 2018; Levandowski, 2023; Levandowski *et al.*, 2023; Zhang *et al.*, 2025). The core of the inversion is Vavryčuk (2014) joint iterative inversion and focal plane selection algorithm. Aleatory uncertainty is estimated in a Monte Carlo fashion and quantified by the distribution of outputs across 200 Monte Carlo realizations for each of seven parameterizations (models 0–6, described below). One realization proceeds as follows. The focal mechanisms are jackknife-downsampled, discarding $n_{data}^{0.5}n$. Each of the retained

TABLE 3
Stress Inversion Results

Stress Model	*n*	Weighting	*AΦ* Mean±1σ... (95% CI)	$\sigma_{H\max}$ Mean±1σ... (95% CI)	Misfit
0—Regional	42	Uniform	1.79 ± 0.02... (1.73–1.85)	N60°E ± 2°... (057–064)	21°
1—Regional	42	Distance^{-1}	1.82 ± 0.03... (1.73–1.86)	N60°E ± 2°... (057–064)	21°
2—Regional	42	Distance^{-1}; GCSZ × 1/3	1.84 ± 0.03... (1.75–1.91)	N68°E ± 2°... (062–072)	21°
3—Sparta and GCSZ	29	Distance^{-1}	1.85 ± 0.03... (1.75–1.96)	N63°E ± 2°... (060–072)	22°
4—Sparta and GCSZ	29	Uniform	1.81 ± 0.03... (1.74–1.88)	N60°E ± 2°... (057–065)	22°
5—Sparta only	17	Uniform	1.89 ± 0.07... (1.78–2.08)	N68°E ± 3°... (061–076)	15°
6—No Sparta	25	Uniform	1.70 ± 0.07... (1.52–1.84)	N61°E ± 3°... (055–067)	21°

CI, confidence interval.

mechanisms is perturbed with up to 15° of noise. This perturbation mimics the uncertainties of individual moment tensors (e.g., Herrmann *et al.*, 2011). For each retained event, one of the noisy nodal plane solutions is chosen at random. The ensemble is inverted for the stress tensor that best minimizes the angular misfit between the associated shear tractions on those planes and the slip vectors (Angelier, 1979). A coefficient of friction is chosen randomly from a uniform distribution of 0.35–1.0. Then, the focal plane choices are revisited: The instability of each plane under the derived stress tensor is computed (see equations 1–3), and the less stable is selected. This revised ensemble is then inverted, and so on for 5 iterations, although nodal plane choices typically stabilize after 2–3 iterations. This process comprises one realization, and then the next jackknife-downsampled, noisy subset of focal mechanisms is inverted, using another randomly selected friction.

The normalized stress tensor determined by these inversions can be described by the directions and relative magnitudes S of the three principal stresses. The stress ratio Φ is given as

$$\Phi = (S_2 - S_3)/(S_1 - S_3), \quad (1)$$

with S_1 the magnitude of the maximum (compressive) stress, S_2 intermediate, and S_3 the minimum. Simpson (1997) combined Φ with the style of faulting (normal/strike slip/reverse, as defined by principal axis plunges; Zoback, 1992) to describe the style of deformation as a quantity $A\Phi$:

$$A\Phi = (n + 0.5) + (-1)^n(\phi - 0.5), \quad (2)$$

with $n = 0$ for normal faulting, 1 for strike slip, and 2 for thrust. Consequently, $A\Phi$ defines a continuum from radial extension ($A\Phi = 0$) to radial contraction ($A\Phi = 3$), passing through uniaxial extension—pure normal faulting ($A\Phi = 0.5$), oblique extension ($A\Phi = 1.0$), horizontal shear–strike slip ($A\Phi = 1.5$), oblique contraction ($A\Phi = 2.0$), and uniaxial contraction—pure reverse faulting ($A\Phi = 2.5$).

Instability I is calculated from Φ and the vector of directional cosines (n_1, n_2, and n_3) defining the inclination of the fault to the principal stress axes (Vavryčuk *et al.*, 2013):

$$I = [\tau + \mu(\sigma + 1)]/[\mu + (1 + \mu^2)^{0.5}], \quad (3)$$

$$\sigma = -n_1^2 + (1 - 2\Phi)n_2^2 + n_3^2, \quad (4)$$

$$\tau = \{n_1^2 + (1 - 2\Phi)^2 n_2^2 + n_3^2 - \sigma^2\}^{0.5}, \quad (5)$$

with weak dependence on friction μ. Of the two nodal planes for each event, the one with greater instability is inferred to be the focal plane. Each Monte Carlo realization is seeded with random choices for the focal planes. The focal/auxiliary determination is made in each of the inversion realizations, offering one of several ways to examine how robust the focal plane choices are.

Because focal mechanisms are not abundant, there is a trade-off between having enough data for robust inversions and capturing small-scale heterogeneity in the stress field using data from only a selected area. For example, Townend and Zoback (2001, 2004) suggest 20–25 focal mechanisms are needed for reliable inversions (although that work did not jackknife downsample, add noise, or iteratively select focal versus auxiliary planes). With this trade-off in mind, inversions are conducted for all 42 regional focal mechanisms and for subsets of them, as well as with different weights (Table 3). The most general inversions (model 0) are the best constrained, whereas the most focused inversions use only the 17 Sparta focal mechanisms (model 5) to allow the highest spatial resolution, albeit at the risk of overfitting. It is also informative to compare the results of inversions using the 25 regional focal mechanisms aside from Sparta (model 6) with the Sparta-only inversions (model 5) to place bounds on how different stress near Sparta could be from its surroundings. Finally, models 1–3 experiment with different weights for the focal mechanisms to test the sensitivity of results to older data (from Giles County (Munsey and Bollinger, 1985)) and to more distant versus closer mechanisms.

The results for all seven parameterizations, in terms of $A\Phi$ and $\sigma_{H\max}$, overlap at 95% confidence interval (Fig. 4a–j, Table 3). All indicate transpression with subhorizontal east-northeast–west-southwest maximum stress $\sigma_{H\max}$ ($A\Phi =$ 1.79–1.89, $\sigma_{H\max}$ N60°E–N68°E). The average angular misfits of 15–22° are acceptable (≪40–44°; Michael, 1991; Hardebeck and Hauksson, 2001).

Quantifying fault-slip potential

In Vavryčuk (2014) approach, normalized instability is used to infer the focal and auxiliary plane for each event. The repeatability of this choice provides one metric for how certain the selection is. Of the 17 focal mechanisms near Sparta, 16 choose the same plane in 96% or more of the inversions (Table 4; Fig. S1). For the final event (ID 13), the dominant plane is selected in 88% of inversions. This consistency across parameterizations and realizations suggests that the focal plane choices are robust.

The algorithm implemented here was also tested on Angelier (1979) dataset of 38 slickensides from Crete, for which the true focal plane is known. The algorithm chose the correct nodal plane in 98.8% of instances (Fig. S2). This fidelity is a second indication that the focal plane choices are reliable.

In addition to instability, fault-slip potential can also be quantified in terms of the Coulomb failure stress change (dCFS; Fig. 4k) expected to initiate frictional slip, which is the magnitude of the frictional resistance minus the shear traction:

$$d\text{CFS} = \text{Friction} \times |\text{Effective normal traction}| - |\text{Shear traction}|$$

$$\text{Effective normal traction} = |\text{Normal traction}| - \text{Pore pressure}$$

$$d\text{CFS} = \mu(S_N - Pp) - \tau, \qquad (6)$$

in which S_N is the normal traction and is the shear traction resolved on the fault plane.

To calculate the magnitudes of shear and normal tractions, the normalized deviatoric stress tensors that result from the inversion are converted to full stress tensors following Walsh and Zoback (2016) and Levandowski, Weingarten, and Walsh (2018): The three equations needed to solve for the three stress magnitudes S_1, S_2, and S_3 are

$$\Phi = (S_2 - S_3)/(S_1 - S_3)$$

$$S_{\text{vertical}} = S_2 \text{ for a strike-slip setting} = \rho g z, \text{ and} \qquad (7)$$

$$(S_1 - P_p)/(S_3 - P_p) = \{\sqrt{\mu^2 + 1} + \mu\}^2. \qquad (8)$$

In equation (8), ρ is the average overburden density, g is 9.8 m/s^2, and z is an arbitrary focal depth. P_p is pore fluid pressure. Equation (9) is a requirement for Mohr circle tangency to the failure envelope (e.g., Zoback, 2010): In other words, that a fault could slip with no stress perturbation, a condition implicitly satisfied by the occurrence of independent (i.e., non-aftershock, natural) earthquakes in the region. Because $\rho g z$ is a piecewise-linear function of depth, and under the assumption that P_p also increases linearly with z, the magnitudes of all three stresses scale linearly with one another, each is a linear function of z, and they can more appropriately be described by stress gradients with depth (e.g., Fig. 4k,l). This treatment obviates a specific z and facilitates analyses of sets of events that occurred at varying depths, so is used here. Nevertheless, because 1 km is a representative depth for Sparta seismicity, the stress values shown in Figure 4k,l are approximately appropriate for hypocentral conditions.

For each of the 1400 stress tensors, pore pressure P_p is sampled from a uniform distribution 9.8 ± 1 MPa/km. Density ρ is $2600 \pm 200\ \text{kg/m}^3$. Friction for each of the 1400 models is the randomly assigned value used in the associated stress inversion. With these magnitudes, the full stress tensor $\boldsymbol{\sigma}$ is defined.

On a fault with normal vector $\mathbf{n}$ subjected to a stress tensor $\boldsymbol{\sigma}$, the traction vector $\mathbf{t}$ is

$$\mathbf{t} = \boldsymbol{\sigma}\mathbf{n}, \qquad (9)$$

$$\text{Normal traction} = \mathbf{t} \cdot \mathbf{n}, \qquad (10)$$

the magnitude of which is used in equation (6). The shear traction vector $\boldsymbol{\tau}$ is the cross product of $\mathbf{n}$ with the normal vector to the plane containing $\mathbf{t}$ and $\mathbf{n}$,

$$\tau = \mathbf{n} \times (\mathbf{t} \times \mathbf{n}). \qquad (11)$$

Equations (11) and (12) provide the values shown in Figure 4l.

Instability and dCFS are linearly related for a given full stress tensor (Fig. 4m):

$$d\text{CFS} = (S_1 - P_p)\mu(I - 1). \qquad (12)$$

It is also worth noting that the pore pressure increase that leads to frictional instability (ΔP_p, e.g., Lundstern and Zoback, 2016; Walsh and Zoback, 2016; Levandowski, Weingarten, and Walsh, 2018; Snee and Zoback, 2018) is also linearly related to dCFS and instability:

$$\Delta P_p = (S_1 - P_p)(I - 1). \qquad (13)$$

Fault-slip potential is quantified probabilistically from the 95% confidence interval upper bound on instability or lower bound on dCFS in Figure 4k. For instance, the dCFS values shown in Figure 4k are sufficient to trigger frictional slip in 5% of the 1400 models. Using the 95% upper bound accounts both for epistemic uncertainty in the stress field, using seven different groupings and weighting schemes for the focal mechanisms, and aleatory uncertainty, by jackknife-downsampling and

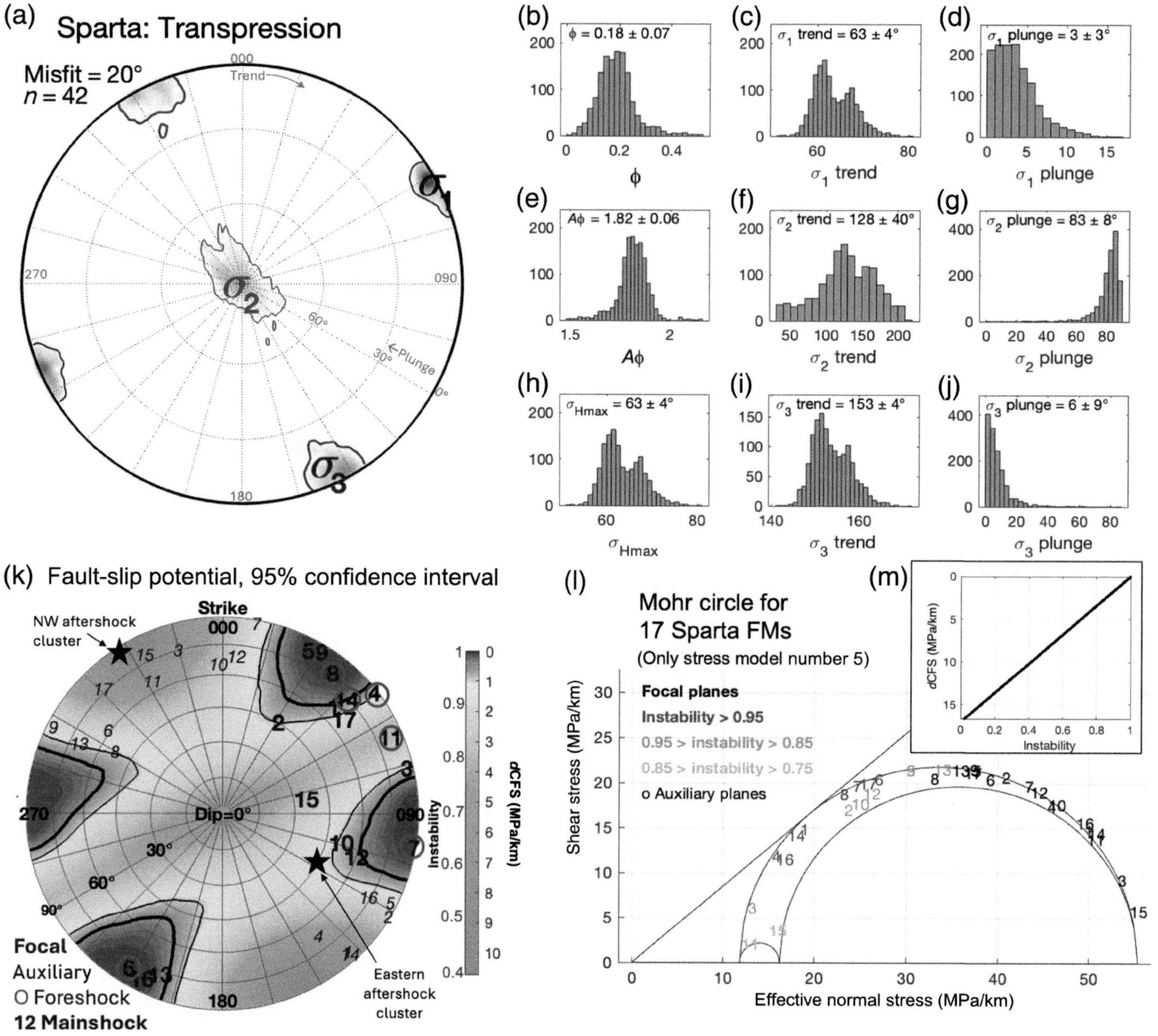

Figure 4. Stress inversion results and fault slip potential. (a) Results of 1400 stress inversions shown as principal stress vectors on a lower hemisphere projection. The solid blue/green/red lines indicate the 95% confidence interval regions for $\sigma_{1/2/3}$ vectors. (b,e) Stress ratio Φ and parameter $A\Phi$ across 1400 stress inversions. Values indicate a strike-slip regime with secondary horizontal compression. (c,d,f–j) Principal axis trends and plunges across 1400 inversions. (k) Fault-slip potential for 17 Sparta focal mechanisms, quantified as normalized instability (Vavryčuk *et al.*, 2013) and Coulomb failure stress gradient (*d*CFS) per kilometer depth. Fault orientations (not poles to planes) are displayed in polar coordinates. Azimuthal coordinate: Fault strike. Radial coordinate: Fault dip. The values shown are the 95% confidence interval lower bound across 1400 realizations (i.e., instability exceeds and *d*CFS is less than this value in 5% of realizations). The numbers indicate the event ID. The bold numbers indicate the preferred focal plane. The italicized numbers indicate the auxiliary plane. The purple circles indicate foreshocks. The stars indicate best-fit planes to two primary aftershock clusters. (l) Mohr circle for 17 Sparta focal mechanisms, using the best-fit stress tensor for the Sparta-only inversions (model 5 in Table 3). The colored numbers indicate preferred focal planes by event ID, colored by instability. The black numbers indicate auxiliary planes. (m) *d*CFS versus instability for arbitrary planes in one of 1400 realizations. *d*CFS is a linear function of instability, so values chosen for density, pore pressure, and other parameters do not affect ranked fault-slip potential. The color version of this figure is available only in the electronic edition.

TABLE 4
Preferred Focal Planes and Instability Results for 17 Sparta Focal Mechanisms

										Instability: Model 5 (Local)					All (Models 0–6)			
											Best-Fit		95% UB		Median		95% UB	
ID	Longitude	Latitude	Type	$S_{H\max}$	Depth	*M*	Strike	Dip	Rake	% NP1	Focal	Auxiliary	Focal	Auxiliary	Focal	Auxiliary	Focal	Auxiliary
1	−81.170	36.448	SS	90	6.9	2.4	45	67	173	100.0	0.98	0.42	0.99	0.64	0.91	0.34	0.98	0.55
2	−81.166	36.447	X (SS)	(67)	7.1	1.6	31	45	179	98.3	0.94	0.71	0.98	0.89	0.87	0.68	0.95	0.83
3	−81.110	36.507	SS	31	0.2	1.7	76	86	15	100.0	0.90	0.24	0.90	0.37	0.89	0.38	0.96	0.52
4	−81.107	36.485	SS	94	5.1	2.0	51	88	158	100.0	0.97	0.55	0.98	0.72	0.88	0.44	0.96	0.65
5	−81.107	36.492	SS	73	2.8	2.7	28	83	176	96.8	0.91	0.78	0.99	0.93	0.97	0.75	1.00	0.89
6	−81.105	36.484	SS	82	4.0	1.9	211	81	151	99.5	0.96	0.73	1.00	0.91	0.99	0.75	1.00	0.86
7	−81.105	36.485	SS	55	4.8	3.3	100	89	2	99.6	0.98	0.64	1.00	0.79	0.97	0.78	1.00	0.88
8	−81.103	36.485	SS	74	0.0	3.4	38	80	−142	96.9	0.99	0.85	1.00	0.98	0.98	0.84	1.00	0.93
9	−81.103	36.510	SS	72	4.0	2.2	28	82	−176	96.4	0.91	0.79	0.99	0.94	0.97	0.78	1.00	0.90
10	−81.102	36.479	TS	56	1.4	3.3	109	53	32	99.6	0.94	0.55	0.98	0.70	0.88	0.68	0.96	0.79
11	−81.100	36.482	SS	106	4.7	2.2	65	83	−155	99.6	0.83	0.39	0.85	0.57	0.77	0.47	0.85	0.59
12	−81.100	36.483	SS	59	1.3	5.1	108	60	24	96.9	0.94	0.62	0.98	0.77	0.89	0.74	0.97	0.85
13	−81.100	36.494	SS	70	2.0	1.6	201	77	159	88.0	0.86	0.82	0.95	0.97	0.93	0.83	0.98	0.92
14	−81.095	36.482	SS	94	4.5	1.9	47	74	176	100.0	0.99	0.41	0.99	0.63	0.91	0.33	0.98	0.53
15	−81.089	36.478	X (SS)	(37)	1.0	1.6	80	36	19	100.0	0.80	0.14	0.80	0.31	0.77	0.22	0.84	0.35
16	−81.073	36.502	SS	75	0.0	2.0	212	81	−164	99.4	0.96	0.45	1.00	0.93	0.99	0.73	1.00	0.89
17	−81.073	36.497	SS	95	0.6	2.2	52	67	−166	100.0	0.96	0.79	0.97	0.69	0.85	0.46	0.95	0.60

Faulting type and maximum horizontal shortening direction $S_{H\max}$ are assigned following Table 2. Unclassified events are listed as X (SS), and their P axis trend is used as a proxy for $S_{H\max}$. Strike, dip, and rake are listed for the preferred focal plane. *M* (magnitude) and depth (in kilometers) are from Neves *et al.* (2024). %NP1, percent of 1400 inversions in which the preferred focal plane was chosen; UB, upper bound.

random parameter choices. By contrast, only results for a single tensor are easily shown on a Mohr Circle; Figure 4l presents the values associated with the best-fit local stress tensor (model 5 in Table 3). Instabilities for each of the 17 Sparta focal mechanisms are listed for several scenarios in Table 4.

Active fault planes

Quantifying *d*CFS is useful because stress transfer of the order ~0.1 MPa is generally responsible for triggering aftershocks (e.g., Stein, 1999). By comparison, the auxiliary planes of the Sparta focal mechanisms are more than ~1 MPa from failure (Fig. 4k) at 1 km depth, which suggests that stress transfer would not cause the auxiliary planes to fail—a third metric that the focal plane determinations are robust. The preferred focal planes for the 17 Sparta focal mechanisms are mostly well aligned in the regional stress field; 15 of 17 could have instability $\gtrsim$0.95 and *d*CFS $\lesssim$ 1 MPa at 1 km depth (Fig. 4k,l; Table 4: all models—95% UB—focal). Neither nodal plane is well oriented for events 11 and 15. Dextral slip on northeast- or south-southwest-striking faults describes most events, including 5 of 6 foreshocks (IDs 4, 6, 8, 11, and 14) and 7 of 10 aftershocks (IDs 1, 2, 5, 9, 13, 16, and 17). This slip allows areas west of the respective fault to move relatively northward. The mainshock (ID 12) and two others within ~500 m of the mainshock (foreshock ID 7 and aftershock ID 10) have preferred strikes ~N110°E and left-lateral slip. The other two remaining events (IDs 3 and 15) also feature left-lateral slip on preferred nodal planes that strike ~N75°E.

Instability—Model 5 (local) refers to stress inversion parameterization 5 (see Table 3), which is based on the 17 Sparta mechanisms: Best-fit is the instability under the best-fit tensor to these 17 mechanisms for both the preferred focal and auxiliary (Aux) planes. 95% UB is the 95% confidence interval upper bound on instability across the 200 inversions for model 5.

Instability—All (models 0–6) refers to results from all 1400 inversions: Median refers to the median instability value for each plane across the 1400 inversions.

Discussion

Slip compatibility of the LRF and aftershocks

The regional stress regime is characterized by strike-slip to reverse-oblique faulting ($A\Phi \sim 1.70$–1.89) with $\sigma_{H\,\max}$ trending 060–068° (Figs. 4 and 5, Table 3). The optimal faults in this stress field are near vertical and strike north-northeast (035 or 215, ±15°) or east (095 or 275, ±15°) (Fig. 4k). The LRF may be quite well aligned for slip, with instability up to 0.97 and *d*CFS as low as 0.55 MPa/km at 95% confidence (Fig. 4m). In addition, 14 of the 16 aftershock focal mechanisms have at least one nodal plane that is well aligned for slip (i.e., 95% confidence interval bounds of instability $\gtrsim$0.9, which equates to *d*CFS $\lesssim$ 1 MPa/km).

The Sparta-only inversions (model 5: $A\Phi = 1.89 \pm 0.07$, $S_{H\,\max}$ 068 ± 3°) produce the highest fault-slip potentials: Increasing compression and clockwise-rotated stress favor reactivation of the LRF. Such a stress regime is intermediate between the strike-slip dominant, 060–064 $\sigma_{H\,\max}$ stress derived for other southern Appalachian data (model 6), and reverse faulting in Central Virginia ($A\Phi = 2.29 \pm 0.04$, $\sigma_{H\,\max}$ 103 ± 2°) and South Carolina ($A\Phi = 2.25 \pm 0.02$, $\sigma_{H\,\max}$ 073 ± 2°).

These findings imply that other faults in the Sparta region with strikes 020–050° or 080–110° (or antipodal) and steep dips are prone to reactivation. These include a plurality (~35%) of brittle faults mapped by Merschat and Carter (2023, their fig. 1C) near Sparta, which suggests that there are other seismically capable faults in the region. However, faults parallel to the dominant regional foliation (063/57°) are not well oriented for slip, nor are faults along the main joint trends (005 and 145).

Aftershock alignments versus active faults

The ~N110°E eastern aftershock cluster may define a well-oriented plane similar to the mainshock on the LRF (Neves *et al.*, 2024). This situation is common: alignments of aftershocks are often used to infer the mainshock fault plane (e.g., Ebel, 2008, 2009, Pennington and Chen, 2017).

By contrast, the northwest aftershock cluster may occupy a pre-existing damage zone, but the 325/88° best-fit plane to the hypocenters might not delineate an active fault. northwest- and southeast-striking planes are unlikely to slip in the modern stress field (e.g., auxiliary planes for IDs 1, 3, 4, 11, 14, 15, 17 in Fig. 4k), especially beyond ~60° dips. For instance, auxiliary planes for events 11 and 15 have instabilities <0.4 and <0.2. The frictional unfavorability of steep northwest-/southeast-striking faults implies that the 325/88° plane fit to the northwest-trending aftershock cluster does not delineate a fault on which those earthquakes are occurring. However, this alignment of aftershocks does parallel the dominant joint trend identified by Merschat and Carter (2023), 145 or 325 (±10°).

If not the 325/88° plane, what faults are active in the northwest cluster? There is only one focal mechanism clearly associated with the northwest cluster (ID 5), which has a steep north-northeast-striking focal plane nearly orthogonal to the northwest trend of the cluster. Nevertheless, the majority of the Sparta focal mechanisms have similar north-northeast–south-southwest-striking preferred focal planes (IDs 1, 2, 4, 5, 6, 8, 9, 13, 14, 16, and 17 in Figs. 4 and 5). Absent additional constraints, it seems most likely that earthquakes in the northwest cluster occur on similar planes. Thus, the northwest aftershocks could be occurring within a damage zone of inherited joints, with slip on highly oblique planes within that damage zone that are well oriented with respect to the regional stress.

Sparta, therefore, may present a cautionary example: Usually, it is assumed that aftershock lineaments delineate the operative fault plane, but the northwest cluster may involve slip on highly oblique faults arrayed along a pre-existing structure. At a broader scale, this situation is analogous to the observation that intraplate deformation often exploits pre-existing

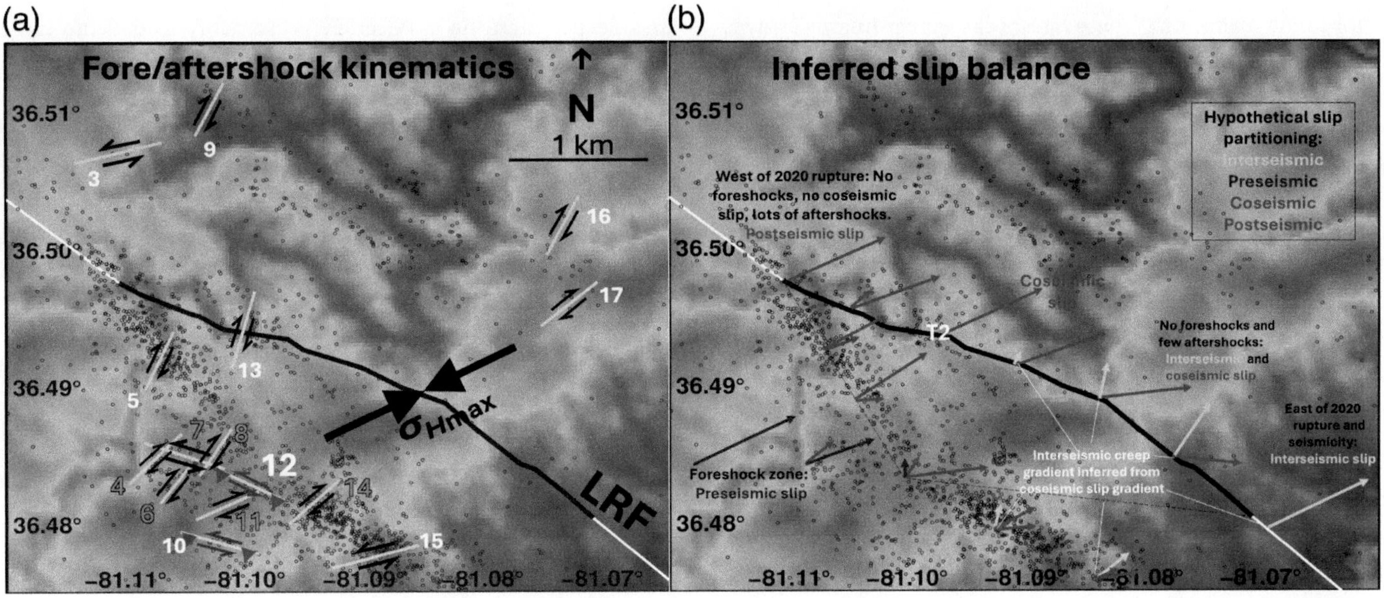

Figure 5. Seismic cycle model. (a) Fault planes and slip senses. The gray indicates inferred fault strike. The black arrows indicate slip sense for strike-slip events. The blue arrows and teeth indicate slip sense for reverse-oblique events. The number 12 indicates the mainshock. The magenta numbers indicate foreshocks. The white lines indicate aftershocks. (b) Hypothetical slip balance across the seismic cycle. The sums of cyan, blue, red, and purple vectors at each location are equal to the peak coseismic vector (at location T2). Coseismic slip vectors (red) are digitized from Szymanski *et al.* (2024, their model CSM Joint) and Pollitz (2023, see Fig. 2d). Where there are no foreshocks or aftershocks (e.g., east of the mainshock), remaining slip is assumed to be interseismic. West of the mainshock, the remaining slip is presumably preseismic in the east-trending foreshock zone and hypothesized to be postseismic elsewhere. The color version of this figure is available only in the electronic edition.

damage zones, even though the faults that are activated may not share the same orientation as the damage zone overall (e.g., Sykes, 1978; Gangopadhyay and Talwani, 2003).

Slip partitioning across the seismic cycle

Elastic rebound theory holds that the total interseismic, preseismic, coseismic, and postseismic motion should be approximately uniform along the LRF. This total slip should be equal to or greater than the maximum coseismic slip from finite-fault models (Pollitz, 2023; Szymanski *et al.*, 2024); thus, the summed interseismic, preseismic, and postseismic motion can be estimated by subtracting coseismic slip vectors from that maximum coseismic slip (Fig. 5b). Focal mechanisms from events surrounding the mainshock (Fig. 5: events 4–8 and 10–15) shed light on the role of pre- and postseismic processes in the overall slip balance.

The relative importance of these four components varies along and across the LRF.

Interseismic slip was presumably dominant east of the mainshock. Beyond the eastern end of the 2020 rupture, there was no coseismic slip, no foreshocks, and no aftershocks. The interseismic slip is thus estimated to at least equal the coseismic slip at T2. Along the surface rupture on the eastern LRF, coseismic deformation was mostly sinistral, and there were few foreshocks or aftershocks, implying that interseismic deformation was mostly reverse: counterclockwise relative to the hypocenter, such that it mirrored the clockwise rotation of the slip patch during the 2020 mainshock (Fig. 2c).

At depth along the eastern LRF (i.e., along the eastern aftershock cluster), abundant aftershocks and a few foreshocks suggest that less interseismic creep had occurred, such that some of the total slip occurred postseismically and to a lesser extent preseismically. Near and east of the mainshock, events 7 (foreshock), 10 and 15 (aftershocks) activated to east-southeast-striking planes grossly similar to the mainshock, albeit with smaller reverse components. These observations are consistent with the conclusion of Neves *et al.* (2024) that seismicity in the eastern cluster occurred along and near the mainshock focal plane. This seismicity could serve to homogenize small-scale coseismic slip variations along and around the focal plane and accommodate any changes or variations in fault-plane orientation.

Because coseismic displacement was greatest near and updip of the hypocenter, it is inferred that this area was locked interseismically.

Points west of the hypocenter experienced little coseismic slip (Fig. 2b,c), yet the division of slip appears to differ between the western part of the slip patch and areas outside of the slip patch. Foreshocks west of and near the mainshock (IDs 4, 6, 8, 11, and 14) chiefly fell along the southern edge and outside of the mainshock slip patch. Focal mechanisms illuminate a preparatory phase of dextral slip on northeast-striking planes in the 37 hr prior to the mainshock. These foreshocks were primarily arrayed along an east–west trend, suggesting an en echelon set of blocks moving areas to the west relatively northeast. There were at least nine foreshocks along this trend, including an M 3.3 and five M 1.9–2.2 earthquakes, which released a total moment of 1.3×10^{14} N · m; this is four orders of magnitude more than the 8.1×10^{9} N · m released by aftershocks in this same area. Because there was also little coseismic slip in this area (Pollitz, 2023; Szymanski *et al.*, 2024), it can be reasoned that most of the slip west of outside of the mainshock slip patch had occurred preseismically. This preparatory phase likely loaded the LRF at the hypocenter, triggering the M_w 5.1 mainshock.

The northwest aftershock cluster delineates the western edge of the coseismic slip patch. There were no foreshocks located within this cluster, little coseismic slip, and abundant aftershocks, which suggests that most slip occurred postseismically. However, focal mechanism 5 (aftershock), within the northwest cluster, is inconsistent with a northwest-striking, near-vertical strike-slip fault: Steep northwest-striking faults are unlikely to slip under east-northeast–west-southwest compression. Rather, the north-northeast-/south-southwest-striking nodal plane of this event is well aligned with respect to modern stress, suggesting activity on north-northeast-striking dextral faults similar to the foreshock sequence (and aftershocks elsewhere, such as event 13). The right-lateral motion on these faults would allow the areas west of T2 and the hypocenter, where there was negligible coseismic slip and no foreshocks, to move north and east relative to the hypocenter, balancing the coseismic slip deficit.

This slip partitioning could also be depth-dependent. The focus of the 2020 mainshock was remarkably shallow at <1.5 km depth, as were most of the aftershocks. Finite-fault models (Pollitz, 2023; Szymanski *et al.*, 2024) show negligible coseismic slip deeper than 1.5 and 2.5 km, respectively. The foreshocks were significantly deeper (5.3 ± 1.3 km), but they were concentrated west of the mainshock. Moreover, travel-time-based relocation places the mainshock at ~3 km depth, and the polarities of these first motions indicate sinistral slip on a steep east-southeast-striking fault (113/88°/1°) (Neves *et al.*, 2024), whereas the overall moment tensor gives a sinistral-reverse solution. This finding comports with Pollitz (2023) finite-fault model, which characterizes a two-phase rupture that begins with a pulse of sinistral slip at the hypocenter (0–0.2 s) that propagates mostly eastward with time, followed by reverse slip at the hypocenter (0.2–0.4 s). This two-phase rupture is also compatible with Figueiredo *et al.* (2022) observations of purely reverse coseismic offsets at the surface. In these ways, the Sparta earthquake resembled two separate events: a sinistral earthquake that did not break the surface and a reverse earthquake that did.

Conclusions

The 2020 M_w 5.1 Sparta, North Carolina, earthquake activated a 3.4 km long portion of the pre-existing, east-southeast-striking Little River fault. A precursory phase of strike-slip west of and deeper than the hypocenter presumably loaded the Little River fault, triggering the mainshock. During the mainshock, a roughly triangular patch of the hanging wall moved east, north, and up relative to the footwall, effectively rotating clockwise around the eastern rupture terminus, where there was negligible slip. Following the mainshock, two distinct alignments of aftershocks emerged. One closely paralleled the mainshock fault plane, possibly accommodating postseismic adjustment and homogenization of slip along and across the fault. The other trended N35°W from the mainshock, approximately along the western edge of the coseismic slip patch and parallel to the dominant regional joint trend.

Stress analyses show that the inherited Little River fault and coplanar aftershocks are suitably aligned for reactivation in the modern stress field, which is characterized by strike slip with N63°E ± 4° maximum compression. By contrast, the best-fit plane to the N35°W trend of aftershocks is not favorable for reactivation. This stress incompatibility suggests that the aligned hypocenters do not delineate the causative aftershock fault plane, as is commonly assumed for aftershock alignments. Rather, the instability criterion indicates that the focal planes for these and for a large majority (75%) of fore- and aftershocks for which focal mechanisms are available are steep, north-northeast– or south-southwest–strike dextral faults. This slip would allow areas to the west (i.e., mainly west of the slip patch) with little or no coseismic slip to move relatively north and east, compensating for their coseismic slip deficit relative to the epicenter. The preferential alignment of epicenters along the western edge of the slip patch and the fact that both parallel the dominant regional joint set suggests a set of en echelon dextral faults that exploit a damage zone inherited from Paleozoic or earlier deformation. In contrast to the inherited Little River fault, however, this damage zone is poorly oriented for slip in the modern stress field, and slip instead occurred on smaller, highly oblique faults. This investigation highlights the utility of stress analyses to understanding fault activity, reactivation potential, and slip partitioning across seismic sequences.

Data and Resources

MATLAB codes are available at github.com/WillLevandowski/ (last accessed November 2025). Scripts associated with this article will be archived as directed by the *SRL* editorial staff. Focal mechanisms shown in Figure 1 are presented in Table S1. https://earthquake.usgs.gov/earthquakes/search/ (last accessed December 2024). The supplemental material for this article contains figures showing the repeatability of focal plane selections for Sparta (Fig. S1) and Angelier (1979) Crete slickensides (Fig.S2).

Declaration of Competing Interests

The authors acknowledge that there are no conflicts of interest recorded.

Acknowledgments

Sara Ashley Lynn (North Carolina Geological Survey) and Kevin Stewart (University of North Carolina) provided comments on an earlier version of this article. Guest Editor Oliver Boyd and two anonymous reviewers are thanked for their reviews. This material is based upon work supported by the U.S. Geological Survey (USGS) under Grant Number G23AP00081.

The views and conclusions contained in this document are those of the authors and should not be interpreted as representing the opinions or policies of the USGS. Mention of trade names or commercial products does not constitute their endorsement by the USGS.

References

Angelier, J. (1979). Determination of the mean principal stresses for a given fault population, *Tectonophysics* **56,** T17–T26.

Carpenter, N. S. (2019). Characterization of linear ground motion site response in the New Madrid and Wabash Valley seismic zones and seismicity in the northern eastern Tennessee seismic zone and Rome trough, eastern Kentucky, *Ph.D. Thesis*, University of Kentucky.

Carpenter, N. S., E. W. Woolery, and Z. Wang (2014). The M_w 4.2 Perry County, Kentucky, earthquake of 10 November 2012: Evidence of the eastern Tennessee seismic zone in southeastern Kentucky, *Seismol. Res. Lett.* **85,** no. 4, 931–939.

Cornou, C., J.-P. Ampuero, C. Aubert, L. Audin, S. Baize, J. Billant, F. Brenguier, M. Causse, M. Chlieh, A. Combey, *et al.* (2021). Rapid response to the M_w 4.9 earthquake of November 11, 2019 in Le Teil, Lower Rhône Valley, France, *C. R. Geosci.* **353,** 441–463.

Dennison, J. M., and K. G. Stewart (2001). Regional structural and stratigraphic evidence for dating Cenozoic uplift of Southern Appalachian highlands, *Geological Society of America, Southeastern Section Meeting, Abstracts with Programs*, Vol. 33.

DePaolis, J., and M. C. Chapman (2018). The mb(Lg) 3.9, September 13, 2017 earthquake on the Virginia—West Virginia border: A significant shock in the Giles county seismic zone, *Seismological Society of America Annual Meeting*, doi: 10.1785/0220180082.

Ebel, J. E. (2008). The importance of small earthquakes, *Seismol. Res. Lett.* **79,** no. 4, 491–493.

Ebel, J. E. (2009). Analysis of aftershock and foreshock activity in stable continental regions: Implications for aftershock forecasting and the hazard of strong earthquakes, *Seismol. Res. Lett.* **80,** no. 6, 1062–1068.

Figueiredo, P., J. Hill, A. Merschat, C. Scheip, K. Stewart, L. Owen, R. Wooten, M. Carter, E. Szymanski, S. Horton, *et al.* (2022) The M_w 5.1, 9 August 2020, Sparta earthquake, North Carolina: The first documented seismic surface rupture in the eastern United States, *GSA Today* **32,** doi: 10.1130/GSATG517A.1.

Figueiredo, P. M., M. W. Carter, B. Cattanach, T. J. Douglas, J. S. Hill, E. Kirby, D. Korte, A. Lynn, A. Merschat, L. A. Owen, *et al.* (2020). Preliminary observations of M_w 5.1 Sparta (North Carolina) surface deformation—A first documented M_w 5 instrumental earthquake surface rupture in eastern USA? *Poster Presentation at 2020 SCEC Annual Meeting*, 14–17 September 2020 (Online).

Frohlich, C., and K. D. Apperson (1992). Earthquake focal mechanisms, moment tensors, and the consistency of seismic activity near plate boundaries, *Tectonics* **11,** no. 2, 279–296.

Gangopadhyay, A., and P. Talwani (2003). Symptomatic features of intraplate earthquakes, *Seismol. Res. Lett.* **74,** no. 6, 863–883.

Hardebeck, J. L., and E. Hauksson (2001). Crustal stress field in southern California and its implications for fault mechanics, *J. Geophys. Res.* **106,** no. B10, 21,859–21,882.

Herrmann, R. (2025) Moment tensors for North American earthquakes, available at https://www.eas.slu.edu/eqc/eqc_mt/MECH.NA/MECHFIG/mech.html (last accessed September 2024).

Herrmann, R. B., L. Malagnini, and I. Munafó (2011). Regional moment tensors of the 2009 L'Aquila earthquake sequence, *Bull. Seismol. Soc. Am.* **101,** 975–993.

Humphreys, E. D., and D. Coblentz (2007). North American dynamics and western US tectonics, *Rev. Geophys.* **45,** no. 3, doi: 10.1029/2005RG000181.

Hill, J. S., B. L. Cattanach, T. J. Douglas, P. M. Figueiredo, E. Kirby, D. M. Korte, A. S. Lynn, A. J. Merschat, L. A. Owen, C. Scheip, *et al.* (2020). Surface rupture of the Little River fault in response to the August 9, 2020 M_w 5.1 earthquake near Sparta, North Carolina, *Poster Presentation at 2020 SCEC Annual Meeting*, 14–17 September 2020 (Online).

Horton, S., M. Withers, C. Cramer, and H. Withers (2021). Source Parameters of the M5.1 Sparta, NC Earthquake of August 9, 2020, , Seismological Society of America Annual Meeting, *Seismol. Res. Lett.* **92,** no. 2B, p. 1439.

Levandowski, W. (2023). Fault slip potential near the deadly 08 September 2023 M_w 6.8 Al Haouz, Morocco earthquake, *Seism. Rec.* **3,** no. 4, 367–375, doi: 10.1785/0320230037.

Levandowski, W., R. B. Herrmann, R. Briggs, O. S. Boyd, and R. Gold (2018). A revised stress map of the continental United States reveals evidence for heterogeneous intraplate stress, *Nat. Geo.* **11.**

Levandowski, W., C. Powell, M. Chapman, and Q. Wu (2023). Anomalous crustal stress in the eastern Tennessee seismic zone, *Seismol. Res. Lett.* **94,** no. 3, 1643–1655.

Levandowski, W., M. Weingarten, and R. Walsh III (2018). Geomechanical sensitivities of injection-induced earthquakes, *Geophys. Res. Lett.* **45,** no. 17, 8958–8965.

Levine, J. S. F., A. J. Mershat, R. J. McAleer, G. Casale, K. R. Quillan, K. I. Fraser, and T. G. BeDell (2018). Kinematic, deformational, and thermchronologic conditions along the Gossan Lead and Fries shear zones: Constraining the western-eastern Blue Ridge boundary in northwestern North Carolina, *Tectonics* **37,** 3500–3523, doi: 10.1029/2017TC004879.

Lundstern, J. E., and M. D. Zoback (2016). State of stress in Texas: Implications for induced seismicity, *Geophys. Res. Lett.* **43,** no. 19, 10-208.

Lundstern, J. E., and M. D. Zoback (2020). Multiscale variations of the crustal stress field throughout North America, *Nat. Commun.* **11,** no. 1, 1951.

Lynn, A. S. (2023). Structural analysis of the seismically active little river fault and its connection to regional brittle structures, *Master's Thesis*, The University of North Carolina, Chapel Hill.

Merschat, A. J., and M. W. Carter (2023). Preliminary map of the surface rupture from the August 9, 2020, M_w 5.1 earthquake near Sparta, North Carolina—The Little River fault and other possible coseismic features, *U.S. Geol. Surv. Rept. No. 2023-1074*.

Michael, A. J. (1991). Spatial variations in stress within the 1987 Whittier Narrows, California, aftershock sequence: New techniques and results, *J. Geophys. Res.* **96,** no. B4, 6303–6319, doi: 10.1029/91JB00195.

Munsey, J. W., and G. A. Bollinger (1985). Focal mechanism analyses for Virginia earthquakes (1978-1984), *Bull. Seismol. Soc. Am.* **75,** no. 6, 1613–1636.

Neves, M., L. Y. Chuang, W. Li, Z. Peng, P. M. Figueiredo, and S. Ni (2024). Complex rupture dynamics of the extremely shallow August 2020 M 5.1 Sparta, North Carolina earthquake, *Nat. Commun. Earth Environ.* **5,** no. 1, 163.

Pennington, C., and X. Chen (2017). Coulomb stress interactions during the Mw 5.8 Pawnee sequence, *Seismol. Res. Lett.* **88,** no. 4, 1024–1031.

Pollitz, F. F. (2023). Shallow fault slip of the 2020 M 5.1 Sparta, North Carolina, earthquake, *Seismol. Res. Lett.* **94,** no. 6, 2831–2839.

Raymond, L. A. (2015). Formal revision of the Ashe and Alligator back Formation names, *Southeast Geol.* **51,** 135–143.

Reinbold, D. J., and A. C. Johnston (1987). Historical seismicity in the southern Appalachian seismic zone, *U.S. Geol. Surv. Open-File Rept. 87-433.*

Richardson, R. M. (1992). Ridge forces, absolute plate motions, and the intraplate stress field, *J. Geophys. Res.* **97,** no. B8, 11,739–11,748.

Sbar, M. L., and L. R. Sykes (1973). Contemporary compressive stress and seismicity in eastern North America: An example of intraplate tectonics, *Geol. Soc. Am. Bull.* **84,** no. 6, 1861–1882.

Simpson, R. W. (1997). Quantifying Anderson's faulting types, *Bull. Seismol. Soc. Am.* **102,** no. B8, 17,909–17,919.

Snee, J. E. L., and M. D. Zoback (2018). State of stress in the Permian Basin, Texas and New Mexico: Implications for induced seismicity, *The Leading Edge* **37,** 127–134.

Stein, R. S. (1999). The role of stress transfer in earthquake occurrence, *Nature* **402,** no. 6762, 605–609.

Stover, C. W., and J. L. Coffman (1993). Seismicity of the United States, 1568-1989 (revised), *U.S. Geol. Surv. Rept. Profess. Pap. 1527,* 17 pp.

Sykes, L. R. (1978). Intraplate seismicity, reactivation of preexisting zones of weakness, alkaline magmatism, and other tectonism postdating continental fragmentation, *Rev. Geophys.* **16,** no. 4, 621–688.

Szymanski, E. D., E. A. Hetland, and P. M. Figueiredo (2024). Imaging left-lateral and reverse near-surface slip of the 2020 M_w 5.1 Sparta, North Carolina, earthquake, *Bull. Seismol. Soc. Am.* **114,** no. 4, 1870–1883.

Talwani, P. (Editor) (2014) *Intraplate Earthquakes*, Cambridge University Press.

Townend, J., and M. D. Zoback (2001). Implications of earthquake focal mechanisms for the frictional strength of the San Andreas fault system, *Geol. Soc. Lond. Sp. Publ.* **186,** no. 1, 13–21.

Townend, J., and M. D. Zoback (2004). Regional tectonic stress near the San Andreas fault in central and southern California, *Geophys. Res. Lett.* **31,** no. 15, doi: 10.1029/2003GL018918.

Vavryčuk, V. (2014). Iterative joint inversion for stress and fault orientations from focal mechanisms, *Geophys. J. Int.* **199,** 69–77.

Vavryčuk, V., F. Bouchaala, and T. Fischer (2013). High-resolution fault image from accurate locations and focal mechanisms of the 2008 swarm earthquakes in West Bohemia, Czech Republic, *Tectonophysics* **590,** 189–195.

Walsh III, F. R., and M. D. Zoback (2016). Probabilistic assessment of potential fault slip related to injection-induced earthquakes: Application to north-central Oklahoma, USA, *Geology* **44,** no. 12, 991–994.

Zhang, Y., W. Levandowski, C. Powell, and C. A. Langston (2025). Transpressive stress throughout the New Madrid seismic zone, with second-order variations: Evidence from focal mechanism inversions, *Tectonics* **44,** no. 5, e2024TC008447, doi: 10.1029/2024TC008447.

Zoback, M. D. (2010). *Reservoir Geomechanics*, Cambridge University Press.

Zoback, M. L. (1992). First-and second-order patterns of stress in the lithosphere: The World Stress Map project, *J. Geophys. Res.* **97,** no. B8, 11,703–11,728.

Manuscript received 11 September 2025
Published online 5 December 2025

Source Complexity and Faulting Heterogeneity of the 2024 M_w 4.8 Zhongdian Earthquake, Yunnan, China

Zhenyu Wang[1], Chunmei Ren[†2], Longtan Wang[†3], Lijun Chang[*1], and Yijian Zhou[*4]

Abstract

Earthquakes in stable continental regions occur less frequently than those at plate boundaries, and their seismic hazards remain poorly understood. In this study, we analyze the source complexity of the M_w 4.8 Zhongdian earthquake in southeastern Tibet, which occurred in an area where no major faults were previously mapped. Notably, the focal mechanism solutions differ significantly between the different approaches: whereas the centroid moment tensor (CMT) indicates oblique-normal faulting, the first-motion (FM) solution suggests purely dip-slip faulting. This discrepancy points to a complex rupture process involving multiple slip modes. Using multi-point-source inversion, we identify two near-simultaneous subevents. The first aligns with the FM dip-slip mechanism, and the second is dominated by strike-slip motion; together, they are consistent with the overall CMT solution. However, source spectral ratio analysis and displacement records show no distinct temporal separation between the subevents. On the other hand, structural complexities are revealed by relocated aftershocks and spatially diverse focal mechanisms, which enable the observed rupture behavior. We further compare the stress fields across multiple scales and find no significant differences in principal stress orientations between the Zhongdian source region and the broader western Chuandian block. Nevertheless, the two subevent areas display contrasting faulting styles, highlighting the influence of localized strain or deformation heterogeneity. These findings suggest that the moderate-size Zhongdian earthquake was governed by both complex fault geometry and heterogeneous faulting behavior.

Cite this article as Wang, Z., C. Ren, L. Wang, L. Chang, and Y. Zhou (2025). Source Complexity and Faulting Heterogeneity of the 2024 M_w 4.8 Zhongdian Earthquake, Yunnan, China, *Seismol. Res. Lett.* **97**, 679–697, doi: 10.1785/0220250259.

Supplemental Material

Introduction

On 9 April 2024, an M_w 4.8 earthquake struck the Deqin-Zhongdian (DQ-ZD) region of the Chuandian block in southeastern Tibet (hereafter referred to as the Zhongdian earthquake). This event was unexpected because it did not rupture a mapped fault, and no historical earthquakes of **M** > 6.5 have been recorded in the source region since 1900 (Fig. 1a). The nearest major fault, the Deqin-Zhongdian-Daju fault (DZDF), is located ~30 km from the epicenter and exhibits a combination of right-lateral strike-slip motion and normal faulting (Chang, 2015). The DZDF also defines the western boundary of the Chuandian block (Fig. 1a, Xu *et al.*, 2003, 2016; Chang, 2015; Wan *et al.*, 2021), which has a relatively slow slip rate (~2 mm/a, Chang, 2015) and infrequent large earthquakes, with recurrence intervals exceeding 1000 yr for events of **M** > 6.5 (Chang *et al.*, 2023). In contrast, the eastern boundary of the Chuandian block, marked by the Xianshuihe-Anninghe fault with a slip rate of 10 mm/a, experiences significantly higher seismic activity (Xu *et al.*, 2005; Wan *et al.*, 2021). The moderate-size Zhongdian earthquake highlights the potential seismic hazard within stable tectonic blocks, which are often overlooked and poorly understood.

Earthquakes within stable continental regions (SCRs) are characterized by low-deformation rates and occur less frequently than those along plate boundaries (Calais and Stein, 2009; Calais *et al.*, 2016; Talwani, 2017). These events are thought to result from transient perturbations in local stress fields associated with certain geological structures, such as rifts and buried plutons, rather than conventional recurrence patterns observed at plate boundaries (Talwani, 2017). In addition, they can occur in

1. Institute of Geophysics, China Earthquake Administration, Beijing, China, https://orcid.org/0000-0002-1555-5346 (ZW); https://orcid.org/0009-0004-1467-3254 (LC); 2. School of Earth Sciences, Yunnan University, Kunming, China, https://orcid.org/0009-0007-3165-0304 (CR); 3. Southern University of Science and Technology, Guangdong, China, https://orcid.org/0000-0003-3630-2927 (LW); 4. Division of Geological and Planetary Sciences, California Institute of Technology, Pasadena, California, U.S.A., https://orcid.org/0000-0002-7205-1769 (YZ)

*Corresponding authors: zhouyj@caltech.edu; ljchang@cea-igp.ac.cn

†These authors contributed equally to this work.

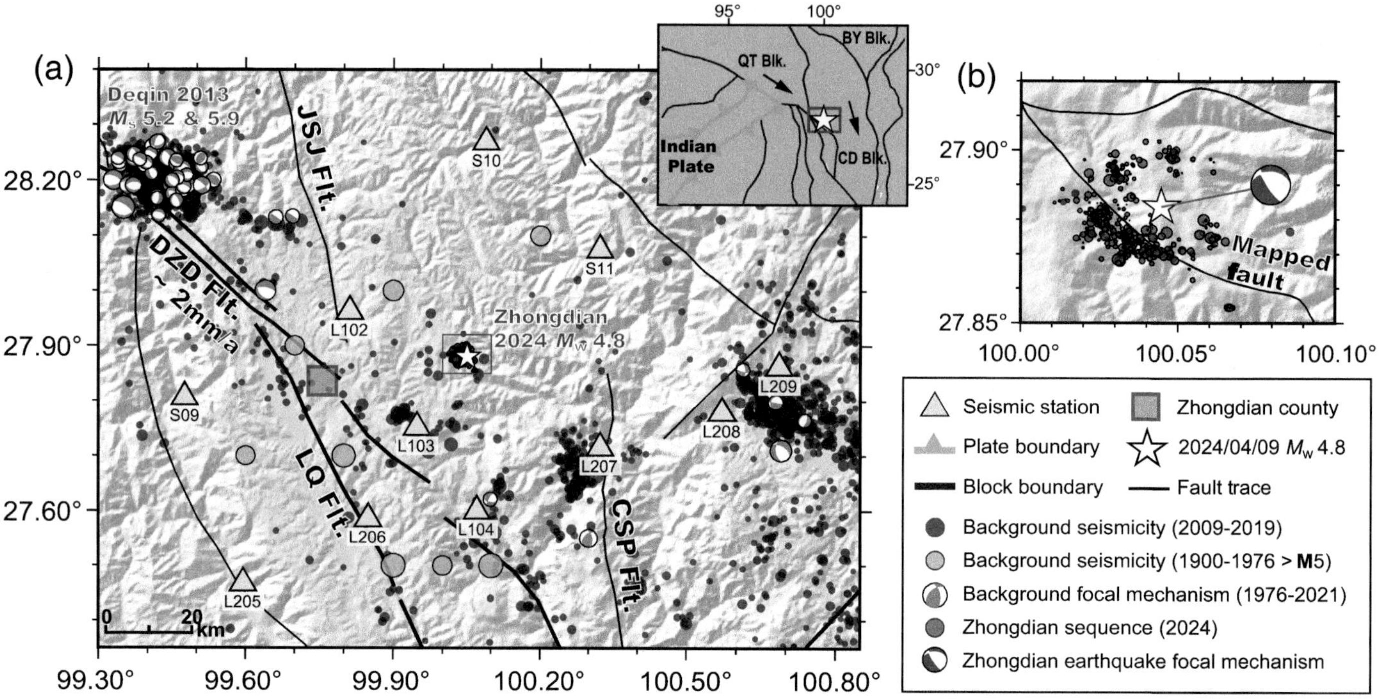

Figure 1. Tectonic setting and seismicity. (a) The inset map shows the major plates and blocks (Zhang *et al.*, 2003) involved in the source region, with arrows indicating the relative motion. The red rectangle indicates the extent of the main map. Black lines indicate active faults, with major faults bolded (Xu *et al.*, 2016). The M_w 4.8 event (white star) is located ~30 km east of Zhongdian County (green square). Circles represent the seismicity in the region with sizes varying with magnitude: the Zhongdian sequence is in red, earthquakes with magnitudes above **M** 5 from 1900 to 1976 (Earthquake Monitoring and Forecasting Department, China Earthquake Administration, 2023) are in orange, earthquakes with magnitudes above **M** 3.5 from 1976 to 2021 (Guo *et al.*, 2022; Global Centroid Moment Tensor [Global CMT]: see Data and Resources) are marked with blue focal spheres, and relocated earthquakes with magnitudes above **M** 1.5 from 2009 to 2019 (IEF, CEA; see Data and Resources) are in blue. Yellow triangles represent the broadband seismic stations. (b) The zoom-in view shows the Zhongdian sequence with mechanism (from multi-point-source [MPS] result in this study) of mainshock aside. Mapped surface fault traces are from Chang *et al.* (2014). BY Blk., Bayan Har block; CD Blk., Chuandian block; CSP Flt., Changsongping fault; DZD Flt., Deqin-Zhongdian-Daju fault; JSJ Flt., Jinshajiang fault; LQ Flt., Longpan-Qiaohou fault; QT Blk., Qiangtang block. The color version of this figure is available only in the electronic edition.

regions with no prior seismicity or surface evidence of strain accumulation (Newman *et al.*, 1999; Calais and Stein, 2009; Calais *et al.*, 2016; Sethanant *et al.*, 2025). These characteristics make traditional probabilistic hazard models less effective in SCRs (Schulte and Mooney, 2005; Talwani, 2017). Moreover, recent studies suggest that SCR earthquakes may exhibit complex rupture behaviors, further complicating seismic hazard assessments (Chapman, 2013; De Novellis *et al.*, 2020; Han *et al.*, 2024; Neves *et al.*, 2024). This is also demonstrated by recorded moderate-size earthquakes in the Chuandian block, such as the 1996 M_w 6.6 Lijiang earthquake (Ma *et al.*, 1998) and the 2021 M_w 6.1 Yangbi foreshock–mainshock sequence (Zhou *et al.*, 2022), which exhibit complex rupture patterns consistent with typical SCR earthquake behavior. These events have caused substantial economic losses and fatalities, underscoring the need for a deeper understanding of their underlying mechanisms.

In this study, we first examine the source complexity of the Zhongdian earthquake by resolving its focal mechanism through both moment-tensor-inversion approaches and first-motion (FM) methods. We then discuss the potential mechanisms causing this complexity through a high-resolution aftershock catalog, source spectral analysis, and stress field inversions.

Focal Mechanism Solutions of the Mainshock

The focal mechanism solution provides essential information for assessing the seismic characteristics and serves as a critical basis for evaluating seismogenic environments. Among the methods for determining seismic focal mechanisms, the centroid moment tensor (CMT) and the FM focal mechanisms represent the kinematic states of the source's spatial–temporal averages and the initial state, respectively (Stein and Wysession, 2003; Wan, 2016). For the Zhongdian earthquake, we use several methods to quantify the differences between these two states and investigate the source complexity.

CMT solution

The cut-and-paste (CAP) method, an advanced waveform-fitting-based double-couple (DC) CMT inversion technique (Zhao and Helmberger, 1994; Zhu and Helmberger, 1996),

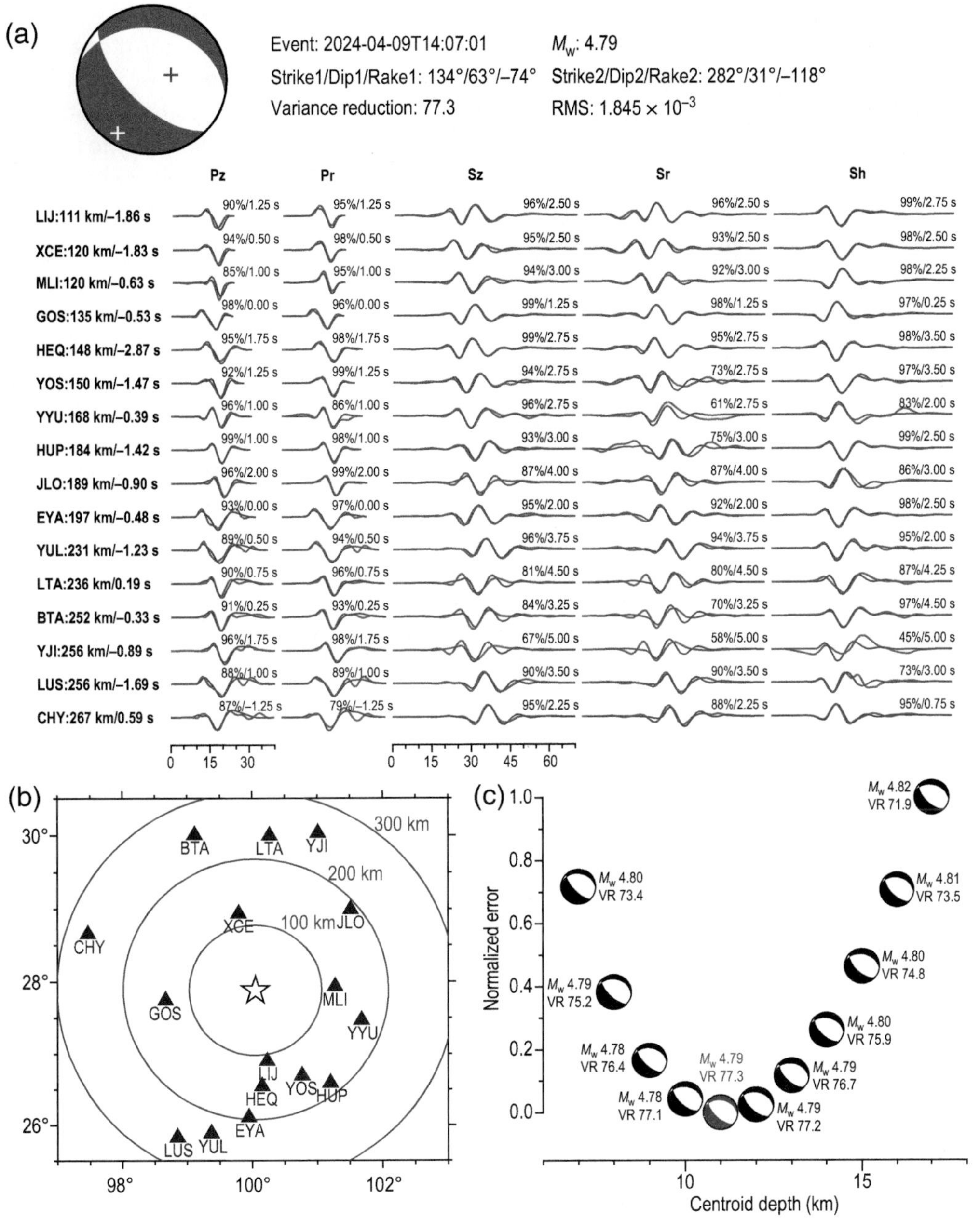

Figure 2. Stations and results from the cut-and-paste (CAP) inversion. (a) The focal mechanism represents the preferred solution. The corresponding comparison of observed (gray) and synthetic (red) waveforms for the Pz, Pr, Sz, Sr, and Sh segments are shown for each station. The station names, epicentral distances (km), and arrival-time differences (s) between observed and synthetic *P* wave are listed on the left side of each. The correlation coefficients (%) and time shifts (s, positive indicate synthetics shifted to the right) are given for each segment. (b) Distribution of stations used in the inversion, with red circles denoting the reference epicentral distances. (c) Normalized waveform fitting errors and solutions for all trial centroid depths. The moment magnitude (M_w) and variance reduction (VR) for each solution are presented. The optimal solution is indicated by a red focal sphere, corresponding to a preferred centroid depth of 11 km. The color version of this figure is available only in the electronic edition.

widely used in numerous studies (Huang *et al.*, 2022; Xu *et al.*, 2023; Su *et al.*, 2024), is used for the Zhongdian earthquake. This method involves conducting a grid search to identify the optimal values for strike, dip, rake angles, centroid depth, and magnitude by minimizing the residuals between synthetic and observed seismograms. The three-component waveforms are divided into five segments: two *P*-wave segments on the vertical and radial components and three *S*-wave (or surface wave) segments on the vertical, radial, and transverse components. Each segment is assigned a specific weight and evaluated separately for the fitting between observed and synthetic data, so that the depth phase can be fully used and the result is not dominated by the higher amplitude *S* waves. Time shifts and cross correlations (CCs) are applied between the synthetic and observed waveforms within each segment to reduce the effects of velocity model errors.

Given the single-point-source assumption inherent to the CAP method, we perform moment tensor inversion for the Zhongdian earthquake using the hypocenter location described in the Comprehensive early aftershock catalog section. Broadband waveforms from regional permanent stations located 100–300 km from the epicenter (Fig. 2b), with well-known and accurate instrument responses, are selected for the inversion. During the inversion process, the window lengths for the *P* and *S* waves are set to 40 and 70 s, respectively. A weight ratio of 2 is applied between the *P* and *S* waves, with distance attenuation factors of 1 and 0.5, respectively. The frequency–wavenumber (*f-k*) method (Zhu and Rivera, 2002) is used to compute the Green's functions based on a 1D velocity model (Table S1, available in the supplemental material to this article) derived from the regional wide-

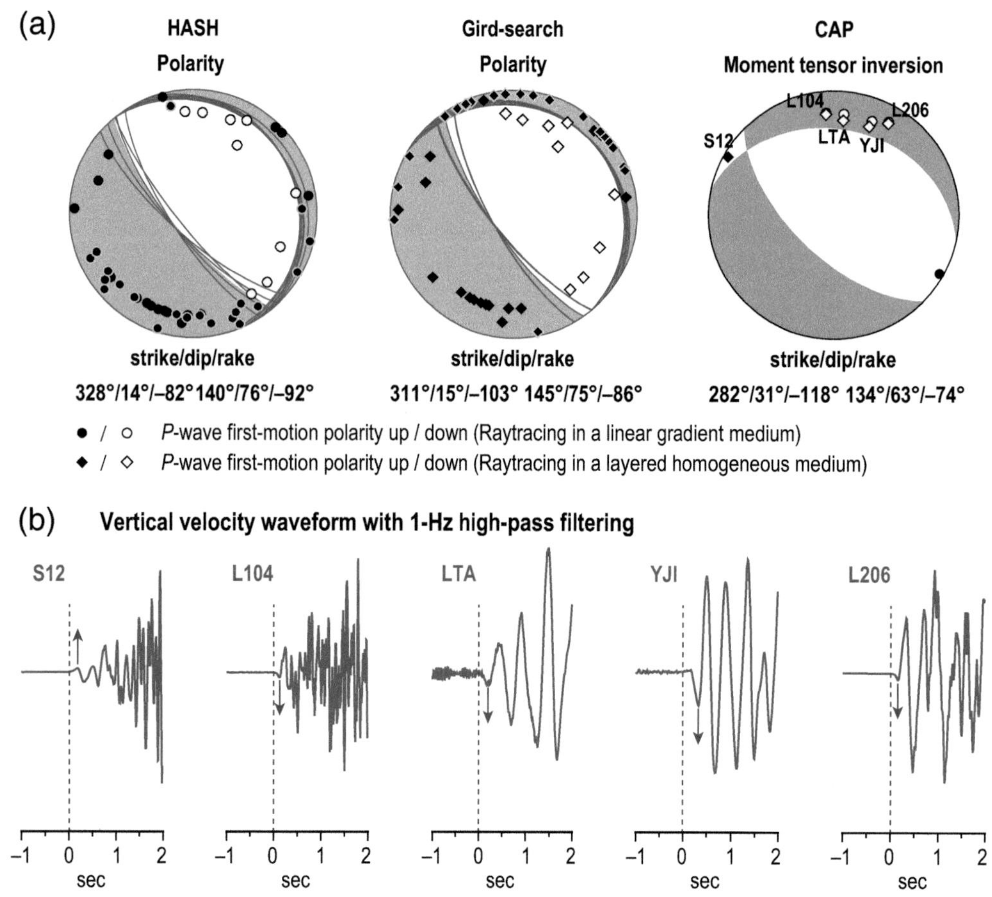

Figure 3. Comparison of focal mechanisms and selected waveforms with inconsistent polarity. (a) Focal mechanisms derived from the HASH, grid-search, and CAP methods are shown from left to right. Positive (black) and negative (white) first-motion (FM) polarities are projected and marked as circles and diamonds, respectively, corresponding to different raytracing methods. Stations with azimuths differing by 180° between the two raytracing methods are highlighted with golden outlines. (b) Five waveforms exhibiting polarities inconsistent with the CAP solution, highlighted after 1-Hz high-pass filtering. The dashed red lines and arrows indicate the *P*-wave arrival times and polarities, respectively. The color version of this figure is available only in the electronic edition.

angle seismic profile (Zhang and Wang, 2009). Both the observed and synthetic seismograms are band-pass filtered to frequency ranges of 0.02–0.15 Hz for *P*-wave windows and 0.02–0.1 Hz for *S*-wave windows. The grid search for strike, dip, and rake angles is conducted with a step of 5°.

The inversion results (Fig. 2a) reveal two nodal planes for the Zhongdian earthquake, with strike, dip, rake angles of 134°, 63°, −74° and 282°, 31°, −118°, repectively. This focal mechanism indicates a combined normal and strike-slip faulting characteristic, suggesting a complex background stress field in the source region. The moment magnitude of the earthquake is estimated to be M_w 4.8, and the optimal centroid depth is determined to be 11 km (Fig. 2c). Given the regional stress field with the minimum principal stress oriented in the northeast–southwest direction (Wang *et al.*, 2019; Su *et al.*, 2024) and the known fault distribution (Fig. 1a,b), the seismogenic fault plane is more likely to align with the one that strikes roughly northwest–southeast.

FM solution

In the waveform fitting of the CAP method, we notice that the initial polarity of some stations does not seem to be quite aligned (Fig. 2a), so the HASH method (Hardebeck and Shearer, 2002, 2003), a widely used technique that combines *P*-wave FM polarities and *S*/*P* amplitude ratios, is used to determine the initial kinematic state for the Zhongdian earthquake. The HASH method uses a grid-search approach to find and evaluate a set of acceptable focal mechanisms, providing a more stable and reliable optimal result while effectively quantifying uncertainties in the hypocenter location, velocity model, and polarity observations during the computation.

We use the HASH method, based on *P*-wave polarity data from 47 stations with full azimuthal coverage (Fig. S1a), to determine the FM solution (i.e., HASH-FM solution) for the Zhongdian earthquake. The *P*-wave polarity is determined by visually inspecting the 1-Hz high-pass filtered vertical-displacement seismogram, which has clear waveforms, making it easy to identify *P*-wave FM polarity. During the HASH inversion, we use the same hypocenter location and velocity model as those adopted in the CAP method. Each solution is computed over 50 trials with a grid-search interval of 1° to ensure calculation accuracy. The angle difference between each acceptable solution and the average focal mechanism (the preferred focal mechanism) must be less than 45°. The HASH solution (Fig. 3a) shows two fault planes with strike, dip, rake angles of 328°, 14°, −82° and 140°, 76°, −92°, respectively, suggesting a clear normal-fault characteristic in contrast to the CMT solution described in the previous section.

Generally, for small to moderate-size earthquakes (**M** < 5), the kinematic properties of the FM and CMT results are usually consistent. A significant discrepancy between the two may indicate the presence of a complex source process (e.g., Sun *et al.*, 2018). To further test the reliability of this discrepancy, we use an alternative Grid-search method with consistent polarity data to recalculate the FM solution (i.e., GS-FM solution; Wan, 2016;

Hu *et al.*, 2023). The method identifies the directions of the P, B, and T axes that best match the observed FM polarity distribution by minimizing the contradiction ratio, and it uses raytracing in a homogeneous 1D layered medium to determine the takeoff angles (Tian and Chen, 2005). This approach differs from the HASH method, which only calculates the takeoff angles using raytracing in a nonhomogeneous 1D layered medium (linear velocity gradient model in this study; Hardebeck and Shearer, 2002). To assess the uncertainty of the solution, we select a set of focal mechanisms with the lowest contradiction ratio. The optimal solution is then determined as the weighted average of these focal mechanisms, with the weight given by weight $= \exp(-15 \times r)$, in which r represents the contradiction ratio. We set the search interval to 5°, and the strike, dip, rake angles of the two nodal planes are estimated to be 311°, 15°, −103° and 145°, 75°, −86°, respectively (Fig. 3a). The result is consistent with the HASH-FM solution, with a Kagan angle of 7° (Kagan, 1991). Although the HASH-FM and GS-FM solutions for the Zhongdian earthquake are similar, we observe that some stations exhibit different takeoff angles on the focal sphere (with Schmidt's lower hemisphere projection), and the azimuths differ by 180° (Fig. 3a). This discrepancy is likely due to raytracing under different velocity models (Fig. S1b).

We find that the polarity distributions observed at five stations are opposite to the predicted results of the CMT solution in both the HASH-FM and GS-FM solutions (Fig. 3). This discrepancy directly supports the notion that the kinematic states of the average and initial source processes differ significantly, implying that a single-point-source mechanism may not adequately capture the source process.

Furthermore, we observe that the nodal planes corresponding to the CMT and FM solutions have similar strike (~140°) and high dip angles (>60°) and significantly different rake angles (Fig. 3a). This indicates that both the average and initial source processes occur on faults with comparable geometric characteristics and that differences in slip may be influenced by variations in deformation states.

Multi-point-source inversion

Considering the differences between the CMT and FM solutions for the single-point-source mechanism, we use the multi-point-source (MPS) inversion technique (Yue and Lay, 2020) to further investigate potential source complexity during the rupture process. Unlike the single-point-source solution, the MPS approach decomposes the entire rupture process into a series of subevents and solves for the spatial–temporal, magnitude, and focal mechanism information for each point source, which enables the identification of potential mechanism variations during the rupture process and has been widely used in source process analysis for both large and moderate-size earthquakes (e.g., Sun *et al.*, 2018; Lo *et al.*, 2019; Zahradník *et al.*, 2022; Ren *et al.*, 2024). In the developed inversion (Yue and Lay, 2020), a priori constraints on potential spatial locations (grid points), search time windows, the shape of the source time functions, and the number of subevents are applied to stabilize the linear iterative process.

In this study, we select 16 stations with relatively evenly distributed azimuths and epicentral distances, most of which are located within 30–100 km of the epicenter (Fig. 4b). This distance range is much smaller than that used in the CAP inversions to resolve the potential rupture complexities (i.e., small subevents) but still fulfills the spatial-point-source assumption, with the epicentral distance larger than ~10 times the source dimension. We define a 10 × 10 grid on the spatial plane, with the plane's geometry derived from the fault model based on the CAP solution (strike, dip = 134°, 63°). The projection of this plane is sufficiently wide to ensure complete coverage of the potential seismic source region for the Zhongdian earthquake. For accurate Green's function calculations at each grid point, we use the *f-k* method based on the same 1D velocity model used in the CAP method. As part of the data preparation, we window the three-component waveforms from each station to a length of 70 s from the onset of the earthquake. To minimize inversion errors arising from imprecise medium characterization, we apply two different filtering frequency bands based on the epicentral distances of the stations. For the four closest stations, we systematically test various upper-end filter frequencies because they tend to exhibit complexities at high-frequency bands (Fig. 4a). Ultimately, we determine the optimal upper-end frequency to be 0.25 Hz based on the L-curve of bandwidth versus root mean square (RMS) error (Fig. S2). For stations located at greater epicentral distances, high-frequency modeling requires a more refined representation of the medium. Consequently, we apply a 0.2 Hz upper-end frequency to these stations. Both the observed and synthetic seismograms are filtered within the same frequency band.

Relying on a single event does not fully capture the variations in the mechanism, as revealed by the FM and CMT solutions, as discussed in the previous section. Given that the Zhongdian mainshock is a relatively small event, we adopt two subevents, the minimum number of subevents (two instead of three or more), to approximate the entire rupture process. During the inversion, we assign potential initial rupture times for each spatial grid using a 0.1 s time interval over a 1 s period to capture the rupture's timing and spatial distribution. It is noteworthy that the real temporal resolution is limited by the filtering band and is much larger than the 0.1 s grid interval. The final results indicate that the Zhongdian mainshock consists of two near-simultaneous subevents (Fig. 4, Table S2). Despite the high-DC component (DC% = 96%; Vavryčuk, 2015) of the summarized tensor, the two subevents exhibit distinct characteristics. Subevent_1 occurs at 0.6 s, near the rupture initiation point (Fig. 4c) and demonstrates normal-faulting behavior. The Kagan angles are 2° and 5°, compared with the HASH and grid-search solutions, respectively, indicating strong consistency with these methods (Fig. 4c). Subevent_2 occurs at 0.8 s, located

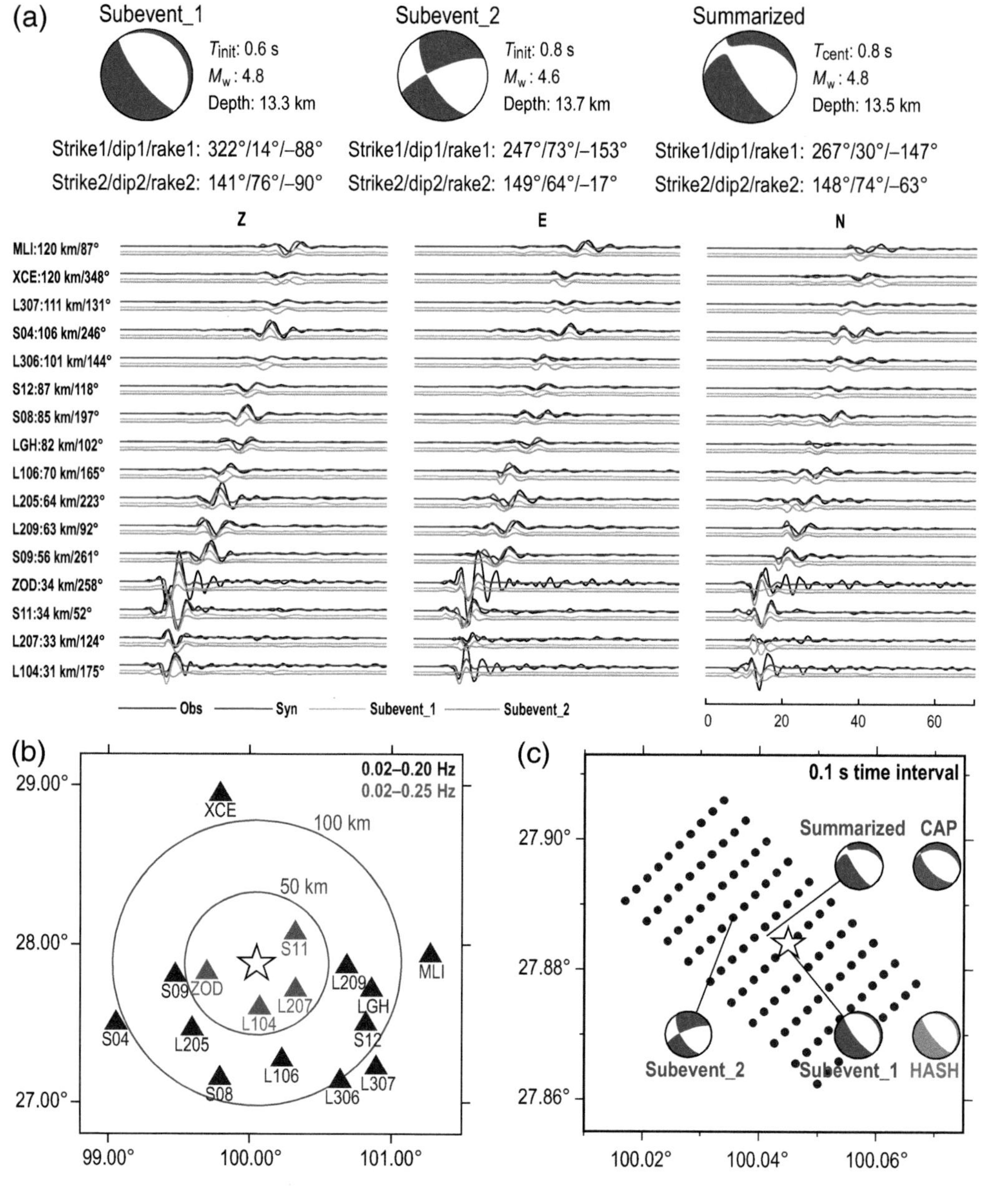

Figure 4. Stations and results from the MPS inversion. (a) From left to right, the three focal mechanism solutions represent subevent_1, subevent_2, and their combination. Relevant source parameters are listed alongside each solution. Below, waveform fits at each station are shown: black traces represent the observed waveforms; red traces show the total synthetic waveforms; and yellow and green correspond to the synthetics from subevent_1 and subevent_2, respectively. The station names, epicentral distances (km), and azimuths (°) are indicated to the left of each waveform group. (b) Distribution of stations used in the MPS inversion, with red circles indicating the different epicentral distances. Note that the waveforms from the blue and purple stations are filtered within the frequency bands of 0.02–0.2 Hz and 0.02–0.25 Hz, respectively. (c) Spatial search grids and distribution of MPS subevents are shown (green), along with comparisons from the CAP (red) and HASH (blue) methods. The color version of this figure is available only in the electronic edition.

to the northwest of subevent_1 and exhibits a left-lateral strike-slip characteristic, similar to aftershock mechanisms along the northwest end of the mapped fault (see the next section). The combination of these two subevents closely matches the CAP result (Kagan angle = 18°), validating the single-point-source solutions, including both the FM and CMT solutions. It also explains the observed differences between the initial and centroid mechanisms, thereby illuminating the inherent complexity of the rupture process.

This type of near-simultaneous spatial complexity has also been documented in other earthquakes, such as the 2017 M_w 6.5 Jiuzhaigou earthquake, in which an M_w 6.3 strike-slip subevent and an M_w 5.6 thrust subevent initiated at a λ-shaped fault system with an indiscernible temporal separation (Sun *et al.*, 2018), and the 2018 M_w 6.4 Hualian earthquake, in which an M_w 5.9 thrust subevent and an M_w 5.5 strike-slip subevent occurred apparently at the same time at a fault junction (Lo *et al.*, 2019). These cases illustrate that subevents with different kinematic characteristics, such as strike slip and dip slip, can occur near simultaneously during a single rupture, revealing the high heterogeneity and complexity inherent in the rupture process.

In summary, the MPS inversion directly analyzes the M_w 4.8 Zhongdian earthquake within SCRs, which involves a complex source process consisting of two near-simultaneous subevents. Specifically, subevent_1 is a purely dip-slip faulting event, whereas subevent_2 contains more strike-slip components, that is, an oblique-normal-faulting event. The correctness of these findings is supported by the FM solution and the CAP solution.

Fault Structure Imaging with Microseismicity

For the Zhongdian earthquake, the MPS inversion (see previous section) suggests that the rupture exhibits diverse focal

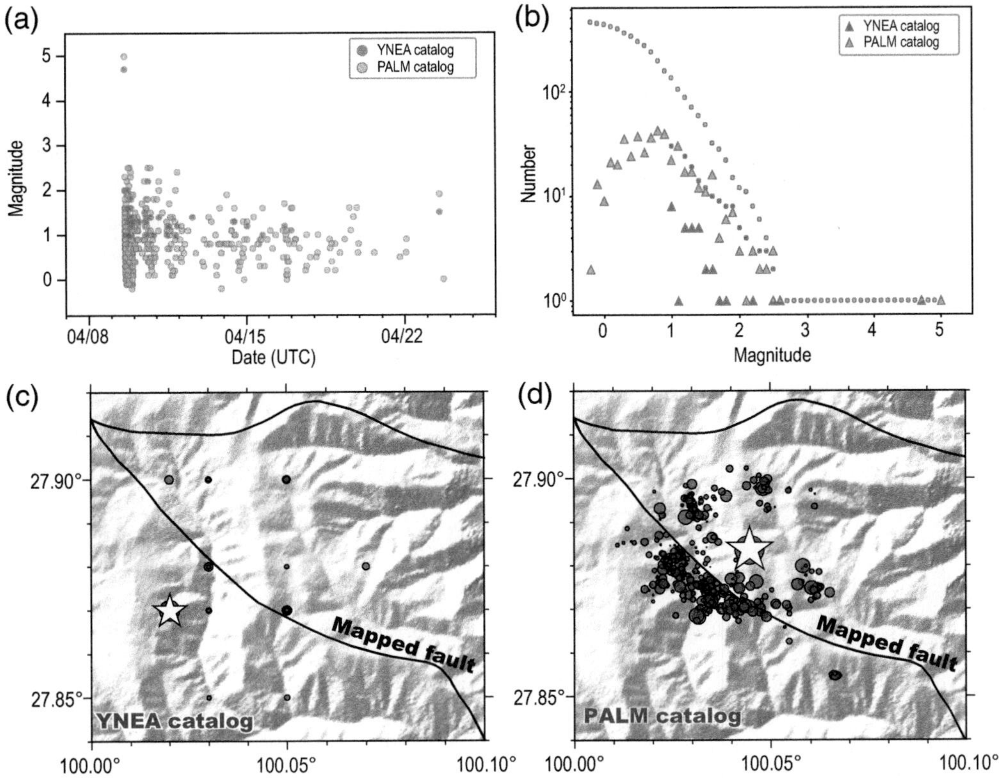

Figure 5. Comparison between the phase picking, association, location, and matched-filter (PALM) catalog and Yunnan Earthquake Agency (YNEA) catalog for the Zhongdian sequence. (a) Magnitude–time sequence. (b) Frequency–magnitude distribution. Blue markers correspond to the YNEA catalog, and orange markers correspond to the PALM catalog. Cumulative and non-cumulative numbers are denoted by dots and triangles, respectively. (c,d) Overall distribution of the Zhongdian sequence according to the YNEA and PALM catalogs. The Zhongdian sequence is represented by red circles, with marker sizes varying according to magnitude. The white star indicates the epicenter. Surface fault traces are shown as in Figure 1b. The color version of this figure is available only in the electronic edition.

mechanisms across different slip patches. This rupture heterogeneity is usually associated with a complex fault geometry (De Novellis *et al.*, 2020; Douilly *et al.*, 2020; Neves *et al.*, 2024). In this section, we use a high-resolution aftershock catalog and focal mechanisms of aftershocks to interpret the local fault structures.

Comprehensive early aftershock catalog

To construct the aftershock catalog, we use a temporary local broadband array (11 stations, located within 60 km of the epicenter) that provides full azimuthal coverage of the Zhongdian sequence from 1 to 23 April 2024 (Fig. 1a, Fig. S3). The PALM (phase picking, association, location, and matched-filter) workflow (Zhou, Yue, *et al.*, 2021) is used to scan the continuous waveforms. It consists of two main components: (1) PAL (picking, association, and location), which uses rule-based algorithms, including short-term average/long-term average (STA/LTA) and the Kurtosis algorithm, to detect *P* and *S* phases, and (2) MESS (match, expand, shift, and stack), an advanced matched-filter method that uses PAL detections as templates to identify smaller events with similar waveforms, which can effectively enhances detection completeness. By leveraging waveform CC, MESS not only enhances detection completeness but also improves relocation precision through sampling-rate-level differential time measurements. This approach has been successfully applied to multiple intense seismic sequences (e.g., Zhou, Ghosh, *et al.*, 2021; Zhou *et al.*, 2022; Ding *et al.*, 2023). For further technical details on the PALM workflow, readers are referred to Zhou, Yue, *et al.* (2021).

For the Zhongdian sequence, the PAL method is applied as follows: a 1–20 Hz band-pass filter is first applied to the continuous waveforms, and the STA/LTA algorithm is used to detect *P* waves, with a trigger threshold of 12 (defined by square amplitude). *S* waves are then searched within a 10 s window following each *P* pick. Event association requires at least four stations, with an origin-time deviation of <2.0 s and a *P*-wave travel-time residual of <1.5 s. Earthquake locations are determined using a 1D velocity model (Table S1), as outlined in the previous section. Absolute locations are obtained using hypoInverse (Klein, 2014), with phase weighting based on epicentral distance and time residuals, tapering from full to zero weight over distances of 20–60 km and residuals of 0.3–0.9 s. This results in a catalog of 107 events, with mean absolute location uncertainties of ~560 m horizontally and 2600 m vertically. Relative relocations are performed using hypoDD (Waldhauser, 2001). Events are linked within a 5 km hypocentral separation (i.e., WDCT = 5 km, in hypoDD terminology, "Distance weighting/cutoff for Catalog Travel-time data"), and four inversion iterations are conducted, yielding a final set of 105 relocated events. The mean relocation uncertainties in hypoDD, based on least-squares inversion, are estimated to be 41 m horizontally and 39 m vertically.

For MESS, the continuous data are filtered between 1 and 20 Hz. The detection window is set to 1 s before and 9 s after the *P*-wave arrival. The window lengths for *P*- and *S*-wave

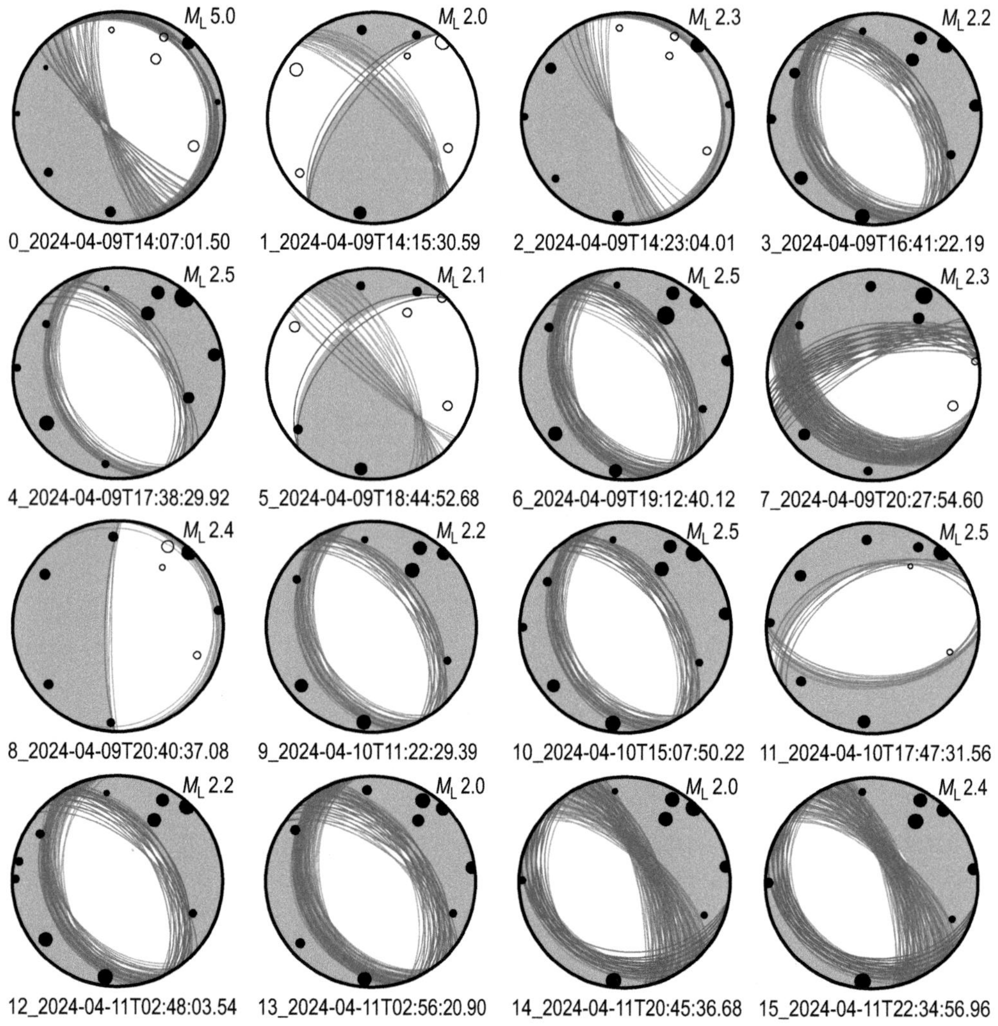

Figure 6. Focal mechanisms of the $M_L \geq 2.0$ events in the Zhongdian sequence. The gray lines represent a set of possible focal mechanisms. The focal mechanism with colored quadrants corresponds to the preferred solution, with detailed information provided in Table S3. Positive and negative polarities are indicated by black and white circles, respectively. The circle size corresponds to the square root of the *P/S* amplitude ratio, following the convention used in the hashpy2 program. The occurrence time and magnitude of each event are marked, with the order corresponding to the event sequence. The color version of this figure is available only in the electronic edition.

differential travel-time measurements are 2 and 3 s, respectively, starting 0.5 s before each phase arrival. During detection, events are required to be associated with at least three stations and have a CC value of ≥0.3. Detections from different templates are grouped as a single event if their origin times are within 2 s. In the hypoDD process, *P*- and *S*-wave differential times are constrained within 0.6 and 1.0 s, respectively, with a maximum hypocentral separation of 2 km (i.e., WDCC = 2 km, in hypoDD terminology, "Distance weighting/cutoff for Cross-Correlation data"). After four iterations of inversion, we obtain a high-precision PALM catalog of 461 events (Fig. 5d), which is approximately four times the number of events in the PAL hypoDD catalog (Fig. S4). The mean relocation uncertainties in hypoDD, based on least-squares criteria, are estimated to be 22 m horizontally and 25 m vertically.

The frequency–magnitude distribution exhibits strong consistency between the PAL and PALM catalogs above the completeness magnitude, confirming the reliability of the MESS detections (Fig. S4b). Notably, the M_w 4.8 mainshock is not relocated because of poor waveform similarity between large and small events. Instead, we use the hypoInverse result for its location: 100.045° E, 27.884° N, at a depth of 13.3 km.

The final PALM catalog significantly improves imaging resolution compared with the routine catalog provided by the Yunnan Earthquake Administration (YNEA), which relies solely on a relatively sparse network of permanent stations (Fig. 5c,d). The PALM catalog contains more than 10 times the number of events recorded in the YNEA catalog and reveals that YNEA missed numerous events above the magnitude of completeness (Fig. 5b).

Notably, the largest aftershock has a magnitude of M_L 2.5, ~2 units lower than the mainshock, deviating from traditional Båth's law (Båth, 1965). Although such a deviation is uncommon, it is possible considering the statistical pattern observed in the continental regions of China (Jiang, 2025), where the magnitude difference between the mainshock and the largest aftershock follows a normal distribution with a mean of 1.7 and a standard deviation of 1.1. The relatively low magnitudes of aftershocks in the 2024 Zhongdian sequence may reflect the low background tectonic stress in the source region (Zhu, 2023), which is in line with the qualitative understanding that the magnitude deviation is negatively correlated with the source region's average fault slip rate (Jiang, 2025). A similar phenomenon was observed in the 1988 M_s 5.5 Ninglang earthquake sequence, in which the largest aftershock had a magnitude of only

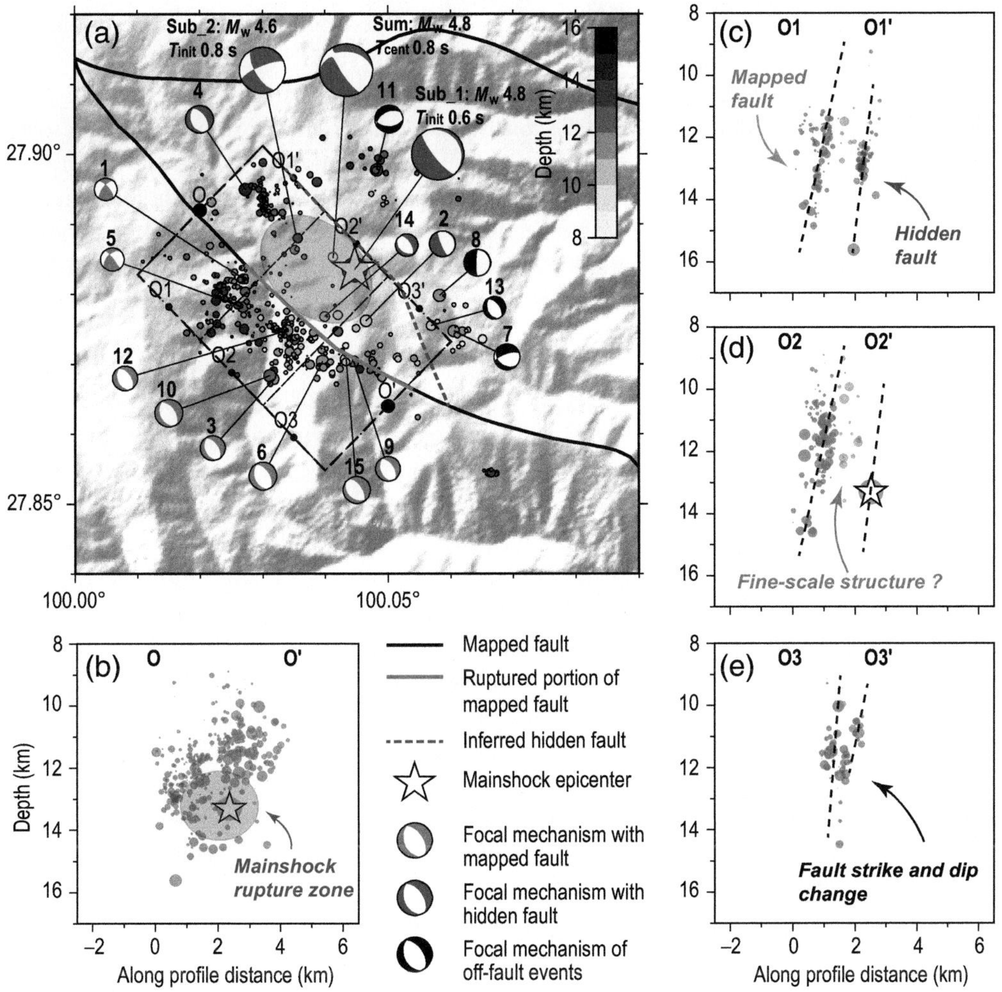

Figure 7. Seismicity distribution and fault structure interpretation of the Zhongdian sequence. (a) Map view of seismicity distribution. The southeast-trending OO′ profile and the northeast-trending O1–O3 profiles are indicated. The color scale represents focal depth. Surface fault traces are shown as in Figure 1b, from Chang *et al.* (2014). Focal mechanisms are the same as in Figures 4 and 6. The solid blue and dashed green lines represent the ruptured portion of mapped faults and the inferred hidden fault from seismicity, respectively. The blue and green focal mechanisms correspond to the faults of the same colors, and the black mechanisms represent off-fault events. (b) Distribution of seismic events along the OO′ profile. The rupture zone of the mainshock is marked with a green shade. (c,d,e) Seismicity distribution along the O1–O3 profiles. The dashed black lines indicate inferred fault structures based on the seismicity. Seismic events associated with the two seismogenic faults are shown in blue and green, respectively. Note the focal depth relative to the ground elevation (2800 m). The mainshock is marked by a star. Event marker sizes vary with magnitude. The color version of this figure is available only in the electronic edition.

M_L 3.5, also located within the Chuandian block (Zhang *et al.*, 1999).

For $M_L \geq 1.5$ events in the PALM catalog, we also calculate their focal mechanisms using the HASH algorithm, constrained by *P*-wave polarity and the *S*/*P* amplitude ratio, with clear waveform records from 11 stations (Fig. 1a). The maximum *S*/*P* amplitude ratio is obtained from the Cartesian summation of the three-component waveform (Bloch *et al.*, 2018; Herrera *et al.*, 2021). The picking windows for the maximum *P*- and *S*-wave amplitudes are set to 1 s before and 2 s after the *P*-wave pick and 10 s after the *S*-wave pick. The acceptable variation in the *S*/*P* amplitude ratio is set to 0.2 on a log10 scale. The other calculation parameters are the same as those detailed in the FM solution section. We obtain 44 reliable results, including 15 $M_L \geq 2.0$ aftershock events and the Zhongdian mainshock (Fig. 6). The Kagan angle between the two types of HASH results for the Zhongdian mainshock is 10° (Figs. 3a,6). The RMS angular difference of the nodal planes from the average for all solutions is <20° (Tables S3, S4), and all meet the quality A standard as defined by Hardebeck and Shearer (2008). The majority of these solutions indicate normal faulting, which is consistent with the extensional regional deformation style in the DQ-ZD region (Zhu, 2023).

Interpretation of fault structure

The high-resolution aftershock catalog reveals two fault segments (Fig. 7), one of which was previously mapped through detailed geological investigations, identified as a Middle–Early Pleistocene active fault (Chang *et al.*, 2014); the other one is a hidden branch associated with the mainshock hypocenter. Both faults strike northwest and dip steeply to the southwest (Fig. 7). The steep dip of the hidden fault is consistent with the focal mechanism of the mainshock (Fig. 3). The mapped fault shows a change in strike across the O3 profile, with the seismicity indicating a steeper dip angle (Fig. 7e).

A comparison of focal mechanism variability between the two faults highlights distinct differences (Fig. 7a): the mapped fault predominantly exhibits normal faulting of consistent nodal plane orientations, except at its northwest end; the hidden fault shows a wider range of strike, dip, and rake angles. The high variability in focal mechanisms along the hidden fault suggests a complex inner structure, which is typically associated with a low cumulative slip (Manighetti *et al.*, 2007; Perrin *et al.*, 2016; Manighetti *et al.*, 2021; Pennington *et al.*, 2022). The northwest portion of both faults likely feature a combination of normal faulting and strike-slip motion (Fig. 7a), suggesting a faulting heterogeneity, which is discussed in later sections.

Notably, for the mapped fault, the dip angle imaged by the aftershock distribution (~75° to southwest) deviates from the nodal planes of the aftershock focal mechanisms. To resolve these discrepancies, we calculate Coulomb failure stress change (ΔCFS) caused by the mainshock with the Coulomb 3.3 software package (Lin and Stein, 2004; Toda *et al.*, 2005). The source fault geometry is determined based on the mainshock hypocenter and MPS source parameters. The coseismic slip (38 cm) and rupture area (3.13 km^2) are derived using spectral ratio analysis (detailed in the Rupture directivity and source parameters section). In the absence of additional constraints, we assume a square faulting area without rupture directivity for the ΔCFS calculation. For the strike, dip, rake angles of the receiver fault, we compare three scenarios: the fault geometry (strike, dip) indicated by aftershock distributions, with the rake derived from the southwest-dipping average nodal planes of aftershock focal mechanisms (140°, 75°, −80°), and both the fault geometry and rake derived from the average nodal planes from aftershock focal mechanisms (Fig. 8a, NP1: 158°, 38°, −80°, NP2: 325°, 53°, −98°), respectively. The elastic parameters applied in the calculations include a friction coefficient of 0.4, a Poisson's ratio of 0.25, and a Young's modulus of 8×10^4 MPa, consistent with typical values used in continental regions (e.g., Stein *et al.*, 1992; Wan and Shen, 2010; Woo *et al.*, 2019).

Results show that the majority of aftershocks on the mapped fault lie in the stress shadow if the source fault dip angle is determined by the aftershock distribution (~75°); a much lower dip angle (~38° to southwest or ~53° to northeast), as suggested by focal mechanisms, results in positive ΔCFS for most of the aftershocks (Fig. 8d,e, Fig. S6). Assuming that the aftershocks are triggered by coseismic stress redistribution, the low dip angle is more likely to be correct. However, we are unable to determine which dip direction of the fault plane is more likely to exist because both correspond to positive ΔCFS distribution. One possible explanation for this discrepancy is that the mapped fault exhibits a set of low-dip subfaults that form a bookshelf structure (Fig. 8b), which could either be a southwest-dipping synthetic bookshelf structure or a northeast-dipping antithetic bookshelf structure. Similar vertical structural complexities in normal fault systems have been observed, as shown in the normal fault system of central Italy, particularly within the Mount Vettore–Mt. Bove and the Mount della Laga fault system (Waldhauser *et al.*, 2021), and the vertical conjugate normal fault system being activated by an M_w 5.3 earthquake in the Western Corinth Rift of Greece (Zahradník *et al.*, 2022). We are unable to confirm or refute this candidate fine-scale structure because of limitations in station distribution and the resolution of seismicity relocation in this study.

In summary, the fault system responsible for the Zhongdian earthquake consists of two faults, both exhibiting certain structural complexities. The hidden fault, where the mainshock nucleated, generates variable focal mechanisms; the mapped fault, which runs nearly parallel to it, may contain a bookshelf structure that is not fully resolved by our catalog. Both faults exhibit a transition from normal faulting to strike-slip motion in their northern end.

Possible Mechanisms Causing the Observed Source Complexity

Results in the previous sections have demonstrated that the Zhongdian mainshock is featured by a multisubevent rupture, which is supported by the geometrical complexities of the local fault system. However, two questions remain: (1) whether temporal complexities also exist, that is, different slip patches of similar focal mechanisms rupture at distinctly different times, and (2) what made the spatial complexity possible, that is, different slip patches rupture in different manners. In this section, we conduct source spectral analysis and compare the focal mechanisms and stress states across different spatial scales to further explore the potential mechanisms behind the source complexities of the M_w 4.8 Zhongdian earthquake.

Source spectra analysis

Spectral ratio calculation. We use source spectral ratio analysis to investigate the temporal complexity of the Zhongdian mainshock and estimate its source parameters. This method uses empirical Green's functions (EGFs) to eliminate the propagation effects and site responses from the seismograms (Chen and Shearer, 2013; Ross and Ben-Zion, 2016; Yoon *et al.*, 2019; Zhou *et al.*, 2022). To ensure similar source locations and deconvolution stability, we select EGFs based on waveform similarity (Abercrombie, 2015). The CC values between candidate EGFs and the target event are calculated within the frequency band of 0.5–4.0 Hz using a *P*-wave window length of 1 s before to 4 s after the *P* pick and an *S*-wave window length of 1 s before to 6 s after the *S* pick. Each EGF must have a CC value >0.4 for both *P*- and *S*-wave segments across at least six stations. Ultimately, we obtain a total of 11 EGFs with magnitudes between M_L 2.0 and 2.5.

In the spectral ratio analysis, we adopt an approach similar to that of Zhou *et al.* (2022). The source spectra are calculated using *S* waves with the multitaper algorithm (Prieto, 2022) for each event–station pair. The *S* wave is windowed from 0.5 s before to 5.5 s after the phase arrival, and a 0.1-Hz high-pass filter is applied. To enhance the stability, we use several strategies, including linear interpolation in the logarithmic frequency space with a spacing of 0.025; a multisliding window strategy (Imanishi and Ellsworth, 2006; Uchida *et al.*, 2007; Yoon *et al.*, 2019) that obtains logarithmic averaged results with offsets

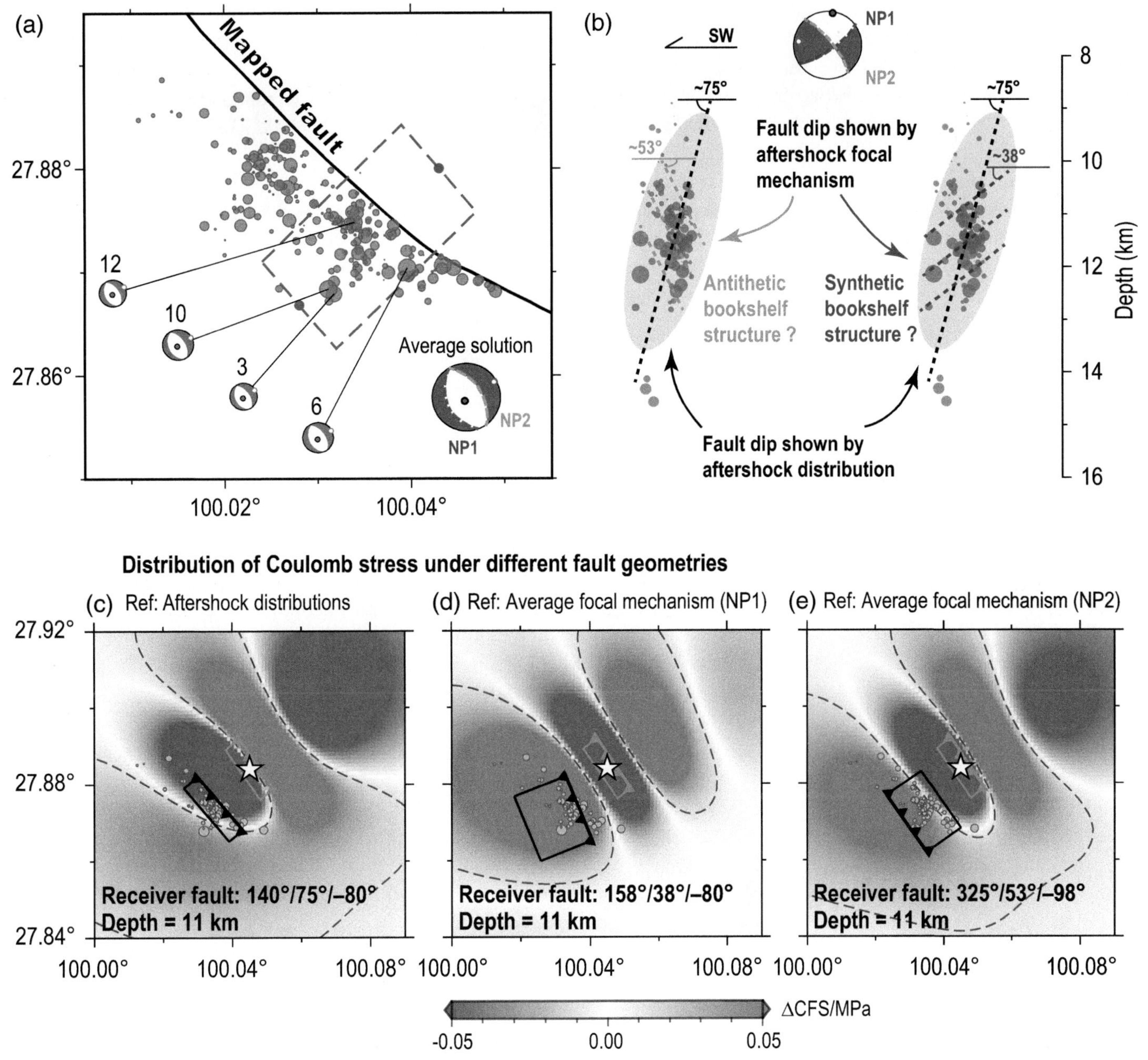

Figure 8. Possible bookshelf structure of the mapped fault and the validation from Coulomb failure stress change (ΔCFS). (a) Map view of seismicity distribution. The seismic events associated with the mapped fault are plotted as blue circles. The dashed gray line indicates the projection range in panel (b), and the gray circles mark the start and end points of the profile. The mapped fault and four aftershock focal mechanisms correspond to those shown in Figure 7a. The gray focal sphere represents the average focal mechanism solution from the four aftershocks (NP: nodal plane). (b) The potential bookshelf structures. The dashed black, red, and orange lines represent the three different dip angles derived from the seismicity distribution and two candidate nodal planes from average focal mechanism. (c–e) Static ΔCFS distributions generated by the M_w 4.8 mainshock on different receiver faults. The green and black rectangles indicate the surface projections of the source and receiver faults, respectively. The receiver fault and depth are shown in the lower left corner of each panel. Seismicity within a ± 0.5 km depth range is plotted. ΔCFS triggering contours are indicated by dashed red lines (0.01 MPa). The color version of this figure is available only in the electronic edition.

of 0, 1, and 2 s to the initial *S* window; and stacking spectra of different EGFs that exhibited similar shapes and amplitudes (Ross and Ben-Zion, 2016). Finally, the spectra obtained from different EGFs at each station demonstrate high consistency (Fig. S8). The final spectral ratio is obtained by dividing the target spectrum with the stacked EGF spectrum.

Rupture directivity and source parameters. We compare the spectral ratios in the along-fault and fault-normal directions (Fig. 9a–d) and find that stations along the mapped fault exhibit a more pronounced high-frequency component (>1 Hz), both when using only aftershock 2 (with a similar focal mechanism to subevent_1, shown in Fig. 6) as the EGF and when using all stacked EGFs, which confirms that the rupture occurred along this fault. Stations located on the northwest and southeast sides (i.e., facing or opposite to the rupture direction) show no significant differences (Fig. 9f). However, we cannot conclusively determine whether the mainshock exhibited bidirectional rupture because waveforms near the epicenter (L102, L103, and S10) are clipped (Fig. S9). Because of the lack of additional stations within 100 km along strike in both directions, we are unable to verify the northwest rupture directivity suggested by the MPS results.

Furthermore, we estimate the source parameters with stations in fault-normal directions (northeast and southwest) to minimize the impact of rupture directivity (Fig. 9e). These fault-normal spectral ratios are first stacked with all EGFs and then fitted to the ω^2-source model (Boatwright, 1980), which assumes a circular rupture and accounts for dynamic rupture effects:

$$\frac{u_{\mathrm{TE}}(f)}{u_{\mathrm{EGF}}(f)} = \frac{M_{0\mathrm{TE}}}{M_{0\mathrm{EGF}}}\sqrt{\frac{1+\left(\frac{f}{f_{c\mathrm{EGF}}}\right)^4}{1+\left(\frac{f}{f_{c\mathrm{TE}}}\right)^4}}, \quad (1)$$

in which TE represents the target event, u is the spectrum, M_0 is the seismic moment, and f_c is the corner frequency. We determine the moment ratio $M_{0\mathrm{TE}}/M_{0\mathrm{EGF}}$ and two corner frequencies $f_{c\mathrm{TE}}$ and $f_{c\mathrm{EGF}}$ by performing a grid search that minimizes the summed difference between predicted and observed spectral ratios between 0.6 and 3.5 Hz. The optimal fit is obtained with the corner frequency of the target event is $f_c = 0.72$ Hz.

We estimate the source radius based on a circular fault model (Madariaga, 1976), with a constant rupture velocity of $0.9V_S$:

$$r = \frac{0.21V_S}{f_{c\mathrm{TE}}}, \quad (2)$$

in which V_S is the local S-wave velocity, set at 3.4 km/s as detailed in Table S1. This results in a rupture radius of ~1 km and a rupture area of ~3.13 km^2, which is consistent with the early aftershock distribution along the hidden branch fault (Fig. 7a).

The average slip on the circular fault is given by

$$D = \frac{M_0}{\mu\pi r^2}, \quad (3)$$

in which μ is the shear modulus, set to 32 GPa, and $M_0 = 10^{(1.5\times M_\mathrm{L}+10.7)}$, with M_L 5.0 representing the local magnitude of the mainshock (Table S3). These parameters give a coseismic slip of 38 cm. The static stress drop is estimated based on the circular fault model (Eshelby, 1957):

$$\Delta\sigma = \frac{7}{16}\frac{M_0}{r^3}, \quad (4)$$

and a stress drop of 16.75 MPa is obtained with the previously determined rupture radius, which is a common value for continental earthquakes (Allmann and Shearer, 2009; Kato, 2009) and is consistent with previous studies on surrounding regions (Zhao *et al.*, 2011; Yang *et al.*, 2024).

Temporal complexity analysis. Previous studies have shown that when moderate-size earthquakes exhibit temporal complexity in their source processes, their source spectra tend to deviate from a simple ω^2-source model (Pennington *et al.*, 2023; Yoshida and Kanamori, 2023). However, the source spectra we obtained for the Zhongdian mainshock are well fit by the ω^2-source model (Fig. 9e), suggesting no observable temporal complexity. This finding is consistent with the MPS inversion, which shows that the two subevents initiated near simultaneously (Table S2). In addition, we did not observe multiple subevents in the displacement waveforms (Fig. S10), further supporting the absence of significant temporal complexity (Yoshida, 2024). Based on these observations, we conclude that the source complexity of the Zhongdian earthquake is primarily spatial rather than temporal. This behavior is probably caused by an overall critical stress state before the mainshock (Zoback and Townend, 2001), which was subsequently triggered by dynamic stress perturbation of the first subevent.

In summary, the source spectra analysis effectively constrains the source parameters of the M_w 4.8 Zhongdian earthquake, but it does not reveal the spatial complex source process, that is, the two near-simultaneous subevents identified by the MPS inversion. This highlights the limitations of source spectra analysis in capturing complex source processes, especially when the temporal resolution is insufficient.

Multiscale stress states and faulting styles

We analyze the focal mechanisms and stress states across different spatial scales to investigate whether the rupture manner of the Zhongdian earthquake requires a heterogeneous stress field or/and faulting styles and whether this heterogeneity exists. Specifically, our analysis covers (1) the large DQ-ZD region (~150 × 150 km); (2) the source regions of two significant earthquake sequences: the Deqin (DQ) source region (~30 × 30 km), which experienced the 2013 M_w 5.0 and 5.6 doublet occurring along the major fault (DZDF, Chang, 2015), and the Zhongdian (ZD) source region (~5 × 5 km) discussed in this study; and (3) the smaller regions associated

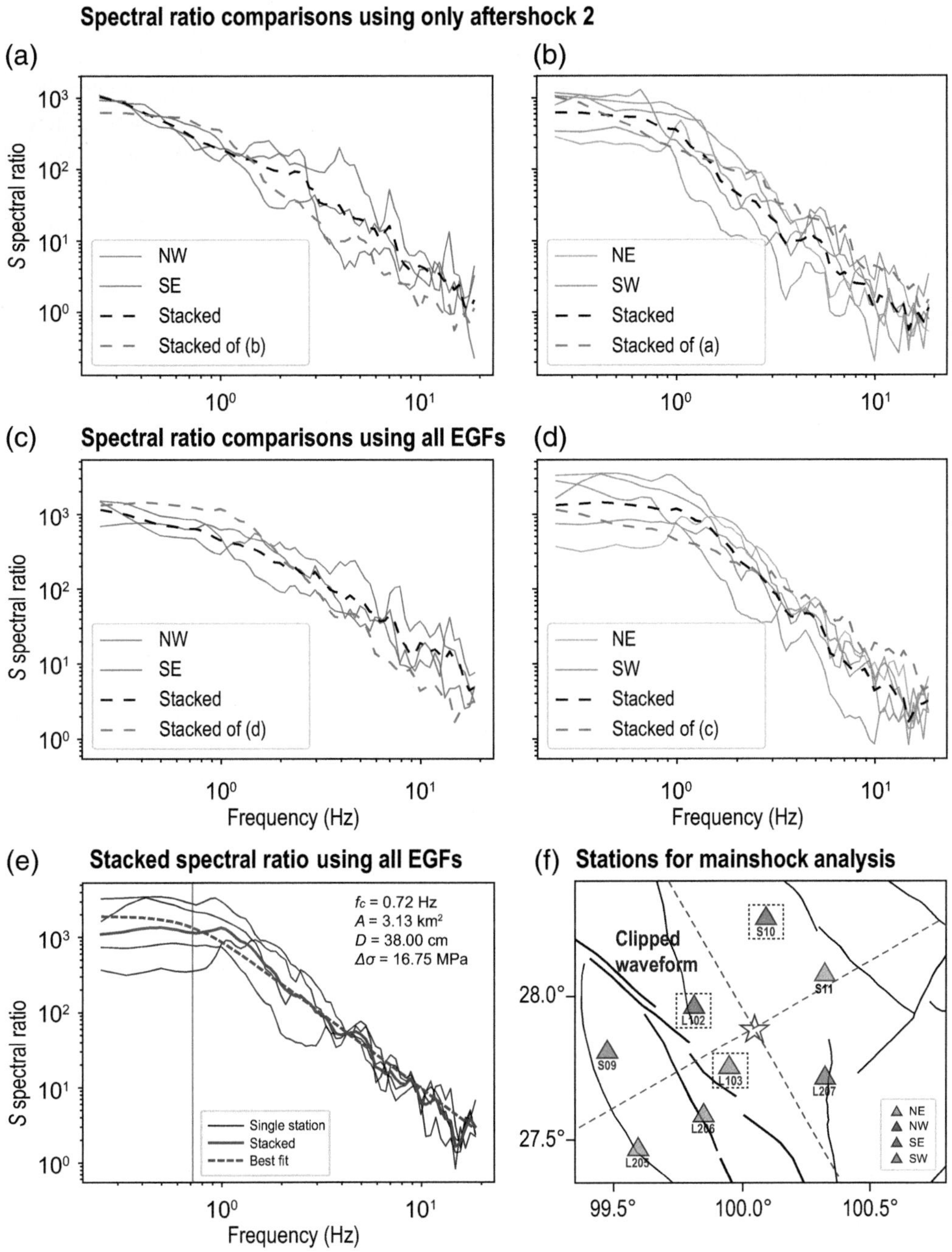

Figure 9. Spectral ratio analysis of the Zhongdian mainshock. (a,b) Spectral ratio comparisons using only aftershock 2 (M_L 2.3 shown in Fig. 6). Two sets of spectral ratio comparisons are made along the fault-parallel and fault-normal directions, respectively. The dashed lines represent the stacked spectral ratios. Note that three stations with clipped waveforms are included, as indicated in panel (f). (c,d) Spectral ratio comparisons using all empirical Green's functions (EGFs), as shown in panels (a,b). (e) The stacked and fitted spectral ratio. The black lines represent individual station spectral ratios, the red-solid line shows the stacked spectral ratio, and the dashed red line represents the best fit of the Boatwright model. The vertical gray line marks the estimated corner frequency. (f) Station distribution. Seismic stations are marked by triangles, with three clipped waveform stations outlined by dashed boxes. The directions are indicated with different colors. Surface fault traces are shown as in Figure 1a. Fault-parallel and fault-normal trends are indicated by dashed red lines. The white star indicates the epicenter. The color version of this figure is available only in the electronic edition.

with the two subevents resolved by MPS analysis within the ZD source region (~2 km spacing).

Local-to-regional stress field. To invert for the regional stress field, we compile one of the most comprehensive focal mechanism datasets for the large DQ-ZD region, including seven FM solutions from 1933 to 1976, 56 CMT solutions from 1976 to 2023 (Tables S5 and S6), and the 44 solutions of the Zhongdian sequence obtained in this study (Tables S2 and S3). A more detailed description of this focal mechanism dataset is provided in Text S1. To reduce potential bias caused by clustered events with similar focal mechanisms, we exclude aftershocks from the analysis of the large DQ-ZD region, retaining only the mainshock of each seismic sequence (i.e., the M_w 5.0 and 5.6 in DQ, and the M_w 4.8 event in ZD; Fig. 10a). According to the classification method of Frohlich (1992), the focal mechanisms in the large DQ-ZD region are predominantly normal and oblique-slip types (36.4%; Fig. 10b), whereas the source regions of DQ and ZD exhibit a high proportion of normal-faulting events (~80%; Fig. 10b). This diversity of focal mechanisms across different scales reflects the spatial variations of stress fields.

In the next step, we use an iterative-joint-inversion method (Vavryčuk, 2014) to resolve the stress fields, including the three principal stress axes (σ_1, σ_2, and σ_3) and the stress ratio R value (defined as $\frac{\sigma_1-\sigma_2}{\sigma_1-\sigma_3}$). This method assumes that earthquakes are shear failures along pre-existing fault nodal planes and uses focal mechanisms to estimate the stress tensor. Unlike traditional stress inversion techniques, this approach incorporates fault instability constraints to identify the correct fault nodal plane, iteratively refines the stress tensor estimation, and accounts for uncertainties in the focal mechanisms, thereby enhancing the robustness and reliability of the stress tensor estimation. In the inversion process, we use three groups of datasets across different scales, each containing >30 focal mechanisms to ensure the reliability of results (Fig. 10b). To optimize the initial estimate of the stress tensor, we generate 10 initial realizations, followed by 20 iterations in each inversion to progressively refine the stress tensor estimate. To assess the uncertainty of the input data, we generate 200 random noise realizations, assuming an average deviation of 10° in the input data. The uncertainties in the principal stress directions and R value estimates are estimated by 95% confidence intervals. Notably, numerical experiments show that the stress directions and R values under high R value stress states, such as the cases in this study, can be accurately reconstructed without relying on the correct identification of the fault nodal plane (Li *et al.*, 2024).

The results show that the large DQ-ZD region exhibits a normal-faulting regime, with the maximum-compressive principal stress (σ_1) being slightly inclined from vertical (~72° plunge). The R value is estimated to be 0.87 (Fig. 10c), suggesting a near-uniaxial extension with $\sigma_2 \approx \sigma_3$. This observation is consistent with previous studies in the DQ-ZD region (Fig. S11, Wang *et al.*, 2019; Su *et al.*, 2024), although the R value and the direction of σ_2 and σ_3 axes differ slightly. This deviation may result from the fact that Wang *et al.* (2019) and Su *et al.* (2024) missed some focal mechanism solutions in certain time periods and magnitude ranges and that they did not exclude the aftershocks of the 2013 DQ sequence. The regional stress field of the DQ-ZD region represents the typical scenario of the western boundary of the Chuandian block, which contrasts with the prominent strike-slip regime along the eastern boundary (Xu *et al.*, 2003; Wan *et al.*, 2021). This extensional stress regime may be linked to the presence of a weak lower crust caused by partial melting or mantle upwelling (Su *et al.*, 2024).

Despite differences in faulting types, the stress fields in the source regions of DQ and ZD are similar to those in the large DQ-ZD region, although the DQ source region shows a more vertical σ_1 and an R value of ~0.8 (Fig. 10c), which is controlled by the local extensional stepover zones (Chang, 2015). Thus, our analysis in this section shows no significant stress heterogeneity down to a ~5 km scale, with the stress fields in the source regions aligning with those of the large DQ-ZD region. In other words, it also indicates that the rupture of Zhongdian mainshock requires no significantly different stress fields in the source region.

Faulting heterogeneity within ZD source region. To investigate whether the faulting style within the ZD source region shows heterogeneity, we divide the region into two smaller parts (<2 km scale; Fig. 10d) that are associated with the two subevents obtained by MPS inversion. Because of the limited number of aftershock fault mechanisms available for the hidden fault, we only calculate the summed potency tensor for these two small regions along the mapped fault (segments 1 and 2; Fig. 10d). Specifically, we examine two types of normalized summed potency tensors $\hat{P}_{ij}^{\mathrm{TOT}}$ and $\hat{P}_{ij}^{\mathrm{SM}}$, which reflect the overall geometric and strain properties of clustered earthquakes (Bailey *et al.*, 2009):

$$\hat{P}_{ij}^{\mathrm{TOT}} = \sum_{k=1}^{N} P_{ij}^{(k)} \Big/ \left\| \sum_{k=1}^{N} P_{ij}^{(k)} \right\|, \tag{5}$$

$$\hat{P}_{ij}^{\mathrm{SM}} = \sum_{k=1}^{N} \hat{P}_{ij}^{(k)} \Big/ \left\| \sum_{k=1}^{N} \hat{P}_{ij}^{(k)} \right\|, \tag{6}$$

in which $\|\cdot\|$ denotes the Euclidean norms. The seismic potency tensor P_{ij} is defined as $P_{ij} = P_0 \hat{P}_{ij}/\sqrt{2}$, in which $\hat{P}_{ij}$ is the source mechanism tensor derived from the faulting directions (strike, dip, and rake; Bailey *et al.*, 2009), and P_0 is the scalar potency calculated using the empirical scaling relation $\log_{10} P_0 = 0.0612 M_{\mathrm{L}}^2 + 0.988 M_{\mathrm{L}} - 4.87$ (Ben-Zion and Zhu, 2002). The CLVD component can be quantified using the intermediate eigenvalues λ_2 of either $\hat{P}_{ij}^{\mathrm{TOT}}$ or $\hat{P}_{ij}^{\mathrm{SM}}$ (Bailey *et al.*, 2009), expressed as

$$r_{\mathrm{CLVD}} = \frac{\sqrt{6}}{2} \lambda_2. \tag{7}$$

The value of r_{CLVD} ranges from −0.5 to 0.5, with the negative and positive values corresponding to mixed normal and reverse faulting within the dominant strike-slip faulting, respectively. The magnitude of r_{CLVD} provides a measure of the geometrical heterogeneity within fault systems in the study area.

Results show that both segments exhibit an overall normal-faulting style, whereas the tensional axes exhibit a trend difference of ~25° (Fig. 10d). The r_{CLVD} values for segments 1 and 2 are determined as positive and negative, respectively, whether the potency of each event is scaled by the magnitude or not (Fig. 10d). Notably, the r_{CLVD} values of segment 2 using $\hat{P}_{ij}^{\mathrm{TOT}}$ reaches −0.293, indicating a high-faulting heterogeneity that is caused by structural complexity and mixed deformation styles. In contrast, the CLVD component of segment 1 is significantly lower, suggesting consistent faulting styles. These observations align with our previous interpretations on fault geometry using the seismicity distribution (see the Interpretation of fault structure section). It is still an open question as to whether the observed faulting heterogeneity suggests different stress states between the two fault segments, but even smaller-scale stress heterogeneity potentially exists, as suggested by the observation by Shearer *et al.* (2024) that a pair of

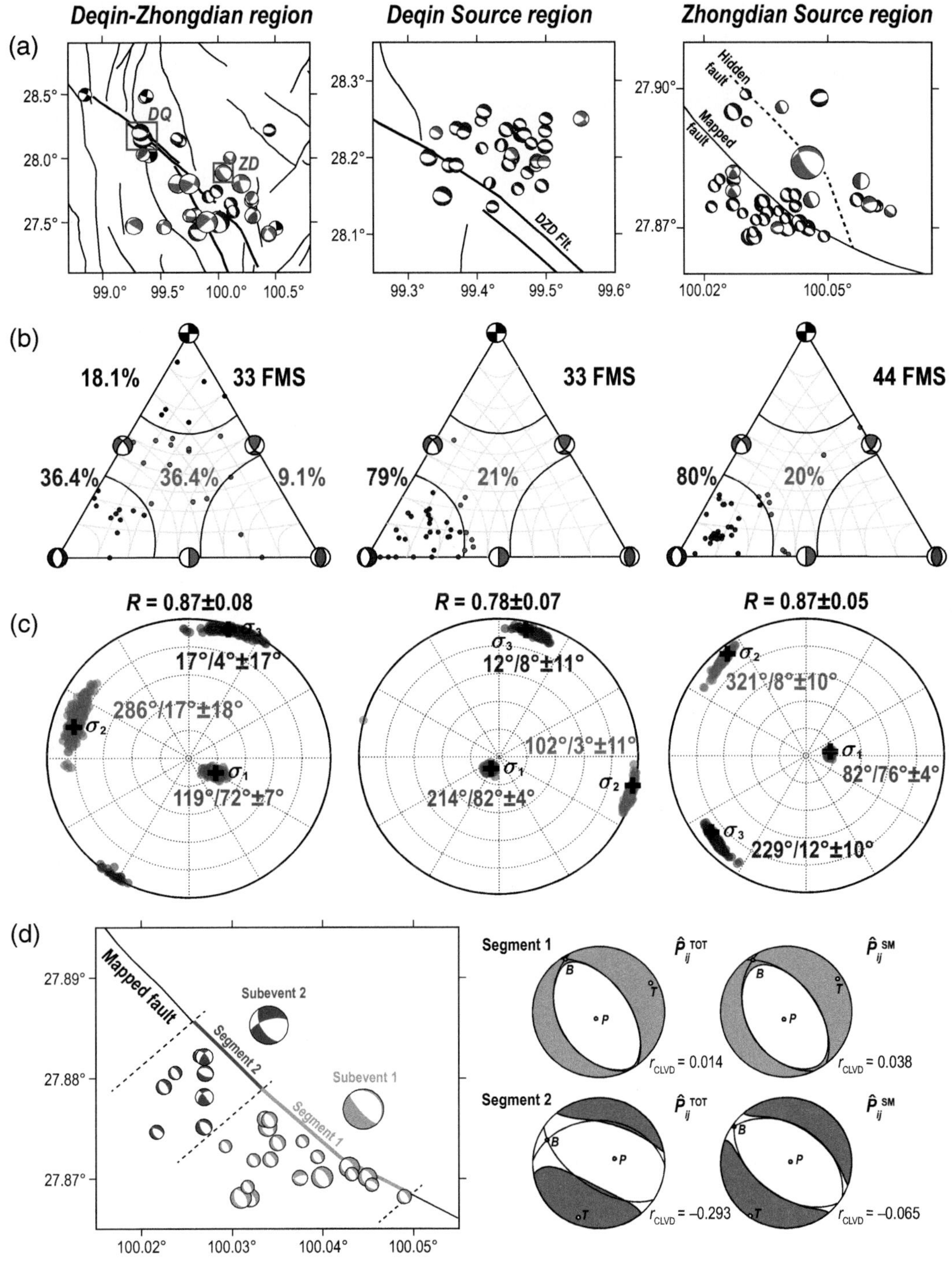

Figure 10. Focal mechanisms and tectonic stress fields at different scales. (a) Spatial distribution of focal mechanisms in regions of different scales. From left to right: Deqin-Zhongdian region, Deqin source region, and Zhongdian source region. The size of the focal spheres scale with magnitude, being twice as large in the Zhongdian source region. Surface fault traces are the same as in Figures 1a and 7a, with major faults highlighted in bold. (b) Classification of focal mechanisms. The order of the subgraphs is the same as in panel (a). Different focal mechanism types are marked in different colors: normal (blue), thrust (red), strike slip (black), and oblique slip (green). The total number of focal mechanisms for each region and the proportion of each type are also shown. (c) Tectonic stress fields. The order of the subgraphs matches panel (a). The three principal stress axes are distinguished by different colors, with azimuth, plunge angles, and uncertainties indicated. The R values and their uncertainties are provided above each result. (d) Normalized summed potency tensor for different segments in Zhongdian source region. The two segments and their corresponding results are marked in orange and purple, respectively. $\hat{P}_{ij}^{\mathrm{TOT}}$ and $\hat{P}_{ij}^{\mathrm{SM}}$ represent the results with and without consideration of the source scale. r_{CLVD} quantifies the degree of fault heterogeneity. The color version of this figure is available only in the electronic edition.

aftershocks from the 2019 Ridgecrest sequence occurring only ~115 m apart exhibited nearly opposite focal mechanisms.

In summary, our analysis in this section demonstrates that the two subevents of the Zhongdian mainshock are associated with two distinct faulting styles: the highly consistent one for which the rupture initiated and a more diverse one that allows for strike-slip faulting like the second subevent. This faulting heterogeneity is more than structural complexity but also includes strain or deformation heterogeneity.

Conclusions

In this study, we investigated the source complexity of the 2024 M_w 4.8 Zhongdian earthquake. The rupture initiated with a pure normal faulting and transitioned into left-lateral strike-slip motion toward the northwest, as revealed by MPS inversion, FM polarities, and CMT analysis. The two subevents occurred near simultaneously, with no discernible temporal separation, as supported by spectral ratio analysis and displacement waveforms.

A multiscale stress field comparison indicates no significant differences in principal stress orientations between the Zhongdian source region and the broader western Chuandian block, suggesting that the observed rupture complexity is driven by localized rather than regional stress variations. The high-resolution aftershock catalog and spatially variable focal mechanisms reveal geometrical complexities in the fault system. In addition, the summed potency tensors of the two subevent regions exhibit contrasting nodal plane orientations and CLVD ratios, indicating heterogeneous faulting styles. These observations suggest that the spatially variable slip behavior during the Zhongdian earthquake was enabled by a combination of complex fault geometry and heterogeneous strain or deformation patterns within the source region.

Data and Resources

The seismic waveforms used in this study can be obtained by contacting the International Earthquake Science Data Center available at http://www.esdc.ac.cn (last accessed December 2024; doi: 10.11998/IESDC). The HypoInverse and HypoDD programs used for earthquake location can be accessed at https://www.usgs.gov/software/hypoinverse-earthquake-location and https://www.ldeo.columbia.edu/~felixw/hypoDD.html, respectively (both last accessed December 2024). The Phase picking, Association, Location, and Matched-filter (PALM) workflow used in this study is available at https://github.com/YijianZhou/PALM (last accessed April 2025). The module used for source spectra analysis can be found at https://github.com/YijianZhou/Manual-Analysis-Helper (last accessed December 2024). The hashpy2 code used for focal mechanism calculation is available at https://github.com/wasjabloch/hashpy2 (last accessed December 2024). The cut-and-paste (CAP) program can be found at https://www.eas.slu.edu/People/LZhu/home.html (last accessed December 2024). The STRESSINVERSE program for stress field inversion is available at https://www.ig.cas.cz/en/stress-inverse (last accessed December 2024). The Coulomb 3.3 program for Coulomb failure stress change (ΔCFS) calculation is available at https://temblor.net/coulomb (last accessed December 2024). The seismic catalog of the Zhongdian sequence constructed in this study is available at https://github.com/YijianZhou/Seismic-Catalog (last accessed April 2025). The Global Centroid Moment Tensor (Global CMT) webpage is available at https://www.globalcmt.org. IEF, CEA website can be accessed at https://www.ief.ac.cn/1068/info/2020/21375.html (last accessed November 2025). The supplemental material for this article includes additional tests on focal mechanism inversion, aftershock location, Coulomb stress calculation, and spectral ratio analysis.

Declaration of Competing Interests

The authors acknowledge that there are no conflicts of interest recorded.

Acknowledgments

The authors thank the *Seismological Research Letters* (*SRL*) editor, the Eastern Section editor, and two anonymous reviewers for their constructive comments on this work. The authors thank the International Earthquake Science Data Center of the Institute of Geophysics, China Earthquake Administration for providing seismic waveforms; Peizhen Su for providing his focal mechanism dataset (Su *et al.*, 2024); and Zhenyue Li and Zhenjiang Liu for their discussions on focal mechanisms, stress field inversion, and Coulomb failure stress change calculation. The maps in this study are primarily generated using the Generic Mapping Tools software package (Wessel *et al.*, 2019). This work is supported by the National Natural Science Foundation of China (Grant Numbers 42374079 and 42074053) and the Basic Research Fund of the Institute of Geophysics, CEA (Grant Numbers DQJB19B30 and JY2024Z01).

References

Abercrombie, R. E. (2015). Investigating uncertainties in empirical Green's function analysis of earthquake source parameters, *J. Geophys. Res.* **120,** no. 6, 4263–4277, doi: 10.1002/2015JB011984.

Allmann, B. P., and P. M. Shearer (2009). Global variations of stress drop for moderate to large earthquakes, *J. Geophys. Res.* **114,** no. B1, doi: 10.1029/2008JB005821.

Bailey, I. W., T. W. Becker, and Y. Ben-Zion (2009). Patterns of co-seismic strain computed from southern California focal mechanisms, *Geophys. J. Int.* **177,** no. 3, 1015–1036, doi: 10.1111/j.1365-246X.2009.04090.x.

Båth, M. (1965). Lateral inhomogeneities of the upper mantle, *Tectonophysics* **2,** no. 6, 483–514, doi: 10.1016/0040-1951(65)90003-X.

Ben-Zion, Y., and L. Zhu (2002). Potency-magnitude scaling relations for southern California earthquakes with $1.0<M_L<7.0$, *Geophys. J. Int.* **148,** no. 3, F1–F5, doi: 10.1046/j.1365-246X.2002.01637.x.

Bloch, W., B. Schurr, J. Kummerow, P. Salazar, and S. A. Shapiro (2018). From slab coupling to slab pull: Stress segmentation in the subducting Nazca plate, *Geophys. Res. Lett.* **45,** no. 11, 5407–5416, doi: 10.1029/2018GL078793.

Boatwright, J. (1980). A spectral theory for circular seismic sources; simple estimates of source dimension, dynamic stress drop, and radiated seismic energy, *Bull. Seismol. Soc. Am.* **70,** no. 1, 1–27.

Calais, E., and S. Stein (2009). Time-variable deformation in the New Madrid seismic zone, *Science* **323,** no. 5920, 1442–1442, doi: 10.1126/science.1168122.

Calais, E., T. Camelbeeck, S. Stein, M. Liu, and T. J. Craig (2016). A new paradigm for large earthquakes in stable continental plate interiors, *Geophys. Res. Lett.* **43,** no. 20, 10,621–10,637, doi: 10.1002/2016GL070815.

Chang, Y., X. Li, Q. Zhou, X. Bai, H. Ran, and W. Luo (2023). The holocene activity evidence of paleo-earthquakes in the northwestern segment of the Deqin-Zhongdian fault, *J. Seismol. Res.* **46,** no. 2, 261–270, doi: 10.20015/j.cnki.ISSN1000-0666.2023.0023 (in Chinese).

Chang, Z. (2015). Seismotectonic background of the 2013 Benzilan M5.9 earthquake, Yunnan province, *Seismol. Geol.* **37,** no. 1, 192–207 (in Chinese).

Chang, Z., Y. Zhang, J. Li, and Y. Zang (2014). The geological and geomorphic characteristic of late quaternary activity of the Degin-Zhongdian-Daju fault, *J. Seismol. Res.* **37,** no. 1, 46–52 (in Chinese).

Chapman, M. C. (2013). On the rupture process of the 23 August 2011 Virginia Earthquake, *Bull. Seismol. Soc. Am.* **103,** no. 2A, 613–628, doi: 10.1785/0120120229.

Chen, X., and P. M. Shearer (2013). California foreshock sequences suggest aseismic triggering process, *Geophys. Res. Lett.* **40,** no. 11, 2602–2607, doi: 10.1002/grl.50444.

De Novellis, V., V. Convertito, S. Valkaniotis, F. Casu, R. Lanari, M. F. Monterroso Tobar, and N. A. Pino (2020). Coincident locations of rupture nucleation during the 2019 Le Teil earthquake, France and maximum stress change from local cement quarrying, *Commun. Earth Environ.* **1,** no. 1, 1–10, doi: 10.1038/s43247-020-00021-6.

Ding, H., Y. Zhou, Z. Ge, T. Taymaz, A. Ghosh, H. Xu, T. S. Irmak, and X. Song (2023). High-resolution seismicity imaging and early aftershock migration of the 2023 Kahramanmaraş (SE Türkiye) MW7.9 & 7.8 earthquake doublet, *Earthq. Sci.* **36,** no. 6, 417–432.

Douilly, R., D. D. Oglesby, M. L. Cooke, and J. L. Hatch (2020). Dynamic models of earthquake rupture along branch faults of the eastern San Gorgonio Pass region in California using complex fault structure, *Geosphere* **16,** no. 2, 474–489, doi: 10.1130/GES02192.1.

Earthquake Monitoring and Forecasting Department, China Earthquake Administration (2023). A compilation of earthquakes with M≥5.0 (Jan.1,1900-Dec.31, 2022), available at https://data.earthquake.cn (last accessed October 2025).

Eshelby, J. D. (1957). The determination of the elastic field of an ellipsoidal inclusion, and related problems, *Proc. Math. Phys. Sci.* **241,** no. 1226, 376–396, doi: 10.1098/rspa.1957.0133.

Frohlich, C. (1992). Triangle diagrams: Ternary graphs to display similarity and diversity of earthquake focal mechanisms, *Phys. Earth Planet. In.* **75,** no. 1, 193–198, doi: 10.1016/0031-9201(92)90130-N.

Guo, X., C. Jiang, L. Han, H. Yin, and Z. Zhao (2022). Focal mechanism data set in Chinese mainland and its adjacent area (2009-2021), doi: 10.12080/nedc.11.ds.2022.0004.

Han, S., W.-Y. Kim, H. Lim, Y. O. Son, M.-S. Seo, J. Y. Park, and Y. Kim (2024). Resolving multi-stage rupture process of the 2021 Mw 4.9 Offshore Jeju Island earthquake from relative source time functions, *Geophys. Res. Lett.* **51,** no. 3, e2023GL106059, doi: 10.1029/2023GL106059.

Hardebeck, J. L., and P. M. Shearer (2002). A new method for determining first-motion focal mechanisms, *Bull. Seismol. Soc. Am.* **92,** no. 6, 2264–2276, doi: 10.1785/0120010200.

Hardebeck, J. L., and P. M. Shearer (2003). Using S/P Amplitude ratios to constrain the focal mechanisms of small earthquakes, *Bull. Seismol. Soc. Am.* **93,** no. 6, 2434–2444, doi: 10.1785/0120020236.

Hardebeck, J. L., and P. M. Shearer (2008). HASH: A FORTRAN program for computing earthquake first-motion focal mechanisms, available at https://www.usgs.gov/node/279393 (last accessed November 2025).

Herrera, C., J. F. Cassidy, S. E. Dosso, J. Dettmer, W. Bloch, C. Sippl, and P. Salazar (2021). The crustal stress field inferred from focal mechanisms in northern Chile, *Geophys. Res. Lett.* **48,** no. 8, e2021GL092889, doi: 10.1029/2021GL092889.

Hu, Y., Z. Li, R. Liu, and Z. Wang (2023). Focal mechanism of Luding M 6.8 earthquake, September 2022 and analysis of the loading role of the tectonic stress on the seismogenic fault, *Earthq. Res. Adv.* **3,** no. 3, 100216, doi: 10.1016/j.eqrea.2023.100216.

Huang, R., L. Zhu, Y. Xu, C. Tang, and H. Wen (2022). The 2014 Zigui earthquake sequence near the Three Gorges Dam in China, *Seismol. Res. Lett.* **93,** no. 4, 2038–2047, doi: 10.1785/0220210356.

Imanishi, K., and W. L. Ellsworth (2006). Source scaling relationships of microearthquakes at Parkfield, CA, determined using the SAFOD pilot hole seismic array, in *Earthquakes: Radiated Energy and the Physics of Faulting*, Abercrombie, R., A. McGarr, H. Kanamori, and G. Di Toro (Editors), American Geophysical Union (AGU), Washington, D.C., 81–90, doi: 10.1029/170GM10.

Jiang, H. (2025). Extended Båth's Law for earthquake sequences with M_S≥5.0 in Chinese Mainland and discussion on primary influencing factors, *Chin. J. Geophys.* **68,** no. 5, 1826–1841, doi: 10.6038/cjg2023R0672 (in Chinese).

Kagan, Y. Y. (1991). 3-D rotation of double-couple earthquake sources, *Geophys. J. Int.* **106,** no. 3, 709–716, doi: 10.1111/j.1365-246X.1991.tb06343.x.

Kato, N. (2009). A possible explanation for difference in stress drop between intraplate and interplate earthquakes, *Geophys. Res. Lett.* **36,** no. 23, doi: 10.1029/2009GL040985.

Klein, F. W. (2014). User's guide to HYPOINVERSE-2000, a Fortran program to solve for earthquake locations and magnitudes, *U.S. Geol. Surv. Open-File Rept. 02-171.*

Li, Z., Y. Wan, X. Guo, and R. Liu (2024). Significance of accurate selection of the seismogenic faults from the earthquake focal mechanisms for stress field reconstruction, *Chin. J. Geophys.* **67,** no. 7, 2612–2624, doi: 10.6038/cjg2023R0193 (in Chinese).

Lin, J., and R. S. Stein (2004). Stress triggering in thrust and subduction earthquakes and stress interaction between the southern San Andreas and nearby thrust and strike-slip faults, *J. Geophys. Res.* **109,** no. B2, 2003JB002607, doi: 10.1029/2003JB002607.

Lo, Y.-C., H. Yue, J. Sun, L. Zhao, and M. Li (2019). The 2018 Mw 6.4 Hualien earthquake: Dynamic slip partitioning reveals the spatial transition from mountain building to subduction, *Earth Planet. Sci. Lett.* **524,** 115729, doi: 10.1016/j.epsl.2019.115729.

Ma, S., Z. Yao, and C. Ji (1998). Preliminary estimation of the double rupture of the February 3, 1996, Lijiang earthquake in Yunnan and related issues, *Acta Seismol. Sin.* no. 1, 19–29 (in Chinese).

Madariaga, R. (1976). Dynamics of an expanding circular fault, *Bull. Seismol. Soc. Am.* **66,** no. 3, 639–666, doi: 10.1785/BSSA0660030639.

Manighetti, I., M. Campillo, S. Bouley, and F. Cotton (2007). Earthquake scaling, fault segmentation, and structural maturity, *Earth Planet. Sci. Lett.* **253,** nos. 3/4, 429–438, doi: 10.1016/j.epsl.2006.11.004.

Manighetti, I., A. Mercier, and L. De Barros (2021). Fault trace corrugation and segmentation as a measure of fault structural maturity, *Geophys. Res. Lett.* **48,** no. 20, e2021GL095372, doi: 10.1029/2021GL095372.

Neves, M., L. Y. Chuang, W. Li, Z. Peng, P. M. Figueiredo, and S. Ni (2024). Complex rupture dynamics of the extremely shallow August 2020 M5.1 Sparta, North Carolina earthquake, *Commun. Earth Environ.* **5,** no. 1, 1–11, doi: 10.1038/s43247-024-01316-8.

Newman, A., S. Stein, J. Weber, J. Engeln, A. Mao, and T. Dixon (1999). Slow deformation and lower seismic hazard at the New Madrid seismic zone, *Science* **284,** no. 5414, 619–621, doi: 10.1126/science.284.5414.619.

Pennington, C. N., T. Uchide, and X. Chen (2022). Slip characteristics of induced earthquakes: Insights from the 2015 M_w 4.0 Guthrie, Oklahoma Earthquake, *J. Geophys. Res.* **127,** no. 5, e2021JB023564, doi: 10.1029/2021JB023564.

Pennington, C. N., Q. Wu, X. Chen, and R. E. Abercrombie (2023). Quantifying rupture characteristics of microearthquakes in the Parkfield Area using a high-resolution borehole network, *Geophys. J. Int.* **233,** no. 3, 1772–1785, doi: 10.1093/gji/ggad023.

Perrin, C., I. Manighetti, J.-P. Ampuero, F. Cappa, and Y. Gaudemer (2016). Location of largest earthquake slip and fast rupture controlled by along-strike change in fault structural maturity due to fault growth, *J. Geophys. Res.* **121,** no. 5, 3666–3685, doi: 10.1002/2015JB012671.

Prieto, G. A. (2022). The *Multitaper* spectrum analysis package in Python, *Seismol. Res. Lett.* **93,** no. 3, 1922–1929, doi: 10.1785/0220210332.

Ren, C., Z. Wang, T. Taymaz, N. Hu, H. Luo, Z. Zhao, H. Yue, X. Song, Z. Shen, H. Xu, *et al.* (2024). Supershear triggering and cascading fault ruptures of the 2023 Kahramanmaraş, Türkiye, earthquake doublet, *Science* **383,** no. 6680, 305–311, doi: 10.1126/science.adi1519.

Ross, Z. E., and Y. Ben-Zion (2016). Toward reliable automated estimates of earthquake source properties from body wave spectra, *J. Geophys. Res.* **121,** no. 6, 4390–4407, doi: 10.1002/2016JB013003.

Schulte, S. M., and W. D. Mooney (2005). An updated global earthquake catalogue for stable continental regions: Reassessing the correlation with ancient rifts, *Geophys. J. Int.* **161,** no. 3, 707–721, doi: 10.1111/j.1365-246X.2005.02554.x.

Sethanant, I., E. Nissen, E. Bergman, S. J. Oliva, L. Pousse-Beltran, E. Karasözen, and P. Pananont (2025). Recent earthquakes on unmapped faults highlight hidden seismic hazards within the Golden Triangle region of Laos, Thailand and Myanmar, *Geophys. J. Int.* **241,** no. 1, 606–627, doi: 10.1093/gji/ggaf061.

Shearer, P. M., N. Shabikay Senobari, and Y. Fialko (2024). Implications of a reverse polarity earthquake pair on fault friction and stress heterogeneity near Ridgecrest, California, *J. Geophys. Res.* **129,** no. 11, e2024JB029562, doi: 10.1029/2024JB029562.

Stein, R. S., G. C. P. King, and J. Lin (1992). Change in failure stress on the southern San Andreas fault system caused by the 1992 magnitude = 7.4 Landers earthquake, *Science* **258,** no. 5086, 1328–1332, doi: 10.1126/science.258.5086.1328.

Stein, S., and M. Wysession (2003). *An Introduction to Seismology, Earthquakes and Earth Structure*, Blackwell Science, Oxford.

Su, P., Y. Luo, and L. Zhao (2024). Regional stress field in the SE margin of the Tibetan Plateau revealed by the focal mechanisms of small and moderate earthquakes, *Tectonophysics* **885,** 230420, doi: 10.1016/j.tecto.2024.230420.

Sun, J., H. Yue, Z. Shen, L. Fang, Y. Zhan, and X. Sun (2018). The 2017 Jiuzhaigou earthquake: A complicated event occurred in a young fault system, *Geophys. Res. Lett.* **45,** no. 5, 2230–2240, doi: 10.1002/2017GL076421.

Talwani, P. (2017). On the nature of intraplate earthquakes, *J. Seismol.* **21,** no. 1, 47–68, doi: 10.1007/s10950-016-9582-8.

Tian, Y., and X. Chen (2005). A rapid and accurate two-point ray tracing method in horizontally layered velocity model, *Acta Seismol. Sin.* **18,** no. 2, 147–154 (in Chinese).

Toda, S., R. S. Stein, K. Richards-Dinger, and S. B. Bozkurt (2005). Forecasting the evolution of seismicity in southern California: Animations built on earthquake stress transfer, *J. Geophys. Res.* **110,** no. B5, 2004JB003415, doi: 10.1029/2004JB003415.

Uchida, N., T. Matsuzawa, W. L. Ellsworth, K. Imanishi, T. Okada, and A. Hasegawa (2007). Source parameters of a M4.8 and its accompanying repeating earthquakes off Kamaishi, NE Japan: Implications for the hierarchical structure of asperities and earthquake cycle, *Geophys. Res. Lett.* **34,** no. 20, doi: 10.1029/2007GL031263.

Vavryčuk, V. (2014). Iterative joint inversion for stress and fault orientations from focal mechanisms, *Geophys. J. Int.* **199,** no. 1, 69–77, doi: 10.1093/gji/ggu224.

Vavryčuk, V. (2015). Moment tensor decompositions revisited, *J. Seismol.* **19,** no. 1, 231–252, doi: 10.1007/s10950-014-9463-y.

Waldhauser, F. (2001). hypoDD–A program to compute double-difference hypocenter locations, *U.S. Geol. Surv. Open-File Rept. 01-113.*

Waldhauser, F., M. Michele, L. Chiaraluce, R. Di Stefano, and D. P. Schaff (2021). Fault planes, fault zone structure and detachment fragmentation resolved with high-precision aftershock locations of the 2016–2017 central Italy sequence, *Geophys. Res. Lett.* **48,** no. 16, e2021GL092918, doi: 10.1029/2021GL092918.

Wan, Y. (2016). *Introduction to Seismology*, Science Press, Beijing, China (in Chinese).

Wan, Y., and Z.-K. Shen (2010). Static Coulomb stress changes on faults caused by the 2008 Mw 7.9 Wenchuan, China earthquake, *Tectonophysics* **491,** nos. 1/4, 105–118, doi: 10.1016/j.tecto.2010.03.017.

Wan, Y., X. Shen, R. Liu, X. Liu, Z. Zheng, Y. Li, Y. Zhang, and L. Wang (2021). Present slip and stress distribution of block boundary faults in the Sichuan-Yunnan region, *Seismol. Geol.* **43,** no. 6, 1614–1637

Wang, H., J. Cao, and H. Xu (2019). Preliminary application of focal mechanism solutions of small and medium-size earthquakes to fault stability analysis in the southeastern Tibetan plateau, *Seismol. Geol.* **41,** no. 3, 633–648 (in Chinese).

Wessel, P., J. F. Luis, L. Uieda, R. Scharroo, F. Wobbe, W. H. F. Smith, and D. Tian (2019). The Generic Mapping Tools Version 6, *Geochem. Geophys. Geosys.* **20,** no. 11, 5556–5564, doi: 10.1029/2019GC008515.

Woo, J.-U., J. Rhie, S. Kim, T.-S. Kang, K.-H. Kim, and Y. Kim (2019). The 2016 Gyeongju earthquake sequence revisited: Aftershock interactions within a complex fault system, *Geophys. J. Int.* **217,** no. 1, 58–74, doi: 10.1093/gji/ggz009.

Xu, D., W. Gong, Z. Zhang, J. Xu, H. Yu, and X. Chen (2023). The 2016 Menyuan earthquake: The largest self-arrested crustal earthquake ever observed, *Geophys. Res. Lett.* **50,** no. 11, e2023GL103556, doi: 10.1029/2023GL103556.

Xu, X., Z. Han, X. Yang, S. Zhang, G. Yu, B. Zhou, F. Li, B. Ma, G. Chen, and Y. Ran (2016). *Seismotectonic Map in China and its Adjacent Regions*, Seismological Press, Beijing, China (in Chinese).

Xu, X., X. Wen, R. Zheng, W. Ma, F. Song, and G. Yu (2003). Pattern of latest tectonic motion and its dynamics for active blocks in Sichuan-Yunnan region, *Sci. China Earth Sci.* no. S1, 151–162.

Xu, X., P. Zhang, X. Wen, Z. Qing, G. Chen, and A. Zhu (2005). Features of active tectonics and recurrence behaviors of strong earthquakes in the western Sichuan province and its adjacent regions, *Seismol. Geol.* no. 3, 446–461 (in Chinese).

Yang, Z., J. Yang, H. Zhang, M. Qin, and Y. Xu (2024). Study on media attenuation, site response and source parameters in Yunnan area, *Acta Sci. Nat. Univ. Pekin.* **60,** no. 4, 615, doi: 10.13209/j.0479-8023.2024.055 (in Chinese).

Yoon, C. E., N. Yoshimitsu, W. L. Ellsworth, and G. C. Beroza (2019). Foreshocks and mainshock nucleation of the 1999 M 7.1 Hector Mine, California, earthquake, *J. Geophys. Res.* **124,** no. 2, 1569–1582, doi: 10.1029/2018JB016383.

Yoshida, K. (2024). Direct evidence for diverse source complexity in small earthquakes (Mw 3.3–5.0) obtained from near-source borehole seismic data, *Seismol. Res. Lett.* **95,** no. 4, 2409–2421, doi: 10.1785/0220230431.

Yoshida, K., and H. Kanamori (2023). Time-domain source parameter estimation of Mw 3–7 earthquakes in Japan from a large database of moment-rate functions, *Geophys. J. Int.* **234,** no. 1, 243–262, doi: 10.1093/gji/ggad068.

Yue, H., and T. Lay (2020). Resolving complicated faulting process using multi-point-source representation: Iterative inversion algorithm improvement and application to recent complex earthquakes, *J. Geophys. Res.* **125,** no. 2, e2019JB018601, doi: 10.1029/2019JB018601.

Zahradník, J., E. M. Aissaoui, P. Bernard, P. Briole, S. Bufféral, L. De Barros, A. Deschamps, P. Elias, C. P. Evangelidis, I. Fountoulakis, *et al.* (2022). An atypical shallow Mw 5.3, 2021 earthquake in the western Corinth Rift (Greece), *J. Geophys. Res.* **127,** no. 9, e2022JB024221, doi: 10.1029/2022JB024221.

Zhang, P., Q. Deng, G. Zhang, J. Ma, W. Gan, W. Min, F. Mao, and Q. Wang (2003). Active tectonic blocks and strong earthquakes in the continent of China, *Sci. China Earth Sci.* **46,** no. 2, 13–24, doi: 10.1360/03dz0002.

Zhang, X., and Y. Wang (2009). Crustal and upper mantle velocity structure in Yunnan, Southwest China, *Tectonophysics* **471,** no. 3, 171–185, doi: 10.1016/j.tecto.2009.02.009.

Zhang, Z., D. Zheng, and J. Xu (1999). *Earthquake Cases in China (1986–1989)*, Seismological Press, Beijing, China (in Chinese with English Abstract and Captions).

Zhao, C., Z. Chen, W. Hua, Q. Wang, Z. Li, and S. Zheng (2011). Study on source parameters of small to moderate earthquakes in the main seismic active regions, China mainland, *Chin. J. Geophys.* **54,** no. 6, 1478–1489 (in Chinese).

Zhao, L.-S., and D. V. Helmberger (1994). Source estimation from broadband regional seismograms, *Bull. Seismol. Soc. Am.* **84,** no. 1, 91–104.

Zhou, Y., A. Ghosh, L. Fang, H. Yue, S. Zhou, and Y. Su (2021). A high-resolution seismic catalog for the 2021 M_S6.4/M_W6.1 Yangbi earthquake sequence, Yunnan, China: Application of AI picker and matched filter, *Earthq. Sci.* **34,** no. 5, 390–398, doi: 10.29382/eqs-2021-0031.

Zhou, Y., C. Ren, A. Ghosh, H. Meng, L. Fang, H. Yue, S. Zhou, and Y. Su (2022). Seismological characterization of the 2021 Yangbi foreshock-mainshock sequence, Yunnan, China: More than a triggered cascade, *J. Geophys. Res.* **127,** no. 8, e2022JB024534, doi: 10.1029/2022JB024534.

Zhou, Y., H. Yue, L. Fang, S. Zhou, L. Zhao, and A. Ghosh (2021). An earthquake detection and location architecture for continuous seismograms: Phase Picking, Association, Location, and Matched filter (PALM), *Seismol. Res. Lett.* **93,** no. 1, 413–425, doi: 10.1785/0220210111.

Zhu, L., and D. V. Helmberger (1996). Advancement in source estimation techniques using broadband regional seismograms, *Bull. Seismol. Soc. Am.* **86,** no. 5, 1634–1641, doi: 10.1785/BSSA0860051634.

Zhu, L., and L. A. Rivera (2002). A note on the dynamic and static displacements from a point source in multilayered media: A note on the dynamic and static displacements from a point source, *Geophys. J. Int.* **148,** no. 3, 619–627, doi: 10.1046/j.1365-246X.2002.01610.x.

Zhu, S. (2023). Present-day crustal deformation based on GPS measurements in southeastern Tibetan Plateau: Implications for geodynamics and earthquake hazard, *Geomat. Nat. Hazards Risk* **14,** no. 1, 2286902, doi: 10.1080/19475705.2023.2286902.

Zoback, M. D., and J. Townend (2001). Implications of hydrostatic pore pressures and high crustal strength for the deformation of intraplate lithosphere, *Tectonophysics* **336,** nos. 1/4, 19–30, doi: 10.1016/S0040-1951(01)00091-9.

Manuscript received 5 August 2025
Published online 2 December 2025

AGMD: A Ground-Motion Database for the Australian Continental Crust

Hadi Ghasemi*[1], Trevor Allen[1], Abhi Sunketa[1], Callum Mckenna[1], and Deepika Mani[1]

Abstract

A ground-motion database is developed for earthquakes occurring in the Australian continental crust. Despite the rich volume of recordings produced by national and regional seismic networks, Australia currently lacks a comprehensive, consistently processed, and openly accessible ground-motion database. Existing datasets are often research-specific, vary in processing standards, and are not broadly reusable. The Australian ground-motion database (AGMD) addresses this gap by collecting and processing earthquake recordings using consistent, repeatable methods and by bringing together detailed information about the earthquakes, recording stations, and waveforms. The AGMD currently includes over 5000 ground-motion records from 270 earthquakes that occurred between 1990 and 2025, recorded by over 1000 stations across 36 different permanent and temporary networks. Each recording is processed using the U.S. Geological Survey "gmprocess" software and saved in structured Hierarchical Data Format workspace files. Ground-motion metrics include peak ground motions for both horizontal and vertical components and pseudo-spectral acceleration, PSA (*T*), for the same components, computed for 21 oscillator periods ranging from 0.01 to 10 s. A cloud-based web portal gives open access to the data, allowing users to search, view, and download both waveforms and calculated ground-motion parameters. The system uses Amazon Web Services to manage large-scale data uploads and a PostgreSQL database for fast and reliable data access. These data will have utility for improving seismic hazard assessments in Australia and analog tectonic regions and will provide engineering practitioners with access to a repository of earthquake time histories that can be used to support engineering design.

Cite this article as Ghasemi, H., T. Allen, A. Sunketa, C. Mckenna, and D. Mani (2026). AGMD: A Ground-Motion Database for the Australian Continental Crust, *Seismol. Res. Lett.* **97**, 698–714, doi: 10.1785/0220250316.

Introduction

The Australian continent is considered to be a stable continental region (SCR), where tectonic activity and seismic hazard are relatively low compared with plate-boundary environments (Johnston, 1994; Leonard, 2008). Nevertheless, the continent has experienced several significant earthquakes capable of causing damage, such as the 2010 M_L 5.0 Kalgoorlie–Boulder, Western Australia, earthquake (Edwards *et al.*, 2010), the 2012 M_w 5.3 Pukatja, South Australia, earthquake (Clark *et al.*, 2014), the 2016 M_w 6.1 Petermann Ranges, Northern Territory, earthquake (King *et al.*, 2021), and the 2021 M_w 5.9 Woods Point, Victoria, earthquake (Mousavi *et al.*, 2023). These events, together with geological evidence for large prehistorical earthquakes (Crone *et al.*, 1997; Clark *et al.*, 2012), underscore the fact that, even in tectonically stable regions, significant earthquakes can and do occur.

One of the largest challenges facing seismic hazard modelers in SCRs is the uncertainty in characterizing earthquake ground motions. This is because large earthquakes that are of significance to hazard are rare, and when they do occur, they are often poorly recorded by sparse monitoring networks. The relative paucity in strong ground motions recorded from Australian earthquakes presents challenges for the characterization of earthquake ground motions and the selection of appropriate ground-motion models (GMMs) for seismic hazard analysis (e.g., Ghasemi and Allen, 2018). These models are commonly adopted from analog tectonic regions. However, there are some unique characteristics for Australian earthquakes and recorded ground motions that make these decisions challenging in the absence of reliable locally developed models and datasets (e.g., Allen, 2020). Globally, there have been recent efforts to compile high-quality earthquake ground-motion datasets for SCRs (e.g., Goulet *et al.*, 2021; Buscetti *et al.*, 2024). However, these datasets are still lacking in data for critical distance and magnitudes of importance to seismic hazard. This highlights the importance of high-quality ground-motion recordings for improving seismic

1. Geoscience Australia, Canberra, Australian Capital Territory, Australia, https://orcid.org/0000-0003-3420-547X (TA)

*Corresponding author: Hadi.Ghasemi@ga.gov.au

hazard assessments and informing risk mitigation strategies in Australia and elsewhere.

Since the 1950s and 1960s, numerous state-, commonwealth-, and university-funded seismic networks have operated within Australia (Leonard, 2008). However, the most significant advances in monitoring occurred following the deadly 1989 Newcastle earthquake (McCue *et al.*, 1990), when seismic networks began transitioning from analog to digital recording. Presently, two primary national-scale networks operate within Australia. These include the Australian National Seismograph Network (ANSN), managed by Geoscience Australia (Geoscience Australia, 2021), and the Australian Seismometers in Schools (AuSIS) network (Balfour *et al.*, 2014; Salmon *et al.*, 2022), part of the global Seismographs in Schools initiative supported by the Seismological Facility for the Advancement of Geoscience (SAGE), operated by the U.S. National Science Foundation.

Formerly established in 1994, the ANSN now consists of over 100 independent seismic stations spanning mainland Australia, offshore territories, and the Australian Antarctic Territory, with a few additional stations located in Papua New Guinea and Niue Island. The network provides essential data for earthquake detection, location, and magnitude estimation (Geoscience Australia, 2021). Most stations are now equipped with both broadband velocity seismometers and strong-motion accelerometers, enabling the capture of a wide dynamic range and vibratory frequency of ground motions.

The AuSIS network, launched in 2011, comprises 50 broadband stations deployed nationwide. Beyond contributing to earthquake monitoring and seismic research, the AuSIS network plays a key role in Earth-science education and public outreach, helping to build awareness and engagement with geophysical sciences (Balfour *et al.*, 2014; Salmon *et al.*, 2022).

In addition to these, two smaller-scale permanent networks, the University of Melbourne Seismic Network (University of Melbourne *et al.*, 2012) and the Australian Support Network (Pickle *et al.*, 2024), are also operating primarily for research purposes. Established in 2012 and 2024, respectively, they currently operate almost 20 broadband stations each. In the private sector, the Seismology Research Centre currently operates a network of approximately 40 stations, which are primarily equipped with short-period sensors and are focused on infrastructure monitoring and commercial applications (e.g., Peck, 2016).

In addition to permanent seismic networks, numerous temporary deployments have been established across Australia to support specific scientific and monitoring objectives. These include baseline seismicity assessments for regions of planned hydrocarbon extraction, such as the seismic monitoring network in the Beetaloo sub-basin (Glanville, 2019); aftershock and earthquake swarm monitoring, including the 2001–2002 Burakin sequence in Western Australia (Allen *et al.*, 2006) and the 2021 Woods Point earthquake aftershock monitoring in Victoria (Velasquez *et al.*, 2024); and investigations into crustal and lithospheric structure. Notable examples of the latter include the Southwest Australia Seismic Network (Miller *et al.*, 2023) and the ongoing Western Australia Array (Murdie *et al.*, 2024). In addition, the Australian Passive Seismic Array (Gorbatov *et al.*, 2020) is a national initiative involving the rolling deployment of broadband arrays across the continent. These networks aim to collect data to support the development of an evolving 3D seismic velocity model of the crust and upper mantle. These models enhance our understanding of Earth's structure and are useful for natural hazard assessment and resource exploration (Gorbatov *et al.*, 2018; Kennett *et al.*, 2023).

Despite the rich volume of recordings produced by these networks, Australia currently lacks a comprehensive, consistently processed, and openly accessible national ground-motion database. Existing datasets are often research-specific, vary in processing standards, and are not broadly reusable. For instance, several regional studies have compiled bespoke ground-motion datasets to examine source and attenuation characteristics, such as Allen *et al.* (2006) in southwestern Australia, Allen *et al.* (2007) in southeastern Australia, Allen (2021) for earthquakes in the Banda Sea affecting the Australian continent, and more recently (Allen, 2025), which provides a continent-wide analysis of ground-motion attenuation and earthquake source parameters. Although valuable, these datasets remain fragmented and are not integrated into a national framework.

To address this gap, Geoscience Australia has developed the Australian ground-motion database (AGMD). This effort involves the systematic and uniform processing of all available ground-motion recordings from significant and well-recorded Australian earthquakes using modern, reproducible workflows (e.g., Thompson *et al.*, 2024). The database includes detailed metadata for recording stations and computes a standardized set of engineering parameters. A companion web portal has also been developed, offering searchable, open access to the data for both seismological and engineering applications (see Data and Resources).

In this article, we present the framework used to compile and process seismic event data, along with an overview of the features and functionality of the associated web portal. The following sections describe the data sources, processing methodologies, and portal design. We conclude with a summary of the resource's significance and potential applications in seismic hazard analysis and research, both for Australia and SCRs globally.

Data Compilation

For this study, we compiled a dataset of close to 8000 ground-motion records from 278 earthquakes that occurred between 1989 and 2025 within the stable continental crust of Australia. These records were collected from 1107 seismic stations operated by 36 permanent and temporary seismic networks across

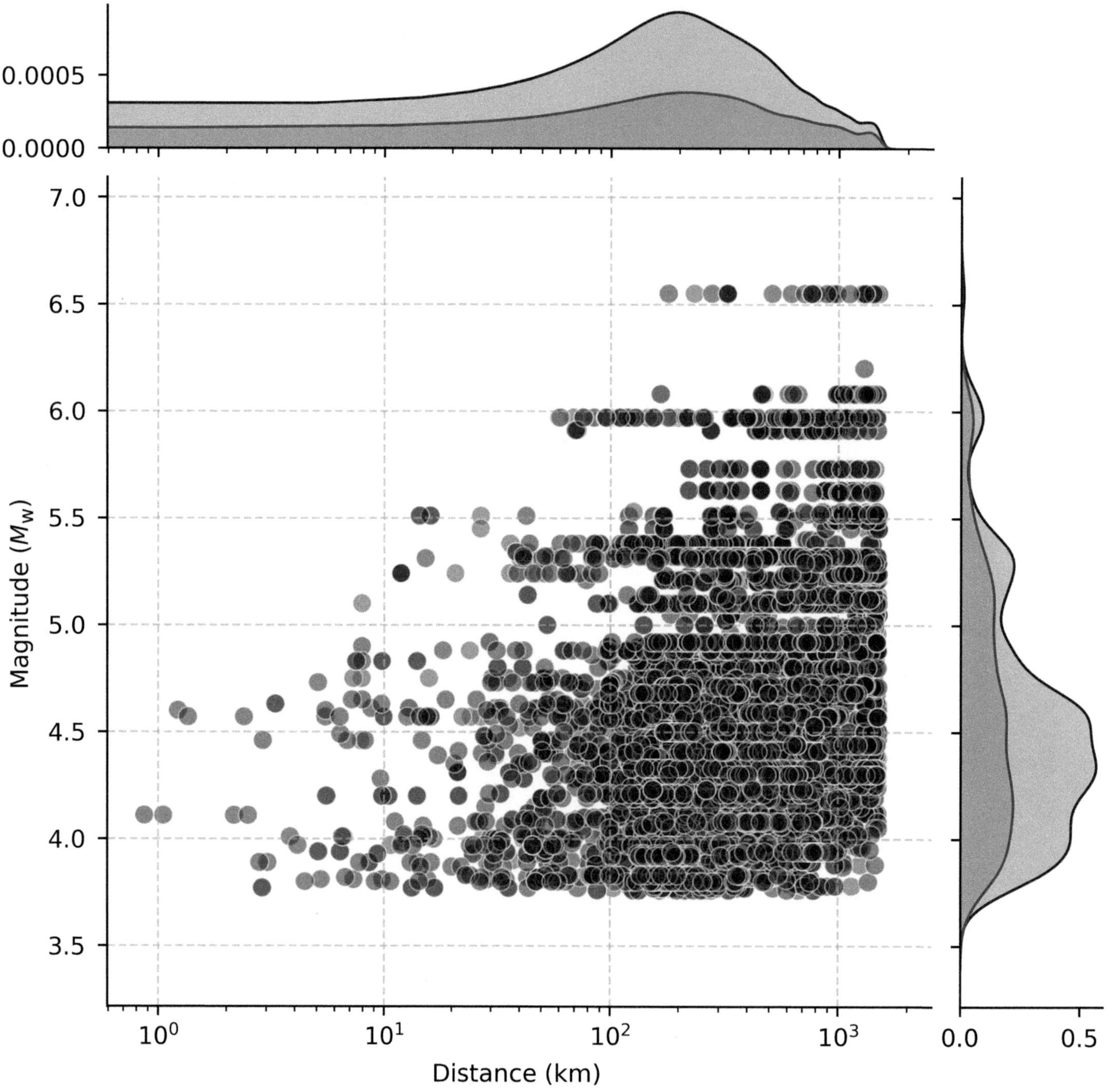

Figure 1. Magnitude–distance distribution of collected earthquake recordings. Recordings that passed quality control checks are shown as blue circles; those that did not are shown as red circles (see the Data Processing section). Marginal kernel density estimate (KDE) plots display the distribution of recordings with respect to magnitude (right panel) and distance (top panel). The color version of this figure is available only in the electronic edition.

the country. Approximately 20% of the dataset consists of co-located and/or duplicate recordings. Co-located recordings refer to instances where multiple instrument types at the same station captured the same seismic event. Duplicate recordings occur when the same instrument records the event at different sampling rates, resulting in multiple versions of the same data.

Figure 1 shows the magnitude–distance distribution of the dataset used in this study. The marginal plots display kernel density estimate curves for each parameter, providing a visual summary of the distribution of earthquake recordings by magnitude and distance. The dataset includes only recordings from earthquakes with moment magnitudes (M_w) ≥ 3.75 and hypocentral distances less than 1500 km. The magnitudes used in this study are derived from the methods developed by Allen (2025).

Using a fixed distance threshold of 1500 km may seem conservative and less ideal, especially for ground-motion

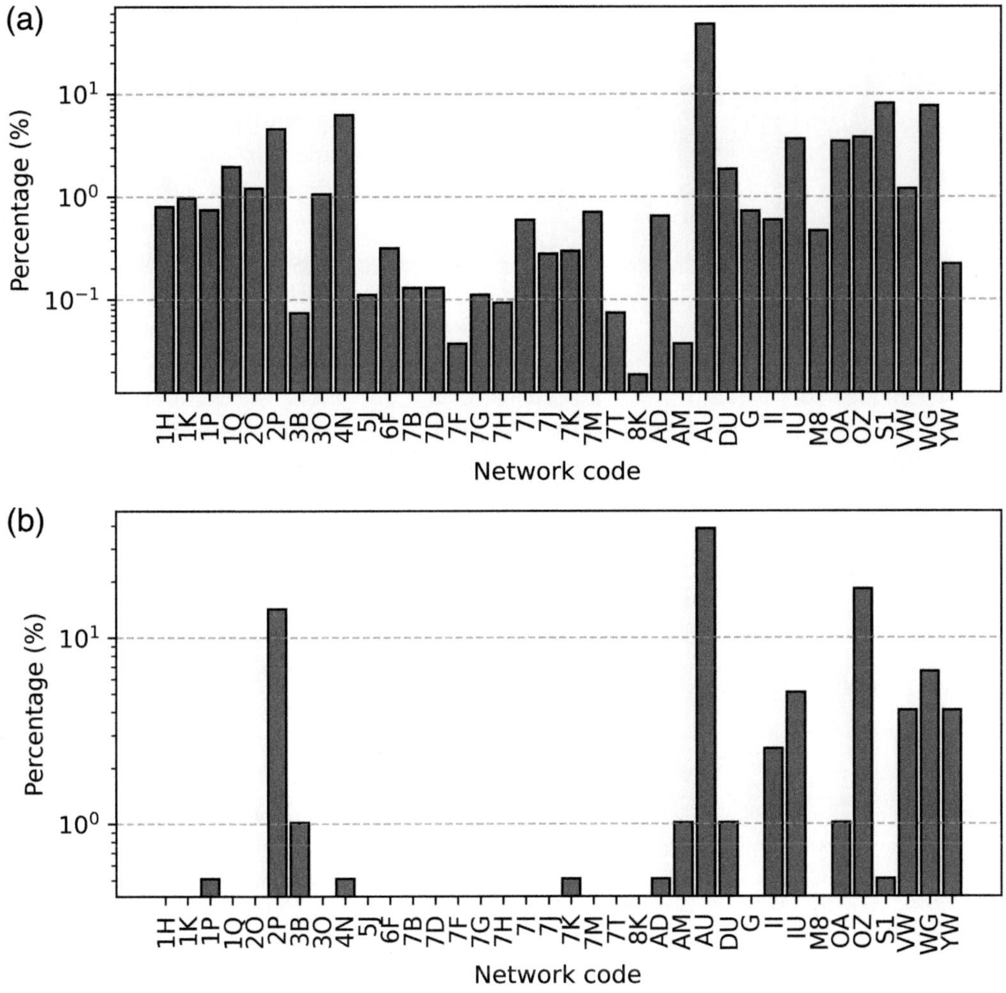

Figure 2. Overview of the compiled earthquake ground-motion database. (a) Contribution of various permanent and temporary seismic networks to the overall dataset (5388 records in total). (b) Network-specific contributions to near-field recordings (epicentral distance < 50 km; 197 records in total). International Federation of Digital Seismograph Networks (FDSN) codes are defined in Data and Resources.

modeling, in which magnitude-dependent distance truncation is often preferred to reduce biases from distant stations with low signal-to-noise ratios (SNRs) (Fukushima and Tanaka, 1990; Zhao *et al.*, 2016). However, this choice was made to maximize the inclusion of high-quality data. Furthermore, the consideration of far-field ground motions is becoming more commonplace in seismic hazard assessment for critical facilities and infrastructure assets, with major ground-motion modeling initiatives requiring the characterization of ground motion up to 1500 km distance or more (Kishida *et al.*, 2017; Goulet *et al.*, 2021).

The chosen magnitude threshold of M_w 3.75 represents a practical compromise: earthquakes above this magnitude are more likely to be of engineering significance in the Australian context (Daniell and Love, 2010; Nievas *et al.*, 2020), whereas smaller events, while valuable for seismological research (e.g., Pilia *et al.*, 2013), are generally less relevant for engineering applications (Kramer, 1996). This threshold also reflects the practical considerations of maintaining the database in Geoscience Australia over time.

Time-Series Data

The ground-motion dataset used in this study is based on the recent compilation by Allen (2025) for continental Australia, which builds on earlier datasets for noncratonic (Ghasemi and Allen, 2023b) and cratonic regions (Ghasemi and Allen, 2021). Waveform data were sourced from continuous recordings by the ANSN, as well as from a range of temporary networks and aftershock deployments (e.g., Leonard, 2002; Gorbatov *et al.*, 2018; Murdie *et al.*, 2022). Additional records were obtained from the Australian Passive Seismic Server (AusPass) and SAGE. Data from the ANSN are typically streamed to the SAGE server at sample rates ranging from 20 to 40 Hz. However, following significant earthquakes, high-sample-rate data (up to 200 Hz) are retrieved by Geoscience Australia on a semiautomated basis. In our dataset, we used these higher-sample-rate recordings from ANSN stations wherever they were available to enhance data quality and usable frequency range.

These publicly available data were further complemented by recordings from private networks (e.g., Peck, 2016), state government agencies (e.g., Love, 2006; Murdie *et al.*, 2024), and university-operated installations (e.g., Saygin and Lumley, 2018; Attanayake *et al.*, 2023). Figure 2a presents a bar chart showing the contribution of various permanent and temporary seismic networks to the overall dataset, whereas Figure 2b illustrates each network's contribution to near-field recordings (recordings with epicentral distances less than 50 km). Although the ANSN (represented by the network code AU) provides the largest single record contribution to the total number of recordings (47%), the remaining 53% comes from a wide range of other networks. Notably, Figure 2b highlights the significant role of temporary and permanent networks other than ANSN in capturing near-field data, demonstrating their importance in addressing, to

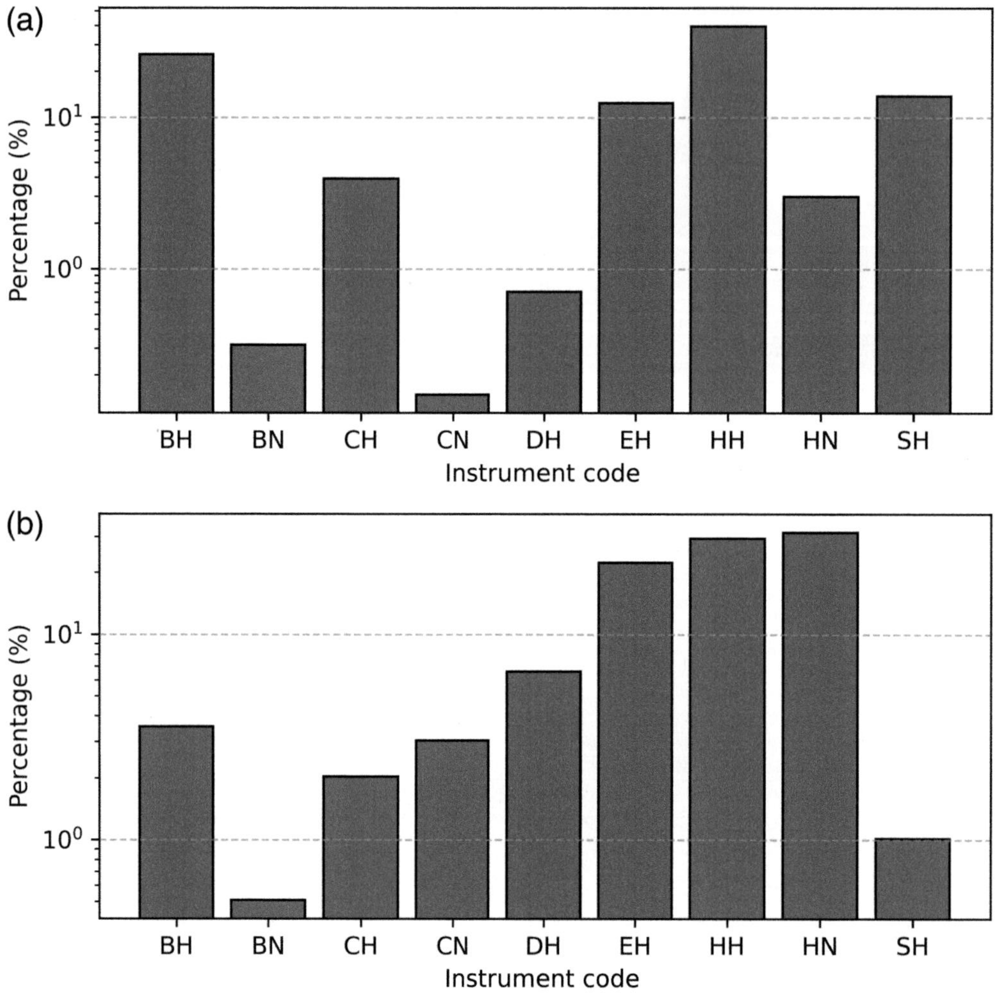

Figure 3. Overview of the compiled earthquake ground-motion database (5388 records in total). (a) Distribution of records by sensor type for the entire dataset. (b) Distribution of records by sensor type for near-field recordings (epicentral distance < 50 km; 197 records in total).

some extent, the sparse coverage of permanent seismic stations across Australia's vast landmass.

In this study, all waveform data were retrieved in, or converted to, raw miniSEED format (Ahern *et al.*, 2009), recorded in units of counts. A series of quality control checks was conducted to ensure that the channel codes in the miniSEED file headers conformed to SEED naming conventions as described in Ringler and Evans (2015), based on the sampling rate and instrument type. When discrepancies were identified, the channel codes were corrected accordingly. For records with missing network codes in the miniSEED file headers, the appropriate codes were added based on the corresponding station metadata as described in the next section. Ground-motion records containing disjointed segments that could not be reliably merged into continuous time series were excluded from the dataset.

Instrument Metadata

The compiled dataset includes records from stations equipped with various types of seismic sensors, namely short-period, broadband, and accelerometer instruments. Figure 3a,b shows the distribution of records by sensor type for the entire dataset and for near-field recordings, respectively. Following the SEED naming convention (Ringler and Evans, 2015), instrument codes "BH," "HH," and "CH" indicate broadband sensors with differing sampling rates, "BN," "HN," and "CN" refer to accelerometers, and the remaining codes correspond to short-period sensors. Although broadband instruments dominate the overall dataset, the contribution of accelerometers is notably higher in the near-field subset.

Although broadband sensors offer high sensitivity and are well suited for detecting weak ground motions from small to moderate earthquakes at mid- to far-field distances, they are less ideal for near-source recordings. Accelerometers, on the well-suited hand, are specifically designed to capture strong ground motions without clipping, typically up to $\pm 2g$ or higher. In contrast, broadband and short-period sensors generally have lower dynamic ranges (often ± 0.1–$0.5g$), making them more susceptible to saturation during intense shaking near the fault (Clinton and Heaton, 2002). This sensor-specific limitation is especially relevant when evaluating the quality of near-field data in the compiled dataset.

Access to station metadata, particularly sensor and digitizer types and configuration parameters, is essential for properly interpreting ground-motion recordings (Scherbaum, 1996). The two main public repositories for such metadata in Australia are the SAGE and AusPass data centers, which collectively cover most of the seismic networks included in this study. However, these repositories are not comprehensive for some legacy networks and may contain inaccuracies. They do not include data from certain private networks or legacy networks managed by state governments. Moreover, the quality of metadata varies both across networks and over time within each network. Older deployments often suffer from incomplete or poorly documented metadata, whereas newer installations tend to be more consistently characterized.

To address these limitations, Allen (2025) compiled an updated list of recording stations across Australia, including sensor and digitizer types and key configuration parameters such as sensitivities and gain factors. This compilation also includes networks not listed in either SAGE or AusPass and incorporates corrections for known metadata discrepancies, particularly for ANSN instruments, in which the SAGE metadata often misrepresent actual configurations.

We converted the revised list by Allen (2025) into a StationXML format (International Federation of Digital Seismograph Networks, 2022) inventory and merged it with metadata from public data centers to create a consolidated, "preferred" metadata inventory for our compiled dataset. During this process, we also addressed several issues with station inventory, including inconsistencies in channel sampling rates within individual instrument streams and incorrect network code assignments for certain stations.

Site Conditions

The local site condition at a recording station is another important component of station metadata because it can significantly influence the recorded ground motions (e.g., Borcherdt, 1970; Singh *et al.*, 1988) and their consequent interpretation. A key parameter commonly used to represent site effects, especially in modern ground-motion models, is V_{S30}, which refers to the time-averaged shear-wave velocity of the upper 30 m of the subsurface (Borcherdt, 1994). Lower V_{S30} values indicate softer or less consolidated materials, which tend to amplify seismic waves and result in higher ground motions during earthquakes. Conversely, higher V_{S30} values typically correspond to stiffer or rock-like conditions that are less susceptible to amplification.

Australia-wide, the V_{S30} parameter can be estimated for any location using either surficial geology (regolith) or topographic slope proxies. The geology-based approach is underpinned by the work of McPherson (2017), who developed an Australia-specific relationship between surficial geology and V_{S30}. This methodology builds on updated geological mapping available at the time and incorporates the weathering intensity index developed by Wilford (2012). These efforts led to the creation of the Australian seismic site conditions map (McPherson, 2017), which classifies site conditions according to National Earthquake Hazards Reduction Program (NEHRP; Wills *et al.*, 2000) site classes. Each class is mapped to a representative V_{S30} value, providing a consistent framework for seismic hazard assessments across the country (e.g., Allen *et al.*, 2023) and underpins the generation of earthquake ShakeMaps for significant earthquakes in Australia (Allen *et al.*, 2019).

The slope-based proxy method estimates V_{S30} by leveraging the empirical correlation between topographic gradient and shear-wave velocity, as established by Wald and Allen (2007). In this study, Shuttle Radar Topography Mission 30 arcsec digital elevation models (Farr and Kobrick, 2000) were used to derive values of maximum gradient, which were then used to infer an alternative V_{S30} at the recording stations included in our dataset.

Although these proxy methods are valuable for regional-scale assessments, site-specific measurements are preferred for detailed evaluations. Prior studies have shown that proxy-based estimates may lack the accuracy needed in areas with complex geology or sparse ground-truth data (e.g., Yong, 2016). In Australia, site-specific shear-wave velocity measurements have been conducted at only a limited number of seismic stations. Kayen *et al.* (2015) reported shear-wave velocity profiles at 50 sites using spectral analysis of surface waves (SASW: Stokoe and Nazarian, 1985). More recently, R. Ebrahimi *et al.* (unpublished report, see Data and Resources) applied the *P*-wave seismogram method (Ni *et al.*, 2014) to estimate V_{S30} at 82 stations across Australia. Single-station and array-based ambient noise techniques have also been applied (Ebrahimi *et al.*, 2022, 2023; Ebrahimi and Allen, 2024) to estimate velocity profiles at selected seismic stations nationwide.

Figure 4a presents the distribution of the methods for which V_{S30} is estimated at Australian recording stations. As expected, the majority of stations rely on proxy-based estimates derived from either surface geology or topographic gradient. For each recording station, a representative V_{S30} estimate was derived by computing a weighted average of the six independent methods, as illustrated in Figure 4a. Each method was assigned a predefined weight reflecting its reliability and relevance. Site-specific measurements were prioritized, with higher weights assigned to SASW-based values (0.8), followed by ambient noise array techniques (0.6), and single-station noise methods (0.4). The *P*-wave method was given a conditional weight of 0.4 if the velocity exceeded 700 m/s, and 0.2 otherwise, following the recommendation of R. Ebrahimi *et al.* (unpublished report, see Data and Resources), who observed improved correlation with measured V_{S30} values above this shear-wave velocity threshold. The proxy geology-based and topographic gradient-based approaches were each assigned a weight of 0.2. Only valid values were included in the calculation, and the final V_{S30} estimate was obtained using a weighted mean of the available inputs. Figure 4b illustrates the distribution of ground-motion records, expressed as percentages, across NEHRP site classes according to their preferred V_{S30} values. It shows that the majority of records are from stations with NEHRP site class C, followed by class B, with minimal representation from classes D, E, and A. This uneven distribution may impose limitations on studying interclass variability in ground-motion recordings due to the limited number of data points available for certain site classes, particularly those less represented.

Data Processing

In this study, we used the U.S. Geological Survey (USGS) "gmprocess" software (Thompson *et al.*, 2024) to assemble previously compiled data, including earthquake parameters, raw

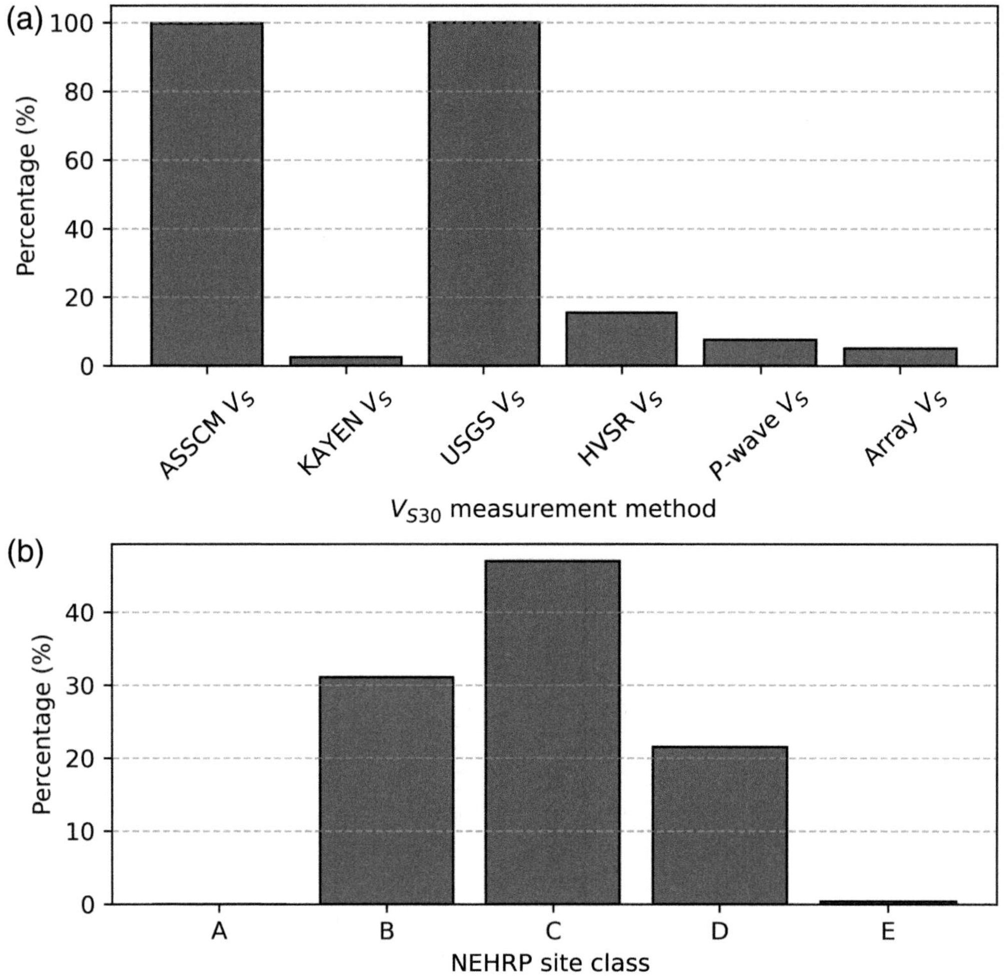

Figure 4. (a) Distribution of recording stations by the method used to estimate V_{S30} and (b) the number of records for each National Earthquake Hazards Reduction Program (NEHRP) site class based on V_{S30} values of corresponding recording stations. NEHRP site class definitions based on V_{S30}: A (>1500 m/s), B (760–1500 m/s), C (360–760 m/s), D (180–360 m/s), and E (<180 m/s). The methods shown along the *x* axis in panel (a) include ASSCM V_S, derived from the Australian Seismic Site Conditions Map (McPherson, 2017); USGS V_S, based on topographic slope proxies (Wald and Allen (2007)); KAYEN V_S, shear-wave velocity profiles from Kayen *et al.* (2015); and site-specific measurements—HVSR V_S, Array V_S, and *P*-wave V_S—obtained using horizontal-to-vertical spectral ratio, array-based ambient noise techniques, and *P*-wave seismogram method, respectively, as reported in recent studies (Ebrahimi *et al.*, 2022, 2023; Ebrahimi and Allen, 2024).

waveform recordings, and associated station metadata, into structured event-specific workspaces. Each earthquake has a dedicated workspace file stored in Hierarchical Data Format (HDF5; Koranne, 2010), a flexible and efficient container format commonly used in scientific computing for managing large, complex datasets. These workspaces adhere to the structure of the adaptable seismic data format (Krischer *et al.*, 2016), which is specifically designed for seismological applications and enables the seamless integration of event metadata, waveform data, and other supporting information within a single, coherent file.

The raw ground-motion data stored in the workspace files is measured in units of digital counts. To convert these to physical units, such as ground acceleration or velocity, the instrument response must be removed. Furthermore, the records often require baseline adjustments and are typically contaminated by low- and high-frequency noise (Boore and Bommer, 2005). The *gmprocess* software provides a comprehensive framework for performing these processing steps, including response removal, filtering, and baseline adjustment. It is built on top of the *ObsPy* Python package (Beyreuther *et al.*, 2010; Megies *et al.*, 2011), which underpins much of its signal processing functionality. In addition to processing, *gmprocess* also supports the calculation of engineering ground-motion parameters such as peak ground acceleration (PGA), peak ground velocity (PGV), peak ground displacement (PGD), and 5% damped pseudospectral accelerations (PSAs), ensuring the processed data are consistent, reproducible, and ready for further analysis.

The processing workflow implemented in this study follows the default scheme used in the *gmprocess* software, as outlined in table 1 of Thompson *et al.* (2024). The key steps in the processing scheme include baseline correction (e.g., removing linear trends from the time series), instrument response removal, and filtering (e.g., Akkar *et al.*, 2010; Paolucci *et al.*, 2011). Instrument response correction is undertaken in the frequency domain by dividing the Fourier amplitude spectrum (FAS) of the waveform data by the instrument's frequency response, using both the waveform data and corresponding metadata retrieved directly from the workspace file. Filtering is also performed in the frequency domain and involves the sequential application of high-pass and low-pass zero-phase Butterworth filters to suppress low- and high-frequency noise components, respectively.

The selection of filter corner frequencies is a critical step in the processing workflow because it determines the frequency range over which the ground-motion records can be reliably used (e.g., Akkar and Bommer, 2006; Douglas and Boore, 2011). Because of the diverse sources of seismic noise, its characteristics can vary not only between recordings from different stations but also across individual channels within the same ground-motion record (e.g., Boore and Bommer, 2005; Cauzzi and Clinton, 2013). As a result, filter corner frequencies are ideally estimated on a trace-by-trace basis. To support this, graphical user interface-based tools have been developed to assist *gmprocess* users in interactively selecting appropriate filter settings (Ghasemi and Allen, 2023a; Ramos-Sepulveda *et al.*, 2023). These tools allow users to visualize the impact of corner frequency choices on the acceleration, velocity, and displacement time series, as well as on the FAS. The long-period portion of the FAS is evaluated for deviations from the expected decay trend, typically proportional to the inverse square of frequency, as predicted by seismological models. Finally, velocity and displacement time histories, obtained through integration and double integration of the filtered acceleration, are visually inspected to ensure they are physically plausible, although such assessments remain somewhat subjective.

With the expansion of regional and national seismic monitoring networks in Australia, alongside improvements in data sharing and accessibility, the volume of available ground-motion recordings has increased substantially. This growing data volume makes manual processing of individual ground-motion records both time-consuming and often impractical. To address this challenge, several studies have introduced automated approaches for selecting filter corner frequencies (e.g., Dawood *et al.*, 2016; Guo *et al.*, 2025), as well as alternative signal processing techniques such as wavelet-based noise reduction (e.g., Ansari *et al.*, 2010; Yang *et al.*, 2024). The *gmprocess* software supports automated selection of filter corner frequencies based on SNR estimates. In this study, we set the SNR threshold to 3.0 and defined the split time between signal and noise windows for each record using the median of P-phase arrival times estimated by five independent detection algorithms implemented in *gmprocess*. These methods include travel-time predictions, amplitude-ratio triggers, and statistical phase-picking techniques. However, the details of these methods are beyond the scope of this article. The noise window was defined from the start of the record to two seconds before the P-phase arrival ($P_{time} - 2.0$), and the signal window from this split time to a duration of $30(M–1.0)$, in which M is the event magnitude. The SNR was calculated by dividing the FAS of the signal window by that of the noise window. Filter corner frequencies were then automatically selected from the frequency range in which the SNR exceeded the prescribed threshold of 3.0, and the waveform data were filtered accordingly.

Despite this automated approach, we observed that long-period noise was not effectively suppressed in some records; in those cases, it was particularly evident in the velocity and displacement time series derived by integration. This issue likely stems from the short noise windows for some recordings (particularly triggered data from legacy datasets), which are often insufficient to capture the true amplitude of long-period noise. Ideally, the noise window should be significantly longer than the noise period itself to yield reliable spectral estimates, but this is not always feasible in practice (Perron *et al.*, 2018).

TABLE 1
Correlation Coefficients Between the Automatically Selected High-Pass Filter Corner Frequency (HPC) and Key Earthquake and Site Parameters

Parameter	Correlation with HPC
Magnitude	−0.58
Distance	0.33
V_{S30}	0.12

Moment magnitude (M_w), epicentral distance, and V_{S30}.

To address this issue, we applied an additional refinement step for selecting the high-pass filter corner frequency using an optimization approach proposed by Ramos-Sepúlveda *et al.* (2025) that is also implemented in *gmprocess*. This method searches for an optimal high-pass corner frequency by satisfying the criterion that the ratio between the maximum of a third-order polynomial fit to the displacement time series and the actual maximum of the displacement time series falls within a user-defined target percentage and tolerance, set to default values of 0.02 and 0.001, respectively. The search is performed within a specified frequency range, starting from a low initial corner (in our case, the high-pass corner frequency determined from the SNR-based method) up to a user-defined maximum cutoff frequency, which in this study was set to the default value of 0.5 Hz.

To explore how key earthquake and station parameters influence the automatically selected high-pass filter corner frequency (HPC), Table 1 presents correlation coefficients between HPC and event size (moment magnitude, M_w), source-to-site distance (epicentral distance), and site condition (V_{S30}). It shows that the HPC is influenced most strongly by earthquake magnitude and, to a lesser extent, by source–site distance, whereas V_{S30} has little effect. Larger events and closer distances tend to produce higher SNRs and longer period energy, leading to lower optimal HPC values.

Random forest regression (Breiman, 2001) confirms these patterns: the baseline model without V_{S30} achieves the coefficient of determination (R^2) of 0.73 (mean square error, MSE = 0.032) with only marginal improvement when V_{S30} is included ($R^2 = 0.75$, MSE = 0.029). Feature importance ranks magnitude highest, followed by distance and then V_{S30}, with interaction terms and record type contributing less. Overall, the automatic HPC selection is primarily governed by event size and source–site distance, with site conditions playing a limited role, indicating that the HPC is more sensitive to source and path effects than to local site properties. This result may also reflect the uncertainty in the current site conditions dataset, in which the majority of V_{S30} estimates are based on proxy methods.

In addition to automated filter corner selection, *gmprocess* incorporates a suite of quality control checks to automatically identify and flag records that do not meet predefined quality criteria. The quality-control checks ensure that each time series meets a minimum sampling rate (20 Hz in this study), is free from clipping, and, for three-component recordings, that all components pass these checks. If any single component fails, the entire record is rejected because this may indicate instrument malfunction or other data quality issues. The clipping check uses the algorithm of Kleckner *et al.* (2021), applying a probability threshold of 0.2 to detect whether any portion of the waveform reaches the instrument's amplitude limit, which can distort the signal and compromise further analysis. The SNR check requires that the SNR within a specified frequency range exceeds the predefined threshold. In this study, the minimum frequency was set to the source corner frequency estimated from the Brune (1970) model, with a maximum corner frequency set to 10 Hz. The Brune corner frequency was calculated assuming a representative stress drop of 2.0 MPa, approximately consistent with median values for earthquakes in Australia (Allen, 2025). Records with a noise window duration shorter than 5 s (user-configurable) are also rejected, as insufficient noise duration can lead to unreliable SNR estimates. In addition, a zero-crossing check is applied, requiring a minimum of 0.1 zero crossings per second (also user-configurable), which helps ensure that the waveform contains sufficient frequency content and is not dominated by long-period noise or baseline offsets. For co-located stations, if multiple records from different instruments at the same site pass all quality checks, only one record is retained based on a predefined sensor preference. In this study, we prioritized broadband sensors over accelerometers due to improved SNR for most recordings, followed by short-period instruments. This preference was manually overwritten for several cases following a detailed review of SNRs for co-located instruments for several recordings. Figure 5 presents the distribution of the automatic record rejections associated with the various quality control checks applied in this study. The bar plot displays the number of records (y axis) that failed each specific check, with failure categories shown along the x axis. Overall, 34% of the records were flagged and rejected, with the SNR check accounting for the largest proportion of failures.

Only those records that satisfy all quality criteria are retained for the subsequent computation of engineering ground-motion parameters. For each accepted time series, we used *gmprocess* to calculate peak ground motions (i.e., PGA, PGV, and PGD) and PSA ordinates at periods ranging from 0.01 to 10 s. Where applicable, we also computed the 50th

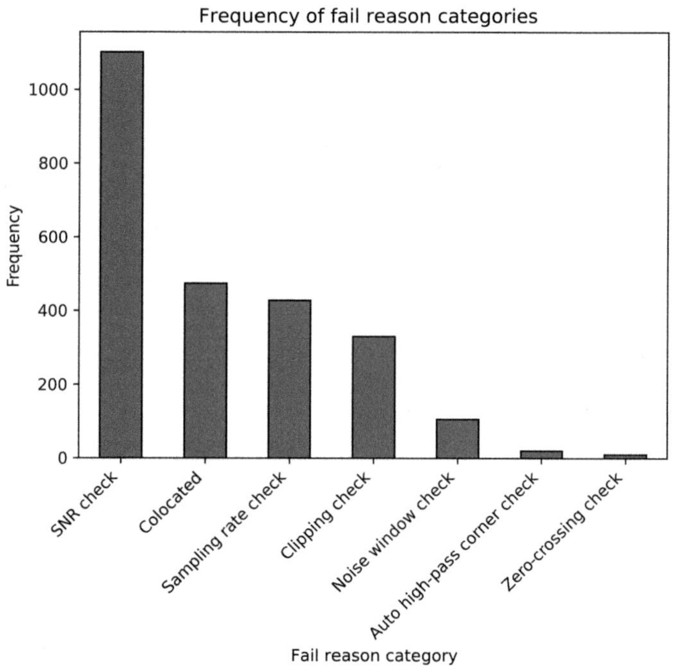

Figure 5. Bar chart summarizing the number of ground-motion records rejected by each quality control criterion applied in this study. Each rejection category is shown along the x axis, with corresponding counts on the y axis. SNR, signal-to-noise ratio.

percentile values of response spectra of the two horizontal components projected onto all nonredundant azimuths (RotD50; Boore, 2010). All processed waveforms, along with the computed ground-motion parameters, are stored in the corresponding event workspace file.

Following the automatic quality checks and automatic processing, a portable document format (PDF) summary file is generated. Before uploading the data into the Amazon Web Services (AWS) Simple Storage Service (S3) bucket, these PDF reports are reviewed for any recordings that erroneously passed quality checks and are manually rejected. Alternatively, high-SNR data that did not pass due to a very short pre-event time window are manually approved. The latter is common for triggered earthquake data in the early digital era. Manual adjustments were also made to the HPC where required.

In addition to computing engineering ground-motion parameters from observed records, for each earthquake–station pair, we also estimated the same parameters using the suite of GMMs evaluated for the 2023 National Seismic Hazard Assessment for Australia (NSHA23, Allen *et al.*, 2023). To support visualization and performance evaluation of these models, similar to Ghasemi *et al.* (2009), all observed ground-motion parameters were normalized to a reference rock-site condition with V_{S30} of 760 m/s using site adjustment factors derived from the GMMs in use. Both the normalized observations and model predictions were stored in a workspace file for later reuse and visualization via the data portal.

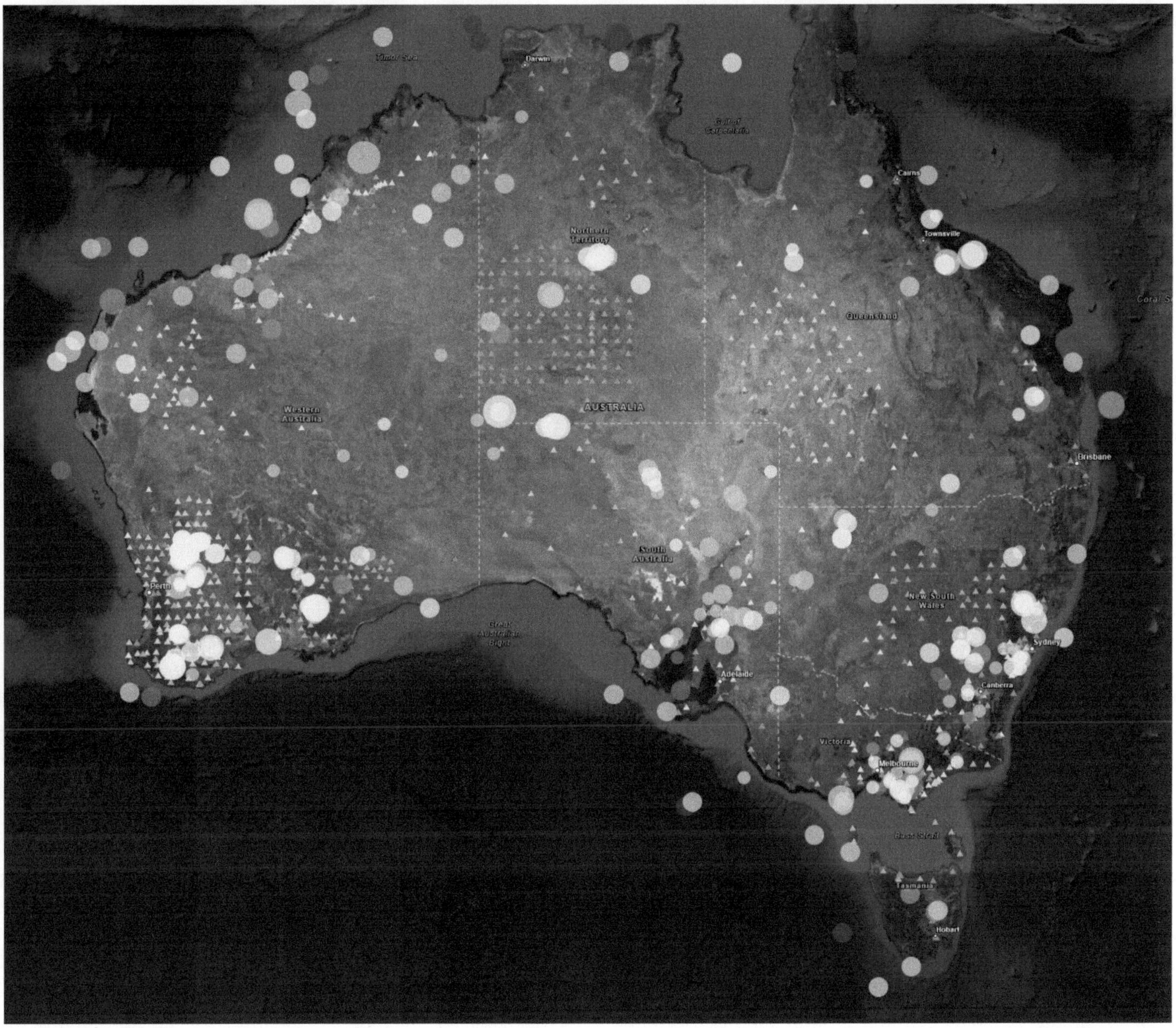

Figure 6. Screenshot of the landing page of the data portal, displaying a spatial map of all earthquakes and seismic stations in the database. Earthquakes are shown as color-coded circles, in which symbol size represents magnitude and color indicates depth. Seismic stations are plotted as triangles, color-coded by network. The color version of this figure is available only in the electronic edition.

Data Portal

To enhance accessibility and utility of the compiled ground-motion records across Australia, we developed an interactive portal that provides a web-based front end for the AGMD. This portal is designed to enable users—from researchers to engineers—to search, visualize, and download earthquake-waveform data and derived engineering ground-motion parameters through an intuitive and map-based user interface.

To enable scalable and efficient ingestion of event-based ground-motion records, the data portal is underpinned by a cloud-based architecture. Event-specific workspace files in HDF5 format are uploaded to an Amazon S3 bucket. These uploads trigger an AWS Lambda function, which subsequently runs the earthquake ground-motion processor to automatically parse the files and extract relevant attributes, including waveform traces, event metadata, and station information. The extracted content is then stored in a PostgreSQL database, which is optimized to manage structured seismic data. This database forms the backend of the data portal, allowing seamless integration between raw data ingestion, waveform processing, and end-user access. The data are then delivered to the portal via GeoServer using formats that comply with standards set by the Open Geospatial Consortium.

Upon loading, the portal displays a spatial map of all earthquakes and seismic stations included in the database, as shown in Figure 6. Earthquakes are represented as color-coded circles, with symbol size proportional to event magnitude and color indicating the estimated hypocentral depth. Seismic stations are plotted as triangles, color-coded by registered International Federation of Digital Seismograph Networks codes (see Data and Resources). The landing map also offers the option to switch between various base layers (e.g., topography, satellite imagery, and street maps) and to overlay several contextual geospatial layers including the Australian seismic site conditions map (McPherson, 2017), the neotectonic domains model (Clark *et al.*, 2011), and seismic hazard maps for Australia, including the map that was published as part of the 1999 Global Seismic Hazard Assessment Program (Giardini *et al.*, 1999; McCue, 1999) and the 2018 National Seismic Hazard Assessment (Allen *et al.*, 2020).

When an event is selected, the map dynamically identifies the associated recording stations and draws connecting lines from the event epicenter to each station with available recordings. A corresponding list of recording stations and section plots of waveforms from that event is also provided. Users can also evaluate how well a suite of candidate GMMs fits the recorded data from an event. The fit is visualized in two ways: (1) a plot showing the GMM mean predictions with ±1 standard deviation as a function of distance, superimposed by observed ground-motion values that have been normalized to a reference rock-site condition ($V_{S30} = 760$ m/s) using site adjustment factors derived from the GMMs in use (Ghasemi *et al.*, 2009), and (2) a residual plot (ln Observed−ln Predicted) versus distance, also including the ±1 standard deviation bounds of the model. In the residual plot, data points are color-coded based on the preferred V_{S30} values assigned to each station (Fig. 7). Through an interactive interface, users can select from a suite of GMMs considered in recent national seismic hazard assessments (e.g., Allen *et al.*, 2023), choose the ground-motion parameter of interest (e.g., PSA at a specified period), and perform systematic comparisons.

To compute predicted ground-motion metrics from the selected GMMs, we assumed a simplified fault plane with dimensions derived from the magnitude–area scaling relationship of Wells and Coppersmith (1994). The earthquake hypocenter was placed at the center of this plane to calculate the source-to-site distance metrics required by the GMMs. Arbitrary values of strike, dip, and rake (45°, 50°, and 0°, respectively) were assigned solely to enable distance calculations within the GMM framework; these do not represent the actual source geometry of the events. Although this simplification should be refined in future work, given the earthquake magnitudes and source-to-station distances in our dataset, we expect minimal influence on GMM predictions because most events can be reasonably approximated as point sources. At this stage, focal mechanism data have not been incorporated into the database. They are available for only a limited number of events, and finite-fault rupture models exist for even fewer cases. A systematic effort to compile focal mechanisms and finite-fault models from reliable sources and integrate them into the database is planned for future portal upgrades.

Clicking on a station reveals its metadata, including network and location information, sensor type, V_{S30} value, and associated photographs (if available). The map then dynamically highlights the earthquakes recorded by the selected station and draws connecting lines from the station to each associated event, allowing users to quickly visualize the spatial relationship between the station and the events it recorded.

The core functionality of the data portal lies in its search and retrieval tools, which allow users to query the database using a wide array of filters related to event parameters (e.g., magnitude, depth, and region), station metadata (e.g., network, station, and sensor type), or ground-motion characteristics (e.g., PGA, PGV, and PSA at specific periods). Searches can be made interactively by drawing a region on the map or using structured forms for more advanced filtering.

Search results are returned as a list or tabular summary, in which each row corresponds to a single ground-motion record. For each record, users can view plots of the waveform and its associated response spectrum, which may also be compared against design spectra specified in AS1170.4–2007 (Standards Australia, 2007) anchored to the PGA 10% chance of exceedance in 50-yr seismic hazard map (McCue, 1999) or the NSHA23 probabilistic uniform hazard spectrum for the same exceedance probability and intensity measure. The waveform data can be downloaded in COSMOS format (Consortium of Organizations for Strong-Motion Observation Systems, 2001), whereas the tabular ground-motion parameters can be exported in standard comma-separated value (CSV) format for further analysis. It should be noted that the parameter values at periods outside the high-pass and low-pass filter corner frequencies applied during ground-motion processing may not be reliable. To help assess data quality, the output CSV file includes the filter corner frequencies, enabling users to identify the valid period range for each record of interest.

A key motivation behind the development of this portal is to support a broad spectrum of end users. In particular, the portal is expected to benefit those involved in seismic hazard analysis, engineering design, structural performance assessment, geotechnical and liquefaction susceptibility assessment, and the ground-motion modeling. By offering straightforward access to consistently processed and well-documented records, the portal lowers the technical barriers for integrating Australian ground-motion data into both research and practice.

Conclusions

The AGMD is the first ground-motion database developed for Australia by systematically collecting and processing earthquake recordings and station metadata from national and regional seismic networks across the continent. Using the open-source USGS *gmprocess* software, all data were uniformly processed and stored in HDF5 workspace files, ensuring

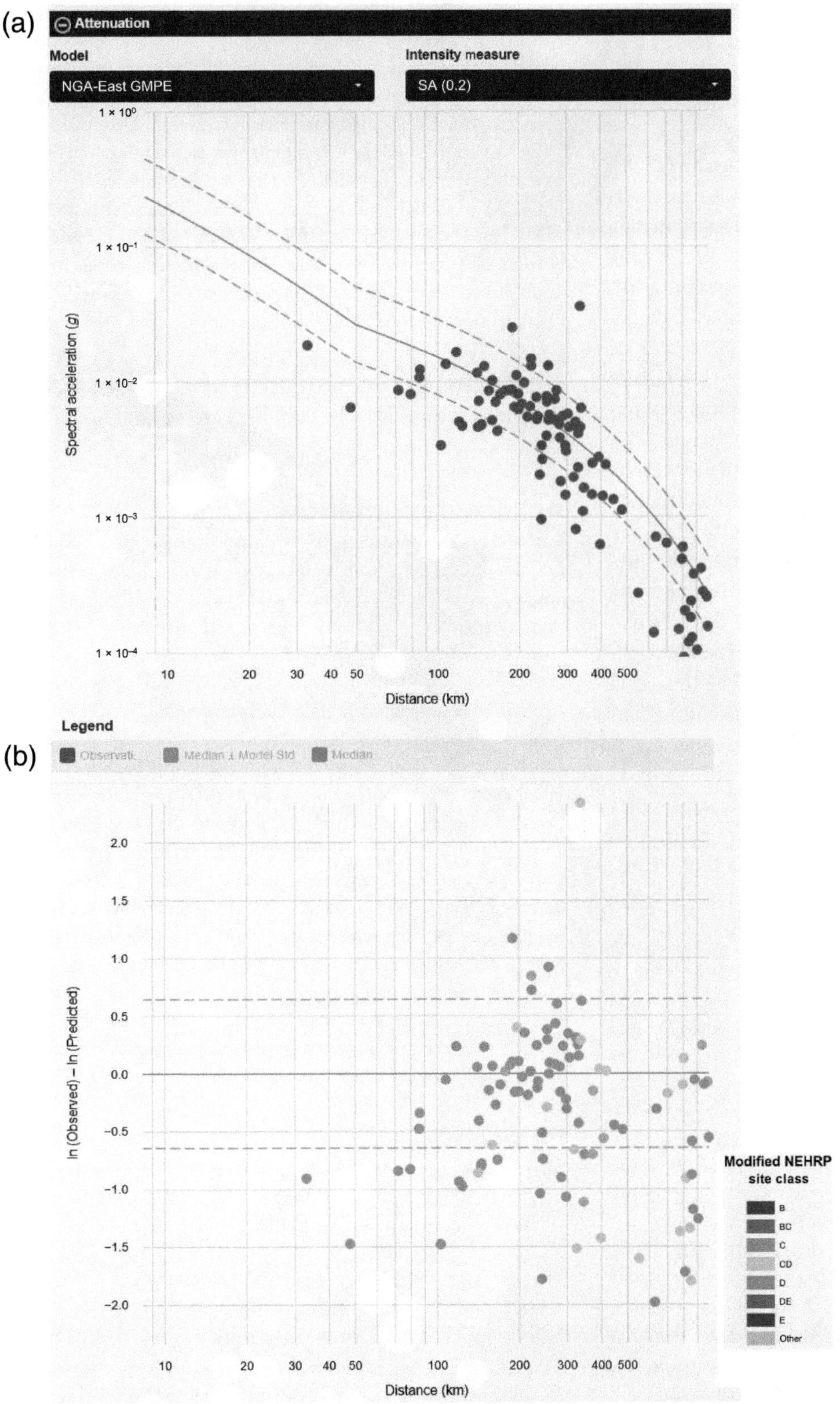

Figure 7. Screenshot from the data portal illustrating the 30 May 2019 M_w 5.2 Southern Tanami, Northern Territory, earthquake. It presents example ground-motion model (GMM) evaluation results for the Next Generation Attenuation (NGA)-East model at pseudo-spectral acceleration (PSA) (0.01 s): (a) predicted mean values with $\pm 1\sigma$ as a function of distance compared with observed ground motions, and (b) residuals (log observation–log prediction) versus distance. Data points are color-coded by V_{S30}. The color version of this figure is available only in the electronic edition.

transparency and repeatability through the inclusion of detailed processing steps and parameters.

The database comprises over 5000 ground-motion records from 270 earthquakes recorded between 1990 and 2025, sourced from more than 1000 stations and from 36 networks. For each record, a comprehensive set of engineering parameters, including peak ground motions and 21 PSAs spanning 0.01–10 s, has been computed and archived. The high-quality data acquired from recent Australian earthquakes now have significant utility to enable more informed choices for the use of GMMs for future hazard assessments and will support future empirical and simulated ground-motion studies for Australia and other SCRs more broadly.

To facilitate broad access and usability, we developed an interactive data portal that serves as the web-based front end to the database. This portal empowers researchers, engineers, and other stakeholders to search, visualize, and download waveform data and derived ground-motion parameters through an intuitive, map-based interface.

Looking ahead, we aim to expand the database by substituting additional high-sample-rate data for lower sample-rate data where available, incorporating additional legacy datasets (e.g., Borleis and Dimas, 2016; Saygin and Lumley, 2018), integrating new recordings from emerging networks and future earthquakes, adding additional site photographs, and refining the portal based on community feedback. Planned enhancements include the addition of event–station-specific metadata such as rupture geometry, if available, and basin depth, as well as ongoing updates to shear-wave velocity metadata because new measurements become available. Data may also be updated periodically if errors in station metadata are identified and updated.

We are also establishing a standard operating procedure (SOP) to ensure the portal remains continuously updated as new earthquakes occur. As outlined here, the procedure involves estimating moment magnitude via Brune spectral fitting (Allen, 2025), processing waveform data, and generating event-specific workspace files for more timely integration into the S3 bucket and publication on the portal for Australian earthquakes with $M_w \geq 3.75$. Initial magnitude estimates (typically M_L) by Geoscience Australia will be converted to M_w using the empirical relationships of Allen *et al.* (2023). If the converted M_w exceeds 3.75, the Allen (2025) method based on the spectral fitting method will be applied to refine the estimate using recorded ground-motion data. For qualifying events, waveform data within a 1500 km radius will be retrieved and processed using *gmprocess* with predefined configuration parameters. The resulting PDF reports will undergo internal review before integration into the database and portal. Non-real-time data, or data embargoed for specific applications, will be ingested on a case-by-case basis because these data become publicly available. These procedures aim to ensure consistent and timely updates, though we acknowledge that maintaining data integrity and fixing issues will be an ongoing task.

Together, these efforts mark a significant step toward building a robust, accessible, and regionally tailored ground-motion resource to improve our collective understanding of seismic hazards, supporting both scientific research and engineering applications in Australia and other SCRs globally.

Data and Resources

Data for this study were gathered from a number of permanent and temporary seismic networks, as shown in Figure 2. The citations for these individual networks, most of which are registered with the International Federation of Digital Seismograph Networks, are as follows: 1H (Rawlinson, 2010), 1K (Tkalčić *et al.*, 2013), 1P (Reading and Rawlinson, 2011), 1Q (Salmon and Kennett, 2016), 2O (Glanville, 2019), 2P (Miller *et al.*, 2020), 3B (Glanville, 2024), 3O (Miller, 2019), 4N (Yuan, 2017), 5J (Salmon and Kennett, 2017), 6F (Rawlinson and Kennett, 2008), 7H (Rawlinson and Kennett, 2001), 7I (Kennett, 2003), 7J (Reading and Kennett, 2005), 7K (Fontaine and Kennett, 2007), 7M (Houseman *et al.*, 1998), AD (Love, 2006), AU (Geoscience Australia, 2021), DU (Seismological Association of Australia Inc., 1995), G (Institut de physique du globe de Paris and École et Observatoire des Sciences de la Terre de Strasbourg, 1982), II (Scripps Institution of Oceanography, 1986), IU (Albuquerque Seismological Laboratory, 1988), M8 (Pickle *et al.*, 2024), OA (Gorbatov *et al.*, 2020), OZ (Peck, 2016), S1 (Salmon *et al.*, 2011), VW (University of Melbourne *et al.*, 2012), WG (Geological Survey of Western Australia, 2022), and YW (Glanville, 2021). Seismic data retrieved from the AusPass archive (http://auspass.edu.au/; Salmon *et al.*, 2020) are used under a Creative Commons Attribution 4.0 International license (CC BY 4.0: https://creativecommons.org/licenses/by/4.0/), as outlined in Geoscience Australia's copyright policy available at https://www.ga.gov.au/copyright. The compiled database used in this study is accessible via the data portal developed as part of this project, available at https://agmd.ga.gov.au. All websites were last accessed in December 2025.

In this study, the V_{S30} measurements based on the *P*-wave method were obtained from unpublished work by Ebrahimi *et al.* (Ebrahimi, R., T. Allen, and H. Ghasemi, 2022, "Site characterization for the Australian National Seismograph Network (ANSN) using the initial portion of P-wave arrivals and HVSR ellipticity curve inversion," unpublished report, Geoscience Australia). This report is available upon request by contacting the first author.

Declaration of Competing Interests

The authors acknowledge that there are no conflicts of interest recorded.

Acknowledgments

The authors acknowledge the traditional owners and custodians of Country throughout Australia and acknowledge their continuing connection to land, waters, and community. The authors pay their respects to the people, the cultures, and the elders, past and present. The authors thank Hugh Glanville and Mustafa Çomoğlu for their internal review of the original article, and Aswin Peris and Bill Farmakis from Geoscience Australia's web development team for their support in developing the data portal. The authors also acknowledge Nova Roosmawati and Carmen Longbottom for their efforts in creating the help page for the portal. In addition, the authors thank Wayne Peck from the Seismological Research Centre and Robert Pickle from the Australian National University for their support of this study. The authors extend their sincere appreciation to Eric Thompson of the U.S. Geological Survey for hosting the first author during the course of this study and for his significant contributions in resolving reported issues and implementing requested features that enhanced the quality of this work. Finally, the authors express their gratitude to Christopher Brooks and the anonymous reviewer for their constructive feedback and insightful comments, which improved the quality of the original submission. This publication is released with the permission of the Chief Executive Officer of Geoscience Australia.

References

Ahern, T., R. Casey, D. Barnes, R. Benson, T. Knight, and C. Trabant (2009). SEED Reference Manual, version 2.4, available at http://www.fdsn.org/seed_manual/SEEDManual_V2.4.pdf (last accessed December 2025).

Akkar, S., and J. J. Bommer (2006). Influence of long-period filter cut-off on elastic spectral displacements, *Earthq. Eng. Struct. Dynam.* **35,** 1145–1165, doi: 10.1002/eqe.577.

Akkar, S., Z. Çağnan, E. Yenier, Ö. Erdoğan, M. A. Sandıkkaya, and P. Gülkan (2010). The recently compiled Turkish strong motion database: Preliminary investigation for seismological parameters, *J. Seismolog.* **14,** 457–479, doi: 10.1007/s10950-009-9176-9.

Albuquerque Seismological Laboratory (1988). *Global seismograph network (GSN - IRIS/USGS)* [Data set], *International Federation of Digital Seismograph Networks*, doi: 10.7914/SN/IU.

Allen, T. (2020). Seismic hazard estimation in stable continental regions: Does PSHA meet the needs for modern engineering design in Australia?, *Bull. New Zeal. Soc. Earthq. Eng.* **53,** 22–36, doi: 10.5459/bnzsee.53.1.22-36.

Allen, T. I. (2021). A far-field ground-motion model for the North Australian craton from plate-margin earthquakes, *Bull. Seismol. Soc. Am.* **112,** 1041–1059, doi: 10.1785/0120210191.

Allen, T. I. (2025). Systematic estimation of earthquake source parameters for continental Australia: Attenuation and stress drop, *Bull. Seismol. Soc. Am.*, doi: 10.1785/0120250054.

Allen, T., A. Carapetis, J. Bathgate, H. Ghasemi, T. Pejić, and A. Moseley (2019). Real-time community internet intensity maps and ShakeMaps for Australian earthquakes, *Australian Earthquake Engineering Society 2019 Conference*, Newcastle, New South Wales, 29 November–1 December 2019.

Allen, T. I., P. R. Cummins, T. Dhu, and J. F. Schneider (2007). Attenuation of ground-motion spectral amplitudes in southeastern Australia, *Bull. Seismol. Soc. Am.* **97,** 1279–1292, doi: 10.1785/0120060172.

Allen, T. I., T. Dhu, P. R. Cummins, and J. F. Schneider (2006). Empirical attenuation of ground-motion spectral amplitudes in southwestern Western Australia, *Bull. Seismol. Soc. Am.* **96,** 572–585, doi: 10.1785/0120040238.

Allen, T. I., J. D. Griffin, D. J. Clark, P. R. Cummins, H. Ghasemi, and R. Ebrahimi (2023). The 2023 National Seismic Hazard Assessment for Australia: Model overview, *Geoscience Australia Record 2023/53*, Canberra, doi: 10.26186/148969.

Allen, T. I., J. D. Griffin, M. Leonard, D. J. Clark, and H. Ghasemi (2020). The 2018 National Seismic Hazard Assessment of Australia: Quantifying hazard changes and model uncertainties, *Earthq. Spectra* **36,** 5–43, doi: 10.1177/8755293019900777.

Ansari, A., A. Noorzad, H. Zafarani, and H. Vahidifard (2010). Correction of highly noisy strong motion records using a modified wavelet de-noising method, *Soil Dynam. Earthq. Eng.* **30,** 1168–1181, doi: 10.1016/j.soildyn.2010.04.025.

Attanayake, J., A. Jones, G. Gibson, and M. Sandiford (2023). Pre-commercial baseline passive seismic monitoring around CarbonNet's Pelican site in the offshore Gippsland basin, Victoria—The first five years, *Int. J. Greenhouse Gas Control* **128,** 103962, doi: 10.1016/j.ijggc.2023.103962.

Balfour, N. J., M. Salmon, and M. Sambridge (2014). The Australian seismometers in schools network: Education, outreach, research, and monitoring, *Seismol. Res. Lett.* **85,** 1063–1068, doi: 10.1785/0220140025.

Beyreuther, M., R. Barsch, L. Krischer, T. Megies, Y. Behr, and J. Wassermann (2010). ObsPy: A Python toolbox for seismology, *Seismol. Res. Lett.* **81,** 530–533, doi: 10.1785/gssrl.81.3.530.

Boore, D. M. (2010). Orientation-independent, nongeometric-mean measures of seismic intensity from two horizontal components of motion, *Bull. Seismol. Soc. Am.* **100,** 1830–1835, doi: 10.1785/0120090400.

Boore, D. M., and J. J. Bommer (2005). Processing of strong-motion accelerograms: Needs, options and consequences, *Soil Dynam. Earthq. Eng.* **25,** 93–115, doi: 10.1016/j.soildyn.2004.10.007.

Borcherdt, R. D. (1970). Effects of local geology on ground motion near San Francisco Bay, *Bull. Seismol. Soc. Am.* **60,** 29–61, doi: 10.1785/BSSA0600010029.

Borcherdt, R. D. (1994). Estimates of site-dependent response spectra for design (methodology and justification), *Earthq. Spectra* **10,** 617–653, doi: 10.1193/1.1585791.

Borleis, E., and V.-A. Dimas (2016). 2015 Fraser Island earthquake sequence, *Australian Earthquake Engineering Society 2016 Conference*, Melbourne, Victoria, 25–27 November 2016.

Breiman, L. (2001). Random forests, *Machine Learn.* **45,** 5–32, doi: 10.1023/A:1010933404324.

Brune, J. N. (1970). Tectonic stress and the spectra of seismic shear waves from earthquakes, *J. Geophys. Res. Solid Earth* **75,** 4997–5009, doi: 10.1029/JB075i026p04997.

Buscetti, M., P. Traversa, V. Perron, P. Rischette, F. Hollender, and H. Shible (2024). Epos-France database of earthquake ground motion for Mainland France: 1996–2021 updated version, *Seismol. Res. Lett.* **96,** 1214–1226, doi: 10.1785/0220240053.

Cauzzi, C., and J. Clinton (2013). A high- and low-noise model for high-quality strong-motion accelerometer stations, *Earthq. Spectra* **29,** 85–102, doi: 10.1193/1.4000107.

Clark, D., A. McPherson, T. Allen, and M. De Kool (2014). Coseismic surface deformation caused by the 23 March 2012 M_w 5.4 Ernabella (Pukatja) earthquake, central Australia: Implications for fault scaling relations in cratonic settings, *Bull. Seismol. Soc. Am.* **104,** 24–39, doi: 10.1785/0120120361.

Clark, D., A. McPherson, and C. D. N. Collins (2011). Australia's seismogenic neotectonic record: A case for heterogeneous intraplate deformation, *Geoscience Australia Record 2011/11*, Canberra.

Clark, D., A. McPherson, and R. Van Dissen (2012). Long-term behaviour of Australian stable continental region (SCR) faults, *Tectonophysics* **566–567,** 1–30, doi: 10.1016/j.tecto.2012.07.004.

Clinton, J. F., and T. H. Heaton (2002). Potential advantages of a strong-motion velocity meter over a strong-motion accelerometer, *Seismol. Res. Lett.* **73,** 332–342, doi: 10.1785/gssrl.73.3.332.

Consortium of Organizations for Strong-Motion Observation Systems (2001). Strong-motion data format, version 1.20, *Consortium of Organizations for Strong-Motion Observation Systems*, available at https://www.strongmotioncenter.org/vdc/cosmos_format_1_20.pdf (last accessed December 2025).

Crone, A. J., M. N. Machette, and J. R. Bowman (1997). Episodic nature of earthquake activity in stable continental regions revealed by palaeoseismicity studies of Australian and North American quaternary faults, *Aust. J. Earth Sci.* **44,** 203–214, doi: 10.1080/08120099708728304.

Daniell, J. E., and D. Love (2010). The socio-economic impact of historic Australian earthquakes, *Australian Earthquake Engineering Society 2010 Conference*, Perth, Western Australia, 26–28 November 2010.

Dawood, H. M., A. Rodriguez-Marek, J. Bayless, C. Goulet, and E. Thompson (2016). A flatfile for the KiK-net database processed using an automated protocol, *Earthq. Spectra* **32,** 1281–1302, doi: 10.1193/071214EQS106.

Douglas, J., and D. M. Boore (2011). High-frequency filtering of strong-motion records, *Bull. Earthq. Eng.* **9,** 395–409, doi: 10.1007/s10518-010-9208-4.

Ebrahimi, R., and T. Allen (2024). Site classification and V_{S30} determination for seismic hazard evaluation in the SWAN seismic network, Western Australia, in R. E. Murdie and M. S. Miller (Editors), *South West Australia Network (SWAN): Passive Seismic Imaging and Hazard Analysis*, Perth, Western Australia, Geological Survey of Western Australia, Report 255, 58–67.

Ebrahimi, R., T. Allen, A. Jones, H. Ghasemi, and J. Attanayake (2023). Site characterisation of 12 seismic monitoring stations in

SE Victoria, Australia, *Australian Earthquake Engineering Society 2023 Conference*, Brisbane, Queensland, 23–25 November 2023.

Ebrahimi, R., H. Ghasemi, and T. Allen (2022). Site characterization for ANSN stations using the ellipticity curve inversion of microtremor data, *Australian Earthquake Engineering Society 2022 Conference*, Mount Macedon, Victoria, 24–25 November 2022.

Edwards, M., M. Griffith, M. Wehner, N. Lam, N. Corby, M. Jakab, and N. Habili (2010). The Kalgoorlie earthquake of the 20th April 2010: Preliminary damage survey outcomes, *Australian Earthquake Engineering Society 2010 Conference*, Perth, Western Australia, 26–28 November 2010.

Farr, T. G., and M. Kobrick (2000). Shuttle Radar Topography Mission produces a wealth of data, *Eos Trans. AGU* **81,** 583–585, doi: 10.1029/EO081i048p00583.

Fontaine, F., and B. Kennett (2007). *SOC - Southern craton* [Data set], *International Federation of Digital Seismograph Networks*, doi: 10.7914/SN/7K_2007.

Fukushima, Y., and T. Tanaka (1990). A new attenuation relation for peak horizontal acceleration of strong earthquake ground motion in Japan, *Bull. Seismol. Soc. Am.* **80,** 757–783, doi: 10.1785/BSSA0800040757.

Geological Survey of Western Australia (2022). *WA Array* [Data set], *International Federation of Digital Seismograph Networks*, doi: 10.7914/xagc-se62.

Geoscience Australia (2021). *Australian National Seismograph Network Data Collection (Version 2.0, September 2018)* [Data set], Commonwealth of Australia, Geoscience Australia, doi: 10.26186/144675.

Ghasemi, H., and T. Allen (2021). Engineering ground-motion database for Western and Central Australia, *Australian Earthquake Engineering Society 2021 Conference*, Virtual Conference, 25–26 November 2021.

Ghasemi, H., and T. Allen (2023a). Development of a web portal for Australian ground-motion data, *Australian Earthquake Engineering Society 2023 Conference*, Brisbane, Queensland, 23–25 November 2023.

Ghasemi, H., and T. Allen (2023b). Ground-motion database for southeastern Australia, *2023 Pacific Conference on Earthquake Engineering*, Vancouver, British Columbia, 25–30 June 2023.

Ghasemi, H., and T. I. Allen (2018). *Selection and Ranking of Ground-Motion Models for the 2018 National Seismic Hazard Assessment of Australia: Summary of Ground-Motion Data, Methodology and Outcomes*, Geoscience Australia Record 2018/29, Canberra, doi: 10.11636/Record.2018.029.

Ghasemi, H., M. Zare, Y. Fukushima, and K. Koketsu (2009). An empirical spectral ground-motion model for Iran, *J. Seismol.* **13,** 499–515, doi: 10.1007/s10950-008-9143-x.

Giardini, D., G. Grünthal, K. M. Shedlock, and P. Zhang (1999). The GSHAP global seismic hazard map, *Ann. Geophys.* **42,** 1225–1230, doi: 10.4401/ag-3784.

Glanville, H. (2019). *Beetaloo seismic monitoring project* [Data set], *International Federation of Digital Seismograph Networks*, doi: 10.7914/SN/2O_2019.

Glanville, H. (2021). *Muswellbrook* [Data set], *International Federation of Digital Seismograph Networks*, doi: 10.7914/SN/YW_2021.

Glanville, H. (2024). *Wyalkatchem temporary network* [Data set], *International Federation of Digital Seismograph Networks*, doi: 10.7914/xy0z-bx66.

Gorbatov, A., K. Czarnota, B. Hejrani, M. Haynes, R. Hassan, A. Medlin, J. Zhao, F. Zhang, M. Salmon, H. Tkalčić, *et al.* (2020). AusArray: Quality passive seismic data to underpin updatable national velocity models of the lithosphere, doi: 10.11636/135284.

Gorbatov, A., K. Czarnota, and T. Kemp (2018). Geoscience Australia's contribution to AusArray - Passive seismic imaging of Australia, *ASEG Extended Abstracts* **2018,** 1–2, doi: 10.1071/ASEG2018abM1_3G.

Goulet, C. A., Y. Bozorgnia, N. Kuehn, L. Al Atik, R. R. Youngs, R. W. Graves, and G. M. Atkinson (2021). NGA-East ground-motion characterization model part I: Summary of products and model development, *Earthq. Spectra* **37,** 1231–1282, doi: 10.1177/87552930211018723.

Guo, W., Y. Ren, T. Kishida, X. Yao, H. Wang, Y. Liu, and R. Wen (2025). An automated protocol for filter processing of strong-motion records: Case study in China, *Earthq. Spectra* **41,** 2436–2459, doi: 10.1177/87552930251332269.

Houseman, G., S. Greenhalgh, and F. Graeber (1998). *LF98* [Data set], *International Federation of Digital Seismograph Networks*, doi: 10.7914/SN/7M_1998.

Institut de physique du globe de Paris and École et Observatoire des Sciences de la Terre de Strasbourg (1982). *GEOSCOPE, French Global Network of broad band seismic stations* [Data set], *Institut de physique du globe de Paris (IPGP), Université de Paris*, doi: 10.18715/GEOSCOPE.G (in French).

International Federation of Digital Seismograph Networks (2022). StationXML version 1.2: XML schema for seismic station metadata, available at https://docs.fdsn.org/projects/stationxml/en/latest/ (last accessed December 2025).

Johnston, A. C. (1994). Seismotectonic interpretations and conclusions from the stable continental region seismicity database, in *The Earthquakes of Stable Continental Regions, Volume 1-Assessment of Large Earthquake Potential*, A. C. Johnston, K. J. Coppersmith, L. R. Kanter, and C. A. Cornell (Editors), Electric Power Research Institute, Palo Alto, California, TR-102261-V1.

Kayen, R. E., B. A. Carkin, T. Allen, C. Collins, A. McPherson, and D. Minasian (2015). Shear-wave velocity and site-amplification factors for 50 Australian sites determined by the spectral analysis of surface waves method, *U.S. Geol. Surv. Open-File Rep. 2014-1264*, doi: 10.3133/ofr20141264.

Kennett, B. (2003). *TASMAL* [Data set], *International Federation of Digital Seismograph Networks*, doi: 10.7914/SN/7I_2003.

Kennett, B. L. N., A. Gorbatov, H. Yuan, S. Agrawal, R. Murdie, M. P. Doublier, C. M. Eakin, M. S. Miller, L. Zhao, K. Czarnota, *et al.* (2023). Refining the Moho across the Australian continent, *Geophys. J. Int.* **233,** 1863–1877, doi: 10.1093/gji/ggad035.

King, T., M. Quigley, D. Clark, A. Zondervan, J.-H. May, and A. Alimanovic (2021). Paleoseismology of the 2016 M_w 6.1 Petermann earthquake source: Implications for intraplate earthquake behaviour and the geomorphic longevity of bedrock fault scarps in a low strain-rate cratonic region, *Earth Surf. Process. Landf.* **46,** 1238–1256, doi: 10.1002/esp.5090.

Kishida, T., D. Di Giacinto, and G. Iaccarino (2017). Comparison of manual and automated ground motion processing for small-to-moderate magnitude earthquakes in Japan, *Earthq. Spectra*, doi: 10.1193/080316EQS124M.

Kleckner, J. K., K. B. Withers, E. M. Thompson, J. M. Rekoske, E. Wolin, and M. P. Moschetti (2021). Automated detection of clipping in broadband earthquake records, *Seismol. Res. Lett.* **93,** 880–896, doi: 10.1785/0220210028.

Koranne, S. (2010). Hierarchical data format 5: HDF5, in *Handbook of Open Source Tools*, Springer, Boston, Massachusetts, 191–200.

Kramer, S. L. (1996). *Geotechnical Earthquake Engineering*, Prentice Hall, Upper Saddle River, New Jersey, pp. 653.

Krischer, L., J. Smith, W. Lei, M. Lefebvre, Y. Ruan, E. S. de Andrade, N. Podhorszki, E. Bozdağ, and J. Tromp (2016). An adaptable seismic data format, *Geophys. J. Int.* **207,** 1003–1011, doi: 10.1093/gji/ggw319.

Leonard, M. (2002). The Burakin WA earthquake sequence Sept 2000 - June 2002, *Australian Earthquake Engineering Society 2002 Conference*, Adelaide, South Australia, 17–18 October 2002.

Leonard, M. (2008). One hundred years of earthquake recording in Australia, *Bull. Seismol. Soc. Am.* **98,** 1458–1470, doi: 10.1785/0120050193.

Love, D. (2006). New Adelaide earthquake monitoring network, *Australian Earthquake Engineering Society 2006 Conference*, Canberra, Australian Capital Territory, 24–26 November 2006, 221–224.

McCue, K. (1999). Seismic hazard mapping in Australia, the southwest Pacific and southeast Asia, *Ann. Geophys.* **42,** 1191–1198, doi: 10.4401/ag-3776.

McCue, K., V. Wesson, and G. Gibson (1990). The Newcastle, New South Wales, earthquake of 28 December 1989, *BMR J. Aust. Geol. Geophys.* **11,** 559–567.

McPherson, A. A. (2017). A revised seismic site conditions map for Australia, *Geoscience Australia Record 2017/12*, Canberra, doi: 10.11636/Record.2017.012.

Megies, T., M. Beyreuther, R. Barsch, L. Krischer, and J. Wassermann (2011). ObsPy – What can it do for data centers and observatories?, *Ann. Geophys.* **54,** 47–58, doi: 10.4401/ag-4838.

Miller, M. (2019). *AKIMBA* [Data set], *International Federation of Digital Seismograph Networks*, doi: 10.7914/SN/3O_2019.

Miller, M., T. Allen, R. Murdie, K. Gessner, H. Yuan, B. Kennett, and R. Pickle (2020). *South West Australia Network* [Data set], *International Federation of Digital Seismograph Networks*, doi: 10.7914/SN/2P_2020.

Miller, M. S., R. Pickle, R. Murdie, H. Yuan, T. I. Allen, K. Gessner, B. L. N. Kennett, and J. Whitney (2023). Southwest Australia Seismic Network (SWAN): Recording earthquakes in Australia's most active seismic zone, *Seismol. Res. Lett.* **94,** 999–1011, doi: 10.1785/0220220323.

Mousavi, S., B. Hejrani, M. S. Miller, and M. Salmon (2023). Hypocenter, fault plane, and rupture characterization of Australian earthquakes: Application to the September 2021 M_w 5.9 Woods Point earthquake, *Seismol. Res. Lett.* **94,** 1761–1774, doi: 10.1785/0220220348.

Murdie, R., R. Pickle, H. Yuan, D. Love, V. Dent, M. S. Miller, and J. Whitney (2022). Observations from the 2022 Arthur River, Western Australia, earthquake swarm, *Australian Earthquake Engineering Society 2022 Conference*, Mount Macedon, Victoria, 24–25 November 2022.

Murdie, R. E., H. Yuan, J. P. O'Donnell, S. P. Johnson, R. Ebrahimi, and M. Rashidifard (2024). WA Array: A high-resolution passive-source seismic survey to image the west Australian lithosphere, *Seismol. Res. Lett.* **95,** 3093–3108, doi: 10.1785/0220230415.

Ni, S., Z. Li, and P. Somerville (2014). Estimating subsurface shear velocity with radial to vertical ratio of local P waves, *Seismol. Res. Lett.* **85,** 82–90, doi: 10.1785/0220130128.

Nievas, C. I., J. J. Bommer, H. Crowley, and J. van Elk (2020). Global occurrence and impact of small-to-medium magnitude earthquakes: A statistical analysis, *Bull. Earthq. Eng.* **18,** 1–35, doi: 10.1007/s10518-019-00718-w.

Paolucci, R., F. Pacor, R. Puglia, G. Ameri, C. Cauzzi, and M. Massa (2011). Record processing in ITACA, the new Italian strong-motion database, in S. Akkar, P. Gülkan, and T. van Eck (Editors), *Earthquake Data in Engineering Seismology: Predictive Models, Data Management and Networks*, Springer Netherlands, Dordrecht, 99–113, doi: 10.1007/978-94-007-0152-6_8.

Peck, W. (2016). An earthquake alarm and situation awareness tool developed for areas of low to moderate seismic hazard: Recent developments and past results, *Australian National Committee on Large Dams/New Zealand Society of Large Dams 2016 Conference*, Adelaide, South Australia, 18–19 October 2016.

Perron, V., A. Laurendeau, F. Hollender, P.-Y. Bard, C. Gélis, P. Traversa, and S. Drouet (2018). Selecting time windows of seismic phases and noise for engineering seismology applications: A versatile methodology and algorithm, *Bull. Earthq. Eng.* **16,** 2211–2225, doi: 10.1007/s10518-017-0131-9.

Pickle, R., M. Miller, R. Murdie, J. P. O'Donnell, A. Gorbatov, and M. Salmon (2024). *Australian Semi-Permanent Support Network* [Data set], *International Federation of Digital Seismograph Networks*, doi: 10.7914/6E8T-6G37.

Pilia, S., N. Rawlinson, N. G. Direen, P. R. Cummins, and N. Balfour (2013). Structural controls on localized intraplate deformation and seismicity in Southern Australia: Insights from local earthquake tomography of the Flinders Ranges, *J. Geophys. Res. Solid Earth* **118,** 2176–2190, doi: 10.1002/jgrb.50168.

Ramos-Sepúlveda, M. E., S. J. Brandenberg, T. E. Buckreis, G. A. Parker, and J. P. Stewart (2025). High-pass corner-frequency selection and review tool for use in ground-motion processing, *Seismol. Res. Lett.* **96,** 3244–3252, doi: 10.1785/0220240265.

Ramos-Sepulveda, M. E., G. A. Parker, E. M. Thompson, S. J. Brandenberg, M. Li, O. Ilhan, Y. M. Hashash, E. M. Rathje, and J. P. Stewart (2023). High-pass corner frequency selection for implementation in the USGS automated ground motion processing tool, *Geo-congress 2023: Geotechnical Data Analysis and Computation*, Los Angeles, California, 26–29 March 2023, 327–335.

Rawlinson, N. (2010). *EAL2* [Data set], *International Federation of Digital Seismograph Networks*, doi: 10.7914/SN/1H_2010.

Rawlinson, N., and B. Kennett (2001). *TIGGER BB* [Data set], *International Federation of Digital Seismograph Networks*, doi: 10.7914/SN/7H_2001.

Rawlinson, S., and B. Kennett (2008). *BILBY* [Data set], *Australian Passive Seismic Server*, doi: 10.7914/SN/6F_2008.

Reading, A., and B. Kennett (2005). *CAPRA - Linkage* [Data set], *International Federation of Digital Seismograph Networks*, doi: 10.7914/SN/7J_2005.

Reading, A., and N. Rawlinson (2011). *Bass Strait* [Data set], *International Federation of Digital Seismograph Networks*, doi: 10.7914/SN/1P_2011.

Ringler, A. T., and J. R. Evans (2015). A quick SEED tutorial, *Seismol. Res. Lett.* **86,** 1717–1725, doi: 10.1785/0220150043.

Salmon, M., and B. Kennett (2016). *AQT* [Data set], *International Federation of Digital Seismograph Networks,* doi: 10.7914/SN/1Q_2016.

Salmon, M., and B. Kennett (2017). *ASR* [Data set], AusPass, doi: 10.7914/SN/5J_2017.

Salmon, M., N. Balfour, and M. Sambridge (2011). *Australian seismometers in schools* [Data set], *AusPass,* doi: 10.7914/SN/S1.

Salmon, M., S. Mousavi, and M. Sambridge (2022). 10 years of Australian seismometers in schools–Education, outreach and research, *Australian Earthquake Engineering Society 2022 Conference,* Mount Macedon, Victoria, 24–25 November 2022.

Salmon, M., R. Pickle, S. Allgeyer, and J. Pfeffer (2020). AusPass, making seismic data stewardship FAIR, *Sub 20 – Inaugural Deep Earth Imaging Conference,* Perth, Western Australia, 12–13 February 2020.

Saygin, E., and D. Lumley (2018). *Passive Seismic Investigations at the SW Hub,* University of Western Australia Australian National Low Emissions Council (ANLEC) R&D Project Number 7-0215-0244, Perth, Western Australia.

Scherbaum, F. (1996). *Of poles and Zeros: Fundamentals of Digital Seismology,* Dordrecht, Kluwer Academic Press, pp. 256.

Scripps Institution of Oceanography (1986). *IRIS/IDA seismic network* [Data set], *International Federation of Digital Seismograph Networks,* doi: 10.7914/SN/II.

Seismological Association of Australia Inc. (1995). *Seismological Association of Australia* [Data set], *International Federation of Digital Seismograph Networks,* doi: 10.7914/SN/DU.

Singh, S. K., E. Mena, and R. Castro (1988). Some aspects of source characteristics of the 19 September 1985 Michoacan earthquake and ground motion amplification in and near Mexico City from strong motion data, *Bull. Seismol. Soc. Am.* **78,** 451–477, doi: 10.1785/bssa0780020451.

Standards Australia (2007). *Structural Design Actions, Part 4: Earthquake Actions in Australia,* Standards Australia AS 1170.4–2007, Sydney, New South Wales.

Stokoe, K., and S. Nazarian (1985). Use of Rayleigh waves in liquefaction studies, in *Measurement and use of Shear Wave Velocity for Evaluating Dynamic Soil Properties,* R. D. Woods (Editor), New York, ASCE, 1–17.

Thompson, E. M., M. Hearne, B. T. Aagaard, J. M. Rekoske, C. B. Worden, M. P. Moschetti, H. E. Hunsinger, G. C. Ferragut, G. A. Parker, J. A. Smith, *et al.* (2024). Automated, near real-time ground-motion processing at the U.S. Geological Survey, *Seismol. Res. Lett.,* doi: 10.1785/0220240021.

Tkalčić, H., B. Kennett, C. Sippl, C. Spaggiari, and K. Gessner (2013). *Albany-Fraser experiment* [Data set], *International Federation of Digital Seismograph Networks,* doi: 10.7914/SN/1K_2013.

University of Melbourne,Jones, A., D. Sandiford, and G. Gibson (2012). *University of Melbourne seismic network* [Data set], *International Federation of Digital Seismograph Networks,* doi: 10.7914/8csc-8z27.

Velasquez, S., D. Ninis, J. Wilcox, W. Peck, and J. La Greca (2024). The 2021 M_W 5.9 Woods Point earthquake and associated seismic sequence: Seismogenic fault zone identification from high-precision relocations of aftershocks, *Australian Earthquake Engineering Society 2024 Conference,* Adelaide, South Australia, 21–23 November 2024.

Wald, D. J., and T. I. Allen (2007). Topographic slope as a proxy for seismic site conditions and amplification, *Bull. Seismol. Soc. Am.* **97,** 1379–1395, doi: 10.1785/0120060267.

Wells, D. L., and K. J. Coppersmith (1994). New empirical relationships among magnitude, rupture length, rupture width, rupture area, and surface displacement, *Bull. Seismol. Soc. Am.* **84,** 974–1002, doi: 10.1785/BSSA0840040974.

Wilford, J. (2012). A weathering intensity index for the Australian continent using airborne gamma-ray spectrometry and digital terrain analysis, *Geoderma* **183–184,** 124-142, doi: 10.1016/j.geoderma.2010.12.022.

Wills, C. J., M. Petersen, W. A. Bryant, M. Reichle, G. J. Saucedo, S. Tan, G. Taylor, and J. Treiman (2000). A site-conditions map for California based on geology and shear-wave velocity, *Bull. Seismol. Soc. Am.* **90,** S187–S208, doi: 10.1785/0120000503.

Yang, H., Y. Li, L. Hu, W. Pan, and S. Ji (2024). New baseline correction method for near-fault ground-motion records based on continuous wavelet transform, *Seismol. Res. Lett.* **95,** 607–625, doi: 10.1785/0220230184.

Yong, A. (2016). Comparison of measured and proxy-based VS30 values in California, *Earthq. Spectra* **32,** 171–192, doi: 10.1193/013114eqs025m.

Yuan, H. (2017). *China-Western Australia seismic array* [Data set], *International Federation of Digital Seismograph Networks,* doi: 10.7914/SN/4N_2017.

Zhao, J., S. Zhou, J. Zhou, C. Zhao, H. Zhang, Y. Zhang, P. Gao, X. Lan, D. Rhoades, *et al.* (2016). Ground-motion prediction equations for shallow crustal and upper-mantle earthquakes in Japan using site class and simple geometric attenuation functions, *Bull. Seismol. Soc. Am.* **106,** doi: 10.1785/0120150063.

Manuscript received 16 September 2025
Published online 12 January 2026

Repeated Large-Magnitude Earthquakes in the Marianna Area of East-Central Arkansas During the Middle-Early Holocene and Possibly the Late Pleistocene

Martitia P. Tuttle*[1], Haydar Al-Shukri[2], Hanan Mahdi[2], Rauf Hussein[3], Taher Ameen[2], Steven L. Forman[4], Kathleen Dyer-Williams[5], Kathleen Tucker[6], Martha Kopper[7], Muntadher Al-Kaabi[2], and Okba R. Al-Qadhi[8]

Abstract

Very large, weathered sand blows and related sand dikes in the Marianna area indicate that large earthquakes were centered there in the past. Radiocarbon (^{14}C) and optically stimulated luminescence dating suggest that the liquefaction features formed during paleoearthquakes about 4.7, 5.4, 6.8, and 9.8 thousand years ago (ka) and possibly during two earlier events about < 19.5 and < 24.3 ka. Many sand blows occur along or near a northwest-oriented tonal lineament—known as the Daytona Beach lineament (DBL)—located southwest of Marianna. Supported by an independent seismic reflection study that identified a fault zone beneath the lineament, the DBL and spatially associated sand blows may be the surface expression of an active fault zone. Sand blows along the lineament at sites DB1, DBSE2, DBNW2, DBNW3, and DBNW5 are elongated in a northwest–southeast direction and have sand dikes with northwest trends. At sites DBSE2 and DBNW2, soft-sediment faults, also with northwest trends, crosscut sand dikes, displacing soil lamellae within the dikes. At one of the sites, small sand dikes were injected along the faults. Northeast of Marianna at site SF500, a compound sand blow composed of multiple depositional units formed about 6.8 ka. Located near the intersection of the White River fault zone and Eastern Reelfoot Rift Margin fault zone, the compound sand blow likely formed as the result of a sequence of large earthquakes, perhaps produced by these fault zones. Liquefaction potential analysis suggests that moment magnitude (M) 6.0–6.5 earthquakes generated by the fault zone beneath the DBL could have induced liquefaction in the Marianna area. However, larger Marianna earthquakes ranging up to M 7.5 would be required to induce liquefaction at distal sites near Blytheville and Marked Tree, Arkansas, and Tunica, Mississippi, where relatively small liquefaction features may have formed during the 4.7, 5.4, and 6.8 ka events.

Cite this article as Tuttle, M. P., H. Al-Shukri, H. Mahdi, R. Hussein, T. Ameen, S. L. Forman, K. Dyer-Williams, K. Tucker, M. Kopper, M. Al-Kaabi, and O. R. Al-Qadhi (2026). Repeated Large-Magnitude Earthquakes in the Marianna Area of East-Central Arkansas During the Middle-Early Holocene and Possibly the Late Pleistocene, *Seismol. Res. Lett.* **97**, 715–729, doi: 10.1785/0220250324.

Supplemental Material

Introduction

Twenty years ago, large weathered sand blows and related sand dikes were discovered in the Marianna area, located about 70 km southwest of Memphis, Tennessee, and 80 km south of the New Madrid seismic zone (NMSZ) (Figs. 1 and 2; Al-Shukri *et al.*, 2005). The discovery came as a surprise since no large historical earthquakes had been reported in the Marianna area, and only a few small earthquakes had been recorded there during the instrumental period, which effectively began in 1974. The sand blows were identified on satellite images and verified in the field. They were excavated and found to be deeply weathered, suggesting that they were thousands of years old. ^{14}C dating indicated that sand blows at the Nancy1 and Nancy2 sites formed about 4.7 and 5.4 ka, respectively (Fig. 2, Fig. S1 in the supplemental material available to this article, Table 1). Given that they were as large as,

1. M. Tuttle & Associates, Georgetown, Maine, U.S.A.; 2. School of Physical Sciences, Physics Program, University of Arkansas at Little Rock, Little Rock, Arkansas, U.S.A., https://orcid.org/0000-0001-9090-1029 (HA-S); https://orcid.org/0000-0002-2747-1465 (HM); https://orcid.org/0000-0002-8083-1191 (TA); https://orcid.org/0009-0000-2594-5260 (MA-K); 3. Parks and Recreation Department, City of Cape Coral, Cape Coral, Florida, U.S.A., https://orcid.org/0000-0002-3441-7600 (RH); 4. Department of Geosciences, Baylor University, Waco, Texas, U.S.A., https://orcid.org/0000-0002-2080-7915 (SLF); 5. VanLeen and Associates, Columbia, Maryland, U.S.A.; 6. PangaeaGIS, Memphis, Tennessee, U.S.A.; 7. Office of the State Geologist of Arkansas, North Little Rock, Arkansas, U.S.A.; 8. Columbus State Community College, Grove City, Ohio, U.S.A.

*Corresponding author: mptuttle@earthlink.net

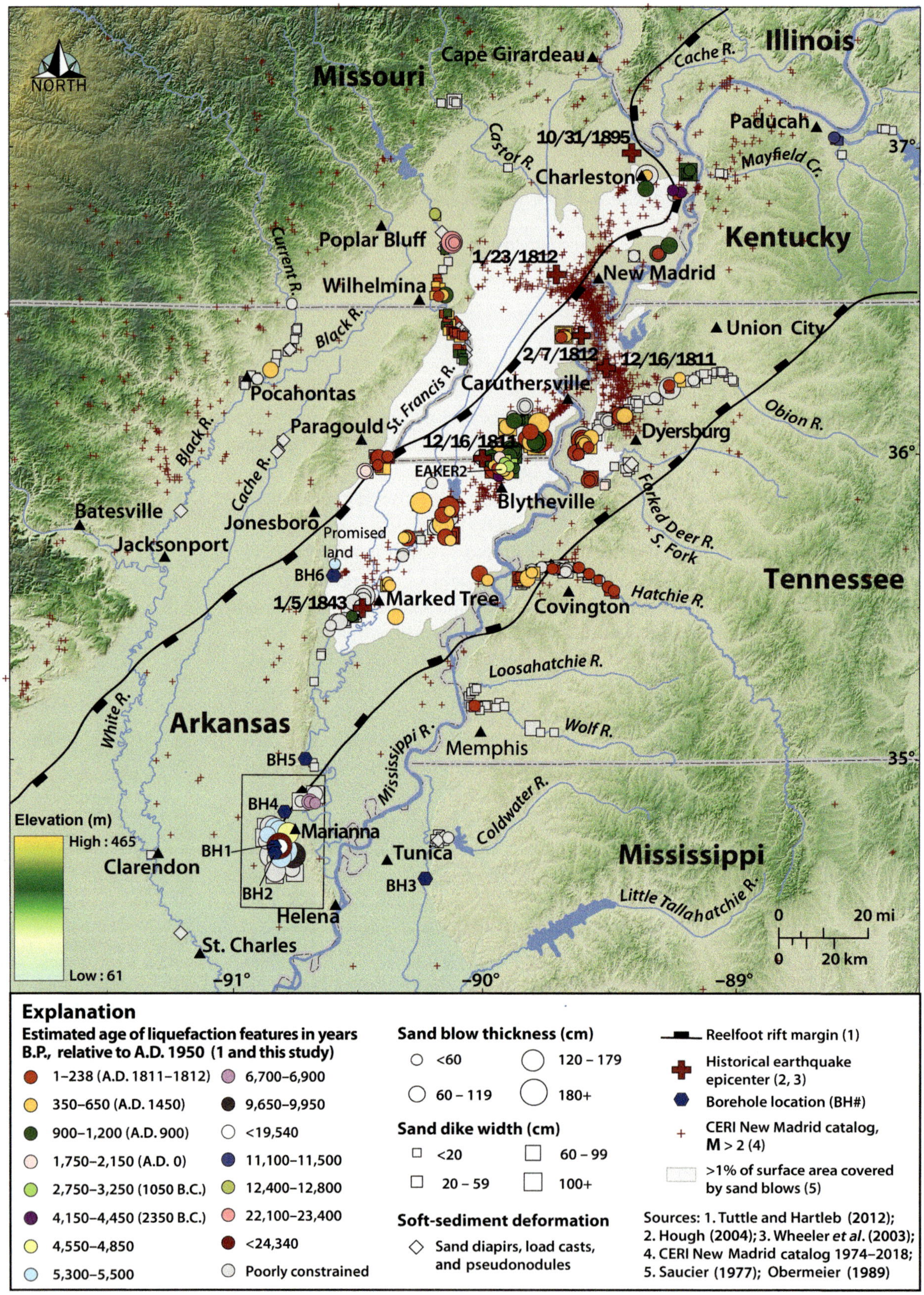

Figure 1. Shaded relief map of the Marianna area (outlined by a black rectangle) and the New Madrid seismic zone (NMSZ) (delineated by seismicity), showing locations, measured sizes, and estimated ages of earthquake-induced liquefaction features. The Marianna area is located near the southern end of the eastern Reelfoot Rift margin fault zone. Sources of information are listed in the Explanation.

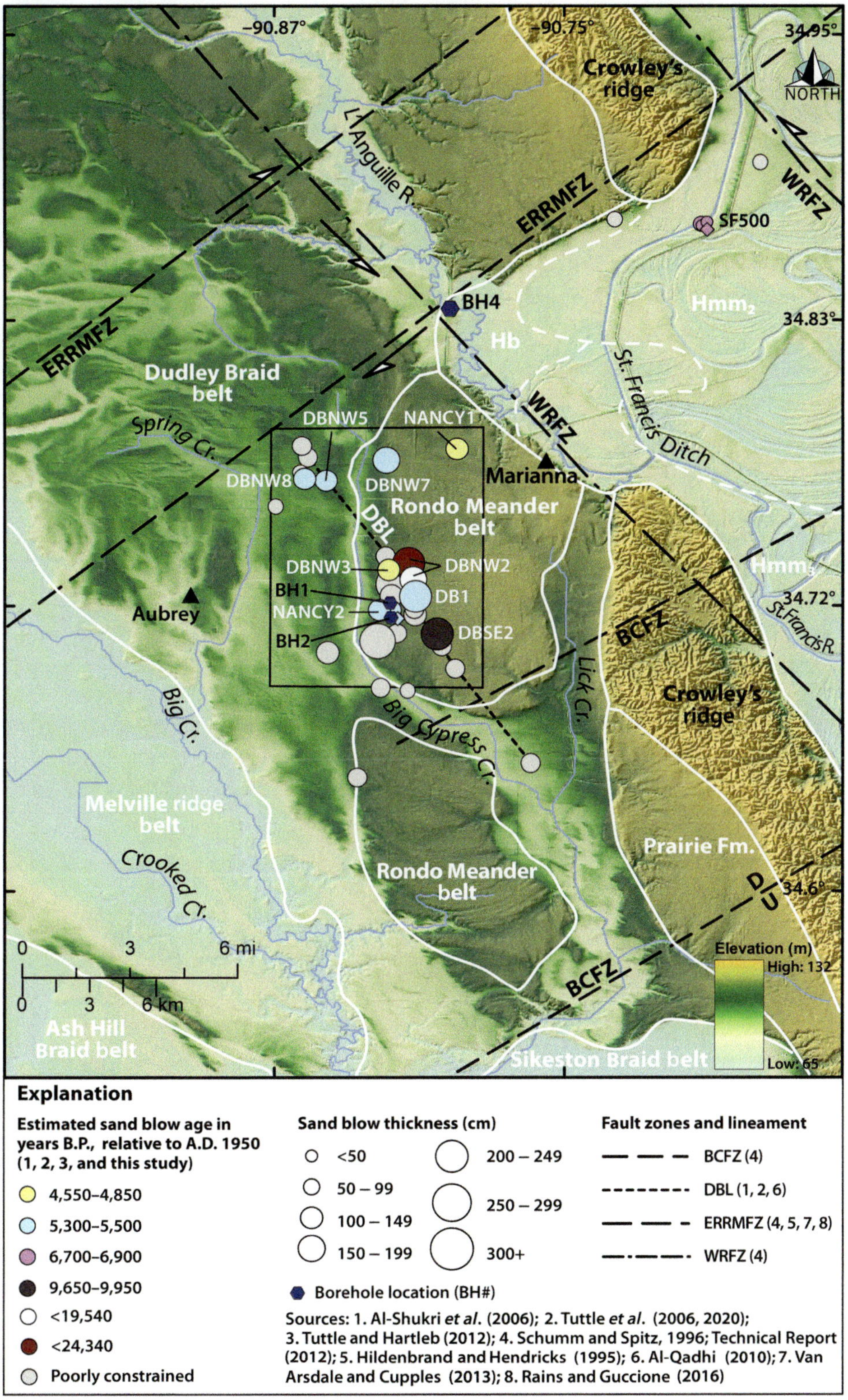

Figure 2. Shaded relief map of the Marianna area (delineated in Fig. 1 with a black rectangle), showing the DBL as well as locations, measured sizes, and estimated ages of sand blows investigated during this and previous studies. Morphostratigraphic units mapped by Rittenour *et al.* (2007) are outlined by white lines. Study sites along the DBL occur in the Pleistocene deposits of the Dudley Braid and Rondo Meander Belts, whereas SF500 occurs in Holocene deposits of the Mississippi River meander belt (Hmm). Borehole abbreviated as BH. Fault zones: BCFZ, Big Creek fault zone; DBL, Daytona Beach lineament; ERRMFZ, eastern Reelfoot rift margin fault zone; and WRFZ, White River fault zone. Sources of information are listed in the explanation.

yet older than, sand blows in the NMSZ, the Marianna sand blows likely formed as the result of large earthquakes centered in the Marianna area (Al-Shukri *et al.*, 2005). A subsequent investigation of a large sand blow at the Daytona Beach 1 (DB1) site corroborated an event about 5.4 ka (Table 1) (Tuttle *et al.*, 2006). The DB1 sand blow and other sand blows were found to occur along a northwest-oriented lineament, named the DBL, which is at least 12 km in length (Al-Qadhi, 2010; Fig. 2, Fig. S1). The DBL is relatively straight, subparallel to the nearby White River fault zone (WRFZ), and might be related to a family of northwest-oriented faults in the region.

To test the hypothesis that the DBL is related to faulting at depth, seismic-reflection data were collected along two transects that crossed the lineament in the vicinity of DB1, Nancy2, and DBSE2 (Odum *et al.*, 2016; see Fig. S1). The seismic-reflection profiles revealed a zone of near-vertical faults directly below the DBL in the 100–1100 m depth range, likely including Eocene through Paleozoic strata (Odum *et al.*, 2016). The seismic-reflection study also found that fault displacements increase with depth, suggesting long-term recurrent faulting. These findings support the interpretation that the DBL and the large sand blows along it are the surface expression of an active fault zone that has repeatedly produced large earthquakes during the Holocene (0–0.0117 million years ago, or Ma; Tuttle *et al.*, 2006, 2020; Al-Shukri *et al.*, 2009, 2015; Cohen *et al.*, 2022).

TABLE 1
Summary of Earthquake-Induced Liquefaction Features, Age Information, and Event Timing

Site Name	Sand Blow Thickness (cm)	Dike Width (cm)	Dike Strike/Dip	Weathering	Age Constraint Yr B.P. (1950)*	Event Timing (ka)
DB1[†]	245	122	N10°W/84° NE	Upper 75–150 cm iron-stained and bioturbated	≤5,440 ± 130	5.4
DBSE2	220	130	N20°W/80° NE, N23°W/78° NE	Iron-stained, redoximorphic features, Fe–Mn nodules, soil lamellae, and silt accumulation	≤9,795 ± 115	9.8
		~500	N35–50°W/73° NE			
		70	N23°W/50° NE			
DBNW2						
S trench	160	640	N43°W/86° NE	Similar but less iron-stained and fewer soil lamellae	≤19,540 ± 1,010	<19.5
N trench	240	450	N36°W/86° NE	Iron-stained, redoximorphic features, 1.5 m section of soil lamellae, silt accumulation	≤24,340 ± 1,790	<24.3
DBNW3						
N trench	75	17, 4	N55°W/86° NE, N41°W/87° NE	Iron-stained, few Fe–Mn nodules and soil lamellae	<4,689 ± 116	4.7
S trench	100	72–100	N39°W/71° NE	Similar	<4,710 ± 215	
DBNW5	140	270	N45°W/steep	Iron-stained, Fe–Mn nodules	≤5,402 ± 75	5.4
DBNW7	150	49	N5°E/79°–90° E	Iron-stained, redoximorphic features, Fe–Mn nodules	≤5,402 ± 75	5.4
DBNW8	105	50–54, 50 and 16	N36°E/37° SE, N21°E/42° SE, N48°E/66° SE	Iron-stained, redoximorphic features, few soil lamellae	≤5,402 ± 75	5.4
Nancy1[‡]	120	20 multiple	NW/90°	Iron-stained and redoximorphic features	<4,825 ± 25	4.7
Nancy2[‡]						
Trench 1	118	15	N25°E/10–15° NW	Iron-stained and redoximorphic features	<5,620 ± 40	5.4
Trench 2	130	20	N35°E/44° NW	Similar	≤5,460 ± 130	
SF500[†]	42, 5, 60, 18, 42	12, 5, 13, 8, 7, 6, 2, 16, 4, 4	Not measured; trending NW	Relatively unweathered due to burial by swamp deposits	≥6,805 ± 95, ~6,810 ± 400	6.8

N, north; NW, northwest; S, south.
*Calibrated ^{14}C ages and optically stimulated luminescence (OSL) ages in years B.P. or before A.D. 1950; < means after, ≤ means during or after, ≥ means during or before, ~ means approximately.
[†]From Tuttle *et al.* (2006).
[‡]From Al-Shukri *et al.* (2005).

About 18 km northeast of the DBL, a compound sand blow was found at site SF500 during reconnaissance along the St. Francis drainage ditch (Fig. 2; Tuttle *et al.*, 2006). The sand blow is composed of five depositional units and related sand dikes, similar to compound sand blows in the NMSZ that formed as a result of the 1811–1812 earthquake sequence. This suggests that the St. Francis features also formed as a result of a sequence of earthquakes. The lower four units are stratigraphically consistent with no intervening soil development or deposition, indicating that they formed over a short period of time, perhaps days to weeks. The uppermost unit is interbedded with the basal portion of the overlying backswamp sediment, indicating a dramatic change in environment from fluvial to backswamp deposition. Geochronology at the site suggests that the liquefaction features formed about 6.8 ka (Tuttle *et al.*, 2006). SF500 is located within the WRFZ and near its intersection with the ERRMFZ. These fault zones are possible sources of the sequence of earthquakes responsible for the formation of the compound sand blow and may have played a role in altering the environment of deposition in the area.

Based on the findings of our paleoliquefaction studies, the Marianna area was recognized as a significant earthquake source and included in the Central and Eastern U.S. Seismic Source Characterization project (CEUS SSCP; Technical Report, 2012) and the 2014 National Probabilistic Seismic Hazard Maps (Petersen *et al.*, 2014). The Marianna source was subsequently retained in the 2023 National Seismic Hazard Model (Thompson Jobe *et al.*, 2022). Paleoliquefaction studies have been ongoing in the Marianna area and include additional investigations of sand blows, dating of liquefaction features to further constrain event timing, and liquefaction potential analysis of scenario earthquakes to help interpret locations and magnitudes of past earthquakes. This article presents the results of these recent studies and updates the interpretation of the earthquake potential of the Marianna area. New information gained about the timing, magnitude, and recurrence of paleoearthquakes in the Marianna area and on the northwest-oriented fault zone beneath the DBL is likely to contribute to the regional assessment of earthquake hazards and the National Seismic Hazard Model. In addition, this article relays important lessons learned about dating old, weathered sand blows, which will contribute to future paleoliquefaction studies in the Marianna area and elsewhere.

Methodology

Site investigations

Numerous large sand blows occur in the Marianna area and appear on satellite images as elliptical, light-colored domains. Sites are identified that have the potential to broaden the spatial and temporal information about earthquake-induced liquefaction in the area. Study sites are visited and test pits excavated to confirm that the light-colored domains are composed of sandy soils, which differ from the surrounding dark-colored, silty soils developed in Late Pleistocene Peoria Loess deposits.

Most study sites in the Western Lowlands west of Marianna occur in the Rondo meander belt, except for study sites DBNW5 and DBNW 8, which are situated to the west in the Dudley braid belt (Fig. 2; Rittenour *et al.*, 2007). Both morphostratigraphic units are characterized by Peoria Loess, deposited about 12–25 ka (McKay, 1979; Ruhe, 1983), overlying fluvial deposits, including sand (Rittenour *et al.*, 2007). Rondo meander belt deposits have a thicker section of loess and finer fluvial section than Dudley braid belt deposits. The Dudley braid belt crosscuts the scroll-bar topography of the Rondo meander belt, suggesting it is younger. Optically stimulated luminescence (OSL) dating of samples collected within the Dudley and Rondo fluvial sections yielded ages of 46–69 ka and 76–90 ka, respectively (Rittenour *et al.*, 2007).

According to The Soil Survey of Lee County, Arkansas (Gray, 1977), the soils mapped on the Rondo and Dudley surfaces west of Marianna are predominantly loamy soils formed in thick loess deposits. The Loring–Memphis–Grenada and Calloway–Henry–Loring soil associations are mapped in the area of the study sites. All these soils are Alfisols, silty, and have profiles generally in the form of A/B/C or A/B horizons, indicating that they formed from one parent material. Also, Marvell and LaGrange soils have been mapped at or very close to the study sites. These soils are also Alfisols, but they are composed of fine sandy loam overlying silt loam and have profiles in the form of A/B/IIB horizons, indicating two different parent materials. We think it is likely that the sandy loam of Marvell and LaGrange soils formed in sand vented from below as a result of earthquake-induced liquefaction; whereas the silt loam below the sandy loam formed in loess deposits like other soils in the area.

If a site appears to be promising and is selected for further evaluation, a ground-penetrating radar (GPR) survey is conducted, usually with a 400 MHz antenna, to determine whether or not the sand deposit is underlain by a sand dike (Fig. 3; Al-Shukri *et al.*, 2006; Chlaib *et al.*, 2014). A sand dike, which marks the fissure through which water and entrained sand vented to the ground surface as a result of earthquake-induced liquefaction, must be present to interpret a sand deposit as a sand blow (Tuttle and Hartleb, 2012; Tuttle, Hartleb, *et al.*, 2019). GPR surveys are also used to determine the extent and dimensions of the sand blows and sand dikes, and to site trenches for further study of the liquefaction features and collection of samples for dating the features.

Trenches are sited so that they cross and expose both sand blows and related sand dikes. Trench walls are cleaned and logged at a scale of 1″ on log = 25 cm or 50 cm of trench wall, depending on the complexity of the liquefaction features (Fig. 4). Liquefaction features and their host sediment are described in terms of sedimentological and weathering characteristics. The size, orientation, vertical and horizontal displacements, and crosscutting relations of liquefaction features are documented. In addition, samples are collected to constrain the ages of the sand blows as narrowly as possible. Organic samples are collected for ^{14}C dating from soils buried by the sand blows and from remnants of soils below the modern plow zone, as well as tree root casts in the upper portions of the sand blows. Sediment samples for OSL dating are collected from sand blows, tops of buried soils, and subsoils.

Dating of sand blows and paleoearthquakes

Beta Analytic, Inc. dated organic samples using accelerator mass spectrometry (AMS). The AMS ages have errors of only ±30 yr and are calibrated using the probability density range method and the INTCAL20 database (Bronk Ramsey, 2009; Reimer *et al.*, 2020). Calibrated ^{14}C ages and calendar dates with error ranges of both 1 standard deviation (68.2% probability) and 2 standard deviations (95.4% probability) are provided in

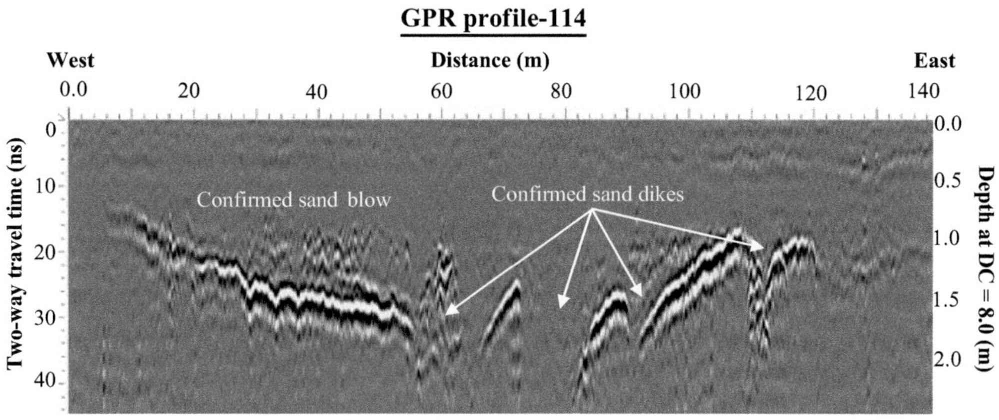

Figure 3. Example of a ground-penetrating radar (GPR) profile, GPR profile-114 from site DBSE2 (see Fig. S2 for location of profile), showing subsurface anomalies associated with a sand blow and related sand dikes (Al-Qadhi, 2010). The black and white bands represent the contact between the overlying sand blow and the underlying buried soil.

Table S1. Results of ^{14}C dating are also presented in the site investigation summaries and on the trench logs, as well as in the supplement.

U.S. Geological Survey (USGS) OSL laboratory in Denver dated sediment samples collected at sites DBSE2 in 2010 and DBNW2 in 2015; whereas Geoluminescence Dating Laboratory at Baylor University dated samples collected later at sites DBNW3, DBNW5, DBNW7, and DBNW8. Systematic and random errors are calculated at one standard deviation (Forman *et al.*, 2000;

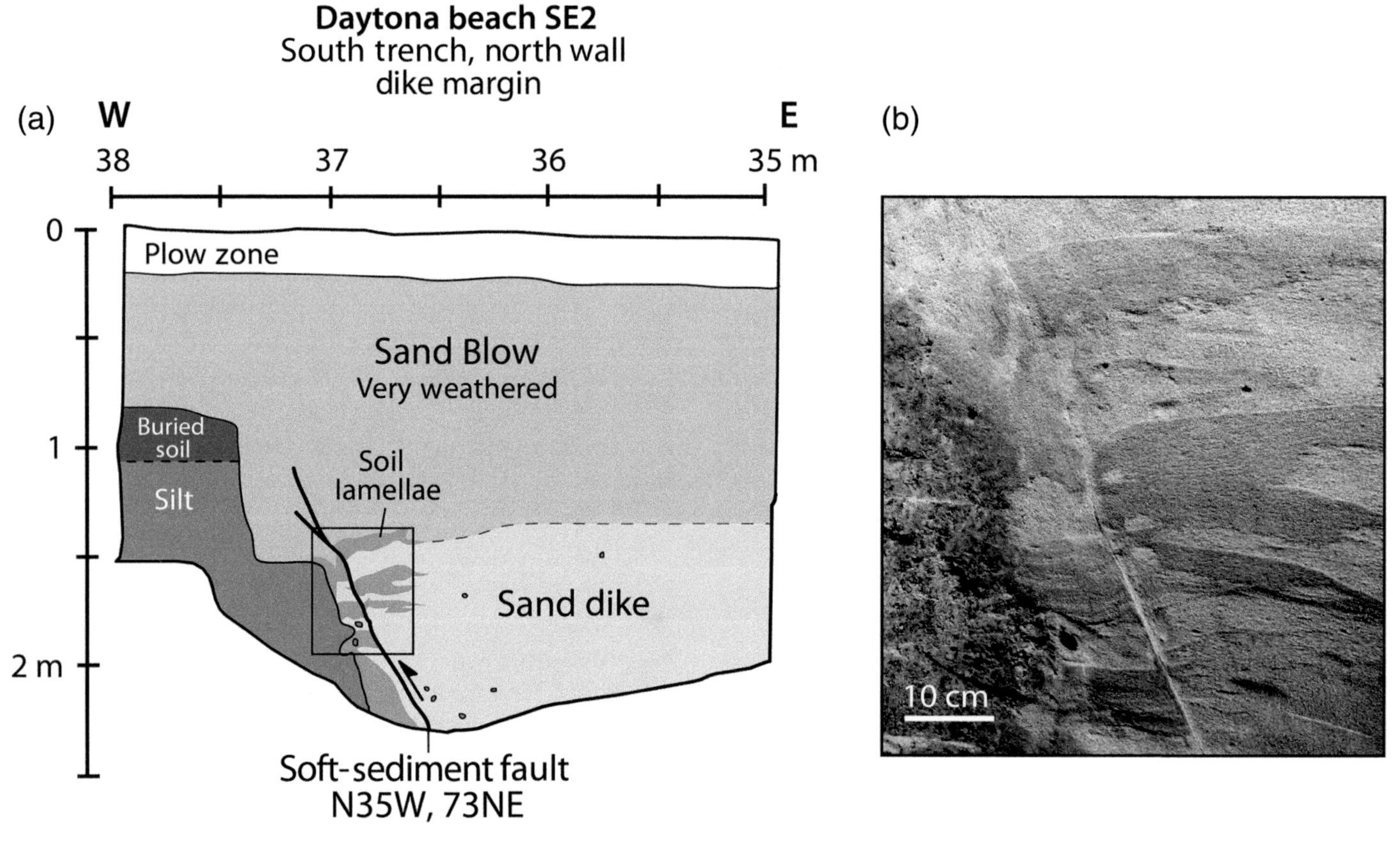

Figure 4. (a) Portion of trench log at site DBSE2 showing a weathered sand blow and the western margin of a sand dike below. Soil lamellae occur along the margin of the sand dike and appear to have been dragged along and offset by a soft-sediment fault (SSF). The fault has a strike and dip of N35°W, 73° NE, and parallels the DBL. (b) Photograph of the SSF along which soil lamellae are dragged and offset. The area of the photograph is outlined with a black rectangle on the adjacent log. Colored versions of the log and photograph are provided in Figure S5.

Liang and Forman, 2019). Results of OSL dating are presented in Tables S2–S5, the site investigation summaries, and trench logs in the supplemental material. Because of improvements in methodology (e.g., algorithms that optimize equivalent dose determinations and more robust statistical analyses to reduce errors) during the course of this study, OSL ages for samples collected at sites DBNW3 and DBNW5 were recalculated (Table S4). OSL ages reflect the statistical mean values with error ranges at 1 standard deviation.

To use both ^{14}C and OSL dating results to estimate the ages of liquefaction features and thus the timing of past earthquakes, ^{14}C ages with error ranges of 1 standard deviation are used in this analysis. Although both ^{14}C and OSL ages are considered in estimating the ages of the liquefaction features, ^{14}C ages are often given preference due to their stratigraphic positions and/or smaller error ranges. Age constraints and age estimates of sand blows, and thus the timing of events, are provided in Table 1 and in site investigation summaries in the supplemental material. ^{14}C and OSL ages are reported as before present (B.P.), meaning before A.D. 1950.

Evaluation of scenario earthquakes

Liquefaction potential analysis is performed for scenario earthquakes of various moment magnitudes (e.g., **M** 5.5, 6.0, 6.5, 7.0, and 7.5) to help assess the magnitudes of the Marianna paleoearthquakes that induced liquefaction in the Marianna area and at distal sites near Marked Tree and Blytheville, Arkansas, and Tunica, Mississippi (Figs. 1 and 2, Table 2). The distal sites of liquefaction were discovered during paleoliquefaction studies in the NMSZ and surrounding region (Tuttle, Wolf, *et al.*, 2019). They include small (10–25 cm thick) sand blows and related sand dikes at the Eaker 2 site north of Blytheville and at the Promised Land site northwest of Marked Tree that are similar in age (4.7 and 5.4 ka, respectively) to large sand blows in the Marianna area (Fig. 1). These liquefaction features are older and smaller than features attributed to New Madrid paleoearthquakes. In addition, three generations of small liquefaction features were found along the Coldwater River east of Tunica, Mississippi (Fig. 1). Two generations of the features overlap with the ages (4.7 and 6.8 ka) of large Marianna sand blows, and therefore, they may have formed as the result of Marianna paleoearthquakes (Tuttle, Wolf, *et al.*, 2019).

The cyclic stress method is used to assess liquefaction potential (e.g., Seed and Idriss, 1971; Juang and Jiang, 2000; Youd *et al.*, 2001; Cetin *et al.*, 2004; Robertson, 2010; Juang *et al.*, 2017), and regionally appropriate ground-motion prediction equations are used to calculate peak ground accelerations for scenario earthquakes (e.g., Atkinson and Boore, 2011; Atkinson and Assatourians, 2012). Geotechnical data used in the analysis were collected by the USGS, the Arkansas Department of Transportation, and the Mississippi Department of Transportation, and their borehole locations are shown in Figures 1 and 2. The geotechnical data were reviewed, and cohesionless sandy sediments between 5 and 20 m below the ground surface and with blow counts (a measure of soil density) of less than 30 were selected for analysis. The results of liquefaction potential analysis for scenario earthquakes are summarized in Table 2.

Results

Site investigations and dating of sand blows

Since 2006, paleoseismic investigations have been conducted at six sites of earthquake-induced liquefaction—DBSE2, DBNW2, DBNW3, DBNW5, DBNW7, and DBNW8—all along or close to the DBL and underlying fault zone (Fig. 2, Fig. S1). The investigations suggest that the fault zone produced large earthquakes about 4.7 ± 0.15 ka, 5.4 ± 0.1 ka, 9.8 ± 0.15 ka, <19.5 ka, and <24.3 ka (Table 1). DBSE2 and DBNW2 occur along the middle portion of the fault zone, and DBNW5, DBNW7, and DBNW8 are located toward the northern end of the fault zone. We have identified likely sand blows along the southern end of the fault zone, but have not been granted permission by property owners to excavate the sites. All the sand blows are very large, ranging from 36–100+m in width and from 60–300+m in length, with sand blows at DBSE2 and DBNW2 in the middle portion of the fault zone being especially large (Table 1).

Sand blows at all the study sites are obvious on satellite images and in the field. GPR surveys at the sites, image large sand blows, and sand dikes delineated by strong reflectors related to contacts between the liquefaction features and the silty soil (see Fig. 3). Trenches were excavated roughly perpendicular to the sand dikes as imaged by the GPR surveys. The trenches reveal sand blows ranging from 1 to 2.4 m thick and sand dikes ranging from 4 cm to 6.4 m wide. All the sand blows are weathered, some more than others (Table 1). Indicators of weathering include redoximorphic features (aka mottles) and related Fe–Mn nodules that form as a result of water-table fluctuations, rubification, or redding of the sand blows due to the release of iron and the formation of iron oxides that coat the sand grains, and soil lamellae, which result from the translocation and accumulation of silt usually along textural boundaries. Soils that would have developed in the sand blows over time are disturbed by plowing, and in some cases, removed by grading, which limits our ability to collect samples that would provide close minimum constraining ages for the sand blows. However, the sand blows bury soils that were at the ground surface at the time of the events; so, dating organic material such as twigs and leaves and residual carbon in the buried soils provides close and fairly close maximum constraining ages for the sand blows. The characteristics and age estimates of sand blows at the six sites are summarized below and in Table 1. More information about the site investigations, including satellite images, geophysical profiles, trench logs, and results of ^{14}C and OSL dating of samples collected at the sites, is provided in the supplemental material.

TABLE 2
Results of Evaluations of Marianna Scenario Earthquakes

Sites*	Map ID	Source-to-Site Distance (km)	Results†
1. Scenario earthquake M 5.5			
Borehole 1	BH1	5	N
Borehole 1	BH1	10	N
Borehole 2	BH2	5	N
Borehole 2	BH2	10	N
L'Anguille River	BH4	13	N
St. Francis River	BH5	37	N
2. Scenario earthquake M 6.0			
Borehole 1	BH1	5	L
Borehole 1	BH1	10	N
Borehole 2	BH2	5	L
Borehole 2	BH2	10	N
L'Anguille River	BH4	13	L
St. Francis River	BH5	37	N
3. Scenario earthquake M 6.5			
Borehole 1	BH1	5	L
Borehole 1	BH1	10	L
Borehole 2	BH2	5	L
Borehole 2	BH2	10	L
L'Anguille River	BH4	13	L
St. Francis River	BH5	37	L
Coldwater River (E. Tunica)	BH3	55	N
Ditch 10 (Promised Land)	BH6	105	N
4. Scenario earthquake M 7.0			
Coldwater River (E. Tunica)	BH3	55	L/N
Ditch 10 (Promised Land)	BH6	105	N
5. Scenario earthquake M 7.5			
Coldwater River (E. Tunica)	BH3	55	L
Ditch 10 (Promised Land)	BH6	105	L

*Liquefaction was observed in the vicinity of these sites.
†L indicates liquefaction likely for 45%–100% of the layers analyzed; L/N indicates marginal because liquefaction is predicted for 24%–44% of the layers analyzed; N indicates liquefaction not likely because liquefaction is predicted for less than 24% of the layers analyzed.

At site DBSE2, the sand blow is about 60 m wide, 140 m long, and 2.2 m thick and connected to at least seven sand dikes ranging in width from 7 cm to possibly as wide as 5 m (Fig. 3, Figs. S2–S4, Table 1). Weathering is especially pronounced in the upper 1 m of the sand blow, though the entire thickness of the sand blow is iron-stained and exhibits redoximorphic features with Fe–Mn nodules (Fig. 4, Fig. S5). Soil lamellae occur along the margins of sand dikes. In addition, fines have accumulated in the lower part of the sand blow above the buried soil and in several of the dikes. A soft-sediment fault (SSF) occurs adjacent to the western margin of a large sand dike and is subparallel to the DBL (Fig. 4, Figs. S4 and S5). Soil lamellae appear to have been dragged along and offset across the fault. Apparent vertical offset of soil lamellae and mismatch of lamellae thickness across the fault suggest reverse and strike-slip components of displacement. ^{14}C dating of charred material, C1, collected from the top of the soil buried by the large sand blow, yielded an age of 9680–9910 yr B.P. (Fig. S4, Tables S1). This represents a close maximum constraining age for the sand blow, indicating that it formed about 9.8 ka. Dating of sediment sample, OSL1, also collected from the buried soil and about 5 cm of the base of the sand blow, yielded an age of 11,940 ± 1,000 yr B.P., consistent with the slightly younger ^{14}C age for charred material collected higher in the buried soil (Fig. S4, Table S2).

At site DBNW2, the sand blow is exceptionally large, exceeding 100 m in width and 300 m in length (Fig. S6). Upon closer inspection, the sand blow is composed of two large sand blows of different ages that formed adjacent to each other along the DBL and underlying fault zone. The sand blow exposed in the south trench is 1.6 m thick and connected to a 6.4-m-wide dike (Figs. S7 and S8, Table 1). The sand blow is very weathered, especially the upper 0.5 m, and exhibits redoximorphic features and manganese staining. Silt has accumulated, and soil lamellae have formed along the eastern margin of the dike. The buried soil below the large sand blow is displaced downward about 1.5 m on the west side of the dike. Dating of sediment samples, OSL1 and OSL2, collected from the buried soil yielded ages of 15,040 ± 4,540 yr B.P. and 19,540 ± 1,010 yr B.P., respectively (Fig. S8, Table S3). The samples were collected from the same context, and their ages overlap at one sigma. However, the age of 19.54 ka for OSL2 has a smaller one sigma error (5%) than does the age of 15.04 ka for OSL1 (30%). Therefore, the age of 19.54 ka has greater significance and is preferred. The overdispersion value, or scatter of the equivalent dose value, is high (33%) for sample OSL2, suggesting that it may not have been completely reset before burial by the sand blow or may include older sediment mixed in from above or below. Therefore, the OSL age is interpreted as a maximum constraining age and suggests that the liquefaction event is younger than about 19.5 ka.

The sand blow exposed in the north trench at DBNW2 is 2.4 m thick and connected to a 4.5-m-wide dike (Fig. S9). The sand blow is extremely weathered, especially the upper 1 m, and exhibits redoximorphic features and iron staining. Silt has accumulated along the base of the sand blow above the buried soil, and a 1.5 m thick sequence of soil lamellae occurs along the eastern margin of the large dike. The buried soil below the sand blow is displaced downward about 1.2 m again on the west side of the dike. Two SSFs, adjacent and subparallel to the eastern margin of the sand dike, appear to offset the sequence of soil lamellae. Several domains of relatively unweathered, loose sand appear to have been injected along the faults. These observations suggest that a second event, including faulting and earthquake-induced liquefaction, occurred thousands of years after the first event responsible for the formation of the large sand blow and dike. The second event may be the same event responsible for the formation of the sand blow in the south trench. Dating of sediment samples, OSL1 and OSL2, collected from the soil buried by the sand blow returned ages of 32,440 ± 1,880 yr B.P. and 24,340 ± 1,790 yr B.P., respectively (Fig. S9, Table S3). Even though the samples were collected from the same context, the OSL ages differ by at least 4430 yr. Overdispersion values are modest (29%) for OSL1 and high (41%) for OSL2. The age for OSL1 may reflect the age of the parent material of the soil, whereas OSL2 may have been mixed sediment or poorly bleached. These ages are not well constrained but represent maximum limiting ages and suggest that the liquefaction event is younger than about 24.3 ka.

At site DBNW3, the sand blow, 52 m wide, 85 m long, and 1 m thick, is connected to at least two sand dikes (Figs. S10 and S11). The sand blow and the main sand dike are exposed in two trenches. The main dike is 17 cm wide in the north trench and up to 1 m wide in the south trench (Figs. S12 and S13). In both trenches, the soil buried by the sand blow is displaced downward on the east side of the dike by 10 cm in the north trench and by 40 cm in the south trench. Weathering is similar in both trenches, with iron staining in the upper 55–90 cm of the sand blow and the upper 15–25 cm of the main sand dike. A few Fe–Mn nodules and soil lamellae have formed in the upper 50 cm of sand blow. In the north trench, ^{14}C dating of charred material, C1, from the buried soil about 13 cm below the sand blow yielded an age of 4573–4805 yr B.P. (Fig. S12, Table S1). This represents a fairly close maximum constraining age of 4.7 ka for the sand blow. Dating of a sediment sample, OSL1, collected from the buried soil 3–5 cm below the sand blow yielded an age of 4710 ± 215 yr B.P. (Fig. S12, Table S4). This age is consistent with the ^{14}C age and supports the age estimate of 4.7 ka for the sand blow. Another sediment sample, OSL3, collected from the subsoil 33–38 cm below the sand blow yielded an OSL age of 13,310 ± 540 yr B.P., probably reflecting the age of the parent material. In the southern trench, a sediment sample, OSL1, collected from the subsoil 32–37 cm below the sand blow yielded an age of 12,500 ± 405 yr B.P., very similar to the age of the sediment sample collected from a similar context in the northern trench (Fig. S13, Table S4). All the sediment samples dated at this site have low overdispersion values (9%, 13%, and 9%), suggesting the sediment was not mixed and lending confidence in the age estimates.

At site DBNW5, the sand blow, 36 m wide, 64 m long, and 1.4 m thick, is connected to a large sand dike about 2.7 m wide (Figs. S14–S16). The sand blow and sand dike were exposed in two trenches, but torrential rain at the time of field work flooded the two trenches and caused them to collapse. The south trench was re-excavated to log the trench wall and to collect samples for dating. In the south trench, large clasts of clayey silt from the subsoil occur in the upper portion of the large sand dike, and the soil buried by the sand blow is displaced downward on the northeast side of the dike by about 1.1 m. Weathering in the sand blow includes iron staining and formation of small to medium Fe–Mn nodules in its upper 40 cm and large nodules above its basal contact with the buried soil. The formation of many small-to-large Fe–Mn nodules is probably related to water-table fluctuations at this relatively wet site. ^{14}C dating of organic-rich sediment samples, SL1 and SL2, from the top of the buried soil on both sides of the large dike provides fairly close maximum constraining ages of 5474–5577 yr B.P. and 5327–5476 yr B.P., respectively (Table S1). Giving preference to the younger ^{14}C age, the sand blow formed about 5.4 ka. Dating of a sediment sample, OSL3, collected from the top of the buried soil on the east side of the dike provides a close maximum constraining age of 5110 ± 120 yr B.P. (Table S5) and is in fairly close agreement with the ^{14}C ages of the organic samples collected in a similar context. A sediment sample, OSL4, collected 16 cm below the top of the buried soil, provides a maximum constraining age of 7475 ± 235 yr B.P. (Table S5). Sediment samples, OSL1 and OSL2, collected from the buried soil higher in the section on the west side of the dike have higher overdispersion values, suggesting that they are more likely to be mixed (Tables S4). Giving preference to the younger of the two ^{14}C ages, the sand blow at this site is estimated to have formed about 5.4 ka.

At site DBNW7, located ~2.4 km east of the DBL, the sand blow is about 45 m wide, 60 m long, and 1.5 m thick and connected to a 49 cm wide sand dike (Figs. S17–S19). A vent structure occurs above the sand dike and is filled with silty, very fine sand, which is finer grained than much of the sand blow and represents the final phase of venting. The sand blow is very weathered with redoximorphic features throughout and several areas of intense iron staining with small Fe–Mn nodules. The soil buried by the sand blow is displaced downward about 0.5 m on the east side of the dike. ^{14}C dating of charred material, C2, collected near the tip of a root cast that extended through the sand blow and into the buried soil below, provides a minimum constraining age for the sand blow of 1179 yr B.P. (Fig. S19, Table S1). Unfortunately, the upper 10 cm of the buried soil was very bioturbated, especially on the west side of the dike, making it difficult to sample an undisturbed portion of the buried soil for dating. Sediment sample, OSL2, collected from the upper 5 cm of the buried soil yielded an age of 41,445 ± 2,060 yr B.P. (Fig. S19,

TABLE 3
Magnitude Estimates for Marianna Paleoearthquakes

Earthquake	DBL*	St. Francis	Coldwater	Ditch 10	Blytheville†
4.7 ka	**M** 6.0–6.5		**M** 7.0–7.5		**M** ≥ 7.2
5.4 ka	**M** 6.0–6.5			**M** 7.5	
6.8 ka		**M** 6.0–6.5	**M** 7.0–7.5		
9.8 ka	**M** 6.0–6.5				
<19.5 ka	**M** 6.0–6.5				
<24.3 ka	**M** 6.0–6.5				

*These magnitude estimates are considered minimum values for earthquakes that could induce liquefaction along the Daytona Beach lineament (DBL). For each of the 9.8, <19.5, and <24.3 ka events, only one liquefaction site so far has been studied along the DBL; these magnitude estimates are also considered minimum values for these three events.
†From Tuttle *et al.* (2019b, 2020).

Table S5). Its overdispersion value (24% ± 3%) is modest, suggesting that the OSL age may reflect the age of the parent material of the soil, rather than the time of burial of the surface by this sand blow. Sediment sample, OSL3, collected 15 cm below the top of the buried soil, in which bioturbation was less severe, yielded an age of 7200 ± 180 yr B.P. Its uncertainty range was relatively small, and the overdispersion value was low (5% ± 1%), lending confidence in the age. The age of this sample is similar to that (7475 ± 235 yr B.P.) of the sample, OSL4, collected 16 cm below the top of the buried soil at site DBNW5 (Fig. S16). This suggests that the sand blow and dike at DBNW7 may have formed at the same time as the liquefaction features at DBNW5 or about 5.4 ka. Sediment samples, OSL1 and OSL4, were collected from the upper portion of the DBNW7 sand blow and yielded ages of 16,285 ± 1,395 yr B.P. and 17,205 ± 1,350 yr B.P., respectively (Fig. S19, Table S5). One of the samples, OSL4, had a low overdispersion value (4% ± 1%). Assuming the sand blow formed about 5.4 ka, the sediment of the upper part of the sand blow is much older. This suggests that luminescence of the sand was not reset during venting, and the sand blow reflects the age of the source layer. This could be due to the rapid deposition of the sand blow.

At site DBNW8, located ~0.5 km west of the DBL, the sand blow is about 65 m wide, 75 m long, and 1.05 m thick (Figs. S20–S22). The sand blow is connected to two sand dikes. The western dike is 54 cm wide, and the eastern compound dike is composed of two phases, 50 and 16 cm wide. Vent structures above the sand dikes are filled with very fine sandy silt, finer grained than much of the sand blow. Similar to DBNW7, the sand blow is very weathered with redoximorphic features common and several areas of intense iron staining. In addition, a few soil lamellae have developed in the sand blow. The soil buried by the sand blow is displaced downward about 0.3 m on the west side of the eastern dike. Dating of a sediment sample, OSL5, collected about 8 cm below the top of the buried soil, yielded an age of 6335 ± 150 yr B.P., which represents a maximum constraining age for the sand blow and related sand dikes (Fig. S22, Table S5). There is confidence in the age estimate of this sample, given its small uncertainty and low overdispersion value of 4% ± 1%. At nearby site DBNW5, sediment samples, OSL3 and OSL4, collected at the top of the buried soil and 16 cm below the sand blow yielded OSL ages of 5110 ± 120 yr B.P. and 7475 ± 235 yr B.P, respectively (Fig. S16). At site DBNW8, the sediment sample, OSL5, which yielded an age of 6335 ± 150 yr B.P. was collected 8 cm below the top of the buried soil, or at a depth halfway between the two samples at DBNW5. Therefore, it seems likely that the sand blow at DBNW8 formed during the same event or about 5.4 ka. Like the samples collected from the sand blow at DBNW7, sediment samples, OSL1 and OSL4, collected from the upper part of the sand blow at DBNW8 yielded ages much older (18,375 ± 495 yr B.P. and 18,605 ± 1,345 yr B.P., respectively) than the soil buried by the sand blow (Fig. S22, Table S5). Also these samples have high dispersion values of 40 ± 8 and 36 ± 6, respectively. Therefore, the sand that vented to the ground surface as a result of liquefaction may not have been solar reset, especially if deposited rapidly.

Liquefaction potential analysis

Considering Marianna scenario earthquakes, an **M** 5.5 earthquake located 5 km below liquefaction site DB1 is not likely to induce liquefaction even at the local geotechnical sites, boreholes 1 and 2 (Figs. 1 and 2, BH1 and BH2; Table 2); whereas an **M** 6.0 earthquake located at 5 km depth, is likely to induce liquefaction at BH1 and BH2 and at the L'Anguille River site, borehole 4 (BH4). An **M** 6.5 earthquake located at 10 km depth is likely to induce liquefaction at those same three sites and at the St. Francis River site, borehole 5 (BH5). An **M** 7.0 earthquake is likely to induce marginal liquefaction at the Coldwater River site east of Tunica, MS, borehole 3 (BH3), but not at the Ditch 10 site near Promised Land, AR, borehole 6 (BH6); whereas an **M** 7.5 earthquake is likely to induce liquefaction at both the Coldwater River and Ditch 10 sites (Table 2).

As discussed earlier, a Marianna paleoearthquake about 4.7 ka produced very large sand blows along the DBL, possibly sand dikes along the Coldwater River east of Tunica, and a small sand blow at Eaker 2 north of Blytheville (Fig. 1; Tuttle, Wolf, *et al.*, 2019; Tuttle, Al-Shukri, and Mahdi, 2020). If so, the 4.7 ka event may have been of **M** 7.0–7.5 according to liquefaction analysis (Table 3). A Marianna paleoearthquake about 5.4 ka produced very large sand blows along the DBL and possibly a small sand blow and related dikes at Promised Land northwest of Marked Tree, Arkansas. If so, this event may have been of **M** 7.5 according to the analysis. In addition, a Marianna paleoearthquake sequence about 6.8 ka produced a compound sand blow along the St. Francis Ditch north of Marianna and possibly a small sand blow and sand dikes along the Coldwater River in Mississippi. If so, the 6.8 ka event may have been of **M** 7.0–7.5 (Table 3). So far, liquefaction features produced by earlier events about 9.8 ka, <19.5 ka, and <24.3 ka have only been documented along the DBL. Therefore, initial magnitude estimates for these events are **M** 6.0–6.5. However, these magnitudes are considered minimum values because the sand blows are very large and likely also formed during very large earthquakes, **M** ≥ 7.

Discussion

Paleoliquefaction investigations

Previously, earthquakes about 4.7 and 5.5 ka were interpreted from large, weathered sand blows and related sand dikes at sites Nancy1, Nancy2, and DB1 west and southwest of the town of Marianna (Fig. 2). These sand blows and other large sand blows occur along a northwest-oriented tonal lineament interpreted as the surface expression of an active fault zone—here named the Daytona Beach fault zone (DBFZ)—and the likely source of the earthquakes responsible for many of the liquefaction features in the area (Al-Shukri *et al.*, 2005, 2006; Tuttle *et al.*, 2006). This interpretation was supported by the results of a subsequent seismic reflection study that identified a fault zone beneath the lineament (Odum *et al.*, 2016). An earthquake sequence about 6.8 ka was interpreted from a compound sand blow at site SF500 northeast of the town of Marianna. This liquefaction site occurs near the intersection of the EMRRFZ and WRFZ, which might have been the sources of the earthquakes.

The more recent investigation at site DBSE2 of a very large sand blow resulted in the identification of an additional paleoearthquakes about 9.8 ka (Table 1). The age estimate for this event is robust, given that it is based on both ^{14}C and OSL ages that are in close agreement. The investigation at site DBNW2 of two very large sand blows with different degrees of weathering, including soil rubification and formation of soil lamellae, suggests two earlier events about <19.5 and <24.3 ka, though their age estimates are not well constrained. The investigation at site DBNW3 corroborated the earlier finding of a paleoearthquake about 4.7 ka. The investigations at DBNW5, DBNW7, and DBNW8 led to a slight revision in the age estimate of the 5.5 ka event to 5.4 ka and a reduction in the uncertainty, or error range, of the event timing (Table 1). The two closely timed events, about 4.7 and 5.4 ka, are distinct. The age estimates for these events do not overlap at the two-sigma error range. In addition, the age estimates for both events are robust, given the close agreement of ^{14}C and OSL ages at sites DBNW3 and DBNW5.

Sites DBSE2, DBNW2, DBNW3, DBNW5, DBNW7, and DBNW8 all occur along the DBL (Fig. 2, Fig. S1). Many of the large sand dikes at these sites strike northwest-southeast, subparallel to the lineament. The DBL cuts across the topography, the Rondo and Dudley morphostratigraphic units, and Big Cypress Creek, and is subparallel to a major fault zone in the area, the WRFZ. As imaged in two seismic reflection lines, an active fault zone, the DBFZ, occurs directly below the DBL (Odum *et al.*, 2016). These relationships support the interpretation that the DBL and the large sand blows along the lineament are the surface expression of faulting of the DBFZ.

At DBSE2 and DBNW2, SSFs with northwest–southeast strikes crosscut large sand dikes and soil lamellae that developed in the dikes (Table 1). SSFs within liquefaction features would normally be attributed to ground failure related to liquefaction during or soon after the event. However, the faults at DBSE2 and DBNW2 clearly formed well after emplacement of the large dikes and sand blows. At DBNW2, a younger generation of sand dikes appears to have been injected along some of the faults during a subsequent event. Though liquefaction-related ground failure cannot be ruled out, an alternative interpretation is that the SSFs at DBSE2 and DBNW2 are fault tips that ruptured the surface, or close to it, during the subsequent events. This seems like a distinct possibility given the occurrence of the two sites along the DBL, the orientation of the SSFs subparallel to the lineament, and the presence of an active fault zone below the DBL (Fig. S1). The SSFs cannot be traced into the overlying sand blows, but this is not surprising given the degree of soil development in these features.

The alternative interpretation of the origin of the SSFs raises the question: could the large sand dikes in which the SSFs occur mark faults that ruptured to the surface during earlier events and were injected by a large volume of water and sand resulting from liquefaction, forming large sand dikes and sand blows that now mask the faults? This question could be tested by conducting additional geophysical surveys to better image the DBFZ in Quaternary deposits. If sites could be identified where the upward termination of faults was not masked by overlying sand blow deposits, the sites could be trenched to directly study the DBFZ and independently evaluate event timing.

On the basis of our current knowledge, the DBFZ repeatedly produced large earthquakes between 4.7 and 9.8 ka, during the Middle and Early Holocene, with recurrence times ranging from 700 to 4400 yr. The fault zone also may have produced two large earthquakes during the last 13,000 yr of the Late Pleistocene (0.0117–0.129 Ma; Cohen *et al.*, 2022). In addition, the EMRRFZ and WRFZ may have produced a sequence of earthquakes about 6.8 ka during the Middle Holocene. Therefore, the Marianna area, or Marianna seismic zone (MSZ), was active for 4000 yr, and possibly 20,000 yr, before entering an apparently

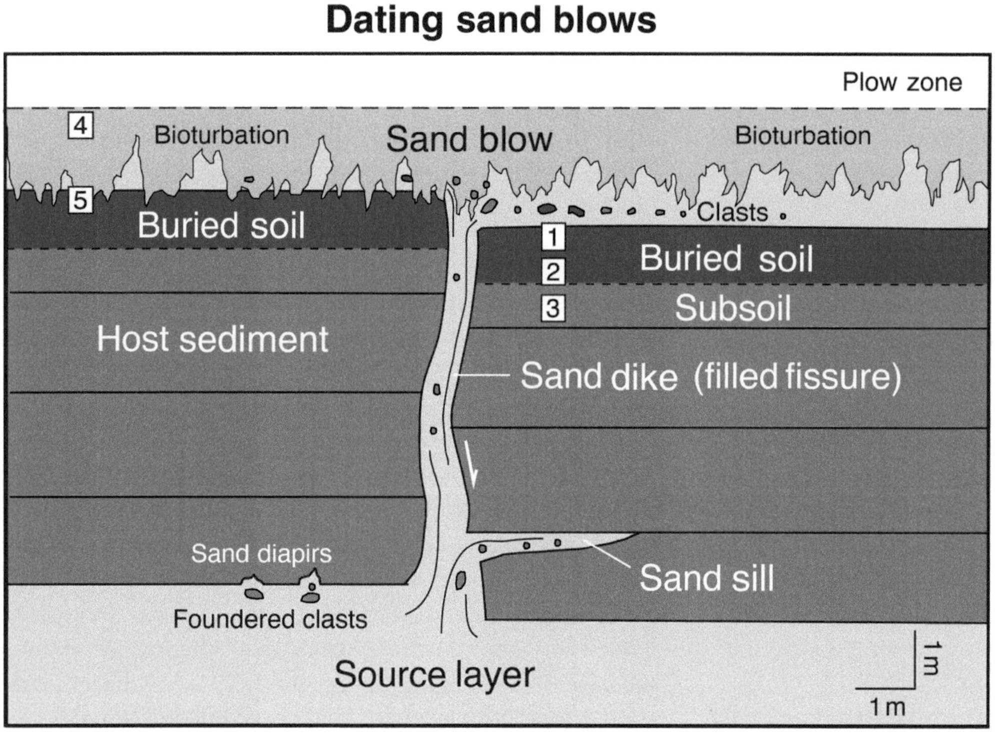

Sample	Description	Age constraint
1	Top of deeply buried soil and below zone of bioturbation: best place to collect 14C and OSL samples; 14C sample likely to be preserved; OSL sample likely to be exposed to sunlight prior to burial and less likely to be reworked	Close maximum
2	Within deeply buried soil and below zone of bioturbation: good place to collect 14C and OSL samples for same reasons given above, but would pre-date liquefaction	Maximum
3	From subsoil: 14C and OSL samples help to establish history of deposition of host sediment; also, provide maximum age constraint of liquefaction if no good samples collected from buried soil	Maximum
4	From sand blow: 14C sample of tree roots grown into sand blow would post-date liquefaction; OSL sample not likely to be exposed to sufficient sunlight to reset luminesence; also, sediment bioturbated	Minimum Maximum; age of source layer
5	Top of less deeply buried soil and within zone of bioturbation: 14C sample less likely to be preserved; OSL sample likely to be reworked	Maximum

Figure 5. Diagram illustrating positions of samples for dating sand blows, descriptions of the effects of depth and bioturbation on the samples, and age constraint provided by the samples.

quiescent period about 4.5 ka. This timing coincides with the beginning of the active period in the NMSZ, suggesting that seismicity shifted from the MSZ to the NMSZ about 4.5 ka. If not, the MSZ may be overdue for a large earthquake.

The chronology of paleoearthquakes in the MSZ is likely to be complete for the Holocene, but incomplete for the Late Pleistocene. There are many more sand blows in the area that could be studied to better understand the Late Pleistocene earthquake history of the MSZ. However, identifying Late Pleistocene sand blows before trenching is challenging. Weathering characteristics of sand blows are useful indicators of age. We have found that the older sand blows and related dikes have deep weathering profiles, including development of rubification and soil lamellae, and accumulation of fines, especially above buried soils. Remote sensing may help differentiate sand blows by their degree of weathering. Currently, various remote sensing techniques are being tested in the MSZ.

A better understanding of the paleoearthquake history of the MSZ would improve our understanding of the recurrence times of large-magnitude earthquakes and the long-term behavior of the Marianna sources. In addition, the Marianna paleoearthquake history, combined with that of other areas, such as the NMSZ, would provide insights regarding the spatial and temporal migration of seismicity across the region. The NMSZ and the MSZ, both sources of repeated large-magnitude earthquakes, are characterized by the northeast-oriented Reelfoot Rift and northwest-oriented Proterozoic fault systems of which the WRFZ is a member, suggesting the two regions are structurally related. If so, their histories of stress buildup and release may be interrelated. Additional paleoliquefaction studies could provide longer-term earthquake chronologies that would test this relationship and improve seismic hazard assessments for the region.

Lessons learned about dating old sand blows

Important lessons have been learned about dating large, weathered sand blows. ^{14}C dating of plant material in the upper few centimeters of soil buried by a sand blow usually provides the best opportunity for establishing a close maximum constraining age for the sand blow, and thus, the causative earthquake (Fig. 5). However, plant material more than 5–10 ka is rarely preserved in buried soils in the Marianna area, especially in buried soils within 0.5–1.0 m of the ground surface. If no plant material can be found, thin (~0.25 cm) slices of the surface of the buried soil can be collected to date residual carbon in the soil. Residual carbon would have accumulated over a period of time, perhaps 10s–100s of years. Therefore, a soil sample can provide a fairly close maximum constraining age for a sand blow, but probably not as close an age as plant material buried immediately below the sand blow.

OSL dating of a buried soil can also provide fairly close maximum constraining ages for sand blows (Fig. 5). For OSL dating to provide a meaningful age estimate of the time of burial by the sand blow, however, the luminescence in the quartz grains has to be completely reset by exposure to the sun, like in buried A horizons. A potential problem is post-event bioturbation of the buried soil by roots, which can mix the soil both with vented sand above and subsoil below, and the OSL age would not reflect the time of burial. For the Marianna sand blows, bioturbation by roots often extends to 1.0–1.5 m below the ground surface. Therefore, samples collected below the zone of bioturbation are more likely to provide meaningful results.

Overdispersion, also known as scatter, is measured during the OSL dating process and often reflects the degree of solar resetting, mixing of grain populations, or variable dose rate environment with burial (Forman *et al.*, 2000; Galbraith and Roberts, 2012; Liang and Forman, 2019). For a sample collected from the A horizon of the buried soil, an OSL age with low overdispersion is more likely to reflect the time of burial by the sand blow. If overdispersion is >20%–25%, the minimum age model is used, which identifies the lowest equivalent dose population for >30 aliquots. This age may be a maximum limiting age. OSL ages of the sand blows are older than the time of their emplacement. Some of the OSL samples collected from the sand blows had high dispersion values, suggesting that they were mixed and/or partially solar reset. In these cases, we surmise that the rapid deposition of the sand blows prohibited complete solar resetting of the vented sand. Other samples yielded overdispersion values of <15%, indicating solar reset, and provided credible estimates of the pre-existing parent material of the soil.

The aeolian loess deposits that cap both Rondo and Dudley morphostratigraphic units were likely to have been solar reset at the time of deposition. Since then, soil formation would have progressed over time. Situated in a forested environment, only the uppermost few centimeters of the A horizons are likely to have been subjected to solar resetting. The Pleistocene terraces experienced little subsequent aeolian or fluvial deposition but were subjected to deformation caused by liquefaction-related ground failures and possibly faulting and to burial by sand blows. Therefore, sand blows are likely to have ages similar to the sandy fluvial deposits from which they were sourced, unless the vented sand was reset or partially reset during deposition.

Liquefaction-potential analysis or evaluation of scenario earthquakes

The sand blows and related sand dikes along the DBL are very large, similar in size to sand blows and dikes in the NMSZ, and their source sands are relatively deep (~12.5 m) (Al-Shukri *et al.*, 2015; Tuttle, Wolf, *et al.*, 2019). Therefore, it is likely that the earthquakes responsible for their formation are very large in the **M** 7.0–7.5 range. Very large earthquakes would be expected to induce liquefaction at considerable distances in sediment that tends to be susceptible to liquefaction, such as Holocene fluvial deposits. Therefore, it seems reasonable to interpret the small sand blows and sand dikes of similar age near Coldwater River, Promised Land, and Blytheville as distal liquefaction features resulting from very large Marianna earthquakes. There are geographical gaps, however, between the MSZ and the distal liquefaction sites, leading to uncertainty in this interpretation. A broader distribution of similar-age features would add confidence in the interpretation of the liquefaction fields and in magnitude estimates for the 4.7, 5.4, and 6.8 ka Marianna events. Therefore, additional reconnaissance for and study of paleoliquefaction features is recommended in the region surrounding the MSZ.

Conclusions

The main findings of this article are as follows:

- The Marianna chronology of paleoearthquakes is revised to about 4.7, 5.4, 6.8, 9.8 ka, and possibly two earlier events about <19.5 and <24.3 ka;
- the age estimates of the Middle-Early Holocene events are robust and have small error ranges of ±0.1–0.15 ka;
- the age estimates of the two possible Late Pleistocene events are not well constrained and require further study to improve confidence in the event timing;
- pre-event surface soils buried by sand blows that are more than 1.5 m thick offer the best opportunity to collect samples for ^{14}C and OSL dating that will provide close or fairly close maximum constraining ages for the sand blows and their causative earthquakes; and
- the DBFZ was the likely source of the about 4.7, 5.4, and 9.8 ka paleoearthquakes, and liquefaction potential analysis suggests that these events were of **M** 7.0–7.5.

Given the recent paleoseismic findings presented here, revisions may be warranted in the characterization of the Marianna earthquake source in the U.S. National Seismic Hazard Model. The revisions might include the addition of the DBFZ as a fault-zone source, reduction in uncertainty of the recurrence times for three Holocene earthquakes, addition of two possible Late

Pleistocene earthquakes, and a shift in magnitude toward very large earthquakes with heavier weighting of **M** 7.5.

Additional reconnaissance for and study of Holocene and Late Pleistocene sand blows in the Marianna area and the surrounding region will improve understanding of liquefaction fields and magnitudes of Marianna earthquakes, recurrence times of large-magnitude earthquakes, long-term behavior of the Marianna source, and spatial and temporal migration of seismicity along the Reelfoot Rift and across the central United States.

Data and Resources

Seismicity shown in Figures 1 and 2 is from the Center for Earthquake Research and Information available at https://folkworm.ceri.memphis.edu/catalogs/html/cat_nm.html. Also shown in Figures 1 and 2 are liquefaction features from this study and other studies conducted by Tuttle and collaborators. Geotechnical data were provided by Tom Holzer of the U.S. Geological Survey and the Arkansas and Mississippi Departments of Transportation. Otherwise, all data included in this article were collected by the authors or derived from other published sources listed in the references. Information about liquefaction sites, liquefaction features, and results of dating have been entered into databases that are available to the public for download as both Excel files and Shapefiles from https://mptuttle.com/databases.html. Both websites were last accessed in December 2025. The supplemental material for this article includes additional information related to the six study sites—DBSW2, DBNW2, DBNW3, DBNW5, DBNW7, and DBNW8—as follows: (1) a map showing ages and sizes of sand blows at the study sites along the Daytona Beach lineament and locations of two seismic-reflection profiles with interpreted fault zones projected to the surface, (2) site investigation summaries including satellite images, geophysical profiles, and trench logs for the sites, (3) tabulated results of radiocarbon (^{14}C) and optically stimulated luminescence dating for samples collected at the sites, and (4) a list of cited references. Satellite imagery used as site base maps is from Esri World Imagery and Google Earth, as noted in the figure captions.

Declaration of Competing Interests

The authors acknowledge that there are no conflicts of interest recorded.

Acknowledgments

The Office of the State Geologist of Arkansas facilitated and paid for the excavation of trenches. ^{14}C and optically stimulated luminescence dating were performed by Beta Analytic, Inc. and Geoluminescence Dating Research Lab at Baylor University or USGS OSL Lab, respectively. Thanks to the property owners and farmers who gave us permission to work at the study sites and to Ross Hartleb and Pilar Villamor for their thorough and thoughtful reviews that improved this article. Research presented in this article was supported by the National Earthquake Hazard Reduction Program managed by the USGS under Grants 1434-07HQGR0069, G12AP20093, G18AP00083, and G22AP00335. The views and conclusions contained in this document are those of the authors and should not be interpreted as representing the opinions or policies of the USGS.

References

Al-Qadhi, O. (2010). Geophysical investigation of paleoseismological features in eastern Arkansas, USA, *Ph.D. dissertation*, University of Arkansas at Little Rock, Little Rock, Arkansas, USA, 235 pp., plus Appendix A.

Al-Shukri, H., H. Mahdi, O. Al-Qadhi, and M. P. Tuttle (2009). Spatial and temporal characteristics of paleoseismic features in the southern terminus of the New Madrid seismic zone in eastern Arkansas, *Final Technical Rept. Prepared for U.S. Geol. Surv. Award 1434-07HQGR0069*, 24 pp.

Al-Shukri, H., H. Mahdi, and M. Tuttle (2006). Three-dimensional imaging of earthquake-induced features with ground penetrating radar, near Marianna, Arkansas, *Seismol. Res. Lett.* **77,** 505–513.

Al-Shukri, H., H. Mahdi, M. P. Tuttle, and K. Dyer-Williams (2015). Geophysical and paleoseismic investigations of large sand blows along a northwest-oriented lineament near Marianna, Arkansas, *Final Technical Rept. Prepared for U.S. Geol. Surv. Award G12AP20093*, 31 pp.

Al-Shukri, H. J., R. E. Lemmer, H. H. Mahdi, and J. B. Connelly (2005). Spatial and temporal characteristics of paleoseismic features in the southern terminus of the New Madrid seismic zone in eastern Arkansas, *Seismol. Res. Lett.* **76,** 502–511.

Atkinson, G., and K. Assatourians (2012). GMPEs for national hazard maps (Miscellaneous resources), available at https://www.seismotoolbox.ca/index.html (last accessed December 2025).

Atkinson, G., and D. Boore (2011). Modification to existing ground-motion prediction equations in light of new data, *Bull. Seismol. Soc. Am.* **101**, 1121–1135.

Bronk Ramsey, C. (2009). Bayesian analysis of radiocarbon dates, *Radiocarbon* **51,** 337–360.

Cetin, K. O., R. B. Seed, A. K. Der Kiureghian, K. Tokimatsu, L. F. Harder Jr., R. E. Kayen, and R. E. S. Moss (2004). SPT-based probabilistic and deterministic assessment of seismic soil liquefaction potential, *J. Geotech. Geoenviron. Eng.* **130,** 1314–1340.

Chlaib, H. K., H. Mahdi, H. J. Al-Shukri, M. Su, A. Catakli, and N. Abd (2014). Using ground penetrating radar to detect small-scale animal burrows, *J. Appl. Geophys.* doi: 10.1016/j.jappgeo.2014.01.011.

Cohen, K. M., S. C. Finney, P. L. Gibbard, and J.-X. Fan (2022). The ICS international chronostratigraphic chart, *Episodes* **36,** 199–204.

Forman, S. L., J. Pierson, and K. Lepper (2000). Luminescence geochronology, *Quat. Geochronol.* **4,** 157–175.

Galbraith, R. F., and R. G. Roberts (2012). Statistical aspects of equivalent dose and error calculation and display in OSL dating: An overview and some recommendations, *Quat. Geochronol.* **11,** 1–27.

Gray, J. L. (1977). Soil survey of Lee County, Arkansas, U.S. Department of Agriculture, Soil Conservation Service and Forest Service, in Cooperation with the Arkansas Agricultural Experiment Station, 94 pp., plus 50 map sheets.

Hildenbrand, T. G., and J. D. Hendricks (1995). Geophysical setting of the Reelfoot Rift and relations between rift structures and the New Madrid seismic zone, *U.S. Geol. Surv. Profess. Pap. 1538-E*.

Hough, S. E. (2004). Scientific overview and historical context of the 1811-1812 New Madrid earthquake sequence, *Ann. Geophys.* **47,** 523–537.

Juang, C. H., and T. Jiang (2000). Assessing probabilistic methods for liquefaction potential evaluation, *Proc. of GeoDenver Conference,*

"Soil Dynamics and Liquefaction 2000", American Society of Civil Engineers, Reston, Virginia.

Juang, C. H., J. Zhang, S. Khoshnevisan, and W. Gong (2017). Probabilistic methods for assessing soil liquefaction and effect, *Geo-Risk 2017: Keynote Lectures*, American Society of Civil Engineers, 122–145, doi: 10.1061/9780784480694.

Liang, P., and S. L. Forman (2019). LDAC: An excel-based program for luminescence equivalent dose and burial age calculations, *Ancient TL* **37,** 21–40.

McKay, E. D., III (1979). Wisconsin loess stratigraphy of Illinois, in *Wisconsinan, Sangamonian, and Illinoian stratigraphy in Central Illinois*, L. R. Follmer, E. D. McKay, J. A. Lineback, and J. A. D. L. Gross (Editors), Illinois State Geological Survey, Champaign, IL, Guidebook, Vol. 13, 95–108.

Obermeier, S. F. (1989). The New Madrid earthquakes: an engineering-geologic interpretation of relict liquefaction features, *U.S. Geol. Surv. Profess. Pap. 1336-B*.

Odum, J. K., R. A. Williams, W. J. Stephenson, M. P. Tuttle, and H. Al-Shukri (2016). Preliminary assessment of a previously unknown fault zone beneath the Daytona Beach sand blow cluster near Marianna, Arkansas, *Seismol. Res. Lett.* **87,** 1453–1464.

Petersen, M. D., A. D. Frankel, S. C. Harmsen, C. S. Mueller, K. M. Haller, R. L. Wheeler, R. L. Wesson, Y. Zeng, O. S. Boyd, D. M. Perkins, *et al.* (2014). Documentation for the 2014 Update of the United States National Seismic Hazard Maps, *U.S. Geol. Surv. Open-File Rept. 2014-1091*, 243 pp.

Rains, D. S., and M. J. Guccione (2016). Formation of the Marianna Gap, a transverse stream valley, through Crowley's Ridge, northern Mississippi alluvial valley, U.S.A., *Seismol. Res. Lett.* **87,** 1442–1452.

Reimer, P. J., W. E. N. Austin, E. Bard, A. Bayliss, P. G. Blackwell, C. Bronk Ramsey, M. Butzin, H. Cheng, R. L. Edwards, M. Frederick, *et al.* (2020). The IntCal20 northern hemisphere radiocarbon age calibration curve (0-55 cal kBP), *Radiocarbon* **62,** 725–757. doi: 10.1017/RDC.2020.41.

Rittenour, T. M., M. D. Blum, and R. J. Goble (2007). Fluvial evolution of the lower Mississippi River valley during the last 100 k.y. glacial cycle: Response to glaciation and sea-level change, *GSA Bull.* **119,** 586–608, doi: 10.1130/B25934.1.

Robertson, P. K. (2010). Evaluation of flow liquefaction and liquefied strength using the CPT, *J. Geotech. Geoenviron. Eng.* **136,** 842–853.

Ruhe, R. V. (1983). Depositional environment of late Wisconsin loess in the midcontinental United States, in *Late-Quaternary Environments of the United States, 1, The Pleistocene*, S. C. Porter (Editor), University of Minnesota Press, Minneapolis, Minnesota, 130–137.

Saucier, R. T. (1977). Effects of the New Madrid earthquake series in the Mississippi alluvial valley, *U.S. Army Corps of Engineers Waterways Experiment Station Misc. Pap. S-77-5*, 10 pp.

Schumm, S. A., and W. J. Spitz (1996). Geological influences on the lower Mississippi River and its alluvial valley, *Eng. Geol.* **45,** 245–261.

Seed, H. B., and I. M. Idriss (1971). Simplified procedure for evaluating soil liquefaction potential, *J. Geotech. Eng. Div.* **97,** 1249–1273.

Technical Report (2012). Central and Eastern United States seismic source characterization for nuclear facilities, EPRI, U.S. DOE, and U.S. NRC, Palo Alto, California.

Thompson Jobe, J., A. Hatem, R. Gold, C. DuRoss, N. Reitman, R. Briggs, and C. Collett (2022). Revised earthquake geology inputs for the central and eastern United States and southeast Canada for the 2023 National Seismic Hazard Model, *Seismol. Res. Lett.* **93,** 3100–3120, doi: 10.1785/0220220162.

Thompson Jobe, J., A. Hatem, R. Gold, C. DuRoss, N. Reitman, R. Briggs, and C. Collett (2022). Revised earthquake geology inputs for the central and eastern United States and southeast Canada for the 2023 U.S. 50-State National Seismic Hazard Model, *Seismol. Res. Lett.* **93,** 3100–3120, doi: 10.1785/0220220162.

Tuttle, M. P., and R. Hartleb (2012). Appendix E. Central and Eastern U.S. paleoliquefaction database, uncertainties associated with paleoliquefaction data, and guidance for seismic source characterization, *The Central and Eastern U.S. Seismic Source Characterization for Nuclear Facilities*, EPRI, U.S. DOE, and U.S. NRC, Palo Alto, California, 135 pp. plus database.

Tuttle, M. P., H. Al-Shukri, and H. Mahdi (2006). Very large earthquakes centered southwest of the New Madrid seismic zone 5,000-7,000 years ago, *Seismol. Res. Lett.* **77,** 664–678.

Tuttle, M. P., H. Al-Shukri, and H. Mahdi (2020). Geophysical and paleoseismic investigations of large sand blows along a northwest-oriented lineament near Marianna, Arkansas, *Final Technical Rept. U.S. Geol. Surv. award G18AP00083*, 31 pp.

Tuttle, M. P., R. Hartleb, L. Wolf, and P. W. Mayne (2019). Paleoliquefaction studies and the evaluation of seismic hazard, *Geosciences* **9,** 61, doi: 10.3390/geosciences9070311.

Tuttle, M. P., L. W. Wolf, K. Dyer-Williams, P. W. Mayne, R. H. Lafferty, K. Hess, M. E. Starr, M. Haynes, J. Morrow, *et al.* (2019). Paleoliquefaction studies in moderate seismicity regions with a history of large earthquakes, *U.S. Nuclear Regulatory Agency, NUREG/CR-7257*, 450 pp.

Van Arsdale, R., and W. Cupples (2013). Late Pliocene and quaternary deformation of the reelfoot rift, *Geosphere* **9,** 1819–1831.

Wheeler, R. L., E. M. Omdahl, R. L. Dart, G. D. Wilkerson, and R. H. Bradford (2003). Earthquakes in the central U.S., 1699–2002, *U. S. Geol. Surv. Geol. Investig. Ser. I-2812*.

Youd, T. L., I. M. Idriss, R. D. Andrus, I. Arango, G. Castro, J. T. Christian, R. Dobry, W. D. L. Finn, L. F. Harder, Jr., and M. E. Hynes, *et al.* (2003). Liquefaction resistance of soils: Summary report from the 1996 NCEER and 1998 NCEER/NSF workshops on evaluation of liquefaction resistence of soils, *J. Geotech. Geoenviron. Eng.* **127,** 817–833.

Manuscript received 19 September 2025
Published online 14 January 2026

The 2023 M_w 6.8 Al Haouz Lower Crustal Earthquake Buried in a Thick Crust Within a Thin Lithosphere Beneath the High Atlas Mountain Range (Morocco)

OPEN ACCESS

Hafid Ouammou*[1,2], Abdelkrim Aoudia[2], Farhan Javed[3], Hari Ram Thapa[4], Abdelilah Tahayt[1], and Hua Wang[5]

Abstract

The High Atlas (HA) forms a major intracontinental belt along the northern margin of the West African craton, stretching from the Atlantic coast of Morocco to the Tunisian Mediterranean across the Saharan Atlas. Global Positioning System data record surface deformation rates below 1 mm/yr, underscoring limited present-day tectonic activity in the framework of the convergence of the Nubian and Eurasian tectonic plates. This study investigates the coseismic deformation following the M_w 6.8 Al Haouz earthquake, combining Interferometric Synthetic Aperture Radar modeling, Coulomb stress change analysis, and the examination of aftershock distribution. We investigate the Earth's structure to understand the earthquake sequence in relation to its regional geodynamics, using ambient noise seismic tomography and *P*-wave coda autocorrelation. Our findings show a west-southwest–east-northeast high-angle blind reverse fault dipping to the northwest that is located beneath a flower structure, with its surface manifestation directly correlating to the documented Tizi n'Test fault. Coulomb failure stress change calculations revealed that the mainshock loaded nearby major faults by ~5 bars, a change that aligns spatially with subsequent aftershock clusters. The resolved Moho and lithosphere–asthenosphere boundary (LAB) depths beneath the western High Atlas revealed a significant increase in Moho depth, which reached 45–50 km in the epicentral region. In contrast, the Moho remains relatively shallow (averaging ~35 km) in the surrounding low-topography areas. Notably, a clear inverse correlation was observed between Moho and LAB depth, with a shallower LAB corresponding to a thicker crust, and vice versa. The Al Haouz earthquake ruptured at least two-thirds of the thick crust that likely compensates the HA topography in a region characterized by a 30 km thin lithospheric mantle at the edge of the western African craton. This suggests that the slow deformation is likely governed by an oblique crustal convergence and a localized asthenospheric uplift caused by a lateral flow of the Canary Plume in interaction with the western African craton.

Cite this article as Ouammou, H., A. Aoudia, F. Javed, H. Ram Thapa, A. Tahayt, and H. Wang (2026). The 2023 M_w 6.8 Al Haouz Lower Crustal Earthquake Buried in a Thick Crust Within a Thin Lithosphere Beneath the High Atlas Mountain Range (Morocco), *Seismol. Res. Lett.* **97**, 730–742, doi: 10.1785/0220250299.

Supplemental Material

Introduction

The Atlas belt system is an Alpine intracontinental orogenic belt that begins with rifting in response to the opening of the Atlantic and Tethys during the Triassic and Jurassic periods (Choubert and Faure-Muret, 1962; Mattauer *et al.*, 1977; Frizon de Lamotte *et al.*, 2000; Gomez *et al.*, 2000; Piqué *et al.*, 2002; Arboleya *et al.*, 2004). This resulted in the formation of normal faults shaping a graben and half-graben structures in the region (Medina, 1995; Zühlke *et al.*, 2004; Hafid *et al.*, 2006; Baudon *et al.*, 2012). Subsequently, the Mesozoic rifting aborted and the Cenozoic inversion took place (Mattauer

1. Research and Development in Applied Geosciences Laboratory, FSTT, Abdelmalek Essaadi University, Tetouan, Morocco, https://orcid.org/0009-0003-5401-124X (HO); https://orcid.org/0000-0003-2734-6266 (AT); 2. Earth System Physics Section, Abdus Salam International Centre for Theoretical Physics, Trieste, Italy; 3. Centre for Earthquake Studies, National Centre for Physics, Islamabad, Pakistan; 4. Department of Environment, Earth, and Geospatial Sciences, North Carolina Central University, Durham, North Carolina, U.S.A., https://orcid.org/0000-0002-6227-2381 (HRT); 5. College of Natural Resources and Environment, South China Agricultural University, Guangzhou, China, https://orcid.org/0000-0002-7546-7591 (HW)

*Corresponding author: hafid.ouammou@etu.uae.ac.ma

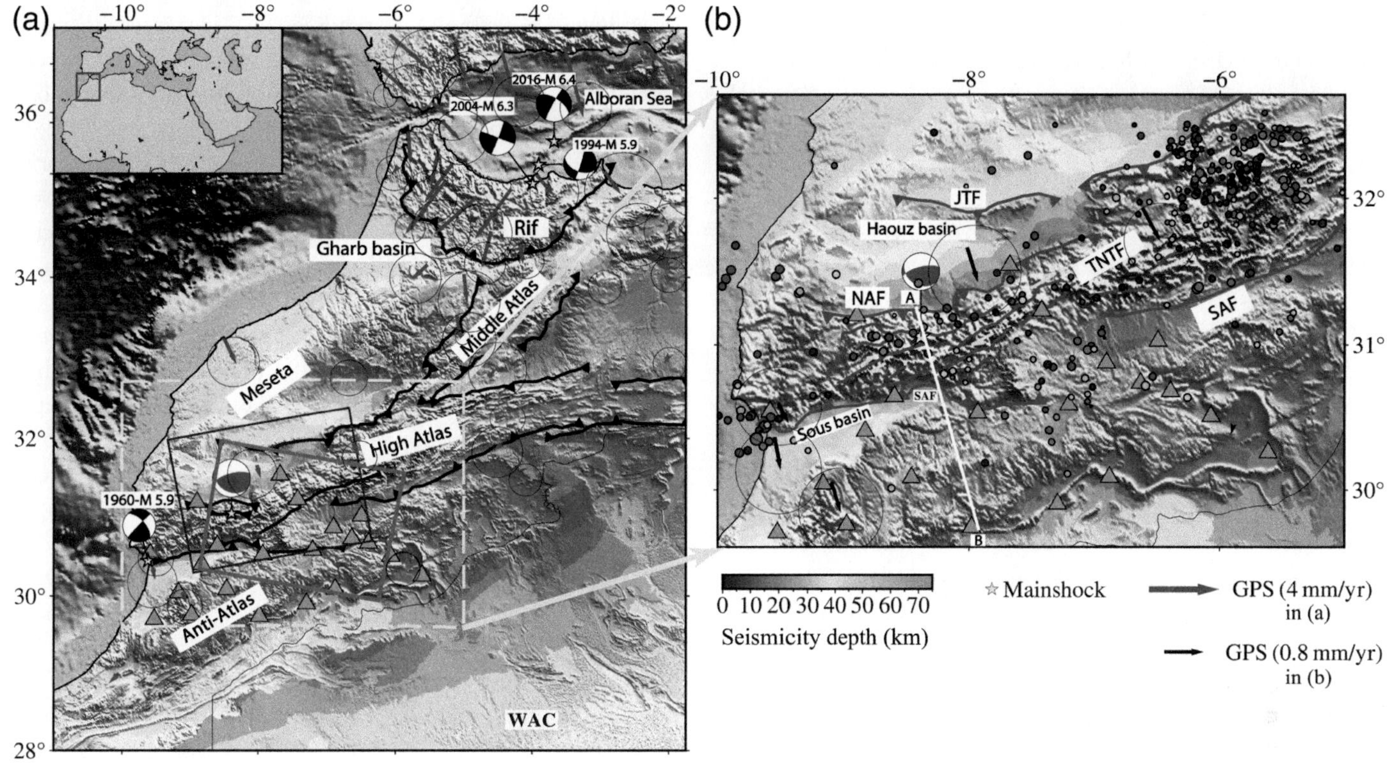

Figure 1. (a) Tectonic map, geological domain, and selected major earthquakes in Morocco (b) Zoom on the High Atlas belt with the main faults from Lanari, Fellin, *et al.* (2020). The red in (a) and black in (b) arrows are Global Navigation Satellite System (GNSS) velocities from Koulali *et al.* (2011). The red–white focal solution is for the 2023 September 8 M_w 6.8 earthquake, and the black–white solutions are for past damaging earthquakes in Morocco. The seismicity in (b) is from the International Seismological Centre (ISC). The brown and blue rectangles represent Sentinel-1A's ascending (T045) and descending (T154) tracks. The green triangles represent the seismic broadband station from two distinct temporary networks: Morocco–Muenster (Thomas, 2010) and CoMITAC Morocco–Bristol (Wookey *et al.*, 2011). The white line AB is the location of the cross-section in the conceptual model (Fig. 5). Abbreviations are: JTF, Jebilet thrust fault; NAF, North Atlas fault; SAF, South Atlas fault; TNTF, Tizi n'Test fault; and WAC, West African craton. The color version of this figure is available only in the electronic edition.

et al., 1977; Frizon de Lamotte *et al.*, 2000; Piqué *et al.*, 2002; Teixell *et al.*, 2003; Tesón *et al.*, 2010) as a result of the ongoing convergence of the African and Eurasian plates (Dewey *et al.*, 1989; Serpelloni *et al.*, 2007). This led to the reactivation of pre-existing paleo-rift normal faults, inverting them to accommodate reverse and strike-slip motion, ultimately giving rise to the formation of a double-verging fold belt (Fekkak *et al.*, 2018; Lanari, Fellin, *et al.*, 2020).

This belt constitutes a principal structural domain, propagating from the Atlantic margin of Morocco eastward to the Mediterranean shoreline of Tunisia and incorporating the Sahara Atlas of Algeria. Overthrust in the north by the Maghrebian belt (Rif-Tell-Kabylia) and overthrusts the Sahara platform in the south. In Morocco, the Atlas system is made up of three major orogenic segments: the anti-Atlas (AA), a belt of massive mountains oriented east-northeast, located on the northern edge of the West African craton (WAC); the Middle Atlas (MA), a segment-oriented northeast; and the High Atlas (HA), aligned east-northeast to east toward the Saharan Atlas. The Jebilet thrust bounds the northern part of the HA, separating the western High Atlas (WHA) from the Coastal Meseta and the Central Meseta, and the North Atlas fault (NAF), with both emergent and blind fault zones (Sébrier *et al.*, 2006; Missenard *et al.*, 2007; Frizon de Lamotte *et al.*, 2008; Fekkak *et al.*, 2018) separating the central and eastern HA from the eastern Meseta. To the south, the belt is mainly bounded by the west-southwest–east-northeast South Atlas fault (SAF), a major tectonic structure extending from Morocco to Tunisia (Bracène *et al.*, 1998) and separating the HA and AA domains (Fig. 1).

In the framework of the convergence of African and Eurasian plates, Global Navigation Satellite System (GNSS) measurements indicate a slowly deforming plate boundary within the western Mediterranean region (Koulali *et al.*, 2011) with estimated movements ranging between ~3.5 and 4.0 mm/yr toward the south-southwest with respect to Africa fixed plate in the Rif belt (Fig. 1a), and movements less than 1 mm/yr across the HA (Fig. 1b). Furthermore, structural studies suggest that WHA is deformed under a transpressional regime (Ellero *et al.*, 2012; Lanari, Fellin, *et al.*, 2020) and estimate the shortening to be limited to between 10% and 25% (Mustaphi *et al.*, 1997; Beauchamp *et al.*, 1999; Teixell *et al.*, 2003; Missenard *et al.*, 2007; Domènech *et al.*, 2016; Fekkak *et al.*, 2018). The high topography of the WHA, exceeding 4 km, remains a subject of debate given the limited crustal shortening and moderate crustal thickness characterizing this belt. This paradox has prompted numerous geodynamic models to point to a significant contribution from mantle upwelling (Teixell *et al.*, 2003, 2005; Zeyen *et al.*, 2005; Missenard *et al.*, 2006; Babault *et al.*, 2008; de Lamotte *et al.*, 2009; Fullea *et al.*, 2010; Jiménez-Munt *et al.*, 2011; Ayarza *et al.*, 2014; Miller and Becker, 2014). Recent GNSS observations revealed that the axial zone of the WHA displays an uplift of 1.1 mm/yr, suggesting that present-day deformation in the WHA is dominated by the reactivation of structurally inherited faults along the mountain range's axial zone (Skikra *et al.*, 2024).

The HA exhibits limited seismic activity confined to the upper crust (within the first 15 km) and low historical seismicity with earthquakes of $M_w < 5$, except for the M_w 5.9 events that correspond to the destructive Agadir earthquake of 29 February 1960 (Tillotson, 1960), that affected the southwest of the current M_w 6.8 earthquake (Fig. 1b). The few focal mechanisms show that, generally, strike-slip mechanisms along steeply dipping fault planes (Medina *et al.*, 2011) and transpression regime drive the kinematics of this region (Soumaya *et al.*, 2018). On 8 September 2023, a strong M_w 6.8 earthquake hit the WHA. Given its unique character in terms of its location in an intraplate context and its deep nucleation, the source mechanism remains debated in spite of several studies since the event (Levandowski, 2023; Yeck *et al.*, 2023; Cheloni *et al.*, 2024; Huang *et al.*, 2024; Malusà *et al.*, 2024; Nouayti *et al.*, 2024; Skikra *et al.*, 2024; Touati *et al.*, 2024; Wu *et al.*, 2024; Yagi *et al.*, 2024). Major discrepancies arise in determining the potential geodynamic origin and source parameters. Although the focal mechanism of the mainshock provided by the seismological catalogs is unanimously accepted, the preferential fault plane is not in complete agreement. Here, we investigated the coseismic deformation following the destructive M_w 6.8 Al Haouz earthquake using a combination of Interferometric Synthetic Aperture Radar (InSAR) deformation modeling, Coulomb failure stress change calculations, and the spatial distribution of aftershocks. We also study the Earth's structure beneath the HA and surrounding regions, to understand the earthquake sequence in relation to its regional geodynamics, using ambient noise seismic tomography (Thapa *et al.*, 2023) and *P*-wave coda autocorrelation (Thapa and Vlahovic, 2025).

Kinematic Inversion of Coseismic Slip and Stress Loading

The destructive 2023 M_w 6.8 Al Haouz seismic event occurred deep in the HA region, outside of any ground-based geodetic observatory. Luckily, spaceborne synthetic aperture radar (SAR) Sentinel-1A was available to record the ground deformation. To measure coseismic deformation, we created the Sentinel-1A ascending (ASC045) and descending (DSC154) interferograms, which were then used to constrain the source parameters. The ascending radar images were acquired on 3 and 15 September; the descending images on 30 August and 11 September 2023. In addition to coseismic deformation, these two pairs also comprise 7 and 3 days of potential postseismic deformation, respectively (Table S1, available in the supplemental material to this article). We used GMTSAR (Sandwell *et al.*, 2011) for interferogram formation and postprocessing (Section 1.1). We estimated the uncertainties in the SAR interferograms using the semi-variogram technique (Table S2, Fig. S1) (Section 1.2). The ascending and descending interferograms show peak-to-peak line-of-sight (LoS) displacements of approximately 180 and 150 mm, respectively (Fig. 2b, Fig. S2). We constrained the geometry of the fault plane (Fig. S3, Table S3) with these interferograms using a Monte Carlo method (Bagnardi and Hooper, 2018) and a rectangular uniform-slip dislocation model (Okada, 1985) (Section 1.3). Assuming a shear modulus of 30 GPa (Hearn and Bürgmann, 2005), the seismic moment of $M_0 = 1.66 \times 10^{19}$ N · m (M_w 6.8) is derived using the best-fit source parameters. The epicentral location and source properties are in agreement with those provided by the U.S. Geological Survey and the German Research Centre for Geosciences (Table S3). This simple model indicates thrust rupturing on a deep fault plane with a strike of 250° ± 12° and dip of 69.5° ± 5°. The fault plane is on the north side of the exposed SAF, buried below the HA Mountains. Furthermore, we estimated spatially variable fault slip and rake (Fig. 2c) using a nonnegative least-squares inversion (Jónsson *et al.*, 2002). We subdivided the uniform-slip model into subfault patches of 2000 m length and 2000 m width, allowing nonzero along-strike and down-dip slip. We used an L-curve (Parker, 1994; Aster *et al.*, 2018) to resolve the trade-off between misfit and roughness (Fig. S4). The distributed-slip model shows that coseismic rupture lies between 10 and 40 km depth, with the maximum displacement of 2 m at 26 km depth.

We next investigated the interaction between this earthquake and the shallow faults through Coulomb stress modeling. For this purpose, we used Coulomb 3.4 (Lin and Stein, 2004; Toda *et al.*, 2005) to resolve the stress on the Tizi n'Test fault (TNTF), Erdouz fault (ERF), SAF, and North Atlas detachment (NAD). Accurately estimating the friction coefficient remains challenging (Hainzl *et al.*, 2009; Toda, Lin, and Stein, 2011; Toda, Stein, and Lin, 2011; Enescu *et al.*, 2012), whereas its variations are known to exert only minor influence on stress perturbations (Harris, 1998; Catalli *et al.*, 2008; Nalbant *et al.*, 2013; Wang *et al.*, 2014). Consequently, we adopt the commonly applied value of 0.4 for this study (King *et al.*, 1994; Stein, 1999; Toda, Stein, Sevilgen, and Lin, 2011) (Fig. S5, Table S4). Coulomb stress changes (ΔCFS) were increased on the SAF fault and partially on TNTF and ERF faults, whereas they decreased on the NAD fault. Furthermore, we simulated the ΔCFS, providing the focal mechanism of the Morocco earthquake (Table S4) as a target fault, and compared it with the

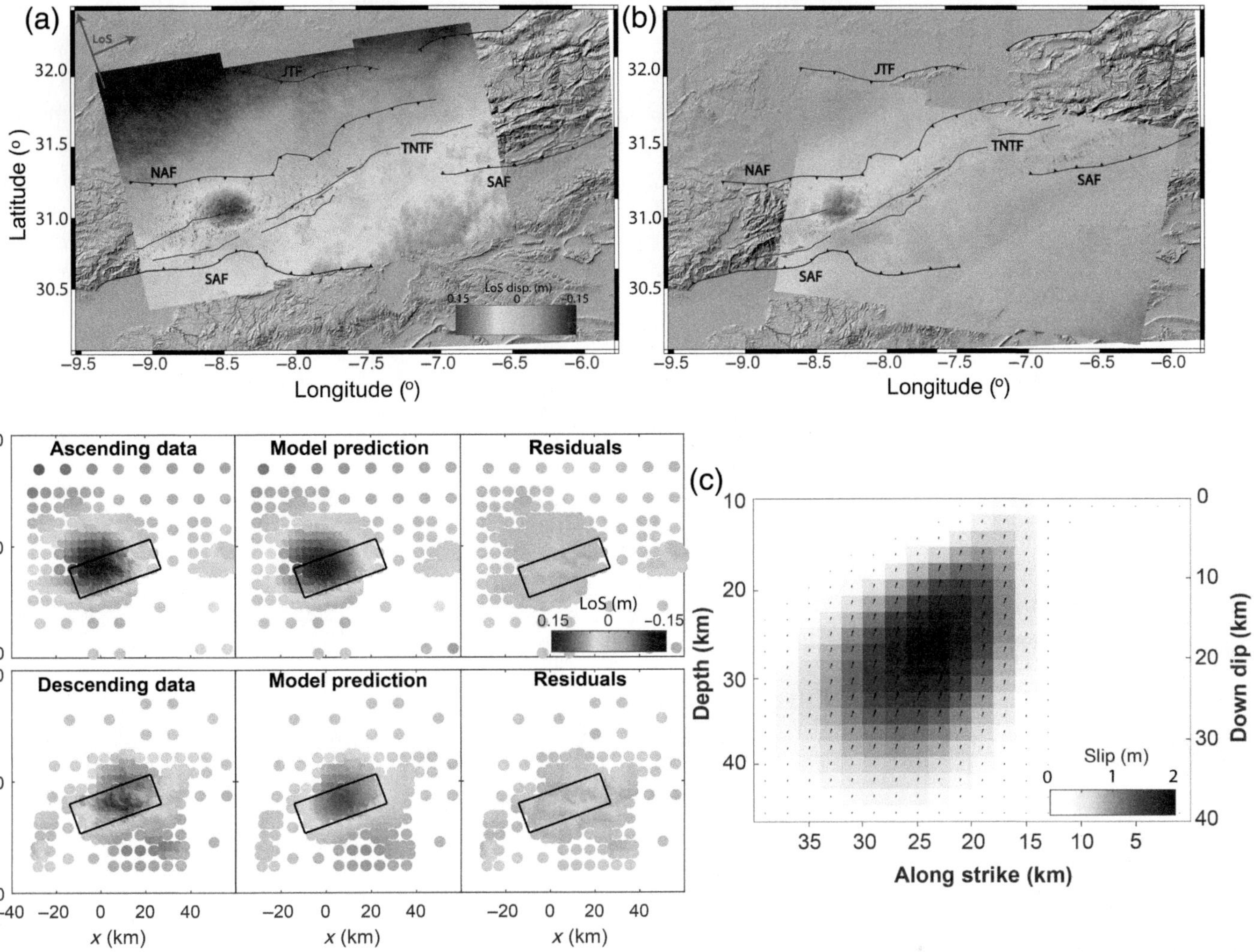

Figure 2. (a) Ascending and (b) descending unwrapped interferogram from Sentinel-1A acquisitions. (c) Finite-slip model using surface deformation measured by Interferometric Synthetic Aperture Radar (InSAR) on ascending and descending tracks. The black rectangle shows the dimensions (40 km × 40 km) of the finite-slip model. The dimension of the uniform slip model is around 20 km × 29 km. The arrows indicate slip directions on the hanging wall, viewing along strike. LoS, line of sight. The color version of this figure is available only in the electronic edition.

spatial distribution of aftershocks. Overall majority of aftershocks were correlated well with the increased ΔCFS, with some aftershocks in the stress shadow region (Fig. 3). The occurrence of aftershocks in the stress shadow region was due to varying dip and orientation of the faults at shallow depth.

Ambient Noise Seismic Tomography and *P*-Wave Coda Autocorrelation

For ambient noise tomography, we utilized continuous time-series data obtained from two distinct networks in Morocco: Morocco–Muenster (Thomas, 2010) and CoMITAC Morocco–Bristol (Wookey *et al.*, 2011). The Morocco–Muenster network operated from 2010 to 2013, whereas CoMITAC Morocco–Bristol was installed from 2011 to 2013. In total, 21 stations were employed, providing dense ray coverage, particularly toward the south and east of the epicenter of the M_w 6.8 Al Haouz earthquake (Fig. S10) that enables us to achieve the highest lateral resolution in the region so far (see Fig. S11). We employed the methodology outlined by (Bensen *et al.*, 2007) to compute cross-correlations between two seismic stations in a pair. For more details, we refer to Text S3.

For *P*-wave coda autocorrelation, we used teleseismic earthquake data (with M_w greater than 5.5) recorded between 2011 and 2013 from the 21 broadband stations (see Fig. 4a). We considered earthquakes with epicentral distances in the range 30°–95°. For details on the *P*-wave autocorrelation and preprocessing steps, we refer to Text S2, Phạm and Tkalčić (2017), and Thapa *et al.* (2025). This method has been successfully applied to estimate the Moho depth beneath the Nepal Himalaya (Thapa, 2021; Thapa *et al.*, 2023), the Ethiopian Volcanic Province (Alemayehu *et al.*, 2023), the Carpathian–Pannonian region (Thapa and Vlahovic, 2025), and the Jammu and Kashmir Himalaya (Thapa *et al.*,

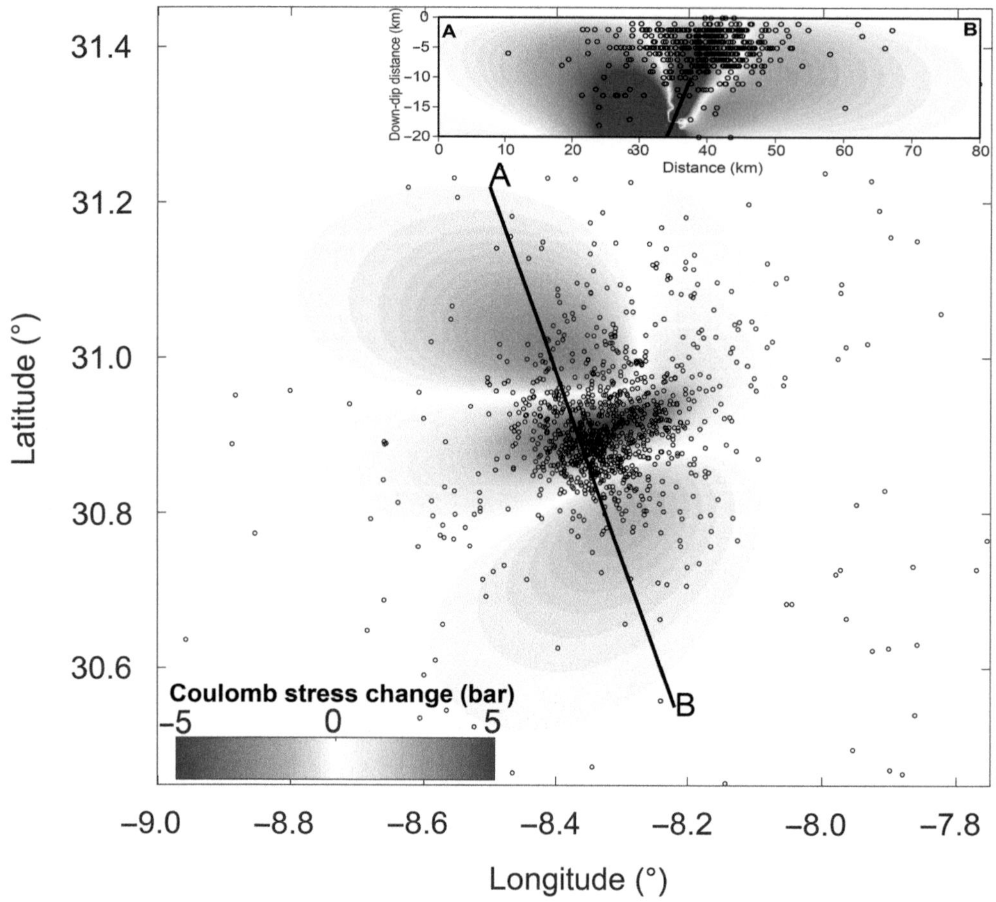

Figure 3. Coulomb stress changes due to the 8 September Al Haouz earthquake resolved on major neighboring faults. The black circles are the aftershock sequence from Institut National de Géophysique–Centre National pour la Recherche Scientifique et Technique (ING-CNRST). AB vertical section perpendicular to the strike 250° fault plane. The color version of this figure is available only in the electronic edition.

2025a,b). We computed the depths of the Moho and lithosphere–asthenosphere boundary (LAB) beneath 21 broadband stations deployed across our study area. The number of vertical and radial components of teleseismic *P*-wave coda used in this study is specified in Table S5. We presented the autocorrelograms and seismic record stacks from the teleseismic dataset for the Moho beneath stations MB17 and MM11 in Figures S13 and S14, and the results observed are mentioned in Text S4. We computed the delay times for the 2*P* and 2*S* reflections from the vertical and radial stacked autocorrelograms of all stations (refer to Fig. S15). The observed delay times were then converted into depths, and the depths of the Moho beneath each station are presented in Table S6. To convert delay time to depth, we used the velocity model obtained from a study by ambient noise tomography to recover the Moho depths. For the LAB, we used the velocity model of Palomeras *et al.* (2017). To convert the observed delay times corresponding to the 2*P* phase to depth, a *P*-wave velocity model is required. The *P*-wave velocity for the crust was derived by multiplying the *S*-wave velocity by the V_P/V_S ratio estimated from the ratio between the delay times of the 2*S* and 2*P* phases. For the upper mantle, we used a fixed V_P/V_S value of 1.81, as suggested by Parera-Portell *et al.* (2024). The Moho depth map is shown in Figure 4b. Near the M_w 6.8 Al Haouz earthquake's epicenter, we observed a significant thickening of the crust, as indicated by a Moho depth increase to 45–50 km. In contrast, the Moho remains substantially shallower in the adjacent regions, and the Moho depth remains relatively constant, approximately 35 km.

In addition, we presented the auto-correlograms and seismic record stacks from the teleseismic dataset for the LAB beneath stations MB17 and MM11 in Figures S16 and S17, and the results observed are mentioned in Text S5. We computed the 2*P* delay times at all stations (refer to Fig. S18) and converted them into depths. The calculated LAB depths beneath each station are presented in Table S6, and the LAB depth distribution is shown in Figure 4c. Notably, we noticed that the LAB is shallower in the area where we noticed a thicker Moho, and vice versa.

The 2D group velocity tomographic maps obtained by applying linearized inversion of group dispersion curves computed for all the station pairs are shown in Figure S19. The results are presented within the 100 km resolution contours. The results related to group velocity tomography is mentioned in Text S6.

We conducted 1D *S*-wave velocity estimation, along with uncertainty determination, as a function of depth up to 50 km by performing inversions of group dispersions obtained at each node within 0.30° × 0.30° grids. The maximum depth was set to 50 km, aligning with the sensitivity of the group dispersion data (3–32 s) used in this study, primarily capturing structural information up to 50 km depth (refer to Fig. S20). The results related to shear-wave structure are mentioned in Text S7.

We computed northwest–southeast profiles of *S*-wave velocity presented in Figure 4e, and other relevant profiles are presented in Figure S23. Figure 4e shows a variation in

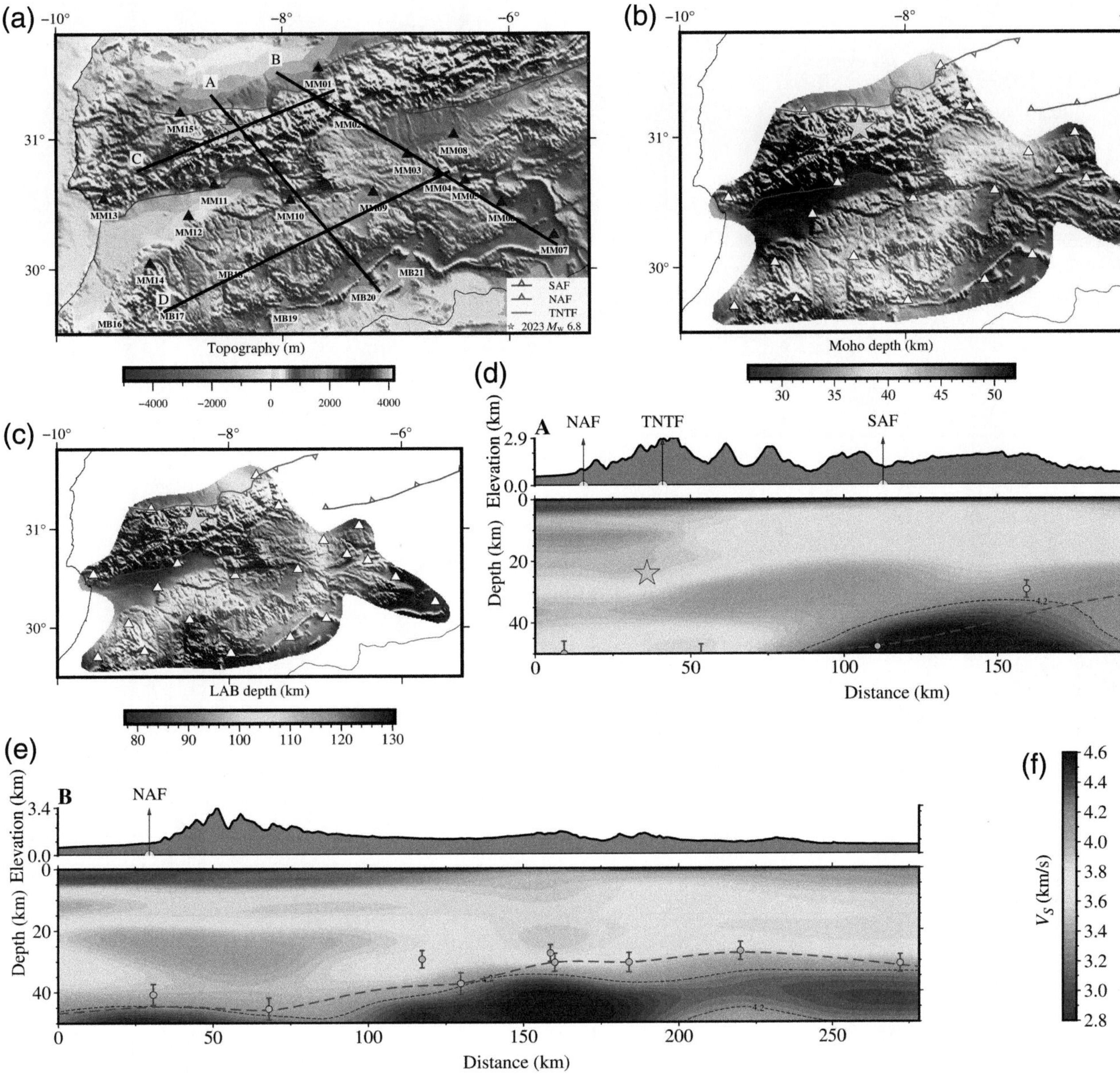

upper and mid-crustal complexity beneath HA and AA. The pronounced feature observed in profile A′ is the low velocity at depths 10–20 km toward the north of the hypocenter of the earthquake. Another pronounced feature that appeared in both profiles is the presence of high velocity ($V_S > 4.2$ km/s) at a depth of 40 km toward the south of SAF, whereas at the same depth, we observed $V_S \sim 3.8$ km/s toward the north of SAF. The Moho depth with error obtained from *P*-wave coda autocorrelation beneath the station closer to the profiles A and B is projected on top of the *S*-wave velocity. The red bar represents the Moho depth with uncertainty, and the red dashed line is the interpolated Moho depth (see Fig. 4e). We projected the Moho depths obtained from autocorrelation onto the shear-wave velocity profiles derived from ambient noise tomography. We found that in profile B, for which the lateral resolution is high, the Moho depth systematically coincides with the $V_S \approx 4.2$ km/s isoline. The average value of crustal V_P/V_S obtained from autocorrelation in this study is 1.75, using this V_P/V_S ratio, the corresponding *P*-wave velocity is approximately 7.4 km/s. This provides evidence that the Moho velocity beneath our study area is 4.2 km/s. Hence, the V_S structure supports the Moho obtained from autocorrelation.

Figure 4. (a) Topographic map of our study area and distribution of seismic stations from two different networks (ZI represented by green and 3D by blue color triangles). (b) Moho depth map and (c) lithosphere–asthenosphere boundary (LAB) depth map across our study area. (d,e) *S*-wave velocity structure as a function of depth along profiles A and B, as shown in (a), with topography on the top. The red dashed line represents the interpolated Moho depth, and red bars indicate the Moho depth with uncertainty obtained from autocorrelation of teleseismic *P*-wave coda. (f) Color palette used for V_S structure in (d) and (e). The color version of this figure is available only in the electronic edition.

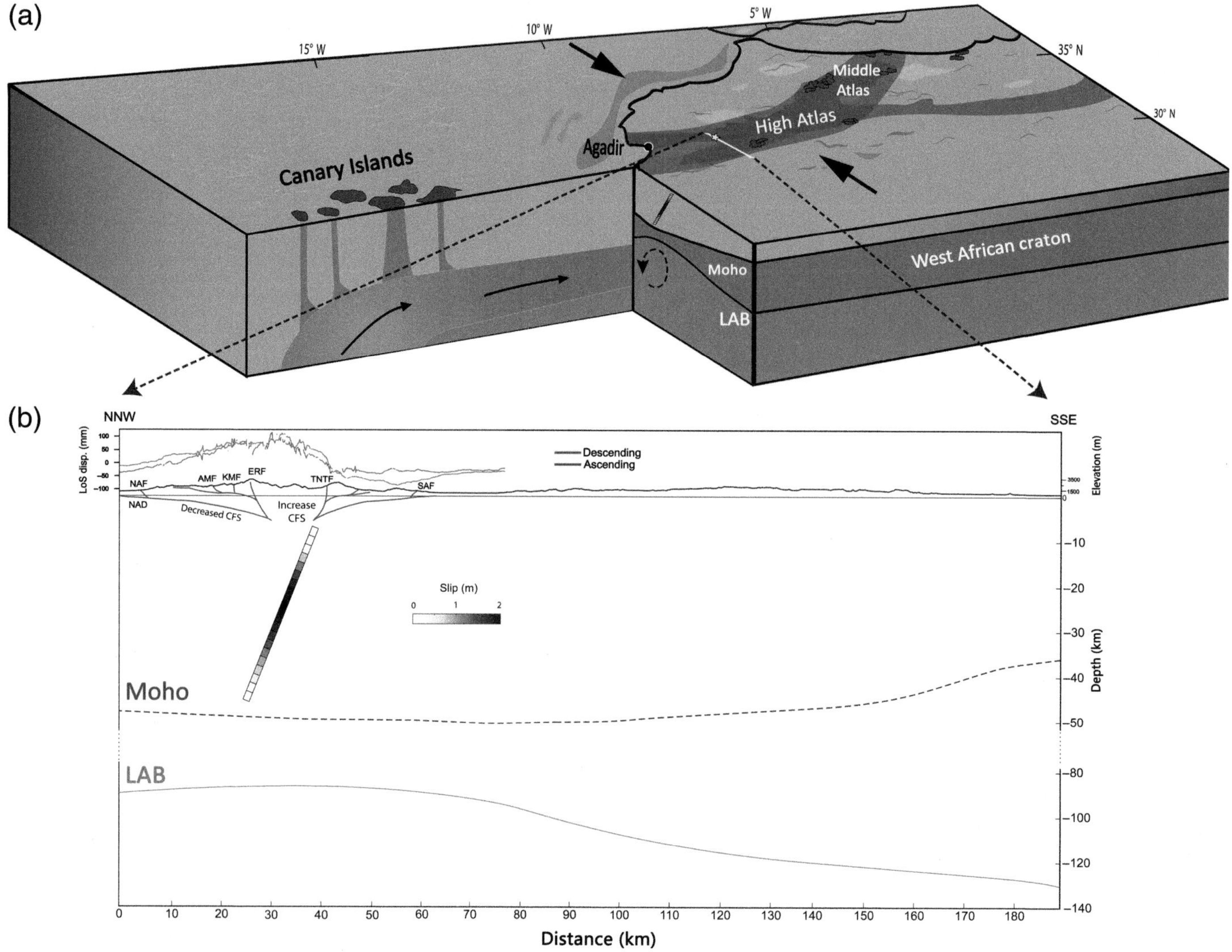

Discussion and Conclusions

Our study has allowed us to investigate the kinematics of the Al Haouz lower crust earthquake and its implications on the crustal deformation and uplift of WHA. The newly computed crust–uppermost mantle structure has allowed us to better constrain the regional geodynamics.

Based on the InSAR modeling of the Al Haouz earthquake, our results support a west-southwest–east-northeast ~250°-striking, blind, reverse-faulting mechanism with a dip of ~69° toward the northwest and a maximum displacement occurring at a depth of approximately 26 km. The distribution of the aftershock sequence coincides with the location of an increase in ΔCFS (reaching up to 5 bars) on different major faults above the Al Haouz rupture. Therefore, our results align with those of Yagi *et al.* (2024) and Yeck *et al.* (2023) and exclude the low-angle thrust fault dipping toward the southwest and related to the NAF as the source of the earthquake following the interpretation of Cheloni *et al.* (2024). Our InSAR LoS surface displacements in ascending and descending tracks (Fig. 5b) show that the southeast flank hosts the sharpest

Figure 5. (a) A conceptual model representing the geodynamic link between the Canary Plume and the Moroccan Hot Line (southwest–northeast green band). It highlights the lateral flow of mantle material from the Canary Plume through the Atlas belt (shown in gray) to the Mediterranean region. The red patches with black outlines illustrate the distribution of Cenozoic alkaline volcanic outcrops. The yellow star indicates the mainshock locations of the Al Haouz earthquake. Moho and LAB are not in scale (b) cross section perpendicular to the ruptured fault of the 2023 M_w 6.8 Al Haouz earthquake showing the slip distribution on our modeled fault plane, the corresponding increase and decrease Coulomb failure stress (CFS) regions, Interferometric Synthetic Aperture Radar (InSAR) line-of-sight (LoS) surface displacements in ascending and descending directions, and Moho and LAB variations in scale. Faults mapped on the cross-section are from Fekkak *et al.* (2018). Abbreviations are: AMF, Adassil–Medinet fault; ERF, Erdouz fault; KMF, Kettou–Makhfamane fault; NAD, North Atlas detachment; NAF, North Atlas fault; and TNTF, Tizi n'Test fault. The color version of this figure is available only in the electronic edition.

displacement changes, consistent with a northwest-dipping fault. In contrast, a southwest-dipping fault model would predict the opposite pattern, namely, the steepest deformation gradients to be located toward the northwest, contrary to what our InSAR data clearly show. The reactivated high-angle reverse fault stands beneath a flower structure, precisely within the axial zone of the WHA (altitudes exceed 4000 m), in which the GNSS data revealed a relatively high interseismic uplift rate of 1.1 mm/yr (Skikra *et al.*, 2024). Even though no surface rupture has been reported, the surface expression of the blind fault coincides with the TNT mapped fault system, in agreement with previous studies (Huang *et al.*, 2024; Nouayti *et al.*, 2024; Skikra *et al.*, 2024). The TNT fault zone has a long record of kinematic studies (Mattauer *et al.*, 1972, 1977; Proust *et al.*, 1977; Binot *et al.*, 1986; Froitzheim *et al.*, 1988; Laville and Pique, 1991; Amrhar, 2002; Qarbous *et al.*, 2003; Laville *et al.*, 2004; Delcaillau *et al.*, 2011) and is known as a structure that has undergone either strike-slip and dip-slip motion during Mesozoic rifting followed by a Cenozoic inversion. Moreover, Lanari, Faccenna, *et al.* (2020) estimated a Cenozoic exhumation rate of about 0.2–0.3 km/Ma, with an acceleration after 6 Ma, and noticed that the uplift of the WHA axial zone involved high-angle faults that are likely controlling the topographic growth of the Atlas. The geometry of the shallow flower structure and its extent above a deeper mid-crust Al Haouz earthquake slip termination (Fig. 5b) may likely imply large-scale folding processes at the surface that contribute both to the regional uplift of the WHA as well to the control of the up-dip coseismic rupture propagation (e.g., Philip and Meghraoui, 1983; Stein and Ekström, 1992; Aoudia *et al.*, 2000). We conclude that the seismological evolution of the Al Haouz lower crust seismogenic fault is likely reflecting the recent structural evolution of the WHA upper crustal flower structure.

Ambient seismic wave tomography and teleseismic *P*-wave coda autocorrelation from a network of 21 broadband stations enabled us to constrain the depth of both the Moho and LAB underlying the WHA region. The low-velocity zone (LVZ) at 10–25 km depth beneath the TNTF (see Fig. 4d), coincides with regions of elevated topography (~3 km) and relatively thick crust (~45–50 km). The projection of the hypocenter of the M_w 6.8 Al Haouz (2023) earthquake shows that it lies at the boundary of this LVZ. The presence of low *S*-wave velocities in the mid-crust likely reflects a mechanically weak layer, which could be caused by fluid accumulation, partial melting, or thermal weakening within the thickened crust. Such a contrast between the LVZ and the surrounding stronger crust may facilitate strain localization, providing a favorable site for earthquake nucleation. These observations suggest that the mid-crustal LVZ not only characterizes the rheological structure beneath the HA but also may play a key role in controlling seismogenic behavior in this region. Our results revealed a significant crustal thickening beneath the epicentral region, as evidenced by Moho depths ranging from 45 to 50 km, therefore compensating the HA topography. Interestingly, we found that LAB is shallower (at 80 km depth) in the region where we observed a thicker Moho, and vice versa, reaching about 130 km depth at the northern edge of WAC (Fig. 5). These tomographic results allow us to constrain the subsurface structure, thereby providing direct context for interpreting the depth extent, localization, and geological setting of the earthquake. On the other hand, our InSAR modeling indicates that the coseismic rupture lies between 10 and 40 km depth. This depth relationship is significant and demonstrates that the earthquake was fully confined to the crust and did not propagate into the mantle or across the Moho. Unlike Huang *et al.* (2024), they suggest that the rupture is localized between depths of 12 and 36 km, displacing the Mohorovičić discontinuity (Moho) to roughly 32 km. The Al Haouz blind earthquake clearly ruptured a minimum of two-thirds of a 45–50 km thick crust and overlies a thin (30–35 km) lithospheric mantle.

The abnormal low lithospheric thickness has been observed beneath CHA (Seber *et al.*, 1996; Missenard *et al.*, 2006; Urchulutegui *et al.*, 2006), confined to a northeast–southwest strip of 150 km wide and 1000 km long beneath the Atlas belt and surrounding area, where LAB reaches minimum depths of 70–80 km (Ayarza *et al.*, 2005; Teixell *et al.*, 2005; Zeyen *et al.*, 2005). This area matches what is known as the Moroccan hot line (de Lamotte *et al.*, 2009), marked by the distribution of Cenozoic alkaline volcanism outcrops with an intraplate chemical affinity (Mokhtari and Velde, 1988; El Azzouzi *et al.*, 2010). Numerous geodynamic models and hypotheses have been proposed to explain this thinning of the lithosphere and its associated volcanism: baby-plume-like or convection cells, delamination with or without Canary mantle plume material flow, subduction process, and edge-driven convection, which involves small-scale convection at the boundary between WAC and the Atlas lithosphere. For more details, we refer to Bezada *et al.* (2013), Civiero *et al.* (2018), Duggen *et al.* (2009), and Missenard and Cadoux (2012).

In light of the earlier, we propose a regional conceptual scheme (Fig. 5a) that integrates our own results (Fig. 5b) into a geodynamic model. We suggest that the lithospheric deformation beneath WHA involves both oblique convergence, as highlighted by a thick active crustal deformation together with a lateral flow of the Canary plume (e.g., Duggen *et al.*, 2009) in interaction with WAC, as highlighted by the strong gradient in LAB thickness. These mechanisms, integrating both external and body forces, led to the reactivation of inherited geological structures like the Al Haouz reverse fault. This suggests that the kinematics of WHA is likely governed by the oblique convergence of tectonic plates and a localized asthenospheric uplift induced by the interaction of the Canary Plume with WAC. Assessing the contribution of body forces within the context of the Africa–Eurasia convergence is of paramount importance to understanding the dynamics of the ongoing deformation.

This earthquake urges us to reconsider hazard estimates across the entire North African intracontinental belt.

Data and Resources

The seismicity catalog was obtained from the International Seismological Centre (ISC), supplemented by the aftershock catalog of the 8 September 2023 Al Haouz earthquake, curated by Institut National de Géophysique—Centre National pour la Recherche Scientifique et Technique, Morocco (ING-CNRST). Continuous seismic recordings were sourced from two temporary deployments: (1) the Morocco–Muenster network (operational 2010–2013; Thomas, 2010; data archived at GFZ Data Services) and (2) the CoMITAC Morocco–Bristol network (operational 2011–2013; Wookey *et al.*, 2011; data available via Incorporated Research Institutions for Seismology Data Management Center). The Synthetic Aperture Radar data used in this study are level-1 single look complex products from ESA's Sentinel-1A satellite, obtained through the Alaska Satellite Facility (ASF) vertex platform. These datasets are publicly available on the ASF data portal at https://search.asf.alaska.edu/#/. The following software tools were used in this study: GMTSAR (Sandwell *et al.*, 2011) for interferogram formation and postprocessing. GMTSAR is openly available at https://topex.ucsd.edu/gmtsar. Geodetic Bayesian Inversion Software (GBIS), MATLAB®-based for geodetic modeling. GBIS is available via https://comet.nerc.ac.uk/gbis/. Coulomb 3.4 for stress change calculations. Coulomb 3.4 is freely accessible at https://pubs.usgs.gov/of/2011/1060/. Autocorrelation code is available at Zenodo (Thapa, 2025). The transdimensional code used in this study is available at Zenodo (Pachhai, 2023). Generic Mapping Tools (GMT) (version 6; Wessel *et al.*, 2019) for figure preparation. GMT is open-source and available at https://www.generic-mapping-tools.org. All websites were last accessed in September 2023. The supplemental material for this article includes a detailed description of the methodology for Interferometric Synthetic Aperture Radar data processing, Bayesian inversion, finite-fault modeling, Coulomb stress change calculations, ambient noise seismic tomography, and *P*-wave coda autocorrelation.

Declaration of Competing Interests

The authors acknowledge that there are no conflicts of interest recorded.

Acknowledgments

This work was supported by the International Centre for Theoretical Physics (ICTP)/International Atomic Energy Agency (IAEA) Sandwich Training Programme, which provided essential resources during this research. All computations were performed on the ICTP Argo cluster. The authors express their sincere gratitude to the Institut National de Géophysique–Centre National pour la Recherche Scientifique et Technique (ING-CNRST) for generously sharing the catalog of aftershocks for this study. H. W. is supported by the National Natural Science Foundation of China (42274001) and the Associates Program by ICTP and the Simons Foundation (284558FY19). H. R. Thapa is supported by the U.S. Department of Defense Grant W911NF2310216. The authors thank the Guest Editor Will Levandowski, Ph.D., the anonymous reviewer, and the handling editor for their thoughtful and constructive comments, which greatly improved the clarity and quality of this article. The authors dedicate this article to the memory of Abdelkrim Aoudia, whose mentorship, generosity, and scientific insight greatly guided and inspired this work.

References

Alemayehu, S., A. Aoudia, A. Ayele, S. Pachhai, H. R. Thapa, C. J. Ebinger, R. Kherchouche, M. Guidarelli, and S. Kim (2023). Structure of the crust-uppermost mantle beneath the Ethiopian volcanic province using ambient seismic noise and teleseismic *P* wave coda autocorrelation, *Tectonophysics* **869,** 230092, doi: 10.1016/j.tecto.2023.230092.

Amrhar, M. (2002). Paléocontraintes et déformations syn-et post-collision Afrique–Europe identifiées dans la couverture mésozoïque et cénozoïque du Haut Atlas occidental (Maroc), *C.R. Geosci.* **334,** no. 4, 279–285, doi: 10.1016/S1631-0713(02)01730-3 (in French).

Aoudia, A., A. Saraò, B. Bukchin, and P. Suhadolc (2000). The 1976 Friuli (NE Italy) thrust faulting earthquake: A reappraisal 23 years later, *Geophys. Res. Lett.* **27,** no. 4, 573–576, doi: 10.1029/1999GL011071.

Arboleya, M. L., A. Teixell, M. Charroud, and M. Julivert (2004). A structural transect through the High and Middle Atlas of Morocco, *J. Afr. Earth. Sci.* **39,** no. 3, 319–327, doi: 10.1016/j.jafrearsci.2004.07.036.

Aster, R. C., B. Borchers, and C. H. Thurber (2018). *Parameter Estimation and Inverse Problems*, Third Ed., Elsevier, Amsterdam, The Netherlands, doi: 10.1016/C2015-0-02458-3.

Ayarza, P., F. Alvarez-Lobato, A. Teixell, M. L. Arboleya, E. Teson, M. Julivert, and M. Charroud (2005). Crustal structure under the central High Atlas Mountains (Morocco) from geological and gravity data, *Tectonophysics* **400,** nos. 1/4, 67–84, doi: 10.1016/j.tecto.2005.02.009.

Ayarza, P., R. Carbonell, A. Teixell, I. Palomeras, D. Martí, A. Kchikach, M. Harnafi, A. Levander, J. Gallart, and M. L. Arboleya (2014). Crustal thickness and velocity structure across the Moroccan Atlas from long offset wide-angle reflection seismic data: The SIMA experiment, *Geochem. Geophys. Geosyst.* **15,** no. 5, 1698–1717, doi: 10.1002/2013GC005164.

Babault, J., A. Teixell, M. L. Arboleya, and M. Charroud (2008). A Late Cenozoic age for long-wavelength surface uplift of the Atlas Mountains of Morocco, *Terra nova* **20,** no. 2, 102–107, doi: 10.1111/j.1365-3121.2008.00794.x.

Bagnardi, M., and A. Hooper (2018). Inversion of surface deformation data for rapid estimates of source parameters and uncertainties: A Bayesian approach, *Geochem. Geophys. Geosyst.* **19,** no. 7, 2194–2211, doi: 10.1029/2018GC007585.

Baudon, C., J. Redfern, and J. Van Den Driessche (2012). Permo-Triassic structural evolution of the Argana Valley, impact of the Atlantic rifting in the High Atlas, Morocco, *J. Afr. Earth Sci.* **65,** 91–104, doi: 10.1016/j.jafrearsci.2012.02.002.

Beauchamp, W., R. W. Allmendinger, M. Barazangi, A. Demnati, M. El Alji, and M. Dahmani (1999). Inversion tectonics and the evolution of the High Atlas Mountains, Morocco, based on a geological-geophysical transect, *Tectonics* **18,** no. 2, 163–184, doi: 10.1029/1998TC900015.

Bensen, G. D., M. H. Ritzwoller, M. P. Barmin, A. L. Levshin, F. Lin, M. P. Moschetti, N. M. Shapiro, and Y. Yang (2007). Processing seismic ambient noise data to obtain reliable broad-band surface wave dispersion measurements, *Geophys. J. Int.* **169,** no. 3, 1239–1260, doi: 10.1111/j.1365-246X.2007.03374.x.

Bezada, M. J., E. D. Humphreys, D. R. Toomey, M. Harnafi, J. M. Dávila, and J. Gallart (2013). Evidence for slab rollback in westernmost Mediterranean from improved upper mantle imaging, *Earth Planet Sci. Lett.* **368,** 51–60, doi: 10.1016/j.epsl.2013.02.024.

Binot, F., G. Dresen, J. Stets, and P. Wurster (1986). Die Tizi-n'Test-Verwerfungszone im Hohen Atlas (Marokko), *Geol. Rundsch.* **75,** 647–664, doi: 10.1007/BF01820638 (in German).

Bracène, R., A. Bellahcene, D. Bekkouche, E. Mercier, and D. F. de Lamotte (1998). The thin-skinned style of the South Atlas front in central Algeria, *Geol. Soc. Lond. Spec. Publ.* **132,** no. 1, 395–404, doi: 10.1144/GSL.SP.1998.132.01.22.

Catalli, F., M. Cocco, R. Console, and L. Chiaraluce (2008). Modeling seismicity rate changes during the 1997 Umbria-Marche sequence (central Italy) through a rate-and state-dependent model, *J. Geophys. Res. Solid Earth* **113,** no. B11, doi: 10.1029/2007JB005356.

Cheloni, D., N. A. Famiglietti, C. Tolomei, R. Caputo, and A. Vicari (2024). The 8 September 2023, M_W 6.8, Morocco earthquake: A deep transpressive faulting along the active high Atlas mountain belt, *Geophys. Res. Lett.* **51,** no. 2, e2023GL106992, doi: 10.1029/2023GL106992.

Choubert, G., and A. Faure-Muret (1962). Le séisme d'Agadir, ses effets et son interprétation géologique, Service de la carte géologique (in French).

Civiero, C., V. Strak, S. Custódio, G. Silveira, N. Rawlinson, P. Arroucau, and C. Corela (2018). A common deep source for upper-mantle upwellings below the Ibero-western Maghreb region from teleseismic *P*-wave travel-time tomography, *Earth Planet Sci. Lett.* **499,** 157–172, doi: 10.1016/j.epsl.2018.07.024.

de Lamotte, D. F., P. Leturmy, Y. Missenard, S. Khomsi, G. Ruiz, O. Saddiqi, F. Guillocheau, and A. Michard (2009). Mesozoic and Cenozoic vertical movements in the Atlas system (Algeria, Morocco, Tunisia): An overview, *Tectonophysics* **475,** no. 1, 9–28, doi: 10.1016/j.tecto.2008.10.024.

Delcaillau, B., M. Amrhar, M. Namous, E. Laville, K. Pedoja, and O. Dugué (2011). Transpressional tectonics in the Marrakech High Atlas: Insight by the geomorphic evolution of drainage basins, *Geomorphology* **134,** nos. 3/4, 344–362, doi: 10.1016/j.geomorph.2011.07.010.

Dewey, J. F., M. L. Helman, S. D. Knott, E. Turco, and D. H. W. Hutton (1989). Kinematics of the western Mediterranean, *Geol. Soc. Lond. Spec. Publ.* **45,** no. 1, 265–283, doi: 10.1144/GSL.SP.1989.045.01.15.

Domènech, M., A. Teixell, and D. F. Stockli (2016). Magnitude of rift-related burial and orogenic contraction in the Marrakech High Atlas revealed by zircon (U-Th)/He thermochronology and thermal modeling, *Tectonics* **35,** no. 11, 2609–2635, doi: 10.1002/2016TC004283.

Duggen, S., K. A. Hoernle, F. Hauff, A. Kluegel, M. Bouabdellah, and M. F. Thirlwall (2009). Flow of Canary mantle plume material through a subcontinental lithospheric corridor beneath Africa to the Mediterranean, *Geology* **37,** no. 3, 283–286, doi: 10.1130/G25426A.1.

El Azzouzi, M., R. C. Maury, H. Bellon, N. Youbi, J. Cotten, and F. Kharbouch (2010). Petrology and K-Ar chronology of the Neogene-quaternary Middle Atlas basaltic province, Morocco, *Bull. Soc. Geol. France* **181,** no. 3, 243–257, doi: 10.2113/gssgfbull.181.3.243.

Ellero, A., G. Ottria, M. G. Malusà, and H. Ouanaimi (2012). Structural geological analysis of the High Atlas (Morocco): Evidences of a transpressional fold-thrust belt, *Tectonics Recent Adv.*, 229–258, doi: 10.5772/50071.

Enescu, B., S. Aoi, S. Toda, W. Suzuki, K. Obara, K. Shiomi, and T. Takeda (2012). Stress perturbations and seismic response associated with the 2011 M 9.0 Tohoku-Oki earthquake in and around the Tokai seismic gap, central Japan, *Geophys. Res. Lett.* **39,** no. 13, doi: 10.1029/2012GL051839.

Fekkak, A., H. Ouanaimi, A. Michard, A. Soulaimani, E. M. Ettachfini, I. Berrada, H. El Arabi, A. Lagnaoui, and O. Saddiqi (2018). Thick-skinned tectonics in a Late Cretaceous-Neogene intracontinental belt (High Atlas Mountains, Morocco): The flat-ramp fault control on basement shortening and cover folding, *J. Afr. Earth. Sci.* **140,** 169–188, doi: 10.1016/j.jafrearsci.2018.01.008.

Frizon de Lamotte, D., B. Saint Bezar, R. Bracène, and E. Mercier (2000). The two main steps of the Atlas building and geodynamics of the western Mediterranean, *Tectonics* **19,** no. 4, 740–761, doi: 10.1029/2000TC900003.

Frizon de Lamotte, D., M. Zizi, Y. Missenard, M. Hafid, M. El Azzouzi, R. C. Maury, A. Charrière, Z. Taki, M. Benammi, and A. Michard (2008). The Atlas system, in *Continental Evolution: The Geology of Morocco: Structure, Stratigraphy, and Tectonics of the Africa-Atlantic-Mediterranean Triple Junction*, A. Michard, O. Saddiqi, A. Chalouan, and D. F. Lamotte (Editors), Vol. 116, Springer, Berlin, Heidelberg, 133–202, doi: 10.1007/978-3-540-77076-3_4.

Froitzheim, N., J. Stets, and P. Wurster (1988). Aspects of western High Atlas tectonics, in *The Atlas System of Morocco: Studies on Its Geodynamic Evolution*, V. H. Jacobshagen (Editors), Vol. 15, Springer, Berlin, Heidelberg, 219–244, doi: 10.1007/BFb0011595.

Fullea, J., M. Fernàndez, J. C. Afonso, J. Vergés, and H. Zeyen (2010). The structure and evolution of the lithosphere–asthenosphere boundary beneath the Atlantic–Mediterranean transition region, *Lithos* **120,** nos. 1/2, 74–95, doi: 10.1016/j.lithos.2010.03.003.

Gomez, F., W. Beauchamp, and M. Barazangi (2000). Role of the Atlas Mountains (northwest Africa) within the African-Eurasian plate-boundary zone, *Geology* **28,** no. 9, 775–778, doi: 10.1130/0091-7613(2000)28<775:ROTAMN>2.0.CO;2.

Hafid, M., M. Zizi, A. W. Bally, and A. A. Salem (2006). Structural styles of the western onshore and offshore termination of the High Atlas, Morocco, *C.R. Geosci.* **338,** nos. 1/2, 50–64, doi: 10.1016/j.crte.2005.10.007.

Hainzl, S., B. Enescu, M. Cocco, J. Woessner, F. Catalli, R. Wang, and F. Roth (2009). Aftershock modeling based on uncertain stress calculations, *J. Geophys. Res. Solid Earth* **114,** no. B5, doi: 10.1029/2008JB006011.

Harris, R. A. (1998). *Introduction to Special Section: Stress Triggers, Stress Shadows, and Implications for Seismic Hazard*, Wiley Online Library, 24347–24358, doi: 10.1029/98JB01576.

Hearn, E. H., and R. Bürgmann (2005). The effect of elastic layering on inversions of GPS data for coseismic slip and resulting stress changes: Strike-slip earthquakes, *Bull. Seismol. Soc. Am.* **95,** no. 5, 1637–1653, doi: 10.1785/0120040158.

Huang, K., G. Wei, K. Chen, N. Zhang, M. Li, and L. Dal Zilio (2024). The 2023 M_w 6.8 Morocco earthquake: A lower crust event triggered by mantle upwelling?, *Geophys. Res. Lett.* **51,** no. 12, e2024GL109052, doi: 10.1029/2024GL109052.

Jiménez-Munt, I., M. Fernandez, J. Vergés, D. Garcia-Castellanos, J. Fullea, M. Pérez-Gussinyé, and J. C. Afonso (2011). Decoupled crust-mantle accommodation of Africa-Eurasia convergence in the NW Moroccan margin, *J. Geophys. Res. Solid Earth* **116,** no. B8, doi: 10.1029/2010JB008105.

Jónsson, S., H. Zebker, P. Segall, and F. Amelung (2002). Fault slip distribution of the 1999 M_w 7.1 Hector Mine, California, earthquake, estimated from satellite radar and GPS measurements, *Bull. Seismol. Soc. Am.* **92,** no. 4, 1377–1389, doi: 10.1785/0120000922.

King, G. C. P., R. S. Stein, and J. Lin (1994). Static stress changes and the triggering of earthquakes, *Bull. Seismol. Soc. Am.* **84,** no. 3, 935–953, doi: 10.1785/BSSA0840030935.

Koulali, A., D. Ouazar, A. Tahayt, R. W. King, P. Vernant, R. E. Reilinger, S. McClusky, T. Mourabit, J. M. Davila, and N. Amraoui (2011). New GPS constraints on active deformation along the Africa–Iberia plate boundary, *Earth Planet. Sci. Lett* **308,** nos. 1/2, 211–217, doi: 10.1016/j.epsl.2011.05.048.

Lanari, R., C. Faccenna, M. G. Fellin, A. Essaifi, A. Nahid, F. Medina, and N. Youbi (2020). Tectonic evolution of the western High Atlas of Morocco: Oblique convergence, reactivation, and transpression, *Tectonics* **39,** no. 3, e2019TC005563, doi: 10.1029/2019TC005563.

Lanari, R., M. G. Fellin, C. Faccenna, M. L. Balestrieri, F. J. Pazzaglia, N. Youbi, and C. Maden (2020). Exhumation and surface evolution of the western high atlas and surrounding regions as constrained by low-temperature thermochronology, *Tectonics* **39,** no. 3, e2019TC005562, doi: 10.1029/2019TC005562.

Laville, E., and A. Pique (1991). La Distension crustale atlantique et atlasique au Maroc au debut du Mesozoique; le rejeu des structures hercyniennes, *Bull. Soc. Geol. France* **162,** no. 6, 1161–1171 (in French).

Laville, E., A. Pique, M. Amrhar, and M. Charroud (2004). A restatement of the Mesozoic Atlasic rifting (Morocco), *J. Afr. Earth. Sci.* **38,** no. 2, 145–153, doi: 10.1016/j.jafrearsci.2003.12.003.

Levandowski, W. (2023). Fault-slip potential near the Deadly 8 September 2023 M_w 6.8 Al Haouz, Morocco, earthquake, *Seism. Rec.* **3,** no. 4, 367–375, doi: 10.1785/0320230037.

Lin, J., and R. S. Stein (2004). Stress triggering in thrust and subduction earthquakes and stress interaction between the southern San Andreas and nearby thrust and strike-slip faults, *J. Geophys. Res. Solid Earth* **109,** no. B2, doi: 10.1029/2003JB002607.

Malusà, M. G., A. Ellero, and G. Ottria (2024). Tectonics of the M_w 6.8 Al Haouz earthquake (Morocco) reveals minor role of asthenospheric upwelling, *Tectonophysics* **891,** 230533, doi: 10.1016/j.tecto.2024.230533.

Mattauer, M., F. Proust, and P. Tapponnier (1972). Major strike-slip fault of late Hercynian age in Morocco, *Nature* **237,** no. 5351, 160–162, doi: 10.1038/237160b0.

Mattauer, M., P. Tapponnier, and F. Proust (1977). Sur les mecanismes de formation des chaines intracontinentales; l'exemple des chaines atlasiques du Maroc, *Bull. Soc. Geol. France* **7,** no. 3, 521–526, doi: 10.2113/gssgfbull.S7-XIX.3.521 (in French).

Medina, F. (1995). Syn-and postrift evolution of the El Jadida–Agadir basin (Morocco): Constraints for the rifting models of the central Atlantic, *Can. J. Earth Sci.* **32,** no. 9, 1273–1291, doi: 10.1139/e95-104.

Medina, F., I. Bensaid, and A. Tangi (2011). Catalogue of focal mechanisms of Moroccan earthquakes for the period 1959-2007; analysis of parameters, *Bull. Inst. Sci. Rabat*, no. 33, 37–46.

Miller, M. S., and T. W. Becker (2014). Reactivated lithospheric-scale discontinuities localize dynamic uplift of the Moroccan Atlas Mountains, *Geology* **42,** no. 1, 35–38, doi: 10.1130/G34959.1.

Missenard, Y., and A. Cadoux (2012). Can Moroccan Atlas lithospheric thinning and volcanism be induced by edge-driven convection?, *Terra Nova* **24,** no. 1, 27–33, doi: 10.1111/j.1365-3121.2011.01033.x.

Missenard, Y., Z. Taki, D. F. de Lamotte, M. Benammi, M. Hafid, P. Leturmy, and M. Sébrier (2007). Tectonic styles in the Marrakesh High Atlas (Morocco): The role of heritage and mechanical stratigraphy, *J. Afr. Earth. Sci.* **48,** no. 4, 247–266, doi: 10.1016/j.jafrearsci.2007.03.007.

Missenard, Y., H. Zeyen, D. Frizon de Lamotte, P. Leturmy, C. Petit, M. Sébrier, and O. Saddiqi (2006). Crustal versus asthenospheric origin of relief of the Atlas Mountains of Morocco, *J. Geophys. Res. Solid Earth* **111,** no. B3, doi: 10.1029/2005JB003708.

Mokhtari, A., and D. Velde (1988). Xenocrysts in Eocene camptonites from Taourirt, northern Morocco, *Mineral Mag.* **52,** no. 368, 587–601, doi: 10.1180/minmag.1988.052.368.04.

Mustaphi, H., F. Medina, H. Jabour, and C. Hoepffner (1997). Le bassin du Souss (Zone de Faille du Tizi n'Test, Haut Atlas occidental, Maroc): Resultat d'une inversion tectonique contrlee par une faille de detachement profonde, *J. Afr. Earth. Sci.* **24,** nos. 1/2, 153–168, doi: 10.1016/S0899-5362(97)00033-X (in French).

Nalbant, S., J. McCloskey, S. Steacy, M. NicBhloscaidh, and S. Murphy (2013). Interseismic coupling, stress evolution, and earthquake slip on the Sunda megathrust, *Geophys. Res. Lett.* **40,** no. 16, 4204–4208, doi: 10.1002/grl.50776.

Nouayti, A., L. El Moudnib, D. Khattach, M. Zeckra, N. Nouayti, O. Saadi, K. Elhairechi, B. Oujane, and H. Iken (2024). Seismic synthesis of the Al Haouz earthquake of September 8th, 2023 by integrating gravimetric and aeromagnetic data from the western High Atlas in Morocco, *Model Earth Syst. Environ.*, 1–20, doi: 10.1007/s40808-024-02148-3.

Okada, Y. (1985). Surface deformation due to shear and tensile faults in a half-space, *Bull. Seismol. Soc. Am.* **75,** no. 4, 1135–1154, doi: 10.1785/BSSA0750041135.

Pachhai, S. (2023). Transdimensional hierarchical Bayesian inversion of phase and group velocity, *Zenodo*, available at https://zenodo.org/records/7825575 (last accessed April 2023).

Palomeras, I., A. Villaseñor, S. Thurner, A. Levander, J. Gallart, and M. Harnafi (2017). Lithospheric structure of Iberia and Morocco using finite-frequency Rayleigh wave tomography from earthquakes and seismic ambient noise, *Geochem. Geophys. Geosyst.* **18,** no. 5, 1824–1840, doi: 10.1002/2016GC006657.

Parera-Portell, J. A., F. Mancilla, J. Morales, and J. Díaz (2024). High-resolution mapping of the mantle transition zone and its interaction with subducted slabs in the Ibero-Maghrebian region, *Earth Planet. Sci. Lett.* **640,** 118798, doi: 10.1016/j.epsl.2024.118798.

Parker, R. L. (1994). *Geophysical Inverse Theory*, Princeton University Press, Princeton, New Jersey.

Phạm, T., and H. Tkalčić (2017). On the feasibility and use of teleseismic P wave coda autocorrelation for mapping shallow seismic discontinuities, *J. Geophys. Res. Solid Earth* **122,** no. 5, 3776–3791, doi: 10.1002/2017JB013975.

Philip, H., and M. Meghraoui (1983). Structural analysis and interpretation of the surface deformations of the El Asnam earthquake of October 10, 1980, *Tectonics* **2,** no. 1, 17–49, doi: 10.1029/TC002i001p00017.

Piqué, A., P. Tricart, R. Guiraud, E. Laville, S. Bouaziz, M. Amrhar, and R. A. Ouali (2002). The Mesozoic–Cenozoic Atlas belt (North

Africa): An overview, *Geodinamica Acta* **15,** no. 3, 185–208, doi: 10.1080/09853111.2002.10510752.
Proust, F., J.-P. Petit, and P. Tapponnier (1977). L'accident du Tizi n'Test et le rôle des décrochements dans la tectonique du Haut Atlas occidental (Maroc), *Bull. Soc. Geol. France* **7,** no. 3, 541–551, doi: 10.2113/gssgfbull.S7-XIX.3.541 (in French).
Qarbous, A., F. Medina, and C. Hoepffner (2003). Le bassin de Tizi n'Test (Haut Atlas, Maroc): Exemple d'évolution d'un segment oblique au rift de l'Atlantique central au Trias, *Can. J. Earth Sci.* **40,** no. 7, 949–964, doi: 10.1139/e03-029 (in French).
Sandwell, D., R. Mellors, X. Tong, M. Wei, and P. Wessel (2011). Open radar interferometry software for mapping surface deformation, *Eos Trans. AGU* **92,** no. 28, 234, doi: 10.1029/2011EO280002.
Seber, D., M. Barazangi, B. A. Tadili, M. Ramdani, A. Ibenbrahim, and D. Ben Sari (1996). Three-dimensional upper mantle structure beneath the intraplate Atlas and interplate Rif mountains of Morocco, *J. Geophys. Res. Solid Earth* **101,** no. B2, 3125–3138, doi: 10.1029/95JB03112.
Sébrier, M., L. Siame, E. M. Zouine, T. Winter, Y. Missenard, and P. Leturmy (2006). Active tectonics in the Moroccan high atlas, *C.R. Geosci.* **338,** no. 1–2, 65–79, doi: 10.1016/j.crte.2005.12.001.
Serpelloni, E., G. Vannucci, S. Pondrelli, A. Argnani, G. Casula, M. Anzidei, P. Baldi, and P. Gasperini (2007). Kinematics of the Western Africa-Eurasia plate boundary from focal mechanisms and GPS data, *Geophys. J. Int.* **169,** no. 3, 1180–1200, doi: 10.1111/j.1365-246X.2007.03367.x.
Skikra, H., A. Fadil, Y. Ouassanouan, K. Lakhouidsi, A. Tahayt, A. Soulaimani, and L. El Moudnib (2024). Seismotectonic assessment of the High Atlas orogen: Implications for the 8 September M_w 6.8 El-Haouz earthquake, *Tectonophysics*, 230573, doi: 10.1016/j.tecto.2024.230573.
Soumaya, A., N. Ben Ayed, M. Rajabi, M. Meghraoui, D. Delvaux, A. Kadri, M. Ziegler, S. Maouche, and A. Braham (2018). Active faulting geometry and stress pattern near complex strike-slip systems along the Maghreb region: Constraints on active convergence in the western Mediterranean, *Tectonics* **37,** no. 9, 3148–3173, doi: 10.1029/2018TC004983.
Stein, R. S. (1999). The role of stress transfer in earthquake occurrence, *Nature* **402,** no. 6762, 605–609, doi: 10.1038/45144.
Stein, R. S., and G. Ekström (1992). Seismicity and geometry of a 110-km-long blind thrust fault 2. Synthesis of the 1982–1985 California earthquake sequence, *J. Geophys. Res. Solid Earth* **97,** no. B4, 4865–4883, doi: 10.1029/91JB02847.
Teixell, A., M. Arboleya, M. Julivert, and M. Charroud (2003). Tectonic shortening and topography in the central High Atlas (Morocco), *Tectonics* **22,** no. 5, doi: 10.1029/2002TC001460.
Teixell, A., P. Ayarza, H. Zeyen, M. Fernandez, and M. Arboleya (2005). Effects of mantle upwelling in a compressional setting: The Atlas Mountains of Morocco, *Terra Nova* **17,** no. 5, 456–461, doi: 10.1111/j.1365-3121.2005.00633.x.
Tesón, E., E. L. Pueyo, A. Teixell, A. Barnolas, J. Agustí, and M. Furió (2010). Magnetostratigraphy of the Ouarzazate Basin: Implications for the timing of deformation and mountain building in the High Atlas Mountains of Morocco, *Geodinamica Acta* **23,** no. 4, 151, doi: 10.3166/ga.23.151-165.
Thapa, H. A. R. I. (2021). Crustal structure and discontinuities beneath the Nepal Himalaya using seismic ambient noise and teleseismic P wave coda autocorrelation, available at https://hdl.handle.net/11368/2996096 (last accessed September 2023).
Thapa, H. R. (2025). Computation of teleseismic P wave coda autocorrelation, in *High-Resolution Moho Depth and Vp/Vs Mapping Beneath the Carpatho–Pannonian Region Using P-Wave Coda Autocorrelation*, Zenodo, doi: 10.5281/zenodo.14655969.
Thapa, H. R., and G. Vlahovic (2025). High-resolution Moho depth and Vp/Vs mapping beneath the Carpatho–Pannonian region using P-wave coda autocorrelation, *J. Geophys. Res. Solid Earth* **130,** no. 5, e2024JB030491.
Thapa, H. R., S. Mitra, A. Aoudia, G. Vlahovic, K. F. Priestley, and S. K. Wanchoo (2025a). Autocorrelation-based imaging of crustal discontinuities including the Main Himalayan thrust and V_P/V_S ratio in the Jammu and Kashmir Himalaya, *ESS Open Archive* doi: 10.22541/essoar.175596919.92774285/v1.
Thapa, H. R., S. Mitra, A. Aoudia, G. Vlahovic, K. F. Priestley, and S. K. Wanchoo (2025b). Imaging crustal discontinuities, including the Main Himalayan thrust, and V_P/V_S ratio using *P*-wave coda autocorrelation in the Jammu and Kashmir Himalaya, *AGU Fall Meeting 2025 (AGU25)*, New Orleans, Louisiana, 15–19 December 2025.
Thapa, H. R., S. Pachhai, A. Aoudia, D. Manu-Marfo, K. Priestley, and S. Mitra (2023). The Main Himalayan thrust beneath Nepal and southern Tibet illuminated by seismic ambient noise and teleseismic P wave coda autocorrelation, *J. Geophys. Res. Solid Earth* **128,** no. 8, doi: 10.1029/2022JB026195.
Thomas, C. (2010). Morocco-Muenster, doi: 10.7914/SN/3D_2010, available at https://www.fdsn.org/networks/detail/3D_2010/ (last accessed September 2023).
Tillotson, E. (1960). The Agadir earthquake of February 29, *Nature* **186,** no. 4720, 199, doi: 10.1038/186199a0.
Toda, S., J. Lin, and R. S. Stein (2011). Using the 2011 M_w 9.0 off the Pacific coast of Tohoku Earthquake to test the Coulomb stress triggering hypothesis and to calculate faults brought closer to failure, *Earth Planets Space* **63,** no. 7, 725–730, doi: 10.5047/eps.2011.05.010.
Toda, S., R. S. Stein, and J. Lin (2011). Widespread seismicity excitation throughout central Japan following the 2011 M = 9.0 Tohoku earthquake and its interpretation by Coulomb stress transfer, *Geophys. Res. Lett.* **38,** no. 7, doi: 10.1029/2011GL047834.
Toda, S., R. S. Stein, K. Richards-Dinger, and S. B. Bozkurt (2005). Forecasting the evolution of seismicity in southern California: Animations built on earthquake stress transfer, *J. Geophys. Res. Solid Earth* **110,** no. B5, doi: 10.1029/2004JB003415.
Toda, S., R. S. Stein, V. Sevilgen, and J. Lin (2011). Coulomb 3.3 Graphic-rich deformation and stress-change software for earthquake, tectonic, and volcano research and teaching—User guide, *U.S. Geol. Surv. Open-File Rept. 1060, No. 2011*, 63.
Touati, B., W. Gu, S. Ni, R. Chu, M. Sheng, Q. Xue, F. Bellalem, S. Maouche, and H. Yahyaoui (2024). The 2023 M_w 6.8 Adassil earthquake (Chichaoua, Morocco) on a steep reverse fault in the deep crust and its geodynamic implications, *Earth Planet. Phys.* **8,** no. 3, 522–534, doi: 10.26464/epp2024019.
Urchulutegui, J. F., M. Fernàndez, and H. Zeyen (2006). Lithospheric structure in the Atlantic–Mediterranean transition zone (southern Spain, northern Morocco): A simple approach from regional elevation and geoid data, *C. R. Geosci.* **338,** nos. 1/2, 140–151, doi: 10.1016/j.crte.2005.11.004.

Wang, J., C. Xu, J. T. Freymueller, Z. Li, and W. Shen (2014). Sensitivity of Coulomb stress change to the parameters of the Coulomb failure model: A case study using the 2008 M_w 7.9 Wenchuan earthquake, *J. Geophys. Res. Solid Earth* **119,** no. 4, 3371–3392, doi: 10.1002/2012JB009860.

Wessel, P., J. F. Luis, L. Uieda, R. Scharroo, F. Wobbe, D. Smith, and D. Tian (2019). The Generic Mapping Tools version 6, *Geochem. Geophys. Geosyst.* **20,** no. 11, 5556–5564, doi: 10.1029/2019GC008515.

Wookey, J., A. Horleston, J. Di Leo, C. Thomas, M. Harnaf, and D. Elouai (2011). CoMITAC Morocco-Bristol Network, doi: 10.7914/SN/ZI_2011.

Wu, W., Y. Zhang, X. Hao, and J. Liu (2024). The source kinematics and slip distribution of the 2023 M_w 6.8 Morocco earthquake, *J. Afr. Earth. Sci.* **220,** 105451, doi: 10.1016/j.jafrearsci.2024.105451.

Yagi, Y., R. Okuwaki, S. Hirano, B. Enescu, M. Chikamori, and R. Yamaguchi (2024). Barrier-induced rupture front disturbances during the 2023 Morocco earthquake, *Seismol. Res. Lett.* **95,** no. 3, 1591–1598, doi: 10.1785/0220230357.

Yeck, W. L., A. E. Hatem, D. E. Goldberg, W. D. Barnhart, J. A. T. Jobe, D. R. Shelly, A. Villaseñor, H. M. Benz, and P. S. Earle (2023). Rapid source characterization of the 2023 M_w 6.8 Al Haouz, Morocco, earthquake, *Seism. Rec.* **3,** no. 4, 357–366, doi: 10.1785/0320230040.

Zeyen, H., P. Ayarza, M. Fernàndez, and A. Rimi (2005). Lithospheric structure under the western African-European plate boundary: A transect across the Atlas Mountains and the Gulf of Cadiz, *Tectonics* **24,** no. 2, doi: 10.1029/2004TC001639.

Zühlke, R., M.-S. Bouaouda, B. Ouajhain, T. Bechstädt, and R. Leinfelder (2004). Quantitative Meso-/Cenozoic development of the eastern central Atlantic continental shelf, western High Atlas, Morocco, *Mar. Pet. Geol.* **21,** no. 2, 225–276, doi: 10.1016/j.marpetgeo.2003.11.014.

Manuscript received 3 September 2025
Published online 10 February 2026

High-Resolution Imaging of the Crust Beneath the Proterozoic Aravalli–Delhi Fold Belt in Northwestern India: Evidence of Anomalous Crustal Thickening

Deepak Nayal[1], Gowthami Bandlamudi[1], and Mohan Gollapally*[1]

Abstract

Evolutionary models for the Proterozoic Aravalli–Delhi fold belt (ADFB) in northwestern India are debatable due to the nonreflective crust resulting in a partially resolved crustal structure, poor imaging of the Moho, and ambiguity in the subduction polarity. Receiver function (RF) analysis was done using ≈5000 RFs from 30 broadband stations spaced at intervals of ≈10 to 12 km along a 250-km-long northwest–southeast traverse across the ADFB. High-resolution common conversion point imaging was performed using the V_P/V_S ratios (κ) and the 1D shear-wave velocity (V_S) models estimated from H–κ stacking and neighbourhood inversion, respectively. The geometry and continuity of the Moho and the intracrustal layers beneath the ADFB are imaged with better resolution than the earlier studies. The Delhi Fold Belt (DFB), located between the Marwar basin (MB) and the Banded Gneissic Complex (BGC), is characterized by an anomalously thick (≈52 km) crust, a southeast-dipping Moho, a domal midcrustal interface, and a mafic lower crust with $V_S \geq 4$ km/s. In contrast, MB is underlain by a thin (≈38 km) felsic crust, and BGC is predominantly characterized by a felsic crust with thickness increasing from ≈38 to ≈45 km toward DFB. The feasible mechanisms of crustal thickening, such as magmatic underplating, relamination, and crustal shortening, are examined within the framework of ensialic and plate tectonic models. The convergence between the Marwar and Aravalli cratons led to the subduction of the intervening oceanic crust, possibly comprising island arcs, which were detached, melted, and relaminated to the base of the crust, followed by crustal accretion and shortening due to collisional tectonics. The mafic residue of the rift-related magma and fractionated melts forms a high-velocity lower crust, resulting in a rheologically strong, thick crust beneath DFB.

Cite this article as Nayal, D., G. Bandlamudi, and M. Gollapally (2026). High-Resolution Imaging of the Crust Beneath the Proterozoic Aravalli–Delhi Fold Belt in Northwestern India: Evidence of Anomalous Crustal Thickening, *Seismol. Res. Lett.* **97**, 743–754, doi: 10.1785/0220250281.

Introduction

The principle of uniformitarianism provides a framework for understanding the past geological events through present day processes. Geochemical evidence indicates that the evolutionary processes varied through time, with the notable mid-Proterozoic eon (1.85–0.85 Ga) being a period of orogenic quiescence relative to the peak times of orogeny associated with the Columbia (2.2–1.5 Ga) and Rodinia (1.3–0.9 Ga) supercontinent assembly (Spencer *et al.*, 2021). The tectonic mode in the Mesoproterozoic period is debated, with hypotheses that include "orogenic quiescence" (Zhu *et al.*, 2022), single-lid tectonics (Stern, 2020), and a different style of hot and thin orogenesis being proposed (Spencer *et al.*, 2021). Based on geological evidence, Stern (2018) proposed that modern plate tectonics began in Neoproterozoic time. Based on seismic studies, Wan *et al.* (2020) suggest that subduction-driven global tectonics was in place by ~2.0 Ga in Proterozoic time. Constraints on the onset of modern plate tectonics can be provided by imaging regions that preserve the complete geological record of Proterozoic activity.

The Aravalli craton in northwestern India (Fig. 1) represents a classic example of the preservation of the geological record of the Precambrian crust over 3 billion years from the Archean to the Neo-Proterozoic (Heron, 1953; Gopalan *et al.*, 1990; Sinha-Roy *et al.*, 1995), which offers a unique opportunity to trace the seismic evidence of the evolution of

1. Department of Earth Sciences, Indian Institute of Technology Bombay, Mumbai, India, https://orcid.org/0009-0002-4116-2674 (DN); https://orcid.org/0000-0001-6126-7735 (GB); https://orcid.org/0000-0003-0100-6001 (MG)

*Corresponding author: gmohan@iitb.ac.in

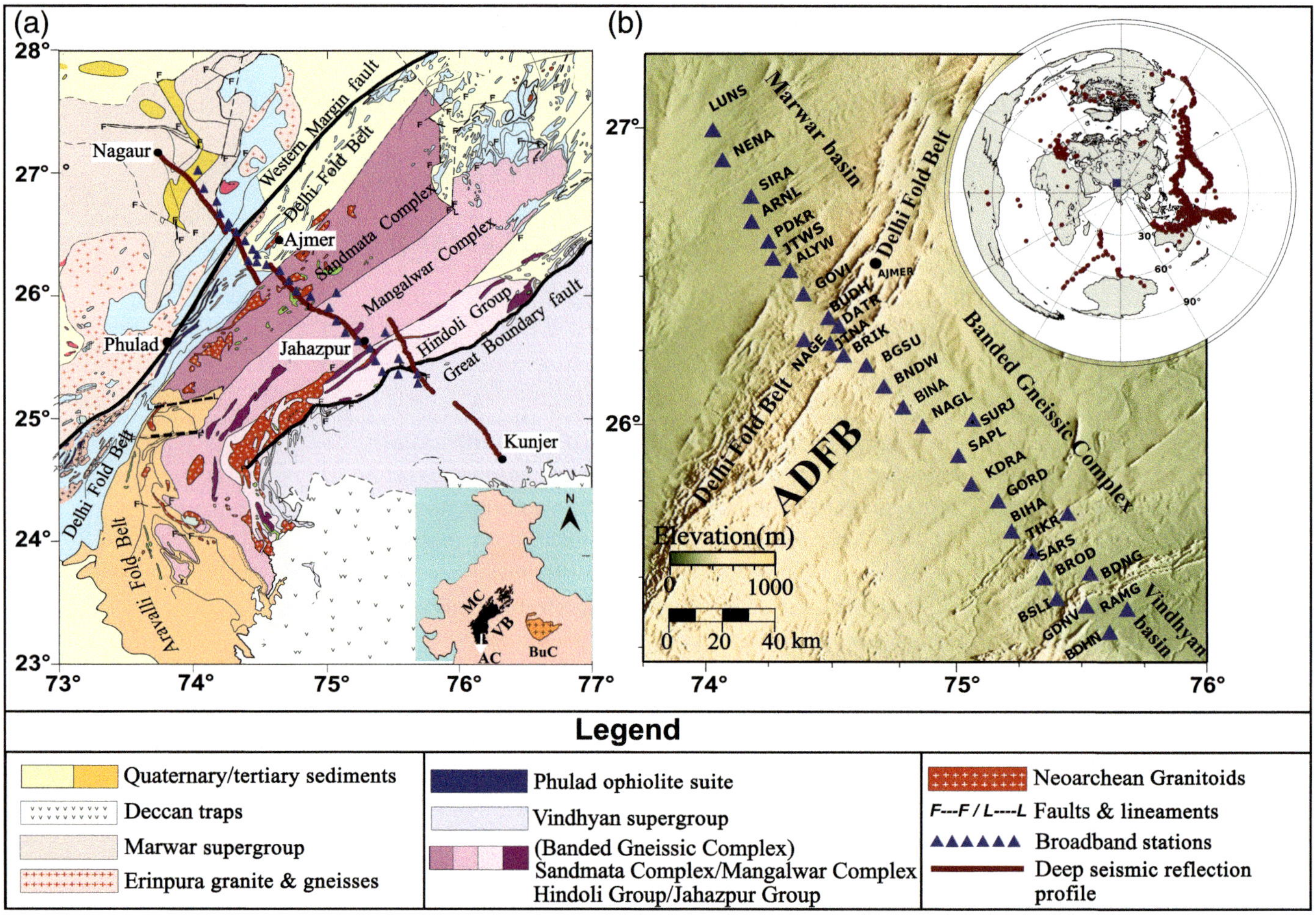

Figure 1. (a) Geological map of the study region (adapted after Geological Survey of India [GSI], 2000) showing the broadband stations deployed along the deep seismic reflection profile (Reddy *et al.*, 1995; Vijaya Rao *et al.*, 2000). The inset map depicts the cratons (AC, Aravalli craton; BuC, Bundelkhand craton; MC, Marwar craton) that converged to form the Aravalli–Delhi fold belt (ADFB). VB denotes the Vindhyan basin. (b) A topographic map showing the location of broadband (BB) seismological stations and the inset shows the back-azimuthal distribution of events used in the study.

the Aravalli–Delhi Proterozoic fold belt. The tectonic history of this region is characterized by the Aravalli and Delhi orogenic events that correlate temporally with the fragmentation and amalgamation of the Columbia and Rodinia supercontinents, respectively (Ghosh *et al.*, 2022). Although diverse tectonic models (Ghosh *et al.*, 2022, and references therein) were proposed for the evolution of the 700 km long, northeast–southwest-trending Aravalli–Delhi Fold Belt (ADFB), there is no consensus on a feasible evolutionary model. The crustal *P*-wave velocity structure and the Moho beneath the various lithounits of the ADFB were partially resolved primarily through several studies using the deep seismic reflection data acquired along a 400-km long, northwest–southeast profile from Nagaur to Kunjer (Fig. 1) across the ADFB (Reddy *et al.*, 1995; Tewari *et al.*, 1997; Vijaya Rao *et al.*, 2000; Krishna and Rao, 2011). The seismic images were enhanced using the common reflection surface (CRS) technique (Mandal *et al.*, 2014); however, due to a nonreflective crust, the Moho beneath the Delhi Fold Belt (DFB) could not be imaged successfully. Although seismic reflection studies have inferred crustal thickening beneath DFB, there remains uncertainty regarding the geometry, continuity, and depth of the Moho, as well as the subduction polarity beneath the ADFB. Thus, there is a knowledge gap in validating the various geological models, ranging from plate tectonic to ensialic, proposed for the evolution of the Proterozoic orogenic belt. Hence, to constrain the feasible evolutionary models for the Proterozoic ADFB, high-resolution receiver function (RF) imaging of the crust beneath a 250-km-long northwest–southeast profile (Fig. 1) coinciding with the deep seismic reflection profile cutting across the ADFB was done.

Geological Setting

The Aravalli craton is a prominent geological feature in northwestern India (Fig. 1), which is separated from the Marwar basin (MB) in the west by the Western Margin fault (WMF) and from the Vindhyan basin in the east by the Great

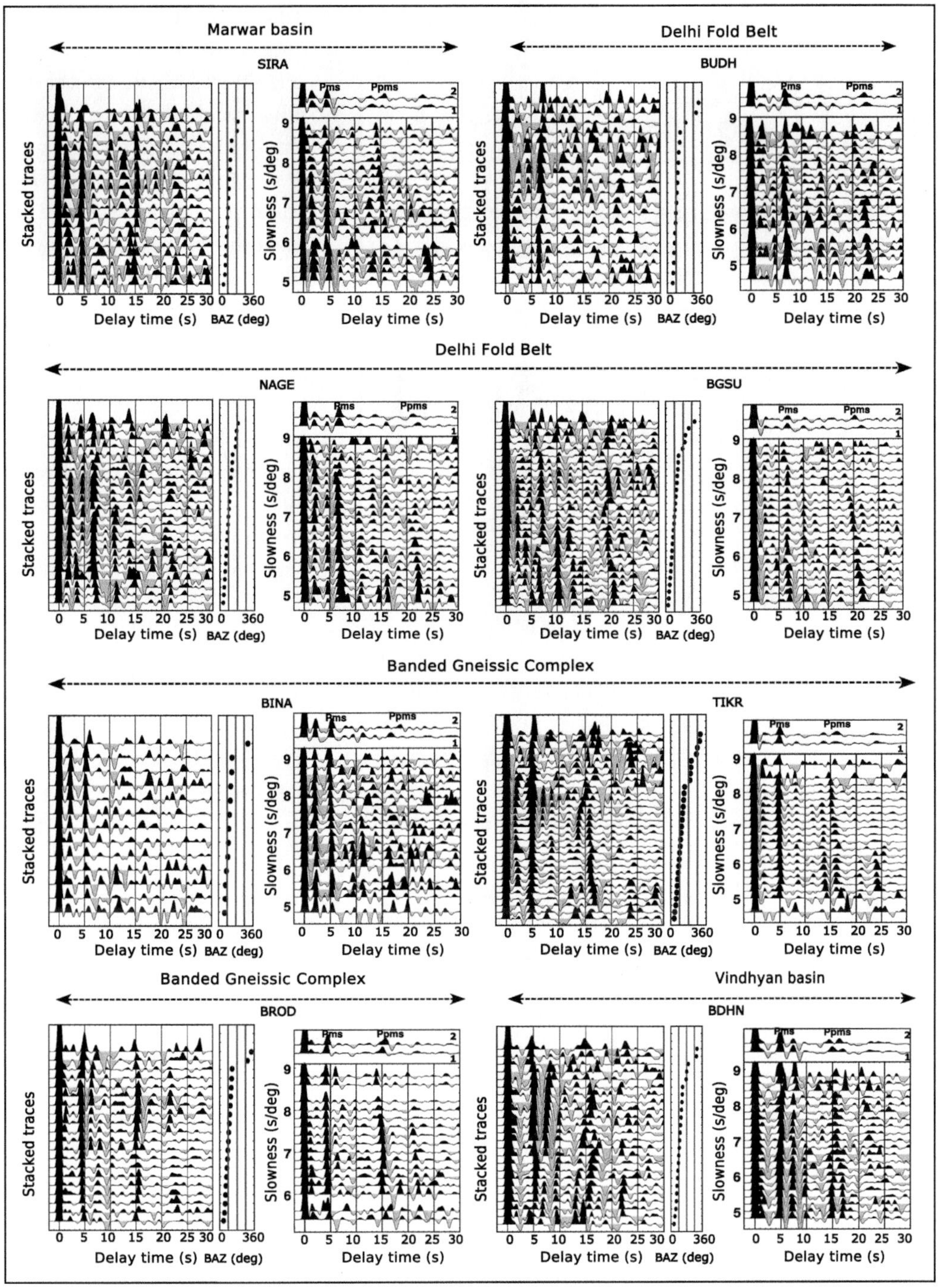

Figure 2. Radial receiver functions (RFs) plotted as a function of back azimuth (left) and slowness (right) at stations in each terrane. The traces were stacked in back-azimuthal bins of 5° and plotted with increasing back azimuth (black dots). In the slowness plots, RFs were binned in intervals of 0.2 s/deg. The top two traces on the slowness plots are the cumulative stacks moveout corrected for (1) *Pms* and (2) *Ppms* phases, respectively. The color version of this figure is available only in the electronic edition.

Boundary fault (GBF). The craton comprises the Archean Banded Gneissic Complex (BGC), which is overlain by the supracrustal sequences of the Paleoproterozoic and Paleoneoproterozoic Aravalli and Delhi Supergroups, which together form the ADFB (Sinha–Roy *et al.*, 1995). The rocks found in BGC were earlier classified into the Hindoli Group (HG), Mangalwar Complex (MC), and Sandmata Complex (SC) based on increasing grade of metamorphism from east to west (Fig. 1), with the former two being later recognized as part of the Aravalli Supergroup (Roy, 1988). It is now widely accepted that a two-stage Proterozoic collisional tectonics led to the formation of the ADFB (Sinha–Roy *et al.*, 1995; Vijaya Rao *et al.*, 2000; Ghosh *et al.*, 2022).

The collision of the Bundelkhand craton with the Aravalli craton formed the Neoarchean granitoids (≈2.5 Ga), followed by Paleoproterozoic rifting and sedimentation west of the granitoid terrane. The subsequent basin closure led to the formation of the Aravalli Fold Belt around 1.8 Ga. The second stage of the evolution of the ADFB involved the development of the DFB in two stages spanning from late Paleoproterozoic to Neoproterozoic time (Sinha-Roy, 1988; McKenzie *et al.*, 2013). In the first stage, the north DFB (north of Ajmer) was formed during ~1.7 to 1.4 Ga, whereas in the second stage, the south DFB was formed during ~1.0 to 0.7 Ga (Ghosh *et al.*, 2022). A zone of mafic–ultramafic rocks, collectively known as the Phulad ophiolite suite (Volpe and Macdougall, 1990; Roy and Jakhar, 2002), is present along the WMF, also referred to as the Phulad shear zone, which marks the suture zone between the Marwar and the Aravalli cratons (Fig. 1). The final thermal event associated with the Delhi orogeny involved intrusion of the Neoproterozoic Erinpura granites in the south DFB and its western foreland (de Wall *et al.*, 2021). The MB evolved during the Late Neoproterozoic

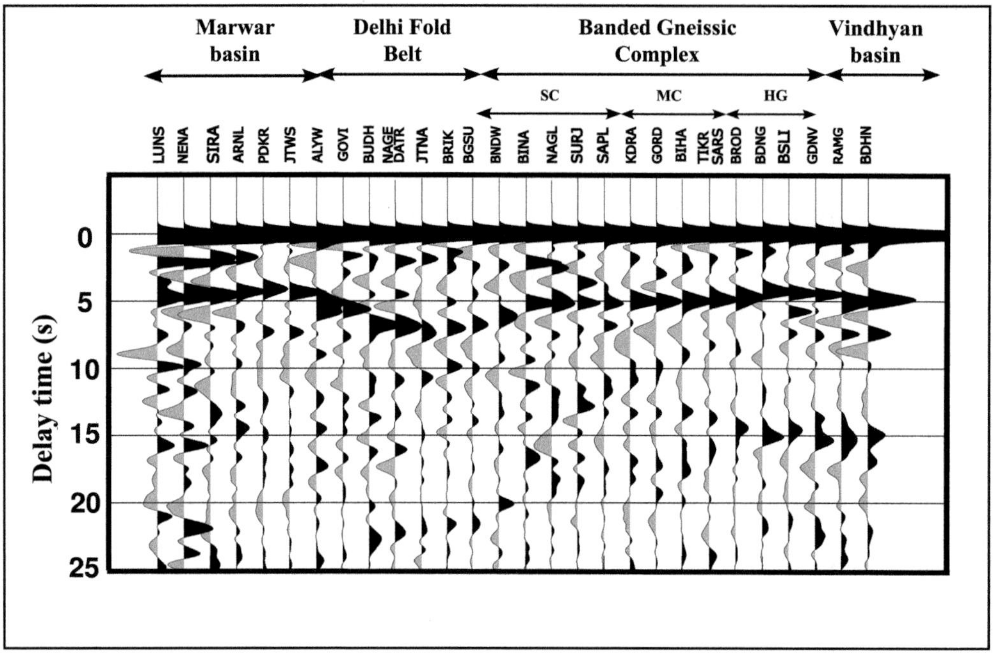

Figure 3. Composite stack of RFs at each station arranged sequentially along the profile from northwest to southeast. The RF stacks were moveout corrected for the *Pms* phase using a reference slowness of 6.4 s/deg. HG, Hindoli Group; MC, Mangalwar Complex; SC, Sandmata Complex.

to Early Cambrian period, and comprises sediments that unconformably overlie the Neoproterozoic Malani igneous suite. The Vindhyan basin is a Mesoproterozoic intracontinental basin located east of the BGC adjoining the GBF.

Data

During the period 2017–2024, broadband stations spaced at intervals of ≈10 to 12 km were established in phases at 30 locations along a 250-km-long northwest–southeast-trending profile overlapping with the deep seismic reflection profile across the ADFB (Fig. 1). The profile cuts across the MB, the south DFB, the BGC, and the Vindhyan basin (VB). Waveforms with a high signal-to-noise ratio (≥2) corresponding to teleseismic events of magnitude ≥5.0, predominantly from back azimuths ranging from 0° to 180°, are utilized (Fig. 1).

RF Methodology

We use the iterative time-domain deconvolution method (Ligorria and Ammon, 1999) that follows the least-squares minimization of the difference between the observed radial seismogram and the predicted signal to generate the radial RFs. The predicted signal is generated by convolving the vertical-component seismogram with the updated, iteratively generated spikes. The high-frequency noise in the RFs was reduced by applying a Gaussian filter with a width of 2.5 on the data. To ensure data quality control, only the RFs that preserved at least 80% of the original signal were used. About 5000 RFs corresponding to 750 teleseismic events were constructed. The RF delay time plots with respect to back azimuth and slowness (Fig. 2) at stations in each terrane exhibit strong positive amplitudes corresponding to the Moho converted *Pms* phase. The first multiple associated with the *Pms* phase is clearly observed in the RFs at most stations in MB, BGC, and VB, but weakly observed at stations in DFB, where the RFs show distinct variation with back azimuth. The *Ps* conversions from the intracrustal high and low-velocity layers are observed as positive and negative pulses, respectively, that arrive earlier than the *Pms* phase.

The composite RF stacks (Fig. 3) moveout corrected to a slowness of 6.4 s/deg exhibit significant variation in the *Pms* delay times across the stations located in different geological terranes. The average *Pms* delay times observed are ≈4.4 s in the MB, ≈6.9 s in the DFB, ≈5.2, ≈5, and ≈4.5 s, respectively, in the three segments of BGC, that is, SC, MC, and HG, and ≈5 s in the Vindhyan basin. The *Pms* delay times at stations in DFB are anomalously large relative to those observed at all other stations.

H–κ Stacking

The bulk crustal thickness (H) and V_P/V_S ratio (κ) are estimated from the RFs using the $H-\kappa$ stacking method (Zhu and Kanamori, 2000) by searching for the combination of H and κ that maximizes the sum of the amplitudes of the *Ps* phase and the associated multiples expressed as

$$S[H,\kappa] = \sum_{n=1}^{N} w_1 r_j(T_{ps}) + w_2 r_j(T_{PpPs}) - w_3 r_j(T_{PpSs},T_{PsPs}), \quad (1)$$

in which w_1, w_2, and w_3 are the stacking weights (0.7, 0.2, and 0.1, for which sum $\sum w_i = 1$) given to the *Ps* phases and the associated multiples (T_{PpPs} and $T_{PpSs} + T_{PsPs}$). The average crustal *P*-wave velocity used was 6.45 km/s for DFB and 6.4 km/s for other terranes, as estimated from seismic reflection studies (Krishna and Rao, 2011). The uncertainties in H and V_P/V_S are estimated by adopting the bootstrap resampling method (Efron and Tibshirani, 1986). $H-\kappa$ analysis yields reliable results for a simple crust; however, for complex structures with gradational or dipping Moho, the κ value may

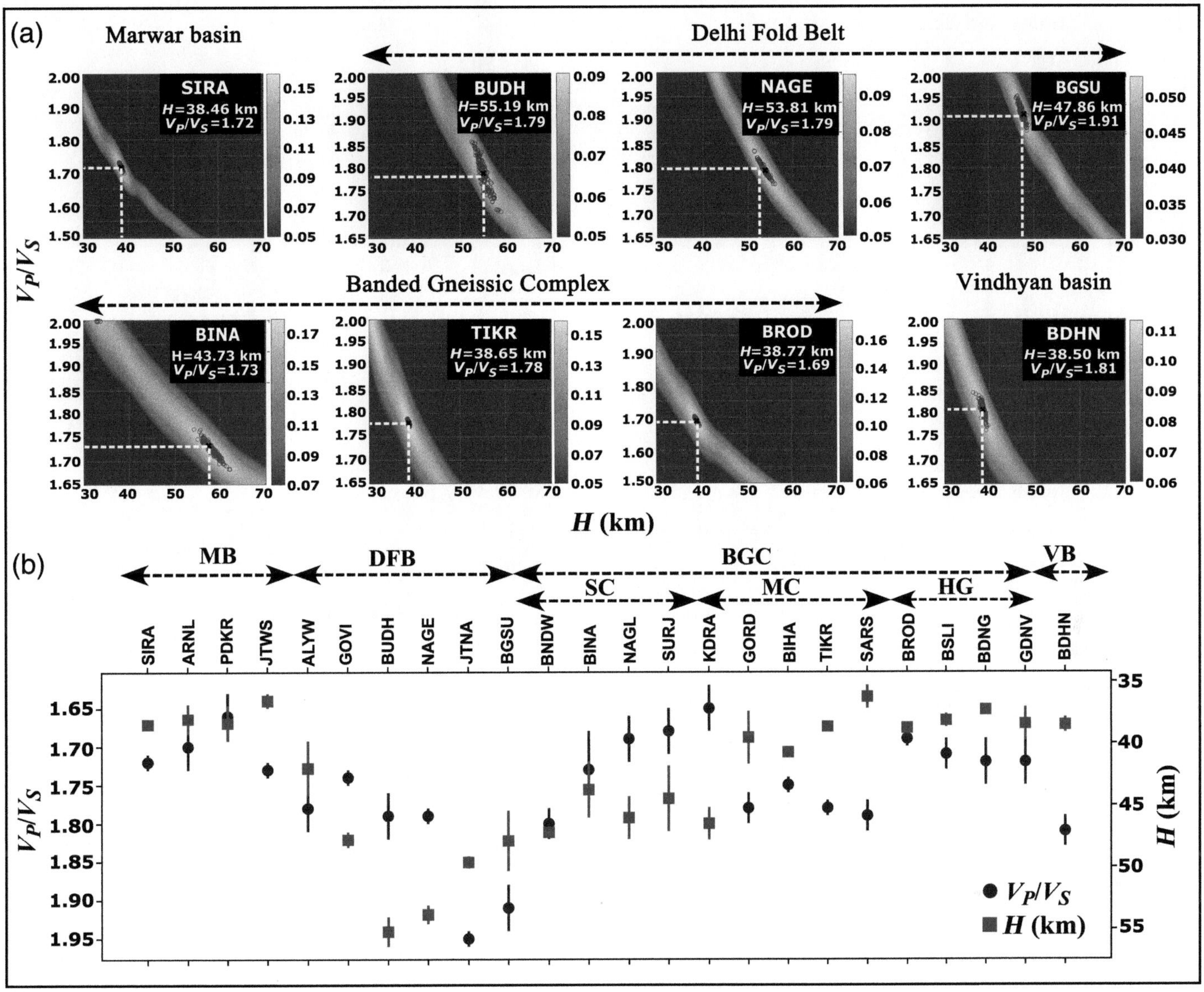

Figure 4. (a) Results of $H - \kappa$ stacking at stations located in different terranes along the profile across ADFB. The black cross in the region with the maximum amplitude (coherency of phases) represents the best H and κ values. The cluster of open circles represents the $H - \kappa$ values estimated from 200 bootstrap iterations. (b) Plot of H and κ values at 24 stations along the profile. BGC, Banded Gneissic Complex; DFB, Delhi Fold Belt; MB, Marwar basin; VB, Vindhyan basin. The color version of this figure is available only in the electronic edition.

be uncertain (Ogden *et al.*, 2019). Ambiguities can be reduced by validating the $H - \kappa$ parameters by carrying out the analysis on RFs constructed using different Gaussian widths (Gws; Ogden *et al.*, 2019), and using the RFs from a narrow back-azimuthal range in the up-dip direction (Wang *et al.*, 2010). $H - \kappa$ stacking was performed on RFs constructed using Gws of 1.6, 2.5, and 5, at all stations, as well as in a narrow back-azimuthal range for stations in DFB to validate the results. The uncertainties from the bootstrap analysis were ≤1 km for H and ≤0.03 for κ at most stations. The $H - \kappa$ plots corresponding to RFs filtered with a Gw of 2.5 are shown for eight stations in Figure 4a. The $H - \kappa$ pairs for 24 stations are plotted station wise in Figure 4b.

Inversion Using Neighbourhood Algorithm

The Neighbourhood algorithm (NA) stochastic inversion technique (Sambridge, 1999) was used to invert the RFs in narrow back-azimuthal and epicentral ranges of 15° at each station. The NA inversion utilizes geometrical constructs known as Voronoi cells to search the multidimensional parameter space and obtain an ensemble of best-fitting models. The inversion is performed over a range of *Ns* and *Nr* values, which represent the number of models generated and the number of Voronoi cells resampled at each iteration (Sambridge, 1999). The final inversion result was chosen based on the convergence of predicted and observed RFs with low misfit. A five-layered crustal model comprising sediments, basement, upper, middle, and

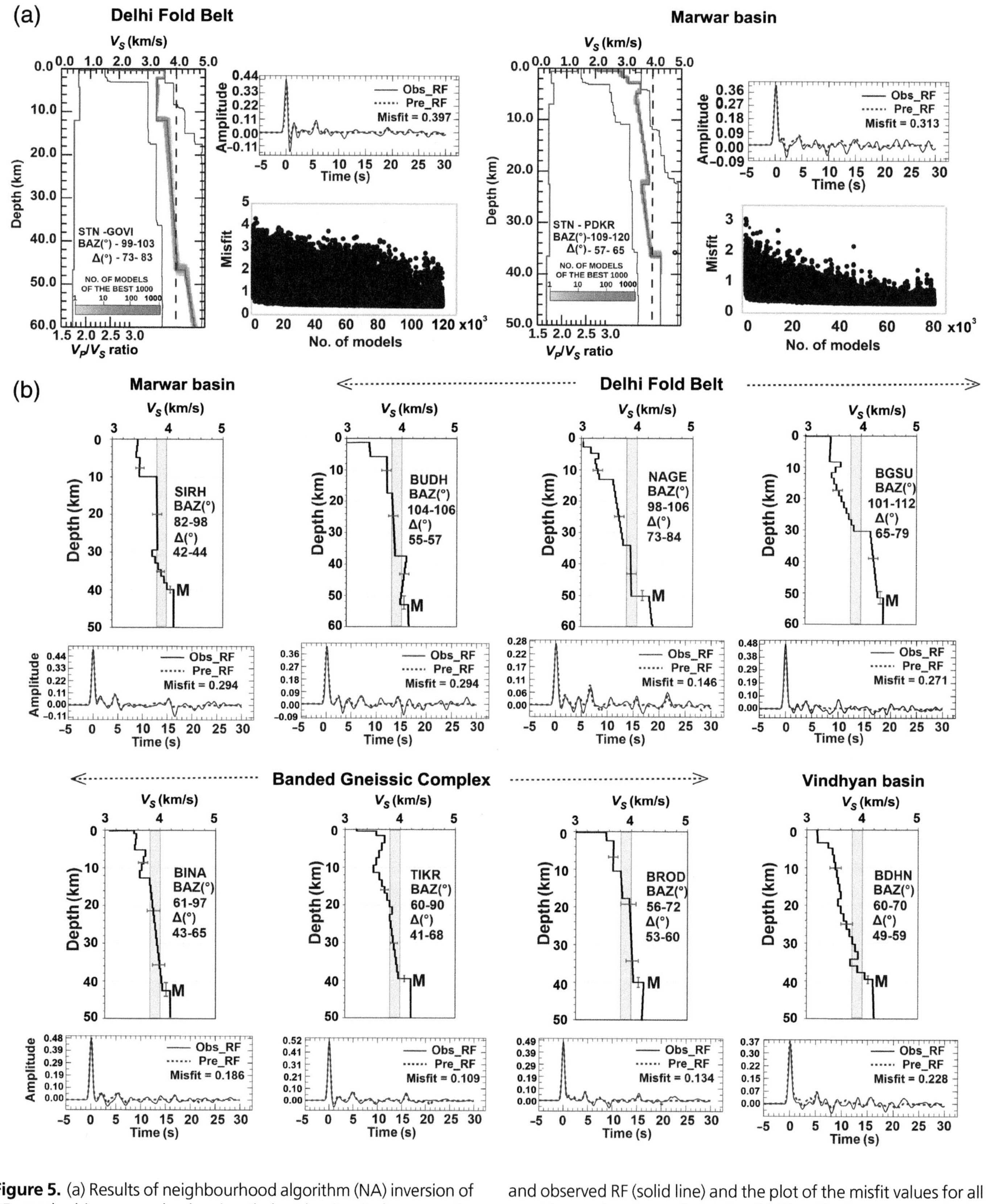

Figure 5. (a) Results of neighbourhood algorithm (NA) inversion of RFs stacked in narrow back-azimuthal and epicentral ranges at two stations. The best-fitting model, the 1000 best-fitting models, and the lower and upper bounds of the ensemble of all models generated are shown. The vertical-dashed line represents the shear-wave velocity (V_S) of 4 km/s. The misfit plots between predicted RF (dashed line) corresponding to the least misfit model and observed RF (solid line) and the plot of the misfit values for all models are shown on the right. (b) The 1D shear-wave velocity models estimated through NA inversion at stations in different terranes. The shaded portion represents V_S ranging from 3.8 to 4 km/s. The misfit plots are shown beneath each model. The color version of this figure is available only in the electronic edition.

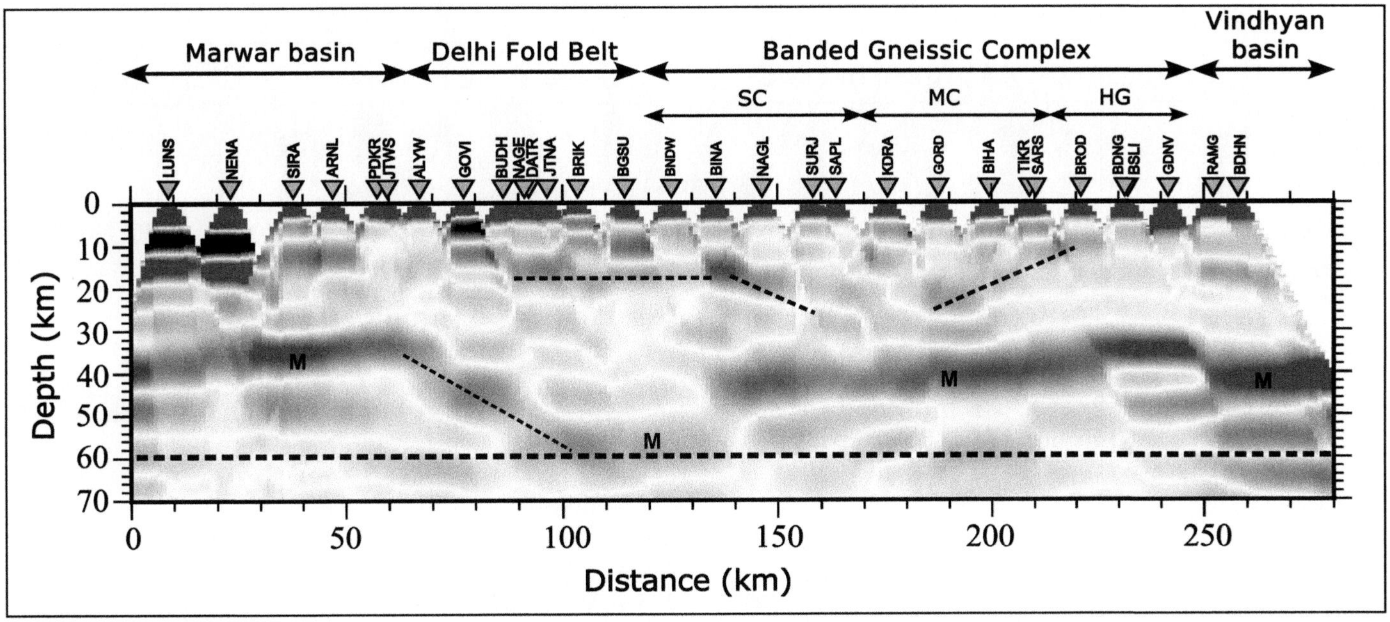

Figure 6. Common conversion point (CCP) image constructed using the standard IASP91 model with $H = 35$ km and $V_P/V_S = 1.73$. M, Moho. The color version of this figure is available only in the electronic edition.

lower crust overlying an upper mantle was considered. In each layer, four parameters were considered, that is, thickness, V_P/V_S ratio, and shear velocities at the top and bottom of each layer, which together formed a 24D parameter space. The inversion results comprising the 1000 best models for two stations and the best-fitting 1D models for eight stations are presented in Figure 5. The uncertainties in the shear-wave velocities (V_S) and crustal thickness estimated from the mean and standard deviation of the 1000 best models are within ±0.1 km/s and ±2 km, respectively.

Common Conversion Point Imaging

The common conversion point (CCP) stacking technique (Zhu, 2000) is adopted to image the lateral variations in the subsurface velocity discontinuities beneath the profile. The depth-domain transformation of the RFs is done by backprojecting the energy along their travel path to the conversion point, using a standard velocity model as a reference, and assuming the energy as *Ps* conversion from a velocity discontinuity. The spatial coherency of the converted phases was enhanced by binning the backprojected amplitudes in bins that are 1 km wide and 0.5 km thick, corresponding to different offsets with depth, and subsequently stacking and projecting them onto a 2D reference plane coinciding with the profile (Zhu, 2000). Initially, the CCP image (Fig. 6) was constructed using the IASP91 velocity model with a 35 km thick, felsic crust having a V_P/V_S ratio (κ) of 1.73. This results in an anomalously thick crust (≈60 km) beneath DFB, which is inconsistent with the average H of ≈52 km, estimated from $H - \kappa$ analysis and NA inversion. Zhu and Kanamori (2000) showed that the uncertainty in the depth to the Moho is ≤1 km for a 4% change in the average crustal P-wave velocity, whereas a similar change in the bulk crustal V_P/V_S ratio results in larger uncertainty of ≈3 km in the depth to the Moho. Because κ plays a dominant role in CCP imaging, the CCP image (Fig. 7b) was reconstructed using the 1D shear-wave velocity models at 18 stations along with the corresponding κ values estimated at each station through $H - \kappa$ analysis. A large variation in the depth to the Moho is observed beneath the profile, with DFB exhibiting an anomalous increase in crustal thickness and V_P/V_S ratio relative to the adjoining terranes.

Results

Significant variations are observed in the H and κ values (Fig. 4b) estimated at stations in different terranes across the ADFB. The H and κ values range from 36 to 55 km and 1.66 to 1.95, respectively. The uncertainties in H are within ±2 km and mostly range from 0.01 to 0.03 for κ. The $H - \kappa$ pairs at stations in the MB are similar to each other and average 38 ± 1 km and 1.70 ± 0.01. DFB is characterized by a significant variation in the $H - \kappa$ pairs, which range from 47 to 55 km and 1.75 to 1.95, respectively. In BGC, the average crustal thickness beneath the western, central, and eastern segments corresponding to SC, MC, and HG is 45, 39, and 38 km, respectively, with the corresponding κ values being 1.71, 1.78, and 1.71, respectively, resulting in an average κ of 1.72 for BGC. The crust beneath the Vindhyan basin is 38 km thick with a V_P/V_S ratio of 1.81.

The CCP image (Fig. 7b) reveals the geometry and continuity of the Moho and intracrustal interfaces beneath the entire profile. The nearly flat Moho beneath MB at a depth of ≈38 km dips to the southeast at the boundary between MB and DFB, and deepens to reach a maximum depth of ≈55 km beneath

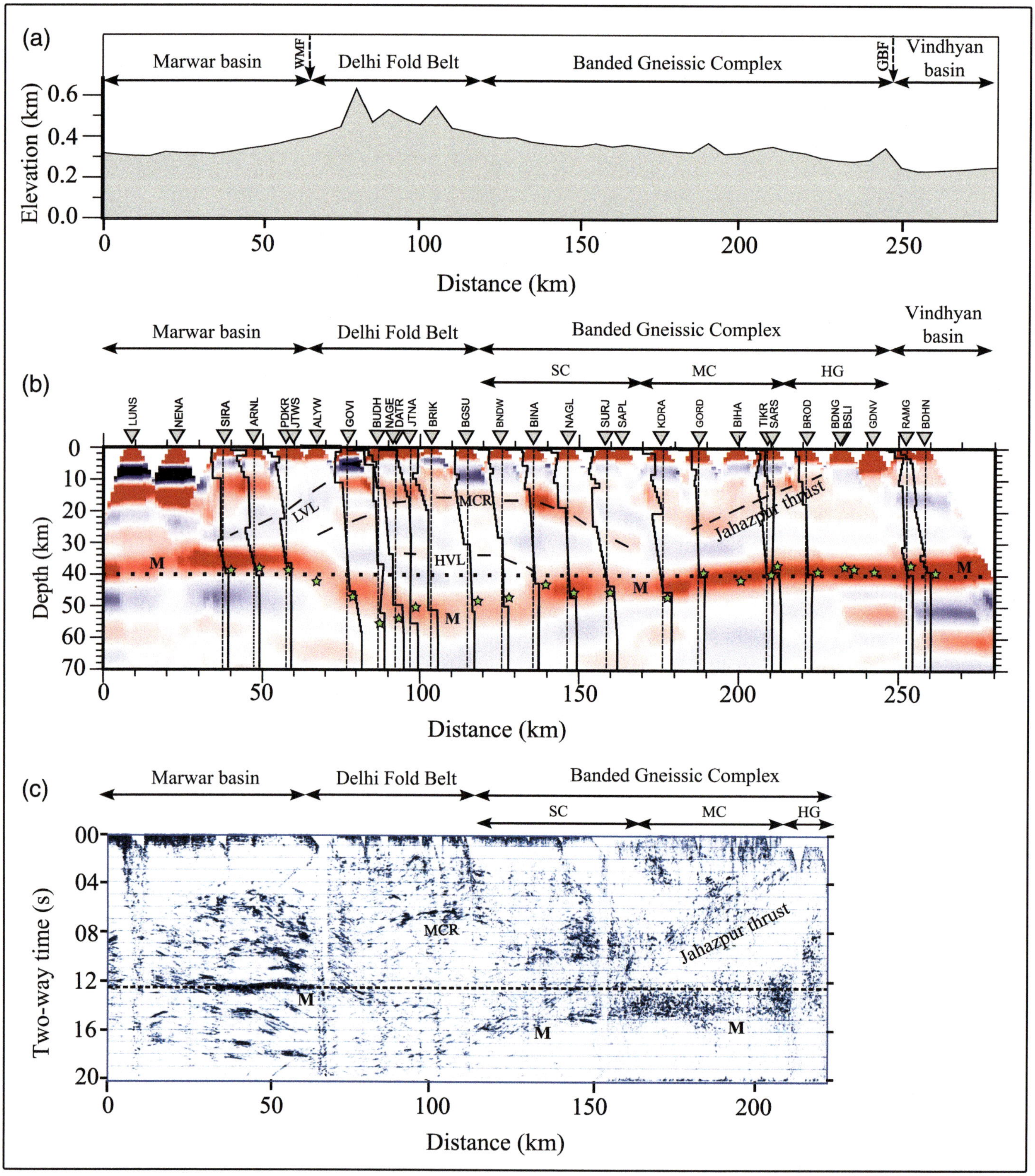

Figure 7. (a) Elevation profile of the RF traverse across ADFB. (b) CCP stacking image of RFs. The red and blue colors denote the positive and negative amplitudes, respectively. The 1D shear-wave velocity (V_S) models (black lines) are plotted beneath each station. The dashed-vertical lines denote $V_S = 4$ km/s. The green stars represent H values estimated from $H - \kappa$ stacking. (c) Common reflection surface (CRS) image generated from deep seismic reflection data adjusted to the scale of the CCP image (adapted after Mandal *et al.*, 2014). GBF, Great Boundary fault; HG, Hindoli Group; HVL, high-velocity layer; LVL, low-velocity layer; M, Moho; MC, Mangalwar Complex; MCR, midcrustal reflector; SC, Sandmata Complex; WMF, Western Margin fault.

DFB. The Moho depth then remains relatively constant for over a distance of ≈50 km and then gradually shallows to a depth of ≈45 km beneath western BGC (SC). Farther east, the Moho shallows gently to reach a depth of ≈38 km at the boundary between BGC and the Vindhyan basin. Superimposing the 1D shear-wave velocity (V_S) models at 18 stations and the corresponding crustal thickness from $H-\kappa$ stacking on the CCP image reveals good correlation with the Moho depth beneath the profile. The upper and middle crust exhibits shear velocities in the range 3.2–3.5 and 3.5–3.8 km/s, respectively, whereas the lower-crustal velocities are ≥3.9 km/s beneath most stations. However, the lower crustal velocities beneath DFB are mostly ≥4 km/s at several stations. The presence of shallow and deep intracrustal interfaces and southeast-dipping Moho beneath DFB, the northwest-dipping low-velocity interface beneath MB, and the northwest-dipping high-velocity interface beneath BGC, which are observed in the CCP image, are validated by the distinct velocity jumps in the shear velocity models (Fig. 7b).

Discussion

Globally, Archean terranes are estimated to have a thinner (≤40 km) crust relative to Proterozoic terranes (40–45 km; Durrheim and Mooney, 1994). The Proterozoic era witnessed a significant increase in crustal growth and the development of a thicker, more stable continental lithosphere. The larger thickness of the Proterozoic crust is primarily due to the high *P*-wave velocity ($V_P \geq 7$ km/s) underplated layer at the bottom of the crust. Another notable difference between the Archean and Proterozoic crusts is the difference in Poisson's ratio (V_P/V_S ratio), which is ≥0.27 ($V_P/V_S \geq 1.78$) for the Proterozoic crust, that is, intermediate composition. In contrast, the Archean crust exhibits a predominantly felsic composition with a Poisson's ratio of ≤0.25 ($V_P/V_S \leq 1.73$). The present results broadly concur with the global observations of a thicker crust with a higher average crustal Poisson's ratio beneath the Proterozoic DFB.

The most significant result of the present study is the well-defined geometry and continuity of the Moho in the CCP image (Fig. 7b), which reveals the variations in the crustal thickness beneath different geological terranes traversed by the profile across the ADFB. Comparing the CCP image with the CRS image (Fig. 7c) constructed by merging and overlapping the CRS sections of the segments (Mandal *et al.*, 2014) of the deep seismic reflection profile (Fig. 1) to the same scale as the CCP image reveals the improvement achieved in imaging the Moho beneath the entire profile. Although the CRS section provides a better image of event continuity than the traditional common midpoint stacking, the Moho beneath DFB remains unidentifiable due to poor reflections, with only short segments of dipping reflectors being faintly visible. In contrast, the CCP image distinctly delineates the southeast-dipping Moho beneath DFB. The Moho beneath the MB correlates with the strong, narrowband of subhorizontal reflections at 12.5 s two-way travel time (TWT) beneath MB.

The Moho depth beneath BGC increases westward from ≈38 to ≈45 km, correlating with the increase in TWT from 14 to 16 s beneath BGC. The shallow high-velocity interface beneath DFB correlates with the prominent convex-shaped midcrustal reflector (MCR) in the CRS. However, unlike the CRS image, the CCP image reveals another deeper high-velocity interface at around 30 km, which is also confirmed by the 1D shear-wave velocity models exhibiting a jump in velocity and correlating with the top of the high-velocity (≈7.1 km/s) zone of short-discontinuous reflectors modeled through seismic reflection studies (Krishna and Rao, 2011). Reinterpretation and remodeling (Mishra and Kumar, 2014) of the Bouguer anomaly over ADFB revealed two distinct high-density layers (2.9 and 3.0 gm/cc) corresponding to the midcrustal layer and the lower-crustal layer, respectively, which concur with the present study. The Jahazpur thrust is well delineated beneath BGC by a northwest-dipping crustal scale interface similar to that in the CRS section. A crustal scale northwest-dipping low-velocity layer (LVL) is distinctly imaged in the CCP image beneath MB but not in the CRS section. The presence of a midcrustal LVL is also reported beneath MB in the *P*-wave velocity model (Krishna and Rao, 2011). The LVL correlates with the northwest-dipping low-density structure delineated in the gravity model (Mishra and Kumar, 2014), which coincides with the location of the felsic, Erinpura granitic belt at the boundary between MB and DFB.

Mechanism for Crustal Thickening

The mechanism for the crustal growth of DFB is discussed in the framework of the ensialic and plate tectonic evolutionary models. Crustal stretching and rifting, accompanied by underplating of magma, compensated for crustal thinning, and led to thermal subsidence, which resulted in the formation of the Delhi basin (DB; Fig. 8a). Subsequently, compressional tectonics caused upliftment and crustal shortening, which together with the mafic underplated layer contributed to an overall increase in the crustal thickness (Fig. 8c). The high shear velocities (≥4 km/s) in the lower crust reflect the presence of mafic intrusives, which also increases the bulk crustal V_P/V_S ratio of DFB. The hypothesis of magmatic underplating supports the ensialic model (Fig. 8a,c), which assumes that rifting was intracratonic and did not result in the development of a full-fledged ocean, contradicting the geological evidence of plate tectonic models (Chatterjee *et al.*, 2025).

Within the plate tectonic framework, extensional related magmatism resulted in the emplacement of granites and gabbroic rocks within the DB (Chatterjee *et al.*, 2025). The continued extension after the formation of the DB separated the western landmass and created an ocean (Chatterjee *et al.*, 2025). A change in the stress regime from extensional to compressional led to intraoceanic subduction, the formation of island arcs (Kaur *et al.*, 2023), followed by the subduction

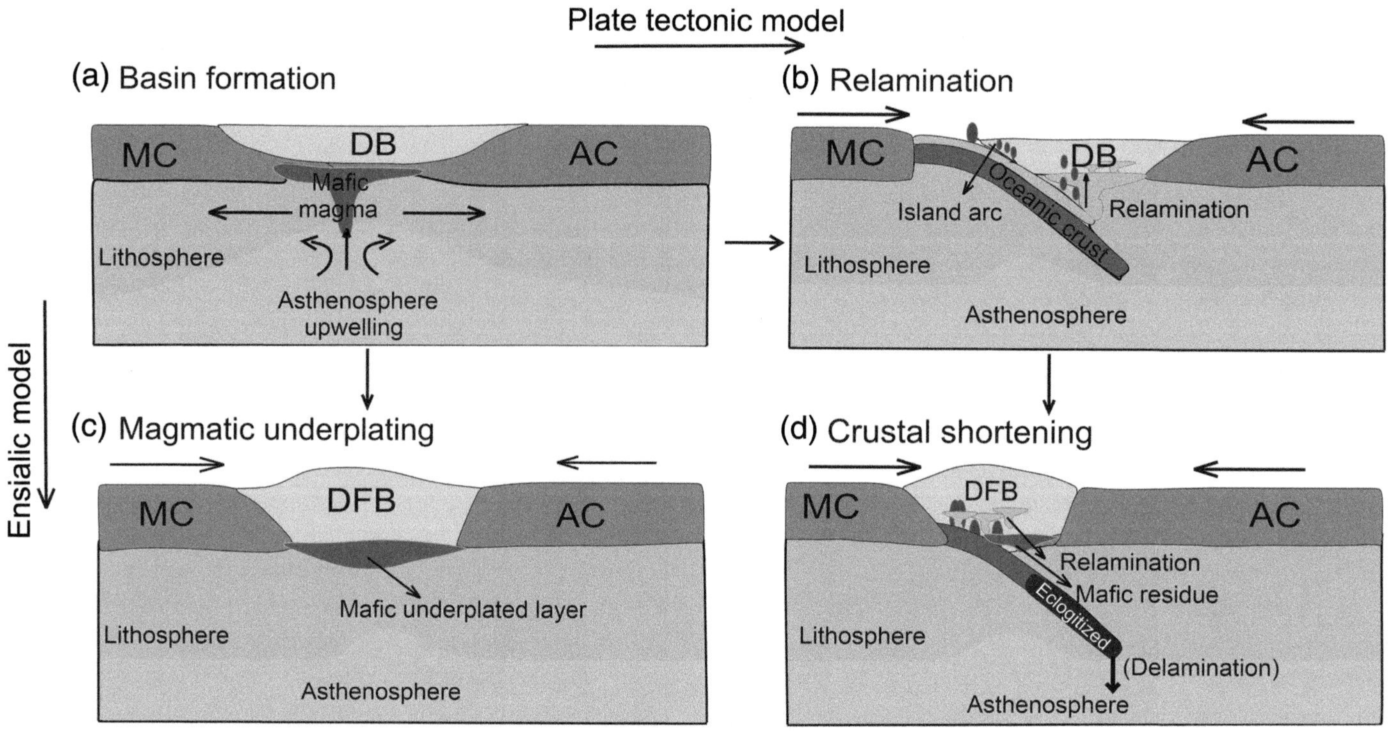

Figure 8. A schematic cartoon of the mechanism of crustal thickening in the framework of (a,c) ensialic and (a,b,d) plate tectonic models. The color version of this figure is available only in the electronic edition.

of the oceanic crust beneath the Aravalli craton. The southeast-dipping Moho, coupled with the tectonic uplift of granites and formation of ophiolites outcropping along the Phulad shear zone on the western margin of DFB (Fig. 1), and evidence of arc magmatism in DFB (Dharma Rao *et al.*, 2013; Ghosh *et al.*, 2022), suggest the subduction of an oceanic plate beneath the Aravalli craton. This interpretation is supported by the mafic volcanism with island arc characteristics, associated sedimentary sequences, and felsic magmatism (Deb and Sarkar, 1990). The buoyant portion of the subducted crust, possibly comprising island arcs which are more mafic than the continental crust, detaches, melts, and ascends to the base of the crust (Fig. 8b), a process known as relamination (Hacker *et al.*, 2011, 2015; Kelemen and Behn, 2016). Fractionation of the intrusions is likely to generate silicic melts, which ascend into the crust, whereas the heavier mafic residues sink and stabilize with cooling, forming a layered structure. The keel-like structure formed by relamination, with a thick, mafic lower crust may be rheologically strong due to its lower silica content (He *et al.*, 2018), and explains the stability of the ancient DFB. The 2D thermomechanical models (Schliffke *et al.*, 2019) of continental collision, combined with petrological data, support the hypothesis of relamination.

After subduction, crustal accretion took place with shortening and underthrusting of the crust under compressional tectonics involving the Marwar and Aravalli cratons, resulting in crustal thickening (Fig. 8d). There is abundant geological evidence of crustal shortening (Ghosh *et al.*, 2022), with thrust faults being well imaged in the CRS sections (Mandal *et al.*, 2014). Because the terranes involved in the crustal shortening process are predominantly felsic, this process cannot explain the relatively higher shear-wave velocity in the crust beneath DFB compared to that beneath the adjoining terranes. However, the relamination and accretion of island arcs could lead to an increase in the shear velocities. Crustal thickening may also lead to densification with lower crustal rocks subjected to high temperature and pressure conditions during continental convergence, resulting in metamorphism and the possible conversion to eclogites. However, the high density (3.0 gm/cc) and high velocity (7.1 km/s) reported for the lower crust beneath DFB are both lower than the density > 3.4 gm/cc and $V_P \approx 7.3$ to 7.4 km/s reported for typical eclogite facies (Buntin *et al.*, 2021). The mafic lower crust (Fig. 8d) may reflect extension related underplated material, or postcollisional magmatism may have led to the influx of mafic material from the mantle, potentially solidifying it into an underplated layer at the bottom of the crust.

A thick crust beneath DFB, a region of low-topographic relief (~0.5 km), is an apparent paradox, as thick-crustal regions are typically associated with elevated topography. This discrepancy can be explained by considering lateral density variations within the crust and the flexural strength of the lithosphere. The Airy isostatic Moho alone cannot fully account for the gravity high observed over DFB, which is modeled in terms of a high-density mafic intrusive in the lower crust (Mishra and Kumar, 2014). The high-density material imposes an additional gravitational load, which is supported by the mechanically strong lithosphere, thereby limiting proportional surface uplift, despite the thicker crust.

Conclusions

This study reveals the diversity in the crustal structure and composition of the different geological terranes across the ADFB. The geometry and continuity of the Moho and the intracrustal layers are distinctly imaged, which resolves the ambiguity in the crustal structure. The DFB is characterized by a southeast-dipping Moho, an anomalously thick (>50 km) crust with a domal midcrustal layer and a mafic lower crust with $V_S \geq 4$ km/s, whereas the adjoining Marwar and BGC terranes are predominantly felsic with a thinner crust. Crustal shortening of the felsic continental crust cannot account for the relatively higher velocities beneath DFB. We propose that apart from crustal shortening, accretion and relamination of island arcs, which have a relatively higher velocity than the continental crust, play an important role in the crustal growth. The thick, rheologically stronger crust beneath DFB is underlain by a high-velocity lower crust formed by the mafic residue of the fractionated melts in the crust and rift-related mafic underplating. The present study provides evidence of significant crustal growth during the period of global orogenic quiescence.

Data and Resources

The receiver function (RF) data used in this study were obtained from a project sponsored by the Ministry of Earth Sciences, Government of India. The authors do not have permission to share the data.

Declaration of Competing Interests

The authors acknowledge that there are no conflicts of interest recorded.

Acknowledgments

This research work was sponsored by the Ministry of Earth Sciences, Government of India. The authors thank Indian Institute of Technology Bombay (IITB) for the research facilities.

References

Buntin, S., I. M. Artemieva, A. Malehmir, H. Thybo, M. Malinowski, K. Högdahl, T. Janik, and S. Buske (2021). Long-lived Paleoproterozoic eclogitic lower crust, *Nat. Commun.* **12,** 6553, doi: 10.1038/s41467-021-26878-5.

Chatterjee, S. M., A. Manna, A. Roy, A. K. Sarkar, S. Das, and U. Dutta (2025). Significance of c. 1Ga granites from the South Delhi Fold Belt, NW India: Implications for paleogeographical reconstructions of Rodinia, *J. Geol. Soc.* **182,** doi: 10.1144/jgs2024-062.

de Wall, H., A. Regelous, B. Schulz, G. Hahn, M. Bestmann, and K. K. Sharma (2021). Neoproterozoic geodynamics in NW India—Evidence from Erinpura granites in the South Delhi Fold Belt, *Int. Geol. Rev.* **64,** 1051–1080, doi: 10.1080/00206814.2021.1907623.

Deb, M., and S. C. Sarkar (1990). Proterozoic tectonic evolution and metallogenesis in the Aravalli-Delhi orogenic complex, northwestern India, *Precambrian Res.* **46,** 115–137.

Dharma Rao, C. V., M. Santosh, S. W. Kim, and S. Li (2013). Arc magmatism in the Delhi Fold Belt: SHRIMP U–Pb zircon ages of granitoids and implications for Neoproterozoic convergent margin tectonics in NW India, *J. Asian Earth Sci.* **78,** 83–99.

Durrheim, R. J., and W. D. Mooney (1994). Evolution of the Precambrian lithosphere: Seismological and geochemical constraints, *J. Geophys. Res.* **99,** no. B8, 15,359–15,374, doi: 10.1029/94jb00138.

Efron, B., and R. Tibshirani (1986). Bootstrap methods for standard errors, confidence intervals, and other measures of statistical accuracy, *Stat. Sci.* **1,** no. 1, doi: 10.1214/ss/1177013815.

Ghosh, S., J. D'Souza, B. R. Goud, and N. Prabhakar (2022). A review of the Precambrian tectonic evolution of the Aravalli Craton, northwestern India: Structural, metamorphic and geochronological perspectives from the basement complexes and supracrustal sequences, *Earth Sci. Rev.* **232,** doi: 10.1016/j.earscirev.2022.104098.

Gopalan, K., J. Macdougall, A. Roy, and A. Murali (1990). Sm-Nd evidence for 3.3 Ga old rocks in Rajasthan, northwestern India, *Precambrian Res.* **48,** no. 3, 287–297, doi: 10.1016/0301-9268(90)90013-g.

Geological Survey of India (GSI) (2000). Seismotectonic atlas of India and its environs, P. Narula, K. Acharyya, and J. Banerjee (Editors), Publishers Director General, Geological Survey of India, Kolkata, India, 87 pp.

Hacker, B. R., P. B. Kelemen, and M. D. Behn (2011). Differentiation of the continental crust by relamination, *Earth Planet. Sci. Lett.* **307,** nos. 3/4, 501–516.

Hacker, B. R., P. B. Kelemen, and M. D. Behn (2015). Continental lower crust, *Annu. Rev. Earth Planet. Sci.* **43,** 167–205, doi: 10.1146/annurev-earth-050212-124117.

He, Y., T. Zheng, Y. Ai, G. Hou, and Q. Chen (2018). Growth of the lower continental crust via the relamination of arc magma, *Tectonophysics* 724-725, 42–50.

Heron, A. M. (1953). *The Geology of Central Rajputana*, Vol. 79, Memoir Geological Survey of India, Delhi, India, 1–389.

Kaur, P., A. Zeh, N. Chaudhri, Manisha, J. K. Tiwana, and P. Dutta (2023). Stenian sediments (<1065 Ma) and Tonian A– and I–type magmatism (1000–970 Ma) along the western margin of the central Aravalli orogen, NW India: Petrogenetic and geodynamic implications, *Gondwana Res.* **117,** 23–40, doi: 10.1016/j.gr.2023.01.006.

Kelemen, P. B., and M.D. Behn (2016). Formation of lower continental crust by relamination of buoyant arc lavas and plutons, *Nature Geosci.* **9,** 197–205.

Krishna, V. G., and V. V. Rao (2011). Velocity modeling of a complex deep crustal structure across the Mesoproterozoic south Delhi Fold Belt, NW India, from joint interpretation of coincident seismic wide–angle and near–offset reflection data: An approach using unusual reflections in wide–angle records, *J. Geophys. Res.* **116,** no. B1, doi: 10.1029/2009jb006660.

Ligorria, J. P., and C. J. Ammon (1999). Iterative deconvolution and receiver–function estimation, *Bull. Seismol. Soc. Am.* **89,** no. 5, 1395–1400, doi: 10.1785/BSSA0890051395.

Mandal, B., M. K. Sen, V. R. Vaidya, and J. Mann (2014). Deep seismic image enhancement with the common reflection surface (CRS) stack method: Evidence from the Aravalli–Delhi fold belt of northwestern India, *Geophys. J. Int.* **196,** no. 2, 902–917, doi: 10.1093/gji/ggt402.

McKenzie, N. R., N. C. Hughes, P. M. Myrow, D. M. Banerjee, M. Deb, and N. J. Planavsky (2013). New age constraints for the Proterozoic Aravalli–Delhi successions of India and their implications, *Precambrian Res.* **238,** 120–128.

Mishra, D. C., and M. R. Kumar (2014). Proterozoic orogenic belts and rifting of Indian cratons: Geophysical constraints, *Geosci. Front.* **5,** no. 1, 25–41.

Ogden, C. S., I. D. Bastow, A. Gilligan, and S. Rondenay (2019). A reappraisal of the H–κ stacking technique: Implications for global crustal structure, *Geophys. J. Int.* **219,** no. 3, 1491–1513, doi: 10.1093/gji/ggz364.

Reddy, P. R., B. Rajendra Prasad, V. Vijaya Rao, P. Khare, G. Kesava Rao, A. S. N. Murty, D. Sarkar, S. Raju, G. S. P. Rao, *et al.* (1995). Deep seismic reflection profiling along Nandsi–Kunjer section of Nagaur–Kunjer transect, preliminary results, in *Continental Crust of NW and Central India*, S. Sinha Roy and K. R. Gupta (Editors), Memoir Geological Society of India, Bangalore, India, Vol. 31, 353–372.

Roy, A. B. (1988). Stratigraphic and tectonic framework of the Aravalli mountain range, in: *Precambrian of the Aravalli Mountain*, A. B. Roy (Editor), Memoir Geological Society of India, Rajasthan, India. Vol. 7, 3–31.

Roy, A. B., and S. R. Jakhar (2002). *Geology of Rajasthan (Northwest India) Precambrian to Recent*, Scientific Publishers, Jodhpur, India, 421 pp.

Sambridge, M. (1999). Geophysical inversion with a neighbourhood algorithm – I. Searching a parameter space, *Geophys. J. Int.* **138,** 479–494, doi: 10.1046/j.1365-246X.1999.00876.x.

Schliffke, N., J. Van Hunen, V. Magni, and M. B. Allen (2019). The role of crustal buoyancy in the generation and emplacement of magmatism during continental collision, *Geochem. Geophys. Geosys.* **20,** no. 11, 4693–4709, doi: 10.1029/2019gc008590.

Sinha-Roy, S. (1988). Proterozoic Wilson Cycles in Rajasthan, in: *Precambrian of Aravalli Mountain, Rajasthan, India*, A. B. Roy (Editor), Vol. 7, Memoir Geological Society of India, Bangalore, India, 95–107.

Sinha-Roy, S., G. Malhotra, and D. S. Guha (1995). A transect across Rajasthan Precambrian terrain in relation to geology, tectonics and crustal evolution of south central Rajasthan, in *Continental crust of NW and Central India*, S. Sinha Roy and K. R. Gupta (Editors), Vol. 31, Memoir Geological Society of India, Bangalore, India, 63–89.

Spencer, C. J., R. N. Mitchell, and M. Brown (2021). Enigmatic mid-proterozoic orogens: Hot, thin, and low, *Geophys. Res. Lett.* **48,** e2021GL093312, doi: 10.1029/2021GL093312.

Stern, R. J. (2018). The evolution of plate tectonics, *Phil. Trans. Roy. Soc. Lond. A* **376,** 20170406, doi: 10.1098/rsta.2017.0406.

Stern, R. J. (2020). The mesoproterozoic single-lid tectonic episode: Prelude to modern plate tectonics, *GSA Today* **30,** no. 12, 4–10.

Tewari, H. C., M. M. Dixit, N. M. Rao, N. Venkateswaralu, and V. V. Rao (1997). Crustal thickening under the palaeo-meso-Proterozoic Delhi Fold Belt in northwestern India: Evidence from deep reflection profiling, *Geophys. J. Int.* **129,** no. 3, 657–668, doi: 10.1111/j.1365-246x.1997.tb04501.x.

Vijaya Rao, V., B. R. Prasad, P. Reddy, and H. Tewari (2000). Evolution of Proterozoic Aravalli Delhi Fold Belt in the northwestern Indian Shield from seismic studies, *Tectonophysics* **327,** nos. 1/2, 109–130, doi: 10.1016/s0040-1951(00)00156-6.

Volpe, A. M., and J. D. Macdougall (1990). Geochemistry and isotopic characteristics of mafic (Phulad Ophiolite) and related rocks in the Delhi Supergroup, Rajasthan, India: Implications for rifting in the Proterozoic, *Precambrian Res.* **48,** 167–191, doi: 10.1016/0301-9268(90)90061-T.

Wan, B., X. Yang, X. Tian, H. Yuan, U. Kirscher, and R. Mitchell (2020). Seismological evidence for the earliest global subduction network at 2 Ga ago, *Sci. Adv.* **6,** no. 32, doi: 10.1126/sciadv.abc5491.

Wang, P., L. Wang, N. Mi, J. Liu, H. Li, D. Yu, M. Xu, X. Wang, and Z. Guo (2010). Crustal thickness and average Vp/Vs ratio variations in southwest Yunnan, China, from teleseismic receiver functions, *J. Geophys. Res.* **115,** no. B11, doi: 10.1029/2009jb006651.

Zhu, L. (2000). Crustal structure across the San Andreas Fault, southern California from teleseismic converted waves, *Earth Planet. Sci. Lett.* **179,** no. 1, 183–190, doi: 10.1016/s0012-821x(00)00101-1.

Zhu, L., and H. Kanamori (2000). Moho depth variation in southern California from teleseismic receiver functions, *J. Geophys. Res.* **105,** no. B2, 2969–2980, doi: 10.1029/1999JB900322.

Zhu, Z., I. H. Campbell, C. M. Allen, J. J. Brocks, and B. Chen (2022). The temporal distribution of Earth's super mountains and their potential link to the rise of atmospheric oxygen and biological evolution, *Earth Planet. Sci. Lett.* **580,** 117391, doi: 10.1016/j.epsl.2022.117391.

Manuscript received 25 August 2025
Published online 12 January 2026

Ground-Motion Simulations for the 2024 M_w 4.8 Tewksbury, New Jersey, Earthquake

OPEN ACCESS

Oliver S. Boyd*[1], Ebru Bozdağ[2], Haiyang L. Kehoe[1,3], and Morgan P. Moschetti[1]

Abstract

Ground-motion simulations of notable earthquakes in the central and eastern United States are limited and typically assume 1D Earth structure. In this study, we use a 3D seismic velocity model to better constrain the depth and focal mechanism of the 5 April 2024, moment magnitude 4.8 Tewksbury earthquake and investigate the spatial variability of earthquake ground motions and the effects of nearby sedimentary basins. We perform earthquake ground-motion simulations up to 0.5 Hz using the 3D spectral-element wave-propagation solver SPECFEM3D over a region 280 km wide by 260 km long by 77 km deep. Topography and subsurface geophysical structure are assigned using the U.S. Geological Survey (USGS) National Crustal Model with a minimum shear-wave velocity of 200 m/s. We use earthquake time series from 13 broadband seismic stations in the region that have a uniform azimuthal distribution and epicentral distances ranging from 76 to 131 km to compare with synthetics and explore the effects of 1D versus 3D seismic structure on focal mechanism and depth solutions. Ground-motion intensity metrics are also presented relative to the Next Generation Attenuation-East Project (NGA-East) ground-motion models (GMMs) currently used in seismic hazard assessments for the region. We find that the 3D model, which reveals a wide spatial variability of period-dependent ground motions, yields better predictions of earthquake ground motions relative to the 1D model and the NGA-East ergodic GMM, with a 76% reduction of residual variance in observed ground motions averaged over 3, 5, 7, and 10 s periods. Use of the 3D model to solve for a focal mechanism yields a shallower focal depth at 4 km and a shallower east-dipping focal plane relative to the USGS regional moment tensor and Global Centroid Moment Tensor. Our study demonstrates that use of 3D seismic velocity models can improve estimates of earthquake focal mechanisms, ground motions, and seismic hazard.

Cite this article as Boyd, O. S., E. Bozdağ, H. L. Kehoe, and M. P. Moschetti (2026). Ground-Motion Simulations for the 2024 M_w 4.8 Tewksbury, New Jersey, Earthquake, *Seismol. Res. Lett.* **97**, 755–766, doi: 10.1785/0220250333.

Introduction

Large earthquakes in the central and eastern United States (CEUS) are relatively infrequent compared with the western United States (WUS) and plate-boundary regions, but the region has experienced notable historical events (e.g., New Madrid, Tuttle *et al.*, 2002; and Charleston, Talwani and Schaeffer, 2001). The lack of instrumentally recorded large earthquakes in the CEUS poses problems for seismic hazard assessments, which depend on an accurate characterization of earthquake sources and the resulting ground motions. With regard to the former, practitioners need to know where the sources are located (along a mapped or unmapped fault and at what depth), fault orientation and slip direction (e.g., focal mechanism), how often the earthquakes occur, and how large they can be. With regard to the latter, earthquake ground motions can exhibit significant spatial variability because of the competence and structure of crustal waveguides and overlying sediments (Ramirez-Guzman *et al.*, 2015), effects that are not captured in ergodic ground-motion models (GMMs; e.g., Goulet *et al.*, 2021).

Recent studies of earthquake ground motions in the Atlantic and Gulf Coastal Plains (hereafter, "Coastal Plains") show that the soft sediments that lie on hard basement rock amplify long-period ground motions and attenuate short-period motions (Guo and Chapman, 2019; Pezeshk *et al.*, 2021). In some cases, resonant peaks may be apparent, especially in the Atlantic Coastal Plain up to 5 s period (Pratt and Schleicher, 2021). Shorter-period (<~1 s) resonant effects are also expected on the glaciated terrains in the northern CEUS where relatively thin layers (<100 m) of soft glacial sediments overlie hard

1. U.S. Geological Survey, Geologic Hazards Science Center, Golden, Colorado, U.S.A., https://orcid.org/0000-0001-9457-0407 (OSB); https://orcid.org/0000-0001-7261-0295 (MPM); 2. Department of Applied Mathematics & Statistics and Department of Geophysics, Colorado School of Mines, Golden, Colorado, U.S.A.; 3. Now at Department of Earth Sciences, University of Oregon, Eugene, Oregon, U.S.A.

*Corresponding author: olboyd@usgs.gov

basement rock (Soller and Garrity, 2018; Pontrelli *et al.*, 2023). In addition to these regions that exhibit complex frequency-dependent site amplification, there exist other sedimentary structures in the CEUS that may give rise to anomalous ground motions, including Paleozoic back-arc basins and Mesozoic rift basins. In our study, these include the Appalachian foreland basin and Newark basin, respectively.

Three-dimensional earthquake simulations of the 2024 M_w 4.8 Tewksbury, New Jersey, earthquake in the eastern United States (Fig. 1) provide a unique opportunity to learn about intraplate earthquake sources and their ground motions. In this study, we use a 3D wave-propagation code to simulate the seismic wavefield from the Tewksbury earthquake for a range of hypocenter locations, focal mechanisms, and subsurface seismic velocity models to assess the impact of these features on earthquake ground motions between the 3 and 10 s shaking period. We are interested to learn how subsurface velocity structure impacts estimates of earthquake focal mechanism and depth and how regional variability in sedimentary strength and structure such as between the Atlantic Coastal Plains, Newark and Appalachian basins, and other types of terrain affect earthquake ground motions. We compare observed and predicted response pseudospectral accelerations (PSAs) at 13 regional broadband seismic stations to determine the best-fitting focal mechanism and depth. This comparison also serves to indicate where the 3D seismic velocity model can be improved.

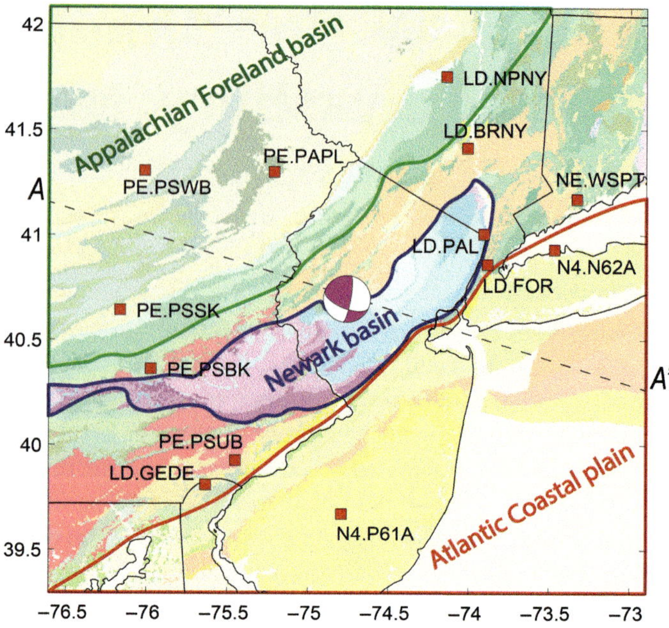

Figure 1. Location of the 2024 M_w 4.8 Tewksbury, New Jersey, earthquake, indicated by the focal mechanism (Global Centroid Moment Tensor [Global CMT]; Dziewonski *et al.*, 1981; Ekström *et al.*, 2012), in relation to surrounding sedimentary structures (Atlantic Coastal Plain—red outline, Newark basin—blue outline, and Appalachian foreland basin—green outline) and seismic stations (red squares). The dashed line from A–A′ indicates the location of the cross section in Figure 3b. Background colors represent bedrock geology (Boyd and Sweetkind, 2025).

Method

We use the 3D spectral-element cartesian wave-propagation code SPECFEM3D (Peter *et al.*, 2011) to simulate earthquake ground motions within a volume 280 km wide by 260 km long by 77 km deep. Within the surface extent of this volume, 13 broadband seismic stations from networks LD (Lamont Doherty Earth Observatory [LDEO], 1970), N4 (Albuquerque Seismological Laboratory/USGS [ASL], 2013), NE (Albuquerque Seismological Laboratory [ASL], 1994), and PE (Penn State University [PENN], 2004) recorded the Tewksbury earthquake. They represent a relatively uniform range of epicentral distances (76–131 km) and back azimuths (Fig. 1). A total of 30 individual 60 s simulations are calculated for each velocity model: five depths (1, 2, 4, 7, and 10 km) and six unit moment-tensor components (M_{rr}, $M_{\theta\theta}$, $M_{\phi\phi}$, $M_{r\theta}$, $M_{r\phi}$, $M_{\theta\phi}$) for each depth. We evaluate the goodness of fit by considering the difference between observed and simulated 5%-damped horizontal (RotD50) response PSA (Boore *et al.*, 2006) between 3 and 10 s period. This metric is chosen because of our interest in seismic hazards, which are typically characterized in terms of response spectra.

Time series up to 120 s after the origin time for the 13 stations are downloaded from the National Science Foundation (NSF) Seismological Facility for the Advancement of Geoscience (SAGE) data archive using ObsPy (Krischer *et al.*, 2015). The instrument response is removed, and time series are converted to displacement. They are detrended, tapered with a 10% cosine taper, and band-pass filtered to between 2- and 50-s period. When calculating PSA, the observed time series are truncated at 60 s after origin time before tapering so that processing of simulated and observed time series is identical. Example time series for stations LD.FOR and N4.P61A is shown in Figure 2. The time series at station N4.P61A are especially notable; it has a significant resonance because of the underlying Atlantic Coastal Plain sediments that cause high amplification on the horizontal components of motion that continue for almost a full minute.

A significant step in applying SPECFEM3D to our problem is the specification of a seismic velocity model. We consider results from (1) the three-layer 1D seismic velocity model developed by Wu *et al.* (2015; Fig. 3a) for the nearby region surrounding the 2011 Mineral, Virginia, earthquake and (2) the U.S. Geological Survey (USGS) National Crustal Model (NCM) for seismic hazard studies (Boyd *et al.*, 2018; NCM, Fig. 3b–d). Tomographic models could also be considered (Schmandt and Lin, 2014; Shen and Ritzwoller, 2016), but their resolution over this spatial footprint would represent an intermediate case between the 1D and 3D models used here.

The NCM is a geology-based 3D seismic velocity model for the conterminous United States consisting of a 1 km by 1 km

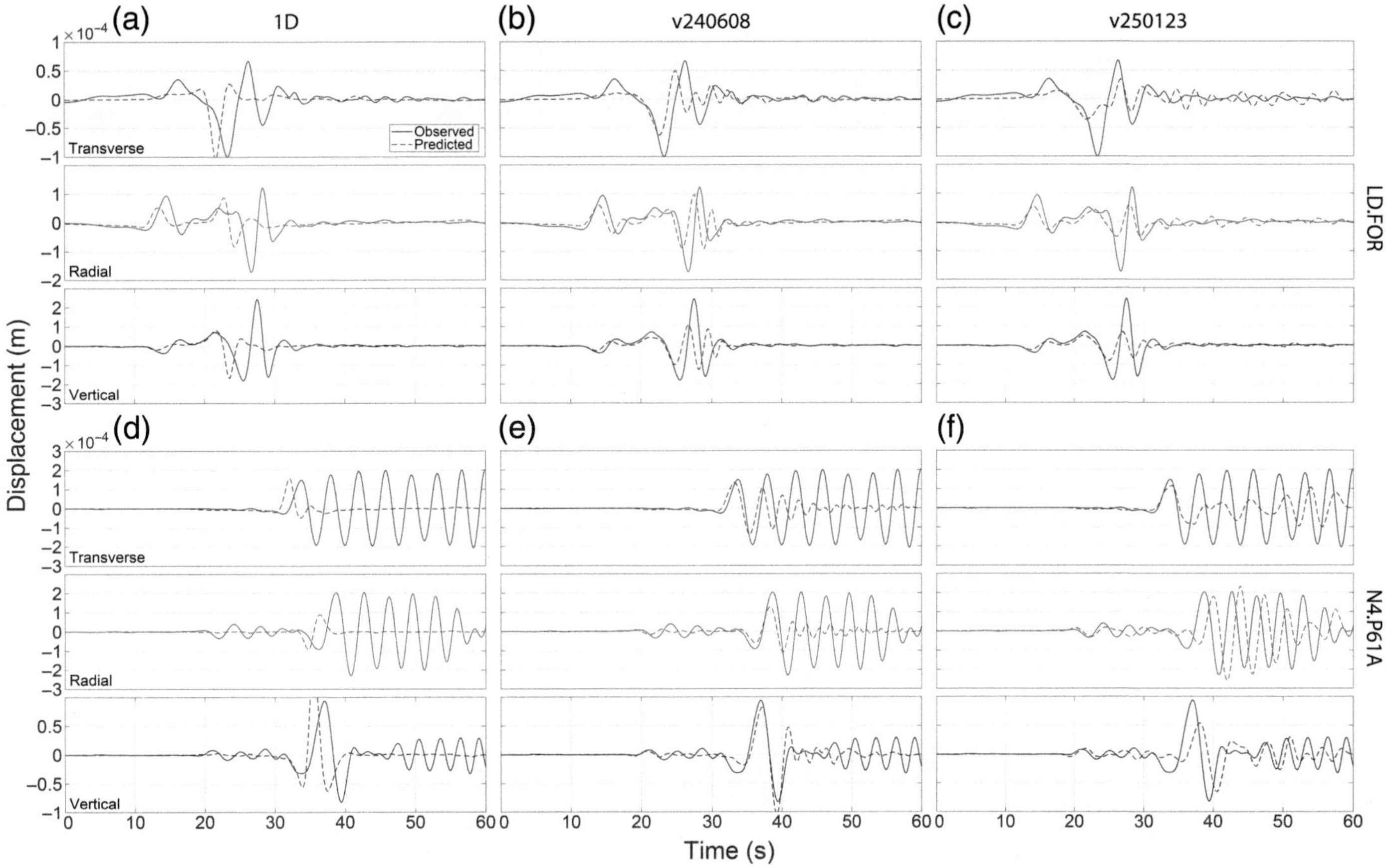

Figure 2. Tangential-, radial-, and vertical-component observed (solid curves) and predicted (dashed curves) time series truncated to 60 s at stations (a–c) LD.FOR and (d–f) N4.P61A for the 2024 M_w 4.8 Tewksbury, New Jersey, earthquake. Whereas the station N4.P61A sits on a thick section of Atlantic Coastal Plain sediments, LD.FOR does not sit on top of an appreciable amount of sediment. Time series is shown for the 1D model of Wu *et al.* (2015) and original (v240608) and updated (v250123) 3D models from the U.S. Geological Survey (USGS) National Crustal Model (NCM). The predicted time series uses the USGS regional moment tensor (MT) at 4 km depth. The color version of this figure is available only in the electronic edition.

grid of analytically derived continuous geophysical vertical profiles. Sedimentary and extrusive volcanic units appear as horizontally layered units, whereas mapped basement geology is extended vertically into the midcrust and truncated by laterally extensive layers of amphibolite, granulite, and peridotite. These features are apparent in Figure 3d and can lead to unusual artifacts in basement seismic velocities (Fig. 3b,c) that can impact the wavefield.

For the two cases considered in this study, topography is included in the ground-motion simulations, and a 3D finite-element volume is constructed using the internal SPECFEM3D mesher. Four doubling layers are implemented to minimize computational requirements and speed up the simulations. The size of the smallest element, comprising the top five mesh layers, is 200 m on each side laterally and ~200 m vertically. Elements are further discretized by the number of Gauss–Lobatto–Legendre points, which is set to 5, yielding an effective length of 40 m. Although this simplified mesh will smooth features of the NCM, this discretization is chosen to resolve Fourier spectral periods down to 2 s for, in the case of the 3D model, a minimum shear wavespeed of 200 m/s. Note that the minimum period resolved in the Fourier domain must be smaller than the response-spectral domain because the amplitude of a given oscillator period in the response-spectral domain is sensitive to shorter period shaking (Bora *et al.*, 2016). In contrast to the low-minimum shear wavespeed in the 3D model, the 1D velocity model has a minimum shear wavespeed of 3530 m/s; the average profile from the 3D velocity model dips below this value above about 6 km depth (Fig. 3a).

Results

Comparisons of the simulated seismic wavefield for a range of oscillator periods, velocity models, and focal depths are presented in Figure 4 and show how 3D variability in seismic velocities, in addition to characteristics of the earthquake source, strongly affect the amplitude and spatial distribution of observed ground motions. In Figure 4a–c, the background color is simulated PSA normalized by that expected using the Next Generation Attenuation-East Project (NGA-East) median GMM (Goulet *et al.*, 2021) with a constant V_{S30} of 300 m/s applied (Stewart *et al.*, 2020). This normalization

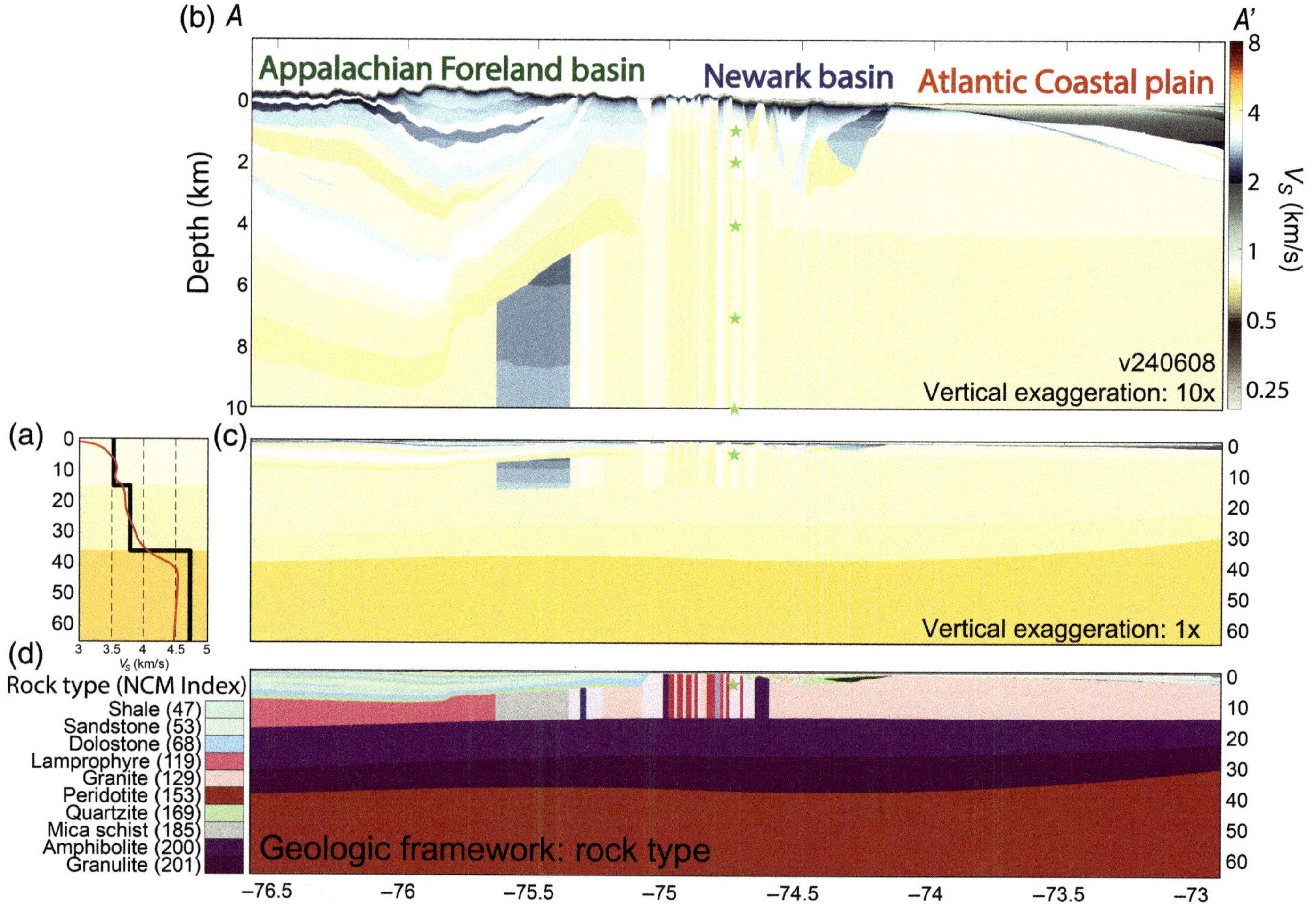

Figure 3. (a) One-dimensional shear-wave velocity model of Wu *et al.* (2015; thick three-layer black curve) overlain with the average shear-wave velocity from the USGS NCM within our modeling domain (thinner red curve; Fig. 1), (b,c) a shear-wavespeed cross section through the NCM along the dashed line A–A′ indicated in Figure 1, and (d) NCM geologic framework along the same cross section. The same background color map of shear wavespeed is used in panels (a–c) and is shown in the color bar to the right of panel (b). The color map in panel (d) represents an index of lithologic type within the NCM (Boyd and Sweetkind, 2025); the top 10 rock types by area in the cross section are presented in the legend to the left of the figure.

removes the effects of earthquake magnitude and epicentral distance (e.g., $\log(\mathrm{PSA}_{\mathrm{Simulated,Observed}}/\mathrm{PSA}_{\mathrm{NGA-East}})$, in which log is the natural logarithm). Each row corresponds to a different shaking period, from 3 s at the top to 10 s at the bottom. In Figure 4a, we show the 1D velocity model results with an earthquake at 4 km depth; in Figure 4b, we show 3D velocity model results with an earthquake at 4 km depth; and in Figure 4c, we show 3D velocity model results with an earthquake at 1 km depth. In Figure 4d, we show the ratio of 3D model results to 1D model results for an earthquake at 4 km depth. Observed normalized ground motions are shown at seismic station locations, indicated by squares. In these simulations, we see the strong impact of the radiation pattern from the earthquake focal mechanism, which in this case assumes the Global Centroid Moment Tensor solution (Global CMT; Dziewonski *et al.*, 1981; Ekström *et al.*, 2012; Table 1). The radiation pattern is especially apparent in the 1D results, for example, in which we observe a decrease in relative ground motion along a corridor from the north-northwest to south-southeast. There are also lobes of stronger ground motion to the west-northwest and east-southeast of the epicenter. But there are no strong differences in the normalized wavefield between periods. For the 3D velocity model with an earthquake at 4 km depth, the radiation pattern is obscured by 3D structure, and lower velocities in the upper kilometers or so generally amplify ground motions. We also observe stronger and frequency-dependent amplifications along the Atlantic Coastal Plain and due north into the Appalachian foreland basin, though the observed shaking at the southernmost station, P61A, is stronger at 5 s period than at 3 s, in contrast to the simulated results. These observations are exemplified by the ratio of 1D to 3D simulated ground motions shown in Figure 4d. Decreasing the earthquake depth to 1 km further increases the ground motions and accentuates the effects of shallow structure. Depending on earthquake depth and the specifics of the subsurface 3D velocity structure, simulated earthquake

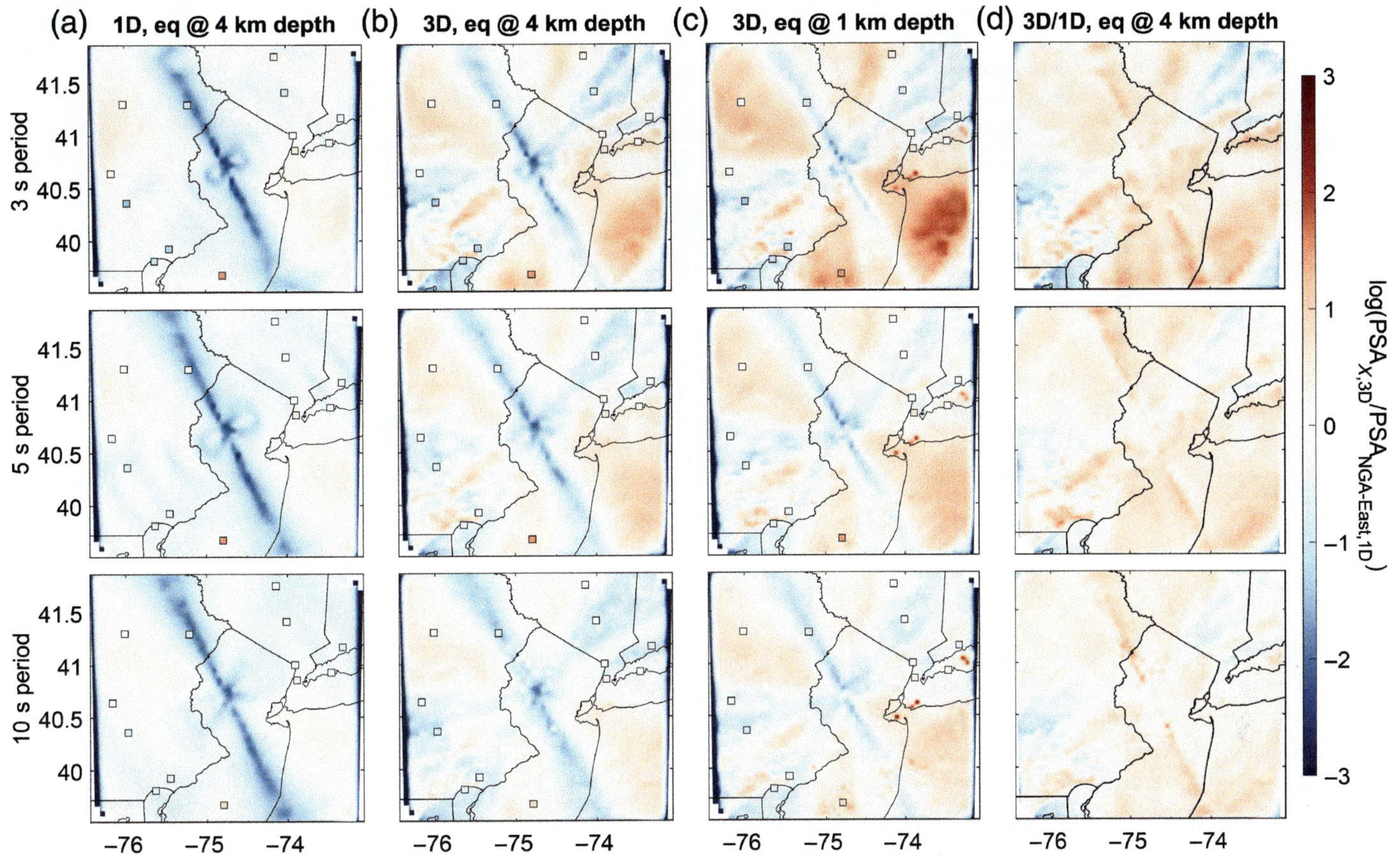

Figure 4. Spatial distribution of RotD50 5%-damped response pseudospectral acceleration (PSA) at 3, 5, and 10 s period (rows) for simulations with the Global CMT normalized by the Next Generation Attenuation-East Project (NGA-East) median ground-motion model (GMM) with a V_{S30} of 300 m/s (a–c) or by simulations with the 1D model ground motions (d). The variable X in the color bar label refers to either the simulated or observed ground motions in columns (a), (b), and (c). Column (a) is for a 1D velocity model with an earthquake at 4 km focal depth, (b) 3D velocity model with an earthquake at 4 km depth, and (c) 3D velocity model with an earthquake at 1 km depth. Column (d) shows the ratio of ground motions resulting from the (b) 3D model to the (a) 1D model for an earthquake at 4 km depth. Observed normalized values are shown at station locations (squares) in panels (a–c).

ground motions can be more than an order of magnitude larger or smaller than predictions from the NGA-East GMM.

In Figure 5a, we show the variance reductions (VarRed) of 3-, 5-, 7-, and 10-s period (T) PSA, defined as

$$\mathrm{VarRed}(T) = 100\left(1 - \frac{\mathrm{Var}(\mathrm{PSA}_{\mathrm{Obs}}(T) - \mathrm{PSA}_{\mathrm{Pred}}(T))}{\mathrm{Var}(\mathrm{PSA}_{\mathrm{Obs}}(T))}\right), \quad (1)$$

in which the predicted ground motions are (1) NGA-East (Goulet *et al.*, 2021; the red bars), accounting for spatial variations in V_{S30} (Stewart *et al.*, 2020) using the USGS V_{S30} mosaic (Heath *et al.*, 2020); (2) the 1D model of Wu *et al.* (2015; the magenta bars); and (3) the 3D velocity model from the USGS NCM (the cyan bars) assuming the Global CMT solution. Note that this figure also includes results from an updated velocity model (blue bars), which are discussed in a later section. We use 13 stations from 76 to 131 km epicentral distance. Because of the epicentral distance range of these stations, there is a limited amount of geometric spreading and therefore a limited predicted amount of variance with the NGA-East GMM, resulting in <13% variance reduction at all periods. Use of the 1D velocity model without a site correction increases the variance at all periods; adding the Stewart *et al.* (2020) site correction using V_{S30} values from the USGS V_{S30} mosaic (Heath *et al.*, 2020) increases the variance reduction from negative values to near zero. However, they generally remain less than the variance reductions for NGA-East, which may indicate that simulations with this 1D velocity model poorly predict true geometric spreading, the source is not properly characterized, or the 1D velocity model cannot adequately capture the spatial variability of the earthquake wavefield. The initial version of the 3D model (v240608) does better at 5 and 7 s shaking period than NGA-East and the 1D model but substantially increases the variance at 10 s.

Sensitivity to focal mechanism and focal depth

We can begin to address the sensitivity to focal mechanism by considering another estimate of the moment tensor: the regional moment tensor produced by the USGS (Herrmann *et al.*, 2011;

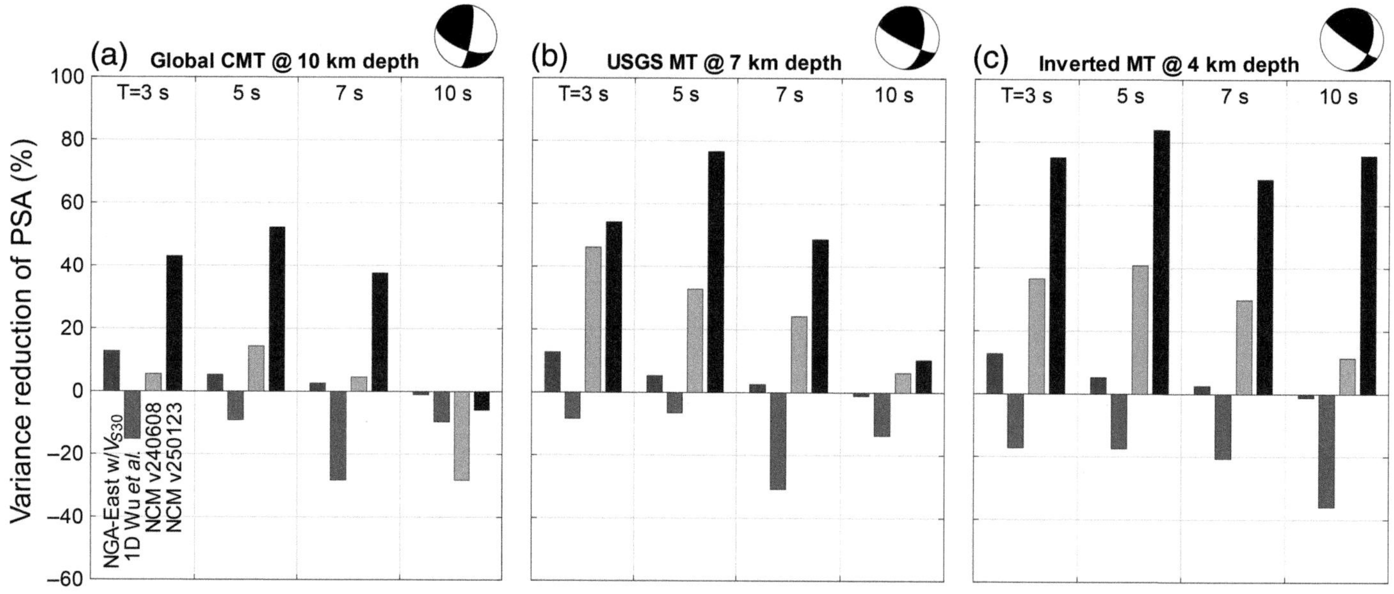

Figure 5. Variance reductions of 3, 5, 7, and 10 s response PSA for (a) the Global CMT but with a 10 km depth, (b) the USGS regional MT at 7 km depth, and (c) the inverted MT from this study at 4 km depth. For each focal mechanism, results are shown for NGA-East (Goulet *et al.*, 2021; the red bars), accounting for spatial variations in V_{S30} using the USGS V_{S30} mosaic (Heath *et al.*, 2020), the 1D model of Wu *et al.* (2015; the magenta bars), and the original (cyan) and revised (blue) 3D velocity model from the USGS NCM. The color version of this figure is available only in the electronic edition.

U.S. Geological Survey Moment Tensor [USGSMT]; Table 1). This mechanism is similar to the Global CMT solution but has less dip on the east-dipping focal plane and greater dip on the southeast-dipping plane. There is also a difference in focal depth, 7 km for the USGSMT versus 12 km for the GCMT. However, we produce simulations for the Global CMT at 10 km depth because we do not expect this event to be ≥12 km deep; all of the relocated aftershocks have a depth of <12 km, and 97% are <10 km (Boyd, Barnhart, *et al.*, 2024). Furthermore, the Global CMT procedure does not solve for focal depths shallower than 12 km (Ekström *et al.*, 2012). Another estimate of the focal mechanism was produced by Han *et al.* (2024). The orientation of focal planes for this mechanism is very similar to the USGS solution, but the focal depth decreases to 5 km. They also find significant rupture directivity toward the east-northeast. For results using the USGSMT, variance reductions do not change appreciably for NGA-East because this GMM is independent of focal mechanism (Fig. 5b; red bars); it remains negative for the 1D velocity model (Fig. 5b; magenta bars) but increases substantially for the 3D model (Fig. 5b; cyan bars). Variance reductions with the 3D model are positive at all periods, ranging from 46% at 3 s to 6% at 10 s.

There is a similar amount of sensitivity to focal depth (Fig. 6). For both the Global CMT and USGSMT, application of the 1D velocity model yields the highest variance reductions for the shallowest focal depth (Fig. 6a,b). Although remaining negative at all depths for the Global CMT, variance reduction rises to nearly 17%, averaged over the four periods, for the USGSMT. Use of the 3D model also yields higher variance reductions for shallower depths (Fig. 6d,e) with the greatest variance reduction, 52% averaged over the four periods, occurring at a focal depth of 2 km for the USGSMT.

These results indicate that the focal mechanism and depth that yield the best match to observed response spectra are

TABLE 1

Focal Mechanism Parameters Including Strike, Dip, Rake, Moment (M_0), and Percent Double Couple (DC) for the Global Centroid Moment Tensor (Global CMT), U.S. Geological Survey (USGS) Moment Tensor Solution, and Inverted Moment Tensor from This Study

	Nodal Plane 1					
Moment Tensor	**Strike (°)**	**Dip (°)**	**Rake (°)**	**M_0 (10^{16} N·m)**	**Percent DC**	**Depth (km)**
Global CMT	10	75	141	1.52	36	12
USGS	11	45	158	1.73	58	7
Inversion	38 ± 6	33 ± 8	−174 ± 13	2.09 ± 0.27	100	4 ± 1

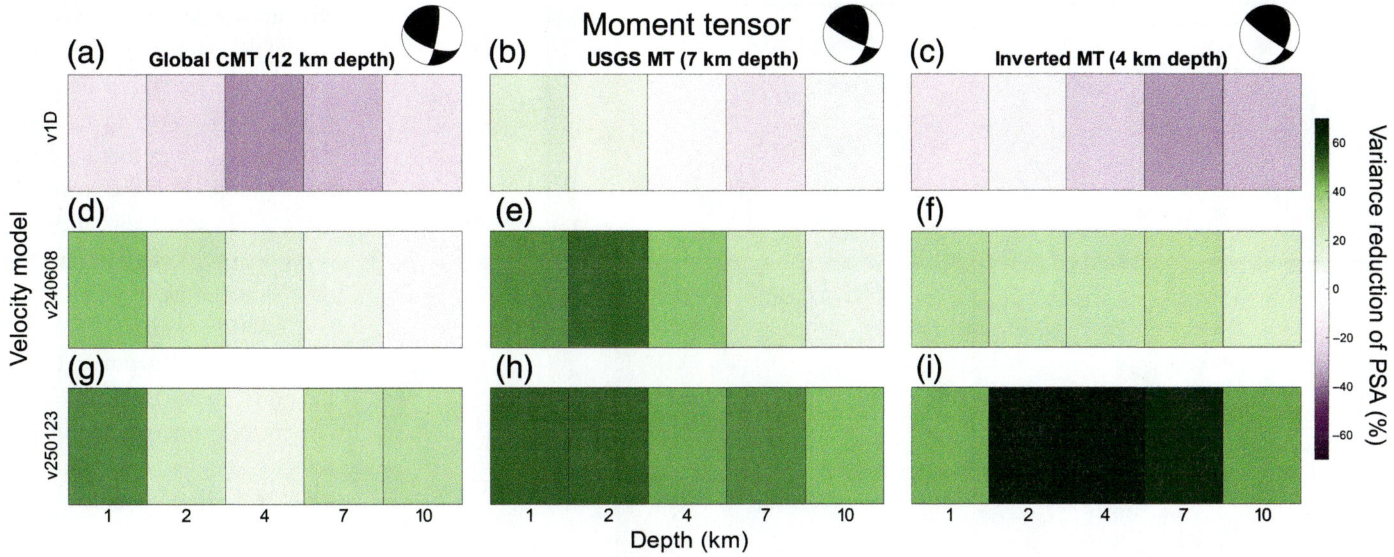

Figure 6. Average variance reductions of 3, 5, 7, and 10 s response PSA as a function of depth for (a,d,g) the Global CMT solution, (b,e,h) the USGS regional MT, and (c,f,i) the inverted MT from this study assuming a (a–c) 1D velocity model and (d–f) initial and (g–i) revised 3D velocity models. Original solution focal depths are shown in parentheses.

dependent on the velocity model. This leads us to two efforts: (1) correct any obvious problems with the 3D velocity model and (2) solve for the focal mechanism and depth that best reproduce observed ground motions.

Velocity model adjustments

The strong resonance observed at station P61A (Fig. 2e; solid line) occurs with a period of ~5 s. In contrast, the resonance in the 3D simulation at this station (Fig. 2e; dashed line) occurs at a shorter period and with smaller amplitude, suggesting that either the Atlantic Coastal Plain sediments are too thin or the seismic wavespeeds are too fast.

Comparison of a recently published sediment thickness surface (Boyd, Churchwell, *et al.*, 2024), which represents the base of Mesozoic for the Atlantic and Gulf Coastal Plains, with the NCM geologic framework indicates that the equivalent surface in the NCM is too shallow. Incorporation of this surface, which had not been done prior to the start of this study, thickens parts of the NCM Coastal Plain sediments in the study area by more than 100% (Fig. 7a). Beneath station P61A, the thickness of Cenozoic and Mesozoic sediments increases by >50%.

Complementing this work, resonant periods T measured from horizontal-to-vertical spectral ratios on broadband seismic stations across the Coastal Plains (Kehoe *et al.*, 2025) are compared to predicted values based on the following relationship:

$$T = \frac{4H}{V_S}, \quad (2)$$

in which H is the thickness of sediments above basement and V_S is the time-averaged shear-wave velocity of these sediments (Urzúa *et al.*, 2017). To match observed resonant periods on average, we find that Cenozoic and Mesozoic sediment and sedimentary rock velocities do not increase as quickly as originally calibrated (Boyd, 2020a). To achieve the lower velocities, the rate of porosity decrease with depth for these units is reduced by 60%, which yields a similar decrease in shear-wave velocity (Fig. 7b). The effect of increasing sediment thickness and decreasing seismic velocities in the Coastal Plain beneath station P61A causes simulated time series from the 3D model to have a similar resonant period to what is observed (Fig. 2f).

We find that the modified velocity model yields a substantial improvement to the variance reductions (Figs. 5a,b and 6g,h), especially for greater focal depths. Period-averaged variance reduction using the Global CMT at 10 km depth is now >30%. For the USGSMT at 7 km depth, variance reduction approaches 50%.

Inverting for a moment tensor

The two moment-tensor products considered thus far assume 1D earth structure that may differ from 1D structure at this location. Inversions for the Global CMT and USGSMT use seismic stations to much greater distance (more than several hundred kilometers) and time series band passed to longer periods (>20 s). Here, we calculate 3D Green's functions for each moment–tensor component over a range of focal depths from 1 to 10 km to solve for the best-fitting moment tensor and focal depth. We assume the moment magnitude reported by the USGS, a double-couple mechanism, and no volume change, which reduces the number of independent variables for each depth from 6 to 3. At each focal depth, we perform an adaptive grid search, successively decreasing the step size to find the best-fitting strike, dip, and rake of one of the focal planes that minimizes the residual variance between observed and synthetic response spectra averaged over 3, 5, 7, and 10 s

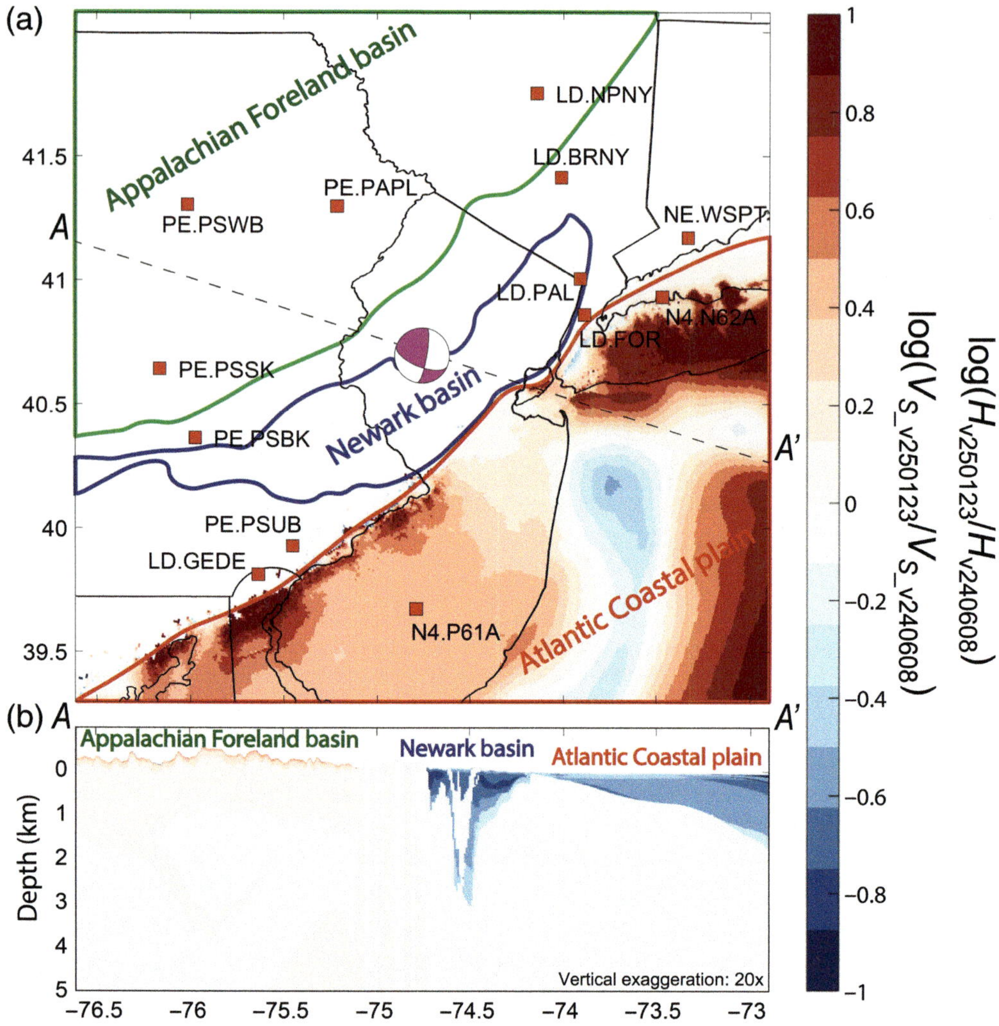

Figure 7. (a) Map view showing the natural logarithm of the ratio of the depth (*H*) to the base of Mesozoic in the Atlantic Coastal Plains in v240608 relative to v250123. Map symbols are the same as those in Figure 1. (b) Cross section from A–A′ depicting the natural logarithm of the ratio of shear-wave velocity (V_S) before and after application of changes to the porosity–depth relationship. In panel (b), the revised geologic framework is used for both velocity versions.

periods. We find that a moment tensor with an even shallower east-dipping focal plane and shallower focal depth closer to 4 km (Table 1) maximizes the variance reductions averaged over the four periods: an average of 76% (Fig. 6i). The original velocity model (v240608) also generates greater variance reduction with the inverted focal mechanism relative to the other two (Fig. 5), but the 1D model continues to increase variance (Fig. 5c).

With this mechanism and focal depth, we adjust the scalar moment to minimize the prediction error, which we define as the absolute difference between observed and synthetic response spectra summed over the 13 available stations and 4 aforementioned periods. This analysis yields a moment ~20% greater than the USGS value and 4% greater than that reported in Han *et al.* (2024). Estimates of moment at the other four depths are all greater than the USGS value by between 29% and 84%. From the curvature of the prediction error at its minimum (Menke, 1989; Aster *et al.*, 2005), we can estimate the uncertainty in these parameters (Table 1). One standard deviation in strike, dip, and rake is on the order of 10°. Our estimate of uncertainty on moment is 2.7×10^{15} N · m (13%), and the hypocentral depth is 1 km. However, note that this does not include uncertainty in the velocity model or deviations from a simple double-couple source, as discussed in the following section.

Discussion

The seismic velocity model clearly plays a crucial role when inverting for earthquake focal mechanisms and modeling regional ground motions. It is also clear that 3D structure is important for understanding the spatial and period-dependent variability in earthquake ground motions. In our case, we have used a geology-based 3D seismic velocity model that was calibrated primarily with velocity profile data in the WUS. Furthermore, this 3D geologic framework is relatively simple below sedimentary and extrusive volcanic deposits where igneous and Precambrian metamorphic rocks extend vertically from where they are mapped at the surface or inferred below younger overburden. This is illustrated by the low-velocity rocks about −75.5° longitude in Figure 3 that are identified as Precambrian mica schist in the geologic framework model and were calibrated with a Cenozoic mica schist in California. The mid to lower crust and upper mantle assume greater simplicity and comprise three rock types that do not include lateral variations in composition.

The inferred lower velocities in the Coastal Plain sediment and sedimentary rock above basement, which are primarily Cenozoic in age, relative to calibrated values in the WUS is accomplished within the NCM by maintaining higher porosity to greater depths. This adjustment could be explained by lower-energy deposition and slower rates of lithification that have been present during the late Mesozoic and Cenozoic

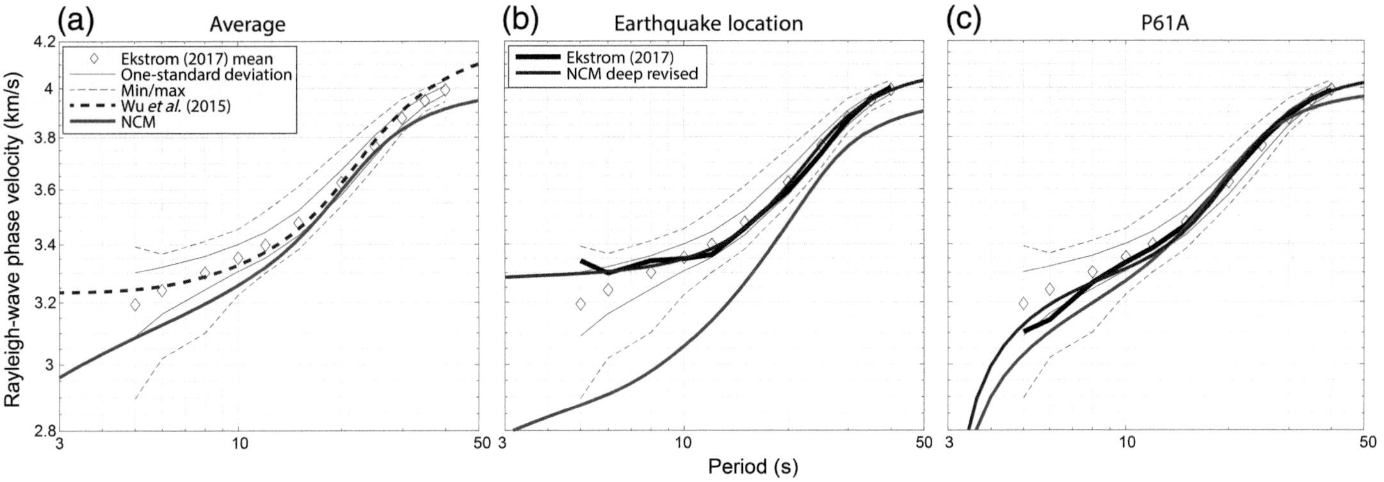

Figure 8. Rayleigh-wave phase velocity from Ekström (2017; diamonds and thin-black curves) within the model region in comparison to the USGS NCM (v250123; thick-red curve), 1D model of Wu *et al.* (2015; thick-dashed blue curve in panel (a), and further adjusted NCM (thick-blue curves) at the (b) earthquake location and (c) station P61A. The thick black curves in panels (b,c) are measured dispersion at those locations. Note that NCM models v240608 and v250123 differ at periods <5 s. The color version of this figure is available only in the electronic edition.

in the stable continental CEUS relative to the tectonically active WUS. The relatively low-topographic gradients in large parts of the CEUS, especially in the Atlantic and Gulf Coastal Plains, lead to better sorting of deposited sediments (Boggs, 2006) and higher porosity (Desmond and Weeks, 2014). Furthermore, accompanying differing rates of tectonic strain and the resulting topography and depositional energy are large differences in heat flow (Blackwell and Richards, 2004). Lower heat flow in the CEUS, reflecting lower temperatures in the upper several kilometers (Blackwell *et al.*, 2011; Boyd, 2020b; Aljubran and Horne, 2024), relative to the WUS reduces rates of cementation in sediments (Ajdukiewicz and Lander, 2010), allowing higher porosities to be maintained to greater depths. We also note that for many rock types, there may be a bias in the NCM calibration toward steeper porosity gradients because of the presence of a residuum layer. Because of this problem, we also apply a similar adjustment for older sedimentary rocks, including those in the Appalachian basin. However, in this case, the porosities are generally much lower such that this adjustment causes near-surface porosities to decrease and velocities to increase (Fig. 7b). The preferred solution to this problem is to separately model a residuum layer in the geologic framework.

We also find evidence for discrepancies in seismic velocities below the Cenozoic sediments and sedimentary rocks. Looking more closely at the time series for the revised 3D velocity model for station P61A (Fig. 2f), we see that the predicted surface waves are delayed, which indicates that the seismic velocities below the sediments along this path in the 3D model are too slow. This might also be supported by the relatively low simulated amplitudes on the transverse component, indicating that the impedance contrast at the base of the sediments is too small, which can also be explained by velocities below the sediments that should be faster. We can test this by comparing period-dependent Rayleigh-wave phase-velocity curves (Ekström, 2017) with predictions from the 3D model (Fig. 8a). At all periods for which surface-wave dispersion is measured (5–40 s) within our model domain, the average of the 3D model lies below the average of observed values, especially at periods >30 s. In contrast, the 1D model more closely matches observed values, more so between 7 and 25 s. Outside of this range, the 1D model tends to overpredict the phase velocities.

The NCM assumes a relatively simple mid to lower crust and upper mantle, consisting of a uniform composition of amphibolite, granulite, and peridotite. Although there are lateral variations in temperature and the depth to these lithologic layers, reasonable adjustments to these quantities consistent with the datasets that were used to produce them are unlikely to quicken velocities to those observed. A more likely explanation is variations in composition.

To consider how the NCM could be adjusted to reproduce observed surface-wave speeds, we investigate two locations: the epicentral location of the New Jersey earthquake and station P61A. Predicted surface-wave speeds at the epicentral location are significantly below measured values at all periods (Fig. 8b) and can be explained by numerous changes, including a decrease in porosity, increase in the mafic content, and relative depletion of the lithospheric mantle. In this case, we speed up the upper-crustal biotite gneiss with a combination of lower porosity and introduction of garnet and speed up the peridotite by increasing forsterite content and introducing garnet. Predicted surface-wave speeds at P61A are only slightly less than observed (Fig. 8c). In this case, we speed up the granite in the basement, again by introducing garnet, slow the granulite by increasing the amount of feldspar relative to pyroxene, and speed up the peridotite by increasing forsterite content. The specific changes applied here are nonunique and are chosen simply to facilitate a match to observed dispersion curves. But it does indicate that spatially variable adjustments could be made to the composition of lithologic units in the NCM to better reflect in situ conditions.

Although tomographic methods can capture spatially variable velocity structure, they generally smooth over fine structure and strong impedance contrasts that may be present in geologic models. Future velocity model improvements in this region and elsewhere could benefit from a combination of geology and tomography-based methods (Tsai *et al.*, 2023). For example, a geology-based model could be used as a starting model in a tomographic inversion. Then the geology-based model could be adjusted to be consistent with the tomographic results. This process could be repeated until a stable solution is found.

It is notable that although predictions of response spectra can be substantially improved with a moment tensor having a shallower focal depth and shallower east-dipping focal plane, this solution seems inconsistent with the distribution of aftershocks, which dip closer to 45° to the east (Boyd, Barnhart, *et al.*, 2024). These aftershocks cover a down-dip length of ~8 km, which is far larger than the ~2 km diameter expected for an M_w 4.8 thrust-type earthquake (Wells and Coppersmith, 1994). There are trends in the relocated aftershocks with shallower dips that might be consistent with our solution. Another explanation that could be further explored is the effect of directivity and how the observed directivity for this event (Han *et al.*, 2024) may have mapped into our estimate of focal mechanism. The east-northeastward directivity could lead to solutions that require greater ground shaking at certain periods to the east of the epicenter, which might be accommodated with a more shallowly dipping focal plane when not accounting for directivity. East-northeastward directivity might also play a role in the relatively large observed amplitude of tangential ground motions at station P61A, which is due south of the epicenter.

Even if we had a perfect velocity model and could perfectly predict the ground motions for a known focal mechanism, by how much could we reduce the uncertainty of seismic hazard estimates in a nonergodic approach to seismic hazard analysis? Part of this problem is related to the ground motions produced by future events. At a given location, will future earthquakes have the same focal mechanism? Will they have the same stress drop, which can significantly affect the level of ground motions above the corner frequency? Certainly, the orientation of principal stresses leading to earthquake mainshocks is unlikely to change appreciably over a period of hundreds to thousands of years, but the range of focal mechanisms consistent with a set of principal stresses could be broad and dependent on the preexisting fracture network. With regard to stress drop, although there are indications that it may be dependent on depth and tectonic environment (Boyd *et al.*, 2017; Huang *et al.*, 2017), the remaining variance is high, and it is difficult to know how much of that variance is caused by measurement uncertainty (Abercrombie *et al.*, 2025). But given the reduction of uncertainty in seismic hazard estimates for nonergodic analyses in the United States based on empirical approaches (Lavrentiadis *et al.*, 2023; Davatgari-Tafreshi and Pezeshk, 2025), our results indicate that an approach based on 3D ground-motion modeling can also be effective.

Conclusions

Simulations of earthquake ground motions for the 2024 M_w 4.8 Tewksbury, New Jersey, earthquake were performed using a range of seismic velocity models, focal mechanisms, and depths to illustrate their impact on ground motions. Whereas the earthquake's focal mechanism and resulting radiation pattern are strongly apparent with the use of a 1D velocity model, there is not a large variance reduction in observed minus predicted ground-motion residuals. 3D seismic velocity structure, on the other hand, distorts the radiation pattern and introduces additional complexity to the wavefield. 3D seismic velocity structure can have a strong impact on earthquake ground motions, increasing or decreasing ground motions by over an order of magnitude relative to ergodic GMMs. We find that ground-motion predictions accounting for 3D earth structure are better able to account for observed values than the use of a 1D model derived for the Mineral, Virginia, area. Although use of the USGS moment tensor solution yields improved results over the Global CMT, knowing that 3D seismic velocity structure affects estimates of focal mechanism leads us to invert for a mechanism that maximizes the variance reduction of ground-motion residuals. The resulting mechanism has a shallower focal depth and shallower east-dipping focal plane. In the process of producing these simulations, we discovered several ways that the USGS's NCM for seismic hazard studies could be improved. These include regional adjustments to porosity–depth relationships and allowing for spatially variable composition. Our results indicate that estimates of earthquake focal mechanism and depth are dependent on the seismic velocity model used to produce the Green's functions. We also find that 3D simulations can be used to improve estimates of earthquake ground motions over a range of oscillator periods that are relevant for nonergodic seismic hazard analyses.

Data and Resources

Time-series data were accessed from the National Science Foundation (NSF) Seismological Facility for the Advancement of Geoscience (SAGE) data archive operated by EarthScope Consortium (https://www.iris.edu, last accessed August 2024; NSF Award Number 1724509) with the Python package ObsPy (https://docs.obspy.org, last accessed August 2024). The U.S. Geological Survey (USGS) National Crustal Model (NCM) is available in Boyd *et al.* (2018), and the codes needed to generate the velocity model are available in Boyd and Clayton (2019). The open-source 3D cartesian spectral-element package SPECFEM3D, which is used for earthquake ground-motion simulations, is freely available via specfem.org (last accessed February 2025).

Declaration of Competing Interests

The authors acknowledge that there are no conflicts of interest recorded.

Acknowledgments

The authors greatly appreciate the reviews by Jeanne Hardebeck, Julian Thurin, and an anonymous reviewer, which improved the content and clarity of this article. O. S. B., H. L. K., and M. P. M. were supported by the U.S. Geological Survey (USGS) Earthquake Hazards Program. E. B. was supported by the U.S. National Science Foundation (NSF) under Award Number OAC-2103621. The authors also thank the Texas Advanced Computing Center (TACC) at the University of Texas at Austin (http://www.tacc.utexas.edu, last accessed February 2025) for providing computational resources on the "Frontera" system (Stanzione *et al.*, 2020). The authors thank the Computational Infrastructure for Geodynamics (CIG) and developers for hosting and maintaining SPECFEM3D.

Any use of trade, firm, or product names is for descriptive purposes only and does not imply endorsement by the U.S. Government.

References

Abercrombie, R. E., A. Baltay, S. Chu, T. A. Taira, D. Bindi, O. S. Boyd, X. Chen, E. S. Cochran, E. Devin, D. Dreger, *et al.* (2025). Overview of the SCEC/USGS community stress drop validation study using the 2019 Ridgecrest earthquake sequence, *Bull. Seismol. Soc. Am.* **115,** no. 3, 734–759, doi: 10.1785/0120240158.

Ajdukiewicz, J. M., and R. H. Lander (2010). Sandstone reservoir quality prediction: The state of the art., *AAPG Bull.* **94,** no. 8, 1083–1091, doi: 10.1306/intro060110.

Albuquerque Seismological Laboratory/USGS (ASL) (2013). Central and eastern US network [Data set], *International Federation of Digital Seismograph Networks*, doi: 10.7914/SN/N4DataCi.

Albuquerque Seismological Laboratory (ASL) (1994). New England seismic network [Data set], *International Federation of Digital Seismograph Networks*, doi: 10.7914/SN/NEDataC.

Aljubran, M. J., and R. N. Horne (2024). Thermal Earth model for the conterminous United States using an interpolative physics⊠informed graph neural network, *Geotherm. Energy* **12,** no. 25, 48, doi: 10.1186/s40517-024-00304-7.

Aster, R. C., B. Borchers, and C. H. Thurber (2005). *Parameter Estimation and Inverse Problems*, Elsevier, San Diego, California, 301 pp.

Blackwell, D., and M. Richards (2004). Geothermal map of North America, American Association of Petroleum Geologists, scale 1:6,500,000, available at https://www.smu.edu/-/media/site/dedman/academics/programs/geothermal-lab/graphics/geothermal_mapna_7x10in.gif (last accessed September 2025).

Blackwell, D., M. Richards, Z. Frone, J. Batir, A. Ruzo, R. Dingwall, and M. Williams (2011). Temperature-at-depth maps for the conterminous U. S. and geothermal resource estimates, *GRC Trans.* **35,** 1545–1550.

Boggs, S. J. (2006). *Principles of Sedimentology and Stratigraphy*, Pearson Education, Upper Saddle River, New Jersey, 774 pp.

Boore, D. M., J. Watson-Lamprey, and N. A. Abrahamson (2006). Orientation-independent measures of ground motion, *Bull. Seismol. Soc. Am.* **96,** no. 4A, 1502–1511, doi: 10.1785/0120050209.

Bora, S. S., F. Scherbaum, N. Kuehn, and P. Stafford (2016). On the relationship between Fourier and response spectra: Implications for the adjustment of empirical ground-motion prediction equations (GMPEs), *Bull. Seismol. Soc. Am.* **106,** no. 3, 1235–1253, doi: 10.1785/0120150129.

Boyd, O. S. (2020a). Calibration of the U.S. Geological Survey National Crustal Model, *U.S. Geol. Surv. Open-File Rept. 2020-1052*, 23 pp., doi: 10.3133/ofr20201052.

Boyd, O. S. (2020b). Temperature Model in support of the U.S. Geological Survey National Crustal Model for Seismic Hazard Studies, *U.S. Geol. Surv. Open-File Rept. 2020-1121*, 15 pp., doi: 10.3133/ofr20191121.

Boyd, O. S., and B. S. Clayton (2019). GeoPhys—Set of utilities is used to extract geophysical information from the National Crustal Model, *U.S. Geol. Surv. Softw. Release*, doi: 10.5066/P9NQ5LNU.

Boyd, O. S., and D. S. Sweetkind (2025). 3D geologic framework for use with the U.S. Geological Survey National Crustal Model for Seismic Hazard Studies, *Lithosphere* **2025,** no. 4, doi: 10.2113/2025/lithosphere_2025_117.

Boyd, O. S., W. D. Barnhart, J. Bourke, M. Chapman, P. S. Earle, G. Huang, J. A. T. Jobe, W.-Y. Kim, F. Link, M. Litherland, *et al.* (2024). Preliminary observations of the 5 April 2024 Mw 4.8 New Jersey earthquake, *Seism. Record* **4,** no. 4, 240–250, doi: 10.1785/0320240024.

Boyd, O. S., D. Churchwell, M. P. Moschetti, E. M. Thompson, M. C. Chapman, O. Ilhan, T. L. Pratt, S. K. Ahdi, and S. Rezaeian (2024). Sediment thickness map of United States Atlantic and Gulf Coastal Plain Strata, and their influence on earthquake ground motions, *Earthq. Spectra* **40,** no. 1, 89–112, doi: 10.1177/87552930231204880.

Boyd, O. S., D. E. McNamara, S. Hartzell, and G. Choy (2017). Influence of lithostatic stress on earthquake stress drops in North America, *Bull. Seismol. Soc. Am.* **107,** no. 2, 856–868, doi: 10.1785/0120160219.

Boyd, O. S., A. K. Shah, D. S. Sweetkind, T. Sowers, and V. E. Langenheim (2018). Components of the USGS National Crustal Model (ver. 2.0, September 2025), *U.S. Geol. Surv. Data Release*, doi: 10.5066/P9T96Q67.

Davatgari-Tafreshi, M., and S. Pezeshk (2025). Analysis of repeatable source and path effects on the ground-motion median and standard deviation based on an empirical dataset from the Central and Eastern United States, *Earthq. Spectra* **41,** no. 4, 3144–3167, doi: 10.1177/87552930251348484.

Desmond, K. W., and E. R. Weeks (2014). Influence of particle size distribution on random close packing of spheres, *Phys. Rev. E* **90,** no. 2, 022204, doi: 10.1103/PhysRevE.90.022204.

Dziewonski, A. M., T.-A. Chou, and J. H. Woodhouse (1981). Determination of earthquake source parameters from waveform data for studies of global and regional seismicity, *J. Geophys. Res.* **86,** no. B4, 2825–2852, doi: 10.1029/JB086iB04p02825.

Ekström, G. (2017). Short-period surface-wave phase velocities across the conterminous United States, *Phys. Earth Planet. In.* **270,** 168–175, doi: 10.1016/j.pepi.2017.07.010.

Ekström, G., M. Nettles, and A. M. Dziewonski (2012). The global CMT project 2004-2010: Centroid-moment tensors for 13,017 earthquakes, *Phys. Earth Planet. In.* **200–201,** doi: 10.1016/j.pepi.2012.04.002.

Goulet, C. A., Y. Bozorgnia, N. Kuehn, L. Al Atik, R. R. Youngs, R. W. Graves, and G. M. Atkinson (2021). NGA-East ground-motion characterization model Part I: Summary of products and model development, *Earthq. Spectra* **37,** no. S1, 1231–1282, doi: 10.1177/87552930211018723.

Guo, Z., and M. C. Chapman (2019). An examination of amplification and attenuation effects in the Atlantic and Gulf Coastal Plain using spectral ratios, *Bull. Seismol. Soc. Am.* **109,** no. 5, 1855–1877, doi: 10.1785/0120190071.

Han, S., W.-Y. Kim, J. Y. Park, M.-S. Seo, and Y. Kim (2024). Rupture model of the 5 April 2024 Tewksbury, New Jersey, earthquake based on regional Lg-wave data, *Seism. Record* **4,** no. 3, 214–222, doi: 10.1785/0320240020.

Heath, D. C., D. J. Wald, C. B. Worden, E. M. Thompson, and G. M. Smoczyk (2020). A global hybrid V_{S30} map with a topographic slope-based default and regional map insets, *Earthq. Spectra* **36,** no. 3, 1570–1584, doi: 10.1177/8755293020911137.

Herrmann, R. B., H. Benz, and C. J. Ammon (2011). Monitoring the earthquake source process in North America, *Bull. Seismol. Soc. Am.* **101,** no. 6, 2609–2625, doi: 10.1785/0120110095.

Huang, Y., W. Ellsworth, and G. Beroza (2017). Stress drops of induced and tectonic earthquakes in the central United States are indistinguishable, *Sci. Adv.* **3,** no. 8, e1700772, doi: 10.1126/sciadv.1700772.

Kehoe, H. L., O. S. Boyd, J. Atterholt, M. P. Moschetti, E. Bozdağ, and E. A. Caylor (2025). TA HVSR curves and peak frequencies, *U.S. Geol. Surv. Data Release*, doi: 10.5066/P13KPX5H.

Krischer, L., T. Megies, R. Barsch, M. Beyreuther, T. Lecocq, C. Caudron, and J. Wassermann (2015). ObsPy: A bridge for seismology into the scientific Python ecosystem, *Comput. Sci. Discovery* **8,** no. 1, 014003, doi: 10.1088/1749-4699/8/1/014003.

Lamont Doherty Earth Observatory (LDEO) (1970). Lamont-Doherty cooperative seismographic network [Data set], *International Federation of Digital Seismograph Networks*, doi: 10.7914/SN/LD.

Lavrentiadis, G., N. A. Abrahamson, and N. M. Kuehn (2023). A non-ergodic effective amplitude ground-motion model for California, *Bull. Earthq. Eng.* **21,** 5233–5264, doi: 10.1007/s10518-021-01206-w.

Menke, W. (1989). *Geophysical Data Analysis: Discrete Inverse Theory*, Academic Press, San Diego, California, 289 pp.

Penn State University (PENN) (2004). Pennsylvania state seismic network [Data set], *International Federation of Digital Seismograph Networks*, doi: 10.7914/SN/PE.

Peter, D., D. Komatitsch, Y. Luo, R. Martin, N. Le Goff, E. Casarotti, P. Le Loher, F. Magnoni, Q. Liu, C. Blitz, *et al.* (2011). Forward and adjoint simulations of seismic wave propagation on fully unstructured hexahedral meshes, *Geophys. J. Int.* **186,** no. 2, 721–739, doi: 10.1111/j.1365-246X.2011.05044.x.

Pezeshk, S., A. Zandeih, and A. Haji-Soltani (2021). A ground-motion model for the Gulf Coast Region of the United States, *Bull. Seismol. Soc. Am.* **111,** no. 1, 242–257, doi: 10.1785/0120200052.

Pontrelli, M., L. Baise, and J. Ebel (2023). Regional-scale site characterization mapping in high impedance environments using soil fundamental resonance (f_0): New England, USA, *Eng. Geol.* **315,** 107043, doi: 10.1016/j.enggeo.2023.107043.

Pratt, T. L., and L. S. Schleicher (2021). Characterizing ground-motion amplification by extensive flat-lying sediments: The seismic response of the eastern U.S. Atlantic Coastal Plain strata, *Bull. Seismol. Soc. Am.* **111,** no. 4, 1795–1823, doi: 10.1785/0120200328.

Ramirez-Guzman, L., K. Olsen, R. Graves, S. Hartzell, O. S. Boyd, and R. A. Williams (2015). Ground motion simulations of 1811–1812 New Madrid earthquakes, Central United States, *Bull. Seismol. Soc. Am.* **105,** no. 4, 1961–1988, doi: 10.1785/0120140330.

Schmandt, B., and F.-C. Lin (2014). P and S wave tomography of the mantle beneath the United States, *Geophys. Res. Lett.* **41,** no. 18, 6342–6349, doi: 10.1002/2014GL061231.

Shen, W., and M. H. Ritzwoller (2016). Crustal and uppermost mantle structure beneath the United States, *J. Geophys. Res.* **121,** no. 6, 4306–4342, doi: 10.1002/2016JB012887.

Soller, D. R., and C. P. Garrity (2018). Quaternary sediment thickness and bedrock topography of the glaciated United States east of the Rocky Mountains, *U.S. Geol. Surv. Sci. Investig. Map 3392*, scale 1:5,000,000, doi: 10.3133/sim3392.

Stanzione, D., J. West, R. T. Evans, T. Minyard, O. Ghattas, and D. K. Panda (2020). Frontera: The Evolution of Leadership Computing at the National Science Foundation, in *Practice and Experience in Advanced Research Computing 2020: Catch the Wave, PEARC '20*, Association for Computing Machinery, Portland, Oregon, 106–111, doi: 10.1145/3311790.3396656.

Stewart, J. P., G. A. Parker, G. M. Atkinson, D. M. Boore, Y. M. A. Hashash, and W. J. Silva (2020). Ergodic site amplification model for central and eastern North America, *Earthq. Spectra* **36,** no. 1, 42–68, doi: 10.1177/8755293019878185.

Talwani, P., and W. T. Schaeffer (2001). Recurrence rates of large earthquakes in the South Carolina Coastal Plain based on paleoliquefaction data, *J. Geophys. Res.* **106,** no. B4, 6621–6642, doi: 10.1029/2000JB900398.

Tsai, V. C., C. Huber, and C. A. Dalton (2023). Towards the geological parametrization of seismic tomography, *Geophys. J. Int.* **234,** no. 2, 1447–1462, doi: 10.1093/gji/ggad140.

Tuttle, M. P., E. S. Schweig, J. D. Sims, R. H. Lafferty, L. W. Wolf, and M. L. Haynes (2002). The earthquake potential of the New Madrid seismic zone, *Bull. Seismol. Soc. Am.* **92,** no. 6, 2080–2089, doi: 10.1785/0120010227.

Urzúa, A., R. Dobry, and J. T. Christian (2017). Is harmonic averaging of shear wave velocity or the simplified Rayleigh method appropriate to estimate the period of a soil profile? *Earthq. Spectra* **33,** no. 3, 895–915, doi: 10.1193/101716eqs174m.

Wells, D., and K. Coppersmith (1994). New empirical relationships among magnitude, rupture length, rupture width, rupture area and surface displacement, *Bull. Seismol. Soc. Am.* **84,** no. 4, 974–1002.

Wu, Q., M. C. Chapman, and J. N. Beale (2015). The aftershock sequence of the 2011 Mineral, Virginia, earthquake: Temporal and spatial distribution, focal mechanisms, regional stress, and the role of Coulomb stress transfer, *Bull. Seismol. Soc. Am.* **105,** no. 5, 2521–2537, doi: 10.1785/0120150032.

Manuscript received 25 September 2025
Published online 15 January 2026

The 2019–2021 Xayaburi, Lao PDR, Intraplate Earthquake Sequence on a Previously Undocumented Active Fault Segment: Source Characteristics, Stress Transfer, and Regional Implications

Pansa Pholsonda[1], Passakorn Pananont[*1,2], Kevin Furlong[3], Patinya Pornsopin[2,4], Kasian Prasertwongphilai[1], and Songsak Muangnoi[1]

Abstract

On 20 November 2019, an M_w 6.3 (M_L 6.4) earthquake occurred in Xayaburi Province, Lao People's Democratic Republic (Lao PDR), about 19 km from the Thai border. Although this earthquake is of a moderate size, it was widely felt across northern Thailand and caused damage to houses and schools on both sides of the border, emphasizing the significance of the seismic hazard from intraplate earthquakes. In this study, we analyzed seismic data recorded by both permanent and temporary seismic networks in Thailand to investigate the earthquake sequence that began with an M_w 5.7 foreshock occurring less than three hours before the mainshock, followed by aftershocks ranging from M_L 0.1 to 5.7 between 20 November 2019 and 31 December 2022. Relocated hypocenters of this earthquake sequence define a north-northwest–south-southeast-trending, 35 km long seismicity zone at roughly 10 km depth, indicating rupture along a previously undocumented active fault segment. The fault mechanisms of the largest 16 earthquakes with M_w 3.8–6.3 in this sequence, including the mainshock, indicate right-lateral strike-slip motion, consistent with other intraplate deformation in the region. Aftershock decay follows Omori's law. Coulomb stress modeling suggests that the foreshock may have stressed the fault patch that occupies the mainshock, and that subsequent stress transfer from the M_w 5.7, 6.3, and 5.6 earthquakes influenced nearby faults, particularly toward the north and south fault extensions and active faults in Thailand. This earthquake sequence provides new seismological evidence of active faulting in northern Lao PDR that had not previously been documented as active in existing geological or seismic hazard map, and highlights the need for regional seismic hazard assessments for both Lao PDR and northern Thailand.

Cite this article as Pholsonda, P., P. Pananont, K. Furlong, P. Pornsopin, K. Prasertwongphilai, and S. Muangnoi (2026). The 2019–2021 Xayaburi, Lao PDR, Intraplate Earthquake Sequence on a Previously Undocumented Active Fault Segment: Source Characteristics, Stress Transfer, and Regional Implications, *Seismol. Res. Lett.* **97**, 767–783, doi: 10.1785/0220250317.

Introduction

On 20 November 2019, at 23:50:47 UTC, an M_w 6.3 (M_L 6.4) intraplate earthquake occurred in Xayaburi (Sainyabuli) Province in the Lao People's Democratic Republic (Lao PDR). This earthquake, with right-lateral strike-slip faulting, was followed by a sequence of aftershocks, with magnitudes as large as M_w 5.6 (M_L 5.7), that continued into December 2022 (U.S. Geological Survey [USGS], 2025). Although this earthquake occurred within the Lao PDR, it generated clear effects over a significant distance into Thailand. The epicenter is 19 km from the boundary of Chaloem Phrakiat district, Nan Province, Thailand, where shaking was strongly felt. The National Disaster Management Office of Lao PDR reported earthquake impact across 11 districts in Xayaburi Province, with estimated damages of about U.S. $278,874. Heaviest losses occurred in 34 villages in Hongsa and Xaysathan districts (AHA Centre, 2019). In northern Thailand, the Department of Mineral

1. SEIS-SCOPE, Department of Earth Sciences, Faculty of Science, Kasetsart University, Bangkok, Thailand, https://orcid.org/0009-0003-3830-0447 (PPh); https://orcid.org/0000-0001-9365-5046 (PPa); https://orcid.org/0009-0002-5958-5376 (SM); 2. Earthquake Research Center of Thailand, National Research Council of Thailand, Bangkok, Thailand, https://orcid.org/0000-0003-3649-8480 (PPo); 3. Department of Geosciences, Pennsylvania State University, Texas, Pennsylvania, U.S.A., https://orcid.org/0000-0002-2674-5110 (KF); 4. Thai Meteorological Department, Bangkok, Thailand

*Corresponding author: fscipkp@ku.ac.th

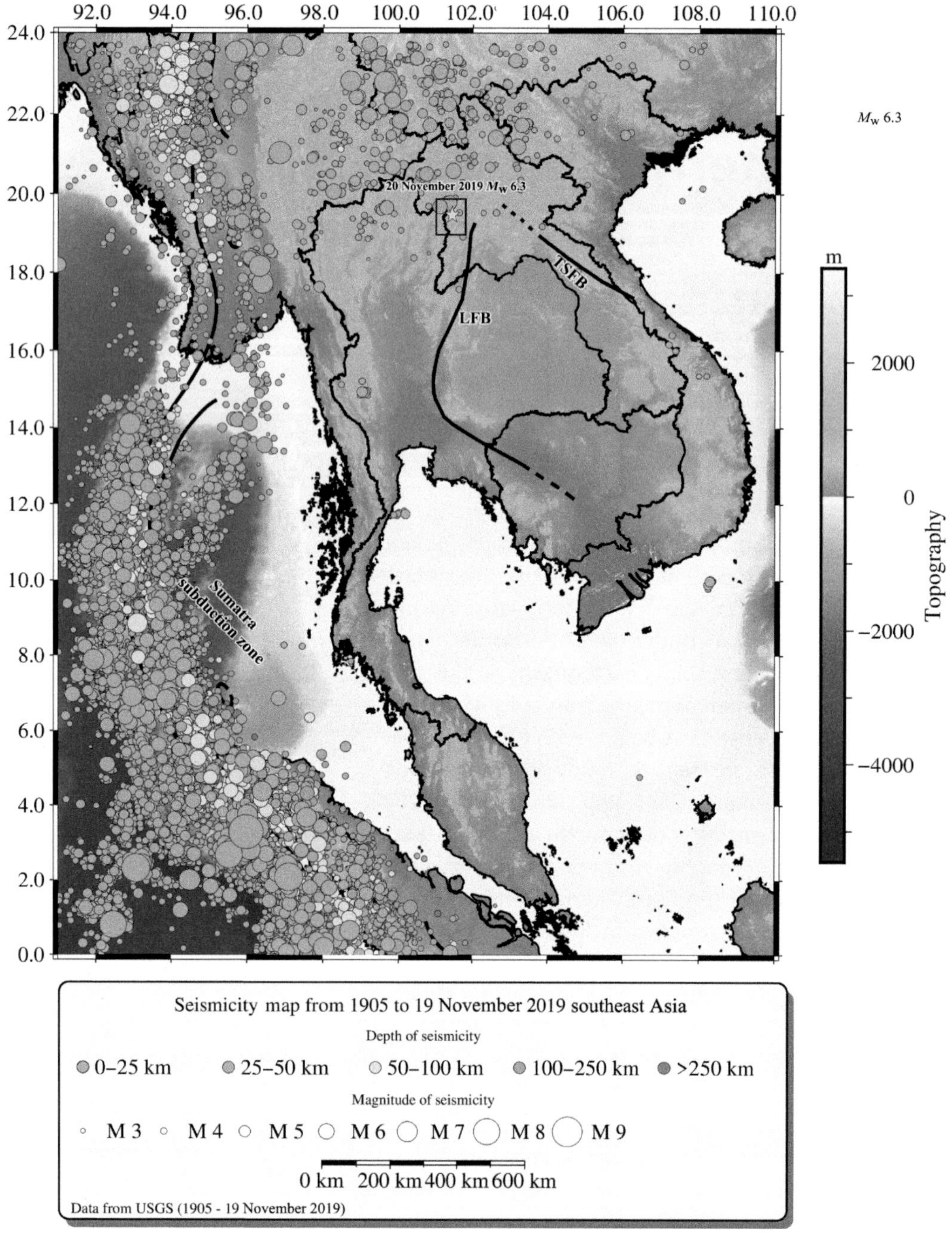

Figure 1. Seismicity and tectonic setting of Southeast Asia between ($M_w \geq 3.0$, 1905–19 November 2019), from the U.S. Geological Survey (USGS) Comprehensive Earthquake Catalog. Thailand is outlined in bold black lines, the Sumatra–Andaman subduction zone, Loei fold belt (LFB) (modified from: Charusiri *et al.*, 2002), the Truong Son fold belt (TSFB) (modified from: Qian *et al.*, 2015), and surrounding active seismic regions. Earthquake symbols are scaled by magnitude and colored by depth. The star marks the M_w 6.3 Xayaburi earthquake of 20 November 2019, located in the Lao People's Democratic Republic (Lao PDR) near the Thai border. The blue box highlights the study area, in which relatively few moderate-to-large earthquakes had been recorded before this event. The color version of this figure is available only in the electronic edition.

Resources (DMR) documented damage to 65 houses in Chaloem Phrakiat District and a school building in Bo Klua District, Nan Province (Department of Mineral Resources [DMR], 2019).

This earthquake is the largest instrumentally recorded earthquake in the region, an area without any previous reports of significant damaging seismicity (Fig. 1). It shows the hazard posed by moderate-magnitude intraplate earthquakes. Classic examples include the 1811–1812 New Madrid earthquake sequence in the central United States, which produced four earthquakes of M_w 7–7.5, causing widespread ground deformation and shaking felt as far as the U.S. East Coast (Johnston and Schweig, 1996) and the 2001 M_w 7.6 Bhuj earthquake in western India, which caused over 19,000 fatalities and severe infrastructure damage (Bilham, 2004). In Southeast Asia, several intraplate earthquakes in the last two decades have shown similar regional damage. The 24 March 2011 M_w 6.8 Tarlay earthquake in eastern Myanmar resulted in at least 74 fatalities, extensive building collapses, and landslides (Tun *et al.*, 2014). More locally, in Thailand, the 5 May 2014 M_w 6.2 Mae Lao earthquake in northern Thailand caused significant damage to more than 15,000 buildings, including houses, temples, and schools in Chiang Rai Province, making it the most damaging instrumentally recorded earthquake within Thailand (Ornthammarath and Warnitchai, 2016; Pananont *et al.*, 2017).

This integrated study of the earthquake sequence, including source characteristics, aftershock behavior, and stress transfer, provides useful information to improve our understanding of the seismic hazard for largely unprepared communities in northern Thailand and the adjacent Lao PDR.

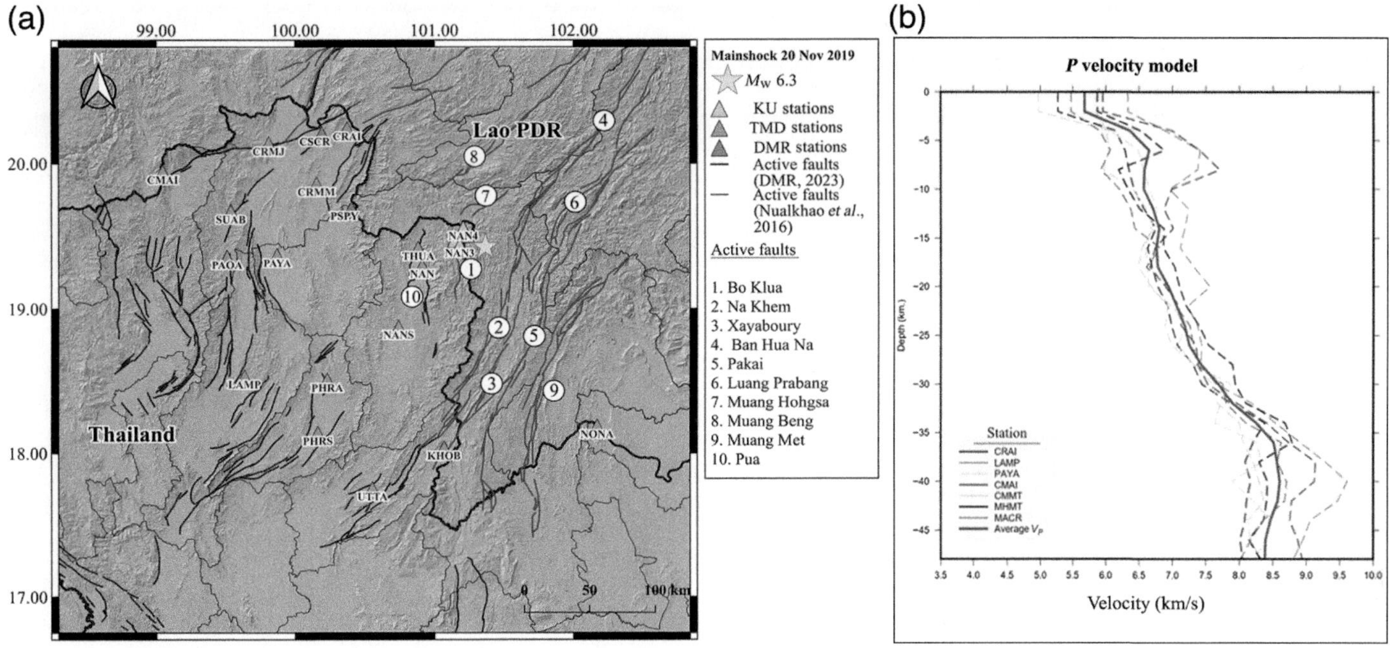

Figure 2. (a) Map of northern Thailand and Lao PDR showing active faults and seismic stations used in this study near the 20 November 2019 M_w 6.3 mainshock in Xayaburi–Hongsa, Lao PDR (yellow star). Fault traces interpreted from digital elevation model (DEM) lineaments (Nualkhao *et al.*, 2016) are shown in red, whereas active faults from the Department of Mineral Resources (DMR) (DMR, 2023) are shown in blue. Seismic stations used in this study include permanent stations from the Thai Meteorological Department (blue triangles) and DMR (orange triangles), together with temporary stations deployed by Kasetsart University (yellow triangles). Numbered faults: (1) Bo Klua, (2) Na Khem, (3) Xayaburi, (4) Ban Hua Na, (5) Pakai, (6) Luang Prabang, (7) Muang Hongsa, (8) Muang Beng, (9) Muang Met, and (10) Pua. (b) *P*-wave seismic velocity models determined for the northern Thailand region from Pananont *et al.*, 2017 (dashed lines). This work used the average northern Thailand *P*-wave seismic velocity model (red line). The color version of this figure is available only in the electronic edition.

Geological Setting

The India–Eurasia collision drives widespread intraplate deformation across much of southeast Asia, producing distributed strike-slip faulting as part of the response to continental extrusion (Tapponnier *et al.*, 1982). The Lao PDR is situated within the central portion of the Indochina composite terrane, a region affected by Paleozoic to Mesozoic tectonic processes. This complex geological terrain is marked by suture zones, fold belts, and widespread magmatism (Tri *et al.*, 2020; Burrett *et al.*, 2021). The intraplate deformation is driven by stresses associated with the India–Eurasia collision and the progressive southeastward extrusion and counterclockwise rotation of Indochina. This movement produced large-scale strike-slip faults trending northwest–southeast (NW–SE) and northeast–southwest (NE–SW) in Yunnan, northern Myanmar, and northern Lao PDR, accommodating intraplate deformation within the Indochina block. This regional stress regime produces distributed intraplate shear, expressed as NW–SE- and NE–NE-SW-trending strike-slip and oblique-slip faulting (Charusiri *et al.*, 2002; Storti *et al.*, 2003; Morley, 2007, 2013; Morley *et al.*, 2011). The tectonics of the western margin, especially the Xayaburi region, are controlled by the Loei fold belt and the Truong Son belt. These belts represent remnants of the Paleo-Tethys Ocean closure and Indochina collision (Kamvong *et al.*, 2014; Zaw *et al.*, 2014). Several major mapped active fault zones across the Lao PDR and adjacent regions are capable of hosting moderate-to-large earthquakes (up to $M_w \sim 6.9$) (Okubo *et al.*, 2021). Although the Lao PDR is generally considered to be an area of relatively low seismicity, recent studies indicate that northern Lao PDR and adjacent Vietnam–southern China fault zones remain seismically active and capable of producing damaging earthquakes (Pailoplee and Charusiri, 2017). In particular, several fault systems are situated in the vicinity of the 2019 Xayaburi earthquake sequence (Fig. 2a): (1) the NE–SW-striking Na Khem fault zone; (2) the NE–SW-trending Xayaburi fault zone; (3) the Ban Hua Na fault that is located within Xayaburi Province; and (4) the Pua and Bo Klua fault zone in Nan Province, Thailand, which trends north–south (NS) (Nualkhao *et al.*, 2016).

Database and Seismic Analysis

Seismic data and network

We studied the Xayaburi earthquake sequence using data from permanent seismic stations operated by the Thai Meteorological Department (TMD) and the DMR in northern Thailand and temporary stations that were installed along the Thai–Lao PDR border by Kasetsart University within 48 hr of the mainshock for a total of 23 stations (Fig. 2a, Table 1).

TABLE 1
Information of Seismic Stations in Northern Thailand Operated by TMD, DMR, and KU for a Total of 23 Stations Used in This Study

No.	Network	Name Station	Latitude	Longitude	Elevation (m)	Start Time (KU Stations)	Channel	Seismometer Type
1	DMR	CSCR	20.1937	100.2217	424	–	HHE, HHN, HHZ	Broadband seismometers
2	DMR	PSPY	19.6842	100.4040	430	–	HHE, HHN, HHZ	Broadband seismometers
3	TMD	CMAI	19.9325	99.0453	1,544	–	HHE, HHN, HHZ	Broadband seismometers
4	TMD	CRAI	20.2289	100.3734	356	–	HHE, HHN, HHZ	Broadband seismometers
5	TMD	CRMJ	20.1266	99.8093	465	–	HHE, HHN, HHZ	Short-period seismometers
6	TMD	CRMM	19.8494	100.1538	383	–	HHE, HHN, HHZ	Short-period seismometers
7	TMD	KHOB	18.0265	101.0689	134	–	HHE, HHN, HHZ	Broadband seismometers
8	TMD	LAMP	18.5226	99.6323	285	–	HHE, HHN, HHZ	Broadband seismometers
9	TMD	NAN	19.2836	100.9116	288	–	SHE, SHN, SHZ	Short-period seismometers
10	TMD	NANS	18.8636	100.7418	264	–	HHE, HHN, HHZ	Broadband seismometers
11	TMD	NONA	18.1751	102.1679	182	–	HNE, HNN, HNZ	Strong-motion accelerometers
12	TMD	PAOA	19.3471	99.5068	543	–	HNE, HNN, HNZ	Strong-motion accelerometers
13	TMD	PAYA	19.3603	99.8692	408	–	HNE, HNN, HNZ	Short-period seismometers
14	TMD	PHRA	18.4989	100.2290	186	–	HHE, HHN, HHZ	Broadband seismometers
15	TMD	PHRS	18.1289	100.1625	166	–	HNE, HNN, HNZ	Short-period seismometers
16	TMD	SUAB	19.6611	99.5346	479	–	HHE, HHN, HHZ	Broadband seismometers
17	TMD	SUAI	19.6610	99.5345	478	–	HNE, HNN, HNZ	Strong-motion accelerometers
18	TMD	THUA	19.4085	100.8825	335	–	HNE, HNN, HNZ	Strong-motion accelerometers
19	TMD	UTTA	17.7443	100.5540	110	–	SHE, SHN, SHZ	Short-period seismometers
20	KU	NAN1	19.5171	101.2250	903	1 December 2019, 13:27:40	CHE, CHN, CHZ	Short-period seismometers
21	KU	NAN2	19.4838	101.1543	840	22 November 2019, 10:28:50	CHE, CHN, CHZ	Short-period seismometers
22	KU	NAN3	19.4296	101.1820	1,014	21 November 2019, 16:55:30	CHE, CHN, CHZ	Short-period seismometers
23	KU	NAN4	19.5475	101.2074	910	25 August 2022, 13:40:50	CHE, CHN, CHZ	Short-period seismometers

Earthquake detection and initial location

We used waveform cross-correlation to improve event detection efficiency. This approach identifies small earthquakes using template waveforms to search for repeating or similar signal patterns within continuous seismic records (Chamberlain *et al.*, 2016; Gao and Kao, 2020). A total of 54 earthquake templates were used. In searching for earthquakes that occurred from November 2019 to December 2022, 1886 earthquake events with a similarity threshold of correlation coefficient (CC) of more than 0.53 were selected. Compared with the TMD's catalog of 492 events, the waveform cross-correlation technique applied in this work triples the number of previously identified earthquakes. Hypocenters were determined with the SEISAN program (Havskov and Ottemöller, 1999), which uses HYPOCENTER (Lienert and Havskov, 1995), using 10,938 P and 2,795 S arrivals and the 1D velocity model for northern Thailand shown in Figure 2b (Pananont *et al.*, 2017). This catalog includes 1886 earthquakes with magnitudes ranging from M_L 0.1 to 6.4. Picking errors averaged about 0.21 s, giving location uncertainties in latitude error ~4.7 km, longitude error ~9.5 km, and depth error ~10.2 km. These relatively large uncertainties reflect the unilateral west-side station distribution (azimuthal gap >180°), a configuration known to produce significant absolute errors due to limited azimuthal coverage and strong trade-offs among epicentral coordinates, depth, and origin time (Bondár *et al.*, 2004). Despite these limitations, the dataset is well-suited for double-difference relocation. The HypoDD method operates on differential travel times, which cancel common timing and velocity-model errors and yield high relative accuracy, even when absolute errors are substantial (Waldhauser and Ellsworth, 2000). Thus, the SEISAN solutions provide a useful starting point for producing precise relative relocations capable of resolving the fault geometry, rupture extent, and internal structure of the sequence.

Magnitude of completeness, *b* value, and aftershock decay analysis

We estimated the magnitude of completeness (M_c) of this earthquake sequence using the method of Wiemer and Wyss (2000), adopting a 95% goodness-of-fit threshold (M_c 95). The *b* values were then calculated from the same earthquake sequence using only earthquakes with magnitudes above the preferred M_c. The catalog used in the earthquake sequence starts from 20 November 2019 to 31 December 2022. We also modeled the aftershock decay using the modified Omori's law (Omori, 1894; Utsu, 1961) using the relationship $n(t) = K/(t + c)^p$, in which $n(t)$ is the aftershock frequency measured over a certain interval of time, K and c are constants and p determines the decay rate, typically in the range ~0.9–1.5 differs from sequence to sequence (Utsu *et al.*, 1995). To avoid ambiguity in the aftershock decay analysis caused by sparse seismicity at later times, we constrained the catalog to the sequence, beginning immediately after the M_w 6.3 mainshock on 20 November 2019 at 23:50:44 to 18 December 2021 at 23:59:59, just before the occurrence of the largest aftershock (M_w 5.6) on the following day. This yielded a total of 1785 events for analysis.

Relative relocation with HypoDD

To improve relative earthquake locations, we applied the double-difference relocation method HypoDD (Waldhauser and Ellsworth, 2000; Waldhauser, 2001) to the initial 1886 HYPOCENTER solutions. HypoDD refines the relative positions of nearby events by minimizing differential travel-time residuals for event pairs recorded at common stations, yielding substantially higher relative accuracy than conventional absolute-location approaches. The dataset comprised 180,284 *P*-wave and 42,685 *S*-wave differential times from 43,399 event pairs, resulting in 1,444 successfully relocated earthquakes. We excluded 442 small earthquakes that did not generate enough differential-time pairs to meet the minimum linkage requirement of at least four pairs per event. These excluded events, although near the Xayaburi clusters, were excluded because they either lacked sufficient differential-time connections or were isolated, causing them to fail to converge in the double-difference inversion. The relocation reduced root mean square residuals by ~50% to 0.108 s. Bootstrap resampling (100 iterations) indicates relative uncertainties of ~374 m horizontally and ~380 m vertically at the 95% confidence level.

Regional moment tensor inversions

We determined the source parameters of the mainshock and the 16 largest foreshocks and aftershocks using regional broadband waveform inversion with the regional moment tensor (RMT) method (Herrmann *et al.*, 2011). Green's functions for the vertical, radial, and transverse components were computed using the Computer Programs in Seismology (Herrmann, 2013) and a 1D velocity model for northern Thailand (Pananont *et al.*, 2017). Waveforms from stations NANS, CRMM, KHOB, CRMJ, SUAB, LAMP, and OMKO, covering an azimuthal range of ~190°–292°, were used in the inversions. Station orientations were corrected following Pornsopin *et al.* (2023). We selected time windows from −5 to +50 s relative to the *P*-wave arrival and applied a 0.04–0.10 Hz band-pass filter to both observed waveforms and Green's functions. All stations within 300 km were assigned equal weighting, with weights decreasing for stations located at greater distances from the hypocenter. The RMT solutions for earthquakes with M_w 3.8–4.1 have a variance reduction of around 0.4, whereas those of the earthquakes with a magnitude greater than M_w 4.1 show a better fit, with variance reductions up to 0.63.

Coulomb stress modeling

We evaluated the Coulomb stress changes (ΔCS) associated with the 2019 Lao PDR sequence using the Hdef software (Herman, 2020) to understand how the sequence of earthquakes redistributes stress, both close to the adjacent faults and in the surrounding region. We used an effective friction coefficient $\mu = 0.5$; a ΔCS of +0.01 MPa (0.1 bar) was taken to be the threshold generally sufficient to promote failure (Stein *et al.*, 1992). Coulomb stress changes were calculated following the methodology of Herman *et al.* (2014, 2016). Source parameters came from our RMT solutions combined with double-difference relocated hypocenters. Each earthquake was represented as a rectangular fault patch with rupture dimensions scaled from magnitude–fault size relations (i.e., Wells and Coppersmith, 1994), with uniform slip derived from the seismic moment at centroid depth. Strike, dip, and rake were assigned from the nodal plane identified as the fault plane. Stress changes were resolved onto the principal fault orientations (target faults) in the region inferred from seismic and geological data. These include strike-slip geometries consistent with the mainshock (342°/70°/−175°) representative of the newly discovered fault, left-lateral faults striking NE (40°/90°/0°) that represent fault systems in Lao PDR, and north-striking normal faults (0°/45°/−90°) that represent active faults in Nan Province, Thailand. These target fault orientations correspond to mapped structures in the region, including the Muang Hongsa, Muang Beng, Ban Hua Na, Bo Klua, and Pua fault zones (Nualkhao *et al.*, 2016; DMR, 2023). Parameters used in the calculations include a *P*-wave velocity (V_P) of 6800 m/s, an *S*-wave velocity (V_S) of 3926 m/s, a density of 3000 kg/m^3, and a shear modulus of 40×10^9 Pa.

Results and Discussions

Characteristics and distribution of the earthquake sequence

A total of 1886 earthquakes (November 2019 to December 2022) with local magnitude (M_L) ranging from M_L 0.1 to 6.4 (M_w 6.3) were relocated.

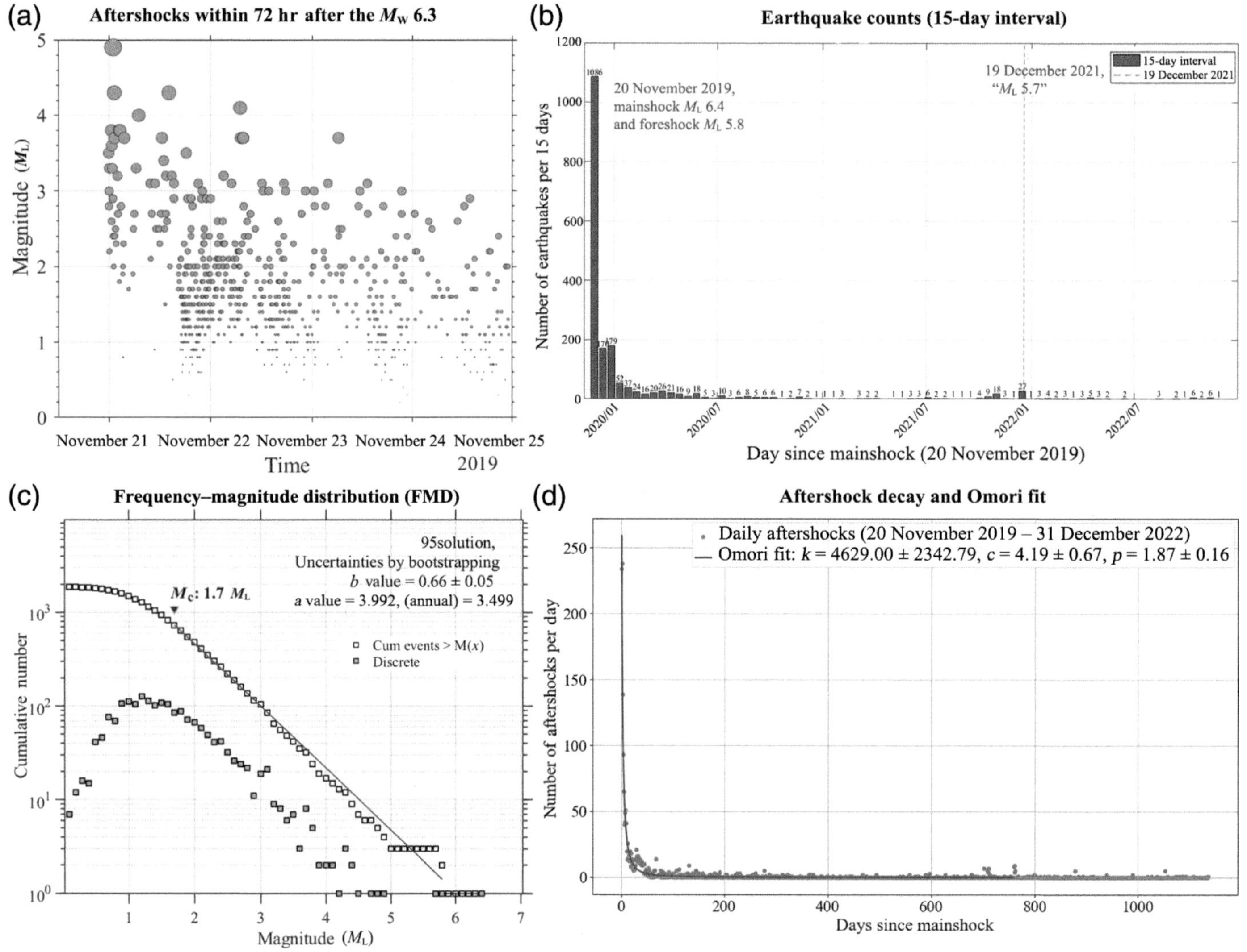

Figure 3. Seismicity characteristics of the 2019 Xayaburi earthquake sequence. (a) A total of 701 aftershocks occurred within 72 hr after the M_w 6.3 mainshock, including eight events with $M_w \geq 3.8$. (b) Earthquake counts in 15-day intervals from 20 November 2019 to 31 December 2022, showing the mainshock (M_L 6.4), foreshock (M_L 5.8), and the later M_L 5.7 earthquake on 19 December 2021. (c) Frequency–magnitude distribution (FMD) with magnitude of completeness (M_c) at M_L 1.7; the cumulative fit yields a b value of 0.66 ± 0.05. (d) Aftershock decay following Omori's law, with p = 1.87 ± 0.16. The color version of this figure is available only in the electronic edition.

The sequence began with an M_w 5.7 (M_L 5.8) foreshock at 21:03 UTC on 20 November, about three hours before the M_w 6.3 (M_L 6.4) mainshock at 23:50 UTC. A total of 701 aftershocks occurred within 72 hr of the M_w 6.3 mainshock, including eight events with $M_w \geq 3.8$ (Fig. 3a). Seismic activity dropped to fewer than five events per day after two months, but continued at a low rate for two years, including an M_w 5.6 (M_L 5.7) earthquake on 19 December 2021 (Fig. 3b). We calculate the b value using the initial catalogue of 1886 earthquakes with magnitudes ranging from M_L 0.1 to 6.4 relocated by SEISAN. The results show a completeness magnitude (M_c) of M_L 1.7, with a b value of 0.66 ± 0.05 (M_c 95) (Fig. 3c). We tested the robustness of M_c and b value calculation by recalculating them using only aftershock data recorded after the first 48 hr, when the local temporary seismic network was completely installed. Recalculation yielded M_c of M_L 1.8 and a b value of 0.76 ± 0.08 (M_c 95). The b value obtained in this study is comparable to those of previous studies in the Thailand–Lao PDR region, in which b values of approximately 0.7–0.8 (Pailoplee and Charusiri, 2016, 2017; Puangjaktha and Pailoplee, 2018a,b) have been reported. When using the entire earthquake catalog, we obtain the initial Omori decay exponent of 1.87 ± 0.16 (Utsu *et al.*, 1995; Fig. 3d). However, when the decay rate is estimated after the first 48 hr, the exponent decreases to 1.10 ± 0.05, which is comparable with a typical decay rate. The initial observation of a relatively low b value and high Omori decay underscores the importance of catalog completeness. Our initial dataset included the first 48 hr, during which the local temporary network was still being installed. The incomplete network in the first 48 hr likely led to an

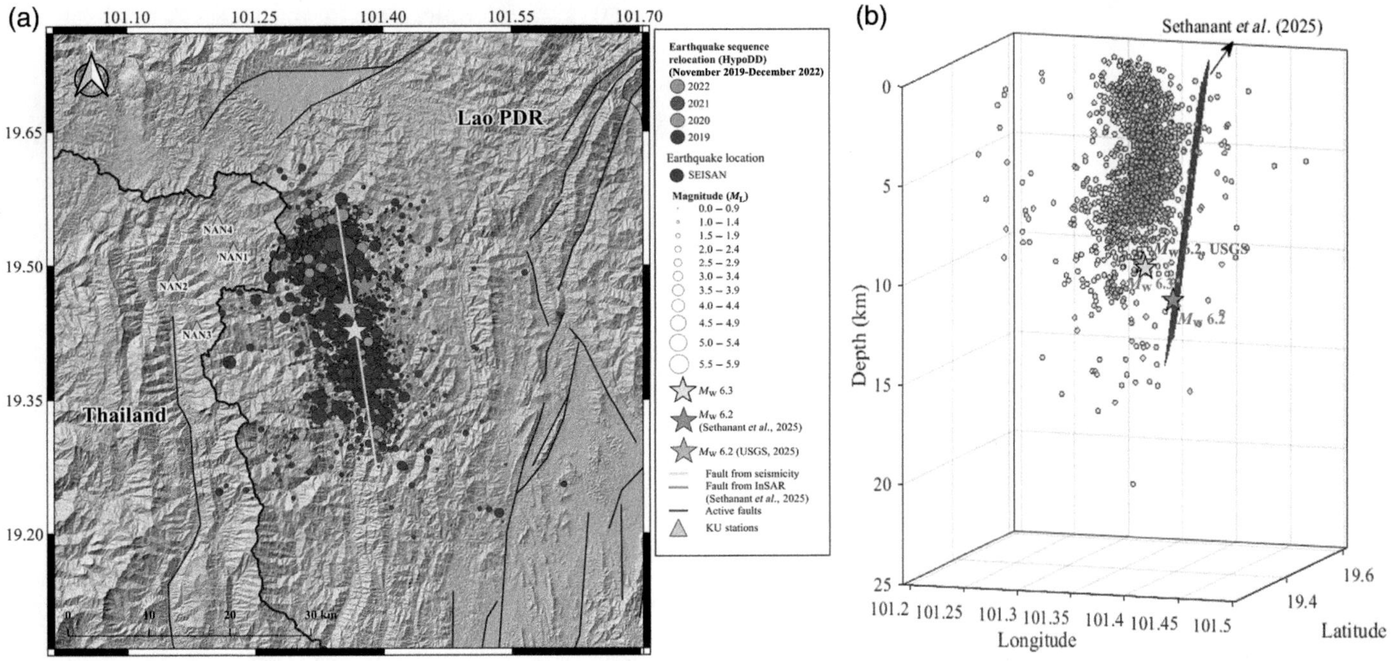

incomplete catalog with a deficiency of smaller events (Kagan, 2004).

The relocated hypocenters define a near-vertical, 35 km long north-northwest (NNW)-striking plane, with the mainshock in the middle (Fig. 4a). Aftershocks extend to depths of 22 km, although most events are shallower than 12 km. Our results show an along-strike length of this earthquake sequence ~10 km longer than the 24 km reported by Sethanant *et al.* (2025) from Interferometric Synthetic Aperture Radar (InSAR) modeling, which may reflect aftershocks extending beyond the rupture zone.

The fault plane derived from our relocated hypocenters aligns well with the mainshock location reported by the U.S. Geological Survey (USGS) (USGS, 2025; Fig. 4b). Relative to the InSAR-derived rupture plane of Sethanant *et al.* (2025), the hypocenters in this study are positioned approximately 4–5 km west of the surface projection of their mapped fault. This discrepancy may be partly an absolute location bias produced by our one-sided seismic network because all stations used in this study are located to the west of the sequence. Networks with azimuthal gaps exceeding 180° can commonly generate systematic horizontal shifts toward the station side due to trade-offs among epicentral coordinates, depth, and origin time (Bondár *et al.*, 2004). Despite this absolute offset, the fault strike, continuity, and ~35 km rupture length defined by our relative relocations remain robust and consistent with the rupture extent inferred from InSAR.

The three largest earthquakes (M_L 5.8, 6.4, 5.7, equivalent to M_w 5.7, 6.3, 5.6, respectively, after RMT inversion in the next section) occurred at 9–14 km depth, suggesting rupture initiated at midcrustal depth and propagated upward (Fig. 5).

Figure 4. (a) Comparison of results from the relocation of earthquakes by different methods: the SEISAN program (gray circles, 1886 earthquakes) and HypoDD (colored circles, 1444 earthquakes). The earthquake sequence distribution shows a north-northwest–south-southeast (NNW–SSE) orientation in Xayaburi, Lao PDR. Earthquake symbols are sized according to magnitude and colored according to the origin time; the colors represent the years in which the earthquakes occurred: red for 2019, sky blue for 2020, purple for 2021, and pink for 2022. The local magnitude (M_L) of each earthquake is indicated by the size of the circle. The locations of the mainshock from this work (yellow star), USGS (purple star), and Sethanant *et al.* (2025) (green star) are plotted as reference. Our inferred fault orientation is indicated with a yellow solid line, compared with that of Sethanant *et al.* (2025) (green solid line). (b) Seismic distribution and hypocenter from this work (yellow star) compared with hypocenters from Sethanant *et al.* (2025) (green star) and USGS (purple star) with the inferred fault plane from Sethanant *et al.* (2025) (dark solid polygon). Please see the discussion in the text. InSAR, Interferometric Synthetic Aperture Radar. The color version of this figure is available only in the electronic edition.

The temporal and spatial migration of aftershocks is clear. Foreshocks are clustered <15 km from the mainshock area, and within 12 hr after the mainshock, seismicity spread along an NNW trend. Between 24 and 72 hr, the aftershock zone extended farther north and south, outlining the fault image. Seismic activity persisted for more than two years at lower rates, remaining concentrated in the upper 15 km of crust. Cross-section views confirm that seismicity is mostly shallow to midcrustal, consistent with rupture along a fault segment within a NNW-trending fault system (Fig. 5).

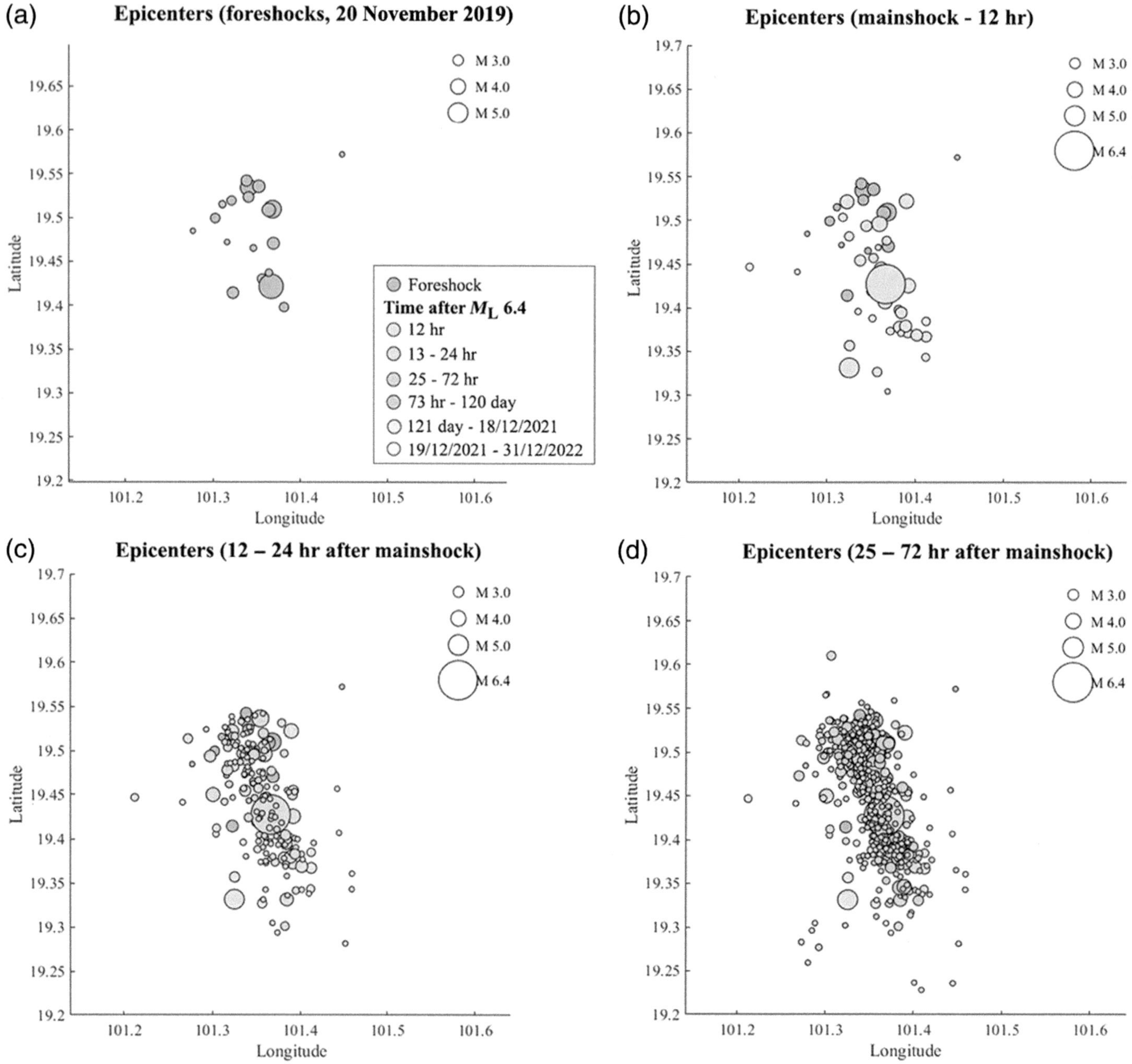

Figure 5. Temporal development of the Xayaburi earthquake sequence is shown in map and cross-section views. Symbol size scales with magnitude, and colors indicate time since the mainshock. (a) Foreshocks within 7 hr before the mainshock (purple). (b) Aftershocks within 12 hr (green). (c) Aftershocks within 24 hr (light blue). (d) Aftershocks within 72 hr (orange). (e) Earthquake sequence from 20 November 2019 to 18 December 2021, before the M_L 5.7 event. The black lines mark cross-section traces. (f) Full earthquake sequence from 20 November 2019 to 31 December 2022. (g) Cross-section A–A′ and (h) cross-section B–B′ show the depth distribution of seismicity for the same time periods and color scheme. The color version of this figure is available only in the electronic edition.

(Continued)

Source mechanisms and fault kinematics from RMT inversion

The result of the RMT inversions of the 16 largest foreshocks and aftershocks is shown in Table 2. Most of the focal mechanisms show right-lateral strike-slip motion on NNW–SSE-trending planes, consistent with the M_w 6.3 mainshock. A few earthquakes show oblique or reverse components, but the overall pattern confirms a dominant strike-slip regime at shallow to mid-crustal depths (9–14 km). The M_w 5.7 foreshock, M_w 6.3 mainshock, and M_w 5.6 aftershock in December

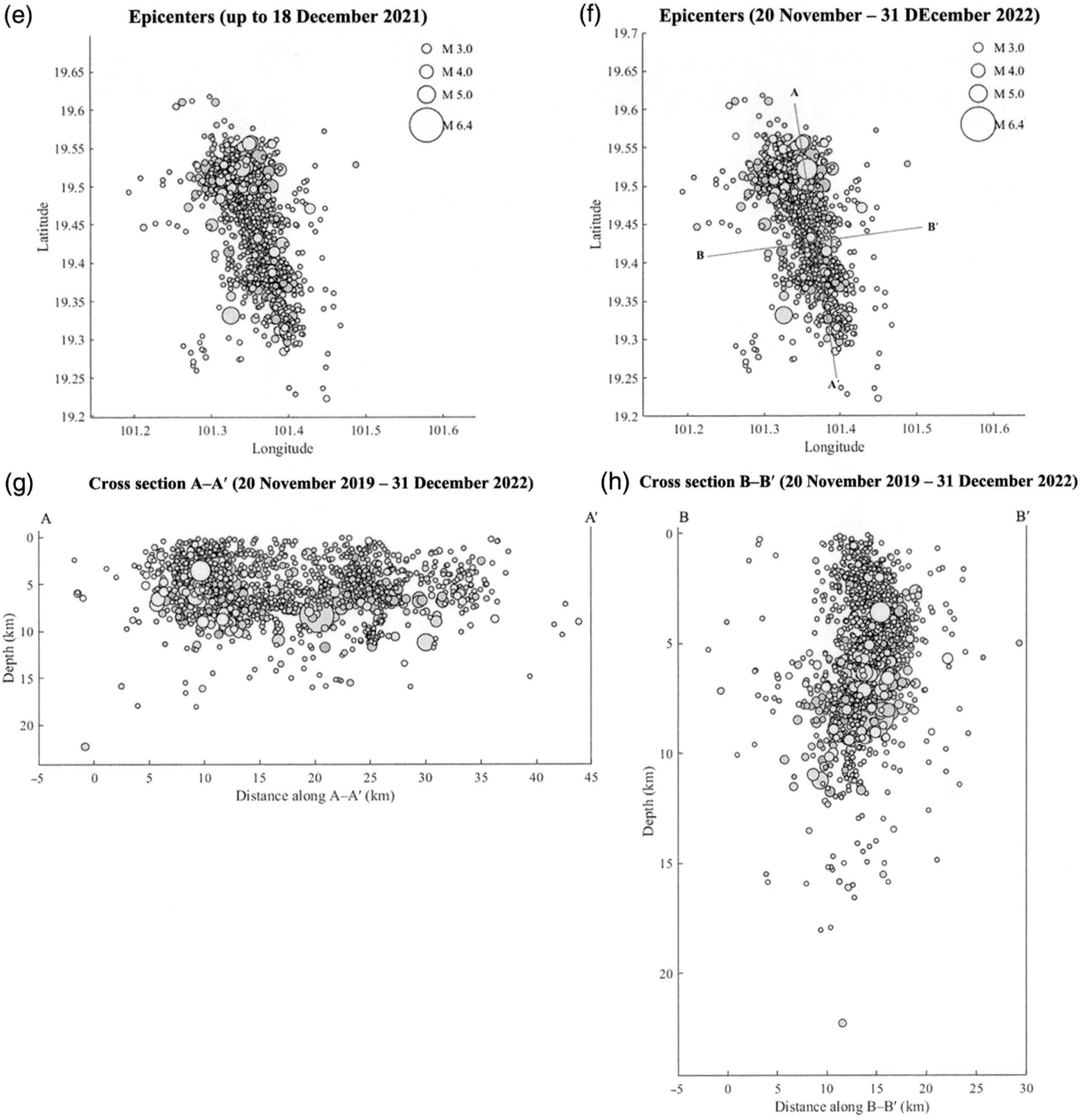

Figure 5. Continued

2021 all share this geometry, highlighting a consistent, but previously unmapped intraplate fault system (Fig. 6a, Table 2).

The sequence of larger events includes an M_w 5.7 foreshock about three hours before the mainshock with a centroid depth of 14 km, and nodal planes defined by strike 15°, dip 65°, and rake −169°. It occurred a few kilometers to the south of the mainshock.

The M_w 6.3 mainshock hypocenter was located at about 10 km depth with a focal mechanism consistent with right-lateral strike-slip motion. Our preferred nodal plane has a strike of 342°, dip of 70°, and rake of −175° (Fig. 6b). This arrangement indicates the best-fitting focal mechanism, showing a reduction of weighted variance of 0.63 at a depth of 10.0 km. Our RMT depth agrees closely with the USGS (M_w 6.2, 10 km

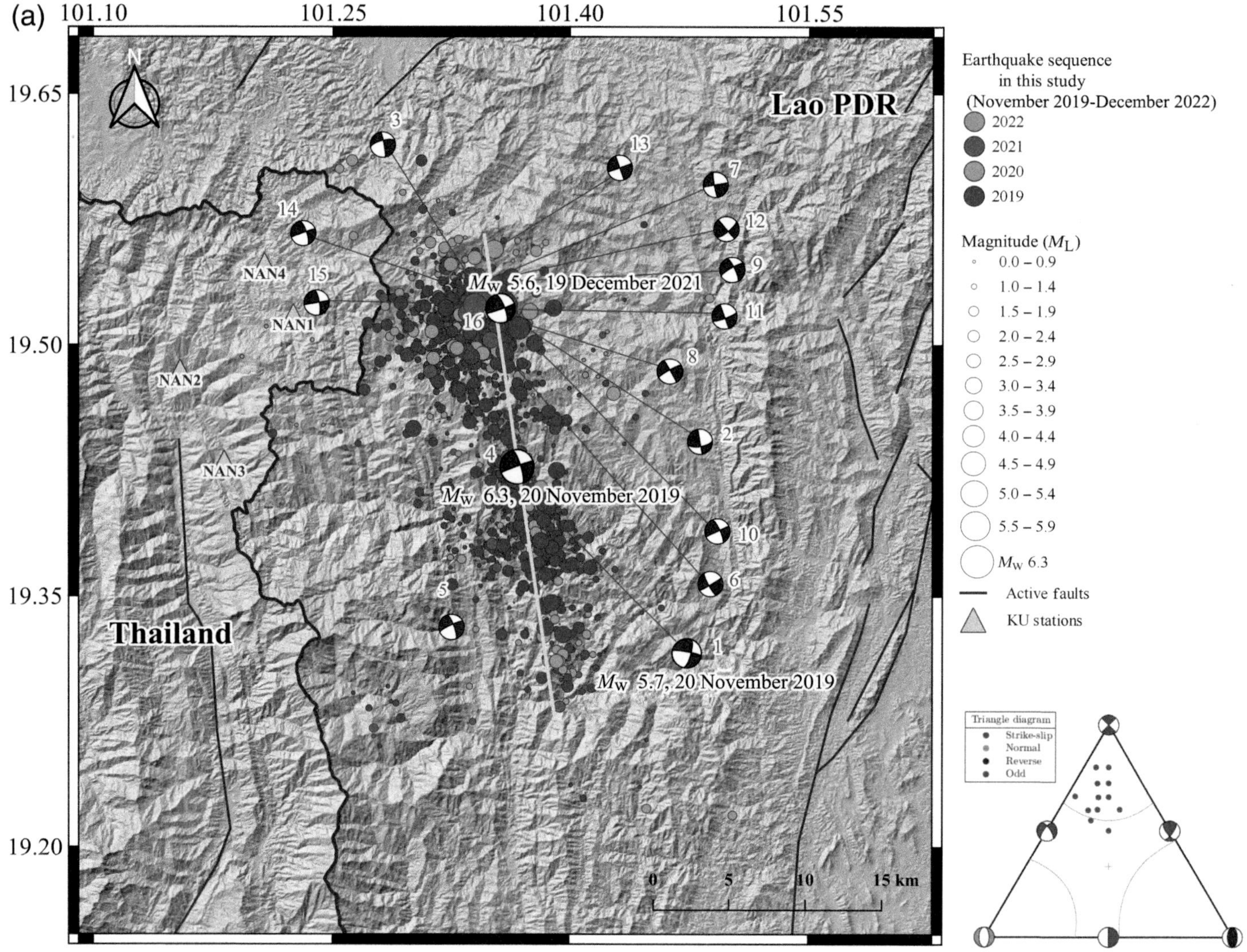

Figure 6. (a) Earthquake sequence from November 2019 to December 2022 relocated with the HypoDD method, showing focal mechanisms from regional moment tensor (RMT) solutions of the 16 biggest earthquakes (M_w 3.8–6.3) that include the M_w 5.7 foreshock, M_w 6.3 mainshock, and M_w 5.6 aftershock. The results indicate a dominant right-lateral strike-slip faulting mechanism along a NNW–SSE-trending fault, with an estimated rupture length of ~35 km. (b) Example of RMT solution for the 20 November 2019 M_L 6.4 (M_w 6.3) mainshock. (A) Observed and synthetic waveforms show a good fit (best-fit value (variance reduction) of 0.63). (B) The solution indicates a focal mechanism of M_w 6.3 at 10 km depth, with strike = 342°, dip = 70°, and rake = −175° (alternate plane: 250°, 85°, −20°), consistent with right-lateral strike-slip motion with a minor normal component. The color version of this figure is available only in the electronic edition. *(Continued)*

depth) and the Global Centroid Moment Tensor (Global CMT) catalog (M_w 6.1, 12 km depth) depths. In addition, Sethanant *et al.* (2025) reported, from a multievent relocation technique and InSAR analysis, right-lateral strike-slip fault movement, with a magnitude of M_w 6.2 at 12 km depth, consistent with our RMT results.

About two years later, on 19 December 2021, a moderate earthquake (M_w 5.6) occurred about 11 km NNW of the mainshock. This event (centroid depth of 9 km and nodal plane parameters of strike 338°, dip 65°, and rake 174°) suggests continued strain release along the same fault system. Our result agrees well with the USGS (M_w 5.5, 10 km depth), Global CMT catalog (M_w 5.5, 12 km depth), and the Sethanant *et al.* (2025) (M_w 5.5, 8 km depth) results.

Coulomb stress transfer, earthquake triggering, and impacts on nearby faults

The M_w 5.7 foreshock, about three hours before the M_w 6.3 mainshock, generated positive ΔCS lobes very close to the position of the mainshock (Fig. 7a,b), suggesting this precursory event may have helped load the fault patch that failed in the mainshock. HypoDD relocations place the foreshock only a few kilometers from the mainshock hypocenter, supporting a possible triggering role. In contrast, Sethanant *et al.* (2025),

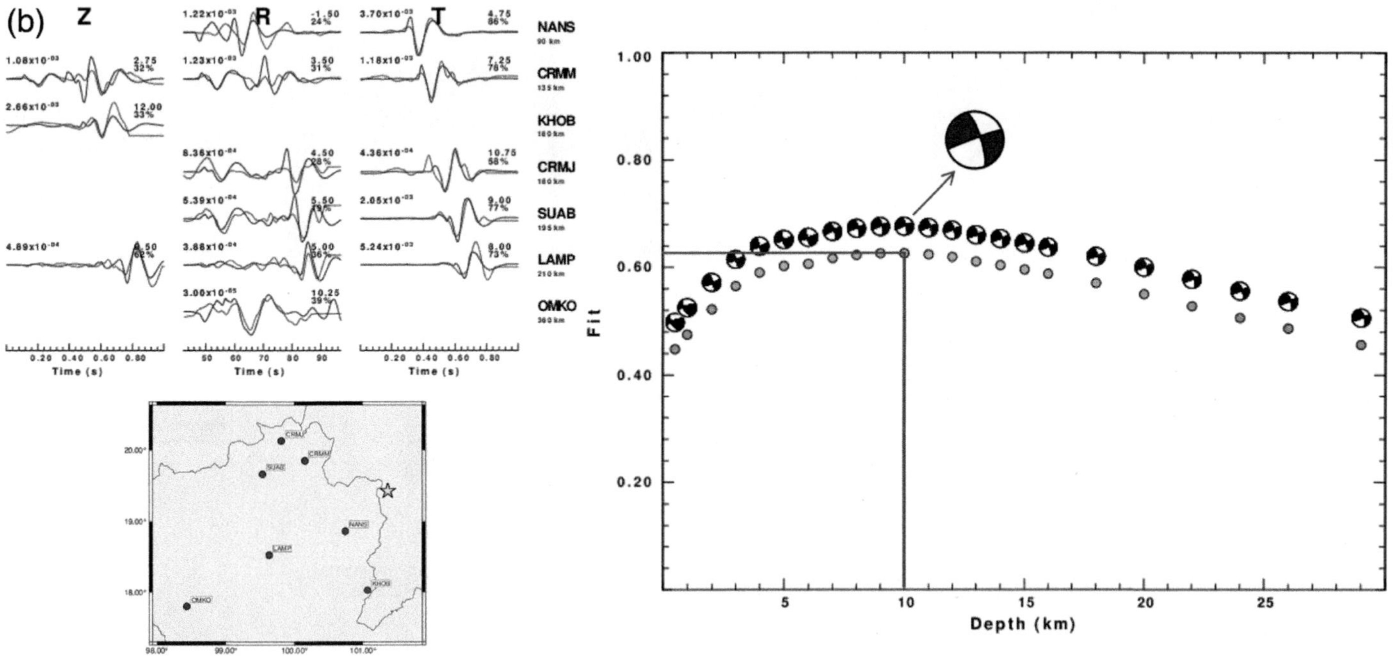

Figure 6. Continued

TABLE 2

Focal Mechanism Solutions for the 16 Largest Earthquakes (M_w≥3.8) in the Xayaburi Sequence (November 2019–December 2022) from This Work, Obtained from Regional Moment Tensor (RMT) Inversion

No	FM	Date (yyyy/mm/dd) Time (hh:mm:ss)	Longitude	Latitude	Depth	Strike/Dip/Rake		Mag (M_w)	Fit
						P1	P2		
1		2019/11/20 21:03:56	101.366520	19.421598	14	15/65/−169	280/80/−25	5.7	0.40
2		2019/11/20 21:19:25	101.367985	19.509668	14	170/90/−145	80/55/0	4.4	0.38
3		2019/11/20 21:33:19	101.340828	19.534393	11	350/81/−150	255/60/−10	4.1	0.33
4		2019/11/20 23:50:44	101.366406	19.427311	10	342/70/−175	250/85/−20	6.3	0.63
5		2019/11/21 00:57:17	101.325317	19.331455	12	340/71/−164	245/75/−20	4.4	0.49
6		2019/11/21 07:00:50	101.359172	19.496065	9	151/75/−175	60/85/−15	4.0	0.37
7		2019/11/21 14:09:58	101.354777	19.536180	13	170/80/−180	80/90/−10	4.1	0.43
8		2019/11/22 06:54:55	101.364380	19.514262	8	331/85/−170	240/80/−5	3.9	0.49
9		2019/11/25 06:58:37	101.356738	19.537103	8	335/71/−164	240/75/−20	4.1	0.55
10		2019/11/27 12:34:19	101.378499	19.500993	6	335/70/−180	245/90/−20	4.0	0.47
11		2019/11/28 23:50:26	101.360213	19.523802	11	160/90/−165	70/75/0	4.4	0.39
12		2019/12/12 09:02:38	101.362703	19.539526	9	140/90/−160	50/70/0	4.6	0.47
13		2020/04/13 22:37:04	101.349561	19.556167	2	340/90/180	70/90/0	3.8	0.34
14		2021/10/29 19:03:29	101.345182	19.525907	10	342/65/−174	250/85/−25	4.5	0.49
15		2021/10/31 03:04:54	101.339933	19.524044	11	350/70/−180	260/90/−20	4.7	0.40
16		2021/12/19 21:06:13	101.355688	19.521940	9	338/65/174	70/85/25	5.6	0.63

The table lists event time, location, depth, magnitude, and nodal plane parameters (strike/dip/rake). FM, focal mechanism; and Mag, Magnitude.

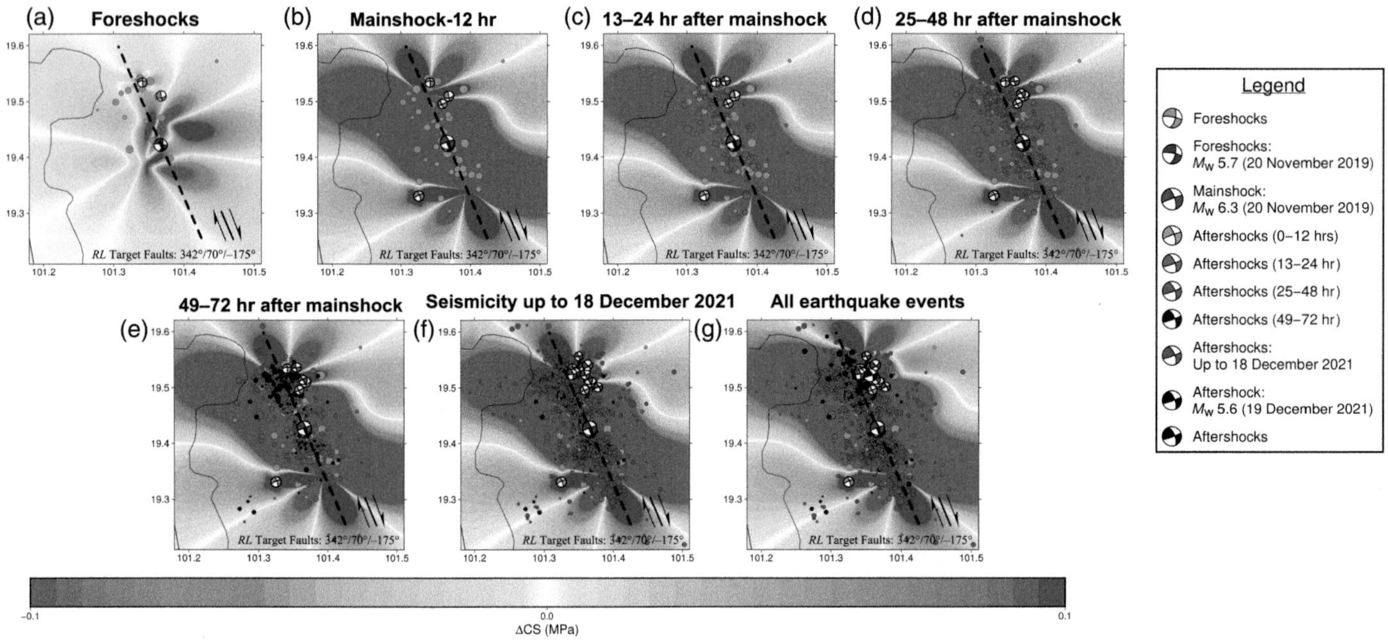

Figure 7. Coulomb stress change (ΔCS) sequence for the 20 November 2019 M_w 6.3 Xayaburi earthquake and its aftershocks, resolved at 10 km depth on the right-lateral strike-slip target fault (strike 342°, dip 70°, and rake −175°) corresponding to the centroid depth of the mainshock. Background colors indicate ΔCS, with red showing positive stress (ΔCS > 0–0.1 MPa) and blue showing negative stress (ΔCS < 0 to − 0.1 MPa). The overall pattern highlights how the M_w 5.7 foreshock helped trigger the mainshock, whereas the mainshock transferred stress northward, sustaining aftershock activity and activating a hidden NNW-trending fault. (a) Foreshocks (green circles), including the M_w 5.7 event, cluster in areas of positive stress close to the fault, suggesting they contributed to loading the mainshock patch (Fig. 9b). (b) The M_w 6.3 mainshock (brown) and its immediate aftershocks within the first 12 hr (pink) fall in zones of enhanced Coulomb stress, consistent with stress transfer along the rupture to the northern end of the fault. (c) Aftershocks during 13–24 hr (gray) extend north and south of the main rupture, tracking stress lobes along the fault zone. (d) Aftershocks in 25–48 hr (purple) broaden in distribution, further delineating the fault geometry. (e) By 49–72 hr (blue), activity remains focused in positive stress regions, showing continued triggering along the NNW fault segment. (f) Seismicity up to 18 December 2019 shows nearly 1800 aftershocks aligned with the rupture, largely confined to stress-enhanced areas. (g) All earthquakes from November 2019 through December 2022, including the M_w 5.6 earthquake on 19 December 2021, illustrate a progressive northward migration of seismicity. The color version of this figure is available only in the electronic edition.

using multievent relocation and InSAR modeling, placed the foreshock on a separate subfault and argued it was not directly linked to the mainshock. These differing interpretations likely reflect (1) variations in datasets, with our work using dense temporary stations and theirs emphasizing InSAR and regional data; (2) differences in relocation methods, with HypoDD refining relative locations within clusters, whereas the multi-event approaches may highlight broader geometry; and (3) an inherent complexity to the fault system, which may involve several closely spaced strands.

The ΔCS generated by the mainshock adjusted stress along the fault system, consistent with the dense aftershock activity that followed. Within the first 12 hr, 56 aftershocks (5 events/hr) were located close to the rupture (Fig. 8b). The number rose to 153 in the 13–24 hr (13 events/hr) period and peaked at 197 events in the 25–48 hr window (8 events/hr), outlining the NNW-trending fault trace (Fig. 7c,d). By 49–72 hr, the sequence was tapering off, but 115 events were still recorded (5 events/hr) (Fig. 7e). The M_w 5.6 aftershock on 19 December 2021 also occurred inside a region of increased Coulomb stress, about 11 km NNW of the mainshock. It fits into the broader pattern of stress transfer, extending seismicity farther north (Fig. 7f,g).

These cumulative effects of the earthquake sequence can modify stresses on nearby faults. Our results reflect that the region of significant ΔCS from the mainshock extends roughly 50 km from the epicenter, with amplitudes above the +0.01 MPa threshold considered significant for earthquake triggering (Fig. 8a–c). When the 16 largest earthquakes of the sequence (M_w 3.8–6.3) are included, this positive stress change footprint is enlarged slightly, but the overall trend remains (Fig. 8d–f). Although the ΔCS changes are small, several mapped faults intersect with the zones of increased stress, highlighting a potential to host future seismic activity. For example, the NNE-trending left-lateral faults to the NE of the rupture in Lao PDR (Fig. 8b, Ban Hua Na and Na Khem faults in Fig. 2a) and the NS normal faults to the west of the main rupture zone in Thailand (Fig. 7c, Pua fault in Fig. 2a) lie at the edge of positive stress change lobes (Fig. 8b,c, respectively).

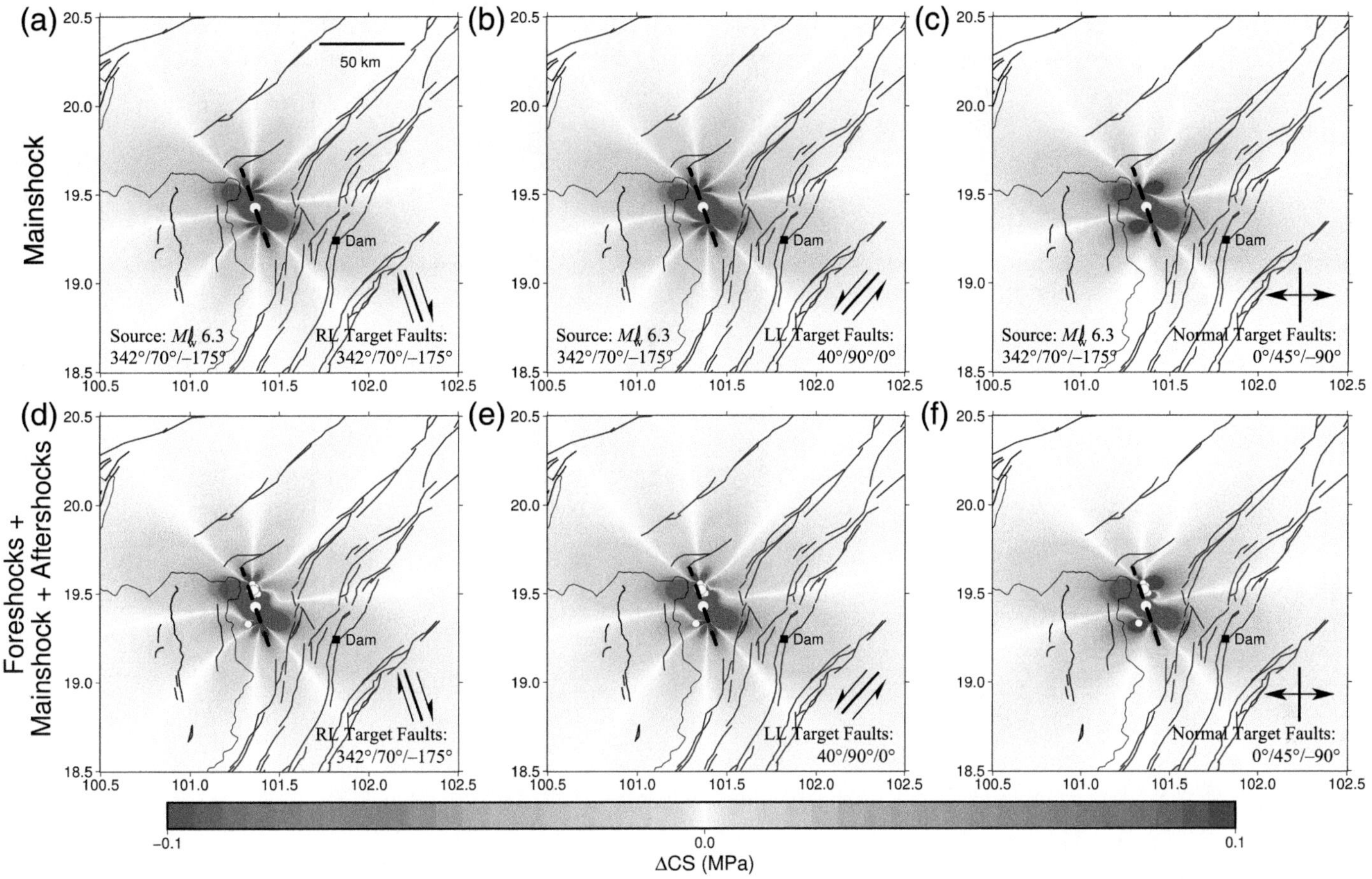

Figure 8. Coulomb stress changes (ΔCS) from the 20 November 2019 M_w 6.3 Xayaburi earthquake and its sequence, resolved on representative target fault geometries in Lao PDR and northern Thailand. Mapped faults with geometries corresponding to each model are highlighted in bold. (a–c) Stress changes from the mainshock alone. (d–f) Stress changes from the combined effects of the foreshock, mainshock, and aftershocks (events with RMT solutions). Panels (a) and (d) show ΔCS resolved on right-lateral strike-slip faults striking 342°. Panels (b) and (e) show ΔCS resolved on left-lateral strike-slip faults striking 40°. Panels (c) and (f) show ΔCS resolved on north-trending normal faults striking 0°. The color version of this figure is available only in the electronic edition.

Earthquake damage distribution and basin amplification effects

Within two days of the main event, a team from Kasetsart University surveyed the damage in the affected area within Thailand, within a radius of approximately 150 km from the epicenter, from 22 to 25 November 2019. The survey locations and seismic intensities at those sites are shown in Figure 9a, and examples of building damage are shown in Figure 9b. There was no evidence of surface rupture. Structural damage ranged from minor cracks in walls to major cracks in buildings (Fig. 9b, A–D). Cracks were mainly found in structural walls and floor tiles (e.g., Fig. 9b, A1,D2). Some buildings had damaged beams and columns (e.g., Fig. 9b, B1,B3), with severe cracks separating the wall from buildings (Fig. 9b, D1). The most damaged area was along the Thai-Lao PDR border, about 20–25 km to the west of the mainshock. However, the ground motion recorded at the strong-motion station in Thung Chang District, Nan Province, about 60 km to the west of the main shock, registered PGA of 0.03*g* (THUA station, an open triangle in Fig. 9a).

The damages from the M_w 6.3 Xayaburi earthquake extended into northern Thailand. In Nan Province, Thailand, a school in Bo Klua District, located 22 km west of the mainshock, suffered severe damage, with ceiling collapse and cracked load-bearing walls (DMR, 2019). Farther away, in Phayao Province, more than 100 km west of the epicenter, a school in Chiang Kham district (19.4° N, 100.4° E) sustained column and wall damage (Fig. 9b, D1–D3). In addition, in the Pua basin (18.7° N, 100.7° E), reported damages were relatively higher than surrounding areas at the same distance from the mainshock. The observed damage at distant locations from the mainshock points to strong basin amplification in Nan and Phayao. Local basin structures in this area likely amplified the ground shaking, although it cannot be ruled out that the abundance of non-earthquake-resistant buildings could also contribute to more damage in the affected area.

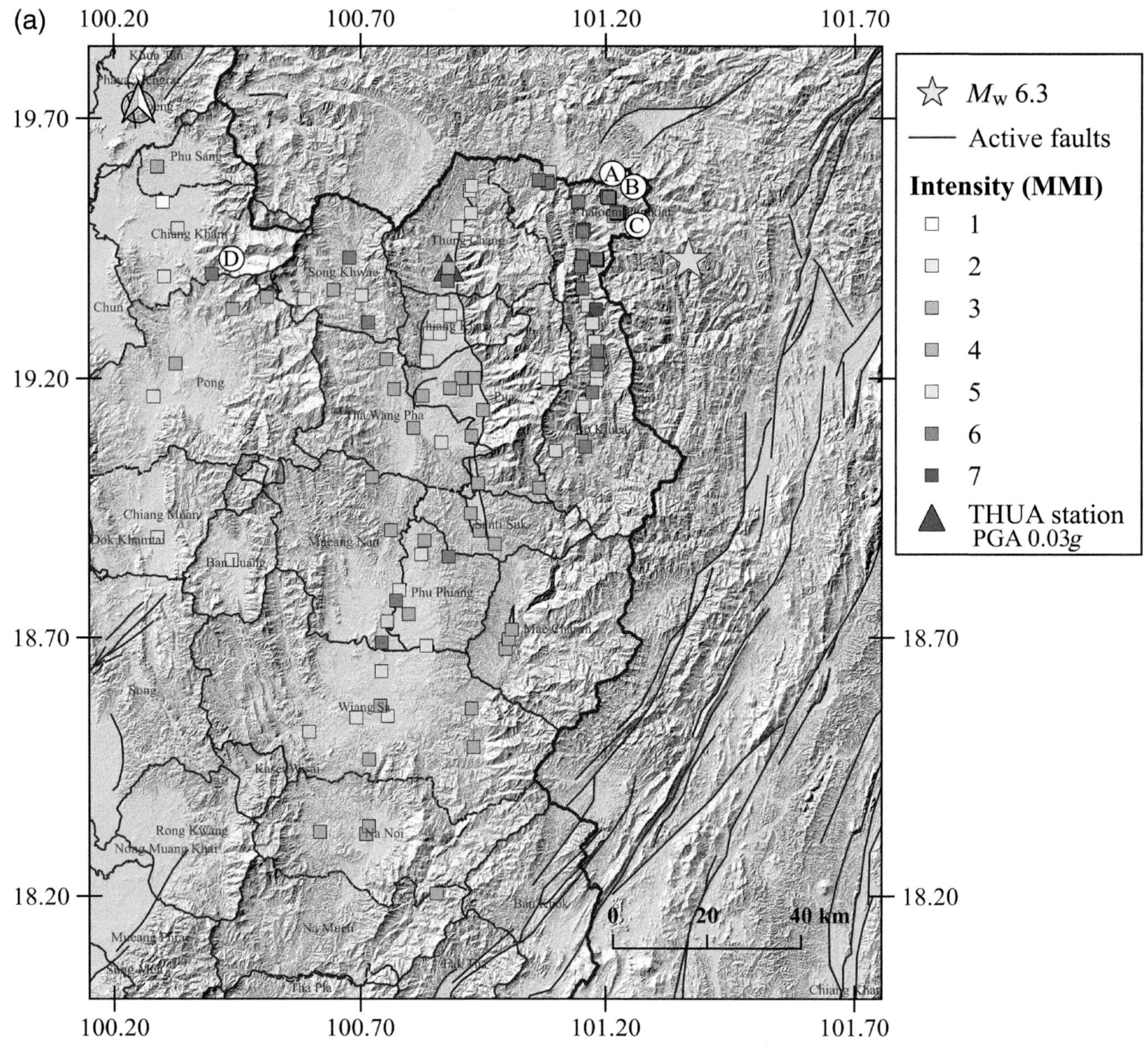

Figure 9. (a) A map showing the seismic intensity from macroseismic surveys within 150 km of the M_w 6.3 mainshock. The boxes show the survey locations and are colored based on the modified Mercalli intensity (MMI) seismic intensity level. Peak ground acceleration (PGA) recorded by the THUA station (purple triangle) registered 0.03g. (b) Examples of structural damage caused by the 20 November 2019 M_w 6.3 Xayaburi earthquake. Locations of each photo group are shown in Figure 8a. (A) School building (reinforced concrete: RC) in Chaloem Phra Kiat district, Nan Province (~20 km from the epicenter) (VI MMI): (A1) diagonal cracks at ~45° around window frames and horizontal cracks along curtain mounts; and (A2–A3) cracks on a wall and structural columns. (B) Residential buildings (RC on the first floor and wooden frame on the second floor) in Ban Nam Chang, Chaloem Phra Kiat District, Nan Province (~20 km from the epicenter) (VI MMI): (B1) large crack at the joint between the RC wall and the second floor wooden support; (B2) broken and fallen window glass; and (B3) crack at the joint between a wooden beam and the concrete column. (C) School building (RC) in Ban Nam Ri, Chaloem Phra Kiat district, Nan Province (~20 km from the epicenter) (VI MMI): (C1–C2) cracks along structural joints (repaired by plaster); and (C3) broken and fallen window glass. (D) School building (RC) in Chiang Kham district, Phayao Province (~100 km from the epicenter) (VI MMI): (D1) major cracks in a column and building walls with visible subsidence; (D2) long crack across tiled floor; and (D3) cracks on wall surfaces and at wall–column joints. The color version of this figure is available only in the electronic edition. *(Continued)*

(b)

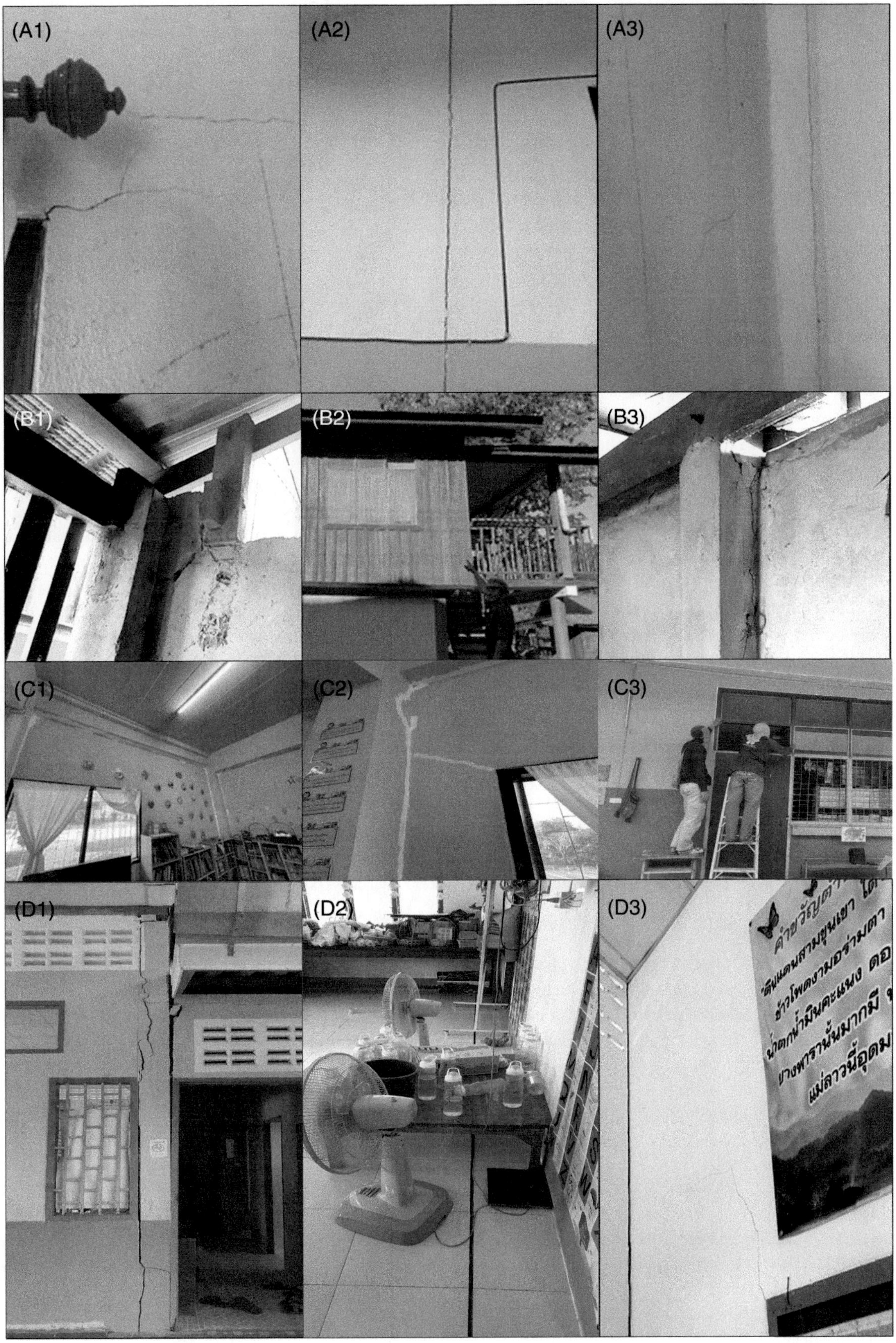

Figure 9. Continued

Conclusions

The 2019 M_w 6.3 Xayaburi earthquake was the largest instrumentally recorded earthquake in northern Lao PDR and along the Lao PDR–Thai border. Although of moderate size, the earthquake produced strong shaking, an extended period of aftershocks, and a broad damage zone. Serious structural damage was reported in both the Lao PDR and Thailand. In Thailand, some of the heaviest losses can be linked to basin amplification effects in Nan and Phayao Provinces.

Our analysis of aftershock relocations and RMTs indicates the rupture occurred on a fault segment of a NNW–SSE trending right-lateral strike-slip fault system. The M_w 5.7 foreshock that occurred a few hours before the mainshock may have modified the stress on the fault that failed in the M_w 6.3 event. Subsegment stress changes from the main event appear to drive a dense aftershock sequence, leading to an M_w 5.6 earthquake in 2021.

Intraplate earthquakes in mainland Southeast Asia, although infrequent, can be damaging with significant negative effects over a long distance, especially in locations where basin effects amplify shaking. The discovery of a fault segment that is presently active in this region indicates a need for more detailed mapping and monitoring. Because the earthquakes affected both the Lao PDR and Thailand, it highlights the importance of joint hazard assessments and cooperation across borders.

Data and Resources

Seismic data for the period November 2019 to December 2022 were collected from 23 stations in northern Thailand, including 17 operated by the Thai Meteorological Department, 2 by the Department of Mineral Resources, and 4 temporary stations installed by Kasetsart University.

Declaration of Competing Interests

The authors acknowledge that there are no conflicts of interest recorded.

Acknowledgments

The authors thank the Thai Meteorological Department and the Department of Mineral Resources, Thailand, for providing earthquake data used in this study. The authors also thank the National Research Council of Thailand for supporting this research through the project "Seismicity of northern Thailand and location delineation and impact assessment of the hidden fault in the Chiang Mai–Lamphun from microseismicity" (Contract Number N25A650425). The Development and Promotion of Science and Technology Talents Project supported graduate study for P. Pholsonda.

References

AHA Centre (2019). Flash Update: No. 01 – M 6.4 in Lao PDR – 21 November 2019, ASEAN Coordinating Centre for Humanitarian Assistance on Disaster Management (AHA Centre), available at https://ahacentre.org/flash-update/flash-update-no-01-m-6-4-in-lao-pdr-21-november-2019/ (last accessed January 2024).

Bilham, R. (2004). Earthquakes in India and the Himalaya: Tectonics, geodesy and history, *Ann. Geophys.* **47,** nos. 2/3, 839–858, doi: 10.4401/ag-3338.

Bondár, I., S. C. Myers, E. R. Engdahl, and E. A. Bergman (2004). Epicentre accuracy based on seismic network criteria, *Geophys. J. Int.* **156,** no. 3, 483–496, doi: 10.1111/j.1365-246X.2004.02070.x.

Burrett, C., J. Hennig-Brett, T. T. Zaw, and M. Udchachon (2021). The Truong Son, Loei-Phetchabun, and Kontum terranes in Indochina: Provenance, rifting, and collisions, *Front. Earth Sci.* **9,** 603565, doi: 10.3389/feart.2021.603565.

Chamberlain, C., C. Boese, and J. Townend (2016). Cross-correlation-based detection and characterisation of microseismicity adjacent to the locked, late-interseismic Alpine fault, South Westland, New Zealand, *Earth Planet. Sci. Lett.* **457,** 1–11, doi: 10.1016/j.epsl.2016.09.061.

Charusiri, P., V. Daorerk, D. Archibald, K. Hisada, and T. Ampaiwan (2002). Geotectonic evolution of Thailand: A new synthesis, *J. Geol. Soc. Thailand* **1,** 1–20.

Department of Mineral Resources (DMR) (2019). Earthquake report: M_w 6.4 Xayaburi Province, Lao PDR, 21 November 2019 (in Thai), Department of Mineral Resources, available at https://www.dmr.go.th/wp-content/uploads/2022/10/article_20191121093251.pdf (last accessed January 2024).

DMR (2023). Active Fault Map Atlas of Thailand, 2023 (Official Edition) (in Thai), Department of Mineral Resources, available at https://anyflip.com/kera/wglh/ (last accessed January 2025).

Gao, D., and H. Kao (2020). Optimization of the match-filtering method for robust repeating earthquake detection: The multisegment cross-correlation approach, *J. Geophys. Res.* **125,** e2020JB019714, doi: 10.1029/2020JB019714.

Havskov, J., and L. Ottemöller (1999). SEISAN: The earthquake analysis software, *Seismol. Res. Lett.* **70,** no. 5, 532–534, doi: 10.1785/gssrl.70.5.532.

Herman, M. W. (2020). mherman09/Hdef: First release of Hdef (v0.0.0), *Zenodo*, doi: 10.5281/zenodo.3894137.

Herman, M. W., K. P. Furlong, G. P. Hayes, and H. M. Benz (2016). Foreshock triggering of the 1 April 2014 M_w 8.2 Iquique, Chile, earthquake, *Earth Planet. Sci. Lett.* **447,** 119–129, doi: 10.1016/j.epsl.2016.04.020.

Herman, M. W., R. B. Herrmann, H. M. Benz, and K. P. Furlong (2014). Using regional moment tensors to constrain the kinematics and stress evolution of the 2010–2013 Canterbury earthquake sequence, South Island, New Zealand, *Tectonophysics* **633,** 1-15, doi: 10.1016/j.tecto.2014.06.019.

Herrmann, R. B. (2013). Computer programs in seismology: An evolving tool for instruction and research, *Seismol. Res. Lett.* **84,** 1081–1088, doi: 10.1785/0220110096.

Herrmann, R. B., H. Benz, and C. J. Ammon (2011). Monitoring the earthquake source process in North America, *Bull. Seismol. Soc. Am.* **101,** no. 6, 2609–2625, doi: 10.1785/0120110095.

Johnston, A. C., and E. S. Schweig (1996). The enigma of the New Madrid earthquakes of 1811–1812, *Annu. Rev. Earth Planet. Sci.* **24,** no. 1, 339–384, doi: 10.1146/annurev.earth.24.1.339.

Kagan, Y. (2004). Short-term properties of earthquake catalogs and models of earthquake source, *Bull. Seismol. Soc. Am.* **94,** 1207–1228, doi: 10.1785/012003098.

Kamvong, T., S. Zaw, D. A. Foster, J. Meffre, T. S. Offler, and T. Yui (2014). Adakites in the Truong Son and Loei fold belts, Thailand and Laos: Genesis and tectonic implications, *Gondwana Res.* **26,** no. 1, 165–184, doi: 10.1016/j.gr.2013.06.011.

Lienert, B. R., and J. Havskov (1995). A computer program for locating earthquakes both locally and globally, *Seismol. Res. Lett.* **66,** no. 5, 26–36, doi: 10.1785/gssrl.66.5.26.

Morley, C. K. (2007). Variations in Late Cenozoic–Recent strike-slip and oblique-extensional geometries, within Indochina: The influence of pre-existing fabrics, *J. Struct. Geol.* **29,** no. 1, 36–58.

Morley, C. K. (2013). Discussion of tectonic models for Cenozoic strike-slip fault-affected continental margins of mainland SE Asia, *J. Asian Earth Sci.* **76,** 137–151, doi: 10.1016/j.jseaes.2012.10.019.

Morley, C. K., P. Charusiri, and I. M. Watkinson (2011). Structural geology of Thailand during the Cenozoic, in *Geology of Thailand,* M. F. Ridd, A. J. Barber, and M. A. Crow (Editors), Geological Society, Special Publications, London, United Kingdom, 273–334.

Nualkhao, P., P. Charusiri, C. Sutiwanich, and S. Pailoplee (2016). Paleoearthquakes along Xaignabouli fault zone in western Lao PDR, *Bull. Geosci.* **7,** 25–32.

Okubo, Y., M. Soe, Y. Takahashi, S. Wongsomsak, and M. Fujita (2021). *Tectonic Interpretation of Active Fault Extending in Myanmar, Laos and China by Relief Map of ASTER GDEM and Harmonized Geological Map*, Geological Society, London, doi: 10.1144/SP501.

Omori, F. (1894). *On After-Shocks of Earthquakes*, Imperial University of Tokyo, Vol. 7, 111–200.

Ornthammarath, T., and P. Warnitchai (2016). 5 May 2014 M_w 6.1 Mae Lao (northern Thailand) earthquake: Interpretations of recorded ground motion and structural damage, *Earthq. Spectra* **32,** 1209–1238, doi: 10.1193/081814EQS129M.

Pailoplee, S., and P. Charusiri (2016). Seismic hazards in Thailand: A compilation and updated probabilistic analysis, *Earth Planets Space* **68,** doi: 10.1186/s40623-016-0465-6.

Pailoplee, S., and P. Charusiri (2017). Analyses of seismic activities and hazards in Laos: A seismicity approach, *Terr. Atmos. Ocean. Sci.* **28,** no. 6, 843–853, doi: 10.3319/TAO.2017.03.23.01.

Pananont, P., M. Herman, P. Pornsopin, K. Furlong, S. Habangkaem, F. Waldhauser, W. Wongwai, S. Limpisawad, P. Warnitchai, S. Kosuwan *et al.* (2017). Seismotectonics of the 2014 Chiang Rai, Thailand, earthquake sequence, *J. Geophys. Res.* **122,** no. 8, 6367–6388, doi: 10.1002/2017jb014085.

Pornsopin, P., P. Pananont, K. P. Furlong, and E. Sandvol (2023). Sensor orientation of the TMD seismic network (Thailand) from P-wave particle motions, *Geosci. Lett.* **10,** 24, doi: 10.1186/s40562-023-00278-7.

Puangjaktha, P., and S. Pailoplee (2018a). Application of the region–time–length algorithm to study of earthquake precursors in the Thailand–Laos–Myanmar borders, *J. Earth Syst. Sci.* 127, doi: 10.1007/s12040-018-0939-y.

Puangjaktha, P., and S. Pailoplee (2018b). Temporal and spatial distributions of precursory seismicity rate changes in the Thailand-Laos-Myanmar border region: Implication for upcoming hazardous earthquakes, *J. Seismol.* **22,** doi: 10.1007/s10950-017-9706-9.

Qian, X., Q. Feng, W. Yang, Y. Wang, C. Chonglakmani, and D. Monjai (2015). Arc-like volcanic rocks in NW Laos: Geochronological and geochemical constraints and their tectonic implications, *J. Asian Earth Sci.* **98,** 342-357, doi: 10.1016/j.jseaes.2014.11.035.

Sethanant, I., E. Nissen, E. Bergman, S. J. Oliva, L. Pousse-Beltran, E. Karasözen, and P. Pananont (2025). Recent earthquakes on unmapped faults highlight hidden seismic hazards within the Golden Triangle region of Laos, Thailand and Myanmar, *Geophys. J. Int.* **241,** no. 1, 606–627, doi: 10.1093/gji/ggaf061.

Stein, R. S., G. C. P. King, and J. Lin (1992). Change in failure stress on the southern San Andreas fault system caused by the 1992 M_w 7.4 Landers earthquake, *Science* **258,** no. 5086, 1328–1332, doi: 10.1126/science.258.5086.1328.

Storti, F., R. Holdsworth, and F. Salvini (2003). *Intraplate Strike-Slip Deformation Belts*, Geol. Soc. Spec. Pub., Vol. 210, 1–14, doi: 10.1144/GSL.SP.2003.210.01.01.

Tapponnier, P., G. Peltzer, A. Y. Le Dain, R. Armijo, and P. Cobbold (1982). Propagating extrusion tectonics in Asia: New insights from simple experiments with plasticine, *Geology* **10,** no. 12, 611–616.

Tri, T., M. Faure, N. Vuong, H. Bui, M. Fyhn, T. Nguyen, C. Lepvrier, T. Thomsen, K. Tani, and P. Charusiri (2020). Neoproterozoic to Early Triassic tectono-stratigraphic evolution of Indochina and adjacent areas: A review with new data, *J. Asian Earth Sci.* **191,** 104231, doi: 10.1016/j.jseaes.2020.104231.

Tun, S. T., Y. Wang, S. N. Khaing, M. Thant, N. Htay, Y. M. M. Htwe, T. Myint, and K. Sieh (2014). Surface ruptures of the M_w 6.8 March 2011 Tarlay earthquake, eastern Myanmar, *Bull. Seismol. Soc. Am.* **104,** no. 6, 2915–2932, doi: 10.1785/0120130321.

U.S. Geological Survey (USGS) (2025). ANSS Comprehensive Earthquake Catalog (ComCat), earthquake data for 20 November 2019 to 31 December 2022, *U.S. Geol. Surv. Earthq. Hazards Program*, available at https://earthquake.usgs.gov/earthquakes/search/ (last accessed January 2024).

Utsu, T. (1961). statistical study on the occurrence of aftershocks, *Geophys. Mag.* **30,** 521–605.

Utsu, T., Y. Ogata, and R. S. Matsu'ura (1995). The centenary of the Omori formula for a decay law of aftershock activity, *J. Phys. Earth* **43,** 1–33, doi: 10.4294/jpe1952.43.1.

Waldhauser, F. (2001). HypoDD—A program to compute double-difference hypocenter location, *U.S. Geol. Surv. Open-File Rept. 01-113*, 25 pp., available at https://pubs.usgs.gov/of/2001/0113/ (last accessed September 2024).

Waldhauser, F., and W. L. Ellsworth (2000). A double-difference earthquake location algorithm: Method and application to the northern Hayward fault, California, *Bull. Seismol. Soc. Am.* **90,** no. 6, 1353–1368, doi: 10.1785/0120000006.

Wells, D. L., and K. J. Coppersmith (1994). New empirical relationships among magnitude, rupture length, rupture width, rupture area, and surface displacement, *Bull. Seismol. Soc. Am.* **84,** no. 4, 974–1002.

Wiemer, S., and M. Wyss (2000). Minimum magnitude of completeness in earthquake catalogs: Examples from Alaska, the western United States, and Japan, *Bull. Seismol. Soc. Am.* **90,** no. 4, 859–869, doi: 10.1785/0119990114.

Zaw, K., M. Meffre, D. A. Foster, T. T. Kamvong, and C. Burrett (2014). Tectonics and metallogeny of mainland Southeast Asia —A review and contribution, *Gondwana Res.* **26,** no. 1, 5–30, doi: 10.1016/j.gr.2013.10.010.

Manuscript received 17 September 2025
Published online 28 January 2026

Characteristic Displacement and Paleoearthquake Activity of the Xiaojiang Fault Mapped from Historical Image Data and Tectonic Implications

Xingao Li[1], Zhongtai He[*1], and Long Guo[1]

Abstract

Understanding the displacement characteristics of active faults is essential for reconstructing the recurrence behavior of large earthquakes and evaluating seismic hazards. Quantifying surface offsets provides key evidence for identifying individual and cumulative rupture events and for testing whether a fault exhibits characteristic slip behavior. In this study, we investigated the northern segment of the Xiaojiang fault, one of the most seismically active strike-slip faults in the southeastern Tibetan Plateau. To evaluate the single- and multievent cumulative offsets of streams along the fault, we analyzed historical aerial photographs from the 1950s and Keyhole satellite images from 1968. Despite extensive recent anthropogenic modification of the landscape, these historical datasets preserve original geomorphic markers that record surface displacements from multiple earthquakes. A cumulative-offset probability density analysis reveals characteristic slip increments of approximately 7 m, corresponding to at least five surface-rupturing events since the Holocene. The results indicate that the northern Xiaojiang fault follows a characteristic slip model with an average recurrence interval of ~1000 yr and a left-lateral slip rate of ~7 mm/yr. These findings enhance our understanding of the fault's long-term behavior and its role in accommodating regional crustal deformation along the southeastern margin of the Tibetan Plateau.

Cite this article as Li, X., Z. He, and L. Guo (2026). Characteristic Displacement and Paleoearthquake Activity of the Xiaojiang Fault Mapped from Historical Image Data and Tectonic Implications, *Seismol. Res. Lett.* **97**, 784–804, doi: 10.1785/0220250326.

Introduction

Situated in the southeastern Tibetan Plateau, the Xiaojiang fault zone separates the active Sichuan–Yunnan block (SYB) from the stable South China block (Cheng *et al.*, 2021) and constitutes a key segment of the Xianshuihe–Xiaojiang left-lateral strike-slip system (Fig. 1). This fault system is crucial for accommodating the block's southeastward lateral movement and its clockwise rotation around the East Himalayan tectonic node (Wang *et al.*, 1998; Shi *et al.*, 2018; Guo *et al.*, 2021) along the SYB's eastern boundary on the southeastern Tibetan Plateau. Since the late Quaternary, the Xiaojiang fault zone has undergone significant deformation and seismicity, forming a key segment of the north–south seismic belt (Deng *et al.*, 2003; Zhang *et al.*, 2013). Together with the Zemuhe and Lianfeng–Zhaotong fault zones, it forms a Y-shaped tectonic configuration analogous to that of the Xianshuihe–Anninghe–Longmenshan system, for which numerous strong earthquakes have occurred. The northern Xiaojiang fault connects to the Zemuhe fault, forming a crucial section of the Y-shaped system. Investigating its tectonic deformation is essential for clarifying the evolution of the Xianshuihe–Xiaojiang fault network and for improving the knowledge of intracontinental deformation across the southeastern Tibetan Plateau.

An effective approach for estimating the magnitudes of potential fault earthquakes is to analyze past surface-rupturing events and identify preserved landforms with measurable offsets along fault traces (Tapponnier *et al.*, 2001; Klinger, 2005; Gold and Cowgill, 2011; Zielke *et al.*, 2012). Clarifying the relationship between single-event and cumulative offsets is essential for characterizing the spatial distribution and patterns of surface slip from major earthquakes (Ren *et al.*, 2015). Cumulative surface dislocations provide information on the rupture history of faults, at least 23 strike-slip faults with geomorphic evidence of multiple earthquakes (Zielke *et al.*, 2015; Reitman *et al.*, 2023a,b). The northern section of the Xiaojiang fault can be characterized in terms of rupture patterns and typical displacements through statistical analysis of cumulative

1. State Key Laboratory of Earthquake Dynamics and Forecasting, Institute of Geology, China Earthquake Administration, Beijing, China

*Corresponding author: hzt@ies.ac.cn

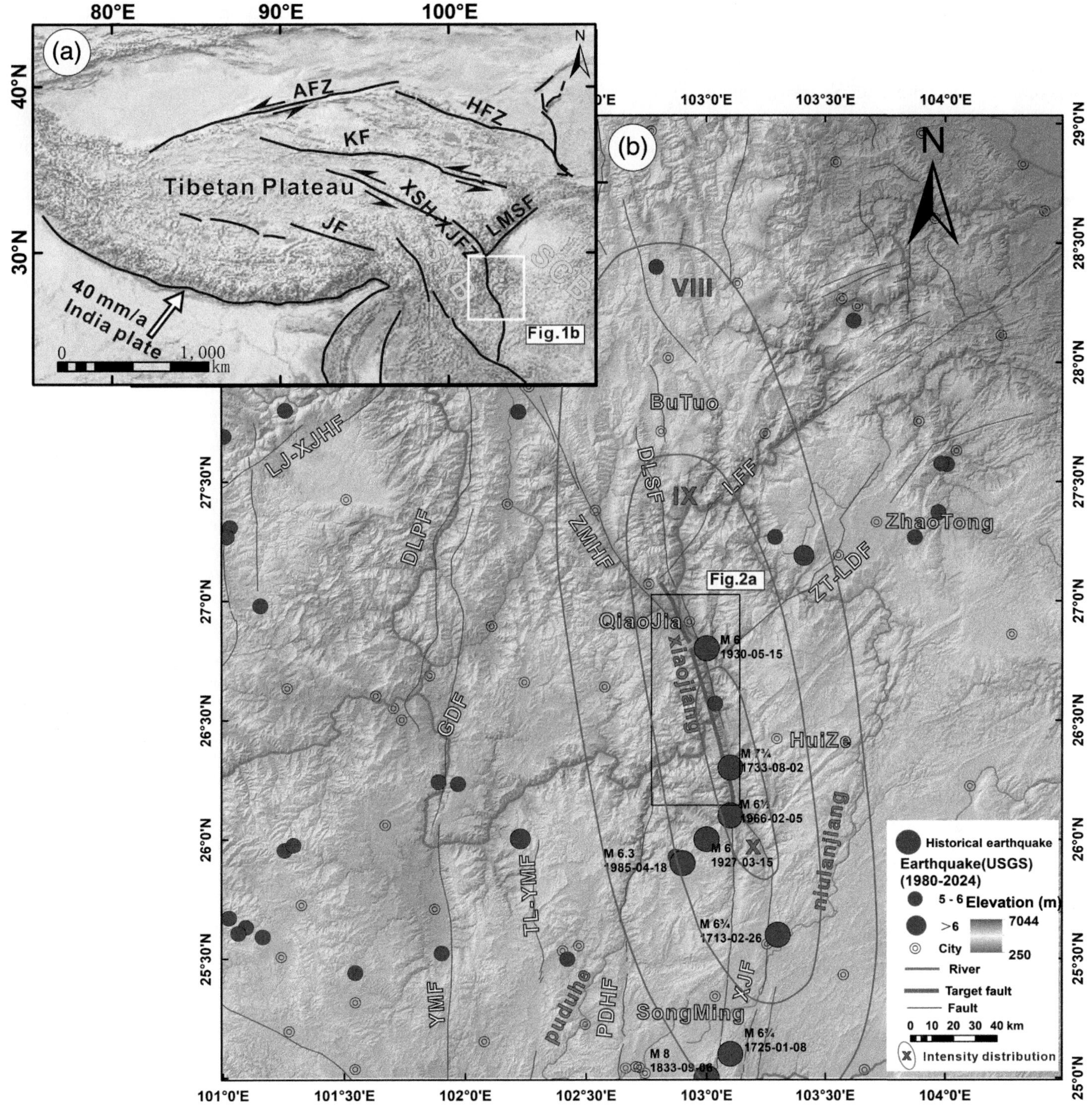

Figure 1. Distribution of active faults and historical seismicity in the northern Xiaojiang fault zone and surrounding areas. (a) Regional tectonic framework showing the locations of the Sichuan–Yunnan block (SYB) and the South China block. (b) Enlarged view of the northern Xiaojiang fault zone showing the detailed traces of the main fault segments and key sites investigated in this study. Fault data were obtained from the China Earthquake Disaster Prevention Center Earthquake Fault Detection Data Center. The earthquake catalog is from the U.S. Geological Survey (USGS). **M**, magnitude. The base data are from the Advanced Spaceborne Thermal Emission and Reflection Radiometer (ASTER) global digital elevation map with a 30 m resolution, and the bold-red lines are the target faults. The bold-red lines represent the target faults: AFZ, Altyn Tagh fault zone; DLPF, Delipu fault; DLSF, Daliangshan fault; HFZ, Haiyuan fault zone; JF, Jiali fault; KF, Kunlun fault; LBF, Leibo fault; LFF, Lianfeng fault; LJ-XJHF, Lijiang–Xiaojinhe fault; PDHF, Puduhe fault; TL-YMF, Tanglang–Yimen fault; XGDF, Xigeda fault; XJF, Xiaojiang fault; XSH-XJFZ, Xianshuihe–Xiaojiang fault zone; YMF, Yuanmou fault; ZMHF, Zemuhe fault; and ZT-LDF, Zhaotong–Ludian fault. The color version of this figure is available only in the electronic edition.

single- and multievent dislocations (Zielke *et al.*, 2010). Understanding a fault's rupture history is crucial for evaluating its future seismic activity and enhancing earthquake risk assessment and prevention efforts along the northern Xiaojiang fault (Zielke *et al.*, 2015).

Submeter-resolution, high-precision remote sensing data, such as digital elevation models derived from airborne light detection and ranging or aerial photogrammetry at the centimeter scale, enable detailed analysis of fault deformations through topographic offsets along entire faults (Cunningham *et al.*, 2006; Arrowsmith and Zielke, 2009; Lin *et al.*, 2013; Zielke *et al.*, 2015; Ma *et al.*, 2022). Over the past 30–40 yr, extensive urbanization in China has greatly modified the original landscape, especially near the Xiaojiang fault, where numerous rivers have vanished because of anthropogenic activities. Pre-urbanization remote sensing imagery thus provides a valuable opportunity to examine undisturbed landforms and clarify the distribution of coseismic offsets along the fault.

Previous studies of surface ruptures and seismic displacements along the Xiaojiang fault have relied primarily on field surveys (Wang, Song, *et al.*, 2013). However, traditional methods are limited in their ability to quantify large-scale, multievent dislocations. In contrast, this study employs historical aerial photographs and Keyhole (KH) satellite imagery, which offer broader spatial coverage and enable more systematic measurements of geomorphic offsets, particularly those resulting from multiple seismic events. This study uses remote sensing to examine single-event and cumulative displacements along the northern Xiaojiang fault. Finally, given the location of this fault segment within a critical Y-shaped tectonic junction, we further examine the regional tectonic dynamics and interactions among fault systems in this area.

Although previous studies have examined the geomorphic expression and late Quaternary slip rate of the Xiaojiang fault, quantitative constraints on its single-event displacement and recurrence behavior remain limited, largely due to the loss of original landforms caused by recent human modification. This study aims to fill this gap by utilizing historical aerial photographs and KH satellite images to identify and measure well-preserved geomorphic offsets along the northern segment of the Xiaojiang fault. Specifically, we seek to (1) quantify single-event and cumulative displacements to reconstruct the history of surface-rupturing earthquakes, (2) test whether the fault exhibits characteristic slip behavior during the Holocene, and (3) evaluate the fault's long-term slip rate and recurrence interval.

Geologic Setting

The SYB, at the southeastern edge of the Tibetan Plateau, borders the stable South China block to the east and moves south-southeast because of Indian–Eurasian plate convergence (Wang and Burchfiel, 2000; Schoenbohm *et al.*, 2006; Fig. 1a). In its southeastern portion, two principal fault sets that differ in orientation have developed: nearly north–south-trending faults (e.g., the Xigeda and Xiaojiang faults) and northwest–west-northwest-trending faults (e.g., the Lijiang–Xiaojinhe and Lianfeng faults; Fig. 1b). The Xiaojiang fault zone extends approximately 400 km in a nearly north–south orientation, exhibiting left-lateral strike-slip movement and intersecting internal faults, which collectively form a broad arc that is slightly convex to the east (Song *et al.*, 1998; Han *et al.*, 2017). Based on Global Positioning System (GPS) inversion results, the Xiaojiang fault zone is primarily characterized by left-lateral strike-slip motion, accompanied locally by compressional components (Shen *et al.*, 2005; Cheng *et al.*, 2012). Remote sensing interpretations also reveal distinct evidence of left-lateral displacement, together with minor vertical offsets (Li *et al.*, 2025). GPS measurements reveal that the SYB moves southeast at 3–5 mm/a, whereas the adjacent South China block extrudes southeast at ~20 mm/a (Burchfiel and Wang, 2003; Zhang *et al.*, 2004).

The Xiaojiang fault zone is the seismically active fault in Yunnan, producing the greatest number of $\mathbf{M} \geq 7.0$ earthquakes in the area (Song *et al.*, 1998; Tan *et al.*, 2023). Historical records since A.D. 1500 report 17 earthquakes of $\mathbf{M} \geq 6.0$ along this zone, including four events of $\mathbf{M} \geq 7.0$ and one event of **M** 8.0. All $\mathbf{M} \geq 7.0$ events in Yunnan occurred here, the largest being the 1833 **M** 8.0 Songming earthquake (Seismological Bureau of Yunnan Province, 1988; Song *et al.*, 1998). The four major earthquakes—the 1500 **M** 7.0 Yiliang, 1733 **M** 7¾ Dongchuan, 1789 **M** 7.0 Huaning, and 1833 **M** 8.0 Songming —were concentrated in the fault zone's northern and central segments (Tan *et al.*, 2023). The 1733 **M** 7¾ Dongchuan earthquake on the northern Xiaojiang fault generated a surface rupture approximately 82 km in length (Wang, Song, *et al.*, 2013; Fig. 1b).

The main objectives of paleoseismic research are to identify or expose sites with large earthquake deformations that are recorded by geologic features; to determine the timing, recurrence characteristics, and parameters such as the coseismic displacements of large earthquakes; and to assess long-term rupture activity and estimate the risk of future large earthquakes (Ran *et al.*, 2012). Research on the surface rupture of the 1733 Dongchuan earthquake suggests a paleoseismic recurrence interval of approximately 2000–2500 yr (Wang, Song, *et al.*, 2013). Recent research has estimated a ~2000 yr recurrence interval for the southern middle Xiaojiang fault (Song *et al.*, 1998; Li, 2015; Li *et al.*, 2015), whereas the southern segment has a longer interval of 2000–4000 yr (Mao, 2017; Guo *et al.*, 2021). Moreover, inversion results of fault locking depth in the Sichuan–Yunnan region, derived from block modeling and dislocation modeling, generally support that the northern segment of the Xiaojiang fault has a relatively high level of seismic hazard (Song *et al.*, 2016; Sun, 2018; Zhang, 2019). These findings suggest that the northern

Xiaojiang fault remains prone to strong earthquakes; however, limited paleoseismic research has left the recurrence interval of major events uncertain.

The Xiaojiang, Zemuhe, and Lianfeng fault zones together form a Y-shaped tectonic system, structurally analogous to the Y-shaped configuration formed by the Xianshuihe, Anninghe, and Longmenshan fault zones. These boundaries outline the Bayan–Kara block, SYB, and Daliangshan sub-block, which experienced significant earthquakes, including the 1955 **M** 7.5 Kangding and 1786 **M** 7.8 Luding events. Recent events include the 2022 M_w 6.8 Luding and 2008 M_s 8.0 Wenchuan earthquakes along the Longmenshan fault zone. Similarly, the Y-shaped tectonic zone formed by the Zemuhe, Xiaojiang, and Lianfeng faults delineates the boundary between the SYB, Daliangshan sub-block, and South China block. This region has experienced notable seismicity, including the 1930 **M** 6.0 Qiaojia, 1733 **M** 7¾ Dongchuan, and 2014 M_s 6.5 Ludian earthquakes. By analogy, the Lianfeng–Zhaotong fault zone was likely active during the Holocene, similar to the Longmenshan fault zone.

Since the Holocene, the Xianshuihe fault has shown strike-slip motion accompanied by thrusting, with a strike-slip rate of approximately 10 mm/a and vertical deformation under 2 mm/a (Xiong *et al.*, 2010). The activity rate of the northwestern section of the fault zone is 10–20 mm/a, and that of the southeastern section is less than 10 mm/a and is approximately 5 mm/a (Xiong *et al.*, 2010). Displacement rate studies of the Anninghe fault zone have primarily targeted its northern section. Ran *et al.* (2008) determined a late Holocene left-lateral slip rate of approximately 6.2 mm/a at the Zima cross section, with an average rate of 3.6–4.0 mm/a since approximately 10 ka, using digital image analysis, total station surveys, trenching, and 14C dating. The slip rate of the northern Anninghe fault zone is ~2.3 mm/a, whereas the late Quaternary left-lateral rate in the southern section is ~4.4 mm/a (Wang *et al.*, 2018).

Combining paleoseismic and slip-rate data to examine the links between the Xiaojiang fault and the Zemuhe and Lianfeng faults is essential for understanding SYB extrusion and slip-rate variations along the fault. The Zemuhe fault, linked to the northern Xiaojiang fault, has exhibited dominant left-lateral strike-slip deformation since the late Quaternary. The latest major earthquake on this fault occurred in A.D. 1850, with a magnitude above M_w 7 and a maximum-coseismic offset near Dajiayangzi of approximately 4 m (Wang *et al.*, 1998; Shi *et al.*, 2018; Guo *et al.*, 2021). Reported slip rates range from 5 to 12 mm/a, but recent studies agree on a left-lateral slip rate of approximately 6.4 mm/a (Li *et al.*, 2021), which aligns with geodetic (5.3 ± 2.4 mm/a) and geological (6.4 ± 0.6 mm/a) findings (Xu *et al.*, 2003; Li *et al.*, 2014). Although the slip rate is approximately 6.4 mm/a, the estimated recurrence intervals for major earthquakes on the fault range from 300 to 3000 yr (Tian *et al.*, 2008; Ren *et al.*, 2010). Trenching and radiocarbon dating at Daqingliangzi yield an average interval of ~2300 yr (Wang, Ran, *et al.*, 2013), confirming repeated large earthquakes during the late Quaternary.

There have been fewer studies on the Lianfeng–Zhaotong fault. Wen *et al.* (2013) reported that the northeast–southwest-trending Lianfeng fault in Zhaotong exhibits dextral strike-slip and retrograde motion, but its activity is controversial. The Zhaotong and Lianfeng faults define the boundary between the SYB and the South China block, dividing the active Daliangshan fault block from the stable South China block (Wen *et al.*, 2013). Recent research verifies Holocene activity on the Lianfeng–Zhaotong fault by reporting a left-lateral slip rate of approximately 2.4 mm/a (Li *et al.*, 2021; Wu *et al.*, 2024). The Daliangshan fault zone exhibits predominantly left-lateral strike-slip activity, with a Holocene slip rate estimated at 3–4 mm/a (Zhou *et al.*, 2003; Wei *et al.*, 2012; Sun *et al.*, 2015).

Overall, the Xiaojiang, Zemuhe, and Lianfeng faults together form a Y-shaped tectonic configuration that defines the boundary between the SYB, Daliangshan sub-block, and the South China block. Regional slip-rate and paleoseismic evidence shows that all three branches of this Y-shaped system have accommodated significant late-Quaternary deformation, with the Zemuhe and Xiaojiang faults exhibiting dominant left-lateral motion and the Lianfeng–Zhaotong fault providing an important but previously under-recognized structural link. The contrasting slip rates and recurrence behaviors of these faults indicate complex strain partitioning around the Y-shaped junction, where deformation from multiple branches is transferred into the northern Xiaojiang fault.

Data and Methods

Data selection

Historical aerial photos and KH satellite images were employed to measure displaced geomorphic features, applying techniques from the Yishu fault study (Jiang *et al.*, 2017). The KH-4B image used in this study was acquired in 1968 and has an approximate spatial resolution of 1.8 m, whereas the selected aerial photographs, taken in the 1950s, have a resolution of approximately 2 m. However, because the historical aerial photograph data were collected long ago, the data are not comprehensive, although they cover most of the area. Both imagery types were georeferenced by manually assigning ground control points. The KH satellite imagery covers the entire study area, whereas the historical aerial photographs cover only a portion of it (Fig. 2).

Recent remote sensing images (Fig. 3c) reveal that the topography has been heavily modified in most areas along the banks of the river and that the washes in some areas of the mountains have been destroyed by road construction. The two historical images (Fig. 3a,b), which document the original landforms present prior to disturbances by urbanization and mechanized agriculture, document more washes, and

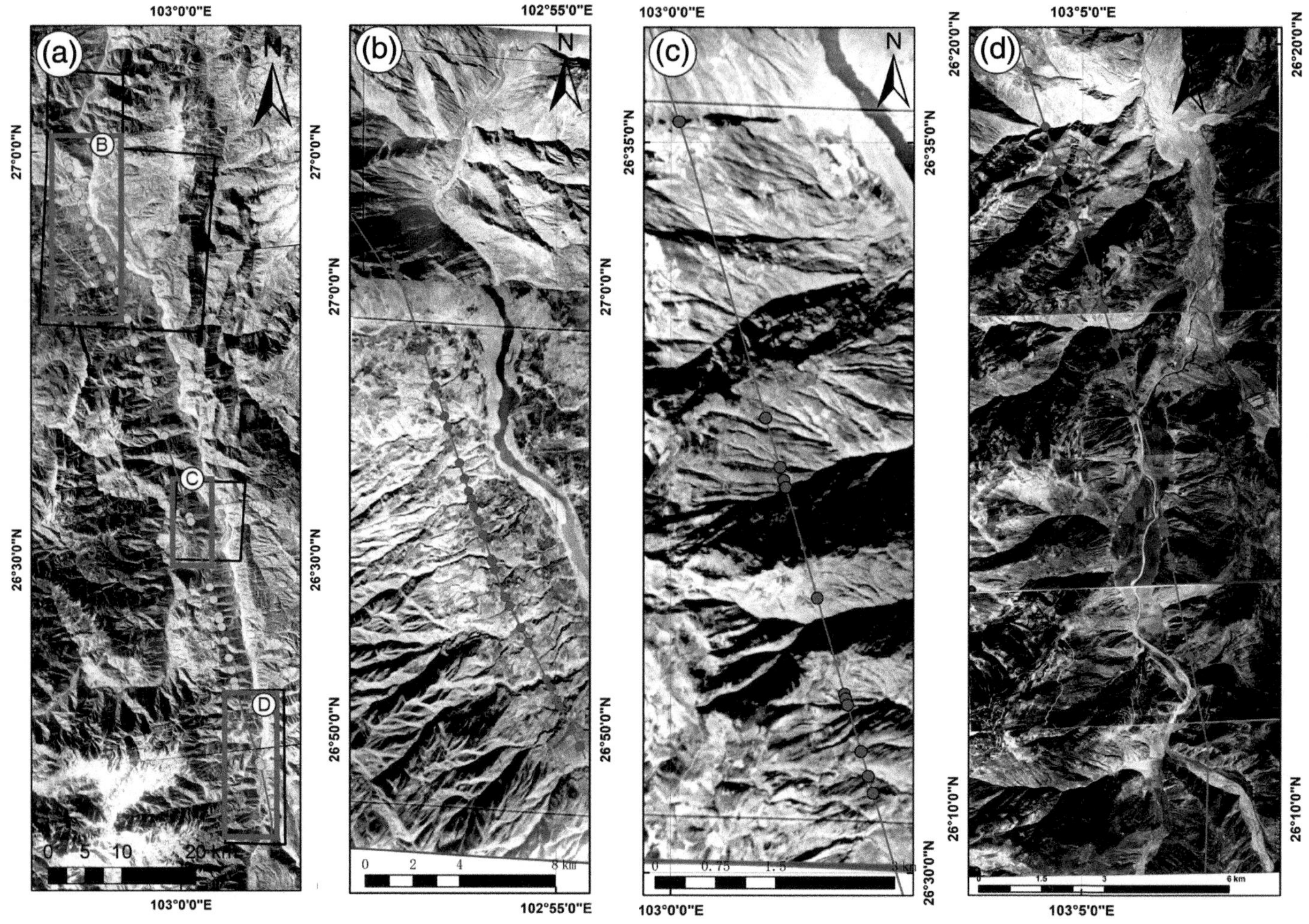

Figure 2. Interpreted points on historical aerial images and Keyhole (KH) images. (a) KH satellite image. (b,c) Historical aerial images. The black boxes in panel (a) show the ranges of the historical aerial images. The green boxes in panel (a) are the locations of panels (b–d). Red lines represent faults. The yellow dots are offset points interpreted on the KH remote sensing images. The blue dots are interpreted as offset points on the aerial images. The color version of this figure is available only in the electronic edition.

the yellow ellipses in Figure 3 illustrate these changes. Using these data, we can identify more dislocated features in the topography, allowing us to measure cumulative dislocations for both single and multiple events. In the comparison map of tectonic geomorphic images (Fig. 4), obvious linear structures can be observed in historical remote sensing images, and the tones on both sides of the faults have changed significantly. Figure 4b interprets a distinct fault slope. The tectonic landforms in the modern image Figure 4b have been destroyed. The left dislocation of the gully in historical images is more obvious. In modern images, the downstream of the gully has been mostly destroyed.

Methods for measuring surface offsets and uncertainty

Estimating single-event and cumulative offsets involves matching geomorphic markers to their original positions along the fault. Features such as stream channels, terraces, and linear landforms intersecting the fault before displacement are key for interpreting fault offset. Accurate offset measurements require matching markers on both fault sides, with factors such as stream geometry and curvature affecting estimate reliability. Zielke *et al.* (2015) detailed methods for matching displaced markers and measuring horizontal offsets. Streams distant from the fault and unaffected by coseismic displacement were excluded.

Two-dimensional river morphologies were analyzed to assess stream dislocations relative to faults, allowing estimation of horizontal displacements from recent seismic events. This includes the 1733 Dongchuan earthquake's single-event offset and cumulative displacements from earlier paleoseismic events. Older geomorphic features generally exhibit larger cumulative offsets, reflecting their exposure to more paleoearthquakes since formation.

Because vertical fault motions are not clearly discernible in 2D imagery, our analysis focused on the horizontal (strike-slip)

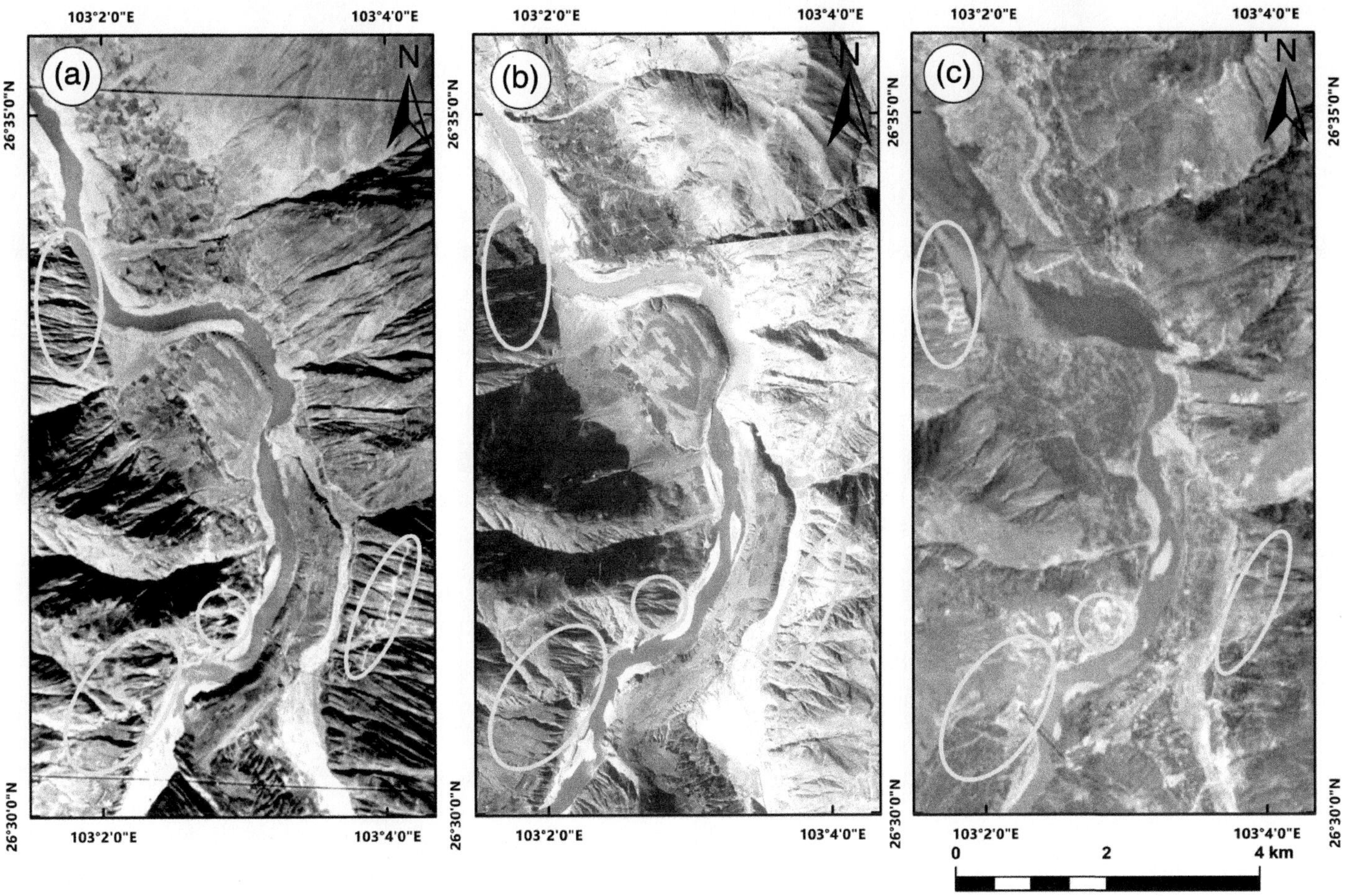

Figure 3. Comparison of historical aerial imagery, KH satellite imagery, and Google imagery for the same location. (a) Historical aerial image (1950s). (b) KH satellite image (1968). (c) Google image (2022). The yellow ellipses highlight the areas of change. The color version of this figure is available only in the electronic edition.

component of displacement. Nevertheless, field observations and previous studies indicate that minor vertical deformation may occur locally along the fault. The surface traces of the Xiaojiang fault (Fig. 2) were mapped through satellite image interpretation and previous study results (Li *et al.*, 2025). Markers used to identify fault locations include left-lateral displacements of topographic features such as rivers, terraces, alluvial fans, and moraines (Ma *et al.*, 2022). In this study, we identified gullies on the basis of visual interpretations of the texture and color features observed in remotely sensed images. We measured only rivers that were left-lateral offset by the fault and were readily identifiable. Deflected rivers and rivers that could not be used to estimate fault displacements were not considered. Streams were graded as follows: G1 for streams that are nearly perpendicular to the fault, G2 for streams that intersect the fault obliquely, and G3 for streams that pass through the fault with a high degree of curvature (Fig. 5). G1 contains offset markers on both sides of the fault with low curvature that intersect it at high or right angles, G2 involves moderately curved offset markers that pass obliquely through the fault, and G3 includes offset markers that have a high degree of curvature or an ill-defined fault trace. We did not consider the G3 rivers in this study because of the low resolution of the historical aerial and KH imagery and the potential for large errors in the G3 measurements.

To evaluate the average coseismic offset and its associated uncertainty, the intersections between riverbeds and terrace uplifts on both sides of the fault were identified as geomorphic markers. The offset of each riser was measured, and the two measurements were then averaged to reconstruct the pre-earthquake morphology for each stream. The offsets at these intersections were measured twice to derive displacement values and error ranges (Jiang *et al.*, 2017). In ArcGIS, geomorphic trend lines were constructed and projected onto the fault trace to quantify displacements across river channels. The displacement measurements for each river are shown in Figure 6. Upstream and downstream river trends were projected onto the fault trace using their linear or near-linear orientations to estimate average stream displacements. These projections used linear or gently curved lineaments on both sides of the fault. Initially, two riverbank lines were drawn from each pixel point, allowing for curvature. Visual fitting was performed according to the delineated

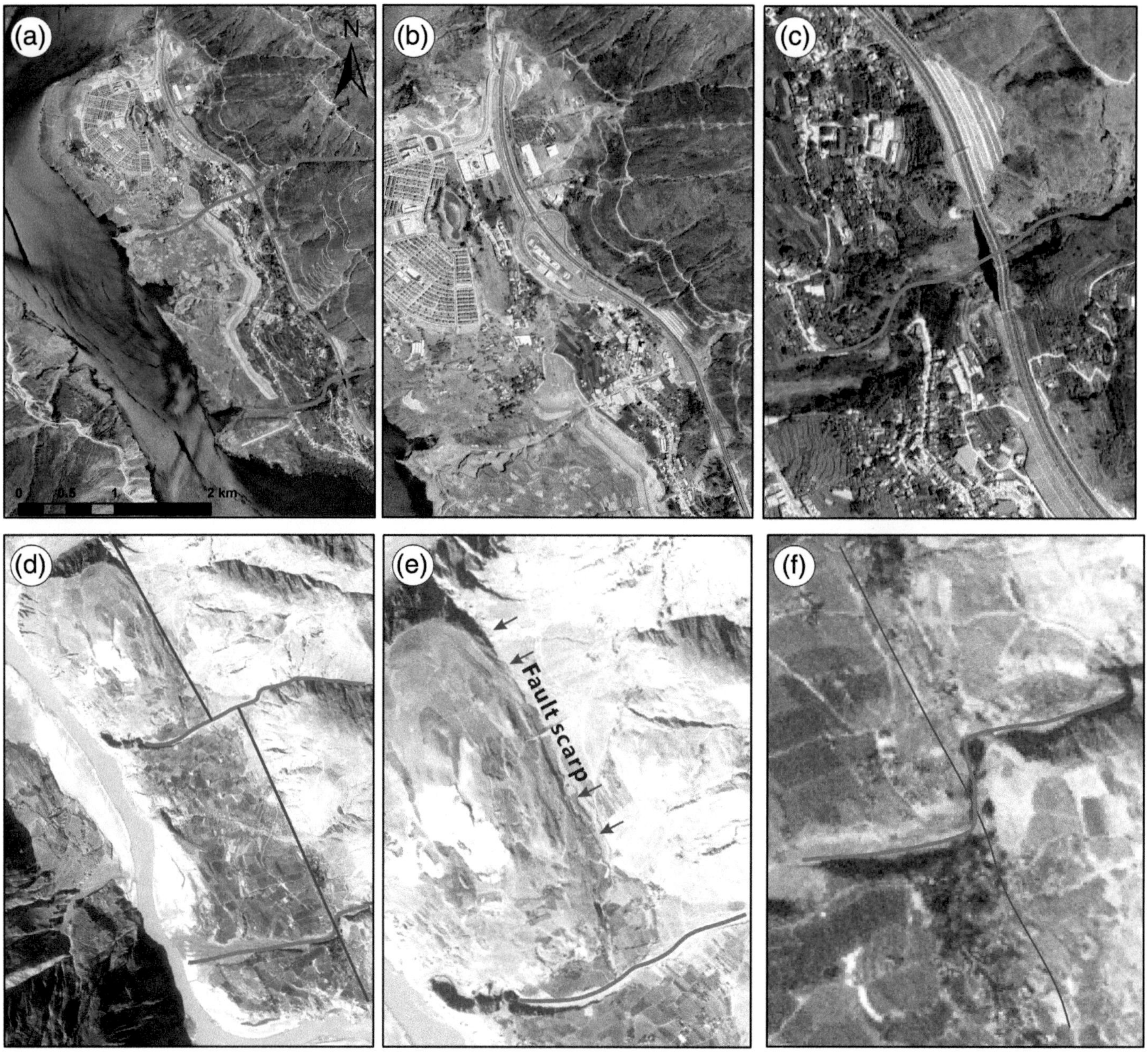

Figure 4. A comparison map of the relevant landforms for fault damage. (a–c) Google image (2022). (d–e) Historical aerial image. The blue lines represent rivers, and the red lines represent faults. The color version of this figure is available only in the electronic edition.

riverbank lines, and the fitting result was a straight line. When both lines were projected onto the fault trace, the effects of adjacent pixels were not considered. A dislocation of 20.9 m is shown in Figure 6b, and the dislocation of 20.5 m is shown in Figure 6c; this resulted in a river dislocation of 20.7 ± 0.2 m. Therefore, the degree of dislocation was estimated to be high. Measurements have focused primarily on terrace risers rather than river channel thalwegs. Because the river itself has a certain width, it is not easy to choose accurate measurement points, and the resulting measurements may produce large errors. We prioritized terrace risers rather than channel thalwegs because riser boundaries are geomorphically sharp and comparatively stable, enabling reproducible projections onto the fault trace. Following established practice, we identified the intersections between the river bed and the terrace risers on both banks as piercing markers; we measured the offset of each riser independently and averaged the two values to reconstruct the pre-earthquake channel geometry (Fig. 5; Jiang *et al.*, 2017). To maximize confidence, we preferentially selected linear to sublinear marker segments that intersect the fault at high angles and lie close to the fault trace, minimizing curvature- and distance-related uncertainties (Jiang *et al.*, 2017). Although thalwegs can in places be visually identifiable, their finite width and potential for lateral migration

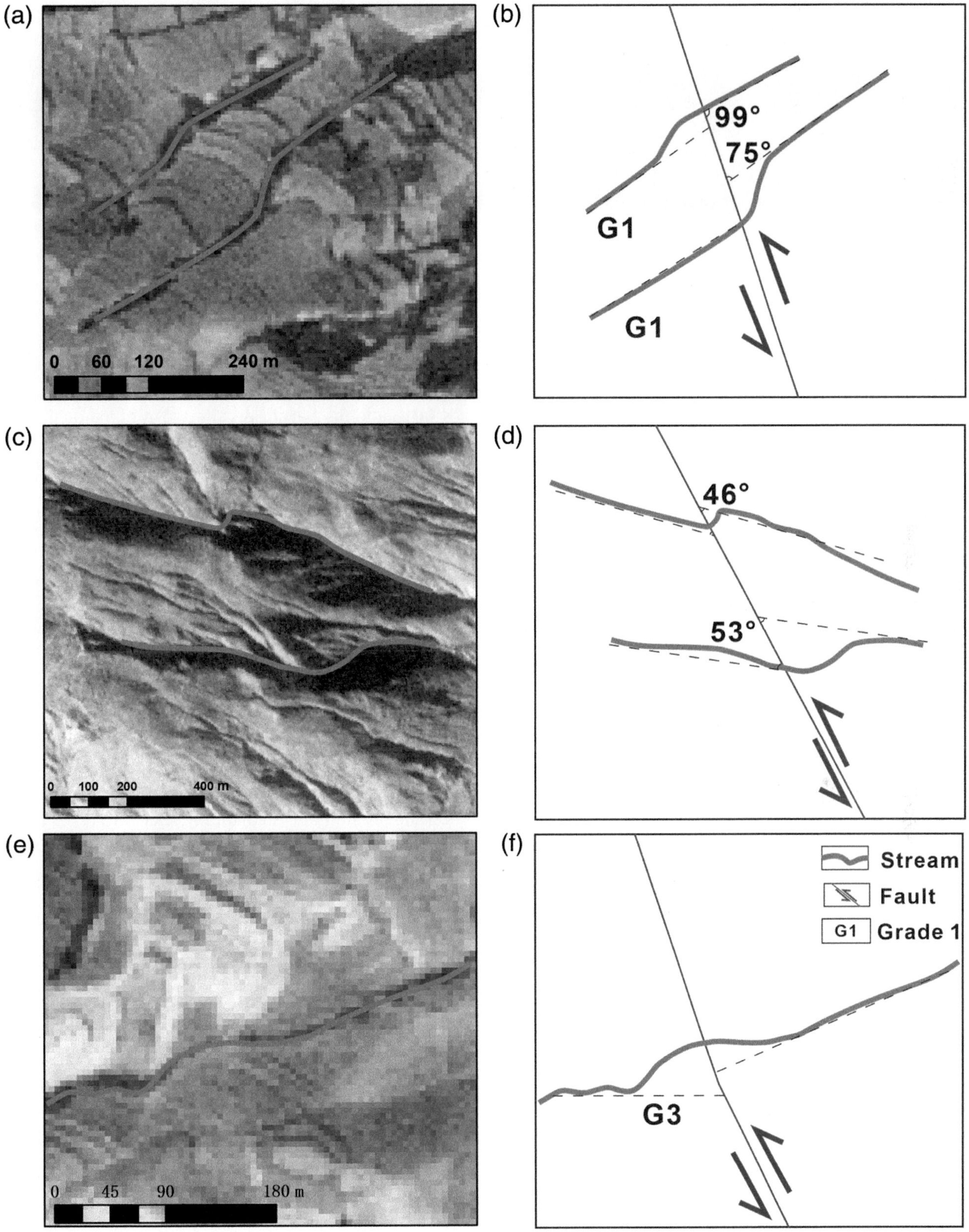

Figure 5. Interpreted the river classification map. (a,b) G1-class rivers. (c,d) G2-class rivers. (e,f) G3-class rivers. The color version of this figure is available only in the electronic edition.

make the precise choice of a single measurement line more subjective than for terrace risers, especially in post-event modified channels; accordingly, thalwegs were not used as primary markers unless terrace risers were absent or poorly preserved. In addition, the distances from selected streams, specifically, their

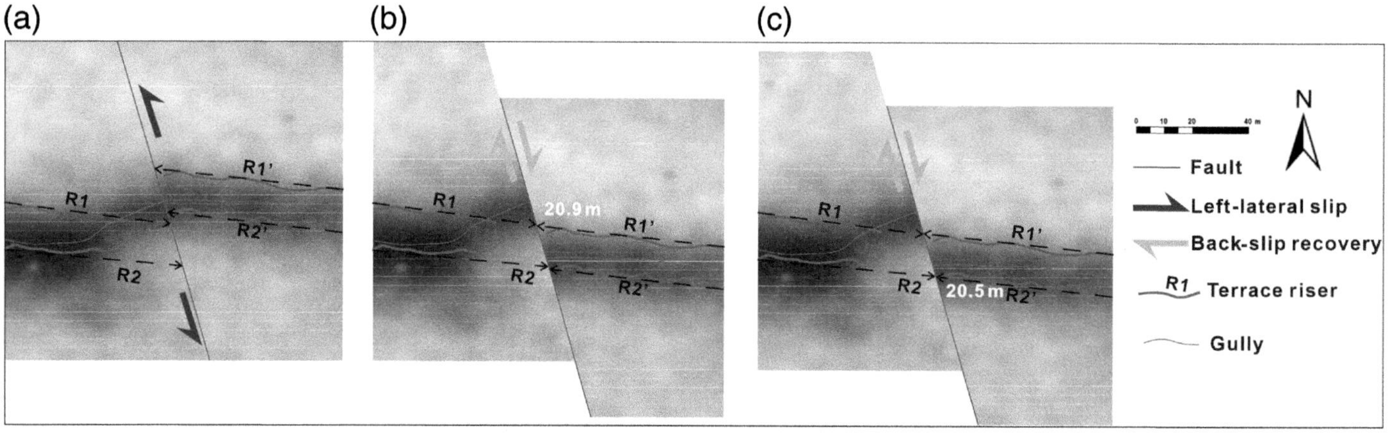

Figure 6. Example map of river dislocation measurement methods. (a) Landforms that are less affected by human activities, with riverbank identification markers. (b) Dislocation recovery based on faults and R1 markers (20.9 m). (c) Dislocation recovery based on faults and R2 markers (20.5 m). The color version of this figure is available only in the electronic edition.

nearest endpoints projected onto the fault, should be minimal relative to the cumulative displacement. Confidence in topographic-offset estimates depends on accurately locating and orienting the fault trace relative to geomorphic markers and reconstructing the markers' original morphology before projection (Zielke *et al.*, 2015; Jiang *et al.*, 2017).

To quantify lateral offsets, we measured each geomorphic feature twice using independent projection lines and marker interpretations. The preferred offset value for each feature was taken as the mean of these two independent measurements, and the uncertainty bounds were defined by the minimum and maximum of the two measurements. This two-measurement approach provides a transparent and internally consistent estimate of the variability introduced by different plausible interpretations of the geomorphic marker geometry.

We note that this approach differs from the more standard method in which multiple analysts or multiple projection geometries are used to determine the preferred, minimum, and maximum offset values for each feature (e.g., Gold *et al.*, 2015; DuRoss *et al.*, 2024). Because the geomorphic markers in this study are generally well defined and unambiguous, additional repeated measurements would not substantially alter the preferred offset but could artificially inflate the uncertainty range. Therefore, our reported uncertainties represent the range of two independent measurements, rather than a statistical 95% confidence interval.

To enhance transparency, several representative examples of offset measurement are presented in Figure 7, showing the geomorphic markers, projection lines, and measurement geometry. These figures allow direct evaluation of the measurement reproducibility and provide visual context for the reported uncertainty estimates.

Previous studies show that displacement measurement uncertainty is largely independent of offset magnitude. Field and remote data reveal that uncertainty remains nearly uniform across different displacement ranges and does not systematically increase with larger offsets (DuRoss *et al.*, 2024). Numerical simulations similarly assume constant relative uncertainties that scale proportionally rather than absolutely with accumulated slip (Zielke, 2018). Hence, most reported uncertainties are method dependent rather than displacement dependent.

In this study, uncertainties were estimated based on two independent measurements for each offset feature. The preferred offset value was determined as the average of the two measurements, and the uncertainty range was defined by their minimum and maximum values. Although this approach yields relatively small uncertainty ranges compared with studies that employ multiple interpreters or replicate measurements, the uncertainties are not systematically related to offset magnitude. This pattern is consistent with previous findings that displacement uncertainty remains nearly uniform and does not increase with larger offsets (Zielke, 2018; Reitman *et al.*, 2023a,b; DuRoss *et al.*, 2024). Therefore, the relatively small uncertainties reported in this study primarily reflect methodological consistency rather than any bias associated with offset size.

Previous studies have shown that displacement measurement uncertainty is largely independent of the offset magnitude. Analyses of field and remote measurements indicate that uncertainty remains nearly uniform across a wide range of displacement values and does not systematically increase with larger offsets (DuRoss *et al.*, 2024). In some cases, fractional uncertainty even decreases slightly as displacement increases, suggesting that the precision of field and remote-sensing techniques remains relatively constant with offset scale.

Model-based investigations further support this observation. Zielke (2018) demonstrated that measurement uncertainty is better represented as a relative value proportional to accumulated slip rather than an absolute value, implying that it does not scale linearly with displacement. Similarly, Reitman *et al.* (2023a,b) emphasized that most variability among repeated offset measurements arises from methodological and interpretative

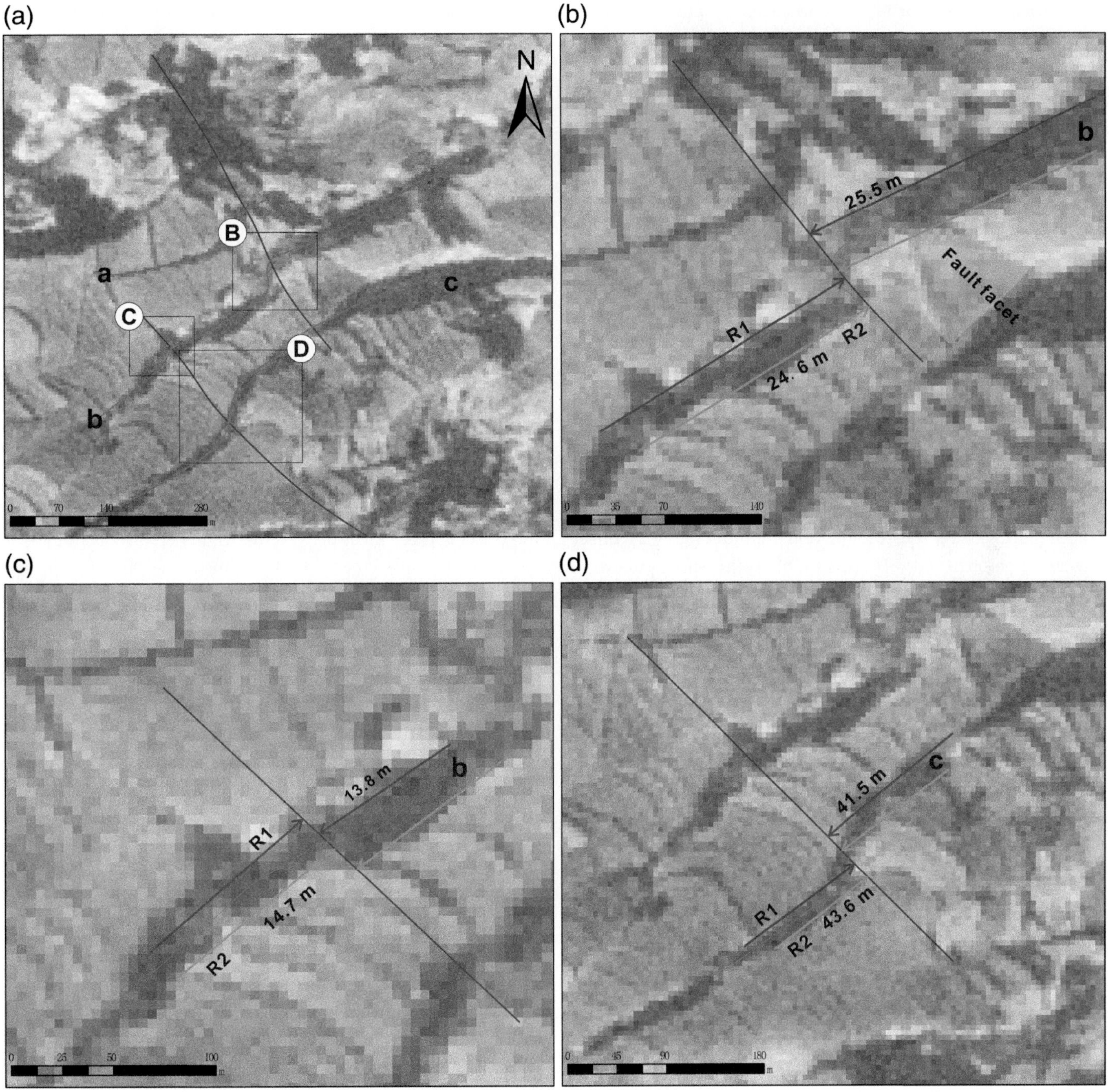

Figure 7. (a) Example map of river dislocation measurement methods. (b) The offset value of river b obtained by the measurement method in Figure 6 is 25.05 ± 0.45. (c) The offset value of river b obtained by the measurement method in Figure 6 is 14.25 ± 0.45 m. (d) The offset value of river c obtained by the measurement method in Figure 6 is 45.55 ± 1.05. The color version of this figure is available only in the electronic edition.

differences rather than from displacement magnitude itself. Therefore, uncertainties reported in offset measurements should be considered primarily method dependent rather than displacement dependent.

Cumulative offset probability and kernel density estimate

Constraining fault rupture histories using geomorphic records assumes that marker formation rates exceed earthquake recurrence intervals (Sieh, 1978; McGill and Sieh, 1991; McGill and Rubin, 1999; Zielke *et al.*, 2015). When more landforms develop prior to an event, a greater number of records preserve surface rupture offsets. If no new landforms develop between two seismic events, the markers record only the cumulative displacement of both events, obscuring individual slips. High-resolution remote sensing can capture these displaced landforms, allowing for separate descriptions and interpretations. Probabilistic analyses of cumulative offsets reveal that peaks in cumulative-offset probability density (COPD) correspond to paleoseismic displacement magnitudes (Zielke *et al.*, 2010; Klinger *et al.*, 2011). Over time, natural and anthropogenic processes degrade or destroy older geomorphic markers, resulting in fewer preserved offset clusters from earlier earthquakes, whereas recent events tend to have abundant preserved markers. Studies (Klinger *et al.*, 2011; Manighetti *et al.*, 2015) have shown that the COPD decreases exponentially with offset. When single-event and cumulative offsets form an arithmetic progression, they reveal a characteristic slip distribution that reflects typical fault rupture behavior (Ren *et al.*, 2015). The 1D COPD was constructed by summing the normalized frequency of measured offsets along the fault and integrating the resulting distribution. To reduce subjectivity, we also applied a kernel density estimate (KDE) to the same dataset, using a Gaussian kernel with an adaptive bandwidth determined by Silverman's rule. The KDE and COPD results were compared to assess the stability and reproducibility of offset clustering patterns. For 2D analysis, offset measurements were projected along the fault trace, and both 2D COPD and KDE maps were generated to visualize spatial variations in offset density (after Reitman *et al.*, 2024). Following established methods (e.g., McGill and Sieh, 1991; Klinger *et al.*, 2011; Zielke *et al.*, 2012), we calculate cumulative offset probability. We also calculate KDEs for each data set in 1D and 2D with Gaussian kernels. KDEs are a type of density estimate using a kernel to make an aggregate probability density function of a data set. The KDE approach is not necessarily better than COPD for earthquake geology because a KDE does not take into account variable measurement uncertainty. We show the KDE plots because they are objective and require no user input and thus are useful as a quick, unbiased treatment of offset measurement data to augment COPD analysis (Reitman *et al.*, 2024). In this article, the calculation of KDE uses the computational program developed by Reitman *et al.* (2023a, b).

Recent studies have refined the interpretation of COPD analysis, showing that not every peak directly corresponds to an individual surface-rupturing earthquake (Zielke, 2018; Lin *et al.*, 2020; Reitman *et al.*, 2024). Numerical simulations indicate that, under typical conditions, only two to three prominent peaks can be confidently linked to distinct paleoearthquakes. However, when the fault exhibits relatively large and uniform single-event slip, low slip variability, high measurement density, and good geomorphic preservation, up to four peaks may reliably record successive seismic events.

Results

Identification of offset rivers

Based on the methodology in the Methods for measuring surface offsets and uncertainty section, 109 horizontal displacements were measured along the ~90 km northern section of the Xiaojiang fault. All horizontal displacement measurements versus the fault strike distance are shown in Figure 8. The horizontal displacements vary, ranging from 1.9 ± 0.4 to 86.2 ± 1.0 m. The presence of both small and large offsets indicates that the dataset includes single-event displacements and cumulative offsets from multiple seismic events. All analyzed streams exhibit notable left-lateral deflections, and corresponding geomorphic features were matched across the fault to reconstruct their original configurations.

Distribution of selected rivers (yellow points identified by KH images and blue points identified by historical aerial images) and Holocene fault breaks along the northern section of the Xiaojiang fault, and the distribution of horizontal offsets along the northern section of the Xiaojiang fault as measured from the left-rotational dislocation geomorphic markers via both images. The location in the figure is consistent with that in Figure 2a.

The uncertainties on the measured offsets are mostly small and nearly uniform across the entire displacement range, which is consistent with the findings of DuRoss *et al.* (2024), who reported that for most displacements, uncertainty is not correlated with displacement. In their meta-analysis of field and remote measurements, uncertainty was found to remain nearly uniform (e.g., 1999 Hector Mine—field data; Zielke *et al.*, 2012; 2016 Kaikōura—remote data; Zinke *et al.*, 2019) or variable (e.g., 2016 Kaikōura—field data; Langridge *et al.*, 2018, 2013 Baluchistan—remote data; Gold *et al.*, 2015), rather than consistently increasing as displacement increases. This pattern indicates that uniform uncertainties, such as those observed in this study, are typical of well-defined geomorphic markers and consistent measurement methods.

COPD and KDE

In this study, historical aerial photographs and KH remote sensing satellite images were analyzed independently. Our analysis of the slip distribution derived from historical aerial photographs reveals four offset probability peaks (Fig. 9a), which occurred at ~7.1, 14.1, 21.4, 28, and 34 m, with a multiplicative relationship for the offset probability density peaks of approximately 7 m. The ~7 m offset probability density peaks are shown in Figure 9a. Our analysis of the slip distribution based on the KH satellite images reveals eight offset probability peaks (Fig. 9b), which occurred at ~7.1, 12.1, 15.8, 25.1, 29.5, 34.5, 56, and 62 m, that is, multiples of seven. Because historical aerial data are not comprehensive, fewer slip distributions were identified, but the comparison with the KH satellite imagery, which contains more comprehensive data, reveals that the incompleteness of the aerial data had little effect on the total offset probability density.

Our statistical data obtained by combining the slip distributions from historical aerial photographs and KH satellite imagery reveal seven offset probability peaks (Fig. 9c), which occurred at ~7.1, 15.2, 21.6, 28.5, 34.5, 49, 55, and 61 m. Many previous studies have shown that the larger offsets

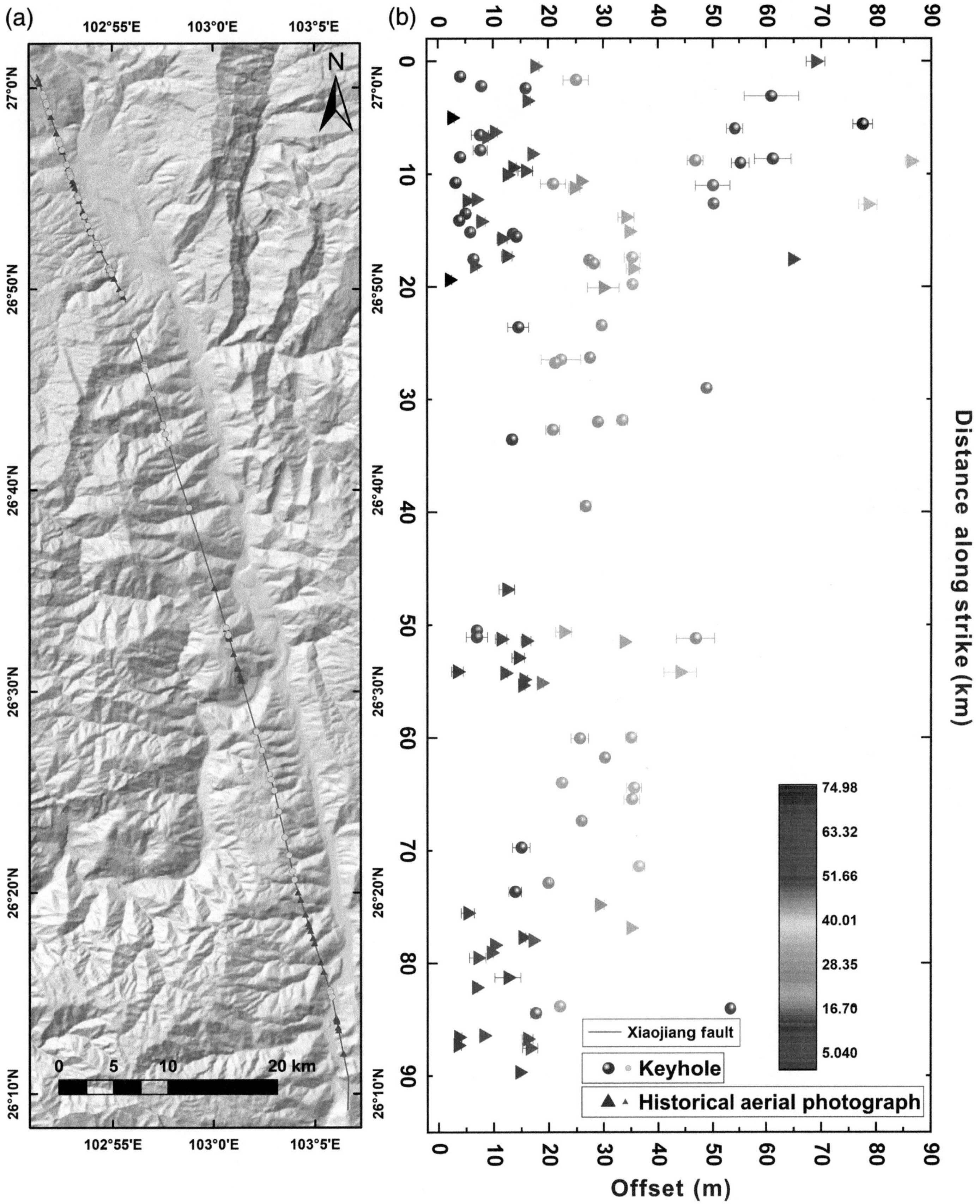

Figure 8. (a) Distribution of the measurement points and (b) values of the measurement points. The color version of this figure is available only in the electronic edition.

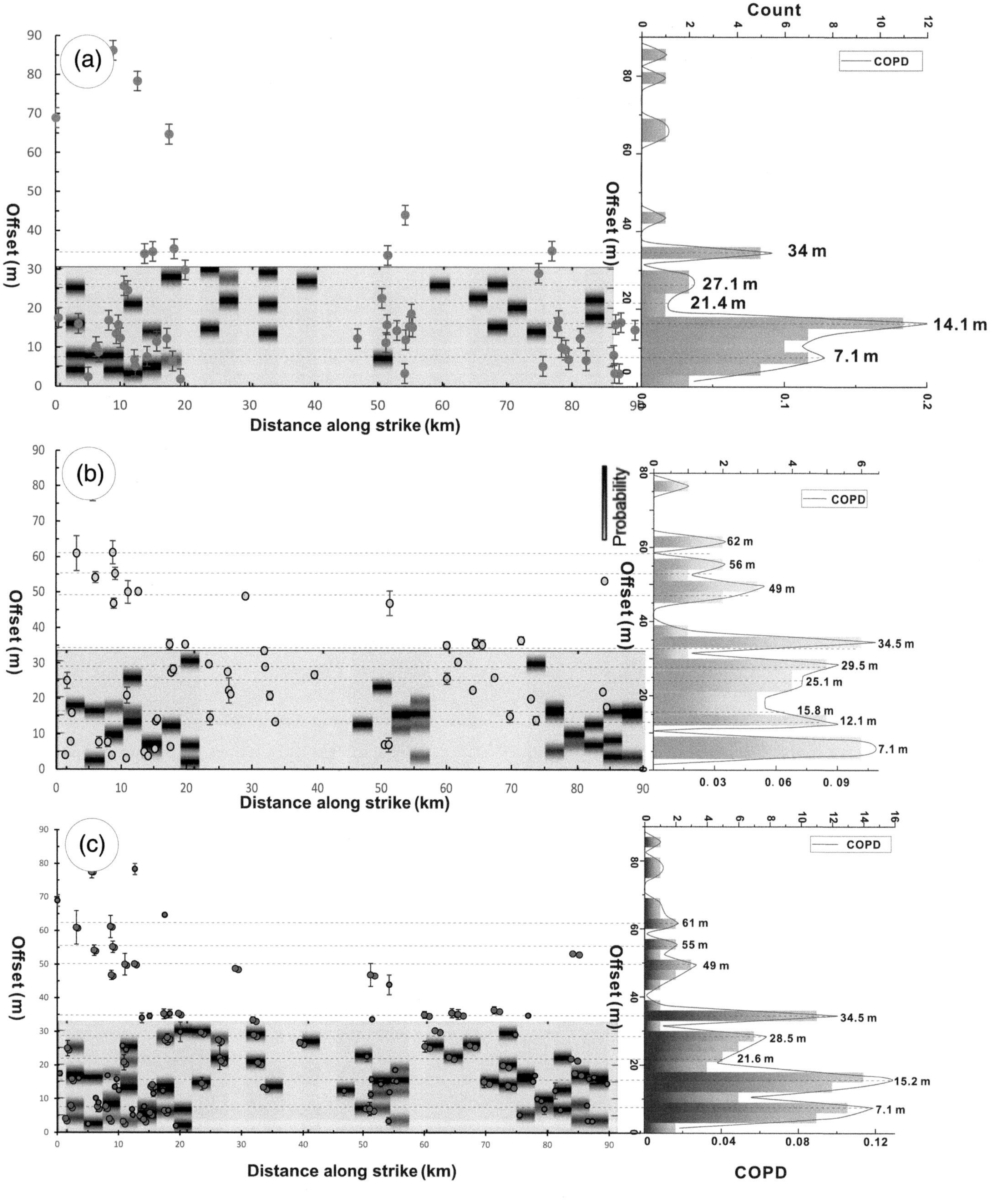

Figure 9. Analysis of the cumulative-offset probability densities (COPDs) obtained from different image types in the northern section of the Xiaojiang fault. (a) Historical aerial image data. (b) KH image data. (c) Merged the results of the two datasets. The color version of this figure is available only in the electronic edition.

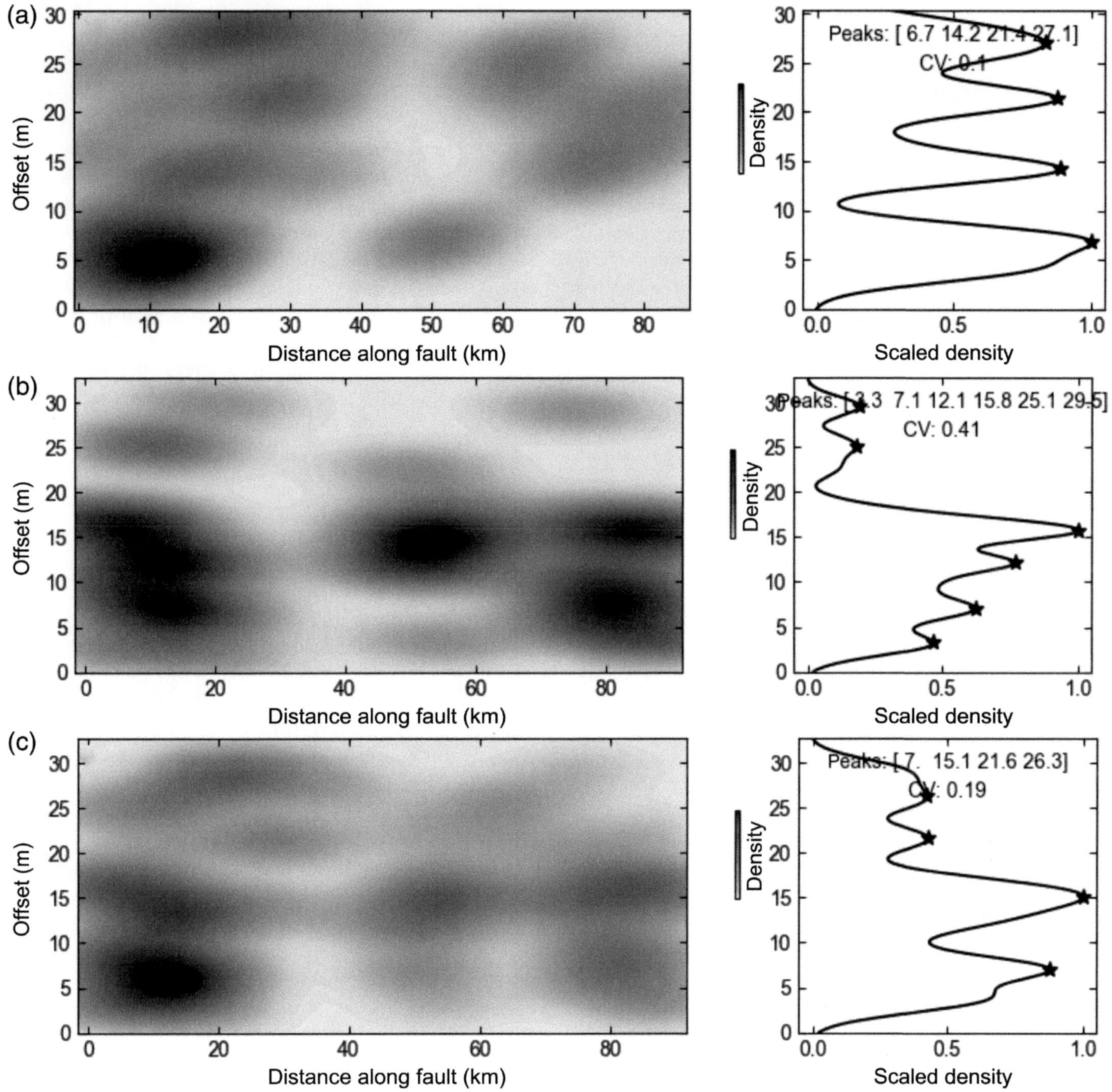

Figure 10. Analysis of the kernel estimation of displacements (KEDs) obtained from different image types in the northern section of the Xiaojiang fault. (a) Historical aerial image data. (b) KH image data. (c) Merged the results of the two datasets. The color version of this figure is available only in the electronic edition.

retained in landscapes with strike-slip faults decay exponentially (Tapponnier *et al.*, 2001; Klinger, 2005; Gold and Cowgill, 2011; Zielke *et al.*, 2012), although recent studies have suggested that they do not always decay exponentially (Bi *et al.*, 2022); this may have been because evidence of offsets along strike-slip faults tends to disappear (Reitman *et al.*, 2019; Reitman *et al.*, 2023a, b). In our study, the COPDs for larger offsets showed a decrease in the number of available displacement measurements, whereas those for offsets <35 m did not display this reduction. We believe that this difference was caused by the lack of resolution of historical aerial photographs and KH satellite imagery, which makes it more difficult to recognize small offsets, resulting in fewer data points to analyze statistically.

The kernel estimation of displacement (KED) method was applied to verify the offsets of gullies identified in different imagery datasets. Previous studies have suggested that this method effectively reduces subjective bias in displacement measurement. Figure 10a shows four displacement peaks at 6.7, 14.2, 21.4, and 27.1 m, respectively. Figure 10b displays six peaks at 3.3, 7.1, 12.1, 15.8, 25.1, and 29.5 m. When all gullies are collectively analyzed using the KED method, four main peaks are identified (Fig. 10c), corresponding to displacements of 7.0, 15.1, 21.6, and 26.3 m.

In this study, four prominent COPD peaks are identified along the northern Xiaojiang fault. The first two peaks (around 7.1 and 15 m) likely represent cumulative slip from the most recent two and three earthquakes, respectively, whereas the larger peaks (around 21 and 28 m) may correspond to older clusters of slip accumulation. This interpretation is consistent with previous modeling results that suggest faults with high slip-per-event and limited deformation distribution can preserve multiple paleoslip distributions. We therefore interpret the four COPD peaks as reflecting distinct phases of large-magnitude surface-rupturing earthquakes, while acknowledging that smaller secondary peaks may reflect partial preservation or measurement noise.

Combining the peak probability densities of each offset, we considered the offset peaks to have a multiplicative relationship of 7 m. Although the COPD shows prominent peaks spaced at approximately 7 m intervals, this interpretation represents an optimal fit to the observed data. Other possible peak combinations, such as overlapping events with variable slip magnitudes or partial preservation of older offsets, cannot be completely excluded. Therefore, although the ~7 m increment provides a reasonable estimate of the characteristic single-event displacement, the interpretation should be regarded as a preferred, but not unique, solution.

Discussion

Paleoearthquake and recurrence cycles

In this study, our statistical data reveal that the slip distributions are multiples of ~7 m. This section has not been systematically studied by previous authors, but this interval is generally consistent with the offset of 6.9 m for the most recent event determined by Wang, Song, *et al.* (2013) in their geologic survey of the 1833 Songming earthquake on the Xiaojiang fault. We interpreted the peak offset probability to be approximately 7 m as the single-event displacement from the 1733 **M** 7¾ Dongchuan earthquake. The COPD peaks at approximately 14 and 21 m likely represent cumulative offsets from the most recent two and three earthquakes, respectively, whereas the larger peaks at 28 m correspond to slip accumulated through four paleoearthquakes. Given that single-event displacements are generally less than 7 m, offsets exceeding this value are interpreted as cumulative displacements along the northern Xiaojiang fault.

According to the results of previous studies, in addition to the 1733 Dongchuan earthquake, the northern section of the Xiaojiang fault is thought to have generated five other paleoseismic events at 2082 ± 85 a, 2807 ± 386 a, 5248 ± 152 a, 7200 ± 155 a, and 9000 a before the present day (Shen *et al.*, 1998; Song *et al.*, 1998). Recent studies have identified the northern section of the Xiaojiang fault as the source of the A.D. 624 Xichang earthquake, and this earthquake may have produced a sinistral dislocation of approximately 13 m across the steep bank of the Heishui River floodplain (Hu *et al.*, 2021). According to our results, the 13 m left-lateral dislocation may have been caused by two earthquakes, that is, the A.D. 624 earthquake and the 1733 Dongchuan earthquake. The 13 m displacement observed along the fault could represent the cumulative slip of two surface-rupturing events, possibly corresponding to the A.D. 624 and 1733 earthquakes. However, this interpretation remains tentative, as direct chronological evidence is still lacking. Additional dating and paleoseismic investigations are required to confirm whether these two events jointly produced the observed cumulative offset. In summary, four seismic events have occurred in the northern section of the Xiaojiang fault since 3000 a, that is, the 2082 ± 85 a event, 2807 ± 386 a event, the Xichang earthquake in A.D. 624, and the Dongchuan earthquake in A.D. 1733. These strong earthquakes occurred at an interval of approximately 1000 yr. In addition, four paleoearthquakes occurred between 9000 a and 2807 ± 386 a, that is, the 9000 a event, 7200 ± 155 a event, 5248 ± 152 a event, and 2807 ± 386 a event; these strong earthquakes occurred at intervals of approximately 2000 yr. To resolve inconsistencies in recurrence intervals, further research is needed to supplement paleoseismic records and establish the Holocene recurrence of strong earthquakes.

Verification of parameters

Wells and Coppersmith (1994) established widely applied empirical relationships that relate earthquake magnitude (**M**), surface rupture length (L), and mean displacement (Dave). Using their regressions—$\mathbf{M} = 5.08 + 1.16 \times \log(L)$ and $\mathbf{M} = 6.93 + 0.82 \times \log(\text{Dave})$—the northern Xiaojiang fault, with a surface rupture length of ~82 km and a mean displacement of ~7 m, yields magnitude estimates of approximately **M** 7.7 (from rupture length) and **M** 7.8 (from mean displacement). An alternative displacement–magnitude relation from the same dataset, $\mathbf{M} = 6.94 + 1.14 \times \log(\text{Dave})$, gives a comparable estimate of **M** 7.8. These values remain consistent with the documented 1733 **M** 7¾ Dongchuan earthquake, suggesting that the measured rupture dimensions are geologically realistic.

Moreover, several later studies provide additional support for the reliability of these estimates on complex continental strike-slip faults such as Xiaojiang. Wesnousky (2008) emphasized that rupture extent and surface slip are strongly controlled by geometric complexity and fault segmentation. The nearly linear geometry of the northern Xiaojiang fault, together with the absence of major releasing or restraining steps, is fully consistent with its ability to host long, throughgoing ruptures approaching 80 km or more. Blaser *et al.* (2010) further demonstrated that strike-slip earthquakes show robust magnitude–length scaling with little evidence for rupture width saturation, particularly when post-1964 datasets are used. Their updated regressions closely resemble those of Wells and Coppersmith

(1994), indicating that W&C relations remain appropriate for large continental strike-slip events, including those in China. Leonard (2014) also showed that self-consistent scaling relations for strike-slip ruptures naturally predict magnitudes in the upper **M** 7 range for faults with rupture lengths on the order of 80–100 km and displacements of several meters, again matching the Xiaojiang case.

Taken together, these independent lines of evidence indicate that the rupture length (~82 km) and average displacement (~7 m) inferred for the northern Xiaojiang fault fall squarely within the expected dimensional range of an M ~7.7 to 7.8 strike-slip earthquake. The consistency among different empirical relations and modern datasets supports the robustness of the reconstructed offsets and implies that the associated geomorphic features have likely preserved their original coseismic expression with only limited postseismic modification.

The dislocation distribution probabilities for the northern Xiaojiang fault indicate that it follows a characteristic slip model. Dividing the ~7 m offset by the ~1000 yr recurrence yields a left-lateral slip rate of 7 mm/a. However, the slip rates determined by previous studies are highly variable, ranging from 5.97 to 17 mm/a (He *et al.*, 2002; Wang *et al.*, 2016). This variation likely stems from uncertainties in fault slip-rate estimates. Some studies have used thermoluminescence dating to derive the ages of geomorphic surfaces (He *et al.*, 2002), but the results of this technique are highly uncertain. Using unmanned aerial vehicle (UAV) photogrammetry and 14C dating of terraces, Hu *et al.* (2023) estimated a late Quaternary slip rate of 10–13 mm/a along the Qiaojia section of the Xiaojiang fault zone. The remaining data were mostly obtained with GPS data or from inversions and were not the actual geologic rates. Paleoseismic data and fault characteristics suggest high-seismic activity on the northern Xiaojiang fault since the late Pleistocene. The fault zone is a major tectonic feature that forms part of the southeastern boundary of the rhomboidal SYB on the southeastern Tibetan Plateau margin (Xu *et al.*, 2003). Given an estimated recurrence interval of 1000–2000 yr and approximately 300 yr since the last major earthquake, reassessing the region's seismic hazard is essential. Paleoseismic recurrence estimates suggest a high likelihood of a major earthquake occurring within the next several thousand years.

Regional tectonic implications

To better understand the regional implications of our results, we discuss the role of fault segmentation and structural connectivity in controlling rupture propagation along the northern Xiaojiang fault system. From the perspective of earthquake rupture segmentation, whether a rupture can propagate across a fault junction is a key factor that controls the final magnitude and destructiveness of an earthquake (Jia *et al.*, 2023). The Xiaojiang and Daliangshan faults lack significant geometric barriers near Qiaojia, where their fault traces exhibit a similar strike, which facilitates coseismic rupture propagation through both faults. This is supported by the intensity distribution of the **M** 7¾ earthquake that occurred near Dongchuan on 2 August 1733 (Fig. 1; Department of Seismic Damage Prevention, 1995). The surface rupture zone of this event was primarily developed near Dongchuan, but the intensity distribution extended northward to Qiaojia without deflecting toward Ningnan. According to earlier research, this observation suggests that the 1733 earthquake did not rupture across the Ningnan–Qiaojia releasing zone toward the Zemuhe fault, but rather connected the northern segment of the Xiaojiang fault with the Jiaojihe segment of the Daliangshan fault. The linkage between the Xiaojiang and Zemuhe faults is likely inhibited by local bending structures and releasing basins, implying that the Ningnan–Qiaojia releasing zone may act as a segmentation boundary that limits rupture propagation. In contrast, the Xiaojiang and Jiaojihe faults are more closely aligned structurally, and their junction shows no obvious geometric segmentation features, making it easier for large earthquakes to rupture across both faults. This structural configuration indicates that the northern Xiaojiang fault and the adjacent Jiaojihe segment of the Daliangshan fault may share similar stress accumulation and release patterns, which could enable multisegment ruptures during large seismic events.

To illustrate the regional deformation pattern, we refer to the Global Navigation Satellite Systems (GNSS) velocity field (Zhao *et al.*, 2015) and the tectonic block model of Li *et al.* (2021), which provide a regional kinematic framework for interpreting the Xiaojiang fault's activity. Overall, these observations highlight that geometric segmentation and structural linkage play a crucial role in controlling earthquake magnitude and rupture continuity along the northern Xiaojiang fault system. Understanding these segmentation boundaries is therefore essential for assessing future rupture scenarios and improving regional seismic hazard evaluation.

GNSS data reveal that the Mabian block is mostly stable, whereas the Daliangshan sub-block moves toward it (Fig. 11a,b). Situated within the arcuate Xianshuihe–Xiaojiang fault system, the Daliangshan fault shows distinct GNSS velocity variations in the northern Xiaojiang segment, which change latitudinally relative to the South China block (Fig. 11b). This contrasts with the northern Anninghe fault in the Y-shaped zone, where slip rates are steady, unlike the increasing rates observed on the northern Xiaojiang fault (Fig. 11c).

The data in Figure 11a,b were generated using data from Li *et al.* (2021). GPS data were obtained from Zhao *et al.* (2015). In Figure 11a,b, the block abbreviations are as follows (Li *et al.*, 2021): BS, Baoshan; DL, Daliang; DZ, Dianzhong; ET, East Tibet; LC, Lancang; LM, Longmenshan; MB, Mabian; RL, Ruili; SC, South China; SM, Simao; XG, Xianggelila; YJ, Yajiang; ZD, Zhongdian; the fault abbreviations are as follows: AHN, Anninghe fault; AZX F., Anninghe–Zemuhe–Xiaojiang fault; DLS, Daliangshan fault; HH F., Honghe fault; LF, Lianfeng fault; LJ F., Lijiang fault; LMS, Longmenshan fault; XJ, Xiaojiang fault; and XSH, Xianshuihe fault; ZMH, Zemuhe fault.

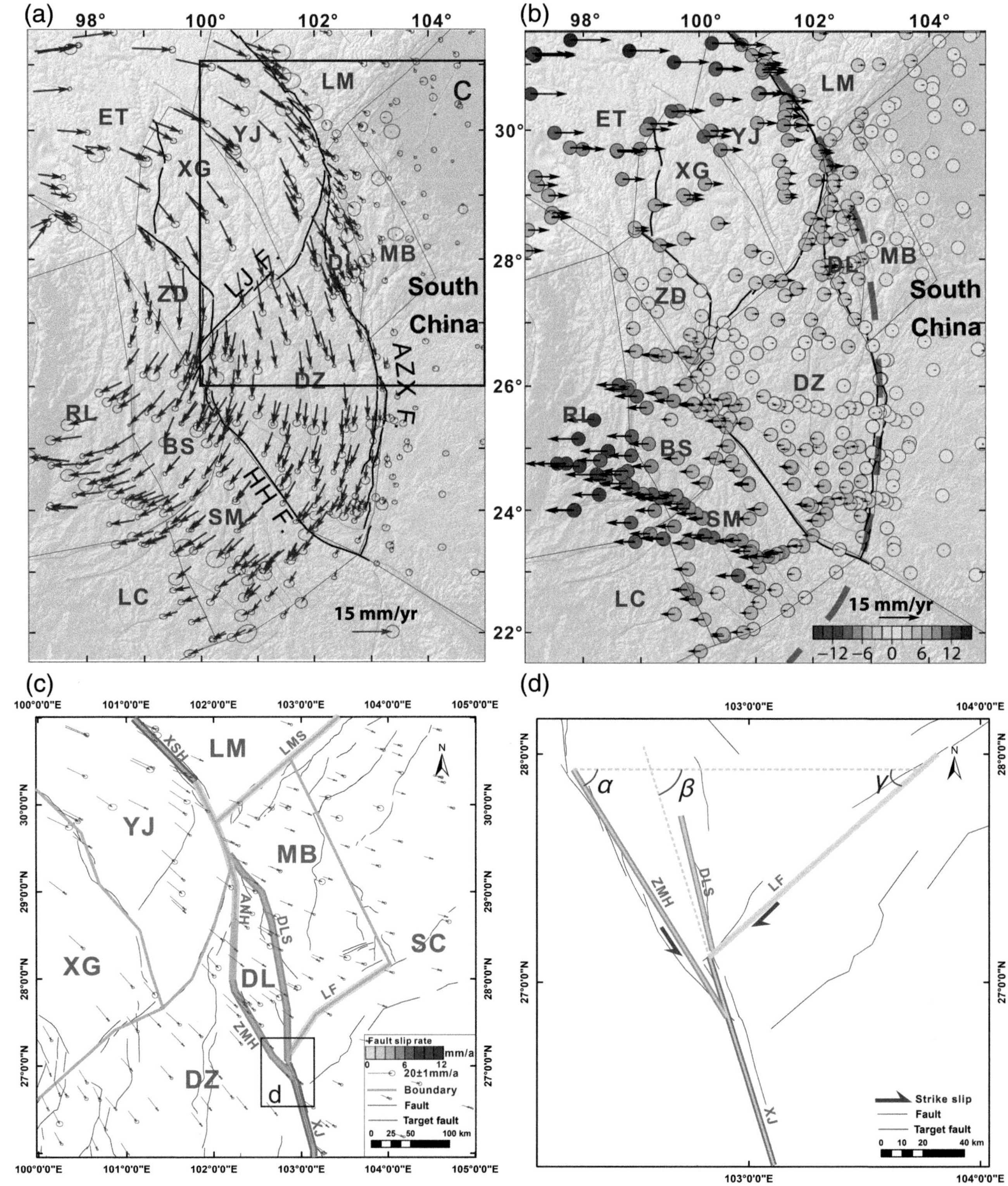

Figure 11. Regional dynamic model. (a) Global Positioning System (GPS) velocities and block divisions relative to the South China block. (b) East–west velocity component of Figure 8a, with gray-dashed lines representing arcuate tectonic zones. (c) Fault slip-rate map. (d) Schematic diagram of the slip-rate calculations for the Xiaojiang fault. The data in Figure 8a,b were generated using data from Li *et al.* (2021). GPS data were obtained from Zhao *et al.* (2015). In Figure 8a,b, the block abbreviations are as follows (Li *et al.*, 2021): BS, Baoshan; DL, Daliang; DZ, Dianzhong; ET, East Tibet; LC, Lancang; LM, Longmenshan; MB, Mabian; RL, Ruili; SC, South China; SM, Simao; XG, Xianggelila; YJ, Yajiang; ZD, Zhongdian; and the fault abbreviations are as follows: AHN, Anninghe fault; AZX F., Anninghe–Zemuhe–Xiaojiang fault; DLS, Daliangshan fault; HH F., Honghe fault; LF, Lianfeng fault; LJ F., Lijiang fault; LMS, Longmenshan fault; XJ, Xiaojiang fault; XSH, Xianshuihe fault; and ZMH, Zemuhe fault. The color version of this figure is available only in the electronic edition.

A comparison of the paleoseismic behavior of the northern Xiaojiang fault with that of the Zemuhe fault clearly reveals that the northern Xiaojiang segment has shorter recurrence intervals for large earthquakes and a higher average left-lateral slip rate. By combining slip rates from the Zemuhe and Lianfeng faults and projecting their components along the Xiaojiang fault's orientation, we infer that its northern segment inherits motion from both sources, that is, $V_{xj} = V_{Lzmh} + V_{Llf}$, in which V_{Lzmh} and V_{Llf} denote the velocity components in the direction of the Xiaojiang fault. The remaining directional components were transferred to the Daliangshan fault. $V_{Lzmh} = V_{zmh} \sin(\alpha)/\sin(\pi - \beta)$, and $V_{Llf} = V_{lf} \sin(\gamma)/\sin(\beta)$, in which V_{zmh} and V_{lf} represent the slip rates in the directions of the Zemuhe and the Lianfeng faults, respectively, and $\alpha = 1/3\pi$, $\beta = 73/180\pi$, and $\gamma = 7/30\pi$ are all angles in radians (Fig. 11d). Using this approach, the slip rate of the northern Xiaojiang fault was estimated to be approximately 7.4 mm/a, closely matching the 7 mm/a derived from the coseismic displacements and recurrence intervals, underscoring the segment's elevated slip rate.

The northern Xiaojiang fault accommodates a left-lateral slip rate of approximately 7 mm/yr, which represents the cumulative motion absorbed from the Zemuhe and Lianfeng faults to the north and east. This indicates that, in a regional kinematic framework, the northern Xiaojiang fault functions as a major transfer structure that channels strain from adjacent fault systems. However, geological and seismological evidence suggests that this slip partitioning does not necessarily translate into throughgoing surface rupture.

From the perspective of rupture segmentation, the connection between the Xiaojiang and Zemuhe faults appears to be inhibited by bending structures and releasing basins in the Ningnan–Qiaojia zone. The 1733 **M** 7¾ Dongchuan earthquake illustrates this segmentation control: although its intensity distribution extended northward to Qiaojia, the surface rupture was confined to the Xiaojiang and Jiaojihe segments of the Daliangshan fault, without propagating toward the Zemuhe fault. This implies that although the long-term slip budget (~7 mm/yr) is distributed among three interconnected faults, coseismic rupture propagation is restricted to the Daliangshan–Xiaojiang linkage, with the Ningnan–Qiaojia releasing zone acting as a persistent structural boundary.

Therefore, the observed discrepancy between slip-rate partitioning and surface rupture extent suggests that only part of the accumulated strain is released through through-going earthquakes along the Xiaojiang–Daliangshan system, whereas the remainder may be accommodated by distributed or aseismic deformation near the segmentation boundary.

Conclusion

In this research, historical aerial photographs and KH satellite imagery were employed to locate and measure numerous geomorphological markers in the northern segment of the Xiaojiang fault zone. Despite extensive anthropogenic modification along the northern Xiaojiang fault zone in recent decades, historical aerial photographs from 1954 and KH satellite imagery from 1969 provide valuable references for identifying and restoring the original geomorphic features and fault-related landforms. We measured the cumulative offsets of a series of gullies showing dislocations along a fault that stretches more than 90 km and calculated the COPDs to analyze the distributions of offsets from recent seismic events. The average single-event offset of the last five seismic events was approximately 7 m. The offset distribution and COPD peaks reveal that recent earthquakes on the northern Xiaojiang fault display characteristic seismic displacement patterns. The high slip rate of the northern Xiaojiang fault likely resulted from combined slip rates inherited from the Zemuhe and Lianfeng faults. We also conclude that the northern section of the Xiaojiang fault inherits the displacement rates of the Zemuhe and Lianfeng faults and propose a corresponding absorption model.

Data and Resources

The KH-4B satellite imagery used in this study is available for download from the U.S. Geological Survey (USGS; https://earthexplorer.usgs.gov/, last accessed January 2024), and historical aerial photographs may be obtained by contacting the corresponding author.

Declaration of Competing Interests

The authors acknowledge that there are no conflicts of interest recorded.

Acknowledgments

This work was supported by grants from the Seismogenic Structure Exploration of Large Earthquakes (Grant Numbers DZ5WTT202501 and Z5WLD202301) and the National Science and Technology Basic Resources Investigation Program of China (Grant Number 2021FY100104). The authors thank the reviewers and editors for their help in improving this article. The authors thank the reviewers and editors for their help in improving the article.

References

Arrowsmith, J. R., and O. Zielke (2009). Tectonic geomorphology of the San Andreas Fault zone from high resolution topography: An example from the Cholame segment, *Geomorphology* **113,** nos. 1/2, 70–81, doi: 10.1016/j.geomorph.2009.01.0.

Bi, H., W. Zheng, P. Zhang, J. Zeng, Y. Shao, Y. Yao, Q. Lei, and H. Peng (2022). Recovering surface slip distribution along the Sertengshan Piedmont Fault (Northern China) from airborne LiDAR data, *Tectonics* **41,** e2021TC007174, doi: 10.1029/2021tc007174.

Blaser, L., F. Krüger, M. Ohrnberger, and F. Scherbaum (2010). Scaling relations of earthquake source parameter estimates with special focus on subduction environment, *Bull. Seismol. Soc. Am.* **100,** no. 6, 2914–2926, doi: 10.1785/0120100111.

Burchfiel, B. C., and E. Wang (2003). Northwest-trending, middle Cenozoic, left-lateral faults in southern Yunnan, China, and their tectonic significance, *J. Struct. Geol.* **25,** 781–792, doi: 10.1016/s0191-8141(02)00065-2.

Cheng, J., X. Xu, J. Ren, S. Zhang, and X. Wu (2021). Probabilistic multi-segment rupture seismic hazard along the Xiaojiang Fault Zone, Southeastern Tibetan Plateau, *J. Asian Earth Sci.* **221,** 104940, doi: 10.1016/j.jseaes.2021.104940.

Cheng, J., X. W. Xu, W. J. Gan, W. T. Ma, W. T. Chen, and Y. Zhang (2012). Block model and dynamic implication from the earthquake activities and crustal motion in the southeastern margin of Tibetan Plateau, *Chin. J. Geophys.* **55,** no. 4, 1198–1212.

Cunningham, D., S. Grebby, K. Tansey, A. Gosar, and V. Kastelic (2006). Application of airborne LiDAR to mapping seismogenic faults in forested mountainous terrain, southeastern Alps, Slovenia, *Geophys. Res. Lett.* **33,** 1–5, doi: 10.1029/2006GL027014.

Deng, Q. D., P. Z. Zhang, Y. K. Ran, X. P. Yang, W. Min, and Q. Z. Chu (2003). Basic characteristics of active tectonics of China, *Sci. China Earth Sci.* **46,** no. 4, 356–372.

Department of Seismic Damage Prevention (1995). *The Catalogue of Chinese Historical Earthquakes*, Seismological Press, Beijing, China.

DuRoss, C. B., N. G. Reitman, A. E. Hatem, H. B. Mason, G. Lavrentiadis, D. Asimaki, C. Milliner, M. Karakaş, and B. Seçen (2024). Are field observations of surface rupture useful? An example from the 2023 Mw 7.8 Pazarcık, Turkey Earthquake, *Seismol. Res. Lett.* **96,** 848–867, doi: 10.1785/0220240280.

Gold, R. D., and E. Cowgill (2011). Deriving fault-slip histories to test for secular variation in slip, with examples from the Kunlun and Awatere faults, *Earth Planet. Sci. Lett.* **301,** 52–64, doi: 10.1016/j.epsl.2010.10.011.

Gold, R. D., M. Stirling, D. Clark, M. C. Quigley, and M. C. Gerstenberger (2015). On- and off-fault deformation associated with the September 2013 Mw 7.7 Balochistan earthquake: Implications for probabilistic fault displacement hazard, *Tectonophysics* **660,** 65–85, doi: 10.1016/j.tecto.2015.08.019.

Guo, P., Z. Han, S. Dong, Z. Mao, N. Hu, F. Gao, and J. Li (2021). Latest quaternary active faulting and paleoearthquakes on the Southern segment of the Xiaojiang Fault Zone, SE Tibetan Plateau, *Lithosphere* **2021,** 7866379, doi: 10.2113/2021/7866379.

Han, Z. J., S. P. Dong, Z. B. Mao, N. Hu, X. B. Tan, R. Yuan, and P. Guo (2017). The Holocene activity and strike-slip rate of the southern segment of Xiaojiang fault in the southeastern Yunnan region, China, *Seismol. Geol.* **39,** 1–19.

He, H. L., Y. Ikeda, F. M. Song, and X. Q. Dong, (2002). Late Quaternary slip rate of the Xiaojiang fault and its implication, *Seismol. Geol.* **24,** 14–26.

Hu, M., Z. Wu, J. Li, and X. Huang, (2023). The late quaternary strike-slip rate of the Qiaojia segment of the Xiaojiang Fault Zone, *Acta Geol. Sin.* **97,** 16–29.

Hu, M., Z. Wu, K. Reicherter, S. Ali, X. Huang, and J. Zuo, (2021). A historical earthquake-induced landslide damming event at the Qiaojia Reach of the Jinsha River, SE Tibetan Plateau: Implication for the seismic hazard of the Xiaojiang fault, *Front. Earth Sci.* **9,** 649543, doi: 10.3389/feart.2021.649543.

Jia, Z., Z. Jin, M. Marchandon, T. Ulrich, A. A. Gabriel, W. Fan, P. Shearer, X. Zou, J. Rekoske, F. Bulut, and A. Garagon (2023). The complex dynamics of the 2023 Kahramanmaraş, Turkey, Mw 7.8–7.7 earthquake doublet, *Science* **381,** no. 6661, 985–990.

Jiang, W., J. Zhang, Z. Han, T. Tian, Q. Jiao, X. Wang, and H. Jiang (2017). Characteristic slip of strong earthquakes along the Yishu Fault Zone in East China evidenced by offset landforms, *Tectonics* **36,** 1947–1965, doi: 10.1002/2016tc004363.

Klinger, Y. (2005). High-resolution satellite imagery mapping of the surface rupture and slip distribution of the Mw 7.8, 14 November 2001 Kokoxili earthquake, Kunlun Fault, Northern Tibet, China, *Bull. Seismol. Soc. Am.* **95,** 1970–1987, doi: 10.1785/0120040233.

Klinger, Y., M. Etchebes, P. Tapponnier, and C. Narteau (2011). Characteristic slip for five great earthquakes along the Fuyun fault in China, *Nature Geosci.* **4,** 389–392, doi: 10.1038/ngeo1158.

Langridge, R. M., W. F. Ries, N. J. Litchfield, P. Villamor, R. J. Van Dissen, D. J. A. Barrell, M. S. Rattenbury, D. W. Heron, S. Haubrock, D. B. Townsend, *et al.* (2018). The New Zealand active faults database, *Bull. Seismol. Soc. Am.* **108,** no. 3B, 1573–1596, doi: 10.1785/0120170130.

Leonard, M. (2014). Self-consistent earthquake fault-scaling relations: Update and extension to stable continental strike-slip faults, *Bull. Seismol. Soc. Am.* **104,** no. 6, 2953–2965, doi: 10.1785/0120140087.

Li, X. (2015). *Study on Fracture Characteristics of Boundary Faults at Different Developmental Stages in Yunnan Region of Sichuan-Yunnan Block*, Institute of Geology, China Earthquake Administration, Beijing, China.

Li, X., Z. He, L. Guo, and L. Li (2025). Using historical remote sensing images for detailed tectonic geomorphological interpretation in the study of active faults: Application to the Xiaojiang fault case study, *Earthq. Res. Adv.* doi: 10.1016/j.eqrea.2025.100376.

Li, X., Y. Ran, L. Chen, F. Wu, X. Ma, and J. Cao (2015). Late quaternary large earthquakes on the Western branch of the Xiaojiang Fault and their tectonic implications, *Acta Geol. Sin. Engl. Ed.* **89,** 1516–1530.

Li, Y., M. Hao, S. Song, L. Zhu, D. Cui, W. Zhuang, F. Yang, and Q. Wang (2021). Interseismic fault slip deficit and coupling distributions on the Anninghe-Zemuhe-Daliangshan-Xiaojiang Fault Zone, Southeastern Tibetan Plateau, based on GPS measurements, *J. Asian Earth Sci.* **219,** 104899, doi: 10.1016/j.jseaes.2021.104899.

Li, Y.-H., M. Hao, L.-Y. Ji, and S.-L. Qin (2014). Fault slip rate and seismic moment deficit on major active faults in mid and South part of the Eastern margin of Tibet Plateau, *Chin. J. Geophys.* **57,** 1062–1078, doi: 10.6038/cjg2014040.

Lin, Z., H. Kaneda, S. Mukoyama, N. Asada, and T. Chiba (2013). Detection of subtle tectonic-geomorphic features in densely forested mountains by very high-resolution airborne LiDAR survey, *Geomorphology* **182,** 104–115, doi: 10.1016/j.geomorph.2012.11.001.

Lin, Z., J. Liu-Zeng, R. J. Weldon, J. Tian, C. Ding, and Y. Du (2020). Modeling repeated coseismic slip to identify and characterize individual earthquakes from geomorphic offsets on strike-slip faults, *Earth Planet. Sci. Lett.* **545,** 11613, doi: 10.1016/j.epsl.2020.116313.

Ma, J., B. Zhou, M. Wang, P. Guo, J. Liu, G. Ha, and J. Fan (2022). Surface rupture and slip distribution along the Zheduotang Fault in the Kangding section of the Xianshuihe Fault Zone, *Lithosphere* **2021,** 6500707, doi: 10.2113/2022/6500707.

Manighetti, I., C. Perrin, S. Dominguez, S. Garambois, Y. Gaudemer, J. Malavieille, L. Matteo, E. Delor, C. Vitard, and S. Beauprêtre (2015). Recovering paleoearthquake slip record in a highly dynamic alluvial and tectonic region (Hope Fault, New Zealand) from airborne lidar, *J. Geophys. Res.* **120,** 4484–4509, doi: 10.1002/2014jb011787.

Mao, Z. (2017). *Study on Late Quaternary Activity in the Southern Section of Xiaojiang Fault Zone*, China University of Geosciences, Beijing, China.

McGill, S., and K. E. Sieh (1991). Surficial offsets on the Central and Eastern Garlock fault associated with prehistoric earthquakes, *J. Geophys. Res.* **96,** no. B13, 21,597–21,621, doi: 10.1130/G50393.1.

McGill, S. F., and C. M. Rubin (1999). Surficial slip distribution on the central Emerson fault during the June 28, 1992, Landers earthquake, California, *J. Geophys. Res.* **104,** no. B3, 4811–4833.

Ran, Y. K., J. W. Cheng, H. L. Gong, and L. C. Chen (2008). Late Quaternary geomorphic deformation and displacement rates of the Anninghe Fault around Zimakua, *Seismol. Geol.* **30,** 86–98.

Ran, Y. K., H. Wang, Y. B. Li, and L. C. Chen (2012). Key techniques and several cases analysis in paleoseismic studies in mainland china: Trenching sites, Layouts and paleoseismic indicators on active strike-slip faults, *Seismol. Geol.* **2,** 197–210.

Reitman, N. G., Y. Klinger, R. W. Briggs, and R. D. Gold (2023a). Climatic influence on the expression of strike-slip faulting, *Geology* **51,** 18–22.

Reitman, N. G., Y. Klinger, R. W. Briggs, and R. D. Gold (2023b). Computational notebook to plot offset measurements along strike-slip faults, *U.S. Geol. Surv. Data Release*, doi: 10.5066/P9UK2UQ1.

Reitman, N. G., Y. Klinger, R. W. Briggs, and R. D. Gold (2024). Limited preservation of strike-slip surface displacement in the geomorphic record, *J. Geophys. Res.* **129,** e2024JB028692, doi: 10.1029/2024JB028692.

Reitman, N. G., K. J. Mueller, G. E. Tucker, R. D. Gold, R. W. Briggs, and K. R. Barnhart (2019). Offset channels may not accurately record strike-slip fault displacement: Evidence from landscape evolution models, *J. Geophys. Res.* **124,** no. 12, 13,427–13,451, doi: 10.1029/2019JB018596.

Ren, Z., A. Lin, and G. Rao (2010). Late Pleistocene–Holocene activity of the Zemuhe Fault on the Southeastern margin of the Tibetan Plateau, *Tectonophysics* **495,** 324–336, doi: 10.1016/j.tecto.2010.09.039.

Ren, Z., Z. Zhang, T. Chen, S. Yan, J. Yin, P. Zhang, W. Zheng, H. Zhang, and C. Li (2015). Clustering of offsets on the Haiyuan Fault and their relationship to paleoearthquakes, *Geol. Soc. Am. Bull.* **128,** 3–18, doi: 10.1130/b31155.1.

Schoenbohm, L. M., B. C. Burchfiel, and C. Liangzhong (2006). Propagation of surface uplift, lower crustal flow, and Cenozoic tectonics of the southeast margin of the Tibetan Plateau, *Geology* **34,** 813–816, doi: 10.1130/g22679.1.

Seismological Bureau of Yunnan Province (1988). *Compilation of Seismological Data in Yunnan Province*, Earthquake Press, Beijing, China.

Shen, J., Y. P. Wang, F. M. Song, and Y. Z. Li (1998). Relative creep rate and characteristic earthquake recurrence interval example from the Xiaojiang Fault Zone in Yunnan, China, *Seismol. Geol.* **20,** no. 4, 328–331.

Shen, Z. K., J. N. Lü, M. Wang, and R. Bürgmann (2005). Contemporary crustal deformation around the southeast borderland of the Tibetan Plateau, *J. Geophys. Res.* **110,** no. B11, doi: 10.1029/2004JB003421.

Shi, X., Y. Wang, K. Sieh, R. Weldon, L. Feng, C. H. Chan, and J. Liu-Zeng (2018). Fault slip and GPS velocities across the Shan Plateau define a curved Southwestward crustal motion around the Eastern Himalayan syntaxis, *J. Geophys. Res.* **123,** 2502–2518, doi: 10.1002/2017jb015206.

Sieh, K. E. (1978). Slip along the San Andreas fault associated with the great 1857 earthquake, *Bull. Seismol. Soc. Am.* **68,** no. 5, 1421–1448.

Song, F. M., Y. P. Wang, W. X. Yu, Z. Cao, X. H. Shen, and J. Shen (1998). *Xiaojiang Active Fault Zone*, Seismological Press, Beijing, China.

Song, J., S. M. Yang, W. Wang, Y. Huang, and M. Lin (2016). Study on the locking characteristics of Anninghe-Zemuhe-Xiaojiang Fault Zone, *J. Geodes. Geodynam.* **36,** 490–494.

Sun, H. Y., H.-L. He, Z. Y. Wei, and W. Gao (2015). Late Quaternary activity of Zhuma Fault on the North segment of Daliangshan Fault Zone, *Seismol. Geol.* **37,** 440–454.

Sun, Y. M. (2018). *Crustal Deformation Characteristics of the Honghe Fault Zone and Its Surrounding Areas Based on GPS Observation Data*, Yunnan Normal University, Kunming, China.

Tan, X., K. Liang, and B. Ma (2023). A review of research progress on the late Quaternary activities of the Xiaojiang Fault Zone, *Technol. Earthq. Disaster Prev.* **18,** 757–772, doi: 10.11899/zzfy20230410.

Tapponnier, P., F. J. Ryerson, J. Van der Woerd, A.-S. Mériaux, and C. Lasserre (2001). Long-term slip rates and characteristic slip: Keys to active fault behaviour and earthquake hazard, *C. R. Acad. Sci. Ser. IIA Earth Planet. Sci.* **333,** 483–494, doi: 10.1016/s1251-8050(01)01668-8.

Tian, Q., Z. K. Ren, and J. L. Zhang (2008). Study of paleoearthquakes by combined trench on Zemuhe Fault around Daqingliangzi, Xichang, Sichuan, *Seismol. Geol.* **30,** 400–411.

Wang, E., and B. C. Burchfiel (2000). Late Cenozoic to Holocene deformation in Southwestern Sichuan and adjacent Yunnan, China, and its role in formation of the Southeastern part of the Tibetan Plateau, *Geol. Soc. Am. Bull.* **112,** 413–423.

Wang, E., B. C. Burchfiel, L. H. Royden, L. Chen, J. Chen, W. Li, and Z. Chen (1998). *Late Cenozoic Xianshuihe-Xiaojiang, Red River, and Dali Fault Systems of Southwestern Sichuan and Central Yunnan, China*, Geological Society of America, Boulder, Colorado.

Wang, H., K. Ran, L. Chen, M. Liang, S. Gao, Y. Li, and L. Xu (2018). Determination of slip rate on the Southern segment of the Anninghe Fault, *Seismol. Geol.* **40,** 967–979.

Wang, H., Y. Ran, Y. Li, F. Gomez, and L. Chen (2013). Holocene palaeoseismologic record of earthquakes on the Zemuhe Fault on the southeastern margin of the Tibetan Plateau, *Geophys. J. Int.* **193,** 11–28, doi: 10.1093/gji/ggs095.

Wang, L. L., Q. H. Wang, Y. Zhang, and Y. Wang (2016). Analysis of current activity of main faults in Yunnan region based on GPS, *J. Inst. Disaster Prev.* **18,** 1–8.

Wang, Y.-P., F.-M. Song, Z.-Q. Cao, X.-H. Shen, J. Shen, W.-X. Yu, H. Xueying, and L. Zhixiang (2013). *Geological Map of Xiaojiang Active Fault Zone: 1:50000*, Seismological Press.

Wei, Z.-Y., H.-L. He, F. Shi, Y.-R. Xu, L.-S. Bi, and H.-Y. Sun (2012). Slip rate on the south segment of Daliangshan Fault Zone, *Seismol. Geol.* **34,** 282.

Wells, D. L., and K. J. Coppersmith (1994). New empirical relationships among magnitude, rupture length, rupture width, rupture area, and surface displacement, *Bull. Seismol. Soc. Am.* **84,** 974–1002, doi: 10.1785/bssa0840040974.

Wen, X.-Z., F. Du, G.-X. Yi, F. Long, J. Fan, P.-X. Yang, R.-W. Xiong, X.-X. Liu, and Q. Liu (2013). Earthquake potential of the Zhaotong and Lianfeng Fault Zones of the eastern Sichuan-Yunnan border region, *Chin. J. Geophys.* **56,** 3361–3372.

\Wesnousky, S. G. (2008). Displacement and geometrical characteristics of earthquake surface ruptures: Issues and implications, *Bull. Seismol. Soc. Am.* **98,** no. 4, 1609–1632, doi: 10.1785/0120070111.

Wu, L., Z. He, D. Xu, L. Li, L. Guo, and X. Li (2024). Study on the late Quaternary activity of the Jinyang-Ningnan segment of the Lianfeng Fault Zone, *J. Struct. Geol.* **178,** 105014, doi: 10.1016/j.jsg.2023.105014.

Xiong, T.-Y., X. Yao, and Y.-S. Zhang (2010). A review on study of activity of Xianshuihe Fault Zone since the Holocene, *J. Geomech.* **16,** 176–188.

Xu, X. W., X. Z. Wen, R. Z. M. Zheng, W. Tao, F. M. Song, and G. H. Yu (2003). Recent tectonic patterns and dynamic sources of active blocks in Sichuan-Yunnan region, *Sci. China Earth Sci.* **33,** 12.

Zhang, P. Z., Q. D. Deng, Z. Q. Zhang, and H. B. Li (2013). Active faults, earthquake hazards and associated geodynamic processes in continental China, *Sci. Sin. Terrae* **43,** no. 10, 1607–1620.

Zhang, P.-Z., Z. Shen, M. Wang, W. Gan, R. Bürgmann, P. Molnar, Q. Wang, Z. Niu, J. Sun, J. Wu, *et al.* (2004). Continuous deformation of the Tibetan Plateau from global positioning system data, *Geology* **32,** 809–812, doi: 10.1130/g20554.1.

Zhang, S. P. (2019). Study on fault activity in Sichuan-Yunnan Region constrained by GPS, Institute of Seismology, China Earthquake Administration, Wuhan, China.

Zhao, B., Y. Huang, C. Zhang, W. Wang, K. Tan, and R. Du (2015). Crustal deformation on the chinese mainland during 1998–2014 based on GPS data, *Geod. Geodynam.* **6,** no. 1, 7–15.

Zhou, R., X. Li, Z. Huang, Y. He, and T. Ge (2003). The late Quaternary average slip rate of the Daliangshan Fault Zone in Sichuan Province, *Seismol. Res.* **26,** 6.

Zielke, O. (2018). Earthquake recurrence and the resolution potential of tectono-geomorphic records, *Bull. Seismol. Soc. Am.* **108,** no. 3A, 1399–1413.

Zielke, O., J. R. Arrowsmith, L. Grant Ludwig, and S. O. Akciz (2012). High-resolution topography-derived offsets along the 1857 Fort Tejon earthquake rupture trace, San Andreas Fault, *Bull. Seismol. Soc. Am.* **102,** 1135–1154.

Zielke, O., J. R. Arrowsmith, L. G. Ludwig, and S. O. Akçiz (2010). Slip in the 1857 and earlier large earthquakes along the Carrizo Plain, San Andreas Fault, *Science* **327,** 1119–1122, doi: 10.1126/science.1182781.

Zielke, O., Y. Klinger, and J. R. Arrowsmith (2015). Fault slip and earthquake recurrence along strike-slip faults—Contributions of high-resolution geomorphic data, *Tectonophysics* **638,** 43–62.

Zinke, R., J. Hollingsworth, J. F. Dolan, and R. Van Dissen (2019). Surface slip and offsets on the Papatea fault during the 2016 Mw 7.8 Kaikōura earthquake from optical image correlation, *GSA Bull.* **131,** 1499–1520.

Manuscript received 22 September 2025
Published online 14 January 2026

A New High-Resolution Seismic Catalog for Southwestern Australia (2020–2025) and Analysis of Long-Term Clustering Behavior

OPEN ACCESS

Robert Pickle*[1], Meghan S. Miller[1], Trevor Allen[2], Sima Mousavi[1], Ping Zhang[1], Huaiyu Yuan[3], and Ruth Murdie[3]

Abstract

We present a new machine-learning-based catalog of southwestern Australia, a stable intraplate zone primarily comprised of the Archean aged Yilgarn craton and the continent's most seismically active region. About 29,000 events were located between 2000 and May 2025 with 43% of these presumed to be related to anthropogenic mining based on location and temporal filtering. Most (75%) events were located following the new SWAN (2P, 2020) and WA Array networks (WG, 2022), which collectively added ~340 stations from 2020 to 2025 and were the first to target this region in detail. We observe a very high degree of spatially correlated clustering, which contains power-law, Omori-type mainshock–aftershock behavior as well as low-volume and low-magnitude atemporal clustering we label as "drip-type" behavior. Drip-type clustering is presumed to reflect the long-tail baseline activity following the cessation of temporally correlated behavior following large earthquakes, but may also be unrelated to past activity. As such, the identification of drip-type clusters could be used to infer the location of prehistoric seismicity and future seismic risk. Three recent significant earthquake sequences were also analyzed in detail: Arthur River (2022), Gnowangerup (2023), and Wyalkatchem (2024), which is still producing significant seismicity as of publication. In each, the distribution of hypocenters is shallow (< 5 km) but mostly disorganized, no clear fault plane could be resolved, and the largest event in the sequence was preceded by a significant but smaller magnitude earthquake by several weeks to months. All three sequences also show centroid moment tensor solutions consistent with the expected west–east compression regime in southwest Australia. "Drip-type" activity preceded both Gnowangerup and Wyalkatchem, but the earthquakes at Arthur River sequence were the first at that location in our catalog.

Cite this article as Pickle, R., M. S. Miller, T. Allen, S. Mousavi, P. Zhang, H. Yuan, and R. Murdie (2026). A New High-Resolution Seismic Catalog for Southwestern Australia (2020–2025) and Analysis of Long-Term Clustering Behavior, *Seismol. Res. Lett.* **97**, 805–821, doi: 10.1785/0220250308.

Supplemental Material

Introduction

The southwestern region of Australia is the county's most seismically active and experiences both persistent low-magnitude seismicity and large damaging events, punctuated by 40+ magnitude 5 or greater earthquakes since 1900, including one of the Australia's most destructive in modern history: 1968 M_w 6.6 Meckering earthquake (Gordon and Lewis, 1980; Vogfjörd and Langston, 1987). This stable continental region also experiences regular short- and long-term earthquake aftershock sequences and other clustered events, including potentially thousands of events in the Burakin region from 2001 to 2002 (Leonard, 2002), 900 recorded events following the Lake Muir sequence in 2018 (Clark *et al.*, 2020; Standen *et al.*, 2021), and 5000 events in the Arthur River region since 5 January 2022 (Murdie *et al.*, 2022). The region is also well known for its vast precious metal and critical mineral reserves, and as such, thousands of mining blasts and other anthropogenic events occur per year.

Seismicity in southwest Australia is decidedly intraplate as the region is ~2000 km from the nearest plate boundary. The source of this activity has been suggested to be the result of east-west-directed compressional stress (Reynolds and Hillis, 2000; Reynolds *et al.*, 2002; Clark and Leonard, 2003;

1. ANU Research School of Earth Sciences, Canberra, Australia, https://orcid.org/0000-0002-8550-5256 (RP); https://orcid.org/0000-0001-5494-2296 (MSM); https://orcid.org/0000-0002-6707-3103 (SM); https://orcid.org/0000-0003-1425-3925 (PZ); 2. Geoscience Australia, Canberra, Australia, https://orcid.org/0000-0003-3420-547X (TA); 3. Department of Mines, Petroleum, and Exploration, Perth, Australia, https://orcid.org/0000-0003-3512-7856 (HY)

*Corresponding author: Robert.pickle@anu.edu.au

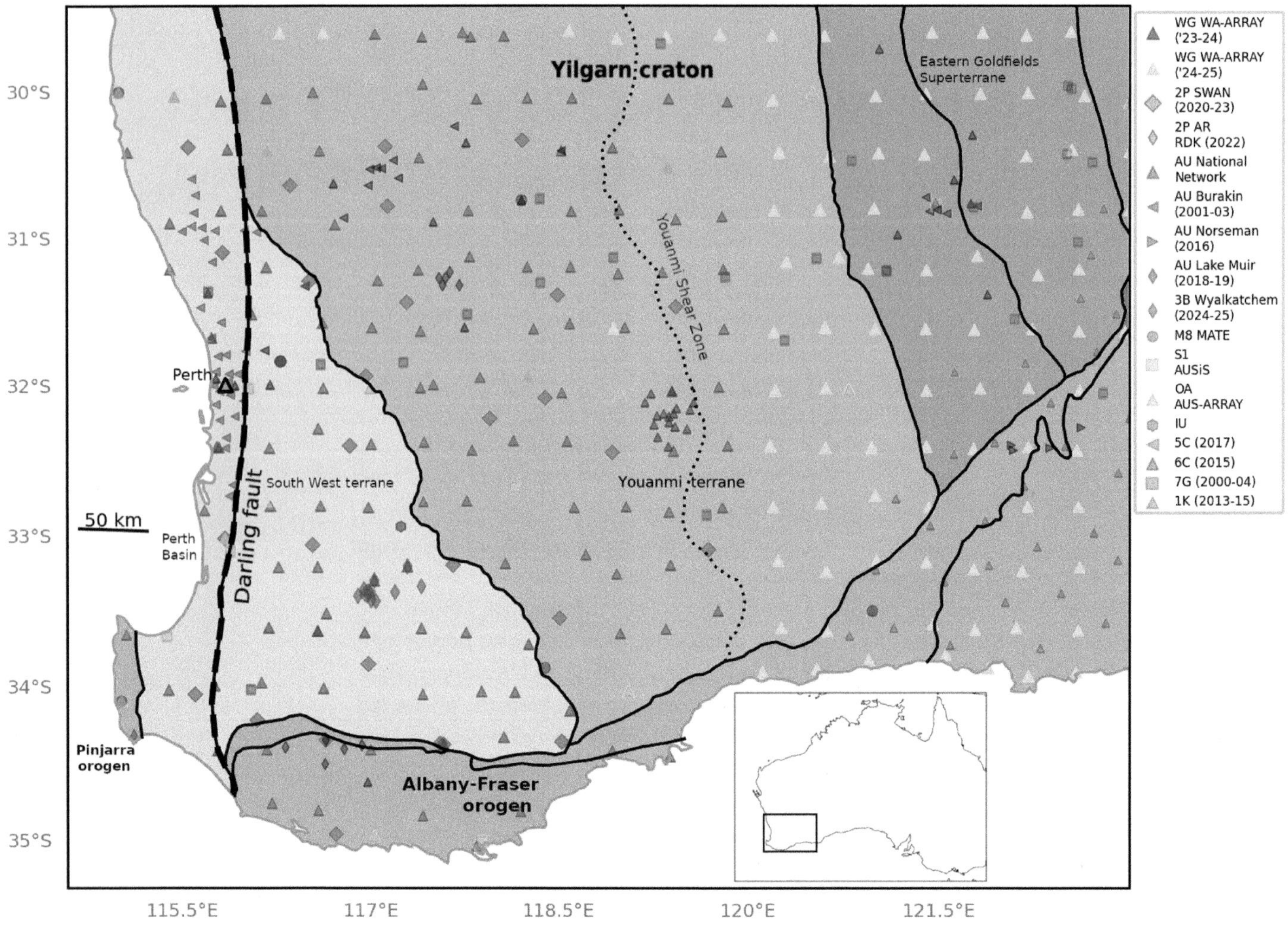

Figure 1. Map of seismic stations and major tectonic units in southwest Australia. The Yilgarn craton (pinks) in the study region comprises the South West terrane (light pink), Youanmi terrane (medium pink), and the Eastern Goldfields Superterrane (dark pink; de Gromard *et al.*, 2021). The Yilgarn craton is bounded by the Perth basin (light green), Pinjarra orogen (dark green, and Albany–Fraser orogen (light blue). The hashed line denotes the Youanmi shear zone–Kawana fault (Martin *et al.*, 2022). The inset shows the zoom-out contextural map of the plotted region. The color version of this figure is available only in the electronic edition.

Sandiford and Egholm, 2008) repartitioned 60° or more from Australia's relative plate motion (UNAVCO), though this is still not well understood. Although earthquakes in continental interiors experiencing long-period, uniform stress is not unusual (e.g., Schulte and Mooney, 2005), this region is unique in that most previously recorded activity occurs in concentrated areas intraterrane within an Archean craton rather than at the margins of major boundaries or within derelict rift structures (e.g., Mooney *et al.*, 2012), suggesting additional localized factors have a significant role in the distribution of seismicity.

Beyond their novelty, earthquakes in this region can be hazardous, and damaging events regularly occur near the metropolitan Perth region (population 2.3M). Investigations of scarp offsets 5–10 Ma have indicated that prehistoric events could approach magnitudes of M_w 7.25 (Leonard and Clark, 2011; Clark *et al.*, 2012), albeit with regional recurrence intervals of ~5000 yr or more (Allen *et al.*, 2023). To better investigate this seismic activity within this region, two significant networks have been deployed here: SWAN (2P, 2020–2023) and WA Array (WG, phases 1 [2022] and 2 [2024]). Before 2020, the region only had limited coverage provided by the Australian Seismometers in Schools (AuSiS, S1) and Australian National Seismic Network (AU), as well as several small temporary networks with various objectives dating to 2000. This study used as much available secondary data as could be found to derive a new machine learning (ML)-based seismic catalog to better understand the nature of the elevated activity within this stable continental interior.

Tectonic Background

The geology of southwest Australia spans billions of years of complex history best described elsewhere (e.g., de Gromard *et al.*, 2021; Murdie *et al.*, 2025), but we attempt to briefly summarize it. The study region is centered by the Archean-aged Yilgarn craton, bounded by the Proterozoic Pinjarra to the west and Albany–Fraser orogens to the south and southeast (Fig. 1).

The Yilgarn craton (2.6–3.7 Ga) consists mostly of granitic and greenstone terranes (Cassidy *et al.*, 2006; de Gromard *et al.*, 2021) for which overall crustal structures are characterized by high Bouguer gravity anomalies and crustal thicknesses averaging 30–45 km (Reading *et al.*, 2003; Kennett *et al.*, 2023). It spans over 1100 km at its widest from west to east. Within this craton, several distinct north-northwest-trending terranes exist, including the aptly named South West terrane, the Youanmi terrane in the center, and the Eastern Goldfields Superterrane further east, which is widely considered a result of the terrane-accretion model that accounts for the formation of the Yilgarn craton in the Archean (Wilde *et al.*, 1996; Reading *et al.*, 2003; Czarnota *et al.*, 2010). Recent geochemical and geophysical studies (Smithies *et al.* 2024; Gauntlett *et al.* 2025; Zhang *et al.* 2025), however, have revealed a dominant northeast- to east-northeast-trending crustal architecture, challenging the conventional terrane accretion model. The craton also features the Corrigin tectonic zone (de Gromard *et al.*, 2021) within the Youanmi terrane along the border of the South West terrane as well as the north–south-trending Youanmi shear zone-Kawana fault (Martin *et al.*, 2022), roughly partitioning the Youanmi terrane in its center. Nine mafic dyke suites from 2615 to 733 Ma are also present, each comprising hundreds of dykes up to hundreds of kilometers in length and all seemingly oriented in disparate directions (Wingate, 2007; Stark *et al.*, 2018, 2019; de Gromard *et al.*, 2021). The Yilgarn craton is also resource-rich and is actively mined for a variety of precious metals and rare earth elements.

South of the Yilgarn craton is the Albany–Fraser orogen, an accretionary Proterozoic basement which has evolved in distinct phases from 1475 Ma to roughly ~1100 Ma (e.g., Bodorkos and Clark, 2004; Spaggiari *et al.*, 2014, 2018). West of the Yilgarn craton is the Perth basin, a 1500+ km long north–south-trending structure likely comprising various accreted terranes accreted across multiple events in the Proterozoic Gondwana assembly era (Fletcher and Libby, 1993; Janssen *et al.*, 2003), which are covered by a thick sequence of sedimentary rocks deposited following the breakup of Gondwana (Myers, 1990, 1995; Thomas, 2018). These Phanerozoic sedimentary materials likely correspond to the strong Bouguer gravity anomaly lows observed here (e.g., Sandwell and Smith, 2009; Sandwell *et al.*, 2014). Separating the Pinjarra orogen and Perth basin with the Yilgarn craton is the 1500+ km long Darling fault, an aseismic west-dipping feature which has likely not been active since the Cenozoic rifting of the proto-Indian continent (Janssen *et al.*, 2003).

Today, southwestern Australia shows no clear sign of intraplate convergence and has a very low deformation rate via Global Navigation Satellite Systems (Featherstone *et al.*, 2004) with strain rates less than 10^{-15}/s (Braun *et al.*, 2009). Despite this, there is abundant ongoing seismicity which appears to manifest itself primarily as west–east compression (Rajabi, Tingay, *et al.*, 2017; Lin *et al.*, 2021).

SWAN and the WA Array

The 27-station SWAN network (Miller *et al.*, 2023) was the first to attempt uniform spatial coverage of the area, and the 160+ station WA Array (phases 1 and 2) expanded on these sites with a roughly 40 km grid spacing. The SWAN, OA, and WA Array sites used broadband sensors of various makes, but all with a corner period of 120 s. After the Arthur River swarm began in early 2022 (Murdie *et al.*, 2022), seven additional SmartSolo BD3C-5 nodes were cyclically deployed for ~11 months to further constrain these earthquakes. In total, over 130,000 station-days of data were analyzed from all networks from January 2000 to May 2025, with over 80% of these accounted, by the SWAN and WA Array networks.

Earthquake Location

ML phase picking

We employed ML-based seismic phase picking using an edited version of the EQTransformer (Mousavi *et al.*, 2020) ML phase picking package. This code is trained on a catalog of ~1.18M global earthquakes from the Stanford Earthquake Dataset (STEAD; Mousavi *et al.*, 2019) and ~0.4M events from the Italian seismic dataset for ML (INSTANCE; Michelini *et al.*, 2021), which has been primarily filtered to exclude events with either a depth or epicentral distance > 300 km. These collections of training data also include 0.23M and 0.13M samples of noise.

We made several significant edits to version 1.61 (current as of publication) of EQTransformer. First, we have changed the waveform data regime to one with a universal sample rate of 50 Hz spanning 60 s data windows from its original 100 Hz, and filtered and downsampled the training datasets to a frequency band of 1–24 and a 50 Hz sample rate. This was done to halve disk requirements, reduce processing time, and allow additional larger-size kernels and filters, and other memory-sensitive enhancements in EQTransformer. In our testing, we did not notice any obvious degradation in model loss or F1 scores relative to a model trained on a 100 Hz dataset, and the time-series resolution loss of 0.01 s is within the training catalog pick time error. Furthermore, the amount of *P*- or *S*-arrival energy contained outside of this band for regional-scale shallow earthquake seismicity was negligible.

Our second significant alteration of the code involved the creation of a dynamic class and sample weighting scheme as required by TensorFlow versions > 2.4. An in-depth review of class weights and sample weights in an ML context is beyond our focus, but it can be briefly said that sample weights offer a means to modulate the achievable model "loss" (i.e., the cost function we are attempting to minimize) by dynamically scaling the loss at each sample relative to the true phase arrival, and class weights provide a mechanism to address class imbalance (e.g., noise or signal) by assigning the appropriate penalty to predictions based on the proportion of noise and signal input training data. In our code, we have defined class weights via a Gaussian-shaped label with a width of 30 samples (±0.15 s) centered at each arrival, and sample weights are a Gaussian label with a width of six samples. Our experiments found that wider class and sample labels produced models with higher F1 scores but typically also resulted in higher loss (i.e., reduced pick accuracy), and conversely, narrower class/sample labels resulted in lower F1 scores but with smaller loss (i.e., increased pick accuracy). Our chosen parameters seemed to be a good compromise between F1 and loss, but we recognize that more work needs to be done in this space.

Our final model had cross-validated *P* and *S* F-scores of 0.64 and 0.56, respectively. An explanation for the relatively low F1 scores is likely some combination of the relatively narrow pick labels (±0.06 s or six samples), as well as the fact that the augmentation done on the training data was expanded to be rather severe to preferentially minimize false positives and increase precision. Because the final picks are determined via the peaks of a probability distribution, these scores do not necessarily reflect what would be returned by the ML picker. Testing our model on the training database yielded *P* and *S* F1 scores of 0.94 (0.99 precision/0.89 recall) and 0.86 (0.99 precision/0.75 recall) with mean picks errors of 0.004 ±0.09 s and 0.0 ± 0.128 s, respectively.

A significant concession for our ML phase picker is that it allows for only one *P* and *S* phase pick per 60 s window. In most instances, this is sufficient, but it is possible that during the early stages of aftershock sequences, events may occur at rates exceeding one per minute. In this instance, the most "probable" looking phase arrival per 60 s window is chosen by the ML algorithm, and any additional arrivals are disregarded. We thereby presume that periods of high seismicity may be underreported.

Association, 3D location, and quality control

Phase picks are initially associated as events using the REAL algorithm (Zhang *et al.*, 2019) using a 1D regional average of the AuSREM crustal model (Salmon *et al.*, 2013). These initial associations were then solved in 3D using NonLinLoc (Lomax and Curtis, 2001; Lomax *et al.*, 2014, 2000) and the full 3D AuSREM model, and then iteratively resolved depending on outcome. About 10% of the catalog was then subjected to manual review and repicking via SeisComP (Helmholtz Centre Potsdam - GFZ German Research Centre for Geosciences and GmbH, 2008) before being double-differenced via the Scrtdd package (Scarabello and Diehl, 2021). Find the full details on these processes in the supplemental material available to this article.

Catalog

Our final catalog comprised ~29,000 events spanning the region in Figure 2. The ~22,000 events from October 2020 had an average latitude, longitude, and depth uncertainty of 1.5 ± 1.4, 1.7 ± 1.5, and 3.0 ± 2.4 km, respectively, an average root mean square error of 0.43 ± 0.20 s, a mean of 30.8 phase picks per event, and a mean of 16.6 stations used per event. Statistics, including the entire catalog span from 2000 onward, predictably have higher uncertainties (latitude, longitude, and depth uncertainty of 2.1 ± 2.0, 2.4 ± 2.6, and 4.0 ± 3.5 km). Double-differencing successfully relocated 57% of our catalog, assuming minimum *P* and *S* correlations of 0.50 for both and a maximum station distance of 160 km. Many of these events, predominantly on the western and eastern margins, likely correspond to quarry blasts associated with resource mining.

We note that this catalog is missing many events before 2020, when permanent station coverage was sparse. The average number of events per year between January 2021 and January 2025 was ~6000, so a complete catalog spanning 24+ yr might include ~150,000 events, assuming similar activity and magnitudes. We also note that this catalog may be missing some larger events before 2020 that are likely otherwise present in Geoscience Australia's national catalog (see Data and Resources, also plotted in Miller *et al.*, 2023). This is because our default event association algorithm was designed for the high-density station network from 2020 onward and did not explicitly search for stations with an epicentral distance greater than 2°. To mitigate this discrepancy, we increased the search radius for periods before 2010 and cross-referenced our catalog with known large events that occurred during periods of sparse station coverage.

Depth uncertainty

Earthquakes in this region are predominantly shallow (2.3 ± 4.3 km) with some important caveats. First, the minimum depth of the velocity model was −1.5 km (i.e., 1500 m above sea level) to best accommodate station elevations of ~500 m amidst a velocity model with 3^2 km grid resolution. Second, we had to estimate a surface ($z = 0$) velocity for the AuSREM model, which begins at 5 km depth. Ultimately, we decided on a surface velocity of 90% of its value at the same longitude and latitude at 5 km depth. This still generated many "air quakes" with depth values of −1.5 km (the top of the model), but less so than if the surface velocity was 80% of its 5 km depth value. Leveraging this catalog to develop a new velocity model to reconcile these inconsistencies and relocate these hypocenters is currently in progress.

The uniformly shallow depth of these events validates the technique of assigning fixed depths for poorly constrained events in this region, especially before 2020. However, there are a few notable areas with deeper than average events. In particular, the Norseman aftershock sequence featured events with an average depth of 14.2 ± 4.7 km. Many events flagged as probable mining explosions also have large depth uncertainty, and we attribute this to the poor quality of *S* picks, as our ML model was not trained with a dataset that included mining activity.

Magnitude calculation and completeness

Both M_{La} (Gaull and Gregson, 1991) and M_{Lv} (the local Richter magnitude M_L using only the vertical component) magnitudes were calculated for each event using the SeisComP *scamp* and

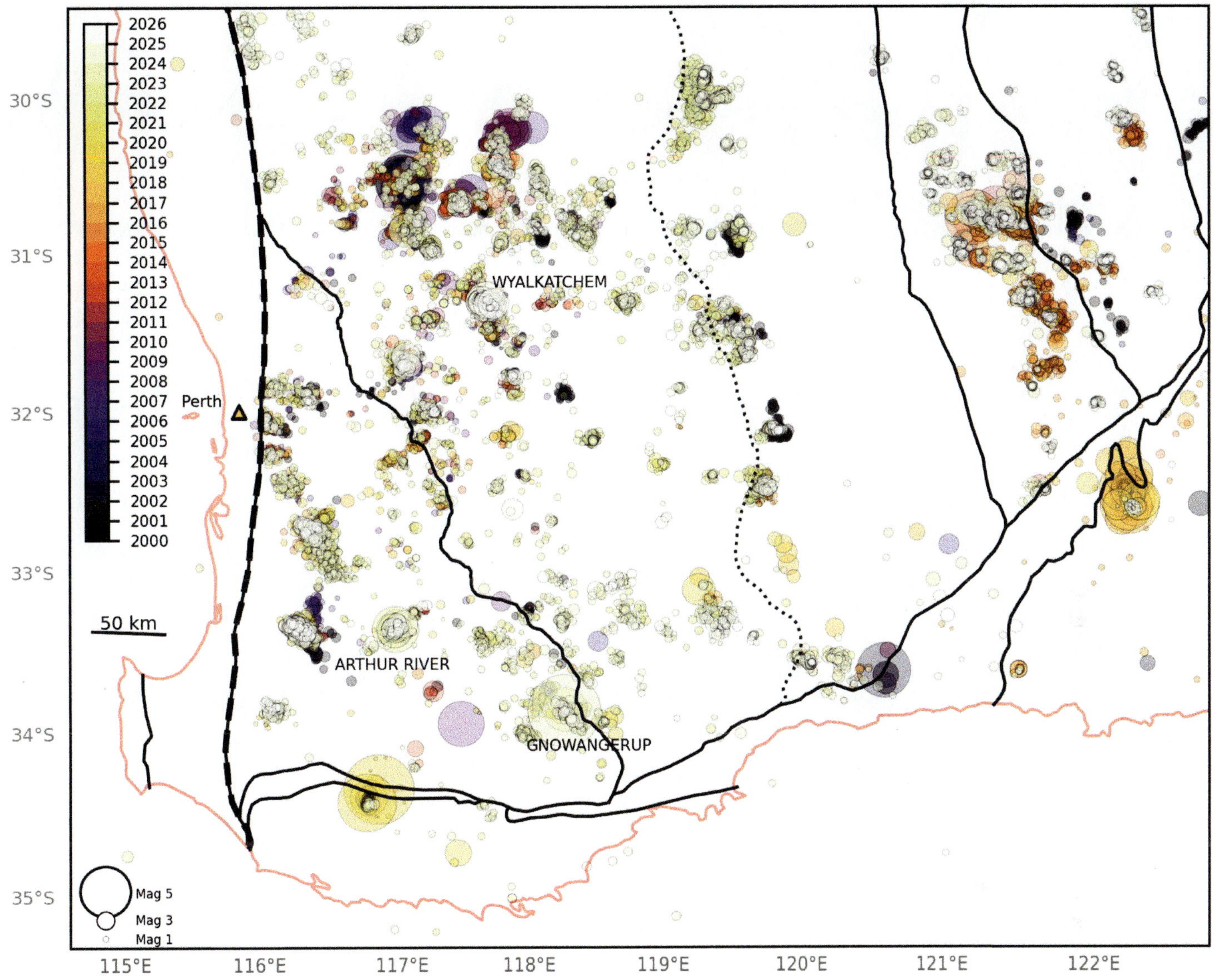

Figure 2. Double-differenced event catalog 2000–2025. Event colors indicate the origin time, as most depths were shallow (<5 km), with magnitude scaled by radius. 75% of our catalog was located following the SWAN (2P) deploy in late 2020. Black lines are terrane boundaries from de Gromard *et al.*, 2021. Three recent earthquake sequences detailed in this work (Athur River, Gnowangerup, and Wyalkatchem) are labeled.

scmag modules. For consistency with the Australian national catalog, M_{La} magnitudes were preferred, but M_{Lv} or m_b were used as a fallback. This technique follows from the original Richter (1935) magnitude formula by removing the instrument response from the signal and replicating the behavior of a Wood–Anderson seismometer. A 1–10 Hz band-pass filter was applied before amplitude calculations, and at least three valid station estimates were required to derive a magnitude. Magnitude estimates were then computed by taking the average of all station solutions with outliers beyond the 12.5th percentile removed.

We conservatively estimate our catalog's magnitude of completeness from the fully instrumented period from October 2020 onward to be ~2.0 M_{La} and note that the events–magnitude distribution (Fig. S4) is likely to be distorted in at least two ways. One, it likely still includes mining explosions between 1.5 and 3 M_{La}, which escaped our time and location filtering. Two, the concentration of extra events in the 0–0.7 M_{La} range is likely due to the disproportionate number of small aftershocks recorded at Arthur River and Wyalkatchem.

Anthropogenic events

Western Australia is one of the most intensively mined regions of the world, with 322 past and present mine sites (courtesy of the Western Australian Department of Mines, Petroleum and Exploration) shown in Figure 3. Above and below-ground explosive quarrying at these mines can generate detectable events and can bias analysis of natural earthquake distributions. We attempted to isolate these events by flagging all with an epicenter within a 10 km radius of any indicated mine site (**X**'s in Fig. 3) and reviewing time, day, and magnitude statistics for any outliers. By location filtering alone, 12,500 events (43%

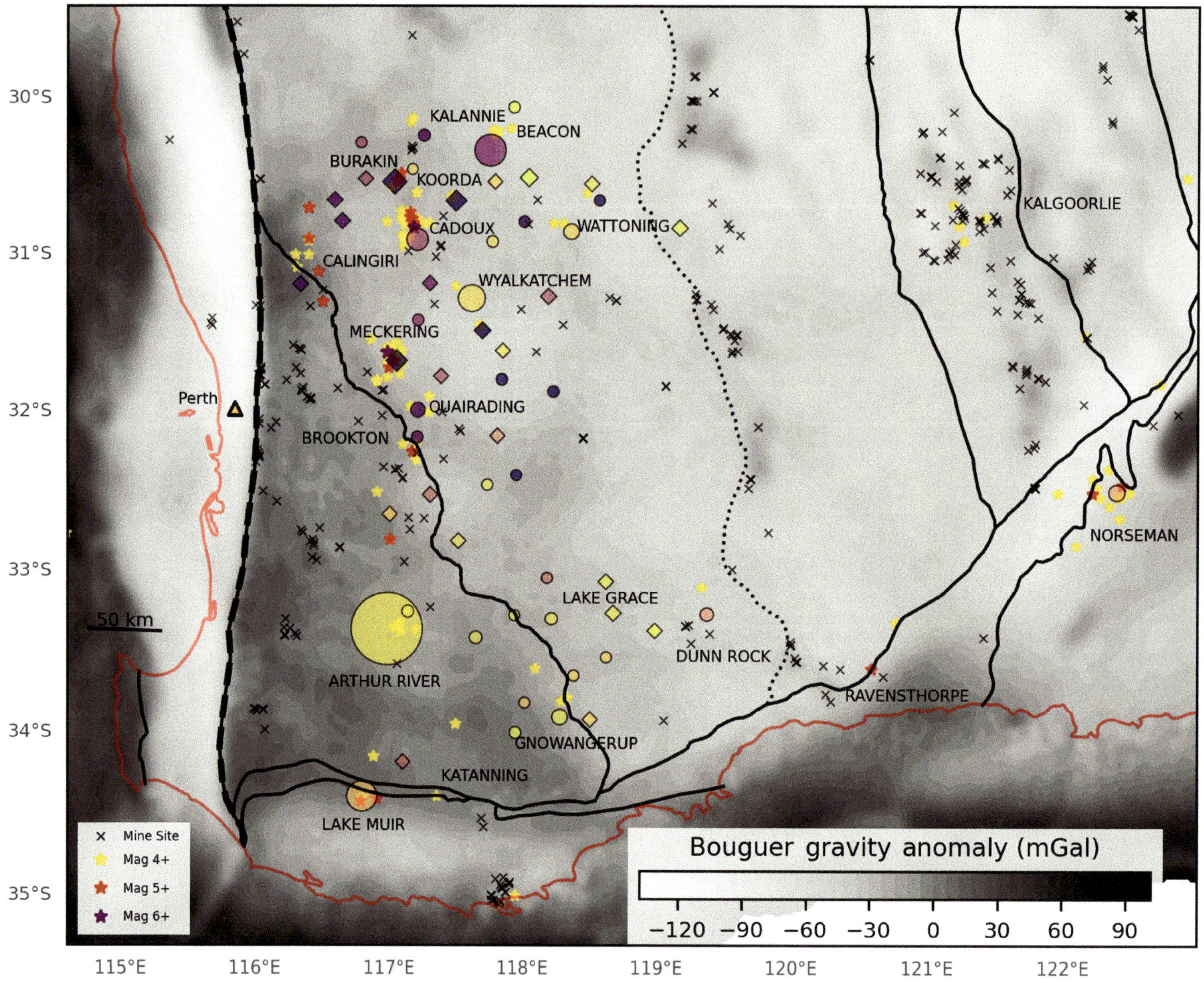

of the catalog) were flagged. Intraday time and day-of-week analysis (Fig. 4) show that blasting schedules in this region are mostly constant throughout the week but have as much as an 8% variance between Friday and Sunday, the busiest and quietest days, respectively. Blasting preferentially occurs at three distinct times: 5:30 a.m., 1:15 p.m., and 5:30 p.m. local time (Perth/AWST) or 21:30, 05:15, and 09:30 UTC. Manual review shows that blasting magnitudes may reach M_{La} 3.0 (M_{Lv} 3.3), for example, at 7 October 2023 09:32 in the northern Kalgoorlie region, as well as in the western Boddington region at 10 January 2025 01:08, with peak blasting periods also having more lower-magnitude events than the background overnight periods. Considering this time distribution, we further refined our suspected mining explosions by only selecting those occurring between 05:00–06:30 and 09:00–18:30 local Perth/AWST time. This additional filter removed an additional ~12% of the events originally flagged, and the remaining have been explicitly labeled as having a "mining explosion" event type in our catalog metadata. Because this filtering technique is unsophisticated, not all mining explosions have certainly been labeled in the final catalog, but the events that are labeled as mining explosions are unlikely to be natural earthquakes. In regions where discrimination is important, such as within the clusters labeled in Figure 3, we also reviewed satellite imagery for evidence of mining in addition to the waveforms

Figure 3. Map showing earthquake clusters (with radius proportional to number of events > 9 events), the location of known-mining activity (X's), and all known-historical seismicity M 4+ dated to 1900 (via Geoscience Australia, 2021) plotted as stars. Notable sequences or regions are labeled. Excluding the 10 largest clusters, the average volume is 43 events. Likely, additional mining areas are not marked. The color of the clusters corresponds to Figure 6. Clusters exclude any events flagged as suspected mining activity. Background is the Bouguer gravity anomaly computed via free air anomaly (Sandwell and Smith, 2009; Sandwell *et al.*, 2014) and satellite topography (Smith and Sandwell, 1997; Becker *et al.*, 2009).

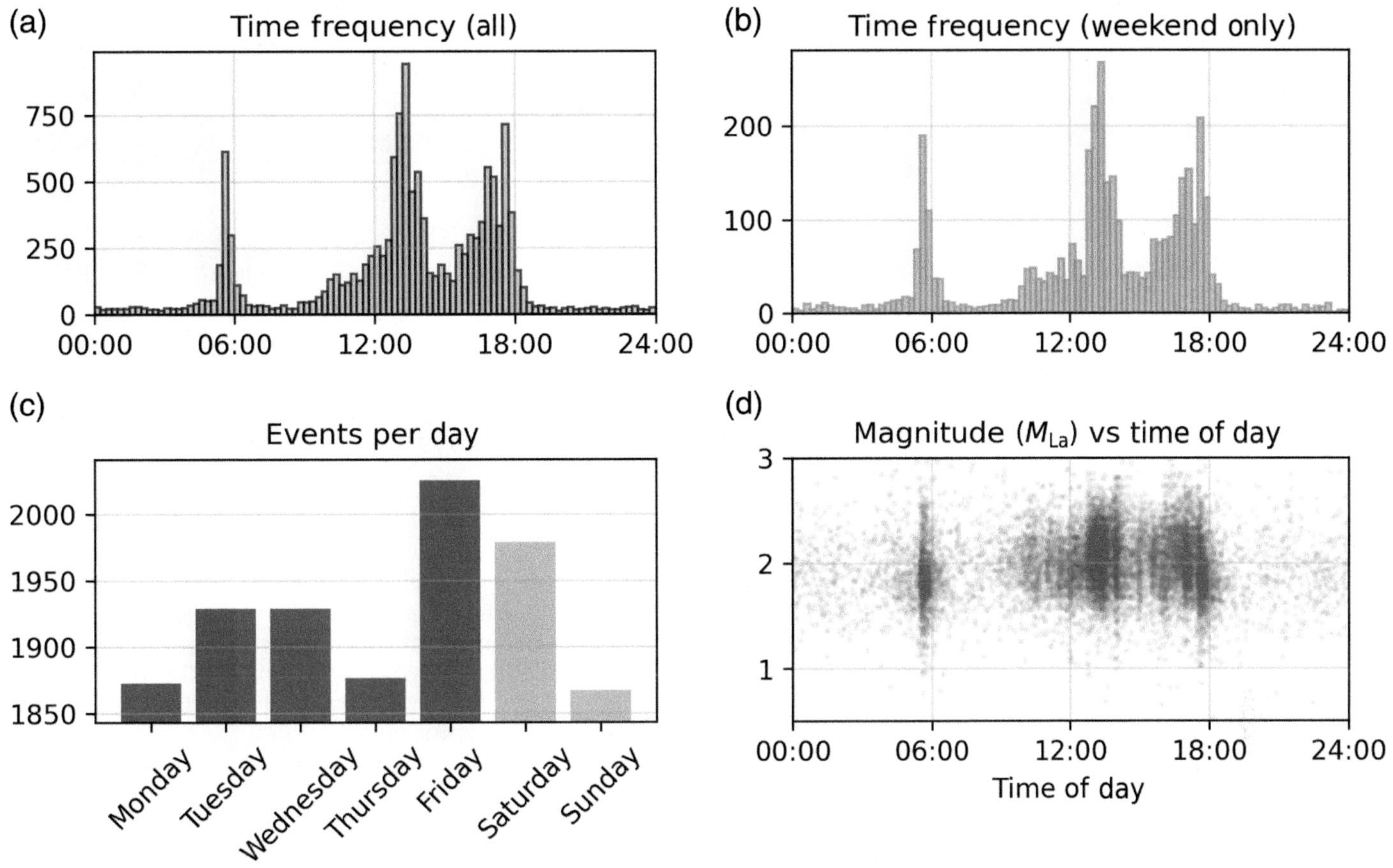

Figure 4. Analysis of initially flagged mining explosions within 10 km of known mining sites and previously defined time windows. (a) Intraday event frequency Monday–Sunday, (b) intraday event frequency (Saturday–Sunday), (c) events per weekday, and (d) M_{La} magnitude per time. All times are local (Perth/AWST). The color version of this figure is available only in the electronic edition.

themselves. Because of the prevalence of mining explosions in our catalog, we henceforth distinguish "events" to mean either natural earthquakes or mining explosions and "earthquakes" to mean only literal earthquakes.

Station distribution bias

Our catalog suffers from a sharp drop in station coverage before the SWAN (2P) experiment beginning in late 2020. According to the metadata available at EarthScope, the earliest permanent stations were IU.NWAO (25 November 1991), AU.RKGY (27 September 1999), AU.KMBL (27 November 2000), and AU.MUN (31 May 2001), with AU.BLDU, AU.KLBR, AU.MORW all installed in mid-2003 to better constrain the activity in the Beacon–Meckering corridor, AU.CARL and AU.MTKN in 2009 in Perth, and the AUSiS (S1) network was gradually coming online, mostly in the south and west coastal areas from 2013. However, we note that the AU network data are only publicly available from EarthScope from ~2005 onward. Aside from the temporary WA craton experiment (7G, 2000–2004) and ALFREX (1K, 2013–2015) networks, most additional stations were short-lived aftershock response deployments or were not designed for locating earthquakes. Lack of coverage greatly limits the ability to uncover M_{La} <2 events and therefore greatly negates the possibility for in-depth analysis of aftershock sequences, given that most rapid response stations rarely cover the entirety of the activity and often miss the first few days or even months of activity. Therefore, we only perform analysis on events from October 2020 where both temporary (2P, WG, and OA) and semipermanent (M8) station coverage began and/or expanded considerably.

The volume of located events relative to the station distribution is shown in Figure 5 and further highlights the dearth of station coverage before 2020. Aside from the labeled significant earthquake aftershock sequences, relatively few events were detected before 2020 (~25% of our catalog despite ~80% of the time span) and fewer still before the ALFREX temporary network in late 2013. The correlation between station coverage and resolved earthquakes implies a minimum of ~10 stations within an average epicentral range of 1°, or at least 20 stations within a range of 2° are required to adequately locate all reasonably detectable (M_{La} >2) events.

Earthquake clustering

Earthquakes in the greater southwest Australia region preferentially occur in proximal (by location) event epicenters, here

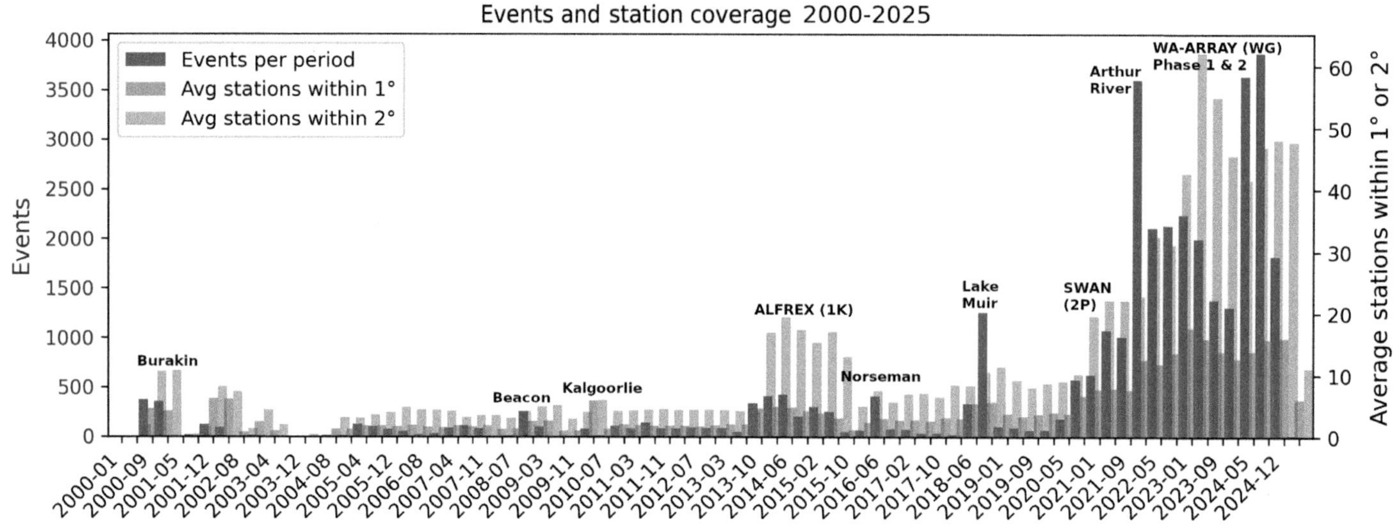

Figure 5. Events (red) and average station coverage within 1° (blue) and 2° (green) of each epicenter between January 2000 and May 2025. Significant earthquake sequences and seismic networks are labeled. Station distributions in 2012 and 2025 are shown in Figure S3. The color version of this figure is available only in the electronic edition.

generalized as "clusters" to include all types and characteristics (Fig. 3). From 1 January 2000, and excluding events flagged as probable mining explosions, 57 of these clusters (median event volume 42) were determined algorithmically via the DBSCAN algorithm (via scikit-learn) assuming a Kernel density estimation bandwidth of 5 km, a maximum distance of 5 km for two events to be considered related, and a minimum of 10 events. Over 74% of our catalog's earthquakes exist in one of these clusters (90% including mining explosions) with an average magnitude of 1.9 ± 0.2 M_{La}. We neglect factoring for or removing background seismicity rates because they are not high nor widespread enough to affect our clustering results and consider the longevity of activity at persistent locations to be critical information.

This catalog also observes several clusters comprising documented earthquake sequences, including the 2001–2002 Burakin (Leonard, 2002), 2009 Beacon (Dent, 2009), 2010 Kalgoorlie (Bathgate *et al.*, 2010), 2016 Norseman (Dent and Love, 2018a,b), Lake Muir (Clark *et al.*, 2020; Standen *et al.*, 2021), 2022 Arthur River (Murdie *et al.*, 2022), and 2024 Wyalkatchem sequences. We also note lesser-recognized or newer sequences, including those at Quairading, Dunn Rock, and Gnowangerup (labeled in Fig. 3), as well as dozens of indiscriminate clusters. We refer the reader to Dent (2016) for a list of notable events in this region before 2000, as well as further details on some of the aforementioned.

Following common nomenclature (e.g., Zaliapin and Ben-Zion, 2016; Zhang and Shearer, 2016) we first attempted to distinguish earthquake clusters into two principal types: burst-type or "Omori-type" clusters, which primarily feature one or more traditional mainshock–aftershock signatures with power-law decay rates, and "swarm-type" clusters without obvious mainshocks but similarly ephemeral, exhibiting both space and time correlation. However, in our catalog, we observe cluster characteristics with spatial correlation but little to no time correlation, making them distinct from both Omori and swarm-type clustering. We propose the term "drip-type" for this owing to their longevity, low activity, low magnitudes, and lack of discernible long-period interevent correlation.

Given the uneven station coverage of both permanent station infrastructure and aftershock deployment kits (e.g., Fig. 5 and Fig. S3), comparing cluster statistics is often unfair due to inconsistent catalog completeness. We note a high degree of station bias in our catalog before 2020 and especially during the ALFREX experiment (1K, 2013–2015), which will bias perceived start and end dates of an event cluster. Fortunately, some fundamental observations that mitigate bias are still possible. Figure 6 shows cluster duration versus magnitude gap (max − mean), mean interevent time, and the logarithm of the ratio of the standard deviation of the interevent time to the mean interevent time. In each, marker size and color are proportional to event volume and earliest event time, respectively. Cluster duration was determined by first removing the 5th and 95th percentiles of origin times within each cluster. Inter-event times were calculated as the *N*th discrete difference in origin times (i.e., NumPy's diff function) after rebinning events at intervals of 1% of each cluster's individual timespan, which effectively applies a low-pass filter. The advantage to this framing is that it is far less sensitive to catalog completeness and can robustly measure both magnitude gap and cluster duration at decadal scales, in addition to getting a reasonable estimate of average interevent time for sparse clusters with variable station availability over long periods.

Low-magnitude clustering is evident at all durations, with little evidence for either transient time correlation or an obvious trend in longer-term interevent times for all but the most recent clusters (Fig. 6). In traditional Omori-like decay

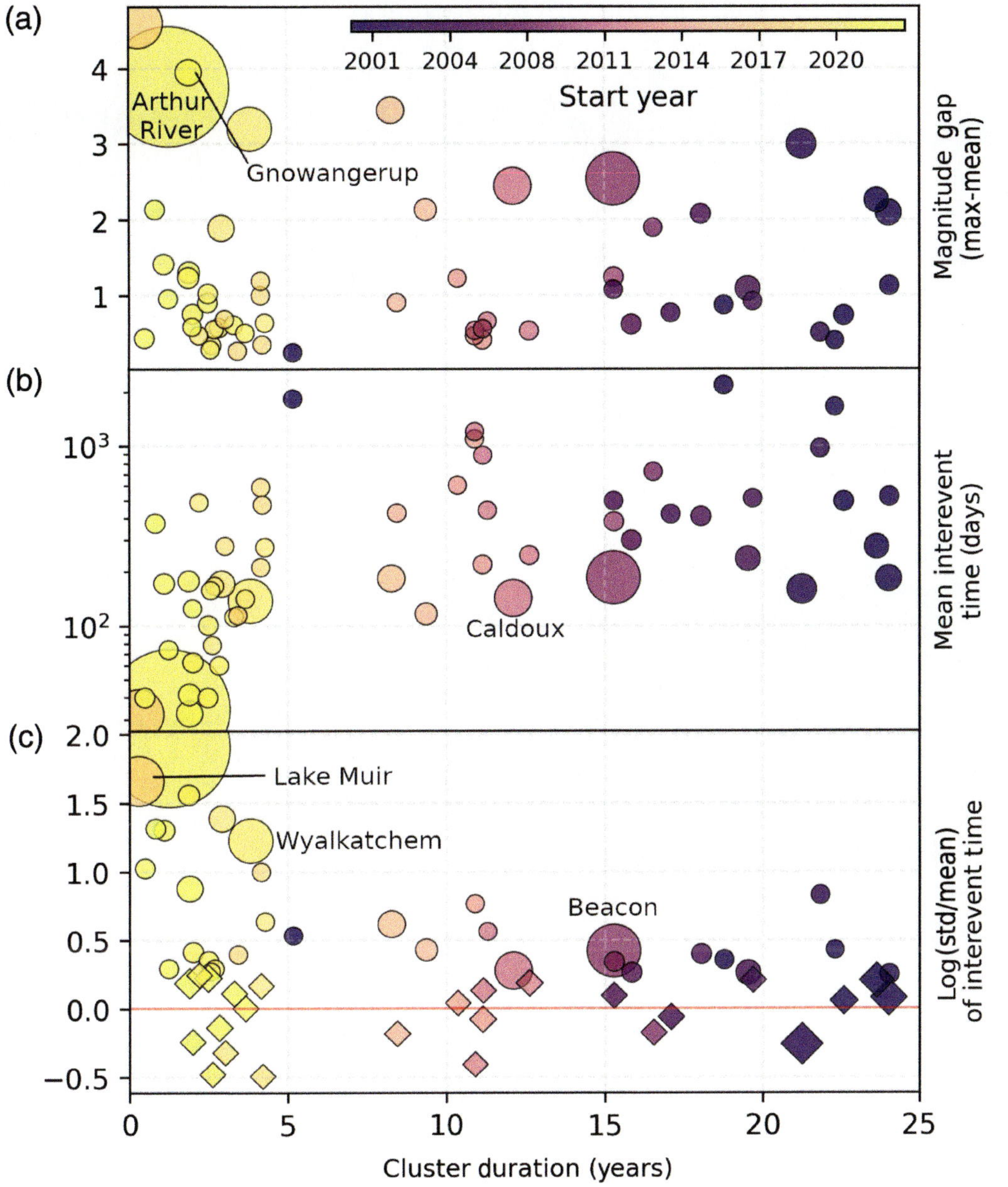

Figure 6. (a) Magnitude gap (max-mean, M_{La}), (b) mean interevent time (days), and (c) Log(std/mean) of interevent time versus cluster duration (years) of 56 clusters containing >9 events from January 2000, excluding suspected mining explosions. Icon size is proportional to the volume of events (largest is Arthur River, 5000+ events), and color corresponds to the first approximate earthquake origin time in each cluster. Clusters with a log(std/mean) < 0.25 are generally assumed to be atemporal and are plotted in diamonds. The minimum of the average cluster magnitude is 0.86 M_{La} and the mean magnitude of all events in the clusters with duration over 20 yr is 1.94 M_{La}. The colors, sizes, and shapes of the dots in this figure correspond to those shown in Figure 3.

patterns, interevent times should increase with age. However, our data show that interevent times become consistent after four years, though we again concede that age estimates may still be affected by station bias (Fig. 5). As most clusters are still active toward the end of our catalog, we assume that clustering in this region is ongoing and continuous in the long term.

The lack of correlation between cluster duration and magnitude gap or interevent times may indicate that clusters with sporadic large-magnitude Omori-type bursts revert to drip-type atemporal activity between episodes. We attempt to quantify the broader time correlation of the events in these clusters by comparing the ratio of the standard deviation of the interevent times with its mean. When the standard deviation of interevent times is equivalent to their mean (i.e., log(std/mean) $\cong$ 0), we interpret events within a cluster to be randomly distributed, with negative values becoming more evenly distributed and positive values increasingly temporally clustered. The bottom section of Figure 6 shows this calculation for each cluster, with about 24 clusters having values 0.25 or lower (standard deviation of these points is 0.5), which we consider to represent "drip-type" temporally declustered sequences. Some long-running, large magnitude gap clusters (e.g., Beacon, Caldoux, and Wyalkatchem), which regularly feature significant burst-type subsequences, marginally escape this label.

Moment tensor calculation

For the centroid moment tensor (CMT) inversion, we used full-waveform data from stations in the 2P, AU, WG, OA, M8, and S1 networks within 0.8°–5° from the earthquake epicenters following the approach of Kikuchi and Kanamori (1991) and modified later by Hejrani and Tkalčić (2020). The CMT solutions in this catalog (Figs. 7–9) exhibit mechanisms consistent with previous CMT solutions for the same region (e.g., Lin *et al.*, 2021) and the present-day crustal stress field (Rajabi, Heidbach, *et al.*, 2017). All measured events located within the Arthur River, Gnowangerup, and Wyalkatchem clusters exhibited predominantly thrust faulting mechanisms with double-couple components exceeding 70%, consistent with simple shear dislocation along reverse faults.

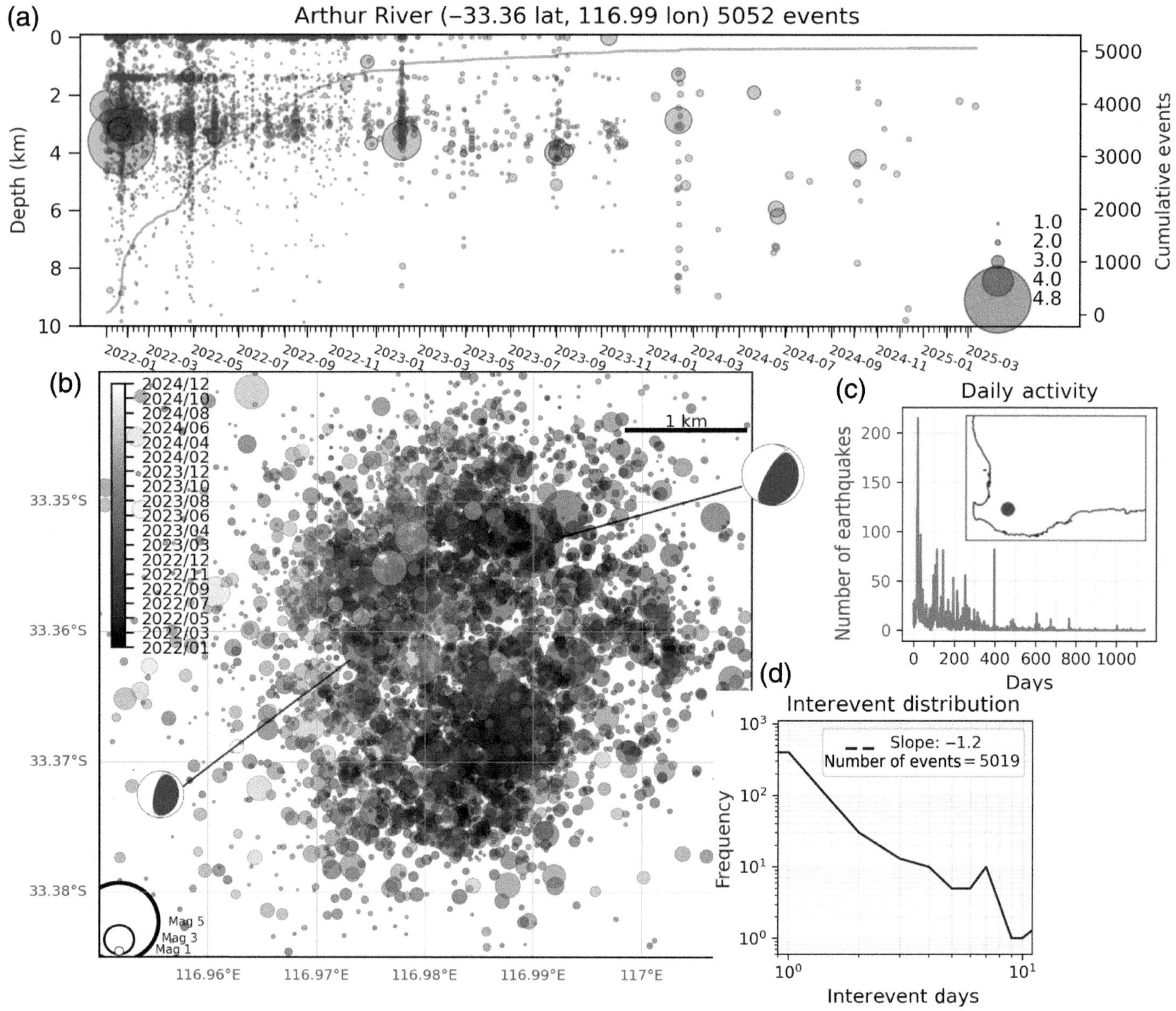

Figure 7. Arthur River sequence (2022, −33.36° latitude, 116.99° longitude). (a) Time series versus depth (with aftershock deploy node removal date indicated), (b) map view with centroid moment tensor (CMT) focal mechanisms, and (c) number of earthquakes per day and interevent frequency distribution. (d) The p value of the interevent distribution is fit between 0 and 10 days. The closest stations are outside this map but shown in Figure 1 as 2P AR RDK. The color version of this figure is available only in the electronic edition.

Arthur River sequence 2022

The SWAN network was fortunate to capture the start of the Arthur River earthquake sequence (Murdie *et al.*, 2022; Miller *et al.*, 2023), which began on 5 January 2022 11:37 with an M_{La} 4.0 (M_{Lv} 4.5) event and was followed by its largest M_{La} 4.8 (M_{Lv} 5.1) event on 24 January 2022 21:24. On 21 January 2022, three days before this largest event, six SmartSolo BD3C-5 nodes were deployed targeting the earthquake swarm and ran in various capacities until roughly November 2022. The SWAN network (Fig. 1) remained in place and was later ingested into the WA Array, which began in earnest in November 2022. Phase 1 of the WA Array was in place until December 2023, after which only the permanent networks remained. Accordingly, the detection of smaller ($M_{La} < 2.0$) events suffered, whereas larger events were still recorded at least up until March 2025.

Over 5000 events were detected within a ~3.0 km radius for the Authur River swarm (Fig. 7) within the South West terrane and with an average depth of 1.8 ± 2.6 km. The events largely exist within six or more Omori-like subsequences (p value of 1.2), each with corresponding large ($M_{La} > 3.0$) events. Neither the 2D nor 3D (not shown) distribution of the events shows any sort of organization, though there may be a subtle (<1 km) north-western migration of epicenters over time, or this could be the result of an evolving distribution of nodes

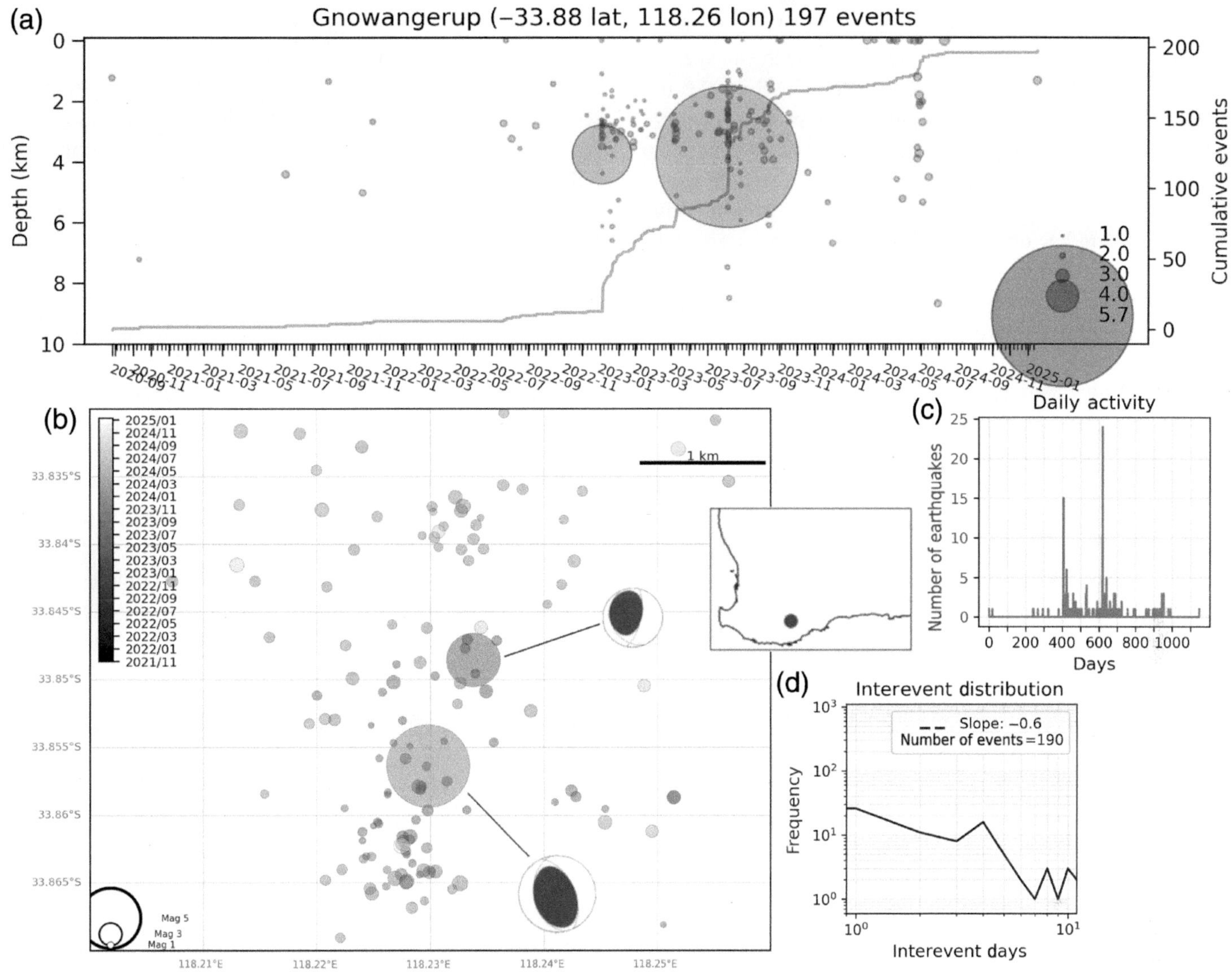

Figure 8. Gnowangerup sequence (2023, −33.88° latitude 118.26° longitude). (a) Time series versus depth (note that plot begins in 2021 to demonstrate preceding drip-type behavior), (b) map view with CMT focal mechanisms and the inset shows the cluster location within southwest Australia, and (c) number of earthquakes per day and interevent frequency distribution. (d) The p value of the interevent distribution is fit between 0 and 10 days The color version of this figure is available only in the electronic edition.

throughout 2022 and the evolution of the seismic network from SWAN to the WA Array in 2023. Focal mechanisms (Fig. 7) preferentially show north-northwest reverse faulting within a disbursed volume of rock consistent with the greater region (e.g., Lin *et al.*, 2021). Before 2022, this region showed very little activity, even relative to other drip-type clusters in the region. This was also the first recorded instance of measurable clustering occurring here in our catalog. Omori-type activity only remained detectable until about 6 December 2023, and there have been fewer than five observed events here in 2024.

The Arthur River sequence does not show a clear temporal–spatial evolution, nor were we able to resolve the events well enough to trace any fault traces or planes. The clustered events appear to have a faint separation between those in the northwest and those in the southwest, but we note that the southwest events are somewhat older in age (blacker in color) and that it is possible that epicenter solutions migrated toward the north-northeast (e.g., black to purple) following the addition of the nodal deploy and the addition of the WA Array sites in 2023. A smaller cluster (both in magnitude and volume) to the northeast outside of the map in Figure 7, but visible in Figure 3, also occurred concurrently with the Arthur River sequence.

Gnowangerup sequence 2023

The Gnowangerup sequence of 2023 began on 5 January 2023 with an M_{La} 4.7 earthquake, which preceded an M_{La} 5.6 event on 5 August 2023, eight months later. These earthquakes occurred on the border of the South West terrane and the Youanmi terrane within the Yilgarn craton. Despite the relatively high station density at the time (primarily via WA Array phase 1) and strength of the event, less than 200 earthquakes were observed within the event sequence (with an average depth of 3.0 ± 1.6 km). Before the earthquakes in 2023, the region was exhibiting slow and steady drip-type cluster behavior with sporadic low-magnitude events occurring back to ~2020 and possibly as far back as 2015, 2005, or 2000, given that few M_{La} <3 events were detected in those years near this area. Shortly following the M_{La} 5.6, the region seemed to resume low-volume drip-type behavior as very few aftershocks were observed. The mainshocks and most of their aftershocks have a general north–south trend.

Wyalkatchem sequence 2024

The Wyalkatchem sequence of 2024 (Fig. 9, the first since 2017) began with two 3.6 and 3.7 M_{La} events six hours apart on 13 July 2024. The largest event in the sequence (M_{La} 4.6) did not occur until 18 August 2024, 36 days later. During the initial earthquake, the WG network was deployed (Fig. 1), but the stations were located outside of the immediate area. Accordingly, the nearest stations were AU.KLBR (36 km) and M8.WATNG (80 km). On 20 August, only two days after the M_{La} 4.6 mainshock event, three additional stations were installed by the Western Australian Department of Mines, Petroleum and Exploration, and two days later, a five-station rapid deploy kit was installed (network code 3B; Glanville, 2024) but removed on 15 January 2025. The addition of these supplement stations increased the volume of found events such that the third $M_{La} \sim 3.7$ event burst in October 2024 recorded more events than the M_{La} 4.6 mainshock.

Similar to the Arthur River sequence, this cluster is primarily comprised of 5–6 individual bursts of events, each beginning with a moderate (M_{La} 2–4) event. Furthermore, both sequences began with smaller events 3–5 weeks before the mainshock. The events in this cluster also have a similar average event depth (2.6 ± 2.1 km), and the event hypocenters show very little cohesion or delineations of any clear fault plane at the surface or in three dimensions. There appears to be a slight migration of events from the north to the south over time, but this likely reflects an evolving station distribution bias. As of November 2025, additional significant seismicity is still occurring in the Wyalkatchem region, with the occurrence of an M_{La} 4.7 earthquake on 29 July 2025, and new temporary aftershock monitoring stations have been installed yet again.

Discussion

Our catalog reaffirms the well-known elevated seismicity in southwest Australia, a stable intraplate region within the Yilgarn craton. It further demonstrates that the overwhelming majority (75%) of suspected earthquakes are correlated spatially into tightly spaced (5 km radius) "clusters," and that these clusters seem to be exclusively Omori-type or drip-type with no evidence for traditional swarm-type activity (see the Catalog section for these distinctions). Figure 6 highlights the similar time spans and lack of temporal correlation of both Omori-type and drip-type clusters, and the extended swarm time series of the Gnowangerup sequence (Fig. 8) shows how drip-type clustering activity can suddenly transition to Omori-type following large events. Other areas of well-known activity (e.g., Wattoning, Quairaiding, Wyalkatchem, Gnowangerup, Beacon, and locations shown in Figs. 2 and 3) show a similar pattern of drip-type activity suddenly experiencing a large earthquake and readopting traditional power-law aftershock characteristics. Other drip-type clusters exist in areas of well-known historic seismicity (e.g., 1968 M_w 6.6 Meckering) but have not recorded significant earthquakes for decades.

We concede that drip-type clusters could be interpreted as long-tail aftershock activity (e.g., Fig. 10) associated with historical and prehistorical earthquake activity (e.g., Stein and Liu, 2009; Toda and Stein, 2018), but still distinguish them in two ways. First, the assumption is that they have reached some form of steady-state background activity with random or even periodic time correlation at the scale of their duration (e.g., Fig. 6), and second, we can label this type of clustering without the assumption of a parent mainshock, as well as leave open the possibility that these clusters could be occurring independently of past seismicity altogether. In a sense, the argument is semantic because their fundamental behavior is the same: both long-tail, steady-state aftershocks and drip-type clustering are presumed to be spatially controlled by relatively weak, geologically heterogeneous, or otherwise highly fractured crust (e.g., Mogi, 1963), and both have the same implications for future hazard potential. Drip-type clustering, of course, has its future hazard potential implied rather than from direct or inferred measurement from past recorded earthquakes or geologically observed fault offsets. The infrequency and low magnitude of the events defining these clusters imply that the current earthquake monitoring infrastructure may be insufficient in southwest Australia and possibly in other global areas of elevated intraplate seismicity.

These drip-type earthquake sequences pose challenges for probabilistic seismic hazard analyses, for which modelers commonly decluster an earthquake catalog of "dependent" events so that it behaves according to the Poisson process; that is, mainshocks occur on a space- and time-independent basis over regional areas with similar seismotectonic characteristics (e.g., Gardner and Knopoff, 1974). Although earthquake clustering is a common occurrence, seismic-hazard modelers may need to rethink classical catalog declustering approaches to allow for hazard contributions from these potentially long-lived earthquake sequences (e.g., Allen *et al.*, 2023).

The three significant Omori-type clusters observed since the influx of instrumentation accompanying the SWAN experiment in 2020 (e.g., Arthur River, Gnowangerup, and Wyalkatchem) all exhibit typical mainshock–aftershock behavior with expected power-law aftershock decay rates. In all three

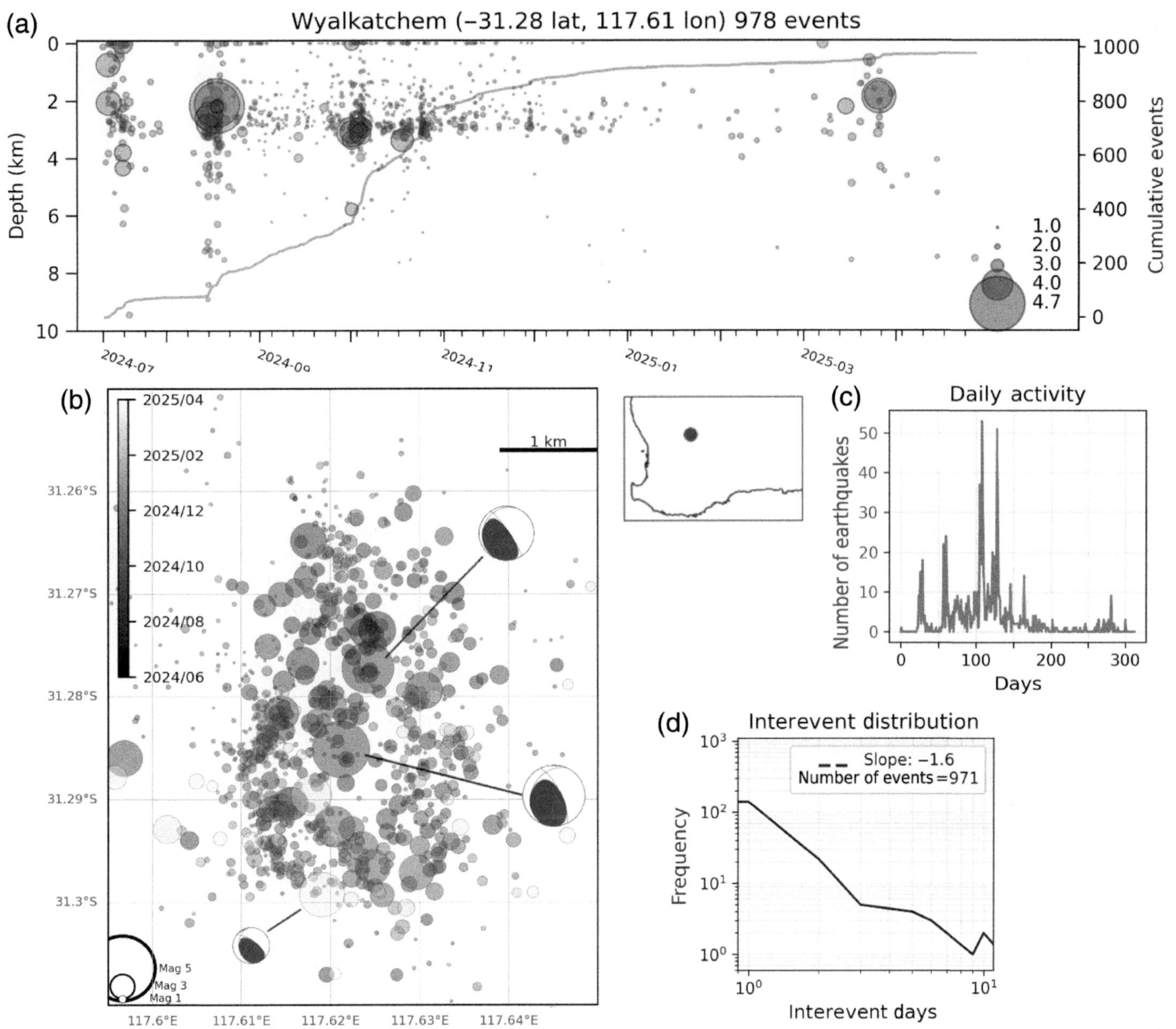

Figure 9. Wyalkatchem sequence (2024, −31.28° latitude 117.61° longitude). (a) Time series versus depth, (b) map view with CMT focal mechanisms and the inset between panels (b) and (c) shows the cluster location within southwest Australia, (c) number of earthquakes per day, and interevent frequency distribution. (d) The p value of the interevent distribution is fit between 0 and 10 days. The closest stations are outside this map but shown in Figure 1 as 3B Wyalkatchem. The color version of this figure is available only in the electronic edition.

clusters, a clear fault plane or event trend could not be observed, with each having a tightly clustered (<1 km) but random event distribution. The lack of a clear fault plane, if not a symptom of poor event hypocenter resolution, may further indicate that the rock mass in these regions is significantly damaged and/or heterogeneous, perhaps having previously experienced significant and persistent seismicity in the past. The occurrence of "air quakes" with negative depth in our catalog at some of these sequences is indicative of a poorly fitting velocity model, which may explain the lack of an observed fault plane; however, the double-differencing process should have helped to alleviate this. Ultimately, an updated velocity model capable of properly fitting nonzero station elevations at a finer resolution than our 3 km^3 model may be needed, along with additional manual picks and review. Both the Gnowangerup and Wyalkatchem clusters (Figs. 8 and 9) also showed ambient drip-type behavior preceding their recent mainshocks.

Notably, this catalog did not record any statistically significant activity between 2000 and 2022, preceding the Arthur River aftershock sequence, which, in combination with Geoscience Australia's historic catalog, might imply that the M_{La} 4.8 earthquake there was the first of its size in that location in modern history. Interestingly, these three earthquake sequences also all feature lower-magnitude precursory earthquakes 2–8 months before the mainshock. The duration of these sequences is each

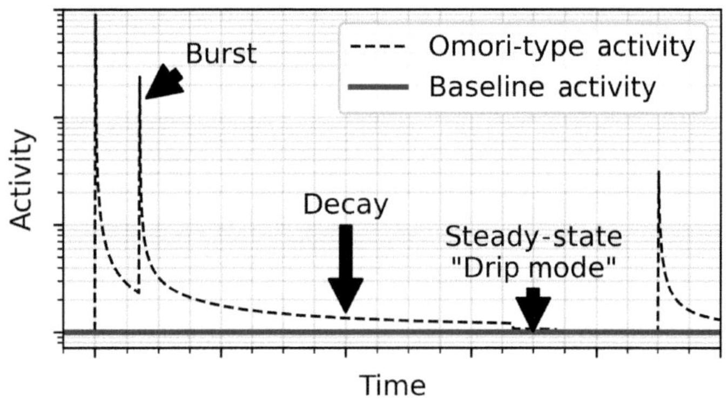

Figure 10. Illustration showing the spectrum of Omori-type earthquake activity. "Drip-type" is assumed when aftershock decay theoretically loses observable time correlation and persists as a temporal background activity. The color version of this figure is available only in the electronic edition.

over a year and consists of 2–10 individual mainshock–aftershock subsequences.

Conclusions

We present a new ML-based seismic catalog spanning January 2000 to May 2025 for the southwest region of Australia based on a customized 50 Hz version of EQTransformer (Mousavi *et al.*, 2020, 2019). Reinforced by new data from the SWAN and WA Array experiments, around 29,000 events were found, with 90% existing within numerically defined spatially correlated clusters. The 12,500 of these events were flagged as probable anthropogenic mining blasts based on a combination of hypocenter locations, time of day, and, in many instances, manual review. Statistically, nil earthquakes were located in the Perth basin or near the Darling fault and relatively few in the Albany–Fraser orogen, with the bulk existing within the Archean Yilgarn craton.

We also show that in addition to traditional Omori-type mainshock–aftershock sequences, long-running, low-magnitude clusters with no clear interevent time correlation are prevalent in the Yilgarn craton. This atemporality makes them distinct from swarm-type clusters and thus proposes the term "drip-type" to characterize them. Drip-type behavior may imply the location of significant past and possibly future seismicity, and we indeed observe instances where drip-type behavior precedes significant mainshocks and Omori-type behavior by several years or more (e.g., Wyalkatchem 2024, Fig. 9).

Three recent Omori-type earthquake sequences were also reviewed: Arthur River (2022), Gnowangerup (2023), and Wyalkatchem (2024). These sequences are primarily comprised of successive shock–aftershock subsequences, each with Omori-like power-law event decays. All three sequences began with smaller foreshocks several months before their mainshock, and both Gnowangerup and Wyalkatchem showed drip-type behavior beforehand.

Data and Resources

In addition to the SWAN (2P, Miller *et al.*, 2020) and phases 1 and 2 of the WA Array (WG, Geologic Survey of Western Australia, 2022) networks, this catalog used available seismic data from temporary networks 7G (Kennett, 2000), 6C (Josip Stipčević *et al.*, 2015), 5C (Murdie *et al.*, 2017), and OA (Gorbatov *et al.*, 2024). In addition, data from the permanent networks S1 (Salmon *et al.*, 2011), AU (Geoscience Australia, 2021), M8 (Pickle *et al.*, 2024), and IU (Albuquerque Seismological Laboratory/USGS, 1988) were used. Data power spectral density and availability plots for all stations available at AusPass can be reviewed via the map at http://auspass.edu.au. Seismic data from post-event rapid response kits, including Burakin (Leonard, 2002), Beacon (Dent, 2009), Kalgoorlie (Bathgate *et al.*, 2010), Norseman (Geoscience Australia), Lake Muir (Clark *et al.*, 2020; Geoscience Australia), and Wyalkatchem (3B, Glanville, 2024), were also used, though the older data were often incomplete and still largely unavailable to the public. Except for some older (<2019) aftershock response data, all seismic data are currently available via the International Federation of Digital Seismograph Networks (FDSN) from the AusPass and/or EarthScope data centers, or at the Geoscience Australia website. The catalog data are available at https:/auspass.edu.au/research/catalogs.html as QuakeML, text, and CSV files. The ObsPy, SeisComP, and Matplotlib packages were instrumental to this work, and the authors thank the contributors to those projects. The Geoscience Australia's national catalog is available at http://earthquakes.ga.gov.au. All websites were last accessed in December 2025. The supplemental material includes the full description of their earthquake location strategy as well as two figures detailing machine learning (ML) phase pick statistics and catalog quality statistics. It also includes a figure showing the map coverage of permanent seismic stations in 2012 and 2025, as well as the source data and cluster locations for the items in Figure 6.

Declaration of Competing Interests

The authors acknowledge that there are no conflicts of interest recorded.

Acknowledgments

This work is supported by the Australian Research Council (Grant Number LP180101118), the Australian National Research Facility for Earth Sounding (ANSIR) enabled by AuScope and the Australian Government via the National Collaborative Research Infrastructure Strategy (NCRIS), and the government of Western Australia. The authors thank their editor and two anonymous reviewers whose suggestions greatly improved this article.

References

Albuquerque Seismological Laboratory/USGS (1988). Global Seismograph Network (GSN - IRIS/USGS), *International Federation of Digital Seismograph Networks*, doi: 10.7914/SN/IU.

Allen, T. I., J. D. Griffin, D. J. Clark, P. R. Cummins, H. Ghasemi, and R. Ebrahimi (2023). The 2023 National Seismic Hazard Assessment for Australia: Model overview, *Geosci. Australia Record 2023/53*, 152 pp., doi: 10.26186/148969.

Bathgate, J., H. Glanville, and C. Collins (2010). The Kalgoorlie earthquake of 20 April 2010 and its aftershock sequence, *Australian Earthquake Engineering Society 2010 Conference*, Perth, Western Australia, 26–28 November.

Becker, J. J., D. T. Sandwell, W. H. F. Smith, J. Braud, B. Binder, J. L. Depner, D. Fabre, J. Factor, S. Ingalls, H. S. Kim, *et al.* (2009). Global bathymetry and elevation data at 30 arc seconds resolution: Srtm30 PLUS, *Mar. Geod.* **32,** no. 4, 355–371.

Bodorkos, S., and D. J. Clark (2004). Evolution of a crustal-scale transpressive shear zone in the Albany–Fraser Orogen, SW Australia: 2. Tectonic history of the coramup gneiss and a kinematic framework for mesoproterozoic collision of the West Australian and Mawson Cratons, *J. Metamorph. Geol.* **22,** no. 8, 713–731.

Braun, J., D. R. Burbidge, F. N. Gesto, M. Sandiford, A. J. W. Gleadow, B. P. Kohn, and P. R. Cummins (2009). Constraints on the current rate of deformation and surface uplift of the Australian Continent from a new seismic database and low-t thermochronological data, *Aust. J. Earth Sci.* **56,** no. 2, 99–110.

Cassidy, K. F., D. C. Champion, B. Krapez, M. E. Barley, S. J. A. Brown, R. S. Blewett, P. B. G. Groenewald, I. M. Tyler, *et al.* (2006). A revised geological framework for the Yilgarn Craton, Western Australia, *Geol. Surv. Western Australia Record* Vol. 8, 15 pp.

Clark, D., and M. Leonard (2003). Principal stress orientations from multiple focal-plane solutions: New insight into the Australian intraplate, in *Evolution and Dynamics of the Australian Plate,* Vol. 372, 91 pp., doi: 10.1130/SPE372.

Clark, D., A. McPherson, and R. Van Dissen (2012). Long-term behaviour of Australian stable continental region (SCR) faults, *Tectonophysics* **566-567,** 1–30, doi: 10.1016/j.tecto.2012.07.004.

Clark, D. J., S. Brennand, G. Brenn, M. C. Garthwaite, J. Dimech, T. I. Allen, and S. Standen (2020). Surface deformation relating to the 2018 Lake Muir earthquake sequence, southwest Western Australia: New insight into stable continental region earthquakes, *Solid Earth* **11,** 691–717, doi: 10.5194/se-11-691-2020.

Czarnota, K., D. C. Champion, B. Goscombe, R. S. Blewett, K. F. Cassidy, P. A. Henson, and P. B. Groenewald (2010). Geodynamics of the eastern Yilgarn Craton, *Precambrian Res.* **183,** no. 2, 175–202.

de Gromard, R. Q., T. J. Ivanic, and I. Zibra (2021). Pre-Mesozoic interpreted bedrock geology of the southwest Yilgarn, 2021, *Accelerated Geoscience Program Extended Abstracts compiled by Geological Survey of Western Australia,* Vol. 2021, Geological Survey of Western Australia Record, 122–144.

Dent, V. F. (2009). The Beacon, WA earthquake swarm commencing January 2009, *Australian Earthquake Engineering Society 2009 Conference,* Newcastle, New South Wales, 11–13 December.

Dent, V. F. (2016). A preliminary map of cluster locations in Southwest Western Australia, 1990–2016, *Joint Conference of the Australian Earthquake Engineering Society and the Asian Seismological Commission,* 25–27 November.

Dent, V. F., and D. N. Love (2018a). An earthquake cluster east of Wyalkatchem, Western Australia, in Late 2017, *Proc. AEES 2017 Conference,* Canberra, Australia.

Dent, V. F., and D. N. Love (2018b). A review of seismicity in the Norseman region of Western Australia, 1970–2018, *Australian Earthquake Engineering Society 2018 Conference,* Perth, Western Australia, 16–18 November.

Featherstone, W. E., N. T. Penna, M. Leonard, D. Clark, J. Dawson, M. C. Dentith, D. Darby, and R. McCarthy (2004). GPS-geodetic deformation monitoring of the south-west seismic zone of Western Australia: Review, description of methodology and results from Epoch-One, *J. R. Soc. Western Australia* **87,** no. 1, 1–9.

Fletcher, I. R., and W. G. Libby (1993). Further isotopic evidence for the existence of two distinct terranes in the southern Pinjarra Orogen, Western Australia, *Geol. Surv. Western Australia Rept. 37,* 81–83.

Gardner, J. K., and L. Knopoff (1974). Is the sequence of earthquakes in southern California, with aftershocks removed, Poissonian? *Bull. Seismol. Soc. Am.* **64,** 1363–1367, doi: 10.1785/BSSA0640051363.

Gaull, B. A., and P. J. Gregson (1991). A new local magnitude scale for Western Australian earthquakes, *Aust. J. Earth. Sci.* **38,** 251–260, doi: 10.1080/08120099108727970.

Gauntlett, M., C. M. Eakin, N. Bishoyi, P. Zhang, J. P. O'Donnell, R. Murdie, M. S. Miller, R. Pickle, and R. Ebrahimi (2025). Seismic anisotropy analysis across Southwestern Australia reveals ENE-trending lithospheric architecture linked to Archean Yilgarn Craton formation, *Geochem. Geophys. Geosys.* doi: 10.1029/2025GC012589.

Geological Survey of Western Australia (2022). WA Array, *International Federation of Digital Seismograph Networks,* doi: 10.7914/XAGC-SE62.

Geoscience Australia (2021). Australian National Seismograph Network Data Collection, Commonwealth of Australia (Geoscience Australia), doi: 10.26186/144675.

Glanville, H. (2024). Wyalkatchem temporary network, *International Federation of Digital Seismograph Networks,* doi: 10.7914/XY0Z-BX66.

Gorbatov, A., B. Hejrani, J. Holzschuh, J. Zhao, R. Hassan, D. Cathro, K. Czarnota, J. Kuoni, M. Sweeney, J. Glowacki, *et al.* (2024). AusArray continent-scale deployment, doi: 10.26186/149640.

Gordon, F. R., and J. D. Lewis (1980). The Meckering and Calingiri Earthquakes, October 1968 and March 1970, Vol. 126, Geol. Surv. West. Australia Bull.

Hejrani, B., and H. Tkalčić (2020). Resolvability of the centroid-moment-tensors for shallow seismic sources and improvements from modeling high-frequency waveforms, *J. Geophys. Res.* **125,** no. 7, e2020JB019643, doi: 10.1029/2020JB019643.

Helmholtz-Centre Potsdam - GFZ German Research Centre for Geosciences and gempa GmbH (2008). The SeisComP seismological software package, *GFZ Data Services,* doi: 10.5880/GFZ.2.4.2020.003.

Janssen, D., A. Collins, and I. Fitzsimons (2003). Structure and tectonics of the Leeuwin complex and darling fault zone Southern Pinjarra Orogen Western Australia-a field guide, *Western Australia Geological Survey, Record: 2003/15.*

Josip Stipčević, C., Sippl, H. Tkalčić, B. Kennett, C. Spaggiari, and K. Gessner (2015). West Australian spiral array, *International Federation of Digital Seismograph Networks,* doi: 10.7914/SN/6C_2015.

Kennett, B. (2000). West Australian cratons, *International Federation of Digital Seismograph Networks,* doi: 10.7914/SN/7G_2000.

Kennett, B. L. N., A. Gorbatov, H. Yuan, S. Agrawal, R. Murdie, M. P. Doublier, C. M. Eakin, M. S. Miller, L. Zhao, K. Czarnota, *et al.* (2023). Refining the Moho across the Australian Continent, *Geophys. J. Int.* **233,** no. 3, 1863–1877.

Kikuchi, M., and H. Kanamori (1991). Inversion of complex body waves—III, *Bull. Seismol. Soc. Am.* **81,** no. 6, 2335–2350.

Leonard, M. (2002). The Burakin WA earthquake sequence Sept 2000 - June 2002, *Australian Earthquake Engineering Society 2002 Conference*, Adelaide, South Australia, 17–18 October.

Leonard, M., and D. Clark (2011). A record of stable continental region earthquakes from Western Australia spanning the late Pleistocene: Insights for contemporary seismicity, *Earth Planet. Sci. Lett.* **309,** nos. 3/4, 207–212.

Lin, X., H. Yuan, M. C. Dentith, R. Murdie, K. Gessner, and A. Nayak (2021). Improved full waveform moment tensor inversion of cratonic intraplate earthquakes in southwest Australia, *Geophys. J. Int.* **227,** no. 1, 123–145.

Lomax, A., and A. Curtis (2001). Fast, probabilistic earthquake location in 3d models using oct-tree importance sampling, *Geophys. Res. Abstr.* **3,** 955.

Lomax, A., A. Michelini, and A. Curtis (2014). Earthquake location, direct, global-search methods, in *Encyclopedia of Complexity and Systems Science*, Springer, New York, New York, 1–33.

Lomax, A., J. Virieux, P. Volant, and C. Berge-Thierry (2000). Probabilistic earthquake location in 3D and layered models: Introduction of a Metropolis–Gibbs method and comparison with linear locations, in *Advances in Seismic Event Location*, Springer Netherlands, Dordrecht, The Netherlands, 101–134.

Martin, D., R. Murdie, D. Kelsey, R. Quentin de Gromard, C. Thomas, H. Cutten, Y. Zhan, Y. Lu, P. Haines, and J. Brett (2022). Compilation and geological implications of the major crustal boundaries map and 3D model of Western Australia, *Geol. Surv. Western Australia Record 2022(7)*, 49 pp.

Michelini, A., S. Cianetti, S. Gaviano, C. Giunchi, D. Jozinović, and V. Lauciani (2021). INSTANCE–the Italian seismic dataset for machine learning, *Earth Syst. Sci. Data* **13,** no. 12, 5509–5544.

Miller, M., T. Allen, R. Murdie, K. Gessner, H. Yuan, B. Kennett, and R. Pickle (2020). South West Australia Network, *International Federation of Digital Seismograph Networks*, doi: 10.7914/SN/2P_2020.

Miller, M. S., R. Pickle, R. Murdie, H. Yuan, T. I. Allen, K. Gessner, B. L. N. Kennett, and J. Whitney (2023). Southwest Australia Seismic Network (SWAN): Recording earthquakes in Australia's most active seismic zone, *Seismol. Res. Lett.* doi: 10.1785/0220220323.

Mogi, K. (1963). Some discussions on aftershocks, foreshocks and earthquake swarms-the fracture of a semi finite body caused by an inner stress origin and its relation to the earthquake phenomena, *Bull. Earthq. Res. Inst.* **41,** 615–658.

Mooney, W. D., J. Ritsema, and Y. K. Hwang (2012). Crustal seismicity and the earthquake catalog maximum moment magnitude (Mcmax) in stable continental regions (SCRs): Correlation with the seismic velocity of the lithosphere, *Earth Planet. Sci. Lett.* **357,** 78–83.

Mousavi, S. M., W. L. Ellsworth, W. Zhu, L. Y. Chuang, and G. C. Beroza (2020). Earthquake transformer—An attentive deep-learning model for simultaneous earthquake detection and phase picking, *Nat. Commun.* **11,** no. 1, 1–12.

Mousavi, S. M., Y. Sheng, W. Zhu, and G. C. Beroza (2019). STanford EArthquake Dataset (STEAD): A global data set of seismic signals for AI, *IEEE Access* **7,** 179,464–179,476.

Murdie, R., R. Pickle, H. Yuan, D. Love, V. Dent, M. S. Miller, and J. Whitney (2022). Observations from the 2022 Arthur River, Western Australia, earthquake swarm, *Australian Earthquake Engineering Society 2022 Conference*, Mount Macedon, Victoria, 24–25 November.

Murdie, R., H. Yuan, and M. Dentith (2017). Perth basin array, *International Federation of Digital Seismograph Networks*, doi: 10.7914/NX28-A367.

Murdie, R. E., T. J. Ivanic, R. Quentin de Gromard, C. M. Thomas, K. Gessner, V. Markwitz, and P. W. Haines (2025). Tectonic setting of southwest Western Australia, in WA array phase 1 – Southwest Western Australia, R. E. Murdie (Editor), *Geol. Surv. Western Australia Rept. 256*, 12–22.

Myers, J. S. (1990). Precambrian tectonic evolution of part of Gondwana, southwestern Australia, *Geology* **18,** no. 6, 537–540.

Myers, J. S. (1995). The generation and assembly of an archaean supercontinent: Evidence from the Yilgarn Craton, Western Australia, *Spec. Publ. Geol. Soc. Lond.* **95,** 143–154.

Pickle, R., M. Miller, R. Murdie, J. P. O'Donnell, A. Gorbatov, and M. Salmon (2024). Australian semi-permanent support network, *International Federation of Digital Seismograph Networks*, doi: 10.7914/6E8T-6G37.

Rajabi, M., O. Heidbach, M. Tingay, and K. Reiter (2017). Prediction of the present-day stress field in the Australian continental crust using 3D geomechanical–numerical models, *Aust. J. Earth Sci.* **64,** no. 4, 435–454.

Rajabi, M., M. Tingay, O. Heidbach, R. Hillis, and S. Reynolds (2017). The present-day stress field of Australia, *Earth Sci. Rev.* **168,** 165–189, doi: 10.1016/j.earscirev.2017.04.003.

Reading, A. M., B. L. N. Kennett, and M. C. Dentith (2003). Seismic structure of the Yilgarn Craton, Western Australia, *Aust. J. Earth Sci.* **50,** no. 3, 427–438.

Reynolds, S. D., and R. R. Hillis (2000). The in situ stress field of the Perth basin, Australia, *Geophys. Res. Lett.* **27,** no. 20, 3421–3424.

Reynolds, S. D., D. D. Coblentz, and R. R. Hillis (2002). Tectonic forces controlling the regional intraplate stress field in continental Australia: Results from new finite element modeling, *J. Geophys. Res.* **107,** no. B7, ETG-1.

Richter, C. F. (1935). An instrumental earthquake magnitude scale, *Bull. Seismol. Soc. Am.* **25,** no. 1, 1–32.

Salmon, M., N. Balfour, M. Sambridge, S. Mousavi, and R. Pickle (2011). Australian Seismometers in Schools, *AusPass*, doi: 10.7914/SN/S1.

Salmon, M., B. L. N. Kennett, and E. Saygin (2013). Australian Seismological Reference Model (AuSREM): Crustal component, *Geophys. J. Int.* **192,** no. 1, 190–206.

Sandiford, M., and D. L. Egholm (2008). Enhanced intraplate seismicity along continental margins: Some causes and consequences, *Tectonophysics* **457,** nos. 3/4, 197–208.

Sandwell, D. T., R. D. Müller, W. H. F. Smith, E. Garcia, and R. Francis (2014). New global marine gravity model from CryoSat-2 and Jason-1 reveals buried tectonic structure, *Science* **346,** no. 6205, 65–67, doi: 10.1126/science.1258213.

Sandwell, D. T., and W. H. F. Smith (2009). Global marine gravity from Retracked Geosat and ERS-1 altimetry: Ridge segmentation versus spreading rate, *J. Geophys. Res.* **114,** no. B1, doi: 10.1029/2008JB006008.

Scarabello, L., and T. Diehl (2021). Swiss-seismological-service/SCRTDD, *Zenodo*, doi: 10.5281/zenodo.5337361.

Schulte, S. M., and W. D. Mooney (2005). An updated global earthquake catalogue for stable continental regions: Reassessing the correlation with ancient rifts, *Geophys. J. Int.* **161,** no. 3, 707–721.

Smith, W. H. F., and D. T. Sandwell (1997). Global sea floor topography from satellite altimetry and ship depth soundings, *Science* **277,** no. 5334, 1956–1962.

Smithies, R. H., K. Gessner, Y. Lu, C. L. Kirkland, T. Ivanic, J. R. Lowrey, D. C. Champion, J. Sapkota, Q. Masurel, N. Thébaud, *et al.* (2024). Geochemical mapping of lithospheric architecture disproves Archean terrane accretion in the Yilgarn craton, *Geology* **52,** no. 2, 141–146, doi: 10.1130/G51707.1.

Spaggiari, C. V., C. L. Kirkland, R. H. Smithies, S. A. Occhipinti, and M. T. D. Wingate (2014). Geological framework of the Albany–Fraser Orogen, in *Albany–Fraser Orogen Seismic and Magnetotelluric (MT) Workshop 2014: Extended Abstracts*, C. V. Spaggiari and I. M. Tyler (Editors), Geological Survey of Western Australia Record, Vol. 6, 12–27.

Spaggiari, C. V., R. H. Smithies, C. L. Kirkland, M. T. Wingate, R. N. England, and Y. J. Lu (2018). Buried but preserved: The proterozoic Arubiddy Ophiolite, Madura province, western Australia, *Precambrian Res.* **317,** 137–158.

Standen, S., M. Dentith, and D. Clark (2021). A geophysical investigation of the 2018 Lake Muir earthquake sequence: Reactivated Precambrian structures controlling modern seismicity, *Aust. J. Earth Sci.* **68,** no. 5, 717–730.

Stark, J. C., X.-C. Wang, S. W. Denyszyn, Z.-X. Li, B. Rasmussen, J.-W. Zi, S. Sheppard, and Y. Liu (2019). Newly identified 1.89 Ga mafic dyke swarm in the Archean Yilgarn Craton, Western Australia suggests a connection with India, *Precambrian Res.* **329,** 156–169.

Stark, J. C., S. A. Wilde, U. Söderlund, Z.-X. Li, B. Rasmussen, and J.-W. Zi (2018). First Evidence of Archean mafic dykes at 2.62 Ga in the Yilgarn Craton, Western Australia: Links to cratonisation and the Zimbabwe Craton, *Precambrian Res.* **317,** 1–13.

Stein, S., and M. Liu (2009). Long aftershock sequences within continents and implications for earthquake hazard assessment, *Nature* **462,** no. 7269, 87–89.

Thomas, C. M. (2018) Regional seismic interpretation and structure of the southern Perth Basin, *Geol. Surv. Western Australia Rept. 184,* 52 pp.

Toda, S., and R. S. Stein (2018). Why aftershock duration matters for probabilistic seismic hazard assessment, *Bull. Seismol. Soc. Am.* **108,** no. 3A, 1414–1426.

Vogfjörd, K. S., and C. A. Langston (1987). The Meckering earthquake of 14 October 1968: A Possible downward propagating rupture, *Bull. Seismol. Soc. Am.* **77,** no. 5, 1558–1578.

Wilde, S. A., M. F. Middleton, and B. J. Evans (1996). Terrane accretion in the southwestern Yilgarn Craton: Evidence from a deep seismic crustal profile, *Precambrian Res.* **78,** nos. 1/3, 179–196.

Wingate, M. T. D. (2007). Proterozoic mafic dykes in the Yilgarn Craton, *Geosci. Australia Record* **14,** 80–83.

Zaliapin, I., and Y. Ben-Zion (2016). A global classification and characterization of earthquake clusters, *Geophys. J. Int.* **207,** no. 1, 608–634.

Zhang, M., W. L. Ellsworth, and G. C. Beroza (2019). Rapid earthquake association and location, *Seismol. Res. Lett.* **90,** no. 6, 2276–2284.

Zhang, P., M. S. Miller, F. Magrini, R. Pickle, H. Y. Yuan, R. Murdie, K. Gessner, and R. Quentin de Gromard (2025) Insights into the Archean to Phanerozoic evolution of southwest Australia from seismic ambient noise tomography, *J. Geophys. Res.* doi: 10.1029/2025JB031274.

Zhang, Q., and P. M. Shearer (2016). A new method to identify earthquake swarms applied to seismicity near the San Jacinto Fault, California, *Geophys. J. Int.* **205,** no. 2, 995–1005, doi: 10.1093/gji/ggw073.

Manuscript received 10 September 2025
Published online 15 January 2026

Rapid Seismicity Monitoring After the March 2023 M_s 4.5 Earthquake Around the Xinfengjiang Reservoir, China

Linyang Xin[1], Ruijia Wang[*1,2,3], Lipeng He[4], Zhen Guo[4], Lichun Yang[1], Zhengtao He[1], and Dixiang Zuo[1]

Abstract

Reservoirs that have experienced induced earthquakes provide ideal inland settings to understand earthquake reactions to fluid loading and migration. The Xinfengjiang Reservoir, one of only four reservoirs documented with $M_L > 6.0$ events after impoundment in the 1960s, has proven to be a critical site for studying reservoir-induced seismicity. On 8 March 2023, an M_s 4.5 earthquake struck the Wudong area in the northwestern sector of the Xinfengjiang Reservoir, a corner previously overlooked because of the rarity of felt-level events. In response, we immediately deployed 29 three-component nodal seismometers to monitor the subsequent seismic sequence following this M_s 4.5 mainshock. Adopting a state-of-the-art machine learning–based seismic detection and location workflow, we constructed a high-precision catalog of 2081 events ($-0.8 < M_L < 2.8$, $M_c = -0.4$) within 21 days. All events are located with hypocenter uncertainties of < 90 m, forming into two earthquake clusters—the Wudong and the Xichang seismic clusters—separated by an ~3 km gap. The Wudong cluster clearly delineated a northwest–southeast-oriented fault (striking at 155° and dipping at 87°) that hosted ~52.5% of our detections. As for the Xichang cluster, evidence of fluid migration from the reservoir bottom to ~10 km depth is supported by the spatiotemporal seismicity pattern and potential non-double-couple components. Using the recently deployed nodal array, our study provides a comprehensive source analysis of the recent M_s 4.5 cluster, promoting further understanding of seismogenic processes beneath the Xinfengjiang Reservoir.

Cite this article as Xin, L., R. Wang, L. He, Z. Guo, L. Yang, Z. He, and D. Zuo (2026). Rapid Seismicity Monitoring After the March 2023 M_s 4.5 Earthquake Around the Xinfengjiang Reservoir, China, *Seismol. Res. Lett.* **97**, 822–831, doi: 10.1785/0220250262.

Supplemental Material

Introduction

Reservoirs are widely distributed across mainland China and play a crucial role in water resource management, flood control, and hydropower production. According to the China Reservoir Dataset (Song *et al.*, 2022), >97,000 reservoirs are currently identified nationwide, with a total maximum inundation area exceeding 50,000 km^2 and a total storage capacity approaching 980 km^3 (Song *et al.*, 2022). The broad geographic spread and complexity of reservoir systems in China have elevated reservoir-triggered seismicity as a key issue for both seismic hazard assessment and the safe planning of water resource infrastructure, demanding focused research and policy attention. Over the past decades, China has witnessed many documented cases of reservoir-triggered seismicity, ranging from low-magnitude microseismic swarms to damaging moderate earthquakes, such as the 1962 M_L 6.1 Xinfengjiang earthquake (Shen *et al.*, 1974; Miao-Yueh *et al.*, 1976; Ding *et al.*, 1983) in the northwest of Heyuan City, Guangdong Province. As one of the only four reservoirs worldwide associated with a reservoir-induced earthquake exceeding M_L 6 (Talwani, 1997; Gupta, 2002; He *et al.*, 2018), Xinfengjiang Reservoir has attracted sustained attention for its seismic triggering environment and risk control (Feng, 1977; Guo *et al.*, 2004; Ye *et al.*, 2017; Zhang, Sun, *et al.*, 2024; He *et al.*, 2025).

Prior to the impoundment of the Xinfengjiang Reservoir, the region experienced limited seismicity with no historical record of damaging earthquakes (Shen *et al.*, 1974; He *et al.*, 2018; Huang *et al.*, 2024). Led by the 1962 M_L 6.1 earthquake,

1. Department of Earth and Space Sciences, Southern University of Science and Technology, Shenzhen, China, https://orcid.org/0000-0002-5779-5479 (LX); https://orcid.org/0000-0002-1757-5113 (RW); https://orcid.org/0000-0003-3736-402X (LY); https://orcid.org/0000-0002-7797-7405 (ZH); https://orcid.org/0000-0003-0863-2072 (DZ); 2. Shenzhen Key Laboratory of Deep Offshore Oil and Gas Exploration Technology, Southern University of Science and Technology, Shenzhen, China; 3. Guangdong Provincial Key Laboratory of Geophysical High-resolution Imaging Technology, Southern University of Science and Technology, Shenzhen, Guangdong, China; 4. Department of Ocean Science and Engineering, Southern University of Science and Technology, Shenzhen, China

*Corresponding author: wangrj@sustech.edu.cn

seismicity around the Xinfengjiang Reservoir remained active until recent years, with $>40 M_L \geq 4$ events documented (He *et al.*, 2018) and elevated regional seismic hazard. Before 2010, seismic activity was initially concentrated around the dam and Heyuan City in the southeastern part of the reservoir (Ding *et al.*, 1983; Wan and Yang, 2011; Guan *et al.*, 2025; He *et al.*, 2025). In 2012–2013, five $M_L > 4$ earthquakes were recorded in the Xichang area, the northwesternmost part of the reservoir, where no significant earthquakes had occurred for more than half a century (Ye *et al.*, 2013; Wang, Wu, and Huang, 2018; Zhang, Sun, *et al.*, 2024; He *et al.*, 2025). This abrupt shift suggests a northwestward migration of seismicity from the dam area (Dong *et al.*, 2022; Huang *et al.*, 2024). Notably, the frequency of large earthquakes in the northwest has surpassed that in the southeast over the past decade (Zhang *et al.*, 2025). Since 2019, although the dam area remained seismically active, the Wudong area, located in the central segment of the reservoir and previously considered seismically quiet, also began to show increasing seismic activity, with several earthquakes exceeding magnitudes of 3. This shift implies an expansion in the spatial extent of active seismic zones, potentially driven by fluid migration and stress accumulation beneath the Xinfengjiang Reservoir (Dong *et al.*, 2022; He *et al.*, 2025). On 8 March 2023, an M_s 4.5 earthquake struck the central part of the Xinfengjiang Reservoir, close to the Wudong area. Widely felt by local residents, this event marks the strongest earthquake recorded in the past decade around the whole reservoir (Jiang *et al.*, 2023; Zhang, Sun, *et al.*, 2024; He *et al.*, 2025; Huang *et al.*, 2025), renewing attention from both the public and experts about the risk of the reservoir-induced seismicity.

Most of the previous studies were conducted focusing on seismic active regions such as the southeast (Heyuan region, where the dam is located) and the northwest (Xichang region), detailing the fault structures (Shen *et al.*, 1974; Ding *et al.*, 1983; He *et al.*, 2018; Wang, Sun, *et al.*, 2018; Wang, Wu, and Huang, 2018), statistical behaviors of recent seismic activity (Wan and Yang, 2011; Ye *et al.*, 2013; Deng and He, 2016), focal mechanisms (Miao-Yueh *et al.*, 1976; Wei *et al.*, 1992; He *et al.*, 2018, 2025), and velocity structures (Yang *et al.*, 2013; Ye *et al.*, 2013, 2016, 2017; He *et al.*, 2018). In contrast, the Wudong area located in the center of the reservoir, where the M_s 4.5 event was reported, remains less explored because of limited seismic station coverage. Therefore, detailed fault structures and the potential fluid conduits or barriers beneath the dam remain unclear, urging further investigation since the occurrence of this M_s 4.5 event. Our team deployed a 29-station seismic array within 24 hr of the mainshock to capture the aftershocks and evaluate the origin of the emerging events.

In this study, we constructed a high-precision microearthquake catalog via a machine learning–based workflow. The results reveal two distinct seismic clusters. First, the cluster in the Wudong area (hereafter, the Wudong cluster) delineates an ~4-km-long northwest–southeast (NW-SE) fault, constrained by both fault-plane fitting and full moment tensor solutions. Second, the cluster in the Xichang area (hereafter, the Xichang cluster) suggests ongoing fluid migration, supported by the presence of potential non-double-couple (non-DC) components and a downward spatiotemporal migration pattern.

Geological Settings and Seismic Data

The Xinfengjiang Reservoir, situated within the active South China block, exhibits complex geological settings, with the main structure emplaced on an east–west (E-W)–trending Late Mesozoic granitic batholith (peraluminous calc-alkaline series). Tectonically, the surrounding region is characterized by multiphase fault systems developed from the Mesozoic to the Cenozoic, accompanied by subordinate folding, reflecting a prolonged history of crustal deformation (Shen *et al.*, 1974). Near our nodal array in the northern reservoir, two main fault systems are observed: the north-northwest (NNW)–trending Shijiao–Xinggang–Baitian fault system in the northeast, consisting of several segments (Ding *et al.*, 1983; Wei *et al.*, 1992), and the north-northeast (NNE)–trending Daping–Yanqian fault system (Cheng *et al.*, 2012; Ye *et al.*, 2013), which manifests as reverse faults near the surface (Fig. 1a). Besides, gravity and electromagnetic imaging have revealed both the Xichang Syncline and the Dakengnan fault near the northwestern edge of the reservoir, suggesting that these structures are likely associated with local seismic activity in the Xichang area (Wang, Wu, and Huang, 2018; Zhang, Sun, *et al.*, 2024).

Our seismic monitoring network involves 29 three-component short-period seismometers (SmartSolo IGU-16HR 3C) partially surrounding the northwest portion of the Xinfengjiang Reservoir (Fig. 1a). With an average spacing of ~1 km, these nodal stations were deployed within 24 hr after the M_s 4.5 mainshock and were recorded continuously for 21 days (i.e., 9–29 March 2023) at a sampling rate of 500 Hz. All stations were shallowly buried at depths of ~20 cm, and their elevations varied between 100 and 289 m, referenced to sea level.

Methodology

Earthquake detection, location, and magnitude calculation

We implemented a popular earthquake detection and location workflow (i.e., LOC-FLOW; Zhang, 2022) that has been successfully applied to many regional-scale detections of both tectonic and induced seismicity (e.g., Wang *et al.*, 2020; Zhang, Wang, *et al.*, 2022, Zhang, Chen, *et al.*, 2024; Yang *et al.*, 2025). The workflow integrates four principal modules and initiates with PhaseNet (Zhu and Beroza, 2019), a machine learning–based phase picker that identifies *P*- and *S*-wave arrivals from continuous waveforms. We applied PhaseNet using the original nodal array sampling rate (i.e., 500 Hz) without downsampling, a strategy previously shown to facilitate the phase detection at such local scales (Wang *et al.*, 2020). With a

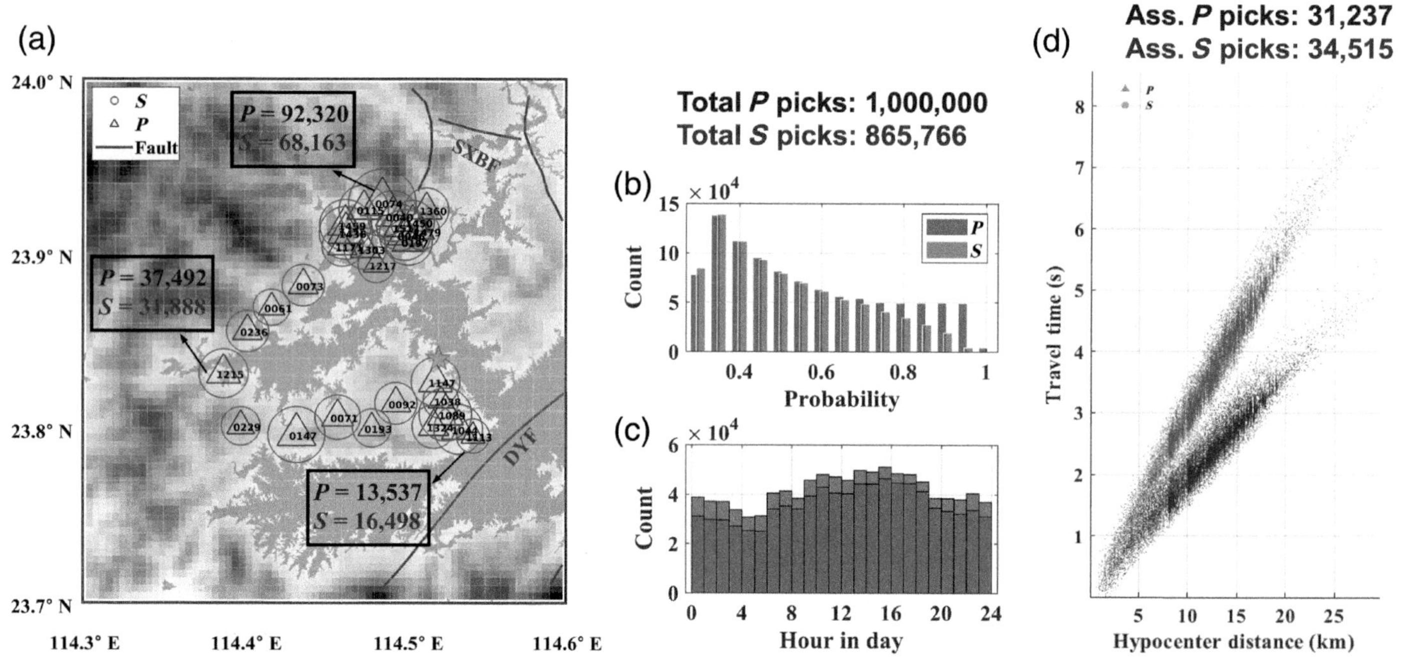

probability threshold of 0.3 (Zhang, Wang, *et al.*, 2022; Wang *et al.*, 2023), this step yields 1,000,000 *P*-phase arrivals and 865,766 *S*-phase arrivals with a relatively low diurnal pattern (Fig. 1b). Subsequent phase association across multiple stations is performed with REAL (Zhang *et al.*, 2019), a grid search–based method to associate and locate earthquakes by minimizing the travel-time residuals of *P* and *S* phases from a range of candidate hypocenter locations. We required a minimum of three *P*- and two *S*-phase picks to define a successful event association and optimized the grid dimensions, search ranges, and other temporal parameters (see Text S1, available in the supplemental material for this article, for details), to accommodate the 30 km × 30 km spatial extent and uneven azimuthal coverage of our nodal array. Details of our regional velocity model are shown in Text S2. Finally, we obtained high-resolution earthquake locations through the remaining two key steps: absolute location using VELEST (Kissling *et al.*, 1995) and relative relocation using hypoDD (Waldhauser and Ellsworth, 2000). The latter combines differential arrival times derived from both phase picks and waveform cross correlation (Zhang, Liu, *et al.*, 2022), enabling robust determination of event hypocenters. Considering that the Xinfengjiang Reservoir is also a popular region for tourism, we suspect the elevated *P*/*S* phase detections during daytime (Fig. 1c) result from local anthropogenic activities that create high-frequency signals, but such phases are not associated into events in the following steps. Therefore, our final catalog still hosts more events at night (when ambient noise levels are lower, Fig. S1b), similar to other local scale detections utilizing shallow-buried nodal arrays (e.g., Wang *et al.*, 2020).

Upon completing the four key LOC-FLOW steps, we addressed the final task of magnitude determination and calibration. After removing instrument responses, we estimated

Figure 1. (a) Overview of the study area and seismic monitoring: The yellow star marks the reported M_S 4.5 mainshock epicenter. The blue triangles (red circles) denote the locations of the 29 seismic stations with symbol sizes scaled by the total number of *P*(*S*)-phase picks with probabilities >0.3 from PhaseNet. The boxes note detailed phase numbers of the most/least and a medium-level station. The geologically identified faults are indicated by the green lines. (b) Total *P*- and *S*-wave phase picks and their probability distribution. (c) *P*/*S*-phase picks by hour (local time UTC + 8). (d) Travel time versus epicentral distance for associated phases (Ass.) after event association. DYF, Daping-Yanqian fault; SXBF, Shijiao-Xingang-Baitian fault. The color version of this figure is available only in the electronic edition.

the event magnitudes based on their peak amplitudes following an empirical relationship (Bullen and Bolt, 1985; Shearer, 2009):

$$M_L = \log_{10}(A) + 2.56 \log_{10}\left(\frac{\text{dist}}{100}\right) + C, \quad (1)$$

in which an effective three-component amplitude *A* is defined as the square root of the summed waveform energy from all three components within a specified event window (i.e., 0.5 s before the *P* arrival and 3 s after *S* arrival) and dist is the epicentral distance in kilometers, following Wang *et al.* (2020) and Zhang, Chen, *et al.*, 2024. The magnitudes were then calibrated using a constant offset *C* of 0.01, defined as the average magnitude difference of the seven largest events between our initial estimates and the moment magnitudes (M_w) derived from NaNDC (Yang and Wang, 2025). Together with the calibrated magnitudes, the constructed catalog was passed for a few statistical analyses (Text S4), including the calculation of *b* values of Gutenberg–Richter (G-R) relationship

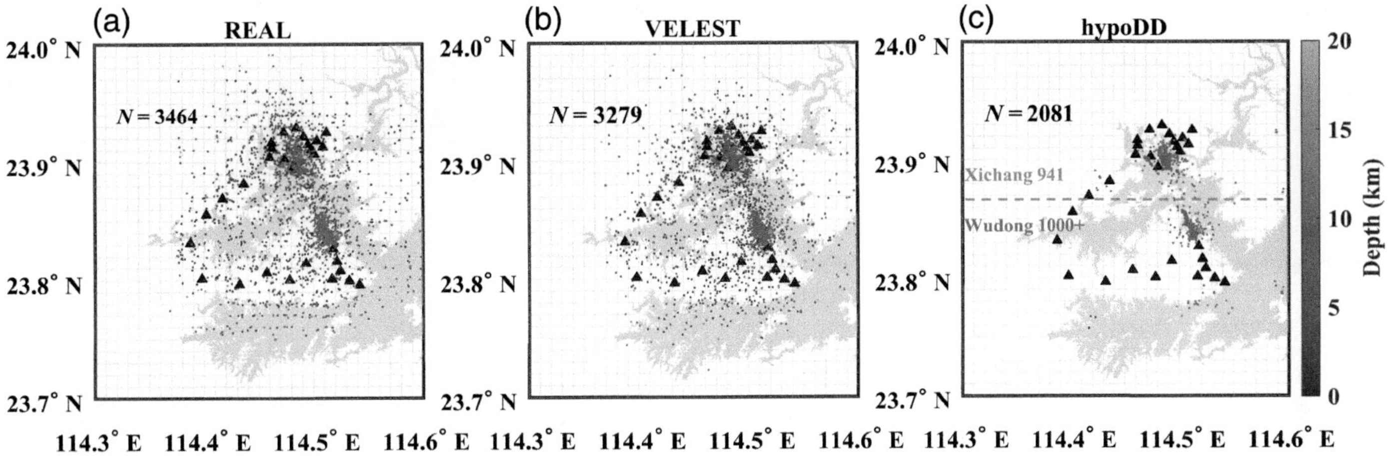

(Gutenberg and Richter, 1944) calculated via the maximum-likelihood approach (Bender, 1983), coefficient of variation (Cv, Kagan and Jackson, 1991; Cochran *et al.*, 2018), and analysis at the nearest-neighbor domain (NND, Zaliapin and Ben-Zion, 2013, 2016).

Figure 2. Spatial distribution of seismicity (dots color coded by depth) obtained via each major step of LOC-FLOW: (a) REAL phase association, (b) VELEST absolute relocation, and (c) hypoDD relative relocation. The yellow star denotes the M_S 4.5 mainshock location. Panel (c) delineates two seismic clusters (Xichang in the northwest part of Xinfengjiang Reservoir and Wudong in the southeast) bounded by orange-dashed contours. The colored numbers (pink and blue) denote the number of events within the two clusters. The color version of this figure is available only in the electronic edition.

Full moment tensors inversion for $M_L > 1$ events

To estimate the magnitude calibration parameter C and investigate potential fluid-related mechanisms, we performed full moment tensor inversion for 45 $M_L > 1$ events using a modified version of the NaNDC algorithm (Yang and Wang, 2025). We first applied a band-pass filter of 4–30 Hz to the waveform data and selected high-quality signals with signal-to-noise ratios (SNRs) >3 for further analysis. The inversion incorporated three types of far-field observations: *P*-wave polarities, *P*-wave amplitudes, and three-component *S*/*P* amplitude ratios. *P*-wave polarities and amplitudes were manually picked and rigorously verified to ensure data quality. Events with <11 valid *P*-wave polarity picks were excluded to avoid large uncertainties caused by poor data quality or insufficient azimuthal station coverage. The *S*/*P* amplitude ratios were calculated following the procedure outlined by Wang *et al.* (2020). Equal weights (set to 1) were assigned to each data type in the inversion.

Subsequently, we adopted a two-step inversion strategy to derive robust full moment tensor solutions. In the first step, we inverted for the best-fitting DC solution. Then, using the optimal DC component as a constraint, we performed a second inversion to resolve the full moment tensor, including the non-DC components. This strategy yields more stable solutions with lower uncertainties in the inversion of three-component waveforms, especially after applying proper regularization.

The inversion uncertainty of non-DC components is quantitatively visualized as confidence regions on the Lune plot (Tape and Tape, 2012), reflecting the misfit landscape around the best-fitting moment tensor solution. The relatively tight error contours indicate a well-constrained inversion, demonstrating both improved model fit and enhanced solution stability. This uncertainty representation in Lune space offers an intuitive and physically meaningful assessment of inversion robustness, which may provide insights into possible fluid-driven processes during the seismic sequence.

Results

Spatiotemporal distribution and statistical characteristics

During the LOC-FLOW processing, an initial set of 3464 seismic events was detected using the REAL algorithm (Fig. 2a), which was reduced to 3279 after absolute relocation with VELEST (Fig. 2b). The final high-resolution catalog, generated through hypoDD relative relocation, comprises 2081 earthquakes. These events are primarily concentrated within two distinct seismic clusters separated by an ~3 km gap: the Wudong cluster, located near the center of the Xinfengjiang Reservoir, contains >1000 events, and the Xichang cluster, situated at the northwestern reservoir edge, includes 941 events (Fig. 2c). The bootstrap resampling of the FDTCC differential times with Gaussian noise $\sigma = 0.1$ s (Text S3) yields mean 1σ uncertainties of ~64 m horizontally and ~88 m in depth, indicating that hypocentral errors are conservatively <90 m (Fig. S4). All three relocation stages yielded small residuals (<0.2 s; Fig. S1a), with focal depths ranging from 0 to 20 km and most events concentrated between 5 and 10 km (Fig. S1c).

The final catalog covers magnitudes from M_L – 0.8 to 2.8, with the M_c being –0.4, and the b value as 0.98 (Fig. 3a). The Cv for interevent times is 2.2 (Fig. 3b), indicating temporal clustering. The NND analysis led to a clear bimodal distribution

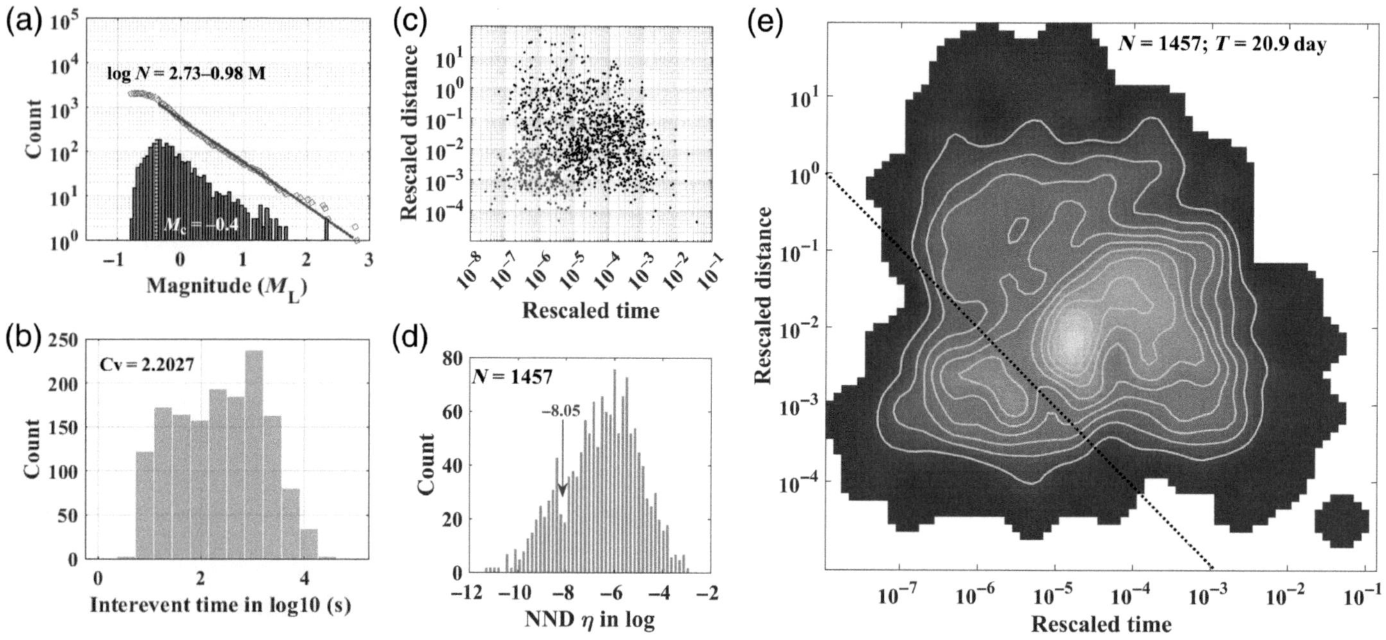

(Fig. 3e), indicating the presence of distinct spatiotemporal characteristics in the study region for compound seismogenic processes.

From the seismicity of spatiotemporal evolution, the Wudong cluster initially nucleated within ~1 km of the M_s 4.5 mainshock and subsequently propagated northwestward along a linear trend before exhibiting a return migration (Fig. S2). Hypocenters are mainly concentrated at depths around 8 km (Fig. S2a). The M_c for this cluster is −0.4, and the corresponding b value is 0.84 (Fig. S6a), implying a relatively low b value characteristic of a relatively mature faulting environment (Maxwell *et al.*, 2009). We also achieved a reasonable Cv value of <2 (Fig. S6b), indicating weak to moderate temporal clustering. The NND analysis in the space-time-magnitude domain shows a unimodal distribution slightly above the best-fitted diagonal line (Fig. S6c–e), suggesting either Poissonian background seismicity driven by possible external influences (i.e., fluid driven, Feng *et al.*, 2024; Zhang, Sun, *et al.*, 2024) or large mainshock clustering (Kothari *et al.*, 2020; Hsu *et al.*, 2024).

As for the Xichang cluster, seismic activity initiated at depths of 5–7 km and gradually extended to ~10 km (Fig. S2a). The recorded magnitudes range from −0.7 to 2.8, with a magnitude of completeness (M_c) of −0.3 and a b value of 1.3 (Fig. S7a), consistent with the occurrence of many small events. The Cv value of 2.71 (Fig. S7b) indicates strong temporal clustering. The NND analysis reveals a pronounced bimodal distribution (Fig. S7c–e), suggesting the Xichang cluster may involve a mixture of triggering processes. The cluster in the lower left of the NND plot reflects short interevent times and distances characteristic of cascading or secondary triggering after a small mainshock (on 15 March, Fig. S3b), and the peak in the upper right suggests a component of external driving forces, such as fluid diffusion or aseismic loading.

Figure 3. Statistical analysis of our final catalog with 2081 events. (a) Gutenberg–Richter distribution. (b) Distribution of the coefficient of variation (Cv) values. (c) Nearest-neighbor distance (NND) analysis on the rescaled time and distance domain, in which red dots denote clustered events and black dots represent background seismicity. (d) Histogram of NND (η) in logarithmic scale, with a threshold of $\eta = -8.05$ chosen to optimally separate clustered and background events. N = 1457 means the number of events larger than the M_c (−0.4). (e) Heat map of the rescaled time–distance domain (same as in panel c), with color intensity indicating event density. The dashed line marks $\eta = -8.05$ that best divides the two modes. The color version of this figure is available only in the electronic edition.

Full moment tensor and variation

Under strict selection criteria (SNR > 3 and P-polarity picks >11), we obtained full moment tensor solutions for 45 events with $M_L > 1$ using the NaNDC algorithm, providing insight into the local seismogenic mechanisms and showing spatial consistency with known and inferred fault structures (Fig. 4a). In the Wudong cluster, 85% of the events display consistent left-lateral strike-slip mechanisms with a normal faulting component, characterized by a mean strike of 150° and a mean dip of 80° (closely matching those of this M_s 4.5 mainshock within ~5°, Jiang *et al.*, 2023; Huang *et al.*, 2025), suggesting rupture along a NW-trending fault plane (further discussed in the next section). In contrast, the Xichang cluster is dominated by normal faulting mechanisms with minor strike-slip components. More than 90% of focal mechanisms show nodal planes that are approximately east–west oriented, parallel to the trace of the inferred Dakengnan fault.

As part of the preparation for reliable full moment tensor inversion of NaNDC, we examine the largest earthquake in each cluster by comparing the P- and S-wave arrival times

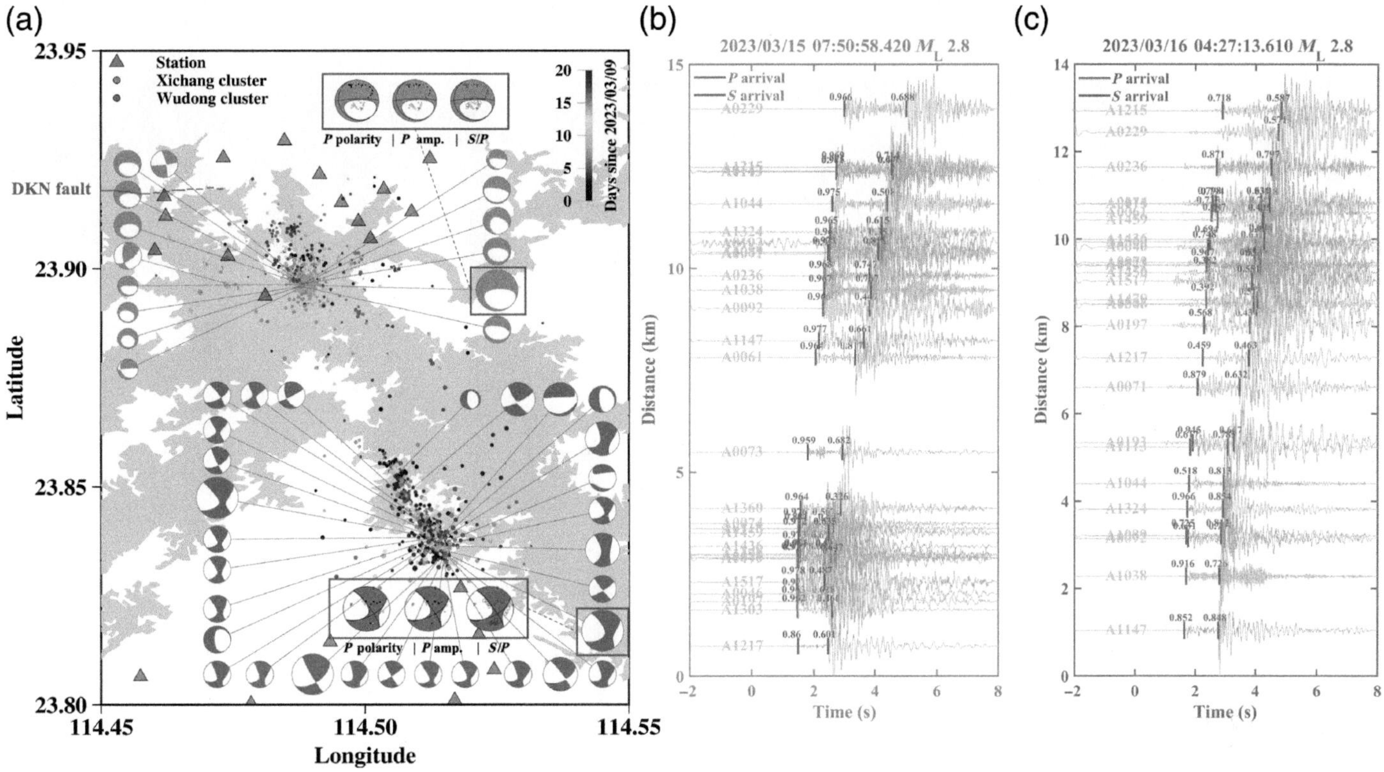

Figure 4. (a) Full moment tensor solutions of the 45 largest events derived using the NaNDC algorithm, overlaid on the distribution of seismicity. The two boxed insets show the waveform fitting for the largest events in each cluster, including *P*-wave polarities, amplitudes, and *S*/*P* amplitude ratios. DKN, Dakengnan fault. (b) Vertical waveform section for the largest event from the Xichang cluster, with *P*- (red) and *S*-wave (blue) arrival picks (numbers denote the picking probability) from 29 stations using PhaseNet. (c) Same as (b), but for the largest event from the Wudong cluster. The color version of this figure is available only in the electronic edition.

derived from PhaseNet on 29 stations (Fig. 4b,c). The picked arrival times show consistent phase alignment across stations, and the waveforms exhibit high SNRs (>3), indicating that the data quality is sufficient for robust full moment tensor inversion.

To evaluate the statistical characteristics of the full moment tensor solutions, we use Lune plots with 95% confidence distribution to illustrate the relative contributions of DC, isotropic (ISO), and compensated linear vector dipole (CLVD) components (Fig. 5a). Most events are dominated by DC components, with a mean contribution of ~76%. The non-DC components show relatively limited variation, with average CLVD and ISO values of ~18% and ~6%, respectively, supporting the overall stability of the inversion results.

At the cluster level, the Wudong cluster exhibits stronger DC dominance (averaging ~80%), alongside moderate CLVD (averaging ~16%) and minor ISO (averaging ~4%). In contrast, the Xichang cluster displays more complex source characteristics, with slightly lower DC (averaging ~67%) and higher CLVD (averaging ~22%) and ISO (averaging ~11%) contributions (Fig. 5b). These distinctions suggest potential regional differences in faulting complexity or seismic source processes.

Discussion

The 4-km-long fault hosted the M_s 4.5 event in the Wudong cluster

Based on the hypocenter locations of the Wudong cluster, E2F (He and Wang, 2025) extracts an ~4-km-long NW-trending fault (strike ≈ 155°, dip ≈ 87°), showing remarkable agreement with the left-lateral strike-slip fault orientations independently resolved via moment tensor inversion (i.e., NaNDC; mean strike ≈ 150°, dip ≈ 80°). These observations are also consistent with the NW–SE aligned earthquake detections based on regional seismic stations distributed at larger scales (Jiang *et al.*, 2023; Huang *et al.*, 2025). Similar strike slip–dominated focal mechanisms were resolved from 12 ($M_L > 1$) earthquakes at the Wudong region in 2021 (He *et al.*, 2025). The consistency between previous events and our result suggest that the regional stress field in the Wudong area has remained stable over recent years.

Furthermore, based on the elevated η values as −6.7 with high event density on the upper right (Fig. S6e), we infer that the seismic sequence following the M_s 4.5 mainshock along the potential fault structure exhibits a more scattered spatial distribution than a typical aftershock sequence, which should concentrate at low-η regions. The relatively low Cv values

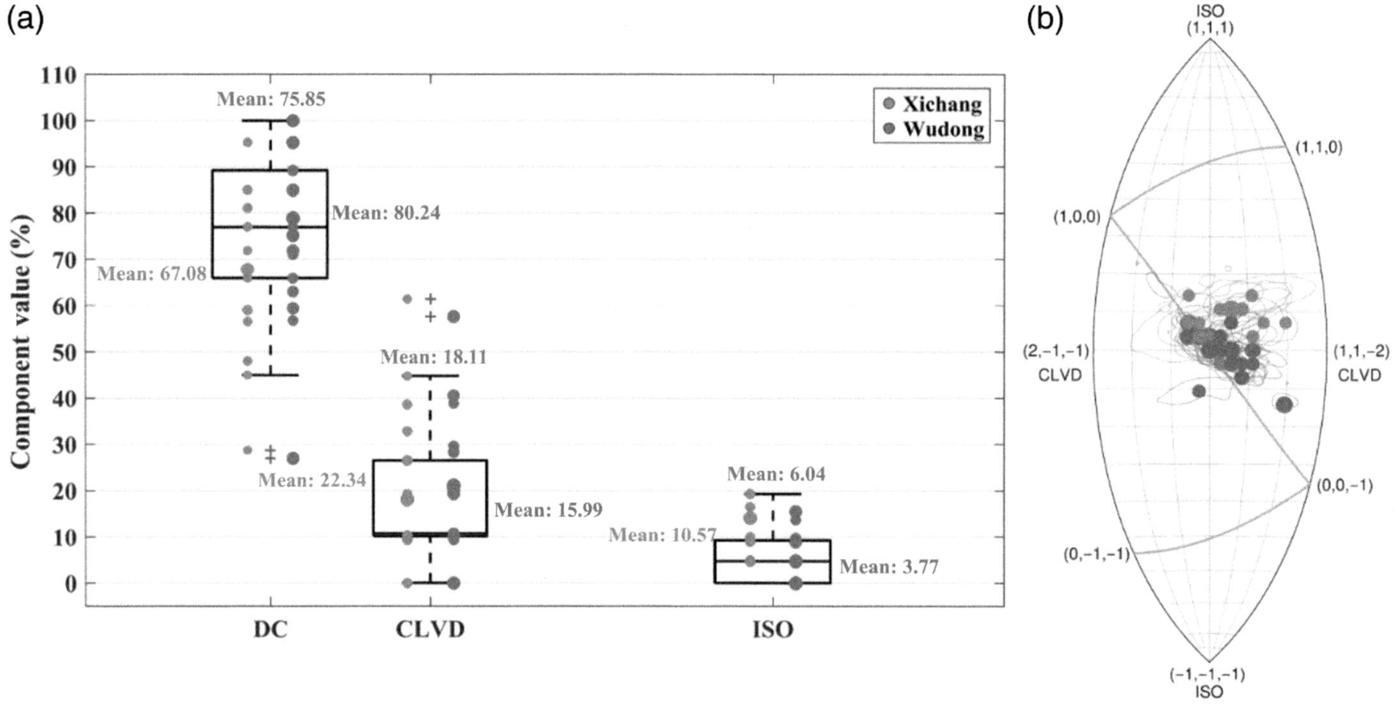

Figure 5. (a) Boxplots showing the percentage contributions of the double-couple (DC), compensated linear vector dipole (CLVD), and isotropic (ISO) components for individual full moment tensor solutions, grouped by region. The horizontal lines indicate the median values, and boxes represent the interquartile range and whiskers for 1.5 × the interquartile range with outliers marked by the red crosses. For each component, the text in gray denotes the mean value for the full dataset (Wudong + Xichang). (b) Lune plot representation of the full moment tensor solutions, showing the distribution of DC, CLVD, and ISO components for the Wudong (blue) cluster and the Xichang (pink) cluster. Contour lines denote confidence intervals at 5% increments from the minimum to maximum misfit, highlighting the inversion uncertainties. The color version of this figure is available only in the electronic edition.

indicate low to moderate clustering and a background-like temporal pattern. In addition, induced seismicity may also exhibit tectonic-like behavior in the NND domain, so these statistical metrics alone cannot rule out fluid diffusion–driven triggering. Earthquake–earthquake triggering has been documented in hydraulic fracturing (Kothari *et al.*, 2020; Zhang, Wang, *et al.*, 2022), wastewater disposal (Wang *et al.*, 2020; Glasgow *et al.*, 2021), and geothermal power production (Feng and Lees, 1998; Zaliapin and Ben-Zion, 2016). However, the limited monitoring time (i.e., 21 days) is likely insufficient to delineate a clear diffusion front for the Wudong cluster, so the sequence cannot be satisfactorily modeled with a simple diffusion-front model.

Regarding our newly constructed catalog at Xinfengjiang, the rescaled distances of events within the Wudong cluster are mostly above 10^{-2} (Fig. S6), indicating that the Wudong sequence may be more similar to a large mainshock cluster mode (Hsu *et al.*, 2024), albeit with a relatively low mainshock magnitude (M_s 4.5). Besides, we did not devote the main effort to explicitly identify which events are aftershocks of the M_s 4.5 mainshock in our study, so the current NND analysis reflects the entire 21-day monitoring period ($\eta = -6.7$ in the Wudong cluster) rather than a clearly isolated sequence, different from the example of large mainshock cluster (i.e., $\eta = -4$) by Hsu *et al.* (2024). In addition, ~90% of the events in the Wudong cluster are located within the mainshock–aftershock grouping, and DC components dominate the focal mechanism solutions, accounting for ~80%. This consistency between spatial clustering and DC-dominant rupture style implies that the seismicity appears to reflect a stress-driven rupture process occurring along a NW-trending fault, characterized by shear failure and aftershock-like clustering. Because of observational limitations, our study was unable to capture the driving mechanism related to fluid processes in the Wudong cluster sequence.

Possible fluid migration revealed by the Xichang cluster

He *et al.* (2025) suggested that a low-permeability body located beneath the aseismic gap between the Wudong and Xichang clusters may have acted as a transient barrier to pore pressure diffusion, possibly explaining the ~3 km separation observed during our study period. To further assess whether the Wudong mainshock could have triggered the Xichang cluster, we performed Coulomb static stress modeling (Coulomb 3.3; Toda *et al.*, 2011). The result indicates that stress changes induced by the M_s 4.5 mainshock remain largely confined to the Wudong fault plane, with negative stress changes in the adjacent Xichang region (Fig. S5a), suggesting limited triggering potential. This is consistent with the minor Coulomb effects previously reported for the same mainshock (Huang *et al.*, 2025).

With no evidence of remote triggering, the two clusters appear to be governed by distinct seismogenic mechanisms. The spatiotemporal evolution of the Xichang cluster sequence and the occurrence of a relatively larger event (M_L 2.8) approximately one week after the M_s 4.5 mainshock (Fig. S3b) suggest that it is more likely an independently initiated sequence that happened to coincide in time rather than one triggered by the M_s 4.5 event. This is also consistent with the NND analysis (Fig. S7e), in which a separate peak in the lower-left portion of the diagram indicates a distinct cascading sequence, likely a small mainshock cluster pattern as interpreted by Hsu *et al.* (2024).

The full moment tensor solutions for the Xichang cluster indicate a steeply dipping (~80°) fault plane, consistent with the four $M_L > 1$ focal mechanisms reported for 2021 events (He *et al.*, 2025) and with historical $M_L > 4$ mechanisms (Wang, Wu, and Huang, 2018; Zhang, Sun, *et al.*, 2024). During the ellipsoid fitting of E2F, the intermediate and minor axes are comparable in length (0.87 km versus 0.60 km) but much shorter than the major axis (2.41 km), indicating a poorly constrained strike orientation compared with the vertical distribution of the Xichang cluster. We therefore infer that the recent dip-slip events most likely reflect reactivation of the down-dip extension of the E-W-trending Dakengnan fault, previously mapped from gravity and magnetic anomaly data (Wang, Wu, and Huang, 2018).

In addition, ~30% non-DC components observed in the moment tensor results consistent with the background components in NND as 27% (Fig. S7c), both indicating the influence of fluid involvement in the seismogenic process, strengthening the possibility of the downward fluid migration trend inferred from the vertical evolution of seismicity (Fig. S2a; He *et al.*, 2025). Similar combinations of downward-migrating seismicity and fluid-related source characteristics have been reported for other reservoir-induced sequences, such as the Baihetan reservoir in southwest China and the Aswan High Dam in Egypt (Saadalla *et al.*, 2020; Duan *et al.*, 2024), indicating that the Xichang cluster is not an isolated case. The relative high b value of the Xichang cluster may further reflect heterogeneous stress conditions and the occurrence of weaker ruptures associated with fluid-related processes.

Conclusion

By integrating high-resolution earthquake relocation, full moment tensor inversion, and fault modeling, we delineate two spatially distinct clusters after the 2023 Wudong M_s 4.5 mainshock in the center of the Xinfengjiang Reservoir. An ~3-km-long gap with markedly reduced seismicity appears between the Wudong and Xichang clusters, consistent with a subsurface low-permeability zone beneath the reservoir as suggested by He *et al.* (2025). With limited Coulomb stress transfer, we propose that the two seismic clusters are relatively independent and driven by different mechanisms. The Wudong cluster aligns along a 4-km-long NW-SE fault that likely hosted the M_s 4.5 event and remained active throughout our study period, evidenced by well-constrained strike-slip focal mechanisms. In contrast, the Xichang cluster, as a seismically active region, may be triggered by persistent fluid infiltration with the evidence of spatiotemporal distribution of seismicity in the vertical direction and the possible non-DC components. Our results provide new constraints to the detailed fault structures beneath the Xinfengjiang Reservoir and underscore the need for continued monitoring in reservoir-induced seismicity to understand triggering processes and seismic hazard potential.

Data and Resources

The mainshock (M_s 4.5) information was obtained from the China Earthquake Networks Center (CENC) database (https://data.earthquake.cn, last accessed August 2025). The waveform data of all events will be archived on Zenodo upon publication. The figures are made with MATLAB (2024a version) and GMT (6.1 version). The supplemental material for this article includes two tables, seven figures, and five texts detailing the parameter optimization during REAL, velocity model used, bootstrap strategy for hypocenter uncertainties, Coulomb stress calculation, and statistical analyses, which support the context in the main text. The earthquake catalog and two movies (showing the spatiotemporal distributions and fault fitting) are uploaded separately.

Declaration of Competing Interests

The authors acknowledge that there are no conflicts of interest recorded.

Acknowledgments

The authors thank two anonymous reviewers and Peng Zhang for their constructive comments. The authors sincerely thank the fieldwork team for their dedication and efforts in data collection for this study. The research is supported by the National Natural Science Foundation of China (Grant Number 42374068), Shenzhen Key Laboratory of Deep Offshore Oil and Gas Exploration Technology (Grant Number ZDSYS20190902093007855), and Guangdong Provincial Key Laboratory of Geophysical High-resolution Imaging Technology (2022B1212010002).

References

Bender, B. (1983). Maximum likelihood estimation of *b* values for magnitude grouped data, *Bull. Seismol. Soc. Am.* **73,** no. 3, 831–851.

Bullen, K., and B. Bolt (1985). *An Introduction to the Theory of Seismology*, Cambridge University Press.

Cochran, E., Z. Ross, R. Harrington, S. Dougherty, and J. Rubinstein (2018). Induced earthquake families reveal distinctive evolutionary patterns near disposal wells, *J. Geophys. Res.* **123,** no. 9, 8045–8055.

Cheng, H., H. Zhang, B. Zhu, Y. Sun, L. Zheng, S. Yang, and Y. Shi (2012). Finite element investigation of the poroelastic effect on the Xinfengjiang Reservoir-triggered earthquake, *Sci. China Earth Sci.* **55,** no. 12, 1942–1952.

Deng, Y., and P. He (2016). Study on the spatiotemporal pattern of b value in Xinfengjiang Reservoir area in Guangdong Province, *South China J. Seismol.* **36,** no. 3, 61–67 (in Chinese).

Ding, Y., J. Pan, A. Xiao, L. Shen, H. Ma, and W. Miao (1983). Tectonic environment of reservoir induced earthquakes in the Xinfengjiang reservoir area, *Seismol. Geol.* **5,** no. 3, 63–74 (in Chinese).

Dong, S., L. Li, L. Zhao, X. Shen, W. Wang, H. Huang, B. Peng, and R. Gao (2022). Seismic evidence for fluid-driven pore pressure increase and its links with induced seismicity in the Xinfengjiang Reservoir, South China, *J. Geophys. Res.* **127,** no. 3, e2021JB023548, doi: 10.1029/2021JB023548.

Duan, M., L. Zhou, C. Zhao, and X. Zhang (2024). Fluid-driven seismicity in the Baihetan reservoir area revealed by 3D seismic tomography based on dense seismic arrays, *Earth Space Sci.* **11,** no. 9, e2023EA003397, doi: 10.1029/2023EA003397.

Feng, R. (1977). On the variations of the velocity ratio before and after the Xinfengjiang reservoir impounding earthquake of M 6.1, *Chin. J. Geophys.* **20,** no. 3, 211–221.

Feng, Q., and J. M. Lees (1998). Microseismicity, stress, and fracture in the Coso geothermal field, California, *Tectonophysics* **289,** nos. 1/3, 221–238.

Feng, T., R. Wang, L. Fang, J. Wu, and T. Yang (2024). Microseismic constraints on the mechanical state of the Anninghe-Daliangshan fault zone, southeastern Tibetan plateau, *Earth Planet. Sci. Lett.* **639,** 118765.

Glasgow, M., B. Schmandt, R. Wang, M. Zhang, S. L. Bilek, and E. Kiser (2021). Raton Basin induced seismicity is hosted by networks of short basement faults and mimics tectonic earthquake statistics, *J. Geophys. Res.* **126,** no. 11, e2021JB022839, doi: 10.1029/2021JB022839.

Guan, H., J. Lei, D. Zhao, and X. Hu (2025). The reservoir-induced 2023 Heyuan earthquake sequence in Guangdong, China and its geodynamic implications, *Tectonophysics* **902,** 230681.

Guo, G., T. Liu, N. Qin, and L. Chen (2004). Analysis on small-earthquake composite fault plane solutions from 1961 to 1999 in Xinfengjiang reservoir area, *Acta Seismol. Sin.* **17,** no. 3, 287–295.

Gupta, H. K. (2002). A review of recent studies of triggered earthquakes by artificial water reservoirs with special emphasis on earthquakes in Koyna, India, *Earth Sci. Rev.* **58,** nos. 3/4, 279–310.

Gutenberg, B., and C. F. Richter (1944). Frequency of earthquakes in California, *Bull. Seismol. Soc. Am.* **34,** no. 4, 185–188.

He, Z., and R. Wang (2025). E2F: Extract fault geometry from earthquake catalogs, *Seismol. Res. Lett.* doi: 10.1785/0220250138.

He, L., Z. Guo, B. Luo, Q. Bai, G. Yin, K. Wu, AG. Osotuyi, and L. Wang (2025). Long-time delays in induced earthquakes caused by low-permeability bodies: Insights from the Xinfengjiang Reservoir, China, *J. Geophys. Res.* **130,** no. 6, e2024JB030579, doi: 10.1029/2024JB030579.

He, L., X. Sun, H. Yang, J. Qin, Y. Shen, and X. Ye (2018). Upper crustal structure and earthquake mechanism in the Xinfengjiang water reservoir, Guangdong, China, *J. Geophys. Res.* **123,** no. 5, 3799–3813.

Huang, R., Y. Deng, Y. Chen, C. Xiong, and Z. Zhang (2025). Source parameters and Stress triggering of 2023 M $\geq$ 4 earthquakes sequence in Heyuan, Guangdong, *Chin. J. Geophys.* **68,** no. 3, 956–969.

Huang, R., X. Sun, P. Zhang, and Y. Deng (2024). Seismicity migration and the upper crustal structure in the Xinfengjiang reservoir, *Seismol. Res. Lett.* **95,** no. 5, 2833–2843.

Hsu, Y., I. Zaliapin, and Y. Ben-Zion (2024). Informative modes of seismicity in nearest-neighbor earthquake proximities, *J. Geophys. Res.* **129,** no. 3, e2023JB027826, doi: 10.1029/2023JB027826.

Jiang, X., Q. Lin, X. Chen, T. Zhu, and M. Liang (2023). The aftershock distribution and focal mechanism solutions characteristics of the Heyuan MS 4.3 and Dongyuan MS 4.5 earthquakes in Guangdong in 2023, *South China J. Seismol.* **43,** no. 4, 126–135.

Kagan, Y., and D. Jackson (1991). Long-term earthquake clustering, *Geophys. J. Int.* **104,** no. 1, 117–133.

Kothari, S., R. Shcherbakov, and G. Atkinson (2020). Statistical modeling and characterization of induced seismicity within the western Canada sedimentary basin, *J. Geophys. Res.* **125,** no. 12, e2020JB020606, doi: 10.1029/2020JB020606.

Kissling, E., U. Kradolfer, and H. Maurer (1995). Program VELEST user's guide-Short Introduction, Institute of Geophysics, ETH Zurich, 22 pp.

Maxwell, S., M. Jones, R. Parker, S. Miong, S. Leaney, D. Dorval, D. D'Amico, J. Logel, E. Anderson, and K. Hammermaster (2009). Fault activation during hydraulic fracturing, *SEG Technical Program Expanded Abstracts 2009*, 1552–1556.

Miao-Yueh, W., Y. Mao-Yuan, H. Yu-Liang, L. Tzu-Chiang, C. Yun-Tai, C. Yen, and F. Jui (1976). Mechanism of the reservoir impounding earthquakes at Hsinfengkiang and a preliminary Endeavour to discuss their cause, *Eng. Geol.* **10,** nos. 2/4, 331–351.

Saadalla, H., A. A. K. Abdel-aal, and K. El-Faragawy (2020). Characteristics of earthquakes recorded around the High Dam Lake with comparison to natural earthquakes using waveform inversion and source spectra, *Pure Appl. Geophys.* **177,** no. 8, 3667–3695, doi: 10.1007/s00024-020-02490-4.

Shearer, P. M. (2009). *Introduction to Seismology*, Second Ed., Cambridge University Press.

Shen, C., H. Chen, C. Zhang, L. Huang, Z. Li, Z. Yang, D. Wang, and X. Luo (1974). Xinfengjiang reservoir earthquakes and its influence on the dam, *Sci. China* **17,** no. 2, 184–205 (in Chinese).

Song, C., C. Fan, J. Zhu, J. Wang, Y. Sheng, K. Liu, T. Chen, P. Zhan, S. Luo, C. Yuan, and L. Ke (2022). A comprehensive geospatial database of nearly 100,000 reservoirs in China, *Earth Syst. Sci. Data* **14,** 4017–4034, 10.5194/essd-14-4017-2022.

Talwani, P. (1997). On the nature of reservoir-induced seismicity, *Pure Appl. Geophys.* **150,** no. 3, 473–492.

Tape, W., and C. Tape (2012). A geometric setting for moment tensors, *Geophys. J. Int.* **190,** no. 1, 476–498.

Toda, S., R. S. Stein, V. Sevilgen, and J. Lin (2011). Coulomb 3.3: Graphic-rich deformation and stress-change software for earthquake, tectonic, and volcano research and teaching—User guide, *U.S. Geol. Surv. Open-File Rept. 2011-1060*, 63 p., available at http://pubs.usgs.gov/of/2011/1060/ (last accessed January 2026).

Waldhauser, F., and W. Ellsworth (2000). A double-difference earthquake location algorithm: Method and application to the northern Hayward fault, California, *Bull. Seismol. Soc. Am.* **90,** no. 6, 1353–1368.

Wan, Y., and M. Yang (2011). Statistic characteristics of Xinfengjiang Reservoir earthquake sequence, *North China Earthq. Sci.* **29,** no. 4, 27–33.

Wang, L., G. Wu, and L. Huang (2018). Focal mechanism inversion of M_L 4.0 earthquakes in Xichang, Xinfengjiang Reservoir by CAP method, *South China J. Seismol.* **38,** no. 3, 1–8.

Wang, R., B. Schmandt, M. Zhang, M. Glasgow, E. Kiser, S. Rysanek, and R. Stairs (2020). Injection-induced earthquakes on complex fault zones of the Raton basin illuminated by machine-learning phase picker and dense nodal array, *Geophys. Res. Lett.* **46,** e2020GL088168, doi: 10.1029/2020GL088168.

Wang, R., D. Yang, Y. Chen, and C. Ren (2023). Lighting up a 1 km fault near a hydraulic fracturing well using a machine learning-based picker, *Seismol. Soc. Am.* **94,** no. 4, 1836–1847.

Wang, S., X. Sun, J. Qin, L. He, and Y. Deng (2018). Fine fault structure of and Xinfengjiang water reservoir area from high-frequency ambient noise tomography, *Chin. J. Geophys.* **61,** no. 2, 593–603.

Wei, B., P. Chen, F. Li, and H. Huang (1992). Focal mechanisms and tectonic stress field of the Xinfengjiang earthquake, *Acta Seismol. Sin.* **5,** no. 3, 539–548.

Yang, L., and R. Wang (2025). NaNDC: Full moment tensor inversion and uncertainty analysis for large-N monitored small earthquakes, *Seismol. Res. Lett.* **96,** no. 2A, 1150–1162.

Yang, Z., B. Liu, Q. Wang, C. Zhao, Z. Chen, and X. Zhang (2013). Tomographic imaging of the upper crustal structure beneath the Xinfengjiang reservoir area, *Chin. J. Geophys.* **56,** no. 4, 1177–1189

Yang, L., J. Zi, R. Wang, and H. Yang (2025). Monitoring induced seismicity in the Weiyuan shale gas field utilizing a dense array, *Tectonophysics*, 230862, doi: 10.1016/j.tecto.2025.230862.

Ye, X., Y. M. Huang, X. M. Hu, and J. Liu (2013). Location of the Dongyuan Ms 4.8 earthquake sequence of Guangdong and 3D P-wave velocity structure in and around source region, *Acta Seismol. Sinica* **35,** no. 6, 809–819 (in Chinese).

Ye, X., Y. Huang, and J. Liu (2016). 3D P-wave velocity structure and active tectonics in the Xinfengjiang area of Guangdong, *Earthq. Res. China* **32,** no. 3, 465–476.

Ye, X., Z. Deng, Y. Huang, J. Liu, X. Wang, J. Liu, and Z. Tan (2017). The characteristics of 3D P-wave velocity structure of middle-upper crust and reservoir water infiltration-diffusion in Xinfengjiang Reservoir of Guangdong, *Chin. J. Geophys.* **60,** no. 9, 3432–3444.

Zaliapin, I., and Y. Ben-Zion (2013). Earthquake clusters in southern California I: Identification and stability, *J. Geophys. Res.* **118,** no. 6, 2847–2864.

Zaliapin, I., and Y. Ben-Zion (2016). Discriminating characteristics of tectonic and human-induced seismicity, *Bull. Seismol. Soc. Am.* **106,** no. 3, 846–859.

Zhang, M. (2022). Dal-mzhang/LOC-FLOW: LOC-FLOW [Software], *Zenodo*, doi: 10.5281/zenodo.5875084.

Zhang, F., Y. Chen, R. Wang, H. Yu, H. Chen, L. Fushen, and S. Xuhua (2024). Integrated analysis of seismic sources and structures: Understanding earthquake clustering during hydraulic fracturing [Dataset], *Zenodo*, doi: 10.5281/zenodo.12683224.

Zhang, F., R. Wang, Y. Chen, and Y. Chen (2022). Spatiotemporal variations in earthquake triggering mechanisms during multistage hydraulic fracturing in western Canada, *J. Geophys. Res.* **127,** no. 8, e2022JB024744, doi: 10.1029/2022JB024744.

Zhang, M., W. Ellsworth, and G. Beroza (2019). Rapid earthquake association and location, *Seismol. Res. Lett.* **90,** no. 6, 2276–2284, doi: 10.1785/0220190052.

Zhang, M., M. Liu, T. Feng, R. Wang, and Z. Weiqiang (2022). LOC-FLOW: An end-to-end machine learning-based high-precision earthquake location workflow, *Seismol. Res. Lett.* **93,** no. 5, 2426–2438, doi: 10.1785/0220220019.

Zhang, P., X. Sun, J. Zong, and Z. Xiao (2025). Research review and future prospect of induced seismicity in the Xinfengjiang Reservoir area, *Geotecton. Metallog.* 49, no. 3, 481–491. doi: 10.16539/j.ddgzyckx.2024.01.143.

Zhang, P., X. Sun, J. Zong, Z. Xiao, and Y. Shen (2024). Microseismicity detection and spatial-temporal migration in the Xinfengjiang reservoir, Guangdong, China, *Phys. Earth Planet. In.* **355,** 107245.

Zhu, W., and G. C. Beroza (2019). PhaseNet: A deep-neural-network-based seismic arrival-time picking method, *Geophys. J. Int.* **216,** no. 1, 261–273, doi: 10.1093/gji/ggy423.

Manuscript received 8 August 2025
Published online 15 January 2026

Focus Section: Intraplate Earthquakes

Coseismic Rupture and Aftershock Migration Governed by Multiple Fault Geometries: The 2022 M_w 6.6 Menyuan Earthquake

Jun Li[1,2], Lihua Fang*[1,3,4], Long Zhang[1], Chaoyong Peng[1], Yijian Zhou[5], Li Zhao[6], and Anne Replumaz[7]

Abstract

Multiple fault geometries, including stepovers and variations in strike and dip angles, play a crucial role in controlling seismic processes. Previous studies have examined individual geometric factors, but integrated analyses of how they jointly govern seismic sequences remain limited. The 2022 M_w 6.6 Menyuan earthquake, located within a complex strike-slip fault system in the northeastern Tibetan Plateau, presents a valuable case study. Here, we combine a high-resolution seismic catalog (~4200 events) with an Interferometric Synthetic Aperture Radar-derived coseismic slip model to elucidate these controls. Our results reveal a multigeometry fault system involving the Tuolaishan fault and the Lenglongling fault, characterized by distinct fault discontinuity features such as fault stepovers, bends, and variations in strike and dip. We observe an aftershock gap of ~5 km at the fault bend, for which the fault's strike and dip change by ~10° to 14°. We demonstrate that these interacting geometries played a dominant role in the coseismic and postseismic process: the coseismic surface rupture successfully propagated across a ~2.5 km stepover but was arrested by the aftershock gap. Meanwhile, the multiple geometries acted as stress concentrators, which likely localized the peak slip to ~3.5 m—an anomalously high value, 2–3 times larger than typical for an M_w 6.6 event. Postseismically, the aftershocks evolved as two independent fronts separated by the variations in strike and dip (fault bend). The detection of repeating earthquakes and the observed "W-shaped" logarithmic migration pattern indicates that aseismic slip and fault discontinuities collectively dominate the path of aftershock expansion. These findings highlight that multiple geometries act as both rupture barriers and stress amplifiers, significantly elevating local seismic hazards.

Cite this article as Li, J., L. Fang, L. Zhang, C. Peng, Y. Zhou, L. Zhao, and A. Replumaz (2026). Coseismic Rupture and Aftershock Migration Governed by Multiple Fault Geometries: The 2022 M_w 6.6 Menyuan Earthquake, *Seismol. Res. Lett.* **97**, 832–844, doi: 10.1785/0220250355.

Supplemental Material

Introduction

Seismic processes are influenced by a range of factors, including loading rates, fault geometry, stress heterogeneity, and the prestress state of involved fault segments (Hamling *et al.*, 2017). Lithology contrasts could also have some minor effect. Among these factors, fault geometry and structural complexity represent particularly important controls because they can influence the initiation, propagation, and termination of earthquake ruptures (Okubo and Aki, 1987; Lee *et al.*, 2024). In most tectonic scenarios, fault geometry complexity can exert a first-order control on rupture propagation and aftershock migration (Wesnousky, 2006; Kato and Obara, 2014; Ren *et al.*, 2024; Zhou *et al.*, 2025). Complex fault systems exhibit multiple geometries and geometric heterogeneity, including fault discontinuities, stepovers, bends, and variations in strike and dip, each affecting rupture dynamics and aftershock distribution (Talwani, 1999; Cowie *et al.*, 2012; Rodriguez Padilla *et al.*, 2024; Roche *et al.*, 2025). In particular, fault geometry

1. Institute of Geophysics, China Earthquake Administration, Beijing, China, https://orcid.org/0009-0003-5020-3885 (JL); https://orcid.org/0000-0002-7379-1355 (LZ); 2. The Second Monitoring and Application Center, China Earthquake Administration, Xi'an, China; 3. Institute of Earthquake Forecasting, China Earthquake Administration, Beijing, China; 4. Key Laboratory of Earthquake Forecasting and Risk Assessment, Ministry of Emergency Management, Beijing, China; 5. Division of Geological and Planetary Sciences, California Institute of Technology, Pasadena, California, U.S.A., https://orcid.org/0000-0002-7205-1769 (YZ); 6. School of Earth and Space Sciences, Peking University, Beijing, China., https://orcid.org/0000-0002-0950-6863 (LZ); 7. ISTerre (Institut des Sciences de la Terre), Université Grenoble Alpes, CNRS, Grenoble, France, https://orcid.org/0000-0002-3707-5722 (AR)

*Corresponding author: fanglihua@ief.ac.cn

complexity exhibits a dual effect. On one hand, it can act as barriers to rupture propagation when the strike-slip stepovers are larger than ~4 to 5 km, thus limiting the magnitudes of the earthquakes (Harris and Day, 1999; Wesnousky, 2006). On the other hand, it can facilitate large-scale ruptures by transferring stresses across adjacent fault segments (Barka and Kadinsky-Cade, 1988; Cowie *et al.*, 2012; Hamling *et al.*, 2017; Ren *et al.*, 2024; Zhao *et al.*, 2025). Meanwhile, variations in strike and dip may influence the distribution of stress and strain on the fault, directly affecting the potential for fault reactivation and cascading earthquake sequences (Sibson *et al.*, 1988; Cowie *et al.*, 2012; Zhang *et al.*, 2025; Zhao *et al.*, 2025). This can either trigger new ruptures or cause the rupture front to self-arrest (Xu *et al.*, 2023, 2024). These mechanisms collectively illustrate that fault geometry exerts a complex influence on seismic activities by controlling the stress and strain distributions. Despite extensive studies, integrated analyses of multiple fault geometry factors simultaneously controlling rupture and aftershock patterns are still limited.

The 8 January 2022 M_w 6.6 Menyuan earthquake occurred within a strain accumulation zone in the northeastern margin of the Tibetan Plateau, a region characterized by frequent large earthquakes. Focal mechanism solutions indicate a coexistence of strike-slip and thrust faulting, reflecting a complex seismotectonic structure (Fig. 1). The 2022 M_w 6.6 Menyuan event ruptured a geometric complex strike-slip fault system, which provides an excellent case for investigating the role of fault geometry in an earthquake sequence. In this study, we construct a high-resolution catalog for the 2022 M_w 6.6 Menyuan earthquake sequence using the matched-filter technique. The new catalog offers a comprehensive picture of the spatial distribution and temporal evolution of aftershocks. By integrating this catalog with an Interferometric Synthetic Aperture Radar (InSAR)-derived slip model, we explore the influence of complex fault geometry on the rupture process. Furthermore, we detect and analyze repeating earthquakes to constrain postseismic deformation, investigating the contribution of aseismic slip to aftershock evolution and the potential influence of fault geometry on the postseismic process. Through a joint analysis of multiple features of fault geometry, the coseismic process and aftershock evolution, we aim to investigate the dominant role of multiple fault geometries in governing coseismic and postseismic processes.

The slip rates of the Tuolaishan and Lenglongling faults (TLSF and LLLF) are from Guo *et al.* (2017) and Huang *et al.* (2022).

Seismotectonic Overview

The 2022 M_w 6.6 Menyuan earthquake occurred near the Haiyuan fault zone on the northeastern margin of the Tibetan Plateau. The Altyn-Tagh-Haiyuan fault system includes the nearly east–west-trending, left-lateral strike-slip faults (Altyn Tagh fault and Haiyuan fault) and the southeast-trending Qilianshan thrust fault system in-between, forming a large-scale push-up structure that accommodates oblique northeast-east convergence and northeast-eastward extrusion of the northeast Tibetan Plateau relative to the Gobi-Alashan (Tapponnier *et al.*, 1990; Avouac and Tapponnier, 1993; Wang and Shen, 2020; Li *et al.*, 2023). This region is one of the most historically seismically active zones in Mainland China, which has experienced several earthquakes greater than *M* 7.0 since A.D 814 (Zheng *et al.*, 2019). In 1920, the *M* 8.5 Haiyuan earthquake caused a surface rupture of approximately 220 km in length (Deng *et al.*, 1986). Seven years later, the 1927 *M* 8.0 Gulang earthquake occurred north of the LLLF. From a geological perspective, this area spans multiple geological eras, including the Ordovician, Devonian, Permian, and Triassic periods (Li *et al.*, 2023). Focal mechanism solutions indicate a coexistence of strike-slip and thrust faulting, reflecting a complex seismotectonic structure (Fig. 1b). According to field surveys and the InSAR analyses, the 2022 M_w 6.6 Menyuan earthquake generated a ~21-km-long surface rupture (Feng *et al.*, 2022). The rupture occurred within a geometric complex fault zone where the LLLF and TLSF intersect, exhibiting fault stepovers, bends, and dip-angle changes (Luo and Wang, 2022; Li *et al.*, 2023; Xu *et al.*, 2024), which provides an excellent case for investigating the role of fault geometry in an earthquake sequence.

Methods and Results

Seismic stations and waveform data

We used seismic records from eight broadband and seven strong-motion stations within an epicentral distance of 130 km, during the period from 8 January 2022 to 8 April 2022. In this 15-station network, there are four broadband stations with epicentral distances less than 80 km and three strong-motion stations within 50 km. The working frequency bands of the broadband and strong-motion instruments are 0.02–50 and 0–100 Hz, respectively.

Aftershock detection and location

We construct the Menyuan aftershock catalog using the phase picking-association-location-matched filter (PALM) workflow (Zhou *et al.*, 2021; Fig. 2), which is based on the matched-filtering technique. Raw continuous waveforms are first preprocessed by removing the mean, detrending and band-pass filtered (1–15 Hz). Then, *P*- and *S*-wave arrivals are identified via a hybrid short-term average/long-term average (STA/LTA)-Kurtosis algorithm. The time windows for detecting potential events and picking *P*- and *S*-wave arrivals are set to [1.0, 10.0 s], [1.0, 2.5 s], and [1.0, 5.0 s], respectively. Phase association is performed using a spatiotemporal clustering with origin-time deviations within 3.0 s, requiring detections ≥3 stations. Local magnitude (M_L) is estimated using *S*-wave amplitudes from all stations, discarding the value with the largest residual and adopting the median of the remaining

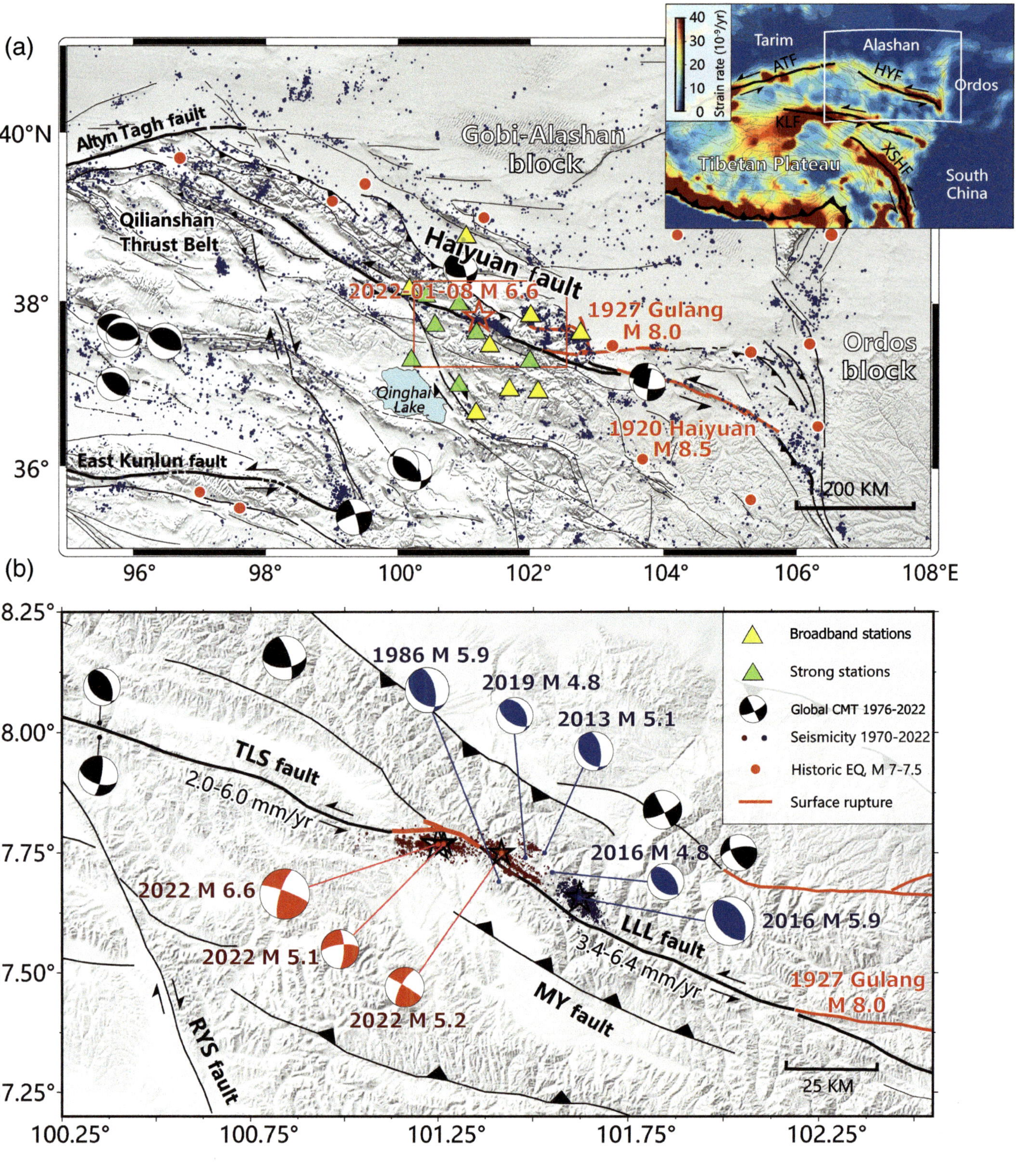

Figure 1. Seismotectonic context of the 2022 M_w 6.6 Menyuan earthquake. (a) Historical $M \geq 7.0$ earthquakes (red circles) and seismicity (blue dots). Yellow and green triangles represent broadband and strong-motion stations, respectively. Top-right inset map shows regional background strain rate from Kreemer *et al.* (2014). (b) Close-up of the rupture zone. Red and blue dots depict aftershocks of the 2022 M_w 6.6 and 2016 M_w 5.9 events, respectively. LLL fault, Lenglongling fault; MY fault, Menyuan fault; RYS fault, Riyueshan fault; TLS fault, Tuolaishan fault. In both panels (a) and (b), focal mechanism plots show focal mechanisms (black and blue: Global Centroid Moment Tensor [Global CMT]; red: Xu *et al.*, 2022). Black and red lines represent active faults (Xu *et al.*, 2017) and surface ruptures (Feng *et al.*, 2022), respectively. The slip rates of the Tuolaishan and Lenglongling faults are from Guo *et al.* (2017) and Huang *et al.* (2022).

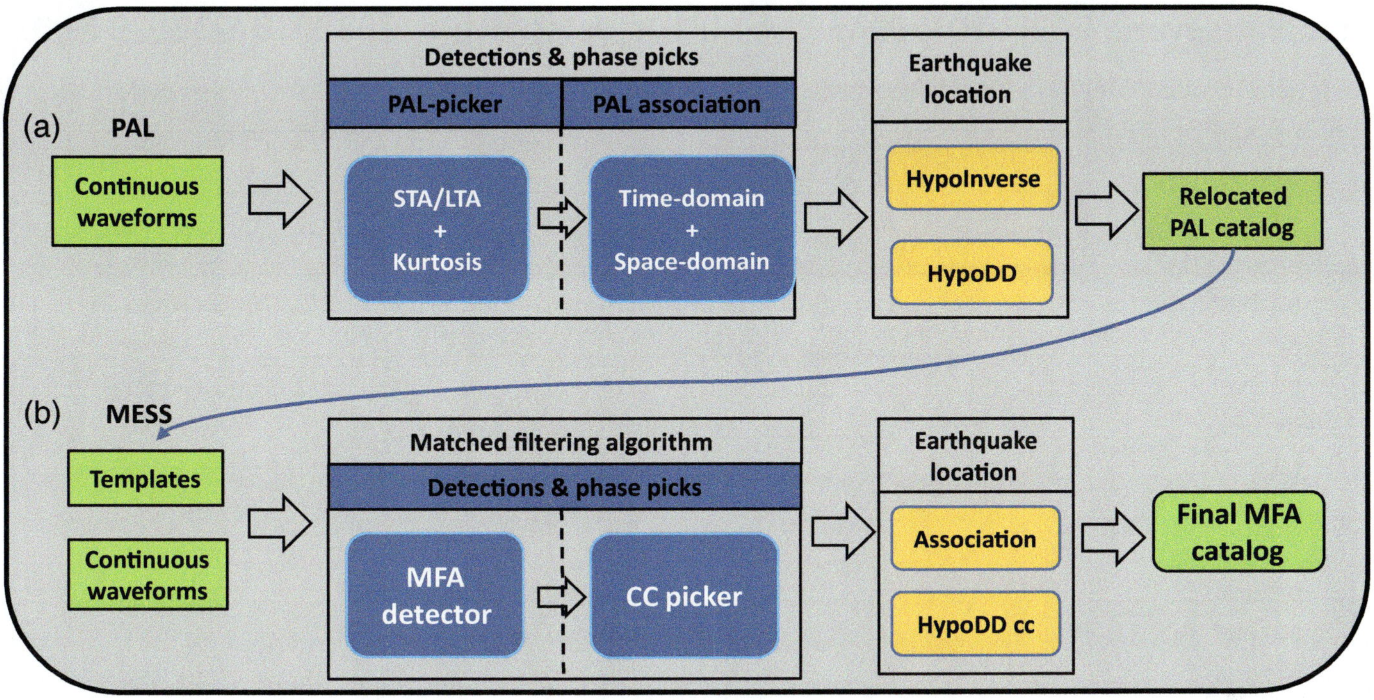

Figure 2. Workflow of the methodology used in this study (modified from Zhou *et al.*, 2021). (a) Phase picking association and location (PAL) module: Event detection and location using short-term average/long-term average (STA/LTA) and Kurtosis algorithms on continuous waveforms to construct an initial template catalog. (b) Match, expand, shift, and stack (MESS) module: Identification of hidden microearthquakes via matched-filter algorithm based on PAL-derived templates, followed by cross-correlation (CC)-based double-difference relocation to construct a final catalog. MFA, matched-filtering algorithm.

values. For aftershocks with $M_L \geq 4.5$, due to the complexity of their source processes, we visually verify the *P*- and *S*-wave arrival times to ensure measurement accuracy. The 1D velocity model used in this study was modified from Jia *et al.* (2019). HypoInverse (Klein, 2002) is used for absolute locations, with several velocity models (Table S1, available in the supplemental material to this article) and inversion parameters tuned for robustness. This yields 1480 well-located aftershocks.

Based on these 1480 template events, we apply the matched-filtering algorithm of the PALM framework to detect more events. Both template and raw continuous waveforms are preprocessed in the same way as in the initial PALM process. The template window is defined as from 1 s before to 20 s after the *P*-wave arrival to contain both *P* and *S* waves (Fig. 3). The cross-correlation coefficient (cc) threshold is set to 0.3. The selection of this threshold is based on the successful applications of cc thresholds in multiple earthquake sequences reported by Zhou *et al.* (2021) and Zhou *et al.* (2022). To ensure higher accuracy, we required that each candidate event be detected by at least three templates. *P*- and *S*-wave arrival times are picked using waveform cross correlation with shorter windows: from 0.5 s before to 2.5 s after the *P* arrival, and from 0.5 s before to 4.0 s after the *S* arrival. Newly detected arrivals are then associated to a new event if their estimated origin times are within 3.0 s. The initial location of each newly detected event is set as the average location of the templates. For relocation, we input the cross-correlation-based differential travel times into HypoDD (Waldhauser and Ellsworth, 2000; Waldhauser, 2001). Stations within 130 km of each event are utilized, and each event pair must have at least six differential times with cc above 0.3 from three stations. We run HypoDD with parameters weight distance of cross correlation (WDCC) = 6 and weight range of cross correlation (WRCC) = 4 for four iterations to relocate the newly detected events. Finally, we constructed a high-resolution catalog of ~4200 events (including the 1480 initial template events), with median location uncertainties of ~32 m (horizontal) and ~138 m (vertical). Our results are generally consistent with previous Menyuan aftershock catalogs, such as those by Fan *et al.* (2022) and Zou and Lei (2023). However, by utilizing a dataset with a longer temporal span and employing an advanced cross-correlation workflow, our catalog exhibits more compact spatial clustering. This improvement is advantageous for resolving fine-scale fault structures and characterizing the postseismic expansion process.

Repeating earthquakes detection

Repeating earthquakes (repeaters) are identified based on waveform similarity, collocation, and rupture overlap. We first pair all events with epicentral distances less than 10 km and recalculate cc coefficients using a time window from 1 s before to 20 s after the *P*-wave arrival. This window contains both *P* and *S*

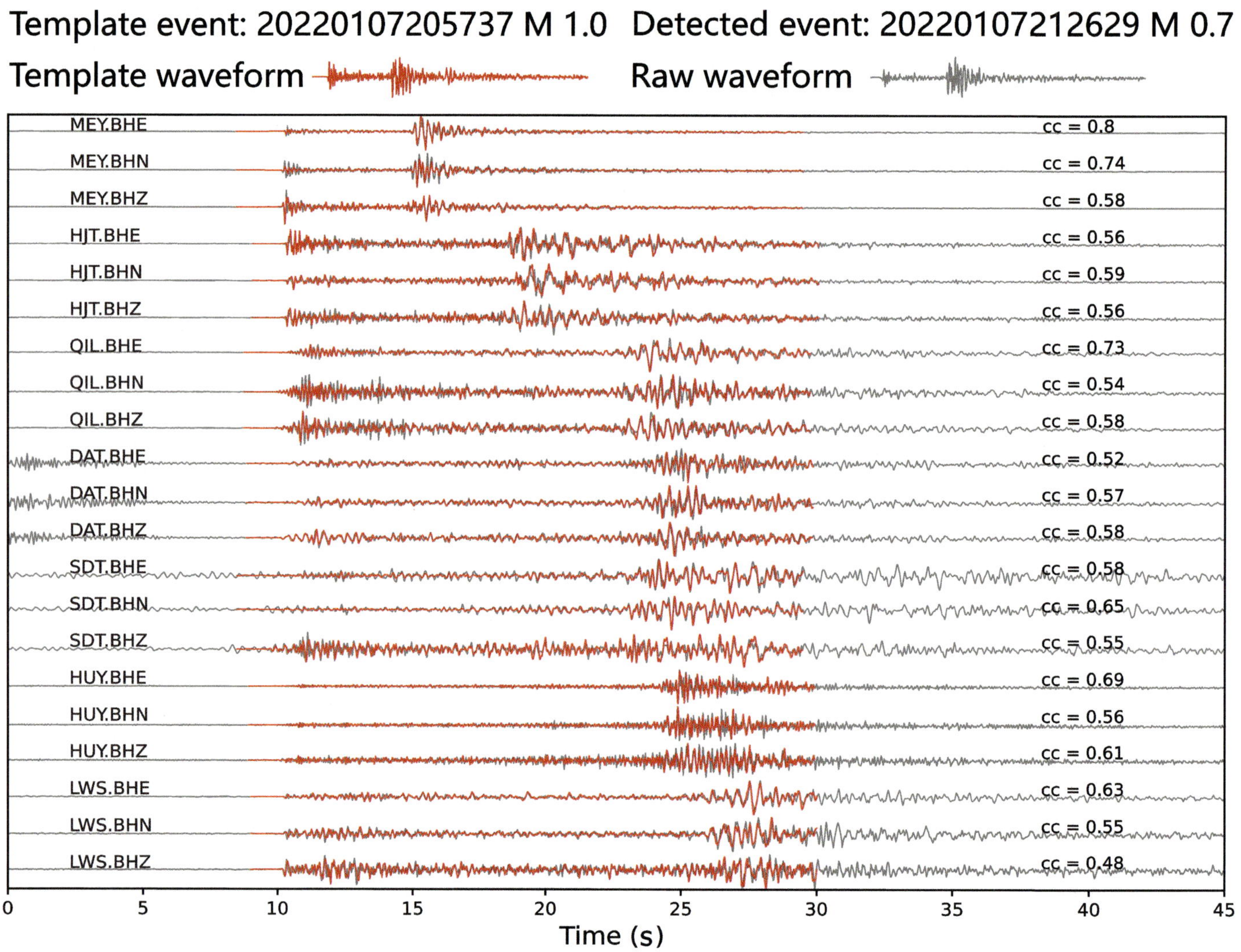

Figure 3. Example of a newly detected event using the MFA. Template and continuous waveforms are shown as red and gray lines, respectively. cc indicates the cross-correlation coefficient between the template and the continuous waveforms. The time window of the templates is from 1 s before to 20 s after the *P*-wave arrival. Both the templates and the continuous waveforms are band-pass filtered between 1 and 15 Hz.

waves, ensuring the same *S–P* time and thus the same hypocentral distance (Uchida, 2019). The raw waveforms are preprocessed by removing the mean and linear trend and applying a 1–10 Hz band-pass filter (Kato *et al.*, 2012; Yamashita *et al.*, 2012; Zhang *et al.*, 2022). Then, we build a distance matrix (dist = 1 − cc) and apply hierarchical clustering (maximum linkage) with dist ≤ 0.1 (cc ≥ 0.9) to obtain candidate similar sequences (Lance and Williams, 1967; Wang and Wang, 2012). To further constrain event similarity, we select sequences with *S–P* differential time $\Delta T_{S-P} \le 0.01$ s (Li *et al.*, 2011) for accurate relocation. The raw waveforms in candidate sequences are resampled to 500 Hz, differential times refined by cross correlation, and relative locations updated with the singular value decomposition (SVD) algorithm in HypoDD, leading to a horizontal uncertainty of ~10 m and a vertical uncertainty of ~20 m. For each sequence, we estimate the seismic moment from M_L ($\log M_0 = 9.8 + M_L$) (Abercrombie, 1996), stress drop ($\log \Delta\sigma = 0.46 \log M_0 - 7.02$; Hua *et al.*, 2013), and rupture radius $r = (7M_0/16\Delta\sigma)^{1/3}$ (Eshelby, 1957). Events are confirmed as repeaters when rupture circles overlap. This process yields two robust repeater sequences (Fig. 4). It is worth noting that we applied strict identification criteria to ensure the reliability of the repeating earthquakes. Therefore, it is likely that additional repeating sequences exist within the aftershock zone that were not captured in this study.

Discussion

Aftershock distribution and fault geometry

Because microearthquakes usually occur along pre-existing fault planes, we can use numerous microearthquakes to reveal the deep geometry of faults (Rubin *et al.*, 1999; Ross *et al.*, 2020; Xie *et al.*, 2021, 2022). The relocation results reveal that the aftershocks are distributed along the intersection of the nearly east–west-trending TLSF and the northwest–southeast-

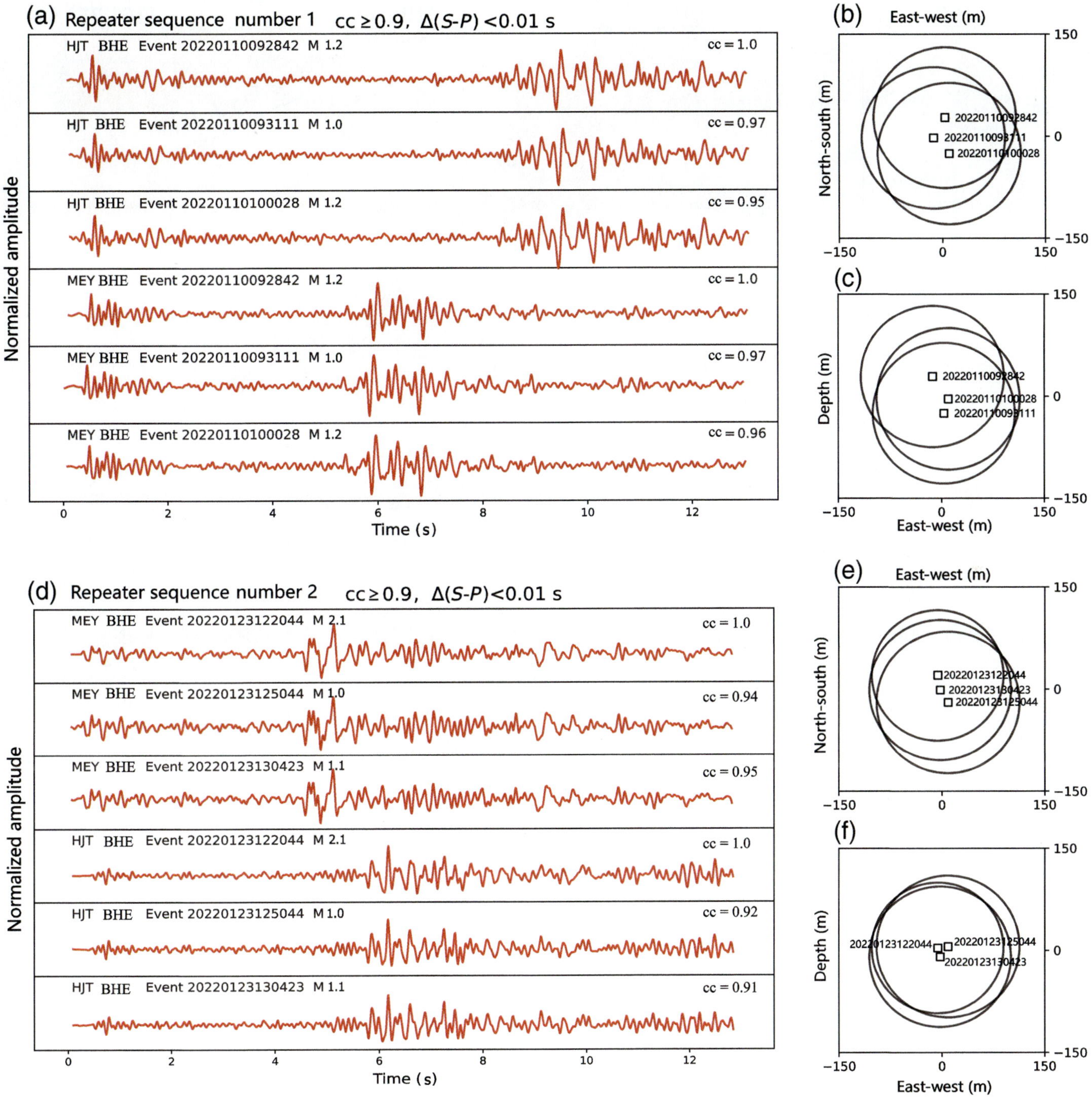

Figure 4. Two repeating earthquake sequences identified in this study. (a,d) Band-pass-filtered (1–10 Hz) waveforms from stations MEY and HJT, showing high similarity (cc ≥ 0.9) and nearly identical *S–P* times ($\Delta T_{S-P} < 0.01$ s). (b,c) Cross-sectional views of locations and estimated rupture radii for repeater sequence number 1. (e,f) Same as panels (b,c) but for repeater sequence number 2.

trending LLLF, extending approximately 30 km (Fig. 5). A prominent feature of relocated seismicity is a ~5 km wide aftershock gap observed near the bend of the LLLF. Although Zou and Lei (2023) also pointed out the presence of a seismic gap, their catalog suggests that the gap was only evident within the first 1.5 hr after the mainshock and subsequently became obscured by aftershocks. This difference may stem from methodological differences because their analysis was based solely on arrival-time data without the use of waveform cross correlation. In contrast, our study utilizes waveform cross correlation, which reduced relative relocation uncertainties by refining the differential travel-time measurements for event pairs (Waldhauser and Ellsworth, 2000). This enhanced resolution allows us to capture fine-scale features. The coseismic surface rupture extends about 21 km in length (Yang *et al.*, 2022), terminating near this aftershock gap.

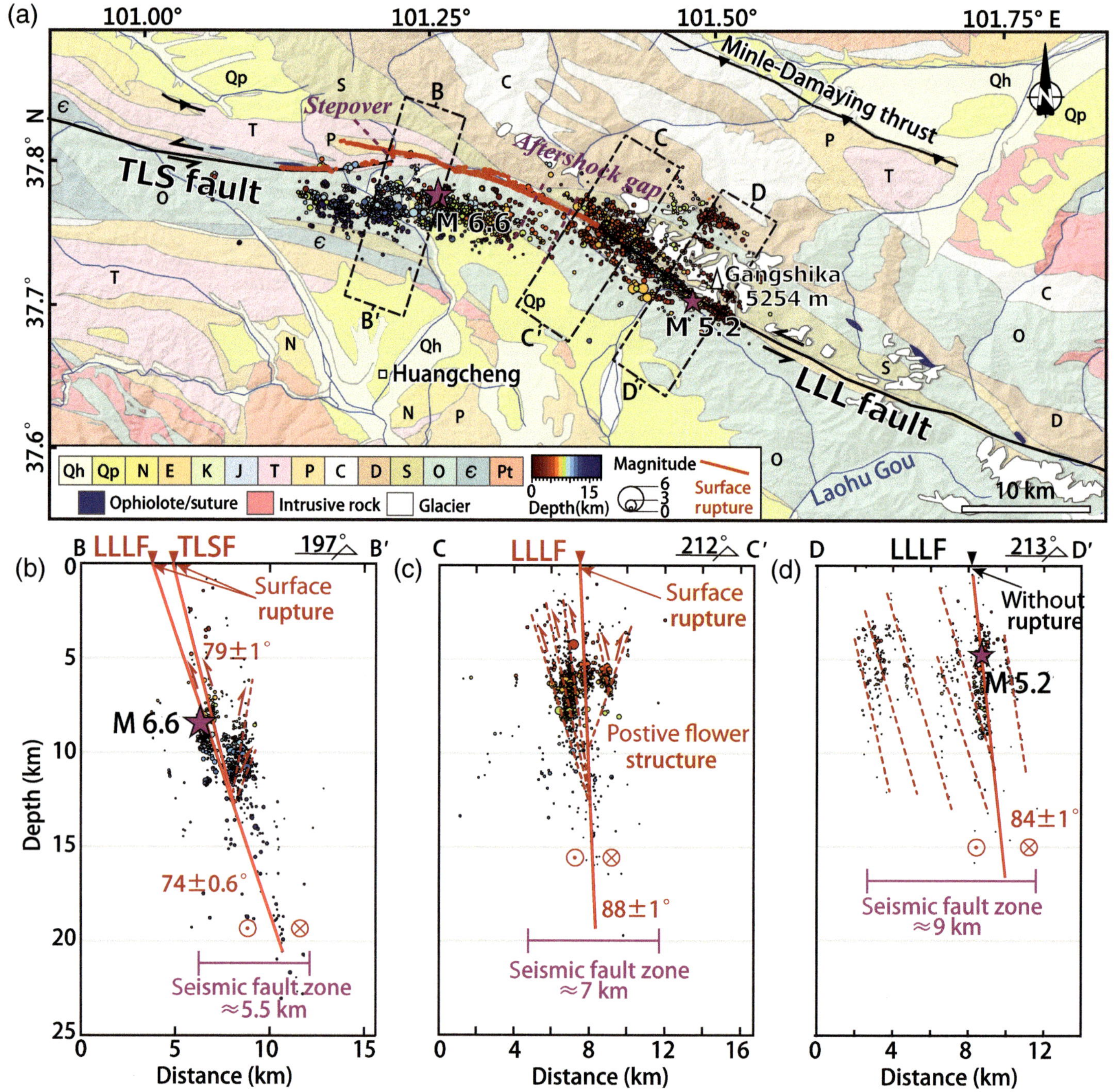

Figure 5. Aftershocks distribution, regional geologic map (1:250,000) and fault geometry. (a) Relocated aftershocks (dots color coded by depth) and surface ruptures (red lines; Feng *et al.*, 2022). Black-dashed rectangles: Cross-section locations in panels (b–d). Colored stars: mainshock and largest aftershock. Purple-dashed lines: aftershock gap. Geoscientific data are available from Li *et al.* (2023). (b–d) Depth sections of aftershocks. Orange-dashed lines: inferred faults.

Based on this gap, we divide the fault system into western and eastern segments for detailed discussion.

On the western segment, field investigations identified a left-lateral stepover of ~2.5 to 2.8 km at the intersection of the TLSF and LLLF (Li *et al.*, 2023; Xu *et al.*, 2024). Our relocated aftershocks reveal that seismicity is not interrupted by this surface stepover; instead, events are continuously distributed across the stepover region, connecting the two fault branches at depth. Furthermore, the InSAR coseismic slip model (Luo and Wang, 2022) also indicates that the coseismic rupture propagated through this fault stepover. Specifically, the aftershocks delineate two branches: one trending east–west and the other northwest. Notably, the epicenters are offset by ~2 to 3 km to the south of the corresponding surface traces. This spatial offset is geometrically consistent with a southward-

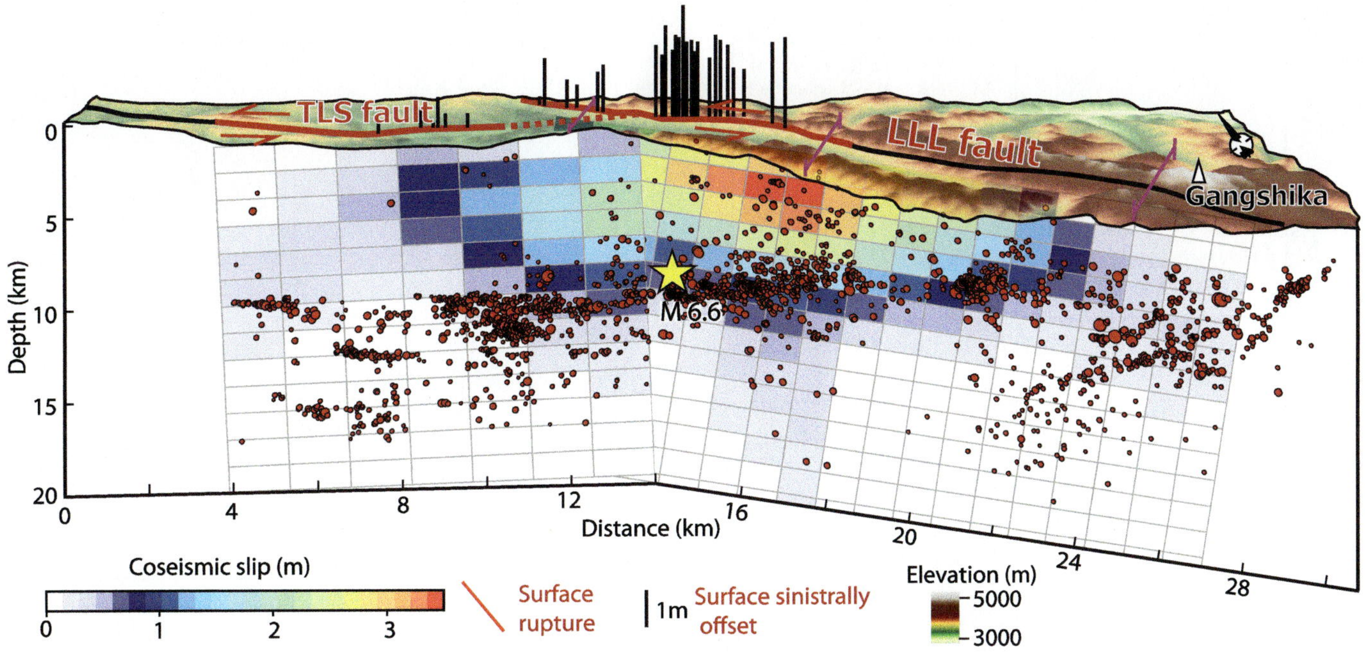

Figure 6. Aftershocks superposed on Interferometric Synthetic Aperture Radar (InSAR) slip model (Luo and Wang, 2022). Red lines represent surface rupture. Black-vertical lines represent surface sinistrally offset. Red dots represent aftershocks. Yellow star is the M_w 6.6 mainshock.

dipping fault plane. Given the ~74° southward dip (Fig. 5b), the surface projection of the fault at the aftershock depth (~10 km) results in a theoretical offset of ~2.9 km, which matches the observed 2–3 km southward shift, supporting the conclusion that these events occurred on the main fault. The linear alignment of aftershocks parallel to the surface traces confirms that the western segment dips to the south, and that the ~2.5 km surface stepover does not extend strictly vertically to depth but rather represents a complex surface expression of a connected fault system at seismogenic depths. Although a ~2.5 km stepover is present on the surface of the western fault segment, it did not impede the propagation of either the coseismic rupture or aftershock migration. The continuous aftershock distribution across the stepover suggests that the two fault branches may be connected at depth, consistent with the interpretation of Li *et al.* (2023).

On the eastern segment, aftershocks delineate multiple subparallel, northwest-trending lineament faults, extending ~15 km and dipping steeply to the southwest. Here, the epicenters are shifted ~3 km north of LLLF surface trace. Given that field geological surveys indicate a northward dip for the LLLF (Feng *et al.*, 2022; Li *et al.*, 2023), these aftershocks likely occurred on subsidiary faults north of the LLLF. At the bend of the LLLF, where the surface rupture terminated, a ~5 km aftershock gap is clearly observed. Depth profiles reveal that the fault dip angle changes by ~14° across this bend (Fig. 5b,c). This observation aligns well with the findings of Luo and Wang (2022), who reported a fault bend of ~10° and a dip angle change of ~10°. Because microearthquakes usually occur along pre-existing fault planes (Rubin *et al.*, 1999), the difference in dip angles between the two fault segments led to this aftershock gap. As illustrated in the depth profiles (Fig. 5b–d), the convergence of these varying dip angles resembles a positive flower structure, a feature commonly observed in strike-slip fault zones (Feng *et al.*, 2022), suggesting that the change in fault geometry plays a critical role in this earthquake sequence.

Relationship between fault geometry and coseismic and postseismic processes

Integrating our high-resolution catalog with the coseismic slip model (Luo and Wang, 2022), surface rupture data (Feng *et al.*, 2022), and the rupture process model (Lv *et al.*, 2022), we infer a bilateral rupture propagation for the mainshock: The event first nucleated on the LLLF, and then the surface rupture propagated eastward before arresting near the geometric bend (the aftershock gap), and westward, jumping across the ~2.5-km-wide stepover onto the TLSF (Fig. 6). The maximum coseismic slip reached up to ~3.5 m, which is 2–3 times greater than the empirically expected value for an M_w 6.6 earthquake, and is concentrated in the region between the stepover and the aftershock gap at depths of 0–8 km. The coseismic slip amplitude was confined within the region bounded by fault discontinuities. This slip distribution suggests that the geometric discontinuities (the bend and dip changes) acted as barriers that confined the rupture, thereby concentrating stress and amplifying slip within the segment.

Postseismically, the sequence exhibits interesting spatiotemporal expansion behaviors. We observed two independent

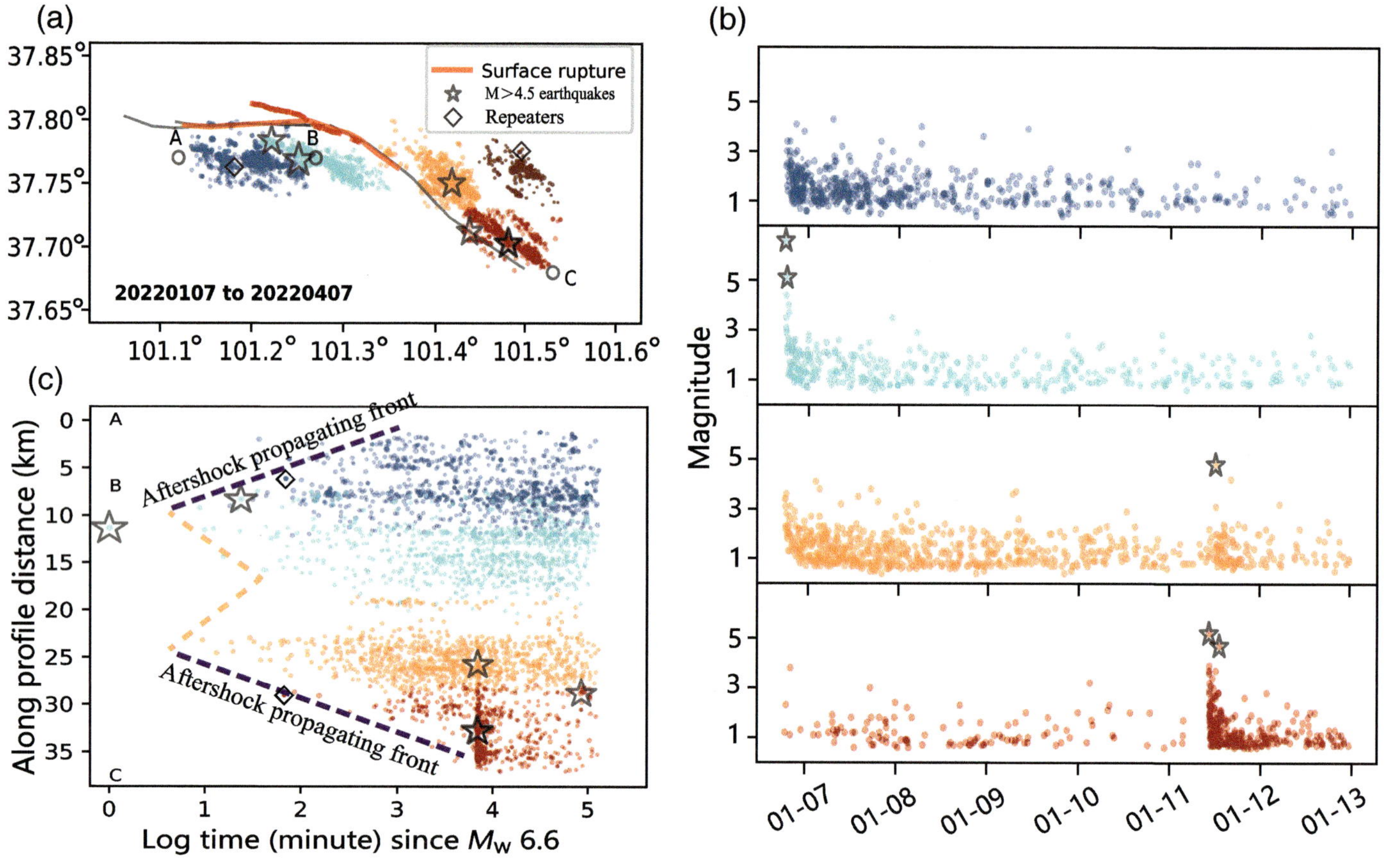

Figure 7. Spatiotemporal aftershock migration. (a) Segmented aftershock distribution with colors indicating fault segments. Stars: $M_W \geq 4.5$ events. (b) Distance-logarithmic time plot showing two expansion fronts (purple- and orange-dashed lines). (c) Event counts per segment over time. The four different colors (blue, cyan, orange, and red) indicate four distinct fault segments identified by the spatial clustering of the aftershock sequence.

aftershock expansion fronts (indicated by purple- and orange-dashed lines in Fig. 7b) and two repeating earthquake sequences (Fig. 4). These observations indicate sustained aseismic slip occurring along the fault plane. Typically, postseismic aseismic slip loads adjacent fault segments, driving aftershocks to expand spatiotemporally with a typical logarithmic time–distance migration pattern that follows Omori's Law (Peng and Zhao, 2009; Kato and Obara, 2014). However, interestingly, the aftershock expansion fronts in this study do not merely follow a simple logarithmic relationship but rather exhibit a "W-shaped" pattern (Fig. 7b). The "trough" of this W-shape occurs at a distance of ~15 to 20 km, spatially coinciding with the aftershock gap and the fault bend. This implies that the postseismic expansion process was not only driven by aseismic slip but was also significantly modulated by variations in fault strike and dip (fault segmentation). It is this fault segmentation that resulted in the observed W-shaped migration pattern. Similar instances of fault geometry controlling aftershock migration have been documented previously. For instance, in the 2007 M_W 6.7 Noto-Hanto earthquake, the observed step-like migration pattern was governed by the inherent segmentation of the geologically complex source region (Kato and Obara, 2014). Two repeating earthquake sequences are located at the edges of the aftershock zone (Fig. 7a). This distribution is consistent with observations from other large earthquakes (Chalumeau *et al.*, 2021), indicating that aseismic slip might be distributed along the periphery of the coseismic rupture zone, driven by stress accumulation at the slip gradient rather than at the slip maxima.

Seven days after the mainshock, the largest aftershock (M_s 5.2) occurred near the eastern termination. Considering the potential for secondary damage caused by the M_s 5.2 aftershock, we evaluated the triggering mechanism of this event. We calculated the Coulomb stress change (ΔCFS) at its focal depth of 4.7 km. To accurately account for the complex fault geometry, we utilized a segmented finite-fault source model consisting of four fault segments (Seg1–Seg4 in Fig. S1), each assigned with specific strike and dip angles based on the inversion results of Luo and Wang (2022). The receiver fault parameters were set according to the focal mechanism of the largest aftershock (strike/dip/rake: 301°/87°/18°). We adopted a friction coefficient of 0.4, a Poisson's ratio of 0.25, and a Young's modulus of 8×10^4 MPa (Toda *et al.*, 2005; Zhang *et al.*, 2023). The results indicate that the mainshock rupture induced a stress increase exceeding the standard triggering threshold of 0.01 MPa (King *et al.*, 1994) at the eastern fault termination. The M_s 5.2 aftershock is located within the zone of positive stress increase, suggesting that its occurrence was possibly triggered by the static Coulomb stress.

Implications of fault geometry on seismic processes

Numerical and statistical models have been used to investigate how individual fault geometric features influence rupture behavior. For instance, strike-slip ruptures are often arrested by stepovers wider than ~4 to 5 km (Harris and Day, 1999; Wesnousky, 2006; Biasi and Wesnousky, 2016; Hu *et al.*, 2016), and fault bends of 10°–25° have approximately 50% chance of stopping rupture propagation (Elliott *et al.*, 2015, 2018; Rodriguez Padilla *et al.*, 2024; Zhao *et al.*, 2025). Reverse-faulting ruptures are more likely to arrest at stepovers, whereas normal and dip-slip ruptures tend to propagate more easily across them. In particular, dip-slip ruptures have been observed to jump across stepovers as wide as 12 km (Biasi and Wesnousky, 2016). If multiple seismic cycles or transfer fault structures are considered, even minor geometric changes, such as along-strike variation in dip angle, can serve as rupture barriers, as observed along the Alpine fault in New Zealand and Altyn Tagh fault (Elliott *et al.*, 2018; Howarth *et al.*, 2021). These insights, while valuable, are largely focused on individual geometric features under specific scenarios. However, in natural fault systems, rupture processes are influenced by the interaction of multiple faults with irregular geometries, making their behaviors more complex and variable. To better understand these interactions, more observational case studies from real earthquakes are needed.

The 2022 Menyuan earthquake provides a compelling case study of these interactions. Specifically, the ~2.5-km-wide stepover on the western segment was insufficient to arrest the rupture, allowing propagation to jump across. In contrast, the combination of geometric complexities on the eastern segment—including a ~10° change in strike, a ~14° variation in dip angle, and the resulting structural discontinuity—effectively terminated the rupture process and led to a ~5 km seismic gap. The confinement of the peak slip (~3.5 m) between these two geometric features highlights how fault geometry can simultaneously act as a barrier to propagation and a concentrator of energy release. Similar barrier and concentration effects induced by fault geometry have been documented in events such as the 2008 Wenchuan earthquake (Shen *et al.*, 2009) and the 2023 Kahramanmaraş, Türkiye, earthquake (Ren *et al.*, 2024; Zhou *et al.*, 2025).

This integrated perspective highlights that the geometric complexities exert a significant control on rupture behavior (Howarth *et al.*, 2021), and the seismic hazard assessment must account not only for individual geometric metrics (such as stepover width) but also for the combined effect of 3D geometric variations (strike and dip changes). Moreover, the influence of fault geometry on seismic processes depends not only on the overall fault geometric complexity and the magnitude of specific geometric variations, but also on the strength of the tectonic stress driving the rupture (Roche *et al.*, 2025). The integrated effect of these variables governs the progression of seismic processes.

Conclusions

In this study, we have constructed a high-resolution aftershock catalog (~4200 events) using the matched-filtering method, delineated the fault geometry, and investigated the influence of multiple geometric features on the coseismic and postseismic processes of the 2022 M_w 6.6 Menyuan earthquake. We have demonstrated that interacting fault geometric complexities—not individual features alone—played a dominant role in this earthquake sequence:

1. Based on the matched-filtering technique, we constructed a high-resolution earthquake catalog containing approximately 4200 events. This catalog reveals that the seismogenic structures involve the nearly east–west-striking, south-dipping TLSF, the northwest–southeast-striking, southwest-dipping LLLF, and their adjacent subsidiary faults. Both main faults are characterized by steep dip angles. Moreover, variations in fault geometry (such as strike and dip) are observed among different fault segments, and a distinct aftershock gap of ~5 km is identified near the fault bend.
2. By integrating our aftershock results with previously published geological surveys, InSAR data, and seismic rupture models, we analyzed the dominant influence of multiple fault geometries on the coseismic process. Our analysis indicates that the coseismic surface rupture propagated across a 2.5 km stepover but was arrested at the ~5 km aftershock gap, a feature coincident with ~10° to 14° changes in both strike and dip angles. This geometric confinement likely contributed to the localization of the peak slip (~3.5 m, as reported by Luo and Wang, 2022), which is 2–3 times larger than empirically expected for an M_w 6.6 event.
3. For the postseismic process, the sequence evolved bilaterally into two independent fronts propagating along the eastern and western segments, separated by the identified aftershock gap. The "W-shaped" pattern and detection of repeating earthquakes imply that aseismic slip and fault segmentation collectively played an important role in dominating aftershock evolution.

Data and Resources

The seismic waveform data are available from the International Earthquake Science Data Center at http://www.esdc.ac.cn (last accessed September 2025; login required). Most figures were generated using the Generic Mapping Tools (GMT; Wessel *et al.*, 2013).

Geoscientific data are available from Li *et al.* (2023). The PALM code is openly available on GitHub at https://github.com/YijianZhou/PALM. The catalog of this study can be downloaded from Github at https://github.com/junlysky/catalog_menyuan. Both websites were last accessed in December 2025. The supplemental material for this article includes additional tests on several velocity model and Coulomb stress calculation.

Declaration of Competing Interests

The authors acknowledge that there are no conflicts of interest recorded. The authors declare that they have no known competing financial interests or personal relationships that could have appeared to influence the work reported in this article.

Acknowledgments

This study is jointly supported by the National Natural Science Foundation of China (NSFC Grant Number 42374081), Key Science and Technology Project of Ministry of Emergency Management of the People's Republic of China (Grant Number 2024EMST040402), Natural Science Basic Research Program Shaanxi Province (2024JC-YBMS-203, 2024JC-YBMS-195, 2024JC-YBQN-0334), and the Special Key Project of the Basic Research Service Fee of the Institute of Earthquake Forecasting, China Earthquake Administration (Grant Number CEAIEF2024030203). The authors thank Baoning Wu, Shiguang Wang, and Yun Zhou for constructive discussions. The authors also thank Teng Wang and Heng Luo for providing coseismic slip data.

References

Abercrombie, R. E. (1996). The magnitude-frequency distribution of earthquakes recorded with deep seismometers at Cajon Pass, southern California, *Tectonophysics* **261,** 1–7, doi: 10.1016/0040-1951(96)00052-2.

Avouac, J., and P. Tapponnier (1993). Kinematic model of active deformation in Central Asia, *Geophys. Res. Lett.* **20,** 895–898, doi: 10.1029/93GL00128.

Barka, A. A., and K. Kadinsky-Cade (1988). Strike-slip fault geometry in Turkey and its influence on earthquake activity, *Tectonics* **7,** 663–684, doi: 10.1029/TC007i003p00663.

Biasi, G. P., and S. G. Wesnousky (2016). Steps and gaps in ground ruptures: Empirical bounds on rupture propagation, *Bull. Seismol. Soc. Am.* **106,** 1110–1124, doi: 10.1785/0120150175.

Chalumeau, C., H. Agurto-Detzel, L. De Barros, P. Charvis, A. Galve, A. Rietbrock, A. Alvarado, S. Hernandez, S. Beck, Y. Font, *et al.* (2021). Repeating earthquakes at the edge of the afterslip of the 2016 Ecuadorian Mw 7.8 Pedernales earthquake, *J. Geophys. Res.* **126,** e2021JB021746, doi: 10.1029/2021JB021746.

Cowie, P. A., G. P. Roberts, J. M. Bull, and F. Visini (2012). Relationships between fault geometry, slip rate variability and earthquake recurrence in extensional settings, *Geophys. J. Int.* **189,** 143–160, doi: 10.1111/j.1365-246X.2012.05378.x.

Deng, Q., S. Chen, F. Song, S. Zhu, Y. Wang, W. Zhang, D. Jiao, B. C. Burchfiel, P. Molnar, L. Royden, *et al.* (1986). Variations in the geometry and amount of slip on the Haiyuan (Nanxihaushan) fault zone, China and the surface rupture of the 1920 Haiyuan earthquake, in *Earthquake Source Mechanics*, S. Das, J. Boatwright, and C. H. Scholz (Editors), Geophysical Monograph Series, Vol. 37, American Geophysical Union, Washington, D. C., 169–182, doi: 10.1029/GM037p0169.

Elliott, A. J., M. E. Oskin, J. Liu-Zeng, and Y. Shao (2015). Rupture termination at restraining bends: The last great earthquake on the Altyn Tagh Fault, *Geophys. Res. Lett.* **42,** 2164–2170, doi: 10.1002/2015GL063107.

Elliott, A. J., M. E. Oskin, J. Liu-Zeng, and Y.-X. Shao (2018). Persistent rupture terminations at a restraining bend from slip rates on the Eastern Altyn Tagh fault, *Tectonophysics* **733,** 57–72, doi: 10.1016/j.tecto.2018.01.004.

Eshelby, J. D. (1957). The determination of the elastic field of an ellipsoidal inclusion, and related problems, *Proc. Math. Phys. Sci.* **241,** 376–396.

Fan, L., B. Li, S. Liao, C. Jiang, and L. Fang (2022). High-precision relocation of the aftershock sequence of the January 8, 2022, Ms 6.9 Menyuan earthquake, *Earthq. Sci.* **35,** 138–145, doi: 10.1016/j.eqs.2022.01.021.

Feng, W., X. He, Y. Zhang, L. Fang, S. Samsonov, and P. Zhang (2022). Seismic faults of the 2022 Mw 6.6 Menyuan, Qinghai earthquake and their implication for the regional seismogenic structures, *Chin. Sci. Bull.* **68,** 254–270, doi: 10.1360/tb-2022-0154 (in Chinese).

Guo, P., Z. Han, W. Jiang, and Z. Mao (2017). Holocene left-lateral slip rate of the Lenglongling fault, northeastern Tibetan Plateau, and its tectonic implications, *Seismol. Geol.* **39,** 323–341, doi: 10.3969/j.issn.0253-4967.2017.02.005.

Hamling, I. J., S. Hreinsdóttir, K. Clark, J. Elliott, C. Liang, N. Litchfield, P. Villamor, L. Wallace, T. J. Wright, E. D'Anastasio, *et al.* (2017). Complex multifault rupture during the 2016 Mw 7.8 Kaikōura earthquake, New Zealand, *Science* **356,** eaam7194, doi: 10.1126/science.aam7194.

Harris, R. A., and S. M. Day (1999). Dynamic 3D simulations of earthquakes on en echelon faults, *Geophys. Res. Lett.* **26,** 2089–2092, doi: 10.1029/1999GL900377.

Howarth, J. D., N. C. Barth, S. J. Fitzsimons, K. Richards-Dinger, K. J. Clark, G. P. Biasi, U. A. Cochran, R. M. Langridge, K. R. Berryman, and R. Sutherland (2021). Spatiotemporal clustering of great earthquakes on a transform fault controlled by geometry, *Nature Geosci.* **14,** 314–320, doi: 10.1038/s41561-021-00721-4.

Hu, F., Z. Zhang, and X. Chen (2016). Investigation of earthquake jump distance for strike-slip step overs based on 3-D dynamic rupture simulations in an elastic half-space, *J. Geophys. Res.* **121,** 994–1006, doi: 10.1002/2015JB012696.

Hua, W., S. Zheng, C. Yan, and Z. Chen (2013). Attenuation, site effects, and source parameters in the Three Gorges Reservoir area, China, *Bull. Seismol. Soc. Am.* **103,** 371–382, doi: 10.1785/0120120076.

Huang, Z., Y. Zhou, X. Qiao, P. Zhang, and X. Cheng (2022). Kinematics of the ~1000 km Haiyuan fault system in northeastern Tibet from high-resolution Sentinel-1 InSAR velocities: Fault architecture, slip rates, and partitioning, *Earth Planet. Sci. Lett.* **583,** 117450, doi: 10.1016/j.epsl.2022.117450.

Jia, S., W. Guo, W. D. Mooney, F. Wang, Y. Duan, J. Zhao, J. Lin, and Z. Liu (2019). Crustal structure of the middle segment of the Qilian fold belt and the coupling mechanism of its associated basin and range system, *Tectonophysics* **770,** 128154, doi: 10.1016/j.tecto.2019.06.024.

Kato, A., and K. Obara (2014). Step-like migration of early aftershocks following the 2007 Mw 6.7 Noto-Hanto earthquake, Japan, *Geophys. Res. Lett.* **41,** 3864–3869, doi: 10.1002/2014GL060427.

Kato, A., K. Obara, T. Igarashi, H. Tsuruoka, S. Nakagawa, and N. Hirata (2012). Propagation of slow slip leading up to the 2011 Mw 9.0 Tohoku-Oki earthquake, *Science* **335,** 705–708, doi: 10.1126/science.1215141.

King, G. C. P., R. S. Stein, and J. Lin (1994). Static stress changes and the triggering of earthquakes, *Bull. Seismol. Soc. Am.* **84,** 935–953.

Klein, F. W. (2002). User's guide to HYPOINVERSE-2000, a Fortran program to solve for earthquake locations and magnitudes, *U.S. Geol. Surv. Open-File Rept. 02-171.*

Kreemer, C., G. Blewitt, and E. C. Klein (2014). A geodetic plate motion and global strain rate model, *Geochem. Geophys. Geosys.* **15,** 3849–3889, doi: 10.1002/2014GC005407.

Lance, G. N., and W. T. Williams (1967). A general theory of classificatory sorting strategies: 1. Hierarchical systems, *Comput. J.* **9,** 373–380, doi: 10.1093/comjnl/9.4.373.

Lee, J., V. C. Tsai, G. Hirth, A. Chatterjee, and D. T. Trugman (2024). Fault-network geometry influences earthquake frictional behaviour, *Nature* **631,** 106–110, doi: 10.1038/s41586-024-07518-6.

Li, K., P. Tapponnier, X. Xu, and W. Kang (2023). The 2022 Ms 6.9 Menyuan earthquake: Surface rupture, Paleozoic suture re-activation, slip-rate and seismic gap along the Haiyuan fault system, NE Tibet, *Earth Planet. Sci. Lett.* **622,** 118412, doi: 10.1016/j.epsl.2023.118412.

Li, L., Q. Chen, F. Niu, and J. Su (2011). Deep slip rates along the Longmen Shan fault zone estimated from repeating microearthquakes, *J. Geophys. Res.* **116,** no. B9, doi: 10.1029/2011JB008406.

Luo, H., and T. Wang (2022). Strain partitioning on the western Haiyuan fault system revealed by the adjacent 2016 Mw 5.9 and 2022 Mw 6.7 Menyuan earthquakes, *Geophys. Res. Lett.* **49,** e2022GL099348, doi: 10.1029/2022GL099348.

Lv, M., K. Chen, H. Chai, J. Geng, S. Zhang, and L. Fang (2022). Joint inversion of InSAR and high-rate GNSS displacement waveforms for the rupture process of the 2022 Qinghai Menyuan M 6.9 earthquake, *Chin. J. Geophys.* **65,** 4725–4738, doi: 10.6038/cjg2022Q0304 (in Chinese).

Okubo, P. G., and K. Aki (1987). Fractal geometry in the San Andreas fault system, *J. Geophys. Res.* **92,** 345–355, doi: 10.1029/JB092iB01p00345.

Peng, Z., and P. Zhao (2009). Migration of early aftershocks following the 2004 Parkfield earthquake, *Nature Geosci.* **2,** 877–881, doi: 10.1038/ngeo697.

Ren, C., Z. Wang, T. Taymaz, N. Hu, H. Luo, Z. Zhao, H. Yue, X. Song, Z. Shen, H. Xu, *et al.* (2024). Supershear triggering and cascading fault ruptures of the 2023 Kahramanmaraş, Türkiye, earthquake doublet, *Science* **383,** 305–311, doi: 10.1126/science.adi1519.

Roche, V., M. van der Baan, and J. Walsh (2025). The role of the three-dimensional geometry of fault steps on event migration during fluid-induced seismic sequences, *J. Geophys. Res.* **130,** e2024JB029476, doi: 10.1029/2024JB029476.

Rodriguez Padilla, A. M., M. E. Oskin, E. E. Brodsky, K. Dascher-Cousineau, V. Herrera, and S. White (2024). The influence of fault geometrical complexity on surface rupture length, *Geophys. Res. Lett.* **51,** e2024GL109957, doi: 10.1029/2024GL109957.

Ross, Z. E., E. S. Cochran, D. T. Trugman, and J. D. Smith (2020). 3D fault architecture controls the dynamism of earthquake swarms, *Science* **368,** 1357–1361, doi: 10.1126/science.abb0779.

Rubin, A. M., D. Gillard, and J.-L. Got (1999). Streaks of microearthquakes along creeping faults, *Nature* **400,** 635–641, doi: 10.1038/23196.

Shen, Z.-K., J. Sun, P. Zhang, Y. Wan, M. Wang, R. Bürgmann, Y. Zeng, W. Gan, H. Liao, and Q. Wang (2009). Slip maxima at fault junctions and rupturing of barriers during the 2008 Wenchuan earthquake, *Nature Geosci.* **2,** 718–724, doi: 10.1038/ngeo636.

Sibson, R. H., F. Robert, and K. H. Poulsen (1988). High-angle reverse faults, fluid-pressure cycling, and mesothermal gold-quartz deposits, *Geology* **16,** 551–555.

Talwani, P. (1999). Fault geometry and earthquakes in continental interiors, *Tectonophysics* **305,** 371–379, doi: 10.1016/S0040-1951(99)00024-4.

Tapponnier, P., B. Meyer, J. P. Avouac, G. Peltzer, Y. Gaudemer, S. Guo, H. Xiang, K. Yin, Z. Chen, S. Cai, *et al.* (1990). Active thrusting and folding in the Qilian Shan, and decoupling between upper crust and mantle in northeastern Tibet, *Earth Planet. Sci. Lett.* **97,** 382–403, doi: 10.1016/0012-821X(90)90053-Z.

Toda, S., R. S. Stein, K. Richards-Dinger, and S. B. Bozkurt (2005). Forecasting the evolution of seismicity in southern California: Animations built on earthquake stress transfer, *J. Geophys. Res.* **110,** no. B5, doi: 10.1029/2004JB003415.

Uchida, N. (2019). Detection of repeating earthquakes and their application in characterizing slow fault slip, *Prog. Earth Planet. Sci.* **6,** 1–21, doi: 10.1186/s40645-019-0284-z.

Waldhauser, F. (2001). hypoDD—A program to compute double-difference hypocenter locations, *U.S. Geol. Surv. Open-File Rept. 01-113.*

Waldhauser, F., and W. L. Ellsworth (2000). A double-difference earthquake location algorithm: Method and application to the northern Hayward fault, California, *Bull. Seismol. Soc. Am.* **90,** 1353–1368, doi: 10.1785/0120000006.

Wang, M., and Z. Shen (2020). Present-day crustal deformation of continental China derived from GPS and its tectonic implications, *J. Geophys. Res.* **125,** e2019JB018774, doi: 10.1029/2019JB018774.

Wang, W.-T., and B.-S. Wang (2012). Quick identification of multi-level similar earthquakes using hierarchical clustering method and its application to Wenchuan northeast aftershock sequence, *Chin. J. Geophys.* **55,** 1952–1962.

Wesnousky, S. G. (2006). Predicting the endpoints of earthquake ruptures, *Nature* **444,** 358–360, doi: 10.1038/nature05275.

Wessel, P., W. H. Smith, R. Scharroo, J. Luis, and F. Wobbe (2013). Generic Mapping Tools: Improved version released, *Eos Trans. AGU* **94,** 409–410, doi: 10.1002/2013EO450001.

Xie, C., B. Zhou, P. Wang, Z. Li, T. Liu, W. Pang, and Z. Cao (2022). The seismogenic structure of the 2017 Mw 6.9 Milin, Tibet, earthquake: A possible newly active fault at the eastern Himalayan syntaxis, *Seismol. Res. Lett.* **93,** 68–75, doi: 10.1785/0220210165.

Xie, C., B. Zhou, F. Yang, Z. Li, Y. Cui, W. Pang, and W. Li (2021). Geological and geomorphological evidence for activity along the Motuo fault, eastern side of the Namche Barwa syntaxis, Tibetan Plateau, *Seismol. Res. Lett.* **92,** 2196–2205, doi: 10.1785/0220200342.

Xu, D., W. Gong, Z. Zhang, J. Xu, H. Yu, and X. Chen (2023). The 2016 Menyuan earthquake: The largest self-arrested crustal earthquake ever observed, *Geophys. Res. Lett.* **50,** e2023GL103556, doi: 10.1029/2023GL103556.

Xu, D., Z. Li, Z. Zhang, H. Yu, J. Xu, Z. Yang, and X. Chen (2024). The 2022 Mw 6.6 Menyuan earthquake: An early-terminated runaway rupture by the complex fault geometry, *Earth Planet. Sci. Lett.* **638,** 118746, doi: 10.1016/j.epsl.2024.118746.

Xu, X., X. Wu, G. Yu, X. Tan, and K. Li (2017). Seismo-geological signatures for identifying M≥7.0 earthquake risk areas and their premilimary application in mainland China, *Seismol. Geol.* **39,** 219–275.

Xu, Y., X. Guo, and L. Feng (2022). Relocation and focal mechanism solutions of the MS 6.9 Menyuan earthquake sequence on January 8, 2022 in Qinghai Province, *Acta Seismol. Sin.* **44,** 195–210, doi: 10.11939/jass.20220008 (in Chinese).

Yamashita, Y., H. Shimizu, and K. Goto (2012). Small repeating earthquake activity, interplate quasi-static slip, and interplate coupling in the Hyuga-Nada, southwestern Japan subduction zone, *Geophys. Res. Lett.* **39,** L08304, doi: 10.1029/2012GL051476.

Yang, H., D. Wang, R. Guo, M. Xie, Y. Zang, Y. Wang, Q. Yao, C. Cheng, Y. An, and Y. Zhang (2022). Rapid report of the 8 January 2022 MS 6.9 Menyuan earthquake, Qinghai, China, *Earthq. Res. Adv.* **2,** 100113, doi: 10.1016/j.eqrea.2022.100113.

Zhang, L., Z. He, S. Wang, Y. Zhang, S. Li, Z. Zhang, and L. Fang (2025). The 2023 Mw 6.0 Jishishan earthquake: A slow unilateral rupture on a blind thrust fault revealed by high-precision earthquake locations and dynamic modeling, *Seismol. Res. Lett.* **96,** 2105–2114, doi: 10.1785/0220240333.

Zhang, L., J. Su, W. Wang, L. Fang, and J. Wu (2022). Deep fault slip characteristics in the Xianshuihe-Anninghe-Daliangshan fault junction region (eastern Tibet) revealed by repeating microearthquakes, *J. Asian Earth Sci.* **227,** 105115, doi: 10.1016/j.jseaes.2022.105115.

Zhang, L., Y. Zhou, X. Zhang, A. Zhu, B. Li, S. Wang, S. Liang, C. Jiang, J. Wu, Y. Li, *et al.* (2023). 2022 Mw 6.6 Luding, China, earthquake: A strong continental event illuminating the Moxi seismic gap, *Seismol. Res. Lett.* **94,** 2129–2142, doi: 10.1785/0220220383.

Zhao, L., E. Nissen, W. Xu, M. Jamalreyhani, E. A. Bergman, D. Zhao, and L. Xie (2025). Variable fault geometry controls the cascading 2023 Herat, Afghanistan multiplet sequence, *Commun. Earth Environ.* **6,** 135, doi: 10.1038/s43247-025-02113-7.

Zheng, W., P. Zhang, D. Yuan, C. Wu, Z. Li, W. Ge, W. Wang, and Y. Wang (2019). Basic characteristics of active tectonic and associated geodynamic processes in continental China, *J. Geomech.* **25,** 699–721, doi: 10.12090/j.issn.1006-6616.2019.25.05.062 (in Chinese).

Zhou, J., Y. Xu, Y. Zhang, W. Feng, T. Taymaz, Y.-T. Chen, C. Xu, B. Xu, R. Wang, F. Shi, *et al.* (2025). Geometric barriers impacted rupture processes and stress releases of the 2023 Kahramanmaraş, Türkiye, earthquake doublet, *Commun. Earth Environ.* **6,** 56, doi: 10.1038/s43247-025-02004-x.

Zhou, Y., H. Yue, L. Fang, S. Zhou, L. Zhao, and A. Ghosh (2021). An earthquake detection and location architecture for continuous seismograms: Phase picking, association, location, and matched filter (PALM), *Seismol. Res. Lett.* **93,** 413–425, doi: 10.1785/0220210111.

Zhou, Y., H. Yue, S. Zhou, L. Fang, Y. Zhou, L. Xu, Z. Liu, T. Wang, L. Zhao, and A. Ghosh (2022). Microseismicity along Xiaojiang fault zone (southeastern Tibetan Plateau) and the characterization of interseismic fault behavior, *Tectonophysics* **833,** 229364, doi: 10.1016/j.tecto.2022.229364.

Zou, K., and J. Lei (2023). Relocation of the 8 January 2022 Menyuan (Ms 6.9), China, earthquake sequence: A conjugated type of rupturing event with a seismic gap in the Qilian-Haiyuan fault in northeast Tibet, *J. Asian Earth Sci.* **258,** 105800, doi: 10.1016/j.jseaes.2023.105800.

Manuscript received 7 October 2025
Published online 21 January 2026

Focus Section: Intraplate Earthquakes

An Intraplate Seismic Swarm in the Karoo Basin, South Africa, Highlights the Presence of Critically Stressed Faults in an Area of Proposed Shale Gas Exploration

OPEN ACCESS

Benjamin A. Whitehead*[1,2], Melody Janse van Rensburg[1,3], Diego A. Quiros[1], R. Alastair Sloan[1], and Beth Kahle[1,4]

Abstract

Stable continental region seismicity is now recognized as a significant source of hazard and the combination of shale gas exploration and wastewater disposal increases the likelihood of failure along critically stressed structures. In this study, we describe a natural swarm of earthquakes that occurred within the Karoo basin, South Africa, in the vicinity of the crustal-scale structure associated with a major long wavelength magnetic anomaly. The cluster began suddenly in 2007, in an area of little prior seismicity, and is characterized by earthquakes with predominantly low magnitudes, however the largest event was M_L 4.8. A short-term geophone deployment characterized the depth extent and trend of microseismicity, which runs west-northwest–east-southeast and spans the lower parts of the sedimentary cover down to, and perhaps into, the upper crystalline basement. Focal mechanisms suggest that the earthquakes involve left-lateral strike-slip motion, similar to the M_w 6.3 Ceres–Tulbagh earthquake that occurred in 1969. Ambient noise tomography reveals a prominent velocity transition concordant to the trend of the microseismicity within the sedimentary units. These results suggest that a critically stressed fault extends from the proposed target for shale gas exploration down to the basement, and so the necessary preconditions for significant induced seismicity may be met. This agrees with worldwide observations that seismicity in stable continental regions often aligns with inherited basement structures. Thus, by carefully considering the depth extent of seismicity and its relationship with these structures it is possible to identify hazardous structures in advance of possible shale gas development.

Cite this article as Whitehead, B. A., M. Janse van Rensburg, D. A. Quiros, R. A. Sloan, and B. Kahle (2026). An Intraplate Seismic Swarm in the Karoo Basin, South Africa, Highlights the Presence of Critically Stressed Faults in an Area of Proposed Shale Gas Exploration, *Seismol. Res. Lett.* **97**, 845–859, doi: 10.1785/0220250325.

Supplemental Material

Introduction

South Africa is an intraplate region characterized by Global Positioning System-derived strain rates on the order of 1 nanostrain per year or less (Malservisi *et al.*, 2013). Consequently, when compared to interplate regions such as the East African Rift system (EARS), it has a relatively low rate of seismic activity. Low strain rates do not however necessarily translate into low maximum earthquake magnitudes. For example, in eastern North America four $M_w > 7$ earthquakes occurred during the 1811–1812 New Madrid earthquake sequence. They occurred in an area which now shows less than 0.2 mm/yr (and indistinguishable from zero) strain accrual (Craig and Calais, 2014). In some cases, such as the 2001 M_w 7.6 Bhuj earthquake in northwest (NW) India these infrequent high-magnitude events have caused considerable devastation (Copley *et al.*, 2011). Within South Africa the most significant events are the 1969 M_w 6.3 Ceres–Tulbagh earthquake (Krüger and Scherbaum, 2014) and a cluster of earthquakes in the vicinity of Koffeefontein the largest of which occurred in 1912 with an $M_w \sim 6.2$ (Ambraseys and Adams, 1991; Strasser *et al.*, 2015). To the south of our study area, trenching suggests even larger Quaternary paleoseismic events have reactivated the Jurassic–Cretaceous basin-bounding Kango fault (Goedhart and Booth, 2016a,b).

1. Department of Geological Sciences, University of Cape Town, Cape Town, South Africa, https://orcid.org/0000-0002-3803-827X (BAW); https://orcid.org/0000-0002-4946-5322 (DAQ); https://orcid.org/0000-0002-1313-6914 (RAS); https://orcid.org/0000-0002-8781-0457 (BK); 2. Department of Geosciences, UiT The Artic University of Norway, Tromsø, Norway; 3. Nanometrics Inc., Milpitas, California, U.S.A.; 4. Department of Earth and Environmental Sciences, Ludwig Maximilian University of Munich, Munich, Germany

*Corresponding author: whtben003@myuct.ac.za

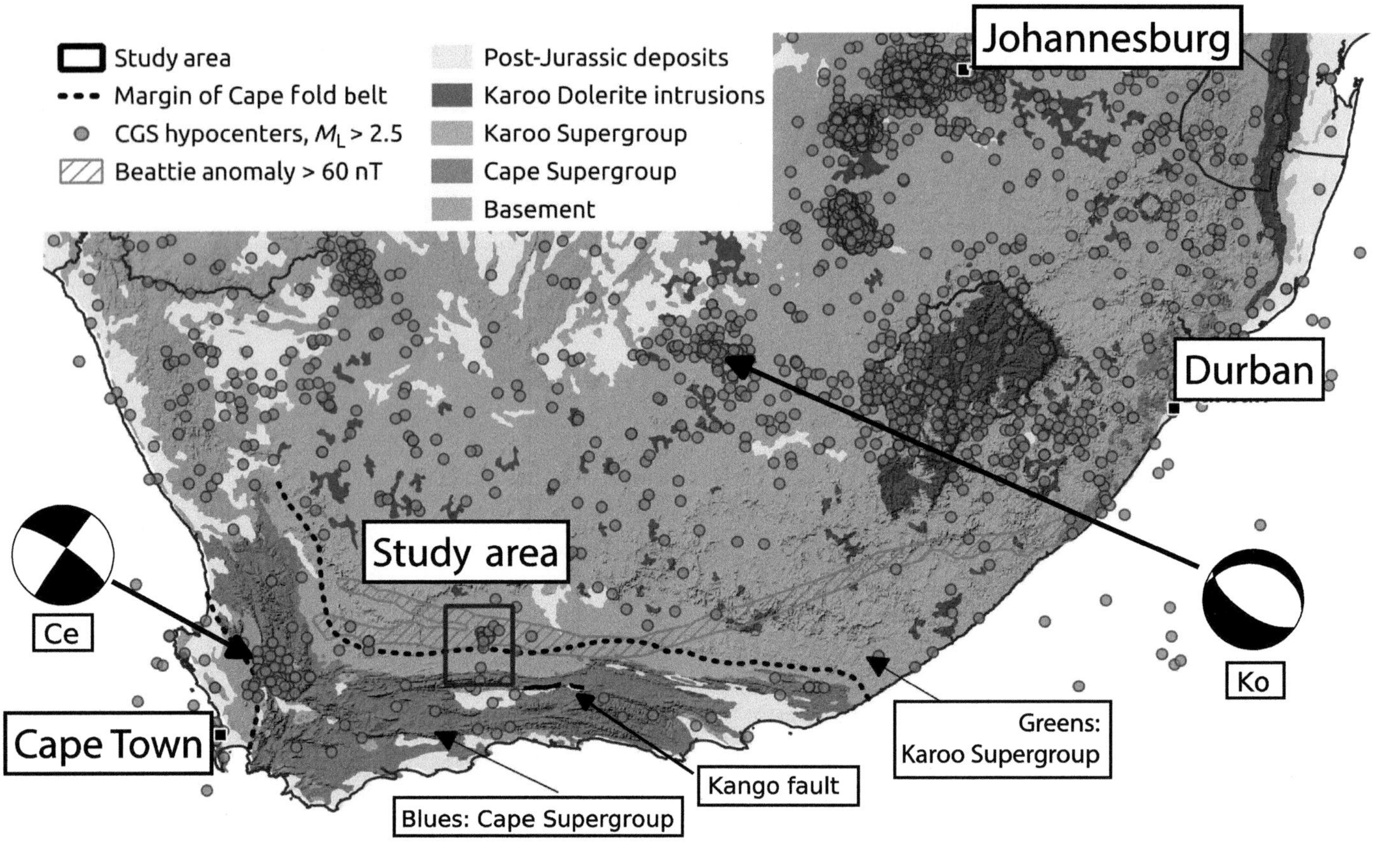

Figure 1. Simplified regional geology of southern Africa by the Council for Geoscience (2018). Earthquakes (red circles) from the CGS catalog (2022) are shown. Because of a sparse national geophone network, depths are poorly constrained. The location uncertainties are not reported but are likely to be significant in the study region. The approximate extent of the Cape fold belt, the location of the Karoo Supergroup, and the Kango fault are shown. The location of the Beattie magnetic anomaly (Beattie, 1909) is indicated (light gray polygon with hatching lines), defined by an increased aeromagnetic total intensity (modified from Scheiber-Enslin *et al.*, 2014). Ce, focal mechanism for the 1969 M_w 6.2 Ceres earthquake (Krüger and Scherbaum, 2014); Ko, focal mechanism for the 1976 M_w 5.8 Koffiefontein earthquake (Foster and Jackson, 1998). The color version of this figure is available only in the electronic edition.

There is no generally accepted model describing where intraplate seismicity is more likely to occur. Many of the largest events do occur on faults associated with ancient rift zones (such as the Kango fault), but many significant events occur in other settings (Schulte and Mooney, 2005), often without any obvious surface expression of faulting. Neither the Ceres–Tulbagh nor the Koffeefontein events have been associated with a clear causative structure at the surface. It has been suggested that major intraplate earthquakes may often be associated with transient stress perturbations emphasizing the importance of understanding the potential for such events in regions where significant anthropogenic stress changes are likely to occur (Calais *et al.*, 2016).

Although earthquakes and earthquake clusters may not be associated with clear surface features, they are often with major crustal structures in the subsurface which are identifiable from geophysical datasets. For instance, earthquake ruptures in Australia and Namibia show a clear correlation with anomalies in aeromagnetic datasets (King *et al.*, 2019; Muir *et al.*, 2023). In this contribution, we examine a cluster of seismicity within the Karoo Foreland basin (a region of potential future shale gas extraction) to try to identify and understand the causative structure. We use a relatively low-cost array of geophones to both better constrain the spatial distribution of seismicity and to determine if subsurface structures can be identified from ambient noise tomography (ANT). Combining these data with a review of existing geophysical datasets we discuss the probable causative structure, the depth extent of faulting and the implications for seismic hazard in the area. The Main Karoo basin (Fig. 1) which covers large parts of the South African interior and that resulted from the deposition of the Late Carboniferous–Early Jurassic Karoo Supergroup (Johnson *et al.*, 1996), provides a useful setting to examine intraplate seismicity within sub-Saharan Africa. The basin is generally described as the foreland basin to the Cape fold-and-thrust belt (Veevers *et al.*, 1994), and most Karoo Supergroup strata are largely undeformed except at the southern and southwestern basin margins affected by the Palaeozoic Cape Orogeny (Newton, 1993).

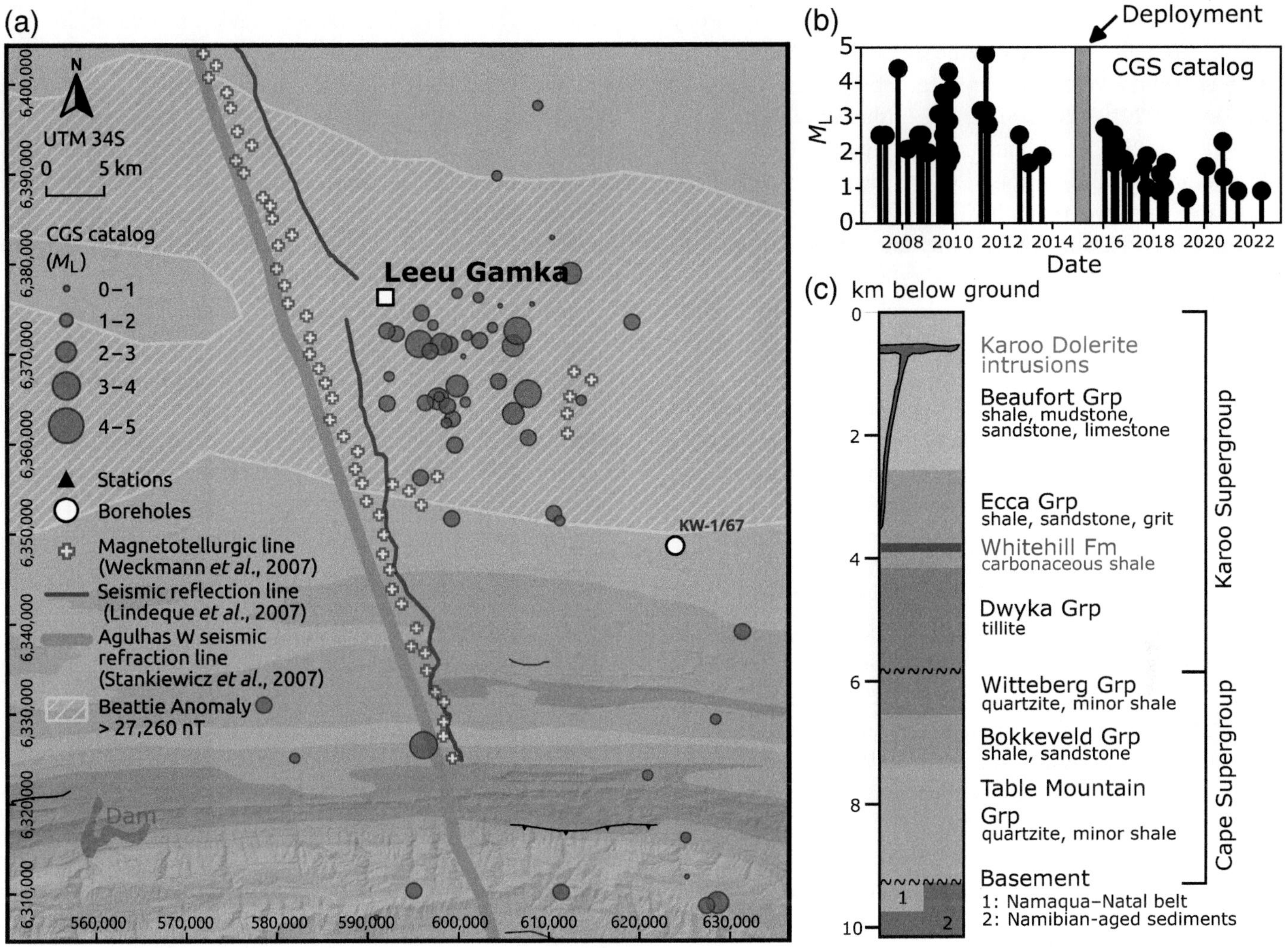

Figure 2. (a) Map of the study area showing the local geology (Council for Geoscience, 2018). Seismicity in the study area (Council for Geoscience, 2022). The Beattie anomaly is now shown as a gray hatched area. (b) Seismic magnitude (M_L) versus time distribution for earthquakes within the study area (Council for Geoscience, 2022), defined by the extent subfigure (a) and the black rectangle in Figure 1. The light gray shading corresponds to the time encompassed by the UCT deployment. (c) Stratigraphic column near Leeu Gamka based on an interpretation of the near-vertical seismic reflection by Lindeque *et al.* (2011). The depths are accurate for a point on the reflection profile with equal latitude as borehole KW-1/76 (Linol *et al.*, 2016), which was used to calibrate the reflection profile. CGS, Council for Geoscience. The color version of this figure is available only in the electronic edition.

Recent seismic clusters in the southern Karoo demonstrate that intraplate faults within the basin can become active. Between 2007 and 2022, the Council for Geoscience (the South African parastatal geological survey) reported 66 earthquakes near Leeu Gamka with a maximum, minimum, and median magnitude of M_L 4.8, 0.7, and 2.0 (Fig. 2a,b). Two of these events were also recorded by the U.S. Geological Survey (USGS) (M_L 4.3 in 2009 and 4.1 in 2011). The cluster highlights that stresses within the plate can reactivate preexisting structures or weak zones, producing locally concentrated seismicity despite the overall stable continental setting.

The Leeu Gamka cluster lies on the Beattie magnetic anomaly, an ~1000 km west-trending lineament defined by an increase in total magnetic field strength (Beattie, 1909) that bifurcates just west of the seismicity in Leeu Gamka. Geophysical transects that pass near the cluster—including seismic refraction (Parsiegla *et al.*, 2007; Stankiewicz *et al.*, 2007, 2008); near-vertical seismic reflection (Bräuer *et al.*, 2007; Lindeque *et al.*, 2007, 2011); and magnetotelluric profiling (Weckmann *et al.*, 2007)—indicate an anomaly in the basement and lower crust that might localize intraplate stresses. The Beattie anomaly's origin is debated, it is generally attributed to an ophiolite terrane (Halbich, 1993) or to mineralized shear zones in the basement (Scheiber-Enslin *et al.*, 2014). Regardless of its exact nature, it likely represents a region of rheological contrast—potentially a highly deformed, fluid-permeable zone—that could focus stress, fluid flow, and therefore intraplate seismicity within the Main Karoo basin.

The Leeu Gamka seismic cluster occurs in a region under exploration for its shale gas potential, specifically in the Karoo

Supergroup's Whitehill formation of the lower Ecca Group (Fig. 2c). Initial investigations began with SOEKOR (now PetroSA) in the 1960s, and more recently by several groups (Geel *et al.*, 2013, 2015; Scheiber-Enslin *et al.*, 2016; de Kock *et al.*, 2017). Although early reports (U.S. Energy Information Administration, 2011) suggested technically recoverable unconventional hydrocarbon reserves of 485 trillion cubic feet, this was subsequently found to be an overestimation due to overmaturation (Geel *et al.*, 2013; 2015). Nonetheless, the possibility that localized economic shale gas reserves are present in the Karoo keeps the region under scrutiny.

Intraplate seismicity has also been observed in other regions undergoing shale gas exploration and extraction, such as Oklahoma, United States, Blackpool, United Kingdom, and Alberta, Canada (e.g., Holland, 2013; Clarke *et al.*, 2014; Schultz *et al.*, 2017). These areas have experienced increased seismicity, with larger events linked to high-volume wastewater disposal in regions with critically stressed faults. For instance, the M_w 5.7 Oklahoma earthquake and its sequence was tied to such activities (Keranen *et al.*, 2013). Induced seismic events are more likely when there are pre-existing basement faults that can be reactivated by increase pore-fluid pressure. This, of course, can significantly increase the calculated seismic hazard in tectonically stable regions (Ellsworth, 2013). Not all fluid injections lead to felt seismicity, but the likelihood of damaging earthquakes appears to increase with the volume of the fluid injected and the geological characteristics of the area (McGarr, 2014). Kolawole *et al.* (2019) showed that the existence of a dominant basement fabric sufficiently well aligned to be reactivated by the current stress regime and the presence of pre-existing, critically stressed basement faults extending up into the sedimentary layers targeted for fluid injection can increase the propensity for felt induced earthquakes. The presence of such faults allows the increase of pore-fluid pressure to affect a greater area and means that relatively small fluctuations in pore-fluid pressure could allow the release of larger stored tectonic stresses resulting in potentially damaging earthquakes.

Within the southern Karoo basin, current seismicity studies aim to identify whether similar conditions exist. This includes examining the presence of faults that could be reactivated under current stress regimes, potentially leading to significant seismic events. The Strategic Environmental Assessment for shale gas development in the Karoo concluded that potentially damaging earthquakes in the area were "not likely" even under the scenario of large-scale extraction (Durrheim *et al.*, 2016). This conclusion was based on the observation that such events only occur in a minority of regions undergoing shale gas extraction, and because the region has experienced few felt earthquakes during the recent instrumental period. However, the assessment acknowledged that interactions between hydraulic fracturing and pre-existing critically stressed faults could lead to damaging earthquakes. Both the environmental assessment and an earlier academic review recommended further research to identify such structures and to better understand the seismic potential in the region (Durrheim *et al.*, 2016; Kijko *et al.*, 2016).

The seismic cluster near Leeu Gamka is the only recent seismic anomaly that falls within the area covered by the Strategic Impact Assessment area and is therefore an important opportunity to determine whether the correct conditions exist to allow potentially damaging induced seismicity in this region. Clusters associated with $M_w > 6$ earthquakes in the Ceres and Koffiefontein areas lie just outside the identified exploration zone. Here, we present results from a temporary seismic network that was deployed to allow a finer spatiotemporal characterization of the seismic cluster. This study focuses on the properties of the seismic cluster as recorded by our instruments and on the 2D shallow Rayleigh-wave group velocity structure from ANT to investigate velocity variations of the Karoo and Cape Supergroups at the Leeu Gamka earthquake cluster.

Leeu Gamka Deployment

Following reports of clustered seismic activity by the Council for Geoscience (CGS), the South African geological survey, in the vicinity of Leeu Gamka, researchers at the University of Cape Town (UCT) Department of Geosciences deployed a temporary seismic network in March 2015 to characterize the local seismicity of the study area. The network consisted of 23 seismic stations (Fig. 2a) distributed over a 60 by 65 km area. Denser spacing was employed near the epicenter locations identified by the CGS (close to stations ACY and AD2) and wider spacing farther away. Each station was equipped with a three-component 4.5 Hz geophone linked to a DiGOS Data-Cube data recorder, capturing continuously at 100 samples per second for up to 95 days. This UCT deployment covered a period during which no seismicity was reported by national or international agencies (Fig. 2b), thus providing a unique catalog of seismic events for that timeframe. Thanks to the network's dense configuration, we were able to detect minor seismic events that larger networks might not be able to detect due to their sparser coverage in this area.

Methods and Results

Local seismicity methodology

The data were examined to identify microseismicity in the area of the earthquake cluster reported by the Council of Geoscience. Events were located using standard methods available in the SEISAN software package (Havskov and Ottemoller, 1999; Havskov *et al.*, 2020), which employed an automated trigger (i.e., short-term average/long-term average) for event detection, followed by manual vetting and repicking. Initial hypocenter locations were estimated with consideration of the velocity structure using HYP. The velocity model was defined to a depth of 17 km below surface level using information from various previous seismic studies (Fatti, 1987;

TABLE 1
Velocity Model Used for the Estimation of Fundamental-Mode Rayleigh-Wave Sensitivity Kernels

Depth (km)	Thickness (km)	V_P (km/s)	V_S (km/s)	Density (kg/m^3)	References
0.5	0.5	5.0	3.13	2.3	Bräuer *et al.* (2007)
1.5	1.0	5.5	3.44	2.5	
1.75	0.25	5.6	3.5	2.55	
2.0	0.25	5.7	3.6	2.6	Stankiewicz *et al.* (2007)
5.0	3.0	6.0	3.75	2.65	
18.0	13.0	6.7	4.19	2.7	
34.0	16.0	7.0	4.38	2.8	Crust1.0 (Laske *et al.*, 2013)
50.0	16.0	8.16	5.1	2.9	

Velocities are constrained by Bräuer *et al.* (2007) for the first kilometer, by Stankiewicz *et al.* (2007) to a depth of 18 km, and by Crust1.0 (Laske *et al.*, 2013) for larger depths.

Lindeque *et al.*, 2007; Stankiewicz *et al.*, 2007; Scheiber-Enslin *et al.*, 2016). At lower depths, the velocity was defined via the Crust1.0 global velocity model (Laske *et al.*, 2013), up to 50 km below the surface (Table 1). Features of the deeper velocity structure (such as the Moho depth) are not critical because no *Pn* arrivals are expected due to the short distances between events and stations. Focal mechanisms were obtained by manually picking the polarity of *P*-wave first arrivals using SEISAN tools, including FOCMEC. The event locations were further refined using double-difference relocation with HYPODD (Waldhauser and Ellsworth, 2000).

Local seismicity results

During the Leeu Gamka deployment, a total of 105 local microearthquakes were detected (Fig. 3a) with magnitudes ranging from M_L − 1.5 to 0.4. These events were sporadically distributed between 6 March and 28 May 2015, with a notable spike in activity on 18 March. In general, this temporal distribution is typical of a seismic swarm (Roland and McGuire, 2009) with no clear dominant event. The locations show that the events originate in the same region as those reported by the National Seismic Network, forming a west-northwest–east-southeast (WNW-ESE)-trending cluster (azimuth ~ 295° from north) near the center of the deployed geophone array. Hypocentral depths range from 2 to 12 km with most events occurring between 5 and 8 km beneath the surface. Both *P*- and *S*-wave arrivals (Fig. 3b) were used to locate seismic events. Using double-difference methods, 96 out of the 105 events were successfully relocated. When the hypocenters and double-difference relocated hypocenters are projected onto vertical planes along profiles A–A′ and B–B′ (Fig. 3c–f), it becomes noticeable that the earthquakes fall on a fault plane. Although the ordinary hypocenters show fall along a broader section of the fault, the relocated hypocenters fall on a smaller cluster, closer to the fault plane. Both the original and relocated events predominantly occurred within the lower Karoo Supergroup and the underlying Cape Supergroup.

In some instances, the polarity of *P*-wave first motions allowed for focal mechanism calculations (Fig. 4). The focal mechanisms generally indicate a dominant oblique strike-slip motion with a gently west-plunging P axis. This suggests left-lateral strike-slip motion when considering a fault plane aligned with the WNW-trending earthquake hypocenters. Although there is no obvious surface expression of such a structure, the seismicity suggests the presence of a subvertical WNW-trending blind fault which is currently experiencing loading consistent with sinistral displacement.

ANT methodology

To investigate possible causative structures of seismicity within the Karoo and Cape Supergroup, we conducted Rayleigh-wave group velocity tomography on the continuous recordings from Leeu Gamka. The theoretical background for ANT emerges from the fluctuation–dissipation theorem (Callen and Welton, 1951; Kubo, 1966) as discussed by Snieder *et al.* (2009). Over the past two decades, the seismological community has adapted these concepts to examine the Earth and other planetary bodies (Campillo and Paul, 2003; Wapenaar, 2003; Shapiro and Campillo, 2004; Larose *et al.*, 2005) within the theoretical and experimental framework of seismic interferometry (SI).

ANT falls within the scope of passive SI, which seeks to extract the empirical Greens function (EGF)—the response to an impulsive source—between two receivers from continuous ground motion records. Most derivations of the noise-correlation property have relied on assumptions such as uniform velocity, isotropic distribution of sources, and energy equipartition. However, these conditions are not typically met in the Earth, leading to potential inaccuracies in the approximated Green's function.

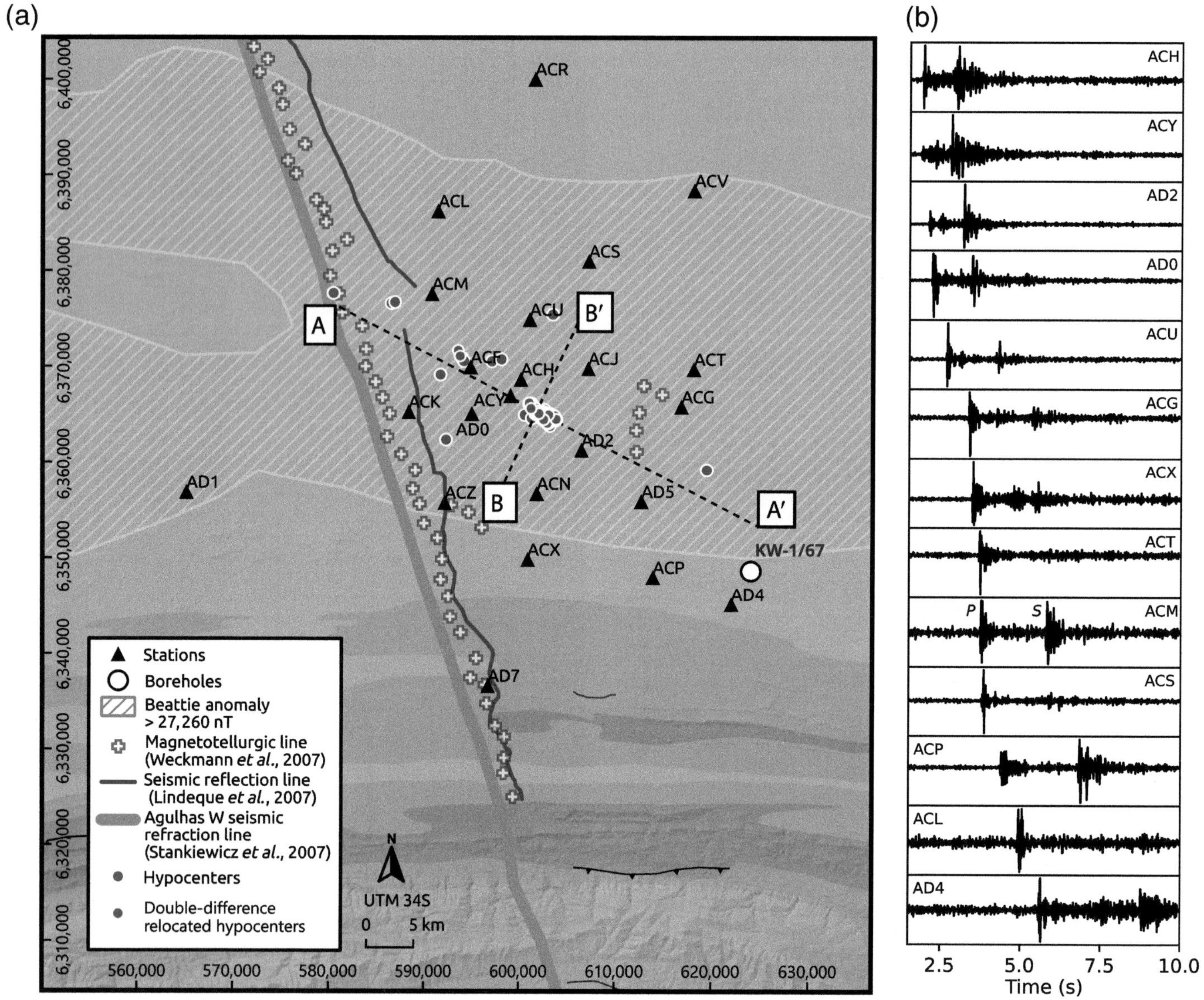

Figure 3. (a) UCT seismic network location (black triangles) and geology of the study area (see Fig. 2 for details). Earthquakes located using the UCT geophone network (see the Discussion section) are plotted as blue circles. The double-difference (DD) relocations are plotted with red circular markers. The Beattie magnetic anomaly shown by a gray hatched area (Scheiber-Enslin *et al.*, 2014). The western Agulhas–Karoo transect composed of a seismic refraction line (Stankiewicz *et al.*, 2007), a near-vertical reflection line (Lindeque *et al.*, 2007), and a magnetotelluric line (Weckmann *et al.*, 2007) are shown. The dashed lines indicate orientation of depth cross sections shown in (c), (d), (e), and (f). Profiles A–A′ and B–B′ have azimuths of 295° and 25° from north, respectively. (b) Example of *P*- and *S*-wave arrivals at all stations in the network. The event occurred midway between stations ACH and AD2 (32.852° S, 22.093° E) at a depth of 6.8 km. Station ACM shows the *P* and *S* arrivals for the event. (c) Depth cross section of seismicity recorded by UCT stations, projected onto vertical plane A–A′. (d) Depth cross section of seismicity recorded by UCT stations projected onto vertical plane B–B′. (e) Depth cross section of double-difference relocations, projected onto a vertical plane A–A′. (f) Depth cross section of double-difference relocations projected onto vertical plane B–B′. The color version of this figure is available only in the electronic edition. (*Continued*)

Of the assumptions noted earlier, the spatial distribution of noise sources deserves particular attention because uneven or transient source distributions can introduce travel-time errors, and result in incomplete amplitude recovery (e.g., Tsai, 2009). Relevant to our array in South Africa, is the work by Davy *et al.* (2015), who investigated sources of secondary microseism (SM) in the Indian Ocean for 2011, and using polarization analysis of records from the SUR broadband station (located 130 km west of our northernmost station, ACR) found dominant SM sources along the southern continental rise and farther offshore at the confluence of the southern Indian and Atlantic oceans (see figs. 6 and 8 in Davy *et al.* 2015). Their

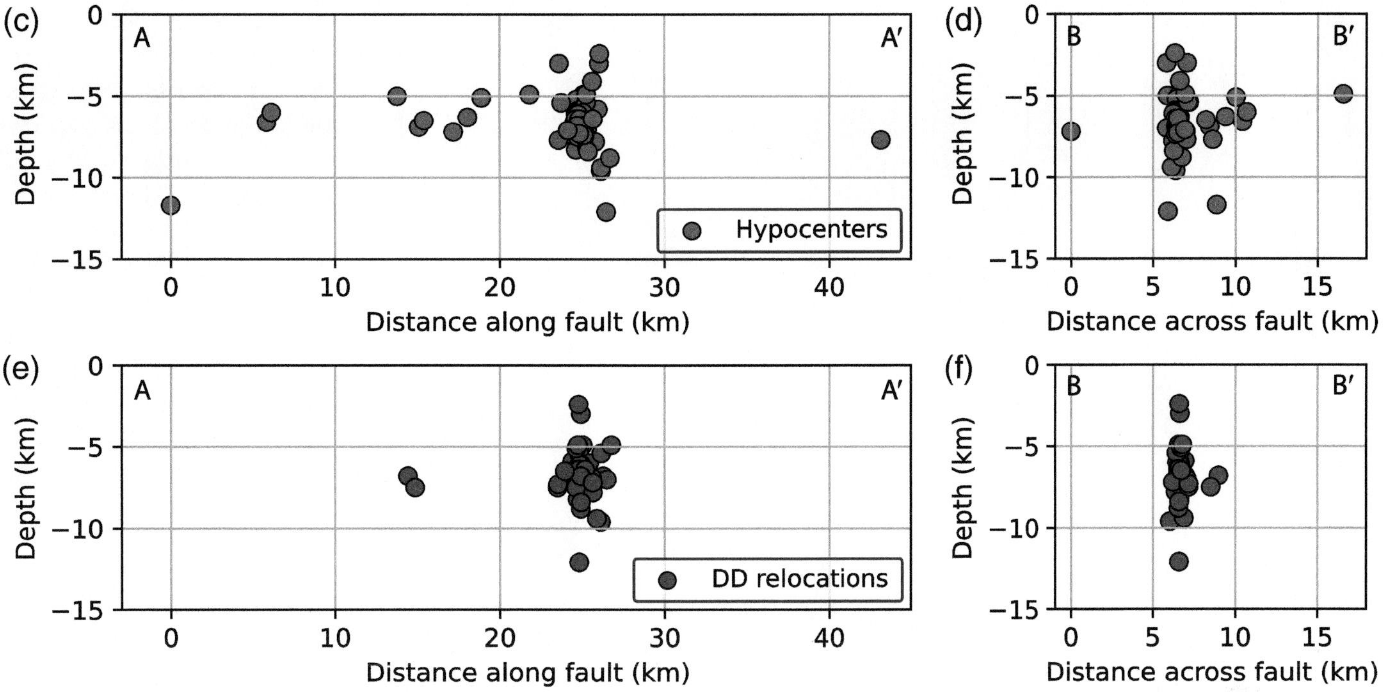

Figure 3. Continued

modeling of SM noise sources using the IOWAGA numerical wave model (Ardhuin *et al.*, 2011) further indicates strong noise sources distributed across the western continental rise of southern Africa and additional sources along the eastern continental rise (see figs. 7 and 8 in Davy *et al.*, 2015). This inference of dominant SM sources to the south with the presence of noise sources to the west and east, is corroborated by Bezuidenhout and Doucouré (2020). Using three different seismic arrays in the Eastern Cape (~300 km east of Leeu Gamka), each deployed for five-week periods (August–September and September–October, 2015, and June–July, 2016), they show SM noise sources to be well distributed relative to their arrays except toward the north. Importantly, their five-week recording intervals imply that even relatively short deployments—such as our three-month record—can sample an adequate SM noise source distribution to effectively retrieve EGFs for station pairs at different orientations, as shown by Bezuidenhout *et al.* (2017) in the Eastern Cape. It is also worth mentioning that other studies, like the work by Yang and Ritzwoller (2008) have determined via synthetic experiments that if noise sources exist over a broad azimuthal range at relatively low levels, accurate EGFs can emerge even when the distribution is far from azimuthally homogeneous

In this study, we focus exclusively on the effectiveness of ANT for revealing significant seismic velocity contrasts associated with structures responsible for the observed microseismicity. Previous analyses (e.g., Davy *et al.*, 2015; Bezuidenhout and

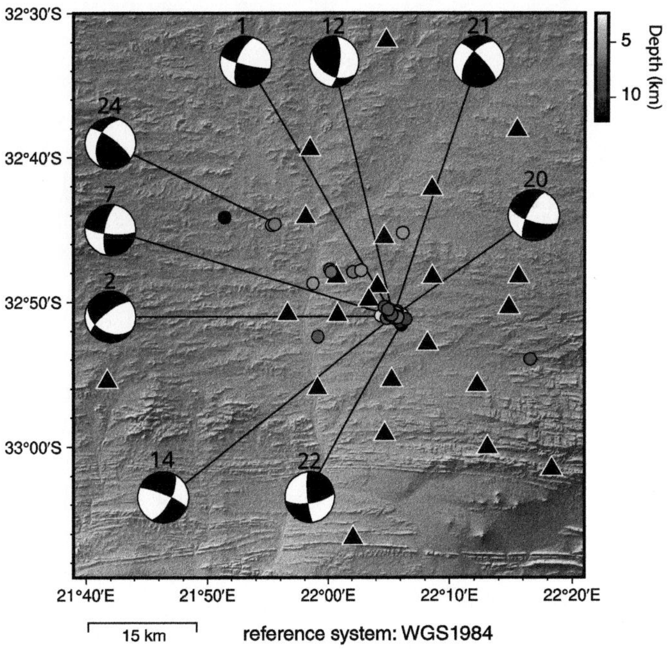

Figure 4. Earthquakes located by the UCT network, with hypocentral depth indicated by shading. Most earthquakes cluster in the center of the network. Depths range from 2 to 12 km with the majority of earthquakes occurring between 5 and 8 km. Focal mechanisms, obtained from *P* arrival polarities are plotted with lines pointing to their respective epicenters. Focal mechanisms are generally concordant with a left-lateral displacement of a steep to subvertical northeast-dipping fault trending at 295°. The color version of this figure is available only in the electronic edition.

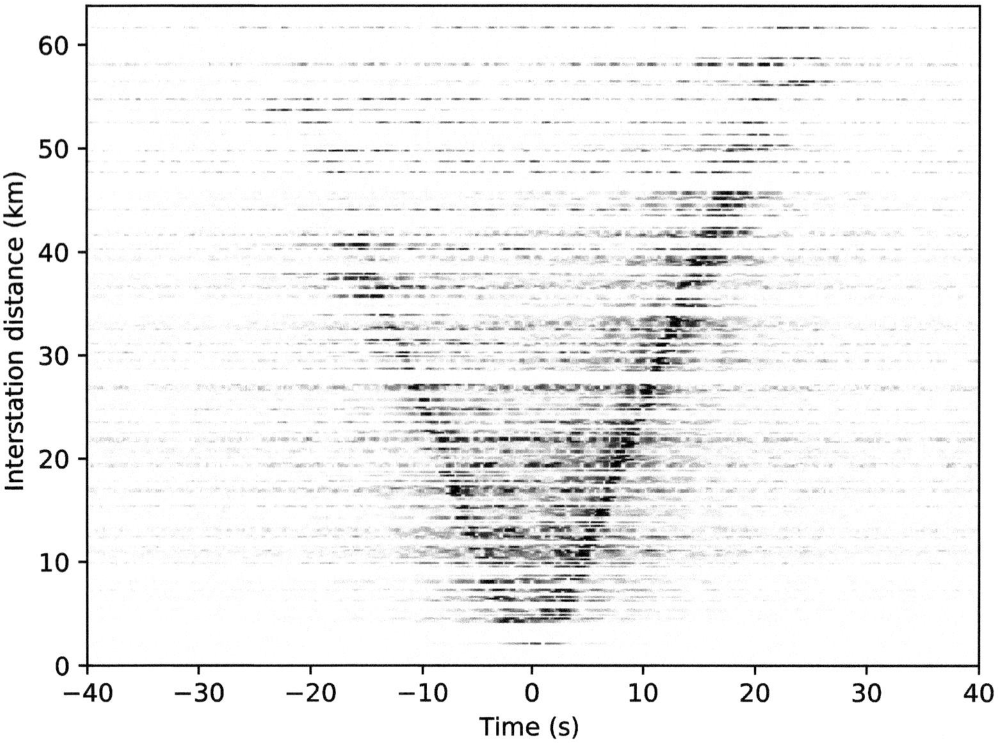

Figure 5. Vertical-component cross correlations for all stations pairs normalized to unity and displayed according to interstation distance. Data were band-pass filtered between 0.08 and 2 Hz. The color version of this figure is available only in the electronic edition.

Doucouré, 2020) indicate that SM noise sources are reasonably well distributed for this purpose. And although additional information—such as temporal velocity variations and seismic wave amplification—could in principle be extracted from studies of time-varying processes (e.g., Brenguier *et al.*, 2008) or from amplitude analyses, the relatively short recording duration and the anisotropic source distribution would complicate the analysis and error estimation. This of course has been noted in the literature because anisotropic source distributions can produce small errors in travel-time and large errors in estimates of amplitude (e.g., Tsai, 2009; Prieto *et al.*, 2011; Tsai *et al.*, 2024). We therefore flag these issues for future work, in which longer records using different instrumentation and targeted strategies to characterize and mitigate source anisotropy (e.g., Tsai *et al.*, 2024) might allow reliable estimates of velocity change and amplification. In this study, we employed an adapted methodology based on Bensen *et al.* (2007) and Goutorbe *et al.* (2015) to generate Rayleigh-wave group velocity maps from ambient seismic noise. The dataset comprises continuous vertical-component recordings collected over the 95-day Leeu Gamka experiment. During preprocessing, we removed the instrument response, the mean, and the trend, then decimated the data to 50 Hz, and applied a band-pass filter between 0.08 and 2 Hz. Amplitude normalization was done via a moving average with a window size of half the maximum period (i.e., 12 s), which yielded slightly better results than one-bit normalization. The EGF was extracted through frequency domain cross correlation, stacked over 215 s windows for each station pair. Figure 5 illustrates the EGFs as a function of inter-station distance band-passed filtered between 0.08 and 2 Hz.

Frequency–time analysis (FTAN) is applied to the folded cross correlations (the sum of negative and positive lags) to extract the frequency-dependent group velocities of Rayleigh waves propagating between stations (e.g., Levshin and Ritzwoller, 2001; Goutorbe *et al.*, 2015). Figure 6 illustrates this process, in which the cross correlation for station pair ACR–AD7 (see inset map in Fig. 6b) is band-pass filtered across different bands to show the velocity dependence on period (Fig. 6a). The subsequent FTAN procedure (Levshin and Ritzwoller, 2001; Bensen *et al.*, 2007) is depicted in Figure 6b. Dispersion curves are selected based on signal-to-noise ratio, the repeatability of a velocity measurement over seven-day intervals, and measurements with an interstation distance (Δ) of at least three wavelengths ($\Delta > 3Tv_\varphi$, in which v_φ is the phase velocity). This results in an effective cutoff period in seconds of $\frac{\Delta}{10}$ (Δ in km), as shown in Figure 6b.

Using the travel times derived from group velocity measurements at each period, we perform a tomographic inversion following Barmin *et al.* (2001). The optimization function for the inversion comprises three terms (Goutorbe *et al.*, 2015):

$$(\boldsymbol{Gm} - \boldsymbol{d})^T \boldsymbol{C}^{-1} (\boldsymbol{Gm} - \boldsymbol{d}) + \alpha^2 \|\boldsymbol{Fm}\|^2 + \beta^2 \|\boldsymbol{Hm}\|^2.$$

G is a function describing surface-wave propagation through a slowness model described by **m**, a vector of slowness perturbations. The vector **d** contains travel-time perturbations. **C** is a covariance matrix, a diagonal matrix containing the standard deviations, obtained from the seven-day dispersion curves. The first term in the optimization function is the misfit. The smoothing term $\alpha^2\|\boldsymbol{Fm}\|^2$ includes a scalar weight α, such that

$$\boldsymbol{F}_{ij} = \begin{cases} 1 & \text{if } i = j \\ -S(\boldsymbol{r}_i, \boldsymbol{r}_j) & \text{if } i \neq j \end{cases},$$

in which elements located outside the diagonal are defined as

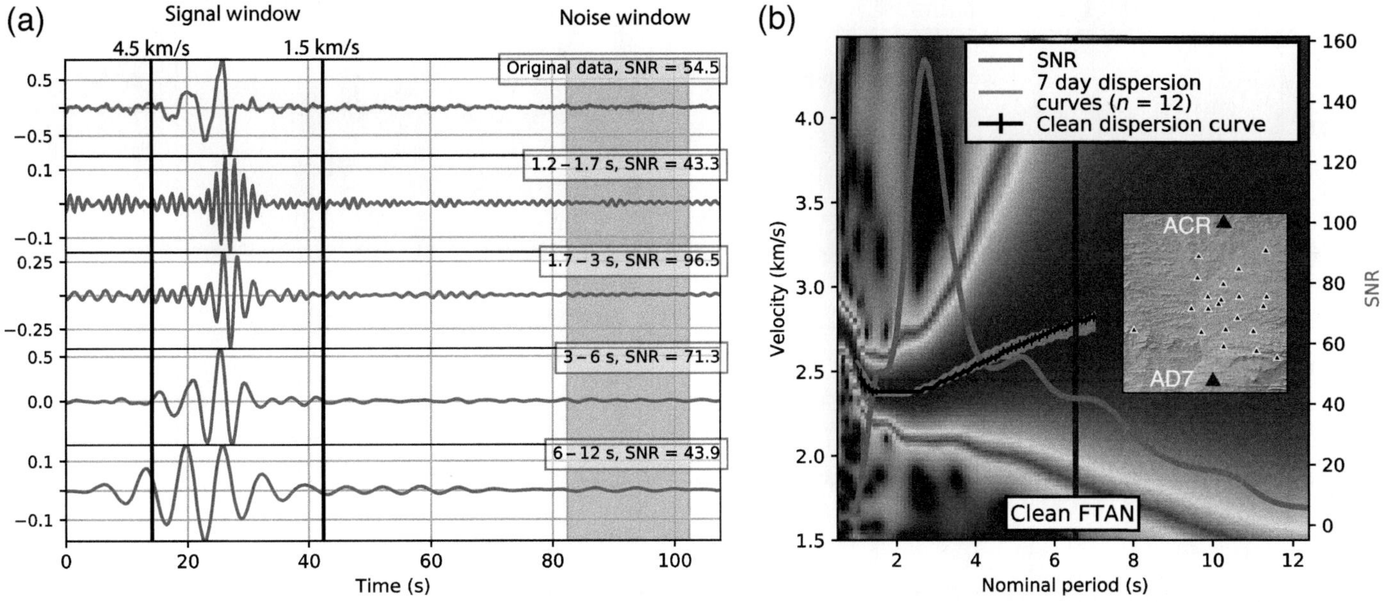

Figure 6. (a) Cross correlation between station pair ACR–AD7 (top panel) subsequently band-pass filtered at different bands to show the velocity dependence on period. The black vertical bold lines delimit the signal window based on predefined velocities. The gray shading indicates the noise window used to estimate the signal-to-noise ratio (SNR). (b) Group velocity dispersion curve (black line) obtained from frequency–time analysis (FTAN). Dispersion curves calculated using seven-day intervals (gray lines). The blue vertical line indicates the effective cutoff period. The inset map shows location of ACR and AD7. Interstation distance is 64 km. The color version of this figure is available only in the electronic edition.

$$S(\boldsymbol{r}_i,\boldsymbol{r}_j) \propto \exp\left(-\frac{\|\boldsymbol{r}_i - \boldsymbol{r}_j\|^2}{2\sigma^2}\right), \sum_{j\neq i} S(\boldsymbol{r}_i,\boldsymbol{r}_j) = 1 \quad \forall i,$$

here $\boldsymbol{r}_i$ is the location of the ith node. The last term penalizes the weighted norm of the model with β also a scalar weight, such that

$$\boldsymbol{H}_{ij} = \exp(-\lambda\rho_i)\delta_{ij},$$

in which λ is a scalar that determines the sharpness of the norm weighting function's decrease, ρ_i is the number of paths crossing the ith node and δ_{ij} is Kronecker delta. The best-fitting model parameters are then given by

$$\hat{\boldsymbol{m}} = (\boldsymbol{G}^T\boldsymbol{C}^{-1}\boldsymbol{G} + \boldsymbol{Q})^{-1}\boldsymbol{G}^T\boldsymbol{d}^{\text{obs}},$$

in which $\boldsymbol{Q}$ is defined as

$$\boldsymbol{Q} = \alpha^2\boldsymbol{F}^T\boldsymbol{F} + \beta\boldsymbol{H}^T\boldsymbol{H},$$

in which $\boldsymbol{d}^{\text{obs}}$ are the observed travel-time perturbations. Parameters α and β are fine-tuned through trial-and-error to minimize artifacts such as specs and streaks in the tomographic maps (Barmin *et al.*, 2001). The inversion is performed via a two-pass procedure to remove outliers. The first pass conducts an overdamped inversion (i.e., extensive spatial smoothing) to remove ray paths with significant residuals that might have bypassed the selection criteria. The second pass produces the final velocity maps.

ANT results

Figure 7 presents the Rayleigh-wave group velocity maps for periods 1.5 and 3.0 s obtained through the ANT methodology described in the previous section. To interpret these maps effectively, depth sensitivity kernels are calculated based on the velocity model compiled from published data in the region spanning various depths (Table 1). Figure 8 illustrates the fundamental-mode Rayleigh-wave sensitivity kernels for periods ranging from 1 to 5 s.

The sensitivity kernels reveal that the 1.5 s period is sensitive to depths between 0.5 and 2.0 km, whereas the 3.0 s period is more sensitive to depths between 1.0 and 4.0 km. The resolution of the tomographic maps, detailed in Figures S2 and S3, available in the supplemental material to this article, indicates that the array geometry is capable of resolving velocity contrasts for the periods of interest (Fig. 7), as well as features with diameters of 6 km and larger. These tomographic maps provide valuable insights into the subsurface structures and stratigraphic units under the array. The specific units and geological structures imaged by these maps are further explored in the Discussion section.

Discussion

The hypocenters identified in this study are located along a subvertical, WNW-ESE-trending plane, with depths ranging

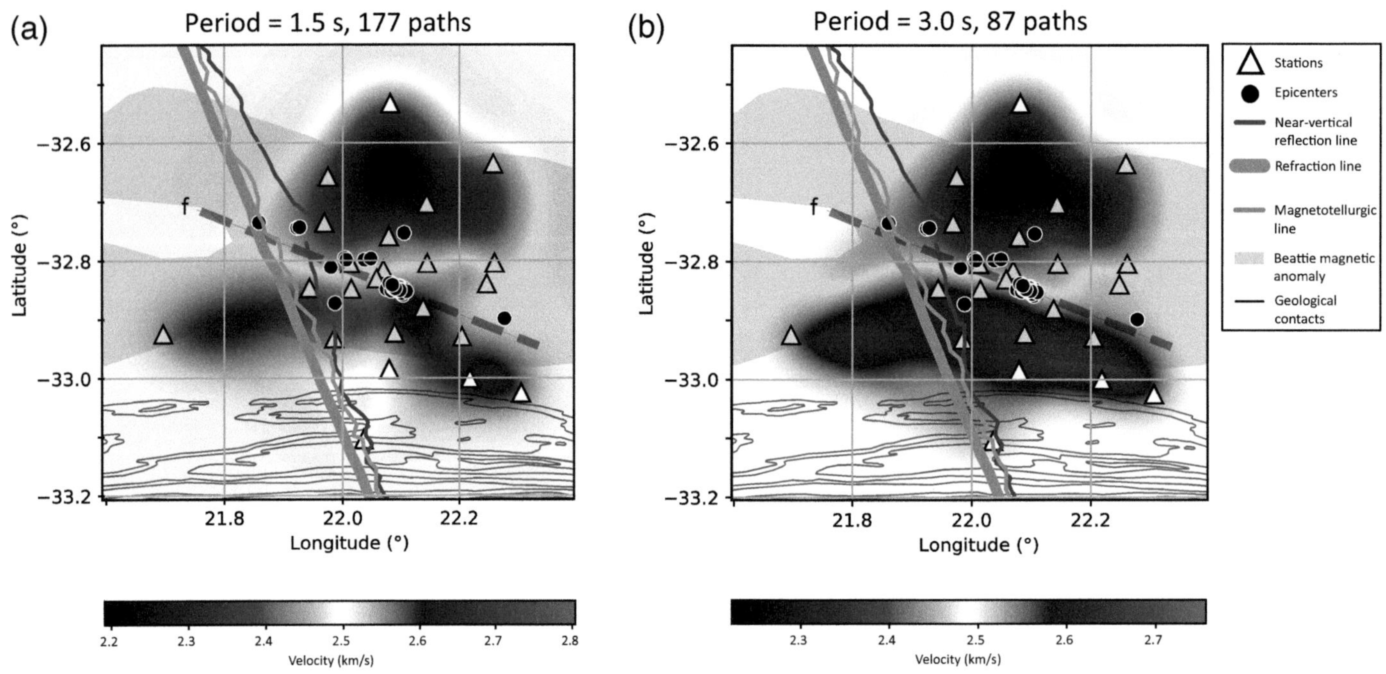

Figure 7. Rayleigh-wave velocity maps for periods (a) 1.5 s and (b) 3.0 s. Locations from this study for microseismic events (black dots), seismic refraction line (dark gray line) (Stankiewicz *et al.*, 2007), seismic reflection line (blue lines) (Lindeque *et al.*, 2007), and magnetotelluric line (green line) (Weckmann *et al.*, 2007), are shown overlaying the Beattie magnetic anomaly (light gray area) (Beattie, 1909; Scheiber-Enslin *et al.*, 2014) and the velocity maps. Also shown are the geologic contacts shown in Figure 2a, and the trace of the presumed seismogenic fault causing the microseismicity. The color version of this figure is available only in the electronic edition.

from 2.4 to 12.1 km below ground level. Most events occur between 5 and 8 km beneath the surface, near the center of the array (Fig. 3). The hypocenters occur in the same region as those reported by the National Seismic Network (Council for Geoscience, 2022), but the reduced location uncertainties enable identification of a planar structure. Tomographic maps show a Rayleigh-wave group velocity increase of ~0.3 km/s consistent with the trend of the plane defined by hypocentral locations (Fig. 7). This corresponds to depth sensitivities of 0.5–2.0 km and 1.0–4.0 km below the surface for periods between 1.5 and 3.0 s, respectively.

The subsurface seismic velocities and geology at the array are constrained by seismic refraction and reflection profiles (Fig. 9) of the Inkaba ye Africa project (de Wit and Horsfield, 2006), which intersect the western margin of the deployed geophone network with a similar location and orientation (Fig. 2a). *P*-wave velocities were obtained from surface to depths of approximately 10–20 km via tomography along the seismic refraction line, and the crustal structure was interpreted using the obtained velocity model (Stankiewicz *et al.*, 2007) and a seismic reflection image (Lindeque *et al.*, 2007).

The Beattie magnetic anomaly was identified as a region of high *P*-wave velocity, and several south-dipping thrust faults associated with the Cape orogeny were identified, including one close to the Leeu Gamka earthquake cluster. More detailed *P*- and *S*-wave velocities for depths less than 2 km have also been reported from the same refraction experiment (Bräuer *et al.*, 2007), indicating a general increase in both *P*- and *S*-wave velocities from north to south at the site of the proposed seismogenic structure. The seismic reflection experiment shows that the base of the Karoo Supergroup ranges from 3.5 km in the north to 5 km in the south of the geophone array, whereas the depth of the unconformity between the Cape Supergroup and the Namaqua–Natal belt crystalline basement ranges from about 5 km in the north to 10 km in the south (Lindeque *et al.*, 2011). Consequently, most seismic activity in this study occurs within the Cape and Karoo Supergroups, although some events may extend into the upper Namaqua–Natal belt crystalline basement. The depth sensitivity of tomographic Rayleigh-wave group velocity maps suggests they effectively image the Karoo and upper Cape Supergroups at depths corresponding to the shallower seismicity.

The persistent microseismicity in the Leeu Gamka region as reported by the National Seismic Network (Council for Geoscience, 2022), along with the hypocentral locations identified in this study, suggests the presence of a structure which is capable of rupturing in the current stress regime.

Focal mechanism solutions derived from first motions (Fig. 4) reveal various faulting types, with a dominant WNW-ESE left-lateral strike-slip motion consistent with the structure inferred from the hypocentral locations. Such a mechanism is similar to that observed for the 1969 Ceres–Tulbagh earthquake (Krüger and Scherbaum, 2014). As with

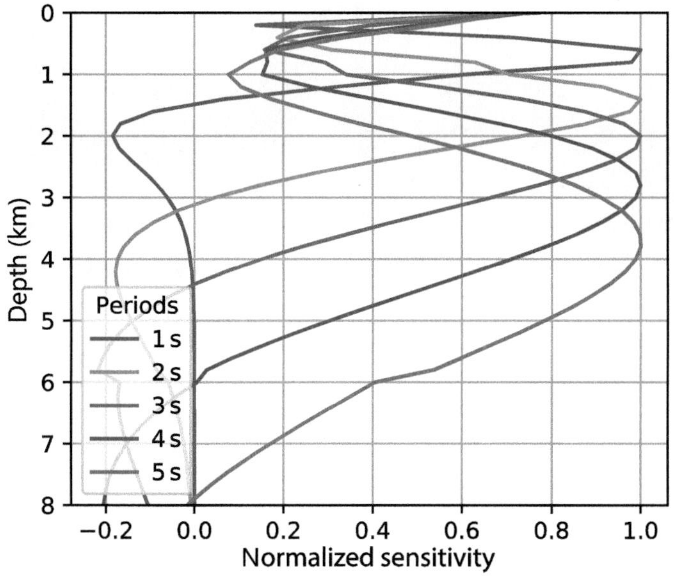

Figure 8. Normalized fundamental-mode Rayleigh-wave group speed sensitivity kernels. The kernels are amplitude normalized, have units of inverse length, and are defined as $\partial c/\partial V_S$, in which c is group speed and V_S is shear wavespeed. The color version of this figure is available only in the electronic edition.

that earthquake, the inferred fault orientation does not clearly align with surface features (Smit *et al.*, 2015).

Tomographic maps derived from Rayleigh waves (Fig. 7) resolve a velocity transition near the center of the Leeu Gamka array, with a decrease of 0.3 km/s from south-southwest (SSW) to north-northeast (NNE). The observed range of velocities is consistent with those reported by Bezuidenhout *et al.* (2017) near Jansenville, Eastern Cape Province, approximately ~250 km east of our array. The position and orientation of the velocity contrast are also consistent with the WNW-ESE-inferred strike of the structure generating the microseismicity. The projection of the seismogenic fault (*f* in Fig. 9) intersects the seismic refraction profile (Stankiewicz *et al.*, 2007) about 90 km from its north-northwest (NNW) edge (Fig. 9a) and the reflection profile (Lindeque *et al.*, 2007) about 50 km from the survey origin (NNW in Fig. 9b). Both profiles detected a horizontal velocity contrast in the top 4 km, aligning with our tomographic maps (Fig. 7) and sensitivity kernels (Fig. 8), interpreted as folding of the Karoo Supergroup by Lindeque *et al.* (2007), and as evidence of a blind thrust fault by Stankiewicz *et al.* (2007).

Given the presence of shallow (<5 km) hypocentral locations (Table S1) within the main seismic cluster, corresponding to the maximum sensitivity of the tomographic maps, it is likely that the same structure has been observed using different methodologies. This study supports previous suggestions (Lindeque *et al.*, 2007; Stankiewicz *et al.*, 2007) that a seismogenic blind fault may exist within the Karoo and Cape Supergroups, potentially extending into the upper Namaqua–Natal belt basement; however, these studies are not in agreement with the fault displacement and our interpretation of fault orientation. Assuming it is a continuous structure, as constrained by the seismicity, the refraction and reflection profiles, and the tomographic maps, the minimum length of the fault is approximately 30 km.

Significantly, this structure associated with seismicity extends into the sedimentary succession, suggesting possible hydraulic connectivity with shale gas target depths. Its dimensions imply (if continuity of the structure is assumed) that it could generate events similar to the M_w 6.3 Ceres–Tulbagh earthquake. This suggests that, in some parts of the Karoo, the necessary preconditions for damaging induced earthquakes may be present (Kolawole *et al.*, 2019). The precise nature and depth extent of the Leeu Gamka structure remain unclear. Previous geophysical interpretations associate shallow velocity contrasts with thin-skinned, low-angle blind thrust faulting and folding from later stages of the Cape orogeny (Fig. 9). However, the focal mechanisms obtained here, along those reported by international catalogues such as the USGS, suggest steeply dipping strike-slip faulting. The Beattie magnetic anomaly that underlies the structure has been interpreted to be caused by an ophiolitic terrane (Halbich, 1993) or a major crustal shear zone (Scheiber-Enslin *et al.*, 2014). Both these interpretations suggest the presence of a structurally weak zone. Elsewhere in Southern Africa ancient shear zones well expressed in aeromagnetic data have been shown to be reactivated in major neotectonic earthquakes (Salomon *et al.*, 2022; Muir *et al.*, 2023). Such a weak zone may have been reactivated both during and since the Cape orogeny.

The earthquake locations, ANT, and previous geophysical surveys of the region demonstrate the presence of a structure which is at least five kilometers long and appears to extend for more than 15 km. The observed microseismicity demonstrates that this structure has the potential to become critically stressed in the current stress field. This suggests that densification of seismic monitoring in the region should precede shale gas exploration, and exclusion zones around human settlements should be considered, especially in the vicinity of such structures. Targeted short-term geophone deployments remain a cost-effective method to detect these potential sources of hazard even in relatively stable low-seismicity environments (e.g., Stevens *et al.*, 2021).

Conclusions

The Leeu Gamka intraplate seismic swarm, with a reported maximum magnitude of $M_L = 4.8$, is linked to left-lateral strike events occurring on a WNW-ESE-trending structure that extends for at least 30 km. ANT indicates a significant velocity change along this structure at depths within the Karoo Supergroup, the lower parts of which are being considered as a target for shale gas exploitation. Microseismicity

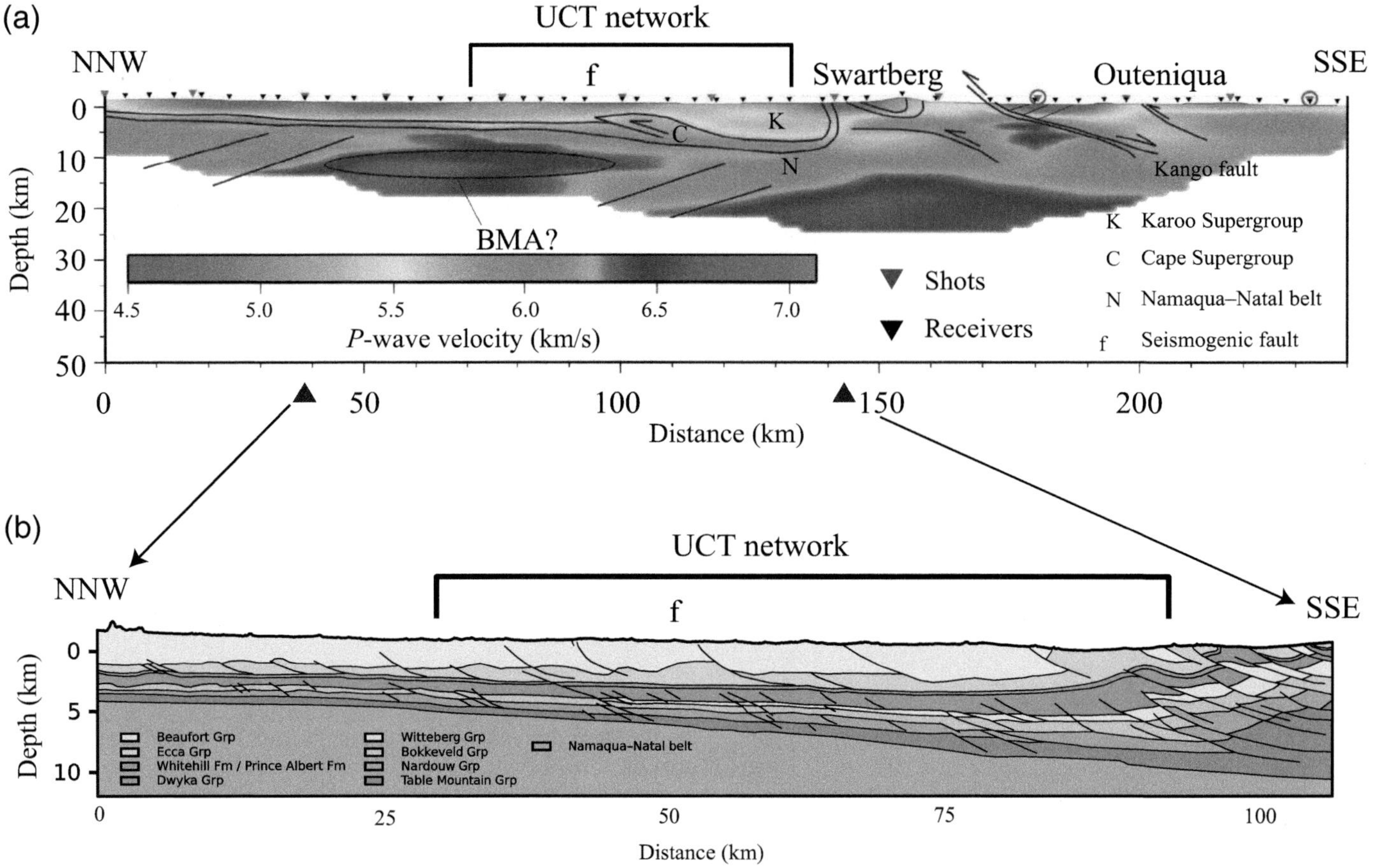

reaches from the lower Karoo through the Cape Supergroup to the Namaqua–Natal basement contact. This area is also associated with the Beattie magnetic anomaly, suggesting a crustal-scale rheological weak zone. These findings imply that critically stressed faults traverse the sedimentary units of the Karoo and Cape Supergroups in this area, highlighting the potentially risk of damaging induced seismicity.

Further research could explore whether similar microseismicity is present elsewhere along the Beattie magnetic anomaly, or in other parts of the southern Karoo basin. Enhanced seismic monitoring and establishing exclusion zones for shale gas exploitation near human settlements, especially around similar velocity anomalies, may be wise until the potential hazards are better understood.

Figure 9. (a) *P*-wave velocity model obtained from a seismic refraction survey near Leeu Gamka (modified from Stankiewicz *et al.*, 2007) part of the Inkaba ye Africa project (de Wit and Horsfield, 2006). The letter C, which refers to Cape Supergroup stratigraphy, is placed at the location of the interpreted blind thrust fault. The blue upright triangles and arrows indicate the extent of reflection profile in (b) with respect to the length of the refraction profile. (b) Interpretation of the near-vertical seismic reflection profile (Lindeque *et al.*, 2007). These profiles constrain the depth of the base of the Karoo Supergroup to ~3.5 km in the north and ~5 km in the south of the deployed network and the base of the Cape Supergroup ranges from ~5 km in the north to ~10 km in the south of the deployed array. The color version of this figure is available only in the electronic edition.

Data and Resources

The supplemental material for this article is accessible through ZivaHub, the University of Cape Town open data institutional repository. Via ZivaHub the following are accessible: the checkerboard tests and ray-path coverage (doi: 10.25375/uct.30119386), station inventory file in xml format (doi: 10.25375/uct.27038296), the earthquake event catalogue with absolute locations in csv format (doi: 10.25375/uct.27061285), the earthquake event double-difference catalog with relative locations in csv format (doi: 10.25375/uct.30758003), the focal mechanism solutions for selected events base on the catalog with absolute locations (doi: 10.25375/uct.30763850), the continuous waveform data (doi: 10.25375/uct.27038233), and the event waveform data in miniseed format (doi: 10.25375/uct.27038191). The program senskernel-1.0 (Levshin, 2018) based on the algorithm by Rodi *et al.* (1975) was used to calculate the sensitivity kernels in Figure 8. The code used to perform the preprocessing, frequency–time analysis (FTAN), and tomography steps described in this study is available in the GitHub repository given in the supporting information by Goutorbe *et al.* (2015).

Declaration of Competing Interests

The authors acknowledge that there are no conflicts of interest recorded.

Acknowledgments

R. A. S. and B. W. acknowledge the The National Research Foundation (NRF) Centre of Excellence (CoE) for Integrated Mineral and Energy Resource Analysis (CIMERA) for funding support. R. A. S., D. Q., and B. W. acknowledge UCT for funding support. B. K. thanks the landowners for providing access (as well as coffee and interesting conversations). The late Chris Hartnady is acknowledged for discussions and encouragement in investigating the Leeu-Gamka swarm. Both "Leeu" and "Gamka" mean lion in Afrikaans and some Khoisan languages, respectively.

References

Ambraseys, N., and R. Adams (1991). Reappraisal of major African earthquakes, south of 20 N, 1900–1930, *Nat. Hazards* **4,** no. 4, 389–419.

Ardhuin, F., E. Stutzmann, M. Schimmel, and A. Mangeney (2011). Ocean wave sources of seismic noise, *J. Geophys. Res.* **116,** no. C9, doi: 10.1029/2011JC006952.

Barmin, M. P., M. H. Ritzwoller, and A. L. Levshin (2001). A fast and reliable method for surface wave tomography, *Pure Appl. Geophys.* **158,** no. 8, 1351.

Beattie, J. C. (1909). *Report of a Magnetic Survey of South Africa*, Cambridge University Press, London.

Bensen, G. D., M. H. Ritzwoller, M. P. Barmin, A. L. Levshin, F. Lin, M. P. Moschetti, N. M. Shapiro, and Y. Yang (2007). Processing seismic ambient noise data to obtain reliable broad-band surface wave dispersion measurements, *Geophys. J. Int.* **169,** no. 3, 1239–1260.

Bezuidenhout, L. J., and C. M. Doucouré (2020). Source azimuth determination of ambient seismic noise in the eastern Cape Karoo, South Africa, *J. Afr. Earth. Sci.* **164,** 103639.

Bezuidenhout, L. J., M. Doucouré, V. Wagener, M. de Wit, A. Mordret, T. Lecocq, and F. Brenguier (2017). Rayleigh group velocity extraction from ambient seismic noise to map the south eastern Cape Karoo region, South Africa, *S. Afr. J. Geol.* **120,** no. 3, 341–350.

Bräuer, B., T. Ryberg, and A. S. Lindeque (2007). Shallow seismic velocity structure of the Karoo basin, South Africa, *S. Afr. J. Geol.* **110,** nos. 2/3, 439–448.

Brenguier, F., M. Campillo, C. Hadziioannou, N. M. Shapiro, R. M. Nadeau, and É. Larose (2008). Postseismic relaxation along the San Andreas fault at Parkfield from continuous seismological observations, *Science* **321,** no. 5895, 1478–1481.

Calais, E., T. Camelbeeck, S. Stein, M. Liu, and T. Craig (2016). A new paradigm for large earthquakes in stable continental plate interiors, *Geophys. Res. Lett.* **43,** no. 20, 10,621–10,637.

Callen, H. B., and T. A. Welton (1951). Irreversibility and generalized noise, *Phys. Rev.* **83,** no. 1, 34.

Campillo, M., and A. Paul (2003). Long-range correlations in the diffuse seismic coda, *Science* **299,** no. 5606, 547.

Clarke, H., L. Eisner, P. Styles, and P. Turner (2014). Felt seismicity associated with shale gas hydraulic fracturing: The first documented example in Europe, *Geophys. Res. Lett.* **41,** no. 23, 8308–8314.

Copley, A., J. P. Avouac, J. Hollingsworth, and S. Leprince (2011). The 2001 M_w 7.6 Bhuj earthquake, low fault friction, and the crustal support of plate driving forces in India, *J. Geophys. Res.* **116,** no. B8.

Council for Geoscience (2018). Geological map of South Africa 1:1 000 000. available at https://www.geoscience.org.za/cgs/systems/publications/cgs-geological-maps/ (last accessed January 2026).

Council for Geoscience (2022). CGS earthquake catalogue, available at https://www.geoscience.org.za/cgs/seismic-events/ (last accessed January 2026).

Craig, T. J., and E. Calais (2014). Strain accumulation in the New Madrid and Wabash Valley seismic zones from 14 years of continuous GPS observation, *J. Geophys. Res.* **119,** 9110–9129.

Davy, C., E. Stutzmann, G. Barruol, F. R. Fontaine, and M. Schimmel (2015). Sources of secondary microseisms in the Indian Ocean, *Geophys. J. Int.* **202,** no. 2, 1180–1189.

de Kock, M. O., N. J. Beukes, E. O. Adeniyi, D. Cole, A. E. Gotz, C. Geel, and F.-G. Ossa (2017). Deflating the shale gas potential of South Africa's Main Karoo basin, *S. Afr. J. Sci.* **113,** nos. 9/10, 1–12–11–12.

de Wit, M., and B. Horsfield (2006). Inkaba yeAfrica project surveys sector of Earth from core to space, *Eos Trans. AGU* **87,** no. 11, 113.

Durrheim, R., M. Doucouré, and V. Midzi (2016). Earthquakes, in *Shale Gas Development in the Central Karoo: A Scientific Assessment of the Opportunities and Risks*, R. Scholes, P. Lochner, G. Schreiner, L. Snyman-Van der Walt, and M. de Jager (Editors), CSIR, Pretoria.

Ellsworth, W. L. (2013). Injection-induced earthquakes, *Science* **341,** no. 6142, 1225942.

Fatti, L. (1987). Reflection seismic surveys in the Karoo basin by Soekor, in *SAGA Yearbook*, South African Geophysical Association (SAGA), Johannesburg, South Africa, 22–30.

Foster, A. N., and J. A. Jackson (1998). Source parameters of large African earthquakes: implications for crustal rheology and regional kinematics, *Geophys. J. Int.* **134,** 422–448.

Geel, C., M. De Wit, P. Booth, H. M. Schulz, and B. Horsfield (2015). Palaeo-environment, diagenesis and characteristics of Permian black shales in the Lower Karoo Supergroup flanking the Cape fold belt near Jansenville, eastern Cape, South Africa: Implications for the shale gas potential of the Karoo basin, *S. Afr. J. Geol.* **118,** no. 3, 249–274.

Geel, C., H.-M. Schulz, P. Booth, M. deWit, and B. Horsfield (2013). Shale gas characteristics of Permian black shales in South Africa: Results from recent drilling in the Ecca Group (eastern Cape), *Energy Procedia* 40, 256–265.

Goedhart, M., and P. Booth (2016a). A palaeoseismic trench investigation of early Holocene neotectonic faulting along the Kango fault, southern Cape fold belt, South Africa–Part I: Stratigraphic and structural features, *S. Afr. J. Geol.* **119,** no. 3, 545–568.

Goedhart, M., and P. Booth (2016b). A palaeoseismic trench investigation of early Holocene neotectonic faulting along the Kango fault, southern Cape fold belt, South Africa–Part II: earthquake parameters, *S. Afr. J. Geol.* **119,** no. 3, 569–582.

Goutorbe, B., D. L. de Oliveira Coelho, and S. Drouet (2015). Rayleigh wave group velocities at periods of 6–23 s across Brazil from ambient noise tomography, *Geophys. J. Int.* **203,** no. 2, 869–882.

Halbich, I. W. (1993). The cape fold belt-Agulhas bank transect, in *Cape Fold Belt-Agulhas Bank Transect Across Gondwana Suture, Southern Africa*, I. W. Halbich (Editor), Vol. 9, American Geophysical Union, Washington, D.C., U.S.A., 1-16–11-16.

Havskov, J., and L. Ottemoller (1999). SEISAN earthquake analysis software, *Seismol. Res. Lett.* **70,** no. 5, 532–534.

Havskov, J., P. H. Voss, and L. Ottemöller (2020). Seismological observatory software: 30 years of SEISAN, *Seismol. Res. Lett.* **91,** no. 3, 1846–1852.

Holland, A. A. (2013). Earthquakes triggered by hydraulic fracturing in south-central Oklahoma, *Bull. Seismol. Soc. Am.* **103,** no. 3, 1784–1792.

Johnson, M. R., C. J. Van Vuuren, W. F. Hegenberger, R. Key, and U. Show (1996). Stratigraphy of the Karoo Supergroup in southern Africa: an overview, *J. Afr. Earth. Sci.* **23,** no. 1, 3–15.

Keranen, K. M., H. M. Savage, G. A. Abers, and E. S. Cochran (2013). Potentially induced earthquakes in Oklahoma, USA: Links between wastewater injection and the 2011 M_w 5.7 earthquake sequence, *Geology* **41,** no. 6, 699–702.

Kijko, A., B. Kahle, A. Smit, S. Esterhuyse, and J. Glazewski (2016). Hydraulic fracturing, wastewater pumping and seismicity, in *Hydraulic Fracturing in the Karoo—Critical Legal and Environmental Perspectives*, J. Glazewski and S. Esterhuyse (Editors), Juta and Company (Pty) Ltd., Cape Town, South Africa, 264–277.

King, T. R., M. Quigley, and D. Clark (2019). Surface-rupturing historical earthquakes in Australia and their environmental effects: New insights from re-analyses of observational data, *Geosciences* **9,** no. 10, 408.

Kolawole, F., C. S. Johnston, C. B. Morgan, J. C. Chang, K. J. Marfurt, D. A. Lockner, Z. Reches, and B. M. Carpenter (2019). The susceptibility of Oklahoma's basement to seismic reactivation, *Nature Geosci.* **12,** no. 10, 839–844.

Krüger, F., and F. Scherbaum (2014). The 29 September 1969, Ceres, South Africa, earthquake: Full waveform moment tensor inversion for point source and kinematic source parameters, *Bull. Seismol. Soc. Am.* **104,** no. 1, 576–581.

Kubo, R. (1966). The fluctuation-dissipation theorem, *Rep. Progr. Phys.* 29, no. 1, 255–284.

Larose, E., M. Campillo, A. Khan, and Y. Nakamura (2005). Lunar subsurface investigated from correlation of seismic noise, *Geophys. Res. Lett.* **32,** no. 16, L16201, doi: 10.1029/2005GL023518.

Laske, G., G. Masters, Z. Ma, and M. Pasyanos (2013). Update on CRUST1. 0—A 1-degree global model of Earth's crust, *EGU General Assembly 2013*, Vienna, 7–12 April 2013.

Levshin, A. L. (2018). SensKernel, available at https://github.com/NoiseCIEI/SensKernel (last accessed January 2026).

Levshin, A. L., and M. H. Ritzwoller (2001). Automated detection, extraction, and measurement of regional surface waves, *Pure Appl. Geophys.* **158,** no. 8, 1531–1545.

Lindeque, A., M. J. de Wit, T. Ryberg, M. Weber, and L. Chevallier (2011). Deep crustal profile across the southern Karoo basin and Beattie magnetic anomaly, South Africa: An integrated interpretation with tectonic implications, *S. Afr. J. Geol.* **114,** nos. 3/4, 265–292.

Lindeque, A., T. Ryberg, J. Stankiewicz, M. H. Weber, and M. J. De Wit (2007). Deep crustal seismic reflection experiment across the southern Karoo basin, South Africa, *S. Afr. J. Geol.* **110,** nos. 2/3, 419–438.

Linol, B., N. Chere, T. Muedi, V. Nengovhela, and M. J. Wit (2016). Deep borehole lithostratigraphy and basin structure of the southern Karoo Basin re-visited, in *Origin and Evolution of the Cape Mountains and Karoo Basin*, B. Linol and M. J. de Wit (Editors), Springer, Cham, Switzerland, 3-16–13-16.

Malservisi, R., U. Hugentobler, R. Wonnacott, and M. Hackl (2013). How rigid is a rigid plate? Geodetic constraint from the TrigNet CGPS network, South Africa, *Geophys. J. Int.* **192,** no. 3, 918–928.

McGarr, A. (2014). Maximum magnitude earthquakes induced by fluid injection, *J. Geophys. Res.* **119,** no. 2, 1008–1019.

Muir, R., B. Whitehead, T. New, V. Stevens, P. Macey, C. Groenewald, G. Salomon, B. Kahle, J. Hollingsworth, and R. Sloan (2023). Exceptional scarp preservation in SW Namibia reveals geological controls on large magnitude intraplate seismicity in southern Africa, *Tectonics* **42,** no. 4, e2022TC007693, doi: 10.1029/2022TC007693.

Newton, A. R. (1993). Thrusting on the northern margin of the Cape fold belt, near Laingsburg, *S. Afr. J. Geol.* **96,** no. 1, 22–30.

Parsiegla, N., K. Gohl, and G. Uenzelmann-Neben (2007). Deep crustal structure of the sheared South African continental margin: first results of the Agulhas-Karoo Geoscience transect, *S. Afr. J. Geol.* **110,** nos. 2/3, 393–406.

Prieto, G. A., M. Denolle, J. F. Lawrence, and G. C. Beroza (2011). On amplitude information carried by the ambient seismic field, *C.R. Geosci.* **343,** nos. 8/9, 600–614.

Rodi, W. L., P. Glover, T. M. C. Li, and S. S. Alexander (1975). A fast, accurate method for computing group-velocity partial derivatives for Rayleigh and Love modes, *Bull. Seismol. Soc. Am.* **65,** no. 5, 1105–1114.

Roland, E., and J. J. McGuire (2009). Earthquake swarms on transform faults, *Geophys. J. Int.* **178,** no. 3, 1677–1690.

Salomon, G. W., T. New, R. A. Muir, B. Whitehead, S. Scheiber-Enslin, J. Smit, V. Stevens, B. Kahle, R. Kahle, F. D. Eckardt, *et al.* (2022). Geomorphological and geophysical analyses of the Hebron fault, SW Namibia: Implications for stable continental region seismic hazard, *Geophys. J. Int.* **229,** no. 1, 235–254.

Scheiber-Enslin, S., J. Ebbing, and S. J. Webb (2014). An integrated geophysical study of the Beattie magnetic anomaly, South Africa, *Tectonophysics* **636,** 228–243.

Scheiber-Enslin, S., S. Webb, and M. Manzi (2016). Seismic imaging of dolerite sills in the Karoo Basin, with implications for shale gas potential, in *Origin and Evolution of the Cape Mountains and Karoo Basin*, B. Linol and M. J. de Wit (Editors), Springer, Cham, Switzerland, 17–26.

Schulte, S. M., and W. D. Mooney (2005). An updated global earthquake catalogue for stable continental regions: Reassessing the correlation with ancient rifts, *Geophys. J. Int.* **161,** no. 3, 707–721.

Schultz, R., R. Wang, Y. J. Gu, K. Haug, and G. Atkinson (2017). A seismological overview of the induced earthquakes in the Duvernay play near Fox Creek, Alberta, *J. Geophys. Res.* **122,** no. 1, 492–505.

Shapiro, N. M., and M. Campillo (2004). Emergence of broadband Rayleigh waves from correlations of the ambient seismic noise, *Geophys. Res. Lett.* **31,** no. 7, L07614, doi; 10.1029/2004GL019491.

Smit, L., Å. Fagereng, B. Braeuer, and J. Stankiewicz (2015). Microseismic activity and basement controls on an active intraplate strike-slip fault, Ceres–Tulbagh, South Africa, *Bull. Seismol. Soc. Am.* **105,** no. 3, 1540–1547.

Snieder, R., M. Miyazawa, E. Slob, I. Vasconcelos, and K. Wapenaar (2009). A comparison of strategies for seismic interferometry, *Surv. Geophys.* **30,** nos. 4/5, 503–523.

Stankiewicz, J., N. Parsiegla, T. Ryberg, K. Gohl, U. Weckmann, R. Trumbull, and M. Weber (2008). Crustal structure of the southern margin of the African continent: Results from geophysical experiments, *J. Geophys. Res.* **113,** no. B10, doi: 10.1029/2008JB005612.

Stankiewicz, J., T. Ryberg, A. Schulze, A. Lindeque, M. H. Weber, and M. J. De Wit (2007). Initial results from wide-angle seismic refraction lines in the southern Cape, *S. Afr. J. Geol.* **110,** nos. 2/3, 407–418.

Stevens, V., R. Sloan, P. Chindandali, L. N. Wedmore, G. Salomon, and R. Muir (2021). The entire crust can be seismogenic: Evidence from southern Malawi, *Tectonics* **40,** no. 6, e2020TC006654, doi: 10.1029/2020TC006654.

Strasser, F., P. Albini, N. Flint, and C. Beauval (2015). Twentieth century seismicity of the Koffiefontein region (Free State, South Africa): Consistent determination of earthquake catalogue parameters from mixed data types, *J. Seismol.* **19,** no. 4, 915–934.

Tsai, V. C. (2009). On establishing the accuracy of noise tomography travel-time measurements in a realistic medium, *Geophys. J. Int.* **178,** no. 3, 1555–1564.

Tsai, V. C., K. Sager, and D. C. Bowden (2024). Towards limited-domain full waveform ambient noise inversion, *Geophys. J. Int.* **237,** no. 2, 965–973.

United States Energy Information Administration (2011). World shale gas resources: An initial assessment of 14 regions outside the United States, available at https://www.eia.gov/analysis/pdfpages/worldshalegasindex.php (last accessed January 2026).

Veevers, J. J., D. I. Cole, and E. J. Cowan (1994). Southern Africa: Karoo basin and Cape fold belt, in *Permian-Triassic Pangean Basins and Foldbelts Along the Panthalassan Margin of Gondwanaland*, J. J. Veevers and C. McA Powell (Editors), Geological Society of America, Boulder, Colorado.

Waldhauser, F., and W. L. Ellsworth (2000). A double-difference earthquake location algorithm: Method and application to the northern Hayward fault, California, *Bull. Seismol. Soc. Am.* **90,** no. 6, 1353–1368.

Wapenaar, K. (2003). Synthesis of an inhomogeneous medium from its acoustic transmission response, *Geophysics* **68,** no. 5, 1756–1759.

Weckmann, U., O. Ritter, A. Jung, T. Branch, and M. De Wit (2007). Magnetotelluric measurements across the Beattie magnetic anomaly and the southern Cape Conductive belt, South Africa, *J. Geophys. Res.* **112,** no. B5, doi: 10.1029/2005JB003975.

Yang, Y., and M. H. Ritzwoller (2008). The characteristics of ambient seismic noise as a source for surface wave tomography, *Geochem. Geophys. Geosys.* **9,** no. 2, doi: 10.1029/2007GC001814.

Manuscript received 22 September 2025
Published online 21 January 2026

Looking for the Possible Epicenters and Magnitudes of Strong Prehistoric Earthquakes Near Boston, Massachusetts

John E. Ebel*[1], Katrin Monecke[2], J. Bradford Hubeny[3], Francine M. G. McCarthy[4], Lindsay Theis[5], and Aaron Alderson[4]

Abstract

This study examines evidence of widespread mass wasting that was found in the sediments of Walden Pond (WP), Concord, Massachusetts, and Sluice Pond (SP), Lynn, Massachusetts, deposited between 1380 and 1520 C.E. and shortly after 1386–1509 C.E., respectively, along with 15 landslides in the sensitive glaciomarine deposits of the Presumpscot Formation in southern Maine, all of which took place between 1221 and 1454 C.E. In addition, the sediments in WP show evidence of mass wasting between 1050 and 1320 C.E., which is not seen in SP or in Maine. Whereas the younger event horizons in WP and SP and possibly the landslides in southern Maine are attributed to an earthquake in ~1400 C.E., the older anomalous layer in WP is attributed to an event in ~1200 C.E. We carried out a modeling analysis to find the range of possible locations and magnitudes of earthquakes that could have disturbed the sediments in the ponds and caused the landslides in Maine. For an earthquake in ~1400 C.E., the area of possible epicenters is in eastern Massachusetts or southeastern New Hampshire, with a possible magnitude range of 5.6 ≤ M_w ≤ 6.7 (±0.3 uncertainty). If the earthquake also caused the landslides in Maine and with a magnitude as small as M_w 4.7 ± 0.3 with an epicenter in eastern Massachusetts if the earthquake did not cause the landslides in Maine. An earthquake in ~1200 C.E. with M_w 4.7 ± 0.3 or a little larger near or west of WP is most likely, although an earthquake as large as M_w 6.2 ± 0.3 and an epicenter as far west of WP as Worcester, Massachusetts, is possible. The results of this study suggest that the seismic hazard in eastern Massachusetts and southeastern New Hampshire might need re-evaluation.

Cite this article as Ebel, J. E., K. Monecke, J. B. Hubeny, F. M. G. McCarthy, L. Theis, and A. Alderson (2026). Looking for the Possible Epicenters and Magnitudes of Strong Prehistoric Earthquakes Near Boston, Massachusetts, *Seismol. Res. Lett.* **97**, 860–876, doi: 10.1785/0220250310.

Supplemental Material

Introduction

Finding geologic evidence of strong prehistoric earthquakes in northeastern North America is very challenging. The last continental glaciation, which retreated from southern New England (including Massachusetts) ~14,000 ^{14}C yr B.P. (Skehan, 2001; Ridge, 2004) and out of northern New England by 10,000 ^{14}C yr B.P. (Borns *et al.*, 2004), scoured the bedrock surface of northeastern North America, likely reshaping and removing Pleistocene and earlier vertical bedrock fault displacements in the process. The retreat of the glacier left widespread till, glaciolacustrine, glaciofluvial, and glaciomarine deposits, which covered bedrock where fault offsets might have occurred. Because most earthquakes in the northeastern United States have reverse focal mechanisms (e.g., Ebel and Kafka, 1991), it is quite possible that a strong earthquake occurred on a blind thrust fault that did not break the earth's surface, thus leaving no direct evidence of surface faulting. Even if faulting in strong earthquakes since the retreat of the last continental glacier did break the surface, the erosion in upland areas and deposition in lowland areas combined with dense vegetation have degraded, buried, and otherwise hidden evidence of postglacial earthquake faulting.

Another way to look for evidence of past earthquakes in regions where primary evidence of earthquake faulting is missing is in the sediments of lakes and ponds, which can provide continuous, undisturbed, and easily datable sediment records that often span multiple millennia and can extend earthquake

1. Weston Observatory, Department of Earth and Environmental Sciences, Boston College, Weston, Massachusetts, U.S.A., https://orcid.org/0000-0003-1064-0629 (JEE); 2. Department of Geosciences, Wellesley College, Wellesley, Massachusetts, U.S.A.; 3. Department of Geological Sciences, Salem State University, Salem, Massachusetts, U.S.A.; 4. Department of Earth Science, Brock University, St. Catharines, Canada, https://orcid.org/0009-0008-8134-7941 (AA); 5. Maine Geological Survey, Augusta, Maine, U.S.A., https://orcid.org/0000-0003-1425-5680 (LT)

*Corresponding author: ebel@bc.edu

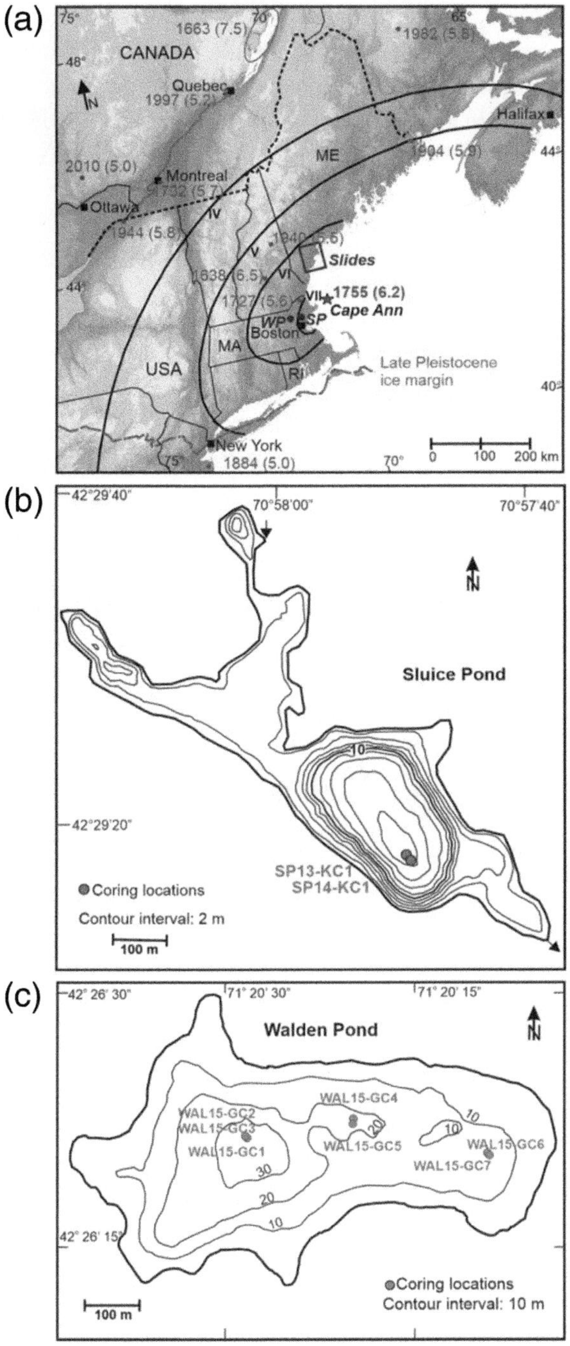

Figure 1. (a) Locations of known or suspected strong historic earthquakes in New England and adjacent areas from 1638 to 2017 with the dates and *Lg* magnitudes (in parentheses) indicated (source: Weston Observatory Northeast Earthquake Maps and Catalogs). Star marks epicenter of 1755 Cape Ann earthquake after Ebel (2006). Isoseismal lines for this event are also shown. Lacustrine study sites Sluice Pond (SP) and Walden Pond (WP) in eastern Massachusetts are shown with circles, and the location of landslides in Southern Maine is indicated with blue. The dashed line marks southernmost extent of Late Pleistocene ice sheet. Modified from Monecke *et al.* (2018). (b) Bathymetric map of SP modified from Hubeny *et al.* (2015) and locations of sediment cores. (c) Bathymetric Map of WP and sediment coring locations modified from Monecke *et al.* (2025). The color version of this figure is available only in the electronic edition.

records well beyond instrumental and historical data (e.g., Moernaut *et al.*, 2014; Kremer *et al.*, 2017; Lu *et al.*, 2020). Earthquake-induced deformation of lake sediments differs depending on the lake basin configuration and the type of lake sediment, but one of the most common features is subaqueous mass wasting (e.g., Shilts and Clague, 1992; Brooks, 2016; Sabatier *et al.*, 2022). Calibration of earthquake-induced deformation is possible when ground-shaking intensities of well-known historic earthquakes can be linked to deformed horizons (e.g., Doig, 1990, 1998; Monecke *et al.*, 2004; Moernaut *et al.*, 2014). Sophisticated dating techniques have been applied in lacustrine settings, including short-lived radionuclides, industrial contaminants, and correlation to historical events for young records; pollen stratigraphy and radiocarbon dating have been used for older records (for a summary, see Sabatier *et al.*, 2022). In conjunction with age-depth modeling software (e.g., Blaauw and Christen, 2011), these datasets can provide robust estimates of when a shaking event took place and how it correlates to other paleoseismic archives in a region.

In this study, we consider the sedimentary records from Sluice Pond (SP) in Lynn, Massachusetts, and Walden Pond (WP) in Concord, Massachusetts. Two prehistoric earthquakes have been inferred from the deposits of WP, one in ~1400 C.E. (1380–1520 C.E.) and the other in ~1200 C.E. (1050–1320 C.E.; Monecke *et al.*, 2025). In SP, Monecke *et al.* (2018) described sedimentary evidence of the 1755 Cape Ann earthquake, the largest historic earthquake in New England. For this study, we measured selected sediment proxies in the older portion of the SP sediment core record and present an updated age model including four new radiocarbon dates. We extend the earthquake record of SP further back in time and present arguments for an older event also in ~1400 C.E. In addition, we consider 15 landslides in the Presumpscot Formation (Spigel, 2020b), a glaciomarine mud deposit of southern Maine that is prone to liquefaction and failure when disturbed. The 15 landslides all took place in ~1400 C.E. and could have been triggered by seismic shaking from the same earthquake that apparently affected the sediments in SP and WP. This article summarizes the sedimentary evidence for the two prehistoric earthquakes in SP and WP, estimates the minimum strength of the ground shaking at each pond necessary to disturb the sediments, summarizes the landslide data in southern Maine and the minimum strength of ground shaking necessary to cause the slides, and then assesses the possible locations and magnitudes of the earthquakes from ~1400 to ~1200 C.E. The implications of the results of this research for the seismic hazard of eastern Massachusetts, which comprises the heavily populated Boston metropolitan area, are discussed.

Evidence of Strong Earthquakes in SP and WP

In eastern Massachusetts, SP and WP represent favorable candidates for paleoseismic investigations (Fig. 1): both lakes are of glacial origin; have deep, undisturbed basins of 20 and 30 m maximum depth, respectively; and are surrounded by steep slopes between 10° and 20° that have been found to be susceptible to subaqueous mass wasting (Strasser *et al.*, 2007; Wilhelm *et al.*, 2016). Furthermore, WP is divided into three sub-basins, which can record independently any large disturbance event, thus providing a strong indicator of a regional event such as an earthquake (Schnellmann *et al.*, 2002). Both ponds are also located close to the epicenter of the *Lg*-wave magnitude M_{Lg} 6.2 (estimated moment magnitude, M_w 5.9) 1755 Cape Ann earthquake, the largest historic earthquake in New England, which caused ground shaking of modified Mercalli intensity (MMI) = VII at the SP site at ~75 km epicentral distance and MMI = VI at WP at ~100 km epicentral distance (Fig. 1, Ebel, 2006).

For paleoseismic work in SP, we recovered two Kullenberg cores of 1.53 and 0.78 m length from the deepest spot of the lake in 2013 and 2014 (Fig. 1). Sediment cores were split lengthwise, described, and photographed. Because the cores show mostly homogeneous organic-rich mud, we used a multiproxy approach combining sedimentological, physical, geochemical, and palynological techniques to characterize the sediments and identify event horizons with anomalous or disturbed sedimentation potentially related to strong ground shaking. Section S1 in the supplemental material gives a more detailed description of the methodology.

For the younger sedimentary record, Crescenzi et al. (2010) and Monecke et al. (2018) developed age-depth models using the sediment surface in the core, radioisotopes ^{137}Cs and ^{210}Pb, and industrial contaminants V and Pb. Older sediments were dated using radiocarbon dates and pollenstratigraphic horizons that trace the vegetation history of New England (Vickers, 1994) . Here, we present an updated age-depth model using the same upper 10 age constrains but obtained four new Accelerator Mass Spectrometry radiocarbon dates from bulk sediment to better confine the lower record. Samples were acid-pretreated and measured at the National Oceanographic Accelerator Mass Spectrometry (NOSAMS) facility at Woods Hole Oceanographic Institution (WHOI, Table 1). We constructed the age-depth model using Bayesian statistics of the age-depth modeling software BACON and calibration curve IntCal20 (Blaauw and Christen, 2011; Reimer *et al.*, 2020; Fig. 2). The model predicts a 2σ age range for each depth in the sediment record as well as a mean age (Fig. 2). In our calculation, we omitted two mass wasting deposits that are discussed subsequently because they represent rapid deposition compared to the typical low-rate background sedimentation.

The younger sediment record of SP of the past ~400 yr is presented in detail by Monecke *et al.* (2018). We are summarizing selected proxies from this study here and present new data that extend the record ~600 yr further back in time (Fig. 3). Sediments of SP from 78 to 50 cm core depth and deposited from ~800 to 1400 C.E. according to our age model consist of dark-brown organic-rich mud with biogenic particles of algal origin dominating the sediment composition. This composition results in low dry bulk densities (DBDs) and relatively low-organic carbon to nitrogen (OC/N) ratios averaging 12.5, indicative of minor terrestrial organic matter input (Meyers, 1994). Mineral grains compose only 5%–10% of the sediment ranging from clay to fine sand with a dominant mode of coarse silt (~35 to 38 μm, Fig. 3). For sediment between 50 and 30 cm depth, deposited from ~1400 C.E. to the mid-eighteenth century, organic carbon content decreases, OC/N ratios increase, and mineral sizes show a higher influx of sediment in the coarse silt range, suggesting an elevated input of terrigenous particles possibly related to a wetter climate proposed for this time period (Hubeny *et al.*, 2011; Marlon *et al.*, 2017). Although there was an initial increase of herbaceous pollen including *Ambrosia* in the late thirteenth century, probably associated with the spread of indigenous Maize agriculture in this region, the abundance of non-arboreal pollen (e.g., *Ambrosia*) increases more rapidly above the European settlement horizon at 39 cm depth, indicating a change from a mostly forested to a cleared landscape. Sediments deposited since the mid-eighteenth century above 30 cm core depth show a complex history of industrialization and land-use change with abundant input of fines in the clay to medium silt range, likely from eroded soils resulting in higher DBD and lower OC content. OC/N ratios averaging 12.6 indicate high productivity within the lake. Above 20 cm core depth and deposited since the early 1900s, a transition to more urban activities around the lake is reflected by a decrease in non-arboreal pollen and a higher influx of terrestrial organic matter (OC/N ratios of ~15.3). Dredging in the shallow areas of the lake in the 1980s and 1990s probably led to deposition of a silty clay layer at 5–4 cm depth (Fig. 3, Monecke *et al.* 2018).

Two intervals that are distinctively different from surrounding sediment occur at 31–29 and 50–45 cm core depth (Fig. 3). Monecke *et al.* (2018) describe the upper layer as a normally graded unit with a distinct geochemical and palynological signature, suggesting mobilization of lacustrine slope sediment and deposition from a turbidity current. With a depositional age of 1740–1810 C.E., Monecke *et al.* (2018) link the deposit to ground shaking and subsequent slope failure during the 1755 Cape Ann earthquake, possibly followed by seiche action because of the abundance of shoreline aquatics within the unit.

We identified a lower interval between 50 and 45 cm depth (Fig. 3) and deposited shortly after 1386–1509 C.E. (2σ age range at 51 cm; Fig. 2) with similar characteristics: The deposit is composed of two normally graded units with the lower unit grading from very fine sands to fine silt and the upper one grading from coarse and medium sands to coarse silts. DBD is high and OC decreases over the interval, indicating a higher input of mineral grains. OC/N ratios are within background values but decrease sharply at the top of the unit, pointing toward incorporation of mostly aquatic organic matter. Palynofacies analysis

TABLE 1

Age Constraints from Radioisotopes, Industrial Contaminants, and Pollenstratigraphic Horizons from Monecke *et al.* (2018) and Radiocarbon Ages and Calibrated Dates Used to Reconstruct Age Model for Sluice Pond Sediments in Figure 2 and Radiocarbon Ages and Calibrated Dates for Landslides in Maine

Sample Type	Depth in Composite Core (cm)	Material	Lab Accession Number	^{14}C Age (yr B.P.)	2σ Calibrated Age (C.E.)	Relative Area Under Distribution (%)	Reference
Sluice Pond							
Core surface	0	Bulk sediment			2014 ± 1		
^{210}Pb correlation 1	5	Bulk sediment			1991 ± 5		Crescenzi *et al.* (2010)
Pb peak	9	Bulk sediment			1979 ± 5		Callender and Rice (2000)
V peak	12	Bulk sediment			1966 ± 5		Chillrud *et al.* (1999)
^{137}Cs peak	12.5	Bulk sediment			1963 ± 5		Crescenzi *et al.* (2010)
^{137}Cs onset	15	Bulk sediment			1950 ± 5		Crescenzi *et al.* (2010)
^{210}Pb correlation 2	20	Bulk sediment			1922 ± 5		Crescenzi *et al.* (2010)
^{210}Pb correlation 3	24	Bulk sediment			1907 ± 5		Crescenzi *et al.* (2010)
Secondary *Ambrosia* increase	28	Pollen			1771 ± 10		Vickers (1994)
Non-arboreal pollen horizon	39	Pollen			1629 ± 10		Vickers (1994)
C14 (core SP13 KC1 30)	46	Bulk sediment	NOSAMS OS-162049	455 ± 25	1422–1459	93.2	Reimer *et al.* (2020)
					1464–1468	1.6	
C14 (core SP13 KC1 41)	57	Bulk sediment	NOSAMS OS-187194	655 ± 25	1283–1322	45	Reimer *et al.* (2020)
					1356–1391	49.7	
C14 (core SP13 KC1 49.5)	65.5	Bulk sediment	NOSAMS OS-162050	805 ± 15	1222–1266	95	Reimer *et al.* (2020)
C14 (core SP13 KC1 70)	86	Bulk sediment	NOSAMS OS-162051	1360 ± 20	645–678	92.4	Reimer *et al.* (2020)
					752–757	2.4	
Southern Maine landslides							
C14 (slide 181)		Wood (twig)	Beta 574360	480 ± 30	1409–1454	95	Reimer *et al.* (2020)
C14 (slide 204)		Wood (twig)	Beta 574375	480 ± 30	1409–1454	95	Reimer *et al.* (2020)
C14 (slide 86)		Plant fragment	Beta 574370	550 ± 30	1321–1358	37	Reimer *et al.* (2020)
					1390–1432	57.8	
C14 (slide 225)		Plant fragment	OS-138872	555 ± 20	1325–1353	35.6	Reimer *et al.* (2020)

(Continued next page.)

TABLE 1 (continued)
Age Constraints from Radioisotopes, Industrial Contaminants, and Pollenstratigraphic Horizons from Monecke *et al.* (2018) and Radiocarbon Ages and Calibrated Dates Used to Reconstruct Age Model for Sluice Pond Sediments in Figure 2 and Radiocarbon Ages and Calibrated Dates for Landslides in Maine

Sample Type	Depth in Composite Core (cm)	Material	Lab Accession Number	^{14}C Age (yr B.P.)	2σ Calibrated Age (C.E.)	Relative Area Under Distribution (%)	Reference
					1394–1422	59.2	
C14 (slide 227)		Wood (twig)	OS-149339	575 ± 20	1319–1360	63.4	Reimer *et al.* (2020)
					1389–1413	31.4	
C14 (slide 58)		Wood w/bark	Beta 574368	580 ± 30	1306–1364	64	Reimer *et al.* (2020)
					1384–1419	30.9	
C14 (slide 218)		Wood charcoal (twig)	Beta 536632	580 ± 30	1306–1364	64	Reimer *et al.* (2020)
					1384–1419	30.9	
C14 (slide 220)		Wood (bark)	OS-149551	580 ± 25	1307–1363	66.6	Reimer *et al.* (2020)
					1386–1412	28.3	
C14 (slide 207)		Wood (twig)	OS-169570	585 ± 20	1310–1361	70.8	Reimer *et al.* (2020)
					1388–1407	24	
C14 (slide 198)		Wood	OS-139265	600 ± 15	1307–1363	77.4	Reimer *et al.* (2020)
					1386–1399	17.6	
C14 (slide 206)		Wood	OS-139259	600 ± 15	1307–1363	77.4	Reimer *et al.* (2020)
					1386–1399	17.6	
C14 (slide 196)		Wood	OS-139262	615 ± 15	1303–1328	39	Reimer *et al.* (2020)
					1335–1367	34	
					1380–1396	21.6	
C14 (slide 185)		Plant fragment	OS-149554	625 ± 20	1299–1327	39	Reimer *et al.* (2020)
					1337–1373	31.8	
					1375–1395	24.3	
C14 (slide 199)		Wood (bark)	OS-139266	725 ± 15	1271–1291	94.5	Reimer *et al.* (2020)
C14 (slide 85)		Wood	OS-144337	810 ± 15	1221–1264	94.1	Reimer *et al.* (2020)

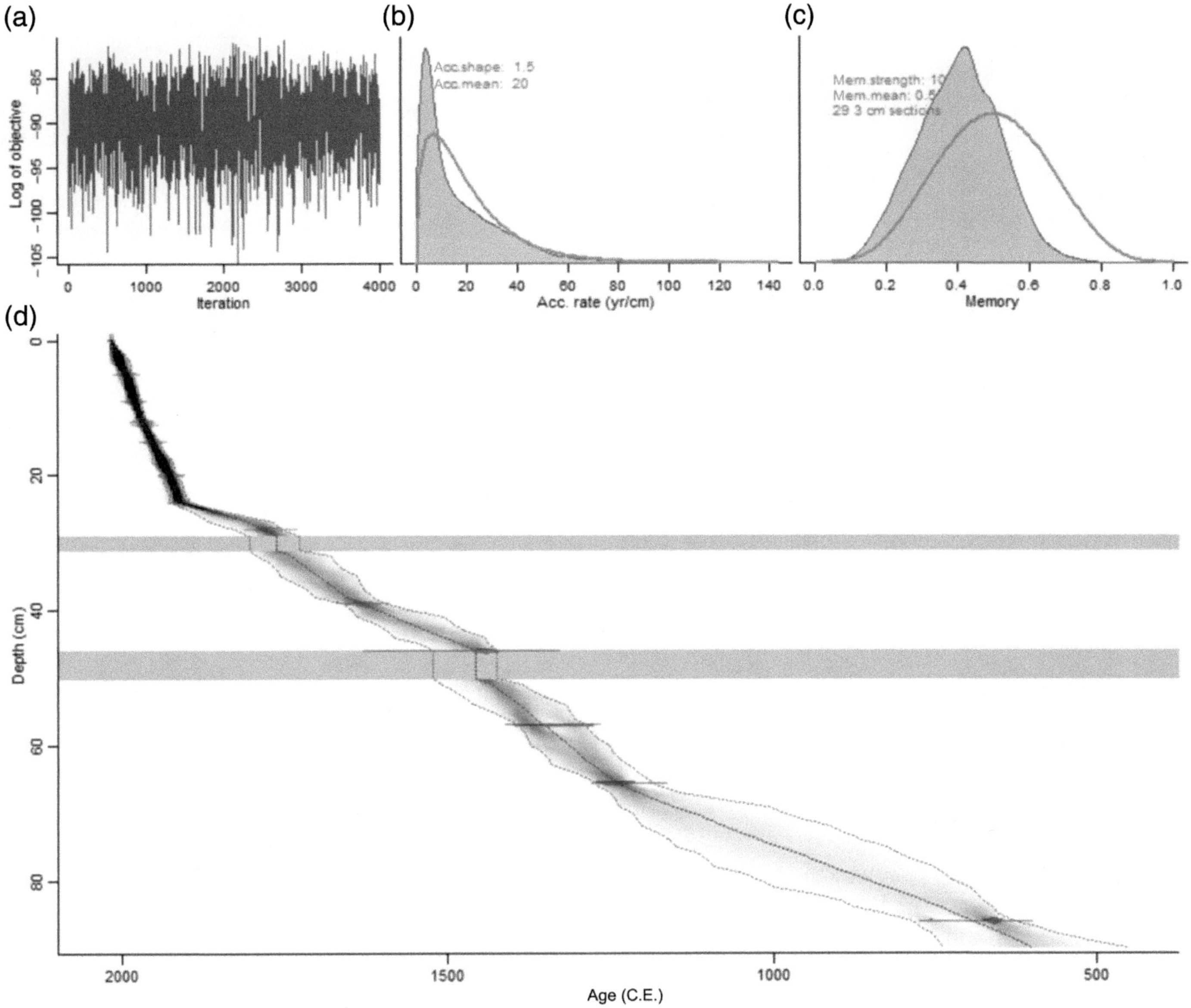

reveals a sudden influx of terrigenous particles and shoreline aquatics such as the spores of *Isoetes* (quillwort) between 50 and 45 cm. In addition, non-pollen palynomorphs (*Botryococcus* and akinetes of *Anabaena* and *Nostoc*) that are common in shoreline settings show sharp increases and an oscillating pattern matching the grain size trends. The palynofacies suggests an even thicker disturbance interval than can be estimated from other proxies. Similar to the upper horizon, we interpret the deposit as a turbidite generated by underwater mass wasting, which mobilized lake sediments along the steep slopes of SP where coarser clastic sediment rich in nearshore vegetation accumulates. A sudden influx of coarse particles in the deep basin is a good indicator of mass-wasting processes along subaqueous slopes within a lake (Sabatier *et al.*, 2022). Similarly, there are palynomorphs of shoreline vegetation such as quillwort (*Isoetes*) as well as acid-resistant remains of benthic algae and resting stages of cyanophytes and dinoflagellates, which are more common in nearshore environments, and their

Figure 2. Age depth model for the sedimentary record of SP using 14 age constraints listed in Table 1 and Bayesian statistics of the BACON 2.2 software package (Blaauw and Christen, 2011). The upper panels depict (a) the Markov Chain Monte Carlo (MCMC) iterations and (b) distributions for sediment accumulation rate, and (c) memory for model run. (d) 2σ age range for each depth with center line marking the mean age. Markers above 40 cm core depth indicate dates and error margins for industrial contaminants, radioisotopes, and pollenstratigraphic horizons used to define the upper sediment record; markers below 40 cm core depth indicate age range of calibrated radiocarbon ages in the lower record. Horizontal gray bars mark depths of two mass wasting deposits associated with the 1755 Cape Ann earthquake and an earlier event further described in the Evidence of Strong Earthquakes in SP and WP section. These were excluded from the age model because they mark instantaneous deposition events. The color version of this figure is available only in the electronic edition.

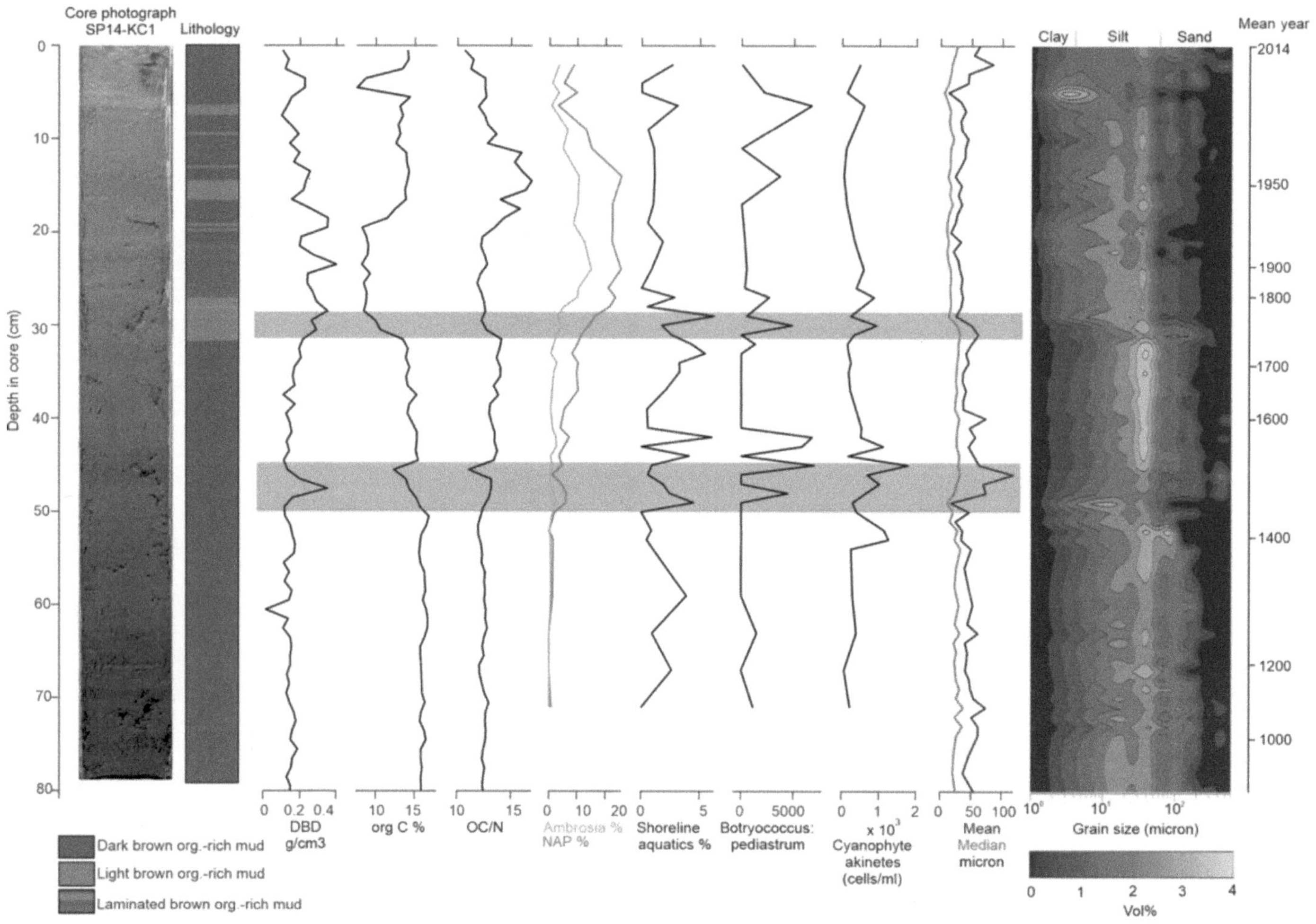

Figure 3. Sedimentary proxies of SP sediments. Mean age is from age model shown in Figure 2. The underlying gray bars mark two mass wasting deposits interpreted to have been triggered by the 1755 Cape Ann earthquake (Monecke *et al.*, 2018) and a prehistoric earthquake in ~1400 C.E. as discussed in the text. The late fourteenth/early fifteenth century age of the older event recorded in sediments of ~50 to 45 cm depth is supported by the initial increase in NAP suggestive of Indigenous agriculture. Multiple peaks in particle size and resedimented palynomorphs suggest episodic shoreline erosion, consistent with seiche activity. DBD, dry bulk density; NAP, non-arboreal pollen; OC, organic carbon. The color version of this figure is available only in the electronic edition.

abundance in deeper-water settings can be evidence of shore erosion (McCarthy *et al.*, 2021).

Because of its similarity to the 1755 deposit, a likely trigger of mass wasting deeper in the core could be evidence of strong ground shaking during a prehistoric earthquake. Turbulence generated during mass failure and mobilization of water-saturated surficial sediments would have been able to throw a large amount of sediment into suspension and transport it to the basin center via a turbidity current (Moernaut *et al.*, 2014, 2017; Vandekerkhove *et al.* 2020). The oscillating character of the deposit could be indicative of the back-and-forth motion of a standing wave or seiche that can be caused by widespread underwater mass wasting in lakes (e.g., Schnellmann *et al.*, 2002) or ground shaking of basin sides (Barberopoulou *et al.*, 2006). Currents under seiches have been found to be strong enough to dislodge nearshore sediment (Avşar *et al.*, 2014), adding to the volume of suspended sediment and explaining the large amount of particles from shoreline vegetation. Other triggers of turbidity currents seem less likely for SP. The scarcity of terrestrial organic matter within the deposit as suggested by its geochemistry and palynofacies excludes an overland flood event as a potential trigger (Fig. 3, e.g., Vandekerkhove *et al.*, 2020). Monecke *et al.* (2018) were also not able to find sedimentary evidence of historic large flood events in the upper record, suggesting that floods do not leave a discernable deposit in this lake because surface water mostly enters the lake as run-off. Large water-level fluctuations linked to wetter and drier periods that could potentially destabilize slopes can also be excluded for the past 1300 yr (Hubeny *et al.*, 2015). SP is only fed by a small creek, leading to minor sediment accumulation in a side arm of the lake (Fig. 1), making a large-scale spontaneous delta collapse because of sediment loading (e.g., Girardclos *et al.*, 2007) unlikely.

WP provides further evidence of the seismic history of eastern Massachusetts. Environmental histories reconstructed from sediments of this lake for the past ~1000 yr show the dramatic change from a mostly forested landscape before the arrival of European settlers in the early seventeenth century to a region influenced by intensive logging for road and home building and increasing industrial needs followed by heavy recreational use since the early 1900s (Winkler, 1993; Köster *et al.*, 2005; Stager *et al.*, 2018; Monecke *et al.*, 2025). Based on a detailed multiproxy analysis of the sedimentary record of all three basins in WP (Fig. 1), Monecke *et al.* (2025) were able to identify three event horizons of mass wasting that are characterized by a sudden influx of coarse sediment typically accumulating on the lake basin slopes closer to shore and high concentrations of non-pollen palynomorphs characteristic of nearshore submerged vegetation. Because all three horizons can be correlated between at least two of the three sub-basins of WP, a regional trigger such as an earthquake is inferred (Monecke *et al.*, 2025). The youngest horizon correlates to the 1755 Cape Ann earthquake within the uncertainties of the age model. Evidence is not consistent through all basins and proxies, likely because of ground shaking of I = VI at the threshold of earthquake-induced deformation in organic-rich lakes (e.g., Wilhelm *et al.*, 2016). However, event horizons with an age of 1380–1520 and 1050–1320 C.E., which are evident across multiple proxies and basins, suggest two larger disturbance events likely triggered by two strong prehistoric earthquakes (Monecke *et al.*, 2025).

Landslides in Southern Maine in ~1400 C.E.

Mass wasting is a common natural hazard in Maine, especially in southern areas of the state where landslides have occurred from early postglacial to modern times (e.g., Morse, 1869; Novak, 1987; Berry *et al.*, 1996; Thompson *et al.*, 2011). Light detection and ranging topographic data recently revealed hundreds of previously unknown prehistoric landslides in Maine that were obscured by thick forest cover (Spigel, 2020a,b). Mass wasting events are possible statewide, but the majority of Maine landslides occur in areas underlain by the Presumpscot Formation —a glaciomarine mud deposited in the late-glacial sea that inundated portions of Maine at the end of the Wisconsinan glaciation (~14,000–12,000 ^{14}C yr B.P.) because of isostatic depression (Bloom, 1960; Borns *et al.*, 2004; Thompson, 2015; Spigel, 2019, 2020b). Isostatic rebound after deglaciation subsequently exposed these deposits with upper portions weathering into a hard, tan crust; deeper unweathered portions appear blue–gray and are stiff to very soft. Informally referred to as "blue clay," the Presumpscot Formation is a variable combination of silt, clay, and sand that is typically present in valleys 15–30 m below the local limit of marine inundation and may occur in combination with other glacial deposits (Amos and Sandford, 1987; Thompson, 2015). Unweathered Presumpscot Formation is a type of "sensitive clay" and poses the risk of unstable terrain because of its low strength, compressibility, and geotechnical sensitivity (Andrews, 1987; Devin and Sandford, 1990). On historical to modern time scales (~1600 C.E. to present), landslides in the Presumpscot Formation tend to occur in spring when consistently wet conditions that add weight and reduce slope shear strength coincide with high stream flow and stream bank or coastal bluff erosion (e.g., Berry *et al.*, 1996; Thompson, 2015; Spigel, 2020a).

The first prehistoric landslide to be studied in southern Maine was found to have occurred in ~13,500 cal yr B.P. (Thompson *et al.*, 2011), which was plausible because of seismic activity related to isostatic rebound and the inherent flux of recently deglaciated terrain. Since the Thompson *et al.* (2011) findings, >40 prehistoric landslide sites have been studied by the Maine Geological Survey, with 37 yielding age estimates of 39 failure events through radiocarbon analysis of organic material that was buried by and preserved in the landslide deposit or had accumulated in postevent wetlands on the deposit surfaces (Spigel, 2019, 2020b; Maine Geological Survey [MGS], 2020). The sampled landslides are a fraction of the >200 landslides that have occurred in Presumpscot Formation deposits, but the primary goal of the original emergency management-funded study was to obtain a general idea of prehistoric landslide ages to better frame future landslide risk in Maine and was constrained by budget and land access. Nonetheless, this study found that these landslides were not constrained to early postglacial times, but rather these events occurred throughout the Holocene, and in fact, many had happened just hundreds of years ago. Of the 39 sites with estimated ages, 15 have two-sigma age ranges between the early thirteenth to the mid-fifteenth centuries (Figs. 4 and 5; Spigel, 2020b). The ages of all events within this temporal cluster were obtained through radiocarbon dating of organic materials from surfaces and soils that were buried by the landslides. The youngest materials, such as herbaceous plant fragments and twigs, were sought out to provide the most accurate age estimate, but overall, these samples represent a maximum age estimate for each event. The landslides dated to ~1400 C.E. in Maine are ~110–150 km from SP and 120–165 km from SP.

Modern landslides in southern Maine are typically related to wet conditions in which water increases overburden weight and reduces overburden shear strength, along with surface water erosion that may lead to unstable Presumpscot Formation exposures in stream banks. A large seismic trigger is more likely for these temporally clustered prehistoric landslide events within ~50 km of each other as noted for similar landslides in the sensitive glaciomarine deposits of eastern Canada (Brooks, 2014). However, supporting primary evidence for a seismic trigger such as offset Quaternary deposits or landforms is lacking in the region (Koons, 1989; Wheeler, 2006).

Correlation of Sedimentary Features Across Archives

To study the potential correlation between the cluster of landslides in southern Maine and mass wasting events in ponds in

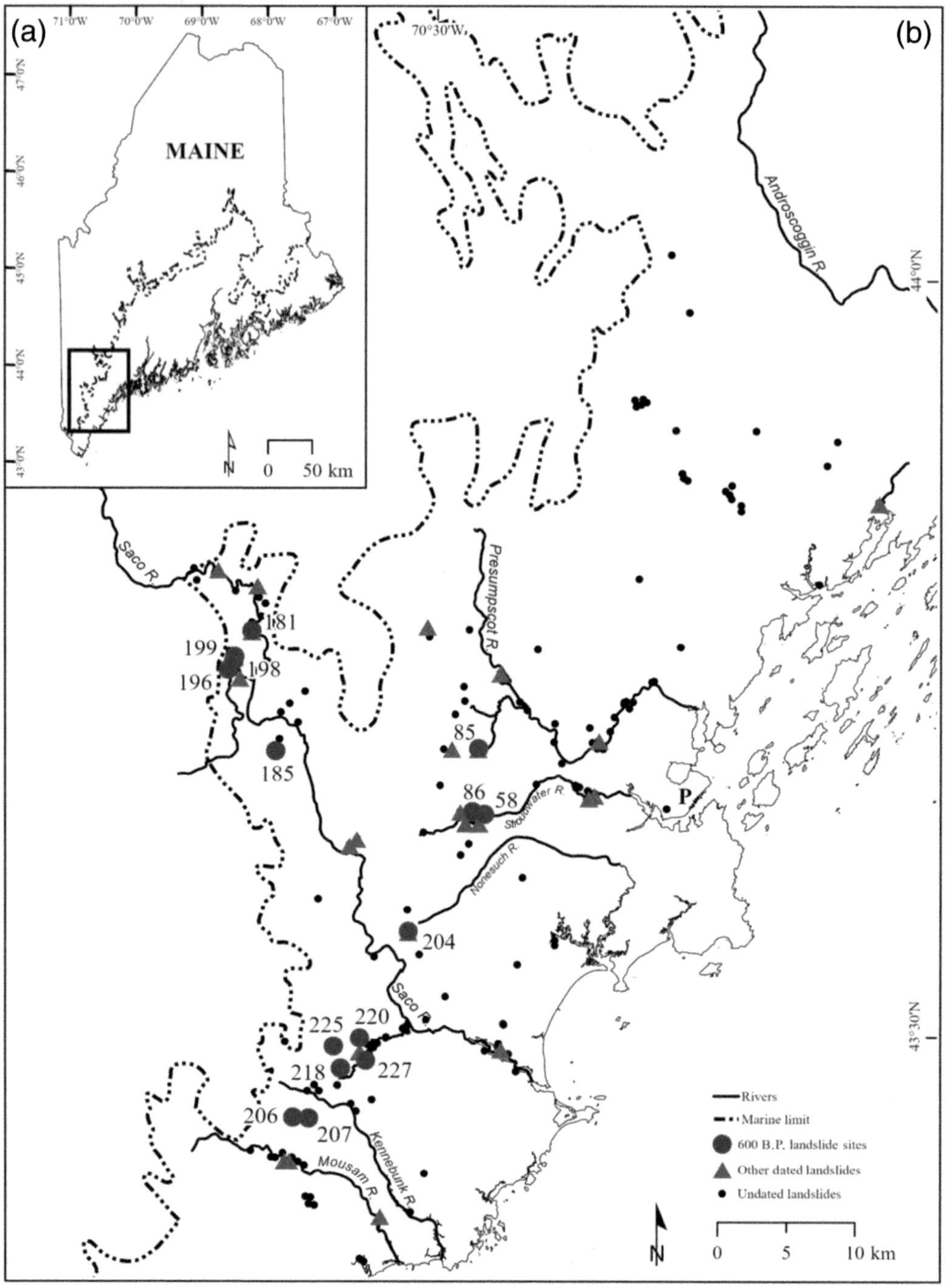

Figure 4. (a) Overview of prehistoric landslide study area in southern Maine. Presumpscot Formation deposits are possible in areas south of the dashed marine limit line. The box marks extent of panel (b), which shows detailed locations of landslide age cluster dated to ~1400 C.E. in southern Maine, along with landslides of other known and unknown ages. Landslides do tend to occur along major river corridors where bank erosion daylights unstable Presumpscot Formation, but many landslides have also happened outside of these corridors. The complete Maine inland landslide inventory can be accessed in MGS (2020). The color version of this figure is available only in the electronic edition.

eastern Massachusetts dating to ~1400 C.E., we analyzed the overlap of age ranges for these features (Fig. 6). Radiocarbon ages for the landslides in Maine were derived from organic material buried by or incorporated into the landslide, thus providing maximum constraining ages that slightly predate the landslides. We used the BACON software package and calibration curve IntCal20 to calibrate those ages (Fig. 6, Table 1; Blaauw and Christen, 2011). Event horizons in lakes were not directly dated; instead, we extracted the 2σ age range from the age models for SP (Fig. 2, Table 1) and the three basins of WP (Monecke *et al.*, 2025) using the BACON software package. To be consistent with the radiocarbon dates for the Maine landslides 2σ age ranges were obtained just below event horizons in the two ponds.

The compiled data show an overlap of the 2σ age range at 1386–1473 C.E. for the prehistoric event in the two ponds. The combined 2σ-age distributions for the landslides in southern Maine lie between 1221 and 1454 C.E. The landslide ages are older possibly because of an inherited age to some of the dated plant debris in contrast to dated lacustrine bulk sediment mostly composed of aquatic organic matter that was likely formed within the lake close to the age of deposition. Because of the irregular shape of the 14C calibration curve between 1300 and 1380 C.E. (Reimer *et al.*, 2020), 11 of the 15 landslides show bimodal or polymodal age distributions, with the youngest peak between 1375 and 1432 C.E., closer to the range in dates of the suspected earthquake horizon in the lacustrine data. Given the uncertainties associated with radiocarbon dating and age-depth modeling, there is no absolute proof that mass wasting at the different sites occurred simultaneously. However, the narrow overlapping age range between all three study areas that are up to 165 km apart from each other supports further investigation of one common trigger.

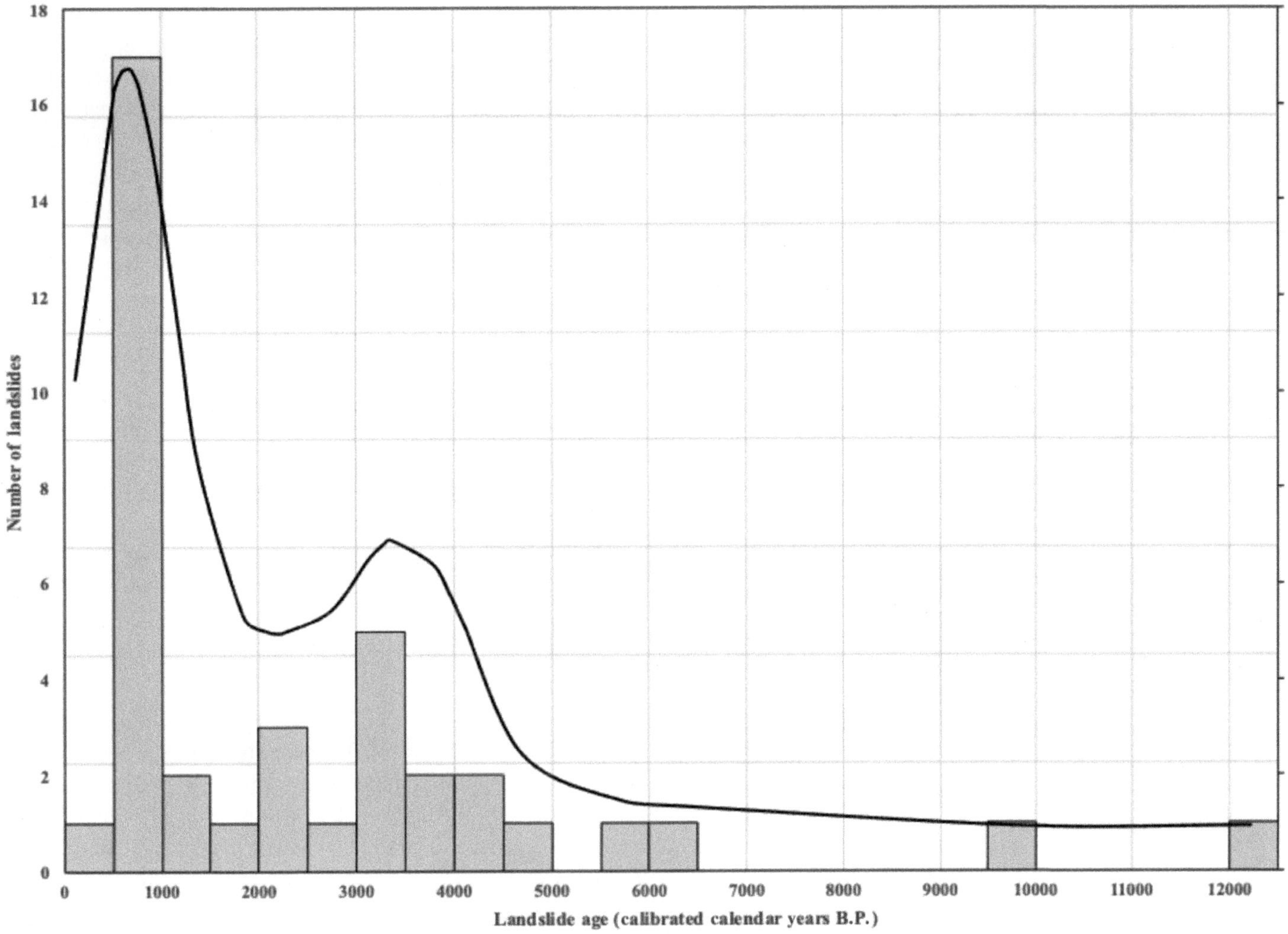

Figure 5. Landslide calibrated calendar age histogram and kernel density plot for the 39 events in southern Maine illustrating a clear cluster of events from ~518 to 715 calendar years B.P. or 1221 to 1454 C.E. This plot uses the median calibrated calendar age for each landslide event. Refer to Figure 6 for more detailed age comparisons of the individual sites and lake sediment records.

Evaluation of Possible Locations and Magnitudes of Prehistoric Earthquakes

Although it is not possible to pinpoint the location and magnitude of either the earthquake that occurred in ~1400 or the one that occurred in ~1200 C.E., it is possible to put constraints on these parameters for both events. To do this, we must estimate the minimum ground motions that will disturb the pond sediments and cause Presumpscot Formation deposits in Maine to fail. In addition, we must identify a ground-motion attenuation relation for the analysis. Each of these items is discussed here, followed by a summary of the calculations to find the range of possible source locations and magnitudes for the earthquakes in ~1400 and ~1200 C.E.

Using ground-shaking attenuation patterns of historic events, thresholds for earthquake-induced deformation as low as ground shaking of intensity I = V 1/2 have been inferred in very sensitive lake settings in Chile (Moernaut *et al.*, 2014), although intensities of I > VI are typically required to induce small-scale soft sediment deformation features (e.g., Lu *et al.*, 2020). Large-scale mass movements in lakes and ponds become the prominent mode of deformation at intensities of I ≥ VII (Monecke *et al.*, 2004; Moernaut *et al.*, 2014). From looking at disturbed lake sediments in the Alps from four historic earthquakes, Monecke *et al.* (2004) reported that ground shaking of at least MMI VI–VII is necessary to affect the sedimentary layers in lakes in Europe, matching observations by Monecke *et al.* (2018) and Monecke *et al.* (2025) of earthquake-induced deformation from the 1755 Cape Ann earthquake in SP and WP, which were situated within the isoseismal lines of VII and VI, respectively (Fig. 1). It is important to note that lake basin configurations, sediment characteristics, and sedimentation rates play large roles in defining the failure threshold caused by ground shaking for individual sites, and these effects might differ between stratigraphic intervals (Wilhelm *et al.*, 2016; Praet *et al.*, 2017; Strupler *et al.*, 2017; Nicovich *et al.*, 2024). For the United States, MMI VI ground

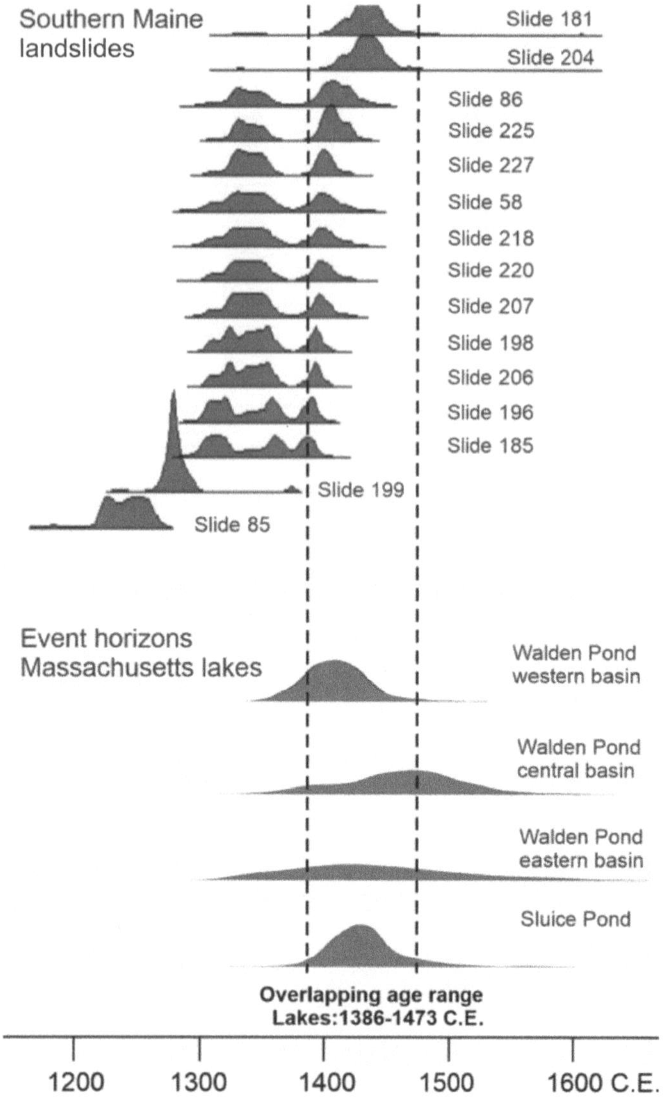

Figure 6. Correlation of landslide cluster in southern Maine with event horizons in SP and in the three basins of WP with a common depositional age around 1400 C.E. Age distributions for event horizons in the three basins of WP are 2-sigma age distributions extracted from age models presented in Monecke *et al.* (2025). Here, 2-sigma age distribution of 1400 C.E. event horizon in SP is extracted from age model in Figure 2.

motion corresponds to a peak ground acceleration (PGA) of ~0.10*g* (Atkinson and Kaka, 2007; Worden *et al.*, 2012). This PGA level is confirmed by Strasser *et al.* (2007), who inferred that PGA levels of ~0.08 and 0.14*g* affected subaqueous slope stability in Lake Lucerne, Switzerland, because of earthquakes in 1601 C.E. and 2220 cal yr B.P. For the purpose of this study, we assumed that a PGA level of at least 0.10*g* is necessary to cause the disturbed sedimentary layers in SP and WP.

The landslides that occurred in ~1400 C.E. in southern Maine all occurred in the geotechnically sensitive Presumpscot Formation. Devin and Sandford (2000) argue that the Presumpscot Formation has a factor of safety (FS) in drained conditions that ranges from 1.13 to 2.08, with a value of FS = 1.0 indicating the material is on the verge of failure and FS < 1.0 meaning that the material is failing. The FS is reduced if the sediments are undrained (i.e., are water saturated), and a geotechnical study by Devin and Sandford (1990) encountered Presumpscot Formation deposits with FS < 1 in an area with known historic and prehistoric landslides, meaning that these sediments are very sensitive and could certainly fail if disturbed by even a small level of ground shaking.

To assess the minimum earthquake PGA value at which the Presumpscot Formation might fail, we consulted the analyses of Jibson and Keefer (1993), Jibson and Harp (2016), and Quinn and Zaleski (2015). Jibson and Keefer (1993) looked at slope failures of two sites in the Mississippi Embayment of shallow-marine deposits of clay and silt that are Eocene in age. These slope failures occurred because of the 1811–1812 New Madrid earthquakes. They estimated that the minimum PGA to generate a landslide at one site is 0.17–0.18*g* with FS (undrained) = 1.57, whereas at the other site the minimum necessary PGA for failure is 0.03–0.05*g* with FS (undrained) = 1.32. Jibson and Harp (2016) compiled a dataset of earthquake-induced landslides in California, Virginia, and Guatemala, and they concluded that the minimum PGA to cause landslides is 0.02–0.08*g* using field data and 0.05–0.11*g* using aerial-photographic data. Quinn and Zaleski (2015) assess the ground motions that caused landslides in sensitive clay in eastern Canada. They found that ground motions as small as 0.02–0.04*g* caused coseismic landslides in low-strength clays because of ground shaking associated with the 1663 M_w 7+ Charlevoix earthquake. Given the low strength of the Presumpscot Formation, we used minimum PGA thresholds of 0.02 and 0.04*g* to cause the sediments to fail in the computations in this study.

The ground-motion attenuation model that was chosen in this study is that of Al Noman and Cramer (2015). It is one of several ground-motion prediction equations (GMPEs) used in the Next Generation Attenuation-East Project (PEER, 2015), and it was selected because it was straightforward to implement for the analyses carried out in this study. This GMPE was calibrated to earthquake data for central and eastern North America along with both instrument and intensity-based PGA estimates for some large earthquakes from other stable cratonic regions. For epicentral distances less than a few hundred kilometers, Al Noman and Cramer (2015) showed that their GMPE gives smaller ground motions than the GMPEs from other investigators that were used in the 2014 U.S. National Seismic Hazard Maps (Petersen *et al.*, 2014). For example, at an epicentral distance of 50 km, Al Noman and Cramer (2015) GMPE gives PGA of 0.06*g* for M_w 6.0, whereas the other GMPEs used by Petersen *et al.* (2014) range up to M_w 6.6 to give this same ground motion. Similarly, at 100 km epicentral distance, the Al Noman and Cramer (2015) GMPE predicts PGA of 0.02*g* for M_w 6.0 with the other GMPEs of Petersen *et al.*

(2014) again ranging up to M_w 6.6. Thus, we assumed in this study that for a given level of ground motion, we need to reduce the PGA given by the Al Noman and Cramer (2015) GMPE by 0.3 magnitude units to get the magnitude value that represents the middle of the magnitudes from the GMPEs of Petersen *et al.* (2014) for a given level of ground motion. We assume that the uncertainties in our magnitude estimate for a given level of ground motion at a given distance are ±0.3 magnitude units.

Because sediments tend to amplify ground shaking compared with nearby rock sites, we must take into account the local site conditions at the two ponds and at the landslide sites in our calculations. Because these are all sites with sedimentary surficial materials, we assumed a V_{S30} value of 250 m/s, typical of soft surficial sedimentary layers, in calculating our PGA values using the Al Noman and Cramer (2015) GMPE.

A grid of points with spacing of 0.1° in latitude and longitude was defined across southeastern New England; at each point, earthquakes of different magnitudes were put into the Al Noman and Cramer (2015) attenuation relation; and the ground motions at the two pond sites in Massachusetts and the 15 landslide sites in Maine were calculated. Earthquake locations and magnitudes at which the minimum ground-motion threshold for failure was exceeded at all sites are considered as possible epicenters and magnitudes that could have triggered the pond disturbances and landslides caused by the earthquake in ~1400 C.E. Evidence for the earthquake in ~1200 C.E. is found clearly in WP but not in SP. For the location and magnitude analysis of this earthquake, it was assumed that the PGA at WP exceeded 0.12*g*, whereas at SP, the earthquake caused PGA <0.08*g*.

For the earthquake in ~1400 C.E., the smallest magnitude earthquake that caused the minimum ground motions at all pond and landslide sites was M_w 5.6 with an epicenter near the Massachusetts–New Hampshire border north of SP, assuming the threshold PGA for the landslides in Maine is 0.02*g*. Figure 7 shows the area of possible epicenters for this PGA threshold if the earthquake is M_w 5.9 and the threshold PGA for landslides in Maine is 0.02*g*. This area is centered approximately between the two ponds in Massachusetts, with possible epicenters anywhere in the greater Boston area and north to the border with New Hampshire. If the threshold PGA for landslides in Maine is increased to 0.04*g*, Figure 7 shows that the area of possible epicenters for an M_w 6.0 earthquake is in northeastern Massachusetts and southeastern New Hampshire. Finally, if the earthquake is M_w 6.7, perhaps near the strongest earthquake that might be expected to take place in southeastern New England, Figure 7 shows that the epicenter could be somewhere in eastern Massachusetts, most of Rhode Island, southeastern and southcentral New Hampshire, or onshore or offshore east and south of the southern tip of Maine. This large area includes the suspected epicenters shown in Figure 1 of the 1755 Cape Ann, Massachusetts, earthquake (M_{Lg} 6.2, Ebel, 2006); the 1727 Newbury, Massachusetts, earthquake (m_b 5.6, Ebel, 2000); and the 1638 Central New Hampshire earthquake (M_{Lg} 6.2–6.5, Ebel 1996).

Of course, it is possible that the landslides in Maine were caused by a different earthquake than the one that caused the disturbances of the sediments in SP and WP in ~1400 C.E. In this case, an earthquake as small as M_w 4.7 ± 0.3 halfway between the two ponds could have disturbed only the sediments in the two ponds. The possible locations of a larger magnitude earthquake to have affected the sediments in both ponds are centered in an elliptical area with the center of the ellipse halfway between the two ponds. For example, the ellipse for an M_w 5.9 in Figure 7 is the same possible source area for an earthquake that could have disturbed the sediments in the two ponds even if the landslides in Maine are not included in the analysis.

There is a small area shown in Figure 7 by a thin solid ellipse for the possible epicentral region of the earthquake in ~1200 C.E. This is because this event was recorded strongly in WP but with no observed effect in SP at the available resolution of our sediment data for that time (Fig. 3). The epicentral area for this earthquake is centered on WP with at least M_w 4.7. This size is close to the lower possible limit of ground shaking because a certain duration and amplitude is required to induce deformation in lake sediments (M_w 5–5.5; e.g., Moretti *et al.*, 1999). However, very sensitive lakes that are located within a few kilometers to the epicenter can show traces of these moderate-size earthquakes as small as M_L 4.9 (Nomade *et al.*, 2005; Wilhelm *et al.*, 2016). With this location and M_w 4.7, the PGA at WP is ~0.19*g* and at SP is ~0.04*g*. If a larger magnitude event is assumed to have occurred, the epicenter must be west of WP. The largest possible magnitude for this earthquake is M_w 6.2 with an epicenter somewhere near Worcester, Massachusetts, ~55 km west of Boston. However, such a strong earthquake would cause PGA at WP just above 0.12*g* and at SP just below 0.08*g*. Given the strong disturbance of the sediments in WP and the apparent lack of sediment disturbance in SP, this M_w 6.2 scenario is much less likely than a smaller magnitude earthquake located closer to WP.

Discussion

As is clear from Figure 7, since 1975 there have been small earthquakes that have occurred throughout the possible source areas of the earthquakes in ~1400 and 1200 C.E. One notable concentration of observed small earthquakes in recent decades is northwest of WP, stretching from just northwest of Littleton to just southwest of Boxborough in Massachusetts (Fig. 8). This has been called the Littleton seismic zone by Ebel and Cipar (2024), and it is the most seismically active zone in southeastern New England, with magnitudes since 1975 ranging up to coda magnitude M_c 3.1. Ebel *et al.* (2000) used the paleoseismicity model of long-lasting aftershock sequences in stable-cratonic regions to estimate that an earthquake of M_w 6.3–6.7 might have taken place in this seismic zone

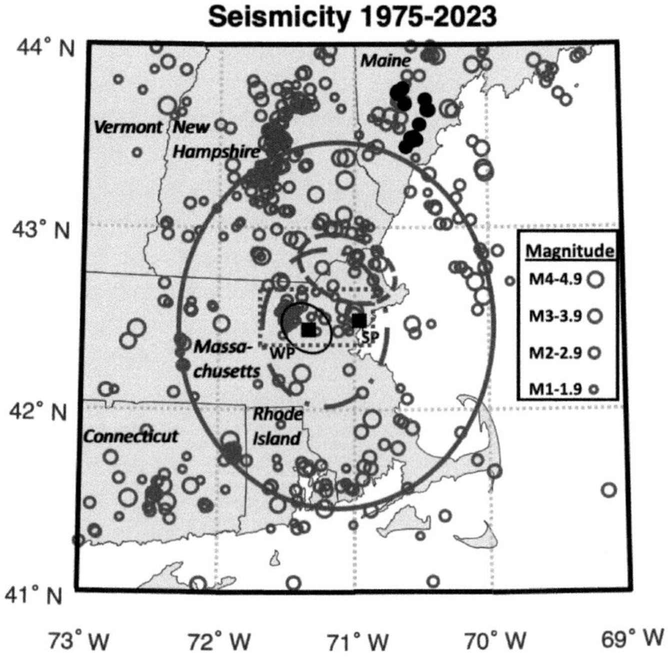

Figure 7. Map of the epicenters of earthquakes in southeastern New England from 1975 to 2023. The filled dots in Maine show the locations of Presumpscot Formation sediments that failed in ~1400 C.E. The filled squares in Massachusetts show the locations of WP and SP. For the earthquake in ~1400 C.E., three contours are shown. The dashed–dotted ellipse shows the area of possible epicenters for an M_W 5.9 earthquake with threshold ground motion for landslides in Maine of 0.02*g*. The dashed ellipse shows the area of possible epicenters for an M_W 6.0 earthquake with threshold ground motion for landslides in Maine of 0.04*g*. The large, thick, solid ellipse shows the area of possible epicenters for an M_W 6.7 earthquake with threshold ground motion for landslides in Maine of either 0.02 or 0.04*g*. For the earthquake in ~1200 C.E., the small, thin, solid ellipse around WP shows the area of possible epicenters for an M_W 4.7 earthquake with threshold ground motion above 0.12*g* for WP and below 0.08 g for SP. The dashed rectangular box in the center of the figure outlines the area shown in Figure 8. The color version of this figure is available only in the electronic edition.

sometime between ~1600 and 1130 C.E., a time period centered around ~1400 C.E. Ground shaking from such an earthquake would have disturbed the sediments in both SP and WP as well as Presumpscot Formation deposits in southern Maine. A somewhat smaller earthquake in or near the Littleton seismic zone in ~1200 C.E. could also explain the disturbance in the sediments of that age in WP but with no disturbance in SP.

Sedimentary evidence for the event in ~1400 C.E. in SP is clearly visible from grain size and palynological characteristics within a 5-cm-thick unit (Fig. 3) compared with WP, where the deposit is thinner and not visible across all proxies (Monecke *et al.*, 2025). This might mean that the epicenter of the earthquake in ~1400 C.E. was closer to SP than to WP, thus favoring the more eastern possible epicenters in Figure 7. However, there is an aspect of sediment disturbances in lakes and ponds that might have contributed to the stronger earthquake signature in SP than in even in WP in ~1400 C.E. if the epicenter of the earthquake in ~1400 C.E. was centered closer to WP. Unlike WP, SP was not visibly affected by the event in ~1200 C.E. Therefore, the slopes of SP may have still been loaded with sediment, making them more likely to fail during the event ~200 yr later (e.g., Strupler *et al.*, 2017).

As noted in the previous section, it is possible that there were different earthquakes with ages ~1400 C.E.—one earthquake that disturbed the sediments in both SP and WP and a different earthquake that caused the landslides in the Presumpscot Formation in southern Maine. The possible source area for an earthquake to have caused the landslides in southern Maine but not affected the sediments of SP and WP is not quantified in this study. Even so, it is clear that a sufficiently strong earthquake with its source location in southern or central Maine could have disturbed Presumpscot Formation deposits in southern Maine without affecting the sediments in WP and SP. Because there have been modern earthquakes distributed across the state of Maine, there is a very wide area near and north of the landslides in ~1400 C.E. in southern Maine, where a separate earthquake could have caused the landslides without disturbing the sediments in SP and WP.

It is important to look for landslides and evidence of earthquakes in the sediments of other lakes in eastern Massachusetts, southeastern New Hampshire, Rhode Island, and southern Maine. Results from such research would test the various postulated the locations and magnitudes of possible strong earthquakes around ~1400 and 1200 C.E. as examined in this study.

If the events in ~1400 and 1200 C.E. prove to be large-magnitude earthquakes with epicenters in the postulated areas in Figure 7, the seismic hazard in eastern Massachusetts and southeastern New Hampshire might be different than previously appreciated. The seismic hazard in the current U.S. National Seismic Hazard Maps for eastern Massachusetts and southeastern New Hampshire is influenced by the 1755 M_{Lg} 6.2 earthquake (Ebel, 2006), which was likely centered ~40 km offshore east of Cape Ann, Massachusetts, and by the 1727 m_b 5.6 earthquake (Ebel, 2000), which was centered near Newburyport, Massachusetts. These epicenters were northeast and north of Boston. Strong prehistoric earthquakes near Littleton, Massachusetts, in the western suburbs of Boston, could mean that a re-evaluation of the seismic hazard for the greater Boston area is needed.

Summary and Conclusions

This study examined the evidence for possible strong earthquake shaking in ~1400 C.E. (1380–1520 C.E.) that was found in the sediments of WP in Concord, Massachusetts (Monecke *et al.*, 2025) and in the sediments of SP in Lynn,

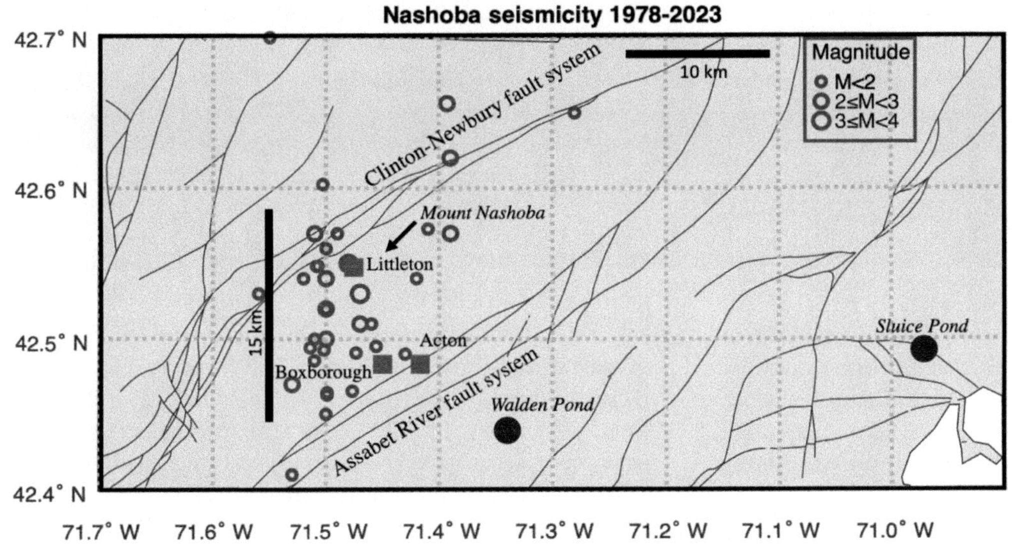

Figure 8. Map of the seismicity from 1978 to 2023 of small earthquakes (open circles) in the Littleton, Massachusetts, seismic zone, discussed by Ebel and Cipar (2024). The towns of Acton, Boxborough, and Littleton are shown as squares on the map. The locations of SP and WP are shown as filled circles. The tip of the arrow in the figure indications the location of Mount Nashoba. Two major Paleozoic faults systems, the Clinton–Newbury fault system and the Assabet River fault system (Skehan, 2001), are labeled. Other faults from the Massachusetts State Bedrock Geology Map of Zen (1983) are shown as solid lines. The earthquakes just to the east of the dashed bar labeled 15 km compose the Littleton seismic zone. The largest earthquake in this zone had coda magnitude M_c 3.1. The color version of this figure is available only in the electronic edition.

Massachusetts, deposited shortly after 1386–1473 C.E. There is evidence of an even earlier earthquake dated to ~1200 C.E. (1050–1320 C.E.) in WP sediments (Monecke *et al.*, 2025) but not in SP sediments. In southern Maine, 15 landslides occurred in the sensitive Presumpscot Formation during or soon after 1221–1454 C.E. These might have been triggered by the same event that caused mass wasting at the two lake sites. Paleoseismic data from other lakes indicate that ground shaking of at least MMI VI–VII is necessary to leave an imprint on the sedimentary record of lakes and ponds. This level of ground shaking corresponds to a PGA value of ~0.10*g*. In Maine, Presumpscot Formation deposits are quite sensitive and could fail if disturbed by even a small level of ground shaking as low as 0.02 and 0.04*g*.

In an effort to constrain the possible range of locations and magnitudes of the earthquakes in ~1400 and 1200 C.E., a modeling analysis was carried out using a modified version of the ground-motion attenuation of Al Noman and Cramer (2015). This modeling effort showed that an earthquake in about1400 C.E. with a range of possible magnitudes of $5.6 \le M_w \le 6.7$ (with an uncertainty of ±0.3 magnitude units) could have both disturbed the sediments in the two ponds in Massachusetts and caused the landslides in Maine. Such an earthquake would have been centered somewhere in eastern Massachusetts, southeastern New Hampshire, or northern Rhode Island. On the other hand, if the landslides in Maine were not caused by the earthquake that disturbed the sediments in WP and SP in ~1400 C.E., then this event could have been as small as M_w 4.7 ± 0.3 and would have been centered somewhere in eastern Massachusetts near the two ponds.

The modeling suggests the earthquake in ~1200 C.E. that disturbed the sediments in WP but not in SP was centered near WP and was at least M_w 4.7 ± 0.3. If the earthquake was larger, the epicenter must be west of WP.

The results of this study suggest that two earthquakes with $M_w \ge 4.7$, a stronger one in ~1400 C.E. and a weaker one about in ~1200 C.E., probably took place somewhere in eastern Massachusetts, with the earthquake in ~1400 C.E. possibly also centered in southeastern New Hampshire or in Rhode Island. Both the earthquakes in ~1400 and 1200 C.E. might have been centered in the Littleton seismic zone in the western suburbs of Boston. The inferred prehistoric earthquakes are large enough to cause damage if they happened today and imply that the seismic hazard in eastern Massachusetts and southeastern New Hampshire might need to be re-evaluated.

Data and Resources

Earthquake epicenters since 1975 come from the regional earthquake catalog maintained at Weston Observatory of Boston College. A copy of these data is available from John Ebel at Weston Observatory. Lake sediment cores are stored at Wellesley College, Wellesley, Massachusetts, and Salem State University, Salem, Massachusetts, and palynological preparations at Brock University, St Catharines, Ontario, and can be viewed on request. Lake sediment proxy data are made publicly available via the National Oceanic and Atmospheric Administration paleoclimate repository (https://www.ncei.noaa.gov/products/paleoclimatology, last accessed January 2026). Radiocarbon lab reports can be made available by the authors. Landslide locations and ages are available in MGS (2020); individual sample data and radiocarbon laboratory reports can be made available by the authors. The supplemental material for this article includes a description of the multiproxy analysis of the lake sediments for this study.

Declaration of Competing Interests

The authors acknowledge that there no conflicts of interest.

Acknowledgments

The authors thank the Walden Pond (WP) State Reservation of the Division of State Parks and Recreation for allowing them to conduct research in WP and the Sluice Pond (SP) Association for their interest and support of their research on SP. Funding for this project was provided by the U.S. Geological Survey (USGS) Earthquake Hazards Program (Collaborative Award Numbers G20AP00062, G20AP00063, and G20AP00064). J. B. H. acknowledges additional funding through the National Science Foundation (NSF; Grant EAR 1126128). Radiocarbon dating of lacustrine samples was conducted at the National Ocean Sciences Accelerator Mass Spectrometry Facility (NOSAMS) at the Woods Hole Oceanographic Institution (WHOI). The authors thank Emma Howey, Michelle Nishimoto, Erynn Lau, and Ilana Levine for help with grain size sample processing. Finally, the authors appreciate the work of special issue editor Sue Hough and of two anonymous reviewers for their thorough reviews of this article.

References

Al Noman, M., and C. H. Cramer (2015). Empirical ground-motion prediction equations for Eastern North America, in *NGA-East: Median Ground-Motion Models for the Central and Eastern North America Region*, PEER Report No 2015/04, Pacific Earthquake Engineering Research Center, Berkeley, California.

Amos, J., and T. C. Sandford (1987). Landslides in the Presumpscot Formation, Southern Maine, *Maine Geol. Surv. Open-File Rept. 87-4*, Augusta, Maine, available at https://digitalmaine.com/mgs_publications/179/ (last accessed January 2026).

Andrews, D. W. (1987). The engineering aspects of the Presumpscot formation, *Geologic and Geotechnical Characteristics of the Presumpscot Formation Maine's Glaciomarine "Clay" Symposium*, D. W. Andrews, W. B. Thompson, T. C. Sandford, and I. D. Novak (Editors), Augusta, Maine, 20 March 1987, variously paginated.

Atkinson, G. M., and S.-L. I. Kaka (2007). Relationships between felt intensity and instrumental ground motion in the Central United States and California, *Bull. Seismol. Soc. Am.* **97,** 497–510, doi: 10.1785/0120060154.

Avşar, U., A. Hubert-Ferrari, M. De Batist, G. Lepoint, S. Schmidt, and N. Fagel (2014). Seismically-triggered organic-rich layers in recent sediments from Göllüköy Lake (North Anatolian Fault, Turkey), *Quaternary Sci. Rev.* **103,** 67–80.

Barberopoulou, A., A. Qamar, T. L. Pratt, and W. P. Steele (2006). Long-period effects of the Denali earthquake on water bodies in the Puget lowland: Observations and modeling, *Bull. Seismol. Soc. Am.* **96,** 519–535.

Berry, H. N., S. M. Dickson, J. T. Kelley, D. B. Locke, R. G. Marvinney, W. B. Thompson, T. K. Weddle, R. T. Reynolds, and D. F. Belknap (1996). The April 1996 Rockland landslide, *Maine Geol. Surv. Open-File Rept. 96-18*, Augusta, Maine, Available at https://digitalmaine.com/mgs_publications/213/ (last accessed January 2026).

Blaauw, M., and J. A. Christen (2011). Flexible paleoclimate age-depth models using an autoregression gamma process, *Bayesian Anal.* **6,** 457–474.

Bloom, A. L. (1960). Late Pleistocene changes of sea level in southwestern Maine, Maine Geological Survey, Augusta, Maine, available at https://digitalmaine.com/mgs_publications/555/ (last accessed January 2026).

Borns, H. W., Jr., L. A. Doner, C. C. Dorion, G. L. Jacobson Jr., M. R. Kaplan, K. J. Kreutz, T. V. Lowell, W. B. Thompson, and T. K. Weddle (2004). The deglaciation of Maine, U.S.A., *Develop. Quat. Sci.* **2,** 89–109, doi: 10.1016/S1571-0866)04)80190-8.

Brooks, G. R. (2014). Prehistoric sensitive clay landslides and paleoseismicity in the Ottawa Valley, Canada, in *Landslides in Sensitive clays: From Geosciences to Risk Management*, J.-S. L'Heureux, A. Locat, S. Leroueil, D. Demers, and J. Locat (Editors), Vol. 36, Advances in Natural and Technological Hazards Research, Springer, Dordrecht, The Netherlands, 119–131.

Brooks, G. R. (2016). Evidence of late glacial paleoseismicity from submarine landslide deposits within Lac Dasserat, northwestern Quebec, Canada, *Quaternay Res.* **86,** 184–199.

Callender, E., and K. C. Rice (2000). The urban environmental gradient: Anthropogenic influences on the spatial and temporal distributions of lead and zinc in sediments, *Environ. Sci. Technol.* **34,** 232–238.

Chillrud, S. N., R. F. Bopp, H. J. Simpson, J. M. Ross, E. L. Shuster, D. A. Chaky, D. C. Walsh, C. C. Choy, L. Tolley, and A. Yarme (1999). Twentieth century atmospheric metal fluxes into Central Park Lake, New York City, *Environ. Sci. Technol.* **33,** 657–662.

Crescenzi, E., J. B. Hubeny, S. B. Moran, and R. P. Kelly (2010). Historic trace metal accumulation in Sluice Pond, MA: Linkages between industry and the environment, *GSA Abstracts with Programs*, Vol. 42, 183 pp.

Devin, S. C., and T. C. Sandford (1990). Stability of natural slopes in the Presumpscot Formation, *Maine Geol. Surv. Open-File Rept. 90-24*, Augusta, Maine, available at https://digitalmaine.com/mgs_publications/203/ (last accessed January 2026).

Devin, S. C., and T. C. Sandford (2000). Shear strength of sensitive clay slopes in Maine, *Slope Stability 2000, Proceedings of Geo-Denver 2000*, American Society of Civil Engineers, 5–8 August 2000, Denver, Colorado.

Doig, R. (1990). 2300 yr history of seismicity from silting events in Lake Tadoussac, Charlevoix, Quebec, *Geology* **18,** 820–823.

Doig, R. (1998). 3000-year paleoseismological record from the region of the 1988 Saguenay, Quebec, earthquake, *Bull. Seismol. Soc. Am.* **88,** 1198–1203.

Ebel, J., and J. J. Cipar (2024). Recent seismicity around Littleton, MA, *Geol. Soc. Am. Abstr. Progr.* **56,** doi: 10.1130/abs/2024NE-397217.

Ebel, J. E. (1996). The Seventeenth Century seismicity of Northeastern North America, *Seismol. Res. Lett.* **67,** 51–68.

Ebel, J. E. (2000). A reanalysis of the 1727 earthquake at Newbury, Massachusetts, *Seismol. Res. Lett.* **71,** 364–374.

Ebel, J. E. (2006). The Cape Ann, Massachusetts earthquake of 1755: A 250th anniversary perspective, *Seismol. Res. Lett.* **77,** 74–86.

Ebel, J. E., and A. L. Kafka (1991). Earthquake Activity in the Northeastern United States, in *Neotectonics of North America*, D. B. Slemmons, E. R. Engdahl, M. D. Zoback, and D. D. Blackwell (Editors), The Geological Society of America, Decade Map, Vol. 1, 277–290.

Ebel, J. E., K.-P. Bonjer, and M. C. Oncescu (2000). Paleoseismicity: Seismicity evidence for past large earthquakes, *Seismol. Res. Lett.* **71,** 283–294.

Girardclos, S., O. T. Schmidt, M. Sturm, D. Ariztegui, A. Pugin, and F. S. Anselmetti, (2007). The 1996 delta collapse and large turbidite in Lake Brienz, *Mar. Geol.* **241,** 137–154.

Hubeny, J. B., J. W. King, and M. Reddin (2011). Northeast US precipitation variability and North American climate teleconnections interpreted from late Holocene varved sediments, *Proc. Natl. Acad. Sci. Unit. States Am.* 108, 17,895–17,900.

Hubeny, J. B., F. M. G. McCarthy, J. Lewis, M. Drljepan, C. Morissette, J. W. King, M. Cantwell, N. M. Hudson, and M. L. Crispo (2015). The paleohydrology of Sluice Pond, NE Massachusetts, and its regional significance, *J. Paleolimnol.* **53**, 271–287.

Jibson, R. W., and E. L. Harp (2016). Ground motions at the outer limits of seismically triggered landslides, *Bull. Seismol. Soc. Am.* **106,** 708–719, doi: 10.1785/0120150141.

Jibson, R. W., and D. K. Keefer (1993). Analysis of the seismic origin of landslides: Examples from the New Madrid seismic zone, *Geol. Soc. Am. Bull.* **105,** 21,536.

Koons, D. (1989). Postglacial bedrock faulting in Maine, in *Neotectonics of Maine*, W. A. Andersonand and H. W. Borns Jr. (Editors), Maine Geological Survey, Augusta, Maine, 149–155.

Köster, D., R. Pienitz, B. B. Wolfe, S. Barry, D. R. Foster, and S. S. Dixit (2005). Paleolimnological assessment of human-induced impacts on Walden Pond (Massachusetts, USA) using diatoms and stable isotopes, *Aquat. Ecosyst. Health Manage.* **8,** 117–131.

Kremer, K., S. B. Wirth, A. Reusch, D. Fäh, B. Bellwald, F. S. Anselmetti, S. Girardclos, and M. Strasser (2017). Lake-sediment based paleoseismology: Limitations and perspectives from the Swiss Alps, *Quaternary Sci. Rev.* **168,** 1–18.

Lu, Y., N. Wetzler, N. Waldmann, A. Agnon, P. Glenn, G. P. Biasi, and S. Marco (2020). A 220,000-year-long continuous large earthquake record on a slow-slipping plate boundary, *Sci. Adv.* **6,** eaba4170, doi: 10.1126/sciadv.aba4170.

Marlon, J. R., N. Pederson, C. Nolan, S. Goring, B. Shuman, A. Robertson, R. Booth, P. J. Bartlein, M. A. Berke, M. Clifford, *et al.* (2017). Climatic history of the northeastern United States during the past 3000 years, *Clim. Past* **13,** 1355–1379.

McCarthy, F. M. G., P. M. Pilkington, O. Volik, A. Heyde, S. L. Cocker, and F. Marret, (2021). Non-pollen palynomorphs in freshwater sediments and their palaeolimnological potential and selected applications, in *Applications of Non-Pollen Palynomorphs: from Palaeoenvironmental Reconstructions to Biostratigraphy*, J. O'Keefe, P. Osterloff, M. Pound, and L. Shumilovskikh (Editors), Vol. 511, Geological Society of London, Special Publication, 121–150.

Meyers, P. A. (1994). Preservation of elemental and isotopic source identification of sedimentary organic matter, *Chem. Geol.* **114,** 289–302.

Maine Geological Survey (MGS) (2020). Maine inland landslides - points [database], Maine Geological Survey, Augusta, Maine, available at https://mgs-maine.opendata.arcgis.com/datasets/maine-inland-landslides-points (last accessed January 2026).

Moernaut, J., M. Van Daele, K. Heirman, K. Fontijn, M. Strasser, M. Pino, R. Urrutia, and M. De Batist (2014). Lacustrine turbidites as a tool for quantitative earthquake reconstruction: new evidence for a variable rupture mode in south central Chile, *J. Geophys. Res.* **119,** 1607–1633.

Moernaut, J., M. Van Daele, M. Strasser, M. A. Clare, K. Heirman, M. Viel, J. Cardenas, R. Kilian, B. Ladrón de Guevara, M. Pino, *et al.* (2017). Lacustrine turbidites produced by surficial slope sediment remobilization: A mechanism for continuous and sensitive turbidite paleoseismic records, *Mar. Geol.* **384,** 159–176.

Monecke, K., F.S. Anselmetti, A. Becker, M. Sturm, and D. Giardini (2004). The record of historic earthquakes in lake sediments of Central Switzerland, *Tectonophysics* **394,** 21–40.

Monecke, K., B. Hubeny, F. McCarthy, A. Alderson, J. Boyce, D. Brabander, R. Veresh, A. Chen, C. Knights, M. Nishimoto, *et al.* (2025). Sedimentation patterns in the three basins of Walden Pond, Concord, Massachusetts, U.S.A. – A multiproxy approach to decipher environmental trends, anthropogenic impacts, and regional events of the last 800 years, *J. Sediment. Res.* **95,** no. 4, 605–626.

Monecke, K., F. G. McCarthy, J. B. Hubeny, J. E. Ebel, D. J. Brabander, S. Kielb, E. Howey, G. Janigian, and J. Pentesco (2018). The 1755 Cape Ann earthquake recorded in lake sediments of Eastern New England: An interdisciplinary paleoseismic approach, *Seismol. Res. Lett.* **89,** 1212–1222.

Moretti, M., P. Alfaro, O. Caselles, and J.A. Canas (1999). Modelling seismites with a digital shaking table, *Tectonophysics* **304,** 369–383.

Morse, E. S. (1869). On the landslides in the vicinity of Portland, Maine, *Boston Society of Natural History Proceedings*, Vol. 12, 235–244.

Nicovich, S. R., C. B. DuRoss, J. A. Thompson Jobe, J. R. Rodysill, R. W. Briggs, A. E. Hatem, M. M. Tan, Y. Gavillot, N. S. Lindberg, L. E. Strickland, *et al.* (2024). Shallow lake, strong shake: Record of seismically triggered lacustrine sedimentation from the 1959 M7.3 Hebgen Lake earthquake within Henrys Lake, Idaho, *Geophys. Res. Lett.* **51,** e2024GL110889, doi: 10.1029/2024GL110889.

Nomade, J., E. Chapron, M. Desmet, J.L. Reyss, F. Arnaud, and V. Lignier (2005). Reconstructing historical seismicity from lake sediments (Lake Laffrey, western Alps, France), *Terra Nova* **17,** 350–357.

Novak, I. D. (1987). Geology of the September 1983 landslide at Gorham, Maine, *Geologic and Geotechnical Characteristics of the Presumpscot Formation Maine's Glaciomarine "Clay" Symposium*,D. W. Andrews, W. B. Thompson, T. C. Sandford, and I. D. Novak, (Editors), March 20, 1987, Augusta, Maine, variously paginated.

PEER (2015). NGA-East: Median Ground-Motion Models for the Central and Eastern North America Region, *PEER Report 2015-04*, Pacific Earthquake Engineering Research Center, University of California, Berkeley, California, available at https://peer.berkeley.edu/sites/default/files/webpeer-2015-04_nga-east-_median_ground-motion_models_for_the_central_and_eastern_north_america_region.pdf (last accessed January 2026).

Petersen, M. D., M. P. Moschetti, P. M. Powers, C. S. Mueller, K. M. Haller, A. D. Frankel, Y. Zeng, S. Rezaeian, S. C. Harmson, O. S. Boyd, *et al.* (2014). Documentation for the 2014 update of the United States national seismic hazard maps, *U.S. Geol. Surv. Open-File Rept. 2014-1091*, 243 pp.

Praet, N., J. Moernaut, M. Van Daele, E. Boes, P. J. Haeussler, M. Strupler, S. Schmidt, M. G. Loso, and M. De Batist (2017). Paleoseismic potential of sublacustrine landslide records in a high-seismicity setting (south-central Alaska), *Mar. Geol.* **384,** 103–119.

Quinn, P., and M. Zaleski (2015). Co-seismic large landslides in sensitive clay in eastern Canada, a search for an initiation threshold, *GeoQuebec 2015*, available at https://members.cgs.ca/documents/conference2015/GeoQuebec/papers/560.pdf (last accessed January 2026).

Reimer, P. J., W. E. N. Austin, E. Bard, A. Bayliss, P. G. Blackwell, C. Bronk Ramsey, M. Butzin, H. Cheng, R. L. Edwards, M. Friedrich, *et al.* (2020). The IntCal20 Northern hemisphere radiocarbon age calibration curve (0–55 cal kBP), *Radiocarbon* **62,** 725–757.

Ridge, J. C. (2004). The Quaternary glaciation of western New England with correlations to surrounding areas, in *Developments in Quaternary Sciences*, J. Ehlers and P. L. Gibbard (Editors), Elsevier, Amsterdam, The Netherlands, 169–199.

Sabatier, P., J. Moernaut, S. Bertrand, M. Van Daele, K. Kremer, E. Chaumillon, and F. Arnaud (2022). A review of event deposits in lake sediments, *Quaternary* **5,** no. 3, 34.

Schnellmann, M., F. S. Anselmetti, D. Giardini, J. A. McKenzie, and S. N. Ward (2002). Prehistoric earthquake history revealed by lacustrine slump deposits, *Geology* **30,** 1131–1134.

Shilts, W. W., and J. J. Clague (1992). Documentation of earthquake-induced disturbance of lake sediments using subbottom acoustic profiling, *Can. J. Earth Sci.* **29,** 1018–1042.

Skehan, J. W. (2001). *Roadside Geology of Massachusetts*, Mountain Press Publishing Company, Missoula, Montana, 379 pp.

Spigel, L. J. (2019). Determining the ages of Maine's prehistoric landslides: Maine geological survey, geologic facts and localities, *Circular GFL-245*, 13 pp., available at https://digitalmaine.com/mgs_publications/587 (last accessed January 2026).

Spigel, L. J. (2020a). Maine landslide guide, *Maine Geol. Surv. Open-File Rept. 20-9*, Augusta, Maine, available at https://digitalmaine.com/mgs_publications/591/ (last accessed January 2026).

Spigel, L. J. (2020b). Characterization of landslides in sensitive clay, southern Maine, USA, *Geol. Soc. Am. Abstr. Progr.* **52,** doi: 10.1130/abs/2020AM-357723.

Stager, J. C., B. Wiltse, J. B. Hubeny, E. Yankowsky, D. Nardelli, and R. Primack (2018). Climate variability and cultural eutrophication at Walden Pond (Massachusetts, USA) during the last 1800 years, *PloS One* **13,** no. 4, e0191755, doi: 10.1371/journal.pone.0191755.

Strasser, M., S. Stegmann, F. Bussmann, F. S. Anselmetti, B. Rick, and A. Kopf (2007). Quantifying subaqueous slope stability during seismic shaking: Lake Lucerne as model for ocean margins, *Mar. Geol.* **240,** 77–97.

Strupler, M., M. Hilbe, F. S. Anselmetti, A. J. Kopf, T. Fleischmann, and M. Strasser (2017). Probabilistic stability evaluation and seismic triggering scenarios of submerged slopes in Lake Zurich (Switzerland), *Geo-Mar. Lett.* **37,** 241–258.

Thompson, W. B. (2015). Surficial geology handbook for southern Maine, *Maine Geol. Surv. Bulletin 44*, Augusta, Maine, available at https://digitalmaine.com/mgs_publications/2/ (last accessed January 2026).

Thompson, W. B., C. B. Griggs, N. G. Miller, R. E. Nelson, T. K. Weddle, and T. M. Kilian (2011). Associated terrestrial and marine fossils in the late-glacial Presumpscot Formation, southern Maine, USA, and the Maine reservoir effect on radiocarbon ages, *Quaternary Res.* **75,** 552–565, doi: 10.1016/j.yqres.2011.02.002.

Vandekerkhove, E., M. Van Daele, N. Praet, V. Cnudde, P. J. Haeussler, and M. De Batist (2020). Flood-triggered versus earthquake-triggered turbidites: A sedimentological study in clastic lake sediments (Eklutna Lake, Alaska), *Sedimentology* **67,** 364–389.

Vickers, D. (1994). *Farmers and Fishermen: Two Centuries of Work in Essex County, Massachusetts, 1630-1850*, The University of North Carolina Press, Chapel Hill, North Carolina.

Wheeler, R. L. (2006). Quaternary tectonic faulting in the eastern United States, *Eng. Geol.* **82,** 165–186, doi: 10.1016/j.enggeo.2005.10.005.

Wilhelm, B., J. Nomade, C. Crouzet, C. Litty, P. Sabatier, S. Belle, Y. Rolland, M. Revel, F. Courboulex, F. Arnaud, *et al.* (2016). Quantified sensitivity of small lake sediments to record historic earthquakes: Implications for paleoseismology, *J. Geophys. Res.* **121,** 2–16.

Winkler, M. G. (1993). Changes at Walden Pond during the Last 600 years: Microfosssil analysis of Walden pond sediments, in *Thoreau's World and Ours: A Natural Legacy*, E. A. Schofieldand and R. C. Baron (Editors), North American Press, Golden, Colorado, 405 pp.

Worden, C. B., M. C. Gerstenberger, D. A. Rhoades, and D. J. Wald (2012). Probabilistic Relationships between ground-motion parameters and modified Mercalli intensity in California, *Bull. Seismol. Soc. Am.* **102,** 204–221, doi: 10.1785/0120110156.

Zen, E. (1983). Bedrock Geologic Map of Massachusetts,R. Goldsmith, N. M. Ratcliffe, P. Robinson, and R. S. Stanley (Editors), U.S. Geological Survey, Reston, Virginia, scale 1:250,000, 3 sheets.

Manuscript received 12 September 2025
Published online 2 February 2026

Earthquake Catalog for the Fairbanks Region of Central Alaska, 2014–2024, Based on Waveform Cross-Correlation

OPEN ACCESS

Nealey E. Sims*[1], Carl Tape[1], Natalia A. Ruppert[2], and Michael E. West[3]

Abstract

The Fairbanks region of central Alaska is part of a broad zone of intraplate crustal deformation, situated north of the Denali fault and north of the ongoing collision and flat-slab subduction of the Yakutat oceanic plateau. Seismicity in the Fairbanks region occurs both in diffuse areas as well as in well-defined lineaments, such as the left-lateral Salcha fault, which hosted the 1937 M_s 7.3 earthquake. Starting with the regional seismicity catalog, we perform waveform cross-correlation, network-matched filtering, and relative relocation to obtain an enhanced seismicity catalog over the time period 2014–2024. Based on the relocated catalog, we interpret a set of 15 fault segments, including two conjugate faults and two new faults east of the previously documented fault system. Considering the combined seismicity in the Minto and Fairbanks regions, the median depth of seismicity decreases from east (6 km) to west (20 km). Our interpreted faults provide guidance for future tectonic modeling and assessment of seismic hazards in this region.

Cite this article as Sims, N. E., C. Tape, N. A. Ruppert, and M. E. West (2026). Earthquake Catalog for the Fairbanks Region of Central Alaska, 2014–2024, Based on Waveform Cross-Correlation, *Seismol. Res. Lett.* **97**, 877–896, doi: 10.1785/0220250342.

Introduction

The discovery of gold in 1902 led to a rush into the Fairbanks region of central Alaska. Two years later, the lone federal judge in the new town of Fairbanks reported earthquake shaking on August 27, 1904: "quite strong for several minutes—no damage but everybody ran outdoors" (Wickersham, 1904, p. 33). Eight years later, earthquake shaking hit the region again, damaging one store and killing one miner in the gold camps north of Fairbanks. Both of these large earthquakes (1904 M_s 7.3 and 1912 M_s 7.2) originated more than 200 km away from Fairbanks (Tape *et al.*, 2017, 2025). In 1937, a M_s 7.3 earthquake struck near Salcha, about 50 km southeast of Fairbanks, which "suffered considerable minor damage," including "broken windows and bottled goods." (Neumann, 1940). Near the epicenter, the earthquake caused ground fissures and landslides, which blocked the main road south of the town for several days.

Three decades later, in 1967, a series of $M_w > 5$ earthquake struck close to the town of Fairbanks, generating modified Mercalli intensity (MMI) 7 shaking and many incidents of damage. Cloud and Knudson (1968) reported: "Minor cracks were observed in a few concrete walls; several chimneys fell; windows broke. The State Court and Office Building reportedly suffered the most extensive damage, with both interior and exterior cracks. Portions of hanging ceilings and some light fixtures fell. Plumbing broke, causing considerable flooding. Cabinets and shelves were overturned, and the building was temporarily closed to the public" (p. 33). The largest of these events was a M_w 5.7, which is 250 times smaller, in terms of seismic moment, than the 1937 earthquake to the southeast. A M_s 7.3 in the epicentral region of 1967 would cause extensive damage in Fairbanks.

The first seismometer in Fairbanks was installed in 1935 on the University of Alaska campus (Heck, 1936). Since that time, seismologists have studied local earthquakes and mapped seismicity patterns with the dual purpose of understanding the faulting regime and documenting seismic hazards to Alaskans. By the 1980s, with the benefit of improved seismic station coverage and computer-based location algorithms, a pattern of northeast-trending seismic zones had emerged in the region surrounding Fairbanks. The seismic zones, from west to east, were named for Minto Flats, Fairbanks, and Salcha (Biswas and Tytgat, 1988). These seismic zone designations were present as recently as Koehler *et al.* (2012) and the review by Koehler and Carver (2018).

1. Geophysical Institute and College of Natural Sciences, University of Alaska Fairbanks, Fairbanks, Alaska, U.S.A., https://orcid.org/0009-0006-0772-7896 (NES); https://orcid.org/0000-0003-2804-7137 (CT); 2. USGS Earthquake Science Center, Seattle, Washington, U.S.A., https://orcid.org/0000-0003-0589-1159 (NAR); 3. Alaska Earthquake Center, University of Alaska Fairbanks, Fairbanks, Alaska, U.S.A.

*Corresponding author: nesims@alaska.edu

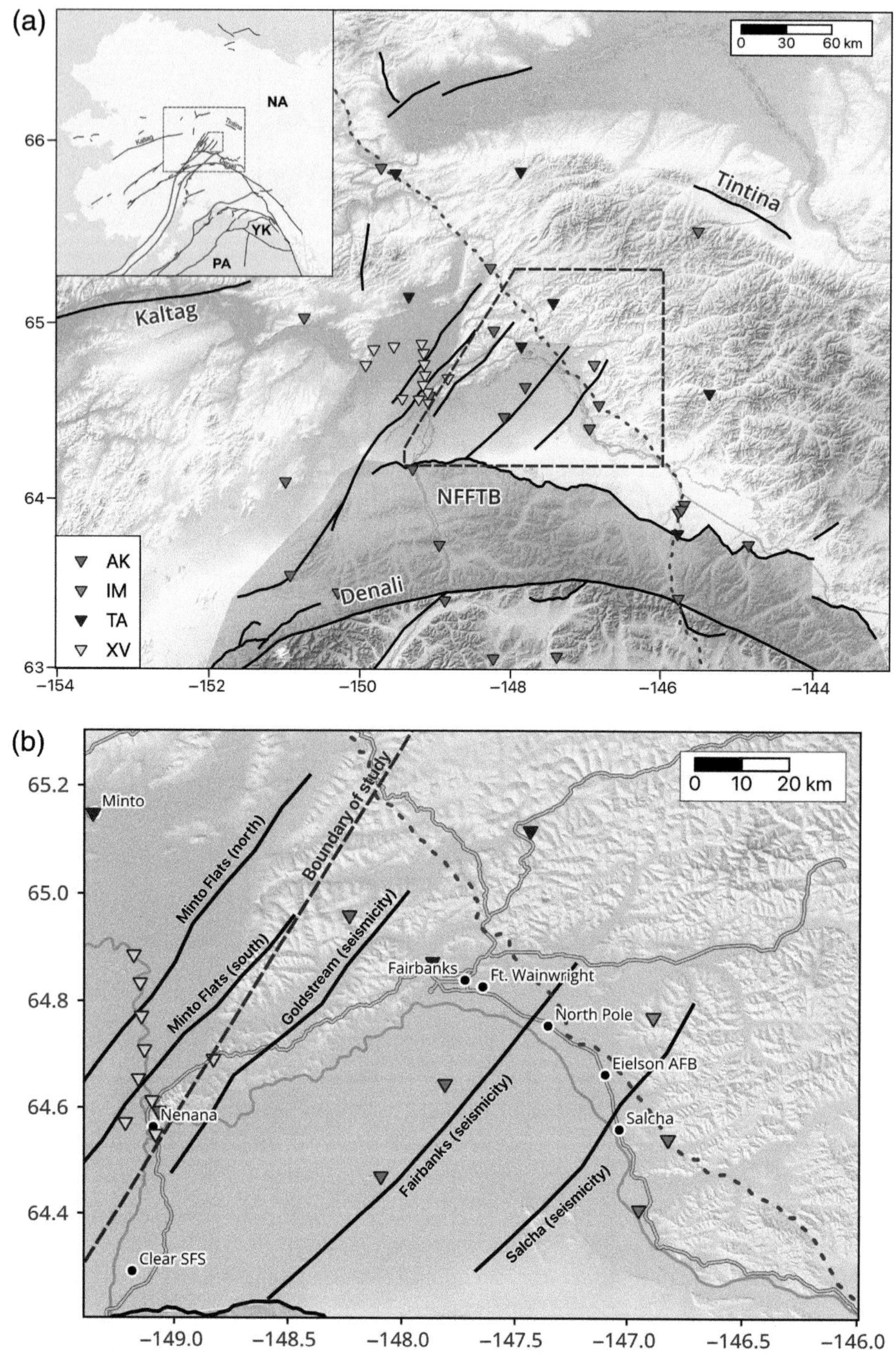

Figure 1. Maps of central Alaska, displaying topography, active faults, and the 47 broadband seismic stations used in this study. (a) Central Alaska, showing the target region of this study as the red dashed pentagon, which is expanded in panel (b). The fault database is from the 2023 National Seismic Hazard Model (NSHM; Haeussler *et al.*, 2025). NFFTB, Northern Foothills fold-and-thrust belt (Bemis and Wallace, 2007; Bemis *et al.*, 2012), which is the shaded region north of the Denali fault. The inset map shows the location of the expanded region as a blue dashed box. The map also includes the NSHM faults (black), plate labels (NA, North America; PA, Pacific), microplate label (YK, Yakutat), the PA-NA plate boundary (southernmost red line: Krabbenhoeft *et al.*, 2018), and subduction interface depth contours at 20, 80, and 140 km as solid-red lines (Hayes *et al.*, 2018). (b) Study region. Also plotted are the road system (yellow) and the Alaska Pipeline (black dashed). The five labeled faults are from Haeussler *et al.* (2025); we use the modified labels MFFZ-W, MFFZ-E, Goldstream fault, Fairbanks fault, and Salcha fault. MFFZ, Minto Flats fault zone. The color version of this figure is available only in the electronic edition.

Since the advent of double-difference relocation methods (Waldhauser and Ellsworth, 2000), there have been efforts to relocate seismicity in the Minto–Fairbanks–Salcha region (Ratchkovski and Hansen, 2002; Ruppert *et al.*, 2008) and the subregion of Minto Flats (Hutchinson, 2015; Tape *et al.*, 2015). There was also a gradual change in perspective on the seismic zones, with some studies assigning discrete faults to the seismicity lineaments (Page *et al.*, 1995; Bemis and Wallace, 2007; Frohman, 2014; Tape *et al.*, 2015), culminating with five faults assigned in the 2023 National Seismic Hazard Model (NSHM; Powers *et al.*, 2024; Haeussler *et al.*, 2025), as shown in Figure 1.

In this study, we present a relocated seismicity catalog for the Fairbanks region spanning 2014–2024, complementing a recent study of the Minto Flats region (Sims *et al.*, 2026). Our main advantage over previously published relocation efforts, the most recent being Ruppert *et al.* (2008), is that we use network matched filtering to obtain an expanded and enhanced relocated catalog. Using the relocated catalog, we interpret a set of 15 fault segments in the Fairbanks region. The faults reveal a trend of deepening seismicity from east to west. There are also conjugate faults that cross-cut the main set of northeast-striking, left-lateral faults that have been interpreted in the context of bookshelf faulting (Page *et al.*, 1995). Our results provide a foundation for a future study to demonstrate how the proposed fault system has evolved in the recent tectonic history.

Tectonic Setting

Much of mainland Alaska is within a broad zone of intraplate deformation (Bird, 2003; Koehler and Carver, 2018). The tectonic setting of our study region is conveyed in the inset map of Figure 1a. The Pacific plate subducts beneath southern Alaska, with flat-slab subduction arising from collision by the Yakutat oceanic plateau (Eberhart-Phillips *et al.*, 2006; Haeussler, 2008; Christeson *et al.*, 2010). In central Alaska, the right-lateral Denali fault and Northern Foothills fold and thrust belt (NFFTB) define a convergent crustal zone overlying the subducting Pacific-Yakutat plate (Fig. 1a).

Based on seismic lineaments, seismic source mechanisms, and geological structures, Page *et al.* (1995) invoked bookshelf faulting to explain the northeast-striking faults in the Fairbanks region, situated between the larger-scale right-lateral "bookshelf" faults of Denali and Kaltag-Tintina. Within the 2023 NSHM, these faults are, from west to east: Minto Flats (north), Minto Flats (south), Goldsteam, Fairbanks, and Salcha (Fig. 1b). The two faults in the Minto Flats fault zone (MFFZ) were designated in Tape *et al.* (2015), and we use their original labels: MFFZ-W and MFFZ-E. These five active faults in the 2023 NSHM are derived from seismicity and have no geological surface evidence. Furthermore, geodetic evidence of interseismic coupling is equivocal due to sparse measurements, low velocities (relative to North America), and complicating influences of coseismic and postseismic deformation from the 2002 M_w 7.9 Denali fault earthquake (Freymueller *et al.*, 2008; Elliott and Freymueller, 2020). Therefore, a primary objective of our study is to obtain an enhanced catalog with the goal of refining the seismicity-based characterization of faults in the Fairbanks region, which will help in understanding this intraplate setting.

Data and Methods

We employ the same workflow described in Sims *et al.* (2026), which integrates network matched filtering, relative relocation, and relative magnitude estimation. We provide a brief summary here, including parameters specific to this study.

Our target region is five-sided (Fig. 1a), defined between latitudes 64.2° and 65.3° and longitudes −149.4° and −146.0° with the northwest corner truncated to reduce the overlap with a previous study of the MFFZ (Sims *et al.*, 2026). Our start date of 2014 is chosen to overlap with the 2014–2019 study of Sims *et al.* (2026). The Alaska Earthquake Center (AEC) catalog contains 11,039 events within our target region and time period (2014-01-01 to 2024-03-17). For each event, we use continuous seismic waveform data from all stations within 90 km of the event. This results in a data set from 47 stations within four networks (see Data and Resources).

There are 10,421 events (out of 11,039) that meet our criteria to be template events (Fig. 2a): events must be recorded on a minimum of six channels with a signal-to-noise ratio of at least 2.0 to be considered for the matched filtering routine performed using EQcorrscan (Chamberlain *et al.*, 2017). For filtering and detection thresholds, we follow the procedures in Sims *et al.* (2026).

After applying the network-matched filtering, we identify a total of 61,219 events (Fig. 2b). A small subset of spurious detections occurs in the vicinity of the Fort Knox Gold Mine (Fig. 2a), which conducts routine blasting that is regularly recorded by the permanent Alaska seismic network. Though most of these quarry blasts are flagged as explosions in the AEC catalog and excluded from our template set, it appears that some blasting signals may slip through the initial identification and filtering process. To avoid the possibility of including quarry blasts in our relocation analysis, we remove all events shallower than 10 km in a small region defined between latitudes 64.96° and 65.06° and longitudes −147.43° and −147.02° (Fig. 2). Following the removal of these potential blasts, we retain 58,590 events for subsequent relocation and magnitude analysis.

We assign the newly detected events to their initial locations at the hypocenters of their matched templates and relocate them using GrowClust (Trugman and Shearer, 2017) with the same settings as those used in Sims *et al.* (2026). Relative magnitudes are estimated using the approach of Schaff and Richards (2014), as implemented in EQcorrscan. Events are retained only if they contain at least two differential time pairs. The final relocated catalog consists of 41,589 events that meet these criteria and are considered high-quality detections.

Results

Our relocated catalog of 41,589 events is displayed in Figure 2b. The catalog is provided in Sims *et al.* (2025) along with two figures showing the spatial variation in uncertainties in epicenter and in depth.

In this section, we explain our assignment of fault segments to features in the seismicity catalog, and we describe the details of the catalog. Our use of the term "fault segment" is different from the geological usage (e.g., dePolo *et al.*, 1991; McAlpin, 2009), which is based on surface ruptures during large earthquakes. Our interpreted fault segments are purely subsurface expressions of seismicity (and source mechanisms). Nevertheless, we consider many of the same questions that geologists would consider for surface ruptures (Wesnousky, 2006; Baize *et al.*, 2019), such as: what is the likelihood that an earthquake rupture will terminate at one segment or jump to another?

Interpretation of fault segments

Our main approach to identifying fault segments is using a Gaussian kernel density estimate of the seismicity, as shown in Figure 3. The calculation of this map (performed using the Python SciPy function gaussian_kde) requires choices in the bandwidth parameter (controlling smoothing) and the color scale limits. We refer to this smoothed seismicity map as a "heat map," with earthquakes more likely in the redder regions.

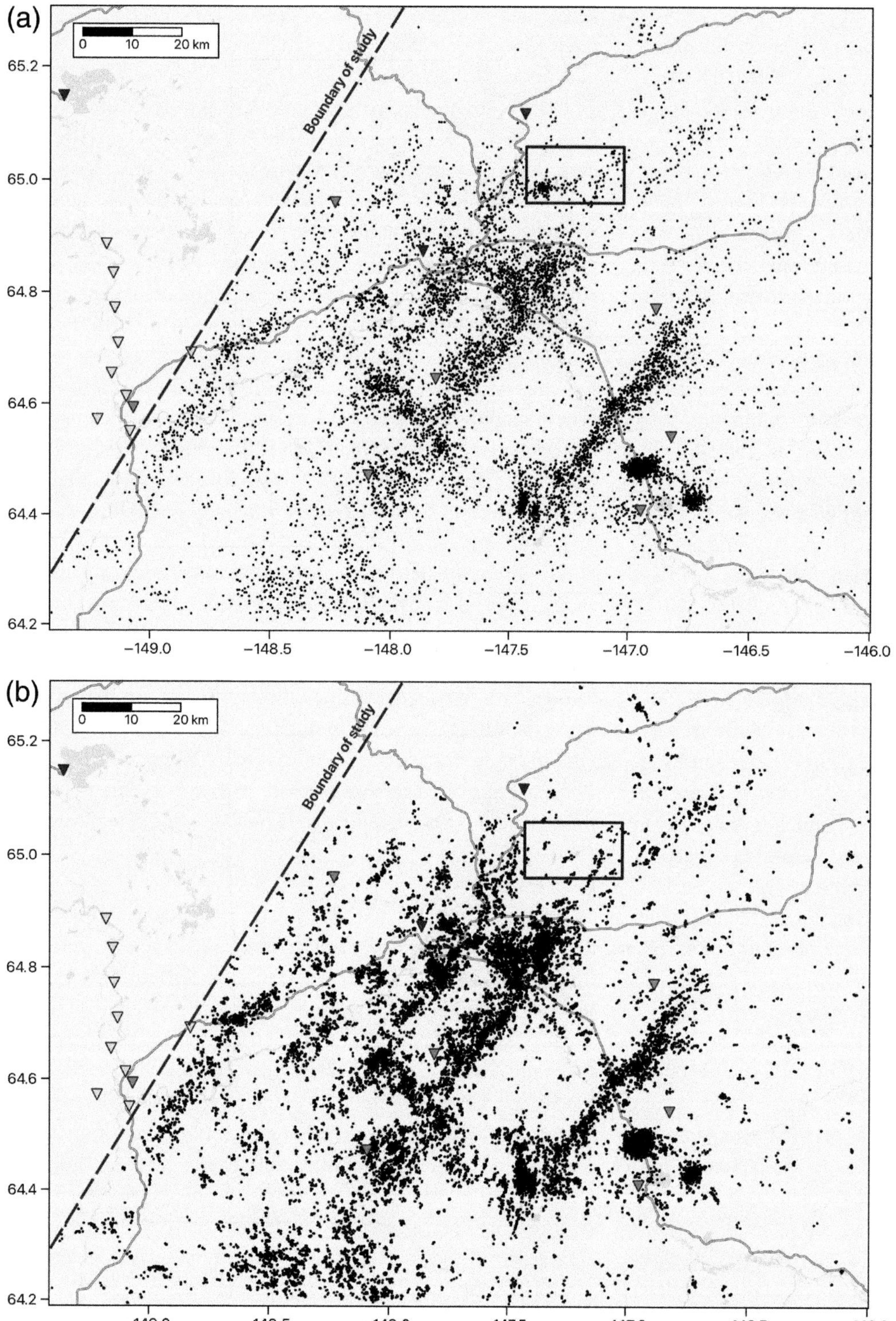

Figure 2. Seismicity in the Fairbanks region, 2014–2024. (a) Events from the Alaska Earthquake Center (AEC) catalog that meet the criteria to become a template for this study. There are 10,421 events spanning 2014-01-01 to 2024-03-17 and within the polygon shown in Figure 1. Triangles depict broadband stations used in this study (see also Fig. 1). The boxed region contains Fort Knox Gold Mine; all events shallower than 10 km in this region were excluded. (b) Final detected and relocated catalog containing 41,589 events. The catalog represents a subset of the 58,590 detections derived from the 10,421 template events shown in panel (a). The color version of this figure is available only in the electronic edition.

A second consideration for assigning fault segments is the depth distribution of seismicity. Breaks in continuity, such as abrupt jumps from shallow to deep seismicity, are used as indicators of possible segmentation. We used this factor in two cases associated with the Salcha fault. The Salcha fault is composed of segments C′, D′, and E′, with the kink segment D′ assigned in part due to the deeper seismicity compared with adjacent segments (Fig. 4a and Table 1). Furthermore, the extent of segment E′ is guided from the depth map (Fig. 4a).

For two regions of diffuse seismicity (segments A′ and B′), we examined the seismicity pattern exhibited by a subset of the larger events ($M_L \geq 1.5$), with the assumption that these are more likely to have occurred in the fault plane.

We assign 15 fault segments, labeled A′–O′, which are listed in Table 1 and shown in Figures 3 and 4a. The sequence of letters follows a similar ordering to that of Sims *et al.* (2026): the northeast–southwest faults from east to west (A′–M′) and then other faults from north to south (N′ and O′). The prime labeling is used to distinguish the fault segments from those in Minto Flats, to the west (A–R: Table 1).

Our assignment of fault segments is based primarily on map-view seismicity. For relocated catalogs determined with dense station coverage, it is possible to estimate fault planes directly from seismicity catalogs (Wang *et al.*, 2013), and this is an active area of research (Rong *et al.*, 2023; Truttmann *et al.*, 2023; Piegari *et al.*, 2024; Alongi *et al.*, 2025; He and

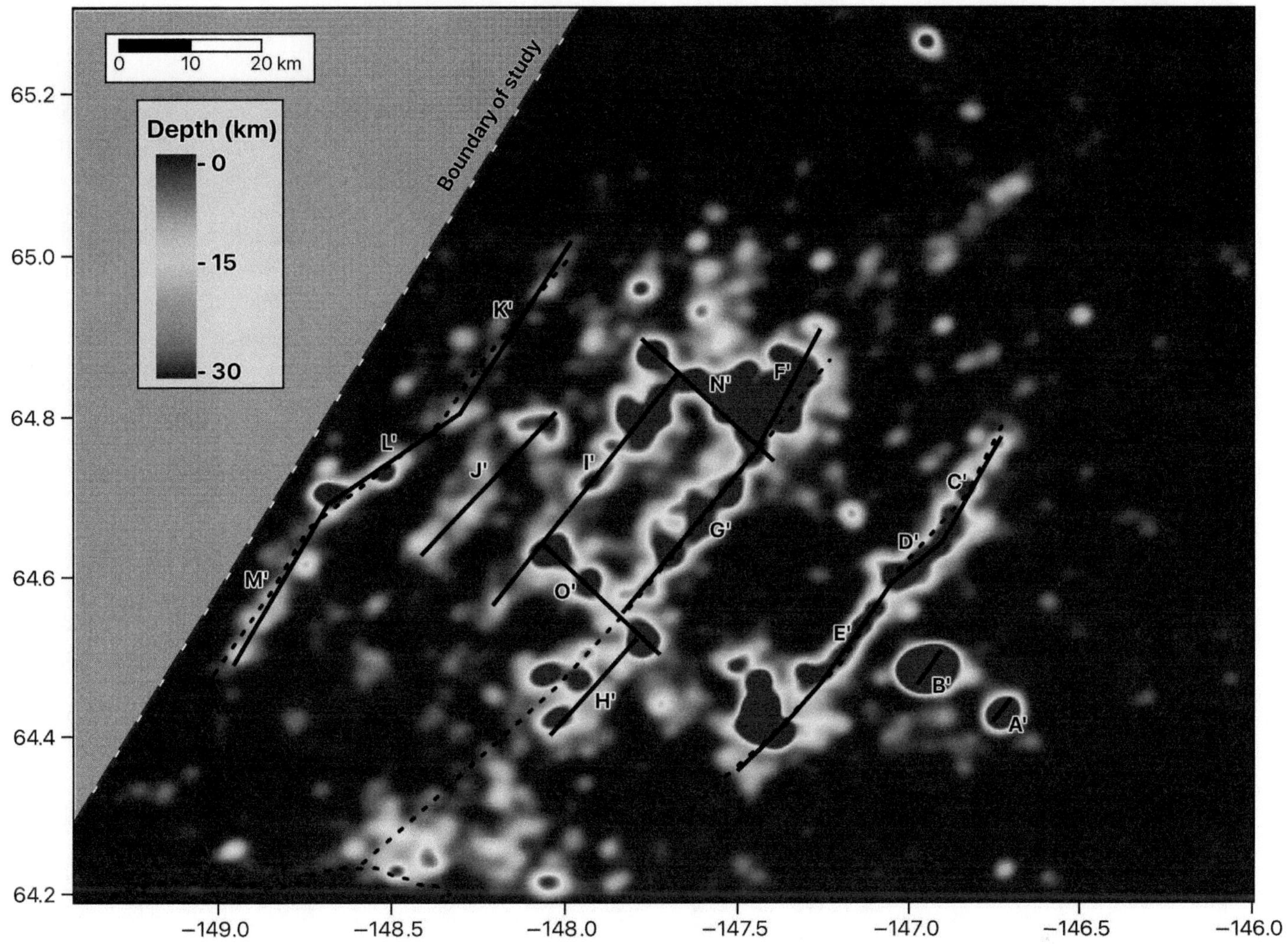

Figure 3. Probability density function for seismicity in our final relocated catalog (Fig. 2b). The interpreted fault segments are plotted as solid lines (Table 1). The NSHM faults are plotted as black dashed lines (Haeussler *et al.*, 2025). The color version of this figure is available only in the electronic edition.

Wang, 2025; Sun *et al.*, 2025). A future goal in central Alaska would be to extend the map-view fault segments to a set of fault surfaces (planar or not), similar to what has been done in southern California (Plesch *et al.*, 2007).

Reference source mechanisms

We obtain a set of high-quality source mechanisms from previous efforts using three-component seismic waveforms. The catalog of Ratchkovski and Hansen (2002, Table 1) contains 38 events, two of which are within our region. The catalog of Smith *et al.* (2023) contains 33 new events, two of which are within our region. The remaining nine events are from the U.S. Geological Survey (USGS) moment tensor catalog (Herrmann *et al.*, 2011; Duputel *et al.*, 2012). The source parameters of these reference events are listed in Tables 2 and 3, and the mechanisms are displayed in Figure 4a.

Seismicity cross-sections

General features of seismicity in the Fairbanks region are readily apparent from different perspectives. First, the basic fault lineaments are apparent, as previously identified and as adopted by the 2023 NSHM and labeled in Figure 1b. Segments C′–D′–E′ align with the Salcha fault, segments F′–G′–H′ align with the Fairbanks fault, and segments K′–L′–M′ align with the Goldstream fault. Second, seismicity generally deepens from east to west. This is apparent in Figure 4a, which, when combined with additional faults to the west, becomes more conspicuous. Third, the reference events—including 11 since 2019—demonstrate the near ubiquity of strike motion in this region, though many segments have no reference event (Fig. 4b).

We examine our relocated seismicity catalog in two sets of vertical cross-sections, one of which is perpendicular to the predominant northwest direction of faults (Fig. 5), the other of which is parallel (Fig. 6). At the top of each vertical cross-section, we label fault segments (in black) if they intersect the cross-section. We also provide the three NSHM faults for

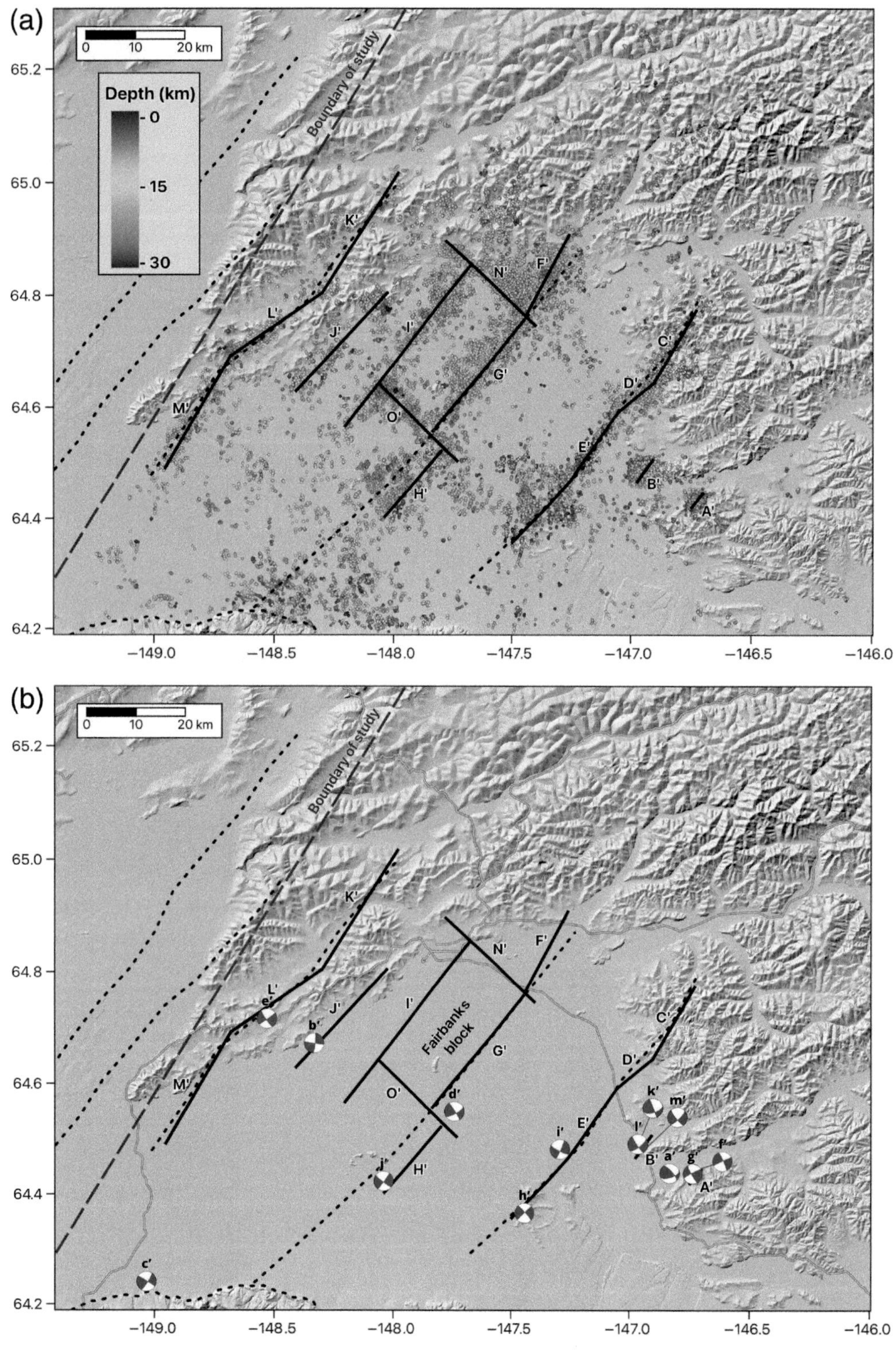

Figure 4. Seismicity, interpreted fault segments, and source mechanisms in the Fairbanks region. (a) Interpreted fault segments overlain on our final relocated seismicity map (Fig. 2b), which is colored by event depth. See also Table 1. The NSHM faults are plotted as black dashed lines (Haeussler *et al.*, 2025). (b) Source mechanisms of 13 reference events in the Fairbanks region (Tables 2 and 3), overlain on faults interpreted from seismicity. The color version of this figure is available only in the electronic edition.

reference, with text labels in red (Go = Goldstream; Fa = Fairbanks; Sa = Salcha) and vertical dashed lines projected downward from their surface positions. In the vertical cross-sections, we display the back hemisphere of each beachball source mechanism, analogous to the convention of plotting the lower hemisphere in map view. A complete set of cross-sections is provided in Sims *et al.* (2025).

The easternmost earthquake activity, represented by segments A′ and B′, is a product of $M_w > 4$ earthquakes in 2021 and 2024. Earlier seismicity (Page *et al.*, 1991) and relocated seismicity (Ruppert *et al.*, 2008) hint at activity east of the Salcha fault, but the 2021 and 2024 events—combined with our enhanced catalog—afford the best opportunity to identify faults in this region.

Figure 7 provides a zoomed-in view of the Salcha region. The heat map (Fig. 3) does not reveal any lineament, even though the Salcha fault (segment E′) is about 10 km west and well defined. This observation suggests that the station configuration, combined with our relocation approach, is capable of identifying lineaments in this region, if they exist. In Figure 7b, we see a slight preference for southwest–northeast alignment within the larger ($M_L \geq 1.5$) events. This direction would imply left-lateral faulting for the reference events in these regions (Fig. 4a). In the broader context, fault segments A′ and B′ represent the easternmost strike-slip faulting within the Fairbanks region.

The cross-section in Figure 5c intersects fault segments A′ and B′, showing

TABLE 1
Seismicity Properties of Fault Segments in the Fairbanks and Minto Regions (See Fig. 8)

Segment	Length (km)	Depth (Median, km)	Depth (MAD, km)	Number of Events	K12	F14	U23
A′	3.6	6.4	1.3	704	–	–	–
B′	5.3	7.0	1.2	4,726	–	–	–
C′	16.6	10.0	2.8	1,204	SSZ	Salcha	Salcha
D′	9.1	11.4	2.5	1,233	SSZ	Salcha	Salcha
E′	33.8	6.7	2.8	3,490	SSZ	Salcha	Salcha
F′	17.5	11.8	2.1	2,727	FSZ	Little Chena	Fairbanks
G′	28.8	11.7	2.2	2,641	FSZ	Little Chena	Fairbanks
H′	17.6	15.0	2.2	1,643	FSZ	Little Chena	Fairbanks
I′	40.6	13.1	2.2	3,127	FSZ	Isabella	–
J′	26.7	10.9	2.2	1,005	FSZ	Chena Ridge	–
K′	28.0	13.5	2.5	450	FSZ	Ester	Goldstream
L′	21.8	14.3	4.0	990	FSZ	Ester	Goldstream
M′	25.8	16.0	2.8	958	–	Ester	Goldstream
N′	24.3	12.9	2.0	2,424	FSZ	–	–
O′	21.9	15.5	2.9	2,262	FSZ	–	–
A	22.0	14.2	2.5	1,024	MFSZ	Minto	Minto south
B	17.5	15.6	1.2	938	MFSZ	Minto	Minto south
C	17.3	15.3	1.4	937	MFSZ	Minto	Minto south
D	8.9	18.5	1.7	1,105	MFSZ	–	–
E	5.8	18.1	1.5	693	MFSZ	–	–
F	13.0	18.6	1.6	987	MFSZ	–	–
G	6.6	20.4	1.3	406	MFSZ	–	Minto north
H	6.0	8.3	3.8	203	MFSZ	–	Minto north
I	14.2	15.4	3.1	522	MFSZ	–	Minto north
J	28.7	19.6	2.1	2,648	MFSZ	–	Minto north
K	6.2	22.7	0.4	334	MFSZ	–	–
L	6.7	23.1	0.7	296	MFSZ	–	–
M	20.9	18.2	2.5	442	MFSZ	–	–
N	10.0	8.6	1.7	791	MFSZ	–	–
O	14.8	10.4	2.3	14,830	MFSZ	–	–
P	7.2	16.7	2.6	392	MFSZ	–	–
Q	9.6	17.3	1.9	1,051	MFSZ	–	–
R	6.3	14.9	1.8	260	MFSZ	–	–

The calculation of median depth uses events having epicenters within 3 km of each segment. Segment names from other studies are in the columns labeled K12 (Koehler *et al.*, 2012), F14 (Frohman, 2014); U23 (U.S. Geological Survey 2023 National Seismic Hazard Model, Haeussler *et al.*, 2025). MAD, median absolute deviation.

their proximity to segment E′ of the Salcha fault. The south-to-north increase in seismicity depth on the Salcha fault is apparent from the fault-parallel view in Figure 6a, as well as the intersecting views between E′ (Fig. 5c) and D′ (Fig. 5d). The southern extent of segment E′ is unclear in the heat map (Fig. 3), and our interpretation is guided in part by the mechanism of reference event h′ (Fig. 4b).

TABLE 2

Source Parameters for the 13 Reference Events Displayed in Figure 4b

ID	Label	Origin Time (yyyy/mm/dd hh:mm:ss)	Longitude (°)	Latitude (°)	Depth (km)	M_w
a′	ruppert2002	1993/12/29 09:34:38	−146.8338	64.4382	11	4.60
b′	ruppert2002	1995/08/25 11:57:12	−148.3338	64.6723	17	4.50
c′	smith2020	2019/01/17 12:13:55	−149.0340	64.2410	17	3.55
d′	smith2020	2019/03/09 23:39:58	−147.7368	64.5498	26	3.60
e′	slm	2020/01/14 20:46:55	−148.5300	64.7160	20	3.59
f′	us	2021/07/23 04:20:19	−146.7704	64.4385	10	4.44
g′	us	2021/09/14 05:56:36	−146.7370	64.4374	4	4.73
h′	us	2021/11/05 22:12:50	−147.4416	64.3663	8	4.06
i′	us	2022/11/17 22:34:41	−147.2927	64.4814	15	4.00
j′	us	2022/12/07 16:21:45	−148.0408	64.4239	21	3.81
k′	us	2023/09/23 11:12:51	−146.9760	64.4772	11	3.70
l′	us	2024/01/19 21:34:35	−146.9641	64.4909	10	5.32
m′	us	2024/01/28 16:56:45	−146.9258	64.4865	11	4.15

See Table 3 for the parameters describing the mechanisms. ruppert2002 = Ratchkovski and Hansen, 2002; smith2020 = Smith *et al.* (2023); slm and us = U.S. Geological Survey regional moment tensor catalog (Herrmann *et al.*, 2011; Duputel *et al.*, 2012).

TABLE 3

Source Parameters for the 13 Reference Events Listed in Table 2 and Displayed in Figure 4b

	Fault Plane 1			Fault Plane 2			Slip Vector		
ID	Strike (°)	Dip (°)	Slip (°)	Strike (°)	Dip (°)	Slip (°)	Azimuth (°)	Plunge (°)	Fault Type
a′	72	52	35	319	63	136	229	27	LL?
b′	7	80	−2	97	88	−170	7	2	LL?
c′	33	77	5	302	85	167	212	5	LL
d′	61	66	6	328	84	156	238	6	LL
e′	55	85	−10	146	80	−175	56	10	LL
f′	246	86	−9	336	81	−176	246	9	LL?
g′	243	79	11	151	80	169	61	10	LL?
h′	227	88	−10	317	80	−178	227	10	LL
i′	25	82	−16	117	74	−172	27	16	LL
j′	37	86	−9	127	81	−176	37	9	LL
k′	73	49	6	339	86	139	249	4	LL?
l′	52	64	−12	147	80	−154	57	10	LL?
m′	46	71	−16	141	75	−161	51	15	LL?

Three angles are listed for each of the two possible fault planes represented by the source mechanisms. The first plane is the one we interpret as the true fault plane. The slip vector angles are based on the chosen fault plane, with the convention of a positive plunge angle. LL? indicates that there is uncertainty in the choice, LL = left-lateral.

The Fairbanks fault is represented by segments F′, G′, and H′. We have interpreted segment H′ as offset from G′; this offset is apparent in earlier (1990–2015) seismicity as well (Tape *et al.*, 2015, their fig. S4). The Fairbanks fault seismicity is deeper than the Salcha fault (Table 1), as shown in the cross sections in Figure 5a–c. The fault-parallel views of Salcha and

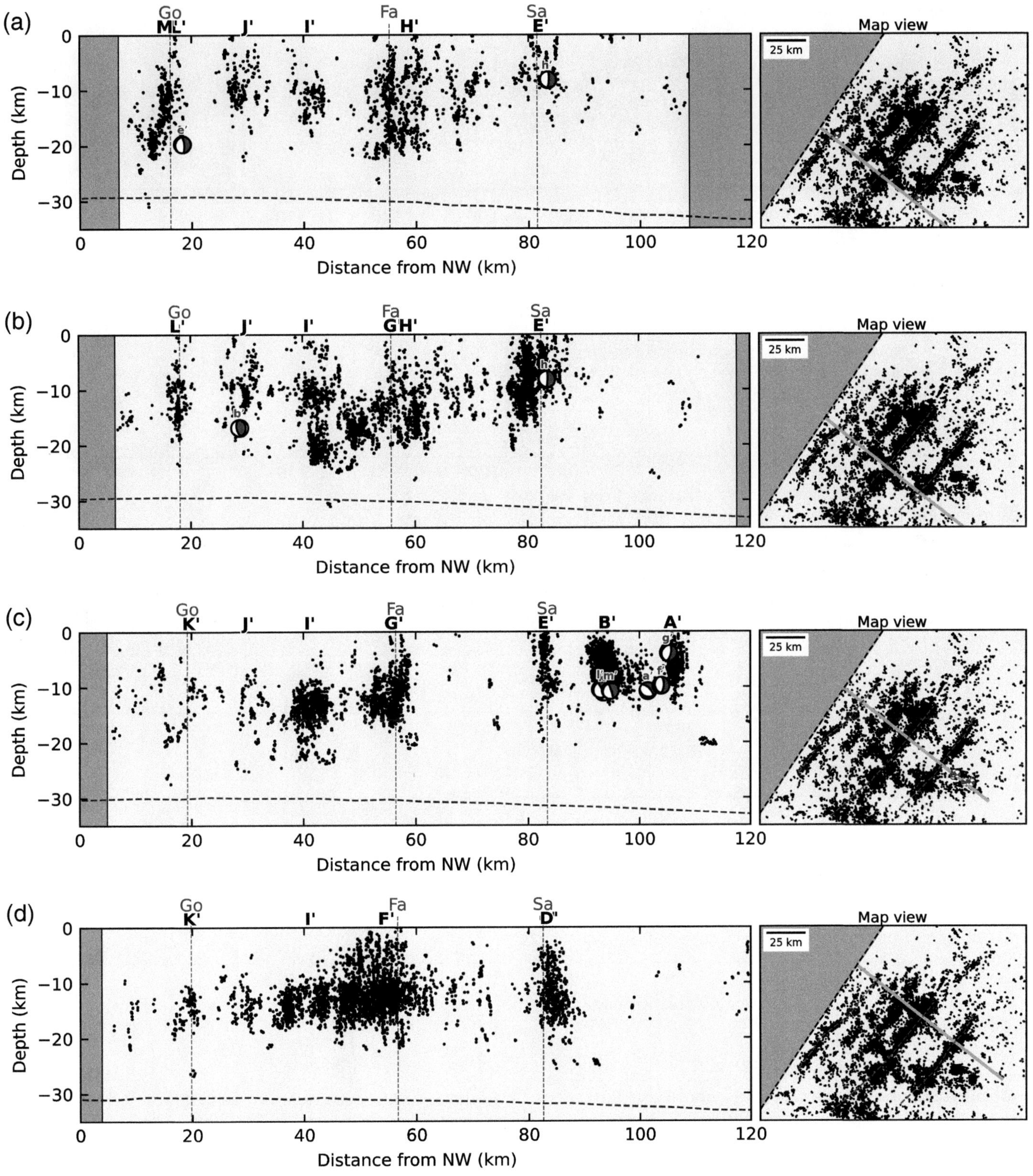

Figure 5. Vertical cross-sections of seismicity perpendicular to the Goldstream (Go), Fairbanks (Fa), and Salcha (Sa) faults, from south to north (a–d). Each cross-section contains all events within 4 km of a vertical plane depicted by the red-solid line in the map view at right. Reference events (Fig. 4b) within 4 km of the fault plane are plotted with lower hemisphere projection in map view (right) and back-hemisphere projection in the vertical cross-section (left). Fault segments intersecting each cross-section are labeled by their letters at the top. The blue dashed line depicts the Moho (Miller and Moresi, 2018). The color version of this figure is available only in the electronic edition.

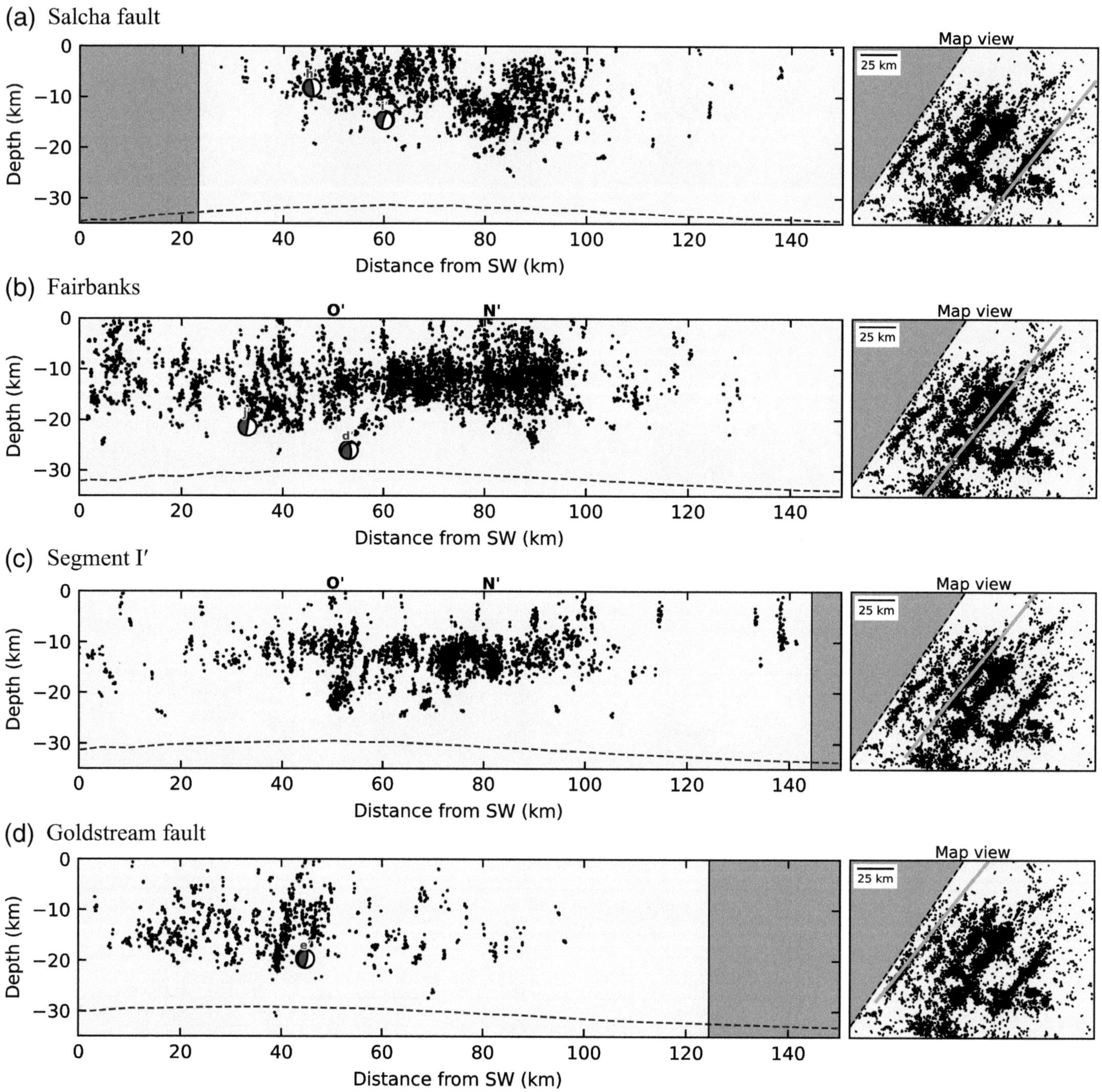

Fairbanks can be compared in Figure 6a,b. Two deep (> 20 km) reference events (d′ and j′: Table 3) occur on or near the Fairbanks fault. Event j′ is interpreted as a left-lateral fault, whereas event d′ could either be left lateral on G′ or H′ or it could be right lateral on O′.

Between the Fairbanks fault (F′–G′–H′) and the Goldstream fault (K′–L′–M′), we identify two subparallel segments, I′ and J′. Segment I′ can be viewed in Figure 5c and in Figure 6c. Segment J′ is visible in Figure 5b; the two fault planes for reference event b′ are not aligned with the interpreted segment (Fig. 4a).

Figure 6. Vertical cross-sections of seismicity parallel to the Salcha, Fairbanks, and Goldstream faults, from southeast to northeast (a–d). Each cross-section contains all events within 4 km of a vertical plane depicted by the red-solid line in the map view at right. Reference events (Fig. 4b) within 4 km of the fault plane are plotted with lower hemisphere projection in map view (right) and back-hemisphere projection in the vertical cross-section (left). Fault segments intersecting each cross-section are labeled by their letters at the top. The blue dashed line depicts the Moho (Miller and Moresi, 2018). The color version of this figure is available only in the electronic edition.

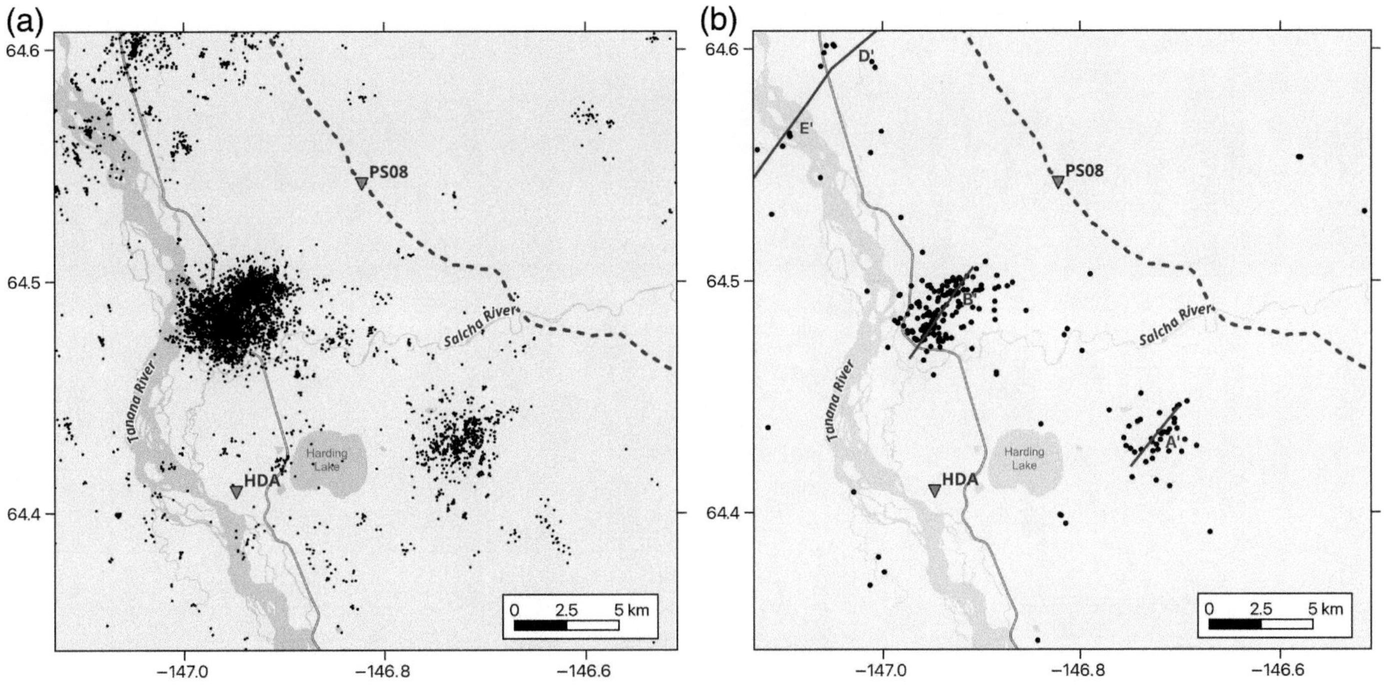

Figure 7. Seismicity in the area of the 2021 and 2024 Salcha earthquakes. The yellow line depicts the Richardson Highway, which is adjacent to the Tanana River. The red dashed line depicts the Alaska Pipeline. The two stations in the region, PS08 (Pump Station 8) and HDA (Harding Lake), are plotted as inverted triangles. (a) Relocated catalog. The western cluster is associated with the 2024-01-19 M_w 5.3 earthquake. The eastern cluster is associated with the 2021-07-23 M_w 4.4 earthquake. (b) Subset of events with $M_L \geq 1.5$. The interpreted fault segments (red lines) are, from east to west, A′, B′, and D′–E′ (Fig. 4a). The Salcha fault (segments C′-D′-E′) was likely the host of the 1937-07-22 M_s 7.3 Salcha earthquake. The color version of this figure is available only in the electronic edition.

The westernmost fault in the Fairbanks region is the Goldstream fault, which is best viewed in Figure 5a and Figure 6d. The central kink segment L′ coincides with reference event e′ (Fig. 4a), which is interpreted as a left-lateral mechanism.

The remaining two fault segments, N′ and O′, are conjugate to the northeast-striking faults. Segment N′ is within a diffuse region of seismicity, as evidenced from both Figure 2b and Figure 4a. A fault-parallel view of N′ can be seen in Figure 5d, where seismicity is clearly extending northwest of segment I′. The fault plane of N′ is intersected by cross-sections in Figure 6b,c. A fault-parallel view of O′ can be seen in Figure 5b, spanning between the letters I′ and H′. The depth extent of seismicity in this plane increases from southeast (right) to northwest, and the seismicity is not laterally continuous. These factors provide uncertainty in the assignment of O′ as a fault plane, though the seismicity on this lineament is also visible in earlier (1990–2015) seismicity as well (Tape *et al.*, 2015, their fig. S4). The fault plane of O′ is intersected by the cross-sections in Figure 6b,c.

We also identify one region of seismicity that was not prominent enough to warrant an assigned fault segment. As seen in Figure 4a, at the southern end of segment E′ of the Salcha fault, there is a north-striking cluster of seismicity that is deeper (median 12.0 km) than the seismicity of segment E′ (6.7 km). This unlabeled cluster is more active than the seismicity of segment E′, as shown in the heat map (Fig. 3). The interpretation of E′ is based more on Figure 4a, which accounts for depth differences, rather than Figure 3.

Discussion

Combining the Fairbanks region result (2014–2024) with the Minto Flats region results (2014–2019; Sims *et al.*, 2026), we obtain a single view of an enhanced high-precision seismicity catalog for central Alaska (Fig. 8a). The northeast-trending lineaments are apparent, as is the westward deepening of seismicity, highlighted in Figure 9. The most prominent conjugate fault features are segments N′ and O′. Figure 8b provides a guide for characterizing the seismicity. The source mechanisms provide valuable information, indicating whether the slip directions from the largest events are consistent with the seismicity lineaments. In this particular region, with the likelihood of conjugate faulting, it is difficult to determine the fault plane.

Our fault segments are summarized in Table 1, which provides a comparison with segments and seismic zones interpreted in three previous compilations: Koehler *et al.* (2012), Frohman (2014), and the 2023 NSHM Haeussler *et al.* (2025). Our study follows several recent efforts to transition from interpreting diffuse seismicity zones to assigning faults to seismic lineaments. Previous studies identified boundaries between the three seismic zones of Minto, Fairbanks, and Salcha (Biswas and Tytgat, 1988; Pulpan, 1988; Page *et al.*, 1991; Fletcher and Christensen, 1996; Koehler *et al.*, 2012;

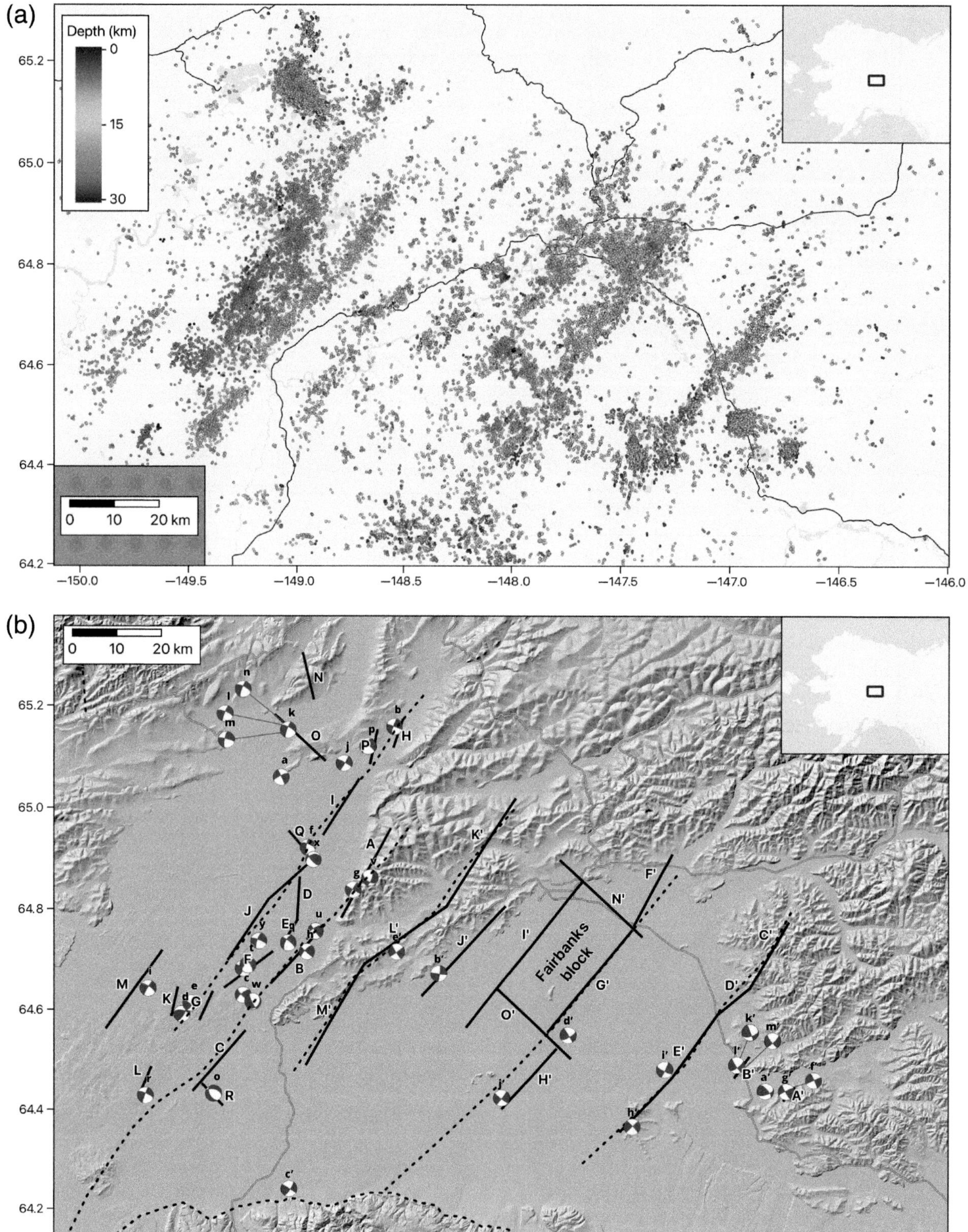

Figure 8. Combined relocated seismicity map for the regions of Minto Flats (2014–2019: Sims *et al.*, 2026) and Fairbanks (2014–2024: this study). (a) Seismicity colored by depth. (b) Interpreted fault segments and reference source mechanisms. Fault segments A–R and source mechanisms a–y are from Sims *et al.* (2026); fault segments A′–O′ and source mechanism a′–m′ are from Tables 1 and 3. The inset maps show the location of the study region as a blue-dashed box. The color version of this figure is available only in the electronic edition.

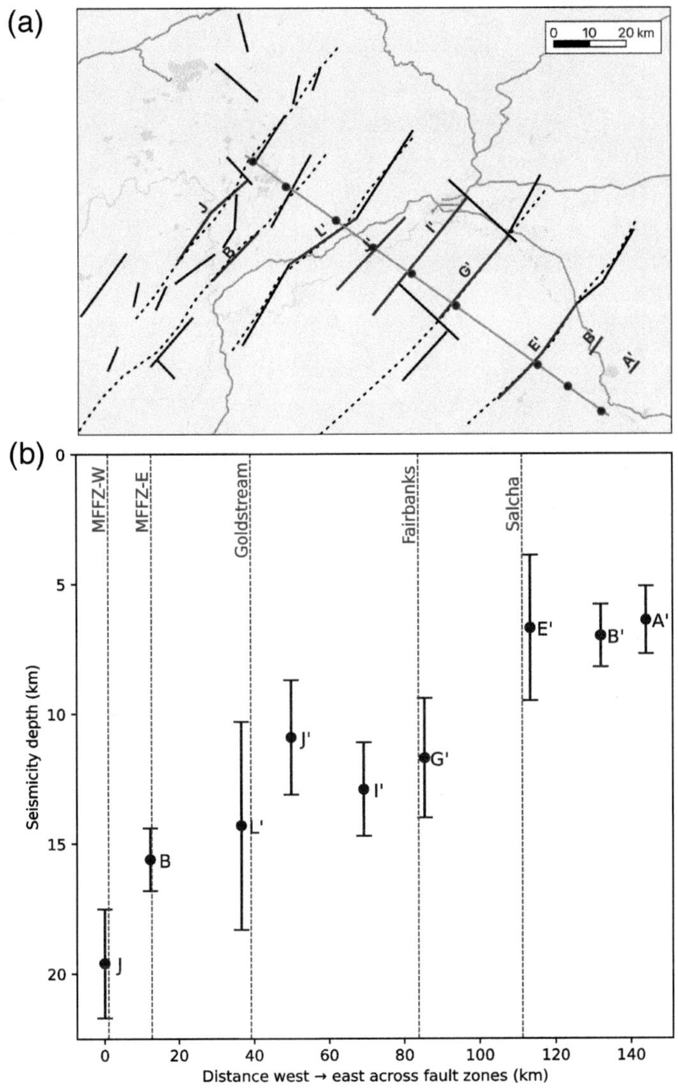

Figure 9. Variation in depth of seismicity across the Minto Flats and Fairbanks regions. (a) Map showing the fault segments (in blue, with letter labels) for which median-depth seismicity (Table 1) is plotted in panel (b). The cyan line with the blue circles, which are projected from the center of each fault segment, defines the horizontal distances in panel (b). (b) Seismicity depth value for each fault, projected onto the cyan line shown in panel (a). The error bars depict the median absolute deviation (MAD) values listed in Table 1. The color version of this figure is available only in the electronic edition.

Koehler and Carver, 2018). These studies overlapped in time with other studies that emphasized the lineaments as faults (Page *et al.*, 1995; Bemis and Wallace, 2007; Frohman, 2014; Dixit and Hanks, 2021), rather than defining boundaries between seismic zones. A detailed seismotectonic study of the Minto Flats seismicity led to the designation of two main faults (Tape *et al.*, 2015). Collectively, these studies of seismicity were influential in the designation of the five NSHM faults shown in Figure 1 (Powers *et al.*, 2024; Haeussler *et al.*, 2025). Our relocated seismicity catalog has led to a more accurate depiction of the five NSHM faults, and it has resulted in the definition of several more faults (and conjugate faults) that are not captured in the 2023 NSHM.

Review of the largest earthquakes

To examine the seismic hazards in the Fairbanks region, we review the largest earthquakes since the start of the instrumental era in 1900. A synoptic view of the fault system and historical earthquakes is provided in Figure 10. For the earthquakes, we have plotted all seven events in the Global Centroid Moment Tensor (Global CMT) catalog and all seven events in the International Seismological Centre-Global Earthquake Model (ISC-GEM) catalog. We note two important considerations. First, the catalog epicenters are probably not as accurate as the epicenters determined using local data. These discrepancies are identified by the red connector lines in Figure 10. Second, the catalog completeness for Global CMT (M_w 5.2) is lower than ISC-GEM. The catalog completeness for ISC-GEM is complete down to 5.6 for events after 1964, and it is above 6.0 for earlier events (Di Giacomo, Bondár, *et al.*, 2015). For the earliest instrumental years of 1900–1903, there are no reported $M_w > 7$ earthquakes for this region (Gutenberg, 1956; Boyd and Lerner-Lam, 1988).

Next, we provide a chronological overview of the largest earthquakes occurring in the Minto and Fairbanks regions since the start of the instrumental era in 1900 (Fig. 10). The first event is 1929-07-04 M_s 6.0, occurring at the southern extent of the Salcha fault (segment E′). Although its epicenter is uncertain, as discussed below, it was felt in Fairbanks, with the front page of the *Fairbanks Daily News-Miner* reporting: "Three earthquake shocks, the first rivaling the tremors felt late January, rocked Fairbanks Wednesday evening… All were of short duration, the longest and most severe lasting probably not more than 15 seconds. Buildings were shaken and suspended objects sent swaying to and fro, but no damage has been reported." The next event, 1937-07-22 M_s 7.3, is the defining earthquake of the entire region, as it demonstrates the $M_w > 7$ potential of this region. The earthquake most likely occurred on the seismicity lineament that defines the Salcha fault (segments C′–D′–E′), which crosses both the Richardson Highway and the Alaska Pipeline (Fig. 10). This event ruptured at the surface and caused landslides that blocked the only highway out of Fairbanks (Bramhall, 1938). Seismic waveforms were examined by Adkins (1940), Fletcher and Christensen (1996), and Doser and Baker (2023), and these studies estimated source parameters indicating strike-slip faulting.

Three decades later, a series of four $M_w > 5$ earthquakes struck close to Fairbanks (Fig. 10), causing extensive minor damage, as well as cases of broken storefront windows and broken chimneys (Cloud and Knudson, 1968; Jordan *et al.*, 1968). The aftershock region (Fig. 10) coincides with segments N′ and F′. Using azimuthally limited local data, Gedney and Berg (1969) estimated a composite strike-slip mechanism for the

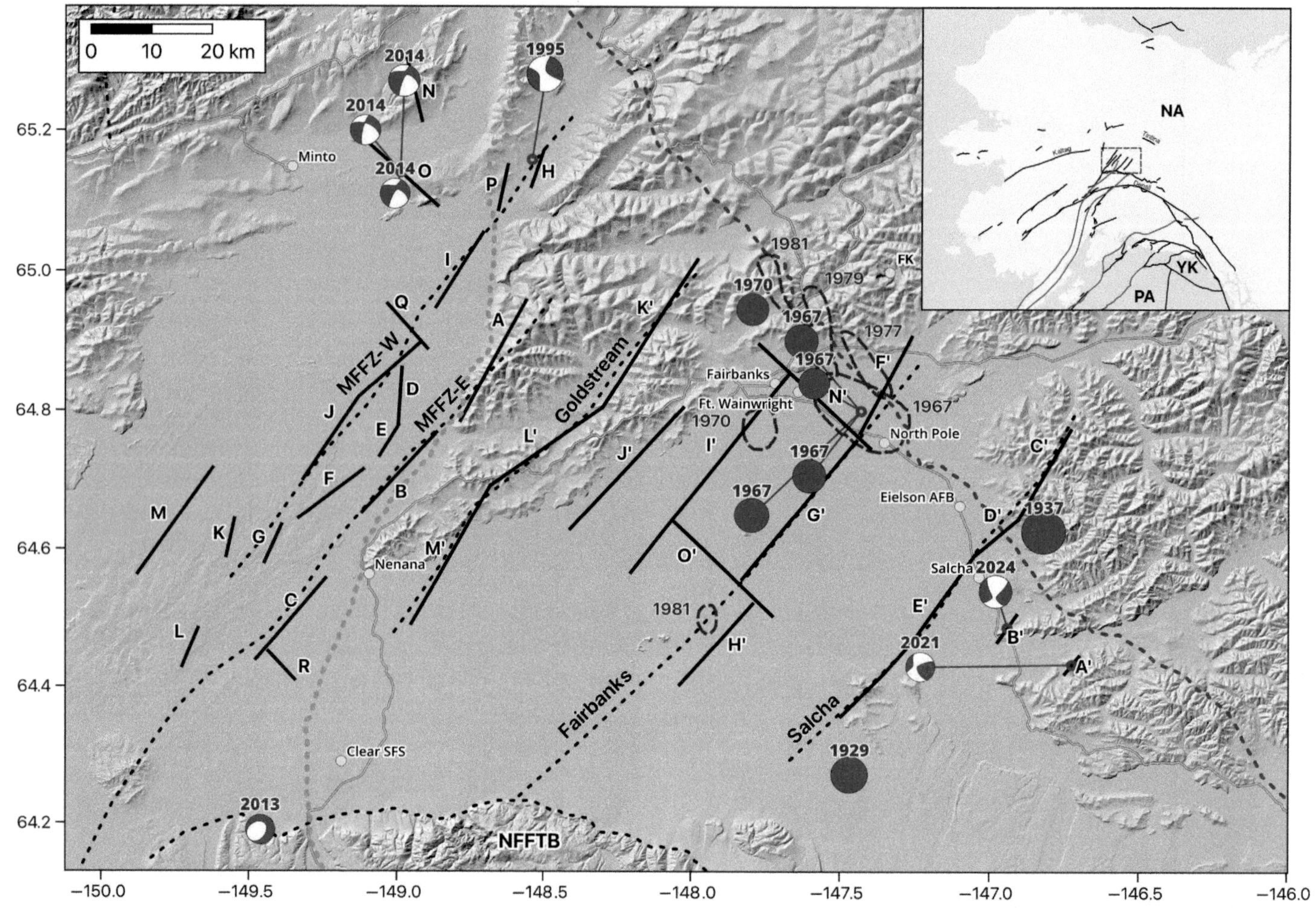

aftershock sequence; the mechanism is consistent with either left-lateral faulting on the Fairbanks fault (F′) or right-lateral faulting on segment N′ (Fig. 10). The 1970-08-14 M_w 5.3 earthquake occurred close to the 1967 events. The annual U.S. seismicity compilation noted: "Int. V at College, Eielson Air Force Base, Fairbanks (minor glass breakage reported by press), and Nenana" (Coffman and von Hake, 1984, p. 31). For this event, we did not find any published epicentral coordinates that used local stations; it does not appear to be associated with the sequence of events that occurred later in 1970, as outlined in Figure 10 (Gedney *et al.*, 1982).

The largest of the seven events from the Global CMT catalog is the 1995-10-06 M_w 6.0 Minto earthquake, which occurred on the northern part of MFFZ (Fig. 10). Finite-source modeling revealed a compact slip patch of about 50 cm at 17 km depth (Tape *et al.*, 2015). Two decades later and 20 km to the west, the 2014-08-31 M_w 5.2 earthquake occurred, illuminating a new fault (segment O) that is conjugate to the main fault zone (Sims *et al.*, 2026). The final three events in the region are the 2021 and 2024 earthquakes in the Salcha region (segments A′ and B′, respectively) and the 2013 M_w 4.9 earthquake at 154 km depth (Fig. 10). The 2013 event is a reminder of the subducting slab, which extends into the Fairbanks region (Hayes *et al.*, 2018).

Figure 10. All 14 events (1904–2025) within the combined catalogs of International Seismological Centre-Global Earthquake Model (ISC-GEM; Di Giacomo, Harris, *et al.*, 2015) and the Global Centroid Moment Tensor (Global CMT; Ekström *et al.*, 2012). Features include the road system (yellow), the Alaska Pipeline (red dashed), the proposed gas pipeline (orange dashed: AGDC, 2025), towns, military bases (Eielson, Fort Wainwright, Clear), and Fort Knox Gold Mine (FK). The solid-black segments are our interpreted faults and the black dashed lines are the 2023 NSHM faults (Fig. 1b). The six blue dashed regions depict seismic sequences between 1967 and 1981 (Gedney *et al.*, 1982). The 1967 sequence encompasses part of segments N′ and F′. The red lines connect the catalog epicenters (beachballs or large red circles) to the epicenters inferred using local data (small red circles). The inset map shows the plate tectonic setting and is described in Figure 1. The color version of this figure is available only in the electronic edition.

It is notable which events are not displayed in Figure 10. The first is the 1904-08-27 M_s 7.3 earthquake, which had been relocated to the Fairbanks region by Boyd and Lerner-Lam (1988) but later determined to have occurred on the Iditarod–Nixon fault, hundreds of kilometers southwest of Fairbanks (Tape *et al.*, 2017). The second is the 1947-10-16 M_s 7.2 earthquake, for which the ISC-GEM epicenter is just south (latitude 64.06°) of the region displayed in Figure 10. Doser and Baker (2023) recently relocated the mainshock and its aftershock, and their epicenters cluster north of the NFFTB boundary near 64.2° latitude. Both the 1904 and 1947 earthquakes appear on earlier compilation maps of the Fairbanks region (Biswas and Tytgat, 1988; Page *et al.*, 1991). Finally, the epicenter of the second two large events in 1929—that of 1929-01-21 M_s 5.75—is south of the region in Figure 10. Doser and Baker (2023) relocated both this event and 1929-07-04 M_s 6.0 within the NFFTB, though uncertainties allowed for the possibility of them occurring in the Fairbanks region.

Implications for seismic hazard assessments

The Fairbanks region, although containing only about 100,000 people, is a hub for much of the northern part of the Alaska. Within the region is a substantial amount of critical infrastructure, as labeled in Figure 10: Eielson Air Force Base, Fort Wainwright, Clear Space Force Station, the open pit Fort Knox Gold Mine, and the Alaska Pipeline. The proposed natural gas pipeline is also displayed.

Prior to the 2023 NSHM, the 2007 seismic hazard maps did not formally include faults within the Minto–Fairbanks–Salcha region. Wesson *et al.* (2007, p. 21) wrote: "Many of the smaller earthquakes in the region are concentrated in three diffuse bands striking north-northeast. These bands have been termed the Minto Flats, Fairbanks, and Salcha seismic zones (Page *et al.*, 1995; Ratchkovski and Hansen, 2002). To date, none of these bands have been clearly associated with a geologic fault." This perspective has evolved, in recognition that not all faults have clear surface expressions, especially in active tectonic regions having significant sedimentation (and erosion). In the case of Minto Flats, the proposed fault feature (Gedney *et al.*, 1972) turned out to be an erosional feature within the Tanana River floodplain Koehler *et al.* (2015).

Considering our newly determined fault segments as well as the occurrence of large $M_w > 5$ earthquakes in the region, we now revisit the faults identified in the 2023 NSHM (Fig. 10). We first examine the southern extent of the five identified faults, which are, from west to east, MFFZ-W, MFFZ-E, Goldstream, Fairbanks, and Salcha. The southern extent of MFFZ-E is determined by Tape *et al.* (2015) and includes reliable source mechanisms and seismicity; it is south of the focus region of Sims *et al.* (2026). The Goldstream fault aligns with our segments K′–L′–M′. This fault exhibits low seismicity relative to Minto Flats (west) and Fairbanks (east) (Fig. 3), it has not hosted a large earthquake during the instrumented era (Fig. 10), though it has hosted one reference event (Fig. 8b).

The Fairbanks fault in the 2023 NSHM extends south to the NFFTB (Fig. 8), whereas we end it at segment H′, excluding the final 30 km. Figure 6b provides a view of the fault-parallel seismicity, including event j′, which is at the southern end of segment H′. Clearly there is seismicity south of this region, but it is not as dense or linear as the regions to the north (Fig. 3). Similarly, the Salcha fault in the 2023 NSHM extends about 10 km further south of our segment E′, into a region exhibiting minimal seismicity.

Our fault assignments (A–R and A′–O′) include finer segmentation and greater geometric detail than those represented in the NSHM. When considering candidate faults for the NSHM, we aggregate our fault segments into larger faults. We pursue a seismic approach to identifying these larger faults, considering three factors: (1) expression of linear (and planar) features within relocated seismicity, (2) fault planes implied by source mechanisms of moderate ($M_w > 3.5$) earthquakes derived using seismic waveforms (with or without using first-motion polarities), and (3) the occurrence of large ($M_w > 5$) earthquakes. Our current study emphasizes the first two factors (Fig. 8), following similar efforts by Tape *et al.* (2015) and Sims *et al.* (2026).

With these considerations, we offer recommendations for updates to the NSHM fault database. First, add three conjugate faults (Fig. 10): O, N′, and O′. Segment O ruptured on 2014-08-31 M_w 5.2. Segments N′ and O′ have no definitive earthquake rupture, though it is possible that N′ hosted one of the 1967 earthquakes (Fig. 10). Segment O′ is the least certain of the three because its seismicity is not laterally continuous. Second, add segment I′, which is more prominent than the existing Goldstream fault (Fig. 3). Third, truncate the southern extents of the Fairbanks and Salcha faults.

What size earthquakes might occur on the main faults in the Minto and Fairbanks regions? Using empirical scaling to relate the length of a strike-slip fault to earthquake magnitude (Thingbaijam *et al.*, 2017), fault lengths of 10, 30, 50, and 70 km have magnitude estimates of 5.8, 6.5, 6.8, and 7.0, respectively. We will discuss the possibilities from east to west (Fig. 10).

The Salcha fault (C′–D′–E′) is 60 km long (Table 1), and it was likely the host of the 1937 M_s 7.3 earthquake. Two reference events (h′ and i′ in Fig. 8b) are consistent with left-lateral motion. The Fairbanks fault (F′–G′–H′) has relatively high seismicity and may have hosted one of the 1967 earthquakes. Its length (Table 1: 64 km) raises the possibility of hosting a M_w 6–7 earthquake. Segments I and N are shorter (41 and 24 km) and extend directly beneath Fairbanks. Segment J′ is the least likely to host a $M_w > 6$ earthquake, given its low seismicity, lack of any historical event, and short length (27 km). The Goldstream fault (K′–L′–M′) has low seismicity and has never hosted a significant historical earthquake, but its length (Table 1: 76 km) raises the possibility of hosting a M_w 6–7 earthquake. In Minto Flats, the 1995 M_w 6.0 earthquake ruptured near segment H, which is short portion of MFFZ-W. As discussed in Tape *et al.* (2015), either or both of the two faults (MFFZ-W and MFFZ-E) could host a $M_w > 7$ earthquake.

Bookshelf faulting

The two new faults (A′ and B′) east of Salcha fault are relevant for several reasons. First, they are close to the highway and pipeline (Fig. 7), and they are about 20 km from Eielson Air Force Base. Second, they are even closer to the Salcha fault, which likely hosted the 1937 M_s 7.3 earthquake. Activity on A′ and B′ could potentially influence activity on the Salcha fault, via static or dynamic triggering. Finally, they represent a newly discovered portion of the central Alaska fault system.

Bookshelf faulting has been identified and examined within laboratory experiments (Mandl, 1987; Cobbold *et al.*, 1989; Dooley and Schreurs, 2012; Koyi *et al.*, 2016), numerical models (Nur *et al.*, 1986; Higgins *et al.*, 2024), and in many geological settings (Ron *et al.*, 1984; Tapponnier *et al.*, 1990; La Femina *et al.*, 2002; Milliner *et al.*, 2021). Overall, our findings in Figure 8 support the basic model of bookshelf faulting proposed by Page *et al.* (1995) for the Minto–Fairbanks region. Nevertheless, we point out that the "books"—defined by northeast-striking faults—clearly do not extend to the "shelves" defined by the Tintina–Kaltag fault in the north and the Denali fault in the south (Fig. 1). In the south there is an active fold-and-thrust belt (NFFTB; Bemis and Wallace, 2007; Bemis *et al.*, 2012; Bender *et al.*, 2023); the NFFTB is bounded to the south by the Denali fault (Fig. 1a), which ruptured in the 2002-11-03 M_w 7.9 earthquake (Eberhart-Phillips *et al.*, 2003). In the north, there is minimal seismic activity, and it is unclear if the Tintina fault itself has produced any large ($M_w > 7$) events in the past centuries. Possibly the upper shelf is fixed, and the bookshelf faulting is entirely driven from the south. If this is true, motion on the northeast-striking faults would decay in proximity to the Tintina fault system. Though motion would be expected to increase on the southern segments of these lineations, as they approach the NFFTB it is hard to predict how strain would be partitioned across these different systems.

It is unclear what the connection is between the Fairbanks region faults and the NFFTB to the south (Doser and Baker, 2023). The northern front of NFFTB (Fig. 1a) is proposed as a south-dipping thrust fault, potentially one that hosted the 1947 M_s 7.2 earthquake (Bender *et al.*, 2023). Reference event c′ (2019-01-17 M_w 3.55) occurred at this southern margin, as shown in Figure 8b. Its depth is 17 km, and its mechanism is strike-slip, which would place it deep below the toe of the NFFTB frontal thrust. Dedicated study of recent and historical earthquakes is needed to unravel the connection between the strike-slip fault system and the NFFTB.

Within the Fairbanks region, there is a 30 km × 15 km block, which we call the "Fairbanks block", with its boundaries defined by fault segments G′, N′, I′, and O′. In essence, the block is defined by the relative absence of seismicity, as shown by the "cold" portion of the heat map (Fig. 3). The kinematic setting (Ratchkovski *et al.*, 2004) implies that I′ and G′ are left lateral (parallel to "books"), whereas N′ and O′ are right lateral (aligned with "shelves"). Future larger earthquakes, as well as dedicated seismicity and geodetic studies, should help refine the geometry of the Fairbanks block and the kinematics at its boundaries.

Time window of seismicity

Our study is based on seismic activity spanning 11 years; and therefore, our interpretation of faults is limited to activity within this time period. For example, a fully locked fault, exhibiting no seismicity, would not be identified as a fault segment. Fortunately, the coverage of seismic stations in the Fairbanks region has been adequate enough for many prior decades to examine whether seismic features in our study have persisted previously, and whether any previous seismic activity is absent during our time period.

We consider three prior views of seismicity in the Fairbanks region. The first is a log-scaled seismicity map in Tape *et al.* (2015, their fig. S4; 1990–2015), the second is the seismicity map in Page *et al.* (1991, their fig. 10; 1982–1985), and the third is the summary of sequences in Gedney *et al.* (1982, their fig. 1; 1967–1982).

Qualitatively, the seismicity features in our relocated catalog are persistent across the decades prior to our study. Examples of features persisting in earlier catalogs include: (1) seismicity in the regions defining segments A′ and B′, (2) the lateral offset between H′ and G′, (3) the unlabeled feature north of the southern end of E′ (Fig. 4a), and (4) the relative absence of seismicity within the Fairbanks block region. The 1967 seismic activity defined by Gedney *et al.* (1982; Fig. 10) coincides with an ongoing region of diffuse seismicity adjacent to segments N′ and F′ (Fig. 8a). The same is true for the 1970 sequence, which coincides with ongoing activity on segment I′ (Fig. 10). Based on these comparisons, we believe that our relocated seismicity catalog and our interpreted fault segments are representative of seismic activity over several decades.

Conclusions

The Fairbanks region is both tectonically and societally relevant. Tectonically, it is an actively deforming intraplate setting, evidenced by earthquakes and GPS displacements (Ruppert *et al.*, 2008). It accommodates convergence that partly originates from subduction and collision of an oceanic plateau (Jadamec *et al.*, 2013; Haeussler *et al.*, 2017). Societally, there are about 100,000 people in the Fairbanks region, as well as critical infrastructure, including the Alaska Pipeline, Eielson Air Force Base, Fort Wainwright, and Clear Space Force Station (Fig. 10). The region hosted large earthquakes in 1937 M_s 7.3 and 1995 M_w 6.0, and the defined fault segments are long enough to host magnitude 7 events.

Our study reinforces the step taken by the 2023 NSHM to label seismicity lineaments as faults, rather than diffuse seismicity zones. From a catalog of 41,589 events, we interpret 15 fault segments (Fig. 8). Together with the findings of Sims *et al.* (2026), we have set the stage for a broader tectonic investigation to understand how the proposed faults interact with each other and within the broader tectonic stress field. Although bookshelf faulting may provide a basic conceptual model (Page *et al.*, 1995), it does not address the southern connection to the thrust system (NFFTB), the westward deepening of seismicity (Figs. 8 and 9), and the development of conjugate faults. New synthesis efforts such as Lesh and Ridgway (2007), Dixit and Hanks (2021), and Doser and Baker (2023)—as well as computational models of deformation (Koons *et al.*, 2010; Jadamec *et al.*, 2013)—are needed to obtain a geodynamical framework that explains both the current tectonic activity as well as the geological evolution to the present day.

Data and Resources

The relocated seismicity catalog is available from Sims *et al.* (2025), which also includes a complete set of cross-sections, including those in Figures 5 and 6. All waveforms used in this study are accessible from the EarthScope Data Management Center (DMC). We ourselves accessed the waveforms from the local databases at the Alaska Earthquake Center (AEC). We used a subset of stations from the following seismic networks (Fig. 1): AK (doi: 10.7914/SN/AK), XV (Tape *et al.*, 2018) (doi: 10.7914/SN/XV_2014), TA (Busby and Aderhold, 2020) (doi: 10.7914/SN/TA), and the ILAR array (generic network code IM) operated by Eielson Air Force Base. The Global Centroid Moment Tensor (Global CMT) catalog in Figure 10 is accessible at https://www.globalcmt.org/ (Ekström *et al.*, 2012). The International Seismological Centre-Global Earthquake Model (ISC-GEM) catalog in Figure 10 is accessible at https://www.isc.ac.uk/iscgem/ (Di Giacomo, Harris, *et al.*, 2015; International Seismological Centre, 2025). We used several open-source software packages, including QGIS (QGIS Development Team, 2025), EQcorrscan (Chamberlain *et al.*, 2017), GrowClust (Trugman and Shearer, 2017), and Pyrocko (Heimann *et al.*, 2019) for plotting moment tensor beachballs in cross-sections. Some of the reference source mechanisms (Fig. 8b) were estimated in previous studies using CAP and MTUQ (Zhu and Helmberger, 1996; Silwal and Tape, 2016; Thurin *et al.*, 2025). Other moment tensors were obtained from the U.S. Geological Survey (USGS) earthquake catalog (https://earthquake.usgs.gov/earthquakes/) and used the methods of Herrmann *et al.* (2011) and Duputel *et al.* (2012). Figures 2a,b, 7, 8a, and 9a, were created in QGIS using ArcGIS basemaps by Esri. For more information about Esri software, please visit www.esri.com. Figure 1 was prepared using OpenTopoMap basemaps (OpenStreetMap contributors, Shuttle Radar Topography Mission [SRTM]). Elevation basemaps generated from USGS 5 m Interferometric Synthetic Aperture Radar (InSAR) digital elevation model (DEM) (Alaska; accessed 2024) and USGS Alaska Mid-Accuracy DEM (accessed 2024). All websites were last accessed in December 2025.

Declaration of Competing Interests

The authors acknowledge that there are no conflicts of interest recorded.

Acknowledgments

The authors are grateful for manuscript reviews by Diane Doser, Rich Koehler, and James Pechmann. This study was supported by Grant Numbers EAR-1645313 and OAC 2104052 (SCOPED project) from the National Science Foundation (NSF). Seismic data recorded by the Alaska Earthquake Center (AEC) are made possible by support from the U.S. Geological Survey (USGS) Advanced National Seismic System (ANSS) program cooperative agreement G25AC00133 and NSF Grant Number OPP-2024208. Stephen Holtkamp, Yoshihiro Kaneko, and Elisabeth Nadin provided helpful discussions.

Any use of trade, firm, or product names is for descriptive purposes only and does not imply endorsement by the U.S. Government.

References

Adkins, J. D. (1940). The Alaskan earthquake of July 22, 1937, *Bull. Seismol. Soc. Am.* **30,** no. 4, 353–376.

AGDC (2025). Alaska gasline development corporation: Alaska LNG, available at https://alaska-lng.com/ (last accessed December 2025).

Alongi, T., A. J. Elliott, R. J. Skoumal, D. R. Shelly, and A. E. Hatem (2025). SURF: An automated method for building nonplanar 3D fault models from earthquake hypocenters, *Seismol. Res. Lett.* doi: 10.1785/0220250126.

Baize, S., F. Nurminen, A. Sarmiento, T. Dawson, M. Takao, O. Scotti, T. Azuma, P. Boncio, J. Champenois, F. R. Cinti, *et al.* (2019). A worldwide and unified database of surface ruptures (SURE) for fault displacement hazard analyses, *Seismol. Res. Lett.* **91,** 499–520.

Bemis, S. P., G. A. Carver, and R. D. Koehler (2012). The Quaternary thrust system of the northern Alaska Range, *Geosphere* **8,** no. 1, 1–10.

Bemis, S. P., and W. K. Wallace (2007). Neotectonic framework of the north-central Alaska Range foothills, in *Tectonic Growth of a Collisional Continental Margin: Crustal Evolution of Southern Alaska*, K. D. Ridgway, J. M. Trop, J. M. G. Glen, and J. M. O'Neill (Editors), Geol. Soc. Am., Boulder, Colorado, Special Paper 431, 549–572.

Bender, A. M., R. O. Lease, T. Rittenour, and J. J. Jones (2023). Rapid active thrust faulting at the northern Alaska Range front, *Geology* **51,** no. 6, 527–531.

Bird, P. (2003). An updated digital model of plate boundaries, *Geochem. Geophy. Geosys.* **4,** 1–52.

Biswas, N. N., and G. Tytgat (1988). Intraplate seismicity in Alaska, *Seismol. Res. Lett.* **59,** no. 4, 227–233.

Boyd, T. M., and A. L. Lerner-Lam (1988). Spatial distribution of turn-of-the-century seismicity along the Alaska-Aleutian Arc, *Bull. Seismol. Soc. Am.* **78,** no. 2, 636–650.

Bramhall, E. H. (1938). The central Alaska earthquake of July 22, 1937, *Bull. Seismol. Soc. Am.* **28,** 71–75.

Busby, R. W., and K. Aderhold (2020). The Alaska Transportable Array: As built, *Seismol. Res. Lett.* **91,** no. 6, 3017–3027.

Chamberlain, C. J., C. J. Hopp, C. M. Boese, E. Warren-Smith, D. Chambers, S. X. Chu, K. Michailos, and J. Townend (2017). EQcorrscan: Repeating and near-repeating earthquake detection and analysis in Python, *Seismol. Res. Lett.* **89,** 173–181.

Christeson, G. L., S. P. S. Gulick, H. J. A. van Avendonk, L. L. Worthington, R. S. Reece, and T. L. Pavlis (2010). The Yakutat terrane: Dramatic change in crustal thickness across the Transition fault, Alaska, *Geology* **38,** no. 10, 895–898.

Cloud, W. K., and C. F. Knudson (1968). Preliminary engineering seismological report, in *The Fairbanks, Alaska, Earthquakes of June 21, 1967*, U.S. Dept. Commerce, Environmental Science Services Admin., Coast and Geodetic Survey, 33–60.

Cobbold, P. R., J. P. Brun, P. Davy, G. Fiquet, C. Basile, and D. Gapais (1989). Some experiments on block rotation in the brittle upper crust, in *Paleomagnetic Rotations and Continental Deformation*, C. Kissel and C. Laj (Editors), Kluwer, Dordrecht, The Netherlands, 145–155.

Coffman, J. L., and C. A. von Hake (1984). United States earthquakes, 1970, *U.S. Geol. Survey Open-File Rept. 84-970*.

dePolo, C., D. G. Clark, D. B. Slemmons, and A. R. Ramelli (1991). Historical surface faulting in the Basin and Range province, western North America: Implications for fault segmentation, *J. Struct. Geol.* **13,** no. 2, 123–136.

Di Giacomo, D., I. Bondár, D. A. Storchak, E. R. Engdahl, P. Bormann, and J. Harris (2015). ISC-GEM: Global Instrumental Earthquake Catalogue (1900–2009), III. Re-computed M_S and m_b, proxy M_W, final magnitude composition and completeness assessment, *Phys. Earth Planet. In.* **239,** 33–47.

Di Giacomo, D., J. Harris, A. Villaseñor, D. A. Storchak, E. R. Engdahl, W. H. K. Lee, and The Data Entry Team (2015). ISC-GEM: Global Instrumental Earthquake Catalogue (1900–2009), I. Data collection from early instrumental seismological bulletins, *Phys. Earth Planet. In.* **239,** 14–24.

Dixit, N., and C. Hanks (2021). Basement structure and styles of active tectonic deformation in central Interior Alaska, *Geosciences* **11,** no. 3, 1–25.

Dooley, T. P., and G. Schreurs (2012). Analogue modelling of intraplate strike-slip tectonics: A review and new experimental results, *Tectonophysics* **574–575,** 1–71.

Doser, D. I., and M. R. Baker (2023). Basement structure of the Northern Foothills Fold and Thrust Belt and southern Fairbanks and Salcha, Alaska Seismic zones and their relation to large (M ≥ 6) earthquakes, *Tectonophysics* **851,** 1–11.

Duputel, Z., L. Rivera, H. Kanamori, and G. Hayes (2012). W phase source inversion for moderate to large earthquakes, *Geophys. J. Int.* **189,** 1125–1147.

Eberhart-Phillips, D., D. H. Christensen, T. M. Brocher, R. Hansen, N. A. Ruppert, P. J. Haeussler, and G. A. Abers (2006). Imaging the transition from Aleutian subduction to Yakutat collision in central Alaska, with local earthquakes and active source data, *J. Geophys. Res.* **111,** 1–31.

Eberhart-Phillips, D., P. J. Haeussler, J. T. Freymueller, A. D. Frankel, C. M. Rubin, P. Craw, N. A. Ratchkovski, G. Anderson, G. A. Carver, A. J. Crone, *et al.* (2003). The 2002 Denali fault earthquake, Alaska: A large magnitude, slip-partitioned event, *Science* **300,** 1113–1118.

Ekström, G., M. Nettles, and A. M. Dziewoński (2012). The global GCMT project 2004–2010: Centroid-moment tensors for 13,017 earthquakes, *Phys. Earth Planet. In.* **200–201,** 1–9.

Elliott, J., and J. T. Freymueller (2020). A block model of present-day kinematics of Alaska and western Canada, *J. Geophys. Res.: Solid Earth* **125,** doi: 10.1029/2019JB018378.

Fletcher, H. J., and D. H. Christensen (1996). A determination of source properties of large intraplate earthquakes in Alaska, *Pure Appl. Geophys.* **146,** no. 1, 21–41.

Freymueller, J. T., H. Woodard, S. C. Cohen, R. Cross, J. Elliott, C. F. Larsen, S. Hreinsdóttir, and C. Zweck (2008). Active deformation processes in Alaska, based on 15 years of GPS measurements, in *Active Tectonics and Seismic Potential of Alaska*, J. T. Freymueller, P. J. Haeussler, R. Wesson, and G. Ekström (Editors), Vol. 179, Geophysical Monograph, American Geophysical Union, Washington, D.C., 1–42.

Frohman, R. A. (2014). Identification and evolution of tectonic faults in the greater Fairbanks area, Alaska, *Master's Thesis*, University of Alaska Fairbanks.

Gedney, L., and E. Berg (1969). The Fairbanks earthquakes of June 21, 1967; aftershock distribution, focal mechanisms, and crustal parameters, *Bull. Seismol. Soc. Am.* **59,** no. 1, 73–100.

Gedney, L., L. Shapiro, and D. VanWormer (1972). Correlation of epicenters with mapped faults, East-Central Alaska, 1968–1971, *U.S. Geol. Surv. Open-File Rept. 72-128*, 7 pp.

Gedney, L. D., S. A. Estes, N. N. Biswas, and D. L. Marshall (1982). A note on further activity in the Fairbanks, Alaska, seismic zone, *Bull. Seismol. Soc. Am.* **72,** no. 4, 1415–1417.

Gutenberg, B. (1956). Great earthquakes 1896–1903, *Eos Trans. AGU* **37,** no. 5, 608–614.

Haeussler, P. J. (2008). An overview of the neotectonics of interior Alaska: Far-field deformation from the Yakutat microplate collision, in *Active Tectonics and Seismic Potential of Alaska*, J. T. Freymueller, P. J. Haeussler, R. Wesson, and G. Ekström (Editors), Vol. 179, Geophysical Monograph, American Geophysical Union, Washington, D.C., 83–108.

Haeussler, P. J., A. M. Bender, P. M. Powers, R. D. Koehler, and D. S. Brothers (2025). Updating the crustal fault model for the 2023 National Seismic Hazard Model for Alaska, in *Tectonics and Seismic Structure of Alaska and Northwestern Canada: EarthScope and Beyond*, N. A. Ruppert, M. A. Jadamec, and J. T. Freymueller (Editors), Vol. 290, Geophysical Monograph, American Geophysical Union, Washington, D.C., 85–127.

Haeussler, P. J., A. Matmon, D. P. Schwartz, and G. G. Seitz (2017). Neotectonics of interior Alaska and the late Quaternary slip rate along the Denali fault system, *Geosphere* **13,** no. 5, 1445–1463.

Hayes, G. P., G. L. Moore, D. E. Portner, M. Hearne, H. Flamme, M. Furtney, and G. M. Smoczyk (2018). Slab2, a comprehensive subduction zone geometry model, *Science* **362,** 58–61.

He, Z., and R. Wang (2025). E2F: Extract fault geometry from earthquake catalogs, *Seismol. Res. Lett.* **96,** 3880–3890.

Heck, N. H. (1936). The seismometer at University of Alaska at College near Fairbanks, *Bull. Seismol. Soc. Am.* **26,** no. 2, 125–127.

Heimann, S., H. Vasyura-Bathke, H. Sudhaus, M. P. Isken, M. Kriegerowski, A. Steinberg, and T. Dahm (2019). A Python framework for efficient use of pre-computed Green's functions in seismological and other physical forward and inverse source problems, *Solid Earth* **10,** 1921–1935.

Herrmann, R. B., H. Benz, and C. J. Ammon (2011). Monitoring the earthquake source process in North America, *Bull. Seismol. Soc. Am.* **101,** no. 6, 2609–2625.

Higgins, M., P. C. La Femina, A. J. Saballos, H. Geirsson, W. Strauch, R. Malservisi, and G. Mattioli (2024). The geodetic signature of bookshelf faulting in Nicaragua, *Tectonics* **43,** no. 5, 1–11.

Hutchinson, L. (2015). Double-difference relocation of earthquakes at Uturuncu Volcano, Bolivia, and Interior Alaska, *Master's Thesis*, University of Alaska Fairbanks, available at http://hdl.handle.net/11122/6093 (last accessed December 2025).

International Seismological Centre (2025). ISC-GEM Global instrumental earthquake catalogue, *Version 12.0, Released on 2025-08-19*.

Jadamec, M. A., M. I. Billen, and S. M. Roeske (2013). Three-dimensional numerical models of flat slab subduction and the Denali fault driving deformation in south-central Alaska, *Earth Planet. Sci. Lett.* **376,** 29–42.

Jordan, J. N., G. J. Dunphy, and S. T. Harding (1968). Preliminary seismological report. In the Fairbanks, Alaska, Earthquakes of June 21, 1967, U.S. Dept. Commerce, Environmental Science Services Admin., Coast and Geodetic Survey, 1–32.

Koehler, R. D., and G. A. Carver (2018). Active faults and seismic hazards in Alaska, *Alaska Div. Geol. Geophys. Surv., Miscellaneous Publication 160*, 59 pp., doi: 10.14509/29705.

Koehler, R. D., R.-E. Farrell, P. A. C. Burns, and R. A. Combellick (2012). Quaternary faults and folds in Alaska: A digital database, *Alaska Div. Geol. Geophys. Surv. Miscellaneous Publication 141*, 31 pp., 1 sheet, scale 1:3,700,000.

Koehler, R. D., R. D. Reger, E. R. Spangler, and A. I. Gould (2015). Investigation of potentially active tectonic faults along the route of the proposed Alaska Stand Alone Pipeline, Livengood to Cook Inlet, Alaska, *Alaska Div. Geol. Geophys. Surv., Report of Investigation 2015-4*, 71 pp.

Koons, P. O., B. P. Hooks, T. Pavlis, P. Upton, and A. D. Barker (2010). Three-dimensional mechanics of Yakutat convergence in the southern Alaskan plate corner, *Tectonics* **29,** 1–17.

Koyi, H., F. Nilfouroushan, and K. Hessami (2016). Modelling role of basement block rotation and strike-slip faulting on structural pattern in cover units of fold-and-thrust belts, *Geol. Mag.* **153,** nos. 5/6, 827–844.

Krabbenhoeft, A., R. von Huene, J. J. Miller, D. Lange, and F. Vera (2018). Strike-slip 23 January 2018 M_w 7.9 Gulf of Alaska rare intraplate earthquake: Complex rupture of a fracture zone system, *Sci. Rep.* **8,** 1–9.

La Femina, P. C., T. H. Dixon, and W. Strauch (2002). Bookshelf faulting in Nicaragua, *Geology* **30,** no. 8, 751–754.

Lesh, M. E., and K. D. Ridgway (2007). Geomorphic evidence of active transpressional deformation in the Tanana foreland basin, south-central Alaska, in *Tectonic Growth of a Collisional Continental Margin: Crustal Evolution of Southern Alaska*, K. D. Ridgway, J. M. Trop, J. M. G. Glen, and J. M. O'Neill (Editors), Geol. Soc. Am., Boulder, Colorado, 573–592, Special Paper 431.

Mandl, G. (1987). Tectonic deformation by rotating parallel faults: The "bookshelf" mechanism, *Tectonophysics* **141,** 277–316.

McAlpin, J. (Editor) (2009). *Paleoseismology*, Second Ed., Academic Press, San Diego, California.

Miller, M. S., and L. Moresi (2018). Mapping the Alaska Moho, *Seismol. Res. Lett.* **89,** no. 6, 2430–2436.

Milliner, C., A. Donnellan, S. Aati, J.-P. Avouac, R. Zinke, J. F. Dolan, K. Wang, and R. Burgmann (2021). Bookshelf kinematics and the effect of dilatation on fault zone inelastic deformation: Examples from optical image correlation measurements of the 2019 Ridgecrest earthquake sequence, *J. Geophys. Res.: Solid Earth* **126,** 1–20.

Neumann, F. (1940). United States Earthquakes 1937, U.S. Department of Commerce.

Nur, A., H. Ron, and O. Scotti (1986). Fault mechanics and the kinematics of block rotations, *Geology* **14,** 746–749.

Page, R. A., N. N. Biswas, J. C. Lahr, and H. Pulpan (1991). Seismicity of continental Alaska, in *Neotectonics of North America, The Geology of North America, Chapter 4*, D. B. Slemmons, E. R. Engdahl, M. D. Zoback, and D. D. Blackwell (Editors), Vol. 1, Geol. Soc. Am., Boulder, Colorado, Decade Map, 47–68.

Page, R. A., G. Plafker, and H. Pulpan (1995). Block rotation in east-central Alaska: A framework for evaluating earthquake potential? *Geology* **23,** no. 7, 629–632.

Piegari, E., G. Camanni, M. Mercurio, and W. Marzocchi (2024). Illuminating the hierarchical segmentation of faults through an unsupervised learning approach applied to clouds of earthquake hypocenters, *Earth Space Sci.* **11,** 1–13.

Plesch, A., J. H. Shaw, C. Benson, W. A. Bryant, S. Carena, M. Cooke, J. Dolan, G. Fuis, E. Gath, L. Grant, *et al.* (2007). Community Fault Model (CFM) for southern California, *Bull. Seismol. Soc. Am.* **97,** no. 6, 1793–1802.

Powers, P. M., J. M. Altekruse, A. L. Llenos, A. J. Michael, K. L. Haynie, P. J. Haeussler, A. M. Bender, S. Rezaeian, M. P. Moschetti, J. A. Smith, *et al.* (2024). The 2023 Alaska National Seismic Hazard Model, *Earthq. Spectra* **40,** no. 4, 2545–2597.

Pulpan, H. (1988). Seismic-hazard analysis of the Nenana agricultural development area, Central Alaska, *Alaska Div. Geol. Geophys. Surv. Report of Investigations 88-1*.

QGIS Development Team (2025). QGIS geographic information system, *Open Source Geospatial Foundation Project*, available at http://qgis.org (last accessed December 2025).

Ratchkovski, N. A., and R. A. Hansen (2002). New constraints on tectonics of interior Alaska: Earthquake locations, source mechanisms, and stress regime, *Bull. Seismol. Soc. Am.* **92,** no. 3, 998–1014.

Ratchkovski, N. A., S. Wiemer, and R. A. Hansen (2004). Seismotectonics of the central Denali fault, Alaska, and the 2002 Denali fault earthquake sequence, *Bull. Seismol. Soc. Am.* **94,** no. 6B, S156–S174.

Ron, H., R. Freund, and Z. Garfunkel (1984). Block rotation by strike-slip faulting: Structural and paleomagnetic evidence, *J. Geophys. Res.* **89,** no. B7, 6256–6270.

Rong, Y., Y. Bai, M. Ren, M. Liang, and Z. Wang (2023). Seismicity-based 3D model of ruptured seismogenic faults in the North-South Seismic Belt, China, *Front. Earth Sci.* **10,** 1–13.

Ruppert, N. A., K. D. Ridgway, J. T. Freymueller, R. S. Cross, and R. A. Hansen (2008). Active tectonics of interior Alaska: Seismicity, GPS, and local geomorphology, in *Active Tectonics and Seismic Potential of Alaska*, J. T. Freymueller, P. J. Haeussler, R. Wesson, and G. Ekström (Editors), Vol. 179, Geophysical Monograph, Am. Geophys. Union, Washington, D.C., 109–133.

Schaff, D. P., and P. G. Richards (2014). Improvements in magnitude precision, using the statistics of relative amplitudes measured by cross correlation, *Geophys. J. Int.* **197,** 335–350.

Silwal, V., and C. Tape (2016). Seismic moment tensors and estimated uncertainties in southern Alaska, *J. Geophys. Res.* **121,** 2772–2797.

Sims, N., C. Tape, N. Ruppert, and M. West (2025). Earthquake catalog and seismicity cross sections for "Earthquake catalog for the Fairbanks region of central Alaska, based on waveform cross-correlation for events 2014–2024" [Data set], *Zenodo*, doi: 10.5281/zenodo.17229905.

Sims, N. E., C. Tape, N. A. Ruppert, and M. E. West (2026). High-precision earthquake catalog for Minto Flats fault zone, central Alaska, reveals complex and conjugate faulting, *Bull. Seismol. Soc. Am.* doi: 10.1785/0120250177.

Smith, K., C. Tape, and V. C. Tsai (2023). Seismic response of Nenana sedimentary basin, central Alaska, *Bull. Seismol. Soc. Am.* **113,** no. 2, 762–781.

Sun, X., R. Lu, W. Wang, F. Yang, and K. He (2025). Automated 3-D modelling of seismic faults using adaptive threshold hierarchical clustering and quantitative assessment, *Geophys. J. Int.* **244,** 1–18.

Tape, C., S. Holtkamp, V. Silwal, J. Hawthorne, Y. Kaneko, J. P. Ampuero, C. Ji, N. Ruppert, K. Smith, and M. E. West (2018). Earthquake nucleation and fault slip complexity in the lower crust of central Alaska, *Nature Geosci.* **11,** 536–541.

Tape, C., A. Lomax, S. P. Bemis, P. J. Haeussler, and J. Ginnaty (2025). The 1912 M_s 7.2 earthquake in the Denali region of central Alaska, *Bull. Seismol. Soc. Am.* doi: 10.1785/0120250150.

Tape, C., A. Lomax, V. Silwal, J. D. Agnew, and B. Brettschneider (2017). The 1904 M_s 7.3 earthquake in central Alaska, *Bull. Seismol. Soc. Am.* **107,** no. 3, 1147–1174.

Tape, C., V. Silwal, C. Ji, L. Keyson, M. E. West, and N. Ruppert (2015). Transtensional tectonics of the Minto Flats fault zone and Nenana basin, central Alaska, *Bull. Seismol. Soc. Am.* **105,** no. 4, 2081–2100.

Tapponnier, P., R. Armijo, I. Manighetti, and V. Courtillot (1990). Bookshelf faulting and horizontal block rotations between overlapping rifts in southern Afar, *Geophys. Res. Lett.* **17,** no. 1, 1–4.

Thingbaijam, K. K. S., P. M. Mai, and K. Goda (2017). New empirical earthquake source-scaling laws, *Bull. Seismol. Soc. Am.* **107,** no. 5, 2225–2246.

Thurin, J., R. Modrak, C. Tape, A. McPherson, F. R. Rodríguez-Cardozo, J. Kintner, L. Ding, Q. Liu, and J. Braunmiller (2025). MTUQ: A framework for estimating moment tensors, point forces, and their uncertainties, *Geophys. J. Int.* **241,** 1373–1390.

Trugman, D. T., and P. M. Shearer (2017). GrowClust: A hierarchical clustering algorithm for relative earthquake relocation, with application to the Spanish Springs and Sheldon, Nevada, earthquake sequences, *Seismol. Res. Lett.* **88,** 379–391.

Truttmann, S., T. Diehl, and M. Herwegh (2023). Hypocenter-based 3D imaging of active faults: Method and applications in the Southwestern Swiss Alps, *J. Geophys. Res. Solid Earth* **128,** 1–23.

Waldhauser, F., and W. L. Ellsworth (2000). A double-difference earthquake location algorithm: Method and application to the Northern Hayward fault, California, *Bull. Seismol. Soc. Am.* **90,** no. 6, 1353–1368.

Wang, Y., G. Ouillon, J. Woessner, D. Sornette, and S. Husen (2013). Automatic reconstruction of fault networks from seismicity catalogs including location uncertainty, *J. Geophys. Res.: Solid Earth* **118,** 5956–5975.

Wesnousky, S. G. (2006). Predicting the endpoints of earthquake ruptures, *Nature* **444,** 358–360.

Wesson, R. L., O. S. Boyd, C. S. Mueller, C. G. Bufe, A. D. Frankel, and M. D. Petersen (2007). Revision of Time-Independent Probabilistic Seismic Hazard Maps for Alaska, *Open-File Rept. 2007-1043.*

Wickersham, J. A. (1904). James Wickersham Diary, Jul. 31, 1904 to Feb. 20, 1905, *MS1907-Diary 08-8/27/1904,* James Wickersham Papers Manuscript Collection, Alaska State Library.

Zhu, L., and D. Helmberger (1996). Advancement in source estimation techniques using broadband regional seismograms, *Bull. Seismol. Soc. Am.* **86,** no. 5, 1634–1641.

Manuscript received 30 September 2025
Published online 2 February 2026

Focus Section: Intraplate Earthquakes

Sub-Basalt Velocity Image of the Main Seismogenic Fault at Koyna, an Intraplate Active Region in Western India, Using Borehole Seismic Network

Dodla Shashidhar*[1], Perugu Mahesh[2], Sandeep Gupta[1], and Kothamasu Mallika[1]

Abstract

We present the first sub-basalt 3D local earthquake tomography of the Koyna seismic zone, western India, using travel-time data from 5325 local earthquakes recorded by a network of eight deep borehole seismometers. These seismometers were installed below the Deccan basalts and within the underlying granite basement. The resulting V_P and V_P/V_S models reveal a well-defined image of the Donachiwada fault (DF), the plausible source of the 10 December 1967 (M 6.3) earthquake—the largest reservoir-triggered event documented globally. These models show clear variations in V_P and V_P/V_S values, from 1 to ~9 km depth, across the DF. At depths (5–9 km), the deeper anomalies spatially correlate with the main zone of seismicity along the DF. These results provide one of the first seismic image of the DF beneath the Deccan basalt and highlights the value of borehole instrumentation for resolving fault-zone structure in basalt-covered regions. The depth extent and seismic signature of the fault zone may have implications for understanding intraplate faulting processes and the long-term persistence of reservoir-triggered seismicity in the Koyna region.

Cite this article as Shashidhar, D., P. Mahesh, S. Gupta, and K. Mallika (2026). Sub-Basalt Velocity Image of the Main Seismogenic Fault at Koyna, an Intraplate Active Region in Western India, Using Borehole Seismic Network, *Seismol. Res. Lett.* **97**, 897–906, doi: 10.1785/0220250319.

Introduction

The Indian subcontinent is prone to significant intraplate seismic activity. Notable intraplate earthquakes include the 1819 M_w 7.8 Kachchh earthquake, 1967 **M** 6.3 Koyna earthquake, 1993 M_w 6.2 Latur earthquake, 1997 M_w 5.7 Jabalpur earthquake, and the 2001 M_w 7.7 Bhuj earthquake (Gupta, 1993; Gupta *et al.*, 2001; Rao *et al.*, 2002). Among these, the Koyna earthquake of 10 December 1967 (**M** 6.3) is an example of a largest intraplate event triggered by an artificial water reservoir. The Koyna region is situated within the Deccan Volcanic Province, which is the world's largest continental flood basalt province, and is one of the prominent global sites of sustained reservoir-triggered seismicity (RTS) (Gupta *et al.*, 2017). At Koyna, RTS have continued to occur for more than five decades following the impoundment of the Shivaji Sagar Lake (Koyna Reservoir) after completion of the Koyna Dam in 1962. A further increase in seismicity in this region was also observed after the filling of a nearby Warna Reservoir (Rastogi *et al.*, 1997) (Fig. 1).

Seismicity in the Koyna region is primarily confined to an $\sim 30 \times 20$ km^2 area and restricted to shallow depths, mostly within 10 km (Rao and Shashidhar, 2016; Gupta *et al.*, 2017). Several geophysical investigations such as gravity and magnetic studies (Kailasam and Murthy, 1971), Landsat imagery analyses (Langston, 1981), seismic refraction profiling (Kaila *et al.*, 1981), aeromagnetic surveys (Negi *et al.*, 1983), local seismicity studies (Gupta, 1992; Chadha *et al.*, 1997; Talwani, 1997; Gahalaut *et al.*, 2004; Shashidhar *et al.*, 2011, 2017; Dixit *et al.*, 2014; Catchings *et al.*, 2015; Rao and Shashidhar, 2016), and airborne light detection and ranging mapping (Arora *et al.*, 2017) have been carried out to map the faults and structural lineaments of the region. These near-surface geophysical and seismological studies, including analyses of seismicity patterns and fault-plane solutions, have primarily imaged structures confined to flood basalt cover and have brought out lineaments trending predominantly northwest–southeast (NW-SE) and north-northeast–south-southwest (NNE–SSW). Whereas, the deeper structure and characteristics of the causative faults remain poorly understood, mainly due to the presence of an approximately 1-km-thick sequence of basaltic lava flows, which attenuates seismic signals and prevent to image subsurface. Borehole core samples indicate that, the flood-basalt pile comprises up to 25 individual flows of

1. CSIR-National Geophysical Research Institute (CSIR-NGRI), Hyderabad, India, https://orcid.org/0000-0003-0553-192X (DS); https://orcid.org/0000-0002-9961-9844 (SG); https://orcid.org/0000-0002-4352-4766 (KM); 2. CSIR-National Institute of Oceanography (CSIR-NIO), Dona Paula, Goa, India

*Corresponding author: shashidhar.ngri@csir.res.in; shashi.geo@gmail.com

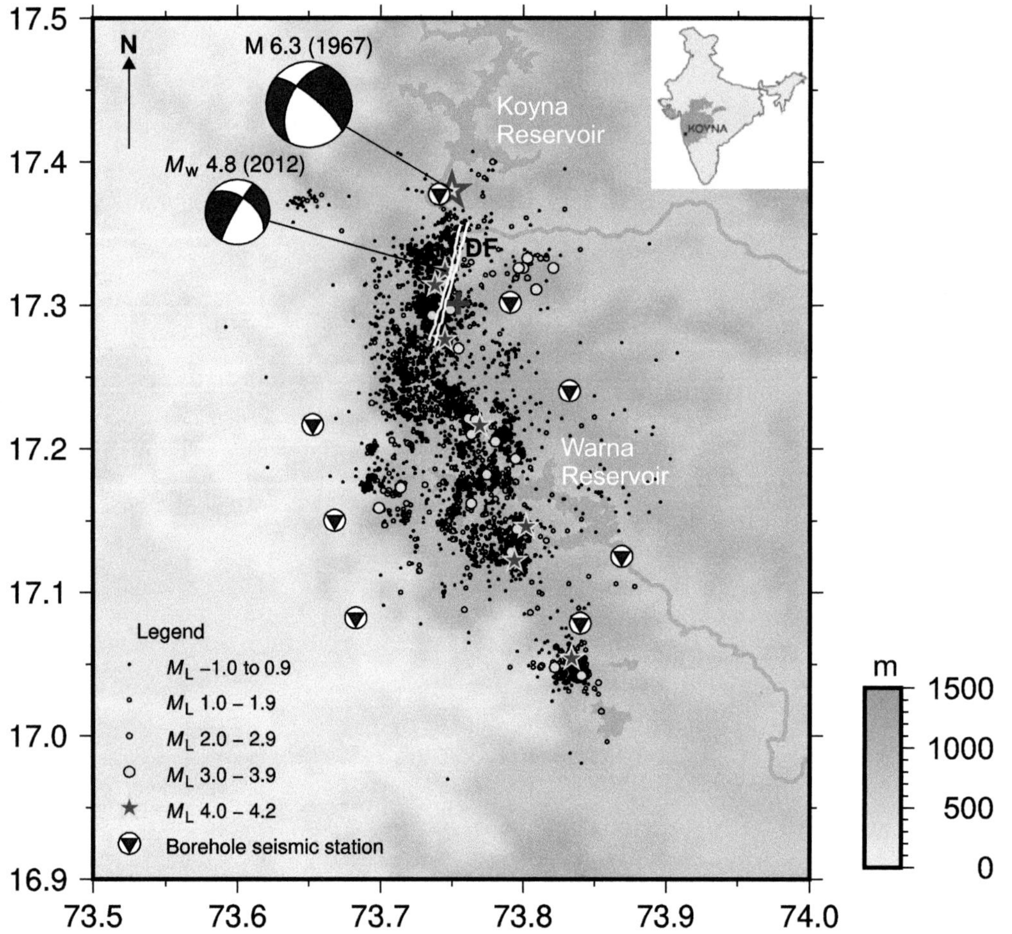

Figure 1. Location of permanent borehole seismic stations (triangles) in the Koyna–Warna region. Seismicity distribution for the period 2016–2024 along with the focal mechanism of the 1967 **M** 6.3 Koyna main earthquake (bigger star) (Chandra, 1976) and the focal mechanism of a well-monitored recent largest earthquake (14 April 2012 M_w 4.8) in the vicinity of Donachiwada fault (DF) (Shashidhar *et al.*, 2013). The lines in white represent the expression of the DF. The "plus" indicates the location of 3 km pilot deep borehole (Goswami *et al.*, 2019). The inset on the top right side indicates the location of the study region situated in the Deccan Volcanic Province (DVP) (shaded portion) of western India. The scale indicates the topography in meters. The color version of this figure is available only in the electronic edition.

varying thickness, each containing both massive and vesicular basalt facies (Gupta *et al.*, 2014).

It is demonstrated that seismic activity in the Koyna region is primarily controlled by a NNE–SSW-trending Donachiwada fault, hereafter referred as DF, which is the main causative structure responsible for the 1967 (**M** 6.3) earthquake. The detailed focal mechanism analysis of a well monitored recent M_w 4.8 earthquake indicating the steep dipping nature of DF (Shashidhar *et al.*, 2013) (Fig. 1). The surface rupture zone produced during the 1967 earthquake corresponds to the DF (GSI, 1968). The region has also experienced several earthquakes of magnitude ~5, most of which are associated with this fault system (Gupta *et al.*, 2017). Recent field investigations by Misra *et al.* (2017), show that the fissures and fractures generated by the 1967 earthquake are still preserved at the surface. Their analysis of core samples from a 1522-m-deep borehole at Rasati, drilled into the granitic basement beneath the Deccan basalts, confirms that these surface fissures extend to significant depths. In spite of many seismological studies in the Koyna region, yet, the subsurface image of this fault is not mapped to its seismogenic depths, to understand its role in Koyna seismicity.

Earlier, few tomographic studies were conducted in the Koyna–Warna region. Rai *et al.* (1999) investigated the crust and uppermost mantle velocity structure. Srinagesh *et al.* (2000) identified relatively high-*P*-wave velocity anomalies in both the upper and lower crust using teleseismic *P*-wave travel times. More recently, Dixit *et al.* (2014) and Catchings *et al.* (2015) developed 3D velocity models for areas near the central Warna reservoir. However, these tomographic studies also did not report the detailed structure of the DF, this could be because of (1) objective of their studies and thus choice of earthquakes and methodology, (2) use of seismic stations, which were deployed on the attenuating and heterogeneous basalt surface, which influenced the arrival-time measurements.

Therefore, in this study we conduct a 3D seismic tomography of the Koyna region to image the sub-basalt seismic structure of the DF, using high-quality borehole seismic data. This approach offers new insight into the geometry and physical properties of this active intraplate fault system and enhances our understanding of the ongoing RTS in the Koyna region.

Data

To monitor seismic activity in the Koyna region, Council of Scientific and Industrial Research (CSIR)–National Geophysical Research Institute (CSIR-NGRI) has deployed eight borehole seismometers at depths ranging from 981 to 1522 m within the granitic basement underlying the Deccan basalts (Fig. 1). Short-period Sunfull borehole seismometers

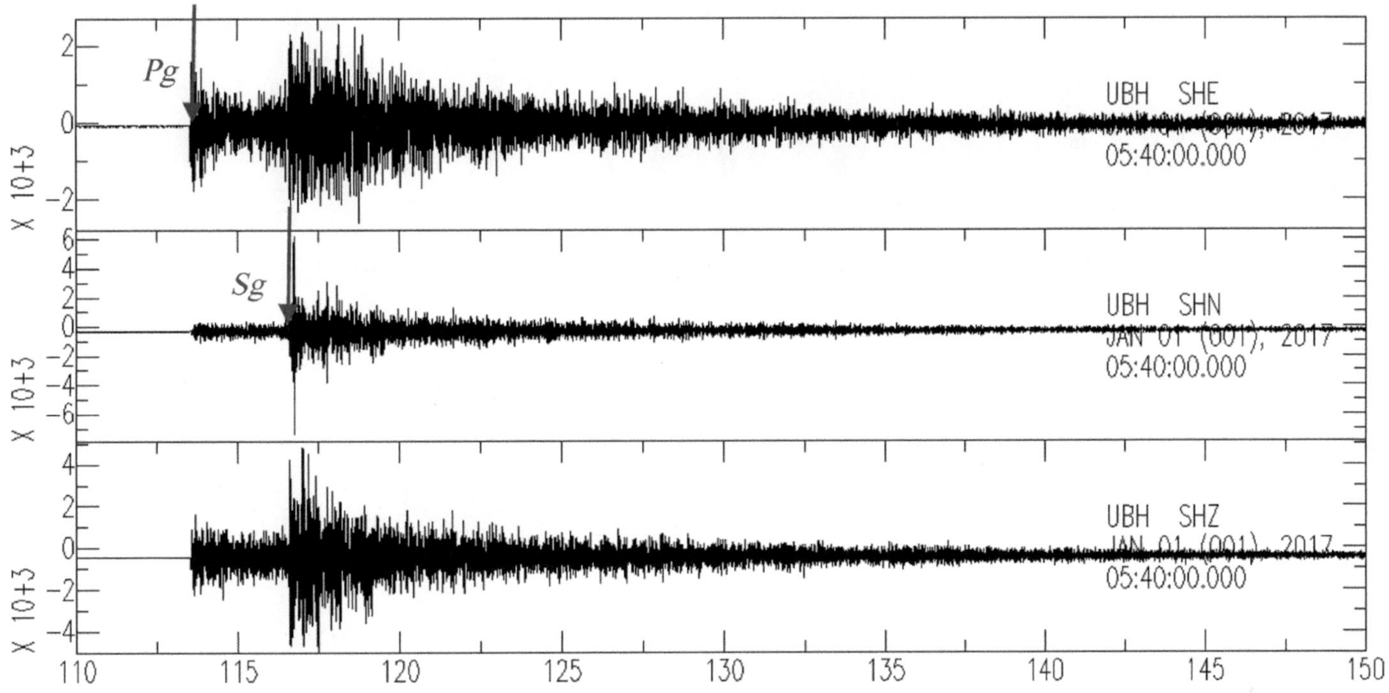

Figure 2. Example of three-component waveforms of an earthquake of magnitude 1.7 that occurred on 1 January 2017 and recorded at UBH borehole seismic station, *P* and *S* phases picked on the waveforms are also shown. The color version of this figure is available only in the electronic edition.

of natural frequency of 4.5 Hz, were connected to REFTEK RT-130 digitizers, which utilize Global Positioning System for accurate time synchronization. The continuous seismic data were recorded at a sampling rate of 250 samples per second. Details of experiment and data recording are provided in Shashidhar *et al.* (2016, 2020). An example seismogram of an M_L 1.7 earthquake recorded by a borehole station is shown in Figure 2. Earthquake locations were determined from the data acquired by these borehole seismic stations and using the HYPOCENTRE algorithm implemented in the SEISAN seismic analysis software package (Lienert *et al.*, 1986; Lienert and Havskov, 1995). The magnitude–frequency distribution, errors in the root mean square (RMS) and the hypocentral locations of earthquakes are shown in Figure 3.

For this study, we utilized 5325 local earthquakes with magnitudes ranging from M_L 0.5 to 4.2 and recorded by eight borehole seismometers between 2016 and 2024 (Fig. 1). Each earthquake used in this study has at least three clear *P*-wave arrivals and three clear *S*-wave arrivals. This resulted in 21,632 *Pg* and 21,500 *Sg* arrival times for the tomographic inversion.

3D Local Earthquake Tomography

To conduct the tomography, we define a model space covering about 40×30 km^2 area bounded by 17.00°–17.40° N and 73.60°–73.90° E, and extending from 0 to 15 km depth, with the grid centered at 17.200° N and 73.750° E. A total of 5325 earthquakes were used in a simultaneous inversion for 3D *P*-wave velocity (V_P), V_P/V_S, and hypocenter locations using the damped, iterative, least-squares algorithm SIMULPS2000 (Thurber and Eberhart-Phillips, 1999). The 1D crustal velocity model derived using the VELEST approach by Shashidhar *et al.* (2011) with an average V_P/V_S value of 1.71 was used as the initial velocity model for the tomography. The seismic ray-path geometry indicates sufficient spatial and depth coverage for the study region (Fig. 4).

To suppress unrealistically large perturbations in V_P and V_P/V_S, damping was applied. Optimal damping values were selected following the empirical procedure of Eberhart-Phillips (1986), in which trade-off curves between data variance and model variance were evaluated using single-step inversions with damping values between 5 and 200 (Fig. 5). Final damping parameters of 15 for *P* phases and 17 for *S* phases were adopted.

Several tomographic tests with varying horizontal spacing and depth layering were performed, after which a grid spacing of 2 km was selected. Vertical nodes were placed at depths of 1, 3.5, 6, 8.5, 12, and 15 km. Following the tomographic inversion, the variance of the arrival-time residuals decreased from 0.007 to 0.003 s^2, and the average RMS residuals improved from 0.08 to 0.03 s, indicating a significant enhancement in the fit of the data.

Quality Assessment

Evaluating the quality of inversion results is a critical component of any tomographic study because it ensures the reliability and interpretability of the derived velocity models. An initial assessment of spatial sampling within the model space can be made using hit count (KHIT) and derivative weight sum (DWS), the latter providing a more representative measure

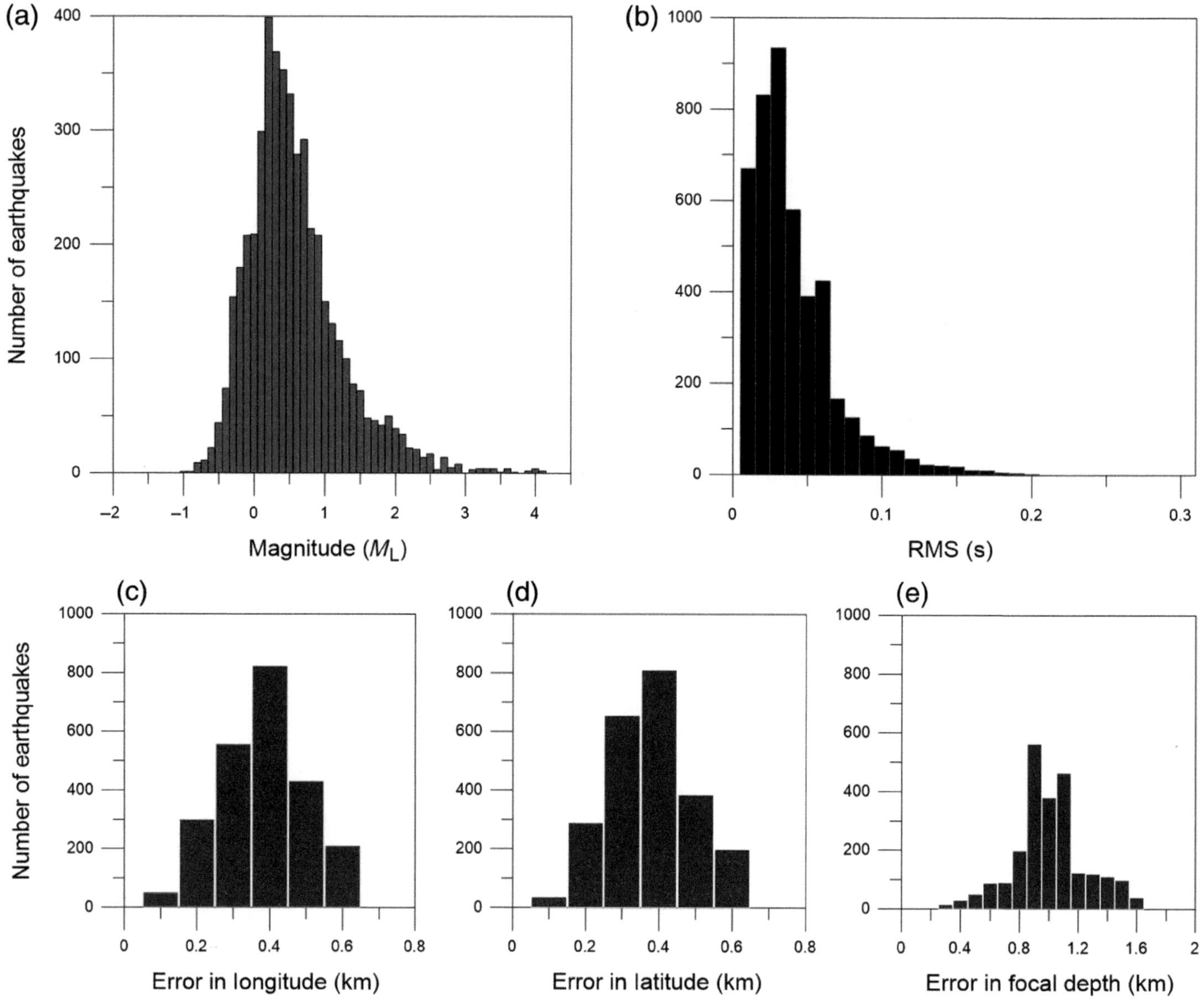

Figure 3. (a) Magnitude–frequency distribution of earthquakes. (b) Travel-time residual root mean square (RMS) error. (c–e) Errors in the estimation of hypocentral parameters of earthquakes using borehole network for the data set of the present study.

of the total ray-path length within each cell. However, these parameters do not fully account for the geometric distribution of ray paths, a limitation better addressed through measures such as the ray-density tensor. The degree of model resolution is more rigorously quantified by the spread value (SV) of the resolution matrix (Toomey and Foulger, 1989; Michelini and McEvilly, 1991), which incorporates all terms of the resolution matrix rather than relying solely on its diagonal elements. A small SV corresponds to a narrow resolving width and therefore indicates a well-resolved parameter.

Figure 6 shows a comparative analysis of resolution diagonal element (RDE) and DWS values for all nodes obtained from the finely gridded velocity model. These diagnostics were used to define an SV threshold beyond which inversion results were considered poorly resolved. Based on empirical evaluation, an SV threshold of 2 was adopted for both V_P and V_P/V_S because nodes exceeding this value consistently exhibited reduced DWS and RDE values, indicating unreliable velocity estimates. Results from the resolution assessments including KHIT, DWS, and SV are presented in Figure 7. After applying the resolution criteria, the main features of the tomographic images, specifically the variations in *P*-wave velocity (V_P) and V_P/V_S within the DF zone region, were interpreted only in the well-resolved portions of the model (Fig. 8).

To further verify the robustness of the derived velocity structures, we performed a synthetic test following the approach of Gupta *et al.* (2022). In this test, phase data were generated from a synthetic velocity model incorporating predefined anomalies. The initial results showed significant variations in both V_P and V_P/V_S, prompting separate tests for each parameter. The synthetic model included a high-V_P

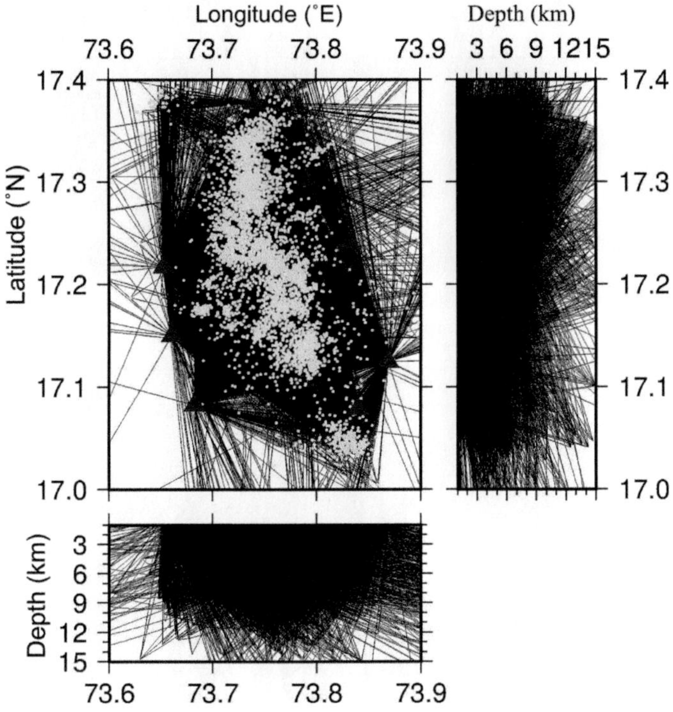

Figure 4. Distribution of seismic ray paths along with the borehole stations (triangles in blue) and earthquakes (yellow dots). The color version of this figure is available only in the electronic edition.

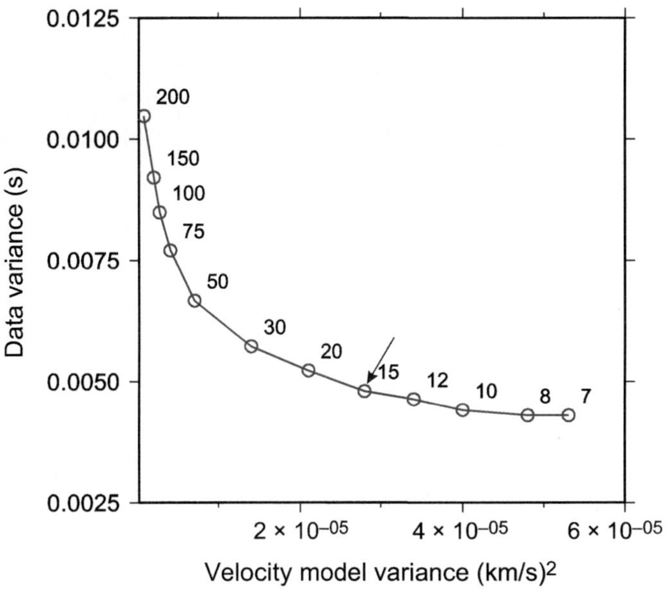

Figure 5. Trade-off curve used to select the optimal damping parameter for V_P (indicated by arrow) to obtain the optimum 3D velocity model. The color version of this figure is available only in the electronic edition.

anomaly (~6.4 km/s) and a low-V_P/V_S(~1.68) anomaly, designed to evaluate the resolving capability and sensitivity of the inversion. Using the same inversion methodology applied to the real dataset, these anomalies were successfully recovered, with minor smearing in both depth and horizontal directions (Fig. 9).

Results and Discussion

3D tomographic images of V_P and V_P/V_S in well-resolved regions (SV < 2) are shown at selected depths in Figure 8a,b, respectively. To correlate with the seismicity in the region, we also projected the earthquakes within 1 km of each depth onto each corresponding depth slices. At ~1 km depth, V_P ranges from 5.2 to 5.6 km/s, whereas V_P/V_S lies between 1.62 and 1.71. At depth ~3.5 km, V_P varies from 5.8 to 6.3 km/s, whereas V_P/V_S is in the same range (1.62–1.71) as observed at 1 km depth. At 6.0 km depth, V_P varies between 6.0 and 6.4 km/s, and V_P/V_S is 1.70–1.74. Further down at 8.5 km depth, the observed V_P is predominantly ~6.4 km/s, though localized regions exhibit slightly lower values (~6.2 km/s). At 8.5 km depth, in general V_P/V_S has larger spread of 1.71–1.78, with larger areas showing $V_P/V_S > 1.74$.

The V_P and V_P/V_S variations, reveal prominent heterogeneity and significant variations in V_P and V_P/V_S across

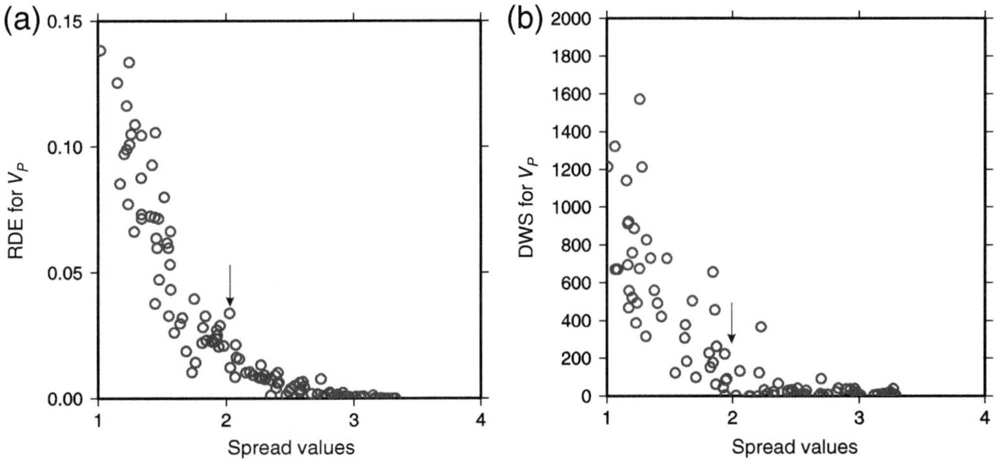

Figure 6. (a) Resolution diagonal element against spread values for V_P. (b) Derivative weight sum against spread values for V_P. In both panels, arrows mark the selected spread value threshold used to distinguish poorly resolved regions in the subsequent velocity models. RDE, resolution diagonal element; DWS, derivative weight sum. The color version of this figure is available only in the electronic edition.

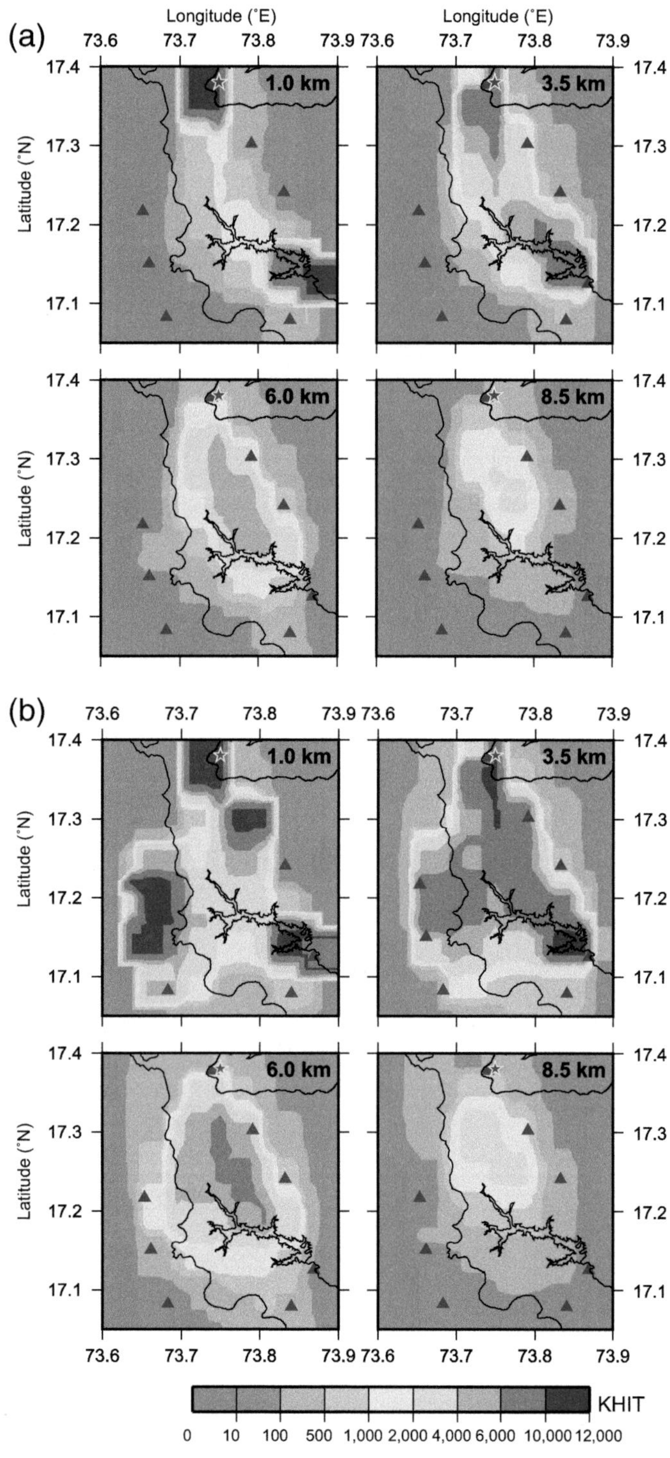

Figure 7. (a,b) Total number of hits per cell (KHIT). (c,d) DWS. (e,f) Spread value (SV) of resolution matrix for V_P and V_P/V_S at different depths respectively. The color version of this figure is available only in the electronic edition. *(Continued)*

the DF (Fig. 8). To better illustrate the structural characteristics of the fault zone, we extract an approximately NW–SE cross-section across the DF and through well-resolved regions of the V_P and V_P/V_S models. The surface trace of the DF is indicated at the top of each V_P and V_P/V_S plots (Fig. 10). These cross

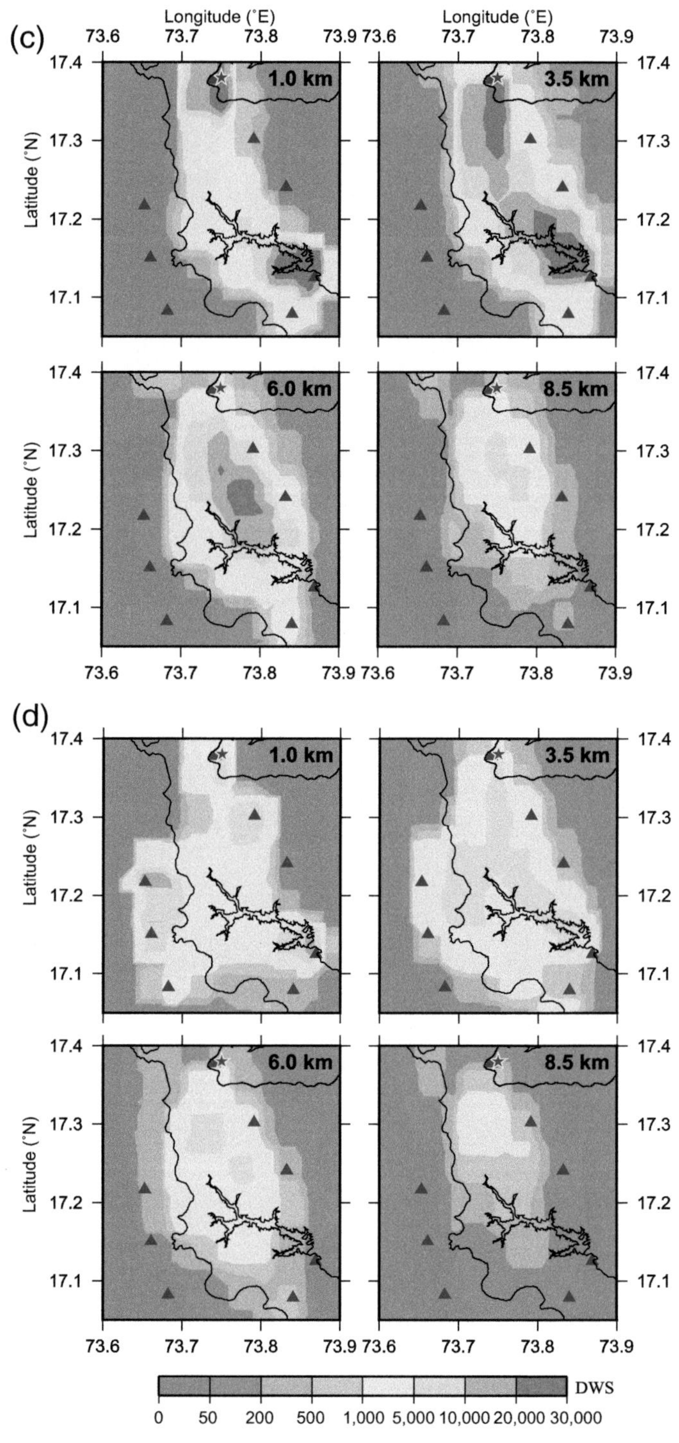

Figure 7. Continued

sections clearly demonstrate variations in both V_P and V_P/V_S across the DF down to a depth of approximately 9 km. Because of limitation of the well-resolved images below 9 km, we are unable to track further depth extent of the DF. In the vicinity of the DF, within the upper 1–4 km, V_P ranges from approximately 5.2 to 5.8 km/s (Fig. 10a), with relatively higher values observed along the eastern flank. The V_P/V_S ratio varies from

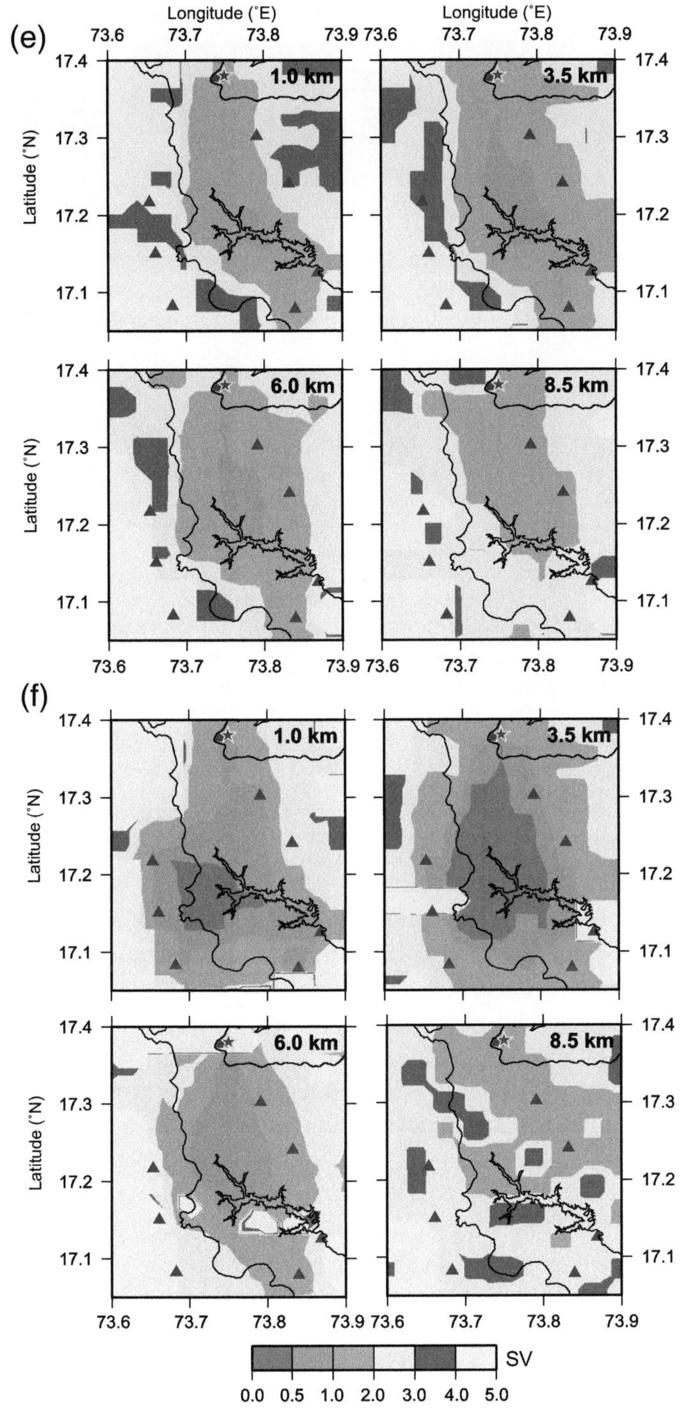

Figure 7. Continued

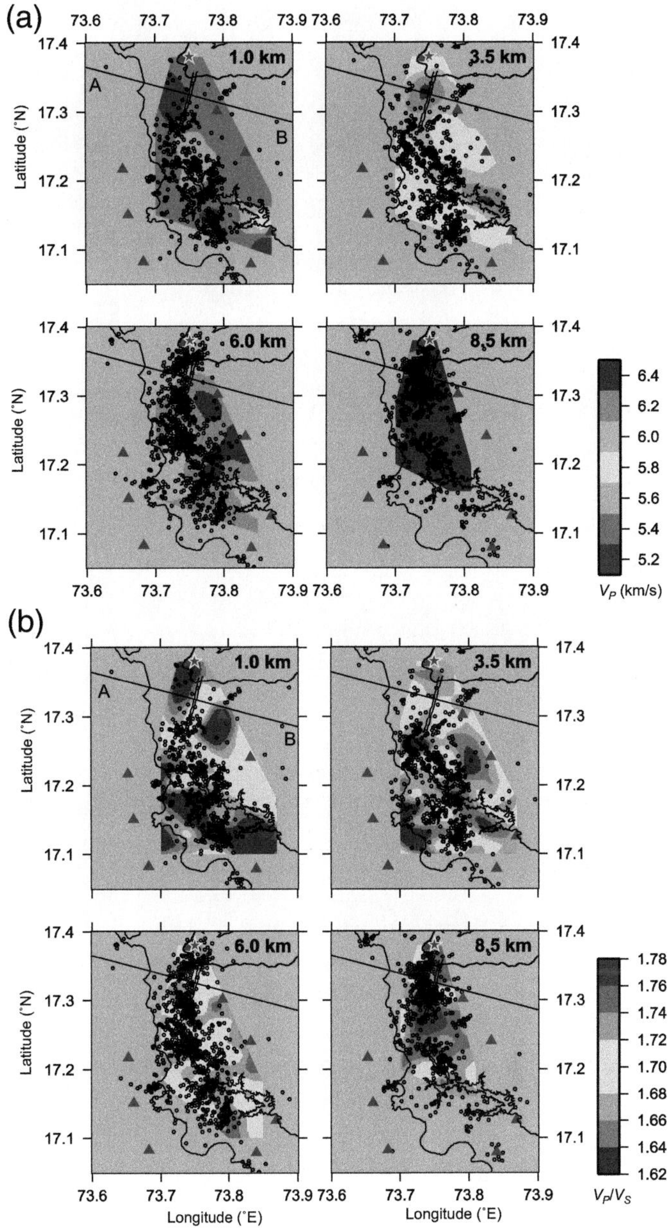

Figure 8. Horizontal depth sections of (a) *P*-wave velocity and (b) V_P/V_S. Locations of earthquakes (small circles) as obtained from tomographic inversion are also plotted. AB indicates the profile across the DF and along which V_P and V_P/V_S are shown. The color version of this figure is available only in the electronic edition.

less than 1.63 on the western flank to greater than 1.65 on the eastern flank (Fig. 10b). No significant seismicity is detected at these depths along the cross section. At depths of 4–10 km, V_P values are below 6.2 km/s on the western flank, whereas these exceed 6.2 km/s and reach up to 6.4 km/s on the eastern flank (Fig. 10a). Within this depth range, the V_P/V_S ratio exhibits distinct variation. On the western flank of the DF, values exceed 1.72, reaching a maximum of 1.75, whereas on the eastern flank, values remain below 1.72 and decrease to as low as 1.65. These pronounced variations in V_P and V_P/V_S persist to depths of approximately 9 km, highlighting strong lateral and vertical heterogeneity within the upper crust along the DF in the Koyna seismic zone. Interestingly, significant microseismicity is concentrated in the western flank of the DF at depths of 6–10 km, whereas the eastern flank exhibits lesser seismicity at this level.

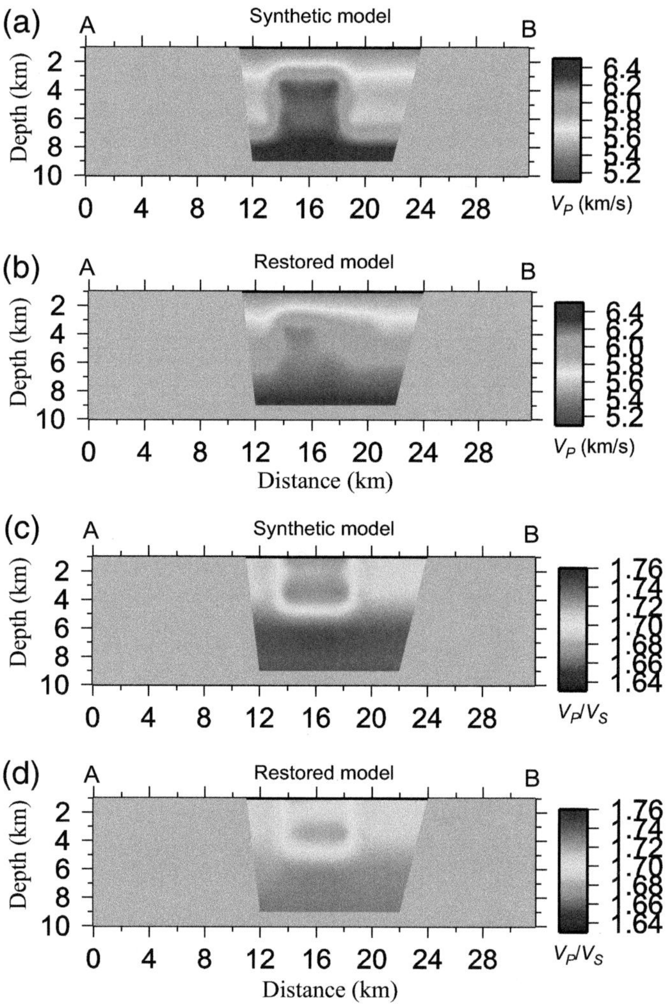

Figure 9. Synthetic and restored models for V_P and V_P/V_S. The color version of this figure is available only in the electronic edition.

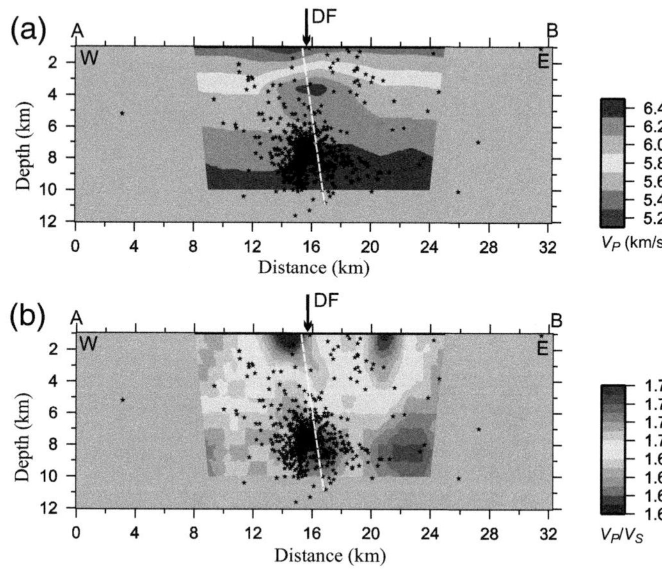

Figure 10. Cross sections across the DF of (a) P-wave velocity and (b) V_P/V_S. Earthquakes within 2 km of the section are shown (stars). The arrow (black) indicates the location of the fault on the profile AB. The dashed line (white) indicates the presence of DF at depths. The color version of this figure is available only in the electronic edition.

The V_P/V_S is directly related to Poisson's ratio, and is a key diagnostic parameter for constraining the petrological properties of crustal rocks (Christensen, 1996). Because of its sensitive to pore-fluid content, V_P/V_S is particularly useful for assessing the role of fluids in earthquake generation. Therefore, taking V_P/V_S in to consideration along with observed V_P and seismicity, we interpret that in the region around DF at shallower depths (<4 km), despite clear signature of variations in V_P and V_P/V_S on its western and eastern sides, the low V_P (<6.0 km/s) and low V_P/V_S (<1.70) (Fig. 10a,b) indicate possible presence of quartz rich felsic rich, such as granite–gneiss. Whereas, at 6–9 km depth, the zone in the western flank of the DF, with lower V_P (<6.2 km/s), higher V_P/V_S (>1.73) and coinciding with the microseismicity could be a fluid saturated zone. Where, due to fluid saturation, pore pressure increases and effective stress reduces to make fault weaker to generate earthquakes (Lees and Nicholson, 1993; Lees, 2007; Gupta *et al.*, 2022).

A pilot scientific borehole, drilled to 3014 m depth in the vicinity of the DF (location shown as plus symbol in Fig. 1) provides direct constraints on the physical and mechanical properties of the basement rocks. Geophysical log data from this borehole indicates the presence of anomalous zones within the granitic basement, interpreted as fault-related damage zones (Goswami *et al.*, 2019). Recent magnetotelluric (MT) investigations along a nearly west–east (W–E) profile close to our tomographic cross section reveals near-vertical conductive and resistive anomalies in the upper crust, and also support our interpretation of fluid-saturated zone in the deeper depths for the Koyna region (Rao *et al.*, 2016; Borah *et al.*, 2023). The observed variation in the V_P and V_P/V_S in this study is consistent with these independent geophysical observations, especially MT and borehole log data. These features likely reflect variations in lithology, fracturing, and fluid content within the brittle upper crust and correlate well with the observed dense seismicity cluster, further supporting the presence of an active, fluid-influenced fault system. Moreover, vertical gravity-gradient and magnetic anomalies along a NW–SE cross section across the DF (Rao *et al.*, 2016) also suggest strong lateral contrasts in density and magnetic susceptibility. Furthermore, the Koyna region forms part of the Western Ghats—a volcanic escarpment associated with intense Quaternary tectonic and magmatic activity (Radhakrishna, 1993) suggesting that deep fluid-rich or altered zones may influence fault behavior here as well.

Similar signatures have also been documented at Aswan RTS site, Egypt (Haggag *et al.*, 2009) in which tomography and geophysical studies reveal strong basement blocks with overlying fractured, fluid-sensitive zones activated by reservoir loading. Collectively, the independent MT, gravity, and magnetic signatures reinforce the interpretation that the DF zone comprises a structurally heterogeneous crustal column reaching up to a depth of ~9 km. To our knowledge, this is the first seismic image of the DF reaching up to a depth of ~9 km. Furthermore, the observed seismicity along the fault is due to presence of fluid within fractured rock, which strongly influences the ongoing intraplate and RTS in the Koyna region.

Conclusion

We presented the first high-resolution 3D local earthquake tomography of the Donachiwada Fault beneath the Deccan basalt in the Koyna region using borehole seismic data. The resulting V_P and V_P/V_S images reveal strong lateral and vertical heterogeneity within the granitic basement, with distinct velocity anomalies across the DF and correlate closely with the seismicity distribution along the DF. Our study suggests that the DF is reaching up to a depth of ~9 km. The seismicity at 5–9 km depth along the DF is related with presence of a fluid-rich or altered zone within the brittle upper crust.

These results provide first subsurface seismic image of the Donachiwada fault and its role in ongoing seismicity in the Koyna region. By resolving the sub-basalt crustal architecture down to ~9 km depth, this study fills a long-standing observational gap left by earlier surface-based seismic investigations. Our findings highlight the importance of borehole instrumentation for imaging fault zone properties in regions obscured by thick volcanic sequences and contribute to a better understanding of intraplate faulting processes within the Indian peninsula.

Data and Resources

The network of short-period borehole seismometers is operated by the Council of Scientific and Industrial Research–National Geophysical Research Institute, Hyderabad, India. Data used in the study can be found at https://rectt.ngri.res.in/data_page/data.out (last accessed January 2026). The authors could not make open data from the year 2020 due to institutional data policy. Figures were made using Generic Mapping Tools (Wessel and Smith, 1998).

Declaration of Competing Interests

The authors acknowledge that there are no conflicts of interest recorded.

Acknowledgments

The authors are thankful to Prakash Kumar, Director, Council of Scientific and Industrial Research–National Geophysical Research Institute (CSIR–NGRI) for his support and encouragement. The authors sincerely acknowledge the invaluable support of colleagues and project staff who contributed to field operations and data processing. The authors are very much grateful to Guest Editor Susan Hough and anonymous reviewer for providing critical and constructive comments to improve the quality of the article. The CSIR–NGRI reference number of the article is NGRI/LIB/2025/Pub-142.

References

Arora, K., R. K. Chadha, Y. Srinu, A. Selles, D. Srinagesh, V. Smirnov, A. Ponomarev, and V. O. Mikhailov (2017). Lineament fabric from airborne LiDAR and its influence on triggered earthquakes in the Koyna–Warna region, western India, *J. Geol. Soc. India* **90,** 670–677.

Borah, U. K., P. K. Patro, K. Raju, K. C. Reddy, N. Babu, and N. P. Rao (2023). Role of fluid on seismicity of an intra-plate earthquake zone in western India: An electrical fingerprint from magnetotelluric study, *Earth Planets Space* **75,** 149, doi: 10.1186/s40623-023-01905-5.

Catchings, R. D., M. M Dixit, R. Goldman, and S. Kumar (2015). Structure of the Koyna-Warna seismic zone, Maharashtra, India: A possible model for large induced earthquakes elsewhere, *J. Geophys. Res.* **120,** 3479–3506, doi: 10.1002/2014JB011695.

Chadha, R. K., H. K. Gupta, H. J. Kumpel, P. Mandal, A. N. Rao, N. Kumar, I. Radhakrishna, B. K. Rastogi, I. P. Raju, C. S. P. Sarma, *et al.* (1997). Delineation of active faults, nucleation process and pore pressure measurements at Koyna (India), seismicity associated with mines, reservoirs and fluid injections, *Pure Appl. Geophys.* **151,** 551–562, doi: 10.1007/978-3-0348-8814-1_11.

Chandra, U. (1976). Focal mechanism of the Koyna, India earthquake of 1967, December 10, *Geophys. J. Int.* **46,** 247–251.

Christensen, N. I. (1996). Poisson's ratio and crustal seismology, *J. Geophys. Res.* **101,** 3139–3156.

Dixit, M. M., S. Kumar, R. D. Catchings, K. Suman, D. Sarkar, and M. K. Sen (2014). Seismicity, faulting, and structure of the Koyna–Warna seismic region, western India, from local earthquake tomography and hypocenter locations, *J. Geophys. Res.* **119,** 6372–6398, doi: 10.1002/2014JB010950.

Eberhart-Phillips, D. (1986). Three-dimensional velocity structure in northern California coast ranges from inversion of local earthquakes, *Bull. Seismol. Soc. Am.* **76,** 1025–1052.

Gahalaut, V. K., Kalpna, and S. K. Singh (2004). Fault interaction and earthquake triggering in the Koyna–Warna region, India, *Geophys. Res. Lett.* **31,** L11614, doi: 10.1029/2004GL019818.

GSI (1968). A geological report on the Koyna earthquake of 11th December, 1967, Satara District, Maharashtra State, *Report Submitted by Officers of the Geological Survey of India*, 273 pp.

Gupta, H. K. (1992). *Reservoir Induced Earthquakes*, Elsevier Publications, New York.

Gupta, H. K. (1993). The deadly Latur earthquake, *Science* **262,** 1666–1667.

Gupta, H. K., N. P. Rao, B. K. Rastogi, and D. Sarkar (2001). The deadliest intraplate earthquake, *Science* **291,** 2101–2102.

Gupta, H. K., K. Arora, N. P. Rao, S. Roy, V. M. Tiwari, P. K. Patro, H. V. S. Satyanarayana, D. Shashidhar, C. R. Mahato, K. N. S. S. S. Srinivas, *et al.* (2017). *Investigations of Continued Reservoir Triggered Seismicity at Koyna, India*, Geological Society of London Special Publications, Vol. 445, 151–188.

Gupta, H. K., N. P. Rao, S. Roy, K. Arora, V. M. Tiwari, B. P. K. Patro, H. V. S. Satyanarayana, D. Shashidhar, K. Mallika, V. V. Akkiraju, *et al.* (2014). Investigations related to scientific deep drilling to study reservoir-triggered earthquakes at Koyna, India, *Int. J. Earth Sci.* **104,** no. 6, 1511–1522.

Gupta, S., P. Mahesh, N. Kanna, K. Sivaram, and A. Paul (2022). 3-D seismic velocity structure of the Kumaun-Garhwal (Central) Himalaya: Insight into the Main Himalayan Thrust and earthquake occurrence, *Geophys. J. Int.* **229,** no. 1, 138–149, doi: 10.1093/gji/ggab449.

Goswami, D., S. Roy, and V. V. Akkiraju (2019). Delineation of damage zones from 3 km downhole geophysical logs in the Koyna seismogenic zone, Western India, *J. Geophys. Res.* doi: 10.1029/2018JB017257.

Haggag, H. M., P. M. Bhattacharya, S. Kamal, and J. R. Kayal (2009). Seismicity and 3D velocity structure in the Aswan Reservoir Lake area, Egypt, *Tectonophysics* **476,** 450–459.

Kaila, K. L., P. R. Reddy, M. M. Dixit, and M. A. Lazarenko (1981). Deep crustal structure at Koyna, Maharashtra indicated by deep seismic soundings, *J. Geol. Soc. India* **22,** 1–16.

Kailasam, L. N., and B. G. K. Murthy (1971). A short note on gravity and seismic investigations in the Koyna area, *Indian J. Power River Val. Develop.*, 27–30.

Langston, C. A. (1981). Source inversion of seismic waveforms: The Koyna, India, earthquakes of 13 September 1967, *Bull. Seismol. Soc. Am.* **71,** 1–24.

Lees, J. M. (2007). Seismic tomography of magmatic systems, *J. Volcanol. Geoth. Res.* **167,** nos. 1/4, 37–56, doi: 10.1016/j.jvolgeores.2007.06.008.

Lees, J. M., and C. Nicholson (1993) Three-dimensional tomography of the 1992 southern California sequence: Constraints on dynamic earthquake ruptures? *Geology* **21,** no. 5, 385–480.

Lienert, B. R., and J. Havskov (1995). A computer program for locating earthquakes both locally and globally, *Seismol. Res. Lett.* **66,** no. 5, 26–36.

Lienert, B. R., E. Berg, and L. N. Frazer (1986). Hypocenter: An earthquake location method using centered, scaled, and adaptively damped least squares, *Bull. Seismol. Soc. Am.* **76,** no. 3, 771–783.

Michelini, A., and T. V. McEvilly (1991). Seismological studies at Parkfield: I. Simultaneous inversion for velocity structure and hypocenters using cubic B-splines parameterization, *Bull. Seismol. Soc. Am.* **81,** 524–552.

Misra, S., S. Roy, V. Bartakke, G. Athavale, and H. K. Gupta (2017) Fissures and fractures in the Koyna seismogenic zone, western India, *J. Geol. Soc. India* **90,** 131–137.

Negi, J. G., P. K. Agarwal, and K. N. N. Rao (1983). Three dimensional model of the Koyna area of Maharashtra state (India) based on the spectral analysis of aeromagnetic data, *Geophysics* **48,** no. 7, 964–974, doi: 10.1190/1.1441522.

Radhakrishna, B. P. (1993). Neogene uplift and geomorphic rejuvenation of the Indian peninsula, *Curr. Sci.* **64,** 787–793.

Rai, S. S., S. K. Singh, P. V. S. Sarma, S. Rajagopal, D. Srinagesh, K. N. S. Reddy, K. S. Prakasam, and Y. Satyanarayana (1999). What triggers Koyna earthquakes? Preliminary results from seismic tomography digital array, *Proc. Indian Acad. Sci.* **108,** 1–14.

Rao, N.P., and D. Shashidhar (2016). Periodic variation of stress field in the Koyna–Warna reservoir triggered seismicity zone inferred from focal mechanism studies, *Tectonophysics* **679,** 29–40.

Rao, N. P., T. Tsukuda, M. Kosuga, S. C. Bhatia, and G. Suresh (2002). Deep lower crustal earthquakes in central India: Inferences from analysis of regional broadband data of the 1997 May 21, Jabalpur earthquake, *Geophys. J. Int.* **148,** 132–138.

Rao, N. P., S. Roy, H. V. S. Satyanarayana, V. M. Tiwari, K. Arora, B. P. K. Patro, A. Babu, T. Seshunarayana, D. Shashidhar, K. Mallika, *et al.* (2016) Geophysical and seismological studies in Koyna-Warna region, *Technical Rept. No. NGRI-2016-SEISM-907.*

Rastogi, B. K., R. K. Chadha, C. S. P. Sarma, P. Mandal, H. V. S. Satyanarayana, I. P. Raju, N. Kumar, C. Satyamurthy, and A. Nageswara Rao (1997). Seismicity at Warna reservoir (near Koyna) through 1995, *Bull. Seismol. Soc. Am.* **87,** no. 6, 1484–1494.

Shashidhar, D., K. Mallika, C. R. Mahato, B. S. Maity, and H. V. S. Satyanarayana (2017). Recent seismicity patterns and microearthquake activity on an active intraplate fault system at Koyna–Warna, western India, *J. Geol. Soc. India* **90,** no. 6, 798–801.

Shashidhar, D., N. P. Rao, and H. K. Gupta (2011). Waveform inversion of broadband data of local earthquakes in Koyna–Warna region, western India, *Geophys. J. Int.* **185,** no. 1, 292–304.

Shashidhar, D., N. P. Rao, D. Srinagesh, H. K. Gupta, H. V. S. Satyanarayana, G. Suresh, and A. Satish (2013). The 14 April 2012 Koyna earthquake of M_w 4.8: Insights into active tectonics of the Koyna region, *J. Seismol.* **17,** no. 4, 345–1353.

Shashidhar, D., I. V. Rodriguez, K. Mallika, D. Kühn, M. Wilks, H. V. S. Satyanarayana, and V. Oye (2020). Relative locations of an earthquake sequence recorded during June 2017 on the Koyna-Warna borehole seismic network of western India, *Bull. Seismol. Soc. Am.* **110,** 3130–3138.

Shashidhar, D., H. V. S. Satyanaryana, C. R. Mahato, K. Mallika, N. P. Rao, and H. K. Gupta (2016). Borehole network at Koyna India, *Seismol. Res. Lett.* **87,** no. 3, 661–667.

Srinagesh, D., S. Singh, K. S. Reddy, K. S. Prakasam, and S. S. Rai (2000). Evidence for high velocity in Koyna seismic zone from *P*-wave teleseismic imaging, *Geophys. Res. Lett.* **27,** 2737–2740.

Talwani, P. (1997). Seismotectonics of the Koyna–Warna area, India, *Pure Appl. Geophys.* **150,** 511–550.

Thurber, C., and D. Eberhart-Phillips (1999). Local earthquake tomography with flexible gridding, *Comput. Geosci.* **25,** 809–818.

Toomey, D. R., and G. R. Foulger (1989). Tomographic inversion of local earthquake data from the Hengill-Grensdalur central volcano complex, Iceland, *J. Geophys. Res.* **94,** 17,497–17,510.

Wessel, P., and W. H. Smith (1998). New, improved version of Generic Mapping Tools released, *Eos Trans. AGU* **79,** no. 47, 579.

Manuscript received 18 September 2025
Published online 23 January 2026

Fault Intersections Control the Extremely Shallow 2020 M_w 5.1 Sparta, North Carolina, Earthquake Sequence

Kaiteng Huang*[1], Sidao Ni[1,2], Jun Xie[2], Xiaohui He[3], and Wangwang Gu[2]

Abstract

Some earthquakes in stable continental regions are very shallow, and their seismogenesis mechanism remains unresolved. Here, we focus on the extremely shallow 2020 M_w 5.1 Sparta earthquake sequence in North Carolina. Joint analysis of short-period surface waves from shallow earthquakes and ambient noise-derived empirical Green's functions reveals a low-velocity zone with strong velocity gradient in the top 3 km of the Sparta-1D velocity model. Furthermore, we validate focal depths in the aftershock catalog with the Rayleigh-wave amplitude spectra method, confirming ~90% of aftershocks occurred within the shallow low-velocity zone, with event rates decreasing at depths at which shear velocity increases. Geological field studies imply that this feature originates from a shallow weak layer containing intersecting fracture network. The velocity structure, aftershock distribution, and mapped near-surface structures in the Sparta region suggest that fault intersections within a shallow weak layer may provide mechanically favorable conditions for extremely shallow earthquakes.

Cite this article as Huang, K., S. Ni, J. Xie, X. He, and W. Gu (2026). Fault Intersections Control the Extremely Shallow 2020 M_w 5.1 Sparta, North Carolina, Earthquake Sequence, *Seismol. Res. Lett.* **97**, 907–917, doi: 10.1785/0220250313.

Supplemental Material

Introduction

Although seismic activity is generally low in stable continental regions (SCRs), destructive earthquakes have occasionally occurred, leading to significant losses and casualties (Gupta, 1993; Greene *et al.*, 2000; Walters *et al.*, 2018). Some of the SCRs are characterized by extremely shallow depths (Klose and Seeber, 2007; Dawson *et al.*, 2008; Ritz *et al.*, 2020; Di *et al.*, 2023; Neves *et al.*, 2024), less than the typical ~10 km observed in active continental regions (ACRs; Scholz, 1998). The shallow depths result in strong ground shaking (Pekeris and Lifson, 1957; Luo *et al.*, 2010). Combined with the weak attenuation of seismic energy with distance in old and cold continental lithosphere, these factors often contribute to more severe surface damage, widespread felt reports, and pronounced societal impacts (Boadu and Long, 1996; Figueiredo *et al.*, 2022; Hilfiker and Ebel, 2025).

In contrast to earthquakes in ACRs, which have well-understood geodynamic driving processes and typically rupture along simple fault systems, the origin of shallow seismicity in SCRs remains an old scientific conundrum. Prior research has proposed various mechanisms for the energy sources of earthquakes in SCRs, including erosion-induced horizontal tension (Mazzotti *et al.*, 2023) and surface process–induced stress perturbations (Steer *et al.*, 2014). Growing observational evidence from extremely shallow earthquakes shows rupture may occur within shallow brittle crust where deformation is accommodated by minor faults or discontinuous fracture zones (Andrews, 1989; Schulte and Mooney, 2005; Martín-González *et al.*, 2023). A subset of well-documented cases indicates that these shallow brittle zones may include linked or intersecting fracture networks that localize strain and promote rupture nucleation (Wetmiller *et al.*, 1984; Seeber and Dawers, 1989; Ritz *et al.*, 2020; Di *et al.*, 2023). Within such settings, the fault intersection hypothesis proposed by Talwani (1988) provides a potential framework for understanding nucleation in structurally intricate intraplate environments, supported by numerical, laboratory, and field observations (Jing and Stephansson, 1990; Ellis, 1991; Gangopadhyay and Talwani, 2005; Talwani, 2017). Complementary observational studies also indicate that structurally irregular fault–fracture networks may promote strain localization, larger stress drops, and fault locking rather than stable aseismic creep (Chu *et al.*, 2021; Malehmir *et al.*, 2022; Lee *et al.*, 2024).

Previous studies on earthquakes in SCRs have primarily focused on surface fault morphology and have identified a clear

1. School of Earth and Space Sciences, University of Science and Technology of China, Hefei, China, https://orcid.org/0009-0005-4175-4946 (KH); https://orcid.org/0000-0003-2988-4850 (SN); 2. State Key Laboratory of Precision Geodesy, Innovation Academy for Precision Measurement Science and Technology, Chinese Academy of Sciences, Wuhan, China, https://orcid.org/0000-0003-1402-4428 (JX); https://orcid.org/0000-0002-2577-8041 (WG); 3. Guangdong Provincial Key Laboratory of Geodynamics and Geohazards, School of Earth Sciences and Engineering, Sun Yat-Sen University, Zhuhai, China, https://orcid.org/0000-0001-8609-4105 (XH)

*Corresponding author: huangkt@mail.ustc.edu.cn

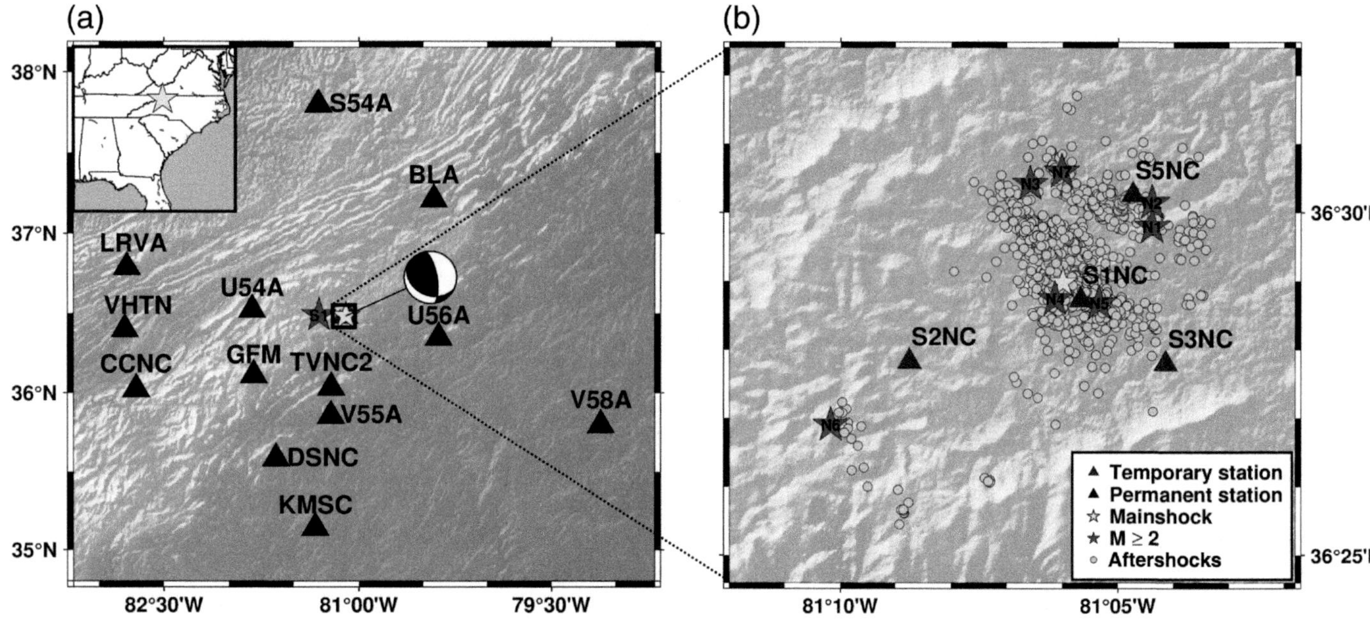

Figure 1. Seismic network and distribution of seismic events in the Sparta region. (a) Map of the Sparta mainshock location and stations used in the study. The inset at the upper left shows Sparta mainshock region within the regional map of the Eastern United States. (b) Zoom-in view of the black box in panel (a), emphasizing the spatial distribution of aftershocks. Symbols used in both panels are consistent: the black triangles indicate permanent seismic stations, the blue triangles represent temporary stations, the yellow star marks the mainshock, the red stars denote earthquakes with $M_w \geq 2.0$ (event names labeled in Table S1), and the ivory-colored circles show the aftershock distribution. The color version of this figure is available only in the electronic edition.

correlation between fault geometry complexity and earthquake behavior (Seeber and Dawers, 1989; Talwani, 1999; King *et al.*, 2019; Yang *et al.*, 2021). However, other studies have shown that fault structures can vary with depth (Ben-Zion *et al.*, 2003; Wei *et al.*, 2011), highlighting the importance of analyzing depth-dependent fault geometry in better understanding earthquake mechanisms. The fault intersection model for extremely shallow earthquake nucleation lacks support from reliable geophysical models because of the difficulty of constructing high-resolution imaging of shallow velocity structures with the sparse seismic network in SCRs. Velocity model provides information of characterizing fault geometry, whereas aftershock locations offer essential constraints for validating fault geometries. Short-period (~1 s) surface waves serve as key data for shallow crustal imaging in SCRs. On 9 August 2020, an M_w 5.1 earthquake with 1.3 km centroid depth ruptured the uppermost crust near the town of Sparta, North Carolina (Fig. 1a; Neves *et al.*, 2024). One day after the mainshock, the Center for Earthquake Research and Information deployed five temporary seismic stations near the epicentral area (four operational; Fig. 1b; Horton *et al.*, 2021), providing a new opportunity for aftershock relocation and subsurface imaging in the mainshock region. Combining deep learning and matched filter earthquake detection, Neves *et al.* (2024) precisely located 1761 earthquakes (Fig. 1b) and found that ~90% of them were concentrated within a diffuse shallow damage zone (<3 km), which they described as "similar to a positive half-flower structure." These findings emphasize the need for improved resolution in shallow velocity models to better constrain both the source mechanisms of extremely shallow earthquakes and the fault-network geometries.

In this study, we aim to characterize the shallow velocity structure of the Sparta mainshock region. We construct a 1D velocity model (Sparta-1D) by jointly inverting short-period surface waves' group velocity dispersion curves from the extremely shallow earthquakes and empirical Green's functions (EGFs) derived from ambient noise. Based on the Sparta-1D model, we further constraint seven aftershocks' depths with $M_w \geq 2.0$ using the Rayleigh-wave amplitude spectra method and assess the accuracy of the earthquake catalog from Neves *et al.* (2024). Finally, by integrating feathers of the velocity model, aftershock distribution, and geological studies, we discuss the relationship between fault distribution and extremely shallow earthquakes, offering new clues for understanding earthquake generation mechanisms in SCRs.

Sparta-1D Velocity Model Inversion

We first extract Rayleigh-wave phase and group velocities in the study area using the ambient noise cross-correlation method. The data comprise 90 days of continuous vertical-component recordings from five permanent and four temporary seismic stations deployed within a 100 km radius of the Sparta mainshock (Fig. 2a). The waveform data are segmented into 2 hr time windows and subjected to standard preprocessing procedures, following the basic processing scheme similar to Yao *et al.* (2006)

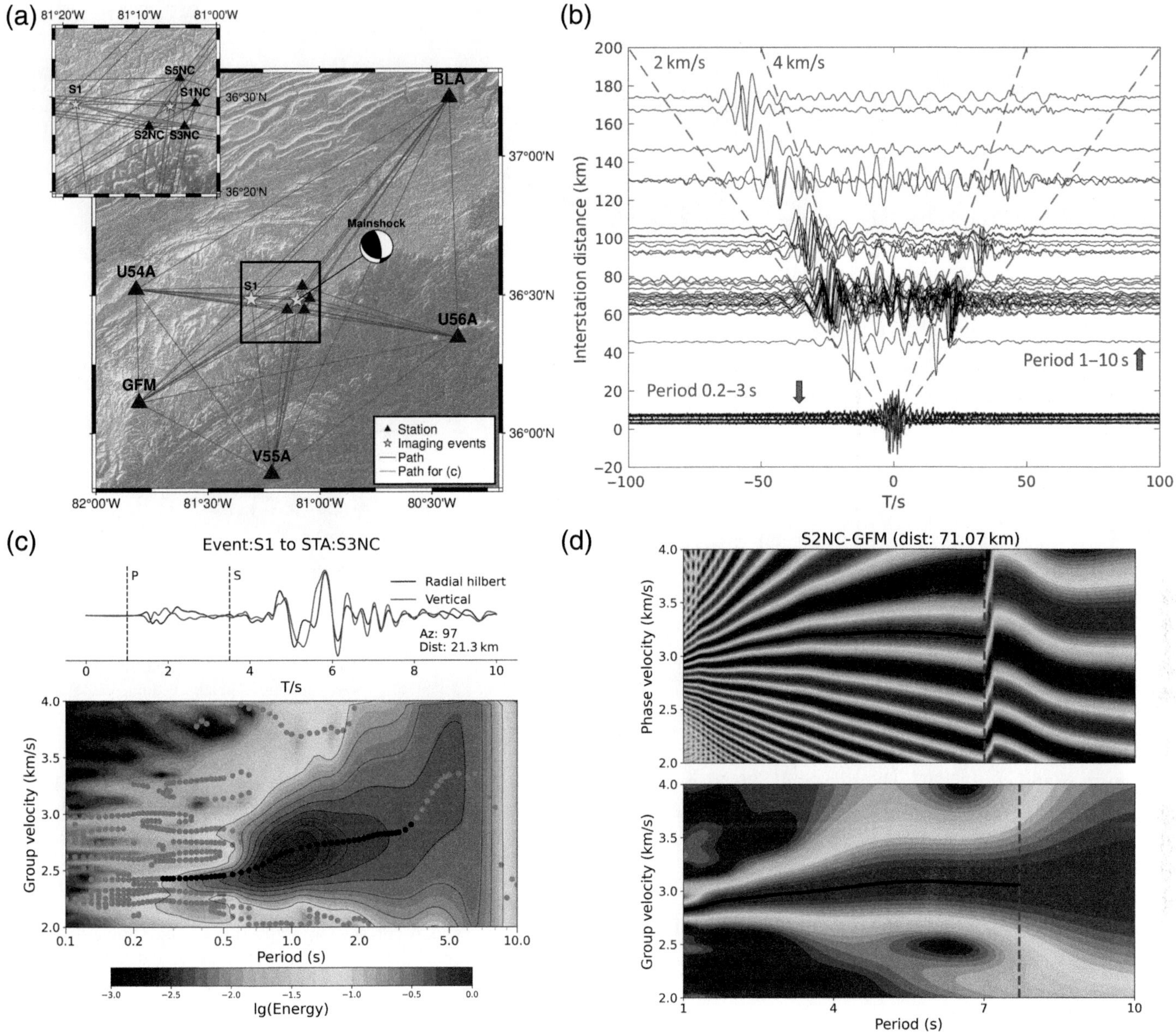

Figure 2. Dispersion curve extraction procedure. (a) Interstation paths and source to station paths used in the analysis. The inset at the upper left shows a zoomed-in view of the black box in the main map. The blue triangles indicate seismic stations, and the yellow stars mark earthquakes for imaging. The red lines represent interstation and source to station paths. The green line highlights the path from event S1 to station S3NC. (b) Plot of noise cross-correlation functions (NCFs) against interstation distance for all selected station pairs in panel (a). The black lines show interstation distance > 20 km filtered over a period range of 1–10 s. The blue lines correspond to interstation distance < 20 km filtered over 0.2–3 s. (c) Example of Rayleigh-wave signals from event S1 recorded at station S3NC, along with the corresponding group velocity dispersion curve for the green path shown in panel (a). The upper panel compares the vertical and radial components, band-pass filtered between 0.3 and 5 Hz. The vertical-component Rayleigh wave (red line) overlaps the radial component after a 90° phase shifting (blue line), indicating a clear Rayleigh-wave signal. (d) Example of Rayleigh-wave dispersion curves extracted from the empirical Green's function (EGF) between stations S2NC and GFM. The upper panel shows phase velocity, and the lower panel shows group velocity, both extracted by image transformation technique (Yao *et al.*, 2006). The vertical red line marks the wavelength corresponding to three times the interstation distance. Results from additional station pairs with interstation distance < 20 km are shown in Figure S1. The color version of this figure is available only in the electronic edition.

and Bensen *et al.* (2007). Cross correlations for all station pairs are computed and stacked to obtain noise cross-correlation functions (NCFs; Fig. 2b). For each station pair, the positive- and the negative-time lags of the NCFs are stacked to form the symmetric component NCFs, which are then converted into the EGFs by correcting for the $\pi/2$ phase shift by Hilbert

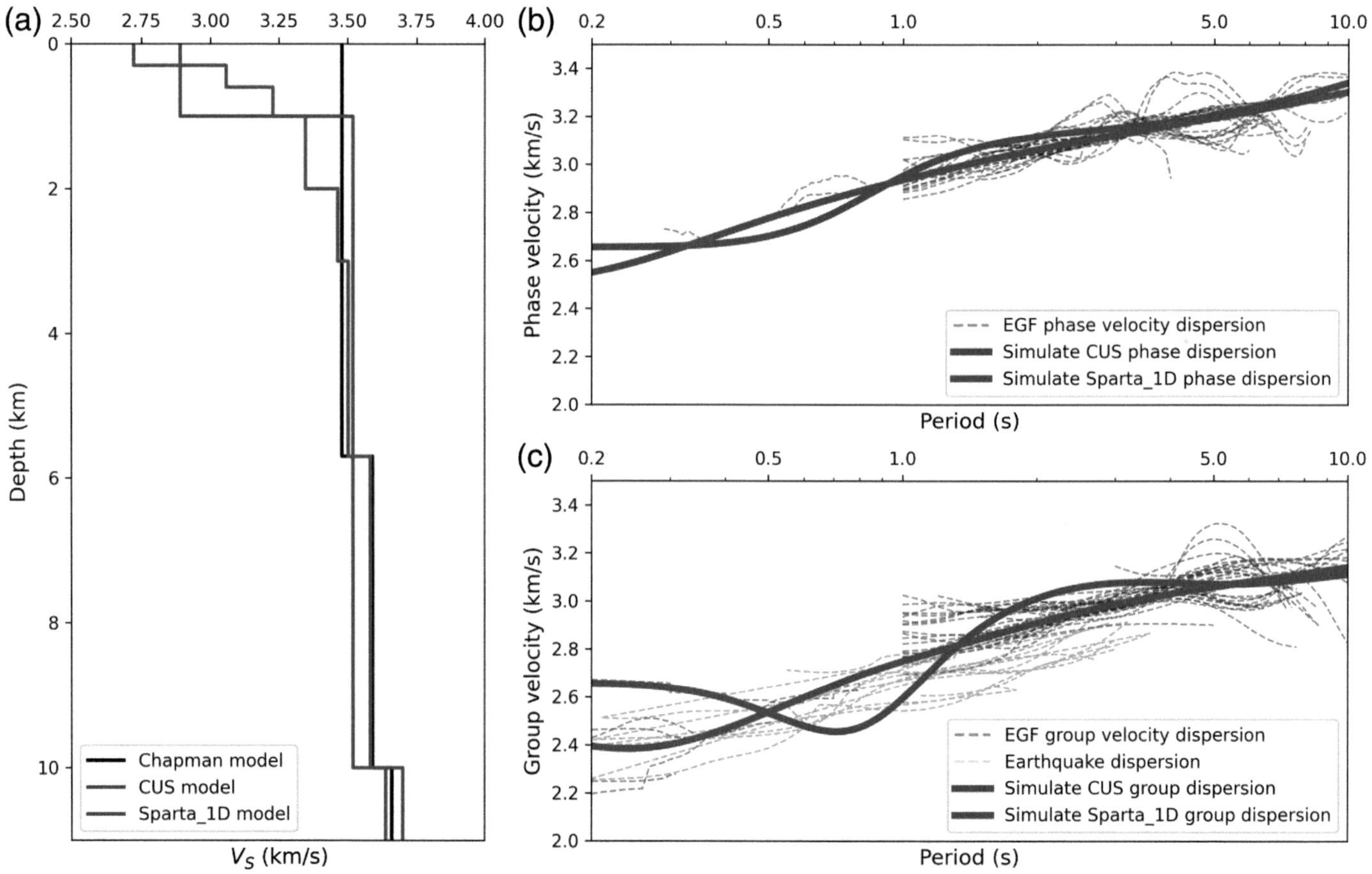

Figure 3. Shear-wave velocity model inversion results. (a) The solid black line represents the initial model from Chapman (2013), the solid red line indicated the final inverted Sparta-1D, and the solid green line shows the Central United States (CUS) model from Herrmann *et al.* (2011). Detail of the Sparta-1D model is listed in Table S1. (b) Observed and theoretical phase velocity dispersion curves. The dashed blue line shows the Rayleigh-wave phase velocity dispersion curve extracted from EGFs, and the solid green and red lines correspond to theoretical simulation based on the CUS model and Sparta-1D model, respectively. (c) Observed and theoretical group velocity dispersion curves. Orange represents observations from earthquake Rayleigh-wave, and the dashed blue lines show the EGFs derived from ambient noise. The solid green and red lines correspond to theoretical group velocity dispersion curves from the CUS model and the Sparta-1D model, respectively. The color version of this figure is available only in the electronic edition.

transform (Yang *et al.*, 2007; Harmon *et al.*, 2008). We select dispersion data over different period bands based on interstation distance. For interstation distances <20 km, we estimate dispersion over 0.2–3 s; for distances ≥20 km, we use 1–10 s. To ensure the reliability of measurements, we impose a minimum-interstation distance of three wavelengths and only retain those with a signal-to-noise ratio (SNR) of the EGF >10. We then apply the image-transformation technique developed by Yao *et al.* (2004, 2005,2006) to extract phase and group velocity dispersion curves by mapping cross-correlation amplitudes into a 2D period–velocity image and picking the dispersion curve along the coherent high-amplitude ridge. Figure 2d presents an example of the dispersion curve of S2NC-GFM station pair, and results for shorter distance interstation pairs are shown in Figure S1, available in the supplemental material to this article. Because of the strict quality control, we retain five group velocity and two phase velocity dispersion curve measurements with incomplete 0.2–3 s coverage (Fig. 3).

Ambient noise EGFs in our study area only provide limited reliable data at short period (≤1 s) from four temporary stations (Fig. 3). Therefore, we incorporate short-period Rayleigh-wave group velocity dispersion from two extremely shallow local earthquakes. These events generate surface waves that develop over short-propagation distances while retaining high-frequency 0.2–3.0 s energy (Fig. 2c; Pekeris and Lifson, 1957; Båth, 1975; Luo *et al.*, 2010; He *et al.*, 2019). Previous studies have mainly used earthquake surface waves to extract long-period dispersion (Yao *et al.*, 2006; Fadel *et al.*, 2020), and extracting dispersion curves from earthquake-generated surface waves requires accounting for source effects (Kanamori and Stewart, 1976; Levshin *et al.*, 1999). Therefore, we conducted synthetic tests to assess the effects of source depth, focal mechanism, and epicentral distance on Rayleigh-wave group velocity measurements (Text S1 and Fig. S2). The results show that short-period dispersion from extremely shallow sources remains more robust and reliable for constraining the shallow velocity structure. Consequently, we include vertical Rayleigh-

TABLE 1
Earthquake Information for the Events Used in This Study

ID	Origin Time (UTC) (yyyy/mm/dd hh:mm:ss)	Longitude (°)	Latitude (°)	Catalog Depth (km)	Magnitude	FDOPM (km)
Mainshock	*2020/08/09 12:07:37*	*–81. 0999*	*36.4830*	*3.067*	*5.14*	–
S1	*2020/10/01 19:53:14*	*–81.3051*	*36.4869*	*4.2 ± 1.6*	*2.63*	–
N1	2020/08/10 08:43:06	–81.0731	36.4966	0.582	2.15	1.47 ± 0.29
N2	2020/08/10 11:10:03	–81.0731	36.5024	0.0	2.21	1.39 ± 0.22
N3	2020/08/11 10:50:17	–81.1098	36.5070	0.042	2.22	0.93 ± 0.33
N4	2020/08/11 20:45:27	–81.1023	36.4790	1.422	2.87	1.57 ± 0.16
N5	2020/09/23 03:01:45	–81.0890	36.4779	1.003	2.19	1.26 ± 0.20
N6	2020/10/13 12:51:07	–81.1696	36.4483	6.908	2.40	8.18 ± 0.60
N7	2020/10/25 03:08:32	–81.1003	36.5099	0.0	2.81	0.58 ± 0.41

Events in italics texts are those that contributed short-period group velocity dispersion curves for velocity model inversion. Other events are $M_w > 2$ earthquakes used to validate depth estimates in the Sparta earthquake catalog (SEC)-Neves catalog. The mainshock location is provided by Neves *et al.* (2024), and the location of event S1 is from the U.S. Geological Survey (USGS). FDOPM denotes the focal depth with optimal period method (He *et al.*, 2023).

wave group velocity dispersion curves from the M_w 5.1 mainshock to five permanent stations and from an M_D 2.6 shallow aftershock (event S1) to both permanent and temporary stations (Fig. 2c and Table 1), with group velocities in the period range 0.2–3 s extracted using the multiple-filter technique (Herrmann, 2013).

Sensitivity kernel analysis confirms that the dispersion measurement in the 0.2–10 s period range is highly sensitive to shallow layer structures (Fig. S3). We use a linear inversion method to jointly invert short-period Rayleigh-wave group velocity dispersion curves from the extremely shallow earthquakes and EGFs derived from ambient noise (Herrmann, 2013). Our initial model is the Chapman (2013) Central Virginia 1D crustal model (Chapman model), developed ~300 km northeast of Sparta. For regional comparison, we also refer the Central U.S. 1D model (CUS model) of Herrmann *et al.* (2011). The initial model is the Chapman model originally developed for the Virginia region, ~300 km from Sparta (Chapman, 2013). The inversion results (named as Sparta-1D) suggest that no significant sedimentary layers are present in the shallow crust beneath the Sparta mainshock region. Although the velocity structure below 3 km aligns with the Chapman and CUS models (Herrmann *et al.*, 2011; Chapman, 2013), the Sparta-1D model provides greater resolution in the upper crust, revealing a V_S (shear velocity) increase from 2.7 km/s at the surface to 3.6 km/s at 3 km depth. As shown in Figure 3b,c, synthetic dispersion curves generated from both the Sparta-1D and CUS model fit the observations well at periods >1 s. However, the Sparta-1D model performs better in fitting the short period (0.2–1.0 s) from both earthquake dispersion curves and EGFs dispersion curves. Considering short-period data were included in the inversion, the Sparta-1D model significantly improves the resolution of the shallow velocity structure and demonstrates better overall fit.

Focal Depth Reliability Assessment

We find a clear correspondence between the low V_S region above 3 km in the Sparta-1D velocity model and the depth distribution of seismicity (Fig. S4). Using deep learning and matched filter techniques, Neves *et al.* (2024) constructed the Sparta earthquake catalog (SEC-Neves) by relocating foreshocks and aftershocks using differential travel times based on the Chapman model. Their results show that 90% of the events in the SEC-Neves catalog occurred at depths shallower than 3 km. Deeper than 1 km, the number of events gradually decreases, showing a negative correlation with the low-velocity and strong velocity-gradient region in the Sparta-1D model. Because of the dense configuration of the temporary seismic array, the SEC-Neves study achieved high accuracy in determining earthquake depths. However, because of discrepancies among velocity models within the top 3 km, we further evaluated the reliability of the source depths by applying the focal depth with optimal period method (FDOPM; He *et al.*, 2023). Specifically, we selected seven $M_w >$ 2.0 aftershocks from SEC-Neves for this analysis (Table 1) using the Sparta-1D model as the velocity model constraint.

FDOPM constrains earthquake source depths by leveraging the near-linear relationship between the optimal period (OP) of Rayleigh-wave amplitude spectra and focal depth. We illustrate the application of this method using event N4 as an example (Fig. 4). Seventeen stations within 200 km of the mainshock are initially considered. Among them, 12 stations with clearly developed surface waves and high SNR are selected for analysis. The amplitude spectra are extracted using the *do_mft* program in the Computer Programs in Seismology (CPS) package (Herrmann, 2013; Fig. 4a,b). To reduce the influence of observational uncertainties, we fit a parabola function to five points near the maxima of each station's amplitude spectrum to measure the OP. The OP systematically increases with epicentral distance

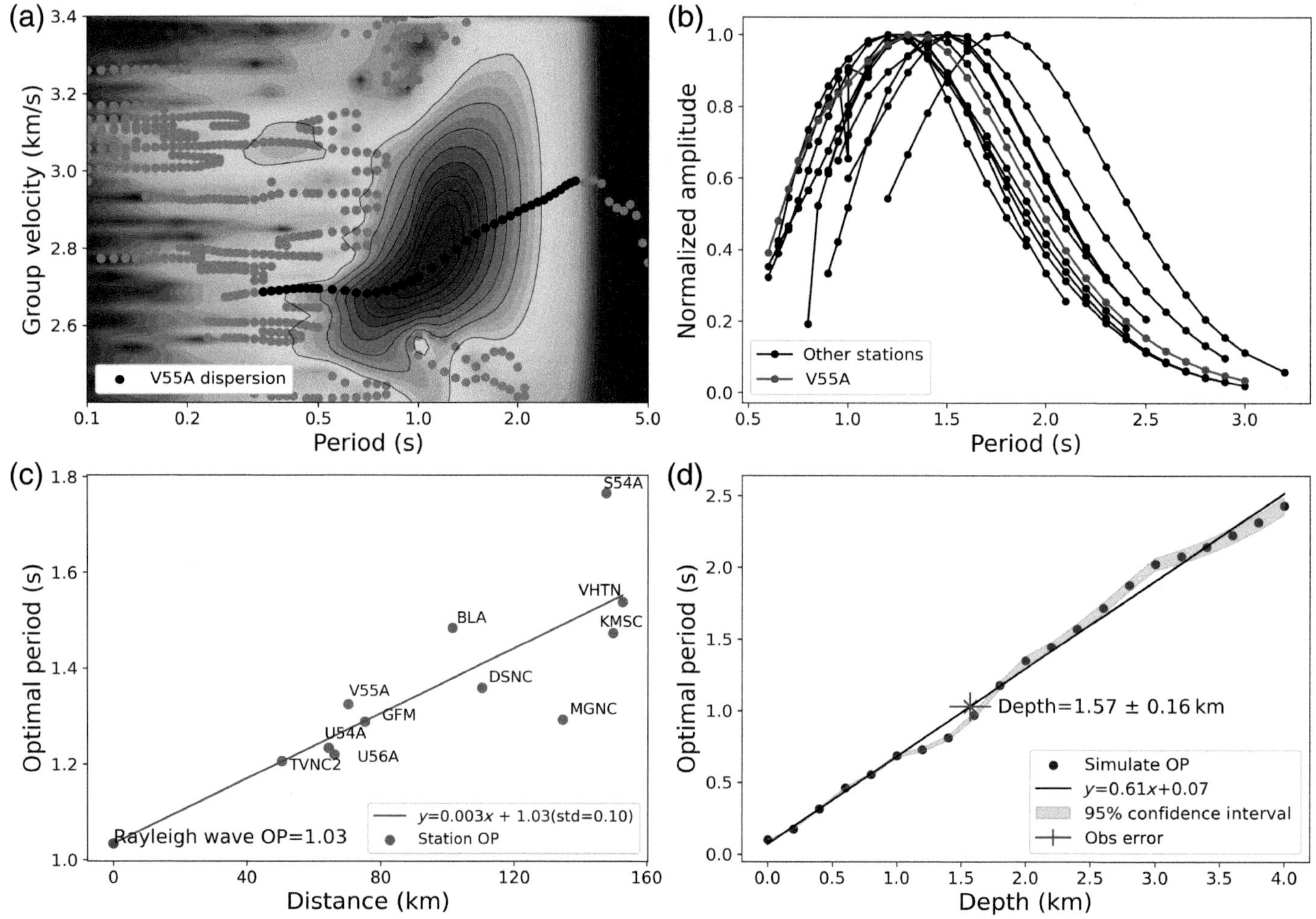

because of either scattering or substantial attenuation in the subsurface, which is strongly influenced by Q factor. Assuming isotropic attenuation, we applied a linear fit to the OP versus distance relationship to estimate the observed OP at the source location, yielding a value of 1.03 ± 0.10 s. Finally, to account for source mechanism uncertainty, we perturbed the strike, dip, and rake angles by ±30° and the azimuth by ±15° based on the focal mechanism catalog of Neves *et al.* (2024), which was derived from P-wave first-motion polarities and S/P amplitude ratios. This gave a 95% confidence range for the theoretical OP. Projecting the observed OP onto the OP–depth relationship yielded a focal depth of 1.57 ± 0.16 km (Fig. 4d).

The results show that the FDOPM depth estimation error is within 0.6 km. Compared with the SEC-Neves catalog, the two datasets of depth estimates exhibit an average deviation of 773 m (Table 1). Considering the discrepancies among shallow velocity model within the top 3 km, this offset is deemed acceptable, confirming the overall reliability of the source depths in the SEC-Neves catalog. Although the SEC-Neves catalog reports three $M_w > 2$ events at depth shallower than 500 m, FDOPM results suggest focal depth closer to 1 km. The discrepancy is potentially explained by topographic influences. Previous studies have shown FDOPM is relatively insensitive to source parameters such as azimuth errors and focal mechanism, with estimated errors <10% (He *et al.*, 2023). Although the method has not been systematically tested in regions with strong topographic relief, we conducted forward simulations using a 3D velocity model of the Sparta region constructed in Specfem3D (Text S2 and Figs. S5–S7), which confirms the theoretical applicability of FDOPM in the study area.

Figure 4. Rayleigh-wave optimal period (OP) and focal depth of event N4. (a) Group dispersion image of vertical-component Rayleigh wave recorded at station V55A. (b) Normalized fundamental model of Rayleigh-wave amplitude spectra observation at selected stations. The red curve is the amplitude spectra extracted from dispersion black dots at V55A in panel (a). (c) Variation of OPs against epicentral distance. The blue dots represent OPs derived from each station and the green dot marks the estimated OP at epicenter. The red line indicates the linear fitting. (d) Relationship between theoretical OP and source depth. The blue dots denote theoretical average OPs calculated at different depths. The shaded gray region indicates the 95% confidence interval obtained from perturbing focal mechanisms and azimuths. The red cross represents the observed OP and its uncertainty projected onto the corresponding depth. The color version of this figure is available only in the electronic edition.

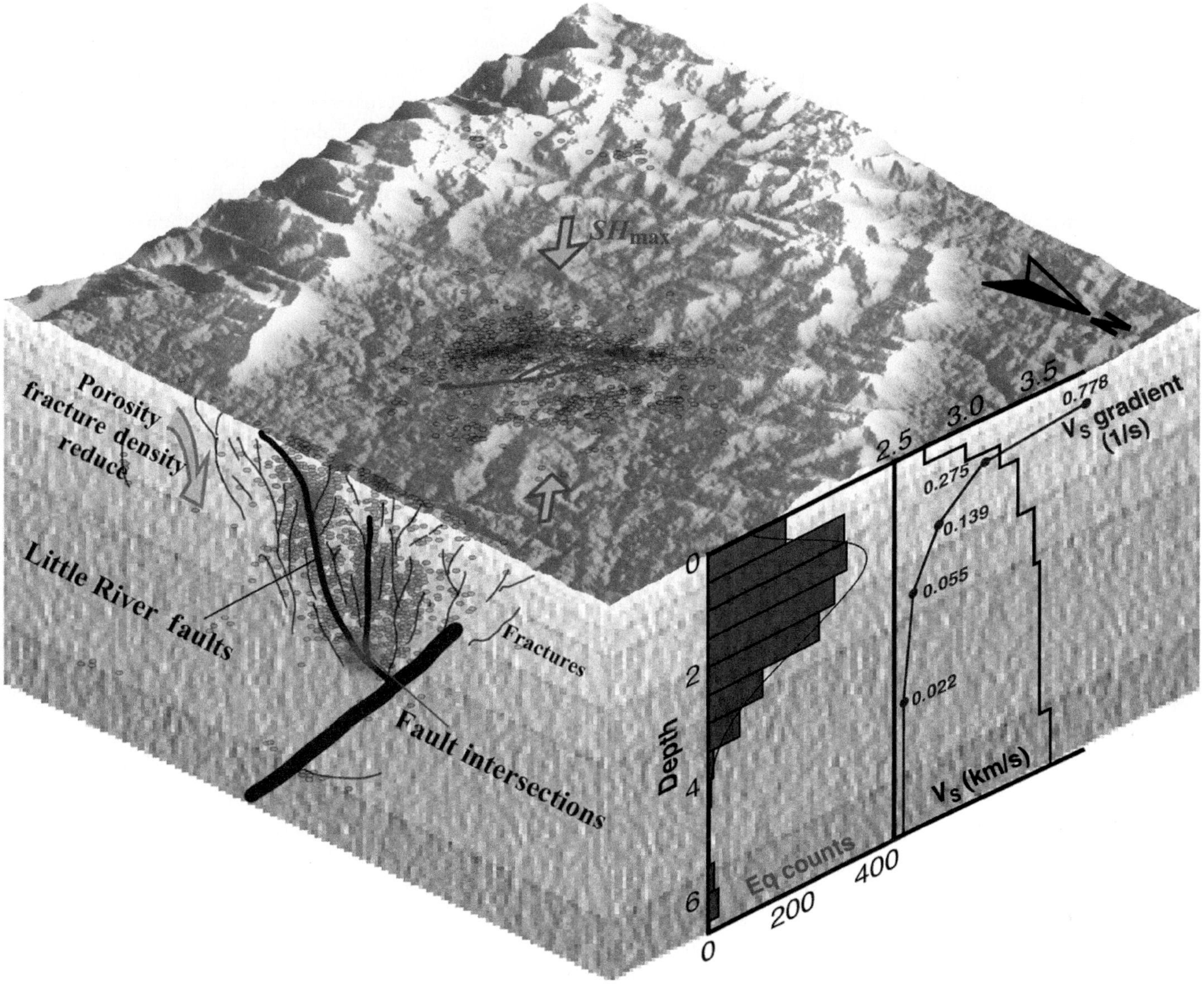

Figure 5. Schematic illustration of earthquake distribution and fault network in the Sparta region. The brown circles represent earthquakes from the Sparta Earthquake catalog (SEC)-Neves catalog, and the red line marks the surface rupture mapped by Merschat and Carter (2023). The left-facing panel of the diagram shows the Little River fault and associated fault-related fractures (black lines) within the shallow weak layer, including intersecting fracture sets inferred from geological mapping. The right-facing panel shows a histogram of aftershock counts versus depth (left) and the Sparta-1D shear-wave velocity profile (black line) and its vertical gradient (blue line) overlaid on a crystalline basement. The color version of this figure is available only in the electronic edition.

Discussion and Conclusions

With the SEC-Neves catalog depth validated, we find that ~90% of the events in the 2020 Sparta sequence occur within the upper ~3 km, coincident with a low-V_S layer that exhibits a strong vertical-velocity gradient in the Sparta-1D model (Fig. 5 and Fig. S4). Deeper than ~1 km, the number of events decreases, and at depths > 3 km, V_S converges toward the CUS and Chapman models while aftershocks become rare. These observations may be attributed to a shallow relatively weak layer associated with a complex system of faults and fractures, where fault intersections exert a key mechanical control on the concentration of seismicity.

Located within the tectonically stable continental interior, the Sparta region shows a largely consistent shallow crustal composition since the late Triassic, dominated by crystalline basement rocks and with little lithologic variation in the upper few kilometers (Hatcher Jr., 2010; Lynn, 2023; Merschat and Carter, 2023; Mahan *et al.*, 2025). This is consistent with a U.S. Geological Survey (USGS) hydrologic well (363002081072701) drilled to ~90 m and completed in mica gneiss, indicating that bulk lithology is unlikely to be the primary control on the shallow low V_S. Within this context, laboratory measurements of intrinsic V_S velocities for representative crystalline rocks are consistent with our V_S estimates, but the strong near-surface velocity gradient is more plausibly attributed to changes in porosity and microcracking with depth (Meltzer and Christensen, 2001; Elbra *et al.*, 2011; Ji *et al.*, 2013; Chawre, 2018). With increasing depth, rising effective confining pressure progressively reduces fracture density and crack porosity, causing V_S to increase toward the intrinsic matrix values of crystalline rocks over the first few kilometers (Price, 1966, 1974; Haxby and Turcotte, 1976; Mavko *et al.*, 2009). This depth-dependent structure produces a strong V_S gradient confined to the upper few kilometers, with the crust below ~3 km behaving more intact and stable and the shallow layer acting as a relatively weakness where strain and rupture preferentially localize.

Geological observations around the Little River fault, the rupturing fault of the 2020 M_w 5.1 Sparta mainshock, provide evidence for intersecting brittle structures. Detailed mapping identifies numerous minor brittle structures at the surface and shows that the main fault is embedded in a narrow structurally controlled corridor of saprolite-hosted brittle deformation that developed before the 2020 rupture (Figueiredo *et al.*, 2022; Lynn, 2023; Merschat and Carter, 2023; Mahan *et al.*, 2025). These structures have formed within an intraplate setting where deformation proceeds at low but finite-strain rates on the order of 10^{-9}–10^{-10} yr^{-1}, yet the upper crust is inferred to be close to its long-term yield strength (Anderson, 1986; Townend and Zoback, 2000; Gan and Prescott, 2001; Zoback *et al.*, 2007). Under such conditions, relatively small stress perturbations, such as those from differential erosion or erosion-driven stress changes, can trigger brittle failure aligned with the prevailing intraplate stress field (Klose and Seeber, 2007; Steer *et al.*, 2014; Calais *et al.*, 2016; Lacombe *et al.*, 2023; Mazzotti *et al.*, 2023), especially in the mechanically weak, mica-rich gneiss (Collettini *et al.*, 2019). Paleostress inversion further reveals a transition from Paleozoic northwest–southeast shortening to a present-day northeast–southwest to east-northeast–west-southwest compression (Lynn, 2023; Merschat and Carter, 2023), producing a shallow brittle system in which fracture sets locally intersect.

This fracture system forms the mechanical environment within which shallow seismicity is focused. In the upper ~3 km, cracks lower the effective strength and provide numerous weak planes for failure. Within such a compliant layer, fault intersections act as localized stress amplifiers (Talwani, 1988, 2008, 2017; Andrews, 1989; Jing and Stephansson, 1990; Ellis, 1991), further enhancing failure potential on subsets of these weak planes. In Sparta, this mechanism likely operated where fault intersections coincide with the shallow weak layer. Coulomb stress changes from the mainshock can preferentially drive failure on pre-existing weak planes within the shallow secondary faults and intersecting fractures rather than intact structures at depth. With increasing depth, confining pressure progressively closes cracks, so both the number of available weak planes and their sensitivity to a given Coulomb stress perturbation are reduced, leading to a decrease in aftershock density below ~3 km. The discrepancy between the observed number of events above 0.5 km and the velocity model can be attributed to two possible factors. First, elevation variability may induce errors in earthquake depth estimates in the top 0.5 km in SEC-Neves catalog, and no events are reliably resolved at depths shallower than 0.5 km using FDPOM. Second, the very low confining pressure near the surface limits the effective normal stress on fault planes, reducing their frictional strength and making brittle failure more difficult.

Similar to many shallow intraplate earthquakes, the Sparta mainshock reactivated a pre-existing shallow brittle splay (the Little River fault) and nucleated near the intersection of two main fault strands (Figueiredo *et al.*, 2022; Lynn, 2023; Merschat and Carter, 2023; Pollitz, 2023; Neves *et al.*, 2024). Similar patterns have been documented for other SCRs earthquakes for which rupture initiates within a shallow brittle layer on inherited faults, including the 2020 Baicheng earthquake (Di *et al.*, 2023), the 2019 Le Teil earthquake (Causse *et al.*, 2021; De Novellis *et al.*, 2020; Ritz *et al.*, 2020), and the 1968 Meckering and 2018 Lake Muir earthquakes in Australia (Langston, 1987; Clark *et al.*, 2020), among others (Walters *et al.*, 2018; Son *et al.*, 2020; Malehmir *et al.*, 2022). Our results further suggest that in Sparta, this fault-intersection-controlled reactivation extends beyond the mainshock, with the aftershock sequence also confined to the weak layer associated with fault intersection, highlighting a potential framework for understanding earthquake generation in SCRs.

Although previous geological studies have documented fault complexity in SCRs through surface observations, dense seismic arrays are essential for resolving finer-scale subsurface structures. Such high-resolution data would enable more direct assessments of depth-dependent fault geometry and its role in earthquake nucleation. Our study employs a joint inversion of short-period Rayleigh-wave group velocity dispersion curves from very shallow events and ambient noise data recorded by a sparse station network. Although this approach successfully resolves the 1D velocity structure, it remains insufficient for imaging lateral heterogeneities. To better capture the complexity of future very shallow events, rapid deployment of dense temporary seismic arrays is essential not only for accurate picking of *P*- and *S*-wave arrivals but also for enabling more comprehensive analyses of surface waves.

Data and Resources

The seismic data are available at Data Management Center (DMC) of the Incorporated Research Institutions for Seismology (IRIS) data center, including the following seismic networks: ET (no DOI is registered for this network), US (Albuquerque Seismological Laboratory [ASL]/USGS, 1990), and N4 (Albuquerque Seismological Laboratory/USGS, 2013). Hydrologic well information is available from the U.S. Geological Survey (USGS) National Water Information System database database (https://waterdata.usgs.gov/nwis/inventory/?site_no=363002081072701&agency_cd=USGS). The figures are made with Matplotlib (Hunter, 2007) and Generic Mapping Tools (GMT; Wessel *et al.*, 2013). The ambient noise cross correlation and dispersion extraction tools developed by Huajian Yao's group (2006) can be accessed via https://yaolab.ustc.edu.

cn/Cas/list.htm. The Computer Programs in Seismology (Herrmann, 2013) used for 1D velocity model inversion, group velocity and amplitude spectrum extraction, and surface waves sensitivity kernel computation are available at https://www.eas.slu.edu/eqc/ComputerPrograms Seismology/index.html. SPECFEM3D Cartesian (Tromp *et al.*, 2008) and the frequency–wavenumber (*f-k*) method (Zhu and Rivera, 2002), available at https://github.com/geodynamics/specfem3d and https://www.eas.slu.edu/People/LZhu/home.html, respectively, are used to theoretically analyze the influence of topographic versus flat models. All websites were last accessed in January 2026. The supplemental material for this article includes discussions of the effects of the extremely shallow seismic source on Rayleigh-wave group velocity dispersion curves and focal depth with optimal period method (FDOPM) applicability in Sparta region, depth sensitivity kernels for Rayleigh wave calculated based on the Sparta-1D model, comparisons with aftershock distributions, and details of the Sparta-1D velocity model.

Declaration of Competing Interests

The authors acknowledge that there are no conflicts of interest recorded.

Acknowledgments

The authors thank reviewer Nano Seeber and one anonymous reviewer for their constructive comments and suggestions, which significantly improved this article. The authors are grateful to Daoyuan Sun for insightful discussions, and the authors thank Steve Horton for providing the temporary aftershock deployment data through the Incorporated Research Institutions for Seismology Data Management Center (IRIS-DMC). This study is supported by National Natural Science Foundation of China (Grant Numbers 42488301, L2424215, and 42474070), the Project on Frontier and Interdisciplinary Research Assessment, Academic Divisions of the Chinese Academy of Sciences (Grant Number 5-XKC2015012), and Chinese Academy of Engineering Local Cooperation Project (Grant Number HB2024B16).

References

Albuquerque Seismological Laboratory (ASL)/USGS (1990). United States National Seismic Network, *International Federation of Digital Seismograph Networks*, doi: 10.7914/SN/US.

Albuquerque Seismological Laboratory/USGS (2013). Central and Eastern US Network, *International Federation of Digital Seismograph Networks*, doi: 10.7914/SN/N4.

Anderson, J. G. (1986). Seismic strain rates in the Central and Eastern United States, *Bull. Seismol. Soc. Am.* **76,** no. 1, 273–290, doi: 10.1785/BSSA0760010273.

Andrews, D. J. (1989). Mechanics of fault junctions, *J. Geophys. Res.* **94,** no. B7, 9389–9397, doi: 10.1029/JB094iB07p09389.

Båth, M. (1975). Short-period Rayleigh waves from near-surface events, *Phys. Earth Planet. In.* **10,** no. 4, 369–376, doi: 10.1016/0031-9201(75)90064-3.

Bensen, G. D., M. H. Ritzwoller, M. P. Barmin, A. L. Levshin, F. Lin, M. P. Moschetti, N. M. Shapiro, and Y. Yang (2007). Processing seismic ambient noise data to obtain reliable broad-band surface wave dispersion measurements, *Geophys. J. Int.* **169,** no. 3, 1239–1260, doi: 10.1111/j.1365-246X.2007.03374.x.

Ben-Zion, Y., Z. Peng, D. Okaya, L. Seeber, J. G. Armbruster, N. Ozer, A. J. Michael, S. Baris, and M. Aktar (2003). A shallow fault-zone structure illuminated by trapped waves in the Karadere-Duzce branch of the North Anatolian Fault, western Turkey, *Geophys. J. Int.* **152,** no. 3, 699–717, doi: 10.1046/j.1365-246X.2003.01870.x.

Boadu, F. K., and L. T. Long (1996). Effects of fractures on seismic-wave velocity and attenuation, *Geophys. J. Int.* **127,** no. 1, 86–110, doi: 10.1111/j.1365-246X.1996.tb01537.x.

Calais, E., T. Camelbeeck, S. Stein, M. Liu, and T. J. Craig (2016). A new paradigm for large earthquakes in stable continental plate interiors, *Geophys. Res. Lett.* **43,** no. 20, 10,621–10,637, doi: 10.1002/2016GL070815.

Causse, M., C. Cornou, E. Maufroy, J.-R. Grasso, L. Baillet, and E. El Haber (2021). Exceptional ground motion during the shallow Mw 4.9 2019 Le Teil earthquake, France, *Comm. Earth Environ.* **2,** no. 1, 14, doi: 10.1038/s43247-020-00089-0.

Chapman, M. C. (2013). On the rupture process of the 23 August 2011 Virginia earthquake, *Bull. Seismol. Soc. Am.* **103,** no. 2A, 613–628, doi: 10.1785/0120120229.

Chawre, B. (2018). Correlations between ultrasonic pulse wave velocities and rock properties of Quartz-Mica Schist, *J. Rock Mech. Geotech. Eng.* **10,** no. 3, 594–602, doi: 10.1016/j.jrmge.2018.01.006.

Chu, S. X., V. C. Tsai, D. T. Trugman, and G. Hirth (2021). Fault interactions enhance high-frequency earthquake radiation, *Geophys. Res. Lett.* **48,** no. 20, 1–10, doi: 10.1029/2021GL095271.

Clark, D. J., S. Brennand, G. Brenn, M. C. Garthwaite, J. Dimech, T. I. Allen, and S. Standen (2020). BSurface deformation relating to the 2018 Lake Muir earthquake sequence, southwest Western Australia: new insight into stable continental region earthquakes, *Solid Earth* **11,** no. 2, 691–717, doi: 10.5194/se-11-691-2020.

Collettini, C., T. Tesei, M. M. Scuderi, B. M. Carpenter, and C. Viti (2019). Beyond Byerlee friction, weak faults and implications for slip behavior, *Earth Planet. Sci. Lett.* **519,** 245–263, doi: 10.1016/j.epsl.2019.05.011.

Dawson, J., P. Cummins, P. Tregoning, and M. Leonard (2008). Shallow intraplate earthquakes in Western Australia observed by interferometric synthetic aperture radar, *J. Geophys. Res.* **113,** no. B11, doi: 10.1029/2008JB005807.

De Novellis, V., V. Convertito, S. Valkaniotis, F. Casu, R. Lanari, M. F. Monterroso Tobar, and N. A. Pino (2020). Coincident locations of rupture nucleation during the 2019 Le Teil earthquake, France and maximum stress change from local cement quarrying, *Comm. Earth Environ.* **1,** no. 1, 20, doi: 10.1038/s43247-020-00021-6.

Di, N., C. Li, T. Li, W. Hu, Z. Chen, Y. Zhang, L. Lü, J. Chen, and X. Shan (2023). The 2021 Mw 5.2 Baicheng earthquake: Implications for the hazards of extremely shallow earthquakes, *Seismol. Res. Lett.* doi: 10.1785/0220220328.

Elbra, T., R. Karlqvist, I. Lassila, E. Hæggström, and L. J. Pesonen (2011). Laboratory measurements of the seismic velocities and other petrophysical properties of the Outokumpu deep drill core samples, eastern Finland, *Geophys. J. Int.* **184,** no. 1, 405–415, doi: 10.1111/j.1365-246X.2010.04845.x.

Ellis, W. L. (1991). Stress distribution in South-Central Oklahoma and its relationship to crustal structure and contemporary seismicity, *The 32nd U.S. Symposium on Rock Mechanics (USRMS)*, p. ARMA-91-073.

Fadel, I., H. Paulssen, M. van der Meijde, M. Kwadiba, O. Ntibinyane, A. Nyblade, and R. Durrheim (2020). Crustal and upper mantle shear wave velocity structure of Botswana: The 3 April 2017 Central Botswana earthquake linked to the East African rift system, *Geophys. Res. Lett.* **47,** no. 4, doi: 10.1029/2019GL085598.

Figueiredo, P. M., J. S. Hill, A. J. Merschat, C. M. Scheip, K. G. Stewart, L. A. Owen, R. M. Wooten, M. W. Carter, E. Szymanski, S. P. Horton, *et al.* (2022). The Mw 5.1, 9 August 2020, Sparta earthquake, North Carolina: The first documented seismic surface rupture in the Eastern United States, *GSA Today* **32,** nos. 3/4, 4–11, doi: 10.1130/GSATG517A.1.

Gan, W., and W. H. Prescott (2001). Crustal deformation rates in Central and Eastern U.S. inferred from GPS, *Geophys. Res. Lett.* **28,** no. 19, 3733–3736, doi: 10.1029/2001GL013266.

Gangopadhyay, A., and P. Talwani (2005). Fault intersections and intraplate seismicity in Charleston, South Carolina: Insights from a 2-D numerical model, *Curr. Sci.* **88,** no. 10, 1609–1616.

Greene, M., C. Godavitarne, F. Krimgold, S. Nikolic-Brzev, and J. Pantelic (2000). Overview of the Maharashtra, India emergency earthquake rehabilitation program, *Proceedings of the 12th World Conference on Earthquake Engineering (WCEE 2000)*, Auckland, New Zealand, Paper No. 2290, 1–8.

Gupta, H. K. (1993). The Deadly Latur earthquake, *Science* **262,** no. 5140, 1666–1667, doi: 10.1126/science.262.5140.1666.

Harmon, N., P. Gerstoft, C. A. Rychert, G. A. Abers, M. S. de la Cruz, and K. M. Fischer (2008). Phase velocities from seismic noise using beamforming and cross correlation in Costa Rica and Nicaragua, *Geophys. Res. Lett.* **35,** no. 19, 1–6, doi: 10.1029/2008GL035387.

Hatcher, R. D., Jr. (2010). The Appalachian orogen: A brief summary, in *From Rodinia to Pangea: The Lithotectonic Record of the Appalachian Region*, R. P. Tollo, M. J. Bartholomew, J. P. Hibbard, and P. M. Karabinos (Editors), Geological Society of America, Boulder, Colorado, doi: 10.1130/2010.1206(01).

Haxby, W. F., and D. L. Turcotte (1976). Stresses induced by the addition or removal of overburden and associated thermal effects, *Geology* **4,** no. 3, 181–184.

He, X., P. Zhang, S. Ni, R. Chu, W. Wu, and K. Zheng (2023). Automatic determination of focal depth with the optimal period of Rayleigh wave amplitude spectra at local distances, *Geophys. J. Int.* **235,** no. 2, 1681–1696, doi: 10.1093/gji/ggad326.

He, X., P. Zhang, S. Ni, and W. Zheng (2019). Resolving focal depth in sparse network with local depth phase sPL: A case study for the 2011 Mineral, Virginia, earthquake sequence, *Bull. Seismol. Soc. Am.* **109,** no. 2, 745–755, doi: 10.1785/0120180221.

Herrmann, R. B. (2013). Computer programs in seismology: An evolving tool for instruction and research, *Seismol. Res. Lett.* **84,** no. 6, 1081–1088, doi: 10.1785/0220110096.

Herrmann, R. B., H. Benz, and C. J. Ammon (2011). Monitoring the earthquake source process in North America, *Bull. Seismol. Soc. Am.* **101,** no. 6, 2609–2625, doi: 10.1785/0120110095

Hilfiker, S. G., and J. Ebel (2025). High-resolution fault geometry and motion of the August 23, 2011, Mw 5.8 Mineral, Virginia, aftershock sequence revealed using double-difference and moment-tensor inversion methods, *Lithosphere* doi: 10.2113/2024/lithosphere_2024_129.

Horton, S., M. M. Withers, C. H. Cramer, and H. Withers (2021). Source parameters of the M5.1 Sparta, NC earthquake of 9 August 2020, *Seismol. Res. Lett.* **92,** 1439.

Hunter, J. D. (2007). Matplotlib: A 2D graphics environment, *Comput. Sci. Eng.* **9,** no. 3, 90–95, doi: 10.1109/MCSE.2007.55.

Ji, S., T. Shao, K. Michibayashi, C. Long, Q. Wang, Y. Kondo, W. Zhao, H. Wang, and M. H. Salisbury (2013). A new calibration of seismic velocities, anisotropy, fabrics, and elastic moduli of amphibole-rich rocks, *J. Geophys. Res.* **118,** no. 9, 4699–4728, doi: 10.1002/jgrb.50352.

Jing, L., and O. Stephansson (1990). Numerical modelling of intraplate earthquake by 2-dimensional distinct element method, *Gerl. Beitr. Zur Geophys.* **989,** no. 5, 463–472.

Kanamori, H., and G. S. Stewart (1976). Mode of the strain release along the Gibbs fracture zone, Mid-Atlantic ridge, *Phys. Earth Planet. In.* **11,** no. 4, 312–332, doi: 10.1016/0031-9201(76)90018-2.

King, T., M. Quigley, and D. Clark (2019). Surface-rupturing historical earthquakes in Australia and their environmental effects: New insights from re-analyses of observational data, *Geosciences* **9,** 408, doi: 10.3390/geosciences9100408.

Klose, C. D., and L. Seeber (2007). Shallow seismicity in stable continental regions, *Seismol. Res. Lett.* **78,** no. 5, 554–562, doi: 10.1785/gssrl.78.5.554.

Lacombe, O., S. Tavani, J. Lamarche, F. Balsamo, and F. Agosta (2023). *Introduction: Faults and Fractures in Rocks: Mechanics, Occurrence, Dating, Stress History and Fluid Flow*, Elsevier, Amsterdam, The Netherlands.

Langston, C. A. (1987). Depth of faulting during the 1968 Meckering, Australia, earthquake sequence determined from waveform analysis of local seismograms, *J. Geophys. Res.: Solid Earth* **92,** no. B11, 11561–11574, doi: 10.1029/JB092IB11P11561.

Lee, J., V. C. Tsai, G. Hirth, A. Chatterjee, and D. T. Trugman (2024). Fault-network geometry influences earthquake frictional behavior, *Nature* **631,** no. 8019, 106–110, doi: 10.1038/s41586-024-07518-6.

Levshin, A. L., M. H. Ritzwoller, and J. S. Resovsky (1999). Source effects on surface wave group travel times and group velocity maps, *Phys. Earth Planet. In.* **115,** nos. 3/4, 293–312, doi: 10.1016/S0031-9201(99)00113-2.

Luo, Y., S. D. Ni, X. F. Zeng, Y. Zheng, Q. F. Chen, and Y. Chen (2010). A shallow aftershock sequence in the north-eastern end of the Wenchuan earthquake aftershock zone, *Sci. China Earth Sci.* **53,** no. 11, 1655–1664, doi: 10.1007/s11430-010-4026-8.

Lynn, A. S. (2023). Structural analysis of the seismically active little river fault and its connection to regional brittle structures, *Masters Thesis*, doi: 10.17615/wrkc-nz08.

Mahan, S. A., E. T. Krolczyk, M. W. Carter, and A. J. Merschat (2025). Luminescence and Radiocarbon data for: Geologic map of the Sparta East, Sparta West, and parts of the Glade Valley and Whitehead 7.5-minute quadrangles, North Carolina and Virginia, and the epicentral area of the August 9, 2020, Mw 5.1 earthquake in Sparta, NC, *U.S. Geol. Surv. Data Release*, doi: 10.5066/P13XJCPS.

Malehmir, A., T. K. Hong, J. Lee, S. Zappalá, B. Brodic, D. Chung, B. Kim, S. Park, J. Lee, and D. Kil (2022). Fault intersections control short period intraplate start-stop seismicity in the Korean Peninsula, *Tectonophysics* **834,** doi: 10.1016/j.tecto.2022.229387.

Martín-González, F., C. Crespo-Martín, S. Cesca, and S. González-Muñoz (2023). Understanding seismicity and seismotectonics in a stable continental region (NW Iberian Peninsula): Implications for the nature of intraplate seismicity, *Glob. Planet. Change* **227,** doi: 10.1016/j.gloplacha.2023.104177.

Mavko, G., T. Mukerji, and J. Dvorkin (2009). *The Rock Physics Handbook: Tools for Seismic Analysis of Porous Media*, Second Ed., Cambridge University Press, Cambridge, United Kingdom, doi: 10.1017/CBO9780511626753.

Mazzotti, S., X. Vergeron, O. Malcles, J. Grosset, and P. Vernant (2023). Impact of long-term erosion on crustal stresses and seismicity in stable continental regions, *Geology* **51,** no. 8, 733–737, doi: 10.1130/G51327.1.

Meltzer, A., and N. Christensen (2001). Nanga Parbat crustal anisotropy: Implications for interpretation of crustal velocity structure and shear-wave splitting, *Geophys. Res. Lett.* **28,** no. 10, 2129–2132, doi: 10.1029/2000GL012262.

Merschat, A., and M. Carter (2023).Preliminary map of the surface rupture from the August 9, 2020, Mw 5.1 earthquake near Sparta, North Carolina—The Little River fault and other possible coseismic features, *Open-File Rept. 2023-1074*, doi: 10.3133/ofr20231074.

Neves, M., L. Y. Chuang, W. Li, Z. Peng, P. M. Figueiredo, and S. Ni (2024). Complex rupture dynamics of the extremely shallow August 2020 M5.1 Sparta, North Carolina earthquake, *Commun. Earth Environ.* **5,** no. 1, 1–11, doi: 10.1038/s43247-024-01316-8.

Pekeris, C. L., and H. Lifson (1957). Motion of the surface of a uniform elastic half-space produced by a buried pulse, *J. Acoust. Soc. Am.* **29,** no. 11, 1233–1238, doi: 10.1121/1.1908753.

Pollitz, F. F. (2023). Shallow fault slip of the 2020 M 5.1 Sparta, North Carolina, earthquake, *Seismol. Res. Lett.* **94,** no. 6, 2831–2839, doi: 10.1785/0220230127.

Price, N. J. (1966). Chapter 1 - Brittle fracture, in *The Commonwealth and International Library: Geology Division*, N. J. Price (Editor), Pergamon Press, Oxford, United Kingdom, 1–56, doi: 10.1016/B978-0-08-011275-6.50006-9.

Price, N. J. (1974). The development of stress systems and fracture patterns in undeformed sediments, *Proc. Third Congress of the International Society for Rock Mechanics*, Denver, Colorado, September 1974.

Ritz, J. F., S. Baize, M. Ferry, C. Larroque, L. Audin, B. Delouis, and E. Mathot (2020). Surface rupture and shallow fault reactivation during the 2019 Mw 4.9 Le Teil earthquake, France, *Commun. Earth Environ.* **1,** no. 1, 1–11, doi: 10.1038/s43247-020-0012-z.

Scholz, C. H. (1998). Earthquakes and friction laws, *Nature* **391,** no. 6662, 37–42, doi: 10.1038/34097.

Schulte, S. M., and W. D. Mooney (2005). An updated global earthquake catalogue for stable continental regions: Reassessing the correlation with ancient rifts, *Geophys. J. Int.* **161,** no. 3, 707–721, doi: 10.1111/j.1365-246X.2005.02554.x.

Seeber, L., and N. Dawers (1989). Characterization of an intraplate seismogenic fault in the Manhattan Prong, Westchester Co., N. Y, *Seismol. Res. Lett.* **60,** no. 2, 71–78, doi: 10.1785/gssrl.60.2.71.

Son, M., C. S. Cho, H. K. Lee, M. Han, J. S. Shin, K. Kim, and S. Kim (2020). Partitioned fault movement and aftershock triggering: Evidence for fault interactions during the 2017 Mw 5.4 Pohang Earthquake, South Korea, *J. Geophys. Res.* **125,** no. 12, doi: 10.1029/2020JB020005.

Steer, P., M. Simoes, R. Cattin, and J. B. H. Shyu (2014). Erosion influences the seismicity of active thrust faults, *Nat. Commun.* doi: 10.1038/ncomms6564.

Talwani, P. (1988). The intersection model for intraplate earthquakes, *Seismol. Res. Lett.* **59,** no. 4, 305–310, doi: 10.1785/gssrl.59.4.305.

Talwani, P. (1999). Fault geometry and earthquakes in continental interiors, *Tectonophysics* **305,** no. 1, 371–379, doi: 10.1016/S0040-1951(99)00024-4.

Talwani, P. (2008). On the nature of intraplate earthquakes, *J. Geophys. Res.* **113,** no. 11, 47–68, doi: 10.1029/2008JB005807.

Talwani, P. (2017). On the nature of intraplate earthquakes, *J. Seismol.* **21,** no. 1, 47–68, doi: 10.1007/s10950-016-9582-8.

Townend, J., and M. D. Zoback (2000). How faulting keeps the crust strong, *Geology* **28,** no. 5, 399–402.

Tromp, J., D. Komatitsch, and Q. Liu (2008). Spectral-element and adjoint methods in seismology, *Comm. Comput. Phys.* **3,** 1–32.

Walters, R. J., L. C. Gregory, L. N. J. Wedmore, T. J. Craig, K. McCaffrey, M. Wilkinson, J. Chen, Z. Li, J. R. Elliott, H. Goodall, *et al.* (2018). Dual control of fault intersections on stop-start rupture in the 2016 Central Italy seismic sequence, *Earth Planet. Sci. Lett.* **500,** 1–14, doi: 10.1016/j.epsl.2018.07.043.

Wei, S., E. Fielding, S. Leprince, A. Sladen, J. P. Avouac, D. Helmberger, E. Hauksson, R. Chu, M. Simons, K. Hudnut, *et al.* (2011). Superficial simplicity of the 2010 El Mayorg-Cucapah earthquake of Baja California in Mexico, *Nature Geosci.* **4,** no. 9, 615–618, doi: 10.1038/ngeo1213.

Wessel, P., W. H. F. Smith, R. Scharroo, J. Luis, and F. Wobbe (2013). Generic mapping tools: Improved version released, *Eos Trans. AGU* **94,** no. 45, 409–410, doi: 10.1002/2013EO450001.

Wetmiller, R. J., J. Adams, F. M. Anglin, H. S. Hasegawa, and A. E. Stevens (1984). Aftershock sequences of the 1982 Miramichi, New Brunswick, earthquakes, *Bull. Seismol. Soc. Am.* **74,** no. 2, 621–653, doi: 10.1785/BSSA0740020621.

Yang, H., M. Quigley, and T. King (2021). Surface slip distributions and geometric complexity of intraplate reverse-faulting earthquakes, *GSA Bull.* **133,** nos. 9/10, 1909–1929, doi: 10.1130/B35809.1.

Yang, Y., M. H. Ritzwoller, A. L. Levshin, and N. M. Shapiro (2007). Ambient noise Rayleigh wave tomography across Europe, *Geophys. J. Int.* **168,** no. 1, 259–274, doi: 10.1111/j.1365-246X.2006.03203.x.

Yao, H., R. D. van der Hilst, and M. V. de Hoop (2006). Surface-wave array tomography in SE Tibet from ambient seismic noise and two-station analysis - I. Phase velocity maps, *Geophys. J. Int.* **166,** no. 2, 732–744, doi: 10.1111/j.1365-246X.2006.03028.x.

Yao, H., G. Xu, X. Xiao, and L. Zhu (2004). A quick tracing method based on image analysis technique for the determination of dual stations phase velocities dispersion curve of surface wave, *Seismol. Geomagn. Observ. Res.* **25,** no. 1, 1–8 (in Chinese).

Yao, H., G. Xu, L. Zhu, and X. Xiao (2005). Mantle structure from inter-station Rayleigh wave dispersion and its tectonic implication in western China and neighboring regions, *Phys. Earth Planet. In.* **148,** no. 1, 39–54, doi: 10.1016/j.pepi.2004.08.006.

Zhu, L., and L. A. Rivera (2002). A note on the dynamic and static displacements from a point source in multilayered media, *Geophys. J. Int.* **148,** no. 3, 619–627, doi: 10.1046/j.1365-246X.2002.01610.x.

Zoback, M. D., S. Hickman, and W. Ellsworth (2007). The role of fault zone drilling, *Treatise Geophys.* **4,** 649–674, doi: 10.1016/B978-044452748-6.00084-5.

Manuscript received 15 September 2025
Published online 21 January 2026

The BELSHAKE Database of Earthquake Ground Motion in Belgium

OPEN ACCESS

Kris Vanneste*[1], Mahsa Onvani[1,2], Giovanni Rapagnani[1], and Koen Van Noten[1]

Abstract

The BELSHAKE database compiles ground-motion data from Belgium and surrounding regions in northwest Europe, a region characterized by low-to-moderate seismicity. It currently contains ~6400 digital records from 344 tectonic and induced earthquakes with $M_L \geq 2$, recorded since 1985 with short-period, broadband, and accelerometric sensors operated by the Royal Observatory of Belgium. The database consists of a waveform archive with the raw and processed seismograms for each event–station pair, and a relational database containing the associated metadata, as well as the derived ground-motion intensity values. All records have been visually inspected to identify, and if possible correct, problematic waveforms. Missing arrival times are computed from the local velocity model and interactively adjusted if necessary. We use a combination of two windowing procedures, one to isolate *P*, *S*, and coda windows, and a more sophisticated method for the noise window. The waveform data were processed in a uniform way using a semiautomated workflow based on schemes in other ground-motion databases. A suite of intensity measures was computed from the processed data that were evaluated as reliable, taking into account the usable frequency range. These are computed for different signal windows and components, including the geometric mean and orientation-independent percentiles. Data consistency was validated using different methods. Fitting a generic ground-motion model (GMM) using mixed-effects regression shows that residuals are well behaved and have a similar range as the database for France. Analysis of the evolution of residuals for each station allowed identifying additional issues related to instrument response and location changes, which were addressed. Finally, we also determined moment magnitudes from displacement spectra for most events. The BELSHAKE database complements existing databases by increasing the coverage of low-seismicity zones. It will not only help evaluating or calibrating GMMs specifically for Belgium but will also be useful for other seismological applications.

Cite this article as Vanneste, K., M. Onvani, G. Rapagnani, and K. Van Noten (2026). The BELSHAKE Database of Earthquake Ground Motion in Belgium, *Seismol. Res. Lett.* **97**, 918–933, doi: 10.1785/0220250321.

Supplemental Material

Introduction

Earthquake ground-motion databases are fundamental resources for the development of ground-motion models (GMMs), which are in turn one of the most crucial ingredients in seismic hazard assessments (SHAs). In the past two decades, several international efforts have collected and disseminated strong-motion data, such as the Next Generation Attenuation project (NGA, Chiou *et al.*, 2008) in the United States, and the follow-up projects NGA-West (Ancheta *et al.*, 2014) and NGA-East (Goulet *et al.*, 2021), the Kiban–Kyoshin network (KiK-net) database in Japan (Dawood *et al.*, 2016), the ITalian ACcelerometric Archive (ITACA) in Italy (Pacor *et al.*, 2011), the RESORCE database for Europe and the Middle East (Akkar *et al.*, 2014), and the worldwide Engineering Strong-Motion (ESM) Database (Luzi *et al.*, 2016). These databases predominantly contain data from the most active regions of the world, where earthquakes, and hence earthquake recordings, are more abundant. A large number of GMMs have been derived from these databases (see overview in Douglas, 2019). However, very few GMMs are valid for intraplate areas like Belgium and more generally northwest (NW) Europe, in which seismicity is much lower, but ground motions may be stronger compared with plate boundaries. Because of the lack of strong-motion data, SHAs in Belgium (e.g., Leynaud *et al.*, 2000) so far

1. Royal Observatory of Belgium (ROB), Brussels, Belgium, https://orcid.org/0000-0003-0044-4421 (KV); https://orcid.org/0000-0002-0685-1506 (MO); https://orcid.org/0000-0001-8933-4426 (KVN); 2. Institute of Mechanics, Materials and Civil Engineering, Université catholique de Louvain (UCLouvain), Louvain-la-Neuve, Belgium

*Corresponding author: kris.vanneste@oma.be

had to rely on GMMs developed for other parts of the world. Although the selection of GMMs has grown more sophisticated over the years and currently consists of 11 GMMs from different regions (Vanneste *et al.*, 2014), their validity for our regions has not been tested and their weighting remains subjective. Considering that in probabilistic SHA, the ground-motion branch of the logic tree is one of the main contributors to dispersion (Sabetta *et al.*, 2005; Bommer and Abrahamson, 2006), there is clearly a need for ground-motion data from lower-seismicity regions, either to evaluate the goodness of fit of existing GMMs, to calibrate regionally adjustable GMMs, or to develop a specific model for the region in question. Although the vast majority of recorded data in these regions concern weak-motion recordings of ground velocity from earthquakes with magnitudes lower than the minimum magnitude considered in SHA ($M_w \cong 4.5$), recent successful projects to model earthquake ground motion in other low-seismicity regions like Switzerland (Edwards and Fäh, 2013) and the United Kingdom (Rietbrock *et al.*, 2013; Rietbrock and Edwards, 2019) or to compile ground-motion databases (e.g., Traversa *et al.*, 2020 in France; Ghasemi *et al.*, 2026 in Australia) have demonstrated that it is not only feasible, but also valuable, to conduct similar studies for Belgium. The currently available seismic data in Belgium are mainly used to detect and locate regional earthquakes, and to determine their main source characteristics (e.g., focal depth, local magnitude, and focal mechanism), but a systematic inventory of these data for the purpose of ground-motion modeling has not been undertaken yet. This provided the rationale to launch a dedicated project, BELSHAKE, with the aim to build a database of earthquake ground motions for Belgium and adjacent areas, and subsequently to use this database to model ground motion produced by earthquakes occurring in Belgium.

Data

The BELSHAKE database aims to collect digital waveforms of local and regional earthquakes recorded by seismometers and accelerometers in and around Belgium. The Royal Observatory of Belgium (ROB) is responsible for monitoring seismic activity in Belgium through the Belgian seismic network (code BE; Royal Observatory of Belgium, 1985), which has been routinely and continuously recording ground motions over the past decades using seismometers and accelerometers. The Belgian seismic network has evolved strongly over time (see Data and Resources). Digital recording started already in 1985, following the damaging M_w 4.7 Liège earthquake on 8 November 1983 (Camelbeeck, 1985), but merely for four stations, and data were only stored for detected events. In subsequent years, the network was gradually expanded and more instruments were equipped with a digital recording system. Simultaneously, instrumentation generally evolved from single-component to three-component short-period seismometers, and subsequently to broadband seismometers. Starting in 1999, the seismic network was complemented with accelerometers, which were installed mainly in the most active areas of Belgium to record strong ground motions. From 2005 onward, increasing storage capacity allowed storing continuous data streams, first for select seismic stations and later for all of them. The accelerometric stations initially operated in triggered mode, but from 2021 onward, they were replaced with instruments capable of continuous recording. The Belgian seismic network (Royal Observatory of Belgium, 1985) currently consists of ~30 seismometers and ~20 accelerometers, the majority of which are streaming in near-real time to the European Integrated Data Archive (Strollo, 2021). Figure 1 shows a map of stations with at least 10 records in the BELSHAKE database. As a result of this network development, the ROB waveform archive is heterogeneous. All waveform data are stored on a server in different formats and folder structures and are accessible through different network services or protocols, depending on sensor type (seismometer or accelerometer) and the year and mode of recording (event records trimmed from originally continuous recordings, triggered records, or continuous streams). Most information related to the instruments and acquisition systems deployed over time in the different stations is stored in the ROB seismic routine database.

To develop the BELSHAKE database, we selected all tectonic and induced earthquakes since 1985 from the ROB earthquake catalog that satisfy two selection criteria: (1) $M_L \geq 2.5$ in a wide rectangular region around Belgium (−1° to 9° E and 49° to 52° N), and (2) $M_L \geq 2.0$ in a more narrow region around Belgium (2.5° to 7° E and 49.25° to 51.5° N). A small number of lower-magnitude events ($M_L \geq 1.0$) were also included because these were recorded at short distances (<10 km). The location of these events and selection regions is shown in Figure 2. The induced earthquakes are mostly due to mining activity in two regions in Germany ($M_L \leq 3.7$), and due to geothermal operations in the north of Belgium ($M_L \leq 2.1$).

The corresponding waveform data were retrieved mostly from the permanent Belgian seismic network (which includes some stations that are currently part of the network of the Grand Duchy of Luxemburg), but for some key events we also obtained data from neighboring networks in Germany (code BQ; Department of Geosciences, Bensberg Observatory, 2016) and The Netherlands (code NL; KNMI, 1993). In addition, we also included data from temporary networks deployed by ROB during some seismic sequences, which provide additional short-distance records. The selection currently contains ~6400 digital seismograms, ~5840 from 327 tectonic earthquakes and ~580 from 17 induced earthquakes. Table 1 lists the most notable events (with $M_L \geq 4.0$) in the database. The largest and hence most important event is the M_w 5.3 Roermond, The Netherlands, earthquake on 13 April 1992, which caused light damage corresponding to intensity VII on the European Macroseismic Scale (EMS-98; Haak *et al.*, 1994) in the border region between The Netherlands, Belgium, and

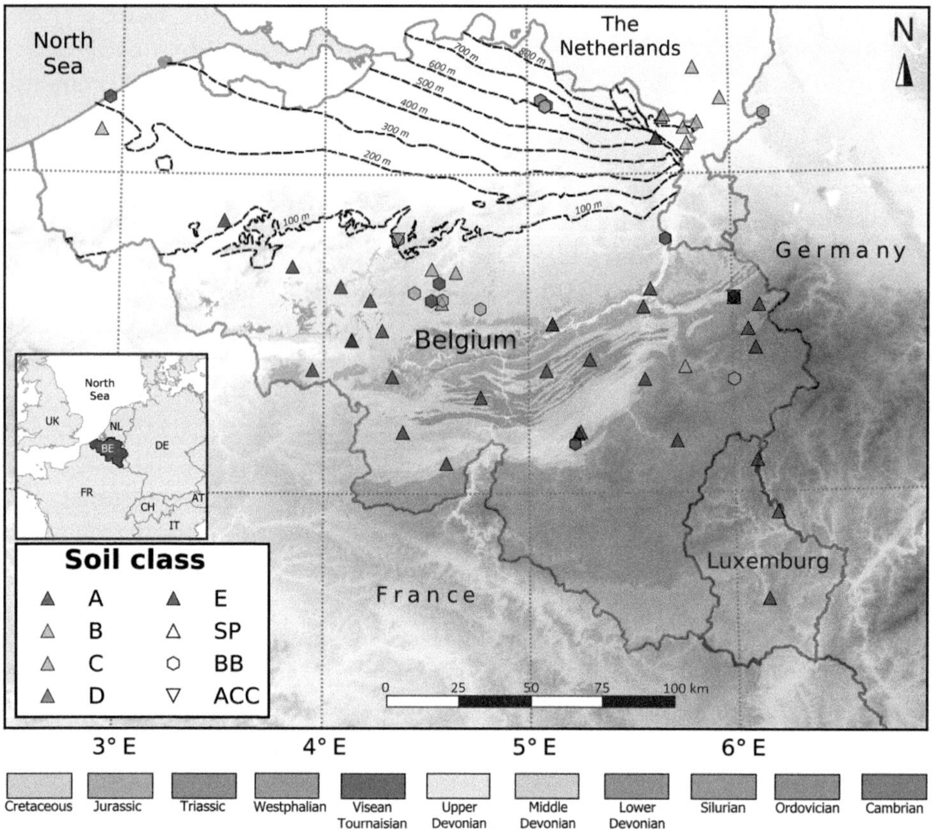

Figure 1. Location of seismic stations with ≥10 records in the BELSHAKE database. Symbol colors correspond to Eurocode 8 (EC8) soil class (A–E) and symbol shapes to instrument type. Background image depicts simplified surface geology, with bedrock in the south and north-northeast-ward thickening sediment layers (100 m contour interval) in the north. Note that some of these stations were deployed in temporary networks, and some stations of the permanent network have been discontinued. ACC, accelerometer; BB, broadband; SP, short-period. The color version of this figure is available only in the electronic edition.

Germany. Unfortunately, most records from this event were clipped because seismometers at the time had limited resolution and were tuned to detect small earthquakes. Furthermore, there were no accelerometers operational at the time. We therefore collected waveform data from networks in France, Germany, the United Kingdom, and Czech Republic for this particular event and its aftershocks. In total, we imported 221 records from 10 different networks into our database. This subset of the database will be described in more detail elsewhere.

The BELSHAKE database consists of two components: (1) a waveform library containing raw and processed waveform data and the associated instrument response information, and (2) an SQL database containing all metadata as well as the derived ground-motion parameters. The waveform library is structured in folders corresponding to each event, containing one file for each station. We opted for the flexible Adaptable Seismic Data Format (ASDF; Krischer *et al.*, 2016), which can contain any number of waveforms in a single file, along with metadata, instrument response information, and auxiliary (non-waveform) data, and is based on existing formats and standards. In our case, we use it to store waveform data, including intermediate processing steps (accessible through different "tags"), along with the instrument response, relevant event and station metadata, and corresponding Fourier and response spectra in a single file for each event–station pair. The SQL database consists of seven main tables, containing (1) event metadata (origin and source parameters); (2) station metadata (physical properties of a seismic station that do not change with time, such as the location, housing, emplacement, and local site conditions); (3) event–station metadata (distances according to different metrics, (back-)azimuth, *P*- and *S*-wave arrival times, and incidence angles); (4) waveform metadata that are common to all components (instrument information, start and end times of different signal windows, identified problems); (5) component-specific waveform metadata (start and end times, sample rate, reliable frequency range, and problems); (6) processing parameters; and (7) calculated ground-motion intensity measures (IMs). We also developed a dedicated Python library (based on ObsPy, Megies *et al.*, 2011), which provides a programming interface with the database and waveform archive, allows reading and writing of metadata, and streamlines data import.

For each selected event–station combination, we calculated a suitable time window to capture the complete event, including pre-event noise and coda wave, and we imported the corresponding raw waveform data, including derived radial and transverse components, into the waveform library. The associated event and station metadata were extracted from the ROB seismic routine database, the corresponding source-to-site parameters were computed, and all these metadata were imported into the BELSHAKE database. Missing *P*- and *S*-wave arrival times were computed from the Belgian velocity model (Camelbeeck, 1993) and, if necessary, manually adjusted during visual inspection. We also attempted

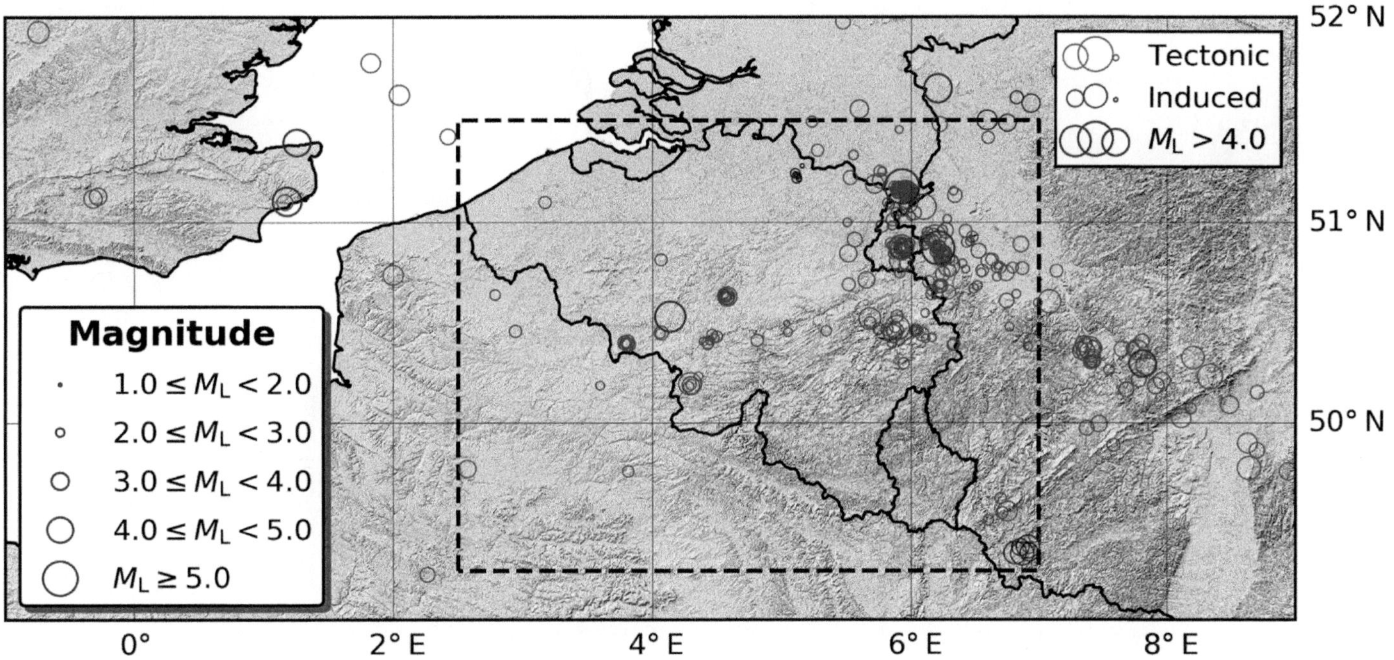

Figure 2. Map showing epicenters of earthquakes included in the BELSHAKE database. The dashed rectangle corresponds to narrow selection area with lower magnitude threshold ($M_L \geq 2.0$). The color version of this figure is available only in the electronic edition.

relocating the selected earthquakes, using handpicked phase arrival times (from multiple agencies) only, by taking the average of 100 runs with the randomly perturbed catalog location as initial location, weighted inversely by the standard deviation of their arrival-time residuals (root mean square error [RMSE]). New solutions for the epicentral locations were only accepted if they yielded significantly lower RMSE (at least 0.05 s) and lower location uncertainties. Thus, we were able to improve the location of ~100 events. Overall, location quality in the BELSHAKE database is very good, with only four events with a total RMSE on the arrival times higher than 2 s. Horizontal and vertical location uncertainties are quite low, with median values of 0.9 and 1.2 km, respectively, and 95th percentile values of 6.7 and 5.7 km, respectively. For six events (four of which came from catalogs of neighboring networks), location quality cannot be assessed due to insufficient phase

TABLE 1
Origin Time, Hypocentral Location, Magnitude, Maximum Macroseismic Intensity (I_{max}), and Number of Records for Main Events in the BELSHAKE Database

Date (yyyy/mm/dd)	Location	Longitude (°)	Latitude (°)	Depth (km)	M_L	M_w	I_{max}	Number of Records
1992/04/13	Roermond, The Netherlands	5.9278	51.1758	16.4	5.8	5.3	VII*	221
1995/06/20	Le Roeulx, Belgium	4.1359	50.5330	26.2	4.5		V†	22
2002/07/22	Alsdorf, Germany	6.2113	50.8731	13.4	4.9	4.6	VI†	25
2007/04/28	Folkestone, United Kingdom	1.1870	51.1040	8.8	4.3		VI‡	28
2011/02/14	Koblenz, Germany	7.8112	50.2992	13.3	4.1		V§	29
2011/09/08	Goch, Germany	6.2116	51.6557	17.7	4.3		IV‖	31
2015/05/22	Ramsgate, United Kingdom	1.2639	51.3910	14.5	4.1		V#	36

*Haak *et al.* (1994)
†Neefs *et al.* (2025)
‡Sargeant *et al.* (2008)
§Hinzen (2019)
‖Van Noten *et al.* (2017)
#Baptie (2017)

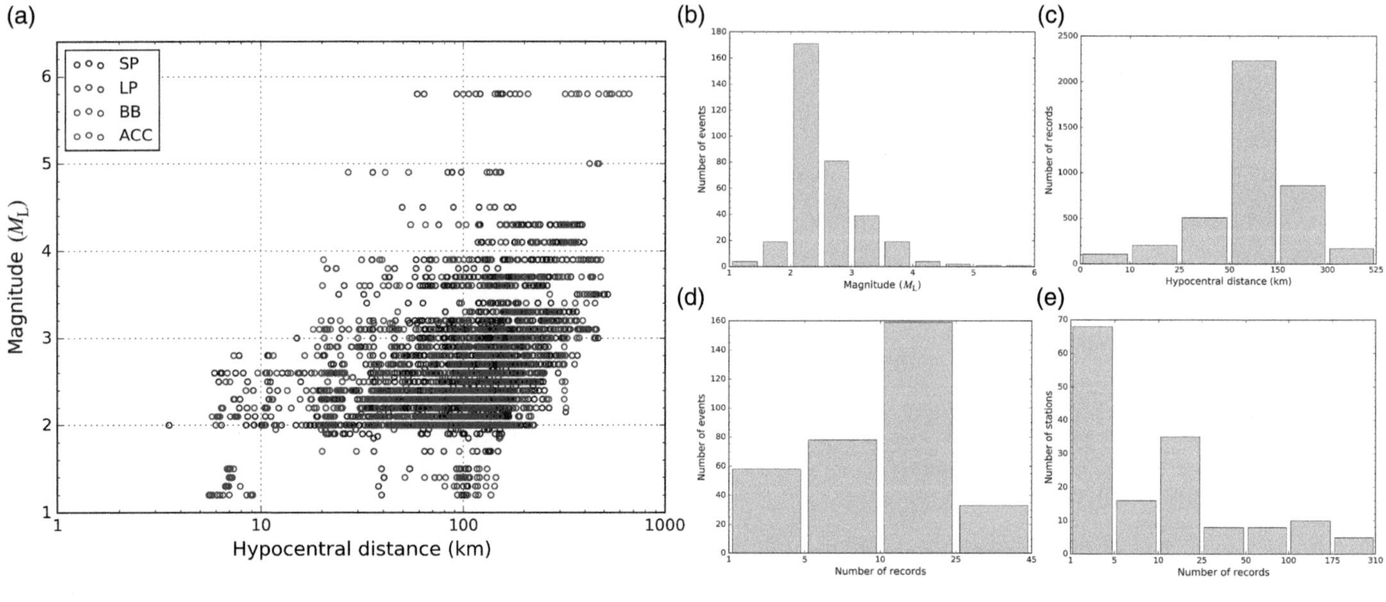

picks. For the largest event, the Roermond earthquake, we also considered a finite-fault solution, assuming that the hypocenter corresponds to the NW bottom edge of the rupture (compare with Gariel *et al.*, 1994), and that the rupture has a strike of 142° similar to the border faults of the Lower Rhine Graben (Vanneste *et al.*, 2013), a southwest (SW)-ward dip of 57°, a length of ∼3.5 km as suggested by the extent of early aftershocks, and an area of 10.6 km^2 (Camelbeeck *et al.*, 1994). Finally, we also recomputed local magnitudes according to the Belgian M_L scale (Camelbeeck, 1985), using the available vertical *S*-wave displacement amplitudes in the ROB seismic routine database. This resulted in slightly lower magnitudes ($\Delta M_L = -0.2$) for only two events. For ∼25 events with insufficient amplitudes, we copied the M_L values from the catalog of the most authoritative neighboring network (depending on location) or used the average of two or more catalogs. This resulted in magnitude differences of $\Delta M_L < -0.3$ for 11 events and $\Delta M_L > 0.3$ for 1 event. The source for each magnitude value was included in the database.

Figure 3 illustrates some distributions of the subset of the BELSHAKE database having horizontal components and acceptable quality of the *S* window (see the Waveform Quality Control section). The magnitude coverage is relatively good up to $M_L = 4.0$ but significantly decreases toward higher magnitudes. Hypocentral distances range mainly between 20 and 300 km, but there are also several records at short distance (<10 km) for lower-magnitude ($M_L < 3.0$) events. Compared with the French Réseau Sismologique et Géodésique Français (RESIF)/Epos-France database (Traversa *et al.*, 2020; Buscetti *et al.*, 2025), the magnitude coverage is sparser in the range $M_L = 4.0 - 5.8$, but the coverage at short distances appears to be better. The other histograms show that many events have been recorded by 10 or more stations (Fig. 3d), most stations have recorded less than 25 events, and a small number of them have recorded more than 100 events (Fig. 3e).

Figure 3. Coverage of records with horizontal components and acceptable quality of the *S* window in the BELSHAKE database. (a) Magnitude–distance plot. Colors correspond to instrument types: SP seismometer, long-period seismometer (LP), BB seismometer, and ACC. (b) Magnitude histogram. (c) Hypocentral distance histogram. (d) Histogram of number of records per event. (e) Histogram of number of records per station. The color version of this figure is available only in the electronic edition.

Instrument Response

A major challenge encountered during the compilation of the database was the lack of instrument response information for older waveform data, which is essential to reconstruct actual ground motion in physical units. After 2005, this information has been systematically collected and maintained in dataless SEED files. However, for data recorded before that time, instrument response information was not readily available. Fortunately, some important parameters are available in the ROB seismic routine database and/or in the headers of the original waveform files. It is possible to combine this information with the response information from similar instruments and/or acquisition systems for other stations or from the Nominal Response Library (see Templeton, 2017) to construct missing instrument response information.

We evaluated the validity of all instrument responses based on different criteria:

- Evolution of energy levels of the noise window in different frequency bands through time;
- consistency of power spectral densities (PSDs) of the noise window within each station deployment (= particular combination and/or configuration of instrument and acquisition system) and between different deployments of the same station; and
- consistency of station–M_L residuals between different deployments of the same station.

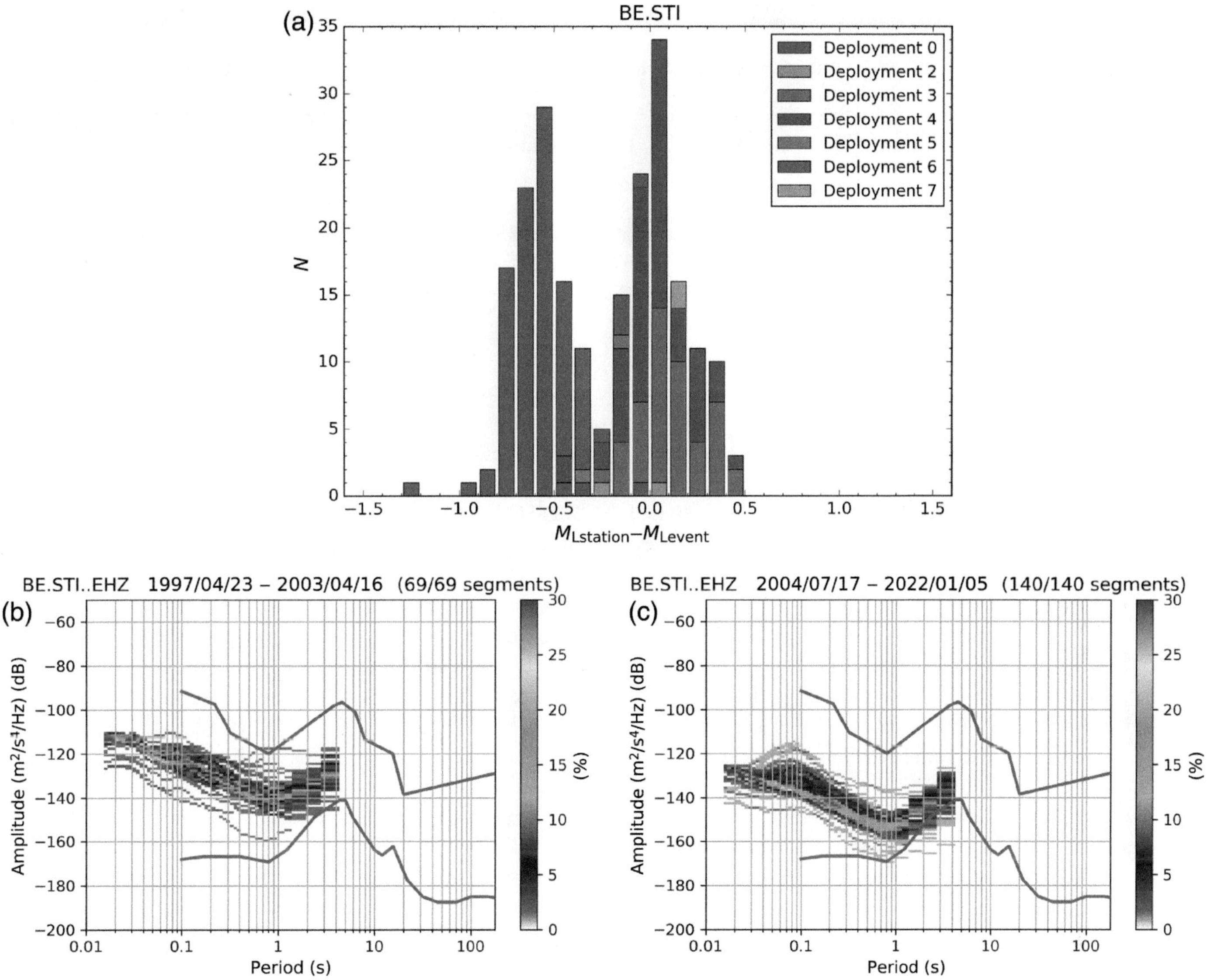

Figure 4. Identification of instrument response problems for one deployment of station BE.STI. (a) Histograms of station, station–M_L residuals for individual deployments of this station. (b,c) Power spectral density (PSD) plots for deployments 4 (left) and 6 (right). The color version of this figure is available only in the electronic edition.

If consistent anomalies were found, that is, anomalously low/high station M_L residuals along with anomalously low-/high-noise levels, we concluded that there was a problem with the instrument response for that particular station deployment. In such a case, we also evaluated the station–M_L residuals and PSDs that would be obtained with the instrument responses constructed from the other information sources mentioned earlier. If one of these yielded station–M_L residuals and PSDs that are in better agreement with the other deployments of the station, we replaced the instrument response in the BELSHAKE waveform library with this alternative response information. The source of the response information of each record is included in the database. In a few cases, problems with total gain were found with instrument responses in the authoritative archive maintained by ROB. We were able to solve most of these issues by examining documentation and hardware. The corresponding dataless files were corrected, and if necessary the ROB seismic routine database as well, and the affected records in the BELSHAKE waveform library were updated. Finally, a number of cases remained in which it was not possible to fix the instrument response. These records were flagged as unreliable in the database, preventing their use in subsequent steps of the project, but keeping them available for possible correction in the future.

We illustrate the instrument response evaluation using one example. Figure 4 shows the identification of a problem for one deployment of station BE.STI. The histogram of station–M_L residuals (top panel) shows a bimodal distribution in which the residuals for deployment 6 are clearly lower (at least 0.5 magnitude units) than the distributions for the other deployments. PSDs (bottom panel) indicate that the noise level during

TABLE 2

Number of Records in the BELSHAKE Database for Different Event Types, Components (H, Horizontal; Z, Vertical), and Quality Categories

Event Type	Component	Good	Intermediate	Bad	Unreliable	Total
Tectonic	Z	3816	869	1156	574	6415
Tectonic	H	5894	1316	1776	422	9408
Induced	Z	300	89	190	16	595
Induced	H	534	158	336	30	1058
All	Z	4116	958	1346	590	7010
All	H	6428	1474	2112	452	10,466

this deployment is significantly lower than in the other ones. Both findings are consistent and indicate that the instrument response for deployment 6, which represents almost 18 yr of operation, was incorrect by a factor of ~2.5. This problem appeared to be due to a wrong value of the shunt resistance and has now been corrected.

Waveform Quality Control

After data selection and before data processing, the waveforms imported in the BELSHAKE database were visually inspected with the interactive seismogram browser in Pyrocko (Heimann *et al.*, 2017) for any of the following problems: timing problems, low signal-to-noise ratio (SNR), presence of spikes, disturbances, data gaps, baseline distortion, resonance, clipping, missing or incomplete phase windows, or presence of fore- or aftershocks in the noise and/or signal windows. Examples of each category are shown in Figure S1, available in the supplemental material to this article. In addition, we also evaluated the presence of 50 Hz hum from Fourier amplitude spectra.

Some of these problems can be, and were, repaired when possible:

- Most timing problems could be fixed by determining the time shift between the *P*-wave onset and the expected *P*-wave arrival, reimporting the data with the time shift applied, and storing the time shift in the database;
- spikes could be removed by replacing them with interpolated values;
- some distortions could be removed by interactive baseline removal or high-pass filtering;
- disturbances that are not affecting the main signal phases (*P* and *S*) could be removed by trimming; and
- 50 Hz hum could be removed by applying a narrow notch filter.

All remaining problems were considered to be irreparable. However, it is interesting to note here that a recent study (Edwards *et al.*, 2025) has demonstrated that it may be possible to reconstruct waveforms that have been clipped down to 10% of their true peak motion using an adaptation of the clipped waveform restoration method (Zhang *et al.*, 2016). The BELSHAKE database contains a number of clipped records for three important events (the first three events listed in Table 1), and it may thus be possible to correct some of these in the near future.

In all cases (except for the timing problems), the original waveform data are kept, and the corrected data are stored with a different tag in the ASDF files. Irreparable records were left as such. The identified problems, and whether or not these have been corrected, are stored in the database, such that they can be queried for any component and signal window. Based on these problem categories and solutions, we defined three different quality classes and developed a method in our programming interface to select only records having a specific minimum quality, at the level of component and window. These quality classes are:

- Good: windows that have no problems, are only slightly curtailed, or with spikes that have been successfully removed or other disturbances that have been successfully trimmed or filtered.
- Intermediate: windows that are noisy or have uncorrected 50 Hz hum.
- Bad: windows that are very noisy, clipped, missing, incomplete, disturbed, interrupted, have no waveform or contain spikes, distortions, or fore- or aftershocks that could not be removed.

Table 2 lists the number of waveform records in each quality category, as well as the number of records with unreliable instrument response, for different event types and components.

Waveform Processing and Calculation of IMs

Following visual quality control, all records in the BELSHAKE database with reliable instrument response were processed using a semiautomated workflow in Python, which is described in more detail in Vanneste and Onvani (2024). With some variations, the processing steps and the order in which they are applied, have been defined in accordance with the processing schemes in existing ground-motion databases, such as RESIF/Epos-France (Traversa *et al.*, 2020), ITACA (Paolucci *et al.*, 2011; Puglia *et al.*, 2014), Pacific Earthquake Engineering Research Center (PEER) NGA-East (Goulet *et al.*, 2014, 2021) and ESM (Luzi *et al.*, 2016). The processing flow is applied to both tectonic and induced earthquake records, and consists of (1) mean removal and linear detrending; (2) two-sided tapering using fixed taper lengths, evaluated separately for both sides; (3) instrument correction to convert to native ground motion (velocity or acceleration); (4) frequency-domain differentiation to acceleration (if required); (5) computation of Fourier amplitude spectra (FAS) and SNR to determine filter corner frequencies (with optional manual adjustment); (6) two-sided tapering; (7) zero-phase band-pass filtering with prior zero-padding; (8) pad-stripping; (9) postprocessing following the PEER NGA procedure, as described in Boore *et al.* (2012), to ensure that acceleration, velocity, and displacement time series are compatible; and (10) splitting of acceleration time series into noise, *P*, *S*, signal (*P* + *S*) and full (*P* + *S* + coda) windows. All processing parameters are stored in a separate table in the database, and the processed waveform data, as well as some intermediate processing steps, are stored with different tags in the ASDF files.

An important part of this workflow is windowing, used to isolate noise, *P*, *S*, and coda portions of the record. Reliable window definitions are required to compute the SNR, which is used to determine the valid frequency range, as well as for computing window-specific IMs. We investigated two windowing approaches applied in other ground-motion databases. To take advantage of their strengths, we combined the PEER NGA-East approach (Goulet *et al.*, 2014) to isolate the *P*, *S*, and coda windows, and the RESIF/Epos-France method (Perron *et al.*, 2018) for the noise window. The latter selects between pre-event, short postevent, and long postevent noise windows, based on available duration and energy level. We refined this method to reduce the number of rejected records and to favor the pre-event noise window.

Following our initial processing (Vanneste and Onvani, 2024), we discovered that several final displacement time series were affected by low-frequency disturbances. This mainly occurred for records with short pre-event noise windows (<1 s). Reprocessing with the PEER NGA-East postprocessing procedure (Goulet *et al.*, 2014) solved this problem. In this procedure, potential drift in displacement time series is avoided by applying left tapering and unconstrained sixth-order polynomial fitting compared with sixth-order polynomial fitting with the zeroth and first coefficients constrained to zero without prior tapering (Boore *et al.*, 2012).

Next, we calculated ground-motion IMs. IMS provide a simplified estimate of the damage potential of earthquake ground motion, which depends, among other factors, on the frequency content of the radiated waves and the natural period of the affected structures. To capture this variability, various IMs have been defined in literature. The most widely used are peak ground motions and response spectra. The other IMs can be categorized as integrals over time histories, integrals over part of the response spectrum, averages over part of the response spectrum, and durations. Table 3 lists and describes all IMs included in the BELSHAKE database. In total, 109 IMs have been calculated, including 92 response spectral periods between 0.01 and 4 s.

All IMs were computed for different component and window combinations. In addition to the physical Z (vertical), E (east), and N (north) components, we also computed IMs for the *T* (transverse) component (equivalent to *SH*-wave motion), the geometric mean (GM) of the horizontal components, and the orientation-independent RotD50 and RotD100, corresponding to the 50th and 100th percentiles, respectively, over all rotation angles of the horizontal components (Boore, 2010). Most ground-motion databases provide IMs for the entire record, but this is not always available due to problems in the *P* or coda windows. We therefore computed IMs for different windows: *P*, *S*, signal (*P* + *S*) and full (*P* + *S* + coda). Because most damage caused by earthquakes is related to the *S*/*Lg* wave, we also define an "auto" window, which corresponds to either the full, the signal, or the *S* window, whichever is available in the given order of preference. Considering all combinations of components and windows, there can be up to 3052 IM values (109 IMs × 7 components × 4 windows) for each record in the database.

We did not compute IMs for components/windows with bad quality. We also did not compute peak ground acceleration (PGA) and peak ground velocity (PGV) for records with low sample rate (<20 Hz). Furthermore, response spectra and derived IMs (Housner intensity [HI], acceleration spectral intensity [ASI], effective peak acceleration [EPA], effective peak velocity [EPV], and effective peak displacement [EPD]) were not computed for

- records for which the full instrument correction was not available (only the total sensitivity);
- records which have been manually corrected; and
- components/windows with intermediate quality.

In total, the BELSHAKE database contains IMs for more than 120,000 record/component/window combinations. It is impossible to show all calculated IMs in a few plots, but as a representative example, Figure 5 shows the distribution of PGA values (RotD50 component, "auto" window) as a function of distance and magnitude. In a first approximation, these results appear quite comparable with the RESIF/Epos-France database (Traversa *et al.*, 2020; Buscetti *et al.*, 2025), showing a consistent relation with respect to distance and magnitude.

Similar to the RESIF/Epos-France database, we limit the range over which response spectra are computed by considering an inward margin of 20% with respect to the reliable

TABLE 3
Definition of Intensity Measures Calculated in BELSHAKE

Category	Code	Intensity Measure	Formula	Unit
Peak ground motion	PGA	Peak ground acceleration	$\max(\lvert a(t)\rvert)$	cm/s^2
	PGV	Peak ground velocity	$\max(\lvert v(t)\rvert)$	cm/s
	PGD	Peak ground displacement	$\max(\lvert d(t)\rvert)$	cm
Response spectra	PSA	Acceleration response spectrum	0.01–4 s/0.25–100 Hz, 5% damping	cm/s^2
	PSV	Pseudospectral velocity	$\mathrm{PSA} * (2\pi f)^{-1}$	c/s
	SD	Spectral displacement	$\mathrm{PSA} * (2\pi f)^{-2}$	cm
Integrals over time series	RMSa	Root mean square acceleration	$\sqrt{1/T_d \int a(t)^2 dt}$	cm/s^2
	AI	Arias intensity	$(\pi/2g) \int^{T_d} a(t)^2 dt$	m/s
	CAV	Cumulative absolute velocity	$\int \lvert a(t)\rvert dt$	g.s
	sCAV	Standardized CAV	CAV of 1-s windows in which PGA ≥ 0.025 *g*	g.s
	bCAV	Bracketed CAV	CAV of portion of *a*(*t*) ≥0.05 *g*	g.s
Integrals over part of response spectrum	HI	Housner intensity	$\int_{T=0.1}^{2.5} \mathrm{PSV}(T)dT$	cm
	ASI	Acceleration spectral intensity	$\int_{T=0.1}^{0.5} \mathrm{PSA}(T)dT$	cm/s
Average over part of response spectrum	EPA	Effective peak acceleration	$\overline{\mathrm{PSA}[0.1 \le T \le 0.5]}/2.5$	cm/s^2
	EPV	Effective peak velocity	$\overline{\mathrm{PSV}[0.7 \le T \le 2]}/2.5$	cm/s
	EPD	Effective peak displacement	$\overline{\mathrm{SD}[2.5 \le T \le 4.0]}/2.5$	cm
Duration	D5_75	Significant (Arias) duration	*T* corresponding to buildup from 5% to 75% of cumulative AI	s
	D5_95	Significant (Arias) duration	*T* corresponding to buildup from 5% to 95% of cumulative AI	s
	D5_95′	Effective duration	2 × *T* corresponding to buildup from 20% to 80% of cumulative AI (Boore and Thompson, 2014)	s
	Db5PcG	Bracketed duration	*T* of portion between first and last occurrence of *a*(*t*) ≥0.05 *g*	s

frequency range of the FAS. As a result, the number of records contributing to each response spectral frequency is different (Fig. 6). At low frequencies, coverage quickly drops below ~0.7 Hz. Because the corner frequency of the source spectrum decreases with magnitude, higher magnitudes ($M_L \ge 4$) contribute relatively more to the lower frequencies, but these are fewer. At high frequencies, coverage drops above ~30 Hz, which is related to the dominant sampling rate of 100 Hz and the associated antialias filters.

Calculation of Moment Magnitudes

Moment magnitudes (M_w) are only available for a few events in the ROB earthquake catalog, from which earthquake source parameters were imported in BELSHAKE. Because it is essential to have reliable M_w values to compare with other ground-motion databases and GMMs, we calculated those with the Python package SourceSpec (Satriano *et al.*, 2016; Satriano, 2025), from displacement spectra derived from the BELSHAKE waveform data. We changed the source code of this program to improve the success rate with the specific data available, which include single-component records, records with short or missing pre-event noise windows, and so forth. These code changes were shared with the author and merged in the main development branch (see Data and Resources). The program was then applied in a semiautomated way to all events with sufficient records, taking advantage of the metadata (component/window quality, reliable frequency range, response reliability, etc.).

The full analysis will be presented in more detail elsewhere, but we summarize the main results here. For each earthquake, we performed up to five computations, depending on the available components and information on the focal mechanism:

- two wave types: *P* wave (on the Z component) and *SH*-wave (on the T component);

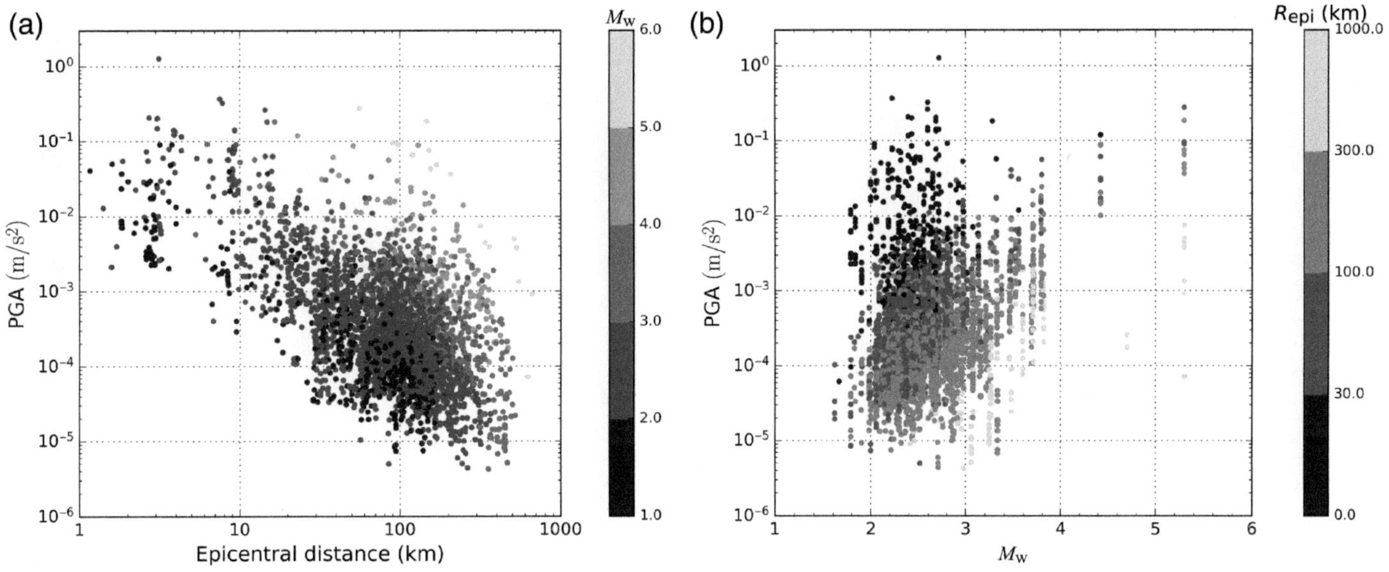

Figure 5. Distribution of peak ground acceleration (PGA) values computed for the RotD50 component and "auto" window in the BELSHAKE database. (a) As a function of epicentral distance, colors represent M_w classes. (b) As a function of magnitude M_w, colors represent epicentral distance classes. The color version of this figure is available only in the electronic edition.

- two radiation patterns: average radiation factor (0.42 for P waves and 0.59 for S waves, compare with Kaneko and Shearer, 2014) and focal mechanism (if available); and
- two geometrical spreading functions: simple $1/R$ and a segmented power law function derived from a recalibration of the local magnitude scale (Vanneste and Camelbeeck, 2025). The latter was only applied for the SH wave and average radiation pattern.

All results are stored in two database tables, one containing the parameters determined for individual stations and the other the averaged solutions for each event.

Comparison of these different computations shows that results based on the P wave and on the SH wave are very consistent for average radiation pattern and simple $1/R$ geometrical spreading (Fig. 7a): the overall difference is small ($\Delta M_{w_{P-SH}} = 0.10$), the variability is quite low ($\sigma = 0.10$), and there are practically no outliers. For the SH wave, the difference between simple $1/R$ geometrical spreading and the segmented spreading function is also very small ($M_w(1/R) - M_w(\text{segm}) = 0.03 \pm 0.05$), but the segmented model yields a lower mean station variability ($\overline{\sigma_{\text{segm}}} = 0.136$) than the simple model ($\overline{\sigma_{1/R}} = 0.149$), indicating a better fit. The differences between values based on focal mechanisms and those based on average radiation pattern are small when P waves are used ($\Delta M_{w_{\text{fm-avg}}} = 0.10$) but significantly higher for the SH wave ($M_{w_{\text{fm-avg}}} = 0.21$). In both cases, the station variability is significantly higher when using focal mechanisms ($\overline{\sigma_{P,\text{fm}}} = 0.244$, $\overline{\sigma_{SH,\text{fm}}} = 0.275$) than when using the average radiation factor ($\overline{\sigma_{P,\text{avg}}} = 0.181$, $\overline{\sigma_{SH,\text{avg}}} = 0.174$), which indicates that solutions based on focal mechanisms are less reliable.

Based on this analysis, we calculate final M_w values for BELSHAKE events as the average (weighted by the number of contributing stations) of the P-wave solution based on simple $1/R$ geometrical spreading and the SH-wave solution based on the segmented spreading model, in both cases using the average radiation factor only and requiring at least four contributing stations. This resulted in direct M_w values for 294 events. The use of both P and S waves should minimize any bias related to the radiation pattern. The median and 95th percentile standard deviations are 0.15 and 0.27, respectively, indicating that these M_w values are well constrained. Our average

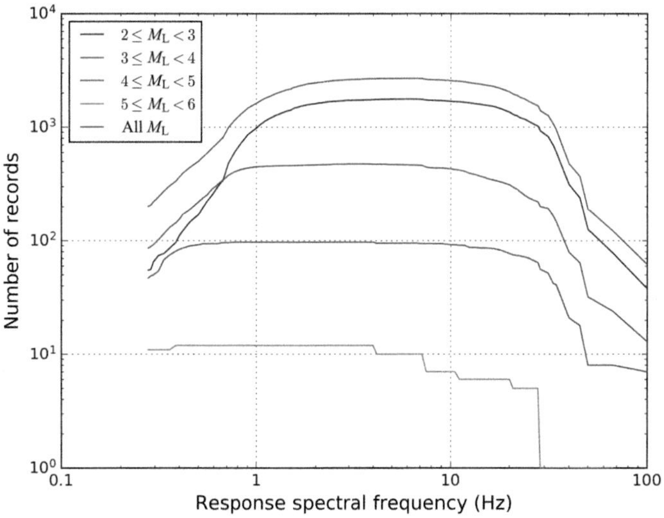

Figure 6. Number of reliable records for each response spectral frequency (GM component, S window) and different magnitude ranges. The color version of this figure is available only in the electronic edition.

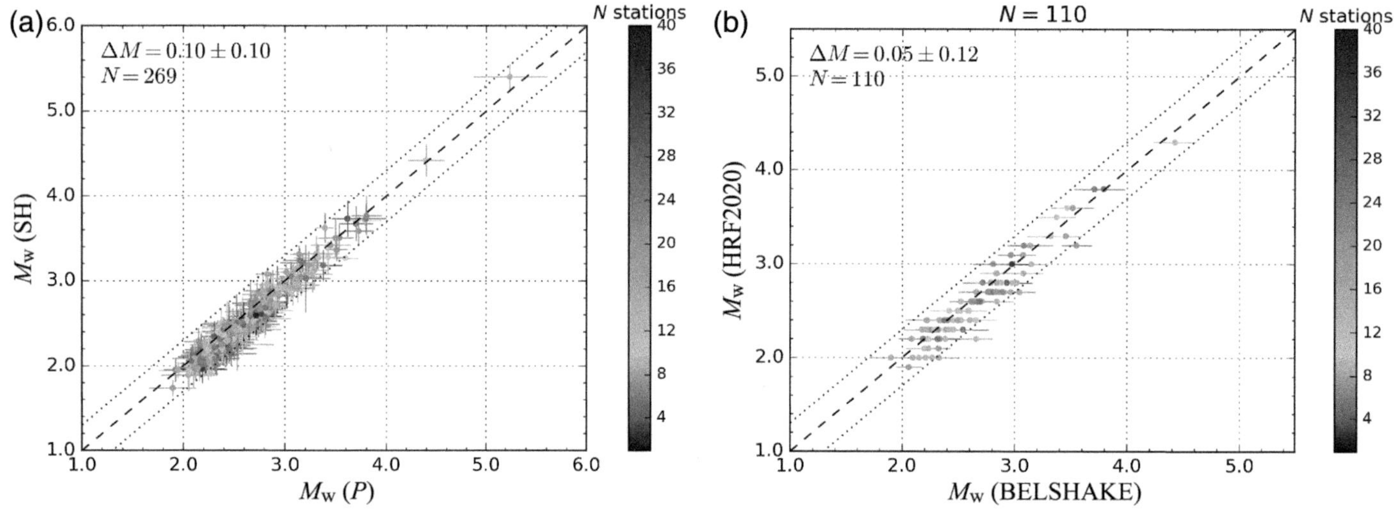

Figure 7. (a) Comparison of M_w values based on the *P* wave and on the *SH* wave, in both cases using average radiation pattern and simple 1/*R* geometrical spreading. (b) Comparison of average M_w values determined from the BELSHAKE database and M_w values in the HRF2020 catalog (Hinzen *et al.*, 2020). Only earthquakes with at least four contributing stations are included. Horizontal and vertical bars indicate standard deviations and symbols are colored according to number of contributing stations. The dashed line indicates 1:1 relation; the dotted line indicates 1:1 relation ±0.3 magnitude units. The color version of this figure is available only in the electronic edition.

M_w values are also in good agreement with those in the catalogs of neighboring agencies, such as the HRF2020 catalog (110 common events) of the Bensberg network for the northern Rhine area (Hinzen *et al.*, 2020) and the French seismic CATalogue FCAT-17 (17 common events) (Manchuel *et al.*, 2018), which have been computed from different waveform data. The comparison with the HRF-2020 catalog is shown in Figure 7b, whereas the comparison with FCAT-17 is shown in Figure S2. The overall difference (M_w(BELSHAKE)–M_w(HRF2020) = 0.05) is small, the standard deviation ($\sigma = 0.12$) is also relatively small, and there is only one minor outlier: a small earthquake near Heerlen (The Netherlands) on 20 December 2000, for which we obtain $M_w = 2.65 \pm 0.14$ (based on 11 stations) compared with M_w 2.2 in HRF2020. We did not find an obvious explanation for this outlier, but it is consistent with the M_L value. Thus, moment magnitudes in the BELSHAKE database are consistent both internally and with respect to independent catalogs. We also compared our direct M_w values with values converted from M_L using the empirical relation of Grünthal *et al.* (2009). The result in Figure S2 shows a relatively wide spread with outliers on both sides. This is particularly the case for $M_w < 3.5$, which is not surprising because the conversion equation was not calibrated for that range. We also note that our standard deviations are generally smaller than those of the conversion equation.

The M_w computations also allowed establishing a new empirical relation with the Belgian M_L scale (Vanneste and Camelbeeck, 2025). We applied it to estimate M_w for the remaining earthquakes in the BELSHAKE database with insufficient number of stations to determine M_w directly.

Station Characterization

Station metadata are an important aspect of ground-motion databases, for example, to link ground motion to site conditions. However, collecting this information is not so straightforward because it has not been systematically maintained in the ROB seismic routine database and many stations have been discontinued since their initial deployment. We tried to complete this information as much as possible for stations of the Belgian seismic network, including: Eurocode 8 (EC8) soil class (Comité Européen de Normalisation [CEN], 2004), time-averaged shear-wave velocity for the top 30 m (V_{S30}), depth to bedrock (h), natural resonance frequency (f_0), lithology, stratigraphic formation, and geological age. For the geotechnical parameters, we included a field to describe the method that was used to determine them. Ten key Belgian stations have been characterized using array measurements (Bruyninx *et al.*, 2023), and for 21 stations information was available from well logging or geophysical investigations, but most of the current and all discontinued stations lacked specific characterization. For those stations, we had to fall back on (1) geological correlation with measured stations, (2) estimation based on other parameters, for example, f_0 converted to bedrock depth h following power law relations designed for specific regions (Van Noten *et al.*, 2022), (3) Rayleigh-wave single-station methods (RayDec; Hobiger *et al.*, 2009), or (4) average values associated with EC8 soil classes. Table 4 lists the different methods used to determine V_{S30}, which is the most important site parameter for ground-motion modeling. For more than half of the stations (68 out of 129), representing 3147 out of 5936 ground-motion records, V_{S30} is based on the EC8 soil class, which is the least reliable method.

TABLE 4
Current Distribution of Methods Used to Determine V_{S30} for Stations of the Belgian Seismic Network in the BELSHAKE Database

V_{S30} Method	Number of Stations	Number of Records
Array measurements	10	1327
Well logging	11	444
Seismic refraction (Camelbeeck, 1993)	5	245
SASW (Camelbeeck, 1993)	3	166
Active seismics using hammer shots	2	181
RayDec	1	55
Estimated from f_0 and h	16	138
Geological correlation with measured station	8	197
Extrapolation based on geological model (Stafleu *et al.*, 2024)	4	30
EC8 soil class	69	3153
Total	129	5936

EC8, Eurocode 8; SASW, spectral analysis of surface waves.

We tested whether it would be possible to improve the V_{S30} values estimated from EC8 by comparing our measured values with values from a global V_{S30} map inferred from topographic slopes (Heath *et al.*, 2020). In flat regions like northern Belgium, slope-derived V_{S30} values are comparable with measured values. However, in hilly areas, such as the Ardennes in southern Belgium where most of our stations are situated, V_{S30} from slope often underestimates (soil class B) the observed V_{S30} (soil class A). This appears to be linked to stations installed in valley floors where the global model expects slower V_{S30} values, whereas our site characterization work shows that these stations should be considered as bedrock stations with EC8 soil class A. This indicates that adopting V_{S30} values from global slope-derived models in southern Belgium would probably lead to overestimation of site amplification.

The EC8 soil class of stations of the Belgian network (having ≥10 records) is shown in Figure 1, superposed on the Belgian geological outcrop map. An interesting result of our analysis so far is that the mean and median V_{S30} for stations situated on rock (soil class A), not including soil-class-derived values, are 1440 and 1100 m/s, respectively. This is significantly higher than the value of 800 m/s that is generally considered for soil class A. Accordingly, we attribute the median V_{S30} value to stations for which no direct information is available and that are situated on soil class A.

We also compiled information on the installation conditions following the classification in the ESM database (Luzi *et al.*, 2016), assigning three codes to each station (whenever possible): housing code (indicating the type of structure the instrument is situated in), installation code (related to the contact surface on which the instrument is installed), and proximity code (indicating proximity to structures). These factors may influence recorded motion compared to free-field conditions.

Data Validation

To ensure the quality and reliability of IMs in the BELSHAKE database, we applied different consistency checks to identify anomalous records. Outliers were examined, and those considered as problematic were either corrected and reprocessed or removed from the database. The following evaluations were performed: (1) evaluation of different component ratios; (2) residual analysis with respect to a generic GMM; (3) comparison of collocated stations; and (4) comparison with events that are also included in the RESIF/Epos-France database.

These different methods and their results are described in more detail in section S3. Here, we only mention the results of residual analysis based on mixed-effects regression. This analysis involved a comparison between IMs (PGA/PGV) in the database and those predicted by a generic GMM fitted to the observations. The advantage of an ad hoc GMM compared to a published model is that its median is centered on the data set, which allows identifying inconsistencies with higher sensitivity (Traversa *et al.*, 2020). We used the same functional form as Traversa *et al.* (2020) in their analysis of the French RESIF/Epos-France database, and we also used the same reference distance ($R_{ref} = 1$ km) and reference magnitude ($M_{ref} = 3.7$), but a different magnitude scale (M_w instead of M_L). Mixed-effects regression (using the Python statsmodels module of Seabold and Perktold, 2010) allows the decomposition of the total residual into different components:

$$\log_{10} Y = F_D(R,M) + F_M(M) + \delta B_e + \delta S2S_s + \epsilon. \quad (1)$$

Y is the ground-motion parameter, that is, PGA or PGV; $F_D(R,M)$ and $F_M(M)$ are the distance and magnitude-scaling components of the GMM, which are considered as the fixed effects (see formulas in Traversa *et al.*, 2020 and in section S3); δB_e and $\delta S2S_s$ are random effects corresponding to between-event and between-station residuals, respectively; ϵ is a lognormally distributed residual term, representing the unexplained or event- and station-corrected residual. This separation gives better insight into the origin of possible inconsistencies (e.g., related to source parameters, station/site parameters, …).

We computed residuals that are similar to or smaller than those in the French RESIF/Epos-France database (Traversa *et al.*, 2020). The results for PGV, RotD50 component and "auto" window are shown in Figure 8. The top panel displays the between-station residuals. These show a relatively good correlation with the V_{S30} values. Stations with $V_{S30} > 1200$ m/s show consistently negative residuals, whereas stations with

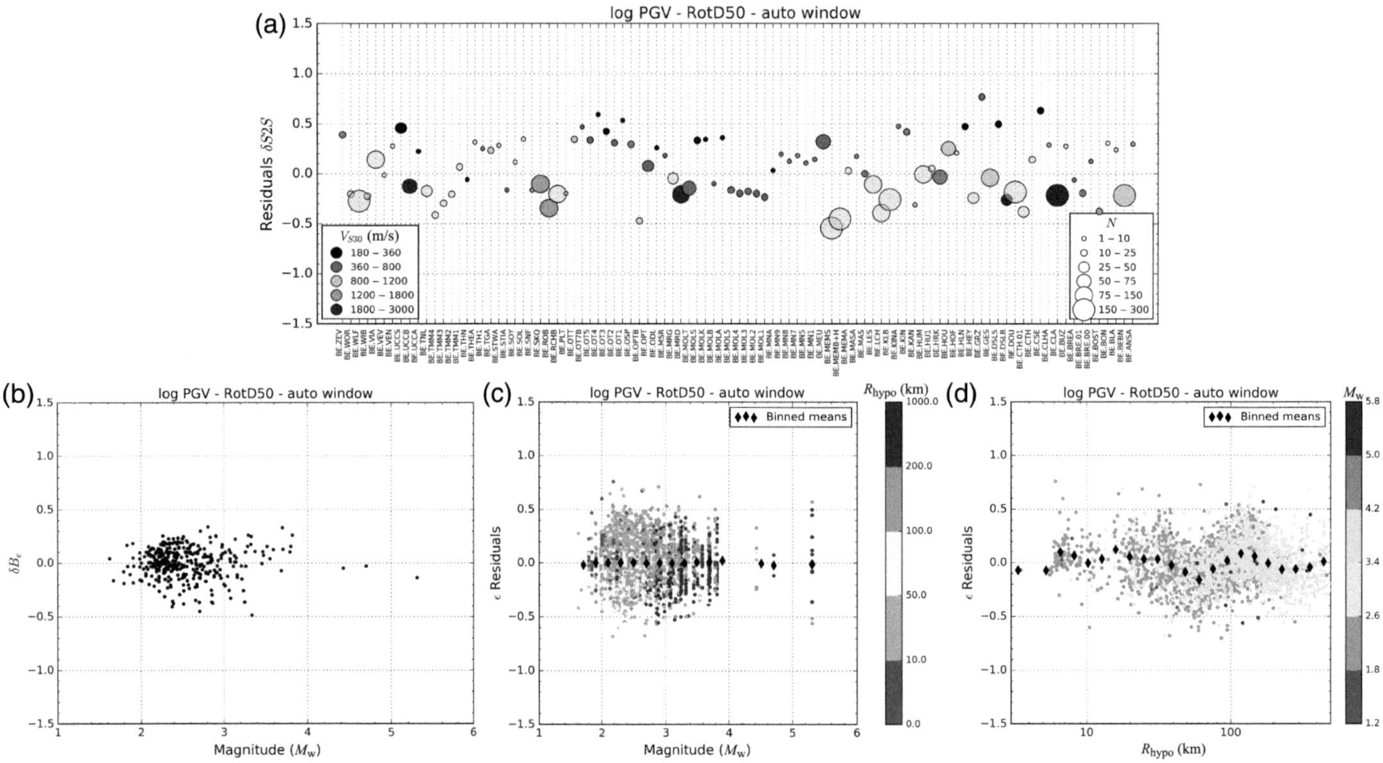

Figure 8. Results of mixed-effects regression for PGV, RotD50 component, "auto" signal window. (a) Station-to-station residuals ($\delta S2S_s$) for stations of the BE network (sorted alphabetically). Colors correspond to V_{S30} and marker sizes to number of records (N); transparent colors correspond to V_{S30} values estimated from EC8 soil class. (b) Between-event residuals (δB_e) as a function of M_w. (c) Unexplained residuals (ϵ) as a function of M_w, color coded by hypocentral distance. (d) ϵ residuals as a function of hypocentral distance, color coded by M_w. The color version of this figure is available only in the electronic edition.

$V_{S30} < 360$ m/s show generally positive residuals. The between-event residuals (bottom left panel) are all within the range −0.5 to +0.5. Data are sparser at higher magnitudes, but there is no obvious bias or trend with respect to magnitude. Outliers may be linked to earthquakes characterized by imprecise magnitude or location estimates but also to unique source characteristics, such as particularly high or low stress drop, which would require further investigation. Considering the good behavior of the between-event residuals, it may be concluded that there are no major problems in that respect in the BELSHAKE database. Finally, the unexplained residuals (bottom panels) fall mostly between −0.5 and +0.5, and entirely between −1 and +1. They show no discernible trend with magnitude, whereas the slight variations with distance are likely related to divergence from the simplified geometrical spreading term in the fitted model.

Analysis of the time evolution of unexplained residuals for each station allowed identifying anomalies that are consistent over a particular period of time. In some cases, as described in section S3, these indicated problems with the instrument response or important changes of the instrument emplacement, which we addressed.

Conclusions and Outlook

We have compiled a new ground-motion database for Belgium and bordering regions, based on waveform data starting from 1985. This database currently contains ~6400 records from 344 tectonic and induced earthquakes with $M_L \geq 2$. These were recorded by a mix of single- and three-component short-period instruments, broadband seismometers, and (to a lesser extent) accelerometers. The only damaging event in the database is the 13 April 1992 M_w 5.3 Roermond, The Netherlands, earthquake. Considerable efforts were undertaken to ensure that both the waveform data, the metadata, and the derived ground-motion data adhere to the standards set by international ground-motion databases. All waveforms and phase picks have been visually inspected, and problems were either corrected or flagged. A unique feature of the BELSHAKE database is that waveform quality of each record can be assessed at the component and signal window level. Depending on the quality, different ground-motion IMs can be computed for each component-window combination. Reconstructing instrument response for older (pre-2000) records proved to be challenging, but different methods were used to check their validity. Records for which instrument response was found to be unreliable were flagged in the database, preventing them to be used in subsequent steps. All reliable records were processed using a semiautomated, uniform workflow. The processing steps and the order in which they are applied have been adapted with slight variations from the processing schemes in existing ground-motion databases such as RESIF/Epos-France (Traversa *et al.*, 2020), ITACA (Paolucci *et al.*, 2011; Puglia *et al.*, 2014), PEER NGA-East (Goulet *et al.*, 2014, 2021), and ESM (Luzi *et al.*, 2016). Subsequently, up to 109 IMs (including 92 response spectral frequencies) were computed from the processed data, for more than 120,000 records and component-window combinations. We also determined moment magnitudes from the waveform data for 294 events in the database and confirmed their reliability by comparing the results of different methods (using *P* or *SH* waves) and comparing with values in other catalogs for a subset of the data. Finally, we performed various consistency checks to ensure the quality and reliability of IMs, including evaluation of different component ratios, residual analysis with respect to a generic GMM, comparison of collocated stations, and comparison with common events in the French RESIF/Epos-France database (Traversa *et al.*, 2020). Anomalous records were analyzed, and those found to be problematic were either corrected or removed. Overall, residuals show no discernible trend with distance or magnitude, and vary in a narrow range that is similar to or even smaller than that in RESIF/Epos-France.

Available ground-motion data in Belgium have so far been underexploited in terms of engineering seismological applications. The BELSHAKE database is a first attempt to bridge this gap. It is clear that the magnitude coverage is too limited to develop a region-specific GMM that can be used in SHA. However, the small uncertainties on epicentral locations and magnitudes and low residuals testify to its high quality. The BELSHAKE database will thus allow evaluating existing GMMs for application in Belgium. It will also contribute to a better assessment of seismic attenuation, which will in turn allow calibrating regionally adaptable models and guide stochastic simulation of earthquake ground motion. On a broader level, it will complement existing databases by increasing the coverage of low-seismicity zones and lower magnitudes. We hope it will also inspire similar initiatives in neighboring regions sharing ground-motion characteristics with Belgium. In addition, the processed waveform data in the BELSHAKE database will serve as a reference data set for many other seismological applications, such as recalibration of the Belgian M_L scale at short distances, stress-drop analysis, and more. To that end, we will continue to improve and extend the database.

Data and Resources

The ground-motion data in the BELSHAKE database have been released as a flatfile (plain text table containing the main IMs and metadata for each record) on Zenodo (doi: 10.5281/zenodo.10669581). The waveform data of the stations of the Belgian seismic network were retrieved from the waveform archive of the Royal Observatory of Belgium (doi: 10.7914/SN/BE). Their size is currently too large to make them available online, but currently they can be requested from the authors. The waveform data of the 1992 M_w 5.3 Roermond earthquake and its aftershocks will be made available as a dedicated data set (location to be determined). Geological information for the site characterization of the Belgian seismic network was taken from the pan-European geological map at 1:1,000,000 from *OneGeologyEurope*, available from the European Geological Data Infrastructure services (http://www.europe-geology.eu/, last accessed September 2023), complemented by local information inferred from Databank Ondergrond Vlaanderen (https://dov.vlaanderen.be/, last accessed September 2023) and the renewed geological mapping of Wallonia (GeolWal; https://geologie.wallonie.be/, last accessed September 2023). The Belgian seismic network can be accessed at http://seismologie.oma.be/en/the-service/seismic-network (last accessed January 2026). The Nominal Response Library can be accessed at https://ds.iris.edu/ds/nrl/ (last accessed July 2025). The contributions to the code for computing moment magnitude were shared at https://github.com/SeismicSource/sourcespec (last accessed December 2025). The supplemental material for this article includes a figure illustrating the various waveform problems that have been encountered during compilation of the BELSHAKE database, a figure comparing direct M_w estimates with values in the FCAT-17 earthquake catalog and with values converted from M_L, and a text (including figures) describing the different data validation steps in more detail than in the main article.

Declaration of Competing Interests

The authors acknowledge that there are no conflicts of interest recorded.

Acknowledgments

The BELSHAKE database was compiled in the frame of the BRAIN-be BELSHAKE project (Contract Number B2/202/P1/BELSHAKE), funded by the Belgian Science Policy Office. The characterization of stations of the Belgian seismic network also benefited from the Epos-BE project "Upgrade of Belgian federal research infrastructure for EPOS" (Contract Number FSIRI/33/EP1), funded by the Belgian Science Policy Office. The authors thank Paola Traversa for inspiration and sharing data and experiences from the RESIF/Epos-France database, and Vincent Perron and an anonymous reviewer for their constructive remarks and language corrections, which improved the article.

References

Akkar, S., M. A. Sandıkkaya, M. Şenyurt, A. Azari Sisi, B. Ö. Ay, P. Traversa, J. Douglas, F. Cotton, L. Luzi, B. Hernandez, *et al.* (2014). Reference database for seismic ground-motion in Europe (RESORCE), *Bull. Earthq. Eng.* **12,** no. 1, 311–339, doi: 10.1007/s10518-013-9506-8.

Ancheta, T. D., R. B. Darragh, J. P. Stewart, E. Seyhan, W. J. Silva, B. S. J. Chiou, K. E. Wooddell, R. W. Graves, A. R. Kottke, D. M. Boore, *et al.* (2014). NGA-West2 database, *Earthq. Spectra* **30,** no. 3, 989–1005, doi: 10.1193/070913EQS197M.

Baptie, B. (2017). Earthquake Seismology 2015/2016, British Geological Survey, Edinburgh, Open Report, OR/17/032, 48 pp.

Bommer, J. J., and N. A. Abrahamson (2006). Why do modern probabilistic seismic-hazard analyses often lead to increased hazard estimates? *Bull. Seismol. Soc. Am.* **96,** no. 6, 1967–1977, doi: 10.1785/0120060043.

Boore, D. M. (2010). Orientation-independent, nongeometric-mean measures of seismic intensity from two horizontal components of motion, *Bull. Seismol. Soc. Am.* **100,** no. 4, 1830–1835, doi: 10.1785/0120090400.

Boore, D. M., and E. M. Thompson (2014). Path durations for use in the stochastic-method simulation of ground motions, *Bull. Seismol. Soc. Am.* **104,** no. 5, 2541–2552, doi: 10.1785/0120140058.

Boore, D. M., A. A. Sisi, and S. Akkar (2012). Using pad-stripped acausally filtered strong-motion data, *Bull. Seismol. Soc. Am.* **102,** no. 2, 751–760, doi: 10.1785/0120110222.

Bruyninx, C., K. Van Noten, F. Bamahry, A. Fabian, M. Zeckra, J. Legrand, G. Rapagnani, B. Frederick, A. Miglio, D. Jacques, *et al.* 2023)). EPOS-BE - Upgrade of Belgian federal research infrastructure for EPOS, Royal Observatory of Belgium, Brussels, Belgium, 51 pp.

Buscetti, M., P. Traversa, V. Perron, P. Rischette, F. Hollender, and H. Shible (2025). Epos-France database of earthquake ground motion for Mainland France: 1996–2021 Updated Version, *Seismol. Res. Lett.* **96,** no. 2A, 1214–1226, doi: 10.1785/0220240053.

Camelbeeck, T. (1985). Some notes concerning the seismicity in Belgium. Magnitude scale. Detection capability of the Belgian seismic stations, in *Seismic Activity in Western Europe, with Particular Consideration to the Liege Earthquake of November 8, 1983*, P. Melchior (Editor), Reidel, Dordrecht, 99–108.

Camelbeeck, T. (1993). *Mécanisme au foyer des tremblements de terre et contraintes tectoniques: le cas de la zone intraplaque belge*, Observatoire Royal de Belgique, Bruxelles (in French).

Camelbeeck, T., T. van Eck, R. Pelzing, L. Ahorner, J. Loohuis, H. W. Haak, P. Hoang-Trong, and D. Hollnack (1994, The 1992 Roermond earthquake, the Netherlands, and its aftershocks, *Geol. Mijnb.* **73,** nos. 2/4, 181–197.

CEN (Comité Européen de Normalisation) (2004). Eurocode 8: Design of structures for earthquake resistance - Part 1: General rules, seismic actions and rules for buildings, European Committee for Standardization, 44 pp.

Chiou, B., R. Darragh, N. Gregor, and W. Silva (2008). NGA project strong-motion database, *Earthq. Spectra* **24,** no. 1, 23–44, doi: 10.1193/1.2894831.

Dawood, H. M., A. Rodriguez-Marek, J. Bayless, C. Goulet, and E. Thompson (2016). A Flatfile for the KiK-net database processed using an automated protocol, *Earthq. Spectra* **32,** no. 2, 1281–1302, doi: 10.1193/071214eqs106.

Department of Geosciences, Bensberg Observatory (2016). Bensberg earthquake network, *International Federation of Digital Seismograph Networks*, doi: 10.7914/SN/BQ.

Douglas, J. (2019). *Ground Motion Prediction Equations 1964 2019*, University of Strathclyde, Glasgow, United Kingdom, 650 pp.

Edwards, B., and D. Fäh (2013). A stochastic ground-motion model for Switzerland, *Bull. Seismol. Soc. Am.* **103,** no. 1, 78–98, doi: 10.1785/0120110331.

Edwards, B., M. Ntinalexis, K. Vanneste, and J. V. Elk (2025). Reconstruction of clipped time-history records, with application to ground motions from the ML 5.8 Roermond, Netherlands, 1992 earthquake, *Seismol. Res. Lett.*, doi: 10.1785/0220250139.

Gariel, J. C., C. Horrent, D. Jongmans, and T. Camelbeeck (1994). Strong ground motion computation of the 1992 Roermond earthquake, the Netherlands, from linear methods using locally recorded aftershocks, *Geol. Mijnb.* **73,** nos. 2/4, 315–321.

Ghasemi, H., T. Allen, A. Sunketa, and C. Mckenna (2026). AGMD: A ground-motion database for the Australian continental crust, *Seismol. Res. Lett* doi: 10.1785/0220250316.

Goulet, C. A., T. Kishida, T. D. Ancheta, C. H. Cramer, R. B. Darragh, W. J. Silva, Y. M. Hashash, J. Harmon, G. A. Parker, J. P. Stewart, *et al.* (2021). PEER NGA-East database, *Earthq. Spectra* **37,** no. 1_suppl, 1331–1353, doi: 10.1177/87552930211015695.

Goulet, C. A., T. Kishida, T. D. Ancheta, C. H. Cramer, R. B. Darragh, W. J. Silva, Y. M. Hashash, J. Harmon, J. P. Stewart, K. E. Wooddell, *et al.* (2014). PEER NGA-east database, Pacific Earthquake Engineering Research Center, Berkeley, California, 98 p.

Grünthal, G., R. Wahlström, and D. Stromeyer (2009). The unified catalogue of earthquakes in central, northern and northwestern Europe (CENEC)—Updated and expanded to the last millennium, *J. Seismol.* **13,** no. 4, 517–541, doi: 10.1007/s10950-008-9144-9.

Haak, H. W., J. A. Van Bodegraven, R. Sleeman, R. Verbeiren, L. Ahorner, H. Meidow, G. Grunthal, P. Hoang-Trong, R. M. W. Musson, P. Henni, *et al.* (1994). The macroseismic map of the 1992 Roermond earthquake, the Netherlands, *Geol. Mijnb.* **73,** nos. 2/4, 265–270.

Heath, D. C., D. J. Wald, C. B. Worden, E. M. Thompson, and G. M. Smoczyk (2020). A global hybrid Vs30 map with a topographic-slope-based default and regional map insets, *U.S. Geol. Surv. Data Release*, doi: 10.5066/P96HFVXM.

Heimann, S., M. Kriegerowski, M. Isken, S. Cesca, S. Daout, F. Grigoli, C. Juretzek, T. Megies, N. Nooshiri, A. Steinberg, *et al.* (2017). Pyrocko - An open-source seismology toolbox and library, *GFZ Data Services*, doi: 10.5880/GFZ.2.1.2017.001.

Hinzen, K. (2019). Engineering seismological parameters of two ML 4.3 intraplate earthquakes in the Northern Rhine Area, Germany, *Seismol. Res. Lett.* **90,** no. 3, 1258–1267, doi: 10.1785/0220180265.

Hinzen, K.-G., S. K. Reamer, and C. Fleischer (2020). Seismicity in the Northern Rhine Area (1995–2018), *J. Seismol.*, doi: 10.1007/s10950-020-09976-7.

Hobiger, M., P.-Y. Bard, C. Cornou, and N. Le Bihan (2009). Single station determination of Rayleigh wave ellipticity by using the random decrement technique (RayDec), *Geophys. Res. Lett.* **36,** no. 14, doi: 10.1029/2009GL038863.

Kaneko, Y., and P. M. Shearer (2014). Seismic source spectra and estimated stress drop derived from cohesive-zone models of circular subshear rupture, *Geophys. J. Int.* **197,** no. 2, 1002–1015, doi: 10.1093/gji/ggu030.

KNMI (1993). *Netherlands Seismic and Acoustic Network*, Royal Netherlands Meteorological Institute, doi: 10.21944/e970fd34-23b9-3411-b366-e4f72877d2c5.

Krischer, L., J. Smith, W. Lei, M. Lefebvre, Y. Ruan, E. S. de Andrade, N. Podhorszki, E. Bozdağ, and J. Tromp (2016). An adaptable seismic data format, *Geophys. J. Int.* **207,** no. 2, 1003–1011, doi: 10.1093/gji/ggw319.

Leynaud, D., D. Jongmans, H. Teerlynck, and T. Camelbeeck (2000). Seismic hazard assessment in Belgium, *Geol. Belg.* **3,** nos. 1/2, 67–86.

Luzi, L., R. Puglia, E. Russo, M. D'Amico, C. Felicetta, F. Pacor, G. Lanzano, U. Çeken, J. Clinton, G. Costa, *et al.* (2016). The engineering strong-motion database: A platform to access Pan-European accelerometric data, *Seismol. Res. Lett.* **87,** no. 4, 987–997, doi: 10.1785/0220150278.

Manchuel, K., P. Traversa, D. Baumont, M. Cara, E. Nayman, and C. Durouchoux (2018). The French seismic CATalogue (FCAT-17), *Bull. Earthq. Eng.* **16,** no. 6, 2227–2251, doi: 10.1007/s10518-017-0236-1.

Megies, T., M. Beyreuther, R. Barsch, L. Krischer, and J. Wassermann (2011). ObsPy - What can it do for data centers and observatories? *Ann. Geophys.* **54,** no. 1, 47–58, doi: 10.4401/ag-4838.

Neefs, B., K. Van Noten, K. Vanneste, and T. Camelbeeck (2025). The Belgian traditional macroseismic (BTM) database of the twentieth century, *J. Seismol.* **29,** no. 5, 1005–1036, doi: 10.1007/s10950-024-10266-9.

Pacor, F., R. Paolucci, L. Luzi, F. Sabetta, A. Spinelli, A. Gorini, M. Nicoletti, S. Marcucci, L. Filippi, and M. Dolce (2011). Overview of the Italian strong motion database ITACA 1.0, *Bull. Earthq. Eng.* **9,** no. 6, 1723–1739, doi: 10.1007/s10518-011-9327-6.

Paolucci, R., F. Pacor, R. Puglia, G. Ameri, C. Cauzzi, and M. Massa (2011). Record processing in ITACA, the new Italian strong-motion database, in *Earthquake Data in Engineering Seismology: Predictive Models, Data Management and Networks*, S. Akkar, P. Gülkan, and T. van Eck (Editors), Springer, 99–113, doi: 10.1007/978-94-007-0152-6_8.

Perron, V., A. Laurendeau, F. Hollender, P.-Y. Bard, C. Gélis, P. Traversa, and S. Drouet (2018). Selecting time windows of seismic phases and noise for engineering seismology applications: A versatile methodology and algorithm, *Bull. Earthq. Eng.* **16,** 2211–2225, doi: 10.1007/s10518-017-0131-9.

Puglia, R., E. Russo, F. Pacor, L. Luzi, and M. D. Amico (2014). A software for the processing of the waveforms of the Italian strong motion database, *Second European Conference on Earthquake Engineering and Seismology Istanbul*, Türkiye, 25–29 August 2014, 1–3.

Rietbrock, A., and B. Edwards (2019). Update of the UK stochastic ground motion model, *SECED 2019 Conference*, Greenwich, London, 9–10 September 2019, 10 pp.

Rietbrock, A., F. Strasser, and B. Edwards (2013). A stochastic earthquake ground-motion prediction model for the United Kingdom, *Bull. Seismol. Soc. Am.* **103,** no. 1, 57–77, doi: 10.1785/0120110231.

Royal Observatory of Belgium (1985). Belgian seismic network, *International Federation of Digitial Seismographic Networks*, doi: 10.7914/SN/BE.

Sabetta, F., A. Lucantoni, H. Bungum, and J. J. Bommer (2005). Sensitivity of PSHA results to ground motion prediction relations and logic-tree weights, *Soil Dynam. Earthq. Eng.* **25,** no. 4, 317–329, doi: 10.1016/j.soildyn.2005.02.002.

Sargeant, S. L., P. J. Stafford, R. Lawley, G. Weatherill, A. J. Weston, J. J. Bommer, P. W. Burton, M. Free, R. M. W. Musson, T. Kuuyuor, *et al.* (2008). Observations from the Folkestone, U.K., earthquake of 28 April 2007, *Seismol. Res. Lett.* **79,** no. 5, 672–687, doi: 10.1785/gssrl.79.5.672.

Satriano, C. (2025). SourceSpec – Earthquake source parameters from P- or S-wave displacement spectra (1.8), doi: 10.5281/ZENODO.3688587.

Satriano, C., A. R. Mejjia Uquiche, and J. M. Saurel (2016). Spectral estimation of seismic moment, corner frequency and radiated energy for earthquakes in the lesser Antilles, *American Geophysical Union, Fall Meeting*, S13A–2518.

Seabold, S., and J. Perktold (2010). statsmodels: Econometric and statistical modeling with python, *9th Python in Science Conference*, Austin, Texas, 28 June–3 July 2010.

Stafleu, J., D. Kraaijpoel, and S. Osinga (2024). Vs30 map of the Netherlands—Update of the proof-of-concept map of 2022, TNO, 30 pp.

Strollo, A. (2021). EIDA: The European integrated data archive and service infrastructure within ORFEUS, *Seismol. Res. Lett.* **92,** no. 3, 1788–1795, doi: 10.1785/0220200413.

Templeton, M. E. (2021). *IRIS Library of Nominal Response for Seismic Instruments*, Incorporated Research Institutions for Seismology, Dataset, doi: 10.17611/S7159Q.

Traversa, P., E. Maufroy, F. Hollender, V. Perron, V. Bremaud, H. Shible, S. Drouet, P. Guéguen, M. Langlais, D. Wolyniec, *et al.* (2020). RESIF RAP and RLBP dataset of earthquake ground motion in Mainland France, *Seismol. Res. Lett.* **91,** no. 4, 2409–2424, doi: 10.1785/0220190367.

Van Noten, K., T. Lecocq, C. Goffin, B. Meyvis, J. Molron, T. N. Debacker, and X. Devleeschouwer (2022). Brussels' bedrock paleorelief from borehole-controlled power laws linking polarised H/V resonance frequencies and sediment thickness, *J. Seismol.* **26,** 35–55, doi: 10.1007/s10950-021-10039-8.

Van Noten, K., T. Lecocq, C. Sira, K. G. Hinzen, and T. Camelbeeck (2017). Path and site effects deduced from merged transfrontier internet macroseismic data of two recent M4 earthquakes in northwest Europe using a grid cell approach, *Solid Earth* **8,** no. 2, 453–477, doi: 10.5194/se-8-453-2017.

Vanneste, K., and T. Camelbeeck (2025). Recalibration of the local magnitude scale of the Belgian seismic network: Improved models of geometrical spreading and path duration, *Seismica*, doi: 10.21203/rs.3.rs-7850272/v1

Vanneste, K., and M. Onvani (2024). Waveform processing in BELSHAKE, the Belgian ground-motion database, *18th World Conf. on Earthquake Engineering* Milano, Italy, 30 June–5 July 2024, 12 pp.

Vanneste, K., T. Camelbeeck, and K. Verbeeck (2013). A model of composite seismic sources for the Lower Rhine Graben, northwest Europe, *Bull. Seismol. Soc. Am.* **103,** no. 2A, 984–1007, doi: 10.1785/0120120037.

Vanneste, K., B. Vleminckx, K. Verbeeck, and T. Camelbeeck (2014). Development of seismic hazard maps for Belgium, in *DGEB Workshop "Seismic Hazard Harmonisation in Europe (SHARE)*, C. Butenweg and D. Kaiser (Editors), DGEB, Frankfurt am Main, Germany, 61–68.

Zhang, J., J. Hao, X. Zhao, S. Wang, L. Zhao, W. Wang, and Z. Yao (2016). Restoration of clipped seismic waveforms using projection onto convex sets method, *Sci. Rep.* **6,** doi: 10.1038/srep39056.

Manuscript received 18 September 2025
Published online 21 January 2026

Seismogenic Crustal Stress in Intraplate North America: Slip Potential of Suspected Quaternary Faults in the Central and Eastern United States

Will Levandowski*[1]

Abstract

Eastern North America has experienced numerous major tectonic events, which have left behind faults of many different orientations. The modern seismogenic potential of these faults depends chiefly on their orientations relative to the local crustal stress field. Here, earthquake focal mechanisms are used to map seismogenic stress across eastern North America. There are large variations, from east-northeast compression and reverse faulting along the Atlantic coast, through transpression and strike slip in the Midcontinent, to trans-tension with widely varying extension directions on the Great Plains, plus important second-order variations. Against this heterogeneous backdrop, the slip potential of 61 suspected Quaternary tectonic features is then quantified in terms of normalized instability and Coulomb failure stress gradient. These analyses provide insight into whether the proposed faults and senses of slip comport with local stress, or if a nontectonic origin for the features is more likely. Of the 61 features, 15 are deemed incompatible with the modern stress field, 7 are misaligned for slip but uncertainties in fault geometry or stress prevent their being ruled out, 10 are suitable for slip but not optimally oriented, 25 are optimally oriented, and there is insufficient information for the remaining four. Slip potential quantification is extended to mapped geologic faults surrounding the features to identify candidate faults for historical earthquakes (e.g., 1886 Charleston, South Carolina; 1727 Newburyport, Massachusetts) or instrumental seismicity (e.g., Moodus, Connecticut; Wabash Valley Seismic Zone), or to highlight regional optimally oriented faults that may slip in future earthquakes (e.g., Ramapo fault system, New Jersey). This new information may aid in interpreting historical accounts, prioritizing paleoseismic targets, and understanding fault-system behavior.

Cite this article as Levandowski, W. (2026). Seismogenic Crustal Stress in Intraplate North America: Slip Potential of Suspected Quaternary Faults in the Central and Eastern United States, *Seismol. Res. Lett.* **97**, 934–956, doi: 10.1785/0220250372.

Supplemental Material

Introduction

Plenty of faults available for reactivation

Eastern North America has experienced two complete Wilson Cycles and a total of around 10 separate tectonic events—collision, suturing, plate-scale transpression and trans-tension, and rifting—with different shortening or extension directions (e.g., King, 1959; Rodgers, 1967; Withjack and Schlische, 2005; Whitmeyer and Karlstrom, 2007). This history of deformation has left behind a tapestry of faults of many orientations. Many of these faults have already been active multiple times because these serial deformation events often exploited the same fault zones (e.g., Sykes, 1978) and reused pre-existing faults, sometimes with a different sense of slip or slip direction (e.g., Levandowski *et al.*, 2017; Thomas and Powell, 2018). These inherited faults may now be prone to reactivation in the modern stress field.

Intraplate earthquakes do typically occur by reactivation of pre-existing faults that are well-oriented for frictional slip under the local stress field (e.g., Zoback and Zoback, 1981; Zoback, 1992a; Worum *et al.*, 2008; McNamara *et al.*, 2015; Walsh and Zoback, 2016). Faults are prone to frictional slip when the shear traction resolved on them reaches a critical magnitude τ_{crit} equal to the frictional resistance to sliding, according to the Mohr–Coulomb failure criterion:

$$\tau_{crit} = (S_N - Pp), \qquad (1)$$

1. Tetra Tech, Inc., Chapel Hill, North Carolina, U.S.A., https://orcid.org/0000-0003-4903-5012 (WL)

*Corresponding author: will.levandowski@tetratech.com

in which μ is the coefficient of static friction, S_N is the magnitude of normal traction, and Pp is pore fluid pressure on the fault. This formulation implies 0 cohesion, consistent with precedent (e.g., Zoback, 1992a; Hurd and Zoback, 2012a,b), to represent a pre-existing fault. The stresses τ_{crit} and S_N are functions of fault orientation relative to the local crustal stress field at seismogenic depth. Quantifying the state of stress is thus paramount to anticipating which of the abundant inherited faults pose seismic hazards.

Variable faulting despite plate-boundary compression

Stress in central and eastern North America (CENA) is dominated by plate-scale processes, even though the nearest plate boundary—the Mid-Atlantic ridge—is 3000–6000 km away. Mid-Atlantic spreading pushes North America west-southwest (WSW; N, north; E, east; S, south; W, west). This ridge push (edge normal traction), the differential motion it causes with the underlying asthenosphere (basal shear traction), or a combination creates a dominant ENE–WSW compressive stress across intraplate eastern North America (e.g., Sbar and Sykes, 1973; Zoback and Zoback, 1980, 1989; Zoback, 1992a; Richardson and Zoback, 1991). The western margin of North America is also compressive, comprising highly oblique transpression along the San Andreas fault system, highly oblique Cascadia subduction, and transpression along the Queen Charlotte fault. Thus, compressive plate boundary tractions encircle North America (e.g., Humphreys and Coblentz, 2007).

Despite this long-wavelength tectonic squeeze, earthquake focal mechanisms (FMs) across North America display variable faulting type (classified following Zoback, 1992b; Table 1) and maximum-horizontal shortening direction, $S_{H\max}$ (Fig. 1). Although FMs indicate faulting type and $S_{H\max}$, these two parameters alone do not constrain stress. For instance, the P axis could lie anywhere within the compressional quadrant (e.g., McKenzie, 1969), and faulting types neither uniquely associate with one stress regime, nor do they constrain relative stress magnitudes.

Combining numerous FMs—20 to 25 (Townend and Zoback, 2001) to 35 or more (Lundstern, 2024)—in a formal stress inversion, however, provides constraints on relative stress magnitudes and the associated stress regime, as well as on principal stress directions. FM-based stress inversions can thus quantify stress variations across North America (Fig. 2).

Known and suspected seismogenic features in the CEUS: Classes A, B, and C

More than 25 yr ago, Crone and Wheeler (2000) cataloged known or suspected Quaternary-active faults or other seismogenic features across the intraplate central and eastern United States (CEUS). They separated the features into those with demonstrable Quaternary faulting (class A), possible Quaternary activity that remains unproven (class B), and equivocal seismogenic origin (class C).

TABLE 1
Focal Mechanism Categorization (Zoback, 1992b)

P Plunge	N Plunge	T Plunge	Type	Inferred $S_{H\max}$
pl ≥ 52°		pl ≤ 35°	Normal (NF)	B trend
40° ≤ pl < 52°		pl ≤ 20°	Oblique normal (NS)	T trend + 90°
pl < 40°	pl ≥45°	pl ≤ 20°	Strike slip (SS)	T trend + 90°
pl ≤ 20°	pl ≥ 45°	pl < 40°	Strike slip (SS)	P trend
pl ≤ 20°		40° ≤ pl < 52°	Oblique reverse (TS)	P trend
pl ≤ 35°		pl ≥ 52°	Reverse (TF)	P trend

To this list, this study adds the epicentral regions of the 2020 M_w 5.1 Sparta, North Carolina, and 2024 M_w 4.8 Tewksbury, New Jersey, earthquakes as class B, because of insufficient evidence for repeated Quaternary tectonism (Jobe *et al.*, 2022; Kolawole *et al.*, 2024, respectively). The eastern Tennessee seismic zone (ETSZ) is added as class A because it is already considered a distinct source zone by the U.S. Geological Survey (USGS) National Seismic Hazard Model (Petersen *et al.*, 2023). Although reverse slip on NNE-trending faults has been proposed (e.g., Warrell *et al.*, 2017; Cox *et al.*, 2022), Jobe *et al.* (2024) examined high-resolution topographic data and conducted field reconnaissance in the ETSZ, finding no evidence of surface-rupturing faults. Repeated Quaternary activity has been documented in the Saline River fault zone (SRFZ), Arkansas (Cox *et al.*, 2013), upgrading it to class A (Jobe *et al.*, 2022).

Stress offers new constraints on seismogenic potential

Available FMs in the CEUS were few (n = 88) and scattered when Crone and Wheeler (2000) were assembling this list, limiting their ability to judge whether features were duly aligned for slip in their local stress field. Rather, their judgments were based mostly on geologic evidence and, in a few cases, seismicity patterns. However, there are serious challenges to geologic studies of CEUS seismotectonics. Low strain and earthquake rates, agriculture, urban and suburban development, glaciation, erosion, and dense vegetation hide or ablate paleoseismic scarps and other signatures of faulting in the CEUS. Moreover, surface ruptures are exceedingly rare in intraplate regions worldwide (e.g., Figueiredo *et al.*, 2022), so even large earthquakes may not leave surficial clues. Meanwhile, seismicity generally does not align with known faults, and liquefaction features due to prehistoric or historic earthquakes can seldom be ascribed to a specific fault. Many suspected CEUS faults have been trenched only to reveal fluvial scarps, collapse features, or other nontectonic origins.

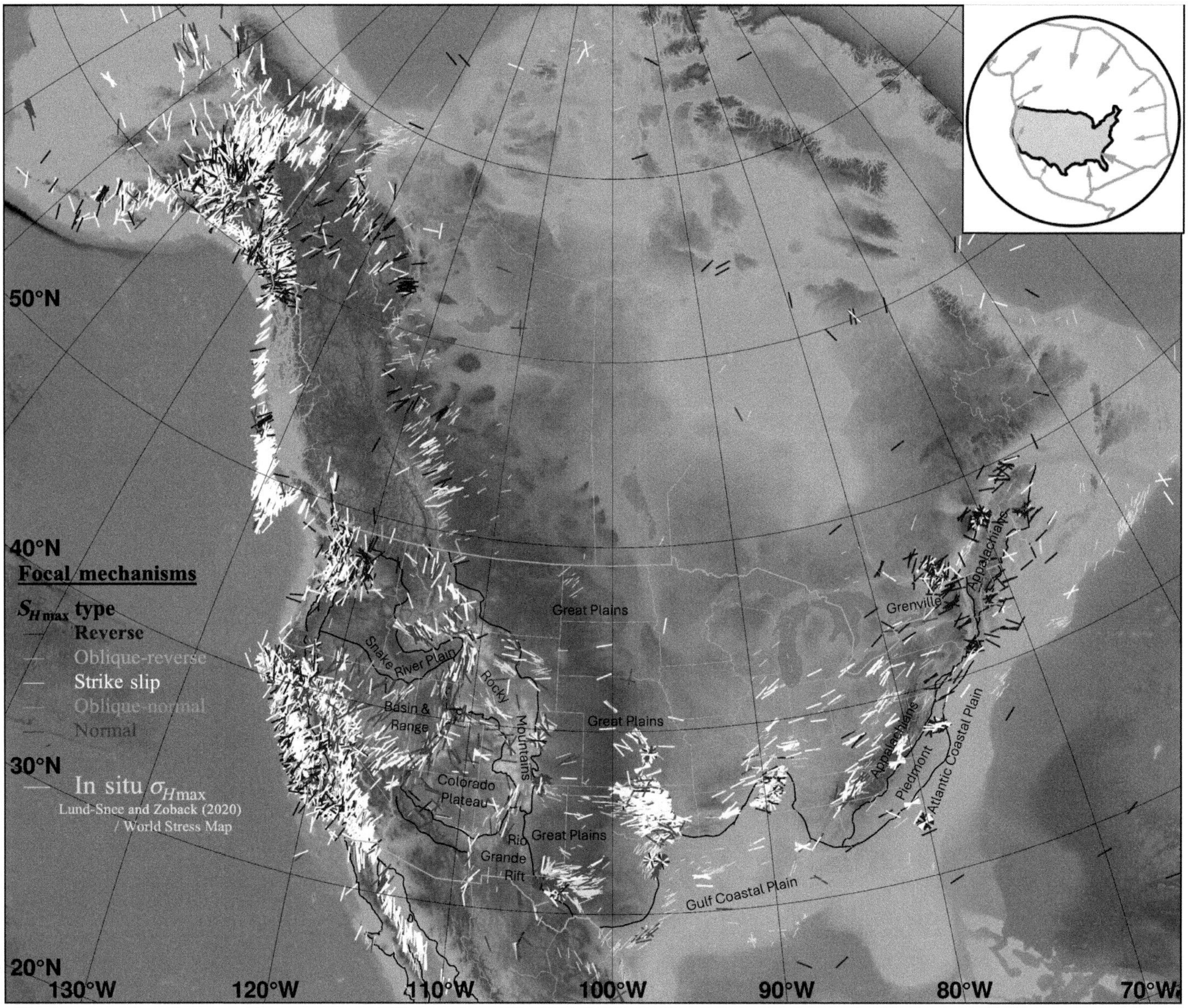

Figure 1. Focal mechanisms (FMs) and in situ stress indicators. Bars: $S_{H\max}$, colored by faulting style (Table 1). Black bars: Maximum-horizontal stress from in situ indicators (World Stress Map/Lundstern and Zoback, 2020). (Inset) Plate boundary tractions on North America. Directions and relative magnitudes from Humphreys and Coblentz (2007). The color version of this figure is available only in the electronic edition.

Geophysical and remote sensing data are increasingly being used to complement geologic investigations of suspected intraplate seismogenic features. Seismic reflection imaging (e.g., Pratt *et al.*, 2022), magnetic and gravity data (Shah *et al.*, 2023), and quantitative geomorphology (Jobe *et al.*, 2022) can highlight candidate structures. Here, quantitative analyses of fault-slip potential (FSP) will provide another complementary tool.

This study aims to document stress variations across the CEUS with a comprehensively updated dataset of earthquake FMs and then to examine in detail stress at each class A, B, and C feature, assessing whether the purported sense of slip and slip direction comply with the site-specific stress models. If a feature is a specific fault, its slip potential (i.e., how well aligned it is for slip) is quantified. Where no specific fault was implicated by Crone and Wheeler (2000), the slip potential of local geologically mapped faults is quantified from their mapped orientation. These new constraints may: indicate that a proposed feature is incompatible with modern stress or confirm that it is; highlight candidate faults for known liquefaction features or historical earthquakes from geologically mapped faults, or categorize suitable and unsuitable fault orientations that may help winnow paleoseismic targets identified from topographic or other datasets.

Data and Methods

FMs and in situ data

Thanks to investments in seismic networks and advances in seismic techniques, the number of FMs available in the

North American crust has grown rapidly over recent years: Figure 1 shows a compilation of 26,879 crustal FMs (Table S1, available in the supplemental material to this article), plus 2210 A–C quality in situ stress direction indicators (e.g., from borehole data; Lund-Snee and Zoback, 2020). The expanded coverage offered by this catalog is most pronounced in the CEUS, which contains 8501 FMs: 5614 in Oklahoma and 2887 from elsewhere in the CEUS. For comparison, early stress maps used ~18 CEUS FMs (Zoback and Zoback, 1980), which grew to ~300 in 2016 (Heidbach *et al.*, 2018). The Transportable Array and other temporary seismic networks enabled later studies 1232 (Lund-Snee and Zoback, 2020) to 1799 FMs (Levandowski, Herrmann, *et al.*, 2018) in the CEUS, with most of the new data in the form of high-quality moment tensor solutions. Ongoing seismicity and installation of networks such as N4 and TexNet have continued this growth, and the 2887 CEUS FMs from outside Oklahoma in the current dataset are double the 1398 in the largest prior compilation (Levandowski, Weingarten, and Walsh, 2018).

The most robust constraints on horizontal-maximum stress directions, especially in low-seismicity regions such as the CEUS, come from wellbore breakouts and other in situ data. These have been used to make high-resolution maps of stress rotations over distances of 10s of kilometers or less, such as in the Permian basin of Texas (Lund-Snee and Zoback, 2016, 2018). Nevertheless, breakouts and other in situ indicators typically contain little information outside of the horizontal plane and therefore do not constrain the stress regime. In other words, most in situ data do not demonstrate whether a region is undergoing horizontal contraction, simple shear, or extension (deformation styles typified by reverse, strike-slip, and normal faulting, respectively). By contrast, FMs directly record faulting style of individual earthquakes (Fig. 1, Table 1), albeit with weak constraints on stress directions (e.g., McKenzie, 1969). Inversions of FMs—which can integrate in situ data—provide a way to quantify both stress directions and the stress regime.

Stress inversion methodology

ere, FMs and in situ data are used to constrain local stress using formal inversions. The core of this inversion is the widely used iterative algorithm from Vavryčuk (2014) widely used iterative algorithm, with modifications to include jackknife downsampling (Levandowski, Weingarten, and Walsh, 2018), plus options for FM weighting (Levandowski *et al.*, 2023; here, by inverse distance from a location of interest), and formal inclusion of in situ horizontal stress direction indicators such as borehole breakouts (following Carlson *et al.*, 2018).

Inversions of fault-slip data, such as FMs, are well established and stem from the axiom that the slip vector on a fault plane (i.e., the rake) parallels the shear traction resolved on that plane. The shear and normal tractions depend on fault orientation (e.g., strike and dip) and the local stress tensor $\boldsymbol{\sigma}$. For a fault with normal vector $\mathbf{n}$, the traction vector $\mathbf{t}$produced by $\boldsymbol{\sigma}$ is

$$\mathbf{t} = \boldsymbol{\sigma}\mathbf{n}. \tag{2}$$

The normal traction vector is

$$\mathbf{t} \cdot \mathbf{n}, \text{ with magnitude } S_N = \mathbf{tn}. \tag{3}$$

The shear traction vector $\boldsymbol{\tau}$ is the cross product of $\mathbf{n}$ with the normal vector to the plane containing $\mathbf{t}$ and $\mathbf{n}$.

$$\tau = \mathbf{n} \times (\mathbf{t} \times \mathbf{n}). \tag{4}$$

This shear traction direction is linearly related to the local stress tensor and fault normal vector (equations 2–4).

With multiple observations from multiple fault planes, this linear system becomes overdetermined and suitable for inversion for the best-fit tensor.

The best-fit tensor minimizes the angular misfit between the slip vectors in the FMs and the predicted shear traction resolved on the associated faults (Wallace, 1951; Bott, 1959; McKenzie, 1969; Angelier, 1979). The underlying assumption is that the earthquakes used in an inversion all occurred in response to the same stress field. In general, inversions of fewer than 20 FMs may be unreliable, and 25 or more are preferable (e.g., Townend and Zoback, 2001).

The resulting tensor defines the three mutually perpendicular principal stress vectors—maximally compressive σ_1, intermediate σ_2, and minimally compressive σ_3. The tensor's shape ratio Φ gives their relative magnitudes $S_{1/2/3}$:

$$\Phi = (S_2 - S_3)/(S_1 - S_3). \tag{5}$$

Simpson (1997) combined Φ and faulting style n in a single quantitative parameter $A\Phi$ to describe the stress regime:

$$A\Phi = (n + 0.5) + (-1)^n(\Phi - 0.5), \tag{6}$$

in which n is the 0/1/2 for normal/strike-slip/reverse faulting, respectively. $A\Phi$ is continuous from radial extension ($A\Phi = 0$) to radial contraction ($A\Phi = 3$), although tectonic stress fields rarely exhibit values less than 0.5 (uniaxial tension) or greater than 2.5 (uniaxial contraction). Integer values of $A\Phi$ imply that two principal stresses are equal in magnitude (Table 2).

The Vavryčuk (2014) algorithm iteratively inverts for the best-fit stress then selects the more likely focal plane from the two nodal planes for each event, based on normalized instability I, which is calculated from Φ and the vector of directional cosines (f_1, f_2, f_3) defining the inclination of the fault to the principal stress axes (Vavryčuk *et al.*, 2013):

$$I = [\tau_0 - \mu(\sigma_0 - 1)]/[\mu + (1 + \mu^2)^{0.5}], \tag{7}$$

TABLE 2
$A\Phi$ Parameter and Stress Regimes

$A\Phi$=0	0.5	1	1.5	2	2.5	3
Radial Extension; Rarely Observed	**Uniaxial Extension, Normal Faulting**	**Oblique Extension/ Oblique-Normal Faulting**	**Simple Shear/ Strike Slip**	**Oblique Contraction/ Oblique-Reverse Faulting**	**Uniaxial Contraction/ Reverse Faulting**	**Radial Contraction; Rarely Observed**
$S_1 = S_V >$, $S_2 = S_{H\max} \approx$, $S_3 = S_{H\min}$	$S_1 = S_V >$, $S_2 = S_{H\max} >$, $S_3 = S_{H\min}$	$S_1 = S_V \approx$, $S_2 = S_{H\max} >$, $S_3 = S_{H\min}$	$S_1 = S_{H\max} >$, $S_2 = S_V >$, $S_3 = S_{H\min}$	$S_1 = S_{H\max} >$, $S_2 = S_V \approx$, $S_3 = S_{H\min}$	$S_1 = S_{H\max} >$, $S_2 = S_{H\min} >$, $S_3 = S_V$	$S_1 = S_{H\max} \approx$, $S_2 = S_{H\min} >$, $S_3 = S_V$

$$\sigma_0 = f_1^2 + (1 - 2\Phi)f_2^2 - f_3^2, \tag{8}$$

$$\tau_0 = \{f_1^2 + (1 - 2\Phi)f_2^2 + f_3^2 - \sigma^2\}^{0.5}, \tag{9}$$

with weak dependence on friction μ. Because μ is seldom known, a value must be assigned; here, randomly from a uniform distribution over the range 0.3–0.9. Instability ranges from 0 to 1, with higher values representing higher FSP.

Uncertainties in the stress inversions are appraised with many Monte Carlo trials. Each trial begins by jackknife-downsampling the FMs, discarding $n_{\text{data}}^{0.5}$ (Levandowski, Weingarten, and Walsh, 2018). Noise is added to each of the remaining FMs from a uniform distribution of 0°–15°, implemented by perturbing each slip vector in a random direction (0°–360°; Vavryčuk, 2014). A random friction of 0.3–0.9 is assigned. One of the nodal planes is chosen at random for each event, and the suite is inverted for the stress tensor that minimizes angular misfit between the shear tractions on the focal planes and the associated slip vectors (Wallace, 1951; Bott, 1959; McKenzie, 1969; Angelier, 1979). Then, the focal plane choices are revisited: I is calculated for both nodal planes for each event, the less stable plane is selected, and this revised ensemble is inverted. This process iterates five times; typically, the focal plane choices stabilize by the second or third iteration. And then a new trial with a new friction and a new jackknifed set of FMs begins.

For the site-specific inversions presented subsequently, 1000 trials are conducted, and the distribution of the output parameters defines their uncertainties.

Including in situ data

In situ data provide strong constraints on local stress directions. Comparing FM inversion results with regional in situ data provides a check on the reliability of the inversions and has been used to check for the possibility of fault-zone-scale stress perturbations (e.g., Mazzotti and Townend, 2010). These uses keep the seismogenic FMs and in situ data separate. Alternatively, in situ data can be integrated in FM inversions, following the formalism developed by Carlson *et al.* (2018). This implementation accounts for the fact that shear stress on a plane perpendicular to $\sigma_{H\max}$ should be zero, and the slip on a vertical plane 45° counterclockwise from $\sigma_{H\max}$ should be right lateral. In essence, the latter amounts to an FM with {strike/dip/rake} = $\{\sigma_{H\max} - 045°/90°/180°\}$. By convention, strike azimuth (000–360) is such that dip is down to the right when looking in the strike direction. Fault strike and dip are expressed as (###/##°).

Joint FM or in situ inversions, used in an automated and unsupervised algorithm, are shown in Figure 2. The purpose of this figure is to illustrate continental-scale stress patterns, as opposed to robustly determining stress at specific locations,

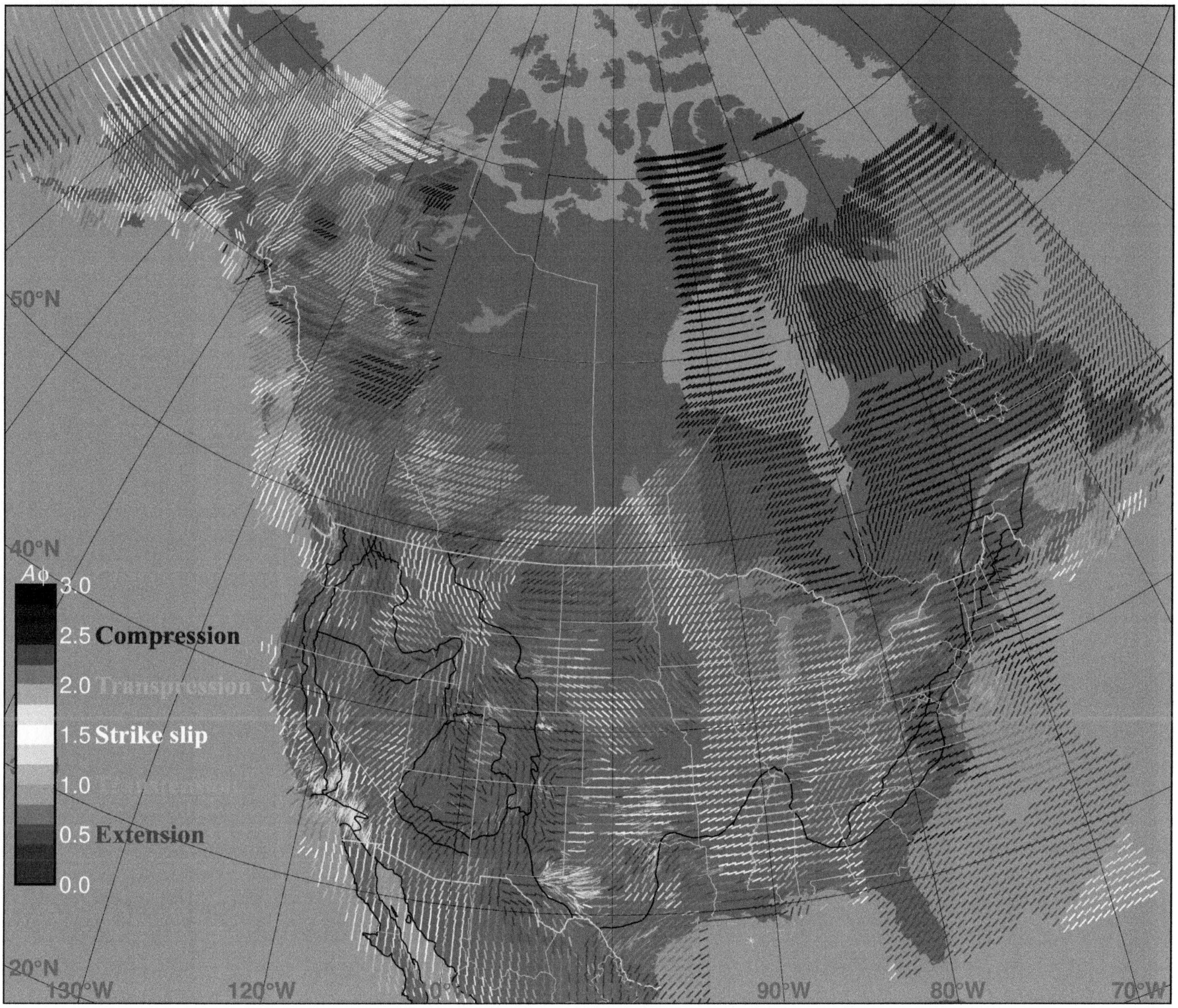

Figure 2. Gridded stress inversions. Bars: $\sigma_{H\,\max}$, colored by $A\Phi$ (Table 2). Yellow bars: maximum-horizontal stress direction from in situ indicators (World Stress Map/Lundstern and Zoback, 2020). Joint inversions of FMs and in situ stress direction indicators are conducted on a 0.5° × 0.5° grid, using at least 25 data for each grid point. Values shown are the median across 100 inversions. Locations with inversion misfit >40° and/or $A\Phi$ variance >0.25 across the 100 inversions are discarded, as are areas without data (e.g., central Canada). The color version of this figure is available only in the electronic edition.

which is the purpose of the site-specific stress models subsequently. For each point on a 0.5° × 0.5° grid, the inversion selects data (FMs plus in situ) from within a radius equal to the distance to the 25th-closest data point plus 5 km. The radius is expanded if needed until it subsumes at least 15 FMs. The data are weighted by inverse-distance and inverted 100 times. Figure 2 represents median values for $\sigma_{H\,\max}$ and $A\Phi$. Uncertainty and goodness-of-fit metrics based on the distributions across the 100 inversions are shown in Figures S1–S4.

Stress inversion validation

When inversions do not integrate in situ data, the two can be compared to validate the inversion results. If the two do not overlap within uncertainty, the inversion may be unreliable, or there may be a local stress perturbation (Mazzotti and Townend, 2010).

Other quality metrics of the inversions are misfit and variance. If the average angular misfit between the predicted shear tractions and slip vectors exceeds ~40°, the FMs might not be coming from a uniform stress field (e.g., Michael, 1991). Alternatively, large misfits may arise because of faulty data, which also may result in poorly resolved stress. These manifest in high variance in Φ or $A\Phi$; Ruppert (2008) suggested a variance threshold of 0.2.

In Figure 2, inversions with $A\Phi$ variance exceeding 0.2 and/or median misfit greater than 40° are omitted.

FSP

The local stress field controls that the faults are well-oriented for frictional slip. There are several metrics to quantify how well aligned faults are—here collectively termed FSP modeling. In general, FSP metrics examine the Mohr–Coulomb failure criterion (equation 1). For a given stress tensor, the shear and normal tractions in equation (1) are functions of fault orientation (e.g., strike and dip). The 1000 separate stress inversion trials for each site (see subsequent sections) provide 1000 stress tensors for use in FSP modeling to fully propagate uncertainty.

There are several metrics for FSP. Normalized instability has been introduced (equations 6–8). The difference between the left and right sides of equation (1) represents the difference from Coulomb Failure Stress (dCFS):

$$\mathrm{dCFS} = \mu(S_N - Pp) - \tau, \tag{10}$$

in which high instability indicates greater FSP, lower dCFS implies greater FSP. An optimally oriented fault has dCFS = 0 MPa.

For application to injection-induced seismicity, it is useful to compute ΔP, the pore pressure increase that would lead to frictional instability:

$$\Delta P = S_N - Pp - \tau/\mu = \mathrm{dCFS}/\mu. \tag{11}$$

On a Mohr circle, dCFS is the vertical distance from the failure envelope, and ΔP is the horizontal distance.

Instability, dCFS, and ΔP are linearly related (Levandowski, 2025):

$$\Delta P = (I - 1)(S_1 - Pp); \mathrm{dCFS} = \mu\Delta P = (I - 1)\mu(S_1 - Pp). \tag{12}$$

Slip tendency (e.g., Rimando and Peace, 2021) and understress (e.g., Qin *et al.*, 2019) are an additive inverse pair, representing the present shear stress τ normalized by the critical shear stress τ_{critical}:

$$\text{Slip tendency } T_s = \tau/\tau_{\mathrm{critical}}, \tag{13}$$

$$\text{Understress} = (\tau_{\mathrm{critical}} - \tau)/\tau_{\mathrm{critical}} = 1 - T_s. \tag{14}$$

These five FSP metrics have their own advantages and disadvantages. Instability is determined directly from the stress inversions and the resultant normalized, deviatoric tensor; the only necessary parameter is friction μ. Moreover, the Vavryčuk (2014) algorithm already requires μ as an input (to compute nodal plane instability). The method used here samples μ for each inversion trial from a uniform distribution 0.3–0.9, and the same randomly selected μ is used in the subsequent FSP model, propagating uncertainty in friction in a self-consistent manner. The other four FSP metrics require estimation of the full stress tensor. Inversions provide four of the six elements of the full stress tensor—the three principal stress directions and the relative magnitude Φ (equation 5). To solve for the absolute magnitudes of the principal stresses, equation (5) is solved simultaneously with equations (15) and (16). The remaining quantities needed to derive the full tensor at a nominal depth z are the average density of overburden ρ and the pore fluid pressure.

From the stress inversion (see equation 5):

$$\Phi \equiv (S_2 - S_3)/(S_1 - S_3).$$

S_{vertical} at depth z beneath the overburden with average density ρ is

$$S_{\mathrm{vertical}} = \rho g z, \tag{15}$$

in which $S_{\mathrm{vertical}} = S_1$ for normal faulting/extension, S_2 for strike slip, or S_3 for reverse faulting/compression.

Tangency of the Mohr circle to the failure envelope implies (Zoback, 2010)

$$(S_1 - Pp)/(S_3 - Pp) = [\sqrt{(\mu^2 + 1)} + \mu]^2. \tag{16}$$

Because the three principal stress magnitudes are linearly related, the depth z is arbitrary because it is for instability, understress, and slip tendency. This characteristic is useful for investigations in which the focal depth varies across events. Therefore, the stress magnitudes ($S_{1/2/3}$), Pp, dCFS, and ΔP are replaced with their derivatives with respect to z: Pp is the pore pressure gradient (9.8 MPa/km at hydrostatic pressure), $S_v = \rho g$, and $S_{1/2/3}$, dCFS, and ΔP have units of MPa/km.

In cases of induced seismicity, ΔP has clear utility (Lund-Snee and Zoback, 2016; Walsh and Zoback, 2016; Levandowski, Weingarten, and Walsh, 2018). For natural and naturally triggered seismicity, dCFS is informative because it is directly comparable to estimates of stress variations due to static stress transfer (e.g., Stein, 1999), reservoir impoundment, or hydrologic loading (e.g., Johnson *et al.*, 2020). These two metrics provide absolute stress magnitudes for subsequent uses such as hydrogeologic modeling or dynamic rupture simulations. By contrast, understress and slip tendency deliver normalized values that make it easy to compare events at different depths, although using stress gradients achieves a similar outcome.

In comparing FSP among faults, it suffices to use boilerplate values for density and other parameters (e.g., Qin *et al.*, 2019; Rimando and Peace, 2021) or sample values from a range (e.g., Walsh and Zoback, 2016; Levandowski, 2023). To further account for regional variations, density can be estimated from seismic velocity models. Here, velocity-based estimates using the Shen and Ritzwoller (2016) V_{sv} model and the Brocher

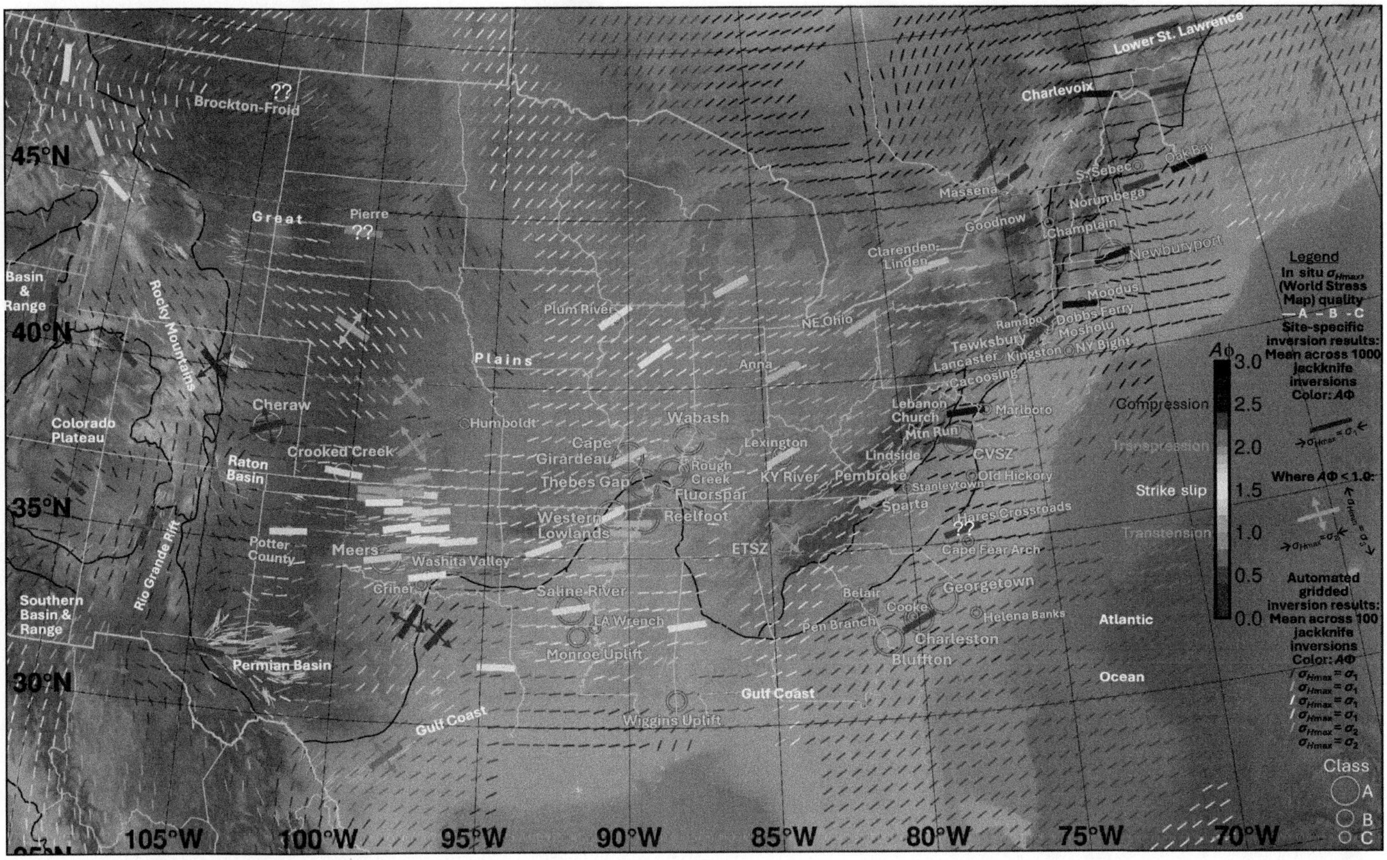

Figure 3. Seismogenic stress in the CEUS. Symbology as in Figures 1 and 2. Thick bars show median results across 1000 site-specific inversions for each class A, B, or C feature, which are labeled in gold. Other locations and features are named in turquoise. The color version of this figure is available only in the electronic edition.

(2005) V_S density relation are refined to also reproduce gravity variations and flexural topography (using the algorithm of Levandowski *et al.*, 2015; Fig. S5). Note that the densities do not affect anything other than the absolute magnitudes of dCFS and ΔP.

Results

Across CENA, the stress regime grades from compression along the Atlantic Coast in the east through strike slip to trans-tension and extension on the Great Plains and in the Rocky Mountains in the west (Figs. 2 and 3).

Principal stress directions are more uniform in the east, with $\sigma_{H\max}$ mainly between NE–SW and E–W, than on the Great Plains, where extension is occurring in many different directions.

These differing stress states control the faults that are prone to slip and influence seismic hazard. To provide more robust constraints on stress conditions than the unsupervised gridded inversions, site-specific inversions are conducted for each of the classes A, B, and C features (thick bars in Fig. 3). Results of the methods used to make Figures 2 and 3 are compared in Figure S4, which shows that the two models agree to less than 0.1 $A\Phi$ units and 10° in $\sigma_{H\max}$, on average. s

Stress map

Eastern North America. Reverse faulting is predominant all along the Atlantic Coast and as far east as roughly −80° longitude (Fig. 3). Near the coast, $\sigma_{H\max}$ trends roughly 090 from the Lower St. Lawrence seismic zone (e.g., Mazzotti and Townend, 2010) as far south as the Central Virginia seismic zone (e.g., Wu *et al.*, 2015). Immediately inland, and in the southern part of the Atlantic Coastal Plain (e.g., South Carolina), $\sigma_{H\max}$ rotates to ~060. In global geodynamic modeling, Ghosh *et al.* (2019) found that including a reduced-viscosity band along the pre-Ordovician Laurentian margin to represent comparatively thin continental lithosphere (their model 3) accomplished much of this 30° rotation. The relation between physiography and this boundary differs from south to north. In the south, the low-viscosity zone comprises the Atlantic Coastal Plain and Piedmont. From approximately New Jersey northward, the viscosity boundary lies west of the Appalachians and may parallel the Grenville Front.

Relative stress magnitudes also change from east to west. The transition from a mainly thrust faulting regime ($A\Phi > 2.0$) to a transpressive regime ($A\Phi < 2.0$) occurs slightly west of the clockwise stress rotation, also cross-cutting the regional northeast-tectonic fabric and physiographic

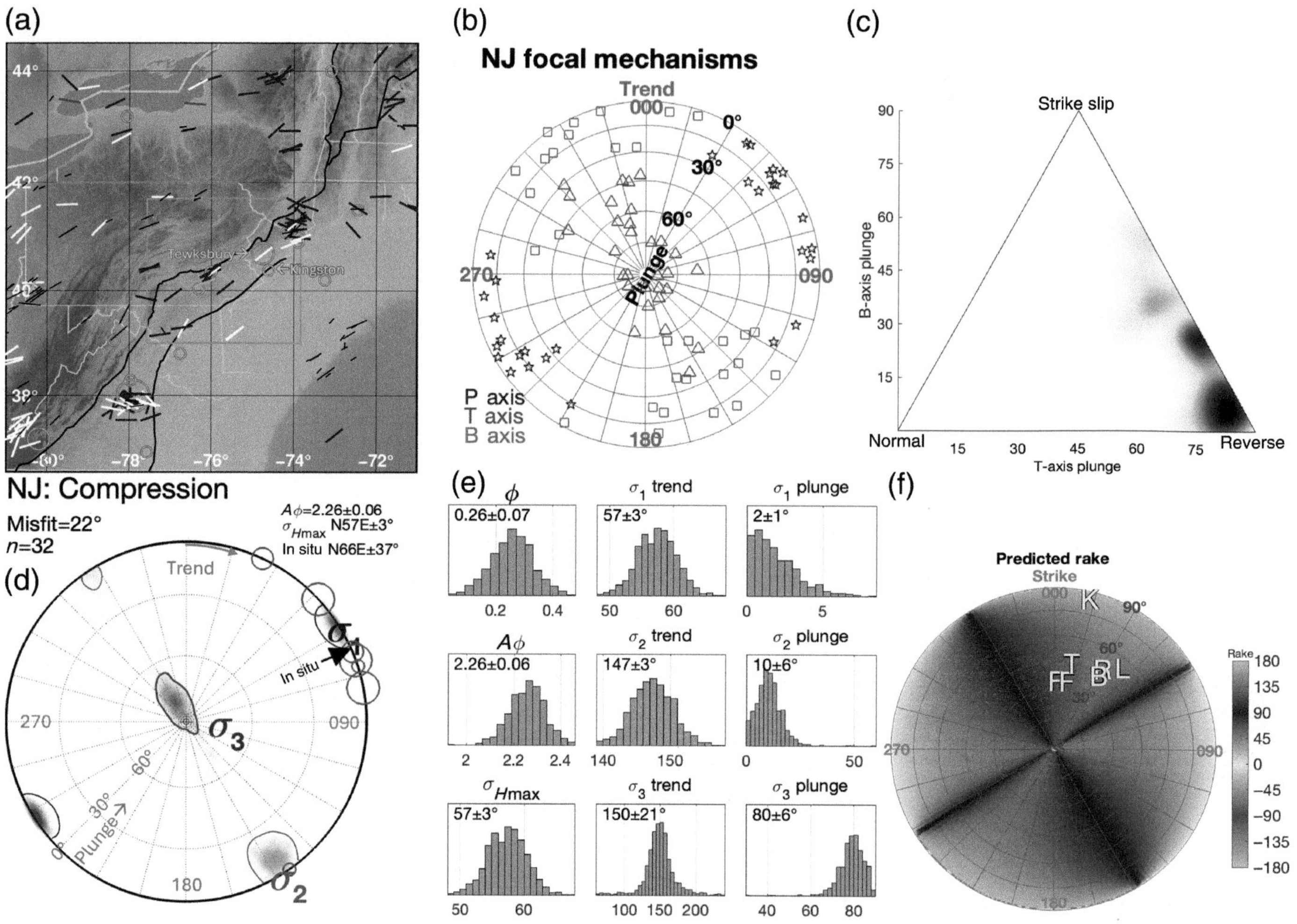

provinces. Transpression becomes dominant in the eastern part of the Great Lakes basin of the Grenville interior, near or west of the Appalachians in central and eastern Pennsylvania (Homman and Nyblade, 2025), east of the Appalachians in the Piedmont between the Central Virginia seismic zone and Giles County seismic zone, and in South Carolina. The westward decrease in stress magnitudes apparent in decreasing $A\Phi$ parallels analytical predications of the decay of stress due to edge normal tractions with distance from the plate boundary (England *et al.*, 1985).

Stress is particularly complicated in the Charlevoix seismic zone; detailed studies of stress in the area (Baird *et al.*, 2009, 2010; Fadugba *et al.*, 2019) have indicated that this complexity is the result of interactions between regional stress, St. Lawrence rift-related faults, and an impact crater.

Midcontinent. Strike-slip earthquakes, slightly transpressive $A\Phi = 1.5$–1.8 and ENE–WSW $\sigma_{H\max}$ prevail from near the eastern front of the Appalachians (e.g., Homman and Nyblade, 2025)] to around 95° W longitude (Fig. 3).

There are at least two important exceptions. Around the New Madrid and Wabash Valley seismic zones, there is more reverse oblique to reverse faulting ($A\Phi = 1.8 - 2.1$) and clockwise-rotated stress, which has been quantified in more than a

Figure 4. Stress inversions and fault-slip potential (FSP) modeling for central New Jersey. (a) Eastern U.S. FMs. Symbology as in Figure 1. The green box represents the region used for central New Jersey stress modeling, containing 32 FMs. (b) FM P/T/B axes. T axes (red) tend to be near vertical and P axes (blue) mainly trend east-northeast–west-southwest. (c) Ternary diagram of faulting style based on principal axis plunges (Frohlich and Apperson, 1993). Reverse to reverse-oblique faulting mechanisms are dominant. (d) Inversion results across 1000 trials. Blue, green, red: $\sigma_{1/2/3}$ vectors from each trial; solid lines show 95% confidence ranges. Circles on the exterior indicate in situ $\sigma_{H\max}$ data from the same region (green box in panel a). Circle size represents World Stress Map quality ranking (a–c). The black arrow indicates the quality-weighted average. (e) Histograms of inversion results show the distribution of stress directions and stress ratios across the 1000 trials. (f) Predicted rake as a function of strike and dip. Strike and dip are mapped to polar coordinates: Strike azimuth is the azimuthal coordinate; dip angle is the radial coordinate, with steeper dips toward the outside. T, 2024 M_w 4.8 Tewksbury focal plane; K, Kingston fault; F, B, R, L, borehole observations of Ramapo fault orientation at Flemington, Bernardsville, Riverdale, and Ladentown, locations shown in Figure 5d. On the Kingston fault (013°/85°), a rake of 170° is predicted, which is at odds with purported normal faulting. By contrast, reverse-oblique faulting (rake 144°) is predicted on the Tewksbury mainshock fault plane, which compares well with the reported 158° rake. The color version of this figure is available only in the electronic edition.

dozen stress studies summarized in Text S7. Numerous studies have also sought to explain the stress rotation and increased $A\Phi$ as the result of mantle flow (recently, Saxena *et al.*, 2021 and Hightower *et al.*, 2024) or gravity-derived stress due to dense, mafic lower crustal intrusions (Grana and Richardson, 1996; Pollitz *et al.*, 2001; Levandowski *et al.*, 2016).

The second hazard-relevant anomaly is oblique extension in the ETSZ surrounded by the otherwise transpressive southeastern United States (e.g., Levandowski *et al.*, 2023). ETSZ extension may be due to flexural rebound from focused erosion (Gallen and Thigpen, 2018), lower crustal to upper-mantle buoyancy (Levandowski *et al.*, 2023), or some other phenomenon. In any case, the extension is particularly hazard relevant because the ETSZ trends 040 for over 300 km along a Proterozoic shear zone (Steltenpohl *et al.*, 2010; Powell and Thomas, 2016). This common origin hints that the seismic zone could be underlain by one continuous fault system (e.g., Ebel, 2008). Such a fault system would not be a concern under the prevailing NE–SW $\sigma_{H\max}$ and a compressive or strike-slip stress regime. However, it is nearly optimally aligned for normal faulting in the ETSZ stress field, and a large number of ETSZ focal planes do strike NE–SW (Levandowski *et al.*, 2023; Fig. S5.1.3). This near-optimal alignment suggests that the possibility of a 300 km long normal fault rupture capable of generating an M 7.5+ earthquake cannot be ruled out.

Great Plains. Strike-slip faulting in Oklahoma is well-documented (e.g., Walsh and Zoback, 2016; Alt and Zoback, 2017; Qin *et al.*, 2019). However, this stress regime differs from its surroundings: Normal to oblique-normal faulting across the Great Plains and Gulf Coast.

Extension in the Great Plains occurs in many different directions. For example, $\sigma_{H\max}$ (perpendicular to the extension direction) varies from NNE–SSW in the Fort Worth basin, Texas (e.g., Quiñones *et al.*, 2018; Hennings *et al.*, 2019) to ~E–W in Oklahoma (e.g., Alt and Zoback, 2015; Walsh and Zoback, 2016; Qin *et al.*, 2019), ENE–WSW in southern Kansas (Amemoutou *et al.*, 2019; Skoumal *et al.*, 2021), NE–SW in central Kansas and SE–NW in northern Kansas and Nebraska (Intfen, 2019). A more detailed summary of stress and extension directions on the Great Plains is provided in Text S9.

Stress rotations of 90° or more are observed over much shorter distances (10s of km) at the western edge of the CEUS near the Rocky Mountain Front, namely in the Permian basin (Lund-Snee and Zoback, 2016, 2018; Quiñones *et al.*, 2018; Huang *et al.*, 2022; Horne *et al.*, 2024) and from the Cheraw fault to the Raton basin (e.g., Levandowski *et al.*, 2017; Zellman *et al.*, 2021; Ostenaa *et al.*, 2022). Because there are no classes A, B, or C features in western Texas, that area is not discussed here; readers are referred to the Lund-Snee and Zoback (2016, 2018) studies of the complex stress field in Texas and other specific studies in the Permian basin (e.g., Huang *et al.*, 2022; Horne *et al.*, 2024).

Stress on the northern Great Plains of North Dakota, South Dakota, and eastern Montana is not well resolved. Although in situ indicators and FM $S_{H\max}$ consistently show either E–W or NE–SW orientations (Lund-Snee and Zoback, 2022), data are insufficient for inversions.

Site-specific stress models for classes A, B, and C features

A site-specific stress inversion is conducted for each of the 61 classes A, B, and C features using a uniform methodology (thick bars in Fig. 3, Tables S2 and S3). Detailed results for each site are presented in Text S1–S10. The uniform process used for each site:

- begins by purposefully delineating a polygonal region surrounding the feature that includes 25–50 FMs with similar faulting styles and/or $S_{H\max}$;
- conducts 1000 Monte Carlo inversion trials using Vavryčuk's iterative algorithm to appraise uncertainty, with random friction, jackknife downsampling, and perturbations up to 15° added to each retained FM in each trial;
- ensures that the inversion misfit is less than 40°, a threshold for homogenous stress (e.g., Michael, 1991; Hardebeck and Hauksson, 2001) and $A\Phi$ variance is less than 0.2 (e.g., Ruppert, 2008), revising the polygonal region if needed based on these metrics; and
- compares the resultant $\sigma_{H\max}$ with in situ data from within the same polygonal region.

This process is illustrated in Figure 4 for the area near the 2024 M 4.8 Tewksbury earthquake, Ramapo fault system, and Kingston fault, New Jersey. An area surrounding the features and containing 32 FMs is delineated (green box in Fig. 4a). Consistency in the P/T/B axes and faulting styles of the events is checked (Fig. 4b,c). Then, the 32 FMs are inverted 1000 times; the results are aggregated in Figure 4d,e. For comparison, the $\sigma_{H\max}$ directions from the seven A- to C-quality in situ data within the same region are plotted as circles on the circumference of the Figure 4d stereonet, with larger circles representing higher-quality $\sigma_{H\max}$ data; the quality-weighted average of the in situ data is indicated by a black arrow. Finally, a single inversion is conducted without jackknife downsampling or adding noise to the FMs, and with a constant friction of 0.6, providing a best-fit stress for all of the FMs; this best-fit tensor is used to predict rake as a function of strike and dip (Fig. 4f), which can be informative when considered together with the purported slip directions of the classes A, B, and C features.

FSP

Using the site-specific stress models, FSP near each of the class A, B, and C features is quantified in terms of instability and dCFS as functions of strike and dip. These FSP models are used to reassess each of the suspected seismogenic features.

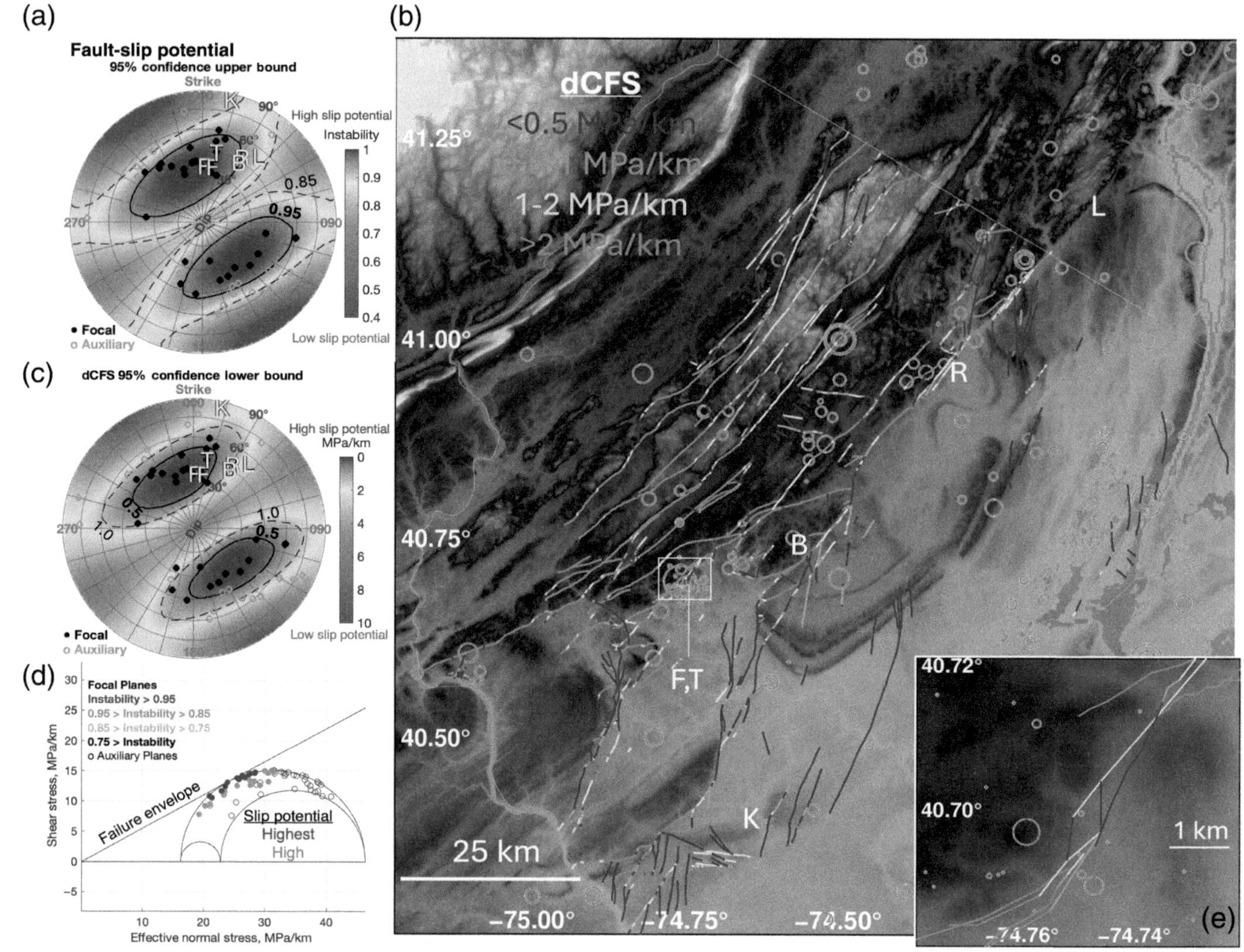

Figure 5. Fault-slip potential modeling for central New Jersey. (a) Instability as a function of fault strike and dip (see panels f and g for additional explanation). Red indicates the highest FSP (highest instability); dark green indicates the lowest FSP (lowest instability). The instability values shown are the 95% confidence limit across the 1000 trials—instability meets or exceeds this value in 5% of the trials. Strike and dip are mapped to polar coordinates: The strike azimuth is the azimuthal coordinate, and the dip angle is the radial coordinate, with steeper dips toward the outside. Black circles: inferred focal planes from the 32 earthquakes used in the stress inversions (see Fig. 4). Gray circles: auxiliary planes. T: 2024 M 4.8 Tewksbury focal plane. K: Kingston Fault. F, B, R, L: Borehole observations of Ramapo fault orientation at Flemington, Bernardsville, Riverdale, and Ladentown, locations shown in panel (d). The Tewksbury focal plane (T) and Ramapo fault system in nearby Flemington (F) are near-optimal orientations. The other Ramapo fault orientations (B/R/L) are suboptimal but still well oriented (instability ~0.9). The Kingston fault is comparatively poorly oriented for slip (instability ~0.8). (b) Difference from Coulomb Failure Stress (dCFS) gradient. Axes and symbology as in panel (a). Low values of dCFS correspond to high FSP. Red indicates the lowest dCFS and highest FSP; dark green indicates the highest dCFS and the lowest FSP. (c) Mohr circle corresponding to the single best-fit stress tensor. Red and orange dots: inferred focal planes from the 32 earthquakes used in the stress inversion, colored according to instability. All 32 focal planes have instability of 0.85 or higher (orange and red dots). Black circles: auxiliary planes of the 32 earthquakes for comparison. (d) Slip potential of New Jersey faults. Red indicates the highest slip potential (lowest dCFS: <0.5 MPa/km); green indicates the lowest slip potential (dCFS >2.0 MPa/km). 4881 segments of 231 faults were digitized from the New Jersey State Geologic Map (Drake *et al.*, 1996). Because dip angle is generally unknown, the values shown correspond to dip with the highest slip potential (highest instability, lowest dCFS) at a given strike. B, Bernardsville; F, Flemington; L, Ladentown; R, Riverdale; and T, Tewksbury. Circles: seismicity M ≥ 2 from U.S. Geological Survey Comprehensive Catalog (see Data and Resources). (e) 2024 Tewksbury epicentral area. The region is indicated by a white box in panel (d). Several near-optimal relay faults are present (indicated by red color), including north-trending strands similar in strike to the 2024 mainshock. (f) Instability as a function of strike and dip in Cartesian coordinates. The same instability values as a function of strike and dip are used in panels (a,f,g). Numbers 1–4 indicate hypothetical faults that are representative of high (1, red), moderate (2, orange to yellow), low (3, green), and very low (4, dark green) FSP. White letters with black outline refer to the same central New Jersey faults as in panels (a,b, d). (g) Instability as a function of fault strike and dip in polar coordinates. Repeated from panel (a), with the representative hypothetical faults (1–4) added. The color version of this figure is available only in the electronic edition. *(Continued)*

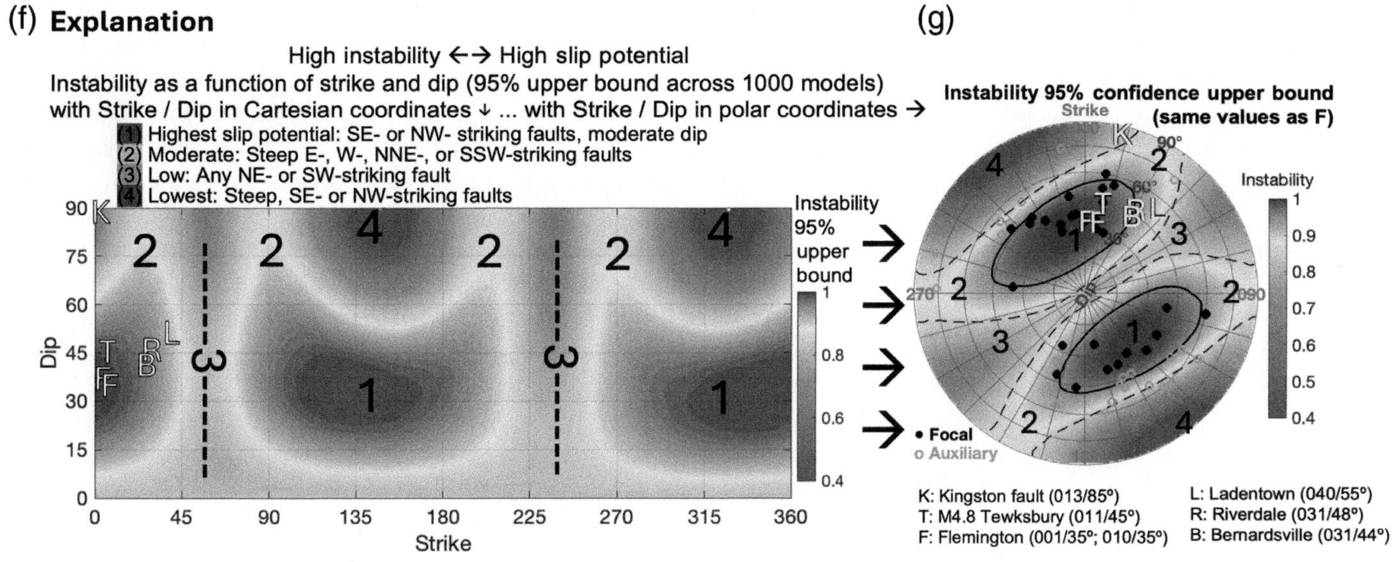

Figure 5. Continued

In a few cases, the implications are straightforward. For example, the class C Kingston fault, New Jersey, was identified as a subvertical, north-striking, east-side-down normal fault, yet the stress field determined for Kingston and the 2024 Tewksbury earthquake ($A\Phi = 2.26 \pm 0.06$; $\sigma_{H\max}$ 057° ± 3°) is compressive, so normal faulting on a plane ~50° from $\sigma_{H\max}$ seems untenable (e.g., Fig. 4f). A similar argument can be made against the purported normal faulting on the Champlain Lowland faults, New York and Vermont.

Example: The 2024 Tewksbury, New Jersey, earthquake and the Ramapo fault system. The central New Jersey stress field also applies to the Ramapo fault system and Tewksbury earthquake (Figs. 4, 5). The 2024 M_w 4.8 Tewksbury earthquake activated a relay fault along the Ramapo system (e.g., Boyd *et al.*, 2024; Beaucé *et al.*, 2025). The system was already well known before 2024, and at more than 100 km long was considered capable of an M 7+ earthquake (e.g., Aggarwal and Sykes, 1978). In the 1980s, the Ramapo fault was investigated with several boreholes (e.g., Burton and Ratcliffe, 1985) and its orientation at depth determined in Flemington (adjacent to Tewksbury), Bedminster, Riverdale, and Ladentown, noted as F, B, R, and L in Figure 5d; T and K denote the Tewksbury mainshock and the Kingston fault.

The focal planes for the M 4.8 mainshock and M 3.7 aftershock, and the two borehole fault orientations at Flemington all strike between 001 and 011, and dip between 35° and 45°. All are nearly optimally oriented, falling in the red-shaded region of Figure 5a,b (instability > 0.95). The Bernardsville, Riverdale, and Ladentown sections of the Ramapo fault system are not as well oriented in the modern stress field but still are slip-compatible (instability ~0.9), indicated by the orange to yellow region of Figure 5a,b.

Because FSP is determined as a function of the fault normal vector, values can be determined for any mapped or hypothetical fault orientation. To assess the slip potential of all of the mapped Triassic extension-related faults similar to the Ramapo, their traces were digitized from the New Jersey state geologic map, local strikes computed from the traces, and FSP calculated, allowing dip to assume the angle with the highest slip potential at that strike. This last point seems ad hoc, but these rift-related faults are often listric, and multiply reactivated intraplate fault systems often feature numerous duplexing strands or flower structures, so any strike observed at the surface is likely to be associated with a wide range of dips at depth. Thus, the assumption of the optimal dip is justified at best and conservative at worst. Figure 5d shows FSP for 4881 segments of 231faults. The most hazardous faults (red) are not the main NE-striking parts of the Ramapo fault system but rather E–W cross faults and N–S relay faults such as the one activated by the 2024 Tewksbury earthquake. Many of the Triassic normal faults east of the Ramapo system are also well oriented, but there is scant associated seismicity. Speculatively, widespread Mesozoic diabase intrusions along them may have restrengthened the faults, dip angles may be too steep, or a combination.

The fact that the longest strands of the Ramapo fault system are not well oriented at any dip suggests that the threat of an M 7+ earthquake within 10s of kilometers of New York City may be limited. Although that is good news, many near-optimal strands, relays, and cross faults exceed 10 km and thus are capable of generating earthquakes exceeding M 6 (Wells and Coppersmith, 1994) that could be very damaging.

Example: The SRFZ—A now-known seismic hazard. Crone and Wheeler (2000) were skeptical about the SRFZ. There was clear evidence of prior tectonic activity as part of the Alabama–Oklahoma transform and some indication of subsequent reactivation of normal faults under transpression, but the area lacked instrumental seismicity, so could it be active? Yes, as demonstrated later by Cox *et al.* (2012, 2013, 2014) and adopted by the National Seismic Hazard Model (Jobe *et al.*, 2022). Therefore, the SRFZ provides a useful check on the methodology employed here: without Cox *et al.*'s documenting Quaternary activity, would the present analysis have identified high slip-potential structures in the SRFZ?

Strike-slip faulting with ENE–WSW to E–W P axes dominates the region surrounding the SRFZ. Stress appears well constrained from regional data ($A\Phi = 1.68 \pm 0.03$; $\sigma_{H\max}$ 080° ± 2°; Fig. 6a) The primary faults in the SRFZ—and those with documented Quaternary faulting—are steep and strike ESE or WNW (~110 to 135), with a smaller NNW–SSE population. Seismic reflection and well log data indicate transpressive flower structures (Cox *et al.*, 2013). Most of the mapped ESE–WNW faults are near optimal ($I \geq 0.95$, red in Fig. 6d), at least where they dip steeply. Consequently, the present analysis would have classified the SRFZ as a high slip-potential feature in need of further investigation.

By contrast, other classes B and C feature in the area.

Example: Hidden historic earthquakes—Charleston, South Carolina, and Newburyport, Massachusetts. Several of the class A, B, or C features are historic earthquakes or prehistoric liquefaction features for which the causative fault is unknown. FSP modeling is useful in these cases to highlight which faults identified by geologic mapping, geophysical investigations, or other means are best oriented for reactivation.

Near Newburyport, Massachusetts, a 1727 M_{we} 4.77 (M_{b} 5.6) broke chimneys, toppled walls, and caused liquefaction. Liquefaction features were located by Tuttle and Seeber (1991; Fig. 7). The mapped geologic fabric comprises ENE-trending primary faults with secondary NNE-trending faults, yet the causative fault was not identified before the Crone and Wheeler (2000) compilation. FSP modeling shows that the main ENE-trending faults are poorly oriented (Fig. 7b), yet several of the secondary NNE structures are nearly optimally aligned (e.g., $I = 1.0$ for a fault oriented 010°/30°). At 3–6 km, these faults are sufficiently long to create an M 5.2–5.6 earthquake (Wells and Coppersmith, 1994). Nevertheless, the liquefaction features align on a NW trend rather than NNE, which suggests that an unmapped fault may be responsible. Ebel (2000) suggested the earthquake occurred on an unmapped NW-trending fault, and Tuttle (2007) sketched a ~N130°E-striking fault collinear with two of three liquefaction features and some small earthquakes. Subsequently, a topographic lineament nearly collocated to the fault proposed by Ebel (2000) and Tuttle (2007) was investigated with *P*-wave refraction, showing a 40° SW-dipping low-velocity zone interpreted as the causative fault and dubbed the Newbury Lineament (Marple *et al.*, 2018). That 130°/40° fault is indeed well oriented for slip ($I = 0.98$; Fig. 7b). So is the parallel Ipswich Lineament (Marple *et al.*, 2018), 5 km SW. Thus, if the Newbury Lineament has indeed been active in damaging historic earthquakes, then the Ipswich Lineament may be hazardous as well.

Identifying the source fault(s) for the 1886 Charleston, South Carolina, earthquake is one of the most vexing mysteries in CEUS seismicity. Whether one or multiple faults, a 50-km-long rupture (33–75 km at 90% confidence, Wells and Coppersmith, 1994) may be needed to generate the M ~7 (Cramer and Boyd, 2014) mainshock. Modern seismicity concentrates near Middleton Place (e.g., Chen *et al.*, 2023), vaguely forming a south-striking, west-dipping plane (186°/43°; Chapman *et al.*, 2016). Nevertheless, potential moderate-to-large magnitude earthquakes along the South Carolina coast are not isolated to Charleston—liquefaction evidence suggests strong shaking both 100 km north and 100 km south (Georgetown and Bluffton, South Carolina; Fig. 8a). Paleoliquefaction data indicate strong shaking every 500–600 yr in coastal South Carolina (Amick and Gelinas, 1991; Talwani and Schaeffer, 2001). Therefore, FSP modeling could inform not only the hunt for the 1886 earthquake but also investigations of prehistoric earthquakes throughout the region.

In Charleston, previous work has searched for the causative fault(s) using geomorphology (Marple and Talwani, 1993), borehole data (Weems and Lewis, 2002), light detection and ranging (Marple and Hurd, 2020), modern seismicity (Durá-Gómez and Talwani, 2009; Talwani and Durá-Gómez, 2009; Chapman *et al.*, 2016), reflection seismic profiles, potential field anomalies, and ground penetrating radar (Chapman and Beale, 2010; Pratt *et al.*, 2022; Shah *et al.*, 2023), and geodetic or anthropogenic uplift markers, deformation features, and engineering records (Bilham and Hough, 2023, 2024; Hough and Bilham, 2024a,b). The proposed faults fall into four categories: NE–SW-striking strike-slip or reverse faults are the most common, followed by NNE–SSW-striking strike-slip faults, NW–SE-striking reverse faults parallel to the Ashley River, and south-striking reverse faults. As in other cases, the dips of faults are typically unknown, with a few exceptions.

NE–SW-striking faults: as noted by Shah *et al.* (2023) and shown in Figure 8d, the abundant NE–SW-striking faults are poorly oriented for slip. The class C Cooke fault (245°/70°) exemplifies these poorly oriented faults (Co in Fig. 8c). It seems unlikely that the Cooke fault or offshore class C Helena Banks fault (HB) would slip in the modern stress field.

NNE–SSW-striking faults: many models have suggested slip on the NNE-trending faults, including the Gants and Woodstock faults (Ga and WM/WW/WT in Fig. 8c). Faults with SSW strikes (dipping west) are unstable at moderate dips ~40° ($I = 0.97$:

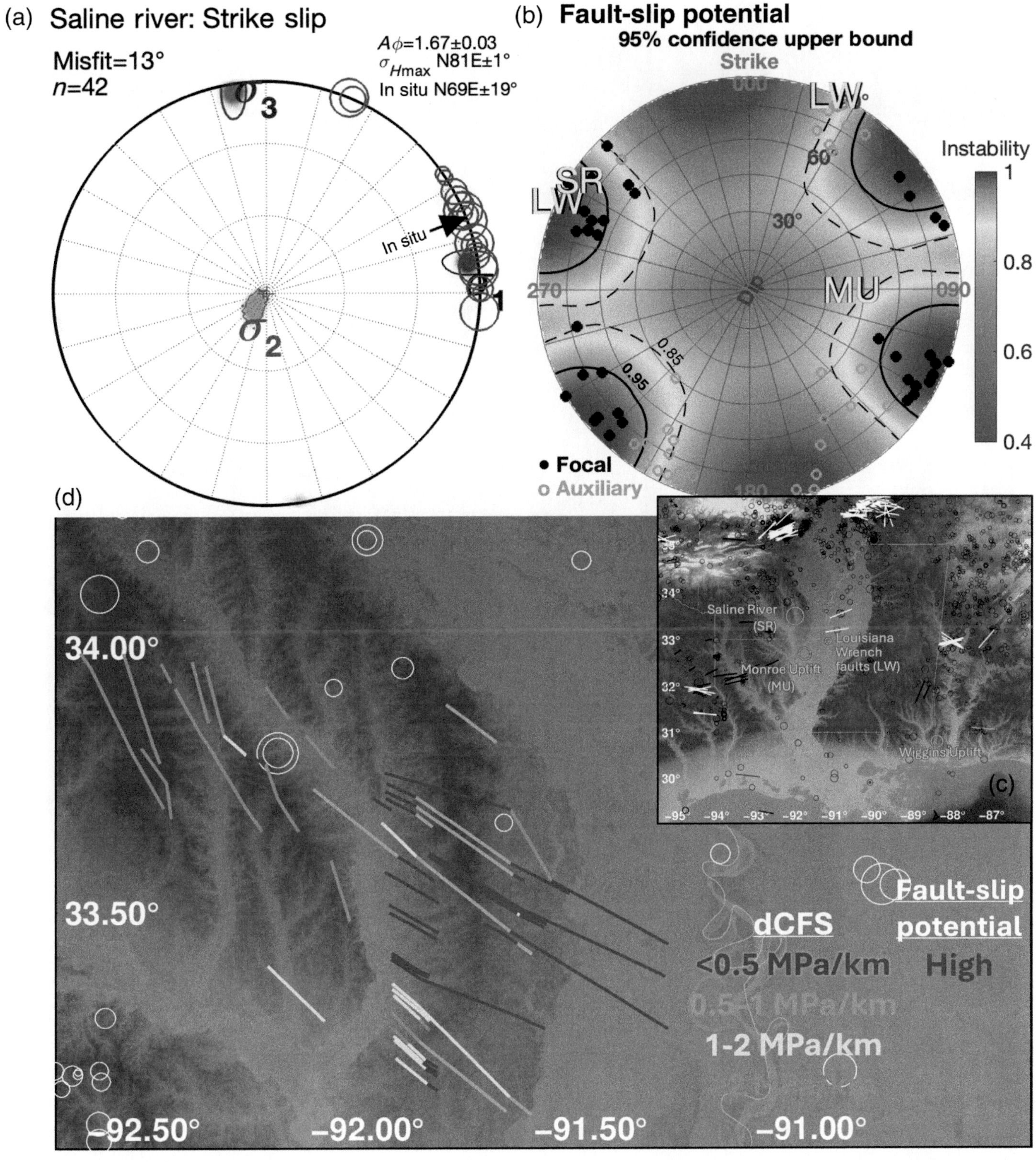

Figure 6. Saline River fault system. (a) Stress inversion results. Symbology and axes as in Figure 4. (b) Instability. Symbology and axes as in Figure 5. LW, Louisiana Wrench faults; MU, Monroe Uplift; SR, Saline River faults. (c) Focal mechanisms in the southern Mississippi Embayment. (d) Fault-slip potential. Faults digitized from Cox *et al.* (2013). The color version of this figure is available only in the electronic edition.

Fig. 8c; dCFS < 1 MPa/km: Fig. 8d). Nevertheless, reprocessed seismic reflection images show that the Gants fault dips ~75° or steeper (Pratt *et al.*, 2022) resulting in $I = 0.7$ (Ga in Fig. 8c). Similarly, there are several different models for a dextral Woodstock Fault (Weems and Lewis, 2002; Marple and Miller, 2006; Durá-Gómez and Talwani, 2009; Talwani and Durá-Gómez, 2009), all proposed to be a near-vertical fault striking

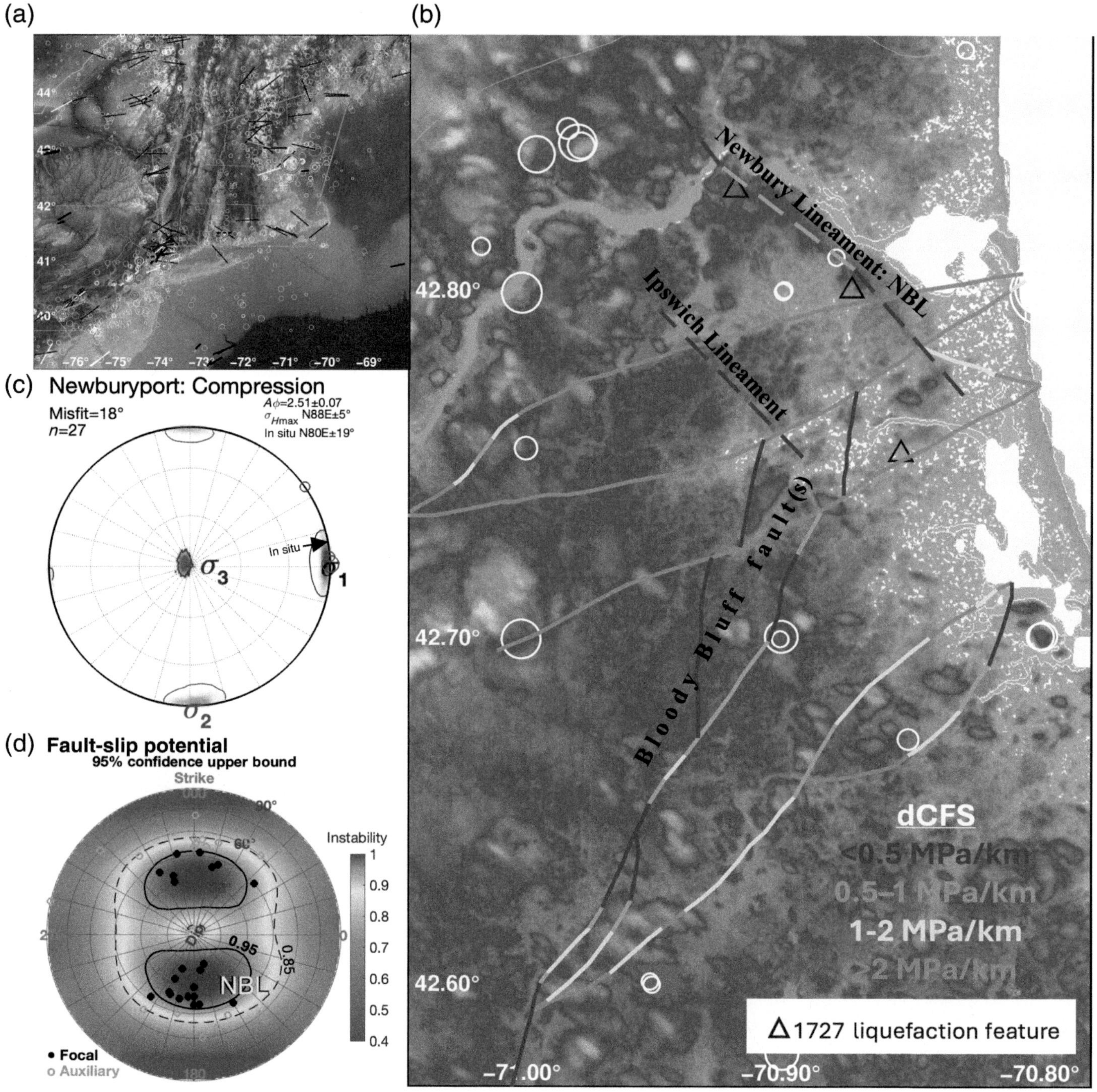

Figure 7. Newbury, Massachusetts. (a) New England focal mechanisms and seismicity. Symbology as in Figure 1. Green polygon: region used for Newbury stress inversion. (b) FSP map. Most of the NBL is near optimal for frictional slip, and it roughly links the three liquefaction features located by Tuttle and Seeber (1991). (c) Stress inversion results. (d) Instability. Newbury Lineament (NBL) proposed by Marple *et al.* (2018); after Ebel (2000) and Tuttle (2007). The color version of this figure is available only in the electronic edition.

between 195 and 220. There are two challenges to this idea. First, a near-vertical fault would be poorly aligned for slip (WM, WT, and WM in Fig. 8c). Second, reflectors are not obviously disrupted because they cross these proposed Woodstock fault traces (Pratt *et al.*, 2022, their fig. 3b).

NW–SE-striking faults: several models show subparallel reverse faults along the Ashley River (striking ~135 or 315) and northeast of the Ashley River (striking ~325; Weems and Lewis, 2002; Marple and Miller, 2006; Talwani and Durá-Gómez, 2009). Allowing for an optimal dip of ~35°, these faults could approach optimal orientation (I = 1 – AR and NE in Fig. 8c). Seismic reflection lines have gaps where

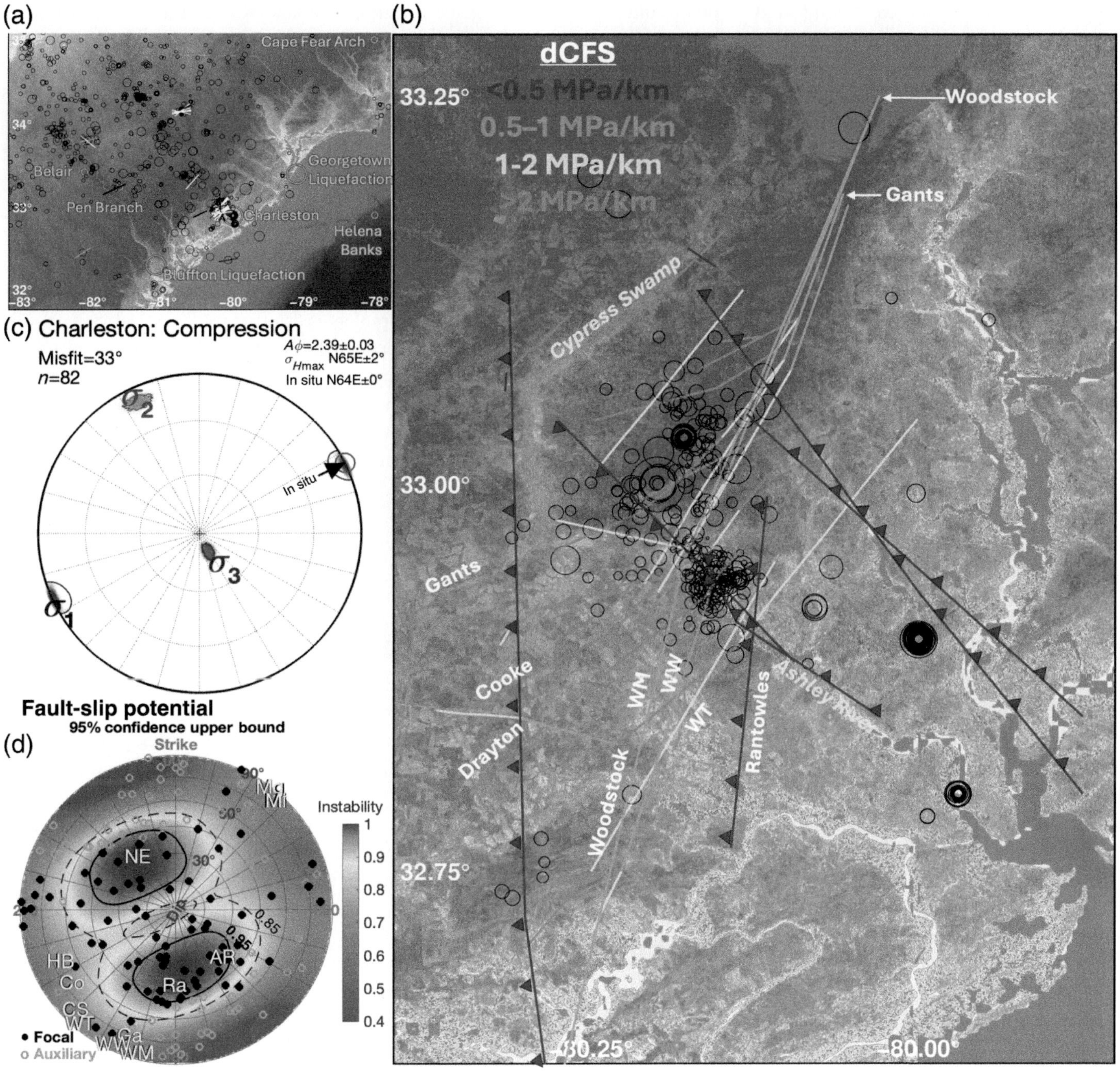

they cross the Ashley River, yet strata equivocally bow upward near the south bank and/or are disrupted near the north bank at the edges of the data gap (Pratt *et al.*, 2022, their fig. 11b). A fault-dipping southwest from that location would pass through the primary modern hypocentral zone near Middleton Place. The longest of the Ashley River faults is ~20 km; however, they may not be sufficient to generate M 7 alone, but a multifault rupture remains a possibility. By contrast, the subparallel faults to the northeast suggested by Marple and Miller (2006) and Weems and Lewis (2002) are up to 50 km long, yet both models indicate northeast dips, away from modern seismicity.

South-striking faults: south-striking, west-dipping faults were proposed by Weems and Lewis (2002) ~10 km west of the seismicity and by Chapman *et al.* (2016) within the modern

Figure 8. Charleston, South Carolina. (a) South Carolina FMs and Seismicity. Symbology as in Figure 1. (b) FSP map. Chapman *et al.* (2016) proposed fault (Rantowles) is near-optimal, as are the other north-trending faults and northwest-trending faults northeast of the Ashley River (Weems and Lewis, 2002; Marple and Miller, 2006). For optimally oriented thrust faults, teeth point down dip. (c) Stress inversion results. (d) Instability. AR, faults along the Ashley River; Co, Cooke fault; CS, Cypress Swamp faults; Ga, northern segment of the Gants fault; HB, Helena Banks fault; Mg, Magnolia fault zone; Mi, Middleton fault; NE, unnamed reverse faults northeast of the Ashley River; Ra, Rantowles fault (186°/43°) plane indicated by seismicity (Chapman *et al.*, 2016). WM, Woodstock fault (Marple and Miller, 2006). WT, Woodstock fault (Talwani and Durá-Gómez, 2009). WW, Woodstock fault (Weems and Lewis, 2002). The color version of this figure is available only in the electronic edition.

hypocentral volume and continuing south to near Rantowles, earning it the moniker Rantowles fault (Ra in Fig. 7d). The former does not align with modern seismicity and dips away from it. The latter was imaged with seismicity; oriented (186°/43°) it has $I \sim 1$, dCFS ~0 MPa/km (Fig. 8c,d). The fault indicated by Pratt *et al.* (2022) is only 25 km long, however, which might be too short to generate the M 7 mainshock (33–75 km, 90% confidence). Above-average stress drop could play a role, as could a multi-segment rupture

Not shown in Figure 8d are dozens of E-to-ESE-trending structures interpreted as Mesozoic rift-related faults by Shah *et al.* (2023); these trend 090–120, with an average of ~100 in their figure 9. Magnetic forward modeling suggested that the features may dip southward (strike E to ESE) at an average of ~40° (25°–60°; Shah *et al.*, 2023). The east-striking segments are not well oriented for slip ($I = 0.84$). The ESE-striking ones may be suitable, if not optimal ($I = 0.92$). In any case, up to ~15 km long, these features are probably not sufficient to account for the M 7 mainshock in isolation. However, a rupture that stepped from one of these faults onto a longer regional fault or vice versa remains a possibility.

In summary, of several fault families proposed near Charleston, the highest slip potentials are on NW–SE reverse faults parallel to the Ashley River and on south-striking reverse faults, whereas the abundant NE–SW-striking faults are poorly oriented. However, the purpose of this discussion is not to advocate for one candidate's fault for the Charleston earthquake. Rather, information from FSP modeling must be synthesized with subsurface data, and—as noted by Pratt *et al.* (2022)—there are abundant subsurface data to constrain, support, or refute models that are not considered here. Nor is evidence considered here from coseismic deformation and historical records (e.g., Bilham and Hough, 2023; 2024). Together, all of these sources of information can inform the search for paleoseismic records of the 1886 faulting.

Summary of classes A, B, or C features. Stress inversion and FSP modeling results are summarized in Figure 9. Stress models, FSP models, and maps similar to Figures 4–8 are presented for each of the class A, B, or C features in the supplemental material. Text S0 summarizes the implications of this analysis for the seismogenic potential of the 61 features and the plausibility that they are of tectonic origin. Text files S1–S10 discuss the features in varying levels of detail, similar to the Example: The 2024 Tewksbury, New Jersey, earthquake and the Ramapo fault system, Example: The SRFZ—A now-known seismic hazard, and Example: Hidden historic earthquakes—Charleston, South Carolina, and Newburyport, Massachusetts, sections, including the stress models, FSP models, and maps.

Slip potential of virtual faults across the CEUS. From the stress tensors that have been derived for the 61 suspected seismogenic features, plus analyses at other well-constrained locations to fill in gaps (Table S2) FSP can be calculated for nearby faults of any orientation (e.g., Figs. 5a–d, 6d, and others). Because stress varies smoothly, assigning these slip potential models to their respective locations allows the seismogenic potential of any fault orientation to be inferred almost anywhere in the CEUS (Fig. 10).

Conclusions

The growth in available FMs and in situ stress direction data in CENA allows for increasingly systematic, quantitative assessment of intraplate crustal stress. Stress varies markedly from ENE compression along the Atlantic coast to transpression and strike slip in the Midcontinent, to trans-tension on the Great Plains with extension in many different directions. Superimposed on these first-order patterns are variations in the relative magnitudes of the principal stresses ($A\Phi$) and in stress directions. Notable anomalies are observed in the New Madrid and Wabash seismic zones, where stress is more compressive and maximum stress approaches E–W, and in the ETSZ, where there is oblique NW–SE extension that is quite different from the surrounding transpressive regime.

The heterogeneous crustal stress field controls what fault orientations are most active and their senses of slip. By developing site-specific stress models for 61 known or suspected Quaternary seismogenic features, their seismogenic potential and expected slip direction—collectively termed FSP—can be quantified. These analyses reveal whether the proposed faults are frictionally favorable for slip and whether the purported slip sense comports with the local stress field, both of which are helpful in gauging whether the features are likely to be tectonic or nontectonic in origin. In addition, the FSP analyses can be used to highlight what mapped faults in a region are well-oriented for slip, providing a means to prioritize targets for shallow geophysical or paleoseismic investigations near historic earthquakes, or to infer which faults are most likely to slip in future earthquakes.

Data and Resources

The focal mechanism (FM) compilation is provided in Table S1. FMs are compiled from Saint Louis University Moment Tensors https://www.eas.slu.edu/eqc/eqc_mt/MECH.NA/MECHFIG/mech.html (last accessed September 2025), the World Stress Map (Heidbach *et al.*, 2018), the Northern California Earthquake Data Center, Oklahoma Geologic Survey (also Qin *et al.*, 2019), and other sources, as listed in Table S1. Stress inversion programs (MATLAB) are available at https://github.com/WillLevandowski/ (last accessed December 2025). The M ≥ 2 from the U.S. Geological Survey (USGS) Comprehensive Catalog (https://earthquake.usgs.gov/earthquakes/search/, last accessed September 2025). The supplemental material includes: Figures S1–S4 showing uncertainties associated with Figure 2; Figure S5 showing the lithospheric density model; and Text S0 provides brief descriptions of the features and their relation to the local stress field, summarizing the

Region	Feature	Class	Lon	Lat	AΦ	std AΦ	Φmax inversion	std Φmax	#FM	Misfit	# of in situ	Φmax in situ	std in situ	Structure: Strike/Dip (###/##°); ?=nominal value	Instability	dCFS
Maine	Norumbega Fault System	C	−69.25	44.4	2.17	0.11	92	4	31	22°	1	20	NaN	Multi-stranded NE-trending system (045/45°?)	1	0
	South Sebec seismic zone	C	−69.08	45.21										Epicentral alignments NW & 250...(315/45°, 250/45°?)	1, 0.98	0.1, 0.75
	Oak Bay fault	C	−67	45	2.25	0.13	78	4	33	23°	35	58	32	NNW, vertical (~345/90°)	0.25	13
Adirondacks	Cornwall - Massena EQ	C	−74.89	44.92	2.17	0.05	71	3	26	20°	0	NaN	NaN	1944 nodal planes (199/42°, 313/70°)	0.98, 0.64	0.6,7.0
	Catlin Lake - Goodnow Pond	C	−74.27	44.02	2.27	0.05	76	3	27	14°	0	NaN	NaN	1983 M4.8 nodal planes (296/32°; 170/70°)	0.97, 0.58	1.3, 8.0
	Champlain Lowlands faults	C	−73.1	44										North-trending normal faults	N/A	N/A
New England	Newbury LF	A	−70.87	42.76	2.58	0.07	82	5	35	22	3	80	19	1727 Mb5.6; (135/40°) [Marple et al., 2018]	0.96	0.8
	Moodus SZ	C	−72.45	41.5	2.52	0.07	91	5	29	24	10	59	19	Shallow seismicity (1–2 km).	1	0.1
NYC	Dobbs Ferry FZ	C	−73.87	41.01	2.37	0.06	65	4	31	23	7	55	18	(315/90°) fault	0.45	10.1
	Mosholu Fault	C	−73.9	40.91										(315/49°,315/89°,315/90°) faults	0.89,0.44,0.45	2.3,10.2,10.1
	New York Bight	C	−73.25	40.2										Vertical NNE fault (025/90°)	0.83	3.8
Mid-Atlantic	Tewksbury EQ / Ramapo FZ	B	−74.75	40.7	2.26	0.06	57	3	32	22	7	66	37	(011/45°) mainshock, (008/36°) aftershock	0.98, 0.99	0.36, 0.07
	Kingston Fault	C	−74.61	40.38										(013,033,358/85°)	0.69, 0.81, 0.50	6.0, 4.6, 9.3
	Lancaster SZ	C	−76.3	40.03	2.14	0.04	59	3	32	22	9	58	36	Epicentral alignment (010/60°) and short faults	0.93	1.3
	Cacoosing EQ	C	−76	40.33										(135/49°) nodal plane	0.93	1.4
	Upper Marlboro Faults	C	−76.75	38.81	2.55	0.06	99	4	31	27	5	54	45	Sketch of 3 faults: app. dips 30–40°; strike unknown.	N/A	N/A
	Lebanon Church Fault	C	−78.37	39.06										(020/57°) fault in outcrop	0.94	1.2
	Central Virginia SZ	A	−77.9	38	2.43	0.05	103	3	27	27	2	88	11	Site of 2011 Mw5.65 Mineral, VA EQ (025/50°)	0.98	0.36
	Mtn. Run - Everona FZ	C	−77.97	38.3										(55/55°,reverse), (40/45?, normal [Pavlides 1994])	1, 1	0.03, 0.04
Piedmont	Old Hickory Faults	C	−77.57	36.91	2.04	0.03	69	2	42	16	0	NaN	NaN	NW/WNW strikes; dip 45–70° (280/45°, 280/70°?)	0.99, 0.99	0.11, 0.14
	Hares Crossroads Fault	C	−78.25	35.67										(007/63°)	0.73	4.7
	Cape Fear Arch	C	−78	35										SE-plunging arch; three faults possible (135/45?)	1	0.04
South Carolina	Charleston	A	−80	32.9	2.37	0.03	61	2	81	32	1	64	NaN	Seismicity (181/40°) [Chapman et al., 2016]	1	0.08
	Georgetown LF	A	−79	34										Scattered liquefaction features.	N/A	N/A
	Bluffton LF	A	−81	32										Scattered liquefaction features.	N/A	N/A
	Helena Banks FZ	C	−78	32.9										(246/70°) offshore	0.75	5.5
	Cooke Fault	C	−80.21	32.95										(235/70°)	0.75	5.2
	Pen Branch Fault	C	−81.8	33.2	2.27	0.02	71	2	96	32	4	59	6	(055/45°)	0.79	5.3
	Belair FZ	C	−82.14	33.43										(030/50°)	0.84	3.1
Appalachia	Sparta/Little River Fault	B	−81.1	36.5	1.82	0.06	69	4	17	13	0	NaN	NaN	(108/60°)	0.98	0.47
	Kentucky River faults	B	−84.4	37.9	1.74	0.04	61	2	39	19	16	60	9	NW/SE strike; dip 25–80°. Trenches: (320/?)x2 & (NW/70°); (320/40°?), (315/70°?)	0.89, 0.67	1.8, 4.6
	Lexington FZ	C	−84.5	38.04										NNE trend, W- and E-dipping, steep: (030/85°?)	1	0.07
	Eastern Tennessee SZ	B	−85	35	0.84	0.03	51	1	60	24	2	64	10	Overall trend 040. (040/60°)	1	0.01
Giles County SZ	Pembroke faults	B	−80.2	37.16	1.82	0.03	58	2	29	22	5	46	11	Five normal faults (046–080/46–70°)...(046/70°, 080/70°?)	0.91, 0.98	2.9, 0.5
	Lindside FZ	C	−80.67	37.45										(065,steep) normal faults. (065,75°?)	0.92	2.8
	Stanleytown-Villa Heights	C	−79.96	36.74										(010/62°), (020,90°) normal faults	0.93, 0.97	1.2, 0.4
Midcontinent	Clarendon-Linden FZ	C	−78.06	43.19	2.05	0.12	74	4	25	19	17	64	13	Iapetan margin; (025/60°?, 000/60°?)	0.96, 0.79	0.65, 3.8
	Northeast Ohio SZ	C	−81.1	41.65	1.82	0.03	60	2	27	12	31	60	11	030 epicentral lineament; FM (025/80°) ... (030/80°?)	1	0.01
	Anna SZ	C	−84.17	40.4	1.89	0.07	70	2	25	10	18	62	12	EQs up to M5.1 (1937). Anna-Champaign fault: west (130/80°), east (110/80°)	0.78, 0.98	3.5, 0.25
	Plum River FZ	C	−90.5	42.15	1.6	0.06	52	2	31	8	6	57	7	(262,80°)	1	0.03
Mississippi Embyament	Wabash Valley LF / SZ	A	−87.5	38.8	1.91	0.1	83	5	25	12	14	85	20	NNE, NE, & SE fault trends; (035/80°) Caborn Fault	0.98	0.3
	Fluorspar / Rough Creek FZ	A	−88.2	37.4	1.92	0.05	97	2	47	23	11	89	21	5 FZs; +&- flower structures... (030/80° & 060/80°)	0.59, 1	6.3, 0
	St. Louis/Cape Girardeau LF	A	−90	38	1.78	0.04	64	2	26	17	4	75	29	LF at 48 sites; 2, 3, or more EQs in 6 kyr	N/A	N/A
	Thebes Gap faults	A	−89.45	37.2	1.92	0.06	69	2	29	18	3	63	26	Long NE faults, shorter E & NW transfer faults; dip <10° to 90°...(030,60°?)	1	0.06
	Reelfoot Scarp	A	−89.45	36.3	2.06	0.02	79	1	111	35	0	NaN	NaN	Reelfoot Fault North (167,30°); South (150,44)	1, 0.98	0.01, 0.2
	Western Lowlands LF	A	−90.6	36.5	1.71	0.03	63	2	27	14	2	76	1	Commerce Geophysical Lineament (042/?)...(042/80°)	0.99	0.12
Gulf Coast	Saline River FZ	A	−91.8	33.6	1.67	0.03	81	1	42	13	20	69	19	284, 290, 307, 320, 326/88° along AOT (300/88°)	0.98	0.18
	Louisiana Wrench faults	C	−91.16	32.97										Four strike-slip faults (024/90?) x 3; (298/90)	0.78, 0.99	2.3, 0.08
	Monroe Uplift	B	−91.75	32.7										E- and W-striking reverse faults ... (090,40°)	0.85	2.85
	Wiggins Uplift	C	−88.4	30.8										Supposed uplift in an area of subsidence & extension	N/A	N/A
Great Plains	Humboldt FZ	C	−96.3	39.8	0.97	0.08	51	2	44	28	0	NaN	NaN	Humboldt (180/90°?).	0.93	0.42
	Nemaha FZ	C	−96.3	38.2	0.91	0.08	50	2	45	32	0	NaN	NaN	Nemaha (196/60°?)	0.97	0.18
	Criner Fault	C	−97.2	34.1	1.44	0.06	83	4	26	25	39	70	29	(320/80°)	0.75	2.6
	Washita Valley Fault	C	−97	34.35	1.52	0.04	86	2	29	17	37	74	21	(120/80°)	1	0.02
	Meers Fault	A	−98.5	34.8	1.76	0.04	82	1	49	11	30	77	15	(114,80°), (118,80°)	1,1	0.06,0.10
	Potter County Fault	C	−102	35.4	1.33	0.05	87	2	34	18	36	93	17	ESE strike? ... (125/80°?)	0.99	0.06
	Crooked Creek	C	−100.3	37.25	0.86	0.16	99	3	25	27	40	93	17	Topographic trough; (208/??°) ... (208/60°?)	0.55	3.6
	Cheraw Fault	A	−103.2	38.4	0.25	0.08	64	14	20	19	41	95	16	(224/66°) average in trenches.	0.99	0.06
	Pierre faults	C	−100.5	44.37	1.0?	0.25?	80	15	NaN	NaN	1	85	NaN	24 faults: 13 normal/5 reverse/6 other. Normal fault strikes: 245,150,015,355,320,325,095,345,045,250	N/A	N/A
	Brockton-Froid FZ	B	−104.7	48.25	0.9?	0.25?	65	10	NaN	NaN	24	78	26	Two or more 055-trending normal faults.	N/A	N/A

Stress constraints favor tectonic origin. Feature is well oriented, and slip sense is compatible with local stress model

Stress constraints may be consistent with tectonic origin. Feature has moderate instability (~0.85<I<0.95) and/or would be near optimal at a different dip.

Stress may be inconsistent with tectonic origin. Low instability (~0.75<I<0.85); poorly resolved stress or dip; moderate instability under optimal conditions (~I<0.9); slip sense that at odds with stress.

Stress constraints are inconsistent with tectonic origin. Feature has the wrong slip sense and/or has low instability (~I<0.75).

No new constraints from stress analysis: Features are not linked to a specific structure or there is insufficient information on the proposed structure.

EQ: Earthquake. SZ: Seismic Zone. FZ: Fault Zone. LF: Liquefaction feature(s).

Figure 9. Summary of stress inversions and FSP modeling for 61 classes A, B, and C features. The color version of this figure is available only in the electronic edition.

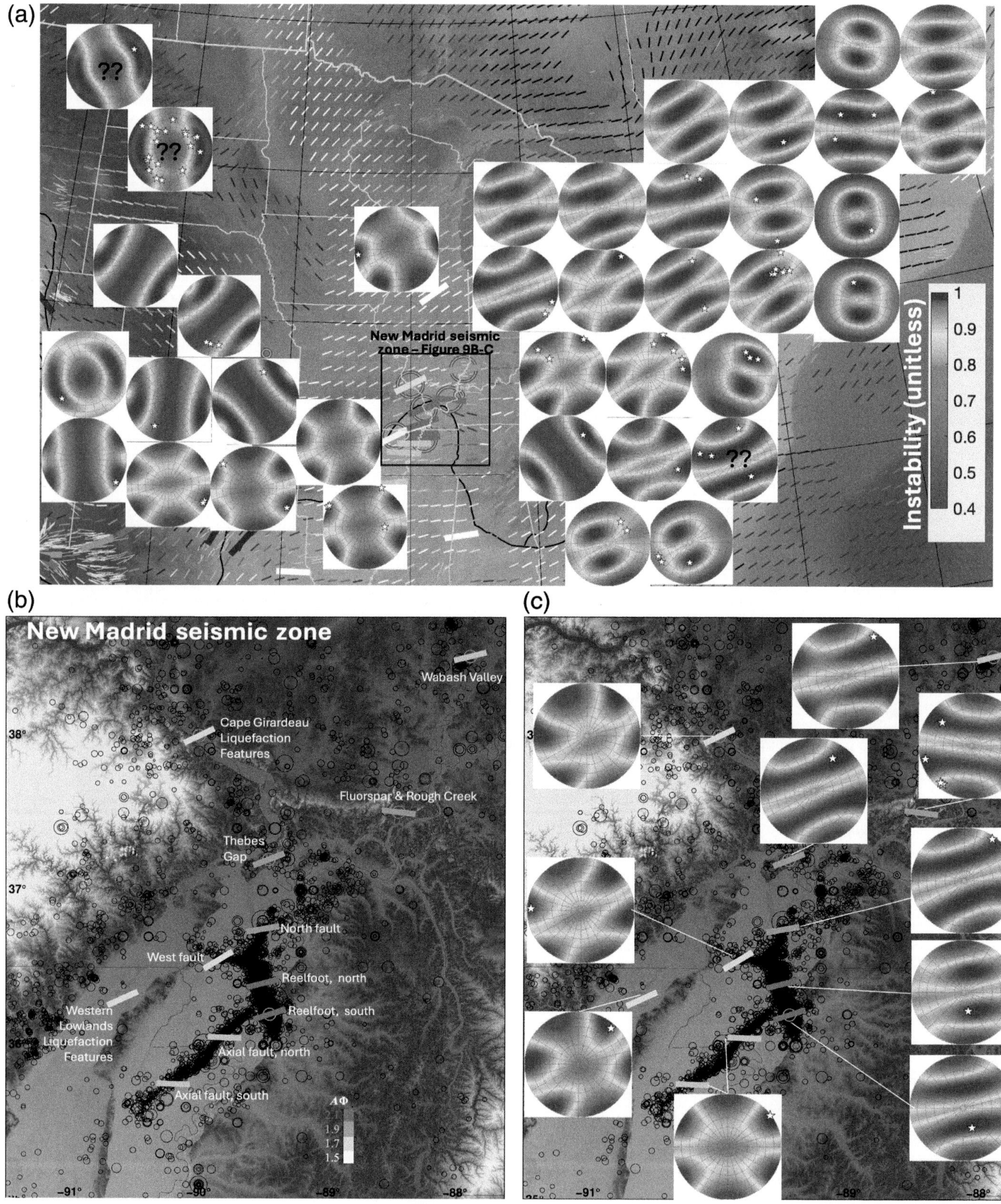

Figure 10. Fault-slip potential across the CEUS. (a) Instability polar plots for the classes A, B, and C features, approximately centered on each feature. Azimuthal coordinate: virtual fault strike. Radial coordinate: virtual fault dip angle, steeper dips toward the outside. Stars: orientations of features of interest (as shown by letters in Figs. 7c, 8c). (b,c) Expanded view of the New Madrid seismic zone. Symbology as in Figures 2–8. The color version of this figure is available only in the electronic edition.

results of fault-slip potential (FSP) modeling. Text S1–S10: reassessing classes A, B, and C potentially seismogenic structures in the central and eastern United States (CEUS), providing details on each of the 61 sites, organized geographically; Table S1: FMs; Table S2: site-specific inversions shown in Figure 3; and Table S3: gridded inversions shown in Figure 2.

Declaration of Competing Interests

The authors acknowledge that there are no conflicts of interest recorded.

Acknowledgments

Comments from two anonymous reviewers greatly improved the presentation of figures and tables. This material is based upon work supported by the U.S. Geological Survey (USGS) under Grant Number G24AP00279.

The views and conclusions contained in this document are those of the authors and should not be interpreted as representing the opinions or policies of the USGS. Mention of trade names or commercial products does not constitute their endorsement by the USGS.t

References

Aggarwal, Y. P., and L. R. Sykes (1978). Earthquakes, faults, and nuclear power plants in southern New York and northern New Jersey, *Science* **200,** no. 4340, 425–429.

Alt, R. C., and M. D. Zoback (2017). In situ stress and active faulting in Oklahoma, *Bull. Seismol. Soc. Am.* **107,** no. 1, 216–228.

Amemoutou, A., P. Martínez-Garzón, G. Kwiatek, J. L. Rubinstein, and M. Bohnhoff (2021). Earthquake source mechanisms and stress field variations associated with wastewater-induced seismicity in Southern Kansas, USA, *J. Geophys. Res.* **126,** no. 7, e2020JB021625.

Amick, D., and R. Gelinas (1991). The search for evidence of large prehistoric earthquakes along the Atlantic seaboard, *Science* **251,** no. 4994, 655–658.

Angelier, J. (1979). Determination of the mean principal directions of stresses for a given fault population, *Tectonophysics* **56,** no. 3–4, T17–T26.

Baird, A. F., S. D. McKinnon, and L. Godin (2009). Stress channelling and partitioning of seismicity in the Charlevoix seismic zone, Québec, Canada, *Geophys. J. Int.* **179,** no. 1, 559–568.

Baird, A. F., S. D. McKinnon, and L. Godin (2010). Relationship between structures, stress and seismicity in the Charlevoix seismic zone revealed by 3-D geomechanical models: Implications for the seismotectonics of continental interiors, *J. Geophys. Res.: Solid Earth* **115,** no. B11, doi: 10.1029/2010JB007521.

Beaucé, E., F. Waldhauser, D. Schaff, W. Y. Kim, and F. Kolawole (2025). The 5 April 2024 Mw 4.8 Tewksbury, New Jersey aftershock sequence resolved with machine-learning-enhanced detection methods, *Geophys. Res. Lett.* **52,** no. 12, e2024GL113598.

Bilham, R., and S. E. Hough (2023). The 1886 Charleston, South Carolina, earthquake: Relic railroad offset reveals rupture, *Seism. Record* **3,** no. 4, 278–288.

Bilham, R., and S. E. Hough (2024). Static and dynamic strain in the 1886 Charleston, South Carolina, earthquake, *Bull. Seismol. Soc. Am.* **114,** no. 5, 2687–2712.

Bott, M. H. P. (1959). The mechanics of oblique slip faulting, *Geol. Mag.* **96,** no. 2, 109–117.

Boyd, O. S., W. D. Barnhart, J. Bourke, M. Chapman, P. S. Earle, G. C. D. Huang, J. A. Thompson Jobe, W.-Y. Kin, F. Link, M. Litherland, *et al.* (2024). Preliminary observations of the 5 April 2024 Mw 4.8 New Jersey earthquake, *Seism. Record* **4,** no. 4, 240–250.

Brocher, T. M. (2005). Empirical relations between elastic wavespeeds and density in the Earth's crust, *Bull. Seismol. Soc. Am.* **95,** no. 6, 2081–2092.

Burton, W. C., and N. M. Ratcliffe (1985). Attitude, movement history, and structure of cataclastic rocks of the Flemington Fault results of core drilling near Oldwick, New Jersey, *U.S. Geol. Surv. Open-File Rept. 1781.*

Carlson, G., K. Johnson, R. Chuang, and J. Rupp (2018). Spatially varying stress state in the central US from Bayesian inversion of focal mechanism and in situ maximum horizontal stress orientation data, *J. Geophys. Res.: Solid Earth* **123,** no. 5, 3871–3890.

Chapman, M. C., and J. N. Beale (2010). On the geologic structure at the epicenter of the 1886 Charleston, South Carolina, earthquake, *Bull. Seismol. Soc. Am.* **100,** 1010–1030, doi: 10.1785/0120090231.

Chapman, M. C., J. N. Beale, A. C. Hardy, and Q. Wu (2016). Modern seismicity and the fault responsible for the 1886 Charleston, South Carolina, earthquake, *Bull. Seismol. Soc. Am.* **106,** no. 2, 364–372.

Chen, W., M. Neves, Q. Zhai, C. Daniels, O. Adeboboye, S. Jaume, and Z. Peng (2023). Preliminary results from a dense short-period seismic deployment around the source zone of the 1886 M 7 South Carolina earthquake, *Seismol. Res. Lett.* **94,** no. 5, 2479–2488.

Cox, R. T., J. L. Hall, and C. S. Gardner (2013). Tectonic history and setting of a seismogenic intraplate fault system that lacks microseismicity: The Saline River fault system, southern United States, *Tectonophysics* **608,** 252–266.

Cox, R. T., R. D. Hatcher, S. L. Forman, R. Counts, J. Vaughn, E. Gamble, J. Glasbrenner, K. Warrell, N. Adhikari, and S. Pinardi (2022). Synthesis of recent paleoseismic research on quaternary faulting in the eastern Tennessee seismic zone, eastern North America: Implications for seismic hazard and intraplate seismicity, *Bull. Seismol. Soc. Am.* **112,** no. 2, 1161–1189.

Cox, R. T., C. Lowe, Y. Hao, and S. A. Mahan (2014). Use of small-scale liquefaction features to assess paleoseismicity: An example from the Saline River fault zone, Southeast Arkansas, USA, *Front. Earth Sci.* **2,** 31.

Cramer, C. H., and O. S. Boyd (2014). Why the New Madrid earthquakes are M 7–8 and the Charleston earthquake is ~M 7, *Bull. Seismol. Soc. Am.* **104,** no. 6, 2884–2903.

Crone, A. J., and R. L. Wheeler (2000). Data for Quaternary faults, liquefaction features, and possible tectonic features in the central and eastern United States, east of the Rocky Mountain Front, *U.S. Depart. Int., U.S. Geol. Surv. Open-File Rept. 2000-260*, 342 p.

Drake, A. A., Jr, R. A. Volkert, D. H. Monteverde, G. C. Herman, H. F. Houghton, R. A. Parker, and R. F. Dalton (1996) Bedrock geologic map of northern New Jersey, *U.S. Geol. Surv. Misc. Geol. Investig. Map I-2540-A*, doi: 10.3133/i2540A.

Durá-Gómez, I., and P. Talwani (2009). Finding faults in the Charleston area, South Carolina: 1. Seismological data, *Seismol. Res. Lett.* **80,** 883–900, doi: 10.1785/gssrl.80.5.883.

Ebel, J. E. (2000). A reanalysis of the 1727 earthquake at Newbury, Massachusetts, *Seismol. Res. Lett.* **71,** no. 3, 364–374.

Ebel, J. E. (2008). The importance of small earthquakes, *Seismol. Res. Lett.* **79,** no. 4, 491–493.

England, P., G. Houseman, and L. Sonder (1985). Length scales for continental deformation in convergent, divergent, and strike-slip environments: Analytical and approximate solutions for a thin viscous sheet model, *J. Geophys. Res.: Solid Earth* **90,** no. B5, 3551–3557.

Fadugba, O. I., E. Choi, and C. A. Powell (2019). Effects of preexisting structures on the seismicity of the Charlevoix seismic zone, *J. Geophys. Res.: Solid Earth* **124,** no. 7, 7370–7386.

Figueiredo, P., J. Hill, A. Merschat, C. Scheip, K. Scheip, C., Stewart, L. Owen, R. Wooten, M. Carter, E. Szymanski, S. Horton, *et al.* (2022). The M_w 5.1, 9 August 2020, Sparta earthquake, North Carolina: The first documented seismic surface rupture in the eastern United States, *GSA Today* **32,** doi: 10.1130/GSATG517A.1.

Frohlich, C., and K. D. Apperson (1992). Earthquake focal mechanisms, moment tensors, and the consistency of seismic activity near plate boundaries, *Tectonics* **11,** 279–296.

Gallen, S. F., and J. R. Thigpen (2018). Lithologic controls on focused erosion and intraplate earthquakes in the eastern Tennessee seismic zone, *Geophys. Res. Lett.* **45,** no. 18, 9569–9578.

Ghosh, A., W. E. Holt, and A. Bahadori (2019). Role of large-scale tectonic forces in intraplate earthquakes of central and eastern North America, *Geochem. Geophys. Geosys.* **20,** no. 4, 2134–2156.

Grana, J. P., and R. M. Richardson (1996). Tectonic stress within the New Madrid seismic zone, *J. Geophys. Res.: Solid Earth* **101,** no. B3, 5445–5458.

Hardebeck, J. L., and E. Hauksson (2001). Crustal stress field in southern California and its implications for fault mechanics, *J. Geophys. Res.: Solid Earth* **106,** no. B10, 21,859–21,882.

Heidbach, O., M. Rajabi, X. Cui, K. Fuchs, B. Müller, J. Reinecker, K. Reiter, M. Tingay, F. Wenzel, F. Xie, *et al.* (2018). The World Stress Map database release 2016: Crustal stress pattern across scales, *Tectonophysics* **744,** 484–498.

Hennings, P. H., J. E. L. Snee, J. L. Osmond, H. R. DeShon, R. Dommisse, E. Horne, C. Lemons, and M. D. Zoback (2019). Injection-induced seismicity and fault-slip potential in the Fort Worth Basin, Texas, *Bull. Seismol. Soc. Am.* **109,** no. 5, 1615–1634.

Hightower, E., M. Gurnis, and W. Mao (2024). Influence of Farallon slab loading on intraplate stress and seismicity in eastern North America in the presence of pre-existing weak zones, *Geochem. Geophys. Geosys.* **25,** no. 6, e2024GC011493.

Homman, K., and A. Nyblade (2025). Moment tensors for small earthquakes and the stress regime in the mid-Atlantic United States, *Tectonophysics* **895,** 230,582.

Horne, E. A., P. Hennings, K. M. Smye, A. Z. Calle, A. P. Morris, and G. C. D. Huang (2024). Interpretation, characterization, and slip hazard assessment of faults in the Midland Basin, west Texas, United States, *AAPG Bulletin* **108,** no. 12, 2313–2346.

Hough, S. E., and R. Bilham (2024a). The 1886 Charleston, South Carolina, earthquake: Intensities and ground motions, *Bull. Seismol. Soc. Am.* **114,** no. 3, 1658–1679.

Hough, S. E., and R. Bilham (2024b). On the provenance of field reports of the 1886 Charleston, South Carolina, earthquake: A seismo historical whodunit, *Seismol. Res. Lett.* **95,** no. 4, 2527–2537.

Huang, G. C. D., E. Horne, F. Kavoura, and A. Savvaidis (2022). Characteristics of seismogenic structures and 3D stress state of the Delaware Basin of West Texas as constrained by earthquake source mechanisms, *Seismol. Res. Lett.* **93,** no. 6, 3363–3372.

Humphreys, E. D., and D. D. Coblentz (2007). North American dynamics and western US tectonics, *Rev. Geophys.* **45,** no. 3, doi: 10.1029/2005RG000181.

Hurd, O., and M. D. Zoback (2012a). Intraplate earthquakes, regional stress and fault mechanics in the Central and Eastern US and Southeastern Canada, *Tectonophysics* **581,** 182–192.

Hurd, O., and M. D. Zoback (2012b). Regional stress orientations and slip compatibility of earthquake focal planes in the New Madrid seismic zone, *Seismol. Res. Lett.* **83,** no. 4, 672–679.

Intfen, J. W. (2019). Evaluation of seismicity trends in Kansas to determine possible source mechanisms using focal mechanism inversion and spectral analysis, *Doctoral Dissertation*, University of Kansas.

Jobe, J. T., R. Briggs, R. Gold, L. Bauer, and C. Collett (2024). Limited evidence of late quaternary tectonic surface deformation in the eastern Tennessee seismic zone, United States, *Bull. Seismol. Soc. Am.* **114,** no. 4, 1920–1940.

Jobe, J. T., A. Hatem, R. Gold, C. DuRoss, N. Reitman, R. Briggs, and C. Collett (2022). Revised earthquake geology inputs for the Central and Eastern United States and Southeast Canada for the 2023 National Seismic Hazard Model, *Seismol. Res. Lett.* **93,** no. 6, 3100–3120.

Johnson, C. W., Y. Fu, and R. Bürgmann (2020). Hydrospheric modulation of stress and seismicity on shallow faults in southern Alaska, *Earth Planet. Sci. Lett.* **530,** 115904.

King, P. B. (1959). *Evolution of North America*, Princeton University Press, Princeton, New Jersey.

Kolawole, F., J. A. Tielke, Z. Foster-Baril, A. Prakash, E. Beaucé, M. Colet, W.-Y. Kim, R. Ajala, C. McCarthy, F. Waldhauser, and L. Seeber (2024). The 2024 M4. 8 New Jersey earthquake: Reactivation of a rough immature fault in frictionally unstable basement rocks, *AGU Fall Meeting Abstracts*, Vol. 2024, 3216, T53B–3216.

Levandowski, W. (2025). Stress constraints on fault activity during the 2020 Mw 5.1 Sparta, North Carolina mainshock and aftershock sequence, *Seismol. Res. Lett.* doi: 10.1785/0220250309.

Levandowski, W. (2023). Fault slip potential near the deadly 08 September 2023 M_w 6.8 Al Haouz, Morocco earthquake, *Seism. Record* **3,** no. 4, 367–375, doi: 10.1785/0320230037.

Levandowski, W., O. S. Boyd, R. W. Briggs, and R. D. Gold (2015). A random-walk algorithm for modeling lithospheric density and the role of body forces in the evolution of the Midcontinent Rift, *Geochem. Geophys. Geosys.* **16,** doi: 10.1002/2015GC005961.

Levandowski, W., O. S. Boyd, and L. Ramirez-Guzmán (2016). Dense lower crust elevates long-term earthquake rates in the New Madrid seismic zone, *Geophys. Res. Lett.* **43,** no. 16, 8499–8510.

Levandowski, W., R. B. Herrmann, R. Briggs, O. S. Boyd, and R. Gold (2018). A revised stress map of the continental United States reveals evidence for heterogeneous intraplate stress, *Nat. Geol.* **11,** 433–437.

Levandowski, W., R. B. Herrmann, W. Shen, R. Briggs, R. Gold, and O. S. Boyd (2017). A new lithospheric density model of the continental United States and implications for intraplate seismicity, *SSA Annual Meeting*, Denver, Colorado, April 2017.

Levandowski, W., C. Powell, M. Chapman, and Q. Wu (2023). Anomalous crustal stress in the eastern Tennessee seismic zone, *Seismol. Res. Lett.* **94,** 1643–1655, doi: 10.1785/0220220364.

Levandowski, W., M. Weingarten, and F. R. Walsh III (2018). Geomechanical sensitivities of injection-induced earthquakes, *Geophys. Res. Lett.* **45,** doi: 10.1029/2018GL077551.

Lund-Snee, J.-E., and M. D. Zoback (2016). State of stress in Texas: Implications for induced seismicity, *Geophys. Res. Lett.* **43,** no. 19, 10,208–10,214, doi: 10.1002/2016GL070974.

Lund-Snee, J. E., and M. D. Zoback (2018). State of stress in the Permian Basin, Texas and New Mexico: Implications for induced seismicity, *The Leading Edge* **37,** no. 2, 127–134.

Lund-Snee, J. E., and M. D. Zoback (2020). Multiscale variations of the crustal stress field throughout North America, *Nat. Comm.* **11,** no. 1, 1951.

Lund-Snee, J. E., and M. D. Zoback (2022). State of stress in areas of active unconventional oil and gas development in North America, *AAPG Bull.* **106,** no. 2, 355–385.

Lundstern, J. E. (2024). Recent advances in characterizing the crustal stress field and future applications of stress data: Perspectives from North America, *Geol. Soc. Lond. Sp. Publ.* **546,** doi: 10.1144/SP546-2023-195.

Lundstern, J. E., and M. D. Zoback (2020). Multiscale variations of the crustal stress field throughout North America, *Nature Comm.* **11,** no. 1, 1951.

Marple, R., and J. Hurd (2020). Interpretation of lineaments and faults near Summerville, South Carolina, USA, using LiDAR data: Implications for the cause of the 1886 Charleston, South Carolina, earthquake, *Atl. Geol.* **56,** 73–95, doi: 10.4138/atlgeol.2020.003.

Marple, R. T., and R. Miller (2006). Association of the 1886 Charleston, South Carolina, earthquake and seismicity near Summerville with a 12 degrees bend in the East Coast fault system and triple-fault junctions, *Southeast. Geol.* **44,** 101–127.

Marple, R. T., and P. Talwani (1993). Evidence of possible tectonic upwarping along the South Carolina Coastal Plain from an examination of river morphology and elevation data, *Geology* **21,** no. 7, 651–654.

Marple, R. T., J. D. Hurd Jr., L. Liu, S. Travis, and R. J. Altamura (2018). Investigation of the 1727 Newbury, Massachusetts, USA, earthquake using LiDAR imagery and P-wave velocity tomography, *Atlantic Geol.* **54,** 267–283.

Mazzotti, S., and J. Townend (2010). State of stress in central and eastern North American seismic zones, *Lithosphere* **2,** no. 2, 76–83

McKenzie, D. P. (1969). The relation between fault plane solutions for earthquakes and the directions of the principal stresses, *Bull. Seismol. Soc. Am.* **59,** 561–601.

McNamara, D. E., H. M. Benz, R. B. Herrmann, E. A. Bergman, P. Earle, A. Holland, R. Baldwin, and A. Gassner (2015). Earthquake hypocenters and focal mechanisms in central Oklahoma reveal a complex system of reactivated subsurface strike-slip faulting, *Geophys. Res. Lett.* **42,** 2742–2749, doi: 10.1002/2014GL062730.

Michael, A. J. (1991). Spatial variations in stress within the 1987 Whittier Narrows, California, aftershock sequence: New techniques and results, *J. Geophys. Res.: Solid Earth* **96,** no. B4, 6303–6319.

Ostenaa, D. A., M. S. Zellman, M. L. Morgan, C. B. DuRoss, R. W. Briggs, R. D. Gold, S. A. Mahan, H. J. Gray, L. Broes, and K. Lindsey (2022). Mid-to Late-Quaternary geomorphic and paleoseismic event history, Cheraw fault, southeastern Colorado, *Bull. Seismol. Soc. Am.* **112,** no. 3, 1742–1772.

Petersen, M. D., A. M. Shumway, P. M. Powers, E. H. Field, M. P. Moschetti, K. S. Jaiswal, K. R. Milner, S. Rezaeian, A. D. Frankel, A. L. Llenos, *et al.* (2023). The 2023 US 50-state national seismic hazard model: Overview and implications, *Earthq. Spectra* **40,** no. 1, 5–88.

Pollitz, F. F., L. Kellogg, and R. Burgmann (2001). Sinking mafic body in a reactivated lower crust: A mechanism for stress concentration at the New Madrid seismic zone, *Bull. Seismol. Soc. Am.* **91,** no. 6, 1882–1897.

Powell, C. A., and W. A. Thomas (2016). Grenville basement structure associated with the Eastern Tennessee seismic zone, southeastern USA, *Geology* **44,** no. 1, 39–42.

Pratt, T. L., A. K. Shah, R. C. Counts, J. W. Horton Jr., and M. C. Chapman (2022). Shallow faulting and folding in the epicentral area of the 1886 Charleston, South Carolina, earthquake, *Bull. Seismol. Soc. Am.* **112,** no. 4, 2097–2123.

Quiñones, L. A., H. R. DeShon, M. B. Magnani, and C. Frohlich (2018). Stress orientations in the Fort Worth Basin, Texas, determined from earthquake focal mechanisms, *Bull. Seismol. Soc. Am.* **108,** no. 3A, 1124–1132.

Qin, Y., X. Chen, J. I. Walter, J. Haffener, D. T. Trugman, B. M. Carpenter, M. Weingarten, and F. Kolawole (2019). Deciphering the stress state of seismogenic faults in Oklahoma and southern Kansas based on an improved stress map, *J. Geophys. Res.: Solid Earth* **124,** no. 12, 12,920–12,934.

Rimando, J. M., and A. L. Peace (2021). Reactivation potential of intraplate faults in the western Quebec seismic zone, eastern Canada, *Earth Space Sci.* **8,** no. 8, e2021EA001825.

Rodgers, J. (1967). Chronology of tectonic movements in the Appalachian region of eastern North America, *Am. J. Sci.* **265,** no. 5, 408–427.

Richardson, R. M., and L. M. Reding (1991). North American plate dynamics, *J. Geophys. Res.: Solid Earth* **96,** no. B7, 12201–12223.

Ruppert, N. (2008). Stress map for Alaska from earthquake focal mechanisms, in *Active Tectonics and Seismic Potential of Alaska*, AGU Monograph, 179, doi: 10.1029/179GM20.

Saxena, A., E. Choi, C. A. Powell, and K. S. Aslam (2021). Seismicity in the central and southeastern United States due to upper mantle heterogeneities, *Geophys. J. Int.* **225,** no. 3, 1624–1636.

Sbar, M. L., and L. R. Sykes (1973). Contemporary compressive stress and seismicity in eastern North America: An example of intraplate tectonics, *GSA Bull.* **84,** no. 6, 1861–1882.

Shah, A. K., T. L. Pratt, and J. W. Horton Jr (2023). Rift basins and intraplate earthquakes: New high-resolution aeromagnetic data provide insights into buried structures of the Charleston, South Carolina seismic zone, *Geochem. Geophys. Geosys.* **24,** no. 5, e2022GC010803.

Shen, W., and M. H. Ritzwoller (2016). Crustal and uppermost mantle structure beneath the United States, *J. Geophys. Res.: Solid Earth* **121,** no. 6, 4306–4342.

Simpson, R. W. (1997). Quantifying Anderson's fault types, *J. Geophys. Res.: Solid Earth* **102,** no. B8, 17,909–17,919.

Skoumal, R. J., E. S. Cochran, K. A. Kroll, J. L. Rubinstein, and D. McPhillips (2021). Characterizing stress orientations in southern Kansas, *Bull. Seismol. Soc. Am.* **111,** no. 3, 1445–1454.

Stein, R. S. (1999). The role of stress transfer in earthquake occurrence, *Nature* **402,** no. 6762, 605–609.

Steltenpohl, M. G., I. Zietz, J. W. Horton Jr, and D. L. Daniels (2010). New York–Alabama lineament: A buried right-slip fault bordering the Appalachians and mid-continent North America, *Geology* **38,** no. 6, 571–574.

Sykes, L. R. (1978). Intraplate seismicity, reactivation of preexisting zones of weakness, alkaline magmatism, and other tectonism postdating continental fragmentation, *Rev. Geophys.* **16,** no. 4, 621–688.

Talwani, P., and I. Durá-Gómez (2009). Finding faults in the Charleston area, South Carolina: 2. Complementary data, *Seismol. Res. Lett.* **80,** 901–919, doi: 10.1785/gssrl.80.5.901.

Talwani, P., and W. T. Schaeffer (2001). Recurrence rates of large earthquakes in the South Carolina Coastal Plain based on paleoliquefaction data, *J. Geophys. Res.: Solid Earth* **106,** no. B4, 6621–6642.

Thomas, W. A., and C. A. Powell (2017). Necessary conditions for intraplate seismic zones in North America, *Tectonics* **36,** no. 12, 2903–2917.

Townend, J., and M. D. Zoback (2001). mplications of earthquake focal mechanisms for the frictional strength of the San Andreas fault system, in *The Nature and Tectonic Significance of Fault Zone Weakening*, R. E. Holdsworth, R. A. Strachan, J. F. Magloughlin, and R. J. Knipe (Editors), Geological Society London, Special Publications.

Tuttle, M., and L. Seeber (1991). Historic and prehistoric earthquake-induced liquefaction in Newbury, Massachusetts, *Geology* **19,** 594–597.

Tuttle, M. P. (2007). Re-evaluation of earthquake potential and source in the vicinity of Newburyport, Massachusetts, *Final Tech. Rept. U.S. Geol. Surv. Award 1434-01HQGR0163*.

Vavryčuk, V. (2014). Iterative joint inversion for stress and fault orientations from focal mechanisms, *Geophys. J. Int.* **199,** no. 1, 69–77.

Vavryčuk, V., F. Bouchaala, and T. Fischer (2013). High-resolution fault image from accurate locations and focal mechanisms of the 2008 swarm earthquakes in West Bohemia, Czech Republic, *Tectonophysics* **590,** 189–195.

Wallace, R. E. (1951). Geometry of shearing stress and relation to faulting, *J. Geol.* **59,** no. 2, 118–130.

Walsh, F. R., III, and M. D. Zoback (2016). Probabilistic assessment of potential fault slip related to injection-induced earthquakes: Application to north-central Oklahoma, USA, *Geology* **44,** no. 12, 991–994, doi: 10.1130/G38275.1.

Warrell, K. F., R. T. Cox, R. D. Hatcher Jr., J. D. Vaughn, and R. Counts (2017). Paleoseismic evidence for multiple Mw≥ 6 earthquakes in the Eastern Tennessee seismic zone during the late quaternary, *Bull. Seismol. Soc. Am.* **107,** no. 4, 1610–1624.

Weems, R. E., and W. C. Lewis (2002). Structural and tectonic setting of the Charleston, South Carolina, region: Evidence from the Tertiary stratigraphic record, *Geol. Soc. Am. Bull.* **114,** 24–42.

Wells, D. L., and K. J. Coppersmith (1994). New empirical relationships among magnitude, rupture length, rupture width, rupture area, and surface displacement, *Bull. Seismol. Soc. Am.* **84,** no. 4, 974–1002.

Whitmeyer, S. J., and K. E. Karlstrom (2007). Tectonic model for the Proterozoic growth of North America, *Geosphere* **3,** no. 4, 220–259.

Withjack, M. O., and R. W. Schlische (2005). A review of tectonic events on the passive margin of eastern North America, in *Petroleum Systems of Divergent Continental Margin Basins*, P. J. Post, N. C. Rosen, D. L. Olson, S. L. Palmes, K. T. Lynos, and G. B. Newton (Editors), SEPM Society for Sedimentary Geology, doi: 10.5724/gcs.05.25.0203.

Worum, G., J. D. van Wees, G. Bada, R. T. van Balen, S. Cloetingh, and H. Pagnier (2004). Slip tendency analysis as a tool to constrain fault reactivation: A numerical approach applied to three-dimensional fault models in the Roer Valley rift system (southeast Netherlands), *J. Geophys. Res.* **109,** no. B2, doi: 10.1029/2003JB002586.

Wu, Q., M. C. Chapman, and J. N. Beale (2015). The aftershock sequence of the 2011 Mineral, Virginia, earthquake: Temporal and spatial distribution, focal mechanisms, regional stress, and the role of Coulomb stress transfer, *Bull. Seismol. Soc. Am.* **105,** no. 5, 2521–2537.

Zellman, M. S., D. A. Ostenaa, and M. P. Brown (2021). Subsurface characterization of the Quaternary active Cheraw fault in southeastern Colorado based on seismic imaging, *Seism. Record* **1,** no. 1, 56–65.

Zoback, M. L. (1992a). Stress field constraints on intraplate seismicity in eastern North America, *J. Geophys. Res.: Solid Earth* **97,** no. B8, 11,761–11,782.

Zoback, M. L. (1992b). First- and second-order patterns of stress in the lithosphere: The World Stress Map Project, *J. Geophys. Res.: Solid Earth* **97,** no. B8, 11,703–11,728.

Zoback, M. D. (2010). *Reservoir Geomechanics*, Cambridge University Press, Cambridge, United Kingdom.

Zoback, M. L., and M. Zoback (1980). State of stress in the conterminous United States, *J. Geophys. Res.: Solid Earth* **85,** no. B11, 6113–6156.

Zoback, M. L., and M. Zoback (1981). State of stress and intraplate earthquakes in the United States, *Science* **213,** no. 4503, 96–104.

Zoback, M. L., and M. D. Zoback (1989). Tectonic stress field of the continental United States, in *Geophysical framework of the continental United States*, L. C. Pakiser and W. D. Mooney (Editors), Geological Society of America Memoir 172, Boulder, Colorado.

Manuscript received 17 October 2025
Published online 9 February 2026

Low Aftershock Productivity and Fault Geometry of the 2017 Delaware Earthquake

Karen M. Pearson*[1], Vedran Lekic[1], and Lara Wagner[2]

Abstract

Central and Eastern United States (CEUS) earthquakes are less common than those in the tectonically active West Coast, but their significance is elevated due to higher population densities, less-attenuating bedrock geology, variable site-amplification effects, and a higher proportion of structures prone to damage from shaking. Associating CEUS earthquake focal mechanisms with causative crustal faults is challenging due to a lack of mapped faults. Aftershock productivity of CEUS earthquakes is difficult to predict because it is highly variable, displaying globally typical behavior in some regions (Wu *et al.*, 2015; Wu and Chapman, 2017) and low decay rates (Stein and Liu, 2009; Calais *et al.*, 2016; Toda and Stein, 2018) in others. Here, we study the aftershock sequence of an unusual M_w 4.24 CEUS earthquake that occurred below the Atlantic Coastal Plain east of Dover, Delaware, in late 2017. We analyze data from a temporary 14-station network and use template matching to search for aftershocks, which we locate using a custom 1D velocity model. We find aftershock locations favoring slip on a northwest–southeast-striking fault oblique to the presumed fault where the mainshock was located. We document an unusually low *a* value and large magnitude difference between the mainshock and the largest aftershock, as well as an average aftershock decay *p* value. Factors proposed to explain variations in aftershock productivity include fault alignment relative to the prevailing stress field (Hardebeck, 2010) and low productivity after a high stress drop (Wetzler *et al.*, 2018). We test these hypotheses in relation to the 2017 Delaware earthquake aftershocks, showing the Delaware earthquake had a stress drop of 35 MPa, normal for an intraplate region (Boyd *et al.*, 2017), and had favorable alignment for aftershock thrust faulting. We therefore propose a small fault of possible pre-Mesozoic origin, limiting the productivity observed.

Cite this article as Pearson, K. M., V. Lekic, and L. Wagner (2026). Low Aftershock Productivity and Fault Geometry of the 2017 Delaware Earthquake, *Seismol. Res. Lett.* **97**, 957–976, doi: 10.1785/0220250322.

Supplemental Material

Background

Introduction

On 30 November 2017, a moment magnitude 4.24 (Kim *et al.*, 2018) earthquake occurred east of Delaware's capital city of Dover. The region has minimal historic seismicity (Stover and Coffman, 1993; Kim *et al.*, 2018) and is in an intraplate location outside of known east coast seismic areas, 80 km from the Lancaster (Pennsylvania) seismic zone, 130 km from the Ramapo fault (New Jersey to New York), and 300 km from the Central Virginia seismic zone (CVSZ) (Fig. 1). This event's epicenter within the Salisbury Embayment of the Atlantic Coastal Plain (ACP) makes it unusual even among east coast earthquakes. As with most of the Central and Eastern United States (CEUS), Delaware and the Salisbury Embayment have no faults recorded in the U.S. Geological Survey (USGS) Quaternary fault database (Data and Resources), and any earthquake that occurs in this region would most likely be due to reactivation of ancient faults.

Other notable earthquakes in Delaware are limited to a modified Mercalli index VII event in 1871 at the Delaware–New Jersey border southeast of Wilmington (Stover and Coffman, 1993) and an M_L 3.8 earthquake in a very similar location southeast of Wilmington in 1973 (Sbar *et al.*, 1975). These are distinct from the 2017 event in that they occurred at the transition from the ACP to the Piedmont (Fig. 1), rather than within the ACP. An earthquake with an estimated magnitude of 3.3 occurred somewhere near Dover in 1879 (Baxter,

1. University of Maryland, College Park, Maryland, U.S.A., https://orcid.org/0000-0002-3548-272X (VL); 2. Carnegie Institution for Science, Washington, D.C., U.S.A.

*Corresponding author: karen.melinda@gmail.com

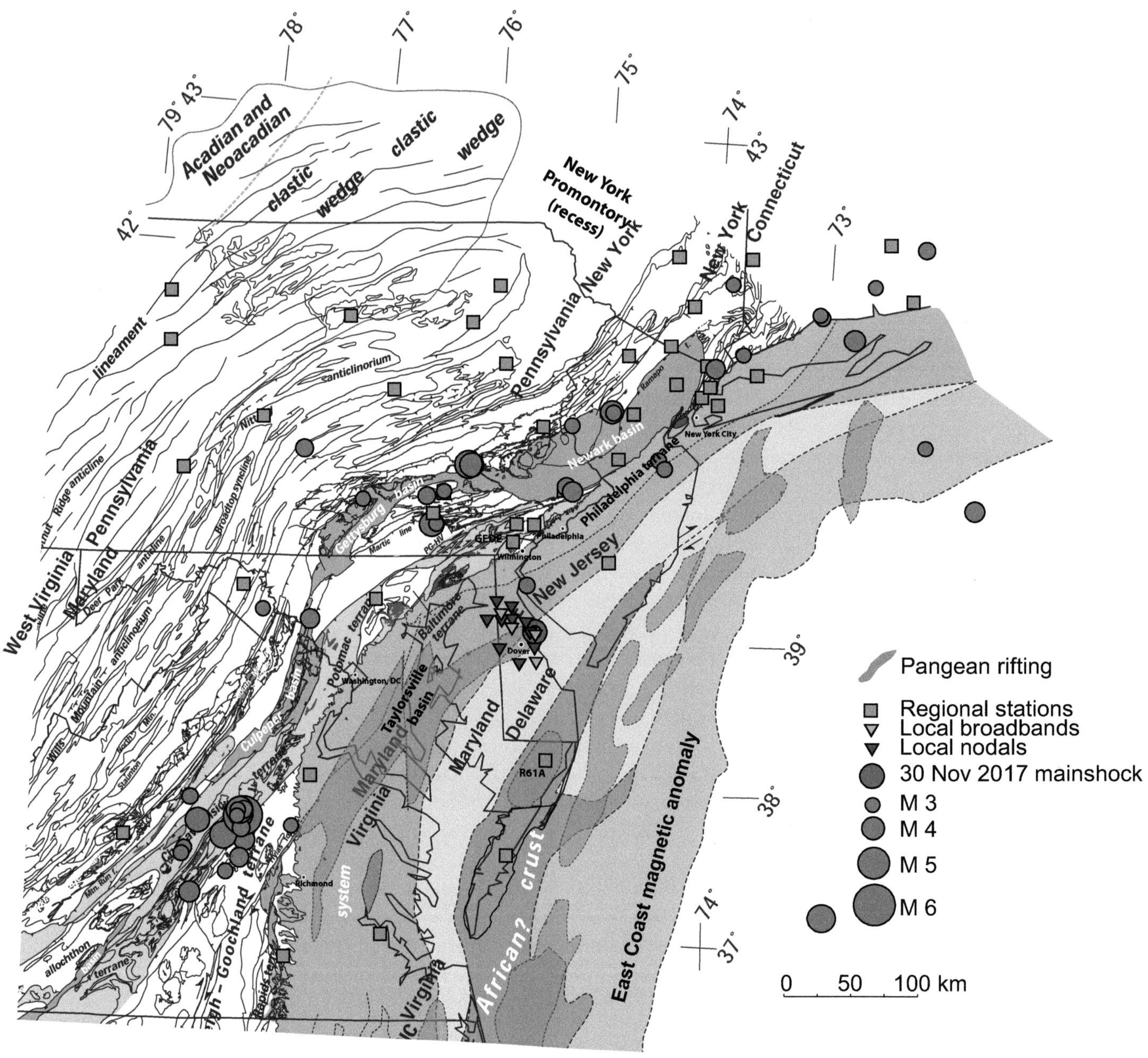

Figure 1. Geologic terrane map of the Mid-Atlantic region of the United States with historic seismicity, regional stations, and local temporary stations. Permanent regional three-component stations at the time of the 2017 Delaware earthquake are shown with green squares. Temporary nodal seismometers are shown with filled red triangles, and temporary broadband seismometers are shown with filled dark gray triangles. The blue circles indicate the locations of all M 3+ earthquakes in the Advanced National Seismic System (ANSS) catalog since 1980, scaled by magnitude (Data and Resources). The epicenter of the 30 November 2017 earthquake is a magenta circle. In Delaware (DE), the green is the Carolina Superterrane, gold is the Brunswick terrane (together these form the Salisbury Embayment), and gray shows the extent of Pangaean rifting. The Culpeper, Gettysburg, and Newark basins shown in light brown are other Triassic–Jurassic basins (Hatcher Jr. *et al.*, 2007; Withjack *et al.*, 2012). Figure modified from Hatcher Jr. *et al.* (2007). The color version of this figure is available only in the electronic edition.

2000; Kim *et al.*, 2018), but primary source information is not accessible to identify an exact source location or felt regions. Beyond Delaware, there have been no other M 4 or greater earthquakes within/under the ACP since 2000 (Advanced National Seismic System [ANSS] Comprehensive catalog, see Data and Resources).

Earthquakes in the CEUS are significant for several reasons. Because of older, colder, and less fractured bedrock geology east of the Rockies, seismic waves can travel much farther while losing less energy than comparable seismic waves in the western U.S. Historic and older, non-retrofitted construction, efficient transmission of seismic waves, and site amplification effects can make even light-to-moderate earthquakes high-risk events within the CEUS. The CEUS has significant aging infrastructure and some of the highest population densities in the country, which could lead to great economic losses and even the potential for human injury if hazards are not properly identified and communicated.

Regional geology and tectonics

East-central Delaware is situated near the northeast end of the estimated extent of the Taylorsville Rift basin, part of the Newark Supergroup of rift basins (Fig. 1; Hatcher Jr. *et al.*, 2007). At the latitude of the Delaware event, this half-graben strikes west-southwest–east-northeast and dips seaward, a result of Triassic rifting (Withjack *et al.*, 1998). The normal faults that formed during the initial rifting of Pangaea shifted to reverse motion during the transition to drifting in the Early Jurassic (Withjack *et al.*, 1998). The southern end of the Taylorsville Rift is exposed in the Piedmont region of central Virginia, and additional extent is inferred from borehole studies, water wells, and geophysical studies (Olsson *et al.*, 1988; LeTourneau, 2003). Seismic surveying in eastern Maryland to the southwest of the mainshock epicenter identified rift basin rocks dipping eastward to the east of the Chesapeake Bay (Hansen, 1988). A graben with a north-northeast strike was also identified about 50 km north of the mainshock location near Delaware City, Delaware (Spoljaric, 1973).

The maximum horizontal stresses in this area strike northeast–southwest (Zoback and Zoback, 1989; Withjack *et al.*, 1998; Heidbach *et al.*, 2018). This is roughly consistent with both the strike of rift structures such as the bounding faults of the Taylorsville basin and the general stress across most of the CEUS, which exhibits a broadly uniform stress field in both magnitude and direction (Zoback and Zoback, 1989; Heidbach *et al.*, 2018). Because the North American plate lacks a subducting edge, the dominant driver of this stress likely comes from ridge push and/or basal drag; Zoback and Zoback (1989) argue that ridge push is the more likely cause of the stress field in the CEUS.

Explanations for seismicity along the east coast of North America have been variably attributed to isostatic rebound from glacial retreat, continental denudation, sediment loading, thermal deformation, plate tectonic sources, crustal thickness variations, and more (see Gardner, 1989, and sources therein; Soto-Cordero *et al.*, 2018). Earthquake locations are often attributed to pre-existing crustal weakness or faults from pre-Quaternary ages (Gardner, 1989).

Previous work

Initial indications in Delaware of a large magnitude difference between the mainshock and the largest aftershock motivated our investigation of parameters governing the detected aftershock sequence. The M_w 4.24 mainshock (Kim *et al.*, 2018) on 30 November 2017 had only one aftershock identified by the USGS (Data and Resources), occurring on 13 December 2017 at 00:45:27 UTC with an estimated local magnitude 1.24 (U.S. Geological Survey [USGS], n.d.a). Preliminary analysis using the regional network and reported in Kim *et al.* (2018) identified one foreshock and eight aftershocks, six of which occurred during this temporary deployment period. The local magnitudes determined by that work for these events ranged from M_L 0.9 to 1.9.

Aftershock sequences are typically described by several statistical "laws," each with one or more characteristic parameters. These parameters are used to quantify the overall productivity, rate of decay, and relative frequency of larger versus smaller magnitude aftershocks. Variations in these parameters can relate to the geologic region being studied, such as the tectonic environment and/or the driving forces of the observed seismicity (i.e., induced earthquakes, volcanic, or geothermal-related).

Ebel (2009) studied a collection of 19 stable continental region (SCR) mainshocks and found the mean magnitude difference between the mainshock and largest aftershock was 1.4 ± 0.7 magnitude units, with a median of 1.3 magnitude units. Those findings were consistent with the difference of 1.2 magnitude units given by Båth's law (Richter, 1958; Båth, 1965).

Factors proposed to explain variations in aftershock productivity include fault alignment relative to the prevailing stress field (Hardebeck, 2010) and low productivity after a high stress drop (Wetzler *et al.*, 2018; Dascher-Cousineau *et al.*, 2020). Productivity for intraplate regions in general has been reported as both lower than the global average (Page *et al.*, 2016) and higher than the global average (Dascher-Cousineau *et al.*, 2020). Dascher-Cousineau *et al.* (2020) observe that productivity is most likely influenced by a combination of stress drop, lithospheric age, and dip (focal mechanism).

Overview of this work

A group of scientists from the University of Maryland, Carnegie Institution for Science, USGS, and others organized a temporary deployment of three-component seismometers installed the day following the mainshock to detect any possible aftershock activity. Here, we report a case study of findings based primarily on data from this temporary deployment, focusing on identifying the fault(s) on which the aftershocks occurred and quantifying the key parameters that characterize the aftershock sequence. We put this sequence into the context of previous observations of aftershock productivity for other earthquakes in SCRs and assess which of the factors above are most likely to apply to this Delaware earthquake.

Data

The nearest permanent seismic station (GEDE/LDSN) is 70 km from the mainshock epicenter and only five stations are within 100 km (Fig. 1). To enable detection of smaller magnitude aftershocks that would not register at those distances, personnel from the Carnegie Institution for Science Department of Terrestrial Magnetism (now Earth and Planets Laboratory), the University of Maryland Department of Geology, and the USGS mobilized the day after the earthquake

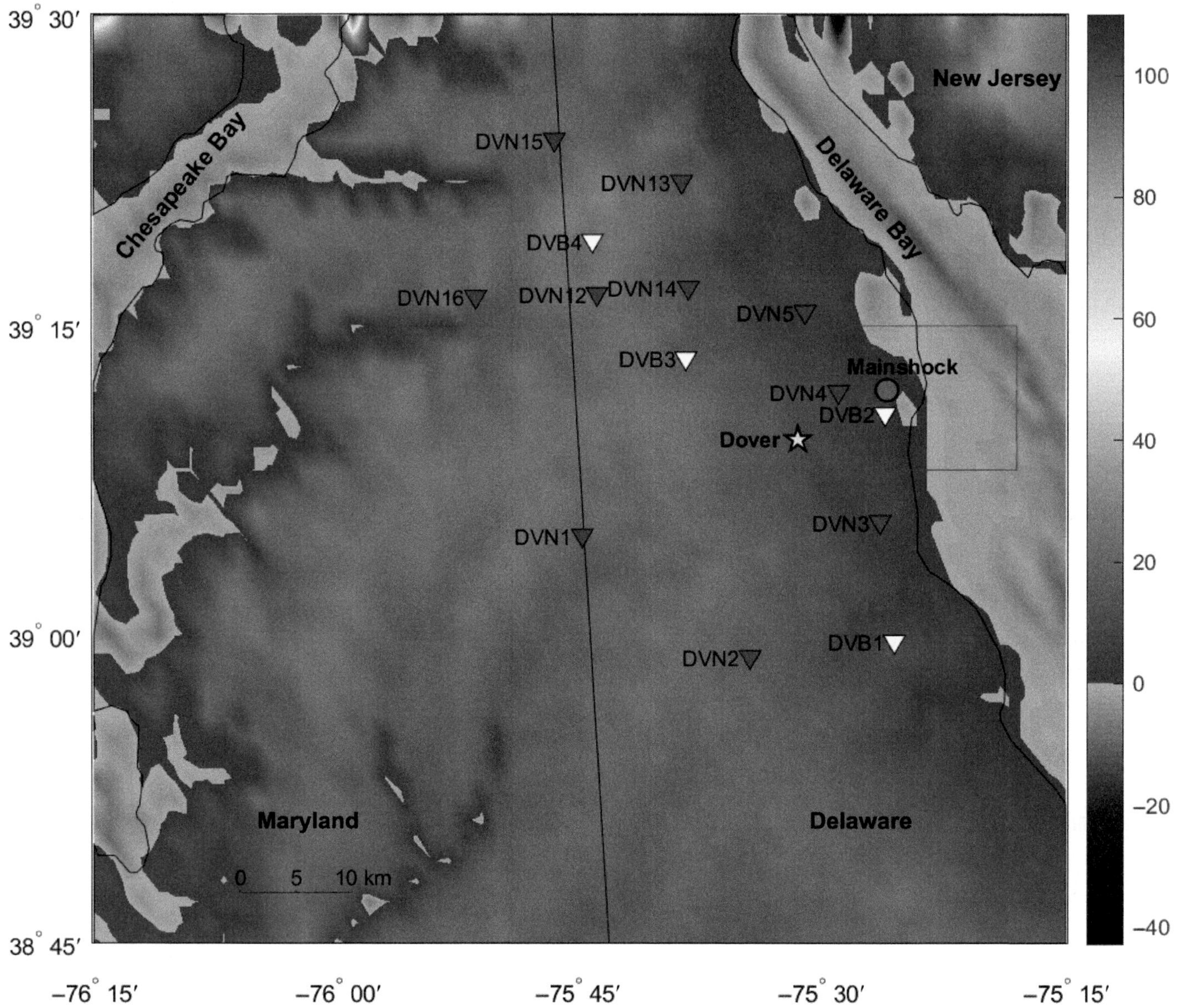

Figure 2. Local portable seismographic station deployment from 1 December 2017 to 11 January 2018. Stations with broadband sensors are plotted by white triangles and designated "DVB"; short-period sensors (nodals) are plotted by red triangles and designated "DVN". The epicenter of the 30 November 2017 earthquake is a magenta circle. The red box indicates the region where aftershocks were detected, and the borders of the map are shown in Figure 6. Note the coast includes significant tidal wetlands, and so the sea level topography does not exactly align with marked state boundaries (black). The color version of this figure is available only in the electronic edition.

(1 December 2017) to install a temporary local network in the epicentral area using a mix of instruments. A total of 14 instruments were installed in central Delaware and eastern Maryland, covering an area approximately 40 km in diameter. Two broadband and two short-period stations were also deployed by Lamont–Doherty Earth Observatory on the north side of Delaware Bay at distances 20 km and greater from the mainshock (Kim *et al.*, 2018). Because of the distance, these stations did not record aftershocks well and were not included in this study. Stations were deployed over a relatively broad area for a moderate-magnitude mainshock. This allowed for location uncertainty in the mainshock location and for no prior expectations on where aftershocks might be located, without defined faults known. Locations were also governed by the ability to gain landowner permission on short notice. The deployment remained in place until 11 January 2018. The temporary local stations that were deployed on 1 December 2017 are shown in detail in Figure 2.

Instrumentation included ten FairfieldNodal ZLand nodes containing three-component 5 Hz geophones provided by the University of Maryland and four Nanometrics Trillium 120 Compact Posthole broadband seismometers provided by the Carnegie Institution for Science. Further details on the deployment are available in Kim *et al.* (2018). Three of the four solar-

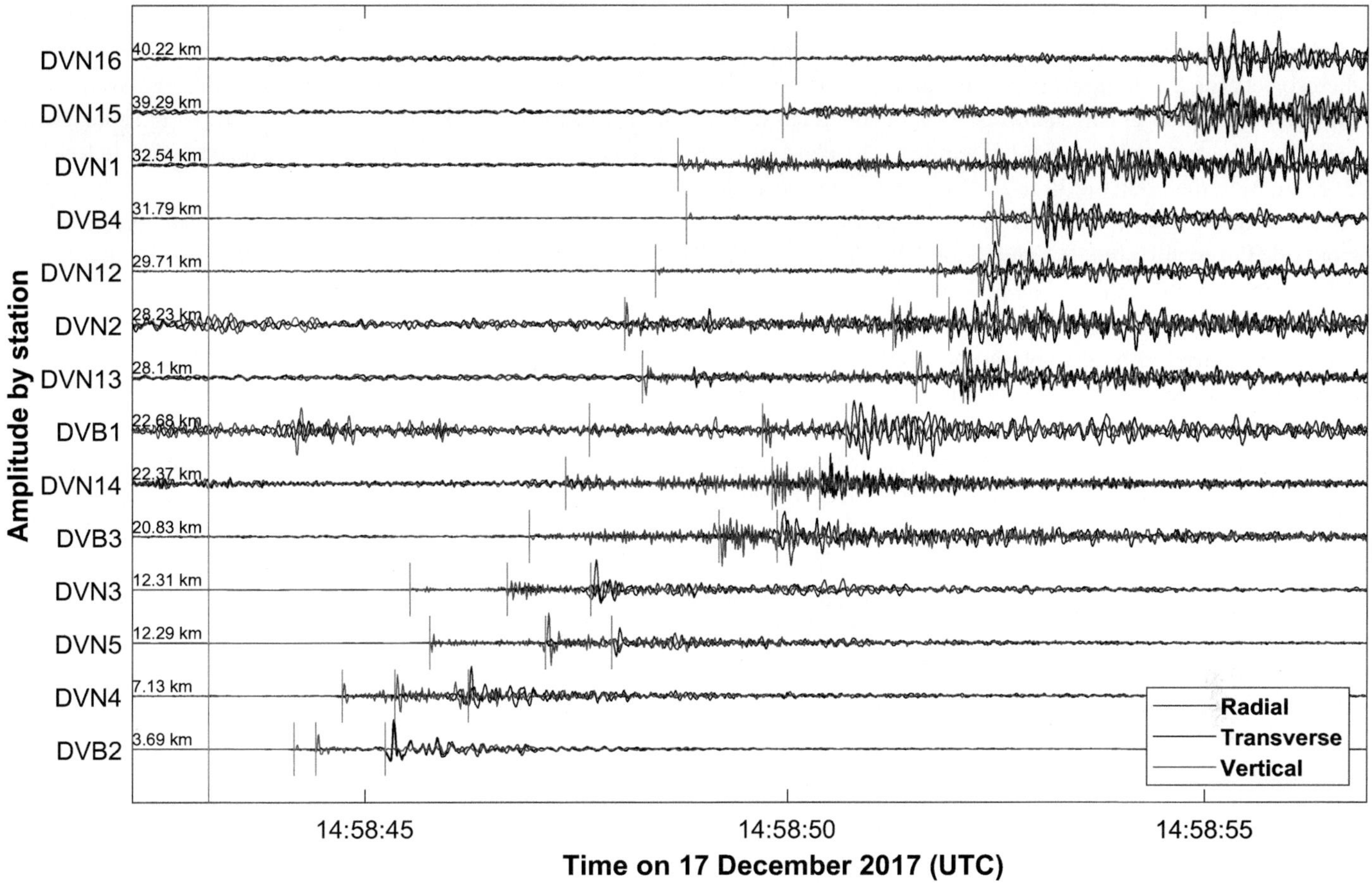

Figure 3. Local station waveforms by distance from the event. Event-to-station distance is given for each station at the start of the trace. The pattern of *Pg*, *SPg*, and *S* arrivals (short gray lines) is exhibited on each station, with the best visibility on the nearer stations. The time between *SPg* and *S* is approximately constant for all distances, and the time between *Pg* and *SPg* lengthens with distance, supporting the interpretation of an *S* wave converting to a *Pg* wave at the sediment layer. The continuous gray line indicates the earthquake origin time. Some marked arrivals are estimated but not used for location determination. Amplitudes for each station are normalized to the maximum recorded for the respective station. The color version of this figure is available only in the electronic edition.

powered compact broadbands, recording 200 samples per second, remained operational until the end of the deployment on 11 January 2018. The ten nodal seismometers, recording 100 samples per second, were battery-operated and remained operational for 37–40 days; locations and end-of-service dates are listed in Table S1, available in the supplemental material to this article.

Methods

Waveform cross-correlation for detection

We used a matched filter waveform correlation technique to identify aftershocks in the data from the temporary deployment (Gibbons and Ringdal, 2006; Schaff and Waldhauser, 2010; Yoon *et al.*, 2015). The largest of the aftershocks detected by Kim *et al.* (2018) was selected as the initial template event. A complete record of the seismograms for the primary template event on 17 December 14:58 at each of the 14 stations is shown in Figure 3.

Using the raw data uncorrected for instrument response, we analyzed the power spectra on each instrument type for a period of 8 s before, during, and after our selected primary template event to ascertain the optimal filtering window and found that the period during the aftershock had elevated power between 4 and 40 Hz relative to nonevent periods for each sensor and component. We therefore used a band-pass filter at 4–40 Hz for raw data from each instrument type. We found the raw waveforms to be more effective at template matching for the high-frequency energy generated by the very small aftershocks we were detecting at close range.

For the initial template, we cut and tapered a waveform segment 12 s long around the *Pg* and *S* arrivals on each data component for each of the 14 deployed stations. The time series for each component (north, east, and vertical) was treated individually in this stage of analysis. Templates were correlated for each of the north, east, and vertical components against all available data for that station, and the algorithm required two components from a given station to be well correlated to their respective templates for that signal to be identified as an aftershock.

Thresholds for each component of data were determined by comparing the distribution of correlation coefficients obtained when correlating the time-reversed template with a day of data, with the distribution of correlation coefficients obtained when correlating the forward, or original, template (Slinkard *et al.*, 2014). In this method, the time-reversed template serves to provide a distribution of correlation coefficients that could be obtained from any random segment of data correlating with that station–component pair. The point at which divergence is observed between the tails of the forward and reverse distributions is considered to be the correlation coefficient threshold for a satisfactory false alarm rate, by removing the false correlations due to noise (which can happen when correlating a waveform in either direction) but retaining the true correlated waveforms of events. Correlation matches are therefore recorded whenever the correlation coefficient exceeds this threshold of divergence from the noise detections. The reader is directed to Slinkard *et al.* (2014) for a more detailed discussion of this approach. We selected a unique correlation threshold for each component and station based on the unique observed noise characteristics. Correlation coefficient thresholds used ranged from 0.4 to 0.6, depending on the station and component, with vertical components accepting lower correlations and the north components requiring the highest correlation to avoid false detections.

In the case of multiple correlation matches recorded for a component within 3 s of each other, the mean time of detection is used as a preliminary event time. To further reduce false alarms, we then compare components for each station with determine when at least two out of three components had detections triggered within 6 s of each other and count these as detections, basing this on the largest measured *S–Pg* arrival times for the template event.

Using the first template, we identified 76 potential aftershocks, which were few enough to allow manual inspection of the waveforms for each. Detection capability was significantly better at station DVB2 than any other in the local network, likely due to a high signal-to-noise ratio (SNR) related to a combination of instrument type, low ambient noise at install location, and proximity to aftershocks. DVB2 was located just south of Bombay Hook National Wildlife Refuge, 3.2 km south-southwest of the mainshock epicenter, and about 1.5 km east of Delaware Route 9—a moderately trafficked road that other proximal stations to the epicenter were located much nearer to (Fig. 2). Other stations' positive detections dropped significantly with distance from the mainshock epicenter and very few unique (nonduplicate) detections were added beyond those from DVB2. Both the closest nodal seismometers and the more distant broadbands exhibited high false positive rates, leading us to focus on station DVB2 for further detections with additional templates.

Because the local stations operated in the near field of the aftershocks, small changes in aftershock epicenters result in a comparatively large difference in azimuth, affecting the detected waveform shape (Fig. 4). We selected an additional ten aftershocks to use as templates for additional event detection. For these templates, we elected to only run the correlation detector on data from DVB2 with a reduced template length of 6 s, due to the shorter travel times for this near-field station. Because of diminishing gains in new event detections with each subsequent template, no further templates were used. With these additional ten templates, there were a total of 108 aftershocks detected during the deployment. Over half of the 108 aftershocks were detected only at station DVB2.

Velocity model development

The peninsula between the Chesapeake Bay and Delaware Bay, colloquially known as "Delmarva" due to its makeup of most of the state of Delaware and portions of the states of Maryland and Virginia, is part of the ACP. It extends approximately 270 km north to south and 100 km east to west at its widest point with an elevation of 31 m above sea level.

Previous geophysical work on the ACP is limited and there are no near-surface crustal velocity models specifically developed for central Delaware that would allow for accurate location estimates for the locatable events. Preliminary aftershock identification for the Delaware earthquake done by Kim *et al.* (2018) used the crustal earth model presented by Herrmann (1979), intended for the central United States and including a 1-km surface layer with moderately low velocity. Other models identified for the CEUS and ACP include work done by Dreiling *et al.* (2017), which established *P*- and *S*-wave crustal velocities for the ACP but recognized the need to separately account for surface site conditions.

Studies of the ACP depth to basement vary in methods and results, with no single study providing conclusive answers at the epicentral location. Work by Pratt (2018) developed a model for V_S in the ACP strata from the fundamental frequencies of horizontal spectral ratios, but is derived from arrays located several hundred kilometers south of Delaware and has a depth to basement of 0.6 km. Studies in the Delmarva region using varied sources including seismic profiles and well data found depth to the crystalline, pre-Cretaceous basement is about 2.35 km at Ocean City, Maryland, to the south on the Atlantic Coast (Olsson *et al.*, 1988; Miller *et al.*, 2017). At Island Beach, New Jersey, to the north and on the Atlantic Coast, depth to basement is about 1.1 km (Olsson *et al.*, 1988) and near Lewes, Delaware, about 50 km south of the mainshock epicenter, depth to basement is about 2 km (Olsson *et al.*, 1988). In addition, receiver function modeling by Cunningham and Lekic (2020) at the TA station nearest to the epicenter of the mainshock (R61A) south-southeast of Dover, Delaware, found the thickness of the surface sediment layer is 2 km. More recently, sediment thickness modeling for the ACP based on well logs from Pope *et al.* (2016) show a 1–1.5 km thick sedimentary layer near the mainshock (Boyd

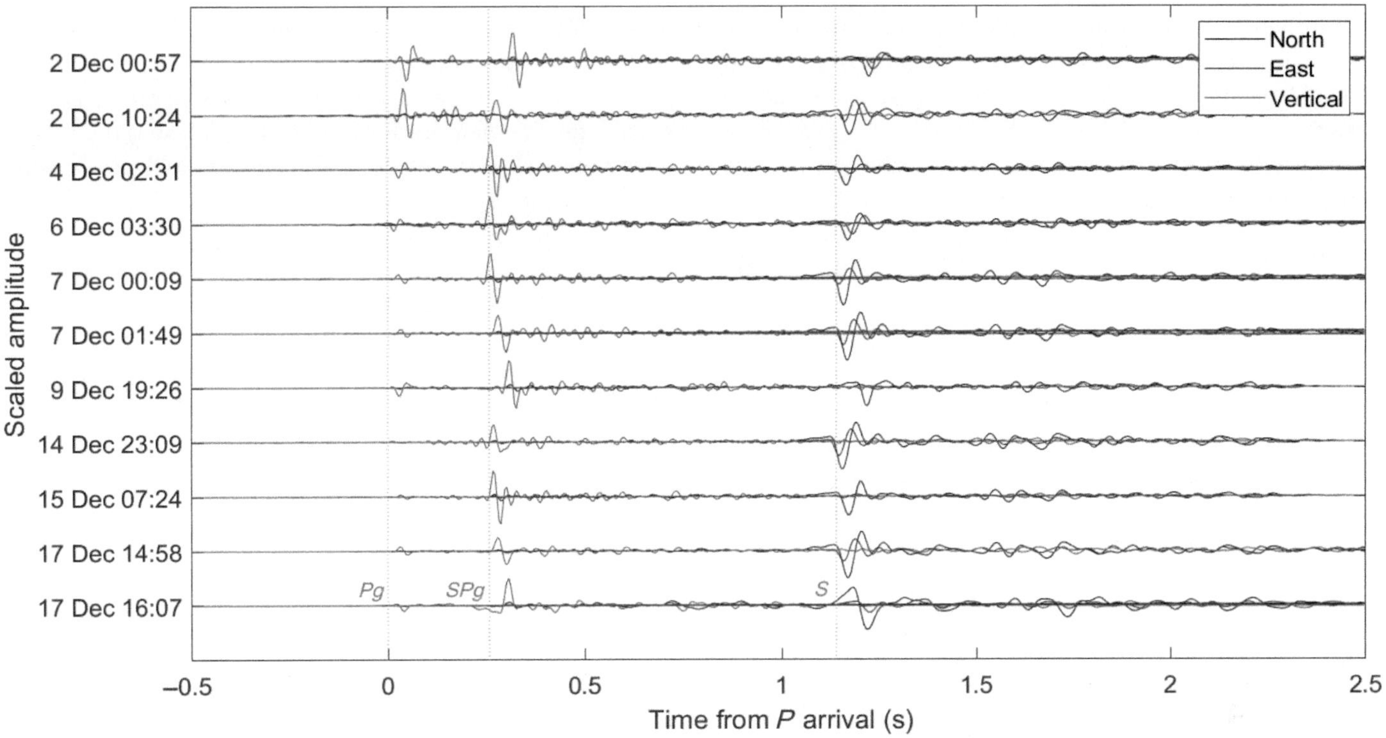

Figure 4. Waveforms for each of the template events at station DVB2 showing north in black, east in blue, and vertical in red. Each event is aligned to have the *Pg* arrival at time 0. The *SPg* converted wave arrival is clear on the vertical component for each of the templates at approximately 0.25 s, marked with a vertical gray line. The *S* wave arrives approximately 1.14 s after the *Pg*, also marked with a vertical gray line. Arrivals are slightly different for each template due to different source locations. Amplitudes for each aftershock are normalized to the maximum recorded for the respective event. The color version of this figure is available only in the electronic edition.

et al., 2024). We chose 2 km as an approximate depth to basement for our location and then determined the appropriate crustal velocities for the upper sediment layers.

We developed a velocity model for use in the location search starting from the model by Dreiling *et al.* (2017). We reduced the top layer of Dreiling *et al.* (2017) ACP model by 2 km corresponding to our surface sediment layer. In the surface sediment layer, the velocities increase rapidly with depth, necessitating thinner layers near the surface and thicker layers deeper down. Therefore, we generate logarithmically spaced points in the sediment pile to define four layers of increasing thickness. Within each layer, the velocities are obtained by computing the harmonic mean of the velocity values within that layer from the continuous velocity profile at the nearest TA station (R61A) from Cunningham and Lekic (2020). Densities for each layer are obtained in the same manner and used solely for model verification. The model was verified by matching waveforms from the M_w 4.24 mainshock observed at the regional station R61A in southern Delaware with synthetic waveforms generated using frequency–wavenumber integration (Saikia, 1994) with the 1D velocity model given in Table 1 (Fig. S1).

TABLE 1

Velocity and Density Model Used for Determining Aftershock Locations and Generating Synthetics Used for Model Verification

Thickness (km)	V_P (km/s)	V_S (km/s)	Density (g/cm^3)
0.030	1.648	0.234	1.7
0.092	2.103	0.549	1.9
0.372	2.611	1.059	2.1
1.506	3.621	1.932	2.3
18	6.0	3.46	2.3
16	6.7	3.87	3.0
∞	8.1	4.68	3.4

The top two kilometers are derived from Cunningham and Lekic (2020) receiver function modeling of crustal sediment at R61A, and the basement layers are from Dreiling *et al.* (2017).

Location search

We manually picked visible *Pg* and *S* arrivals when visible for each of the 108 aftershocks at all temporary local stations. A subset of 39 events was identified as locatable, defined as having at least three stations with waveforms that allowed a seismic analyst to pick body-wave arrival times, with a minimum of three *Pg*-arrival times and one *S*-arrival time. The stations most distant from the mainshock location only detected the largest few aftershocks; some stations recorded low SNR and we could not pick a *Pg* arrival—only an *S* arrival could be picked.

To determine event locations, an iterative grid-search method was used (supplement). The grid center was located southeast of the mainshock by about 3 km just offshore in the Delaware Bay. We used grid spacing of 100 m laterally and 100 m in depth and an overall search region extending 15 km in each direction. Optimal locations for each depth increment were determined based on the minimum residual between the observed travel times and the predicted travel times from each grid location to a station using our crustal velocity model. The residuals for all depth increments were compared and the depth with the least residual was determined to be the optimal depth, with the grid location for that depth as the optimal epicenter.

Source parameters

For all events large enough to locate, we determined a local magnitude using the relation for M_L calibrated for eastern North America (ENA) intraplate events (Kim, 1998):

$$M_L = \log_{10} A + 1.55 \log_{10} X - 0.22 + C, \qquad (1)$$

in which C is a station correction term and X is the epicentral station-to-event distance in kilometers. The amplitude A is determined by removing instrument response and convolving the signal with the Wood–Anderson seismograph response, then measuring the maximum horizontal-component body-wave amplitude (in mm). The station correction, given in the Table S1, is calculated from the mean of the station residuals following the method given in Kim (1998).

Using these magnitudes, we obtained the Gutenberg–Richter relation between magnitude and number of events detected while the local network was deployed, $\log_{10} N(\geq m) = A - bm$. We performed an iterative search for the linear portion of the fit to the log-cumulative frequency-magnitude counts adjusting both the lower (M_c) and upper limits of the magnitude range in 0.1 magnitude increments. We selected the magnitude range which minimized the error of the least-squares fit, so that fitting is only done within the magnitude range in which the observed frequency-magnitude relationship is close to linear.

To test the hypothesis of high stress drop causing the low productivity observed for the Delaware aftershock sequence, we determined the stress parameter estimate for the M_w 4.24 mainshock using the Brune model (Brune, 1970) for a circular rupture. The choice of constant k in this model can lead to stress parameter estimates differing by more than a factor of five (Brune, 1970; Madariaga, 1976; Kaneko and Shearer, 2014). We use the value for k derived by Kaneko and Shearer (2014), which models a dynamic rupture with no singularities and results in stress parameter estimates between those of Brune and Madariaga. We fit the model to the *P*-wave and *S*-wave spectra for the mainshock and our primary template aftershock at regional stations, computed the corner frequency for the mainshock model fit by modeling the best-fit power spectral ratio between the mainshock and largest aftershock, and used the resulting value to calculate the stress parameter and rupture radius (supplement).

Aftershock productivity analyses

We used a Bayesian Markov Chain Monte Carlo (MCMC) simulation (supplement) to further constrain the parameters a and b noted above, but now also including c and p as described in the Omori decay rate equation:

$$\lambda(t, M_{\min}) = 10^{a+b(M_{\text{main}}-M_{\min})}(t + c)^{-p}, \qquad (2)$$

(Omori, 1895; Utsu, 1961; Reasenberg and Jones, 1989). We use the ensemble model of solutions to quantify the posterior likelihood for each parameter, and their tradeoffs with one another.

Results

Near-surface phase conversion

We observed a strong secondary arrival on the vertical component before horizontal arrivals, which we interpreted to be an *S*-to-*Pg* (*SPg*) wave arriving due to conversion at the ray-path transition for the sediment layer occurring in the ACP (Fig. 3). A wave conversion at the sediment layer has previously been reported in the Mississippi Embayment by Chen *et al.* (1996). Daniels *et al.* (2019) observed wave conversion in South Carolina, where the upgoing S-wave converted to a horizontally propagating *P* wave. However, we do not interpret the ray path as horizontally propagating in our case because our *SPg* arrival is strongest on the vertical component rather than the radial throughout the array (Figs. 3 and 4). Furthermore, the time between arrival of the *SPg* and *S* phases is more consistent than that of *Pg* and *SPg*, suggesting the upgoing ray travels as an *S* wave until it converts and traverses the shallow sediment layer vertically as a *P* wave (Fig. 3). The thinning of the sediment layer of the ACP moving westward from the coast appears in the closer spacing between the observations for the *SPg* and *S* phase arrivals (Fig. 5; see Fig. 2 for station location reference), further supporting our hypothesis that this arrival is an *SPg* phase.

Aftershock locations

A total of 39 out of the 108 detected aftershocks had sufficient phase picks to allow event location. Aftershocks are located primarily just offshore and below the Delaware Bay, with depths ranging from 0.5 to 6.5 km (Table 2, Fig. 6). There did not appear to be any temporal progression in aftershock locations. The northeast group of aftershocks are almost exclusively 2.1 km in depth, just below the sediment layer. The

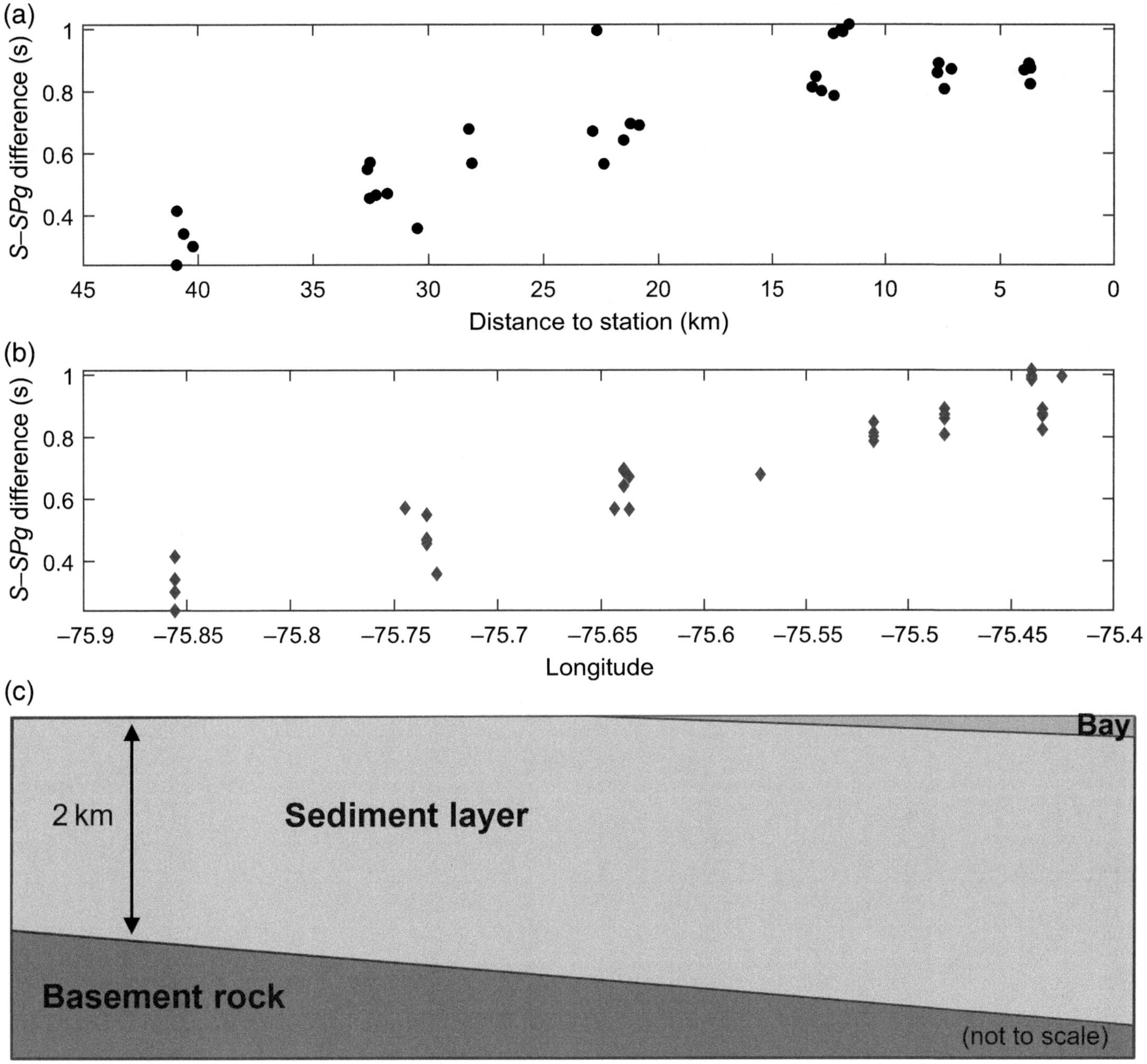

Figure 5. Difference in phase arrival time *S–SPg* relative to event-to-station distance (a) and to longitude (b). There is a stronger correlation between *S–SPg* time and longitude (b) than between *S–SPg* and distance (a), corresponding to the thickening of the sediment layer moving toward the coast (eastward). Note in (a) the reversed axis because events are located near the coast or beneath the Delaware Bay, and thus distance increases both westward and north/southward. Notional diagram of the thickening sediment wedge is depicted in (c). The color version of this figure is available only in the electronic edition.

majority of aftershocks fall on a plane striking northwest–southeast and dipping to the southwest (Fig. 5). The southwestern shallow aftershocks with depths from 0.5 to 2 km appear to originate in the sediment. We find aftershock epicenters somewhat farther to the east as well as a slightly different strike than Kim *et al.* (2018). Similarly, the mainshock may have been located a few kilometers farther east, had it been located with this network. These discrepancies may be due to the addition of more local seismic data in our analyses.

The one-sigma error contours for all located aftershocks are shown in Figure S2 in the supplemental material, and the maximum $1-\sigma$ radial errors are listed in Table 2. Depth uncertainty is constrained to the aftershock location in either the sediment layer or basement rock (Table 2, Fig. S3) and thus is variable in the shallower and deeper sections. Our evaluations of uncertainty are limited to the depths included in the grid search (0.5–8.0 km). Figure 6 shows the one-sigma

TABLE 2
Dates, Times (UTC), Epicentral Locations, Depths, Local Magnitudes, Horizontal Location 1-σ Error, and 90% Confidence Bounds for Depth of 39 Located Aftershock Events

Date (yyyy/mm/dd) Time (hh:mm:ss.s)	Latitude	Longitude	Depth (km)	M_L	σ Error (km)	90% Depth Confidence (km)
2017/12/01 21:41:33.6	39.218	−75.362	2.1	−0.60	0.35	2.1–4.3
2017/12/01 23:27:32.1	39.201	−75.368	2.1	−0.07	0.55	2.1–4.9
2017/12/02 00:57:40.1	39.165	−75.476	2.0	−0.24	0.44	0.5–2.0
2017/12/02 10:24:44.6	39.197	−75.352	2.1	0.07	0.81	2.1–5.8
2017/12/02 14:36:14.6	39.199	−75.367	2.1	0.39	1.15	2.1–6.9
2017/12/02 18:38:43.1	39.211	−75.365	2.1	0.95	0.68	2.1–5.3
2017/12/04 02:31:26.2	39.236	−75.368	2.1	0.41	0.92	2.1–7.3
2017/12/04 12:13:39.5	39.193	−75.370	2.1	0.81	1.06	2.1–6.9
2017/12/05 01:23:59.3	39.206	−75.364	2.1	0.20	1.16	2.1–6.3
2017/12/06 03:30:09.0	39.166	−75.389	0.5	−0.73	0.07	0.5–1.2
2017/12/07 00:09:27.2	39.159	−75.373	5.7	−0.97	0.07	5.65–5.75
2017/12/07 00:44:01.6	39.203	−75.372	2.1	0.20	0.90	2.1–6.0
2017/12/07 01:49:06.0	39.151	−75.391	6.5	0.69	0.19	6.4–6.6
2017/12/07 18:53:52.7	39.187	−75.358	2.1	0.33	0.94	2.1–6.3
2017/12/07 19:39:39.2	39.211	−75.364	2.1	1.01	1.08	2.1–6.9
2017/12/08 12:17:48.4	39.202	−75.352	2.1	0.82	1.13	2.1–7.1
2017/12/08 14:19:49.3	39.172	−75.486	0.5	0.42	0.45	0.5–2.0
2017/12/09 19:26:58.6	39.204	−75.357	2.1	1.01	0.98	2.1–6.7
2017/12/09 20:26:18.2	39.161	−75.392	1.4	−0.19	0.11	0.5–2.0
2017/12/11 22:02:39.9	39.193	−75.397	6.4	1.29	1.31	3.7–8.0
2017/12/12 04:24:57.5	39.145	−75.454	0.6	−0.16	0.07	0.5–1.3
2017/12/13 00:45:24.4	39.193	−75.393	6.4	1.62	1.19	3.5–8.0
2017/12/14 17:50:51.3	39.168	−75.392	2.0	−0.02	0.07	1.7–2.0
2017/12/14 23:09:51.0	39.171	−75.426	5.2	−0.81	1.20	2.1–8.0
2017/12/15 07:24:09.7	39.197	−75.358	2.1	0.34	0.78	2.1–5.5
2017/12/17 14:58:43.3	39.198	−75.400	5.9	1.75	1.06	2.1–8.0
2017/12/17 16:07:04.7	39.190	−75.394	6.0	1.31	1.40	3.0–8.0
2017/12/19 10:34:59.3	39.207	−75.360	2.1	0.14	0.79	2.1–5.9
2017/12/23 00:57:46.0	39.200	−75.345	2.1	−0.01	1.03	2.1–6.9
2017/12/23 13:29:50.9	39.186	−75.397	4.8	0.56	1.41	2.9–6.6
2017/12/23 16:21:51.6	39.207	−75.387	2.5	0.25	0.90	2.1–6.2
2017/12/27 14:11:44.7	39.211	−75.370	2.1	0.59	0.86	2.1–6.0
2017/12/27 14:32:23.1	39.169	−75.484	0.5	0.29	0.15	0.5–2.0
2017/12/28 05:39:22.7	39.186	−75.367	2.6	−0.40	0.63	2.1–5.2
2017/12/28 09:42:24.9	39.209	−75.367	2.1	−0.12	0.87	2.1–6.0

(Continued next page.)

TABLE 2 (continued)
Dates, Times (UTC), Epicentral Locations, Depths, Local Magnitudes, Horizontal Location 1–σ Error, and 90% Confidence Bounds for Depth of 39 Located Aftershock Events

Date (yyyy/mm/dd) Time (hh:mm:ss.s)	Latitude	Longitude	Depth (km)	M_L	σ Error (km)	90% Depth Confidence (km)
2017/12/30 12:48:56.7	39.193	−75.397	0.5	−0.66	0.07	0.5–2.0
2017/12/31 00:11:18.9	39.203	−75.358	2.1	0.72	1.13	2.1–7.2
2018/01/01 22:37:39.2	39.204	−75.377	4.6	0.51	1.07	2.1–7.5
2018/01/02 05:36:19.3	39.207	−75.367	2.1	0.43	0.72	2.1–5.7

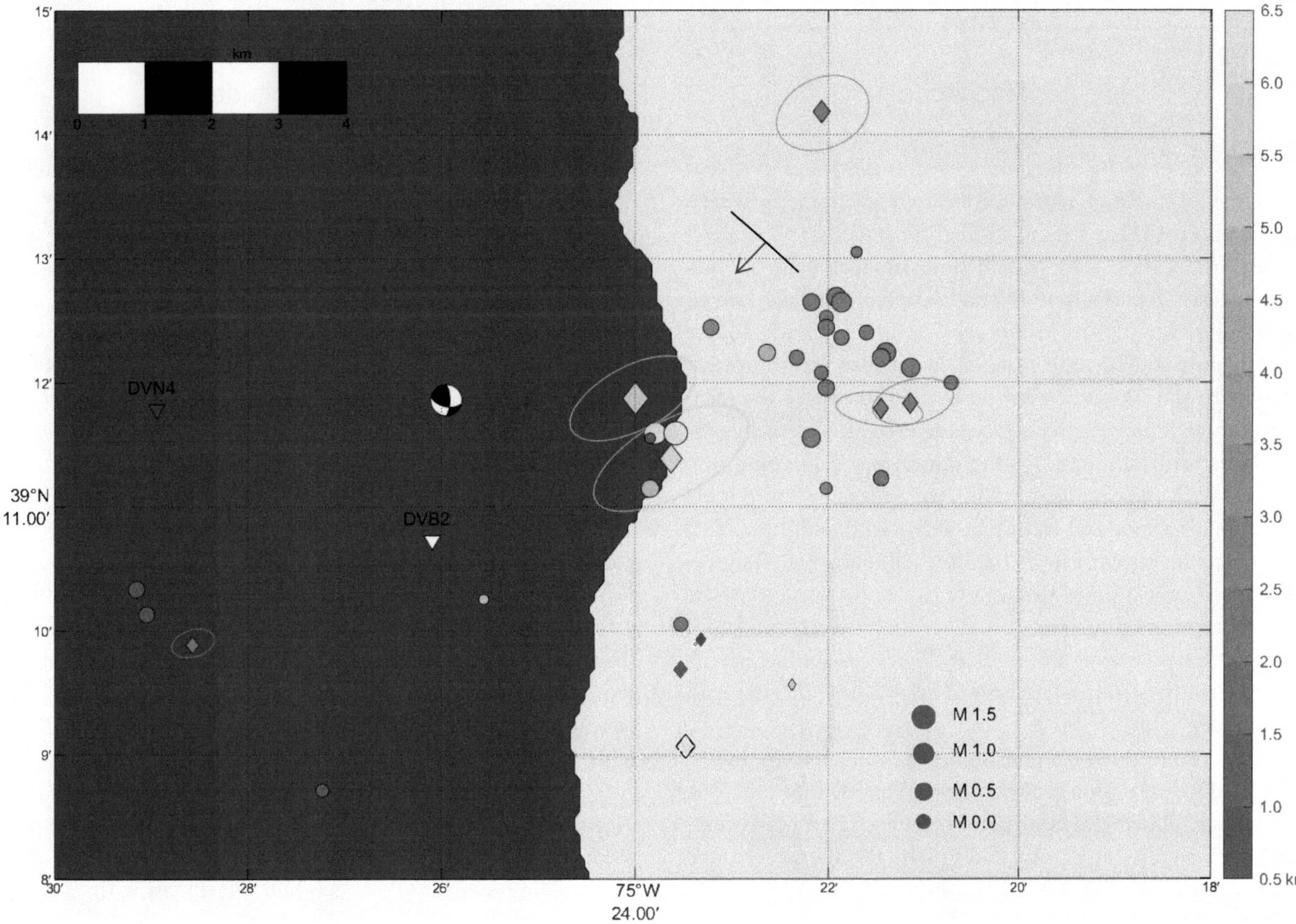

Figure 6. Locations of aftershocks. Shading corresponds to the depth of the event. The size of the marker is proportional to the event's local magnitude; see key for scale. Diamond-shaped markers indicate the events used as templates for aftershock detection and are shown with their one-sigma horizontal error contour. The mainshock location and moment tensor are from Kim *et al.* (2018) and had an approximate depth of 3 km and horizontal location error of ±2.5 km. Only the two nearest stations of the local deployment are visible in this projection; see Figure 2 for the context of location in Delaware. The color version of this figure is available only in the electronic edition.

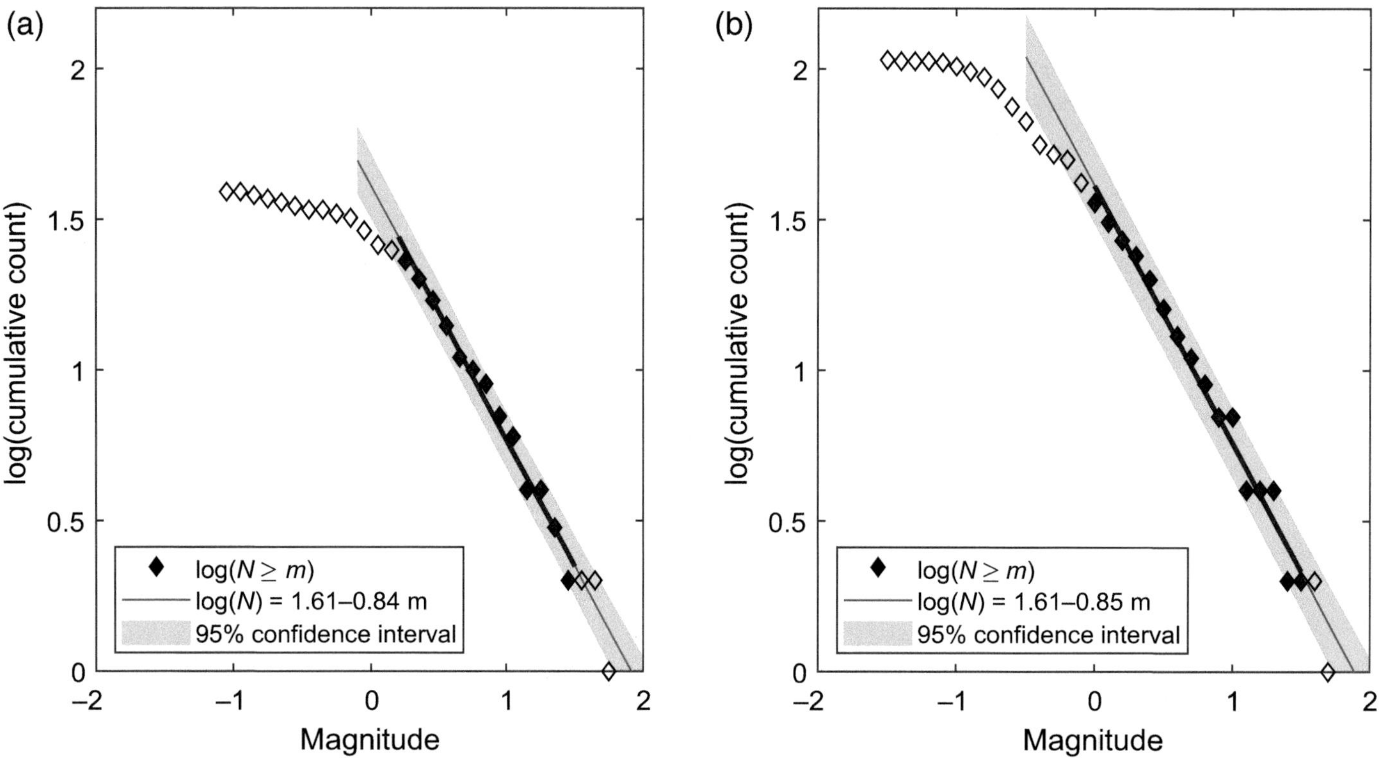

Figure 7. Gutenberg–Richter relation showing relative frequency versus magnitude of located aftershocks during the deployment period of the local network (a). Local magnitudes are calculated using Kim (1998) formula for eastern North America (ENA). Filled counts are those used for determining the best-fit linear regression. The light blue shading shows the 95% confidence of the fit regression. (b) As in (a), but for all 108 detected aftershocks using magnitudes determined from extrapolated distance for those without location. The color version of this figure is available only in the electronic edition.

error contours for the aftershocks used as templates as a representative example of errors for location accuracy. However, we also observed that for the small-magnitude template aftershocks, the location error was at times smaller than the pictured marker. Although additional data are generally known to reduce error, the overdetermined solution for 3D source location plus source time resulted in smaller errors present for the aftershocks, with fewer picks used to resolve the location. Although the χ-square function used to determine the one-sigma error accounts for the number of data going into it (in this case, the number of valid *P* or *S* picks), we find there is additional unmodeled error that grows with additional data used from the more distant stations. The larger aftershocks using more arrival times from more distant stations are more sensitive to errors due to using a 1D crustal velocity model for the 3D sediment wedge of the ACP (Fig. 5), as well as having greater sensitivity to human error in arrival-time picking with lower SNRs.

Locations are generally consistent when the velocity model is adjusted to use a 1-km sediment layer (Fig. S4, Table S2). The distribution follows the same pattern, indicating a northwest–southeast-, southwest-dipping fault plane for aftershocks, but epicenters are up to 1 km farther east and south under the Delaware Bay. The shallower events have depths near the new sediment–basement transition (1.1–1.7 km instead of 2.1–2.6 km), and the deeper events shift to hypocenters about 0.2 km deeper on average. The changes in epicenters result in absolute changes in local magnitude averaging 0.2 units, though the distribution of positive and negative changes is sufficiently even such that the average change is near 0.

Aftershock magnitudes

Local magnitudes for the 39 located aftershocks are given in Table 2. Our aftershock magnitude estimates are consistent with those found by Kim *et al.* (2018). The largest magnitude aftershock was M_L 1.75, resulting in the difference between the mainshock and largest aftershock $\Delta m = 2.45$, more than twice the typical difference $\Delta m = 1.2$ given by Båth's law (Richter, 1958; Båth, 1965).

The detection magnitude of completeness is approximately $M_c = 0.2$ (Fig. 7a), and the *b* value of the best-fit least-squares model for $0.2 \le M \le 1.5$ is 0.84, with a corresponding *A* value of −1.61. Using the Aki (1965) method of estimating the *b* value for the 39 earthquakes located, we obtain a value of 0.83, with a standard error of 0.14 determined using the method of Shi and Bolt (1982).

We extrapolated magnitudes for the remaining 69 detected aftershocks as described in the supplemental material using the relationship between *S*–*Pg* arrival time versus event-to-station distance for located events (Fig. S5). We were able to use the total catalog of 108 aftershocks and lower our magnitude of completeness to $M_c = 0$. We again applied Aki (1965) method for b value estimation and plotted the Gutenberg–Richter relation (Fig. 7b) to compare it with the smaller sample size above. In this case, the estimate using the Aki (1965) method was $b = 0.86$, with standard error (Shi and Bolt, 1982) equal to 0.11, which overlaps substantially with the estimate for 39 events and is very close to the least-squares estimate of $b = 0.85$ for 108 events, with $A = -1.61$.

Stress-drop estimation

We fit the power spectral ratio model (supplement) to the P-wave and S-wave spectra for the mainshock and our primary template aftershock at several nearby regional stations (see Fig. 1 for locations; see Data and Resources). A table of the best-fit corner frequencies by station and body-wave type is provided in Table S3. An example of the mainshock and aftershock spectra and spectral ratio modeling for the station GEDE is shown in Figure 8.

We determine the mean stress drop was 41 MPa with one standard deviation of ±35 MPa, and the median stress drop is 35 MPa, and the median rupture radius is 323 m. Because of the difficulty in measuring the corner frequency at different stations, our estimates have a high uncertainty level, making it difficult to draw firm conclusions about our stress drop (Abercrombie and Baltay, 2025). In addition, values for k in the circular rupture model are not always reported, contributing to the difficulty in making meaningful comparisons with other studies. For completeness, we note that the estimated stress drop appears typical for an intraplate earthquake in the ENA (Boyd *et al.*, 2017). In comparison, the 2011 M_w 5.7 Mineral, Virginia, earthquake stress drop was variably reported as unusually high (50–75 MPa) (Ellsworth *et al.*, 2011; Wu and Chapman, 2017), even by ENA standards, and as a more usual ENA value of 15–25 MPa (Hartzell *et al.*, 2013) or 17–39 MPa (Boyd *et al.*, 2017). The 2024 M_w 4.8 Tewksbury, New Jersey, earthquake had a stress drop of 2.3–18 MPa and 13–104 MPa for the Brune and Madariaga models, respectively (Beaucé *et al.*, 2025).

A study of global seismicity shows intraplate earthquakes have stress drops about two times higher than for interplate events (Allmann and Shearer, 2009), and a study of North American seismicity found stress drops in ENA around three times higher than central and western North America on average (Boyd *et al.*, 2017). Considering the stress drop of 35 MPa is within the typical range, we therefore do not attribute stress drop as the cause for the low aftershock productivity in Delaware and do not examine this further.

Aftershock productivity parameters

Our MCMC inversions determined optimal values for a, b, c, and p, as shown in Figure 9. For all four parameters, our ensemble mean and median were within 3% of each other. Because we are interested in quantifying the uncertainty of the specific aftershock parameters on their own without making assumptions about preferred values of other model variables, the distributions shown in Figure 9 integrate out all the other parameters to obtain the marginal probability that accounts for uncertainty arising from the tradeoffs with the estimates of the other parameters (Fig. S6). The estimates are compared in Table 3 to values from Page *et al.* (2016) and Ebel (2009).

Discussion

Productivity

The 30 November 2017 M_w 4.24 Delaware mainshock was followed by a maximum M_L 1.75 aftershock on 17 December 2017 (Table 2), giving $\Delta m = 2.45$, much higher than Båth's law's nominal value of 1.2 (Richter, 1958; Båth, 1965). Båth's law indicates that the largest aftershock generally has about 50 times less energy than the mainshock, given a 1.2 magnitude unit difference. In the case of the 2017 Delaware earthquake, the largest aftershock was an additional 1.25 magnitude units lower than expected, indicating it had 125 times less energy than expected and 10,000–15,000 times less energy produced than the mainshock.

To compare the magnitudes on a more equal basis, we convert the mainshock's moment magnitude to the local magnitude scale. Using the scaling for $4.3 < m_b(Lg) < 6.0$ in Rigsby *et al.* (2014) for M_w 4.24, this gives an $m_b(Lg)$ of 4.7. This is in line with the published value of 4.6 in ComCat (Data and Resources). In Kim (1998), he provides the relation between his local magnitude and $m_b(Lg)$, which results in M_L 4.54. Using this to compare with the Delaware earthquake's M_L 1.75 largest aftershock, we find the mainshock–aftershock difference to be $\Delta m = 2.79$ (Table 4), an even larger value than the uncorrected $\Delta m = 2.45$, and an even greater difference from the expected $\Delta m = 1.2$ (Richter, 1958; Båth, 1965). Using Kim (1998) to convert the largest aftershock magnitude to $m_b(Lg)$, we find a difference of $\Delta m = 2.95$.

Båth's law is based on measurements of earthquake magnitudes using the surface-wave magnitude, M_s. The M_s magnitude scale is not suitable for small, local events (Chung and Bernreuter, 1981). An empirical relationship between m_b and M_s is challenging to define, given the inherently different wave types and frequencies used for each (Chung and Bernreuter, 1981). Chung and Bernreuter (1981) provide a regression between m_b and M_s for western U.S. data with an m_b correction for eastern U.S. data, but this is used for magnitudes 4.5 and greater. Lienkaemper (1984) also has a conversion from m_b to M_s, yet it is intended for magnitudes 7 and greater. The values we calculated for $m_b(Lg)$ can be taken as equivalent to m_b magnitudes (Nuttli, 1973; Chung and Bernreuter, 1981), and we use this with the Lienkaemper (1984) formula to estimate M_s for the Delaware mainshock and aftershock.

Table 4 shows the magnitude differences between the mainshock and aftershock using M_L, $m_b(Lg)$, M_s, and M_w for comparison. The M_s difference is very large, but the formula used

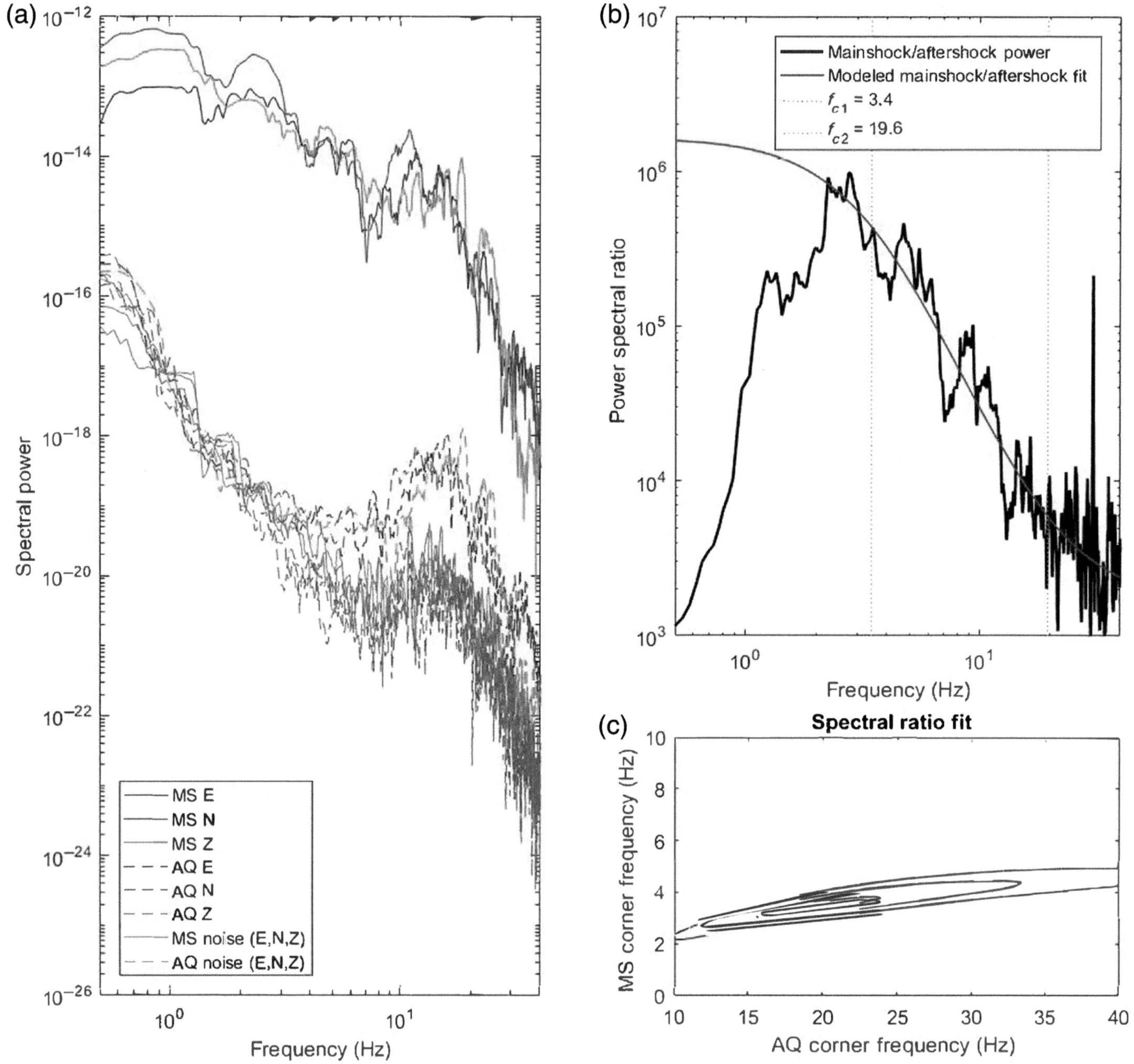

Figure 8. (a) Mainshock ("MS") *P*-wave spectral power (solid lines) and M_L 1.75 aftershock ("AQ") on 17 December 14:58 (dashed lines) at station GEDE. For both events, blue is east, red is north, and green is vertical-component data. Noise windows before each event are gray. (b) The mainshock spectral power to aftershock spectral power ratio is shown in solid black. The best-fit spectral ratio model using these two events is shown in red. Thin gray lines indicate the two corner frequencies. (c) The spectral ratio tradeoff between mainshock and aftershock corner frequencies for the optimal coefficient a (see supplement for details on fit modeling). The color version of this figure is available only in the electronic edition.

in that case may not be applicable. The M_w difference is smaller, though still above the nominal 1.2-unit difference for Båth's law. Taken together, the range of possibilities for Δm using different calculated magnitudes for this event's mainshock and aftershock indicates that the difference $\Delta m = 2.45$ is likely not a bad estimate for the true value of the difference.

Page *et al.* (2016) presented SCR parameters for five aftershock sequences that followed M ≥ 6.4 mainshocks between 1990 and 2015. Ebel (2009) investigates SCR aftershock parameters for 13 aftershock sequences following M ≥ 5 mainshocks between 1968 and 2008. Both Page *et al.* (2016) and Ebel (2009) used the Reasenberg and Jones (1989) formulation for Omori decay, consistent with this study, but their methods for calculating the parameters vary. They both also include global

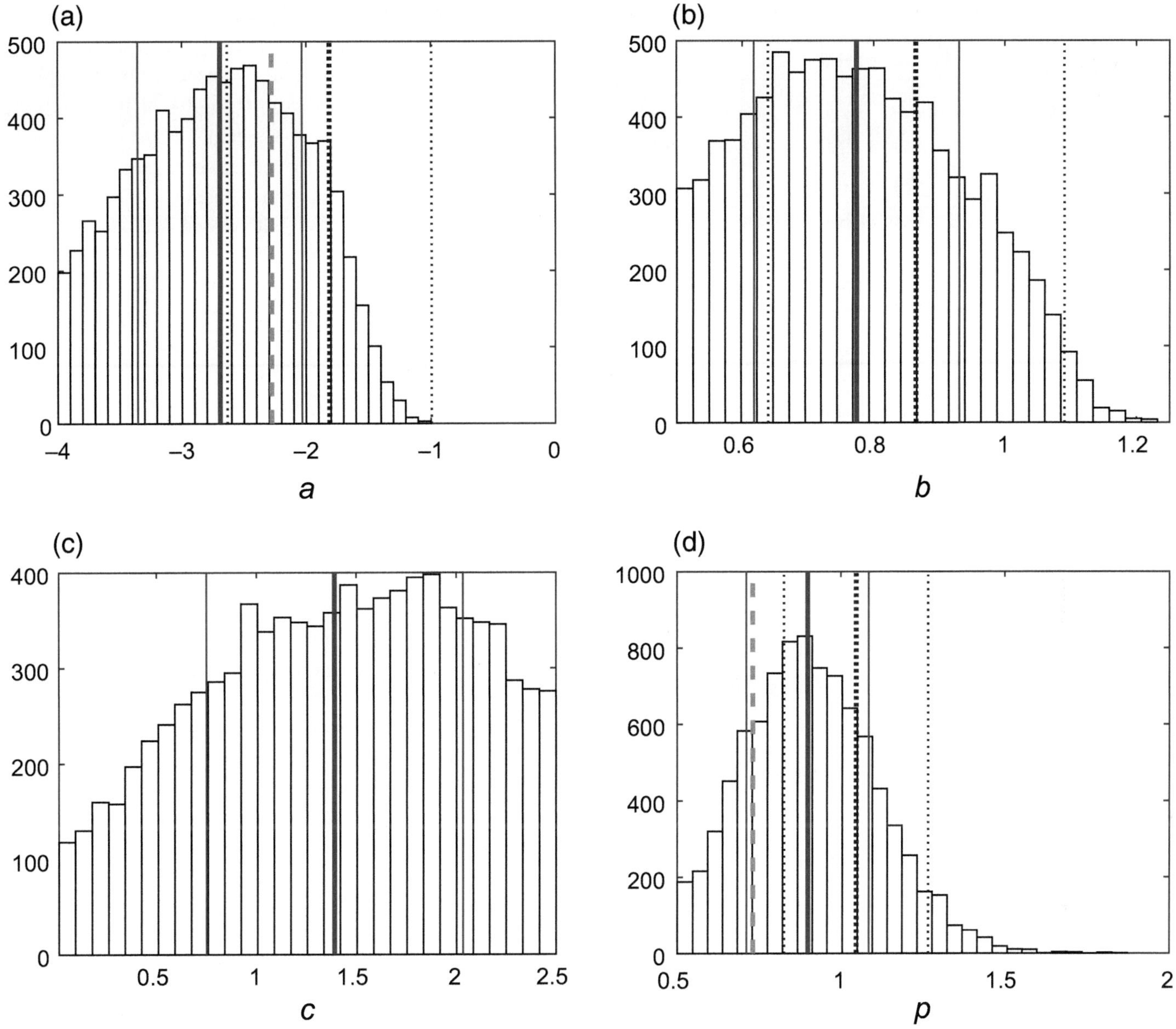

Figure 9. (a–d) Histograms showing the distribution of values for each parameter in the ensemble of model solutions for the Omori decay rate equation. The red solid lines show the mean and standard deviation of the best 10% of ensemble solutions to Bayes modeling for each parameter. The blue-dotted lines show the mean and standard deviation of parameter estimates for stable continental regions (SCRs) by Ebel (2009). The green-dashed lines show the mean estimates for parameters provided by Page *et al.* (2016). The color version of this figure is available only in the electronic edition.

earthquakes with larger minimum magnitudes in their studies of SCR aftershock sequences. Magnitude types were varied in Ebel (2009), and Page *et al.* (2016) used National Earthquake Information Center catalog magnitudes.

Prior work in SCRs has shown the observed catalog value for a median 10-day Båth's law is $\Delta m = 1.9$ (Page *et al.*, 2016), but the authors observe that the median values are larger than the means. In addition, this study only used events within 10 days of the mainshock. This may fail to capture larger aftershocks, artificially making the mainshock–aftershock difference look larger (Page *et al.*, 2016), and in turn making the difference in Delaware more unusual.

Our MCMC inversion results in parameter values $a = -2.694 \pm 0.660$, $b = 0.774 \pm 0.157$, $c = 1.391 \pm 0.642$, $p = 0.898 \pm 0.186$ for the modified Omori decay equation (equation 2). Although some of these values are similar to those found in previous results, others differ significantly.

Our mean a value, indicating overall productivity, does not fall within one standard deviation of the a value given by Ebel (2009) (Table 3). Our mean a value is also lower than that from Page *et al.* (2016). We note, however, that our a value is approximately halfway between the Page *et al.* (2016) SCR value (−2.28) and the stable oceanic regions value of −2.98.

TABLE 3
Aftershock Productivity Parameters

Parameter Set	a	b	c	p
Bayesian MCMC solution	−2.694 ± 0.660	0.774 ± 0.157	1.391 ± 0.642	0.898 ± 0.186
Page *et al.* (2016)	−2.28	–	0.018	0.73
Ebel (2009)	−1.815 ± 0.82	0.865 ± 0.226	0.05	1.046 ± 0.221

Mean and standard deviation ($\pm\sigma$) for the ensemble of model solutions for parameters {*a*, *b*, *c*, *p*}, compared with results from Page *et al.* (2016) and Ebel (2009). Values for standard deviation for {*a*, *p*} were not provided in Page *et al.* (2016). Both reference studies used fixed values for c. Parameter c is in days, other parameters are unitless. MCMC, Markov Chain Monte Carlo; SCR, stable continental region.

TABLE 4
Derived Magnitudes for the Mainshock and Aftershock in Different Scales

Magnitude	Mainshock	Aftershock	Δm
M_L	4.54	**1.75**	2.79
$m_b(Lg)$	4.70	1.84	2.86
M_s	4.04	0.12	3.92
M_w	**4.24**	2.27	1.97

The mainshock magnitude originally used was M_w; the aftershock magnitude used was M_L (listed in bold). Conversion between M_L and $m_b(Lg)$ is from Kim (1998), conversion from $m_b(Lg)$ to M_w is from Rigsby *et al.* (2014), and conversion from $m_b(Lg)$ to M_s is from Lienkaemper (1984). M_L, local magnitude; $m_b(Lg)$, computed short-period *Lg* magnitude; M_s, computed 20-s surface-wave magnitude; M_w, moment magnitude; Δm, mainshock–aftershock magnitude difference.

The proximity of the continental shelf may play a role in this factor and is an area for further research.

The *b* value found with Bayesian modeling is consistent with the value $b = 0.863 \pm 0.111$ we found for the maximum-likelihood estimate (Aki, 1965). It is below the global average of ~1 (Frohlich and Davis, 1993), but consistent with values for SCRs (Ebel, 2009) as well as *b* values for California aftershock sequences observed by Reasenberg and Jones (1989).

The *c* value, or time offset between the mainshock and the sequence of aftershocks, is the most poorly resolved parameter in the MCMC inversion (Fig. 9, Fig. S6), but also the least relevant for aftershock interpretation. Ebel (2009) uses a fixed value $c = 0.05$ days, which is drawn from Reasenberg and Jones (1989) but not explained. Page *et al.* (2016) used a fixed value $c = 0.018$ days for fitting to SCR aftershocks, in which *c* was the result of the global fit for all tectonic regimes. We fix the value of $c = 1.526$ days based on $t(\text{main}) - t(\text{first aftershock} \geq M_c)$ for our dataset. This value is larger than in Page *et al.* (2016) and Ebel (2009) because the data we used were from stations deployed after the mainshock, and not from permanent stations that would have been able to record aftershocks that occurred immediately after the mainshock. Inverting for *a*, *b*, and *p*, we obtain similar results of $a = -2.732 \pm 0.662$, $b = 0.790 \pm 0.156$, and $p = 0.920 \pm 0.180$. If instead we fix $c = 0.05$, the MCMC inversion results in $a = -2.896 \pm 0.594$, $b = 0.772 \pm 0.141$, and $p = 0.762 \pm 0.132$. The *b* value remains stable independent of variations in *c* value, and changes in *a* value are within one standard deviation of one another. The *p* value shows a positive correlation to changes in *c* (Fig. S6), which is most likely due to the MCMC inversion trying to compensate for the lack of detected aftershocks in the first 1.5 days after the mainshock through a low decay value. Because we know there was at least one aftershock on 1 December 2017 prior to our network deployment (Kim *et al.*, 2018), our results with $c = 1.391$ days account for this time delay.

The value we find for *p*, or the rate of aftershock sequence decay, is higher than that found by Page *et al.* (2016) but on the low end of the range given by Ebel (2009). This is not surprising, given the limited sample sizes for both prior studies, and we find our value to be generally consistent with both studies.

Despite the observed differences in Båth's law Δm and Omori *a* values, the subsequent aftershock magnitude distribution followed a typical SCR Gutenberg–Richter distribution. Other related values appear consistent with those reported in previous studies (Ebel, 2009; Page *et al.*, 2016). Our *b* value, indicating the relative proportion of smaller and larger aftershocks, was consistent with values for SCRs (Ebel, 2009). Similarly, we found a *p* value for the Omori decay exponent (Utsu, 1961; Reasenberg and Jones, 1989) that is also consistent with prior studies for SCR earthquakes (Ebel, 2009; Page *et al.*, 2016), indicating that the decay in frequency with time of Delaware aftershocks was nominal.

To compare, the 2011 M_w 5.8 Mineral, Virginia, aftershock sequence had a *b* value of 0.86, a value for the Omori *p* near 1, and a typical $\Delta m = 1.5$ (Wu *et al.*, 2015; Wu and Chapman, 2017), all consistent with findings for stable continental earthquakes with $M \geq 5$. The M_w 4.8 Tewksbury, New Jersey, earthquake in 2024 had a much higher $b = 1.19 \pm 0.03$ and a typical $\Delta m = 1.1$ (Beaucé *et al.*, 2025). Their estimate of the *p* value ranged from 0.25 to 0.80, corresponding to a slower-than-usual decay; however, the highly heterogeneous local network for detection makes this estimate hard to interpret or compare with other sequences (Beaucé *et al.*, 2025).

Other work has suggested that low-to-moderate-magnitude earthquakes may not be consistent with Båth's parameter for maximum aftershock magnitude (Utsu, 1969; Vere-Jones, 1969; Console *et al.*, 2003). Low aftershock productivity has also been reported for moderate-magnitude earthquakes in South Carolina (Daniels *et al.*, 2019) and Maine (Quiros *et al.*, 2015) (M_w 4.1 and 4.0 respectively) and observed in

Michigan (M_w 4.24) (USGS, n.d.b). Although individually these sequences are not unusual, the occurrence of multiple low productivity sequences among the relatively small pool of M 4+ earthquakes in the CEUS is intriguing. This suggests that aftershock behavior in the intraplate CEUS may not be well modeled by parameters from generic worldwide SCRs and is an avenue for additional research.

In contrast to our work and other previous studies, Dascher-Cousineau *et al.* (2020) evaluated relative productivity for different tectonic settings, source effects, and focal mechanisms; however, their work did not evaluate productivity directly from the Omori a value. They argued that an intraplate location could lead to higher-than-average productivity, in contrast to Page *et al.* (2016), but also that this could be mitigated by other factors. In Delaware, these include the primarily strike-slip mechanism of the mainshock and the lithospheric age of the CEUS (Dascher-Cousineau *et al.*, 2020), possibly in combination with the stress drop above the global average (Boyd *et al.*, 2017; Wetzler *et al.*, 2018; Dascher-Cousineau *et al.*, 2020).

Potential causes of Delaware seismicity

One potential contributing factor to seismicity in passive margins is the existence of inherited faults or planes of weakness along which earthquakes might be more likely to occur. Hatcher Jr. *et al.* (2007, Fig. 1) provide a detailed map of the surface geology units in the Salisbury Embayment region. The location of the M_w 4.24 mainshock is approximately at the interface of the Carolina superterrane and the Brunswick (Charleston) terrane in east-central Delaware (Hatcher Jr. *et al.*, 2007). This terrane boundary strikes northeast–southwest at this latitude. It is also the inferred northern end of the Taylorsville rift basin, a Mesozoic rift zone produced by the rifting process that broke up Pangaea in the Triassic–Jurassic (Olsen, 1990; Withjack *et al.*, 1998). The half-graben remaining from the Taylorsville rift has an east-northeast–west-southwest trend (Olsen, 1990; Hatcher Jr. *et al.*, 2007; Withjack *et al.*, 2012). Kim *et al.* (2018) proposed a west-northwest–east-northeast-striking, *S*-dipping fault based on their estimated aftershock alignment and suggested the nodal plane at 103° was the likely fault plane for the mainshock. Although this is not exactly aligned with the orientation of the rift margin, we cannot rule out that rift-related faults were a contributing factor to the generation of the mainshock. However, the northeast–southwest orientation of the terrane boundaries is more oblique to the nodal planes of the mainshock and is therefore less likely to be responsible for this seismicity.

The aftershock locations we find in this article fall along an apparent northwest–southeast striking, southwest-dipping fault (Fig. 6). This plane is oblique to both the nodal planes of the mainshock and the known rift basin structures and terrane boundaries (Withjack *et al.*, 1998; Hatcher Jr. *et al.*, 2007; Kim *et al.*, 2018). There is no known geological structure that strikes parallel to our observed aftershock fault plane. Given that the fault plane evidenced by our aftershocks is otherwise undefined in the local geological maps, it is difficult to constrain what fault properties might be responsible for the low aftershock productivity. However, we can evaluate the combined effect of a northwest–southeast striking, southwest-dipping fault plane with the ambient stress field.

The moment tensor for the mainshock in our study has three consistent solutions: the National Earthquake Information Center, Saint Louis University (USGS, n.d.), and Kim *et al.* (2018). The strikes of the two nodal planes were approximately 0° and 100° for each of these moment tensors (Kim *et al.*, 2018). This would imply a maximum stress direction of ~55°. Delaware has an overall northeast–southwest (~45°)-striking stress field, as does the majority of the CEUS (Gardner, 1989; Zoback and Zoback, 1989; Heidbach *et al.*, 2018). This is broadly consistent with the compressive stress inferred from the focal mechanism of the mainshock. Both of these give evidence of a regional stress field characterized by a maximum compressive stress direction oriented northeast–southwest, roughly orthogonal to our observed dipping fault plane. This might suggest that these events are therefore caused by thrusting along the previously unidentified northwest–southeast-striking, southwest-dipping fault. However, given that little is known about this fault, it is difficult to assess the geological contributing factors that might produce our observed low aftershock productivity. It is possible that the mainshock triggered seismicity on a pre-existing, optimally oriented fault zone caused by any one of the earlier repeated episodes of orogenesis and rifting to which the eastern United States has been subjected. The low aftershock productivity may simply reflect the small size of this obliquely oriented fault.

Conclusions

The M_w 4.24 mainshock was the largest earthquake under the ACP in the twenty-first century (ANSS ComCat, Data and Resources). The use of a local network increased the total number of detected aftershocks during the period from late on 1 December to 11 January 2018 by an order of magnitude and lowered the magnitude of completeness for detected events by approximately one magnitude unit, relative to detections with regional stations reported by Kim *et al.* (2018). We observed a lower-than-average aftershock productivity for this sequence, characterized by a high $\Delta m = 2.45$ that is more than twice Båth's law expected difference of $\Delta m = 1.2$ (Richter, 1958; Båth, 1965), and a low a value for the Omori decay rate (Reasenberg and Jones, 1989). Our observed a value is substantially lower than the mean of other SCR aftershock sequences (Ebel, 2009; Page *et al.*, 2016).

We do not find an unusual stress drop for the Delaware earthquake relative to CEUS events and therefore do not consider stress drop to be a primary factor for the low number of aftershocks. The apparent aftershock fault plane is well aligned for shear failure for thrust faulting (Hardebeck, 2010), but its orientation orthogonal to Mesozoic rift margins may indicate a very small obliquely oriented fault of differing origin. This may be pre-Mesozoic, or may be a splay fault off of the rift bounding faults. The likely small size may contribute toward lower-than-usual aftershock productivity. Our results contribute to our body of knowledge concerning aftershock sequences in SCRs and hold implications for predicting hazards due to aftershock occurrence in intraplate settings.

Data and Resources

Nodal data used in this deployment were gathered on instruments owned by the University of Maryland and is available at: Vedran Lekic and Karen M. Pearson (2017). *Dover, Delaware Aftershock Nodal Deployment* [Data set], International Federation of Digital Seismograph Networks, doi: 10.7914/3gq2-3h19. Broadband data used in this deployment were gathered on instruments owned by the Carnegie Institution for Science and are available at Lara Wagner and Diana Roman (2017). *Delaware 2017 Aftershock Study* [Data set], International Federation of Digital Seismograph Networks, doi: 10.7914/SN/Y3_2017. Regional data used for stress parameter estimation were accessed through the Incorporated Research Institutions for Seismology (now EarthScope) Data Services. These included data from the LD and PE networks: Lamont Doherty Earth Observatory (LDEO), Columbia University (1970). *Lamont–Doherty Cooperative Seismographic Network* [Data set]. International Federation of Digital Seismograph Networks, doi: 10.7914/SN/LD. Penn State University (2004). *Pennsylvania State Seismic Network* [Data set], International Federation of Digital Seismograph Networks, doi: 10.7914/SN/PE. Reference data from the U.S. Geological Survey included: USGS, Earthquake Hazards Program, 2017, Advanced National Seismic System Comprehensive Catalog of Earthquake Events and Products: Various, doi: 10.5066/F7MS3QZH. USGS, Quaternary fault and fold database for the United States available at https://www.usgs.gov/natural-hazards/earthquake-hazards/faults (last accessed February 2021). The supplemental material for this article includes details on the algorithms for location grid search, locations using a 1 km sediment model, stress-drop modeling, magnitude extrapolation for events without locations, and Bayesian Markov Chain Monte Carlo simulation.

Declaration of Competing Interests

The authors acknowledge that there are no conflicts of interest recorded.

Acknowledgments

The authors would like to thank Erin Cunningham, Chao Gao, Steven Golden, Phillip Goodling, Quancheng Huang, Helen Janiszewski, Pete Meehan, Diana Roman, Lisa Schleicher, and Thomas Pratt, who assisted with the installation and retrieval of the temporary deployment of sensors. The authors thank two external reviewers, John Ebel and Andrea Llenos, as well as the Focus Section Guest Editor Oliver Boyd, for insightful comments and feedback that contributed to the article. The authors thank Thomas Pratt for conversations and input to improve the article. The authors thank Nicholas Schmerr for assistance in the archiving of the nodal data. Funding for this work came from the David and Lucille Packard Foundation Fellowship to V. L.

References

Abercrombie, R. E., and A. S. Baltay (2025). Magnitude, depth, and methodological variations of spectral stress drop within the SCEC/USGS community stress drop validation study using the 2019 Ridgecrest earthquake sequence, *Bull. Seismol. Soc. Am.* **115,** no. 6, 2741–2768, doi: 10.1785/0120250056.

Aki, K. (1965). Maximum likelihood estimate of b in the formula log $N = a\text{-}bM$ and its confidence limits, *Bull. Earthq. Res. Inst.* **43,** 237–239.

Allmann, B. P., and P. M. Shearer (2009). Global variations of stress drop for moderate to large earthquakes, *J. Geophys. Res.* **114,** no. 1, 1–22, doi: 10.1029/2008JB005821.

Båth, M. (1965). Lateral inhomogeneities of the upper mantle, *Tectonophysics* **2,** no. 6, 483–514, doi: 10.1016/0040-1951(65)90003-X.

Baxter, S. J. (2000). Catalog of earthquakes in Delaware, *Delaware Geol. Surv. Open File Rept. No. 42,* Delaware Geological Survey, Newark.

Beaucé, E., F. Waldhauser, D. Schaff, W. Y. Kim, and F. Kolawole (2025). The 5 April 2024 M_w 4.8 Tewksbury, New Jersey aftershock sequence resolved with machine-learning-enhanced detection methods, *Geophys. Res. Lett.* **52,** no. 12, doi: 10.1029/2024GL113598.

Boyd, O. S., D. Churchwell, M. P. Moschetti, E. M. Thompson, M. C. Chapman, O. Ilhan, T. L. Pratt, S. K. Ahdi, and S. Rezaeian (2024). Sediment thickness map of United States Atlantic and Gulf Coastal Plain strata, and their influence on earthquake ground motions, *Earthq. Spectra* **40,** no. 1, 89–112, doi: 10.1177/87552930231204880.

Boyd, O. S., D. E. McNamara, S. Hartzell, and G. Choy (2017). Influence of lithostatic stress on earthquake stress drops in North America, *Bull. Seismol. Soc. Am.* **107,** no. 2, 856–868, doi: 10.1785/0120160219.

Brune, J. N. (1970). Tectonic stress and the spectra of seismic shear waves from earthquakes, *J. Geophys. Res.* **75,** no. 26, 4997–5009, doi: 10.1029/JB075i026p04997.

Calais, E., T. Camelbeeck, S. Stein, M. Liu, and T. J. Craig (2016). A new paradigm for large earthquakes in stable continental plate interiors, *Geophys. Res. Lett.* **43,** no. 20, 10,621–10,637, doi: 10.1002/2016GL070815.

Hatcher, R. D., Jr., M. P. Carlson, J. H. McBride, and J. R. M. Catalán (2007). Geologic terranes of the south-eastern U. S., in *4-D Framework of Continental Crust*, R. D. Hatcher, M. P. Carlson, J. H. McBride, and J. R. M. Catalán (Editors), Geological Society of America, doi: 10.1130/MEM200.

Chen, K.-C., J.-M. Chiu, and Y.-T. Yang (1996). Shear-wave velocity of the sedimentary basin in the upper Mississippi embayment using S-to-P converted waves, *Bull. Seismol. Soc. Am.* **86,** no. 3, 848–856.

Chung, D. H., and D. L. Bernreuter (1981). Regional relationships among earthquake magnitude scales, *Rev. Geophys.* **19,** no. 4, 649–663, doi: 10.1029/RG019i004p00649.

Console, R., A. M. Lombardi, M. Murru, and D. Rhoades (2003). Båth's law and the self-similarity of earthquakes, *J. Geophys. Res.* **108,** no. B2, doi: 10.1029/2001jb001651.

Cunningham, E., and V. Lekic (2020). Constraining properties of sedimentary strata using receiver functions: An example from the

Atlantic Coastal Plain of the southeastern United States, *Bull. Seismol. Soc. Am.* **110,** no. 2, 519–533, doi: 10.1785/0120190191.

Daniels, C., Z. Peng, Q. Wu, S. Ni, X. Meng, D. Yao, L. S. Wagner, and K. M. Fischer (2019). The 15 February 2014 M_w 4.1 South Carolina earthquake sequence: Aftershock productivity, hypocentral depths, and stress drops, *Seismol. Res. Lett.* **91,** no. 1, 452–464, doi: 10.1785/0220190034.

Dascher-Cousineau, K., E. E. Brodsky, T. Lay, and T. H. W. Goebel (2020). What controls variations in aftershock productivity? *J. Geophys. Res.* **125,** no. 2, doi: 10.1029/2019JB018111.

Ebel, J. E. (2009). Analysis of aftershock and foreshock activity in stable continental regions: Implications for aftershock forecasting and the hazard of strong earthquakes, *Seismol. Res. Lett.* **80,** no. 6, 1062–1068, doi: 10.1785/gssrl.80.6.1062.

Ellsworth, W. L., K. Imanishi, J. H. Luetgert, J. Kruger, and J. Hamilton (2011). The M_w 5.8 Virginia earthquake of August 23, 2011 and its aftershocks: A shallow high stress drop event, *AGU Fall Meeting Abstracts*, p. S14B-05.

Frohlich, C., and S. D. Davis (1993). Teleseismic *b* values; Or, Much ado about 1.0, *J. Geophys. Res.* **98,** no. B1, 631–644.

Gardner, T. W. (1989). Neotectonism along the Atlantic passive continental margin: A review, *Geomorphology* **2,** nos. 1/3, 71–97, doi: 10.1016/0169-555X(89)90007-X.

Gibbons, S. J., and F. Ringdal (2006). The detection of low magnitude seismic events using array-based waveform correlation, *Geophys. J. Int.* **165,** no. 1, 149–166, doi: 10.1111/j.1365-246X.2006.02865.x.

Hansen, H. J. (1988). Buried rift basin underlying coastal plain sediments, central Delmarva Peninsula, Maryland, *Geology* **16,** no. 9, 779–782.

Hardebeck, J. (2010). Aftershocks are well aligned with the background stress field, contradicting the hypothesis of highly heterogeneous crustal stress, *J. Geophys. Res.* **115,** no. 12, doi: 10.1029/2010JB007586.

Hartzell, S., C. Mendoza, and Y. Zeng (2013). Rupture model of the 2011 Mineral, Virginia, earthquake from teleseismic and regional waveforms, *Geophys. Res. Lett.* **40,** no. 21, 5665–5670, doi: 10.1002/2013GL057880.

Heidbach, O., M. Rajabi, X. Cui, K. Fuchs, B. Müller, J. Reinecker, K. Reiter, M. Tingay, F. Wenzel, F. Xie, *et al.* (2018). The World Stress Map database release 2016: Crustal stress pattern across scales, *Tectonophysics* **744,** 484–498, doi: 10.1016/j.tecto.2018.07.007.

Herrmann, R. B. (1979). Surface wave focal mechanisms for eastern North American earthquakes with tectonic implications, *J. Geophys. Res.* **84,** no. 8, 3543–3552, doi: 10.1029/JB084iB07p03543.

Kaneko, Y., and P. M. Shearer (2014). Seismic source spectra and estimated stress drop derived from cohesive-zone models of circular subshear rupture, *Geophys. J. Int.* **197,** no. 2, 1002–1015, doi: 10.1093/gji/ggu030.

Kim, W. (1998). The ML scale in eastern North America, *Bull. Seismol. Soc. Am.* **88,** no. 4, 935–951.

Kim, W. Y., M. Gold, J. Ramsay, A. Meltzer, D. Wunsch, S. Baxter, V. Lekic, P. Goodling, K. Pearson, L. Wagner, *et al.* (2018). The M_w 4.2 Delaware earthquake of 30 November 2017, *Seismol. Res. Lett.* **89,** no. 6, 2447–2460, doi: 10.1785/0220180124.

LeTourneau, P. M. (2003). Stratigraphic architecture and paleomagnetic reversal stratigraphy of the Late Triassic Taylorsville basin, Virginia and Maryland, in *The Great Rift Valleys of Pangea in Eastern North America*, LeTourneau, P. M., and P. E. Olsen (Editors), Vol. 2, Columbia University Press, New York, 12–58.

Lienkaemper, J. J. (1984). Comparison of two surface-wave magnitude scales: M of Gutenberg and Richter (1954) and Ms of "Preliminary Determination of Epicenters," *Bull. Seismol. Soc. Am.* **74,** no. 6, 2357–2378.

Madariaga, R. (1976). Dynamics of an expanding circular fault, *Bull. Seismol. Soc. Am.* **66,** no. 3, 639–666, doi: 10.1086/622062.

Miller, K. G., J. V. Browning, P. J. Sugarman, D. H. Monteverde, D. C. Andreasen, C. Lombardi, J. Thornburg, Y. Fan, and R. E. Kopp (2017). Lower to mid-Cretaceous sequence stratigraphy and characterization of CO2 storage potential in the Mid-Atlantic U.S. Coastal Plain, *J. Sedimentary Res.* **87,** no. 6, 609–629, doi: 10.2110/jsr.2017.33.

Nuttli, O. W. (1973). Seismic wave attenuation and magnitude relations for eastern North America, *J. Geophys. Res.* **78,** no. 5, 876–885, doi: 10.1029/jb078i005p00876.

Olsen, P. E. (1990). Tectonic, climatic, and biotic modulation of Lacustrine ecosystems—Examples from Newark supergroup of eastern North America, in *Lacustrine Basin Exploration: Case Studies and Modern Analogs*, B. Katz (Editor), American Association of Petroleum Geologists, 209–224.

Olsson, R. K., T. G. Gibson, H. J. Hansen, and J. P. Owens (1988). Geology of the northern Atlantic coastal plain: Long Island to Virginia, in *The Atlantic Continental Margin: U.S.*, R. E. Sheridan and J. A. Grow (Editors), The Geological Society of America, Boulder, Colorado, 87–105.

Omori, F. (1895). On the aftershocks of earthquakes, *J. Coll. Sci. Imp. Univ. Jpn.* **7,** no. 2, 111–200.

Page, M. T., N. van Der Elst, J. Hardebeck, K. Felzer, and A. J. Michael (2016). Three ingredients for improved global aftershock forecasts: Tectonic region, time-dependent catalog incompleteness, and intersequence variability, *Bull. Seismol. Soc. Am.* **106,** no. 5, 2290–2301, doi: 10.1785/0120160073.

Pope, J. P., D. C. Andreasen, E. R. Mcfarland, and M. K. Watt (2016). Digital elevations and extents of regional hydrogeologic units in the Northern Atlantic Coastal Plain aquifer system from Long Island, New York, to North Carolina, *U.S. Geol. Surv.*, Reston, Virginia, doi: 10.3133/ds996.

Pratt, T. L. (2018). Characterizing and imaging sedimentary strata using depth-converted spectral ratios: An example from the Atlantic Coastal Plain of the eastern United States, *Bull. Seismol. Soc. Am.* **108,** no. 5A, 2801–2815, doi: 10.1785/0120180046.

Quiros, D. A., A. Cabolova, L. D. Brown, C. Chen, J. E. Ebel, and J. Starr (2015). Aftershock imaging with dense arrays (AIDA) following the M_w 4.0 Waterboro earthquake of 16 October 2012 Maine, U.S.A., *Seismol. Res. Lett.* **86,** no. 3, 1032–1039, doi: 10.1785/0220140169.

Reasenberg, P. A., and L. M. Jones (1989). Earthquake hazard after a mainshock in California, *Science* **243,** no. 4895, 1173–1176, doi: 10.1126/science.243.4895.1173.

Richter, C. F. (1958). *Elementary Seismology*, W.H. Freeman, San Francisco, doi: 10.5408/0022-1368-7.1.21.

Rigsby, C., R. B. Herrmann, and H. Benz (2014). An investigation of *MbLg* versus M_w for eastern North America, *Seismol. Res. Lett.* **85,** no. 3, 625–630.

Saikia, C. K. (1994). Modified frequency-wavenumber algorithm for regional seismograms using Filon's quadrature: Modelling *Lg* waves in eastern North America, *Geophys. J. Int.* **118,** 142–158.

Sbar, M. L., R. R. Jordan, C. D. Stephens, T. E. Pickett, K. D. Woodruff, and C. G. Sammis (1975). The Delaware-New Jersey earthquake of February 28, 1973, *Bull. Seismol. Soc. Am.* **65,** no. 1, 85–92.

Schaff, D. P., and F. Waldhauser (2010). One magnitude unit reduction in detection threshold by cross correlation applied to Parkfield (California) and China seismicity, *Bull. Seismol. Soc. Am.* **100,** no. 6, 3224–3238, doi: 10.1785/0120100042.

Shi, Y., and B. A. Bolt (1982). The standard error of the magnitude-frequency *b* value, *Bull. Seismol. Soc. Am.* **72,** no. 5, 1677–1687.

Slinkard, M., D. Schaff, N. Mikhailova, S. Heck, C. Young, and P. G. Richards (2014). Multistation validation of waveform correlation techniques as applied to broad regional monitoring, *Bull. Seismol. Soc. Am.* **104,** no. 6, 2768–2781, doi: 10.1785/0120140140.

Soto-Cordero, L., A. Meltzer, and J. C. Stachnik (2018). Crustal structure, intraplate seismicity, and seismic hazard in the mid-Atlantic United States, *Seismol. Res. Lett.* **89,** no. 1, 241–252, doi: 10.1785/0220170084.

Spoljaric, N. (1973). Normal faults in basement rocks of the northern coastal plain, Delaware, *Bull. Geol. Soc. Am.* **84,** no. 8, 2781–2784.

Stein, S., and M. Liu (2009). Long aftershock sequences within continents and implications for earthquake hazard assessment, *Nature* **462,** no. 7269, 87–89, doi: 10.1038/nature08502.

Stover, C. W., and J. L. Coffman (1993). *Seismicity of the United States, 1568-1989,* United States Government Printing Office, Denver.

Toda, S., and R. S. Stein (2018). Why aftershock duration matters for probabilistic seismic hazard assessment, *Bull. Seismol. Soc. Am.* **108,** no. 3, 1414–1426, doi: 10.1785/0120170270.

U.S. Geological Survey (USGS) (n.d.a). Event page M 4.1–3 km NNE of Little Creek, Delaware, available at https://earthquake.usgs.gov/earthquakes/eventpage/us1000bjkn/executive#executive (last accessed December 2025).

USGS (n.d.b). Event page M 4.2–5 km S of Galesburg, Michigan, available at https://earthquake.usgs.gov/earthquakes/eventpage/us20002avh/executive (last accessed October 2025).

Utsu, T. (1961). A statistical study on the occurrence of aftershocks, *Geophysics* **30,** 521–605.

Utsu, T. (1969). Aftershocks and earthquake statistics: Some parameters which characterize an aftershock sequence and their interrelations, *J. Faculty Sci. Hokkaido Univ.* **3,** no. 3, 129–195.

Vere-Jones, D. (1969). A note on the statistical interpretation of Bath's law, *Bull. Seismol. Soc. Am.* **59,** no. 4, 1535–1541.

Wetzler, N., T. Lay, E. E. Brodsky, and H. Kanamori (2018). Systematic deficiency of aftershocks in areas of high coseismic slip for large subduction zone earthquakes, *Sci. Adv.* **4,** no. 2, 1–10, doi: 10.1126/sciadv.aao3225.

Withjack, M. O., R. W. Schlische, M. L. Malinconico, and P. E. Olsen (2012). *Rift-Basin Development: Lessons from the Triassic-Jurassic Newark Basin of Eastern North America,* Geological Society of Special Publication, Vol. 369, 301–321, doi: 10.1144/SP369.13.

Withjack, M. O., R. W. Schlische, and P. E. Olsen (1998). Diachronous rifting, drifting, and inversion on the passive margin of central eastern North America: An analog for other passive margins, *Am. Assoc. Pet. Geol. Bull.* **82,** no. 5A, 817–835.

Wu, Q., and M. C. Chapman (2017). Stress-drop estimates and source scaling of the 2011 Mineral, Virginia, mainshock and aftershocks, *Bull. Seismol. Soc. Am.* **107,** no. 6, 2703–2720, doi: 10.1785/0120170098.

Wu, Q., M. C. Chapman, and J. N. Beale (2015). The aftershock sequence of the 2011 Mineral, Virginia, earthquake: Temporal and spatial distribution, focal mechanisms, regional stress, and the role of Coulomb stress transfer, *Bull. Seismol. Soc. Am.* **105,** no. 5, 2521–2537, doi: 10.1785/0120150032.

Yoon, C. E., O. O'Reilly, K. J. Bergen, and G. C. Beroza (2015). Earthquake detection through computationally efficient similarity search, *Sci. Adv.* **1,** 1–13, doi: 10.1126/sciadv.1501057.

Zoback, M. L., and M. D. Zoback (1989). Tectonic stress field of the continental United States, in *Geophysical framework of the continental United States,* L. C. Pakiser and W. D. Mooney (Editors), Geological Society of America, Boulder, Colorado, 523–539, doi: 10.1130/MEM172-p523.

Manuscript received 18 September 2025
Published online 4 February 2026

Coseismic Slip of the 2024 M_w 7.3 Hualien Earthquake Constrained by GNSS Observations and Its Implications for Fault Interactions

Chengfang Sang[1], Yan Hu[*1,2], Siyuan Yang[1], Kai Wang[1], and Xin Cui[1]

Abstract

On 2 April 2024, an M_w 7.3 thrust earthquake occurred in Hualien City, Taiwan. In this study, we examined three coseismic models, that is model 1 (an east-dipping fault), model 2 (a west-dipping fault), and model 3 (a combination of an east-dipping and a west-dipping fault). For each model, the geometry of the fault plane(s) and coseismic fault slip were determined through a Bayesian method based on the coseismic Global Navigation Satellite Systems (GNSS) displacements. Although models 1 and 2 both produce reasonable fits to GNSS data, with corresponding average root mean square (rms) misfits of 16.4 and 20.0 mm, respectively, model 3 better reproduces the first-order pattern of the GNSS data and achieves a smaller average rms misfit of 15.2 mm. Based on the rms misfit, Akaike information criterion, and Bayesian information criterion, model 3 is identified as the optimal model. Model 3 features thrust slips on the east-dipping fault, with a maximum slip of 1.45 m. The Longitudinal Valley and Milun faults undergo a coseismic Coulomb stress increase of up to 21 and 5 bars, respectively, increasing the seismic potential in the future.

Cite this article as Sang, C., Y. Hu, S. Yang, K. Wang, and X. Cui (2025). Coseismic Slip of the 2024 M_w 7.3 Hualien Earthquake Constrained by GNSS Observations and Its Implications for Fault Interactions, *Seismol. Res. Lett.* **97**, 977–985, doi: 10.1785/0220250013.

Supplemental Material

Introduction

The island of Taiwan is an orogen located in the plate boundary region between the Eurasian plate (EP) and the Philippine Sea plate (PSP, Fig. 1a). Taiwan is the junction region of continental collision between the PSP and EP at the East Luzon arc and the subduction of the PSP beneath the EP along the Ryukyu trench. The island undergoes continuous oblique convergence at a rate of about 9 cm/yr in the northwest direction between the EP and PSP since 5 Ma (Huang *et al.*, 2012). To the south of Taiwan, the EP subducts beneath the PSP along the Manila trench. To the north of Taiwan, on the contrary, the PSP is subducting beneath the EP along the Ryukyu trench, inducing large-scale extensions of about 4 cm/yr in the back-arc region (Shyu *et al.*, 2005; Thomas *et al.*, 2014). The complicated geological settings and intense tectonic movements in and around Taiwan have resulted in a highly elusive fault system with high seismicity and many destructive earthquakes. Hualien City, located in eastern Taiwan, is prone to strong seismic hazards due to its unique tectonic setting, for example, this region has been struck by three earthquake sequences (1951, 1986–1992, and 2018–2022) since the midtwentieth century (Kao *et al.*, 1998; Shyu *et al.*, 2007; Chung *et al.*, 2008; Huang and Wang, 2022; Jian and Wang, 2022). Therefore, earthquake studies in this region are important for seismic hazard mitigation and the understanding of tectonic processes.

On 2 April 2024 23:58 (UTC), an M_w 7.3 earthquake struck the south of Hualien City, causing more than 1100 casualties (KYODO NEWS, 2024). More than 1400 aftershocks were recorded within one month after the mainshock (see Data and Resources). This earthquake is the largest earthquake since the 1999 Chi-Chi earthquake in this region and provides an opportunity to study the tectonics and seismicity in Taiwan. The focal mechanisms determined by the U.S. Geological Survey (USGS), the Global Centroid Moment Tensor (Global CMT) Project, and the Broadband Array in Taiwan for Seismology (BATS) all confirm that this event occurred on a northeast–southwest-striking reverse fault in the off-shore region of northern Coastal Mountain Range (Table S1, available in the supplemental material to this article; Fig. 1b). However, the complicated fault systems make it difficult to determine the precise fault structure in the coseismic region, for example, the epicenter locations and focal depths. Thus,

1. School of Earth and Space Sciences, University of Science and Technology of China, Hefei, China, https://orcid.org/0009-0000-4495-4971 (CS); https://orcid.org/0000-0002-5704-4827 (YH); https://orcid.org/0009-0000-6596-0377 (SY); https://orcid.org/0000-0001-5223-6291 (KW); https://orcid.org/0000-0002-4807-7061 (XC); 2. Institute of Deep Space Sciences, Deep Space Exploration Laboratory, Hefei, China

*Corresponding author: yanhu11@ustc.edu.cn

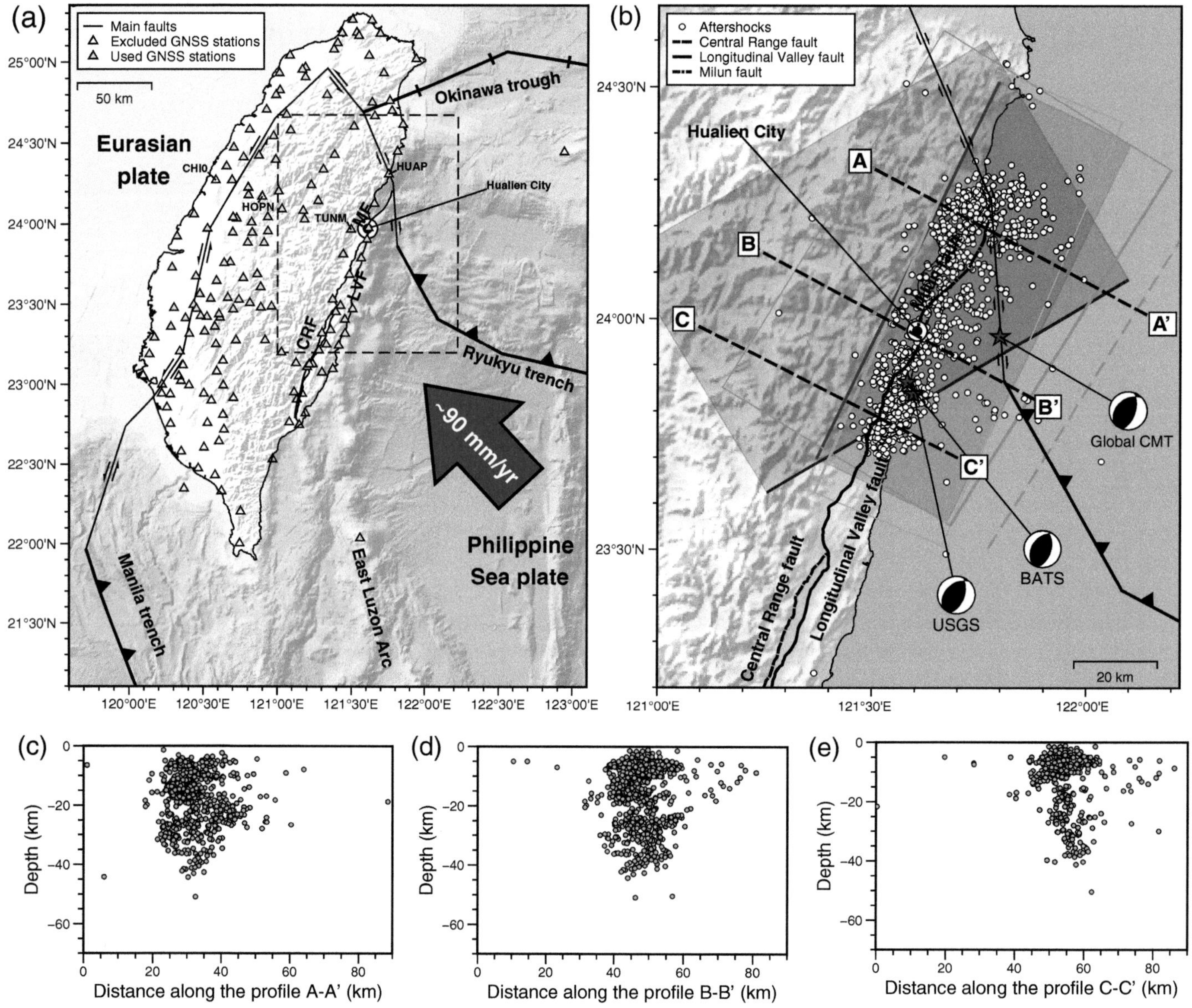

Figure 1. (a) Tectonic background of Taiwan orogeny (Hasterok *et al.*, 2022) and the distribution of Global Navigation Satellite Systems (GNSS) stations. Solid-yellow triangles represent the location of GNSS stations used in the Bayesian sampling whereas the open triangles are the stations excluded from the sampling. The main faults shown by solid-black lines are the Milun fault (MF), Longitudinal Valley fault (LVF), and Central Range fault (CRF; Shyu *et al.*, 2016, 2020). The black-dashed rectangle outlines the region plotted in panel (b). (b) The close-up view of the coseismic region. The red- and blue-transparent shaded areas are the surface projections of the F3 and F4 in model 3, respectively. The thick red and blue lines show the upper boundaries of the F3 and F4, respectively. The orange and green rectangles show the surface projection of F1 in model 1 and F2 in model 2, respectively. The orange- and green-thick solid lines denote the upper boundary of F1 and F2, respectively. The green-dashed line indicates the intersection of F2 with the surface. (c–e) The aftershock distributions along profile A–A′, B–B′, and C–C′. The color version of this figure is available only in the electronic edition.

there are large differences between the focal mechanisms of different agencies, for example, the focal depth from the BATS is considerably shallower than that of the USGS and Global CMT.

Unlike inland faults in Taiwan for which detailed locations and geometries have been well studied and determined (Shyu *et al.*, 2016, 2020), offshore faults in the coseismic region of the 2024 earthquake are poorly constrained due to the absence of offshore observations and the complex geological structures and fault system. This poses a significant challenge to the coseismic slip inversion of this event.

In this work, we first derive the coseismic displacements from continuous Global Navigation Satellite Systems (GNSS) time series available at the Nevada Geodetic Laboratory (NGL). We then use a Bayesian inference method to estimate the fault location and geometrical parameters, including strike direction, dip angle, and rake angle. We carry out Bayesian sampling of the coseismic displacement to obtain the coseismic fault slip model by setting the fault location and geometry to the optimal fault solution from the Bayesian inference. Finally, we calculate the Coulomb stress change over active faults due to this event and assess the potential impact of this event.

GNSS Data and Method

The coseismic displacements of the 2024 Hualien earthquake are well recorded by GNSS stations across the Taiwan Island. We used the GNSS time series (5-min final solutions) processed by NGL (Blewitt *et al.*, 2018) in the International Terrestrial Reference Frame 2014 (ITRF, 2014). We chose 5-min time series rather than 24-hr final solutions because the 24-hr final solutions suffer substantial data gaps in the studied region after the 2024 mainshock, which could include significant postseismic deformation signals and introduce a large bias in coseismic displacement estimations. We remove multipath signals and diurnal variations from the 5-min time series (Text S1) following the method of Itoh *et al.* (2022, 2023). We removed outliers and estimated common mode errors (Text S2) from the time series to produce the cleaned time series for all GNSS stations (Köhne *et al.*, 2023). We fit the cleaned time series from 30 days before to 1 day after the mainshock with a least-squares method with a model combination consisting of an offset and a linear trend. The largest aftershock of M_w 6.4 occurred only 13 min after the mainshock. Given the temporal proximity, excluding the effects of the largest aftershock is not feasible when using 5-min GNSS data. Other aftershocks within 12 hr are mostly below M_w 5.0, for which contribution to surface deformation is expected to be minor. Therefore, the derived coseismic offsets from 5-min GNSS solutions used in this work represent the cumulative effects of the mainshock and one-day large aftershocks. During the Bayesian samplings, the displacements were weighted based on the uncertainties, which ensures that observations with smaller uncertainties contribute more significantly to the results. We used displacements all across Taiwan (solid-yellow triangles in Fig. 1a) except those in southern Taiwan because there are no obvious coseismic displacements. We excluded two stations, CHI0 and HOPN (Fig. 1a), because displacements at these two stations are not consistent with those at their surrounding stations and probably result from local conditions. In the end, we selected the GNSS data of 121 stations.

Because the geometry of the coseismic fault is not clear, we have employed a two-step procedure in this work. First, we search the geometrical parameters of the ruptured fault through a Bayesian method. With the obtained geometrical parameters as prior information, we then do finite-fault slip inversion through a Bayesian method. During the Bayesian sampling of the fault property, considered parameters include the strike direction, dipping and rake angles, length and width of the fault plane, as well as the fault slip. In addition, we searched for the positions of fault planes defined by the depth of the fault upper boundary (defined as fault depth hereinafter) and the position in eastern and northern directions of the center of the fault upper boundary relative to the epicenter (defined as east shift and north shift, respectively, hereinafter). Because the coseismic displacements may be explained by both east-dipping or west-dipping faults, we examined three models (Fig. 1b), that is model 1 (an east-dipping fault, F1), model 2 (a west-dipping fault, F2), and model 3 (a combination of an east-dipping F3 and a west-dipping fault F4). Models 1 and 2 were inspired by the focal mechanisms as shown in Figure 1b. Model 3 is proposed based on the complicated fault system reported by previous studies (Huang *et al.*, 2014; Lee *et al.*, 2018; Wen *et al.*, 2019; Huang and Wang, 2022) and aftershock distribution. We conducted Bayesian searches using the open-source software Bayesian earthquake analysis tool (BEAT) for geometrical parameters of faults in the three models (Heimann *et al.*, 2019; Vasyura-Bathke *et al.*, 2020). In the BEAT, a sequential Monte Carlo method is employed to do the Bayesian sampling of higher dimensional seismic problems (Vasyura-Bathke *et al.*, 2020). This method effectively samples complex distributions and avoids becoming trapped in local modes by combining importance sampling, tempering, and a large collection of the Markov chain Monte Carlo chains that run in parallel (Moral *et al.*, 2006).

We invert for coseismic slip from both horizontal and vertical coseismic GNSS displacements through a Bayesian method with the location and geometrical parameters of the fault from the maximum a posterior (MAP) solutions of the Bayesian estimations as prior information. We extend the length and width of the fault plane during the inversion to avoid potential boundary artifacts. The length and width of F1 and F2 are assumed to be 110×80 and 100×70 km, respectively. Both F1 and F2 are discretized to 5×5 km patches, resulting in 352 (22×16) and 280 (20×14) patches, respectively. For model 3, the lengths and widths of F3 and F4 are the same, with a length of 100 km and a width of 80 km. To stabilize the inversion, the patch size is increased to 10×10 km, resulting in 160 patches. Because inverse problems are often ill-posed, we apply regularization with Laplacian smoothness constraints to avoid unstable solutions. In Bayesian sampling, smoothing regularization can be implemented through a Gaussian prior, for which Cholesky decomposition is equivalent to a discrete Laplacian operator (Vasyura-Bathke *et al.*, 2020). In the BEAT, all hyperparameters, including the smoothing parameter, are jointly sampled with other model parameters. The optimal smoothing parameters are obtained from the posterior (MAP used in this work). During the inversion, we sample model space for the rake-parallel and rake-perpendicular slip of all patches of the fault planes. The corresponding standard deviations of the slips can be calculated from the posterior probability density. BEAT assumes a layered model based on the ak135 reference model for subsurface structure during the calculation of Green's functions for static displacement data (Heimann *et al.*, 2019; Vasyura-Bathke *et al.*, 2020).

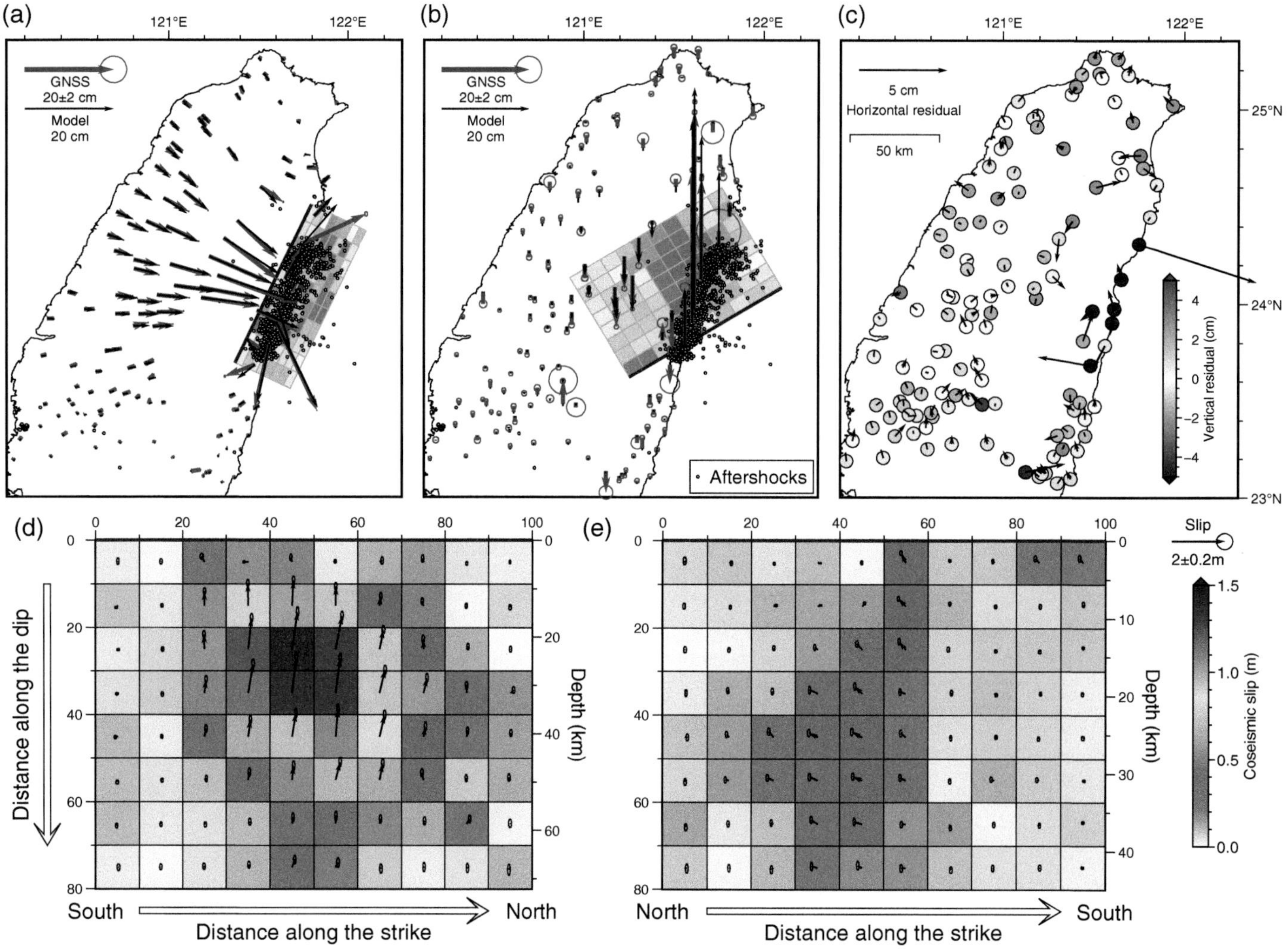

Figure 2. Bayesian sampling results of model 3 (F3 and F4). (a) Horizontal GNSS data fitting and inverted finite-fault slip of F3. The colored patches show the surface projection of F3 with the color denoting the total slip of the patches. The thick-blue line represents the upper boundary of F3. Red and black arrows represent GNSS observations and model predictions, respectively. (b) Similar to panel (a), vertical GNSS data fitting and inverted finite-fault slip of F4. The colored patches show the surface projection of F4 with the color denoting the total slip of the patches. The thick-blue line represents the upper boundary of F4. (c) Horizontal (black arrows) and vertical (colored circles) residuals between GNSS observations and model predictions. Inverted finite-fault slip of (d) F3 and (e) F4. The color of the patches shows the total slip. Black arrows represent the slip vector with one standard deviation. The thick-blue line denotes the upper boundary of the fault plane. The color version of this figure is available only in the electronic edition.

Results

Coseismic displacement

The derived coseismic displacements show overall eastward motions up to 22 cm (Fig. 2a and Fig. S1). The near-field horizontal motions are characterized by dextral strike-slip movement north of the epicenter but sinistral strike-slip motion south of the epicenter. This may be due to the complex fault system and fault interactions (Huang and Wang, 2022). The vertical displacements along the eastern coastal region (i.e., the near field) show substantial uplift, of up to about 45 cm, except for one station TUNM, that exhibits a subsidence of 9.1 cm (Fig. 2b and Fig. S2). In the far field, the vertical displacements show overall small subsidence with the magnitude decreasing with the distance to the epicenter.

Fault geometry

For models 1 and 2, the parameter space is explored by 1040 Markov chains (MCs) with 500 steps each over 16 stages, which results in 8.32 million forward evaluations. For model 3, the parameter space is explored by 2080 MCs with 500 steps each over 21 stages, which results in 21.84 million forward evaluations. The search range, the mean of the posterior distribution, and the mode of the posterior distribution (MAP) of the geometrical parameters of models 1–3 are summarized in Tables S2–S4.

The strike direction, dipping, and rake angles as well as their standard deviations of F1 from the MAP solutions are 22.7 ± 0.57°, 65.7 ± 0.67°, and 82.5 ± 0.85°, respectively (Fig. S3 and Table S2). For F2, the strike direction, dipping, and rake angles, and the corresponding standard deviations from the MAP solutions are 211.6 ± 0.88°, 25.0 ± 0.82°, and 98.3 ± 0.80°, respectively (Fig. S4 and Table S3). The steep east-dipping and gentle west-dipping fault structure are consistent with the focal mechanisms from USGS, Global CMT, and BATS, and also coincide well with the seismogenic structure revealed by the analyses of the 3D crustal velocity model and the relocated earthquake hypocenters (Huang and Wang, 2022). For both models 1 and 2, trade-offs among some parameters exist, for example, between the slip and fault depth. Despite the trade-offs, the positions, the strike directions, and the dipping and rake angles are well constrained as indicated by the small standard deviations of parameter samples, providing good prior information for subsequent finite-fault Bayesian inference.

For model 3, the strike direction, the dipping, and rake angles along with their standard deviation of F3 (F4) from the MAP solutions are 25.5 ± 0.80° (239.2 ± 2.18°), 64.4 ± 0.74° (34.1 ± 3.43°), and 82.8 ± 0.89° (148.4 ± 3.71°), respectively (Figs. S5, S6 and Table S4). The results for F3 are similar to those of F1, whereas the optimal parameters of F4 are different from those of F2. Similar to models 1 and 2, the positions, the strike directions, and the dipping and rake angles of F3 and F4 are tightly constrained to small parameter spaces quantified by relatively small standard deviations.

Coseismic fault slip

For model 1, the main slip area on F1 is determined to be at depths 10–60 km and the along-strike length is 60 km with the maximum slip of 1.79 m (Fig. S3). The slips are primarily dip slips, with minor sinistral strike slips on some patches in the main slip area, except for the shallow left section that exhibits a small dextral strike slip. This may be the consequence of a bilateral strike slip observed near the coast (e.g., Fig. 2a). The equivalent moment corresponds to an M_w 7.29 event (Table S1). The data fit of model 1 performs well in the far field in the horizontal direction. However, there are significant residuals in the horizontal direction at several GNSS stations in the near field, including HUAP, YENL, TUNM, and DNFU. In the vertical direction, data misfits are worse than those in the horizontal direction and large residuals remain at several near-field stations, such as HUAP, SCH7, HHUA3, and YENL (Figs. S7 and S8).

For model 2, the main slip area is confined between 25 and 85 km along the strike direction and about 10–25 km in depth (Fig. S4). The largest slip is 1.85 m and the estimated magnitude is M_w 7.27. There are both thrust slips and strike slips in the main slip area. Most patches in the main slip area exhibit a dextral strike-slip component. However, the slips in the north section of the fault gradually rotate clockwise toward the shallow parts, eventually evolving into a sinistral component. Similar to model 1, the data fit is more accurate in the far field than in the near field in the horizontal direction, with noticeably larger residuals observed at some near-field stations. Specifically, relatively large horizontal residuals are observed at stations HUAP, SCH7, TUNM, YENL, SLI1, and DNFU. For the vertical component, the data fit in the far field is poorer than in the horizontal direction, and there are significant residuals (up to 22 cm) at stations NAAO, HUAP, SCH7, TUNM, and DNFU in the near field (Figs. S7 and S8).

For model 3, the coseismic slip essentially concentrated on F3 with the largest slip of 1.45 m (Fig. 2). The main slip on F3 is between about 10 and 50 km in depth, with an along-strike length of 60 km. The slip on F4 is smaller with a maximum slip of 0.43 m. The estimated seismic moment is equivalent to an M_w 7.3 event. Slips on F3 are mostly thrust motion, whereas there are more strike slips on F4. Rake direction variations on F3 and F4 are less significant than those of F1 and F2.

Models 1–3 all successfully predict the first-order pattern of GNSS observations, both in the horizontal and vertical directions. The residuals in the near field are larger than those in the far field, possibly due to the simple plane geometry and coarse fault discretization used. The root mean square (rms) misfits for models 1 and 2 are 16.4 and 20.0 mm, respectively. The slip inversion result of model 3 indicates that a steep east-dipping fault may be the main structure hosting the most coseismic slip. Besides, the rms misfits of models 1 and 2 also confirm that an east-dipping fault better explains the GNSS observations. Model 1 better reproduces the clockwise rotation of coseismic displacements south of the epicenter (Fig. S3a) and the subsidence at TUNM (Fig. S3b). For model 3, the data fitting is better than that of models 1 and 2, with a smaller rms of 15.2 mm. In addition, model 3 better reproduces the coseismic displacements south of the epicenter. Among F3 and F4, the finite-fault sampling result indicates that F3 released the most energy (about 72%) of this event and accounted for the most displacements in the dip direction, whereas F4 accounted for both the strike slip and thrust components at the same time.

Discussion

For models 1–3, we perform a detailed analysis of residuals at nine near-field GNSS stations. Among these stations, the model 1 performs better than the model 2 at seven stations (NAAO, SCH7, TUNM, HUA3, SLI1, SHUL, and DNFU) in the horizontal direction (Fig. S7). For the remaining two stations (HUAP and YENL), the residuals of the model 1 are comparable with those of the model 2. When compared with model 1 and model 2, model 3 exhibits smaller horizontal residuals at eight stations (NAAO, SCH7, HUA3, TUNM, YENL, SHUL, SLI1, and DNFU). Notably, all three models fail to accurately reproduce the observed coseismic displacement at station HUAP. In the vertical direction (Fig. S8), models 1–3 demonstrate similar data-fitting performance at stations NAAO, SHUL, SLI1, and HUA3. Model 2 performs better at stations YENL and HUAP, whereas model 3 shows a lower misfit at TUNM and DNFU. Overall, the vertical data fitting for models 1–3 is comparable in the near field, making it challenging to identify a better model based only on vertical residuals. However, taking into consideration both horizontal and vertical GNSS observations, the model 3 shows generally improved performance.

In addition to data misfit, we evaluate model performance with the Akaike information criterion (AIC) and Bayesian Information Criterion (BIC). Both AIC and BIC provide a relative measure of model quality based on both the goodness of fit (prediction error) and model complexity (number of parameters), with lower values indicating better models. The AICs are calculated by

$$AIC = 2k - 2\ln(L), \tag{1}$$

in which k denotes the number of model parameters, and L represents the likelihood reflecting the model's fit to the data. The BICs are calculated by

$$BIC = k2\ln(n) - 2\ln(L), \tag{2}$$

in which n is the number of observations. Compared to AIC, BIC imposes a stronger penalty on model complexity. We calculate the AICs and BICs of models 1–3 (Table S5). The results show significant differences in AIC and BIC values among models 1–3, with model 3 achieving the lowest AIC and BIC. Given this result, model 3 demonstrates the best balance between explanatory ability and complexity. In conclusion, based on analyses of near-field residuals, AICs, and BICs of models 1–3, model 3 is our optimal model for the 2024 Hualien earthquake.

The 2024 Hualien earthquake involved an east-dipping fault (F3) and a west-dipping fault (F4) according to the preferred coseismic slip model in the previous section. Although our preferred model explains most GNSS observations, horizontal and vertical residuals at some stations are up to 7 and 13.6 cm, respectively (Figs. S7 and S8). We attribute those large residuals to the simple plane fault geometry. Moreover, coarse fault discretization of model 3 may potentially induce large near-field residuals. To investigate the impact of the discretized patch size of F3 and F4 in model 3 on the data misfitting, we performed Bayesian finite-fault inversions with uniform patch sizes ranging from 10 km × 10 km down to 6 km × 6 km. We compare the residuals and use the AICs and BICs of the models to assess which patch size is optimal among the three uniform patch sizes tested. Both AICs and BICs of the tested models demonstrate that the model with a patch size of 10 km × 10 km achieves the balance of model complexity and relatively good data fit (Table S6). Finer discretization, which increases parameter numbers, does not significantly improve the data fit when penalized for the added complexity. Nevertheless, the patch size of 10 km in this work is thus already fine enough for the data resolution.

The effect of the smoothing hyperparameter is assessed by varying (increasing or decreasing) the best-smoothing hyperparameter by 1 or 2 (Text S3). The trade-off relationship between the two-norm of inverted fault slips (model roughness) and the weighted rms (data misfit) exhibits a characteristic L-shaped curve (Figs. S9–S11). Our optimal smoothing hyperparameter is located in the corner region of the curve, which suggests that the smoothing hyperparameter used in model 3 is appropriate and the smoothing level used is reasonable.

For on-land major faults in Taiwan, their structures have been determined by the multidisciplinary Taiwan earthquake model (TEM) project, including several major faults, such as the Longitudinal Valley fault (LVF), the Central Range fault (CRF), and the Milun fault (MF) in the coseismic region of this event (Shyu *et al.*, 2016, 2020). However, for the TEM, fault geometries are available only for the onshore portion of the faults, but not for the northern segment of the CRF, which is located offshore. For the LVF and MF, only the geometry of the top portion shallower than 20 km is available, but the focal mechanism of this earthquake indicates the rupture depths of 35.5 and 32.4 km according to the USGS and Global CMT, respectively (Table S1). Extending the fault from known shallow depths to unknown greater depths can be arbitrary and potentially misleading. On the other hand, it is not clear whether the LVF and CRF were both involved in this event because there is no obvious surface rupture along these faults and the northern segment of the CRF is located offshore. Therefore, we decided to solve for our own fault geometries in models 1–3 in this work rather than directly using these fault models.

Earthquakes with multiple ruptured faults have been previously reported in this region (Huang and Huang, 2018; Lee *et al.*, 2018, 2023; Yang *et al.*, 2018). This behavior may be due to the unique tectonic settings in the study area characterized by numerous faults. Strain rates computed from GNSS data show that the Longitudinal Valley is undergoing significant contraction, whereas the region northeast of Hualien shows large extensions (Hsu *et al.*, 2009). In addition, the orientations of the extension show significant clockwise rotation north of Hualien (Hsu *et al.*, 2009; Ching *et al.*, 2011). In a geological context, the coseismic region is located in a transition zone from the collision between the EP and PSP to the northward subduction of the PSP beneath the Ryukyu trench (Ching *et al.*, 2011). This manifests as contraction along the LVF, the extension north of Hualien, and the clockwise rotation of strain-rate axes (Ching *et al.*, 2011). F3 and F4 in our preferred model have different rake directions. This suggests that F3 may accommodate the most convergence between the EP and PSP, whereas F4 may be more related to the variation of subduction of the PSP. More than 1400 aftershocks occurred near the coseismic region within one month after the earthquake according to the aftershock catalog from the Central Weather Administration Seismological Center (CWASC). Analyses of spatial positions of aftershocks and seismogenic zones on F3 and F4 show that the aftershock distribution roughly follows F3 (Figs. 2a,b, 3). Despite being

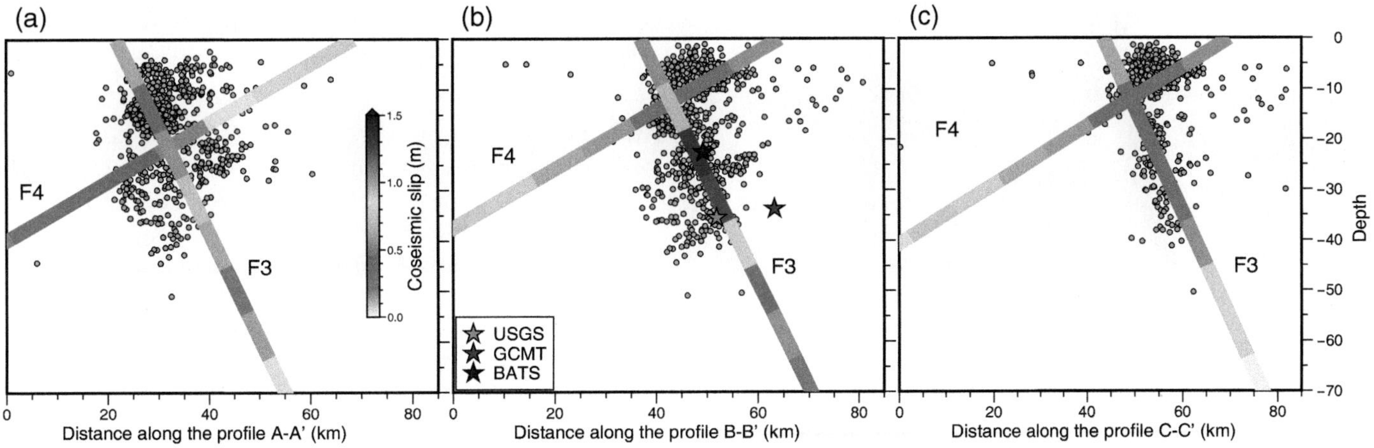

Figure 3. Cross sections of slip on F3 and F4 in model 3, as well as the aftershock distributions along (a) profile A–A′, (b) profile B–B′, and (c) profile C–C′ for which locations are shown as thick-black dashed lines in Figure 1b. Stars in panel (b) represent the hypocenter locations of the 2024 Hualien earthquake provided by U.S. Geological Survey (USGS; green), Global Centroid Moment Tensor (Global CMT; red), and Broadband Array in Taiwan for Seismology (BATS; blue). The color version of this figure is available only in the electronic edition.

oblique to the distribution of aftershocks, F4 may nevertheless correspond to those aftershocks occurring at greater distances from F3. This weak correlation between F4 and aftershocks could also be explained by the smaller slip observed on F4, which is likely to have produced fewer aftershocks. This could also be attributed to the large uncertainties of the aftershocks catalog without a relocation. Nevertheless, both the tectonic setting and the distribution of aftershocks provide additional support for the fault configuration in our preferred model (Fig. 3, Figs. S12 and S13). The intense aftershock activity in the up-dip regions of F3 and F4 (Fig. 3) suggests that afterslips may also contribute to the aftershock activity. We calculate the Coulomb stress change on major active crustal faults (Fig. 4) in this region (Okada, 1992; King *et al.*, 1994; Moore *et al.*, 2019) on the basis of model 3. The coseismic Coulomb stress increases on the LVF and MF are up to 21 and 5 bars, respectively, which makes these faults more susceptible to failure. The Coulomb stress change on the south LVF and CRF are negligible. Coulomb stress change analyses indicate that the mainshock increases the earthquake potential on the north tip of the LVF and MF.

The GNSS and Interferometric Synthetic Aperture Radar (InSAR) observations for the 2024 Hualien earthquake have previously been analyzed by Qiu *et al.* (2024). Based on the observed pattern of coseismic surface displacements, they explore the geometrical parameters of the coseismic fault that is assumed to be west dipping using a Bayesian search method. In this work, we tested both west-dipping and east-dipping fault models with the GNSS in models 1 and 2. Our results show that although all three test models provide a reasonable first-order fit to GNSS data, model 3, which includes a west-dipping fault as well as an east-dipping fault, produces the best data fit. Tang *et al.* (2024) also inverted the coseismic finite-fault slip based on both GNSS and InSAR (Sentinel-1 data) observations. In their work, they incorporate two simple coseismic models, each consisting of a single fault plane: one model with an east-dipping fault and another model with a west-dipping fault. Their results indicate that the west-dipping fault is better than the east-dipping fault because the rms misfit of the west-dipping fault (17.5 mm) is smaller than that of the east-dipping fault (32.1 mm), with a large residual reduction of 14.6 mm. However, analyses of data fitting to GNSS observations of the F1 and F2 in this work show that an east-dipping fault performs better than a west-dipping fault if the earthquake only ruptured one single fault. This may be attributed to the fact that InSAR observations usually record more short-period postseismic deformations mainly induced by rapid afterslips and poroelastic rebound. Furthermore, InSAR observations suffer from poor coherence possibly caused by the lush vegetation in this region. Based on misfit analyses, we prefer that the coseismic model (model 3) with an east-dipping fault and a west-dipping fault is better than single-fault models (models 1 and 2).

Conclusions

We obtained the geometrical parameters and coseismic slip models by inverting GNSS observations through the Bayesian method for three fault scenarios: an east-dipping fault (F1), a west-dipping fault (F2), and a combination of an east-dipping fault and a west-dipping fault (F3 and F4). Based on the data fitting, the coseismic model with F3 and F4 is our preferred model, with an average rms misfit of 15.2 mm. Among the two faults, F3 is the primary ruptured fault contributing to about 72% moment release. The maximum slip is 1.45 m on F3 and 0.43 m on F4. Coulomb stress change analyses indicate that this event makes the LVF and MF more prone to rupture and increases the seismic risk in this region.

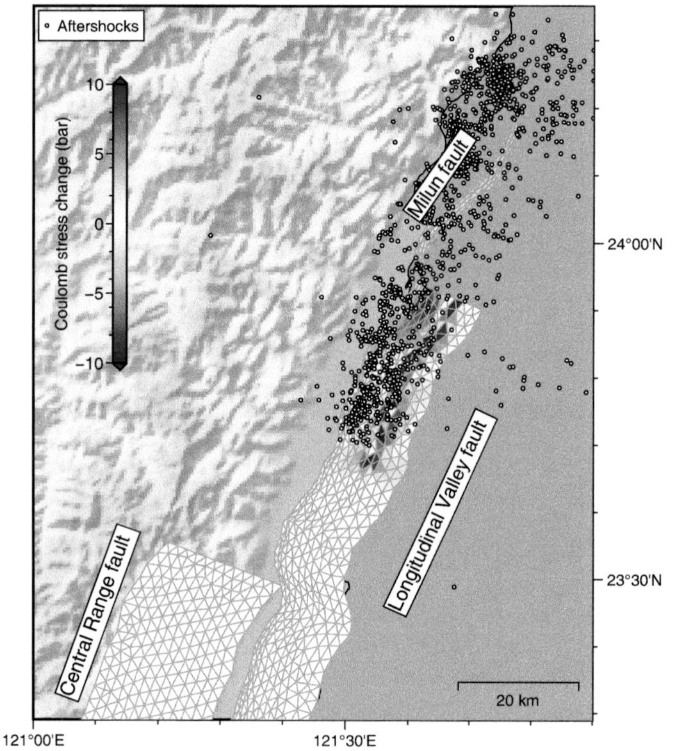

Figure 4. Coulomb stress change on the LVF, MF, and CRF calculated from model 3. The friction coefficient is assumed to be 0.4. The white circles show aftershocks from 2 April to 14 May. The color version of this figure is available only in the electronic edition.

Data and Resources

Global Navigation Satellite Systems (GNSS) time series used in this work are available at http://geodesy.unr.edu/NGLStationPages/GlobalStationList (last accessed June 2024). The aftershock catalog is obtained from the Central Weather Administration Seismological Center (CWASC) at https://scweb.cwa.gov.tw/en-us/earthquake/data (last accessed May 2024). The code for Bayesian inference is available at https://github.com/hvasbath/beat (last accessed December 2024). The supplemental material for this article includes 3 texts, 7 tables, and 13 figures to show the details of data processing, the Bayesian search results of models 1–3, the slip inversion results of models 1 and 2, the comparison of models 1–3, and the effects of regularization.

Declaration of Competing Interests

The authors acknowledge that there are no conflicts of interest recorded.

Acknowledgments

The authors would like to thank Hannes Vasyura-Bathke for the help on using Bayesian earthquake analysis tool (BEAT). The authors thank Renier Viltres and two anonymous reviewers for their comments to improve the article. This work was funded by the National Key R&D Program (2022YFF0800704) and the Strategic Priority Research Program of Chinese Academy of Sciences (XDB42020104). The numerical calculations in this article have been done on the supercomputing system in the Supercomputing Center of University of Science and Technology of China.

References

Blewitt, G., W. Hammond, and C. Kreemer (2018). Harnessing the GPS data explosion for interdisciplinary science, *Eos* **99,** doi: 10.1029/2018EO104623.

Ching, K.-E., R.-J. Rau, K. M. Johnson, J.-C. Lee, and J.-C. Hu (2011). Present-day kinematics of active mountain building in Taiwan from GPS observations during 1995–2005, *J. Geophys. Res.* **116,** no. B9, doi: 10.1029/2010JB008058.

Chung, L.-H., Y.-G. Chen, Y.-M. Wu, J. B. H. Shyu, Y.-T. Kuo, and Y.-N. N. Lin (2008). Seismogenic faults along the major suture of the plate boundary deduced by dislocation modeling of coseismic displacements of the 1951 M7.3 Hualien–Taitung earthquake sequence in eastern Taiwan, *Earth Planet. Sci. Lett.* **269,** no. 3, 416–426, doi: 10.1016/j.epsl.2008.02.035.

Hasterok, D., J. A. Halpin, A. S. Collins, M. Hand, C. Kreemer, M. G. Gard, and S. Glorie (2022). New maps of global geological provinces and tectonic plates, *Earth Sci. Rev.* **231,** 104069, doi: 10.1016/j.earscirev.2022.104069.

Heimann, S., H. Vasyura-Bathke, H. Sudhaus, M. P. Isken, M. Kriegerowski, A. Steinberg, and T. Dahm (2019). A Python framework for efficient use of pre-computed Green's functions in seismological and other physical forward and inverse source problems, *Solid Earth* **10,** no. 6, 1921–1935, doi: 10.5194/se-10-1921-2019.

Hsu, Y.-J., S.-B. Yu, M. Simons, L.-C. Kuo, and H.-Y. Chen (2009). Interseismic crustal deformation in the Taiwan plate boundary zone revealed by GPS observations, seismicity, and earthquake focal mechanisms, *Tectonophysics* **479,** no. 1, 4–18, doi: 10.1016/j.tecto.2008.11.016.

Huang, H.-H., J. B. H. Shyu, Y.-M. Wu, C.-H. Chang, and Y.-G. Chen (2012). Seismotectonics of northeastern Taiwan: Kinematics of the transition from waning collision to subduction and postcollisional extension, *J. Geophys. Res.* **117,** no. B1, doi: 10.1029/2011JB008852.

Huang, H.-H., and Y. Wang (2022). Seismogenic structure beneath the northern Longitudinal Valley revealed by the 2018–2021 Hualien earthquake sequences and 3-D velocity model, *Terr. Atmos. Ocean. Sci.* **33,** no. 1, 17, doi: 10.1007/s44195-022-00017-z.

Huang, H.-H., Y.-M. Wu, X. Song, C.-H. Chang, S.-J. Lee, T.-M. Chang, and H.-H. Hsieh (2014). Joint Vp and Vs tomography of Taiwan: Implications for subduction-collision orogeny, *Earth Planet. Sci. Lett.* **392,** 177–191, doi: 10.1016/j.epsl.2014.02.026.

Huang, M., and H. Huang (2018). The Complexity of the 2018 Mw 6.4 Hualien Earthquake in East Taiwan, *Geophys. Res. Lett.* **45,** no. 24, doi: 10.1029/2018GL080821.

Itoh, Y., Y. Aoki, and J. Fukuda (2022). Imaging evolution of Cascadia slow-slip event using high-rate GPS, *Sci. Rep.* **12,** no. 1, 7179, doi: 10.1038/s41598-022-10957-8.

Itoh, Y., A. Socquet, and M. Radiguet (2023). Largest aftershock nucleation driven by afterslip during the 2014 Iquique sequence, *Geophys. Res. Lett.* **50,** no. 24, e2023GL104852, doi: 10.1029/2023GL104852.

Jian, P.-R., and Y. Wang (2022). Applying unsupervised machine-learning algorithms and MUSIC back-projection to characterize 2018–2022 Hualien earthquake sequence, *Terr. Atmos. Ocean. Sci.* **33,** no. 1, 28, doi: 10.1007/s44195-022-00026-y.

Kao, H., S. J. Shen, and K.-F. Ma (1998). Transition from oblique subduction to collision: Earthquakes in the southernmost Ryukyu arc-Taiwan region, *J. Geophys. Res.* **103,** no. B4, 7211–7229, doi: 10.1029/97JB03510.

King, G. C. P., R. S. Stein, and J. Lin (1994). Static stress changes and the triggering of earthquakes, *Bull. Seismol. Soc. Am.* **84,** no. 3, 935–953.

KYODO NEWS (2024). Taiwan quake injured toll rises to 1,100 with 15 missing, 10 dead, available at https://english.kyodonews.net/news/2024/04/c5a7af48577c-taiwan-quake-injured-toll-rises-to-1050-with-30-missing-9-dead.html (last accessed December 2024).

Köhne, T., B. Riel, and M. Simons (2023). Decomposition and inference of sources through spatiotemporal analysis of network signals: The DISSTANS python package, *Comput. Geosci.* **170,** 105247, doi: 10.1016/j.cageo.2022.105247.

Lee, S., T. Lin, T. Liu, and T. Wong (2018). Fault-to-fault jumping rupture of the 2018 Mw 6.4 Hualien earthquake in Eastern Taiwan, *Seismol. Res. Lett.* **90,** no. 1, 30–39, doi: 10.1785/0220180182.

Lee, S.-J., T.-Y. Liu, and T.-C. Lin (2023). The role of the west-dipping collision boundary fault in the Taiwan 2022 Chihshang earthquake sequence, *Sci. Rep.* **13**, no. 1, 3552, doi: 10.1038/s41598-023-30361-0.

Moore, J. D. P., S. Barbot, L. Feng, Y. Hang, V. Lambert, E. Lindsey, T. Matsuzawa, J. Muto, P. Nanjundiah, R. Salman, *et al.* (2019). jdpmoore/unicycle: Unicycle, *Zenodo*, doi: 10.5281/zenodo.5688288.

Moral, P. D., A. Doucet, and A. Jasra (2006). Sequential Monte Carlo samplers, *J. Roy. Stat. Soc. Ser. B Stat. Methodol.* **68,** no. 3, 411–436, doi: 10.1111/j.1467-9868.2006.00553.x.

Okada, Y. (1992). Internal deformation due to shear and tensile faults in a half-space, *Bull. Seismol. Soc. Am.* **82,** no. 2, 1018–1040, doi: 10.1785/BSSA0820021018.

Qiu, J., L. Ji, L. Zhu, Y. Li, C. Liu, and Q. Zhao (2024). Coseismic deformation and seismogenic structure of the 2024 Hualien Earthquake measured by InSAR and GNSS, *Earthq. Res. Adv.* 100328, doi: 10.1016/j.eqrea.2024.100328.

Shyu, J. B. H., Y.-R. Chuang, Y.-L. Chen, Y.-R. Lee, and C.-T. Cheng (2016). A new on-land seismogenic structure source database from the Taiwan earthquake model (TEM) project for seismic hazard analysis of Taiwan, *Terr. Atmos. Ocean. Sci.* **27,** no. 3, 311, doi: 10.3319/TAO.2015.11.27.02(TEM).

Shyu, J. B. H., L.-H. Chung, Y.-G. Chen, J.-C. Lee, and K. Sieh (2007). Re-evaluation of the surface ruptures of the November 1951 earthquake series in eastern Taiwan, and its neotectonic implications, *J. Asian Earth Sci.* **31,** no. 3, 317–331, doi: 10.1016/j.jseaes.2006.07.018.

Shyu, J. B. H., K. Sieh, Y.-G. Chen, and C.-S. Liu (2005). Neotectonic architecture of Taiwan and its implications for future large earthquakes, *J. Geophys. Res.* **110,** no. B8, doi: 10.1029/2004JB003251.

Shyu, J. B. H., Y.-H. Yin, C.-H. Chen, Y.-R. Chuang, and S.-C. Liu (2020). Updates to the on-land seismogenic structure source database by the Taiwan Earthquake Model (TEM) project for seismic hazard analysis of Taiwan, *Terr. Atmos. Ocean. Sci.* **31,** no. 4, 469–478, doi: 10.3319/TAO.2020.06.08.01.

Tang, X., R. Guo, L. Li, Y. Xu, J. Xu, Y. Zheng, and H. Sun (2024). Earthquake interactions in Eastern Taiwan: Insight from the 2024 Mw 7.3 Hualien Earthquake, *Seismol. Res. Lett.* doi: 10.1785/0220240230.

Thomas, M. Y., J.-P. Avouac, J. Champenois, J.-C. Lee, and L.-C. Kuo (2014). Spatiotemporal evolution of seismic and aseismic slip on the Longitudinal Valley Fault, Taiwan, *J. Geophys. Res.* **119,** no. 6, 5114–5139, doi: 10.1002/2013JB010603.

Vasyura-Bathke, H., J. Dettmer, A. Steinberg, S. Heimann, M. P. Isken, O. Zielke, P. M. Mai, H. Sudhaus, and S. Jónsson (2020). The Bayesian earthquake analysis tool, *Seismol. Res. Lett.* **91,** no. 2A, 1003–1018, doi: 10.1785/0220190075.

Wen, S., Y.-Y. Wen, K.-E. Ching, Y.-L. Yeh, and Y.-H. Lee (2019). Tectonic implications on the 2018 Hualien earthquake, *Terr. Atmos. Ocean. Sci.* **30,** no. 3, 389–398, doi: 10.3319/TAO.2019.01.28.01.

Yang, Y.-H., J.-C. Hu, H. Tung, M.-C. Tsai, Q. Chen, Q. Xu, Y.-J. Zhang, J.-J. Zhao, G.-X. Liu, J.-N. Xiong, *et al.* (2018). Co-seismic and postseismic fault models of the 2018 Mw 6.4 Hualien earthquake occurred in the junction of collision and subduction boundaries offshore Eastern Taiwan, *Remote Sens.* **10,** no. 9, 1372.

Manuscript received 8 January 2025
Published online 30 September 2025

Coseismic Deformation and Slip Distribution of the 2024 M_w 7.0 Wushi, Xinjiang, Earthquake from High-Rate GNSS

Zhicai Li*[1], Zhi Chen[1], Xiaodong Huang[2], Junli Wu[3], and Kaihua Ding[4]

Abstract

On 23 January 2024, at 02:09:05 a.m. Beijing time, a magnitude M_w 7.0 earthquake struck Wushi County in Aksu Prefecture, Xinjiang. This study utilized high-frequency (1 Hz) observation data from six Global Navigation Satellite System (GNSS) stations near the epicenter to investigate its coseismic deformation. The data were processed using Pride PPP-AR 3.0 software, revealing maximum coseismic displacements (east: 10.3 mm, north: 55.7 mm, and up: −5.5 mm) represent component-specific extremes observed across the network, with each maximum originating from distinct stations. To extract more precise coseismic signals, we decomposed the high-rate GNSS time series using the complete ensemble empirical mode decomposition with adaptive noise method, and combined wavelet threshold denoising and multiscale permutation entropy (MPE) techniques to effectively remove static offsets, nonlinear trends, and low-frequency noise from the original time series. The resulting reconstruction significantly improved the precision and accuracy of coseismic deformation extraction, demonstrating that this approach presents a novel methodology for high-rate GNSS seismic analysis. Using the 1 Hz GNSS coseismic displacements as constraints, we applied the particle swarm optimization algorithm with the Okada model to invert fault geometry parameters. The results indicate that the fault responsible for the Wushi earthquake has a strike of 238°, a dip of 53°, and a rake of 20°. We further integrated the inverted fault geometry with GNSS observed surface deformation data to perform a distributed fault-slip inversion using the steepest descent method. The inversion results show that the coseismic rupture was confined to depths of less than 23 km, with no surface rupture observed. The maximum slip of 1.1 m occurred at a depth of 11 km, ~18 km northeast of the mainshock. The energy released is consistent with a moment magnitude of M_w 7.0, corroborating findings from seismological analyses.

Cite this article as Li, Z., Z. Chen, X. Huang, J. Wu, and K. Ding (2025). Coseismic Deformation and Slip Distribution of the 2024 M_w 7.0 Wushi, Xinjiang, Earthquake from High-Rate GNSS, *Seismol. Res. Lett.* **97**, 986–997, doi: 10.1785/0220250048.

Introduction

On 23 January 2024, at 02:09:05 a.m. Beijing time, a magnitude 7.0 earthquake, referred to as the Wushi earthquake, struck Wushi County in Aksu Prefecture, Xinjiang Province, China. The earthquake's hypocenter was located at 41.26° N latitude and 78.63° E longitude, with a depth of 22 km. The epicenter is located in a high-altitude region, which is sparsely populated, with no densely inhabited areas within a 20 km radius. Despite the earthquake's high magnitude and strong shaking intensity, it fortunately caused minimal casualties and property damage because the area lacks densely populated regions. The epicenter was ~6 km from the Maidan fault, situated within the tectonically active Tianshan seismic belt (Wu *et al.*, 2014; Zhang, Qian, *et al.*, 2024).

Shortly after the event, several research groups conducted detailed analyses of its focal mechanism. The U.S. Geological Survey (USGS) derived source parameters from seismic wave data, identifying strikes of 236° and 110°, dips of 48° and 57°, and rakes of 47° and 127°. Guo Xiangyun's team, using regional waveform data, determined the earthquake was primarily a thrust event, providing focal mechanism solutions with strikes of 241° and 127°, dips of 63° and 51°, and rakes of 45° and 144° (see Data and Resources). Zhang, Fang, *et al.* (2024), analyzing far-field body-wave data, characterized the Wushi earthquake as a thrust

1. School of Geoscience and Surveying Engineering, China University of Mining and Technology-Beijing, Beijing, China; 2. Xinjiang Uyghur Autonomous Region Academy of Surveying and Mapping, Urumqi, China; 3. Geodesy Department, National Geomatics Center of China, Beijing, China; 4. School of Geography and Information Engineering, China University of Geosciences, Wuhan, China, https://orcid.org/0000-0002-4383-2654 (KD)

*Corresponding author: zcli@cumtb.edu.cn

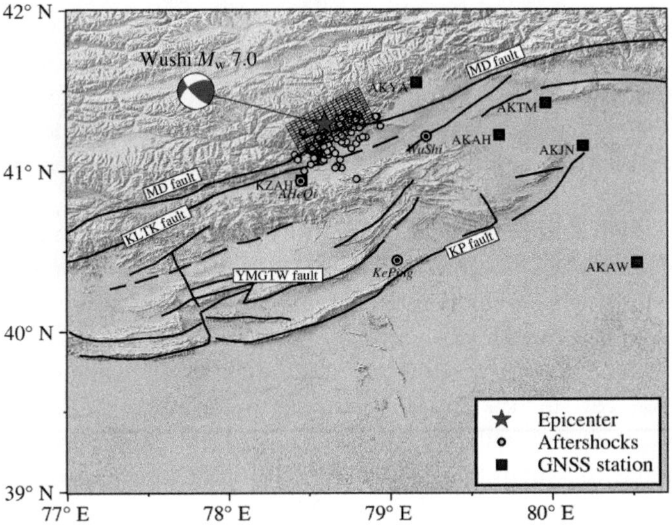

Figure 1. Regional geological background and distribution of Global Navigation Satellite System (GNSS) stations. The light-blue circles represent aftershocks with a magnitude of 3.0 or higher following this earthquake. The blue rectangles are the high-frequency continuous GNSS observation stations used in this study. The red star marks the location of the mainshock of the Wushi earthquake. The black grid indicates the fault range for the subsequent distributed slip inversion. The black dots indicate the county. KLTK, fault-KaLaTieKe fault; KP, fault-KePing fault; MD, fault-MaiDan fault; YMGTW, fault-YiMuGanTaWu fault. The color version of this figure is available only in the electronic edition.

event with a minor strike-slip component. Their findings indicated a rupture process lasting less than 20 s, with a rupture length of ~25–30 km, potentially reaching the surface. The moment magnitude (M_w) was estimated at 7.0, with a centroid depth of 20 km. Inversion of centroid moment tensor data yielded fault parameters of strikes 250° and 109°, dips 42° and 55°, and rakes 59° and 115°. As of 7 February 2024, at 05:00 p.m., the China Earthquake Data Center recorded 183 aftershocks, including 175 with magnitudes between 3.0 and 4.9 and 8 of magnitude 5.0, with the strongest event of M_w 5.7 (see Data and Resources). These aftershocks were predominantly distributed in a northeast-eastward direction (Fig. 1). Although the Tianshan seismic belt is a region of high seismic activity in China, the Maidan Fault itself exhibits relatively low activity (Wang *et al.*, 2022). The Wushi earthquake is the first recorded event of magnitude 7.0 along this fault, making a detailed investigation into the fault's geometry and slip distribution critical for understanding the tectonic dynamics of the Tianshan seismic belt (Nai *et al.*, 2024).

Advances in Global Navigation Satellite System (GNSS) technology have greatly enhanced geodetic seismology, particularly in detecting coseismic deformation and analyzing earthquake source mechanisms (Shan *et al.*, 2019; Wen *et al.*, 2019; Ding *et al.*, 2022; Li *et al.*, 2022, 2024; Zang *et al.*, 2022; Yuan *et al.*, 2023; Meng *et al.*, 2024; Ren *et al.*, 2024). High-rate GNSS stations can capture both instantaneous and permanent coseismic deformations in real time (Xu *et al.*, 2013; Michel *et al.*, 2017; Hohensinn *et al.*, 2020; Dittmann *et al.*, 2022), facilitating rapid determination of earthquake source parameters. For instance, following the 2021 Maduo earthquake, Li *et al.* (2021) combined near-field high-frequency and far-field low-frequency GNSS data to derive the coseismic deformation field and invert fault parameters using an elastic dislocation model. Similarly, Wu *et al.* (2023) used high-rate GNSS data to analyze the coseismic deformation of the 2022 Luding earthquake, revealing its kinematics and performing an inversion of its fault rupture mode and stress changes. Zhang, Ji, *et al.* (2024) applied the Helmert similarity transformation model to unify velocity fields from different studies, combining GNSS and Interferometric Synthetic Aperture Radar (InSAR) data to create a 3D deformation field for the Jishishan earthquake. The Wushi earthquake occurred in a high-altitude, sparsely populated region with limited GNSS infrastructure. Because of the lack of extensive GNSS coverage, only high-rate (1 Hz) GNSS data from six stations within 200 km of the epicenter were available for this study—five stations to the east and one to the west of the epicenter (Fig. 1). These data were managed by the local surveying and mapping authorities and are not publicly accessible. Despite these data limitations, this study provides a detailed analysis of the coseismic deformation field, including the fault geometry and slip distribution of the causative fault. The challenges posed by the sparse station distribution and limited data coverage are addressed through advanced inversion techniques, making this study one of the first to analyze the Wushi earthquake's coseismic slip in such a data-constrained environment. This analysis offers valuable insights into the earthquake's source mechanism and contributes to a deeper understanding of the tectonic processes in the Tianshan seismic belt.

Geological Background Associated with the Wushi Earthquake

The Tianshan seismic belt, located in central Asia, lies between the Pamir plateau and the Tarim basin to the south, and the Kazakhstan platform and Junggar basin to the north. Since the Cenozoic era, this region has experienced sustained and intense tectonic collision between the Indian plate and the Eurasian plate. This collision has transformed the Tianshan seismic belt into one of the largest intracontinental orogenic belts on the Eurasian continent. Defined by pronounced north–south compressive deformation, it is one of the most seismically active regions in China (Molnar and Tapponnier, 1975; Molnar and Stock, 2009).

The primary fault responsible for the Wushi earthquake is the Maidan fault (Fig. 1), a complex fault system composed of a network of subsidiary faults. Extending ~400 km in length and 15–17 km in width, the fault trends northeast and dips west-northwest, with dip angles ranging from 30° to 80° (Jia *et al.*, 2015). Although the Maidan fault itself exhibits low instrumental seismicity (no $M_w \geq 6.0$ events directly on the fault trace since 1716 C.E.) detailed measurements and chronological studies by Wu (2017) have identified the Maidan fault as an active Holocene fault, predominantly characterized by thrust motion with a minor left-lateral strike-slip component. The thrust slip rate has been estimated at 1.24 ± 0.20 mm/yr, whereas the left-lateral strike-slip rate is 1.74 ± 0.61 mm/yr. Notably, four $M_w \geq 8.0$ megathrust earthquakes have occurred within 300 km of the fault since 1716 (China Earthquake Administration, 2022), suggesting strain transfer capability to adjacent. Yang *et al.* (2008) used Global Positioning System data collected from 400 stations across the Tianshan region between 1992 and 2006 to calculate movement rates along major active faults. Their findings revealed slip rates of 10–13 mm/yr along the primary detachment fault on the southwestern Tianshan front. Similarly, Zhu *et al.* (2021) utilized GNSS data from 1999 to 2015 to assess slip rates and seismic moment deficits in the Tianshan seismic belt and adjacent areas. They reported a shortening rate of −6.3 ± 1.9 mm/yr for the Maidan fault, highlighting a significant seismic moment deficit and the potential for generating earthquakes of magnitude 7.0 or greater.

Data and Methods

GNSS data processing

This study employed the Pride PPP-AR 3.0 software, developed by Wuhan University, to dynamically process the 1 Hz high-rate GNSS data (Geng *et al.*, 2019). The software is based on precise point positioning with ambiguity resolution (PPP-AR) technology, enabling real-time acquisition of single-epoch solutions for high-frequency data sets. The processing methodology integrates precise orbit products, ionospheric corrections, pseudorange bias corrections, and various ancillary files, including receiver and satellite phase center models, provided by Wuhan University. To optimize processing efficiency, an undifferenced and uncombined solution strategy was adopted. In addition, a satellite elevation cutoff angle of 15° was applied to minimize the impact of multipath effects, ensuring both the reliability and precision of the processed GNSS data.

Decomposition and MPE method

To address challenges such as low signal-to-noise ratios (SNRs), nonstationarity in high-rate GNSS coseismic displacements, and limitations in accuracy, adaptability, and error susceptibility in extracting coseismic deformation, this study investigated the use of modal decomposition methods for signal detection and extraction. The objective is to improve the precision and stability of coseismic information derived from high-rate GNSS data. Modal decomposition methods are particularly effective for adaptively analyzing and decomposing nonstationary and nonlinear signals, making them well suited for identifying and extracting coseismic signals. These methods have been successfully applied in various geophysical processes, such as extracting coseismic signals from well-water level observations (Sun *et al.*, 2018) and isolating gravity tide signals (Yu *et al.*, 2019). Given that high-rate GNSS data similarly exhibit nonstationary and nonlinear characteristics, modal decomposition is an appropriate approach for isolating high-frequency seismic signals.

This study employs the complete ensemble empirical mode decomposition with adaptive noise (CEEMDAN) method to evaluate its feasibility for detecting high-frequency coseismic signals. Originally proposed by Torres (Torres *et al.*, 2011), CEEMDAN was developed to address the mode mixing issues inherent in the empirical mode decomposition (EMD) method. By combining the strengths of ensemble empirical mode decomposition (EEMD) and complementary ensemble empirical mode decomposition (CEEMD), CEEMDAN effectively resolves the residual white noise problem. CEEMDAN addresses these challenges through two key innovations: (1) instead of directly adding Gaussian white noise to the original signal, it introduces auxiliary noise to the intrinsic mode function (IMF) components after EMD decomposition. (2) Upon extracting the first IMF component, CEEMDAN calculates the overall mean immediately to finalize the IMF1 component. This process is repeated iteratively for the subsequent components. Unlike EEMD and CEEMD, which average all modes after EMD processing, CEEMDAN reduces the transfer of white noise from high to low frequencies, enhancing signal clarity (Liang and Gao, 2023). Xu *et al.* (2023) applied CEEMDAN to denoise 1 Hz GNSS data for slope deformation monitoring. Their results demonstrated that CEEMDAN outperformed EMD in terms of correlation coefficients, SNRs, root mean square errors (rmse), and overall denoising performance, making it a superior method for processing high-rate GNSS signals.

In this study, the coseismic displacement time series of the Wushi earthquake in Xinjiang is analyzed using the CEEMDAN method for signal decomposition. The method was implemented with the following parameter settings: a noise coefficient of 0.2, 500 noise realizations, and a maximum of 5000 iterations. After decomposing the signal, the multiscale permutation entropy (MPE) method was applied to classify the decomposed IMF components into different frequency bands, following the approach of Ma and Wang (2020). Based on MPE values, the IMF components were categorized into two groups: those with MPE values greater than 0.6 were identified as high-frequency components, whereas those with MPE values less than 0.6 were categorized as low-frequency components. The threshold of MPE = 0.6 was chosen based on empirical analysis of GNSS data characteristics, where MPE values greater than 0.6 typically correspond to noiselike behavior, whereas values less than 0.6 are usually associated with more stable, low-frequency signals linked to coseismic deformation. Although there is no theoretical justification for this threshold, it has proven effective in distinguishing between high-frequency and low-frequency

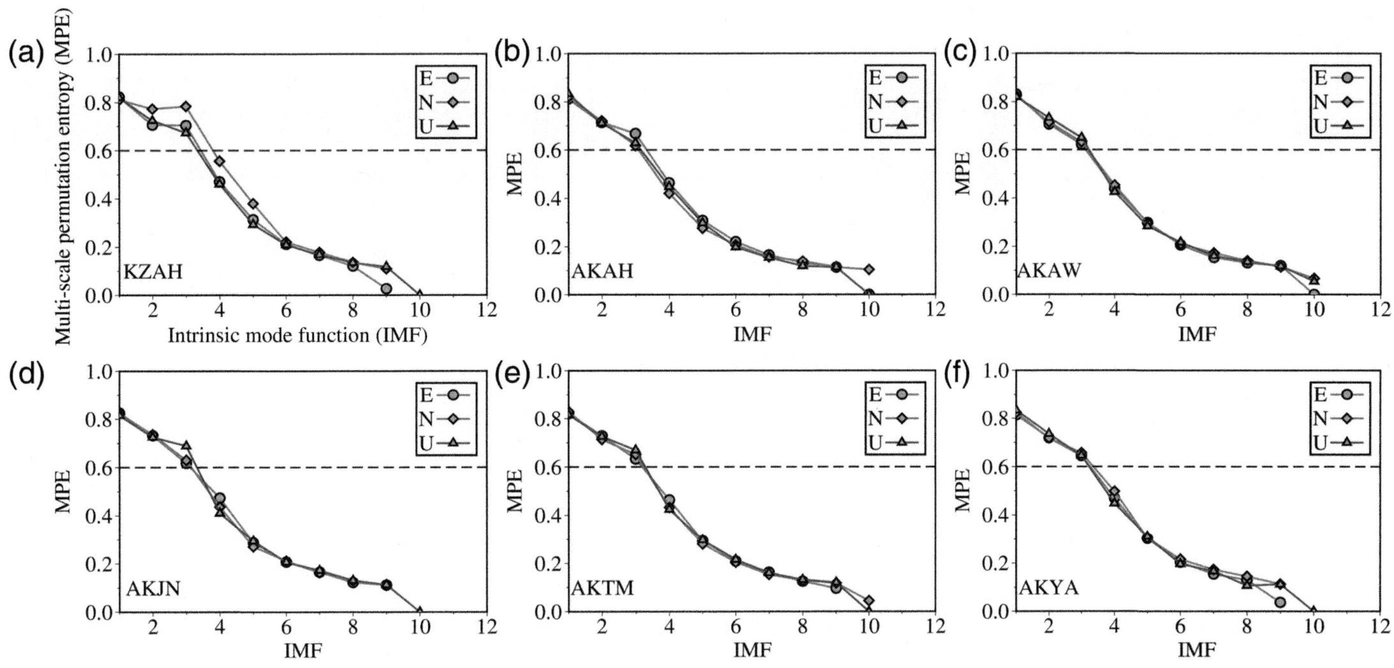

components in our analysis. We will further clarify this choice in the article, providing a more detailed explanation of the rationale behind using this threshold (Fig. 2).

Figure 2. (a–f) Multiscale permutation entropy (MPE) of the intrinsic mode function (IMF) components at the station. E, east; N, north; U, up. The color version of this figure is available only in the electronic edition.

Fault parameter and fault-slip distribution inversion method

Based on the GNSS-derived surface coseismic displacements, we performed a nonlinear inversion to determine the seismogenic fault parameters for the Wushi earthquake with the particle swarm optimization (PSO) algorithm, introduced by Kerdphol *et al.* (2016). PSO algorithm is a stochastic optimization method inspired by the social behaviors of birds flocking or fish schooling. It is particularly useful for solving complex, nonlinear, and high-dimensional optimization problems. In PSO, a swarm of particles, each representing a potential solution, moves through the solution space by adjusting its position and velocity based on two key factors: the particle's own best position (personal best, **pbest**) and the best position found by the entire swarm (global best, **gbest**). The velocity update rule is given by

$$\mathbf{v}_i(t+1) = w\mathbf{v}_i(t) + c_1 r_1(\mathbf{pbest}_i - \mathbf{x}_i(t)) + c_2 r_2(\mathbf{gbest} - \mathbf{x}_i(t)),$$

in which ω is the inertia weight, and c_1, c_2 are acceleration coefficients. Each particle adjusts its position according to its velocity, and the process is iterated to minimize an objective function, typically the misfit between observed and theoretical displacements in the case of fault parameter inversion. PSO's advantage lies in its ability to avoid local minima by balancing exploration and exploitation, making it suitable for nonlinear seismic inversion problems in which traditional methods may fail. The algorithm converges efficiently to an optimal solution, providing accurate fault parameters, such as fault strike, dip, depth, and slip distribution, from GNSS-derived surface displacements.

Using the GNSS-derived coseismic deformation field and the fault geometric parameters, specifically a strike of 238° and a dip of 54°, obtained in this study, we constructed a simplified fault geometry model. The fault-plane dimensions were set at 45 km along the strike and 30 km along the dip, and the plane was discretized into a uniform grid with 3 km by 3 km. To determine the fault's slip distribution, we employed the steepest descent method program, with a slip angle search range for each subfault spanning from −180° to 180°. The Green's functions were calculated using an elastic half-space homogeneous medium dislocation model, based on the foundational works of Wang, Diao, and Hoechner (2013), Okada (1985, 1992), and further developed by Wang, Parolai, *et al.* (2013). The inversion process followed the least-squares criterion and utilized the steepest descent algorithm, as outlined by Wang, Parolai, *et al.* (2013).

Results and Analysis

GNSS coseismic time series and coseismic deformation field

Using the described processing strategy, dynamic precise point positioning (PPP) analysis was performed on GNSS observations from six stations located within 200 km of the earthquake epicenter. Figure 3 presents the east, north, and vertical displacement components at each station, covering 100 epochs before and 200 epochs after the earthquake. The time series reveals distinct coseismic signals triggered by the arrival of seismic wavefronts at the stations. The KZAH station, located

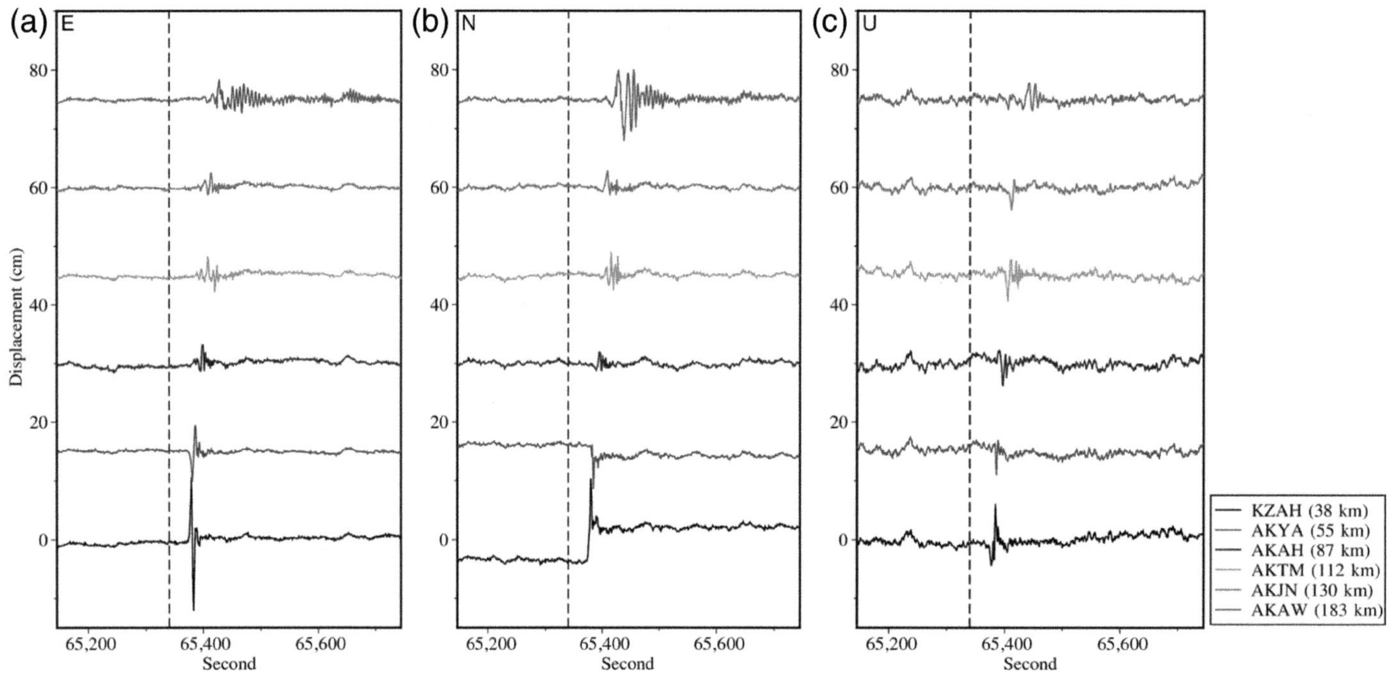

Figure 3. (a–c) Displacement time series during the period from 18:07:20 to 18:12:20 (UTC) on 22 January 2024. The color version of this figure is available only in the electronic edition.

38 km from the epicenter, was the first to detect the seismic signal and recorded the largest horizontal displacements, with instantaneous deformations of ~110 mm eastward, 140 mm northward, and 50 mm vertical. The AKYA station, situated 55 km from the epicenter, experienced instantaneous deformations of about 50 mm in the east, north, and vertical directions. Other stations recorded varying degrees of seismic deformation. Postearthquake stabilization showed significant permanent deformations at the KZAH, AKYA, and AKAH stations. In contrast, most stations farther from the epicenter largely returned to their original positions, exhibiting no significant permanent deformations. As shown in Figure 3, the earthquake caused notable coseismic deformation in both horizontal and vertical dimensions. Considering the regional geological context, this event is inferred to have been caused by thrust faulting, consistent with previous studies (Nai *et al.*, 2024).

Given the pronounced fluctuations in the high-rate GNSS time series induced by the Wushi earthquake, this study adopts a methodology similar to that employed by Li *et al.* (2021) for extracting coseismic displacements following the 2021 Maduo earthquake. To minimize the influence of dynamic seismic wave arrivals, data exhibiting strong transient motions were excluded. Instead, the analysis focused on a window of 100 epochs before and after the earthquake origin time. For each station, mean positions were computed within these pre- and postevent intervals, and the coseismic displacements were obtained by differencing the postearthquake and pre-earthquake means. Table 1 summarizes the calculated coseismic displacements and their associated uncertainties, which were estimated using the error propagation method outlined by Tan *et al.* (2023). Significant permanent displacements were observed at the KZAH, AKYA, and AKAH stations. Specifically, KZAH recorded displacements of ~8.53 mm eastward, 55.77 mm northward, and 3.76 mm vertically. At AKYA, displacements of −1.93 mm (east), −18.24 mm (north), and −5.49 mm (vertical) were observed, and AKAH registered displacements of 10.27 mm (east), −5.68 mm (north), and −2.99 mm (vertical). The remaining stations exhibited comparatively smaller displacements. As shown in Table 1, the uncertainties in horizontal components are generally less than 3 mm, indicating a high SNR for horizontal measurements. In contrast, vertical uncertainties are predominantly greater than 3 mm, reflecting the lower precision of vertical GNSS positioning and the relatively higher noise in the vertical time series. A joint interpretation of Table 1 and Figure 4 indicates that the amplitude of coseismic displacement decreases with increasing distance from the epicenter. Figure 4a shows that stations located north and south of the epicenter exhibit approximately symmetric horizontal motions perpendicular to the fault trace, consistent with thrust-dominated deformation. In contrast, stations east of the epicenter display northwestward displacement vectors, implying a minor left-lateral component. Figure 4b further reveals uplift on the hanging wall and subsidence on the footwall, providing additional support for a predominantly thrust-faulting mechanism. The western segment of the rupture zone exhibits primarily dip-slip motion, and the eastern segment transitions to oblique slip, involving both thrust and strike-slip components. However, due to the absence of stations directly north of the epicenter, some uncertainty remains in resolving the full displacement field. Based on the observed fault-

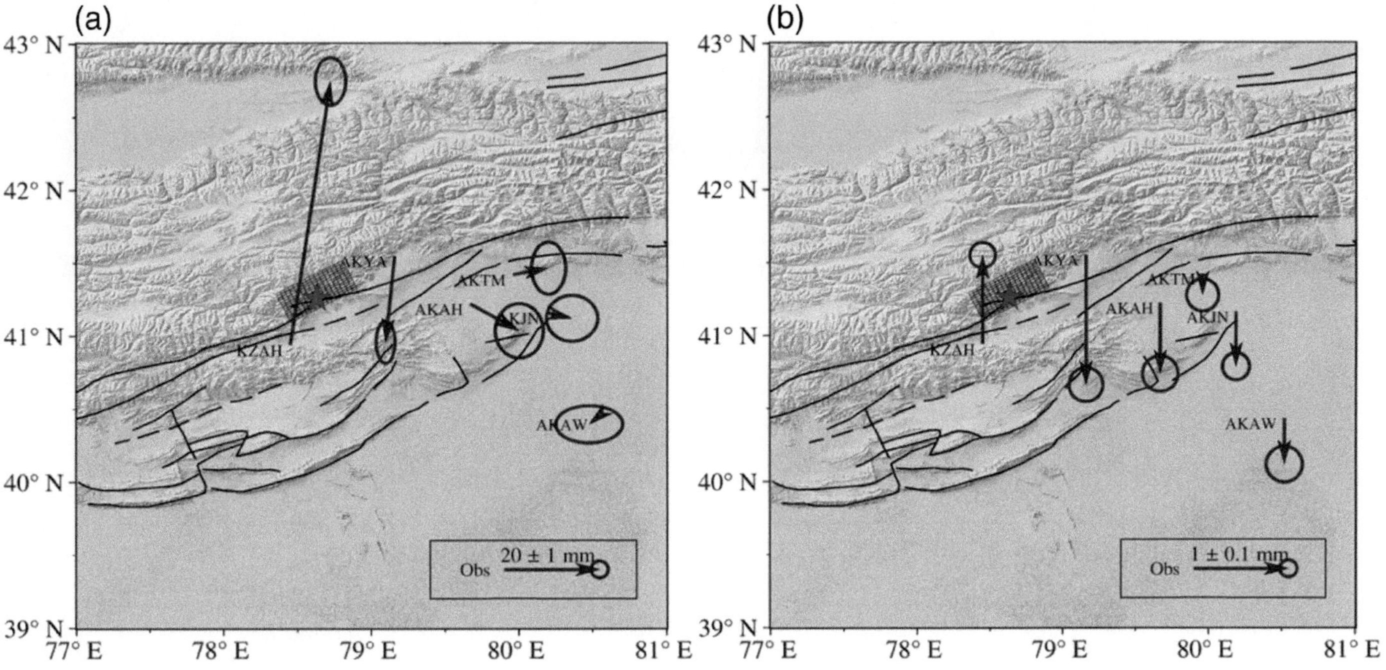

Figure 4. Horizontal (a) and vertical (b) GNSS-derived coseismic deformation field. The blue arrows represent the magnitude and direction of coseismic deformation, and the red star represents the epicenter. The error ellipses represent 80% confidence. The color version of this figure is available only in the electronic edition.

perpendicular horizontal displacements and widespread vertical offsets, the Wushi earthquake is interpreted as a thrust-dominated event with localized left-lateral slip concentrated in its eastern sector.

Modal decomposition and signal reconstruction

Because of space constraints, this study focuses on the north (N) component time series from the AKAH station as a representative example, as shown in Figure 5. The first to ninth time series correspond to the intrinsic mode function (IMF) components, and the tenth represents the residual component. Because the decomposition progressed, the signals became progressively smoother, with decreasing frequencies. Among these components, IMF1 to IMF3 were identified as high-frequency components. Notably, IMF2 exhibited the highest resolution in capturing the instantaneous seismic changes, with minimal noise interference. In contrast, IMF1 demonstrated a lower resolution for earthquake-induced displacements and a higher noise level, and IMF3 showed the lowest resolution for capturing such changes. The majority of information related to the instantaneous changes induced by the earthquake was contained in IMF1 and IMF2, with IMF3 contributing only a limited amount of useful data. Consequently, IMF1 through IMF3 were retained for further analysis. Beyond IMF4, the resolution of high-frequency oscillations was significantly diminished. IMF5 through IMF7 exhibited periodic variations, and IMF8, IMF9, and the residual

TABLE 1
Coseismic Deformation at the High-Rate Global Navigation Satellite System (GNSS) Stations

Station	Longitude (°)	Latitude (°)	E (mm)	N (mm)	U (mm)	Se (mm)	Sn (mm)	Su (mm)
AKAH	79.67	41.22	10.27	−5.68	−2.99	2.8	2.6	2.1
AKTM	79.96	41.42	7.48	1.41	−0.90	2.0	3.0	2.9
AKYA	79.16	41.55	−1.93	−18.24	−5.49	1.1	2.5	3.0
KZAH	78.45	40.94	8.53	55.77	3.76	1.5	2.8	1.8
AKAW	80.52	40.43	−1.28	−1.09	−1.95	2.9	2.2	3.1
AKJN	80.19	41.16	5.27	−1.21	−2.31	3.0	2.7	3.6

Se, Sn, and Su represent the standard errors of the east, north, and up components, respectively. E, east; N, north; U, up.

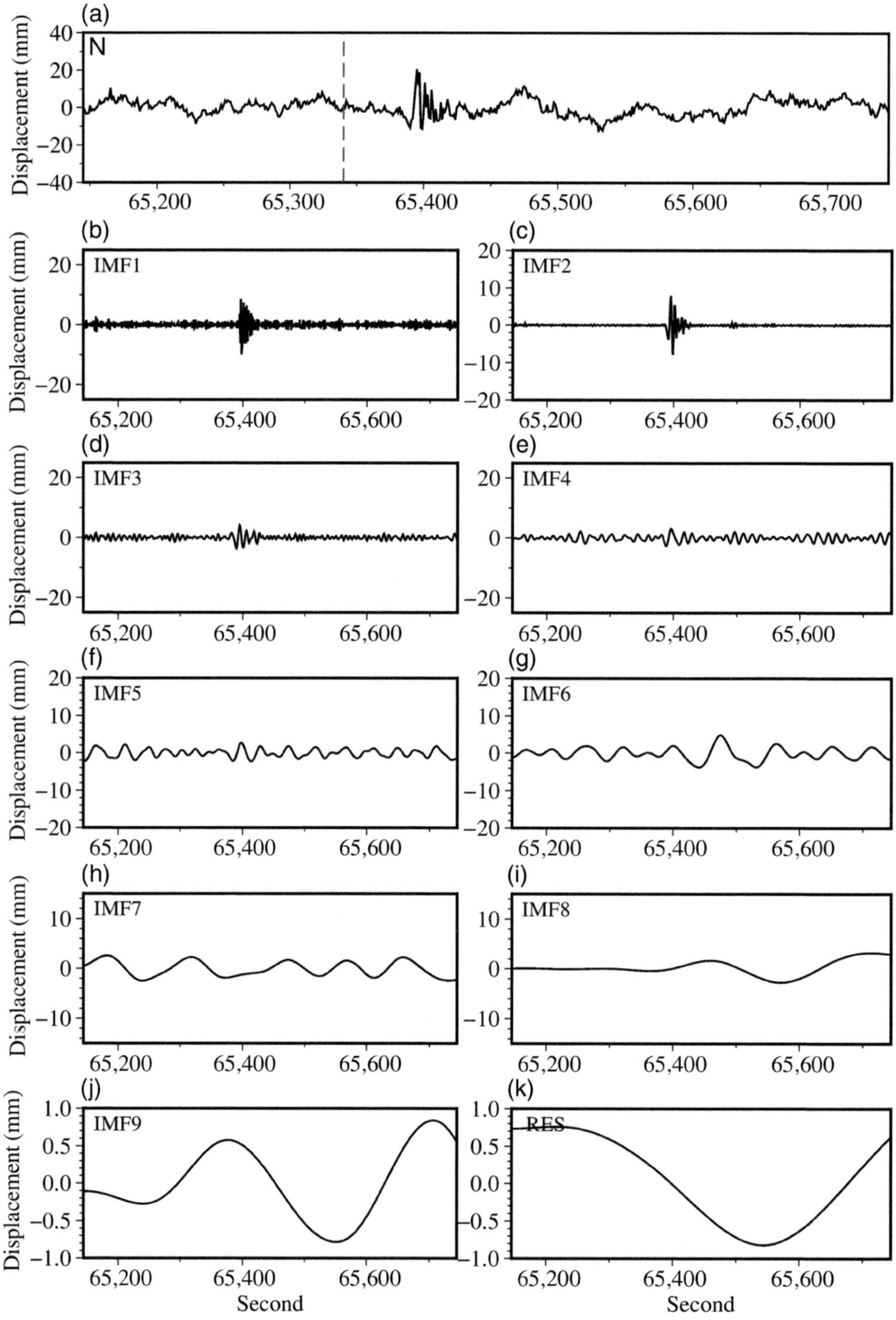

Figure 5. (a–k) Complete ensemble empirical mode decomposition with adaptive noise (CEEMDAN) decomposition results at AKYA station in the N direction during the Wushi earthquake. The color version of this figure is available only in the electronic edition.

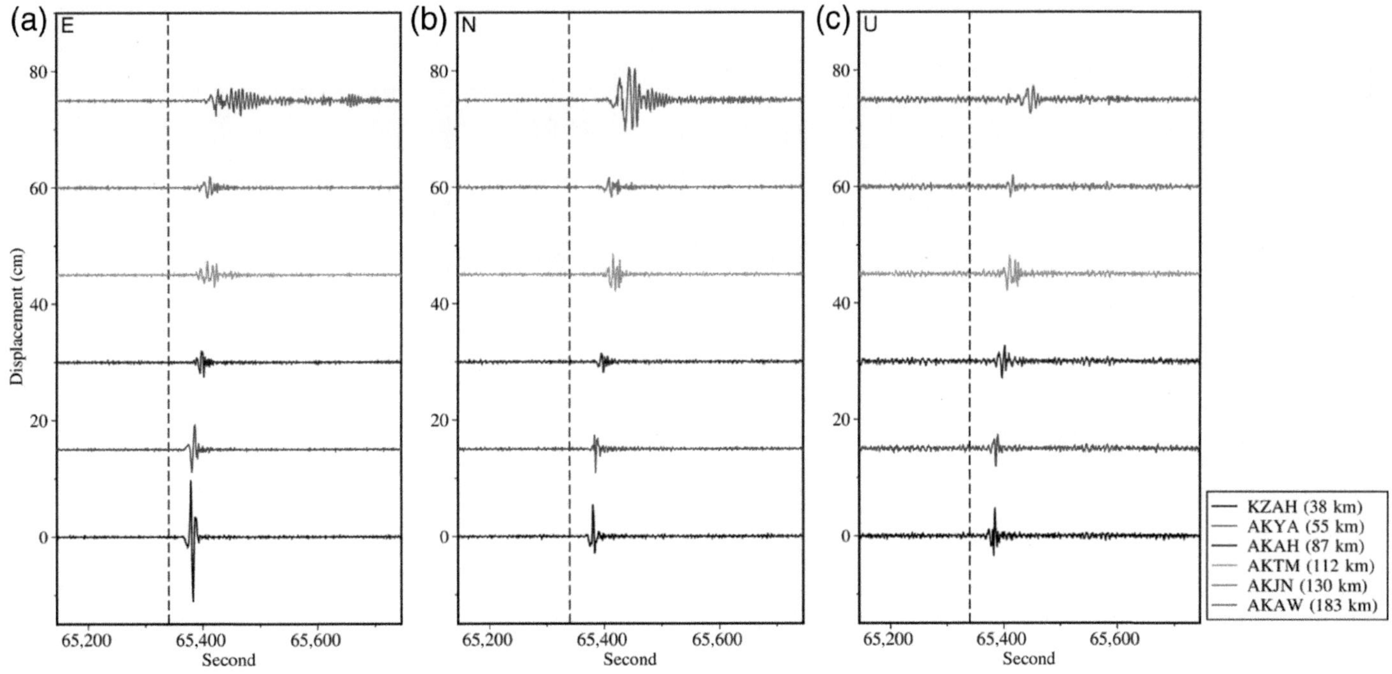

Figure 6. (a–c) Reconstructed high-frequency GNSS seismic displacements at GNSS stations. The color version of this figure is available only in the electronic edition.

component represented low-frequency components, primarily reflecting the static displacements resulting from the earthquake.

Using the high-frequency components (IMF1 to IMF3) extracted through the MPE method, wavelet thresholding was applied for noise reduction. The denoised components were then reconstructed to derive the GNSS seismic displacements, as shown in Figure 6. This approach revealed significant seismic responses in the east (E), north (N), and vertical (U) directions across the six GNSS stations. The stations exhibited strong coseismic responses to the Wushi earthquake in all three directions, with the displacement amplitude inversely correlated with the distance from each station to the epicenter. Notably, both the KZAH and AKYA stations, located near the epicenter, recorded substantial instantaneous deformations. However, the displacement at KZAH, situated southwest of the epicenter, was considerably larger than that at AKYA. This discrepancy suggests that the KZAH station may be located along the fault rupture path of the earthquake. Nonetheless, further field investigations are required to confirm this hypothesis.

Figures 4 and 6 collectively show that the coseismic responses at the AKAW station, located farther northeast and at a greater epicentral distance, are similar to those observed at the closer AKAH, AKTM, and AKJN stations. This similarity may be attributed to the direction of the rupture, which will be further investigated through field observations. In addition, Figure 6 demonstrates that coseismic signals at GNSS stations within 200 km of the epicenter can be effectively detected using the CEEMDAN decomposition and MPE method. Compared to the original displacement waveforms, the reconstructed signal is free from low-frequency noise and static offsets. In future studies, this approach could be applied to reconstruct waveform signals, offering more reliable high-frequency coseismic information by efficiently filtering out noise. Moreover, it has the potential to extend the monitoring capabilities of continuously operating reference stations (CORS) for coseismic signals, allowing for more comprehensive data collection from surrounding stations. This expanded network could provide valuable data for seismic research, including seismic phase identification, fault rupture mechanisms, and fault-slip distribution, among other critical aspects.

Fault geometry parameter inversion

We used source mechanism solutions from various institutions, including Global Centroid Moment Tensor (Global CMT), USGS, and GeoForschungsZentrums (GFZ) (as summarized in Table 2), alongside the GNSS-derived coseismic deformation, to identify the best-fitting fault parameters. These parameters included a strike angle ranging from 220° to 260°, a dip angle from 30° to 70°, and a rake angle from 0° to 90°. Within these parameter spaces, fault models were stochastically generated, and forward calculations were performed to simulate the theoretical coseismic deformation at each GNSS station. The residuals between the simulated and observed values were calculated, and the optimization process iteratively converged toward the best-fitting set of fault parameters when the residuals reached their minimum. After conducting 100 model inversion experiments, we selected the set of parameters with the minimal error and the best fit between observed and forward-modeled values (Fig. 7): a strike of 238°, a dip of 54°, and a rake of 20°. These

TABLE 2
Focal Mechanism for the Wushi Earthquake

	Epicenter Location			Focal Mechanism			
	Longitude (°)	**Latitude (°)**	**Depth (km)**	**Strike (°)**	**Dip (°)**	**Rake (°)**	M_w
Global CMT	78.57	41.19	14	236/110	48/57	47/127	7.0
USGS	78.65	41.27	13	235/113	45/62	42/126	7.0
GFZ	78.70	41.27	15	251/92	38/53	72/72	7.0
Nai *et al.* (2024)	78.64	41.23	6.6 ± 1.39	230.27 ± 0.23	57.49 ± 3.65	41.67 ± 1.59	7.00
This study	78.59	41.29	11	238	54	20	7.0

GFZ, GeoForschungsZentrums; Global CMT, Global Centroid Moment Tensor; USGS, U.S. Geological Survey.

strike and dip angles are in close agreement with those reported by Global CMT, USGS, and Nai *et al.* (2024), as shown in Table 2. However, there are notable discrepancies in the rake angle and depth parameters. The rake angle of 20° obtained in this study deviates from the 72° reported by GFZ and the 48° and 45° reported by Global CMT and USGS, respectively. This variation may stem from the limited GNSS data used in this study, which resulted in less stringent constraints and thus led to some differences in the inversion results. Furthermore, the depth of 11 km obtained in this study differs significantly from the 6.6 ± 1.39 km depth reported by Nai *et al.* (2024) using InSAR data, though it aligns more closely with the seismic wave results from Global CMT and USGS. This suggests that the fault parameters inverted in this study are consistent with the overall fault model of the earthquake rupture.

Slip distribution inversion

A smoothing factor of 0.1 was carefully chosen based on the trade-off curve, which balances the smoothness of the fault-slip distribution with the residual fitting value, as shown in Figure 8. This methodology resulted in the best-fitting fault-slip distribution.

Using the calculated GNSS-derived coseismic displacements and a fixed smoothing factor, the slip distribution for the Wushi earthquake was inverted, as shown in Figure 9. The results reveal two distinct slip concentrations within the coseismic rupture model: one primarily occurring at depths ranging from 7.0 to 17.0 km, northeast of the epicenter, and another deeper patch in the lower-right corner of the model, which may be an inversion artifact. The maximum slip, reaching 1.1 m, is located about 8 km northeast of the epicenter at a depth of 11 km. This value is lower than the maximum slip of 2.37 m, derived from InSAR measurements by Zhao *et al.* (2024). Notably, the rupture did not reach the surface. The calculated moment magnitude (M_w) of the coseismic slip distribution model was 7.0, which is consistent with the values reported by Global CMT, USGS, and GFZ. The spatial relationship between the mainshock epicenter and the coseismic slip distribution suggests that the rupture likely propagated bilaterally, with a preferred northeastward propagation. Although the slip distribution primarily indicates northeastward propagation, the possibility of southwestward propagation should not be ruled out, considering that the GNSS observation stations in this study were largely located northeast of the epicenter, with fewer stations to the southwest. This unbalanced spatial distribution of GNSS stations may influence the inversion, potentially underrepresenting the slip distribution to the southwest of the epicenter. Given these factors, future research will focus on expanding the observational data set to further refine and improve the accuracy of the slip distribution model.

Conclusion

On 23 January 2024, a magnitude 7.0 earthquake struck Wushi County, Xinjiang. GNSS data from six stations within 200 km of the epicenter were analyzed to investigate coseismic deformation, fault geometry, and slip distribution. Significant permanent deformations were recorded at KZAH, AKYA, and AKAH stations, with thrust faulting and a minor left-lateral strike-slip component dominating the seismic behavior.

By combining CEEMDAN decomposition, wavelet threshold denoising, and the MPE method, we effectively removed static displacements and nonlinear trends from the GNSS time series, enabling the reconstruction of high-frequency coseismic signals. This methodology improves coseismic information precision, facilitates the detection of distant signals (up to 200 km from the epicenter), and enhances future CORS-based seismic monitoring.

Using the PSO algorithm with the Okada model, fault parameters for the Wushi earthquake were determined: strike 238°, dip 54°, and rake 20°. Discrepancies in the rake angle compared to USGS and Global CMT may reflect data limitations. However, the modeled GNSS deformation closely matches observed data, confirming the inversion results.

The constructed slip distribution model showed lateral rupture, with maximum slip (1.1 m) at 11 km depth, 8 km northeast of the epicenter, and no surface rupture. The model aligns with

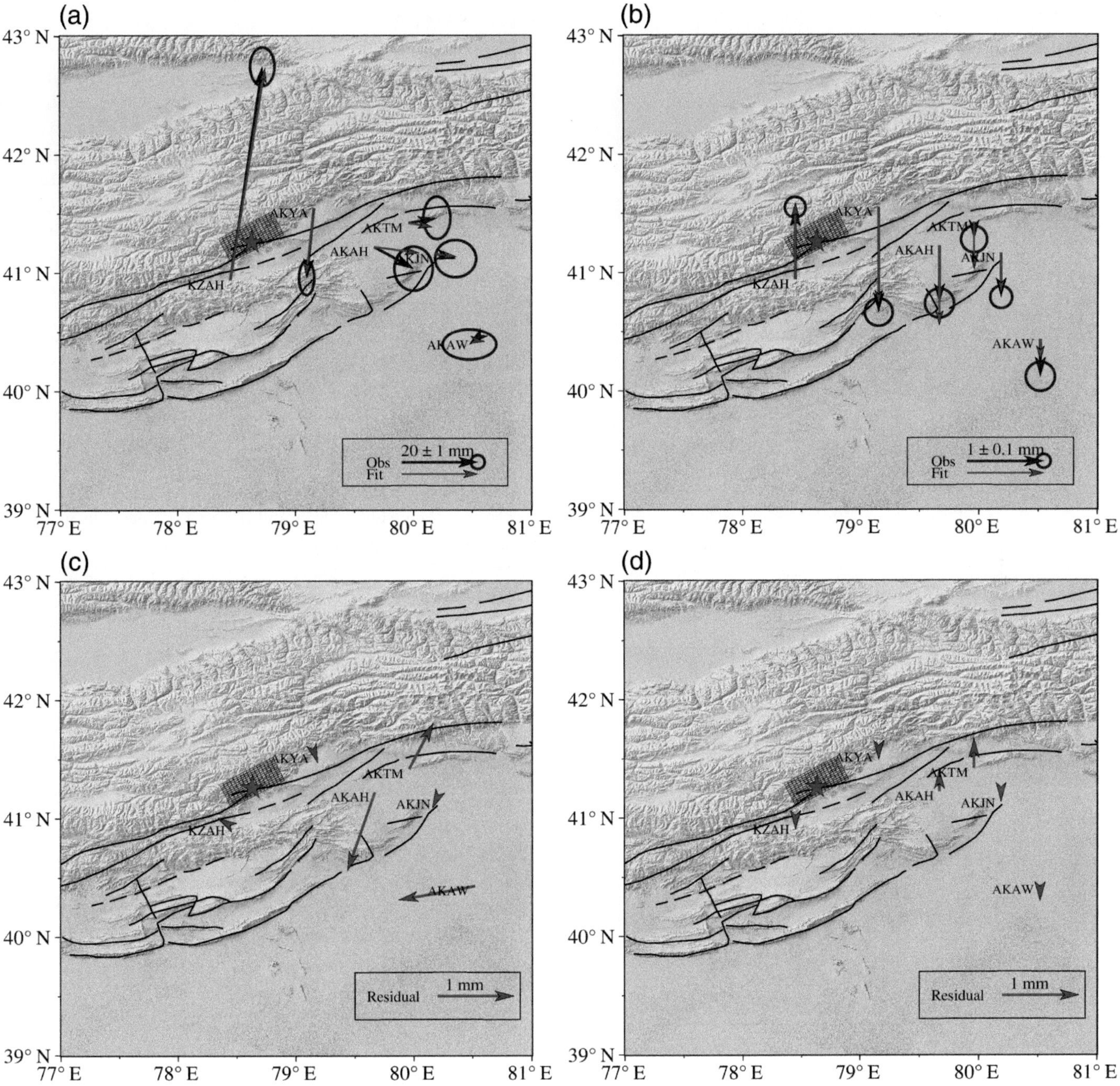

Figure 7. The observed and simulated coseismic deformation field in (a) horizontal and (b) vertical, as well as their (c,d) corresponding residuals. The color version of this figure is available only in the electronic edition.

the seismic moment magnitude of M_w 7.0, consistent with global seismic databases. Future improvements in the model accuracy will require additional data, particularly to address the southwestern slip distribution gap.

Data and Resources

Guo, Zhang, and Xu *et al.* provided the source mechanism solution at https://www.cea-igp.ac.cn/kydt/. The aftershock sequence of the M_w 7.0 Wushi earthquake is available at https://www.xjdzj.gov.cn/yztj/. The U.S. Geological Survey (USGS) database is available at https://www.usgs.gov/. The Global Centroid Moment Tensor (Global CMT) database is available at https://www.globalcmt.org/. The database of the GFZ is available at https://www.gfz-potsdam.de/en/. The regional waveform data are available at https://www.cea-igp.ac.cn/kydt/280467.html. The data to China Earthquake Data Center are available at https://data.earthquake.cn/20240123yzxx/info/2024/334671436.html. All the websites were last accessed in July 2024.

Declaration of Competing Interests

The authors acknowledge that there are no conflicts of interest recorded.

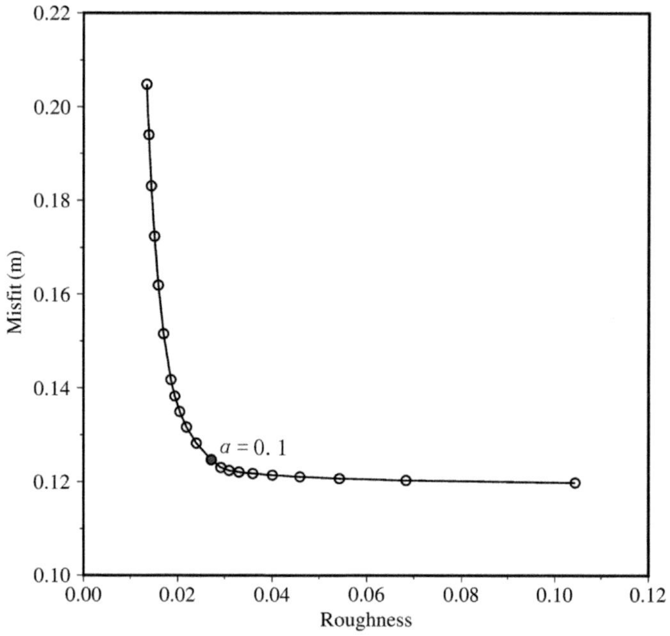

Figure 8. Trade-off curve between GNSS fitting residuals and the smoothness of coseismic slip distribution on fault plane. The color version of this figure is available only in the electronic edition.

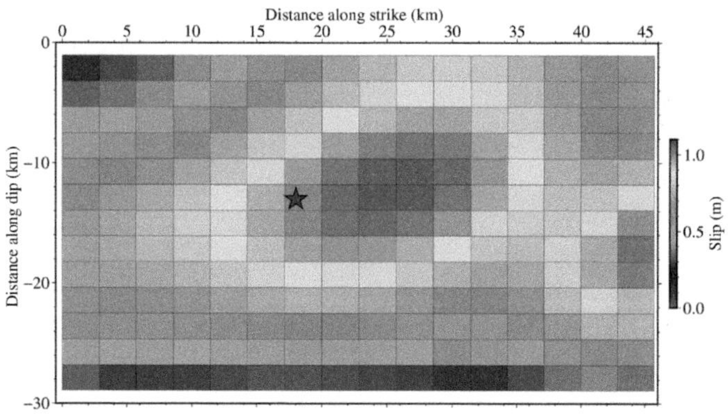

Figure 9. Inverted slip distribution of the causative fault. (Strike from left to right is southwest to northeast, Strike: 238°). The color version of this figure is available only in the electronic edition.

Acknowledgments

The authors would like to thank anonymous reviewers for their constructive comments to improve the article. The authors are grateful to their collaborators for collecting and providing high-rate Global Navigation Satellite System (GNSS) data from CMONOC. This work is supported by Special project on National Science and Technology Basic Resources Investigation (Grant Number 2024FY101103); National Natural Science Foundation of China (Grant Number 42174012); and National Key Research and Development Program of China (Grant Number 2023YFB3907101).

References

China Earthquake Administration (2022). *China Historical Earthquake Catalog*, Seismological Press, Beijing, China.

Ding, K., Q. Wang, Z. Li, P. He, P. Zhang, J. Chen, X. You, and L. Zhao (2022). Rapid source determination of the 2021 M_w 7.4 Maduo earthquake by a dense high-rate GNSS network in the Tibetan plateau, *Seismol. Res. Lett.* **93,** no. 6, 3234–3245, doi: 10.1785/0220210307.

Dittmann, T., H. Kathleen, M. Jade, M. David, and M. Glen (2022). Comparing sensitivities of geodetic processing methods for rapid earthquake magnitude estimation, *Seismol. Res. Lett.* **93,** no. 3, 1497–1509, doi: 10.1785/0220210265.

Geng, J., X. Chen, Y. Pan, S. Mao, C. Li, J. Zhou, and K. Zhang (2019). PRIDE PPP-AR: An open-source software for GPS PPP ambiguity resolution, *GPS Solut.* **23,** no. 91, 1–10, doi: 10.1007/s10291-019-0888-1.

Hohensinn, R., H. Simon, and G. Alain (2020). Dynamic displacements from high-rate GNSS: Error modeling and vibration detection, *Measurement* **157,** 107,655, doi: 10.1016/j.measurement.2020.107655.

Jia, Q., C. Wu, J. Shen, G. Wu, and R. Pen (2015). Evidence of left-lateral strike-slip along the Aheqi segment of Maidan fault in southwest Tianshan Mountains, China and its latest activity, *China Earthq. Eng. J.* **37,** no. 1, 222–227.

Kerdphol, T., K. Fuji, Y. Mitani, M. Watanabe, and Y. Qudaih (2016). Optimization of a battery energy storage system using particle swarm optimization for stand-alone microgrids, *Int. J. Elec. Power* **81,** 32–39, doi: 10.1016/j.ijepes.2016.02.006.

Li, Z., Z. Chen, J. Wu, X. Zhou, M. Zhang, L. Zhao, B. Yu, J. Zhou, and S. Zhang (2024). Co-seismic deformation of the Jishishan 6.2 earthquake in Gansu Province based on high-rate GNSS observation, *Geomat. Inf. Sci. Wuhan Univ.* doi: 10.13203/j.whugis20240004.

Li, Z., K. Ding, P. Zhang, Y. Wen, L. Zhao, and J. Chen (2021). Coseismic deformation and slip distribution of 2021 M_w 7.4 Madoi earthquake from GNSS observation, *Geomat. Inf. Sci. Wuhan Univ.* **46,** no. 10, 1489–1497, doi: 10.13203/j.whugis20210301.

Li, Z., J. Zang, S. Fan, Y. Wen, C. Xu, F. Yang, X. Peng, L. Zhao, and X. Zhou (2022). Real-time source modeling of the 2022 M_w 6.6 Menyuan, China earthquake with high-rate GNSS observations, *Remote Sens.* **14,** no. 21, 5378, doi: 10.3390/rs14215378.

Liang, A., and S. Gao (2023). Application of CEEMDAN and wavelet packet analysis in noise reduction of seismic signals[J], *Seismol. Geomagn. Obs. Res.* **44,** no. 5, 29–36.

Ma, X., and W. Wang (2020). Partial discharge recognition based on synchrosqueezing wavelet transform and multi-scale permutation entropy[J], *Comput. Meas. Control.* **28,** no. 2, 131–135, doi: 10.16526/j.cnki.11-4762/tp.2020.02.027.

Meng, J., T. Kusky, W. D. Mooney, E. Bozkurt, M. N. Bodur, and L. Wang (2024). Surface deformations of the 6 February 2023 earthquake sequence, eastern Türkiye, *Science* **383,** no. 6680, 298–305, doi: 10.1126/science.adj3770.

Michel, C., K. Kelevitz, N. Houlié, B. Edwards, P. Psimoulis, Z. Su, J. Clinton, and D. Giardini (2017). The potential of high-rate GPS for strong ground motion assessment, *Bull. Seismol. Soc. Am.* **107,** no. 4, 1849–1859, doi: 10.1785/0120160296.

Molnar, P., and J. M. Stock (2009). Slowing of India's convergence with Eurasia since 20 Ma and its implications for Tibetan mantle dynamics, *Tectonics* **28,** TC3001, doi: 10.1029/2008TC002271.

Molnar, P. H., and P. E. Tapponnier (1975). Cenozoic tectonics of Asia: Effects of a continental collision: Features of recent continental tectonics in Asia can be interpreted as results of the India-Eurasia collision, *Science* **189,** no. 4201, 419–426, doi: 10.1126/science.189.4201.419.

Nai, Y., B. Han, Z. Liu, Z. Li, C. Song, C. Yu, S. Li, and J. Peng (2024). Coseismic surface displacements and source model of the 2024 M_w 7.0 Wushi (Xinjiang, China) earthquake revealed by InSAR observations, *Geomat. Inf. Sci. Wuhan Univ.* doi: 10.13203/j.whugis20240037.

Okada, Y. (1985). Surface deformation due to shear and tensile faults in a half-space, *Bull. Seismol. Soc. Am.* **75,** no. 4, 1135–1154, doi: 10.1785/BSSA0750041135.

Okada, Y. (1992). Internal deformation due to shear and tensile faults in a half-space, *Bull. Seismol. Soc. Am.* **82,** no. 2, 1018–1040, doi: 10.1785/BSSA0820021018.

Ren, C., Z. Wang, T. Taymaz, N. Hu, H. Luo, Z. Zhao, H. Yue, X. Song, Z. Shen, H. Xu, *et al.* (2024). Supershear triggering and cascading fault ruptures of the 2023 Kahramanmaraş, Türkiye, earthquake doublet, *Science* **383,** no. 6680, 305–311, doi: 10.1126/science.adi1519.

Shan, X., H. Yin, X. Liu, Z. Wang, C. Qu, G. Zhang, Y. Zhang, Y. Li, C. Wang, and Y. Jiang (2019). High-rate real-time GNSS seismology and early warning of earthquakes, *Chin. J. Geophys.* **62,** no. 8, 3043–3052, doi: 10.6038/cjg2019M0076.

Sun, H., M. Zhang, J. Xu, X. Chen, and C. Liu (2018). Extraction and study of the gravity pole tide using EEMD[J], *Chin. J. Geophys.* **61,** no. 2, 521–530 (in Chinese).

Tan, M., Y. Fan, K. Lv, S. Hao, T. Xu, G. Cai, J. Zhang, and Z. Li (2023). Co-seismic deformation extraction and accuracy analysis of the Maduo earthquake based on the combined of different global navigation satellite systems, *Bull. Surv. Mapp.* **0,** no. 7, 80–84, doi: 10.13474/j.cnki.11-2246.2023.0205.

Torres, M., M. Colominas, G. Schlotthauer, and P. Flandrin (2011). A complete ensemble empirical mode decomposition with adaptive noise, *2011 IEEE International Conference on Acoustics, Speech and Signal Processing (ICASSP)*, Prague, Czech Republic, 22–27 May 2011, 4144–4147, doi: 10.1109/ICASSP.2011.5947265.

Wang, R., F. Diao, and A. Hoechner (2013). SDM-A geodetic inversion code incorporating with layered crust structure and curved fault geometry, *Proc. of the EGU General Assembly*, Vienna, Austria, 7 April 2013, Conference Abstracts EGU2013-2411.

Wang, R., S. Parolai, M. Ge, M. Jin, T. R. Walter, and J. Zschau (2013). The 2011 M_w 9.0 Tohoku earthquake: Comparison of GPS and strong-motion data, *Bull. Seismol. Soc. Am.* **103,** no. 2B, 1336–1347, doi: 10.1785/0120110264.

Wang, Z., H. Zhang, Q. Meng, and Y. Shi (2022). Finite element simulation of deformation and stress changes of Kalpin-Kemin fault system in the southwest Tianshan orogenic belt, *Sci. China Earth Sci.* **103,** no. 5, 863–873, doi: 10.1007/s11430-021-9875-y.

Wen, Y., Z. Guo, C. Xu, G. Xu, and C. Song (2019). Coseismic and postseismic deformation associated with the 2018 M_w 7.9 Kodiak, Alaska, earthquake from low-rate and high-rate GPS observations, *Bull. Seismol. Soc. Am.* **109,** no. 3, 908–918, doi: 10.1785/0120180246.

Wu, C. (2017). Late Quaternary activity characteristics of NE-trending fault in southwest Tianshan Mountains and its role in Tianshan tectonic deformation, *Recent Dev. World Seismol.* **47,** no. 9, 46–48.

Wu, C., L. Alimujiang, X. Dai, G. Wu, and J. Chen (2014). Discovery of late-quaternary activity along the eastern segment of Maidan fault in southwest Tianshan and its tectonic implication, *Seismol. Geol.* **36,** no. 4, 976–990, doi: 10.3969/j.issn.0253-4967.2014.04.004.

Wu, W., G. Meng, T. Liu, C. Wei, and X. Wei (2023). Coseismic displacement field and slip distribution of the 2022 Luding M 6.8 earthquake derived from GNSS observations, *Chin. J. Geophys.* **66,** no. 6, 2306–2321, doi: 10.6038/cjg2023Q0826 (in Chinese).

Xu, H., F. Meng, and C. Yu (2023). Research on denoising methods for GNSS deformation monitoring data of slopes, *Geomat. Tech. Equip.* **25,** no. 3, 31–36, doi: 10.20006/j.cnki.61-1363/P.2023.03.006.

Xu, P., C. Shi, R. Fang, J. Liu, X. Niu, Q. Zhang, and T. Yanagidani (2013). High-rate precise point positioning (PPP) to measure seismic wave motions: An experimental comparison of GPS PPP with inertial measurement units, *J. Geodes.* **87,** 361–372, doi: 10.1007/s00190-012-0606-z.

Yang, S., J. Li, and Q. Wang (2008). Study on present deformation and fault activity in Tianshan Mountains by GPS, *Sci. China Earth Sci.* **38,** no. 7, 872–880.

Yu, D., C. Liu, X. Wang, X. Han, and X. Huang (2019). Application of ensemble empirical mode decomposition (EEMD) in underground fluid data processing[J], *Earthq. Res. China* **35,** no. 2, 337–346.

Yuan, D., H. Xie, R. Su, Z. Li, Y. Wen, G. Si, S. Xue, G. Chen, B. Liu, S. Liang, *et al.* (2023). Characteristics of co-seismic surface rupture zone of Menyuan MS6.9 earthquake in Qinghai Province on January 8, 2022 and seismogenic mechanism, *Chin. J. Geophys.* **66,** no. 1, 229–244, doi: 10.6038/cjg2022Q0093 (in Chinese).

Zang, J., Y. Wen, Z. Li, C. Xu, K. He, P. Zhang, G. Wen, and S. Fan (2022). Rapid source models of the 2021 M_w 7.4 Maduo, China, earthquake inferred from high-rate BDS3/2, GPS, Galileo and GLONASS observations, *J. Geodes.* **96,** no. 9, doi: 10.1007/s00190-022-01641-w.

Zhang, B., L. Qian, T. Li, J. Chen, J. Xu, Y. Yao, L. Fang, C. Xie, J. Chen, G. Liu, Z. Hu, W. Yang, J. Zhang, and W. Pang (2024). Geological disasters and surface ruptures of January 23, 2024 Ms7.0 Wushi earthquake, Xinjiang, China, *Seismol. Geol.* **46,** no. 1, 220–234, doi: 10.3969/j.issn.0253-4967.2024.01.013.

Zhang, W., L. Ji, Y. Chen, C. Liu, and J. Xu (2024). Analysis of crustal deformation of the 2023 Ms 6.2 Jishishan earthquake in Gansu Province, *Inf. Sci. Wuhan Univ.* doi: 10.13203/j.whugis20240012.

Zhang, Z., L. Fang, K. Chen, R. Liu, Y. Wang, and X. Guo (2024). The rapid output parameters of the Wushi M7.0 earthquake in Aksu, Xinjiang on January 23, 2024, *Progr. Earthq. Sci.* **54,** no. 3, 221–228, doi: 10.19987/j.dzkxjz.2024-037.

Zhao, L., Z. Chen, L. Xie, Z. Zhu, and W. Xu (2024). Coseismic deformation and slip model of the 2024 M_w 7.0 Wushi earthquake obtained from InSAR observation, *Rev. Geophys. Planet. Physics.* **55,** no. 4, 453–460, doi: 10.19975/j.dqyxx.2024-010.

Zhu, S., H. Liang, W. Wei, and J. Li (2021). Slip rates and seismic moment deficits on major faults in the Tianshan region, *Seismol. Geol.* **43,** no. 1, 249–261, doi: 10.3969/j.issn.0253-4967.2021.01.015.

Manuscript received 12 February 2025
Published online 23 September 2025

Increased Stress Along the Sumpur and Northern Sianok Segments of Sumatran Fault Due to the 25 February 2022 M_w 6.1 Pasaman, Indonesia, Earthquake

OPEN ACCESS

Endra Gunawan[1,2], Nanang T. Puspito[1,2], Andri Dian Nugraha[1,2], Sri Widiyantoro[1,2], Risya Fauziyyah[3], Medina Apriani[3], Nuraini Rahma Hanifa[4], Ekbal Hussain*[5], Bayu Triyogo Widyantoro[6], and Sidik Tri Wibowo[6]

Abstract

On 25 February 2022, a destructive M_w 6.1 earthquake struck western Sumatra in the early hours of the morning. The earthquake shaking was focused around the Pasaman Regency and resulted in 25 fatalities. Coseismic displacements were recorded by an existing network of Global Navigation Satellite System (GNSS) sensors managed by the Geospatial Information Agency of Indonesia. The GNSS data show a maximum of 2.0 cm of displacement with a right-lateral sense of motion across a northwest–southeast-trending fault. An investigation into the responsible fault producing the earthquake is performed through a series of coseismic slip inversions on a rectangular fault plane, comparing two fault models: (a) a fault segment that is an extension of the already identified Sianok segment of the Sumatran fault zone, and (b) the recently identified Talamau segment. The maximum slip of 14 cm occurred at 4 km depth, 13 km away from the epicenter. The mainshock is associated to a seismic moment of 1.58×10^{25} N·m, or equivalent to M_w 6.1. Our results indicate increased stress along the Sumpur segment and the northern Sianok segment. With no historical earthquakes reported along the Sumpur and northern Sianok segments since 1892, our analysis using a scaling relationship between fault length and earthquake magnitude indicates that a rupture in these areas could potentially generate an earthquake with a magnitude of 6.7.

Cite this article as Gunawan, E., N. T. Puspito, A. D. Nugraha, S. Widiyantoro, R. Fauziyyah, M. Apriani, N. R. Hanifa, E. Hussain, B. T. Widyantoro, and S. T. Wibowo (2025). Increased Stress Along the Sumpur and Northern Sianok Segments of Sumatran Fault Due to the 25 February 2022 M_w 6.1 Pasaman, Indonesia, Earthquake, *Seismol. Res. Lett.* **97**, 998–1007, doi: 10.1785/0220240476.

Supplemental Material

Introduction

Accurate detection of fault slip and deformation is crucial for understanding the full cycle of strain accumulation and release in an earthquake (Wang *et al.*, 2012; Wright, 2016). Global Navigation Satellite Systems (GNSS) have been widely employed to study tectonic processes in various earthquake cases (e.g., Bürgmann *et al.*, 2013; Nishimura *et al.*, 2014; Feng *et al.*, 2015; Larson, 2019). In these cases, the coseismic surface deformation recorded by the GNSS sensors is inverted, often assuming an elastic half-space (e.g., Tanaka *et al.*, 2019; Gunawan, Gualandi, *et al.*, 2024), to determine the magnitude and distribution of slip on the fault plane.

Sumatra, one of the world's most tectonically active regions, experiences frequent earthquakes due to the interplay between the dip-slip component of the Sumatra subduction zone and the strike-slip component of the Sumatran fault (McCaffrey, 2009). The Sumatran fault is a major right-lateral fault zone running for 1900 km along the entire length of the island with an average slip rate of 15–16 mm/yr (Ito *et al.*, 2012; Bradley *et al.*, 2017). Of the 42 total Sumatran fault segments, which pose a threat to everyone living on the west coast of the island, seven are located in West Sumatra Province (Irsyam *et al.*, 2020).

On 25 February 2022, at 01:39 UTC, an M_w 6.1 earthquake occurred at Pasaman, West Sumatra, Indonesia, with a shallow depth of 4 km (Supendi *et al.*, 2023). The Indonesian National

1. Global Geophysics Research Group, Faculty of Mining and Petroleum Engineering, Institut Teknologi Bandung, Bandung, Indonesia, https://orcid.org/0000-0002-4844-8723 (ADN); https://orcid.org/0000-0002-8941-7173 (SW); 2. Research Center for Disaster Mitigation, Institut Teknologi Bandung, Bandung, Indonesia; 3. Geophysical Engineering Study Program, Faculty of Mining and Petroleum Engineering, Institut Teknologi Bandung, Bandung, Indonesia; 4. Research Center for Geological Disaster, National Research and Innovation Agency, Bandung, Indonesia, https://orcid.org/0000-0002-8012-5385 (NRH); 5. British Geological Survey, Nottingham, United Kingdom, https://orcid.org/0000-0001-6921-2843 (EH); 6. Geospatial Information Agency, Cibinong, Indonesia, https://orcid.org/0000-0001-5117-2740 (BTW); https://orcid.org/0009-0002-6816-5920 (STW)

*Corresponding author: ekhuss@bgs.ac.uk

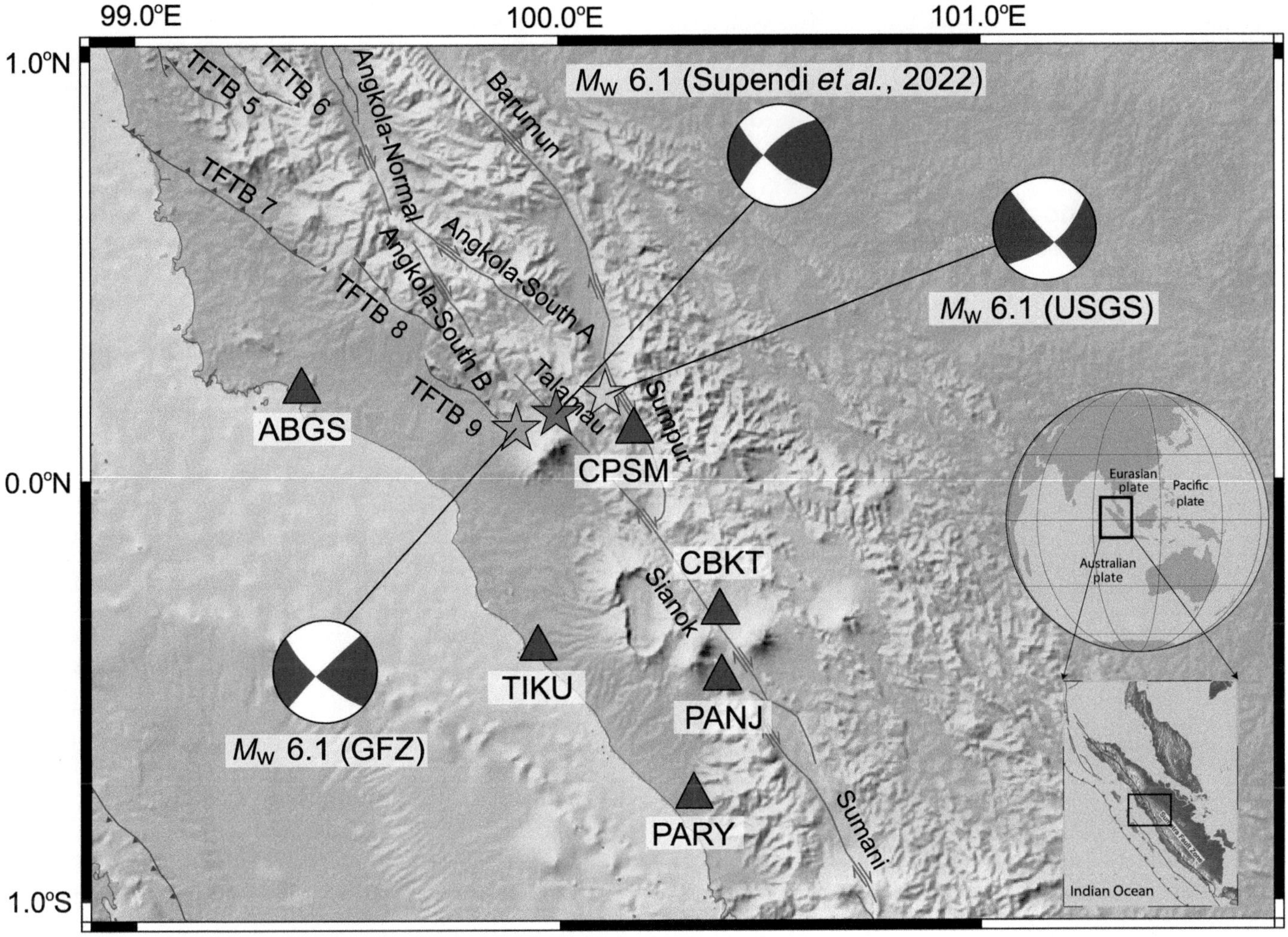

Board for Disaster Management reported 25 fatalities, at least 465 injuries, and the displacement of over 16,000 people. According to the U.S. Geological Survey (USGS) earthquake catalog, the epicenter was located northeast of Mount Talamau, positioned south of the Angkola segment, west of the Sumpur segment, and north of the Sianok segment of the seismically active Sumatran fault (Fig. 1). The hypocenter's location, not closely associated with any known Sumatran fault segments, raises intriguing questions about the fault source of the earthquake.

Supendi *et al.* (2023) conducted a relocation of the foreshock, mainshock, and aftershocks, with a total of 201 seismic events ranging in magnitude from 1.4 to 6.1. These seismic events, which included a foreshock, mainshock, and aftershocks, were recorded over the 12-day period from 25 February to 8 March 2022. The aftershocks revealed a previously unidentified section of the Sumatran fault. This newly discovered segment, which Supendi *et al.* (2023) named the Kajai fault segment, is approximately 20 km long and characterized by right-lateral strike-slip movement. The fault has a strike orientation of N132°E and a dip angle of 72° to the southwest. This fault is approximately 15 km to the west of the currently identified Sumpur segment. However, the USGS catalog suggested that

Figure 1. Tectonic setting of the study area. Locations of the Global Navigation Satellite System (GNSS) stations used in this study are shown by blue triangles. The epicenter location of the 25 February 2022 Pasaman earthquake with focal mechanisms is from the U.S. Geological Survey (USGS) catalog (yellow star), GeoForschungsZentrums (GFZ) catalog (green star), and Supendi *et al.* (2023; purple star). The solid red lines indicate the identified fault trace of the Sumatran fault based on the National Center for Earthquake Studies of Indonesia (2024). Inset shows the regional map. The color version of this figure is available only in the electronic edition.

the epicenter is located at the Sumpur segment. These two different epicenter locations raised questions about which is the responsible fault segment of the 2002 Pasaman earthquake.

This study investigates the coseismic deformation of the 25 February 2022 Pasaman earthquake using GNSS data to determine the responsible fault segment of the earthquake. We apply a Bayesian inversion model to calculate the coseismic slip using two fault model scenarios (e.g., Fukahata and Wright, 2008; Li *et al.*, 2015). We also explore the stress transfer impacts of the earthquake on nearby faults. We analyze the

Coulomb stress change to investigate the potential seismic risk along the Sumatran fault (e.g., Toda and Stein, 2003). Finally, we discuss the implications of our coseismic slip model on earthquake scaling relationships, which are often used in seismic hazard analysis.

Data and Method

GPS

This study utilizes GNSS data, which is recorded as part of the Indonesia Continuously Operating Reference Station (Ina-CORS; Gunawan *et al.*, 2022), and provided by the Geospatial Information Agency of Indonesia, and the Sumatran Global Positioning System (GPS) Array (SuGAr), which is maintained by the Earth Observatory of Singapore and National Research and Innovation Agency of Indonesia (BRIN; e.g., Feng *et al.*, 2015). There are three GNSS stations from the Ina-CORS network available in the region; in Bukittinggi (CBKT), West Pasaman (CPSM), and Padang Panjang (PANJ). Meanwhile, another three GNSS data from SuGAR network are in West Pasaman (ABGS), Agam (TIKU), and Padang Pariaman (PARY). The location of these GNSS stations is shown in Figure 1.

GNSS data from the Ina-CORS network were processed using GAMIT (Herring *et al.*, 2010a,b), and daily solutions were obtained through a three-stage process (e.g., Gunawan *et al.*, 2022). First, daily positions were estimated using atmospheric zenith delays and loose constraints at each station, incorporating prior GNSS phase observations with fixed orbit and earth-orientation parameters. Next, these positions and their covariance were combined with global GNSS solutions from Massachusetts Institute of Technology (MIT)'s International GNSS Service (IGS) processing. The loosely constrained solution was then transformed into a well-constrained reference frame by minimizing position and velocity differences between selected stations and their prior IGS14-defined values within the International Terrestrial Reference Frame (ITRF) 2014 (Altamimi *et al.*, 2016). The final position time series was subsequently estimated.

Meanwhile, the GNSS data from the SuGAr network are downloaded in a RINEX format (see Data and Resources), which is collected over a 30 s interval. This data are processed using the GipsyX software (Bertiger *et al.*, 2020), by employing a precise point positioning technique to estimate the daily solutions of the GNSS data (Gunawan *et al.*, 2023). The Jet Propulsion Laboratory's reanalysis of the final set of the IGS 2014 (IGS14) orbit and clock product was utilized to actualize the ITRF2014 reference (Altamimi *et al.*, 2016). Five iterations of fiducial-free processing were also employed, with the elevation cutoff angle set at 15°. In addition, the ocean-loading parameters of the GOT4.8 model obtained from the Onsala Space Observatory were also used.

Fault-plane model

The 2022 Pasaman earthquake epicenter occurred in a region with no previously identified segment of the Sumatran fault. Thus, we investigate two possible fault-plane models to estimate the coseismic slip of the mainshock. The first fault-plane model, named model 1, built by extending the Sianok segment of the Sumatran fault (Fig. 1) to the northwest direction toward the epicenter. Our approach is based on the assumption that the mainshock occurred along the Sianok segment. We construct a fault with length of 103 km, width of 32 km, strike of 327°, and dip of 90° (Fig. 2). Along length, we divide the fault into nine subfaults, in which length is varied from 5 to 25 km. Along width, we divide the fault into four subfaults, in which the width is 8 km.

The second fault-plane model, named model 2, is constructed using the information from the USGS catalog. We construct a fault with strike 319°, dip of 90°, length of 20 km, and depth of up to 32 km (Fig. 3). Fault length is obtained based on the earthquake scaling relationship proposed by Gunawan (2021). In this model, we divided the fault into subfaults with size of 4 km in length and 8 km in width.

Coseismic slip modeling

Using the daily solutions data, we calculate the coseismic displacement by subtracting the average displacement from five-day intervals after—with before—the mainshock. Our calculation involves three components of the GNSS data: the easting, northing, and vertical components. The standard deviation is obtained by averaging the error of the daily solutions data at each station.

We estimated the coseismic slip distribution using a Bayesian inversion approach developed by Yabuki and Matsu'ura (1992), based on observed coseismic displacements. The slip is computed using the equation: $s(m) = (d - Gm)^T E^{-1} (d - Gm) + \alpha^2 m^T Lm$. In this formulation, G represents the Green's function derived from an elastic dislocation model (Okada, 1992) with a Poisson's ratio of 0.25, E denotes the measurement variance–covariance matrix, α^2 is a hyperparameter, and L is a Laplacian smoothing matrix. We determined the optimal hyperparameter using Akaike's Bayesian information criterion (ABIC; e.g., Gunawan, Gualandi, *et al.*, 2024). In our procedure, diagonal elements of the covariance matrix are also calculated.

Processing Result

Coseismic displacements

Our results indicate that the largest coseismic displacement was recorded at the CPSM station, with a displacement of 2.0 cm to the east. Similarly, the CBKT station also experienced displacement in the same direction, albeit with a smaller magnitude of 0.4 cm. In contrast, three stations (ABGS, TIKU, and PARY) exhibited coseismic displacements toward the northwest, with magnitudes of 0.5, 0.4, and 0.2 cm, respectively. The smallest displacement, measuring 0.1 cm, was directed

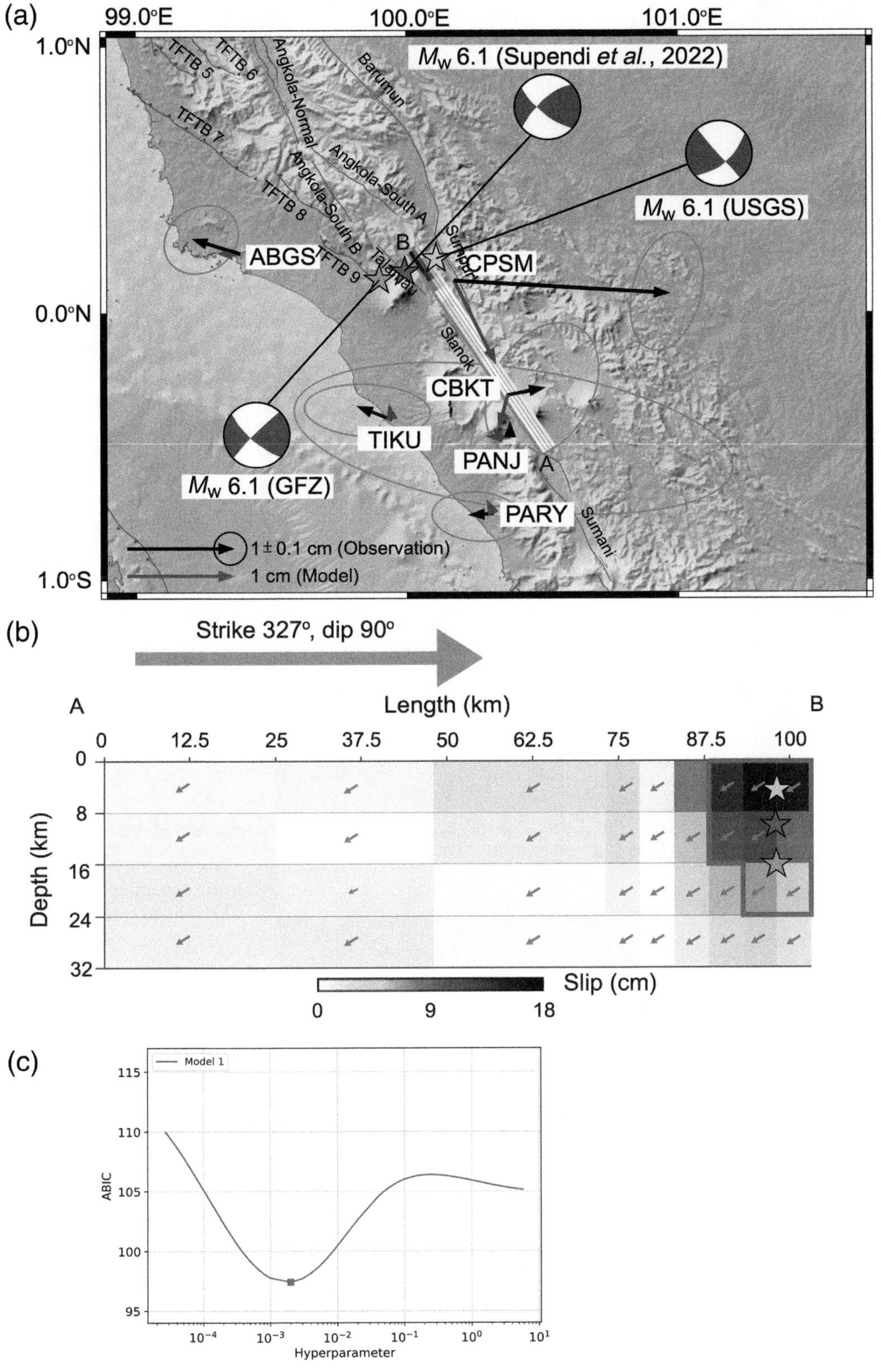

Figure 2. Coseismic deformation analysis on a fault with a length of 103 km, width of 32 km, and fault strike and dip of 327° and 90°, respectively (model 1). (a) Coseismic displacements of the 2022 Pasaman earthquake, which is shown by black vectors. Red vectors indicate the modeled coseismic displacements. (b) The inferred coseismic slip of the 2022 Pasaman earthquake using a fault geometry of model 1. Gray vectors indicate the rake direction. Slip within the blue polygons indicates where the estimated uncertainty is lower than the absolute value of the predicted slip. (c) Hyperparameter as a function of Akaike's Bayesian information criterion (ABIC) with best-fit parameter shown by the blue square (see Fig. 1 for a detailed description of the figure legend). The color version of this figure is available only in the electronic edition.

toward the north and was recorded at the PANJ station. The spatial patterns of these displacements are visually represented in Figures 2 and 3.

Coseismic slip

Coseismic slip is estimated by employing the α^2 hyperparameter for which the ABIC is minimum. The best-fit ABIC parameter that is used for final model in model 1 is 97.42 (Fig. 2), whereas in model 2 is 95.43 (Fig. 3). Inverted GPS data on model 1 show that the maximum slip is around 16 cm, which is focused at 4 km deep, located approximately 9 km from the Pasaman earthquake epicenter (Fig. 2). In model 2, the inversion data indicate that the maximum slip is about 14 cm at the same depth as the previous model, located at 13 km away from the epicenter (Fig. 3). The region where the estimated slip uncertainty is lower than the absolute value of the predicted slip is shown in Figures 2 and 3.

The misfit between coseismic displacement data and inversion data is calculated using the mean absolute error (MAE), defined as follows: $\mathrm{MAE} = 1/n \sum_{i=1,n} |\mathrm{data}_i - \mathrm{model}_i|$, in which n is the total number of data consisting of east, north, and up components. We found that model 1 had a misfit of 4 mm, whereas model 2 had a smaller misfit of 2 mm. Calculating the seismic moment from the coseismic slip result, we found that model 1 corresponds to 7.26×10^{24} N · m, equivalent to M_w 5.8 when assuming a shear modulus of 33 GPa. Meanwhile, model 2 is associated with 1.58×10^{25} N · m,

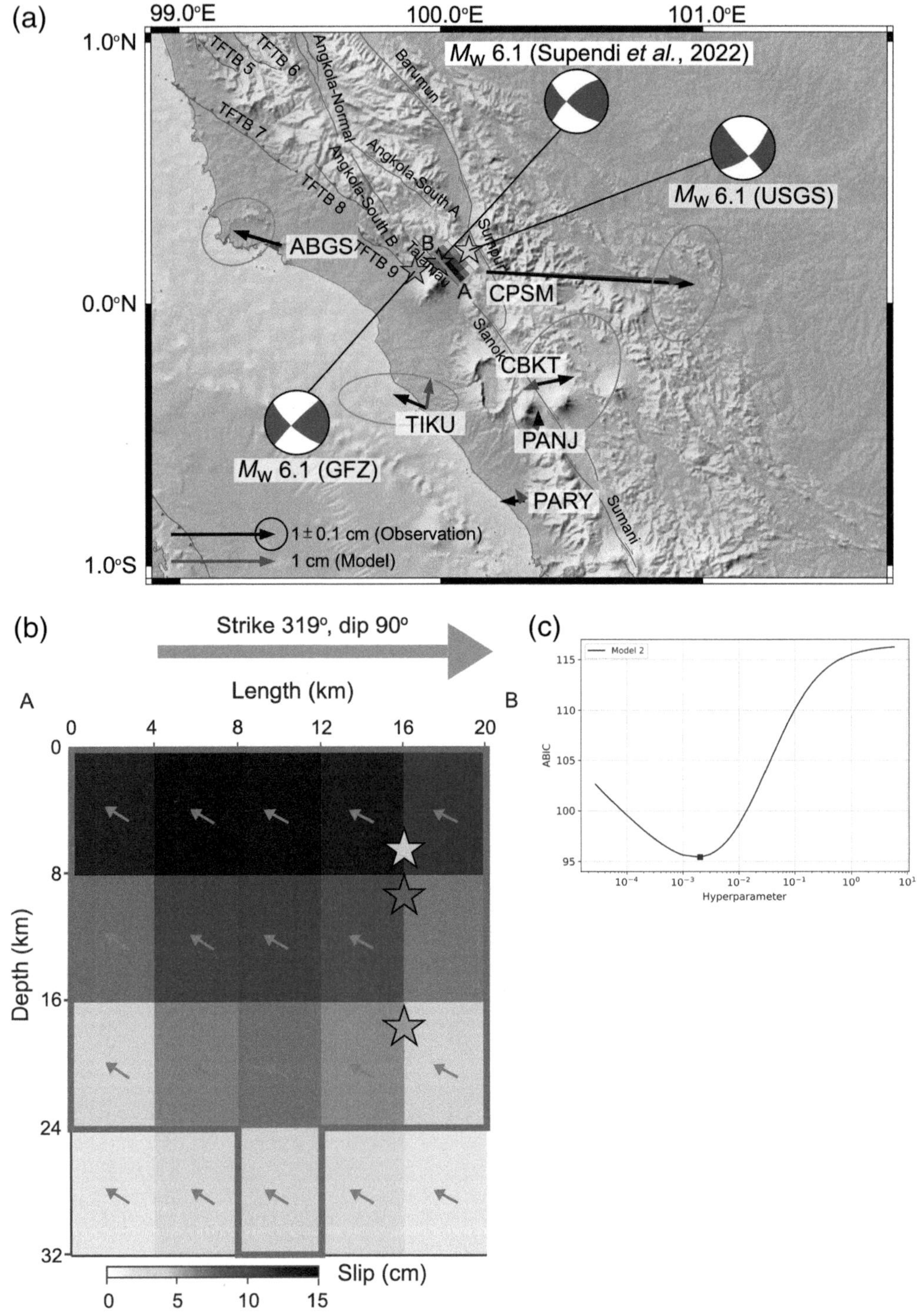

Figure 3. Coseismic deformation analysis on a fault with a length of 20 km, width of 32 km, and fault strike and dip of 319° and 90°, respectively (model 2). (a) Coseismic displacements of the 2022 Pasaman earthquake, which is shown by black vectors. Red vectors indicate the modeled coseismic displacements. (b) The inferred coseismic slip of the 2022 Pasaman earthquake using a fault geometry of model 2. Gray vectors indicate the rake direction. Slip within the blue polygons indicates where the estimated uncertainty is lower than the absolute value of the predicted slip. (c) Hyperparameter as a function of ABIC with best-fit parameter shown by the red square (see Fig. 1 for a detailed description of the figure legend). The color version of this figure is available only in the electronic edition.

or equivalent to M_w 6.1, if we use the same shear modulus value.

Discussion

Identification of the ruptured fault segment

The epicenter location from USGS catalog showed that the earthquake may have occurred along Sumpur segment (Fig. 1). If this is true, then the coseismic displacements at CPSM station, which is located in the western part of the Sumpur segment, should exhibit northwest motion. Instead, the coseismic displacement at this station has a southeast direction, suggesting that this station is located on the eastern part of the fault.

Following Supendi *et al.* (2023), the epicenter of the 2022 Pasaman earthquake occurred in a previously unknown fault segment, located between the Angkola segment and the Sianok segment. By having the epicenter at this location, the coseismic displacements at the right part of the fault segment should exhibit a southeast direction, which is what we see in the coseismic displacements data at CPSM. Thus, we conclude that the mainshock did not occur along the Sumpur segment; instead, it occurred on an unknown fault segment between the Angkola segment and the Sianok segment, validating the inferences of Supendi *et al.* (2023).

The National Center for Earthquake Studies (2024) defined this unknown fault segment as the Talamau segment (Fig. 1). In our model 1, although we include the Sinaok segment, our result showed that maximum slip occurred near the epicenter, closer to the Talamau segment. Nonetheless, with the inclusion of Sianok segment in the process, model 1 failed to predict GNSS station observations closest to the epicenter, CPSM (Fig. 2). On the other hand, model 2 successfully predicts the coseismic displacements at CPSM by modeling only using a fault with a length of 20 km. In terms of error, model 2 also produces a smaller MAE than model 1. For these reasons, we consider model 2 as our preferred model and use it for further analysis.

Model 2 suggests that coseismic slip extends to a depth of approximately 24 km. In line with this, Prawirodirdjo *et al.* (2000) investigated the fault slip rate and locking depth along the Sumatran fault using historical triangulation and GNSS data. They found that the locking depth of the Sianok segment is also around 24 km. Our coseismic slip results are therefore consistent with their earlier estimates.

We compare our preferred coseismic slip model 2 with the coseismic slip model from the arrival-time dataset by Supendi *et al.* (2023). Their study showed that aftershock distributed extending ~20 km northwest–southeast parallel to the Sumatran fault, which they named the Kajai segment. The location of Kajai and Talamau segments is identical. Thus, both segments are similar, only differing in naming. Finally, our GNSS-based investigation of the 2022 Pasaman earthquake rupture along Talamau segment is supported by the seismic investigation.

Potential seismic hazard along the Sumatran fault

Aftershocks can be triggered by the stress generated from preceding mainshocks, with their spatial patterns being particularly challenging to forecast. Although shear stress change provides a better measure of potential earthquake triggering, Coulomb failure stress remains one of the most widely used criteria to explain the spatial distribution of aftershocks (e.g., DeVries *et al.*, 2018).

The friction coefficient of rocks exhibits a strong dependence on normal stress at typical crustal depths. For Coulomb stress calculations, the typical assumption is that frictional resistance is linearly proportional to the effective normal stress (King *et al.*, 1994). Barbot (2024) suggests that there may be a time-dependent, nonlinear relationship between friction and normal stress and attributes this to heterogeneities in the fault geology and asperity distribution. However, in this study, we do not have geological information and produce slip distribution to the level of detail required to disentangle this effect, and therefore, we maintain the assumption of a linear relationship between friction and normal stress.

The Coulomb stress change imparted by the 2022 Pasaman earthquake rupture could be used to determine if a neighboring fault is brought closer to failure and, thus, provide information on the possible region where earthquakes may occur in the future (e.g., Toda *et al.*, 2011; Gunawan *et al.*, 2022).

In this study, we compute the Coulomb stress change (ΔCFF) using the equation $\Delta \mathrm{CFF} = \Delta\tau + \mu' \Delta\sigma$, in which $\Delta\tau$ represents the change in shear stress on a specific fault plane (with positive values indicating promotion of slip along the receiver fault), μ' denotes the effective friction coefficient on the receiver fault, and $\Delta\sigma$ represents the change in normal stress acting on the fault plane (for which positive values signify unclamping or reduction in normal stress). This methodology aligns with approaches outlined in previous research (e.g., King *et al.*, 1994; Hardebeck *et al.*, 1998; Lin and Stein, 2004; Toda *et al.*, 2005). In our calculation, we used a Poisson ratio of 0.25, Young's modulus of 8×10^5 bar, and a friction coefficient of 0.8.

To see the variation of stress along the receiver faults consisting of the Barumun, Sumpur, Angkola, Sianok, and Sumani segments, a fault model was created from the coseismic slip model 2. Our result suggests that the M_w 6.1 2022 Pasaman earthquake increased stress along the Sumpur segment and the northern Sianok segment by approximately 0.4 and 0.3 bar, bringing these segments closer to failure (Fig. 4). Hurukawa *et al.* (2014) reported that no historical earthquake has been reported along the Sumpur and northern Sianok segments since at least 1892. If these segments rupture, it may generate an earthquake with a magnitude of 6.7 (National Center for Earthquake Studies, 2024).

Meade *et al.* (2017) suggest that maximum shear stress and the magnitudes of the second and third invariants of the stress tensor are higher by 10% in explaining aftershocks compared to Coulomb stress. Regardless, Coulomb stress still satisfactorily explains seismicity in various cases, such as the Rangely oil field in Colorado (Byrne *et al.*, 2020), the 2016 Mie offshore earthquake in Japan (Yoshida *et al.*, 2020), the 2020 Samos earthquake (Lentas *et al.*, 2022), the 2022 Chihshang earthquake (Murase *et al.*, 2025), the 2021 Fukushima earthquake (Zhang *et al.*, 2023), and many other studies. Nonetheless, further investigation is needed to explore the role of maximum shear stress and the magnitudes of the second and third invariants of the stress tensor in the context of the 2022 Pasaman earthquake.

Implication of coseismic slip model to earthquake scaling relationship

Empirical relationships between fault geometry and earthquake magnitude (e.g., Wells and Coppersmith, 1994) have been widely used in earthquake magnitude estimation in seismic hazard analysis (e.g., Irsyam *et al.*, 2020). We use the earthquake scaling relationships for the tectonic region of Indonesia (Gunawan, 2021) for strike-slip faulting regimes, which proposed a relationship between fault length and earthquake magnitude. We further analyze this empirical function with the case of the 2022 Pasaman earthquake and five other large earthquakes on the Sumatran fault based on the work of Gunawan *et al.* (2018), Gunawan *et al.* (2020), and Salman *et al.* (2020). Those major earthquakes are the 2007 M_w 6.3 Sianok earthquake at the southern segment, 2007 M_w 6.4 Sumani earthquake, 2009

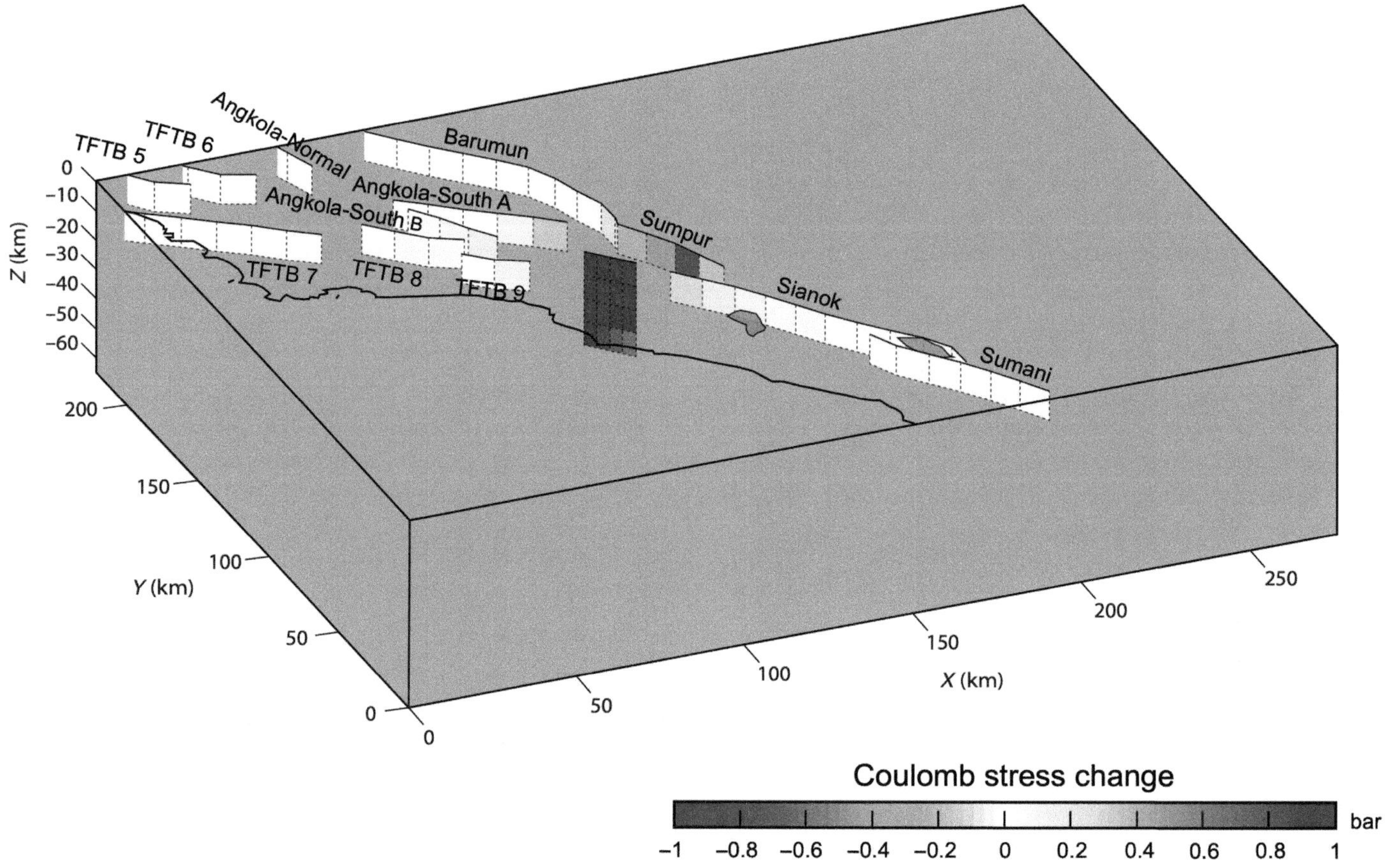

Figure 4. Stress imparted by the fault rupture of model 2 to the surrounding active faults. Except for the Talamau segment, the top and bottom depths of the active faults are set to 0 and 10 km, respectively. The color version of this figure is available only in the electronic edition.

M_w 6.6 Dikit earthquake (Salman *et al.*, 2020), 2013 M_w 6.1 Aceh earthquake, and 2016 M_w 6.5 Aceh earthquake. Another major strike-slip earthquake, that is the 2018 M_w 7.6 Palu Donggala earthquake (Socquet *et al.*, 2019), was also used as a comparison. Figure 5 shows the comparison between parameters of those earthquakes (magnitude and fault length) with the earthquake scaling relationship model of Gunawan (2021).

By comparing the earthquake scaling relationship model and these major strike-slip earthquakes, we show that the 2022 Pasaman earthquake follows the empirical function satisfactorily (Fig. 5). The fault length of model 1 did not follow the earthquake scaling relationship, resulting in a poor prediction of the GNSS displacements. Thus, estimating an earthquake magnitude from fault length information can be a simple but rapid way to estimate future earthquake potential.

Marliyani *et al.* (2016) showed that the Cimandiri fault, in western Java, Indonesia, consists of six segments, where each segment may generate earthquakes between 6.5 and 6.9. However, the case of the 2018 M_w 7.6 Palu Donggala earthquake showed that crustal earthquakes in Indonesia could reach up to M_w 7.6. Thus, assuming a similar case to the Cimandiri fault, it could reach a magnitude of up to M_w 7.3. The 2022 Cianjur earthquake in western Java showed that it did not necessarily need a magnitude 7 class earthquake to be devastating (Gunawan, Hanifa, *et al.*, 2024). An M_w 5.6 is enough to generate damage to ~56,548 buildings, and more than 300 fatalities. In such cases, the background seismicity is key to conducting seismic hazard assessment. However, defining the minimum magnitude is a challenge that needs to be considered based on the completeness of the recorded seismicity in each region.

Conclusion

This study has investigated the responsible fault segment of the 2022 Pasaman earthquake using GNSS data. We found that the mainshock ruptured a newly recognized segment of the Sumatran fault named by the National Center for Earthquake Studies as the Talamau segment. The maximum slip of 14 cm in our best-fit model occurred at 4 km depth, 13 km away from the epicenter. Assuming the shear modulus of 33 GPa, we found that the earthquake was associated with a seismic moment of 1.58×10^{25} N · m, or equivalent to M_w 6.1. We also explore the impact of the earthquake on nearby faults. Using the Coulomb stress change investigation, we found that the 2022 M_w 6.1 Pasaman earthquake increased stress along the

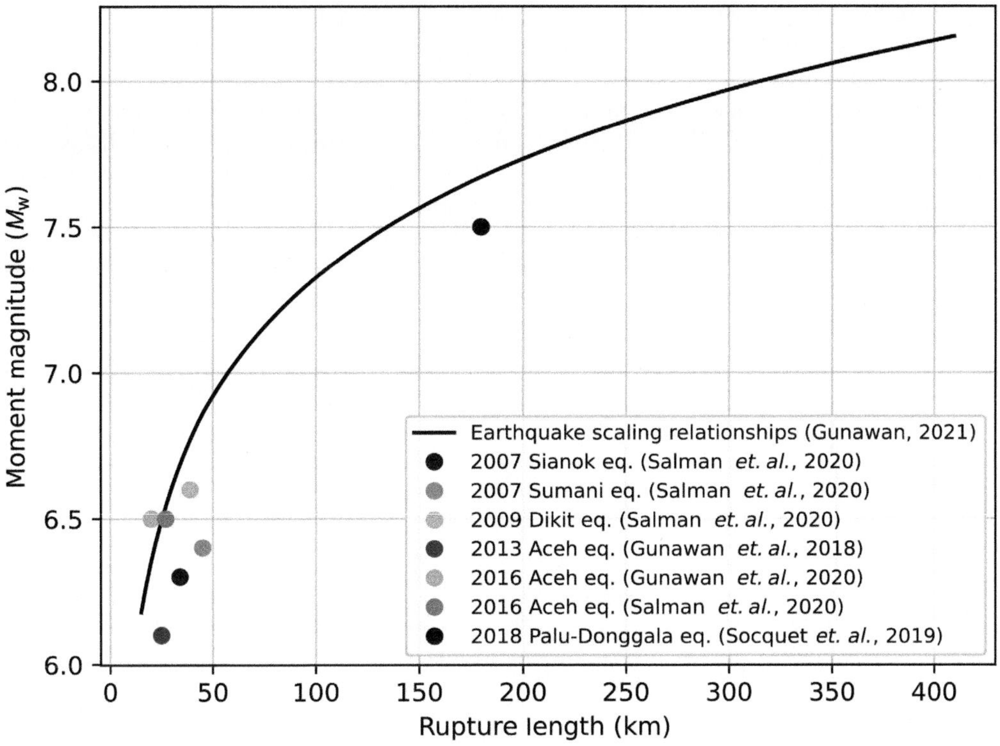

Figure 5. Rupture length as a function of moment magnitude. A solid black line indicates the earthquake scaling relationship for rupture length and moment magnitude based on Gunawan (2021). Color dots represent various earthquake cases from Socquet *et al.* (2019), Salman *et al.* (2020), and Gunawan *et al.* (2018, 2020). The color version of this figure is available only in the electronic edition.

Sumpur and the northern Sianok segments by approximately 0.4 and 0.3 bar bringing these closer to failure. Given that no historical earthquake has been reported along Sumpur and northern Sianok segments since at least 1892, an earthquake with a magnitude of 6.7 may occur if these segments were to rupture. Finally, we show that the 2022 Pasaman earthquake follows the empirical earthquake scaling relationship between fault length and earthquake magnitude for active regions in Indonesia developed by Gunawan (2021). Thus, estimating an earthquake magnitude from fault length information is a simple but rapid way of estimating future earthquake potential on faults with otherwise little information.

Data and Resources

The data and materials used and/or analyzed during the current study are available from the corresponding author on reasonable request. The ocean-loading parameters were obtained from the Onsala Space Observatory (http://holt.oso.chalmers.se/loading/, last accessed September 2024). Earthquake focal mechanisms were taken from the U.S. Geological Survey (USGS) catalog (https://earthquake.usgs.gov/earthquakes/eventpage/us6000gzyg/executive, last accessed September 2024) and GeoForschungsZentrums (GFZ) catalog (https://geofon.gfz.de/old/eqinfo/event.php?id=gfz2022dwpy, last accessed September 2024). The information about the Earth Observatory of Singapore is available at ftp://ftp.earthobservatory.sg/SugarData/ (last accessed October 2024). The supplemental material includes a description of the inversion procedure, the Global Navigation Satellite System (GNSS) data used in the study, and a summary of the slip distribution model 2.

Declaration of Competing Interests

The authors acknowledge that there are no conflicts of interest recorded.

Acknowledgments

The authors thank two anonymous reviewers, Romain Jolivet and Editor-in-Chief Allison Bent, for their critical comments and constructive suggestions, which help improve the quality of this article. This study is supported by the 2025 Excellent Research of Institut Teknologi Bandung, the 2024 Research and Innovation for Advanced Indonesia program supported by the National Research and Innovation Agency of Indonesia (BRIN) and Indonesia Endowment Fund for Education Agency (LPDP), and the Center for Excellence Research and Research Centers (RU3P; Riset Unggulan Pusat dan Pusat Penelitian) of Institut Teknologi Bandung. Ekbal Hussain is supported by the British Geological Survey International NC programme "Geoscience to tackle Global Environmental Challenges," NE/X006255/1. Ekbal Hussain publishes with permission from the Executive Director of the British Geological Survey. Figures were generated using the Generic Mapping Tools (GMT) software (Wessel *et al.*, 2019).

References

Altamimi, Z., P. Rebischung, L. Métivier, and X. Collilieux (2016). ITRF2014: A new release of the International Terrestrial Reference Frame modeling nonlinear station motions, *J. Geophys. Res.* **121,** no. 8, 6109–6131.

Barbot, S. (2024). Transient and steady-state friction in non-isobaric conditions, *Geochem. Geophys. Geosys.* **25,** no. 2, e2023GC011279, doi: 10.1029/2023GC011279.

Bertiger, W., Y. Bar-Sever, A. Dorsey, B. Haines, N. Harvey, D. Hemberger, M. Heflin, W. Lu, M. Miller, A. W. Moore, and D. Murphy (2020). GipsyX/RTGx, a new tool set for space geodetic operations and research, *Adv. Space Res.* **66,** no. 3, 469–489.

Bradley, K. E., L. Feng, E. M. Hill, D. H. Natawidjaja, and K. Sieh (2017). Implications of the diffuse deformation of the Indian

Ocean lithosphere for slip partitioning of oblique plate convergence in Sumatra, *J. Geophys. Res.* **122,** no. 1, 572–591.

Bürgmann, R., W. Thatcher, and M. E. Bickford (2013). Space geodesy: A revolution in crustal deformation measurements of tectonic processes, *Geol. Soc. Am. Spec. Pap.* **500,** 397–430.

Byrne, H., J. A. Silva, A. Plesch, R. Juanes, and J. H. Shaw (2020). The groundbreaking experiment in earthquake control at Rangely, Colorado, revisited, *Geophys. Res. Lett.* **47,** no. 11, e2020GL088257, doi: 10.1029/2020GL088257.

DeVries, P. M., F. Viégas, M. Wattenberg, and B. J. Meade (2018). Deep learning of aftershock patterns following large earthquakes, *Nature* **560,** no. 7720, 632–634.

Feng, L., E. M. Hill, P. Banerjee, I. Hermawan, L. L. Tsang, D. H. Natawidjaja, B. W. Suwargadi, and K. Sieh (2015). A unified GPS-based earthquake catalog for the Sumatran plate boundary between 2002 and 2013, *J. Geophys. Res.* **120,** no. 5, 3566–3598.

Fukahata, Y., and T. J. Wright (2008). A non-linear geodetic data inversion using ABIC for slip distribution on a fault with an unknown dip angle, *Geophys. J. Int.* **173,** no. 2, 353–364.

Gunawan, E. (2021). An assessment of earthquake scaling relationships for crustal earthquakes in Indonesia, *Seismol. Res. Lett.* **92,** no. 4, 2490–2497, doi: 10.1785/0220200267.

Gunawan, E., R. Amey, J. Elliott, S. Widiyantoro, N. T. Puspito, N. R. Hanifa, Syamsuddin, and E. Hussain (2023). Coseismic deformation of the 19 August 2018 Mw 7.2 Lombok earthquakes, Indonesia, estimated through InSAR and GPS observations, *Nat. Hazards* **119,**545–558, doi: 10.1007/s11069-023-06142-3.

Gunawan, E., A. Gualandi, N. Rawlinson, S. Widiyantoro, M. Kholil, P. Supendi, G. H. Pramono, and S. T. Wibowo (2024). Complex fault system associated with the Molucca Sea Divergent double subduction zone revealed by the 2019 Mw 6.9 and Mw 7.1 earthquakes, *Tectonophysics* 230493, doi: 10.1016/j.tecto.2024.230493.

Gunawan, E., N. R. Hanifa, D. H. Natawidjaja, T. Nishimura, S. Widiyantoro, B. Sugiarto, A. F. Shomim, and M. Ohzono (2024). Early postseismic slip of the 21 November 2022 Mw 5.6 Cianjur, Indonesia, earthquake based on GPS measurements, *New Zeal. J. Geol. Geophys.* doi: 10.1080/00288306.2024.2402254.

Gunawan, E., W. Kongko, M. Kholil, B. T. Widyantoro, S. Widiyantoro, P. Supendi, N. R. Hanifa, I. M. Anjasmara, C. Pratama, and A. R. Gusman (2022). The 2019 Mw 7.0 Banten, Indonesia, intraslab earthquake: Investigation of the coseismic slip, tsunami modelling and Coulomb stress change, *Geoenviron. Disast.* **9,** no. 14, doi: 10.1186/s40677-022-00215-4.

Gunawan, E., T. Nishimura, S. Susilo, S. Widiyantoro, N. T. Puspito, D. P. Sahara, N. R. Hanifa, S. Hidayati, A. Omang, and A. Agustan (2020). Fault source investigation of the 6 December 2016 Mw 6.5 Pidie Jaya, Indonesia, earthquake based on GPS and its implications of the geological survey result, *J. Appl. Geodes.* **14,** no. 4, 405–412.

Gunawan, E., S. Widiyantoro, S. Rosalia, M. R. Daryono, I. Meilano, P. Supendi, T. Ito, T. Tabei, F. Kimata, Y. Ohta, and N. Ismail (2018). Coseismic slip distribution of the 2 July 2013 Mw 6.1 Aceh, Indonesia, earthquake and its tectonic implications, *Bull. Seismol. Soc. Am.* **108,** no. 4, 1918–1928.

Hardebeck, J. L., J. J. Nazareth, and E. Hauksson (1998). The static stress change triggering model: Constraints from two southern California aftershock sequences, *J. Geophys. Res.* **103,** no. B10, 24,427–24,437.

Herring, T. A., R. W. King, and S. C. McClusky (2010a). *GAMIT Reference Manual Release 10.4, Report*, Massachusetts Institute Technology, Cambridge, Massachusetts, 1–171.

Herring, T. A., R. W. King, and S. C. McClusky (2010b). *GLOBK Reference Manual: Global Kalman filter VLBI and GPS Analysis Program, Release 10.4, Report*, Massachusetts Institute Technology, Cambridge, Massachusetts, 1–95.

Hurukawa, N., B. R. Wulandari, and M. Kasahara (2014). Earthquake history of the Sumatran fault, Indonesia, since 1892, derived from relocation of large earthquakes, *Bull. Seismol. Soc. Am.* **104,** no. 4, 1750–1762.

Irsyam, M., P. R. Cummins, M. Asrurifak, L. Faizal, D. H. Natawidjaja, S. Widiyantoro, I. Meilano, W. Triyoso, A. Rudiyanto, S. Hidayati, and M. Ridwan (2020). Development of the 2017 national seismic hazard maps of Indonesia, *Earthq. Spectra* **36,** no. 1_suppl, 112–136, doi: 10.1177/8755293020951206.

Ito, T., E. Gunawan, F. Kimata, T. Tabei, M. Simons, I. Meilano, Agustan, Y. Ohta, I. Nurdin, and D. Sugiyanto (2012). Isolating along-strike variations in the depth extent of shallow creep and fault locking on the northern Great Sumatran Fault, *J. Geophys. Res.* **117,** no. B6, doi: 10.1029/2011JB008940.

King, G. C., R. S. Stein, and J. Lin (1994). Static stress changes and the triggering of earthquakes, *Bull. Seismol. Soc. Am.* **84,** no. 3, 935–953.

Larson, K. M. (2019). Unanticipated uses of the global positioning system, *Annu. Rev. Earth Planet. Sci.* **47,** no. 1, 19–40.

Lentas, K., C. G. Gkarlaouni, N. Kalligeris, and N. S. Melis (2022). The 30 October 2020, MW= 7.0, Samos earthquake: Aftershock relocation, slip model, Coulomb stress evolution and estimation of shaking, *Bull. Earthq. Eng.* **20,** no. 2, 819–851.

Li, M., S. Zhang, C. Zhang, and Y. Zhang (2015). Fault slip model of 2013 Lushan earthquake retrieved based on GPS coseismic displacements, *J. Earth Sci.* **26,** 537–547.

Lin, J., and R. S. Stein (2004). Stress triggering in thrust and subduction earthquakes and stress interaction between the southern San Andreas and nearby thrust and strike-slip faults, *J. Geophys. Res.* **109,** no. B2, doi: 10.1029/2003JB002607.

Marliyani, G. I., J. R. Arrowsmith, and K. X. Whipple (2016). Characterization of slow slip rate faults in humid areas: Cimandiri fault zone, Indonesia, *J. Geophys. Res.* **121,** no. 12, 2287–2308.

McCaffrey, R. (2009). The tectonic framework of the Sumatran subduction zone, *Annu. Rev. Earth Planet. Sci.* **37,** no. 1, 345–366.

Meade, B. J., P. M. DeVries, J. Faller, F. Viegas, and M. Wattenberg (2017). What is better than Coulomb failure stress? A ranking of scalar static stress triggering mechanisms from 105 mainshock-aftershock pairs, *Geophys. Res. Lett.* **44,** no. 22, 11–409.

Murase, M., N. Matta, T. Ishiyama, C. H. Lin, W. Chen, J. Y. Yen, J. B. H. Shyu, J. Lin, Y. Nishikawa, I. C. Yen, and F. R. Widiatmoko (2025). Effects of the 2022 Mw 7.0 Chihshang earthquake on the shallow creeping of the Central Longitudinal Valley Fault in Eastern Taiwan: Insights from precise leveling measurements, *Seismol. Res. Lett.* **96,** no. 3, 1521–1531.

Nishimura, T., M. Sato, and T. Sagiya (2014). Global Positioning System (GPS) and GPS-Acoustic observations: Insight into slip along the subduction zones around Japan, *Annu. Rev. Earth Planet. Sci.* **42,** no. 1, 653–674.

Okada, Y. (1992). Internal deformation due to shear and tensile faults in a half-space, *Bull. Seismol. Soc. Am.* **82,** no. 2, 1018–1040.

Prawirodirdjo, L., Y. Bock, J. F. Genrich, S. S. O. Puntodewo, J. Rais, C. Subarya, and S. Sutisna (2000). One century of tectonic deformation along the Sumatran fault from triangulation and Global Positioning System surveys, *J. Geophys. Res.* **105,** no. B12, 28,343–28,361.

Salman, R., E. O. Lindsey, L. Feng, K. Bradley, S. Wei, T. Wang, M. R. Daryono, and E. M. Hill (2020). Structural controls on rupture extent of recent Sumatran Fault Zone earthquakes, Indonesia, *J. Geophys. Res.* **125,** no. 2, e2019JB018101, doi: 10.1029/2019JB018101.

Socquet, A., J. Hollingsworth, E. Pathier, and M. Bouchon (2019). Evidence of supershear during the 2018 magnitude 7.5 Palu earthquake from space geodesy, *Nature Geosci.* **12,** no. 3, 192–199.

Supendi, P., N. Rawlinson, B. S. Prayitno, D. Sianipar, A. Simanjuntak, S. Widiyantoro, K. H. Palgunadi, A. Kurniawan, H. A. Shiddiqi, A. D. Nugraha, and D. P. Sahara (2023). A previously unidentified fault revealed by the February 25, 2022 (Mw 6.1) Pasaman earthquake, West Sumatra, Indonesia, *Phys. Earth Planet. In.* **334,**106973, 10.1016/j.pepi.2022.106973.

Tanaka, Y., Y. Ohta, and S. I. Miyazaki (2019). Real-time coseismic slip estimation via the GNSS carrier phase to fault slip approach: A case study of the 2016 Kumamoto earthquake, *Geophys. Res. Lett.* **46,** no. 3, 1367–1374.

Toda, S., and R. Stein (2003). Toggling of seismicity by the 1997 Kagoshima earthquake couplet: A demonstration of time-dependent stress transfer, *J. Geophys. Res.* **108,** no. B12, doi: 10.1029/2003JB002527.

Toda, S., J. Lin, and R. S. Stein (2011). Using the 2011 Mw 9.0 off the Pacific coast of Tohoku Earthquake to test the Coulomb stress triggering hypothesis and to calculate faults brought closer to failure, *Earth Planets Space* **63,**725–730.

Toda, S., R. S. Stein, K. Richards-Dinger, and S. B. Bozkurt (2005). Forecasting the evolution of seismicity in southern California: Animations built on earthquake stress transfer, *J. Geophys. Res.* **110,** no. B5, doi: 10.1029/2004JB003415.

Wang, K., Y. Hu, and J. He (2012). Deformation cycles of subduction earthquakes in a viscoelastic Earth, *Nature* **484,** no. 7394, 327–332.

Wells, D. L., and K. J. Coppersmith (1994). New empirical relationships among magnitude, rupture length, rupture width, rupture area, and surface displacement, *Bull. Seismol. Soc. Am.* **84,** no. 4, 974–1002.

Wessel, P., J. F. Luis, L. A. Uieda, R. Scharroo, F. Wobbe, W. H. Smith, and D. Tian (2019). The generic mapping tools version 6, *Geochem. Geophys. Geosys.* **20,** no. 11, 5556–5564.

Wright, T. J. (2016). The earthquake deformation cycle, *Astron. Geophys.* **54,** no. 7, 4–20.

Yabuki, T., and M. Matsu'ura (1992). Geodetic data inversion using a Bayesian information criterion for spatial distribution of fault slip, *Geophys. J. Int.* **109,** no. 2, 363–375.

Yoshida, S., T. Maeda, and N. Kato (2020). Earthquake triggering model based on normal-stress-dependent Nagata law: Application to the 2016 Mie offshore earthquake, *Earth Planets Space* **72,** 1–13.

Zhang, Y., H. Bao, Y. Aoki, and A. Hashima (2023). Integrated seismic source model of the 2021 M 7.1 Fukushima earthquake, *Geophys. J. Int.* **233,** no. 1, 93–106.

Manuscript received 11 December 2024
Published online 10 October 2025

Crustal Rheology and Fluid Migration Control the 2008 M_w 7.9 Wenchuan, China, Earthquake

Xingpeng Dong[1], Dinghui Yang[*2], and Weijuan Meng[3]

Abstract

The 2008 M_w 7.9 Wenchuan earthquake caused widespread devastation, prompting in-depth investigations into its underlying mechanisms. Benefiting from the dense seismograph deployments of the ChinArray project, we conducted an innovative Wasserstein-based full-waveform inversion in the Longmenshan region. Our results reveal significant rheological contrasts across the region: a mechanically weak plateau west of the Longriba fault (LRBF), characterized by low-seismic velocity and high-Poisson's ratio; a moderately stronger zone between the LRBF and Longmenshan fault (LMSF), exhibiting intermediate velocity and low-Poisson's ratio; and a highly rigid Sichuan basin with high velocity and low-Poisson's ratio. This rheological architecture suggests enhanced crustal strength surrounding the LMSF, facilitating significant strain accumulation prior to rupture. Notably, the elevated Poisson's ratio beneath the earthquake's hypocenter indicates fluid-rich zones, where the migration of fluids into the seismogenic zone may have increased the likelihood of mainshock fault failure. These findings provide new insights into the physical mechanisms driving the Wenchuan earthquake and offer broader implications for understanding the generation of devastating earthquakes worldwide.

Cite this article as Dong, X., D. Yang, and W. Meng (2025). Crustal Rheology and Fluid Migration Control the 2008 M_w 7.9 Wenchuan, China, Earthquake, *Seismol. Res. Lett.* **97**, 1008–1017, doi: 10.1785/0220250040.

Supplemental Material

Introduction

The Tibetan Plateau, the largest and highest continental collision zone on Earth, has been undergoing uplift since the Cenozoic, representing one of the most significant geodynamic phenomena globally (Yin and Harrison, 2000; Tapponnier *et al.*, 2001). Global positioning system (GPS) measurements reveal large-scale tectonic extrusion across the plateau, driven by the ongoing collision between the Indian and Eurasian plates (Kreemer *et al.*, 2014; Wang and Shen, 2020). This extrusion is particularly pronounced along the southeastern margin, where it manifests as a clockwise rotation around the Eastern Himalayan syntaxis (EHS; Fig. 1a). In contrast, extrusion is less prominent along other margins due to the presence of rheologically strong terranes, such as the Tarim basin (TB), Alxa block (AB), Ordos block (OB), and Sichuan basin (SB). The Longmenshan fault (LMSF), which marks the boundary between the eastern Tibetan Plateau and the SB, exhibits the steepest topographic gradient among all plateau margins (Royden *et al.*, 1997).

The 2008 M_w 7.9 Wenchuan earthquake ruptured the LMSF along approximately 300 km, resulting in nearly 70,000 fatalities, widespread destruction, and significant economic losses, making it China's most devastating earthquake since the 1976 Tangshan earthquake (Xu *et al.*, 2009; Zhang *et al.*, 2010). Despite extensive research, the fundamental mechanics underlying this earthquake remain enigmatic and hotly debated. Balanced geological cross sections derived from seismic reflection data suggest that crustal shortening was the principal mechanism driving uplift in the Longmenshan region and the primary cause of the Wenchuan earthquake (Hubbard and Shaw, 2009). Alternatively, other studies argue that crustal thickening beneath the eastern Tibetan Plateau is predominantly driven by ductile deformation in the low-viscosity deep crust, with the Wenchuan earthquake representing a manifestation of this prolonged tectonic process (e.g., Burchfiel *et al.*, 2008). Resolving this debate necessitates a refined 3D crustal model, which is now possible through the application of advanced full-waveform inversion (FWI) techniques, aided by dense seismic networks across the Longmenshan region.

Recent advances in computing power, signal processing, numerical modeling, and optimization techniques have significantly enhanced the capability of FWI to image high-resolution

1. State Key Laboratory of Earthquake Dynamics and Forecasting, Institute of Geology, China Earthquake Administration, Beijing, China; 2. Department of Mathematical Sciences, Tsinghua University, Beijing, China; 3. Institute of Geophysics, China Earthquake Administration, Beijing, China, https://orcid.org/0000-0002-9622-7781 (WM)

*Corresponding author: ydh@tsinghua.edu.cn

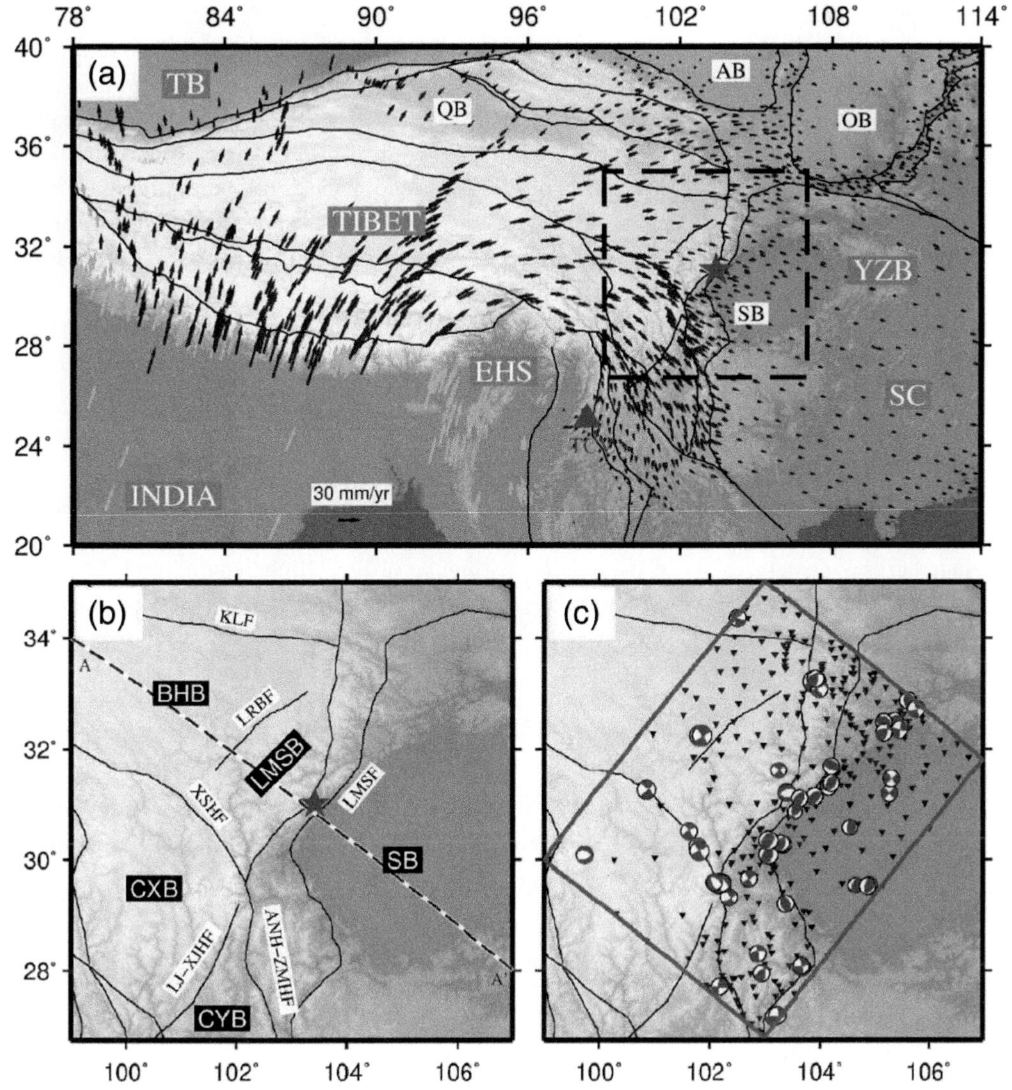

Figure 1. Tectonic map of the Tibetan Plateau and adjacent regions. (a) Location of the study region within the Tibetan Plateau and surrounding regions, (b) tectonic units and major faults within the study region, and (c) seismic events and stations utilized in the inversion. The blue-inverted triangles denote portable stations, the black-inverted triangles denote permanent stations, and the red focal mechanism plots represent earthquake focal mechanisms. The red star marks the 2008 Wenchuan earthquake, and the red triangle marks the Tengchong volcano. AB, Alxa block; ANH-ZMHF, Anninghe-Zemuhe fault; BHB, Bayan Har block; CXB, Chuanxibei sub-block; CYB, Central Yunnan sub-block; EHS, Eastern Himalayan syntaxis; KLF, Kunlun fault; LJ-XJHF, Lijiang-Xiaojinhe fault; LMSB, Longmenshan block; LMSF, Longmenshan fault; LRBF, Longriba fault; OB, Ordos block; QB, Qaidam basin; SB, Sichuan basin; SC, South China plate; TB, Tarim basin; TCV, Tengchong volcano; XSHF, Xianshuihe fault; YZB, Yangtze block. The blue-dashed line indicates cross-section A–A′. The blue and light-blue arrows represent the global positioning system (GPS) velocity field with respect to the stable Eurasian plate, from Wang and Shen (2020) and Kreemer *et al.* (2014), respectively. The color version of this figure is available only in the electronic edition.

subsurface structures (e.g., Fichtner *et al.*, 2009; Tape *et al.*, 2009; Chen *et al.*, 2015; Tao *et al.*, 2018; Zhu *et al.*, 2020; Gao *et al.*, 2021; Chow *et al.*, 2022; Zhang and Zhu, 2023; Dong and Yang, 2025; Yang *et al.*, 2025). Traditionally, the L2 norm has been used as the objective function in FWI. However, this approach, based on point-by-point comparisons, is highly nonconvex with respect to time shifts, making it susceptible to local minima, especially when significant time shifts (e.g., greater than half the wave period) exist between observed and synthetic seismograms (Virieux and Operto, 2009).

Mathematically, FWI can be formulated as a partial-differential-equation-constrained optimization problem, for which the critical challenge lies in addressing the nonconvexity rather than merely the nonlinearity (Rockafellar, 1993). To improve stability and convergence, it is essential to adopt a metric that enhances the convexity of the misfit function in the associated inverse problem (Métivier *et al.*, 2016). The quadratic Wasserstein (W2) metric, derived from optimal transport theory, has emerged as a promising alternative to mitigate the nonconvexity inherent in the conventional L2 norm (Engquist and Froese, 2014; Engquist *et al.*, 2016). Previous studies have demonstrated that the W2 metric offers several advantages, including enhanced convexity with respect to time shifts and partial amplitude variations (Qiu *et al.*, 2017; Yang *et al.*, 2018). Furthermore, in contrast to the L2 norm, which is sensitive to noise, the W2 metric exhibits notable robustness, making it particularly suited for large-scale, earthquake-based tomographic studies for which data noise is unavoidable and often significant (Qiu, 2021; Engquist and Yang, 2022).

In this study, we employ W2-based FWI to develop a high-resolution, multiparameter 3D crustal model of the Longmenshan region and its surroundings. This model is constructed using high-quality, three-component seismograms recorded by both permanent and portable seismic arrays (Zheng *et al.*, 2009). The resulting images, which include seismic velocities, Poisson's ratio, and radial anisotropy, provide critical new insights into the crustal architecture, highlighting variations in rheology and potential deep fluid anomalies. These findings enhance our understanding of the physical processes underlying the 2008 Wenchuan earthquake and offer valuable constraints for mitigating seismic hazards in the densely populated regions along the LMSF.

Data and Methods

The ChinArray project deployed a dense network of portable seismic stations across the Longmenshan region and its surroundings (denoted by blue-inverted triangles in Fig. 1c), supplemented by sparser permanent stations from the China Digital Seismograph Network (black-inverted triangles in Fig. 1c). Combined with the frequent occurrence of moderate-to-large earthquakes, this network offers an optimal observational framework for imaging the detailed crustal structures of the region using W2-based FWI.

To focus the imaging efforts on the LMSF, we selected earthquakes and seismic stations within a rectangular region, with the long axis of the rectangle aligned approximately parallel to the trend of the LMSF (Fig. 1c). We collected seismic waveforms from 51 regional earthquakes, recorded by 59 permanent and 247 portable stations. The selected events, with magnitudes ranging from M_w 4.5 to 6.5, were chosen to balance maintaining a sufficient signal-to-noise ratio (SNR) while minimizing finite-source effects (Fichtner *et al.*, 2013; Chen *et al.*, 2015).

Traditional L2-norm-based FWI is often hindered by the cycle-skipping problem, a significant challenge resulting from the limitations of its local metric (Virieux and Operto, 2009). This issue can lead the inversion process into local minima, reducing the accuracy of subsurface imaging and undermining the reliability of geological interpretations. In contrast, the W2 metric, as a global measure, provides improved convexity with respect to model parameters, making it a more attractive objective function for comparing seismic signals in FWI (Yang, 2018).

The initial model was derived from the corresponding region of the FWEA18 model, which is a large-scale background anisotropic velocity model for East Asia (Tao *et al.*, 2018). Seismic waveform inversions were performed across two frequency bands: 20–40 and 8–40 s. The inversion result from the lower frequency band served as the initial model for the higher frequency band (Tape *et al.*, 2007; Blom *et al.*, 2020). We utilized FLEXWIN software to select appropriate waveform windows, within which the misfit function and corresponding adjoint source were calculated (Maggi *et al.*, 2009). The selection process is based on a comparison of the three-component observed and synthetic seismograms according to several quantitative criteria. The primary criteria for selecting waveform windows include: (1) the cross-correlation coefficient between the observed and synthetic waveforms must be ≥0.85; (2) the amplitude discrepancy between the observed and synthetic waveforms must be ≤1.0; (3) the travel-time residual must be ≤8.0 s; and (4) the SNR, calculated as the ratio of the maximum amplitude within the time window to the root mean square amplitude of the pre-event noise window, must be ≥3.0. It is important that all calculations of these parameters are performed independently within each candidate time window, with no averaging applied across components or windows. These stringent criteria ensure the reliability of the selected waveform segments, particularly by excluding those dominated by noise.

The W2-based misfit function between the observed (g) and synthetic (f) seismograms within a selected waveform window is defined as follows (Yang *et al.*, 2018; Dong *et al.*, 2019):

$$W_2^2(f,g) = \int_0^{T_0} |t - G^{-1}(F(t))|^2 f(t)\mathrm{d}t, \tag{1}$$

in which T_0 is the recording time length, and G and F are cumulative distribution functions of the observed and synthetic waveforms, respectively.

$$F(t) = \int_0^t f(\tau)\mathrm{d}\tau, G(t) = \int_0^t g(\tau)\mathrm{d}\tau. \tag{2}$$

The W2-based misfit function $\chi(\boldsymbol{m})$ for the current Earth model $\boldsymbol{m}$ encompassing all selected windows is expressed as follows (Dong *et al.*, 2022):

$$\chi(\boldsymbol{m}) = \frac{1}{N_\omega}\sum_{e=1}^{E}\sum_{i=1}^{N_\omega^e}\int_{T_{i,\mathrm{start}}}^{T_{i,\mathrm{end}}} |t - G^{-1}(F(t))|^2 f(t)\mathrm{d}t, \tag{3}$$

in which $T_{i,\mathrm{start}}$ and $T_{i,\mathrm{end}}$denote the starting and ending times of the time window, respectively.N_ω^e denotes the number of time windows for each earthquake$e$, E indicates the overall number of earthquakes, and $N_\omega = \sum_{e=1}^{E} N_\omega^e$encompasses all selected windows. The total misfit variation can be expressed as a volume integral involving the relative perturbations of three model parameters, as established and applied in previous studies (Tromp *et al.*, 2005; Liu and Tromp, 2006, 2008; Fichtner *et al.*, 2008; Zhu *et al.*, 2012):

$$\delta\chi = \int (K_{V_c}\delta\ln V_c + K_{V_{sv}}\delta\ln V_{sv} + K_{V_{sh}}\delta\ln V_{sh})\mathrm{d}^3x, \tag{4}$$

in which K_{V_c}, $K_{V_{sv}}$, and $K_{V_{sh}}$represent the Fréchet kernels for the compressional wave speed (V_c), vertically polarized *SV*-wave (V_{SV}), and horizontally polarized *SH*-wave (V_{SH}), respectively. Rather than directly inverting for mass density (ρ), we scaled it to isotropic shear-wave speed perturbations by a factor of 0.33, in which the isotropic shear-wave speed is defined as $V_S = \sqrt{\frac{2V_{SV}^2+V_{SH}^2}{3}}$ (Panning and Romanowicz, 2006). The adjoint-state method was used to efficiently calculate the misfit gradient. The adjoint-source term for each

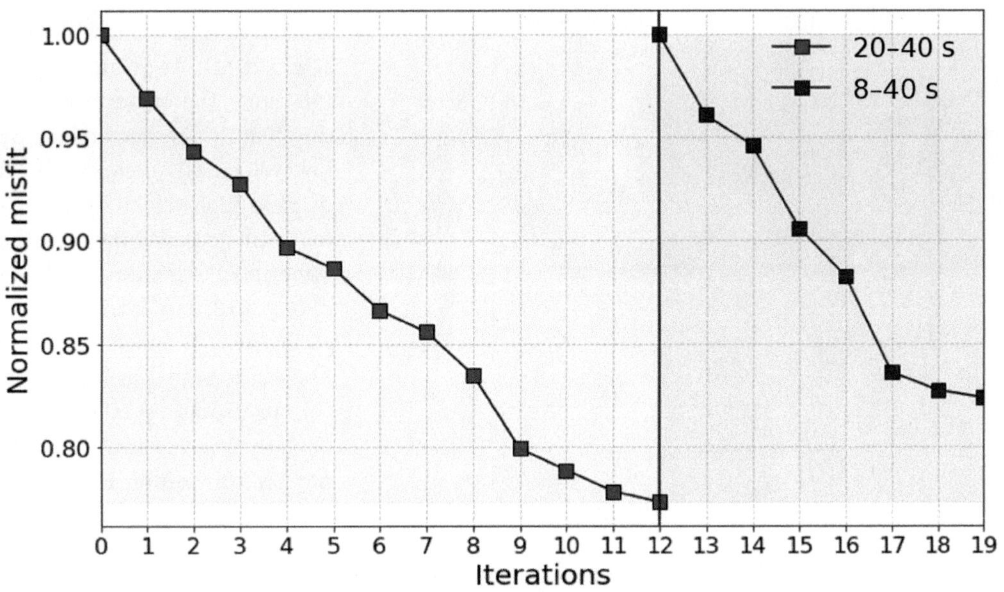

Figure 2. Evolution of the normalized misfit across iterations for the 20–40 s frequency band (red squares) and the 8–40 s frequency band (blue squares). The color version of this figure is available only in the electronic edition.

waveform window is expressed as follows (Yang *et al.*, 2018; Dong *et al.*, 2019):

$$\nabla W_2^2(t) = \left[-2\Gamma \mathrm{diag}\left(\frac{f\Delta t}{g(\mathrm{G}^{-1}\bigcirc \boldsymbol{F}(t))}\right) + \mathrm{diag}(t - \mathrm{G}^{-1}\bigcirc \boldsymbol{F}(t))\right](t - \mathrm{G}^{-1}\bigcirc \boldsymbol{F}(t)), \quad (5)$$

in which Γ represents an upper-triangular matrix with nonzero elements equal to 1. Here, "$\bigcirc$" denotes function composition, such that $\mathrm{G}^{-1}\bigcirc\mathrm{F}(t) = \mathrm{G}^{-1}(\mathrm{F}(t))$ and Δt represents the temporal sampling interval.

The spectral-element software SES3D was used to simulate seismic wave propagation in radially anisotropic media and numerically compute the Fréchet derivatives (Gokhberg and Fichtner, 2016). Attenuation is considered in the forward modeling using a smoothed version of the QL6 model (Durek and Ekström, 1996), with the *Q* parameter remaining fixed during the inversion process. The conjugate gradient method was then applied to iteratively update the model parameters, excluding the *Q* parameter. The iteration process was terminated once the reduction in data misfit between consecutive iterations became negligible—defined here as less than 0.5%. Specifically, this convergence criterion was met after the 12th iteration for the first frequency band (20–40 s) and the 7th iteration for the second frequency band (8–40 s), as shown in Figure 2. This stopping condition provides a pragmatic balance between misfit reduction and computational efficiency and aligns with established practices in large-scale FWI studies (e.g., Chen *et al.*, 2015).

Resolution Test

The checkerboard test is commonly used in large-scale seismic tomography to assess the spatial resolution of imaging results. However, it is less suitable for seismic-wave equation-based FWI due to the substantial computational demands, which are comparable to those of an actual structural inversion (Zhu *et al.*, 2012; Chen *et al.*, 2015). Because the gradient of the misfit function guides model parameter updates, analyzing the spatial distribution of this gradient provides a viable alternative for evaluating the resolution of inversion results, particularly when a local gradient-based optimization method is employed in the inversion.

To assess the reliability of the imaging results, we performed a series of spatial resolution tests in eight key regions: the Wenchuan earthquake epicenter, a site near the LRBF, the northern part of the western SB, the southern Longmenshan block (LMSB), the northern LMSF, the southern part of the western SB, the central part of the western SB, and the region west of the LRBF, at depths of 15 and 35 km. A 5% low-velocity perturbation of size 0.5° × 0.5° was introduced into the *SV*-wave velocity, whereas the *P*- and *SH*-wave velocities remained unchanged. The results show that the gradient pattern of the *SV* velocity closely matches the location of the low-velocity anomaly, indicating that the inversion process effectively captures the primary *SV* velocity anomalies (Figs. S1–S16, available in the supplemental material to this article). Moreover, the gradient values for the *P*- and *SH*-wave velocities are significantly smaller than those for the *SV*-wave velocity, suggesting minimal trade-off between the *P*-, *SH*-, and *SV*-wave velocities (Figs. S1–S16). To further validate the reliability of our inversion results, we compared observed seismograms with synthetic seismograms generated from both the initial and final models for an earthquake that occurred on 10 April 2011, at 09:02:44 (UTC) at stations SC.YYC and T2.S113, as shown in Figures S17 and S18. The synthetic seismograms from the final model show significant improvements in fitting the observed seismograms compared to those from the initial model.

Results and Discussion

The Longmenshan region presents a unique example of an active convergent mountain belt, characterized by minimal relative motion relative to the adjacent SB (Chen *et al.*, 2000;

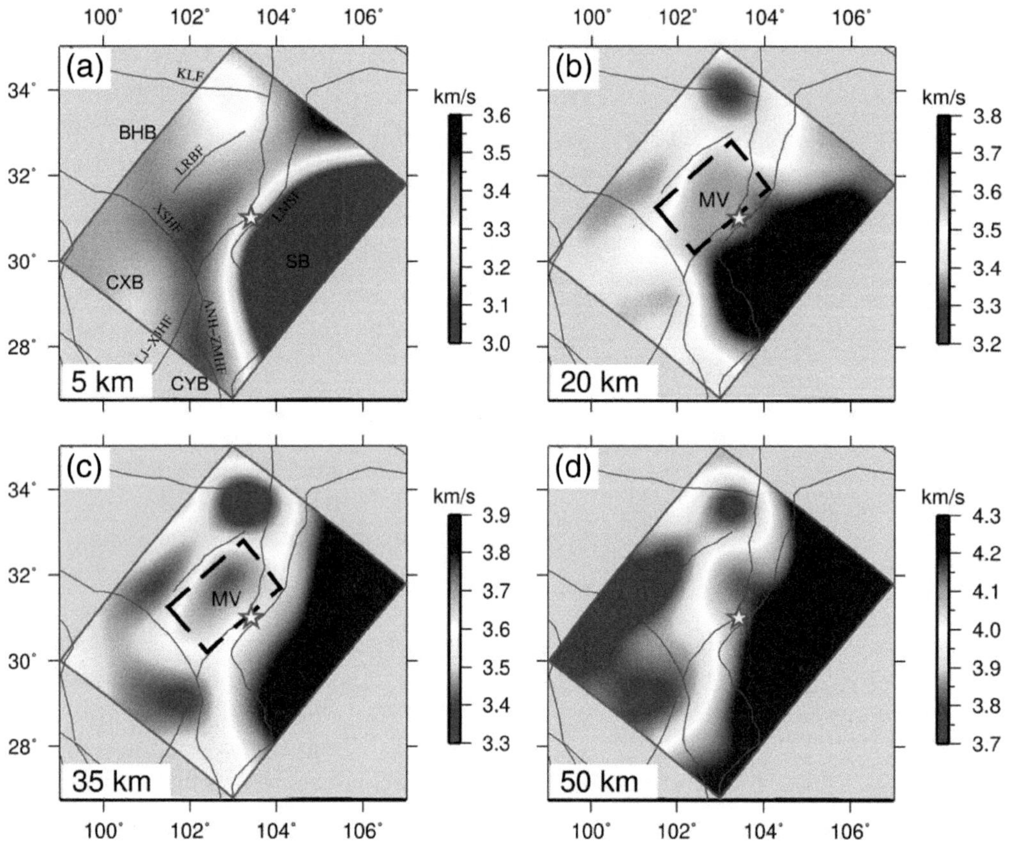

Figure 3. Isotropic *S*-wave velocity distributions in the study region at different depths: (a) 5, (b) 20, (c) 35, and (d) 50 km. The white star denotes the Wenchuan earthquake. MV, moderate velocity. The color version of this figure is available only in the electronic edition.

Shen *et al.*, 2005; Meade, 2007). Despite extensive tomographic studies in this region, most have focused on either *P*- or *S*-wave velocity distributions, derived independently from different datasets and seismic frequencies, making joint interpretation difficult (e.g., Yao *et al.*, 2006, 2008; Lei and Zhao, 2009; Wei *et al.*, 2010; Huang *et al.*, 2018; Zhang *et al.*, 2018; Liu *et al.*, 2021). Consequently, there is a pressing need for comprehensive, high-resolution, crustal-scale tomographic models that can accurately capture the detailed rheology and deformation features of this earthquake-prone area.

Here, we present a new multiparameter seismic model that incorporates the isotropic *S*-wave velocity, Poisson's ratio (v), and radial anisotropy ($\xi = \frac{V_{SH}-V_{SV}}{V_S}$). Figure 3 illustrates that the lateral *S*-wave velocity distributions at various depths. At shallow depths (5 km), the SB is characterized by a pronounced low-velocity anomaly, consistent with its thick sedimentary layer, whereas the surrounding regions exhibit relatively high velocities (Wei *et al.*, 2010). In the mid-lower crust (20 and 35 km), three distinct velocity patterns are observed from the Bayan Har block (BHB) to the SB: a low-velocity BHB (part of the Tibetan Plateau), a moderate-velocity central region, and a high-velocity SB. The central region, bounded by the Longriba fault (LRBF) to the west and the LMSF to the east, is referred to as the LMSB (Guo *et al.*, 2014). At greater depths (50 km), the plateau is predominantly characterized by low velocities, whereas the SB displays high velocities, consistent with its position within the uppermost mantle (Zhang *et al.*, 2018; Liu *et al.*, 2021).

Figure 4 illustrates the Poisson's ratio distributions at various depths, revealing a particularly low-Poisson's ratio in the LMSB. Combined with its moderate seismic velocity, this suggests a rheological structure characterized by moderate-to-strong rigidity. Notably, a remarkably high-Poisson's ratio is observed in the deep crust beneath the Longmenshan range (Fig. 4c,d). To further explore depth-dependent structural variations, a vertical profile along section A–A′ is presented in Figure 5. Significantly, the hypocenter of the 2008 Wenchuan earthquake is precisely located within a transition zone characterized by substantial structural variations. This zone exhibits sharp contrasts, including the juxtaposition of high velocities associated with the SB against the moderate velocities of the Longmenshan region, a transition from positive to negative radial anisotropy, and a shift from a low-Poisson's ratio above the hypocenter to a high-Poisson's ratio below it.

Previous studies have examined the relationship between subsurface structural variations and large earthquakes, primarily focusing on seismic velocity structures such as *P*- and *S*-wave velocities (Huang *et al.*, 2002; Mishra *et al.*, 2007; Lei and Zhao, 2009; Zhao *et al.*, 2010). Expanding on this, our study incorporates additional geophysical parameters, including radial anisotropy and Poisson's ratio, which provide deeper insights into deformation processes and rheological behavior. By integrating these parameters, we highlight the pronounced crustal rheological heterogeneity associated with the 2008 Wenchuan earthquake, offering an enhanced understanding of the mechanisms driving such devastating seismic events.

The region west of the LRBF, within the Tibetan Plateau, with crustal thickness of ~60 km inferred from receiver function analysis, exhibits prominent low-velocity anomalies, strong positive radial anisotropy, and elevated Poisson's ratios, indicative of intense deformation and ductile mid-lower crustal flow (Clark

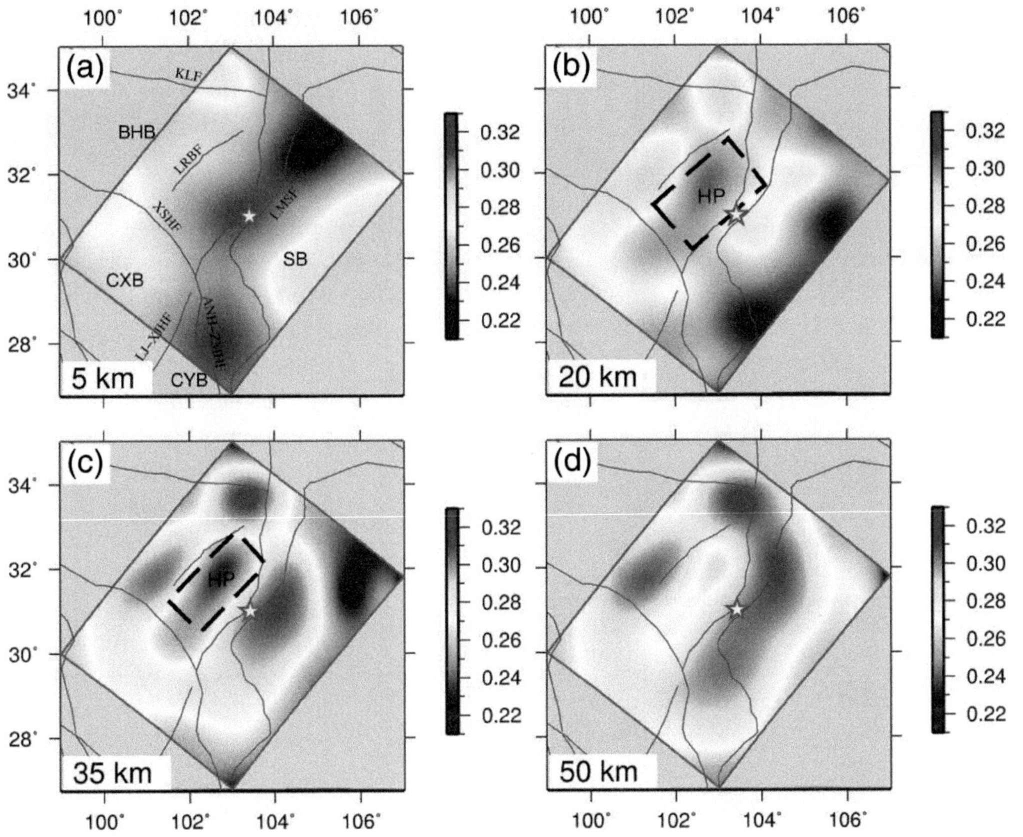

Figure 4. Poisson's ratio distributions in the study region at different depths: (a) 5, (b) 20, (c) 35, and (d) 50 km. The white star denotes the Wenchuan earthquake. HP, high-Poisson's ratio. The color version of this figure is available only in the electronic edition.

et al., 2005; Royden *et al.*, 2008; Wang *et al.*, 2010, 2016). In contrast, the LMSB shows distinctly different seismic velocities and Poisson's ratios. Specifically, seismic velocity in the LMSB is higher than in the plateau to the west but lower than in the SB to the east. In addition, the LMSB has a lower Poisson's ratio, whereas the plateau west of the LRBF exhibits a significantly higher Poisson's ratio. These observations suggest a transition in rheological structure from the plateau to the SB, with a weaker plateau to the west, a relatively stronger LMSB, and a strong SB.

GPS measurements reveal a steep velocity gradient approximately 150 km west of the LMSF, where the eastward motion of the Tibetan Plateau decreases sharply from ~12 to ~3 mm/yr over a distance of less than 10 km (Lv *et al.*, 2003; Shen *et al.*, 2005). This velocity gradient coincides with the LRBF, which likely accommodates stress and modifies the eastward displacement of the Tibetan Plateau (Xu *et al.*, 2008; Ren *et al.*, 2013). The seismic structural pattern revealed in our study suggests that the LMSB may not be part of the eastern Tibetan Plateau but rather linked to the Yangtze block, formed by the extension of the Yangtze crystalline basement from the SB into the easternmost Tibetan Plateau (Guo *et al.*, 2015).

This rheological structure implies that both the LMSB and the SB possess relatively high rock strength on either side of the LMSF, enabling substantial strain energy to accumulate while experiencing minimal deformation under the ongoing compression from the eastern Tibetan Plateau. This configuration explains the lack of significant relative motion between the SB and the Longmenshan region prior to the Wenchuan earthquake (Xu *et al.*, 2005; Zhang *et al.*, 2008), and provides insights into why such a large-magnitude, catastrophic event occurred in this area.

Furthermore, a notable observation is the presence of a distinct high-Poisson's ratio anomaly beneath the hypocenter of the 2008 Wenchuan earthquake, with values exceeding 0.30 (Fig. 5). Several studies have suggested that Poisson's ratio greater than 0.30 in continental crustal rocks are indicative of fluid presence or partial melting (Watanabe, 1993; Zandt and Ammon, 1995; Owens and Zandt, 1997). This anomalous region may be linked to crustal thickening, resulting from ductile crustal channel flow and/or magmatic underplating in the uppermost mantle. A prominent anomaly of low-seismic velocities (V_P, V_S) and a high-V_P/V_S ratio beneath the hypocenter was also identified through traditional ray-theory-based travel-time tomography, interpreted as evidence of fluid infiltration, likely related to partial melting associated with viscous crustal flow from the Tibetan Plateau (Wang *et al.*, 2021). Magnetotelluric imaging further reveals a low-resistivity zone near the Wenchuan hypocenter, suggesting a fluid-rich environment (Zhao *et al.*, 2012). In addition, high-resolution Q_{Pg} tomography indicates a prominent low-Q anomaly region, which spatially coincides with the region of high-Poisson's ratio beneath the hypocenter of the 2008 Wenchuan earthquake, further suggesting significant fluid presence (Li *et al.*, 2023). Given the significantly lower density of crustal fluids compared to surrounding materials, these fluids are likely to migrate upward from deep anomalous regions into the shallow brittle seismogenic layer, either through thin pores (aspect ratio ~0.01) or via cracks that open due to high pore pressure accumulation from persistent crustal flow in Tibet (Rutter and Brodie, 1998; Pei *et al.*, 2019; Wang *et al.*, 2021).

Fluid intrusion into the seismogenic layer plays a critical role in earthquake generation and rupture (O'connell and

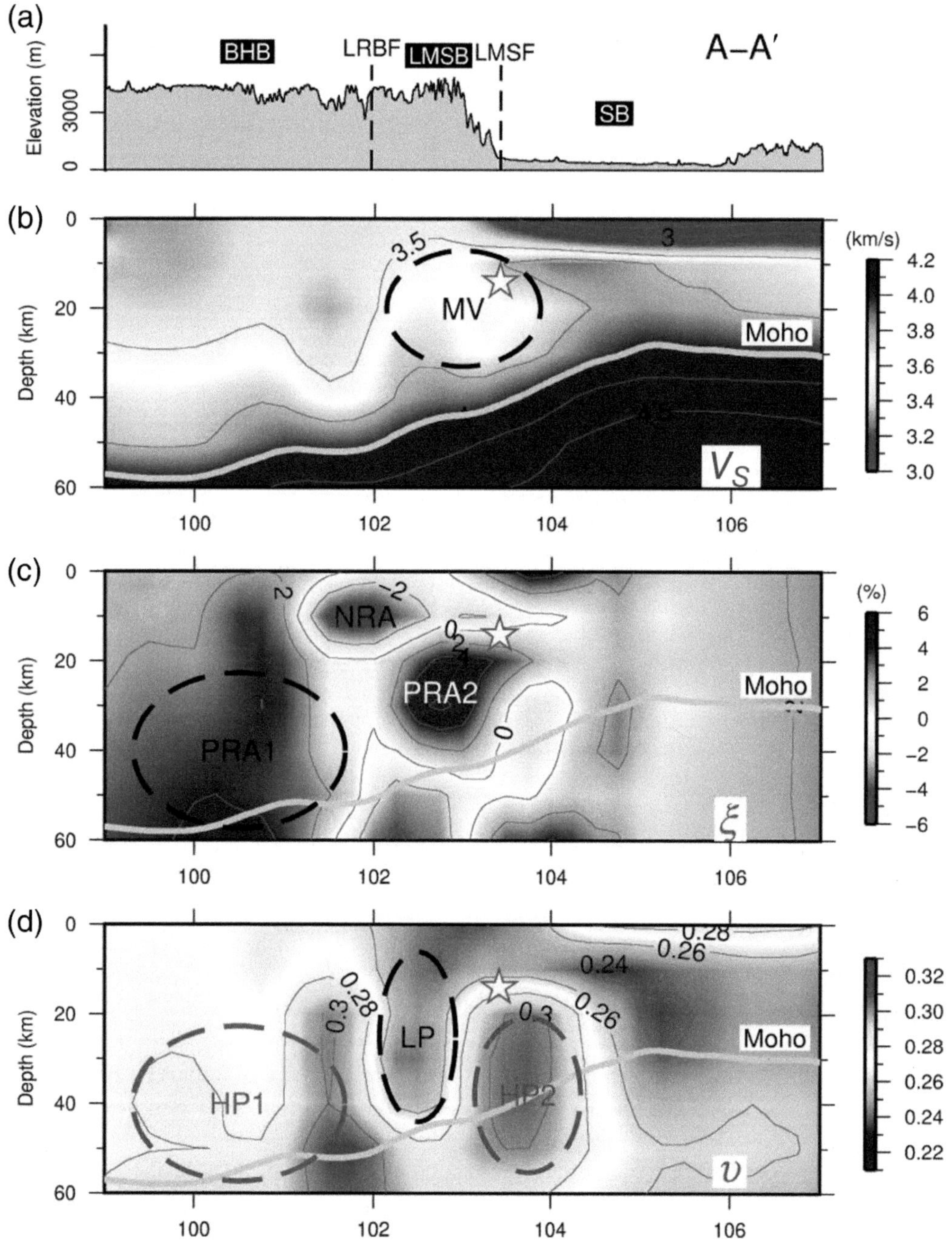

Figure 5. (a) Topographic elevation, (b) isotropic *S*-wave velocity, (c) radial anisotropy, and (d) Poisson's ratio distribution along vertical profile A–A′. The white star indicates the Wenchuan hypocenter. The gray line denotes the Moho discontinuity derived from an isotropic *S*-wave velocity of 4.0 km/s. HP, high-Poisson's ratio; LP, low-Poisson's ratio; MV, moderate velocity; NRA, negative radial anisotropy; PRA, positive radial anisotropy. The color version of this figure is available only in the electronic edition.

Budiansky, 1974). The presence of fluids can significantly influence the long-term structural and compositional evolution of fault zones, affecting fault strength and the local stress regime (Sibson, 1982; Hickman *et al.*, 1995; Wang *et al.*, 2006). In the LMSF region, continuous fluid intrusion, resulting from ductile crustal flow outward from the Tibetan Plateau, would accumulate high pore pressure in seismic zones, weakening the mechanical strength of the rock matrix and potentially altering the local shear-stress field (Wang *et al.*, 2011). In addition, fluid pressure, along with chemical interactions, can enhance stress concentration within the seismogenic layer, leading to mechanical failure of strong asperities (Zhao *et al.*, 2004). Therefore, we conclude that the upward migration of fluids from deep crustal anomalies may have played a significant role in triggering the 2008 Wenchuan earthquake. Similar processes have been linked to other major seismic events, such as the 1995 Kobe earthquake in Japan (Zhao *et al.*, 1996), the 1976 Tangshan earthquake in China (Lei *et al.*, 2008), and the 2019 Ridgecrest earthquake sequence in the United States (Tong *et al.*, 2021).

Conclusions

Utilizing an advanced W2-based FWI technique, we have developed a high-resolution, multiparameter 3D crustal model beneath the Longmenshan region and its surroundings. Our model indicates that the hypocenter of the 2008 Wenchuan earthquake lies within a transition zone characterized by significant contrasts in seismic velocities, radial anisotropy, and Poisson's ratios. This observation suggests that the earthquake likely initiated at the edge of structural anomalies, a region prone to stress concentration. In addition, we identified significant lateral variations in crustal rheology, with the BHB west of the LRBF being weaker, the LMSB relatively strong, and the SB strong. This configuration likely promoted substantial strain energy accumulation along the LMSF, facilitated by the increased strength of the crustal rocks.

The high rheological strength on either side of the LMSF also offers an explanation for the previously puzzling lack of significant relative motion between the Longmenshan region and the SB before the 2008 Wenchuan earthquake, as well as for the occurrence of such a large-magnitude event along this fault. Furthermore, the upward migration of fluids likely played a crucial role in triggering the earthquake by increasing pore pressure and weakening fault interfaces. These results provide new insights into the mechanical processes that governed the 2008 Wenchuan earthquake and highlight the importance of incorporating detailed rheological heterogeneity and crustal fluids into fault risk and seismic hazard assessments, particularly in seismically active regions such as Longmenshan.

Data and Resources

The waveform data utilized in this study are available from doi: 10.6084/m9.figshare.26830315.v1. The numerical modeling of seismic-wave propagation was conducted using the open-source spectral element code SES3D, accessible at http://www.cos.ethz.ch/software/production/ses3d.html. For the automatic selection of waveform windows, we employed the open-source software FLEXWIN, which is accessible at https://geodynamics.org/resources/flexwin. Both websites last accessed in January 2025. The supplemental material for this article includes figures of resolution tests and waveform comparisons.

Declaration of Competing Interests

The authors acknowledge that there are no conflicts interest recorded.

Acknowledgments

The authors thank Editor-in-Chief Allison Bent, the associate editor, and the two anonymous reviewers for their constructive suggestions and insightful comments, which have significantly improved the quality of the article. This research was supported by the National Natural Science Foundation of China (Grant Number 42374115). The authors gratefully acknowledge the International Earthquake Science Data Center at the Institute of Geophysics, China Earthquake Administration (CEA; doi: 10.11998/IESDC), for providing the waveform data.

References

Blom, N., A. Gokhberg, and A. Fichtner (2020). Seismic waveform tomography of the Central and Eastern Mediterranean upper mantle, *Solid Earth* **11**, 669–690.

Burchfiel, B. C., L. H. Royden, R. D. van der Hilst, B. H. Hager, Z. Chen, R. W. King, C. Li, J. Lü, H. Yao, and E. Kirby (2008). A geological and geophysical context for the Wenchuan earthquake of 12 May 2008, Sichuan, People's Republic of China, *GSA Today* **18**, 4–11, doi: 10.1130/GSATG18A.1.

Chen, M., F. Niu, Q. Liu, J. Tromp, and X. Zheng (2015). Multiparameter adjoint tomography of the crust and upper mantle beneath East Asia: 1. Model construction and comparisons, *J. Geophys. Res.* **120**, 1762–1786.

Chen, Z., B. C. Burchfiel, Y. Liu, R. W. King, L. H. Royden, W. Tang, E. Wang, J. Zhao, and X. Zhang, 2000). Global positioning system measurements from eastern Tibet and their implications for India/Eurasia intercontinental deformation, *J. Geophys. Res.* **105**, 16,215–16,227.

Chow, B., Y. Kaneko, C. Tape, R. Modrak, N. Mortimer, S. Bannister, and J. Townend (2022). Strong upper-plate heterogeneity at the Hikurangi subduction margin (North Island, New Zealand) imaged by adjoint tomography, *J. Geophys. Res.* **127**, e2021JB022865, doi: 10.1029/2021JB022865.

Clark, M. K., J. W. M. Bush, and L. H. Royden (2005). Dynamic topography produced by lower crustal flow against rheological strength heterogeneities bordering the Tibetan Plateau, *Geology* **162**, 575–590.

Dong, X., and D. Yang (2025). Crustal flow-induced earthquake revealed by full-waveform tomography and implications for prehistoric civilization destruction, *J. Geophys. Res.* **130**, e2024JB029745, doi: 10.1029/2024JB029745.

Dong, X., D. Yang, and F. Niu (2019). Passive adjoint tomography of the crustal and upper mantle beneath eastern Tibet with a W2-norm misfit function, *Geophys. Res. Lett.* **46**, 12,986–12,995.

Dong, X., D. Yang, H. Zhu, and Y. Chen (2022). Geometry-preserving full-waveform tomography and its application in the Longmen Shan area, *Sci. China. Earth. Sci.* **65**, no. 3, 437–448.

Durek, J., and G. Ekström (1996). A radial model of anelasticity consistent with long-period surface-wave attenuation, *Bull. Seismol. Soc. Am.* **86**, 144–158.

Engquist, B., and B. Froese (2014). Application of the Wasserstein metric to seismic signals, *Commun. Math. Sci.* **12**, 979–988.

Engquist, B., and Y. Yang (2022). Optimal transport based seismic inversion: Beyond cycle skipping, *Commun. Pure. Appl. Math.* **75**, no. 10, 2201–2244.

Engquist, B., B. Froese, and Y. Yang (2016). Optimal transport for seismic full waveform inversion, *Commun. Math. Sci.* **14**, 2309–2330.

Fichtner, A., B. Kennett, H. Bunge, and H. Igel (2008). Theoretical background for continent and global scale full-waveform inversion in the time-frequency domain, *Geophys. J. Int.* **175**, 665–685.

Fichtner, A., B. Kennett, H. Igel, and H. Bunge (2009). Full seismic waveform tomography for upper-mantle structure in the Australasian region using adjoint methods, *Geophys. J. Int.* **179**, 1703–1725.

Fichtner, A., E. Saygin, T. Taymaz, P. Cupillard, Y. Capdeville, and J. Trampert (2013). The deep structure of the North Anatolian Fault Zone, *Earth Planet. Sci. Lett.* **373**, 109–117.

Gao, Y., F. Tilmann, D.-P. Herwaar der van, S. Thrastarson, A. Fichtner, B. Heit, X. Yuan, and B. Schurr (2021). Full waveform inversion beneath the Central Andes: Insight into the dehydration of the Nazca slab and delamination of the back-arc lithosphere, *J. Geophys. Res.* **126**, e2021JB021984, doi: 10.1029/2021JB021984.

Gokhberg, A., and A. Fichtner (2016). Full-waveform inversion on hetrogeneous HPC systems, *Comput. Geosci.* **89**, 260–268.

Guo, X., R. Gao, X. Xu, G. R. Keller, A. Yin, and X. Xiong (2015). Longriba fault zone in eastern Tibet: An important tectonic boundary marking the westernmost edge of the Yangtze block, *Tectonics* **34**, doi: 10.1002/2015TC003880.

Guo, X., G. R. Keller, R. Gao, X. Xu, H. Wang, and W. Li (2014). Irregular western margin of the Yangtze block as a cause of variation in tectonic activity along the Longmen Shan fault zone, eastern Tibet, *Int. Geol. Rev.* **56**, 473–480.

Hickman, S., R. Sibson, and R. Bruhn (1995). Introduction to special section: Mechanical involvement of fluids in faulting, *J. Geophys. Res.* **100**, 12,831–12,840, doi: 10.1029/95JB01121.

Huang, J., D. Zhao, and S. Zheng (2002). Lithospheric structure and its relationship to seismic and volcanic activity in southwest China, *J. Geophys. Res.* **107,** 2255, doi: 10.1029/2000JB000137.

Huang, Z., L. Wang, M. Xu, and D. Zhao (2018). P wave anisotropic tomography of the SE Tibetan Plateau: Evidence for the crustal and upper mantle deformations, *J. Geophys. Res.* **123,** 8957–8978.

Hubbard, J., and J. H. Shaw (2009). Uplift of the Longmen Shan and Tibetan plateau, and the 2008 Wenchuan (M = 7.9) earthquake, *Nature* **458,** 194–197.

Kreemer, C., G. Blewitt, and E. Klein (2014). A geodetic plate motion and Global Strain Rate Model, *Geochem. Geophys. Geosys.* **15,** 3849–3889.

Lei, J., and D. Zhao (2009). Structural heterogeneity of the Longmenshan fault zone and the mechanism of the 2008 Wenchuan earthquake (Ms 8.0), *Geochem. Geophys. Geosys.* **10,** Q10010, doi: 10.1029/2009GC002590.

Lei, J., F. Xie, C. Lan, C. Xing, and S. Ma (2008). Seismic images under the Beijing region inferred from P and PmP data, *Phys. Earth Planet. In.* **168,** 134–146, doi: 10.1016/j.pepi.2008.06.005.

Li, R., L. Zhao, X. Xie, and Z. Yao (2023). Crustal deformation in the southeastern margin of the Tibetan Plateau: Insights from broad-band Pg-wave attenuation tomography, *Geophys. J. Int.* **235,** 2870–2886.

Liu, Q., and J. Tromp (2006). Finite-frequency sensitivity Kernels based upon adjoint methods, *Bull. Seismol. Soc. Am.* **96,** no. 6, 2383–2397.

Liu, Q., and J. Tromp (2008). Finite-frequency sensitivity kernels for global seismic wave propagation based upon adjoint methods, *Geophys. J. Int.* **174,** no. 1, 265–286.

Liu, Y., H. Yao, H. Zhang, and H. Fang (2021). The Community Velocity Model V.1.0 of Southwest China, constructed from joint body- and surface-wave travel-time tomography, *Seismol. Res. Lett.* **92,** 2972–2987.

Lv, J. N., Z. K. Shen, and M. Wang (2003). Contemporary crustal deformation and active tectonic block model of the Sichuan-Yunnan region, China (in Chinese with English abstract), *Seismol. Geol.* **25,** 543–554.

Maggi, A., C. Tape, M. Chen, D. Chao, and J. Tromp (2009). An automated time-window selection algorithm for seismic tomography, *Geophys. J. Int.* **178,** 257–281.

Meade, B. J. (2007). Present-day kinematics at the India-Asia collision zone, *Geology* **35,** 81–84.

Métivier, L., R. Brossier, Q. Mérigot, E. Oudet, and J. Virieux (2016). Increasing the robustness and applicability of full-waveform inversion: An optimal transport distance strategy, *The Leading Edge* **35,** 1060–1067.

Mishra, O. P., J. R. Kayal, G. K. Chakrabortty, O. P. Singh, and D. Ghosh (2007). Aftershock investigation in the Andaman-Nicobar Islands of India and its seismotectonic implications, *Bull. Seismol. Soc. Am.* **97,** no. 1A, S71–S85, doi: 10.1785/0120050629.

O'connell, R. J., and B. Budiansky (1974). Seismic velocities in dry and saturated cracked solids, *J. Geophys. Res.* **79,** no. 35, 5412–5426.

Owens, T. J., and G. Zandt (1997). Implications of crustal property variations for model of Tibetan Plateau evolution, *Nature* **387,** 37–43.

Panning, M., and B. Romanowicz (2006). A three-dimensional radially anisotropic model of shear velocity in the whole mantle, *Geophys. J. Int.* **167,** no. 1, 361–379.

Pei, S., F. L. Liu, Y. Ben-Zion, Q. Sun, Y. B. Liu, X. T. Xue, J. Su, and Z. Shao (2019). Seismic velocity reduction and accelerated recovery due to earthquakes on the Longmenshan fault, *Nature Geosci.* **12,** 387–392.

Qiu, L. (2021). Analysis of seismic inversion with optimal transportation and softplus encoding. *Inverse Probl.* **37,** 095004, doi: 10.1088/1361-6420/ac1511.

Qiu, L., J. Ramos-Martìnez, A. Valenciano, Y. Yang, and B. Engquist (2017). Full-waveform inversion with an exponentially encoded optimal-transport norm, *SEG Technical Program Expanded Abstracts 2017*, 1286–1290.

Ren, J. J., X. W. Xu, R. S. Yeats, and S. M. Zhang (2013). Latest Quaternary paleoseismology and slip rates of the Longriba fault zone, eastern Tibet: Implications for fault behavior and strain partitioning, *Tectonics* **32,** 216–238, doi: 10.1002/tect.20029.

Rockafellar, R. T. (1993). Lagrange multipliers and optimality. *SIAM Rev.* **35,** 183–283.

Royden, L. H., B. C. Burchfiel, R. W. King, E. Wang, Z. Chen, F. Shen, and Y. Liu (1997). Surface deformation and lower crustal flow in Eastern Tibet, *Science* **321,** 788–790.

Royden, L. H., B. C. Burchfiel, and R. D. van der Hilst (2008). The geological evolution of the Tibetan Plateau, *Science* **276,** 1054–1058.

Rutter, E. H., and K. H. Brodie (1998). Experimental "Syntectonic" dehydration of serpentinite under conditions of controlled pore water pressure, *J. Geophys. Res.* **93,** no. B5, 4907–4932.

Shen, Z. K., J. N. Lu, M. Wang, and R. Burgmann (2005). Contemporary crustal deformation around the southeast borderland of the Tibetan Plateau, *J. Geophys. Res.* **110,** 11409, doi: 10.1029/2004JB003421.

Sibson, R. (1982). Fault zone models, heat flow and the depth distribution of earthquakes in the continental crust of the United States, *Bull. Seismol. Soc. Am.* **72,** 151–163.

Tao, K., S. Grand, and F. Niu (2018). Seismic structure of the upper mantle beneath eastern Asia from full waveform seismic tomography, *Geochem. Geophys. Geosys.* **19,** 2732–2763.

Tape, C., Q. Liu, A. Maggi, and J. Tromp (2009). Adjoint tomography of the southern California crust, *Science* **325,** 988–992.

Tape, C., Q. Liu, and J. Tromp (2007). Finite-frequency tomography using adjoint methods—Methodology and examples using membrane surface waves, *Geophys. J. Int.* **168,** 1105–1129.

Tapponnier, P., Z. Xu, F. Roger, B. Meyer, N. Arnaud, G. Wittlinger, and J. Yang (2001). Oblique stepwise rise and growth of the Tibet plateau, *Science* **294,** 1671–1677.

Tong, P., J. Yao, Q. Liu, T. Li, K. Wang, S. Liu, Y. Cheng, and S. Wu (2021). Crustal rotation and fluids: Factors for the 2019 Ridgecrest earthquake sequence? *Geophys. Res. Lett.* **48,** e2020GL090853, doi: 10.1029/2020GL090853.

Tromp, J., C. Tape, and Q. Liu (2005). Seismic tomography, adjoint methods, time reversal and banana-doughnut kernels, *Geophys. J. Int.* **160,** 195–216.

Virieux, J., and S. Operto (2009). An overview of full-waveform inversion in exploration geophysics, *Geophysics* **74,** no. 6, WCC1–WCC26.

Wang, C., Y. Li, and H. Lou (2016). Issues on crustal and upper-mantle structures associated with geodynamics in the northeastern Tibetan Plateau, *Chin. Sci. Bull.* **61,** 2239–2263.

Wang, C., L. Zhu, H. Lou, B. Huang, Z. Yao, and X. Luo (2010). Crustal thicknesses and Poisson's ratios in the eastern Tibetan Plateau and their tectonic implications, *J. Geophys. Res.* **115,** no. B11, doi: 10.1029/2010JB007527.

Wang, M., and Z. K. Shen (2020). Present-day crustal deformation of continental China derived from GPS and its tectonic implications, *J. Geophys. Res.* **125,** e2019JB018774, doi: 10.1029/2019JB018774.

Wang, Z., J. Wang, Z. Chen, Y. Liu, R. Huang, S. Pei, Q. Zhang, and W. Tang (2011). Seismic imaging, crustal stress and GPS data analyses: Implications for the generation of the 2008 Wenchuan Earthquake (M7.9), China, *Gondwana Res.* **19,** no. 1, 202–212.

Wang, Z., J. Wang, and X. Yang (2021). The role of fluids in the 2008 Ms8.0 Wenchuan earthquake, China, *J. Geophys. Res.* **126,** e2020JB019959, doi: 10.1029/2020JB019959.

Wang, Z., D. Zhao, O. P. Mishra, and A. Yamada (2006). Structural heterogeneity and its implications for the low frequency tremors in Southwest Japan, *Earth Planet. Sci. Lett.* **251,** 66–78.

Watanabe, T. (1993). Effects of water and melt on seismic velocities and their application to characterization of seismic reflectors, *Geophys. Res. Lett.* **20,** 2933–2936.

Wei, W., R. M. Sun, and Y. L. Shi (2010). P-wave tomographic images beneath southeastern Tibet: Investigating the mechanism of the 2008 Wenchuan earthquake, *Sci. China. Earth. Sci.* **40,** no. 7, 831–839.

Xu, X., X. Wen, G. Yu, G. Chen, Y. Klinger, J. Hubbard, and J. Shaw (2009). Coseismic reverse- and oblique-slip surface faulting generated by the 2008 Mw 7.9 Wenchuan earthquake, China, *Geology* **37,** 515–518.

Xu, X., P. Zhang, X. Wen, Z. Qin, G. Chen, and A. Zhu (2005). Features of active tectonics and recurrence behaviors of strong earthquakes in the western Sichuan province and its adjacent regions, *Seismol. Geol.* **27,** no. 3, 446–461.

Xu, X. W., X. Z. Wen, G. H. Chen, and G. H. Yu (2008). Discovery of the Longriba fault zone in eastern Bayan Har Block, China and its tectonic implication, *Sci. China Earth Sci.* **51,** 1209–1223.

Yang, D., X. Dong, J. Huang, Z. Fang, X. Huang, S. Liu, M. Liu, and W. Meng (2025). High-resolution full waveform seismic imaging: Progresses, challenges, and prospects, *Sci. China Earth Sci.* **68,** no. 2, 315–342.

Yang, Y. (2018). *Optimal Transport for Seismic Inverse Problem*, The University of Texas, Austin Texas.

Yang, Y., B. Engquist, J. Sun, and B. Hamfeldt (2018). Application of optimal transport and the quadratic Wasserstein metric to full-waveform inversion, *Geophysics* **83,** R43–R62.

Yao, H., R. D. van der Hilst, and M. V. de Hoop (2006). Surface-wave array tomography in SE Tibet from ambient seismic noise and two-station analysis: I - Phase velocity maps, *Geophys. J. Int.* **166,** 732–744.

Yao, H. J., C. Beghein, and R. D. van der Hilst (2008). Surface wave array tomography in SE Tibet from ambient seismic noise and two-station analysis-II. Crustal and upper-mantle structure, *Geophys. J. Int.* **173,** no. 1, 205–219.

Yin, A., and T. M. Harrison (2000). Geologic evolution of the Himalayan–Tibetan orogeny, *Annu. Rev. Earth Planet. Sci.* **28,** 211–280.

Zandt, G., and C. J. Ammon (1995). Continental crust composition constrained by measurements of crustal Poisson's ratio, *Nature* **374,** 152–154.

Zhang, F. X., Q. J. Wu, and Z. F. Ding (2018). A P-wave velocity study beneath the eastern region of Tibetan Plateau and its implication for plateau growth, *Chin. Sci. Bull.* **63,** 1949–1961 (in Chinese).

Zhang, P., X. Wen, Z. Shen, and J. Chen (2010). Oblique, high-angle, Listric-reverse faulting and associated development of strain: The Wenchuan earthquake of May 12, 2008, Sichuan, China, *Annu. Rev. Earth Planet. Sci.* **38,** 353–382.

Zhang, P., X. Xu, X. Wen, and Y. Ran (2008). Slip rates and recurrence intervals of the Longmen Shan active fault zone, and tectonic implications for the mechanism of the May 12 Wenchuan earthquake, 2008, Sichuan, China, *Chin. J. Geophys.* **51,** no. 4, 1066–1073.

Zhang, S., and H. Zhu (2023). Constructing a 3-D radially anisotropic crustal velocity model for Oklahoma using full waveform inversion, *J. Geophys. Res.* **128,** e2023JB026992, doi: 10.1029/2023JB026992.

Zhao, D., H. Kanamori, H. Negishi, and D. Wiens (1996). Tomography of the source area of the 1995 Kobe earthquake: Evidence for fluids at the hypocenter? *Science* **274,** no. 5294, 1891–1894.

Zhao, D., M. Santosh, and A Yamada (2010). Dissecting large earthquakes in Japan: Role of arc magma and fluids, *Island Arc* **19,** no. 1, 4–16.

Zhao, D., H. Tani, and O. P. Mishra. (2004). Crustal heterogeneity in the 2000 western Tottori earthquake region: Effect of fluids from slab dehydration, *Phys. Earth Planet. In.* **145,** 161–177, doi: 10.1016/j.pepi.2004.03.009.

Zhao, G., M. J. Unsworth, Y. Zhan, L. Wang, X. Chen, A. G. Jones, J. Tang, Q. Xiao, J. Wang, J. Cai, *et al.* (2012). Crustal structure and rheology of the Longmenshan and Wenchuan Mw 7.9 earthquake epicentral area from magnetotelluric data, *Geology* **40,** no. 12, 1139–1142.

Zheng, X., B. Ouyang, D. Zhang, Z. Yao, J. Liang, and J. Zheng (2009). Technical system construction of Data Backup Center for China Seismograph Network and the data support to researches on the Wenchuan earthquake, *Chin. J. Geophys.* **52,** no. 5, 1412–1417 (in Chinese).

Zhu, H., E. Bozdağ, D. Peter, and J. Tromp (2012). Structure of the European upper mantle revealed by adjoint tomography, *Nature Geosci.* **5,** 493–498.

Zhu, H., R. Stern, and J. Yang (2020). Seismic evidence for subduction-induced mantle flows underneath Middle America, *Nat. Commun.* **11,** 2075, doi: 10.1038/s41467-020-15492-6.

Manuscript received 3 February 2025
Published online 17 September 2025

The East Helanshan Fault: Revisiting the 1739 M 8 Pingluo Event and Earthquake Scenarios

Boyang Sun[†1,2], Yilong Li[†3], Zijia Wang[*4], Baizhou An[2,5], Xudong Zhou[4], and Zhenguo Zhang[4,6]

Abstract

The 1739 M 8 Pingluo earthquake is the largest seismic event recorded in the Yinchuan basin, located in Ningxia Hui Autonomous Region, China. The East Helanshan fault (EHF), a prominent active normal fault, was suggested as its causative fault. This study inferred a reasonable combination of dynamic parameters for the EHF by revisiting the 1739 event from dynamic rupture to disaster assessment. The dynamic model agreed well with surface rupture observations and previous damage investigations. The magnitude of this earthquake is about M_w 7.6. Subsequently, four distinct epicenters were chosen as earthquake scenarios for the EHF. Our simulation revealed that earthquakes nucleated at the northeast segment of the EHF can always trigger cascading rupture of two fault segments, reaching a moment magnitude of 7.6. In contrast, earthquakes nucleated at the southwest segment of the EHF only have a magnitude of M_w 7.0. Furthermore, we estimated the potential fatalities and economic losses in the study area if these scenarios occur in the current year. For the four M_w 7.6 scenarios, the highest probability (~52% to 56%) of the economic loss range is RMB 1000–10,000 billion yuan, and the probability of resulting in more than 1000 deaths is close to 90%. The overall impact of hypocenter-dependent scenarios on economic losses is significantly smaller than that on fatalities. This phenomenon likely related to the spatial characteristics of population and fixed asset exposure. Yinchuan, Shizuishan, and Wuhai were identified as high-seismic risk regions. Our physics-based simulations provide additional insights into the complex seismic hazard mechanisms of hanging-wall effect coupled with basin amplification. This work also established a valuable framework for assessing potential seismic hazards in basin areas governed by normal faults.

Cite this article as Sun, B., Y. Li, Z. Wang, B. An, X. Zhou, and Z. Zhang (2026). The East Helanshan Fault: Revisiting the 1739 M 8 Pingluo Event and Earthquake Scenarios, *Seismol. Res. Lett.* **97**, 1018–1031, doi: 10.1785/0220250207.

Supplemental Material

Introduction

The East Helanshan fault (EHF) is located at the boundary of the Ordos active block, an important tectonic unit in eastern China (Fig. 1). The Ordos block covers an area of approximately 370,000 square kilometers. Historically, this region has experienced more than five earthquakes of magnitude 8.0 or greater (Bureau of Earthquake Damage Protection, China Earthquake Administration, 1995), indicating its high-seismic activity. The Ordos block is surrounded by multiple fault zones, creating a complex geological structure. The EHF is a significant active northeast–southwest-striking normal fault situated along its western edge.

The formation of the EHF is closely related to the tectonic setting of the Ordos block. This fault lies between the Alxa block and the Ordos block, both are stable, rigid blocks, whereas its southwestern boundary adjoins the northeastern edge of the Qinghai-Tibet block (Lei *et al.*, 2024, Fig. 1). Since the Cenozoic, the ongoing subduction of the Indian plate beneath the Eurasian plate has led to the uplift of the Qinghai-Tibet block and its northeastward compression, resulting in significant changes in the regional stress field (Zhang *et al.*,

1. School of Resources and Geosciences, China University of Mining and Technology, Xuzhou, China; 2. Geophysical Geochemical Survey Institute of Ningxia Hui Autonomous Region (Deep Earth Exploration Center of Ningxia Autonomous Region), Yinchuan, China; 3. School of National Safety and Emergency Management, Beijing Normal University, Zhuhai, China, https://orcid.org/0000-0002-3427-9471 (YL); 4. Department of Earth and Space Sciences, Southern University of Science and Technology, Shenzhen, China, https://orcid.org/0000-0002-2909-2741 (ZW); https://orcid.org/0009-0003-1960-893X (XZ); https://orcid.org/0000-0002-0059-1766 (ZZ); 5. Institute of Geology and Geophysics, Chinese Academy of Sciences, Beijing, China; 6. Key Laboratory of Earthquake Forecasting and Risk Assessment, Ministry of Emergency Management, Southern University of Science and Technology, Shenzhen, China

*Corresponding author: wangzj2022@mail.sustech.edu.cn

†These authors contributed equally to this work.

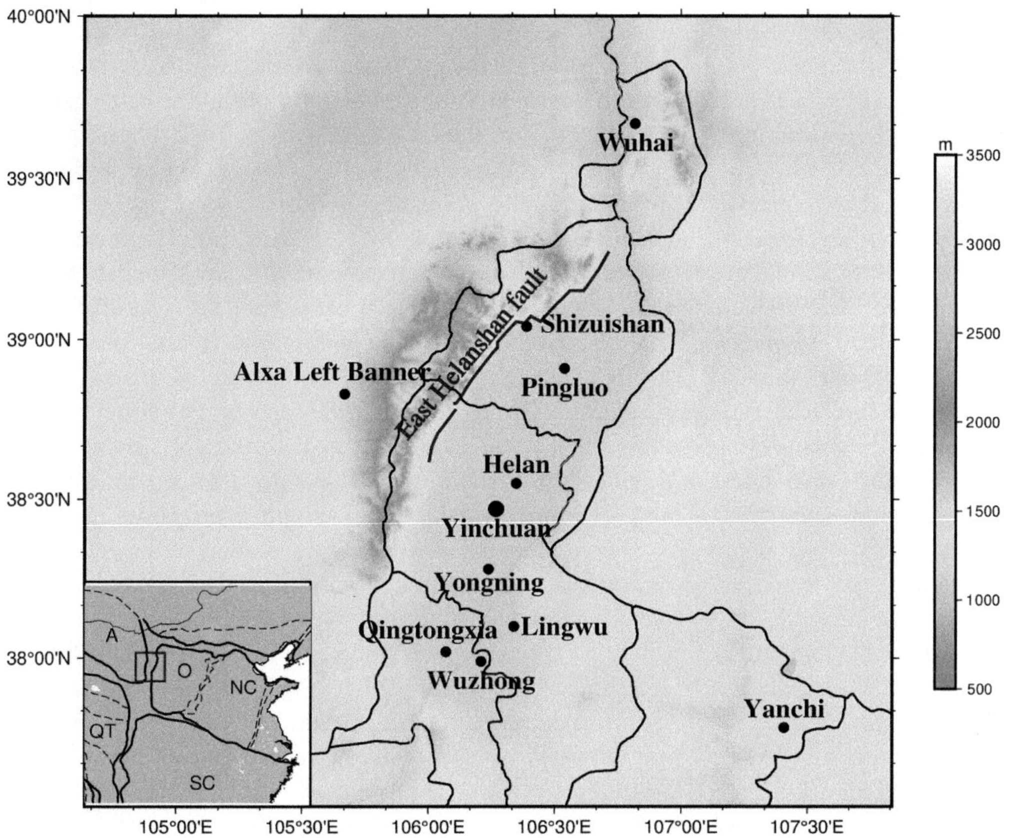

Figure 1. Map view of the research region. Blue line represents the fault surface trace of the East Helanshan Fault. Some major cities are marked on the map. Inset is the location of the research region (blue rectangle). The capital letters in the inset represent the block names, in which A, Alxa block; O, Ordos block; NC, North China block; SC, Sourth China block; QT, Qinghai-Tibet block. The solid and dotted-black lines in the inset represent the primary and secondary block boundaries, respectively. The block boundary data are from Wang *et al.* (2003). The color version of this figure is available only in the electronic edition.

1990; Deng *et al.*, 1999). Under this stress regime, the Yinchuan graben has experienced continuous subsidence (Zhao *et al.*, 2007), whereas the EHF controls the western boundary of the Yinchuan graben, with the Helan Mountains to its west. Since the Cenozoic, this fault has exhibited intense activity, with a high frequency and severity of seismic events throughout history (Deng and Liao, 1996). Its strong tectonic activity has a significant impact on regional seismic hazards.

In addition, as the core region of the Yinchuan graben, the Yinchuan basin contains extremely thick (7 km) Cenozoic sediments (Feng *et al.*, 2011), which can amplify seismic waves and significantly increase the risk of seismic hazards, making seismic activity in this area more destructive. The basin amplification effect has been the subject of extensive research (e.g., Olsen, 2000; Day *et al.*, 2008; Smith and Tape, 2019; Wirth *et al.*, 2019). The 1739 Pingluo earthquake, the magnitude of which is estimated to be 8 according to the recorded damage, is the largest seismic event recorded in the Yinchuan basin (Lee *et al.*, 1976), and its destructive power is closely related to the thick sedimentary layers of the basin. Typically, the intensity decreases with the distance from the causative fault. However, the area with the highest intensity of the Pingluo earthquake did not coincide with the EHF but was in the Yinchuan basin (Bureau of Earthquake Damage Protection, China Earthquake Administration, 1995; Bai and Jiao, 2005). This led to controversy about causative faults.

Some scholars propose that the Yinchuan-Pingluo fault was the causative fault of the earthquake (Li and Wan, 1984; Lin *et al.*, 2013). They argue that the surface projection of this concealed fault trends north-northeast to south-southwest, crossing directly beneath the city of Yinchuan, which appears to coincide with the highest intensity region. Lin *et al.* (2015) suggest that the Huanghe fault might be the causative fault based on recent microearthquake locations and fault scarp detection results. However, the Hongguozi Great Wall offset strongly supports that the EHF is the causative fault (Zhang *et al.*, 1986; Deng and Liao, 1996; Lei *et al.*, 2015). Middleton *et al.* (2016) used radiocarbon dating of fault scarps along the EHF and demonstrated that the formation of these scarps coincides closely with the 1739 Pingluo earthquake, further verifying this view. At the same time, a lot of drilling (Lei *et al.*, 2008, 2014), seismic exploration (Liu *et al.*, 2008,2017; Fang *et al.*, 2009), and imaging work (Wang, Cai, *et al.*, 2023) has been carried out in Yinchuan basin, revealing the complex structure in this area: the eastward dipping and shovel-shaped EHF intersects the Yinchuan-Pingluo fault and the Yellow River fault at a depth of about 20 and 28 km, respectively (Fang *et al.*, 2009; Liu *et al.*, 2017; Wang, Cai, *et al.*, 2023). Furthermore, for the Yinchuan-Pingluo fault and Huanghe fault, the Holocene fault length, late Quaternary cumulative displacements, average slip rates, and coseismic displacements do not support the possibility of an **M** 8 earthquake occurring (Chai *et al.*, 2007; Fang *et al.*, 2009; Lei *et al.*, 2015). In summary, it is reasonable to conclude that the 1739 Pingluo earthquake occurred on the EHF.

At present, we have a plausible interpretation of the tectonic background of the 1739 Pingluo earthquake, but its coseismic physical process still remains poorly understood. Moreover, a significant seismic moment deficit (equivalent to M_w 7.8) in the fault zones northwest of the Ordos block (Huang *et al.*, 2018) suggests that the region still poses a high-seismic risk. Therefore, in-depth research on the Pingluo earthquake not only aids in understanding its physical process but also provides a scientific basis for modern seismic hazard assessments. Through numerical simulations of historical earthquakes (Lozos, 2016; Yu *et al.*, 2022, 2023; Wang, Li, *et al.*, 2022), it is possible to optimize the dynamic parameters of faults, better predict the rupture processes and strong ground motion of future potential earthquakes on the same fault, and estimate fatalities and economic losses under various seismic scenarios (Li *et al.*, 2024). Then, we can provide crucial insights for the formulation of seismic design strategies and emergency response plans, facilitating a shift from passive disaster relief to proactive disaster mitigation.

In this work, following the methodology demonstrated by Wang, Li, *et al.* (2022) for paleoearthquake research, we inferred the dynamic parameters of the EHF by simulating the dynamic rupture process of the 1739 Pingluo earthquake. Surface rupture data and intensity distributions are used to constrain the dynamic model. We then conduct physical-based scenario earthquake simulations with four different nucleation locations, calculating intensity distributions and estimating fatalities and economic losses in the study area. Finally, we identify the regions most vulnerable to seismic disasters surrounding the EHF and point out the danger of superposition of the hanging-wall effect and basin amplification effect.

Materials and Methods

Model setup

The surface trace data of the EHF are provided by China's "Seismic Active Fault Survey Data Center" (see Data and Resources). Based on the fault scarp identification results (Middleton *et al.*, 2016), we construct two nonplanar fault segments (blue lines in Fig. 1). The total fault length is about 108 km. As we mentioned in the Introduction, the EHF is a shovel-shaped normal fault. Thus, the fault dip angle varies with depth (from shallow to deep, from 66° to 39°, Middleton *et al.*, 2016, Fig. S1, available in the supplemental material to this article). The fault width is set to 36 km, with the maximum depth reaching 25.37 km.

Based on the focal mechanism analysis of small earthquakes, the minimum principal compressive stress direction in the Yinchuan region is about N137°E (Fan *et al.*, 2003). The stress shape ratio R is about 0.6 (Huang *et al.*, 2013; Deng and Sheng, 2015), which is defined as $R = (S_H - S_h)/(S_v - S_h)$, in which S_H is the maximum principal stress, S_h is the minimum principal stress, and S_v is the vertical stress. For a normal fault, the values of three principal stresses satisfy $S_v > S_H > S_h$. Higher values of the stress ratio R correspond to an increased strike-slip component of the fault. Through trial and error comparing simulated surface slip and intensity to observations, we set the value of triaxial principal stresses as $S_v = 54$ MPa, $S_H = 44.4$ MPa, and $S_h = 30$ MPa (Fig. S2a). By solving the principal stress tensor onto our nonplanar fault, we can obtain the heterogeneous initial stress distribution (Fig. 2a–c).

The slip weakening friction law (Ida, 1972) is applied in our dynamic rupture simulation, with static and dynamic friction coefficients set as 0.42 and 0.16, respectively. The value of slip weakening distance D_c and cohesion C_0 are depth dependent (Fig. S2b,c). These frictional parameters are also inferred by trial and error, following the same criteria as stress parameters. Xu *et al.* (2024) showed an example of the effect of these parameters. Figure 2d shows the ratio (μ_0) of shear stress to the normal stress. The closer μ_0 is to the static friction coefficient, the closer the initial shear stress is to shear strength, and the more favorable it is for rupture propagation.

Determining the exact epicenter location of the paleoearthquake is almost impossible due to the lack of seismic data records more than hundreds of years ago. However, we can calculate the intensity distribution of different epicenter locations and compare them with the intensity distribution inferred from the damage degree recorded in historical documents to determine the approximate location of the epicenter. Thus, we finally set the epicenter near the northeast end of the EHF (106.825° E, 39.082° N). Seismic imaging results suggested that two faults (EHF and Yinchuan-Pingluo fault) may intersect at 20 km depth, and this depth is also a high low-velocity transition zone, where stress tends to accumulate and cause major earthquakes (Wang, Cai, *et al.*, 2023). In all of our simulations, the focal depth is set at about 21 km. The radius of the nucleation zone is 2.2 km. The strategy of overload nucleation is used to trigger the rupture, with the shear stress set to exceed the shear strength by 0.1%.

In this work, a 3D complex medium is considered in the dynamic rupture and strong ground motion simulations. The *P*- and *S*-wave velocities are obtained from the interpolation of model China Seismological Reference Model 1.0 (CSRM1.0) (see Data and Resources, Xiao *et al.*, 2024). The horizontal and vertical resolution of the original data are 0.2° and 500 m, respectively. An empirical formula (Brocher, 2005) is used to approximate the density. Figure 3 shows the *S*-wave velocity structure of the research region. The minimum *S*-wave velocity in the research region is 1.066 km/s.

Numerical simulation and disaster loss assessment methods

We use the curved-grid finite-difference method (CGFDM, Zhang *et al.*, 2014, 2020) to simulate the dynamic rupture process of the EHF. This method solves the first-order velocity–stress equation in the curvilinear coordinate system, which significantly increases the flexibility of the traditional finite-difference method. It has been verified by benchmark models (Harris *et al.*, 2018) and widely used in simulations of paleoearthquakes (Wang, Li, *et al.*, 2022; Yu *et al.*, 2022, 2023;

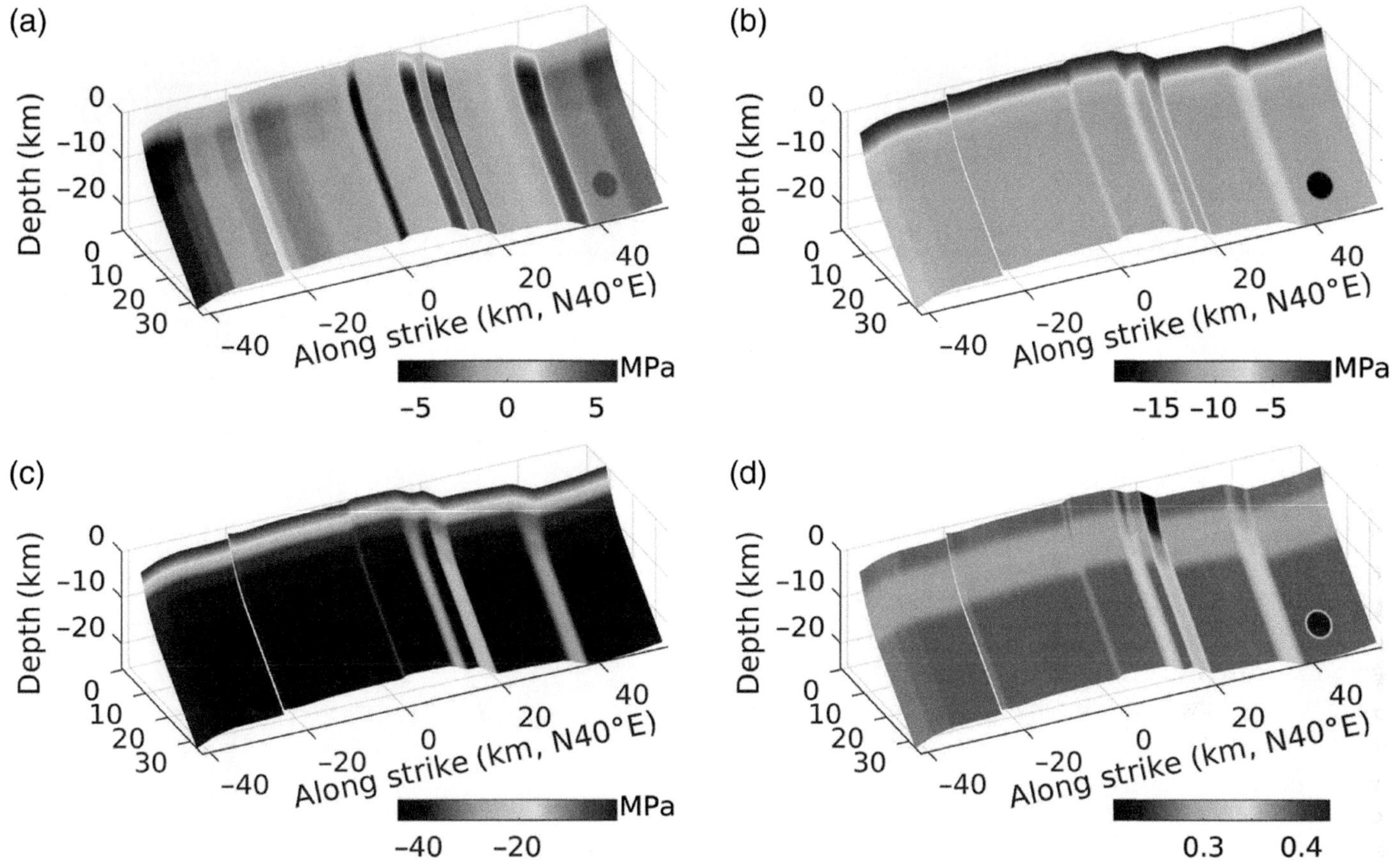

Figure 2. Stress distributions of the East Helanshan fault (EHF). (a) Shear stress of strike-slip component, a negative value indicates the right-lateral direction. (b) Shear stress of dip-slip component, a negative value indicates the normal direction. (c) Normal stress. (d) Distribution of the ratio μ_0 between the shear stress and the normal stress. The contrasting circle on the bottom northeast corner of the fault is the nucleation zone. The color version of this figure is available only in the electronic edition.

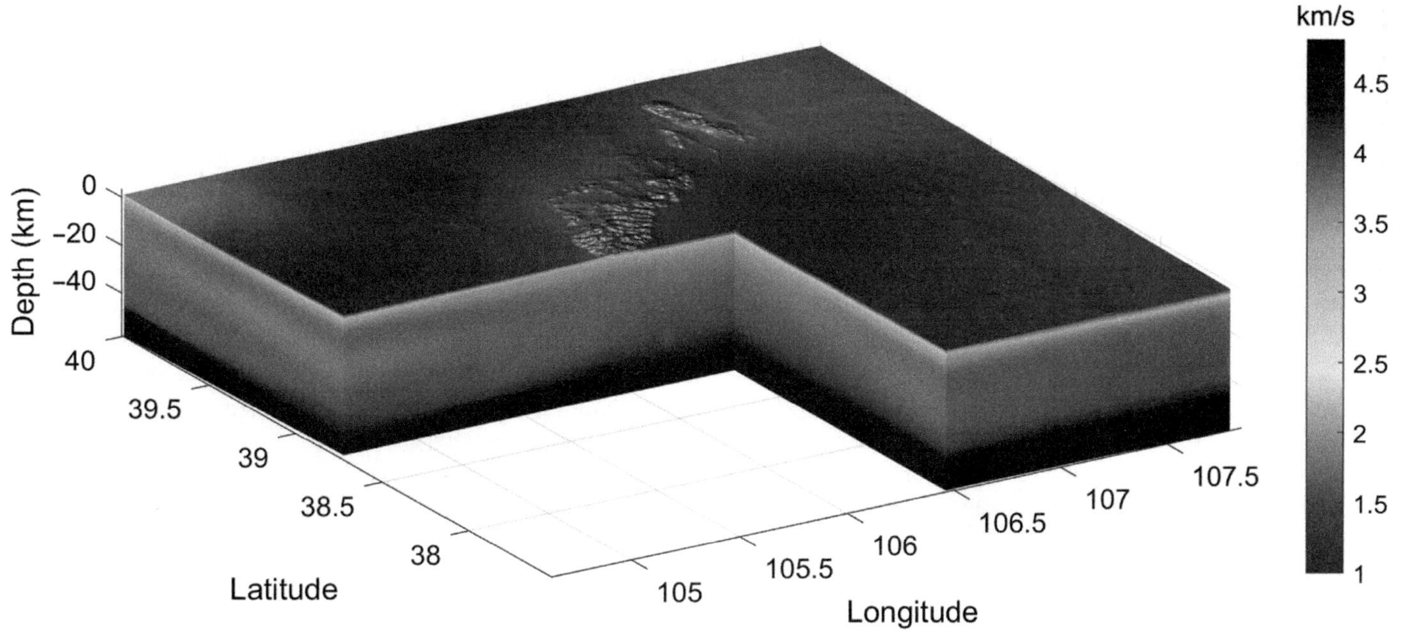

Figure 3. *S*-wave velocity structure (Xiao *et al.*, 2024) of the research region. The color version of this figure is available only in the electronic edition.

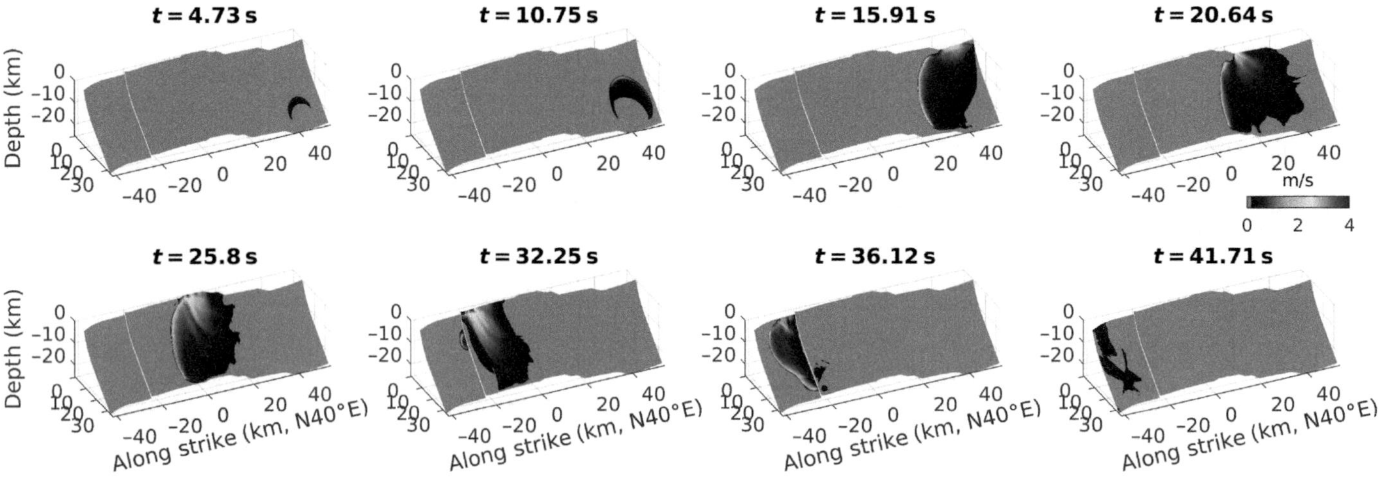

Figure 4. Dip-slip rate snapshots of the 1739 Pingluo earthquake. The normal dip-slip rate is indicated as positive values. The color version of this figure is available only in the electronic edition.

Sunilkumar *et al.*, 2024) and scenario earthquakes (Zhang *et al.*, 2017; Li *et al.*, 2024). In our dynamic simulation, the grid scale is 300 × 1128 × 410, with a uniform spatial step of 100 m. This mesh size can ensure about five points in the cohesive zone to resolve the rupture (Day *et al.*, 2005). The timestep is 0.0043 s and the total simulation time is 47.945 s.

CGFDM3D-EQR (Wang, Zhang, *et al.*, 2022), a rapid earthquake disaster response platform, is used to conduct strong ground motion simulations. This software is also developed based on the CGFDM (Zhang and Chen, 2006; Zhang *et al.*, 2012), which can consider the complex 3D medium and accurately describe the topography. The source time function of each subfault obtained from dynamic rupture models is input to the platform to simulate the ground motions. After obtaining the peak ground velocity (PGV) from the strong ground motion simulation, we can convert it to the intensity distribution based on the Chinese Seismic Intensity Scale (Standardization Administration of the People's Republic of China [SAC], 2020). Then, we can further estimate the earthquake disaster losses. The Shuttle Radar Topography Mission (SRTM) terrain data SRTM90 (SRTM90, Reuter *et al.*, 2007) and 3D complex media CSRM1.0 (Xiao *et al.*, 2024) are considered in the simulation. The grid scale is 1400 × 1400 × 300, with a grid size of 200 m. The time step is 0.0144 s, and the total simulation time is 175.7 s. Our maximum calculation frequency is about 0.89 Hz, which is calculated by $f_{\max} = v_{\min}/(\mathrm{PPW} \times dh)$, in which dh is the grid size, PPW is the point per wavelength needed in the simulation, for CGFDM, PPW = 6. $v_{\min}$ is the minimum *S*-wave velocity of the simulation region (1.066 km/s).

For Mainland China, Li *et al.* (2021) and Li, Xin, *et al.* (2023) developed the earthquake fatality estimation and economic loss estimation models, respectively. Using these models, we can not only quickly estimate the postearthquake losses (Wang, Li *et al.*, 2023), but also quantitatively analyze the loss distribution under potential earthquake scenarios, so as to make the earthquake prevention and disaster reduction work more targeted (Li *et al.*, 2024, 2025). Specifically, the earthquake disaster estimation model follows the following equations:

$$E_i = \sum_{\mathrm{Int}} r(\mathrm{Int}) \times \left(\frac{\mathrm{HDI}_{\text{regression-year}}}{\mathrm{HDI}_{\text{event-year}}}\right)^h \times \text{per capita Exposure}_{(\text{Int,event-year})} \times \mathrm{PE}_{(\text{Int,event-year})}, \quad (1)$$

$$P(a < \text{loss} \le b) = \Phi\left[\frac{\ln b - \ln(E_i)}{\xi}\right] - \Phi\left[\frac{\ln a - \ln(E_i)}{\xi}\right], \quad (2)$$

in which E_i is the estimated fatalities or economic losses in an earthquake. $r(\mathrm{Int})$ is a loss ratio function dependent on seismic intensity Int. The Human Development Index (HDI) allows us to consider the social development impacts in the earthquake disaster estimation. Per capita $\mathrm{Exposure}_{(\text{Int,event-year})}$ represents the per capita exposure quantity at each intensity. For economic losses, this term is the per capita fixed asset value calculated by the perpetual deposit method (Zhang, 2008; Xin *et al.*, 2025). For fatality estimation, it can be ignored. $\mathrm{PE}_{(\text{Int,event-year})}$ is the number of people exposed at each intensity. The probability of loss between a and b is calculated by the difference between two normal cumulative distribution functions Φ. $\ln(E_i)$ and ξ are the mathematical expectation and standard deviation of Φ, respectively. The detailed process of constructing model parameters and uncertainty analysis can be referred to Li *et al.* (2021) and Li, Xin, *et al.* (2023).

Results

The 1739 M 8 Pingluo event

The rupture process of the 1739 event is shown in Figure 4 and Movie S1. It can be seen that the initial stage of the rupture is relatively slow with a small slip rate. After about 10 s, the rupture began to accelerate. The southern segment of the EHF is triggered at about 32.2 s. Figure 5a,b shows the slip distributions of

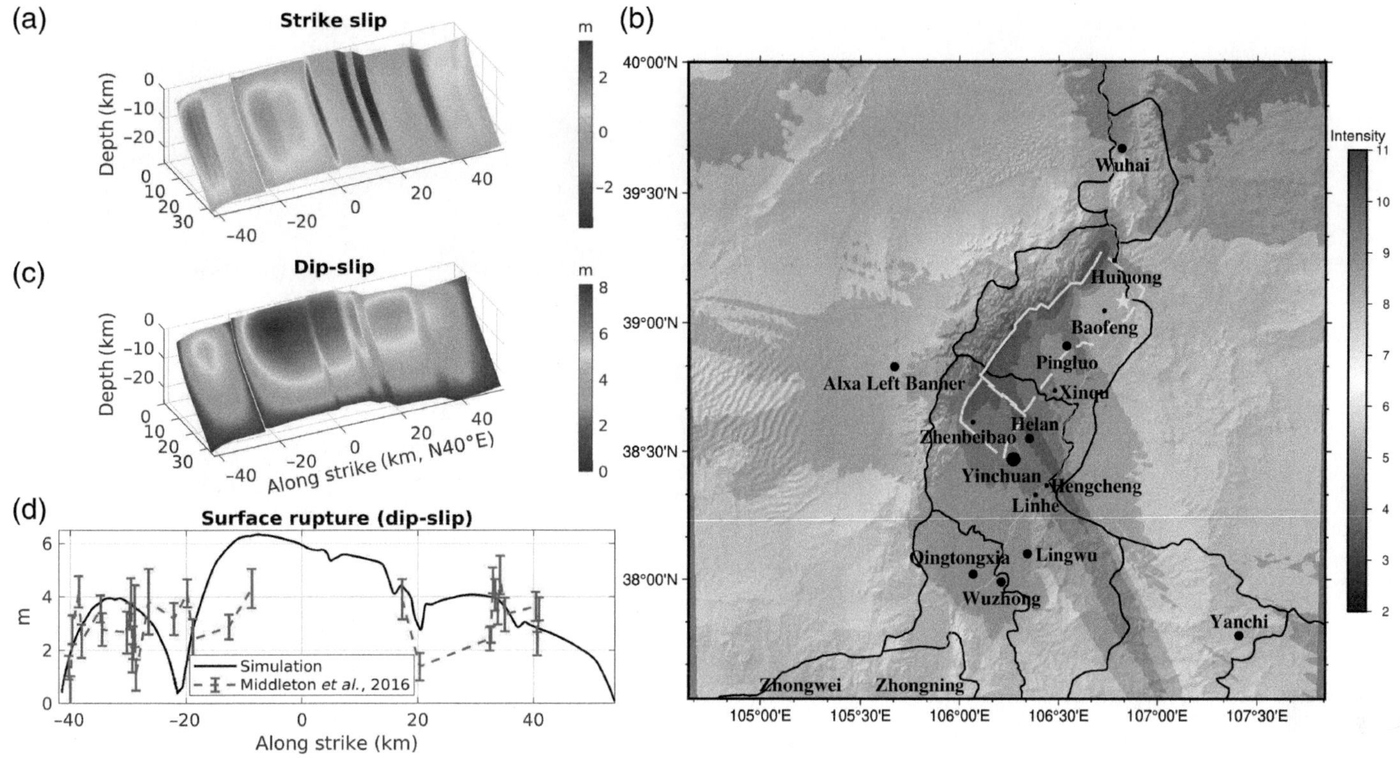

Figure 5. Simulation results of the 1739 Pingluo earthquake. (a) Strike-slip and (b) dip-slip distributions on the fault surface. The right-lateral strike-slip and normal dip-slip are indicated as positive values. (c) Comparison between our simulation results and the fault vertical offsets measured by Middleton *et al.* (2016). (d) The simulated intensity distribution. The yellow lines are surface traces of the EHF, whereas yellow-dotted lines show the down-dip extent of the fault. The yellow star marks the epicenter. The color version of this figure is available only in the electronic edition.

our dynamic model. Our results show that the maximum dip-slip exceeds 8 m, and the strike-slip motion is strongly affected by the fault strike. To verify our dynamic model, we compare the surface rupture (dip-slip component) with the fault scarp measurement results conducted by Middleton *et al.* (2016; Fig. 5c). The two results show good consistency at the northeastern and southwestern segments of the fault. In the middle segment, our surface rupture result may be slightly larger; however, there is also a lack of observation data to constrain the dynamic model.

Based on the dynamic source model, we simulate the strong ground motion of the Pingluo earthquake. The seismic-wave propagation process can be found in Movie S2. Figure 5d illustrates the intensity distribution converted from the PGV based on the Chinese seismic intensity scale (Standardization Administration of the People's Republic of China [SAC], 2020). The obvious amplification effect can be observed in Yinchuan basin. Combined with the hanging-wall effect, the Yinchuan basin suffered serious damage. Furthermore, the intensities of most cities or villages are consistent with the previous investigation (Table 1, Bureau of Earthquake Damage Protection, China Earthquake Administration, 1995). The intensity X zones simulated in this study are not all located in Yinchuan basin as previously investigated, which is mainly due to the limited accuracy of the velocity model in the Yinchuan basin, the lack of consideration of site effects, and the limited calculation frequency.

Middleton *et al.* (2016) estimated the moment magnitude of the Pingluo earthquake to be between 7.1 and 7.6 based on their surface rupture measurements. Our results are in line with their estimates (M_w 7.6). It should be noted that the "**M** 8" we often use is estimated by the recorded damage and can be regarded as the surface-wave magnitude M_s. We have selected two virtual stations with epicenter distance of 1° in our ground motion simulation region to calculate the M_s. Two virtual stations are located at (106.825° E, 38.082° N) and (105.825° E, 39.082° N), respectively. According to the M_s formula of China (Guo and Pang, 1981), their calculated M_s are 7.797 and 8.271. The average value is 8.0, which is well consistent with the estimated 8.0.

Then, we estimate fatalities for the 1739 Pingluo earthquake. The detailed process and parameters of fatality estimation are listed in the supplemental material. The highest probability of fatality range is 10,000–100,000 and the mathematical expectation is 49,463 (Fig. S3). This result closely aligns with the Lou (1996) estimate of 50,000, derived from rough historical records.

In summary, the consistency of intensity distribution and estimated fatalities with historical documents further verifies our dynamic model of the 1739 Pingluo earthquake. On this basis, we can carry out scenario earthquake simulations and provide further suggestions for earthquake prevention and disaster reduction in the surrounding areas of the EHF.

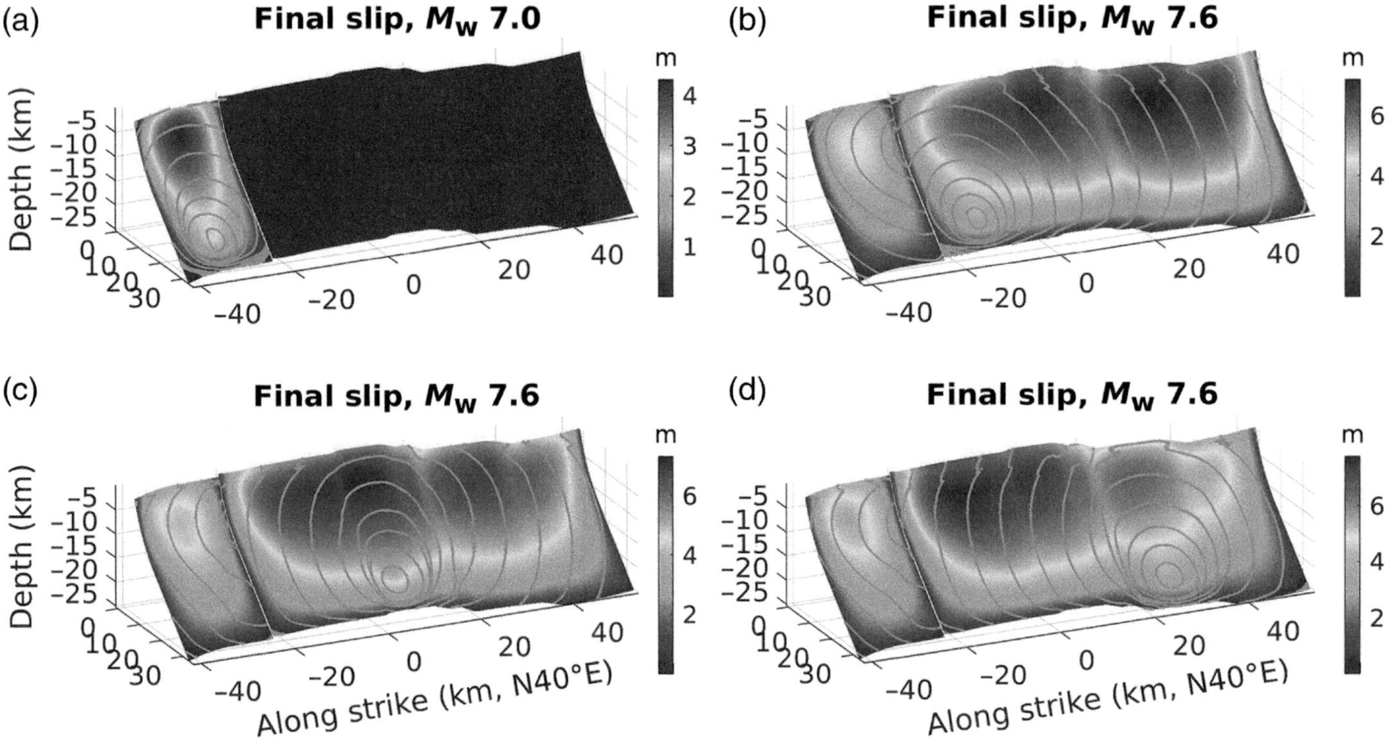

Earthquake scenarios of the EHF

We select four different epicenter locations and simulate their dynamic rupture process as earthquake scenarios of the EHF (Fig. 6a–d, Movies S3–S6, corresponding to scenarios 1–4, respectively). Together with the preferred model for the 1739 event, there are five earthquake scenarios in total.

As shown in Figure 6, if the rupture nucleates in the northeast segment of the EHF, it always triggers a cascading rupture in the southwest segment, and the final moment magnitude reaches M_w 7.6. The location of maximum slip is affected by the location of the epicenter. The shallow part of the fault far away from the epicenter tends to produce greater slip due to the rupture directivity. In contrast, the earthquake nucleated in the southwest segment of the EHF cannot trigger cascading rupture, with a magnitude of only M_w 7.0 (Fig. 6a).

In general, a long-rupture acceleration distance is conducive to the rupture passing through the stepover (Hu *et al.*, 2016). We can expect the southwest segment of EHF to rupture in scenarios 3 and 4 (Fig. 6c,d). However, for scenarios 1 and 2 (Fig. 6a,b), the rupture acceleration distance is about 10 km, and one rupture jumping does not occur (Movie S3) but the other does with a few seconds' delay (Movie S4). To explore the physical process, we calculate the shear and normal stress changes at the secondary fault (the fault segment without nucleation zone, Fig. 7). Similar to the results of strike-slip stepover (Wang and Zhang, 2025), the shear stress change mode is similar, but the normal stress disturbance mode is different in different stepover types, which results in different cascading rupture behavior. Specifically, for the EHF, a dipping normal fault, the reflection phase of free surface can bring a

Figure 6. Dynamic rupture processes of earthquake scenarios (a–d) 1–4 of the EHF. The gray lines in panels (a–d) are rupture isochrons with an interval of 2 s. Scenario 5 is the same as the 1739 event (see Fig. 4). The color version of this figure is available only in the electronic edition.

TABLE 1
Comparison of Intensity of Some Regions

Region	Bureau of Earthquake Damage Protection, China Earthquake Administration (1995)	This Work
Pingluo	X	IX
Yinchuan	X	IX
Helan	X	X
Xinqu	X	IX
Baofeng	X	VII
Zhenbeibao	IX	IX
Hengcheng	IX	IX
Linhe	IX	IX
Huinong	VIII	VIII
Lingwu	VII	VIII
Yanchi	VII	VII
Zhongning	VII	VII
Zhongwei	VI–VII	VI–VII

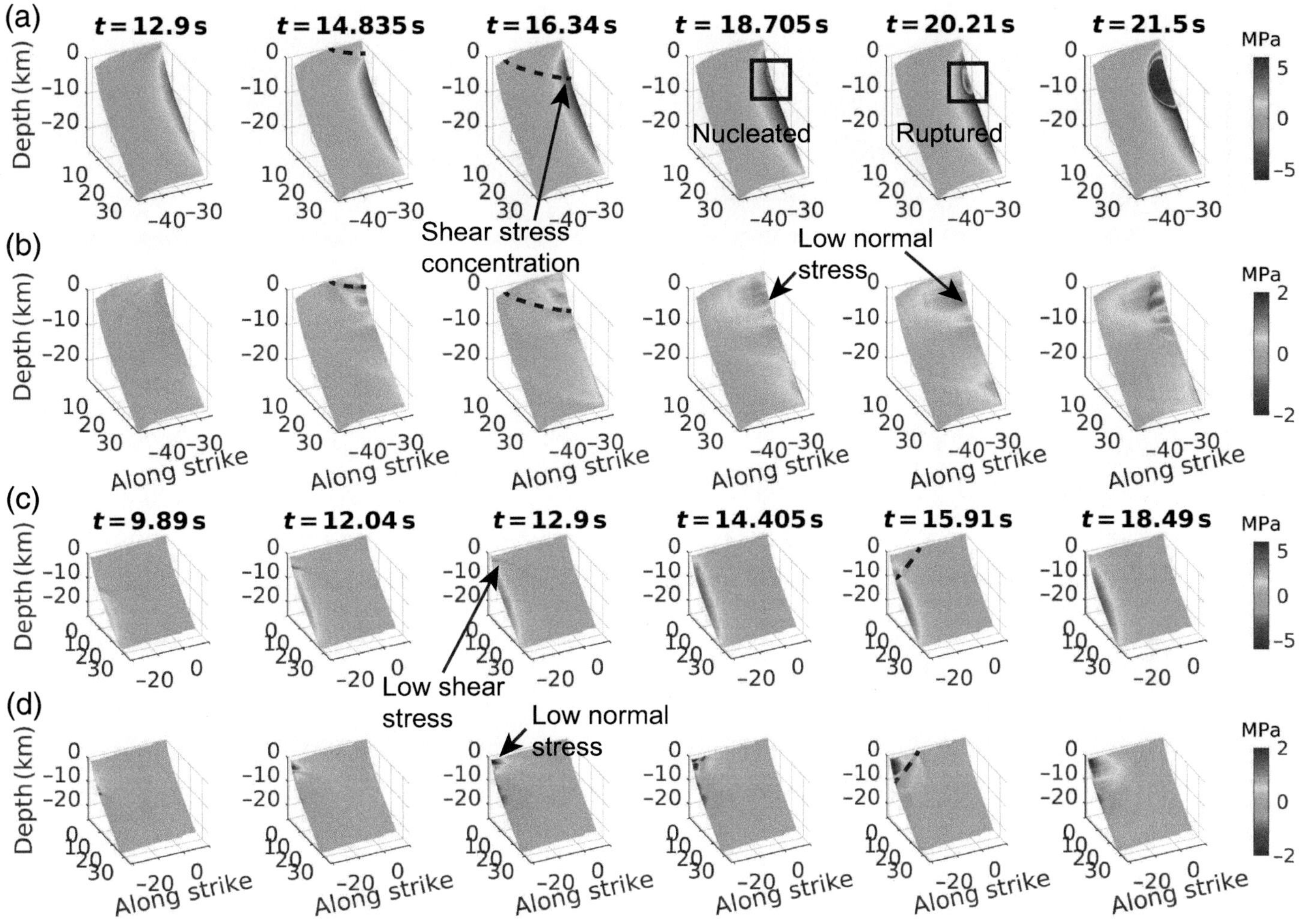

Figure 7. (a,c) Shear stress change and (b,d) normal stress change snapshots at six different times of the secondary fault. Panels (a) and (b) are scenario 2; in this case the southwest segment of the EHF is the secondary fault. Although panels (c) and (d) are scenario 1, in this case the northeast segment of the EHF is the secondary fault. We only illustrate the −20 to 10 km portion of the EHF along the fault strike. The dotted lines indicate the reflection phase of free surface. The color version of this figure is available only in the electronic edition.

high-dynamic shear stress (dotted lines in Fig. 7a and 7c) and generate a shear stress concentration near the fault edge. This shear stress concentration needs to work together with low normal stress to nucleate the rupture. Therefore, cascading rupture occurs in scenario 2 but due to the very short rupture acceleration distance, the slow nucleation stage (see the snapshot $t = 18.705$ s in Fig. 7a) cause the observed triggering delay. For scenario 1, the normal stress also reduces near the free surface, the relatively low shear stress and increased cohesion (Fig. S2c) lead to the nucleation failed. At the depth where rupture nucleated in scenario 2, the normal stress of the secondary fault in scenario 1 increases and the shear stress disturbance is weaker than that in scenario 2. Thus, the cascading rupture cannot occur. For other detailed rupture dynamics of dip-slip faults, refer to Oglesby *et al.* (2000) and Aochi (2018).

The four dynamic rupture source models are input to the CGFDM3D-EQR platform (Wang, Zhang, *et al.*, 2022) to simulate the ground motions and obtain the intensity distributions. Scenario 1 has a small magnitude and a limited range of high-intensity areas (Fig. 8a). For scenarios 2–5, earthquakes of the same magnitude lead to different intensity distributions due to the rupture directivity (Figs. 8b–d, 5d). However, as we mentioned in The 1739 **M** 8 Pingluo event section, the superposition of the hanging-wall effect and basin amplification effect always causes the Yinchuan basin to have higher intensity in different earthquake scenarios. Within the basin, the intensity is always above VII and, even in most areas, the intensity is above VIII in scenarios 3 and 4. Compared with above the source, the amplification effect of the area far from the source in the basin is more obvious, which is consistent with previous studies (Olsen, 2000; Wirth *et al.*, 2019).

Direct economic losses and fatalities assessment

Finally, we perform an assessment and risk analysis of direct economic losses and fatalities in the study area based on earthquake scenarios initiated in the EHF. The first and third panels

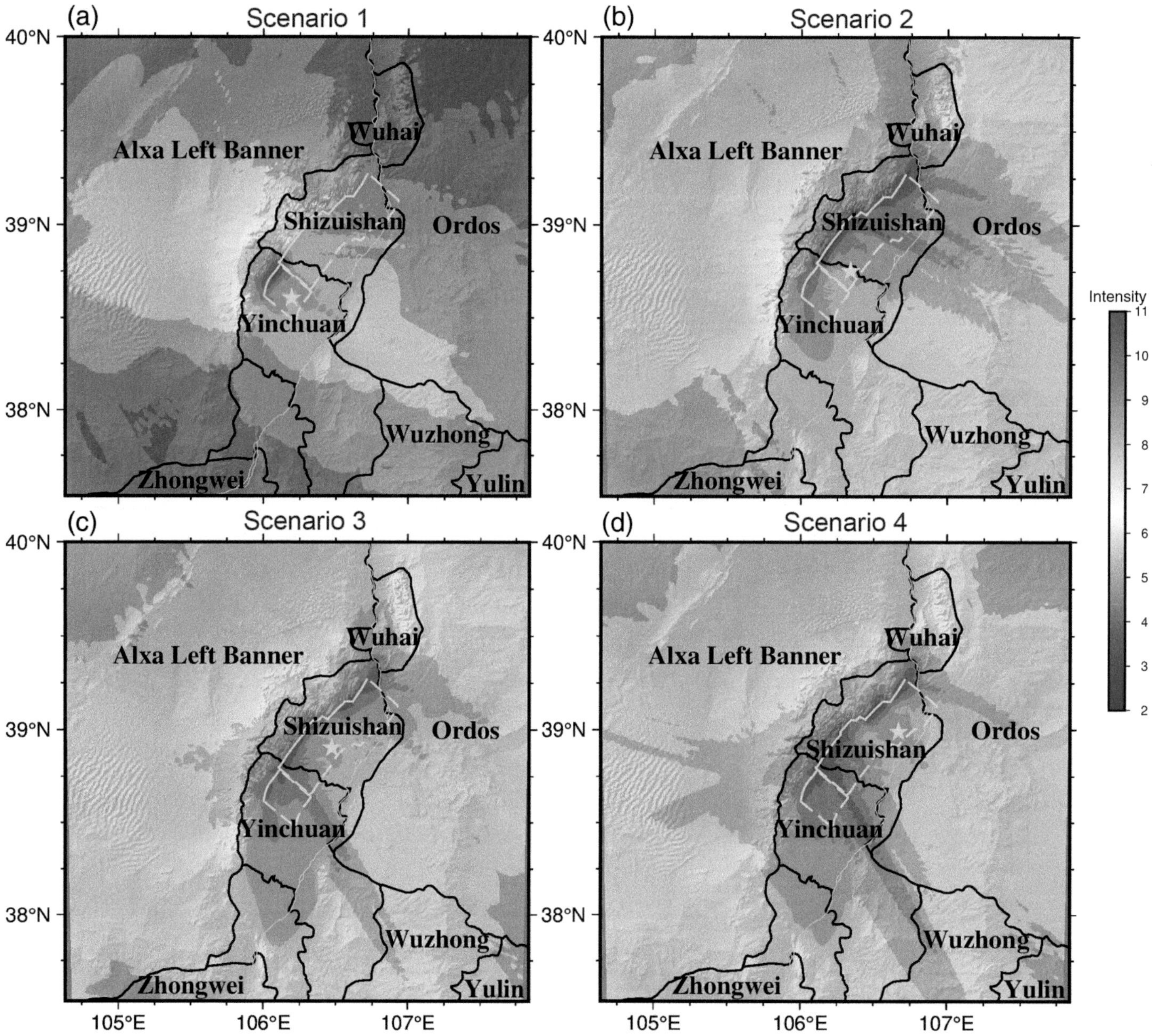

Figure 8. Intensity distributions of earthquake scenarios (a–d) 1–4 of the EHF. The yellow stars represent the epicenters. The yellow lines are surface traces of the EHF, whereas dotted-yellow lines show the down-dip extent of the fault. Scenario 5 is the same as the 1739 event (see Fig. 5d). The color version of this figure is available only in the electronic edition.

of each subplot in Figure 9 illustrate the risk distribution of direct economic losses and fatalities across the major impacted cities. The bar charts (the second and fourth panels) represent the relative likelihood of total losses falling within designated loss ranges (*x* axis). Overall, scenario 1 has a smaller loss scale than the other scenarios due to its smaller magnitude and intensity distribution. Scenarios 2–5 exhibit similar economic loss scales, relative probabilities {~52% to 56% probability of losing RMB 1000-10,000 billion yuan [1 USD = RMB 7.16 yuan (at 26 June 2025)]} and economic loss spatial distributions (Fig. 9) although their epicenters differ significantly (Fig. 6), leading to distinct ground motion distributions (Fig. 8). This observation aligns with our previous findings (Li *et al.*, 2024, 2025), suggesting that when dynamic rupture dimensions and slip distributions are similar on the same fault, the overall economic loss scale and probability are roughly equivalent, even with different epicenter locations. This is because the spatial variation of asset exposure is relatively small. High risk areas for economic losses are primarily concentrated in Yinchuan, Shizuishan, and Wuhai.

Compared to assessing economic losses, the uncertainty surrounding population loss assessment results—both in terms of loss scale and probability distribution—is significantly greater (Fig. 9). This finding also aligns with our earlier research (Li *et al.*, 2024, 2025). The phenomenon can be closely linked to

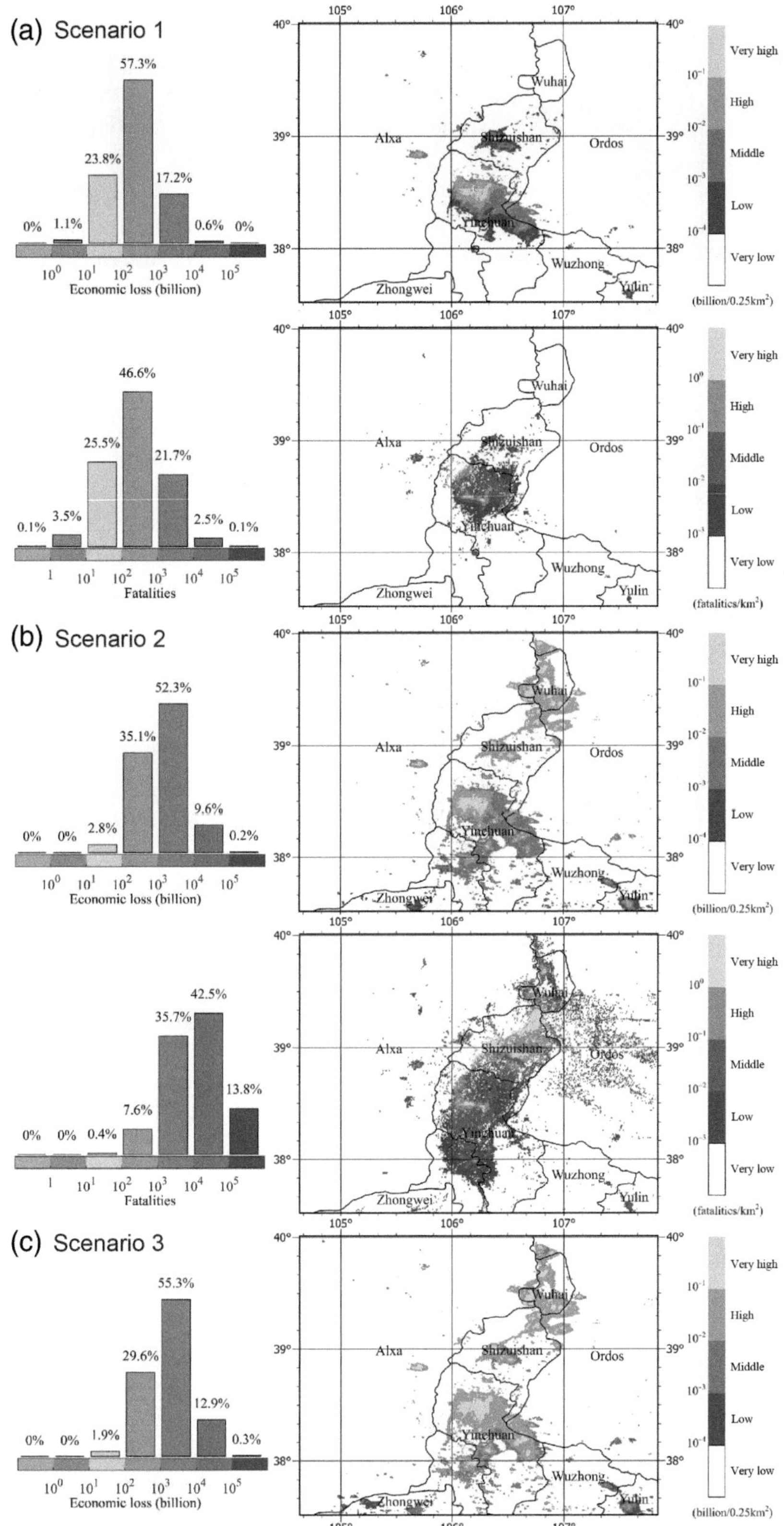

Figure 9. (a–e) Estimation results of economic loss and fatality in earthquake scenarios of the EHF. Among them, scenario 5 is the recurrence of the 1739 event. In each subplot, the first column is the histograms of direct economic losses and fatalities. Bar charts illustrate the relative probabilities of total losses occurring within various ranges. The colors of the bars indicate the severity of the losses, progressively intensifying from green to red. The second column is the risk distributions of direct economic losses and fatalities across the major impacted cities. The color version of this figure is available only in the electronic edition. (*Continued*)

the spatial characteristics of population exposure versus fixed asset exposure. Specifically, the difference between the maximum and minimum fixed asset values within a given spatial range is much smaller than the variations in population exposure. For scenario 1, the highest probability (46.6%) indicates a population loss scale of 100–1000 people. Scenarios 2–5 also show similar loss scales and probability distributions (the likelihood of losing 1000–10,000 people or 10,000–100,000 people is close), although there are some differences. We can draw certain conclusions that the earthquake scenario triggered by the northeast segment of the EHF has nearly a 90% probability of resulting in more than 1000 deaths, which classifies it as an extreme catastrophic earthquake event. The areas at highest risk for population loss are Yinchuan and Shizuishan, followed by the western and southern regions of Wuhai. In summary, the northeastern segment of the EHF poses substantially greater potential seismic risk to human society than its southwestern counterpart.

Discussion and Conclusion

In this work, we revisit the 1739 **M** 8 Pingluo earthquake from dynamic rupture to fatality estimation. Our dynamic model shows good agreement with surface rupture observations and previous damage investigations. As discussed by Wang, Li, *et al.* (2022), various data uncertainties, such as initial stress, epicenter location, fault geometry, and friction parameters, can affect historic earthquake simulation results. Nevertheless, we can still

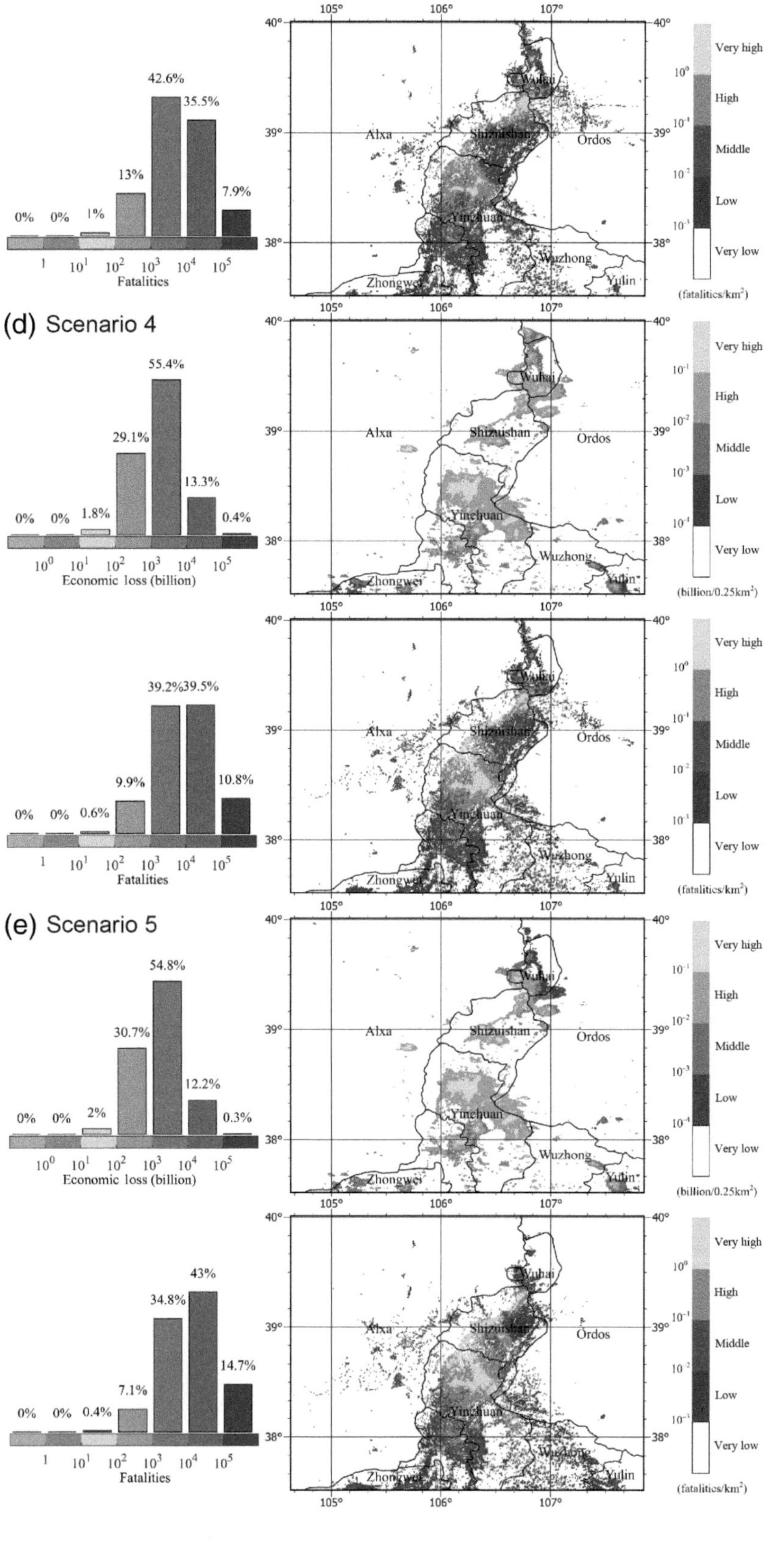

Figure 9. Continued

construct a reasonable dynamic model of historic, preinstrumental earthquakes based on the existing information. Future work can further incorporate site effects and the effect of plasticity (Gabriel *et al.*, 2013). Scenario earthquake simulations demonstrate that earthquakes nucleated at the southwest segment of the EHF may have a magnitude of M_W 7.0, whereas those nucleated at the northeast segment of the EHF can trigger a cascading rupture of two fault segments and reach a moment magnitude of 7.6. We find that the overall impact of hypocenter-dependent scenarios on economic losses is significantly smaller than on population losses, likely due to the spatial characteristics of risk exposure, for which the variation in fixed assets within a given area is much smaller than that of population exposure. Based on four M_W 7.6 earthquake scenarios of the EHF, we conclude that Yinchuan, Shizuishan, and Wuhai may suffer the most serious seismic disaster in potential earthquakes. Previous researches (Bray and Rodriguez-Marek, 2004; An *et al.*, 2021; Li, Gabriel, *et al.*, 2023; Li *et al.*, 2024, 2025) have emphasized the importance of considering the rupture directivity, whereas this work focusses on normal faults and highlights the disastrous consequences caused by the superposition of hanging-wall effect and basin amplification effect.

In addition, the limited resolution of basin velocity structures may result in underestimating shaking amplification (Olsen, 2000). Although the Yinchuan graben is characterized by a low-velocity zone in the CSRM velocity model (Xiao *et al.*, 2024), the resolution of the basin margin may be insufficient. Our results may just partially reflect the basin effect on ground motion. It is not excluded that the disaster of the actual earthquake scenario is more serious than our simulation results. Nevertheless, integrating physics-based simulation into seismic disaster assessment is of great significance and is developing rapidly. For further discussion in this aspect, refer to Petrone *et al.* (2021) and Xin and Zhang (2021).

Our work, through physics-based simulations, provides additional insights into the complex seismic hazard mechanisms (hanging-wall effect coupled with basin amplification) specific to normal-fault-bounded basins like Yinchuan. We also establish a valuable framework for assessing potential earthquake scenarios and their impacts in similar basins globally.

Data and Resources

Fault surface trace data are obtained from Seismic Active Fault Survey Data Center (https://www.activefault-datacenter.cn/map, last accessed November 2024). The *P*- and *S*-wave velocity data are obtained from China Seismological Reference Model 1.0 (CSRM1.0; http://chinageorefmodel.org/, last accessed November 2024). The topographic data are obtained from Shuttle Radar Topography Mission (SRTM, https://srtm.csi.cgiar.org/srtmdata/, last accessed December 2024). The graphic processing units (GPU)-based dynamic rupture software curved-grid finite-difference method (CGFDM) is available at https://github.com/Zijia-Wang/CGFDM (last accessed December 2024). The strong ground-motion simulation software CGFDM3D-EQR is available at https://github.com/wenqiangwangsustech (last accessed December 2024). The supplemental material for this article includes the detailed process of fatality estimation of the 1739 Pingluo earthquake, a figure of fault geometry (dip-angle distribution), a figure of dynamic parameter settings, rupture process (slip rate) of the 1739 Pingluo earthquake (Movie S1), seismic-wave propagation process (*Vz*) of the 1739 Pingluo earthquake (Movie S2), and rupture process (slip rate) of the other four earthquake scenarios (Movies S3–S6).

Declaration of Competing Interests

The authors acknowledge that there are no conflicts of interest recorded.

Acknowledgments

The authors thank Timothy A. Middleton and Richard T. Walker for providing the fault offset measurement data. This work is supported by the Ningxia Natural Science Foundation (Grant Number 2023AAC03754), the Fundamental Research Funds for the Central Universities (2243300007), the Shenzhen Science and Technology Program (JCYJ20241202125759001), and the Interdisciplinary Intelligence Super Computer Center of Beijing Normal University at Zhuhai. The authors thank Editor-in-Chief Allison Bent, an anonymous Associate Editor and Baoning Wu for their constructive and insightful suggestions and comments.

References

An, Z., J. Xie, Y. Zhang, X. Li, and Z. Wen (2021). Rupture directivity effect on strong ground motion during the 12 May 2008 Mw7.9 Wenchuan earthquake, *Earthq. Sci.* **34,** 234–245.

Aochi, H. (2018). Dynamic asymmetry of normal and reverse faults due to constrained depth-dependent stress accumulation, *Geophys. J. Int.* **215,** 2134–2143, doi: 10.1093/gji/ggy407.

Bai, M., and D. Jiao (2005). The historical analysis for M=8 earthquake in 1739 at Yinchuan-Pingluo area, *Northwestern Seismol. J.* **27,** 135–140 (in Chinese).

Bray, J. D., and A. Rodriguez-Marek (2004). Characterization of forward-directivity ground motions in the near-fault region, *Soil Dynam. Earthq. Eng.* **24,** 815–828.

Brocher, T. M. (2005). Empirical relations between elastic wavespeeds and density in the earth's crust, *Bull. Seismol. Soc. Am.* **95,** 2081–2092, doi: 10.1785/0120050077.

Bureau of Earthquake Damage Protection, China Earthquake Administration (1995). *Compilation of Earthquake Disaster Losses in China Mainland (23rd Century BC - 1911)*, Seismological Press, Beijing, China (in Chinese).

Chai, C., G. Meng, P. Du, Y. Wang, B. Liu, W. Shen, Q. Lei, Y. Liao, C. Zhao, S. Feng, *et al.* (2007). Comprehensive multi-level exploration of buried active faults: An example of the Yinchuan buried active fault, *Earthq. Res. China.* **21,** 225–235 (in Chinese).

Day, S. M., L. A. Dalguer, N. Lapusta, and Y. Liu (2005). Comparison of finite difference and boundary integral solutions to three-dimensional spontaneous rupture, *J. Geophys. Res.* **110,** no. B12, doi: 10.1029/2005JB003813.

Day, S. M., R. Graves, J. Bielak, D. Dreger, S. Larsen, K. B. Olsen, A. Pitarka, and L. Ramirez-Guzman (2008). Model for basin effects on long-period response spectra in southern California, *Earthq. Spectra* **24,** 257–277.

Deng, Q., and Y. Liao (1996). Paleoseismology along the range-front fault of Helan Mountains, north central China, *J. Geophys. Res.* **101,** 5873–5893, doi: 10.1029/95jb01814.

Deng, Q., S. Cheng, W. Min, G. Yang, and D. Ren (1999). Discussion on Cenozoic tectonics and dynamics of Ordos block, *J. Geomech.* **5,** 13–21 (in Chinese).

Deng, S., and S. Sheng (2015). The crustal stress field around the Ordos Block, *North China Earthq. Sci.* **33,** 55–62 (in Chinese).

Fan, J., J. Ma, and G. Diao (2003). Contemporary tectonic stress field around the Ordos Fault Block inferred from earthquake focal mechanisms, *Seismol. Geol.* **25,** 88–99 (in Chinese).

Fang, S., C. Zhao, C. Chai, B. Liu, S. Feng, M. Liu, Q. Lei, and H. Liu (2009). Seismic evidence of crustal structures in the Yinchuan faulted basin, *Chin. J. Geophys.* **52,** 1768–1775 (in Chinese).

Feng, S., R. Gao, C. Long, S. Fang, C. Zhao, K. Kou, Y. Tan, and H. He (2011). The compressive stress field of Yinchuan Garben: Deep seismic reflection profile, *Chinese J. Geophys.* **54,** 692–697 (in Chinese).

Gabriel, A. A., J. P. Ampuero, L. A. Dalguer, and P. M. Mai (2013). Source properties of dynamic rupture pulses with off-fault plasticity, *J. Geophys. Res.* **118,** 4117–4126, doi: 10.1002/jgrb.50213.

Guo, L., and M. Pang (1981). Surface-wave magnitude of earthquakes and its station correction, *Acta Seismol. Sin.* **3,** 312–320.

Harris, R. A., M. Barall, B. Aagaard, S. Ma, D. Roten, K. Olsen, B. Duan, D. Liu, B. Luo, K. Bai, *et al.* (2018). A suite of exercises for verifying dynamic earthquake rupture codes, *Seismol. Res. Lett.* **89,** 1146–1162, doi: 10.1785/0220170222.

Hu, F., Z. Zhang, and X. Chen (2016), Investigation of earthquake jump distance for strike-slip step overs based on 3-D dynamic rupture simulations in an elastic half-space, *J. Geophys. Res.* **121,** 994–1006, doi: 10.1002/2015JB012696.

Huang, X., W. Shi, H. Li, L. Chen, and M. Cen (2013). Cenozoic tectonic evolution of the Yinchuan Basin: Constraints from the deformation of its boundary faults, *Earth Sci. Front.* **20,** 199–210 (in Chinese).

Huang, Y., Q. Wang, M. Hao, and S. Zhou (2018). Fault slip rates and seismic moment deficits on major faults in Ordos constrained by GPS observation, *Sci. Rep.* **8,** 16,192, doi: 10.1038/s41598-018-34586-2.

Ida, Y. (1972). Cohesive force across the tip of a longitudinal-shear crack and Griffith's specific surface energy, *J. Geophys. Res.* **77,** 3796–3805, doi: 10.1029/JB077i020p03796.

Lee, W. H. K., F. T. Wu, and C. Jacobsen (1976). A catalog of historical earthquakes in China compiled from recent Chinese publications, *Bull. Seismol. Soc. Am.* **66,** 2003–2016, doi: 10.1785/bssa0660062003.

Lei, Q., C. Chai, P. Du, J. Yu, Y. Wang, and X. Xie (2015). The seismogenic structure of the M8.0 Pingluo earthquake in 1739, *Seismol. Geol.* **37,** 413–429 (in Chinese).

Lei, Q., C. Chai, G. Meng, P. Du, Y. Wang, X. Xie, and X. Zhang (2008). Composite drilling section exploration of Yinchuan buried fault, *Seismol. Geol.* **30,** 250–263 (in Chinese).

Lei, Q., C. Chai, W. Zheng, P. Du, X. Xie, Y. Wang, J. Cui, and G. Meng (2014). Activity and slip rate of the northern section of Yellow River Fault revealed by drilling, *Seismol. Geol.* **36,** 464–477 (in Chinese).

Lei, Q., W. Zheng, Y. Wang, S. Yu, X. Shen, and M. Hao (2024). The compilation of 1:500,000 seismotectonic map of the Ordos active block and boundary zone, *Prog. Earthq. Sci.* **54,** 65–74, doi: 10.19987/j.dzkxjz.2023-059 (in Chinese).

Li, B., A. A. Gabriel, T. Ulrich, C. Abril, and B. Halldorsson (2023). Dynamic rupture models, fault interaction and ground motion simulations for the segmented Húsavík-Flatey Fault Zone, Northern Iceland, *J. Geophys. Res.* **128,** e2022JB025886, doi: 10.1029/2022jb025886.

Li, M., and Z. Wan (1984). Characteristics of the earthquake-generating structures for magnitude 8.0 Pingluo earthquake of 1739 and the process of its preparation, *Seismol. Geol.* **6,** 23–28 (in Chinese).

Li, Y., Z. Wang, Z. Zhang, Y. Gu, and H. Yu (2024). A physics-based seismic risk assessment of the Qujiang Fault: From dynamic rupture to disaster estimation, *Int. J. Disast. Risk Sci.* **15,** 165–177, doi: 10.1007/s13753-024-00542-0.

Li, Y., D. Xin, and Z. Zhang (2021). A rapid-response earthquake fatality estimation model for mainland China, *Int. J. Disast. Risk Reduct.* **66,** 102618, doi: 10.1016/j.ijdrr.2021.102618.

Li, Y., D. Xin, and Z. Zhang (2023). Estimating the economic loss caused by earthquake in Mainland China, *Int. J. Disast. Risk Reduct.* **95,** 103708, doi: 10.1016/j.ijdrr.2023.103708.

Li, Y., H. Yu, M. Wang, X. Ye, K. Liu, Z. Zhang, W. Zhang, and X. Chen (2025). The physics-based deterministic scenarios for earthquake hazards and losses of the Zhujiangkou fault in southern China, *npj Nat. Hazards.* **2,** doi: 10.1038/s44304-024-00054-3.

Lin, A., J. Hu, and W. Gong (2015). Active normal faulting and the seismogenic fault of the 1739 M ~8.0 Pingluo earthquake in the intracontinental Yinchuan Graben, China, *J. Asian Earth Sci.* **114,** 155–173, doi: 10.1016/j.jseaes.2015.04.036.

Lin, A., G. Rao, J. Hu, and W. Gong (2013). Reevaluation of the offset of the Great Wall associated with the ca. M 8.0 Pingluo earthquake of 1739, Yinchuan graben, China, *J. Seismol.* **17,** 1281–1294, doi: 10.1007/s10950-013-9391-2.

Liu, B., C. Chai, S. Feng, C. Zhao, and H. Yuan (2008). Seismic exploration method for buried fault and its up-break point in Quaternary sediment area - An example of Yinchuan buried active fault, *Chin. J. Geophys.* **51,** 1475–1483 (in Chinese).

Liu, B., S. Feng, J. Ji, S. Wang, J. Zhang, H. Yuan, and G. Yang (2017). Lithospheric structure and faulting characteristics of the Helan Mountains and Yinchuan Basin: Results of deep seismic reflection profiling, *Sci. China Earth Sci.* **60,** 589–601, doi: 10.1007/s11430-016-5069-4.

Lou, B. (1996). *A Comprehensive Compilation of Historical and Recent Earthquake Disaster Status in China*, Seismological Press, Beijing, China (in Chinese).

Lozos, J. C. (2016). A case for historic joint rupture of the San Andreas and San Jacinto faults, *Sci. Adv.* **2,** e1500621, doi: 10.1126/sciadv.1500621.

Middleton, T. A., R. T. Walker, B. Parsons, Q. Lei, Y. Zhou, and Z. Ren (2016). A major, intraplate, normal-faulting earthquake: The 1739 Yinchuan event in northern China, *J. Geophys. Res.* **121,** 293–320, doi: 10.1002/2015jb012355.

Oglesby, D. D., R. J. Archuleta, and S. B. Nielsen (2000). The three-dimensional dynamics of dipping faults, *Bull. Seismol. Soc. Am.* **90,** 616–628, doi: 10.1785/0119990113.

Olsen, K. B. (2000). Site amplification in the Los Angeles basin from three-dimensional modeling of ground motion, *Bull. Seismol. Soc. Am.* **90,** S77–S94.

Petrone, F., N. Abrahamson, D. McCallen, and M. Miah (2021). Validation of (not-historical) large-event near-fault ground-motion simulations for use in civil engineering applications, *Earthq. Eng. Struct. Dynam.* **50,** 116–134, doi: 10.1002/eqe.3366.

Reuter, H. I., A. Nelson, and A. Jarvis (2007). An evaluation of void filling interpolation methods for SRTM data, *Int. J. Geogr. Inf. Sci.* **21,** 983–1008.

Standardization Administration of the People's Republic of China (SAC) (2020). The Chinese seismic intensity scale, *GB/T 17742-2020*, available at https://openstd.samr.gov.cn/bzgk/gb/newGbInfo?hcno=6FD8F9071FAC980D5B2A636A9EA79DE9 (last accessed January 2025).

Smith, K., and C. Tape (2019). Seismic response of Cook Inlet sedimentary basin, Southern Alaska, *Seismol. Res. Lett.* **91,** 33–55, doi: 10.1785/0220190205.

Sunilkumar, T. C., Z. Zhang, Z. Wang, W. Wang, and Z. He (2024). Unveiling the mechanisms of the 1819 M 7.7 Kachchh Earthquake, India: Integrating physics-based simulation and strong ground motion estimates, *Earth Space Sci.* **11,** e2023EA003308, doi: 10.1029/2023ea003308.

Wang, H., G. Zhang, Y. Wu, and H. Ma (2003). The deformation of active crustal-blocks on the Chinese Mainland and its relation with seismic activity, *Earthq. Res. China* **19,** 243–254 (in Chinese).

Wang, W., G. Cai, G. Lai, X. Zeng, J. Bao, L. Zhang, J. Su, and M. Chen (2023). Three-dimensional S-wave velocity structure of the crust and upper mantle for the normal fault system beneath the Yinchuan Basin from joint inversion of receiver function and surface wave, *Sci. China Earth Sci.* **66,** 997–1014, doi: 10.1007/s11430-022-1059-y.

Wang, W., Y. Li, Z. Zhang, D. Xin, Z. He, W. Zhang, and X. Chen (2023). Rapid estimation of disaster losses for the M6.8 Luding earthquake on September 5, 2022, *Sci. China Earth Sci.* **66,** 1334–1344, doi: 10.1007/s11430-022-1078-6.

Wang, W., Z. Zhang, W. Zhang, H. Yu, Q. Liu, W. Zhang, and X. Chen (2022). CGFDM3D-EQR: A platform for rapid response to earthquake disasters in 3D complex media, *Seismol. Res. Lett.* **93,** 2320–2334, doi: 10.1785/0220210172.

Wang, Z., and Z. Zhang (2025). Unexpected rupture triggering behavior of subshear and free-surface-induced supershear ruptures on stepover, *Earth Planet. Sci. Lett.* **664,** 119457, doi: 10.1016/j.epsl.2025.119457.

Wang, Z., Y. Li, W. Wang, W. Zhang, and Z. Zhang (2022). Revisiting paleoearthquakes with numerical modeling: A case study of the 1679 Sanhe–Pinggu earthquake, *Seismol. Res. Lett.* **94,** 720–730, doi: 10.1785/0220220208.

Wirth, E. A., J. E. Vidale, A. D. Frankel, T. L. Pratt, N. A. Marafi, M. Thompson, and W. J. Stephenson (2019). Source-dependent amplification of earthquake ground motions in deep sedimentary basins, *Geophys. Res. Lett.* **46,** 6443–6450, doi: 10.1029/2019GL082474.

Xiao, X., S. Cheng, J. Wu, W. Wang, L. Sun, X. Wang, J. Ma, Y. Tong, X. Liang, X. Tian, *et al.* (2024). CSRM-1.0: A China Seismological Reference Model, *J. Geophys. Res.* **129,** e2024JB029520, doi: 10.1029/2024jb029520.

Xin, D., and Z. Zhang (2021). On the comparison of seismic ground motion simulated by physics-based dynamic rupture and predicted by empirical attenuation equations, *Bull. Seismol. Soc. Am.* **111,** 2595–2616, doi: 10.1785/0120210077.

Xin, D., J. E. Daniell, Z. Zhang, F. Wenzel, S. S. Wang, and X. Chen (2025). A grid-level fixed-asset model developed for China from 1951 to 2020, *Nat. Hazards Earth Syst. Sci.* **25,** 1597–1620, doi: 10.5194/nhess-25-1597-2025.

Xu, D., Z. Li, Z. Zhang, H. Yu, J. Xu, Z. Yang, and X. Chen (2024). The 2022 Mw 6.6 Menyuan earthquake: An early-terminated runaway rupture by the complex fault geometry, *Earth Planet. Sci. Lett.* **638,** 118746, doi: 10.1016/j.epsl.2024.118746.

Yu, H., F. Hu, J. Xu, Z. Zhang, and X. Chen (2022). Dynamic rupture simulation of the 1833 Songming, Yunnan, China, M 8.0 earthquake: Effects from stepover location and overlap distance, *Earth Space Sci.* **9,** e2021EA002100, doi: 10.1029/2021ea002100.

Yu, H., Z. Zhang, F. Hu, D. Xu, and X. Chen (2023). Estimation of the nucleation location and rupture extent of the 1850 Xichang, Sichuan, China, earthquake by dynamic rupture simulations on a multi-segment stepover structure, *Earth Space Sci.* **10,** e2022EA002775, doi: 10.1029/2022ea002775.

Zhang, B., Y. Liao, S. Guo, R. E. Wallace, R. C. Bucknam, and C. H. Thomas (1986). Fault scarps related to the 1739 earthquake and seismicity of the Yinchuan Graben, Ningxia Huizu Zizhiqu, China, *Bull. Seismol. Soc. Am.* **76,** 1253–1287.

Zhang, J. (2008). Estimation of China's provincial capital stock (1952–2004) with applications, *J. Chin. Econ. Business Stud.* **6,** 177–196.

Zhang, P., B. C. Burchfiel, P. Molnar, W. Zhang, D. Jiao, Q. Deng, Y. Wang, R. Leigh, and F. Song (1990). Late Cenozoic tectonic evolution of the Ningxia-Hui Autonomous region, China, *Geol. Soc. Am. Bull.* **102,** 1484–1498.

Zhang, W., and X. Chen (2006). Traction image method for irregular free surface boundaries in finite difference seismic wave simulation, *Geophys. J. Int.* **167,** 337–353, doi: 10.1111/j.1365-246X.2006.03113.x.

Zhang, W., Z. Zhang, and X. Chen (2012). Three-dimensional elastic wave numerical modelling in the presence of surface topography by a collocated-grid finite-difference method on curvilinear grids, *Geophys. J. Int.* **190,** 358–378, doi: 10.1111/j.1365-246X.2012.05472.x.

Zhang, W., Z. Zhang, M. Li, and X. Chen (2020). GPU implementation of curved-grid finite-difference modelling for non-planar rupture dynamics, *Geophys. J. Int.* **222,** 2121–2135.

Zhang, Z., W. Zhang, and X. Chen (2014). Three-dimensional curved grid finite-difference modelling for non-planar rupture dynamics, *Geophys. J. Int.* **199,** 860–879.

Zhang, Z., W. Zhang, X. Chen, P. E. Li, and C. Fu (2017). Rupture dynamics and ground motion from potential earthquakes around Taiyuan, China, *Bull. Seismol. Soc. Am.* **107,** 1201–1212, doi: 10.1785/0120160239.

Zhao, H., C. Liu, F. Wang, J. Wang, Q. Li, and Y. Yao (2007). Uplifting time and evolution of Helan Mountain, *Sci. China Earth Sci.* **37,** 185–192 (in Chinese).

Manuscript received 26 June 2025
Published online 13 October 2025

Automated Classification of Volcanic Earthquakes Using Transformer Encoders: Insights into Data Quality and Model Interpretability

Yugo Suzuki[1], Yohei Yukutake[2], Takao Ohminato[2], Masami Yamasaki[1], and Ahyi Kim[*1]

Abstract

Precisely classifying earthquake types is crucial for elucidating the relationship between volcanic earthquakes and volcanic activity. However, traditional methods rely on subjective human judgment, which requires considerable time and effort. To address this issue, we developed a deep learning model using a transformer encoder for a more objective and efficient classification. Tested on Mount Asama's diverse seismic activity, our model achieved high F1 scores (0.930 for volcano tectonic, 0.931 for low-frequency earthquakes, and 0.980 for noise), superior to a convolutional neural network-based method. To enhance interpretability, attention weight (AW) visualizations were analyzed, revealing that the model focuses on key waveform features similarly to human experts. However, inconsistencies in training data, such as ambiguously labeled B-type events with *S* waves, were found to influence classification accuracy and AW distributions. Experiments addressing data selection and augmentation demonstrated the importance of balancing data quality and diversity. In addition, stations within 3 km of the crater played an important role in improving model performance and interpretability. These findings highlight the potential of transformer-based models for automated volcanic earthquake classification, particularly in improving efficiency and interpretability. By addressing challenges such as data imbalance and subjective labeling, our approach provides a robust framework for understanding seismic activity at Mount Asama. Moreover, this framework offers opportunities for transfer learning to other volcanic regions, paving the way for enhanced volcanic hazard assessments and disaster mitigation strategies.

Cite this article as Suzuki, Y., Y. Yukutake, T. Ohminato, M. Yamasaki, and A. Kim (2025). Automated Classification of Volcanic Earthquakes Using Transformer Encoders: Insights into Data Quality and Model Interpretability, *Seismol. Res. Lett.* **97**, 1032–1047, doi: 10.1785/0220240494.

Supplemental Material

Introduction

Active earthquake swarms are frequently associated with volcanic activity in volcanic regions. Monitoring these earthquakes is crucial for assessing current volcanic activity and providing insights into the physical processes of volcanic fluids, such as magma and hydrothermal fluids (Chouet, 1988; McNutt, 1996; Nishimura and Iguchi, 2011). Minakami *et al.* (1970) proposed that volcanic earthquakes could be classified into four types based on waveform characteristics, source location, and their relationship with surface activity: A-type (tectonic earthquakes), B-type earthquakes (commonly referred to as low-frequency earthquakes, although shallow earthquakes at Mount Asama can be classified as B-type regardless of their waveform characteristics, implying some B-type events do not strictly exhibit low-frequency features), volcanic tremors, and explosion earthquakes. Although the frequency components of these four types of earthquakes vary by volcano and may be further subdivided or include other types, a typical pattern before eruptions begin is an increase in A-type earthquakes, followed by an increase in B-type earthquakes and volcanic tremors (Oikawa *et al.*, 2006; Iguchi, 2013). We note that A- and B-type classifications commonly used in Japan correspond to volcanotectonic events and long-period events, respectively, as is more common internationally (Chouet, 1996, 2003). These seismic events often indicate changes in subsurface magmatic and hydrothermal activity, making them crucial for monitoring volcanic hazards. However, the exact relationship between these earthquakes and their subsequent

1. Yokohama City University, Yokohama City, Kanagawa Prefecture, Japan, https://orcid.org/0009-0001-7948-5332 (YS); https://orcid.org/0000-0002-0605-0397 (AK); 2. Earthquake Research Institute, The University of Tokyo, Yayoi Bunkyo-ku, Tokyo, Japan

*Corresponding author: ahyik@yokohama-cu.ac.jp

eruptions remains unclear, particularly due to inconsistencies in classification methods. Developing precise classification criteria for A-type and B-type earthquakes is essential not only for improved understanding of these processes but also for enhancing eruption forecasting and developing more effective disaster mitigation strategies.

Traditional methods classify volcanic earthquakes based on visual observations of the seismic wave amplitude, dominant frequency, duration, and related surface activity evaluated by experts, which are time-consuming and expensive. In addition, the classification criteria may need to be standardized across observers and institutions.

Permana *et al.* (2022) aimed to automate classification specifically for volcanic tremors and B-type earthquakes based on seismic correlation analysis, distinguishing them from continuous seismic recordings. Consequently, they analyzed continuous data from six seismic stations at Sakurajima volcano, Japan, from April to September 2017, correctly classifying ~80% of the volcanic earthquakes and 75% of the B-type earthquakes reported in the Japan Meteorological Agency catalog. However, this method relies on the correlation of seismic waveforms, and the issue of reduced classification accuracy persists for signals impacted by noise or lacking sufficient coherence.

Several machine learning models have also been proposed for the automatic classification of volcanic earthquakes and tremors. Unsupervised learning methods include hidden Markov models (Bebbington, 2007), self-organizing maps (Langer *et al.*, 2009, 2011; Köhler *et al.*, 2010), Gaussian mixture models (Hammer *et al.*, 2012), and principal component analysis (Unglert *et al.*, 2016). Ida and Ishida (2022) developed a method combining k-means clustering and dynamic time warping to classify volcanic earthquake waveforms, applying it to data from the day when magma ascent was observed beneath the active crater of Sakurajima volcano, demonstrating its validity. However, unsupervised learning faces challenges in interpretation and the need for manual labeling by human experts in the final classification.

In contrast, supervised learning models include the work of Malfante *et al.* (2018), who used support vector machines to classify six types of seismic events with 92% accuracy. Titos *et al.* (2018) employed convolutional neural networks (CNNs) to classify volcanic earthquakes, demonstrating that these methods can be applied even in areas with relatively few observational data through transfer learning. Because of the significant influence of source mechanisms on spectral characteristics, some studies have used time–frequency representations with 2D CNNs (e.g., Canário *et al.*, 2020; Lara *et al.*, 2021). Nakano *et al.* (2022) showed that there is no significant difference in performance between the two because even in a 1D CNN with only a temporal domain, the frequency components are accounted for when extracting features in the convolution layer. Although deep learning has significantly improved the performance of earthquake type classification and reduced human effort and time costs, the lack of transparency in the classification rationale remains a challenge.

In this study, we propose a method using a transformer encoder to overcome these challenges. The transformer can learn features directly from raw data, greatly simplifying the preprocessing and feature extraction process; its flexibility allows it to adapt to different volcanic and seismic environments. In addition, by visualizing the attention weights (AWs), we aimed to render a portion of the classification process interpretable, enabling us to examine whether the model follows similar criteria to human experts or if it uses unique classification criteria. The use of transformer architectures in seismology has been explored previously by Mousavi *et al.* (2020), who developed EQTransformer for simultaneous earthquake detection and phase picking. Although their model focuses on tectonic earthquakes, our study employs a transformer encoder specifically for classifying volcanic earthquakes, addressing the unique characteristics of A- and B-type events and enhancing interpretability for volcanic monitoring purposes.

Methods

Model architecture overview

We developed a neural network for classifying seismic events that combines a 1D convolutional front-end with a transformer encoder backend (Fig. 1). The input to the model is a three-component seismic waveform segment of length 3000 samples (30 s at 100 Hz). First, a 1D convolution layer with a kernel size of 50, a stride of 10, input channels = 3 (for the three components: east–west [EW], north–south [NS], and up–down [UD]), and output channels = 150 processes the waveform. This convolution segments the waveform into overlapping 50-sample frames and outputs 150 features per frame. With the given stride, the convolution produces a sequence of 296 feature vectors of length 150 each, preserving temporal order while reducing sequence length for efficiency. We apply batch normalization and a Rectified Linear Unit (ReLU) activation to the convolutional outputs. Using a larger kernel to capture longer temporal patterns and a larger stride (instead of a pooling layer) to achieve dimension reduction, we retain important temporal information while efficiently reducing sequence length, similar to the approach in Gulati *et al.* (2020).

Next, we insert a special classification token (CLS) at the beginning of the sequence of convolutional features, immediately following positional embedding (Fig. 1), as a learnable summary representation for classification. The sequence length thereby becomes 297 (296 feature vectors plus one CLS token). This sequence (CLS + features) is fed into three stacked transformer encoder layers. Finally, the transformer output from the CLS token embedding is passed through a fully connected layer (linear layer) followed by a softmax function to obtain class probabilities for A-type, B-type, or noise event classes. Without the

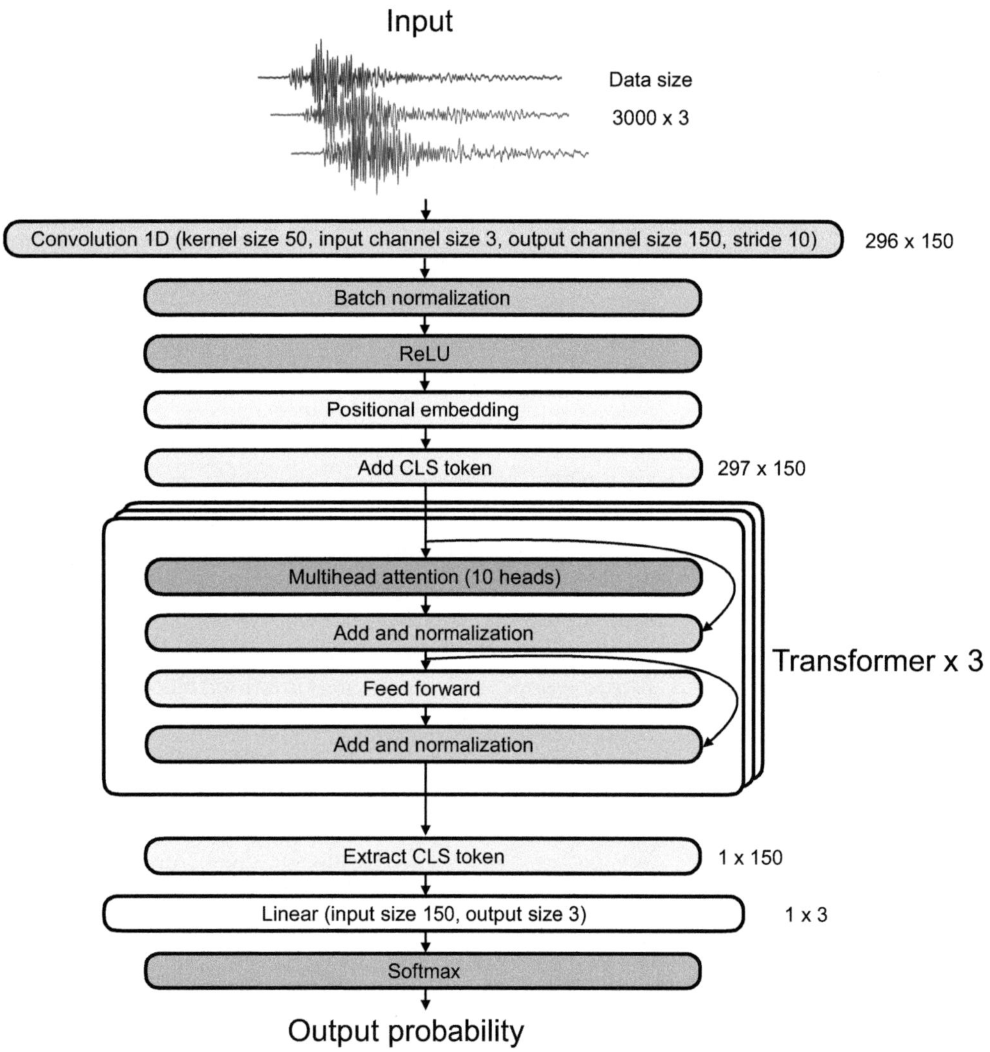

Figure 1. Network architecture. Three-component seismic waveforms are passed through a 1D convolution layer (kernel size: 50; input channel size: 3; output channel size: 150; and stride: 10), followed by batch normalization, ReLU activation, and positional embedding. A classification token (CLS) is added to the input sequence and processed through three stacked Transformer encoder layers, each consisting of 10 multi-head attention mechanisms, feedforward sublayers, and residual connections. The CLS token output is extracted and passed through a linear transformation to classify A- and B-type events, as well as noise. The color version of this figure is available only in the electronic edition.

CLS token, the model would need to aggregate sequence information through alternative methods such as average or maximum pooling over all feature vectors. However, these pooling methods might discard critical contextual information needed for accurate classification. The CLS token explicitly provides a dedicated, learnable summary representation, allowing the model to effectively capture and integrate global sequence information via the self-attention mechanism. Before model training, we prepared seismic waveform data from Mount Asama, consisting of A-type and B-type earthquake waveforms, as well as noise segments (see Fig. 2 for waveform examples and event distribution). Training was conducted for 60 epochs using a minibatch size of 200 and a multiclass cross-entropy loss function. We utilized the AdamW optimizer (Loshchilov and Hutter, 2017), which incorporates weight decay into Adam (Kingma and Ba, 2014), with a learning rate of 0.001 and weight decay of 0.01. These hyperparameters were selected through parameter tuning to balance model performance and computational efficiency. The minibatch size was set to the maximum feasible value that could fit within the memory of the graphic processing units, ensuring stable and efficient training. The learning curves shown in Figure 3 represent the entire 60 epochs of training, demonstrating consistent convergence without overfitting. Note that the CLS token is a single vector with the same dimensionality (150) as each of the convolutional feature vectors. This single CLS vector is prepended once at the very beginning of the entire sequence (not separately to each of the 150 channels), resulting in a sequence of dimension 297 × 150.

Transformer encoder and self-attention

Our model uses only the encoder component of the transformer architecture (Vaswani *et al.*, 2017) because our task involves encoding input sequences into representative vectors for classification. A key feature of the transformer encoder is the self-attention mechanism, which weights the relevance of every input position relative to others. Each token (vector) x_i(dimension $d_{\mathrm{model}} = 150$) is projected into three vectors: query (q_i), key (k_i), and value (v_i):

$$q_i = x_i W^Q, \quad k_i = x_i W^K, \quad v_i = x_i W^V, \tag{1}$$

in which W^Q, W^K, and W^V are parameter matrices, each of dimension (150 × 15), with 150 corresponding to d_{model} and the column size of 15 was determined by dividing d_{model} by

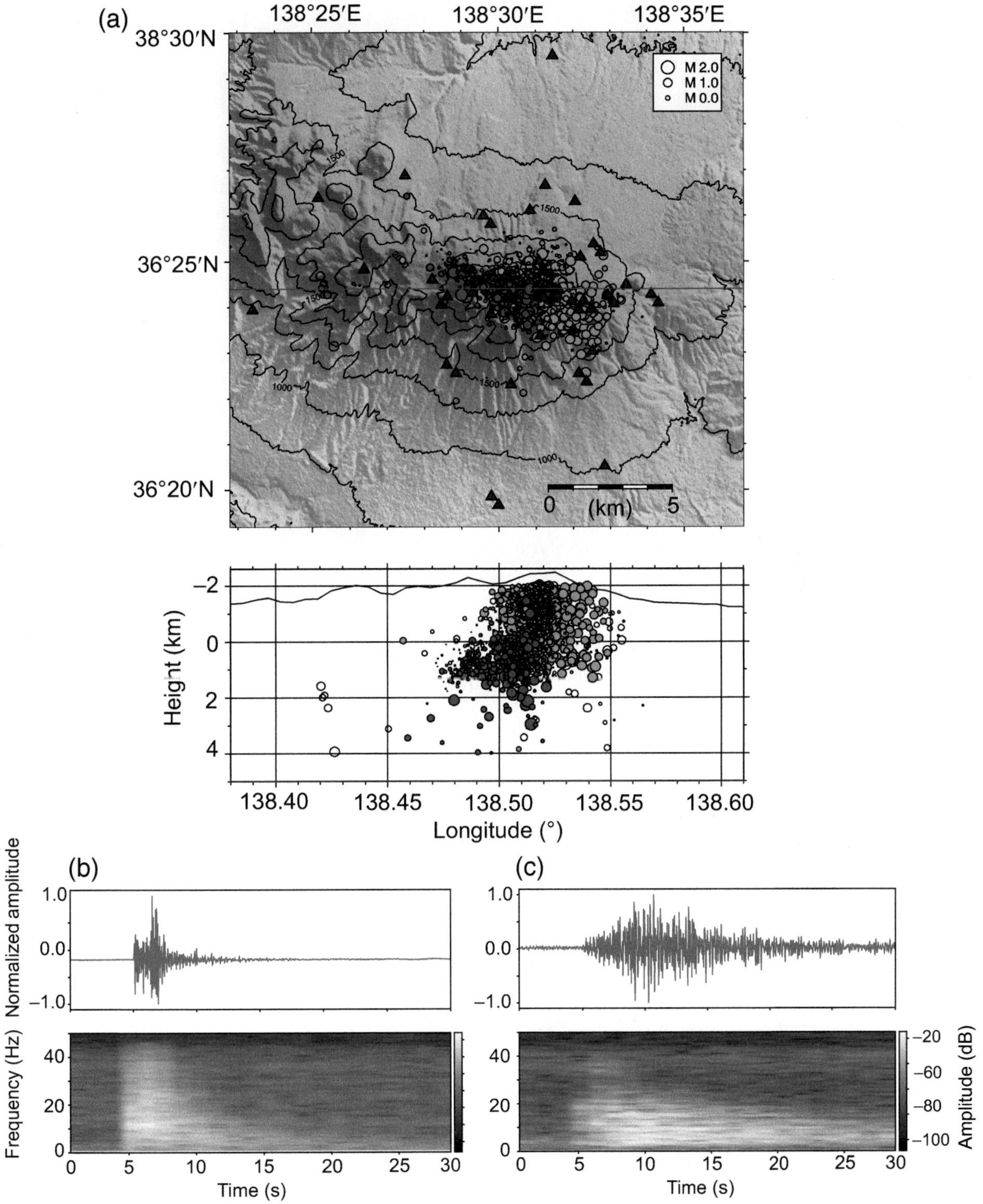

Figure 2. Distribution of earthquakes and stations, and examples of input data. Earthquakes detected between January 2003 and October 2022, only with location determination errors less than 100 m in horizontal and depth directions (based on the earthquake catalog from the Earthquake Research Institute, The University of Tokyo), were plotted. (a) Distribution of earthquakes (circles) and stations (blue triangles) at Mount Asama. The red circles represent A-type events, green circles represent B-type labeled events, and open circles represent earthquakes that do not belong to either type. The top image is a map view, and the bottom image is a cross-sectional view along the red line in the map view. In the cross section, "Height" represents elevation relative to sea level, with positive values indicating depth below the surface. The "0" on the vertical axis indicates the surface level. (b) An example of an A-type earthquake. The top panel shows the seismic waveform, and the bottom image shows the spectrogram. (c) Same as panel (b), but representing an example of a B-type earthquake. The color version of this figure is available only in the electronic edition.

the number of attention heads (10 heads), thus 150/10 = 15. The vectors, q_i, k_i, are v_i form matrices Q, K, V, respectively, each with dimensions (297 × 15):

$$Q,K,V \in \mathbb{R}^{L \times d_{\text{model}}}, \tag{2}$$

in which $L = 297$ is the sequence length (296 convolutional feature vectors plus 1 CLS token), and $d_{\text{model}} = 150$. The AWs computed from the dot product of Q and K thus form a square matrix of dimensions $(L \times L) = (297 \times 297)$.

Intuitively, q_i represents a query (what information the token seeks), k_i a key (the information held by each token), and v_i the value (the actual content at each token). These projected vectors (q_i, k_i, and v_i) and subsequent attention calculations are performed within the "Multi-Head Attention" block of the transformer encoder, as illustrated in Figure 1. We set 10 attention heads ($h = 10$), making each head's dimension $d_k = 15$ because $h \times d_k = 150$. Multi-head attention enables capturing diverse aspects of information simultaneously because each head learns to focus on different patterns or features within the waveform data.

The attention score e_{ij} between tokens i and j is calculated by the scaled dot product of query and key vectors:

$$e_{ij} = \frac{q_i \cdot k_j}{\sqrt{d_k}}. \tag{3}$$

These scores are normalized by the softmax function to obtain AWs a_{ij}:

$$a_{ij} = \frac{\exp(e_{ij})}{\sum_{m=1}^{L} \exp(e_{im})}, \tag{4}$$

in which L is the sequence length, which in this study is 297 (296 feature vectors from convolution plus 1 CLS token).

The scaling by $\sqrt{d_k}$ in the attention calculation prevents excessively large dot-product values (q_i) as d_k increases. This ensures that the softmax function does not produce overly peaked distributions, which would otherwise result in saturated gradients and unstable training (Vaswani *et al.*, 2017).

Finally, the attention output z_i for token i is the weighted sum of value vectors:

$$z_i = \sum_{j=1}^{L} a_{ij} v_{ij}. \tag{5}$$

In matrix form, this is represented concisely as

$$\text{Attention}(Q,K,V) = \text{softmax}\left(\frac{QK^T}{\sqrt{d_k}}\right)V. \tag{6}$$

Multi-head attention. Our model employs multi-head attention with 10 heads to simultaneously capture multiple aspects of information. Each head performs the attention mechanism independently with its own projection matrices W_m^Q, W_m^K, and W_m^V, each sized 150 × 15. Each head's output (size $L \times 15$) is concatenated into an $L \times 150$ matrix and linearly transformed by W^O (150 × 150):

$$\text{Multihead}(Q,K,V) = \text{Concat}(\text{head}_1, \cdots, \text{head}_{10}) W^O. \tag{7}$$

Each transformer encoder layer also includes a position-wise feed-forward network (FFN), consisting of two linear layers with a ReLU activation:

$$(x) = \text{ReLU}(xW_1 + b_1)W_2 + b_2, \tag{8}$$

in which W_1 is 150 × 2048, W_2 is 2048 × 150, b_1 is 2048 × 1, and b_2 is 150 × 1. Both the attention and FFN sublayers utilize residual connections and layer normalization:

$$\text{Output} = \text{LayerNorm}(x + \text{SubLayer}(x)), \tag{9}$$

in which SubLayer is either multi-head attention or FFN.

Positional information and relative positional embedding

Because the transformer encoder does not inherently capture token order, we incorporate positional information via relative positional embeddings (Huang, 2018). We adopted this relative positional embedding because, for seismic waveform classification, capturing the relative timing between waveform features (such as the delay between observed P waves and S waves) is critical, whereas absolute timestamps within the waveform window are less informative. A trainable embedding vector r_k represents each possible relative displacement k. This relative positional embedding vector r_k has dimension $d_k = 15$, matching the dimension used for queries and keys within each attention head. A relative positional bias term $S_{i,j}^{\text{rel}}$ is computed as the dot product between the query vector q_i at token position I and the relative positional embedding vector r_{j-i}, corresponding to the displacement $j - i$:

$$S_{i,j}^{\text{rel}} = q_i \cdot r_{j-i}. \tag{10}$$

This bias term $S_{i,j}^{\text{rel}}$ is then added to attention scores based on token positions i and j. To efficiently construct S^{rel}, we use the Skew algorithm introduced by Huang (2018). The Skew algorithm first pads the matrix obtained by multiplying queries by relative positional embeddings with an additional dummy column. Next, this padded matrix is flattened into a vector. A dummy row of length $N - 1$ is then appended. Finally, the resulting vector is reshaped into a matrix of size $(N + 1, 2N - 1)$, and each subsequent row is shifted (skewed) by one position relative to the previous row. After removing excess elements introduced during padding, the resulting matrix S^{rel} provides efficient computation of relative positional biases without explicitly calculating each pairwise positional displacement. The modified attention mechanism with relative position embedding is thus:

$$\mathrm{Attention}_{\mathrm{rel}}(Q,K,V) = \mathrm{softmax}\left(\frac{QK^T + S^{\mathrm{rel}}}{\sqrt{d_k}}\right)V. \tag{11}$$

In this study, positional information is captured exclusively through these learned relative positional embeddings, without absolute positional encoding.

Classification token and output layer

To aggregate sequence information into a single vector, we prepend a classification token (CLS). Unlike pooling, the CLS token is learnable and dynamically aggregates relevant information. Initially, the CLS embedding is the average of the convolutional outputs, then refined by transformer layers. After the final encoder layer, the CLS token output vector (150D) is passed through a fully connected layer (150 × 3), producing logit scores for the three classes (A-type, B-type, and noise). A softmax function converts these logits into class probabilities. Training uses cross-entropy loss, and at inference time, the class with the highest probability is selected. No reshaping or pooling of features is needed before the transformer input.

Data

To validate the classification model, we selected Mount Asama, an active andesitic volcano in central Japan, as our test site (Fig. 2a). This volcano is known for frequent occurrences of both A-type (tectonic) and B-type (low-frequency) earthquakes, making it an ideal site to evaluate the model's ability to distinguish between these types of seismic events. Historical studies (Oikawa *et al.*, 2006; Takeo *et al.*, 2022) show that Mount Asama exhibits a typical pre-eruption seismic pattern, with an increase in A-type earthquakes followed by B-type events. The frequent occurrences of both earthquake types allow us to test the accuracy of our model in classifying seismic signals. Seismic observations have been conducted on Mount Asama for more than 100 yr. Since the establishment of a modern observation network around the volcano in 2003, a network consisting of 30 seismometers, including 19 with broadband sensors, has been installed by institutions such as the Earthquake Research Institute, Japan Meteorological Agency, and National Research Institute for Earth Science and Disaster Resilience (Fig. 2a) up to 2017.

Volcanic earthquakes on Mount Asama have been classified based on their source locations and waveform characteristics (Minakami *et al.*, 1970). Recent observations and research have identified several types of volcanic earthquakes on Mount Asama. B-type earthquakes, typically located directly beneath the crater, are characterized by lower frequency components and unclear *P*- and *S*-wave onsets. A-type earthquakes, situated slightly westward and at greater depths than the B-type distribution area, exhibit clearer *P*- and *S*-wave onsets and higher frequency components (Fig. 2). In addition, F-type earthquakes occur on the flanks of the volcano away from the crater, whereas N-type earthquakes occur within the B-type source area, but are distinguished by decaying oscillatory waveforms (Oikawa *et al.*, 2006). Currently, these events are further categorized into 12 specific types. However, A- and B-type earthquakes are of particular interest because they are commonly observed at many volcanoes and often follow a pre-eruption pattern in which A-type activity increases first, followed by an increase in B-type events (Oikawa *et al.*, 2006). Thus, this study focused on classifying A-type and B-type earthquakes to establish a robust classification model that can serve as a basis for future generalization studies to other volcanoes while also contributing to a broader understanding of Mount Asama's seismic activity. Because our model was trained and tested exclusively on three waveform categories (A-type, B-type, and noise), waveforms belonging to other seismic event types identified at Mount Asama (e.g., the other ten types) were not included in this study, partly due to their limited sample sizes. Thus, potential misclassification for these event types has not yet been assessed. Incorporating additional event types into future training datasets would be an important next step toward developing a more generalizable classification model.

Figure 2b,c, respectively, shows waveforms and spectrograms of A- and B-type earthquakes. A-type earthquakes have distinct *P* and *S* waves, whereas B-type earthquakes often have unclear *P*-wave onsets and indistinguishable *S* waves. B-type earthquakes tend to have longer durations and lower dominant frequencies than A-type earthquakes. Therefore, this study aimed to classify A- and B-type earthquakes and differentiate them from noise. We used a seismic catalog between January 2003 and October 2022, developed by the ERI Asama Volcano Observatory, to construct the classification model. The earthquake types in this catalog were manually classified based on visual waveform inspection. Figure 2a shows only those with horizontal and depth source errors within 100 m for 900 A- and 3191 B-type earthquakes. To ensure comprehensive model training, all detected earthquakes, including those with relatively large location errors, were used. This comprises 1,027 A-type earthquakes (8,318 waveforms) and 4,090 B-type earthquakes (37,196 waveforms), with *P*- and *S*-wave arrival times manually selected. As shown in Figure 2, the volcanic earthquakes at Mount Asama, especially B-type earthquakes, are concentrated in shallow regions in the vicinity of the crater. Therefore, most seismic waveforms used in this study were observed at ~20 stations located within 3 km of the crater. However, the number of stations historically varied due to differences in operational duration, relocations, and data availability. Such variability, combined with issues of waveform quality and operational gaps at these stations, explains the discrepancy between the actual number of waveforms used and

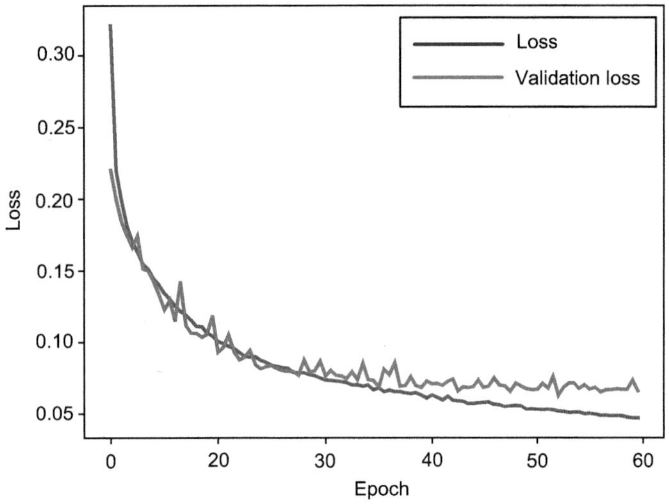

Figure 3. Learning curves for the model constructed in this study. The blue and red lines represent the training and validation losses, respectively. The color version of this figure is available only in the electronic edition.

the theoretical maximum. The onsets of the *P*- and *S*-wave arrival times for these earthquakes were manually selected. Each dataset consisted of three channels (two horizontal and one vertical). We decimated the waveforms of stations recorded at 200 Hz such that the sampling frequency of all waveforms was 100 Hz. Each waveform was initially extracted from a segment of 9001 points. For A- and B-type earthquakes, the starting point was randomly selected from 150 to 1000 points before the *P*-wave arrival time, and 3000 points were extracted for use. Noise data were obtained from a time interval with no earthquake signals. All waveform data were standardized before model training and testing by subtracting the mean and dividing by the standard deviation.

Results

Model performance

To construct the dataset, we included 112,852 noise waveforms derived from segments before the *P*-wave arrival in seismic records. This number exceeds the total waveforms for A- and B-type earthquakes because it also includes waveforms from events that do not belong to either class (A- or B-type). Importantly, the noise dataset does not include any waveforms overlapping with A-type, B-type, or any other categorized seismic events. For model evaluation, a fixed test set consisting of 1663 waveforms for each class (A-type, B-type, and noise) was used across all experiments. The remaining waveforms were used for training. Detailed information on the dataset composition is provided in Table S1, available in the supplemental material to this article. The training curves (Fig. 3) indicate that learning progressed without overfitting.

The model's performance was compared with that of a CNN-based model constructed following the architecture used by Nakano and Sugiyama (2022), consisting of four CNN layers and two fully connected layers (Fig. S1). This CNN model was trained entirely using our dataset (Table 1).

TABLE 1
Classification Performance of Models with and without Data Augmentation

Model	BACC	Event Type	Precision	Recall	F1 Score
This study	0.947	A	0.976	0.889	0.930
		B	0.900	0.964	0.931
		Noise	0.972	0.989	0.980
CNN*	0.921	A	0.949	0.855	0.899
		B	0.869	0.935	0.901
		Noise	0.952	0.975	0.963
This study (data augmentation)	0.968	A	0.984	0.935	0.959
		B	0.940	0.975	0.957
		Noise	0.982	0.993	0.987
CNN* (data augmentation)	0.910	A	0.977	0.784	0.870
		B	0.826	0.962	0.889
		Noise	0.953	0.984	0.968

BACC, balanced accuracy.
*A convolutional neural network (CNN) model was created using the method described in Nakano and Sugiyama (2022).

The evaluation metrics calculated were the balanced accuracy (BACC), precision, recall, and F1 score, as expressed as follows:

$$\text{BACC}: \frac{\frac{\text{TP}}{\text{TP+FN}} + \frac{\text{TN}}{\text{TN+FP}}}{2}, \tag{12}$$

$$\text{Precision}: \frac{\text{TP}}{\text{TP} + \text{FP}}, \tag{13}$$

$$\text{Recall}: \frac{\text{TP}}{\text{TP} + \text{FN}}, \tag{14}$$

$$\text{F1 score}: \frac{2\text{TP}}{2\text{TP} + \text{FP} + \text{FN}}. \tag{15}$$

in which TP, TN, FP, and FN represent true positives, true negatives, false positives, and false negatives, respectively. Compared with CNN-based models, our classification model demonstrated consistently higher classification performance across all metrics, underscoring its effectiveness in classifying volcanic earthquakes (Table 1). The recognition accuracy for the A-type was lower than that for the B-type for both methods, likely due to the smaller amount of training data available for the A-type. To address the imbalanced data issue, we applied data augmentation techniques. Specifically, we augmented A- and B-type earthquake data to match the number of noise samples (111,189) using two methods: (1) randomly adjusting the *P*-wave arrival times with random temporal shifts and (2) rotating the waveforms randomly by ±15° in 3D space (involving EW, NS, and UD components). These methods preserved the waveform characteristics while introducing variability, enhancing the model's robustness (Fig. S2 illustrates an example of a rotated waveform). Data augmentation was applied only to the training set, and the validation set remained unaltered to accurately evaluate the model's generalization performance. The augmented dataset significantly improved classification performance compared with the imbalanced dataset, as listed in Table 1. For instance, the BACC improved from 0.949 to 0.968, and the F1 scores for A-type, B-type, and noise also showed marked increases. In contrast, the CNN model exhibited a slight decrease in certain metrics, such as precision for the A-type, following data augmentation. This reduction may indicate underfitting of the CNN because data augmentation increased the training set size without increasing the number of training epochs.

AW visualization

Similar to the creation of many volcanic earthquake catalogs, the classification of earthquake types at Mount Asama was performed visually by humans based on the clarity of the *P*- and *S*-wave onsets and hypocenter depth. However, the classification processes of deep learning models are generally considered a "black-box," making it difficult to identify features that the model uses for classification. We therefore attempted to visualize which parts of the waveform the model attends to during classification by utilizing the AWs calculated within the model.

We explored a method for directly visualizing the AWs by extracting the AWs from the multi-head self-attention mechanism within the transformer encoder. Each transformer layer consists of 10 attention heads; each head calculates its own set of AWs for every timestep in the input sequence. The AW dimension (297 × 297) corresponds directly to the sequence length entering the transformer encoder, which is reduced from the original 3000 waveform samples down to 296 convolutional feature vectors, plus one CLS token, resulting in a total of 297 tokens. To obtain the final visualization, the AWs from all 10 heads are concatenated and then processed to compute the maximum value at each timestep. This approach ensures that the most significant attention values are highlighted, providing a clear representation of where the model is focusing during the classification process.

The visualization results showed that AWs tended to concentrate mainly on the earthquake signal (Fig. 4a). This suggests that our model focuses on features of seismic waveforms, such as how humans classify earthquakes. However, many cases were observed wherein the AW was dispersed across the entire waveform despite high confidence in the classification (Fig. 4b).

We extracted the AW for two specific time intervals: 0.1 s before to 5 s after the *P* wave, and from the start of the waveform to 1 s before the *P* wave. The average AW within each interval was calculated, and the ratio of these averages was defined as the attention weight ratio (AWR). This ratio provides insight into the relative concentration of AWs around the *P*-wave region compared to earlier parts of the waveform. The visualization showed that many values were concentrated at ∼1, indicating the dispersion of the AW (Fig. 4c).

When examining data with an AWR below 1.2, we identified several examples of ambiguous or potentially mislabeled events, as illustrated in Figure 5. Although we did not explicitly quantify the proportion across the entire dataset, these examples suggest that low-AWR data may contain waveforms that complicate clear classification. These examples represent typical cases of misclassifications observed in our analysis. They included cases of multiple earthquakes within a single dataset, time inversion errors, large nonearthquake signals, and earthquakes labeled as B-type that exhibit clear characteristics of A-type events, such as distinct *P* and *S* waves. Such data may lead to a dispersion of AWs across the waveform, diminishing the interpretability of the model by introducing noise. In addition, we found that a significant subset of B-type earthquakes contained manually labeled *S*-wave arrivals that were not clear or typical for this type. This introduces further ambiguity in the classification process, suggesting the need for enhanced data quality control and potential automation in labeling to ensure the reliability of training data.

Discussion

The quality of training data, which hinders effective learning, is presumed to be a significant reason for the divergence in AWs. Generally, B-type earthquakes are characterized by indistinct *P* and *S* waves. However, for Mount Asama, shallow earthquakes can be classified as B-type, regardless of their waveform characteristics. To investigate how data selection influences model performance, we conducted several experiments, including removing B-type events with *S*-wave labels, balancing the dataset through data augmentation, and training the model for four classes (A-type, B-type with *S* wave, B-type without *S* wave, and noise). These experiments were designed to address the challenges associated with data quality and imbalance, providing insights into the factors that affect classification accuracy and interpretability (Table 2). First, when B-type events with *S*-wave labels were removed, we observed an improvement in the AW distribution, which became more localized around the seismic signals (Fig. 6a,b). Note that the waveforms presented in Figure 6a are identical to those shown previously in Figure 4b, illustrating how AW distributions changed due to

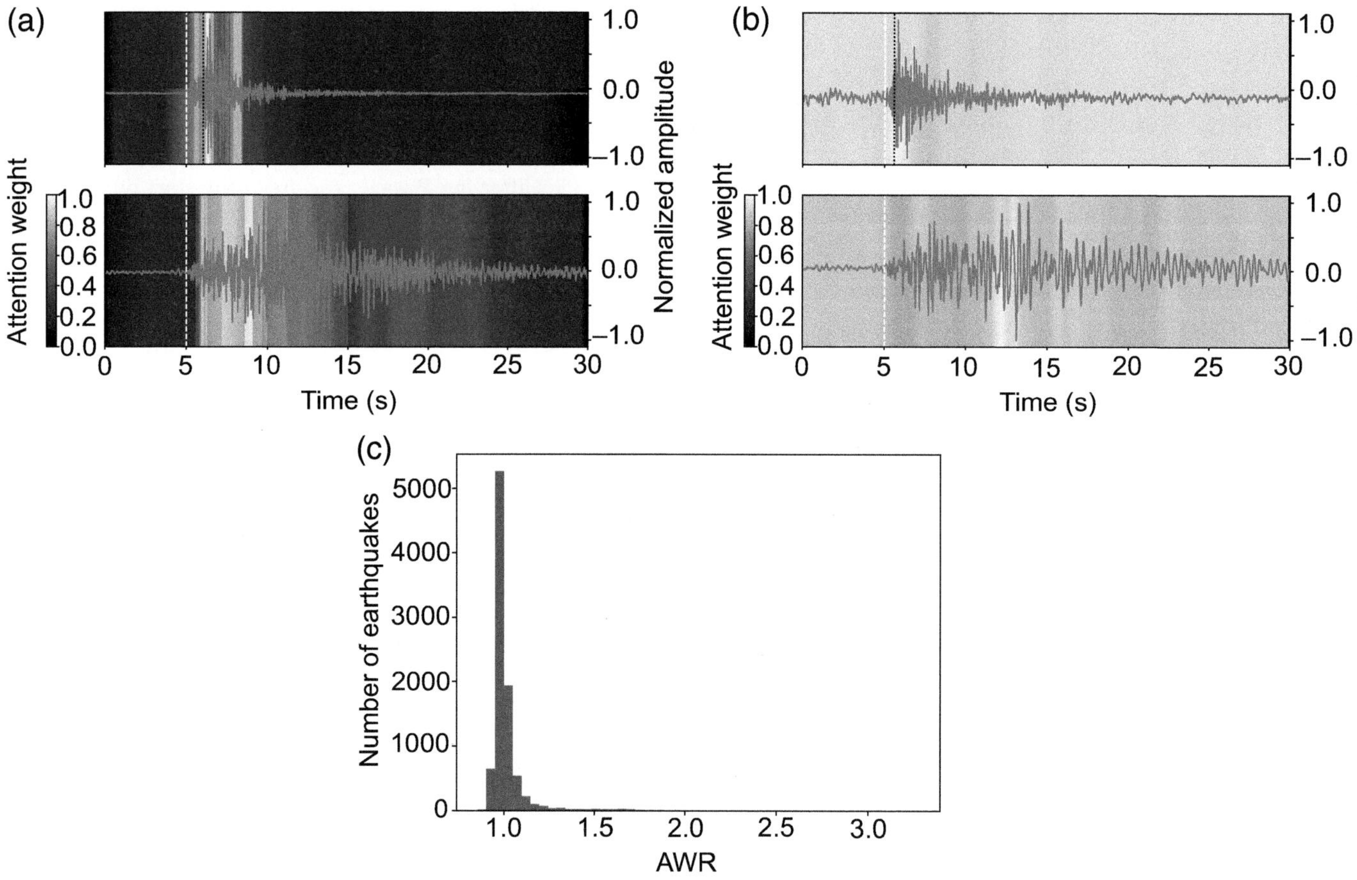

Figure 4. Prediction results from the validation data. (a) An example where a high attention weight (AW) is focused on the seismic signal. The upper figure shows a waveform classified as an A-type earthquake, and the lower figure shows one classified as a B-type earthquake. The AW is normalized between 0 and 1.0. (b) Examples of dispersed AW. The upper figure shows a waveform classified as an A-type earthquake, and the lower figure shows one classified as a B-type earthquake. The white- and black-dotted lines in the waveforms represent the onset of *P* and *S* waves selected by experts, respectively. (c) The number of earthquakes plotted against the attention weight ratio (AWR). The color version of this figure is available only in the electronic edition.

the removal of B-type events labeled with *S*-wave arrivals. The increase in AWR could result from removing ambiguous labels; however, the decreased performance likely resulted from insufficient training due to fewer data points. Indeed, an additional experiment in which we randomly reduced waveforms to match the number before removing *S*-labeled events resulted in improved model performance, supporting the conclusion that there is a meaningful relationship between AWR and model accuracy. Figure S3 shows separate histograms illustrating the distribution of AWR values for A-type and B-type earthquakes. We found no clear or significant difference between the AWR distributions for these two event types, suggesting that the attention weight distributions are largely independent of earthquake type (A-type versus B-type) in our dataset. The model trained on the modified dataset, even with data augmentation to balance the dataset, demonstrated lower performance compared with the original dataset that included *S*-wave labeled B-type events (Table 2). This suggests that removing *S*-wave labeled B-type events may inadvertently exclude important waveform characteristics, reducing the diversity and representativeness of the B-type class. In addition, training the model with four classes resulted in poor classification accuracy for distinguishing between B-type events with and without *S* waves. Detailed inspection revealed that some B-type events labeled with *S* wave arrivals did not exhibit clearly distinguishable *S* waves, potentially due to subjective labeling by human analysts (Fig. 7). This overlap in waveform characteristics likely hindered the model's ability to effectively differentiate between the two subcategories of B-type events. These findings highlight the challenges of using subjective labels in training data. Note that although the validation datasets for A-type and noise events were consistent across all experimental configurations, the validation data for B-type events differed in the four-class classification scenario because B-type events were explicitly separated into those with and without *S*-wave labels (see Table S1). Consequently, caution is required when directly comparing classification accuracy for the B-type class between three-class and four-class experiments.

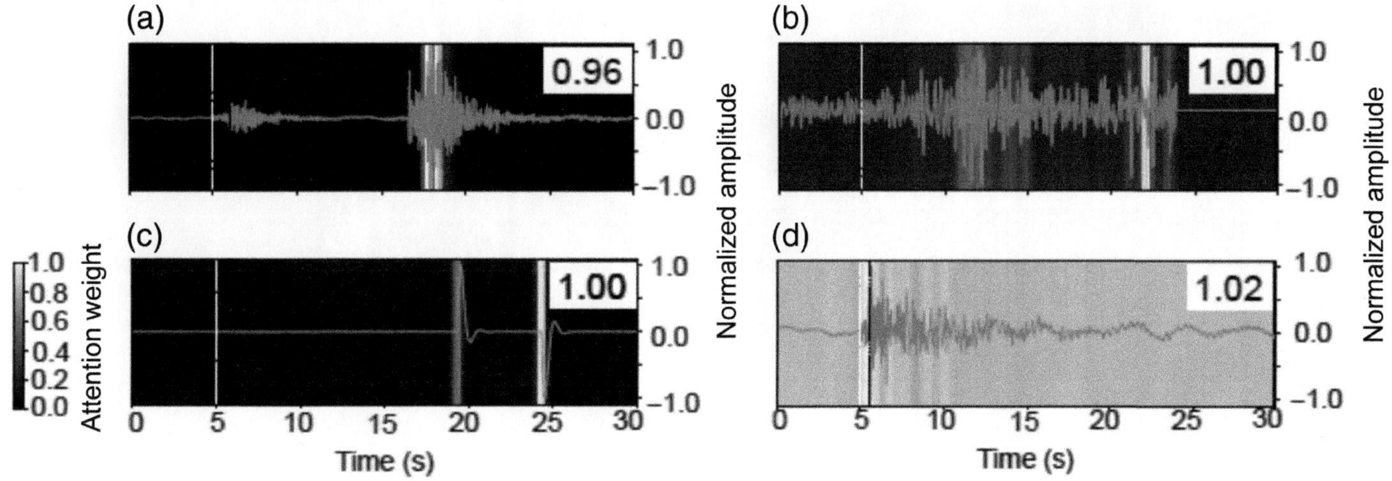

Figure 5. Examples of inappropriate data within the dataset, with the maximum AWR values displayed in the upper-right corner of each panel. These waveforms represent typical examples of misclassifications resulting from data quality issues or ambiguous waveform characteristics. (a) A waveform containing multiple earthquakes within a single dataset. (b) A case of time-inverted data. (c) A waveform dominated by a large non-earthquake signal. (d) A waveform labeled as a B-type earthquake but exhibiting characteristics more consistent with an A-type event. Signal amplitude and AW are normalized between 0 and 1.0, respectively. The white- and black-dotted lines in the waveforms indicate the onset of *P* and *S* waves selected by experts, respectively. The color version of this figure is available only in the electronic edition.

A slight tendency for a higher AWR at shorter source–receiver distances was observed (Fig. 8a). Because many earthquakes occur beneath the crater, stations within 3 km of the crater inevitably recorded more seismic events and may also have higher signal-to-noise ratios due to their proximity to shallow hypocenters. These factors collectively provided the transformer architecture with richer waveform data, allowing it to better learn distinctive local features and thereby enhancing both classification performance and interpretability (Fig. 8b). Furthermore, by overlaying the distribution of all data from each station with the distribution of data from sites with a prediction probability >99%, these distributions matched. This trend remained unchanged even after removing the waveforms of events with large location errors, which is defined in the previous section (Fig. 8c).

In this study, waveform classification was conducted independently at each seismic station. Although an explicit event-level classification integrating results from multiple stations was not performed, we confirmed that classifications were highly consistent across stations for individual events in our validation set. Developing a robust method for aggregating station-based classifications into event-level decisions will be addressed in future research.

Misclassifications are most likely to occur under certain conditions, such as high-noise levels, ambiguous waveform characteristics, or overlapping features between classes. Such misclassifications could delay hazard assessments or lead to incorrect interpretations of volcanic processes. Therefore, it is essential

TABLE 2
Classification Performance across Different Data Configurations

Model	**Data without *S****			**Data without *S* with Data Augmentation†**			**Four Class Classification‡**			
BACC	0.938			0.957			0.780			
Event Type	**A**	**B**	**Noise**	**A**	**B**	**Noise**	**A**	**B with *S***	**B without *S***	**Noise**
Precision	0.904	0.950	0.961	0.942	0.972	0.958	0.934	0.749	0.569	0.956
Recall	0.934	0.888	0.992	0.951	0.929	0.990	0.865	0.434	0.832	0.987
F1 score	0.919	0.918	0.976	0.947	0.950	0.974	0.898	0.549	0.676	0.971

BACC, balanced accuracy.
*Training data exclude B-type events with *S*-wave labels, with no data augmentation applied.
†Training data exclude B-type events with *S*-wave labels, with data augmentation applied to balance the dataset to the number of noise samples.
‡Training conducted using four categories: A-type, B-type with *S* wave, B-type without *S* wave, and noise.

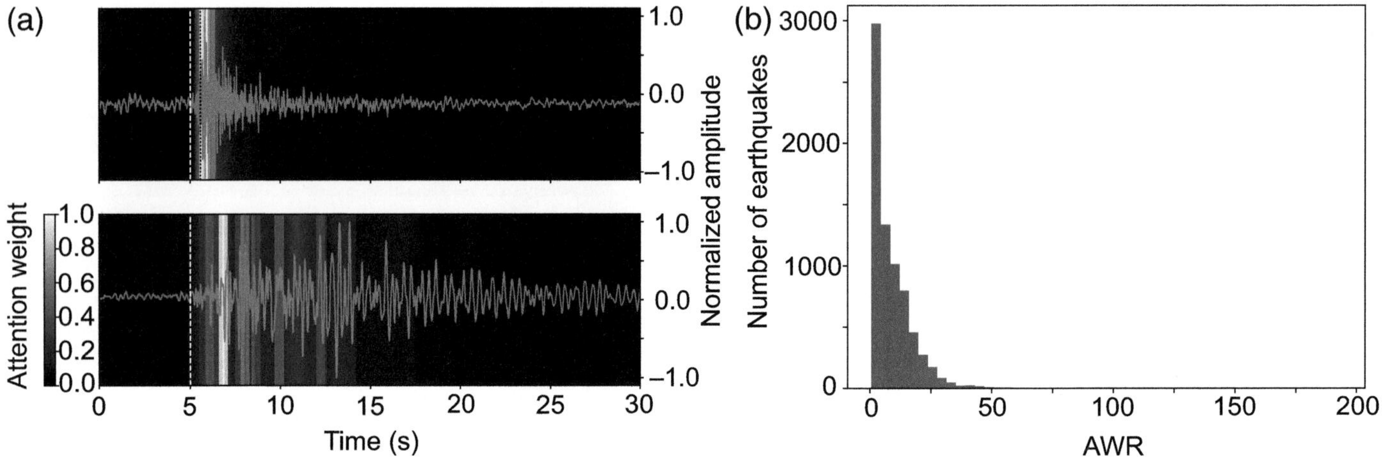

Figure 6. Evaluations using a model trained by excluding events with *S*-wave detection from B-type training data. (a) The same data are shown in Figure 4b. (b) Number of earthquakes relative to the AWR. The color version of this figure is available only in the electronic edition.

to further analyze the conditions under which misclassifications arise. To this end, we analyzed confusion matrices generated from the testing data. The confusion matrix for the transformer model trained with data augmentation (Table 3) shows that most misclassifications occurred between A- and B-type earthquakes. Specifically, 92 true B-type events were misclassified as A-type, and 26 true A-type events were misclassified as B-type. These misclassifications likely stem from overlapping waveform characteristics between certain subcategories of A- and B-type earthquakes. In addition, noise waveforms were classified with high accuracy, suggesting that the variability of noise characteristics had a limited impact on the model's performance in this dataset. For comparison, the confusion matrix for the CNN model (Table 3) reveals a higher rate of misclassification. Specifically, the CNN model misclassified 313 true A-type events as B-type and 47 true A-type events as noise. This highlights the transformer model's superior ability to handle the complexity of waveform data and its robustness against misclassification under similar conditions.

Notably, when the B-type events without S labeling were used, our model exhibited a slight increase in misclassification between A- and B-type events, compared with the original dataset (Table 3). This suggests that the exclusion of *S*-wave labeled B-type events may have reduced the diversity of the B-type class, making it more difficult for the model to generalize effectively. The CNN model's confusion matrix for the same dataset further emphasizes its difficulty in handling the reduced dataset, with a noticeable decline in classification performance (Table 3). This discrepancy may be attributed to differences in how the two architectures handle increased data variability introduced through augmentation. Although the CNN model may have been more sensitive to the augmented data, potentially interpreting the variability as noise, transformers benefited from the increased data diversity and volume, demonstrating their scalability with larger datasets (Kaplan *et al.*, 2020). This property, combined with their ability to effectively leverage augmented data, makes transformers particularly well-suited for volcanic earthquake classification tasks. Addressing data imbalance through augmentation and employing architectures capable of harnessing the enhanced datasets are critical for improving classification accuracy in scenarios for which available data for each class are highly imbalanced, such as in volcanic earthquake classification.

In the four-class classification experiment, misclassifications were concentrated between *S*-wave labeled and unlabeled B-type events (Table 3). This result aligns with earlier discussion and highlights the need for further waveform scrutiny and feature validation to effectively distinguish between these subcategories. These results collectively emphasize the importance of balancing data quality and diversity in building robust classification models. Although the inclusion of *S*-wave labeled B-type events introduces noise, it also contributes essential variability that aids in generalization. Addressing the overlap between subcategories through more objective feature extraction methods, such as autoencoders, could reduce subjectivity and improve classification accuracy. Integrating clustering methods or connecting the bottleneck layer of an autoencoder to a transformer encoder could further enhance the interpretability and performance of classification models (e.g., Kong *et al.*, 2021). In future research, employing autoencoder-based methods may allow for effective extraction of essential features even from sparse datasets, facilitating the development of volcano-specific classification models. This approach could further reduce the human and time resources required for manual labeling, thus significantly enhancing the efficiency and reproducibility of volcanic earthquake classification workflows. In addition, clarifying these subtle distinctions explicitly not only highlights the subjective challenges inherent in manual labeling but also underscores the broader necessity

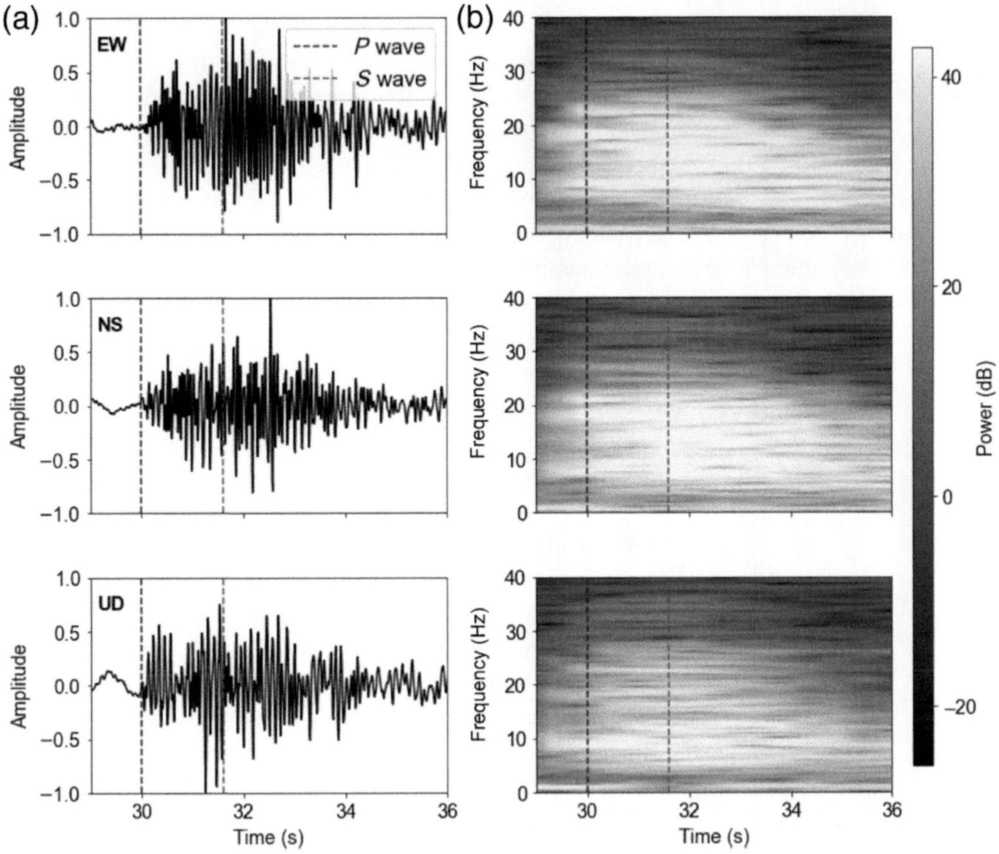

Figure 7. Example of a B-type event manually labeled with an *S*-wave arrival, which exhibits ambiguous or indistinct *S*-wave features. (a) Three-component (east–west [EW], north–south [NS], and up–down [UD]) waveforms, each normalized to its maximum amplitude. The blue- and red-dashed lines represent manually labeled *P*- and *S*-wave arrivals, respectively. (b) Corresponding spectrograms (frequency range: 0–40 Hz) clearly illustrate spectral characteristics consistent with a typical B-type earthquake (compare to Fig. 1c). Despite the manual *S*-wave label, both waveform and spectral content indicate indistinct *S*-wave energy, highlighting inherent ambiguities and subjectivity in traditional manual labeling approaches. The color version of this figure is available only in the electronic edition.

of developing objective, reproducible classification methods. This clarity can directly benefit future studies and practical earthquake monitoring efforts by promoting consistent, reliable classification and deeper mechanistic insights.

Finally, our study demonstrated the effectiveness of using a transformer encoder for volcanic earthquake classification. However, applying this model to other volcanic regions presents additional challenges. Because the model incorporates features influenced by geological structures, source–receiver distances, and source characteristics, it may require retraining or adaptation through transfer learning to ensure effectiveness in new regions. Furthermore, achieving comparable performance in new regions will likely necessitate large datasets or data augmentation using synthetic or cross-regional data.

To evaluate the suitability of spectral metrics such as frequency index (FI) for distinguishing volcanic earthquake types, we examined the FI distributions of manually labeled A-type and B-type earthquakes (Fig. 9). Following Yukutake *et al.* (2023), which builds upon the definitions proposed by Buurman and West (2010) and Matoza *et al.* (2014), we calculated FI as the logarithmic ratio of mean spectral amplitudes between high-frequency (10–15 Hz) and low-frequency (1–4 Hz) bands, derived from the Fourier transforms of vertical-component waveforms. Although this definition is commonly used, FI performance in our dataset might potentially improve by evaluating a higher-frequency band, such as 20–30 Hz or 30–40 Hz because energy is notably depleted above 30 Hz (Fig. 2). Nevertheless, significant overlap observed in FI values clearly indicates that using a spectral metric alone is insufficient for robust earthquake classification at Mount Asama. As explicitly illustrated in Figure 9, some B-type events exhibit frequency indices overlapping with A-type events, and the FI distribution for B-type events appears bimodal, concentrating around FI values of ~−1.3 and −0.2. This bimodal distribution may reflect inherent variability within B-type earthquakes themselves, possibly due to differences in source processes or propagation paths. In addition, classification practices at Mount Asama contribute significantly to this overlap. Human analysts at Mount Asama classify shallow earthquakes beneath the crater primarily based on hypocenter depth and event location, rather than strictly waveform clarity or frequency characteristics. Consequently, even events exhibiting clearer *P*- and *S*-wave arrivals and higher FI values—features typically associated with A-type events—are sometimes classified as B-type. This practice introduces inherent ambiguity and complexity into classification, further contributing to the observed overlap between these two event types. Thus, waveform characteristics among events with similar FI values can differ substantially, highlighting the difficulty of using frequency-domain information alone for robust classification.

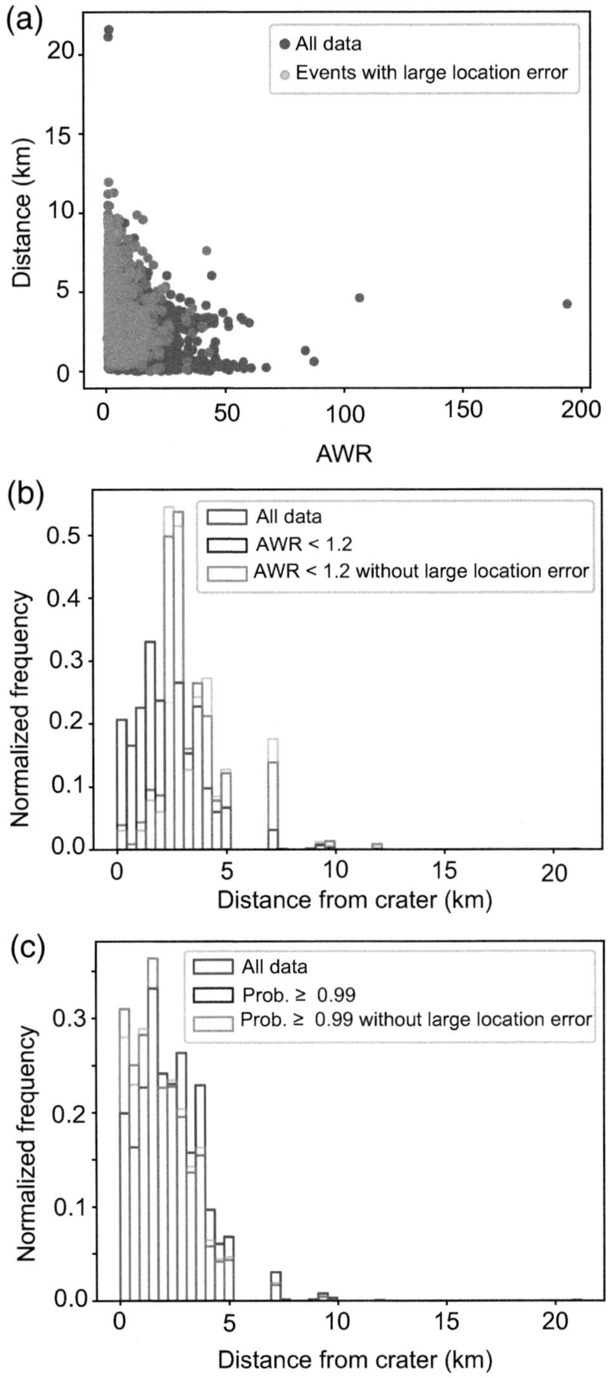

Figure 8. (a) Source–receiver distance relative to the AWR. The red circles indicate events with large location errors, and blue circles represent all other events. (b) Histograms of distances from the crater (latitude: 36.4, longitude: 138.52) to each station. Displays all test data (red), data with AWR < 1.2 (blue), and data with AWR < 1.2 excluding large location errors. Total data are normalized to sum to one. (c) Horizontal axis and red histogram are as described in (b). The blue represents the data histogram with a prediction probability > 99%, and green denotes the data histogram with a prediction probability > 99%, excluding events with large location errors. Total data are normalized to sum to one. The color version of this figure is available only in the electronic edition.

Our transformer-based model addresses this limitation by leveraging waveform characteristics beyond simple spectral ratios. Specifically, the transformer extracts and utilizes nonlinear and temporal waveform features, such as envelope shape, duration, and arrival patterns of seismic phases, which are critical for accurate classification but are not represented adequately by FI or similar single-parameter spectral indices. Consequently, our approach achieves high classification performance, as evidenced by high F1 scores of 0.959 and 0.957 for A-type and B-type events, respectively, clearly demonstrating the benefit of employing deep learning techniques to classify volcanic earthquakes.

Finally, our results highlight the broader relevance of advanced artificial intelligence methodologies, such as transformer architectures, in volcanic seismology. Deep learning models with interpretability tools (e.g., attention visualizations) can systematically reveal ambiguities and inconsistencies in traditional earthquake classifications, thus guiding improvements in data quality and labeling practices (Mousavi *et al.*, 2020; Kong *et al.*, 2021). Nevertheless, operational implementation of these AI techniques requires careful validation and clear demonstration of interpretability to ensure trust and practical utility in volcanic monitoring contexts (Rudin, 2019). Future studies should further refine these approaches and rigorously evaluate their applicability to diverse volcanic environments.

Conclusion

In this study, we developed a transformer-based deep learning model capable of accurately classifying volcanic earthquakes at Mount Asama into A-type, B-type, and noise categories, achieving high F1 scores (~0.96) that significantly surpass conventional CNN-based methods. Our model effectively handled imbalanced data through augmentation strategies, substantially enhancing classification accuracy.

Visualization of AW revealed that the transformer model consistently attends to physically meaningful waveform features, primarily around *P*-wave arrivals, thereby providing interpretability and insight into the model's decision-making process. Analysis of the AWR highlighted critical issues with data quality, such as ambiguous labeling and waveform inconsistencies, serving as a practical tool to identify problematic data.

Our results also underscore the importance of strategically positioned seismic stations near volcanic craters, significantly enhancing model accuracy and interpretability. Ensuring high-quality, consistent datasets is essential for reliable automated volcanic earthquake classification. By systematically addressing ambiguity in manual classification, our transformer-based approach provides objective and reproducible criteria, benefiting volcano monitoring operations by reducing subjectivity and enhancing efficiency. Future research, including advanced waveform feature extraction methods and robust transfer learning frameworks, is needed to expand this approach's applicability to other volcanic regions.

TABLE 3
Unified Confusion Matrices for Various Experimental Conditions

Model/Condition	Predicted A-type	Predicted B-type	Predicted Noise	Predicted B-Type (with *S*)	Predicted B-Type (without *S*)
This study (data augmentation)					
True A-type	1555	92	16		
True B-type	26	1622	15		
True noise	0	12	1651		
CNN (data augmentation)					
True A-type	1303	313	47		
True B-type	29	1600	34		
True Noise	2	25	1636		
This study (B-type without *S*)					
True A-type	1582	36	45		
True B-type	91	1545	27		
True noise	7	9	1647		
CNN (B-type without *S*)					
True A-type	1538	86	39		
True B-type	115	1531	17		
True noise	11	18	1634		
This study (four classes)					
True A-type	1438		33	36	156
True B-type (with *S*)	61		7	721	874
True B-type (without *S*)	38		36	205	1384
True noise	3		1642	1	17
CNN (four classes)					
True A-type	1371		31	48	213
True B-type (with *S*)	59		10	645	949
True B-type (without *S*)	48		28	200	1387
True noise	10		1613	1	39

Four-class models (transformer and convolutional neural network [CNN]) include the following categories: A-type, B-type with S-wave, B-type without *S-wave*, and noise.

Data and Resources

Waveform data were obtained from Hinet (https://hinetwww11.bosai.go.jp/auth/?LANG=en), the Earthquake Research Institute, and the Japan Meteorological Agency via the JVDN system (https://jvdn.bosai.go.jp/app/pages/index.html?root=publicDataList&lang=en). The model developed in this study, training data, and seismic station lists were downloaded from our GitHub page (https://github.com/yugosuz/Volcanic-Earthquake-Classification-using-Transformer-Encoder). All websites were last accessed in June 2025. The supplemental material includes dataset configurations, convolutional neural network (CNN) model architecture, examples of augmented waveforms, and attention weight ratio (AWR) histograms (Table S1, Figs. S1–S3).

Declaration of Competing Interests

The authors acknowledge that there are no conflicts of interest recorded.

Acknowledgments

The authors sincerely thank Editor-in-Chief Allison Bent, the Associate Editor, and the three anonymous reviewers for their careful reading and insightful comments, which greatly improved the quality and clarity of our article. The waveform data and earthquake catalogs used in this study were collected and created by the Asama Volcano Observatory at the University of Tokyo. Waveforms were recorded by stations operated by the Earthquake Research Institute (ERI), National Research

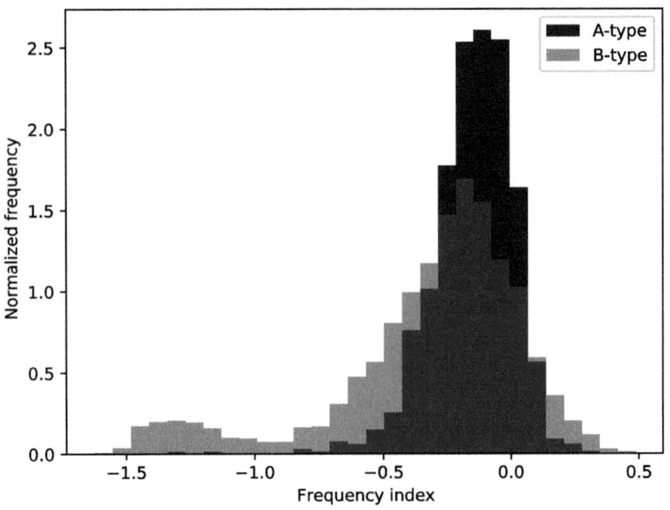

Figure 9. Frequency index (FI) distributions for manually labeled A-type (blue) and B-type (red) earthquakes at Mount Asama, shown as probability density functions (PDFs). Histograms are normalized so that the total area under each equals 1, allowing clear visual comparison of distribution shapes. FI was calculated following Yukutake *et al.* (2023), which builds upon the definitions proposed by Buurman and West (2010) and Matoza *et al.* (2014), using the logarithmic ratio of mean spectral amplitudes between high-frequency (10–15 Hz) and low-frequency (1–4 Hz) bands, as described explicitly in the Discussion section. The significant overlap indicates the difficulty of accurately classifying earthquake types based solely on FI. The color version of this figure is available only in the electronic edition.

Institute for Earth Science and Disaster Resilience (NIED), and Japan Meteorological Agency (JMA). Maps were prepared using Geophysical Mapping Tools (Wessel *et al.*, 2019), and other figures were created using Matplotlib, a Python module. This study was supported by JSPS KAKENHI (Grant Numbers 22K03752 and 15KK0171) and the Next Generation Volcano Research and Human Resource Development Project of the Ministry of Education, Culture, Sports, Science, and Technology of Japan.

References

Bebbington, M. S. (2007). Identifying volcanic regimes using Hidden Markov models, *Geophys. J. Int.* **171,** no. 2, 921–942, doi: 10.1111/j.1365-246X.2007.03545.x.

Buurman, H., and M. West (2010). Seismic precursors to volcanic explosions: The 2006 eruption of Augustine Volcano, *J. Volcanol. Geotherm. Res.*, **191,** 1–14, doi: 10.1016/j.jvolgeores.2009.11.005.

Canário, J. P., R. Mello, M. Curilem, F. Huenupan, and R. Rios (2020). In-depth comparison of deep artificial neural network architectures on seismic events classification, *J. Volcanol. Geotherm.* **401,** 106,881, doi: 10.1016/j.jvolgeores.2020.106881.

Chouet, B. (1988). Resonance of a fluid-driven crack: Radiation properties and implications for the source of long-period events and harmonic tremor, *J. Geophys. Res.* **93,** 4375–4400, doi: 10.1029/JB093iB05p04375.

Chouet, B. A. (1996). Long-period seismicity: Its source and use in eruption forecasting, *Nature* **380,** 309–316.

Chouet, B. A. (2003). Volcano seismology, *Pure Appl. Geophys.* **160,** 739–788.

Gulati, A., J. Qin, C. Chiu, N. Parmar, Y. Zhang, J. Yu, W. Han, S. Wang, Z. Zhang, Y. Wu, and R. Pang (2020). Conformer: Convolution-augmented transformer for speech recognition, doi: 10.48550/arXiv.2005.08100.

Hammer, C., M. Ohrnberger, and U. Wegler (2012). Pattern recognition of volcanic earthquakes and its application to the monitoring of volcano activity, *J. Volcanol. Geotherm. Res.* **243/244,** 91–104, doi: 10.1016/j.jvolgeores.2012.06.012.

Huang, Y. (2018). Earthquake rupture in fault zones with along-strike material heterogeneity, *J. Geophys. Res.* **123,** no. 11, 9884–9898, doi:10.1029/2018JB016354.

Ida, Y., and M. Ishida (2022). Analysis of seismic activity using self-organizing map: Implications for earthquake prediction, *Geophys. J. Int.* **229,** no. 2, 1077–1091, doi: 10.1093/gji/ggab476.

Iguchi, M. (2013). Magma movement from the deep to shallow Sakurajima volcano as revealed by geophysical observations, *Bull. Volcanol. Soc. Jpn.* **58,** no. 1, 1–18.

Kaplan, J., S. McCandlish, T. Henighan, T. B. Brown, B. Chess, R. Child, S. Gray, and A. Radford (2020). Scaling laws for neural language models, arXiv preprint, https://arXiv:2001.08361 (last accessed June 2025).

Kingma, D. P., and J. Ba (2014). Adam: A method for stochastic optimization, arXiv preprint, https://arXiv:1412.6980 (last accessed June 2025).

Köhler, C. M., T. J. Kouwenhoven, and K. Kuijken (2010). The effect of the Galactic tide on local stellar streams, *Astron. Astrophys.* **519,** A13, doi: 10.1051/0004-6361/201014147.

Kong, Q., A. Chiang, A. C. Aguiar, M. G. Fernández-Godino, S. C. Myers, and D. D. Lucas (2021). Deep convolutional autoencoders as generic feature extractors in seismological applications, *Artif. Intell. Geosci.* **2,** 96–106, doi: 10.1016/j.aiig.2021.12.002.

Langer, H., S. Falsaperla, and R. Campanini (2011). Automatic classification and identification of volcanic tremor sources based on support vector machines, *Geophys. Res. Lett.* **38,** no. 19, L19304, doi: 10.1029/2011GL049065.

Langer, H., S. Falsaperla, M. Masotti, R. Campanini, S. Spampinato, and A. Messina (2009). Synopsis of supervised and unsupervised pattern classification techniques applied to volcanic tremor data at Mt Etna, Italy, *Geophys. J. Int.* **178,** no. 2, 1132–1144, doi: 10.1111/j.1365-246X.2009.04211.x.

Lara, F., R. Lara-Cueva, J. C. Larco, E. V. Carrera, and R. León (2021). A deep learning approach for automatic recognition of seismo-volcanic events at the Cotopaxi volcano, *J. Volcanol. Geotherm.* **409,** 107,142, doi: 10.1016/j.jvolgeores.2020.107142.

Loshchilov, I., and F. Hutter (2017). Decoupled weight decay regularization, aXiv preprint. arXiv:1711.05101.2017.

Malfante, M., M. D. Mura, J. I. Mars, J. P. Metaxian, O. Macedo, and A. Inza (2018). Automatic classification of volcano seismic signatures, *J. Geophys. Res.* 123, 10,645–10,658.

Matoza, R. S., P. M. Shearer, and P. G. Okubo (2014). High-precision relocation of long-period events beneath the summit region of Kīlauea volcano, Hawaiʻi, from 1986 to 2009, *Geophys. Res. Lett.* **41,** no. 10, 3413–3421.

McNutt, S. R. (1996). Seismic monitoring and eruption forecasting of volcanoes: A review of the state-of-the-art and case histories, in *Monitoring and Mitigation of Volcano Hazards 99–146,*

R. Scarpa and R. I. Tilling (Editors), Springer, Berlin, Heidelberg, doi: 10.1007/978-3-642-80087-0_3.

Minakami, T., S. Utibori, S. Hiraga, T. Miyazaki, N. Gyoda, and T. Utsunomiya (1970). Seismometrical studies of volcano Asama, Part I. Seismic and volcanic activities of Asama during 1934-1969, *Bull. Earthq. Res. Inst.* **48,** 235–301.

Mousavi, S. M., W. L. Ellsworth, W. Zhu, L. Y. Chuang, and G. C. Beroza (2020). Earthquake transformer—An attentive deep-learning model for simultaneous earthquake detection and phase picking, *Nat. Commun.* **11,** 3952.

Nakano, M., and D. Sugiyama (2022). Discriminating seismic events using 1D and 2D CNNs: Applications to volcanic and tectonic datasets, *Earth Planets Space* **74,** 134, doi: 10.1186/s40623-022-01696-1.

Nishimura, T., and M. Iguchi (2011). *Volcanic Earthquakes and Tremor in Japan*, Kyoto University Press, Kyoto, Japan, ISBN: 4876989796.

Oikawa, J., Y. Ida, and H. Tsuji (2006). Precise hypocenter determination for volcanic earthquakes observed at Asama Volcano, Japan, *Bull. Volcanol. Soc. Jpn.* **51**, no. 2, 117–124.

Permana, T., T. Nishimura, H. Nakahara, and N. Shapiro (2022). Classification of volcanic tremors and earthquakes based on seismic correlation: Application at Sakurajima volcano, Japan. *Geophys. J. Int.* **229,** no. 2, 1077–1091, doi: 10.1093/gji/ggab476.

Rudin, C. (2019). Stop explaining black box machine learning models for high stakes decisions and use interpretable models instead, *Nat. Mach. Intell.* **1,** 206–215.

Takeo, M., Y. Aoki, and T. Koyama (2022). Recent volcanic activity at the Asama volcano and long-period seismic signals, *Proc. Jpn. Acad. Ser. B* **98**, no. 8, 416–438, doi: 10.2183/pjab.98.022.

Titos, M., A. Bueno, L. Garcia, and C. Benitez (2018). A deep neural networks approach to automatic recognition systems for volcano-seismic events, *IEEE J. Sel. Top. Appl. Earth Obs. Remote Sens.* **11**, no. 5, 1533–1544, doi: 10.1109/JSTARS.2018.2803198.

Unglert, K., A. M. Jellinek, and R. P. Hoblitt (2016). Patterns of precursory volcanic tremor and earthquake swarms preceding eruptions at Redoubt Volcano, Alaska, *J. Volcanol. Geotherm. Res.* **325,** 116–135, doi: 10.1016/j.jvolgeores.2016.06.008.

Vaswani, A., N. Shazeer, N. Parmar, J. Uszkoreit, L. Jones, A.N. Gomez, L. Kaiser, and I. Polosukhin (2017). Attention is all you need, *Adv. Neural. Inf. Process. Syst.* **30,** 6000–6010.

Wessel, P., J. F. Luis, L. Uieda, R. Scharroo, F. Wobbe, W. H. F. Smith, and D. Tian (2019). The generic mapping tools version 6, *Geochem. Geophys.* **20,** no. 11, 5556–5564, doi: 10.1029/2019GC008515.

Yukutake, Y., A. Kim, and T. Ohminato (2023). Reappraisal of volcanic seismicity at the Kirishima volcano using machine learning, *Earth Planets Space* **75**, 183.

Manuscript received 27 December 2024
Published online 19 September 2025

Ambient Noise Analyses at Broadband Ocean-Bottom Seismometers: Data Quality and Transfer Function Corrections

Helen A. Janiszewski*[1] and Joshua B. Russell[2]

Abstract

Seismic ambient noise tomography has revolutionized regional crustal and upper-mantle imaging for broadband ocean-bottom seismometer (BBOBS) studies. However, the ocean poses unique challenges including tilt and compliance noise, and interface waves with considerable water-column sensitivity. Transfer function (TF) noise removal techniques enable separation of fundamental Scholte waves from overtone Rayleigh waves, but such noise removal strategies do not always provide the expected signal improvement. Here, we leverage data from recent U.S.-led BBOBS deployments to evaluate variability in ambient-noise surface-wave quality and efficacy of TF corrections across different oceanic environments and instrumentation. We examine the 15–30 and 3–10 s period bands that are typically used in lithospheric imaging. We find that water depth, sediment thickness, instrument design, and ocean basin characteristics are the primary factors influencing ambient-noise data quality and effectiveness of TF corrections. In the 3–10 s period band, enhancement of higher-mode Rayleigh waves is most successful in deep waters with thin sediments. In the 15–30 s period band, signal is improved both in shallow waters likely due to infragravity wave removal, and in instances of high tilt noise. Our results provide new insights into the environmental conditions and instrument designs that shape ambient noise tomography performance, offering practical guidance for optimizing future BBOBS studies as well as novel seafloor-sensing technologies.

Cite this article as Janiszewski, H. A., and J. B. Russell (2025). Ambient Noise Analyses at Broadband Ocean-Bottom Seismometers: Data Quality and Transfer Function Corrections, *Seismol. Res. Lett.* **97**, 1048–1066, doi: 10.1785/0220250106.

Supplemental Material

Introduction

In the past two decades, seismic ambient noise tomography has become a useful tool for imaging regional crustal and upper-mantle structure (Shapiro and Campillo, 2004). The increasing availability of broadband ocean-bottom seismometer (BBOBS) data has enabled the expansion of ambient noise tomography in marine environments (Harmon *et al.*, 2007; Takeo *et al.*, 2014; Lin *et al.*, 2016; Russell *et al.*, 2019). This method relies on cross correlations of continuous seismic recordings between stations to estimate empirical Green's functions, and it is well suited for the oceans where the microseism sources are strongest. Marine studies provide some of the highest quality images of the lithospheric mantle, partly due to the relatively thin, homogenous oceanic crust compared to the thicker and more heterogeneous continental crust. Typically, fundamental-mode Rayleigh waves extracted from the primary microseism band (12–30 s) are used to image the oceanic crust and upper mantle. Ocean-bottom data also often display clear overtone Rayleigh-wave energy in the secondary microseism band (3–12 s) that can be used to probe the crust and uppermost mantle in extraordinary detail (Bowden *et al.*, 2016; Yang *et al.*, 2020; Russell *et al.*, 2022), unlike typical continental settings, which often exhibit complex scattering and directional noise sources and, thus, lower signal-to-noise ratios (SNRs) in this band.

However, the ocean also poses unique challenges. Because BBOBS are deployed at the boundary between the ocean and solid Earth, interface waves primarily sensitive to the water column and shallow sedimentary layers are commonly observed in interstation noise cross-correlation functions (CCFs) at short periods (Fig. 1a). These are high-amplitude phases that travel at or below the sound speed of water (~1.5 km/s) are visible on vertical (Z), pressure (P), and radial (R) components (Fig. S1, available in the supplemental material to this article), and may be the most prominent arrivals before mitigation (Harmon *et al.*, 2007; Yao *et al.*, 2011; Takeo *et al.*, 2014; Yeck *et al.*, 2017). They are fundamental-mode interface waves trapped at the seafloor interface (Ruan *et al.*, 2014) and are typically observed only at periods <~10 s. Interface waves at

1. Department of Earth Sciences, University of Hawai'i at Mānoa, Honolulu, Hawaii, U.S.A., https://orcid.org/0000-0003-1425-7969 (HAJ); 2. Department of Earth and Environmental Sciences, Syracuse University, Syracuse, New York, U.S.A., https://orcid.org/0000-0003-3251-2919 (JBR)

*Corresponding author: hajanisz@hawaii.edu

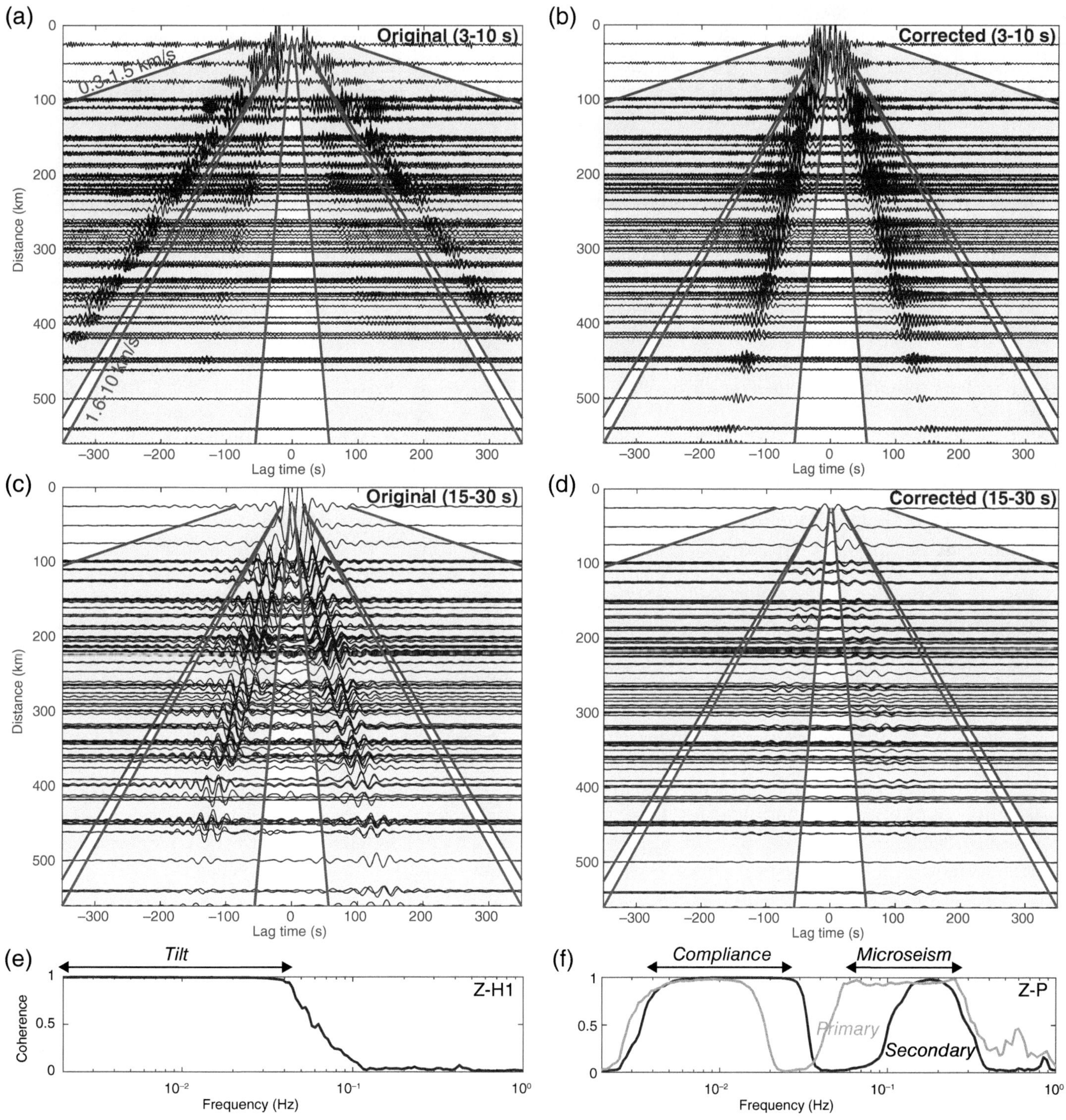

Figure 1. Example of ambient noise Z-Z cross-correlation functions (CCFs) from the NoMelt deployment filtered between 3 and 10 s (a) before and (b) after transfer function (TF) corrections, and filtered between 15 and 30 s (c) before and (d) after TF corrections. The same amplitude normalization factor is used in all panels, so amplitudes can be directly compared. Red and blue regions indicate the 1.6–10 and 0.3–1.5 km/s group velocity windows, which represent the solid- and water-velocity windows, respectively. (e) Coherence between Z and H1 components on station YO.X02, which exhibits strong tilt noise indicated by the high coherence at frequencies <0.1 Hz. (f) Coherence between Z and P components on stations 7D.M07A (black) and 2D.OBS07 (gray). At lower frequencies high coherence indicates strong compliance noise. High coherence at shorter periods is due to the microseism, which may be focused either within the secondary frequency band, or may span across the primary and secondary bands. The color version of this figure is available only in the electronic edition.

this solid–fluid boundary consist of a combination of Scholte waves and leaky Rayleigh waves (Scholte, 1947; Zhu and Popovics, 2006), both of which have elliptical particle motion similar to Rayleigh waves but with displacements highly focused at this interface. They are distinguished from one another by their predominant sensitivity to either sediments or the water column (Zhu and Popovics, 2006). Seismic ambient noise tomography literature uses a variety of terminology to refer to these waves, including Rayleigh waves, Scholte waves, or Rayleigh–Scholte waves (Nolet and Dorman, 1996; Ruan *et al.*, 2014; Le *et al.*, 2017; Adimah and Padhy, 2019; Hable *et al.*, 2019; Williams *et al.*, 2019). Herein, for simplicity we refer to these collectively as "fundamental-mode Scholte waves," because the distinction between these waves depends on the shallow subsurface structure, which is often poorly constrained.

Short-period CCFs (<~10 s) can also contain overtones sensitive to solid–earth structure. In contrast to the fundamental-mode Scholte waves, overtones are observed only on the Z-Z and R-R CCFs, and are characterized by faster velocities (Harmon *et al.*, 2007; Fig. S1). Typically, the first overtone is the most prominent, and we refer to these as "first-overtone Rayleigh waves." At longer periods (> ~15 s), fundamental-mode Rayleigh waves predominantly sensitive to solid–earth mantle structure dominate the Z-Z CCFs (Fig. 1c). Studies may use these longer periods to avoid the complications of multiple modes at shorter periods (Janiszewski *et al.*, 2019; Doran and Laske, 2020; Pinzón *et al.*, 2023). Although technically these are also fluid–solid interface waves, their sensitivity to the water column and sediment is negligible. Thus, here we refer to them as "fundamental-mode Rayleigh waves."

Oceanographic noise can also degrade ambient noise CCFs (Tian and Ritzwoller, 2017). On the Z component, two predominant noise sources are tilt and compliance (Crawford and Webb, 2000). The former is due to bottom currents acting on a tilted Z component, identified via spectral coherence between Z and horizontal (H1, H2) components (Fig. 1e), and is typically observed at periods >10 s (Webb, 1998). The latter is due to infragravity waves displacing the seafloor and is identified via spectral coherence between Z and P components (Fig. 1f). Its period range depends on water depth; at a depth of 5000 m compliance noise is only present at periods > ~56 s, whereas at a depth of 100 m it exists at periods > ~8 s (Crawford *et al.*, 1991; Webb and Crawford, 2010).

Both tilt and compliance noise can be reduced on the Z component via transfer function (TF) corrections (Crawford and Webb, 2000; Bell *et al.*, 2015; Janiszewski *et al.*, 2019). These are traditionally only applied at periods longer than the limits for each respective noise source and can improve the quality of Z-component ambient noise CCFs (Tian and Ritzwoller, 2017; Russell and Gaherty, 2021). High spectral coherences between the Z and P components of BBOBS are also routinely observed between ~3 and 10 s period in the secondary microseism band (Janiszewski *et al.*, 2023; Fig. 1f). P-Z TF corrections applied to 3–10 s ambient noise CCFs reduce or remove the fundamental Scholte wave (Fig. 1b) and either preserve or amplify the first-overtone Rayleigh wave (Bowden *et al.*, 2016; Adimah *et al.*, 2024). This is because the fundamental Scholte wave is well recorded on both the Z- and P-component CCFs in this period band, whereas the first-overtone Rayleigh wave is only recorded on the Z component (Yang *et al.*, 2020; Kawano *et al.*, 2023; Fig. S1). We note that high spectral coherence due to the microseism can sometimes extend to longer periods (Fig. 1f), although precisely what causes this variability remains unclear (Janiszewski *et al.*, 2023). To distinguish from the infragravity-induced compliance correction, we refer to TF corrections between P and Z components in the microseism band as the "microseism correction" in our discussion (Ruan *et al.*, 2014).

A variety of BBOBS ambient noise studies have characterized observations of the fundamental-mode Scholte wave, first-overtone or fundamental-mode Rayleigh wave, and the effects of TF corrections in coastal and open-ocean environments in the Pacific, Atlantic, and Indian Oceans (Harmon *et al.*, 2007; Yao *et al.*, 2011; Takeo *et al.*, 2014; Bowden *et al.*, 2016; Takeo *et al.*, 2016; Yeck *et al.*, 2017; Adimah and Padhy, 2019; Hable *et al.*, 2019; Yang *et al.*, 2020; Wolf *et al.*, 2021; Kawano *et al.*, 2023; Pinzón *et al.*, 2023). Unfortunately, these studies often use different preprocessing and noise-mitigation strategies, precluding direct comparisons. They also focus on individual BBOBS deployments, which typically have similar noise characteristics due to their limited environmental and instrumental variability (Janiszewski *et al.*, 2023).

Here, we use data from a subset of recent U.S.-led BBOBS deployments to compare self-consistently calculated ambient noise CCFs both pre- and post-noise mitigation via TFs. We focus on the 3–10 and 15–30 s period bands, which are commonly used for crustal and upper-mantle tomography, respectively. These bands typically exhibit phase- and group-velocity curves that are relatively flat, resulting in comparatively simple CCFs. In contrast, the 10–15 s band spans the transition between Scholte and Rayleigh waves and is characterized by a steep phase- and group-velocity gradient, which complicates the resulting CCFs. In addition, microseism noise amplitudes peak within these bands, typically yielding high-quality CCFs (McNamara and Buland, 2004; Bensen *et al.*, 2007). Although ambient noise tomography at periods shorter than 3 s or longer than 30 s is possible, these analyses at modern BBOBS arrays can be limited by array density or aperture, respectively. Within our selected period bands, we compare the results systematically across deployments and assess the features and quality of the CCFs in the context of environment, instrumentation, and noise properties. This provides new insights into the key variables affecting data quality, and practical guidance for improving future BBOBS ambient noise tomography. Such observations are relevant not only for traditional BBOBS arrays but also for emerging methodologies such as dense ocean-bottom nodal

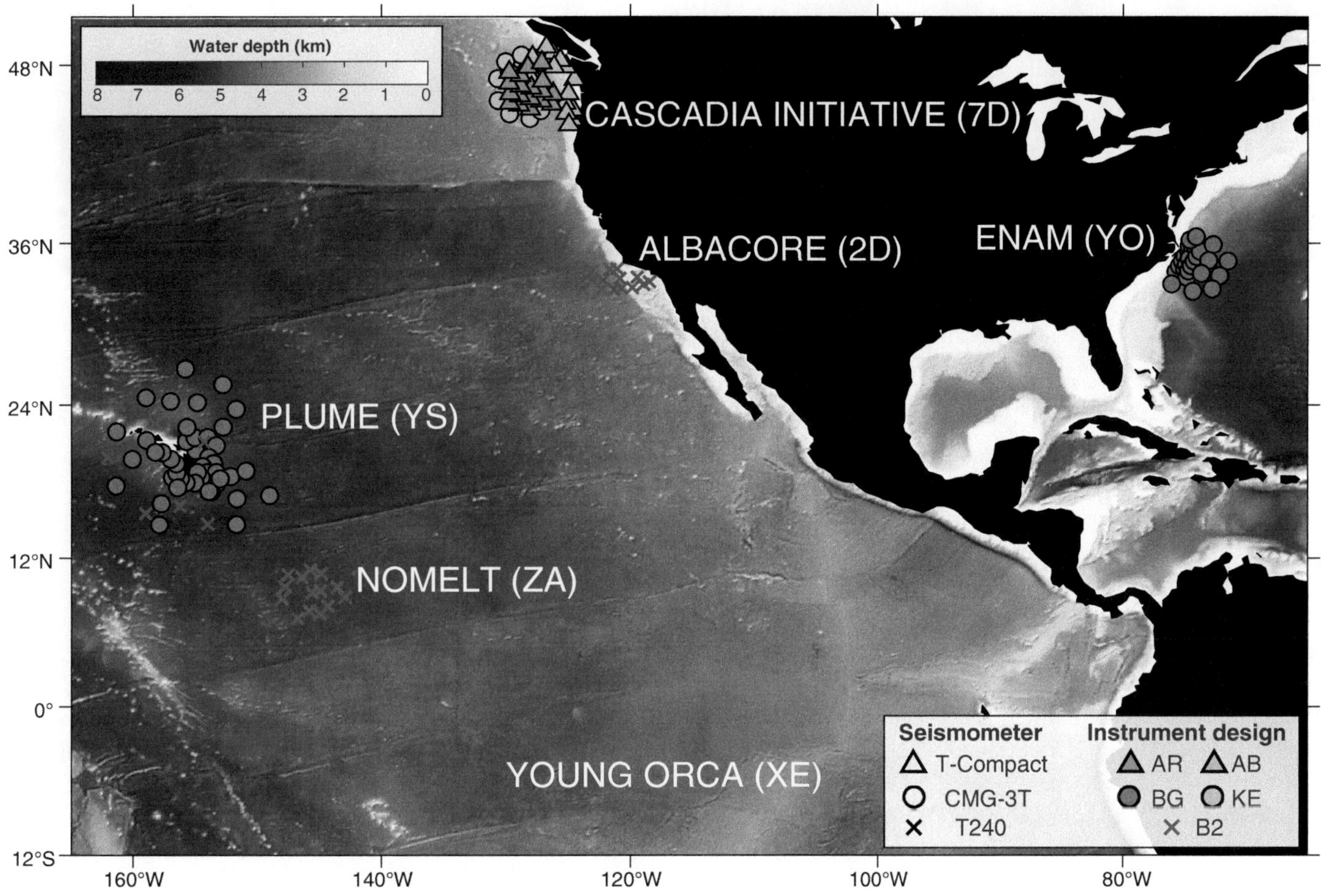

Figure 2. Map of stations analyzed and their corresponding deployments with names and network codes. Symbols and colors indicate seismometer type and instrument design as detailed in Table 1. The color version of this figure is available only in the electronic edition.

deployments, distributed acoustic sensing (DAS), and long-term cabled seafloor instrumentation.

Data and Methods

Deployments and instrumentation

We examine data from six BBOBS deployments (Fig. 2): (1) PLUME (Wolfe *et al.*, 2009); (2) ALBACORE (Lin *et al.*, 2015); (3) the Juan de Fuca portion of Cascadia Initiative (Toomey *et al.*, 2014); (4) NoMelt (Lin *et al.*, 2016); (5) ENAM (Lynner *et al.*, 2019); and (6) Young ORCA (Eilon *et al.*, 2021). Each was deployed with instrumentation from the Ocean-Bottom Seismic Instrument Pool (OBSIP) or Ocean-Bottom Seismic Instrument Center (OBSIC) between 2005 and 2020 (Aderhold *et al.*, 2019). Detailed site and instrument metadata are assembled by Janiszewski *et al.* (2023). For each deployment, BBOBS are equipped with a three-component broadband seismometer and a pressure gauge yielding a total of four individual components per instrument. The dataset contains 193 BBOBS, although not all instruments have four operational components.

These BBOBS sample a variety of parameters that are known to affect noise in our period bands of interest. Janiszewski *et al.* (2023) find that water depth, seismometer type, and instrument design play significant roles regulating tilt and compliance noise properties. Our included BBOBS are deployed at water depths between ~50 and 6000 m. Each uses one of three types of seismometers: Güralp CMG-3T (CMG-3T), Nanometrics Trillium Compact (T-Compact), and Nanometrics Trillium 240 (T-240). All instruments also include a differential pressure gauge (DPG). Our dataset incorporates five distinct instrument designs (Table 1).

Similarly, primary and secondary microseism noise sources are impacted by water depth, ocean basin characteristics, and subsurface structure, although less is known about how this impacts their viability for imaging. The primary microseism is caused by the interaction of waves with small-scale seafloor topography at shallow water depth, and large-scale slopes near coastlines (Ardhuin *et al.*, 2015). On the shallow continental shelf, the primary microseism is amplified relative to the open ocean, and relative to the secondary microseism (Webb and Crawford, 2010). The secondary microseism is caused by interacting waves either from oblique intersection, coastline reflection, or storm-generated swell interactions (Ardhuin *et al.*,

TABLE 1
Instrument Design Details

Abbreviation	Design Institution	Seismometer	Pressure Gauge	Instrument Name
AB	SIO	T-Compact	DPG	Abalone
B2	SIO	T-240	DPG	SIO unshielded broadband
AR	WHOI	T-Compact	DPG	WHOI ARRA
BG	WHOI	CMG-3T	DPG	WHOI BBOBS
KE	WHOI	CMG-3T	DPG	WHOI KECK

ARRA and KECK refer to instruments on the OBSIC website; BBOBS, broadband ocean-bottom seismometer; DPG, differential pressure gauge; SIO, Scripps Institution for Oceanography; WHOI, Woods Hole Oceanographic Institution.

2011). Systematic differences in the amplitude and frequency range of the secondary microseism power spectral density (PSD) peak are observed between the Pacific and Atlantic basins (Babcock *et al.*, 1994). Furthermore, Ruan *et al.* (2014) show that sedimentary thickness and velocity structure also impact seismometer response in the secondary microseism band. To investigate these factors, our dataset includes BBOBS in both coastal and open-ocean environments, in the Pacific and Atlantic Oceans, and with sedimentary thicknesses from ~0 to 8000 m.

Unfortunately, we cannot completely isolate these variables with existing BBOBS datasets (Janiszewski *et al.*, 2023). For example, shallow coastal regions often are heavily sedimented and require shielded BBOBS designs. However, to our knowledge this represents the most comprehensive assembled dataset for systematic analysis of the quality of ambient noise CCFs observed on BBOBS to date.

TFs

The TF describes the linear relationship between common signals present on any two components of a BBOBS, which can be used to identify and remove coherent noise (Crawford and Webb, 2000). This is particularly valuable because it does not require a full understanding of the noise source—only that the noise appears coherently across components. Here, we summarize the TF theory and terminology relevant to this study.

We define the cross spectrum between two components $x(t)$ and $z(t)$ as: $G_{ZX}(f) = Z^*(f)X(f)$, in which $Z(f)$ is the Fourier transform of $z(t)$ and $Z^*(f)$ is its complex conjugate. Similarly, the power spectrum of $x(t)$ is defined as: $G_{XX}(f) = X^*(f)X(f)$. Using the cross spectrum of any two components and the power spectrum of the reference component, a TF can be calculated that describes the linear mapping of signals common to both components. Treating Z as the component of interest we want to correct, and X as the component containing noise, we define the TF T_{ZX} as

$$T_{ZX}(f) = \frac{G_{ZX}(f)}{G_{XX}(f)}. \quad (1)$$

This TF can then be used to correct the Z component for the common noise present on the X component in the frequency domain:

$$Z_{\mathrm{corr}}(f) = Z(f) - T^*_{ZX}(f)X(f). \quad (2)$$

Ambient noise CCFs

Z-component ambient noise CCFs are calculated following the procedure of Russell and Gaherty (2021). We divide daily displacement seismograms into 15 three-hour windows with 50% overlap. The cross-spectral coherence $\rho_{ij}(f)$ between two stations i and j is calculated in the frequency domain for each time window k and summed over all N windows of the deployment:

$$\rho_{ij}(f) = \frac{1}{N}\sum_{k=1}^{N}\frac{Z^*_{ik}(f) \times Z_{jk}(f)}{|Z_{ik}(f)| \times |Z_{jk}(f)|}, \quad (3)$$

in which $Z(f)$ is the vertical displacement spectrum at frequency f, and $Z^*(f)$ is its complex conjugate. This definition of the CCF results in spectral whitening, and we do not apply additional time-domain normalization or other spectral conditioning. By stacking many short-time windows, transient signals such as earthquakes do not need to be removed as any individual windows containing such signals have a small influence on the overall CCF stack.

We remove coherent H1, H2, and P energy from the daily Z records using the TF approach as implemented by automated tilt and compliance removal (ATaCR) package (Janiszewski *et al.*, 2019). We use a modified code that does not include quality control steps for removing anomalous TFs (see Data and Resources). We calculate mean daily spectra from 24-hr seismograms by dividing each day into 20 windows of length 6000 s with ~50% overlap. Mean H1-Z, H2-Z, and P-Z TFs are then calculated for each 24-hr segment of data. For each record, H1-Z and H2-Z TF corrections are applied first to target the tilt correction, followed by P-Z TF corrections to target the compliance and microseism corrections across all periods. Using these corrected seismograms, we recalculate the CCFs using equation (3). These corrected CCFs show noticeable changes in the amplitude of the fundamental-mode Scholte, first-overtone Rayleigh, and fundamental-mode Rayleigh waves (Fig. 1, Fig. S2).

To quantify differences between the original and corrected CCFs, we define metrics for the change in SNR of expected interface wave arrivals for the two period bands of interest. In the 3–10 s period band, we calculate SNR in two group velocity windows: 1.6–10 km/s to target the faster first-overtone Rayleigh wave, and 0.3–1.5 km/s to target the slower fundamental-mode Scholte wave. We term the faster and slower velocity windows as the "solid-velocity" and "water-velocity" window, respectively. In the 15–30 s period band, we isolate the expected fundamental Rayleigh wave using a group velocity window of 1.6–10 km/s. We ignore the water-velocity window because we do not expect to observe a Scholte wave in this band (Nolet and Dorman, 1996). In each case, the windowed portion of the seismogram is considered the signal u_s and SNR is calculated as

$$\mathrm{SNR} = \frac{N_s^{-1}\sum^{N_s} u_s^2}{N_n^{-1}\sum^{N_n} u_n^2}, \tag{4}$$

in which u_n is the noise defined between 4000 and 5000 s lag time. Finally, for each period band and group velocity window, we calculate the change in SNR between the original and TF corrected CCFs as

$$\Delta\mathrm{SNR} = \log_{10}\frac{\mathrm{SNR_{corr}}}{\mathrm{SNR_{orig}}}, \tag{5}$$

in which positive values indicate SNR improvement after correction and negative values indicate SNR decline.

Noise spectral properties

To understand causes of variability in the CCF SNRs and the effect of TF corrections, we examine these results in the context of spectral properties for each BBOBS. We use the PSD and cross-component admittance, coherence, and phase for each station from Janiszewski *et al.* (2023); details of the methodology are given therein. Components with data dropouts, glitches, or other anomalies are discarded. We require that BBOBS have four operational components, producing a total of 155 instruments used for subsequent analyses. In particular, we use spectral coherence as a metric to compare with the ΔSNR of the CCFs. Because coherence ranges from 0 to 1, it facilitates comparisons across instruments as it is indifferent to gain or polarity. Generally, where coherence is low, TF removal has little effect and vice versa; thus, we expect to observe a strong relationship between coherence and ΔSNR. We octave-average the coherence function in 1/16 intervals following McNamara and Buland (2004) and then calculate mean coherence in the 15–30 and 3–10 s period bands. Here, we use PZ coherence to refer to the coherences after tilt noise has already been removed.

Results

After we apply H1-Z, H2-Z, and P-Z TF corrections in the 3–10 s band, the mean ΔSNR is positive in the solid-velocity window, and negative in the water-velocity window (Fig. 3a,b). This is consistent with the expected behavior for the first-overtone Rayleigh wave and the fundamental-mode Scholte wave. Although the mean improvement of the first-overtone Rayleigh-wave signal is small, ~63% of the CCFs are improved, in some cases exceeding a factor of 10 increases in SNR. However, the remainder of CCFs shows a decrease in SNR after correction in this window, indicating that TF corrections in some instances reduce data quality. By contrast, nearly all measurements (~99%) of the fundamental-mode Scholte wave have a reduced SNR, indicating that the TFs reliably remove this wave from CCFs. After only horizontal TFs, ΔSNR changes minimally in both velocity windows (Fig. S3a,b), consistent with the minimal tilt noise expected in this band. After applying the H1-Z, H2-Z, and P-Z TF corrections in the 15–30 s band, the mean ΔSNR is negative; however, ~22% of the CCFs improve (Fig. 3c). Thus, the correction reduces the fundamental-mode Rayleigh-wave SNR for the majority of the CCFs. The horizontal correction alone results in no change in the mean ΔSNR; however, at some stations ΔSNR increases (Fig. S3c), which is expected if the TF correction successfully removes tilt noise. This is consistent with the previous observation that tilt noise only dominates on a subset of instrument types (Bell *et al.*, 2015; Janiszewski *et al.*, 2023).

Although the mean behavior of ΔSNR aligns with expectations, there is significant variability in the effect of corrections, particularly for the Rayleigh waves. To investigate the cause of this variability, we calculate covariance between the following: SNR of the original CCFs, ΔSNR, PZ coherence, water depth, and interstation pair distance (Fig. 4). For the coherence and water depth, we use the mean of each station pair, and water depth is a positive value.

In the 3–10 s band, the $\Delta\mathrm{SNR_{solid}}$ for the first-overtone Rayleigh wave is positively correlated with PZ coherence and water depth, with values of 0.45 and 0.60, respectively. This indicates that the correction is most effective for higher PZ coherences and deeper stations (Fig. 3d, Fig. S4a). In contrast, $\Delta\mathrm{SNR_{water}}$ for the fundamental-mode Scholte wave is not highly correlated with these (Fig. 3e, Fig. S4b) but instead is negatively correlated (−0.72) with its original SNR. This indicates that a higher SNR fundamental-mode Scholte wave in the original CCF is more effectively removed via TF corrections. The $\Delta\mathrm{SNR_{water}}$ for the fundamental-mode Scholte wave is also negatively correlated (−0.59) with the original SNR of the first-overtone Rayleigh wave; however, this is likely driven by a high-positive correlation (0.88) between the original SNRs in the solid- and water-velocity windows. Finally, the original SNR of both the fundamental-mode Scholte wave and first-overtone Rayleigh wave is negatively correlated with interstation distance (−0.69 and −0.67, respectively), likely due to

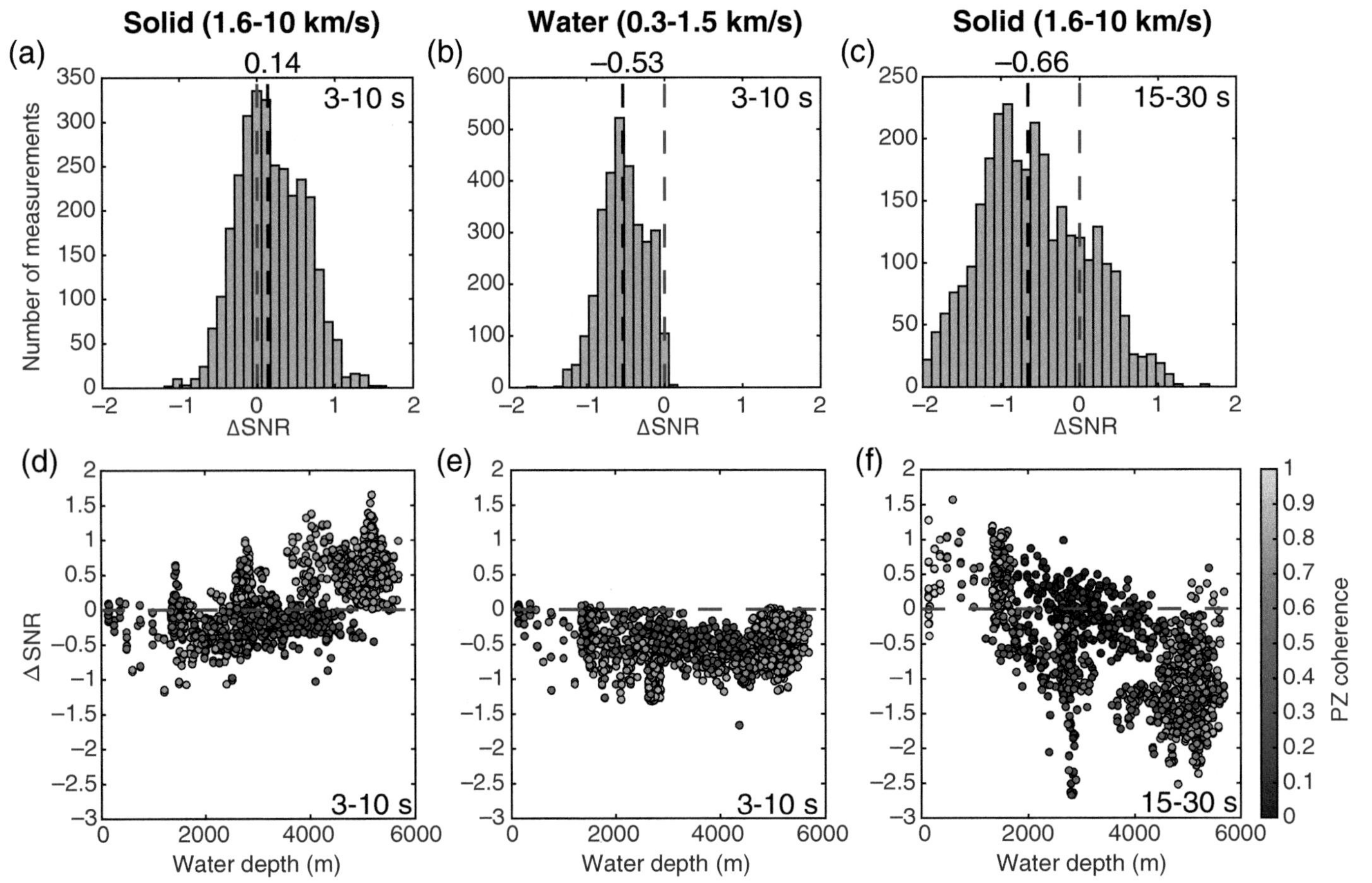

geometrical spreading and attenuation effects (Harmon *et al.*, 2007).

In the 15–30 s band, the ΔSNR_{solid} for the fundamental-mode Rayleigh wave has a −0.62 correlation coefficient with water depth. This is opposite in direction but similar in magnitude to the correlation observed with water depth in the 3–10 s band, instead indicating that the correction is more successful in shallow water (Fig. 3f). The ΔSNR_{solid} is only weakly correlated (−0.16) with PZ coherence in the 15–30 s band (Fig. S4c), substantially weaker than the correlation in the 3–10 s band. The ΔSNR_{solid} for the fundamental-mode Rayleigh wave has a negative correlation coefficient (−0.64) with the original SNR, which indicates that the TF correction either reduces signal if the original CCF has high SNR (e.g., Fig. 1) or reduces noise if the original CCF has low SNR. Furthermore, the original SNR of the fundamental-mode Rayleigh wave has a positive correlation coefficient of 0.45 with water depth, indicating that deeper stations generally have higher original SNR values before corrections. Finally, a negative correlation of −0.42 is observed between the original SNR and interstation distance. This is weaker than the correlation observed in the 3–10 s band, consistent with lower attenuation for the same distances at longer periods.

In summary, water depth and, to a lesser extent, PZ coherence are strongly related to ΔSNR for both the first-overtone and fundamental-mode Rayleigh waves (i.e., waves within the solid-velocity window) at 3–10 and 15–30 s. It is somewhat surprising that water depth yields a higher correlation coefficient than PZ coherence in both bands because PZ coherence is directly incorporated into the TF corrections. There are several limitations to our covariance analysis. First, using the mean value of parameters for each station pair obscures relationships. For example, a pair of stations both at ~2000 m water depth has a similar mean as a station pair with 100 and 4000 m water depths, respectively. Second, we cannot investigate relationships with qualitative parameters such as instrument design, seismometer, ocean basin, or deployment. Third, the covariance analysis is ill suited for relationships for which variables are not evenly sampled across our dataset. For example, sediment thickness is highly unevenly distributed with most

Figure 3. Histograms of the change in signal-to-noise ratio (ΔSNR) for the CCFs for the (a) solid-velocity window at 3–10 s, (b) water-velocity window at 3–10 s, and (c) solid-velocity window at 15–30 s. The red dashed line indicates the zero axis, or no change. The black dashed line indicates the mean ΔSNR. Here, H1-Z, H2-Z, and P-Z TFs are applied. Scatter plots of the ΔSNR for each CCF as a function of mean water depth for the panel (d) solid-velocity window at 3–10 s, (e) water-velocity window at 3–10 s, and (f) solid-velocity window at 15–30 s. Color indicates mean PZ coherence for each station pair. The color version of this figure is available only in the electronic edition.

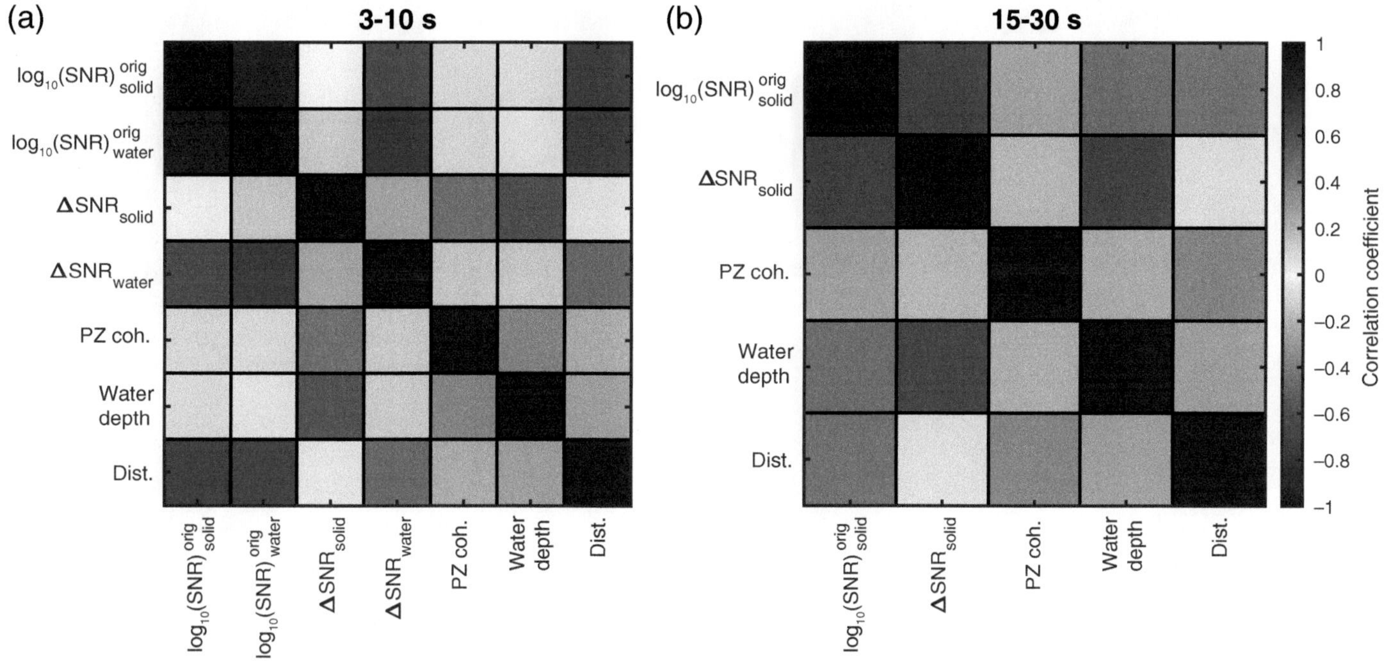

Figure 4. Correlation coefficients for listed variables for (a) 3–10 and (b) 15–30 s periods. The color version of this figure is available only in the electronic edition.

stations having thicknesses <1000 m but with ENAM stations sampling thicknesses up to ~8000 m. Instead, we undertake a more targeted investigation, and discuss our observations in the context of expectations for seismic and oceanographic noise behavior.

Discussion

Effects of water depth

There are two mechanisms that are likely responsible for the relationship between water depth and the effectiveness of TF corrections on the ambient noise CCFs. First, the frequency below which infragravity waves appear, and thus where compliance noise is present, is given by the dispersion relationship:

$$f \approx \sqrt{\frac{g}{2\pi d}}, \tag{6}$$

in which g is the gravity and d is the water depth (Crawford *et al.*, 1998). Because the water depth of each instrument is known, so too is this frequency. Importantly, infragravity waves result in high-PZ coherence below this cutoff frequency, particularly once tilt has been removed (Crawford and Webb, 2000). Second, variations in bathymetry, and sediment thickness and velocity impact the frequency range at which fundamental-mode Scholte waves are observed (Webb, 1992; Harmon *et al.*, 2007; Ruan *et al.*, 2014). In general, these waves extend to lower frequencies in deeper water. Increasing sediment thickness or decreasing velocity also result in their extension to lower frequencies. Because this depends on both the water depth and shallow seismic velocities beneath interstation paths, which are variably constrained for our dataset, it is difficult to predict the precise frequency transition for individual station pairs. Here, we examine the ΔSNR for the solid-velocity window in both the 3–10 and 15–30 s period bands as compared with the water depth and PZ coherence of each member of a station pair (Fig. 5). We focus on the maximum ΔSNRs in our discussions because these provide an insight into the maximum signal improvement at a given water depth or PZ coherence.

At 3–10 s, infragravity waves only significantly affect the shallowest stations (<~150 m). For example, the shallowest station in our dataset is deployed at 126 m water depth, which corresponds to an infragravity cutoff at 9 s. Thus, much of the 3–10 s band does not record infragravity waves, even at the shallowest stations. When either member of a station pair is deployed at <150 m water depth, the maximum ΔSNR is <~0.5, indicating little to no improvements in the data after TF corrections (Fig. 5a). These correspond to relatively low-PZ coherences because the infragravity signal overlaps with only a small portion of the target period range. Because these waves arrive within the solid-velocity window, they are Rayleigh waves predominantly sensitive to solid–earth structure; however, it is unclear if they are fundamental or first-overtone phases. Although most solid-velocity arrivals are first overtones at 3–10 s, the transition between modes should shift to shorter periods in shallow water (Ruan *et al.*, 2014; Tian and Ritzwoller, 2017).

The most significant improvements of the CCFs in the solid-velocity window in the 3–10 s band occur in deeper water

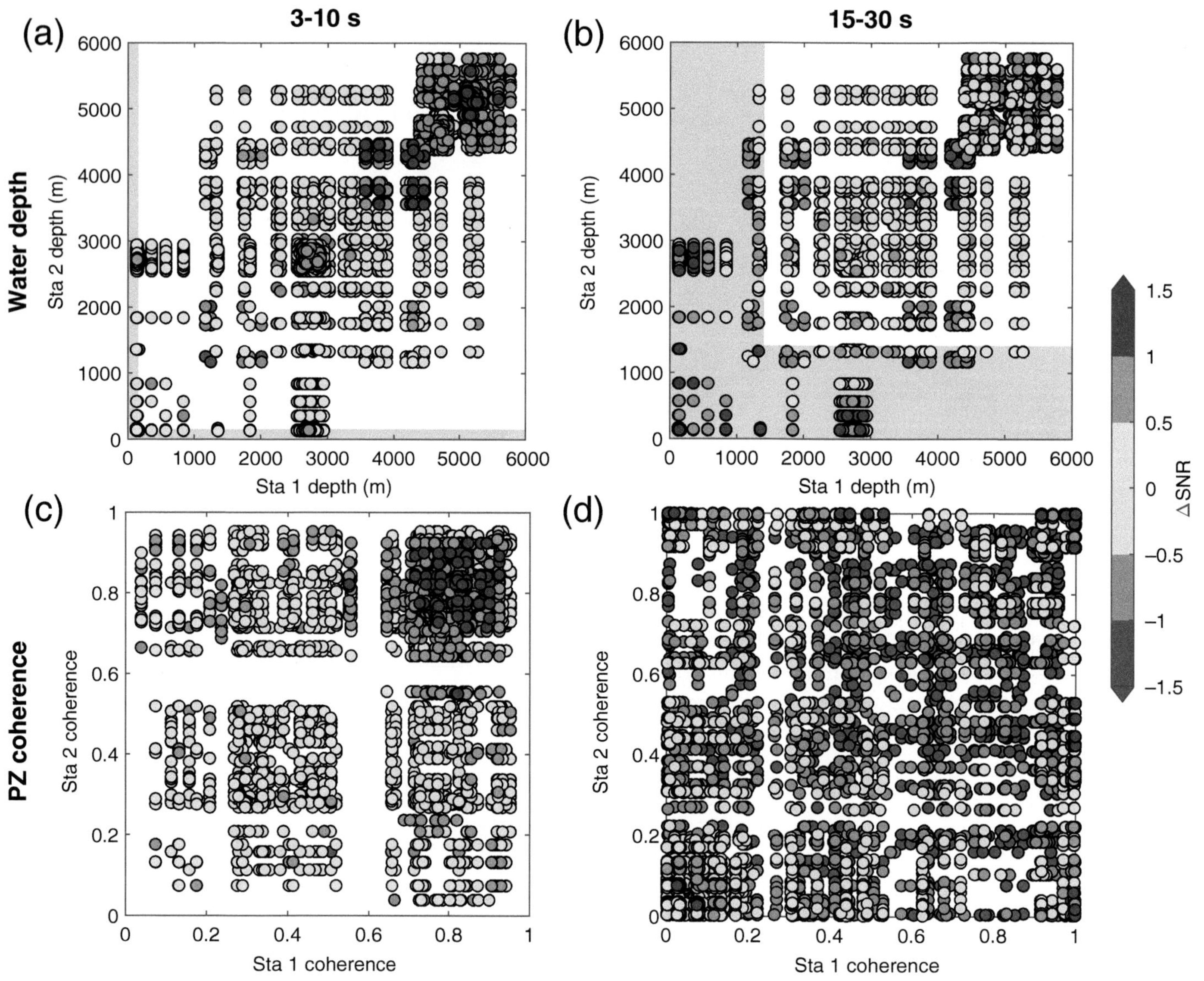

Figure 5. Scatter plots showing ΔSNR in the solid-velocity window as a function of (a,b) the water depth and (c,d) the PZ coherence of each member of a station pair for (a,c) 3–10 and (b,d) 15–30 s period bands. For water depth, gray shading indicates depth range overlapping with the infragravity band at (a) 10 and (b) 30 s. Note that individual points overlap; points with the highest ΔSNR values are plotted on top. The color version of this figure is available only in the electronic edition.

(> ~3500 m), and where both stations in a pair have similar water depths (< ~1000 m difference). These pairs typically have high-PZ coherence (> ~0.7), which is due to the secondary microseism and not the infragravity signal (Fig. 5c). Corrections applied under these conditions yield ΔSNR > 1 (Fig. 5a), reflecting enhanced detection of the first-overtone Rayleigh mode. In contrast, station pairs with shallower depths or large depth differences tend to have smaller or negative ΔSNR values, despite varying levels of PZ coherence. This indicates that high coherence alone is not sufficient for successful correction (Fig. S4a). Although there is a general positive correlation between ΔSNR and mean water depth or PZ coherence, these results emphasize that both absolute depth and interstation depth differences are critical for improving first-overtone Rayleigh-wave signals after TF corrections. Notably, some deployments deviate from this trend: ENAM stations consistently show lower ΔSNRs values, even for water depths >3500 m and station pair depth differences <1000 m (Fig. S5).

We observe markedly different behaviors at 15–30 s. At 30 s period, the infragravity wave is observable on stations at water depths < ~1400 m. For station pairs with at least one station in this depth range, the corrections effectively remove infragravity wave noise, resulting in the greatest signal improvements of ΔSNR > 1 (Fig. 5b). This is likely the primary improvement previously observed at the Cascadia Initiative experiment by Tian and Ritzwoller (2017). These predominantly correspond to station pairs where PZ coherence is very high (> ~0.95) on at least one station, although we note that the accompanying station may have coherences as low as ~0 (Fig. 5d). In contrast, most station pairs deployed at depths >1400 m show reduced signal quality (ΔSNR < 0). This is consistent with the negative correlation coefficient between ΔSNR and mean water depth (Fig. 4b), supporting the dominant role of infragravity wave removal at these periods. In addition, station pairs at water depths >1400 m have ΔSNR < 0 even when PZ coherence is high (Fig. 5d, Fig. S5). High-PZ coherences at these water depths cannot arise from infragravity waves, and instead are driven by the presence of primary microseism-generated Rayleigh waves (e.g., Fig. 1f). The resulting negative ΔSNRs indicate that the TF corrections remove part of the desired fundamental-mode Rayleigh-wave signal.

We also observe moderate improvements (0 < ΔSNR < 1) at some stations with water depths >1400 m, most of which correspond to low-PZ coherences (<0.2) on both stations (Fig. 5d). This bimodal relationship between PZ coherence and ΔSNR is markedly different than observations in the 3–10 s band (Fig. 5c), and the cause of this variability is not explained by infragravity waves. Only three deployments—ENAM, Cascadia Initiative, and PLUME—contain instruments with positive ΔSNRs at >1400 m water depth, and the majority of high ΔSNRs (>0.5) that are accompanied by low-PZ coherence are restricted to ENAM (Fig. S5). Overall, these results highlight the complex interplay between water depth, noise sources, and the success of TF corrections, emphasizing the importance of considering both station depth and pair configuration when deciding how to analyze CCFs.

Effects of tilt noise

We posit that positive ΔSNRs at water depths >1400 m in the 15–30 s period band are instead driven by the correction of tilt noise on the CCFs. Previous analyses of BBOBS noise properties demonstrate that tilt noise is highly dependent on the seismometer and instrument design (Bell *et al.*, 2015; Janiszewski *et al.*, 2023). To investigate the influence of tilt noise on the CCFs, we examine the difference between the mean PZ coherence and HZ coherence for each station pair (Fig. 6). We define the HZ coherence as the maximum of the H1-Z and H2-Z coherences. When tilt noise is present and stronger than compliance noise, the HZ coherence should be high (Crawford and Webb, 2000). Because we do not rotate the horizontals into the maximum tilt direction, the HZ coherence should not necessarily equal one at a high tilt station. However, in the absence of tilt noise, the H1-Z and H2-Z coherences should both be close to zero (Bell *et al.*, 2015); thus, a nonzero HZ coherence should serve as a reasonable diagnostic for tilt noise. After tilt noise is removed, the PZ coherence increases substantially within the infragravity band due to compliance noise (Bell *et al.*, 2015). The PZ coherence due to the microseism may also moderately increase if its frequency range overlaps with the tilt noise (Janiszewski *et al.*, 2023). We can distinguish between high-PZ coherence due to the infragravity wave versus the microseism using the water-depth cutoff-frequency relationship in equation (6).

By differencing the PZ and HZ coherence, we examine the relative strength of tilt, compliance, and coherent microseism noise. Negative values indicate higher HZ coherence (stronger tilt noise), whereas positive values indicate higher PZ coherence (stronger compliance or coherent microseism noise). Near-zero values indicate either similar magnitudes of HZ and PZ coherences (comparable tilt, and compliance or microseism noise) or an absence of any coherence. We discriminate between these possibilities by comparing PZ-HZ coherence with PZ coherence (Fig. 6c,d). The subset of stations with low-PZ coherence but high ΔSNR in the 15–30 s band (Fig. 5d) corresponds to the most negative PZ-HZ coherence values (Fig. 6d). Because these station-pair water depths are >1400 m, this indicates they have high tilt noise accompanied by a lack of PZ microseism coherence. Thus, the increase in ΔSNR is driven primarily by the removal of tilt noise from the CCFs. In contrast, at <1400 m water depth positive ΔSNRs accompany positive PZ-HZ coherences due to the removal of strong compliance noise.

Negative PZ-HZ values occur only at deployments with instrument designs that use CMG-3T seismometers (i.e., ENAM, Cascadia Initiative, and PLUME; Fig. S6), which have been shown to have systematically higher tilt noise than other seismometer types and instrument designs before TF corrections (Bell *et al.*, 2015; Janiszewski *et al.*, 2023). Among these deployments, ENAM shows the most negative PZ-HZ values, which are accompanied by high ΔSNRs for stations with >1400 m water depth (Figs. S5, S6). This indicates that ENAM uniquely experiences high tilt noise accompanied by lower PZ coherence in the primary microseism band. Thus, the high ΔSNRs observed at the ENAM deployment arise not only from tilt noise removal but also from a lack of removal of the fundamental-mode Rayleigh wave due to low-PZ microseism coherence. Improvement of CCFs due to tilt removal at ENAM was previously demonstrated by Russell and Gaherty (2021), and they interpreted the remarkably high tilt noise as a result of the strong Gulf Stream current. At the Cascadia Initiative and PLUME deployments, PZ microseism coherence is higher and therefore potential improvements in signal quality due to tilt noise removal are reduced due to degradation of the fundamental-mode Rayleigh wave. Here, tilt noise removal alone may yield higher ΔSNRs. Negative PZ-HZ coherences do not occur in the 3–10 s band. This is consistent with the expectation that tilt noise is absent at periods <10 s (Crawford and Webb, 2000). Instead, the PZ-HZ metric is almost entirely driven by the PZ coherence (Fig. 6c).

Impact of sediments and other factors

Although water depth has a primary control on the ΔSNR of the first-overtone Rayleigh wave in the 3–10 s band, sediment

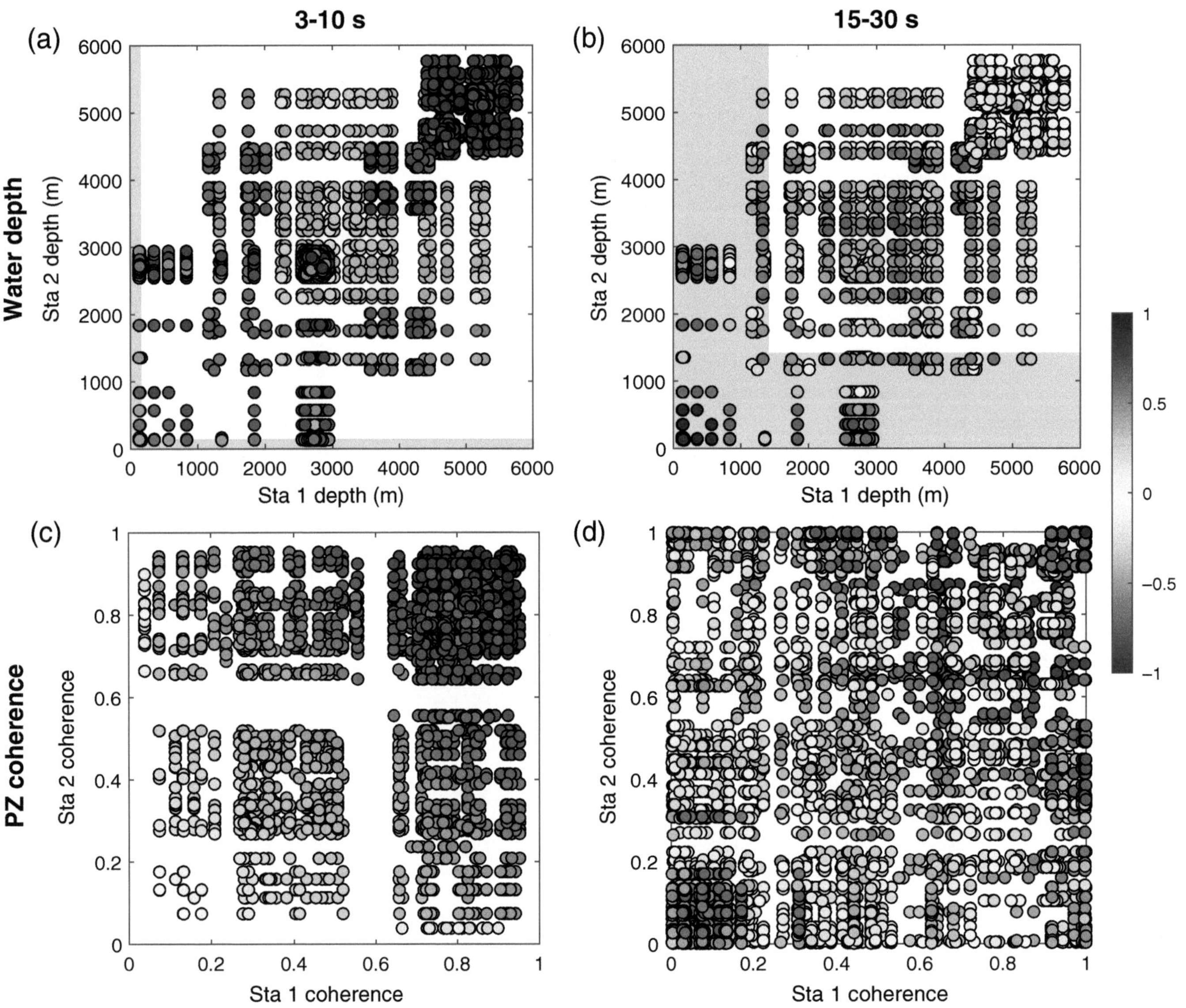

Figure 6. Scatter plots showing PZ–HZ coherence as a function of (a,b) the water depth and (c,d) the PZ coherence of each member of a station pair for (a,c) 3–10 and (b,d) 15–30 s period. The gray shading is the same as in Figure 5. Note that we use the same plotting order as Figure 5 for direct comparison; that is, points with the highest ΔSNR values are plotted on top. The color version of this figure is available only in the electronic edition.

structure should also play a role (Nolet and Dorman, 1996; Zhu and Popovics, 2006; Ruan *et al.*, 2014). These two factors are often interrelated—thicker sediments are typically found on continental shelves at shallower water depths, whereas thinner layers are more common in deeper ocean basins (Straume *et al.*, 2019). ENAM is the only deployment in our analysis with sediment thickness >2000 m, reaching ~8000 m beneath some stations. It is also the only deployment with relatively deep stations (>3000 m), where the TF correction produces maximum ΔSNRs < 0 for the first-overtone Rayleigh wave. Thus, it is possible that these anomalous observations on the ENAM deployment are driven by thick sedimentary layers.

To understand the role of sediments, we explore the theoretical behavior of interface waves for two layered models: one with sediments and one without (Fig. 7a). The sediment-free model contains a 4 km thick water layer, underlain by oceanic crust (divided into a 2 km thick upper crust and 5 km thick lower crust) and mantle using velocities based on Ruan *et al.* (2014). The second model is identical to the first, but includes a 2 km layer of sediment on top of the upper oceanic crust. Surface-wave dispersion, eigenfunctions, and ellipticity values are calculated using the SURF96 software (Herrmann, 2013). Here, we define the relative polarity of the P and Z components such that a decrease in pressure due to an uplift in ground displacement results in a ±180° phase separation. Polarity conventions for DPG responses can differ, so we adjust these for consistency across deployments. Using this convention, the P and Z records of fundamental-mode Scholte and Rayleigh waves are out of phase, and the amplitude of the

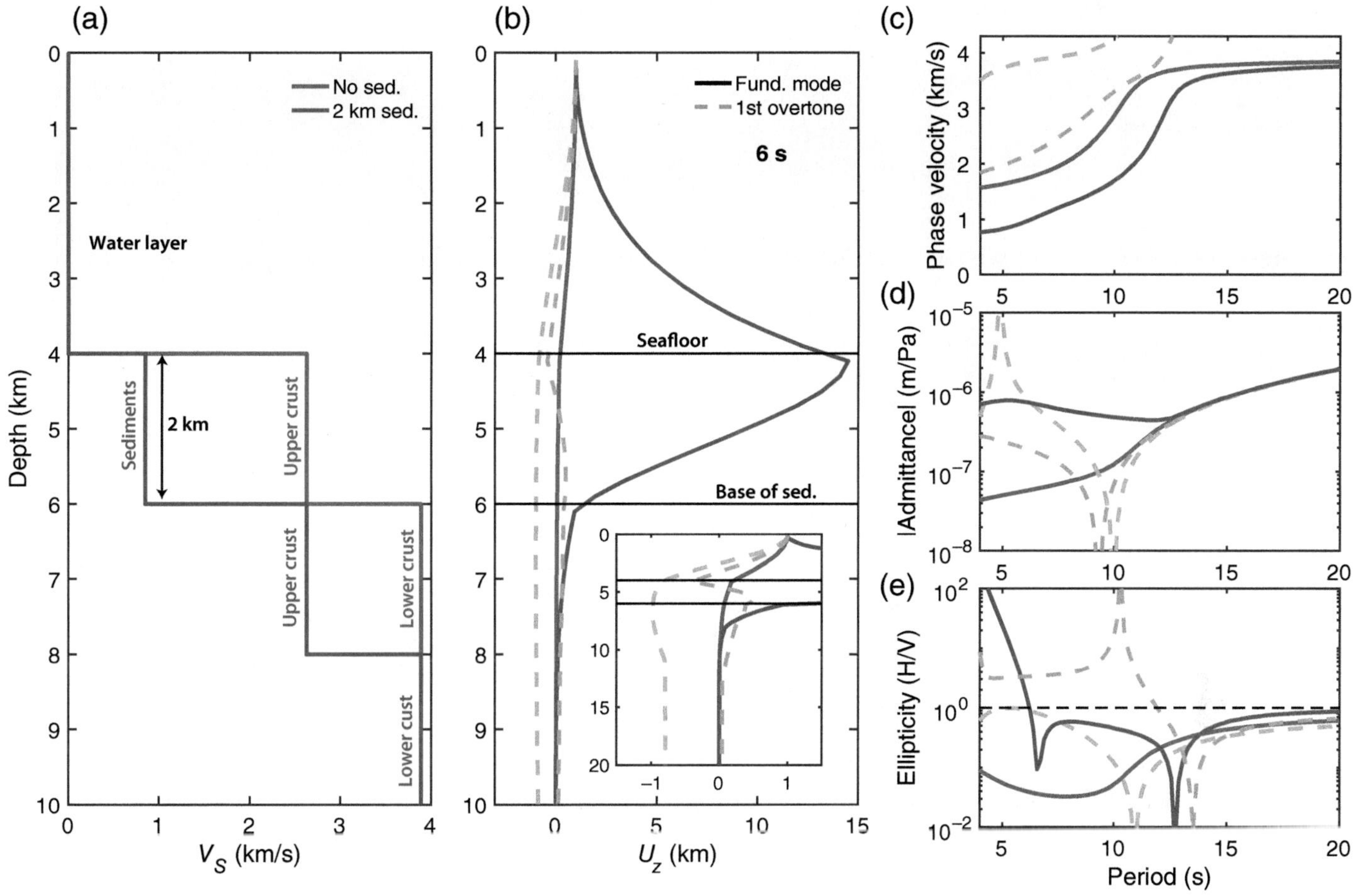

Figure 7. Synthetic Scholte and Rayleigh-wave calculations for a model containing no sediments (blue) and a model containing a 2-km-thick sediment layer (red). (a) Shear velocity model, (b) vertical displacement eigenfunctions at 6 s period, (c) phase velocity dispersion, (d) admittance, and (e) ellipticity. The fundamental mode and first overtone are indicated by solid and dashed lines, respectively. The color version of this figure is available only in the electronic edition.

TF (or admittance) is calculated as the ratio of the vertical displacement eigenfunction U_z to the vertical stress eigenfunction (proportional to the spatial gradient of displacement) τ_{zz} at the seafloor (Ruan *et al.*, 2014):

$$T_{ZP}(f) = \frac{U_z(f)}{\tau_{zz}(f)} = \frac{U_z(f)}{K\left[\frac{\partial U_x}{\partial x(f)} + \frac{\partial U_z}{\partial z(f)}\right]}, \quad (7)$$

in which K is the incompressibility of water and U_x is the horizontal displacement eigenfunction.

Based on our synthetic tests, interface wave sensitivity strongly differs in the presence of thick sediments, resulting in differences in phase velocity dispersion, seafloor admittance, and wave ellipticity (Fig. 7). In the absence of sediments, the fundamental-mode Scholte wave is largely sensitive to the water column, as shown by the vertical displacement eigenfunctions (Fig. 7b). This wave is sometimes described as a leaky Rayleigh wave, distinguished from a Scholte wave on the basis of the subsurface shear velocity and wave ellipticity (Zhu and Popovics, 2006). Its sensitivity to the water column is reflected in the phase velocity dispersion, which approaches the acoustic water wavespeed (1.5 km/s) at periods <10 s (Fig. 7c). In contrast, the first-overtone Rayleigh wave samples deeper into the crust and uppermost mantle down to ~40 km depth, and phase velocities are 3.5–4.2 km/s at these periods. For thick sediments, the fundamental-mode Scholte-wave energy is trapped predominantly in the sediment layer (Fig. 7b), leading to phase velocities <1.5 km/s at short periods, approaching sediment shear velocity. The first overtone also shows significant sensitivity to the sediments as well as the upper crust, resulting in phase velocities that are comparable to that of the sediment-free fundamental Scholte mode at periods <10 s. Slower velocities and less separation of the mode branches in the presence of thick sediments implies potentially stronger overtone interference and hence more difficulty isolating mode branches.

To validate these findings, we analyzed real data from the NoMelt experiment, which features relatively thin sediments (~250 m; Mark *et al.*, 2019; Russell *et al.*, 2019), resembling the sediment-free model (Fig. 7). We apply a linear Radon transform to P-P and Z-Z CCFs to extract multimode

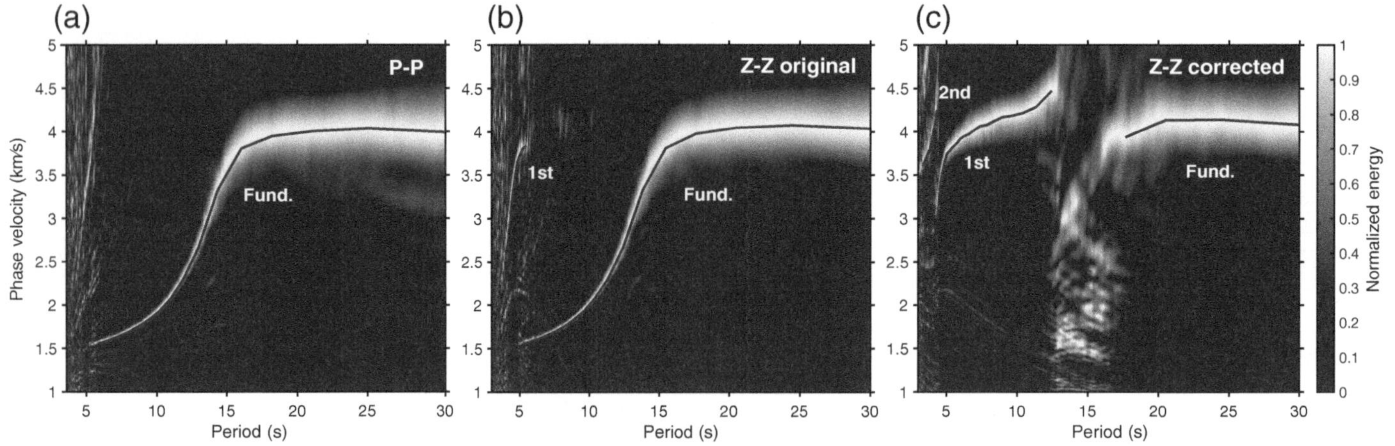

Figure 8. Linear Radon transform panels displaying array-average dispersion at the NoMelt deployment obtained from ambient noise CCFs. (a) P-P component, (b) original Z-Z component without TF corrections applied, and (c) corrected Z-Z component with TF corrections applied. Red lines indicate high-quality dispersion branches extracted from the Radon panels. The color version of this figure is available only in the electronic edition.

dispersion characteristics (Luo *et al.*, 2008, 2015; Russell, 2021; Fig. 8). In this setting, the P-P component captures only the fundamental-mode branch (Fig. 8a), whereas the original Z-Z component reveals both fundamental-mode and first-overtone energy (Fig. 8b). After applying TF corrections, the fundamental Scholte wave is removed from the Z-Z component, the first overtone becomes more prominent between ~5 and 12 s, and the second overtone emerges at periods <5 s (Fig. 8c). These overtones are sensitive to the crust and shallow lithospheric mantle, and offer potential for high-resolution imaging. Although the second overtone has been observed in earlier studies (Russell, 2021; Phillips *et al.*, 2023), to our knowledge it has not yet been used for structural imaging of the oceanic lithosphere using passive broadband seismic arrays. Overall, the observed dispersion aligns well with predictions from the sediment-free model.

Unfortunately, a similar analysis for a deployment with thick sediments (i.e., ENAM) results in a Radon transform largely absent of distinct dispersion curves due to the poor quality of the CCFs, and heterogeneous water depth and sediment structure (Russell and Gaherty, 2021). However, noise properties of the ENAM deployment are consistent with higher-mode interference at 3–10 s period due to thick sediments. At deployments excluding ENAM, we observe high-PZ coherences over this band (Fig. 9a). At water depths >~4500 m, distinct minima in PZ coherence are observed, although these are primarily restricted to periods <5 s. Furthermore, coherence values remain > ~0.5 at these minima. In contrast, ENAM stations have lower overall PZ coherence values in this period band (Fig. 9b). Distinct coherence minima begin at ~3000 m water depth, reaching near-zero values. We also examine the phase relationship between the P and Z components as a function of period where the PZ coherence is >0.7. Excluding ENAM, the P and Z components are mostly directly out of phase (±180°), as expected given our polarity conventions (Fig. 9c). We observe scatter at some stations, particularly at periods with reduced coherences. These subsequently return to phase separations of ±180° at higher coherence values at most stations. In contrast, ENAM consistently shows a distinct pattern of 180° phase flips as a function of period (Fig. 9d). At a single station, longer period high-PZ coherence peaks have a phase separation of ±180°, followed by a flip to a phase of 0° at shorter periods. These phase flips are separated by the distinct minima in PZ coherence (Fig. 9b,d).

Significant decreases in PZ coherence at BBOBS at periods <10 s, particularly accompanied by a ±180° change in phase, can indicate interference from higher order modes (Ruan *et al.*, 2014). This may also result from a transition from retrograde to prograde elliptical particle motion at the seafloor for the fundamental mode and first overtone. Onshore, fundamental-mode Rayleigh waves can exhibit prograde particle motion in the presence of very thick sedimentary layers with slow surface velocities (Tanimoto and Rivera, 2005). Similar observations for higher modes are also documented at sedimentary basins on land (Ma *et al.*, 2016; Nayak and Thurber, 2020). Changes from retrograde to prograde particle motion should be accompanied by sharp minima in ellipticity, as seen in our thick sediment model (Fig. 7e). Measurements of Rayleigh-wave ellipticity on BBOBS instruments are often hindered by high noise levels on horizontal components (Janiszewski *et al.*, 2023); thus, a detailed analysis is outside the scope of our current study. However, the ENAM observations are consistent with expectations for mode interference in the presence of thick sediments. Combined with their uniqueness relative to other deployments, and the anomalously thick sediments beneath ENAM, we suggest that complex particle motion and mode interference play a significant role in the CCFs of this deployment at periods <10 s.

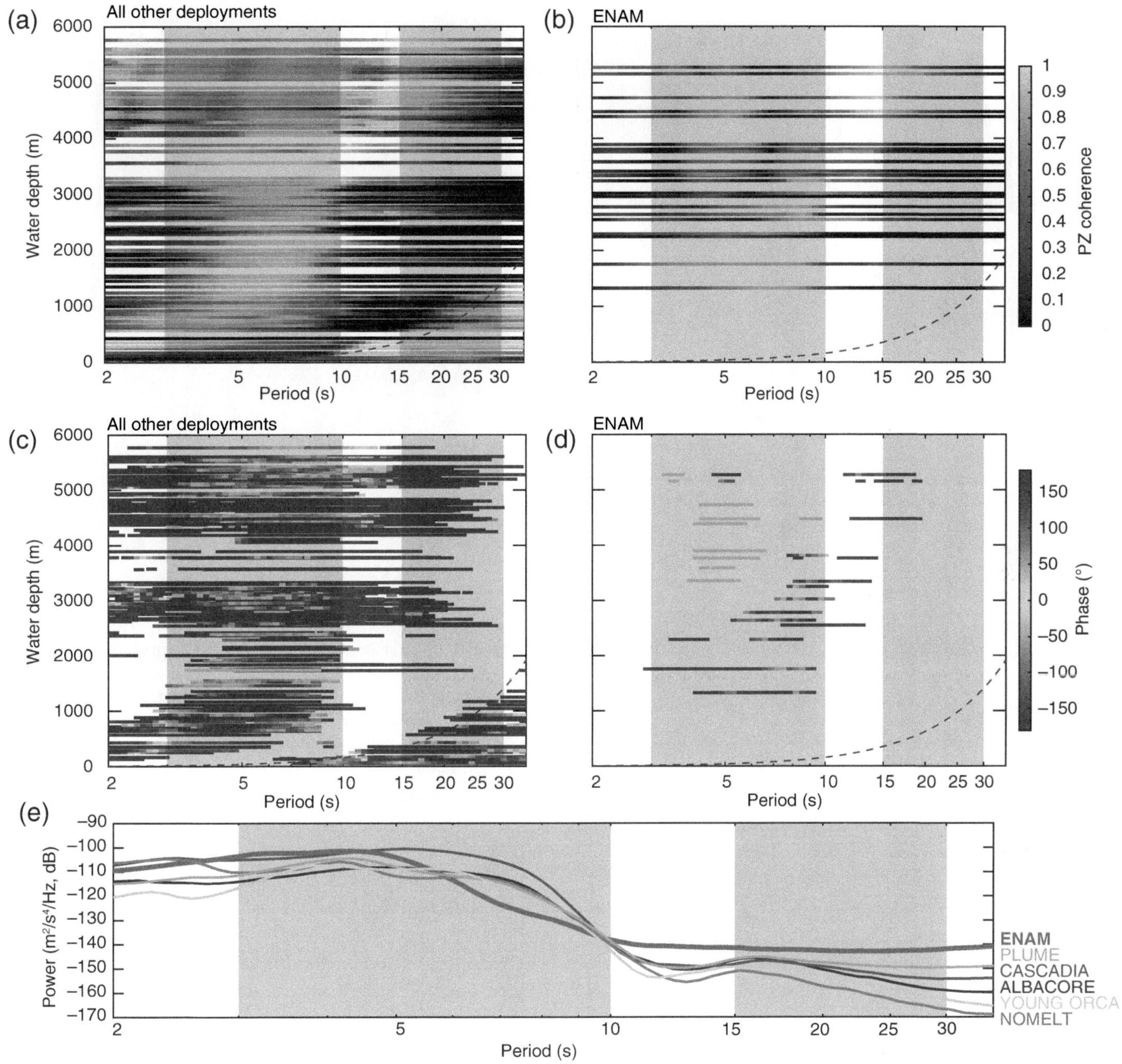

Additional environmental factors may also influence microseism amplitudes. For example, BBOBS in the Atlantic Ocean are expected to record weaker microseism signals at periods >7 s compared to those in the Pacific due to differences in wind regimes (Webb, 1992; Babcock *et al.*, 1994). We observe this pattern when comparing mean Z-component power spectra across deployments (Fig. 9e), excluding shallow-water (<500 m) stations, as these have distinct microseism noise characteristics (Webb, 1992; Janiszewski *et al.*, 2023). ENAM, located in the western Atlantic, indeed shows reduced secondary microseism energy at longer periods relative to Pacific deployments. Furthermore, ENAM's location within the strong Gulf Stream current likely contributes to its unique

Figure 9. P-Z coherence plotted as a function of broadband ocean-bottom seismometer (BBOBS) water depth for (a) all analyzed deployments excluding ENAM and (b) ENAM. P-Z phase relationship plotted as a function of BBOBS water depth for (c) all analyzed deployments excluding ENAM and (d) ENAM. Phase is only plotted at periods where PZ coherence exceeds 0.7. Individual horizontal lines represent a single BBOBS, gray shaded areas indicate the 3–10 and 15–30 s period bands, and the red-dashed line indicates the predicted infragravity cutoff as a function of water depth. (e) Average Z-component noise power spectral density functions calculated as the mean of each deployment. Stations with water depths shallower than 500 m are excluded. The color version of this figure is available only in the electronic edition.

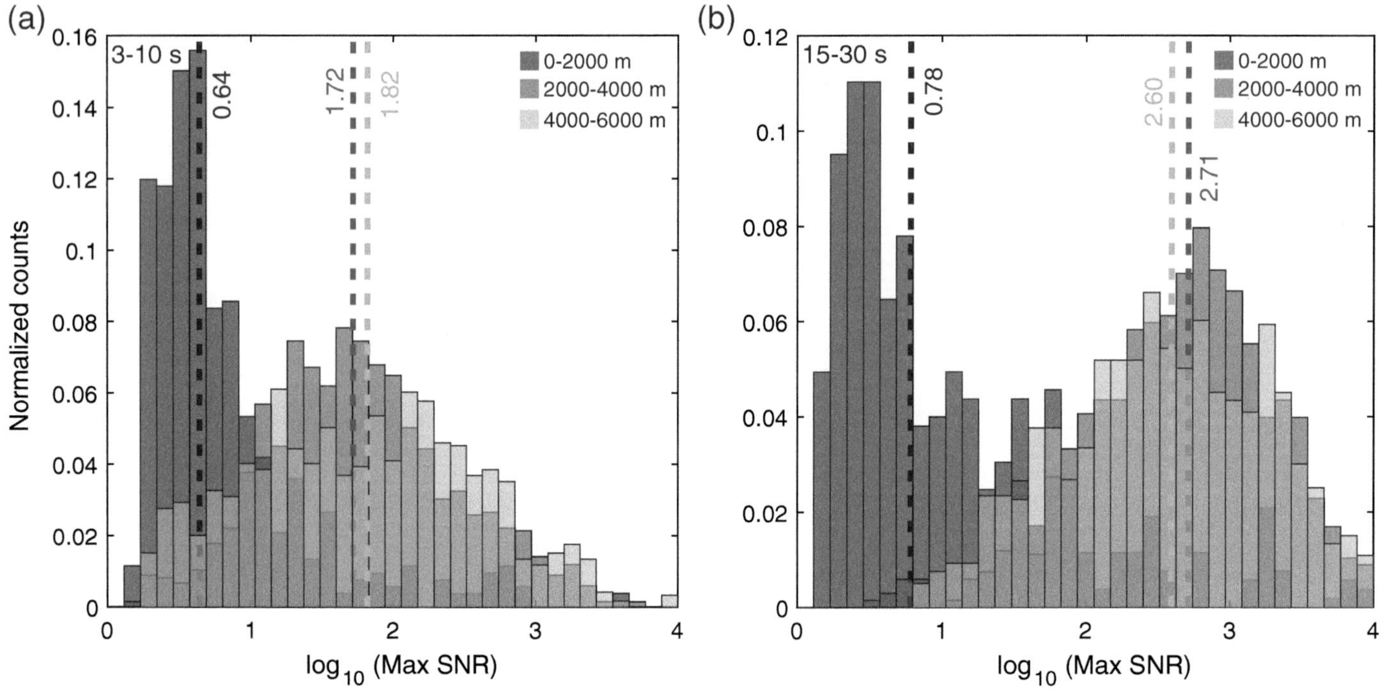

Figure 10. Histograms of maximum CCF signal-to-noise ratios (SNRs; e.g., the maximum SNR out of the original and TF corrected CCF for each station pair) in the solid-velocity window grouped by water depth for the (a) 3–10 and (b) 15–30 s period band. Median values for each water depth group are shown by dashed lines. The color version of this figure is available only in the electronic edition.

noise environment (Russell and Gaherty, 2021), adding to the complexity of its seismic recordings.

Criteria for success

The effectiveness of TF corrections on ambient noise CCFs depends on environmental conditions and instrumentation. In the 3–10 s band, these corrections are most reliable at deep, open-ocean stations. Specifically, we observe that the first-overtone Rayleigh-wave signal is consistently enhanced for station pairs when both their mean water depth exceeds ~4000 m and PZ coherence is > ~0.5 (Fig. 3d). In all other cases, the impact of the TF corrections becomes less predictable. Under these conditions, it may be beneficial to compare CCFs before and after correction, and select the highest quality version for further analysis.

In the 15–30 s band, several important considerations arise. First, the PZ TF correction should only be applied at periods that are within the expected infragravity wave band for a given station's water depth. Applying it outside this range risks removing the fundamental-mode Rayleigh wave, which carries valuable structural information. Some studies have proposed using coherence thresholds to avoid such issues (e.g., Tian and Ritzwoller, 2017), and we emphasize the importance of distinguishing whether the observed coherence stems from microseism activity or infragravity waves. By contrast, tilt noise corrections show more variable outcomes across different settings. Although they can improve ΔSNR, their effect is not consistently tied to water depth or other environmental factors (Fig. S3, Fig. 6). This is likely due to the stronger relationship between tilt noise and instrumentation (Janiszewski *et al.*, 2023). Therefore, tilt corrections should be applied routinely, but CCFs should be evaluated post-correction to confirm that data quality has improved. Overall, these findings suggest that no single preprocessing workflow will work equally well in all environments, especially outside of deep, open-ocean environments. Finally, thick sediments can significantly complicate short-period ambient noise analyses.

To evaluate the overall usability of ambient noise data, we examine the distribution of maximum SNR value of either the original or corrected CCFs across all station pairs (Fig. 10, Fig. S7). This approach does not distinguish cases for which tilt corrections alone might yield the highest SNRs, but it provides a general overview of data quality trends. As expected, SNR values are generally high, with ~75% of observations exceeding an SNR of 10 in the 3–10 s band and ~89% in the 15–30 s band. However, quality drops sharply for station pairs with mean water depths <2000 m, where median SNRs fall to 4.4 (3–10 s) and 6.0 (15–30 s). In deeper waters, median SNRs exceed 50 and 400 in the respective bands. This contrast highlights that fewer sufficient-quality CCFs are likely in shallow water, although it is important to emphasize that the maximum range of SNRs for shallow water stations is similar to all water depths. In addition, SNR levels are consistently higher in the 15–30 s band than in the 3–10 s band, especially at water depths >2000 m. This difference may reflect greater attenuation of shorter-period signals or increased noise contamination.

Conclusions

Systematic analysis of ambient noise CCFs across six BBOBS deployments demonstrates that water depth, sediment thickness, ocean basin characteristics, and instrumentation impact data quality and effectiveness of TF corrections. In the 15–30 s period band, signal quality is primarily governed by infragravity wave and tilt noise, which vary with water depth and instrument design, respectively. Applying TF corrections within the appropriate period bands for these noise sources improves CCFs, but using them outside these ranges can unintentionally remove the fundamental-mode Rayleigh wave, which is critical for structural imaging. These relationships likely continue at longer periods where tilt and compliance noise remain the dominant noise sources (Tian and Ritzwoller, 2017). In the 3–10 s period band, CCFs are shaped by the properties of the fundamental-mode Scholte wave and first-overtone Rayleigh wave. The velocities and period ranges of these waves are primarily related to water depth and sediment structure.

Our results highlight both the challenges and opportunities in using ambient noise for imaging in marine environments, particularly at shorter periods. The results in the 3–10 s band emphasize that shallow structure significantly affects how interface waves propagate, influencing the success of ambient noise techniques traditionally used to image deeper crustal and lithospheric structure. Covariance of environmental and deployment parameters remains a persistent barrier to isolate relationships, and viable directions for future research may include analysis of non-US-led deployments or targeted pilot deployments to better quantify the role of specific variables (Janiszewski *et al.*, 2023). It is notable that Janiszewski *et al.* (2023) do not find a significant relationship between sediment thickness and BBOBS noise properties, likely due to their broad focus on periods longer than 1 s. Our CCF results demonstrate that bandlimited investigations motivated by specific use cases for BBOBS data can yield additional insights, further clarifying directions for future investigations.

Our results also demonstrate that at 3–10 s interface waves can be highly sensitive to the water column and shallow sediment structure, potentially representing relatively novel directions for broadband ambient noise imaging studies. Scholte waves are more commonly analyzed to constrain sediment velocities in marine active-source experiments and typically use periods shorter than 1 s facilitated by denser instrument spacing than passive, broadband arrays (Nolet and Dorman, 1996; Bohlen *et al.*, 2004; Kugler *et al.*, 2007; Nguyen *et al.*, 2009). Recent ocean-bottom nodal and DAS deployments show that ambient noise generated Scholte waves can also image the sedimentary layer, in some cases extending to periods >1 s (Tomar *et al.*, 2016; Lior *et al.*, 2022; Girard *et al.*, 2024). Developments in long-term seafloor cabled observations (e.g., Kelley *et al.*, 2014; Shinohara *et al.*, 2021; Howe *et al.*, 2022) open additional opportunities for monitoring changes in seismic velocity over time using ambient noise observations. Such techniques typically focus on periods from ~0.25 to 10 s (Lee *et al.*, 2024), overlapping with the band where we observe complex interface wave properties. The overlap of these diverse approaches suggests that further exploration of the utilization of both Scholte and Rayleigh waves in passive, broadband ambient noise imaging studies may yield new insights. However, our results demonstrate that leveraging both Scholte and Rayleigh waves will require careful identification of different mode branches and modeling of depth sensitivities. Although simple 1D modeling approaches (e.g., Herrmann, 2013) yield useful insights, more computationally robust methodologies that incorporate 2D or 3D heterogeneity and better represent the full waveform may improve accuracy of interpretations. Addressing these challenges will be key to unlocking the full potential of ambient noise imaging in marine settings.

Data and Resources

The seismic and pressure time-series data are available for download through the EarthScope Data Management Center (DMC; https://ds.iris.edu/ds/nodes/dmc/) under the following network codes: 2D.2010, 7D.2011, XE.2018, YO.2014, YS.2004, and ZA.2011. The codes for broadband ocean-bottom seismometer (BBOBS) noise transfer function (TF) calculations and corrections are based on the MATLAB version (www.mathworks.com/products/matlab) of the ATaCR code part of the OBStool package (Audet and Janiszewski, 2020), and are available for download via GitHub (https://github.com/helenjanisz/ATaCR). A modified version of ATaCR used in this article for ambient noise applications can be found here: https://github.com/jbrussell/ATaCR/tree/correct_noise. Calculation of the ambient noise cross-correlation functions (CCFs) and array dispersion measurements uses the MATnoise code available for download via GitHub (https://github.com/jbrussell/MATnoise). All websites were last accessed in March 2025. The supplemental material contains figures of additional parameters and data separated by individual deployments.

Declaration of Competing Interests

The authors acknowledge that there are no conflicts of interest recorded.

Acknowledgments

The data analyzed herein were collected on instruments maintained by ocean-bottom seismic instrument center (OBSIC) and the ocean-bottom seismograph instrument pool (OBSIP), and in deployments supported by the University National Oceanographic Laboratory System (UNOLS) funded by the National Science Foundation (NSF). The facilities of EarthScope Consortium were used for access to waveforms, related metadata, and/or derived products used in this study. These services are funded through the NSF's Seismological Facility for the Advancement of Geoscience (SAGE) Award under Cooperative

Agreement EAR-1724509. Figures were made using the M_Map code package (Pawlowicz, 2020), and the Scientific Color Maps package (Crameri, 2018). The article benefited from conversations with Spahr Webb, Jim Gaherty, Nick Harmon, and Robert Dunn. The authors acknowledge the thoughtful contributions of two anonymous reviewers and the editor whose feedback greatly improved this article. This work was partially supported by funds from the Gordon and Betty Moore Foundation Award GBMF10787, and NSF Award EAR-1952702.

References

Aderhold, K., R. Woodward, and A. Frasetto (2019). Ocean bottom seismography instrument pool, *Final Report*, doi: 10.5281/zenodo.3524424.

Adimah, N. I., and S. Padhy (2019). Ambient noise Rayleigh wave tomography across the Madagascar Island, *Geophys. J. Int.* **220,** no. 3, 1657–1676, doi: 10.1093/gji/ggz542.

Adimah, N. I., Y. J. Tan, and J. B. Russell (2024). Shear-wave velocity structure of the Blanco oceanic transform fault zone, *Geophys. J. Int.* **239,** no. 2, 1287–1312, doi: 10.1093/gji/ggae318.

Ardhuin, F., E. Stutzmann, M. Schimmel, and A. Mangeney (2011). Ocean wave sources of seismic noise, *J. Geophys. Res.* **116,** no. C9, doi: 10.1029/2011jc006952.

Ardhuin, F., L. Gualtieri, and E. Stutzmann (2015). How ocean waves rock the Earth: Two mechanisms explain microseisms with periods 3 to 300 s, *Geophys. Res. Lett.* **42,** no. 3, 765–772, doi: 10.1002/2014gl062782.

Audet, P., and H. Janiszewski (2020). OBStools: Software for processing broadband ocean-bottom seismic data, *Zenodo*, doi: 10.5281/zenodo.3905412.

Babcock, J. M., B. A. Kirkendall, and J. A. Orcutt (1994). Relationships between ocean bottom noise and the environment, *Bull. Seismol. Soc. Am.* **84,** no. 6, 1991–2007, doi: 10.1785/bssa0840061991.

Bell, S. W., D. W. Forsyth, and Y. Ruan (2015). Removing noise from the vertical component records of ocean-bottom seismometers: Results from year one of the Cascadia initiative, *Bull. Seismol. Soc. Am.* **105,** no. 1, 300–313, doi: 10.1785/0120140054.

Bensen, G. D., M. H. Ritzwoller, M. P. Barmin, A. L. Levshin, F. Lin, M. P. Moschetti, N. M. Shapiro, and Y. Yang (2007). Processing seismic ambient noise data to obtain reliable broad-band surface wave dispersion measurements, *Geophys. J. Int.* **169,** no. 3, 1239–1260.

Bohlen, T., S. Kugler, G. Klein, and F. Theilen (2004). 1.5D inversion of lateral variation of Scholte-wave dispersion Scholte-wave inversion, *Geophysics* **69,** no. 2, 330–344, doi: 10.1190/1.1707052.

Bowden, D. C., M. D. Kohler, V. C. Tsai, and D. S. Weeraratne (2016). Offshore Southern California lithospheric velocity structure from noise cross-correlation functions, *J. Geophys. Res.* doi: 10.1002/2016jb012919.

Crameri (2018). Scientific colour maps, *Zenodo*, doi: 10.5281/zenodo.1243862.

Crawford, W. C., and S. C. Webb (2000). Identifying and removing tilt noise from low-frequency (<0.1Hz) Seafloor vertical seismic data, *Bull. Seismol. Soc. Am.* 952–963.

Crawford, W. C., S. C. Webb, and J. A. Hildebrand (1991). Seafloor compliance observed by long-period pressure and displacement measurements, *J. Geophys. Res.* **96,** no. B10, 16,151–16,160, doi: 10.1029/91jb01577.

Crawford, W. C., S. C. Webb, and J. A. Hildebrand (1998). Estimating shear velocities in the oceanic crust from compliance measurements by two-dimensional finite difference modeling, *J. Geophys. Res.* **103,** no. B5, 9895–9916, doi: 10.1029/97jb03532.

Doran, A. K., and G. Laske (2020). Melt-affected ocean crust and uppermost mantle near Hawaii—Clues from ambient-noise phase velocity and seafloor compliance, *Geophys. J. Int.* **224,** no. 2, 843–857, doi: 10.1093/gji/ggaa470.

Eilon, Z. C., J. B. Gaherty, L. Zhang, J. Russell, S. McPeak, J. Phillips, D. W. Forsyth, and G. Ekström (2021). The Pacific OBS Research into Convecting Asthenosphere (ORCA) experiment, *Seismol. Res. Lett.* **93,** no. 1, 477–493, doi: 10.1785/0220210173.

Girard, A. J., J. Shragge, M. Danilouchkine, C. Udengaard, and S. Gerritsen (2024). Observations from the seafloor: Ultra-low-frequency ambient ocean-bottom nodal seismology at the Amendment field, *Geophys. J. Int.* **239,** no. 1, 17–36, doi: 10.1093/gji/ggae249.

Hable, S., K. Sigloch, E. Stutzmann, S. Kiselev, and G. Barruol (2019). Tomography of crust and lithosphere in the western Indian Ocean from noise cross-correlations of land and ocean bottom seismometers, *Geophys. J. Int.* **219,** no. 2, 924–944, doi: 10.1093/gji/ggz333.

Harmon, N., D. Forsyth, and S. Webb (2007). Using ambient seismic noise to determine short-period phase velocities and shallow shear velocities in young oceanic lithosphere, *Bull. Seismol. Soc. Am.* **97,** no. 6, 2009–2023, doi: 10.1785/0120070050.

Herrmann, R. B. (2013). Computer programs in seismology: An evolving tool for instruction and research, *Seismol. Res. Lett.* **84,** no. 6, 1081–1088, doi: 10.1785/0220110096.

Howe, B. M., M. Angove, J. Aucan, C. R. Barnes, J. S. Barros, N. Bayliff, N. C. Becker, F. Carrilho, M. J. Fouch, B. Fry, *et al.* (2022). SMART subsea cables for observing the earth and ocean, mitigating environmental hazards, and supporting the blue economy, *Front. Earth Sci.* **9,** doi: 10.3389/feart.2021.775544.

Janiszewski, H. A., J. B. Gaherty, G. A. Abers, H. Gao, and Z. C. Eilon (2019). Amphibious surface-wave phase-velocity measurements of the Cascadia subduction zone, *Geophys. J. Int.* **217,** no. 3, 1929–1948, doi: 10.1093/gji/ggz051.

Janiszewski, H. A., Z. Eilon, J. B. Russell, B. Brunsvik, J. B. Gaherty, S. G. Mosher, W. B. Hawley, and S. Coats (2023). Broad-band ocean bottom seismometer noise properties, *Geophys. J. Int.* **233,** no. 1, 297–315, doi: 10.1093/gji/ggac450.

Kawano, Y., T. Isse, A. Takeo, H. Kawakatsu, M. Morishige, H. Shiobara, N. Takeuchi, H. Sugioka, Y. Kim, H. Utada, *et al.* (2023). Seismic structure of the lithosphere-asthenosphere system beneath the oldest seafloor revealed by Rayleigh-wave dispersion analysis, *J. Geophys. Res.* **128,** no. 6, doi: 10.1029/2023jb026529.

Kelley, D. S., J. R. Delaney, and S. K. Juniper (2014). Establishing a new era of submarine volcanic observatories: Cabling axial seamount and the Endeavour segment of the Juan de Fuca Ridge, *Mar. Geol.* **352,** 426–450, doi: 10.1016/j.margeo.2014.03.010.

Kugler, S., T. Bohlen, T. Forbriger, S. Bussat, and G. Klein (2007). Scholte-wave tomography for shallow-water marine sediments, *Geophys. J. Int.* **168,** no. 2, 551–570, doi: 10.1111/j.1365-246x.2006.03233.x.

Le, B. M., T. Yang, Y. J. Chen, and H. Yao (2017). Correction of OBS clock errors using Scholte waves retrieved from cross-correlating hydrophone recordings, *Geophys. J. Int.* **212,** no. 2, 891–899, doi: 10.1093/gji/ggx449.

Lee, M. K., Y. J. Tan, J. B. Russell, M. Tolstoy, and F. Waldhauser (2024). Relative seismic velocity variations at axial seamount observed with ambient seismic noise capture transition point in volcanic inflation, *Geophys. Res. Lett.* **51,** no. 10, doi: 10.1029/2024gl108883.

Lin, F., M. D. Kohler, P. Lynett, A. Ayca, and D. S. Weeraratne (2015). The 11 March 2011 Tohoku tsunami wave front mapping across offshore Southern California, *J. Geophys. Res.* **120,** no. 5, 3350–3362, doi: 10.1002/2014jb011524.

Lin, P.-Y. P., J. B. Gaherty, G. Jin, J. A. Collins, D. Lizarralde, R. L. Evans, and G. Hirth (2016). High-resolution seismic constraints on flow dynamics in the oceanic asthenosphere, *Nature* **535,** no. 7613, 538–541, doi: 10.1038/nature18012.

Lior, I., E. D. Mercerat, D. Rivet, A. Sladen, and J.-P. Ampuero (2022). Imaging an underwater basin and its resonance modes using optical fiber distributed acoustic sensing, *Seismol. Res. Lett.* **93,** no. 3, 1573–1584, doi: 10.1785/0220210349.

Luo, Y., J. Xia, R. D. Miller, Y. Xu, J. Liu, and Q. Liu (2008). Rayleigh-Wave dispersive energy imaging using a high-resolution linear radon transform, *Pure Appl. Geophys.* **165,** no. 5, 903–922, doi: 10.1007/s00024-008-0338-4.

Luo, Y., Y. Yang, Y. Xu, H. Xu, K. Zhao, and K. Wang (2015). On the limitations of interstation distances in ambient noise tomography, *Geophys. J. Int.* **201,** no. 2, 652–661, doi: 10.1093/gji/ggv043.

Lynner, C., J. A. Van Avendonk, H. Bécel, A. Christeson, G. L. Dugan, B. Gaherty, J. B. Harder, S. Hornbach, M. J. Lizarralde, D. Long, *et al.* (2019). The Eastern North American margin community seismic experiment: An amphibious active- and passive-source dataset, *Seismol. Res. Lett.* **91,** no. 1, 533–540, doi: 10.1785/0220190142.

Ma, Y., R. W. Clayton, and D. Li (2016). Higher-mode ambient-noise Rayleigh waves in sedimentary basins, *Geophys. J. Int.* **206,** no. 3, 1634–1644, doi: 10.1093/gji/ggw235.

Mark, H. F., D. Lizarralde, J. A. Collins, N. C. Miller, G. Hirth, J. B. Gaherty, and R. L. Evans (2019). Azimuthal seismic anisotropy of 70-Ma Pacific-plate upper mantle, *J. Geophys. Res.* **79,** no. 26, 4011–4021, doi: 10.1029/2018jb016451.

McNamara, D. E., and R. P. Buland (2004). Ambient noise levels in the Continental United States, *Bull. Seismol. Soc. Am.* **94,** no. 4, 1517–1527, doi: 10.1785/012003001.

Nayak, A., and C. H. Thurber (2020). Using multicomponent ambient seismic noise cross-correlations to identify higher mode Rayleigh waves and improve dispersion measurements, *Geophys. J. Int.* **222,** no. 3, 1590–1605, doi: 10.1093/gji/ggaa270.

Nguyen, X. N., T. Dahm, and I. Grevemeyer (2009). Inversion of Scholte wave dispersion and waveform modeling for shallow structure of the Ninety east Ridge, *J. Seismol.* **13,** no. 4, 543–559, doi: 10.1007/s10950-008-9145-8.

Nolet, G., and L. M. Dorman (1996). Waveform analysis of Scholte modes in ocean sediment layers, *Geophys. J. Int.* **125,** no. 2, 385–396, doi: 10.1111/j.1365-246x.1996.tb00006.x.

Pawlowicz, R. (2020). M_Map: A mapping package for MATLAB, version 1.4m, available at www.eoas.ubc.ca/~rich/map.html (last accessed March 2025).

Phillips, J., J. Gaherty, J. Russell, Z. Eilon, D. Forsyth, and J. Byrnes (2023). Spatial variation in anisotropic shear velocity of old oceanic lithosphere-asthenosphere in the southwest pacific, *AGU Fall Meeting Abstracts*, San Francisco, California.

Pinzón, J. I., S. Custódio, G. Silveira, F. Krüger, J. Mata, and L. Matias (2023). Crustal and uppermost mantle structure near the Gloria Fault, North Atlantic, from ocean bottom seismometer surface wave observations, *Geophys. J. Int.* **236,** no. 1, 1–13, doi: 10.1093/gji/ggad405.

Ruan, Y., D. W. Forsyth, and S. Bell (2014). Marine sediment shear velocity structure from the ratio of displacement to pressure of Rayleigh waves at seafloor, *J. Geophys. Res.* doi: 10.1002/(issn)2169-9356.

Russell, J. B., and J. B. Gaherty (2021). Lithosphere structure and seismic anisotropy offshore Eastern North America: Implications for continental breakup and ultra-slow spreading dynamics, *J. Geophys. Res.* **126,** no. 12, doi: 10.1029/2021jb022955.

Russell, J. B., J. B. Gaherty, H. F. Mark, G. Hirth, L. N. Hansen, D. Lizarralde, J. A. Collins, and R. L. Evans (2022). Seismological evidence for girdled olivine lattice-preferred orientation in oceanic lithosphere and implications for mantle deformation processes during seafloor spreading, *Geochem. Geophys. Geosys.* **23,** no. 10, doi: 10.1029/2022gc010542.

Russell, J. B, J. B. Gaherty, P.-Y. P. Lin, D. Lizarralde, J. A. Collins, G. Hirth, and R. L. Evans (2019). High-resolution constraints on Pacific Upper Mantle Petrofabric inferred from surface-wave anisotropy, *J. Geophys. Res.* **124,** no. 1, 631–657, doi: 10.1029/2018jb016598.

Russell, J. B. (2021). Structure and evolution of the oceanic lithosphere-asthenosphere system from high-resolution surface-wave imaging, *Ph.D. Thesis*, Columbia University, doi: 10.7916/d8-33w6-f908.

Scholte, J. G. (1947). The range of existence of Rayleigh and Stoneley waves, *Geophys. J. Int.* **5,** 120–126, doi: 10.1111/j.1365-246x.1947.tb00347.x.

Shapiro, N. M., and M. Campillo (2004). Emergence of broadband Rayleigh waves from correlations of the ambient seismic noise, *Geophys. Res. Lett.* **31,** no. 7, doi: 10.1029/2004gl019491.

Shinohara, M., T. Yamada, K. Uehira, S. Sakai, H. Shiobara, and T. Kanazawa (2021). Development and operation of an ocean bottom cable seismic and tsunami (OBCST) observation system in the source region of the Tohoku-Oki earthquake, *Earth Space Sci.* **8,** no. 3, doi: 10.1029/2020ea001359.

Straume, E. O., C. Gaina, S. Medvedev, K. Hochmuth, K. Gohl, J. M. Whittaker, R. Abdul Fattah, J. C. Doornenbal, and J. R. Hopper (2019). GlobSed: Updated total sediment thickness in the World's Oceans, *Geochem. Geophys. Geosys.* **20,** no. 4, 1756–1772, doi: 10.1029/2018gc008115.

Takeo, A., H. Kawakatsu, T. Isse, K. Nishida, H. Sugioka, A. Ito, H. Shiobara, and D. Suetsugu (2016). Seismic azimuthal anisotropy in the oceanic lithosphere and asthenosphere from broadband surface wave analysis of OBS array records at 60 Ma seafloor, *J. Geophys. Res.* **121,** no. 3, 1927–1947, doi: 10.1002/2015jb012429.

Takeo, A., D. W. Forsyth, D. S. Weeraratne, and K. Nishida (2014). Estimation of azimuthal anisotropy in the NW Pacific from seismic ambient noise in seafloor records, *Geophys. J. Int.* **199,** no. 1, 11–22, doi: 10.1093/gji/ggu240.

Tanimoto, T., and L. Rivera (2005). Prograde Rayleigh wave particle motion, *Geophys. J. Int.* **162,** no. 2, 399–405, doi: 10.1111/j.1365-246x.2005.02481.x.

Tian, Y., and M. H. Ritzwoller (2017). Improving ambient noise cross-correlations in the noisy ocean bottom environment of the Juan de Fuca plate, *Geophys. J. Int.* **210,** no. 3, 1787–1805, doi: 10.1093/gji/ggx281.

Tomar, G., N. M. Shapiro, A. Mordret, S. C. Singh, and J.-P. Montagner (2016). Radial anisotropy in Valhall: Ambient noise-based studies of Scholte and Love waves, *Geophys. J. Int.* **208,** no. 3, 1524–1539, doi: 10.1093/gji/ggw480.

Toomey, D., R. Allen, A. Barclay, S. Bell, P. Bromirski, R. Carlson, X. Chen, J. A. Collins, R. P. Dziak, B. Evers, *et al.* (2014). The Cascadia initiative: A sea change in seismological studies of subduction zones, *Oceanography* **27,** no. 2, 138–150, doi: 10.5670/oceanog.2014.49.

Webb, S. C., and W. C. Crawford (2010). Shallow-Water_Broadband_OBS_Seismology.pdf, *Bull. Seismol. Soc. Am.* **100,** no. 4, 1770–1778, doi: 10.1785/0120090203.

Webb, S. C. (1992). The equilibrium oceanic microseism spectrum, *J. Acoust. Soc. Am.* **92,** no. 4, 2141–2158, doi: 10.1121/1.405226.

Webb, S. C. (1998). Broadband seismology and noise under the ocean, *Rev. Geophys.* **36,** no. 1, 105–142.

Williams, E. F., M. R. Fernández-Ruiz, R. Magalhaes, R. Vanthillo, Z. Zhan, M. González-Herráez, and H. F. Martins (2019). Distributed sensing of microseisms and teleseisms with submarine dark fibers, *Nat. Commun.* **10,** no. 1, 5778, doi: 10.1038/s41467-019-13262-7.

Wolf, F. N., D. Lange, A. Dannowski, M. Thorwart, W. Crawford, L. Wiesenberg, I. Grevemeyer, and H. Kopp (2021). 3D crustal structure of the Ligurian Basin revealed by surface wave tomography using ocean bottom seismometer data, *Solid Earth* **12,** no. 11, 2597–2613, doi: 10.5194/se-12-2597-2021.

Wolfe, C. J., S. C. Solomon, G. Laske, J. A. Collins, R. S. Detrick, J. A. Orcutt, D. Bercovici, and E. H. Hauri (2009). Mantle shear-wave velocity structure beneath the Hawaiian hot spot, *Science* **326,** no. 5958, 1388–1390, doi: 10.1126/science.1180165.

Yang, X., Y. Luo, H. Xu, and K. Zhao (2020). Shear wave velocity and radial anisotropy structures beneath the central Pacific from surface wave analysis of OBS records, *Earth Planet. Sci. Lett.* **534,** 116086, doi: 10.1016/j.epsl.2020.116086.

Yao, H., P. Gouédard, J. A. Collins, J. J. McGuire, and R. D. van der Hilst (2011). Structure of young East Pacific Rise lithosphere from ambient noise correlation analysis of fundamental- and higher-mode Scholte-Rayleigh waves, *C. R. Geosci.* **343,** nos. 8/9, 571–583, doi: 10.1016/j.crte.2011.04.004.

Yeck, W. L., A. F. Sheehan, J. C. Stachnik, and F.-C. Lin (2017). Offshore Rayleigh group velocity observations of the South Island, New Zealand, from ambient noise data, *Geophys. J. Int.* **209,** no. 2, 827–841, doi: 10.1093/gji/ggx054.

Zhu, J., and J. S. Popovics (2006). Analytical study of excitation and measurement of fluid-solid interface waves, *Geophys. Res. Lett.* **33,** L09603, doi: 10.1029/2006GL026068.

Manuscript received 25 March 2025
Published online 16 September 2025

Probing the Dead Sea Fault with the First Wireline-Free Hybrid DAS-Accelerometer Array in an Abandoned Well

Ariel Lellouch*[1] and Nadav Wetzler[2]

Abstract

We deployed the first-of-its-kind wireline-free collocated vertical distributed acoustic sensing (DAS) fiber and borehole accelerometer in a 750-m-deep abandoned oil well near the Dead Sea Fault, an active plate boundary. A dense active-source survey combining surface geophones and DAS reveals the dynamics of the DAS signal. We observe seismic phases with moderate-to-high signal-to-noise ratio in the fluid-filled section of the borehole. Prominent tube waves are visible in its open portion. First-arrival tomography, in conjunction with surface sources and geophones, indicates high near-surface velocities, consistent with logging reports of shallow high-velocity basaltic layer overlying more heterogeneous sedimentary sequences. Our 10-day-long temporary installation enabled the detection of multiple previously uncatalogued microearthquakes ($M_L \approx 1$), using a PhaseNet automatic phase picker manually validated by DAS data. These results demonstrate that low-effort vertical DAS deployments in abandoned boreholes can enhance seismic imaging and microseismic monitoring at active tectonic regions, offering a high-resolution complementary scope to traditional borehole sensors.

Cite this article as Lellouch, A., and N. Wetzler (2025). Probing the Dead Sea Fault with the First Wireline-Free Hybrid DAS-Accelerometer Array in an Abandoned Well, *Seismol. Res. Lett.* **97**, 1067–1077, doi: 10.1785/0220250179.

Supplemental Material

Introduction

Borehole seismometry provides an exceptional tool to filter natural and anthropogenic seismic noise, which mostly propagates as surface waves (Carter *et al.*, 1991; Peterson, 1993; Shapiro *et al.*, 2005). In addition to lower noise levels compared with surface sensors, the seismic signal improves thanks to a shorter source–receiver distance and the seismic wavefronts not traveling through the highly dissipative shallow subsurface. The improved signal-to-noise ratio (SNR) allows for the detection of faint subsurface events, well below the magnitude completeness level of regional seismic networks (Boettcher *et al.*, 2009; Kwiatek *et al.*, 2010; Prevedel *et al.*, 2015; Bohnhoff *et al.*, 2018; Hofstetter *et al.*, 2020), and potentially even detecting otherwise missed foreshocks (Malin *et al.*, 2018). Borehole seismometers also yield significantly more robust source parameter estimations (Abercrombie, 1995; Ide *et al.*, 2003; Stork and Ito, 2004; Lin *et al.*, 2012, 2016), mostly thanks to avoiding anelastic and scattering losses in the dissipative shallow subsurface (Bethmann *et al.*, 2012), which alter the frequency content of the upgoing seismic events.

The usage of borehole distributed acoustic sensing (DAS) for seismological studies has been shown in several recent studies (Lellouch *et al.*, 2021; Glubokovskikh *et al.*, 2023; Lellouch, 2024; Ma *et al.*, 2024; Nayak *et al.*, 2024), following its more extensive industry-driven use in monitoring microseismic activity during hydraulic stimulation (Stork *et al.*, 2020; Lellouch and Biondi, 2021; Huot *et al.*, 2022). DAS is a new sensing technology (Zhan, 2020; Lindsey and Martin, 2021) that transforms any optical fiber into a dense seismic array by means of optical time-domain interferometry (Hartog, 2017). Its main benefits are long-term resilience in harsh underground conditions, continuous measurement of the seismic wavefield along the entire borehole as opposed to discrete points, and a wide-frequency response that can span up to 17 octaves (Paitz *et al.*, 2021). Nonetheless, DAS also suffers from inherent limitations (Lellouch, 2024). First, it yields a unidirectional measurement along the direction of the fiber, as opposed to three-component inertial sensors. This limits the ability of event location and moment tensor estimation, depending on the specific well trajectory (Lellouch *et al.*, 2021; Shimony and Lellouch, 2024, 2025). When comparing a single measurement point in space, DAS measurements are significantly noisier than inertial sensors. DAS also measures strain or strain rate instead of particle displacement, velocity, or acceleration and does so over an average distance called the gauge length instead of a point measurement. These require the adaptations

1. Department of Geophysics, Tel Aviv University, Tel Aviv, Israel, https://orcid.org/0000-0002-9913-7191 (AL); 2. Geological Survey of Israel, Jerusalem, Israel, https://orcid.org/0000-0002-7552-0866 (NW)

*Corresponding author: ariellel@tauex.tau.ac.il

of traditional seismological methods (Lior *et al.*, 2021; Luo *et al.*, 2021; Lior, 2024; Nayak *et al.*, 2024) to DAS data. In cases of large strain, especially for long gauge lengths, saturation of the DAS measurements and ensuing loss of phase coherency might happen, depending on the phase unwrapping algorithm used in the optical interrogator (Willis *et al.*, 2019; Willis, 2022).

A particular challenge with DAS measurements is that their quality strongly depends on the fiber installation and coupling method. Most reported seismological studies using downhole DAS rely on behind-casing fibers, installed along the casing of the well before cementing (Hartog, 2020). These installations are costly and are contingent on drilling a new well. Significant efforts, mostly driven by the industry, have been made to leverage existing wells that are not equipped with fiber optics through temporary wireline-type deployments (Henninges *et al.*, 2021; Lellouch and Biondi, 2021; Martuganova *et al.*, 2022; Aldawood *et al.*, 2023). Whereas the SNR was much lower than for behind-casing installations, such setups have been used for active surveys and subsurface imaging after dedicated denoising procedures (Martuganova *et al.*, 2021).

The goal of our study is to test a relatively low-cost deployment of a wireline-free, hybrid, collocated DAS-borehole seismometer apparatus for seismological studies, aiming to leverage their individual strengths. We deployed a custom-made apparatus in an abandoned oil well drilled vertically more than 40 yr ago and located on the periphery of an active plate boundary. We show results from active imaging and passive monitoring, illustrating that even in seemingly unfavorable conditions, valuable data can be obtained. We also draw conclusions regarding the choice of well, installation method, and data processing, which would be valuable in planning future similar deployments.

Geological Background and Regional Seismicity

The Dead Sea Fault is a seismically active fault system representing the plate boundary between the African and the Sinai subplate. Geodetic measurements indicate a relatively low tectonic plate motion of 5 mm/yr (Sadeh *et al.*, 2012), which is consistent with the mean geological displacement of 105 km since the Miocene (Quennell, 1959; Freund *et al.*, 1970). The relatively low tectonic plate motion is compatible with a moderate seismicity rate of an average of one–two earthquakes per month above the completeness level M_w 2.1 (Engelberg *et al.*, 2025). With a single M 5 earthquake recorded within the region of the seismic network during the past 30 yr (Hofstetter *et al.*, 2008), hazard estimation is difficult to assess due to the narrow range of observable magnitudes in the earthquake catalog. During the past decade, few deep borehole seismometers were deployed along the Dead Sea Fault, including two seismometers in the Dead Sea basin (Hofstetter *et al.*, 2020), and two at the Kinneret basin (Hofstetter and Malin, 2018).

The Belvoir-1 oil well (Fig. 1) is located southeast of the Kokhav HaYarden National Park, operated by the Israel Nature and Parks Authority. The name of the well is taken from the archaeological site, the Belvoir Fortress, which was built by the Crusaders from the stones of earlier Israelite (twelfth century B.C.) and Jewish settlements (second and sixth centuries B.C.). The site is topographically elevated (at ~290 m above sea level), with a sharp incline from the eastward Jordan Valley at an elevation of −200 m (Fig. 1b). The borehole is ~7 km away from the Dead Sea Fault. Regional seismicity at the periphery of the Belvoir oil well is mostly localized along the Dead Sea Fault (Fig. 1a), with spatial clustering at the northwestern part of the Sea of Galilee, mostly associated with the 2018 earthquake sequence (Wetzler *et al.*, 2019).

The Belvoir-1 well has been associated with evidence of oil shows, indicating the potential presence of hydrocarbons, but it was ultimately classified as a dry hole (Belvoir-1 completion report). The borehole was drilled to a total depth of 2280 m, 85 m in the Upper Jurassic limestone, by the North America-Israel Oil Exploration, during March to June 1983. The extracted geological section presented stratigraphic units between the Quaternary, Neogene, Cretaceous, and Jurassic sediments. The top 60 m of the section includes the Pleistocene Cover Basalt. Below is the Pliocene–Upper Miocene Bira Formation (60–153 m), and underneath (153–313 m) is the Hordos Formation (Upper Miocene). Below is the Upper Miocene, Lower Basalt section (313–998 m) with interchanging basaltic lava flows. Below are the Santonian–Campanian (998–1002 m), Turonian–Cenomanian (dolomites, 1002–1275 m), and Lower Cretaceous (1275–2187 m) units, which are associated with the Judea Group (Kj; Fig. 1b). The repeated basalts indications are mostly associated with magmatic flow and intrusions from regional volcanic activity (Rozenbaum *et al.*, 2016). During the Miocene, tectonic and volcanic activity shaped the landscape, leading to the formation of the Lower Basalt, Umm Sabune, and Bira Formations (Fig. 1). In the Pliocene, cover basalt flows occurred alongside normal faulting, with post-Miocene tectonic processes uplifting the Galilee Mountains (Rozenbaum *et al.*, 2016). The repeated basalts observed in the lithological sections are expected to yield high seismic velocities in the region. Groundwater is mostly fed by rain precipitation, flowing eastward where they are drained by wellsprings at the valleys. Water level at the periphery of the Belvoir-1 well is associated with the southern Galilee aquifer with an average level of ~60 m above sea level (Fig. S1, available in the supplemental material to this article), or ~350 m below the wellhead.

Experimental Layout

We commissioned the design and manufacturing of a specialized hybrid fiber-optic and copper-wire cable that can withstand high pressures (Fig. S2). It was built by Teldor Inc. as 6 single-mode optical fibers, around which are 12 insulated copper conductors protected by double aramid braid reinforcement, steel braid armoring, and water-resistant jacketing. The cable was designed to withstand hydrostatic pressure down to

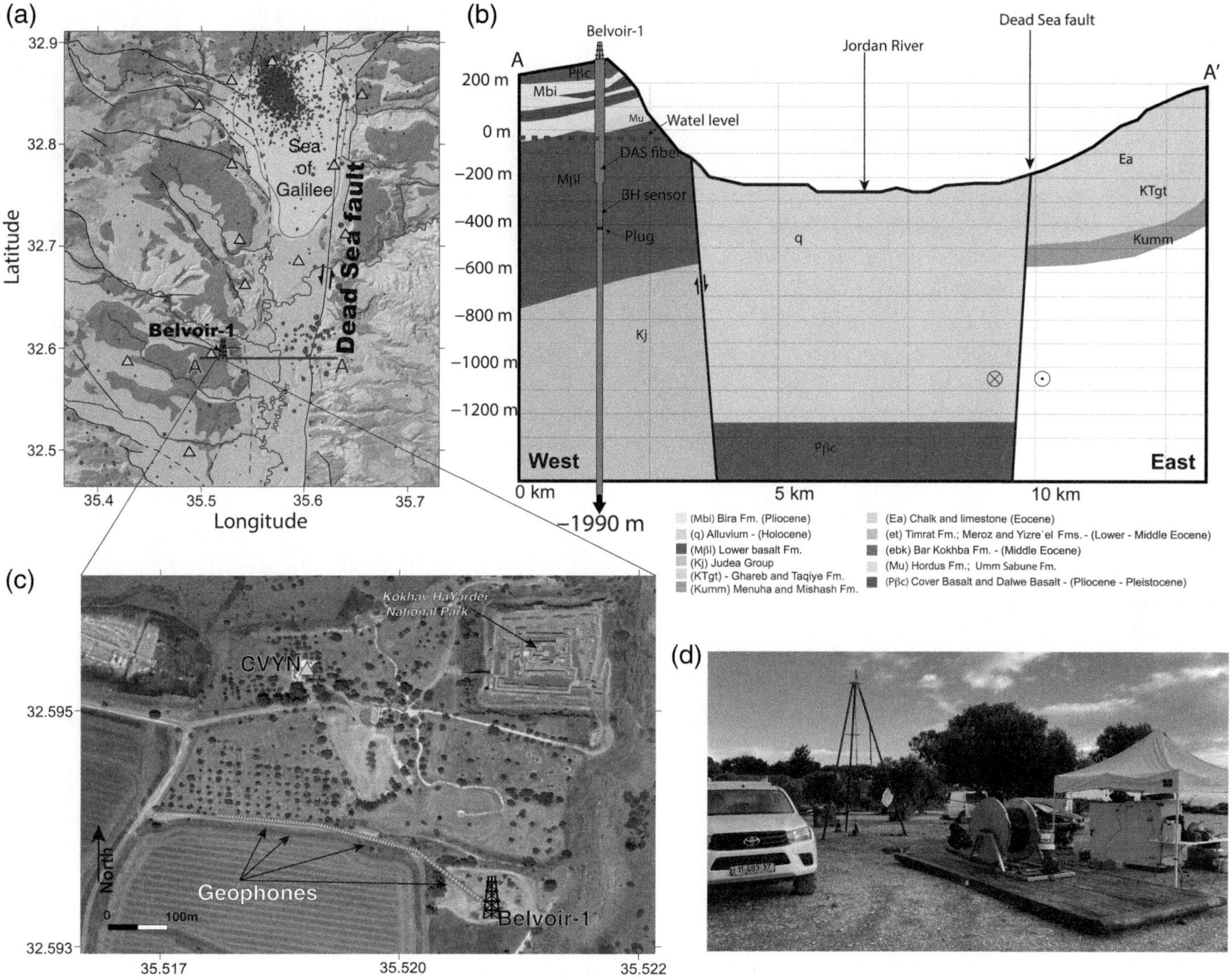

Figure 1. Regional to local view of the experiment. (a) Regional geological units are overlaid on a topographic map, with the regional seismicity in red dots, and mapped surface (solid dark lines) and subsurface (dashed dark lines) faults, following Sneh and Weinberger (2014). The Belvoir-1 oil well is marked by a green triangle, and the TRUAA seismic stations (Nof and Kurzon, 2020) are in yellow triangles. A cross section is taken along A–A′ (magenta). (b) Depth west–east cross section (A–A′) shows the main stratigraphic units at the periphery of the borehole (BH) following Möller *et al.* (2012). Main geological units are marked below. Depth is measured relative to sea level. The total depth of the Belvoir-1 well is 2280 m, with the wellhead at an elevation of 290 m. (c) Zoomed-in view of the experiment, with geophone and active source locations in yellow–green triangles. The nearby CVYN station is marked by a large yellow triangle. (d) Field photo of actual deployment and acquisition site. DAS, distributed acoustic sensing; Fm., formation. The color version of this figure is available only in the electronic edition.

1.5 km depth and support its own weight and that of the accelerometer. The cable was spooled on a wooden drum that we reinforced with steel plates and attached to a motor for lowering and retrieving the cable (see Fig. 1d). At one end of the cable, we attached a triaxial optical-interference accelerometer (model ABB, sensitivity of 60 V/g, manufactured by ASIR Inc.). We use a Centaur (Nanometrics) data logger at the surface after analog signal transmission through the cable. There is no wireline, and the apparatus was gravitationally pulled while maintaining tension using the cable drum. This significantly simplifies deployment operations and costs compared with industry solutions such as the one described in Henninges *et al.* (2021). The cable and attached accelerometer were lowered (Fig. S3) into the Belvoir-1 well, originally drilled to a total depth of 2280 m (Fig. 1a). Because of the regulations, the well was plugged at a depth of ~750 m from the wellhead, which is the reference depth we use throughout the article. The surface end of the cable was connected to a Silixa iDAS v. 2 interrogator, with a 1 m channel spacing and 10 m gauge length. Data were recorded at 500 Hz. The equipment was operational for about 10 days in November–December 2024, in a climate-controlled cabinet, with electric supply from the nearby national park visitor center. There is a strong-motion monitoring station (CVYN; Fig. 1c) that is part of the TRUAA network (Nof and Kurzon, 2020) located about 370 m away from the well.

The orientation of the downhole accelerometer is unknown. Because of severe electrical interference during the active survey, the known surface sources were poorly recorded by the accelerometer. We assume that the spooled cable was the major source of noise because it was located close to a power line. Therefore, we had to calibrate the accelerometer orientation using two catalogued earthquakes with known locations. We analyze horizontal hodograms from the onset *P*-wave arrival window, picked manually, and average their rotation matrices to yield a single rotation matrix (Fig. S4). We assume that the accelerometer is vertical, which is not necessarily correct but is only assumed for comparison between DAS and the vertical component of the accelerometer. Anyhow, the horizontal rotation is only approximately correct because it assumes no lateral velocity variation between the catalogued earthquakes and the borehole station, as well as the correct location of the earthquakes.

Active Survey and Imaging

The seismic survey was conducted along 100 locations spaced ~3 m apart along a general west-northwest azimuth (Fig. 1c). At each location, we deployed a three-component SmartSolo autonomous geophone and generated five acceleration-triggered accelerated weight drops (Fig. S5), which were later summed for improved SNR. This number was chosen based on the averaged number of shot points and available time window for active surveying. The same seismic survey was conducted twice. The first run was for a cable deployment down to a depth of ~600 m, for which the cable was under full tension. The second was after the downhole sensor had been lowered to its maximal depth. Thus, the tension on the cable decreased as the weight of the sensor was supported by the plug and sediments accumulated above it. We were continuously monitoring tension and immediately stopped the cable when the tension drop was detected by locking the rotating drum. Therefore, we expect introduced slack to be on the order of less than 1 m. However, the second survey suffered from significantly lower SNR, probably due to rain that affected source coupling, as well as triggering issues that prevented us from obtaining reliable timing for most of the shots. Thus, we show results from the cable under tension, down to ~600 m depth. Whereas we do not expect significant differences compared with the final acquisition configuration, additional tests are required for validation. Examples of common shot and receiver gathers are in Figure 2. There are very strong tube waves down to a depth of about 420 m, although their nature changes at about 350 m in terms of slope and phase continuity. For a source located 90 m away, the *S*-wave conversion is highly indicative of a change in the tube wave nature. Below 420 m, the first arrival is dominated by seismic arrivals that travel through the formation and not the borehole. Therefore, they are more visible at farther offsets, where there is better temporal separation between seismic and tube waves, as well as lower tube wave energy. For near-well shots (less than 30–40 m), it is impossible to clearly differentiate between the tube waves and direct arrivals. For most distant sources, the direct arrivals are faster than the tube waves and can be picked. Common receiver gathers indicate slight issues (<0.05 ms) with triggering timing. Figure S6 shows a common-shot gather for the survey in the final deployment configuration, with a clear signal of the direct downgoing *P* arrival down to ~675 m depth.

We conduct a *P*-wave, ray-based first-arrival travel-time tomography following Zhang and Toksöz (1998) using surface geophones and DAS, which minimizes travel-time differences between picked and predicted arrivals. For the 100 sources, we manually pick 3489 DAS and 4705 surface geophone travel times. All these picks are used for a 2D *P*-wave velocity inversion with a 2 × 2 m grid spacing. The initial model is chosen to be unrealistic with an extremely steep linear gradient $V_z = 500 + 25Z$ to avoid influencing the final solution. We also apply 2D smoothing (25 m in X, 4 m in Z) and recompute ray paths at each iteration. The resulting model and its interpretation (Fig. 2d) support the existence of cover basalt, manifesting as a high-velocity layer, in the near surface. Below it, low-velocity marl is visible, below which the velocity primarily increases, as expected from the geological structure. We note that tomography using solely surface geophones resolves the subsurface structure down to ~50 m, and the shallowest DAS pick is at about 420 m, due to masking by tube waves. We tried removing tube energy using simple frequency–wavenumber analysis but failed because the seismic signal has a similar velocity range. Despite the limited coverage of the 50–420 m depth range, the combination of the two data sets yields a geological reliable model. Using only the downhole DAS picks fails to resolve the structure above 420 m, and we thus conclude that the deployment of surface geophones is necessary.

Earthquake Monitoring

To detect small uncatalogued earthquakes, we apply a PhaseNet (Zhu and Beroza, 2019) automatic picking to the borehole accelerometer and several nearby surface strong-motion stations that are part of the TRUAA network (Nof and Kurzon, 2020), retaining picks with a confidence level ≥0.3. Picks undergo association and initial location with Gaussian Mixture Model Association (Zhu *et al.*, 2022). After manual inspection, we cross-validate detections with DAS data to reject erroneous events by visually confirming that the event propagates upward along the DAS fiber, indicating that they originate from a subsurface earthquake. We also estimate the local magnitude of these events based on the nearby CVYN station and the estimated event location. We chose not to use the borehole accelerometer as its coupling, inclination, and the transfer function of the borehole and plug, is unknown.

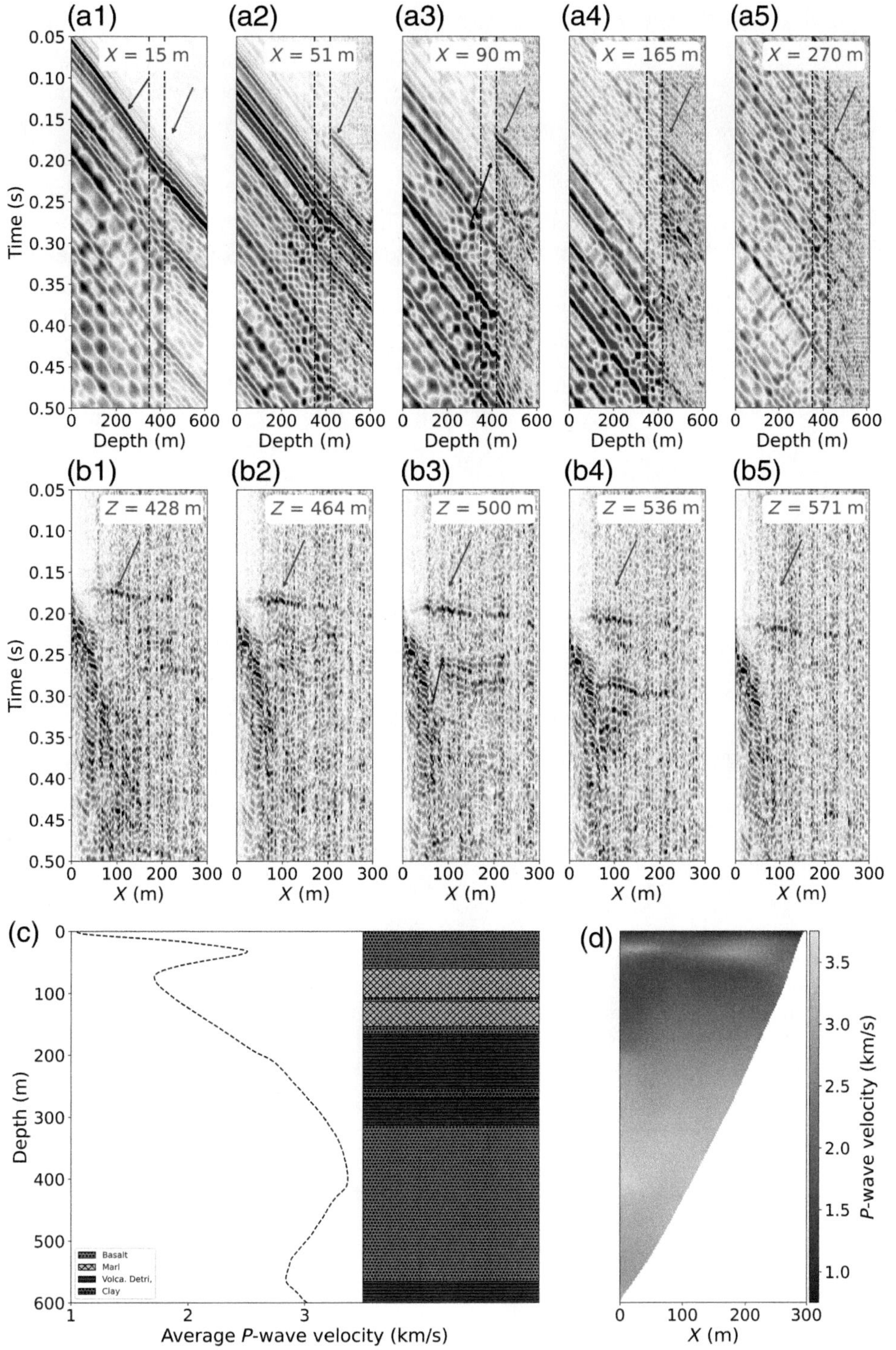

Figure 2. Active survey and imaging results. Depth measured from wellhead. (a1–a5) Common shot records, at increasing distances from the DAS borehole. The red arrows at fixed locations indicate the approximate timing of the first break. The purple arrow indicates the approximate location of tube waves in (a1). The blue arrow indicates a *P–S* conversion in (a3). Depths of 350 and 420 m, indicative of a change in the nature of tube waves, are marked in black dashed lines. (b1–b5) Common receiver gathers, for DAS channels at different depths. The red arrows at fixed locations indicate the approximate timing of the first break, which is clearly delayed with depth. The blue arrow indicates the *P–S* conversion. (c) Average velocity model derived from tomography (d), along with cuttings log information color coded by formation type. (d) 2D *P*-wave velocity tomography derived from surface geophones and downhole DAS. Volca. Detri; volcanic detritus. The color version of this figure is available only in the electronic edition.

The CVYN station is located ~340 m northwest of the wellhead and is equipped with a calibrated Nanometrics Titan strong-motion accelerometer, as a part of the TRUAA early warning system (Fig. 1c). Therefore, we use the CVYN station for magnitude estimation. We compute the local magnitude by double integration of the acceleration data to displacement followed by a conversion to a Wood–Anderson seismometer using the ObsPy simulation tool. The maximum amplitude of 20 s before and after the *S* arrival time (A) is used to compute $M_L = \log_{10}(A) + 1.11 \times \log_{10}(r) + 0.00189 \times 4 - 2.09$, in which A is measured in meters and r is the 3D distance from the earthquake, measured in kilometers. Although the coefficients of the formula are based on a specific region for southern California (Hutton and Boore, 1987), they provide a relatively reliable representation for the magnitude estimation. We apply an additional correction of the local site effects at CVYN that may bias estimations. We compare the computed M_L magnitude values at CVYN with the M_w magnitude values calculated by the Geological Survey of Israel using the entire network for earthquakes that have an SNR >1.5 at CVYN. We find that from the 5233 events recorded in the original catalog (black dots Fig. S9), 435 earthquakes were recorded at CVYN with SNR >1.5. By linear regression, we find that the M_L estimates at CVYN are systematically higher by 0.4 magnitude units (on average) compared with the M_w of the catalog, and use this value to

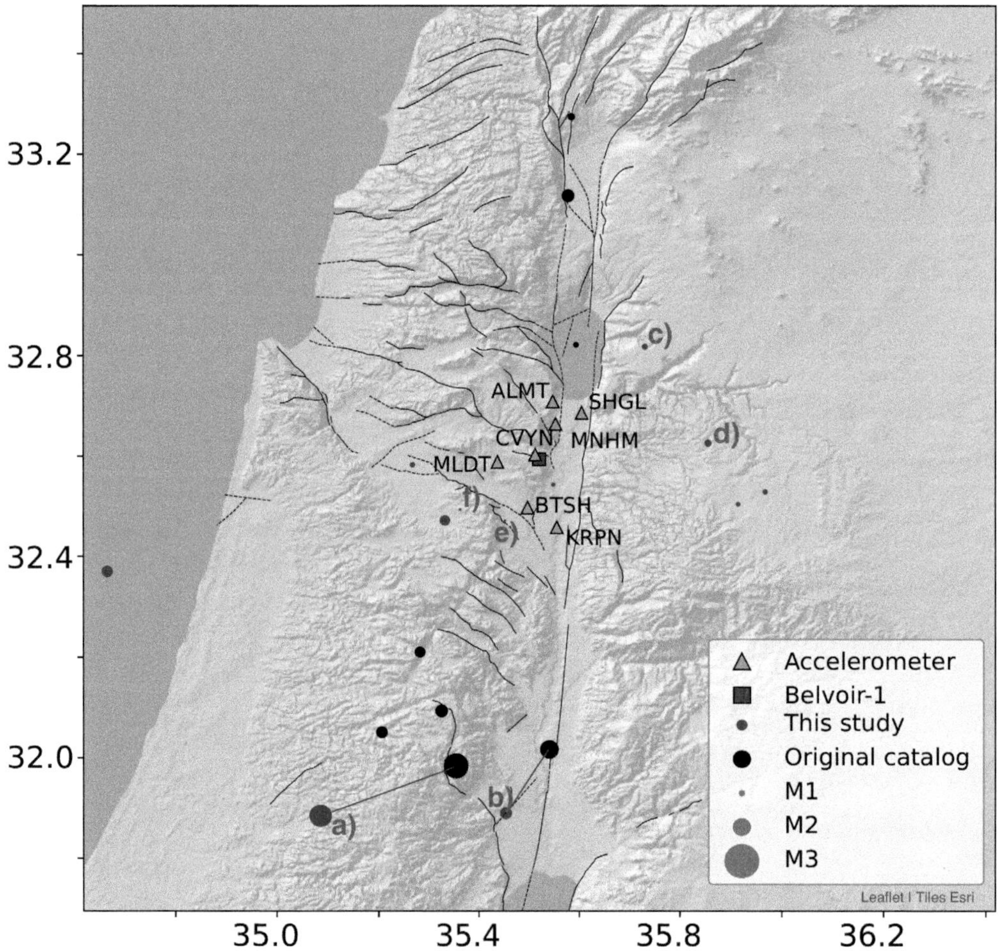

Figure 3. Seismic activity detected during the experiment by accelerometers (olive green triangles) and borehole accelerometer (green square). Validated earthquakes are in red and catalogued earthquakes are in black, along with their estimated location. If both exist, a red line connects the two points. Event sizes are proportional to the estimated local magnitude. Six earthquakes marked a)–f) are shown in detail in Figure 4. Solid lines denote faults visible at the surface and dashed lines denote inferred subsurface faults. The color version of this figure is available only in the electronic edition.

correct our M_L computed values (Fig. S7). In any case, we acknowledge that these values are only correct as a first approximations. We show validated events and their estimated magnitudes, all of which have been automatically detected in the borehole accelerometer, in Figure 3.

We show borehole records of several earthquakes in Figure 4. We compare DAS data (in strain-rate units) with the borehole accelerometer and nearby strong-motion accelerometer (in acceleration units). The scaling factor between strain rate and acceleration is phase velocity (Lellouch *et al.*, 2019), which we do not attempt to correct for due to difficulties in its precise measurement (Lior *et al.*, 2021). Therefore, whereas amplitude mismatches are possible, the kinematics are expected to match. We generate a single DAS channel from the stack of the 11 channels at depths 15–5 m above the borehole accelerometer. Therefore, the nominal vertical distance between the single DAS channel compared with the accelerometer is 10 m. We also note that the accelerometer is assumed to be vertical, which is not necessarily the case, whereas the DAS data are practically vertical. Overall, we observe a very good kinematic match between the deepest DAS channels and the vertical component of the downhole accelerometer (Fig. 4). More importantly, we can coherently track the seismic phases because they propagate along the borehole, with velocities that match the *P*- and *S*-wave velocities in the area.

In addition, as can be seen in the lower magnitude, uncatalogued events (Fig. 4c–f), there is visible, coherent, and temporally continuous noise that also propagates upward with velocities within the range of seismic waves. As it also shows, albeit relatively weaker, on the vertical component of the accelerometer, we are certain that it is not due to the DAS recording or fiber layout. We do not know its origin, but thanks to the DAS measurement, we know it is not a local, site-driven disturbance, which would show with a downward slope because it originates at the surface. We suspect that it is due to a nearby pump-storage hydroelectric station, located several kilometers away from the borehole because the noise pattern is irregular over the duration of the experiment and can be potentially tied to pumping or unloading phases.

Discussion

We propose a cost-efficient solution for borehole deployments. Whereas previous studies have shown similar deployments over wireline, we suggest the simplest possible deployment in which only the cable itself, used for sensing and power, is lowered into the borehole. Whereas data quality may be lower than what can be achieved over wireline, which can also support an accelerometer string instead of a single sensor, we believe that our approach is valuable for academic groups around the world.

Active surveying was conducted with two different deployment configurations. Both cases, including cable under full

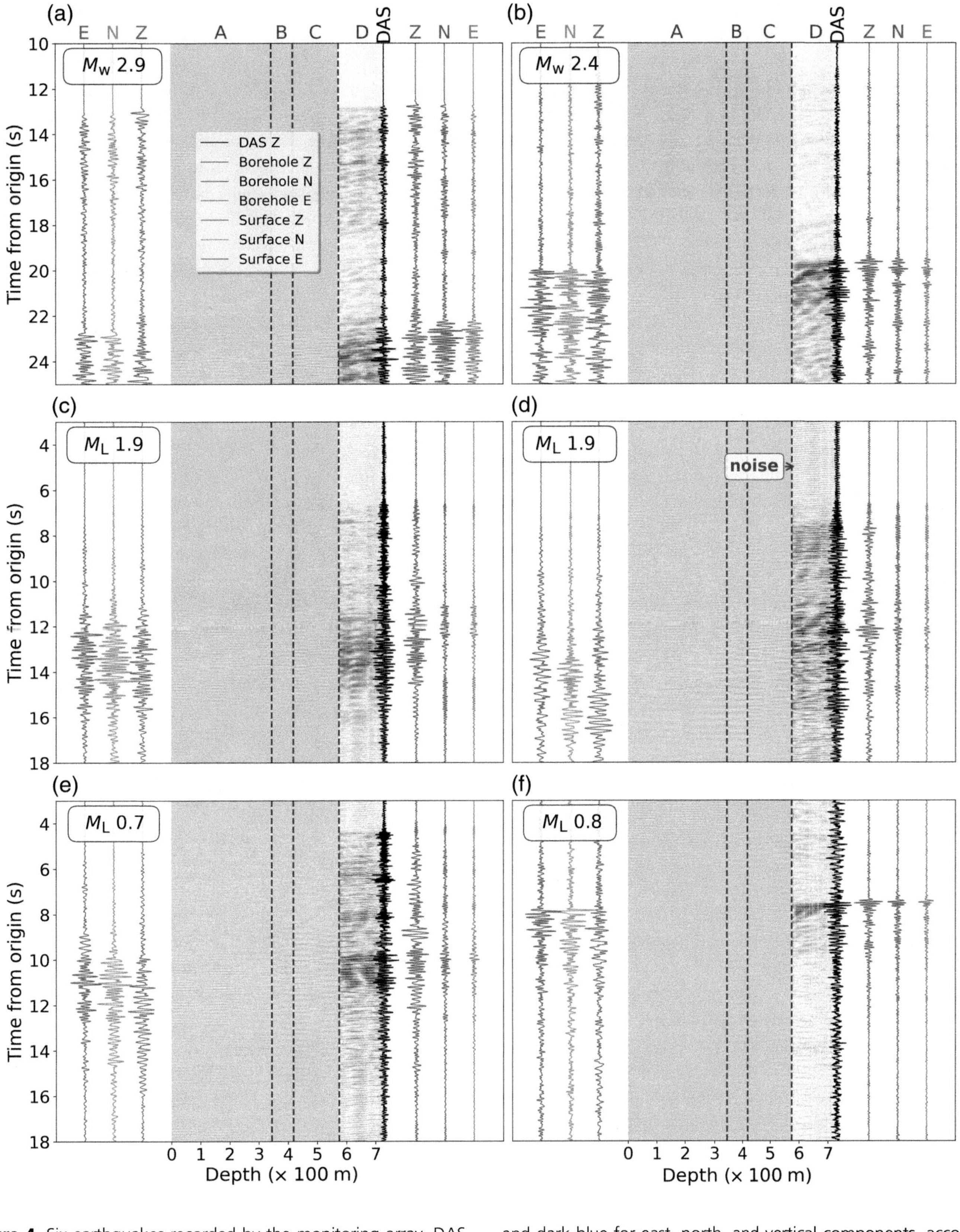

Figure 4. Six earthquakes recorded by the monitoring array. DAS data are shown only for 575 m and deeper (section D—see the Discussion section). The colored background shows strain-rate measurements, with areas of poor coupling grayed out. A single average DAS channel is in black. The rotated borehole accelerometer is in blue, red, and pink for vertical, north, and east, accordingly. The nearby CVYN station is in magenta, dark red, and dark blue for east, north, and vertical components, accordingly. (a,b) Catalogued events with known moment magnitude M_w. Events (c–f) are uncatalogued, and we denote their estimated M_L. An example of coherent noise is marked in (d). The dashed green lines separate the DAS data into four sections, A–D. The color version of this figure is available only in the electronic edition.

tension and accelerometer reaching the plugged section of the well, show that the DAS coupling in a vertical well can be obtained in the fluid-filled section. In the dry section of the borehole, we obtained only very weak signals in certain strong earthquakes, but it is generally less useful due to the prominence of tube waves. We note that it is also possible to achieve coupling through the imperfect vertical nature of the borehole (Fichtner *et al.*, 2025). In this study, for which the borehole inclination is unknown, the presence of fluid played a major part in improving the coupling between cable and borehole, leading to a drastic improvement in the quality of seismic data.

For reasons that are still unknown to us, we encountered coupling issues during the passive monitoring phase at intermediate DAS depths, after the accelerometer was deployed to its maximal depth. Because these issues were not present during the active surveying, conducted ~12 hr before the first recorded earthquake, it is difficult to study their cause. One potential reason is that the deployment along a cliff significantly influences the upgoing wavefronts reaching the array and that upgoing/downgoing waves behave differently. Alternatively, the coupling of the DAS cable itself, rather than geological or borehole conditions, may have temporally changed. We observe through low-frequency DAS analysis (Text S1) a period of ~12 hr after deployment in which strong, low-frequency signals originating at or below the bottom of the cable appear in the records (Figs. S8–S10), with the first 3–4 hr being the most dominant. These events have propagation velocities of meters per second or less and frequencies of below 0.01 Hz. They subsided 12–24 hr after deployment, after which they reach a relatively stable rhythm of an event every few hours. We do not know the origin of these events but attribute them at least partially to the cable deployment process, which requires a stabilization time after the bottom of the well is reached. For further examination of the noise patterns, we separate the DAS array into four main sections, as shown in the unmasked version of Figure 4a in Figure S11. The phase behavior in section C includes unexplained polarity flips and a very high apparent propagation velocity that likely exceeds that of seismic wave propagation through geological formations. Section B exhibits plausible moveouts, but the arrival time at 419 m appears to be earlier than that at 575 m (bottom of section D), again indicating that wave propagation in the 419–575 m range cannot be explained by seismic wave propagation through geological formations. Section A is generally contaminated by tube waves, although some arrivals can be seen in its deeper section. Overall, we conclude that direct lowering of the recording apparatus yielded good coupling between 575 m and the maximal depth, poor coupling at depths of 419–575 m, and reasonable coupling at ~344 m (water table, consistent with Fig. S1) to 419 m. Nonetheless, because we cannot explain the wave propagation in the 419–575 m range, we discard the 344–419 m range from further analysis. We know from cuttings log about a sharp lithological transition around 565 m, from basalts (above) to weathered volcanic rocks (below). It could thus potentially explain high-velocity moveouts at depths of 419–575 m, but not their polarity flips or the timing of arrivals in section B, which appear to precede section D. Whereas we cannot draw definite conclusions on the reasons for poor coupling in some portions of the well, which could also be due to the specific borehole location near a cliff, we do recommend to closely monitor cable behavior in the 12–24 hr following the deployment. A single active survey is not a sufficient guarantee because it appears that cable movements have significantly altered coupling. Instead, we recommend conducting a survey of several shot points, ideally located 50–100 m away from the well, to detect changes in fiber coupling over time and potentially readjust the deployment if needed.

Deploying an analog accelerometer proved to be a significant issue. Whereas we cannot directly quantify signal loss along the cable, the amount of electrical noise picked up by the drum-mounted cable was significant, both due to nearby power grid transmission lines and the current used for alimentation of the experimental setup, especially during active surveys. Whenever possible, we recommend using a downhole data logger, fed by electric wires but with data transfer via one of the fiber-optic strands.

The resulting 2D tomography model from active imaging using surface geophones and downhole DAS is consistent with the general subsurface geology surrounding the borehole. The immediate surface layer consists primarily of basalts and tuffs, associated with the Pleistocene Cover basalt, which in this region reaches a thickness of ~100 m. The tomographic results reveal a relatively high *P*-wave velocity, which sharply increases to ~2.2 km/s at a depth of 50 m, marking the transition into a more coherent basalt. This measured velocity is significantly lower than the regional averages reported for thicker basalt sequences in the central and northern Golan Heights, where basalt layers exceed 800–1100 m in thickness and exhibit velocities in the range of 4–5 km/s (Meiler *et al.*, 2011). In contrast, basalts in the southern Golan, where thicknesses are typically much lower (tens to a few hundred meters), show velocities between 3–3.5 km/s. The relatively low velocity observed in our model likely reflects the thin and possibly weathered or heterogeneous fracturing of the basalt at this location. This pattern is consistent with regional trends that show seismic velocity increases with basalt thickness, due to greater compaction, structural coherence, and lithologic continuity in thicker sequences.

Overall, there is relatively sparse seismic activity during the experiment, due to the relatively low tectonic rate of the Dead Sea Fault, commending longer recording campaigns. Nonetheless, passive monitoring results show the benefits of hybrid DAS–accelerometer monitoring. We were able to quickly detect uncatalogued events using the downhole accelerometer, leveraging a machine learning-based approach. With DAS, we can directly validate the seismic nature of the events and rule out inconsistent picks erroneously attributed by automatic processing. In more detailed analysis, DAS data can help separate secondary *P* and *S* phases based on their slope because they propagate upward through the array, which is impossible to do using a single accelerometer. Whereas in this study the recording segment was rather short, the quality of such separation increases with DAS depth coverage. We emphasize that automatic detection was carried out using a combination of nearby accelerometer stations and the borehole accelerometer. Therefore, events had to be above the detection threshold in at least one surface station. However, detection with only the borehole accelerometer is also possible and can potentially extend the range of detectable earthquakes even farther than this study, at the cost of having to filter out more local noise events. Validating through DAS data would be mandatory in such cases. It is also possible to apply the detection on DAS data using either beamforming or channel-by-channel picking approaches (Lellouch *et al.*, 2021; Zhu *et al.*, 2023), in conjunction with accelerometer data processing. Given longer recording periods, template matching methods (Ross *et al.*, 2019) would be invaluable, especially when combining DAS and accelerometer data. So far, we have not applied this approach due to coherent noise patterns that have phase arrivals similar to earthquakes.

Estimating the magnitude of uncatalogued events is challenging due to unknown and probably frequency-dependent coupling of borehole accelerometer and DAS, and relatively short recording period, which does not allow for sufficient statistical regression using catalogued earthquakes. Therefore, we had to use a nearby surface station. Based on available data, we can detect uncatalogued local earthquakes with magnitudes in the range of $M_L 0.5 - 2$, although there is significant uncertainty in the estimation and insufficient data to estimate statistically significant magnitude constraints.

The active surveying plays an important role in calibrating the orientation of the downhole accelerometer. In this study, electrical interference invalidated this option, although all sources were strong enough to be visible along the vertical component. We rotate the accelerometer to the best of our ability using two catalogued earthquakes, but we do not judge it sufficiently accurate because they are quite distant. More catalogued earthquakes would be helpful in better constraining the rotation process but are not expected to be as good as an active survey calibration. Once the orientation, ideally in both azimuth and dip, is established, the combination of DAS and downhole accelerometer can be used for location. The DAS data can reliably estimate event dip assuming knowledge of the velocity model, obtained from active surveying (Lellouch *et al.*, 2019), whereas the borehole accelerometer can reasonably estimate dip and azimuth based on hodogram analysis.

We conclude that whereas this first-of-its-kind deployment has its shortcomings, along with experimental errors, hybrid deployment in abandoned wells is possible thanks to fluid-induced coupling. The acquired data, although statistically limited, indicate that they can push the boundaries of low-magnitude seismology. Longer recording periods, ideally recording in multiple boreholes and in conjunction with dense surface arrays, are necessary to quantify the benefits more accurately. Nonetheless, the economic viability of this approach makes it attractive for medium-size research projects. Whereas borehole access can be challenging depending on the region, relatively shallow wells drilled for hydrological or mining purposes can also be leveraged for such deployments, in addition to abandoned exploration wells.

Data and Resources

Seismic data, auxiliary information, and existing catalogs are provided by the Geological Survey of Israel. They can be accessed using standard ObsPy routines with the client defined as https://seis.gsi.gov.il/ (last accessed July 2025) and station code BLVR for the borehole accelerometer. Distributed acoustic sensing (DAS) data used for the active imaging and plotting of Figure 4 can be accessed via Lellouch (2025). Additional figures about the experiment, calibration, and extended data analysis are in the supplemental material.

Declaration of Competing Interests

The authors acknowledge that there are no conflicts of interest recorded.

Acknowledgments

The authors are grateful to the Geological Survey of Israel (GSI) for the incorporation of this temporary deployment into the TRUAA seismic network. The authors thank Pavel Sinitsyn for his valuable help with planning, fieldwork, and active data processing. The authors are grateful to Moshe Reshef for valuable discussions, advice, and generously sharing geophysical equipment. Aleksei Nelaev helped with geological interpretation and active data processing. The authors thank Omer Shamir, Jonathan Levy, Shachar Yahav, and Uri Wygodny for their help in fieldwork. The authors thank the technical team of the GSI, and specifically Pavel Portnov, for the connections of the cable with the borehole sensor, Alex Shvartsburg and Vadim Giller for field assistance, and Avi Bar-Natan and Andrey Polozov for coordination, telemetry, and data storing. The authors thank Yuval Moran from the Kokhav HaYarden National Park, the Israel Nature and Parks Authority, for providing them access and electricity. The authors also thank the Nuclear Research Center for their financial support and Yael Radziner and Dorian Golriz for useful discussions and field assistance during the experiment. This research was supported by the Israeli Science Foundation under Grant Number 2775/21. This study was supported by the Israeli government under GSI Dead Sea Project 40946.

References

Abercrombie, R. E. (1995). Earthquake source scaling relationships from −1 to 5 M using seismograms recorded at 2.5-km depth, *J. Geophys. Res.* **100,** no. B12, 24,015–24,036.

Aldawood, A., A. Shaiban, E. Alfataierge, and A. Bakulin (2023). Acquiring and processing deep dual-well DAS walkaway VSP in an onshore desert environment, *The Leading Edge* **42,** no. 10, 676–682.

Bethmann, F., N. Deichmann, and P. Martin Mai (2012). Seismic wave attenuation from borehole and surface records in the top 2.5 km beneath the city of Basel, Switzerland, *Geophys. J. Int.* **190,** no. 2, 1257–1270.

Boettcher, M. S., A. McGarr, and M. Johnston (2009). Extension of Gutenberg-Richter distribution to MW -1.3, no lower limit in sight, *Geophys. Res. Lett.* **36,** no. 10.

Bohnhoff, M., P. Malin, J. ter Heege, J.-P. Deflandre, and C. Sicking (2018). Suggested best practice for seismic monitoring and characterization of non-conventional reservoirs, *First Break* **36,** no. 2, 59–64.

Carter, J. A., N. Barstow, P. W. Pomeroy, E. P. Chael, and P. J. Leahy (1991). High-frequency seismic noise as a function of depth, *Bull. Seismol. Soc. Am.* **81,** no. 4, 1101–1114.

Engelberg, S., N. Wetzler, and A. Agnon (2025). Earthquake swarms and seismic gaps along the Dead Sea fault system. *Seismol. Res. Lett.* **96,** no. 4, doi: 10.1785/0220240414.

Fichtner, A., C. Hofstede, B. L. N. Kennett, A. Svensson, J. Westhoff, F. Walter, J.-P. Ampuero, E. Cook, D. Zigone, D. Jansen, and O. Eisen (2025). Hidden cascades of seismic ice stream deformation, *Science* **387,** no. 6736, 858–864.

Freund, R., Z. Garfunkel, I. Zak, M. Goldberg, T. Weissbrod, B. Derin, F. Bender, F. E. Wellings, and R. W. Girdler (1970). The shear along the Dead Sea rift [and Discussion]. *Phil. Trans. Roy. Soc. Lon. A* **267,** no. 1181, 107–130.

Glubokovskikh, S., P. Shashkin, S. Shapiro, B. Gurevich, and R. Pevzner (2023). Multiwell fiber optic sensing reveals effects of CO2 flow on triggered seismicity, *Seismol. Res. Lett.* **94,** no. 5, 2215–2230.

Hartog, A. H. (2017). *An Introduction to Distributed Optical Fibre Sensors*, CRC Press, Boca Raton, Florida.

Hartog, A. H. (2020). Distributed sensors in the oil and gas industry, in I. D. Villar and I. R. Matias (Editors), *Optical Fibre Sensors,* John Wiley & Sons, 151–191.

Henninges, J., E. Martuganova, M. Stiller, B. Norden, and C. M. Krawczyk (2021). Wireline distributed acoustic sensing allows 4.2 km deep vertical seismic profiling of the Rotliegend 150°C geothermal reservoir in the North German basin, *Solid Earth* **12,** no. 2, 521–537.

Hofstetter, R., and P. E. Malin (2018). Dead Sea Fault area microearthquake observations from 4 borehole stations, *AGU Annual Meeting*, S11D-0386.

Hofstetter, R., Y. Gitterman, V. Pinsky, N. Kraeva, and L. Feldman (2008). Seismological observations of the northern Dead Sea basin earthquake on 11 February 2004 and its associated activity, *Isr. J. Earth Sci.* **57,** no. 2, 101–124.

Hofstetter, R., P. Malin, and Z. Ben-Avraham (2020). Seismic observations of microearthquakes from the Masada deep borehole, *Seismol. Res. Lett.* **91,** no. 4, 2298–2309.

Huot, F., A. Lellouch, P. Given, B. Luo, R. G. Clapp, T. Nemeth, K. T. Nihei, and B. L. Biondi (2022). Detection and characterization of microseismic events from fiber-optic DAS data using deep learning, *Bull. Seismol. Soc. Am.* **93,** no. 5, 2543–2553.

Hutton, L. K., and D. M. Boore (1987). The ml scale in southern California, *Bull. Seismol. Soc. Am.* **77,** no. 6, 2074–2094.

Ide, S., G. C. Beroza, S. G. Prejean, and W. L. Ellsworth (2003). Apparent break in earthquake scaling due to path and site effects on deep borehole recordings, *J. Geophys. Res.* **108,** no. B5.

Kwiatek, G., K. Plenkers, M. Nakatani, Y. Yabe, G. Dresen, and JAGUARS- Group (2010). Frequency-magnitude characteristics down to magnitude −4.4 for induced seismicity recorded at Mponeng Gold Mine, South Africa, *Bull. Seismol. Soc. Am.* **100,** no. 3, 1165–1173.

Lellouch, A. (2024). Seismological applications of downhole distributed acoustic sensing, in *Distributed Acoustic Sensing in Borehole Geophysics*, 431–443, American Geophysical Union (AGU), New Jersey, U.S.A.ISBN 978-1-394-17927-5.

Lellouch, A. (2025). Raw DAS data for GRL paper submission [Data set], *Zenodo* doi: 10.5281/zenodo.15396449.

Lellouch, A., and B. L. Biondi (2021). Seismic applications of downhole DAS, *Sensors* **21,** no. 9, 2897.

Lellouch, A., R. Schultz, N. J. Lindsey, B. L. Biondi, and W. L. Ellsworth (2021). Low-magnitude seismicity with a downhole distributed acoustic sensing array—Examples from the FORGE geothermal experiment, *J. Geophys. Res.* **126,** no. 1, e2020JB020462.

Lellouch, A., S. Yuan, W. L. Ellsworth, and B. Biondi (2019). Velocity-based earthquake detection using downhole distributed acoustic sensing—Examples from the San Andreas fault observatory at depth, *Bull. Seismol. Soc. Am.* **109,** no. 6, 2491–2500.

Lin, Y.-Y., K.-F. Ma, H. Kanamori, T.-R. Alex Song, N. Lapusta, and V. C. Tsai (2016). Evidence for non-self-similarity of microearthquakes recorded at a Taiwan borehole seismometer array, *Geophys. J. Int.* **206,** no. 2, 757–773.

Lin, Y.-Y., K.-F. Ma, and V. Oye (2012). Observation and scaling of microearthquakes from the Taiwan Chelungpu-fault borehole seismometers, *Geophys. J. Int.* **190,** no. 1, 665–676.

Lindsey, N. J., and E. R. Martin (2021). Fiber-optic seismology, *Annu. Rev. Earth Planet. Sci.* 309–336.

Lior, I. (2024). Accurate magnitude and stress drop using the spectral ratios method applied to distributed acoustic sensing, *Geophys. Res. Lett.* **51,** no. 1, e2023GL105153, doi: 10.1029/2023GL105153.

Lior, I., A. Sladen, D. Mercerat, J.-P. Ampuero, D. Rivet, and S. Sambolian (2021). Strain to ground motion conversion of distributed acoustic sensing data for earthquake magnitude and stress drop determination, *Solid Earth* **12,** no. 6, 1421–1442.

Luo, B., G. Jin, and F. Stanek (2021). Near-field strain in distributed acoustic sensing-based microseismic observation, *Geophysics* **86,** no. 5, P49–P60.

Ma, K.-F., S. von Specht, L.-W. Kuo, H.-H. Huang, C.-R. Lin, C.-J. Lin, C.-S. Ku, E.-S. Wu, C.-Y. Wang, W.-Y. Chang, and P. Jousset (2024). Broad-band strain amplification in an asymmetric fault zone observed from borehole optical fiber and core, *Commun. Earth Environ.* **5,** no. 1, 1–13.

Malin, P. E., M. Bohnhoff, F. Blümle, G. Dresen, P. Martínez-Garzón, M. Nurlu, U. Ceken, F. T. Kadirioglu, R. F. Kartal, T. Kilic, and K. Yanik (2018). Microearthquakes preceding a M 4.2 earthquake offshore Istanbul, *Sci Rep* **8,** no. 1, 16,176.

Martuganova, E., M. Stiller, K. Bauer, J. Henninges, and C. M. Krawczyk (2021). Cable reverberations during wireline distributed acoustic sensing measurements: Their nature and methods for elimination, *Geophys. Prospect.* **69,** no. 5, 1034–1054.

Martuganova, E., M. Stiller, B. Norden, J. Henninges, and Charlotte M. Krawczyk (2022). 3D deep geothermal reservoir imaging with wire-line distributed acoustic sensing in two boreholes, *Solid Earth* **13,** no. 8, 1291–1307.

Meiler, M., M. Reshef, and H. Shulman (2011). Seismic depth-domain stratigraphic classification of the Golan Heights, central Dead Sea Fault, *Tectonophysics* **510,** no. 3, 354–369.

Möller, P., C. Siebert, S. Geyer, N. Inbar, E. Rosenthal, A. Flexer, and M. Zilberbrand (2012). Relationship of brines in the Kinnarot Basin, Jordan-Dead Sea Rift Valley, *Geofluids* **12,** no. 2, 166–181.

Nayak, A., J. Correa, and J. Ajo-Franklin (2024). Seismic magnitude estimation using low-frequency strain amplitudes recorded by DAS arrays at far-field distances, *Bull. Seismol. Soc. Am.* **114,** no. 4, 1818–1838.

Nof, R. N., and I. Kurzon (2020). TRUAA—Earthquake early warning system for Israel: Implementation and current status, *Seismol. Res. Lett.* **92,** no. 1, 325–341.

Paitz, P., P. Edme, D. Gräff, F. Walter, J. Doetsch, A. Chalari, C. Schmelzbach, and A. Fichtner (2021). Empirical investigations of the instrument response for distributed acoustic sensing (Das) across 17 octaves, *Bull. Seismol. Soc. Am.* **111,** 1, 1–10.

Peterson, J. R. (1993). Observations and modeling of seismic background noise, *Technical Report*, U.S. Geological Survey.

Prevedel, B., F. Bulut, M. Bohnhoff, C. Raub, R. F. Kartal, F. Alver, and P. E. Malin (2015). Downhole geophysical observatories: Best installation practices and a case history from Turkey, *Int. J. Earth Sci.* **104,** no. 6, 1537–1547.

Quennell, A. M. (1959). Tectonics of the Dead Sea rift, *Proc. 20th International Geological Congress*, Mexico, 385–403.

Ross, Z. E., D. T. Trugman, E. Hauksson, and P. M. Shearer (2019). Searching for hidden earthquakes in southern California, *Science* **771,** 767–771.

Rozenbaum, A. G., A. Sandler, E. Zilberman, M. Stein, B. R. Jicha, and B. S. Singer (2016). 40Ar/39Ar chronostratigraphy of late Miocene-early Pliocene continental aquatic basins in SE Galilee, Israel, *GSA Bulletin* **128,** nos. 9/10, 1383–1402.

Sadeh, M., Y. Hamiel, A. Ziv, Y. Bock, P. Fang, and S. Wdowinski (2012). Crustal deformation along the Dead Sea transform and the Carmel fault inferred from 12 years of GPS measurements, *J. Geophys. Res.* **117,** no. B8.

Shapiro, N. M., M. Campillo, L. Stehly, and M. H. Ritzwoller (2005). High-resolution surface-wave tomography from ambient seismic noise, *Science* **307,** no. 5715, 1615–1618.

Shimony, E., and A. Lellouch (2024). Microseismic event location with dual vertical DAS arrays: Insights from the FORGE 2022 stimulation, *Seismol. Res. Lett.* **95,** no. 4, 2290–2304.

Shimony, E., and A. Lellouch (2025). Wave equation moment tensor inversion of microseismic events using multiwell distributed acoustic sensing recording, *Geophysics* **90,** no. 3, L99–L114.

Sneh, A., and R. Weinberger (2014). *Major Geological Structures of Israel and Environs, 1: 500,000 Scale*, Geological Survey of Israel, Jerusalem.

Stork, A. L., and H. Ito (2004). Source parameter scaling for small earthquakes observed at the western Nagano 800-m-deep borehole, Central Japan, *Bull. Seismol. Soc. Am.* **94,** no. 5, 1781–1794.

Stork, A. L., A. F. Baird, S. A. Horne, G. Naldrett, S. Lapins, J.-M. Kendall, J. Wookey, J. P. Verdon, A. Clarke, and A. Williams (2020). Application of machine learning to microseismic event detection in distributed acoustic sensing data, *Geophysics* **85,** no. 5, KS149–KS160.

Wetzler, N., E. Shalev, T. Göbel, F. Amelung, I. Kurzon, V. Lyakhovsky, and E. E. Brodsky (2019). Earthquake swarms triggered by groundwater extraction near the Dead Sea fault, *Geophys. Res. Lett.* **46,** no. 14, 8056–8063.

Willis, M. E. (2022). *Distributed Acoustic Sensing for Seismic Measurements - What Geophysicists and Engineers Need to Know*, Society of Exploration Geophysicists, Tulsa, Oklahoma, ISBN 978-1-56080-384-3 978-1-56080-385-0.

Willis, M. E., X. Wu, W. Palacios, and A. Ellmauthaler (2019). Understanding cable coupling artifacts in wireline-deployed DAS VSP data, *SEG Technical Program Expanded Abstracts*, San Antonio, Texas, 15–20 SEptember 2019, 5310–5314.

Zhan, Z. (2020). Distributed acoustic sensing turns fiber-optic cables into sensitive seismic antennas, *Seismol. Res. Lett.* **91,** no. 1, 1–15.

Zhang, J., and M. N. Toksöz (1998). Nonlinear refraction traveltime tomography, *Geophysics* **63,** no. 5, 1726–1737.

Zhu, W., and G. C. Beroza (2019). PhaseNet: A deep-neural-network-based seismic arrival-time picking method, *Geophys. J. Int.* **216,** no. 1, 261–273.

Zhu, W., E. Biondi, J. Li, J. Yin, Z. E. Ross, and Z. Zhan (2023). Seismic arrival-time picking on distributed acoustic sensing data using semi-supervised learning, *Nat. Commun.* **14,** no. 1, 8192.

Zhu, W., I. W. McBrearty, S. M. Mousavi, W. L. Ellsworth, and G. C. Beroza (2022). Earthquake phase association using a Bayesian Gaussian mixture model, *J. Geophys. Res.* **127,** no. 5, e2021JB023249, doi: 10.1029/2021JB023249.

Manuscript received 1 June 2025
Published online 2 October 2025

Meter- and Second-Scale Spatiotemporal Analysis of Anthropogenic Seismic Noise Source Distributions Using Deep Learning

Jie Zhou[1], Binbin Mi[*1], and Jianghai Xia[1]

Abstract

Man-made activities contribute to the ambient seismic wavefield. Locating these anthropogenic seismic noise sources at a high spatiotemporal resolution becomes vital for identifying human activities, understanding source mechanisms, and imaging subsurface geological structures. Existing noise source localization methods based on array analysis face challenges in time-lapse monitoring of the source distribution due to the computational cost. Here, we introduce an efficient approach of using deep learning to monitor the change of seismic noise source locations. The neural network extracts noise source locations from noise cross-correlation functions. The network model is trained with abundant simulated data at a low cost, and then it is sustained for monitoring the changes of noise source distribution in a survey area. We propose a comprehensive framework to ensure prediction accuracy and stability, which allows us to monitor the noise source distribution at a high spatiotemporal resolution. Field data examples acquired by small nodal arrays in the urban area of Hangzhou, China, suggest that the anthropogenic noise sources can be monitored at meter and second scales. The results reveal spatiotemporal variations of the vehicle traffic distribution along a road and two drilling machines working at a construction site. Our study demonstrates an approach to develop deep learning models for real-time monitoring of the distribution of seismic noise sources associated with human activities.

Cite this article as Zhou, J., B. Mi, and J. Xia (2025). Meter- and Second-Scale Spatiotemporal Analysis of Anthropogenic Seismic Noise Source Distributions Using Deep Learning, *Seismol. Res. Lett.* **97**, 1078–1088, doi: 10.1785/0220250171.

Supplemental Material

Introduction

Human activities make a contribution to the ambient seismic wavefield (Díaz *et al.*, 2017; Hong *et al.*, 2020). Different from the natural seismic phenomena like earthquakes (Simons *et al.*, 2011; Li *et al.*, 2018; Zhan *et al.*, 2021; McPherson *et al.*, 2022) and volcanoes (Brenguier *et al.*, 2007; Zali *et al.*, 2024; Goebel *et al.*, 2025), human activities such as vehicle traffic (Bonnefoy-Claudet *et al.*, 2006; Green *et al.*, 2017; Xie *et al.*, 2025), engineering constructions, and even conflict attacks (Dando *et al.*, 2023) exhibit intricate spatiotemporal distributions at a small scale and generate strong seismic noise at high frequencies. Understanding these man-made seismic noise sources is critical for identifying human activities. During COVID-19 lockdowns, Lecocq *et al.* (2020) observed a global reduction in the energy of high-frequency seismic noise. Regionally, a 50% reduction in vehicle-related seismic signals in a commuter sector was revealed using the distributed acoustic sensing, although traffic persisted near-critical infrastructure such as hospitals (Lindsey *et al.*, 2020). The observed seismic noise reduction in Tokyo during the COVID-19 pandemic did not indicate city-wide quieting, but rather reflected localized decreases in school-related activities (Hayashida *et al.*, 2023). The high-density deployments of seismometers have allowed us to monitor train and traffic circulation, aircraft landings, and other man-made activities (Riahi and Gerstoft, 2015; Meng and Ben-Zion, 2018).

The anthropogenic seismic noise sources have been used for imaging and monitoring subsurface geological structures (Nakata *et al.*, 2011; Brenguier *et al.*, 2019; Fang *et al.*, 2020; Mi *et al.*, 2022; Cheng *et al.*, 2023; Liu *et al.*, 2025). Different from the seismic monitoring using low-frequency random ambient noise (Brenguier *et al.*, 2008; Lecocq *et al.*, 2017; Mao *et al.*, 2022), the use of anthropogenic high-frequency seismic noise sources gives the change of seismic velocities in the shallower subsurface. The intricate spatiotemporal distributions of the anthropogenic seismic noise sources, however, may produce errors in the retrieval of seismic signals (Mi *et al.*, 2025) and make challenges in the accurate estimation of subsurface changes.

To locate these anthropogenic seismic noise sources, the array analysis methods such as the matched field processing

1. School of Earth Sciences, Zhejiang University, Hangzhou, China, https://orcid.org/0009-0001-4961-5343 (JZ); https://orcid.org/0000-0002-4317-3732 (BM)

*Corresponding author: mibinbin1991@126.com;mibinbin@zju.edu.cn

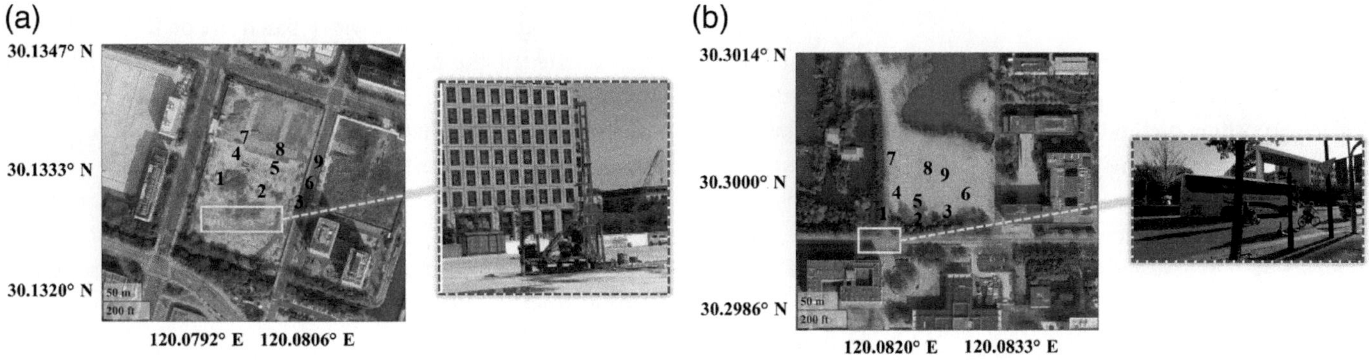

Figure 1. (a) Experimental setup at the construction site with drilling machines working at the site (highlighted by the yellow rectangle). (b) Experimental setup at the park site, close to a road with heavy traffic (highlighted by the yellow rectangle). The triangles denote the receiver arrays. The color version of this figure is available only in the electronic edition.

(MFP) (Kuperman and Turek, 1996; Corciulo *et al.*, 2012; Walter *et al.*, 2015; Gal *et al.*, 2018; Zhang *et al.*, 2022) have been proposed by matching the theoretical phase of surface waves at different frequencies, phase velocities, and source locations to the field data. This method directly derives the distribution of seismic sources from observed data. To enhance coherent surface-wave signals, the cross-correlation-based seismic interferometry method has been utilized (Weaver and Lobkis, 2001; Snieder, 2004; Yang *et al.*, 2007; Saengduean *et al.*, 2024). The waveform of the cross-correlation functions contains information on the source and subsurface structures, which can be inverted for the source information (Tromp *et al.*, 2010; Hanasoge, 2014; Fichtner *et al.*, 2017; Xu *et al.*, 2019, 2020). Unlike the MFP, the waveform inversion allows for a more detailed depiction of noise source distributions because it is not affected by the array response (Xu and Mikesell, 2022). Although the MFP and waveform inversion methods can achieve reliable localization results with long-term noise segments, the application to time-lapse monitoring with high temporal resolution is limited due to the computational inefficiency and lower temporal resolution.

Recently, deep learning-based artificial intelligence has begun to revolutionize seismology, providing new solutions to long-standing challenges (Yu and Ma, 2021). The deep learning methods have emerged as powerful tools for detecting and characterizing urban seismic data (Snover *et al.*, 2021). Zhou *et al.* (2024) introduced a novel deep learning framework for locating ambient seismic noise sources. The neural network extracts noise source locations from noise cross-correlation functions, and it is trained with abundant simulated data at a low cost (Zhou *et al.*, 2024). It has been demonstrated that the method is robust for locating stable and static noise sources. However, the distribution of anthropogenic seismic noise sources often changes rapidly both in time and space. Tracking the spatiotemporal variations in noise source distributions with a high resolution becomes challenging.

In the monitoring of seismic noise source distributions, the cross-correlation functions of short-term ambient noise recordings are inherently unstable. The low-signal-to-noise-ratio (SNR) data severely impact the prediction accuracy of the source location. Here, building upon the deep learning-based noise source localization method proposed by Zhou *et al.* (2024), we develop a comprehensive workflow that integrates deep learning and the quality control methods to enable reliable monitoring of spatiotemporal variations of noise source distributions. The SNR and asymmetry of the noise cross-correlation waveforms are analyzed to control the quality of the prediction results. The combined use of the deep learning and quality control methods ensures the stability and efficiency, facilitating high-resolution spatiotemporal monitoring of noise source distributions. We apply the workflow to monitor vehicle traffic and engineering constructions in the urban area of Hangzhou, China, at meter and second scales. The accuracy of the predicted source locations using deep learning is further evaluated by the comparison of noise cross-correlation waveforms between synthetic and observed data.

Data

Field data

The field data were collected in the city of Hangzhou, eastern China. To characterize the spatiotemporal changes of the anthropogenic seismic noise source distributions, we deployed two nodal arrays at two sites: one was in a construction area, and the other one was in a small park close to a busy road (Fig. 1a,b). Each array consisted of nine seismic nodes including 5 Hz geophones with about tens of meters of interstation distance. At the construction site, seismic data were continuously recorded between 07:00 and 07:30 a.m. on 1 June 2020. During this period, there were drilling machines working at the site (Fig. 1a). In the roadside case, data were collected from 10:40 to 11:45 a.m., on 27 November 2023, coinciding with heavy traffic of buses, cars, bikes, and so on (Fig. 1b). The seismic noise recordings at each site were divided into time windows and then cross-correlated between different stations because the input of the deep learning network for monitoring the anthropogenic seismic noise source locations.

Training data

The deep learning network was trained by synthetic data. The synthetic noise data were generated using a surface-wave wavefield superposition method (Park and Miller, 2008) with the fixed array geometry under the assumption of a known layered earth model at the site. In the construction case, the phase velocity dispersion curve of surface waves was calculated from the model obtained by borehole measurements (Fig. S1a, available in the supplemental material to this article), and the training dataset used here is same as that used in Zhou *et al.* (2024). In the roadside case, the surface wave phase velocities were derived from active seismic data at the site (Fig. S2b). Each of the survey area was discretized into a grid of 128*128 points with a spacing of 3 m, which provided sufficient spatial resolution for localizing high-frequency (>5 Hz) urban noise sources. This aperture configuration balances the demand of high spatial resolution and computational efficiency, and can be adapted to larger-scale noise source monitoring by increasing the grid spacing accordingly. Random noise sources at the grid points were activated and the peak frequency of the source wavelet was chosen depending on the field data frequency band. We utilized an 8 Hz Ricker wavelet as the source function in the construction case and a 10 Hz wavelet was used for the roadside case. The cross-correlation functions were extended by zero-padding to make sure the sampling is 128*128 with a 2-ms timestep for the training and field data. The synthetic noise data with a fixed receiver array associated with the noise sources at four adjacent grid points were cross-correlated and stacked as the one training sample for the network. Totally 127*127 samples were generated for each case. The network learns the relationship between cross-correlation functions and the noise source location.

Method

Deep learning-based noise source localization

The cross-correlation function of seismic noise recorded by different receivers (Fig. 2a,b) contains information on the noise source distribution as well as the earth model structures. The neural network can extract the noise source location from the cross-correlation functions under the assumption of a known layered earth model (Zhou *et al.*, 2024). The U-net deep learning architecture is deployed including the convolutional kernel (3×3) and the max-pooling window (2×2) (Fig. 2c). The input data of the network are noise cross-correlation functions (Fig. 2a), and the output is a sparse matrix representing the probability of the noise source location (Fig. 2d).

The network model is trained with synthetic data at a low cost. We randomly choose 80% of the synthetic data sets for training and 20% for validation. A weighted binary cross-entropy loss function is used for evaluating the performance of the network during training, which can make sure that the trained neural model is robust and has a high spatial resolution in predicting the source locations (Zhou *et al.*, 2024). We train the model using the Adam optimizer (Kingma and Ba, 2017) and a learning rate of 0.0001 with a batch size of 32. The training is terminated if the loss of two consecutive epochs does not decrease any more. For the construction site case, we directly used the model that had been trained by Zhou *et al.* (2024), and the training process is shown in Figure S2a. For the roadside case, we trained a new model and the loss changes with the increasing epochs of training and validation are shown in Figure S2b. The well-trained network predicts the noise source location from the observed noise cross-correlation functions.

Quality control

For a high-temporal-resolution monitoring of noise source distributions, the quality of the noise cross-correlation functions from short-time noise segments is evaluated based on the SNR values. The cross-correlation data with a higher SNR make the prediction result more reliable. Besides, the asymmetry of the causal and acausal parts of the cross-correlation function is adopted for the quality control (Fig. 2b). The asymmetry corresponds to the distribution of noise sources in real-world scenarios (Ermert *et al.*, 2016). By analyzing the asymmetry of the cross-correlation function between causal and acausal parts, we can determine whether noise sources are nonuniformly distributed. The cross-correlation data with a higher asymmetry are more beneficial for predicting strong isolated noise sources. The asymmetry is described as (Ermert *et al.*, 2016; Zhou *et al.*, 2018)

$$\text{Asymmetry} = \ln\left(\frac{E_{\text{signal}}}{E_{\text{symmetric}}}\right), \quad (1)$$

in which E_{signal} denotes the average amplitude in the signal window of the cross-correlation functions, and $E_{\text{symmetric}}$ represents the average amplitude in the symmetric part of the signal window in the cross-correlation function. The signal window is reestimated according to the predicted source location. If the asymmetry is much larger than zero, it indicates that strong isolated noise sources can be accurately located. The low-SNR cross-correlation data or the uniformed noise source distribution makes the value of the asymmetry below or close to zero, which suggests that the source localization results are inaccurate.

Workflow

We propose the following workflow to monitor the spatiotemporal changes of anthropogenic seismic noise source distributions, which combines the continuous localization of the noise sources using deep learning and a quality control technique (Fig. 2):

1. continuously record the seismic noise data in a survey area using a fixed array (Fig. 1a,b);
2. split the noise recordings into time windows of seconds and calculate the cross-correlation functions (Fig. 2a);
3. develop a deep learning network using synthetic data according to the known earth model parameters and the fixed seismic array (Fig. 2c);

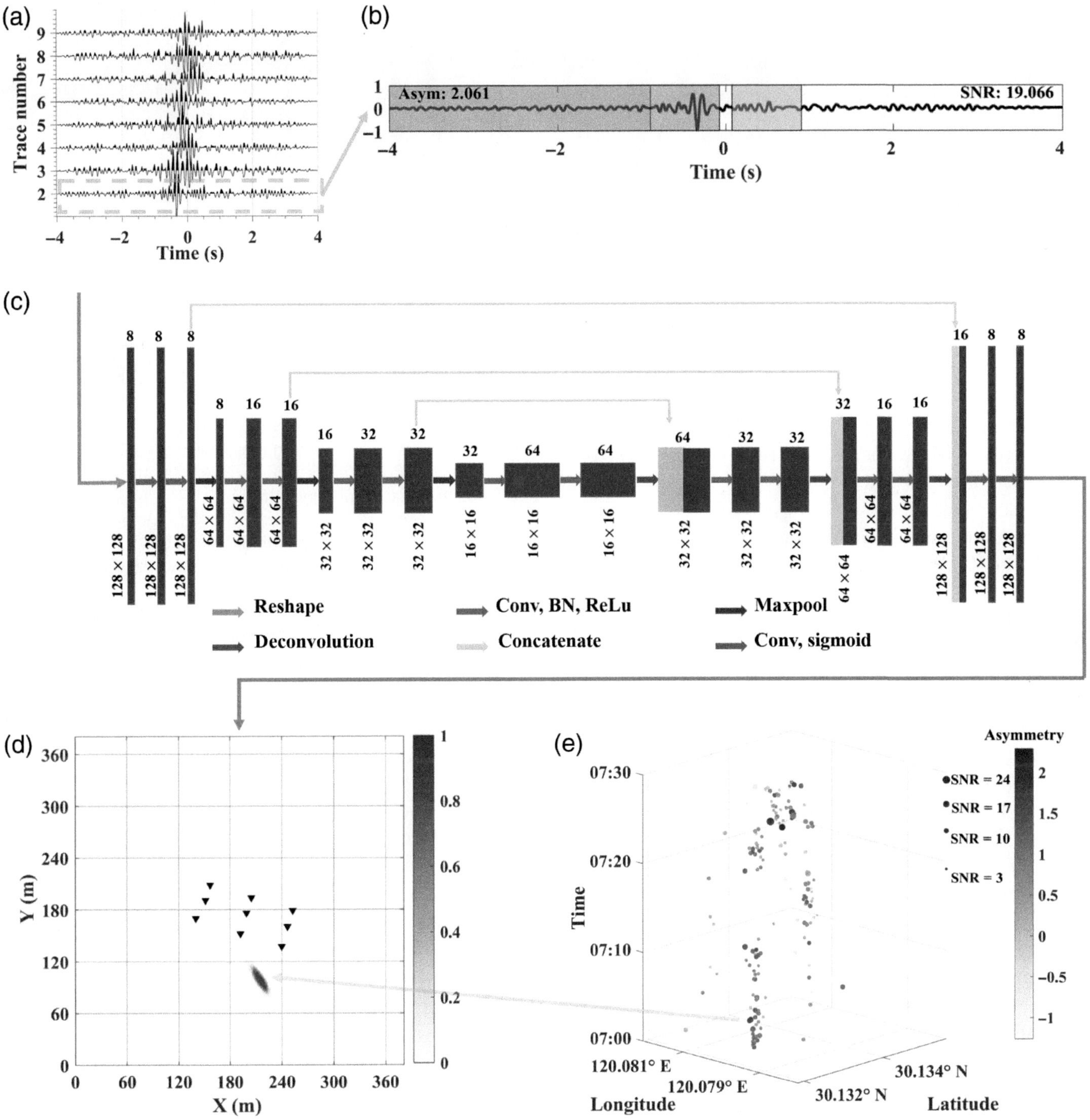

Figure 2. (a) Cross-correlation results from a 4 s noise segment obtained at the construction site with the first station as the reference. (b) An example of one cross-correlation function with the signal (in red) and noise (in blue) windows for the signal-to-noise ratio (SNR). The window in yellow is the symmetric part of the signal window, used for the estimation of the asymmetry (Asym). (c) The U-net deep learning architecture including the convolution layer (conv), the batch normalization layer (BN), and the rectified linear unit layer (ReLu). The input data of the network are the noise cross-correlation functions in panel (a). (d) The output presenting the noise source location and the color scale represents the probability distribution of the noise source. (e) Spatiotemporal changes of the noise source distributions monitored using deep learning (maximum prediction probability >0.5). The color scale represents the average asymmetry values of the input cross-correlation data and the size of the dots is proportional to the average SNR values, which are used for the quality control. The color version of this figure is available only in the electronic edition.

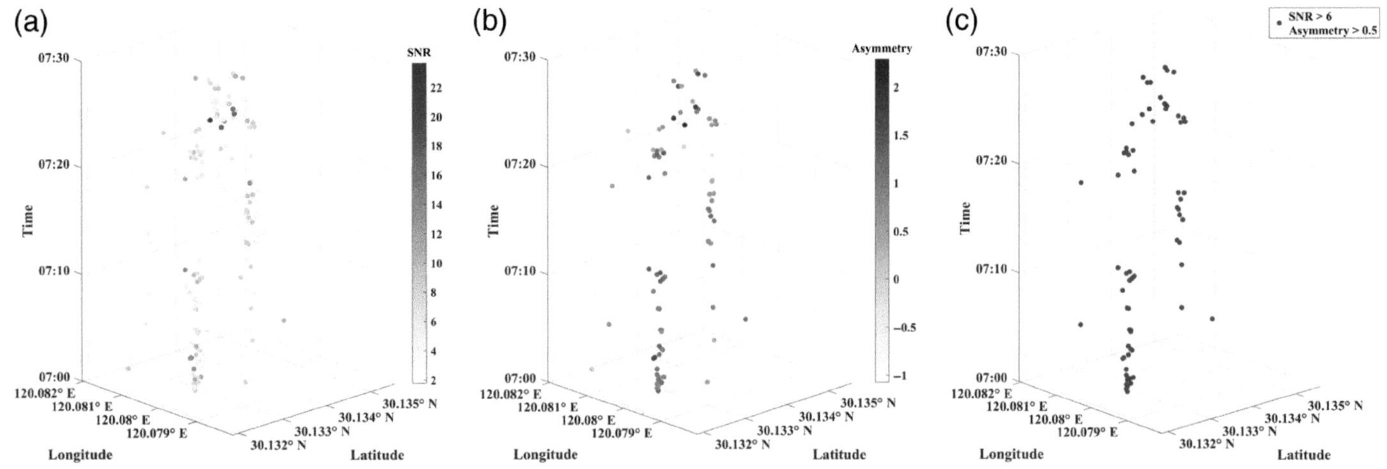

Figure 3. Spatiotemporal changes of the noise source distribution monitored using deep learning (probability >0.5) at the construction site with the analysis of the SNR in (a), the asymmetry in (b), and the final monitoring result in (c). The noise data from 07:00 to 07:30 a.m. were divided into 4 s segments. Dots in (a) give the prediction results with different SNRs. Dots in (b) give the prediction results with different asymmetry values (the results with SNR less than 6 are removed). Dots in (c) represent the distribution of the predicted source locations with the SNR > 6 and asymmetry > 0.5 for the construction case. The color version of this figure is available only in the electronic edition.

4. predict the noise source distribution using deep learning from the cross-correlation functions of each segment (Fig. 2d);
5. calculate the SNR and asymmetry for the quality control (Fig. 2b); and
6. monitor the spatiotemporal changes of the noise source distribution (Fig. 2e).

The SNR and asymmetry shown in Figure 2(e) are averaged from all cross-correlation functions of each segment, and a threshold value is given to ensure the accuracy and reliability of the monitoring results.

Results

Construction site

The half-hour seismic noise data acquired at the construction site were divided into 4 s segments. The cross-correlation functions from each segment were put into the trained network model. We kept the prediction results with the maximum probability value larger than 0.5. The locations of predicted noise sources on the ground surface were plotted as a function of time (Fig. 3). The average SNRs and asymmetry values of the cross-correlation functions from each segment were analyzed (Fig. 3a,b). In Figure 3(c), we show the results with the SNR higher than 6 and the asymmetry larger than 0.5, which present a reliable distribution of the noise sources in space and time. From Figure 3c, we notice that the noise sources were dominantly located at two positions. It was observed that there were drilling machines working at the site during the data collection (Fig. 1a). The noise source monitoring results at the construction site give two drilling machines working (not all the time) at two locations. One can recognize when the drilling machine was working from the monitoring results (Fig. 3c). Figure 4 shows two examples of the cross-correlation data and the predicted source locations from two noise segments at different time. The cross-correlation data (Fig. 4a,b) have high SNRs and asymmetry values. The predicted results show that one drilling machine was in the southeast corner of the site (Fig. 4c) and the other one was in the southwest (Fig. 4d). The high SNR and asymmetry values suggest that the locations of two drilling machines are accurately estimated.

Roadside park site

In the roadside case, the raw data were also divided into 4 s windows. The cross-correlation functions obtained from a 4 s segment had a very low SNR. We stacked the cross-correlation functions in one minute as the input data for a more reliable prediction result. The average SNRs and asymmetry values of the stacked cross-correlation functions were analyzed (Fig. 5a,b). The roadside data were in relatively low SNRs even stacking the cross-correlation results in one minute. We show the monitoring results with the SNR higher than 4 and the asymmetry larger than 0.2 (Fig. 5c). It is noticed that only in a few moments the strong isolated noise sources were predicted. We further show two examples of the stacked cross-correlation data and the predicted source locations at two moments (Fig. 6). Comparing the predicted results with the site condition (Fig. 1b), one noise source was located at an intersection of the main road (Fig. 6c), which was probably caused by the heavy traffic. The other one appeared after 11:15 a.m. at the entrance of a parking lot (Fig. 6d), suggesting the rush hour in the parking lot. The monitoring of the noise source distribution presents the spatiotemporal changes of the vehicle traffic near the site.

Discussion

The accuracy of the anthropogenic seismic noise distribution monitored by the deep learning network is mainly affected

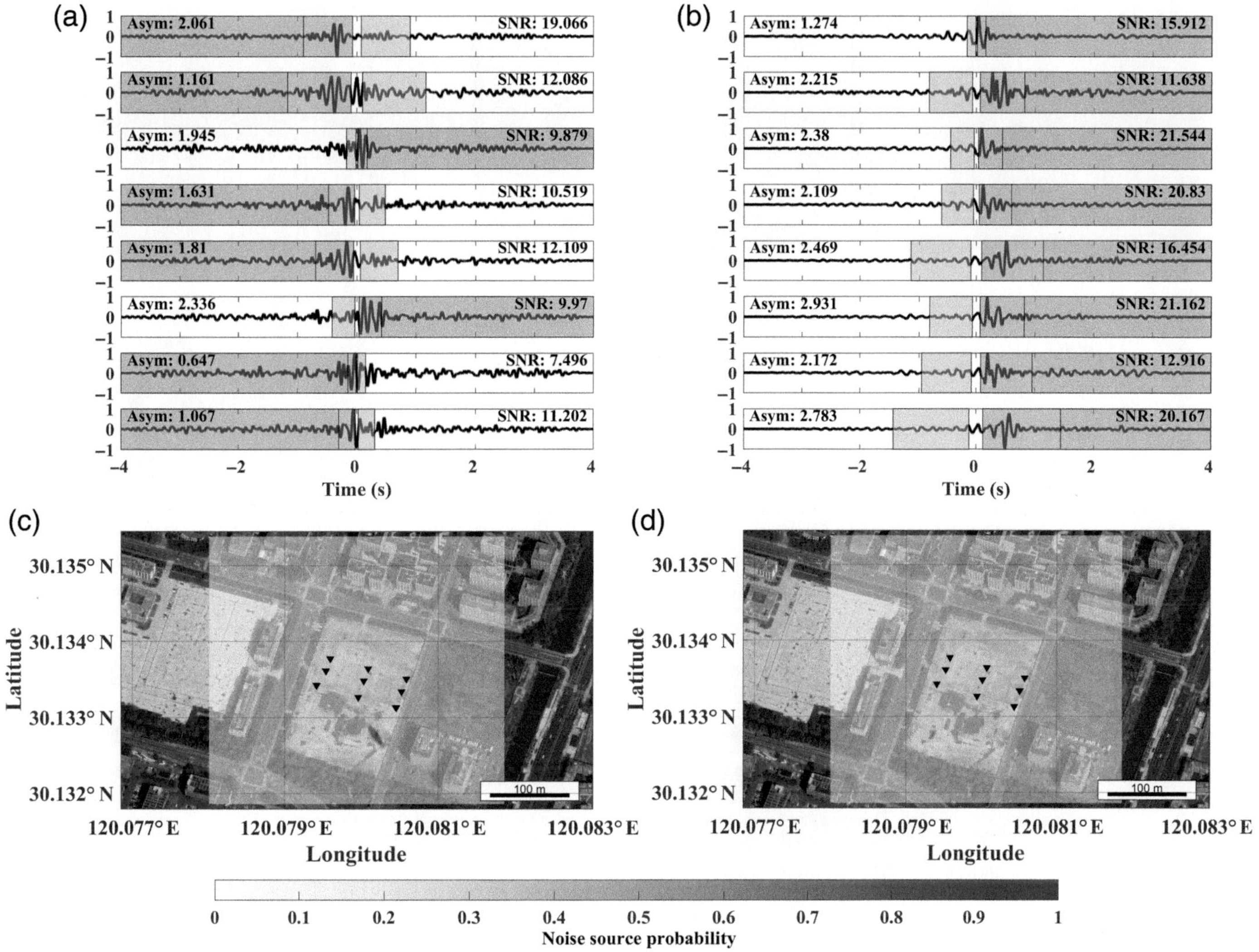

Figure 4. Examples of the cross-correlation data (a,b) and the predicted source locations (c,d) from the noise segments at the construction site. The data were from 07:03:04 to 07:03:08 on 1 June 2020 in (a) and (c), and from 07:25:56 to 07:26:00 on 1 June 2020 in (b) and (d). The SNR and Asym of the cross-correlation functions are analyzed with the signal windows in red, noise windows in blue, and the symmetric windows of the signals in yellow. The triangles in (c) and (d) denote the receiver array. The color scale represents the probability distribution of the noise source. The color version of this figure is available only in the electronic edition.

by the quality of the noise cross-correlation function, which in our study has been controlled by the analysis of the SNR and asymmetry values. We further verify the results by forward modeling of the cross-correlation functions according to the predicted noise source location and comparing the synthetic data with the observed cross-correlation waveforms (Figs. 7 and 8). The synthetic data with each of the two drilling machines at the construction site agree well with the observed data in phase (Fig. 7), which confirms that the two drilling machines were monitored accurately in space and time. In the roadside case, the synthetic cross-correlation functions according to the traffic noise sources at the intersection of the main road are consistent with the field data (Fig. 8a). For the traffic sources at the entrance of the parking lot, the forward modeling data exhibit a few differences due to the low SNRs of the observed data (Fig. 8b). The waveform comparisons between the forward modeling and observed data confirm the accuracy of the spatiotemporal distributions of the anthropogenic seismic noise sources monitored by the deep learning network.

We applied the MFP to the same short-time noise segments analyzed in Figures 4c,d and 6c,d to assess the performance of the proposed deep learning-based localization workflow. As shown in Figure S3, the MFP generally reproduced similar localization results but with lower spatial resolution. In the construction noise example, MFP results from 4 s time windows exhibited unstable localization with scattered noise energy (Fig. S3b), whereas the predictions using the deep learning-based localization method remained stable and focused (Fig. 4d). In the traffic noise example with low SNRs, the MFP gave diffuse localization images with insufficient resolution to identify strong sources. The comparisons with the MFP results highlight the advantage of our approach in terms of

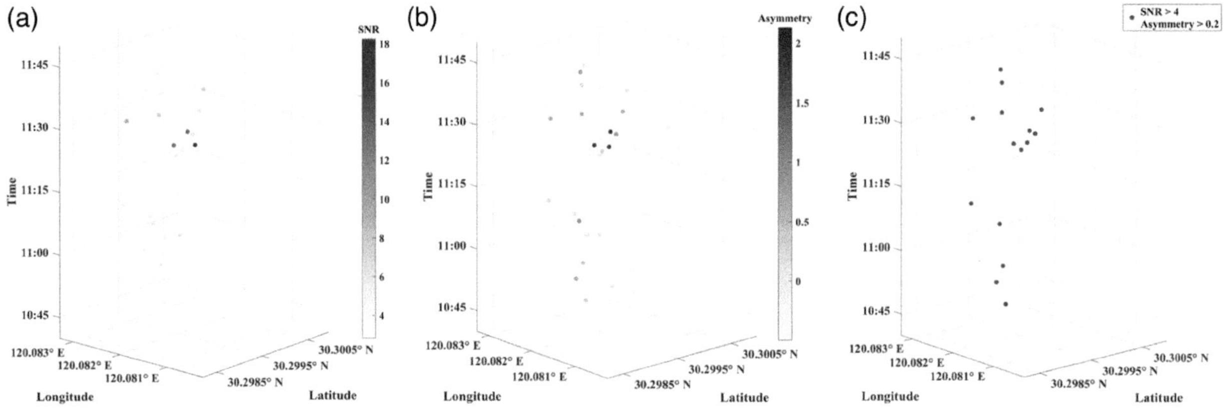

Figure 5. Spatiotemporal changes of the noise source distribution monitored using deep learning (probability >0.5) at the roadside park site with the analysis of the SNR in (a), the asymmetry in (b) and the final monitoring result in (c). The noise data from 10:40 to 11:45 a.m. were divided into 4 s segments for the cross-correlation functions and then stacked in 1 min as the input data. Dots in (a) give the prediction results with different SNRs. Dots in (b) give the prediction results with different asymmetry values (the results with SNR less than 4 are removed). Dots in (c) represent the distribution of the predicted source locations with the SNR > 4 and asymmetry > 0.2 for the roadside case. The color version of this figure is available only in the electronic edition.

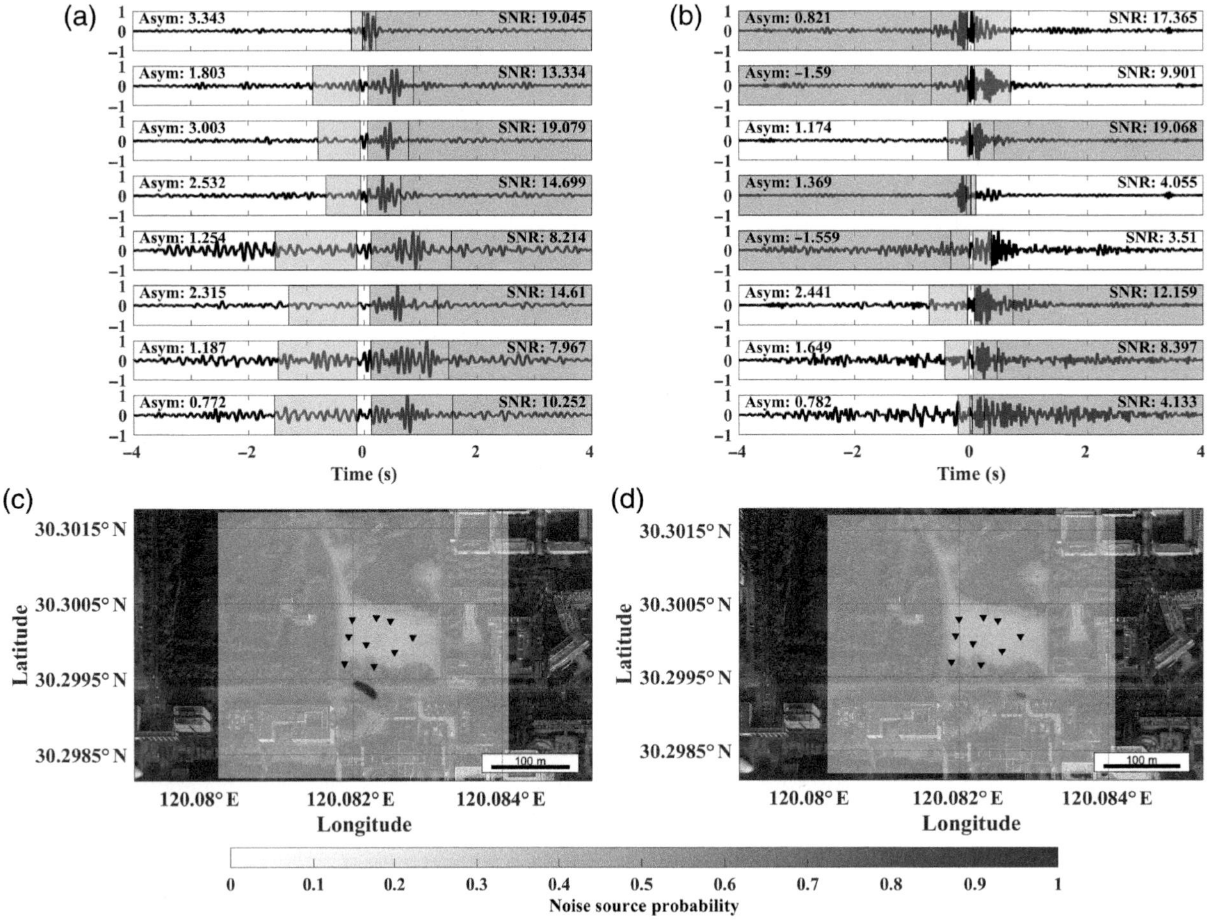

Figure 6. Examples of the stacked cross-correlation data (a,b) and the predicted source locations (c,d) at the roadside site. The data were from 11:25 to 11:26 a.m. on 27 November 2023 in (a) and (c), and from 11:28 to 11:29 a.m. on 27 November 2023 in (b) and (d). The SNR and Asym of the stacked cross-correlation functions are analyzed with the signal windows in red, noise windows in blue, and the symmetric windows of the signals in yellow. The triangles in (c) and (d) denote the receiver array. The color scale represents the probability distribution of the noise source. The color version of this figure is available only in the electronic edition.

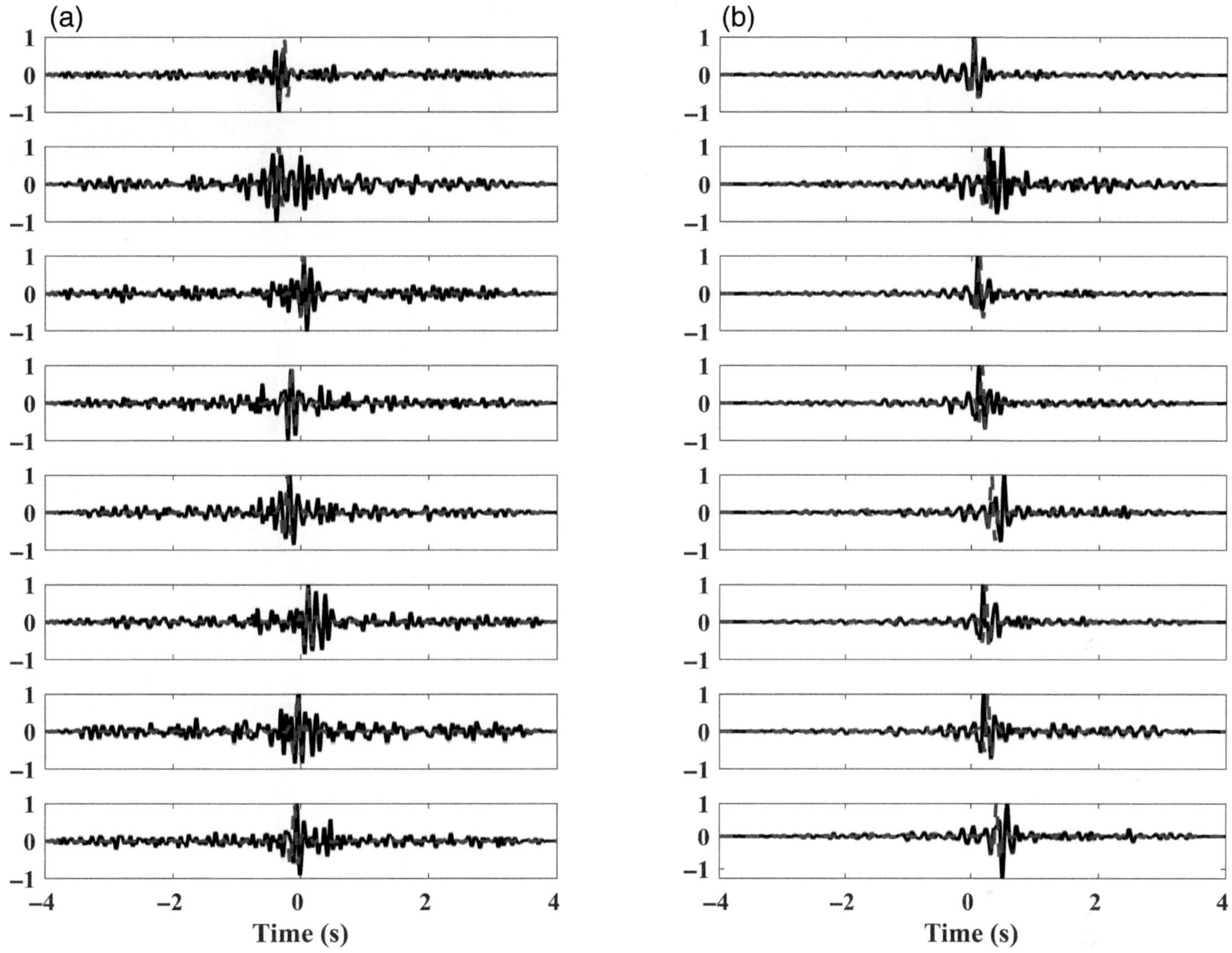

Figure 7. Comparative analysis of the observed (black) and forward modeling (red) data according to the southeast (a) and the southwest (b) drilling machines predicted at the construction site. The color version of this figure is available only in the electronic edition.

resolution and robustness for noise source localization with short-time segments.

Compared to the previous work on noise source localization with long-term noise recordings (Zhou *et al.* 2024), our study expands the deep learning-based framework to use short-term noise segments for high-temporal-resolution monitoring of noise source distributions. This advancement allows us to capture the spatiotemporal dynamics of both transient and persistent sources. The use of quality control based on SNR and asymmetry makes the prediction from short segments reliable, which is a key step for variable anthropogenic noise source monitoring.

In the deep learning noise source monitoring, it is assumed that, (1) the earth model in the survey area is horizontally homogenous and the model parameters are known, (2) seismic sources are distributed on the free surface and generate surface waves dominating the wavefields, and (3) the receiver array is fixed on the ground surface. Although estimation errors in surface-wave phase velocities bias the source estimation (Zhou *et al.*, 2024), these conditions are not particularly stringent and are generally met in various scenarios of anthropogenic or even natural seismic sources. To address the model's generalization limitations, Zhou *et al.* (2024) has explored transfer learning method, in which a pretrained model is retrained using new training data from a different site. This approach reduces training cost by nearly 50%. Our synthetic training data are generated using the wavefield superposition method, which enables rapid simulation of surface-wave-dominated ambient noise recordings. This ensures that both the dataset generation and the retraining using transfer learning processes are computationally efficient, thereby facilitating the adaptation of the framework to new field data. The receiver array can be composed of either seismic nodes or optical fibers with

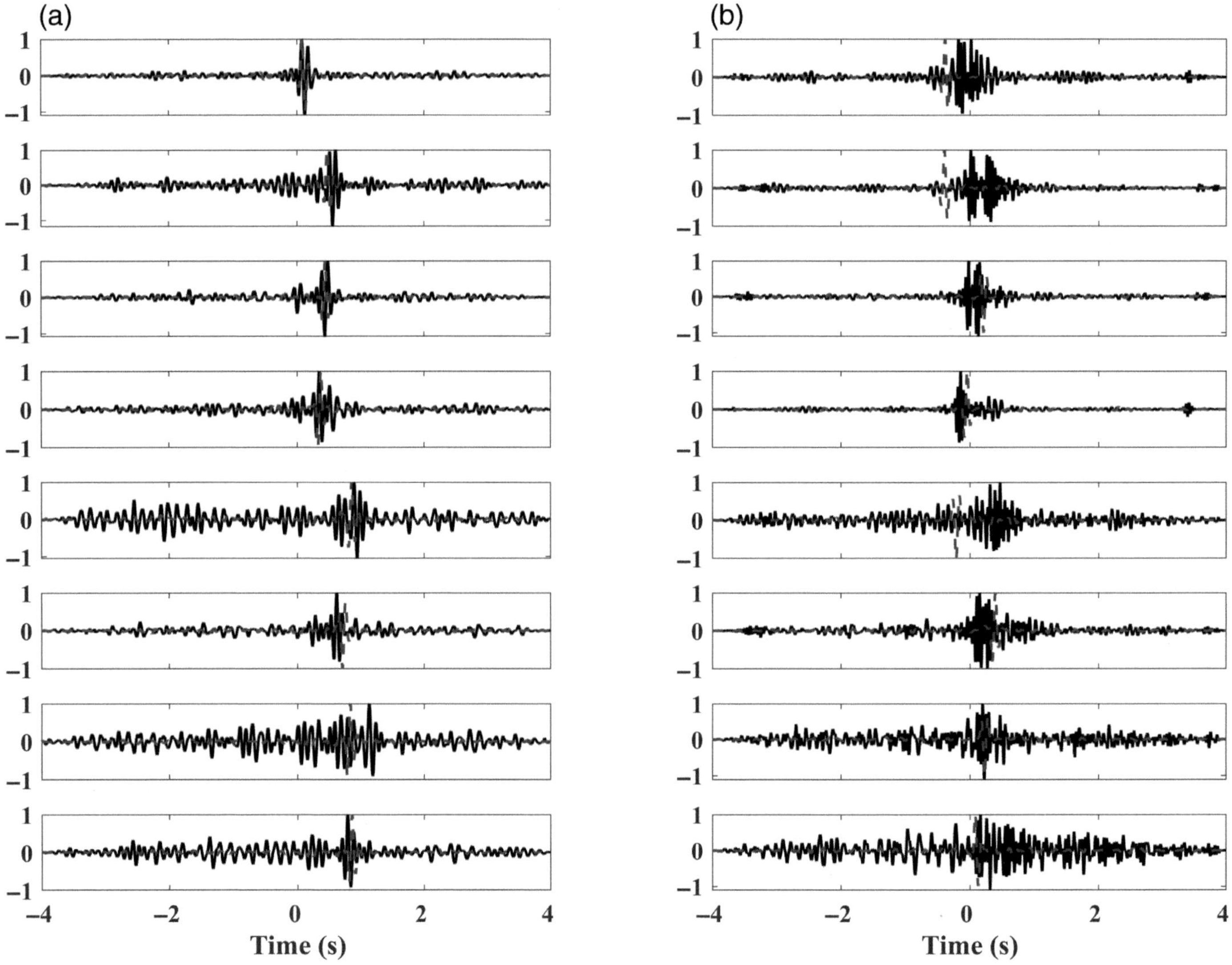

Figure 8. Comparative analysis of the observed (black) and forward modeling (red) data according to the traffic noise sources predicted at the intersection of the main road (a) and the entrance of the parking lot (b). The color version of this figure is available only in the electronic edition.

distributed acoustic sensing. This allows us not only to monitor the man-made activities, but also to detect natural and environmental sources such as active volcanoes, glaciers, landslides, windstorm and so on.

The current framework is designed for single-source localization with short-term noise segments. In real scenarios, multiple sources may be simultaneously activated, which increase the complexity of the cross-correlation wavefields and may challenge the accuracy of source localization. By avoiding simultaneous sources in a very short time, the monitoring workflow may mitigate the influence of multiple sources to a certain extent. In the future work, it is a compelling direction to extend the method for locating multiple noise sources. In practice, nonuniformly distributed noise sources can significantly bias the extracted dispersion energy maps, often leading to overestimated phase velocities. By monitoring noise source distributions, we can correct the inaccurate dispersion energy image caused by the change of source locations under a reference subsurface velocity model. This capability is particularly valuable for calibrating the results of time-lapse imaging with variable noise source distributions and improving monitoring results of subsurface changes.

Conclusion

We present an innovative workflow for monitoring seismic noise source distributions in urban environments using deep learning-based localization techniques. By training models on simulated datasets and applying them to field cross-correlation results from Hangzhou, we successfully tracked spatiotemporal variations of anthropogenic noise sources. Our quality control strategies, based on the SNR and asymmetry analysis, ensured reliable noise source localization. The results reveal a direct correlation between seismic noise and human activities, showcasing the method's capability to monitor anthropogenic noise sources at meter- and second-scale resolution when adequate seismometers are deployed. Compared to conventional camera-based monitoring systems in urban areas, which offer rich visual information, seismic array analysis combined with deep learning provides a complementary approach for tracking isolated noise sources, especially in environments with lighting conditions or line-of-sight constraints. This approach offers promising applications for long-term, high-resolution spatiotemporal monitoring of both anthropogenic and natural noise source distributions.

Data and Resources

The field data used in the study are available at Zenodo (doi: 10.5281/zenodo.15039872). The deep learning and quality control codes used in the study are available at Zenodo (doi: 10.5281/zenodo.15039912). The supplemental material includes Figures S1–S3.

Declaration of Competing Interests

The authors acknowledge that there are no conflicts of interest recorded.

Acknowledgments

This study is supported by the National Natural Science Foundation of China (Grant Number 42374177). The authors thank the team from the Subsurface Imaging and Sensing Laboratory of Zhejiang University for the help in field data collection. And the authors would like to thank reviewers and the editor for detailed reviews of an early version of this work.

References

Bonnefoy-Claudet, S., F. Cotton, and P.-Y. Bard (2006). The nature of noise wavefield and its applications for site effects studies, *Earth Sci. Rev.* **79,** nos. 3/4, 205–227, doi: 10.1016/j.earscirev.2006.07.004.

Brenguier, F., P. Boué, Y. Ben-Zion, F. Vernon, C. W. Johnson, A. Mordret, O. Coutant, P.E. Share, E. Beaucé, D. Hollis, *et al.* (2019). Train traffic as a powerful noise source for monitoring active faults with seismic interferometry, *Geophys. Res. Lett.* **46,** no. 16, 9529–9536, doi: 10.1029/2019GL083438.

Brenguier, F.., N. M. Shapiro, M. Campillo, V. Ferrazzini, Z. Duputel, O. Coutant, and A. Nercessian (2008). Towards forecasting volcanic eruptions using seismic noise, *Nat. Geosci.* **1,** no. 2, 126–130, doi: 10.1038/ngeo104.

Brenguier, F., N. M. Shapiro, M. Campillo, A. Nercessian, and V. Ferrazzini (2007). 3-D surface wave tomography of the Piton de la Fournaise volcano using seismic noise correlations, *Geophys. Res. Lett.* **34,** no. 2, 2006GL028586, doi: 10.1029/2006GL028586.

Cheng, F., J. B. Ajo-Franklin, and V. Rodriguez Tribaldos (2023). High-resolution near-surface imaging at the basin scale using dark fiber and distributed acoustic sensing: Toward site effect estimation in Urban environments, *J. Geophys. Res.* **128,** no. 9, e2023JB026957, doi: 10.1029/2023JB026957.

Corciulo, M., P. Roux, M. Campillo, D. Dubucq, and W. A. Kuperman (2012). Multiscale matched-field processing for noise-source localization in exploration geophysics, *Geophysics* **77,** no. 5, KS33–KS41, doi: 10.1190/geo2011-0438.1.

Dando, B. D. E., B. P. Goertz-Allmann, Q. Brissaud, A. Köhler, J. Schweitzer, T. Kværna, and A. Liashchuk (2023). Identifying attacks in the Russia–Ukraine conflict using seismic array data, *Nature* **621,** no. 7980, 767–772, doi: 10.1038/s41586-023-06416-7.

Díaz, J., M. Ruiz, P. S. Sánchez-Pastor, and P. Romero (2017). Urban seismology: On the origin of earth vibrations within a city, *Sci. Rep.* **7,** no. 1, 15,296, doi: 10.1038/s41598-017-15499-y.

Ermert, L., A. Villaseñor, and A. Fichtner (2016). Cross-correlation imaging of ambient noise sources, *Geophys. J. Int.* **204,** no. 1, 347–364, doi: 10.1093/gji/ggv460.

Fang, G., Y. E. Li, Y. Zhao, and E. R. Martin (2020). Urban near-surface seismic monitoring using distributed acoustic sensing, *Geophys. Res. Lett.* **47,** no. 6, e2019GL086115, doi: 10.1029/2019GL086115.

Fichtner, A., L. Stehly, L. Ermert, and C. Boehm (2017). Generalized interferometry–I: Theory for interstation correlations, *Geophys. J. Int.* **208,** no. 2, 603–638, doi: 10.1093/gji/ggw420.

Gal, M., A. M. Reading, N. Rawlinson, and V. Schulte-Pelkum (2018). Matched field processing of three-component seismic array data applied to Rayleigh and love microseisms, *J. Geophys. Res.* **123,** no. 8, 6871–6889, doi: 10.1029/2018JB015526.

Goebel, T. H. W., N. Thapa, S. Rinty Marium, S. Delgado Andino, A. Martinez-Coto, J. Rivera, and B. Henriquez-Miranda (2025). A community seismic network for the early detection of seismic activity close to active volcanoes in western El Salvador, *Seismol. Res. Lett.* **96,** 2241–2252, doi: 10.1785/0220240343.

Green, D. N., I. D. Bastow, B. Dashwood, and S. E. J. Nippress (2017). Characterizing broadband seismic noise in Central London, *Seismol. Res. Lett.* **88,** no. 1, 113–124, doi: 10.1785/0220160128.

Hanasoge, S. M. (2014). Measurements and kernels for source-structure inversions in noise tomography, *Geophys. J. Int.* **196,** no. 2, 971–985, doi: 10.1093/gji/ggt411.

Hayashida, T., M. Yoshimi, H. Suzuki, S. Mori, T. Kagawa, K. Ichii, and M. Yamada (2023). Tracking the effect of human activity on MeSO-net noise using seismic data traffic—Did seismic noise in Tokyo truly decrease during the COVID-19 state of emergency? *Seismol. Res. Lett.* **94,** no. 6, 2750–2764, doi: 10.1785/0220230015.

Hong, T.-K., J. Lee, G. Lee, J. Lee, and S. Park (2020). Correlation between ambient seismic noises and economic growth, *Seismol. Res. Lett.* **91,** no. 4, 2343–2354, doi: 10.1785/0220190369.

Kingma, D. P., and J. Ba (2017). Adam: A method for stochastic optimization, doi: 10.48550/arXiv.1412.6980.

Kuperman, W. A., and G. Turek (1996). Matched field acoustics, *Mech. Syst. Sig. Process.* **1,** no. 11, 8, doi: 10.1006/mssp.1996.0066.

Lecocq, T., L. Longuevergne, H. A. Pedersen, F. Brenguier, and K. Stammler (2017). Monitoring ground water storage at mesoscale using seismic noise: 30 years of continuous observation and thermo-elastic and hydrological modeling, *Sci. Rep.* **7,** no. 1, 14,241, doi: 10.1038/s41598-017-14468-9.

Lecocq, T., S. P. Hicks, K. Van Noten, K. Van Wijk, P. Koelemeijer, R. S. M. De Plaen, F. Massin, G. Hillers, R. E. Anthony, M. T. Apoloner, *et al.* (2020). Global quieting of high-frequency seismic noise due to COVID-19 pandemic lockdown measures, *Science* **369,** no. 6509, 1338–1343, doi: 10.1126/science.abd2438.

Li, Z., M.-A. Meier, E. Hauksson, Z. Zhan, and J. Andrews (2018). Machine learning seismic wave discrimination: Application to earthquake early warning, *Geophys. Res. Lett.* **45,** no. 10, 4773–4779, doi: 10.1029/2018GL077870.

Lindsey, N. J., S. Yuan, A. Lellouch, L. Gualtieri, T. Lecocq, and B. Biondi (2020). City-scale dark fiber DAS measurements of infrastructure use during the COVID-19 pandemic, *Geophys. Res. Lett.* **47,** no. 16, e2020GL089931, doi: 10.1029/2020GL089931.

Liu, J., H. Li, S. Yuan, H. Y. Noh, and B. Biondi (2025). Characterizing vehicle-induced distributed acoustic sensing signals for accurate urban near-surface imaging, *Seismol. Res. Lett.* **96,** 2867–2880, doi: 10.1785/0220240344.

Mao, S., A. Lecointre, R. D. Van Der Hilst, and M. Campillo (2022). Space-time monitoring of groundwater fluctuations with passive seismic interferometry, *Nat. Commun.* **13,** no. 1, 4643, doi: 10.1038/s41467-022-32194-3.

McPherson, R. C., J. R. Patton, M. Hellweg, S. W. Smith, L. Dengler, A. Lomax, and D. S. Dreger (2022). Large repeating gorda intraplate earthquakes occurring along an inherited weak zone near the mendocino triple junction, *Seismol. Res. Lett.* **96,** 3179–3188, doi: 10.1785/0220250005.

Meng, H., and Y. Ben-Zion (2018). Characteristics of airplanes and helicopters recorded by a dense seismic array near Anza California, *J. Geophys. Res.* **123,** no. 6, 4783–4797, doi: 10.1029/2017JB015240.

Mi, B., J. Xia, G. Tian, Z. Shi, H. Xing, X. Chang, C. Xi, Y. Liu, L. Ning, T. Dai, *et al.* (2022). Near-surface imaging from traffic-induced surface waves with dense linear arrays: An application in the urban area of Hangzhou, China, *Geophysics* **87,** no. 2, B145–B158, doi: 10.1190/geo2021-0184.1.

Mi, B., J. Xia, and H. Zhang (2025). Surface-wave imaging with nonrandom traffic seismic sources, *Earthq. Sci.* **38,** 253–262, doi: 10.1016/j.eqs.2025.01.003.

Nakata, N., R. Snieder, T. Tsuji, K. Larner, and T. Matsuoka (2011). Shear wave imaging from traffic noise using seismic interferometry by cross-coherence, *Geophysics* **76,** no. 6, SA97–SA106, doi: 10.1190/geo2010-0188.1.

Park, C. B., and R. D. Miller (2008). Roadside passive multichannel analysis of surface waves (MASW), *J. Environ. Eng. Geophys.* **13,** no. 1, 1–11, doi: 10.2113/JEEG13.1.1.

Riahi, N., and P. Gerstoft (2015). The seismic traffic footprint: Tracking trains, aircraft, and cars seismically, *Geophys. Res. Lett.* **42,** no. 8, 2674–2681, doi: 10.1002/2015GL063558.

Saengduean, P., R. Snieder, and M. B. Wakin (2024). Weighted compressive sensing applied to seismic interferometry: Wavefield reconstruction using prior information, *Seismol. Res. Lett.* **95,** no. 4, 2221–2228, doi: 10.1785/0220230066.

Simons, M., S. E. Minson, A. Sladen, F. Ortega, J. Jiang, S. E. Owen, L. Meng, J. P. Ampuero, S. Wei, R. Chu, *et al.* (2011). The 2011 magnitude 9.0 Tohoku-Oki earthquake: Mosaicking the megathrust from seconds to centuries, *Science* **332,** no. 6036, 1421–1425, doi: 10.1126/science.1206731.

Snieder, R. (2004). Extracting the Green's function from the correlation of coda waves: A derivation based on stationary phase, *Phys. Rev. E* **69,** no. 4, 046610, doi: 10.1103/PhysRevE.69.046610.

Snover, D., C. W. Johnson, M. J. Bianco, and P. Gerstoft (2021). Deep clustering to identify sources of urban seismic noise in long beach, California, *Seismol. Res. Lett.* **92,** no. 2A, 1011–1022, doi: 10.1785/0220200164.

Tromp, J., Y. Luo, S. Hanasoge, and D. Peter (2010). Noise cross-correlation sensitivity kernels: Noise cross-correlation sensitivity kernels, *Geophys. J. Int.* **183,** no. 2, 791–819, doi: 10.1111/j.1365-246X.2010.04721.x.

Walter, F., P. Roux, C. Roeoesli, A. Lecointre, D. Kilb, and P.-F. Roux (2015). Using glacier seismicity for phase velocity measurements and Green's function retrieval, *Geophys. J. Int.* **201,** no. 3, 1722–1737, doi: 10.1093/gji/ggv069.

Weaver, R. L., and O. I. Lobkis (2001). Ultrasonics without a source: Thermal fluctuation correlations at MHz frequencies, *Phys. Rev. Lett.* **87,** no. 13, 134301, doi: 10.1103/PhysRevLett.87.134301.

Xie, D., X. Wu, Z. Guo, H. Hong, B. Wang, and Y. Rong (2025). Intelligent traffic monitoring with distributed acoustic sensing, *Seismol. Res. Lett.* **96,** 2477–2488, doi: 10.1785/0220240298.

Xu, Z., and T. D. Mikesell (2022). Estimation of resolution and covariance of ambient seismic source distributions: Full waveform inversion and matched field processing, *J. Geophys. Res.* **127,** no. 6, e2022JB024374, doi: 10.1029/2022JB024374.

Xu, Z., T. D. Mikesell, G. Gribler, and A. Mordret (2019). Rayleigh-wave multicomponent cross-correlation-based source strength distribution inversion. Part 1: Theory and numerical examples, *Geophys. J. Int.* **218,** no. 3, 1761–1780, doi: 10.1093/gji/ggz261.

Xu, Z., T. D. Mikesell, J. Umlauft, and G. Gribler (2020). Rayleigh-wave multicomponent crosscorrelation-based source strength distribution inversions. Part 2: A workflow for field seismic data, *Geophys. J. Int.* **222,** no. 3, 2084–2101, doi: 10.1093/gji/ggaa284.

Yang, Y., M. H. Ritzwoller, A. L. Levshin, and N. M. Shapiro (2007). Ambient noise Rayleigh wave tomography across Europe, *Geophys. J. Int.* **168,** no. 1, 259–274, doi: 10.1111/j.1365-246X.2006.03203.x.

Yu, S., and J. Ma (2021). Deep learning for geophysics: Current and future trends, *Rev. Geophys.* **59,** no. 3, e2021RG000742, doi: 10.1029/2021RG000742.

Zali, Z., S. M. Mousavi, M. Ohrnberger, E. P. S. Eibl, and F. Cotton (2024). Tremor clustering reveals pre-eruptive signals and evolution of the 2021 Geldingadalir eruption of the Fagradalsfjall Fires, Iceland, *Commun. Earth Environ.* **5,** no. 1, 1, doi: 10.1038/s43247-023-01166-w.

Zhan, Z., M. Cantono, V. Kamalov, A. Mecozzi, R. Müller, S. Yin, and J. C. Castellanos (2021). Optical polarization–based seismic and water wave sensing on transoceanic cables, *Science* **371,** no. 6532, 931–936, doi: 10.1126/science.abe6648.

Zhang, H., B. Mi, C. Xi, Y. Liu, B. Guan, and L. Ning (2022). Extraction of surface-wave phase velocities from ambient noise in the presence of local noise sources based on matched-field processing, *J. Appl. Geophys.* **204,** 104755, doi: 10.1016/j.jappgeo.2022.104755.

Zhou, C., C. Xi, J. Pang, and Y. Liu (2018). Ambient noise data selection based on the asymmetry of cross-correlation functions for near surface applications, *J. Appl. Geophys.* **159,** 803–813, doi: 10.1016/j.jappgeo.2018.09.033.

Zhou, J., B. Mi, J. Xia, H. Zhang, Y. Liu, X. Chen, B. Guan, Y. Hong, and Y. Ma (2024). Noise source localization using deep learning, *Geophys. J. Int.* **238,** no. 1, 513–536, doi: 10.1093/gji/ggae171.

Manuscript received 21 May 2025
Published online 8 October 2025

Imaging Shallow Complex V_S Structure Using F–J Surface-Wave Tomography with Partition Similarity Test: A Case Study at the San Jacinto Fault Zone

Shuhao Song[1], Zhengbo Li[1,2,3], Juqing Chen[1], Fengjiang Ju[1], Chunquan Yu[1,2,3], and Xiaofei Chen*[1,2,3]

Abstract

Dense seismometer arrays offer new opportunities for refining the exploration of near-surface near-fault structures. By deploying regional dense seismic arrays, seismologists have significantly advanced their insights into structures, rupture processes, and dynamic behaviors for fault systems. However, achieving high-resolution shear-wave velocity structures remains challenging. This study applies the frequency–Bessel transform (F-J) method, a multimodal surface-wave tomography technique, to image complex subsurface systems. The F-J method enables broad frequency band dispersion curves, overtone extraction, and improved resolution. To address challenges in reliable subarray selection for 3D complex subsurface imaging when using this array-based method, we introduce a partition similarity test to quantitatively and adaptively generate suitable subarrays. We apply this method to image the Sagebrush flat site along the Clark fault branches of the San Jacinto fault zone, demonstrating its effectiveness in mitigating the branched dispersion phenomenon that appears in the traditional workflow of the F-J method. The high-resolution imaging results reveal two low-velocity anomalies, a trapping structure, an inferred fault, and significant lateral velocity variations along the Clark fault branches.

Cite this article as Song, S., Z. Li, J. Chen, F. Ju, C. Yu, and X. Chen (2025). Imaging Shallow Complex V_S Structure Using F–J Surface-Wave Tomography with Partition Similarity Test: A Case Study at the San Jacinto Fault Zone, *Seismol. Res. Lett.* **97**, 1089–1103, doi: 10.1785/0220240465.

Supplemental Material

Introduction

In the past decade, ambient noise data has been recorded by many regional dense arrays consisting of portable short-period seismometers to explore refined structures (Ben-Zion *et al.*, 2015; Hansen and Schmandt, 2015; Nakata *et al.*, 2015; Chang *et al.*, 2016; Wei *et al.*, 2018). Surface-wave dispersion is an essential observation to constrain velocity structure (Trampert and Woodhouse, 1995; Shapiro and Ritzwoller, 2002; Shapiro *et al.*, 2005; Yao *et al.*, 2006). It can be cheaply and broadly extracted from the empirical Green's functions calculated from cross-correlated ambient noise (Campillo and Paul, 2003; Shapiro and Campillo, 2004). Numerous studies have applied ambient noise surface-wave tomography to regional dense seismic array data to obtain detailed near-surface structures. (Lin and Ritzwoller, 2011; Chang *et al.*, 2016; Roux *et al.*, 2016; Liu *et al.*, 2017; Wang *et al.*, 2018; Mordret *et al.*, 2019; Fu *et al.*, 2022).

State-of-the-art ambient noise surface-wave tomography has provided valuable insights into complex near-surface systems (Roux *et al.*, 2016; Mordret *et al.*, 2019). However, methodological challenges persist in resolving shallow-depth shear-wave velocity (V_S) structures with high resolution (Share *et al.*, 2020). These include (1) insufficient resolution related to a narrow frequency range in dispersion spectrograms, particularly for complex velocity (Cheng *et al.*, 2023), and (2) the reliance on fundamental-mode surface waves alone cannot always provide sufficient constraints for inversion (Wiggins, 1972; Nolet and Panza, 1976; Maraschini *et al.*, 2010; Yokoi, 2010; Tomar *et al.*, 2018; Pan *et al.*, 2019).

Extracting high-quality phase velocity dispersion curves is essential to surface-wave methods. Numerous techniques have been developed for fundamental-mode extraction, including

1. Department of Earth and Space Sciences, Southern University of Science and Technology, Shenzhen, China, https://orcid.org/0009-0006-2319-5594 (SS); https://orcid.org/0000-0002-1243-8355 (ZL); https://orcid.org/0000-0003-4622-5988 (JC); https://orcid.org/0009-0000-0174-5870 (FJ); https://orcid.org/0000-0001-8681-8572 (CY); 2. Shenzhen Key Laboratory of Deep Offshore Oil and Gas Exploration Technology, Southern University of Science and Technology, Shenzhen, China; 3. Guangdong Provincial Key Laboratory of Geophysical High-Resolution Imaging Technology, Southern University of Science and Technology, Shenzhen, China

*Corresponding author: chenxf@sustech.edu.cn

the spatial autocorrelation method (Aki, 1957), the frequency–wavenumber (*f-k*) method (Capon, 1969; Lacoss *et al.*, 1969), the phase velocity image analysis (Yao *et al.*, 2006), and double beamforming (Roux *et al.*, 2016; Mordret *et al.*, 2019). To obtain dispersion curves with overtones, multichannel recording transformations such as the Radon transform method (RTM; Luo *et al.*, 2008) and the multichannel analysis of surface-wave (MASW) method (Park and Miller, 2008; Pan *et al.*, 2016) have been developed. With uniformly distributed stations, the *f-k* method can also extract overtones (Gabriels *et al.*, 1987; Mordret *et al.*, 2014). Wang *et al.* (2019) introduced the F-J method to extract Rayleigh dispersion curves with higher modes from ambient noise. This method is effective in resolving both Rayleigh- and Love-wave overtones (Hu *et al.*, 2020) from earthquakes (Zhou *et al.*, 2023) and ambient noise sources (Wang *et al.*, 2019; Li and Chen, 2020), and numerous studies updated this method from its original version (Dong *et al.*, 2021; Gao *et al.*, 2021; Song *et al.*, 2021, 2022; Xi *et al.*, 2021; Zhang *et al.*, 2022; Zhou and Chen, 2022). Applications of this method now include shallow subsurface exploration (Fu *et al.*, 2022; Li *et al.*, 2023) and continental lithosphere tomography (Wu *et al.*, 2020; Zhan *et al.*, 2020; Chen *et al.*, 2022; Wang *et al.*, 2024).

Several advantages drive our continued development of the F-J method for complex subsurface tomography. Although methods like *f-k*, MASW, and RTM can extract overtones, they depend on a 2D plane-wave assumption. In contrast, the F-J method, grounded in 3D wave propagation in a flat multilayered isotropic elastic model (Wang *et al.*, 2019), offers enhanced reliability for subsurface imaging. In addition, as noted by Share *et al.* (2020), travel-time-based imaging methods such as beamforming (Roux *et al.*, 2016; Mordret *et al.*, 2019) struggle to image low-velocity features because travel-time data are predominantly sensitive to higher velocity structures. This limitation underscores the value of non-travel-time-based methods such as the F-J method for complex structure tomography.

Similar to other surface-wave methods, dispersion extraction by the F-J method assumes a layered velocity structure. By applying the F-J transform to cross-correlation functions (CCFs) of an array, dispersion curves can be extracted to estimate the 1D velocity structure at the centroid of the array. This array-based nature requires dividing the array into subarrays for 3D modeling. Each subarray provides a local 1D velocity estimate and is then merged and interpolated to construct a 3D velocity model for the entire array. However, challenges in subarray selection persist. The subarray must be large enough to capture high-quality overtones and low-frequency dispersion curves but small enough to achieve adequate horizontal resolution and avoid the coverage of the subarray crossing two different 1D velocity structures.

The traditional array subdivision strategy of the F-J method tests various sizes and shapes, such as circular (Fu *et al.*, 2022) or square (Chen *et al.*, 2022), to identify suitable choices for specific research areas. Based on the test results, the array is subdivided into overlapping fixed-size and fixed-shape subarrays covering the entire area. Another method proposed by Li *et al.* (2023) estimates dispersion curves by stacking results of randomly generated subarrays. Although these methods can effectively find good subarrays for large-scale lithospheric tomography (Chen *et al.*, 2022; Ma *et al.*, 2022) and relatively uniform shallow structures (Fu *et al.*, 2022; Li *et al.*, 2023), they face challenges when imaging complex structures. The F-J method assumes a flat multilayered isotropic velocity structure, valid only when lateral velocity variations within the coverage of individual subarrays are sufficiently small. A synthetic test by Li and Chen (2020) demonstrated that when the F-J method is applied to subarrays covering two different layered structures, the resulting dispersion spectrogram combines dispersions from both structures, which is referred to as branched dispersion curves.

To find suitable subarrays adaptively instead of manual selection, which brings substantial workloads (Wang *et al.*, 2024; Yuan and Chen, 2024), we developed partition similarity test (PST). This method uses the dispersion similarity of different smaller subarrays to quantitatively measure structural homogeneity, judging their suitability to be combined into a larger subarray. Though the generated subarrays require rationale support by further research into the potential bias introduced by irregular shapes, this array subdivision approach offers a solution for applying the F-J method to complex environments.

Here, we apply the F-J method with subarrays generated by the PST the ambient noise data recorded at the Sagebrush flat site along the Clark fault branches of the San Jacinto fault zone (Ben-Zion *et al.*, 2015) to image the V_S structure. Numerous geophysical research have already been applied to study this array (Ben-Zion *et al.*, 2015; Hillers *et al.*, 2016; Roux *et al.*, 2016; Meng and Ben-Zion, 2018; Qin *et al.*, 2018; Mordret *et al.*, 2019; Share *et al.*, 2020; Touma *et al.*, 2021, 2022). Among these, the V_S structure (Mordret *et al.*, 2019) shows a divergence in a shallow low-velocity area compared to the V_P and resistivity inversion results (Share *et al.*, 2020). Our refined V_S model resolves this discrepancy and is consistent with the shallow structure review (Share *et al.*, 2020) at the low-velocity anomaly on both sides of the Clark fault and the trapping structure observed northeast of the Clark fault (Ben-Zion *et al.*, 2015; Qin *et al.*, 2018). This model images the underlying structure of a fault that is not field observed but inferred by topographic survey (Bevis *et al.*, 2005), and reveals clear lateral velocity variations along the Clark fault branches. Our case study demonstrates the ability of the new method in high-resolution imaging of shallow complex structures. The developed array subdivision method can be generally applied to adaptively identify suitable subarrays in dense arrays of various sizes and configurations.

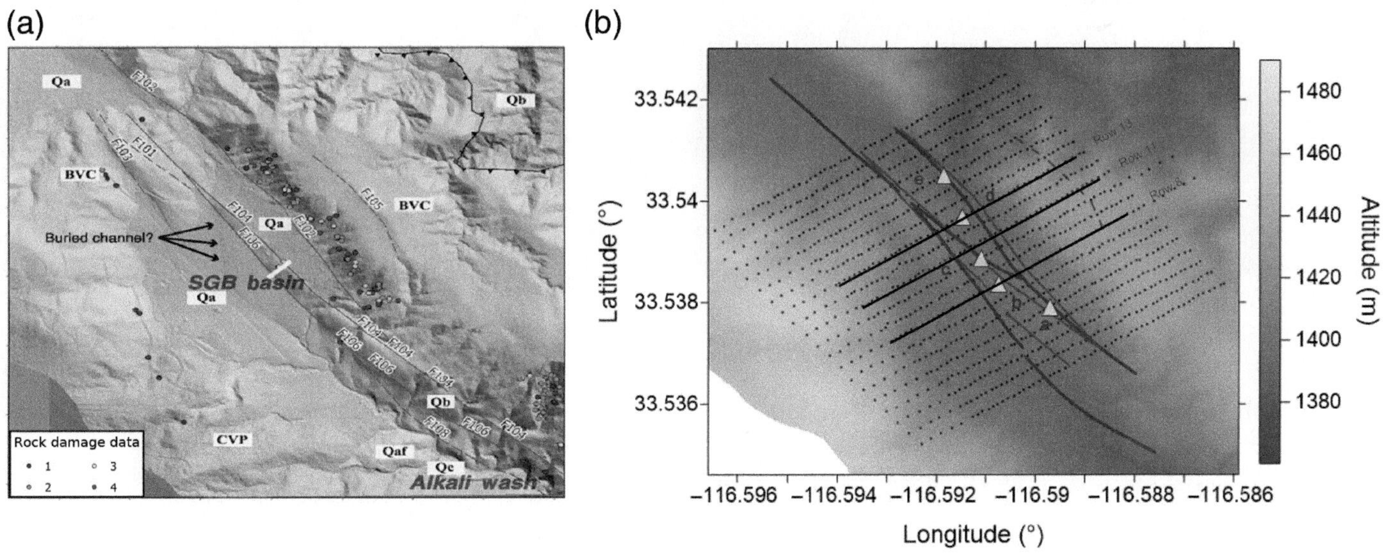

Figure 1. Geological and topographic data are analyzed here. (a) Lithology and damage intensity mapping at the surface modified from (Share *et al.*, 2020). The main geological/lithological units are Coahuila Valley Pluton (CVP, pink), Burnt Valley Complex (BVC, green), Quaternary sediments (Qa, gray), and Plio-Pleistocene Bautista Formation (Qb, brown). More differentiated sediments are alluvial fan (Qaf, gray) and colluvium (Qc, gray). The "buried channel?" indicates an inferred buried drainage channel containing more microfluids and conductive sediments than the rest of the Qa-SW unit. The colored dots indicate the damage intensity of the rock. The red solid line represents the strike-slip fault observed from the field by Wade (2018), and the red-dashed line represents the inferred faults not observed in the field. (b) Distribution of the dense seismic array used in this study. The background color is the relief calculated within a 10 m radius and topography from the B4 light detection and ranging (lidar) project (Bevis *et al.*, 2005). The blue solid lines are the surface traces for the Clark fault, referred to as F106, F104, and F102 from left to right by U.S. Geological Survey (USGS) (2006). The red solid lines are the same traces evaluated by Wade (2018) after a joint analysis of different research. The red dashed line represents the inferred fault trace. The black solid lines tagged by row numbers indicate the reference locations in Figure 10. The yellow filled triangles indicate the locations of the five stations we used for model validation in Figure S5. The color version of this figure is available only in the electronic edition.

Data and Methods

Sagebrush flat array

This study uses ambient noise data recorded by a dense nodal array with 1108 geophones in an ~600 m × 600 m configuration around the Clark fault branches of the San Jacinto fault zone at the Sagebrush flat (SGB) site for tomography. The array had an average 10 m row interstation and 30 m row separation and recorded vertical waveforms continuously at 500 Hz for about 1 month in 2014 (Ben-Zion *et al.*, 2015). After cutting the raw ambient noise data into hour-long segments, the CCFs between all station pairs were calculated by the open-source Python package CC-FJpy (Li *et al.*, 2021). Spectrum whitening was applied to reduce the effects of earthquakes and nonstationary noise sources (Bensen *et al.*, 2007). All hour-long CCF segments were stacked to improve the signal-to-noise ratio.

Bevis *et al.* (2005) conducted a high-resolution topographic survey of the San Andreas and San Jacinto fault zones in southern California to assess near-field ground deformation, with the relief details at the SGB site shown in Figure 1b. Wade (2018) analyzed the lithology and surface fault traces at the SGB site based on the V_S properties (Mordret *et al.*, 2019) and surface geological mapping results, as shown in Figure 1a (edit from Share *et al.*, 2020). Based on these analyses, three exposed branches of the Clark fault (F102, F104, F106) cross the array from northwest to southeast, whereas an inferred fault (F105) is situated to the northeast from the topographic survey (Bevis *et al.*, 2005).

F-J method

The CCF of ambient noise record is defined as

$$\tilde{C}(\boldsymbol{r},\omega) = U_1(\boldsymbol{x_1},\omega) * U_2(\boldsymbol{x_2},\omega), \tag{1}$$

in which $U_1(\boldsymbol{x_1},\omega)$ and $U_2(\boldsymbol{x_1},\omega)$ are the vertical component of seismic records at $\boldsymbol{x_1}$ and $\boldsymbol{x_2}$ in the frequency domain, ω is the angular frequency, and $\boldsymbol{r} = \boldsymbol{x_1} - \boldsymbol{x_2}$. Under the equipartition assumption (Campillo and Paul, 2003), the ambient seismic noise field is isotropic and stationary in space and time. Consequently, $\tilde{C}(r,\omega) = \tilde{C}(\boldsymbol{r},\omega)$, and $r = |\boldsymbol{r}|$ is the distance between two stations.

Similar to other ambient noise methods, the F-J method assumes a flat multilayered isotropic elastic model (Wang *et al.*, 2019). The CCFs are first retrieved from z-component ambient noise records, and a frequency–wavenumber transform is applied to CCFs to obtain the dispersion spectrogram $I(\omega,k)$, also known as the F-J spectrogram (Wang *et al.*, 2019):

$$I(\omega,\boldsymbol{k}) = \frac{1}{2\pi}\int_{-\infty}^{+\infty}\int_{-\infty}^{+\infty} \tilde{C}(r,\omega)e^{i\boldsymbol{k}\,\boldsymbol{r}}d\Sigma(\boldsymbol{r}). \tag{2}$$

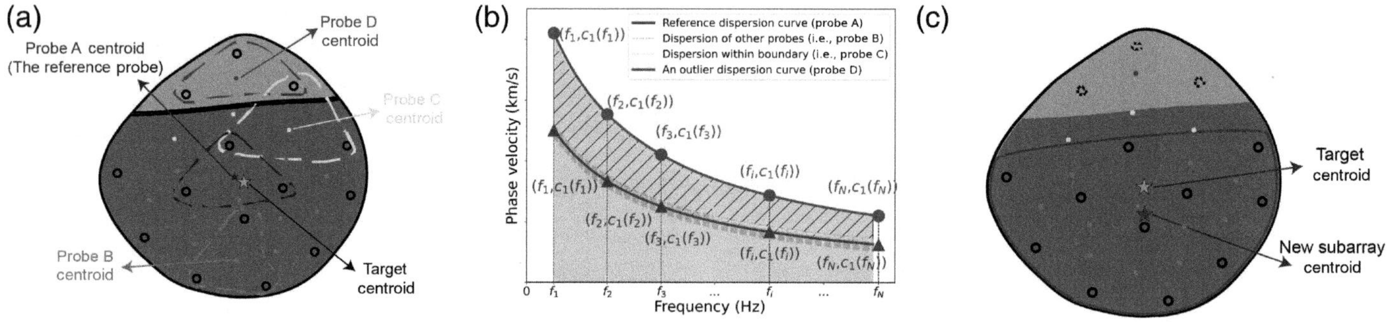

Figure 2. Illustration of the partition similarity test concept. (a) Target and probe definition: in the frequency–Bessel (F-J) method, the cross-correlation functions (CCFs) of a seismic station array are used to estimate the velocity structure at its centroid. Suppose there are some seismic stations (black hollow circles), and the covered area crosses two 1D velocity structures (orange and green background regions). The "target" refers to a relatively large seismic station array (in this case, all seismic stations are included). The target can be divided into smaller subarrays, called "probes" (e.g., three-station groups in this case), which enable localized dispersion curve extraction around the target centroid. Among these, the probe closest to the target centroid is designated as the reference probe (probe A). The relative error (RE) of all other probes is calculated with respect to probe A. Probes with the same velocity structure as probe A are marked in cyan, those crossing two structures are marked in yellow, and those covering a different structure are marked in red. (b) RE calculation: This panel illustrates the RE calculation and a hypothetical fundamental mode dispersion curve distribution of the probes in panel (a). The red dots and blue triangles represent dispersion points from an outlier and the reference probe, respectively. The slashed area denotes the absolute error (AE) between the curves. Dividing the AE by the entire gray area is defined as the RE, as approximated by equation (4). (c) New subarray formation: probes with similar dispersion curves (cyan centroids in panel a and corresponding cyan curves in panel b) are combined to form a new subarray. Note that this process excludes certain stations from the target, causing a centroid shift in the new subarray. The color version of this figure is available only in the electronic edition.

By transforming from Cartesian to cylindrical coordinates and assuming axial symmetry, the integral representation of zero-order Bessel function, $\frac{1}{2\pi}\int_0^{2\pi} e^{ikr\cos\theta}d\theta = J_0(kr)$, simplifies (2) to a 1D integral over the interstation distances (Wang *et al.*, 2019):

$$I(\omega,c) = \int_0^{+\infty} \tilde{C}(r,\omega)J_0\left(\frac{\omega}{c}r\right)rdr. \tag{3}$$

Here,$I(\omega,c)$ represents the F-J spectrogram for a given angular frequency ω and velocity c. Under the assumption that the CCF approximates the imaginary part of the Green's function in a flat multilayered elastic half-space, the Rayleigh-wave dispersion curves can be extracted as peak values of $I(\omega,c)$. Notably, this method retrieves not only the fundamental mode, but also overtone dispersion curves (Chen *et al.*, 2022) and even leaking modes (Li *et al.*, 2022). This study uses CC-FJpy (Li *et al.*, 2021) to implement the F-J method.

Criteria of similarity between two dispersion curves

To objectively evaluate the similarity between dispersion curves, a relative error (RE) is defined as follows:

$$\mathrm{RE} = \frac{\sum_{i=1}^{N} |c_1(f_i) - c_2(f_i)|}{\sum_{i=1}^{N} \max[c_1(f_i),c_2(f_i)]}, \tag{4}$$

in which f_1 to f_N represent the N picked frequency points for two dispersion curves, and $c_1(f_i)$ and $c_2(f_i)$ represent the corresponding phase velocity at f_i. Figure 2b illustrates the setup for equation (4), which quantitatively estimates the dissimilarity of dispersion curves on a scale from 0 to 1. Small RE indicates less discrepancy, whereas large RE indicates more discrepancy.

PST

The F-J method uses a subarray to estimate its centroid 1D velocity structure locally. The idea of the PST is to divide the subarray for more local estimation within the coverage of this subarray. A new subarray is generated by eliminating stations that produce dissimilar dispersion curves. The workflow consists of four steps:

First, the shape and size of "targets" and "probes" should be established, as shown in Figure 2a. A "target" refers to a relatively large subarray that is usually directly used for dispersion extraction in the traditional workflow of the F-J method (Chen *et al.*, 2022; Fu *et al.*, 2022). The shape of targets and probes can be tuned to the array distribution, such as a circle or square. Appropriate sizes of targets need to be tested to produce a better dispersion spectrogram (Chen *et al.*, 2022; Fu *et al.*, 2022). A helpful starting point is applying the F-J method to the entire array, with the first branched fundamental-mode dispersion point revealed by the dispersion spectrogram indicating the lower limit of the resolvable frequency range. Targets are fixed-shape subarrays with sufficient aperture to capture the phase velocity at the minimum frequency (f_{min}). The suitable aperture (r_{max}) of the array can be estimated by the minimum target frequency $f_{\min}$, which is considered at least half of the wavelength ($\lambda_{\max}$) at the $f_{\min}$ in this study:

$$r_{\max} \geq \frac{\lambda_{\max}}{2} = \frac{c(f_{\min})}{2f_{\min}}, \quad (5)$$

in which c is the phase velocity of the surface-wave fundamental mode. "Probes" are smaller subarrays with centroids located within a target. These provide more local dispersion estimations within the target coverage. The probe size is determined by the branched frequency range, that is, f_1 to $f_N$of the target dispersion spectrogram (Fig. 2b), ensuring accurate dispersion extraction using the same criteria as in equation (5). In addition, the aperture of the probe will be the smallest resolvable structural unit of the obtained velocity model.

Second, the RE of each probe is calculated within the target by comparing its dispersion curve against that of the reference probe, the one nearest to the centroid of the target (probe A in Fig. 2a). As shown in Figure 2a,b, probes with similar velocity models will produce comparable dispersion curves (e.g., probe B in Fig. 2a), whereas dissimilar ones (e.g., probes C and D in Fig. 2a) will exhibit larger RE values.

Third, an error threshold is established, and probes with small RE values are combined into a new, larger subarray. For this study, probes in cyan in Fig. 2c represent those with RE values below the empirically determined threshold of 0.05, forming the refined subarray. The robustness of this threshold is discussed in section 4.3.

Fourth, quality control is applied to remove or adjust unsatisfactory subarrays. In transition zones, some probes may still show branched dispersion curves in their dispersion spectrograms (e.g., when probe C in Fig. 2a serves as the reference probe as probe A), resulting in the acceptance of only a few or disconnected probes. Therefore, only subarrays formed by more than four adjacent probes are retained for analysis. In addition, the dispersion spectrograms of these new subarrays are examined manually to confirm that there is no branched dispersion. For those generated subarrays that remain having branched dispersion curves on their dispersion spectrograms, error thresholds between 0.03 and 0.08 will be applied and tested again.

Multimodal dispersion picks and inversion

This study employs a quasi-Newton method to invert 1D V_S model based on the Broyden–Fletcher–Goldfarb–Shanno (BFGS) correction (Byrd *et al.*, 1995). Pan *et al.* (2019) presented the misfit function for multimodal surface-wave dispersion as follows:

$$f(V_S) = \frac{1}{m}\sum_j A_j\left\{\sum_i (c^s_{ij}(V_S) - c^0_{ij})^2\right\} + \alpha||\nabla \cdot V_S||, \quad (6)$$

in which V_S represents the shear-wave velocity model, i is the frequency sampling point, j is the mode of the dispersion curve, c^s_{ij} is the synthetic phase velocity, c^0_{ij} is the observed phase velocity, and A_j is the weight of the jth mode. $||\nabla \cdot V_S||$ is the derivate damping term, which is the L2 norm of the spatial Laplacian of V_S, and α is set to be 0.1 based on the L-curve criteria (Pan *et al.*, 2019). We adopt a layered model with a 5 m thickness for each layer, inverting to a depth of 300 m. To ensure robust convergence and avoid local minima, we perform multimodal dispersion curve inversion using 80 randomized starting models, with velocity varying of each layer by up to 0.8 km/s from a reference model, following Mordret *et al.* (2019).

A careful overtones selection is essential because an inversion of spurious estimates often results in more significant misfits and worse dispersion fitness (Li *et al.*, 2022). Limited by the complex velocity structures and strong crossed artifacts caused by insufficient space sampling for dispersion curves of high frequency (Cheng *et al.*, 2023), continuous overtones cannot be directly determined for each subarray, and some modes are missing or mixed. Given the stability and broader frequency range coverage of the fundamental mode, overtones are auxiliary information to refine details. Therefore, we assign weights of four to the fundamental mode and one to each overtones in equation (6), while implementing a conservative dispersion-curve picking and examination strategy: first, only the fundamental dispersion is picked and inverted for a reference velocity referred to as V_S^{fund}. Next, theoretical overtones are calculated from V_S^{fund}, identifying relevant overtone strips in the dispersion spectrogram. A joint inversion of fundamental mode and overtones is performed to obtain a new velocity structure referred to as V_S^{over}. Finally, the misfit of V_S^{over} compared to V_S^{fund} and the fit of the fundamental mode are assessed to examine the quality of the overtone data.

Workflow of FJ-PST

The process of integrating the FJ method with PST (FJ-PST) to obtain a 3D V_S model involves four main steps, as illustrated in Figure 3 for the application in the SGB array. First, subarrays are adaptively generated using the PST method. To determine an appropriate target size, the entire array is initially analyzed using the F-J method. The dispersion spectrogram of the entire array (Fig. S1b1, available in the supplemental material to this article) showed that the first branch is around 3 Hz, indicating the minimum resolvable frequency band. Based on the maximum phase velocity of ~900 m/s observed in Figure S1b1, the minimum aperture of the subarray estimated by equation (5) is about 150 m. Given the approximately square shape of the array and its uniform station spacing, square-shaped targets with a side length of 120 m (an aperture of 170 m) were selected (yellow dots in Fig. 3a).

Probes are set to squares of 60 m because branching typically occurs between around 9 and 16 Hz (Fig. S1b2), requiring a subarray aperture of around 50 m by equation (5), based on the highest phase velocity of ~800 m/s observed among all targets at 9–10 Hz. Setting probes to squares of 60 m (brown dots in Fig. 3a) ensures accurate extraction of dispersion curves for

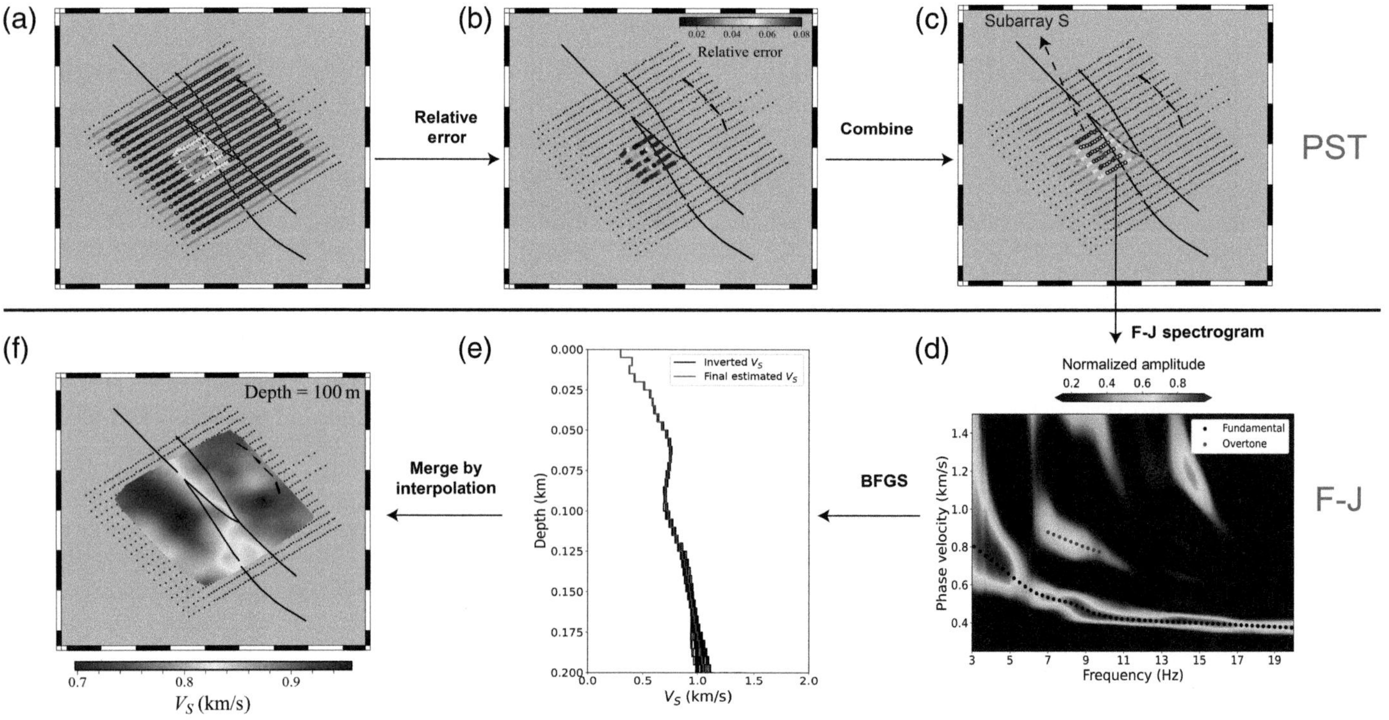

Figure 3. Illustration of the 3D V_S model retrieval from ambient noise data using FJ-PST in this study. (a) The set of targets and probes. The black dots represent array stations, solid lines indicate fault branches, and dashed lines mark inferred faults, as shown in Figure 1a. The green dots and hollow blue circles indicate the centroids of all targets and probes, respectively, used in this study. The yellow triangles represent stations of a sample target, and brown triangles represent stations of a sample probe used to test this target. The centroid of the sample target and probe is marked with a red star and a red cross, respectively. (b) The distribution of RE for probes within this target. (c) A generated subarray "S" for the sample target. The yellow dots show stations of the sample target, green dots represent stations from all probes for the target, and blue dots mark stations in the generated subarray. (d) The dispersion spectrogram calculated from CCFs of subarray S. (e) 1D V_S model from the inversion of multimodal dispersion curves with the Broyden–Fletcher–Goldfarb–Shanno method. (f) A depth slice at 100 m of the final 3D V_S model by merging 1D V_S models at all reference locations by Kriging interpolation. The color version of this figure is available only in the electronic edition.

this frequency range. Subsequently, all possible targets and probes are generated to maximize data utilization and enhance lateral resolution, as shown in Figure 3a–c.

Second, the F-J transform is applied to the CCFs of each subarray to obtain dispersion spectrograms (Fig. 3d). Third, multimodal dispersion curves are picked and examined, and the BFGS method is used to invert these curves to derive the 1D V_S structure for each subarray (Fig. 3e). Finally, all 1D V_S structures are merged using Kriging interpolation to construct the final 3D V_S model (Fig. 3f).

Results

Phase velocity

Figure 4a–c shows the Rayleigh-wave fundamental-mode phase velocity at 4, 8, and 15. At 8 and 15 Hz, two significant low-velocity anomalies are present on either side of the Clark fault. The anomaly on the northeast side persists at 4 Hz, whereas the southwestern anomaly diminishes at this frequency. The southwestern and northwestern corners remain at high velocities within all presented frequency ranges. The observed highest mode for each subarray is plotted in Figure 4d. The overall fundamental-mode phase velocity distribution aligns well with the geological units.

3D shear-wave velocity structure

Representative vertical slices of the final 3D V_S model are shown in Figure 5, offering perspectives from southwest and southeast. Representative depth slices of the final 3D V_S model are presented in Figure 6.

From 10 to 40 m depth, the Clark fault is characterized by high velocity. At the same time, the V_S structure contains two low-velocity anomalies on both sides of the fault branches (Figs. 5a and 6a). The patterns of these two low-velocity anomalies gradually diminish from 50 to 100 m (Fig. 6b). In contrast, two other low-velocity anomalies emerge on the northeast side of the Clark fault, one at the southeast corner ranging from 50 to 100 m, whereas another underneath the northeast of the Clark fault ranges from 70 to 100 m (Fig. 6b,c). Lower than 80 m, two low-velocity anomalies are located at the center of the Clark fault and beneath the inferred fault, respectively (Figs. 5b and 6c).

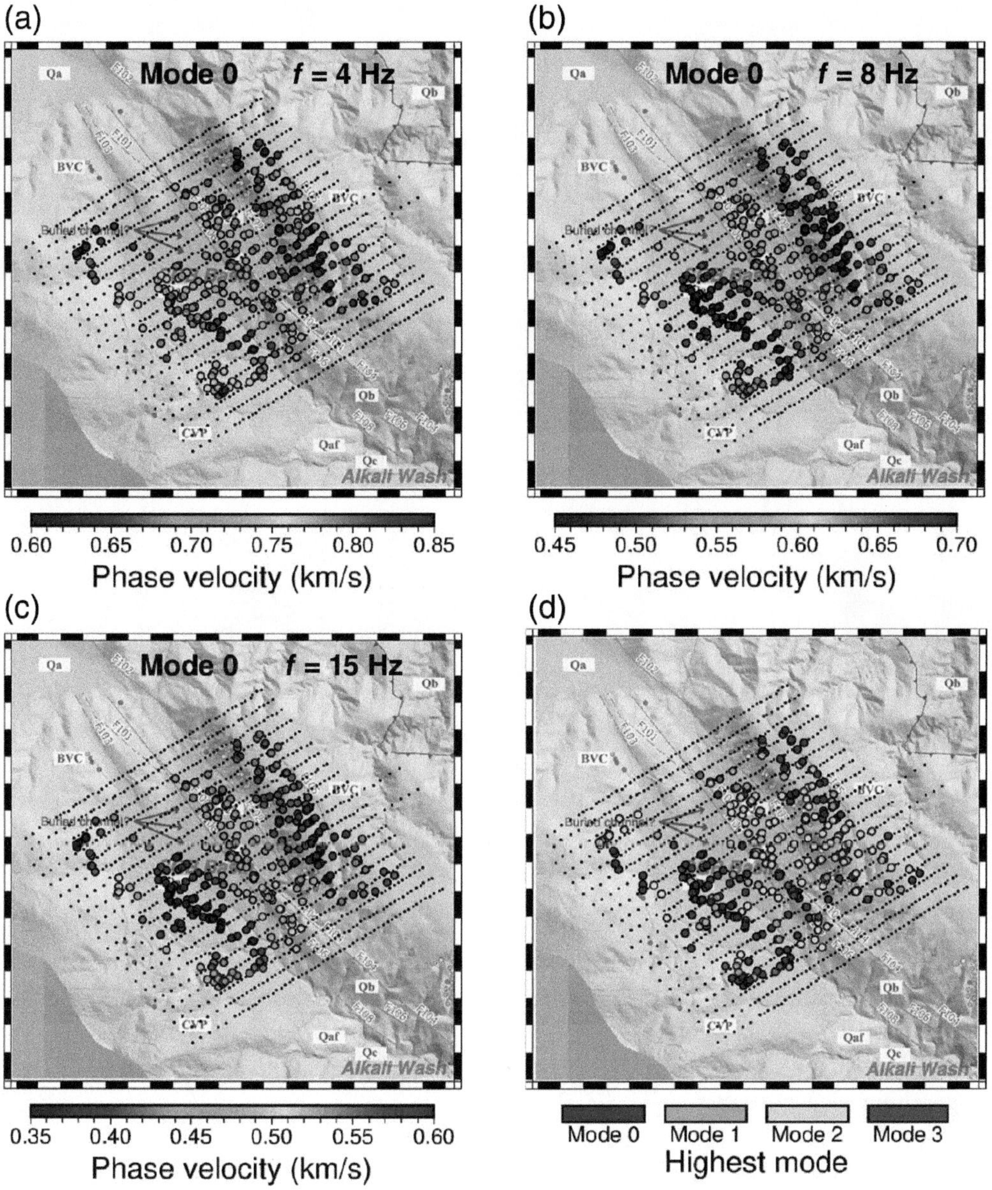

Figure 4. The phase velocity maps for the Rayleigh-wave fundamental mode at (a) 4 Hz, (b) 8 Hz, and (c) 15 Hz. The highest mode extracted for each subarray is shown in (d). The background image for each figure is edited from Share *et al.* (2020). The color version of this figure is available only in the electronic edition.

Discussion

Effectiveness of overtones

Overtones of dispersion curves offer additional constraints for inversion alongside the fundamental mode. In this study, due to the complex geological structures and prominent crossed artifacts, many overtones can only be identified in limited segments, as the example presented in Figure 3d. Figure 7 compares inversion results obtained using the fundamental mode alone with those incorporating multiple modes for the representative subarray "S" (shown in blue dots of Fig. 3c) and a sensitivity analysis. Even when integrating only a short segment of overtones, the resulting velocity structure captures more detailed features in the shallow structure (from 30 to 100 m), and the standard deviation is significantly reduced, demonstrating the value of overtone inclusion.

Comparison between FJ-PST and the traditional F-J method

The synthetic test by Li and Chen (2020) has demonstrated the importance of subarray selection when applying the F-J method to complex structures, highlighting the issue caused by subarrays crossing two different layered velocity structures. Here, we illustrate the effectiveness of FJ-PST by comparing it to the dispersion spectrogram of the traditional F-J method in this array. As shown in Figure 8, the traditional F-J method with fixed-shaped subarrays results in branched fundamental-mode dispersion curves, whereas FJ-PST effectively identifies boundaries and adaptively adjusts subarrays to mitigate this issue. More cases across different areas of the array and the corresponding improvement of FJ-PST can be found in Figure S2.

Error threshold

One primary step in the PST is combining the accepted probes into a new subarray. Although the 0.05 threshold used in this study is empirical, it is important to emphasize the robustness of the F-J method: the removal or addition of certain seismic stations has a negligible impact on dispersion extraction as long as the structure can be treated as a 1D layered velocity model. Therefore, the goal of PST is not to identify the "best" subarray for a given target, but to select suitable probes by excluding stations that would create an array over different 1D velocity structures. Because probes across different structures typically show significant dispersion dissimilarity, a wide range of error thresholds can effectively detect and eliminate unwanted probes.

Figures S3 and S4 present error threshold tests for two subarrays: one exhibiting branched dispersion curves and

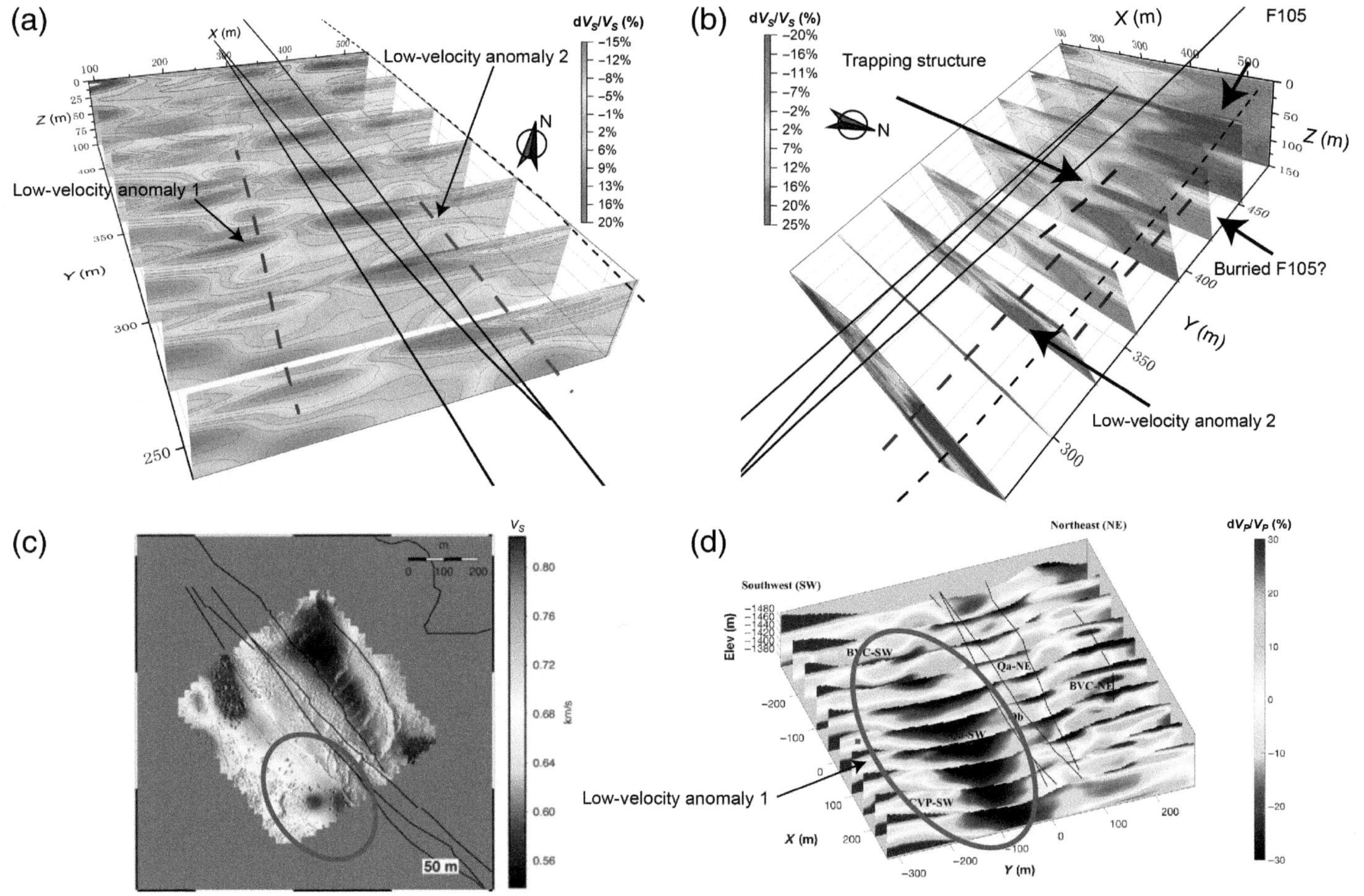

Figure 5. Representative vertical slices of the final 3D V_S perturbation model from the inversion of multimodal dispersion curves, shown from two perspectives: (a) southwest and (b) southeast. The black solid lines indicate fault traces evaluated by USGS (2006), and the black dashed line marks the inferred fault trace F105 Wade (2018). The red dashed lines in (a) denote two low-velocity anomalies identified in the model, and blue dashed lines in (b) mark features including a trapping structure, low-velocity anomaly 2, and a buried F105. The "?" in (b) points to "Burried F105," which indicates the possible location of an inferred fault (F105) identified by sharp lineaments in the topographic survey (Bevis *et al.*, 2005). (c) The V_S velocity map obtained from Mordret *et al.* (2019) at 50 m depth (edited from Share *et al.*, 2020). (d) The V_P velocity perturbation model obtained by Share *et al.* (2020). The red ellipses mark the velocity discrepancy between (c) and (d). The color version of this figure is available only in the electronic edition.

one without. In both cases, although some differences in subarrays occur when thresholds are set between 0.03 and 0.08, these variations have minimal impact on the dispersion extraction of the dispersion spectrogram. Most importantly, in all scenarios, the subarrays effectively avoid stations that could negatively affect the new dispersion spectrogram (i.e., cause branched dispersion curves).

Subarray distributions

Current state-of-the-art surface-wave theories are based on the flat multilayered isotropic structure assumption, which complicates the extraction of dispersion curves in geologically interesting transition zones where the velocity structure changes laterally. Although it is possible to extract low-quality dispersion curves in these areas, they may yield biased interpretations of the underlying structures. Further research is needed to develop methods to capture velocity structures in these transitional regions accurately.

In this study, the PST method offers an alternative solution by enabling array-based methods to avoid direct measuring phase velocities within transition zones and instead estimate these areas through interpolation. However, the interpolated structures lack the same reliability as directly measured data, and, here, we introduce a model credibility assessment.

Because the dispersion curve extracted from each subarray provides a local 1D estimate of the velocity structure at its centroid location, a higher density of centroids within a given area yields richer observational data. In contrast, regions containing fewer subarrays or lacking observations likely correspond to structural boundaries and are estimated via interpolation. Consequently, areas with denser observations yield more reliable velocity estimates. We quantify this observation density as follows: first, the model coverage is defined as the area of the

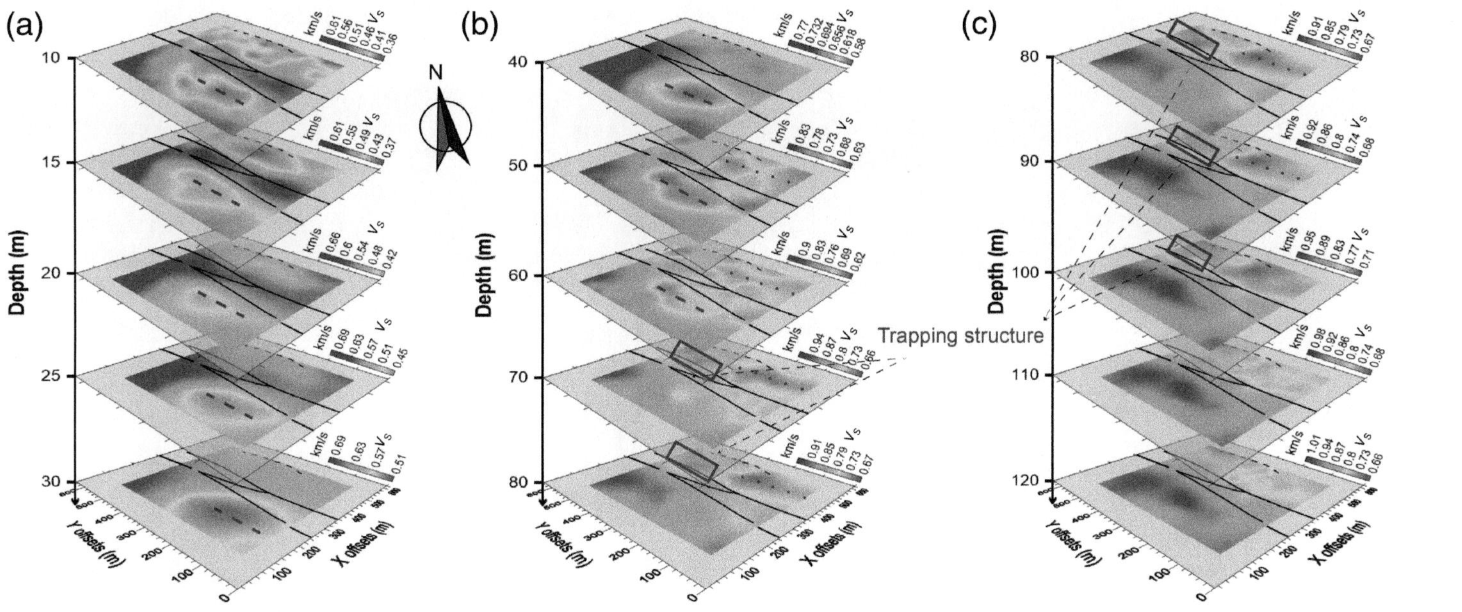

Figure 6. Depth slices of the final 3D V_S model from multimodal dispersion curve inversion at three depth ranges: (a) 10–30 m, (b) 40–80 m, and (c) 80–120 m. The red dashed line represents the low-velocity anomaly 1; the red dotted line indicates low-velocity anomaly 2; and the red rectangles indicate the low-velocity trapping structure inferred by fault zone trapped waves (Qin *et al.*, 2018). The color version of this figure is available only in the electronic edition.

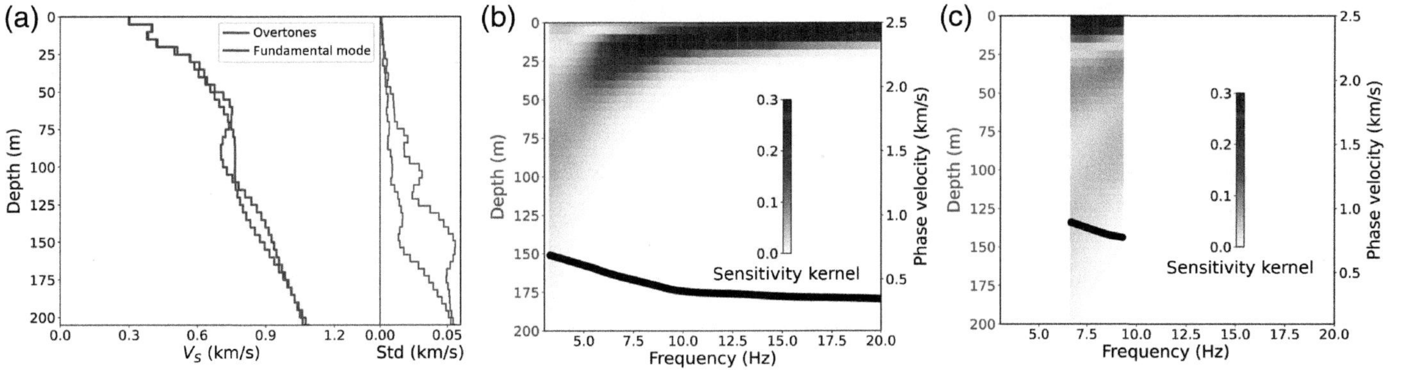

Figure 7. The effectiveness of overtone and dispersion sensitivity analysis. (a) Comparison of the 1D V_S model inverted with and without overtones extracted in Figure 3d. (b) The sensitivity kernel of the dispersion curve for the fundamental mode, and (c) the overtone. The red-shaded areas illustrate the sensitivity distributions as a function of depth and frequency, and the black points indicate the selected dispersion curves for each mode, as shown in Figure 3d. The values for each dispersion curve are shown on the right-side vertical axes. The color version of this figure is available only in the electronic edition.

V_S model derived from inversion and interpolation. To simplify calculations, we compute the density only at the locations of stations within this coverage (see black dots within the colored area in Fig. 9a). For the location of each station, we count the number of subarrays for which centroids fall within a unit aperture of 60 m (the side length of the probe), which serves as the resolution unit for this model. Next, we determine the maximum number of such subarrays across the entire region. Finally, we normalize the counts across the region by this maximum value and define them as the subarray density.

The density plot is illustrated in Figure 9a. As anticipated, the density within each unit is higher, whereas the unit boundaries (transitional zones) exhibit low density. The V_S model in regions identified with low subarray density (e.g., structural boundaries or near-fault blind spots; see Fig. 9b and Fig. S6) relies more heavily on interpolation and carries higher uncertainty. This is exemplified by the bimodal low-density area on the southeast, which corresponds to the boundaries between the Burnt Valley Complex (BVC), Coahuila Valley Pluton (CVP), and southwestern Quaternary sediments (Qa-SW)

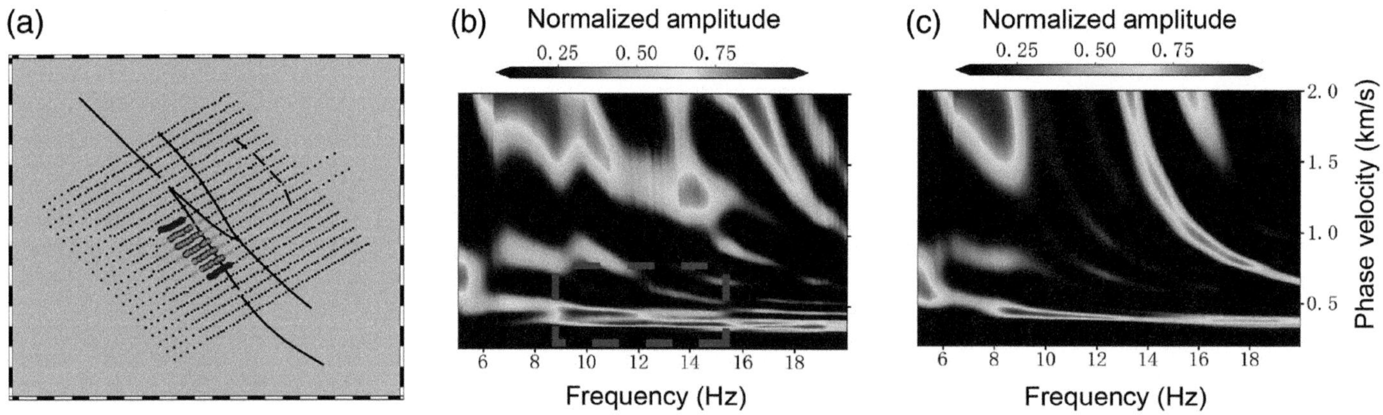

Figure 8. Comparison between FJ-PST and the traditional F-J for the dispersion spectrogram improvement. (a) Subarrays of FJ-PST (blue) and the nearest subarrays of traditional F-J (green). (b) Dispersion spectrogram calculated by the F-J for the green subarrays in panel (a), with red-dashed squares indicating the branched fundamental mode. (c) Dispersion spectrogram calculated by the F-J for the blue subarrays in panel (a). The color version of this figure is available only in the electronic edition.

units. Similarly, the curved low-density region on the right edge aligns with the abrupt velocity change across F105. These observations demonstrate that the PST is sensitive to boundaries between geological units without requiring prior information.

A further comparison between the phase velocity distribution of the Rayleigh-wave fundamental mode at 15 Hz and the observed geological units is presented in Figure 9b. Significant phase velocity contrasts are observed across different units. For instance, the BVC units in the northwestern corner exhibit very high phase velocities, whereas the Qa-SW and BVC units in the northeastern region show very low phase velocities. However, within each individual unit, the velocity variations are relatively minor. This explains why the PST can effectively detect boundaries because phase velocities typically undergo dramatic changes when transitioning between different geological units.

A significant low-density region is identified at the top edges of Figure 9a, which we designate as the northwestern complex zone (CPZ-NW). Geological observations in Figure 9b indicate that the CPZ-NW is linked to two inferred fault traces, F101 and F103, and a mixture of BVC and Qa rock units. The complex geological morphologies will likely result in significant velocity variations, making them unsuitable for applying the F-J method with the current probe and target sizes. Consequently, the PST accepted only a few subarrays in this region. Figure 9e,f provides examples of two subarrays located in the CPZ-NW (subarrays B and C in Fig. 9c). The corresponding dispersion spectrograms indicate low-quality dispersion curves and significant branched fundamental modes in multiple frequency bands, beginning at around 9 Hz. Figure S6 provides five probes within the CPZ-NW; the corresponding dispersion spectrogram still has branched dispersion curves within the tested band. These are the cases when probe C in Figure 2a serves as the reference probe and thus does not find nearby probes with small RE.

The continuous high density observed along the Clark fault branches in Figure 9a raises an interesting point because the PST is expected to result in a low-density area along the middle three fault branches as other geological boundaries. This indicates neither a failure of the PST nor the absence of F104 because the analysis was limited to the 3–16 Hz frequency band. Extensively branched dispersion is primarily observed between 9 and 16 Hz for the regular-shape subarrays (targets, i.e., Fig. 8b), motivating us to perform PST within this frequency range. Zooming-in on the phase measurements at 15 Hz in Figure 9b, the differences between the two sides of F104 exist but are relatively small compared to those observed across other boundaries.

As indicated by a subarray located at the trifurcated branches (the subarray A in Fig. 9c), the obtained dispersion spectrogram (Fig. 9d) does not have severe branched dispersion curves between 9 and 16 Hz but begins from 17 Hz. This higher branched band is sensitive to a shallower variation that is beyond the vertical resolution here. A different test band and probe size should be used for PST if a dispersion higher than 16 Hz is wanted, and show that the shallow part in this area (<60 m) does not exhibit significant changes compared to other geological boundaries, and prominent variations become apparent deeper than 80 m. This relatively uniform shallow velocity provides F-J with more accepted subarrays at the Clark fault, revealing a deeper variation with higher resolution.

Important shallow geology structures

Based on the 3D V_S model, several primary geological structures are observed:

1. Low-velocity anomaly 1: As illustrated in Figures 5a and 6a,b, a buried low-velocity channel is situated in the southwest (referred to as low-velocity anomaly 1), ranging in depths from 10 to 60 m. Previous research highlighted this

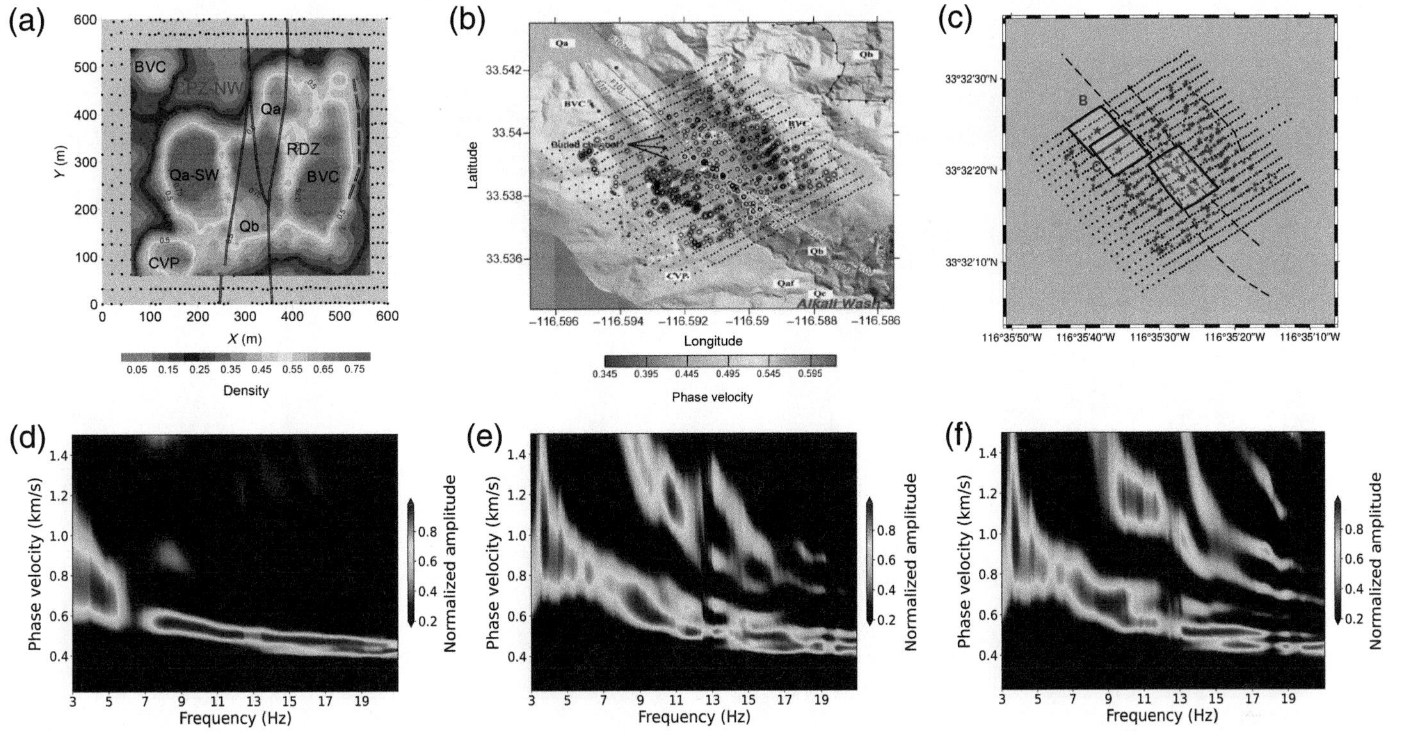

Figure 9. The relationship between geological units and partition density. (a) The partition density plot for the model coverage. The main geological units are marked in black, and the RDZ is marked in blue. A significant low-density area is highlighted in red: CPZ-NW. (b) The phase velocity distribution of Rayleigh-wave fundamental mode at 15 Hz is plotted at the original geology unit plot by Share *et al.* (2020). (c) Example subarrays: subarray A is located within the Clark fault, and subarrays B and C are located in the CPZ-NW. The subarrays consist of stations (black dots) covered by yellow areas, with the red star indicating the centroid of each subarray. (d–f) The dispersion spectrograms obtained by the F-J method for subarrays A, B, and C, respectively. The color version of this figure is available only in the electronic edition.

pattern by a *P*-wave low-velocity anomaly (Fig. 5d) and a low-resistivity feature (Share *et al.*, 2020). However, the previous V_S model obtained by Mordret *et al.* (2019) in the depth slice at 50 m (Share *et al.*, 2020) does not depict this structure (Fig. 5c), and our tomography results resolve this discrepancy.

2. Low-velocity anomaly 2: As depicted in Figures 5b and 6b,c, another deeper low-velocity anomaly (referred to as low-velocity anomaly 2) is situated on the right side of the middle fault traces, ranging from 50 to 90 m. The V_S model of Mordret *et al.* (2019) exhibits a general pattern consistent with this observation (Fig. 5c).
3. The trapping structure: Ben-Zion *et al.* (2015) and Qin *et al.* (2018) noted a low-velocity trapping structure to the northeast of the fault traces. Our results exhibit this pattern at depths from 70 to 100 m, as shown in Figures 5b and 6b,c. We find it interconnects with low-velocity anomaly 2 but displays a lower velocity anomaly and offsets horizontally and vertically.
4. The inferred fault F105: Identified by sharp lineaments from the topographic survey (Bevis *et al.*, 2005), an inferred fault trace (F105 in Fig. 1a) is situated in the northeastern corner of the array. Our V_S tomography confirms its presence, revealed by the northeastern low-velocity anomaly from 10 to 25 m in Figure 6a. Interestingly, this structure becomes less distinct below 30 m but gradually becomes more pronounced after 100 m (Fig. 6c). We attribute this depth-dependent resolution to the combined effects of low-velocity anomaly 2 and the trapping structure, which obscure the fault expression at intermediate depths.

Structures within the branches of Clark fault at the SGB site

To better visualize the lateral variation of the Clark fault at the SGB site, we plot three vertical V_S slices where three fault branches (F106, F104, and F102) intersect (Fig. 10), with black reference lines in Figure 1b indicating their locations. Evaluations of two surface fault traces are marked in gray and black dashed lines (Dor *et al.*, 2006; U.S. Geological Survey [USGS], 2006). Our results show significant along-strike variations along branch F104 below 60 m depth. The southern segment (rows 8-11) exhibits particularly strong velocity contrasts, which become weaker in the direction northward (row 13).

We use the waveform simulation method proposed by Lu and Ben-Zion (2022) to validate this high-resolution variation. We choose five stations distributed along and within the fault

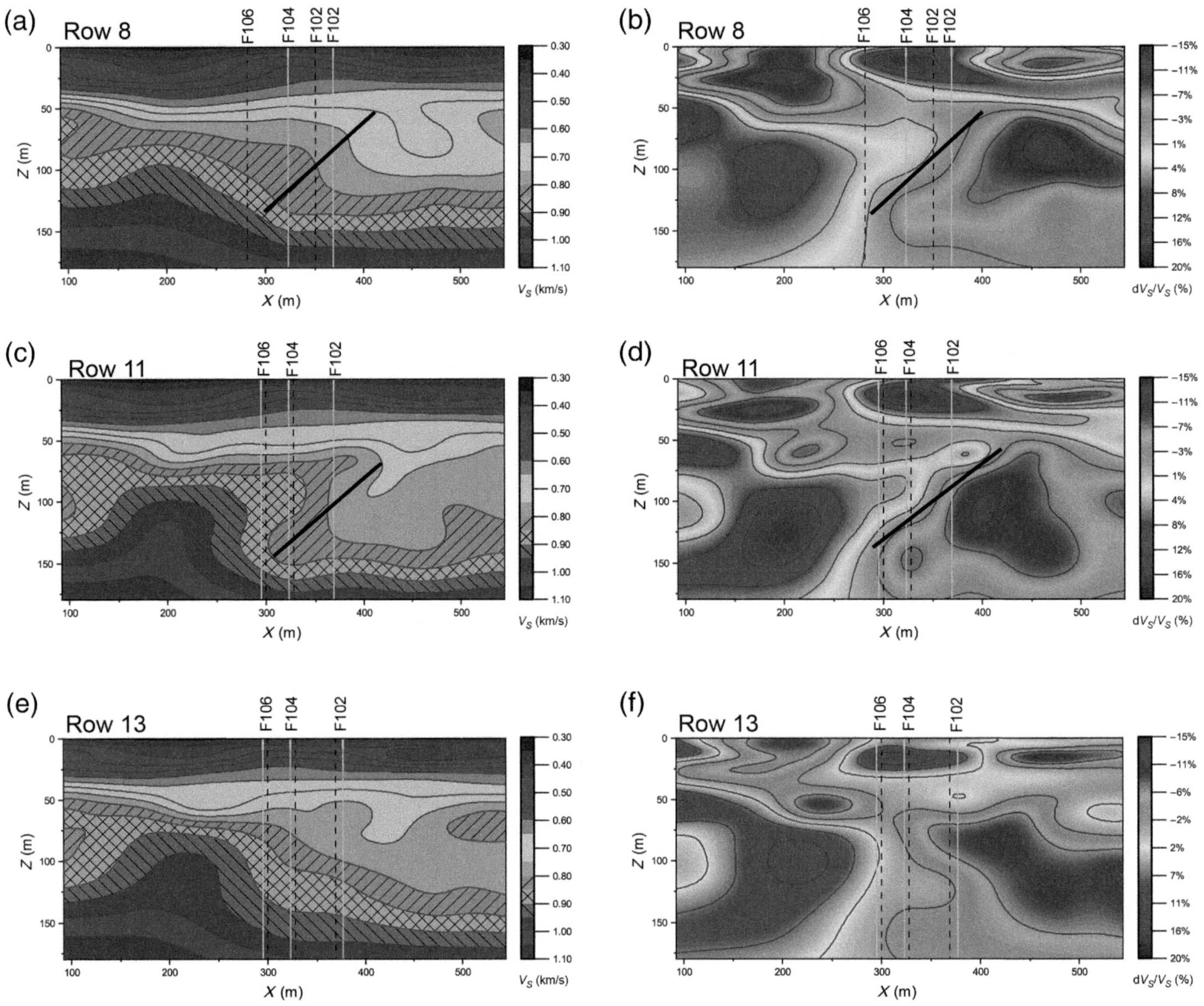

Figure 10. Vertical slices of (a,c,e) V_S model and (b,d,f) V_S perturbation within the mixture branches of F106, F104, and F102 (referenced in Fig. 1b as rows 8, 11, and 13). The black dashed vertical lines and gray solid lines in each plot represent the fault traces estimated by USGS (2006) and Wade (2018), respectively. Three velocity contours are typically marked in panels (a) as different filling lines to visualize the variations better. The black solid lines indicate the high-resolution variation along the fault branches under F104. The color version of this figure is available only in the electronic edition.

branches (reference locations in Fig. 1b) to synthesize the CCFs using the finite-difference method (Zhang and Chen, 2006; Zhang *et al.*, 2012). The synthesized CCFs are compared with the observed in three different frequency bands (3–7 Hz, 7–12 Hz, and 10–15 Hz). As illustrated in Figure S5, while slight time delays and waveform mismatches exist, the synthetic CCFs align well with the observed data, supporting the accuracy of our inferred model.

Conclusions

In this study, we propose a quantitative PST to adaptively address the branch dispersion phenomenon of the dispersion spectrogram when applying the F-J method to complex structures. To validate its effectiveness, the method is utilized to image the V_S structure at the SGB site, located along the Clark fault branches of the San Jacinto fault zone. The PST generates subarrays that extract continuous Rayleigh-wave fundamental modes from 3 to 16 Hz and fragmental overtones. The inversion result resolves a discrepancy between the V_S model and other geophysical observations, presenting higher resolution geological characteristics and revealing detailed structures of the Clark fault at shallow depths. The density information of subarray centroids is employed to evaluate the model credibility and guide further improvements, such as exploring different targets and probes or conducting joint analyses with other methods. Based on this case study, we consider this method a valuable tool for overtone surface-wave tomography in imaging complex subsurface structures. The developed array subdivision method can be applied to adaptively identify suitable subarrays in dense arrays of various sizes and configurations beyond the scope of this case study.

Data and Resources

The seismic data used in this article can be obtained from the Data Management Center (DMC) of the Incorporated Research Institutions for Seismology (IRIS) and Broadband Seismic Data Collection Center (Vernon *et al.*, 2014) via doi: 10.7914/SN/ZG_2014, and the IRIS DMC via https://ds.iris.edu/mda/9A/156/. The CC-FJpy (Li *et al.*, 2021) which was used for cross correlation and F-J calculation can be obtained from https://github.com/ColinLii/CC-FJpy. Both websites were last accessed in December 2023. The supplemental material includes a detailed comparison of dispersion spectrograms for different subarray sizes, improved examples of spectrograms using the FJ-PST method, and error threshold tests. Additionally, it presents the results of waveform fitting for different virtual sources and provides dispersion spectrograms of probes located within the CPZ-NW.

Declaration of Competing Interests

The authors acknowledge that there are no conflicts of interest recorded.

Acknowledgments

The authors thank two anonymous reviewers for their constructive comments and suggestions. This work was supported by the National Key Research and Development Program of China (2022YFC3003504), the Guangdong Provincial Key Laboratory of Geophysical High-resolution Imaging Technology (2022B1212010002), and the Shenzhen Key Laboratory of Deep Offshore Oil and Gas Exploration Technology (ZDSYS20190902093007855). The numerical calculations were supported by Center for Computational Science and Engineering at Southern University of Science and Technology.

References

Aki, K. (1957). Space and time spectra of stationary stochastic waves, with special reference to microtremors, *Bull. Earthq. Res. Inst.* **35,** 415–456.

Bensen, G. D., M. H. Ritzwoller, M. P. Barmin, A. L. Levshin, F. Lin, M. P. Moschetti, N. M. Shapiro, and Y. Yang (2007). Processing seismic ambient noise data to obtain reliable broad-band surface wave dispersion measurements, *Geophys. J. Int.* **169,** no. 3, 1239–1260, doi: 10.1111/j.1365-246X.2007.03374.x.

Ben-Zion, Y., F. L. Vernon, Y. Ozakin, D. Zigone, Z. E. Ross, H. Meng, M. White, J. Reyes, D. Hollis, and M. Barklage (2015). Basic data features and results from a spatially dense seismic array on the San Jacinto fault zone, *Geophys. J. Int.* **202,** no. 1, 370–380, doi: 10.1093/gji/ggv142.

Bevis, M., K. Hudnut, R. Sanchez, C. Toth, D. Grejner-Brzezinska, E. Kendrick, *et al.* (2005). The B4 project: Scanning the San Andreas and San Jacinto fault zones, *Paper Presented at the AGU Fall Meeting Abstract*, available at https://ui.adsabs.harvard.edu/abs/2005AGUFM.H34B..01B/abstract (last accessed August 2025).

Byrd, R. H., P. Lu, J. Nocedal, and C. Zhu (1995). A limited memory algorithm for bound constrained optimization, *Siam J. Sci. Comput.* **16,** no. 5, 1190–1208, doi: 10.1137/0916069.

Campillo, M., and A. Paul (2003). Long-range correlations in the diffuse seismic coda, *Science* **299,** no. 5606, 547–549, doi: 10.1126/science.1078551.

Capon, J. (1969). High-resolution frequency-wavenumber spectrum analysis, *Proc. IEEE* **57,** no. 8, 1408–1418, doi: 10.1109/PROC.1969.7278.

Chang, J. P., S. A. L. de Ridder, and B. L. Biondi (2016). High-frequency Rayleigh-wave tomography using traffic noise from Long Beach, California, *Geophysics* **81,** no. 2, B43–B53, doi: 10.1190/GEO2015-0415.1.

Chen, J., L. Pan, Z. B. Li, and X. Chen (2022). Continental reworking in the eastern South China block and its adjacent areas revealed by F-J multimodal ambient noise tomography, *J. Geophys. Res.* **127,** no. 11, doi: 10.1029/2022JB024776.

Cheng, F., J. Xia, and C. Xi (2023). Artifacts in high-frequency passive surface wave dispersion imaging: Toward the linear receiver array, *Surv. Geophys.* **44,** no. 4, 1009–1039, doi: 10.1007/s10712-023-09772-1.

Dong, S., Z. Li, X. Chen, and L. Fu (2021). Dispernet: An effective method of extracting and classifying the dispersion curves in the frequency-Bessel dispersion spectrum, *Bull. Seismol. Soc. Am.* **111,** no. 6, 3420–3431, doi: 10.1785/0120210033.

Dor, O., T. K. Rockwell, and Y. Ben-Zion (2006). Geological observations of damage asymmetry in the structure of the San Jacinto, San Andreas and Punchbowl faults in southern California: A possible indicator for preferred rupture propagation direction, *Pure Appl. Geophys.* **163,** no. 2, 301–349, doi: 10.1007/s00024-005-0023-9.

Fu, L., L. Pan, Z. Li, S. Dong, Q. Ma, and X. Chen (2022). Improved high-resolution 3d Vs model of Long Beach, California: Inversion of multimodal dispersion curves from ambient noise of a dense array, *Geophys. Res. Lett.* **49,** no. 4, doi: 10.1029/2021GL097619.

Gabriels, P., R. Snieder, and G. Nolet (1987). Insitu measurements of shear-wave velocity in sediments with higher-mode Rayleigh-waves, *Geophys. Prospect.* **35,** no. 2, 187–196, doi: 10.1111/j.1365-2478.1987.tb00812.x.

Gao, L., W. Zhang, Z. Zhang, and X. Chen (2021). Extraction of multimodal dispersion curves from ambient noise with compressed sensing, *J. Geophys. Res.* **126,** no. 6, doi: 10.1029/2020JB021472.

Hansen, S. M., and B. Schmandt (2015). Automated detection and location of microseismicity at Mount St. Helens with a large-N geophone array, *Geophys. Res. Lett.* **42,** no. 18, 7390–7397, doi: 10.1002/2015GL064848.

Hillers, G., P. Roux, M. Campillo, and Y. Ben-Zion (2016). Focal spot imaging based on zero lag cross-correlation amplitude fields: Application to dense array data at the San Jacinto fault zone, *J. Geophys. Res.* **121,** no. 11, 8048–8067, doi: 10.1002/2016JB013014.

Hu, S., S. Luo, and H. Yao (2020). The frequency-Bessel spectrograms of multicomponent cross-correlation functions from seismic ambient noise, *J. Geophys. Res.* **125,** no. 8, e2020JB019630, doi: 10.1029/2020JB019630.

Lacoss, R. T., E. J. Kelly, and M. N. Toksoz (1969). Estimation of seismic noise structure using arrays, *Geophysics* **34,** no. 1, 21–38, doi: 10.1190/1.1439995.

Li, Z., and X. Chen (2020). An effective method to extract overtones of surface wave from array seismic records of earthquake events, *J. Geophys. Res.* **125,** no. 3, e2019JB018511, doi: 10.1029/2019JB018511.

Li, Z., S. Dong, C. Shi, L. Fu, L. Pan, J. Wang, and X. Chen (2023). Multiple Voronoi partition improves multimodal dispersion imaging from ambient noise: A case study of Lasso dense array, *J. Geophys. Res.* **128,** no. 5, e2022JB026081, doi: 10.1029/2022JB026081.

Li, Z., C. Shi, H. Ren, and X. Chen (2022). Multiple leaking mode dispersion observations and applications from ambient noise cross-correlation in Oklahoma, *Geophys. Res. Lett.* **49,** no. 1, e2021GL096032, doi: 10.1029/2021GL096032.

Li, Z., J. Zhou, G. Wu, J. Wang, G. Zhang, S. Dong, L. Pan, Z. Yang, L. Gao, Q. Ma, *et al.* (2021). Cc-Fjpy: A Python package for extracting overtone surface-wave dispersion from seismic ambient-noise cross correlation, *Seismol. Res. Lett.* **92,** no. 5, 3179–3186, doi: 10.1785/0220210042.

Lin, F.-C., and M. H. Ritzwoller (2011). Helmholtz surface wave tomography for isotropic and azimuthally anisotropic structure, *Geophys. J. Int.* **186,** no. 3, 1104–1120, doi: 10.1111/j.1365-246X.2011.05070.x.

Liu, Y., F. Niu, M. Chen, and W. Yang (2017). 3-D Crustal and uppermost mantle structure beneath Ne China revealed by ambient noise adjoint tomography, *Earth Planet. Sci. Lett.* **461,** 20–29, doi: 10.1016/j.epsl.2016.12.029.

Lu, Y., and Y. Ben-Zion (2022). Validation of seismic velocity models in southern California with full-waveform simulations, *Geophys. J. Int.* **229,** no. 2, 1232–1254, doi: 10.1093/gji/ggab534.

Luo, Y., J. Xia, R. D. Miller, Y. Xu, J. Liu, and Q. Liu (2008). Rayleigh-wave dispersive energy imaging using a high-resolution linear Radon transform, *Pure Appl. Geophys.* **165,** no. 5, 903–922, doi: 10.1007/s00024-008-0338-4.

Ma, Q., L. Pan, J. Wang, Z. Yang, and X. Chen (2022). Crustal S-wave velocity structure beneath the northwestern Bohemian massif, central Europe, revealed by the inversion of multimodal ambient noise dispersion curves, *Front. Earth Sci.* **10,** 838,751, doi: 10.3389/feart.2022.838751.

Maraschini, M., F. Ernst, S. Foti, and L. Socco (2010). A new misfit function for multimodal inversion of surface waves, *Geophysics* **75,** no. 4, G31–G43, doi: 10.1190/1.3436539.

Meng, H., and Y. Ben-Zion (2018). Detection of small earthquakes with dense array data: Example from the San Jacinto fault zone, southern California, *Geophys. J. Int.* **212,** no. 1, 442–457, doi: 10.1093/gji/ggx404.

Mordret, A., M. Landes, N. M. Shapiro, S. C. Singh, and P. Roux (2014). Ambient noise surface wave tomography to determine the shallow shear velocity structure at Valhall: Depth inversion with a neighbourhood algorithm, *Geophys. J. Int.* **198,** no. 3, 1514–1525, doi: 10.1093/gji/ggu217.

Mordret, A., P. Roux, P. Boué, and Y. Ben-Zion (2019). Shallow three-dimensional structure of the San Jacinto fault zone revealed from ambient noise imaging with a dense seismic array, *Geophys. J. Int.* **216,** no. 2, 896–905, doi: 10.1093/gji/ggy464.

Nakata, N., J. P. Chang, J. F. Lawrence, and P. Boue (2015). Body wave extraction and tomography at Long Beach, California, with ambient-noise interferometry, *J. Geophys. Res.* **120,** no. 2, 1159–1173, doi: 10.1002/2015JB011870.

Nolet, G., and G. F. Panza (1976). Array analysis of seismic surface waves: Limits and possibilities, *Pure Appl. Geophys.* **114,** no. 5, 775–790, doi: 10.1007/BF00875787.

Pan, L., X. Chen, J. Wang, Z. Yang, and D. Zhang (2019). Sensitivity analysis of dispersion curves of Rayleigh waves with fundamental and higher modes, *Geophys. J. Int.* **216,** no. 2, 1276–1303, doi: 10.1093/gji/ggy479.

Pan, Y., J. Xia, Y. Xu, Z. Xu, F. Cheng, H. Xu, and L. Gao (2016). Delineating shallow S-wave velocity structure using multiple ambient-noise surface-wave methods: An example from western Junggar, China, *Bull. Seismol. Soc. Am.* **106,** no. 2, 327–336, doi: 10.1785/0120150014.

Park, C. B., and R. D. Miller (2008). Roadside passive multichannel analysis of surface waves (Masw), *J. Environ. Eng. Geophys.* **13,** no. 1, 1–11, doi: 10.2113/JEEG13.1.1.

Qin, L., Y. Ben-Zion, H. Qiu, P. Share, Z. Ross, and F. Vernon (2018). Internal structure of the San Jacinto fault zone in the Trifurcation area southeast of Anza, California, from data of dense seismic arrays, *Geophys. J. Int.* **213,** no. 1, 98–114, doi: 10.1093/gji/ggx540.

Roux, P., L. Moreau, A. Lecointre, G. Hillers, M. Campillo, Y. Ben-Zion, D. Zigone, and F. Vernon (2016). A methodological approach towards high-resolution surface wave imaging of the San Jacinto fault zone using ambient-noise recordings at a spatially dense array, *Geophys. J. Int.* **206,** no. 2, 980–992, doi: 10.1093/gji/ggw193.

Shapiro, N. M., and M. Campillo (2004). Emergence of broadband Rayleigh waves from correlations of the ambient seismic noise, *Geophys. Res. Lett.* **31,** no. 7, doi: 10.1029/2004gl019491.

Shapiro, N. M., and M. H. Ritzwoller (2002). Monte-Carlo inversion for a Global shear-velocity model of the crust and upper mantle, *Geophys. J. Int.* **151,** no. 1, 88–105, doi: 10.1046/j.1365-246X.2002.01742.x.

Shapiro, N. M., M. Campillo, L. Stehly, and M. H. Ritzwoller (2005). High-resolution surface-wave tomography from ambient seismic noise, *Science* **307,** no. 5715, 1615–1618, doi: 10.1126/science.1108339.

Share, P. E., P. Taborik, P. Stepancikova, J. Stemberk, T. K. Rockwell, A. Wade, J. Arrowsmith, A. Donnellan, F. Vernon, and Y. Ben-Zion (2020). Characterizing the uppermost 100 M structure of the San Jacinto fault zone southeast of Anza, California, through joint analysis of geological, topographic, seismic and resistivity data, *Geophys. J. Int.* **222,** no. 2, 781–794, doi: 10.1093/gji/ggaa204.

Song, W., X. Feng, G. Wu, G. Zhang, Y. Liu, and X. Chen (2021). Convolutional neural network, Res-Unet++, -based dispersion curve picking from noise cross-correlations, *J. Geophys. Res.* **126,** no. 11, e2021JB022027, doi: 10.1029/2021JB022027.

Song, W., X. Feng, G. Zhang, L. Gao, B. Yan, and X. Chen (2022). Domain adaptation in automatic picking of phase velocity dispersions based on deep learning. *J. Geophys. Res.* **127,** no. 6, e2021JB023389, doi: 10.1029/2021JB023389.

Tomar, G., E. Stutzmann, A. Mordret, J. P. Montagner, S. C. Singh, and N. M. Shapiro (2018). Joint inversion of the first overtone and fundamental mode for deep imaging at the Valhall oil field using ambient noise, *Geophys. J. Int.* **214,** no. 1, 122–132, doi: 10.1093/gji/ggy122.

Touma, R., T. Blondel, A. Derode, M. Campillo, and A. Aubry (2021). A distortion matrix framework for high-resolution passive seismic 3-D imaging: Application to the San Jacinto fault zone, California, *Geophys. J. Int.* **226,** no. 2, 780–794, doi: 10.1093/gji/ggab133.

Touma, R., A. Aubry, Y. Ben-Zion, and M. Campillo (2022). Distribution of seismic scatterers in the San Jacinto fault zone, southeast of Anza, California, based on passive matrix imaging, *Earth Planet. Sci. Lett.* **578,** 117304, doi: 10.1016/j.epsl.2021.117304.

Trampert, J., and J. H. Woodhouse (1995). Global phase velocity maps of Love and Rayleigh waves between 40 and 150 seconds, *Geophys. J. Int.* **122,** no. 2, 675–690, doi: 10.1111/j.1365-246X.1995.tb07019.x.

U.S. Geological Survey (USGS) (2006). Quaternary Fault and Fold Database for the United States, available at https://earthquake.usgs.gov/hazards/qfaults/ (last accessed January 2017).

Vernon, F., Y. Ben-Zion, and D. Hollis (2014). Sage Brush flats nodal experiment [Dataset], *International Federation of Digital Seismograph Networks. Other/Seismic Network*, doi: 10.7914/SN/ZG_2014.

Wade, A. M. (2018). *Geologic and Structural Characterization of Shallow Seismic Properties Along the San Jacinto Fault at Sage Brush Flat, Southern California (Mscthesis)*, Arizona State University, Arizona.

Wang, G., X. Tian, L. Guo, J. Yan, and Q. Lyu (2018). High-resolution crustal velocity imaging using ambient noise recordings from a high-density seismic array: An example from the Shangrao section of the Xinjiang basin, China, *Earthq. Sci.* **31,** nos. 5/6, 242–251, doi: 10.29382/eqs-2018-0242-4.

Wang, J., G. Wu, and X. Chen (2019). Frequency-Bessel transform method for effective imaging of higher-mode Rayleigh dispersion curves from ambient seismic noise data, *J. Geophys. Res.* **124,** no. 4, 3708–3723, doi: 10.1029/2018JB016595.

Wang, P., J. Chen, X. Feng, L. Pan, and X. Chen (2024). Crust and upper mantle S wave velocity structure in eastern Turkey based on ambient noise tomography, *Tectonophysics* **876,** 230,267, doi: 10.1016/j.tecto.2024.230267.

Wei, Y., X. Tian, Y. Duan, and X. Tian (2018). Imaging the topography of crust-mantle boundary from a high-density seismic array beneath the Middle-Lower Yangtze River, eastern China, *Seismol. Res. Lett.* **89,** no. 5, 1690–1697, doi: 10.1785/0220180045.

Wiggins, R. A. (1972). The general linear inverse problem: Implication of surface waves and free oscillations for earth structure, *Rev. Geophys.* **10,** no. 1, 251–285, doi: 10.1029/RG010i001p00251.

Wu, G., L. Pan, J. Wang, and X. Chen (2020). Shear velocity inversion using multimodal dispersion curves from ambient seismic noise data of Usarray transportable array, *J. Geophys. Res.* **125,** no. 1, e2019JB018213, doi: 10.1029/2019JB018213.

Xi, C., J. Xia, B. Mi, T. Dai, Y. Liu, and L. Ning (2021). Modified frequency-Bessel transform method for dispersion imaging of Rayleigh waves from ambient seismic noise, *Geophys. J. Int.* **225,** no. 2, 1271–1280, doi: 10.1093/gji/ggab008.

Yao, H., R. D. van der Hilst, and M. V. de Hoop (2006). Surface-wave array tomography in Se Tibet from ambient seismic noise and two-station analysis - I. Phase velocity maps, *Geophys. J. Int.* **166,** no. 2, 732–744, doi: 10.1111/j.1365-246X.2006.03028.x.

Yokoi, T. (2010). New formulas derived from seismic interferometry to simulate phase velocity estimates from correlation methods using microtremor, *Geophysics* **75,** no. 4, doi: 10.1190/1.3454210.

Yuan, Y., and X. Chen (2024). Efficient array partitioning method for F-J transform to extract multimode dispersion curves from ambient noise data, *Chin. J. Geophys. (in Chinese)* **67,** no. 2, 492–502, doi: 10.6038/cjg2023R0274.

Zhan, W., L. Pan, and X. Chen (2020). A widespread mid-crustal low-velocity layer beneath northeast China revealed by the multimodal inversion of Rayleigh waves from ambient seismic noise, *J. Asian Earth Sci.* **196,** 104,372, doi: 10.1016/j.jseaes.2020.104372.

Zhang, W., and X. Chen (2006). Traction image method for irregular free surface boundaries in finite difference seismic wave simulation, *Geophys. J. Int.* **167,** no. 1, 337–353, doi: 10.1111/j.1365-246X.2006.03113.x.

Zhang, G. H., Q. Liu, and X. F. Chen (2022). Enhancing the frequency–Bessel spectrogram of ambient noise cross-correlation functions, *Bull. Seismol. Soc. Am.* **113,** no. 1, 361–377, doi: 10.1785/0120220124.

Zhang, W., Z. Zhang, and X. Chen (2012). Three-dimensional elastic wave numerical modelling in the presence of surface topography by a collocated-grid finite-difference method on curvilinear grids, *Geophys. J. Int.* **190,** no. 1, 358–378, doi: 10.1111/j.1365-246X.2012.05472.x.

Zhou, J., and X. Chen (2022). Removal of crossed artifacts from multimodal dispersion curves with modified frequency-Bessel method, *Bull. Seismol. Soc. Am.* **112,** no. 1, 143–152, doi: 10.1785/0120210012.

Zhou, J., Z. Li, and X. Chen (2023). Extending the frequency band of surface-wave dispersion curves by combining ambient noise and earthquake data and self-adaptive normalization, *J. Geophys. Res.* **128,** no. 5, e2022JB026040, doi: 10.1029/2022JB026040.

Manuscript received 30 November 2024
Published online 17 September 2025

Surface-Wave Tomography with Transfer Learning and Moho Constraints: Method and Application to China Mainland

Feiyi Wang[1,2], Xuezhen Zhang[2,3], and Xiaodong Song[*2,4]

Abstract

We develop a novel method based on deep learning to simultaneously obtain shear-wave velocity (V_S) structure, sedimentary layer thickness, and Moho depth from Rayleigh-wave phase and group velocities. Compared with previous studies, the proposed method constrains the inversion process through forward information to enhance the physical interpretability and uses transfer learning to significantly improve the accuracy of the inversion results. Furthermore, to alleviate the multiple solution problem in surface-wave inversion, we constrain it by introducing Moho information. We have fully considered the influence of the parameter settings in the inversion process, and selected appropriate parameters during the inversion, such as sedimentary layer, attenuation, density, V_P/V_S ratio. The effectiveness and robustness of the proposed method are demonstrated through synthetic tests. Using recently measured surface-wave dispersion data, we obtained the lithospheric V_S structure in East Asia based on the proposed approach. Results from application of our model to observed data show consistency with previous research, fit to known geological structure, and result in a smaller misfit. Our findings support our method as an impactful tool for V_S structure inversion. In the mantle, the tearing of the Indian plate beneath the Tibetan Plateau (TP) can be seen at approximately 85° and 90° E. The high-velocity block outlines the possible subduction of the Indian plate, extending as far as about 35° N position. The lithosphere in the western Sichuan basin may have been modified by plateau material from the southeastern edge of the TP, showing low-velocity anomalies at a depth of about 100 km.

Cite this article as Wang, F., X. Zhang, and X. Song (2025). Surface-Wave Tomography with Transfer Learning and Moho Constraints: Method and Application to China Mainland, *Seismol. Res. Lett.* **97**, 1104–1122, doi: 10.1785/0220240437.

Supplemental Material

Introduction

Machine learning is increasingly being applied in the field of geophysics to enhance data analysis and automate various tasks such as removing noise and improving the signal-to-noise ratio (Zhang *et al.*, 2017; Yu *et al.*, 2019; Zhu *et al.*, 2019; Feng and Li, 2022), phase picking (Zhu and Beroza, 2019; Yang *et al.*, 2020; Soto and Schurr, 2021; Liao *et al.*, 2022; Münchmeyer *et al.*, 2022), phase association (McBrearty *et al.*, 2019; Ross *et al.*, 2019), earthquake forecasting (Wang *et al.*, 2017; Devries *et al.*, 2018; Mignan and Broccardo, 2020), event detection (Mousavi *et al.*, 2020; Duan *et al.*, 2023), and structure inversion (Meier *et al.*, 2007; Yang and Ma, 2019; Wang *et al.*, 2022).

Surface waves exhibit dispersion, meaning that their velocity varies with frequency. Dispersion curves are a representation of the relationship between velocity and frequency. They contain valuable information about the subsurface and are therefore widely used to determine the Earth's subsurface shear-wave velocity (V_S) structure (e.g., Zheng *et al.*, 2008; Shen *et al.*, 2016). The inversion typically involves finding a V_S model of the subsurface for which predictions best fit the observed dispersion curves. Various inversion methods are used to estimate the subsurface V_S structure. These methods include traditional techniques such as linear inversion (Sun *et al.*, 2010; Herrmann, 2013; Bao *et al.*, 2015; Li *et al.*, 2022) and nonlinear inversion (Wathelet, 2008; Xu *et al.*, 2013; Li *et al.*, 2017) as well as more advanced approaches such as Bayesian inversion (Shen *et al.*, 2013; Roy and Romanowicz, 2017). Deep learning (DL), a significant branch of machine learning, is highly effective at extracting features from

1. School of Mathematics, Harbin Institute of Technology, Harbin, China; 2. State Key Laboratory of Deep Earth and Mineral Exploration, School of Earth and Space Sciences, Peking University, Beijing, China, https://orcid.org/0009-0009-8919-7105 (XZ); https://orcid.org/0000-0002-5932-6916 (XS); 3. Institute of Theoretical and Applied Geophysics, Peking University, Beijing, China; 4. Center of Artificial Intelligence Geosciences, Institute for Artificial Intelligence, Peking University, Beijing, China

*Corresponding author: xiao.d.song@gmail.com

observational data (Yu *et al.*, 2019; Feng and Li, 2022; Wang *et al.*, 2023). These features may be direct representations of the raw data or high-level abstract representations obtained through various transformations or learning processes. Consequently, DL has been applied to surface-wave inversion (Hu *et al.*, 2020; Cai *et al.*, 2022; Wang *et al.*, 2023).

For conventional supervised or semi-supervised DL, surface-wave inversion can be roughly divided into the following steps (Hu *et al.*, 2020; Cai *et al.*, 2022; Wang *et al.*, 2023). The first step is to generate a large number of synthetic velocity models as labels, which can be directly derived from existing regional velocity models (Hu *et al.*, 2020; Cai *et al.*, 2022) or generating representative velocity models through a certain method (Wang *et al.*, 2023). Hu *et al.* (2020) found poor performance of DL surface-wave inversion when applied to a different region than that of the training dataset. Cai *et al.* (2022) utilized the structure of generative adversarial networks (GANs; Goodfellow *et al.*, 2014) to alleviate the dependence on the training dataset used in the network training process and obtain better V_S results than conventional machine learning methods. However, GAN suffers from training instability as well as the mode collapse problem. These concerns remain open-challenging issues for GANs and become more complex in the case of cycle-consistent adversarial network (cycle-GAN; Jabbar *et al.*, 2020; Ding *et al.*, 2022; Vandana *et al.*, 2022). Wang *et al.* (2023) completely used a spline-based method to generate the training dataset, without referring to any existing regional velocity models. Systematic synthetic data tests and observed data applications prove that the DL model trained based on this training dataset has high generalization and is faster and more accurate than traditional methods (Wang *et al.*, 2023). The second step is to perform forward modeling to obtain the dispersions, that is, to obtain the data corresponding to the label in the training process. The third step is to design a suitable neural network and train it using the large amount of data obtained in the first two steps. The purpose is to perform an inversion using the powerful data mining capabilities of deep networks to learn complex mappings from dispersion to 1D V_S structure. The last step is application, feeding the observed dispersion curves into the trained DL model, and outputting its corresponding 1D V_S structure (Fig. S1, available in the supplemental material to this article).

The synthetic velocity model generated in the Wang *et al.* (2023) account for key parameter assumptions such as sedimentary layer, attenuation and density, which have significant impacts on the inversion results (Zhang and Song, 2024). In this study, we comprehensively consider the parameter assumptions in the surface-wave inversion and generate a representative training dataset using a spline-based approach. Transfer learning, a technique in which a pretrained model is adapted for a new but related task, is utilized in our approach. Referring to the cycle-consistent network, the forward information (implemented via a forward subnetwork [FwNet]) is used to constrain the inversion process. This process introduces physical constraints and significantly improves the accuracy of the inversion. In addition, the introduction of FwNet can incorporate observation data into transfer learning, improving the agreement between model predictions and observed data. Training is divided into two steps. The first step is pretraining that completely uses synthetic data. After pretraining, we introduce Moho depth to constrain the preliminary inversion results. The second step is a transfer learning that uses observed data. Finally, the Monte Carlo Dropout technique is used to estimate the uncertainty of the inversion results to illustrate the reliability of the results. Synthetic tests and observed data applications show that compared with conventional supervised learning methods, the new method can further improve the quality of inversion. In addition to the V_S structure that is consistent with previous studies, we also obtain sedimentary layers and Moho depth distributions corresponding to the surface structure (e.g., Tibetan Plateau [TP], Sichuan basin, Tarim basin, and North China plain; Jia and Wei. 2002; Royden *et al.*, 2008; Lei *et al.*, 2020).

Methods and Data

V_S structure in training dataset

The quality of training dataset is crucial to the performance of DL methods (Deng *et al.*, 2009; Hu *et al.*, 2020). If the observed dispersion curve is significantly different from the dispersion curves in the training dataset, the network may not predict the correct results, which is called the generalization problem. Wang *et al.* (2023) demonstrated that the training dataset constructed using the spline-based method has high generalization, and its application on observed data can obtain results consistent with the traditional method and has smaller data misfits with the observed data. In this study, we also use the spline-based method to generate the training dataset. Based on Wang *et al.* (2023), we add the sedimentary layer for the 1D V_S structure and each V_S structure is divided into three parts: sedimentary layer, crust, and mantle.

There are two styles of sedimentary layers: one in which velocity increases linearly with depth and the other remains constant within the layer. The thickness of the sediment layer is randomly generated between 0 and 15 km, and the velocity range is 1.5–3 km/s. Specifically, we assume that the sedimentary layer is divided into two approaches. In the first approach, once the sedimentary layer thickness, starting velocity, and final velocity are determined, the velocity within the sedimentary layer increases uniformly with depth. In the second approach, after determining the sedimentary layer thickness, a fixed velocity is assigned throughout the layer. The velocities of both the crust and mantle are regulated by the use of cubic spline. The number of nodes in the crust spline is randomly selected, ranging from 4 to 10, whereas the number of nodes in the mantle spline remains fixed at 10. The number of nodes is set by referring to Li *et al.* (2017) and Wang *et al.* (2023).

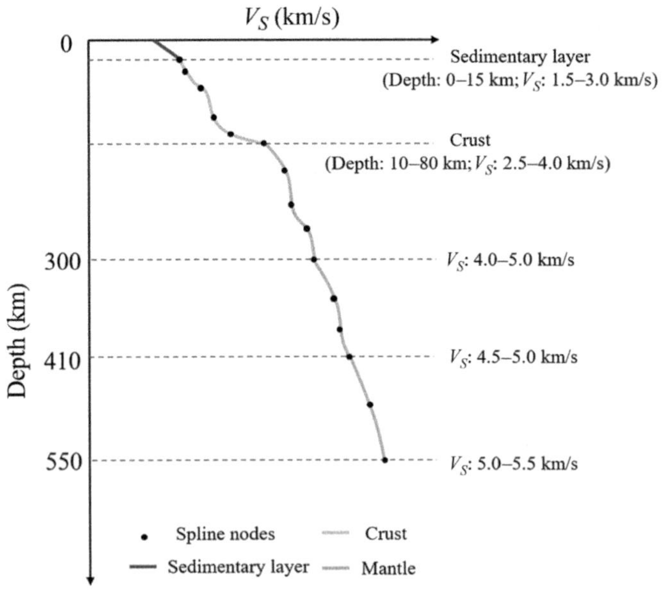

Figure 1. Schematic diagram of value distribution when constructing V_S models. The color version of this figure is available only in the electronic edition.

In fact, as long as the constructed training dataset accurately represents the true distribution of underground media, the network can learn useful information from it. Previous works have confirmed the reliability of using a similar number of nodes (Li *et al.*, 2017; Wang *et al.*, 2023). The final node of the crustal spline is assigned the same value as the initial node of the mantle spline, serving as the connecting node. This connecting node's depth is referred to as the Moho depth and is set at a random value between 10 and 80 km. We maintain a uniform node spacing for the crust. To simulate either a gradual or sharp Moho transition, we further adjust the node spacing in the mantle using a stretching function. We refer to three global 1D models (preliminary reference Earth model [PREM], IASP91, and AK135; Dziewonski and Anderson, 1981; Kennett and Engdahl, 1991; Kennett *et al.*, 1995) to obtain an appropriate general range and set the different ranges of values of V_S corresponding to different depths (Fig. 1). After generating the velocity model, we perform resampling. The total number of resampling points is 195 and the resampling intervals are: 0.5 km from 0 to 80 km, 2 km from 80 to 120 km, 10 km from 120 to 200 km, and 50 km from 200 to 550 km. Finally, we generate 100,000 V_S structures for training and the model space of generated training dataset is shown in Figure S2.

Assumptions in the forward modeling

In addition to V_S structure, Zhang and Song (2024) extensively explored the influence of various parameters on the results of surface-wave inversion. These parameters include the presence of sedimentary layers, V_P/V_S ratio, density, attenuation, and the definition of Moho thickness, which are necessary to be considered in surface-wave inversion. Therefore, these parameters should also be considered when constructing training dataset in DL method.

Zhang and Song (2024) demonstrated that the assumption on the sedimentary layer can affect the inversion result of both shallow and deep structures. The sedimentary layer is characterized by a lower V_S and a higher V_P/V_S ratio. The main constituents of the sedimentary layers encompass clastic particles, carbonate, silicate minerals, and organic matter. The V_P/V_S ratio in such rock types is influenced by factors such as porosity, saturation, and cementation level, typically resulting in a higher V_P/V_S ratio (1.8–2.4; Castagna *et al.*, 1993; Garia *et al.*, 2020). The V_P/V_S ratio of the sedimentary layer in the Sichuan basin obtained from the receiver functions and joint inversion of body-wave arrival times and surface-wave dispersion data is approximately 1.87–2.2 (Wang, Chen, and Yao, 2021; Han *et al.*, 2022). We construct training datasets for testing under the conditions of sedimentary layer V_P/V_S ratios of 1.8 and 2.2, and the results of applying observed data on two different datasets showed that there was little difference in the thickness and distribution of the sedimentary layers. Therefore, in the end we take the average value to be 2, which was also adopted by previous studies (Shen *et al.*, 2016; Li *et al.*, 2017). For V_P/V_S ratio in crystalline crust, tests in Zhang and Song (2024) showed that different assumptions resulted in a maximum difference in V_S of about 1% in the inversion network (InvNet) model. Brocher (2005) made statistics on a wide range of lithologies, including sandstone, shale, biotite, gabbro, calcium-rich rocks (dolomite and syenite), and other crystalline rocks, and derived the V_P–V_S empirical relationship (equation 1), which can represent the average physical properties of crustal rocks over a large depth range. However, this relationship only applies to the crust. Luo *et al.* (2022) extended this relationship to the mantle (equation 2) by combining three 1D global models PREM, IASP91, and AK135 (Dziewonski and Anderson, 1981; Kennett and Engdahl, 1991; Kennett *et al.*, 1995):

$$V_P = 0.9409 + 2.0947V_S - 0.8206V_S^2 + 0.2683V_S^3 - 0.0251V_S^4, \quad (1)$$

$$V_P = 0.9098 + 2.211V_S - 0.8984V_S^2 + 0.2786V_S^3 - 0.02412V_S^4. \quad (2)$$

Choosing a reasonable density model is crucial to surface-wave inversion process (Zhang and Song, 2024). Through synthetic data testing, Zhang and Song (2024) found that when constant relative density changes are applied solely to the crust or mantle, the impact on the inversion results is significant. The commonly used relationship in the crust for calculating density is obtained through V_P (equation 3; Brocher, 2005).

Although Luo *et al.* (2022) also obtained a new relationship in mantle by combining the aforementioned three 1D global models, there is almost no difference between it and Brocher's relationship. Therefore, in both the crust and mantle we use Luo's relationship to get V_P and Brocher's relationship to calculate density:

$$\rho = 1.6612V_P - 0.4721V_P^2 + 0.0671V_P^3 - 0.0043V_P^3 + 0.000106V_P^5. \quad (3)$$

The effect of attenuation should also be considered in surface-wave inversion. In sedimentary rocks, the pores and cementation degree have an important impact on attenuation. In this study, we set the attenuation value of sedimentary layer is to 80, consistent with that of AK135. The crust is generally considered to have relatively small attenuation (Kanamori and Anderson, 1977). The Q_s value in the crust is fixed at 600 in models such as AK135 (Kennett *et al.*, 1995) and PREM (Dziewonski and Anderson, 1981). Therefore, we also fix the attenuation value in the crust to 600. Dalton *et al.* (2008) analyzed a large dataset of fundamental-mode Rayleigh-wave amplitudes and derived a new global 3D model of upper-mantle shear-wave attenuation. Amplitude observations span a period from 50 to 250 s and are derived from earthquakes with $M_w > 6.0$, occurring between 1993 and 2005. The attenuation coefficient of each model in our training dataset is randomly obtained from this 3D model (Dalton *et al.*, 2008). The V_P, density, and attenuation aforementioned are only used to calculate theoretical dispersion and will not be input into the subsequent neural network.

Zhang and Song (2024) demonstrated that if the Moho assumption of the initial model is inconsistent with the true model, the inversion results will have a maximum deviation of 8%. Therefore, a reasonable Moho setup is very necessary. The range of Moho in our training dataset is 10–80 km, completely covering the possible Moho in the entire East Asia (including offshore). Once the model is built, we use Computer Programs in Seismology (CPS) to calculate the theoretical dispersion (Herrmann, 2013). When generating the training dataset, we directly output the sedimentary layer thickness and Moho depth corresponding to each velocity as labels for the network to learn. When the model is well trained, the Moho thickness can be inferred directly from the dispersion curves, thus avoiding the need to make Moho assumptions before inversion.

Pretraining architecture

Supervised DL algorithms are typically data-driven and commonly employed to find optimal transformations from input data to their corresponding labels. Subsequently, these trained DL models are utilized to make predictions on new data. For surface-wave inversion, the input data are the dispersion curve and the output is the velocity structure. What the neural network needs to learn is the one-way mapping relationship from the dispersion curve to the velocity structure.

To enhance the physical interpretability and further improve the performance of the common DL method, we follow the concept of Cycle-GAN (Zhu *et al.*, 2017) to construct a cycle-consistent inversion network, which uses forward modeling data to constrain the inversion process. The purpose of this design is to make the inverted velocity satisfy the physical constraints of the forward process as much as possible. What the neural network learns is the bidirectional mapping relationship between dispersion and velocity structure. In other hand, the observed data can also be introduced into the training process as the transfer learning in this framework. We completely use synthetic data for the pretraining. In addition, to ensure smoothness in the depth direction, we introduce a smooth term (equation 7) to further constrain the output of the inversion network. Finally, the loss function of the pretraining network consists of three parts: the inverse term, the forward term, and the smoothing term (equations 4–7). The setting of weights will be explained in the next section (see the Moho constraints and transfer learning section):

$$L(E_{\text{inv}},E_{fw}) = E[v,\text{inv}(d)] + E\{d,fw[\text{inv}(d)]\} + S[\text{inv}(d)], \quad (4)$$

$$E[v,\text{inv}(d)] = \lambda_1(v - v')^2 + \lambda_2(\text{sedi} - \text{sedi}')^2 + \lambda_3(\text{Moho} - \text{Moho}')^2, \quad (5)$$

$$E\{d,fw[\text{inv}(d)]\} = \lambda_4(d - d')^2, \quad (6)$$

$$S[\text{inv}(d)] = \lambda_5 \sum_{i=2}^{N-1}(v'_{i+1} + v'_{i-1} - 2v'_i)^2, \quad (7)$$

in which v, d, sedi, and Moho are the ground-truth values of velocity, dispersion, sedimentary thickness, and Moho depth, respectively. v',d',sedi$'$, and Moho$'$ are the predicted values of velocity, dispersion, sedimentary thickness, and Moho depth by neural network, respectively. $E(*,*)$ stands for the measurement of the difference between two input data. inv(*) stands for the inversion neural network operator to generate V_S structure from the dispersion. *fw*(*) stands for the forward neural network operator to generate dispersion from the inv(d). S[inv(d)] stands for the smoothing term. N is the number of layers of a V_S structure. The sedimentary thickness and Moho depth are designed to be two 1D vectors in the form of Gaussian distributions and the peaks represent the thicknesses, similar to the definition of Moho depth in Wang *et al.* (2022).

Moho constraints and transfer learning

The inverse problem to obtain a V_S structure from surface-wave dispersion data is inherently pathological, nonlinear, and hybrid deterministic, with no unique solution

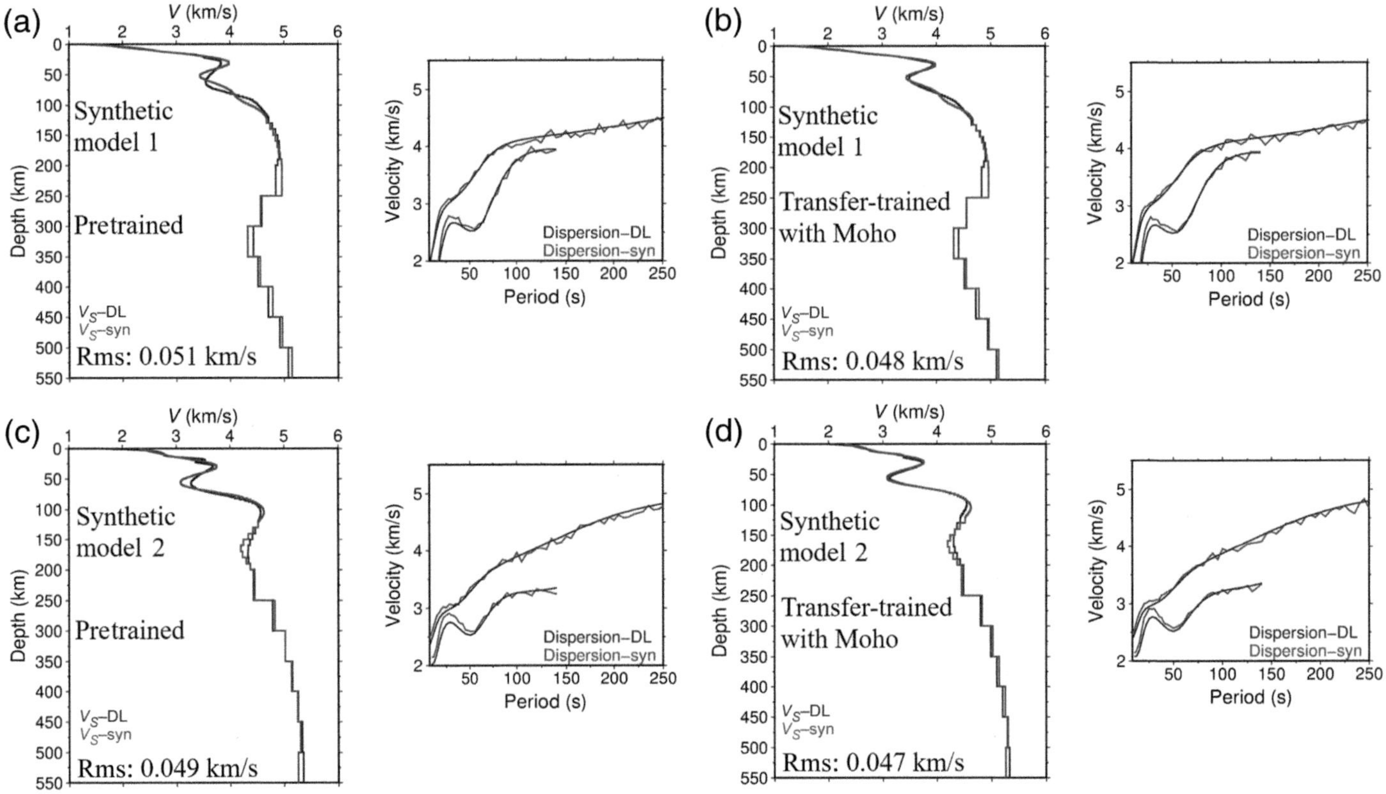

Figure 2. Synthetic tests on pretrained model and transfer-learned model with prior knowledge of Moho depth. (a) Result of synthetic model 1 on pretrained model. (b) Result of synthetic model 1 on transfer-trained model with prior knowledge of Moho depth. (c) Result of synthetic model 2 on pretrained model. (d) Result of synthetic model 2 on transfer-trained model with prior knowledge of Moho depth. The dispersions in the figure refer to Rayleigh-wave phase and group velocities. Rms, root mean square. The color version of this figure is available only in the electronic edition.

(Foti *et al.*, 2009; Cercato, 2011). Because dispersion data are not as sensitive to discontinuities of velocity structure as receiver functions, to alleviate the problem of multiple solutions, we introduce the prior Moho depth to constrain the Moho obtained by the inversion, thereby improving the overall inversion results. The Crust1.0 model is derived from dispersion, free oscillation, and body-wave arrival data and has been widely used as a reference model for crustal thickness (Laske *et al.*, 2012). Therefore, we use the Moho information from Crust1.0 as a reference when applying the proposed method to observed data.

The method of introducing Moho information into the training process is as follows. After the pretraining is completed, we generate a set of possible InvNet models by adding subtle noise to the observed dispersion data during inference. The subtle noise are randomly generated following the uniform probability distribution $\delta v \sim U(-0.005\ \mathrm{km/s}, 0.005\ \mathrm{km/s})$. Then compare the Moho depth of this set of possible models with the prior Moho depth, and find the model with the smallest difference as the initial model for transfer learning. It should be noted that the amplitude of the subtle noise determines the difference of inversion velocities. The amplitude of the subtle noise added here cannot be too large; otherwise, the inversion velocities will deviate too far from the true value. However, if it is too small, it cannot match the appropriate velocity as the initial model. Tests on synthetic data show that adding prior Moho depth information and transfer learning will aid the inversion of surface-wave dispersion to find the correct V_S model (Fig. 2). We consider two models to illustrate the impact of pretraining and transfer learning. Both models have distinct sedimentary layers and low-velocity layer in the crust. The second adds low-velocity layers to the mantle. The two input dispersions (Rayleigh-wave phase and group velocities) for each example were calculated by CPS based on the same model and added different Gaussian noise of the same amplitude. These two cases show that although the dispersions calculated by the different InvNet models can correspond well to the observed dispersions, the inversion introducing Moho depth leads to better recovery of the input V_S model, especially near the Moho depth (~70 km). There are relatively many existing global Moho models, so it is not difficult to obtain a prior Moho information before inversion. Because the Moho in most areas is continuous, even if the resolution of the prior Moho information is not enough, we can still obtain the required resolution through interpolation.

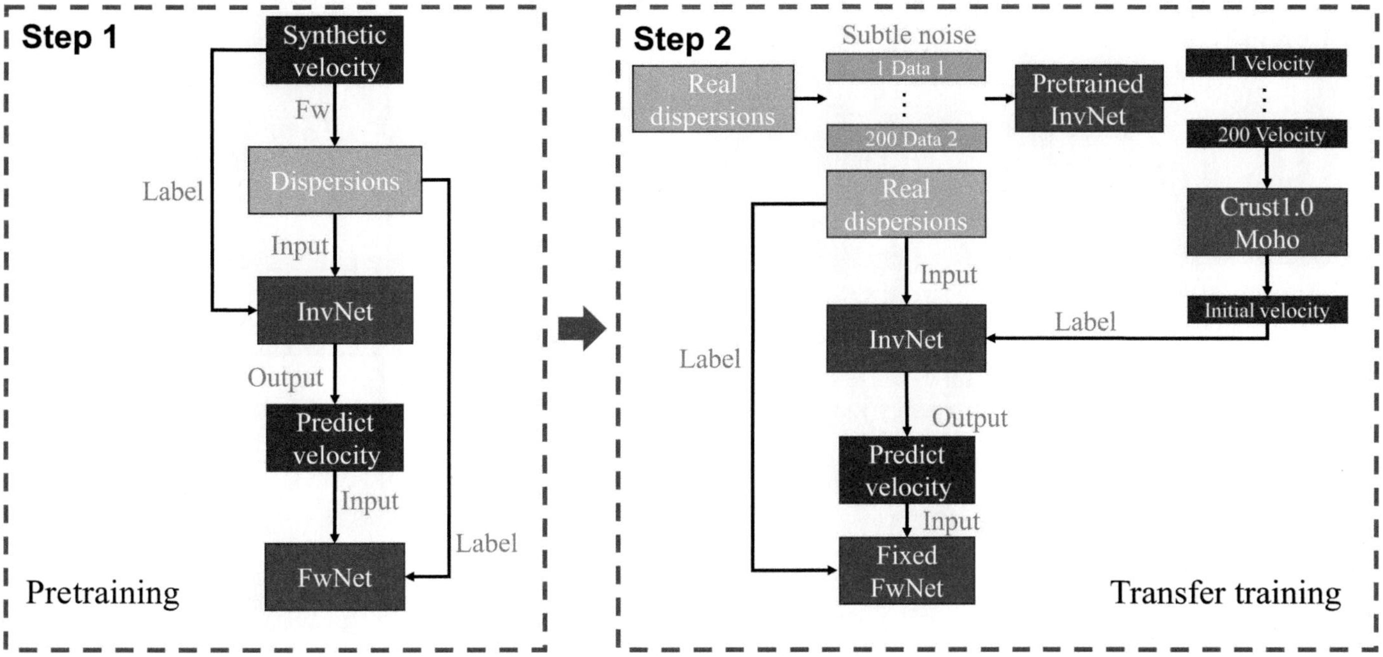

Figure 3. Workflow of the proposed method. FwNet, forward subnetwork; InvNet, inversion network. The color version of this figure is available only in the electronic edition.

We train the InvNet model using the initial velocity model (i.e., inversion results of pretrained model with prior Moho constraints) as the label to compute the loss as part of the total loss in transfer learning. We also use the predicted model of InvNet as the input fed to FwNet model, calculate the difference of the observed dispersion and predicted dispersion by FwNet as another part of the total loss. In this step, we fix the parameters of the FwNet. In other words, the FwNet is trained entirely on synthetic data because there is a one-to-one correspondence between velocity and dispersion in synthetic data. Although in transfer learning, we do not know the true velocity structure corresponding to the observed data. Our purpose in this step is to make the velocity predicted by the InvNet satisfy the forward relationship learned during the pretraining process. During the pretraining process, our focus is to find the inversion and FwNet models at the same time, so the weights of the forward and inversion terms in the loss function are relatively large. But in transfer learning, first, our initial velocity is not so accurate, and second, our purpose is to match the observation data, so we increase the weight of the dispersion label and reduce the weight of the velocity label. We experiment with different values and use $\lambda_1 = 1.0$, $\lambda_2 = 0.1$, $\lambda_3 = 0.1$, $\lambda_4 = 1.0$, and $\lambda_5 = 0.2$ in pretraining process and $\lambda_1 = 0.2, \lambda_2 = 0.1, \lambda_3 = 0.1, \lambda_4 = 0.8$, and $\lambda_5 = 0.2$ in transfer learning process. Figure 3 is the workflow of the proposed method. When applying to new data, we only need to perform the second step of transfer learning. We conduct 100 training epochs in the pretraining and transfer training, performing validation after each epoch to monitor the training effect. We use open-source libraries TensorFlow and Keras to support all of the aforementioned DL concepts and optimization algorithms. All computations are performed on two NVIDIA V100 graphic processing units with 32 GB memory. The pretraining time is approximately 8 hr and the transfer training time is approximately 1 hr.

Structure of the DL models

Because the neural networks have powerful mapping fitting capabilities, different networks have been proposed to perform inversion tasks, such as convolutional neural networks (CNNs) by Hu *et al.* (2020) and Wang *et al.* (2022), fully connected networks by Wang, Song, and Zhang (2021), and Cycle-consistent GAN by Cai *et al.* (2022). In this article, considering that the dispersion of different periods is more or less sensitive to the velocity structure of different depths, we mainly use the gate recurrent unit (GRU) to design the forward and InvNet (Chung *et al.*, 2014). Unlike CNN, the output of a GRU at each timestep not only depends on the current input (i.e., surface-wave velocity at current period), but also on the previous input (surface-wave velocities at previous periods). After GRU, we introduce a fully connected neural network to fuse the learned features and map them into the required dispersion or velocity data. A detailed introduction to GRU and fully connected layers can be found in Text S1. Finally, we use a two-layer GRU network with two fully connected layers to build the FwNet and InvNet (Fig. 4). The number of sampling points of phase velocity dispersions was 56 at periods of 8–250 s. The number of sampling points of group velocity dispersions was 33 at periods of 10–140 s. For storage convenience, we zero-pad the number of group velocity sampling points to 56.

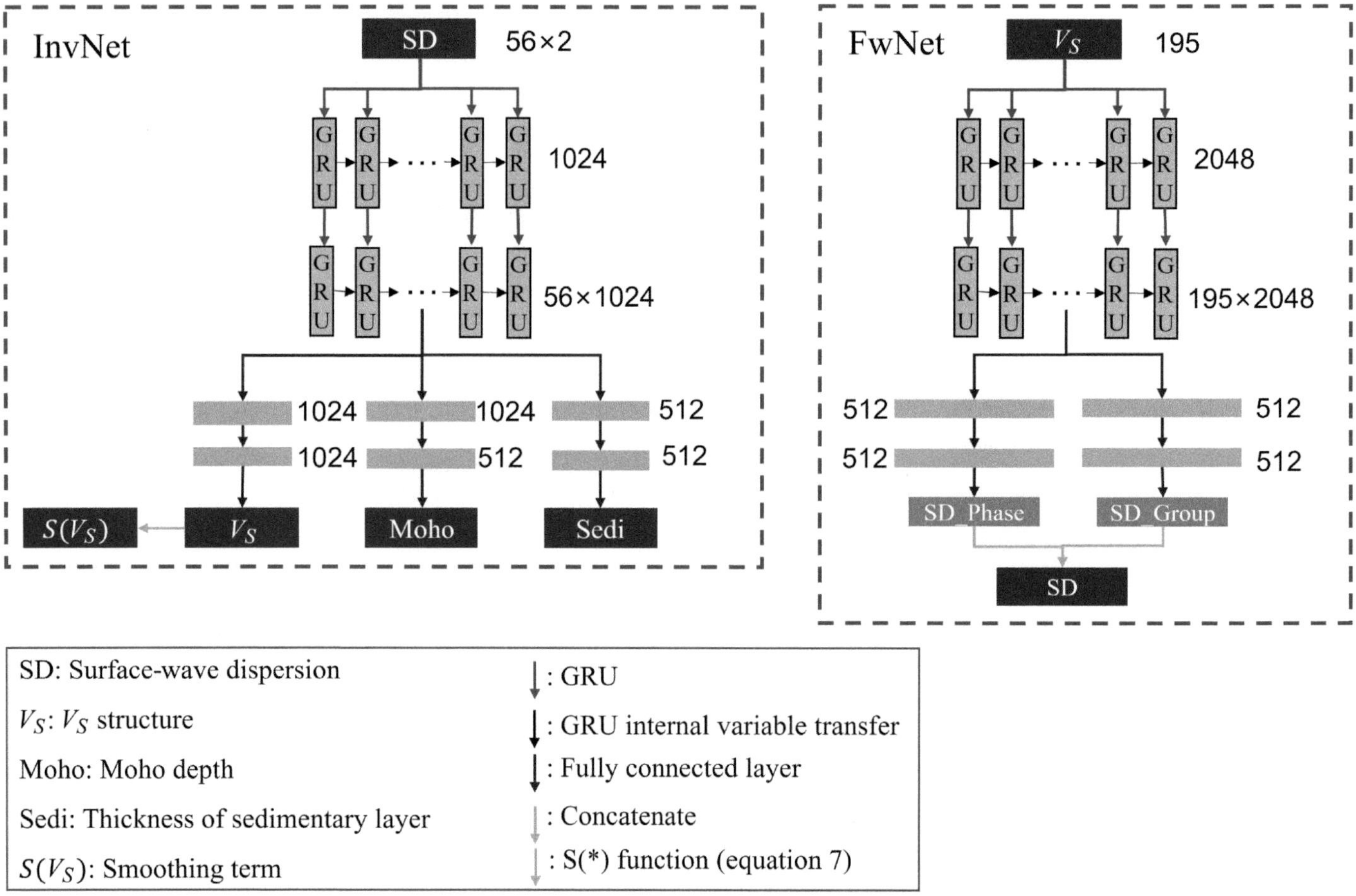

Figure 4. Structure of the FwNet and InvNet. The orange rectangular block represents a gate recurrent unit (GRU) in Figure S3. The color version of this figure is available only in the electronic edition.

Results

Synthetic tests

We test the proposed method using V_S models from Li *et al.* (2022), which includes 5700 individual models in the East Asian. We use CPS to calculate the theoretical dispersion (Herrmann, 2013). We use root mean square (rms) error (equation 8), correlation coefficient (CC; equation 9), and Jensen–Shannon divergence (JSD; equations 10 and 11) on both depth and horizontal directions of the input and inversion V_S models to evaluate the results of the proposed method. CC is used to judge the similarity between the perturbation patterns of each pair of models. The value of CC is between −1 and 1. The closer to 1, the higher the similarity of the perturbation patterns. JSD is often used in machine learning to measure the similarity of two distributions. The value is between 0 and 1. The closer to 0, the closer the two distributions are. We calculate the results of three DL models, namely the pretraining model, the transfer learning model (transfer learning A in Table 1), and the transfer learning model after adding Moho constraints (transfer learning B in Table 1). The results are shown in Table 1, Figure 5, and Figures S4–S7. The depth of Li's model only reaches 300 km. From 300 to 550 km

TABLE 1
Performances of Different Deep Learning Models

DL Models	V_S Rms (km/s)	Moho Rms (km)	CC (Vertical)	CC (Horizontal)	JSD (Vertical)	JSD (Horizontal)
Pretraining	0.052	1.805	0.995	0.956	2.3×10^{-5}	1.9×10^{-5}
Transfer-learning A	0.049	1.722	0.995	0.962	2.1×10^{-5}	1.6×10^{-5}
Transfer-learning B	**0.047**	**0.771**	**0.996**	**0.967**	$\mathbf{2.0 \times 10^{-5}}$	$\mathbf{1.4 \times 10^{-5}}$

The best results are in bold font. CC, correlation coefficient; DL, deep learning; JSD, Jensen–Shannon divergence; and rms, root mean square.

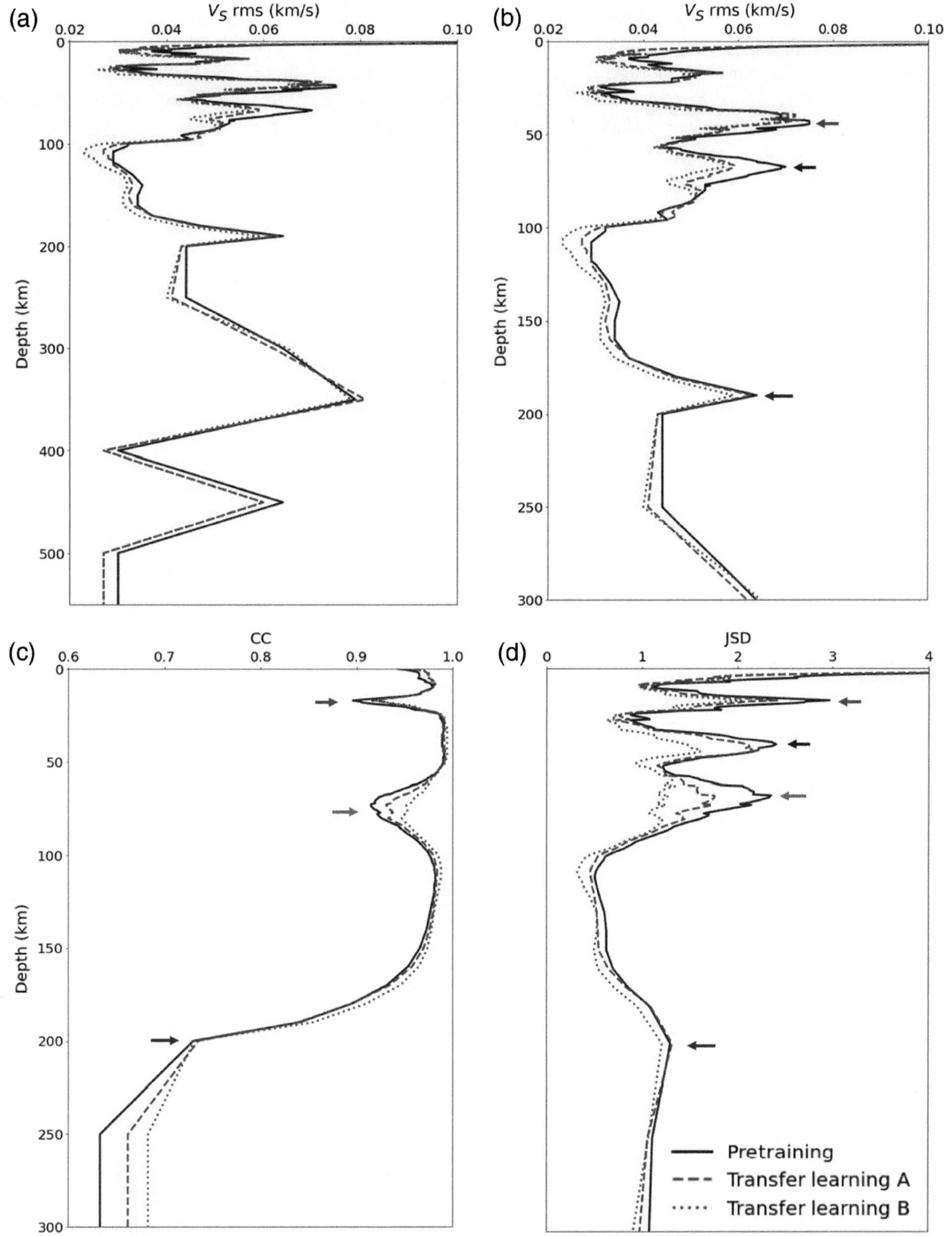

Figure 5. Results of synthetic tests based on the three DL models used the Vs structure from Li *et al.* (2022). (a) The rms error at all depths, (b) the rms error for depth above 300 km, (c) the correlation coefficient (CC) for depth above 300 km, and (d) the Jensen–Shannon divergence (JSD) for depth above 300 km with the input V_S models. The red, blue, green, and brown arrows correspond to relatively poor inversion results at depths of 17, 42, 67, and 190 km, respectively. Transfer learning A is transfer learning without Moho constraints and transfer learning B is transfer learning with Moho constraints. The color version of this figure is available only in the electronic edition.

deep, we uniformly use the 1D AK135 model. Therefore, we first show the V_S rms errors at all depths in Figure 5a, and then show the V_S rms errors and similarity measures for 0–300 km depth in Figure 5b–d. In Li's results, only the Moho depth is clearly given, but not the thickness of the sedimentary layer. Therefore, we compare the inverted Moho and the input Moho without comparing the predictions of sedimentary layer thickness. When calculating dispersion curves as input to the network, we consider the layer in which V_S is less than 3 km/s to be the sedimentary layer (i.e., a V_P/V_S ratio of 2.0 is used to calculate V_P when V_S is less than 3 km/s)

$$E_{\mathrm{rms}} = \sqrt{\frac{1}{N}\sum_{n=1}^{N}\sum_{l=1}^{L}\left\| x_{\mathrm{ln}}^{\mathrm{pred}} - x_{\mathrm{ln}}^{\mathrm{true}} \right\|_2^2}, \quad (8)$$

$$\mathrm{CC} = \frac{\sum[(x_i^{\mathrm{pred}} - \bar{x}^{\mathrm{pred}})(x_i^{\mathrm{true}} - \bar{x}^{\mathrm{true}})]}{\sqrt{\sum(x_i^{\mathrm{pred}} - \bar{x}^{\mathrm{pred}})^2 \sum(x_i^{\mathrm{true}} - \bar{x}^{\mathrm{true}})^2}}, \quad (9)$$

$$\mathrm{KLD}(x\|y) = \sum x_i \log\frac{x_i}{y_i}, \quad (10)$$

$$\mathrm{JSD}(x\|y) = \frac{1}{2}\mathrm{KLD}\left(x^{\mathrm{pred}} \middle\| \frac{x^{\mathrm{pred}} + x^{\mathrm{true}}}{2}\right) + \frac{1}{2}\mathrm{KLD}\left(x^{\mathrm{true}} \middle\| \frac{x^{\mathrm{pred}} + x^{\mathrm{true}}}{2}\right), \quad (11)$$

in which N denotes the number of test models and L denotes the number of layers. x^{pred} denotes the prediction of the DL model, and x^{true} denotes the ground truth. KLD is the Kullback–Leibler divergence.

The rms error of the all three DL models remains at approximately 0.05 km/s (Table 1). The average CC of the single model is closed to 1 and the JSD is close to 0 in both horizontal and vertical directions, which demonstrate that our methods are powerful and effective. A careful comparison of the three methods shows that transfer learning can further improve the accuracy of the inversion, especially after the introduction of Moho constraints; all indicators have achieved the best results (Table 1). The addition of Moho constraints will not only improve the inversion results near the Moho depth, but also improve the inversion at the entire depth (Fig. 5). It should be noted that at approximately 17, 42, and 67 km (red, blue, and green arrows in Fig. 5), relatively large errors appear in both the rms error and JSD of the inversion result V_S. However, CC only drops at 17 and 67 km, and still maintains a high similarity at 42 km. The reason is that the dispersion data are not sensitive to velocity discontinuities, so the inverted V_S have a large error near the Moho depth. In addition, 17, 42, and 67 km correspond to the shallowest (northeast coast) of the input model, continental crust except for the TP, and the deepest (TP) Moho depth, respectively. Therefore, for 17 and 67 km, this error will systematically affect the average value in the CC calculation, causing its value to decrease. But for 42 km, because it is around the average crustal thickness, this error will be canceled out positively and negatively, resulting in no systematic change in the average velocity, so the calculated CC still has a high value. In addition, there is also a large inversion error at about 190 km (reddish-brown arrows line in Fig. 5), which is speculated to be related to the asthenosphere interface. Below about 190 km, CC dropped significantly, but the rms error and JSD still performed well. It may be because compared with the shallow part, the fluctuation range of the V_S value below 190 km is smaller. Therefore, under the same absolute inversion error, CC will decrease.

Figures S4–S7 show that our method can reconstruct the input model well at different depths. The main geological structures can clearly correspond to the input model, such as the extremely thick crust of the TP and the relatively low-velocity sedimentary layers of the Sichuan and Tarim basins. It is worth noting that although surface-wave dispersions are not sensitive to velocity discontinuities, we can still invert relatively accurate Moho depth. This is because the Moho we invert here does not only represent the velocity discontinuity but also represents the Moho definition specified in the training dataset. In other words, in addition to the large discontinuity in the velocity value itself, the network can also determine the Moho depth through other features, such as the changes in attenuation coefficient near Moho and velocity value of approximately 4 km/s (Xu *et al.*, 2013; Bao *et al.*, 2015; Li *et al.*, 2017).

Application to observed data

The observed data (Rayleigh phase velocities with period range of 8–250 s and Rayleigh group velocities with period range of 10–140 s) we used also come from Li *et al.* (2022). They utilized seismic event data gathered from over 1000 seismic stations, including national and global and permanent and temporary networks located in and surrounding Mainland China (CEArray, Program for the Array Seismic Studies of the Continental Lithosphere, and Global Seismographic Network). The geological background, stations, and event distribution of the study area are shown in Figure 6. The dataset allows us to construct a 3D S-wave velocity model extending to 550 km depth for East Asia, encompassing both the lithosphere and underlying mantle regions. This compilation of data offers a notably consistent and possibly the most extensive coverage of the study region using surface waves. Resolution tests show that the 1° × 1° checkboard can be recovered in the most part of study region at periods of 30 and 60 s, even at 90 s. The 2° × 2° checkboard can be recovered at periods larger than 90 s (Li *et al.*, 2022).

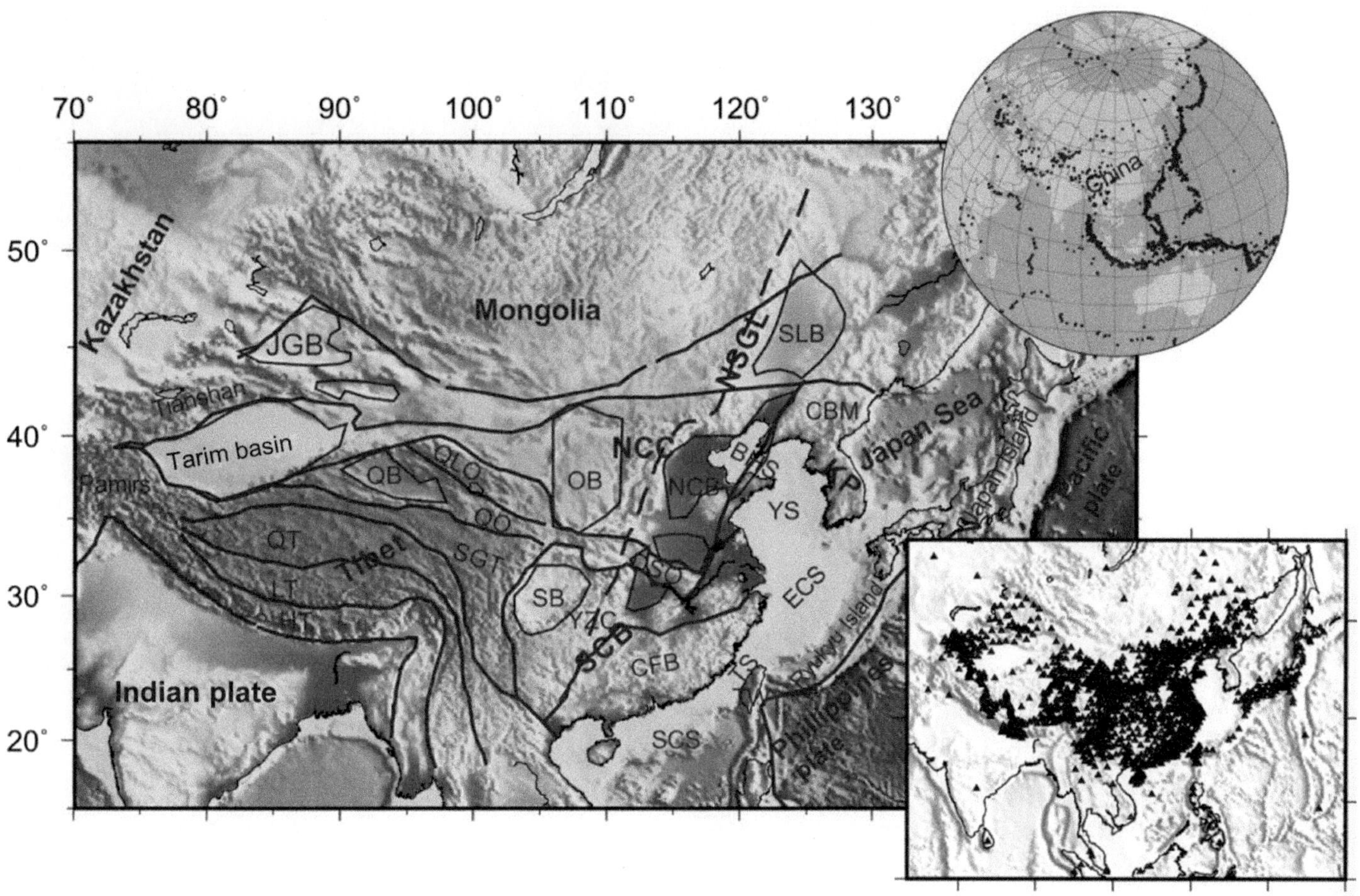

It can be seen from the distribution of sedimentary layers that the inversion results correspond well to main basins (Sichuan, Ordos, Tarim, Qaidam, Junggar, and Songliao basins) and North China plain (Fig. S8a). Among them, the Tarim basin has the most widely distributed and deepest sedimentary layers. Several factors have contributed to the accumulation of thick sedimentary layers in the Tarim basin. First, the Tarim basin is situated at the convergence of several tectonic plates, including the Eurasian plate, the Indian plate, and the Pacific plate. These tectonic interactions have led to the subsidence and deformation of the basin over time, creating favorable conditions for sediment deposition. Second, the Tarim basin is surrounded by several major mountain ranges, including the Kunlun Mountains to the south and the Tian Shan Mountains to the north. These mountains act as a source of sediment due to erosion. The eroded material, such as sand, silt, and clay, is transported into the basin by rivers and wind, contributing to the accumulation of sedimentary layers. Third, the Tarim basin has a predominantly arid and dry climate, which limits the erosional processes that might otherwise remove sediments. In wetter climates, sediments can be eroded and transported away more easily, but in an arid climate, they tend to accumulate and remain in place (Mather, 2007; Li and Fang, 2016; Chen *et al.*, 2021; Mandel *et al.*, 2024). Finally, the Tarim basin is a closed basin, meaning that it does not have an outlet to the sea. This lack of an outlet inhibits the removal of sediments by flowing water, allowing sediments to accumulate over time. The Moho thickness distribution can clearly correspond to China's three-level stepped terrain from west to east (Fig. S8b). The TP in the west has the highest elevation, exceeding 4 km, and its corresponding Moho depth is the greatest, reaching over70 km. The thickness

Figure 6. Topographic map of the study area showing the main tectonic units in the East Asia region, and the distributions of seismic stations (blue triangles) and earthquakes (blue dots). The thick-blue lines represent the boundaries of geological units (from Liang *et al.*, 2004, which is modified from the original map by Zhang *et al.*, 1984). (Top-right inset) Detailed distribution of earthquakes (blue dots). (Bottom-right inset) Detailed distribution of seismic stations (blue triangles). The abbreviations are BHS, Bohai Sea; CBM, Changbai Mountain range; CFB, Cathaysia Fold Belt; DSO, Dabie-Sulu orogen; ECS, East China Sea; HT, Himalaya terrane; JGB, Jungger basin; LT, Lhasa terrane; NCB, North China basin; NCC, North China craton; NSGL, North South gravity line; OB, Ordos block; QB, Qaidam basin; QLO, Qilian orogen; QO, Qinling orogen; QT, Qiang-Tang terrane; SB, Sichuan basin; SCB, South China block; SCS, South China Sea; SGT, Songpan-Ganzi terrane; SLB, Songliao basin; TS, Taiwan Strait; TW, Taiwan Island; YS, Yellow Sea; YZC, Yangtze craton. Modified from Li *et al.* (2022). The color version of this figure is available only in the electronic edition.

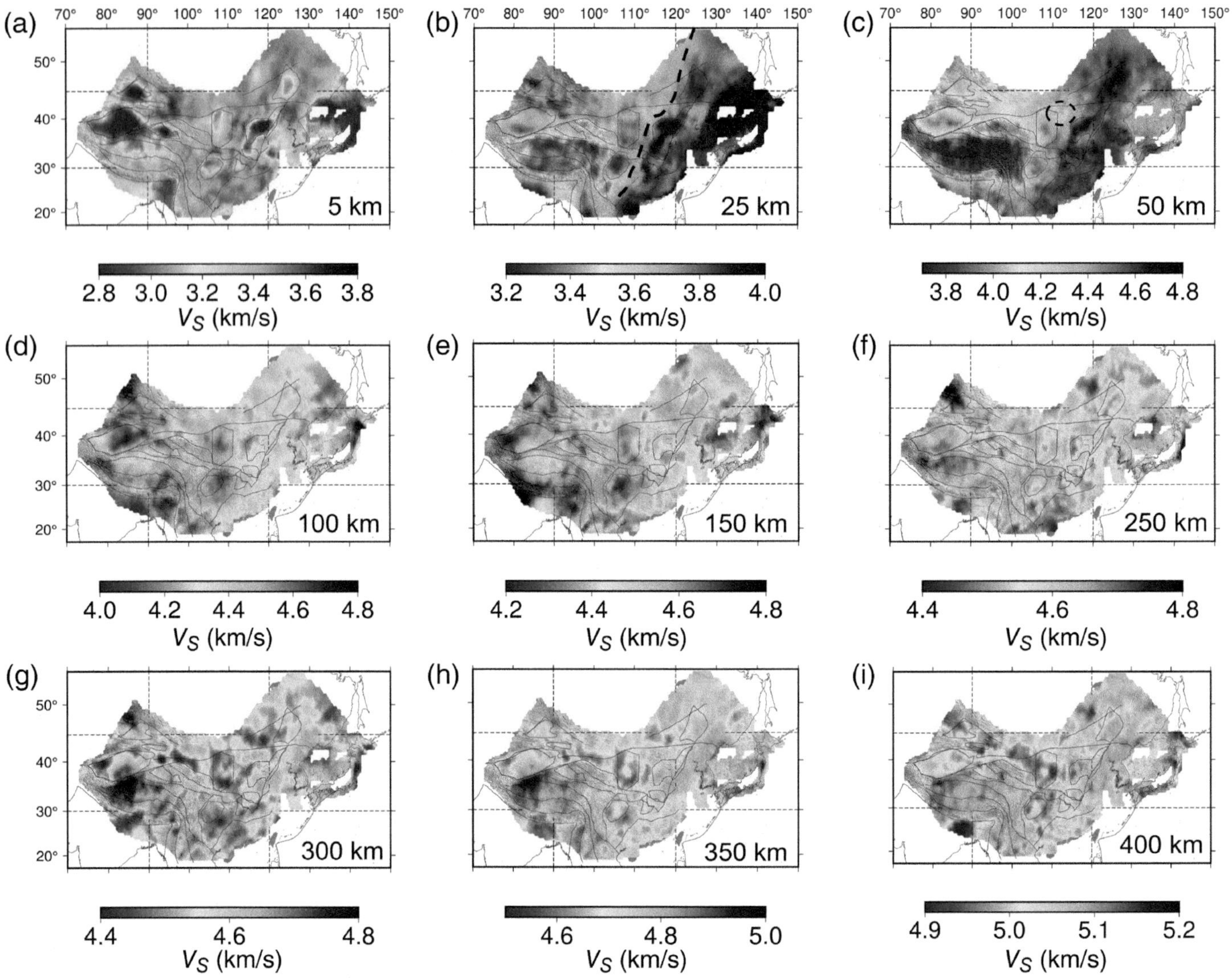

Figure 7. Depth slices of V_S structure obtained at (a) 5, (b) 25, (c) 50, (d) 100, (e) 150, (f) 250, (g) 300, (h) 350, and (i) 400 km. The black dotted line in panel (b) represents the north–south gravity line, and the black dotted circle in panel (c) corresponds to the Datong volcanic area. The color version of this figure is available only in the electronic edition.

of the crust gradually becomes thinner toward the east, and the crust along the eastern coast is only about 30 km deep.

Figure 7 shows velocity slices at different depths. The velocity at 5 km depth corresponds well to the surface structure (Fig. 7a). The basin area is still in the sedimentary layer and the velocity is low. Among them, the structure of the Ordos block is relatively complex, and the velocity in the eastern part of the Ordos basin is higher than that in the western part, indicating that it is subject to stronger erosion, causing the sedimentary layers to be denuded.

At a depth of 25 km (Fig. 7b), a sharp velocity dividing line can be seen between the north and south gravity lines (black-dashed lines in Fig. 7b). Areas east of the dividing line, such as the North China plain, the Yangtze block, the Northeast region, and the Sea of Japan, all exhibit high velocities. West of the dividing line, low velocities dominate, especially the TP. Sichuan, Tarim, and Ordos basins show high velocities compared with the surrounding geological blocks. The crust beneath these basins is mainly composed of harder blocks (Hu *et al.*, 2008; Wang *et al.*, 2019). The low-velocity feature in the TP is more obvious at a depth of 50 km (Fig. 7c). The majority of the study area extends into the uppermost mantle. However, the TP is still in the crust and therefore exhibits lower velocities. A marked low-velocity anomaly is identified in the Datong volcanic region (black dotted circle in Fig. 7c). This low-velocity feature aligns with findings from previous regional surface and *P*-wave tomographic studies (Zhao *et al.*, 2011; Chen *et al.*, 2014), suggesting the potential upwelling of melt materials from the deeper mantle.

At depths of 100 and 150 km (Fig. 7d,e), the TP still shows relatively low velocities, whereas the basins exhibit relatively high velocities. However, because all areas are within the mantle, the contrast is less pronounced. Overall, velocities are lower

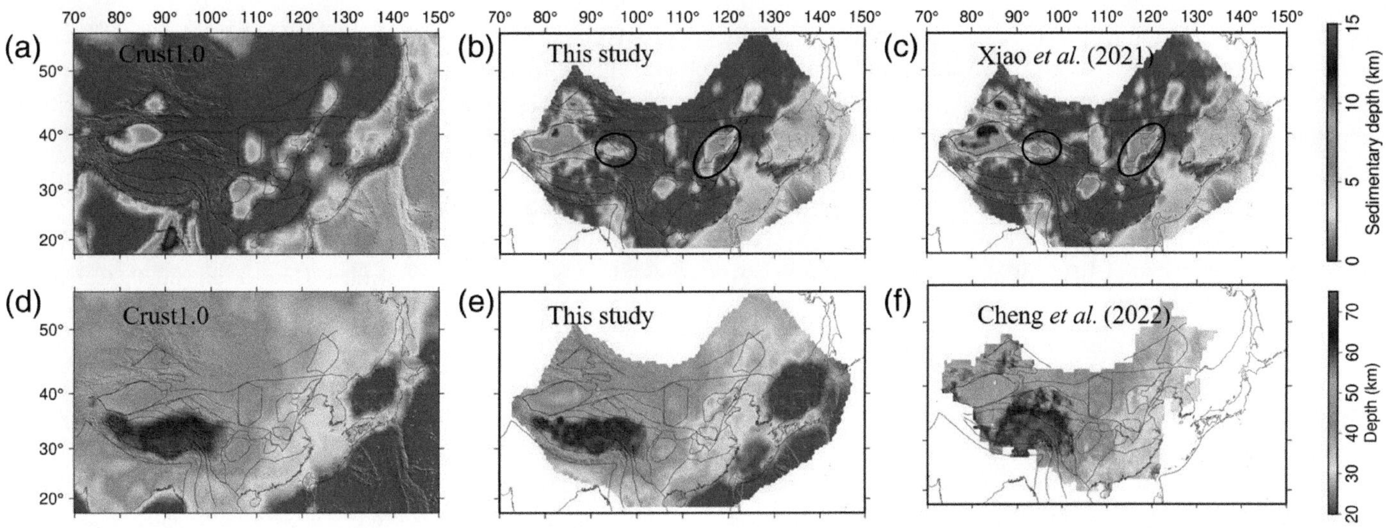

Figure 8. Comparison of sedimentary layer thickness and Moho depth with previous results. (a) Sedimentary layer thickness and (d) Moho depth of Crust1.0. (b) Sedimentary layer thickness and (e) Moho depth of this study. (c) Sedimentary layer thickness of Xiao *et al.* (2021) and (f) Moho depth of Cheng *et al.* (2022). The black circles in panel (b) mark the Qaidam basin and the North China plain. The color version of this figure is available only in the electronic edition.

in the eastern region and higher in the west. At the 250 km depth, because eastern China lies within the asthenosphere, while the TP has a thicker lithosphere. Consequently, the TP exhibits higher velocities, and the overall velocity distribution becomes significantly more complex. Below 300 km (Fig. 7g–7i), low-velocity zones (LVZs) occur in the Sichuan basin, the Qilian Mountain Belt-Ordos basin, and the Yangtze plate, where the TP exhibits higher velocities.

Based on the inversion velocity model, we calculate the theoretical dispersions and compare them with the observed dispersions, as shown in Figures S9–S11. It can be seen that the misfit in most areas is smaller than 0.05 km/s. Compared with the west, the misfit in the east is smaller. There are obvious errors in the northwest end of Altai Mountain. We check the data of this location and found obvious error in the measured dispersion (Fig. S12). Overall, the rms errors of group velocity and phase velocity are 0.043 and 0.045 km/s, respectively, which prove the correctness of the velocity structure obtained by the inversion to a certain extent. It is important that despite the bias in the observational data, we deliberately refrain from applying any quality control to ensure a fair comparison with Li's results. Because the inversion is performed at a single station, data from problematic areas do not affect the results at other locations.

The results we obtain are consistent with the previous study by Li *et al.* (2022), as shown in Figure S13. Although we use the same dispersion data, differences still exist between our results and those of Li *et al.* (2022) due to different assumptions and methods. We calculate the average V_S models and CC between the two results, as shown in Figure S14. As can be seen from Figures S13 and S14, both results have a high consistency in 0–150 km. Compared with the shallow part, the difference between the two becomes larger in the deep part (>150 km). The location of relatively large errors is similar to that in the synthetic test (Fig. 5c), and they all exist at the locations where discontinuities appear in the V_S structure. Based on the two results, we calculate the corresponding dispersions and compare them with the observed dispersions (Fig. S14c). Compared with the results of Li *et al.* (2022), our dispersion curves correspond better to the observations, especially at long periods. Because the long-period dispersions are more sensitive to the velocity in the deep part, our results may be more reliable in the deep part. However, it should be noted that although we introduced Moho information to improve spatial smoothness, the new results are still not as smooth as Li's results. This may be due to the fact that Li *et al.* (2022) is based on the same initial model when inverting the velocity of each grid point, whereas the velocity at each grid point in DL is completely independent.

Discussion

Comparison of sedimentary layer and Moho with previous results

We compare and analyze the obtained sedimentary layer thickness and Moho depth with the previous results, as shown in Figure 8. Crust1.0 provides global crustal velocity structure information and is also the source of the Moho constraints in this study (Laske *et al.*, 2012). Xiao *et al.* (2021) used *P*-wave polarization, Rayleigh-wave ellipticity, and receiver function to invert the shallow velocity structure of China, including the distribution of sedimentary thickness. Cheng *et al.* (2022) used 150,543 receiver functions to invert the distribution of crustal thickness across the China.

The three sedimentary layer distributions exhibit certain similarities, particularly in regions corresponding to main basins. It is worth noting that the sedimentary layers in the Tarim basin are the most widely distributed and thickest. In addition, distinct sedimentary layers are evident in the Sichuan, Ordos, and Songliao basins. Different from Crust1.0, results of the proposed method in this study and Xiao *et al.* (2021) show significant sedimentation distribution in the Qaidam basin and North China plain (black circles in Fig. 8). The North China plain stands as one of the largest plains in China, situated in the middle and lower reaches of the Yellow River. Over time, the Yellow River has bestowed this region with abundant river sediments through erosion and deposition, giving rise to fertile soil conducive to agricultural development (Liu *et al.*, 2021; Du *et al.*, 2024). In contrast, the Qaidam basin, positioned in northwest China, represents an inland basin shaped by prolonged geological processes. Within the basin, sedimentary layers primarily result from the deposition processes occurring over time. Historically, the Qaidam basin hosted ancient lakes, such as the Kuqa basin, contributing to the formation of sedimentary layers comprised of lake sediments and Salt Lake deposits. In addition, the basin's arid climate fosters the transport of fine particles by wind, depositing them within the basin and leading to the formation of wind-borne deposits (Heermance *et al.*, 2013; Lu *et al.*, 2018). It should be noted that, compared with Xiao *et al.* (2021), we only use surface-wave data, whereas Xiao also used *P*-wave polarization and receiver functions.

We also compare Moho to the results of Crust1.0 and Cheng *et al.* (2022; Fig. 8d–f). First, all three results show significant lateral variations, with the TP having the thickest crust, whereas the crust in the eastern region, especially along the coast, is thinner. Second, our crustal thickness map exhibits a strong correlation with surface geology. The three steps of China's topography are clearly defined by a pronounced crustal thickness gradient. Figure S15 shows the Moho depth before and after adding the Moho information of Crust1.0 as a constraint. In the pretraining results (Fig. S15a), the Moho depth has maintained good consistency with Crust1.0 on a large scale but is slightly insufficient in lateral continuity (especially in the TP). After adding the Moho constraint, the lateral continuity is greatly enhanced, which reflects the advantage of adding constraints. In comparison to Crust 1.0, our results more clearly delineate the coastline by highlighting the transition zone in crustal thickness within the land-sea interaction area. An important reason for the difference between our result and that of Cheng *et al.* (2022) is that, unlike the surface-wave data we used, Cheng *et al.* (2022) used receiver functions entirely for inversion. Because of the diverse data types employed in the inversion process, it is not feasible to determine which results are superior. The results provided here are intended for reference only.

The aforementioned comparison results show that although our geological constraint information is taken from Crust1.0, the new method can mine deeper information from the observed data (surface-wave dispersions), and can obtain more reasonable inversion results than the Crust1.0 and similar to the recent research results, which shows the superiority of the new method.

Importance of the new framework

Surface-wave inversion methods based on DL have been proposed in some previous studies (Hu *et al.*, 2020; Cai *et al.*, 2022; Wang *et al.*, 2023), and systematic synthetic tests have proven that the DL-based method is more accurate and efficient than the traditional nonlinear inversion method (Wang *et al.*, 2023). However, unlike the method proposed in this study, previous studies did not introduce forward modeling data or Moho information to constrain the inversion process. Conventional inversions based on DL often use synthetic velocity as labels, and the dispersion curves corresponding to each velocity obtained by forward modeling as input, and then train the designed network to find the mapping relationship from dispersion to velocity. To further verify the improvement of the proposed method, we compare it with the conventional DL method (CDM) that only includes an InvNet without FwNet, transfer-learning or Moho information. To exclude the performance differences brought by network structures, the same structure of InvNet and training dataset as in Figure 4 is used in CDM. The workflow of CDM is shown in Figure S16.

Figures S17 and S18 show the test results of CDM and the new method proposed in this study on synthetic tests. The input models of the synthetic tests are the same as in the Synthetic tests section. Compared with CDM, the V_S model inverted by the proposed method is significantly better in all indicators. Judging from the slices at 20 km depth because this depth approximately corresponds to the thickness of the oceanic crust, and surface-wave dispersion is not sensitive to velocity discontinuities, there is obviously a large error in the CDM results in the Sea of Japan. Because of the introduction of Moho constraints, the method we proposed can recover the input model well in this area. In addition, the new method also enhances the spatial smoothness of the results, such as in the Tarim and Jungar basins. Similarly, from the slices at 75 km depth, the results obtained by the proposed method are smoother and more continuous in the TP region and major basin areas. These comparisons show that the new framework improves the prediction quality of DL methods.

Uncertainty estimation

Standard neural networks lack the ability to provide reliable certainty estimates and often exhibit issues of overconfidence or underconfidence, displaying poor calibration. In response to this challenge, numerous researchers have been dedicated to exploring and quantifying uncertainty within the predictions of neural networks. Consequently, various forms and origins of uncertainty have been recognized, leading to the development of diverse methodologies to assess and measure

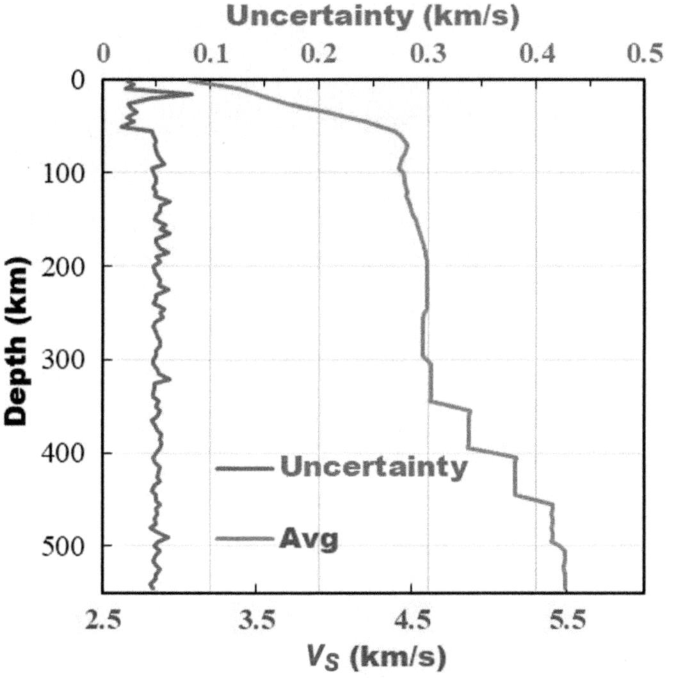

Figure 9. The average V_S structure and uncertainty along depth of all grid points. The blue line denotes the average V_S structure. The gray line denotes the uncertainties of V_S structure calculated as one standard deviation. The color version of this figure is available only in the electronic edition.

uncertainty in neural networks (Gawlikowski *et al.*, 2021). Several factors such as noise in measurement and errors in the model structure may cause uncertainty and affect DL's predictions. Because Li *et al.* (2022) did not explicitly give the uncertainty of the measured dispersions, we estimate the uncertainty of the inversion results from the perspective of the network model.

We use Monte Carlo dropout (MC dropout) to estimate the uncertainty of the inversion results (Gal and Ghahramani, 2016). MC dropout is a method of estimating uncertainty using the dropout layer of a neural network at inference time. Gal and Ghahramani (2016) demonstrated that the properties of the dropout layer can be exploited to simulate the posterior distribution by running forward propagation multiple times. Dropout is a technique that randomly turns off some neurons in a neural network during training to prevent overfitting. MC dropout uses the properties of dropout during inference to obtain the distribution predicted by different models by sampling the dropout state multiple times, thereby estimating the uncertainty of the model. In this study, we refer to Gal and Ghahramani (2016), by setting the number of forward iterations to 100 and setting the dropout probability to 0.1 of the last two fully connect layers. The result shown in Figure 9 indicates that the overall uncertainty is about 0.05 km/s. The uncertainty for depths less than 50 km, which is approximately equal to the average crustal thickness of the study area, is relatively small, whereas the uncertainty for the mantle is relatively large. This may be due to the relatively poor quality of long-period dispersion data that are sensitive to mantle structure. Furthermore, large uncertainties are also shown at depths around 20 km, which is roughly equivalent to the thickness of oceanic crust.

TP

TP is the youngest and highest plateau in the world. The current common view is that about 50 million years ago, the Indian plate collided with the Eurasian plate, leading to the birth of the TP (Harrison *et al.*, 1992; Rohrmann *et al.*, 2012). Figure 10 shows three representative profiles of the lithospheric structure under the TP.

Section A crosses the TP, and the hugely thick crust and the widely distributed LVZs can be clearly seen. There are several possible causes for these LVZs. First, due to continental collisions, the temperature at the bottom of the crust increases, which may lead to partial melting, manifesting as LVZs (Rodgers and Schwartz, 1998; Schilling and Partzsch, 2001). In addition, intense compression and extension within the TP lead to significant crustal deformation, forming structures such as fractures and thrusts that are associated with low-velocity anomalies (Hu and Wang, 2018; Wang *et al.*, 2018). In the mantle (yellow-dotted lines in Fig. 10b), there are obvious high- and low-velocity separation phenomena at about 85° and 90° E, which is consistent with Li and Song (2018). Section B traverses the TP, Tarim basin, Tianshan Mountains, and Junggar basin. There are extensive sedimentary layers in the upper crust of the Tarim and Junggar basins, which exhibit low-velocity characteristics. High-velocity anomalies in the upper mantle of the TP outline the possible subduction of the Indian plate, extending approximately 34° N. A similar situation is observed in profile C, for which the Indian slab extends as far as approximately 35° N (red-dotted lines in Fig. 10c,d). During the subduction process, the torn Indian plate detached and entered the upper mantle. The stress release during the tearing caused the formation of many rift valleys on the TP.

Sichuan basin

The Sichuan basin (SB), located in southwest China and on the southeastern edge of the TP, is one of the largest sedimentary basins in China. The SB is also an important compressional structural basin. To the west of the Longmenshan fault zone, the SB is subject to compression from the TP. The southeastward flow of material from the TP has caused significant deep and large faults in the western SB, such as Xianshuihe fault, Longmenshan fault, and Anninghe fault, leading to frequent seismic activity.

We display the lithospheric structure of the SB from two profiles: northeast–southwest and southeast–northwest, as

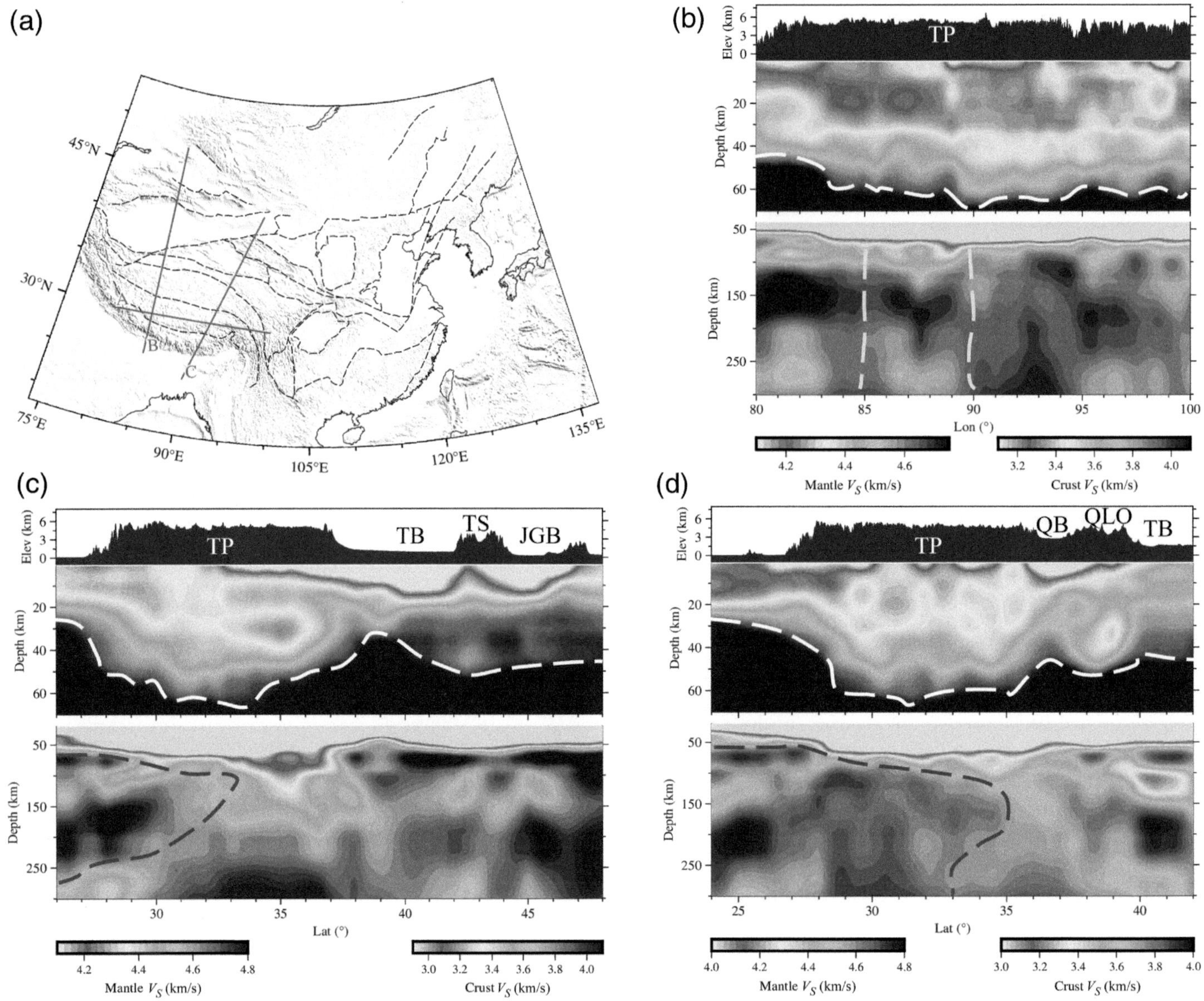

Figure 10. Profiles across the TP lithosphere. Panel (a) shows the study area, with the three profile locations (b–d) marked by purple lines. The white, yellow, and red dotted lines represent Moho, the possible location of plate tearing, and the shape of downward thrust of the Indian plate, respectively. JGB, Junggar basin; QB, Qaidam basin; QLO, Qilian orogenic; TB, Tarim basin; TP, Tibetan Plateau; and TS, Tianshan Mountains. The color version of this figure is available only in the electronic edition.

shown in Figure 11. The thickness of the crust gradually decreases from west to east. The thickest is the northeastern edge of the Songpan-Ganzi terrane (SGT) located on the TP, which is about 55 km, whereas the thickness of the crust beneath the SB is about 40 km, which is consistent with previous results obtained from the receiver function (Xu *et al.*, 2012). There are obvious sedimentary layers under the SB, showing low-velocity characteristics, with a thickness of up to 10 km. Under the sedimentary layer, the lower crust shows obvious high-velocity characteristics, which may be caused by the uplift of the upper mantle (Gong *et al.*, 2022).

Compared with the SB, the crustal material on the northeastern edge of the SGT has a lower velocity, indicating that the strength of the middle and lower crust of the SB is significantly higher. The hard middle and lower crust of the SB can block the eastward escape of the SGT. It is worth noting that at the top of the upper mantle in the SB, the two profiles show very similar shapes, and there are obvious gradient changes with depth. In the western SB, there is an obvious low-velocity anomaly at a depth of about 100 km (black dotted line in Fig. 11b,c). This implies that during the eastward escape of plateau material from the TP, in addition to being blocked by the hard material of the crust of the SB, it is likely to also affect the upper mantle of the SB, thereby transforming the lithosphere. In other words, after the eastward escape flow of material in the plateau area encounters the rigid obstruction of the SB area, it splits into two branches. One-part escapes to the southeast and northeast around the SB, and the other part dives downward.

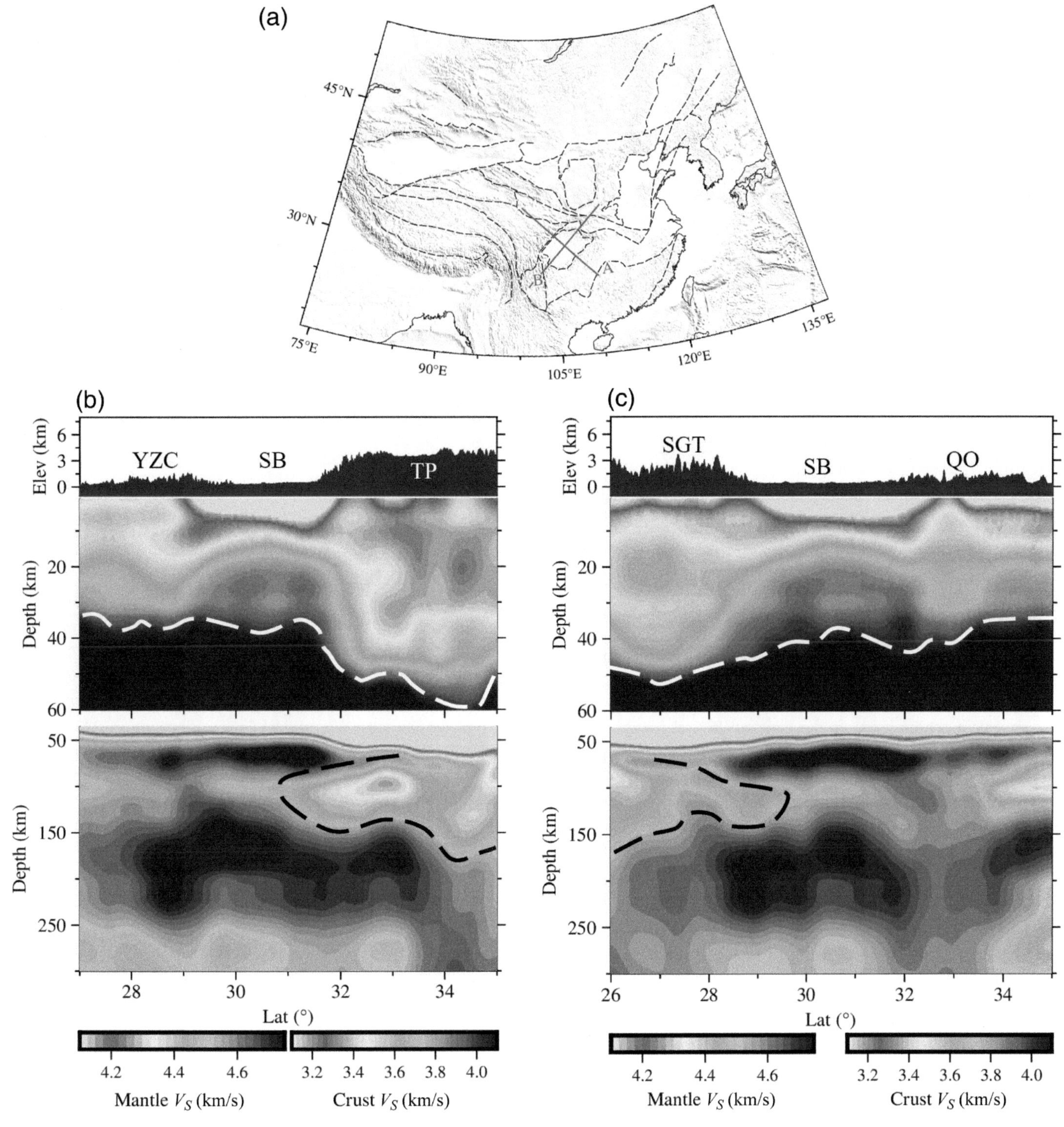

Figure 11. Profiles across the SB lithosphere. Panel (a) shows the study area, with the two profile locations (b,c) marked by purple lines. The white and black dotted lines represent Moho and the shape of material from the TP after diving into the mantle, respectively. QO, Qinling orogenic; SB, Sichuan basin; SGT, Songpan-Ganzi terrane; TP, Tibetan Plateau; and YZC, Yangtze craton. The color version of this figure is available only in the electronic edition.

Conclusion

We propose a new method to derive the V_S structure from surface-wave dispersion based on DL, while also determining the sedimentary layer thickness and Moho depth. In addition to the impact of V_S itself on dispersion, we consider more reasonable parameter assumptions during the inversion, and constructed a training data set through a spline-based method to improve the generalization of the method. To enhance physical interpretability, we use forward modeling data to constrain the inversion process. Moho information is introduced to alleviate the multiple solutions of the inversion problem and enhance spatial smoothness, and observed data are used to perform transfer learning on the pretrained model to further improve the quality of the inversion results.

Tests on synthetic data show that our method can effectively invert the V_S structure, sedimentary layer thickness, and crustal thickness. Compared with CDMs, the proposed method can better recover the input V_S structure, especially in the area near the Moho depth and on the lateral continuity. We apply the proposed method to observed data of East Asia. The V_S structure is generally consistent with previous work that used the same observed data (Li *et al.*, 2022). However, the new method can simultaneously output reasonable sedimentary layer thickness and Moho depth, which are comparable to recent studies. Compared with the V_S result of traditional inversion, our misfit of the observed data is significantly reduced, especially for long periods. In future research, we will focus on improving the lateral smoothness of the inversion results. In addition, developing more accurate and physically meaningful uncertainty estimates warrants further investigation.

Data and Resources

The surface-wave dispersions used in this study were from Li *et al.* (2022; doi: 10.1016/j.eqs.2022.05.004). Some figures were plotted with the Generic Mapping Tools (GMT) 4.5.18 software (https://www.generic-mapping-tools.org/download/; Wessel and Smith, 1998). The dataset can be obtained upon request from the authors or directly from Zenodo (https://zenodo.org/records/14840247). Both websites were last accessed in September 2025. The supplemental material for this article includes details on the model space of training dataset, comparing misfit to observations and figures of different results obtained by different methods.

Declaration of Competing Interests

The authors acknowledge that there are no conflicts of interest recorded.

Acknowledgments

The authors thank two anonymous reviewers for constructive and insightful comments, which helped improve the article greatly. This work was by the China National Science and Technology Major Project (Grant Number 2024ZD1001101) and the Heilongjiang Postdoctoral Found (LBH-Z24163).

References

Bao, X., X. Song, and J. Li (2015). High-resolution lithospheric structure beneath Mainland China from ambient noise and earthquake surface-wave tomography. *Earth Planet. Sci. Lett.* **417,** 132–141, doi: 10.1016/j.epsl.2015.02.024.

Brocher, T. M. (2005). Empirical relations between elastic wavespeeds and density in the earth's crust, *Bull. Seismol. Soc. Am.* **95,** no. 6, 2081–2092, doi: 10.1785/0120050077.

Cai, A., H. Qiu, and F. Niu (2022). Semi-supervised surface wave tomography with Wasserstein cycle-consistent GAN: Method and application on Southern California Plate Boundary Region, *J. Geophys. Res.* doi: 10.1002/essoar.10505230.1.

Castagna, J. P., M. L. Batzle, and T. K. Kan (1993). Rock physics: The link between rock properties and AVO response, in *Offset-Dependent Reflectivity - Theory and Practice of AVO Analysis (investigations in Geophysics)*, J. P. Castagna and M. M. Backus (Editors), SEG, Tulsa, Oklahoma, Vol. 8, 135–171.

Cercato, M. (2011). Global surface wave inversion with model constraints. *Geophys. Prospect.* **59,** no. 2, 210–226.

Chen, H., L. Zhu, Q. Wang, P. Zhang, and Y. Yang (2014). S-wave velocity structure of the North China from inversion of Rayleigh wave phase velocity, *J. Asian Earth Sci.* **88,** 178–191.

Chen, X., Y. Song, Y. Li, Y. Huang, X. Zhou, and Y. Fan (2021). Provenance of sub-aerial surface sediments in the Tarim Basin, Western China, *Catena* **198,** 105,014.

Cheng, S., X. Xiao, J. Wu, W. Wang, L. Sun, X. Wang, and L. Wen (2022). Crustal thickness and Vp/Vs variation beneath continental China revealed by receiver function analysis, *Geophys. J. Int.* **228,** no. 3, 1731–1749.

Chung, J., C. Gulcehre, K. Cho, and Y. Bengio (2014). Empirical evaluation of gated recurrent neural networks on sequence modeling, doi: 10.48550/arXiv.1412.3555.

Dalton, C. A., G. Ekström, and A. M. Dziewoński (2008). The global attenuation structure of the upper mantle, *J. Geophys. Res.* **113,** no. B9, doi: 10.1029/2007JB005429.

Deng, J., W. Dong, R. Socher, L. J. Li, K. Li, and L. Fei-Fei. (2009). Imagenet: A large-scale hierarchical image database, *2009 IEEE Conf. on Computer Vision and Pattern Recognition*, 248–255.

Devries, P. M. R., F. Viegas, M. Wattenberg, and B. J. Meade (2018). Deep learning of aftershock patterns following large earthquakes, *Nature* **560,** no. 7720, 632–634.

Ding, Z., S. Jiang, and J. Zhao (2022). Take a close look at mode collapse and vanishing gradient in GAN, *2022 IEEE 2nd International Conference on Electronic Technology, Communication and Information (ICETCI)*, Changchun, China, 597–602, doi: 10.1109/ICETCI55101.2022.9832406.

Du, T., W. Zhang, B. Li, L. Liu, Y. Li, Y. Ge, and S. Yu (2024). Sedimentary evidence for the diversion of the Yellow River onto the North China Plain 3000–2600 years ago, *Palaeogeogr. Palaeoclimatol. Palaeoecol.* **634,** 111,909.

Duan, L., C. Zhao, X. Du, and L. Zhou (2023). Machine learning-based automatic construction of earthquake catalog for reservoir areas in multiple river basins of Guizhou province, China, *Earthq. Sci.* **36,** no. 2, 132–146, doi: 10.1016/j.eqs.2023.03.002.

Dziewonski, A. M., and D. L. Anderson (1981). Preliminary reference Earth model. *Phys. Earth Planet. In.* **25,** 297–356.

Feng, Q., and Y. Li (2022). Denoising deep learning network based on singular spectrum analysis—DAS seismic data denoising with multichannel SVDDCNN, *IEEE Trans. Geosci. Remote Sens.* **60,** 1–11, doi: 10.1109/TGRS.2021.3071189.

Foti, S., C. Comina, D. Boiero, and L. V. Socco (2009). Non-uniqueness in surface-wave inversion and consequences on seismic site response analyses, *Soil Dynam. Earthq. Eng.* **29,** no. 6, 982–993.

Gal, Y., and Z. Ghahramani (2016). Dropout as a Bayesian approximation: Representing model uncertainty in deep learning, *International Conference on Machine Learning*, PMLR, 1050–1059.

Garia, S., A. K. Pal, A. M. Nair, and K. Ravi (2020). Elastic wave velocities as indicators of lithology-based geomechanical behaviour of sedimentary rocks: An overview, *Appl. Sci.* **2,** 1–21.

Gawlikowski, J., C. R. N. Tassi, M. Ali, J. Lee, M. Humt, J. Feng, A. Kruspe, R. Triebel, P. Jung, R. Roscher, *et al.* (2021). A survey of uncertainty in deep neural networks, doi: 10.48550/arXiv.2107.03342.

Gong, M., J. Lv, Y. Zheng, Z. J. Xie, S.-Z. Sheng, and X.-M. Zhang (2022). Three-dimensional S-wave velocity distribution based on ambient noise analysis in south China block and its adjacent areas, *Seismol. Geol.* **44,** no. 4, 1011–1028.

Goodfellow, I. J., J. Pouget-Abadie, M. Mirza, B. Xu, D. Warde-Farley, S. Ozair, A. Courville, and Y. Bengio (2014). Generative adversarial networks, *Adv. Neur. Inform. Process. Syst.* **27.**

Han, S., H. Zhang, H. Xin, W. Shen, and H. Yao (2022). Ustclitho2.0: Updated unified seismic tomography models for continental China lithosphere from joint inversion of body-wave arrival times and surface-wave dispersion data, *Seismol. Res. Lett.* **93,** 201–215.

Harrison, T. M., P. Copeland, W. S. F. Kidd, and A. N. Yin (1992). Raising Tibet, *Science* **255,** no. 5052, 1663–1670.

Heermance, R. V., A. Pullen, P. Kapp, C. N. Garzione, S. Bogue, L. Ding, and P. Song (2013). Climatic and tectonic controls on sedimentation and erosion during the Pliocene-Quaternary in the Qaidam Basin (China), *Geol. Soc. Am. Bull.* **125,** nos. 5/6, 833–856.

Herrmann, R. B. (2013). Computer programs in seismology: An evolving tool for instruction and research, *Seismol. Res. Lett.* **84,** no. 6, 1081–1088, doi: 10.1785/0220110096.

Hu, J., H. Qiu, H. Zhang, and Y. Ben-Zion (2020). Using deep learning to derive shear-wave velocity models from surface-wave dispersion data, *Seismol. Res. Lett.* **91,** no. 3, 1738–1751, doi: 10.1785/0220190222.

Hu, J., H. Yang, and H. Zhao (2008). Structure and significance of S-wave velocity and Poisson's ratio in the crust beneath the eastern side of the Qinghai-Tibet Plateau, *Pure Appl. Geophys.* **165,** 829–845.

Hu, Y., and Z. Wang (2018). Plate interactions, crustal deformation and magmatism along the eastern margins of the Tibetan Plateau, *Tectonophysics* **740,** 10–26.

Jabbar, A., X. Li, and B. Omar (2020). A survey on generative adversarial networks: Variants, applications, and training, *ACM Computing Surveys (CSUR)* **54,** no. 8, 1–49.

Jia, C., and G. Wei (2002). Structural characteristics and petroliferous features of Tarim Basin, *Chin. Sci. Bull.* **47,** 1–11.

Kanamori, H., and D. L. Anderson (1977). Importance of physical dispersion in surface wave and free oscillation problems: Review, *Rev. Geophys.* **15,** no. 1, 105–112.

Kennett, B. L. N., and E. R. Engdahl (1991). Travel times for global earthquake location and phase identification. *Geophys. J. Int.* **105,** 429–465.

Kennett, B. L. N., E. R. Engdahl, and R. Buland (1995). Constraints on seismic velocities in the Earth from traveltimes, *Geophys. J. Int.* **122,** 108–124.

Laske, G., G. Masters, Z. Ma, and M. E. Pasyanos (2012). CRUST1.0: An updated global model of Earth's crust, *EGU General Assembly Conference Abstracts*, Vienna, Austria, 22–27 April 2012.

Lei, X., J. Su, and Z. Wang (2020). Growing seismicity in the Sichuan Basin and its association with industrial activities, *Sci. China Earth Sci.* **63,** 1633–1660.

Li, J., and X. Song (2018). Tearing of Indian mantle lithosphere from high-resolution seismic images and its implications for lithosphere coupling in southern Tibet, *Proc. Natl. Acad. Sci. Unit. States Am.* **115,** no. 33, 8296–300.

Li, J., X. Song, L. Zhu, and Y. Deng (2017). Joint inversion of surface wave dispersions and receiver functions with P velocity constraints: Application to Southeastern Tibet, *J. Geophys. Res.* **122,** 7291–7310, doi: 10.1002/2017JB014135.

Li, M., X. Song, J. Li, and X. Bao (2022). Crust and upper mantle structure of East Asia from ambient noise and earthquake surface wave tomography, *Earthq. Sci.* **35,** doi: 10.1016/j.eqs.2022.05.004.

Li, Z., and H. Fang (2016). Impacts of climate change on water erosion: A review. *Earth Sci. Rev.* **163,** 94–117.

Liang, C., X. Song, and J. Huang (2004). Tomographic inversion of Pn travel times in China. *J. Geophys. Res.* **109,** no. B11.

Liao, W., E. Lee, D. Mu, and P. Chen (2022). Toward fully autonomous seismic networks: Backprojecting deep learning-based phase time functions for earthquake monitoring on continuous recordings, *Seismol. Res. Lett.* **93,** 1880–1894.

Liu, H., H. Guo, O. Pourret, Z. Wang, and M. Liu (2021). Distribution of rare earth elements in sediments of the north china plain: A probe of sedimentation process, *Appl. Geochem.* **134,** nos. 3/4, doi: 10.1016/j.apgeochem.2021.105089.

Lu, H., J. Ye, L. Guo, J. Pan, S. Xiong, and H. Li (2018). Towards a clarification of the provenance of Cenozoic sediments in the northern Qaidam Basin, *Lithosphere,* **11,** no. 2, 252–272, doi: 10.1130/L1037.1.

Luo, S., H. Yao, Z. Zhang, and T. Bem (2022). High-resolution crustal and upper mantle shear-wave velocity structure beneath the central-southern Tanlu fault: Implications for its initiation and evolution, *Earth Planet. Sci. Lett.* **595,** doi: 10.1016/j.epsl.2022.117763.

Mandel, R. D., P. Goldberg, and V. T. Holliday (2024). Site formation processes, in *Encyclopedia of Geoarchaeology*, A. S. Gilbert (Editor), Springer International Publishing, Cham, Switzerland, 1–20.

Mather, A. (2007). Arid environments, in *Environmental Sedimentology*, C. Perry and K. Taylor (Editors), Blackwell Publishing, Oxford, 144–189.

McBrearty, I. W., A. A. Delorey, and P. A. Johnson (2019). Pairwise association of seismic arrivals with convolutional neural networks, *Seismol. Res. Lett.* **90,** no. 2A, 503–509.

Meier, U., A. Curtis, and J. Trampert (2007). Global crustal thickness from neural network inversion of surface wave data, *Geophys. J. Int.* **169,** no. 2, 706–722, doi: 10.1111/j.1365-246X.2007.03373.x.

Mignan, A., and M. Broccardo (2020). Neural network applications in earthquake prediction (1994–2019): Meta-analytic and statistical insights on their limitations, *Seismol. Res. Lett.* **91,** 2330–2342.

Mousavi, S. M., W. L. Ellsworth, W. Zhu, L. Y. Chuang, and G. C. Beroza (2020). Earthquake transformer—An attentive deep-learning model for simultaneous earthquake detection and phase picking, *Nat. Commun.* **11,** no. 1, 3952.

Münchmeyer, J., J. Woollam, A. Rietbrock, F. Tilmann, D. Lange, T. Bornstein, T. Diehl, C. Giunchi, F. Haslinger, D. Jozinović, *et al.* (2022). Which picker fits my data? A quantitative evaluation of deep learning based seismic pickers, *J. Geophys. Res.* **127,** e2021JB023499, doi: 10.1029/2021JB023499.

Rodgers, A. J., and S. Y. Schwartz (1998). Lithospheric structure of the Qiangtang Terrane, northern Tibetan Plateau, from complete regional waveform modeling: Evidence for partial melt, *J. Geophys. Res.* **103,** no. B4, 7137–7152.

Rohrmann, A., P. Kapp, B. Carrapa, P. W. Reiners, J. Guynn, L. Ding, and M. Heizler (2012). Thermochronologic evidence for plateau formation in central Tibet by 45 Ma, *Geology* **40,** no. 2, 187–190.

Ross, Z. E., Y. Yue, M. A. Meier, E. Hauksson, and T. H. Heaton (2019). PhaseLink: A deep learning approach to seismic phase association, *J. Geophys. Res.* **124,** no. 1, 856–869.

Roy, C., and B. A. Romanowicz (2017). On the implications of a priori constraints in transdimensional Bayesian inversion for continental lithospheric layering, *J. Geophys. Res.* **122,** no. 12, 10,118–10,131, doi: 10.1002/2017JB014968.

Royden, L. H., B. C. Burchfiel, and R. D. van der Hilst (2008). The geological evolution of the Tibetan Plateau, *Science* **321,** no. 5892, 1054–1058.

Schilling, F. R., and G M. Partzsch (2001). Quantifying partial melt fraction in the crust beneath the Central Andes and the Tibetan plateau, *Phys. Chem. Earth* **26,** nos. 4/5, 239–246.

Shen, W., M. H. Ritzwoller, D. Kang, Y. Kim, F. C. Lin, J. Ning, W. Wang, Y. Zheng, and L. Zhou (2016). A seismic reference model for the crust and uppermost mantle beneath China from surface wave dispersion, *Geophys. J. Int.* **206,** 954–979.

Shen, W., M. H. Ritzwoller, V. Schulte-Pelkum, and F. C. Lin (2013). Joint inversion of surface wave dispersion and receiver functions: A Bayesian Monte-Carlo approach, *Geophys. J. Int.* **192,** no. 2, 807–836, doi: 10.1093/gji/ggs050.

Soto, H., and B. Schurr (2021). Deepphasepick: A method for detecting and picking seismic phases from local earthquakes based on highly optimized convolutional and recurrent deep neural networks, *Geophys. J. Int.* **227,** 1268–1294.

Sun, X. L., X. D. Song, S. H. Zheng, Y. J. Yang, and M. H. Ritzwoller (2010). Three dimensional shear wave velocity structure of the crust and upper mantle beneath China from ambient noise surface wave tomography, *Earthq. Sci.* **23,** no. 5, 449–463.

Vandana, B., B. Bhaskar, and S. K. Kumar (2022). EMOCGAN: A novel evolutionary multiobjective cyclic generative adversarial network and its application to unpaired image translation, *Neural Comput. Appl.* **34,** 21,433–21,447.

Wang, F., X. Song, and J. Li (2022). Deep learning-based H-κ method (HkNet) for estimating crustal thickness and Vp/Vs ratio from receiver functions, *J. Geophys. Res.* doi: 10.1029/2022JB023944.

Wang, F., X. Song, and M. Li (2023). A deep-learning-based approach for seismic surface-wave dispersion inversion (SfNet) with application to the Chinese mainland, *Earthq. Sci.* **36,** no. 2, 147–168, doi: 10.1016/j.eqs.2023.02.007.

Wang, Q., Y. Guo, L. Yu, and P. Li (2017). Earthquake prediction based on spatio-temporal data mining: A LSTM network approach, *IEEE Trans. Emerging Top. Comput.* **8,** 148–158.

Wang, S., B. Liu, X. Tian, B. Liu, X. Song, X. Deng, Y. Sun, C. Ma, and Y. Yang (2018). Crustal P-wave velocity structure in the northeastern margin of the Qinghai-Tibetan Plateau and insights into crustal deformation, *Sci. China Earth Sci.* **61,** no. 9, 1221–1237.

Wang, X., L. Chen, and H. Yao (2021). A new body-wave amplitude ratio-based method for imaging shallow crustal structure and its application in the Sichuan basin, southwestern China, *Geophys. Res. Lett.* **48,** no. 18, doi: 10.1029/2021GL095186.

Wang, X., J. Zhang, W. Jiang, and D. Wang (2019). Gravity field and deep seismogenic environment in the Longmen Shan and adjacent regions, Eastern Tibetan Plateau, *J. Asian Earth Sci.* **176,** 79–87.

Wang, Y., X. Song, and X. Zhang (2021). Research on nonlinear inversion of seismic surface waves based on artificial neural network algorithm, *Oil Geophys. Prospect.* **56,** no. 5, 979–991.

Wathelet, M. (2008). An improved neighborhood algorithm: Parameter conditions and dynamic scaling, *Geophys. Res. Lett.* **35,** no. 9, doi: 10.1029/2008GL033256.

Wessel, P., and W. H. Smith (1998). New, improved version of Generic Mapping Tools released, *Eos Trans. AGU* **79,** no. 47, 579.

Xiao, X., S. Cheng, J. Wu, W. Wang, L. Sun, X. Wang, and L. Wen (2021). Shallow seismic structure beneath the continental China revealed by P-wave polarization, Rayleigh wave ellipticity and receiver function, *Geophys. J. Int.* **225,** no. 2, 998–1019.

Xu, X., J. Li, F. Lin, and F. Zhao (2012). Analysis of crust-mantle structure profile with S receiver functions in Sichuan region, *J. Yunnan Univ.* **34,** no. S2, 33–39.

Xu, Z., X. Song, and S. Zheng (2013). Shear velocity structure of crust and uppermost mantle in china from surface wave tomography using ambient noise and earthquake data, *Earthq. Sci.* **26,** 267–281, doi: 10.1007/s11589-013-0010-7.

Yang, F., and J. Ma (2019). Deep-learning inversion: A next generation seismic velocity-model building method, *Geophysics* **84,** 1–133.

Yang, S., J. Hu, H. Zhang, and G. Liu (2020). Simultaneous earthquake detection on multiple stations via a convolutional neural network, *Seismol. Res. Lett.* **92,** no. 1, 246–260.

Yu, S., J. Ma, and W. Wang (2019). Deep learning for denoising. *Geophysics* **84,** no. 6, V333–V350, doi: 10.1190/geo2018-0668.1.

Zhang, K., W. Zuo, S. Gu, and L. Zhang (2017). Learning deep CNN denoiser prior for image restoration, *IEEE Conf. on Computer Vision and Pattern Recognition*, 2808–2817.

Zhang, X., and X. Song (2024). Assessing the effects of model parameter assumptions on surface-wave inversion results, *Earthq. Sci.* **37,** no. 6, 529–545.

Zhang, Z. M., J. G. Liou, and R. G. Coleman (1984). An outline of the plate tectonics of China, *Geol. Soc. Am. Bull.* **95,** no. 3, 295–312.

Zhao, D., S. Yu, and E. Ohtani (2011). East Asia: Seismotectonics, magmatism and mantle dynamics, *J. Asian Earth Sci.* **40,** no. 3, 689–709.

Zheng, S. H., X. L. Sun, X. D. Song, Y. Yang, and M. H. Ritzwoller (2008). Surface wave tomography of China from ambient seismic noise correlation, *Geochem. Geophys. Geosys.* **9,** no. 5, doi: 10.1029/2008GC001981.

Zhu, J. Y., T. Park, P. Isola, and A. A. Efros (2017). Unpaired image-to-image translation using cycle-consistent adversarial networks, *2017 IEEE International Conference on Computer Vision (ICCV)*, IEEE.

Zhu, W., and G. C. Beroza (2019). Passive seismic imaging of subwavelength natural fractures: Theory and 2-D synthetic and ultrasonic data tests, *Geophys. J. Int.* **216,** 1831, doi: 10.1093/gji/ggy529.

Zhu, W., S. M. Mousavi, and G. C. Beroza (2019). Seismic signal denoising and decomposition using deep neural networks, *IEEE Trans. Geosci. Remote Sens.* **57,** no. 11, 9476–9488, doi: 10.1109/tgrs.2019.2926772.

Manuscript received 31 October 2024
Published online 10 October 2025

Present-Day Segmented Kinematic Characteristics of the Keping Nappe System, Tian Shan, Inferred from Intensive GPS Observations

Ling Zhang[1], Shiming Liang[*1], Rui Li[1], and Jie Li[2]

Abstract

The M 7.1 Wushi earthquake unexpectedly struck the eastern tail of the Keping nappe system (KNS) in the southwest Tianshan Mountains, highlighting the complex tectonic activities in this region. Traditionally, this area has only experienced moderate earthquakes with a notable scarcity of large earthquakes. The Maidan fault, the seismogenic fault, is situated within a region characterized by intense stress, yet it exhibits an exceptionally low long-term slip rate. The aim of this study is to elucidate the previously underestimated seismic risk by analyzing the strain accumulation processes of seismogenic faults and their influence on fault activities. The latest Global Positioning System data prior to the Wushi earthquake have been utilized to construct a rational block model. The results reveal that the western part of the KNS absorbs most of the crustal deformation at its southern boundary, whereas crustal deformation in the corresponding eastern part is primarily concentrated along the northern boundary. The Piqiang fault acts as a passive, inheritable tectonic boundary bisecting the KNS and accommodating differential block rotation. The Wushi earthquake may have been facilitated by slip deficits on key active faults, emphasizing the importance of understanding regional tectonics for assessing seismic risks and providing insights into the unbalanced dynamic processes shaping the KNS.

Cite this article as Zhang, L., S. Liang, R. Li, and J. Li (2025). Present-Day Segmented Kinematic Characteristics of the Keping Nappe System, Tian Shan, Inferred from Intensive GPS Observations, *Seismol. Res. Lett.* **97**, 1123–1135, doi: 10.1785/0220240406.

Supplemental Material

Introduction

According to the report of the China Earthquake Networks Centre (CENC), at 02:09 on 23 January 2024, local time, an M 7.1 earthquake struck the Wushi county, Akesu Prefecture, Xinjiang, China (hereafter called the Wushi earthquake), with its hypocenter at the northern edge of the Keping nappe system (KNS), that is, the southern piedmont of the Tianshan Mountains (Fig. 1, Zhang *et al.*, 2024). This earthquake broke the record that no large earthquake of magnitude 7 or above occurred in the KNS since the historical records were established, and its location was farther away from the southern boundary of the nappe system with frequent moderately strong earthquakes in the past.

Before the Wushi earthquake, although the KNS had experienced a large amount of seismic moment release, earthquake magnitudes were primarily around 6 (Lü *et al.*, 2021). The 1997–1998 Jiashi earthquake cluster, which included nine moderately strong earthquakes with magnitudes ≧6.0, 2003 M_w 6.2 Bachu-Jiashi earthquake, and 2020 M_w 6.0 Jiashi earthquake all occurred along the southern edge of the KNS, on the western side of the Piqiang fault (Yao *et al.*, 2020; He *et al.*, 2021). In contrast, in the eastern part of the nappe system, there have been no earthquakes with magnitude > 6 in the past 20 yr, except for the 1987 M 6.4 and 2005 M 6.2 earthquakes in Wushi County. The marked difference in earthquake occurrence characteristics between the eastern and western sides of the KNS prompts us to investigate whether there are significant differences in seismogenic faults and strain accumulation processes. The regional crustal deformation field prior to the Wushi earthquake represents an important window for studying its potential seismogenic tectonic, and relevant research can provide vital insights into earthquake occurrence patterns during the growth of the active thrust nappe system. This research will also prompt a new understanding of earthquake

1. State Key Laboratory of Earthquake Dynamics and Forecasting, Institute of Geology, China Earthquake Administration, Beijing, China, https://orcid.org/0000-0002-5892-1545 (LZ); https://orcid.org/0000-0002-0196-5934 (SL); 2. Urumqi Institute of Central Asia Earthquake, China Earthquake Administration, Urumqi, China

*Corresponding author: liangshiming@ies.ac.cn

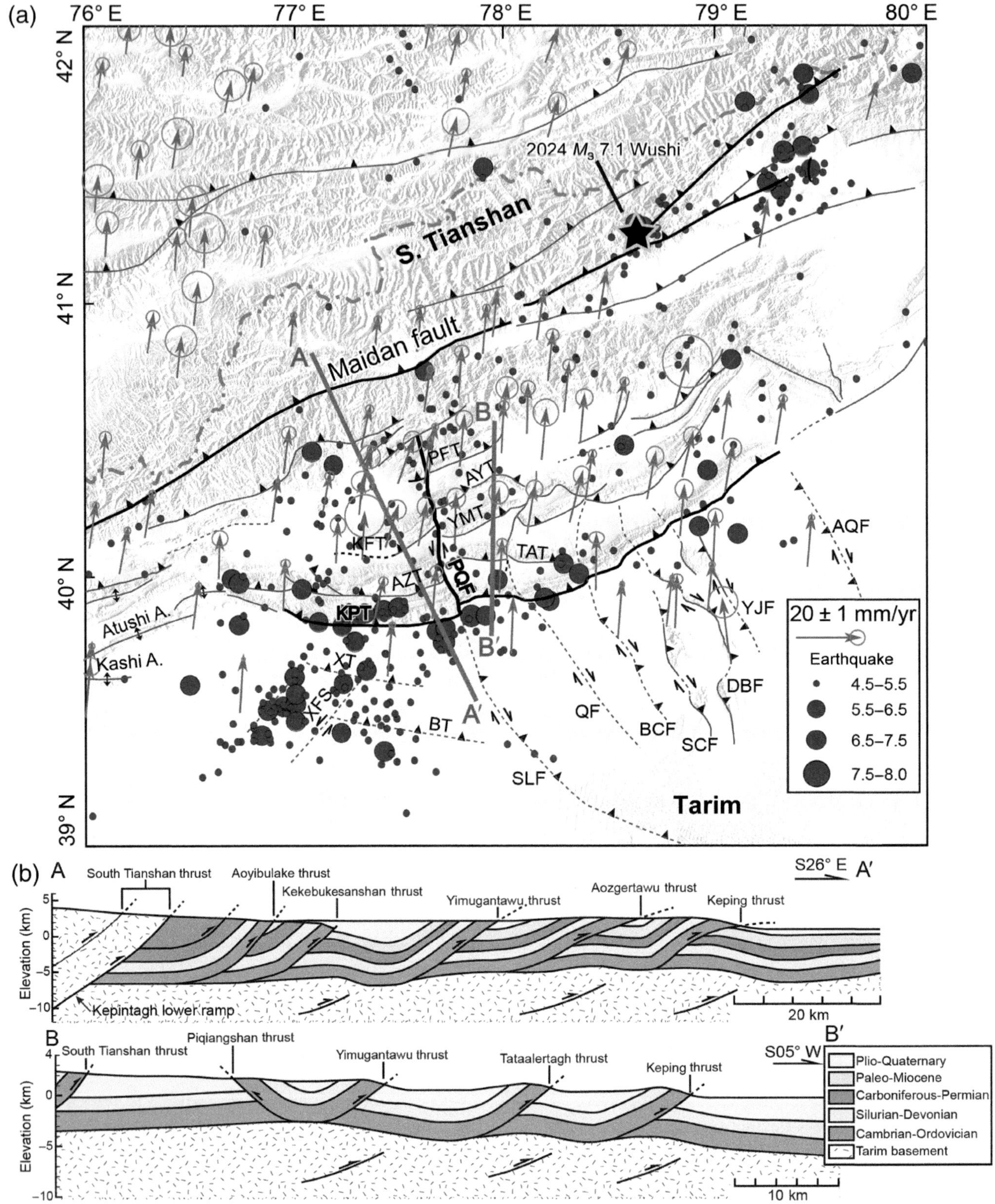

Figure 1. (a) Topography, main active faults, and earthquakes ($M \geq 4.5$, during 1900–2023) in the Jiashi-Kepingtage and its adjacent areas. The Global Positioning System (GPS) velocity field is relative to the stable Eurasian frame of reference. AQF, Aqia fault; AYT, Aoyibulake thrust fault; AZT, Aozigertawu thrust fault; BCF, Bachu fault; BT, Bashituopu thrust; DBF, Dabantagh fault; KFT, Kekebuke front thrust fault; KPT, Keping thrust fault; PFT, Piqiangshan front thrust; PQF, Piqiang fault; QF, Quxugai fault; SCF, Sanchakou fault; SLF, Selibuya fault; TAT, Tataiertagh thrust fault; XFS, Xiasuhong fault system; XT, Xikekur thrust; YJF, Yijianfang fault; YMT, Yimugantawu thrust fault. (b) Structural cross sections illustrating the outcropping Kepintagh thrust imbricates (locations shown in panel a; modified from Allen *et al.*, 1999; Zhang *et al.*, 2019; Lü *et al.*, 2021). The color version of this figure is available only in the electronic edition.

risk in the trailing edge of the thrust nappe system, where earthquakes have been relatively rare in the past.

In this study, based on the Global Positioning System (GPS) velocity field with dense data coverage of the KNS and its adjacent area prior to the Wushi earthquake, we first develop a reasonable block model. We then use the TDEFNODE software (McCaffrey, 2009) to estimate the regional interseismic block deformation characteristics and the kinematic parameters of the faults that dominate regional crustal deformation. These parameters include slip sense, slip rate, locking coefficient, and slip-rate deficit. The structural framework controlling the current deformation characteristic of the KNS is subsequently established. Finally, we discuss the potential seismic risk and tectonic implications relevant to this area.

Tectonic Background

The Tianshan Mountains is a young orogenic belt that is still growing under the influence of the remote pushing effect of Indo-Eurasian plate collision since the late Cenozoic. Numerous high-angle, basement-rooted thrusts, and foreland thrust belts are well developed on its northern and southern piedmonts (e.g., Molnar and Tapponnier, 1975; Tapponnier and Molnar, 1979; Zhang *et al.*, 1996; Burchfiel *et al.*, 1999; Deng *et al.*, 2000; Qu *et al.*, 2003; Li *et al.*, 2022; Fig. 1a). The high crustal-shortening rate, reaching up to ~20 mm/yr across the Tianshan Mountains, leads to the frequent occurrence of large earthquakes with magnitudes ≥ 7.5 (e.g., Abdrakhmatov *et al.*, 1996; Thompson *et al.*, 2002; Zubovich *et al.*, 2010; Wang and Shen, 2020).

The KNS, located between the southern Tianshan Mountains to the north and the Tarim basin to the south, is a typical thin-skinned foreland thrust belt and consists of 5–7 east–northeast-trending surface-expressed thrust imbricates (e.g., Yin *et al.*, 1998; Allen *et al.*, 1999; Yang *et al.*, 2006, 2016; Turner *et al.*, 2011; Zhang *et al.*, 2019, Fig. 1). Integrated interpretation of surface mapping data and seismic profiles indicate that these thrust imbricates produce prominent topographic relief on their hanging wall and, at depth, are generally parallel to the hanging-wall bedding (e.g., Turner *et al.*, 2011; Zhang *et al.*, 2019). These structures flatten downward to a basal detachment that coincides with the Lower–Middle Cambrian evaporites (e.g., Allen *et al.*, 1999; Yang *et al.*, 2006; Turner *et al.*, 2011).

The north-northwest—south-southeast-striking Piqiang fault, which bisects the KNS, is a prominent complex fault composed of a deep thrust fault and a shallow sinistral strike-slip (tear) fault (Yang *et al.*, 2008). Its orientation is subparallel to the thrust transport direction, and it can be traced for over 70 km on the ground surface (e.g., He *et al.*, 2002; Yang *et al.*, 2006, 2008; Turner *et al.*, 2011; Yang *et al.*, 2016). It likely initiated as a major normal fault during a period of regional extension or transtension in the Early Permian, coinciding with widespread magmatism and the emplacement of northwest-trending mafic dikes in the Tarim basin (Turner *et al.*, 2011). It was reactivated as a strike-slip fault during the Late Cenozoic in response to the development of the KNS (Yang *et al.*, 2006, 2008; Turner *et al.*, 2011; Yang *et al.*, 2016). It is segmented, with different segments exhibiting varying faulting mechanisms. The northern segment displays pure strike-slip behavior, whereas the central segment acts as a lateral ramp, completely decoupling the KNS (Turner *et al.*, 2011). In addition, the Piqiang fault accommodated significant horizontal displacement in the north–south direction, with satellite images indicating offsets of ~3.8 and 0.8 km in its northern and southern segments, respectively (Turner *et al.*, 2011). Its recent activities are evidenced by a prominent scarp within Quaternary sediments near Piqiang village, indicating ongoing tectonic activity related to the India–Asia collision and the outward propagation of the Tianshan to the Tarim basin (Lü *et al.*, 2021).

The existence of the Piqiang fault causes significant east–west variations in the number and spacing of thrust imbricates, the thickness of north-dipping Cambrian-Quaternary strata (Turner *et al.*, 2011, Fig. 2): (1) There are five thrust imbricates in the west and three to four thrust imbricates in the east; (2) because both the Carboniferous-Permian and the Paleogene-Neogene strata are absent in the eastern segment, the overburden strata above the deep detachment in the west are nearly 3000–4000 m thicker than those in the east (Turner *et al.*, 2011; Zhang *et al.*, 2019); (3) the depth of the main detachment of the KNS is ~9–10 km in the west and 5–6 km in the east (e.g., Yang *et al.*, 2006; Lü *et al.*, 2021). The deep thrust fault of the Piqiang fault is the northwestern extension of the Selibuya fault. These two faults are naturally connected at the surface and share a similar evolutionary history (Yang *et al.*, 2008).

Farther south, the Bachu Uplift, situated in the western portion of the central uplift belt of the Tarim basin, is a significant fold belt composed of a series of northwest/northwest-west-trending fold structures. To the west, it is connected to the northeast-trending Keping fault. To the south and north, it is connected to Mageti slope and the Awati depression, and bounded by the Selibuya-Mazatage fault belt and the Acha-Tumuke fault belt, respectively (Yang *et al.*, 2008). The Bachu uplift extends northwestward beneath the KNS, dividing it into three sections in the east–west direction, namely, the Xikel, Keping, and Aksu regions (Yang *et al.*, 2006, 2016). The current topography of the Bachu uplift is higher in the west and lower in the east. It has been tectonically active since the Paleozoic and its essential geological structural configuration was formed by the end of the Miocene. During the Pliocene–Holocene period, the fault zone along its southern margin has become nearly inactive, whereas its northern margin continues to exhibit activity, albeit with significantly reduced intensity (Yang *et al.*, 2006, 2016).

Fault Kinematic Parameters Inferred from GPS Measurements

GPS data

To obtain a relatively reliable GPS velocity field and subsequent block rotation estimation, we endeavored to collect as much data

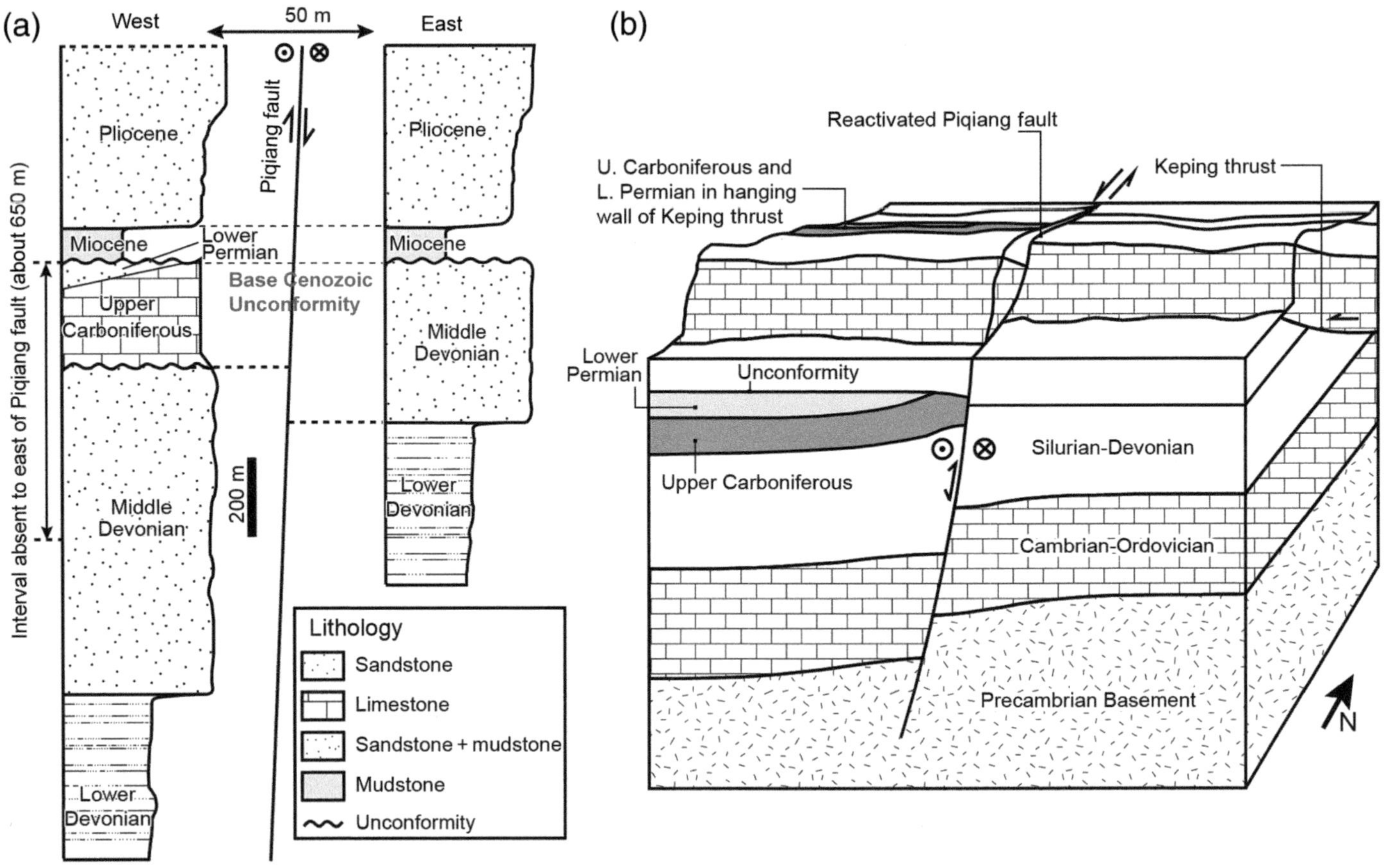

as possible. The GPS velocities used as a priori inputs for the following inversion are derived from 522 GPS observation stations (Table 1), which represent a complication of intensive observations around the Tianshan and Tarim regions from different research institutions (e.g., Kreemer *et al.*, 2014; Ge *et al.*, 2015; Wang *et al.*, 2017; Zheng *et al.*, 2017; Metzger *et al.*, 2020; Wang and Shen, 2020; Li *et al.*, 2022). The data set of Li *et al.* (2022) includes 54 new self-built stations, which significantly improve the spatial resolution of the current crustal deformation field on the piedmont of the South Tianshan Mountains. The majority of these stations were established in 2008 and have an average observation period of six epochs.

Figure 2. (a) Stratigraphic correlation across the southern segment of the Piqiang fault, near the Mystery Canyon Tourist Centre, showing the net loss of about 650 m Late Paleozoic stratigraphy from west to east, beneath the base-Cenozoic unconformity (modified from Turner *et al.*, 2011). (b) Late Cenozoic evolution of the Keping thrust fault and reactivation of the Piqiang fault as a strike-slip (tear) fault (modified from Turner *et al.*, 2011).

Owing to the differences in data processing strategies and reference frames, the GPS velocity fields from different sources invariably exhibit some degree of discrepancy. To reconcile these

TABLE 1
Summary of the Information of GPS Observation Stations (~74°–90° E, ~35.5°–44° N)

Number of GPS Stations Used	Number of Common Stations	Euler Vector Ω (Ω_x, Ω_y, Ω_z) (mas/yr)	Reference
207	/	/	Wang and Shen (2020)
33	/	/	Kreemer *et al.* (2014)
5	/	/	Ge *et al.* (2015)
54	13	0.0075, 0.0305, 0.0251	Li *et al.* (2022)
8	5	0.0124, 0.0537, 0.0487	Metzger *et al.* (2020)
197	207	−0.0020, −0.0029, −0.0027	Wang *et al.* (2017)
18	271	0.0017, 0.0064, 0.0072	Zheng *et al.* (2017)

contradictions, we integrated all velocities mentioned above into a stable Eurasian reference framework by applying rigid-body rotation transformations that minimize the residual misfit of GPS velocities for common stations (Wang and Shen, 2020; Zhang *et al.*, 2021). The discrepancies among different GPS velocity fields mentioned earlier are evaluated to be all within 1 mm/yr, with a maximum root mean square (rms) difference of 1.17 mm/yr (Table S1, available in the supplemental material to this article, in the appendix). Among these, the GPS velocity field from Li *et al.* (2022) exhibits a relatively low rms error of less than 1 mm/yr.

Specifically, to ensure the accuracy of the inversion model results, it is necessary to carefully adjust the contributions of velocity vectors from different sources to the velocity field. Because the data from Wang and Shen (2020), with an average velocity error of ~4 mm/yr, has the highest observation quality, the largest number of stations, and the broadest coverage area compared to other data sources, their corresponding velocity field is taken as reference. The data from Li *et al.* (2022) are assigned a threefold amplification factor to adjust the velocity error. This approach reduces the weight of low-quality velocity vectors in the calculations, thereby achieving more reasonable constraints on the kinematic parameters of the blocks.

Block definition and modeling

Based on the high-resolution GPS velocity field described earlier, we employed TDEFNODE (McCaffrey, 2009) to construct an elastic block model for analyzing the regional kinematic characteristics of active faults during the interseismic period. The interseismic geodetic surface velocities are modeled as arising from a combination of crustal block rotations, elastic strain rates from locked faults, and distributed permanent strain rates. The surface deformation resulting from fault locking is calculated according to the elastic half-space dislocation model (Okada, 1985). The key block parameters are systematically presented in the Appendix (Tables S2–S4). The estimated parameters include the rotational angular velocities of the blocks and the locking coefficient of block-bounding faults. Combined, these parameters can be used to calculate the interseismic slip rate and slip deficit rates.

Each fault-slip rate represents the rate of relative motions of the blocks bounded by the fault and is typically expressed in millimeter per year. Suppose two blocks, block A and block B, are separated by a fault with the angular velocities ωA and ωB, respectively. At a point on the fault plane, the velocities VA and VB for block A and block B can be determined. The relative movement rate, that is, the slip rate, is given by the difference between VA and VB. The fault locking coefficient is defined as the ratio of the relative motion between two blocks along their boundary fault (McCaffrey, 2002), and the slip-rate deficit is calculated by multiplying the fault slip rate by the locking coefficient (McCaffrey *et al.*, 2007).

Because the TDEFNODE program only requires the stations within the blocks involved in solving the problem, stations outside these blocks were not included in the calculations. A total of 73 stations were used in the modeling (Table S5 in the Appendix).

We synthesized field surveys (e.g., He *et al.*, 2002; Yang *et al.*, 2006, 2008, 2016; Turner *et al.*, 2011), 3D structure (e.g., Lü *et al.*, 2021), and current crustal deformation characteristics (Li *et al.*, 2022) of the KNS to define the boundaries of blocks and the geometry of faults in the inversion (Fig. 3). Fault planes are represented in 3D by nodes distributed on them, with positions given by longitude, latitude, and depth (McCaffrey *et al.*, 2007). The average interval between fault nodes along strike was ~30 km, with five rows of nodes down-dip (Fig. 2b). The depth, dip angle, and locking coefficient of nodes are set in advance. The locking coefficient is simultaneously Laplacian smoothed in both the strike and dip directions of the fault to avoid short-wavelength artefacts in the locking solution.

The main faults in our model actually include the Keping fault, the Maidan fault, and the Piqiang fault. These faults divide the study area into four main blocks: the east Keping, the west Keping, the Tarim, and the Tianshan blocks (Fig. 3). The geometric parameters of these faults in the model have been determined according to their actual fault geometries: (1) Based on seismic reflection profiles, the Keping fault is configured with a ramp-flat geometry extending to depth (Yao *et al.*, 2020), characterized by a maximum dip angle in its shallow part that gradually decreases with increasing depth. (2) Although its dip angle varies along different segments, the Maidan fault is characterized as a moderate-to-high-angle reverse fault (Wu *et al.*, 2019). It is set as a segmented planar fault with a 70° dip angle, consistent with the setting in Wang and Shen (2020). (3) Considering the planar structural intersection between the Piqiang fault and other east–west-trending thrust belts in the KNS, as well as its actual fault attitude near the Earth's surface, the Piqiang fault is configured as a vertical, northwest-trending planar fault in the modeling process. Simultaneously, the relocation of aftershocks from the 2020 M_w 6.0 Jiashi earthquake, as recorded by the local seismic network (Zhang *et al.*, 2024), indicates that these aftershocks are primarily concentrated within the crystalline basement at a depth less than 22 km. Considering that the depth distribution of seismic activity partly represents the seismogenic environment and that some redundancy is required during the modeling process, we set the maximum depth of all faults to 25 km.

The latest GPS velocity field profile shows that prominent nonlinear elastic deformation gradient, caused by the low-angle thrust structure, is mainly concentrated at the southern front of the KSN, near the fault trace on the ground surface (Li *et al.*, 2022). Conversely, the surface deformation away from this leading edge varies linearly, which can be explained by block rotation. Meanwhile, the east and west Keping blocks, both accompanied by limited GPS stations, are relatively small in area. This fact prompts us to ignore the imponderable internal deformation within the blocks. For the eastern segment of

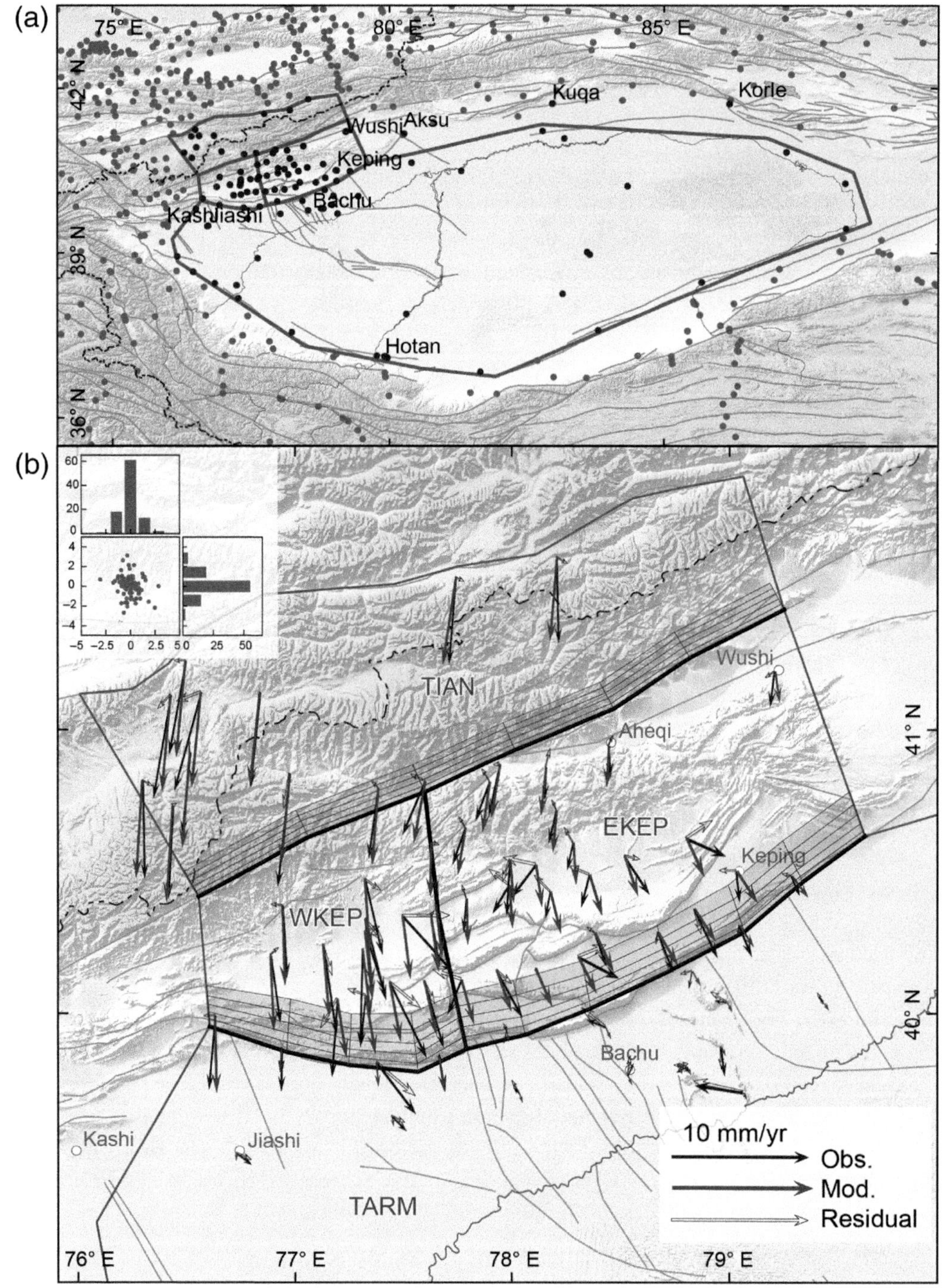

Figure 3. Global Positioning System (GPS) stations and blocks around the Tarim basin (a) and the GPS velocity field relative to the stable Tarim basin (b). The black thick lines and red thin lines delineate the boundaries of blocks. The former one represents the faults for which elastic locking parameters were estimated. The blue points are the GPS stations involving in inversion calculation. The green-shaded grids represent the surface projection of the fault-plane set in the model, with depth contours in black thin lines. The blue and red arrows represent the horizontal velocity vectors from observation and those predicted by the block model, respectively. Scatter diagram showing distribution of residual velocity components derived from the inversion calculation of block model, and top and right histograms revealing north and east residual velocity components percentage with respect to overall velocities. EKEP, east Keping block; TARM, Tarim block; TIAN, Tianshan block; WKEP, west Keping block. The inset in (b) shows the fitting residuals of the observed values. The color version of this figure is available only in the electronic edition.

the Maidan fault, the sparse GPS station distribution cannot guarantee the reliability of the locking depth and coefficient calculated along the fault due to the trade-off relationships between multiple parameters in the absence of necessary constraints (Fig. 3). Therefore, we adopt the assumption that the locking depth and locking coefficient are constant along this segment. Through continuous testing, the kinematic parameters of the blocks and their boundary faults are finally constrained when χ_n^2 tends to be the minimum value:

$$\chi_n^2 = (\mathrm{Sum}(r^2)/(sF)^2)/\mathrm{dof}.$$

Here, r denotes the residual, s represents the standard deviation, F is the scaling factor just described, and dof refers to the degrees-of-freedom (number of observations minus number of free parameters). The Sum means that the summation is taken over all data.

Results

The preferred block model illustrates the interblock convergence deformation between the Tianshan Mountain and the Tarim basin through the rigid rotation of the east and west Keping blocks (Fig. 4a), the relative movement rate along the boundary faults of blocks (Fig. 4b), and the slip deficit rate of the boundary faults (Fig. 4c). The observed and modeled velocity vectors exhibit good agreement in both magnitude and direction, with no significant deviations. The residual GPS velocities, defined as the difference between the observed and modeled velocities, display a typical normal

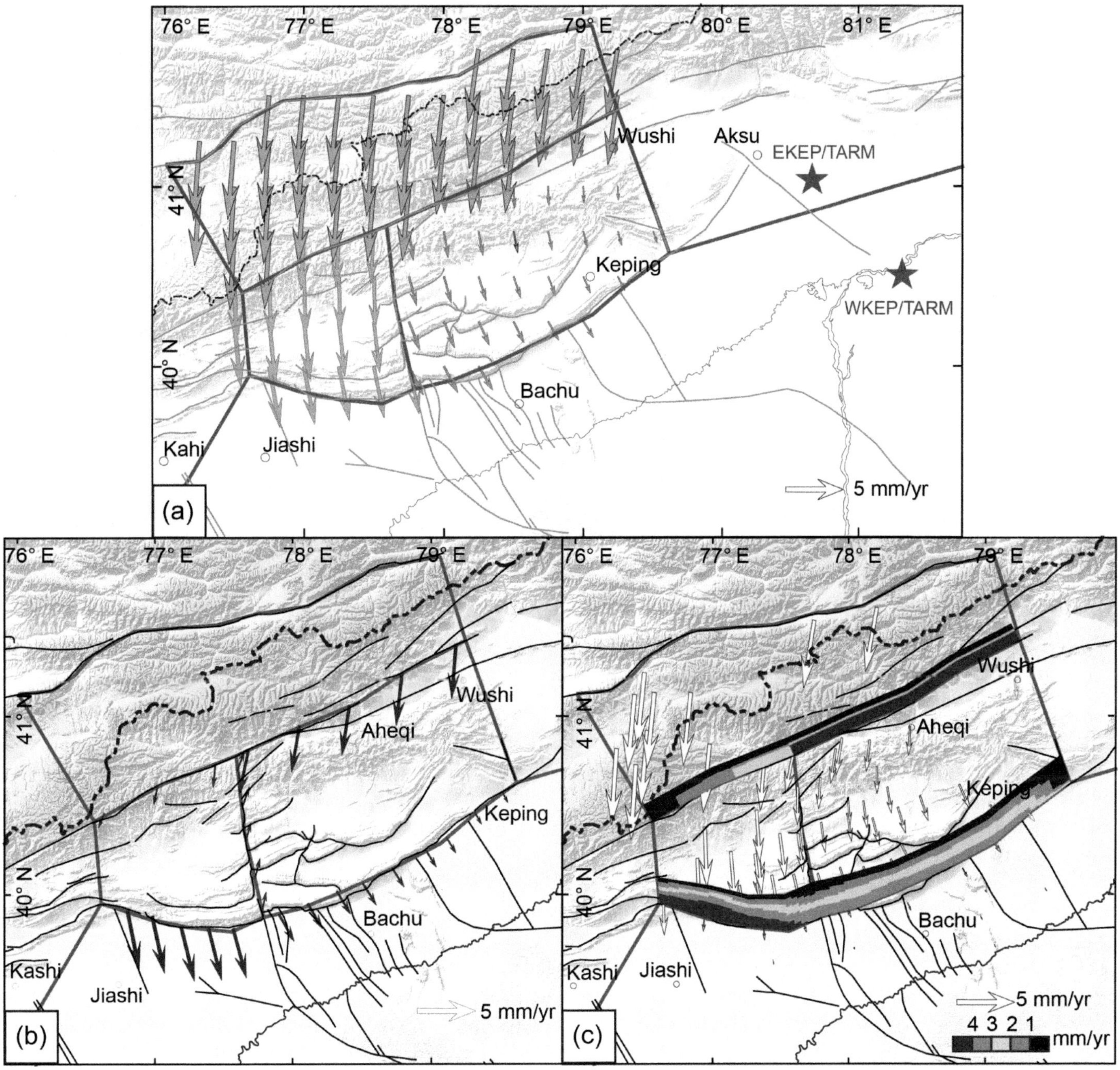

Figure 4. (a) Rigid rotations of the Tianshan (orange), west Keping (green), and east Keping (light blue) blocks relative to the stable Tarim block. Two red stars represent the Euler rotation poles of the east and west Keping blocks with respect to the stable Tarim block. (b) The relative velocity between adjacent blocks on their boundary faults. (c) The slip-rate deficit of the Maidan fault and the Keping thrust fault indicated by the color-coded bar legend and the horizontal velocity vectors predicted by the block model represented by the white arrows. The color version of this figure is available only in the electronic edition.

distribution with a standard deviation of ~1.5 mm/yr (Fig. 3b). This suggests that our model is a statistically feasible representation of reality.

Figure 4a shows the rigid rotations of the Tianshan, west Keping, and east Keping blocks relative to the stable Tarim block, demonstrating progressive convergence between the Tianshan Mountains and the Tarim basin. Two remarkable differential rotations are evident: one between the Tianshan and the two Keping blocks, and another one showing that the rotational velocities of the blocks decrease to zero after passing through the KSN from north to south. These features are more intuitively presented by the Euler rotation poles of blocks: the Euler rotation poles of the east and west Keping blocks are adjacent to each other and located near the Aksu city, but farther away from that of the Tianshan block. This characteristic is consistent with the visible regional structural framework in which the Tianshan Mountains, the KNS, and the Tarim basin are three clearly defined tectonic units.

The distribution of rotation velocities relative to the stable Tarim block in Figure 4a indicates that the west Keping block moves more rapidly than the east Keping block. The western segment of the Keping thrust fault, located at the southern margin of the KNS, absorbs most of the crustal convergence deformation between the Tianshan Mountains and the Tarim basin, whereas the eastern segment of the Maidan fault on the north side plays an equivalent role (Fig. 4b). The Piqiang fault thus serves as an important tectonic boundary accommodating differential rotation between the west and east Keping blocks. Under the pattern of slip partition and constraints from near-field GPS stations, it is inferred that more remarkable slip-rate deficits occur on the western segment of the Keping thrust fault and the eastern segment of the Maidan fault, with the typical value being ~4 mm/yr (Fig. 4c).

Discussion

Permanent strain within the east Keping block

Substantial discrepancies are observed between the observed and modeled GPS velocities within the east Keping block, warranting further clarification (Fig. 3b). Although block subdivision represents a conventional solution, the following analysis may suggest an alternative explanation.

In this study, the velocity field is constructed by integrating data from multiple sources, with data from the Crust Movement Observation Network of China (CMONOC) stations serving as the core component. Since its inception (phase I: 1999; phase II: 2009), the CMONOC has generated a data set on current crustal motion that is widely recognized as the most reliable in China (Wang and Shen, 2020). Within our research area, these high-quality data from CMONOC stations are complemented by GPS data from Li *et al.* (2022), which have been collected since 2014.

Notably, the four CMONOC stations within the east Keping block exhibit exceptionally high data quality, with postinversion residuals remaining below 1 mm/yr (Table S6, Fig. S1). This remarkable consistency indicates that the east Keping block behaves as a coherent unit, exhibiting no internal permanent deformation.

However, we observed that certain stations within the east Keping block display relatively large velocity residuals, which are predominantly concentrated in the aforementioned basin. This pattern suggests the potential presence of internal permanent strain within the east Keping block. To address the issue of these excessive residuals, we independently calculated the internal strain within the east Keping block. Specifically, we employed the method proposed by Gan *et al.* (2007) to estimate the uniform internal permanent strain of the basin, based on the residual velocities observed within it. It is important to note that we deliberately refrained from using TDEFNODE for the calculation of internal permanent strain. This decision was made because TDEFNODE treats the divided block as a single rigid unit in its computational approach, which would fail to adequately capture localized strain variations within the basin.

The inset in Figure 5 demonstrates how incorporating internal permanent deformation within the basin significantly improves the fit to the residuals in both east- and north-component velocity fields. Statistical analysis indicates that the average residual velocity is as low as 0.91 mm/yr, which is below the reported uncertainty of the velocity field by Li *et al.* (2022). Our calculations result in a maximum principal strain rate (E1) of 24.6×10^{-9}/yr and a minimum principal strain rate (E2) of 19.5×10^{-9}/yr, with the maximum principal strain oriented at 102.2° (Fig. 5). This strain pattern indicates east–west extension coupled with north–south compression. Notably, this uniformly distributed principal strain field exhibits excellent kinematic consistency with the focal mechanisms of two earthquakes in the east Keping block (an M_w 6.1 earthquake on 25 April 2007 at 40.36° N, 77.78° E, and an M_w 4.2 earthquake on 25 June 1992 at 40.58° N, 78.51° E) (Lü *et al.*, 2021), thereby demonstrating the feasibility of independently calculating the internal permanent strain.

Resolution test

We utilized the checkerboard test to evaluate the resolution of our inversion model results, following the methodology of Zhao *et al.* (2025) (Fig. 6). The validation process involved subdividing the fault plane into regularly spaced patches along both strike and dip directions, with alternating locked and unlocked segments. Synthetic GPS velocities were generated through forward modeling, and subsequently used to invert for slip rates. Resolution was assessed by comparing input and output models. Each patch was defined by 2–3 vertices along the strike direction and 1–2 vertices along the dip direction.

The test result indicates satisfactory resolution for the western segment of the Keping fault in both strike and dip directions. However, for its eastern segment, although resolution in the strike direction remains acceptable, resolution in depth deteriorates, especially toward the easternmost part. The Maidan fault exhibits reasonable resolution at shallow depths, but estimates of coupling at greater depths remain uncertain. These resolution limitations primarily arise from inadequate near-field GPS station coverage. The strategic placement of additional GPS stations at both local and regional scales would markedly enhance model reliability and resolution.

Current differential movements of the east and west Keping blocks and the occurrence of Wushi earthquake

The preferred model in this article reveals prominent characteristics of complex current crustal deformation on the piedmont of the South Tianshan Mountains, specially within

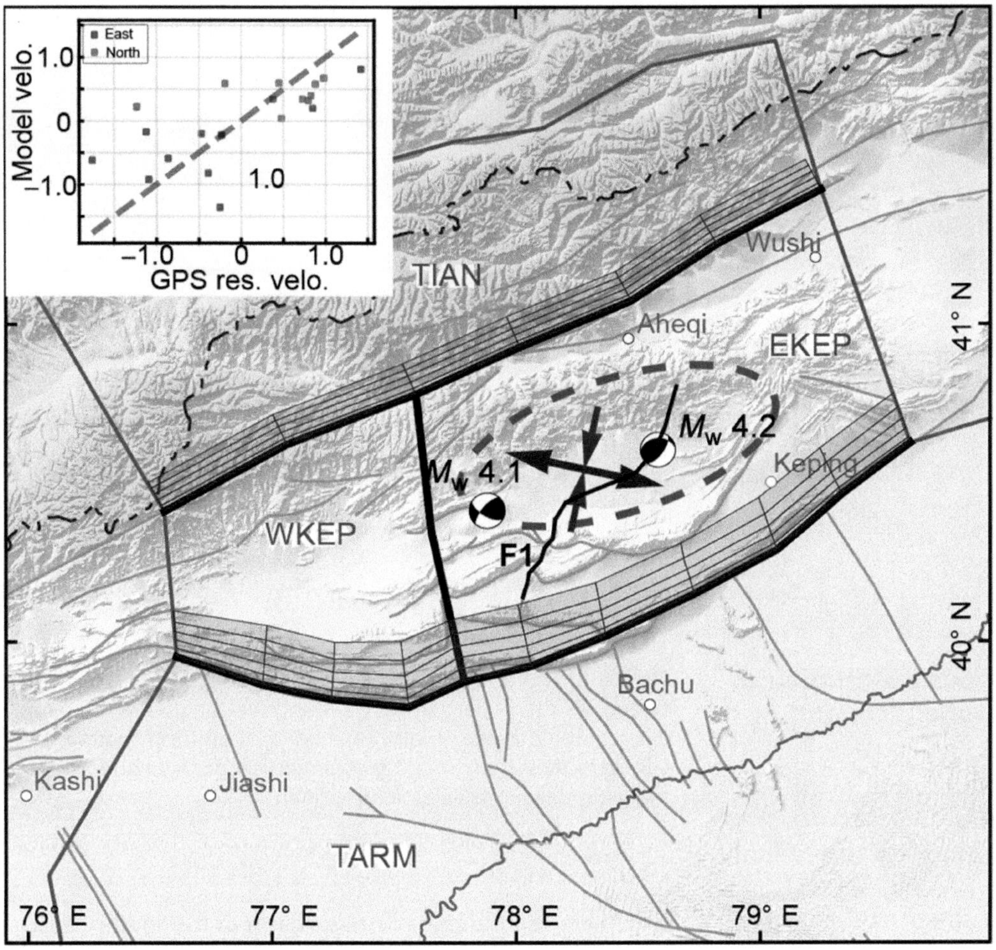

Figure 5. Internal strain and the focal mechanisms of two small earthquakes in the east Keping block. The inset shows the fitting between the observed values and the model values. The color version of this figure is available only in the electronic edition.

the KSN: (1) relative to the Tarim block, although the Euler poles of the east and west Keping blocks are both located in the vicinity of Aksu, the counterclockwise angular velocity of the west Keping block is significantly greater than that of the east Keping block. This phenomenon indicates that the lateral heterogeneity of the present-day crustal deformation in the southwestern piedmont basin of the Tianshan Mountains. (2) Most current crustal relative displacement is accommodated by the southern boundary fault of the west Keping block and the northern boundary fault of the east Keping block, namely, the western segment of the Keping thrust fault and the eastern segment of the Maidan fault (Fig. 4b). It can be inferred that the present-day crustal deformation in the western KSN has migrated farther southward, that is, toward the Tarim basin, whereas the major deformation in the eastern part is concentrated in the trailing edge of the KSN.

The heterogeneous distribution of current crustal deformation in the KSN serves as a reminder of the seismic risk associated with large active thrust faults, particularly those with low slip rate.

First, earthquakes typically arise from the abrupt instability and rupture of active faults once accumulated strain surpasses the strength threshold of the surrounding medium (e.g., Scholz, 1998). Essentially, slip deficits on faults, contributing to strain accumulation, only develop when a fault remains fully or partially locked. The strain continues to build until it is released through an earthquake or aseismic creep, marking the beginning of the next seismic cycle (Wallace *et al.*, 2004). Therefore, earthquakes are more likely to occur in fault segments with larger slip rates and greater locking ratios (e.g., Li *et al.*, 2016). In the KSN, the slip-rate deficits of the main faults, constrained by the GPS velocity field, are most pronounced at the western segment of the Keping fault belt and the eastern segment of the Maidan fault (Fig. 4), indicating locally high seismic risk. This assessment is supported by the occurrence of the 2020 M_w 6.0 Jiashi earthquake and the subsequent 2024 Wushi earthquake.

Second, the Maidan fault, which is closely related with the Wushi earthquake, exhibits a low long-term shortening rate (1.19 ± 0.25 mm/yr) and sinistral strike-slip rate (1.56 ± 0.64 mm/yr) (Wu *et al.*, 2019). The absence of strong earthquakes and low long-term slip rate of the Maidan fault had previously led to an underestimation of the potential for future strong earthquakes prior to the Wushi earthquake. This underestimation may be attributed to limited GPS observations that do not cover the entire earthquake cycle. Meanwhile, the seismogenic fault of the Wushi earthquake and its aftershocks likely involves multiple shallow active faults, among which the total crustal shortening is partitioned. They are simplified to the Maidan fault in our modeling. Because the number of GPS stations within the KNS increases, especially between different active faults, comparisons of slip rates on different timescales may become more reliable and actionable in the future.

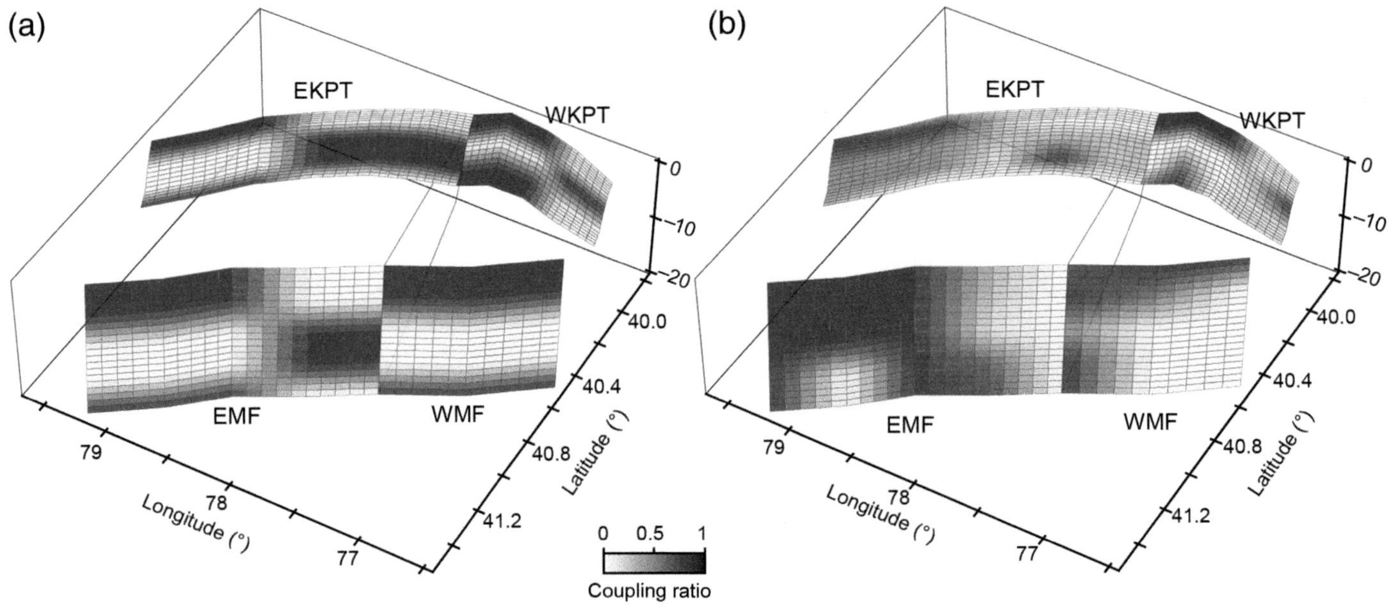

Figure 6. The synthetic checkerboard model of coupling distribution for the Keping thrust fault and the Maidan fault (a) and the recovered coupling distributions for them from synthesized GPS velocity vectors (b). The color version of this figure is available only in the electronic edition.

Implications of the heterogeneous distribution of current crustal deformation on the piedmont of the South Tianshan Mountains

In a broad sense, during the continuous growth of the nappe system in the foreland direction, thrust faults at the trailing edge tend to gradually become inactive, whereas new major thrust faults continuously form ahead of them and absorb crustal shortening as the primary mechanism (Jamison, 1987; Mitra *et al.*, 1988; Gosen, 1992). These major thrust faults are parallel to one another at the Earth's surface and root into a common detachment at depth. In other words, current crustal shortening tends to be concentrated at the leading edge of the nappe system.

Yang *et al.* (2006) ever used the balanced cross-section technique to constrain the total crustal shortening of the west and east Keping blocks as 45 and 40 km in the north–south direction since the initiation of the KSN (~20 Ma) to the present, respectively. The long-term crustal shortening between the Tianshan Mountains and the Tarim basin is relatively consistent in the east–west direction, indicating that the long-term effect of tectonic stress maintains horizontal uniformity. This is also verified from the multiple rows of fold-and-thrust belts, which are located approximately parallel within the KSN. In other words, the total crustal deformation over long timescales is roughly equivalent between the eastern and western parts of the KNS. However, present-day crustal deformation exhibits significant differences between these two sides, promoting us to consider the significance of the differences in inherited structure.

The current distribution of main active thrust fault zones revealed in this article supports the notion that the west Keping block developed in a north-to-south sequence, that is, a forward propagation sequence, following the collision between the Tianshan Mountain and the Tarim basin. This is consistent with observations in foreland basins worldwide, such as the Rocky Mountains foreland basin in the Canadian Cordillera and the Kuqa foreland basin in the South Tianshan Mountains. In contrast, the east Keping block exhibits a different growth pattern, with the southern boundary fault of the South Tianshan Mountains being part of an active out-of-sequence thrust fault system. Other active out-of-sequence thrust faults have also been reported, such as those located in the central Nepalese Himalaya (e.g., Wobus, 2005) and the Plio-quaternary ones in the northern Tunisia (Azizi *et al.*, 2024). Mukherjee *et al.* (2012) proposed that out-of-sequence thrusting could arise randomly within a deforming crustal wedge. The presence of an ancient fault block, lateral shifts in the mechanical characteristics of detachment horizons, and additional buttressing processes are all conceivable triggers for such thrusting (e.g., Wobus, 2005; Larson *et al.*, 2010).

We have developed a simple conceptual model to illustrate the current crustal deformation characteristics of the KSN (Fig. 7). The occurrence of active out-of-sequence thrust faults in the east Keping block can be attributed to the pre-existence of the Piqiang fault and the structure difference between the west and east Keping blocks. First, the Piqiang fault is an active, deep-seated fault that cuts into the basement and also breaks through to the surface (e.g., He *et al.*, 2002; Yang *et al.*, 2006, 2008, 2016; Turner *et al.*, 2011; Li *et al.*, 2022). Second, an ancient heave developed beneath the Cenozoic sediments is located in the southern front of the east Keping block (e.g., Yang *et al.*, 2006, 2008, 2016; Lü *et al.*, 2021). As a result, the east Keping block was strongly hindered when the KSN absorbed

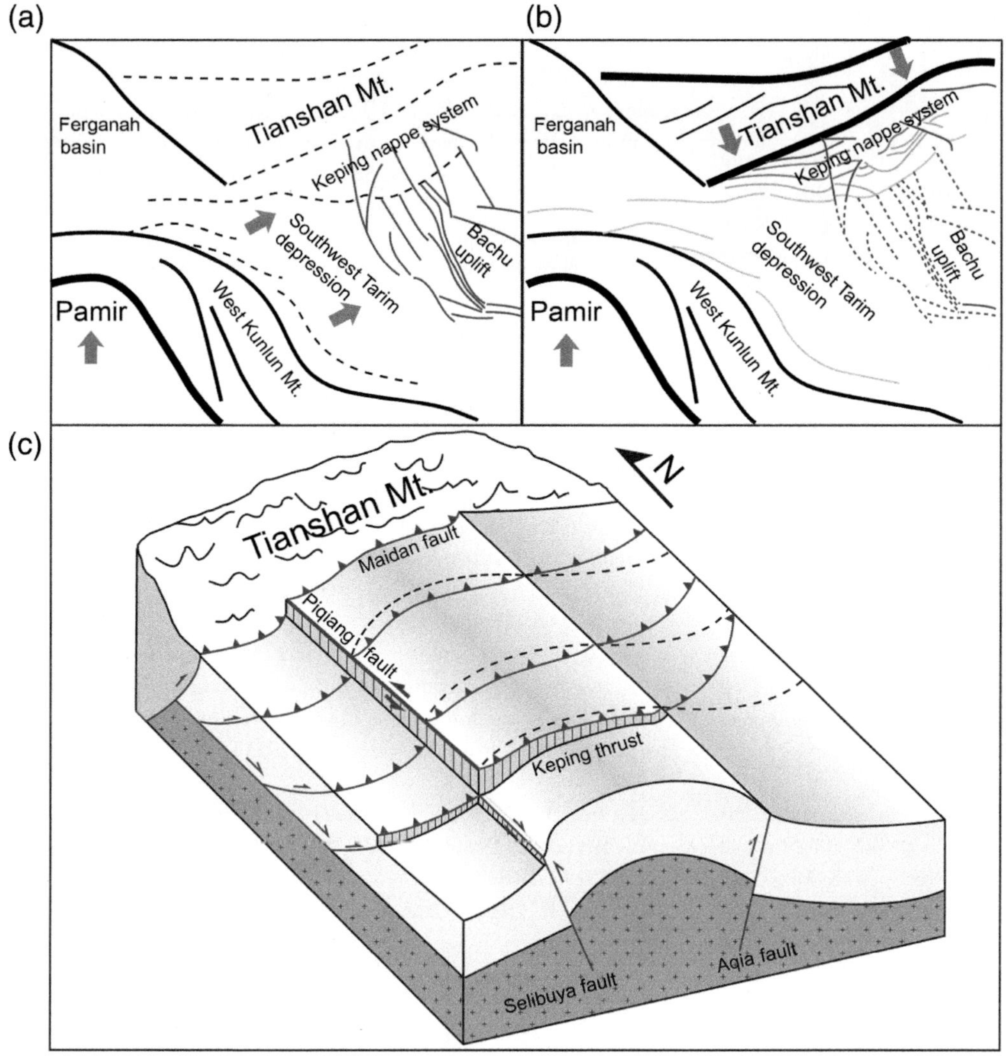

Figure 7. (a) Distribution of the faults within and around the Keping thrust nappe (KNS) system in early Miocene. During this period, the Tianshan Mountains had not yet rapidly uplifted, and the nearly north–south-trending faults began to develop in the Keping–Bachu area. The dashed lines represent the terrain structure lines that have not yet appeared on the Earth's surface. (b) The Keping nappe thrust system continued to propagate forward. During this period, the Piqiang fault began to show sinistral strike-slip movement, and several parallel north–south-trending faults, such as the Selibuya fault, were covered by the late Quaternary sediments at the edge of the Tarim basin. (c) Conceptual diagram of current kinematic characteristics of the Keping thrust nappe system. The color version of this figure is available only in the electronic edition.

crustal shortening between the Tianshan Mountains and the Tarim basin during deformation propagation. The Piqiang fault plays a role similar to that of a transform fault (Turner *et al.*, 2011; Zhang *et al.*, 2021), and its sinistral strike-slip movement reconciles the differences in movement between the east Keping block and west Keping block.

Conclusions

Based on the current kinematic characteristics, the KSN can be divided into the east and west Keping blocks, which exhibit significant differential rotating. In the west Keping block, most of the intense crustal shortening is absorbed by the Keping thrust, whereas in the east Keping block, it is absorbed by the Maidan fault. The absence of earthquake with a magnitude of 7 or greater in the KNS, particularly in the east block, can be attributed to the relatively short duration of observational records compared to the seismic cycles of such large events. The occurrence of the Wushi earthquake helps fill this observational gap. The relatively higher intensity of fault activity along the Keping thrust and the Maidan fault supports the notion that the west Keping block has developed through a north-to-south sequence, that is, a forward propagation sequence, over a much longer timescale. In contrast, the east Keping block appears to be characterized by an active out-of-sequence thrust fault system.

Data and Resources

Epicenter data are downloaded from the U.S. Geological Survey Seismic Catalog (http://earthquake.usgs.gov/earthquakes/, last accessed January 2024). Global Positioning System (GPS) data were obtained from Ge *et al.* (2015), Goudarzi *et al.* (2014), Kreemer *et al.* (2014), Wang *et al.* (2017), Metzger *et al.* (2020), Wang and Shen (2020), Li *et al.* (2022), and Zheng *et al.* (2017). The supplemental material lists GPS stations and horizontal velocity vectors retained for modeling. To balance reproducibility with research efficiency, we provide all model parameters in a concise tabular format. These tables include the coordinates defining block boundaries and the fault planes of the West Keping Thrust, Maidan, and Piqiang Faults. Velocities and associated uncertainties for selected CMONOC stations within the EKEP block (Wang and Shen, 2020) and representative sites from Li *et al.* (2022) are also given in the supplemental material.

Declaration of Competing Interests

The authors acknowledge that there are no conflicts of interest recorded. And they declare that they have no known competing financial interests or personal relationships that could have appeared to influence the work reported in this article.

Acknowledgments

All the figures were plotted and generated using the following tools and applications: Generic Mapping Tools (version 6.3.0, https://www.generic-mapping-tools.org/), QGIS (version 3.32.1, https://www.qgis.org/), and Python Matplotlib (version 3.5.2, URL: https://matplotlib.org/). All websites were last accessed in March 2025. This research was funded by the National Key Research and Development Program of China (Grant Number 2022YFC3003702).

References

Abdrakhmatov, K. Y., S. A. Aldazhanov, B. H. Hager, M. W. Hamburger, T. A. Herring, K. B. Kalabaev, V. I. Makarov, P. Molnar, S. V. Panasyuk, M. T. Prilepin, *et al.* (1996). Relatively recent construction of the Tien Shan inferred from GPS measurements of present-day crustal deformation rates, *Nature* **384,** 450–453, doi: 10.1038/384450a0.

Allen, M. B., S. J. Vincent, and P. J. Wheeler (1999). Late Cenozoic tectonics of the Kepingtage thrust zone: Interactions of the Tien Shan and Tarim basin, northwest China, *Tectonics* **18,** no. 4, 639–654, doi: 10.1029/1999TC900019.

Azizi, R., A. Barhoumi, and A. Mancini (2024). New insight on the structural architecture of northern Tunisia with a multidisciplinary approach: Association of Miocene piggy-back basin and active Plio-quaternary out-of-sequence thrusts, *Mar. Pet. Geol.* **160,** 106,639, doi: 10.1016/j.marpetgeo.2023.106639.

Burchfiel, B. C., E. Brown, Q. Deng, and X. Feng (1999). Crustal shortening on the margins of the TienShan, Xinjiang, China, *Int. Geol. Rev.* **41,** no. 8, 665–700, doi: 10.1080/00206819909465164.

Deng, Q., X. Feng, P. Zhang, X. Xu, X. Yang, S. Peng, and J. Li (2000). Active Tectonics of the Tian Shan Mountains, Seismology Press, Beijing, 399 pp. (in Chinese with English abstract).

Gan, W., P. Zhang, Z. K. Shen, Z. Niu, M. Wang, Y. Wan, D. Zhou, and J. Cheng (2007). Present-day crustal motion within the Tibetan plateau inferred from GPS measurements, *J. Geophys. Res.* **112,** no. B8, doi: 10.1029/2005JB004120.

Ge, W., P. Molnar, Z. Shen, and Q. Li (2015). Present-day crustal thinning in the southern and northern Tibetan plateau revealed by GPS measurements, *Geophys. Res. Lett.* **42,** no. 13, 5227–5235, doi: 10.1002/2015GL064347.

Gosen, W. (1992). Structural evolution of the Argentine Precordillera: The Rio San Juan section, *J. Struct. Geol.* **14,** no. 6, 643–667, doi: 10.1016/0191-8141(92)90124-F.

Goudarzi, M. A., M. Cocard, and M. C. Santerre (2014). EPC: Matlab software to estimate Euler pole parameters, *GPS Solut.* **18,** no. 1, 153–162, doi: 10.1007/s10291-013-0354-4.

He, W., J. Li, X. Qian, and D. Zheng (2002). Analysis of fault structures in the Kalpin fault uplift, Tarim basin, *Geol. China* **29,** no. 1, 37–43 (in Chinese with English abstract).

He, Y., T. Wang, L. Fang, and L. Zhao (2021). The 2020 M_w 6.0 Jiashi earthquake: Coinvolvement of thin-skinned thrusting and basement shortening in shaping the Keping-Tage fold-and-thrust belt in southwestern Tian Shan, *Seismol. Res. Lett.* **93,** no. 2A, 680–692, doi: 10.1785/0220210063.

Jamison, W. R. (1987). Geometric analysis of fold development in overthrust terranes, *J. Struct. Geol.* **9,** no. 2, 207–219, doi: 10.1016/0191-8141(87)90026-5.

Kreemer, C., G. Blewitt, and E. C. Klein (2014). A geodetic plate motion and Global strain rate model, *Geochem. Geophys. Geosys.* **15,** no. 10, 3849–3889, doi: 10.1002/2014GC005407.

Larson, K. P., L. Godin, W. Davis, and D. W. Davis (2010). Out-of-sequence deformation and expansion of the Himalayan orogenic wedge: insight from the Changgo culmination, south central Tibet, *Tectonics* **29,** no. 4, TC4013, doi: 10.1029/2008TC002393.

Li, J., Y. Yao, R. Li, S. Yusan, G. Li, J. T. Freymueller, and Q. Wang (2022). Present-day strike-slip faulting and thrusting of the Kepingtage fold-and-thrust belt in southern Tianshan: Constraints from GPS observations, *Geophys. Res. Lett.* **49,** no. 11, e2022GL099105, doi: 10.1029/2022GL099105.

Li, Y., X. Shan, X. Song, Y. Jiang, W. Gan, C. Qu, and Z. J. Wang (2016). Fault locking and slip rate deficit on the middle and southern segment of the Tancheng-Lujiang fault inverted from GPS data, *Chin. J. Geophys.* **59,** no. 11, 4022–4034, doi: 10.6038/cjg20161108 (in Chinese with English abstract).

Lü, L. X., T. Li, Z. Chen, J. Chen, J. T. Jobe, and L. Fang (2021). Active structural geometries and their correlation with moderate (M 5.5-7.0) earthquakes in the Jiashi-Keping region, Tian Shan Southwestern front, *Tectonics* **40,** e2021TC006760, doi: 10.1029/2021tc006760.

McCaffrey, R. (2002). *Crustal Block Rotations and Plate Coupling*, Geodynamics Series, AGU, Washington, D.C., 101–122, doi: 10.1029/GD030p0101.

McCaffrey, R. (2009). Time-dependent inversion of three-component continuous GPS for steady and transient sources in northern Cascadia, *Geophys. Res. Lett.* **36,** L07304, doi: 10.1029/2008GL036784.

McCaffrey, R., A. I. Qamar, R. W. King, R. Wells, G. Khazaradze, C. A. Williams, C. W. Stevens, J. J. Vollick, and P. C. Zwick (2007). Fault locking, block rotation and crustal deoformation in the Pacific Northwest, *Geophys. J. Int.* **169,** no. 3, 1315–1340, doi: 10.1111/j.1365-246X.2007.03371.x.

Metzger, S., A. Ischuk, Z. Deng, L. Ratschbacher, M. Perry, S. Kufner, R. Bendick, and M. Moreno (2020). Dense GNSS profiles across the northwestern tip of the India-Asia collision zone: Triggered slip and westward flow of the Peter the First Rang, Pamir, into the Tajik depression, *Tectonics* **39,** no. 2, e2019TC005797, doi: 10.1029/2019TC005797.

Mitra, G., J. M. Hull, W. A. Yonkee, and G. M. Protzman (1988). Comparison of mesocopic and microscopic deformational styles in the Idaho-Wyoming thrust belt and the Rocky Mountain foreland, in *Interaction of the Rocky Mountain Foreland and the Cordilleran Thrust Belt*, C. J. Schmidt and W. J. Perry Jr. (Editors), Geological Society of America, Memoir 171, doi: 10.1130/MEM171-p119.

Molnar, P., and P. Tapponnier (1975). Cenozoic tectonics of Asia: Effects of a continental collision, *Science* **189,** no. 4201, 419–426, doi: 10.1126/science.189.4201.419.

Mukherjee, S., H. A. Koyi, and C. J. Talbot (2012). Implications of channel flow analogue models for extrusion of the Higher Himalayan shear zone with special reference to the out-of-sequence thrusting, *Int. J. Earth Sci.* **101,** no. 1, 253–272, doi: 10.1007/s00531-011-0650-6.

Okada, Y. (1985). Surface deformation due to shear and tensile faults in a half-space, *Bull. Seismol. Soc. Am.* **75,** no. 4, 1135–1154.

Qu, G., Y. Li, and J. Chen (2003). Geometry, kinematic and tectonic evolution of Kepingtage thrust system, *Earth Sci. Front.* **10,** no. z1, 142–152, doi: 10.3321/j.issn:1005-2321.2003.z1.021 (in Chinese with English abstract).

Scholz, C. H. (1998). Earthquakes and friction laws, *Nature* **391,** no. 6662, 37–42, doi: 10.1038/34097.

Tapponnier, P., and P. Molnar (1979). Active faulting and Cenozoic tectonics of the Tien Shan, Mongolia, and Baykal regions, *J. Geophys. Res.* **84,** no. B7, 3425–3459.

Thompson, S. C., R. J. Weldon, C. M. Rubin, K. Abdrakhmatov, P. Molnar, and G. W. Berger (2002). Late quaternary slip rates across the central Tien Shan, Kyrgyzstan, central Asia, *J. Geophys. Res.* **107,** no. B9, 2203, doi: 10.1029/2001JB000596.

Turner, S. A., J. G. Liu, and J. W. Cosgrove (2011). Structural evolution of the Piqiang fault zone, NW Tarim basin, China, *J. Asian Earth Sci.* **40,** 394–402, doi: 10.1016/j.jseaes.2010.06.005.

Wallace, L. M., C. Stevens, E. Silver, R. McCaffrey, W. Loratung, S. Hasiata, R. Stanaway, R. Curley, R. Rosa, and J. Taugaloidi (2004). GPS and seismological constraints on active tectonics and arc-continent collision in Papua New Guinea: Implications for mechanics of microplate rotations in a plate boundary zone, *J. Geophys. Res.* **109,** no. B5, doi: 10.1029/2003JB002481.

Wang, M., and Z. Shen (2020). Present-day crustal deformation of continental China derived from GPS and its tectonic implications, *J. Geophys. Res.* **125,** no. 2, e2019JB018774, doi: 10.1029/2019JB018774.

Wang, W., X. Qiao, S. Yang, and D. Wang (2017). Present-day velocity field and block kinematics of Tibetan plateau from GPS measurements, *Geophys. J. Int.* **208,** no. 2, 1088–1102, doi: 10.1093/gji/ggw445.

Wobus, C. (2005). Geomorphic and thermochronologic signature of active tectonics in the Central Nepalese Himalaya, *Ph.D. Thesis*, Massachusetts Institute of Technology, 1–207.

Wu, C., W. Zheng, P. Zhang, Z. Zhang, Q. Jia, J. Yu, H. Zhang, Y. Yao, J. Liu, G. Han, *et al.* (2019). Oblique thrust of the Maidan fault and Late Quaternary tectonic deformation in the southwestern Tian Shan, northwestern China, *Tectonics* **38,** 2625–2645, doi: 10.1029/2018TC005248.

Yang, G., X. Shi, C. Jia, J. Zhang, C. Zhang, and D. He (2008). Spatial relationship between Piqiang fault and Selibuya fault in Keping-Bachu district, northwest Tarim basin, *Uranium Geol.* **24,** no. 4, 201–207, doi: 10.3969/j.issn.1000-0658.2008.04.003 (in Chinese with English abstract).

Yang, X. P., Y. K. Ran, F. M. Song, X. W. Xu, J. W. Cheng, W. Min, Z. J. Han, and L. C. Chen (2006). The analysis for crust shortening of Kalpin thrust tectonic zone, south-western Tianshan, Xinjiang, China, *Seismol. Geol.* **28,** no. 2, 194–204 (in Chinese with English abstract).

Yang, Y., L. Tang, Y. Guo, and D. Xie (2016). Cenozoic structural evolution characteristics of Piqiang fault, Kalpin thrust belt, *J. China Univ. Mining Technol.* **45,** no. 6, 1204–12210 (in Chinese with English abstract).

Yao, Y., S. Wen, T. Li, and C. Wang (2020). The 2020 M_w 6.0 Jiashi earthquake: a fold earthquake event in the southern Tian Shan, northwest China, *Seismol. Res. Lett.* **92,** 859–869, doi: 10.1785/0220200146.

Yin, A., S. Nie, P. Craig, T. M. Harrison, F. J. Ryerson, Q. Xianglin, and Y. Geng (1998). Late Cenozoic tectonic evolution of the southern Chinese Tian Shan, *Tectonics* **17,** no. 1, 1–27, doi: 10.1029/97TC03140.

Zhang, B. X., L. Qian, T. Li, J. Chen, J. Xu, Y. Yao, L. Fang, C. Xie, J. Chen, and G. Liu (2024). Geological disasters and surface ruptures of January 23, 2024 M_s 7.1 Wushi earthquake, Xinjiang, China, *Seismol. Geol.* **46,** no. 1, 220–234, doi: 10.3969/j.issn.0253-4967.2024.01.013 (in Chinese with English abstract).

Zhang, L., S. Liang, X. Yang, W. Gan, and C. Dai (2021). Geometric and kinematic evolution of the Jiali fault, eastern Himalayan Syntaxis, *J. Asian Earth Sci.* **212,** 104722, doi: 10.1016/j.jseaes.2021.104722.

Zhang, P., Q. Deng, X. Yang, S. Peng, X. Xu, and X. Feng (1996). Late Cenozoic tectonic deformation and mechanism along the Tianshan Mountain, northwestern China, *Earthq. Res. China* **12,** no. 2, 127–140 (in Chinese with English abstract).

Zhang, Y., S. Yang, H. Chen, Y. Dilek, X. Cheng, X. Lin, C. Wang, and T. Zhu (2019). The effect of overburden thickness on deformation mechanisms in the Keping fold-thrust belt, southwestern Chinese Tian Shan Mountains: Insights from analogue modeling, *Tectonophysics* **753,** 79–92, doi: 10.1016/j.tecto.2019.01.005.

Zhao, S., P. R. Cummins, S. McClusky, and M. S. Miller (2025). Interseismic coupling along the Java-Timor subduction-collision zone at East Indonesia, *Geophys. Res. Lett.* **52,** no. 6, e2024GL112563, doi: 10.1029/2024GL112563.

Zheng, G., H. Wang, T. J. Wright, Y. Lou, R. Zhang, W. Zhang, C. Shi, J. Huang, and N. Wei (2017). Crustal deformation in the India-Eurasia collision zone from 25 years of GPS measurements, *J. Geophys. Res.* **122,** no. 13, 9290–9312, doi: 10.1002/2017JB014465.

Zubovich, A. V., X. Wang, Y. G. Scherba, G. G. Schelochkov, R. Reilinger, C. Reigber, O. I. Mosienko, P. Molnar, W. Michajljow, V. I. Makarov, *et al.* (2010). GPS velocity field for the Tien Shan and surrounding regions, *Tectonics* **29,** no. 6, TC6014, doi: 10.1029/2010tc002772.

Manuscript received 11 October 2024
Published online 12 September 2025

Late Pleistocene Kinematics of the Great Southern Puerto Rico Fault Zone, Puerto Rico

Emerson M. Lynch*[1], Jessica Thompson Jobe[1], Rich Briggs[1], M. Morow Tan[2], Victor Ortega Díaz[3], and K. Stephen Hughes[3]

Abstract

Several onshore faults in southern Puerto Rico have recently been recognized as Quaternary active. However, the kinematics of these faults, particularly any lateral component, remain largely unconstrained. It is difficult to characterize low strain-rate faults, partially due to extensive erosional and anthropogenic landscape modification, steep relief, and frequent landsliding, limiting the preservation of geomorphic features that could serve as recorders of fault motion. Here, we constrain the kinematics along sections of the Great Southern Puerto Rico Fault Zone (GSPRFZ) on the southern coastal plain of Puerto Rico. We integrate ~1-m-resolution light detection and ranging (lidar)-derived topography, historical air photos, and field mapping to identify a series of ~50–1200-m-long fault scarps and lineaments that trend northwest–southeast and extend for ≥ 25 km across the southern coastal plain. Fault scarps are primarily south facing, cut across topography, and displace Quaternary deposits and landforms. We document multiple offset geomorphic markers, including channel thalwegs and interfluves formed in deposits previously mapped as Quaternary piedmont alluvial plain. We observe both vertical (south-side-down) and right-lateral meter-scale displacements, which indicate that the GSPRFZ accommodates right-lateral oblique motion in the late Pleistocene, consistent with northeast motion of the Puerto Rico and the Virgin Islands microplate away from the Hispaniola block.

Cite this article as Lynch, E. M., J. Thompson Jobe, R. Briggs, M. M. Tan, V. Ortega Díaz, and K. S. Hughes (2025). Late Pleistocene Kinematics of the Great Southern Puerto Rico Fault Zone, Puerto Rico, *Seismol. Res. Lett.* **97**, 1136–1155, doi: 10.1785/0220250116.

Supplemental Material

Introduction

Identification and characterization of potentially active low-slip-rate faults is typically achieved by integrating remote observations of fault-related geomorphology on high-resolution topography (e.g., light detection and ranging [lidar]) with detailed field verification and mapping (e.g., Lin *et al.*, 2013; Khajavi *et al.*, 2014; Ntokos *et al.*, 2016; Morell *et al.*, 2017; Meghraoui *et al.*, 2000; Pánek *et al.*, 2020; Thompson Jobe, Gold, *et al.*, 2020; Thompson Jobe, Briggs, Hughes, 2024). However, the subtle geomorphic record of fault slip in regions obscured by variable vegetation cover, anthropogenic modification, and steep relief often results in uncertainty in both remote (e.g., Cunningham *et al.*, 2006; Lin *et al.*, 2013; Thompson Jobe, Gold, *et al.*, 2020) and field (e.g., Morell *et al.*, 2017; Thompson Jobe, Philibosian, *et al.*, 2020) identification of fault-related features. Moreover, determining the kinematics of low-slip-rate faults can be difficult, particularly in environments with dense or variable vegetation, steep relief, and rapid landscape modification, where preservation of reliable geomorphic markers can be challenging (e.g., Khajavi *et al.*, 2014; Duvall and Tucker, 2015; Marliyani *et al.*, 2016; Morell *et al.*, 2017; Parrino *et al.*, 2022). For example, the low-slip-rate Neodani Fault through the mountains in central Japan was obscured by dense vegetation and steep relief, but higher resolution lidar data and different terrain visualizations were used to reveal a longer-than-expected left-lateral strike-slip fault (Lin *et al.*, 2013). Similarly, in the dense temperate rainforest of Vancouver Island, BC, Canada, high-resolution lidar data and detailed field mapping were used to identify the Quaternary-active oblique Leech River Fault (Morell *et al.*, 2017). Finally, landscape evolution models and field studies indicate that low-slip-rate strike-slip faults may not hold a complete record of lateral offsets from recent

1. U.S. Geological Survey, Geologic Hazards Science Center, Golden, Colorado, U.S.A., https://orcid.org/0000-0003-1419-1373 (EML); https://orcid.org/0000-0001-5574-4523 (JTJ); https://orcid.org/0000-0001-8108-0046 (RB); 2. Department of Geological Sciences, University of Colorado Boulder, Boulder, Colorado, U.S.A., https://orcid.org/0000-0003-2959-5733 (MMT); 3. Department of Geology, University of Puerto Rico Mayagüez, Mayagüez, Puerto Rico, U.S.A., https://orcid.org/0009-0005-1301-158X (VOD); https://orcid.org/0000-0001-9820-3188 (KSH)

*Corresponding author: elynch@usgs.gov

earthquakes (e.g., Hetzel *et al.*, 2002; Reitman *et al.*, 2019, 2023), complicating the interpretation of lateral offsets in the context of their fault slip histories.

Puerto Rico is a prime example of an environment where identifying and characterizing low-slip-rate faults faces similar challenges. Geodetic data indicate ~3 mm/yr of differential motion between Puerto Rico and Hispaniola (Fig. 1b, Jansma *et al.*, 2000; Jansma and Mattioli, 2005; Calais *et al.*, 2016), implying that individual faults distributed across deformation zones may have slip rates <1 mm/yr. The low-slip-rate faults in Puerto Rico are located across both humid and semiarid landscapes that have been heavily modified by anthropogenic development, agriculture, erosion, and landsliding. These processes have obscured fault scarps in many places, especially through the mountainous interior of the island. Regardless, several active faults have been identified onshore Puerto Rico, primarily along the semiarid, low-relief southern and western coasts (e.g., Prentice and Mann, 2005; Piety *et al.*, 2018; Thompson Jobe, Briggs, Hughes, *et al.*, 2024). For example, the South Lajas Fault in southwestern Puerto Rico (Fig. 1c) was the first fault recognized onshore (Prentice and Mann, 2005) and was the only onshore fault included in the 2003 National Seismic Hazard Model (NSHM) update for Puerto Rico and the U.S. Virgin Islands (PRVI; e.g., Mueller *et al.*, 2003, 2010). The advance of high-resolution topography techniques facilitated the identification and characterization of additional active faults (Roig-Silva *et al.*, 2013; Piety *et al.*, 2018; Weilert and Laó-Dávila, 2023). Toward this end, Thompson Jobe, Briggs, Hughes, *et al.* (2024) mapped active faults onshore Puerto Rico from lidar-derived topography and field observations for inclusion in the 2025 NSHM update for PRVI (Fig. 1c; Thompson Jobe, Briggs, ten Brink, *et al.*, 2024).

Although seven active faults have been identified on the southern and western coasts of Puerto Rico, the kinematics and slip histories of these low-slip-rate faults remain largely unconstrained. The Great Southern Puerto Rico Fault Zone (GSPRFZ), for example, has been proposed to accommodate lateral motion, but discrepancies exist between the bedrock and surficial geologic records. Based on paleoseismic trench data, Piety *et al.* (2018) proposed that the Quaternary-active GSPRFZ has some component of lateral displacement but were unable to determine whether strike slip was right- or left-lateral. In contrast, Eocene bedrock faults show left-lateral displacement (e.g., Glover, 1971; Erikson *et al.*, 1990). Whereas the field evidence for left-lateral displacement in the bedrock is limited, fault orientation inversions strongly support left-lateral transpression (Erikson *et al.*, 1990). However, Quaternary fault movement may or may not be the same as the long-term record (e.g., Loveless *et al.*, 2010; Regalla *et al.*, 2017).

In this study, we document late Pleistocene to Holocene fault activity and kinematics on parts of the low-slip-rate GSPRFZ. We focus on the southern coastal plain of the island where the Quaternary-active GSPRFZ has the clearest landscape expression in a semiarid, low-relief environment. To better determine the timing and kinematics of faulting, we map surficial deposits where the GSPRFZ parallels a prominent ridge and offsets multiple generations of Quaternary landforms. We use lidar-derived topography, historical air photos, satellite imagery, and field observations to map tectonic lineaments, including fault scarps, and topographic and tonal lineaments. Field surveys and lidar-derived topographic profiles of laterally and vertically offset geomorphic features show oblique displacements of ~4–14 m in late Pleistocene to Holocene deposits. These observations document the first detailed evidence indicative of right-lateral displacement of Quaternary deposits along the GSPRFZ. We also document the offset of bedrock units along strike from faulted surficial deposits. We integrate these observations and interpret that parts of the GSPRFZ were reactivated in the modern strain field, may accommodate right-lateral normal motion, and may have hosted multiple earthquakes in the late Pleistocene to Holocene.

Geologic Setting

Tectonic setting

The boundary between the Caribbean Plate and North American Plate is a broad zone of deformation with complex kinematics, termed the North Caribbean Plate Boundary Zone (Fig. 1a; e.g., Dolan *et al.*, 1998). Puerto Rico is moving ~17–20 mm/yr relative to the North American Plate toward the east-northeast (Fig. 1a; e.g., DeMets *et al.*, 2000; Jansma *et al.*, 2000). The plate boundary is accommodating oblique subduction of the North American Plate underneath the Caribbean Plate at the Puerto Rico Trench located ~150 km north of the island. Puerto Rico is in a transitional zone between subduction to the east and partitioned subduction and left-lateral motion to the west on the island of Hispaniola (Fig. 1a; Dolan *et al.*, 1998).

Geodetic data show ~3 mm/yr of differential motion between Hispaniola and PRVI (Fig. 1b; Jansma *et al.*, 2000; Jansma and Mattioli, 2005; Calais *et al.*, 2016). The Mona Rift to the northwest of Puerto Rico (Fig. 1b) likely forms the northern part of the western boundary of the PRVI microplate, but the continuation of that boundary southward is unclear. The Cabo Rojo Rift offshore southwestern Puerto Rico and the Yuma Rift offshore southeastern Hispaniola are two possible candidates for the PRVI-Hispaniola boundary (Fig. 1b; e.g., Symithe *et al.*, 2015; Calais *et al.*, 2016), but the Mona Rift appears to curve toward the southeast as it approaches Puerto Rico, forming Desecheo Ridge and a series of east–west-oriented faults that continue eastward on the island (e.g., Hippolyte *et al.*, 2005). Faults across southwestern Puerto Rico could be actively accommodating the differential motion between PRVI and Hispaniola (Fig. 1b; e.g., Jany *et al.*, 1990; ten Brink *et al.*, 2022).

Crustal faults onshore Puerto Rico

Potentially active onshore crustal faults in Puerto Rico have been recognized for several decades. Previous active fault

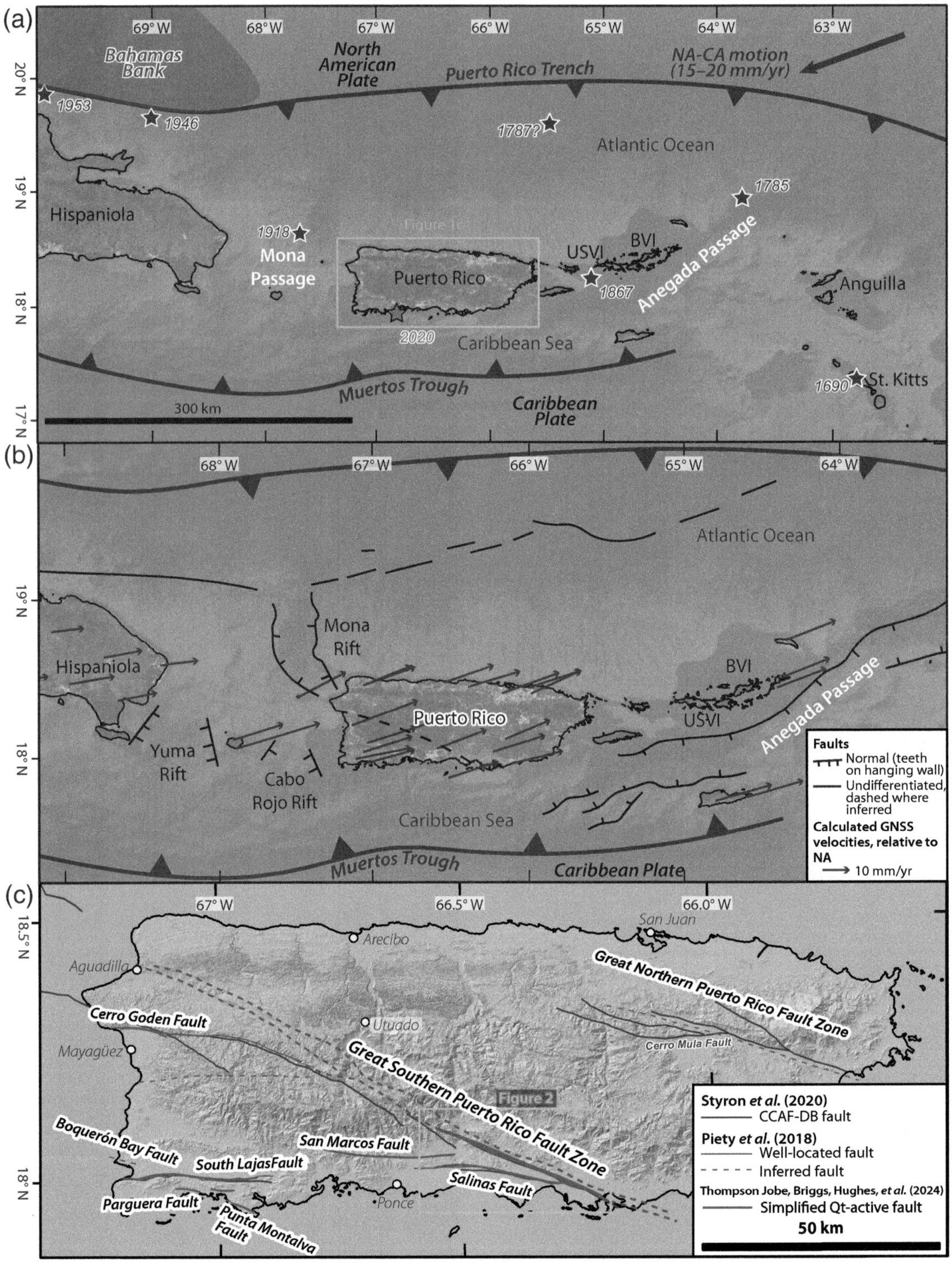

Figure 1. Regional tectonic setting showing the location of Puerto Rico within the northern Caribbean Plate Boundary Zone (NCPBZ). The shaded bathymetry (panels a and b) and topography (panel b) are from the 10 m National Elevation Dataset (available in Data and Resources). (a) Plate boundaries and major structures around the Puerto Rico-Virgin Islands (PRVI) microplate. Locations of earthquakes shown in green (historical) and purple (2019–ongoing sequence) after U.S. Geological Survey Comprehensive Catalog (ComCat; U.S. Geological Survey, 2017). North America-Caribbean Plate motion vector after Calais *et al.* (2016). The yellow box shows the location of panel (c). "?" indicates that the location is approximate. (b) Faults that have been proposed as boundaries of the PRVI microplate. Also shown are GNSS velocity vectors relative to the North American Plate for Hispaniola and PRVI, after Calais *et al.* (2016) and Solares Colón (2019), respectively. (c) Mapped Quaternary-active faults onshore Puerto Rico. The yellow box shows the location of Figure 2. BVI, British Virgin Islands; CA, Caribbean Plate; CCAF-DB, Central Caribbean active faults database; GNSS, Global Navigation Satellite System; NA, North American Plate; Qt, Quaternary; USVI, U.S. Virgin Islands. The color version of this figure is available only in the electronic edition.

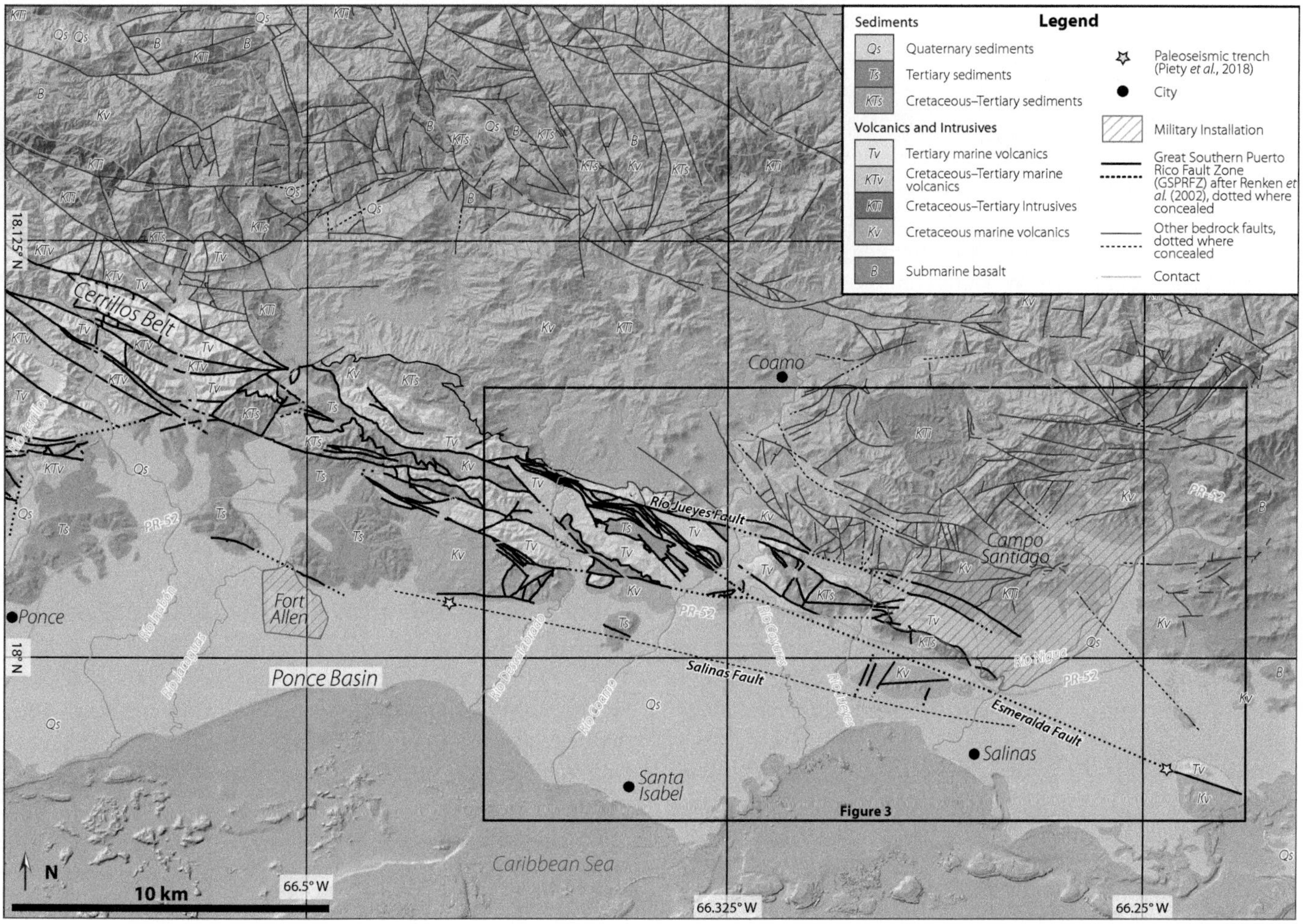

Figure 2. Bedrock geology of south-central Puerto Rico. Mapping is overlain over the 10 m National Elevation Dataset (available in Data and Resources) and a combination of 10 m National Ocean Service bathymetry and variable resolution BlueTopo bathymetry (both available in Data and Resources). Bedrock mapping after Bawiec *et al.* (2001); faults included in the Great Southern Puerto Rico Fault Zone after Renken *et al.* (2002). The black box shows the location of Figure 3. The color version of this figure is available only in the electronic edition.

studies have primarily focused on the South Lajas, Salinas, and Punta Montalva Faults and sections of the GSPRFZ in southern Puerto Rico (Fig. 1c; Mann, Hippolyte, *et al.*, 2005; Prentice and Mann, 2005; Roig-Silva *et al.*, 2013; Piety *et al.*, 2018; Weilert and Laó-Dávila, 2023; Thompson Jobe, Briggs, Hughes, *et al.*, 2024), in addition to the Cerro Goden Fault in the Río Grande de Añasco valley in western Puerto Rico (Fig. 1c; Hippolyte *et al.*, 2005; Mann, Prentice, *et al.*, 2005; Zachariasen and von Hillebrandt-Andrade, 2005; Thompson Jobe, Briggs, Hughes, *et al.*, 2024). At a larger spatial scale, Styron *et al.* (2020) remotely mapped onshore potentially active faults (Fig. 1c) for use in a regional probabilistic seismic hazard assessment. More recently, Thompson Jobe, Briggs, Hughes, *et al.* (2024) used ~1-m-resolution lidar collected in 2018 after Hurricane Maria to complete a preliminary neotectonic map of Puerto Rico to assess potentially new and existing fault sources for inclusion in the 2025 PRVI NSHM (Fig. 1c; Thompson Jobe, Briggs, ten Brink, *et al.*, 2024).

Although the GSPRFZ has been recognized as a Quaternary-active fault (e.g., Mann, Hippolyte, *et al.*, 2005; Piety *et al.*, 2018; Thompson Jobe, Briggs, Hughes, *et al.*, 2024), the fault location and kinematics appear to be different over million-year and millennial timescales. For example, the bedrock GSPRFZ has been mapped as a northwest–southeast-striking, ~10–30-km-wide zone of deformation, composed of at least 12 distinct faults (Rodríguez-Martínez, 2007). On the southern coastal plain of Puerto Rico, the bedrock GSPRFZ is bound by the Río Jueyes Fault to the north, and the Esmeralda Fault to the south (Figs. 1b and 2). Renken *et al.* (2002) considered all bedrock faults in a zone that widens toward the southern coast and includes the coastal plain from Ponce to east of Salinas to be part of the GSPRFZ (faults shown in bold in Fig. 2). Eocene shortening resulted in a fold-and-thrust belt preserved in a narrow portion of the Cerrillos Belt along the GSPRFZ (Fig. 2; Renken *et al.*, 2002; Mann, Hippolyte, *et al.*, 2005). Previous field studies document a lateral component of slip on the constituent faults of the GSPRFZ (Glover, 1971; Krushensky and Monroe, 1975), supported by fault orientation inversions (Erikson *et al.*, 1990). The strike-slip motion is assumed to be contemporaneous with the thrusting (e.g., Erikson *et al.*, 1990), and faulting may have occurred during the middle Eocene to early Oligocene, ending by the early Miocene (e.g., Glover, 1971; Krushensky and Monroe, 1978; McCann, 1985; Erikson *et al.*, 1990; Renken *et al.*, 2002).

Both Piety *et al.* (2018) and Thompson Jobe, Briggs, Hughes, *et al.* (2024) proposed that Quaternary activity within the GSPRFZ may accommodate a substantial component of strike slip in the late Pleistocene or Holocene, but the sense of strike slip is debated. Piety *et al.* (2018) based their interpretation on straight scarps within the GSPRFZ with both northeast- and southwest-facing directions and varying vertical separation. In a paleoseismic trench across a scarp within the GSPRFZ, Piety *et al.* (2018) identified evidence for two paleoearthquakes that likely occurred in the late Pleistocene or Holocene, based on correlating stratigraphy to a trench on the nearby Salinas Fault. They observed different fault strands with varying amounts of vertical separation and mismatched stratigraphy across the fault zone, which they interpreted as evidence for lateral motion. Although they referenced the bedrock left-lateral displacement documented by Glover (1971), Piety *et al.* (2018) did not document any evidence for a slip sense in the Quaternary. Thompson Jobe, Briggs, Hughes, *et al.* (2024) suggested that the GSPRFZ hosts right-lateral oblique slip, based on potentially right-laterally offset or deflected channels observed on lidar-derived topography. In their trench across the Salinas Fault, Piety *et al.* (2018) similarly interpreted a lateral component of slip from mismatched stratigraphy across the fault zone, steep fault dips, and the lack of scarp-derived colluvium. They note that there is no consistent pattern of drainage deflections, but they interpret that a sharp bend in Río Cayures (Fig. 2) indicates left-lateral motion on the Salinas Fault.

There are a few dated Quaternary deposits on the southern coastal plain of Puerto Rico. A large carbonate platform, topped by middle Miocene to Pliocene Ponce Limestone (Renken *et al.*, 2002; Rodríguez-Martínez, 2007), forms the base of the Ponce Basin (Ponce to Santa Isabel, Fig. 2). During the middle to late Tertiary subsidence that formed the Ponce Basin, large alluvial fans and well-developed fluvial terraces buried portions of the carbonate platform (e.g., Glover, 1971; Renken *et al.*, 2002; Mann, Hippolyte, *et al.*, 2005). Renken *et al.* (2002) mapped a Miocene to Pliocene fan delta in the Ponce Basin (stratigraphically below Quaternary sediments; *Qs* in Fig. 2). These fans are relatively thin (~10–30 m thick at their proximal margins) and have undergone fluvial degradation since the last Holocene transgression, which likely occurred before the formation of a relict shoreline around ~3.0–1.5 ka (Renken *et al.*, 2002). Piety *et al.* (2018) dated ~16.4–2.3 ka fluvial deposits and ~10.6–2.5 ka eolian deposits in their trench on the Salinas Fault (Fig. 2). The shallow subsurface ages from Piety *et al.* (2018) support late Pleistocene to Holocene deposition for similar surficial deposits along the southern coastal plain.

Methods

Lineament mapping

We mapped fault-related features across the south coast and into the interior of Puerto Rico to determine the extent and kinematics of potentially active faulting associated with the GSPRFZ. We used a 2018 ~1-m-scale bare-earth lidar digital elevation model (DEM) and derivatives, historical air photos, and recent satellite imagery to remotely map scarps, topographic lineaments (steps or benches and changes in slope), and tonal lineaments (vegetation lineaments, linear trends in color patterns, and tonal contrasts). Details of these publicly available data are in Data and Resources. Historical aerial images were mosaiced together in Agisoft Metashape following a workflow simplified from Knuth *et al.* (2023). Using the lidar-derived DEM, shaded relief, and slope map, we mapped scarps that offset the surface or juxtapose different surfaces or landforms. We identified topographic lineaments from lidar-derived aspect and slope maps, and identified tonal lineaments from historical and recent aerial images, adding to and refining the prior mapping of Thompson Jobe, Briggs, Hughes, *et al.* (2024) and Piety *et al.* (2018). Historical aerial images were also used to check for evidence of landscape modification (e.g., landslides, anthropogenic modification such as ephemeral farm roads). At each lineament, we noted whether there was evidence of vertical displacement, lateral displacement, or both. Fault-related features were then field-checked where possible.

Surficial mapping

We mapped surficial and bedrock geology in an area where a prominent scarp within the GSPRFZ is well expressed and continuous for ~1 km along the southern slope of Cerro Respaldo, which we refer to as the Hacienda Las Carolinas site (Fig. 3). We identified offset deposits and landforms, and developed a relative chronology of these features. Using the lidar DEM and its derivatives, historical aerial images, and field mapping, we distinguished between different deposits using surface morphology and sedimentary characteristics (Table S1, available in the supplemental material to this article). For surface morphology, we described the roughness, dissection, remnant bar and swale morphology, inset and burial relationships, and relative elevation and position on slope for each deposit. We also described the sedimentary characteristics of each unit where exposed, primarily along road cuts, following Schoeneberger *et al.* (2012). We did not describe areas of extensive anthropogenic modification, and instead classified these areas as "disturbed." Our assessment of the extent of disturbed areas was aided by historical aerial imagery.

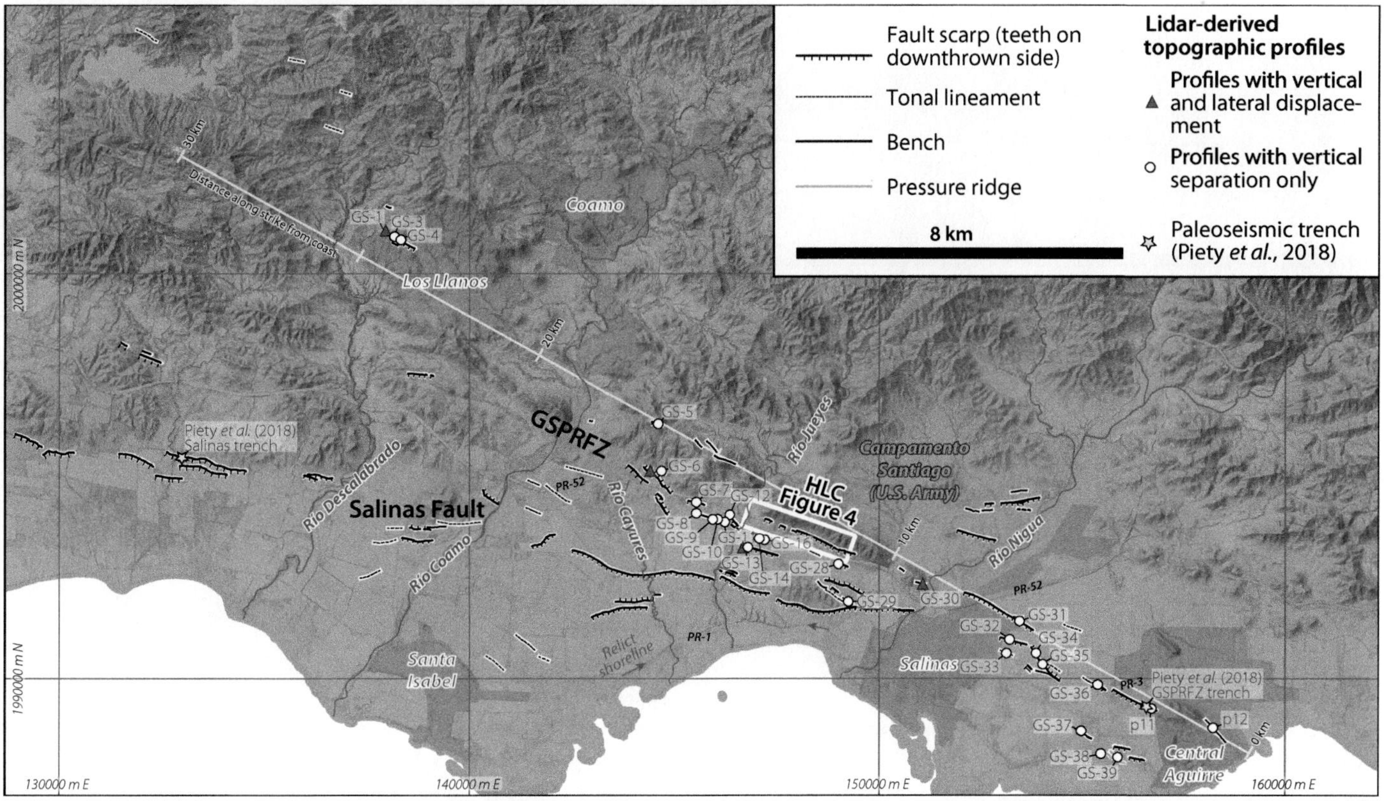

Figure 3. Fault-related features of south-central Puerto Rico, including the Great Southern Puerto Rico Fault Zone (northwest–southeast) and the Salinas Fault (east–west). Mapping is overlain on an ~1-m-resolution light detection and ranging (lidar)-derived relief map generated in QGIS (3D Elevation Program, see Data and Resources). Lineament mapping in this figure is updated and refined from Thompson Jobe, Briggs, Hughes, *et al.* (2024), and is available in Lynch, Thompson Jobe, *et al.* (2025). The white box shows the location of the Hacienda Las Carolinas site in Figure 4. Also shown are the locations of previous paleoseismic trenches (Piety *et al.*, 2018), and locations of lidar-derived profiles outside of Figure 4 coverage (GS- profiles collected in this study, p# profiles from Thompson Jobe, Briggs, Hughes, *et al.*, 2024). The brown shading represents urban areas; red shading represents an area of restricted access at Camp Santiago (U.S. Army). The blue arrows indicate a relict Holocene shoreline. Unannotated lidar-derived relief map shown in Figure S1. The color version of this figure is available only in the electronic edition.

Displacements

To quantify the amount and kinematics of Quaternary motion on different fault sections within the GSPRFZ, we collected topographic surveys in the field and extracted topographic profiles from lidar DEMs across mapped scarps. We used the field topographic surveys, supplemented with lidar-derived topographic profiles, to calculate vertical and lateral displacements. We also used straight-line topographic profiles from lidar to calculate vertical separation across scarps. In the field, we identified correlative linear geomorphic features (e.g., channel margins) across the fault trace. We projected the features into the fault and measured the lateral displacement of our preferred, minimum, and maximum projections with a flexible tape measure draped across the ground surface. We also collected differential Global Navigation Satellite Systems (GNSS) surveys of these features using a Trimble Geo7x rover and Zephyr 3 antenna with ≤5 cm horizontal and vertical precision after postprocessing. We calculated dip slip, strike slip, and oblique slip using the SCARP-3D script from Lynch *et al.* (2025a,b). For these calculations, we used a local strike measured from lidar or calculated from surveyed scarp midpoints, and an average dip of 80° south. The 80° south dip was calculated using a modified three-point approach regressing a fault plane through surveyed fault scarp midpoints (SCARP-3D; Lynch *et al.*, 2025a,b) and is consistent with the 60°–90° fault dip measured by (Piety *et al.*, 2018) in their trench site within the GSPRFZ. SCARP-3D then uses the input fault strike, dip, and surveyed topographic profiles in a Monte Carlo simulation. Each simulation randomly selects a linear regression for a geomorphic piercing line on each side of the fault from the 95% confidence interval for each regression, and randomly selects a fault-plane geometry from distributions around the input fault strike and dip. SCARP-3D then calculates the intersection points between the profile regressions and the fault plane, and calculates dip slip, strike slip, oblique slip, and the trend and plunge of the slip vector, reporting the mean and standard deviation of the suite of Monte Carlo simulations. At locations where we identified lateral displacements, but could not visit or

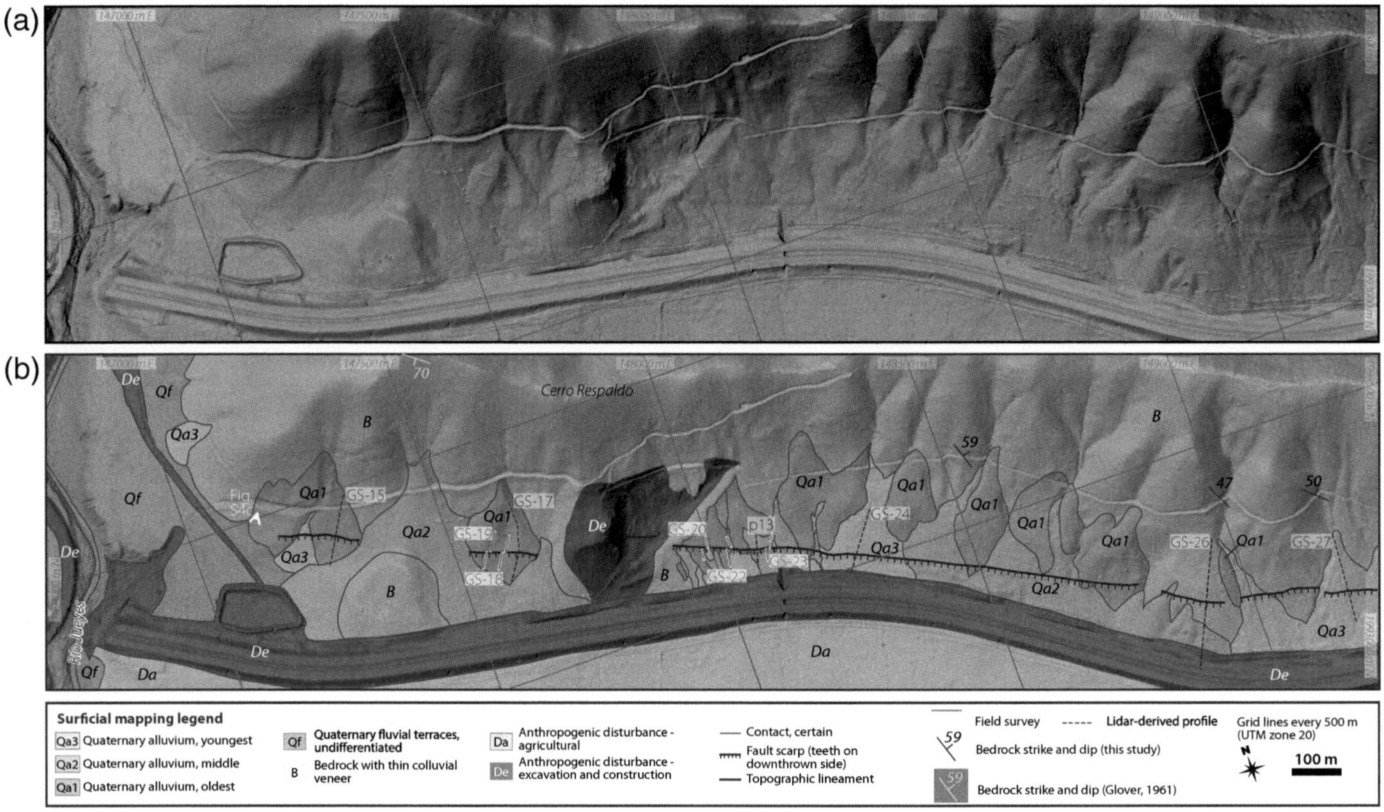

measure in the field, we extracted topographic profiles from the lidar DEM and calculated displacements using SCARP-3D. At locations where there were vertical displacements but no linear geomorphic features to record lateral displacements, we extracted linear profiles from lidar and calculated vertical separation following DuRoss *et al.* (2019). Using recent satellite imagery, we excluded from our surface regressions portions of linear profiles that represented post-deposition, but nontectonic, modification (e.g., channel dissection, roads, and irrigation ditches).

Figure 4. (a) 1-m-resolution lidar-derived shaded relief map of the Hacienda Las Carolinas site on the southern face of Cerro Respaldo (3D Elevation Program, see Data and Resources). (b) Surficial geology and topographic profiles at Hacienda Las Carolinas. South-facing fault scarps offset channels incised into multiple generations of alluvial deposits (Qa1, Qa2, and Qa3), as well as locations where bedrock is covered with a thin colluvial veneer (B). The color version of this figure is available only in the electronic edition.

Bedrock fault description

We leveraged a large anthropogenic exposure of a bedrock fault zone to place the Quaternary activity within the GSPRFZ in the context of the bedrock faulting history of southern Puerto Rico. This exposure, located in the middle of our surficial mapping area (Fig. 4), was created during the construction of highway PR-52 in the 1970s, documented by historical air photos (Data and Resources). We used a DJI Mavic Air 2S drone to take 1423 of photos of the exposure and surrounding landscape and then created a 3D structure-from-motion model and orthophoto following the methods of Reitman *et al.* (2015). Ground control points were surveyed with Emlid Reach RS and RS2 RTK GNSS receivers. In the field, we described each bedrock unit and measured bedding where accessible. We also measured the strikes and dips of exposed fault planes, and the rake or trend and plunge of lineations on those planes.

Limitations and challenges in characterizing faults in low-slip-rate settings

Identifying and calculating displacements on low-slip-rate faults faces several uncertainties and challenges. Here, we discuss these general challenges, followed by a summary of how we have addressed these challenges on the GSPRFZ. First, identifying and measuring offset linear features in the field can be ambiguous due to the influence of erosional and depositional processes. For example, channel margins surveyed in the field may be broad and uncertain (e.g., Cowgill, 2007; Scharer *et al.*, 2014). Geomorphic features such as ridgelines are not as clearly defined as young channel margins, and this ambiguity in feature geometry may increase the uncertainty, especially when mapping and measuring displacements using remote data. In addition, work by Reitman *et al.* (2023) shows that lateral offsets in wet, humid climates are modified quickly and that low-slip-rate faults in wet regions are, for the most part, missing from the geomorphic record. The south coast of Puerto Rico receives <100–125 cm/yr of precipitation

(PRISM Climate Group, 2019), which the Holzapfel (2008) aridity index classifies as wet or extremely wet. These faults are more likely to preserve a mix of smaller offsets recording the most recent event and larger offsets that record cumulative slip over multiple events than those in arid climates (Reitman *et al.*, 2023). The wetter climate typically results in channels that are incised, vegetated, established in the landscape, and sparsely spaced, resulting in ideal conditions to better preserve cumulative slip (Reitman *et al.*, 2023). In addition, scarp diffusion can affect apparent vertical displacement (e.g., Thompson Jobe and Reitman, 2025), and, therefore, the ratio of vertical to lateral slip. Second, offsets derived from remote measurements (e.g., lidar-derived offsets) may not record the offset of correlative surfaces. Vertical separation measurements may be affected by lateral juxtapositions of different surfaces or topography, and lateral displacements could reflect apparent lateral motion. Third, small offsets may be overlooked, and offsets derived from remote measurements may have larger uncertainties due to the resolution of the datasets. For example, a lidar dataset with ~1-m-pixel resolution typically requires lateral offsets of at least several pixels to be identifiable. In addition, the geometry of linear features mapped with lidar may be more uncertain than those mapped in the field due to the sublinear and temporally evolving character of a ridgeline subject to hillslope diffusion, landsliding, or other surface processes. Finally, the largest source of uncertainty in slip-rate estimates is often the age of the offset landform.

Along the GSPRFZ, there has been modification of the landscape due to agriculture, including planting, cattle grazing, and irrigation projects, as well as the construction of the PR-52 expressway. Frequent storm events in Puerto Rico cause erosion and landsliding (e.g., Bessette-Kirton *et al.*, 2019; Hughes and Schulz, 2020), which may modify offset landforms. We used the following methods to address the limitations discussed earlier.

First, to account for geomorphic uncertainty, we modified SCARP-3D to include 1 m uncertainty on individual survey point locations (easting and northing), resulting in a wider distribution of profile regressions used in the Monte Carlo simulation. Second, we limited our offsets from remote measurements to those we could not access or confidently survey in the field. We used slope, aspect, and relief DEM derivatives, historical air photos, and satellite imagery to assess whether our profiles represented the same surface or landform on either side of the fault. Finally, we acknowledge that the uncertainty in landform ages remains substantial. Because there is no geochronology specific to our study site, we assume that the landforms we survey correlate to regional ages. We discuss the impact of this assumption further in the Slip-rate approximations section.

Results

Lineament mapping

We mapped Quaternary-active features within the GSPRFZ in a northwest–southeast-trending zone ≥25 km long and ~1–2 km wide (Fig. 3). We found 71 fault-related features across the south coastal plain of Puerto Rico and into the interior of the island that we associate with the GSPRFZ (Lynch, Thompson Jobe, *et al.*, 2025). Lineaments are discontinuous and include 43 scarps, 9 topographic lineaments, 4 pressure ridges and topographic highs, and 15 tonal lineaments on air photos. Individual lineaments trend ~100°–130°, and the zone overall trends ~120°. Fault scarps are ~50–1900 m long, and ~0.5–3 m tall. Scarps face both southwest ($n = 30$) and northeast ($n = 11$), and are mostly straight, cutting across contours.

Surficial mapping

We mapped surficial geology in a 600 × 2600 m area near the city of Salinas (Hacienda Las Carolinas; Figs. 3 and 4; Table S1). This map area covers the south-facing slope of Cerro Respaldo and alluvial fans at the base of the range in the transition to the coastal plain. In the northwestern part of the map area is the incised Río Jueyes and associated terraces. Autopista Luís A. Ferré (PR-52) crosses the southwestern part of the map area and separates the relatively unmodified pasture area in the northeast from agricultural fields in the southwest.

Our new detailed mapping identified three generations of alluvial fans at Hacienda Las Carolinas along the southern side of Cerro Respaldo. The oldest group of these alluvial fans (Qa1) consists of smooth, convex fans with apexes in bedrock channels in the upper half of the rangefront. The surface is brushy with little grass, and includes cobbles and boulders, both distributed on the surface and within cobble lags. Qa1 is a poorly to moderately sorted, clast-supported deposit of sub-angular to rounded pebbles to boulders. Clasts consist of crystalline limestone, fossiliferous limestone, sandstone, siltstone, and conglomerate. There is broadly slope-parallel weak stratification in places, and weak reverse grading is present in one exposure. Exposures of Qa1 are very weathered, with caliche crust developed on clasts and a loss of clast cohesion. There is weak pavement development with overturned clasts in places. The distal portions of Qa1 are buried by younger deposits.

The next oldest alluvial fans (Qa2) consist of a broad surface draping across the base of the rangefront. The fan apexes are in bedrock channels, but the fans are primarily inset into alluvial deposits higher on the rangefront. Qa2 is a very poorly sorted, clast-supported deposit of sub-angular to sub-rounded pebbles to boulders. Clasts consist primarily of fossiliferous limestone in an indurated matrix with possible reverse grading. Exposures of Qa2 are weathered with abundant lichen, but no distinct carbonate chips or carbonate overprinting are present. Qa2 is inset into Qa1 and is buried by Qa3.

The youngest alluvial fans (Qa3) consist of individual and coalescing convex fan-shaped deposits with remnant bar and swale morphology in places. There are some inset surfaces and very few exposures. Qa3 is a poorly sorted, matrix-supported deposit of sub-angular to sub-rounded pebbles to boulders. Clasts are predominantly limestone and sandstone cobbles, with uncommon boulders of cobble-rich conglomerate. Soil development obscures any stratification, and there are no distinct carbonate chips or carbonate overprinting. Cobbles and boulders are exposed on the surface, including one location where boulders are ponded against trees. Based on these observations, we interpret that Qa3 forms the active alluvial fans.

We also mapped fluvial terraces (Qf) as broad, flat surfaces separated by 5–15-m-tall risers along Río Jueyes. Qf is a moderately sorted, clast-supported deposit of sub-angular to rounded pebbles with uncommon cobbles. Clasts consist of limestone, both fossiliferous and crystalline, sandstone, and finely laminated siltstone, with rare intrusive rocks. There are distinct pebble beds and matrix-rich beds, with small cobbles in the top ~20–30 cm of the exposure. The long axes of cobbles throughout the exposure are predominantly sub-horizontal. Cobbles of various lithologies are exposed on the surface within well-developed grass and tall shade trees.

Two anthropogenically disturbed areas are present along the southern margin of the map area. First, the surface south of PR-52 has been extensively modified for agriculture (Da). We also mapped several areas of disturbance from excavation (De). The map area is used for cattle grazing, and flow was channelized across the surface of Qf to a holding pond. PR-52 was constructed between 1968 and 1975, partially from materials excavated from Cerro Respaldo. We used air photos collected in 1977 and 1983 (publicly available from EarthExplorer) to determine the extent of disturbance from excavation, highway construction, and the construction of roads and drainage tunnels under the highway.

We mapped bedrock with thin colluvial cover as B (bedrock). This colluvial cover ranges from <20-cm-thick soil to ~3-m-thick colluvium. Within the mapped bedrock unit, we observe limestone, sandy conglomerate, and siltstone in exposures uphill of the alluvial deposits, ranging from ~4-cm-thick to massive, dipping northeast (Fig. 4). There are carbonate coatings present and slope-parallel carbonate development. Previous geologic maps of the region show Tertiary Cuevas Limestone along the top of the range and describe it as a pale pink limestone with calcareous algal fragments and sandy interbeds (Glover, 1961a, 1971). We interpret that the limestone bedrock is likely the Cuevas Limestone, and the epiclastic bedrock is likely the Raspaldo Formation mapped on the north face of Cerro Respaldo (Fig. 2; Glover, 1971). Previous geologic maps also include a generalized Quaternary piedmont alluvial plain deposit and a Quaternary terraced alluvium deposit (Glover, 1961a,b, 1971), consistent with our more detailed mapping.

Displacements

We collected topographic surveys and extracted topographic profiles from lidar at multiple locations along the GSPRFZ. These profiles are numbered GS-1 through GS-39, from northwest to southeast. We also include the lidar-derived topographic profiles p11, p12, and p13 from Thompson Jobe, Briggs, Hughes, *et al.* (2024). We discuss first the 32 straight-line profiles extracted from lidar and used to calculate vertical separation (Figs. 3 and 5; Table S2). Second, we discuss the five field surveys of laterally offset linear geomorphic features (Table 1). Finally, we discuss the two lidar-derived topographic profiles of laterally offset linear geomorphic features (Table 1).

We calculated vertical separation across scarps from lidar-derived straight-line topographic profiles at 32 locations (Figs. 3 and 5). These profiles show up to ~1.7 m primarily south-side-down vertical separation, with a mean and standard deviation of 0.7 ± 0.4 m (Table S2). Eight of these straight-line profiles are across north- or northeast-facing scarps, whereas 22 are across south- or southwest-facing scarps. The two remaining profiles are across symmetrical pressure ridges (Fig. 3).

Our five field surveys, GS-18, GS-19, GS-20, GS-22, and GS-23 (Figs. 4, 6, and 7, Fig. S2) were collected within our surficial mapping area. We describe these field surveys from northwest to southeast, and list preferred, minimum, and maximum offsets in Table 1. The first field survey, GS-19, is of an offset cobble lag on the surface of a Qa1 fan (Fig. 6, Fig. S2). The margin of the cobble lag is sinuous, so we projected it to a straight line in the field (Fig. 6g, Fig. S5). Survey GS-19 showed 0.3 ± 0.2 m south-side-down displacement and 4.7 ± 1.1 m right-lateral displacement of the cobble lag, though we note that its sinuosity results in more interpretation uncertainty beyond the measurement uncertainty we report. Adjacent to GS-19, ~30 m east, is GS-18—a channel incised into the surface of the Qa1 fan (Fig. 6, Fig. S2). Survey GS-18 showed 0.4 ± 0.2 m south-side-down displacement and 5.4 ± 1 m right-lateral displacement of the channel margin.

East of GS-18 and GS-19, on the other side of the large exposure created during PR-52 construction (mapped as De, Fig. 4), we surveyed two offset channel margins (Fig. 7). GS-20 is a survey of an offset channel margin incised into both Qa1 and Qa2. The downthrown part of the channel curves to the east as it nears the scarp, so we consider only the portion of the downthrown channel that is parallel to the upthrown channel in our offset calculations. GS-20 shows negligible vertical displacement of the base of the channel margin, but 6.6 ± 0.9 m right-lateral displacement. The next channel margin, ~50 m east, surveyed as GS-22, is incised into Qa1 (Fig. 7). GS-22 also shows negligible vertical displacement of the base of the channel margin but ~7.2 ± 1.2 m right-lateral displacement. However, the upthrown and downthrown sections of the channel are not parallel, so this right-lateral displacement may be an overestimate not captured in the reported error.

Approximately 70 m farther east is a beheaded channel incised into Qa2, surveyed as GS-23 (Fig. 7). The upthrown section of this channel has a pronounced curve as it approaches the fault, so we consider only the portion of the survey that is parallel to the downthrown section. The channel is offset by 0.4 ± 0.2 m south-side-down vertical separation and 7 ± 1.7 m of right-lateral displacement.

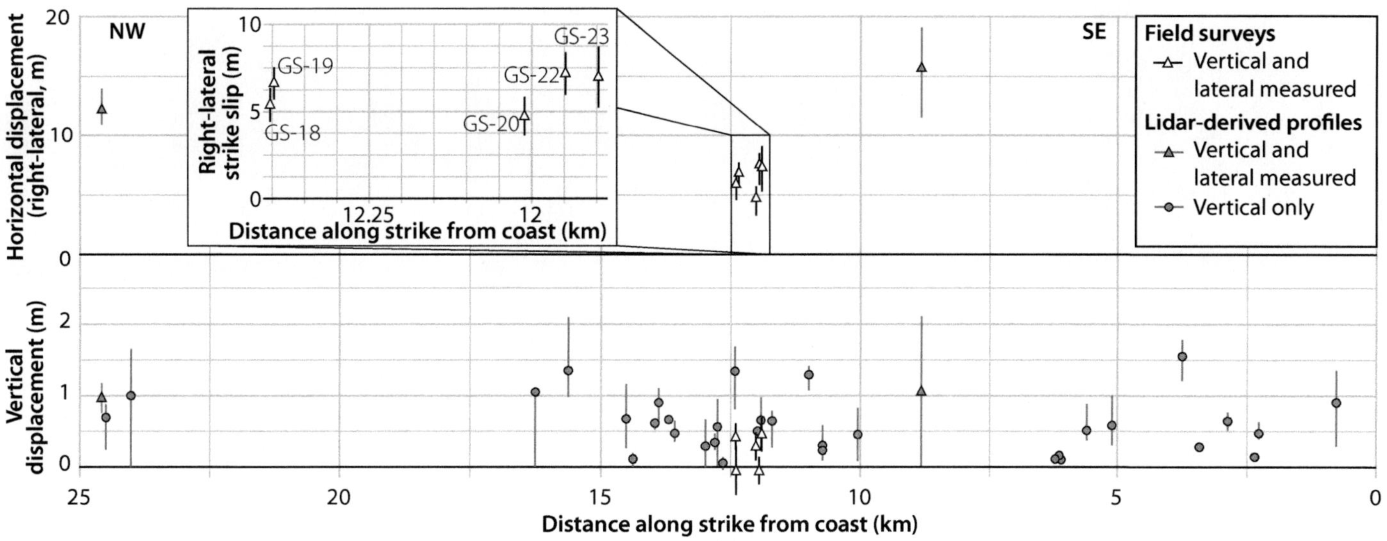

Figure 5. Strike slip (above) and vertical displacement (below) along the Great Southern Puerto Rico Fault Zone. Distance along strike from the coast at Central Aguirre is shown in Figure 3. Field surveys are shown with hollow markers; topographic profiles extracted from lidar are shown with filled markers. The triangles denote profiles used for both vertical and lateral displacements with error bars representing 1σ uncertainty following Lynch *et al.* (2025a,b); the circles denote profiles used for vertical separation only following DuRoss *et al.* (2019), with error bars showing minimum and maximum. Vertical displacement is fairly consistent along strike and is generally ≤1.5 m. Right-lateral displacement at Hacienda Las Carolinas ranges from 5 to 8 m, with higher amounts in lidar-derived profiles GS-1 and GS-30 (refer to Figs. S2 and S3). The inset shows the strike-slip displacement of the field surveys in more detail.

Our topographic profiles of laterally offset linear geomorphic features GS-1 and GS-30 were extracted from lidar-derived DEMs at sites that were not easily accessible in the field (Fig. 3, Figs. S2 and S3). In the northwest, GS-1 shows a channel wall that is right-laterally displaced at a scarp that offsets an adjacent agricultural field (GS-3, 0.7 m north-side-down displacement; Fig. S2). GS-1 shows 1 ± 0.2 m north-side-down displacement and 13.5 ± 1.4 m right-lateral displacement of the base of the channel wall. The farthest southeast site of our lateral displacements, GS-30, is the crest of a broad ridge that is crossed by a topographic lineament within Camp Santiago (Fig. 3, Fig. S3e–h). GS-30 shows 1.1 ± 1 m of south-side-down displacement and 16.2 ± 3.4 m right-lateral displacement of the ridgeline. We note that in all of our 3D

TABLE 1
Field Measurements and Calculations of Displacements Across the Great Southern Puerto Rico Fault Zone (GSPRFZ)

		Dip Slip (m)	Right-Lateral Slip (m)		Oblique Slip (m)	Ratio of Strike Slip to Dip Slip
Profile Name	**Distance from Coast Along Strike (km)***	**SCARP-3D†**	**SCARP-3D†**	**Field Right Lateral**	**SCARP-3D†**	**SCARP-3D**
GS-1	24.6	1.0 ± 0.2	13.5 ± 1.4	–	13.6 ± 1.4	15:1
GS-18	12.4	0.4 ± 0.2	5.4 ± 1.0	~3.4	5.4 ± 1.0	3:1
GS-19	12.4	0.3 ± 0.2	4.7 ± 1.1		4.7 ± 1.1	14:1
GS-20	12.0	0 ± 0.3	6.6 ± 0.9	6.5 (3.5–9.2)‡	6.6 ± 0.9	66:1
GS-22	11.9	−0.1 ± 0.2	7.2 ± 1.2	6.9 (4.7–10)‡	7.2 ± 1.2	24:1
GS-23	11.9	1.4 ± 0.2	7.0 ± 1.7	7.1 (4–8.8)‡	7.0 ± 1.7	20:1
GS-30	8.9	1.1 ± 1.1	16.2 ± 3.4	–	16.2 ± 3.4	22:1

*Refer to Figure 3 for the location along a transect from the coast.
†Mean and 1σ uncertainty.
‡Preferred projections, with minimum and maximum in parentheses.

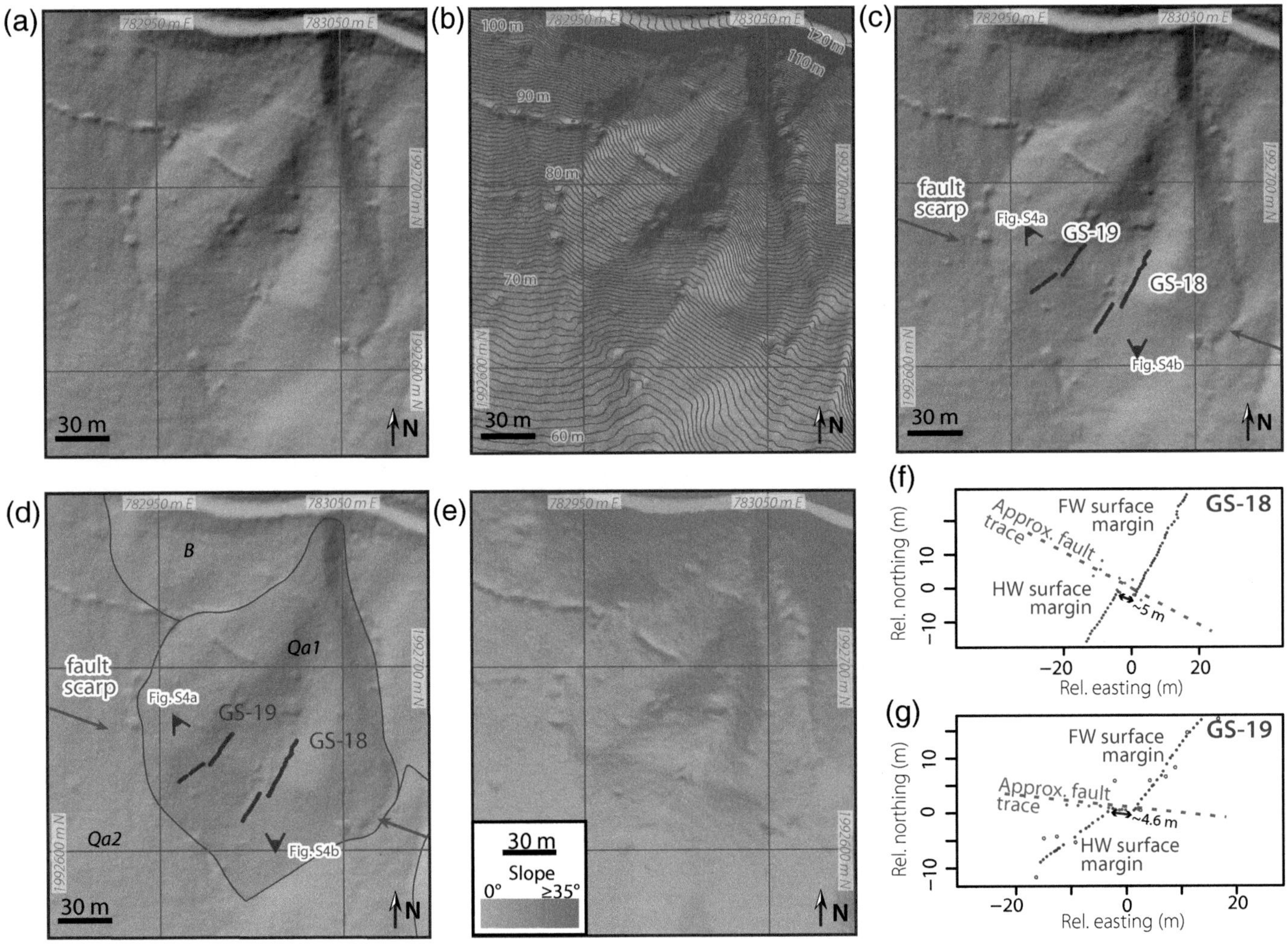

offsets, the vertical component is so small relative to the right-lateral component that the oblique displacement and right-lateral displacements are the same within uncertainty.

Bedrock fault

A large outcrop in the middle of our surficial mapping area exposes a bedrock fault zone along strike from our mapped scarps (Figs. 4 and 8). We describe four broader units in this outcrop, which we term units B1–B4. The first unit, B1, is well-bedded buff to orange limestone interbedded with beds of a finer grain size. Beds are centimeter-to-meter scale and exhibit folding in the upper section (Fig. 8). Unit B1 dips 20°–70° toward the north. Below unit B1 is unit B2—a reddish-brown conglomerate with cobble- to boulder-size sub-rounded to angular clasts and massive bedding at the outcrop scale. Unit B3 is juxtaposed against unit B2 and is a gray, moderately sorted sandstone with uncommon pebbles. Unit B3 has steeply-dipping (345°/70° northeast) compositional foliation. Approximately 3 m south of unit B3 is unit B4, a reddish-purple volcaniclastic breccia with abundant calcite veining and mineralization around basalt and greenstone clasts. Unit B4

Figure 6. Right-lateral displacement of two surveys (GS-18 and GS-19) on the southern face of Cerro Respaldo. Coordinates are WGS84, UTM zone 19. Annotated photos of GS-18 and GS-19 are in Figure S3a,b. (a) 1-m-resolution lidar-derived relief map (3D Elevation Program, see Data and Resources). (b) 1-m-resolution lidar-derived relief map with 0.5 m contours. (c) 1-m-resolution lidar-derived relief map with blue arrows showing the locations of GS-18 and GS-19, and the blue dots showing the surveyed profiles and fault scarps. The red arrows show the location of the south-facing fault scarp. (d) Surficial mapping of panel (a), with the same annotations as panel (b). Refer to Figure 4 for the surficial mapping legend. (e) Lidar-derived slope shade of panel (a). (f) Plan view of GS-18, showing the right-lateral displacement along the 132°-striking fault trace. The red dots show surveyed scarp crest, toe, and midpoints. (g) Plan view of the GS-19 survey, showing the right-lateral displacement along the 096°-striking fault trace. Hollow dots show surveyed surface-margin points projected to the profile. The red dots show surveyed scarp midpoints. Approx., approximate; B, bedrock; FW, footwall; HW, hanging wall; Rel., relative; Qa1, Quaternary alluvium, oldest; Qa2, Quaternary alluvium, middle. The color version of this figure is available only in the electronic edition.

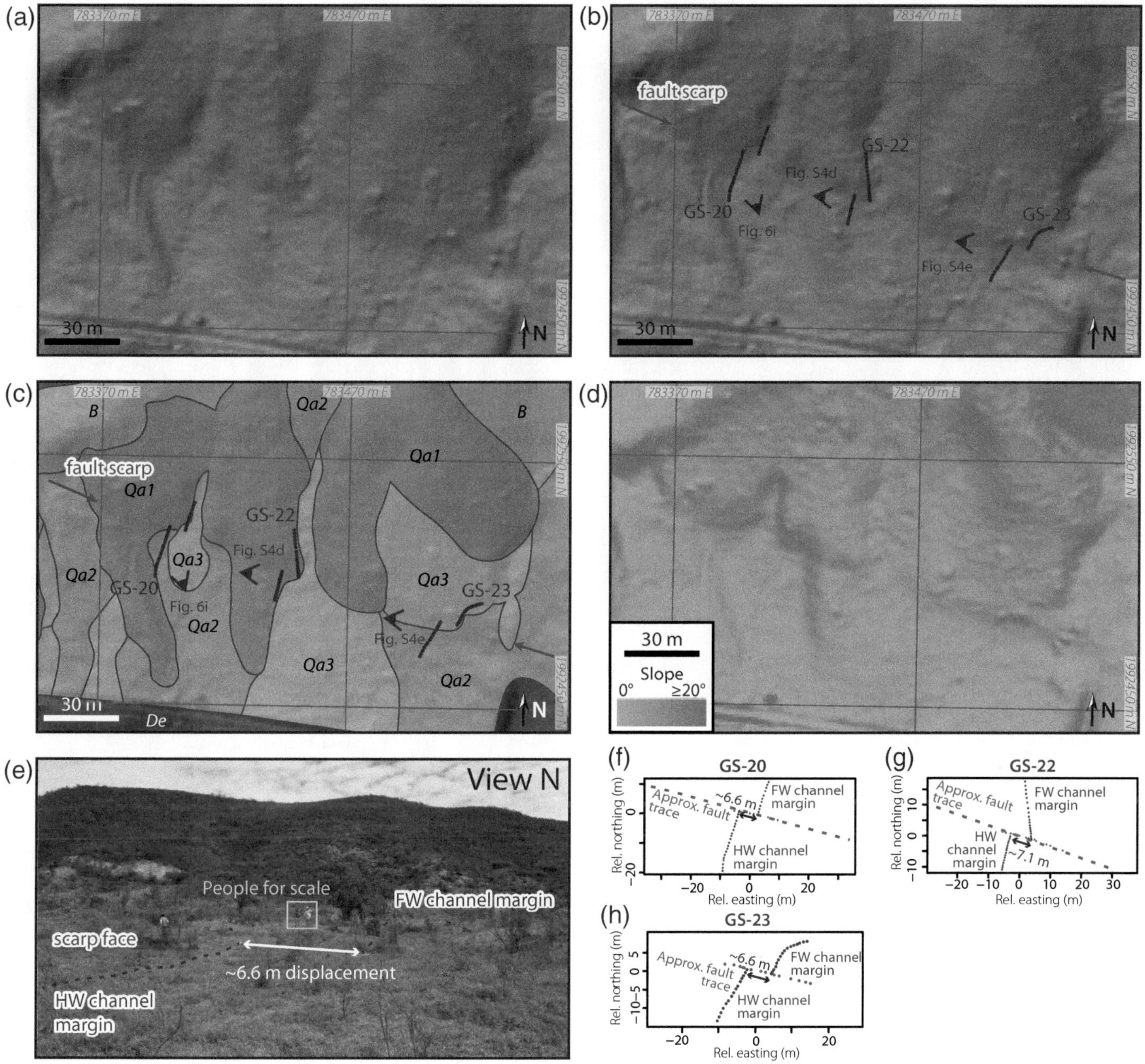

Figure 7. Right-lateral displacement of three surveys (GS-20, GS-22, and GS-23) on the southern face of Cerro Respaldo. Coordinates are WGS84, UTM zone 19. (a) 1-m-resolution lidar-derived relief map (3D Elevation Program, see Data and Resources). (b) 1-m-resolution lidar-derived relief map of panel (a) with blue arrows showing the locations of GS-20, GS-22, and GS-23, and blue dots showing surveyed profiles. The red arrows show the location of the south-facing fault scarp. (c) Surficial mapping of panel (a) with the same annotations as panel (b). Refer to Figure 4 for the surficial mapping legend. (d) Lidar-derived slope shade of panel (a). (e) An annotated photo of GS-20, an offset channel margin incised into the oldest and middle Quaternary alluvium (Qa1 and Qa2, respectively). The white arrow shows the ~6.6 m of right-lateral displacement. The blue-dashed lines show the hanging-wall and footwall projections of the surface margin; the red-shaded area shows the scarp face. People for scale. Annotated photos of GS-22 and GS-23 are in Figure S3d,e. (f) Plan view of GS-20, showing the right-lateral displacement along the 104°-striking fault trace. The red dots show surveyed scarp midpoints. (g) Plan view of GS-22, showing the right-lateral displacement along the 107°-striking fault trace. The red dots show surveyed scarp midpoints. (h) Plan view of GS-23, showing the right-lateral displacement along the 103°-striking fault trace. The red dots show surveyed scarp midpoints. Approx., approximate; FW, footwall; HW, hanging wall; Rel., relative. The color version of this figure is available only in the electronic edition.

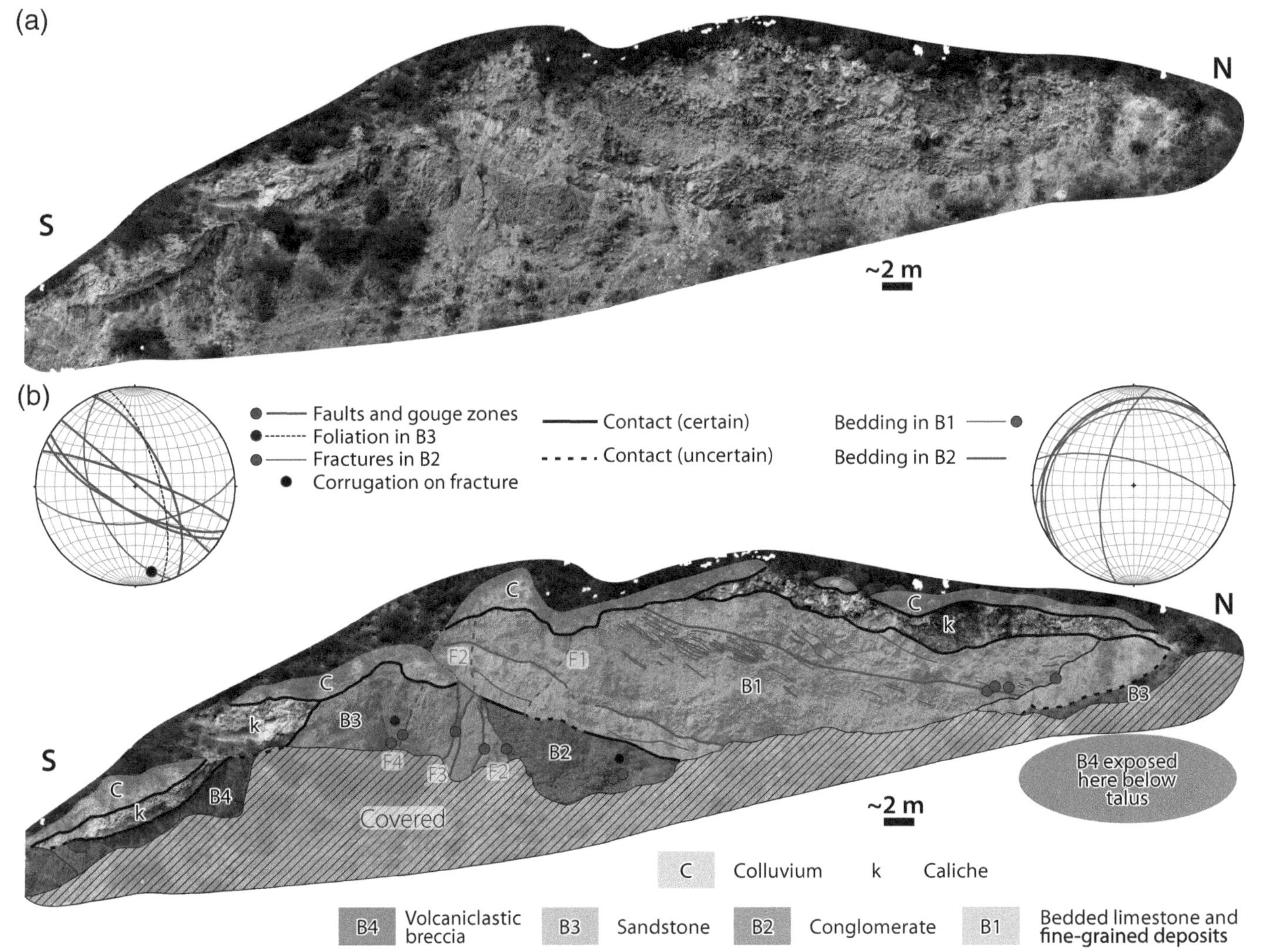

Figure 8. Unannotated (a) and annotated (b) photomosaic of bedrock fault exposure along strike from the active GSPRFZ fault scarp. A package of bedded limestone and fine-grained deposits (B1) and conglomerate (B2) is juxtaposed against sandstone (B3) above a volcaniclastic breccia (B4). Inset equal-area southern hemisphere stereonets show the orientations of faults and gouge zones labeled F1–F4 in panel (b), foliation, fractures, and corrugations (left), and bedding (right). The circles on the annotated photomosaic show the locations of structural measurements, with colors corresponding to those on the stereonets. The fine blue lines show internal stratigraphy within unit B1, which dips moderately northward in the center of the outcrop, shallowing toward the north. At the far northern end of the outcrop are sub-horizontal beds and a few beds that dip gently southward. The color version of this figure is available only in the electronic edition.

is located below unit B3 on the outcrop (Fig. 8), but we were unable to observe the contact between the two units due to colluvial cover. The top ~1–3 m of the northern and southern ends of the outcrop are modified by a well-developed caliche layer (k) with slope-parallel stratification. There is also patchy colluvium (C) in the top >50 cm of the exposure.

Units B1 and B2 are not laterally continuous, and are juxtaposed against units B3 and B4, in what we interpret as an ~10-m-wide fault zone based on the presence of multiple shear planes, a gouge zone, corrugations, and slickenlines (Fig. 8). This fault zone is subvertical, with multiple subsidiary faults and gouge zones dipping both north and south. There is one fault that has been eroded that extends through units B1 and B2 (F1 in Fig. 8). Unit B2 is sheared with fractured clasts and calcite veining. The main fault between units B2 and B3, F2, has an ~10-cm-wide core with gouge and a zone of brecciation. There is a slight corrugation to the fault plane, which is oriented 291°/82° NE, with a branching fault into unit B3 that is oriented 117°/70° SW. We observed F2 extending up through unit B1 in the field; in Figure 8, the orthorectification is such that the colluvium (C) obscures the upper part of F2. Another fault plane within unit B3 (F3) has been eroded and is oriented 312°/88° NE. South of F3, unit B3 is heavily fractured with purple and white slickensides present on some fractures. An ~1-m-wide fault zone (F4) in unit B3 is bounded to the north by a fault plane oriented 122°/70° SW and to the south by a gouge zone oriented 335°/64° NE (Fig. 8). The clasts within unit B4 are heavily fractured, and several clasts are entrained within a gouge zone at the far southern end of the outcrop.

We correlate our observations of the bedrock in the outcrop with bedrock mapping on previous geologic maps. These maps show Tertiary Cuevas Limestone on the southern face of Cerro Respaldo, deposited disconformably over Tertiary Raspaldo Formation to the north, and faulted against Cretaceous Robles Formation to the south (Glover, 1961a,b, 1971). The Raspaldo Formation is named for its type locality on Cerro Respaldo (Fig. 3; Glover, 1971) but is based on an earlier misspelling of the Spanish word. The similarities in our observations of unit B1 with descriptions of the Cuevas Limestone (Glover, 1971) support our interpretation that unit B1 is Cuevas. However, units B2, B3, and B4 do not match the Cuevas description. Based on our observations, unit B2 may correlate with the Cretaceous Coamo Formation, a red-matrix wacke conglomerate, or the Raspaldo Formation, which includes tuffaceous conglomerate with rounded cobbles and weathers yellowish brown (Glover, 1971). We interpret unit B2 to be the Raspaldo based on its depositional contact with unit B1 (Cuevas Limestone). We interpret that unit B3 is the Tertiary Juana Díaz Formation because our observations of unit B3 are similar to Glover's description (1971)of the Juana Díaz as a gray calcareous litharenite with indistinct stratification. In addition, the Juana Díaz Formation is the only sandstone mapped along the southern coastal plain. Based on previous geologic mapping (Glover, 1971), unit B4 should be the Robles Formation. However, the volcanic breccia of the Robles Formation is characterized by clear thin bedding and a green–gray color (Glover, 1971). In contrast, unit B4 is a massive and reddish-purple volcaniclastic breccia. Our observations are more similar to the Coamo Formation, which Glover (1971) described as a coarse, massive volcaniclastic unit with reddish matrix in places. Therefore, we interpret unit B4 to be the Coamo Formation.

Discussion

Quaternary kinematics

Offset sublinear geomorphic features within the GSPRFZ are consistent with right-lateral-oblique kinematics. We document right-lateral offset or deflection of linear geomorphic features at 10 locations. We document five right-lateral offsets of channel margins and linear ridges (profiles in Fig. 4), and five right-lateral deflections or not field-confirmed offsets (triangles in Fig. 3; Figs. S2, S3e–h, and S4c). These right-lateral offsets and deflections primarily occur on the southern coastal plain, including the base of Cerro Respaldo where channels incised into multiple generations of inferred Quaternary fan surfaces are offset (Fig. 4). We also observe right-lateral offsets northwest along strike into the interior of the island, where a channel wall is right-laterally offset at Finca Los Llanos (GS-1; Fig. 3, Fig. S2).

The geomorphic expression of the mapped lineaments is also consistent with right-lateral-oblique kinematics. Vertical separation across scarps (circles in Fig. 3) is predominantly southwest-down ($n = 36$), but there are also 12 profiles with northeast-down displacement. These uphill- and downhill-facing scarps that cut across contours are consistent with a minor amount of extension on a steeply southwest-dipping fault, as documented by Piety *et al.* (2018) and indicated by our fault-plane regressions. The far-field displacements across our mapped scarps are primarily south-side-down, indicating net extension across the fault system.

Relationship to bedrock faulting. We interpret that the bedrock fault outcrop at Hacienda Las Carolinas exposes a subvertical fault zone that juxtaposes Tertiary Cuevas Limestone and Raspaldo Formation against late Cretaceous Coamo Formation and Tertiary Juana Díaz Formation (Fig. 8). The fault zone is directly along strike from the mapped Quaternary scarps and exhibits north-side-up displacement (on a north-dipping fault) consistent with observed southwest-side-down Quaternary dip slip (on a southwest-dipping fault). We note that apparent changes between reverse and normal kinematics have been observed on steeply dipping fault systems where individual fault planes may have different dip directions (e.g., Naylor *et al.*, 1986; Keller *et al.*, 1995) and do not necessarily reflect a change in stress state. At Hacienda Las Carolinas, the bedrock north-side-up displacements result in the same landscape record of faulting as the southwest-side-down displacement of the active fault. The complex bedrock faulting described by Renken *et al.* (2002) and that we document here includes both north- and south-dipping fault planes. One of the south-dipping fault planes may have been reactivated in the current stress field.

The fault zone juxtaposes shallow marine Cuevas Limestone against the beach and terrestrial facies within the Coamo and the Juana Díaz, which is mapped ~7 km to the west (Glover, 1971). There may have been some component of lateral displacement to translate Juana Díaz east to Hacienda Las Carolinas. Lateral displacement is also supported by the presence of subhorizontal corrugations on the fault planes (Fig. 8). However, we are unable to constrain the sense of lateral motion from a single exposure. Previous work has suggested that the GSPRFZ has experienced left-lateral displacement since the Eocene (Glover, 1971; Krushensky and Monroe, 1975). The right-lateral transtension that we observe in the Quaternary sediments indicates that there has been a substantial change in the tectonic setting since the left-lateral transpression in the Eocene to early Miocene (Erikson *et al.*, 1990).

We are unable to determine the timing of the most recent fault movement from the outcrop observations alone. The surface above the outcrop is not clearly offset; however, any scarp may have been degraded during highway construction, and the surface records overlapping excavator tracks on the lidar-derived topography. Notably, the well-developed caliche observed at the northern and southern margins of the outcrop is missing above the fault zone (Fig. 8). This lack of caliche above the fault zone could result from fault movement disrupting the existing caliche or could have been removed during excavation.

Evidence for progressive vertical and lateral offset

The magnitude and variation in displacement support an interpretation that the GSPRFZ has hosted multiple surface-rupturing earthquakes in the Quaternary. In the island interior, the channel wall at Finca Los Llanos (GS-1) is offset right-laterally by 13.5 ± 1.4 m (Fig. 5, Fig. S2). The surveys collected at Hacienda Las Carolinas yield right-lateral displacements of 4.5–7.2 m; to the southeast, a ridge is offset by 16.2 ± 3.4 m right-laterally (GS-30; Fig. 5; Table 1). At these sites, vertical separations are <7% of the total displacement. The straight-line profiles elsewhere along strike record up to ~1.7 m vertical separation. If we assume the ratio of vertical to right-lateral displacement is consistent along strike, we might expect up to ~24 m of right-lateral displacement at these sites if there were linear features to record such offsets. However, our 3D displacements (Table 1) indicate the ratios are not consistent and, in fact, vary by an order of magnitude. Our straight-line profiles may therefore be in locations where the fault accommodates more dip-slip motion. In addition, many of these straight-line profiles are in agricultural fields on the relatively low-relief coastal plain. Incised channels that could record lateral displacement may not have existed at these sites, or any channels may have been modified by agriculture or by high erosion rates relative to slip rates due to the wet climate in Puerto Rico (e.g., Reitman *et al.*, 2023). We note that the interior of the island, where GS-1 is located, is in a tropical rainforest with different vegetation and significantly more precipitation than the semiarid savanna on the southern coastal plain. Glover (1971) documented a broad zone of bedrock faulting incorporating different fault orientations and slip senses; these preexisting structural discontinuities may also affect how the active GSPRFZ is expressed along strike.

The small fans, and therefore the channels that are incised into the fans, are likely to be of the latest Pleistocene to Holocene in age. Piety *et al.* (2018) dated fluvial deposits in their trench on the Salinas Fault to ~16.4–2.3 ka, and Renken *et al.* (2002) described Holocene fluvial degradation of an older fan delta on the southern coastal plain. However, we do not know the relative ages of the channel margins we surveyed in the field, as they are incised into deposits of multiple ages and could have been incised any time after deposition (e.g., Hatem *et al.*, 2025).

Within Hacienda Las Carolinas, the amount of lateral offset does not appear to correlate with deposit age; older deposits do not record higher amounts of lateral offset than younger deposits, which we interpret to mean that these deposits are all relatively close in age and/or all record the same recent earthquakes. Recurrence intervals on the Salinas and South Lajas Faults are ~4 and >20 kyr, respectively (Prentice and Mann, 2005; Piety *et al.*, 2018; Thompson Jobe, Briggs, Hughes, *et al.*, 2024), so if the Hacienda Las Carolinas deposits are all Holocene, it is reasonable to expect that they have all experienced the same 1 or 2 earthquakes. However, right-lateral offsets measured remotely using lidar-derived topography are two to three times greater outside Hacienda Las Carolinas, indicating that (1) sites along different strands of the GSPRFZ record more slip and hence more earthquakes or (2) these sites are older geomorphic features or landforms than the fans at Hacienda Las Carolinas.

Recent surface ruptures of strike-slip and transtensional faults show that lateral slip is variable on different strands of the fault zone (e.g., 1999 M_w 7.1 Hector Mine earthquake, Treiman *et al.*, 2002; 2019 M_w 7.1 Ridgecrest earthquake, DuRoss *et al.*, 2020). Because the GSPRFZ is composed of multiple fault strands, each strand may record different amounts of slip during each earthquake or cumulatively. Two sites with higher lateral offsets are located on different strands of the GSPRFZ. One of these sites, GS-30, is located ~2 km southeast of Hacienda Las Carolinas on a broad ridge down a hillslope (Fig. 3). This ridge crosses a northern strand of the GSPRFZ, which may have experienced larger offsets than the strand at Hacienda Las Carolinas. The second site, GS-1 at Finca Los Llanos, is located ~10 km northwest of Hacienda Las Carolinas (Fig. 3), and records a channel wall laterally offset by a different strand of the GSPRFZ. Alternatively, these two sites may also record higher displacements because they are older geomorphic features. There are considerably fewer age controls on Quaternary deposits in the interior of the island than on the southern coastal plain, and the deposits that are offset at GS-1 may be older than those at Hacienda Las Carolinas and thus may record more earthquakes.

Multiple scaling relationships indicate that the mapped length of the GSPRFZ, ≥25 km, is consistent with the expected surface rupture length from a moment magnitude (M_w) 6.7–7.0 earthquake (Wells and Coppersmith, 1994; Wesnousky, 2008). Earthquakes of this magnitude typically produce 0.75–2.5 m average total displacement (Wells and Coppersmith, 1994), significantly less than the smallest oblique displacements of 4.2 m at GS-19. If we consider the entire mapped length of the onshore bedrock GSPRFZ, 111 km, scaling relationships indicate that the GSPRFZ could host earthquakes up to M_w 7.1–8.0 with ~1–2.5 m of average right-lateral displacement, still less than half of the smallest oblique displacements observed. One possible explanation is that earthquake(s) on the GSPRFZ could have had larger-than-average displacement, which has been observed in recent surface ruptures. For example, scaling relationships predict maximum displacements of ~2.7 m for the 2016 M_w 7.8 Kaikōura earthquake in New Zealand, but offsets up to 12 m were observed locally (e.g., Litchfield *et al.*, 2018; Nicol *et al.*, 2018; Zinke *et al.*, 2019). If the GSPRFZ continues offshore to the northwest and southeast, as suggested by Mann, Hippolyte, *et al.* (2005) and Grindlay *et al.* (2005), its total length could be ≥180 km. Such a length would be consistent with M_w 7.2–8.3 earthquakes and maximum displacements of ~1.3–6.3 m (Wells and Coppersmith, 1994; Wesnousky, 2008).

Although we acknowledge that a single 180-km-long rupture could have produced the displacements we observe, we propose it is more likely that these displacements likely result from multiple earthquakes. The 4.2 m of oblique displacement observed at GS-19 would be consistent with ≥4 M_w 6.7–7.0 earthquakes or ≥2 island-wide M_w 7.8 earthquakes. Not every earthquake is clearly recorded in the geomorphology, especially in areas with rapid landscape modification (e.g., Reitman *et al.*, 2023, 2024); therefore, the GSPRFZ may have hosted additional events we do not observe in the geomorphology.

Slip-rate approximations

Without directly dating the offset deposits and landforms along the GSPRFZ, we can only estimate a slip rate based on regional geomorphic and age correlations. Although there are no ages available for the deposits at Hacienda Las Carolinas, regional mapping (e.g., Renken *et al.*, 2002) and ages from similar deposits along the south coast indicate that the alluvial fans are likely late Pleistocene to Holocene (e.g., Prentice and Mann, 2005; Piety *et al.*, 2018; Thompson Jobe, Briggs, Hughes, *et al.*, 2024). In a paleoseismic trench on the nearby Salinas Fault (Fig. 3), Piety *et al.* (2018) dated fluvial and eolian deposits to ~16.4–2.3 ka and ~10.6–2.5 ka, respectively. If we assume that the deposits at Hacienda Las Carolinas are of similar ages, the 4.5–7.2 m displacements at the site would yield slip rates of ~0.3–≥3 mm/yr. However, geodetic data indicate total motion of 3 mm/yr between PRVI and Hispaniola (e.g., Jansma *et al.*, 2000; Jansma and Mattioli, 2005; Calais *et al.*, 2016), so we favor the lower end of this range because there are multiple active faults onshore Puerto Rico that each likely accommodate a portion of this total motion. In the 2025 National Seismic Hazard Model update, the GSPRFZ was assigned a slip-rate bin of 0–0.5 mm/yr (Thompson Jobe, Briggs, ten Brink, *et al.*, 2024) based on a 0.2 mm/yr minimum slip rate determined from vertical separation magnitudes and estimated Holocene ages of the offset deposits (Thompson Jobe, Briggs, Hughes, *et al.*, 2024). Our observations are consistent with this assigned slip-rate bin.

Implications for regional seismotectonics

Instrumental seismicity is concentrated in southwestern Puerto Rico (e.g., Asencio, 1980; Huérfano *et al.*, 2005), including the 2019–2025 (ongoing at time of publication) sequence (e.g., Blasweiler *et al.*, 2022; ten Brink *et al.*, 2022; Yoon *et al.*, 2023). Moment tensors for this sequence show a variety of fault strikes and kinematics, but in general the sequence can be simplified as left-lateral displacement on a series of northwest–southeast-striking faults (e.g., Yoon *et al.*, 2023), and a north-northeast–south-southwest-oriented extension direction (ten Brink *et al.*, 2022). The southwestern Puerto Rico sequence is ~50 km southwest of the GSPRFZ, on a set of faults offshore (ten Brink *et al.*, 2022). Although this extension is consistent with our observations of extension across the GSPRFZ, left-lateral displacement on faults parallel to the GSPRFZ is inconsistent with our geomorphic observations of right-lateral displacement.

The mismatch of left-lateral moment tensors to the southwest with apparent right-lateral geomorphic markers along the GSPRFZ raises the possibility that the apparent landscape record of faulting is incorrect. For example, geomorphic observations might be misleading due to channel aliasing, causing apparent right lateral in a left-lateral system (e.g., Reitman *et al.*, 2019, 2021). With progressive offset of channels, stream capture may occur, resulting in channels that appear offset in the direction opposite to fault movement (e.g., Huang, 1993; Replumaz *et al.*, 2001; Walker and Allen, 2012). Huang (1993) concluded that stream capture was more likely with channels that are displaced by at least half the channel spacing. At our primary study site (Hacienda Las Carolinas), we measured five neighboring channels that are spaced an order of magnitude farther apart (~30–400 m) than the observed offsets (4–7 m), indicating that stream capture may be unlikely along this short section of the fault, and channels may accurately record fault movement. However, not all channels along this section of the fault record right-lateral offset, possibly because of channel formation after the most recent earthquake, or an incomplete or misleading geomorphic record. If the geomorphic record is correct, our observations are consistent with past studies that indicate only 30%–80% of channels may accurately record offset in the same direction as fault movement (Gaudemer, 1989; Walker and Allen, 2012).

Northeastward-directed geodetic motion of Puerto Rico relative to North America (Fig. 1; e.g., Solares Colón, 2019) is consistent with right-lateral displacement on the GSPRFZ. Some models for PRVI microplate movement (e.g., Speed and Larue, 1991; Hippolyte *et al.*, 2005) show the southwestern PRVI boundary extending across the southern coastal plain, accommodated by the east–west-striking South Lajas and Salinas Faults, and then extending offshore via the GSPRFZ to connect to the faults in Anegada Passage (Fig. 1). This model requires reconciling the disparate lateral slip senses on either side of the microplate boundary. Other models (e.g., Mann and Burke, 1984; Jany *et al.*, 1990; ten Brink and Lin, 2004) connect the Mona Rift to the Anegada Passage through a continuous Cerro Goden-GSPRFZ boundary across Puerto Rico (Fig. 1b). If this is the case, it is plausible that faults in southwestern Puerto Rico may have a different slip sense than the GSPRFZ. A possible cause of the shift from Miocene left-lateral motion to Quaternary right-lateral motion observed on Puerto Rico is the collision of the Bahamas Bank with Hispaniola in the late Miocene to early Pliocene (Fig. 1a), effectively pinning Hispaniola in place and allowing PRVI to move independently and rotate counterclockwise (e.g., Mann *et al.*, 1995; Dolan *et al.*, 1998; Mann, Hippolyte, *et al.*, 2005).

Conclusions

We mapped fault scarps and topographic and tonal lineaments of the GSPRFZ in a zone ~25 km long and ~1–2 km wide across the southern coastal plain of Puerto Rico, using high-resolution lidar elevation data, satellite imagery, and historical air photos. Our surface observations are consistent with the interpretation that the GSPRFZ is a right-lateral oblique fault with primarily south-side-down normal motion. Surveys of offset geomorphic features document ~4.5–7.2 m of right-lateral displacement of young (likely late Pleistocene or Holocene) alluvial fans with up to ~1.5 m down-to-south vertical separation. Scaling relations indicate that the GSPRFZ is capable of hosting M_w 6.7–7.0 earthquakes, and our observations are consistent with the 0–0.5 mm/yr slip rate implemented in the 2025 PRVI NSHM (Thompson Jobe, Briggs, ten Brink, *et al.*, 2024). The apparent late Pleistocene and Holocene right-lateral transtensional kinematics of the GSPRFZ raise questions regarding the kinematics of other faults onshore Puerto Rico and the role of the GSPRFZ in accommodating PRVI motion.

Data and Resources

The 10 m National Elevation Dataset and 3D elevation program light detection and ranging (lidar) data are available at https://apps.nationalmap.gov/viewer (last accessed May 2024). The authors used air photos from throughout the twentieth century, including: 1:10,000 air photos from 1930, publicly available at https://prgeoref.weebly.com/1930-y-1936.html (López Marrero *et al.*, 2017). 1:20,000 air photos from 1940, from U.S. Army Topographic Command (1940), publicly available from the Puerto Rico GIS Portal at https://gis.pr.gov/descargaGeodatos/FotosAereasHistoricas/Pages/default.aspx. 1:20,000 air photos from 1958 to 1977, and 1:42,000 air photos from 1983, publicly available on EarthExplorer at https://earthexplorer.usgs.gov/. The authors also used recent satellite imagery, publicly available from Bing Maps and the Maxar Open Data program. All field photographs are by Emerson M. Lynch, U.S. Geological Survey (USGS). The SCARP-3D script from Lynch *et al.* (2025a) is available at doi: 10.5061/dryad.nvx0k6dvc. The data to Figures 1, 2, 3, 6, and 7 were available at nationalmap.gov, and for Figure 2 at coast.noaa.gov/dataviewer. The supplemental material includes additional figures and tables. All data presented in this study (shapefiles of the geomorphic and neotectonic mapping, topographic field surveys, and structure-from-motion orthomosaic) are available from Lynch, Thompson Jobe, *et al.* (2025).

Declaration of Competing Interests

The authors acknowledge that there are no conflicts of interest recorded.

Acknowledgments

Funding was provided by the U.S. Geological Survey Earthquake Hazards Program. The authors thank Hacienda Las Carolinas for land access. This article benefited from comments from Nadine Reitman, Sean Bemis, and Alex Morelan.

Any use of trade, firm, or product names is for descriptive purposes only and does not imply endorsement by the U.S. Government.

References

Asencio, E. (1980). Western Puerto Rico seismicity, *U.S. Geol. Surv. Open-File Rept. 80-192.*

Bawiec, W., S. Marsh, R. Learned, R. Krushensky, and J. Schellekens (2001). Geology, geochemistry, geophysics, mineral occurrences, and mineral resource assessment for the Commonwealth of Puerto Rico, *U.S. Geol. Surv. Open-File Rept. 98-38.*

Bessette-Kirton, E., C. Cerovski-Darriau, W. Schulz, J. A. Coe, J. W. Kean, J. W. Godt, M. A. Thomas, and K. S. Hughes (2019). Landslides triggered by Hurricane Maria: Assessment of an extreme event in Puerto Rico, *GSA Today* **29,** no. 6, 4–10.

Blasweiler, M., M. W. Herman, F. Houtsma, and R. Govers (2022). Tectonic context and possible triggering of the 2019–2020 Puerto Rico earthquake sequence, *Seismol. Res. Lett.* **93,** no. 2A, 584–593.

Calais, E., S. Symithe, B. Mercier De Lépinay, and C. Prépetit (2016). Plate boundary segmentation in the northeastern Caribbean from geodetic measurements and Neogene geological observations, *C. R. Geosci.* **348,** no. 1, 42–51.

Cowgill, E. (2007). Impact of riser reconstructions on estimation of secular variation in rates of strike-slip faulting: Revisiting the Cherchen River site along the Altyn Tagh fault, NW China, *Earth Planet. Sci. Lett.* **254,** no. 3, 239–255.

Cunningham, D., S. Grebby, K. Tansey, A. Gosar, and V. Kastelic (2006). Application of airborne LiDAR to mapping seismogenic faults in forested mountainous terrain, southeastern Alps, Slovenia, *Geophys. Res. Lett.* **33,** no. 20, L20308, doi: 10.1029/2006GL027014.

DeMets, C., P. E. Jansma, G. S. Mattioli, T. H. Dixon, F. Farina, R. Bilham, E. Calais, and P. Mann (2000). GPS geodetic constraints on Caribbean-North America plate motion, *Geophys. Res. Lett.* **27,** no. 3, 437–440.

Dolan, J. F., H. T. Mullins, and D. J. Wald (1998). Active tectonics of the north-central Caribbean: Oblique collision, strain partitioning, and opposing subducted slabs, in *Active Strike-Slip and Collisional Tectonics of the Northern Caribbean Plate Boundary Zone*, J. F. Dolan and P. Mann, Vol. 326, Geological Society of America Special Paper, Boulder, Colorado, 1–61.

DuRoss, C. B., M. P. Bunds, R. D. Gold, R. W. Briggs, N. G. Reitman, S. F. Personius, and N. A. Toké (2019). Variable normal-fault rupture behavior, northern Lost River fault zone, Idaho, USA, *Geosphere* **15,** no. 6, 1869–1892.

DuRoss, C. B., R. D. Gold, T. E. Dawson, K. M. Scharer, K. J. Kendrick, S. O. Akciz, S. J. Angster, J. Bachhuber, S. Bacon, S. E. Bennett, *et al.* (2020). Surface displacement distributions for the July 2019 Ridgecrest, California, earthquake ruptures, *Bull. Seismol. Soc. Am.* **110,** no. 4, 1400–1418.

Duvall, A. R., and G. E. Tucker (2015). Dynamic ridges and valleys in a strike-slip environment, *J. Geophys. Res.* **120,** no. 10, 2016–2026.

Erikson, J. P., J. L. Pindell, and D. K. Larue (1990). Mid-Eocene-early Oligocene sinistral transcurrent faulting in Puerto Rico associated with formation of the northern Caribbean plate boundary zone, *J. Geol.* **98,** no. 3, 365–384.

Gaudemer, Y. (1989). River offsets across active strike-slip faults, *Ann. Tecton.* **3,** 55–76.

Glover, L. (1961a). Preliminary report on the geology of the Coamo quadrangle, Puerto Rico, *U.S. Geol. Surv. Misc. Invest. Series Map I-335.*

Glover, L. (1961b). Preliminary report on the geology of the Salinas quadrangle, Puerto Rico, *U.S. Geol. Surv. Misc. Invest. Series Map I-337.*

Glover, L. (1971). Geology of the Coamo area, Puerto Rico, and its relation to the volcanic arc-trench association, *U.S. Geol. Surv. Profess. Pap. 636.*

Grindlay, N. R., P. Mann, J. F. Dolan, and J.-P. van Gestel (2005). Neotectonics and subsidence of the northern Puerto Rico–Virgin Islands margin in response to the oblique subduction of high-standing ridges, in *Active Tectonics and Seismic Hazards of Puerto Rico, the Virgin Islands, and Offshore Areas*, P. Mann (Editor), Vol. 385, Geological Society of America Special Paper, Boulder, Colorado.

Hatem, A. E., R. W. Briggs, and R. D. Gold (2025). How does the onset of offset influence geologic slip rates? *Seismol. Res. Lett.* **96,** no. 1, 363–376.

Hetzel, R., S. Niedermann, M. Tao, P. W. Kubik, S. Ivy-Ochs, B. Gao, and M. R. Strecker (2002). Low slip rates and long-term preservation of geomorphic features in Central Asia, *Nature* **417,** no. 6887, 428–432.

Hippolyte, J.-C., P. Mann, and N. R. Grindlay (2005). Geologic evidence for the prolongation of active normal faults of the Mona Rift into northwestern Puerto Rico, in *Active Tectonics and Seismic Hazards of Puerto Rico, the Virgin Islands, and Offshore Areas*, P. Mann (Editor), Vol. 385, Geological Society of America Special Paper, Boulder, Colorado, 161–171.

Holzapfel, C. (2008). Deserts, in *Encyclopedia of Ecology*, S. E. Jørgensen and B. D. Fath, Academic Press, Oxford, 879–898.

Huang, W. (1993). Morphologic patterns of stream channels on the active Yishi fault, southern Shandong Province, eastern China: Implications for repeated great earthquakes in the Holocene, *Tectonophysics* **219,** no. 4, 283–304.

Huérfano, V., C. von Hillebrandt-Andrade, and G. Báez-Sanchez (2005). Microseismic activity reveals two stress regimes in southwestern Puerto Rico, in *Active Tectonics and Seismic Hazards of Puerto Rico, the Virgin Islands, and Offshore Areas*, P. Mann (Editor), Vol. 385, Geological Society of America Special Paper, Boulder, Colorado, 81–101.

Hughes, K. S., and W. Schulz (2020). Map depicting susceptibility to landslides triggered by intense rainfall, Puerto Rico, *U.S. Geol. Surv. Open-File Rept. 2020-1022.*

Jansma, P. E., and G. S. Mattioli (2005). GPS results from Puerto Rico and the Virgin Islands: Constraints on tectonic setting and rates of active faulting, in *Active Tectonics and Seismic Hazards of Puerto Rico, the Virgin Islands, and Offshore Areas*, P. Mann (Editor), Vol. 385, Geological Society of America Special Paper, 13–30.

Jansma, P. E., G. S. Mattioli, A. Lopez, C. DeMets, T. H. Dixon, P. Mann, and E. Calais (2000). Neotectonics of Puerto Rico and the Virgin Islands, northeastern Caribbean, from GPS geodesy, *Tectonics* **19,** no. 6, 1021–1037.

Jany, I., K. M. Scanlon, and A. Mauffret (1990). Geological interpretation of combined Seabeam, Gloria and seismic data from Anegada passage (Virgin Islands, north Caribbean), *Mar. Geophys. Res.* **12,** no. 3, 173–196.

Keller, J. V. A., S. H. Hall, C. J. Dart, and K. R. McClay (1995). The geometry and evolution of a transpressional strike-slip system: The Carboneras fault, se Spain, *J. Geol. Soc.* **152,** no. 2, 339–351.

Khajavi, N., M. Quigley, and R. M. Langridge (2014). Influence of topography and basement depth on surface rupture morphology revealed from LiDAR and field mapping, Hope fault, New Zealand, *Tectonophysics* **630,** 265–284.

Knuth, F., D. Shean, S. Bhushan, E. Schwat, O. Alexandrov, C. McNeil, A. Dehecq, C. Florentine, and S. O'Neel (2023). Historical structure from motion (HSfM): Automated processing of historical aerial photographs for long-term topographic change analysis, *Remote Sens. Environ.* **285,** 113,379.

Krushensky, R., and W. Monroe (1975). Geologic map of the Ponce quadrangle, Puerto Rico, *U.S. Geol. Surv. Misc. Invest. Series Map I-863.*

Krushensky, R., and W. Monroe (1978). Geologic map of the Peñuelas and Punta Cuchara quadrangles, Puerto Rico, *U.S. Geol. Surv. Misc. Invest. Series Map I-1042.*

Lin, Z., H. Kaneda, S. Mukoyama, N. Asada, and T. Chiba (2013). Detection of subtle tectonic–geomorphic features in densely forested mountains by very high-resolution airborne LiDAR survey, *Geomorphology* **182,** 104–115.

Litchfield, N. J., P. Villamor, R. J. V. Dissen, A. Nicol, P. M. Barnes, D. J. Barrell, J. R. Pettinga, R. M. Langridge, T. A. Little, J .J. Mountjoy, *et al.* (2018). Surface rupture of multiple crustal faults in the 2016 M_w 7.8 Kaikōura, New Zealand, earthquake, *Bull. Seismol. Soc. Am.* **108,** no. 3B, 1496–1520.

López Marrero, T., M. A. Lorenzo Pérez, C. F. Riviera López, A. C. González Toro, D. Rivera Santiago, H. N. Crespo, and P. H. Gonzalez (2017). Porto Rico 1930 georeferenced: A coastal mosaic, Interdisciplinary Center for Coasetal Studies, University of Puerto Rico, Mayagüez, available at https://prgeoref.weebly.com/1930-y-1936.html (last accessed May 2024).

Loveless, J. P., R. W. Allmendinger, M. E. Pritchard, and G. González (2010). Normal and reverse faulting driven by the subduction zone earthquake cycle in the northern Chilean fore arc, *Tectonics* **29,** no. 2, 1–16.

Lynch, E. M., C. Regalla, K. D. Morell, N. Harrichhausen, and L. J. Leonard (2025a). Evidence for an active transtensional Beaufort Range fault in the northern Cascadia forearc, *Seismica* **2,** no. 4, 25.

Lynch, E. M., C. Regalla, K. D. Morell, N. Harrichhausen, and L. J. Leonard (2025b). Three-dimensional offsets of geomorphic piercing lines displaced by the Quaternary-active Beaufort Range fault, northern Cascadia forearc, BC, Canada, *DRYAD*, dataset, doi: 10.5061/dryad.nvx0k6dvc.

Lynch, E. M., J. Thompson Jobe, R. W. Briggs, M. M. Tan, V. Ortega Díaz, and K. Stephen Hughes (2025). Supporting data for "Late Pleistocene kinematics of the Great Southern Puerto Rico fault zone, Puerto Rico", *U.S. Geol. Surv.*, Data Release, doi: 10.5066/P18SPREU.

Mann, P., and K. Burke (1984). Neotectonics of the Caribbean, *Res. Geophys. Space Phys.* **22,** no. 4, 309–362.

Mann, P., J.-C. Hippolyte, N. R. Grindlay, and L. J. Abrams (2005). Neotectonics of southern Puerto Rico and its offshore margin, in *Active Tectonics and Seismic Hazards of Puerto Rico, the Virgin Islands, and Offshore Areas*, P. Mann (Editor), Vol. 385, Geological Society of America Special Paper, Boulder, Colorado, 173–214.

Mann, P., C. S. Prentice, J.-C. Hippolyte, N. R. Grindlay, and L. J. Abrams (2005). Reconnaissance study of Late Quaternary faulting along Cerro Goden fault zone, western Puerto Rico, in *Active Tectonics and Seismic Hazards of Puerto Rico, the Virgin Islands, and Offshore Areas*, P. Mann (Editor), Vol. 385, Geological Society of America Special Paper, Boulder, Colorado, 115–138.

Mann, P., F. Taylor, R. L. Edwards, and T.-L. Ku (1995). Actively evolving microplate formation by oblique collision and sideways motion along strike-slip faults: An example from the northeastern Caribbean plate margin, *Tectonophysics* **246,** nos. 1/3, 1–69.

Marliyani, G. I., J. R. Arrowsmith, and K. X. Whipple (2016). Characterization of slow slip rate faults in humid areas: Cimandiri fault zone, Indonesia, *J. Geophys. Res.* **121,** no. 12, 2287–2308.

McCann, W. R. (1985). On the earthquake hazards of Puerto Rico and the Virgin Islands, *Bull. Seismol. Soc. Am.* **75,** no. 1, 251–262.

Meghraoui, M., T. Camelbeeck, K. Vanneste, M. Brondeel, and D. Jongmans (2000). Active faulting and paleoseismology along the Bree fault, lower Rhine graben, Belgium, *J. Geophys. Res.* **105,** no. B6, 13,809–13,841.

Morell, K. D., C. Regalla, L. J. Leonard, C. B. Amos, and V. Levson (2017). Quaternary rupture of a crustal fault beneath Victoria, British Columbia, Canada, *GSA Today* **27,** nos. 3/4, 4–10.

Mueller, C., A. Frankel, M. Petersen, and E. Leyendecker (2010). New seismic hazard maps for Puerto Rico and the U.S. Virgin Islands, *Earthq. Spectra* **26,** no. 1, 169–185.

Mueller, C., A. D. Frankel, M. D. Petersen, and E. Leyendecker (2003). Documentation for 2003 USGS Seismic Hazard Maps for Puerto Rico and the U.S. Virgin Islands, *U.S. Geol. Surv. Open-File Rept. 03-379*.

Naylor, M., G. Mandl, and C. Supesteijn (1986). Fault geometries in basement-induced wrench faulting under different initial stress states, *J. Struct. Geol.* **8,** no. 7, 737–752.

Nicol, A., N. Khajavi, J. R. Pettinga, C. Fenton, T. Stahl, S. Bannister, K. Pedley, N. Hyland-Brook, T. Bushell, I. Hamling, *et al.* (2018). Preliminary geometry, displacement, and kinematics of fault ruptures in the epicentral region of the 2016 M_w 7.8 Kaikōura, New Zealand, earthquake, *Bull. Seismol. Soc. Am.* **108,** no. 3B, 1521–1539.

Ntokos, D., E. Lykoudi, and T. Rondoyanni (2016). Geomorphic analysis in areas of low-rate neotectonic deformation: South Epirus (Greece) as a case study, *Geomorphology* **263**, 156–169.

Pánek, T., J. Minár, L. Vitovič, and M. Břežný (2020). Post-LGM faulting in central Europe: LiDAR detection of the >50 km-long sub-Tatra fault, western Carpathians, *Geomorphology* **364,** 107,248.

Parrino, N., F. Pepe, P. Burrato, G. Dardanelli, M. Corradino, C. Pipitone, M. G. Morticelli, A. Sulli, and C. Di Maggio (2022). Elusive active faults in a low strain rate region (Sicily, Italy): Hints from a multidisciplinary land-to-sea approach, *Tectonophysics* **839,** 229,520.

Piety, L. A., J. R. Redwine, S. A. Derouin, C. S. Prentice, K. I. Kelson, R. E. Klinger, and S. Mahan (2018). Holocene surface ruptures on the Salinas fault and southeastern Great Southern Puerto Rico fault zone, south coastal plain of Puerto Rico, *Bull. Seismol. Soc. Am.* **108,** no. 2, 619–638.

Prentice, C. S., and P. Mann (2005). Paleoseismic study of the South Lajas fault: First documentation of an onshore Holocene fault in Puerto Rico, in *Active Tectonics and Seismic Hazards of Puerto Rico, the Virgin Islands, and Offshore Areas*, P. Mann (Editor), Vol. 385, Geological Society of America Special Paper, Boulder, Colorado, 215–222.

PRISM Climate Group (2019). Puerto Rico, Oregon State University, available at https://prism.oregonstate.edu/ (last accessed March 2024).

Regalla, C., D. M. Fisher, E. Kirby, D. Oakley, and S. Taylor (2017). Slip inversion along inner fore-arc faults, eastern Tohoku, Japan, *Tectonics* **36,** no. 11, 2647–2668.

Reitman, N. G., S. E. Bennett, R. D. Gold, R. W. Briggs, and C. B. DuRoss (2015). High-resolution trench photomosaics from image-based modeling: Workflow and error analysis, *Bull. Seismol. Soc. Am.* **105,** no. 5, 2354–2366.

Reitman, N. G., Y. Klinger, R. W. Briggs, and R. D. Gold (2023). Climatic influence on the expression of strike-slip faulting, *Geology* **51,** 18–22.

Reitman, N. G., Y. Klinger, R. W. Briggs, and R. D. Gold (2024). Limited preservation of strike-slip surface displacement in the geomorphic record, *J. Geophys. Res.* **129,** no. 11, e2024JB028692, doi: 10.1029/2024JB028692.

Reitman, N. G., K. J. Mueller, and G. E. Tucker (2021). Surface slip variability on strike-slip faults, *Earth Surf. Process. Landf.* **47,** no. 4, 908–935.

Reitman, N. G., K. J. Mueller, G. E. Tucker, R. D. Gold, R. W. Briggs, and K. R. Barnhart (2019). Offset channels may not accurately record strike-slip fault displacement: Evidence from landscape evolution models, *J. Geophys. Res.* **124,** no. 12, 13,427–13,451.

Renken, R. A., W. C. Ward, I. P. Gill, F. Gómez-Gómez, and J. Rodríguez-Martínez (2002). Geology and hydrogeology of the Caribbean Islands aquifer system of the Commonwealth of Puerto Rico and the U.S. Virgin Islands, *U.S. Geol. Surv. Profess. Pap. 1419*.

Replumaz, A., R. Lacassin, P. Tapponnier, and P. H. Leloup (2001). Large river offsets and Plio-Quaternary dextral slip rate on the Red River fault (Yunnan, China), *J. Geophys. Res.* **106,** no. B1, 819–836.

Rodríguez-Martínez, J. (2007). Stratigraphy, structure, and geologic and coastal hazards in the Penuelas to Salinas area, southern Puerto Rico: A compendium of published literature, *U.S. Geol. Surv. Open-File Rept. 2007-1259*.

Roig-Silva, C., E. Asencio, and J. Joyce (2013). The northwest trending North Boqueron Bay-Punta Montalva fault zone; A through going active fault system in southwestern Puerto Rico, *Seismol. Res. Lett.* **84**, 538–550.

Scharer, K., J. Salisbury, R. Arrowsmith, and T. Rockwell (2014). Southern San Andreas fault evaluation field activity: Approaches to measuring small geomorphic offsets–challenges and recommendations for active fault studies, *Seismol. Res. Lett.* **85**, 68–76.

Schoeneberger, P., D. Wysocki, E. Benham, and , and Soil Survey Staff (2012). Field book for describing and sampling soils, Version 3.0.

Solares Colón, M. (2019). New constraints on crustal deformation within the Puerto Rico-Virgin Islands microplate using two decades of GPS data, *Master's Thesis*, University of Puerto Rico Mayagüez, Mayagüez, Puerto Rico.

Speed, R. C., and D. K. Larue (1991). Extension and transtension in the plate boundary zone of the northeastern Caribbean, *Geophys. Res. Lett.* **18,** no. 3, 573–576.

Styron, R., J. García-Pelaez, and M. Pagani (2020). CCAF-DB: the Caribbean and Central American active fault database, *Nat. Hazards Earth Syst. Sci.* **20,** no. 3, 831–857.

Symithe, S., E. Calais, J. B. de Chabalier, R. Robertson, and M. Higgins (2015). Current block motions and strain accumulation on active faults in the Caribbean, *J. Geophys. Res.* **120,** no. 5, 3748–3774.

ten Brink, U., and J. Lin (2004). Stress interaction between subduction earthquakes and forearc strike-slip faults: Modeling and application to the northern Caribbean plate boundary, *J. Geophys. Res.* **109,** no. 12, 1–15.

ten Brink, U. S., E. A. Vanacore, E. J. Fielding, J. D. Chaytor, A. M. López-Venegas, W. E. Baldwin, D. S. Foster, and B. D. Andrews (2022). Mature diffuse tectonic block boundary revealed by the 2020 southwestern Puerto Rico seismic sequence, *Tectonics* **41,** no. 3, e2021TC006896, doi: 10.1029/2021TC006896.

Thompson Jobe, J., R. Briggs, K. S. Hughes, J. Joyce, R. Gold, S. Mahan, H. Gray, and L. Strickland (2024). Neotectonic mapping of Puerto Rico, *Seismica* **3,** no. 1, 1–34.

Thompson Jobe, J., R. W. Briggs, U. ten Brink, T. L. Pratt, K. S. Hughes, A. E. Hatem, C. B. DuRoss, N. G. Reitman, J. A. Herrick, S. Nicovich, *et al.* (2024). Geologic input databases for the 2025 Puerto Rico—U.S. Virgin Islands National Seismic Hazard Model update: Crustal faults component, *Seismol. Res. Lett.* **96,** no. 2A, 1–27.

Thompson Jobe, J. A., and N. G. Reitman (2025). Timescales of surface faulting preservation in low-strain intraplate regions from landscape evolution modeling and the geomorphic and historical record, *J. Geophys. Res.* **130,** no. 6, e2024JB029966, doi: 10.1029/2024JB029966.

Thompson Jobe, J. A., R. D. Gold, R. W. Briggs, R. A. Williams, W. J. Stephenson, J. E. Delano, A. Shah, and B. Minsley (2020). Evidence for late quaternary deformation along Crowleys ridge, New Madrid seismic zone, *Tectonics* **39,** no. 4, e2019TC005746, doi: 10.1029/2019TC005746.

Thompson Jobe, J. A., B. Philibosian, C. Chupik, T. Dawson, S. E. K. Bennett, R. Gold, C. DuRoss, T. Ladinsky, K. Kendrick, E. Haddon, *et al.* (2020). Evidence of previous faulting along the 2019 Ridgecrest, California, earthquake ruptures, *Bull. Seismol. Soc. Am.* **110,** no. 4, 1427–1456.

Treiman, J. A., K. J. Kendrick, W. A. Bryant, T. K. Rockwell, and S. F. McGill (2002). Primary surface rupture associated with the M_w 7.1 16 October 1999 Hector Mine earthquake, San Bernardino County, California, *Bull. Seismol. Soc. Am.* **92,** no. 4, 1171–1191.

U.S. Army Topographic Command (1940). Puerto Rico aerial survey, *U.S. Army Map Service.*

U.S. Geological Survey (2017). Advanced National Seismic System (ANSS) comprehensive catalog of earthquake events and products, *U.S. Geol. Surv.*, available at https://earthquake.usgs.gov/earthquakes/search/ (last accessed May 2024).

Walker, F., and M. B. Allen (2012). Offset rivers, drainage spacing and the record of strike-slip faulting: The Kuh Banan Fault, Iran, *Tectonophysics* **530–531,** 251–263.

Weilert, L., and D. A. Laó-Dávila (2023). Fault structure and segmentation of the Punta Montalva fault in southwestern Puerto Rico using high-resolution digital elevation models, *Tectonophysics* **860,** 229,921.

Wells, D. L., and K. J. Coppersmith (1994). New empirical relationships among magnitude, rupture length, rupture width, rupture area, and surface displacement, *Bull. Seismol. Soc. Am.* **84,** no. 4, 974–1002.

Wesnousky, S. G. (2008). Displacement and geometrical characteristics of earthquake surface ruptures: Issues and implications for seismic-hazard analysis and the process of earthquake rupture, *Bull. Seismol. Soc. Am.* **98,** no. 4, 1609–1632.

Yoon, C. E., E. S. Cochran, E. A. Vanacore, V. Huerfano, G. Báez-Sánchez, J. D. Wilding, and J. Smith (2023). A detailed view of the 2020–2023 southwestern Puerto Rico seismic sequence with deep learning, *Bull. Seismol. Soc. Am.* **113,** no. 6, 2377–2415.

Zachariasen, J., and C. G. von Hillebrandt-Andrade (2005). Holocene faulting of the Cerro Goden fault, western Puerto Rico, *U.S. Geol. Surv. /NEHRP Final Technical Rept.*, University of Puerto Rico Mayagüez, 27.

Zinke, R., J. Hollingsworth, J. F. Dolan, and R. Van Dissen (2019). Three-dimensional surface deformation in the 2016 M_w 7.8 Kaikōura, New Zealand, earthquake from optical image correlation: Implications for strain localization and long-term evolution of the Pacific-Australian plate boundary, *Geochem. Geophys. Geosys.* **20,** no. 3, 1609–1628.

Manuscript received 8 April 2025
Published online 2 October 2025

Crustal Unloading as a Possible Source of Seismicity at Plainfield, Connecticut

John E. Ebel*[1], Sean Kondas[2], Parker Aubin[3], Justin Starr[4], and Jay J. Pulli[1]

Abstract

In 2014–2015, an extended swarm of small earthquakes occurred at Wauregan in the town of Plainfield, Connecticut, with epicenters around the Wauregan Tilcon bedrock quarry, which was closed about four years before the swarm occurred. Dozens of earthquakes were felt or heard by the residents near the quarry. Following the M_{Lg} 3.1 thrust mainshock, which occurred very early in the swarm, four portable seismic instruments were installed in the epicentral area. More than 180 microearthquakes were confirmed with the portable instrument data, and as many as 200 more possible events were detected by the portable instruments. The mainshock and most of the swarm events immediately following the mainshock appear to be spatially associated with the west-dipping Lake Char fault. Later events in the swarm occurred within about 500 m of a projected steeply dipping NW–SE-striking unnamed fault to the NW of the quarry. Modeling of the perturbation of the local stress field due to the removal of rock from the quarry suggests that most of the events took place where the local Coulomb failure stress was increased on thrust faults throughout the area and on left-lateral, vertical strike-slip faults west of the quarry. The delay of about 4 yr between the end of quarrying and the earthquake swarm, perhaps can be explained if static fatigue due to the past quarrying may have led to the earthquake swarm. Because of some previous studies at other quarries, it might be possible that quarrying operations can trigger seismic activity in settings with a favorable stress regime, fault orientations, and rock characteristics. However, this study does not indicate that quarrying can trigger an earthquake large enough to be damaging.

Cite this article as Ebel, J. E., S. Kondas, P. Aubin, J. Starr, and J. J. Pulli (2026). Crustal Unloading as a Possible Source of Seismicity at Plainfield, Connecticut, *Seismol. Res. Lett.* **97**, 1156–1173, doi: 10.1785/0220250129.

Supplemental Material

Introduction

Industrial activities such as oil and gas production, impoundment of manmade reservoirs, and mining and quarrying can generate earthquakes of magnitude $M_w > 5.8$, which can cause millions of dollars of damage to the built environment (Foulger *et al.*, 2018). The largest events induced by human activities, for example, the 1967 Koyna earthquake of M 6.3, can lead to loss of human life (Gupta, 2002). Many research efforts currently focus on earthquakes caused by fluid injection because of the recent surge in seismic activity surrounding wastewater injection in Oklahoma, Texas, and other areas (Weingarten *et al.*, 2015). However, other physical processes, including fluid removal, hydraulic fracturing, and mass loading/unloading, must be considered for a complete understanding of the seismic hazards caused by industrial activity (Doglioni, 2018). Globally, more than 90 sites have been identified where earthquakes have been triggered by the filling of water reservoirs, that is, mass loading (Gupta, 2002), whereas only a few sites have been identified in the published literature where earthquakes have been triggered by mass unloading through quarrying operations (Pomeroy *et al.*, 1976; Gibowitz, 1982; Seeber *et al.*, 1998).

The most recent investigation of seismicity induced by mass unloading in the United States was published in 1998 after an M_{bLg} 4.6 earthquake occurred within the upper 2.5 km of the crust underneath a large quarry in Cacoosing Valley, Pennsylvania (Seeber *et al.*, 1998). In the months following the mainshock, a swarm of aftershocks clustered around the periphery of a tabular 3 × 3 km zone that was interpreted to outline the mainshock rupture. The Seeber *et al.* (1998) study showed that the event occurred as the result of an oblique-thrusting mechanism with left-lateral slip, and that roughly

1. Weston Observatory, Department of Earth and Environmental Sciences, Boston College, Weston, Massachusetts, U.S.A., https://orcid.org/0000-0003-1064-0629 (JEE); 2. Newtown, Connecticut, U.S.A.; 3. Infrasense, Woburn, Massachusetts, U.S.A.; 4. Slingerlands, New York, U.S.A.

*Corresponding author: ebel@bc.edu

TABLE 1
Earthquakes Located by the Regional Seismic Network

Date (yyyy/mm/dd) Origin Time (hh:mm:ss) (UTC)	Latitude (°N)	Longitude (°E)	Depth (km)	M_{Lg}	M_c
2014/10/13 09:16:51	41.79	−71.88	2.45	0.9	1.6
2014/11/09 10:42:24	41.83	−71.91	5.54	0.6	1.3
2014/11/09 10:43:38	41.72	−71.95	2.46	0.9	1.0
2015/01/08 14:28:01	41.77	−71.90	5.89	2.0	2.2
2015/01/12 11:33:15	41.76	−71.89	0.43	1.1	1.8
2015/01/12 11:34:27	41.77	−71.92	1.37	1.0	1.6
2015/01/12 11:36:39	41.76	−71.90	0.68	3.1	3.0
2015/01/12 11:50:06	41.76	−71.89	3.59	2.0	2.4
2015/01/12 17:03:17	41.78	−71.88	3.79	1.3	2.0
2015/01/12 18:04:15	41.79	−71.87	1.24	1.2	1.9
2015/01/13 12:27:07	41.75	−71.91	2.71	2.1	2.2
2015/01/14 11:33:45	41.76	−71.89	1.54	1.7	2.3
2015/01/14 13:10:22	41.75	−71.89	1.04	1.1	1.6
2015/01/15 09:39:38	41.74	−71.89	3.07	1.9	2.2
2015/02/24 14:13:46	41.73	−71.88	1.25	0.9	1.3
2015/02/24 14:18:27	41.74	−71.88	3.67	1.5	2.0

$2 million of damage occurred in the surrounding area due to this earthquake, which at that time was the highest amount of damage caused by an earthquake in the eastern United States since 1944. In the years following the Cacoosing Valley event, the focus of induced seismicity research has largely shifted toward injection-induced seismicity following the development of unconventional hydrocarbon resource extraction in the mid-2000s. However, the continued improvement in our understanding of the relationship between quarrying operations and seismic activity is warranted. The relative paucity of published examples of seismicity, perhaps induced by crustal mass unloading, suggests that a new contribution to the investigation of this topic is useful.

In early 2015, an extended swarm of small earthquakes took place in eastern Connecticut in the Wauregan section of the town of Plainfield. The swarm was preceded by three small earthquakes in the same epicentral area in the fall of 2014. The earthquake swarm was of special seismological interest because the events were located around and beneath the Wauregan Tilcon bedrock quarry, which had been closed about four years before the swarm took place. Excavation at the Wauregan Tilcon quarry began around 1970, with crushed stone being produced from a local orthogneiss rock body. Over the approximately 40 yr that the quarry was in operation, a total of approximately 4.05×10^6 m^3 of rock was removed (Kondas, 2020). The quarry extends about 225 m in the east–west (E-W) direction and 600 m in the north–south (N-S) direction, with a maximum depth of about 20–30 m.

Because of the large number of small earthquakes that were felt or heard by the local residents, public interest in this earthquake swarm was quite high. Weston Observatory of Boston College responded to the largest event of this swarm by installing four portable seismographs in the area where the residents were feeling and hearing the events. These instruments, which were operated until July 2015, recorded between 180 and 380 microearthquakes over several months during which they operated. Regional seismic network stations also detected the earthquakes above about M_{Lg} 0.6 in the swarm. Later, Weston Observatory conducted a gravity and magnetic survey in the area of the swarm to help identify the possible geologic structure or structures on which the seismic events may have taken place. It is the analyses of these data, along with local stress modeling due to the presence of the rock quarry, that are the subjects of this article.

Time History of the Plainfield Swarm

Although the Plainfield swarm began in January 2015, there were three earlier small earthquakes in fall 2014 that were detected by regional seismic stations in southern New England (Table 1; see Fig. 1 for the locations of the closest regional seismic network stations). On 13 October 2014, an earthquake of M_{Lg} 0.9 was located in Plainfield. On 9 November 2014, two additional small earthquakes (M_{Lg} 0.6 and 0.9) were located at approximately the October epicenter. The swarm itself began in earnest on 8 January 2015 with an M_{Lg} 2.0 event that took place at 14:28

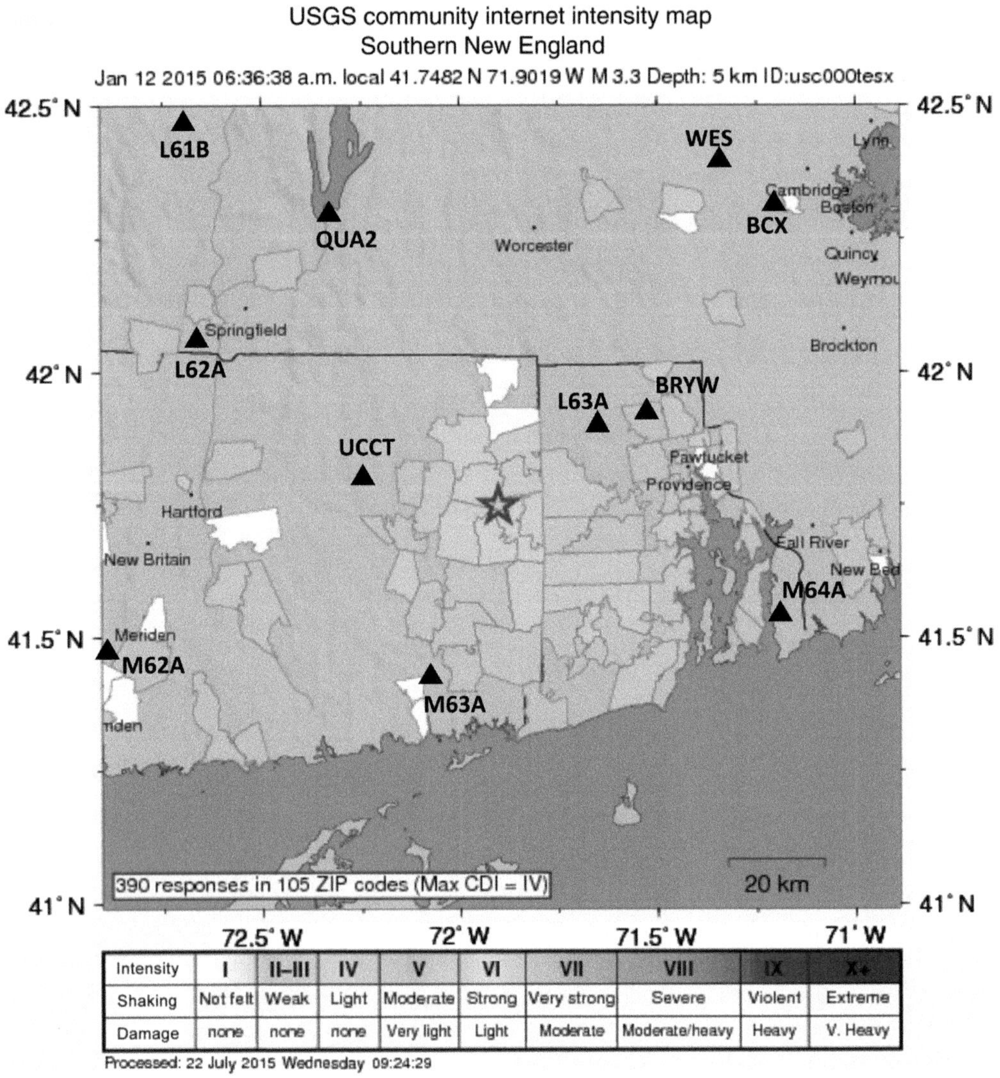

Figure 1. Felt modified II-IV Mercalli shaking intensities seen throughout Connecticut, Rhode Island, and Massachusetts as a result of the 2015 M_{Lg} 3.1 earthquake in Plainfield. Mainshock location represented by a red star. The triangles show the closest regional seismic network stations to the event epicenter. The color version of this figure is available only in the electronic edition.

UTC, which was 09:28 a.m. local time, and which was reportedly felt by some local residents. The following day at 15:36 UTC (10:36 a.m. local time), many residents of the Wauregan section of Plainfield reported another small earthquake. Although the seismic signals of this second event were too weak to be recorded by enough of the regional seismic network stations to allow for an independent computation of its epicenter, the similarity of its seismic waveforms to the earthquake of the previous day at the closest seismic stations confirmed that this event had approximately the same hypocenter as the event of the previous day and had an M_{Lg} 0.4. The Wauregan residents next started feeling and hearing earthquakes on the morning of 12 January 2015, with a noticeable event of M_{Lg} 1.1 at 11:33 UTC (06:33 a.m. local time) (Table 1). Within the next few minutes, another smaller event took place, followed by the largest earthquake of the sequence, an M_{Lg} 3.1 event at 11:36 UTC (06:36 a.m. local time). The M_{Lg} 3.1 event was felt throughout most of Connecticut and Rhode Island and across their borders at several towns in Massachusetts (Fig. 1), although no damage was reported anywhere due to this seismic event. Numerous small earthquakes were felt and/or heard throughout the rest of 12 January 2015 and during the subsequent days by residents in Wauregan, and the local residents were clearly spooked by hearing and feeling the frequent small earthquakes, something that they had not previously experienced. The observation that earthquakes of very small magnitude can be heard or felt in New England is a common one (Ebel, 2019). For example, in swarms of small earthquakes at Moodus, Connecticut, events as small as M_c 1.0 were felt and as small as M_c − 1.0 were heard (Ebel *et al.*, 1982; Ebel, 1989). In an earthquake swarm at McAdam, New Brunswick, in 2015, events as small as M_L 0.1 were felt (Bent *et al.*, 2017). Even outside New England and New Brunswick, similar observations have been made. For example, at Columbus, Georgia, in 1982, many residents living within 2 km of the epicenters of M_D 3.1 and 2.9 mainshocks heard and felt many aftershocks (Jones *et al.*, 1985) during the 10 days following the mainshocks. Portable earthquake monitoring of the aftershocks found that none of the aftershocks that were heard and felt exceeded M_D 0.0.

On 13 January 2015, a team from the Weston Observatory of Boston College installed four broadband portable seismographs in the Wauregan area to record the events that were taking place (Table 2). During the several hours that the Weston Observatory team was in the Wauregan area, they heard two small events, both of which had M_{Lg} 0.5 and were too small to be seen on seismographs outside of the closest couple of regional seismic network stations. Over the next few days, local Wauregan residents continued to report hearing

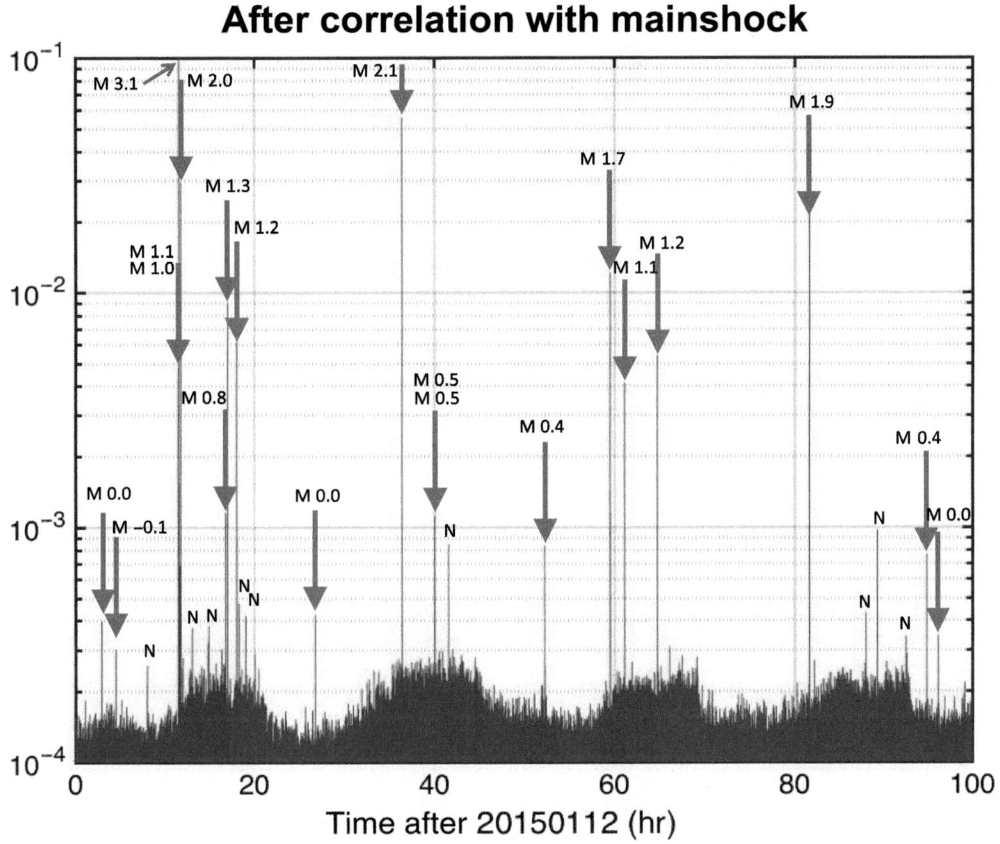

Figure 2. Microearthquake detections using a matched filter analysis of the seismic trace from the closest regional seismic network station to the swarm (EarthScope Transportable Array [TA] station L63A, see Fig. 1) for the first 100 hr of the swarm, starting at 00 UTC on 12 January 2015. The waveform of the M_{Lg} 3.1 earthquake on 12 January was used as the template waveform in this analysis (see Fig. 3). The vertical axis is the normalized cross-correlation coefficient value. The magnitude values shown in the figure assume that a reduction of a factor of 10 in cross-correlation value corresponds to a reduction of 1 magnitude unit relative to the M_{Lg} 2.1 event at hour 38. Peaks labeled N are judged to be noise correlations due to vehicular traffic. The color version of this figure is available only in the electronic edition.

and sometimes feeling the events that were taking place. Although the portable instruments detected a large number of microearthquakes that took place after 15 January 2015, none of the events were large enough for an absolute epicentral determination using only the regional seismic network station data, except for two events of M_{Lg} 0.9 and 1.5 on 24 February 2015. The last microearthquake of the swarm was detected by the portable instruments on 19 July 2015, even though the portable seismographs were not removed until 2 October 2015.

To learn about the history of the smaller earthquakes of the swarm during the time period before the portable instruments were installed, a matched filter analysis of the seismic trace from the closest regional seismic network station to the swarm (EarthScope Transportable Array, network code TA, station L63A, epicentral distance 26 km) was carried out (Pulli, 2016). A frequency band of 1–18 Hz in a three-pole Butterworth filter was applied in forward and reverse time to eliminate phase shifts due to the filter to all seismograms in this analysis. A 15 s window, starting 5 s before the first P arrival, of the M_{Lg} 3.1 mainshock waveform was used as the template waveform in the cross-correlation analysis, and this template was tapered with a 20% cosine taper at the two ends of the waveform. The template waveform was cross-correlated with successive 2-hr time seismogram time windows from 1 June 2014 to 1 June 2015 to look for possible seismic events. For all cross-correlation peaks above the background cross-correlation values, the template waveform was visually compared to the section of the seismogram with the cross-correlation match to ensure that the correlated section of the seismogram looked like a seismic event similar to that of the mainshock. This analysis discovered cross-correlation peaks above the background correlation level of what are likely two small foreshocks early on 12 January 2015 as well as several small aftershocks during the time period after the mainshock and before the portable seismographic instruments were installed starting about 30 hr after the mainshock (Fig. 2). No other small events were found on L63A between 8 and 12 January using this matched filter method other than the events on 8 and 9 January already noted in Table 1. Figure 3 shows the

TABLE 2
Locations of Portable Seismographs

Station Name	Latitude (°N)	Longitude (°E)
9CCD	41.7460	−71.89588
B680	41.75612	−71.90191
B235	41.74940	−71.90984
AAC3	41.73284	−71.87988

Sensors: Güralp CMG-40T broadband three-component seismometer (frequency range 10–0.03 Hz). Digitizers: Reftek 130 24-bit digitizer with a sampling rate of 100 Hz.

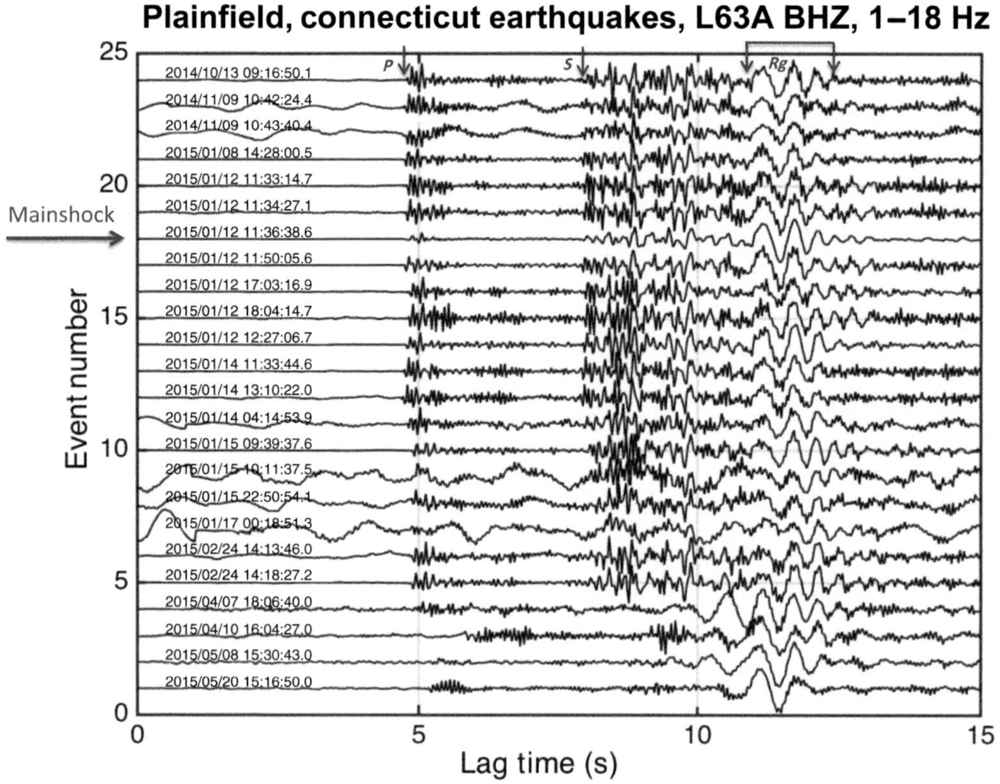

Figure 3. Vertical-component waveforms from N4 network station L63A (epicentral distances of about 26 km, azimuths about 57° from the event locations) band-pass filtered from 1 to 18 Hz. The arrows show the arrival times of the *P* and *S* waves, and the waveform band delineated by the arrows shows the window in which the *Rg* waves arrive. All of the waveforms have been aligned at the first *P*-wave arrival time. *Rg* waves suggesting shallow focal depths are seen for all of these events. Location and magnitude parameters for events numbered 1, 2, 6, and 8–20 are found in Table 1. Location and magnitude parameters for events numbered 3–5 are found in Table 3. There is no hypocentral computation for event 7, but it is the event with M 0.4 in Figure 2 at about 52 hr. Event 14 on 12 January 2015 at 11:36:38.6 labeled mainshock is the template waveform for the cross-correlation analysis shown in Figure 2. The color version of this figure is available only in the electronic edition.

mainshock waveform that was used for the template matching, along with the 23 other waveforms of foreshocks and aftershocks detected by the matched filter analysis.

Because the portable seismic stations were deployed in a tight spatial cluster in the area of the epicenters, they detected what appeared to be hundreds of microearthquakes associated with the swarm. After manual review of the seismographic data filtered in a 3–15 Hz band, more than 180 microearthquakes were confirmed based on their detection by more than one portable seismograph and by the similarity of their waveforms with larger events. Another 200 or so events that appear on at least one of the portable seismographs may also have been microearthquakes. In many cases, these possible events were only detected by one portable instrument. In some cases, background noise (probably local vehicular traffic) interfered with what appeared to be small events. Figure 4 shows a timeline of all events of a swarm of M − 1.0 and greater. The magnitudes of the events in Figure 4 were computed using a linear regression of the maximum vertical amplitudes of the events at portable station 9CCD with the computed M_{Lg} magnitudes of the larger events from the regional seismic network given in Table 1 (see S1, available in the supplemental material to this article, for details). For a large majority of the swarm events, station 9CCD was the closest station to the epicenters, and hence it typically had the strongest signal of any of the portable station recordings.

Locations of the Plainfield Swarm Events

Because of the installation of the four portable seismographs within about 2 km of the locations of the swarm events, absolute hypocentral locations with precisions of 500–1500 m in both epicenter and focal depth were determined for a number of the aftershocks using only the data from the portable seismic stations (Table 3). The events in Table 3 comprise all of the local earthquakes for which there were clear event detections on the records from all four of the portable seismic instruments. Initially, *P* and *S* arrival-time readings from the four stations were used to compute hypocenters of these events using the program HYPO2000 (Klein, 2002) and using a seismic velocity model for Connecticut (Ebel, 1985; supplement S2). The root mean square (RMS) fit of the predicted and observed *P* and *S* arrival times for these hypocentral determinations ranged from 0.03 to 0.19 s, with half the events having an RMS value ≥ 0.10 s. After some trial and error, it was discovered that, with one exception, locating the events using only the arrival times for stations B680, B235, and AAC3 yielded hypocentral locations with RMS values no more than 0.04 s, with only three events having an RMS value greater than 0.02 s. Apparently, the Global Positioning System clock at station 9CCD lost synchronization with the satellites during most of its operation. For one event (event 25 in Table 3), station AAC3 apparently lost the GPS synchronization of its clock and could not be used to locate that event. Fortunately, the clock

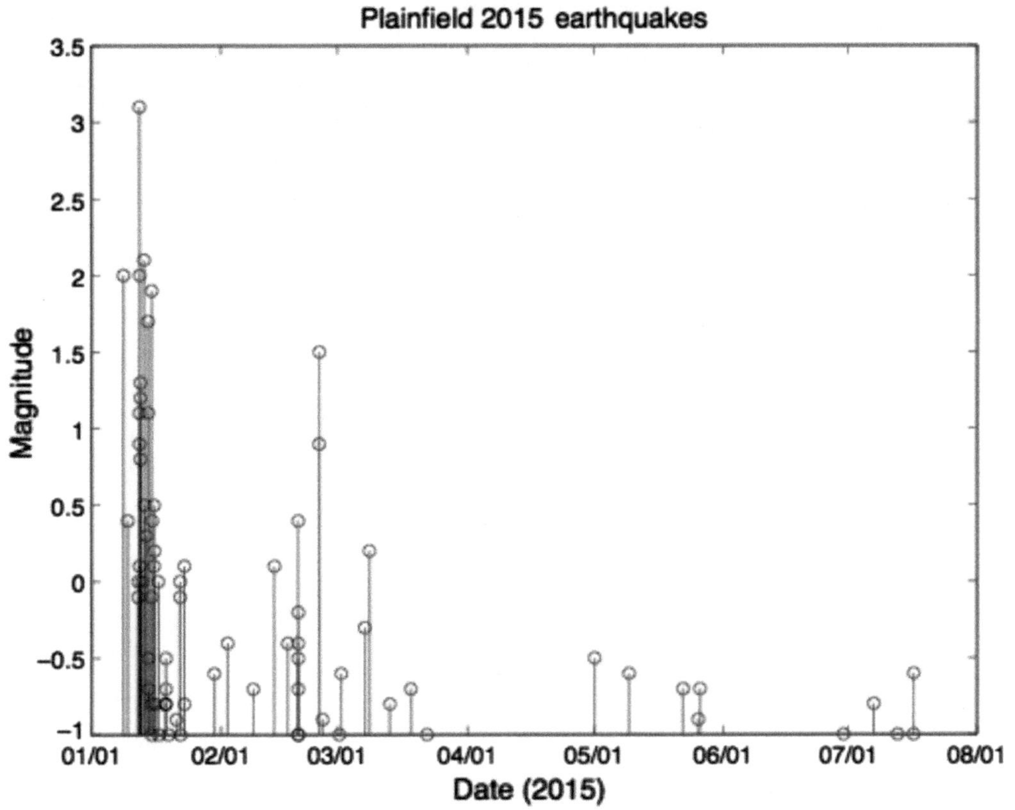

Figure 4. Timeline of all swarm events of M−1.0 and greater. Magnitudes computed using a linear regression of the maximum amplitudes of the events at portable station 9CCD with the computed magnitudes of the larger events from the regional seismic network (see section S.1). The color version of this figure is available only in the electronic edition.

at station 9CCD appears to have been synchronized at that time, meaning that a location with an RMS of 0.02 s could be computed using the arrival-time readings from stations B680, B235, and 9CCD. Table 3 shows the computed hypocenters for each of the events, all of which were determined using the *P* and *S* arrival times from three of the portable stations.

The focal depths of all of the events in Table 3 are less than 1.7 km, with many of the events having focal depths less than 1.0 km. These shallow focal depths are confirmed by very strong *Rg* waves (short-period Rayleigh waves) that were recorded at the regional seismic network stations for the swarm events (e.g., Fig. 4). As shown by Kafka (1990), *Rg* waves are only observed if the focal depth of an event is less than about 4 km, with higher amplitude *Rg* waves for shallower focal depths. The high-amplitude *Rg* waves seen in Figure 3 confirm the very shallow focal depths listed in Table 3.

Figure 5a–c shows maps of the locations of the events in Table 3. Also shown in the three maps of Figure 5 is the location of the mainshock relative to the location of event 4 in Table 3 using the method of Ebel *et al.* (2008). The relative-location method of Ebel *et al.* (2008) utilizes relative *P* and *S* arrival times computed using waveform cross-correlations to compute a highly precise hypocenter of one event relative to that of another event. The great precision of the relative locations is achieved by ignoring the absolute locations of the events in the analysis. The mainshock epicenter in Figure 5 was computed using the *P* and *S* waveforms from regional seismic network stations L63A, UCCT, BRYW, M63A, M62A, and HRV (listed here in order of increasing epicentral distance from 26 to 84 km). The relative epicentral uncertainty is about 50 m. The mainshock was computed to have a focal depth that was about 125 ± 96 m shallower than that of event 4, suggesting that the mainshock took place very close to the surface of the earth.

The events in Table 3 are broken into three different time periods in Figure 5 to emphasize their spatial variation with time. Figure 5a shows the locations of the first eight events from Table 3, covering a time period spanning the first five days after the mainshock. Events 3–8 clearly have a strong north-northeast–south-southwest (NNE-SSW) trend that follows the Lake Char fault. This trend is parallel to that of the nodal planes of the mainshock focal mechanism (Fig. 6), the only event of the swarm for which a constrained focal mechanism could be computed. Events 1 and 2 occurred farther to the west, off of this NNE-SSW trend. In contrast, in Figure 5b, events 10–18 from 23 January to 1 March spread along a west-northwest–east-southeast (WNW-ESE) trend and encompassed the locations of events 1 and 2. Figure 5c shows the last events (after 8 March) in the swarm from Table 3. With the exceptions of events 19 and 20, these events also follow the WNW-ESE trend seen in Figure 5b. In Figure 5a, events 3–7 occurred in the vicinity of the mainshock epicenter, whereas event 8 occurred to the SSW of these events. In Figure 5b, events 9–11 occurred very close to each other (and very close to the epicenters of events 1 and 2), but then the swarm events appear to have spread in both the WNW and ESE directions. The SSW end of the trend of the events in Figure 5a and the ESE end of the trend of the events in Figure 5b,c appear to coincide.

TABLE 3.
Earthquakes Located Using the Portable Seismographic Data

Event Number	Date (yyyy/mm/dd) Time (hh:mm)	Latitude (°N)	Longitude (°E)	Depth (km)	RMS (s)	Magnitude*
1	2015/01/14 11:33	41.7450	−71.8937	1.07	0.01	1.7
2	2015/01/14 13:10	41.7455	−71.8932	1.22	0.02	1.1
3	2015/01/15 09:33	41.7480	−71.8850	0.71	0.01	−0.1
4	2015/01/15 09:39	41.7517	−71.8807	0.13	0.02	1.9
5	2015/01/15 10:11	41.7480	−71.8827	0.64	0.01	0.4
6	2015/01/15 22:50	41.7452	−71.8850	0.93	0.01	0.5
7	2015/01/16 00:09	41.7458	−71.8845	0.72	0.00	0.2
8	2015/01/17 00:18	41.7383	−71.8878	0.84	0.01	0.0
9	2015/01/22 04:39	41.7447	−71.8942	0.04	0.03	0.0
10	2015/01/23 05:16	41.7422	−71.8930	1.48	0.01	−0.8
11	2015/01/23 05:36	41.7452	−71.8937	0.40	0.02	0.1
12	2015/02/13 20:33	41.7493	−71.8975	0.32	0.01	0.1
13	2015/02/17 09:21	41.7480	−71.9005	0.88	0.01	−1.1
14	2015/02/19 12:55	41.7407	−71.8878	0.46	0.00	0.4
15	2015/02/19 13:08	41.7423	−71.8930	1.52	0.01	−0.2
16	2015/02/19 15:13	41.7433	−71.8925	1.46	0.01	−1.0
17	2015/02/25 09:33	41.7467	−71.9000	0.72	0.00	−0.9
18	2015/03/01 10:08	41.7418	−71.8852	0.68	0.01	−1.0
19	2015/03/08 13:34	41.7530	−71.8927	1.19	0.03	0.2
20	2015/03/22 08:51	41.7448	−71.8820	0.07	0.04	−1.0
21	2015/05/01 04:01	41.7417	−71.8967	0.01	0.01	−0.5
22	2015/05/03 23:14	41.7428	−71.8910	0.99	0.02	−1.3
23	2015/05/08 10:16	41.7440	−71.8955	1.68	0.01	−1.2
24	2015/05/09 09:34	41.7442	−71.8962	0.43	0.02	−0.6
25	2015/05/22 07:36	41.7467	−71.8995	0.79	0.02	−0.7
26	2015/07/13 04:35	41.7408	−71.8888	0.35	0.01	−1.2

*Magnitude computed from the maximum amplitude at station 9CCD. RMS, root mean square.

There was a sufficient number of first-motion readings across the regional seismic network stations, including EarthScope TA stations, that a well-constrained focal mechanism from *P*-wave first motions only for the mainshock could be computed. That focal mechanism, shown in Figure 6, indicates that the mainshock was a thrust earthquake on an NNE-SSW-striking fault plane. As can be seen in Figure 5, the Lake Char fault trends NNE-SSW in the Wauregan area, and the fault dips toward the west (Skehan, 2008). Thus, the mainshock location, its focal mechanism, and the locations of six of the first eight aftershocks in Table 1 and Figure 5a are all consistent with a segment of one strand of the Lake Char fault being active during this earthquake sequence. In contrast, the later events that align in a WNW-ESE direction do not plot on a mapped fault, although they are on-strike with a WNW-striking fault that has been mapped farther to the NW of the quarry in Connecticut. The SE end of that fault, as shown on the bedrock map of Connecticut (Rodgers, 1985), can be seen in Figure 5 just to the NW of Wauregan.

Earthquake Sounds and Infrasound Observation

One aspect that generated much public interest in this earthquake swarm was the large number of events that were heard or felt by the residents of Wauregan, particularly those who lived the closest to the area where the events were centered.

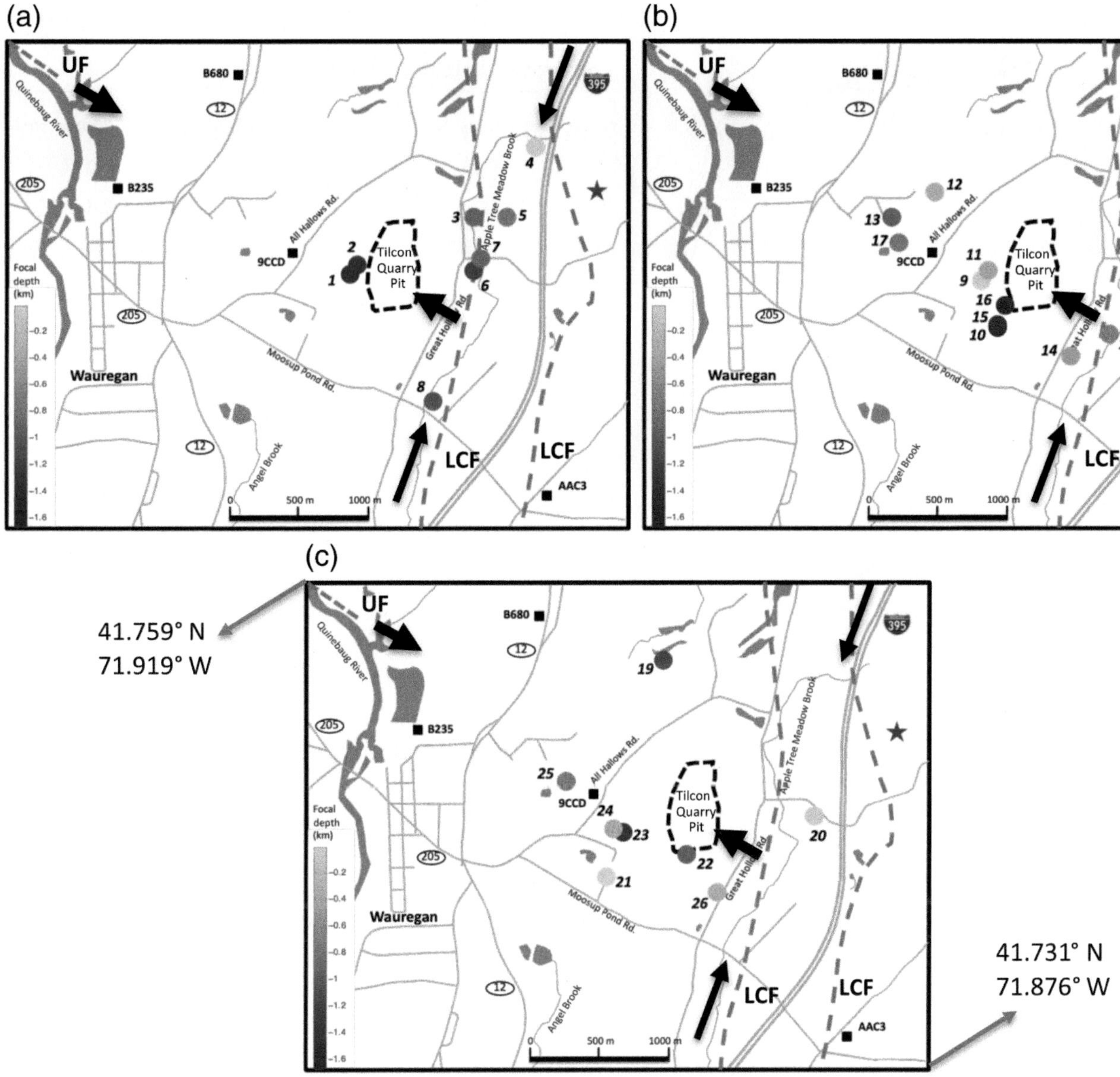

Figure 5. Accurately located hypocenters of aftershocks (Table 3) following the M_{Lg} 3.1 mainshock (blue star) in Plainfield, Connecticut, in 2015. The circles represent hypocenter locations numbered chronologically because they occurred throughout the months following the mainshock. Spatiotemporal development is seen along the Lake Char fault system (a; trend shown by longer, thinner arrows), along a possible SE-trending fault (b; trend shown by the shorter, thicker arrows), and somewhat randomly distributed but including the SE trend (c). The black squares represent locations of installed portable seismograph stations. Quarry area outlined in a black dashed line. Mapped faults are outlined in brown-dashed lines, with the two strands of the Lake Char fault system labeled LCF and the unnamed fault in the northwestern corner of the plot labeled UF. The mainshock location on this figure was computed relative to the location of event 4 in (a). Map (a) shows the seismicity to 17 January 2025; map (b) shows the seismicity from 22 January to 1 March 2025; and map (c) shows the seismicity from 8 March to 13 July 2025. The color version of this figure is available only in the electronic edition.

Those residents were especially spooked because the larger shocks on 8, 9, 12, and 13 January took place within a couple of hours of sunrise, suggesting to them a pattern in the event occurrences. In contrast, the microearthquakes that were detected by the portable seismic instrumentation occurred at all times of the day and night and did not show an association with local sunrise.

Although it was impossible to obtain a complete record of which events of the swarm were felt and heard, Weston Observatory staff did receive many reports with specific times when local earthquakes were felt and heard by persons living in Wauregan near the quarry. These are listed in Table 4. There were many additional felt and heard reports received by Weston Observatory for which no specific date and/or time were given. It was not possible to include these reports in Table 4, and hence the reports listed reflect only a fraction of the total number of felt and heard reports received at Weston Observatory from the Wauregan area during the time

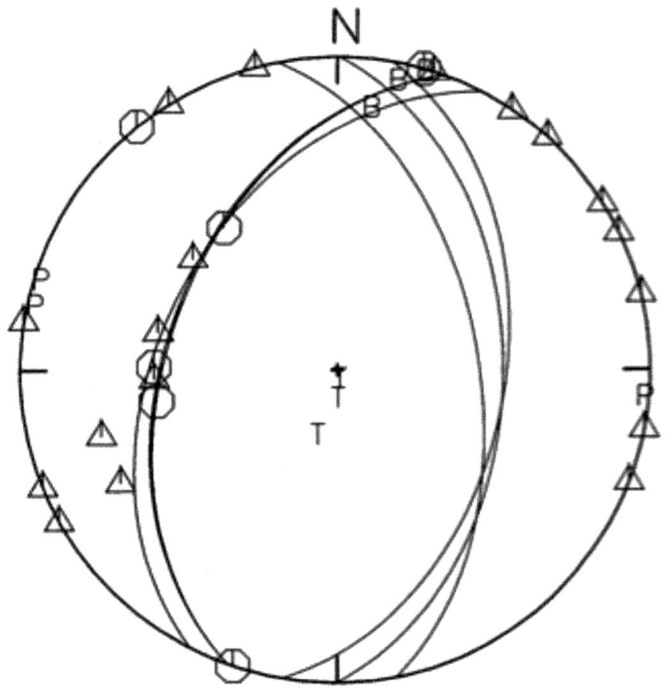

Figure 6. *P*-wave first-motion focal mechanism for the M_{Lg} 3.1 Plainfield, Connecticut, event on 12 January 2015 at 11:36 UTC. The circles indicate compressional first arrivals, and triangles represent dilatational first arrivals. Locations of the P, T, and B axes for the different possible fault-plane solutions are shown. The focal mechanism indicates thrust faulting on a fault oriented in a north-northeast–south-southwest (NNE-SSW) direction.

TABLE 4
Confirmed Felt/Heard Reports

Date (yyyy/mm/dd) Time (hh:mm) (UTC)	Magnitude
2015/01/08 14:28	2.0
2015/01/09 15:26	0.4
2015/01/12 11:36	3.1
2015/01/13 16:04	0.5
2015/01/13 16:04	0.5
2015/01/14 11:33	1.7
2015/01/14 13:10	1.1
2015/01/15 09:36	−1.0
2015/01/15 10:11	0.4
2015/01/15 18:17	−1.3
2015/01/15 22:50	0.5
2015/01/15 22:54	0.1
2015/01/16 00:09	0.2
2015/01/30 10:16	−0.6
2015/02/17 09:21	−1.1
2015/02/19 12:55	0.4

Magnitude is M_{Lg} for magnitude ≥1.1 events, and M is computed from the maximum amplitude on portable station COLI for smaller events.

of the swarm. It is can be confirmed from Table 4 that events with $M < -1.0$ were heard by local residents. Shocks at night as small as M 0.4 appear to have awakened some persons, according to reports from the residents. These thresholds are very similar to those that were reported in some shallow microearthquake swarms at Moodus, Connecticut, in the 1980s (Ebel, 1989). In the Moodus swarms, Ebel (1989) reported that events as small as coda magnitude $M_c - 1.0$ were heard and as small at M_c 1.0 were felt by persons living within about 2 km of the epicenters, with the largest events in those swarms, those above about M_c 2.0, being felt at greater epicentral distances. Although the coda magnitude scale used at Moodus has not been calibrated to the amplitude magnitudes computed for the Plainfield swarm, broadly speaking, it appears that the felt and heard magnitude thresholds for both swarms were approximately similar. Both swarms occurred within about 2.4 km of the Earth's surface, which is a strong indication that the felt and heard magnitude thresholds are controlled by the very shallow focal depths of the events.

Another indication of the sounds generated by these earthquakes comes from an infrasound recording of the M_{Lg} 3.1 earthquake on 12 January at the closest EarthScope TA station L63A (Fig. 7) at an epicentral distance of 26 km. The infrasound instrument detected small signals associated with the passages of the *P*, *S*, and *Lg* waves, and then it detected a much larger acoustic signal at the time the sound wave from the event reached the station (Fig. 7). This confirms that the events at Wauregan were putting significant acoustic energy into the atmosphere, something that is not unusual for events with depths of focus of about 2 km or less in the New England region (Ebel, 2019).

Analyses of Local Gravity and Magnetic Data

We conducted a gravity survey over a roughly 60 km^2 area around the quarry to investigate the subsurface structure near the site of the 2015 Plainfield earthquake swarm. A total of 113 measurements are recorded with ~600 m spacing along public roads. Relative gravity measurements are obtained with a LaCoste and Romberg model G-1189 gravimeter with an Aliod100 upgrade. The system has a range of ±50 mGal with a resolution of 0.01 mGal. Elevations were determined to 1-m accuracy using available light detection and ranging elevation data for the area. Base station recordings are taken every two hours to account for instrumental drift and diurnal variation associated with sun and moon tides. The gravity data were reduced with drift, latitude, free-air, and simple Bouguer corrections.

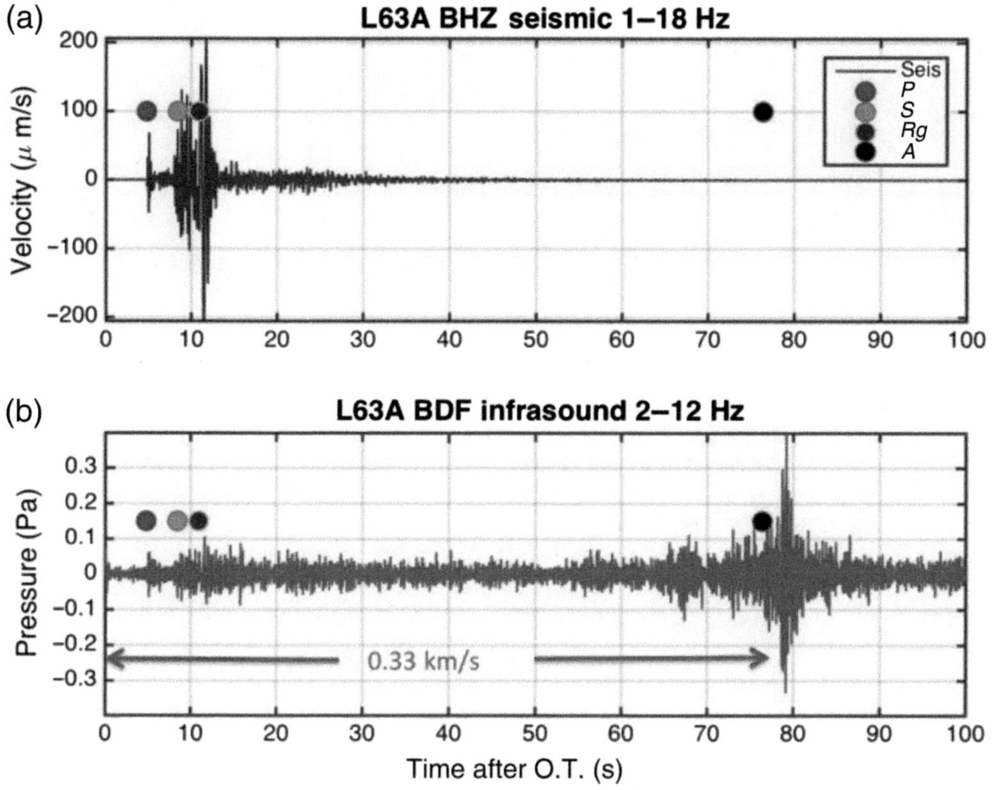

Figure 7. (a) Seismic velocity and (b) infrasound measurements at N4 station L63A for the M_{Lg} 3.1 Plainfield, Connecticut, event on 12 January 2015 at 11:36 UTC. The top trace is the vertical-component seismogram, whereas the bottom is the infrasound signal. On both traces, the times of the *P*, *S*, *Rg*, and sound arrivals are indicated. The color version of this figure is available only in the electronic edition.

A contour map of the reduced gravity data is shown in Figure 8a. The gravity data were interpolated using an inverse distance weighting (IDW) interpolation technique, an ArcMap 3D analyst tool. Also shown in Figure 8b is a map of local aeromagnetic field data from Zietz *et al.* (1974). On both maps, faults from Rodgers, 1985 and Dixon (1965, 1968) are shown.

The calculated relative gravity values in Figure 8a tend to decrease from west to east across the survey area. The maximum gravity value is seen in the SW corner of the area surveyed, and the minimum value is in the NE. The southwestern part of the map in Figure 8a likely shows increased gravity values due to the mapped presence of a diopside-rich layer of the Black Hill Member, which is a fine-grained oligoclase schist of the Quinnebaug Formation (Dixon, 1965). This part of the Black Hill Member outcrops just south of the southwestern extent of the survey area, but it probably lenses out to the north (N) and south (S). The formation on the east side of the Lake Char fault is primarily composed of the medium-grained Alaskite gneiss, which is likely of lower density than most of the Quinnebaug Formation, based on its relatively light mineral content. A lower gravity region is apparent on the east side of Figure 8a and appears to trend N-S, approximately on strike with the Lake Char fault system. Profile AB in Figure 8a across the extrapolated extent of the NW-SE-trending unnamed fault shows a strong gravity gradient from SW to NE, perhaps suggesting a steeply dipping fault on-strike with the fault mapped farther to the NW. The dip angle of the Lake Char fault is not clearly defined using the gravity data, but based on published information, its dip is probably about 25° to the west in this part of Connecticut (Castle *et al.*, 1976).

The data in Figure 8a,b provide evidence that the SE-trending unnamed fault in this area may extend all the way to the Wauregan quarry, as inferred in Figure 8. The gravity gradient along profile AB is consistent with a steeply dipping fault, as noted in the previous paragraph. The regional aeromagnetic data of Figure 8b has a magnetic ridge just west of the Wauregan quarry that appears to be sinistrally offset along the SE projection of this fault, although a sinistral offset is not apparent in the magnetic field farther to the NW. Melvin *et al.* (1995) noted that in this part of Connecticut, there are some NW-SE-trending, steeply dipping faults that are younger than the older Lake Char fault system. The gravity and magnetic data of Figure 8 suggest that the WNW-ESE fault mapped to the NW of Wauregan could be a steeply dipping fault that extends SE all the way to the Wauregan quarry.

Modeling Stress Changes on Faults near Wauregan Tilcon Quarry

Changes in the shear and normal stresses on thrust and strike-slip faults near the quarry in Plainfield as a result of crustal unloading have been investigated in this study. Because the removal of the rock due to the quarrying operations left a negative surface load at the quarry, Boussinesq's problem, which computes the stress tensor in an elastic half-space due to a vertical surface point load, can be used (Selvadurai, 2001). As given by Athanasopoulos (2021) and using the geometry shown in Figure 9, the following equations were used to calculate the normal and shear stresses in cylindrical coordinates at a point X beneath the surface due to a point force P at coordinates (0, 0, 0) on the earth's surface:

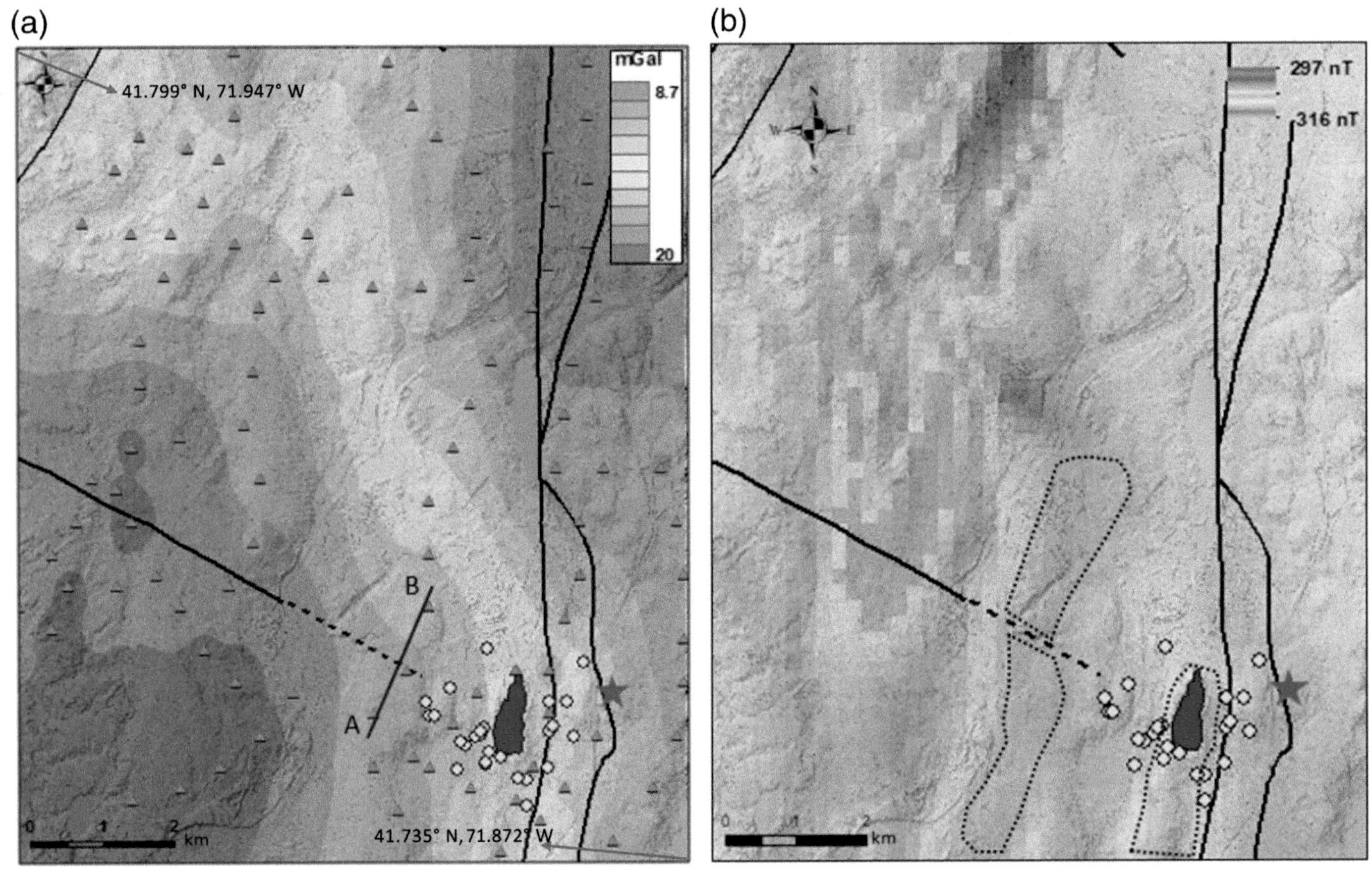

$$\sigma_z = \frac{3P}{2\pi z^2} \times \left[\frac{1}{1 + (r/z)^2}\right]^{5/2} = \frac{P}{z^2} \times P_z, \tag{1}$$

$$P_z = \frac{3}{2\pi} \times \left[\frac{1}{1 + (r/z)^2}\right]^{\frac{5}{2}}, \tag{2}$$

$$\sigma_r = \frac{P}{2\pi} \times \left[\frac{3r^2 z}{(r^2 + z^2)^{\frac{5}{2}}} - \frac{1 - 2v}{r^2 + z^2 + z(r^2 + z^2)^{\frac{1}{2}}}\right], \tag{3}$$

$$\sigma_\theta = -\frac{P}{2\pi}(1 - 2v) \times \left[\frac{z}{(r^2 + z^2)^{3/2}} - \frac{1}{r^2 + z^2 + z(r^2 + z^2)^{1/2}}\right], \tag{4}$$

$$\tau_{rz} = \frac{3P}{2\pi} \times \left[\frac{rz^2}{(r^2 + z^2)^{\frac{5}{2}}}\right], \tag{5}$$

in which v is the Poisson's ratio of the earth. Note that $\tau_{\theta z} = 0$ and $\tau_{r\theta} = 0$ in the cylindrical coordinate system of the calculations, as shown in Figure 9.

Figure 8. (a) Simple Bouguer anomaly over a hillshade map processed from the 113 gravity measurements (green triangles) collected in the area of Wauregan, Connecticut. The gravity data along line AB are the gravity profile used to calculate the dip of the northwest–southeast (NW-SE)-trending fault. Note that the lowest gravity value is 8.7 mgal and the highest value is 20 mgal. (b) Historic aeromagnetic data (Zietz *et al.*, 1974) over a hillshade map around the survey area in Wauregan, Connecticut. The black-dotted lines enclose a local high in the aeromagnetic field that appears to be sinistrally offset. Note that the lowest magnetic value is 297 nT and the highest magnetic value is 316 nT. In both plots, the black-solid lines represent mapped faults from Rodgers (1985), and the black-dashed line is the proposed southeastern extent of the NW-SE-trending fault based on the geophysical data in these two figures. Strands of the Lake Char fault are labeled LCF, and the unnamed fault to the NW of the quarry is labeled UF. The arrow with the letters WTQ points to the Wauregan Tilcon quarry site. In both maps, the epicenters are those from Kondas (2020). The color version of this figure is available only in the electronic edition.

The total surface load of the quarried rock can be represented as a set of vertical point loads distributed over the quarry area. For each position in the subsurface, the stress tensor due to a point load P on the surface can be calculated using equations (1)–(5), and then the stress tensor for that subsurface position can be rotated into a coordinate system that is common for all of the subsurface positions. Because of linearity, the stress tensors due to the individual point forces at different surface

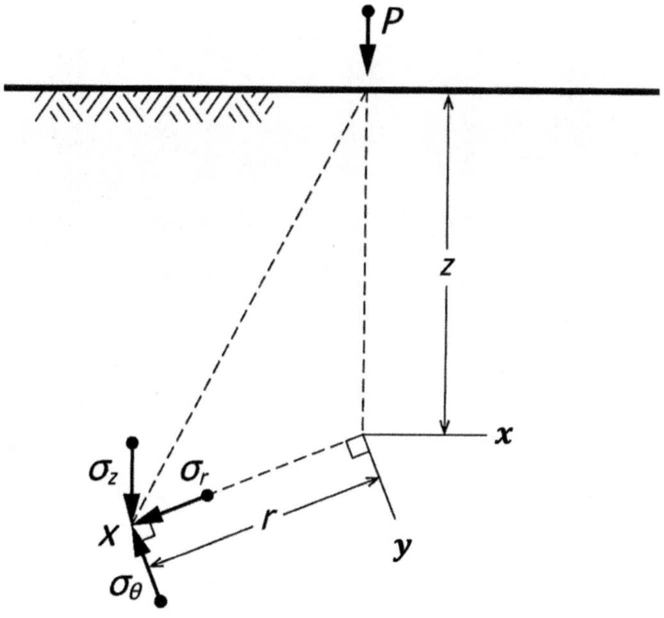

Figure 9. Cylindrical coordinate system for the calculation of the stresses at a subsurface point X at coordinates (r, θ, z). The origin of the coordinate system is at the surface of the earth beneath the arrow with the z coordinate being positive downward. The directions of the normal stresses σ_r, σ_θ, and σ_z are also shown in the figure. From Athanasopoulos (2021).

locations can be added together at each subsurface position to find the total stress tensor from the distributed surface load at that subsurface position. At each subsurface position, the total stress tensor can then be rotated to find the shear and normal stresses for any fault orientation at that spot in the earth. The resulting stresses represent the changes in the stress tensor, and therefore the shear and normal stresses, due to the entire surface load for that fault orientation.

The Wauregan Tilcon quarry covers an area of approximately 1.6×10^5 m^2, from which about 4.05×10^6 m^3 of rock was removed. Using a rock density of 2.79 Mg/m^3, it is estimated that the total rock load removed during quarrying operations is approximately 1.1×10^{11} N. To model the removed rock load in the quarry with surface point sources, the area of the quarry was approximated by a rectangular shape 250-m wide (in the E-W direction) and 500-m long (in the N-S direction). A total of 1326 point source locations (26 × 51 source locations) were used, with each location having a downward force of -8.37×10^7 N, in which the negative sign represents an upward force due to the rock removal. Stress tensors were computed at 10-m increments across an area of 3500 m E-W and 2500 m N-S, with the quarry near the center of this area and from the surface to a depth of 2000 m to cover the depth range of all of the events in Table 3. For the stress calculations, a Poisson's ratio of 0.25 was assumed. The stresses that are calculated in this study are in addition to the regional stresses in this area (Ebel and Kafka, 1991), with the maximum horizontal stress $S_{H\max}$ oriented approximately E-W, the minimum horizontal stress $S_{h\min}$ oriented approximately N-S, and the vertical stress being the least principal stress for the thrust earthquake focal mechanisms in this region.

Two different sets of calculations were carried out. In the first set, the shear and normal stresses for faults parallel to the orientation of the Lake Char fault were calculated. The fault is assumed to dip at 25° to the west (Castle *et al.*, 1976), and the stresses for pure thrust faulting were found. An E-W depth section of the change in shear stress is shown in Figure 10a down to a depth of 200 m, with Figure 10b showing that the normal stress decreases by a value approximately four times that of the shear stress decrease (promoting thrust failure) along a substantial portion of the Char Lake fault. This means that at most points beneath and to the east of the quarry, the Coulomb stress change moves the rock closer to failure on some thrust faults, like the Lake Char fault, if the static friction is assumed to be 0.7. Beneath and east of the quarry, thrust faulting on faults parallel to the Lake Char fault is enhanced, with the greatest enhancements taking place in the immediate vicinity of the quarry itself. The greatest changes in shear and normal stresses are approximately 28 and 65 MPa, respectively, at the quarry itself, and these changes in stress decay rapidly as depth increases (Fig. 10b). At 2000 m depth, the stress change due to the extraction of the rock from the quarry is about 20% of the maximum stress changes at the quarry itself. These calculations indicate that the extraction of the rock from the quarry would move the stress field closer to failure in thrust earthquakes on Lake Char-parallel faults beneath and east of the quarry, with the greatest chance for such earthquakes being closest to the quarry.

The second set of stress calculations looked at the stress enhancements for faults parallel to the projected WNW-ESE vertical unnamed fault that is mapped NW of the quarry assuming that this fault runs in the subsurface to the quarry itself (i.e., Fig. 8). Such faults could be reactivated as left-lateral strike-slip events if the removal of the quarry load reduces $S_{h\min}$ enough that its magnitude drops below the vertical stress. The shear stress modeling in Figure 11a shows that the events west of the quarry appear to be approximately equally distributed between areas of enhanced left-lateral movement and areas of enhanced right-lateral movement on surfaces parallel to the projected WNW-ESE vertical unnamed fault. Similarly, the normal stress modeling in Figure 11b shows that the events west of the quarry appear to be approximately equally distributed between areas of enhanced fault-normal compression and areas of enhanced fault-normal extension on surfaces parallel to the projected WNW-ESE vertical unnamed fault. Thus, it does not appear that the rock removal from the quarry enhanced left-lateral shear motion on the projected WNW-ESE vertical unnamed fault.

The stress modeling shown in Figures 10 and 11 suggests that subsurface stress changes due to rock removal from the quarry could explain thrust faulting on faults parallel to the Lake Char fault east of and beneath the quarry, but it cannot

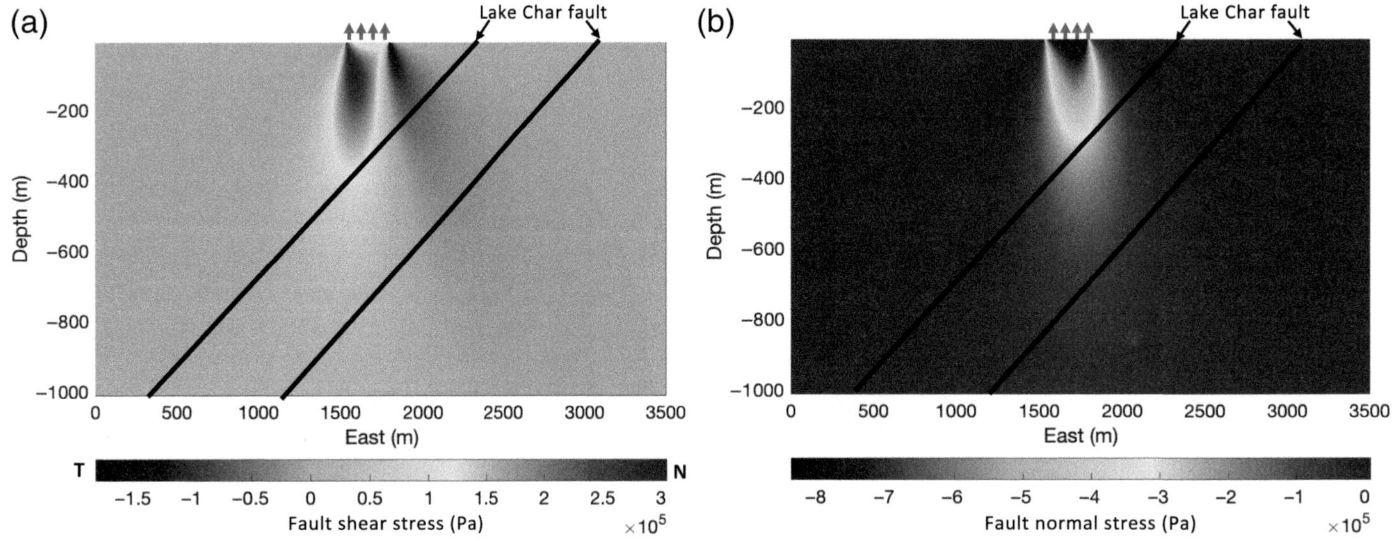

Figure 10. (a) Modeled cross-section of the change of shear stress on 25° west-dipping faults parallel to the west-dipping Lake Char fault for a negative load of 1.1×10^{11} N due to removal of surface rock at the quarry site. The upward arrows show the location of the quarry. A negative shear stress indicates enhanced thrust faulting due to the removal of the rock in the quarry. The two strands of the Lake Char fault shown in Figure 5 are projected into this cross section (note the great vertical exaggeration). (b) Modeled cross-section of the change of normal stress on 25° west-dipping faults parallel to the west-dipping Lake Char fault for a negative load of 1.1×10^{11} N due to removal of surface rock at the quarry site. The upward arrows show the location of the quarry. A negative normal stress indicates reduced normal stress on fault surfaces parallel to the Lake Char fault due to the removal of the rock in the quarry. The two strands of the Lake Char fault shown in Figure 5 are projected into this cross section (note the great vertical exaggeration). The color version of this figure is available only in the electronic edition.

explain the events that are located west of the quarry as either thrust motion on Lake Char-parallel faults or strike-slip motion on vertical faults west of the quarry. According to King *et al.* (1994), it appears that static Coulomb stress changes as low as 10 kPa can trigger seismicity. Given this criterion, thrusting movement on faults parallel to the trend of the Lake Char fault might have been induced anywhere out to about 1 km east of the quarry and to a depth of about 1600 m due to rock extraction. For the seismicity west of the quarry, the stress analysis of Figure 11 does not suggest that strike-slip faulting would have been induced by the extraction of rock from the quarry. In addition, the stress analysis does not support stress changes that could have induced thrust faulting on surfaces parallel to the Lake Char fault west of the quarry. On the other hand, thrust faulting west of the quarry might have been induced on fault surfaces that dip toward the east, although no such fault surfaces have been reported in the geological literature.

Discussion

The possibility that the Wauregan swarm was induced by the quarry

It is clear from Figure 5 that the earthquakes of the 2015 Plainfield swarm took place immediately around the abandoned Wauregan Tilcon quarry. The quarry, which produced crushed stone for road construction, was closed in 2011 after about 40 yr of operation and had been inactive since then. Recent images of the quarry on Google Maps show that the bottom of the quarry is dry. The possibility that quarries might induce some earthquakes in the northeastern United States has been a consideration since the study of Pomeroy *et al.* (1976) of a small earthquake that took place beneath a surface quarry in Wappinger Falls, New York, in 1974.

M. Chapman (personal comm., 2024) reported on a swarm of earthquakes near a quarry in Columbus, Georgia, in 1982. An article by Jones *et al.* (1985) discusses this swarm, but that article does not link the swarm to the quarry. On the other hand, M. Chapman (in an email to the first author dated 25 July 2024) had gone to the quarry during the swarm and was informed by the quarry employees that a large crack had formed in the floor of the quarry at the time of the earthquakes. M. Chapman heard and felt some of the swarm events during his time visiting the quarry, and the local residents were convinced that the largest event of the swarm had originated from the quarry itself. In many ways, the swarm of earthquakes at Columbus, Georgia, in 1982 is similar to the 2015 Plainfield earthquake swarm. In the same email just discussed, M. Chapman (personal comm., 2024) stated that an earthquake swarm in December 2017 apparently originated at a limestone quarry near Dickensonville, Virginia. There is no published article on that swarm, but seismic instrumentation installed at the quarry confirmed that the swarm was centered on the quarry property. In both of these cases, the earthquake swarms took place at active quarries.

It is interesting to compare the seismicity at the Wauregan quarry with earthquake activity suspected to have been induced by quarrying at Wappingers Falls in 1974 (Pomeroy *et al.*, 1976),

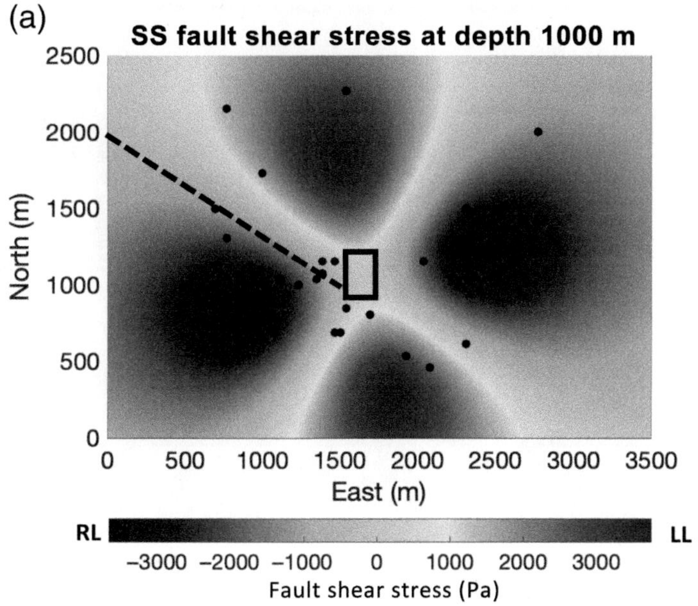

Figure 11. Modeled map view of the stress changes on vertical faults parallel to the projected NW-SE fault (dashed line) into the area of the quarry. The calculated stress changes are due to the negative load of 1.1×10^{11} N from the removal of surface rock at the quarry site (black rectangle). The dots in the figure show the epicenters of the well-located earthquakes of the swarm as shown in Figure 5 and listed in Table 3. (a) Horizontal shear stress changes at a depth of 1000 m on vertical faults parallel to the projected NW-SE fault. A negative shear stress indicates enhanced right-lateral strike-slip (SS) faulting (RL), whereas a positive shear stress indicates enhanced left-lateral strike-slip faulting (LL). (b) Horizontal normal stress changes at a depth of 1000 m on vertical faults parallel to the projected west-north-west–east-southeast (WNW-ESE) fault. A positive normal stress indicates increased normal stress on WNW-ESE vertical faults, whereas a negative normal stress indicates decreased normal stress on NW-SE vertical faults. The color version of this figure is available only in the electronic edition.

at Cacoosing Valley, Pennsylvania, in 1994 (Seeber *et al.*, 1998), and at a cement quarry in Le Teil, France, in 2019 (De Novellis *et al.*, 2020). The magnitude of the largest of the Wappingers Falls earthquakes was m_b 3.3, at Cacoosing was $m_b(Lg)$ 4.6, and at Le Teil was M_w 4.9. The Wappingers Falls and Cacoosing earthquakes were followed by very active aftershock sequences, whereas only a few aftershocks and one foreshock were reported by De Novellis *et al.* (2020) around the time of the Le Teil earthquake. Almost all of the aftershocks following the largest event at Wappingers Falls and Cacoosing were located beneath each quarry at depths of about 2 km or less, whereas the aftershocks of the Le Teil earthquake were located outside the quarry limits.

Table 5 lists some of the characteristics of the quarrying activities at the four quarries at the time of the earthquakes. The Le Teil quarry had the largest volume of extracted rock and the largest earthquake, whereas the smallest volume of extracted rock and the smallest magnitude was at the Wauregan and Cacoosing quarries. The average surface stress change due to the removed rock is nearly the same for the Wappingers Falls and the Wauregan quarries, and it is larger for the Le Teil quarry but smaller for the Cacoosing quarry. For Le Teil, Wappingers Falls, and Wauregan, the epicenters of the largest events were located outside the quarries by 1500–3000 m, although it is not known whether this reflects the actual event locations or is simply due to biases in the event locations using data from regional seismic network stations. Seeber *et al.* (1998) do not present the location of the mainshock epicenter at Cacoosing. Quarrying operations were ongoing at the Le Teil and Wappingers Falls quarries at the time of the earthquakes, whereas they had stopped at Cacoosing and Wauregan before the largest earthquakes occurred. Of these four quarries, only the Cacoosing had filled with water, and the largest earthquakes took place about the time that the quarry had completed filling with water, about 1.5 yr after the quarry stopped mining operations.

From Table 5, it appears that for the three dry quarries, the size of the largest earthquakes is related to the amount of rock excavated. On the other hand, although the amount of rock excavated from the Cacoosing and Wauregan quarries was comparable and less than the rock taken from the other two quarries, the largest earthquake at Cacoosing was much larger than the largest earthquake at either Wauregan or Wappingers Falls. The size of the largest earthquake at Cacoosing is perhaps due to an increase in subsurface pore pressure from the water that had filled the Cacoosing quarry (Seeber *et al.*, 1998). In addition, it should be noted that the earthquakes at Wappingers Falls, Cacoosing, and Wauregan were followed by very active aftershock sequences, with the events all being within about 2 km of the surface and being within 100s of meters or so beneath the quarries in all three cases. De Novellis *et al.* (2020) do not discuss the aftershock activity at Le Thiel. Finally, the earthquakes at Le Teil and Wauregan appear to have taken place on local

TABLE 5
Quarry Characteristics at Time of Earthquake

Quarry Parameter	Le Teil ~1830–Present*	Cacoosing 1934–1992†	Wappingers Falls ~1910–Present‡	Wauregan ~1970–2011§
Dates of quarrying, surface area of quarry (m^2)	1×10^6	8×10^5	1×10^6	1.6×10^5
Volume of extracted rock (m^3)	4.2×10^7	4×10^6	2.5×10^7	4.0×10^6
Total force of extracted rock (N)	1.1×10^{12}	1.1×10^{11}	7×10^{11}	1.1×10^{11}
Average stress (total force/quarry area) (kPa)	1100	138	700	690
Magnitude of the largest earthquake	M_w 4.9	$m_b(Lg)$ 4.6	m_b 3.3	M_{Lg} 3.1
Distance to the largest event epicenter (m)	3000	0–1000	1500	1500

*De Novellis *et al.* (2020).
†Seeber *et al.* (1998).
‡Pomeroy *et al.* (1976).
§This study.

geologic structures that are favorably oriented for failure in the local modern stress fields. The earthquakes at Cacoosing have focal mechanisms that suggest failures on a fault plane that is parallel to a local minor fracture set. Pomeroy *et al.* (1976) do not find any local faults or other geologic structures to explain the fault orientation for the Wappingers Falls earthquake, although they note that the event's focal mechanism is similar to the focal mechanisms of earthquakes in other parts of the same region.

At Wauregan, the delay of the 2015 seismicity until after the quarrying activities had ceased needs to be explained if the earthquakes were induced by the rock removal from the quarry. One possible explanation is that the delayed swarm following the cessation of quarry operations might have been due to failure by static fatigue associated with the removal of the rock during earlier quarrying (e.g., Cruden, 1974; Amitrano and Helmstetter, 2006; Cerfontaine and Collin, 2017). Studies of rocks stressed up to but just below their failure stress show that the rocks can fail at some time in the future due to diffuse micro-fracturing and decohesion of the rock structure (Cerfontaine and Collin, 2017). The time delay between the application of the constant stress load and the failure of the rock depends on how far below the failure stress the constant stress load is, with the smaller the difference between these two stresses, the shorter the time between the application of the stress load and rock failure. Static fatigue might explain the time difference between the end of quarrying operations and the 2015 earthquake swarm. Static fatigue has long been a concern for mining activities, particularly underground mining (Zhou *et al.*, 2021).

One final point to note is that the evidence from Wappingers Falls, Cacoosing, and Le Teil suggests that quarrying does not trigger continuous earthquake activity, but rather, for quarries that operate over many decades, earthquakes occur sporadically with periods of quiescence between the events. At Wappingers Falls, before the 1974 earthquake, there were events in 1926, 1951, and 1952 (Pomeroy *et al.*, 1976). At Le Teil, no earthquakes within about 30 km of the mine before 2019 are known during the almost 190 yr that the mine has been active (De Novellis *et al.*, 2020). At Cacoosing, Seeber *et al.* (1998) noted that the only previous earthquakes were in 1954–1955, which they argue may have been on the same fault as the 1994 events and may have been triggered by the onset of large-scale rock removal in the early 1950s.

Pomeroy *et al.* (1976), Seeber *et al.* (1998), and De Novellis *et al.* (2020) all implicate the stress perturbation due to the removal of the rock load during quarrying activities as their explanation of the earthquake activity at the respective quarries that they studied. The same implication could be drawn in this study for the 2015 earthquake activity around the Wauregan Tilcon quarry. The evidence from these four quarries suggests that if quarrying does induce earthquakes, it does not generate continuous earthquake activity but rather is associated with episodic earthquakes that can be separated in time by several decades.

Association with the local geology

As noted earlier, the 2015 Plainfield mainshock and most of the aftershocks during the first few days after the mainshock appear to align with the local orientation of the surface trace of the Lake Char fault. As described by Goldstein and Hepburn (1999), the Lake Char fault system divides late Precambrian gneisses and quartzites from metasedimentary and metavolcanic rocks that are probably of early Paleozoic age. With a dip to the west in the Plainfield area, the fault appears to have originally been a thrust fault but was reactivated in late Paleozoic time with normal faulting. Some later-stage normal faulting may also have taken place on this fault. The NNE-SSW strike of the Lake Char fault in the Plainfield area means that the fault has an optimal orientation to be reactivated today as a thrust fault in the modern regional stress field, which exhibits a maximum stress direction that is approximately E-W in southeastern New England (Ebel and Kafka, 1991). On the other hand, regional seismic network monitoring since 1975 has detected no other earthquakes from the vicinity of the Lake Char fault other than the events in 2014 and 2015, all of which took place around the Wauregan Tilson quarry. Based on this evidence, it is difficult to argue that the Lake Char fault could be seismically active.

As seen in Figure 5b,c, the WNW-ESE trend of the later events in the Wauregan swarm suggests that a WNW-ESE unnamed fault may also have been active during the swarm. These events align on-strike with a fault that runs from Stetson Corner to Wauregan, as shown in the Connecticut state bedrock map (Rodgers, 1985). The evidence in the gravity and magnetic field analyses of Figure 8, combined with the location of some of the 2015 seismicity, supports the argument that this fault extends farther to the SE than shown on the state bedrock map, based on the WNW-ESE lineation of the events in Figure 5b,c. This fault appears to be a steeply dipping fault that may have some left-lateral displacement on it. Unfortunately, focal mechanisms cannot be determined for any of the 2015 events in this WNW-ESE trend, and so the style of faulting associated with these events is unknown.

Implications for seismic hazard

The results of the analyses of the Plainfield earthquake swarm reported in this study have implications for assessments of the seismic hazard of northeastern North America. One implication comes from the possible association of the earthquake swarm with the Wauregan Tilcon quarry in Connecticut in 2015 and its similarity to the earthquakes at Cacoosing Valley in Pennsylvania in 1994 that appear to have been associated with a quarry there. In both cases, it is possible that stress perturbations were sufficient to induce the earthquake activity. If the shear stresses at these two quarries are very close to the failure stress of the rock, then the horizontal stress may be very close to the fracture stress in the upper crust throughout the region, something that has been inferred in other studies in the region (Hurd and Zoback, 2012). This would mean that small temporal perturbations in the local stress field anywhere in the region might be sufficient to trigger earthquakes. At Plainfield, Connecticut, the largest earthquake in that swarm was M_{Lg} 3.1, and at Cacoosing Valley, Pennsylvania, the largest earthquake was $m_b(Lg)$ 4.6. Even if very small shear-stress perturbations triggered the earthquake activity at these two quarries, it is not known if such small stress perturbations could have triggered larger earthquakes than the ones that took place.

A second implication for seismic hazard comes from the shallow focal depths of the earthquakes in the Plainfield and Cacoosing Valley swarms. The shallow focal depths imply that a high horizontal stress in the rocks must extend upward through the crust all the way to the surface. The 1989 Ungava Peninsula, Quebec, earthquake (M_s 6.3, M_w 5.3) was an earthquake that had surface faulting (Adams *et al.*, 1991) and that had a hypocentral depth of about 3 km (Bent, 1994). Similarly, the M_w 5.1 Sparta, North Carolina, earthquake in August 2020 was a shallow earthquake with observed surface faulting (Neves *et al.*, 2024). Clearly, these two earthquakes with surface faulting must have occurred in areas with a high horizontal stress within 3 km of the surface of the earth. One implication of these shallow, surface-rupturing events is that an earthquake of at least M_w 5.1 and perhaps larger might be considered possible in the uppermost crust of this part of Connecticut and probably more broadly in the northeastern United States.

The 2015 Plainfield earthquake swarm is far from the only such swarm to have taken place in northeastern North America, and several of these have been studied in some detail. There were four shallow earthquake swarms at Moodus, Connecticut, in the 1980s, each consisting of more than 100 events and lasting for a few to several months (Ebel, 1989). The largest event in these swarms was M_c 2.9, and the swarm events all took place within 2.4 km of the Earth's surface. There was an earthquake swarm at Bar Harbor, Maine, in 2006–2007 that was studied by Ebel *et al.* (2008). There were 41 events detected by the regional seismic network in this swarm, with the largest event being M_{Lg} 4.2. The events had high-amplitude *Rg* waves, and absolute focal depths for two of the shocks determined from portable instruments over the epicenters were less than 2 km. Ebel (2016) reported on a swarm of 21 small earthquakes, the largest of which was M_{Lg} 1.7, near Searsport, Maine, in 2011. These events had focal depths less than 2.7 km. More vigorous earthquake swarms were detected from McAdam, New Brunswick, in 2012 and 2015–2016 (Bent *et al.*, 2017). Over 150 earthquakes with magnitudes up to M_N 3.3 were detected from McAdam in these swarms. As with the other swarms mentioned here, the McAdam swarms were confined to a small volume of rock about 1–2 km on a side in lateral extent and no more than 1.2 km deep. Ebel (2022) reported on several other swarms of small, shallow earthquakes in Maine. In contrast to these shallow swarms, Jacobi and Ebel (2019) reported on several earthquake swarms that took place near Albany, New York, from 2007 to 2011. Each of these swarms consisted of a few to a couple of dozen events. The focal depths of these swarms were 6–24 km. None of these other swarms took place near quarries, indicating that earthquake swarms are part of the natural seismicity that occurs in the northeastern United States.

In addition to these onshore earthquake swarms, there was a swarm of 16 earthquakes offshore south of Nova Scotia and east of New England in 2012 that was detected by the onshore regional seismic networks. Napoli and Ebel (2017) studied this swarm and determined that the events had focal depths between 12 and 18 km. The spatial extent of these hypocenters was 2.7 by 2.4 km.

In all of the earthquake swarms described here, the swarm events appeared to spread out with time from the locations of the initial events. This suggests a growing zone of deformation in the fault zone that was active during each of the earthquake swarms. For all of these swarms, the maximum spatial extents of the swarms spread over a fault distance that would have given an earthquake of about M_w 5 if the entire fault zone had failed in a single large earthquake. Why each of these localities experienced several small shocks that spread out with time, rather than failing in one larger earthquake, is not known. It is also not known if a larger earthquake is possible at any of these localities.

Conclusions

The 2014–2015 Plainfield swarm of over 180 small earthquakes took place in the area immediately around the Wauregan Tilcon quarry. The earthquake occurred within about 2.0 km of the earth's surface, and events as small as M 0.0 were felt, and M −1.0 were heard by the local residents. The focal mechanism computed from the mainshock suggests thrusting on a plane that is parallel to the Lake Char fault system and subperpendicular to the regional maximum principal stress. The distribution of accurately located aftershocks appears to delineate rupture geometries corresponding to two subperpendicular trends: the shallowly west-dipping Lake Char fault complex that strikes 15°, and a steeply dipping fault trending WNW-ESE that strikes 123°. Results from a gravity survey are consistent with the notion that the Lake Char fault separates higher density metaigneous island arc rocks in the west from the Precambrian Alaskite gneiss to the east. Gravity and aeromagnetic data provide an updated estimate of the extent of the WNW-ESE-trending fault, supporting the interpretation that the fault may extend SE all the way to the quarry.

Subsurface stress change modeling due to the removal of the surface rock load in the quarrying process suggests that thrusting shear stresses would have been enhanced on fault surfaces parallel to the west-dipping Lake Char fault within about 1 km east of the quarry and down to a depth of about 1600 m. Under the assumption that the change in Coulomb failure stresses near the quarry exceeded the threshold of 10 kPa at which earthquakes might be induced. The stress modeling of the earthquakes west of the quarry cannot explain those events as being due to Coulomb stress changes, inducing strike-slip faulting on vertical faults or thrust faulting on west-dipping faults parallel to the trend of the Lake Char fault. Increased Coulomb stress for thrust faulting on east-dipping faults west of the quarry might be possible, but no such faults are reported in the geological literature. The delay of the Plainfield swarm until a few years after quarrying operations ended might be explained by the rock failure being caused by static fatigue.

In agreement with past studies, the results of this study show that seismic activity can occur near or at quarrying operations in specific settings with a favorable stress regime, fault orientations, and rock characteristics such as those that exist in the northeastern United States. On the other hand, this study does not show conclusive evidence that the quarrying operations induced the earthquakes or that quarrying operations can trigger a significant, damaging earthquake if indeed the smaller earthquakes can be induced by rock removal in the quarry.

Data and Resources

Regional seismic network data used in this work came from the Earthscope Data Management Center and are freely available from that center. Seismographic data from the four portable seismic instruments were collected by Weston Observatory of Boston College. The availability of those seismographic data is currently unclear. The gravity data for this project were collected by Weston Observatory of Boston College. The original gravity data can be acquired by contacting the first author of this article. All other data came from published sources. The supplemental material includes descriptions of the magnitude scales and seismic velocity models used in the analyses.

Declaration of Competing Interests

The authors acknowledge that there are no conflicts of interest recorded.

Acknowledgments

The authors have many people to thank for their participation in the data acquisition and data analysis. First, the authors thank Margaret Thomas, former State Geologist in Connecticut, whose office provided many logistical details for their field work and regularly visited the portable seismic instrumentation to collect the data from the instruments. Second, the authors thank those students who assisted with the installation of the portable instruments (Seun Fadubga and Steve Hilfiker) and who helped collect the gravity data (Achille Monad and Thomas Vezmar, both of whom were visiting interns from the University of Strasbourg in France). Third, the authors thank Bob Wintsch, who provided information about the local geology in the area of the earthquake swarm. Fourth, Ivan Wong and two anonymous reviewers, along with AE Oliver Boyd, for their careful and thoughtful reviews of several earlier versions of this article. Fifth, the authors want to say a special thanks to all the residents of the Wauregan area who provided Weston Observatory with information on the dates and times when small seismic events were felt and heard. This is a great example of citizen science at its best.

References

Adams, J., R. J. Wetmiller, H. S. Hasegawa, and J. Drysdale (1991). The first surface faulting from a historical intraplate earthquake in North America, *Nature* **352,** 617–618.

Amitrano, D., and A. Helmstetter (2006). Brittle creep, damage, and time to failure in rocks, *J. Geophys. Res.* **111,** B11201, doi: 10.1029/2005JB004252.

Athanasopoulos, G. A. (2021). Online lecture notes on soil mechanics, doi: 10.48246/GEOENG-EDU-001.

Bent, A. L. (1994). The 1989 (Ms 6.3) Ungava, Quebec, earthquake: A complex intraplate event, *Bull. Seismol. Soc. Am.* **84,** 1075–1088.

Bent, A. L., S. Halchuk, V. Peci, K. E. Butler, K. B. S. Burke, J. Adams, N. Dahal, and S. Hayek (2017). The McAdam, New Brunswick earthquake swarms of 2012 and 2015-2016: Extremely shallow, natural events, *Seismol. Res. Lett.* **89,** 1586–1600.

Castle, R. O., H. R. Dixon, E. S. Grew, A. Griscom, and I. Zietz (1976). Structural dislocations in eastern Massachusetts, *U.S. Geol. Surv. Bulletin 1410*, Washington, D.C.

Cerfontaine, B., and F. Collin (2017). Cyclic and fatigue behaviour of rock materials: Review, interpretation and research perspectives, *Rock Mech. Rock Eng.* doi: 10.1007/s00603-017-1337-5.

Cruden, D. M. (1974). The static fatigue of brittle rock under uniaxial compression, *Int. J. Rock Mech. Min. Sci. Geomech.* **11,** 67–73.

De Novellis, V., V. Convertito, S. Valkaniotis, F. Casu, R. Lanari, M. Tobar, and N. A. Pino (2020). Coincident locations of rupture nucleation during the 2019 Le Teil earthquake, France and maximum stress change from local cement quarrying, *Commun. Earth Environ.* **1,** 20, doi: 10.1038/s43247-202-00021-6.

Dixon, H. R. (1965). Bedrock geologic map of the Plainfield quadrangle, Windham and New London Counties, Connecticut, *U.S. Geol. Surv.*, Geologic Quadrangle Map GQ-481, scale 1:24,000.

Dixon, H. R. (1968). Bedrock geologic map of the Danielson quadrangle, Windham County, Connecticut, *U.S. Geol. Surv.*, Geologic Quadrangle Map GQ-696, scale 1:24,000.

Doglioni, C. (2018). A classification of induced seismicity, *Geosci. Frontiers* **9,** 1903–1909.

Ebel, J. E. (1985). A study of the seismicity and tectonics in New England, *U.S. Nuclear Regulatory Commission NUREG/CR-4354*, Washington, D.C., 88 pp.

Ebel, J. E. (1989). A comparison of the 1981, 1982, 1986 and 1987-1988 microearthquake swarms at Moodus, Connecticut, *Seismol. Res. Lett.* **60,** 177–183.

Ebel, J. E. (2016). An enigmatic little earthquake swarm near Searsport, Maine, *Seismol. Res. Lett.* **87,** 207–214.

Ebel, J. E. (2019). *New England Earthquakes: The Surprising History of Earthquakes in the Northeast*, Globe Pequot Press, Guilford, Connecticut, 304 pp.

Ebel, J. E. (2022). The earthquake swarms of eastern Maine and nearby New Brunswick, available at https://www.seismosoc.org/wp-content/uploads/2022/10/ES-SSA2022_ProgramAbstracts-1.pdf (last accessed September 2025), p. 14.

Ebel, J. E., and A. L. Kafka (1991). Earthquake activity in the northeastern United States, in *Neotectonics of North America*, D. B. Slemmons, E. R. Engdahl, M. D. Zoback, and D. D. Blackwell (Editors), The Geological Society of America, Decade Map, Boulder, Colorado, Vol. 1, 277–290.

Ebel, J. E., A. M. Moulis, D. Smith, and M. Hagerty (2008). The 2006-2007 earthquake sequence at Bar Harbor, Maine, *Seismol. Res. Lett.* **79,** 457–468.

Ebel, J. E., V. Vudler, and M. Celata (1982). The 1981 microearthquake swarm near Moodus, Connecticut, *Geophys. Res. Lett.* **9,** 397–400.

Foulger, G. R., M. P. Wilson, J. G. Gluyas, B. R. Julian, and R. J. Davies (2018). Global review of human-induced earthquakes, *Earth Sci. Rev.* **178,** 438–514, doi: 10.1016/j.earscirev.2017.07.008.

Gibowitz, S. J. (1982). The mechanism of large mining tremors in Poland, in *Proceedings of the International Congress on Rockbursts and Seismicity in Mines*, First Ed., N. C. Gay and E. H. Wainwright (Editors), 17–28.

Goldstein, A., and J. C. Hepburn (1999). Possible correlations of the Norumbega fault system with faults in southeastern New England, in *Norumbega Fault System in of the North Appalachians*, A. Ludman and D. P. West Jr. (Editors), Geological Society of America, Special Paper 331, Boulder, Colorado.

Gupta, H. K. (2002). A review of recent studies of triggered earthquakes by artificial water reservoirs with special emphasis on earthquakes in Koyna, India, *Earth Sci. Rev.* **58,** 279–310.

Hurd, O., and M. D. Zoback (2012). Intraplate earthquakes, regional stress and fault mechanics in the Central and Eastern U.S. and Southeastern Canada, *Tectonophysics* **581,** 182–192.

Jacobi, R. D., and J. B. Ebel (2019). Seismotectonic implications of the Berne earthquake swarms west-southwest of Albany, NY, *Lithosphere* **11,** 750–764, doi: 10.1130/L1066.1.

Jones, F. B., L. T. Long, K.-H. Zelt, and M. C. Chapman (1985). Columbus, Georgia, earthquakes of October 31, 1982, *Seismol. Res. Lett.* **56,** no. 2, 55–61, doi: 10.1785/gssrl.56.2.55.

Kafka, A. L. (1990). *Rg* as a depth discriminant for earthquakes and explosions: A case study in New England, *Bull. Seismol. Soc. Am.* **80,** 373–394.

King, G. C. P., R. S. Stein, and J. Lin (1994). Static stress changes and the triggering of earthquakes, *Bull. Seismol. Soc. Am.* **84,** 935–953.

Klein, F. W. (2002). User's Guide for HYPOINVERSE-2000, a Fortran program to solve for earthquake locations and magnitudes, *U.S. Geol. Surv. Open-File Rept. 02-171.*

Kondas, S. M. (2020). Crustal unloading as a source of induced seismicity in Plainfield, Connecticut, *Master's Thesis*, Department of Earth and Environmental Sciences, Boston College, 63 pp.

Melvin, R. L., J. R. Stone, P. A. Craft, and J. W. Lane Jr. (1995). Geohydrology of the Gallup's Quarry area, Plainfield, Connecticut, *Water-Resources Investig. Rept. 93-4138*, U.S. Geological Survey.

Napoli, V. J., and J. E. Ebel (2017). Relative location analysis and moment tensor inversion of the 2012 Gulf of Maine earthquake swarm, *Seismol. Res. Lett.* **89,** 229–240.

Neves, M., L. Y. Chuang, W. Li, Z. Peng, P. M. Figueiredo, and S. Ni (2024). Complex rupture dynamics of the extremely shallow August 2020 M 5.1 Sparta, North Carolina earthquake. *Commun. Earth Environ.* **5,** 163, doi: 10.1038/s43247-024-01316-8.

Pomeroy, P. W., D. W. Simpson, and M. L. Sbar (1976). Earthquake triggered by surface quarrying, the Wappinger Falls, New York, sequence of June 1974, *Bull. Seismol. Soc. Am.* **66,** 685–700.

Pulli, J. J. (2016). Analysis of the January, 2015, Plainfield, CT, earthquake sequence using waveform correlation techniques, *Seismol. Res. Lett.* **87,** 252.

Rodgers, J. (1985). Bedrock geological map of Connecticut, Connecticut Geological and Natural History Survey, Connecticut Natural Resources Atlas Series, scale 1:125,000, 2 sheets.

Seeber, L., J. G. Armbruster, W.-Y. Kim, N. Barstow, and C. Scharnberger (1998). The 1994 Cacooing Valley earthquakes near reading, Pennsylvania: A shallow rupture triggered by quarry unloading, *J. Geophys. Res.* **103,** 24,505–24,521.

Selvadurai, A. P. S. (2001). On Boussinesq's problem, *Int. J. Eng. Sci.* **39,** 317–322.

Skehan, J. W. (2008). *Roadside Geology of Connecticut and Rhode Island*, Mountain Press Publishing Company, Missoula, Montana.

Weingarten, M., S. Ge, J. W. Godt, B. A. Bekins, and J. L. Rubinstein (2015). High-rate injection is associated with the increase in U.S. mid-continent seismicity, *Science* **348,** 1336–1340.

Zhou, X., X. Pan, and F. Berto (2021). A state-of-the-art review on creep damage mechanics of rocks, *Fatigue Fract. Eng. Mater. Struct.* **45,** 627–652, doi: 10.1111/ffe.13625.

Zietz, I., J. R. Kirby Jr., and F. P. Gilbert (1974). Aeromagnetic map of Connecticut, *U.S. Geol. Surv. Geophys. Investig. Map GP-897*, scale 1:125,000.

Manuscript received 28 April 2025
Published online 6 January 2026

Electronic Seismologist

OPEN ACCESS

SURF: An Automated Method for Building Nonplanar 3D Fault Models from Earthquake Hypocenters

Travis Alongi*[1], Austin J. Elliott[1], Robert J. Skoumal[1], David R. Shelly[2], and Alexandra E. Hatem[2]

Abstract

Accurately characterizing 3D fault geometry is vital for improving our understanding of earthquake behavior and informing the development of seismic hazard models. Despite their importance, subsurface fault structures tend to be poorly constrained because of limitations in observational data. Improvements to the seismic networks and earthquake detection algorithms have increased the precision and volume of earthquake catalogs, which help illuminate detailed subsurface fault structure and provide the most direct information available about fault geometries at depth. We present a Python package to automate generating 3D fault geometries directly from hypocentral seismicity patterns. This method begins with clustering events based on their spatial density, identifying coherent patterns. Nearby clusters are then merged based on the similarity of their orientations. We fit nonplanar surfaces using support vector regression to balance surface accuracy with minimal deviations from planarity. The fault models are output as quadrilateral meshes at user-defined resolution. In the process of generating the 3D fault surfaces, we compute the spatial density of seismicity around the surface and the planarity as quantitative metrics of the model outputs.

As a proof of concept, we apply this approach to the San Andreas–Calaveras fault junction region and the 2019 Ridgecrest earthquake sequence, both in California, which contain complex subparallel faults well defined at the Earth's surface and abundant microseismicity. These case studies demonstrate the method's ability to model complex fault structures, including long continuous fault surfaces, crossing faults, variably dipping segments, and subparallel faults. We test the method on both standard network catalogs and double-difference relocated catalogs. We find that our seismicity-based fault model results align with published 3D models that incorporate additional constraints and interpretations (Plesch *et al.*, 2020; Aagaard and Hirakawa, 2021). This workflow provides a low-user-input solution for estimating fault geometries at depth from earthquake catalogs.

Cite this article as Alongi, T., A. J. Elliott, R. J. Skoumal, D. R. Shelly, and A. E. Hatem (2025). SURF: An Automated Method for Building Nonplanar 3D Fault Models from Earthquake Hypocenters, *Seismol. Res. Lett.* **97**, 1174–1190, doi: 10.1785/0220250126.

Supplemental Material

Introduction

The spatial distribution and magnitude of earthquakes depend on 3D fault structure, yet it is rarely known in detail. Earthquake hazard assessments rely on representations of fault locations and areas (Field *et al.*, 2014). Currently, the representations of faults, in many cases, are based on mapped surface traces and have limited dip information. This presents a problem because natural faults are nonplanar, are multistranded, and have variable dip both along strike and depth (Segall and Pollard, 1980; Carena *et al.*, 2002; Fletcher *et al.*, 2016; Ulrich *et al.*, 2019; Chu *et al.*, 2021; Alongi *et al.*, 2022, 2024). Furthermore, faults are often geometrically complex, featuring roughness, stepovers, and curvature (Willemse and

1. Earthquake Science Center, U.S. Geological Survey, Moffett Field, California, U.S.A., https://orcid.org/0000-0002-0865-8064 (TA); https://orcid.org/0000-0001-5924-7268 (AJE); https://orcid.org/0000-0002-5627-6239 (RJS); 2. Geologic Hazard Science Center, U.S. Geological Survey, Golden, Colorado, U.S.A., https://orcid.org/0000-0003-2783-5158 (DRS); https://orcid.org/0000-0001-7584-2235 (AEH)

*Corresponding author: talongi@usgs.gov

Pollard, 2000; Candela *et al.*, 2012; Candela and Brodsky, 2016) that can play an essential role in earthquake nucleation, propagation, and arrest (Poliakov *et al.*, 2002; Wesnousky, 2006; Lozos *et al.*, 2011; Hatem *et al.*, 2015; Cattania and Segall, 2021). Limited knowledge of 3D fault geometry restricts the predictive capabilities of earthquake hazard models and highlights the need for improved methods that can estimate fault geometry at depth.

Existing methods

The importance of 3D fault models has driven efforts such as the Statewide California Earthquake Center's Community Fault Model (CFM), which uses data that include surface traces, hypocentral distributions, well penetrations, seismic reflection profiles, and geologic cross sections to build 3D fault surfaces (Plesch *et al.*, 2007). However, these data-intensive models are often limited to well-studied regions such as southern California and require interpretive expertise. In less well-studied areas, seismicity trends can provide a uniform and data-driven alternative for identifying faults at depth.

Previous studies have explored various methods for determining 3D fault orientations from seismicity. Ouillon *et al.* (2008) laid the groundwork for this using clustering and principal component analysis to define planes. Subsequent work introduced Gaussian mixture models, probabilistic clustering, and Bayesian information criterion to improve fault detection accuracy (Wang *et al.*, 2013). Other studies have incorporated stochastic plane-fitting approaches to overcome shortcomings inherent to regression (e.g., L1- and L2-norm fits) as a way to better represent faults (Kaven and Pollard, 2013; Skoumal *et al.*, 2019). Other work has used Monte Carlo simulations to account for hypocentral uncertainty and focal mechanisms to assess fault orientation reliability (Truttmann *et al.*, 2023). Recently, the normal vectors of the nearest-neighbor events have been included in the clustering step (Sawaki *et al.*, 2025) as well as strain-rate-based fault reconstructions (Jourdon *et al.*, 2025). Although these methods have advanced fault characterization, they produce numerous small, disconnected planes, limiting their ability to capture larger, more continuous structures. Importantly, to our knowledge, existing methodologies assume planarity, preventing them from accurately representing the nonplanarity of typical fault surfaces. Our method directly addresses these limitations by building larger faults from small clusters of seismicity and applying a flexible nonplanar surface fitting technique.

Fault zones

Although nonplanar surfaces improve the representation of faults, it remains important to evaluate whether the modeled surfaces conform to what is known about fault zone structure. Fault zones are recognized as volumes of inelastic deformation, recorded both geologically—through features such as secondary fractures, cracks, and deformation bands—and geophysically via observations of rock properties and seismic velocity structure at depth (Caine *et al.*, 1996; Fialko, 2004; Li *et al.*, 2004; Chester *et al.*, 2005; Cochran *et al.*, 2009; Choi *et al.*, 2016; Alaei and Torabi, 2017; Scott *et al.*, 2018; Antoine *et al.*, 2021; Atterholt *et al.*, 2022; Cocco *et al.*, 2023). A consistent observation across studies is that the intensity of deformation, often approximated by fracture density or seismicity, tends to decay with distance from the principal slip zone (Shipton and Cowie, 2001; Berg and Skar, 2005; Faulkner *et al.*, 2010; Powers and Jordan, 2010; Savage and Brodsky, 2011; Perrin *et al.*, 2021; Alongi *et al.*, 2022, 2024; Rodriguez Padilla, Oskin, *et al.*, 2022). These patterns have been described using exponential or power law functions and provide a quantitative framework for assessing off-fault deformation. In this study, we use the decay of seismicity density with distance from a modeled fault surface as a proxy for deformation localization, enabling an appraisal of how well our surface-fitting method reproduces known fault zone characteristics.

This study

Many previous efforts to generate 3D fault representations have largely concentrated on improving clustering techniques and addressing hypocentral aleatory uncertainty. Here, we introduce the Seismicity Utilized for Reconstructing Faults (SURF) algorithm (Alongi and Skoumal, 2025) (see Data and Resources) for determining fault geometries from seismicity patterns. We build on prior work (Ouillon *et al.*, 2008; Kaven and Pollard, 2013; Wang *et al.*, 2013; Skoumal *et al.*, 2019), introducing a low-user-input approach to estimate fault geometries from seismicity patterns. Our method focuses on generating fault surfaces from numerous small, nearly coplanar clusters, which are then merged based on nearest-neighbor coplanarity. This approach allows us to model faults that are spatially continuous with variable geometry over large distances. We fit 3D nonplanar, semiparametric surfaces to the data, and the events near the modeled surface do not impact the misfit and effectively account for a finite damage zone width and location uncertainty. The result is a set of nonplanar fault geometries generated from seismicity patterns and requiring minimal user input. The detailed fault geometries and locations can be used to model rupture scenarios and may contribute to improving hazard assessments in both well-studied and underresearched regions.

Methods

The SURF algorithm is designed to build on and overcome the limitations of previous methods (Ouillon *et al.*, 2008; Kaven and Pollard, 2013; Wang *et al.*, 2013; Skoumal *et al.*, 2019), which produce numerous small and purely planar fault surfaces. Inspired by traditional mapping approaches, our method identifies clusters of seismicity based on spatial density and merges nearby clusters with similar orientations to create longer and more continuous faults. Unlike prior techniques that simplify fault geometries as planes, our approach

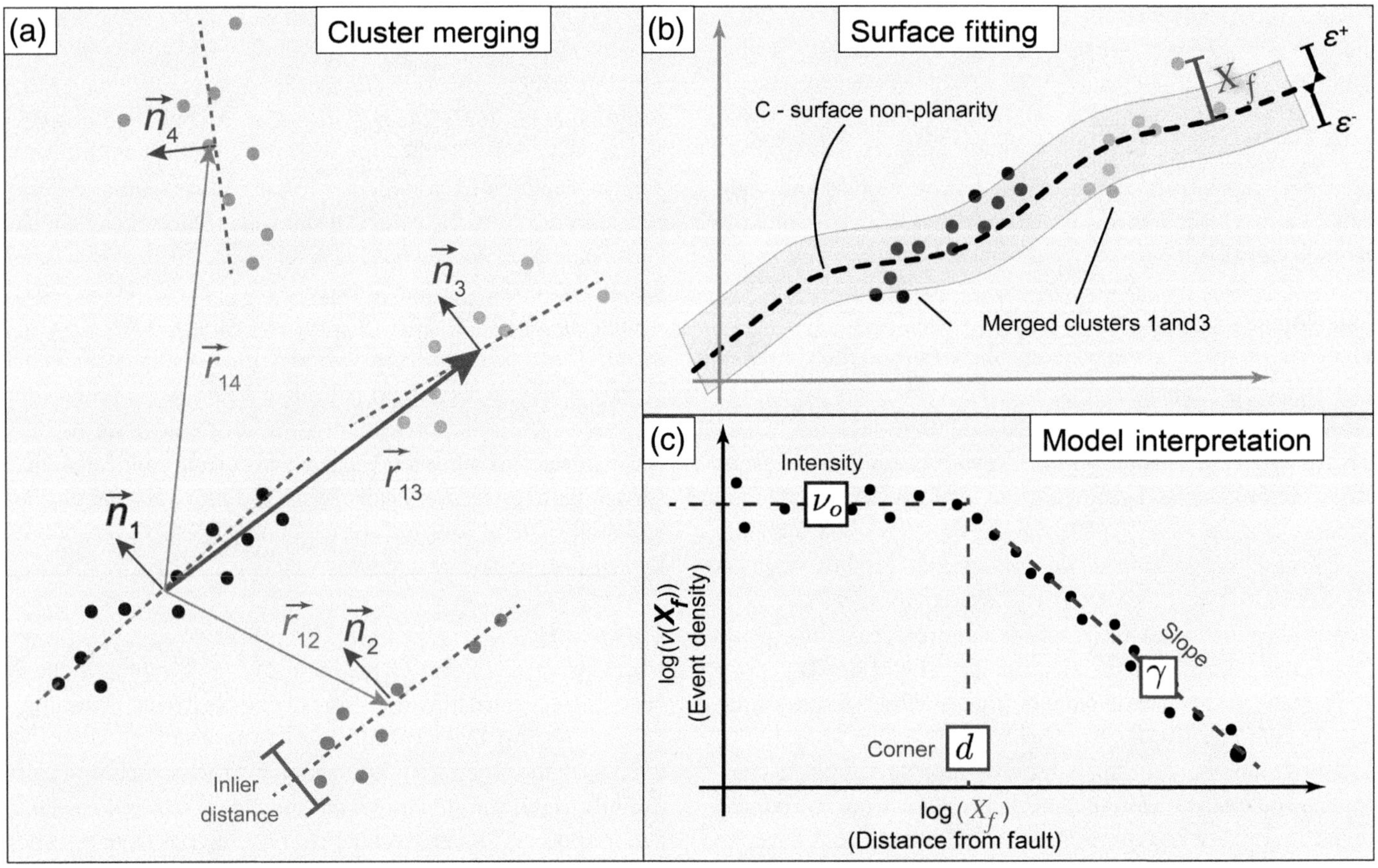

Figure 1. Schematic illustrating the key aspects of the seismicity utilized for reconstructing faults (SURF) algorithm. (a) The earthquake cluster merging process. First, each initial cluster (indicated by color) is fit with a plane using random sampling consensus to determine its normal vector $\vec{n}_i$. Next, the k, nearest-neighbor clusters ($k = 3$ in this example) are identified, and the direction vector $\vec{r}_{ik}$ to the kth cluster is calculated. Finally, normal vectors and direction vectors are used to construct the measurement matrix **M** (from equation 3), which quantifies the coplanarity of neighboring clusters and informs the merging process; see the main text for more details. (b) An illustration to help build intuition about the support vector regression (SVR) parameters C and ϵ. C describes how nonplanar the modeled fault surface is, with higher values indicating greater nonplanarity. Here, ϵ describes the length scale near the surface where points do not impact the fit. (c) A schematic to build intuition about the quality indicator parameters in equation (4). The equation fits a modified power law to the earthquake density as a function of distance from the fault surface (in log space). The color version of this figure is available only in the electronic edition.

independently fits each cluster with a nonplanar surface, allowing for more realistic fault geometries without imposing prior assumptions about their shape (Fig. 1).

Density-based clustering

The first step is to generate a spatial framework to build the faults around that is tied to active structures that are identified by where seismicity is spatially localized and clustered. To identify clusters, we use the hierarchical density-based spatial clustering of applications with noise (HDBSCAN) algorithm (Campello *et al.*, 2013) from the scikit-learn Python package (Pedregosa *et al.*, 2011). HDBSCAN is chosen for its ability to identify diverse, fault-like shapes, and it requires only one parameter, the minimum number of events to be considered a unique cluster. We find that setting the minimum cluster size to between 20 and 40 events ensures that clusters can be oriented while remaining small enough to merge in the next step. Note that clusters typically contain many more events than the minimum number, and this depends on the dataset. In our tests, the median number of events per cluster in is typically around 70–90.

Cluster merging

To extend fault lengths, we merge clusters with similar orientation that are nearly coplanar. Refer to Figure 1 for a schematic of the following steps.

Orientation assessment. To assess the coplanarity of clusters, we determine their orientations using a planar approximation. Here, we use a 3D implementation of the random sampling consensus algorithm (Fischler and Bolles, 1981). This stochastic method iteratively selects three earthquake hypocenters to create two vectors and compute their cross product, providing trial plane-normal vectors. Next, to assess which iteration provides the best fit, points are classified as inliers or outliers based on the distance from the trial plane. In this study, we use a distance threshold of 500 m, which is a typical absolute hypocentral depth uncertainty in California (typically greater than the horizontal location uncertainty) (Thurber *et al.*, 2003). The iteration with the greatest number of inliers is selected as the best fit. These best-fit orientations and the direction vectors to its nearest neighbors (calculated using k-dimensional [KD] tree; Bentley, 1975) provide a measure of coplanarity.

Coplanarity determination. To quantitatively assess coplanarity, we use the cluster's nearest-neighbor's normal vectors and direction vectors to calculate the following:

$$\vec{N} = \vec{n}_i \cdot \vec{n}_{jk}, \quad (1)$$

$$\vec{D} = \vec{n}_i \cdot \vec{r}_{jk}. \quad (2)$$

Here, $\vec{N}$ is the scalar dot product of the normal vector for the ith cluster with the normal vector j of k nearest neighbors. The value of $\vec{N}$ describes how similar the orientations of each cluster are with its nearest neighbors. $\vec{D}$ is the scalar dot product of the ith normal vector with the direction vector to k nearest neighbors; this quantity describes the coplanarity of pairs of clusters. Combining equations (1) and (2) provides a measure of coplanarity given by

$$\mathbf{M} = |\vec{N}| \times (1 - |\vec{D}|), \quad (3)$$

$\mathbf{M}$ ranges from 0 to 1, in which a value of 1 means that the pair i, k clusters are coplanar and 0 indicates that clusters are orthogonal, are on an adjacent parallel feature, or a combination of the two. We put a threshold on $\mathbf{M}$ to determine which clusters to combine. Clusters that do not meet the threshold are retained but are neither discussed nor displayed in this study.

Surface fitting

After merging clusters, we again use scikit-learn (Pedregosa *et al.*, 2011), this time to fit nonparametric surfaces to the data using support vector regression (SVR), a machine learning method based on support vector machines (SVMs) (Smola and Schölkopf, 2004; Bishop and Nasrabadi, 2006). Originally developed for classification, SVMs identify optimal decision boundaries by maximizing the margin between data classes. SVR extends this approach to regression tasks, predicting continuous values from inputs while allowing a margin of tolerance epsilon (ϵ) around the true values. The goal is to find a function that is as flat as possible while allowing deviations from the data within a specified distance ϵ and points outside this margin are penalized. The trade-off between flatness and tolerance for deviation is controlled by the parameter C. A small ϵ allows tighter fits to the data, whereas a larger C permits more complex surfaces that better capture outliers at the cost of smoothness.

We chose SVR for several reasons. It is nonparametric, meaning the surface is not restricted to a predefined shape and is instead guided directly by the data, avoiding assumptions about fault geometry. In addition, SVR's objective of maximizing flatness leads to smooth and simple surfaces that reflect the minimum complexity required to fit the data. During fitting, earthquakes that fall within the distance ϵ do not affect the regression, reducing sensitivity to location uncertainty and to diffuse seismicity within the broader damage zone. Moreover, the parameters C and ϵ can be selected through cross validation—a procedure in which the data are partitioned into training and validation sets to identify the values that generalize best to unseen data—minimizing the need for user tuning and reducing the risk of overfitting. Finally, the resulting surface can be discretized at any desired resolution and extrapolated beyond the data, making it a flexible tool for modeling fault geometry.

Model interpretation and hypocentral distributions

To help interpret the SURF algorithm's outputs, we measure the distribution of seismicity around the modeled fault surfaces. Measuring the hypocentral event density as a function of distance from the modeled surface may provide insights into the suitability or appropriateness of representing a volume of seismicity as a discrete fault surface. Specifically, we fit the distributions of seismicity around the modeled surfaces with a modified inverse power law relationship used in previous studies (Powers and Jordan, 2010; Perrin *et al.*, 2021; Rodriguez Padilla, Oskin, *et al.*, 2022; Rodriguez Padilla and Oskin, 2023). For each fault surface, we fit the equation first introduced in Powers and Jordan (2010) given by

$$v(x) = v_o \left(\frac{d^m}{|x|^m + d^m} \right)^{\frac{\gamma}{m}}. \quad (4)$$

Following Rodriguez Padilla, Oskin, *et al.* (2022), we use logarithmically spaced bins for x, in which $v(x)$ is the number of earthquakes in each bin, normalized by the bin width. The parameter d represents the distance from the fault where the inverse power law applies. The parameter m, controlling the sharpness of the distribution's corner at d, is set to 2, which is consistent with previous studies (Powers and Jordan, 2010; Rodriguez Padilla, Oskin, *et al.*, 2022). The power law exponent gamma (γ) describes the nonlinear decrease in event density with increasing distance from the fault to build some intuition (see the illustration in Figure 1). We fit equation (4) using maximum-likelihood estimation (MLE), assuming that $v(x)$ follows a Poisson distribution (Boettcher and Jordan, 2004; Powers and Jordan, 2010).

We evaluate the goodness of fit using mean relative error (MRE), which normalizes the misfit at each point by its estimated value,

$$\mathrm{MRE} = \frac{1}{n}\sum_{i=1}^{N}\frac{|v_{\mathrm{obs},i} - v_{\mathrm{fit},i}|}{v_{\mathrm{fit},i}}, \quad (5)$$

in which v_{obs} represents the data and v_{fit} is the MLE fit of the power law to the data. This provides a quantitative measure of the fit quality and is one component in discrimination between modeled faults with seismicity patterns that adhere to the power law scaling from those that do not. In addition to using the error in the fit to assess the modeled fault quality, we compare the parameters of the fit γ and d with what has been documented previously. Furthermore, we use the parameter C and ϵ from the SVR fit to provide information about the modeled surface as additional way to assess the quality. For more details about how modeled faults may be assessed, please refer to the Interpretation and evaluation section.

Results and Discussion

We applied the SURF algorithm to two different locations in California to test the robustness and versatility of our method. We find that the algorithm successfully identified long and continuous plate-boundary faults where epicenters are closely aligned with mapped surface traces. In addition, we find that documented subparallel fault strands are identified with the algorithm. The modeled results also feature several previously undocumented smaller secondary and variably oriented faults that are delineated by the seismicity patterns at depth.

San Juan Bautista, California

Our first test case focuses on the region south of the San Francisco Bay Area near the San Andreas fault (SAF) and Calaveras fault (CF) junction (Fig. 2). These two major faults creep variably within the bounds of the study region (e.g., Lienkaemper *et al.*, 2014). Two other faults are documented as active within the past 15,000 yr in the U.S. Geological Survey (USGS) Quaternary Fault and Fold Database (see Data and Resources), the Sargent fault and the Quien Sabe fault, and have seismicity associated with them (Fig. 2). This location features abundant well-located seismicity, and we used ~80,000 double-difference relocated hypocenters over 1984–2021 the time period provided by the Waldhauser and Schaff (2021) catalog. (The geographic boundary encloses about 10% of the total catalog.)

Running the catalog through the SURF workflow, described in the Methods section, we set the minimum cluster size to 40, which results in 357 unique clusters. We then merge clusters by comparing the plane orientation and directions to nine nearest neighbors using equation (3) and merging clusters that have an **M** value >0.75. This orientation merging step results in 13 consolidated clusters that are displayed as red surfaces in Figure 2 and Video S1, available in the supplemental material to this article. Only 34 of the initial clusters were not coplanar with their nearest neighbors and therefore not merged or shown.

Comparisons. SURF successfully identifies the four faults that have been active within the past 15,000 yr, each of which has 3D representations in two existing fault models. One model is the USGS's Bay Area Velocity Model (BAVM) (Aagaard and Hirakawa, 2021), which features detailed 3D faults created by integrating surface geology, seismicity, and gravity data. This model serves as the basis for the current iteration of the Statewide California Earthquake Center's (SCEC) CFM 7.0 (Plesch *et al.*, 2007). The second model is the third Uniform California Earthquake Rupture Forecast (UCERF3), which provides simplified representations of USGS quaternary fault trace points that are extruded to depth at fixed dip and dip direction (Field *et al.*, 2014). Although UCERF3 offers general agreement with our findings, its level of detail is lower than that of the BAVM/CFM.

We evaluate the consistency between our modeled fault surfaces and the CFM because it provides a comparable level of detail and a meaningful basis for evaluation. To accomplish this comparison, we resample the SAF and CF modeled fault surfaces from this study at 50 m increments. We apply the same gridding process to the CFM's CF and the composite San Andreas sections "Creeping," "Loma Prieta," and "Southern Peninsula." We then calculate the distance between points on our modeled fault surface and the points on the existing fault model. These distances are then binned, and we subsequently fit using the equation

$$N = \kappa 10^{-x/x_0}, \quad (6)$$

in which x is the interfault distance, x_0 is the decay distance that characterizes the distribution, and κ is a constant that is related to the count at the fault location. The decay distance x_0 represents the characteristic length scale over which the counts decrease, such that ~90% of all points are less than x_0 from the fault. Figure 3 highlights the distribution of distances between these results and SCEC CFM. What stands out is that our results closely match those generated by the SCEC CFM experts, even though we rely solely on seismicity. These figures show the distribution of distances between our results and the CFM's SAF and CF. In both cases, the models agree within 1 km, a value substantially lower than what might be expected given the lack of shallow (<4 km depth) seismic constraints.

Ridgecrest, California

Our next test case focuses on the 2019 Ridgecrest earthquake sequence, which included an M_w 6.4 earthquake followed by an M_w 7.1 event that occurred the next day. Previous studies have generated relocated earthquake catalogs that have informed

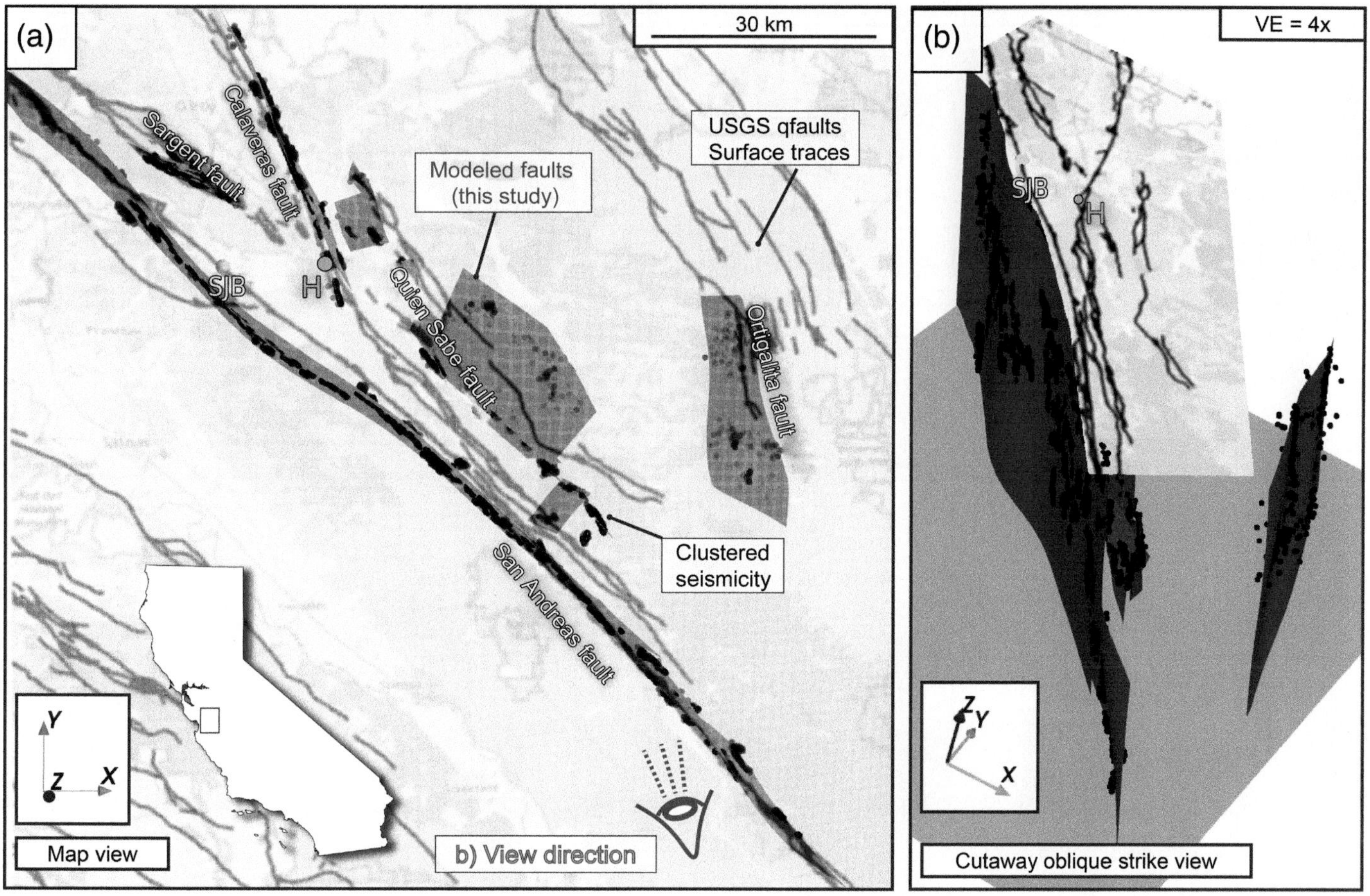

Figure 2. 3D rendering of the modeled fault surfaces in the San Juan Bautista region, California. The red surfaces represent modeled faults, and the black lines indicate the U. S. Geological Survey's Quaternary Fault and Fold Database, where the labeled fault zones are active in the latest Quaternary (<15,000 yr) and are included as fault sources in U.S. National Seismic Hazard Model (Petersen *et al.*, 2024). The black dots mark epicentral locations used to develop the fault planes. Towns mentioned in the main text, San Juan Bautista (SJB) and Hollister (H), are denoted with yellow and orange, respectively. (a) Map view of fault surfaces, where the semitransparent base map is overlain to highlight the agreement between modeled faults and the location of the mapped surface traces. The inset map shows the study region in California. The blue eye indicates the viewing direction for (b). (b) An oblique cutaway view looking northwest with 4× vertical exaggeration (VE) to highlight the geometry of the San Andreas fault. See Video S1 for a rotating animation of this model, which provides a complete 360° perspective on fault geometry and seismicity. The color version of this figure is available only in the electronic edition.

detailed interpretations of fault geometries at depth. A unique aspect of this sequence is the near-orthogonal orientation of the activated fault structures (Liu *et al.*, 2019; DuRoss *et al.*, 2020; Pollitz *et al.*, 2020; Fialko and Jin, 2021; Nevitt *et al.*, 2023), which poses challenges for distinguishing intersecting faults using focal mechanisms because the nodal planes are also orthogonal. The spatial distribution of aftershock hypocenters also reflects orthogonal features (Ross *et al.*, 2019; Lomax, 2020; Shelly, 2020b).

For this study, we use the double-difference relocated earthquake catalog by Shelly (2020a), which includes the foreshock sequence and the first 10+ days of the aftershocks following the M 7.1 mainshock. This catalog was generated using ~13,500 cataloged events as waveform templates, detecting and locating >34,000 events that provide insight into this complex fault system. We apply the SURF algorithm to the catalog and use similar parameters as those in the San Juan Bautista example. However, in this case, we set the minimum cluster size to 35, resulting in 100 unique clusters. These initial clusters are then combined and merged by comparing orientations and direction to the five nearest neighbors as described by equation (3). Clusters with **M** >0.75 were merged. This process resulted in 15 merged clusters; 34 remain unmerged. The merged results are then fit and are displayed as a warm color map (indicating depth) in Figure 4a and red surfaces in Figure 4b,c.

Comparison. The resulting fault model shown in Figure 4a demonstrates general agreement with the surface rupture trace locations from DuRoss *et al.* (2020). The modeled fault surfaces that correspond to the foreshock surface rupture traces (southwest section in Fig. 4a) exhibit steep and variable dips. In this region, the modeled faults highlight the method's

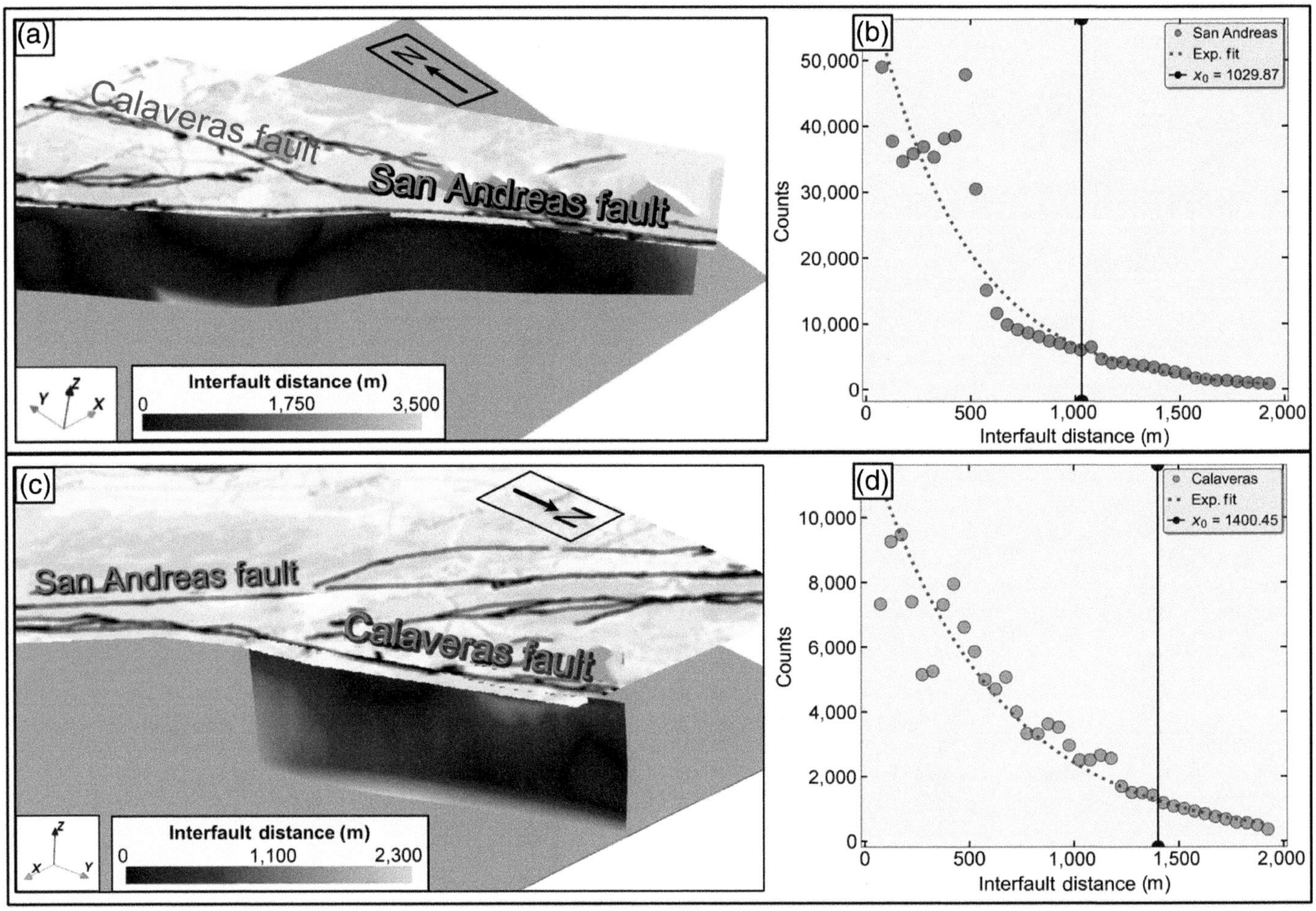

Figure 3. Comparison of the modeled fault surfaces from this study with the Statewide California Earthquake Center's Community Fault Model (CFM) v.7.0 (Plesch *et al.*, 2007), which approximates the Bay Area Velocity Model's fault surfaces (Aagaard and Hirakawa, 2021). Both datasets were resampled to a uniform 50 m node spacing, and the minimum distance between the faults was calculated. (a,b) Results for the San Andreas fault. (c,d) Results for the Calaveras fault. (a,c) The modeled fault result rendered, where the faults are colored from purple to yellow, indicating the distance between the modeled result and the CFM. (b,d) The distribution of interfault distances these results versus CFM and fit with exponential from equation (6) in which x_0 indicates the decay distance. The color version of this figure is available only in the electronic edition.

ability to delineate subparallel faults, as illustrated in Figure 4b and Video S2. Further evidence of these subparallel fault delineations can also be seen in the southeasternmost extent of the mainshock rupture, where modeled faults are offset from the surface mapping by 1–2 km. In addition, it is notable that the modeled fault of the mainshock is not continuous at the intersection with the foreshock, as can be seen in Figure 4b.

The most significant deviation in the fault model compared to previous mapping efforts (DuRoss *et al.*, 2020; Hudnut *et al.*, 2020; Pierce *et al.*, 2020; Rodriguez Padilla, Quintana, *et al.*, 2022; Young *et al.*, 2024) occurs at the northwestern tip of the mainshock rupture near the Coso volcanic field. In our model, the fault is characterized by a shallow dip to the southeast, contrasting with the steeply dipping horsetail-like features mapped at the surface in previous studies. This discrepancy may stem from fitting a continuous surface through a diffuse cloud of seismicity that lacks indications of fault network structure. Although the horsetail-like lineations are difficult to distinguish visually at depth, focal mechanisms suggesting vertical strike-slip features are abundant (Plesch *et al.*, 2020; Wang and Zhan, 2020; Fialko, 2021). Further discussion of the distribution of seismicity and the modeled fault results is provided in the Interpretation and evaluation section.

Interpretation and evaluation

We present SURF, a method for semiautomated 3D mapping based on hypocentral locations. The two test cases described in the Results and Discussion sections demonstrate the potential for applying this method in regions with existing 3D fault models and in areas where such models are lacking. These results raise several fundamental questions: (1) What are the limitations of using this novel yet simplistic approach? (2) How will the method perform in regions without relocated catalogs? (3) When is it appropriate to fit a plane through a diffuse cloud

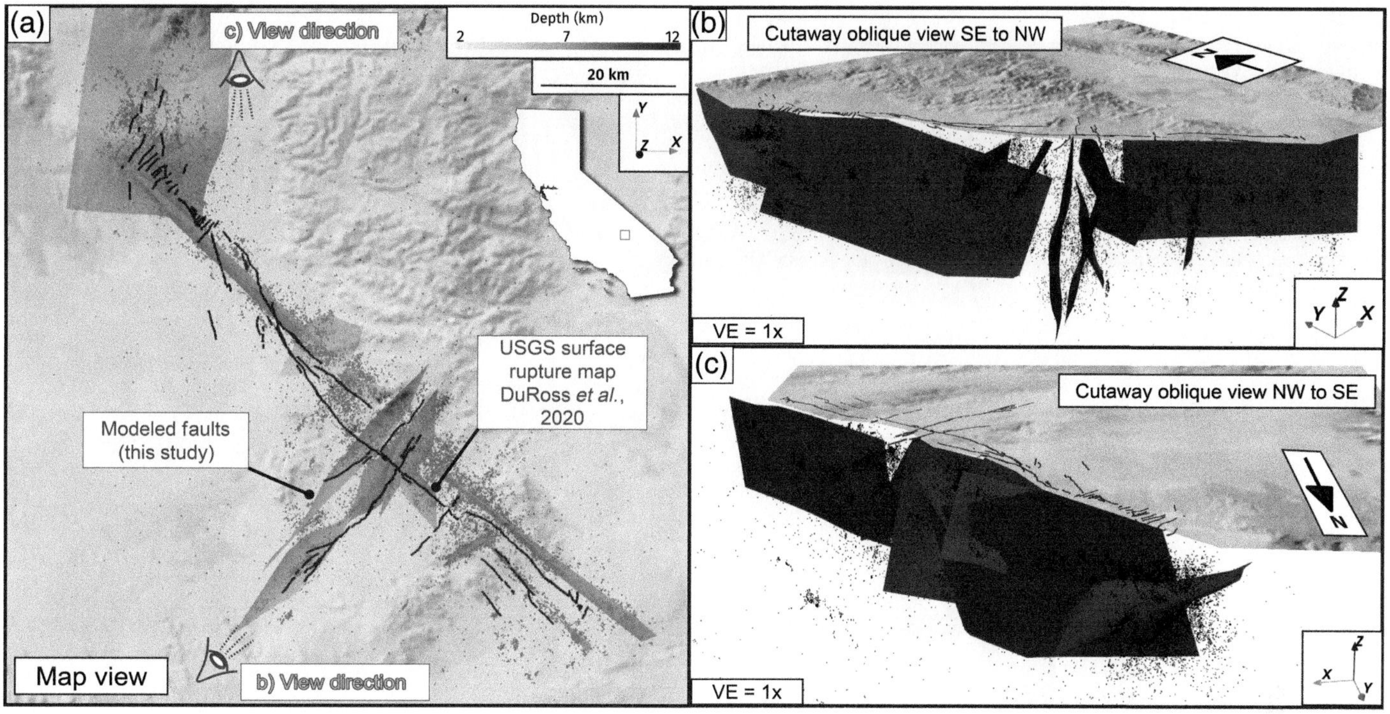

of seismicity? (4) What are our suggested best practices for implementation, and what do the model outputs mean? All of these questions are explored in the following subsections.

Limitations. The SURF algorithm proposed in this study takes a simplistic and flexible approach to modeling 3D faults. To minimize user-defined parameter choices, the code does not impose strict assumptions about the distances that nearest-neighbor clusters should or should not be merged. However, this could be problematic if clusters are farther apart than the user would like to allow merging to occur. In such scenarios, the clusters must be coplanar and have similar orientations. Although our tests have not encountered issues, we acknowledge that the current approach could produce unrealistic results in some scenarios. If needed, adding a distance cutoff parameter would be a straightforward modification.

The model outcomes are inherently dependent on the density and accuracy of the input earthquake catalog in the region of interest. Reliable results cannot be obtained in areas with sparse seismicity or where the events lack a discernible trend. Both case studies presented here have abundant relocated seismicity where near-linear trends are observable. We find that in some cases, modeled surfaces extrapolated to Earth's surface align with the mapped surface traces, but others do not (Figs. 2 and 4). For example, the modeled SAF surface near San Juan Bautista (SJB) is offset from the surface trace by up to 2 km, whereas farther south, in the creeping section, the discrepancy is reduced to a few hundred meters. Notably, these deviations persist across all tested earthquake catalogs, including double-difference, standard-network, and double-difference tomographic results (Zhang and Thurber, 2006). This suggests

Figure 4. 3D fault model for the 2019 Ridgecrest earthquake sequences. The modeled fault surfaces from this study are shown in 3D renderings. The purple lines represent surface traces mapped by DuRoss *et al.* (2020). (a) Map view of the fault surfaces, colored by depth (yellow indicates shallow, and red indicates deep). The light blue eye icons indicate view directions for (panels b and c) and labeled accordingly. (b) Southern region of the sequence, showing the M_w 6.4 foreshock and near-orthogonal surfaces with subparallel strands extending to depth. (c) Northern region near the Coso volcanic field, where the fault model diverges from the existing model. No VE is applied to any 3D renderings. See Video S2 for a rotating animation of this model, which provides a complete 360° perspective on fault geometry and seismicity The color version of this figure is available only in the electronic edition.

that variable offset of seismicity from the surface trace is a feature of the earthquake catalog rather than an error in the method. One possible explanation is an abrupt change in dip near Earth's surface (Fig. 2). Alternatively, the offsets may stem from errors in the absolute locations, an issue that is debated in the literature (e.g., Thurber *et al.*, 1997; McGuire and Ben-Zion, 2005; Zaliapin and Ben-Zion, 2011). The CFM features the same offset of the fault at depth as in our results, but the fault is constructed to connect to the surface trace. This requires that the CFM here feature a slightly shallower dip than our results, as well as a shallowing of the dip of the fault near the surface.

Network versus relocated catalogs. The results from the test cases presented in this study use double-difference catalogs from highly instrumented regions of California. Although this represents an ideal scenario, it raises the question: how do the

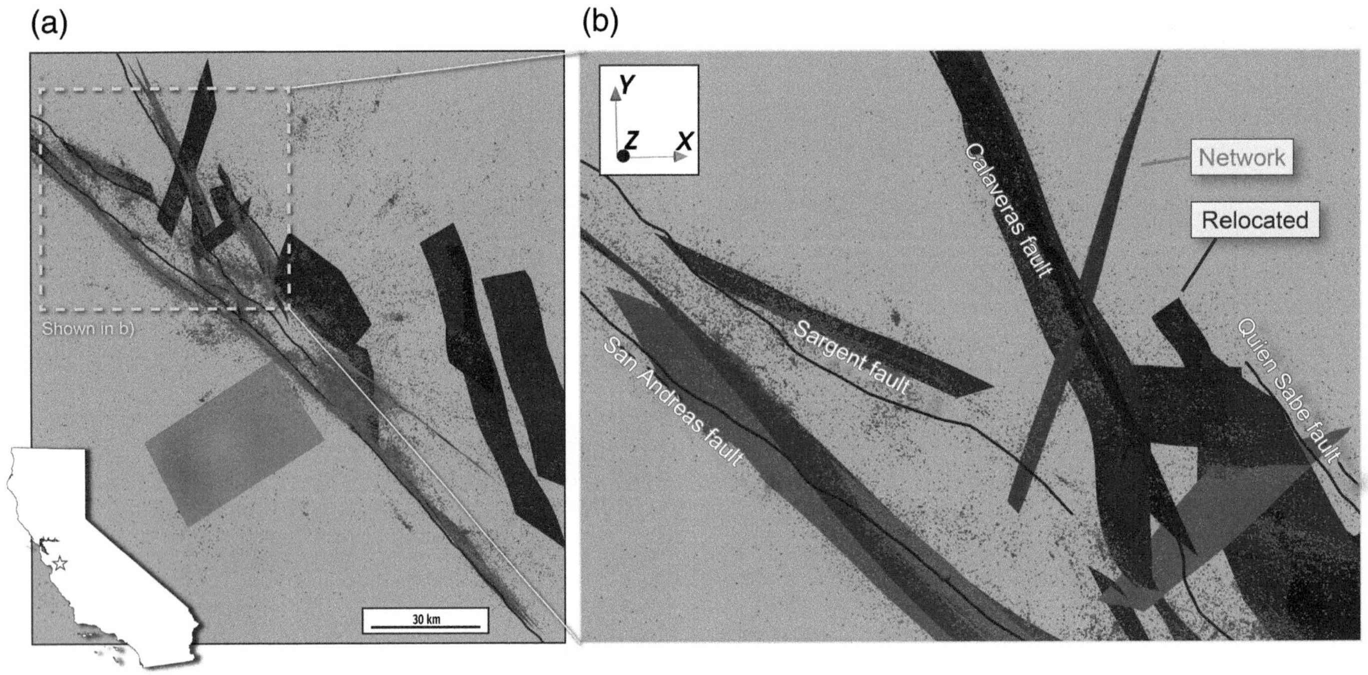

results change when a routine network catalog is used that has not been relocated? To address this, we modeled the fault system near SJB (discussed in San Juan Bautista, California) using the standard Northern California Earthquake Data Center's Northern California Seismic System catalog, which covers the same coordinates and time frame (1984–2021) as the double-difference catalog results discussed in San Juan Bautista, California. These two different datasets (double difference and network) have relative errors that vary by roughly an order of magnitude, tens of meters for the double-difference versus hundreds of meters for the network catalog ($e_m \approx \text{rmse}_t \cdot v_{\text{avg}}$), in which rmse is root mean square error; see Figure S1 for the error distributions. For a visual comparison of the algorithm's results for the different datasets, refer to Figure 5 and Video S3. Qualitatively, the general model outputs for the double-difference catalog and the network catalog are somewhat consistent; however, there are second-order differences. We find that model results corresponding to the location of the SAF and Sargent fault are very similar for both network and relocated catalog results. However, results diverge near the SAF and CF junction, close to SJB and Hollister. Here, the network catalog yields a greater number and more complex fault shapes and morphologies that we attribute to the diffuse distribution of hypocenters. In addition, the network results for the CF are more nonplanar and have more intersecting faults than the double-difference results. These features of the CF have not been documented in other studies. In our interpretation, the double-difference catalog results better agree with existing models and are more physically realistic. When double-different catalogs are available, they will likely produce the best results, which is an intuitive result given the structural clarity that more precise hypocentral locations generally provide.

Figure 5. Fault model results for the San Juan Bautista region of central California. The orange surfaces and spheres are the model results using "network" catalog using Northern California Earthquake Data Center's (NCEDC's) Northern California Seismic System (1984–2021). The blue surfaces and spheres are the results using the "relocated" double-differenced catalog during the same timeframe (Waldhauser and Schaff, 2021). Note that these surfaces are the same as what is shown in Figure 2. (a) The region of interest where the relocated and network catalogs broadly agree along the San Andreas and Quien Sabe faults. (b) A zoom in of the junction region of the highlighting how Calaveras and Sargent faults (labeled) where the model results differ; the network results include rougher surfaces and some results that may be erroneous. See Video S3 for a rotating animation of this model, which provides a complete 360° perspective on fault geometry and seismicity. The color version of this figure is available only in the electronic edition.

Quality assessment, diffuse seismicity, and interpretation. A key challenge in fault modeling is determining when a surface approximately represents the underlying seismicity. In both the SJB and Ridgecrest examples, we observe regions where seismicity is broadly distributed and lacks indicators of continuous throughgoing fault structures. These regions include the SAF–CF junction near SJB, where seismicity is diffused and the algorithm generates variably oriented surfaces (Fig. 2), and the northwestern tip of the Ridgecrest mainshock rupture, near Coso volcanic field, where seismicity is confined to a narrow depth range but lacks clear fault structure (Fig. 4). These examples highlight the fundamental questions of when is it justifiable to fit planes or surfaces through diffuse clouds of seismicity, and how should model results be interpreted?

One approach for assessing model quality is comparing the spatial distribution of seismicity around the modeled fault

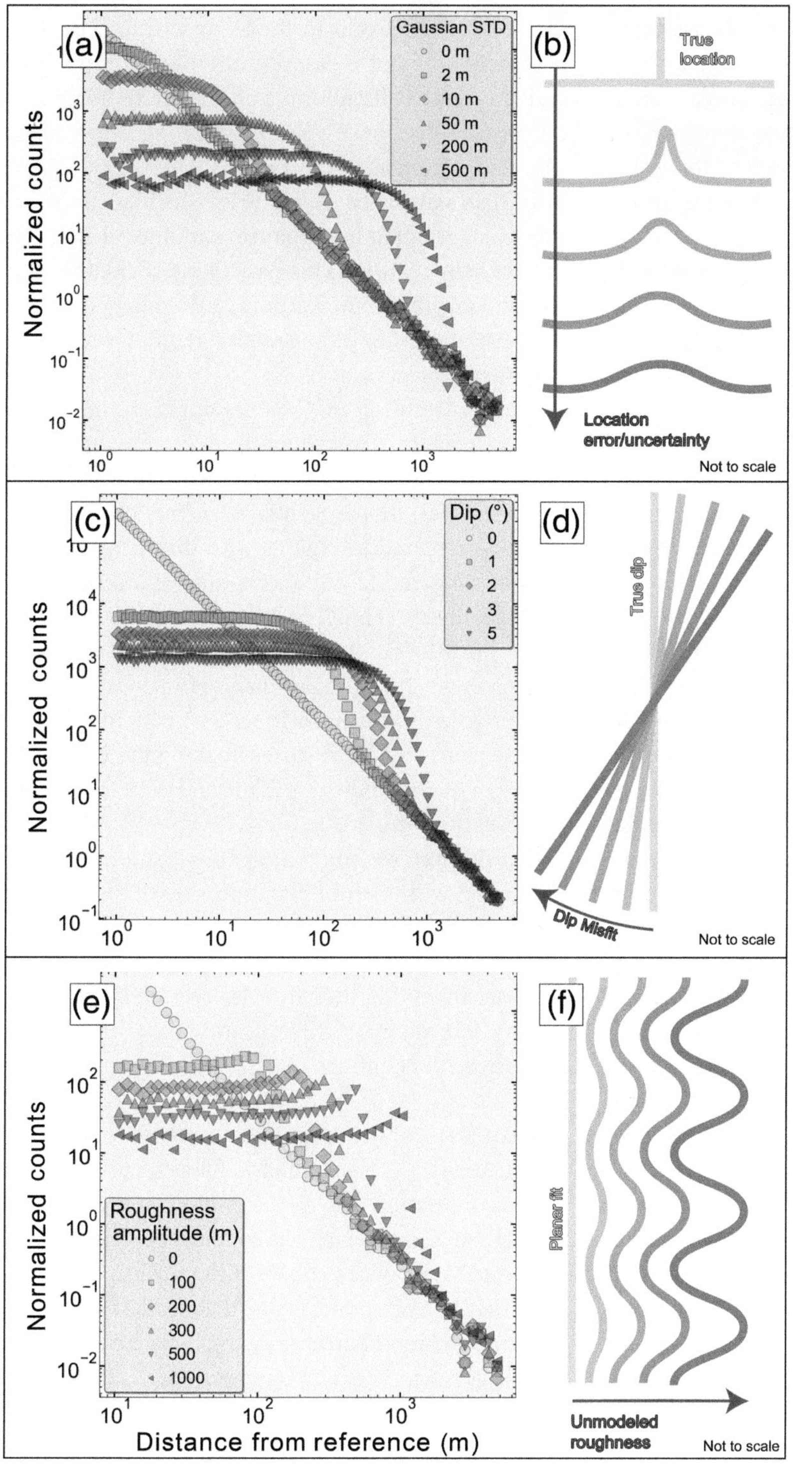

Figure 6. Impact of misfit and unmodeled complexity on the corner d and slope γ on the power law relationship equation (4). The points (green circles) are distributed in an idealized pattern around the fault, with lateral distances following a power-law distribution from a central line, and positions along the fault length and depth following a Gaussian distribution. (a) The figure shows how earthquake location uncertainty impacts the power law distribution. (b) The impact on the power law relationship when modifying the dip of the reference measured surface while holding the points fixed and measuring distances to the rotated reference surface. (c) The effect of unmodeled surface roughness modeled by superimposing a sine wave to the prescribed distribution of points and then measuring the distances with respect to the original planar fit. (d–f) Schematics illustrating the synthetic perturbations that are plotted to the left. Note that examples feature a similar result of moving the corner of the power law farther from the fault with increasing unaccounted for fault complexity or fit errors. The color version of this figure is available only in the electronic edition.

surfaces to the known tendency for the number of earthquakes to decrease as a function of distance from the fault in an inverse power law relationship (introduction). By fitting equation (4) to the observed hypocentral distribution around the modeled fault surfaces and evaluating the misfit using the MRE (equation 5), we identify regions where the distribution of seismicity aligns well with the modeled faults.

Faults such as the San Andreas, Quien Sabe, and portions of the CF exhibit low MRE misfit (<0.5), indicating that the seismicity distribution follows the expected power law decay. However, in regions with diffuse seismicity, the power law deteriorates, suggesting that a single fault surface may not fully capture the underlying fault structure (Figs. S2 and S3).

Interpreting fit parameters d and γ in power law distributions. Beyond overall misfit, the fit parameters d and γ in equation (4) offer additional insight into how well the modeled fault surfaces represent seismicity. The parameter d, which defines the characteristic corner in the power law distribution of earthquake density with distance, can be particularly informative when also considering hypocentral location uncertainty. In the SJB double-difference catalog, location uncertainties are lognormally distributed and range from ≈5 to 50 m (Fig. S1). In this study, where the fits for d significantly exceed the location uncertainty (Figs. S2 and S3), it may indicate real unmodeled fault complexity or orientation misfit, as shown in Figure 6b,c.

Previous studies have proposed a link between d and hypocentral uncertainty in power law observations (Goebel *et al.*, 2014; Rodriguez Padilla and Oskin, 2023). However, our analysis finds little to no correlation between the mean hypocentral location uncertainty and the parameters discussed in this subsection (Fig. S4), reinforcing the idea that d may capture structural complexity beyond location errors.

To further explore the interpretation of d, we conducted synthetic tests simulating fault-like seismicity distributions while systematically perturbing the fault geometry. In these simulations, we generate a simplified 1D linear and vertical strike-slip fault by distributing points (representing hypocenters) along its length with a Gaussian depth profile, a reasonable assumption for California (Fig. S5). We then prescribe an idealized power law decay of distances from the line, after which we introduced controlled geometric perturbations. To model fault misfit, we incrementally rotate the line. To model surface roughness, we superimpose a sine wave on the "fault" line, representing unresolved surface complexity (Fig. 6).

These results demonstrate that even slight deviations, such as a rotation of just a few degrees or adding a low-amplitude sine wave, are sufficient to introduce a measurable corner d where none initially existed. We interpret d as a characteristic length scale that reflects the distance between the modeled fault and the true underlying geometry. For example, the magnitude of d scales with the amplitude of the imposed sine wave, as shown in Figure 6, and we observe that $d \approx \sigma * \tan \delta$ in which σ is the standard deviation of the normal distribution along the synthetic fault length, and δ is the dip misfit. These synthetic examples suggest that d captures the effect of unmodeled complexity or geometric misfit and may be used as a diagnostic measure of the relative accuracy of the modeled fault (Fig. 7).

In some cases, we find anomalously low values of the power law exponent γ, with values <0.8 (Powers and Jordan, 2010; Rodriguez Padilla, Oskin, *et al.*, 2022; Rodriguez Padilla and Oskin, 2023) (Fig. 7). Such low γ values indicate a more gradual decrease in seismicity density with distance from the fault, implying a broader spatial distribution of earthquakes than typically observed for well-defined faults. We interpret these low γ values as evidence that the seismicity is diffusely distributed around the modeled fault rather than tightly localized along a discrete structure. This suggests that in some regions, a single fault surface may not fully capture the true underlying fault structure. Consequently, low γ values serve as an additional metric for evaluating whether a modeled fault surface is a meaningful representation of the observed seismicity.

Machine learning surface fit parameters. A complementary approach to interpreting the modeled faults is to examine the SVR fit parameters, which provide additional insight into the structural characteristics of the modeled surfaces, as discussed in the Surface fitting section. The SVR parameters C and ϵ describe the nonplanarity of the surface and the spatial distribution of seismicity, respectively.

We find that low C values, indicating nearly planar surfaces, sometimes coincide with regions where modeled surface is fit to diffuse seismicity clouds (Fig. 8). In such cases, the low C values suggest that incorporating additional curvature does not improve the SVR fit. This may imply that either the seismicity is uniformly distributed around a genuinely planar fault or that the spatial trends of seismicity do not provide meaningful structural constraints.

The distribution of C values appears bimodal, and we use Gaussian mixture modeling to determine a separation threshold as $C = 0.35$ between the two distributions (see Figure S6). In our test cases, model results from the low C population generally correspond to regions with diffuse seismicity. However, before using the C value as a quality indicator, the expected fault geometry should be considered. In this study, we have prior knowledge that the fault geometries are nonplanar (Plesch *et al.*, 2020; Aagaard and Hirakawa, 2021). In contrast, some studies, particularly in regions with induced earthquakes, feature nearly planar features, making the C value less informative as a quality indicator (Skoumal *et al.*, 2019; Cochran *et al.*, 2020; Park *et al.*, 2022).

In addition, we find that the SVR parameter ϵ is moderately correlated with d from equation (4) with a correlation coefficient of $R^2 = 0.61$ (Fig. S7). This is unsurprising because both metrics provide information about the distribution of near-fault seismicity. Although ϵ lacks a clear physical basis as a quality indicator, its correlation with d suggests that it offers complementary information.

Synthesis: A multimetric approach to fault model evaluation. No single metric fully captures the modeled fault surface uncertainty, but by integrating multiple measures, d, γ, C, ϵ, and MRE, model reliability may be cautiously interpreted. Whereas the goodness-of-fit to the inverse power law distribution (MRE) highlights faults that exhibit expected seismicity trends, deviations, particularly in γ, suggest cases in which a single surface may not fully represent the fault system. In cases in which hypocentral location uncertainty is low, the corner parameter d captures unmodeled fault complexity, with higher values indicating either systematic misfits or genuine small-scale structural variations. Similarly, the SVR parameter C helps distinguish between well-constrained and poorly constrained fault surfaces, in which low values often coincide with diffuse seismicity clouds, potentially indicating a lack of clear structural trends. By considering these parameters together, we can develop a more comprehensive perspective on when and where fault surfaces can be confidently interpreted and where model-based structural interpretations should be treated with caution. This framework provides a systematic way of interpreting fault models and highlights anomalous areas that may justify further investigation.

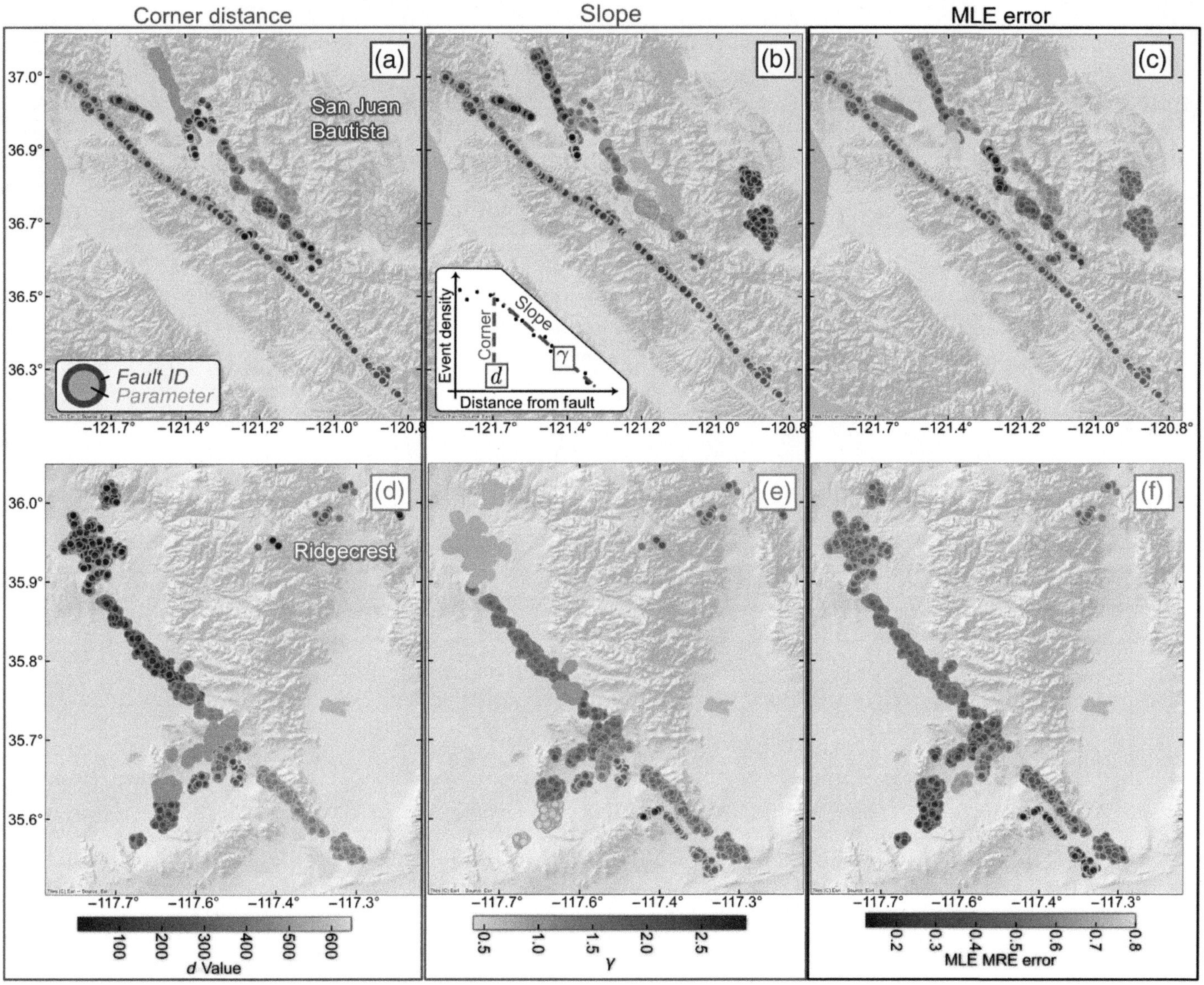

Recommendations for implementation

It is important to note that several key parameters influence the outcome of the algorithm. For example, we found that setting the minimum cluster size to 30–40 events allows for the generation of longer faults. Using large minimum cluster sizes either omits small dense clusters or lumps them together and reduces the resolution. Conversely, using minimum cluster sizes that are too small often produces unstable results because cluster orientation calculations become uncertain with few data points. In some rare cases, clustering may produce two clusters, with one containing a large portion of events and another cluster with few events. This issue can be resolved by reclustering the large cluster and breaking it down into smaller clusters.

The merging thresholds also impact the results. In these examples, we use a threshold value for **M** 0.75 from equation (3), which produces results that agree with previous models (Figs. 3 and 4). Increasing the merging threshold to higher values reduces the likelihood of merging. Another important parameter is the number of nearest neighbors used for comparing directions and orientations. As may be expected, increasing the number of neighbors may result in merging over large distances, which typically increases fault continuity.

Figure 7. Map view display of the output of power law fit parameters d (a,d), γ (b,e), and the mean relative error (MRE) of the maximum-likelihood estimated (MLE) (c,f) fit to equation (4), for the two example datasets. The markers indicate the location of the earthquake cluster centroids used to generate the fault surfaces, the fill color indicates the parameter value, and the marker edge color indicates the merged clusters fault ID used to generate the modeled fault. The color map for the markers ranges from yellow to purple, where the yellower colors indicate potentially problematic fault surfaces. (a–c) Results for the San Juan Bautista region of California. (d–f) The parameter values for the 2019 Ridgecrest, California, earthquake sequence. The color version of this figure is available only in the electronic edition.

We also define ranges of the two parameters C and ϵ that control the SVR fit surface. Optimal values for these parameters are selected using cross-validation with a randomized search over

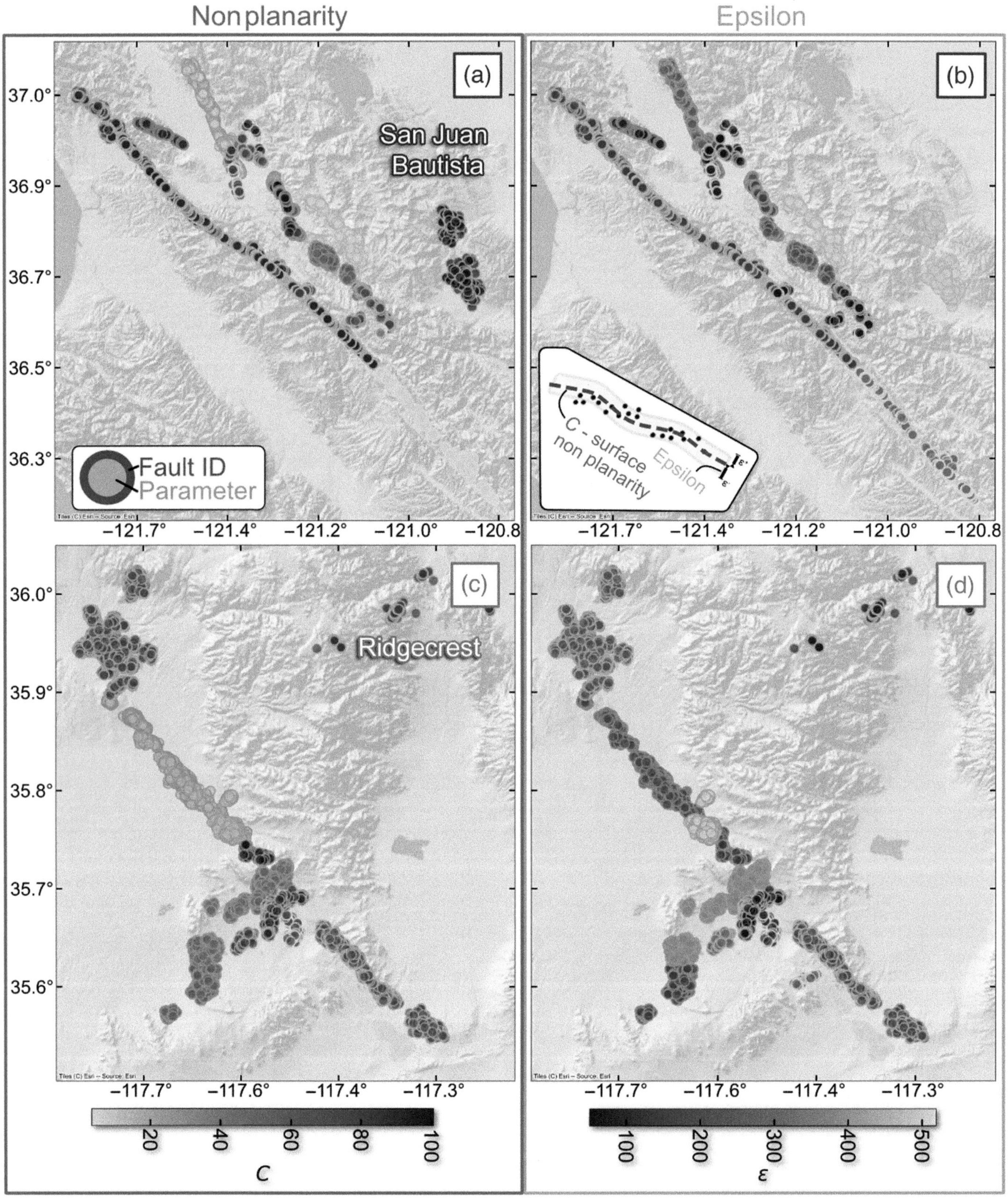

Figure 8. Map view display of the parameter outputs: *C*, that describes the surface nonplanarity (a,c) and ϵ (b,d) for the two example datasets. The markers indicate the location of the earthquake cluster centroids used to generate the fault surfaces, the fill color indicates the parameter value, and the marker edge color indicates the merged cluster's fault ID that was used to generate the modeled fault using the method presented in the text. (a,b) Results for the San Juan Bautista region of California. (c,d) The parameter values for the 2019 Ridgecrest, California, earthquake sequence. The color version of this figure is available only in the electronic edition.

a uniform distribution for both parameters. The tolerance zone ϵ around the fitted surface, where errors are not penalized, accommodates location errors and microseismicity that occurs within the fault damage zone. Because the length scale of absolute hypocentral location uncertainties (Fig. S1) and damage zone dimensions are generally on the order of hundreds of meters, we set ϵ to range from 1 to 500 m; this may be adjusted for other use cases. For example, larger permissible ϵ may be required in regions with sparse or asymmetric seismic station coverage that yield different uncertainty ellipsoids. Conversely, smaller values might be appropriate for very precise near source studies. The parameter C controls the model's complexity and tolerance for errors when larger values correspond to a greater degree of nonplanarity (see Fig. S8). In our tests, we find a range of 1–100 for C balances model complexity and smoothness, with 1 yielding near-planar outputs and 100 allowing for reasonable surface detail. Larger C values can be applied as needed depending on expected fault geometry and data intricacies.

The method presented in this study offers a semiautomated and uniform approach to 3D fault modeling. This uniform approach offers scalability and consistency across different regions. Our results may provide complementary, alternative, or additional information to expertly interpreted fault model studies. We suggest that the method presented here may be a good starting point for 3D fault mapping and that a hybrid approach that includes some additional quality controls and user interpretation is likely best. In addition, the method can be modified based on the desired use cases and information available, such as using surface traces information to shift fault surfaces in space or incorporating focal mechanism information into the clustering step.

Conclusion

The SURF algorithm presented in this study provides a novel, low-user-input approach for constructing 3D fault geometries from seismicity patterns. By integrating density-based clustering with spatially constrained cluster merging, this workflow effectively models continuous fault surfaces, crossing faults, and subparallel fault structures. A key advantage of this approach is that it fits fault surfaces to the data without imposing a priori assumptions about their shape. To objectively assess model reliability, we evaluate the spatial distribution of seismicity around the modeled surfaces, ensuring alignment with established fault zone characteristics.

When applied to the SAF–CF junction and the 2019 Ridgecrest earthquake sequence, the SURF algorithm produces fault geometries that closely match previously published models. This agreement highlights its effectiveness in delineating complex fault structures using only earthquake catalogs. The simplicity and scalability of this workflow make it a promising tool for further fault modeling applications, offering an efficient, data-driven alternative for understanding subsurface fault structures and improving seismic hazard assessments.

Although the method performs well in the case studies presented, its applicability to regions with sparser seismicity or more diffuse fault structures warrants further investigation. Future improvements could incorporate additional geophysical constraints, such as geodetic data or geological mapping, to enhance model accuracy. In addition, refining clustering and merging criteria may improve fault delineation in complex settings, particularly where fault intersections and diffuse seismicity clouds are present. Beyond fault modeling, this workflow could aid in real-time seismic monitoring efforts by providing rapid estimates of fault geometry following significant earthquake sequences.

Data and Resources

The SURF software Alongi and Skoumal (2025) is publically available. Python (https://www.python.org), the NumPy package (https://numpy.org), the Pandas package (https://pandas.pydata.org), the SciPy package (https://scipy.org), the PyVista package (https://docs.pyvista.org), the pyproj package (https://pyproj4.github.io/pyproj), the scikit-learn package (https://scikit-learn.org), and the Networkx package (https://networkx.org) were used. These websites were last accessed in March 2025. The northern California double-difference earthquake catalogs for the Bay Area were obtained from Lamont–Doherty Earth Observatory, Columbia University California Data Center, https://nocaldd.ldeo.columbia.edu/catalog (last accessed December 2024). Northern California Earthquake Data Center, NCSS catalog for this study were accessed through the Northern California Earthquake Data Center (NCEDC), doi: 10.7932/NCEDC (last accessed December 2024). Ridgecrest catalog was obtained from the U.S. Geological Survey (USGS) data release that may be accessed at doi: 10.5066/P9JN6H0N. Mapped fault traces used in figures were obtained from the Quaternary Fault and Fold Database (https://www.usgs.gov/programs/earthquake-hazards/faults). See the supplemental material for additional figures and animations that support main article.

Declaration of Competing Interests

The authors acknowledge that there are no conflicts of interest recorded.

Acknowledgments

Stations used in this study are operated by the U.S. Geological Survey; the University of California, Berkeley; and the California Division of Mines and Geology. Ole Kaven, Ruijia Wang, and an anonymous reviewer provided helpful reviews and comments that helped improve the article. The authors give thanks to Tim Clements for testing and helping to improve the seismicity utilized for reconstructing faults (SURF) algorithm.

Any use of trade, firm, or product names is for descriptive purposes only and does not imply endorsement by the U.S. government.

References

Aagaard, B., and E. Hirakawa (2021). San Francisco bay region 3D seismic velocity model v21. 1, *U.S. Geol. Surv. Data Release* [Data Set], doi: 10.5066/P9TRDCHE.

Alaei, B., and A. Torabi (2017). Seismic imaging of fault damaged zone and its scaling relation with displacement, *Interpretation* **5,** no. 4, SP83–SP93, doi: 10.1190/INT-2016-0230.1.

Alongi, T., E. E. Brodsky, J. Kluesner, and D. Brothers (2022). Using active source seismology to image the Palos Verdes fault damage zone as a function of distance, depth, and geology, *Earth Planet. Sci. Lett.* **600,** 117,871, doi: 10.1016/j.epsl.2022.117871.

Alongi, T., E. E. Brodsky, J. Kluesner, and D. Brothers (2024). Characteristics of the fault damage zone from high-resolution seismic imaging along the Palos Verdes fault, California, *AGU Adv.* **5,** no. 4, e2023AV001155, doi: 10.1029/2023AV001155.

Alongi, T., and R. Skoumal (2025). SURF: A python package for reconstructing faults from seismicity patterns (Version 1.0.0), *U.S. Geol. Surv. Soft. Rel.* doi: 10.5066/P1MM9HMW.

Antoine, S. L., Y. Klinger, A. Delorme, K. Wang, R. Bürgmann, and R. D. Gold (2021). Diffuse deformation and surface faulting distribution from submetric image correlation along the 2019 Ridgecrest, California, ruptures, *Bull. Seismol. Soc. Am.* **111,** no. 5, 2275–2302.

Atterholt, J., Z. Zhan, and Y. Yang (2022). Fault zone imaging with distributed acoustic sensing: Body-to-surface wave scattering, *J. Geophys. Res.* **127,** no. 11, e2022JB025052, doi: 10.1029/2022JB025052.

Bentley, J. L. (1975). Multidimensional binary search trees used for associative searching, *Commun. ACM* **18,** no. 9, 509–517.

Berg, S. S., and T. Skar (2005). Controls on damage zone asymmetry of a normal fault zone: Outcrop analyses of a segment of the Moab fault, SE Utah, *J. Struct. Geol.* **27,** no. 10, 1803–1822, doi: 10.1016/j.jsg.2005.04.012.

Bishop, C. M., and N. M. Nasrabadi (2006). *Pattern Recognition and Machine Learning*, Vol. 4, Springer, New York, New York.

Boettcher, M. S., and T. Jordan (2004). Earthquake scaling relations for mid-ocean ridge transform faults, *J. Geophys. Res.* **109,** no. B12, doi: 10.1029/2004JB003110.

Caine, J. S., J. P. Evans, and C. B. Forster (1996). Fault zone architecture and permeability structure, *Geology* **24,** no. 11, 1025, doi: 10.1130/0091-7613(1996)024<1025:FZAAPS>2.3.CO;2.

Campello, R. J., D. Moulavi, and J. Sander (2013). Density-based clustering based on hierarchical density estimates, *Pacific-Asia Conf. on Knowledge Discovery and Data Mining*, 160–172.

Candela, T., and E. E. Brodsky (2016). The minimum scale of grooving on faults, *Geology* **44,** no. 8, 603–606.

Candela, T., F. Renard, Y. Klinger, K. Mair, J. Schmittbuhl, and E. E. Brodsky (2012). Roughness of fault surfaces over nine decades of length scales, *J. Geophys. Res.* 117, doi: 10.1029/2011JB009041.

Carena, S., J. Suppe, and H. Kao (2002). Active detachment of Taiwan illuminated by small earthquakes and its control of first-order topography, *Geology* **30,** no. 10, 935–938.

Cattania, C., and P. Segall (2021). Precursory slow slip and foreshocks on rough faults, *J. Geophys. Res.* **126,** no. 4, e2020JB020430, doi: 10.1029/2020JB020430.

Chester, J. S., F. M. Chester, and A. K. Kronenberg (2005). Fracture surface energy of the Punchbowl fault, San Andreas system, *Nature* **437,** no. 7055, 133–136.

Choi, J.-H., P. Edwards, K. Ko, and Y.-S. Kim (2016). Definition and classification of fault damage zones: A review and a new methodological approach, *Earth Sci. Rev.* **152,** 70–87, doi: 10.1016/j.earscirev.2015.11.006.

Chu, S. X., V. C. Tsai, D. T. Trugman, and G. Hirth (2021). Fault interactions enhance high-frequency earthquake radiation, *Geophys. Res. Lett.* **48,** no. 20, e2021GL095271, doi: 10.1029/2021GL095271.

Cocco, M., S. Aretusini, C. Cornelio, S. B. Nielsen, E. Spagnuolo, E. Tinti, and G. Di Toro (2023). Fracture energy and breakdown work during earthquakes, *Annu. Rev. Earth Planet. Sci.* **51,** no. 1, 217–252.

Cochran, E. S., Y.-G. Li, P. M. Shearer, S. Barbot, Y. Fialko, and J. E. Vidale (2009). Seismic and geodetic evidence for extensive, long-lived fault damage zones, *Geology* **37,** no. 4, 315–318, doi: 10.1130/G25306A.1.

Cochran, E. S., R. J. Skoumal, D. McPhillips, Z. E. Ross, and K. M. Keranen (2020). Activation of optimally and unfavourably oriented faults in a uniform local stress field during the 2011 Prague, Oklahoma, sequence, *Geophys. J. Int.* **222,** no. 1, 153–168.

DuRoss, C. B., R. D. Gold, T. E. Dawson, K. M. Scharer, K. J. Kendrick, S. O. Akciz, S. J. Angster, J. Bachhuber, S. Bacon, S. E. Bennett, *et al.* (2020). Surface displacement distributions for the July 2019 Ridgecrest, California, earthquake ruptures, *Bull. Seismol. Soc. Am.* **110,** no. 4, 1400–1418.

Faulkner, D., C. Jackson, R. Lunn, R. Schlische, Z. Shipton, C. Wibberley, and M. Withjack (2010). A review of recent developments concerning the structure, mechanics and fluid flow properties of fault zones, *J. Struct. Geol.* **32,** no. 11, 1557–1575, doi: 10.1016/j.jsg.2010.06.009.

Fialko, Y. (2004). Evidence of fluid-filled upper crust from observations of postseismic deformation due to the 1992 M_w 7.3 Landers earthquake, *J. Geophys. Res.* **109,** doi: 10.1029/2004JB002985.

Fialko, Y. (2021). Estimation of absolute stress in the hypocentral region of the 2019 Ridgecrest, California, earthquakes, *J. Geophys. Res.* **126,** no. 7, e2021JB022000, doi: 10.1029/2021JB022000.

Fialko, Y., and Z. Jin (2021). Simple shear origin of the cross-faults ruptured in the 2019 Ridgecrest earthquake sequence, *Nature Geosci.* **14,** no. 7, 513–518.

Field, E. H., R. J. Arrowsmith, G. P. Biasi, P. Bird, T. E. Dawson, K. R. Felzer, D. D. Jackson, K. M. Johnson, T. H. Jordan, C. Madden, *et al.* (2014). Uniform California earthquake rupture forecast, version 3 (UCERF 3)—The time-independent model, *Bull. Seismol. Soc. Am.* **104,** no. 3, 1122–1180.

Fischler, M. A., and R. C. Bolles (1981). Random sample consensus: A paradigm for model fitting with applications to image analysis and automated cartography, *Communications of the ACM* **24,** no. 6, 381–395.

Fletcher, J. M., M. E. Oskin, and O. J. Teran (2016). The role of a keystone fault in triggering the complex El Mayor-Cucapah earthquake rupture, *Nature Geosci.* **9,** no. 4, 303–307.

Goebel, T., T. Candela, C. Sammis, T. Becker, G. Dresen, and D. Schorlemmer (2014). Seismic event distributions and off-fault damage during frictional sliding of saw-cut surfaces with pre-defined roughness, *Geophys. J. Int.* **196,** no. 1, 612–625.

Hatem, A. E., M. L. Cooke, and E. H. Madden (2015). Evolving efficiency of restraining bends within wet kaolin analog experiments, *J. Geophys. Res.* **120,** no. 3, 1975–1992.

Hudnut, K. W., B. A. Brooks, K. Scharer, J. L. Hernandez, T. E. Dawson, M. E. Oskin, J. Ramon Arrowsmith, C. A. Goulet, K. Blake, M. L. Boggs, *et al.* (2020). Airborne lidar and electro-optical imagery along surface ruptures of the 2019 Ridgecrest earthquake sequence, southern California, *Seismol. Res. Lett.* **91,** no. 4, 2096–2107, doi: 10.1785/0220190338.

Jourdon, A., D. A. May, J. N. Hayek, and A.-A. Gabriel (2025). 3D reconstruction of complex fault systems from volumetric geodynamic shear zones using medial axis transform, *Geochem. Geophys. Geosys.* **26,** no. 6, e2025GC012169, doi: 10.1029/2025GC012169.

Kaven, J. O., and D. D. Pollard (2013). Geometry of crustal faults: Identification from seismicity and implications for slip and stress transfer models, *J. Geophys. Res.* **118,** no. 9, 5058–5070.

Li, Y.-G., J. E. Vidale, and E. S. Cochran (2004). Low-velocity damaged structure of the San Andreas fault at Parkfield from fault zone trapped waves: Low-velocity damaged structure of the San Andreas fault, *Geophys. Res. Lett.* **31,** no. 12, doi: 10.1029/2003GL019044.

Lienkaemper, J. J., F. S. McFarland, R. W. Simpson, and S. J. Caskey (2014). Using surface creep rate to infer fraction locked for sections of the San Andreas fault system in northern California from alignment array and GPS data, *Bull. Seismol. Soc. Am.* **104,** no. 6, 3094–3114.

Liu, C., T. Lay, E. E. Brodsky, K. Dascher-Cousineau, and X. Xiong (2019). Coseismic rupture process of the large 2019 Ridgecrest earthquakes from joint inversion of geodetic and seismological observations, *Geophys. Res. Lett.* **46,** no. 21, 11,820–11,829.

Lomax, A. (2020). Absolute location of 2019 Ridgecrest seismicity reveals a shallow M_w 7.1 hypocenter, migrating and pulsing M_w 7.1 foreshocks, and duplex M_w 6.4 ruptures, *Bull. Seismol. Soc. Am.* **110,** no. 4, 1845–1858.

Lozos, J. C., D. D. Oglesby, B. Duan, and S. G. Wesnousky (2011). The effects of double fault bends on rupture propagation: A geometrical parameter study, *Bull. Seismol. Soc. Am.* **101,** no. 1, 385–398.

McGuire, J., and Y. Ben-Zion (2005). High-resolution imaging of the bear valley section of the San Andreas fault at seismogenic depths with fault-zone head waves and relocated seismicity, *Geophys. J. Int.* **163,** no. 1, 152–164.

Nevitt, J. M., B. A. Brooks, J. L. Hardebeck, and B. T. Aagaard (2023). 2019 M 7.1 Ridgecrest earthquake slip distribution controlled by fault geometry inherited from independence dike swarm, *Nat. Commun.* **14,** no. 1, 1546.

Ouillon, G., C. Ducorbier, and D. Sornette (2008). Automatic reconstruction of fault networks from seismicity catalogs: Three-dimensional optimal anisotropic dynamic clustering, *J. Geophys. Res.* **113,** doi: 10.1029/2007JB005032.

Park, Y., G. C. Beroza, and W. L. Ellsworth (2022). Basement fault activation before larger earthquakes in Oklahoma and Kansas, *Seism. Rec.* **2,** no. 3, 197–206.

Pedregosa, F., G. Varoquaux, A. Gramfort, V. Michel, B. Thirion, O. Grisel, M. Blondel, P. Prettenhofer, R. Weiss, V. Dubourg, *et al.* (2011). Scikit-learn: Machine learning in python, *J. Machine Learn. Res.* **12,** 2825–2830.

Perrin, C., F. Waldhauser, and C. H. Scholz (2021). The shear deformation zone and the smoothing of faults with displacement, *J. Geophys. Res.* doi: 10.1029/2020JB020447.

Petersen, M. D., A. M. Shumway, P. M. Powers, E. H. Field, M. P. Moschetti, K. S. Jaiswal, K. R. Milner, S. Rezaeian, A. D. Frankel, A. L. Llenos, *et al.* (2024). The 2023 US 50-State National Seismic Hazard Model: Overview and implications, *Earthq. Spectra* **40,** no. 1, 5–88.

Pierce, I., A. Williams, R. D. Koehler, and C. Chupik (2020). High-resolution structure-from-motion models and orthophotos of the southern sections of the 2019 M_w 7.1 and 6.4 Ridgecrest earthquakes surface ruptures, *Seismol. Res. Lett.* **91,** no. 4, 2124–2126.

Plesch, A., J. H. Shaw, C. Benson, W. A. Bryant, S. Carena, M. Cooke, J. Dolan, G. Fuis, E. Gath, L. Grant, *et al.* (2007). Community fault model (CFM) for southern California, *Bull. Seismol. Soc. Am.* **97,** no. 6, 1793–1802, doi: 10.1785/0120050211.

Plesch, A., J. H. Shaw, Z. E. Ross, and E. Hauksson (2020). Detailed 3D fault representations for the 2019 Ridgecrest, California, earthquake sequence, *Bull. Seismol. Soc. Am.* **110,** no. 4, 1818–1831.

Poliakov, A. N., R. Dmowska, and J. R. Rice (2002). Dynamic shear rupture interactions with fault bends and off-axis secondary faulting, *J. Geophys. Res.* **107,** no. B11, ESE-6.

Pollitz, F. F., J. R. Murray, J. L. Svarc, C. Wicks, E. Roeloffs, S. E. Minson, K. Scharer, K. Kendrick, K. W. Hudnut, J. Nevitt, *et al.* (2020). Kinematics of fault slip associated with the 4-6 July 2019 Ridgecrest, California, earthquake sequence, *Bull. Seismol. Soc. Am.* **110,** no. 4, 1688–1700.

Powers, P. M., and T. H. Jordan (2010). Distribution of seismicity across strike-slip faults in California, *J. Geophys. Res.* **115,** doi: 10.1029/2008JB006234.

Rodriguez Padilla, A. M., and M. E. Oskin (2023). Displacement hazard from distributed ruptures in strike-slip earthquakes, *Bull. Seismol. Soc. Am.* **113,** no. 6, 2730–2745.

Rodriguez Padilla, A. M., M. E. Oskin, C. W. Milliner, and A. Plesch (2022). Accrual of widespread rock damage from the 2019 Ridgecrest earthquakes, *Nature Geosci.* **15,** no. 3, 222–226.

Rodriguez Padilla, A. M., M. A. Quintana, R. M. Prado, B. J. Aguilar, T. A. Shea, M. E. Oskin, and L. Garcia (2022). Near-field high-resolution maps of the Ridgecrest earthquakes from aerial imagery, *Bull. Seismol. Soc. Am.* **93,** no. 1, 494–499.

Ross, Z. E., B. Idini, Z. Jia, O. L. Stephenson, M. Zhong, X. Wang, Z. Zhan, M. Simons, E. J. Fielding, S.-H. Yun, *et al.* (2019). Hierarchical interlocked orthogonal faulting in the 2019 Ridgecrest earthquake sequence, *Science* **366,** no. 6463, 346–351.

Savage, H. M., and E. E. Brodsky (2011). Collateral damage: Evolution with displacement of fracture distribution and secondary fault strands in fault damage zones, *J. Geophys. Res.* **116,** doi: 10.1029/2010JB007665.

Sawaki, Y., T. Shiina, K. Sagae, Y. Sato, H. Horikawa, A. Miyakawa, K. Imanishi, and T. Uchide (2025). Fault geometries of the 2024 M_w 7.5 Noto peninsula earthquake from hypocenter-based hierarchical clustering of point-cloud normal vectors, *J. Geophys. Res.* **130,** no. 4, e2024JB030233, doi: 10.1029/2024JB030233.

Scott, C. P., J. R. Arrowsmith, E. Nissen, L. Lajoie, T. Maruyama, and T. Chiba (2018). The *M* 7 2016 Kumamoto, Japan, earthquake: 3-D deformation along the fault and within the damage zone constrained from differential lidar topography, *J. Geophys. Res.* **123,** no. 7, 6138–6155, doi: 10.1029/2018JB015581.

Segall, P., and D. Pollard (1980). Mechanics of discontinuous faults, *J. Geophys. Res.* **85,** no. B8, 4337–4350.

Shelly, D. R. (2020a). A high-resolution seismic catalog for the initial 2019 Ridgecrest earthquake sequence, doi: 10.5066/P9JN6H0N.

Shelly, D. R. (2020b). A high-resolution seismic catalog for the initial 2019 Ridgecrest earthquake sequence: Foreshocks, aftershocks, and faulting complexity, *Seismol. Res. Lett.* **91,** no. 4, 1971–1978.

Shipton, Z. K., and P. A. Cowie (2001). Damage zone and slip-surface evolution over mm to km scales in high-porosity Navajo sandstone, Utah, *J. Struct. Geol.* 20, doi: 10.1016/S0191-8141(01)00035-9.

Skoumal, R. J., J. O. Kaven, and J. I. Walter (2019). Characterizing seismogenic fault structures in Oklahoma using a relocated template-matched catalog, *Seismol. Res. Lett.* **90,** no. 4, 1535–1543.

Smola, A. J., and B. Schölkopf (2004). A tutorial on support vector regression, *Stat. Comput.* **14,** 199–222.

Thurber, C., S. Roecker, W. Ellsworth, Y. Chen, W. Lutter, and R. Sessions (1997). Two-dimensional seismic image of the San Andreas fault in the northern Gabilan range, central California: Evidence for fluids in the fault zone, *Geophys. Res. Lett.* **24,** no. 13, 1591–1594.

Thurber, C., S. Roecker, K. Roberts, M. Gold, L. Powell, and K. Rittger (2003). Earthquake locations and three-dimensional fault zone structure along the creeping section of the San Andreas fault near Parkfield, CA: Preparing for SAFOD, *Geophys. Res. Lett.* **30,** no. 3, doi: 10.1029/2002GL016004.

Truttmann, S., T. Diehl, and M. Herwegh (2023). Hypocenter-based 3D imaging of active faults: Method and applications in the southwestern Swiss Alps, *J. Geophys. Res.* **128,** no. 6, e2023JB026352, doi: 10.1029/2023JB026352.

Ulrich, T., A.-A. Gabriel, J.-P. Ampuero, and W. Xu (2019). Dynamic viability of the 2016 M_w 7.8 Kaikōura earthquake cascade on weak crustal faults, *Nat. Commun.* **10,** no. 1, 1–16.

Waldhauser, F., and D. P. Schaff (2021). A comprehensive search for repeating earthquakes in northern California: Implications for fault creep, slip rates, slip partitioning, and transient stress, *J. Geophys. Res.* **126,** no. 11, e2021JB022495, doi: 10.1029/2021JB022495.

Wang, X., and Z. Zhan (2020). Seismotectonics and fault geometries of the 2019 Ridgecrest sequence: Insight from aftershock moment tensor catalog using 3-D Green's functions, *J. Geophys. Res.* **125,** no. 5, e2020JB019577, doi: 10.1029/2020JB019577.

Wang, Y., G. Ouillon, J. Woessner, D. Sornette, and S. Husen (2013). Automatic reconstruction of fault networks from seismicity catalogs including location uncertainty, *J. Geophys. Res.* **118,** no. 11, 5956–5975.

Wesnousky, S. G. (2006). Predicting the endpoints of earthquake ruptures, *Nature* **444,** no. 7117, 358–360, doi: 10.1038/nature05275.

Willemse, E. J., and D. D. Pollard (2000). Normal fault growth: Evolution of tipline shapes and slip distribution, in *Aspects of Tectonic Faulting: In Honour of Georg Mandl,* F. K. Lehner and J. L. Urai (Editors), Springer, Berlin, Heidelberg, 193–226.

Young, E. K., M. E. Oskin, and A. M. Rodriguez Padilla (2024). Reproducibility of remote mapping of the 2019 Ridgecrest earthquake surface ruptures, *Seismol. Res. Lett.* **95,** no. 1, 288–298.

Zaliapin, I., and Y. Ben-Zion (2011). Asymmetric distribution of aftershocks on large faults in California, *Geophys. J. Int.* **185,** no. 3, 1288–1304.

Zhang, H., and C. Thurber (2006). Development and applications of double-difference seismic tomography, *Pure Appl. Geophys.* **163,** 373–403.

Manuscript received 22 April 2025
Published online 8 October 2025

Subduction Zone Earthquake Catalog Separation Tool: Implementation in the USGS 2025 Puerto Rico and U.S. Virgin Islands National Seismic Hazard Model

Kirstie L. Haynie*[1], Eric M. Thompson[1], Mike Hearne[1], Gavin P. Hayes[2], David R. Shelly[1], Allison M. Shumway[1], Andrea L. Llenos[1], Andrew J. Michael[3], and Peter M. Powers[1]

Abstract

The U.S. Geological Survey (USGS) periodically releases updates to National Seismic Hazard Model (NSHM) for the United States and its territories leveraging current scientific knowledge and methodologies to guide public policy, building codes, and risk assessments regarding potential ground shaking due to earthquakes that may result in infrastructure damage. In subduction zones, there is a need to separate the earthquake catalog into tectonic regimes to create specific seismicity models for which the most appropriate ground-motion models are then applied. Here, we describe newly developed methods and software, called CatSep, that classifies subduction zone events into three primary tectonic regimes: crustal, interface, and intraslab. This method incorporates information about the location of the earthquake relative to the subducting slab, the depth of the Mohorovičić discontinuity, and the earthquake's moment tensor. Applying this method is a first step in the NSHM workflow for regions covering U.S. subduction zones. Results using this subduction zone earthquake catalog separation tool for the 2025 Puerto Rico and U.S. Virgin Islands NSHM earthquake catalog are presented and analyzed.

Cite this article as Haynie, K. L., E. M. Thompson, M. Hearne, G. P. Hayes, D. R. Shelly, A. M. Shumway, A. L. Llenos, A. J. Michael, and P. M. Powers (2025). Subduction Zone Earthquake Catalog Separation Tool: Implementation in the USGS 2025 Puerto Rico and U.S. Virgin Islands National Seismic Hazard Model, *Seismol. Res. Lett.* **97**, 1191–1200, doi: 10.1785/0220250078.

Introduction

The U.S. Geological Survey (USGS) creates National Seismic Hazard Models (NSHM) to evaluate hazard, mitigate loss, improve safety, and reduce risk from earthquakes in the United States (U.S.) and its territories. These models and related products are updated approximately every six years (corresponding to building code update cycles) to include new data, methods, and tools. Gridded seismicity models and ground-motion models are core parts of the NSHM development process, and it is important that appropriate data and algorithms are used for each tectonic regime. In the case of subduction zones, the earthquake catalog used as input for an NSHM must be sorted into subcatalogs, where each catalog represents a tectonic regime, such as crustal (within the overriding plate's crust), interface (in the interplate region between the overriding and subducting plates), or intraslab (within the subducting plate). Previously, this sorting was done by establishing a depth cutoff for which earthquakes below this depth were labeled as intraslab and earthquakes above were labeled as interface or crustal (e.g., Wesson *et al.*, 2007). The 2024 Alaska NSHM and the 2025 Puerto Rico and U.S. Virgin Islands (PRVI) NSHM updates adopted a new method that uses the Slab2 global subduction zone models (Hayes *et al.*, 2018) to more precisely separate earthquakes.

Because of the reliance on the Slab2 model, earthquake location, and focal mechanisms, each of which is an approximation, it can be difficult to classify all events in a subduction

1. U.S. Geological Survey, Geologic Hazards Science Center, Golden, Colorado, U.S.A., https://orcid.org/0000-0001-9930-6736 (KLH); https://orcid.org/0000-0002-6943-4806 (EMT); https://orcid.org/0000-0002-8225-2396 (MH); https://orcid.org/0000-0003-2783-5158 (DRS); https://orcid.org/0000-0003-1142-7141 (AMS); https://orcid.org/0000-0002-4088-6737 (ALL); https://orcid.org/0000-0003-2124-6184 (PMP); 2. U.S. Geological Survey, Natural Hazards Mission Area, Golden, Colorado, U.S.A., https://orcid.org/0000-0003-3323-0112 (GPH); 3. U.S. Geological Survey, Earthquake Science Center, Moffett Field, California, U.S.A., https://orcid.org/0000-0002-2403-5019 (AJM)

*Corresponding author: khaynie@usgs.gov

zone earthquake catalog accurately via an automated approach. Therefore, this article describes a practical solution that takes advantage of the most accurate data coupled with ramp functions to calculate plausibility scores to determine the most likely tectonic classification (refer to the Earthquake Classification Methods section). The methods used in this earthquake classification tool, CatSep, and results from the 2025 PRVI NSHM catalog are presented. The procedure and results presented here expand on those used in the Alaska NSHM which are described in Llenos *et al.* (2024) and Powers *et al.* (2024).

Earthquake Classification Methods

We devised an earthquake classification scheme to classify earthquakes in a subduction zone earthquake catalog into crustal, interface, and intraslab regimes for each Slab2 subduction region (refer to Hayes *et al.*, 2018, for details on the Slab2 regions). This method follows the heuristic approach in the USGS product ShakeMap (Worden *et al.*, 2024), which uses the SeismoTectonic Regime Earthquake Calculator (STREC). STREC is based on the methods described in García *et al.* (2012), by employing a ramp function that scales between two values, p_1 and p_2, where the total plausibility score, $P(x)$, is given by

$$P(x) = \begin{cases} p_1 & \text{for } x < x_1, \\ p_1 + \frac{p_2-p_1}{x_2-x_1}(x - x_1) & \text{for } x_1 \le x \le x_2, \text{ or} \\ p_2 & \text{for } x > x_2, \end{cases} \quad (1)$$

in which x is a variable representing an earthquake-related parameter, x_1 and x_2 are associated parameters that define the ramp, and p_1 and p_2 give the associated scoring values for those parameters (Fig. 1). Parameters used in this methodology are earthquake depth, slab surface depth at the location of the earthquake, Moho (Mohorovičić discontinuity) depth (Laske *et al.*, 2013) at the location of the earthquake, seismogenic zone depth (Hayes *et al.*, 2018), and, when focal mechanisms are available, an angle of rotation between the fault plane and orientation of the slab surface at the location of the earthquake (Table 1).

The subduction zone earthquake catalog classification algorithm reads in a subduction zone earthquake catalog and evaluates every event by calculating a plausibility score, between 0.0 and 1.0, for each tectonic regime. Each event is then assigned the tectonic regime with the highest plausibility score. By default, the code only classifies events that are within a Slab2 region, discarding events that occur outside this region. However, an option is available to classify earthquakes that occur outside the Slab2 subduction region bounds; these events are classified as falling in the outerrise tectonic regime.

The catalog separation process starts by determining the plausibility score that an earthquake occurred along the subduction interface. The total plausibility score that the earthquake occurred along the interface ($P_{\text{interface}}$) consists of three parameters: p_{flex}, p_{sz}, and p_{kagan}. p_{flex} gives the plausibility score that the event occurred within the interface, which is defined by a buffer called the flex zone ±15 km above and below the slab surface (Fig. 2b,c). This flex zone value was determined from heuristic testing using a global subduction zone catalog (refer to the Heuristic procedure section). p_{sz} is the plausibility score that the event occurred within the seismogenic zone, and p_{kagan} is used when moment tensor information is provided by analyzing how similar the fault plane and slab orientation are.

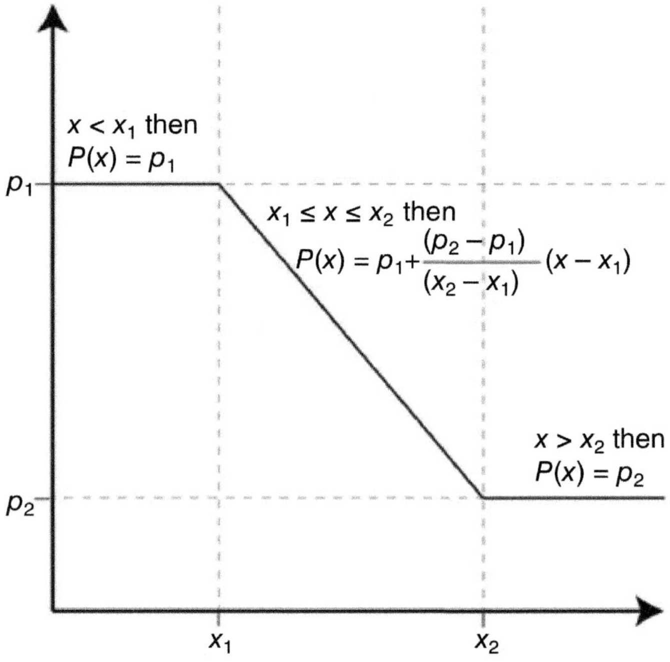

Figure 1. Graphical representation of the ramp function described in equation (1). Corresponding values used in the CatSep algorithm discussed here are provided in Table 1.

Because of the uncertainties in earthquake depth (which the algorithm currently does not consider) and slab depth, as well as the tectonic complications of the accretionary prism and mantle wedge regions, depending on where the earthquake occurred with respect to slab depth, seismogenic zone depth, and Moho depth, a specific p_{flex} is applied. The three possible options for p_{flex} are described subsequently:

1. If the earthquake occurred within the interface flex zone of ±15 km from the Slab2 surface and no deeper than the seismogenic zone limit, as defined from Slab2 (Hayes *et al.*, 2018), plus 15 km (referred to here as maximum seismogenic zone depth), p_{flex} is 1.0 (this is the area within the purple lines and above the red-dashed line marking the maximum seismogenic zone depth, Max. SZ, in Fig. 2b). This is to take into account the combined uncertainties in earthquake and slab depths, as well the uncertainty of seismogenic zone thickness. Note that a ramp function calculation is not used in this case.

TABLE 1
Parameters Used in the Ramp Functions Within the Earthquake Classification Code

Parameter	x	x_1	x_2	p_1	p_2
p_{sz}	Earthquake depth	SZ depth	Maximum SZ depth	1.0	0.0
p_{flex}	Earthquake depth	Moho depth	Top interface flex zone	0.0	0.4
p_{kagan}	Kagan angle	30	53	1.0	0.25
p_{diff}	Earthquake depth – slab depth	−20	20	1.0	0.0
p_{moho}	Earthquake depth	Moho depth	Slab depth	1.0	0.0

SZ, seismogenic zone depth; p_{sz}, plausibility score that the event occurred within the seismogenic zone; p_{flex}, plausibility score that the earthquake occurred within the interface flex zone (Fig. 2); p_{kagan}, plausibility score that the angle of rotation between a provided moment tensor and the orientation of the slab are similar; p_{diff}, plausibility score that the earthquake is within the crust; p_{moho}, scoring value that the earthquake is above the Moho (Mohorovičić discontinuity).

2. If earthquake depth is less than the top of the interface flex zone (denoted by 'Top flex zone' in Fig. 2b) and deeper than Moho depth (yellow solid line in Fig. 2) from CRUST1.0 (Laske *et al.*, 2013) at the location of the earthquake, a ramp function between these two parameters is used to determine p_{flex}. An example is given in Figure 2b where p_{flex} ranges from 0.0 at the Moho and 0.4 at the top of the flex zone. This p_{flex} ramp function is used to address the use case where an earthquake occurs between the crust and the mantle wedge. Although this area is near the interface, the event is most likely not an interface event, but instead crustal or mantle. As a result, the assigned plausibility values for the event being classified as interface are lower when this ramp function is applied.
3. If the earthquake occurred within the interface flex zone and shallower than Moho depth at the location of the earthquake, p_{flex} is 1.0. Note that a ramp function calculation is not used in this case. This determination is used to address the case when the event occurs in the accretionary prism, which represents a complicated tectonic regime that this method does not cover. Instead, because material within the accretionary prism is formed by sediments and rocks scraped off of the downgoing plate where the underlying fault here is a décollement, or the plate boundary interface, these events are assumed to be interface.

p_{sz} is used to account for uncertainty of the seismogenic zone limit, or interface fault depth. This is done by determining a plausibility score that the earthquake occurs between the seismogenic zone limit (red solid line in Fig. 2c), which is assigned a plausibility score of 1.0, and maximum seismogenic zone limit (red-dashed line in Fig. 2c), which is assigned a plausibility score of 0.0 (Table 1).

The final plausibility score that the earthquake occurred within the interface is then given by

$$P_{interface} = p_{flex} \times p_{sz}. \quad (2)$$

The general idea here is that the more confidence an earthquake is within the interface flex zone and also above the seismogenic zone limit, the more confident we are that it is an interface event.

The last parameter, p_{kagan}, used in the total interface calculation involves the earthquake's moment tensor. If available, the plausibility score indicating the similarity between the Kagan angle (Kagan, 1991), or angle of rotation, of the fault plane and the orientation of the slab surface at the earthquake location is determined (Table 1). Thus, p_{kagan} represents a plausibility score for how similar the earthquake's moment tensor is to the moment tensor that would be expected for an earthquake occurring at this location. For this case, the final plausibility score that the earthquake occurred within the interface is given by

$$P_{interface} = p_{flex} \times p_{sz} \times p_{kagan}. \quad (3)$$

Next, the plausibility score determining if the event occurred within the crust ($P_{crustal}$) is calculated. This is determined by first calculating the plausibility score that the depth difference between the earthquake and Slab2 surface at the location of the earthquake is within ±20 km (p_{diff}; Table 1 and Fig. 2d). To account for the fact that we are not using depth to the base of the upper lithospheric plate, a probabilistic ramp function, p_{moho}, from the CRUST1.0 Moho depth (Laske *et al.*, 2013), where anything occurring shallower than that has p_{moho} equal to 1.0, to the depth of the Slab2 surface, where p_{moho} is 0.0, is calculated (yellow line where $p_{moho} = 1.0$ at the Moho and $p_{moho} = 0.0$ at the slab surface in Fig. 2d). This ramp function ensures a higher plausibility score for events that occur within the upper plate crust, with plausibility decreasing with depth, such that events within the upper lithospheric mantle or upper mantle are assigned a lower p_{moho}. Total crustal value is then given by

$$P_{crustal} = (1 - P_{interface}) \times p_{diff} \times p_{moho}. \quad (4)$$

Finally, the plausibility score that the event occurred within the subducting plate is

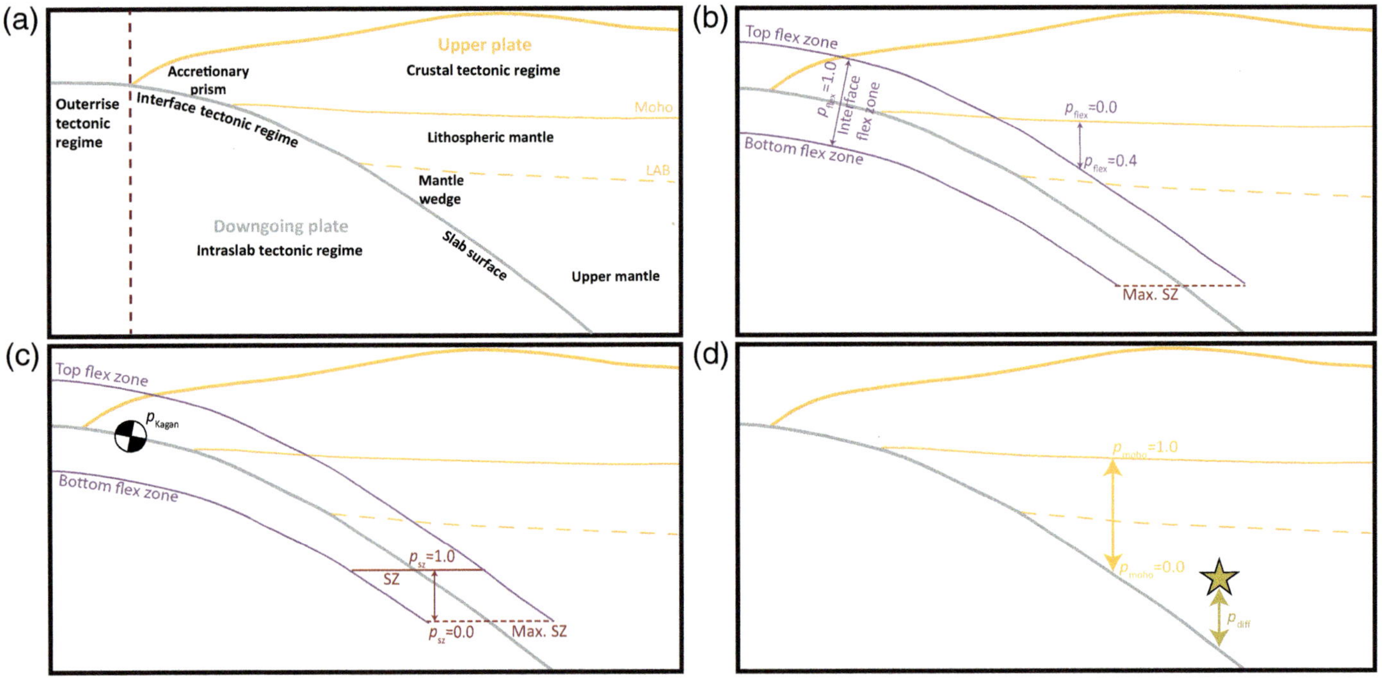

$$P_{\text{slab}} = 1 - (P_{\text{interface}} + P_{\text{crustal}}). \tag{5}$$

It is essential to note that the calculation of the intraslab plausibility score lacks a logical framework. Instead, CatSep prioritizes the accurate classification of interface events, which may introduce a potential bias.

Earthquakes occurring outside the Slab2 surface, below the Moho, and below the maximum depth of the seismogenic zone have the potential to be flagged as mantle events. These events are flagged after the plausibility score for each tectonic regime are calculated and is only determined for events that were not classified as interface. This mantle flag is given to an event if it occurred below the maximum seismogenic zone depth but above the Slab2 slab surface depth plus the Slab2 depth uncertainty given at the location of the earthquake.

Earthquakes that are assigned equal probabilities are also flagged. This is uncommon. However, if an equal plausibility score that an earthquake occurred in specific tectonic regimes is assigned, additional criteria are assessed to determine the most likely classification. In addition, a quality is assigned to each classification. These range from "A," meaning there is high confidence that the earthquake was classified correctly, to "D," meaning there is low confidence that the earthquake was classified correctly. This quality grade is determined by the plausibility score assigned to the classification and whether a moment tensor is provided for the earthquake. If there is a moment tensor, the quality is given by

$$\text{Quality} = \begin{cases} A & \text{when } P(x) \geq 0.8, \\ B & \text{when } 0.6 \leq P(x) < 0.8, \\ C & \text{when } 0.4 \leq P(x) < 0.6, \text{ or} \\ D & \text{when } P(x) < 0.4. \end{cases} \tag{6}$$

Figure 2. Cartoon displaying the parameters and associated scoring ramps used in the classification algorithm (refer to equation 1, Table 1, and the Earthquake Classification Methods section for more details). (a) Subduction zone cross-section cartoon with features used in the algorithm and tectonic regimes labeled. The red-dashed line indicates the bounds of the subduction zone region which separates the outerrise regime from the other tectonic regimes. (b) Parameters used in the interface plausibility score calculation for p_{flex}, which gives the plausibility score that the earthquake occurred within the interface flex zone. (c) Parameters used in the remainder of the interface plausibility score calculation. p_{sz} gives the plausibility score that the event occurred within the seismogenic zone. p_{Kagan} is only used when a moment tensor is available with ramp values provided in Table 1. (d) Parameters used in the crustal plausibility score calculation, where p_{diff} is based on the difference between earthquake depth (gold start) and slab depth (values provided in Table 1) and p_{moho} is determined based on how close the earthquake is to the Moho versus the slab's depth. LAB, lithosphere asthenosphere boundary; Max. SZ, maximum seismogenic zone depth; Moho, Mohorovičić discontinuity; SZ, seismogenic zone depth. Cartoon is not drawn to scale.

Because moment tensors provide additional data that improve the classification of interface events, for earthquakes without moment tensors, the quality grades are lower,

$$\text{Quality} = \begin{cases} B & \text{when } P(x) \geq 0.8, \\ C & \text{when } 6 \leq P(x) < 0.8, \text{ or} \\ D & \text{when } P(x) < 0.6. \end{cases} \tag{7}$$

By default, outerrise, mantle, or equally scored earthquakes are given a quality grade of "D." Such classifications are flagged and assigned a quality so that the user is aware and can

TABLE 2
Confusion Matrix Illustrating How CatSep Predictions Compare to Actual Results

	Predicted Values		
Actual Values	**Crustal (32 Total)**	**Interface (49 Total)**	**Intraslab (26 Total)**
Crustal (28 total)	28	3	0
Interface (57 total)	3	40	6
Intraslab (22 total	1	6	20

perform manual inspection of the result to best determine in which regime the earthquake resides.

Heuristic procedure

These methods were informed using 107 global events that were manually classified into crustal, interface, and intraslab. These global events are all within Slab2 subduction regions. Because moment tensors provide a higher quality score (i.e., higher confidence) for determining interface plausibility, it is important that the majority of the test catalog events contain moment tensors. Of the 107 global test events, 95 events (54 interface, 20 crustal, and 21 intraslab) contain moment tensors, and 12 (2 interface and 10 crustal) do not. This test catalog was used to determine the best values for each parameter in the probabilistic earthquake classification method (Table 1) by minimizing the Brier score, which is a goodness-of-fit metric for probabilistic predictions given by

$$\text{Brier Score} = \frac{1}{N}\sum_{t=1}^{N}(p_t - o_t)^2, \quad (8)$$

in which N is the number of items used in the Brier score calculation, p_t is the predicted result, and o_t is the observed, or actual, result.

In this scoring method, a value of 0.0 means the prediction matches reality and is completely accurate, whereas a Brier score of 1.0 means the prediction is inaccurate. Thus, Brier scores closer to 0.0 indicate a higher accuracy prediction. The aforementioned methodology and values utilized in Table 1 yield Brier scores of 0.010 for the crustal test events, 0.155 for the interface test events, and 0.097 for the intraslab test events. This analysis suggests that interface and intraslab events have a higher chance of being misclassified than crustal events.

A confusion matrix used to visualize the performance of the algorithm is provided in Table 2. This illustrates how CatSep predictions compare to actual results. For example, of the 107 global test events, CatSep classified 32 events as crustal, although 3 are interface and 1 is intraslab; 49 events as interface, though 3 are crustal and 6 and intraslab; and 26 events as intraslab, with 6 being interface. This analysis indicates that the interface classification has the highest rate of false positives. However, the positive predictive values are 87.5% for crustal, 81.6% for interface, and 76% for intraslab, suggesting that events classified as intraslab have the lowest accuracy in this classification method. This may in part be due to the lack of any logical framework in the intraslab calculation (refer to the Earthquake Classification Methods for more details).

Earthquake Classification Code: CatSep

The subduction zone catalog separation code, referred to as CatSep (Haynie, 2024), is written in Python and is optimized to run in parallel to handle earthquake catalogs with tens of thousands of events. The code relies heavily upon the USGS Slab2 subduction zone model (Hayes *et al.*, 2018) using Slab2 seismogenic zone depths, querying the Slab2 depth, depth uncertainty, dip, and strike grid files, as well as, by default, only classifying the provided earthquake catalog to within the bounds of the specified Slab2 region.

Running CatSep

Any default values and probabilities associated with the ramp function calculations (Table 1) used in CatSep (Haynie, 2024) were determined by the heuristic approach defined in the Heuristic procedure subsection. These values can be fine-tuned to a specific subduction zone or updated as needed by the user before running the code. Because CatSep relies heavily upon Slab2 data and the Slab2 catalog input format, the CatSep code repository includes Slab2 model files and input catalogs. It is recommended to use the default values and ramp parameters when running the code using Slab2 data. CatSep can be run for using the following command,

```
python catalog_sep/src/classify_catalog.py
<slab> <path-to-csv>
```

in which `<slab>` is the name of the Slab2 region to use, and `<path-to-csv>` is the path to the input catalog file.

CatSep determines the number of central processing units (CPUs) to utilize based on what is available on the user's machine. Depending on the number of CPUs and the input catalog size, the parallelized code may take a few minutes to a few hours to run. Once finished, the results are saved as a comma-separated value (CSV) file. This file can then be filtered into subcatalogs for each tectonic regime using a utility script (`separate_csv.py`) provided in the repository (Haynie, 2024).

To utilize CatSep for a user-specified earthquake catalog (i.e., not a Slab2 input catalog), the catalog must first be converted into the Slab2 input catalog format. This can be done manually or by following instructions in the documentation for the USGS slab models repository (see Data and Resources). Note that the earthquake catalog must be associated with a Slab2 subduction region.

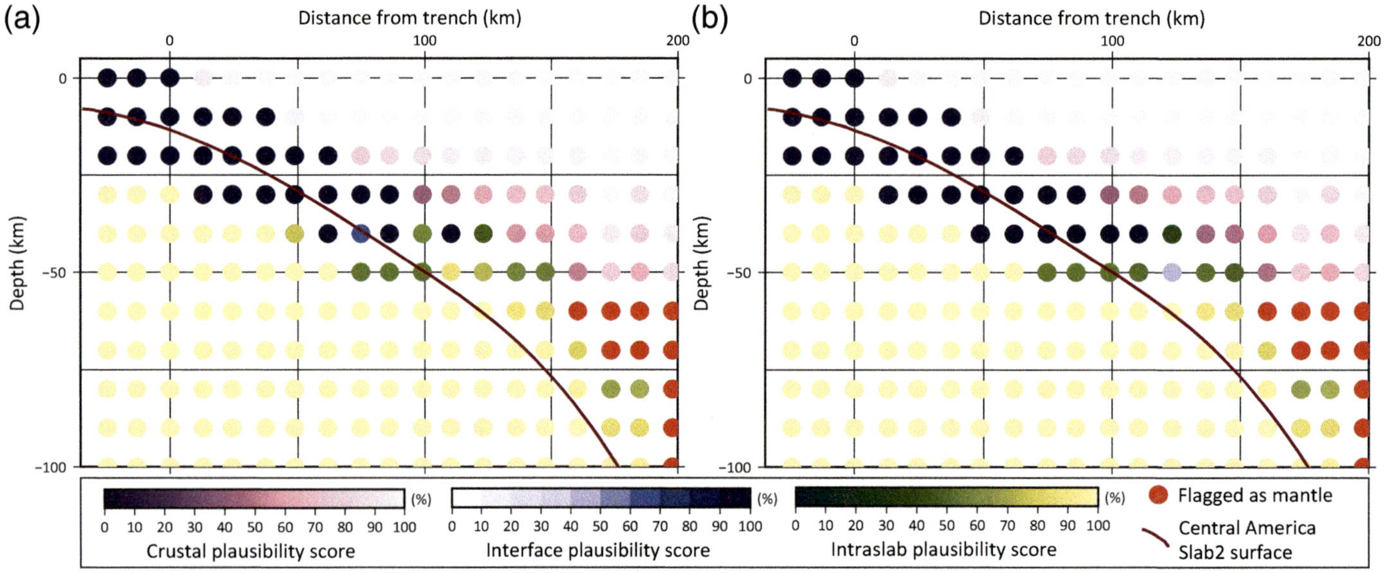

Figure 3. Cross sections through the central America subduction zone at 267° E longitude and 14° N latitude. Earthquakes are projected onto the cross section from 30 km on either side of the cross-section line. (a) Results from CatSep using a test earthquake catalog with moment tensors. (b) Results from CatSep using the same test catalog in (a), but without moment tensors. Plausibility scores are plotted as a percentage. Slab2 surface is plotted in dark red from Hayes *et al.* (2018).

A user can add moment tensors to their catalog. Although moment tensors are not required for running the classification code, the inclusion of this data type is intended to lead to better constrained interface events. The CatSep repository provides a script to retrieve moment tensors (`get_mt.py`) from the Advanced National Seismic System (ANSS) Comprehensive Catalog (ComCat) hosted by the U.S. Geological Survey, Earthquake Hazards Program (2017). Figure 3 illustrates the difference between using an earthquake catalog with and without moment tensors for the central America Slab2 subduction region. This gridded central America test catalog was generated using moment tensors from interface, crustal, and intraslab events and was taken directly from the test catalog used in the heuristic testing (section Heuristic procedure). Results from running the same earthquake catalog with and without moment tensors are very similar, with the most notable difference occurring for interface events at a depth of 40 km (Fig. 3). At this depth, results show more uncertainty between interface and intraslab events, with the catalog containing moment tensors (Fig. 3a) providing a lower plausibility score for interface classification than the catalog without moment tensors (Fig. 3b).

Earthquake classification for USGS NSHMs. Classifying USGS NSHM subduction zone earthquake catalogs requires a few updates to the classification process. In general, the NSHM requires that all earthquakes in the input catalog are classified. As a result, the classification code does not impose the Slab2 subduction region bounds, nor does it flag earthquakes as mantle, and all quality rankings are considered. Earthquakes that occur outside the Slab2 subduction region bounds are assigned the tectonic regime "outer-rise." Such earthquakes are then classified according to procedures and results determined during the gridded seismicity process (refer to Llenos *et al.*, 2025). In reality, these events are likely crustal, intraslab, or outerrise depending on various factors such as depth, focal mechanism, and location. Nonetheless, employing these methods ensures that every event in the provided NSHM catalog is classified into an appropriate tectonic regime that is used to create seismicity models that are then assigned a specific ground-motion modeling equation. To follow these guidelines, the `-nshm True` flag can be used when running the code.

2025 Puerto Rico and U.S. Virgin Islands NSHM Earthquake Catalog and Classification

2025 NSHM PRVI earthquake catalog

The 2025 NSHM PRVI earthquake catalog was sourced from two catalogs: (1) ANSS ComCat and (2) a corrected catalog from the Puerto Rico Seismic Network (PRSN, Huérfano and Lin, 2022). These input catalogs contained a mixture of magnitude types. Events without a moment magnitude, M_w, were converted to M_w using conversion equations following NSHM methods in Mueller (2019). For the PRSN catalog, a duration magnitude, M_D, to M_w conversion was performed using an orthogonal distance regression equation provided by the PRSN (refer to Llenos *et al.*, 2025, for more details).

The ANSS ComCat catalog query spanned a region of 72°–60° W longitude and 12°–23° N latitude, and from 1 January 1600 to 31 December 2023 for all earthquakes greater than or equal to a magnitude of 2, for all magnitude types. The final ANSS ComCat catalog contained 14,358 earthquakes from 1615 to 2023 with M_w 2+. The corrected PRSN catalog was queried for **M** 2+ within 69°–63.5° W longitude and 17°–20° N latitude. This resulted in a catalog with 67,052 events of M_w 2+ from 1986 to 2021.

To create the 2025 NSHM PRVI earthquake catalog, the ANSS ComCat and PRSN catalogs were merged. The PRSN catalog was taken as authoritative, such that PRSN data were used for any duplicate events. Nontectonic events as well as duplicates were removed, resulting in a final catalog with 81,410 events for M_w 2+ from 8 September 1615 to 31 December 2023. Finally, specifically for the catalog separation procedure, moment tensor information was obtained from ANSS ComCat for events where a moment tensor had been calculated. Moment tensors were available for 167 earthquakes.

Because earthquake depth is essential in the CatSep algorithm, depth values for events that were assigned default depths (e.g., 15, 25, or 33 km) were replaced. Values from Doser *et al.* (2005) and Russo and Villaseñor (1995) were used for 11 historic earthquakes spanning 1900–1946. For other default depth events, the depth distribution of nearby hypocenters since 1973 with $M_w \geq 4$ were used to estimate the plausibility scores. Plausibility scores were calculated using that depth distribution at the epicenter of the default depth event. The resulting plausibility scores were then averaged providing a more realistic estimate on tectonic regime plausibility score. More details are available in Llenos *et al.* (2025).

CatSep specifications for the 2025 PRVI NSHM

The Puerto Rico and U.S. Virgin Islands NSHM has additional complexities that the classification code handles. Specifically, this NSHM region contains two subduction zones: the (1) Muertos trough and (2) Caribbean subduction zone. The classification code is able to handle catalogs that span two user-specified Slab2 subduction regions, using the `-second_slab` argument, by determining which slab is vertically closest to each earthquake in the catalog. The respective Slab2 properties are then used to determine the earthquake's classification. If an earthquake is equidistant to both slabs, the first user-supplied slab region is used. Because the code only uses the vertical distance between the earthquake's hypocenter and the Slab2 surfaces, this case would only occur if the earthquake is below one slab surface and above another slab surface, implying that the earthquake is most likely an intraslab event and the assumption of which slab to use is inconsequential. With the seismogenic zone depth being poorly constrained by Slab2 for both the Muertos and Caribbean slabs, the code assumes a seismogenic zone depth of 40 km for the Muertos slab and 50 km for the Caribbean slab based on values reported in Slab2 (Hayes *et al.*, 2018). Other parameter values used for the PRVI NSHM classification process are specified in Table 1.

CatSep results for the 2025 NSHM PRVI catalog

The catalog separation code separated all 81,410 events from the 2025 NSHM PRVI earthquake catalog into four tectonic regimes: crustal, interface, intraslab, and outerrise. 41,634 earthquakes were classified as crustal, 17,856 as interface, 20,852 as intraslab, and 1,068 as outerrise. No equal probabilities were assigned. 116 events were given a quality rank of "A," 76,582 a quality of "B," 2,039 a quality of "C," and 2,673 a quality of "D," where 1,068 of those were outerrise and by default were given this quality ranking. 34,815 earthquakes were classified as having occurred within the Muertos subduction region, and 46,595 were classified as having occurred within the Caribbean subduction region.

All earthquakes classified as interface occur along the shallow portion of the slabs down to depths of 55 km for the Muertos slab and 65 km for the Caribbean slab (Figs. 4 and 5). Events that occur deeper than that, either below the slab surface, above the slab surface and within the slab depth uncertainty, or in-between the two slabs are classified as intraslab. Shallow earthquakes as well as earthquakes above the slab surface and interface are marked as crustal. Earthquakes that occur outside of the Slab2 regions are tagged as outerrise. A strong linear cutoff between outerrise and non-outerrise events is clearly seen (e.g., cross section E in Fig. 5). This is because CatSep strictly classifies any event outside of a Slab2 region as outerrise. In some cross sections, crustal earthquakes occur along the same depth resulting in a horizontal line of crustal earthquakes (e.g., cross sections B, G, and H in Fig. 5). This is not a result of the CatSep process, but instead is likely due to seismic networks setting a default depth for events that are poorly constrained.

Future Considerations for CatSep

Although the USGS subduction zone earthquake catalog separator code is effective at classifying large earthquake catalogs into various subduction zone tectonic regimes, there are several areas for improvement that future enhancements to the code could consider. Small enhancements include incorporating other subduction-related tectonic regimes, such as volcanic, and improving default variables (e.g., thickness of the buffer zone used for constraining interface events), as well as fine-tuning parameters to best suit specific subduction zones. Another ramp function that tapers Kagan angle parameter values could also be included so that if focal mechanisms are similar to a thrust mechanism a higher plausibility score is given. CatSep currently uses vertical distance to query slab properties. However, for steep slabs the closest distance from the earthquake to the slab may be the horizontal distance, which may result in misclassifications. The closest, perhaps perpendicular, distance to the slab could be considered in future updates. A more involved enhancement is to take various steps to make the code fully probabilistic. This updated method may consider taking into account all uncertainties with moment tensors,

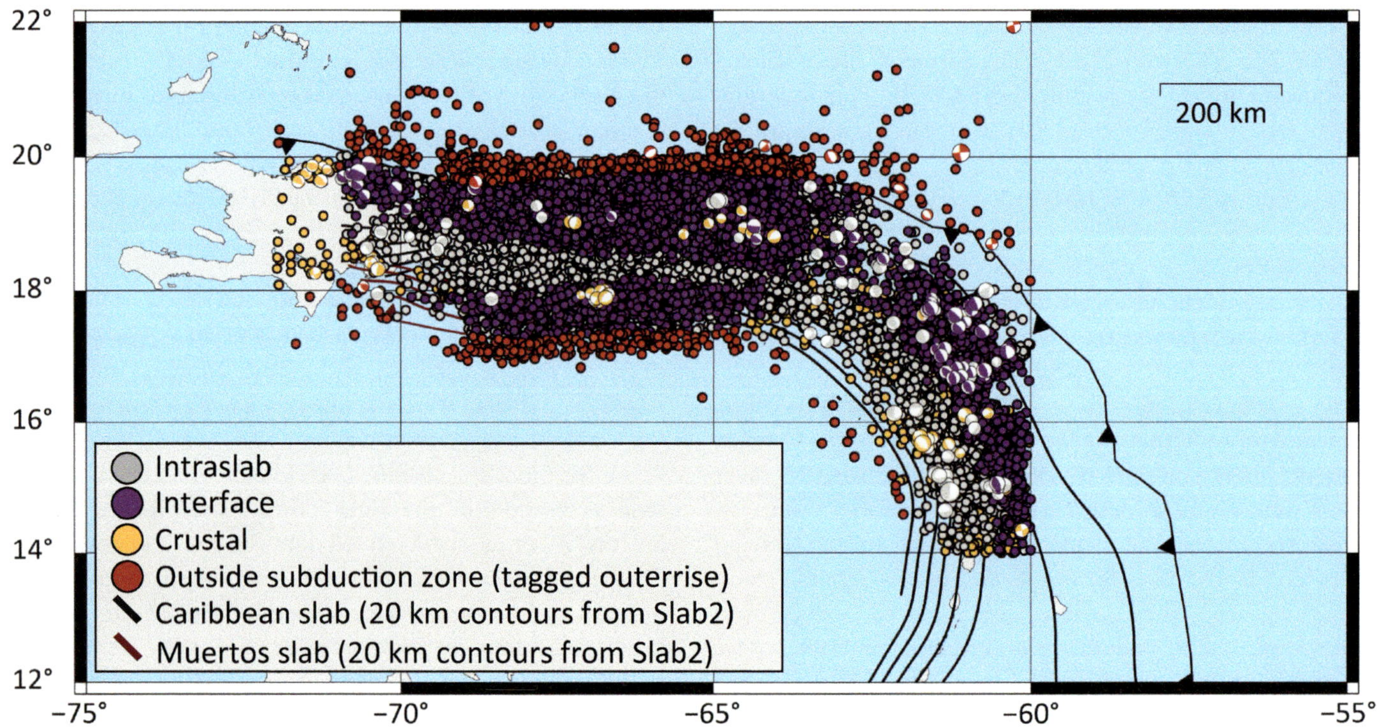

Figure 4. Map view of the 2025 PRVI NSHM earthquake catalog separated into tectonic regimes using the CatSep software (Haynie, 2024). Intraslab events are plotted in gray, interface events in purple, crustal events in orange, and events tagged as outerrise in red. Slab2 contours are plotted in 20 km intervals for the Caribbean (black) and Muertos (maroon) slabs. Crustal events make up majority of the separated catalog and are plotted below the intraslab and interface events so that these events can be clearly depicted. Refer to Figure 5 to view crustal events in cross section.

earthquake location, and slab properties using probability distribution functions.

Summary

An earthquake catalog separation methodology and code was developed for classifying subduction zone earthquake catalogs into tectonic regimes. The USGS NSHM is employing this new methodology in subduction zone regions so that appropriate seismicity models for each tectonic regime are created such that appropriate ground-motion models are then applied. The catalog separation code uses a simple ramp function with parameter values determined via a heuristic approach. The parallel Python CatSep code is open source and available via Haynie (2024). Users can apply this tool to their own subduction zone catalogs and fine-tune variables to best suit their subduction zone of interest. The default variables and methods described here for NSHM purposes were applied to the 2024 Alaska and 2025 Puerto Rico and U.S. Virgin Islands NSHM earthquake catalogs. Running the 2025 PRVI NSHM earthquake catalog through CatSep gives results that are expected, where interface events occur to the maximum seismogenic zone depth and within a buffer region around the shallow slab. Intraslab events occur below the Slab2 surface, and crustal events occur above the Slab2 surface and interface buffer zone.

Data and Resources

The 2025 National Seismic Hazard Model (NSHM) Puerto Rico and U.S. Virgin Islands (PRVI) earthquake catalog and separated catalogs are available in Shumway *et al.* (2025). The version of the U.S. Geological Survey (USGS) Earthquake Catalog Separation code, CatSep, used for the 2025 PRVI NSHM is available through Haynie (2024). The SeismoTectonic Regime Earthquake Calculator (STREC) code mentioned in the Earthquake Classification Methods section is available at https://code.usgs.gov/ghsc/esi/strec. Documentation on how to use the USGS slab modeling code for generating input files is available at https://ghsc.codepages.usgs.gov/esi/usgs-slab-models/index.html (last accessed June 2024).

Declaration of Competing Interests

The authors acknowledge that there are no conflicts of interest recorded.

Acknowledgments

The authors thank Zachary Cloutet for code reviews, as well as Bruce Worden, Kiran Kumar Thingbaijam, and an anonymous reviewer for their literature reviews. Generic Mapping Tools version 6 was used for plotting (Wessel *et al.*, 2019).

Any use of trade, firm, or product names is for descriptive purposes only and does not imply endorsement by the U.S. Government.

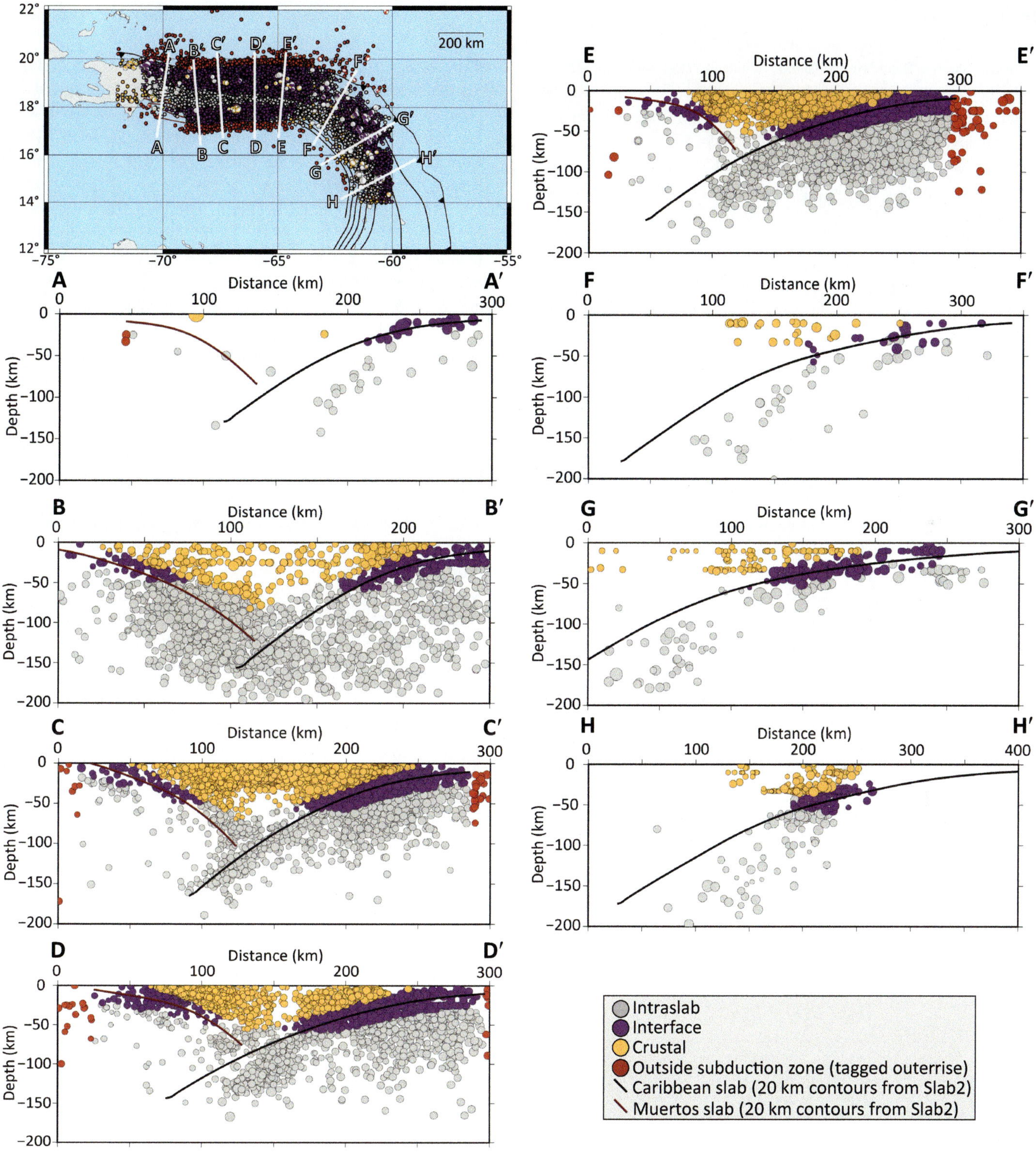

Figure 5. Cross sections through the classified 2025 PRVI NSHM earthquake catalog. Slab2 (Hayes *et al.*, 2018) geometries for the Muertos and Caribbean slabs are plotted in maroon and black, respectively. Earthquakes are projected from 20 km on either side of each cross section.

References

Doser, D. I., C. M. Rodriguez, and C. Flores (2005). Historical earthquakes of the Puerto Rico–Virgin Islands region (1915–1963), in *Active Tectonics and Seismic Hazards of Puerto Rico, the Virgin Islands, and Offshore Areas*, P. Mann (Editor), Vol. 385, Geological Society of America Special Papers, Boulder, Colorado, 103–114.

García, D., D. J. Wald, and M. G. Hearne (2012). A global earthquake discrimination scheme to optimize ground-motion prediction equation selection, *Bull. Seismol. Soc. Am.* **102**, no. 1, 185–203.

Hayes, G. P., G. L. Moore, D. E. Portner, M. Hearne, H. Flamme, M. Furtney, and G. M. Smoczyk (2018). Slab2, a comprehensive subduction zone geometry model, *Science* **362,** no. 6410, 58–61.

Haynie, K. L. (2024). Subduction zone earthquake catalog separation code, *U.S. Geol. Surv. Software Release v1.0.0*, doi: 10.5066/P13E7CAY.

Huérfano, V. A., and G. Lin (2022). Characteristics of seismicity in Puerto Rico and the U.S. Virgin Islands: Collaborative research with University of Miami, and University of Puerto Rico in Mayagüez, *Final Technical Rept.*, 67 pp., available at https://earthquake.usgs.gov/cfusion/external_grants/reports/G21AP10252.pdf (last accessed February 2025).

Kagan, Y. (1991). 3-D rotation of double-couple earthquake sources, *Geophys. J. Int.* **106,** no. 3, 709–716.

Laske, G., G. Masters, Z. Ma, and M. Pasyanos (2013). Update on CRUST1.0—A 1-degree global model of Earth's crust, *EGU General Assembly 2013*, Vol. 15, 2658.

Llenos, A. L., A. J. Michael, K. L. Haynie, A. M. Shumway, and J. A. Herrick (2025). Using gridded seismicity to forecast the long-term spatial distribution of earthquakes for the 2025 Puerto Rico and U.S. Virgin Islands National Seismic Hazard Model, *Seismol. Res. Lett.*

Llenos, A. L., A. J. Michael, A. M. Shumway, J. L. Rubinstein, K. L. Haynie, M. P. Moschetti, J. M. Altekruse, and K. R. Milner (2024). Forecasting the long-term spatial distribution of earthquakes for the 2023 US National Seismic Hazard Model using gridded seismicity, *Bull. Seismol. Soc. Am.* **114,** no. 4, 2028–2053.

Mueller, C. S. (2019). Earthquake catalogs for the USGS National Seismic Hazard Maps. *Seismol. Res. Lett.* **90,** no. 1, 251–261.

Powers, P. M., J. M. Altekruse, A. L. Llenos, A. J. Michael, K. L. Haynie, P. J. Haeussler, A. M. Bender, S. Rezaeian, M. P. Moschetti, J. A. Smith, *et al.* (2024). The 2023 Alaska National Seismic Hazard Model, *Earthq. Spectra* **40,** no. 4, 2545–2597.

Russo, R. M., and A. Villaseñor (1995). The 1946 Hispaniola earthquakes and the tectonics of the North America-Caribbean plate boundary zone, northeastern Hispaniola, *J. Geophys. Res.* **100,** no. B4, 6265–6280.

Shumway, A., K. Milner, J. Altekruse, J. Herrick, M. Llenos, K. Haynie, R. Briggs, and K. Jaiswal (2025). Data release for the 2025 USGS National Seismic Hazard Model for Puerto Rico and the U.S. Virgin Islands: Overview of model and hazard results, *U.S. Geol. Surv. Data Release*, doi: 10.5066/P14ATJLJ.

U.S. Geological Survey, Earthquake Hazards Program (2017). Advanced National Seismic System (ANSS) comprehensive catalog of earthquake events and products, doi: 10.5066/f7ms3qzh.

Wessel, P., J. F. Luis, L. Uieda, R. Scharroo, F. Wobbe, W. H. F. Smith, and D. Tian (2019). The Generic Mapping Tools version 6, *Geochem. Geophys. Geosys.* **20,** no. 11, 5556–5564.

Wesson, R. L., O. S. Boyd, C. S. Mueller, C. G. Bufe, A. D. Frankel, and M. D. Petersen (2007). Revision of time-independent probabilistic seismic hazard maps for Alaska, *U.S. Geol. Surv. Open-File Rept. 2007-1043*, 33 pp., doi: 10.3133/ofr20071043.

Worden, C. B., E. M. Thompson, M. G. Hearne, and D. J. Wald (2024). ShakeMap Manual Online: Technical manual, user's guide, and software guide, doi: 10.5066/F7D21VPQ.

Manuscript received 3 March 2025
Published online 15 October 2025

Demise of the Pilgrimage Town of Philippi (Northern Greece): Structural, Hydrogeological, Historical, and Seismological Implications of an Unrecorded, Seventh Century Strong Earthquake in a Low-Seismicity Region

Stathis C. Stiros*[1]

Abstract

Philippi, a small Greek and then Roman town in Northern Greece, became a flourishing pilgrimage center in the fourth century, commemorating the first Christian community in Europe established by St. Paul. After the sixth century, impressive churches and other buildings of the town were turned into ruins, currently registered in the UNESCO World Heritage. The reasons and timing of the demise of the town are unclear, and several scenarios have been proposed to explain them. Analysis of excavation data indicates no signs of invasion by Slavs or Avars, but sitewide destruction, which can be assigned to a major unrecorded earthquake that occurred probably within approximately 15 yr after 615, as numismatic data (hiatus in coin circulation) reveal. This result is important because Philippi is in a low-seismicity region, whereas an earthquake alone cannot easily explain the demise of a town with a millennium-long history. However, it was found that the destructive earthquake had produced an up to 10 m drop in a karstic spring feeding a low-gradient aqueduct, depriving Philippi of a main infrastructure of a Roman and Byzantine town, especially of a pilgrimage center. This, in combination with the overall sociopolitical situation, hindered the town's postseismic recovery. The destruction pattern and extent, as well as the structural characteristics of the destroyed buildings, testify to a strong earthquake of intensity IX or X (MMS) from a nearby source. Two nearby known active normal faults are candidates for the earthquake source, but the Xanthi fault, well marked in the topography, and especially its continuation offshore, is more likely, because it runs mid-distance (about 20 km) from Philippi and the Town of Thasos, another site for which seismic damage at the same period was claimed.

Cite this article as Stiros, S. C. (2025). Demise of the Pilgrimage Town of Philippi (Northern Greece): Structural, Hydrogeological, Historical, and Seismological Implications of an Unrecorded, Seventh Century Strong Earthquake in a Low-Seismicity Region, *Seismol. Res. Lett.* **97**, 1201–1214, doi: 10.1785/0220250226.

Introduction

The wider Aegean region is recognized as a broad zone of distributed seismicity, faulting, and deformation, within which some regions of limited seismicity exist. The central part of the Aegean Sea is one of them. A second one extends north of the North Aegean trough (NAT, continuation of the North Anatolian fault), covering the provinces of Eastern Macedonia and Thrace in the Greek territory. In this region, a few moderate earthquakes have been recorded by seismographs (Fig. 1), and a few poorly constrained, even dubious earthquakes are known from historical sources (e.g., Guidoboni *et al.*, 1994; Papazachos and Papazachou, 1997; Ambraseys, 2009; Albin *et al.*, 2013; Stiros, 2025). Low seismicity correlates with rarity of active faults (Caputo *et al.*, 2012) and minimal internal deformation derived from geodetic observations (Mouslopoulou *et al.*, 2014).

1. Department of Civil Engineering, Patras University, Patras, Greece, https://orcid.org/0000-0002-6451-5375 (SCS)

*Corresponding author: stiros@upatras.gr

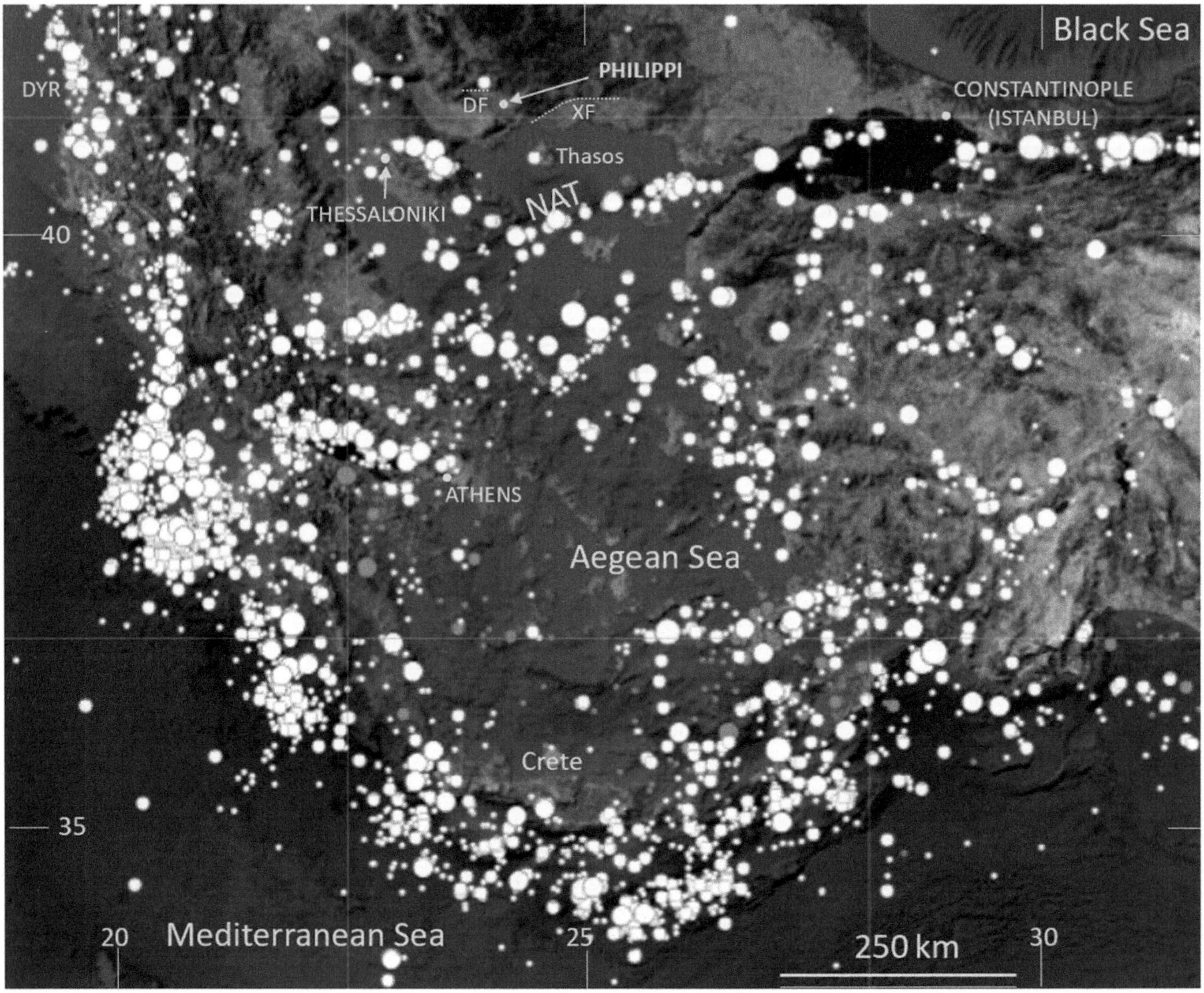

Figure 1. Earthquake epicenters in Greece and adjacent regions, 1900–2015, **M** > 4.5 (after U.S. Geological Survey, with additions). Philippi is located in one of the zones of low seismicity in the broader Aegean region. It was also located on the Via Egnatia (Road) crossing the Balkan peninsula, from Dyrrachium (DYR) to Byzantium, later Constantinople, and still later Istanbul. This road, passing through Thessaloniki, connected Rome with the eastern provinces. Two yellow-dashed lines indicate the active faults in the vicinity of Philippi, the Drama fault (DF) and Xanthi fault (KV; simplified after Caputo *et al.*, 2012). The color version of this figure is available only in the electronic edition.

In these conditions, the most promising way to understand active tectonics is palaeoseismology, especially archaeoseismology, based on the study of earthquakes that have left traces on ancient constructions, widespread in this region. Still, this is not an easy task because, despite the large number of archaeological remains, the evidence of seismic damage is limited and is essentially ignored by Earth scientists.

This study focuses on the ancient town of Philippi, at the center of this low-seismicity zone of northeast Greece (Fig. 1). Philippi is mainly known as the town that hosted the first Christian church in Europe, founded in about A.D. 50 by St. Paul who is broadly recognized as an Apostle, though he was not one of the 12 Apostles. For this reason, it became an important pilgrimage center.

Since the seventh or eighth century, major public and other buildings were ruined, and the town was essentially abandoned (Sève, 2000; Fournier, 2016; Mentzos, 2016). The conditions and reasons for the demise of Philippi are unclear, and several scenarios have been proposed to explain it, mostly earthquake and invasion scenarios, representing *deus ex machina* explanations, common for Archaeology (Rapp, 1986; Stiros, 1996).

Evidence presented here favors the scenario of an earthquake-induced demise. Still, this raises an important question. In antiquity, the towns in the broader region had a long history, were resilient, and could survive destructive earthquakes

for millennia (Di Vita, 1996; Mentzos, 2016, p. 258). Hence, if an earthquake marks the end of the Late Roman-Early Byzantine period of Philippi, what was the particularity of this earthquake? An answer to this problem is given based on the hydrogeological impacts of the ancient earthquake on the aqueduct of Philippi.

Figure 2. Topography of the central (downtown) part of Philippi. Ancient remains are marked on a Google Earth Pro background. In inset, the plan and cross section of the sixth century Basilica B, in the left part of the figure, after Lemerle (1945). This Basilica, approximately 100 m long and 35 m high, was a fine example of early, major vaulted churches and gives an impression of the importance of the site. The color version of this figure is available only in the electronic edition.

Ancient Town of Philippi

Philippi was a small mining Greek town, which, in Roman times, was found in a strategic position on Via Egnatia, a road connecting the Adriatic with the Eastern provinces of the Empire (Fig. 1). A battle next to its walls in 42 B.C., marking the defeat of the republicans by the imperial forces, made Philippi a benchmark in the imperial history of Rome, and then a privileged Roman colony, a miniature of Rome. This town also became a benchmark for Christianity because of the first Christian community in Europe, established by St. Paul, who was imprisoned in this town and later addressed one of his Epistles to its Christian community (Philippians). For this reason, since the fourth or fifth century, Philippi became a flourishing pilgrimage center, culminating in the sixth century (Fig. 2). The main characteristic of this town was a network of at least four imposing churches and of other religious buildings, very close to each other, a quite unusual situation for a small town in the early Christian period. Pilgrims followed a tour of these sites, probably dedicated to different events in the life of St. Paul in this town (Mentzos, 2005).

Since 1914, numerous excavations have brought to light the remains of major churches, various public buildings, and the ancient Greek theater. Because of these findings, Philippi is inscribed among the United Nations Educational, Scientific and Cultural Organization (UNESCO) World Heritage Convention sites. Illustrative information and reconstructions of the ancient town and its monuments can be found in webpages 1–4 (see Data and Resources).

The archaeological excavations also revealed that since the seventh or eighth century, the late Roman-Early Byzantine town, previously flourishing, was characterized by generalized destruction and partial abandonment until a new wave of building works partly revitalized the pilgrimage town a few centuries later (Sève, 2000; Fournier, 2016; Mentzos, 2016).

Previous Scenarios for the Demise of Philippi

Four main scenarios have been proposed for the demise of Philippi.

First, Lemerle (1945), one of the first excavators of Philippi, assigned the demise of the early Byzantine town to the Slavic expansion in the area in the 580s, during a period of weakness of the Late Roman-Early Byzantine Empire.

A second scenario was inspired by an earthquake that caused much damage to Thessaloniki in 1978 (Papazachos and Papazachou, 1997). According to this hypothesis, proposed mainly by Bakirtzis (1989), in about the year 620, a Thessaloniki earthquake destroyed Philippi, but the town was not abandoned. Other investigators proposed earlier or later dates for the earthquake destruction.

A third scenario was proposed by Sève (2021), who argued that the town was depopulated because of a sixth century pest epidemic, and could not recover after the earthquake about the year 620.

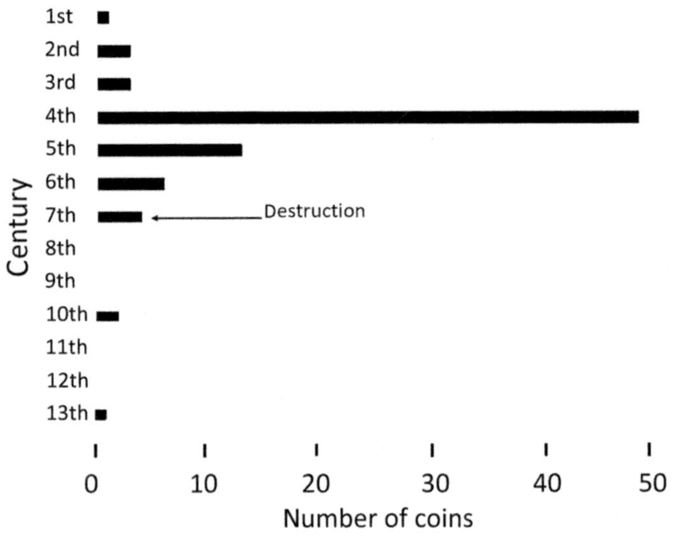

Figure 3. Datable stray (randomly lost) coins from the fourth sector of the Thessaloniki University excavation at Philippi (for location see Fig. 2), apparently representative of the wider town. A hiatus in coin circulation after 614 to 615 defines a lower bound for the destruction layer. Partial recovery in the tenth century is also derived. Based on data of Gounari (2016).

A fourth scenario was proposed by Poulou (2019–2020), who questioned the seismic destruction and suggested that the observed changes in buildings indicate an intentional reorganization of the urban space of Philippi since the seventh century (Poulou, 2019–2020, p. 136).

Limitations of Proposed Scenarios

The Slavic invasion scenario was essentially based on an ancient sermon, "*The Miracles of St Demetrius*." This sermon claims that most of the present-day Northern Greece was occupied by Slavic tribes, and only Thessaloniki, the second major town in the Balkans after Constantinople, had remained free because of certain miracles of its protector, St Demetrius. This information seems to be supported by additional, vague, and exaggerated information that in the 580s, and possibly also in the 590s, the Slavs raided the Balkan peninsula (Blondé *et al.*, 1984), conquering some castles and destroying and burning towns (e.g., *John of Ephesus, Eccles. History, VI,25*), so some authors hypothesize that Philippi was among them. Still, no signs of fires, looting, or a different culture (pottery, etc.) have been found in Philippi (Zachariadis, 2014; Poulou-Papadimitriou, 2000; Poulou, 2019–2020) to justify an invasion. In addition, the only significant archaeological argument for the invasion scenario was that no Byzantine coins later than 585 were found in the broader area because it was detached from the Byzantine Empire (Lemerle, 1979, p. 401). However, this argument proved incorrect because more recent coins have been found in Philippi (Fig. 3) and the broader region to the northeast (Gandila and Hristov, 2023), whereas newer analysis discards the possibility of Slavic occupation of Macedonia (Curta, 2012). Interestingly, an earthquake was included in this scenario to explain the collapse of the dome of a major church in Philippi about the year 550 (Lemerle, 1945, p. 139, 289).

The earthquake scenario, which was adopted by many investigators (e.g., Kourkoutidou-Nikolaïdou, 1995; Gounaris and Velenis, 1996; Sève, 2000; Fournier, 2016), is presented in different versions, with earthquake damage dated between approximately the years 600 and 850 (Gounaris, 1988; Bakirtzis, 1989; Mentzos, 2016; Mentzos *et al.*, 2016, p. 259). Another earthquake at around 500 was also postulated (Sève, 2000). The unclear earthquake chronology and the possibility of recurrence of destructive earthquakes in a region of low seismicity (Fig. 1) are major problems with this scenario.

The association of damage to Philippi with inferred seismic damage to Thessaloniki about the year 620, in particular, is not justified, because the evidence comes from "*The Miracles…*": This sermon mentions an earthquake that affected Thessaloniki, causing a cloud of dust from the collapse of walls and buildings, which triggered a Slavic raid. Still, when the Slavs approached for looting, to their surprise, they found the town unharmed, because of a miracle of St Demetrius, and they retreated (*Mir. S. Dim, 222*). This postulated earthquake, indirectly dated only, is ignored or discarded in most earthquake catalogs (Guidoboni *et al.*, 1994; Ambraseys, 2009), and it probably derives from the memory of another earthquake, possibly distant, earlier, or later.

The third scenario tries to explain the unusual demise of an ancient town as a result of a combination of an epidemic and an earthquake, but it has some difficulties. An epidemic is expected to have led to mass burials, for which there exists some evidence because many burials were found around and inside the ruins of Basilica B. Still, one of these graves, perhaps the only well-described one, was assigned to an earthquake victim (Gounaris, 1984).

Finally, the fourth scenario, which emphasizes a reorganization of the urban space of Philippi, does not explain the cause of the destruction or replacement of impressive churches and other buildings of a pilgrimage center without any change in the religion of the town or region.

These problems in the previous scenarios for the demise of Philippi call for a detailed analysis of the existing evidence, coming mostly after excavations in the last decades, and this is the focus of the following section.

Archaeological Background of the Demise of Philippi

Existing archaeological evidence is used to provide answers to four questions arising from the hypotheses proposed for the history of Philippi after sixth century: (1) whether the demise of the town was produced by a major destruction, (2) whether it was a seismic effect, (3) when it occurred, and (4) what its implications were for the history of the town.

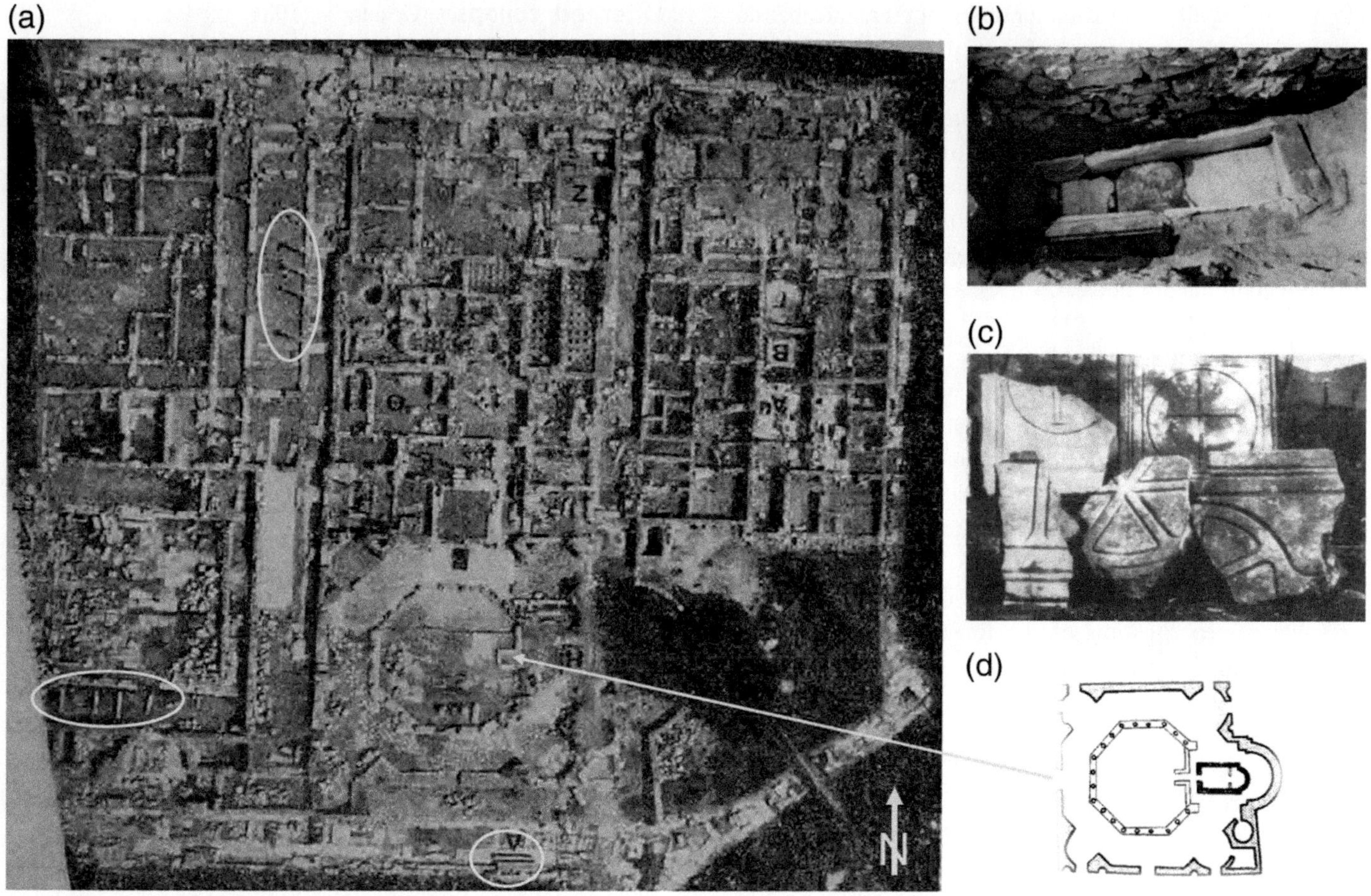

Figure 4. Evidence of large-scale seismic destruction and post-seismic recovery in the area of the Octagon church. (a) Excavation balloon photo, after Bakirtzis (1989), showing ruins all around the Octagon church. Ellipses mark columns toppled down in parallel, usually indicating seismic collapse. A circle at the bottom marks three 4-m-long columns, which were moved from the destroyed Octagon and deposited in a main street. (b) A cist-type (box-type) grave, possibly of an earthquake victim, a church minister, or an eminent citizen, in the area of the church. The grave was made of fragments of sculpted marble panels from the church, some shown in panel (c). (d) On top of the ruins of the church, a modest chapel, shown in solid lines, was built. Its remains were removed before the balloon photo was taken. Sources: (a,c) Bakirtzis (1989), modified. (b,c) Excavations archives, shown in Pelekanidis (1958) and Poulou (2019–2020). The color version of this figure is available only in the electronic edition.

Evidence of a townwide destruction layer

The excavations in different parts and building complexes of the town cover a large part of the center of the ancient town (Fig. 2), and testify to the same pattern: vast and luxurious buildings from the period Philippi was thriving as a pilgrimage town (fifth and sixth centuries), churches and their subordinate structures, various public buildings and houses were turned into ruins. Above the ruins, later poor construction testifies to new building phases (Fig. 4; see also Poulou, 2019–2020). For example, a modest chapel was built above the ruins of the Octagon church, dedicated to St. Paul (Fig. 4d), whereas surviving parts of other major churches were transformed into small chapels (Sève, 2000, Mentzos, 2016). Buildings of poor quality, including warehouses, were constructed on top of the ruins using material from destroyed buildings (Fig. 5), after the debris was partly cleared and moved to depositories inside the destroyed building complexes (Bakirtzis, 1989). Cemeteries were established in the center of the town (Sève, 2000). The second or third century aqueduct feeding the downtown part of the town was abandoned, and one of its principal cisterns was used much later as a shrine, regarded as the prison of St. Paul when at Philippi (Mentzos, 2005; Stiros, 2025), whereas wells were opened to serve the basic need for water (Mentzos *et al.*, 2016).

The aforementioned data provide clear evidence of large-scale destruction, especially of well-built religious buildings, and a major discontinuity in the town history.

The question is whether observed destruction corresponds to a single phase or recurrent events within 200–300 yr, as the spread of proposed datings of the earthquake (between approximately 600 and 850, as previously stated) may imply. It is difficult to assume that the destruction and essential abandonment of all monumental churches in this pilgrimage center was a multiphase event. A single major destruction event is likely, followed by a gradual collapse of structurally weakened buildings. Reoccupation of the space of ruins, on the other hand, could not have been a single-phase event, but a sequence of phases of repair, occupation for different uses, and abandonment, giving the impression of recurring destructive events. Still, the details of these interventions remain unknown because of limitations in datable material. Bakirtzis (1989), for instance, argued that four, 4-m-long columns deposited at the edge of a street (Fig. 4a) indicate efforts at postseismic recovery. This is a reasonable hypothesis, but in the absence of a clear stratigraphic context, the timing and hence significance of these columns are unclear.

Evidence of seismic destruction

Three possible explanations can be proposed for the destruction of Philippi. First, it reflects long-lasting, gradual decay that followed the abandonment of the town. Second, the town was radically restructured. Third, the destruction reflects dynamic effects, implying either a natural catastrophe or deliberate destruction by invaders.

The first possibility can be readily rejected because of the evidence of reoccupation of the town and because it was impossible that a prosperous, fortified pilgrimage town on Via Egnatia would have been left a ghost town for centuries. The second possibility can also be readily rejected. The pilgrimage character of the town rules out any deliberate, organized transformation of the town center to an essentially trade and workshop town with modest chapels; this could have been the case only after a major catastrophe or a change of the Christian regime.

The possibility of deliberate destruction can also be discarded. In a period before the advent of explosives, any catastrophic invasion by Slavs, Avars, and so forth, would have left signs of conflagration, typically accompanying such events in other towns (compare with *John of Ephesus VI 25*), and signs of a different culture. Local signs of fire were only found (Gounaris, 1984, p. 49), but they were expected during the reoccupation of the sites, or they may have been produced by localized, earthquake-triggered fires. Finally, there is no reason to assume that the invaders spent years trying to demolish all buildings; this is a case known only once or twice in the long history of the Mediterranean, for example, in Carthage, after its defeat by the Roman Army in 146 B.C.E.

Among the natural catastrophes, flooding, tornadoes, and earthquakes could have a destructive impact on the town, lying at the upper reaches of a swampy plain. Flooding can be excluded because the main town buildings were made with rock, brick, and strong mortar, thus resisting transient flooding. In addition, there are no signs of foundation instability in the building remains, which could have led to the collapse of their superstructure, even for Basilica A, which was built on an artificial terrace. Tornadoes can produce localized damage in the region, but the failure of an underground aqueduct is not explained. The only reasonable explanation is a strong earthquake. This result is supported by the following specific evidence.

Oriented collapse. Gounaris (1984, p. 49; 1988, p. 400) mentions that the columns and overlying structural elements of the Octagon complex were found toppled in a direction from northeast to southwest, a motion assigned to "the direction of the earthquake." Still, in another sector of the town, building walls and columns were reported to have been toppled toward northwest (Gounaris and Velenis, 1996, p. 531–532). This difference in the direction of collapse does not negate the possibility of seismic destruction because structural failure usually follows several cycles of seismic oscillation, not the "first push," implying the direction of the epicenter, whereas the direction of toppling depends on various factors, especially the orientation of the collapsed structure and its coupling with other structures.

Examination of the balloon photo of the early excavations of the broader Octagon area indicates columns lying on the ground parallel to each other (Fig. 4a); this pattern ("oriented collapse") represents evidence for seismic destruction if foundation instability and localized effects can be ruled out (as mentioned earlier).

Broken sculpted marble panels from Balisica B used in graves. Excavations brought to light a kind of cemetery, established within the remains of a major church complex, close to the Forum (Fig. 4); this is an extraordinary situation for a Roman town, indicating a dramatic change in its evolution. Broken marble panels separating the nave from the inner church of Basilica B were found in at least one of the graves, which were explained as the grave of an earthquake victim, a church minister, or another prominent citizen (Gounaris, 1984; Fig. 4b,c). An earthquake is the only reasonable explanation for the combination of a cemetery in the center of the town and of broken panels for a major church (compare with Koumousi-Vgenopoulou, 1996–1998; Stamati and Stiros, 2018).

In summary, evidence of generalized destruction, local signs of probable earthquake activity, and alternative explanations rejected, satisfy the criteria for a safe identification of an earthquake as the only reasonable explanation for the demise of Philippi (compare with Stiros, 1996).

Dating of the seismic destruction

The precise dating of destruction layers and building phases in the Christian period of Philippi is not clear for two reasons. First, the building style in Late Antiquity did not change, making stylistic dating very difficult. Second, the gradual collapse of destroyed buildings and the gradual reoccupation of parts of the town produced stratigraphic complexities.

Apart from radiometric dating, which is not available, the main possibilities for detailed dating of remains of this period are using inscriptions, which are unavailable, stray coins (numismatic dating), and some kinds of dated seals, which are rare.

(a)

(b)

(c)

Figure 5. Evidence of destruction and reconstruction in civic buildings in sector 4 (see Fig. 2). (a) A vast luxury building with columns and fine mosaics was destroyed and transformed into workshops and warehouses. About 80 large pottery jars were stored in it, with their bases fitting in circular holes opened in the mosaic floor. Poorly constructed walls correspond to efforts of postseismic recovery. (b,c) Details of poorly constructed walls built using material from the collapsed building, a fragment of a column (sector 6), and on top of the remains of a colonnade (sector 4). Source: excavations archives, shown by Poulou (2019–2020). The color version of this figure is available only in the electronic edition.

Stray coins were coins of small value in everyday use (not savings hoards), randomly lost within archaeological layers (occasional losses). Because of the frequent change of authorities in Late Antiquity, these coins were produced nearly every year in various production centers, and they were stamped with the details of their production, town and year of minting, referring to the honored authority. These coins were of smaller value and poor quality, and they usually rapidly decayed (worn). For this reason, well-preserved stray coins in Late Antiquity provide a lower bound chronology for the layer in which they were found. In cases of large samples of coins, the most recent mints can date a stratigraphic level, especially a destruction level due to an earthquake or another disaster, with an accuracy of up to one year (Metcalf, 1991; Stiros and Papageorgiou, 2001).

In Philippi, for reasons that are not well understood, the number of stray coins found is limited; perhaps the civil infrastructure (houses, roads, etc.) was new or at an excellent level of preservation because of the character of the town, so that coins could not be easily lost in floor or street fissures in the central part of the town. Luckily, there exist detailed statistics of stray coins for sector 4 of the excavation area of Thessaloniki University (for location see Fig. 2); Figure 3 indicates the distribution of stray coins in this sector, which is believed to be representative of the whole downtown area (compare with Poulou, 2019–2020). This figure indicates a continuity in coin circulation for centuries, and a gap of about 2–3 centuries after the first decades of the seventh century. The last coins before this gap were issued in 614 to 615, and for the reasons discussed earlier, they indicate that the highest probability is that the seismic destruction of the town occurred shortly after 614/615.

The aforementioned dating is with one reservation. Since approximately the end of the sixth century, coin circulation in the Byzantine Empire was highly reduced (Curta, 2005), and coins may have been in use for longer than in previous periods. However, it is unlikely that these coins were in use for more than 10–15 yr after their minting. This implies that the destruction of Philippi occurred between 614 to 615 and approximately 630, before an influx of coins after the victory of Emperor Heraclius against the Persians (compare with Gandila and Hristov, 2023). It is probably only a coincidence that this dating is consistent with the dating proposed by Bakirtzis (1989) based on the inferred dating of the postulated Thessaloniki earthquake mentioned in "*The Miracles....*"

Implications for the history of Philippi

Just before the destructive earthquake, Philippi was a fortified pilgrimage center, a station in a major road, but also the administrative center of the broader agrarian area, for which little information exists. After the earthquake, there have been efforts at cleaning debris and building a new generation of humble chapels and buildings to cover the needs of the remaining population. Pilgrimage was annulled, various parts of the town remained beyond the access of people who could leave numismatic (coin) traces, and life continued at a very primitive level, using locally produced goods. This is mainly reflected in the pottery style, with imported fine pottery replaced after the destruction by locally produced coarse jars for everyday use (Poulou-Papadimitriou, 2000; Zachariadis, 2014). Therefore, the earthquake marked the transition to the Middle Ages. This situation lasted for centuries, until a new phase of partial restoration of Philippi as a pilgrimage center in the tenth century, mainly reflected in repairs in major churches (Sève, 2000; Fournier, 2016).

Earthquake Resilience and Demise of Ancient Towns

Ancient towns in the Eastern Mediterranean had a long history, were adapted to the environment using principles developed in the broader region, and were resilient to natural disasters, including earthquakes (compare with Di Vita, 1996; Mentzos, 2016, p. 258–259). Hence, the question arising is how to explain the long demise of Philippi.

Insecurity in traveling along the Via Egnatia and the limited resources of the Empire during the seventh century were two good reasons. But in the same period, the Emperor had funded the postseismic recovery of Gortyn, capital of Crete (Di Vita, 1996), whereas Philippi was a small provincial town. Still, Philippi was important for the essentially theocratic Byzantine regime, and, in addition, it was a station on the Egnatia Road, offering protection and support to passengers and administrative activities, hence critical for the connection of Constantinople with the western provinces. This means that an additional reason for the demise existed.

Towns in the Roman and Byzantine periods had two main requirements: security (fortifications) and water supply for baths and other activities. Fortifications of Philippi, probably damaged during the earthquake, could have been repaired. But the aqueduct that supplied water to the town, especially necessary for the pilgrimage, could not be repaired.

The Philippi Aqueduct, the Kefalari Spring, and the Seventh Century Earthquake

The needs for water for civic and religious reasons in Philippi, high because of its pilgrimage character, were covered by an aqueduct, as in most major Roman towns, in which local sources (wells, minor springs, and rainwater stored in small house cisterns) could offer limited amounts of water and usually of lower quality. Information for the Philippi aqueduct comes mainly from archaeological excavations (Kranioti, 1989; Iliadis, 2010; Provost, 2011; Dadaki *et al.*, 2016; Oulkeroglou *et al.*, 2019). Based on several surviving or excavated segments, the aqueduct trace, about 8 km long, can be reconstructed from Philippi to the Kefalari spring (Fig. 6), a major karstic spring, currently feeding all modern towns and villages in the wider area. Locally, remains of a second, smaller aqueduct next to the main aqueduct have been observed (Oulkeroglou *et al.*, 2019), probably to increase the capacity of the main aqueduct.

The aqueduct was a closed underground channel, 1.2–1.5 m high and 0.5–1.0 m wide (Fig. 6), with several service shafts. The conduit was lying on a layer of pottery tiles, with the bottom and walls covered with hydraulic plaster. It was a typical Roman structure of the second century of the cut-and-cover type (in a covered trench), fully adapted to the topography; it roughly followed the 80 m contour (approximately between 84 and 78 m, Provost, 2011), with a gradient of about 1/1000. Its capacity is estimated to be 150 m^3/hr and was feeding two main cisterns with a capacity of 400 m^3 next to or near Basilica A (Dadaki *et al.*, 2016). This nearly horizontal aqueduct served only the lower part of Philippi, where the religious and administrative center of the town was located.

After the seventh century earthquake, the aqueduct was put out of use, and hence, baths and pools for civic and religious use (baptism, etc.) were not possible anymore using local sources. Later on, one of the abandoned cisterns of the useless aqueduct next to Basilica A, was transformed into a shrine, because it was regarded as the prison of St. Paul (Mentzos, 2005, p. 147). This was in analogy to the Mamertine prison, at the foot of the Capitol Hill, a former cistern in Rome, where both St. Peter and St. Paul had been detained before their deaths (Stiros, 2025).

A strong earthquake may have damaged the buried aqueduct because of landslides or ground fissures, or even faulting (e.g., Galli *et al.*, 2019). Still, these represented repairable problems for this aqueduct.

The reason for the abandonment of the aqueduct can be found in the situation at the spring, noticed by Iliadis (2010) and Dadaki *et al.* (2016); near the spring, the aqueduct is at an elevation of 80 m, whereas the modern spring is at an elevation of 70 m, at the bottom of a polished surface on marble. Because the aqueduct was rendered out of use after the earthquake, it is plausible to assign a major part of this about 10 m drop of the spring level to the seventh century strong motion (Fig. 7). Given that the cisterns in Philippi were at a level only about 6 m below the pre-earthquake spring level (84–78 m, as mentioned earlier), it was neither possible to construct a new aqueduct to convey water to the town, nor did there exist any other sources of water to exploit (Vergis, 1985). After the earthquake, only very basic needs for water in the town could be satisfied through wells that were opened (Mentzos *et al.*, 2016).

On these grounds, the following scenario can be proposed for the earthquake that affected Philippi: strong ground

Figure 6. Approximate path of the 8-km-long Philippi subhorizontal aqueduct, fed from the Kefalari karstic spring. In inset, a cross section of the aqueduct south of the spring (top, uncovered during the excavation) and when crossing the west walls of Philippi (bottom). Based on data of Iliadis (2010), Dadaki *et al.* (2016), and Oulkeroglou *et al.* (2019). The color version of this figure is available only in the electronic edition.

shaking formed tensile cracks and induced a fracture-related vertical anisotropic permeability (Rojstaczer *et al.*, 1995; Wang *et al.*, 2004) in calcareous rocks, tending to lower the basal level of the spring. This is a process known from other cases, in which springs dried up after an earthquake or were shifted to other areas (Amoruso *et al.*, 2011; Petitta *et al.*, 2018; Sanz de Ojeda *et al.*, 2019; Wang and Manga, 2021). Earthquake effects on springs have been reported by various ancient authors (Ambraseys and Melville, 1982; Guidoboni *et al.*, 1994; Ambraseys, 2009) and are a scenario examined in palaeoseismology (Guidoboni and Ebel, 2009, p. 384–385).

Earthquake Evidence in Nearby Sites

Numerous archaeological sites exist around Philippi, but only for a few among them a reference to earthquakes was made, such as for Kipia, as well as for the town of Thasos, at the northernmost part of Thasos Island (Fig. 8).

At Kipia, a 25 × 17 m wide Palaeochristian Basilica was excavated. The original structure was damaged; the roof, a three-apse wall separating the entrance (narthex) from the main space, and a corner next to the sacred space were destroyed. According to the excavator, the scale of destruction testifies to an earthquake. The church was repaired, but it was destroyed again. Later, above its remains, a modest chapel, about 5 times smaller than the earlier structure, was built. No direct dating of any of the two destruction phases is available, but the excavator correlated them with destruction in Philippi and Thasos in about the years 575 and 620 (Bakirtzis, 1988).

The Town of Thasos (present-day Limenas), at the northernmost coast of Thasos Island, was an important ancient town with a long history, mainly flourishing from quarrying

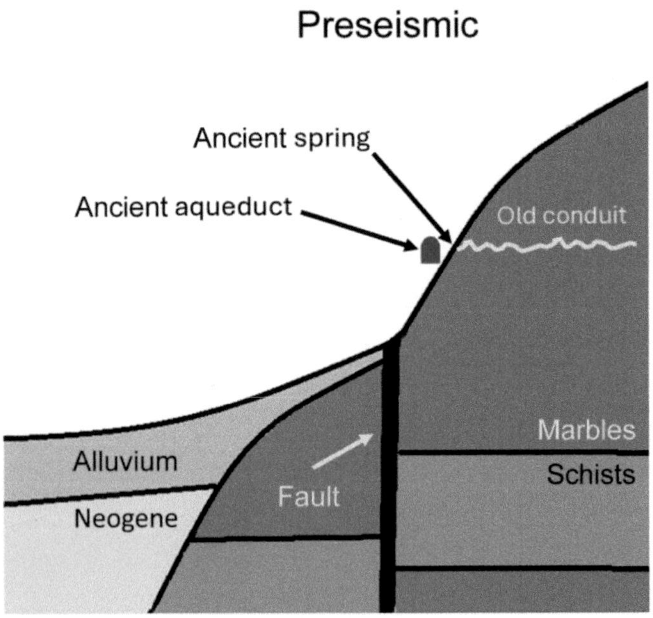

Figure 7. Geological cross section at the Kefalari spring (based on Vergis, 1985; Institute of Geology and Mineral Exploration [IGME], unpublished data) and schematic representation of the spring level drop after the seventh century earthquake. The aqueduct was adapted to the preseismic spring level and became useless after its level dropped. The color version of this figure is available only in the electronic edition.

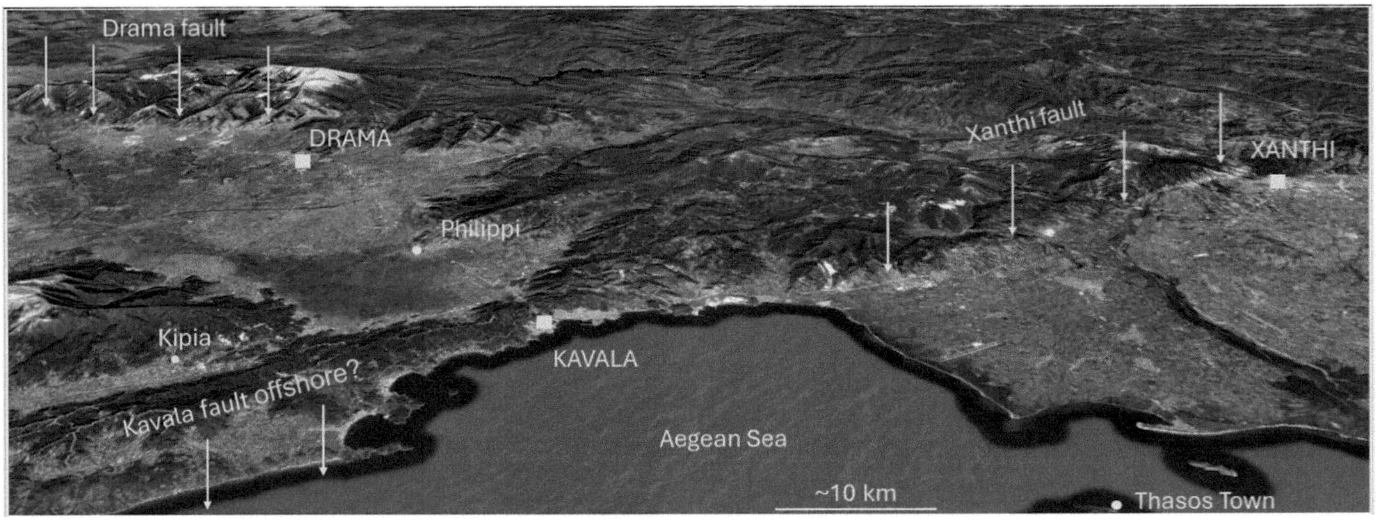

Figure 8. Oblique, Google Map Pro view of the area around Philippi, marked with the known active faults in the area (after Caputo *et al.*, 2012), showing also the location of Kipia and the Town of Thasos, for which there have been archaeological reports of seismic destruction about the year 620. The scale is approximate and decreases to the upper part of the figure. The color version of this figure is available only in the electronic edition.

and exportation of marble. There is evidence that the town was abandoned or destroyed shortly after 615, possibly around 620. The demise of Thasos was first assigned to a Slavic invasion and later to an earthquake (Bakirtzis, 1986; Sodini, 2011), but no consensus exists among archaeologists (Sève, 2000, p. 204). Given the rarity of earthquakes in the region, should the earthquake scenario for the end of the Town of Thasos prove reliable (a study is in progress), the destruction of both Philippi and Thasos could be related to the same seismic sequence.

About 50 km southwest of Philippi, in the remains of the archaeological site of Amphipolis, signs of an earthquake after 650 have been reported by Syrides *et al.* (2017). This seems to have been a different, later event, possibly associated with the seismic zone east of Thessaloniki (Fig. 1).

Seismological Implications

The town-wide destruction in Philippi implies an earthquake of minimum intensity IX or X (MMS) and high accelerations in spectral frequencies resonant with those of large churches, structures with colonnades, and smaller buildings. Accelerations were probably amplified or modified because of interaction with the thin layer of alluvium at the rims of the plain next to the Acropolis hill, on which the town was built (Fig. 2).

Using a classical approximate formula of Gutenberg and Richter (1956) connecting seismic intensity and magnitude

$$\mathbf{M} = 1 + 0.66 I_o, \tag{1}$$

in which **M** is the magnitude and I_o is the IX, max intensity (MMS), an earthquake of magnitude of the order of 7+ is obtained, which seems to represent an upper bound for an earthquake in this area. Because this estimate comes from a single site, it is safer to think of an earthquake magnitude of the order of 6.7 associated with a fault about 30 km long (Caputo *et al.*, 2012; Roumelioti *et al.*, 2017).

Two lines of evidence point to an earthquake with an epicenter within a few tens of kilometers of Philippi.

First, peak ground accelerations in the region are rapidly attenuated away from the fault or epicenter (Theodulidis and Papazachos, 1992).

Second, destroyed or damaged structures in Philippi were essentially high-frequency structures (small, well-built structures with fundamental frequencies >1–2 Hz), vulnerable (resonant) to high-frequency seismic ground accelerations. The main frequencies of the major churches, which represented the largest and typically more slender structures in Philippi, were between 2 and 6–10 Hz (Stiros *et al.*, 2025). In fact, among the large buildings of Philippi, only Church (Basilica) B, 50 m long, 40 m wide, and about 35 m high (if the dome had not collapsed, see earlier), was close to the 2 Hz value.

The aforementioned results point to an earthquake deriving from the reactivation of a fault in the vicinity of Philippi. Databases of active faults in Greece (Caputo *et al.*, 2012; Ganas *et al.*, 2013; Ganas, 2024) include two normal faults a few tens of kilometers away from Philippi, the Drama fault or the Xanthi fault (Fig. 8). Philippi is roughly at the same distance from the two faults; hence, both of these faults are candidates for the seventh century earthquake. The possibility is higher for the Xanthi fault, especially its offshore continuation offshore Kavala, given the potential for coeval seismic destruction of Thasos: Thasos and Philippi are roughly at the same distance from the Xanthi fault, and hence they could have been both damaged during its reactivation. On the contrary, the distance of Thasos from the Drama fault is much larger than that of Philippi, and it is not easy for the two towns to have been destroyed by reactivation of this fault. Of course, the possibility of reactivation of another unrecognized, probably buried fault cannot be ruled out.

Discussion and Conclusions

Analysis of archaeological data indicates that a highly destructive earthquake affected Philippi, probably between 615 and 630, and the inferred coseismic fall of the level of a karstic spring feeding its low-gradient aqueduct deprived Philippi of a major infrastructure. If this earthquake had occurred in a different period, characterized by political stability and a strong economy, imperial funds would have permitted the reconstruction of the town, and certain technical solutions, some described by the Roman engineer Vitruvius in his work *De Architectura,* could have been adopted to bring water back to the town. This indicates that the demise of this town was not a simple, direct process of the type stimulus-response, but a product of complex, conditional processes, schematically summarized in Figure 9.

Was the case of Philippi unique in the history of the broader region? The answer is no. The scale of destruction in Philippi is reminiscent of several towns in Crete destroyed after the 365 earthquake (Stiros and Papageorgiou, 2001). This last earthquake had probably a moderate impact on Gortyn, the capital of Roman Crete, which was seriously damaged by later earthquakes. An earthquake about the year 560 destroyed the water supply system of Gortyn, but the problem was solved with an aqueduct funded by a donor. An earthquake in about the year 620 ruined the town, but imperial funding permitted its recovery. Gortyn was essentially abandoned after an earthquake about the year 670; the scale of damage, the presence of the Arabs, the interruption of the commerce with the west, and the limited funds of the Empire shaped the background that led to the death of Gortyn after a millennium-long life (for details and references see Di Vita, 1996).

Impacts of a combination of earthquake destruction and earthquake-induced hydrogeological effects have also been described in other regions. For example, Qumis (modern Damgan) in Northern Iran was reported to have been destroyed by a highly destructive earthquake in 856 and was abandoned, possibly because the earthquake caused the drying up of springs and underground aqueducts (qanats; Ambraseys and Melville, 1982). Still, this information comes mostly from later historical sources, and it may reflect a fusion of information from three different earthquakes (Berberian, 2014) and possibly memories of other seismic events.

Another example is the ancient town of Aigeira, close to the Gulf of Corinth. At about the year 250, the town was abandoned, as was inferred mostly from the abrupt interruption of an architectural modification of its imposing ancient Greek theater.

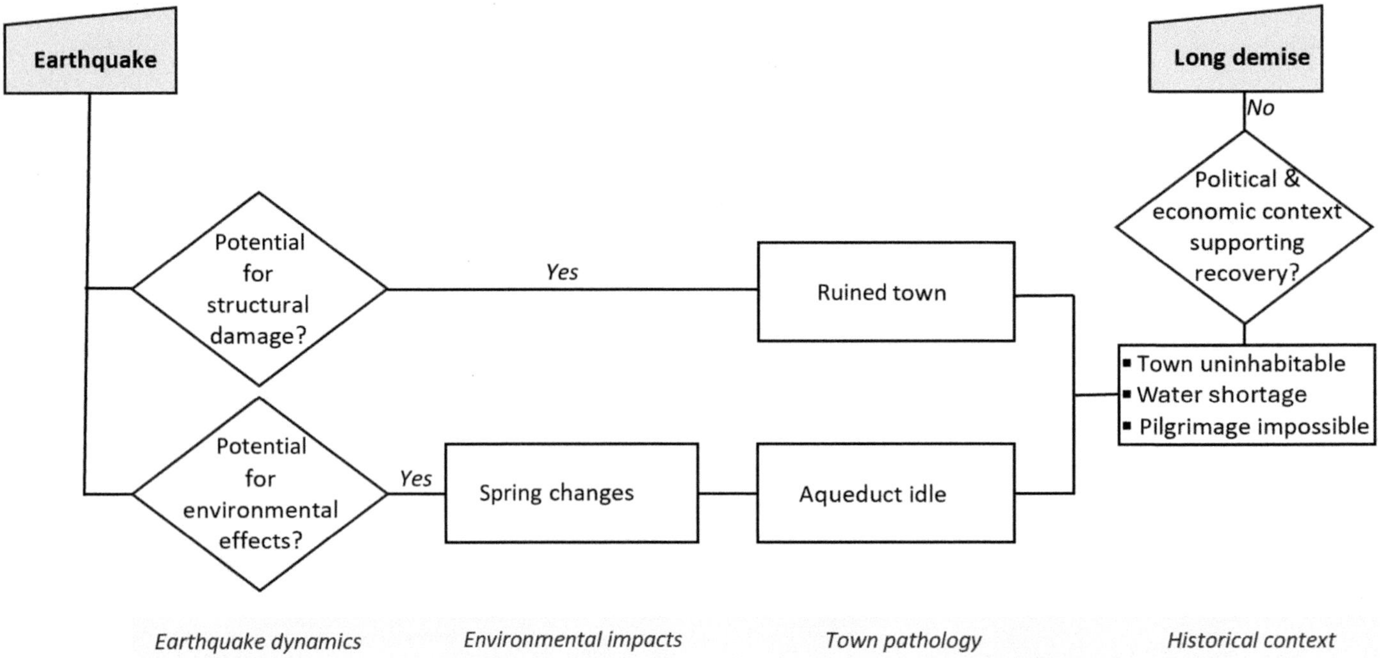

Figure 9. A flowchart-type explanation for the demise of Philippi after the earthquake about the year 620. Input and output are shaded. The town demise does not reflect a direct response to a seismic shock, but a complex, conditional process, controlled by earthquake dynamics, the environmental and structural response to the strong motion, and the political, social, and economic background of the Empire at the time of the earthquake. This figure can be modified to cover other environmental effects, for example, coastal changes that may influence a harbor. The color version of this figure is available only in the electronic edition.

Changes aimed to remodel the theater so that during performances it could be temporarily transformed into a water basin to simulate naval battles, according to the fashion of this period. The project was abruptly interrupted, building material was abandoned in the orchestra (circular, flat part of the theater for the chorus and actors), and this impressive theater was never reused. This implies the end of Aigeira as an organized Roman town, and this end was vaguely assigned to a crisis of the Roman Empire (Gogos, 1992). However, the study of the coast of the town showed that its abrupt decline is consistent with an environmental effect, a seismic land uplift that destroyed Aigeira's harbor, transforming it into dry land, and after this loss, the ancient town never recovered (Stiros, 1998). The flowchart of Figure 9 can be easily modified to cover this case.

The destruction of Philippi, and possibly of other towns in the area, testifies to a minimum intensity IX-X (MMS) and points to a strong earthquake from a nearby source. Two known active normal faults are known candidates for this earthquake, the Drama fault, or more probably the Xanthi fault and its continuation offshore (Fig. 8).

Data and Resources

Data used come from field observations and bibliographic investigations from the sources indicated in the references, in their striking majority accessible online. Figures 2 and 8 are based on Google Earth Pro material. Illustrative information and reconstructions of the ancient town and its monuments are found in the following webpages: (1) https://whc.unesco.org/en/list/1517/gallery/, (2) https://greekunescomonuments.s3.eu-central-1.amazonaws.com/wp-content/uploads/2023/07/18_Filippoi-1.pdf, (3) https://kavala.citypedia.gr/seitepos-itan-i-arxaia-poli-ton-philippon-1500-xronia-prin/, and (4) https://www.visitkavala.gr/sightseeing/arxaiologikos-xoros-filippon/. All websites were last accessed in July 2025.

Declaration of Competing Interests

The author acknowledges that there are no conflicts of interest recorded.

Acknowledgments

Inspirational comments and careful reviewing by Associate Editor J. Ebel and an anonymous reviewer are highly appreciated. S. Papageorgiou (Ministry of Culture, Greece) is thanked for information on Thasos, and V. Kontogianni (EAGME, formerly Institute of Geology and Mineral Exploration [IGME], Athens) is thanked for her help with IGME hydrogeological data.

References

Albini, P., M. Locati, A. Rovida, and M. Stucchi (2013). European archive of historical earthquake data (AHEAD), *Istituto Nazionale di Geofisica e Vulcanologia (INGV)*, doi: 10.6092/ingv.it-ahead.

Ambraseys, N. (2009). *Earthquakes in the Mediterranean and the Middle East*, Cambridge University Press, Cambridge, United Kingdom.

Ambraseys, N., and C. P. Melville (1982). *A History of Persian Earthquakes*, Cambridge University Press, Cambridge, United Kingdom, 219 pp.

Amoruso, A., L. Crescentini, M. Petitta, S. Rusi, and M. Tallini (2011). Impact of the April 6, 2009 L'Aquila earthquake on groundwater flow in the Gran Sasso carbonate aquifer central Italy, *Hydrol. Processes* **25**, 1754–1764.

Bakirtzis, C. (1986). What happened to Thasos at the beginning of the 7th century?, *Philia Epi to George E. Mylonas*, to commemorate his sixty years as an excavator, Vol. 3, 339–341 & plate 88 (in Greek).

Bakirtzis, C. (1988). Excavation of a Palaeochristian Basilica at Kipia Paggaiou, in *The Archaeological Work in Macedonia and Thrace*, Vol. 2, Archaeological Museum of Thessaloniki and Thessaloniki University, Thessaloniki, 433–437 (in Greek).

Bakirtzis, C. (1989). The day after the destruction in Philippi, *Proc. of the Int. Conf. on the Everyday Life in Byzantium*, 695–710 (in Greek).

Berberian, M. (2014). Earthquakes and coseismic surface faulting on the Iranian Plateau: A historical, social, and physical approach, in *Developments in Earth Surface Processes*, Vol. 17, Elsevier, 776 pp.

Blondé, F., A. Muller, and D. Mulliez (1984). Thasos, 2-Terrain Valma, *Bulletin de Correspondance Hellenique* **108**, 872–878.

Caputo, R., A. Chatzipetros, S. Pavlides, and V. Sboras (2012). The Greek Database of Seismogenic Sources (GreDaSS): State-of-the-art for northern Greece, *Ann. Geophys.* **55**, 859–894.

Curta, F. (2005). Byzantium in Dark-Age Greece. The numismatic evidence in its Balkan context, *Byz. Modern Greek Stud.* **29**, 113–146.

Curta, F. (2012). Were there any Slavs in seventh-century Macedonia? *J. Hist.* **XLVII**, 61–74.

Dadaki, S., E. Iliadis, and I. Iliadis (2016). Distance water carriers in the Roman period. The case of Philippi and Neapolis-Kavala, *Revista Santuários*, 1–12.

Di Vita, A. (1996). Earthquakes and civil life at Gortyn (Crete) in the period between Justinian and Constant II (6-7th century AD), in *Archaeoseismology*, S. Stiros and R. Jones (Editors), Fitch Lab Occ paper 7, British School at Athens, IGME (Athens), Oxford, 45–50.

Fournier, J. (2016). Introduction in Philippes, de la préhistoire à Byzance. Études d'archéologie et d'histoire, *Bull. Corr. Hell. Suppl.* **55**, 15–19.

Galli, P., A. Galderisi, M. Martino, G. Mugnozza Scarascia, and F. Bozzano (2019). The coseismic faulting of the San Benedetto tunnel (2016, Mw 6.6 central Italy earthquake), in *Tunnels and Underground Cities. Engineering and Innovation Meet Archaeology, Architecture and Art*, D. Peila, G. M. B. Viggiani, and T. B. Celestino (Editors), Taylor & Francis Group, London, United Kingdom, 805–811.

Ganas, A., I. Oikonomou, and C. Tsimi (2013). NOAfaults: A digital database for active faults in Greece, *Bull. Geol. Soc. Greece* **47**, 518–530.

Ganas, A. (2024). NOAFAULTS KMZ layer Version 6.0 (version 6.0), *Zenodo*, doi: 10.5281/zenodo.13168947.

Gandila, A., and I. Hristov (2023). Collapse in the Balkans? Three 7th-century AD coin hoards from Hrisosotira on the Black Sea Coast (Bulgaria), *Ancient West & East*, **22**, 133–157.

Gogos, S. (1992). Das Theater von Aigeira: Ein Beitrag zum antiken Theaterbau, Sonderschriften des Oesterreichischen Archaeologisches Institut, Wien, 21 pp. (in German).

Gounari, E. (2016). Architecture and urban space design in Philippi: The case of the fourth urban sector, *Ph.D. Thesis*, University of Athens, 487 pp. (in Greek).

Gounaris, G. (1984). Bronze buckles from the Octagon in Philippi and Central Macedonia, *Byzantina* **4**, 47–59 (in Greek).

Gounaris, G. (1988). The finds of the University excavation at Philippi in 1988, in *The Archaeological Work in Macedonia and Thrace*, Vol. 2, Archaeological Museum of Thessaloniki and Thessaloniki University, Thessaloniki, 395–408 (in Greek).

Gounaris, G., and G. Velenis (1996). University excavation at Philippi 1988–1996, in *Archaeological Work in Macedonia and Thrace*, Vol. 10, Archaeological Museum of Thessaloniki and Thessaloniki University, Thessaloniki, 719–733 (in Greek).

Gutenberg, B., and C. Richter (1956). Earthquake magnitude, intensity, energy, and acceleration (Second paper), *Bull. Seismol. Soc. Am.* **46**, 105–145.

Guidoboni, E., and J. Ebel (2009). *Earthquakes and Tsunamis in The past. A Guide to Techniques in Historical Seismology*, Cambridge University Press, 590 pp.

Guidoboni, E., A. Comastri, and G. Traina (1994). Catalogue of Earthquakes in the Mediterranean Region up to the 10th Century, *Istituto Nazionale di Geofisica*, 504 pp.

Iliadis, I. (2010). Philippi: Water supply of the ancient town, *Archaeol. Arts* **116**, 58–62 (in Greek).

Koumousi-Vgenopoulou, A. (1996–1998). Excavation "evidence" for the AD552 earthquake at Patras, *Archaeologika Analekta ex Athinon* **XXIX–XXXI**, 51–56 (in Greek).

Kourkoutidou-Nikolaïdou, E. (1995). Philippi, from the Paleochristian to the Byzantine town, *Proc. of the Int. Symp. Byzantine Macedonia AD324-1430*, Thessaloniki, Greece, 1992, 171–182 (in Greek).

Kranioti, L. (1989). Ancient aqueduct at Kefalari Dramas, in *Archaeologikon Ergon in Macedonia and Thrace*, Vol. 3, Archaeological Museum of Thessaloniki and Thessaloniki University, Thessaloniki, 475–482 (in Greek).

Lemerle, P. (1945). Philippos et la Macédoine orientale à l'époque chrétienne et byzantine, Recherches d' histoire et d' archéologie. Bibliothèque des Écoles françaises d' Athènes et de Rome, 158 pp., Paris and LXXXII plates (in French).

Lemerle, P. (1979). Les anciens recueils des miracles de saint Démétrius et l'histoire de la péninsule balkanique, *Bull. Classe Lett. Sci. Moral. Politiques* **65**, 395–415, doi: 10.3406/barb.1979.55425 (in French).

Metcalf, D. (1991). Avar and Slav invasions into the Balkan peninsula (c.575-625): The nature of the numismatic evidence, *J. Roman Archaeol.* **4**, 140–148.

Mentzos, A. (2005). Problems of the topography of ancient Philippi, *Egnatia* **9**, 101–156 (in Greek).

Mentzos, A. (2016). Les complexes ecclésiastiques à l'époque mésobyzantine: Renaissance ou survivance? *Bull. Corr. Hell. Suppl.* **55**, 245–260 (in French).

Mentzos, A., M. Paisidou, and P. Papadopoulou (2016). Preliminary conclusions on the transition of Philippi from Late Antiquity to the Middle Ages, in *Archaeologikon Ergon in Macedonia and Thrace*, Vol. 30, 531–540 (in Greek).

Mouslopoulou, V., V. Saltogianni, M. Gianniou, and S. Stiros (2014). Geodetic evidence for tectonic activity on the Strymon Fault System, northeast Greece, *Tectonophysics* **633**, 246–255.

Oulkeroglou, A., S. Papadopoulos, and I. Giamali (2019). The Roman aqueduct of Philippi, *J. Greek Archaeol.* **4**, 229–251.

Papazachos, B., and K. Papazachou (1997). *The Earthquakes of Greece*, Zitis, Thessaloniki, Greece.

Pelekanidis, S. (1958). Excavation at Philippi, *Praktika Archaeologikis Etaireias*, 84–89 & Plates 62–66 (in Greek).

Petitta, M., L. Mastrorillo, E. Preziosi, F. Banzato, M. D. Barberio, A. Billi, C. Cambi, G. De Luca, G. Di Carlo, and D. Di Curzio, *et al.* (2018) Water-table and discharge changes associated with the 2016–2017 seismic sequence in central Italy: Hydrogeological data and a conceptual model for fractured carbonate aquifers. *Hydrogeol. J.* **26,** 1009–1026.

Poulou-Papadimitriou, N. (2000). La céramique montée à la main est-elle forcement barbare? *Dossiers d'archeologie* **256,** 35 (in French).

Poulou, N. (2019–2020). Philippi towards the early Medieval period: A reconsideration of the archaeological data, *Byzantina* **37,** 113–156 (in Greek).

Provost, S. (2011). Réparations et transformations des installations hydrauliques à Philippes, in *Les réseaux d'eau courante dans l'Antiquité, Réparations, modifications, réutilisation, abandon, recuperation*, C. Abadie, *et al.* (Éditor), Presses Universitaires de Rennes, Rennes, 217–230 (in French).

Rapp, G., Jr. (1986). Assessing archaeological evidence for seismic catastrophies, *Geoarchaeology* **1,** 365–379.

Rojstaczer, S., S. Wolf, and R. Michel (1995). Permeability enhancement in the shallow crust as a cause of earthquake-induced hydrological changes, *Nature* **373,** no. 6511, 237–239.

Roumelioti, Z., A. Kiratzi, B. Margaris, and A. Chatzipetros (2017). Simulation of strong ground motion on near-fault rock outcrop for engineering purposes: The case of the city of Xanthi (northern Greece), *Bull. Earthq. Eng.* **15,** 25–49.

Sanz de Ojeda, A., I. Alhama, and E. Sanz (2019). Aquifer sensitivity to earthquakes: The 1755 Lisbon earthquake, *J. Geophys. Res.* **124,** 8844–8866.

Sève, M. (2000). De la naissance à la mort d'une ville: Philippes en Macédoine (IVe siècle av. J.-C.-VIIe siècle ap. J.-C.), *Histoire Urbaine* **1,** 187–204, doi: 10.3917/rhu.001.0187 (in French).

Sève, M. (2021). Varia Philippica, 3. Que s'est-il passé à Philippes dans la seconde moitié du VIe s. apr. J.-C.? *Bull. Correspondance Hellénique* **145,** no. 1, 47–63, doi: 10.4000/bch.1256 (in French).

Sodini, J.-P. (2011). Thasos protobyzantine, *C. R. Séances Acad. Inscr Belles-Lett.* **155,** no. 2, 1161–1207.

Stamati, A.-V., and S.C. Stiros (2018). Destruction layers, urban evolution, and earthquakes in Roman Patras, Greece, *Geoarchaeology* **33,** 13–23.

Stiros, S. (1996). Identification of earthquakes from archaeological data: Methodology, criteria and limitations, in *Archaeoseismology*, S. Stiros and R. Jones (Editors), Fitch Lab Occ paper 7, British School at Athens and IGME (Athens), Oxford, 129–152.

Stiros, S. (1998). Archaeological evidence for unusually rapid Holocene uplift rates in an active normal faulting terrain: Roman Harbour of Aigeira, Gulf of Corinth, Greece, *Geoarchaeology* **13,** 731–741.

Stiros, S. C. (2025). The Philippi (Eastern Macedonia, Greece) earthquake ca. AD50: New evidence for a debated event and implications for ancient earthquakes assigned to divine intervention, *J. Seismol.* doi: 10.1007/s10950-025-10323-x.

Stiros, S., D. Antoniou, and V. Kontogianni (2025). Palaeoseismological information from church repairs dated by inscriptions: Evidence from 18th century Greece. *Seismol. Res. Lett.* **96,** no. 5, 3253–3264.

Stiros, S. C., and S. Papageorgiou (2001). Seismicity of Western Crete and the destruction of the town of Kisamos at AD 365: Archaeological evidence, *J. Seismol.* **5,** 381–397.

Syrides, G., S. Pavlides, and A. Chatzipetros (2017). The geological structure of Kastas hill archaeological site, Amphipolis, eastern Macedonia, Greece, *Bull. Geol. Soc. Greece* **51,** 39–51.

Theodulidis, N., and B. Papazachos (1992). Dependence of strong ground motion on magnitude-distance, site geology and macroseismic intensity for shallow earthquakes in Greece: I, Peak horizontal acceleration, velocity and displacement, *Soil Dynam. Earthq. Eng.* **11,** 387–402.

Vergis, S. (1985). Inventory of karstic springs of Greece. Hydrological Sector of Thrace, *Unpublished Rept. 28/VII*, Institute of Geology and Mineral Exploration (IGME), Athens, Greece (in Greek).

Wang, C.-Y., C.-H. Wang, and M. Manga (2004). Coseismic release of water from mountains: Evidence from the 1999 (Mw = 7.5) Chi-Chi, Taiwan, earthquake, *Geology* **32,** 769–772.

Wang, C., and M. Manga (2021). Stream flow, in *Water and Earthquakes, Lecture Notes in Earth System Sciences*, Springer, 201–230.

Zachariadis, S. (2014). Pottery from the workshop building, in the early Byzantine city of Philippi, Greece, *4th Conference on Late Roman Coarse Wares, Cooking Wares and Amphorae in the Mediterranean: Archaeology and Archaeometry (LRCW 4), Mediterranean: A Market Without Borders*, Thessaloniki, Greece, 7–11 April 2011, BAR international Series 2616, 705–713.

Manuscript received 7 July 2025
Published online 10 October 2025

Data Mine

Nodal Seismic Deployment on Mauna Loa Volcano, Hawai'i: Dataset and Preliminary Insights

Xusong Yang*[1], Guoqing Lin[1], Ninfa Bennington[2], and Elisabeth Gallant[3]

Abstract

Mauna Loa is the largest active volcano on Earth, comprising ~51% of the Island of Hawai'i's landmass and posing significant risks to the island's communities, infrastructure, and natural environment. Historical eruptions have produced lava flows that have reached the ocean in as little as 3 hr. The timing and location of such lava flows in the past 200 yr underscore how critical determination of the location and geometry of magma storage and structure is for volcanic hazard assessment and eruption forecasting. Now, after nearly 38 yr of volcanic quiescence, Mauna Loa has erupted again. On 27 November 2022, fissures initiated within the summit caldera and then migrated to the northeast rift zone, where they generated a large lava flow that threatened a major highway. To improve our understanding of the geometry of this magma system, we deployed a temporary nodal array on Mauna Loa in the summer of 2024. This increased our seismic coverage sufficiently to image this magmatic system. This nodal array consists of 33 seismometers distributed on and around the volcano and was deployed for over three months to record seismic signals. The primary objective of this project is to resolve the high-resolution seismic velocity structure and characterize seismic features associated with magma storage and ascent pathways. In this article, we present an overview of the deployment, evaluate the quality of the data, and show example recordings to evaluate the suitability of the data set for future seismic investigations, including earthquake relocation, seismic tomography, and receiver function analysis. Comparisons with nearby permanent broadband and short-period seismic stations demonstrate that the nodal array recorded high-quality waveforms, making it a valuable resource for constraining the magmatic system beneath Mauna Loa at multiple scales.

Cite this article as Yang, X., G. Lin, N. Bennington, and E. Gallant (2025). Nodal Seismic Deployment on Mauna Loa Volcano, Hawai'i: Dataset and Preliminary Insights, *Seismol. Res. Lett.* **97**, 1215–1226, doi: 10.1785/0220250232.

Supplemental Material

Introduction

Mauna Loa, situated on the Island of Hawai'i, is the largest active volcano on Earth, comprising more than half of the island's landmass and rising to an elevation of 4169 m above sea level (Fig. 1a). On 27 November 2022, at ~11:30 p.m. local time, lava erupted within Moku'āweoweo, the volcano's summit caldera, marking the end of nearly 38 yr of volcanic quiescence. Within several hours, eruptive activity migrated to the northeast rift zone (NERZ), where it persisted for 13 days before ceasing on 10 December. This eruption produced a 19-km-long lava flow that advanced in a north-northeast direction, crossing the Mauna Loa Weather Observatory access road and halting within 2.8 km of the Daniel K. Inouye Highway (Saddle Road), the main highway connecting the east and west sides of the island (Downs *et al.*, 2023; Mulliken *et al.*, 2024) (Fig. 1b). The 2022 Mauna Loa eruption was accompanied by sustained seismic tremor, which began ~30 min prior to the surface breakout and continued for several days after the lava effusion had ended (Maher *et al.*, 2023).

Although Mauna Loa has remained relatively quiet in recent decades, it has a well-documented history of frequent volcanic activity. Prior to the 2022 eruption, Mauna Loa had erupted 33 times since 1843. Most of these eruptions occurred before 1950 at an average recurrence interval of 3.6 yr (Barnard, 1995). Since 1950, however, the eruption frequency has markedly declined, with only three eruptions: in 1975, in 1984, and in 2022. Historically, eruptions typically initiated in the summit

1. Rosenstiel School of Marine, Atmospheric, and Earth Science, University of Miami, Miami, Florida, U.S.A., https://orcid.org/0000-0001-8137-3674 (XY); 2. U.S. Geological Survey, Hawaiian Volcano Observatory, Hilo, Hawai'i, U.S.A., https://orcid.org/0000-0003-3230-6744 (NB); 3. Department of Geology, University of Hawai'i at Hilo, Hilo, Hawai'i, U.S.A.

*Corresponding author: xxy458@miami.edu

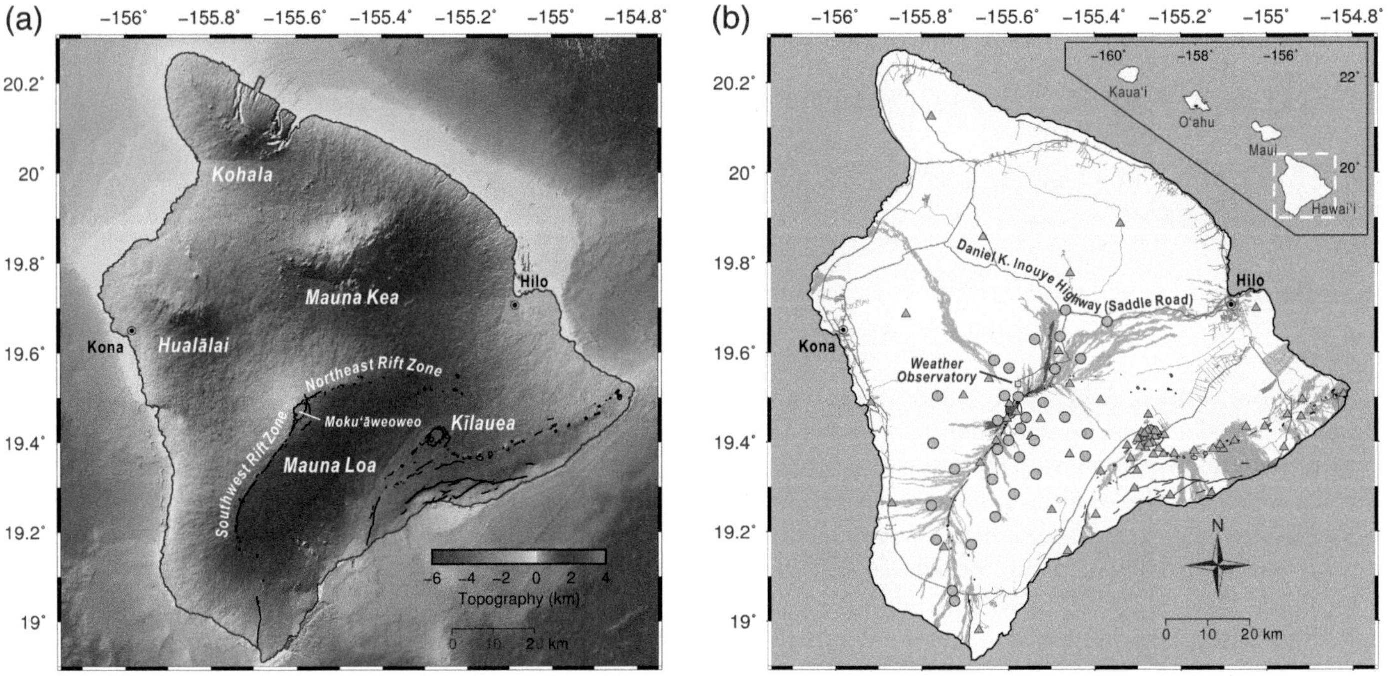

Figure 1. (a) Topography and major geological features of the Island of Hawai'i. (b) Distribution of historical lava flows (gray shading), with the 2022 Mauna Loa lava flow highlighted in red. The Hawaiian Volcano Observatory (HVO) permanent seismic stations (network code HV) are depicted as triangles, and the temporarily deployed nodal array sites are shown as circles. Active faults are delineated by black lines, and primary roads are indicated in blue, including the Daniel K. Inouye Highway (Saddle Road). The Mauna Loa Weather Observatory is marked by a yellow box. The inset in panel (b) illustrates the location of the Island of Hawai'i. The color version of this figure is available only in the electronic edition.

caldera, and approximately half of them then migrated to either the NERZ or to the southwest rift zone (SWRZ), as shown in Figure 1 (Lockwood and Lipman, 1987). Eruptions along the SWRZ pose a greater threat because steeper slopes allow lava to rapidly reach populated coastal areas, severing roads and utilities along the way (Gregg *et al.*, 2004; Trusdell and Zoeller, 2017). For example, the 1950 flows from Mauna Loa's SWRZ reached the ocean in ~3 hr (Finch and Macdonald, 1953). Mauna Loa is likely to erupt again, and the risk associated with future eruptions only increases because the population on the island grows and development expands on the flanks of the volcano. Therefore, it is imperative to improve our spatial understanding of the subsurface magma reservoirs and pathways to better mitigate the volcanic hazards they represent.

In contrast to the more recently frequently active southeastern neighbor Kīlauea, Mauna Loa, has been less extensively investigated due to its sheer size, steep topography, and high elevation. Of the 97 seismic instruments currently operated by the U.S. Geological Survey (USGS), Hawaiian Volcano Observatory (HVO) on the Island of Hawai'i, only 13 are located within 20 km of Mauna Loa's summit (Fig. 1b). To improve seismic data coverage and enhance imaging of Mauna Loa's magmatic plumbing system, we deployed a temporary nodal array on Mauna Loa from July to November 2024 (Fig. 1b). The project was a collaborative effort led by the University of Miami (UM; Lin and Yang) and the USGS HVO (Bennington). The primary goal of this deployment is to investigate the magmatic system, characterize potential magma bodies, and to assess their roles in the 2022 eruption. We plan to jointly analyze the data from this nodal array and the existing HVO network to enhance regional earthquake catalogs and produce high-resolution 3D images of the subsurface velocity structure. The detailed structural framework, combined with patterns of local seismicity, together promise to provide critical insights into the distribution of magma storage zones and the pathways of magma ascent. Comparisons with previous and future studies will facilitate temporal comparisons that improve our understanding of magma transport processes and eruption precursors at Mauna Loa.

Instrument Deployment

The nodal array was designed with reference to a permanent, campaign Global Navigation Satellite System (GNSS) network deployed annually by HVO. Seismic nodes were placed within ±5 m of the GNSS coordinates to optimize installation conditions and account for terrain constraints. To differentiate these temporary deployment sites from the GNSS stations, each node was named with an "S" prefix.

In this experiment, we successfully deployed 33 SmartSolo IGU-BD3C-5 nodal seismometers along the summit region of Mauna Loa, as well as the NERZ and SWRZ (Fig. 1b). These

(a)

(b)

Figure 2. (a) Example of a fully deployed site, showing a node connected to an external battery and covered with a 10 lb sandbag. (b) Helicopter used for field operations. The color version of this figure is available only in the electronic edition.

instruments are owned and maintained by HVO and have previously been used for dense nodal array deployments in the vicinity of the 2022 Pāhala earthquake swarm (Janiszewski *et al.*, 2024) and across Kaluapele, the caldera floor within Kīlauea volcano's summit (Denlinger *et al.*, 2024). Each node is a three-component seismometer with a response corner frequency of 5 s, and integrates a Global Positioning System (GPS), onboard data storage, digitizer, and a lithium-ion battery. To extend the duration of continuous recording, each node was connected to an external battery (Fig. 2a). Ground motion was recorded at a sampling rate of 400 samples per second. To account for the high wind speeds at the Mauna Loa summit and the relatively weak instrument–ground coupling of the deployment method (as described subsequently), the gain was set to 0 dB to reduce the potential for amplitude clipping in the seismic records.

Because the majority of the sites were located on shelly pāhoehoe lava flows, the seismometers were neither buried nor anchored with ground spikes. Instead, we adopted a deployment strategy proven effective in the 2022 Pāhala nodal array (Janiszewski *et al.*, 2024), in which each instrument was covered with a 10-pound sandbag to improve ground coupling (Fig. 2a). Of the 33 successfully deployed nodes, 29 were inaccessible by road and required helicopter support for both installation and retrieval (Fig. 2b).

Overall Data Availability

Of the 33 deployed instruments, data from one node were unrecoverable, yielding 32 functional datasets. Site SKFLT (marked by a white circle in Fig. 3a) was found with its external battery cable severed, and both the battery and the node showed visible scratches. This damage was likely caused by heavy machinery, such as a mower or brush cutter. Because of extensive physical damage, data from this site were unrecoverable. In addition, six nodes were found tilted upon retrieval (Fig. 3). Except for the node at the Mauna Loa summit (SMLSW), the remaining five were located near publicly accessible roads, where they were likely disturbed by human activity or wild animals such as feral hogs or cattle.

Detailed operational information, including battery voltage, GPS status, and tilt angle, was continuously recorded in the log files of each nodal instrument. These logs are valuable for assessing the operational status and overall health of the nodes throughout the deployment. In the previous 3-month Pāhala deployment by Janiszewski *et al.* (2024), nodes equipped with external batteries operated for an average of 93.2 days, with many remaining functional upon retrieval, indicating their potential for even longer field durations. By the end of our 4-month deployment, all nodes had exhausted their power supplies. This outcome offers a valuable opportunity to assess the operational limits of the instruments under field conditions and provides practical insights for optimizing future deployment strategies. Overall, the recorded operational durations for the nodes in this deployment ranged from 31 to 109 days, with an average runtime of 90.5 days (Fig. 3b). According to the instrument log files, five nodes were deployed with depleted external batteries, and one node failed to switch to its internal

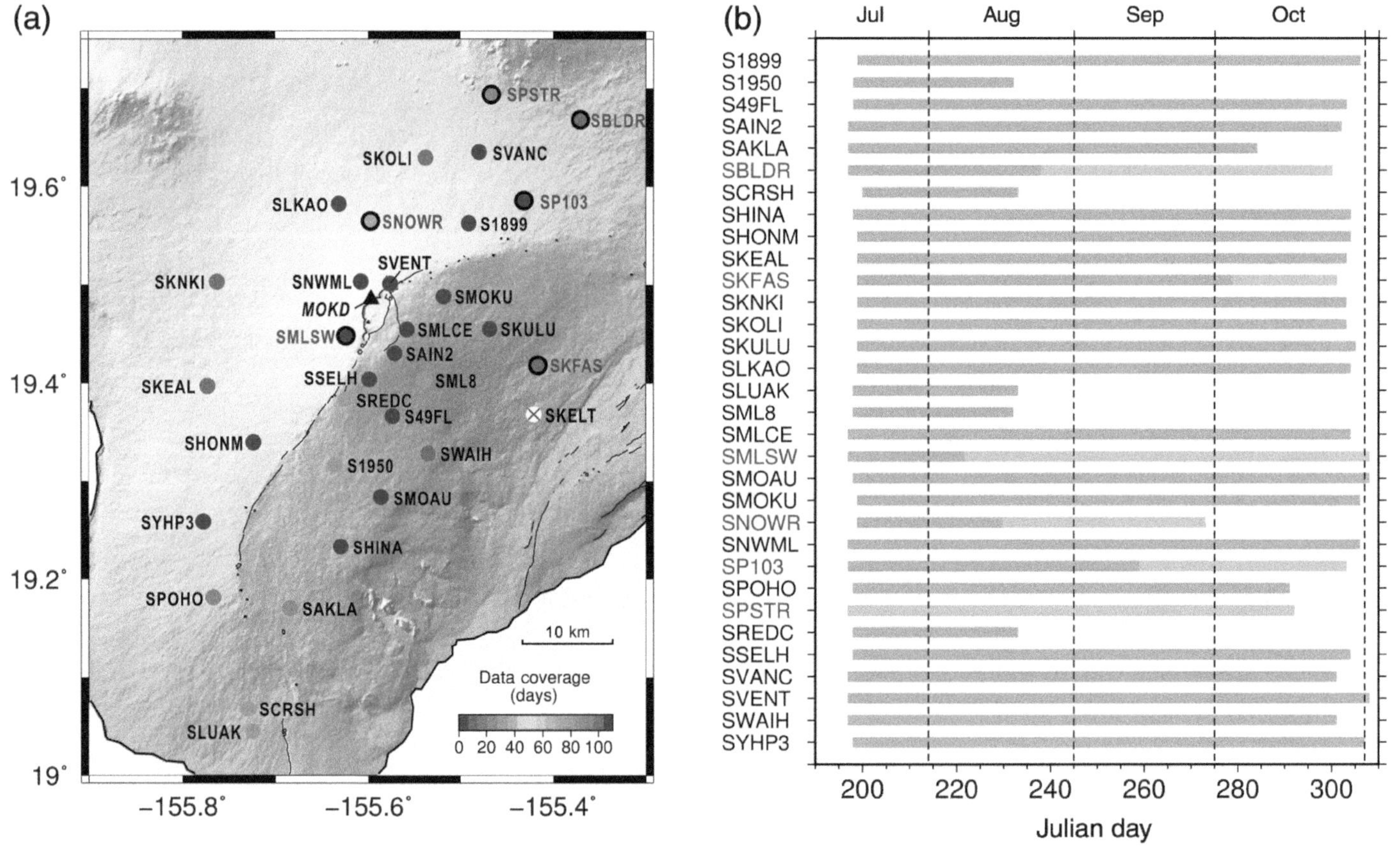

Figure 3. (a) Map summarizing the deployment and data coverage of the nodal seismic array (colored circles). Nodes that were found to be tilted upon retrieval are marked with black rings and red labels, and the white circle with a red cross indicates the node for which no data were recovered. (b) Timeline depicting data coverage and tilt status for each nodal instrument. Station names shown in red correspond to nodes identified as tilted upon retrieval. Each horizontal bar represents the operational period of an individual node, with gray segments denoting intervals when the node remained upright and light peach segments indicating periods of tilt, as determined from instrument log files. The color version of this figure is available only in the electronic edition.

battery after the external battery was depleted (Fig. S1, available in the supplemental material to this article). Excluding these six instruments that experienced power issues at either end of the deployment, the remaining 26 nodes achieved an average operational duration of 102.5 days, with only three operating for fewer than 100 days. Further analysis revealed that the external batteries had an average runtime of 72.6 days, with most lasting within ±3 days of this mean, although a few remained active for up to 90 days. The internal batteries had a maximum runtime of 34 days and an average of 30 days, with three instruments operating for fewer than 15 days. Detailed battery life information for each node is shown in Figure S1.

Data Quality Assessment

Tilt-angle information was extracted from the instrument log files to identify data segments affected by tilt (Fig. 3b). For all nodes found to be tilted upon retrieval, the onset of tilt was clearly documented in the logs and occurred at various times throughout the deployment. Notably, node SPSTR tilted within the first two hours after installation. At present, we have not identified or validated a reliable method for robustly recovering usable signals from these intervals. Therefore, in our analyses, data recorded during periods of tilt were excluded to prevent contamination. We recommend that users evaluate these intervals with care and make informed decisions regarding their inclusion in further analyses. Even with the exclusion of tilt-affected periods, the dataset maintains strong spatial and temporal coverage across the summit caldera and rift zones of Mauna Loa.

Apart from the tilt-related issues, no additional malfunctions were identified in this dataset, such as the flatlined segments reported in previous deployments (Janiszewski *et al.*, 2024). Compared with the HV stations, the amplitudes of the nodal array records closely match those of the HV stations at periods shorter than 5 s but are higher at periods longer than 5 s. A detailed comparison of amplitudes across different seismograms is presented in the Seismic Waveform Examples section subsequently.

To assess data quality, we computed power spectral densities (PSDs) using the probability density function (PDF)–PSD module of the Incorporated Research Institutions for Seismology (IRIS) Noise Toolkit (Incorporated Research Institutions for

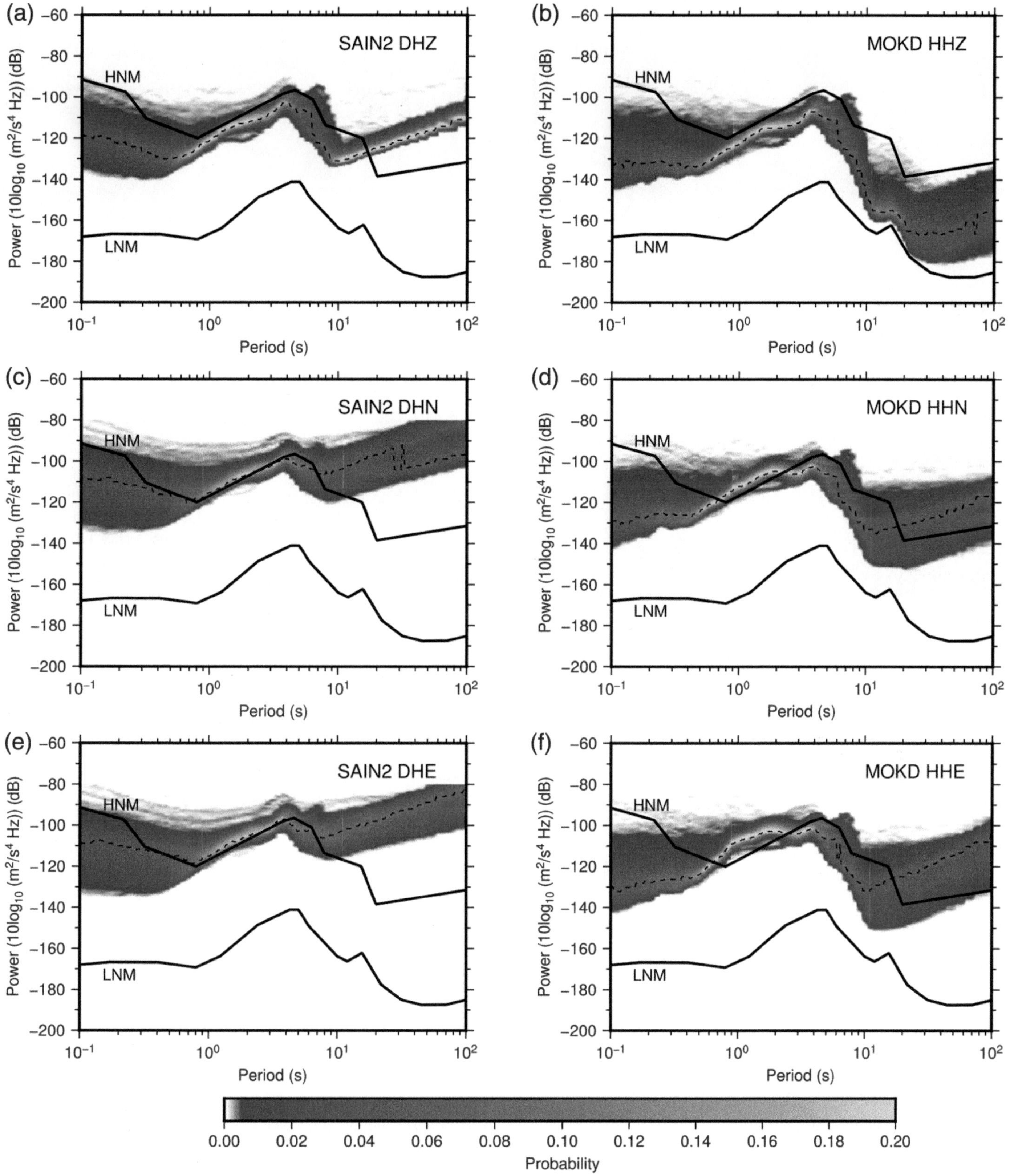

Figure 4. Probability density functions (PDFs) of power spectral densities (PSDs) for the three components at node station SAIN2 (a,c,e) and HVO broadband station MOKD (b,d,f). The locations of both stations are shown in Figure 3a. Primary PDF modes are shown as dashed lines. The black thick lines indicate the Peterson (1993) nominal high noise model (HNM) and low noise model (LNM). The color version of this figure is available only in the electronic edition.

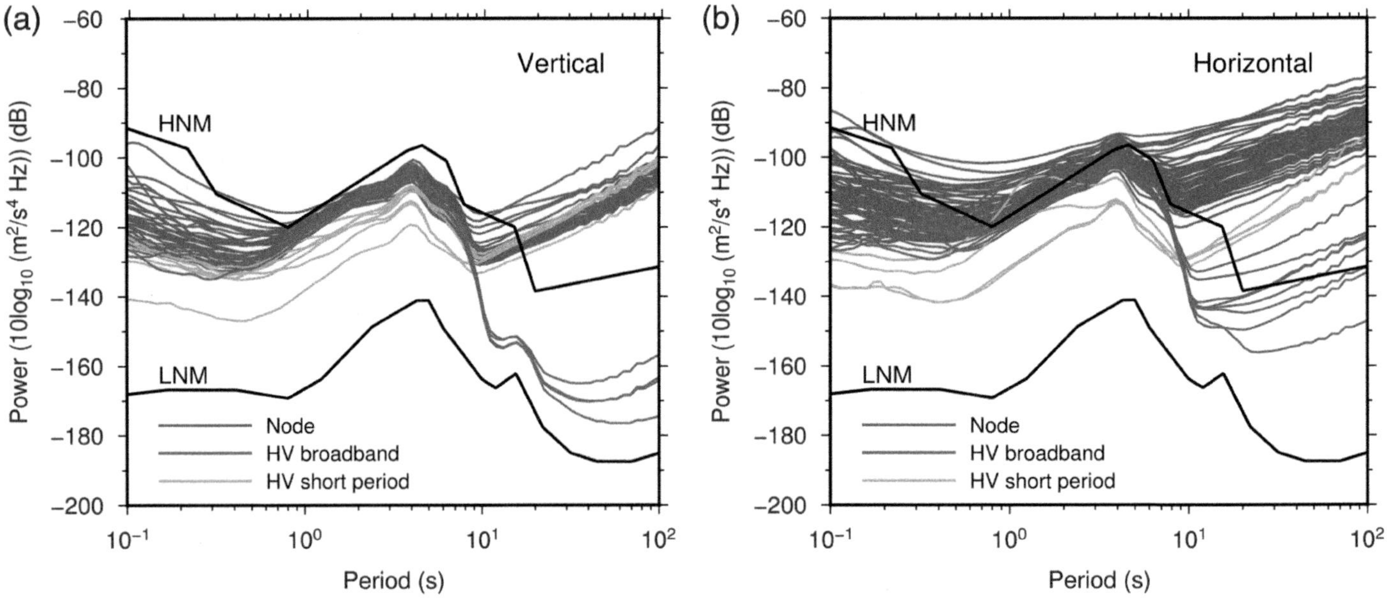

Figure 5. Mean PSDs for all nodes (blue) compared with nearby HV broadband (rose) and short-period (lavender) instruments for the (a) vertical and (b) horizontal components. HNM, high noise model; LNM, low noise model. The color version of this figure is available only in the electronic edition.

Seismology [IRIS], 2014). We first calculated PSD segments of 1-hr time windows with a 0.5-hr overlap, and then extracted mean PSDs and PDFs from them. Processing followed the methodology of McNamara and Buland (2004). For comparison, mean PSDs and PDFs were similarly extracted for nearby permanent HVO stations, including broadband and short-period instruments, from 15 July to 27 October 2024. Figure 4 shows PDFs for nodal station SAIN2 and broadband HVO station MOKD, both located near the summit of Mauna Loa (station locations shown in Fig. 3a). Overall, the primary modes of the PDFs of both instruments lie close to the nominal high noise model (HNM; Peterson, 1993), indicating relatively noisy conditions at the high-elevation summit area. In addition, noise levels for the nodal data at periods shorter than ~5–10 s are comparable to broadband stations for both vertical and horizontal components, whereas at periods longer than 10 s, nodal data exhibit elevated noise. This characteristic is also evident in comparisons of mean PSDs (Fig. 5). Across all periods, vertical-component noise levels of nodal data are comparable with those of HVO short-period instruments, whereas horizontal-component noise levels are slightly higher (Fig. 5). These observations align well with those reported in previous nodal deployments (Janiszewski *et al.*, 2024).

Initial Observations

Ambient noise characteristics

In addition to evaluating instrument performance, PSDs also characterize the ambient noise levels at each site. According to the mean PSDs, both seismic nodes and HV stations exhibit noise levels near the nominal HNM (Fig. 5), consistent with the previous Pāhala deployment (Janiszewski *et al.*, 2024) and indicative of generally noisy conditions across the Island of Hawaiʻi. We assess ambient noise characteristics in two period bands: 1–10 s, which overlaps with frequencies typically analyzed for teleseismic body waves, and 0.2–1 s, relevant for local seismicity analyses. To capture diurnal variability, we selected two 1-hr windows representing day (12:00–13:00 HST) and night (00:00–01:00 HST) periods, respectively.

Overall, noise levels on the horizontal components are consistently higher than those on the vertical components across both period bands (Fig. 6), likely due to weaker ground coupling from surface deployment without burial or anchoring. In the 1–10 s period, elevated noise levels are primarily observed at sites near the Mauna Loa summit and its northern flank, with a few exceptions near major roads, such as at SBLDR adjacent to Saddle Road (Fig. 6). Noise levels in the 0.2–1 s period show a similar spatial distribution to those in the 1–10 s period. Sites near the summit exhibit minimal diurnal variation in both period bands, whereas those at lower elevations display much stronger fluctuations, particularly in the 0.2–1 s period (Fig. 7).

Seismic background noise can generally be classified into natural sources, including ocean wave activity and wind, and anthropogenic (cultural) sources associated with human activity. Cultural noise typically dominates at periods shorter than 1 s and exhibits pronounced diurnal variability (Ringdal and Bungum, 1977; McNamara and Buland, 2004; Sheen, Shin, and Kang, 2009; Sheen, Shin, Kang, and Baag, 2009). Although natural noise may also show diurnal fluctuations at longer periods (e.g., 30–50 s), such variability is generally not observed in the short-period bands (<10 s) analyzed in this study (Stutzmann *et al.*, 2000). In this context, sites at lower

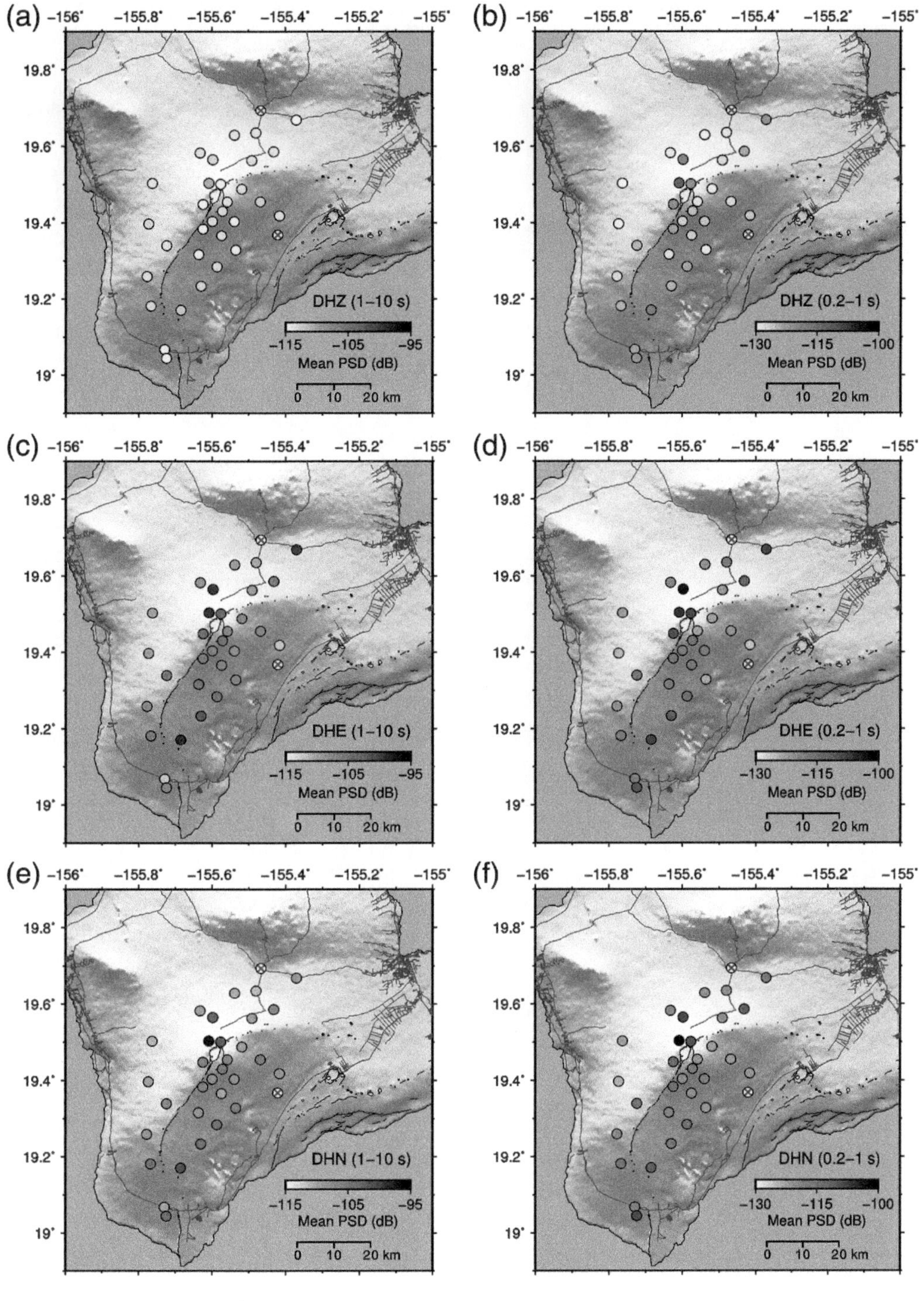

Figure 6. Map view of mean power spectral density (PSD) values for the three seismic components in the (a,c,e) 1–10 s and (b,d,f) 0.2–1 s period bands for the nodal array (circles). The colors represent the mean PSD values for each period band. Nodal stations with no data retrieved (SKFLT) or that became tilted shortly after installation (SPSTR) are shown as white circles with a red cross. The gray lines denote primary roads on the Island of Hawai'i. The color version of this figure is available only in the electronic edition.

elevations generally exhibit stronger diurnal variation, consistent with the expectation that cultural noise contributes more significantly in these areas. Moreover, the particularly pronounced variability observed in the 0.2–1 s period at these sites, compared to the 1–10 s band, further supports the interpretation that cultural noise is the dominant source in this frequency range. A representative example is site SBLDR, located near Saddle Road. During the daytime, the average PSD in the 0.2–1 s period reaches ~−102 dB, decreasing to about −114 dB at night, resulting in a difference of 12 dB (Fig. S3).

In contrast to low-elevation sites, summit sites exhibiting minimal diurnal variability are more likely influenced by natural sources. At periods shorter than 10 s, such natural noise is typically attributed to secondary microseisms generated by ocean wave interactions (Longuet-Higgins, 1950; Ardhuin *et al.*, 2011), wave–coastline interactions (Webb, 1998; Poppeliers and Mallinson, 2015), and wind-induced ground vibrations (De Angelis and Bodin, 2012; Lott *et al.*, 2017; Dybing *et al.*, 2019). The first two mechanisms tend to produce stronger signals near coastlines, which contrasts with the observed spatial pattern. This suggests that wind-induced ground motion is more likely the dominant source of natural noise in the summit region.

To evaluate this hypothesis, we compared the PSD spectrograms at site SNWML, located at the Mauna Loa summit, with wind speed data from a nearby National Oceanic and Atmospheric Administration (NOAA) weather station over a three-week interval (Fig. 8). Two intervals of elevated wind speed were identified: 22–24 July and 2–6 August. During these periods, seismic noise levels increased significantly across nearly all periods. In addition, during relatively stable wind conditions from 25 July to 1 August and from 7 to 11 August, fluctuations in noise levels were observed at periods longer than 30 s and shorter than 2 s,

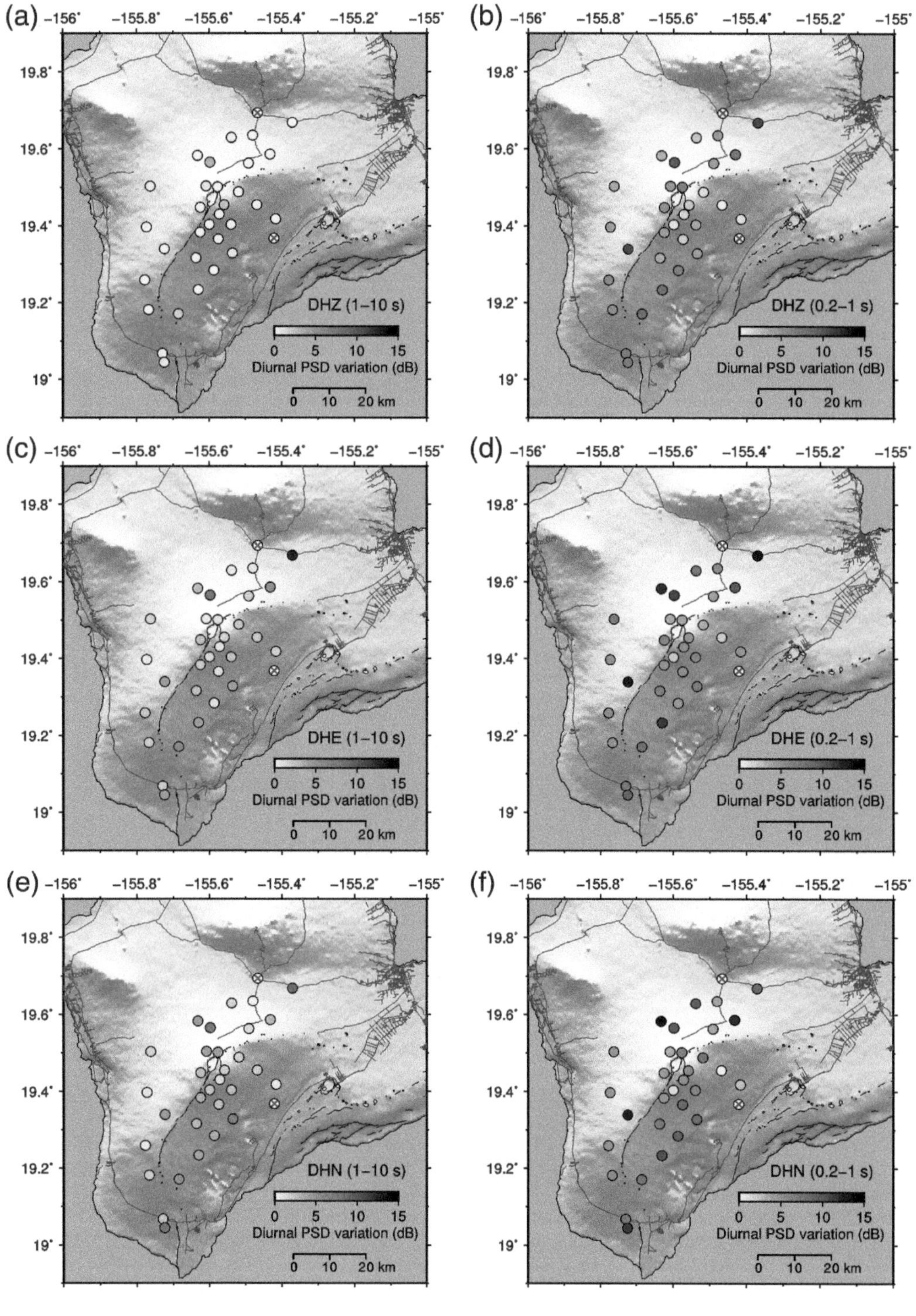

Figure 7. Same as Figure 6 but showing the variation in PSD between daytime and nighttime. Detailed mean PSD maps for daytime and nighttime are presented in Figures S2 and S3. The color version of this figure is available only in the electronic edition.

showing a strong correspondence with the wind speed changes. Previous studies have shown that ambient seismic noise generally correlates well with wind speed at periods longer than 30 s (De Angelis and Bodin, 2012; Ji and Dunham, 2024), whereas such correlations tend to weaken at higher frequencies due to increasing contributions from cultural sources (Lott *et al.*, 2017; Dybing *et al.*, 2019). However, in the Mauna Loa summit area, we find that wind speed correlates well with seismic noise levels at both long and short periods (Fig. 8). This suggests that wind is the dominant source of seismic noise at the summit. In addition, we find that noise levels on the northern flank of Mauna Loa are generally higher than those on the southern flank (Fig. 6), which may reflect variations in local wind conditions. Verification of this hypothesis will require additional wind speed data.

Seismic waveform examples

This section presents example waveforms primarily recorded by the nodal array and compares them with data from nearby permanent HVO stations. During the deployment, 341 teleseismic earthquakes with magnitudes greater than M_b 5.5 occurred at epicentral distances between 30° and 100°, a range commonly used for receiver function analysis (Langston, 1977). Of these, 77 events took place while all 31 functional nodes (excluding SPSTR) were operating stably and free of tilt disturbances.

Figure 9 shows waveforms from a teleseismic event on 19 July 2024, at 01:50:48.571 UTC (18 July, 15:50:48.571 local time), with an epicentral distance of 95.5° and back azimuth of 161° from Mauna Loa. Prior to comparison with HVO data, we removed instrument responses, downsampled the waveforms to 50 Hz, applied a zero-phase band-pass filter (0.5–20 s), and rotated horizontal components to radial and transverse directions. The resulting records exhibit high signal-to-noise ratios for both *P* and *S* waves, even at this long distance. As expected, vertical-component *P*-wave arrivals align well with those at HVO stations (Fig. S4). Spectral analysis of the vertical-component *P* wave (first 50 s) demonstrates

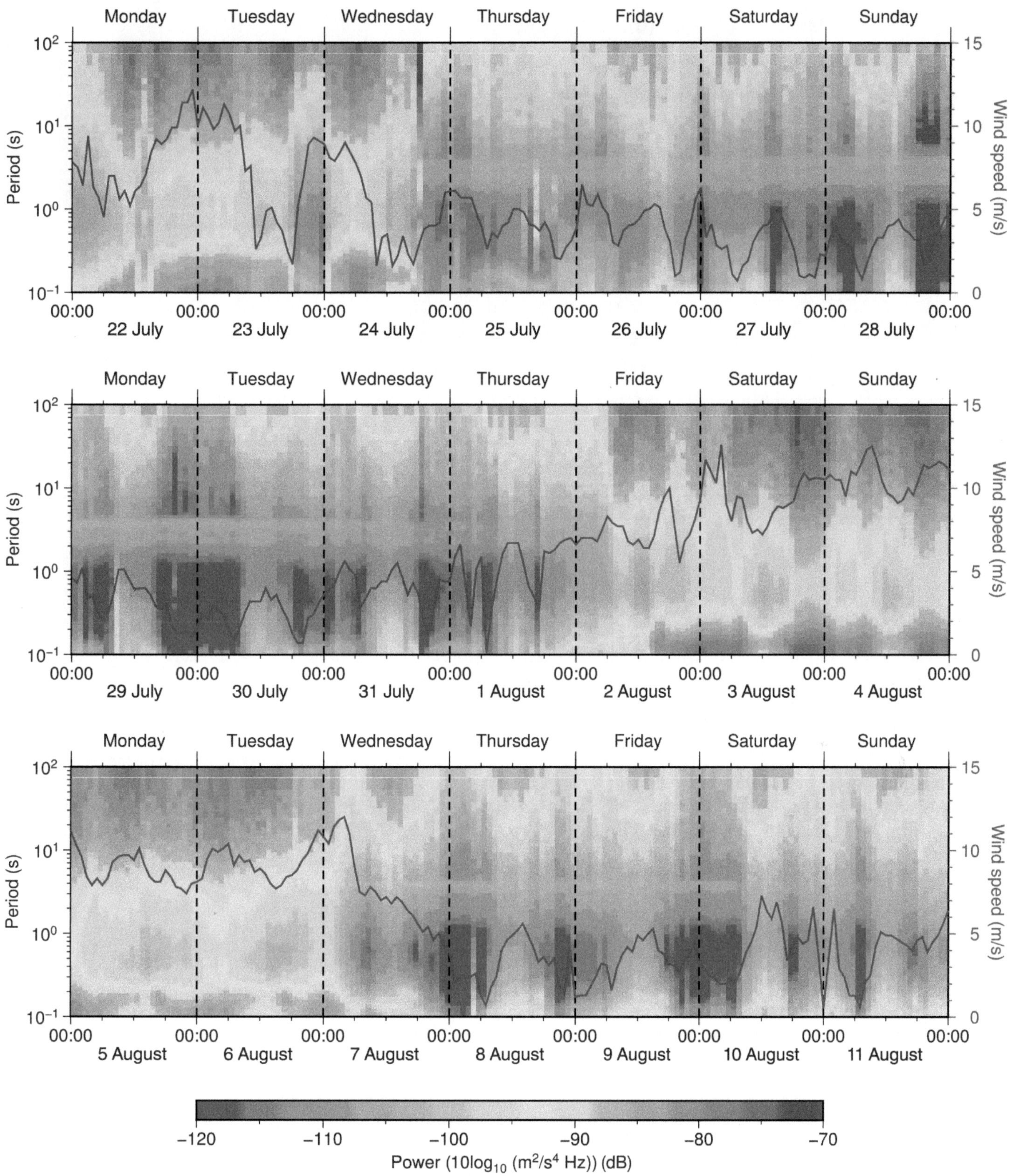

that the amplitudes of the nodal array records closely match those of the HV stations at periods shorter than 5 s, whereas they are systematically higher at longer periods (Fig. S5).

The nodal array also captured abundant local and regional earthquakes, with over 1400 events ($M_b > 1.4$) reported in the

Figure 8. Spectrograms over a three-week period showing the PSD of the E component at node SNWML (Fig. 3a). The red curve indicates wind speed recorded at the nearby Mauna Loa Weather Observatory (Fig. 1b). All times are shown in local time (HST). The color version of this figure is available only in the electronic edition.

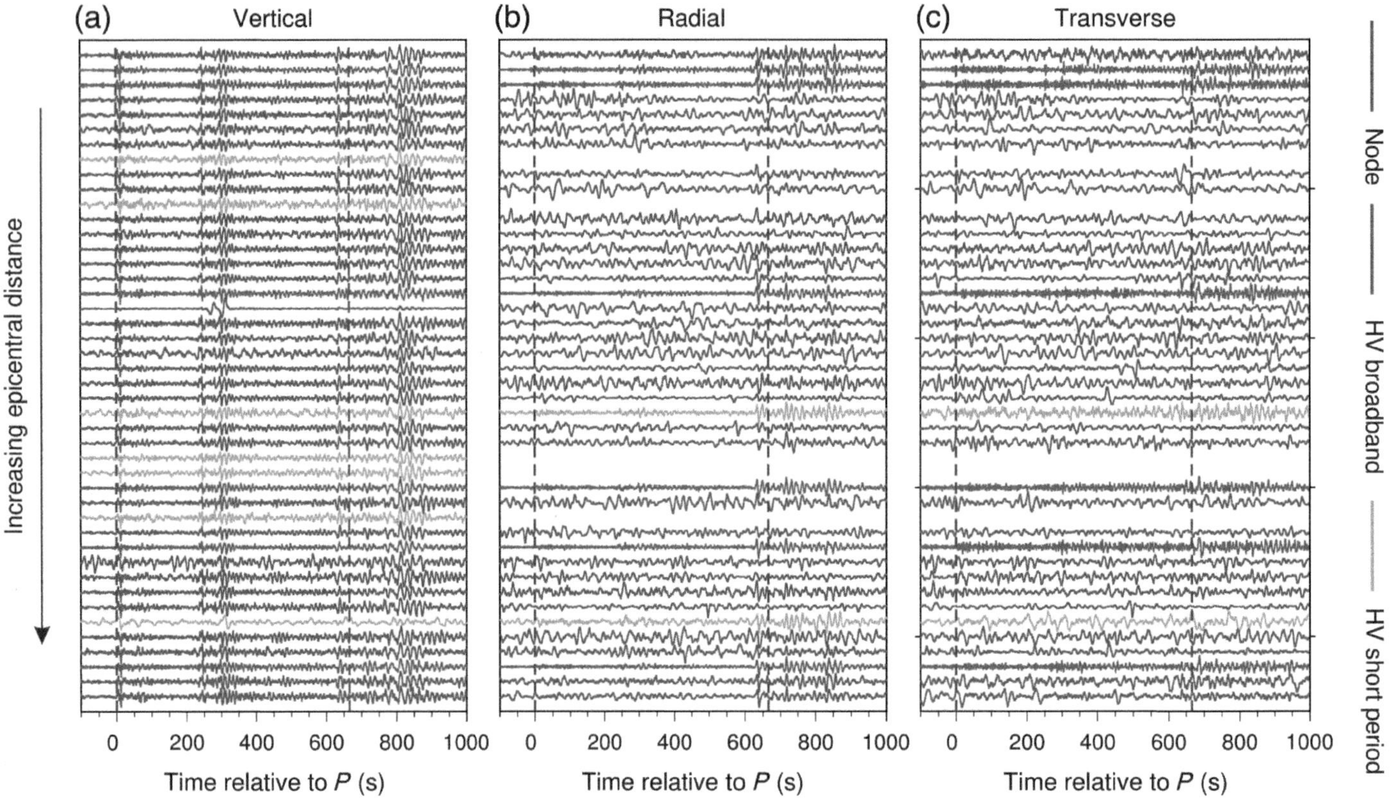

HVO catalog between 15 July and 1 November 2024, including five with magnitudes above 3.5. Additional events are likely to be detected using matched-filter techniques (Comte *et al.*, 2019). Figure 10 displays waveforms from a local earthquake on 6 August 2024, at 12:00:41 UTC (6 August 02:00:41 local time), with a depth of 7.5 km. Data were processed as above, with band-pass filtering between 0.5 and 3 Hz. The event is clearly recorded across the array, with distinct *P*- and *S*-wave arrivals.

These examples highlight the array's ability to capture high-quality waveforms from both teleseismic and local events. The dataset supports a broad spectrum of seismic analyses, including body- and surface-wave tomography, receiver function imaging, earthquake relocation, shear-wave splitting, and full waveform inversion. It may also contribute to ambient noise imaging and joint inversion efforts combining ambient noise with other geophysical observables such as receiver functions.

Figure 9. Examples of (a) vertical, (b) radial, and (c) transverse seismograms generated from an M_w 7.4 earthquake that occurred on 19 July 2024 at 01:50:48.571 UTC, as recorded by the nodal deployment and nearby permanent stations. Traces are color coded by the instrument type, as indicated in the key at right. In each panel, seismograms are aligned by the predicted *P*-wave arrival time based on the IASP91 global model (Kennett and Engdahl, 1991) and are ordered by increasing epicentral distance. Predicted arrival times for the *P* and *S* waves are indicated by gray-dashed lines. All seismograms have been instrument-response corrected and band-pass filtered between 0.05 and 2 Hz. Horizontal components have been rotated into radial and transverse directions. For clarity, the amplitude of each trace is normalized by its own maximum. The color version of this figure is available only in the electronic edition.

Summary

From July to November 2024, we deployed a temporary array of 33 nodal seismometers on Mauna Loa to augment seismic coverage and investigate its subsurface magmatic system. This array significantly increases ray-path density beneath the summit caldera and rift zones, complementing the permanent HVO seismic network, and allowing us to image underlying structure using a broad range of seismic analyses. This deployment provides a critical foundation for future high-resolution imaging of Mauna Loa's magmatic plumbing system and advances efforts to improve eruption forecasting for the Island of Hawai'i.

Data and Resources

The data from the new nodal array will be under a two-year moratorium following the retrieval of the final instruments from the field (estimated release of 31 December 2026) and will then be made publicly available. The network code 5O (2024-2024) has been assigned by the International Federation of Digital Seismograph Networks (FDSN; doi: 10.7914/axw2-7n89). Wind speed data were obtained from the National Oceanic and Atmospheric Administration (NOAA; https://www.noaa.gov/). Noise power spectral densities (PSDs) and their associated probability density functions (PDFs) were computed using the Incorporated Research Institutions for Seismology (IRIS)

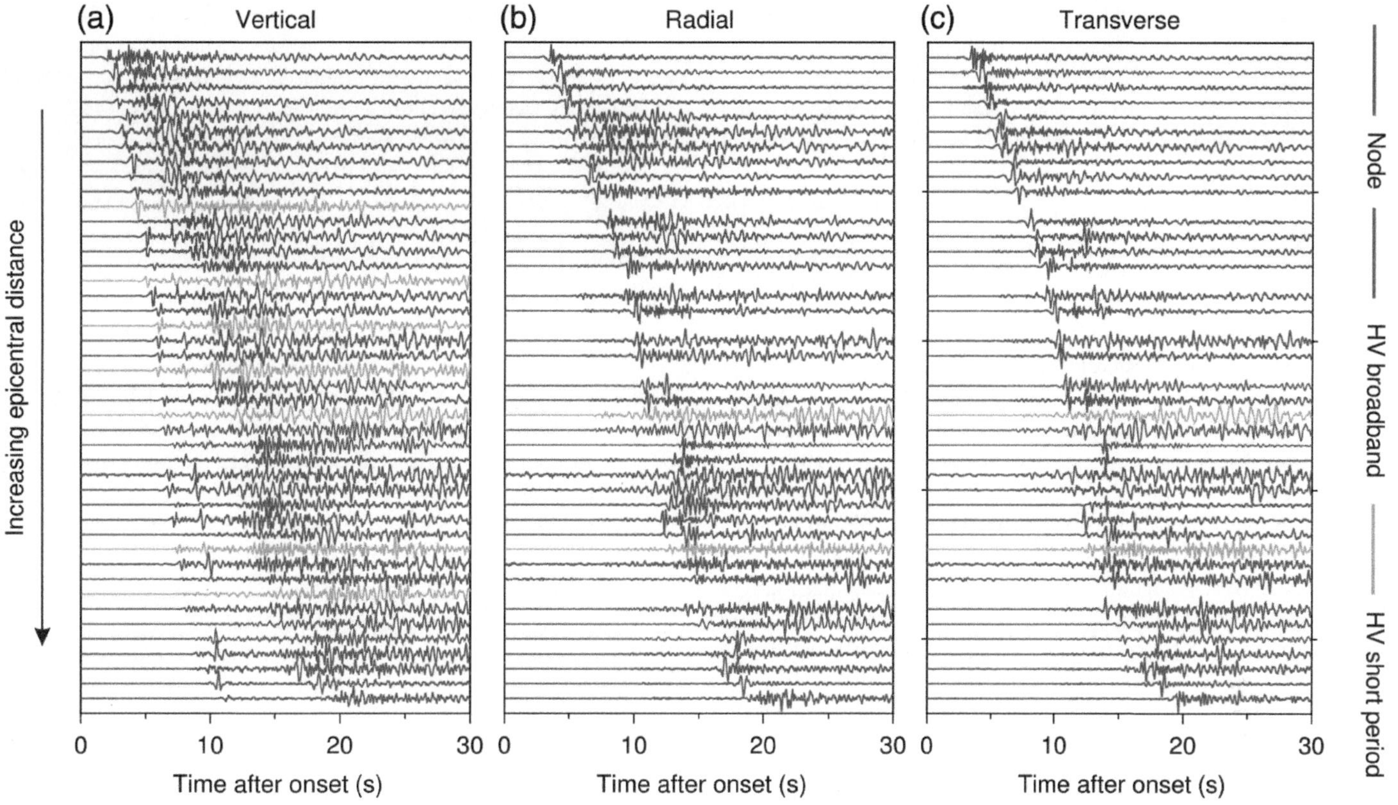

Figure 10. Examples of (a) vertical, (b) radial, and (c) transverse seismograms generated from a local earthquake with M_b 4.0, a depth of 7.5 km, and an onset time of 6 August 2024 12:00:41 (UTC) recorded by the nodal deployment, as well as nearby permanent stations. Traces are color coded by the instrument type, as indicated in the key at right. In each panel, time zero corresponds to the earthquake origin time, and seismograms are ordered by increasing epicentral distance. Seismograms are band-pass filtered between 0.5 and 3 Hz. Amplitudes are plotted as relative values normalized by the maximum absolute amplitude for all traces on each component. The color version of this figure is available only in the electronic edition.

Noise Toolkit PDF–PSD software (http://ds.iris.edu/ds/products/noise-toolkit-pdf-psd/). All websites were last accessed in June 2025. Figures were generated using the Generic Mapping Tools (GMT) (Wessel *et al.*, 2013), and data processing was conducted using the Seismic Analysis Code (SAC). The supplemental material includes figures showing battery life summaries, PSDs, seismograms, and spectrograms.

Declaration of Competing Interests

The authors acknowledge that there are no conflicts of interest recorded.

Acknowledgments

The authors thank Hawai'i Volcanoes National Park, Elizabeth Vinarski, Liliana DeSmither, and Andria Ellis for all the support during our field survey. The authors thank the U.S. Geological Survey (USGS) and the Hawaiian Volcano Observatory (HVO) for maintaining and providing access to seismic data. Seismic waveform data from the HVO permanent stations were obtained via EarthScope's Data Services (formerly Incorporated Research Institutions for Seismology Data Management Center [IRIS DMC]). This work was supported by the National Science Foundation under Grant EAR-2317687. Computational resources were provided by Bridges-2 at the Pittsburgh Supercomputing Center through allocation EES240060 from the Advanced Cyberinfrastructure Coordination Ecosystem: Services and Support (ACCESS, Boerner *et al.*, 2023) program.

Any use of trade, firm, or product names is for descriptive purposes only and does not imply endorsement by the U.S. Government.

References

Ardhuin, F., E. Stutzmann, M. Schimmel, and A. Mangeney (2011). Ocean wave sources of seismic noise, *J. Geophys. Res. Oceans* **116,** no. C9.

Barnard, W. M. (1995). Mauna Loa volcano: Historical eruptions, exploration, and observations (1779-1910), *Geophys. Monogr. Ser.* **92,** 1–19.

Boerner, T. J., S. Deems, T. R. Furlani, S. L. Knuth, and J. Towns (2023). Access: Advancing innovation: NSF's advanced cyberinfrastructure coordination ecosystem: Services and support, in *Practice and Experience in Advanced Research Computing 2023: Computing for the Common Good*, Association for Computing Machinery, p. 173–176.

Comte, D., M. Farias, S. Roecker, and R. Russo (2019). The nature of the subduction wedge in an erosive margin: Insights from the analysis of aftershocks of the 2015 m_w 8.3 illapel earthquake beneath the Chilean coastal range, *Earth Planet. Sci. Lett.* **520,** 50–62.

De Angelis, S., and P. Bodin (2012). Watching the wind: Seismic data contamination at long periods due to atmospheric pressure-field-induced tilting, *Bull. Seismol. Soc. Am.* **102,** no. 3, 1255–1265.

Denlinger, R., D. O'Connell, G. Lin, S. Roecker, and N. Bennington (2024). An unprecedented experiment to map Kīlauea's summit magma system, *Eos* 105.

Downs, D., F. Trusdell, K. Lynn, J. Schmith, J. Chang, C. Gansecki, S. Lundblad, N. Deligne, T. Orr, E. Gallant, *et al.* (2023). Sample details and near-real-time ed-xrf, grain size, and grain shape data collected during the November–December 2022 eruption of Mauna Loa volcano, island of Hawai'I, U.S. Geological Survey Data Release, doi: 10.5066/P9NA7GU3.

Dybing, S. N., A. T. Ringler, D. C. Wilson, and R. E. Anthony (2019). Characteristics and spatial variability of wind noise on near-surface broadband seismometers, *Bull. Seismol. Soc. Am.* **109,** no. 3, 1082–1098.

Finch, R. H., and G. A. Macdonald (1953). Hawaiian volcanoes during 1950, *Technical Report,* U.S. Government Printing Office, 27–89.

Gregg, C. E., B. F. Houghton, D. Paton, D. A. Swanson, and D. M. Johnston (2004). Community preparedness for lava flows from Mauna Loa and Hualālai volcanoes, Kona, Hawai'i, *Bull. Volcanol.* **66,** 531–540.

IRIS, D. (2014). Data services products: Noise toolkit pdf-psd noise toolkit pdf, *PSD bundle.*

Janiszewski, H., N. Bennington, and J. Wight (2024). A seismic nodal deployment to understand magmatic structure in the vicinity of the Pāhala earthquake swarm, *Seismol. Res. Lett.* **95,** no. 5, 3082–3092.

Ji, Q., and E. M. Dunham (2024). Ambient noise from the atmosphere within the seismic hum period band: A case study of hurricane landfall, *Earth Planet. Sci. Lett.* **629,** 118,589.

Kennett, B., and E. Engdahl (1991). Traveltimes for global earthquake location and phase identification, *Geophys. J. Int.* **105,** no. 2, 429–465.

Langston, C. A. (1977). The effect of planar dipping structure on source and receiver responses for constant ray parameter, *Bull. Seismol. Soc. Am.* **67,** no. 4, 1029–1050.

Lockwood, J. P., and P. W. Lipman (1987). Holocene eruptive history of Mauna Loa volcano, *U.S. Geol. Surv. Profess. Pap. 1350,* no. 1, 509–535.

Longuet-Higgins, M. S. (1950). A theory of the origin of microseisms. *Phil. Trans. Roy. Soc. Lond. A* **243,** no. 857, 1–35.

Lott, F. F., J. R. Ritter, M. Al-Qaryouti, and U. Corsmeier (2017). On the analysis of wind-induced noise in seismological recordings: approaches to present wind-induced noise as a function of wind speed and wind direction, *Pure Appl. Geophys.* **174,** 1453–1470.

Maher, S. P., P. Dawson, A. Hotovec-Ellis, W. A. Thelen, A. Jolly, N. Bennington, J. C. Chang, and P. Dotray (2023). Characterizing and locating seismic tremor during the 2022 eruption of Mauna Loa volcano, Hawai'i, with network covariance, *Seism. Rec.* **3,** no. 3, 228–238.

McNamara, D. E., and R. P. Buland (2004). Ambient noise levels in the continental United States, *Bull. Seismol. Soc. Am.* **94,** no. 4, 1517–1527.

Mulliken, K. M., J. P. Kauahikaua, D. Swanson, and M. H. Zoeller (2024). Chronology of recent volcanic activity on the island of Hawai'i, Hawaii. Data Release, U.S. Geological Survey Asset Identifier Service, AIS.

Peterson, J. R. (1993). Observations and modeling of seismic background noise, *Technical Report, U.S. Geological Survey.*

Poppeliers, C., and D. Mallinson (2015). High-frequency seismic noise generated from breaking shallow water ocean waves and the link to time-variable sea states, *Geophys. Res. Lett.* **42,** no. 20, 8563–8569.

Ringdal, F., and H. Bungum (1977). Noise level variation at norsar and its effect on detectability, *Bull. Seismol. Soc. Am.* **67,** no. 2, 479–492.

Sheen, D.-H., J. S. Shin, and T.-S. Kang (2009). Seismic noise level variation in South Korea, *Geosci. J.* **13,** 183–190.

Sheen, D.-H., J. S. Shin, T.-S. Kang, and C.-E. Baag (2009). Low frequency cultural noise, *Geophys. Res. Lett.* **36,** no. 17.

Stutzmann, E., G. Roult, and L. Astiz (2000). Geoscope station noise levels, *Bull. Seismol. Soc. Am.* **90,** no. 3, 690–701.

Trusdell, F. A., and M. H. Zoeller (2017). Lava inundation zone maps for Mauna Loa, island of hawai 'i, hawaii. *U.S. Geol. Surv. Sci. Investig. Map 3387,* 12.

Webb, S. C. (1998). Broadband seismology and noise under the ocean, *Rev. Geophys.* **36,** no. 1, 105–142.

Wessel, P., W. H. Smith, R. Scharroo, J. Luis, and F. Wobbe (2013). Generic mapping tools: Improved version released, *Eos Trans. AGU* **94,** no. 45, 409–410.

Manuscript received 9 July 2025
Published online 29 October 2025

Erratum

Erratum to Automated Classification of Volcanic Earthquakes Using Transformer Encoders: Insights into Data Quality and Model Interpretability

Yugo Suzuki[1], Yohei Yukutake[2], Takao Ohminato[2], Masami Yamasaki[1], and Ahyi Kim[*1]

In the published article (Suzuki *et al.*, 2025), one in-text citation and several bibliography entries were incorrect due to a late-stage bibliography merge and reference manager mapping errors. These corrections do not affect the results, analyses, or conclusions. The authors sincerely apologize for these mistakes. On the second page, the in-text citation "Ida and Ishida (2022)" should read "Ida *et al.* (2022)".

References

Bebbington, M. S. (2007). Identifying volcanic regimes using Hidden Markov models, *Geophys. J. Int.* **171,** no. 2, 921–942, doi: 10.1111/j.1365-246X.2007.03559.x.

Buurman, H., and M. E. West (2010). Seismic precursors to volcanic explosions during the 2006 eruption of Augustine volcano: Chapter 2, in *The 2006 Eruption of Augustine Volcano, Alaska* J. A. Power, M. L. Coombs, and J. T. Freymueller (Editors), *U.S. Geol. Surv. Profess. Pap. 1769*, 41–57, doi: 10.3133/pp17692.

Gulati, A., J. Qin, C.-C. Chiu, N. Parmar, Y. Zhang, J. Yu, W. Han, S. Wang, Z. Zhang, Y. Wu, *et al.* (2020). Conformer: Convolution-augmented transformer for speech recognition, *Interspeech* **2020,** 5036–5040, doi: 10.48550/arXiv.2005.08100.

Hammer, C., M. Beyreuther, and M. Ohrnberger (2012). A seismic-event spotting system for volcano fast-response systems, *Bull. Seismol. Soc. Am.* **102,** 948–960, doi: 10.1785/0120110167.

Ida, Y., E. Fujita, and T. Hirose (2022). Classification of volcano-seismic events using waveforms in the method of k-means clustering and dynamic time warping, *J. Volcanol. Geotherm. Res.* **429,** 107616, doi: 10.1016/j.jvolgeores.2022.107616.

Kaplan, J., S. McCandlish, T. Henighan, T. B. Brown, B. Chess, R. Child, S. Gray, A. Radford, J. Wu, and D. Amodei (2020). Scaling laws for neural language models, doi: 10.48550/arXiv.2001.08361.

Kingma, D. P., and J. Ba (2014). Adam: A method for stochastic optimization, doi: 10.48550/arXiv.1412.6980.

Köhler, A., M. Ohrnberger, and F. Scherbaum (2010). Unsupervised pattern recognition in continuous seismic wavefield records using self-organizing maps, *Geophys. J. Int.* **182,** no. 3, 1619–1630, doi: 10.1111/j.1365-246X.2010.04709.x.

Langer, H., S. Falsaperla, M. Masotti, R. Campanini, S. Spampinato, and A. Messina (2009). Synopsis of supervised and unsupervised pattern classification techniques applied to volcanic tremor data at Mt Etna, Italy, *Geophys. J. Int.* **178,** 1132–1144, doi: 10.1111/j.1365-246X.2009.04179.x.

Langer, H., S. Falsaperla, A. Messina, S. Spampinato, and B. Behncke (2011). Detecting imminent eruptive activity at Mt Etna, Italy, in 2007–2008 through pattern classification of volcanic tremor data, *J. Volcanol. Geotherm. Res.* **200,** no. 1, 1–17, doi: 10.1016/j.jvolgeores.2010.11.019.

Loshchilov, I., and F. Hutter (2017). Decoupled weight decay regularization, doi: 10.48550/arXiv.1711.05101 (presented at ICLR 2019).

Permana, T., T. Nishimura, H. Nakahara, and N. Shapiro (2022). Classification of volcanic tremors and earthquakes based on seismic correlation: Application at Sakurajima volcano, Japan, *Geophys. J. Int.* **229,** no. 2, 1077–1097, doi: 10.1093/gji/ggab517.

Suzuki, Y., Y. Yukutake, T. Ohminato, M. Yamasaki, and A. Kim (2025). Automated classification of volcanic earthquakes using transformer encoders: insights into data quality and model interpretability, *Seismol. Res. Lett.* **97,** 1032–1047, doi: 10.1785/0220240494.

Unglert, K., V. Radic, and A. M. Jellinek (2016). Principal component analysis vs. self-organizing maps combined with hierarchical clustering for pattern recognition in volcano seismic spectra, *J. Volcanol. Geotherm. Res.* **320,** 58–74, doi: 10.1016/j.jvolgeores.2016.04.014.

Manuscript received 3 November 2025
Published online 9 December 2025

1. Yokohama City University, Yokohama, Japan, https://orcid.org/0009-0001-7948-5332 (YS); https://orcid.org/0000-0002-0605-0397 (AK); 2. Earthquake Research Institute, The University of Tokyo, Bunkyō, Japan

*Corresponding author: ahyik@yokohama-cu.ac.jp

Cite this article as Suzuki, Y., Y. Yukutake, T. Ohminato, M. Yamasaki, and A. Kim (2025). *Erratum to* Automated Classification of Volcanic Earthquakes Using Transformer Encoders: Insights into Data Quality and Model Interpretability, *Seismol. Res. Lett.*, **xx**, 1227–1227, doi: 10.1785/0220250392.

SSA News and Notes

A Year of Support

Throughout 2025, members of the Seismological Society of America (SSA) stepped forward to mentor and teach one another. They raised their voices to advocate for federal support of seismology and made generous financial gifts to aid the Society's mission.

Together, we advanced seismology through:

$88,600+ in grants supporting our community's scientific efforts, including 3 Community Grants, 2 Paul Andrew Spudich Travel Grants, 7 Global Travel Grants, 23 2025 Annual Meeting Travel Grants, and 2 Travel Grants for the fall Environmental Seismology Conference.

400+ papers published in our three peer-reviewed journals that continue to have a major impact in seismology.

50+ interactions with U.S. policymakers/their staff to advocate for federal support of seismology and other outreach efforts, including letters to Congress and a new policy statement on the link between seismic research/monitoring and U.S. defense.

1+ new international partnership to support the International Conference on Intraplate and Himalayan Seismology.

Nine complimentary courses/mentoring sessions offered to members, including Signal, Not Noise: Crafting a High-Clarity LinkedIn Profile (Sarah Pietraszek-Mattner), Effective Scientific Public Speaking, Slides and Poster Design (Ross Stein), Engage! Steps to Contact Congress Right Now (Elizabeth Duffy), Navigating Career Transitions (Ross Stein and Ellen Shulman), How to Submit a Session Proposal for the Annual Meeting (Peggy Hellweg and Will Levandowski), All About SSA Grants (Nicola Perlwitz), Career and Academic Advice for Members (Ericka Alinne Solano, Andy Michael, and Doyeon Kim) and Networking to Find Collaborators and Build Your Career (Emily Brodsky, Paula Figueiredo, Paul Friberg, and Victor Tsai).

Two Society meetings, SSA 2025 and the topical conference on environmental seismology, focused on strengthening connections and sharing science in our international community.

226 free introductory SSA memberships provided to students through Society exhibitions at scientific conferences worldwide, including this year's American Geophysical Union Meeting, European Geosciences Union General Assembly, International Meeting for Applied Geoscience and Energy, and Comprehensive Nuclear-Test-Ban Treaty Organization Science and Technology Conference.

Four awards presented at SSA 2025, honoring pioneering scientists, including the late Jeffrey Given, and inspiring others to aim high in their professional endeavors.

Donor Generosity = Record Number of Grant Recipients

A record number of SSA members received travel grants to attend the **2026 Annual Meeting**, including the first to receive a new Society grant for U.S.-based regular members. The grants were made possible through generous contributions to the **General Fund, Annual Meeting Travel Fund,** and **Kanamori Fund.**

Student Recipients:

- Bartu Bilgen, Middle East Technical University
- Yuly Rave Bonilla, University of South Florida
- Hilary Chang, Lamont-Doherty Earth Observatory
- Sifang Chen, University of Chicago
- Julia Grossman, University of Washington
- Yuriko Iwasaki, University of California, Santa Cruz
- Albert Kabanda, Northwestern University
- Carlos Montalvo Lara, Victoria University of Wellington
- David Naranjo, Delft University of Technology
- Batul Bilal Peralta Nemr, The Institute of Earth Sciences (ISTerre)
- Victor Timilehin Olawoyin, Boston College
- Grant Spraker, University of Utah
- Kathrine Udell-Lopez, University of Maryland
- Guglielmo Vullo, University of Pisa
- Zoë Zawol, National Park Service, Scientists-in-Parks; University of California, Berkeley

Early-Career Recipients:

- Valeria Cortés Rivas, Pontifical Catholic University of Chile
- Jiaxuan Li, University of Houston
- Irene Liou, GFZ Helmholtz Centre for Geosciences
- Boris Rösler, Center for Scientific Research and Higher Education at Ensenada (CICESE)
- Israporn Sethanant, University of Melbourne

International Recipients:

- Raul Castro, Center for Scientific Research and Higher Education at Ensenada (CICESE)
- Constantinos Charalambous, Imperial College London
- John Londono, Colombia Geological Survey
- Thanh-Son Pham, Australian National University

European Seismological Commission/SSA Recipients:

- Silvia Beretta, University of Bologna

- Pavlos Bonatis, Aristotle University of Thessaloniki
- Chuanbin Zhu, Northumbria University

Regular Domestic Recipients:

- Xiaotao Yang, Purdue University
- Asiye Aziz Zanjani, New Mexico Institute of Mining and Technology

A record number of grant recipients from across SSA's global community will connect at the 2026 Annual Meeting. The color version of this figure is available only in the electronic edition.

Francisco José Sánchez-Sesma Selected as 2026 Joyner Lecturer

Universidad Autónoma de Mexico Professor Francisco José Sánchez-Sesma is the 2026 recipient of the William B. Joyner Lecture Award.

Francisco José Sánchez-Sesma, 2026 Joyner Lecturer The color version of this figure is available only in the electronic edition.

Sánchez-Sesma will deliver his lecture, "Seismic Wave Propagation in Complex Geological Domains: From Site Effects in Ground Motion to Diffuse Fields in Passive Seismology," at the 2026 SSA Annual Meeting and the 13th National Conference on Earthquake Engineering.

The lecture will reflect on his decades of research aimed at understanding and modeling seismic-wave propagation in complex geological media and its manifestations in ground motion, from strong shaking during large earthquakes to weak ambient vibrations such as microtremors and seismic noise.

The lectureship is jointly awarded by Earthquake Engineering Research Institute (EERI) and SSA to those who have provided outstanding earth science contributions to the theory and practice of earthquake engineering or outstanding earthquake engineering contributions to the direction and focus of earth science research, together with demonstrated skills of communication at the interface of earthquake science and earthquake engineering.

Manuscript received 31 December 2025
Published online 10 February 2026

Meeting Reports

2025 SSA Environmental Seismology Meeting Report

Environmental Seismology: Earth's Surface and Subsurface Hazards, Dynamics and Resources was held in Denver, Colorado, on 14–18 October 2025. The meeting, the fourth topical conference convened by the Seismological Society of America, was co-chaired by Rick Aster of Colorado State University and Siobhan Niklasson of New Mexico Tech. The meeting included 139 participants from 88 institutions and 16 countries.

Aster and Niklasson proposed the meeting to acknowledge the tremendous advances in research topics now falling under the umbrella of environmental seismology, from cryoseismology to groundwater and fluvial dynamics, landslides, ocean signals, extreme weather events, subsurface monitoring and imaging, and urban seismology. As Aster said in his remarks to open the meeting, "Elastic waves are ubiquitous, and I think the breadth of this conference really shows the great reach of seismology."

On Tuesday, 14 October, the meeting opened with a reception and the keynote address "Environmental Forcing of Faults and Slow-moving Landslides" by Roland Bürgmann of the University of California, Berkeley Department of Earth and Planetary Science, and the Berkeley Seismological Laboratory. Bürgmann shared examples of how environmental processes such as hydrological variations across various timescales impact the tectonics of California's San Andreas Fault and slow-moving landslides such as the Slumgullion Earthflow in southern Colorado.

Bürgmann suggested that these forcing studies could not only help researchers understand environmental phenomena also "but actually learn something about tectonic faults, about their mechanical behavior and properties and about landslides, the dynamics of slope movement in landslides, by seeing how they respond to these external changes in stress and conditions."

The Wednesday through Friday sessions featured keynote and invited presentations, poster sessions open at breakfast and during session breaks, and morning and afternoon oral sessions. At the end of each oral session, speakers participated in a panel discussion with the audience.

The Wednesday, 15 October keynote speakers were Fabian Walter of Swiss Federal Institute for Forest, Snow and Landscape Research WSL on "News from the Dark: Portable and Distributed Seismic Sensors Shed Light on Subglacial Processes" and Victor Tsai of Brown University on "Using Seismology for Non-earthquake Signals."

On Thursday, 16 October, keynote speakers included Domniki Asimaki of the California Institute of Technology on "Machine-Learning Ground Motions for Infrastructure Risk Reduction" and Andreas Fichtner of ETH Zürich on "Integrated Fiber-optic Sensing—Technological Developments and Potentials for Environmental Applications."

The meeting concluded on Friday, 17 October with a keynote address by Jean-Philippe Avouac of the California Institute of Technology on "Recent Advances in the Understanding and Forecasting of Induced Seismicity" and a closing session on the seismic investigation of mass movements.

Some of the themes that emerged during the four days of presentations included the need for greater integration of seismic data with other types of relevant environmental data collected at study sites; attention to the timescales and temporal patterns of interest for each research question; the ability to identify and study precursor events; and the need for better understanding and modeling of the fundamental physics behind some of the smaller high-frequency signals studied in this discipline.

Speakers also emphasized the importance of collaboration with experienced engineers to provide the types of multisensors and stable power sources, data telemetry, and other components needed for long-term deployment in challenging environments such as glaciers and riverbeds, as well as hungry polar fox hunting grounds. Another key challenge mentioned often was the need for better data storage and cataloging so that the vast amounts of information collected can be searchable and tagged for machine learning analysis.

Attendees discussed ways to reach out to a broad range of funding agencies and facilities that could support multidisciplinary research required for the field's success. Several attendees noted the absence of U.S. federal agency and lab colleagues, who could not attend the topical conference because of a U.S. government shutdown.

On Saturday, 18 October, 37 meeting attendees participated in a field seminar on seismic sources and environmental conditions associated with landslides, glaciers, and ice in Rocky Mountain National Park, which included hiking to 10,240′ elevation Lake Haiyaha for a view of the 28 June 2022 $>1\ Mm^3$ Chaos Canyon landslide site. The seminar was led by Jon Achuff, geoscientist and president of Black Spruce Inc., along with Aster and Niklasson. Field seminar planning was carried out by USGS scientists Kate Allstadt, Rob Anthony, and Jeff Coe, who were unfortunately unable to attend the event.

Figure 1. SSA 2025 Environmental Seismology Co-Chairs Siobhan Niklasson (left) and Rick Aster. Credit: SSA. The color version of this figure is available only in the electronic edition.

Figure 2. SSA 2025 Environmental Seismology attendees on field seminar at Dream Lake, Colorado. Credit: Siobhan Niklasson. The color version of this figure is available only in the electronic edition.

Generous donations to SSA's General Fund made it possible to offer complimentary registration and a travel stipend to the following attendees: Taylor Kenyon of the University of Waterloo and the U.S. National Park Service and Samara Omar of the Colorado School of Mines.

SSA and the meeting co-chairs thank Colorado State University Geosciences, Güralp, and Nanometrics for their sponsorship of the conference.

The supplemental material consists of the topical meeting program, which was accurate as of 27 October 2025.

Declaration of Competing Interests

The authors acknowledge that there are no conflicts of interest recorded.

Manuscript received 18 November 2025
Published online 26 December 2025

In Recognition

Seismological Society of America (SSA) is glad to acknowledgethe following individuals for their service as peer reviewers in 2025.SSA's journals are known for their rigorous peer review and for thevaluable reviewer feedback that helps authors improve the qualityof their publications. Thank you for contributing your expertise tothis vital component of the publication process. Your volunteer effortshelp us further our mission of advancing earthquake science worldwide.

John Townend
Chair of SSA Publications Committee

Brad Aagaard
Alice Abbate
Paul Abbott
Medhat Abdelaziz
Mohamed Abdelmeguid
Fatemeh Abdi
Niloofar Abedi
Francesc Abella Sans
Rachel Abercrombie
Norman Abrahamson
Elliot Abt
A. Omar Abubaker
Nicholas Ackerley
A. Enrique Acosta Gio
Guy Adami
John Adams
Oluwaseyifunmi Adeboboye
Kasey Aderhold
Hafsa Affendi
Kelvin Afrashtehfar
Anita Agarwal
Mohit Agrawal
Jorge Aguirre
Sarah Aguirre
Bushra Ahmad
Moni Ahmadian
Yinshuang Ai
Chastity Aiken
Amir Akbari
Aybige Akinci
Sinan Akkar
Bahadir Aktug
Takeshi Akuhara
Linda Al Atik
Lama Alabdulaaly
Alev Alaçam
Abdullah Alalyani
Judith Albino
Ziad Al-Dwairi
Roger Alexander
Richard Alfaro-Diaz
Trishul Allareddy
Carl Allen
Trevor Allen
Paul Allison
Travis Alongi
Aurelio Alonso
Elizabeth Alpert
Hosam Alraqiq
Mona Al-Sane
Mishali Alsharief
Don Altman
José Álvarez-Gómez
Abla Ahmed Mohamed Aly
Brandon Ambrosino
Gabriele Ameri
Ghada Amin Khalifa
Jean-Paul Ampuero
Fotini Anagnostopoulos-King
Ryosuke Ando
Sérgio Andrade
Jennifer Andrews
Solene Antoine
Antonio Antunes
Uzonna Anyiam
Chukwuemeka Anyikwa
Hideo Aochi
Johan Aps
Tariq Anwar Aquib
Ana Cecilia Aranha
Ralph Archuleta
Oscar Arevalo
Sherwin Arman
Roland Arnold
Ramon Arrowsmith
Stephen Arrowsmith
Mario Arroyo-Solórzano
Pietro Artale Harris
Kimiyuki Asano
Saeed Asgary
Aysegul Askan
Jelle Assink
Michael Asten
Richard Aster
Rodrigo Astroza
Gail Atkinson
Jane Atkinson
Januka Attanayake
James Atterholt
Douglas Auld
David Avenetti
Jérôme Azzola
Zhenning Ba
Jose Badal
James Bader
Milad Bader
Victor Badner
Ling Bai
Alan Baird
Laurie Baise
Stephane Baize
Jack Baker
Arifa Bakerywala
Rohit Baal Balasundaram
Ben Balevi
Annemarie Baltay
Sepideh Banava
Xuewei Bao
Xueyang Bao
Sylvain Barbot
Andrew Barbour
Pierre-Yves Bard
Steven Barefoot
Serif Baris
Adnan Barkat
Carla Barnaba
Patricia Barros
Noel Barstow
Olivia Bartholomew
Santanu Baruah
Roberto Basili
Meghan Bastin
Urbi Basu

Gary Bauman
Roxanne Bavarian
Curt Bay
Jeff Bayless
Kirsty Bayliss
Stephen Bayne
Eric Beaucé
Celine Beauval
Dirk Becker
Tracy Becker
Raman Bedi
Mahmoud Belal
Tena Belinic Topic
Eugenio Beltrán-Aguilar
Sean Bemis
Steven Bender
Beatriz Benjumea
Rob Berg
Felix Bernauer
Eric Bernstein
Gregory Beroza
Al Best
Maximiliano Bezada
Ruchi Bhandari
Harsha Bhat
Glenn Biasi
Lidong Bie
Umair Bin Waheed
Dino Bindi
Ettore Biondi
Peter Bird
Sigmund Birkeland
Yesim Biro
Jordan Bishop
Saptadeep Biswas
Som Biswas
Quentin Bletery
Paul Bodin
Thomas Bodin
Carolin Boese
Ian Boggero
Julian Bommer
Anna Alessandri Bonetti
Jessie Bonner
David Boore
Sanjay Bora
Pollyanna Borges
Hrishikesh Borgikar
Carolina Bosso Andre
Remy Bossu
Michael Bostock
Lea Bouffaut
Daniel Bowman
James Boynton
Peter Bradford
Grace Bradley
Pier Luigi Bragato
Stanton Braid
Wolter Brands
Jochen Braunmiller
Romina Brignardello-Petersen
Warren Brill
Christopher Brooks
John Brooks
Megan Brown
Ronald Brown
Jared Bryan
Ayşe Bulut
Erin Bumann
Kerin Burdette
Roland Bürgmann
Jan Burjánek
Katherine Burkett
Jill Burns
Jason Buschman
Antony Butcher
Ashly Cabas
Recep Cakir
Eric Calais
Giovanna Calderoni
Scott Callaghan
Jake Callahan
Sara Camañes-Gonzalvo
Michel Campillo
Alexandre Canitano
Daniel Caplan
Jacqueline Caplan-Auerbach
Camila Cardoso
Elisa Caredda
Clifton Carey
Trevor Carey
Joshua Carmichael
N. Seth Carpenter
Alonso Carrasco-Labra
Antonio Carrassi
Caroline Carrico
Eunice Carrilho
Jerry A. Carter
Paul Casamassimo
Emmanuel Castillo
Raul Castro
Laura Cataldi
Rufus Catchings
Mathieu Causse
Carlo Cauzzi
Vanessa Cavalli
Monica Cayouette
Laura Ceballos
Malcon Celorio Murillo
Maximiliano Cenci
Chengping Chai
Megha Chakraborty
Caroline Chalumeau
David Chambers
Derrick Chambers
Chanthujan Chandrakumar
Arun Chandu
Jih-Hsin Chang
Sung-Joon Chang
Yucheng Chang
Zhiwang Chang
Shu-Hsien Chao
Martin Chapman
Marinos Charalampakis
Avigyan Chatterjee
Daniele Cheloni
Baokui Chen
Chi-Wen Chen
Da-Yi Chen
Guan Chen
Haiyan Chen
Jing Chen
Jiu-Hui Chen
Kate Chen
Kejie Chen
Xiaowei Chen
Yangkang Chen
Ying-Nien Chen
Yunfeng Chen
Feng Cheng
Guo-Liang Cheng
Jia Cheng
Yifang Cheng
Zhan Chengxiang
Ivor Gordon Chestnutt
Monique Cheung
Kristen Chiama
Andrea Chiang
Christine Chiao
Judith R. Chin
Katherine Chin
Kuo Ching
Brett Chiquet
Malgorzata Chmiel
Bryant Chow
Annemarie Christophersen
C.H. Chu
Shanna Chu
Ray Chuang
Evelyn Chung
Joohyun Chung
Sarah Clark
Bill Claytor
Timothy Clements
Charles Cobb
Elizabeth Cochran
James Coll
Simona Colombelli
Donald Coluzzi
Juliann Colwell
Valerio Comerci

Mustafa Comoglu
Todd Connell
Vincenzo Convertito
Giovanni Costa
Samuel Costa
Giuseppe Costantino
Sanne Cottaar
Fabrice Cotton
Paulo Couto-Souza
David Covell
Brady Cox
Darren Cox
Gemma Cremen
Philip Crotwell
Helen Crowley
Yasmi Crystal
Xin Cui
Arianna Cuius
Giovanna Cultrera
Phil Cummins
G. Frans Currier
Susana Custódio
Christie Custodio-Lumsden
Sebastiano D'amico
Manon Dalaison
Luis Angel Dalguer
David Dall'osto
Peter Damiano
Laurentiu Danciu
Anil Kumar Danda
David Danesh
Kalmár Dániel
Bob Darragh
Ananda Dasanayake
Mehran Davatgari-Tafreshi
Joern Davidsen
Andres Davila
Victoria Dawson
Steven M. Day
Raquel De Carvalho
Jose De La Hoz
Reny De Leeuw
Raffaele De Risi
Valerio De Rubeis
Francesca De Santis
Abdelilah Dekayir
Andrew Delorey
Christina Demopoulos
Yangfan Deng
Roger Denlinger
Donald Denucci
Boumédiène Derras
Paul Desjardins
Yadab Dhakal
Vineet Dhar
Domenico Di Giacomo
John Dale Dianala
Jordi Diaz
Julien Diaz
Michele Diniz
Rocco Ditommaso
John Dmytryk
Ramin Dokht
James Dolan
Mark Donaldson
Dongdong Dong
Kevin Donly
Bruce Donoff
Claire Doody
Diane Doser
Douglas Dreger
Pierre Dublanchet
Peter Duda
Eric Dunham
Zacharie Duputel
Cecilia Duran
Virginie Durand
Christopher Duross
Anne Dutfoy
Sydney Dybing
Bruce Dye
Caroline Eakin
John Ebel
George Eckert
Hafsteinn Eggertsson
Frederick Eichmiller
Zachary Eilon
Ellen Eisenberg
Satheesh Elangovan
Ahmed E. Elbanna
Tarek El-Bialy
Maria Elkins
Omar El-Mowafy
Ali El-Solh
Alexey Emanov
Kentaro Emoto
Mark Engebretson
Dennis Engel
Tugce Ergun
Eric Everett
Läslo Evers
Sezim Ezgi Güvercin
Islam Fadel
Licia Faenza
Giuseppe Falcone
Wenyuan Fan
Hongjian Fang
Lihua Fang
Julie Farmer
John Featherstone
Joshua Fein
Cecile Feldman
Jikun Feng
Wanpeng Feng
Theekshana Fernando
Leticia Ferreira Cabido
Aaron Ferris
Gaetano Festa
Yuri Fialko
Andreas Fichtner
Anna Figlioli
Paula Figueiredo
James Fine
John Firriolo
Izabel Regina Fischer Rubira-Bullen
Sarah Fitzpatrick
Eleanor Fleming
Jason Flores
Andres Flores Hidalgo
Carlos Flores-Mir
Jonas Folesky
Heather Ford
Sean Ford
Alan Formicola
Thomas Forstner
Robert Foss
Chelsea Fosse
Ioannis Fountoulakis
Katherine France
Inchingolo Francesco
William Frank
Sarah Franklin
Julie Frantsve-Hawley
Jeff Fraser
William Frazer
William Frazier
Sylvia Frazier-Bowers
Andrew Frederiksen
Jeffrey Freymueller
Paul Friberg
Reid Friesen
Zhen Fu
Antonio Fuggi
Eiichi Fukuyama
Sydney Gable
Alice-Agnes Gabriel
Nimita Gaggar
Aaron Gallant
Maria Giovanna Gandolfi
Dawei Gao
Kai Gao
Ke Gao
Raul Garcia
Franklin Garcia-Godoy
Antonio Garcia-Jerez
Nadia Gargouri
Chet Gary
Paolo Gasperini
Filippo Gatti
Melissa Gaydos
Zengxi Ge

Hassem Geha
Stefania Gentili
Elisabetta Giampiccolo
Steven Gibbons
Jennifer L. Gibbs
Brad Gibson
Kathy Gibson
Sophie Giffard-Roisin
Florent Gimbert
Russell A. Giordano
Joseph Giovannitti Jr.
Aaron Girard
Subha Giri
Cédric Giry
Daniel Givan
Sarah Glass
Michael Glick
Robert Glickman
David Glotzer
Joan Gluch
Katsuichiro Goda
Thomas Goebel
Anita Gohel
Dara Goldberg
James Goltz
Eudes Gondim Jr.
�?lvaro González
Sara Gordon
Yuancong Gou
Kenny Graham
Vladimir Graizer
Anupama Grandhi
Lisa Grant-Ludwig
Ronni Grapenthin
Joseph Graskemper
Robert Graves
John Grbic
David Green
Michael Greenfield
Nick Gregor
David Grembowski
Jonathan Griffin
Francesco Grigoli
Iason Grigoratos
Eric Grin
Yu Gu
Philippe Gueguen
John Gunsolley
Yicun Guo
Zhen Guo
Hamid Haddadi
Mohamed Hamdache
Kimberly Hammersmith
William Hammond
Peng Han
Sangwoo Han
Catherine Hanagan
Annabel Händel
Matthew Haney
Katrin Hannemann
Jeanne Hardebeck
Prashanth Haribabu
Thanu Harnpattanapanich
Stephen Harrel
Nicolas Harrichhausen
David Harris
Ruth Harris
Johannes Hart
Ross Hartleb
J. Renate Hartog
James Hartsfield
Stephen Hartzell
Elizabeth Hatfield
Paul V. Hatton
Jens Havskov
Helen Hawkey
Takafumi Hayashi
Catherine Hayes
Ping He
Xiaohui He
Lisa Heaton
Gary Heir
John Hellstein
Kadek Hendrawan Palgunadi
Pasan Herath
Andre Herrero
Marcus Herrmann
Robert Herrmann
Elliot Hersh
György Hetényi
Ross Heyburn
Clément Hibert
Ryley Hill
Gregor Hillers
Linda Himmelberger
Klaus-G. Hinzen
Evan Hirakawa
Naoshi Hirata
Takanobu Hirosawa
Rich Hirschinger
Yoshiaki Hisada
Adam Hiscock
Maritzabel Hogge
Joanna Holmgren
Jennifer Holtzman
Kyle Homman
Keiichi Hosaka
Alicia Hotovec-Ellis
Xiaolin Hou
Susan Hough
Jamie Howarth
Brian Howe
Pavla Hrubcova
Roman Hryciw
Ming-Che Hsieh
Ting Yu Hsu
Ya-Ju Hsu
Yungting Hsu
Jinjun Hu
Yan Hu
Zongkai Hu
Hsin-Hua Huang
Shulamite Huang
Wen-Jeng Huang
Xing Huang
Yihe Huang
Kenneth Hudson
Patrick Hupe
Allen Husker
Fahmida Hussain
Sean Hutchings
Jesse Hutchinson
Lorraine Hwang
Antonio Giovanni Iaccarino
Tsuyoshi Ichimura
Gene Ichinose
Nadine Igonin
Matt Ikari
Makbule Ilgac
Kentaro Imai
Peter Imrey
Afifa Imtiaz
Yigit Isbiliroglu
Md Mohimanul Islam
Jennie Ison
Yoshihiro Ito
Asako Iwaki
Tomotaka Iwata
Bernadette Jaeger
Poonam Jain
Helen Janiszewski
Marcos Antônio Japiassú Resende Montes
Jorge Jara
Steven Jaume
R. Jayangondaperumal
Hyeran Jeon
Seokho Jeong
Seongju Jeong
Chen Ji
Ke Jia
Peiru Jian
Changsheng Jiang
Chengxin Jiang
Junle Jiang
Wenbin Jiang
Wenliang Jiang
Sebin John
David Johnsen
Christopher Johnson
Kaj Johnson
Asbjorn Jokstad

Kenneth D. Jones Jr.
Sigurjon Jonsson
Roslyn Joseph
Dario Jozinović
Jordi Julia
Joaquin Julve
M. Marianne Jurasic
Emanuel Kaestle
Michael Kahn
James Kaklamanos
Preetish Kakoty
Özkan Kale
Mythili Kalladka
Daniel Kalmar
John Kalmar
Ronnie Kamai
Jyotima Kanaujia
Tae-Seob Kang
Nagaraju Kanna
Piranit Kantaputra
Kamila Rosamilia Kantovitz
Ezgi Karasozen
Sadegh Karimpouli
Shaghayegh Karimzadeh
Glen Karunanayake
Ghabi Kaspo
Mirna Kassem
Linda Kaste
Akshay Katara
Pranav Kataria
Hiroshi Kawase
Nobuyuki Kawashima
Jesse Kearse
Martha Ann Keels
Sabrina Keil
David Keith
Robert Kerstein
Tom Kettlety
Namita Khandelwal
Navid Kheirdast
Zohaib Khurshid
Debi Kilb
Ahyi Kim
Byungmin Kim
Doyeon Kim
Hyejeong Kim
Ji Hwan Kim
Keehoon Kim
Seong-Gon Kim
Seongryong Kim
Young Ho Kim
Brian Kinard
Danielle Kinkel
Jannes Kinscher
Jonas Kintner
Konstantin Kislov
Gary Klasser
Elliot Klein
Dushanka Kleinman
Mustafa Kockar
Yuki Kodera
Rich Koehler
Andreas Köhler
Meetu Kohli
Roshan Koirala
Tamaribuchi Koji
Michal Kolaj
Balaji Kolasani
Ahu Komec Mutlu
Fansheng Kong
Qingkai Kong
Keith Koper
Manuela Köpfli
Dorota Kopycka-Kedzierawski
Meera Kota
Sreeram Reddy Kotha
Albert Kottke
Jill M. Kramer
Ashley Kranz
Zoe Krauss
Corne Kreemer
Jozef Kristek
Pauline Kruiver
Wenhuan Kuang
Hisahiko Kubo
Gajanan Kulkarni
Utpal Kumar
Vikas Kumar
Felipe Kuncar
Bhaskar Kundu
Ban-Yuan Kuo
Chun-Hsiang Kuo
Yu-Ting Kuo
Hao Kuo-Chen
Ayodeji Kuponiyi
Zoya Kurago
Sam Thomas Kuriadom
Tevfik Özgür Kurtulmuş
Seema Kurup
Matheus Kury
Giusy Rita Maria La Rosa
Guijuan Lai
Ssu-Ting Lai
Voon Hui Lai
Rajesh V. Lalla
Ernest Lam
Sophie Lambotte
Cornelius Langenbruch
Nadege Langet
Charles A. Langston
Pablo Lara
Franc Larsonnier
Cesar Lascala
Joel Laudenbach
Aurore Laurendeau
Vincent Lavoie
Grigorios Lavrentiadis
Ghida Lawand
Maryline Le Beon
Ronan Le Bras
Kecia Leary
Chun-Teh Lee
Duhyeong Lee
Helen Lee
Hsin-Yu Lee
Jae-Hyun Lee
Jessica Lee
Jian-Cheng Lee
Peggy Lee
Robin Lee
Thomas Lee
Won Sang Lee
Jonathan Lees
Ariel Lellouch
Kelly Lemke
Yiu Yan Leung
Will Levandowski
Mitchell Levine
Felipe Leyton
Bo Li
Chenyu Li
Duo Li
Hongjie Li
Ji Li
Jiangtao Li
Jing Li
Junlun Li
Kang Li
Tao Li
Wenda Li
Xiaodong Li
Yong Li
Yujiang Li
Yunyue Elita Li
Zefeng Li
Chao Liang
Lee Liberty
Frank Licari
Adriano Lima
Nareudee Limpuangthip
Fan-Chi Lin
Guan-Wei Lin
Jianmin Lin
Jiun-Ting Lin
Shih Wei Lin
Yen-Yu Lin
Yi-Ling Lin
Nathaniel Lindsey
Itzhak Lior
Frank Lippert
Eugenio Lippiello

Chengli Liu
Chujie Liu
Jihong Liu
Lihua Liu
Min Liu
Qinya Liu
Tianze Liu
Yingci Liu
Andrea Llenos
Edward Lo
Philippe Lognonné
Anthony Lomax
Steven London
Peter Loomer
Alberto Lopez-Venegas
John Louie
John Loveless
Julian Lozos
Cai-Ping Lu
Antoine Lucas
John Ludlow
Bjorn Lund
Bin Luo
Haipeng Luo
Heng Luo
Huabin Luo
Karen Lythgoe
Chao Lyu
Kuo-Fong Ma
Shuo Ma
Tao Ma
Xiaolong Ma
Zhangfeng Ma
William Maas
Jonathan Maccarthy
Jorge Macedo
Michael Macentee
Kenneth Macpherson
Ross Maguire
Alireza Babaie Mahani
P. Martin Mai
Ian Main
Gisele Mainville
Hany Makkawy
Alberto Malacarne
Luca Malagnini
Sanjay Mallya
Brassnavy Manzunzu
Savvas Marcou
Valentin Marguin
Mariam Margvelashvili-Malament
Sadia Marium Rinty
David Marsan
Evan Marschall
Teresa Marshall
Stacey Martin
Fernando Martinelli
Patricia Martinez Garzon
Evgeniia Martuganova
Samson Marty
Warner Marzocchi
Claudia Mascandola
Ana Karina Mascarenhas
Henry Mason
Kathryn Materna
Kavita Mathu-Muju
Jukka Matinlinna
Robin Matoza
Takanori Matsuzawa
Eric Matzel
Brett Maurer
Jeremy Maurer
Julie Maury
Melanie Mayberry
Ian Mcbrearty
John H. Mcbride
Sara Mcbride
David Mccallen
Arthur Mcgarr
Jeffrey Mcguire
Kathleen Mckee
Greg Mclaskey
Mustapha Meghraoui
Albert Mehl
Timothy Melbourne
Haoran Meng
Shuai Meng
William Menke
Arthur Merschat
Diana Messadi
Sabrina Metzger
Beau Meyer
Wenpei Miao
Andrew Michael
Sylvain Michel
Alberto Michelini
Peter Milgrom
Craig Miller
Douglas Miller
Meghan Miller
Kevin Milner
Mark Mintline
Roberto Miranda
Pratishtha Mishra
Hiroyuki Miura
Hiroe Miyake
Masatoshi Miyazawa
Leila Mizrahi
Peter Moczo
Kami Mohammadi
Gonzalo Montalva
Jean Moore
Maria Mora
Frederick More
Alexander Morelan
Isabel Moreno-Hay
Emily Morton
Ilaria Mosca
Morgan Moschetti
Francesco Mosconi
Mark Moss
Robb Moss
Stephen Moss
Caroline Mouchon
Seyed Mostafa Mousavi
Sima Mousavi
James Muirhead
Hiroshi Murata
Carol Anne Murdoch-Kinch
Jessica Murray
Daniel Myers
Steve Myers
Aparna Naidu
S.M. Hashim Nainar
Kenichi Nakano
Masaru Nakano
Romesh Nalliah
Makoto Naoi
Lucia Nardone
Chiara Nardoni
Aline Bou Nassif
Romina Ñaupari-Villasante
Sergio M. Navarro
Mahvash Navazesh
Avinash Nayak
James Neely
Kamil Henryk Nelke
Travis Nelson
Ana Neumann
Miguel Neves
Michael Newman
Man Wai Ng
Sidao Ni
Yiyu Ni
Shiying Nie
Alireza Niksejel
Stuart Nippress
Govinda Niroula
Yuanyuan Niu
Kirk Noraian
Ahmed Nouibat
Andri Nugraha
Ceri Nunn
Chukwuebuka Nweke
Andrew Nyblade
Kelly O'Brien
Colin O'Rourke
Enihomo Obadan-Udoh
Kazushige Obara
Paul Ogwari
Matthias Ohrnberger

Diptee Ojha
Taro Okamoto
Tomohisa Okazaki
Sergio Olate
Maria Jose Oliveros
Kim Olsen
Tolulope Olugboji
Galal Omami
Daniel Oreadi
Daniel Orr Li
Bar Oryan
Mitsutaka Oshima
Sarah Ostrander
Lars Ottemöller
Adepitan A. Owosho
Volker Oye
David Ozar
Lorraine Ozar
Volkan Ozsarac
Francesca Pacor
Ricardo Padilla
Marco Pagani
Morgan Page
Benjamin Palla
Paulo J. Palma
Jiawei Pan
Francesco Panzera
Enrico Paolucci
Athena Papas
Jeongwon Park
Ji Man Park
Sun-Cheon Park
Yongsoo Park
Grace Parker
Tom Parsons
Nicole Passia
Cesar Pasten
Michael Pasyanos
Jay Patel
Paras Patel
Amey Patil
Julie Patris
Lauren Patton
Spyros Pavlides
James Pechmann
Cecilia Pedroso Turssi
Shunping Pei
Tanja Pejic
Carlos Peña
Andres Peña Castro
Chaoyong Peng
Zhigang Peng
Colin Pennington
Andrea Perez-Silva
Mahesh Perguru
Theodorus Permana
Vincent Perron
Patricia Persaud
Ove Peters
Laura Petrescu
Giuseppe Petrillo
Anatoly Petukhin
Shahram Pezeshk
Thanh-Son Pham
Robert Pickle
Matteo Picozzi
Camilo Ignacio Pinilla Ramos
Andres Pinto
Marta Pischiutta
Piero Poli
Deborah Polk
Fred Pollitz
Angeliki Polymeri
Hernan Porras Espinoza
Robert Porritt
Peter Powers
Meghna Prakash
Raj Prasanna
Carlo Prati
Thomas Pratt
David Preble
Renmin Pretell
Jeffery Price
Keith Priestley
German Prieto
Janire Prudencio
Wuchuan Pu
Nelson Pulido
Prinya Putthapiban
Shadi Qasem
Hongrui Qiu
Wei Qu
Carlos Quiñonez
Lori Rainchuso
Johnson Rajasingh
Kusala Rajendran
Mario Ramos
Ryan Rasanen
Sarah Raskin
Nicholas Rawlinson
Kenneth Reed
Julie Regnier
Sven M. Reich
John Reith
Nadine Reitman
Yefei Ren
Alexandra Renouard
Michael Rethman
Mark Reynolds
David Rhoades
Paul G. Richards
D. Brad Rindal
Adam Ringler
Douglas Risk
Johannes Ristau
Luis Rivera
Thibault Roch
Thomas Rockwell
Arthur Rodgers
R.C.M. Rodrigues Garcia
Alba Rodriguez Padilla
Veronica Rodriguez Tribaldos
Adrian Rodriguez-Marek
Chris Rollins
Yufang Rong
Steven Roser
Boris Rösler
Michael Ross
Yara Rossi
Renata Rotondi
Baptiste Rousset
Tao Ruan
Rajesh Rupakhety
Natalia Ruppert
James Rutledge
Laxmikanth S M
Omar Saad
David Saftner
Saadet Sa�lam Atsü
Amrit Saini
James Salisbury
Michelle Salmon
Nooshin Saloor
Francisco Sanchez-Sesma
Abdullah Sandikkaya
Linda Sangalli
Divesh Sardana
Sergio Sargenti Neto
Alexandra Sarmiento
Karina Sarmiento
Elise Sarvas
Jessie Saunders
Jean-Marie Saurel
Martha Savage
Alexandros Savvaidis
Caroline Sawicki
Erdinc Saygin
Paola Sbarra
Taís Scaramucci
William Scarfe
David P. Schaff
Rebecca Schaffer
Martin Schimmel
Lisa Schleicher
Nico Schliwa
Brandon Schmandt
Douglas Schmitt
Jean Schmittbuhl
Max Schneider
Frederic Schoenberg
Christopher Scholz

Ryan Schultz
Michele Schultz-Robins
Scott Schwartz
Johannes Schweitzer
Lezize Şebnem Türkün
Leonardo Seeber
Helena Seivane Ramos
Claudia Serna
Frank Setzer
Emel Seyhan
Sara Sgobba
Sonal Shah
Mohammad Shahvar
Nader Shakibay Senobari
Sharmin Shamsalsadati
Pieter-Ewald Share
Bruce Shaw
Robert Shcherbakov
Peter Shebalin
David Shelly
Wenhao Shen
Xuzhang Shen
Zheng-Kang Shen
Zhichao Shen
Yixiao Sheng
Elizabeth Sherrill
Lei Shi
Peidong Shi
Qibin Shi
Xuhua Shi
Yaozhong Shi
Hussein Shible
Elizabeth Shick
Takahiro Shiina
Thomas Shipley
Brian Shiro
Taghi Shirzad
Azusa Shito
David Shonberg
Madhu Shrestha
Poojan Shrestha
Sarah Shueb
Vladimir Shumila
Michael Siegel
Elizabeth Silber
Jan Šílený
Vitor Silva
Marushka Silveira
Michael Simmons
Lisa Simon
Steven Singer
A. P. Singh
Arun Singh
Chandrani Singh
Krittanon Sirorattanakul
Robert Skoumal
Lyubov Slashcheva
Robert Smalley Jr.
Chris Smiley
Derek Smith
Molly Smith
Krystyna Smolinski
Katie Smye
Maria Sobral
Georgios Sokratis Chatzopoulos
Margarita Solares-Colon
Kazuhiro Somei
Susan Somerset
Minkyung Son
Chao Song
Jindong Song
Seok Goo Song
Xiaohan Song
Zilin Song
Carlos Sousa Oliveira
Manoel Damião Sousa-Neto
Heiko Spallek
Ilaria Spassiani
Vemula Sreenath
Tony Alfredo Stabile
Samantha Stanley
Ross Stein
Seth Stein
Andreas Steinberg
Rene Steinmann
William Stephenson
Jeffry Stevens
Jonathan Stewart
Mark Stirling
Dan Stoeckel
Dmitry Storchak
Katherine Strafford
Ronald Strauss
Claudio Strumia
Brian Stump
Richard Styron
Gerardo Suarez
Kurt Summersgill
Danielle Sumy
Hongyu Sun
Li Sun
Muchen Sun
Wei-Fang Sun
Ya Sun
Yudong Sun
Chih-Hsuan Sung
Eric Swirsky
Eric Szymanski
Ricardo Taborda
Taka'aki Taira
Ryota Takagi
Fengzhou Tan
Yen Joe Tan
Yuyang Tan
Yifu Tang
Yuxiang Tang
Daranee Tantbirojn
Hakan Tanyas
Carl Tape
Matteo Taroni
Izidor Tasic
Ruben Tatevossian
Tuncay Taymaz
Uri Ten Brink
Sarat Thikkurissy
Kiran Kumar Thingbaijam
Eric Thompson
Stephen Thompson
John Thornley
Julien Thurin
Lei Tian
Xiao Tian
Xiaobo Tian
Rigobert Tibi
Norman Tinanoff
Hrvoje Tkalcic
Shinji Toda
Scott Tomar
Takashi Tonegawa
Ping Tong
Gabriel Toro
Riva Touger-Decker
Matthias Troeltzsch
Edmond Truelove
Daniel Trugman
Tomohiro Tsuji
Süleyman Tunç
Abidin Tuncer
Sebnem Turkun
Martitia Tuttle
Donald Tyndall
Takahiko Uchide
Kristin Ulmer
Thomas Ulrich
Jasbir Upadhyaya
Janelle Urata
Sergio Uribe
Olivia Urquhart
Pinar Usta
Piamkamon Vacharotayangul
Gianluca Valensise
Alessandro Valentini
Martin Vallée
Eduardo Valmaseda-Castellón
Denise Van Diermen
Russ Van Dissen
Janneke Van Ginkel
Koen Van Noten
Elizabeth Vanacore
Ian Vandevert
Gianfranco Vannucci

Joseph Vantassel
Richard Vargo
Elisa Varini
Daria Vasilyeva
Vaclav Vavrycuk
Analia Veitz-Keenan
Brandon Veremis
Jean-Noel Vergnes
Felipe Vicencio
John Vidale
Nadarajah Vigneswaran
Handially Vilela
Alessandro Villa
Pilar Villamor
Renier Viltres
Cinzia Viroli
Francesco Visini
Arjan Vissink
Hsingchi Von Bergmann
Sebastian Von Specht
Ray Wagner
Rosie Wagner
Damien Walmsley
Laurence J. Walsh
Tanya Walsh
Jack Walter
William Walter
Maureen Walton
Richard Walton
Baoshan Wang
Dehua Wang
Dun Wang
Jieh-Jiuh Wang
Kaiwen Wang
Kang Wang
Kelin Wang
Li Wang
Mao-Xin Wang
Qing-Yu Wang
Rui Wang
Ruijia Wang
Shiguang Wang
Shuai Wang
Teng Wang
Ting Wang
Wei Wang
Weilai Wang
Xin Wang
Yan Wang
Yongfei Wang
Zhi Wang
Chun Wang Chau
Wendy Ward
John Warren
Graeme Weatherill
Darien Weatherspoon
Thomas Weber
George Wehby
Carolyn Wehler
Shengji Wei
Pan Wen
Yangmao Wen
Huihui Weng
Rod Wentworth
Maximilian Werner
Michael West
Sri Widiyantoro
John Wilding
Ethan Williams
Jacob Williams
Amy Williamson
Anne Wilson
David Wilson
Sam Wimpenny
J. Paul Winberry
Mitch Withers
Christine Wittich
Jochen Woessner
Mark Wolff
Ivan Wong
Jeong-Ung Woo
Sook-Bin Woo
Liam Wotherspoon
Tanya Wright
Baoning Wu
Chuanyong Wu
Jing Wu
Kungang Wu
Sin-Mei Wu
Andreas Wuestefeld
Patrice Wunsch
Mang Xiao
Lei Xie
Min Xu
Tao Xu
Wenbin Xu
Xiaohua Xu
Yuji Yagi
Masumi Yamada
Hongfeng Yang
Lei Yang
Liuqing Yang
Shaobo Yang
Tingwei Yang
Xiaotao Yang
Yan Yang
Yi Yang
Yinghui Yang
Yuanhong Yang
Dongdong Yao
Jiayuan Yao
Suli Yao
Cemil Yavas
William Yeck
Te-Yang Yeh
Juan Yepes
Kyuho Yi
Ollie Yiru Yu
Alan Yong
Kyunghyeon Yoo
Keisuke Yoshida
Chunquan Yu
Ellen Yu
Guiping Yu
Hongyu Yu
Congcong Yuan
Rm Yuan
Shihao Yuan
Yohei Yukutake
Naidan Yun
Davide Zaccagnino
Jiri Zahradnik
Hongyu Zeng
Xiangfang Zeng
Ronald Zentz
Domenick Zero
Hao Zhang
Hongcai Zhang
Ji Zhang
Jiaming Zhang
Jinhai Zhang
Miao Zhang
Wei Zhang
Wenqiang Zhang
Xiong Zhang
Yan Zhang
Yayun Zhang
Yijun Zhang
Ying Zhang
Yong Zhang
Zhendong Zhang
Zhenguo Zhang
Ziqi Zhang
Bin Zhao
Dezheng Zhao
Guo-Chen Zhao
Lian-Feng Zhao
Xiong Zhao
Mengje Zheng
Wenjun Zheng
Yong Zheng
Yiyuan Zhong
Suzanne Y. Zhou
Yatong Zhou
Yijian Zhou
Chuanbin Zhu
Gaohua Zhu
Jun Zhu
Tieyuan Zhu
Weiqiang Zhu
Jiancang Zhuang

Jinping Zi
Vincent Ziccardi
Olaf Zielke
Paolo Zimmaro
Gert Zöller
Bingshuang Zou
Kawtar Zouaidi
Can Zulfikar
Samuel Zwetchkenbaum

Corporate Members, Seismological Society of America

ExxonMobil
Sara Gates
22777 Springwoods Village Parkway
Spring, TX 77389
www.corporate.exxonmobil.com

GeoSIG Ltd
Talhan Biro
Wiesenstrasse 39
8952 Schlieren
Switzerland
www.geosig.com

Guralp Systems
James Lindsey
3 Midas House, Calleva Park Aldermaston
Berkshire RG7 8EA
United Kingdom
www.guralp.com

ISTI
Paul Friberg
5 Case Street
Saratoga Springs, NY 12866
www.isti.com

Kinemetrics, Inc.
Veronica Vera
222 Vista Avenue
Pasadena, CA 91107
www.kinemetrics.com

Lettis Consultants International, Inc.
Jeffrey Unruh
1981 N Broadway
Suite 330
Walnut Creek, CA 94596
www.lettisci.com

Moody's
Nilesh Shome
7575 Gateway Boulevard
Newark, CA 94560
www.moodys.com

Nanometrics
Alyssa Parks
250 Herzberg Road
Kanata, ON K2K 2A1
Canada
www.nanometrics.ca

Puerto Rico Strong Motion Program
Dr. José Martinez-Cruzado
Call Box 9000-Civil Engineering
Mayaguez, Puerto Rico 00681
www.prsmp.uprm.edu

Reftek Systems Inc.
Leonid Zimakov
75 MacDonald Avenue
Dartmouth, NS B3B 1T8
Canada
www.reftek.com

Seismology Research Centre
Adam Pascale
141 Palmer Street
Richmond, VIC 3121
Australia
www.src.com.au

SSA
Seismological
Society of America